S
FOOTBALL YEARBOOK 1983–84

EDITOR: TONY WILLIAMS

QUEEN ANNE PRESS
MACDONALD & CO
LONDON and SYDNEY

A QUEEN ANNE PRESS BOOK

First published in Great Britain in 1983 by
Queen Anne Press
Macdonald & Co (Publishers) Ltd
London & Sydney

A BPCC plc Company

Front cover photograph: Manchester United's teenage hero Norman Whiteside evades a tackle by Alan Hanson of Liverpool during the Milk Cup Final at Wembley.

Photographs courtesy of Colorsport, Sporting Photos.

ISBN 0356 09726 9 (cased)
0356 09727 7 (limp)

Filmset, printed and bound in Great Britain by
Hazell Watson & Viney Ltd, Aylesbury, Bucks

CONTENTS

THE FA CUP

SCOTTISH FOOTBALL

INTERNATIONAL FOOTBALL

EUROPEAN FOOTBALL

IRISH AND WELSH FOOTBALL

NON-LEAGUE SECTION

INFORMATION SECTION

FOREWORD FROM ROTHMANS OF PALL MALL

The season under review in the 14th edition of the Rothmans Football Yearbook will be remembered as the year Bob Paisley retired from the job of managing Liverpool after guiding the club to their 14th League title win.

There were many who thought the retirement of the late Bill Shankly may bring a halt to the continuing triumphs of the Merseyside Club. It did not, and this time fewer people are willing to assume that a change of manager will halt the progress of the team which has won the Football League four times in the past five seasons.

European success went to Aberdeen in a season which saw the Scottish domination of Rangers and Celtic brought to an end, whilst in Wales and Northern Ireland the International spotlight moved from the World Cup to the European scene.

The Chester Committee re-emerged with new proposals for the future of football and the questions of shirt sponsorship and television coverage exercised the minds of many involved in the sport.

Despite the gloom-makers, soccer lives on as our national game and the Rothmans Football Yearbook again provides the facts and figures to satisfy the enthusiast.

Full details of every English and Scottish League Clubs are given, illustrated for the first time with team photographs. Tony Williams is also editor of our other soccer annual, the Rothmans F.A. Non League Football Yearbook, and we are sure that you will find much pleasure in both.

INTRODUCTION

Major changes of format have been made in this, the fourteenth Rothmans Football Yearbook but no club features have been left out, while many new statistics have been included.

With photographs added and the club section certainly more comprehensive than ever before, it is hoped that readers will soon find their way around the new features and enjoy the lively presentation of this, the 1983–84 edition.

Figures such as Football League/Milk Cup and FA Cup appearances and goals are added to players' career records for the first time, as are birthdates and transfer fees (which of course are not official).

Features such as past 'Home' International teams, included in the last four issues, will be used intermittently in the future and every season new statistical ideas will be presented.

The advice of individual members of The Association of Football Statisticians has been gratefully received this year and Ray Spiller has been of great assistance in introducing them to the Yearbook administration.

Once again the book has been given enthusiastic co-operation from The Home Countries Football Associations, The Football League and the Scottish League, while special thanks also go to Tony Pullein and Barry Hugman (Domestic Competitions), Leslie Vernon (Overseas Football) and Dick Donnelly and Ray Hepburn (Scottish Football) for their invaluable contributions.

ACKNOWLEDGEMENTS

The Editor would like to thank the following individuals and organisations for their cooperation, encouragement and support: Glynis Firth, Mike Foster, Chris J. Whalley, Debbie Singleton, Patricia Callon (all from the Football League); Adrian Titcombe, MIke McNamara, Steve Clark, David Barber, Glen Kirton (The Football Association); The Scottish Football Association, The Welsh Football Association, The Scottish League, the secretaries of all Football League and Scottish League clubs, Malcolm Brodie, A. Rice (The English Schools FA), W. P. Goss (AFA), Maurice Galsworthy, Ken Goldman, Peter Dunk, Bill Mitchell, J. & M. Blackstock, L. Coaker, Lindsay MacLeod, Roy Peskett, Rod McLeod, and all agencies who supplied photographs, including: Press Association, Mark Leech, Sportapics Ltd, Kemsley Picture Services, Ian Peebles Publications, M. Ward, Central Press Photos, John Rooney, Oldham Chronicle, Hanley Sports Photographics, Varley Picture Agency, Sporting Pictures (UK) Ltd, Bob Thomas, Colorsport, Universal Pictorial Press, Newsport Press.

EDITORIAL

Anyone reading the day by day diary of last November could be forgiven for thinking that the professional game in this country had decided to devote itself to an all out 'kamakasi' course of self destruction. Reading the daily football disasters; of discrepancies of club funds, rows between players and managers, deception between chairmen and managers, club to club arguing, take over 'coups', record total of dismissals, organised gangs of thugs in the stands, and clubs in terrible debt, it was, to say the least, very sad for all who dearly loved the game.

We had started the season with a new interpretation of the laws which discouraged defenders from deliberately cheating, with body checks, trips and handball. This should have given spectators and the game in general a tremendous boost. Forwards could now push a ball past, or chip a ball over defenders and rely on skill and pace to triumph. Well, that was the idea, as John Barnes, Mark Chamberlain and Paul Walsh tore into defences in a spectacular start to the season. However, we read more about massive totals of dismissals and complaining managers than we did about the extra goals, entertainment, and the emphasis on quality and skill. It appeared that legal defensive play was a forgotten art which had to be re-learnt, but as pressure was put on referees to 'ease off', the game tended to lose that glorious free expression we enjoyed in those early weeks.

Perhaps the next degrading and boring aspect of the game to be elimated should be kicking the ball away after committing an infringement. If this unpleasantness were to be outlawed it would surely help the game to stand comparison with other spectator sports. There is nothing wrong with the game itself however, and last season, despite the unsavoury aspects already mentioned, football proved itself bigger than these problems and gave us plenty of wonderful memories. Huge crowds poured back over the Christmas holiday period and many clubs produced some outstanding entertainment. The sheer attacking brilliance, in completely different styles, of Liverpool (with Kenny Dalglish supreme), Watford and Luton Town in particular was also matched at times by practically all the First Division clubs, with the quality of many goals proving quite breathtaking.

All the good aspects of British professional football were seen by massive world wide T.V. audiences at the Milk and F.A. Cup Final matches. The drama, pace and skill enjoyed in a refreshingly happy atmosphere was really displaying our game at its best. There is no doubt that a successful Manchester United 'lifts' the domestic competitions and they certainly made a great contribution to the season. The emotional departure of Bob Paisley was also a reassuring reminder that great managers do not have to be constantly hitting the controversial headlines; a good job can still be done with the minimum of fuss and publicity.

There were lesser-known success stories, however, which proved that the fans are still about; more discerning perhaps, but still wanting to be attracted back to support worthwhile football at their local grounds. The excitement and rejoicing at Wolverhampton, Leicester, Portsmouth, Huddersfield, Cardiff and Hull, where comparitively recent gloom had been lifted, was most moving, and the sheer joy showed by local inhabitants at their club's promotion celebrations proved their pride in 'their town' clubs.

Aberdeen showed the whole of Britain how a club can be deliberately built into a disciplined, well-organised and successful organisation both on and off the field. They have also proved that by treating their supporters with respect, they in turn are rewarded by loyal, enthusiastic and well-behaved followers. England's team under Bobby Robson started quietly, developed into a very promising outfit and then through unfortunate circumstances proved once again that no-one will be attracted to the sport at any level if matches, like those in Australia are played by players appearing to lack the enthusiasm and technique to display the game at its best.

With wages and transfer fees more realistic, more footballers realising that only the completely dedicated will stay in the game, and outside The Football League there are more players playing the game than ever before, the sport has surely weathered the worst of the storm. Clubs have been forced to face life more realistically and the coming season could see a new refreshing attitude to attract the supporters who still yearn for the game to be played in a sporting, uninhibited and exciting fashion, in a happy and relaxed atmosphere.

TONY WILLIAMS

Rothmans Football Awards 1970–1982

For the first five years of publication The Rothmans Football Yearbook presented awards to a British 'Golden Boots XI. All these awards were of course based on the previous season's form and were selected by a panel of leading journalists.

It's interesting to note that the first three 'sides' were selected in 4-2-4 formation and that only Billy Bremner held his place for all five seasons.

David Hay, originally selected at Right Back in the first 'team' made an impressive comeback in mid-field four years later, and the 'Young Players of the Year' all lived up to their original promise by winning a number of 'full' caps for England between them.

When the awards were changed to six special presentations, some interesting names appeared; Dickie Guy for his heroic penalty save for Wimbledon in their 0-0 F.A. Cup draw at Leeds; Geoffrey Green for all the pleasure his writing brought us through 'The Times' and for his eloquence on the radio; Liverpool became the first club to win an award and then Billericay Town followed them as the first club from outside The Football League; then last season Corinthian Casuals won an award in their centenary year for their success despite a pure amateur policy.

No doubt in another fourteen years it will be equally interesting to look back and see which personalities and teams hold these coveted awards.

Rothmans Golden Boot Awards

1970–71 Book (4-2-4)

Gordon Banks (Stoke C); **David Hay** (Celtic), **Mike England** (Tottenham H), **Bobby Moore** (West Ham U), **Terry Cooper** (Leeds U); **Billy Bremner** (Leeds U), **Alan Ball** (Everton); **Jimmy Johnstone** (Celtic), **Ron Davies** (Southampton), **Geoff Hurst** (West Ham U), **George Best** (Manchester U).

1971–72 Book (4-2-4)

Gordon Banks (Stoke C); **Chris Lawler** (Liverpool), **Frank McLintock** (Arsenal), **Bobby Moore** (West Ham U), **Terry Cooper** (Leeds U); **Billy Bremner** (Leeds U), **Martin Peters** (Tottenham H); **George Best** (Manchester U), **Martin Chivers** (Tottenham H), **Ron Davies** (Southampton), **Francis Lee** (Manchester C). *Substitute:* **Peter Storey** (Arsenal).
Young Player of the Year: **Ray Kennedy** (Arsenal).

1972–73 Yearbook (4-2-4)

Gordon Banks (Stoke C); **Paul Madeley** (Leeds U), **Roy McFarland** (Derby Co), **Bobby Moore** (West Ham U), **Terry Cooper** (Leeds U); **Billy Bremner** (Leeds U), **Johnny Giles** (Leeds U); **Jimmy Johnstone** (Celtic), **Martin Chivers** (Tottenham H), **Francis Lee** (Manchester C), **Eddie Gray** (Leeds U). *Substitute:* **Peter Simpson** (Arsenal).
Young Player of the Year: **Kevin Keegan** (Liverpool).

1973–74 Yearbook (4-3-3)

Pat Jennings (Tottenham H); **Paul Madeley** (Leeds U), **Bobby Moore** (West Ham U), **Roy McFarland** (Derby Co), **Emlyn Hughes** (Liverpool); **Billy Bremner** (Leeds U), **Alan Ball** (Arsenal), **Johnny Giles** (Leeds U); **Peter Lorimer** (Leeds U), **Mick Channon** (Southampton), **Allan Clarke** (Leeds U). *Substitute:* **Colin Todd** (Derby Co).
Young Player of the Year: **John Richards** (Wolverhampton W).

1974–75 Yearbook (4-3-3)

Pat Jennings (Tottenham H); **Paul Madeley** (Leeds U), **Roy McFarland** (Derby Co), **Norman Hunter** (Leeds U), **Alec Lindsay** (Liverpool); **Billy Bremner** (Leeds U), **Emlyn Hughes** (Liverpool), **David Hay** (Celtic); **Kevin Keegan** (Liverpool), **Mick Channon** (Southampton), **Tommy Hutchinson** (Coventry C). *Substitute:* **Colin Todd** (Derby Co).
Young Player of the Year: **Kevin Beattie** (Ipswich T).

1975 **Alan Mullery** (Fulham), **Alan Taylor** (West Ham U), **Mike Smith** (Manager, Wales), **Dickie Guy** (Wimbledon), **Colin Todd** (Derby Co), **'Dixie' McNeil** (Hereford U).

1976 **Emlyn Hughes** (Liverpool), **Geoffrey Green** (*Times* Football Correspondent), **Don Masson** (Q.P.R.), **Alex Stepney** (Manchester U), **Terry Paine** (Hereford U), **Mick Channon** (Southampton).

1977 **Liverpool F.C.**, **Martin Buchan** (Manchester U), **Peter Ward** (Brighton & HA), **Danny McGrain** (Celtic), **Jack Taylor** (F.I.F.A. Referee), **Laurie Cunningham** (W.B.A.).

1978 **Kenny Dalglish** (Liverpool), **Bob Latchford** (Everton), **John McGovern** (Nottingham F), **Bobby Robson** (Ipswich T, Manager), **John Greig** (Rangers), **Billericay Town F.C.**.

1979 **Liam Brady** (Arsenal), **Ray Clemence** (Liverpool), **Brian Clough** (Manager, Nottingham F), **Ross Jenkins** (Watford), **Danny McGrain** (Celtic), **John Toshack** (Player/Manager, Swansea C).
1980 **Bobby Clark** (Aberdeen), **Harlow Town F.C.**, **Huddersfield Town F.C.**, **David Johnson** (Liverpool), **John Robertson** (Nottingham F), **Dave Watson** (Southampton).
1981 **John Bond** (Manager, Manchester C), **Enfield F.C.**, **Tony Kellow** (Exeter C), **Jim Mclean** (Manager, Dundee U), **Mick Mills** (Ipswich T), **Bryan Robson** (W.B.A.).
1982 **Keith Burkenshaw** (Manager, Tottenham H), **Billy McNeill** (Manager, Celtic), **Corinthian Casuals F.C.**, **Aston Villa F.C.**, **Keith Edwards** (Sheffield U), **Graeme Souness** (Liverpool).

Rothmans Football Awards 1983

ABERDEEN FOOTBALL CLUB. To win a European trophy deserves recognition in itself, but to win the European Cup-Winners' Cup with such style, backed by an administrative department known to be second to none and supporters whose good behaviour made them the pride of Scotland, adds up to a superb all-round club performance. One impressive novelty to be admired in Alec Ferguson's side is the way he and his staff have harnessed the natural Scottish aggression and talent to disciplined teamwork. But all aspects of the club are thought out, even the inside of the roofs covering the all-seater stadium have been painted in light colours to give the impression of cheerfulness. Yes, the sun shines all the time at Pittodrie these days, and where is it more deserved?
DEREK DOUGAN. The name of Wolverhampton Wanderers was only a minute away from being taken off The Football League's membership list last summer. In stepped Derek Dougan, an ex-Wolves player, who in his time had upset a few people in the game with his articulate outspokenness. This time he put money and action where his mouth was and has followed through to lead his beloved Wolves back to the First Division through his own brand of leadership by example and shrewd selection of club staff. Last season saw Wolves provide the League with one of it's special fairy stories and other struggling clubs with the inspiration to get their house in order.
CHARLIE NICHOLAS. The amazing flow of exciting football talent that finds its way out of Scotland and into the Football League must be resented by those who watch the game North of the border. He has followed his idol, Kenny Dalglish, into the Celtic and Scotland sides and now he will be competing against him for Arsenal in the First Division. Charlie may take time to settle in strange surroundings, but anyone capable of scoring the type of goal he registered as his first for Scotland, on his debut against Switzerland, must be a success at any level of football.
SHREWSBURY TOWN. At a time when most small town clubs are pleading poverty and complaining about the recession, little Shrewsbury Town Football Club not only held their own in Division Two but hovered on the fringe of the promotion race and finally finished in their best ever position in the Football League. Graham Turner has enjoyed his 'giant killing' feats with 'The Town' during the last few seasons but last season, through a sensible wage structure, wise manipulation of the transfer market and a sound youth policy he and the directors of the club proved the perfect example to the rest of football. Successful, happy, 'little' clubs can still enjoy their role in the Football League, if their housekeeping is orderly and the right characters are at the helm.
GRAHAM TAYLOR. Another perfect example of 'team work' off the field and on it, has seen Watford leap from the Fourth Division to runners-up position in Division One. A storybook rise, but one that is hardly surprising when you see the quality of the men looking after their Chairman's generous backing. Eddie Plumley, their Chief Executive, adviser Bertie Mee and the man who is responsible for achieving the necessary results to reward all the back room hard work, Graham Taylor. The club's popular team manager is a very intelligent, articulate and sensible personality who gives the image of football managers a much appreciated boost every time he is quoted or interviewed.
TOMMY TYNAN (Newport County). Following Tony Kellow and Keith Edwards, another experienced professional who has never played in the First Division, Tommy Tynan of Newport County, scored more goals than anyone else and has been chosen to win an Award. He has always given value for money with an all-action style that has brought him goals for Swansea (loan), Sheffield Wednesday, Lincoln City and Newport County. Having had the disappointment of not making the grade at his home town club of Liverpool, his success last season in a very good Newport side and this award may well inspire him to help in a promotion run in the coming season.

MILESTONES DIARY 1982–83

Derek Dougan by Rod McLeod

August 1982

1 Arsenal leave for a pre-season tournament in West Germany and reveal that **Pat Jennings** and **Graham Rix** had been granted weekly contracts.

2 **Brian Winston**, Orient chairman, resigns. **Neville Ovendon** – a former Director is reappointed to the board. Notts County's proposal to play West Ham United on Sunday, December 19th is voted down by the Hammers' players. **Gordon Milne** appointed manager of Leicester City and warns of the drastic pruning that will be necessary because the club is overstaffed. **Ian Greaves** states he will probably have to apply for his own job as manager of Wolves now that a company headed by **Derek Dougan** has taken over. **Dougan** announces plans to make Molyneux a multi-faction sports complex and appoints a former Aston Villa commercial manager – **Eric Woodward** – as general manager. Aldershot 1 Manchester United 3 is the result of a friendly to raise money for the South Atlantic fund. **Billy Steel**, 30 Scottish Caps and once the costliest player in Britain, dies in the USA at the age of 59.

3 **Colin Todd** agrees to leave Birmingham City and join Nottingham Forest. **Peter Barnes** agrees a one year contract with Spanish First Division club Real Betis. Leeds United will receive £110,000 plus further £170,000 should Real keep him for a further two years. **Jim Bailey** leaves Middlesbrough for Sheffield Wednesday in a £100,000 deal – substantially less than Boro's original valuation. **Malcolm Allison** who led Sporting Lisbon to a League and Cup double in his first season with them is suspended by the club. After a meeting with **Derek Dougan**, **Ian Greaves** leaves Wolves. Home Office denies blocking or delaying **Ricky Villa**'s return to White Hart Lane after he had spent the summer in his native Argentina.

4 Former defender **Graham Hawkins** (36) succeeds Ian Greaves as Manager at Wolves. **Jack Taylor** – former world cup referee – loses his post as commercial manager.

6 Liverpool and Shrewsbury Town swap goalkeepers **Steve Ogrizovic** and **Bob Wardle**. Yugoslav FA block move of **Vladimir Petrovic** from Red Star to Arsenal. **Peter Barnes** opts to remain with Leeds United and turns down the move to Real Betis.

7 Manchester United and Glasgow Rangers are reported to be well advanced with plans for a pools amalgamation. Rangeman Promotions Ltd set up to organise fund raising on a national basis. Another 'U' turn from **Peter Barnes** who decided to join Real Betis after all. Nottingham Forest lose 1-3 in Spain to Atletico Bilbao in a 'friendly' and have **Fashanu** and **Robertson** sent off.

8 Sporting Lisbon announce the dropping of all disciplinary proceedings against **Malcolm Allison**. Ipswich Town protest to Colchester United over their signing of **Kevin Beattie** as player-coach. Ipswich Town had previously paid up his contract and staged a testimonial for him when he retired from the game because of a knee injury. **Gary Mabbutt** – £150,000 signing from Bristol Rovers – scores the only goal, after 60 seconds, for Spurs in a challenge match with Scottish League Cup winners Rangers at Ibrox. European XI 3 Rest of the World XI 2 in a FIFA all star match in the Giants Stadium, New Jersey.

9 Arsenal Manager, **Terry Neill**, discusses **Petrovic** transfer impasse with the Yugoslavian Ambassador but FA President **Thomas Thomasovic** is adamant that the player will not be allowed to move until January. **David Johnson** agrees to re-join his original club – Everton.

11 **David Hodgson** (22) joins Liverpool from Middlesbrough. Stoke City Manager **Richie Barker** bans **Chapman**, **Dodd** and **McManus** who have all refused new contracts and

are training with Port Vale. Keeper **Jim Blyth** moves from Coventry City to Birmingham City on a free transfer. Sixteen-year-old **Andy**, younger son of **Jimmy Greaves**, signs apprentice forms for Southend United where he joins older brother **Danny** (19). FA announce a new system and code of disciplinary points. League tribunal decide that Manchester City must pay West Ham United £135,000 for **David Cross**. City's original offer had been £150,000 against the Hammers' valuation of £300,000. League tribunal fix a fee of £150,000 on the move of **Trevor Aylott** from Barnsley to Millwall. Barnsley valuation had been £400,000. Should Millwall receive more than the set fee for the player within the next 3 years half the excess is payable to Barnsley. **Peter Borota** signs a one-month contract with Brentford.

12 Another one for the tribunal to decide, as Arsenal sign Stoke City's unsettled striker **Lee Chapman** but refuse to accept Stoke's valuation of £600,000. **Brian Bason** leaves Crystal Palace to join Reading on a free transfer. FA Commission decide that WBA and Leeds United were not to blame for the crowd disturbances in their match at the Hawthorns last season, but nevertheless, Leeds must print warning notices in their programmes in the coming season. California dance instructor, **Karen Thomas**, recruited by Southend United to put their squad through additional fitness routines.

13 Announced that Orient relegated from the Second Division last season – have secured substantial sponsorship for the forthcoming season from brewers Taylor-Walker. Stoke City keeper, **Eric McManus** turns down a 3 month loan to Bradford City.

14 New punishments for 'professional' fouls immediately a controversial topic for debate. Reading beat Oxford United 2-1 in the league trophy but, after losing **Doherty** with a suspected broken nose, substitute **Lawrie Sanchez** is quickly sent off for finger tipping a shot around the post. Trophy gates are about 25% down on the corresponding matches for last season (Group Cup). Wigan Athletic draw 1-1 with the touring national China team. In the Scottish League Cup Rangers draw 1-1 away with Hibs and Celtic hit 6 without reply at home to Dunfermline.

16 **Brian Clough** denies speculation that he is interested in **Pat Jennings** following **Peter Shilton**'s move to Southampton and expresses his confidence in youngster **Steve Sutton**. **Ron Atkinson** reported as being unable to meet the terms required by **Kevin Keegan**. Wolves' Secretary, **Phil Shaw**, is the latest to part company with the club in the shake-out at Molyneux. Director of Public Prosecutions is considering a Fraud Squad report on the finances involved in Aston Villa's new office buildings. Blackburn Rovers report the worst financial year in the history of the club after losing over £¼ last season.

17 Swansea City beat Sporting Braga (Portugal) 3-0 in their 1st leg preliminary round Cup Winners' Cup tie at Vetch Field. **Ricky Villa**'s visa problems resolved and he returns to training with Spurs. Luton Town announce a 4 year sponsorship deal with Bedford Trucks who have already provided a purpose built team coach which incorporates a treatment bench.

18 Aberdeen chalk up a 7-0 win against Sion (Switzerland) in their 1st leg Preliminary Round Cup Winners' Cup tie. Newcastle United emerge as likely favourites to sign **Kevin Keegan**. Norwich City's striker **Ross Jack** hits a second half hat trick in 20 minutes to help turn a half-time 1-2 deficit into a resounding 6-2 win over Peterborough United in the League Trophy. Newport County hit 5 goals against Exeter City and Reading 4 in their match with AFC Bournemouth.

19 **Kevin Keegan** duly signs for Newcastle United. **Keith Burkinshaw** states categorically that **Ricky Villa** stays with Spurs as **Steve Foster** and **Mike Robinson** of Brighton submit transfer requests.

20 **Mark Aizleworth** signs a new contract with Luton Town on settlement of their pay dispute. Chelsea agree terms with **Tony McAndrew** of Middlesbrough but ask the league tribunal to set a provisional fee.

21 Injury hit Spurs beaten 1-0 at Wembley by Liverpool in a lack-lustre Charity Shield match. First Division Watford and Norwich City both win comfortably to lead their Sections in the League Trophy.

22 The unconventional **Peter Borota** departs to join Benfica after a month at Brentford.

23 Relief at injury-ridden White Hart Lane with the news that **Graham Roberts** is suffering ligament strain and will not require a cartilage operation as had been feared. Stoke City agree to sign **Micky Thomas** from Brighton. Striker **Alan Biley** of Everton rejects terms offered by Middlesbrough and is set to join Portsmouth. Football League reveal that 282 players released on free transfers at the end of last season have not yet found new clubs. Despite his previously stated confidence in keeper **Steve Sutton**, **Brian Clough** is reported to be interested in Dutch keeper **Hans Van Breukelen** of Utrecht.

24 **Bob Paisley** announces that he will retire from his manager's post at Liverpool next May. Chairman **John Smith** adds that **Bob** will continue with the club in another capacity. After 11 years **Sit Matt Busby** resigns his directorship at Old Trafford for 'personal reasons'.

25 League Tribunal set a fee of £500,000 on Stoke City's **Lee Chapman** – double Arsenal's original offer.

26 FA after much deliberation by a special commission announce that no action is to be taken against **Jimmy Hill** in respect of the abortive South African tour. **Hans Van Breukelen** joins Nottingham Forest. European Truck Manufacturers IVECO who sponsor Bayern Munich and Avellino in Italy are to provide £400,000 of sponsorship over 3 years to Watford. Aldershot reveal that they have taken out insurance to cover the costs of bonuses payable to their players should they gain promotion at the end of the season. **Justin Fashanu** is signed by Southampton on a month's loan.

28 League programme opens with Liverpool beating WBA 2-0 and Manchester United 3-0 winners over Birmingham City. **Kevin Keegan** hits the only goal of the match on his debut for Newcastle United against QPR. Newly-promoted Luton Town hold Spurs at White Hart Lane and Watford beat Everton 2-0 in their first-ever Division 1 match.

28 Thirty-seven goals were scored in Division 3 with Brentford leading the list as they hit 5 against Bristol Rovers.

30 Aston Villa's pay rebellion ends as all the players bar one accept the new package deal on bonuses. Arsenal will not be taking disciplinary action against **Lee Chapman** booked in the 4th minute of his debut game against former club Stoke City.

31 Speculation arises that Newcastle United are negotiating to sign **Mick Channon** to team up with **Kevin Keegan** at St James's. Grimsby Town and Leeds United are at loggerheads over Leeds' share of previous Saturday's gate after Elland Road supporters had caused £6,000 of damage at the Grimsby ground. It is announced that officials are to meet in London in an attempt to smooth out disputes at Lincoln City and Southend United arising from proposals to cut bonuses now that the issue has reached a stage where players have threatened strike action. In Division 1, Birmingham City hold champions Liverpool to a goal-less draw whilst newcomers Watford run out 4-1 winners at the Dell. Spurs win 2-1 at Ipswich and Everton take the scoring honours with 5-0 trouncing of Villa. Eight goals are scored in the Milk Cup match at Bury where Burnley win 5-3.

September 1982

1 Leeds United chairman, **Manny Cussins**, spells out the dire financial plight of the club and stresses that any heavy fines in ground closure imposed for hooliganism might necessitate the calling in the receiver. Fee which Chelsea must pay Middlesbrough for **Tony McAndrew** is assessed by the League Tribunal at £92,500 against Boro's valuation of £300,000. FIFA announce that they will await the FA report before deciding on any possible action in respect of players involved in the South African tour. Manchester United win 3-0 at Nottingham Forest with all the goals coming after the sending off of **Colin Todd** for deliberate handling. WBA beat Brighton 5-0. In Division 2 **Keegan** scores again in Newcastle United's away 2-1 win at Blackburn Rovers.

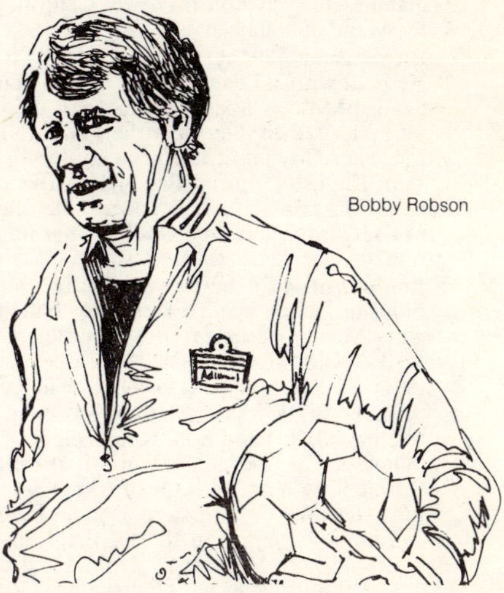

Bobby Robson

2 **Brian Clough** states that Forest need help in order to pay the £300,000 fee to buy **Gary Birtles** whom they sold to Manchester United for £¼ million a couple of years ago. FIFA are to seek a number of assurances from Colombia in the proposed hosting of the 1986 World Cup.

3 Football League order Sheffield United, Lincoln City, Southend United, Chester,

Wrexham and Hartlepool United (all in dispute with their players) to honour existing match bonus agreements. League rejected suggestions that the tribunal is depressing transfer fees as a matter of policy.

4 In a full League programme 8 players were sent off bringing the season's total already to 15. Manchester City maintain their 100% record with a 1-0 win over hitherto unbeaten Watford. Full back **Bobby McDonald** took over in goal after 3 minutes when **Joe Corrigan** dislocated a shoulder. Liverpool win 2-0 at Highbury. First Division hat-tricks by **Latchford** (Swansea City) and **Walsh** (Luton Town). **Kevin Keegan** nets a penalty but Newcastle United lose 1-3 at Bolton Wanderers. Sheffield Wednesday head the Second Division after winning 3-0 at Charlton Athletic. **Billy Bonds** equals **Bobby Moore**'s 544 League appearances for West Ham United as they lose 1-0 at Sunderland. Gates are down almost 44,000 on corresponding games for last season.

6 **David Harvey** returns to Leeds United after 3 seasons with Vancouver Whitecaps.

7 Brighton and Hove Albion gain first win of the season as they beat Arsenal 1-0; 'The Gunners' have still to win after 4 games. Watford contrive to impress with a 2-1 win over Swansea City. Liverpool came back from a half time 2-3 deficit to beat Forest 4-3. Wolves maintain their unbeaten run with a 5-0 win over Charlton Athletic. League leaders Manchester City lose their 100% record 0-1 against Notts County.

8 Spurs lose **Glen Hoddle** with a knee injury as they slam Southampton 6-0. Aston Villa move off the bottom of the table with a 4-1 win over Luton Town. **Mick Channon** scores on his debut for Newcastle United in the 1-1 draw at Middlesbrough. **Mick Mills** delays a decision about joining Leicester City to consider other offers.

9 Reports suggest that **John Bond** would like **Mick Mills** at Maine Road but Leicester City, Southampton and Watford are all also believed to be interested.

10 Doncaster Rovers achieve their biggest victory in 13 years by beating Exeter City 6-1. **John Robertson** and **Fashanu** (now on loan to Southampton) get 2 match suspensions for their pre-season dismissals in Spain, but **Willie Young**'s sending off is to be the subject of further enquiries.

11 Watford head the First Division after a 3-0 victory over WBA. Luton Town hold Liverpool 3-3 at Anfield using three different goalkeepers in the game. Port Vale score their first League goals of the season in a 2-0 win at Mansfield. Unsettled **Mike Robinson** (Brighton and Hove Albion) talks over a possible move to Sunderland with **Alan Durban**. Darlington head the 4th Division after their 3rd League win. Birmingham City lose 5-0 at Upton Park and have now conceded 14 goals in their last three matches.12 Plymouth Argyle Chairman – **Stuart Dawe** – warns that the club is on the verge of collapse.

13 Birmingham City agree a fee of £35,000 for Aston Villa reserve defender **Noel Blake**. Arsenal with 1 League point from 4 games leave for their UEFA Cup 1st leg match against Moscow Spartak. Swansea City are banned from further signings in the transfer market until they clear their debt to Everton in respect of the **Gary Stanley** move. Leicester City and Coventry City set up an exchange deal involving **Jim Melrose** and **Tom English**. Injured **Bruno Conti** is expected to miss both legs of Romas UEFA Cup tie against Ipswich Town. Leicester City withdraw from negotiations for **Mick Mills**. Cardiff City sign **Godfrey Ingram** from San Jose Earthquakes for a club record of £200,000.

14 **Bobby Robson** names 19 players in his first England squad for the European Championship match against Denmark. Notable omissions are **Mick Mills** and **Kevin Keegan**. Arsenal (2 up after 30 minutes) concede a last minute goal to lose 3-2 in the UEFA Cup against Spartak. Three more sendings off in the seven Milk Cup ties played. Exeter City again concede six goals as they lose to Newport County.

15 A night of European action. Swansea City hit twelve goals without reply against Sliema (Malta) and no less than eight of their players get on the score sheet in a Cup Winners' Cup tie. Spurs win 3-0 in Ireland against Coleraine. In the European Cup Aston Villa beat Besiktas (Turkey) 3-1 in an empty Villa Park – punishment for the misbehaviour of their supporters in Belgium last season. Celtic are held at home to a 2-2 draw by Ajax. In the UEFA Cup Ipswich Town go under 3-0 to Roma whilst Southampton, Manchester United and Dundee United all draw at home. Rangers get a goal-less draw away to Dortmund. Cardiff City, Lincoln City, Oxford United, Peterborough United and Bristol Rovers all go through to the 2nd round in the Milk Cup. FA to pay £750 compensation to League clubs for each player selected for England International squads. New signing **Godfrey Ingram** withdrawn from Cardiff City's side at Hereford United following objection by Luton Town who claim they are still owed much of the £80,000 for which they sold the player to San Jose last March.

16 **Eric Gates** requests a tranfer at Ipswich Town who are still seeking their first League win of the season.

17 Former Middlesbrough striker **Billy Woof** on a month's trial at Cardiff City walked out on the club after being left out of the side in a midweek game at Hereford.

18 **Malcolm Poskett** scores all Carlisle United's goals in their 4-1 defeat of Crystal Palace. **Brian Stein** hits a hat-trick in Luton Town's 5-0 thrashing of Brighton and Hove Albion. **Kevin Lock** took over when Fulham keeper, **Gerry Peyton**, sustained a serious head injury after just 2 minutes play at Middlesbrough. Fulham won 4-1. Four more sendings-off bring the season's tally to 34. Ipswich Town lose yet again (2-3 at home to Stoke City). A spectator in clown's outfit who rushed onto the pitch at Nottingham Forest's home game was collared and bundled off by **Brian Clough**. Change of fortune for Birmingham City who notched their first win (1-0 against Coventry City). Nottingham Forest announce a loss of £319,000 for the year ending 31st May. They also owe £1 million on their stand and have an overdraft of £800,000. Manchester United win 1-0 at the Dell to lead the First Division – a point clear of Liverpool who win 3-0 at Swansea. Wolves retain top spot in Division 2 with a win at Bolton.

19 Scottish FA Secretary **Ernie Walker** declares that Scotland will not follow the English FA in paying clubs compensation for every player released for international matches. Northampton Town thrash Bristol City 7-1. In contrast the only other Sunday game was the score-less draw between Scunthorpe United and York City. League secretary, **Graham Kelly**, refuses to comment on the problem of falling attendances after Saturday's total of 390,451 is revealed as the lowest for any full programme in September since the war and was 71,000 down on the corresponding day of last season. The only gate to top 25,000 was at Maine Road.

20 Liverpool Chairman **John Smith** calls for a 'Super League' and agrees with the idea supported by Arsenal and Spurs that the Premier Division should only contain sixteen clubs.

21 England complete a remarkable Under-21 double. Last year's team winning the home leg of the 1980–82 Final, 3-1 against West Germany and this season's youngsters start the new European Championship with a 4-1 victory in Denmark.

22 Denmark, playing brilliantly, equalise late to draw at home to England 2-2, but **Peter Shilton** had previously kept England in the game. Wales beat Norway with a goal from **Ian Rush** but Eire lose away to Holland 1-2. Luton Town announce plan to move into a £7 million sports complex near the M1 on the Luton/Dunstable border. **Frank Lord** becomes the season's first casualty among managers as Hereford United relieve him of his duties. The disgraceful behaviour of English supporters in Copenhagen may persuade UEFA to ban English fans from travelling to away matches.

24 Middlesbrough secretary for the last 21 years (**T. H. C. Green**) is to retire because of ill health. **Alan Brazil** signs a new contract for Ipswich Town which adds two years to his existing three-year contract.

25 The First Division programme produced 50 goals with Watford registering a staggering 8-0 victory over Sunderland. **Luther Blissett** scored four in this win but Reading's **Kerry Dixon**, who also scored four, finished on the losing side at Doncaster where the score was 7-5. An overall League total of 151 goals with hat-tricks plentiful and 8 'professional' fouls being strictly punished by dismissals makes one wonder if defenders can really defend successfully without cheating. Certainly the entertainment is improving every week and attendances are rising as a result.

27 FA Secretary, **Ted Croker**, calls for a new law for the Government to make it illegal for travel agents to organise unofficial trips for fans to follow England abroad. Fulham have given the go-ahead for the installation of a £250,000 'Cellsystem' pitch of synthetic natural grass for next season.

28 Liverpool eliminate Dundalk 5-1 on aggregate in the European Cup and Spurs beat Coleraine 7-0 over two games in the Cup Winners' Cup. **Terry McDermott** returns to Newcastle United for a £100,000 fee.

29 A disastrous night for English clubs in European competitons. Manchester United fans bring more discredit to England as their team loses 1-2 to Valencia and Arsenal are given an incredible thrashing (2-5) at home by Moscow Spartak. However, Celtic, Dundee United, Rangers, Aberdeen and Swansea City cheered Scottish and Welsh fans while holders Aston Villa drew 0-0 to knock out Greek champions Besiktas with an aggregate of 3-1. Colchester striker **Kevin Bremner** goes to Birmingham City on trial. Middlesbrough manager **Bobby Murdoch** resigns.

30 Chelsea financial director **Martin Spencer** announces that the club lost £531, 225 but now under the guidance of new Chairman, **Ken Bates**, he felt that the crisis had

passed. **Mick Channon**'s spell at Newcastle comes to an end after only four games. Everton's **Mike Walsh** joins Norwich City on loan.

First Division

		pts
Liverpool	7	17
Manchester U	7	16
Watford	7	15
Norwich C	7	6
Southampton	7	4
Birmingham C	7	4

Second Division

		pts
Grimsby T	7	19
Wolves	7	17
Sheffield W	7	15
Cambridge U	8	4
Derby Co	6	4
Middlesbrough	7	2

Third Division

		pts
Lincoln C	7	18
Oxford U	7	16
Cardiff C	7	15
Doncaster R	7	7
Exeter C	7	6
Walsall	7	5
Reading	7	5

Fourth Division

		pts
Bury	8	15
Colchester U	7	15
Torquay U	7	14
Wimbledon	7	13
Rochdale	7	5
Tranmere R	7	5
Bristol C	7	5
Hereford U	7	1

Scottish Premier

		pts
Celtic	4	8
Rangers	4	6
Dundee U	4	6
Hibernian	4	3
Kilmarnock	4	3
Motherwell	4	1

October

1 **Ossie Ardiles**' club Paris St Germain are drawn against Swansea City in the European Cup Winners' Cup. Aston Villa have been guaranteed £90,000 by Toyota, the sponsors of the World Club Championship match against the South American champions.

2 **Kevin Keegan** scores four goals for Newcastle United at Rotherham and repeats that he is not available for England as he was so disappointed at **Bobby Robson** failing to let him know that he had been dropped. **Kerry Dixon** scores two more goals for Reading but the club attract their smallest ever League attendance of 1,713. Seven more sending-offs brings the total to 55 against 20 at the same time last season.

Kevin Keegan

4 Scotland regulars **Kenny Dalglish**, **Danny McGrain**, **Joe Jordan**, **Alan Rough** and **Asa Hartford** are dropped from the squad to face West Germany. **Mark Chamberlain**, Stoke City's exciting coloured winger has made the impressive rise from Fourth Division football with Port Vale last season to the full England squad in just eight games. In fact four young players in the squad, **Mark**, **John Barnes**, **Luther Blissett** and **Gary Mabbutt** have only played 35 First Division games between them.

5 Reading Football Club is put up for sale and an ex-player **Roger Smee**, now a successful businessman, is the favourite to take over. Canada could be challenging Brazil and the United States as the next hosts for the World Cup.

6 **Allan Simonsen** seems to be set to join Charlton Athletic for £300,000. AFC Bournemouth's coach **Harry Redknapp**, recalled to played at Manchester United in the Milk Cup because of the club's injury problems, after four and a half years' retirement, scores in his own goal within twenty-eight minutes! Nottingham Forest score six in the Milk Cup against WBA, Notts County win 2-1 at Aston Villa and Brighton and Hove Albion draw at Tottenham through a **Ray Clemence** 'own goal'.

7 Barcelona keep Charlton Athletic waiting on the **Simonsen** deal.

8 Due to inflated transfer fees Manchester United announce a loss of £2,282,007 but Charlton Athletic get their man and pay out a quarter of a million for **Simonsen** who gets £82,000 a season for two years. Rock star **Ian Gillan**, a keen amateur footballer,

hopes to buy Reading but Chairman **Waller** doesn't give the impression that he wants to deal with him or **Roger Smee**.

10 After an entertaining and sporting game at Upton Park, **Bob Paisley** joked that the 1-3 defeat and fifth position in the league didn't worry him, perhaps they should move us down to twelve and we'll start again' . . . many a true word . . .!! The Minister of Sport calls for a 'who's who of hooliganism' in a desperate bid to get grips with the problem. Manchester United Chairman, **Martin Edwards**, says he is unhappy about the £1,350 fine for the trouble caused by United's fans in Valencia, but he would not be appealing.

11 Ipswich Town directors have reluctantly agreed to striker **Eric Gates**'s transfer request.

12 England win the UEFA Under-21 European Championship by beating West Germany 3-2 in Bremen; a total aggregate of 5-4 enabled **Sammy Lee** to collect the trophy, the first won by England at this level. Scotland Under-21 beat East Germany 2-0 at Tynecastle.

13 England lose to West Germany 1-2 but Scotland balance matters with a 2-0 win over East Germany.

14 **Mick Mills** has refuted any suggestions that he might take on the job as Derby County manager.

15 Derby County appear to be ready for a take over. Referees are completely baffled by the FA's decision no longer to regard deliberate hand ball as a sending-off offence. The **Simonsen** saga goes on as Barcelona block the transfer until they have received a banker's guarantee for £100,000.

16 Liverpool and Manchester United draw 0-0 and goals are scarce compared with previous weeks. Two Wigan Athletic players were sent off at Bristol Rovers where Graham Withey, a signing from Alliance League Bath City, scored with his first touch, as substitute, and added another in a 4-0 win. Allan Simonsen has been 'seen' by the Charlton Athletic fans but he won't make his debut until next Saturday.

17 Bristol Rovers sign **Mick Channon** on a year's contract paid for by a Director's firm.

18 **Sir Norman Chester** is appointed by The Football League to make another report on the state of the game. **Peter Ward** may return to Brighton and Hove Albion where he enjoyed his most successful days.

19 It is announced that England will have to play their international against Greece in Salonika as the Greek FA do not want English supporters in their National Olympic stadium. HJK Helsinki beat Liverpool 1-0 with an ex-Harlow and Charlton Athletic goalkeeper **Wood** starring as he keeps a clean sheet against the English champions. **Peter Ward** returns to Brighton and Hove Albion on loan from Nottingham Forest.

20 Aston Villa get a good 2-0 victory in Rumania against Dinamo Bucharest and Aberdeen beat Poland's Lech Poznan 2-0 at home. Rangers and Dundee United also win but Spurs only draw at home to Bayern Munich and Swansea City lose at home to Paris St Germain. Celtic also lose 0-2 away to Real Sociadad. A mixed day for Britain! Liverpool put **Craig Johnston** on the transfer list.

21 Pop star **Ian Gillan**'s take over bid at Reading seems to be fading out. Ipswich Town made a loss of £173,395 last year. Plymouth Argyle Chairman **Robert Daniel**, 48, has resigned through ill health. Bristol City have slumped from the top six in the First Division to bottom of the Fourth Division in three years. Charlton Athletic are given a final demand by Barcelona in connection with the long drawn out **Simonsen** transfer saga.

22 The Greek FA switch their International against England back to Athens. Charlton Athletic directors are fuming over the **Simonsen** affair; he still has not signed for the club.

23 **Malcolm Allison** is back. He takes over at Middlesbrough and with new chairman, **Mike McCullagh**, gives Ayrsome Park an exciting and fresh atmosphere after a disappointing start to the season. Another chairman takes over at Derby, where millionaire snooker promoter **Mike Watterson** faces up to a difficult job of reviving County's fortunes. Plenty of goals are scored again in the League programme, but nine more players are sent off, including **Paul Mariner**. The day's biggest crowd (57,334 at Old Trafford) watched the 105th Manchester 'Derby', where two **Frank Stapleton** goals pegged back City after the visitors had taken a surprise two goal lead.

25 Notts County team manager, **Howard Wilkinson**, is favourite to be offered a full time position as manager to England's Under-21 squad.

26 Corinthians celebrate their 100th birthday. Columbia officially give up their chance of holding the next World Cup finals. On a night when most of the big clubs ease through

another round of the Milk Cup, England and Manchester United skipper **Ray Wilkins** breaks a cheek bone and will be out of the game for about six weeks.

27 Two stories that seem to have been with us all season continue to feature on the sports pages – **Allan Simonsen** still has not become a Charlton Athletic player despite constant bargaining by Chairman **Mark Hulyer**. It now looks as if Barcelona may call the whole deal off. The future of Reading appears to be most likely in the hands of ex-player **Roger Smee** who has moved ahead of pop star **Ian Gillan** in the running. However, does Chairman **Waller** really want to sell? England's European Championship match in Greece has had its venue changed yet again – it will now be played in Salonika! Poor **Trevor Brooking**, who has suffered so much from injury, is to have a groin operation. **Max Briggs**, Oxford United's defender, was sent off for the second time in four days. WBA's lowest attendance for 25 years (6,536) watch Albion play Nottingham Forest in the Milk Cup.

28 **Mick Mills** is 'linked' with Chelsea; and **Archie Gemmill** is expected back to help in the 'Derby revival'. Football League President, **Jack Dunnett**, has spoken out against the idea of reducing the number of clubs in the First Division.

29 **Justin Fashanu** finishes his loan spell at Southampton to be welcomed back into the Forest third team! **Alan Ball** announces he is definitely retiring as a player in the Football League and **Allan Simonsen** still doesn't know whether he will become a Charlton Athletic player.

30 **Kevin Keegan** is hit by a coin while playing for Newcastle United at Leeds. **Alan Ball** plays his last game for Southampton. **Ashley Grimes** is sent off for pulling the referee round by the shoulder during Manchester United's game at West Ham.

31

First Division		*pts*	**Second Division**		*pts*
Liverpool	12	22	Sheffield W	12	26
West Ham U	12	22	QPR	13	26
Manchester U	12	22	Fulham	12	24
Sunderland	12	13	Bolton W	12	8
Norwich C	12	11	Derby Co	12	8
Birmingham C	12	8	Cambridge U	12	7

Third Division		*pts*	**Fourth Division**		*pts*	**Scottish Premier**		*pts*
Lincoln C	13	30	Bury	14	29	Celtic	9	15
Bristol R	13	26	Wimbledon	13	28	Dundee U	9	14
Newport Co	13	25	Port Vale	13	27	Aberdeen	9	12
			Scunthorpe U	13	26			
Reading	13	12				Hibernian	9	6
Walsall	13	11	Halifax T	13	11	Motherwell	9	5
Orient	13	11	Hereford U	13	11	Kilmarnock	9	4
Doncaster R	13	10	Bristol C	13	11			
			Crewe Alex	13	10			

November

1 **Jock Stein** announces that he will probably stand down as Scotland's manager in two years' time. Ipswich Town, already annoyed by **Kevin Beattie**'s comeback with Colchester United, having paid up his contract and given him a testimonial, feel that if he is now fit enough to join Middlesbrough he should be worth £100,000 to them. **Mick Mills** talks to a consortium of businessmen at Reading with a view to joining the Third Division club.

Ian Rush

2 Two wealthy businessmen take over struggling clubs. **Neville Ovenden** returns to the Orient board but retains chairman of ten weeks, **Adrian Harding**, and former Chairman, **Brian Winston**, and snooker promoter **Mike Watterson** warns there may be unpopular decisions to come at Derby County.

Trevor Brooking goes into hospital for a groin operation. Police officers in South Yorkshire have been instructed to arrest players whose behaviour on the pitch could inflame crowd troubles. It was suggested that arrests should be made at the end of the game rather than on the field of play! Liverpool cruise to a 5-1 aggregate European Cup victory over HJK Helsinki.

3 **Graham Taylor** is appointed as Manager in charge of the England Youth team with Notts County's **Howard Wilkinson** taking over from **Dave Sexton** and **Terry Venables** with the Under-21 side. **Dario Gradi** is appointed as Youth development officer at Orient. Aston Villa, Aberdeen and Dundee United make European progress but Celtic, Rangers, Tottenham Hotspur, Swansea City and Shamrock Rovers are all eliminated. The FA announce that no tickets for England's away match in Greece will be sold in this country.

4 Brentford declare a £240,000 loss for the last financial year. **Ashley Grimes**, sent off while playing for Manchester United at West Ham last Saturday, is to be charged with bringing the game into disrepute.

5 Success story at Oxford United! A profit of £101,542 is announced for the year ending 30 June after nearly going into liquidation last January. The match account showed a £93,181 profit compared with a deficit of £67,671 the previous season. Attendances had jumped by 45% and gate receipts had risen by £113,647. Spurs Manager **Keith Burkinshaw**, disappointed with his club's heavy European Cup Winners' Cup defeat at the hands of Bayern Munich, considers that the size of our First Division and the exhausting competitive pressures put on our schoolboy stars, give our players very little chance to develop techniques to challenge the continentals.

6 RAOC soldier **Phil Stant** is 'called up' by Reading having just returned from service in the Falklands and scores in his side's 4-2 victory over Newport County. **David Webb**, AFC Bournemouth's player-manager, plays his first game for two years, his 553rd in the league, but takes himself off after 68 minutes as 'The Cherries' lose 0-1 at home to Huddersfield Town. Millwall chairman **Alan Thorne** suspends his manager, **Peter Anderson**, and **Terry Long**, the Assistant Manager, for 72 hours. The long running **Simonsen** saga seems to be coming to an end as Charlton Athletic announce that the former European Footballer of the Year will be playing for the Reserves on Wednesday. **Ian Rush** scores four in Liverpool's impressive 5-0 victory in the local 'Derby' at Goodison Park. These games are of course usually much closer fought affairs as the overall scoreline suggests: Liverpool 45 Everton 44 with 38 draws. Middlesbrough, obviously warming to **Malcolm Allison**'s presence, beat Barnsley in front of their largest gate of the season – 11,787. Bolton Wanderers on the other hand played in front of their lowest gate for 35 years – 4,879.

7 It is announced from Derby County that **John Newman** has been relieved of his Managerial duties and **Peter Taylor** is expected to return.

8 Millwall manager **Peter Anderson** is officially sacked. Sunderland manager **Alan Durban** is extremely upset, having set up a Press conference to welcome 'new signing' **Mick Mills** only to be told by England's World Cup captain that he had changed his

mind at the last moment and would be signing for Southampton. Coventry City's young full back, **Danny Thomas**, becomes the seventh black player to be called up by England's full International squad. **Sammy Lee** also gets the chance of a first 'cap'. **Peter Taylor** is officially re-instated as Manager of Derby County.

9 **Jimmy Dickinson** dies at the age of 57. At the time of his retirement as a player he held the record of 764 appearances for one club – his beloved Portsmouth. He then became the club's PRO, secretary, Manager and finally Pompey's Chief Executive. Jimmy also won 48 England caps and was one of the games most popular personalities. **Kenny Dalglish** returns to the Scotland squad for their European Championship match in Switzerland.

10 Nottingham Forest crash seven goals past Watford in a ten goal Milk Cup treat for the fans.

11 Tranmere Rovers, preparing for a close down on 27th November hear that a wealthy businessman based in America, **Billie McAteer**, has pledged his support. **Justin Fashanu** refuses a move to Derby County. The local council, much to manager **Graham Taylor**'s disappointment, has turned down a £2 million plan to turn the Vicarage Road ground into a 35,000 all seater de luxe stadium. Bradford City Manager **Roy McFarland** is awaiting permission from his Chairman to talk to Derby County about a possible move back to rejoin **Peter Taylor**.

12 Tranmere Chairman **Gerry Gould** announced that a deal to save the club had fallen through and it looked as if the club would have to be closed down at the end of the month. Colombia formally withdraw as hosts of the 1986 World Cup.

13 **Allan Simonsen** makes his long awaited debut for Charlton Athletic in front of 10,807. He scores but Middlesbrough win 3-2 at the Valley. With **Kevin Keegan** scoring two for Newcastle United, two ex-European Footballers of the Year played in Division 2. Watford's annual accounts show that their Chairman, **Elton John**, has provided the club with more than £1 million in interest free, unsecured loans. **Ian Rush** follows last week's four with a hat-trick at home to Coventry City. **Terry Venables** was reported to the FA by referee **John Deakin** after the QPR manager had run onto the field to protest against a controversial Blackburn Rovers goal. Lincoln City's **Marshall Burke** became the 100th player to be sent off this season and the total at the end of the day was 103. **Bobby Davison** scored Halifax Town's first hat-trick for nine years when he registered three away at Wimbledon.

14 An extremely angry **Brian Clough** bans **Justin Fashanu** because he won't go on loan to Derby County. **Fashanu** just wants to play his way back into the Forest side and is upset by the idea of going on loan to different clubs.

15 **Terry Butcher** pulls out of the England squad and is replaced by Manchester City's **Tommy Caton**. **Malcolm Allison** is quoted as saying that English football is all predictable and extremely boring. No players seem to have the technique or ability to do anything original. Britain's Professional Footballers give the thumbs down to the idea of a super league and secretary **Gordon Taylor** said that if necessary he would instruct his members to go for complete freedom of contract and therefore abolish the Transfer system, which would stop a breakaway. The players' invitation to League Referees and Linesmen's Secretary to speak about the new law interpretations proved a great success.

16 England Under-21 lose 0-1 in Greece but Scotland beat Switzerland 4-3 at Aarau in the same competition. Sutton United beat Leatherhead 11-1 in a Servowarm Isthmian League match and **Micky Joyce** scored 9 goals with his first five coming within twenty minutes of the start. Tranmere Rovers need to raise £66,000 immediately if they are to continue. Manchester United fail to secure Ipswich Town's unsettled striker **Alan Brazil**.

17 **Sammy Lee** wins his first England Cap and scores in an excellent 3-0 victory in Greece. **Tony Woodcock** scores the other two. Scotland lose 2-0 in Switzerland and Eire gain a thrilling 3-3 draw after trailing 1-3 at home to Spain. Northern Ireland take the honours, however, with a 1-0 victory over West Germany.

18 **Justin Fashanu** is ejected from the ground, having reported for training after **Brian Clough** had banned him from the club. Police were called to remove the young striker and his case is to be considered by the PFA. **Kevin Keegan** is said to be recovering well after sustaining an eye injury in **John Craggs**'s testimonial match. Rumours suggest that a shock take over of Tottenham Hotspur will take place at next month's annual meeting of shareholders.

19 Middlesbrough announce that they will be organising a Testimonial match for their two famous English Internationals of the 'fifties', **Wilf Mannion** and **George Hardwick**. **Justin Fashanu** reports for training after talks with the PFA. Chelsea Chairman

Ken Bates warns his players that, unless there is an improvement in their attitude and results, they will be replaced.

20 A record twelve players are dismissed during the FA Cup First Round ties and Altrincham, Boston United, Bishops Stortford, North Shields and Slough Town beat League opposition. Crowd trouble was inflamed by players fighting at Slough, and a wall collapsed at Wokingham where Cardiff City supporters like their counterparts from Millwall completely ruined their non-league opposition's big day.

21 Charlton Athletic manager, **John Craggs**, reports that his chairman has told him his job is safe for the time being.

22 **Gordon Taylor** calls upon his PFA members to follow a strict code of conduct and not exaggerate fouls, feign injury, show dissent or retaliate. In a week when the game's credibility is being severely tested, **Roy McFarland** and his coach **Mick Jones** resign just under 72 hours before Bradford City's Milk Cup replay with Manchester United, much to the consternation of City chairman **Bob Martin**, who feels his staff have been illegally approached by Derby County. And the FA feel that no good will come from punishing Leeds United for the misdemeanours of the well-organised bunch of thugs masquerading under the colours of the Yorkshire club. This leniency is not appreciated fully as the football public in general are desperately anxious for these hooligans to be hounded out of the game. **Ken Craggs** is sacked at Charlton Athletic to complete a horrific week as far as the game's image is concerned.

23 **Joe Gallagher**, Wolves' £450,000 signing from Birmingham City, is told he is no longer wanted by the club. **Ashley Grimes** is fined a record £750 and banned for two games following his man-handling of referee **Dennis Hedges** earlier in the month at West Ham. **Roy McFarland** and **Mick Jones** sign on for Derby County. Tranmere Rovers have been given an extended safety deadline of 16th December.

24 **Justin Fashanu** takes his case to the Football League and wins as there is insufficient evidence to support Nottingham Forest's ban. The public is completely confused by **Brian Clough**'s scathing remarks about a player for whom he paid a million pounds.

25 Tottenham Hotspur's accounts appear to show that £52,000 was missing and that one player earned between £95,000 and £100,000 during the year. Rumours of a board room coup grow stronger. Derby County are fined £10,000 for 'poaching' **Roy McFarland** and **Mick Jones** from Bradford City but Chairman **Mike Watterson** threatens to drag the case through every court in the country. **Justin Fashanu** turns down a move to Manchester City on loan.

26 Tottenham Hotspur's battle hots up as **Irving Scholar** bids to take over control from club chairman **Arthur Richardson**. European Champions, Aston Villa, could also be up for sale, as the **Bendall** family are prepared to sell the 45% of shares they own. **Trevor Francis**'s unflattering remarks about Italian marking methods upset the Italian football establishment. **John Hollins** is linked with the vacant Millwall job.

27 Scottish International goalkeeper, **Alan Rough**, leaves Partick Thistle for Hibernian. **Mike Bailey** despairs after Brighton and Hove Albion's pathetic showing at home against Notts County and brands the performance as 'an absolute disgrace'.

28 Referees promise not to ease up in their bid to discourage the game's cheats at a meeting in the presence of PFA Chairman, **Steve Coppell**. Total dismissals for the season now stand at 120.

League Positions on the last Saturday of the month are:

First Division		*pts*
Liverpool	16	34
Watford	16	30
Nottingham F	16	29
Birmingham C	16	16
Norwich C	16	14
Sunderland	16	14

Second Division		*pts*
QPR	17	34
Fulham	16	33
Sheffield W	16	30
Cambridge U	17	13
Bolton W	16	13
Derby Co	16	11

Third Division		*pts*
Lincoln C	16	36
Huddersfield T	17	32
Newport Co	17	31
Orient	17	15
Preston NE	17	14
Walsall	17	14
Doncaster R	17	12

Fourth Division		*pts*
Bury	18	38
Scunthorpe U	17	35
Swindon T	17	34
Hull C	17	32
Hereford U	17	15
Tranmere R	17	14
Bristol C	17	14
Crewe Alex	16	13

Scottish Premier		*pts*
Celtic	13	23
Dundee U	13	20
Aberdeen	13	19
Morton	13	8
Hibernian	13	7

29 **Kevin Keegan** resumes training after being out of action for two weeks with his eye injury. Leading Fulham goalscorer **Gordon Davies** is linked with Manchester United. Boardroom negotiations hot up at Spurs and Villa.

30 At the end of a damaging month in which the credibility and reputation of professional football can hardly ever have been dragged so low, matters can surely only get better!

December

Diego Maradona

1 **Doug Ellis** takes over as Chairman of Aston Villa for the third time. **Pat Jennings** has talks with **Ron Wylie** to discuss a possible move to WBA. The Irving Scholar take over group at Tottenham give **Keith Burkinshaw** a pledge of support and say there will be no Board interference. Sunderland sign the much-travelled **Frank Worthington** for £50,000. Stoke City consider bidding for **Alan Brazil**.

2 **Harry Parkes** withdraws his injunction against new Villa Chairman **Doug Ellis** who can now take control of the available shares. Spurs officially under new leadership as the old board of **Mr Arthur Richardson** steps down.
Brian Clough announces that a new deal for **Justin Fashanu** could soon be official and a move to neighbours County seems most likely.

3 Brazil declared 80% certain of taking Colombia's place as the next World Cup hosts. The FA are worried by the trend for Directors selling their shares in clubs for big profits.

4 Coventry City, Swansea City and Everton have their lowest ever attendances in the First Division – 8,054, 9,556 and 13,703 respectively. Tranmere Rovers, living each day as if their last, record their first away win of the season at Port Vale. Leeds United, with their terraces closed as a punishment for their supporters' behaviour, recorded their lowest home gate for nineteen years (11,528) but their all-seater receipts were similar to those taken from a normal 17,000 crowd. Celtic win the Scottish League Cup for the first time for eight years.

6 **Mike Bailey** leaves Brighton and Hove Albion and **Alan Mullery** and **Ron Greenwood** are linked with the vacant position. The FA are to spend £40,000 on advertising the visit of Luxembourg to Wembley on 15th December. **George Graham** takes over as Manager of Millwall. Television announces record profits of £1¾ from selling recordings of football to about 40 countries.

7 ITV chief **John Bromley** warns football that there will be only limited money for screening League football in the future and advertising on shirts may not be allowed. Arsenal's goalkeeper **George Wood** is sent off against Aston Villa but **Pat Jennings** announces he will stay with the club. Chairman of Brighton and Hove Albion, **Mike Bamber**, acting in a General Manager's role pledges his side will produce no more of the 'boring' performances that have lost **Mike Bailey** his job and kept the fans at home. **Francois Van der Elst** hits top form with a hat-trick for West Ham United at Notts County in the Milk Cup.

8 Dundeed United qualify for the Quarter-Finals of the UEFA Cup by drawing 1-1 with Werder Bremen in West Germany (Aggregate 3-2). Forty applications are received for the Brighton and Hove Albion Manager's job. 'Atari' are to sponsor a six-a-side tournament at the National Exhibition Centre in January, and this may be a forerunner of an even more significant sponsorship deal. Little Reading beat high riding Watford 5-3 in the quarter-finals of the League Trophy. Oxford win the 'Varsity' match at Wembley by beating Cambridge 4-2.

9 The game's battered image has persuaded Charlton Athletic's sponsors, FADS, to take their initials from the team's shirts and two massive multi-million pound sponsorship deals may fall through for the same reason. Tottenham's financial and administrative controller, **Jim Prentice**, is not retained by the new board of directors.

10 **David Webb** is dismissed from the AFC Bournemouth Manager's job. Luxembourg FA are worried about crowd control for their home match with England and offer to play both European Championship ties in England. But this would not be allowed by

UEFA. **Jimmy Melia** as head coach, and **George Aitkin** are given team responsibility at Brighton and Hove Albion for the time being.

11 Only three non-league clubs go into the draw for the third round: Bishop's Stortford, Worcester City (2-1 victors over Wrexham) and the heroes of the round, Weymouth, who came back from a 0-2 half-time deficit to win 3-2 at Cardiff City. But all three are drawn away. The most intriguing tie is **Peter Taylor**'s Derby County v **Brian Clough**'s Nottingham Forest.

12 Aston Villa lose 0-2 to Penarol (Uruguay) in the World Club Championship in Tokyo's National Stadium.

13 **Frank McLintock** returns to one of the clubs he played for – QPR – as Reserve and Youth team coach.

14 **Luther Blissett** is selected for his full International and **Pat Jennings** is selected to return to Albania for Northern Ireland, 17 years since he played there for his country in 1965. Scotland Under-21 defeat Belgium 2-1 in Ghent.

15 England score 9 v Luxembourg and **Blissett** scores three; Belgium beat Scotland 3-2 in Brussels; Wales draw 4-4 in Yugoslavia and Northern Ireland draw 0-0 in Albania. Plans are drawn up to spend £5 million on a gradual face lift for Wembley Stadium.

16 Northern Ireland announce a £¼ million profit from the World Cup but Manchester City have to report a loss for the year of £960,992. **Diego Maradona** is out of football for three months with hepatitis. **Peter Reid**, Bolton Wanderers' England Under-21 International, may be moving to Everton for £60,000. Two years ago he refused a move to his home town club when he was priced at £600,000.

17 **Justin Fashanu** prepares to make his debut for Notts County, having moved across from Forest for £150,000. **Peter Reid** also moves for £60,000 to Everton. The FA clear Oxford United who had been charged with crowd misconduct after coin throwing on 3rd November.

18 The Pools panel sit, and the usual poor attendances for the Saturday before Christmas reduce attendances dramatically.

19 **Trevor Francis** is cleared of writing 'obnoxious comments' about the Italian football scene in his very popular autobiography.

20 FIFA announce that the host nation for the next World Cup will be announced in May. England are to withdraw from the 'Friendly' International originally planned for their Summer tour, but hope to arrange alternative fixtures.

21 **Mick Channon** moves on to his third club of the season – Newcastle United, Bristol Rovers and now Norwich City. The PFA want a Government backed 'Football Council' to tackle the game's many problems. **Cyrille Regis** reassures West Bromwich Albion that he is happy to sign a new contract with them despite rumours to the contrary. Bristol Rovers' Directors donate over £100 of club souvenirs to be given away by the players at hospitals throughout Bristol.

22 Russia offer to play England in the Summer. Reading's future is still unsure, as their Chairman, **Mr Waller**, having offered to stand down, has frustrated efforts by pop singer **Ian Gillan** to take over and also appears to be unwilling to discuss business with **Roger Smee**, a local property millionaire who used to play for the club.

.23 Following a meeting at the Football Association, FIFA have given Football League Referees the all clear to carry on their 'clean up' campaign.

27 The best attendances since Boxing Day 1978 lifted the hearts of all football officials. 708,044 people attended which was 212,337 more than the season's previous best, recorded on the opening day of the season. Seven First Division clubs had their best home attendances with Arsenal topping the lot with 51,497 and Birmingham City doubling their previous home gate by attracting 43,864. Luton Town with 21,145, had their largest crowd at Kenilworth Road for ten years.

28 **Paolo Rossi** wins the European Footballer of the Year award. Another bumper day for attendances and **Mick Channon** scores the winner on his debut for Norwich City. Attendances for the week-end topped the million mark.

29 **Vladimir Petrovic** flew in to sign for Arsenal having been forced to wait for half a season by the Yugoslav football authorities but **Ossie Ardiles** is only delayed by 24 hours due to the weather before he is due back at the Spurs club.

30 **Brian Clough** warns Nottingham Forest players that any arguing amongst themselves on the field will be severely punished through their wage packets.

31 Although **Ray Wilkins** is now fit following a broken jaw; there is no place for him in the side and of course he has lost the captaincy of both United and England to **Bryan Robson**.

First Division		pts	Second Division		pts
Liverpool	21	44	Wolves	21	43
Nottingham F	21	38	QPR	22	43
Watford	21	36	Fulham	21	38
Brighton & HA	21	22	Cambridge U	22	21
Birmingham C	21	21	Burnley	21	15
Sunderland	21	19	Derby Co	21	15

Third Division		pts	Fourth Division		pts	Scottish Premier		pts
Lincoln C	20	43	Bury	22	45	Celtic	16	29
Portsmouth	21	40	Hull C	22	43	Dundee U	16	26
Huddersfield T	21	39	Swindon T	21	41	Aberdeen	17	25
			Port Vale	21	41			
Doncaster R	21	19				Morton	17	10
Walsall	21	19	Darlington	20	19	Motherwell	17	9
Preston NE	21	18	Bristol C	22	18	Kilmarnock	17	9
Millwall	21	17	Herford U	21	16			
			Crewe Alex	21	14			

January 1983

Ossie Ardiles

1 Spectators pack onto the terraces and goals crash into the back of the net! It's a great start to the Year for football. FA Cup heroes Weymouth put next week's tie at Cambridge at stake by striking over an expenses squabble with the club's directors. Celtic win 2-1 at Ibrox Park – their first New Year's Day victory, away from home, for 62 years.

2 **Frank Lord**, who was the first manager to lose his job this season, is appointed coach to Penang state team in Malaysia.

3 It is announced that England's World Cup profit is less than £100,000 after expenses.

4 Arsenal threaten to ban TV cameras from Highbury if 'live' soccer is introduced on television next season. **Paul Walsh** scores a fine hat-trick to give Luton Town a 3-2 away win at West Ham.

3 Liverpool take a ten points lead at the top of the League and **Kenny Dalglish**'s performance in their 3-1 defeat of Arsenal prompts **Bob Paisley** to describe him as the best Liverpool player of all time.

4 Weymouth players go back to work.

5 Swansea City suspend **Ray Kennedy** and **John Toshack** strips him of the club captaincy. The French FA have agreed that **Ossie Ardiles** will be available to play for Spurs on 15th January but due to an administrative mix up he is not available for Saturday's cup tie. Coventry City's sky blue stand is damaged by storms and will be closed for the cup tie against Worcester City.

6 FA Cup fever sets in as Bishop's Stortford, Worcester City and Weymouth prepare for their away trips to attempt some 'giant killing' at League Club grounds. Poor **Tommy Williams**, Leicester City's full back who broke a leg in last season's semi-final, breaks it again while preparing for the Third Round tie.

7 Little Weymouth offer their players £100 per man to beat Cambridge United away.

8 The FA Cup produces the most unlikely hero once again – Bishop's Stortford reserve mid-field player **Richard Bradford** scores two second half goals to equalise at Middlesbrough. **Peter Taylor**'s Derby County beat **Brian Clough**'s Nottingham Forest but there are no outstanding surprises.

10 The Cup draw gives Spurs yet another home draw, against WBA, but most of the favourites avoid each other.

11 Arsenal's £500,000 signing from Stoke City, **Lee Chapman**, undergoes a cartilage operation. Middlesbrough beat Bishop's Stortford despite trailing 9-1 to a **Lyndon**

Lynch goal at half time. Bury's chairman for four years **Ron Clarke**, resigns and hands over to **Terry Robinson**. **Mr Clarke** will stay on the board.

12 Brighton and Hove Albion pull off a fine replay win in front of 32,134 at Newcastle to qualify for a home time with Manchester City in the fourth round. **Peter Bodak** is to leave United and join Manchester City on a free transfer. Seattle Sounders sack **Alan Hinton**, their manager, who took them to the finals of the 1982 North American Soccer League Bowl.

13 Bayern Munich show interest in Spurs' **Glen Hoddle** whose contract finishes at the end of the season.

14 Heavy winds cause £5,000 worth of damage at Watford's Vicarage Road ground. The Football League are confident that this season's total of arrests at grounds will show a substantial improvement. The Alliance Premier League has put its own ideas forward for the future structure of football. Streamlined First, Second and Third Divisions with two regional (North and South) Fourth Divisions made up of full-time or part-time players.

15 **Allan Simonsen** scores both goals in a 2-1 victory for Charlton Athletic but, overall, goals and attendances take a drop although there is a pleasing reduction in dismissals (only two). **Ossie Ardiles** returns to the Spurs first team and shows great character in playing well despite pressures from the crowd at Luton and criticism from home.

14 **Kenny Swain** returns to Aston Villa after a happy period on loan at Nottingham Forest. The Nottingham club's budget apparently is preventing a transfer.

15 Blackpool have two points deducted by The Football League for playing an ineligible player in a Milk Cup tie. The forms were delayed in the post but ironically the club is the nearest (three miles) from the League's Lytham headquarters.

17 **Kerry Dixon**, Reading's striker who leads the national scoring lists with 27 goals, may be out for two months before his three-week old pelvic injury clears up.

18 Liverpool and Arsenal go through in Fifth Round Milk Cup ties. Brighton and Hove Albion plan a new £7 million American-style stadium to be opened in two years' time. Colchester United's player-manager **Allan Hunter** gives up the job as he just can't stand it! As 'it is impossible to be completely honest' as a manager he feels it only right to stand down.

19 On the day of his club's quarter-final Milk Cup tie at Spurs, **Brian Miller** is relieved of his duties as Manager of Burnley. **Frank Casper** stands in and his side records a fine 4-1 victory at White Hart Lane. Manchester United also qualify with a 4-0 home win over Nottingham Forest.

20 **Garrincha**, one of Brazil's most famous players, dies aged 49, after a long illness. **Rene Courte**, Press and Public Relations Officer for FIFA since 1969, has resigned. **Paul Breitner** announces his retirement in West Germany for the end of the season.

22 Leeds United followers cause thousands of pounds worth of damage at Derby but Chelsea fans behave well at Wolverhampton despite their bad reputation. A quiet day generally in the League but poor **Graham Roberts** who gave away two 'own goals' last week follows up by conceding a penalty against Sunderland. Only seventeen goals are scored in the First Division and six of those are at Brighton where Luton Town win 4-2. Attendances are the best for eleven weeks, other than 'Boxing Day'.

23 A unanimous call goes out from the press for drastic action to be taken against the louts using Leeds United as their excuse to cause chaos at Football grounds.

24 Ipswich Town drop **Alan Brazil**. Brighton and Hove Albion's chairman **Mike Bamber** confidently states that his club can go all the way in the FA Cup. **Paul Futcher** joins Derby County from Oldham Athletic. **John Robertson**, Nottingham Forest's international winger has a cartilage operation.

25 Derby County have lost £7,500 worth of Sponsorship because of hooliganism. The Football League are recommending that two substitutes should be allowed next season. 'Soccer 6' proves a great success again at the Birmingham National Exhibition Centre. It is sponsored by Atari who may be prepared to add their financial support to the whole League competition in the future.

26 Aston Villa gain a great 3-0 victory over Barcelona to win the Super Cup 3-1 after extra time. **Alan Ball** moves to help **Bobby Gould** at Bristol Rovers. **Stuart Boam** is sacked as Manager at Mansfield Town.

27 Atari are reported to be willing to inject £3 million into the Football League subject to TV negotiations and action to curb hooliganism. **Jeff Powell** of the *Daily Mail* is named Sports Reporter of the Year.

28 **Don Howe** confirms he will continue as Arsenal coach. The FA confirm that they will donate £2 million towards the £5 million needed to give Wembley a new look.

29 FA Cup attendances are up compared with last season. Brighton and Hove Albion

crash in four against Manchester City, **Kenny Dalglish** scores his 300th goal at club level and **Kevin Wilson**, a Derby County reserve, scores both goals in his side's 2-1 win over Chelsea whose supporters attempt to emulate the Leeds louts at the battered Baseball Ground.

30 Everton beat Shrewsbury Town in the FA Cup tie postponed to avoid clashing with Liverpool's match. **Ron Greenwood** is honoured at a special dinner organised by The Football Writers Association and is presented with an antique statuette of a footballer by Italian Manager **Enzo Bearzot**. **Ian Greaves** takes over as Manager of Mansfield Town. **'Dixie' McNeil**, one of the game's most prolific goalscorers (239) retires.

31 Spurs refuse to play their next FA Cup tie on a Sunday as requested by Everton. Derby County lose their appeal against a 'poaching' charge for luring **Roy McFarland** and **Mick Jones** from Bradford City. With Spurs away from London for the first time in three years, **Jimmy Melia**, Brighton and Hove Albion's caretaker manager and ex-Liverpool star himself, gets a glamour trip to Anfield in the fifth round.

First Division		*pts*	**Second Division**		*pts*
Liverpool	25	56	Wolves	25	53
Manchester U	25	46	QPR	25	49
Watford	25	43	Fulham	25	47
Norwich C	25	26	Cambridge U	25	27
Brighton & HA	25	24	Burnley	25	22
Birmingham C	25	23	Derby Co	25	20

Third Division		*pts*	**Fourth Division**		*pts*	**Scottish Premier**		*pts*
Lincoln C	25	53	Hull C	28	56	Celtic	21	36
Cardiff C	26	52	Port Vale	27	54	Aberdeen	22	34
Portsmouth	26	49	Bury	28	53	Dundee U	21	31
			Wimbledon	27	49			
Reading	27	27				St Mirren	22	15
Chesterfield	26	26	Darlington	26	23	Morton	22	15
Millwall	26	25	Crewe Alex	27	23	Kilmarnock	22	12
Preston NE	26	22	Bristol C	27	23			
			Hereford U	27	23			

February 1983

Pat Jennings

1 Watford knock out Fulham from the FA Cup at Craven Cottage thanks to goals from **Lohman** and **Barnes**. The match was watched by 22,206, Fulham's best of the season. Over 8,000 people watch a Blackpool select XI play Liverpool to raise funds for a drowning disaster fund.

2 Arsenal manage a draw at Leeds with a last minute goal by **Graham Rix** in extra time of their Fourth Round replay but Norwich City knock out Coventry City also in extra time. Brentford decide to carry on at Griffin Park despite £100,000 worth of damage to the main stand caused by a fire. Scunthorpe United manager **John Duncan** is replaced by **Allan Clarke**. Bristol Rovers' goalkeeper **Martin Thomas**, who failed to agree terms with Spurs after a loan period at White Hart Lane, joins Southend United, also on loan.

3 **John Bond**, frustrated at Manchester City's lack of form and the disastrous defeat in the cup at Brighton, resigns and **John Benson** takes over as caretaker manager.

4 **John Jackson** is signed on by Brighton and Hove Albion as goalkeeping cover at the age of 40. The FA find both Derby County and Leeds United 'guilty' of not taking reasonable precautions to avoid crowd troubles at their recent Second Division match at the Baseball Ground.

5 **Mick Channon** returns to the Dell with Norwich City only to lose 0-4; **Alan Ball** scores

for Bristol Rovers. **Allan Simonsen** scores his seventh for Charlton Athletic and **Kevin Keegan** his 15th for Newcastle United. Despite these famous names on the score sheet, attendances were low but only one player was sent off.

7 First Division Managers deny that they are withholding their youngsters from England's Youth team training sessions. Spurs consider bringing American Football to Wembley. **Peter Ward**, who has been on loan at Brighton and Hove Albion for a major part of the season, looks set to leave Nottingham Forest for Seattle Sounders, for £125,000.

8 Despite losing 0-3 to Liverpool in the end, Burnley shake the Champions with a spirited performance in the first leg of the Milk Cup semi-final.

9 Swansea City chairman, **Malcolm Struel**, is to be 'rebuked' for calling the Welsh FA 'bumbling amateurs'. Ipswich Town, who opened their new pioneer stand at the week-end, have launched an economy drive. Arsenal beat Leeds United at the third attempt and qualify for a fifth round FA cup tie at Middlesbrough. Attendances for the Fourth Round of the cup were 95,436 up on last year.

10 Derby County and Leeds United given a stern warning regarding crowd behaviour by the FA. **Peter Withe** is suspended for two games by the FA and will miss Aston Villa's next cup tie.

11 UEFA fine Barcelona £20,000 for their violent behaviour against Aston Villa in the Super Cup. **Leighton Phillips**, Charlton Athletic's player coach, leaves the club by mutual consent.

12 Snow and ice cut down the league programme and the pools panel sit. But Liverpool play and their 1-0 win over Ipswich Town takes them to a 15-point lead at the top of Division One. An incredible week-end result in the European Championships! – Cyprus draw 1-1 with Italy in Limassol!

13 Seven uncapped players are selected for the England squad to play Wales. **Thomas** (Coventry City), **Statham** and **Bennett** (WBA), **Stein** (Luton Town), **Caton** (Manchester City), **Barnes** (Watford) and **Cowans** (Aston Villa). **Gary Brooke** is severely injured after a car crash. The young Spurs forward was said to be in a 'stable' condition.

15 Manchester United produce a brilliant performance to win 4-2 on a frozen Highbury pitch in their Milk Cup semi-final first leg, while little Burnley beat Liverpool 1-0 but lose overall 1-3.

16 Portsmouth go top in the Third Division after a superb 3-0 away win at Lincoln City. **Neil Whatmore** is set to sign for Oxford United for £25,000 only 18 months after Birmingham City had paid £330,000 for him from Bolton Wanderers.

17 **Michael Robinson** is fined £250 and banned for one match after his 'assault' on Watford goalkeeper **Steve Sherwood** had been seen on TV. It is announced that England training squads would use the excellent Bisham Abbey sports facilities instead of five star hotels, whenever possible in the future.

18 It is reported that Argentine footballers offered Polish players £15,000 a man incentive to play well against Italy in the 1974 World Cup at a time when Poland had already qualified and were considering the use of reserves for the match.

19 Spurs are out of the FA Cup for the first time in three years, losing 0-2 at Goodison Park, but most of the favourites go through. The quarter-finals are made up of Everton, Aston Villa, Norwich C, Sheffield Wednesday and Manchester United with Arsenal and Burnley expected to win home replays and Liverpool and Brighton and Hove Albion yet to meet.

20 One of the season's most famous victories is recorded at Anfield where lowly Brighton and Hove Albion, inspired by their scouse extrovert manager, **Jimmy Melia**, and another ex-Red, **Jimmy Case**, win 2-1 against Liverpool.

21 **Gordon Cowans** and **Derrick Statham** are picked to win their first 'caps'.

22 The future of Soccer on Television becomes a talking point throughout the country and **Brian Clough** suggests the game should be banned from the screens for three years.

23 England beat Wales on an icy Wembley pitch in front of only 24,000. **Bryan Robson**, playing for Manchester United in their 2-1 Milk Cup victory over Arsenal, damages ligaments in his ankle and expects to be out for at least a month. United reach the final however with a 6-3 aggregate.

24 Deadlock is reached as the League club chairmen vote unanimously to reject the TV companies' new offer of £5·3 million. But the FA and The Football League are to try television advertising to attract better attendances at Internationals and basic league games.

25 Luton Town consider Milton Keynes as a new home for the club. Bradford City decide

not to appeal for more than the £55,000 awarded to them as compensation for Derby County's 'poaching' of their manager and coach. Lincoln City's players are upset at the club board's apparent lack of ambition at a time when the club is poised to push for promotion to Division Two.

26 **Pat Jennings** plays his 1,000th senior First team match in Spurs' 0-0 draw at home to Norwich City. Liverpool draw at Old Trafford and leave United with a massive task if they are to catch them.

27 Charlton Athletic reluctantly announce that the **Allan Simonsen** signing was a costly mistake. An inquest into what appeared to be planned hooliganism at little Ilkeston is to be held. Hundreds of local youngsters from the Derby area turned up in a uniform of green berets and systematically tried to call a halt to the FA Trophy tie at the town's ground as Enfield cruised to a 5-1 lead. The club's biggest ever day in its history was ruined and the same louts had previously caused damage at Barnet during Ilkeston's last round match.

28 Arsenal and Burnley duly win their FA Cup replays and move on to face Aston Villa and Sheffield Wednesday respectively. Two former Lincoln City Chairmen appear to be preparing to inject money into the club and enable the manager to buy the players he needs for the promotion run in.

First Division		*pts*
Liverpool	28	63
Watford	27	49
Manchester U	27	48
Birmingham C	27	27
Norwich C	27	27
Brighton & HA	28	25

Second Division		*pts*
Wolves	28	56
QPR	28	56
Fulham	28	52
Cambridge U	28	28
Burnley	27	26
Derby Co	27	26

Third Division		*pts*
Portsmouth	31	64
Cardiff C	32	62
Lincoln C	30	55
Chesterfield	31	33
Doncaster R	31	30
Millwall	30	28
Preston NE	30	24

Fourth Division		*pts*
Port Vale	30	63
Hull C	32	62
Wimbledon	31	59
Bury	33	58
Hartlepool U	31	31
Crewe Alex	30	30
Darlington	30	29
Hereford U	32	26

Scottish Premier		*pts*
Aberdeen	25	40
Celtic	24	39
Dundee U	24	35
Motherwell	24	18
Morton	25	16
Kilmarnock	25	12

March 1983

1 **John Hollins** is linked with the vacant Colchester United manager's position. Missed penalties make the headlines for the evening matches. **John Burridge** saves two from Sheffield Wednesday's **Gary Bannister** for Wolves, in their 1-0 win, **Stuart Beavon** misses a first minute penalty for Reading in their 0-0 draw at Cardiff and **Colin Sullivan** becomes the sixth Portsmouth player to miss from the spot this season as Portsmouth's run of seven victories is ended in a 0-0 draw with Wigan Athletic.

George Best

2 A first minute goal from **Rossi** helps Juventus to a 2-1 first leg victory at Villa Park and Liverpool go down 0-2 in Poland against Widzew Lodz to complete a bad night for England in the European Cup. Aberdeen gain a superb 0-0 draw away to Bayern Munich and Dundee United come back with only a one goal deficit from Prague.
Luton Town sign Charlton Athletic's **Paul Elliott** for £150,000. Oxford United's new

signing from Birmingham City **Neil Whatmore** scores a hat-trick against Bradford City.

3 **Colin Murphy** has asked for £25,000 to keep up his Lincoln City side's challenge at the top of Division Three as they suffer their third consecutive defeat with a side badly depleted by injury. The Bedfordshire County Council offer Luton Town some hope, as they suggest they could re-route the proposed link road to avoid the Kenilworth Road ground. **Bobby Gould**, Bristol Rovers' manager, fines himself £200 for making remarks to the referee after his side had lost to Bradford City in a recent League match.

4 **George Graham**, Millwall's new manager, orders six players back for extra training in the afternoon as he considers players who have lost their first team place should work twice as hard to regain their form.

5 Liverpool score five against Stoke City and Manchester City lose their lead over neighbours United to lose 1-2 at home. Notts County register an impressive 3-0 victory over injury-hit Spurs who slip to 13th position. Chelsea's hopes of signing **Bob Latchford** are dashed as Mrs Latchford decides she doesn't want to move to London. **Terry Neill** apologises to the spectators for the lack of entertainment in Arsenal's home goalless draw with Nottingham Forest.

7 Liverpool sign eighteen-year-old **Michael Laudrup**, Denmark's 'Footballer of the Year', for £275,000. Fulham announce that they now have a club debt of over £1 million.

8 Leeds United with a £1·5 million debt are to increase share capital. **Billy Kellock**, a Luton Town mid-field player, signs for Wolves for £20,000.

9 **Don Megson** is appointed manager by the new four man consortium in charge at AFC Bournemouth. The Football League have agreed to make 12th October 1984 a clear Saturday in which First Division clubs will not play in preparation for England's important European Nations Championship qualifying match away to Hungary the following week. **Harry Gregg**'s two month spell as assistant coach at Swansea comes to an end as he walks out after a policy disagreement.

10 **John Wile** is wanted by Peterborough United as manager but although his move is agreed he will not be leaving WBA until the end of the season.

12 Arsenal and Manchester United move into the semi-finals as expected, although Everton put up a tremendous battle at Old Trafford and it is **Jimmy Case** who is again the hero of Brighton and Hove Albion as they reach the semi-finals for the first time. Sheffield Wednesday draw at Burnley in an excellent cup-tie. St Mirren, Aberdeen, Celtic and Rangers reach the Scottish Cup semi-finals.

14 Cup draws bring together the giants in England and Scotland as Arsenal are drawn to play Manchester United for the second time in a major semi-final this season and Aberdeen face Celtic.

15 Sheffield Wednesday storm into the semi-final with a 5-0 victory over Burnley.

16 Sad night for English football as Liverpool win 3-2 but lose 3-4 over two legs to Widzew Lodz in the European Cup. The Kop gain in stature once more however as they stay to applaud the Polish victors; Aston Villa lose in Turin 1-3 and 2-5 overall to Juventus. Aberdeen come back from behind twice to record a brilliant and spectacular 3-2 victory over Bayern Munich but Dundee United only draw 0-0 at home to Bohemians Prague and lose 0-1 on aggregate. **Jimmy Melia** is officially named as manager of Brighton and Hove Albion.

17 The FA and the Wembley Stadium officials hold up their plans for the Stadium's £5 million face lift as deadlock is reached over the contributions each party should make. **Sandy Clark** is sold by West Ham United to Glasgow Rangers for £150,000.

18 Aberdeen are drawn at home to Waterschei in the first leg of the European Cup Winners' Cup Semi-Final. **Carlos Alberto Pereira**, Kuwait's manager in the last World Cup, is appointed as Brazil's new manager.

19 **Alan Brazil**, Spurs' £500,000 signing from Ipswich Town, sets up their winning goal at Watford but skipper **Steve Perryman** is sent off. **Tony Woodcock** scores his first hat-trick for Arsenal and **Steve Moran** also gets three for Southampton. **Bobby Gould** warns his Bristol Rovers supporters that if they ever come on the field again he will take his team off and concede the match. **Allan Simonsen** plays his last game for Charlton Athletic and moves back to Denmark.

21 **Laurie Cunningham** signs on for Manchester United on loan from Real Madrid. **David Swindlehurst** joins West Ham United from Derby County for £200,000. **George Kerr** takes over as Manager of Rotherham United.

22 Brighton and Hove Albion swap **Andy Ritchie** for Leeds United's **Terry Connor**.

Trevor Brooking makes his first appearance for nine months, in West Ham United's reserve side. **Bryan Robson**'s bid to be fit for the Milk Cup Final fails.

23 Southampton sign Carlisle United striker **Bob Lee** and Portsmouth add West Ham United's **Nicky Morgan** to their squad. Little Caernarfon draw 0-0 with Wrexham in the Welsh Cup semi-final second leg but lose 0-2 overall. Ilkeston Town are cleared following an inquiry into crowd troubles during their FA Trophy match with Enfield.

24 The London and Liverpool Trust, who provide pub entertainment through Telejector screens, are prepared to set up 25,000 screens in a £8 million pound deal which will provide football for clubs and pubs instead of on television. **George Best** makes yet another 'comeback', this time with AFC Bournemouth, who have obtained his clearance from San José Earthquakes. **Emlyn Hughes**, having been relieved of his managerial duties at Rotherham, has joined Hull City as a player. **Kevin Dillon** joins Portsmouth from Birmingham City for £175,000; and 'Blues' also sell **Alan Curbishley** to neighbours Aston Villa for £100,000 while a number of other transfers just beat the deadline.

25 The Scottish FA are unhappy about a letter from the Hearts Chairman following a disciplinary hearing to consider **Willie Johnston**'s 19th dismissal!

26 Liverpool beat Manchester United 2-1 in a thrilling Milk Cup Final which went to extra time; and **Bob Paisley** collects the Cup on his last visit to Wembley. AFC Bournemouth get over twice their average 'gate' 9,121 to see **George Best**'s latest comeback.

27 **Kenny Dalglish** wins the PFA Player of the Year with **Ian Rush** being named Young Player of the Year and **Bob Paisley** receiving a special merit award to make it a clean sweep for Liverpool. A Football League plan to allow two substitutes next season has been voted out by the clubs as they feel it would be an extra expense.

28 The Chester Report on the State of Football, as requested by The Football League, is published. The main suggestions include a reduction of clubs in the First Division with Third and Fourth Divisions split into four region groups of sixteen clubs, the home club keeping its gate money and the League's constitution to be changed so that a three-fifths majority would be needed to approve changes instead of the present three-quarters. Watford play Corinthian Casuals for The Sheriff of London's Shield to commemorate the amateur club's centenary.

29 Wales confirm that they will be playing Brazil on 11th June. England Under-21 beat Greece 2-1 and Scotland defeat Switzerland Under-21 by the same score. **Kenny Dalglish** is picked to win his 90th Scottish cap alongside Celtic's **Charlie Nicholas** who is making his debut against Switzerland.

30 Scotland's comeback from a two-goal deficit to draw with Switzerland is highlighted by a brilliant goal from **Charlie Nicholas** but English fans are badly let down by a poor performance in a 0-0 draw against the Greeks. The Football League recommend the go-ahead for the £8 million pub and club Telejector deal.

31 FIFA Executive Committee announce that they will only consider Mexico's request to hold the next World Cup.

First Division		*pts*
Liverpool	32	71
Watford	33	58
Manchester U	31	55
Luton T	31	34
Birmingham C	32	33
Brighton & HA	33	31

Second Division		*pts*
QPR	33	68
Wolves	33	63
Fulham	32	58
Rotherham U	33	35
Derby Co	32	33
Burnley	30	29

Third Division		*pts*
Portsmouth	36	70
Newport Co	37	68
Cardiff C	37	68
Chesterfield	37	36
Preston NE	36	35
Doncaster R	36	34
Millwall	35	31

Fourth Division		*pts*
Hull C	37	72
Wimbledon	35	71
Port Vale	35	68
Bury	38	67
Rochdale	35	39
Hartlepool U	37	38
Crewe Alex	37	35
Hereford U	37	34

Scottish Premier		*pts*
Aberdeen	28	34
Celtic	28	42
Dundee U	28	41
Motherwell	29	22
Morton	29	17
Kilmarnock	29	14

April

Brian Robson

1 Good Friday football brings Brentford their best attendance of the season for the visit of Portsmouth (12,593) and nearly 9,000 watch the local 'derby' at Plymouth where Argyle beat neighbours Exeter City 1-0. Manchester City register their first win under new management by beating WBA 2-0 and at Old Trafford **Frank Stapleton** scores his 100th league goal. The FA announce that they might put in a bid to stage the 1986 World Cup finals. Brighton and Hove Albion's **Chris Ramsey** loses his place in the semi-final through being sent off and Spurs' **Tony Galvin** receives a 'rocket' from his manager for unprofessional behaviour after his dismissal in the same match.

4 **Jimmy Bloomfield**, whose career as a player and manager spanned 29 years dies at the age of 49 after a long illness. Spurs crash five goals past Arsenal to record their most decisive victory over their local rivals for 71 years. Blackburn Rovers and Burnley are to be reported for bad crowd behaviour which stopped their match for 16 minutes. **Bobby Charlton** takes over as 'caretaker' manager at Wigan after the sacking of **Larry Lloyd**, who carries on as a player. **John Sainty** takes over as the new manager at Chester. West Ham United score 5 at Swansea and Carlisle United also get five at home to Bolton Wanderers.

6 Maidstone United are the latest soccer club to have a Rugby League club accepted into the National Championship; the club will be called 'Kent Invicta'. Four senior clubs, Liverpool, Manchester United, Arsenal and Tottenham Hotspur all condemn the idea of pub 'Telejector' soccer. Aberdeen book their place in the Final of the European Cup Winners' Cup by beating Waterschei 5-1 in great style in their first leg semi-final match.

7 The League and TV companies are no nearer to solving their contractual problems as the right for clubs to display advertising on their shirts becomes a stumbling block to negotiations. Over 8,000 supporters cheer Norwich City's Youth team into the Final of the FA Youth Cup after a 0-0 draw has given them a 3-1 aggregate victory over Luton Town. **George Best**, who had been 'missing' from Bournemouth for the last week, resumes training.

8 **Vladimir Petrovic** seems certain to leave Arsenal after only half a season as all concerned admit that he has not been able to adapt to the pace and physical demands of the Football League. The TV companies are expected to make another offer in a bid to keep soccer on the screens next season.

9 England and Manchester United captain **Bryan Robson** returns to the United side after the injury that kept him out of the Milk Cup Final. An average of over three goals a match cheered the fans but at Walsall, where the visiting Bristol Rovers fans had been given free travel by the Rovers Directors as a 'thank you' for their support in the rain the previous week, the home team again put a dampener on the proceedings by scoring five times.

11 Seventeen First Division and eight Second Division Chairmen attend a meeting chaired by **Jimmy Hill** at Coventry to discuss football's problems and find a way for the game to survive healthily.

12 Luton Town beat Birmingham City 3-1 in a vital battle in the relegation zone. The TV tug-of-war goes on and a decision by the main board of Governors at the BBC on shirt advertising may be the deciding factor. **Steve Coppell** will miss the rest of the season as he is going into hospital for operations on his left knee.

13 **Alf Grey** who has been nominated to referee the FA Cup Final states that the FA's crackdown on cheats in football has certainly helped the game to become more attractive and produced more goals; he feels that the rest of the world would do well to follow our example. **Arnold Muhren** pulls out of Manchester United's semi-final side with a calf injury. **Henry Kissinger** is given the job of persuading FIFA that USA should be allowed to host the 1986 World Cup finals.

14 **Gerry Hitchens**, the former Aston Villa and England centre-forward who also enjoyed a successful spell in Italy with Inter Milan, dies at the age of 48. **Eric Houghton**, one of his managers, describes him as 'the perfect professional'. **Jimmy Hill** has expressed

his willingness to stand down from the Chairmanship of Coventry City if a younger man wishes to step in and invest £250,000 in the club.

16 **Robert Maxwell**, Chairman of Oxford United, announces that he has bought a controlling interest in Reading Football Club and that he plans to merge the two clubs and form a new club called Thames Valley Royals. Brighton and Hove Albion reach Wembley for the first time, with **Jimmy Case** again a goalscoring hero, and Manchester United knock out Arsenal at the semi-final stage for the second time in the season. Italy continue their disastrous form since the World Cup by losing in Rumania.

17 Immediate reaction for supporters of both Oxford United and Reading is to fight the proposed merger. It is announced that FA Cup ties this season have produced over £1 million more than last season in receipts. Hungary beat Luxembourg 6-2 in Budapest.

18 **Dino Zoff** announces his retirement from International football after winning 111 caps. Wigan Athletic are the latest club to announce that they are in serious financial trouble. A break away by top clubs is again a distinct possibility as the big clubs are determined to receive a larger share of gate receipts and television payments.

19 Liverpool win their fourteenth championship as Everton beat their nearest rivals Manchester United 2-0. **Ray Wilkins** is recalled to the England squad. Wimbledon win Capital Radio's £25,000 prize for becoming London's first League club to score 80 league goals. Aberdeen, although beaten 0-1, defeat Waterschei 5-2 on aggregate and qualify for the European Cup Winners' Cup Final.

20 **Peter Withe** and **Graham Rix** are called up to join the England squad. Juventus and Hamburg will contest the European Cup Final.

21 The Football League announce that if Oxford United and Reading merge then five clubs will be promoted from Division Four and **Mr Maxwell**'s plans are given full support by the Oxford United board.

22 Opponents of the Thames Valley merger are wasting their time says **Mr Maxwell** as his plans are outlined at a Press Conference held at The Football Association. Mexico once again emerges as the favourite venue for the 1986 World Cup.

24 Leicester City win at Fulham to open up the Second Division promotion race. A 'sit in' on Oxford United's ground holds up the kick-off while home supporters demonstrate against the planned merger. Norwich City's great charge up the table continues as they win at Liverpool – 2-0. **Terry Venables**, having taken QPR up to the First Division plans to buy the club from out-going Chairman, **Jim Gregory**.

26 **Bobby Robson** is upset that a number of players failed to report their unavailability through injuries after Saturday's League games, but **Trevor Francis** is available after scoring a hat-trick for Sampdoria. Norwich City win 3-2 in the FA Youth Cup Final first leg against Everton. **Sir Norman Chester**'s report is given little support by club chairmen although some of the points will be voted upon at the League's AGM.

27 **Trevor Francis** and **Peter Withe** both play well and score the goals that beat Hungary 2-0. Wales beat Bulgaria 1-0 to go top of their group but Scotland cannot qualify following Belgium's 2-1 defeat of East Germany. Northern Ireland beat Albania 1-0 but Eire lose in Spain 0-2. Telejector pull out of their proposed deal with the Football League leaving the way open for a new TV deal for the clubs.

28 A strike at Hartlepool United is averted as disgruntled players are promised their wages after a three week 'freeze' by chairman **Vince Barker**.

29 The TV saga goes on as Television authorities ask for more 'live' football on the screens but the Football League insists on shirt advertising and better fees.

31 **Steve Foster** is booked and according to FA rules will automatically miss the Cup Final. Reading supporters parade a coffin around the town and ground before the Millwall match, but having led 3-0 and having two opponents sent off the home side allowed a spirited revival to achieve a 3-3 draw. Doncaster Rovers and Chesterfield are relegated to Division Four. VS Rugby having lost to their West Midland colleagues twice in the league and once in the league cup beat Halesowen 1-0 to win the FA Vase.

First Division		*pts*	**Second Division**		*pts*
Liverpool	39	81	QPR	38	78
Watford	39	67	Wolves	39	73
Manchester U	37	64	Fulham	39	66
Birmingham C	39	43	Chelsea	39	42
Brighton & HA	39	39	Rotherham U	40	41
Swansea C	39	38	Burnley	37	36

Third Division

		pts
Portsmouth	42	81
Cardiff C	43	79
Huddersfield T	43	78
Exeter C	43	47
Millwall	43	46
Doncaster R	43	37
Chesterfield43		36

Fourth Division

		pts
Wimbledon	42	88
Hull C	44	86
Port Vale	42	84
Bury	44	80
Aldershot	43	45
Hartlepool U	43	42
Crewe Alex	44	41
Hereford U	43	41

Scottish Premier

		pts
Dundee U	34	52
Celtic	34	51
Aberdeen	33	50
Motherwell	34	26
Morton	34	20
Kilmarnock	34	16

May 1983

1 Oxford City Council are reported to have offered Oxford United a site for a new stadium; **Robert Maxwell** says merger with Reading is still 'on' but he will consider the offer. FA say that there is no hope for Brighton and Hove Albion's **Steve Foster**, whose 31 disciplinary points reached on Saturday mean that he must miss the Cup Final.

2 Arsenal beat Manchester United in a League match, but worse still for United is the dismissal near the end of the match of **Remi Moses**. **Jimmy Hill** may sell off £1·5 million Sky Blue Connexion to cover Coventry City's overdraft. The Denmark Football authorities apologise for a press release describing 'sex crimes' by Greek players – it was now said to be nonsense.

Dino Zoff

3 **Jimmy Hill** resigns from Coventry City. His likely successor is **Iain Jamieson**, a former player. Burnley win at Shrewsbury Town and improve their chances of remaining in the Second Division.

4 Newcastle United give themselves an outside chance of promotion from Second Division by winning 5-0 at Barnsley; **Keegan** is one of the scorers, **McDonald** and **Varadi** scoring twice each.

5 Further talks between the Football League and TV companies fail; which could affect Canon's sponsorship next season.

7 The penultimate Saturday of the season sees Brighton and Hove Albion and Swansea City relegated to Division Two. Other issues settled are promotion from the Third for Portsmouth, Cardiff City and Huddersfield Town with Doncaster Rovers and Chesterfield descending from the same Division to be replaced by Wimbledon, Port Vale, Hull City and one other. Crewe Alexandra and Hereford United must seek re-election yet again. Luton Town lose at home to Everton and are plunged back into relegation trouble whilst Manchester City's surprise win at Brighton and Hove Albion gives them hope but seals the Seagulls' fate at the same time. **Bob Paisley** says his farewells to the fans in Liverpool's last home match.

8 Millwall give themselves a chance of escaping relegation to the Fourth by scoring the only goal at home to Brentford – **Bremner** is the hero. The ladies have their own 'Wembley' at Lincoln where Doncaster Belles win their F.A. Cup with a thrilling win 3-2) over St Helens.

9 Luton Town's chances of escaping the 'drop' are badly undermined at Old Trafford where they lose 3–0 to United, whose **McGrath** does his Wembley chances no harm by scoring twice. The FA Youth Cup is on its way to Norwich after they win a replay at Goodison Park; **Clayton** is the scorer in front of 20,562 fans – mostly Everton supporters. Stockport County and Hartlepool United are saved from extinction sought by the Tax Man. Stockport County have a payment offer accepted, whilst the North-Easterners having paid their debt hear their adversary's petition against them dismissed.

10 **Ron Atkinson** will not appeal against the FA charge of bringing the game into disrepute following incidents at Highbury on 2nd May. Second Division relegation worries for Middlesbrough (2-0 victors over Crystal Palace) are virtually eliminated but Burnley's win (2-1) over QPR (the Champions) merely increases their chances. Portsmouth score a single goal at Fratton Park which makes them Third Division Champions and Swansea City look like achieving Europe again as a consolation for being relegated – they win the first leg of the Welsh FA Cup Final at Wrexham (2-1). West Ham United's European ambitions disappear with their home defeat against Arsenal, whose best player in their win (3-1) is **Petrovic**, but he will not be back next season!

11 In dreadful conditions in Gothenburg Aberdeen score the odd goal in three against Real Madrid and take the Cup-Winners' Cup. **Eric Black** scores early in the game, **Juanito** equalises soon after from a penalty and after considerable pressure in the second half and throughout extra time **John Hewitt** heads home a **McGhee** cross for victory.

12 It is announced that **Steve Foster** is to go to the High Court on Monday to seek an injunction to set aside his suspension, so that he can play in the Cup Final on the 21st.

13 The UEFA International Youth Tournament starts with England beating Spain (1-0) but they have **Simmonds** harshly sent off near the end. Scotland (the holders) beat USSR (3-0). **Graham Taylor** says his Watford duties will prevent him from continuing as Youth Manager after the tournament. The Reading merger with Oxford United seems to be off – finally. Reading Chairman (**Frank Waller**) and two directors resign leaving the way free for **Roger Smee** to become Chairman and end **Robert Maxwell**'s bid to form Thames Valley Royals. The latter says he will leave Oxford United if the council in that city fails to provide a site for a new stadium.

14 The final Saturday of the League campaign! Most issues are settled but a few remain in abeyance including the final promotion place from Division Two, where Leicester City think they have won promotion after a goalless draw with Burnley, but Fulham's match with Derby ended 78 seconds early owing to crowd encroachment. Other unsettled issues are the last relegation place from Division Two (Burnley of Crystal Palace) and a single re-election place in the Fourth. Luton Town's Yugoslav substitute, **Radi Antic**, scores the only goal at Maine Road four minutes from time so down go Manchester City to Division Two, whose ranks lose Bolton Wanderers and Rotherham United to the Third. Reading beat Wrexham in their final match, but both clubs descend to the Fourth because Millwall and Orient both win and Exeter City draw. The final promotion place from the Fourth goes to Scunthorpe United, who win at Chester whilst Bury lose at home to the Champions, Wimbledon. In Scotland the Final Day sees Dundee United lift the Flag for the first time, hotly pursued by Celtic and Aberdeen; all three win well. Hearts join St Johnstone in replacing Morton and Kilmarnock in the Premier Division whilst the replacements in that league for Dunfermline Athletic and Queen's Park have already been decided – Brechin City and Meadowbank Thistle with the former confirmed as Second Division Champions today. **Bob Paisley**'s final match as Liverpool's Manager ends with defeat at Watford, who finish second with Manchester United third. Also going into Europe (UEFA Cup) are Nottingham Forest with Aston Villa waiting on the Cup Final result to ascertain their own position. Finally, Telford United win the FA Trophy at Wembley after a fine second half against Northwich Victoria (score – 2-1).

15 England's Youth team beat Scotland (4-2) and are favourites to progress in their group. England's ladies make it a double by winning their UEFA Championship match in Belfast (4-0). Hungary lose in Budapest against Greece which makes England's qualifying chances in Group 3 look excellent; only a late rally brings a respectable score (2-3). Sweden (5-0 home winners over Cyprus) and Spain (3-2 victors in Valetta) also score points.

16 **Steve Foster** loses in the High Court and is still suspended from the Cup Final, whilst the Football League reject Fulham's request for a replay against Derby County so Leicester are promoted to Division One. Tranmere Rovers and Rochdale fail to provide a goal at Prenton Park, but both escape having to apply for re-election; Blackpool are almost certain to be the fourth unlucky team since only a 9-0 home defeat for Darlington in their final match (v Peterborough United) can save them!

17 **Crystal Palace** stay in the Second Division by defeating **Burnley** 1-0 at Selhurst Park but the little Lancastrian club having enjoyed two superb cup runs in the season, are relegated. **Graham Roberts** is called up for the England squad, Everton's **Steve McMahon** discusses a move to Aston Villa and Brighton & Hove Albion accept that their captain **Steve Foster** will not be able to lead them out at Wembley. The England Youth team lose 0-2 to Russia but qualify in their group for the semi-final.

18 **Gary Howlett**, a 20-year-old Eire Youth International, is selected for Brighton & Hove Albion's cup final team in only his 11th senior match. Aston Villa sign **Steve McMahon** for £400,000 despite Liverpool's interest in the Under 21 International mid-field player.

19 **Kenny Dalglish** receives his Football Writers' 'Footballer of the Year' award from Pele at the Cafe Royal. **George Wood** signs for Crystal Palace. Manchester United emerge as early favourites to sign **Charlie Nicholas**.

20 **Alan Davies**, A Welsh Under-21 international gets the last place in United's Cup Final team pipping Laurie Cuningham and Ashley Grimes. Mexico are officially named as hosts for the next World Cup. England Youth team lose on penalties in their European Youth cup semi-final against Czechoslovakia. Bobby Robson selects uncapped players, **Mark Barham**, **Nigel Spink**, **John Gregory** and **Paul Walsh** for the tour of Australia.

21 A great day for Brighton & Hove Albion as they take an early lead, then equalise in the closing minutes of normal time and miss a good chance of winning near the end of extra time! Like the Milk Cup Final, the FA Cup Final proves to be a superb advertisement for British Football. Aberdeen complete a memorable Cup Double by Winning the Scottish Cup Final 1-0 after extra time against Rangers.

22 **Gary Stevens**' Cup Final 'Man of the Match' performance makes him the week end's talking point and it is accepted by Brighton & Hove Albion that he will be moving on. England's ladies beat Scotland (2-0) at Leeds and qualify for further possible honours in Europe.

23 It is to be **Joe Fagan** at Liverpool; he takes over from **Bob Paisley**, thus maintaining the club's custom of promoting from their own boot room. **Joe** is 62. **John Hollins** goes back to Chelsea as Assistant First Team Coach.

24 The Home International Championships continue with a goalless draw at Hampden Park between Scotland and Northern Ireland – neither side being at full strength. Will **Gordon Cowans** go to Napoli? It is still not known. As **Ron Atkinson** is let off with a warning by the FA he will be on his club's bench at Wembley for the Cup Final Replay.

25 Hamburg take the European Cup with a single goal win over a disappointing Juventus – the veteran **Magath** being the scorer after nine minutes. Fulham's appeal to have their match at Derby County replayed fails before the League Board of Appeal, whilst Brighton and Hove Albion make only one change of personnel for the Replay bringing in **Foster** (as expected) for the injured **Ramsey**, but there will be a reshuffle of the defence. Manchester United are unchanged. **Gordon Cowans** still does not know whether he goes to Napoli or not.

26 It is Manchester United all the way at Wembley with victory by four clear goals over gallant Brighton and Hove Albion. The scorers are **Robson** (2), **Whiteside** and **Muhren** (penalty).

27 **Jack Charlton** – not unexpectedly – resigns at Hillsborough and is replaced for the moment by **Maurice Setters**; the parting is 'amicable' but **Jack** is clearly disappointed at his failure to bring Wednesday First Division football.

28 The Home Championship bumbles on with Scotland good winners at Cardiff over Wales with two goals by **Andy Gray** and **Alan Brazil**, whilst Northern Ireland and England fail to score in Belfast.

31 Aston Villa are announced as having signed Swindon Town's very promising **Paul Rideout** at a reported fee of £200,000. Northern Ireland again fail to score in the Home Championships, but **Gordon Davies** does chalk up one for Wales in Belfast, whilst among the Semi-Pros in Scarborough England start well against Italy (2-0) and Holland and Scotland share six goals.

June 1983

1 England are Home Champions. Bobby Robson's men efficiently beat a strangely subdued Scottish line-up. The two goals are scored (one in each half) by **Bryan Robson** (before retiring injured) and **Cowans**. Aston Villa's **Peter Withe** also retires injured and is almost certainly out of England's trip to Australia.

2 England take a mighty step towards regaining the Semi-Pro title in Scarborough by thrashing Holland by six clear goals; Scotland beat Italy (3-1).

4 England win the Semi-Pro Tournament in Scarborough beating Scotland 2-1 with a last minute winner from **Colin Williams** of Telford United; a draw would have been enough, but the 100% record is good. Holland beat Italy (3-2) in the other match. In Swaziland Cup Winners, Manchester United, beat Spurs (2-1) with **Stapleton** scoring

a late goal to supplement a penalty equaliser from **Muhren**; **Archibald** scored for Tottenham.

5 The World Youth Tournament has started in Mexico and Scotland beat South Korea (2-0), but Nigeria provide a shock by beating Russia by a solitary, last minute goal. In matches in Africa, Coventry are 5-2 winners against Zimbabwe whilst a combined Spurs and Manchester United side score six with only a single response against Swaziland.

6 The International Youth Tournament continues with Scotland losing in Mexico (1-2) to Australia. In the same tournament the United States beat Ivory Coast by a lone goal and the African team have three players ordered off for dissent.

7 **John Benson's** short spell as Manager of Manchester City is over; a relegation victim. Russia depart from the World Youth Tournament losing (3-2) to Holland, whilst Ivory Coast lose one player (Lucien Kassy) for a year for referee-assault yesterday; three others are suspended for shorter periods.

9 **Charlie Nicholas** seems set to join Arsenal and is thought likely to announce the fact to-morrow – the fee around £650,000! In a rowdy match (the crowd being the problem) in Mexico City, Scotland through **Clarke**, score once against the home team and this win puts the home team out and sees the Scots through to a quarter-final match against Poland.

10 The Football League A.G.M. Sees all the bottom four clubs in Division Four re-elected; Maidstone are within ten votes of the lowest of those four, Hartlepool. The Football League introduce seeding in the Milk Cup and home clubs are to retain gate receipts. **Gordon Cowans** is not now going to Napoli, but **Glenn Hoddle** might yet end up with A.C. Milan or one of Italy's other promoted clubs. Bobby Robson announced four new caps for England's first match against Australia in Sydney on Sunday, the lucky ones being **Barham** of Norwich, **Steve Williams**, **Danny Thomas** and Q.P.R's **John Gregory**. Various 'words' are passed between the two camps – probably to arouse public interest in the game.

11 At Wembley the Under-15's of England and Scotland share six goals with the Scots scoring two late counters in a brave recovery. Their youths are less fortunate in Mexico and lose by a solitary, early goal to Poland in the quarter-finals.

12 In Australia, England fail to score in a bore at Sydney, where the home team show no ambition and also are scoreless, but Wales through a **Flynn** goal score early in Cardiff against Brazil, whose second half reply gives them a scarcely deserved draw.

13 Scotland in Canada beat the home country (2-0) through a **Strachan** penalty in the first half and one after the interval from substitute **Mark McGhee**; the performance is unconvincing.

14 **John Bond** goes as Manager to Burnley. Who goes with him? **John Benson** perhaps? **John Duncan** (ex Scunthorpe Manager) leaves Hartlepool for the 'hot-seat' at Chesterfield.

15 Ten Thousand fans see England score a goal in Brisbane against the home country; the second half scorer is Luton's **Paul Walsh** after a dubious cross from **Gregory** (QPR), which may or may not have been over the by-line. Grasshoppers of Zurich win the Swiss Cup.

16 Scotland retain their unbeaten record in Canada beating the Dominion in Edmonton (3-0). **Charlie Nicholas, Richard Gough** (his first for Scotland) and **Graeme Souness** are the scorers. Referee **Ben Fusco's** attempt to star has mixed fortunes; he books three Scots, but also whistles for half-time four minutes early!

17 The South Korea President's Cup is won by PSV Eindhoven, who beat the home country (3-2) with third place going to Ghana who gave the United States a resounding five-nil thrashing. Brazil continue in Europe with a win in Switzerland (2-1). The **Rubin Brothers** having taken over Southend United sack the Manager, **Dave Smith**, whilst the latter is on holiday in Tenerife.

19 In Melbourne England's scratch team are held by Australia (1-1) with **Francis** scoring the goal, missing a twice-taken penalty and being booked. **Phil Neal** (own goal) is the unlucky scorer for the home team. England debuts are made by **Pickering** (Sunderland) and **Spink** (Aston Villa), the substitute goalkeeper. Scotland's **Andy Gray** scores twice in the first half in Toronto as Canada go down again to the visitors without scoring once during the three matches.

20 Brazil win the World Youth Cup in Mexico by a single early goal against Argentina from a penalty (**Silva**). The win is deserved and there is no violence this time. Poland had already clinched third place by beating much improved South Korea (2-1). **Frank Barlow** leaves Chesterfield after eleven years there; he decides against joining the new manager, **John Duncan**, as his assistant.

THE FOOTBALL LEAGUE

Featuring full details of each of the 92 clubs in the Football League.

Officials, statistics, ground information, full1982–83 League record and career details of theplayers.

THE FOOTBALL LEAGUE OFFICIALS

President

J. J. Dunnett MA (Cantab), LLB, MP
(*Notts County*)

Vice-Presidents

R. Wragg F Inst BM, FIOR (*Sheffield United*)
J. F. Wiseman (*Birmingham City*)

Management Committee

R. Daniel (*Plymouth Argyle*)
Dr C. S. Grossmark MB, BS, MRCS, LRCP (*Gillingham*)
G. H. C. Needler MA, FCA (*Hull City*)
J. W. Smith CBE, DL, JP (*Liverpool*)
Sir Arthur South JP (*Norwich City*)

Life Members

Sir Matt Busby CBE, KCSG
E. M. Gliksten
L. T. Shipman CBE
The Rt Hon Lord Westwood JP, FCIS
F. A. Would

Secretary

R. H. G. Kelly FCIS

INTRODUCTION TO CLUB SECTION

The four pages given to each of the ninety-two Football League clubs have all been changed a little this season. The statistics featured are mostly self-explanatory but hopefully the details given below will help readers to enjoy the section to the full.

Club Page One: The introduction of a team photo has necessitated a move for some of the club statistics. 'Honours' and 'League Records' are now on page 3 and standing club records such as 'largest victory' and 'most capped player' have their own sections later in the book. In the past, all players have had their league records tabulated in detail and now thanks to the team photo, faces can be put to facts, and even club shirt designs will also be recorded through the years.

Club Pages Two and Three: A match by match league record still dominates these pages but referees' names have been added for the first time.

Over the years there have been a number of queries raised concerning the attendance figures which appear on these pages. Those which feature on page two of each club are taken from press sources at the time of the match or from estimated figures. But the final attendance figures for the season, which also incorporate the club's average crowd at home, are those officially supplied by the Football League.

Appearances shown on page three of the club section are those provided officially by the Football League. In past years it has been pointed out that the actual shirt number worn by a player in a particular match has varied with that published. Whilst every care has been taken, it sometimes happens that the team sheets completed by clubs have been at variance with the team numbering published at the time of the match.

Club Page Four: Club data for this page is set at the beginning of the close season and is based on the Football League Retain/Release document produced in mid-May 1983. All close season transfer activities will be recorded in the next yearbook.

For the first time ever, career Football League Cup/Milk Cup and FA Cup appearances and goals have been listed. As official goalscorers have never been tabulated in this way before and even appearances in these competitions have not always been fully audited, members of The Association of Football Statisticians have kindly helped with statistics. However in this, the first compilation of such comprehensive appearances (and substitute appearances) and goalscoring records, any extra information that has eluded the team of compilers will be welcomed with interest.

Players' details are recorded in similar fashion to previous years:

Positions vary season by season but club advisers in the Association of statisticians will be keeping up with players' changes.

Names: Christian names are usually those by which players are known within their clubs.

Honours: The player's senior International honours is recorded: i.e. E = Full England International, E'B' = England 'B' International, E U21 = England Under 21 International, E'Y' = England Youth International and E'S' = England Schools International. Other internationals initials are those used on the International caps pages.

Height, Weight and birthdates are included where known and the *birthplace* column is above any transfer details. *Transfer fees* are based on figures given to the Press by clubs but while giving a rough indication of a player's value during his career, we respect the fact that some clubs do not wish to disclose exact details of their transactions. Free transfers are shown by F/T, player exchange by P/E and shows that there was no fee involved or it was a loan transfer.

Loan transfers are shown where appearances were made and an (A) behind a club's name indicates that the player was an apprentice at the club. Where a player played for a number of 'non-league' clubs before joining a league club only the last one is shown.

Non-Contract Players are shown only when making appearances for season 1982–83 and being retained for the following season. If a N/C player plays during the season but is not retained, his entry will appear amongst players released since May 1982.

Players Released since May 1982 includes all players who have been released from the club and have left The Football League.

Hopefully this section will be of great interest and will once again give the most comprehensive and enjoyable guide to Football League clubs and their players. I am most appreciative of the support and interest given to us by Ray Spiller and his Association of Football Statisticians and the tremendous work put in by Barry Hugman and Tony Pullien while helping Tony Williams compile these pages.

ALDERSHOT Division 4

Back row (left to right): Len Walker (Manager), Ian Wood, Mark Sanford, Clive Holmes, Murray Brodie, Ian Gillard (Player/Coach), Dale Banton, John Anderson (Trainer).
Front row: Stuart Robinson, Ian McDonald, Brian Lucas, Peter Scott, Glen Johnson, Joe Jopling, Les Briley, Paul Shrubb, Colin Fielder.

Chairman: R. J. Driver.

Vice-Chairman: F. G. Wiltshire FSVA.

Directors: R. H. Lamarre, A. English, L. Kennett, Major A. Dobson MBE.

Team Manager: Len Walker.

Secretary/Commercial Manager: M. A. Cosway.

Year Formed: 1926. ***Turned Professional:*** 1927. ***Ltd Co.:*** 1927.

Previous Managers since 1946: Bill McCracken, Gordon Clark, Harry Evans, Dave Smith, Tommy McAnearney, Jimmy Melia, Cliff Huxford, Tommy McAnearney (8).

Recreation Ground, High St, Aldershot GU11 1TW. Telephone Aldershot (0252) 20211. ***Record attendance:*** 19,138 v Carlisle U, FA Cup 4th rd replay, 28 January, 1970. ***Record receipts:*** £11,850 v Shrewsbury T, FA Cup 5th rd, 20 February, 1979. ***Ground capacity:*** 16,000 (14,000 under cover).

Directions to Ground: Aldershot railway station is on the main line from London's Waterloo; the ground is five minutes walk from the station. Many buses run from the town centre on match days.

Match tickets: Can be booked in advance by telephoning ground. Available two weeks prior to match.

Car parking: Car parks within ¾ mile of the ground.

Entertainments/catering facilities: Vice-Presidents' club, Sportsman's club.

Club shop: Run by Supporters' Club; sells all types of souvenirs.

Handbooks/programmes: Programmes only available on sale.

Address of Supporters Club: 213 High St, Aldershot.

Note: Full club statistical records are on pages 416–455.

ALDERSHOT 1982–83 LEAGUE RECORD

Match No.	Date	Venue	Opponents	Result	H/T Score	Lg. Pos.	Goalscorers	Attendance
1	Aug 28	H	Tranmere R	W 1-0	1-0	—	Goddard	1653
2	Sept 4	A	Scunthorpe U	D 1-1	0-1	7	Shrubb	1309
3	8	A	Torquay U	L 2-4	1-4	—	Banton, Goddard	2198
4	11	H	Peterborough U	W 2-0	1-0	6	Banton, Goddard	1691
5	18	A	Halifax T	W 3-1	1-0	3	Brodie, Wood (og), Banton	2243
6	25	H	Hull C	L 1-2	0-1	8	Goddard	2345
7	28	H	Port Vale	L 1-4	0-2	—	Goddard	1781
8	Oct 2	A	Northampton T	D 1-1	1-0	13	Goddard	1706
9	9	A	Wimbledon	L 1-6	1-2	14	Banton	2440
10	16	H	Stockport Co	W 2-1	2-1	12	McDonald, Banton	1417
11	19	H	Crewe Alex	W 2-1	1-1	—	McDonald, Goddard	1574
12	23	A	Hartlepool U	D 1-1	0-0	8	Sanford	1412
13	30	H	Bristol C	D 0-0	0-0	8		2826
14	Nov 2	A	Darlington	D 1-1	1-1	—	Smith, K. (og)	1453
15	6	A	York C	L 0-4	0-2	11		1743
16	13	H	Chester	L 1-2	1-2	13	Storton (og)	1675
17	27	H	Blackpool	W 2-1	0-0	10	Banton, Wood	2,003
18	Dec 4	A	Bury	L 1-3	0-2	13	Sanford	2482
19	18	A	Rochdale	L 1-3	0-2	13	Banton	1003
20	27	H	Swindon T	D 1-1	0-0	15	Goddard	5087
21	28	A	Colchester	D 0-0	0-0	16		2463
22	Jan 1	H	Mansfield	W 2-1	1-0	14	Brodie, Lucas	2235
23	3	A	Hereford U	L 1-2	0-1	15	Banton (pen)	1992
24	22	H	Torquay U	W 2-1	0-1	16	Lucas, Gillard	1706
25	25	A	Tranmere R	D 1-1	0-0	—	McDonald	1509
26	29	A	Peterborough U	D 0-0	0-0	15		2841
27	Feb 5	A	Hull C	D 2-2	2-0	16	Banton, McDonald	6758
28	12	H	Northampton T	W 3-0	2-0	13	Banton 2 (1 pen), Goddard	1761
29	15		Crewe Alex	D 0-0	0-0			2349
30	19	H	Wimbledon	D 1-1	0-1	13	Banton (pen)	2720
31	26	A	Stockport Co	L 1-2	1-0	14	Banton	1853
32	Mar 1	H	Darlington	L 1-6	0-1	—	Robinson	1400
33	5	H	Hartlepool U	L 0-2	0-1	15		1439
34	12	A	Bristol C	L 0-2	0-1	16		4239
35	15	H	Scunthorpe U	D 1-1	1-1	—	Gillard	1422
36	19	H	York C	L 2-3	2-2	16	Barton 2	1528
37	26	A	Chester	D 1-1	0-1	18	McDonald	1197
38	Apr 2	H	Colchester U	L 0-1	0-1	19		1670
39	4	A	Swindon T	L 0-2	0-0	—		3494
40	9	H	Bury	D 1-1	0-0	19	Brodie	1426
41	16	A	Port Vale	L 1-2	1-0	21	Senior	5624
42	23	H	Rochdale	W 6-4	3-1	18	Senior 3, Banton 3	1651
43	30	A	Blackpool	L 1-4	1-1	20	McDonald	1994
44	May 2	H	Hereford U	W 2-1	2-1	20	Senior 2	1653
45	7	H	Halifax T	W 6-1	2-1	16	Banton 5, Robinson	1701
46	14	A	Mansfield T	L 1-4	1-2	17	Banton	1786

Final League Position: 18

GOALSCORERS

League (61): Banton 24 (3 pens), Goddard 9, McDonald 6, Senior 6, Brodie 3, Gillard 2, Lucas 2, Robinson 2, Sanford 2, Shrubb 1, Wood 1, own goals 3.
Milk Cup (0).
FA Cup (7): Banton 4 (2 pens), Briley 1, Brodie 1, Sanford 1.
Football League Trophy (6): McDonald 2, Sanford 2, Banton 1, Shrubb 1.

Milk Cup	First Round	Colchester U (a)	0-2
		(h)	0-1
FA Cup	First Round	Wimborne (h)	4-0
	Second Round	Portsmouth (a)	3-1
	Third Round	Swindon T (a)	0-7
Football League Trophy		AFC Bournemouth (a)	2-2
		Oxford U (h)	1-3
		Reading (h)	3-3

Johnson	Andruszewski	Gillard	Briley	Wood	Jopling	Shrubb	Banton	Goddard	McDonald	Brodie	Sanford	Scott	Lucas	Fielder	Wooler	Robinson	Whitlock (L)	Senior (L)	Referees	Match No.
1	2	3	4	5	6	7	8	9	10	11									D. Brazier	1
1	2	3	4	5	6	7	8	9*	10	11	12								N. Midgley	2
1	2	3*	4	5	6	7	8	12	10	11	9								D. Lloyd	3
1	2	3	4	5	6	7	8	9	10	11									A. Gunn	4
1		3		5	6	7	8	9	10	11	4	2							R. Bridges	5
1		3	4	5	6	7*	8	9	10	11	12	2							E. Scales	6
1	2*	3	4	5	6		8	9	10	11		12	7						K. Salmon	7
1	2	3	4	5			8	9	10	11	7	6							D. Civil	8
1	2	3				4	8	9	10	11	7	5		6					L. Robinson	9
1	2	3			6	7	8	9	10	11		4			5				M. Bodenham	10
1	2	3			6	7	8	9	10	11*	12	4			5				B. Stevens	11
1	2	3*		7	6	12	8	9	10		11	4			5				A. Challinor	12
1	2	3			6		8	9	10	11	7	4			5				B. Hill	13
1	2	3		7	6		8	9	10	11		4			5				A. Robinson	14
1	2	3		8	6*	7	12	9	10	11		4			5				R. Banks	15
1		3	4		6	7	8	9	10	11		2			5				E. Read	16
1	4			5	6	7	8		10	11*	9	2	12		3				D. Axcell	17
1		3	4		6	7	8		10	11	9	2			5				J. Key	18
1		3		5		7	8	4	10	11*	9		2	12	6				D. Hutchinson	19
1		3		6		2	7	8	10	11*	9		4	12	5				J. Moules	20
1		3			6	2	8	4	10		9		7		5	11			J. Deakin	21
1		3	4		6	2	8	9	10	11			7		5				A. Crickmore	22
1		3			6	2	8		10	11*	9	4	7	12	5				C. Thomas	23
1		3*			6	2	8		10	11	9	4	7		5	12			B. Daniels	24
1	12	3*			6	4	8		10	11	9	2	7		5				G. Newsome	25
1	5	3				2	10		7	11	9	6	8		4				J. Bray	26
1	5				6	2	10		7	11	9*	3	8		4	12			D. Richardson	27
1	2	3			6	7*	8	9	10	11		4			5				H. King	28
1	3		4		6*	7	8	9	10			2			5	11			T. Fitzharris	29
1	2		4		6	7	8*	9	10	11		3			5				L. Burden	30
1	2		4		6	7	8*	9	10	11		3			5				K. Hackett	31
1	6	3	4			7	8		10*			2	9	12	5	11			T. Ward	32
1	6		4			2	8	12	10		9	3	7			11	5*		T. Glasgow	33
1	2	3	4		6	7	8	9	10				12			11*	5		A. Hamil	34
1	2	3	4		6	7	8	9	10							11	5		M. Bodenham	35
1	2	3	4		6	7	8	9	10							11	5		K. Salmon	36
1	12	3	4		6*	7	8		10	11		2					5	9	M. Peck	37
1		3	4		6	7	8		10	11*		2	12				5	9	M. Robinson	38
1		3	4		6*	12			10	11	8	2	7				5	9	V. Callow	39
1		3	4		6		8		10	11		2	7				5	9	K. Cooper	40
1			4		6		8		10	11*		2	7	3		12	5	9	K. Barrett	41
1		3	4		6		8		10			2	7			11	5	9	R. Milford	42
1		3	4		6	2	8		10				7			11	5	9	F. Roberts	43
1		3	4		6	2	8		10	11			7				5	9	M. Dimblebee	44
1		6	4			3	8		10			2	7	12		11	5*	9	M. Taylor	45
1		6	4			3	8		10			2	7			11	5	9	R. McGinlay	46
46	25	39	28	14	37	37	44	26	46	34	18	32	20	2	23	11	14	10		
	+ 2s					+ 2s	+ 1s	+ 2s			+ 3s	+ 1s	+ 3s	+ 5s		+ 3s				

FOOTBALL LEAGUE RECORD

1932 Elected to Division 3(S); 1958–73 Division 4; 1973–76 Division 3; 1976– Division 4.

HONOURS

Football League: best season: 8th, Division 3, 1973–74. *FA Cup:* best season: 5th rd, 1932–33, 5th rd replay, 1978–79. *Football League Cup:* never past 2nd rd.

COLOURS

Red and blue striped shirts, blue edge on collar and cuffs, blue shorts, red stockings with two blue hoops.
Change colours: White shirt, red edge on collar and cuffs, white shorts with blue stripe, white stockings with two blue hoops.

ALDERSHOT

Players Names Ht, Wt, D.o.B.	Birthplace Transfer Fee	Clubs	Appearances F.L. A & S	Appearances F.L.C. A & S	Appearances F.A.C. A & S	Goals F.L.	Goals F.L.C.	Goals F.A.C.
Goalkeepers								
Glen Johnson (EY)	Barron	Arsenal						
6 2, 13 6, 7.3.52	F/T	Doncaster R	95	4	3			
	—	Walsall (loan)	3					
	F/T	Aldershot	424	19	24			
Defenders								
†Joe Jopling*	South Shields	Aldershot	35	2	6	2		1
6 0, 12 13, 21.4.51	£30,000+2 players	Leicester C	2+1					
	—	Torquay U (loan)	6					
	£13,500	Aldershot	297+9	15	21	11		1
Manny Andruszewski*	Eastleigh	Southampton (A)	82+1	7	6+1	3		
5 10, 11 9, 4.10.55		Tampa Bay R						
	F/T	Aldershot	25+2	2				
Peter Scott* (NI)	Liverpool	Everton (A)	42+2	1	5	1		1
5 10, 11 4, 19.9.52	—	Southport (loan)	4					
	£11,000	York C	99+1	8	6	4		
	£30,000	Aldershot	114+7	3	7+1	2		
Ian Gillard (E)	Hammersmith	QPR (A)	403+5	32	36	9	1	1
6 1¾, 13 7, 9.10.50	F/T	Aldershot	39	2	2			
Ian Wood	Kirkby	Mansfield T (A)	135+14	9+1	10	9	2	
5 10, 10 7, 24.5.58	F/T	Aldershot	14	2	1	1		
Midfield								
Les Briley	Lambeth	Chelsea (A)						
5 6, 9 11, 2.10.56	F/T	Hereford U	60+1	3+1	2	2		
	£18,000	Wimbledon	59+2	4+1	8+1	2		
	£43,000	Aldershot	121	8	5	2		1
Stuart Robinson*	Middlesbrough	Newcastle U (A)	11+1		2	2		1
5 7, 10 5, 16.1.59	F/T	Aldershot	71+6	3+1	5	10	1	1
Colin Fielder*	Winchester	Aldershot (A)	3+5					
Ian McDonald	Barrow	Barrow (A)	30+5	1	2	2		
5 7, 10 5, 10.5.53	£3000	Workington	42	2	1	4	1	
	£35,000	Liverpool						
	—	Colchester U (loan)	5			2		
	£19,000	Mansfield T	47+9	6+1	6	4	3	1
		York C	175	9	11	29	1	1
	P/E	Aldershot	77	2	6	9		1
Paul Shrubb	Guildford	Fulham (A)	1					
5 8, 10 4, 1.8.55	F/T	Hellenic						
	F/T	Brentford	170+12	9	6+1	8		
	F/T	Aldershot	37+2	2	3	1		
Forwards								
Brian Lucas	Farnborough	Aldershot	92+10	4+2	3+1	14	1	
5 10, 10 12, 31.1.61								
Mark Sanford*	London	Aldershot	72+12	7	2	23		1
6 0, 11 8, 10.9.63								
Murray Brodie*	Glasgow	Cumbernauld U						
6 0, 12 13, 26.9.50		Leicester C	3			2		
	P/E	Aldershot	450+11	16+2	32	84	2	7
•Dale Banton	Kensington	West Ham U (A)	2+3	1		24		4
5 10, 10 5, 15.5.61	F/T	Aldershot	44+1	2	3	24		4

Club Coach: Ian Gillard
Physiotherapist: John Anderson *Chief Scout:*
Association of Football Statisticians Club Adviser to Yearbook: P. Worrall.

Players released since May 1982: Paul Bennett, D. (R S Southampton); Colin Garwood, F. (Boston U); Paul Hampshire, F. (N/K); Alex McGregor, F. (Farnborough); Wayne Wanklyn, M. (Basingstoke); Alan Wooler, D. (N/K); Clive Holmes, G. (Aldershot N/C); Howard Goddard, M. (Finland).
†Captain
•Supporters player of the season

ARSENAL Division 1

Back row (left to right): Tony Woodcock, Peter Nicholas, John Hawley, Chris Whyte, Pat Jennings, George Wood, David O'Leary, Brian Talbot, Stewart Robson, Graham Rix
Front row (left to right): Alan Sunderland, John Devine, Raphael Meade, Brian McDermott, Lee Chapman, John Hollins, Paul Vaessen, Kenny Sansom, Paul Davis

Chairman: P. D. Hill-Wood.

Directors: Sir Robert Bellinger CBE, DSC, S. C. McIntyre MBE, FCIS, The Rev N. F. Bone TD, A. Wood, R. G. Gibbs, C. E. B. L. Carr, R. C. L. Carr, K. J. Friar.

Manager: Terry Neill. ***Managing Director:*** K. J. Friar.
Assistant Secretary: David Miles.

Assistant Manager/Chief Scout: Wilf Dixon.

Chief Coach: Don Howe. ***Club Nickname:*** 'Gunners'.

Formed: 1886. ***Turned Professional:*** 1891.

Ltd Co.: 1893.

Former Names: 1886–91, Royal Arsenal; 1891–1914, Woolwich Arsenal.

Club Nickname: 'Gunners'.

Former Grounds: 1886–87, Plumstead Common; 1887–88, Sportsman Ground; 1888–90, Manor Ground; 1890–93, Invicta Ground; 1893–1913, Manor Ground; 1913– Highbury.

Previous Managers since 1946: George Allison, Tom Whittaker, Jack Crayston, George Swindin, Billy Wright, Bertie Mee (6).

Arsenal Stadium, Highbury, London N5. Telephone 01-226 0304. ***Ground Capacity:*** 60,000. ***Record attendance:*** 73,295 v Sunderland, Div 1, 9 March, 1935. ***Record receipts:*** £116,498 v Juventus, Cup-Winners' Cup semi-final, 9 April, 1980. ***Telegraphs:*** 'Gunneretic London N5.' ***Pitch measurements:*** 110yd×71yd.

Directions to Ground: Arsenal Underground Station (Piccadilly Line) is within one minute of the ground. Finsbury Park (Piccadilly and Victoria) and Drayton Park are also within walking distance. Buses 4a, 19, 106, 141a, 236. ***Shop*** in Avenell Road, Highbury. Mon–Fri 9.30 am–5 pm.

Match tickets: Postal application one calendar month prior to the match. Prices and availability of tickets can be checked with the club on their Ansafone Service 01-359 0131.

Car parking: Parking is allowed in the adjacent streets under the control of the Police.

Entertainments/catering facilities: East & West Stand restaurants are open Mon–Fri for the general public and on match days for East Stand Upper tier ticket holders. Reservations for both restaurants can be made by telephoning 01-226 4968. There are also extensive refreshment bars around the ground.

Handbooks/programmes: Programmes on subscription from club shop.

ARSENAL 1982–83 LEAGUE RECORD

Match No.	Date	Venue	Opponents	Result	H/T Score	Lg. Pos.	Goalscorers	Attendance
1	Aug 28	A	Stoke C	L 1-2	0-1	—	Sunderland	15,504
2	31	H	Norwich C	D 1-1	0-0	—	Woodcock	22,650
3	Sept 4	H	Liverpool	L 0-2	0-1	18		36,429
4	7	A	Brighton & HA	L 0-1	0-1	—		13,507
5	11	A	Coventry C	W 2-0	1-0	19	Chapman, Woodcock	10,245
6	18	H	Notts Co	W 2-0	1-0	15	Rix, Hollins (pen)	20,556
7	25	A	Manchester U	D 0-0	0-0	14		43,198
8	Oct 2	H	West Ham U	L 2-3	1-2	18	Talbot, Davis	30,484
9	9	A	Ipswich T	W 1-0	0-0	14	Woodcock	20,792
10	16	H	WBA	W 2-0	2-0	12	Sunderland, Woodcock	21,666
11	23	A	Nottingham F	L 0-3	0-1	14		17,161
12	30	H	Birmingham C	D 0-0	0-0	13		20,699
13	Nov 6	A	Luton T	D 2-2	0-0	16	Rix, Talbot	16,597
14	13	H	Everton	D 1-1	0-1	17	McDermott	23,067
15	20	A	Swansea C	W 2-1	0-0	13	Woodcock, Chapman	12,389
16	27	H	Watford	L 2-4	1-1	14	Robson, Talbot	34,287
17	Dec 4	A	Manchester C	L 1-2	0-0	16	McDermott	23,057
18	7	H	Aston Villa	W 2-1	2-1	—	Whyte, Woodcock	17,384
19	18	A	Sunderland	L 0-3	0-1	16		11,753
20	27	H	Tottenham H	W 2-0	1-0	15	Sunderland, Woodcock	51,497
21	28	A	Southampton	D 2-2	1-0	16	Woodcock, Chapman	22,025
22	Jan 1	H	Swansea C	W 2-1	2-0	14	Sunderland, Woodcock	25,237
23	3	A	Liverpool	L 1-3	0-1	14	Talbot	37,713
24	15	H	Stoke C	W 3-0	2-0	13	Rix, Petrovic, Hollins (pen)	19,428
25	22	A	Notts Co	L 0-1	0-0	14		9731
26	Feb 5	H	Brighton & HA	W 3-1	2-1	12	Rix, Meade 2	17,972
27	26	A	WBA	D 0-0	0-0	14		13,923
28	Mar 5	H	Nottingham F	D 0-0	0-0	15		21,698
29	15	A	Birmingham C	L 1-2	0-0	—	Sunderland	11,276
30	19	H	Luton T	W 4-1	3-0	14	Woodcock 3, Davis	23,987
31	22	H	Ipswich T	D 2-2	2-0	—	Rix, Whyte	17,639
32	26	A	Everton	W 3-2	0-1	12	Robson, Sunderland, Woodcock	16,318
33	Apr 2	H	Southampton	D 0-0	0-0	11		24,911
34	4	A	Tottenham H	L 0-5	0-3	—		43,642
35	9	H	Coventry C	W 2-1	2-0	12	Rix, Woodcock	19,152
36	20	A	Norwich C	L 1-3	1-1	—	Davis	16,858
37	23	H	Manchester C	W 3-0	1-0	12	Talbot 3	16,810
38	30	A	Watford	L 1-2	0-0	12	McDermott	20,043
39	May 2	H	Manchester U	W 3-0	1-0	11	O'Leary, Talbot 2	23,602
40	7	H	Sunderland	L 0-1	0-0	13		18,053
41	10	A	West Ham U	W 3-1	3-0	—	Petrovic, Whyte, McDermott	28,930
42	14	A	Aston Villa	L 1-2	0-1	10	Davis	24,647

Final League Position: 10

GOALSCORERS

League (58): Woodcock 14, Talbot 9, Rix 6, Sunderland 6, Davis 4, McDermott 4, Chapman 3, Whyte 3, Hollins 2 (2 pens), Meade 2, Petrovic 2, Robson 2, O'Leary 1.
Milk Cup (14): Sunderland 5 (1 pen), Woodcock 3, Davis 2, Hollins 1, Meade 1, Nicholas 1, Robson 1.
FA Cup (13): Rix 4, Woodcock 4, Davis 2, Petrovic 1, Sunderland 1, Talbot 1.
UEFA Cup (4): Chapman 2, Robson 1, own goal 1.

Milk Cup	Second Round	Cardiff C (h)	2-1
		(a)	3-1
	Third Round	Everton (a)	1-1
		(h)	3-0
	Fourth Round	Huddersfield T (h)	1-0
	Fifth Round	Sheffield W (h)	1-0
	Semi-final	Manchester U (h)	2-4
		(a)	1-2
FA Cup	Third Round	Bolton W (h)	2-1
	Fourth Round	Leeds U (h)	1-1
		(a)	aet 1-1
		(h)	2-1
	Fifth Round	Middlesbrough (a)	1-1
		(h)	3-2
	Sixth Round	Aston Villa (h)	2-0
	Semi-final	Manchester U	1-2
UEFA Cup	First Round	Moscow Spartak (a)	2-3
		(h)	2-5

Wood	Hollins	Sansom	Talbot	O'Leary	Whyte	Robson	Sunderland	Chapman	Woodcock	Rix	Davis	Devine	Hawley	O'Shea	Jennings	McDermott	Nicholas	Petrovic	Meade	Kay	Hill	Referees	Match No.
1	2	3	4	5	6	7	8*	9	10	11	12											C. Thomas	1
1	2	3*	4		6	7	8	10	9	11	5	12										L. Burden	2
1	2		4	5	6	7		9	10	11	8	3										J. Martin	3
1	2		4*	5	6	7		9	10	11	8	3	12									Alan Robinson	4
1	2	3	4	5	6	8		9	10	11	7											R. Nixon	5
1	2	3	4	5	6	8		9	10	11	7											T. Spencer	6
1	2	3	4	5	6	8		9	10	11	7											P. Willis	7
1	2	3	4	5	6		8	9	10	11	7											T. Bune	8
1	2*	3	4	5	6	9	8		10	11	7		12									J. Hunting	9
1		3	4	5	6	9	8		10	11	7	2										B. Hill	10
1	2	3	4	5	6	9*	8	12	10	11	7											G. Courtney	11
1		3	4	5	6	9	8	12	10*	11	7			2								M. Bodenham	12
1		3	4	5	6	9	8		10	11	7			2								E. Read	13
		3	4	5*	6	9		8	10	11	7			2	1	12						A. Grey	14
1		3	4	5	6	9	8	12	10*	11	7			2								G. Napthine	15
1		3	4	5	6	9	8		10	11	7			2								A. Hamil	16
1		3	4	5	6	10	8	9		11	7			2*		12						D. Lloyd	17
1	2	3	4	5	6	9	8		10	11	7											D. Letts	18
	2	3	4	5	6	9	8	12	10	11	7*				1							K. Hackett	19
	2	3	4	5		9	8		10	11	7				1		6					L. Shapter	20
	2	3	4	5		9	8	12	10*	11	7				1		6					K. Baker	21
	2	3	4	5		6	8*	12	10	11	7				1			9				D. Hedges	22
	2	3	4	5		6		8	10	11					1		7	9				A. Saunders	23
	2	3	12	5*	4		8		10	11	7				1		6	9				M. James	24
	2	3	12	5		4	8		10	11	7*				1		6	9				R. Banks.	25
	2	3	7	5		4				11	10				1		6	9	8			D. Civil	26
		3	12		5	4			10	11	8	7			1		6		9	2		N. Wilson	27
	2	3	7		5	4	9		10	11	8				1		6		12			H. King	28
	2	3	12		5	4	9		10	11	8				1		6	7*				T. Jones	29
		3	7	2*	5	4	9		10	11	8				1		6		12			C. Thomas	30
1	2	3	7		5		9		10	11	8	4					6					J. Deakin	31
1		3	7	5	4	2	9		10	11	8						6					J. Lovatt	32
1		3	7	5	4		9		10	11	8						6			2		I. Borrett	33
1		3	7	5	4*	2	9		10	11	8						6	12				Alan Robinson	34
1		3	7		4	2		12	10	11	8						6*	9		5		A. Glasgow	35
1	12	3	4	5	6			10		11*	9					7				2	8	D. Axcell	36
		7	8	3	4				10*		9		12		1	11	6			5	2	D. Brazier	37
		3	7	5	4						8		10*		1	9	6	12		2	11	M. Scott	38
		3	7	5	4						8	2	9		1	10	6	12			11*	E. Read	39
		3	7	5	4						8	2*	12		1	10	6	9			11	T. Spencer	40
		3	7	5	4						8				1	10	6	9		2	11	A. Gunn	41
		3	7	5	4						8	2			1	9	6	10			11	N. Ashley	42
23	22	40	38	36	36	31	25	12	34	36	40	8	2	6	19	7	21	10	2	7	7		
	+ 1s		+ 4s					+ 7s			+ 1s	+ 1s	+ 4s			+ 2s		+ 3s	+ 2s				

FOOTBALL LEAGUE RECORD

1893 Elected to Division 2; 1904–13 Division 1; 1913–19 Division 2; 1919– Division 1.

HONOURS

Football League: Division 1 – Champions 1930–31, 1932–33, 1933–34, 1934–35, 1937–38, 1947–48, 1952–53, 1970-71; Runners-up 1925–26, 1931–32, 1972–73; Division 2 – Runners-up 1903–04. *FA Cup:* Winners 1929–30, 1935–36, 1949–50, 1970–71, 1978–79; Runners-up 1926–27, 1931–32, 1951–52, 1971–72, 1977–78, 1979–80. *Double Performed:* 1970–71. *League Cup:* Runners-up 1967–68, 1968–69. **European Competitions:** *Fairs Cup:* 1963–64, 1969–70 (winners), 1970–71; *European Cup:* 1971–72; *UEFA Cup:* 1978–79, 1981–82, 1982–83; *European Cup-Winners' Cup:* 1979–80 (runners-up).

COLOURS

Red shirts with white sleeves, white shorts, red and white stockings.
Change colours:

ARSENAL

Players Names Ht. Wt. D.o.B.	Birthplace Transfer Fee	Clubs	*Appearances* F.L. A & S	F.L.C. A & S	F.A.C. A & S	*Goals* F.L.	F.L.C.	F.A.C.
Goalkeepers								
Pat Jennings (NI)	Newry	Newry T						
6 0, 12 6, 12.6.45	£6500	Watford	48	1	3			
	£25,000	Tottenham H	472	39	43			
	£50,000	Arsenal	184	25	37			
Rhys Wilmot (WU21)	Newport	Arsenal (A)						
6 1, 12 0, 21.2.62	—	Hereford U (loan)	9					
George Wood* (S)	Douglas	East Stirling						
6 3, 14 0, 26.9.52	£7000	Blackpool	117	8	4			
	£140,000	Everton	103	13	4			
	£150,000	Arsenal	60	4	1			
Defenders								
†David O'Leary (EI)	London	Arsenal (A)	272	33	37	9	1	1
5 11, 11 3, 2.5.58								
John Devine* (EI)	Dublin	Arsenal (A)	86+3	25	6			
5 10½, 12 0, 11.11.58								
Chris Whyte (EU21)	London	Arsenal (A)	68	10	5	5		
6 1, 11 10, 2.9.61								
Kenny Sansom (E)	Camberwell	Crystal Palace (A)	172	11	17	3		1
5 6, 11 8, 26.9.58	£800,000	Arsenal	124	17	10	3		
Danny O'Shea	Stoke Newington	Arsenal (A)	6	3		1		
6 0, 12 8, 26.3.63								
John Kay	Sunderland	Arsenal (A)	7					
5 10, 11 6								
Midfield								
Graham Rix (E)	Doncaster	Arsenal (A)	228+5	30	36+1	30		4
5 9, 11 0, 23.10.57								
Brian Talbot (E)	Ipswich	Ipswich T (A)	177	12	23	25	1	3
5 10, 12 0, 21.7.53	£450,000	Arsenal	182+4	23	17	24	1	2
•John Hollins* (E)	Guildford	Chelsea (A)	436	43	50	47	7	4
5 8, 11 7, 16.7.46	£80,000	QPR	148+3	11+2	10+1	5		1
	£75,000	Arsenal	123+4	19+1	12	9	3	
Stewart Robson	Billericay	Arsenal (A)	51	9	9	4	1	
5 11, 11 13								
Peter Nicholas (W)	Newport	Crystal Palace(A)	127	10	7	7		
5 8½, 11 8, 10.11.59	£400,000	Arsenal	57+3	8	8	1	1	1
Paul Gorman	Dublin	Arsenal (A)	4					
5 10, 11 8, 6.8.63								
David Cork	Doncaster	Arsenal (A)						
5 9, 11 8, 28.10.62								
Tony Rees		Arsenal (A)						
5 5, 10 1								
Forwards								
Alan Sunderland (E)	Mexborough	Wolverhampton W (A)	139+19	13+1	16	29	4	
5 9, 11 7, 1.7.53	£320,000	Arsenal	193+1	22	34	51	12	15
Brian McDermott (EY)	Slough	Arsenal (A)	32+16	3+1	+1	10		
5 8, 10 0, 8.4.61	—	Fulham (loan)	+3					
Paul Vaessen*	Gillingham	Arsenal (A)	23+9	10+1		6	4	
16.10.61								
Brian Sparrow	London	Arsenal (A)	17			1		
5 7, 10 2, 24.6.62	—	Wimbledon (loan)						
Paul Davis (EU21)	London	Arsenal (A)	87+4	10+2	6+1	9	2	2
5 8, 9 7, 9.12.61								
John Hawley*	Withernsea	Hull C	101+13	10+1	5	22	2	1
6 0, 13 12, 8.5.54	£75,000	Leeds U	30+3	6	3	16	1	
	£200,000	Sunderland	25	3	3	11		
	£50,000	Arsenal	14+6	1		3		
	—	Orient (loan)	4			1		
	—	Hull C (loan)	3			1		
Colin Hill	Uxbridge	Arsenal (A)	7					
5 11, 11 11								
Tony Woodcock (E)	Nottingham	Nottingham F (A)	125+4	21	14	36	12	10
5 10, 11 0, 6.12.55	—	Lincoln C (loan)	2+2			1		
	—	Doncaster R (loan)	6			2		
	£650,000	Cologne						
	£500,000	Arsenal	34	8	8	14	3	4
Lee Chapman (EU21)	Lincoln	Stoke C	95+4	5	3	34	3	1
6 1½, 13 5, 5.12.59	—	Plymouth Arg (loan)	3+1					
	£500,000	Arsenal	12+7	+2		3		
Raphael Meade	London	Arsenal (A)	10+10	3	1	6	1	
5 10, 11 9, 22.11.62								
Terry Lee		Arsenal (A)						
5 11, 11 3								

Commercial Manager: A. J. Kelsey (01-226 9562). *Club Coach:* Don Howe.
Association of Football Statisticians Club Adviser to Yearbook: J. Waters.

Players (non-appearance) granted free transfer: Mark Gerbaldi.
Players released since May 1982: James Watt, D. (Hendon); Vladimir Petrovic, M. (Antwerp).

ASTON VILLA

Division 1

Back row (left to right):
Mark Jones
Colin Gibson
Allan Evans
Ken McNaught
Pat Heard
Middle row:
Jim Williams (Physio)
Gordon Cowans
Andy Blair
Nigel Spink
Jimmy Rimmer
David Geddis
Gary Williams
Roy MacLaren
(Assistant Manager)
Front row:
Tony Morley
Des Bremner
Ken Swain
Tony Barton (Manager)
Dennis Mortimer
Peter Withe
Gary Shaw.

Chairman: H. D. Ellis.

Directors: J. H. Kartz, A. T. Gill.

Manager: Tony Barton. ***Secretary:*** Steven Stride.

Commercial Manager: Tony Stephens.

Year Formed: 1874.

Turned Professional: 1885. Ltd Co.: 1896.

Previous Grounds: 1874–76, Aston Park; 1876–97, Perry Barr; 1897– Villa Park.

Club Nickname: 'The Villans'.

Previous Managers since 1946: Alex Massie, George Martin, Eric Houghton, Joe Mercer, Dick Taylor, Tommy Cummings, Tommy Docherty, Vic Crowe, Ron Saunders (9).

Villa Park, Trinity Rd, Birmingham B6 6HE. Telephone 021-327 6604. 24-hour answering service 021-328 1722. ***Telegraphic Address:*** 'Villa, Birmingham 6'. ***Ground capacity:*** 48,000. ***Record attendance:*** 76,588 v Derby Co, FA Cup 6th rd, 2 March, 1946. ***Record receipts:*** £211,155, FA Cup semi-final, Arsenal v Manchester U, 16 April, 1983. ***Club record:*** £165,481 European Cup semi-final v Juventus, 2 Mar, 1983. ***Pitch measurements:*** 115yd×75yd.

Directions to Ground: Bus 5 from Corporation Street to Witton Square. Special buses from Priory Ringway and Hall of Memory (city centre). Birmingham New Street railway station is near the centre. The ground is ½ mile from link to the motorway.

Match tickets: Applications for any games can be made by post or in person, any time during the season.

Car parking: Asda Car Park in Aston Hall Road. Side-street parking also available.

Entertainments/catering facilities: Many refreshment points around the ground.

Club shop: Adjacent to the ground; sells all types of souvenirs.

Handbooks/programmes: Programmes available on seasonal subscription.

Note: Full club statistical records are on pages 416–455.

ASTON VILLA 1982–83 LEAGUE RECORD

Match No.	Date	Venue	Opponents	Result	H/T Score	Lg. Pos.	Goalscorers	Attendance
1	Aug 28	H	Sunderland	L 1-3	1-0	—	Cowans	22,945
2	31	A	Everton	L 0-5	0-3	—		24,026
3	Sept 4	A	Southampton	L 0-1	0-1	22		17,943
4	8	H	Luton T	W 4-1	3-0	—	Mortimer, Withe, Cowans 2 (2 pens)	18,823
5	11	H	Nottingham F	W 4-1	2-1	16	Mortimer, Withe 2, Cowans (pen)	21,224
6	18	A	Manchester C	W 1-0	1-0	10	Shaw	28,650
7	25	H	Swansea C	W 2-0	2-0	8	Mortimer, Evans	21,246
8	Oct 2	A	WBA	L 0-1	0-0	9		25,300
9	9	A	Notts Co	L 1-4	0-2	11	Shaw	8990
10	16	H	Watford	W 3-0	1-0	9	Withe, Morley 2	21,572
11	23	A	Norwich C	L 0-1	0-0	11		15,761
12	30	H	Tottenham H	W 4-0	0-0	10	Cowans 2 (1 pen), Morley, Shaw	25,992
13	Nov 6	A	Coventry C	D 0-0	0-0	10		12,076
14	13	H	Brighton & HA	W 1-0	0-0	7	Withe	18,834
15	20	H	Manchester U	W 2-1	1-1	6	Shaw, Withe	35,487
16	27	A	Stoke C	W 3-0	1-0	6	Parkin (og), Shaw 2	18,886
17	Dec 4	H	West Ham U	W 1-0	0-0	3	Cowans (pen)	24,658
18	7	A	Arsenal	L 1-2	1-2	—	McNaught	17,384
19	18	H	Liverpool	L 2-4	2-3	5	Shaw, Withe	34,568
20	27	A	Birmingham C	L 0-3	0-1	7		43,864
21	29	H	Ipswich T	D 1-1	1-1	7	Withe	21,912
22	Jan 1	A	Manchester U	L 1-3	1-1	8	Cowans (pen)	41,545
23	3	H	Southampton	W 2-0	1-0	7	Cowans (pen), Evans	19,925
24	15	A	Sunderland	L 0-2	0-1	7		16,052
25	22	H	Manchester C	D 1-1	1-1	7	Shaw	20,415
26	Feb 5	A	Nottingham F	W 2-1	1-1	9	Withe 2	16,532
27	12	H	Everton	W 2-0	1-0	6	Morley, Withe	21,117
28	26	A	Watford	L 1-2	1-1	5	Walters	19,318
29	Mar 5	H	Norwich C	W 3-2	1-1	5	Withe, Deacy, Shaw	18,624
30	8	H	Notts Co	W 2-0	1-0	—	Withe, Shaw	17,452
31	19	H	Coventry C	W 4-0	3-0	4	Shaw, Withe 2, Evans	20,509
32	23	A	Tottenham H	L 0-2	0-1	—		22,455
33	26	A	Bighton & HA	D 0-0	0-0	4		14,657
34	Apr 2	A	Ipswich T	W 2-1	1-1	4	Shaw, Withe	19,912
35	4	H	Birmingham C	W 1-0	0-0	—	Shaw	40,897
36	9	A	Luton T	L 1-2	1-1	4	Shaw	10,924
37	19	H	WBA	W 1-0	1-0	—	Mortimer	26,921
38	23	A	West Ham U	L 0-2	0-0	4		21,822
39	30	H	Stoke C	W 4-0	1-0	4	Cowans, McNaught, Morley, Evans	20,944
40	May 2	A	Swansea C	L 1-2	1-1	5	Shaw	9173
41	7	A	Liverpool	D 1-1	1-0	5	Shaw (pen)	39,939
42	14	H	Arsenal	W 2-1	1-0	6	Shaw, Gibson	24,647

Final League Position: 6

GOALSCORERS

League (62): Shaw 17 (1 pen), Withe 16, Cowans 10 (7 pens), Morley 5, Evans 4, Mortimer 4, McNaught 2, Deacy 1, Gibson 1, Walters 1, own goal 1.
Milk Cup (1): Withe 1.
FA Cup (6): Cowans 1, Gibson 1, Morley 1, Shaw 1, Walters 1, Withe 1.
European Cup (10): Shaw 5, Withe 2, Cowans 1, Morley 1, Mortimer 1.
European Super Cup (3): Cowans 1, McNaught 1, Shaw 1.

Milk Cup	Second Round	Notts Co (h)	1-2
		(a)	0-1
FA Cup	Third Round	Northampton T (a)	1-0
	Fourth Round	Wolverhampton W (h)	1-0
	Fifth Round	Watford (h)	4-1
	Sixth Round	Arsenal (a)	0-2

European Champions Cup	First Round	Besilatas (h)	3-1
		(a)	0-0
	Second Round	Dynamo Bucharest (a)	2-0
		(h)	4-2
	Quarter-final	Juventus (h)	1-2
		(a)	1-3
European Super Cup		Barcelona (a)	0-1
		(h)	3-0
World Club Championship		Penarol	0-2 (in Tokyo).

Rimmer	Swain	Williams	Evans	McNaught	Mortimer	Bremner	Walters	Withe	Cowans	Morley	Heard	Shaw	Jones	Blair	Geddis	Hopkins	Gibson	Deacy	Spink	Curbishley	Walker	Referees	Match No.
1	2	3	4	5	6	7	8	9*	10	11	12											H. King	1
1	2	3	4*	5	6	7	9		10	11	12	8										A. Challinor	2
1				5	6	4		9	10	11	3		2	7	8							C. Downey	3
1				5	6	4	12	9	10	11	3	8*	2	7								D. Owen	4
1		2	12	5	6	4		9	10	11	3	8*		7								R. Bridges	5
1		3	4	5	6	7		9	10	11		8	2									F. Roberts	6
1		3	4	5	6	7		9	10	11		8	2									T. Fitzharris	7
1		3	4	5	6	7		9	10	11		8	2									T. Mills	8
1		3*	4		6	5		9	10	12	11	8	2			7						D. Hutchinson	9
1			4	5	6	7		9	10	11		8	2				3					R. Banks	10
1		12	4*	5	6	7			10	11		8	2		9		3					K. Salmon	11
1		2	4	5	6	7		9	10	11		8					3					C. Thomas	12
1		2	4	5	6	7		9	10	11		8						3				J. Deakin	13
1		3	4	5	6	7	12	9	10	11		8*						2				J. Lovatt	14
1		3	4	5	6	7		9	10	11		8	2									B. Hill	15
1		3	4	5	6	7		9	10	11		8	2									D. Scott	16
1		3	4	5	6*	7	12	9	10	11		8	2									E. Read	17
1		3	4	5		7	12	9	10	11	6*	8	2									D. Letts	18
1		3	4	5	6	7	11	9	10			8	2									M. Scott	19
1		3	4	5	6	7	11	9	10			8	2									R. Lewis	20
		2*	4	5	6	7	11	9	10	12		8					3		1			R. Milford	21
		2	4	5	6	7	11	9	10			8					3		1			G. Tyson	22
		3	4	5	6	7		9	10	11		8	2						1			D. Shaw	23
		3	4	5	6	7	8	9	10	11			2						1			N. Wilson	24
		2	4	5	6	7		9	10	11		8					3		1			D. Reeves	25
		2	4	5		7		9	10	11		8		6			3		1			D. Allison	26
		2	4	5	6			9	10	11*		8		7			3		1			B. Stevens	27
		2	4	5	6		9		10	11		8		7			3		1			M. James	28
			4	5	6	7	11	9*	10			8					3	2	1			J. Worrall	29
			4	5	6*	7	11	9	10			8		12			3	2	1			R. Nixon	30
		2	4	5	6	7	11	9	10	12		8*					3		1			T. Spencer	31
		2	4	5	6	7	11	9	10	12		8*					3		1			D. Axcell	32
		2	4	5	6	7	11	9	10			8					3		1			T. Glasson	33
		2	4	5	6	7	11	9	10			8					3		1			E. Scales	34
		2	4	5	6	7*	11	9	10			8					3		1	12		N. Midgeley	35
		2	4	5	6	7	11	9	10			8					3		1			L. Burden	36
		2	4	5	6			9	10	11		8					3		1	7		L. Shapter	37
		2	4	5				9	10	11		8					3		1	7	6	C. Thomas	38
		2	4	5	6	12	9		10	11		8					3		1	7*		C. Downey	39
		2	4	5	6		9		10	11		8					3		1	7		D. Hedges	40
		2*	4	5	6	7			10	11		8			12		3		1	9		C. Seel	41
			4	5	6	7			10	11*		8	2		12		3		1	9		N. Ashley	42
20	2	35	39	41	39	36	18	35	42	29	5	39	17	6	2	1	23	4	22	6	1		
		+ 1s	+ 1s			+ 1s	+ 4s			+ 4s	+ 2s			+ 1s	+ 2s					+ 1s			

FOOTBALL LEAGUE RECORD

1888 Original Member of the League; 1936–38 Division 2; 1938–59 Division 1; 1959–60 Division 2; 1960–67 Division 1; 1967–70 Division 2; 1970–72 Division 3; 1972–75 Division 2; 1975– Division 1.

HONOURS

Football League: Division 1 – Champions 1893–94, 1895–96, 1896–97, 1898–99, 1899–1900, 1909–10, 1980–81; Runners-up 1888–89, 1902–03, 1907–08, 1910–11, 1912–13, 1913–14, 1930–31, 1932–33; Division 2 – Champions 1937–38, 1959–60; Runners-up 1974–75; Division 3 – Champions 1971–72. *FA Cup:* Winners 1887, 1895, 1897, 1905, 1913, 1920, 1957 (7 wins stands as the record); Runners-up 1892, 1924. *Double Performed:* 1896–97. *Football League Cup:* Winners 1961, 1975, 1977; Runners-up 1963, 1971. **European Competitions:** *European Cup:* 1981–82 (winners), 1982–83; *UEFA Cup:* 1975–76, 1977–78. *World Club Championship:* 1982–83; *European Super Cup:* 1982–83 (winners).

COLOURS

Claret shirts with light blue sleeves and trim, claret shorts with light blue trim, blue stockings.
Change colours: White shirt with faint yellow/claret hoops, white shorts with yellow/claret stripe and white stockings with yellow/claret hoops.

ASTON VILLA

Players Names Ht, Wt, D.o.B.	Birthplace Transfer Fee	Clubs	Appearances F.L. A & S	 F.L.C. A & S	 F.A.C. A & S	Goals F.L.	 F.L.C.	 F.A.C.
Goalkeepers								
Nigel Spink	Chelmsford	Chelmsford C						
6 1, 13 10, 8.8.58	£6000	Aston Villa	23		4			
Jimmy Rimmer (E)	Southport	Manchester U (A)	34	3	6			
5 11, 11 12, 10.2.48	—	Swansea C (loan)	17					
	£40,000	Arsenal	124	10	12			
	£70,000	Aston Villa	229	23	12			
Kevin Poole	Bromsgrove	Aston Villa (A)						
5 10½, 11 6, 21.7.63								
Defenders								
Colin Gibson (EU21)	Bridport	Aston Villa (A)	106+4	13	11	3	1	
5 8, 10 10, 6.4.60								
Ken McNaught	Kirkcaldy	Everton (A)	64+2	10	10	3		
5 11, 11 1, 11.1.55	£200,000	Aston Villa	207	17	13	8		
Allan Evans (S)	Dunfermline	Dunfermline Ath						
6 0, 11 12, 12.10.56	£30,000	Aston Villa	196+2	17	14	28		2
Gary Williams	Wolverhampton	Aston Villa (A)	106+5	11	8			
5 9, 11 7, 17.6.60	—	Walsall (loan)	9					
Mark Jones	Warley	Aston Villa (A)	19	2	1			
5 6, 10 1, 22.10.61								
Ray Walker	North Shields	Aston Villa (A)	1					
5 10, 11 9, 28.9.63								
Paul Birch	Birmingham	Aston Villa (A)						
5 6, 10 6, 20.11.62								
Dean Glover	West Bromwich	Aston Villa (A)						
5 10, 11 2, 29.12.63								
Midfield								
†Dennis Mortimer (EB)	Liverpool	Coventry C (A)	179+14	11	8+1	10		
5 10, 12 0, 5.4.52	£175,000		274	31	19	26		1
Gordon Cowans (E)	Durham	Aston Villa (A)	247+9	17+3	18+1	41	4	3
5 8, 9 2, 27.10.58								
Brendan Ormsby (EY)	Birmingham	Aston Villa (A)	35+2	3+1	1+1			
5 10½, 11 3, 1.10.60								
Eamonn Deacy (EI)	Galway	Galway R						
5 8½, 10 10, 1.10.58		Aston Villa	15+5	2+2	1			
Des Bremner (S)	Aberchirer	Hibernian						
5 10, 11 11, 17.9.52	£275,000	Aston Villa	152+1	13	12	8	1	
Alan Curbishley (EU21)	Forest Gate	West Ham U (A)	78+7	3	5	5		
5 9, 11 6, 8.11.57	£275,000	Birmingham C	128+2	12	10	11	3	1
	£100,000	Aston villa	6+1					
Andy Blair (SU21)	Bedworth	Coventry C (A)	90+3	11	8	6	1	2
5 9, 10 9, 18.12.59	£300,000	Aston Villa	15+10	+2	3			
Mark Hutchinson	Stoke	Aston Villa (A)						
5 8, 10 0, 2.11.63								
Steve McMahon (EU21)	Liverpool	Everton (A)	99+1	11	9	11	3	
5 7, 10 7, 20.8.61	£300,000	Aston Villa						
David Norton		Aston Villa (A)						
5 7½, 10 12								
Forwards								
Gary Shaw (EU21)	Birmingham	Aston Villa (A)	135+1	12+1	9	53	4	4
5 10, 11 9, 12.1.61								
Mark Walters (EY)	Birmingham	Aston Villa (A)	18+5		2+1	1		1
5 9, 10 12, 2.6.64								
David Geddis (EB)	Carlisle	Ipswich T (A)	26+17	+1	2+1	5		1
5 10½, 12 2, 12.3.58	—	Luton T (loan)	9+4			4		
	£300,000	Aston villa	43+4	4	4+1	12		4
	—	Luton T (loan)	4					
Tony Morley (E)	Ormskirk	Preston NE (A)	78+6	8	6+1	15	3	2
5 8½, 11 8, 26.8.54	£100,000	Burnley	78+13	3+1	3+2	5	1	1
	£200,000	Aston Villa	122+8	13	8	24	3	1
Peter Withe (E)	Liverpool	Southport	3					
6 2, 12 0, 30.8.51	—	Barrow	1					
	—	Arcadia Shepherds						
	—	Wolverhampton W	12+5			3		
	£50,000	Birmingham C	35	3	2	9		
	£40,000	Nottingham F	74+1	21	14	28	12	10
	£225,000	Newcastle U	76	3	4	25		2
	£500,000	Aston Villa	106	10	6	46	4	1
Paul Kerr		Aston Villa (A)						
5 8½, 11 2								
Tony Rees		Aston Villa (A)						
5 8½, 11 10								

Commercial Manager: Tony Stephens. (Tel. No. 021 327 5399).
Assistant Manager: Roy MacLaren. *Chief Scout:* Malcolm Beard.
Physiotherapist: Jim Williams *Club Statistician:*
Association of Football Statisticians Club Adviser to Yearbook: D. Hodges

Players released since May 1982: Gary Stirland, M., (Gloucester C); Martin McKenzie, M., (N/K).

BARNSLEY Division 2

Back row (left to right): Paul Longden, Derrick Parker, Ian Banks, Winston Campbell, Don Souter.
Middle row: Norman Rimmington (Physiotherapist), Nicky Law, Mick McCarthy, Bobby Horn, Ian Evans, Garry Pierce, Ronnie Glavin, Alan Birch, Bobby Collins (Youth Coach).
Front Row: Colin Walker, Phil Chambers, Norman Hunter (Manager), Stewart Barrowclough, Joe Joyce, Jimmy Mann.

Chairman: G. Buckle LLB.

Directors: A Raynor JP, R. F. Potter, G. Pallister, N. W. B. Moody JP, C. Williams, J. Steele.

Secretary: Michael Spinks. ***Team Manager:*** Norman Hunter.

Year Formed: 1887. ***Turned Professional:*** 1888. ***Ltd Co.:*** 1899.

Previous Name: Barnsley St Peter's.

Club Nickname: 'The Tykes' or 'Reds'.

Previous Managers since 1946: Angus Seed, Tim Ward, Johnny Steele, John McSeveney, Jim Iley, Allan Clarke (6).

Oakwell Ground, Grove St, Barnsley. Telephone Barnsley (0226) 295353. ***Ground Capacity:*** 35,554 (15,000 under cover). ***Record attendance:*** 40,255 v Stoke C, 15 Feb, 1936, FA Cup 5th rd. ***Record receipts:*** £16,146 v Rotherham U, 16 Dec, 1978, FA Cup 2nd rd. ***Pitch measurements:*** 111yd×75yd.

Directions to Ground: Fairly frequent train service from Sheffield and Leeds to Exchange Station Barnsley. No special buses, just the normal services, and no buses from town centre because the ground is so close.

Match tickets: Stand seats bookable two weeks in advance.

Car parking: Two official club parks adjacent to the ground holding 1200 cars; parking fee 25p. There is a free public park in Queens Road, two minutes from the ground. The M1 runs approximately two miles from the ground.

Entertainments/catering facilities: Football club social club is adjacent to the ground. Seven tea bars sited around the ground sell refreshments; three of them sell alcoholic drinks.

Club shop: Inside the ground; sells all types of souvenirs.

Handbooks/programmes: Programmes available on subscription.

Note: Full club statistical records are on pages 416–455.

BARNSLEY 1982–83 LEAGUE RECORD

Match No.	Date	Venue	Opponents	Result	H/T Score	Lg. Pos.	Goalscorers	Attendance
1	Aug 28	A	Crystal Palace	D 1-1	1-1	—	Airey	7549
2	Sept 4	H	Oldham Ath	D 1-1	0-0	16	Futcher (og)	11,909
3	7	A	Cambridge U	D 1-1	0-1	—	Parker	3314
4	11	A	Wolverhampton W	L 0-2	0-0	17		15,065
5	18	H	Burnley	W 3-0	2-0	13	Glavin 2, Parker	11,938
6	25	A	Newcastle U	W 2-1	2-1	8	Glavin, Parker	24,511
7	Oct 2	H	Fulham	W 4-3	1-3	8	Banks 2, Glavin, Cunningham	12,582
8	9	H	QPR	L 0-1	0-0	11		13,270
9	16	A	Rotherham U	L 0-1	0-1	12		13,791
10	19	H	Derby Co	D 1-1	0-1	—	Airey	10,343
11	23	A	Bolton W	W 2-0	1-0	8	Glavin (pen), Birch	7339
12	30	H	Shrewsbury T	D 2-2	2-2	8	Glavin, Parker	11,150
13	Nov 6	A	Middlesbrough	L 0-2	0-1	11		11,787
14	13	H	Chelsea	D 1-1	0-1	12	Glavin	13,286
15	20	A	Grimsby T	W 2-1	0-0	9	Glavin, Cunningham	7500
16	27	H	Leeds U	W 2-1	1-1	7	Campbell, Glavin (pen)	21,530
17	Dec 4	A	Blackburn R	D 1-1	0-0	9	Campbell	6769
18	11	H	Carlisle U	D 2-2	2-1	10	Barrowclough, Banks	10,226
19	18	A	Charlton Ath	L 2-3	1-2	10	Glavin, Cunningham	4942
20	27	H	Sheffield W	D 0-0	0-0	11		23,275
21	28	A	Leicester C	L 0-1	0-1	14		14,838
22	Jan 1	H	Grimsby T	W 4-0	3-0	11	Banks, Parker 2, Birch	12,318
23	3	A	Oldham Ath	D 1-1	0-1	11	Parker	8382
24	15	H	Crystal Palace	W 3-1	2-0	9	Glavin 2, Cunningham	10,120
25	22	A	Burnley	L 1-3	0-2	10	Joyce	10,275
26	Feb 5	H	Wolverhampton W	W 2-1	1-1	7	Banks, Parker	13,535
27	19	A	QPR	L 0-3	0-2	11		10,271
28	26	H	Rotherham U	W 2-1	0-0	8	Birch, Parker	13,941
29	Mar 5	H	Bolton W	W 3-1	1-1	7	Birch, McCarthy, Ronson	10,400
30	12	A	Shrewsbury T	L 1-3	1-0	9	Parker	4024
31	19	H	Middlesbrough	W 2-0	0-0	7	Birch, Campbell	10,681
32	26	A	Chelsea	W 3-0	1-0	5	Hales (og), Cunningham, Parker	7223
33	Apr 2	H	Leicester C	L 1-2	0-1	8	McGuire	13,278
34	4	A	Sheffield W	W 1-0	0-0	—	Glavin	22,427
35	9	H	Cambridge U	L 2-3	2-0	7	Cunningham, Glavin	9934
36	16	A	Derby Co	D 1-1	0-1	8	Cunningham	14,861
37	19	A	Fulham	L 0-1	0-0	—		9003
38	23	H	Blackburn R	D 2-2	0-0	9	Glavin 2	7617
39	30	A	Leeds U	D 0-0	0-0	10		15,344
40	May 4	H	Newcastle U	L 0-5	0-1	—		10,958
41	7	H	Charlton Ath	D 0-0	0-0	9		6457
42	14	A	Carlisle U	D 1-1	0-0	10	Glavin	5898

Final League Position: 10

GOALSCORERS

League (57): Glavin 17 (2 pens), Parker 11, Cunningham 7, Banks 5, Birch 5, Campbell 3, Airey 2, Barrowclough 1, Joyce 1, McCarthy 1, McGuire 1, Ronson 1, own goals 2.
Milk Cup (8): Glavin 3, Banks 1, Birch 1, McCarthy 1, own goals 2.
FA Cup (1): Glavin 1.

Milk Cup	Second Round	Cambridge U (h)	2-1
		(a)	3-1
	Third Round	Sheffield U (a)	3-1
	Fourth Round	Sheffield W (a)	0-1
FA Cup	Third Round	Bradford C (a)	1-0
	Fourth Round	Cambridge U (a)	0-1

Commercial Manager: Gerald Whewall (Tel. No. Barnsley 86718).
Club Coach: Ian Evans. *Chief Scout:* Phil Chambers.
Physiotherapist: N, Rimmington. *Club Statistician:* G. Firth.
Association of Football Statisticians Club Adviser to Yearbook: A. Bower.

Horn	Joyce	Chambers	Ronson	Banks	McCarthy	Souter	Walker	Airey	Mann	Campbell	Parker	Law	Barrowclough	Evans	Birch	Glavin	Cunningham	Ainscow (L)	Pierce	Hunter	Wilkes	Moores (L)	McGuire	Cross	Longden	Shutt	Goodison	*Referees*
1	2	3	4	5	6	7	8*	9	10	11	12																	I. Borrett
1	2	3	4	5	6	7		9	10	11	8																	G. Napthine
1		3	4		6			9	10	12	8	2	5	7*	11													A. Grey
1		3	4		6	12		9	10	7*	8	2	5		11													A. Ward
1		3	10	5*	6	7	9				8	2	12		11	4												M. Scott
1		3	10	5	6	7					8	2			11	4	9											D. Richardson
1		3	10	5	6	7					8	2			11	4	9											M. Robinson
1		3	10	5	6	7					8	2	12		11*	4	9											R. Chadwick
1		3	10	5	6	7					8	2	12		11*	4	9											K. Redfern
1	2	3	10	5	6	7		12		8*			4		11		9											N. Midgley
1	2	3	10	5	6	7				8					11	4	9											F. Roberts
1	2	3	10	5	6	7				9*	8				11	4	12											A. Saunders
1	2	3	10	5	6	7				8	9*				11	4	12											N. Glover
1	2	3	10	5	6	7				8	9				11	4												P. Willis
1	2	3		5	6	7			10	8			11			4	9											J. Bray
1	2	3		5	6	7				8			11			4	9	10										N. Ashley
1	2	3	10		6	7				8			11			4	9	5										D. Shaw
1	2	3	10	5	6	7				8	12		11*			4	9											D. Owen
	2	3	9	5	6	7				8					11	4	10		1									D. Letts
	2	3	10	5	6						8	7			11	4	9		1									G. Courtney
	2	3	9	5	6						8	7			11	4	10		1									E. Scales
	2	3	9	5							8	7	12		11	4	10		1	6*								R. Guy
	2	3	9	5	6						8	7			11	4	10		1									N. Peck
	2	3	9	5	6						8	7			11	4	10		1									D. Civil
	2	3	9	5	6			10			8	7			11*	4			1		12							V. Callow
	2	3	9	5	6						8	7	11			4			1			10						N. Wilson
	2	3	9	5	6*		12				8	7	11			4			1			10						M. Taylor
	2	3	9*	5	6					12	8	7			11	4			1			10						A. Seville
	2	3	9	5	6*					10	8	7			11	4			1									K. Barratt
	2	3	9	5		12				10	8	7		6*	11	4			1									J. Hough
	2	3	9	5		6				10*	8	7	12		11	4			1									J. Lovatt
	2	3	9	5	6						8	7			11		10		1				4					H. King
		3	9	5	6	2					8	7			11*	12	10		1				4					T. Fitzharris
	2	3	9	5	6						8*	7	11			12	10		1				4					M. Heath
	2		9	5	6						12	7	11			8	10		1				4	3*				D. Allison
	2		9	5	6						8	7	11		12	4*	10		1						3			A. Cooper
		3	9	5	6						8		2		11		10		1							4	7	Alan Robinson
		3	9	5	6			8				7	11			4	10		1								2	R. Nixon
	2	3	9		6			8				7	11			4	10		1				5					J. Hunting
	2	3	9		6			8				7	11*			4	10		1		12		5					H. Taylor
1	2	3		5	6			9								4	10				11		8				7	G. Tyson
1	2	3	8	5	6			9				7				4	10				11							D. Scott
20	32	40	39	37	39	19	2	10	5	15	29	28	16	2	26	33	27	2	22	1	2	3	7	1	1	1	3	
						+ 2s	+ 1s	+ 1s		+ 2s	+ 3s		+ 5s		+ 1s	+ 2s	+ 2s				+ 2s							

FOOTBALL LEAGUE RECORD

1898 Elected to Division 2; 1932–34 Division 3(N); 1934–38 Division 2; 1938–39 Division 3(N); 1946–53 Division 2; 1953–55 Division 3(N); 1955–59 Division 2; 1959–65 Division 3; 1965–68 Division 4; 1968–72 Division 3; 1972–79 Division 4; 1979–81 Division 3; 1981– Division 2.

HONOURS

Football League: best season: 3rd, Division 2, 1914–15, 1921–22; Division 3(N) – Champions 1933–34, 1938–39, 1954–55; Runners-up 1953–54; Diision 3 – Runners-up 1980–81; Division 4 – Runners-up 1967–68; Promoted 1978–79. *G Cup:* Winners 1912; Runners-up 1910. *Football League Cup:* best season: 5th rd, 1981–82.

COLOURS

Red shirts, white shorts, red stockings. **Change colours:** White shirts, black shorts, white stockings.

Players (non-appearance) granted free transfer: Philip Watkin, M.; John Bukovina, F.; Ernie Heseltine; Ron Wakefield. *Players released since May 1982:* Ian Hughes, M. (N/K); Gary Walters, M. (N/K); Martin New, G. (N/K); David Glover, D. (N K); Philip Dunstone, D. (N K).

BARNSLEY

			Appearances			Goals		
Players Names	*Birthplace*	*Clubs*	*F.L.*	*F.L.C.*	*F.A.C.*	*F.L.*	*F.L.C.*	*F.A.C.*
Ht. Wt. D.o.B.	*Transfer Fee*		*A & S*	*A & S*	*A & S*			
Goalkeepers								
Gary Pierce*	Bury	Mossley						
6 1, 12 9, 2.3.51		Huddersfield T	23	1				
	£40,000	Wolverhampton W	98	6	5			
	£40,000	Barnsley	81	4	4			
Bobby Horn	Westminster	Crystal Palace (A)						
6 1, 14 1, 15.12.61		Barnsley	62	13	1			
Ian Ironside		Barnsley						
Andy Rhodes		Barnsley (A)						
6 10, 12 9								
Defenders								
Phil Chambers (ES)	Barnsley	Barnsley (A)	399+1	27	22	6		
5 7½, 11 1, 10.11.53								
Mick McCarthy	Barnsley	Barnsley (A)	260	26	16	7	3	
6 1½, 13 3, 7.2.59								
Joe Joyce	Consett	Barnsley	92+1	13+1	9	1	1	
5 9, 10 5, 18.3.61								
Ian Evans (W)	Egham	Q.P.R. (A)	39		3	2		
6 2½, 12 6, 30.1.52	P/E	Crystal Palace	137	10	16	14		2
	£80,000	Barnsley	102	14	6	3	2	
Nicky Law	Greenwich	Arsenal (A)						
6 0, 13 5, 8.9.61	F/T	Barnsley	47	2	2			
Paul Longden*	Wakefield	Barnsley (A)	5					
5 7, 10 3, 28.9.62								
Don Soutar*	Hammersmith	Ipswich T (A)						
5 11, 11 8, 1.12.61	F/T	Barnsley	19	5				
Mark Fletcher		Barnsley (A)						
5 8, 11 0								
Wayne Goodison		Barnsley (A)	3					
5 8, 11 7								
Midfield								
Ian Banks	Mexborough	Barnsley (A)	158+6	20	11	37	3	
5 10½, 12 2, 9.1.61								
• Ronnie Glavin (S)	Glasgow	Celtic						
5 10, 12 6, 27.3.51	£40,000	Barnsley	137+4	21+1	9	62	15	4
Winston Campbell	Sheffield	Barnsley (A)	22+4	5	+1	3		
5 8, 11 6, 9.10.62	—	Doncaster R (loan)	3					
David Wilkes	Barnsley	Barnsley (A)	4+2					
5 8, 10 2, 10.3.64	—	Halifax T (loan)	4					
Dean Whitehouse	Mexborough	Barnsley (A)						
5 5, 9 1, 3.10.63								
Alan Birch	West Bromwich	Walsall (A)	158+13	9	9	23	1	
5 6, 10 5, 12.8.56	£25,000	Chesterfield	90	8	8	35	4	1
	£200,000	Wolverhampton W	13+2	2	1			
	£100,000	Barnsley	43+1	4	2	10	1	
Mick McGuire (EY)	Blackpool	Coventry C	60+12	3	5	1		
5 7, 10 5, 4.9.52	£50,000	Norwich C	172+10	11	7+1	10		
	£30,000	Barnsley	7			1		
Billy Ronson	Fleetwood	Blackpool (A)	124+4	10	4	12	1	
5 6, 9 9, 22.1.57	£135,000	Cardiff C	90	9	3	4		
	£100,000	Wrexham	31+1		4	1	1	
	£50,000	Barnsley	39	5	2	1		
Forwards								
Stewart Barrowclough (EU23)*	Barnsley	Barnsley (A)	9		1			
5 9, 10 5, 29.10.51	£40,000	Newcastle U	201+18	14+3	13+6	20		2
	P/E	Birmingham C	26+3	1		2		
	£100,000	Bristol R	60+1	6	3	14	1	2
	£50,000	Barnsley	46+6	7+1	1+1	1	1	
Derrick Parker	Wallsend	Burnley (A)	5+1			2		
5 9½, 11 8, 7.2.57	F/T	Southend U	129	8	12	43	1	7
	F/T	Barnsley	104+3	15	6	33	4	3
Carl Airey	Barnsley	Barnsley (A)	10+1	+1		2		
5 11, 11 6, 6.2.65								
Tony Cunningham	Jamaica	Stourbridge						
6 1, 13 2, 12.11.57	£20,000	Lincoln C	111+12	13	5+1	32	7	
	£30,000	Barnsley	27+2		1	7		
Steve Shutt		Barnsley (A)	1					
5 10, 10 4								
Non-contract Players								
Norman Hunter (E)	Middlesbrough	Leeds U	541	70	57+1	18		
5 11½, 12 6, 29.10.43	£40,000	Bristol C	108	2	3	14		
	F/T	Barnsley	28+3	1	2			
Apprentices								
Paul Cross	Barnsley	Barnsley (A)	1					
5 7, 9 6, 31.10.65								

BIRMINGHAM CITY Division 1

Back row (left to right): Graham Diog *(Physio)*, Kevin Sommerfield, Geoff Scott, Tony Van Mierlo, Kevin Dillon, Jeff Wealands, Tony Coton, Phil Hawker, Mick Harford, Pat Van den Hene, Jim Hagan, Keith Leonard *(Coach)*
Front row: Stuart Gibson, Les Phillips, Alan Curbishley, Kevin Broadhurst, Ron Saunders *(Manager)*, Tony Evans, Dave Langan, Mark Dennis, Neil Whatmore, Ian Handysides

Chairman: C. K. Coombs.

Vice Chairman: J. F. Wiseman.

Directors: N. B. A. Bosworth LLB, D. M. Coombs, R. Burman, H. Parkes, G. Greaves.

Manager: Ron Saunders.

Year Formed: 1875. ***Turned Professional:*** 1885. ***Ltd Co.:*** 1888.

Previous Grounds: Waste ground near Arthur St, 1875; Muntz St, Small Heath, 1877; St Andrew's, 1906.

Previous Names: 1875–88, Small Heath Alliance; 1888, dropped 'Alliance'; became Birmingham 1905; became Birmingham City 1945.

Club Nickname: 'Blues'.

Previous Managers since 1946: Ted Goodier, Harry Storer, Bob Brocklebank, Arthur Turner, Pat Beasley, Gil Merrick, Joe Mallett, Stan Cullis, Fred Goodwin, Willie Bell, Sir Alf Ramsey, Jim Smith (12).

St Andrews, Birmingham B9 4NH. Telephone 021-772 0101/2689, (Information Service) 021-773 7161. ***Ground capacity:*** 44,500 (9,009 seats). ***Record Attendance:*** 66,844 v Everton, FA Cup 5th rd, 11 Feb, 1939. ***Record receipts:*** £48,505 v Aston Villa, Division 1, 11 Oct, 1980. ***Pitch measurements:*** 115yd×75yd. ***Match tickets:*** Bookable three weeks in advance.

Directions to Ground: Buses 97 from Carr's Lane, City Centre, 98, 99 from Bus Station, 58, 60 from High Street; Specials from Albert Street and Hall of Memory, Broad Street. Nearest railway station, Birmingham New Street. By road; via M1, M45, and A45 to Small Heath area of Birmingham and via Cattell Road (sixth turning on the right past Small Heath Park) to the ground; via M6 (exit 6, Gravelly Hill) and A38M (Aston Expressway at first exit), left into Dartmouth Street, and then via Lawley Street and Watery Lane onto the Coventry Road. Turn left and then take left fork into Cattell Road.

Address of Supporters Club: St Andrew's Club, St Andrew's, Birmingham 9.

Car parking: Public car park in Coventry Road and Cattell Road.

Entertainments/Catering facilities: Catering points inside the ground.

Address of the Club Shop or Boutique: City Souvenirs, 26 Cattell Road, Birmingham 9.

BIRMINGHAM CITY 1982–83 LEAGUE RECORD

Match No.	Date	Venue	Opponents	Result		H/T Score	Lg. Pos.	Goalscorers	Attendance
1	Aug 28	A	Manchester U	L	0-3	0-0	—		48,673
2	31	H	Liverpool	D	0-0	0-0	—		20,176
3	Sept 4	H	Stoke C	L	1-4	0-4	20	Curbishley	14,412
4	8	A	Norwich C	L	1-5	1-3	—	Broadhurst	13,860
5	11	A	West Ham U	L	0-5	0-2	22		18,754
6	18	H	Coventry C	W	1-0	1-0	21	Evans	11,681
7	25	A	Brighton & HA	L	0-1	0-0	21		9845
8	Oct 2	H	Watford	D	1-1	0-1	22	Summerfield	13,870
9	Oct 9	H	Luton T	L	2-3	0-0	22	Langan (pen), Brazier	13,772
10	16	A	Nottingham F	D	1-1	1-0	22	Bremner	14,548
11	23	H	Ipswich T	D	0-0	0-0	22		12,051
12	30	A	Arsenal	D	0-0	0-0	22		20,699
13	Nov 6	H	WBA	W	2-1	0-1	22	Dillon (pen), Blake	18,520
14	13	A	Notts Co	D	0-0	0-0	21		9118
15	20	A	Manchester C	D	0-0	0-0	22		23,174
16	27	H	Sunderland	W	2-1	1-0	20	Ferguson, Evans	12,375
17	Dec 4	A	Everton	D	0-0	0-0	21		13,703
18	11	H	Southampton	L	0-2	0-0	21		11,199
19	18	A	Tottenham H	L	1-2	0-0	22	Langan	20,546
20	27	H	Aston Villa	W	3-0	1-0	21	Blake, Hardysides, Ferguson	43,864
21	29	A	Swansea C	D	0-0	0-0	21		11,840
22	Jan 1	H	Manchester C	D	2-2	1-1	21	Ferguson 2	16,362
23	Jan 3	A	Stoke C	D	1-1	1-0	22	Phillips	15,428
24	15	H	Manchester U	L	1-2	0-0	22	Dillon (pen)	19,333
25	22	A	Liverpool	L	0-1	0-1	22		30,986
26	Feb 5	H	West Ham U	W	3-0	1-0	20	Harford, Ferguson, Gayle	12,539
27	26	H	Nottingham F	D	1-1	1-0	20	Harford	12,987
28	Mar 5	A	Ipswich T	L	1-3	0-0	27	Dennis	16,436
29	15	H	Arsenal	W	2-1	0-0	—	Van den Hauwe, Dillon	11,276
30	19	A	WBA	L	0-2	0-1	21		20,794
31	22	A	Watford	L	1-2	0-0	—	Ferguson	14,229
32	26	H	Notts Co	W	3-0	2-0	20	Ferguson 2 (1 pen), Harford	11,744
33	Apr 2	H	Swansea C	D	1-1	0-0	20	Stevenson (pen)	13,591
34	4	A	Aston Villa	L	0-1	0-0	—		40,897
35	9	H	Norwich C	L	0-4	0-2	22		11,733
36	12	A	Luton T	L	1-3	0-3	—	Hopkins	12,868
37	16	A	Coventry C	W	1-0	0-0	21	Phillips	10,420
38	23	H	Everton	W	1-0	0-0	20	Hopkins	11,045
39	30	A	Sunderland	W	2-1	0-1	20	Blake (pen), Harford	14,818
40	May 2	H	Brighton & HA	D	1-1	1-0	19	Handysides	15,977
41	7	H	Tottenham H	W	2-0	1-0	18	Halsall, Harford	18,947
42	14	A	Southampton	W	1-0	0-0	17	Harford	20,327

Final League Position: 17

GOALSCORERS

League (40): Ferguson 8 (1 pen), Harford 6, Blake 3 (1 pen), Dillon 3 (2 pens), Evans 2, Handysides 2, Hopkins 2, Langan 2 (1 pen), Phillips 2, Brazier 1, Bremner 1, Broadhurst 1, Curbishley 1, Derris 1, Gayle 1, Halsall 1, Stevenson 1 (pen), Summerfield 1, Van den Hauwe 1.
Milk Cup (10): Curbishley 3, Handsides 3, Dillon 2 (1 pen), Evans 2.
FA Cup (1): Summerfield 1.

Milk Cup	Second Round	Shrewsbury T (a)	1-1
		(h)	4-1
	Third Round	Derby Co (h)	3-i
	Fourth Round	Burnley (a)	2-3
FA Cup	Third Round	Walsall (a)	0-0
		(h)	1-0
	Fourth Round	Crystal Palace (a)	0-1

Blyth	Langan	Hawker	Scott	Van den Hauwe	Broadhurst	Van Mierlo	Carrodus	Harford	Curbishley	Francis	Hagan	Evans	Dillon	Dennis	Summerfield	Phillips	Stevenson	Blake	Handysides	Brazier	Bremner (L)	Coton	Ferguson (L)	Gayle (L)	Halsall	Hopkins	*Referees*
1	2	3	4	5	6	7	8	9	10	11																	M. Peck
1	2*	3	4	5	6	7	11	9	10		12	8															D. Vickers
1	2	3	4	5	6	7	11	9	10				8														D. Allison
1	2		4*	5	6		11	9	10		12		8	3	7												J. Martin
1		4		5*		7	11	9	10		2		8	3	12	6											M. James
1	2								10	12	7	8		3*		6	4	5	11								D. Richardson
1	2						7		10	12	3	8*				6	4	5	11								D. Reeves
1	2			3	6		7		10				8		12		4	5	11*	9							P. Tyldesley
1	2			3	6				10				8				4	5	11	9	7						D. Scott
1					6		12		10*		3		7				4	5	11	9	8						N. Midgley
1				3	6				10				7				4	5	11	9	8						N. Ashley
				3	6*				10		2	8	7				4	5	11	9	12	1					M. Bodenham
				3	6				10		2		7				4	5	11	8		1	9				J. Worrall
				3	6				10	8	2		7					5	11	4		1	9				A. Saunders
				3*	6				10	12	2		7				4	5	11	8		1	9				D. Shaw
1					6				10		2	8	7	3			4	5	11				9				D. Owen
				3	6				10			8	7				4	5	11	2		1	9				G. Courtney
				3	6*				10		2	8	7				4	5	11	12		1	9				R. Dixon
	10			3	6			8			2		7	11			4	5	12			1	9*				L. Burden
	2			3	6			9	10				7				4	5	11			1	8				R. Lewis
	2			3	6			8	10				7				4	5	11			1	9				A. Glasson
	2				6			8	10		4		7	3				5	11			1	9				H. King
	2				6			9	10				7	3		8	4	5	11			1					D. Hutchinson
					6			9	10		2		7	3	8		4	5	11			1					C. Thomas
					6			9	10		2		7	3	12			5	11*	4		1		8			J. Howell
	2				6			9	10				11	3			4	5				1	8	7			T. Fitzharris
					6			9	10		2		11	3			4	5				1	8	7*			M. Heath
				12	6			9	10		2		11	3			4	5				1	8	7*			D. Letts
				6				9	10		2		11	3			4	5	8			1		7			T. Jones
				6				9	10		2		11				4	5				1		7	8		R. Chadwick
								9	10		2		11	3			4	5				1	8	7	6		M. Taylor
				6				9			2			3			4	5				1	8	7	10	11	B. Daniels
				6				9			2			3		8	4	5	12			1		7*	10	11	R. Bridges
				6				9			2			3			4	5				1	8	7	10	11	N. Midgeley
				6	2			9			3					12	4	5	7*			1	8		10	11	J. Moules
				2	6*			9			3					12	4	5				1	8	7	10	11	A. Grey
				2				9			4			3		6		5	12			1	8*	7	10	11	J. Martin
1				2	12			9			4			3		6		5	8					7*	10	11	K. Cooper
				2	7			9			4			3		6		5	8			1			10	11	K. Walmsley
1				2				9			4			3		6	12	5	7				8*		10	11	L. Shapter
				7				9			2			3		6	4	5	8			1			10	11	A. Challinor
				7				9			2			3		6	4	5	8			1				11	D. Hedges
14	14	4	4	30	28	4	7	29	30	2	30	7	27	23	2	11	30	37	26	10	3	28	20	13	12	11	
				+ 1s	+ 1s		+ 1s			+ 3s	+ 2s				+ 3s	+ 2s	+ 1s		+ 3s	+ 1s	+ 1s						

Also played: Whatmore (no. 9, matches 6, 7); Mumford (no. 2, matches 10, 11); Kuhl (no. 3, match 30; no. 10, match 42).

FOOTBALL LEAGUE RECORD

Division One: 1894–96; 1901–02; 1903–08; 1921–39; 1948–50; 1955–65; 1972–79; 1980–. Division 2: 1892–94; 1896–1901; 1902–03; 1908–21; 1946–48; 1950–55; 1965–72; 1979–80.

HONOURS

Football League: Division 1 best season: 6th, 1955–56; Division 2 – Champions 1892–93, 1920–21, 1947–48, 1954–55; Runners-up 1893–94, 1900–01, 1902–03, 1971–72. *FA Cup:* Runners-up 1931, 1956. *Football League Cup:* Winners 1963. **European Competitions:** *European Fairs Cup:* 1955–58, 1958–60 (runners-up), 1960–61 (runners-up), 1960-62.

COLOURS

Royal blue shirts with three white vertical stripes on sleeves, white shorts with blue trim, white stockings with blue hoops on turn over.

Change colours: Yellow shirts with three blue vertical stripes on sleeves, yellow shorts with blue trim, yellow stockings with blue hoops on turn over.

BIRMINGHAM CITY

Players Names Ht, Wt, D.o.B.	Birthplace Transfer Fee	Clubs	Appearances F.L. A & S	 F.L.C. A & S	 F.A.C. A & S	Goals F.L.	 F.L.C.	 F.A.C.
Goalkeepers								
Tony Coton	Tamworth	Mile Oak R						
6 1, 11 10, 19.5.61		Birmingham C	46	2	5			
Jeff Wealands*	Darlington	Wolverhampton W (A)						
6 0½, 12 0, 26.8.51	F/T	Darlington	28	1	2			
	£10,000	Hull C	240	19	11			
	£30,000	Birmingham C	102	10	5			
	—	Manchester U (loan)	5					
Jim Blyth (S)	Perth	Preston NE (A)	1					
6 1¼, 13 3, 28.7.44	£30,000	Coventry C	151	13	10			
	—	Hereford U (loan)	7					
	F/T	Birmingham C	14	2				
Defenders								
Mark Dennis (EU-21)	Streatham	Birmingham C (A)	130	8	7	1		
5 9, 10 8, 2.5.61								
Pat Van Den Hauwe	Dendermonde	Birmingham C (A)	71+4	4		1		
5 10, 10 6, 16.12.60	Belgium							
Kevan Broadhurst	Dewsbury	Birmingham C (A)	126+5	7	8	9		
5 9½, 11 2, 3.6.59	—	Walsall (loan)	3					
David Langan (EI)	Dublin	Derby Co (A)	143	6	6	1		
5 10, 11 2, 15.2.57	£350,000	Birmingham C	92	6	4	3		
Kevin Rogers	Mertlye	Aston Villa (A)						
5 9, 11 3,	F/T	Birmingham C						
Jim Hagan	Monkstown	Larne						
5 11, 11 9, 10.8.56	£25,000	Coventry C	12+1		3			
	—	Torquay U (loan)	7					
	F/T	Birmingham C	29+2	2				
Noel Blake	Jamaica, WI	Walsall (N/C)						
6 0, 13 5, 12.1.62	—	Aston Villa	4					
	—	Shrewsbury T (loan)	6					
	£55,000	Birmingham C	37	4	3	3		
Wayne Mumford	Rhymn	Manchester C (A)						
	F/T	Birmingham C	2	1				
Martin Kuhl	Frimley	Birmingham C (A)	2					
Mike Halsall	Bootle	Liverpool (A)						
5 10, 11 4, 21.7.61	F/T	Birmingham C	12			1		
Midfield								
Robert Hopkins	Birmingham	Aston Villa (A)	1+2			1		
5 7, 10 5, 25.10.61		Birmingham C	11			2		
Carl Francis	West Ham	Birmingham C (A)	2+3					
5 11, 10 9, 21.8.62								
Duncan McDowall*	Paddington	Birmingham C (A)	2					
6 1, 12 0,								
Ian Handysides	Jarrow	Birmingham C (A)	40+17	4+1	2+2	2	3	
5 6, 10 6, 14.12.62								
Frank Carrodus*	Manchester	Altrincham						
5 9, 10 11, 31.5.49		Manchester C	33+9	3	1+1	1		1
	£95,000	Aston Villa	151	28	9	7	3	
	£70,000	Wrexham	97	6	7	6		
	F/T	Birmingham C	7+1	+1				
Les Phillips	Lambeth	Birmingham C (A)	18+6	+1	1	3		
5 8, 10 6, 7.1.63								
Byron Stevenson (W)	Llanelli	Leeds U (A)	88+7	7+1	6	4	3	1
6 1, 11 0, 7.9.56	P/E	Birmingham C	42+1	4	2	1		
Forwards								
Tony Evans	Liverpool	Formby						
5 8, 11 7, 11.1.54		Blackpool	4+2					
	F/T	Cardiff C	120+4	6+1	8	47	6	4
	£175,000	Birmingham C	62+4	5	1+1	28	3	1
Mike Sturridge	Birmingham	Birmingham C (A)						
5 11, 11 0, 18.9.62								
Mick Harford	Sunderland	Lincoln C	109+6	8	3	4	5	
6 1, 12 4, 12.2.59	£180,000	Newcastle U	18+1			4		
	£160,000	Bristol C	30	5	5	11	1	2
	£100,000	Birmingham C	41		2	15		

Commercial Manager:
Club Coach: Keith Leonard
Supporters Player of the Season 1982–83: Tony Coton
Physiotherapist: Graham Doig
Club Captain 1982–83: Kevan Broadhurst
Chief Scout: Norman Bodell
Club Statistician: John Garrard
Association of Football Statisticians Club Adviser to Yearbook: D. Drage

Players (non-appearance) granted free transfer: Derek McKay, M.; Nigel Winterburn, D.
Players released since May 1982:
Geoff Craig, (N/K); Gary Fillery, (N/K); Terry Goode, F. (Kettering T); Tony Hinchey, (N/K); Tony Knight, (N/K); John Whitehouse, (N/K); Brian Stewart, M. (N/K); Tony Van Miello, F. (Willem II, Holland); Bud Brocken, F. (Groningen, Holland); Tony McGarr, D. (N/K).

BLACKBURN ROVERS Division 2

Back row (left to right):
Mick Rathbone
Vince O'Keefe
Paul Comstive
Terry Gennoe
Derek Fazakerley
Middle row:
David Mail
Colin Randall
Kevin Stonehouse
Norman Bell
Donal Murphy
Front row:
Noel Brotherston
Ian Miller
Jim Brannigan
Simon Garner
David Hamilton

President: W. H. Bancroft.

Chairman: W. Fox.

Vice-Chairman: R. D. Coar BSC.

Directors: T. W. Ibbotson LLB, A. Sharples, Dr M. Jeffries TD, K. C. Lee.

Secretary: John W. Howarth AAAI. ***Manager:*** Bobby Saxton.

Year Formed: 1875. ***Turned Professional:*** 1880. ***Ltd Co.:*** 1897.

Previous Grounds: 1875, Brookhouse Ground; 1876, Alexandra Meadows; 1881, Leamington Road; 1890, Ewood Park.

Previous Name: Blackburn Grammar School OB.

Club Nickname: 'Blue and Whites'.

Previous Managers since 1946: Eddie Hapgood, Will Scott, Jack Bruton, Jackie Bestall, John Carey, Dally Duncan, Jack Marshall, Eddie Quigley, John Carey, Ken Furphy, Gordon Lee, Jim Smith, Jim Iley, Howard Kendall (14).

Ewood Park, Blackburn BB2 4JF. Telephone Blackburn (0254) 55432/55433. ***Telegraphic Address:*** 'Rovers, Blackburn'. ***Ground capacity:*** 23,400. ***Record attendance:*** 61,783 v Bolton W, FA Cup 6th rd, 2 Mar, 1929. ***Record receipts:*** £60,612 v Liverpool, FA Cup 3th rd, 8 Jan, 1983. ***Pitch measurements:*** 116yd 2ft×72yd 2ft.

Directions to Ground: Blackburn is the nearest railway station and Corporation buses run from there to the ground.

Note: Full club statistical records are on pages 416–455.

BLACKBURN ROVERS 1982–83 LEAGUE RECORD

Match No.	Date	Venue	Opponents	Result	H/T Score	Lg. Pos.	Goalscorers	Attendance
1	Aug 28	A	Wolverhampton W	L 1-2	1-0	—	Garner	15,605
2	Sept 1	H	Newcastle U	L 1-2	0-2	—	Bell	14,421
3	4	H	Cambridge U	W 3-1	2-1	13	Garner 2, Bell	4562
4	7	A	Grimsby T	L 0-5	0-2	—		7567
5	11	A	Crystal Palace	L 0-2	0-0	19		7529
6	18	H	Leicester C	W 3-1	1-0	15	Garner, Bell, Barton	4963
7	25	A	Derby Co	W 2-1	0-0	11	Garner, Hamilton	9361
8	Oct 2	H	Sheffield W	L 2-3	1-1	15	Garner, Stonehouse (pen)	10,362
9	9	A	Fulham	L 1-3	1-2	17	Brotherston	5698
10	16	H	Chelsea	W 3-0	1-0	14	Garner 2, Stonehouse	6062
11	23	H	Leeds U	D 0-0	0-0	14		12,040
12	30	A	Charlton Ath	L 0-3	0-0	17		5276
13	Nov 6	H	Carlisle U	W 3-2	2-1	16	Garner 2, Hamilton	5204
14	13	A	QPR	D 2-2	1-1	15	Miller, Bell	9149
15	20	H	Bolton W	D 1-1	0-0	16	Stonehouse (pen)	7428
16	27	A	Middlesbrough	W 5-1	1-0	14	Stonehouse, Brotherston 2, Bell, Randell	10,821
17	Dec 4	H	Barnsley	D 1-1	0-0	12	Brotherston	6769
18	Dec 11	A	Shrewsbury T	D 0-0	0-0	13		4833
19	18	H	Rotherham U	W 3-0	0-0	11	Garner, Miller, Randell	6333
20	27	A	Burnley	W 1-0	1-0	9	Garner	20,283
21	29	H	Oldham Ath	D 2-2	2-1	10	Garner 2	10,121
22	Jan 1	H	Bolton W	L 0-1	0-0	12		11,481
23	3	A	Cambridge U	L 0-2	0-1	14		3471
24	15	H	Wolverhampton W	D 2-2	2-0	13	Branagan, Keeley	7401
25	22	A	Leicester C	W 1-0	1-0	11	Lowey	8361
26	Feb 5	H	Grimsby T	W 2-1	2-1	8	Arnott, Miller	4724
27	15	A	Sheffield W	D 0-0	0-0	—		11,648
28	19	H	Fulham	D 0-0	0-0	8		6141
29	26	A	Chelsea	L 0-2	0-1	10		6982
30	Mar 5	A	Leeds U	L 1-2	1-1	12	Lowey	12,280
31	13	H	Charlton Ath	W 2-0	0-0	—	Lowey, Miller	5493
32	19	A	Carlisle U	L 1-3	1-3	12	Brotherston	4756
33	26	H	QPR	L 1-3	1-2	12	Garner (pen)	5317
34	Apr 1	A	Oldham Ath	D 0-0	0-0	—		7966
35	4	H	Burnley	W 2-1	0-0	—	Garner 2 (2 pens)	13,431
36	9	A	Newcastle U	L 2-3	0-2	11	Keeley 2	17,788
37	16	H	Crystal Palace	W 3-0	2-0	11	Garner 2, Lowey	4635
38	23	A	Barnsley	D 2-2	0-0	11	Garner, Keeley	7617
39	30	H	Middlesbrough	D 1-1	1-0	11	Lowey	4083
40	May 2	H	Derby Co	W 2-0	1-0	11	Garner, Brotherston	5619
41	7	A	Rotherham U	L 1-3	0-2	10	Bell	5871
42	14	H	Shrewsbury T	W 1-0	1-0	11	Garner	3797

Final League Position: 11

GOALSCORERS

League (58): Garner 22 (3 pens), Bell 6, Brotherston 6, Lowey 5, Keeley 4, Miller 4, Stonehouse 4 (2 pens), Hamilton 2, Randell 2, Arnott 1, Barton 1, Branagan 1.
Milk Cup (2): Fazackerley 1, Stonehouse 1.
FA Cup (1): Garner 1.

Milk Cup	Second Round	Brentford (a)	2-3
		(h)	0-0
FA Cup	Third Round	Liverpool (h)	1-2

Gennoe	Branagan	Rathbone	Randell	Barton (L)	Fazackerley	Miller	Stonehouse	Bell	Garner	Brotherston	Hamilton	Mail	Lowey	O'Keefe	Arnott (L)	Comstive	Keeley	Metcalfe	Devine	*Referees*	*Match No.*
1	2	3	4	5	6	7	8	9	10	11										E. Read	1
1	2	3	4	5	6	7	8	9	10	11										F. Roberts	2
1	2	3		5	6	7	8	9	10	11	4									J. Hough	3
1	2	3		5	6	7	8	9	10	11	4									T. Mills	4
1	2	3	4	5	6	7	8	9	10	11										L. Burden	5
1	2	3	4	5	6		8	9	10	11	7									A. Saunders	6
1	2	3	4		6		8	9	10	11	7	5								B. Hill	7
1	2	3	4		6	12	8	9	10	11	7*	5								N. Ashley	8
1	2	3		7	6		8	9	10	11		5	4							A. Glasson	9
1	2	3	4	5*	6	7	9		10	11	12		8							J. Lovatt	10
1	2	3	4		6	7	9*	12	10	11	8	5								G. Newsome	11
1	2	3	4		6	7		9	10	11	8	5								B. Stevens	12
1	2	3	4		6	7		9	10	11	8	5								M. Heath	13
	2	3	4		6	7		9	10*	11	8	5		1	12					J. Deakin	14
	2	3	4		6	7	12	9	10*	11	8	5		1						G. Tyson	15
1	2	3	4		6	7	10	9		11	8	5								D. Hutchinson	16
1	2	3	4		6	7	10*	9	12	11	8	5								D. Shaw	17
1	2	3	4		6	7		9	10	11	8	5								M. Robinson	18
1	2	3	4		6	7		9	10	11	8	5								D. Civil	19
1	2	3	4		6	7		9	10	11	8	5								A. Hamil	20
1	2	3			6	7		9	10	11	8	5			4					P. Willis	21
1	2	3	4		6	7		9	10	11	8	5								K. Baker	22
1	2	3			6	7		9	10	11		5	8		4					J. Moules	23
1	2	3				7	4*	9	10			5	11		8	12	6			A. Challiner	24
1	2	3	4*		6	7		9	10			5	11		8		12			M. Dimblebee	25
	2	3				7		9	10	11		5	4	1	8		6			R. Bridges	26
	2	3			6	7		9*	10	11	12	5	4	1	8					M. Scott	27
	2	3			6	7			10	11	9	5	4	1	8					T. Holbrook	28
	2*	3			6	7		12	10	11	9	5	4	1	8					D. Letts	29
		3	4		6	7			10*	11	2	5	9	1	8		12			V. Kellow	30
		3	4		6	7			10	11	2	5	9*	1	8		12			G. Courtney	31
		3	4			7			10	11	2	5	9	1	8		6			K. Redfern	32
1	2	3	4			7		12	10	11	8	5	9				6*			C. Seel	33
1	2	3	4		6	7			10	11	8	5	9							J. Hough	34
1	2	3	4		6	7*		12	10	11	8	5	9							D. Hutchinson	35
1	2	3	4		6			7	10		8*	5	9				12	11		A. Challiner	36
1	8	3	4		6			9	10	7		2	11				5			P. Tyldesley	37
1	8	3	4		6			9	10	7		2	11				5			R. Nixon	38
1		3	4		6			9	10	7	8	2	11				5			D. Owen	39
1		3	4		6				10	7	8	2	11				5		9	F. Roberts	40
1	12	3	4		6*			9	10	7	8	2	11				5			T. Jones	41
1	2	3	4		6			9	10	7	8		11				5			M. Peck	42
33	36	42	32	8	38	31	14	31	40	39	30	34	22	9	11	0	10	1	1		
	+ 1s					+ 1s	+ 1s	+ 4s	+ 1s		+ 2s					+ 1s	+ 1s	+ 4s			

FOOTBALL LEAGUE RECORD

1888 Original Member of the League; 1936–39 Division 2; 1946–47 Division 1; 1947–57 Division 2; 1957–66 Division 1; 1966–71 Division 2; 1971–75 Division 3; 1975–79 Division 2; 1979–80 Division 3; 1980– Division 2.

HONOURS

Football League: Division 1 – Champions 1911–12, 1913–14; Division 2 – Champions 1938–39; Runners-up 1957–58; Division 3 – Champions 1974–75; Runners-up 1979–80. *FA Cup:* Winners 1884, 1885, 1886, 1890, 1891, 1928; Runners-up 1882, 1960. *Football League Cup:* Semi-final 1961–62.

COLOURS

Blue and white halved shirts, white shorts, blue stockings with red and white tops.
Change colours:

BLACKBURN ROVERS

Players Names Ht. Wt. D.o.B.	Birthplace Transfer Fee	Clubs	Appearances F.L. A & S	 F.L.C. A & S	 F.A.C. A & S	Goals F.L.	 F.L.C.	 F.A.C.
Goalkeepers								
Terry Gennoe	Shrewsbury	Bury	3					
6 2½, 13 5, 16.3.53		Halifax T	78	8	8			
	£40,000	Southampton	36	10	5			
	—	Crystal Palace (loan)	3					
	£60,000	Blackburn R	68	4	2			
Michael Salmon*	Leyland	Blackburn R	1					
6 2,	—	Chester (loan)	16		2			
Vince O'Keefe	Birmingham	Birmingham C						
6 0, 11 0, 2.4.57	F/T	Walsall						
	F/T	AP Leamington						
		Exeter C	53	11	3			
	£30,000	Torquay U	108	4	6			
	£20,000	Blackburn R	9					
Defenders								
Glen Keeley (EY)	Basildon	Ipswich T (A)	4					
5 10, 12 0, 1.9.54	£70,000	Newcastle U	43+1	10	7	2	2	
	£50,000	Blackburn R	223+5	12	13	12		
	—	Everton (loan)	1					
Mike Rathbone (EY)	Birmingham	Birmingham C (A)	17+3	1	2			
5 10, 11 13, 6.11.58	£40,000	Blackburn R	151+2	5	7	2		
Jim Branagan	Barton	Oldham Ath	24+3	2				
5 10, 11 5, 3.7.55	F/T	Cape Town						
	F/T	Huddersfield T	37+1	+1				
	£20,000	Blackburn R	149+1	8	10	3		
David Mail	Bristol	Aston Villa (A)						
12.9.62	F/T	Blackburn R	34	2	1			
Derek Fazackerley	Preston	Blackburn R (A)	472+2	28	29	14	1	1
5 11, 11 6, 5.11.51								
David Byrom	Padiham	Blackburn R (A)						
Midfield								
Noel Brotherston (NI)	Belfast	Tottenham H (A)	1					
5 8½, 10 8, 18.11.56	F/T	Blackburn R	223+3	13	13+1	31	2	1
Paul Comsitive*	Southport	Blackburn R	3+3					
25.11.61	—	Rochdale (loan)	9	1		2		
Simon Barker	Farnworth	Blackburn R (A)						
David Hamilton	South Shields	Sunderland (A)						
5 7½, 9 12, 7.11.60	F/T	Blackburn R	46+6	4		2		
Donal Murphy*	Dublin	Coventry C (A)	33+10	2	5	10		1
5 11, 11 0, 23.2.55	—	Millwall (loan)	3					
	£10,000	Torquay U	81+4	6	6	20	1	1
	£65,000	Plymouth Arg	44+4	2+1	3	9		2
	—	Torquay U (loan)	2+1					
	F/T	Blackburn R	1+2					
Colin Randell (WU23)	Skewen	Coventry C (A)						
5 9, 10 8, 12.12.52		Plymouth Arg	137+2	10	8	9		2
	£10,000	Exeter C	78	5	5	4		2
	£60,000	Plymouth Arg	110	12	3	8		
	£40,000	Blackburn R	32	2	1	2		
Forwards								
Norman Bell	Sunderland	Wolverhampton W (A)	58+22	+2	14+4	17		7
6 0¼, 13 2, 16.11.55	£70,000	Blackburn R	56+4	2	2	10		
Simon Garner	Boston	Blackburn R (A)	152+11	12+2	7+1	57	3	4
5 8, 11 3, 23.11.59								
John Lowey	Manchester	Manchester U (A)						
5 11, 12 7, 7.3.58	F/T	California Stings						
	F/T	Blackburn R						
	F/T	Port Vale						
	F/T	California Stings						
	F/T	Sheffield W	35+7	1	7	4		2
	£25,000	Blackburn R	53+2	2		8	1	
Ian Miller	Perth	Bury	9+6	1			1	
5 9, 11 7, 13.5.55		Nottingham F						
	P/E	Doncaster R	124	10	4	14		
	£25,000+player	Swindon T	123+4	19+1	12	9	2	2
	£67,000	Blackburn R	73+1	3+1	2	7		
Peter Devine	Chorley	Chorley						
		Bristol C	19+2	1+1	5	1		
		Blackburn R	1					

Reserve Team Manager: Jim Furnell
First Team Coach: Tony Parkes
Supporters Player of the Season 1982–83: Derek Fazackerley
Physiotherapist: Tony Long
Association of Football Statisticians Club Adviser to Yearbook: H. Berry

Club Captain 1982–83: Jim Branagan
Club Statistician:

Players (non-appearance) granted free transfer: Gary Butcher, F.
Players released since May 1982: Phil Williamson, D. (N/K); Kim Walters, M. (N/K).

BLACKPOOL Division 4

Back row (left to right):
Colin Greenall
Dave Bamber
Iain Hesford
Lloyd Scott
Steve Hetzke
Nigel Hart (on loan to Crewe Alex)
Middle row:
Jack Chapman
Paul Stewart
Dave Serella
Sam Ellis (Manager)
Dave Hockaday
Billy Jeffrey
Alan Smith
Front row:
John Deary
Gordon Simmonite
Steve Trainor
Terry Pashley
Peter Noble
Bobby Downes
Andy Brockbank

Chairman: K. Chadwick LLB.

Directors: G. Bloor, M. H. Melling, R. P. Gibrail, T. White.

Manager: Sam Ellis. ***Secretary:*** D. Johnson.

Year Formed: 1887. ***Turned Professional:*** 1887. ***Ltd Co.:*** 1896.

Club Nickname: 'The Seasiders'.

Previous Grounds: 1887, Raikes Hall Gardens; 1897, Athletic Grounds; 1899, Raikes Hall Gardens; 1899, Bloomfield Road.

Previous Name: 'South Shore' combined with Blackpool in 1899, twelve years after the latter had been formed on the breaking up of the old 'Blackpool St John's club.

Previous Managers since 1946: Joe Smith, Ron Suart, Stan Mortensen, Les Shannon, Jimmy Meadows, Bob Stokoe, Harry Potts, Allan Brown, Jimmy Meadows, Bob Stokoe, Stan Ternent, Alan Ball Jnr, Allan Brown (13).

Bloomfield Rd Ground, Blackpool FY1 6JJ. Telephone Blackpool (0253) 404331. ***Telegraphic address:*** 'Football Blackpool'. ***Ground capacity:*** 18,000. ***Record attendance:*** 39,118 v Manchester U, Division 1, 19 April, 1952. ***Record receipts:*** £28,986.52 v Everton, League Cup 2nd rd, 2nd leg, 3 Sept, 1980. ***Pitch measurements:*** 111yd×73yd.

Directions to Ground: Coliseum bus station, Lytham Road, 10 minutes' walk. Railway: South station (a few minutes' walk from ground) and North station.

Match tickets: Bookable four weeks in advance of the match.

Car parking: Car park for 1,000 cars. Street parking available.

Entertainments/catering facilities: Refreshment and licensed bars. Entertainment after the game at the Supporters' Club by prior arrangement.

Club shop: In Bloomfield Road sells all types of souvenirs.

Handbooks/programmes: Programmes available from the development shop.

Note: Full club statistical records are on pages 416–455.

BLACKPOOL 1982–83 LEAGUE RECORD

Match No.	Date	Venue	Opponents	Result	H/T Score	Lg. Pos.	Goalscorers	Attendance
1	Aug 28	A	Mansfield T	L 1-2	0-2	—	Hockaday	2627
2	Sept 4	H	Swindon T	W 2-1	1-1	9	Pashley (pen), Bamber	3593
3	7	H	Bury	D 1-1	1-0	—	Bamber	4292
4	11	A	Bristol C	D 0-0	0-0	13		4681
5	18	H	Wimbledon	D 1-1	0-0	14	Hockaday	3929
6	25	A	Colchester U	L 1-4	1-2	11	Pashley (pen)	2918
7	29	A	Chester	W 2-1	1-1	—	Bamber, Deary	2256
8	Oct 2	H	Darlington	W 2-0	1-0	10	Hockaday, Bamber	4059
9	9	H	Halifax T	D 0-0	0-0	11		4150
10	16	A	Rochdale	L 1-3	1-1	14	Bamber	2001
11	19	H	York C	D 1-1	1-0	—	Deary	2765
12	23	H	Hereford U	W 5-1	2-0	9	Downes (pen), Stewart 2, Bamber 2	3405
13	30	A	Port Vale	L 0-1	0-0	9		5449
14	Nov 2	H	Torquay U	W 1-0	0-0	—	Bamber	2734
15	6	H	Crewe Alex	W 2-0	2-0	8	Mayo, Bamber	3443
16	13	A	Northampton T	L 1-2	0-1	9	Hockaday	1893
17	27	A	Aldershot	L 1-2	0-0	9	Downes (pen)	2003
18	Dec 4	H	Hull C	D 1-1	1-1	9	Pashley	3395
19	18	H	Scunthorpe U	W 3-1	0-0	9	Hockaday, Downes, Bamber (pen)	2860
20	27	A	Stockport Co	L 0-3	0-2	12		3673
21	28	H	Tranmere R	L 0-2	0-1	12		3563
22	Jan 1	A	Hartlepool U	L 1-2	1-1	15	Jeffrey	1569
23	3	H	Peterborough	L 0-3	0-1	17		2388
24	15	H	Mansfield T	W 2-1	0-0	14	Woodhead (og), Richardson I.	2217
25	22	A	Bury	L 1-4	0-2	18	Richardson I.	3263
26	29	H	Chester	D 1-1	0-0	17	Stewart	2054
27	Feb 5	H	Colchester U	L 1-2	0-0	18	Hetzke	1747
28	15	A	York C	L 0-2	0-0			2937
29	18	A	Halifax T	L 0-2	0-0	—		2366
30	26	H	Rochdale	W 1-0	1-0	18	McNiven	2373
31	Mar 2	A	Torquay U	W 3-1	3-1	—	Hockaday, Noble, Deary	1802
32	5	A	Hereford U	D 0-0	0-0	17		1755
33	12	H	Port Vale	W 2-0	0-0	15	Noble, Hetzke	4519
34	19	A	Crewe Alex	L 1-3	0-1	17	Stewart	2538
35	26	H	Northampton T	D 0-0	0-0	19		2054
36	Apr 1	H	Stockport Co	D 0-0	0-0	—		3126
37	2	A	Tranmere R	D 1-1	1-1	17	Pritchett	1831
38	9	A	Hull C	L 1-3	1-3	18	Deary	8555
39	12	A	Darlington	W 1-0	1-0	—	Stewart	1333
40	16	H	Bristol C	L 1-4	1-1	16	McNiven	2209
41	19	A	Swindon T	D 3-3	3-2	—	McNiven, Hockaday, Deary	2408
42	23	A	Scunthorpe U	L 3-4	2-1	17	McNiven 2, Greenall	2791
43	30	H	Aldershot	W 4-1	1-1	16	Senior (og), Hockaday, Deary, Stewart	1994
44	May 4	A	Peterborough U	L 1-3	1-3	—	Stewart	1636
45	7	A	Wimbledon	L 0-5	0-3	18		2717
46	14	H	Hartlepool U	L 1-2	1-2	19	Serella	2184

Final League Position: 21

GOALSCORERS

League (55): Bamber 10 (1 pen), Hockaday 8, Stewart 7, Dreary 6, McNiven 5, Downes 3 (2 pens), Pashley 3 (2 pens), Richardson, I. 2, Hetzke 2, Noble 2, Greenall 1, Jeffrey 1, Mayo 1, Pritchett 1, Serella 1, own goals 2.
Milk Cup (12): Bamber 4, Pashley 2 (1 pen), Serella 2, Deary 1, Hetzke 1, Stewart 1, Downes 1 (pen).
FA Cup (4): Bamber 1, Brockbank 1, Deary 1 (pen), Pashley 1.

Milk Cup	First Round	Chester (a)	2-1
		(h)	5-1
	Second Round	Northampton T (a)	1-1
		(h)	2-1
	Third Round	Luton T (a)	2-4
FA Cup	First Round	Horwich RMI (h)	3-0
	Second Round	Preston NE (a)	1-2

Hesford	Simmonite	Brockbank	Deary	Hetzke	Greenall	Noble	Hockaday	Bamber	Pashley	Downes	Stewart	Serella	Butler	Hart	Jeffrey	Mayo (L)	Bardsley	Pritchett	Richardson P. (L)	Scott	Richardson I. (L)	McNiven	Bramhall	Referees	Match No.
1	2	3	4	5	6	7*	8	9	10	11	12													N. Hough	1
1	2	3	4	5		7*	8	9	10	11	12	6												P. Willis	2
1	2	3	4	5			8	9	10	11	7	6												G. Courtney	3
1	2	3	4	5		7	8		10		9	6	11											A. Crickmore	4
1	2	3	4	5		7	11	9	10		8	6												T. Jones	5
1	2	3	4	5		7	11	9	10		8	6												I. Borrett	6
1	2		4	5			8	9	10	11	7	6		3										A. Hamil	7
1	2			5			7	9	10	11	8	6		3	4									R. Nixon	8
1	2		5		6	12	7	9	10	11	8*			3	4									N. Ashley	9
1	2		10		5		7	9	3	11		6	12		4	8*								F. Roberts	10
1	2		4	5			7	9	10	11	8	6		3										M. Peck	11
1	2		4	5			7	9	10	11	8	6		3										K. Hackett	12
1	2		4	5			7	9	10	11		6		3		8								J. Key	13
1	2		4	5			7	9	10	11		6		3		8								J. Worrall	14
1	2		4	5			7	9	10	11	12	6*		3		8								K. Redfern	15
1	2		4	5			7	9	10	11	12	6		3		8*								J. Martin	16
1			4	5			7	9	10	11		6			8		2	3						D. Axcell	17
1			4*	5		12	7	9	10	11		6			8		2	3						G. Seel	18
1		3	4	5		12	7*	9	10	11		6			8		2							D. Owen	19
		3	4	5		12		9	10	11*		6			8		2		7	1				M. Robinson	20
			4	5				9	10		11	6			8		2	3	7	1				T. Holbrook	21
1			4	5			7*	9	10		11	6			8		2	3			12			D. Hutchinson	22
1			4	5				9	10	11	7	6			8		2	3						M. Heath	23
1			4	5					10	11	9	6					2	3	7		8			J. Lovatt	24
1			4	5			10		2	11	9	6						3	7		8			K. Baker	25
1			4	5	12		7		10	11*	9	6					2	3			8			A. Saunders	26
1			4*	5	6	12	7		10	11	9						2	3			8			P. Tyldesley	27
1			4	5*	6	9	7		11		10				8		2	3						G. Tyson	28
1			4*	5	6	10	7		11		9	12			8		2	3						T. Jones	29
1			4	5	6	10*	8		11		9						2	3				7		H. Glover	30
1			4	5	6	8	7*		11		9						2	3				10		T. Bune	31
1*			4	5	6	10	7		11		9				12		2	3				8		C. Newsome	32
1			4	5	6	10	7		11		9				12		2	3*				8		T. Mills	33
1			4	5	6	10	7		11	3	9						2					8		A. Seville	34
1			4	5	6	10	7		11		9		3				2					8		R. Nixon	35
1			4	5	6	10	7		11		9						2	3				8		P. Willis	36
1			4	5	6*	10	7		11	9							2	3				8	12	A. Hamil	37
1			4		5	10	7		6	11	9						2	3				8		J. Bray	38
1			4	5	6	10	7		11		9						2	3				8		J. Hough	39
1			4	5	6	10*	7	12	11		9						2	3				8		D. Shaw	40
1			4	5	6		7	10	11		9						2	3				8		R. Lewis	41
1			4	5	6	10	7		11		9						2	3				8		V. Callow	42
1			4	5	6	10	7		11		9						2	3				8		F. Roberts	43
1			4	5	6		7		11	12	9		10*				2	3				8		D. Brazier	44
1			4		6			7	11	10	9	5					2	3				8	12	B. Daniels	45
1			4	7	6	10		11*	2		9	5						3				8	12	D. Owen	46
44	16	8	45	42	23	21	40	25	46	26	34	26	3	9	12	5	28	26	4	2	4	17	0		
					+ 1s	+ 5s		+ 1s		+ 1s	+ 4s	+ 1s	+ 1s		+ 2s						+ 1s		+ 3s		

FOOTBALL LEAGUE RECORD

1896 Elected to Division 2; 1899 Failed Re-election; 1900 Re-elected; 1900–30 Division 2; 1930–33 Division 1; 1933–37 Division 2; 1937–67 Division 1; 1967–70 Division 2; 1970–71 Division 1; 1971–78 Division 2; 1978–81 Division 3; 1981– Division 4.

HONOURS

Football League: Division 1 – Runners-up 1955–56; Division 2 – Champions 1929–30; Runners-up 1936–37, 1969–70. *FA Cup:* Winners 1953; Runners-up 1948, 1951. *Football League Cup:* Semi-final 1962. *Anglo-Italian Cup:* Winners 1971; Runners-up 1972.

COLOURS

Tangerine shirts with white stripe on sleeves, white collar and cuffs, white shorts, tangerine stockings with white tops. **Change colours:** White shirts, tangerine shorts and stockings.

BLACKPOOL

Players Names Ht, Wt, D.o.B.	Birthplace Transfer Fee	Clubs	Appearances F.L. A & S	 F.L.C. A & S	 F.A.C. A & S	Goals F.L.	 F.L.C.	 F.A.C.
Goalkeepers								
Iain Hesford (EU21)	Noola, Kenya	Blackpool (A)	203	14	13			
6 1½, 14 2, 4.3.60								
Defenders								
John Butler	Salford	Blackpool (A)	4+1	2	1			
5 9, 10 10,								
David Bardsley	Manchester	Blackpool (A)	29		2			
5 10, 10 0,								
Terry Pashley (ES)	Chesterfield	Burnley (A)	16+2					
5 8, 12 0, 11.10.56		Blackpool	201	15	13	7	2	1
Colin Greenall	Billinge	Blackpool (A)	50+4	3	1	1		
5 11, 11 10, 30.12.63								
Steve Hetzke	Marlborough	Reading (A)	254+7	28	8+3	23	5	1
6 2, 11 10, 3.6.55	£12,500	Blackpool	42	4	2	2	1	
Dave Serella	Kings Lynn	Nottingham F (A)	65+3	2	7			
5 9, 10 10, 24.9.52		Walsall	265+2	17	21	12	1	
	F/T	Blackpool	26+1	4	2	1	2	
Keith Pritchett	Glasgow	Wolverhampton W						
5 9¼, 11 5, 8.11.53	F/T	Doncaster R	6					
	F/T	QPR	4					
	F/T	Brentford	11	2		1		
	£4000	Watford	133+7	18	10	9	2	
	F/T	Blackpool	26			1		
Midfield								
John Deary	Ormskirk	Blackpool (A)	45	4	2+1	6	1	1
5 8, 11 2, 18.10.62								
Bobby Downes	Bloxwich	WBA						
5 7½, 11 4, 18.8.49	F/T	Peterborough U	23+3		1	3		1
	F/T	Rochdale	164+10	9	8+1	10		2
	£10,000	Watford	192+7	21+1	9	19	4	
	£10,000	Barnsley	43	6	6	1		
		Blackpool	26+1	4	2	3	1	
Peter Noble*	Newcastle	Consett						
5 9, 10 7, 19.8.44	£1000	Newcastle U	22+3			7		
	£10,000	Swindon T	212+4	18	10+1	62	7	2
	£40,000	Burnley	241+2	19	14	63	8	1
	£25,000	Blackpool	92+5	4	7	14		
Forwards								
David Hockaday*	Billingham	Blackpool	131+16	18+1	10+2	23		2
5 10, 10 9, 9.11.57								
David Bamber	St Helens	Manchester Univ						
6 3, 13 10, 1.2.59	—	Blackpool	81+5	6	7+1	29	5	2
Paul Stewart	Manchester	Blackpool (A)	43+9	4		10	1	
5 11, 11 10,								
David McNiven	Stonehouse	Leeds U (A)	15+7	1		6		
5 6, 11 4, 9.9.55	£25,000	Bradford C	202+10	22	11	64		2
		Blackpool	17			5		
Apprentices								
Neil Bramhall		Blackpool (A)	+3					
6 10, 11 7,								

Commercial Manager: Mrs. D. Howarth (Tel.)
Player Coach: R. Downes
Supporters Player of the Season 1982–83:
Physiotherapist: A. Smith
Club Captain 1982–83:
Chief Scout:
Club Statistician:
Association of Football Statisticians Club Adviser to Yearbook:

Players released since May 1982:
Wayne Harrison, M. (Workington); Willie Morgan, M. (N/K); Steve Trainor, (N/K); Alan McAvoy, F. (N/K); Andy Brockbank, D. (N/K); Lloyd Scott, G. (N/K).

BOLTON WANDERERS Division 3

Front row (left to right):
Dave Hoggan
Wayne Foster
John McGovern (Player-Manager)
Jeff Chandler
Peter Reid
Ray Deakin.
Middle row:
Charlie Wright (Coach)
Mick Bennett
Neil Berry
Chris Thompson
Mike Doyle
Vernon Allatt
Tony Henry
Walter Joyce (Coach)
Back row:
Gerry McElhinney
Paul Jones
Jim McDonagh
Simon Farnworth
Ian Moores
Steve Whitworth.

President: J. Battersby. ***Chairman:*** T. Edge.

Vice-Chairman: N. Riley.

Directors: G. Ball, G. Hargreaves, S. Jones, G. Seymour, G. Warburton.

Player Manager: John McGovern. ***Secretary:*** Des McBain.

Year Formed: 1874. ***Turned Professional:*** 1880. ***Ltd Co.:*** 1895.

Previous Grounds: Park Recreation Ground and Cockle's Field before moving to Pike's Lane Ground 1881; Burnden Park 1895.

Previous Name: 1874–77, Christ Church FC; 1877 became Bolton Wanderers.

Club Nickname: 'The Trotters'.

Previous Managers since 1948: Walter Rowley, Bill Ridding, Nat Lofthouse, Jimmy McIlroy, Jimmy Meadows, Nat Lofthouse, Jimmy Armfield, Ian Greaves, Stan Anderson, George Mulhall (10).

Burnden Park, Bolton BL3 2QR. Telephone Bolton (0204) 389200. Information Service: Bolton 21101. ***Ground capacity:*** 43,000. ***Record attendance:*** 69,912 v Manchester C, FA Cup 5th rd, 18 Feb, 1933. ***Record receipts:*** £53,931 v Everton, League Cup, semi-final 2nd leg, 15 Feb, 1977. ***Pitch measurements:*** 113yd×76yd.

Directions to the Ground: Local buses 8, 524, 523, 542, 543. The nearest station is Trinity St in the town centre.

Match tickets: Bookable in advance.

Car parking: Private car parking only on Burnden forecourt. Large park only 200 yards from the ground. Limited street parking in the vicinity. Multi-storey parks in the town centre.

Entertainments/catering facilities: Prerecorded programmes of news, interviews, and record requests. Refreshment bars in each section of the ground.

Club shop: On main car park. Open Mon–Sat. Send SAE for mail order list.

Handbooks/programmes: Programmes available on subscription from club shop.

Address of Supporters' Club: Supporters' Club, Burnden Park, Manchester Road, Bolton.

Address of the Club Shop or Boutique: 'The Happy Shop', Burnden Park, Bolton.

Note: Full club statistical records are on pages 416–455.

BOLTON WANDERERS 1982–83 LEAGUE RECORD

Match No.	Date	Venue	Opponents	Result		H/T Score	Lg. Pos.	Goalscorers	Attendance
1	Aug 28	A	Burnley	D	0-0	0-0	—		10,527
2	Sept 4	H	Newcastle U	W	3-1	3-0	7	Henry 2 (1 pen), Reid	17,707
3	7	A	Sheffield W	L	1-3	0-1	—	Henry	17,307
4	11	A	Fulham	L	0-4	0-2	15		5688
5	18	H	Wolverhampton W	L	0-1	0-0	18		9264
6	25	A	Grimsby T	L	0-1	0-0	19		7583
7	28	H	Oldham Ath	L	2-3	2-2	—	Henry, Moores	5605
8	Oct 2	H	Crystal Palace	W	1-0	1-0	19	Hoggan	5804
9	9	H	Rotherham U	D	2-2	2-1	19	Thompson, Moores	6577
10	16	A	Middlesbrough	L	0-1	0-0	19		5521
11	23	H	Barnsley	L	0-2	0-1	20		7339
12	30	A	QPR	L	0-1	0-0	20		9363
13	Nov 6	H	Shrewsbury T	L	1-4	0-1	21	Henry (pen)	4879
14	13	A	Derby Co	D	0-0	0-0	21		10,999
15	20	A	Blackburn R	D	1-1	0-0	21	Chandler	7428
16	27	H	Leicester C	W	3-1	2-0	21	Foster, Doyle, Thompson	5060
17	Dec 4	A	Cambridge U	D	0-0	0-0	22		3000
18	11	H	Charlton Ath	W	4-1	2-1	19	Chandler, Whatmore 2, Foster	5645
19	18	A	Chelsea	L	1-2	0-1	19	Henry	6903
20	27	H	Carlisle U	W	1-0	0-0	19	Jones	8171
21	28	A	Leeds U	D	1-1	0-0	19	Whatmore	16,180
22	Jan 1	H	Blackburn R	W	1-0	0-0	19	Henry	11,481
23	3	A	Newcastle U	D	2-2	1-0	18	Foster, Thompson	23,455
24	15	H	Burnley	W	3-0	2-0	17	Henry, Hoggan, McDonagh	8894
25	22	A	Oldham Ath	W	3-2	1-1	15	Thompson C., Chandler, Foster	8510
26	Feb 5	H	Fulham	L	0-1	0-0	15		6748
27	19	A	Rotherham U	D	1-1	1-1	16	Chandler	5646
28	22	A	Crystal Palace	L	0-3	0-2	—		4456
29	26	H	Middlesbrough	W	3-1	2-0	14	Deakin, Hoggan 2	5598
30	Mar 5	A	Barnsley	L	1-3	1-1	15	Rudge	10,400
31	12	H	QPR	W	3-2	2-1	14	Doyle, Henry, Rudge	6373
32	19	A	Shrewsbury T	L	0-1	0-1	14		4163
33	26	H	Derby Co	L	0-2	0-0	15		7041
34	Apr 2	H	Leeds U	L	1-2	0-1	16	Rudge	10,784
35	5	A	Carlisle U	L	0-5	0-3	—		5615
36	9	H	Sheffield W	L	0-2	0-2	21		6408
37	16	A	Wolverhampton W	D	0-0	0-0	20		12,723
38	23	H	Cambridge U	W	2-0	1-0	19	Hoggan 2	4636
39	30	A	Leicester C	D	0-0	0-0	17		13,959
40	May 2	H	Grimsby T	D	0-0	0-0	16		5866
41	7	H	Chelsea	L	0-1	0-0	19		8687
42	14	A	Charlton Ath	L	1-4	0-0	22	Moores	8720

Final League Position: 22

GOALSCORERS

League (42): Henry 9 (2 pens), Hoggan 6, Chandler 4, Foster 4, Thompson C. 4, Moores 3, Rudge 3, Whatmore 3, Doyle 2, Deakin 1, Jones 1, McDonagh 1, Reid 1.
Milk Cup (9): Doyle 2, Henry 2, Hoggan 2, Moores 2, McGovern 1.
FA Cup (1): Whatmore 1.

Milk Cup	First Round	Carlisle U (a)	3-3
		(h)	4-0
	Second Round	Watford (h)	1-2
		(a)	1-2 (aet)
FA Cup	Third Round	Arsenal (a)	1-2

McDonagh	Whitworth	Bennett	McGovern	Jones	Doyle	Chandler	Henry	Moores	Reid	Hoggan	Berry	McElhinney	Rudge	Deakin	Foster	Thompson C. D.	Whatmore (L)	Redfean	Gray	Borrows (L)	Joyce	Thompson S. J.	Referees	Match No.
1	2	3	4	5	6	7	8	9	10*	11	12												K. Hackett	1
1	2	3	4	5	6	7	8	9	10	11													J. Lovatt	2
1	2	3	4	5	6	7	8	9	10	11													P. Willis	3
1	2	3	4	5		7	8	9	10	12	11	6*											C. Thomas	4
1	2	3	4	5	6	7	8	9	10		11*		12										D. Hutchinson	5
1	2	3	4	5		7	8	9	10			6	11										G. Courtney	6
1	2	3	4	5		7	8	9	10			6	11										D. Civil	7
1	2		4	5		7	8		10	11		6	9	3									T. Holbrook	8
1	2*		4	5		7	8	11				6	9	3	12	10							M. Peck	9
1		2	4	5		7	8	9	10			6		3		11							T. Mills	10
1	2	3		5		7	8	9	4	11		6	10										F. Roberts	11
1		3	4	5			10	9			2	6	8		7	11							J. Martin	12
1		3	4	5		12	10	9*			2	6	8		7	11							G. Seel	13
1	2	12		5	4*	11	7		8				10	3	9							6	D. Reeves	14
1	2		4	5	6	7	8		10					3	9	11							G. Tyson	15
1	2		4	5	6	7	8		10					3	9	11							R. Bridges	16
1	2	3		5		7	4		10					5	9	11	8						B. Daniels	17
1	2			5	6	7	4		10					3	9	11	8						G. Napthine	18
1				5	6	7	4			10	2			3	9	11	8						R. Milford	19
1	2			5	6	7	4			10				3	9	11	8						A. Challiner	20
1	2			5	6	7	4			10				3	9	11	8						H. Taylor	21
1	2			5	6*	7	4	12		10				3	9	11	8						K. Baker	22
1	2	3		5		7	4			10				6	9	11	8						J. Key	23
1	2			5	6	7	4			10				3	9	11	8						M. Robinson	24
1	2			5*	6	7	4	12		10				3	9	11	8						A. Seville	25
1	2			5	6	7	4			10				3	9	11	8						D. Hutchinson	26
1	2	3		5		7	8			10				6	9			4				11	M. Heath	27
1	2	11		5	6	7	4			8			12	3	9*			10					A. Crickmore	28
1	2			5	6	7	10			11			8	3	9			4					D. Lloyd	29
1	2			5	6	7	10	12		11			8	3	9*			4					K. Barratt	30
1	2			5	6	7	10	9		11			8	3				4					K. Redfern	31
1	2			5	6	7		9		10			8	3				4				11*	H. King	32
1	2			5	6	7		9		10	3		8					4	11				A. Saunders	33
1	2				6	7		9		11	5		8					4	10	3			P. Scott	34
1	2				6	7*					5		8	3	9			4	10	11	12		G. Tyson	35
1	2				6			9				5	8	3	10*			4	11	7	12		D. Owen	36
1	2				6			9		11		5	8	3					4	7	10		N. Ashley	37
1	2				6	7		9		10		5*	8	3					4	11	12		K. Hackett	38
1	2				6			9		10		5	8	3					4	11	7		K. Salmon	39
1	2				6			9		10		5	8	3	12				4	11*	7		B.Newsome	40
1	2				6	12		9		10		5	8	3					4	11*	7		T. Holbrook	41
1	2				6	8		9		10		5		3	12				4	11	7*		C. Thomas	42
42	38	15	14	33	30	35	31	23	15	27	8	16	21	30	21	16	10	10	10	9	5	3		
		+ 1s				+ 2s		+ 3s		+ 1s	+ 1s		+ 2s		+ 3s						+ 3s			

FOOTBALL LEAGUE RECORD

1888 Founder Member of the League; 1899–1900 Division 2; 1900–03 Division 1; 1903–05 Division 2; 1905–08 Division 1; 1908–09 Division 2; 1909–10 Division 1; 1910–11 Division 2; 1911–33 Division 1; 1933–35 Division 2; 1935–64 Division 1; 1964–71 Division 2; 1971–73 Division 3; 1973–78 Division 2; 1978–80 Division 1; 1980–83 Division 2; 1983– Division 3.

HONOURS

Football League: Division 1 best season: 3rd, 1891–92, 1920–21, 1924–25. Division 2 – Champions 1908–09, 1977–78; Runners-up 1899–1900, 1904–05, 1910–11, 1934–35. Division 3 – Champions 1972–73. *FA Cup:* Winners 1923, 1926, 1929, 1958; Runners-up 1894, 1904, 1953. *Football League Cup:* Semi-final 1976–77.

COLOURS

White shirts, navy blue shorts, white stockings.
Change colours: Red shirts, white shorts, red stockings.

BOLTON WANDERERS

Players Names Ht, Wt, D.o.B.	Birthplace Transfer Fee	Clubs	Appearances F.L. A & S	 F.L.C. A & S	 F.A.C. A & S	Goals F.L.	 F.L.C.	 F.A.C.
Goalkeepers								
Jim McDonagh (EI)	Rotherham	Rotherham (A)	121	5	9			
6 0, 13 9, 6.10.52	£10,000	Bolton W	161	13	10			
	£250,000	Everton	40	3	5			
	£90,000+player	Bolton W	81	6	3	1		
Simon Farnworth	Chorley	Bolton W (A)						
5 11, 10 11,								
Defenders								
Paul Jones*	Ellesmere Port	Bolton W (A)	440+4	30	31	38	4	1
6 1½, 12 9, 13.5.53								
Mike Bennett* (EY)	Bolton	Bolton W (A)	62+3	5	3	1		
5 7, 10 0, 24.12.62								
Gerry McElhinney	Londonderry	Distillery						
6.2, 13 0, 19.9.56	£25,000	Bolton W	51+1	3	4	1		
	—	Rochdale (loan)	20			1		
Neil Berry* (SY)	Edinburgh	Bolton W (A)	10+2	2+2			1	
5 11, 10 4, 6.4.63								
Steve Whitworth (E)	Coalville	Leicester C (A)	352+1	18	29			
6 0, 12 0, 20.3.52	£125,000	Sunderland	83	8	3			
	£25,000	Bolton W	67	3	3			
Mike Doyle* (E)	Manchester	Manchester C (A)	441+7	43	44	32	4	2
6 0, 12 2, 25.11.46	£50,000	Stoke C	115	8	5	5	1	
	£10,000	Bolton W	40	2		2	2	
Brian Borrows	Liverpool	Everton	27	2				
5 10, 10 12, 20.12.60	£6000	Bolton W	9					
Midfield								
David Hoggan (SU-21)	Falkirk	Bolton W (A)	83+10	7	3+1	11	2	2
5 9, 10 0, 10.8.61								
Ray Deakin	Liverpool	Everton (A)						
5 8, 11 1, 19.6.59	F/T	Port Vale	21+2	4		6	1	
	F/T	Bolton W	30	1	1	1		
John McGovern (SU-23)	Montrose	Hartlepool U (A)	68+3	2	2	5	2	
5 10, 10 13, 28.10.49	£7000	Derby Co	186+4	14	17	16	2	1
	£65,000	Leeds U	4					
	£60,000	Nottingham F	249+4	33	17+1	6	3	1
	F/T	Bolton W	14	4			1	
Warren Joyce	Oldham	Bolton W	5+3					
5 8½, 11 5,								
Neil Redfearn	Dewsbury	Nottingham F (A)						
5 10, 11 6,		Bolton W	10					
Steve Thompson	Oldham	Bolton W (A)	3					
5 8½, 11 0,								
Fowards								
Chris Thompson* (EY)	Walsall	Bolton W (A)	66+7	3+1	3+1	18	1	1
5 10, 11 6, 24.1.60	—	Lincoln C (loan)	5+1					
Wayne Foster (EY)	Leigh	Bolton W (A)	41+6	1	3	6		1
5 8½, 11 0								
Jeff Chandler (EI)	Hammersmith	Blackpool (A)	31+6	2+1	+1	7		1
5 7, 10 1, 19.6.59		Leeds U	21+5	1	1	2		
	£40,000	Bolton W	67+3	3	3	6		
Ian Moores (EU-23)	Chesterton	Stoke C (A)	40+10	2	4+1	14		1
6 2, 13 8, 5.10.54	£70,000	Tottenham H	25+4	3		6	2	
	£60,000	Orient	110+7	2+1	12	26	2	3
	F/T	Bolton W	23+3	3+1		3	2	
	—	Barnsley (loan)	3					
Steve Saunders	Warrington	Bolton W (A)						
5 7½, 10 6,								
Simon Rudge	Warrington	Bolton W (A)	21+2	2		3		
5 6½, 10 6,								

Commercial Manager: Alf Davies (Tel. 389200)
Club Coach: Charlie Wright
Supporters Player of the Season 1982–83: Paul Jones
Physiotherapist: Peter Nightingale
Club Captain 1982–83: Paul Jones
Chief Scout:
Club Statistician:
Association of Football Statisticians Club Adviser to Yearbook: S. Marland

Players released since May 1982:
David Kay, M. (Leigh RFC); Barry Taylor, M. (N/K); Geoff Langley, F. (N/K)

AFC BOURNEMOUTH Division 3

Back row (left to right): Ivan Golac, Nigel Spackman, Phil Brignull, Tom Heffernan, John Impey, Kenny Allen, Ian Leigh, Trevor Morgan, Trevor Lee, Derek Dawkins, Steve Carter.
Front row: Tony Funnell, Kevin Dawtry, Harry Redknapp (Manager), Mark Nightingale, Keith Williams, Milton Graham. *Inset:* Chris Sulley.

Chairman: H. G. Walker LLB.

Directors: E. G. Keep, P. W. Hayward, W. J. L. Mackeen, D. R. Lever, G. P. Pound, S. A. Latter, A. W. R. Stock, M. C. McDonagh, R. J. C. Barton.

Secretary: Mrs C. B. Dowsett. ***Manager:*** Don Megson.

Commercial Manager: D. Dowsett. ***Club Nickname:*** 'Cherries'.

Year Formed: 1899. ***Turned Professional:*** 1912. ***Ltd Co.:*** 1914.

Previous Names: Boscombe St Johns, 1890–99; Boscombe FC, 1899–1923; Bournemouth & Boscombe Ath FC, 1923–71.

Previous Grounds: 1899–1910, Castlemain Road, Pokesdown; 1910, Dean Court.

Previous Managers since 1948: Harry Kinghorn, Harry Lowe, Jack Bruton, Freddie Cox, Don Welsh, Bill McGarry, Reg Flewin, Freddie Cox, John Bond, Trevor Hartley, John Benson, Alec Stock, David Webb (13).

Dean Court Ground, Bournemouth. Telephone Bournemouth (0202) 35381. ***Telegraphic address:*** 'Football Bournemouth'. ***Ground capacity:*** 19,175. ***Record attendance:*** 28,799 v Manchester U, FA Cup 6th Rd, 2 March, 1957. ***Record receipts:*** £24,145 v Portsmouth, Division 3, 26 Feb, 1983. ***Pitch measurements:*** 112yd×75yd.

Directions to the Ground: Nearest station Bournemouth on the main line from London (Waterloo). Corporation bus 25.

Car parking: Adequate parking for 1500 cars.

Entertainments/catering facilities: Refreshment points around the ground.

Club shop: Sells all types of souvenirs.

Handbooks/programmes: All souvenir/programme enquiries to Keith MacAlister c/o Club shop.

Extra information: The club did not compete in the FA Cup in 1923–24, their first League season, because their election came too late for them to be exempt from the preliminary rounds.

Address of Club Shop: The Cherry Bees Shop, Dean Court, Bournemouth, BH7 7AF.

Note: Full club statistical records are on pages 416–455.

AFC BOURNEMOUTH 1982–83 LEAGUE RECORD

Match No.	Date	Venue	Opponents	Result		H/T Score	Lg. Pos.	Goalscorers	Attendance
1	Aug 28	H	Walsall	W	3-0	0-0	—	Funnell 2, Spackman	5330
2	Sept 4	A	Oxford U	L	0-2	0-0	7		4729
3	8	A	Millwall	L	0-2	0-2	—		3012
4	11	H	Sheffield U	D	0-0	0-0	16		6424
5	18	A	Wigan Ath	W	2-1	2-0	12	Funnell 2	4866
6	25	H	Exeter C	W	2-0	0-0	8	Beck, Morgan	7547
7	28	H	Southend U	L	0-2	0-0	—		4502
8	Oct 2	A	Wrexham	L	0-1	0-1	12		2046
9	9	H	Cardiff C	W	3-1	2-0	12	Morgan, Graham 2	5818
10	16	A	Portsmouth	W	2-0	0-0	10	Funnell, Heffernan	10,961
11	19	A	Plymouth Arg	L	0-2	0-1	—		2525
12	23	H	Gillingham	L	0-1	0-0	13		5528
13	30	A	Preston NE	W	1-0	1-0	12	Heffernan	3589
14	Nov 2	H	Bristol R	D	0-0	0-0	—		6263
15	6	H	Huddersfield T	L	0-1	0-0	12		5194
16	13	A	Newport Co	L	1-5	0-3	14	Brignull	4071
17	27	H	Bradford C	D	2-2	1-1	16	Morgan 2	4025
18	30	A	Bristol R	D	1-1	0-0	—	Dawtry	4358
19	Dec 4	A	Chesterfield	D	0-0	0-0	14		2226
20	18	A	Lincoln C	L	0-9	0-2	15		3597
21	27	H	Reading	D	1-1	1-0	15	Lee	6118
22	28	A	Orient	L	0-5	0-2	16		3718
23	Jan 1	H	Brentford	W	4-3	1-1	15	Brignull, Spackman 2, Dawtry	5593
24	3	A	Doncaster R	L	1-2	0-1	16	Morgan	3298
25	15	A	Walsall	L	1-3	1-2	18	Lee	2735
26	22	H	Millwall	W	3-0	1-0	18	Heffernan 3 (1 pen)	4707
27	29	A	Sheffield U	D	2-2	1-1	17	Funnell, Heffernan (pen)	11,614
28	Feb 1	H	Oxford U	W	2-0	0-0	—	Morgan, Spackman	3776
29	5	A	Exeter C	L	2-4	1-1	16	Morgan 2	3008
30	12	H	Wrexham	D	1-1	0-0	14	Hefferman (pen)	3827
31	19	A	Cardiff C	D	1-1	0-0	16	Hefferman	4878
32	26	H	Portsmouth	L	0-2	0-1	18		13,406
33	Mar 5	A	Gillingham	W	5-2	1-0	18	Lee 2, Dawtry 2, Beck	3485
34	12	H	Preston NE	W	4-0	1-0	15	Lee, Hefferman (pen), Morgan 2	4407
35	15	H	Plymouth Arg	W	1-0	1-0	—	Nightingale	4258
36	19	A	Huddersfield T	D	0-0	0-0	14		8630
37	26	H	Newport Co	L	0-1	0-1	14		9121
38	Apr 2	H	Orient	W	2-0	0-0	14	Morgan, Beck	7039
39	4	A	Reading	L	1-2	1-1	—	Morgan	4424
40	9	H	Chesterfield	W	2-1	1-1	13	Morgan, Beck	5227
41	16	A	Southend U	D	0-0	0-0	14		4275
42	23	H	Lincoln C	W	1-0	1-0	13	Morgan	5018
43	30	A	Bradford C	W	3-2	0-0	12	Dawtry, Lee, Morgan	3455
44	May 2	H	Doncaster R	D	2-2	1-0	12	Sulley, Hefferman (pen)	3995
45	7	H	Wigan Ath	D	2-2	2-0	13	Nightingale, Morgan	4523
46	14	A	Brentford	L	1-2	0-2	14	Lee	6191

Final League Position: 14

GOALSCORERS

League (59): Morgan 16, Hefferman 10 (5 pens), Lee 7, Funnell 6, Dawtry 5, Beck 4, Spackman 4, Brignull 2, Graham 2, Nightingale 2, Sulley 1.
Milk Cup (5): Morgan 2, Brignull 1, Compton 1, Funnell 1.
FA Cup (0).

Milk Cup	First Round	Plymouth Arg (a)	0-2
		(h)	3-0 (aet)
	Second Round	Manchester U (a)	0-2
		(h)	2-2
FA Cup	First Round	Southend U (h)	0-2
Football League Trophy		Aldershot (h)	2-2
		(a)	2-4
		(h)	3-0

Allen	Hefferman	Sulley	Spackman	Brignull	Impey	Carter	Williams	Morgan	Funnell	Dawtry	O'Donnell	Graham	Crawford	Dawkins	Beck	Compton	Mundee	Leigh	Aitken	Nightingale	Golac	Lee	Neighbour (L)	Madden (L)	*Referees*	*Match No.*
1	2	3	4*	5	6	7	8	9	10	11	12														A. Crickmore	1
1	2	3	4	5	6*	7		9	10		8	12	11												R. Lewis	2
1	2	5	6*	3	4	9		11	10		7			12	8										I. Borrett	3
1	2	3		5		7	8	9	10		4					6	11								K. Cooper	4
1	2	3		5		7	8	9	10		4					6	11								K. Hackett	5
1	2	3		5		7	8	9	10		4				11	6									B. Daniels	6
1	2	3		5		7	8	9	10		11*			12	4	6									E. Read	7
1	2	3	11	5		7	8	9*	12				10		4	6									N. Midgley	8
	2	3	4	5			8	9	10			11				6		1							A. Ward	9
	2	3	4	5		7	8	9	10			11				6		1							K. Salmon	10
	2	3	4	5		7	8	9	10	12		11*				6		1							V. Callon	11
	2	3	4	5		7*	8	9	10	12		11				6		1							H. King	12
	2	3	4	5		7	8	9	12	11		10*				6		1							D. Hutchinson	13
	2	3	4	5		7		9		11		12	10*	8		6		1							M. Bodenham	14
	2	3	4	5		7		9		11		12	10			6		1							T. Bune	15
	2	3	4	5		7		9	10*			11				6		1	8	12					T. Jones	16
1		3	4	5	6	7		9		11										8	2	10			M. James	17
1		3	4	5	6	7		9		11										8	2	10			D. Brazier	18
1		3		5	6	7		9		11		4								8	2	10			J. Lovatt	19
1	2	3		5	6	7*		9		11		4					12			8		10			N. Ashley	20
1	2	3	4	5	6	7	8	9				11*								12		10			Alan Robinson	21
1	2	3	4	5	6	7	8	9				11										10			A. Grey	22
1	2	3	4	5			6	9	7	11										8		10			L. Shapter	23
1	2	3	4	5			8*	9	7			12					11			6		10			A. Robinson	24
1	2	3	4	5	6			9	11													10	7	8	J. Deakin	25
	2	3	4	5				9	10	11								1			6		7	8	J. Martin	26
	2	3	4	5				9	10									1		11	6		7	8	P. Willis	27
	2	3	4	5				9	10	11								1			6	12	7	8*	R. Milford	28
	3	6	4	5				9	10*									1		11	2	12	7	8	J. Bray	29
1	2	3*	4	5	6	11		9				12									8	10	7		D. Axcell	30
	2	3	4	5*	6			9		7		8						1		11	8				D. Hedges	31
	2	3	4	5	6			9		7		10			8*			1		11		12			C. Downey	32
	2	3	4	5	6			9		7					8			1		11		10			T. Ward	33
	2	3	4	5	6			9		7					8			1		11		10			A. Crickmore	34
	2	3	4	5	6	7*		9				12			8			1		11		10			M. Robinson	35
	2	3	4	5	6			9		7					8			1		11		10			K. Walmsley	36
	2	3	4	5	6					11		12			8			1		10*		9			D. Reeves	37
	2	3	4	5	6			9		7					8			1		11		10			M. Bodenham	38
	2	3	4	5	6			9		7*		12			8			1		11		10			B. Stevens	39
	2	3	4	5	6			9		12					8			1		11		10			S. Bates	40
	2	3	4	5	6			9							8			1		11		10			K. Salmon	41
	2	3	4	5	6			9							8			1		11		10			A. Gunn	42
	2	3	4	5	6		8	9		7								1		11		10			J. Heath	43
	2	3	4	5	6		8	9		7			12					1		11		10*			J. Moules	44
	2	3	4	5	6			9		12								1		11*		10			E. Scales	45
	2	3	4	5	6		12	9		7								1		11		10			E. Reid/R. Smith	46
18	43	46	40	46	27	23	17	45	19	22	6	12	4	1	15	13	3	28	1	24	9	24	6	5		
							+ 1s		+ 2s	+ 2s	+ 1s	+ 8s	+ 1s	+ 2s			+ 1s			+ 2s		+ 3s				

Also played: Redknapp (no. 7, match 9); Webb (no. 8*, match 15); Shaw (no. 8, matches 45, 46); Best (no. 7, matches 37, 40, 41, 42, 45).

FOOTBALL LEAGUE RECORD

Elected to Division 3(S), 1923. Remained a Third Division Club for record number of years until 1970; 1970–71 Division 4; 1971–75 Division 3; 1975–82 Division 4; 1982– Division 3.

HONOURS

Football League: Division 3 best season: 3rd, 1961–62, 1971–72; Division 3(S) – Runners-up 1947–48. Promotion from Division 4 1970–71 (2nd), 1981–82 (4th). *FA Cup:* best season: 6th rd, 1956–57. *Football League Cup:* best season: 4th rd, 1962, 1964.

COLOURS

All red with single white stripe under arm and down side.
Change colours: All white with red stripe under and arm and down side.

AFC BOURNEMOUTH

Players Names Ht. Wt. D.o.B.	*Birthplace Transfer Fee*	*Clubs*	*Appearances* F.L. A & S	F.L.C. A & S	F.A.C. A & S	*Goals* F.L.	F.L.C.	F.A.C.
Goalkeepers								
Kenny Allen*	Thornaby	Bath C						
6 4, 13 8, 12.1.52		Bournemouth	152	9	8			
Ian Leigh	Ilfracombe	Swaythling						
5 11, 12 3, 11.6.62		Bournemouth	64	1	4			
Defenders								
John Impey	Exeter	Cardiff C (A)	13+8		+2			1
6 0, 11 12, 11.8.54	F/T	Bournemouth	280+4	12	16+1	7		
Paul Compton	Stroud	Trowbridge T						
6 1½, 13 1, 6.6.63	£10,000	Bournemouth	64	5	2		1	
Phil Brignull (ES)	Stratford	West Ham U (A)	10+1					
6 0, 11 2, 2.10.60	F/T	Bournemouth	75	4	3	4	1	
Chris Suiley	Camberwell	Chelsea (A)						
5 8, 10 0, 3.12.59		Bournemouth	99+1	6	5	1		
Midfield								
John Beck	Edmonton	QPR (A)	32+8	2	4	1		
	£40,000	Coventry C	60+9	5	3	6		
	£80,000	Fulham	113+1	6	6	13	1	
	F/T	Bournemouth	15			4		
Tom Heffernan	Dublin	Dunleary						
6 2, 12 7, 30.4.55		Tottenham H						
	F/T	Bournemouth	152+2	8	6	21		
Keith Williams	Burtwood	Aston Villa (A)						
5 9, 11 7, 12.4.57		Northampton T	128+3	8	2+1	6	1	
	F/T	Bournemouth	53+2	6	5	1		1
Milton Graham	Tottenham							
5 10½, 12 6,		Bournemouth	17+8	1	+1	5		
Tony Funnell*	Eastbourne	Eastbourne U						
5 6½, 10 10, 20.8.57		Southampton	13+4	1+1	+1	8	1	
	£50,000	Gillingham	27+6	2+1	+1	10		
	£50,000	Brentford	29+3		2+1	8		2
	£5000	Bournemouth	59+5	2+1	5	22	1	2
Trevor Lee	London	Epsom & Ewell						
5 11, 11 7, 3.7.54	—	Millwall	99+9	10+2	5	23	2	2
	£15,000	Colchester	95+1	6	13	35	1	3
	£90,000	Gillingham	43+4	3	2	14		
	—	Orient (Loan)	5					
	£5000	Bournemouth	24+1			7		
Brian Mundee*	London	Hungerford T						
5 10, 10 12,		Bournemouth	3+1	1				
Forwards								
Andy Crawford*	Filey	Derby Co (A)	16+5	1+1		4	1	
5 7, 10 4, 30.1.59	F/T	Blackburn R	56	4	9	21		5
	£35,000	Bournemouth	31+2	1	4	10		1
Steve Carter	Yarmouth	Manchester C (A)	4+2			2		
5 8, 10 10, 23.4.53	£18,000	Notts Co	172+16	10+3	10+2	21	3	
	P/E	Derby Co	32+1	1	1			
	—	Notts Co (N/C)						
	F/T	Bournemouth	38+1	3	1	1		
Nigel Spackman	Romsey	Andover						
6 1, 12 4, 2.12.60		Bournemouth	118+1	5	7	10		
Trevor Morgan	Forest Gate	Leytonstone						
6 1, 13 1, 30.9.56	£3000	Bournemouth	53	2	2	13		2
		Mansfield T	12		1	6		
		Bournemouth	59	6	3	20	2	2
George Best* (NI)	Belfast	Manchester U	361	12	39	137	6	21
5 8½, 11 3, 22.5.46		Stockport C (Loan)	3			2		
		Los Angeles A						
		Fulham	42	3	2	8	2	
		Golden Bay						
		Bournemouth	5					
Non-contract Players								
Chris Shaw		Bournemouth	2					
Kevin Dawtry	Southampton	Southampton (A)	+1					
5 6, 9 10, 15.6.58	F/T	Crystal Palace						
		Bournemouth	36+2	3	3	6		
	F/T	Reading	4					
	F/T	Bournemouth	22+3	1	1	5		
Mark Nightingale (EY)	Salisbury	Bournemouth (A)	44+5	2	8	4		
5 10, 10 7, 1.2.57		Crystal Palace						
		Norwich C	28+7	2				
	F/T	Bournemouth	24+2			2		

Commercial Manager: Dickie Dowsett (Tel. B'mth 37777)
Club Coach: Harry Redknapp
Club Captain 1982–83: John Impey
Supporters Player of the Season 1982–83:
Chief Scout:
Physiotherapist:
Club Statistician:
Association of Football Statisticians Club Adviser to Yearbook: N. Treleven.

Players released since May 1982: Dean Mooney, F. (N/K); Graham Ray, D. (N/K); Kevin Green, (N/K); Jeremy Judd, (N/K); Derek Dawkins, D. (N/K); Harry Redknapp, F. (N/C–Bournemouth Coach).

BRADFORD CITY Division 3

Back row (left to right): Peter Jackson, Barry Gallagher, Cyril Podd, Garry Watson, Eric McManus, Ian Mellor, Bobby Campbell, Joe Cooke, Mike Lester
Front row: Mick Jones (Coach), John Black, Stuart McCall, Terry Gray, Roy McFarland (Manager), David McNiven, Mark Ellis, Les Chapman, Bryan Edwards (Physio).

Chairman: R. Martin. ***Vice-Chairman:*** J. H. Garside.

Directors: E. Sutcliffe, R. Stead. ***Manager:*** Trevor Cherry.

Secretary: T. F. Newman. ***Club Nickname:*** 'The Bantams'.

Year Formed: 1903. ***Turned Professional:*** 1903. ***Ltd Co.:*** 1908.

Previous Managers since 1948: Jack Barker, John Milburn, David Steele, Ivor Powell, Peter Jackson, Bob Brocklebank, Bill Harris, Willie Watson, Grenville Hair, Jimmy Wheeler, Bryan Edwards, Bobby Kennedy, John Napier, George Mulhall, Roy McFarland (15).

Valley Parade Ground, Bradford BD8 7DY. Telephone Bradford (0274) 306062. ***Ground capacity:*** 16,000. ***Record attendance:*** 39,146 v Burnley, FA Cup 4th rd, 11 March, 1911. ***Record receipts:*** £27,000 v Southampton, FA Cup 6th rd, 6 March, 1976. ***Pitch measurements:*** 110yd×76yd.

Directions to Ground: Ground situated approximately ¾ mile from city centre along Manningham Lane. Corporation buses 23–26 from Cheapside plus specials. West Yorkshire buses from Chester St bus station. The nearest railway station is Bradford Exchange. By road, the ground is approximately ¼ mile from Ring Road towards Bradford.

Car parking: Street parking in most side-streets. No parking in Valley Parade or South Parade.

Entertainments/catering facilities: Hot drinks, pies, crisps, etc. available at snack bars in the ground.

Club shop: Adjacent to ground entrance; sells all types of souvenirs.

Handbooks/programmes: Programmes will be sent on receipt of remittance and SAE c/o City Shop, Valley Parade.

Note: Full club statistical records are on pages 416–455.

BRADFORD CITY 1982–83 LEAGUE RECORD

Match No.	Date	Venue	Opponents	Result	H/T Score	Lg. Pos.	Goalscorers	Attendance
1	Aug 28	H	Reading	W 3-2	2-2	—	Campbell, Mellor, Gallagher	5001
2	Sept 4	A	Orient	W 1-0	0-0	3	Gray	2565
3	7	A	Wigan Ath	L 2-3	0-0	—	Campbell, Mellor	5339
4	11	H	Newport Co	W 4-2	1-0	4	Campbell, Jackson, Cooke, Gallagher	4793
5	18	A	Millwall	D 1-1	0-0	4	Campbell	3558
6	25	H	Southend U	W 1-0	1-0	3	Campbell	5150
7	29	H	Walsall	D 1-1	0-0	—	Cooke	4648
8	Oct 2	A	Bristol R	L 1-4	0-2	7	Campbell	4451
9	9	H	Plymouth Arg	W 4-0	1-0	2	Campbell 2, Gallagher (pen), Gray	4690
10	16	A	Chesterfield	L 0-3	0-2	7		3850
11	19	A	Cardiff C	L 0-1	0-1	—		5007
12	23	H	Doncaster R	W 1-0	1-0	9	Campbell	5526
13	30	A	Lincoln C	L 0-1	0-0	11		5296
14	Nov 3	H	Oxford U	W 3-2	2-1	—	McNiven, Campbell 2	6171
15	6	A	Brentford	W 2-0	1-0	7	McNiven, Jackson	6669
16	13	H	Exeter C	D 3-3	2-2	7	Campbell, Mellor (pen), Lester	4576
17	27	A	AFC Bournemouth	D 2-2	1-1	8	McNiven, Ellis	4025
18	Dec 4	H	Portsmouth	D 2-2	1-0	9	Gray 2	4961
19	27	A	Preston	D 0-0	0-0	10		7238
20	28	H	Wrexham	D 0-0	0-0	10		5542
21	Jan 1	A	Huddersfield T	L 3-6	2-2	10	Podd, Campbell, Ellis	18,438
22	3	H	Gillingham	D 1-1	1-1	10	Mellor	4294
23	12	H	Orient	L 2-3	1-1	—	Campbell, Gray	3315
24	15	A	Reading	L 1-2	0-1	13	McCall	2050
25	22	H	Wigan Ath	L 0-1	0-1	14		4741
26	29	A	Newport Co	D 1-1	1-0	13	Gray	3397
27	Feb 5	A	Southend U	D 1-1	1-1	14	Black (pen)	2858
28	12	H	Bristol R	W 2-0	0-0	12	Campbell, McNiven	4261
29	16	H	Cardiff C	W 4-2	2-0		Campbell 2, Black, Cooke	3786
30	19	A	Plymouth Arg	L 1-3	0-1	11	Cooke	3644
31	26	H	Chesterfield	W 1-0	0-0	10	Black (pen)	4033
32	Mar 2	A	Oxford U	L 1-5	1-4	10	Campbell	4064
33	5	A	Doncaster R	W 2-1	2-0	—	McCall, Cooke	3473
34	12	H	Lincoln C	D 1-1	0-0	10	Lampkin	5026
35	19	H	Brentford	L 0-1	0-0	12		3828
36	26	A	Exeter C	L 1-2	0-1	13	Campbell	2639
37	Apr 2	A	Wrexham	W 4-0	2-0	12	Campbell 2, Gray 2	2808
38	4	H	Preston NE	L 1-2	1-0	—	Campbell	4357
39	9	A	Portsmouth	W 1-0	1-0	12	McCall	12,198
40	16	H	Millwall	D 0-0	0-0	12		3953
41	23	A	Sheffield U	L 1-2	1-0	14	Campbell	9375
42	30	H	AFC Bournemouth	L 2-3	0-0	15	Campbell, Hill	3455
43	May 3	A	Gillingham	L 0-3	0-2	—		2716
44	7	A	Walsall	D 1-1	1-1	15	Campbell	3322
45	8	H	Sheffield U	W 2-0	2-0	—	Cavener 2	4576
46	14	H	Huddersfield T	W 3-1	2-0	12	McCall, Jackson, Ellis	10,375

Final League Position: 12

GOALSCORERS

League (68): Campbell 25, Gray 8, Cooke 5, McCall 4, McNiven 4, Mellor 4 (1 pen), Black 3 (2 pens), Ellis 3, Gallagher 3 (1 pen), Jackson 3, Cavener 2, Hill 1, Lampkin 1, Lester 1, Podd 1.
Milk Cup (9): Campbell 3, Cooke 2, Gallagher 2, Ellis 1, Mellor 1.
FA Cup (5): Campbell 2, Gray 1, Lester 1, McNiven 1.
Football League Trophy (6): Campbell 3, Gray 1, Lester 1, Watson 1.

Milk Cup	First Round	Mansfield T (h)	1-0
		(a)	2-0
	Second Round	Rochdale (a)	1-0
		(h)	4-0
	Third Round	Manchester U (h)	0-0
		(a)	1-4
FA Cup	First Round	Port Vale (a)	1-0
	Second Round	Mansfield T (a)	1-1
		(h)	3-2
	Third Round	Barnsley (h)	0-1
Football League Trophy		Halifax T (h)	1-0
		Hartlepool U (a)	4-0
		Hull C (a)	0-0
	Quarter-final	Millwall (a) (lost on penalties)	1-1

McManus	McCall	Chapman	Watson	Cooke	Jackson	Gray	Gallagher	Campbell	McNiven	Mellor	Lester	Podd	McFarland	Ellis	Cherry	Yorath	Ramsbottom	Black	Abbot	Lampkin	Cavener (L)	McGovern	Hill	Fee	Referees	Match No.
1	2	3	4	5	6	7	8	9	10	11															D. Allison	1
1	2	3		5	6	7	8	9	10	11	4														M. Taylor	2
1	2	3		5	6	7	8	9	10	11	4														T. Holbrook	3
1		3		5	12	7	8	9	10*	11	4	2	6												F. Roberts	4
1		3		5		7	8	9		11	4	2	6	10											B. Stevens	5
1		3		5	12	7	8	9	10*	11	4	2	6												R. Bridges	6
1		3		5	12	7	8		9	11	4	2	6	10*											P. Tyldesley	7
1		3		5	12	7	8	9	10	11*	4	2	6												C. Newsome	8
1		3		5		7	8	9		11	4	2	6	10											D. Shaw	9
1		3	12	5	6	7	8*	9		11	4	2		10											A. Seville	10
1		3		6	5	8		9	10	11	4	2		7											D. Lloyd	11
1		3		6	12	7		9*	10	11	4	2	5	8											N. Midgley	12
1		3		6	12	7		9	10*	11	4	2	5	8											D. Brazier	13
1		3		5	12	7*		9	10	11	4	2	6	8											T. Fitzharris	14
1		3		5	8			9	10	11	4	2	6	7											A. Crickmore	15
1	12	3		5	6	8		9	10	11*	4	2		7											K. Redfern	15
1	4	3		5	6	8		9	10	11		2		7											M. James	17
1		3		5	6	8		9	10	11	4	2		7											N. Glover	18
1		3		9	5	7	12		10	11*	4	2		8	6										T. Jones	19
1		3		9	5	8			10	11	4	2		7	6										M. Peck	20
1		3		10	5*	8		9	11	12	4	2		7	6										J. Hough	21
1		3		5	12	8		9	10	11*	4	2		7	6										P. Tyldesley	22
1		3			5	8		9	11	12	4*	2		7	6	10									R. Nixon	23
	12	3			5	8		9	10*	11	4	2			6	7	1								I. Borrett	24
	12	3		10	5	7		9		11	4	2			6	8*	1								N. Ashley	25
	8	3		10*	5	7		9	12	11	4	2			6		1								D. Letts	26
	7	3			5	8		9	10		4	2			6		1	11							T. Ward	27
	7	3		8	5			9	10		4	2			6*		1	11							J. Lovatt	28
	7	3		8	5	12		9*			4	2		11	6		1	10							G. Courtney	29
	7	3		8*	5	12		9			4			11	6		1	10	2						T. Bune	30
	7*	3		8	5	10	12	9			4				6		1	11	2						A. Robinson	31
	7	3		8	5	10		9*			4				6		1	11	2						T. Spencer	32
	7	3		8	5	10		9			4*				6		1	11	2	12					R. Chadwick	33
	7	3			5	4	8	9							6		1	10	2	11					R. Guy	34
	7	3			5	4	8*	9		12					6		1	10	2	11					D. Owen	35
	7	3		8	5	10		9				4			6		1	12		11	4				V. Callow	36
	10	3			5	7		9				2			6		1	8		11	4				G. Napthine	37
	10	3	12		5	7		9				2			6		1	8		11*	4				C. Seel	38
	10	11	3		5	7		9				2			6		1	8			4				E. Scales	39
	7	11	3		5	8		9		12		2			6		1	10*			4				M. Scott	40
	4	11	3		5			9		12		2		10	6		1	7			8*				M. Midgley	41
	4	11	8		5			9				3		10	6		1		2			7*	12		J. Head	42
1	4	11	3							10		2		9	6				8		7*		12	5	Alan Robinson	43
1	4	11	3	7				9				2		10	6				8					5	K. Salmon	44
1	7	3		8								2		11	6				10		4		9	5	K. Walmsley	45
1	4	3		8	6							2		11	7				10		5		9		G. Tyson	46
27	25	46	7	34	33	36	12	40	23	25	31	37	10	25	28	3	19	14	11	5	9	1	2	3		
	+ 3s		+ 2s		+ 8s	+ 2s	+ 2s		+ 1s	+ 5s									+ 1s		+ 1s			+ 2s		

FOOTBALL LEAGUE RECORD

1903 Elected to Division 2; 1908–22 Division 1; 1922–27 Division 2; 1927–29 Division 3(N); 1929–37 Division 2; 1937–61 Division 3; 1961–69 Division 4; 1969–72 Division 3; 1972–77 Division 4; 1977–78 Division 3; 1978–82 Division 4; 1982– Division 3.

HONOURS

Football League: Division 1 best season: 5th, 1910–11; Division 2 – Champions 1907–08; Division 3(N) – Champions 1928–29. *FA Cup:* Winners 1911 (first holders of the present trophy). *Football League Cup* best season: 5th rd, 1965.

COLOURS

White shirts with claret and amber shoulder panels, claret shorts, white stockings.
Change colours: Amber shirts with white and claret shoulder panels, amber shorts and stockings.

BRADFORD CITY

Players Names Ht, Wt, D.o.B.	Birthplace Transfer Fee	Clubs	Appearances F.L. A & S	 F.L.C. A & S	 F.A.C. A & S	Goals F.L.	 F.L.C.	 F.A.C.
Goalkeepers								
Eric McManus (NIAM)	Limavady	Coleraine						
6 1, 12 12, 14.11.50	—	Coventry C	6					
	£3000	Notts Co	229	13	9			
	£85,000	Stoke C	4					
	—	Lincoln C (loan)	21					
	£15,000	Bradford C	27	6	4			
Defenders								
Peter Jackson	Bradford	Bradford C (A)	128+11	15	5+1	13		
6 1, 12 0, 6.4.61								
Roy McFarland (E)	Liverpool	Tranmere R	35					
5 11½, 11 4, 5.4.48	£25,000	Derby Co	434	36	33	44		
	F/T	Bradford C	40	4	2	1		
Gary Watson	Bradford	Bradford C (A)	242+17	18+2	9+1	28	2	
5 8, 10 6, 7.10.55	—	Doncaster R (loan)	13					
Cyril Pond	St Kitts, WI	Bradford C	464+8	31+1	28	3		
5 9, 10 0, 7.8.52								
Trevor Cherry (E)	Huddersfield	Huddersfield T	184+2	7	13	10	1	1
5 9, 11 6, 23.2.48	£90,000	Leeds U	393+6	36	28+1	24	4	1
	£10,000	Bradford C	28		1			
Greg Abbott		Coventry C (A)						
	F/T	Bradford C	11					
Greg Fee	Halifax	Bradford C	3					
Midfield								
Les Chapman*	Oldham	Oldham Ath	75+1	5	1	9		1
5 7, 10 4, 27.9.48	£20,000	Huddersfield T	120+3	8	11	8		2
	£10,000	Oldham Ath	186+1	9	11	11		1
	F/T	Stockport Co	32	4	1	1		
	£10,000	Bradford C	137+2	14+1	6	3		1
John Black*	Helensburgh	Wolverhampton W (A)	5+1					
5 8, 10 11, 10.11.57	F/T	Bradford C	50+5	4	1	13	2	
Terry Yorath (W)	Cardiff	Leeds U (A)	120+23	10+1	18+2	10		1
6 0, 12 3, 27.3.50	£135,000	Coventry C	99	7	3	3		
	£300,000	Tottenham H	44+4	7	7	1		
	£140,000	Vancouver W						
	F/T	Bradford C	3		1			
Stuart McCall	Leeds	Bradford C (A)	25+3	2		4		
Forwards								
Terry Gray (EY)	Bradford	Ashley Road						
5 8, 10 0, 3.6.54	—	Huddersfield T	146+17	7+2	9	36	3	2
	£45,000	Southend U	106+4	8	2	28	1	1
	F/T	Bradford C	36+2	5	3	8		1
Bobby Campbell (NI)	Belfast	Aston Villa (A)	7+3	1		1		
5 11, 12 7, 13.9.56	—	Halifax T (loan)	14+1					
	F/T	Huddersfield T	30+1	3		9	1	
	£10,000	Sheffield U	35+2	1		11		
	F/T	Huddersfield T	7			3		
	F/T	Halifax T	19+3		1	3		
	F/T	Brisbane C						
	F/T	Bradford C	147+1	15	6	76	9	2
Mark Ellis	Bradford	Bradford C	44+3	7	4+1	4	1	
5 7, 10 5, 6.1.62								
Joe Cooke	Dominica, WI	Bradford C (A)	184+20	10+1	15	62	5	4
5 11, 12 7, 15.2.55	£40,000	Peterborough U	18			5		
	£50,000	Oxford U	71+1	5	2	13		
	£25,000	Exeter C	17	3	1	3	2	
	£10,000	Bradford C	56	6	4	6	2	4
Ian Mellor	Sale	Wythenshawe Ams						
6 2, 11 12, 19.2.50	—	Manchester C	36+4	1+1	2+1	7		
	£70,000	Norwich C	28+1	5+1	1	2	4	
	£40,000	Brighton	116+6	14+3	10+1	31	1	3
	£30,000	Chester	38+2	4	3	11	1	3
	£60,000	Sheffield W	54+16	5+1	2+1	11		
	F/T	Bradford C	25+5	6	3	4	1	
Steve Lampkin		Bradford C	5+1			1		
Non-Contract Players								
Simon McGovern		Bradford C	1					
Dave Hill		Bradford C	2+2			1		

Commercial Manager: Mike Ryan (Tel.)
Club Coach: Terry Yorath
Supporters Player of the Season 1982–83: Bobby Campbell
Physiotherapist: Brian Edwards
Association of Football Statisticians Club Adviser to Yearbook: T. Frost
Club Captain 1982–83: Joe Cooke
Chief Scout: Maurice Lindley
Club Statistician: David Markham

Players released since May 1982:
John Hanson, F. (Scarborough); Alan Hebditch, D. (N/K); Billy Ingham, M. (Accrington); Neil Ramsbottom, G. (N/K).

BRENTFORD Division 3

Back row (left to right): F. Callaghan (Manager), S. Bowles, J. McNichol, A. Whitehead, P. Borota, R. Booker, K. Bowen, G. Johnson, E. Lyons (Physiotherapist), R. Harris (Player-Coach)
Front row: G. Roberts, T. Hurlock, A. Mahoney, F. Joseph, C. Kamara, T. Rowe, B. Tucker, G. Wilkins, P. Walker.

Chairman: M. M. Lange.

Directors: R. J. J. Blindell LLB, E. J. Radley-Smith MS, FRCS, LRCP, D. Tana.

Manager: Fred Callaghan.

Chief Development Executive: Miss C. Mathews.

Press Officer /Programme Editor: Eric White (01-574 3047).

Year Formed: 1889. ***Turned Professional:*** 1899. Ltd Co.: 1901.

Previous Grounds: Clifden Road 1889–91; Benns Fields, Little Ealing 1891–95; Shotters Field 1895–98; Cross Road, S. Ealing 1898–1900; Boston Park 1900–04; Griffin Park 1904.

Previous Managers since 1948: Harry Curtis, Jackie Gibbons, Jimmy Bain, Tom Lawton, Bill Dodgin (Snr), Malcolm McDonald, Tommy Cavanagh, Billy Gray, Jimmy Sirrel, Frank Blunstone, Mike Everitt, John Docherty, Bill Dodgin (Jnr) (13).

Griffin Park, Braemar Rd, Brentford, Middlesex TW8 0NT. Telephone 01-560 2021. ***Ground capacity:*** 37,000 (30,500 under cover). ***Record attendance:*** 39,626 v Preston NE, FA Cup 6th rd, 5 March, 1938. ***Record receipts:*** £16,799 v Fulham, Division 3, 13 Sept, 1980. ***Pitch measurements:*** 114yd×75yd.

Directions to the Ground: South Ealing (Underground, Piccadilly line). Southern Region trains from waterloo to Brentford Central. Buses 91, 65, 117, E1, E2, 267. The ground is within a mile of the M4 and A4 roads.

Match tickets: Admission mainly by cash through the turnstiles on the day but tickets for Block B only are available a fortnight prior to each match. Postal applications should include SAE.

Car parking: Confined to streets around the ground.

Entertainments /catering facilities: Catering kiosks in the ground. A members' social club, the 'Centre Circle' in Braemar Road.

Club shop: Applications for price lists, etc., should be sent to the Commerical Manager, Brentford FC, Braemar Road, Brentford, Middlesex, TW8 0NT, accompanied by SAE.

Handbooks /programmes: Programmes not available on subscription.

Address of Supporters Club: Same as Football Club. ***Address of the Club Shop or Boutique:*** c/o the Club.

Note: Full club statistical records are on pages 416–455.

BRENTFORD 1982–83 LEAGUE RECORD

Match No.	Date	Venue	Opponents	Result		H/T Score	Lg. Pos.	Goalscorers	Attendance
1	Aug 28	H	Bristol R	W	5-1	2-0	—	Mahoney, Joseph 2, Roberts 2	5542
2	Sept 4	A	Wigan Ath	L	2-3	1-2	6	Mahoney, Joseph	5019
3	8	A	Reading	D	1-1	0-1	—	Joseph	3555
4	11	H	Southend U	W	4-2	1-0	5	Mahoney 2, Joseph, Roberts	5604
5	18	A	Orient	D	3-3	0-1	8	Mahoney, Roberts, Booker	3458
6	25	H	Millwall	D	1-1	0-0	10	McNichol	6455
7	28	H	Newport Co	W	2-0	1-0	—	Joseph, Mahoney	5706
8	Oct 2	A	Walsall	L	1-2	0-0	10	Kamara	2723
9	9	H	Chesterfield	W	4-2	1-1	7	Hurlock, Joseph 2, Bowles (pen)	5706
10	16	A	Doncaster R	D	4-4	1-1	8	Mahoney, McNichol, Roberts, Booker	3265
11	20	A	Oxford U	D	2-2	1-1	—	Joseph, Mahoney	6113
12	23	H	Lincoln C	W	2-0	1-0	8	Joseph Bowen	8017
13	30	A	Plymouth Arg	L	0-2	0-0	9		4036
14	Nov 2	H	Preston NE	W	3-1	0-0	—	McNichol, Kamara, Roberts	6142
15	6	H	Bradford C	L	0-2	0-1	10		6669
16	13	A	Huddersfield T	L	0-2	0-0	12		10,034
17	27	A	Sheffield U	W	2-1	2-1	9	Booker, Joseph	10,202
18	Dec 4	H	Wrexham	W	4-1	1-1	7	Kamara, Mahoney, Joseph 2	5606
19	18	H	Exeter C	W	4-0	3-0	7	Bowles, Walker, Whitehead, Booker	5296
20	27	A	Portsmouth	L	1-2	1-1	8	Joseph	14,476
21	28	H	Gillingham	D	1-1	0-0	8	Joseph	7796
22	Jan 1	A	AFC Bournemouth	L	3-4	1-1	9	Roberts, Joseph 2	5593
23	3	H	Cardiff C	L	1-3	0-2	9	Bowles (pen)	7602
24	8	H	Wigan Ath	L	1-3	0-2	9	Roberts	4939
25	15	A	Bristol R	L	0-2	0-0	11		5449
26	22	H	Orient	W	5-2	1-1	9	Booker 2, Bowles (pen), Roberts, Hurlock	5209
27	29	A	Southend U	L	2-4	0-2	11	Kamara, Roberts	3074
28	Feb 6	A	Newport Co	D	0-0	0-0	—		3401
29	12	H	Reading	L	1-2	0-2	11	Bowles (pen)	6273
30	19	A	Chesterfield	L	1-2	1-0	14	Cassells	2291
31	26	H	Doncaster R	W	1-0	0-0	13	Bowles (pen)	4413
32	Mar 1	A	Preston NE	L	0-3	0-2	—		3669
33	5	A	Lincoln C	L	1-2	1-1	14	Cassells	3698
34	11	H	Plymouth Arg	W	2-0	0-0	—	Joseph, Kamara	4967
35	19	A	Bradford C	W	1-0	0-0	13	Cassells	3828
36	22	H	Oxford U	D	1-1	1-0	—	Bowles	5086
37	26	H	Huddersfield T	W	1-0	1-0	11	Bowles (pen)	6277
38	Apr 1	H	Portsmouth	D	1-1	1-0	—	Joseph	12,593
39	2	A	Gillingham	D	2-2	1-1	11	Kamara 2	4168
40	8	A	Wrexham	W	4-3	3-3	—	Kamara, Cassells 2, Joseph	2104
41	16	H	Walsall	L	2-3	1-2	11	Bowles (pen), Cassells	4868
42	23	A	Exeter C	W	7-1	3-0	10	Kamara 2, Joseph 2, Cassells 2, Roberts	2759
43	30	H	Sheffield U	W	2-1	0-1	9	Hurlock, Roberts	4987
44	May 2	A	Cardiff C	L	1-3	0-1	10	Kamara	9112
45	8	A	Millwall	L	0-1	0-1	—		9097
46	14	H	AFC Bournemouth	W	2-1	2-0	9	Joseph, Bowles (pen)	6191

Final League Position: 9

GOALSCORERS

League (88): Joseph 23, Roberts 12, Kamara 11, Bowles 10 (8 pens), Cassells 8, Mahoney 9, Booker 6, Hurlock 3, McNichol 3, Bowen 1, Walker 1, Whitehead 1.
Milk Cup (9): Mahoney 3, Roberts 3, Bowles 1 (pen), Hurlock 1, Joseph 1.
FA Cup (10): Mahoney 3, Hurlock 2, Roberts 2, Bowen 1, Joseph 1, McNichol 1.
Football League Trophy (5): Roberts 2, Johnson 1, Joseph 1, Mahoney 1.

Milk Cup	First Round	Wimbledon (a)	1-1
		(h)	2-0
	Second Round	Blackburn R (h)	3-2
		(a)	0-0
	Third Round	Swansea C (h)	1-1
		(a)	2-1
	Fourth Round	Nottingham F (a)	0-2

FA Cup	First Round	Windsor & Eton (a)	7-0
	drawn away but played at Griffin Park.		
	Second Round	Swindon T (a)	2-2
		(h)	1-3 (aet
Football League Trophy		Crystal Palace (h)	2-2
		Millwall (a)	0-3
		Wimbledon (a)	3-1

Roche	Tucker	Wilkins	McNichol	Whitehead	Hurlock	Kamara	Joseph	Mahoney	Bowles	Roberts	Booker	Johnson	Rowe	Spencer	Salman	Bowen	Harris	Walker	Strong (L)	Holmes	Cassells	Referees	Match No.
1	2	3	4	5	6	7	8	9	10	11												J. Martin	1
1	2	5		3	6	7	10	9	8	11*	4	12										G. Tyson	2
1	2	3		5	6	7	8	9	10	11	4											J. Bray	3
1	2	3		5	6	7*	8	9	10	11	4	12										L. Shapter	4
1	3		4		6	7	8*	9	10	11	5		2			12						J. Hunting	5
1		5	3		8	7	9	10	6	11	4		2									C. Thomas	6
1		3*	4	5	6	7	8	9	10	11	12		2									A. Gunn	7
1		3	4	5	6	7	8	9*	10	11	12		2									R. Guy	8
1		2	5	4	6	7*	8	9	10	11	12			3								D. Hedges	9
1		3	4		6	7	8	9	10	11	5				2*	12						D. Richardson	10
1		3	4		6	7	8	9	10	11	5		2									H. Taylor	11
1		3*	4	5	6	7	8	9	10	11			2			12						Alan Robinson	12
1			4	5	6	7		9	10	11	8		2			12	3*					R. Milford	13
1			4	5	6	7		9	10	11			2	3		8						L. Burden	14
1			4	5	6	7	8	9	10	11			2	3								A. Crickmore	15
1		3	4	5	6	7	8*	9		11	12		2				10					M. Heath	16
1		3	4*	5		7	8	9	10	11	6	12	2									R. Nixon	17
1		3		5		7	8	9	10	11	4		2					6				B. Hill	18
1		3		5	6	7	8		10		4	9	2					11				K. Baker	19
1		3		5	6	7	8		10*	11	4	9						12	2			M. James	20
1		3		5		7	8		10	11	4	9*				12		6	2			B. Stevens	21
1				5			8		10	11	4	12	3			9	6*	7	2			L. Shapter	22
1				5	6		8		10	11	4	9	2					7	3			A. Grey	23
1				5	6	7	8			11			2	4		9		10	3			M. Bodenham	24
1		3		5	6	7	8		10	11*	4		2			12		9				H. King	25
1				5	6	7	8		10	11	4		2				3	9				A. Glasson	26
1				5	6	7	8		10	11	4		2			12	3	9*				G. Napthine	27
1			4	5	6	7	8		10	11*			2			9				3		M. Robinson	28
1		2	4	5	6	7	8		10	11	12									3	9*	J. Deakin	29
1			4	5	6	7	8		10	11	2			3		12					9*	N. Midgley	30
1*			4	5	6	7	8		10	11	12		2							3	9	A. Gunn	31
1			4	5*	6	7	8		10	11	12		2			9				3		N. Ashley	32
1		3	4	5	6	7	8		10	11	12		2								9*	T. Holbrook	33
1		3	4	5	6	7	8		10	11			2								9	D. Brazier	34
1		3		5		7	8		10	11	4		2				6				9	D. Owen	35
1		3	4	5		7	8		10	11	6		2*					12			9	D. Axcell	36
1			4	5	6	7	8		10	11	3		2								9	R. Milford	37
1			4	5	6	7	8		10	11	3		2								9	H. Taylor	38
1			4	5	6	7	8			11	3		2				10				9	B. Daniels	39
1		12	4	5	6	7	8		10	11	3		2								9*	K. Hackett	40
1		3*	4	5		7			10	11	8		2				6	12			9	L. Burden	41
1			4		6	7	8		10	11	5		2	3							9	C. Newsome	42
1			4	5	6	7*	8		10	11	2			3				12			9	T. Bune	43
1			4	5	6	7	8		10*	11	2			3				12			9	A. Hamil	44
1			4	5	6	7	8			11	2		3				10*	12			9	Alan Robinson	45
1			4	5*	6	7	8		10	11	9		2	3				12				E. Read/R. Smith	46
46	5	24	32	41	39	44	43	18	42	45	31	4	34	9	1	5	9	9	5	4	16		
		+ 1s									+ 8s	+ 4s				+ 8s		+ 7s					

FOOTBALL LEAGUE RECORD

1920 Original Member of Division 3; 1921–33 Division 3(S); 1933–35 Division 2; 1935–47 Division 1; 1947–54 Division 2; 1954–62 Division 3(S); 1962–63 Division 4; 1963–66 Division 3; 1966–72 Division 4; 1972–73 Division 3; 1973–78 Division 4; 1978– Division 3.

HONOURS

Football League: Division 1 best season: 5th, 1935–36; Division 2 – Champions 1934–35; Division 3(S) – Champions 1932–33; Runners-up 1929–30, 1957–58; Division 4 – Champions 1962–63. *FA Cup* best season: 6th rd, 1938, 1946, 1949. *Football League Cup* best season: 4th rd, 1982–83.

COLOURS

Red and white striped shirts, black shorts, black stockings with red and white hooped tops. **Change colours:** All blue.

BRENTFORD

Players Names Ht, Wt, D.o.B.	Birthplace Transfer Fee	Clubs	Appearances F.L. A & S	 F.L.C. A & S	 F.A.C. A & S	Goals F.L.	 F.L.C.	 F.A.C.
Goalkeepers								
David McKellar	Irvine	Ipswich T (A)						
6 0, 11 8, 22.5.56	F/T	Ardrossan W						
	£2500	Derry Co	41		2			
	£30,000	Brentford	84	2	5			
Pat Roche (EI)	Dublin	Shelbourne						
6 1, 11 9, 4.1.51	£15,000	Manchester U	46	5				
	F/T	Brentford	46	7	3			
Defenders								
Barry Tucker*	Swansea	Northampton T (A)	209+5	10	10	3		
5 6, 10 12, 28.8.52	£10,000	Brentford	168+1	6	5	5		
	—	Northampton T (loan)	37		1	4		
Jim McNicholl (SU-21)	Glasgow	Ipswich T (A)						
6 0, 12 10, 9.6.58	F/T	Luton T	13+2					
	£30,000	Brentford	132+3	7	8	18		1
Alan Whitehead	Bury	Bury	98+1	6	10	13		2
6 3, 12 0, 20.11.56	£65,000	Brentford	83+1	9	6	4		
Terry Rowe	Fulham	Brentford	44	6	3			
5 7, 9 7,								
Graham Wilkins	Hillingdon	Chelsea (A)	136+1	7	3	1		
5 6½, 10 2, 28.6.55	F/T	Brentford	24+1	2	2			
Ranis Salman (EY)	Famagusta	Brentford (A)	212+9	10	10	5		
5 10, 11 8,	Cyprus							
Tony Spender		Brentford (A)	12	1				
Midfield								
Terry Hurlock	Hackney	Leytonstone						
5 9, 13 2, 22.9.58	£6000	Brentford	121	7	8	9	1	1
Stan Bowles* (E)	Manchester	Manchester C(A)	15+2	1+2		2	2	
5 10, 11 4, 24.12.48	—	Bury (loan)	5	1				
	F/T	Crewe Alex	51	1	3	18		1
	£12,000	Carlisle U	33	1	2	12		1
	£110,000	QPR	255	27	25	70	7	8
	£250,000	Nottingham F	19		1	2		
	£100,000	Orient	46	3	1	7		
	£30,000	Brentford	73	7	5	16	1	
Chris Kamara	Middlesbrough	Portsmouth (A)	56+7	1	4	7		1
6 1, 12 0, 25.12.57	£20,000	Swindon T.	133+14	18+4	14	21	1	4
	£50,000	Portsmouth	11	3			1	
	P/E	Brentford	75	7	6	16		
Bob Booker	Watford	Bedmond Soc						
6 2¼, 12 4, 25.1.58	—	Brentford	92+24	7+1	7+1	23		1
Forwards								
Gary Roberts	Rhyl	Wembley T.						
6 0, 11 6, 5.4.60	£6000	Brentford	98+6	9	5	23	3	3
Tony Mahoney	Barking	Fulham (A)	53+6	4	8+2	10	1	5
6 0, 11 12, 29.9.59	F/T	Brentford	18	7		9	3	
Francis Joseph	London	Hillingdon Bor						
5 10, 12 0, 6.3.60	£1000	Wimbledon	42+9	2	1	14		
	£30,000	Brentford	43	7	3	23	1	1
Keith Tonge*		Brentford (A)	1					
Keith Cassells	London	Wembley T.						
5 10, 11 12, 10.7.57	£500	Watford	6+6	2	1+1			
	—	Peterborough U (loan)	8					
	£5000	Oxford U	43+2	5	8	13	4	7
	£115,000	Southampton	13+6	5	1	4	1	
	£25,000	Brentford	16			8		
Non-Contract Players								
Ron Harris (EU-23)	Hackney	Chelsea (A)	646+9	45+2	63	13		
5 8, 11 7, 13.11.44	F/T	Brentford	57+1	4	1			

Commercial Manager:
Club Coach: Ron Harris
Supporters Player of the Season 1982–83:
Physiotherapist:
Association of Football Statisticians Club Adviser to Yearbook: G. Haynes

Club Captain 1982–83:
Chief Scout:
Club Statistician:

Players released since May 1982:
Paul Priddy, G. (retired); Paul Walker, M. (PG Rangers, South Africa); Gary Johnson, F. (PG Rangers, South Africa).

BRIGHTON & HOVE ALBION Division 2

Back row (left to right): John Collins (1st team coach), Neil McNab, Andy Ritchie, Sammy Nelson, Graham Moseley, Perry Digweed, Steve Foster, Gordon Smith, Tony Grealish, Mike Yaxley (Physiotherapist)
Front row: Mickey Thomas, Jimmy Case, Gary Stevens, Gerry Ryan, Mike Bailey (Manager), Don Shanks, Steve Gatting, Mike Robinson, Neil Smillie.

Chairman: M. K. Bamber.

Vice-Chairman: K. Wickenden, MP.

Directors: N. J. Hyams, T. Appleby.

Manager: Jimmy Melia.

Secretary: Kenneth Calver.

Year Formed: 1900. ***Turned Professional:*** 1900. ***Ltd Co.:*** 1904.

Previous Name: Brighton & Hove Rangers.

Previous Grounds: 1900, Withdean; 1901, County Ground; 1902, Goldstone Ground.

Club Nickname: 'The Seagulls'.

Previous Managers since 1948: Charles Webb, Tommy Cook, Don Welsh, Billy Lane, George Curtis, Archie Macaulay, Freddie Goodwin, Pat Saward, Brian Clough, Peter Taylor, Alan Mullery MBE, Mike Bailey (12).

Goldstone Ground, Old Shoreham Rd, Hove, Sussex BN3 7DE. Telephone Brighton (0273) 739535. ***Ground capacity:*** 32,500. ***Record attendance:*** 36,747 v Fulham, Division 2, 27 December, 1958. ***Pitch measurements:*** 112yd×75yd.

Directions to the Ground: Buses 5, B5, 9, 26, 40, 55, 19 from Old Steyne and 11 via Brighton station and Old Shoreham Rd. Hove station is five minutes walk from the ground.

Match tickets: Postal bookings for tickets four weeks in advance if available.

Car parking: Car parking facilities are available a few minutes away at the Greyhound Stadium, Neville Road, and in Hove Station Goods Yard, Sackville Road. There is limited parking adjacent to the stadium.

Entertainments/catering facilities: Bars and tea stands around the ground.

Club shop: At the ground; sells all types of souvenirs.

Handbooks/programmes: Programmes available by post from the club shop.

Address of Supporters Club: Albion Shop, Goldstone Ground, Hove.

Note: Full club statistical records are on pages 416–455.

BRIGHTON & HOVE ALBION 1982–83 LEAGUE RECORD

Match No.	Date	Venue	Opponents	Result		H/T Score	Lg. Pos.	Goalscorers	Attendance
1	Aug 28	H	Ipswich T	D	1-1	1-1	—	Ritchie	13,641
2	Sept 1	A	WBA	L	0-5	0-0	—		11,546
3	4	A	Nottingham F	L	0-4	0-2	21		13,709
4	7	H	Arsenal	W	1-0	1-0	—	Ryan	13,507
5	11	H	Sunderland	W	3-2	0-2	18	Smith, Ryan, Grealish	10,264
6	18	A	Luton T	L	0-5	0-1	18		11,342
7	25	H	Birmingham C	W	1-0	0-0	11	Gatting	9845
8	Oct 2	A	Everton	D	2-2	1-1	11	Robinson, Case	17,539
9	9	H	Swansea C	D	1-1	1-0	12	Foster	11,050
10	16	A	Stoke C	L	0-3	0-2	16		13,936
11	23	H	West Ham U	W	3-1	1-0	12	Smith, Gatting, Robinson	20,490
12	30	A	Liverpool	L	1-3	1-3	14	Ryan	27,929
13	Nov 6	H	Manchester U	W	1-0	0-0	12	Ward	18,398
14	13	A	Aston Villa	L	0-1	0-0	15		18,834
15	20	A	Watford	L	1-4	0-1	17	Ryan	16,529
16	27	H	Notts Co	L	0-2	0-1	17		10,008
17	Dec 4	A	Coventry C	L	0-2	0-2	18		8054
18	11	H	Norwich C	W	3-0	1-0	18	Case, Ritchie, Robinson	9994
19	18	A	Manchester C	D	1-1	0-1	18	Ritchie	20,615
20	27	H	Southampton	L	0-1	0-0	19		21,794
21	28	A	Tottenham H	L	0-2	0-1	19		23,994
22	Jan 1	H	Watford	D	1-1	0-0	20	Ward	15,139
23	3	H	Nottingham F	D	1-1	0-1	18	Robinson	10,402
24	15	A	Ipswich T	L	0-2	0-1	21		17,092
25	22	H	Luton T	L	2-4	0-2	21	Ritchie, Grealish	11,705
26	Feb 5	A	Arsenal	L	1-3	1-2	22	Robinson	17,972
27	12	H	WBA	D	0-0	0-0	22		9902
28	26	H	Stoke C	L	1-2	1-2	22	Ritchie	14,937
29	Mar 1	A	Swansea C	W	2-1	1-1	—	Robinson, Case	8825
30	5	A	West Ham U	L	1-2	0-0	21	Ryan	16,850
31	19	A	Manchester U	D	1-1	1-0	22	Gatting	36,700
32	22	H	Liverpool	D	2-2	2-0	—	Robinson, Howlett	25,030
33	26	H	Aston Villa	D	0-0	0-0	22		14,657
34	Apr 2	H	Tottenham H	W	2-1	0-1	22	Gatting, Ryan	20,359
35	5	A	Southampton	D	0-0	0-0	—		18,253
36	9	H	Everton	L	1-2	0-1	21	Smith (pen)	14,534
37	19	A	Sunderland	D	1-1	1-1	—	Smith	13,414
38	23	H	Coventry C	W	1-0	0-0	21	Connor	14,676
39	30	A	Notts Co	L	0-1	0-0	21		7349
40	May 2	A	Birmingham C	D	1-1	0-1	22	Smith	15,977
41	7	H	Manchester C	L	0-1	0-0	22		17,794
42	14	A	Norwich C	L	1-2	0-1	22	Smith	20,306

Final League Position: 22

GOALSCORERS

League (38): Robinson 7, Ryan 6, Smith 6 (1 pen), Ritchie 5, Gatting 4, Case 3, Grealish 2, Ward 2, Connor 1, Foster 1, Howlett 1.
Milk Cup (1): Grealish 1.
FA Cup (13): Case 4, Robinson 3, Ritchie 1, Ryan 1, Smillie 1, Smith 1, Stevens 1, Ward 1.

Milk Cup	Second Round	Tottenham H (a)	1-1
		(h)	0-1
FA Cup	Third Round	Newcastle U (h)	1-1
		(a)	1-0
	Fourth Round	Manchester C (h)	4-0
	Fifth Round	Liverpool (a)	2-1
	Sixth Round	Norwich C (h)	1-0
	Semi-final	Sheffield W	2-1
	Final	Manchester U	2-2 (aet)
		Manchester U	0-4

Digweed	Shanks	Pearce	Grealish	Stevens	Gatting	Smillie	Ritchie	Robinson	McNab	Smith	Foster	Ryan	Case	Nelson	Stille	Moseley	Ring	Ward (L)	Ramsey	Howlett	Connor	O'Reagan	Rodon	Referees	Match No.
1	2	3	4	5	6	7	8*	9	10	11		12												D. Hedges	1
1	2	3*	4	5	6	7	8	9	10	11	12													N. Glover	2
1	2	3*	4	11	6	12	8	9	10		5		7											C. Thomas	3
1	2		4	5	6	12	8			11		9	7	3	10*									Alan Robinson	4
	2		4	5	6		8			11		9	7	3	10	1								B. Daniels	5
	2		4	5	6		8*			11		9	7	3	10	1	12							R. Milford	6
			4*	2	6		8	12		11	5	9	7	3	10	1								D. Reeves	7
	3		4	2	6		8	9	10	11	5		7			1								C. Seel	8
	3		4*	2	6	12	8	9	10	11	5		7			1								D. Vickers	9
		3	4	2	6		8	9	10	11	5		7			1								A. Challinor	10
		3		2	6			9	8	11	5	12	7*		4	1		10						L. Burden	11
	2	3	4		6			9	8	11	5	7*			12	1		10						L. Robinson	12
			4	2	6			9	8	11	5	7		3		1		10						T. Spencer	13
			4	2	6			9	8	11	5	7*		3	12	1		10						J. Lovatt	14
				2	6	11		9	8		5	12	7	3	4*	1		10						A. Seville	15
				2	6	11*	12	9	8		5	4	7	3		1		10						A. Ward	16
1	2		4	6	11			9	8*		5	12	7	3				10						M. Heath	17
1			4	6	11		8	9			5		7	3				10	2					M. Taylor	18
1			4	6	11		8	9			5		7	3				10	2					V. Callow	19
1			4	6	11		8*	9			5	12	7	3				10	2					M. Dimblebee	20
1			4	6	11		8	9			5		7	3				10	2					K. Barratt	21
1		3	4	6	11			9			5	10	7					8	2					J. Hunting	22
1		3	4	6			12	9			5	10*	7		11			8	2					D. Axcell	23
		3	4	6	5	11	10	9		12			7			1		8*	2					J. Bray	24
		3*	4	6		11	12	9		10	5		7			1		8	2					D. Letts	25
1			4	6	3	11*	8	9		10	5	12	7						2					D. Civil	26
1			4	6	3	11	8	9		10	5		7						2					E. Scales	27
1			4	6	3	11	9				5	10	7					8	2					J. Moules	28
			4	6	3	11	8	9			5	10	7			1			2					A. Crickmore	29
			4	6	3	11	8	9			5	10	7			1			2					J. Deakin	30
			4	6	3	11	8	9		12	5	10*	7			1			2					R. Saunders	31
			4	6	3	11		9		8	5		7			1			2	10				K. Salmon	32
			4*	6	3	11		9		12	5		7			1			2	10	8			T. Glasson	33
		4		6	3			9		10	5	12	7			1			2	11*	8			V. Callow	34
			4	6	3	11		9		10	5	12	7			1			2		8*			D. Reeves	35
		12	4	6	3	11		9		10	5	8*	7			1			2					C. Thomas	36
1			4	6	3	11*		9		10	5		7						2	8	12			D. Richardson	37
			4	6	3	11		9		10	5		7*			1			2	8	12			E. Read	38
			4	6	3	11			7	10	5					1			2	8	9			N. Wilson	39
			4	6	3	11		9		10	5	12				1			2	8*	7			L. Shapter	40
		2	4	6	3	11		9		10	5	12	7			1				8*				L. Burden	41
		3	4	5	6	11				10*		9	7			1				8		2	12	A. Ward	42
15	10	13	38	41	40	22	21	35	14	26	35	16	35	13	7	27	0	16	23	9	5	1	0		
		+ 1s				+ 3s	+ 3s	+ 1s		+ 3s	+ 1s	+ 10s			+ 2s		+ 1s				+ 2s		+ 1s		

FOOTBALL LEAGUE RECORD

1920 Original Member of Division 3; 1921–58 Division 3(S); 1958–62 Division 2; 1962–63 Division 3; 1963–65 Division 4; 1965–72 Division 3; 1972–73 Division 2; 1973–77 Division 3; 1977–79 Division 2; 1979–83 Division 1; 1983– Division 2.

HONOURS

Football League: Division 1 best season: 16th, 1979–80; Division 3(S) – Champions 1957–58; Runners-up 1953–54, 1955–56; Division 3 – Runners-up 1971–72, 1976–77; Division 4 – Champions 1964–65. *FA Cup* best season: Finalists 1982–83. *Football League Cup* best season: 5th rd, 1978–79.

COLOURS

Blue shirts with red and white trim, white shorts with blue trim, blue stockings with white trim.
Change colours: White shirts, blue shorts, white stockings.

BRIGHTON & HOVE ALBION

Players Names *Ht, Wt, D.o.B.*	*Birthplace* *Transfer Fee*	*Clubs*	*Appearances* *F.L.* *A & S*	 *F.L.C.* *A & S*	 *F.A.C.* *A & S*	*Goals* *F.L.*	 *F.L.C.*	 *F.A.C.*
Goalkeepers								
Graham Moseley (EY)	Manchester	Blackburn R (A)				—		
6 0, 11 8, 16.11.53	£18,000	Derby Co	32	4	4	—		
	—	Aston Villa (loan)	3			—		
	—	Walsall (loan)	3			—		
	£20,000	Brighton	137	14	15			
Perry Digweed	London	Fulham (A)	15			—		
6 0½, 11 4, 26.10.59	£150,000	Brighton	42		1			
Defenders								
Gary Stevens (EU21)	Hillingdon	Brighton (A)	120+13	6+1	11+1	2		1
5 11, 11 10, 30.3.62								
Steve Foster (E)	Portsmouth	Portsmouth (A)	101+8	10	8	6		2
6 0, 12 8, 24.9.57	£150,000	Brighton	155+1	13	13	5	2	
Chris Ramsey	Birmingham	Bristol C (N/C)						
5 9, 10 12, 28.4.62	F/T	Brighton	26		6			
Sammy Nelson (NI)	Belfast	Arsenal	245+10	27	33	10	1	1
5 10, 11 0, 1.4.49	£30,000	Brighton	40	2	3			
Steve Gatting	Willesden	Arsenal (A)	50+8	3	9	5		1
5 11, 11 11, 25.9.59	£200,000	Brighton	79	5	10	7	1	
Graham Pearce	London	Barnet						
5 9, 11 0,	£10,000	Brighton	13+1	1	5			
Mark Fleet (EIY)	Southport	Brighton (A)						
Eric Young		Slough T						
6 3,	£10,000	Brighton						
Keiran O'Reagan	Cork	Tramore Ath						
5 7, 10 8, 9.11.63		Brighton	1					
Gerry McTeague	Queensferry	Brighton (A)						
Midfield								
Giles Stille	London	Kingstonian						
5 9, 11 9, 10.11.58	£3000	Brighton	19+6		2	4		
Neil McNab (SU21)	Greenock	Morton						
5 7, 10 10, 6.6.57	£75,000	Tottenham H	63+9	5	2	3		
	£250,000	Bolton W	33+2	2	2	4		
	£220,000	Brighton	100+3	3	5	4		1
	—	Leeds U (loan)	5		1			
Tony Grealish (EI)	Paddington	Orient (A)	169+2	6+1	17	10		
5 7, 11 7, 21.9.56	£300,000	Luton T	78	5	3	2		
	£100,000	Brighton	72+3	4	11	3	2	
Jimmy Case (EU23)	Liverpool	South Liverpool						
5 9, 12 7, 18.5.54	£500	Liverpool	170+16	21+1	20+1	23	3	7
	£350,000	Brighton	68	4	10	6		4
Gary Howlett (EIY)	Dublin	Home Farm						
5 8, 10 4, 2.4.63		Coventry C						
	F/T	Brighton	9		3	1		
Matthew Wiltshire	Brighton	Brighton (A)						
Forwards								
Mike Ring	Brighton	Brighton (A)	1+1	1				
5 10, 10 6, 13.2.61								
Gerry Ryan (EI)	Dublin	Bohemians						
5 10, 10 12, 4.10.55	£50,000	Derby Co	30	2	2	4		1
	£80,000	Brighton	94+33	3+5	6+3	21	1	2
Michael Robinson (EI)	Leicester	Preston NE (A)	45+3	4	2	15	1	
6 0, 13 4, 12.7.58	£750,000	Manchester C	29+1	4	1	8	1	
	£400,000	Brighton	111+2	8	12	37	3	3
Gordon Smith (SU21)	Kilwinning	Rangers						
5 11, 12 0, 29.12.54	£400,000	Brighton	86+8	7	5+1	18		1
Neil Smillie	Barnsley	Crystal Palace (A)	71+12	7	7	7		1
5 6, 10 7, 19.7.58	—	Brentford (loan)	3					
	P/E	Brighton	22+3	1	6+1			1
Terry Connor (E.Y.)	Leeds	Leeds U (A)	83+13	4+2	5	19	1	1
5 7, 10 0, 9.11.62	P/E	Brighton	5+2			1		
Chris Rodon	Swansea	Pontadawe						
6 1, 12 7,		Brighton	+1					

Commercial Manager: Ron Pavey (Tel. 778230)
Club Coach: George Aitken
Supporters Player of the Season 1982–83: G. Stevens
Physiotherapist: Michael Yaxley
Association of Football Statisticians Club Adviser to Yearbook: T. Carder.
Club Captain 1982–83: S. Foster
Chief Scout:
Club Statistician:

Players (non-appearance) granted free transfer: Danny Deans, F.
Players released since May 1982: Tommy Mason, D.(Seattle S.); Jacob Cohen, D.(Bethsheba, Israel); Don Shanks, D.(Eastern, Hong Kong)

BRISTOL CITY Division 4

Back row (left to right):
Colin Freeman
Simon Panes
Kevin Slabber
Steven Palmer
Ian Bowdige
Standing:
Alex Lockhart (Physio)
Paul Stevens
Gary Williams
Jon Economou
John Shaw
Garry Smith
Russell Musker
Wayne Bray
Terry Cooper (Manager)
Seated:
Steve Thompson
Ricky Chandler
Alan Nicholls
Terry Boyle
Tom Ritchie
Robert Newman
Alan Crawford
Glyn Riley
Front row:
Mark Jones
Nigel Smith
Colsten Gwyther
Andy Llewellyn

Chairman: D. Williams. ***Vice-Chairman:*** L. J. Kew.

Directors: D. N. Coller, K. J. Sage, O. W. Newland, W. I. Williams, B. Boyd, B. Marshall. ***Commercial Manager:*** B. White.

Manager: Terry Cooper. ***Secretary:*** J. Lillington.

Year Formed: 1894. ***Turned Professional:*** 1897.

Ltd Co.: 1897. BCFC (1982) PLC.

Previous Grounds: 1894, St John's Lane; 1904, Ashton Gate.

Previous Name: 1894–97, Bristol South End. ***Club Nickname:*** 'Robins'.

Previous Managers since 1948: Bob Hewison, Bob Wright, Pat Beasley, Peter Doherty, Fred Ford, Alan Dicks, Bob Houghton, Roy Hodgson (8).

Ashton Gate, Bristol BS3 2EJ. Telephone Bristol (0272) 632812 (5 lines). ***Telegraphic address:*** 'City Bristol'. ***Ground capacity:*** 30,868. ***Record attendance:*** 43,335 v Preston NE, FA Cup 5th rd, 16 Feb, 1935. ***Record receipts:*** £45,000 v Aston Villa, FA Cup 4th rd, 23 Jan, 1982. ***Pitch measurements:*** 115yd×75yd.

Directions to the Ground: Buses 79, 59. Parsons St station is available within walking distance for special trains. Also certain scheduled trains stop there.

Match tickets: Tickets can be booked any length of time before the match; Postal applications must include remittance and SAE. Personal applications not accepted until four weeks before the match.

Car parking: Season-ticket holders can obtain season car park parking tickets. Coach, parking at Cannons Marsh. There is limited street parking around the ground.

Entertainments/catering facilities: Social club in the main stands. Tea bars in the ground. Alcoholic beverages only obtainable by members of a bona-fide Supporters' Club. There is a wide variety of pre-match entertainment, and some matches are sponsored, so throw-away gifts to the crowd, and programme prizes, are a regular feature.

Club shop: One of the biggest in the country, sells all types of souvenirs, clothing and many other items.

Handbooks/programmes: Programmes available on subscription postal applications are accepted.

Extra information: Indoor bowling area in the main stand. Large room available for functions caters for 200 people.

Address of Supporters Club: Supporters Club, Bristol City FC, Ashton Gate, Bristol BS3 2EJ.

Address of the Club Shop or Boutique: City Shop, Ashton Gate, Bristol BS3 2EJ.

Note: Full club statistical records are on pages 416–455.

BRISTOL CITY 1982–83 LEAGUE RECORD

Match No.	Date	Venue	Opponents	Result	H/T Score	Lg. Pos.	Goalscorers	Attendance
1	Aug 28	H	Hull C	W 2-1	1-0	—	Riley, Musker	4877
2	Sept 4	A	Tranmere R	D 2-2	0-2	4	Ritchie 2	1534
3	7	A	Crewe Alex	L 1-4	0-1	—	Ritchie (pen)	1409
4	11	H	Blackpool	D 0-0	0-0	15		4681
5	19	A	Northampton T	L 1-7	0-3	17	Riley	3017
6	25	H	Scunthorpe U	L 0-2	0-0	21		3890
7	28	H	Torquay U	L 0-1	0-1	—		3041
8	Oct 2	A	Peterborough U	L 0-3	0-2	23		2739
9	9	H	York C	D 2-2	1-1	22	Crawford, Chandler	3680
10	16	A	Hartlepool	L 1-3	1-2	23	Riley	1449
11	19	A	Halifax T	D 2-2	1-2	—	Ritchie, Newman	1465
12	23	H	Wimbledon	W 4-2	3-0	22	Nicholls, Riley 3	4723
13	30	A	Aldershot	D 0-0	0-0	23		2823
14	Nov 2	H	Chester	D 0-0	0-0	—		3942
15	6	H	Stockport Co	D 2-2	0-0	21	Riley, Chandler	4645
16	13	A	Mansfield T	D 1-1	1-0	22	Riley	1979
17	27	H	Colchester U	L 0-2	0-1	23		4310
18	Dec 4	A	Rochdale	L 0-1	0-0	24		1307
19	11	A	Chester	L 0-1	0-0	24		1163
20	18	A	Bury	D 2-2	0-0	23	Chandler, Crawford	2196
21	27	H	Port Vale	L 1-3	0-1	23	Phillipson-Masters	6729
22	28	A	Hereford U	W 3-1	3-1	23	Chandler 2, Kelly N.	3548
23	Jan 1	H	Swindon T	D 1-1	0-0	22	Riley	9002
24	3	A	Darlington	D 2-2	2-2	22	Chandler, Garland	1425
25	15	A	Hull C	L 0-1	0-0	23		7035
26	18	H	Tranmere R	W 1-0	0-0	—	Riley	3344
27	22	H	Northampton T	L 1-3	1-2	21	Ritchie (pen)	4855
28	Feb 5	A	Scunthorpe U	D 1-1	0-0	23	Nicholls	3624
29	12	H	Peterborough U	W 1-0	1-0	21	Ritchie (pen)	3959
30	15	H	Halifax T	W 3-0	2-0	—	Ritchie, Economou, Cooper	3169
31	19	A	York C	L 0-3	0-0	20		2879
32	26	H	Hartlepool U	W 2-0	1-0	17	Ritchie (pen), Economou	4194
33	Mar 5	A	Wimbledon	L 1-2	0-2	20	Kelly E.	2541
34	12	H	Aldershot	W 2-0	1-0	20	Crawford, Riley	4239
35	18	A	Stockport Co	D 2-2	1-1	—	Riley, Ritchie	2036
36	20	A	Torquay U	W 2-0	1-0	—	Crawford, Riley	3094
37	26	H	Mansfield T	W 3-1	0-1	15	Riley, Williams P., Crawford	4919
38	Apr 2	H	Hereford U	D 1-1	1-1	15	Ritchie	6264
39	4	A	Port Vale	D 1-1	1-1	—	Riley	6573
40	9	H	Rochdale	D 0-0	0-0	15		4772
41	16	A	Blackpool	W 4-1	1-1	14	Hetzke (og), Ritchie (pen), Riley, Crawford	2209
42	23	H	Bury	W 2-1	0-1	15	Breckin (og), Nicholls	5298
43	29	A	Colchester U	L 1-3	1-2	—	Ritchie (pen)	2196
44	May 2	H	Darlington	D 2-2	1-2	15	Crawford, Phillipson-Masters	4788
45	7	H	Crewe Alex	W 2-1	0-0	14	Newman 2	4700
46	14	A	Swindon T	L 0-2	0-1	14		5103

Final League Position: 14

GOALSCORERS

League (59): Riley 16, Ritchie 12 (6 pens), Crawford 7, Chandler 6, Newman 3, Nicholls 3, Economou 2, Phillipson-Master 2, Garland 1, Kelly E. 1, Kelly N. 1, Musker 1, Williams P. 1, own goals 2.
Milk Cup (5): Boyle 2, Chandler 1, Newman 1, Ritchie 1.
FA Cup (1): Johnson 1.
Football League Trophy (3): Chandler 1, Economou 1, Ritchie 1.

Milk Cup	First Round	Swindon T (a)	1-2
		(h)	2-0
	Second Round	Sheffield W (h)	1-2
		(a)	1-1 (aet)
FA Cup	First Round	Orient (a)	1-4
Football League Trophy		Exeter C (a)	1-2
		Torquay U (h)	1-0
		Newport Co (h)	1-4

Shaw	Stevens	Williams G.	Newman	Boyle	Riley	Economou	Musker	Cooper	Ritchie	Crawford	Bray	Thompson	Chandler	Nicholls	Panes	Johnson (L)	Phillipson-Masters	Kelly E.	Llewellyn	Garland	Smith	Williams P.	Palmer	Jones	Kelly N.	Referees	Match No.
1	2	3	4	5	6	7	8	9	10	11																K. Cooper	1
1	2	4	3	5	6	7		9	10	11	8															P. Tyldesley	2
1	2	4	3	5	6	7*		9	10	11	8	12														R. Banks	3
1	2	4	3	5	6	7*		8	10	11	9		12													A. Crickmore	4
1	2	4	3	5	6			9	10	12	8	11	7*													K. Salmon	5
1	2	4	7*	5	6	8		9	10	11				3	12											T. Holbrook	6
1	2	3	8	5	10	6			9	11*		7		4	12											D. Vickers	7
1	2*	4	11	5	6	7			10			8	12		9	3										K. Baker	8
1			2	5	10	7				11	6	8	9	4		3										C. Thomas	9
1		8	2		6			7	5	11		10*	9	4		3									12	J. Key	10
1		10	2	5	6			7	8	11			9	4		3										M. Scott	11
1			2	5	6	7		10	8	11			9	4		3										D. Civil	12
1			2	5	6	7		9		11		8	10	4		3										B. Hill	13
1		12	2	5	7	8		6		11		9*	10	4		3										L. Shapter	14
1		8	2	5	6	7		9		11			10*	4		3									12	C. Downey	15
1	5	8	2		6	7		10	9	11				4		3										D. Owen	16
1	2		7		6			9		11		8	10*	4		3	5								12	T. Bune	17
1			7		6			10		11		8	9	4		3	5		2							A. Challinor	18
1			7		6			10		11		8		4	9*	3	5		2	12						D. Allison	19
1			8		9	6		2	7	11			10	4		5	3									J. Lovatt	20
1			2		6*	9		7	8	11			10	4		3	5			12						A. Glasson	21
1			2					9	8	11			10	4		3	5			6					7	A. Seville	22
1			2		12			7	6	11			10*	4		3	5			9					8	M. Robinson	23
1		2	12		6			9	8	11			10	4		3	5*			7						D. Scott	24
1		2			6			9	8	11			10	4		3	5			7						T. Mills	25
1		2	5		6	9			7	11			8	4		3				10						J. Martin	26
1		2	5		6	9		12	7	11			10	4		3				8*						R. Lewis	27
1		3	2		6	9			7	11			10	4			5			8						R. Chadwick	28
1		3	2		6	8	10	9	7	11				4			5									L. Burden	29
1		3	2		6*	9	10	7	8	11			12	4			5									B. Daniels	30
1		3	2		6	8*	10		7	11	12		9	4			5									J. Hough	31
1		3	2		6	8	10	9	7	11				4			5									J. Bray	32
1		3	2		6	8	10		7	11				4			5	9								M. Dimblebee	33
1		3	2		6	10		9		11				4			5	8*	12		7					A. Hamil	34
1		3	5		6	7		10	8	11				4					2			9*	12			F. Roberts	35
1		3	2		6	7		10	8	11				4			5					9*	12			C. Thomas	36
1		3	2		6	10		9	7*	11				4			5					8	12			T. Spencer	37
1		3			6			9	7	11	10*			4			5		2			8	12			B. Stevens	38
1		3	2		6			9	8	11	7			4			5					10				A. Robinson	39
1		3	2		6	10		9		11	7*			4			5					8			12	D. Hedges	40
1		3	2		6	7		9	8	11				4			5					10				D. Shaw	41
1		3	2		6	10		9*	7	11				4			5	12				8				J. Deakin	42
1		3	2		6	10			7	11				4			5	9*				8	12			T. Ward	43
1		3	2		8	10		4	6	11							5	7*				9	12			K. Barratt	44
1		3	2		11	9		5	7	6				4					12		8*		10			M. James	45
1		3				8		9	7	11	6*			4					2			10	5	12		L. Shapter	46
46	10	35	42	14	43	34	6	37	37	44	9	10	20	39	2	20	25	4	5	7	2	11	2	0	2		
		+ 1s	+ 1s		+ 1s			+ 1s		+ 1s	+ 1s	+ 1s	+ 3s		+ 2s			+ 1s	+ 2s	+ 2s			+ 6s	+ 1s	+ 4s		

FOOTBALL LEAGUE RECORD

1901 Elected to Division 2; 1906–11 Division 1; 1911–22 Division 2; 1922–23 Division 3(S); 1923–24 Division 2; 1924–27 Division 3(S); 1927–32 Division 2; 1932–55 Division 3(S); 1955–60 Division 2; 1960–65 Division 3; 1965–76 Division 2; 1976–80 Division 1; 1980–81 Division 2; 1981–82 Division 3; 1982– Division 4.

HONOURS

Football League: Division 1 – Runners-up 1906–07; Division 2 – Champions 1905–06; Runners-up 1975–76; Division 3(S) – Champions 1922–23, 1926–27, 1954–55; Runners-up 1937–38; Division 3 – Runners-up 1964–65. *FA Cup:* Runners-up 1909. *Football League Cup:* Semi-final 1970–71. *Welsh Cup:* Winners 1934. *Anglo-Scottish Cup:* Winners 1977–78.

COLOURS

Red shirts, white shorts, red and white stockings. **Change colours:** White shirts, black shorts, black stockings.

BRISTOL CITY

Players Names Ht, Wt, D.o.B.	Birthplace Transfer Fee	Clubs	Appearances F.L. A & S	F.L.C. A & S	F.A.C. A & S	Goals F.L.	F.L.C.	F.A.C.
Goalkeepers								
John Shaw	Stirling	Leeds U (A)						
6 1, 13 7, 4.2.54	F/T	Bristol C	208	7	8			
Defenders								
Forbes Phillipson-Masters	Bournemouth	Southampton (A)	9					
6 1, 12 10, 14.11.55	—	Exeter C (loan)	6					
	—	Bournemouth (loan)	7			2		
	—	Luton T. (loan)	10					
	£50,000	Plymouth Arg	119	8	6			
	F/T	Bristol C	25			2		
Paul Stevens	Bristol	Bristol C (A)	71	7	7	1		
5 7, 9 9, 4.4.60								
Alan Nicholls	Plymouth	Bristol C (A)	79	2	3	5		
6 2, 12 0, 10.2.63								
Gary Williams	Bristol	Bristol C (A)	77+1	4	6	1		
5 8, 10 1, 8.6.63								
Terry Cooper (E)	Castleford	Leeds U (A)	239+10	21	30+1	7	2	
5 7½, 10 9, 12.7.44	£50,000	Middlesbrough	105	11	7	1		
	£10,000	Bristol C	11					
	F/T	Bristol R	53+6	6+1	2			
	F/T	Doncaster R	20		3			
	F/T	Bristol C	37+1	3	1	1		
Midfield								
Joe Economou	London	Bristol C (A)	51+2	3	1	3		
5 6, 10 6, 25.10.61								
Wayne Bray		Bristol C (A)	28+1	2+1		2		
Rob Newman		Bristol C (A)	57+17	4	1	6	1	
6 2, 12 0								
John Palmer		Weston S.M.						
6 2½, 13 8	—	Bristol C	2+4					
Forwards								
Russell Musker	Plymouth	Bristol C (A)	42+1	3	3	1		
5 7, 10 0, 10.7.62								
Tom Ritchie	Edinburgh	Bridgend Th						
5 11, 12 8, 2.1.52	—	Bristol C	308+13	21+1	17+1	77	2	2
	£185,000	Sunderland	32+3	2	3	8	2	
	—	Carlisle U (loan)	14+1					
	F/T	Bristol C	37	3		12	1	
Alan Crawford	Rotherham	Rotherham U (A)	233+4	17	15	49	6	9
5 7¼, 9 10, 30.10.53	—	Mansfield T (loan)	1+1					
	£30,000	Chesterfield	88+6	7	6	20	1	1
	F/T	Bristol C	44+1	3	1	7		
Glyn Riley	Barnsley	Barnsley (A)	103+27	9	5	16	2	1
5 10, 11 11, 24.7.58	—	Doncaster R (loan)	7+1			2		
	F/T	Bristol C	43+1	4		16		
Errington Kelly	St. Vincent, WI	Ledbury T						
5 8, 11 7,	£1000	Bristol R	12+6	2+1		3		
	F/T	Lincoln C (N/C)	+2					
	—	Bristol C	4+1			1		
Paul Williams		Ottery St Mary						
6 0, 11 8		Bristol C	11			1		
Non-Contract Players								
Nyrere Kelly		Bristol C	2+4	+4		1		
Apprentices								
Mark Jones		Bristol C (A)	+1					
5 6, 9 6								
Nigel Smith		Bristol C (A)	2					
6 0, 10 9								
Andy Llewellyn		Bristol C (A)	5+1					
5 7, 11 12								

Commercial Manager: Brian White (Tel. 632812)
Club Coach: Clive Middlemass
Supporters Player of the Season 1982–83: John Shaw
Physiotherapist: Alex Lockhart
Association of Football Statisticians Club Adviser to Yearbook:
Club Captain 1982–83: Tom Ritchie
Chief Scout: Jock Rae
Club Statistician: David Woods

Players released since May 1982:
Billy Down, D. (Torrington); Mark Smith, M. (N/K); Ray Perlee, D. (USA); Ricky Chandler, M. (Bath C); Simon Panes, F. (Mangotsfield); Colin Freeman (Frome T); Gary Smith, F. (N/K); Steve Wherry, F. (N/K); Les Carter, F. (N/K); David Mogg, G. (N/K).

BRISTOL ROVERS Division 3

Back row (left to right): Steve Bailey, Tim Parkin, Ray Cashley, Graham Withey, Phil Kite, Keith Curle, David Smith. *Middle row:* Steve Balcombe, Archie Stephens, Mark Hughes, Paul Randall, Aidan McCaffery, Neil Slatter, Nick Platnauer. *Front row:* Ian Holloway, Errington Kelly, Brian Williams, David Williams, Mike Barrett, Geraint Williams, Jeff Sherwood.

President: Duke of Beaufort. ***Vice-Presidents:*** E. W. H. Godfrey, H. E. L. Brown.

Chairman: Martin R. Flook.

Directors: C. A. L. Stevens, G. A. Holmes, A. Palmer, G. H. Hole, N. Roydon, B. W. Bradshaw.

Player-Manager: David Williams. ***Hon. Company Secretary:*** A. E. Hill FCA.

Chief Executive: G. J. Bennett.

Year Formed: 1883. ***Turned Professional:*** 1897. ***Ltd Co.:*** 1896.

Club Nickname: 'Pirates'.

Previous Names: 1883, Black Arabs; 1884, Eastville Rovers; 1897, Bristol Eastville Rovers; 1898, Bristol Rovers.

Previous Grounds: Purdown, Three Acres, Ashley Hill, Rudgeway.

Previous Managers since 1946: Brough Fletcher, Bert Tann, Fred Ford, Bill Dodgin (Snr), Don Megson, Bobby Campbell, Harold Jarman, Terry Cooper, Bobby Gould (9).

Bristol Stadium, Eastville, Bristol BS5 6NN. Telephone Bristol (0272) 573687. ***Ground capacity:*** 12,500 (7,500 covered). ***Record attendance:*** 38,472 v Preston NE, FA Cup 4th rd, 30 Jan, 1960. ***Record receipts:*** £23,275 v Southampton, FA Cup 4th rd, 28 Jan, 1978. ***Pitch measurements:*** 110yd×70yd.

Directions to Ground: Buses 51 from Temple Meads Station to Stapleton Rd, five minutes from ground. By car, leave M4 or M5 at M32 junction; M32 runs direct to the ground.

Match tickets: Stand tickets available two weeks prior to the match.

Car parking: Large car parks at Stapleton Rd and Muller Rd entrances.

Entertainments/catering facilities: Bar open to the public in stand. Tea bar on the terraces.

Club shop: In Stapleton Rd; sells all types of souvenirs.

Handbooks/programmes: Handbooks and programmes available from club shop; programmes can be ordered on subscription.

Address of Supporters Club: 468 Stapleton Road, Bristol.

Address of the Club Shop or Boutique: The Rovers Shop, 468 Stapleton Road, Bristol 5.

NB All correspondence should be sent to Hambrook Training Ground, Filton Road, Hambrook, Bristol BS16 1JG. Telephone Bristol 566756.

Note: Full club statistical records are on pages 416–455.

BRISTOL ROVERS 1982–83 LEAGUE RECORD

Match No.	Date	Venue	Opponents	Result	H/T Score	Lg. Pos.	Goalscorers	Attendance
1	Aug 28	A	Brentford	L 1-5	0-2	—	Randall	5542
2	Sept 4	H	Doncaster R	W 2-0	0-0	15	Barrett, Kelly	3617
3	7	H	Gillingham	W 2-1	2-1	—	Randall, Curle	3688
4	11	A	Chesterfield	D 0-0	0-0	8		1990
5	18	H	Lincoln C	L 1-2	1-1	13	Randall	4177
6	25	A	Preston NE	D 2-2	1-2	12	Barrett, Williams G.	3880
7	28	A	Plymouth Arg	W 4-0	0-0	—	Randall 2, Kelly, Williams D.	3543
8	Oct 2	H	Bradford C	W 4-1	2-0	6	Randall 2, Parkin, Williams D.	4451
9	9	A	Newport Co	L 0-2	0-1	11		5912
10	16	H	Wigan Ath	W 4-0	0-0	6	Withey 2, Randall, Williams G.	4439
11	19	H	Millwall	W 4-0	2-0	—	Williams D. 2, McCaffery, Holloway	7241
12	23	A	Orient	W 5-1	1-0	2	Holloway 2, Williams D. (pen), Randall, Withey	2534
13	30	H	Reading	W 3-0	1-0	2	Williams D. 2, Withey	7270
14	Nov 2	A	AFC Bournemouth	D 0-0	0-0	4		6263
15	5	A	Southend U	L 0-1	0-0	—		3480
16	13	H	Portsmouth	W 5-1	3-0	4	Stephens, Parkin, Williams D., McCaffery, Holloway	9389
17	27	A	Huddersfield T	L 1-3	1-1	5	Holloway	8251
18	30	H	AFC Bournemouth	D 1-1	0-0	—	Parkin	4358
19	Dec 4	H	Walsall	W 2-0	2-0	2	Stephens, Kelly	4822
20	18	H	Wrexham	W 4-0	0-0	2	Williams D., Holloway, Williams G., Williams B.	4607
21	27	A	Oxford U	L 2-4	1-2	3	McCaffery, Stephens	9551
22	29	H	Exeter C	D 4-4	4-2	5	Randall 2, Holloway, Viney (og)	8160
23	Jan 1	A	Cardiff C	L 1-3	0-2	6	Bradd	11,050
24	8	A	Doncaster R	W 2-1	1-0	6	Stephens, Randall	3234
25	15	H	Brentford	W 2-0	0-0	4	Carter, Randall	5449
26	22	A	Lincoln C	L 1-2	1-1	5	Platnauer	5342
27	29	H	Chesterfield	W 3-0	2-0	4	Platnauer 2, Randall	6066
28	Feb 5	H	Plymouth Arg	W 2-0	0-0	3	Platnauer, Ball	6556
29	12	A	Bradford C	L 0-2	0-0	4		4261
30	19	H	Newport Co	L 1-3	1-2	5	Randall	6812
31	26	A	Wigan Ath	W 5-0	2-0	5	Randall 2, Withey 2, Platnauer	3288
32	Mar 5	H	Orient	W 2-1	1-1	5	Randall, Withey	5642
33	12	A	Reading	W 2-1	0-0	4	Withey 2	4270
34	19	H	Southend U	D 2-2	0-0	6	Barrett, Stephens	6025
35	26	A	Portsmouth	L 0-1	0-1	6		17,828
36	29	H	Sheffield U	W 2-1	2-0	—	Williams B., Platnauer	6595
37	Apr 2	A	Exeter C	W 1-0	1-0	4	Randall	5741
38	5	H	Oxford U	L 0-1	0-0	—		8190
39	9	A	Walsall	L 0-5	0-2	5		4559
40	12	A	Millwall	D 1-1	1-0	—	Curle	4873
41	16	H	Preston NE	W 3-2	0-1	5	Barrett, Randall, Stephens	5189
42	22	A	Wrexham	D 0-0	0-0	—		2053
43	30	H	Huddersfield T	W 1-0	0-0	5	Ball	8919
44	May 2	A	Sheffield U	L 1-2	1-0	5	Withey	7694
45	7	A	Gillingham	L 0-1	0-1	6		4024
46	14	H	Cardiff C	D 1-1	0-1	7	Platnauer	10,731

Final League Position: 7

GOALSCORERS

League (84): Randall 20, Withey 10, Williams D. 9 (1 pen), Holloway 7, Platnauer 7, Stephens 6, Barrett 4, Kelly 3, McCaffery 3, Parkin 3, Williams G. 3, Ball 2, Curie 2, Williams B. 2, Bradd 1, Carter 1, own goal 1.
Milk Cup (7): Randall 2, Barrett 1, Parkin 1, Platnauer 1, Stephens 1, Williams d. 1.
FA Cup (3): Williams D. 2, Stephens 1.

Milk Cup	First Round	Torquay U (h)	2-2
		(a)	4-0
	Second Round	Swansea C (h)	1-0
		(a)	0-3
FA Cup	First Round	Wycombe W (h)	1-0
	Second Round	Plymouth Arg (h)	2-2
		(a)	0-1

Kite	Stephens	Slatter	Williams G.	Hughes	McCaffery	Curle	Williams D.	Randall	Kelly	Barratt	Withey	Williams B.	Parkin	Platnauer	Sherwood	Holloway	Channon	Pulis	Carter (L)	Bradd (L)	Ball	Adams	Referees	Match No.
1	2	3	4	5*	6	7	8	9	10	11	12												J. Martin	1
1	9*	2	4		6	7	8	10	12	11		3	5										V. Callow	2
1	9	2	4		6	7	8	10*	12	11		3	5										A. Glasson	3
1	9*	3	4		6	7	8	10	12	11		2	5										A. Robinson	4
1	12	2	4		6		8	10	9	11		3	5	7*									J. Moules	5
1	10	2*	4		6		8		9	11		3	5		12	7							A. Challinor	6
1		2	4		6		8	10	9*	11		3	5		12	7							Alan Robinson	7
1	12	2	4		6		8	10	9*	11		3	5			7							C. Newsome	8
1		2	4	12	6		8	10	9*	11		3	5			7							M. Heath	9
1	9*	2	4		6		8	10		11	12	3	5			7							K. Cooper	10
1		2	4		6		8	10*		11	9	3	5			7	12						T. Bune	11
1		2	4		6		8	10*		11	9	3	5			7	12						B. Hill	12
1			4		6		8	10		11	9*	3	5		2	12	7						T. Spencer	13
1			4		6		8	10			9*	3	5	11	2	12	7						M. Bodenham	14
1			4		6		8	12			9	3	5	10*	2	11	7						A. Grey	15
1	9	2	4		6		8	10		11		3	5			7							D. Civil	16
1	9	2	4		6		8	10*		11		3	5			7	12						F. Roberts	17
1	9	2	4		6			10	12	11*		3	5			7	8						D. Brazier	18
1	9	2	4		6		8		10*	11		3	5			7	12						D. Vickers	19
1	9	2	4		6		8*			11	10	3	5			7	12						C. Downey	20
1	9	2	4		6				10*	11		3	5	8		7		12					D. Letts	21
1	9*	2	4		6		8	10		11		3	5	12		7							D. Reeves	22
1	12		4		6			10		11		3	5		2	7*			8	9			R. Barratt	23
1	9				6	7*		10		12		3	5	11	2			4	8				R. Nixon	24
1	9	3			6	7		10		11			5	12	2			4*	8				H. King	25
1		3			6	7	12	9	10*				5	11	2			4	8				J. Hunting	26
1		3			6		8	10		9		2	5	11		4					7		K. Salmon	27
1		2			6		8	10		11		3	5	9		4					7		E. Scales	28
1	12	2	4		6*		8	10		11		3	5	9							7		J. Lovatt	29
1	9	2			6		8*	10		11		3	5	12		4*					7		T. Ward	30
1		2	8		6			10			9	3	5	11		12		4			7*		G. Napthine	31
1		2	4		6			10*			9	3	5	11		12		8*			7		C. Thomas	32
1		2	4	8	6	11		10			9	3	5*			12					7		T. Holbrook	33
1	12	2	4		6			10		11	9	3	5			8*					7		L. Burden	34
1	12		4		6			10			9	3	5	11	2			8*			7		L. Shapter	35
1	12		4		6			10*			9	3	5	11	2			8			7		B. Daniels	36
1	12		4		6			10			9*	3	5	11	2			8			7		A. Gunn	37
1	12		4		6			10			9*	3	5	11	2			8			7		A. Seville	38
1	9			5	6			10		12		3		11	2	8		4			7*		P. Tyldesley	39
1		5			6	7		12		11	10	3		9*	2	8		4					K. Baker	40
1	12	2			6	7*		10		11	9	3			5	4		8					D. Hedges	41
1	12	2			6			10		11	9*	3			5	8		4			7		H. Taylor	42
1		2						10*		11	12	3	6	9	5	8		4			7		R. Lewis	43
1		2	7		6	12				11	9	3	5	10		8*		4					D. Civil	44
1	11	2	8		6					12	10	3	5*	9				4			7		B. Hill	45
1	10	2	8		6	4		9*				3	5	11							7	12	D. Lloyd	46
46	19	36	35	3	45	11	24	38	9	32	19	43	41	21	16	26	4	16	4	1	17	0		
	+ 11s			+ 1s		+ 1s	+ 1s	+ 2s	+ 4s	+ 3s	+ 3s			+ 3s	+ 2s	+ 5s	+ 5s	+ 1s				+ 1s		

FOOTBALL LEAGUE RECORD

1920 Original Member of Division 3; 1921–53 Division 3(S); 1953–62 Division 2; 1962–74 Division 3; 1974–81 Division 2; 1981– Division 3.

HONOURS

Football League: Division 2 best season: 6th, 1955–56, 1958–59; Division 3(S) – Champions 1952–53; Division 3 – Runners-up 1973–74. *FA Cup* best season: 6th rd, 1950–51, 1957–58. *Football League Cup* best season: 5th rd, 1970–71, 1971–72.

COLOURS

Blue and white quartered shirts, blue shorts, white stockings with two blue rings on top.
Change colours:

BRISTOL ROVERS

Players Names Ht, Wt, D.o.B.	Birthplace Transfer Fee	Clubs	Appearances F.L. A & S	 F.L.C. A & S	 F.A.C. A & S	Goals F.L.	 F.L.C.	 F.A.C.
Goalkeepers								
Martin Thomas (WU21)	Senghenydo	Bristol R (A)	162	12	9			
6 1, 13 0, 28.11.59	—	Cardiff C (loan)	15	4				
	—	Southend U (loan)	6					
	—	Newcastle (loan)	3					
Ray Cashley	Bristol	Bristol C	227	16	3			
5 10, 11 0	—	Hereford U (loan)	20					
	F/T	Bristol R						
Phil Kite (EY)	Bristol	Bristol R (A)	77	8	5			
6 1½, 14 7, 26.10.62								
Defenders								
Mark Hughes (WY)	Port Talbot	Bristol R (A)	64+1	9+1	3	3		
6 0, 11 4, 3.2.62	—	Torquay U (loan)	9		3	1		1
Aidan McCaffery (EY)	Newcastle	Newcastle U (A)	57+2	3+1	5	4		1
5 11, 11 2, 30.8.57	£25,000	Derby Co	31+6	4		4		
	£40,000	Bristol R	63	7	3	8	1	
	—	Bristol C (loan)	6			1		
	F/T	Bristol R	48+4	4	3			
Tim Parkin	Penrith	Blackburn R (A)	13	3			1	
6 2, 13 3, 31.12.57	£25,000	Malmo						
	£15,000	Bristol R	80+1	4	3	5	1	
Neil Slatter (WU-21)	Cardiff	Bristol R (A)	67+1	6	3	1		
5 11, 10 10, 30.5.64								
John McDowell (EU-23)	East Ham	West Ham U (A)	243+6	21	19	8	1	
5 10, 12 4, 7.9.51	£90,000	Norwich C	40+1	1	2	1		
	F/T	Bristol R						
Jeff Sherwood	Bristol	Bath C						
5 10, 11 5,	—	Bristol R	16+2					
Mark Waite (WY)	Cwmbran	Cwmbran T						
5 9, 10 0,	—	Bristol R						
Mike Adams		Bristol R (A)	+1					
Midfield								
David Williams (WU-21)	Cardiff	Bristol R	287+4	27	14+1	57	4	6
5 10, 11 8, 11.3.55								
Geraint Williams (WY)	Cwmpark	Bristol R (A)	77+2	5	5	4		2
5 7, 10 8, 5.1.62								
Ian Holloway	Kingswood	Bristol R (A)	29+6	2	2	7		
5 7, 9 12, 12.3.63								
Brian Williams	Salford	Bury (A)	148+11	11	12	19		
5 8, 12 12, 5.11.55	£70,000	QPR	9+10	1+1	+2			
	£50,000	Swindon T	89+10	14	9	8	1	1
	P/E	Bristol R	80+2	5	4	6		
Steve Bailey	Bristol	Bristol R (A)	15+1			1		
5 10, 11 7, 12.3.64								
Alan Ball (E)	Farnworth	Blackpool (A)	116	6	5	41	3	1
5 6, 10 5, 12.5.45	£110,000	Everton	208	10	21	66	3	5
	£220,000	Arsenal	177	12	28	45		7
	£60,000	Southampton	132	12	17	9		2
	F/T	Vancouver W						
	F/T	Blackpool	30	3		5		
	F/T	Southampton	63	3	1	2		
	F/T	Bristol R	17			2		
Tony Pulis	Newport	Bristol R (A)	78+7	7+1	5	3		
5 10, 11 8, 16.1.58	F/T	Happy Valley, HK						
	F/T	Bristol R	16+1					
Forwards								
Mike Barrett	Bristol	Shirehampton						
5 10, 10 6, 12.9.59		Bristol R	86+7	8	4	9	1	1
Paul Randall	Liverpool	Frome T						
5 11, 12 6, 16.2.58		Bristol R	49+3	2	4	37		
	£180,000	Stoke C	38+8	2+2	1	35	2	
	£55,000	Bristol R	87+5	7	3	35	2	
Archie Stephens	Liverpool	Melksham T						
5 11, 12 7, 19.5.54	£3000	Bristol R	54+15	4+2	4	17	2	1
Keith Curle	Bristol	Bristol R (A)	21+11	3	1	4		
6 0, 11 9, 14.11.63								
Nick Platnauer	Leicester	Bedford T						
5 11, 12 10,	£5000	Bristol R	21+3	1	+1	7	1	
Graham Withey	Bristol	Bath C						
6 1, 11 12,	£5000	Bristol R	19+3	1	1+1	10		
Paul Wheeler		Bristol R (A)						

Club Coach:
Club Captain 1982–83:
Supporters Player of the Season 1982–83:
Chief Scout:
Association of Football Statisticians Club Adviser to Yearbook: M. Jay

Players released since May 1982:
Shaun Penny, F. (Bath C.); Kevin Westaway, D. (Clevedon); Steve Williams, F. (Barry T); Don Gillies, D. (Paulton R.)

BURNLEY Division 3

Back row (left to right): Paul McGee, David Miller, Kevin Young, Steve Taylor, Billy Hamilton, Mark Allen. *Middle row:* David Holt, Vince Overson, Billy O'Rourke, Michael Phelan, Alan Stevenson, Paul Dixon, Trevor Steven. *Front row:* Billy Wright, Lee Dixon, Andy Wharton, Martin Dobson (with Div 3 Championship trophy), Phil Cavener, Derek Scott, Brian Laws.

Chairman: J. E. Jackson.

Vice-Chairman: Dr R. D. Iven MRCS(Eng), LRCP (Lond), MRCGP.

Directors: J. Eglin, D. Gill, A. R. Hutchinson.

Team Manager: John Bond.

Secretary: Albert Maddox. ***Deputy Secretary:*** Robert Bradshaw.

Commercial Manager: Bill Read.

Year Formed: 1882. ***Turned Professional:*** 1883. ***Ltd Co.:*** 1897.

Club Nickname: 'Clarets'.

Previous Name: 1881–82, Burnley Rovers.

Previous Grounds: 1881, Calder Vale; 1882 Turf Moor.

Previous Managers since 1946: Cliff Britton, Frank Hill, Alan Brown, Billy Dougall, Harry Potts, Jimmy Adamson, Joe Brown, Harry Potts, Brian Miller, Frank Casper (caretaker) (10).

Turf Moor, Burnley BB10 4BX. Telephone: Office: Burnley (0282) 27777/38021; ***Ticket Office and Shop:*** Burnley 27777 and 38021. ***Ground capacity:*** 23,000. ***Record attendance:*** 54,775 v Huddersfield T, FA Cup 3rd rd, 23 Feb, 1924. ***Pitch measurements:*** 115yd×73yd.

Directions to Ground: Central bus station and the Central railway station are both within 5 minutes' walk of the ground, which is near the town centre.

Match tickets: None. Pay at turnstiles.

Car parking: Parks in Church St and Fulledge Recreation Ground are both chargeable. Each holds about 500 cars, and both are about 5 minutes' walk from the stadium.

Entertainments/catering facilities: 'Centre Spot' Social Club underneath Bob Lord Stand. Seating for 300. Members and bona-fide guests only on match days. Snack, licensed bars are sited around the ground and under the stands.

Club shop: Attached to the Development Office in Brunshaw Rd, Burnley. Telephone: Burnley 27777 and 38021.

Handbooks/programmes: Centenary Handbook on sale £1.50. There is a subscription list for League programmes on a seasonal basis; enquiries c/o Club shop.

Note: Full club statistical records are on pages 416–455.

BURNLEY 1982–83 LEAGUE RECORD

Match No.	Date	Venue	Opponents	Result	H/T Score	Lg. Pos.	Goalscorers	Attendance
1	Aug 28	H	Bolton W	D 0-0	0-0	—		10,527
2	Sept 4	A	Middlesbrough	W 4-1	3-0	6	Dobson, Laws, Young, Hamilton	8074
3	7	H	Carlisle U	W 4-1	3-0	—	Hamilton 3 (1 pen), McGee	7645
4	11	H	Rotherham U	L 1-2	0-1	10	Steven	9099
5	18	A	Barnsley	L 0-3	0-2	12		11,938
6	25	H	Shrewsbury T	L 1-2	1-1	14	Wharton	6436
7	Oct 2	A	QPR	L 2-3	2-0	18	Steven 2	9145
8	9	H	Crystal Palace	W 2-1	0-1	14	Taylor, Hamilton	6429
9	16	A	Charlton Ath	L 1-2	1-1	17	Phelan	5940
10	20	A	Leeds U	L 1-3	1-2	—	Muir	13,827
11	23	A	Fulham	L 1-3	1-1	18	Laws (pen)	9040
12	30	H	Oldham Ath	L 1-2	1-0	19	Hamilton	7197
13	Nov 6	A	Newcastle U	L 0-3	0-1	20		20,996
14	13	H	Cambridge U	W 2-1	1-0	20	Taylor 2	6020
15	20	A	Sheffield W	D 1-1	1-1	19	Steven	16,117
16	27	H	Derby Co	D 1-1	1-0	19	McGee	7484
17	Dec 4	A	Chelsea	L 1-2	1-2	19	Laws (pen)	8184
18	11	H	Leicester C	L 2-4	1-1	20	Steven, Taylor	6457
19	18	A	Grimsby T	L 2-3	2-2	21	Laws (pen), Moore K. (og)	5448
20	27	H	Blackburn R	L 0-1	0-1	21		20,283
21	28	A	Wolverhampton W	L 0-2	0-0	22		21,961
22	Jan 1	H	Sheffield W	W 4-1	2-0	21	Taylor 3, Hamilton	9644
23	3	H	Middlesbrough	D 1-1	1-0	21	Scott	9139
24	15	A	Bolton W	L 0-3	0-2	21		8894
25	22	H	Barnsley	W 3-1	2-0	21	Hamilton, Steven, Taylor (pen)	10,275
26	Feb 5	A	Rotherham U	D 1-1	1-0	21	Taylor	6079
27	26	H	Charlton Ath	W 7-1	2-1	21	Taylor 3, Hamilton 3, Steven	7022
28	Mar 5	H	Fulham	W 1-0	1-0	19	Flynn	8828
29	19	H	Newcastle U	W 1-0	0-0	21	Donovan	13,900
30	26	A	Cambridge U	L 0-2	0-0	22		3549
31	Apr 2	H	Wolverhampton W	L 0-1	0-1	22		9593
32	4	A	Blackburn R	L 1-2	0-0	—	Scott	13,431
33	9	H	Leeds U	L 1-2	1-1	22	Steven	12,149
34	12	A	Oldham Ath	L 0-3	0-2	—		6126
35	16	A	Carlisle U	D 1-1	0-0	22	Phelan	5081
36	23	H	Chelsea	W 3-0	1-0	22	Hamilton 2, Donovan (pen)	7393
37	30	A	Derby Co	L 0-2	0-2	22		14,674
38	May 3	A	Shrewsbury T	W 2-1	0-0	—	Phelan, Donovan	3537
39	7	H	Grimsby T	D 1-1	1-1	22	Donovan (pen)	7083
40	10	H	QPR	W 2-1	2-0	—	Donovan 2	7191
41	14	A	Leicester C	D 0-0	0-0	21		29,376
42	17	A	Crystal Palace	L 0-1	0-0	21		22,714

Final League Position: 21

GOALSCORERS

League (56): Hamilton 13 (1 pen), Taylor 12 (1 pen), Steven 8, Donovan 6 (2 pens), Laws 4 (3 pens), Phelan 3, McGee 2, Scott 2, Muir 1, Flynn 1, Dobson 1, Coharton 1, Young 1, own goals 1.
Milk Cup (22): Hamilton 4, McGee 4, Laws 2 (1 pen), Phelan 2, Scott 2, Steven 1, Taylor 1, Wharton 1, Young 1, own goals 4.
FA Cup (10): Hamilton 2, Steven 2, Taylor 2 (1 pen), Cassidy 1, Flynn 1, Laws 1 (pen), Wharton 1.

Milk Cup	First Round	Bury (a)	5-3
		(h)	3-1
	Second Round	Middlesbrough (h)	3-2
		(a)	1-1
	Third Round	Coventry C (a)	2-1
	Fourth Round	Birmingham C (h)	3-2
	Fifth Round	Tottenham H (a)	4-1
	Semi-final	Liverpool (a)	0-3
		(h)	1-0

FA Cup	Third Round	Carlisle U (a)	2-2
		(h)	3-1
	Fourth Round	Swindon T (h)	3-1
	Fifth Round	Crystal Palace (a)	0-0
		(h)	1-0
	Sixth Round	Sheffield W (h)	1-1
		(a)	0-5

Stevenson	Laws	Ray	Scott	Phelan	Holt	Dobson	Steven	Hamilton	McGee	Young	Wharton	Taylor	Cassidy	Cavener	Muir (L)	Donachie	Flynn	O'Rourke	Walsh (L)	Miller	Donovan	Overson	Dixon	*Referees*	*Match No.*
1	2	3	4	5	6	7	8	9	10	11														K. Hackett	1
1	2		4	5	6	7	8	9	10	11	3													C. Seel	2
1	2		4	5	6	7	8	9	10	11	3													J. Key	3
1	2		4*	5	6	7	8	9	10	11	3	12												G. Courtney	4
1	2		4	5	6	7	8	9	10*		3	12	11											M. Scott	5
1	2		4	5	6	7	8	9	10		3	12	11*											R. Nixon	6
1	2		4	5	6	7	8	9		11	3	10												H. King	7
1	2		4	5	6	7		9		11	3	10		8										J. Lovatt	8
1	2		4	5	6	7*		9		11	3	10		8	12									M. Taylor	9
1	2		4	5	6	7		9		11	3			8	10									P. Willis	10
1	2		4*	5	6	7	12	9		11	3	10		8										E. Read	11
1	2		10	5	6	7*	8	9	4	11	3			12										J. Hunting	12
1	2		6	4	5	7	8	9	10	11	3													A. Challinor	13
1	2		6	3		4	7		10	9		11	8			5								R. Bridges	14
1	2		12	5		7	8	9	11			10	4			3*	6							D. Lloyd	15
1	2			5		7	8	9	11		3	10	4				6							K. Redfern	16
1	2		12	5*		7	8	9	11		3	10	4				6							J. Martin	17
1	2			5	3	7	8	9	11			10	4				6							G. Tyson	18
1	2			5	3	7	8	9	11			10	4				6							I. Borrett	19
	2			5	3	7	8	9				10	4				6	1	11					A. Hamil	20
	2		11	5	3	7	8	9				10	4				6	1						K. Salmon	21
	2		11*	5		7	8	9				10				3	6	1	4	12				A. Saunders	22
	2		11	5	7		8	9				10				3	6	1	4					N. Ashley	23
	2		7	5	4		8	9		11	12	10*				3	6	1						L. Robinson	24
1			2	4		5	8*	9		11	12	10		7		3	6							V. Callow	25
1	2		7	4		5	8	9		11*		10	12			3	6							D. Brazier	26
1	2		7	4		5	8	9		11		10				3	6							D. Owen	27
1	2			4*		5	8	9		11		10	7			3	6				12			M. Heath	28
1	2		7	4		5	8	9		11						3	6				10			D. Civil	29
1	2		7	4		5	8			11		9				3	6				10			D. Vkckers	30
1	2		4	5		6	8			11*		9				3	7				10	12		T. Mills	31
1	2		7	4		5	8	9		11		10				3	6							D. Hutchinson	32
1	2		4	5		6	8	9		11*			12			3	7				10			F. Roberts	33
1	2		7*	4		5	8	9				12				3	6				10	11		A. Challinor	34
1	2			4		5	8	9			11		7			3	6				10			J. Hough	35
1	2		11	4		5	8	9					7			3	6				10			M. Peck	36
1	2		11	4		5	8	9					7			3	6				10			M. Dimblebee	37
	2		11	4		5	8	9					7*			3	6	1			10	12		J. Bray	38
	2		11	4		5	8	9					7*			3	6	1			10	12		A. Seville	39
			11	4			8	9	12	7*						3	6	1			10	5	2	J. Worrall	40
			11	4		5	8	9		7						3	6	1			10		2	D. Shaw	41
			11	4		5*	8	9			7					3	6	1			10	12	2	D. Axcell	42
32	38	1	34	42	19	39	38	39	14	24	16	22	16	5	1	23	28	10	3	0	13	2	3		
			+ 2s				+ 1s		+ 1s		+ 2s	+ 4s	+ 2s	+ 1s	+ 1s					+ 1s	+ 1s	+ 4s			

FOOTBALL LEAGUE RECORD

1888 Original Member of the Football League; 1897–98 Division 2; 1898–1900 Division 1; 1900–13 Division 2; 1913–30 Division 1; 1930–47 Division 2; 1947–71 Division 1; 1971–73 Division 2; 1973–76 Division 1; 1976–80 Division 2; 1980–82 Division 3; 1982–83 Division 2; 1983– Division 3.

HONOURS

Football League: Division 1 – Champions 1920–21, 1959–60; Runners-up 1919–20, 1961–62; Division 2 – Champions 1897–98, 1972–73; Runners-up 1912–13, 1946–47; Division 3 – Champions 1981–82. Record 30 consecutive Division 1 games without defeat 1920–21. *FA Cup:* Winners 1913–14; Runners-up 1946–47, 1961–62. *Football League Cup:* semi-final 1960–61, 1968–69. *Anglo-Scottish Cup:* Winners 1978–79. **European Competitions:** *European Cup:* 1960–61; *European Fairs Cup:* 1966–67.

COLOURS

Claret shirts with light blue sleeves, white shorts and stockings.
Change colours: All yellow.

BURNLEY

Players Names Ht, Wt, D.o.B.	Birthplace Transfer Fee	Clubs	Appearances F.L. A & S	 F.L.C. A & S	 F.A.C. A & S	Goals F.L.	 F.L.C.	 F.A.C.
Goalkeepers								
Alan Stevenson* (EU23)	Staveley	Chesterfield	104	4	8			
6 1, 12 3, 6.11.50	£50,000	Burnley	438	36	33			
Billy O'Rourke	Nottingham	Burnley (A)	14		1			
6 0,12 7, 2.4.60								
Marcus Phelan		Burnley (A)						
Defenders								
Andy Wharton	Rossendale	Burnley (A)	56+2	5	6+3	6	1	1
5 5½, 10 6, 21.12.61								
Mickey Phelan	Nelson	Burnley (A)	79+2	10	9	6	2	
5 10½, 11 11, 24.9.62								
Brian Laws	Wallsend	Burnley (A)	125	14	15	12	2	1
5 8, 11 0, 14.10.61								
Vince Overson	Kettering	Burnley (A)	99+4	2	11	5		
6 0, 13 0, 15.5.62								
David Miller	Burnley	Burnley (A)	+1					
5 10½, 10 3,	—	Crewe Alex (loan)	3					
Willie Donachie (S)	Glasgow	Manchester C	347+4	40	21	2		
5 9, 11 5, 5.10.51	£200,000	Portland Timbers						
	£200,000	Norwich C	11	2				
	£200,000	Portland Timbers						
	F/T	Burnley	23	3	7			
Lee Dixon	Manchester	Burnley	3					
5 9½,								
Philip Ray	Wallsend	Burnley (A)	1					
Midfield								
Paul Dixon*	Londonderry	Burnley (A)	23+1		5	1		
5 11, 10 10, 22.2.60								
Martin Dobson (E)	Blackburn	Bolton W	—					
5 9, 11 7, 14.2.48	F/T	Burnley	220+4	16	12	43	2	5
	£300,000	Everton	190	22	13	29	8	2
	£100,000	Burnley	158	17	15	16	2	1
Tom Cassidy* (NI)	Belfast	Coleraine						
5 11, 12 5, 18.11.50	£15,000	Newcastle U	170+10	15+1	20+1	22	3	1
	£30,000	Burnley	70+2	8+2	8+1	4	2	1
Kevin Young	Sunderland	Burnley (A)	112+6	10+1	17+1	11	1	
5 9, 10 9, 12.8.61								
Brian Flynn (W)	Port Talbot	Burnley (A)	115+5	11+1	5	8	2	1
5 4, 12 3, 12.10.55	£175,000	Leeds U	152+2	12	6+1	11		
	—	Burnley (loan)	2					
	£60,000	Burnley	28	4	7	1		1
Trevor Steven	Berwick	Burnley (A)	74+2	10	13	11	1	4
5 10, 11 7, 21.9.63								
Derek Scott (ES)	Gateshead	Burnley (A)	212+5	19	18	19	3	
5 8, 11 12, 8.2.58								
Forwards								
Phil Cavener*	South Shields	Burnley (A)	55+14	6+1	5+1	4		
5 8, 10 7, 2.6.61		Bradford C (loan)	9			2		
Billy Hamilton (NI)	Belfast	Linfield						
6 1, 12 0, 9.5.57	£25,000	QPR	9+3		1	2		
	£38,000	Burnley	154	14	17	40	5	7
Steve Taylor*	Royton	Bolton W (A)	34+6	7	1	16	4	
5 10, 10 9, 18.10.55	—	Port Vale (loan)	4			2		
	£40,000	Oldham Ath	45+2		2	25		1
	£50,000	Luton T	15+5			1		
	£50,000	Mansfield T	30+7	5	3	7	3	
	£35,000	Burnley	80+6	11+2	12	37	1	5
Billy Wright*	Corbridge	Burnley						
6 0, 10 11, 4.11.62	—	Crewe Alex (loan)	3			1		
Mark Allen*	Newcastle	Burnley (A)	+2			1		
5 11, 11 3,								
Paul McGee* (EI)	Dublin	Sligo R						
5 10, 13 4, 19.6.54	F/T	Hereford U						
	F/T	Toronto						
		QPR	32+8	3	1+1	7	1	
	£100,000	Preston NE	62+4	7	1+1	13	2	1
	£25,000	Burnley	33+1	5	2	9	4	2
Terry Donovan (EI)	Liverpool	Louth U						
5 11, 10 2, 27.2.58		Grimsby T	52+12	6	3	23	2	2
	£75,000	Aston Villa	17		6	6	3	
	—	Oxford U (loan)	3					
	£25,000	Burnley	13+1		+2	6		

Club Coach:
Club Captain 1982–83:
Supporters Player of the Season 1982–83:
Chief Scout:
Physiotherapist:
Club Statistician:
Association of Football Statisticians Club Adviser to Yearbook: W. G. Chadwick.

Players released since May 1982: Garnwett Cromie, D. (N/K); Martin Lowe, F. (N/K); David Holt, D. (retired)

BURY Division 4

Back row (left to right): Jim Iley (Manager), Francis Firth, Chris Cutler, Paul Hilton, David Brown, John Bramhall, John Platt, Steve Kenworthy, Steve Johnson, Paul Jones, Wilf McGuiness
Front row: Paul Cruickshank, Paul Gardner, John Hughes, Joe Jakub (Captain), Tommy Gore, Craig Madden, Mark Comley.

Chairman: T. Robinson.

Vice-Chairman: Canon J. R. Smith MA.

Directors: G. A. Black, A. Metcalfe, Mrs A. Allen, R. A. Clarke, I. Pickup.

Team Manager: Jim Iley. ***Secretary:*** John Heap.

Year Formed: 1885. ***Turned Professional:*** 1885. ***Ltd Co.:*** 1897.

Club Nickname: 'Shakers'.

Previous Managers since 1946: Norman Bullock, John McNeil, Dave Russell, Bob Stokoe, Bert Head, Les Shannon, Jack Marshall, Les Hart, Colin McDonald, Tommy McAnearney, Allan Brown, Bobby Smith, Bob Stokoe, Dave Hatton, Dave Connor (15).

Gigg Lane, Bury BL9 9HR. Telephone 061-764 4881/2. ***Ground capacity:*** 22,500. ***Record attendance:*** 35,000 v Bolton, FA Cup 3rd rd, 9 Jan, 1960. ***Record receipts:*** £22,000 v Nottingham F, League Cup quarter-final, 17 Jan, 1978. ***Pitch measurements:*** 112yd×72yd.

Directions to Ground: Buses 35, 472, 481, 488, 524 from Kay Gardens to within walking distance. The nearest railway station is Bury. Buses run from the station to the ground.

Match tickets: 500 seats in the Reserved Chair section of the main stand may be booked two weeks before the match.

Car parking: Season-ticket holders only may use the car park on match days. But there is ample parking space in the side-streets around the ground.

Entertainments/catering facilities: Social club open during normal licensing hours.

Club shop: At the ground; sells all types of souvenirs (061-764 7475).

Handbooks/programmes: Programmes available from club shop.

Extra information: The social club has large dance hall, lounge, and cocktail bars. These facilities may be hired for private functions; tel: 061-764 6771.

Note: Full club statistical records are on pages 416–455.

BURY 1982–83 LEAGUE RECORD

Match No.	Date	Venue	Opponents	Result	H/T Score	Lg. Pos.	Goalscorers	Attendance
1	Aug 28	H	Hereford U	W 3-2	1-1	—	Hilton P., Gore, Bramhall	2138
2	Sept 4	A	Port Vale	D 0-0	0-0	5		2888
3	7	A	Blackpool	D 1-1	0-1	—	Madden	4292
4	11	H	Crewe Alex	L 0-1	0-0	14		2164
5	18	A	Peterborough U	D 1-1	0-1	15	Gore	2828
6	21	A	Northampton T	W 3-0	1-0	—	Johnson, Firth, Madden	2792
7	25	H	Halifax T	W 2-0	2-0	2	Potts, Johnson	2244
8	28	H	Tranmere R	W 3-0	2-0	—	Johnson, Madden, Hilton P.	1796
9	Oct 2	A	Rochdale	D 0-0	0-0	3		3207
10	9	A	Mansfield T	W 4-1	1-1	2	Bramhall, Firth, Hilton P., Madden	2415
11	16	H	Swindon T	D 0-0	0-0	2		2497
12	19	H	Stockport Co	W 3-2	1-1	—	Hilton, Firth, Johnson	2447
13	23	A	Darlington	W 2-1	0-1	1	Madden, Hilton	1240
14	30	H	Colchester U	W 1-0	0-0	1	Parker	2653
15	Nov 2	A	Hull C	L 1-2	0-2	—	Madden	6101
16	6	A	Chester	W 1-0	1-0	2	Parker	2023
17	13	H	Torquay U	W 3-0	2-0	1	Madden, Hilton P., Parker	2735
18	27	A	Scunthorpe U	W 1-0	1-0	1	Hilton P.	6335
19	Dec 4	H	Aldershot	W 3-1	2-0	1	Gore (pen), Parker, Bramhall	2482
20	18	H	Bristol C	D 2-2	0-0	1	Madden, Parker	2196
21	27	A	York C	L 1-3	0-1	1	Madden	5174
22	28	H	Hartlepool U	W 4-0	2-0	1	Madden 3 (1 pen), Potts	3275
23	Jan 1	A	Wimbledon	L 1-2	0-0	2	Parker	2467
24	3	H	Northampton T	D 1-1	0-1	2	Gore (pen)	3398
25	8	H	Port Vale	L 0-1	0-0	3		4748
26	15	A	Hereford U	W 2-0	0-0	3	Madden 2	1920
27	22	H	Blackpool	W 4-1	2-0	2	Hetzke (og), Firth, Jakub, Bramhall	3263
28	29	A	Crewe Alex	D 3-3	2-3	3	Parker, Madden, Johnson	2642
29	Feb 5	A	Halifax T	L 0-1	0-0	3		4021
30	12	H	Rochdale	D 0-0	0-0	3		4376
31	14	A	Stockport Co	L 1-2	1-1	—	Gore (pen)	3058
32	19	H	Mansfield T	W 1-0	0-0	3	Bramhall	2304
33	26	A	Swindon T	D 1-1	1-1	4	Johnson	4692
34	Mar 1	H	Hull C	L 2-3	1-1	—	Bramhall, Madden	4239
35	5	H	Darlington	W 3-0	1-0	4	Gore (pen), Jakub, Madden	1926
36	12	A	Colchester U	L 1-2	0-2	4	Potts	3357
37	19	H	Chester	W 3-2	1-1	4	Gore, Johnson, Jakub	2453
38	26	A	Torquay U	W 3-2	1-0	4	Parker (pen), Johnson, Cantello	1565
39	Apr 2	A	Hartlepool U	W 1-0	0-0	3	Johnson	1285
40	4	H	York C	W 2-1	0-1	—	Madden 2	3543
41	9	A	Aldershot	D 1-1	0-0	4	Potts	1426
42	16	H	Peterborough U	W 1-0	1-0	4	Gore (pen)	2761
43	23	A	Bristol C	L 1-2	1-0	4	Johnson	5298
44	30	H	Scunthorpe U	W 1-0	0-0	4	Madden	4739
45	May 7	A	Tranmere R	D 1-1	1-1	4	Potts	2623
46	14	H	Wimbledon	L 1-3	0-2	5	Parker	6760

Final League Position: 5

GOALSCORERS

League (74): Madden 20 (1 pen), Johnson 10, Parker 9 (1 pen), Gore 8 (5 pens), Hilton P. 7, Bramhall 6, Potts 5, Firth 4, Jakub 3, Cantello 1, own goals 1.
Milk Cup (4): Cruickshank 1, Gore 1, Jakub 1, Madden 1.
FA Cup (1): Hilton P. 1.

Milk Cup	First Round	Burnley (h)	3-5
		(a)	1-3
FA Cup	First Round	York C (a)	1-3

Platt	Gardner	Hilton P.	Bramhall	Kenworthy	Potts	Gore	Jakub	Parker	Madden	Firth	Brown	Johnson	Cruickshank	Hughes	Davies (L)	Halliday	Cutler	Breckin (L)	McHale (L)	Cantello	Hilton M.	Referees	Match No.
1	2	5	6	3	11	4	10	9	8	7												A. Saunders	1
	2	5	6	3		4	10	8	7		1	9	11									K. Hackett	2
	2	5	6	3	12	4	10	8	7		1	9*	11									G. Courtney	3
	2	3	4	5	9	6	8*	10	11		1	12	7									T. Mills	4
	2		5	3	7	4	10		8	11	1	9	6									D. Axcell	5
	2	5	6	3	7	4	10		8	11	1	9										R. Lewis	6
	2	3	4	5	8	6	7		9	11*	1	10	12									M. Peck	7
	2*	3	4	5		6	8	12	9	11	1	10	7									M. Heath	8
	2	5	6	3		4	10		8	7	1	9	11									P. Willis	9
	2	5	6	3		4	10		8	7	1	9	11									T. Holbrook	10
	2	4	3	5		6	8	12	9	11	1	10	7*									D. Owen	11
	2	3	4	5		6*	8	12	9	11	1	10	7									D. Civil	12
	2	5	6	3		4	10	12	8	7*	1	9	11									C. Seel	13
	2	3	4	5*		6	8	12	9	11	1	10	7									G. Tyson	14
	2	5	6		7	4	10	3	9		1	9*	11	12								J. Hunting	15
	2	5	6			4	10	9	8	7	1		11		3							G. Napthine	16
	2	3	4		12	6	8	10	9	11	1		7*		5							N. Ashley	17
	2	5	6			4	10	9	8	7	1				3	11						M. Scott	18
	2	5	6		12	4	10	9	8	7*	1				3	11						J. Key	19
	2	7	3*		12	6	8	10	8	11	1				5	4						J. Lovatt	20
	2		5		11	4	10	9	8	7	1				3	6						H. Taylor	21
	2		3		6	7	8	10*	9	11	1	12			5	4						C. Newsome	22
	2		5		11*	4	10	9	8	7	1				3	6	12					Alan Robinson	23
	2		4		6*	7	8	9	10	11	1				5	3	12					F. Roberts	24
	2		4		6*	7	8	10	9	11	1				5	3	12					K. Redfern	25
	2		5		11*	4	10	9	8	7	1				3	6	12					J. Martin	26
	2		3		6	7	8	10	9	11	1				5	4						K. Baker	27
	2		5		11*	4	10	9	8	7	1	12			3	6						M. Robinson	28
	2		5		11*	4	10	9	8	7	1	12			3	6						V. Callow	29
	2		3*			6	8	10	9	11	1	12				4		5	7			D. Allinson	30
	2		5		7	4	10		8		1*	9				6		3	11			R. Bridges	31
	2		4*			6	8		9	11	1	10				3		5	7			G. Courtney	32
	2		5*			4	10		8	7	1	9				6		3	11			A. Hamil	33
	2		5			4	10		8	7*	1	9				6		3	11			R. Nixon	34
	2		4			6	8		9	11	1	10				3		5*	7			J. Bray	35
	2		5		11	4	10	8		7*	1	9				6	12	3				M. Dimblebee	36
	2		4		6	7	8	9		11*	1	10				3		5		12		T. Mills	37
	2		5		11		10	8		7	1	9				6		3		4		D. Hedges	38
	2		5		11	4	10*	8	12		1	9				6		3		7		K. Hackett	39
	2		5		11	4	10	8*	12		1	9				6		3		7		N. Ashley	40
	2		5*		11	4	10	8	12		1	9				6		3		7		K. Cooper	41
	2		4		9	6	8		11		1	10				3		5		7		D. Hutchinson	42
	2		5		11		10	12	8		1	9				6		3		7*	4	J. Deakin	43
	2*		4		9	6	8	12	11		1	10				3		5		7		M. Peck	44
	2		5		11	4	10		8		1	9				6		3		7		J. Lovatt	45
	2		4		9	6	8	12	11		1	10				3		5			7	A. Saunders	46
1	46	19	46	14	27	44	46	26	40	33	45	29	14	0	14	29	0	17	6	8	2		
					+ 4s			+ 8s	+ 3s			+ 5s	+ 1s	+ 1s			+ 5s			+ 1s			

FOOTBALL LEAGUE RECORD

1894 Elected to Division 2; 1895–1912 Division 1; 1912–24 Division 2; 1924–29 Division 1; 1929–57 Division 2; 1957–61 Division 3; 1961–67 Division 2; 1967–68 Division 3; 1968–69 Division 2; 1969–71 Division 3; 1971–74 Division 4; 1974–80 Division 3; 1980– Division 4.

HONOURS

Football League: Division 1 best season: 4th, 1925–26; Division 2 – Champions 1894–95; Runners-up 1923–24; Division 3 – Champions 1960–61; Runners-up 1967–68. *FA Cup:* Winners 1900, 1903. *Football League Cup:* Semi-final 1963.

COLOURS

White shirts, royal blue shorts, white stockings. **Change colours:** All yellow.

BURY

Players Names Ht, Wt, D.o.B.	Birthplace Transfer Fee	Clubs	Appearances F.L. A & S	Appearances F.L.C. A & S	Appearances F.A.C. A & S	Goals F.L.	Goals F.L.C.	Goals F.A.C.
Goalkeepers								
David Brown	Hartlepool	Horden CW						
6 1, 12 8, 28.1.57		Middlesbrough	10					
	—	Plymouth Arg (loan)	5					
	£40,000	Oxford U	21	2				
	£5000	Bury	72	1	5			
John Platt*	Ashton	Ashton U						
5 10, 11 7, 22.8.54	—	Oldham Ath	109	3	9			
	F/T	Bury	20	3				
Defenders								
Steve Kenworthy*	Wrexham	Wrexham	19+1		5			
6 1, 12 8, 6.11.59	F/T	Bury	14	2				
John Bramhall	Warrington	Tranmere R	164+6	16	8	7	1	
6 2, 13 6, 20.11.56	£10,000	Bury	55	1	1	6		
Paul Gardner	Southport	Blackpool (A)	149+3	14	5	1		
5 9, 12 6, 22.9.57	F/T	Bury	46	2	1			
John Breckin*	Sheffield	Rotherham U (A)	405+4	31	27+1	8	1	3
5 9½, 11 9, 27.7.53	—	Darlington (loan)	4					
		Bury	17					
Bruce Halliday*	Sunderland	Newcastle U (A)	32	2	4	1		
5 11, 11 2, 3.1.61	—	Darlington (loan)	7					
	F/T	Bury	29					
Midfield								
Joe Jakub	Falkirk	Burnley (A)	42	2				
5 6, 9 6, 7.12.56	£19,000	Bury	123+2	3	10	6	1	1
Tommy Gore*	Liverpool	Tranmere R (N/C)						
5 7, 11 8, 26.11.53	£12,000	Wigan Ath	102	9	7	14	4	4
	£20,000	Bury	118+1	4	9	15	1	
Paul Cruikshank*	Oldham	Blackpool (A)						
5 11, 11 1, 15.1.60	F/T	Bury	14+1	2			1	
Frauny Firth*	Dewsbury	Huddersfield T (A)	26+1	4		4		
5 10, 11 0, 27.5.56	F/T	Halifax T	157+1	6	7	19		
	F/T	Bury	33	1	1	4		
Eric Potts	Liverpool	Oswestry T						
5 6, 10 5, 16.3.50	£5000	Sheffield W	143+17	12+1	8+2	21	4	
	£14,000	Brighton	19+14	6	1+1	5	1	1
	£37,000	Preston NE	50+7	2+1	2	5	1	
		Burnley	48+8	2	4+1	5	1	1
	F/T	Bury	27+4	2	1	5		
Mark Hilton*	Middleton	Oldham Ath (A)	48+2	2	+1	2		
5 9, 10 3, 15.1.60	F/T	Bury	29+3		1	3		1
Forwards								
Craig Madden	Manchester	Northern Nomads						
5 8, 10 2, 25.9.58	—	Bury	152+19	9	8+1	75	4	6
Paul Hilton (E.S)	Oldham	Bury	117+12	2+3	16	33		4
6 1, 11 6, 8.10.59								
Steve Johnson	Liverpool	Altrincham						
6 0, 12 9, 23.6.57	—	Bury	139+15	8+1	14+1	52	5	4
Chris Cutler*	Manchester	Bury	+7					
5 11, 11 0,								
Stuart Parker*	Preston	Blackpool (A)	10+6	2		2		
6 1, 11 9, 16.2.54	F/T	Southend U	62+2	4	9	23		7
		Chesterfield	30+4	1		8		
	£20,000	Sparta Rotterdam						
		Blackburn R	5+4	1		1		
	F/T	Frecheville Com						
	F/T	Bury	26+8	2	1	9		
Non-contract Player								
Len Cantello (EU23)	Newton Heath	WBA (A)	297+4	21	20	13	3	3
5 10, 11 13, 11.9.51	£350,000	Bolton W	89+1	5	3	3		
	F/T	Altrincham						
	F/T	Hereford U (N/C)	1					
	F/T	Bury	8+1			1		

Commercial Manager: Mr G. Harrison (Tel. 061-764 7475)
Club Coach: Wilf McGuinness
Club Captain 1982–83:
Supporters Player of the Season 1982–83:
Chief Scout:
Physiotherapist: J. Cunningham
Club Statistician:
Association of Football Statisticians Club Adviser to Yearbook: P. Greenlees.

Players (non-appearance) granted free transfer: Mark Comley, M.; Steve Guest, F.
Players released since May 1982: Mick Butler, F. (Retired); David Constantine, D. (Altrincham); Brian Edwards, D. (N/K); Pat Howard, D. (N/K); Steve Mullen, D. (Darwen); Jim Woodyer, (St Helens); John Hughes, D. (N/K).

CAMBRIDGE UNITED Division 2

Back row (left to right): Dave Donaldson, Martin Goldsmith, Jamie Murray, Steve Fallow, Keith Lockhart, Floyd Streete, Les Cartwright
Middle row: Joe Mayo, Chris Turner, Lindsay Smith, Richard Key, Dean Greygoose, Malcolm Webster, Andy Beattie, George Reilly
Front row: Tom Finney, Tommy O'Neill, Steven Pyle, Steven Spriggs, Graham Watson, Derek Christie, Ray Nicholls.

President: A. E. Harris.

Chairman: D. A. Ruston. ***Vice-Chairman:*** A. R. Douglas.

Directors: C. R. Brett, J. E. Cooke, N. H. Benton, B. Peacock.

Manager: John Docherty. ***Secretary:*** L. S. Holloway.

Year Formed: 1919. ***Turned Professional:*** 1946. ***Ltd Co.:*** 1948.

Club Nickname: 'United'.

Previous Name: Abbey United until 1949.

Previous Managers since 1946: Bill Whittaker, Gerald Williams, Bert Johnson, Roy Kirk, Alan Moore, Bill Leivers, Ron Atkinson (7).

Abbey Stadium, Newmarket Rd, Cambridge. Telephone Teversham 0223-241237. ***Ground capacity:*** 12,000. ***Record attendance:*** 14,000 v Chelsea, Friendly, 1 May, 1970. ***Record receipts:*** £22,075 v Sheffield Wednesday, FA Cup 5th rd, 19 Feb, 1983. ***Pitch measurements:*** 110yd×74yd.

Directions to Ground: Nearest railway station: Cambridge. Buses 180 and 181 run from the station to the town centre; then buses 182 and 183 to the ground, which is situated on the east side of the city.

Match tickets: Reserved seats bookable fortnight in advance. Postal applications must be accompanied by remittance and SAE.

Car parking: Limited parking at main entrance; off-street parking allowed, and at Coldhams Common.

Entertainments/catering facilities: Entertainments each evening organised by Supporters' Club. Three canteens open in the ground on match days.

Club shop: Two shops, one at the main entrance, the other inside the ground.

Handbooks/programmes: Handbooks not available.

Address of Supporters Club: 530 Newmarket Rd, Cambridge.

Note: Full club statistical records are on pages 416–455.

CAMBRIDGE UNITED 1982–83 LEAGUE RECORD

Match No.	Date	Venue	Opponents	Result	H/T Score	Lg. Pos.	Goalscorers	Attendance
1	Aug 28	H	Chelsea	L 0-1	0-0	—		8124
2	31	A	QPR	L 1-2	0-1	—	Reilly	9686
3	Sept 4	A	Blackburn R	L 1-3	1-2	20	Mayo	4562
4	7	H	Barnsley	D 1-1	1-0	—	Nicholls	3314
5	11	H	Charlton Ath	W 3-2	0-2	14	Streete, Reilly 2	3162
6	18	A	Rotherham U	L 0-2	0-1	17		6654
7	25	H	Carlisle U	D 1-1	0-1	18	Reilly	3051
8	28	A	Shrewsbury T	L 1-2	1-1	—	Streete	2974
9	Oct 2	A	Leeds U	L 1-2	1-1	20	Reilly	14,910
10	9	A	Derby Co	D 1-1	1-1	21	Streete	8135
11	16	H	Sheffield W	D 2-2	0-0	20	Streete, Turner	5677
12	30	A	Grimsby T	L 0-1	0-0	22		5738
13	Nov 2	H	Wolverhampton W	W 2-1	1-0	—	Lockhart, Reilly	4571
14	6	H	Leicester C	W 3-1	3-1	19	Lockhart, Reilly, Finney	5011
15	13	A	Burnley	L 1-2	0-1	19	Smith	6020
16	20	H	QPR	L 1-4	0-2	20	Smith	5685
17	27	A	Newcastle U	L 0-2	0-2	20		20,360
18	Dec 4	H	Bolton W	D 0-0	0-0	20		3000
19	11	A	Oldham Ath	L 0-3	0-1	22		7127
20	17	H	Middlesbrough	W 2-0	1-0	—	Fallon, Mayo	2533
21	27	A	Fulham	D 1-1	1-0	20	Reilly	9105
22	28	H	Crystal Palace	W 1-0	0-0	20	Cannon (og)	4822
23	Jan 3	H	Blackburn R	W 2-0	1-0	20	Mayo, Reilly	3471
24	15	A	Chelsea	L 0-6	0-2	20		7808
25	22	H	Rotherham U	W 2-0	1-0	20	Mayo, Turner	3090
26	Feb 5	A	Charlton Ath	L 1-2	0-0	20	Cartwright	4592
27	12	H	Leeds U	D 0-0	0-0	20		6909
28	26	A	Sheffield W	L 1-3	0-2	20	Mayo	12,815
29	Mar 5	A	Wolverhampton W	D 1-1	0-0	20	Mayo	13,204
30	12	H	Grimsby T	W 1-0	1-0	20	Spriggs	3337
31	15	H	Derby Co	D 0-0	0-0	—		4476
32	19	A	Leicester C	L 0-4	0-1	19		8305
33	26	H	Burnley	W 2-0	0-0	16	Sinton 2	3549
34	Apr 2	A	Crystal Palace	D 0-0	0-0	17		5495
35	5	H	Fulham	W 1-0	0-0	—	Christie	6249
36	9	A	Barnsley	W 3-2	0-2	13	Sinton, Goldsmith, Reilly	9934
37	16	H	Shrewsbury T	D 0-0	0-0	12		3615
38	23	A	Bolton W	L 0-2	0-1	12		4636
39	30	H	Newcastle U	W 1-0	1-0	12	Cooke	7591
40	May 3	A	Carlisle U	D 2-2	1-1	—	Sinton, Christie	4630
41	7	A	Middlesbrough	W 1-0	1-0	11	Cooke	9879
42	14	H	Oldham Ath	L 1-4	0-0	12	Sinton (pen)	3948

Final League Position: 12

GOALSCORERS

League (42): Reilly 10, Mayo 6, Sinton 5 (1 pen), Streete 4, Christie 2, Cooke 2, Lockhart 2, Smith K. 2, Turner 2, Cartwright 1, Fallon 1, Finney 1, Goldsmith 1, Nicholls 1, Spriggs 1, own goal 1.
Milk Cup (2): Christie 1, Finney 1.
FA Cup (3): Mayo 1, Reilly 1, Turner 1.

Milk Cup	Second Round	Barnsley (a)	1-2
		(h)	1-3
FA Cup	Third Round	Weymouth (h)	1-0
	Fourth Round	Barnsley (h)	1-0
	Fifth Round	Sheffield W (h)	1-2

Commercial Manager:
Club Coach:
Supporters Player of the Season 1982–83:
Physiotherapist:
Club Captain 1982–83:
Chief Scout:
Club Statistician:
Association of Football Statisticians Club Adviser to Yearbook: C. Faiers

Webster	Donaldson	Murray	Smith L.	Fallon	Reilly	Cartwright	Spriggs	Mayo	Streete	Nicholls	O'Neill	Finney	Key	Turner	Lockhart	Christie	Smith K.	Goldsmith	Sinton	Fisher	Cooke	Pyle	*Referees*	*Match No.*
1	2	3	4	5	6	7	8*	9	10	11	12												H. Taylor	1
1	2	3	4	5	9	8*		10	6	11	7	12											R. Milford	2
	2	3	4	5	6	7		9*	10	12	8		1	11									J. Hough	3
	2	3		5	6	7			10	9	8		1	11	4								A. Gray	4
1	2	3		5	9	7			10	11	8	6		4									K. Barratt	5
1	2	3		5	9	7			10*	11	8	6		4			12						D. Shaw	6
1	2	3	11	5	9						8	6		4		7	10						A. Ward	7
1	2	3	6	5	9				10			11		4	12	7*	8						D. Scott	8
1	2	3		5	9				12	11		8		4	6	7	10*						R. Chadwick	9
1	2	3		5	9				10	7	8	11		4	6								N. Glover	10
1	2	3		5					10	12	8	11		4	6	7		9*					D. Vickers	11
1	2	3		5	9		8		10			11		4	6	7							A. Robinson	12
1	2	3		5	9	7	12					11		4	6		10		8*				A. Gunn	13
1	2	3		5	9	7	12			8*		11		4	6		10						M. James	14
1	2	5		4	11	9	12			6*		8		3	7		10						R. Bridges	15
1	12	3		5	9	7*	2					11		4	6	8	10						I. Borrett	16
1		3		5	9	7	8			12		11		4	6		10*			2			N. Midgley	17
1		3		5	9	7*	8			10		11		4	6			12		2			B. Daniels	18
1	7	3		5	9	12	8							4	6			11	10*	2			A. Saunders	19
1	2	3		5	9	7	8	10			6			4						11			K. Salmon	20
1	2	3		5	9	7	8	10			6			4						11			L. Burden	21
1	2	3		5	9	7	8	10			6			4						11			D. Hedges	22
1		3		5	9	7	8	10			6	11		4						2			J. Moules	23
1	2	3		5		7		10		12	6	9		4*					8	11			B. Stevens	24
1	2	3		5	9	7	8	10			6			4						11			D. Axcell	25
1	2	3		5	9	7		10	8		6			4						11			K. Cooper	26
1	2	3		5*		7		10	8		6	9		4				12		11			R. Lewis	27
1	2	3		5	9	7		10*				8		4						11	6		H. Taylor	28
1	2	3		5	9	12		10				6		4		7*				11	8		T. Fitzharris	29
1	2	3		5	9		8	10			7	6		4							11		M. Taylor	30
1	2	3		5	9		8				7	6		4						10	11		C. Downey	31
1	2	3		5	9		8				7	6		4						10	11		J. Key	32
1	2	3		5	12							6		4		7*		9	8	10	11		D. Vickers	33
1		3		5	12							6		4		7		9	8	2	11	10*	D. Axcell	34
1		3		5	10							6		4		7		9	8	2		11	J. Bray	35
		3		5	10							6	1	4		7		9	8	2		11	D. Allison	36
1		3		5	10							6		4		7		9	8	2		11	M. Bodenham	37
1		3			5				12			6		4		7		9*	8	2	10	11	K. Hackett	38
1		3		5*	9		7					6		4		11	12		8	2	10		D. Brazier	39
1		3		5	9			10				6		4		7			8	2	11		N. Glover	40
1		3		5	9					7	6			4		11			8	2	10		K. Walmsley	41
1		3		5	9*	7					6			4		11	12		8	2	10		T. Bune	42
39	29	42	5	41	37	22	15	15	12	11	21	30	3	40	12	17	8	8	13	25	12	5		
	+ 1s				+ 2s	+ 2s	+ 3s		+ 2s	+ 4s	+ 1s	+ 1s			+ 1s		+ 3s	+ 2s						

FOOTBALL LEAGUE RECORD

1970 Elected to Division 4; 1973–74 Division 3; 1974–77 Division 4; 1977–78 Division 3; 1978– Division 2.

HONOURS

Football League: Division 2 best season: 8th, 1979–80. Division 3 – Runners-up 1977–78; Division 4 – Champions 1976–77. *FA Cup* best season:. *Football League Cup:* 4th rd, 1980–81.

COLOURS

Amber shirts with black trim, amber shorts with black trim, stocking amber with black trim.
Change colours: All white.

CAMBRIDGE UNITED

Players Names *Ht. Wt. D.o.B.*	*Birthplace* *Transfer Fee*	*Clubs*	*Appearances* *F.L.* *A & S*	*F.L.C.* *A & S*	*F.A.C.* *A & S*	*Goals* *F.L.*	*F.L.C.*	*F.A.C.*
Goalkeepers								
Malcolm Webster (EY)	Rossington	Arsenal (A)	3	2				
5 10½, 12 6, 12.11.50		Fulham	95	5	3			
	£12,000	Southend	96	4	8			
	F T	Cambridge U	239	17	10			
Richard Key*	Coventry	Coventry C (AM)						
6 0, 12 4, 13.4.56	—	Exeter C	109	3	8			
	£10,000	Cambridge U	52	2	2			
	—	Northampton T (loan)	2					
Dean Greygoose		Cambridge U (A)						
Defenders								
Steve Fallon	Whittlesey	Kettering T						
6 1, 12 7, 3.8.56	—	Cambridge U	333+5	17	14	24	1	1
Jamie Murray	Glasgow	Rivet Sports						
5 9, 10 12, 27.12.58	—	Cambridge U	189+16	9+2	9+2	3		
Dave Donaldson (ES)	London	Arsenal (A)						
5 10, 13 0, 12.11.54	F T	Millwall	215+1	24	17+1	1		1
	£50,000	Cambridge U	117+1	8	4			
Chris Turner	St Neots	Peterborough U	308+4	16+1	33	37	3	3
6 1, 14 0, 3.4.51	£100,000	Luton T	30	4		5		
	£90,000	New England TM						
	F T	Cambridge U	15+4		3			1
	F T	New England TM						
	F T	Swindon T	+3					
	F T	Cambridge U	59+3	3	3	3		1
Bobby Fisher	Wembley	Orient (A)	302+6	19+1	26	4	1	
5 8, 11 2, 3.8.56	F T	Cambridge U	25		3			
Midfield								
Floyd Streete*	West Indies	Rivet Sports						
6 1, 13 11, 5.5.59		Cambridge U	111+14	10+2	5+1	19	1	
Steve Spriggs	Doncaster	Huddersfield T(A)	2+2	1				
5 3, 1 2, 16.2.56	F T	Cambridge U	292+4	19	12	44	2	1
Les Cartwright (W)	Aberdare	Coventry C	50+18	8	7+4	3	2	
5 9, 10 13, 4.3.52	£40,000	Wrexham	111+4	14	14	6	1	2
	F T	Cambridge U	36+5		3	1		
Andy Beattie	Lincoln	Cambridge U (A)						
6 2, 11 6								
Ray Nicholls	Peterborough	Cambridge U (A)	16+4	1		1		
5 6, 10 6,								
Tom O'Neill*	Glasgow	Ipswich T (A)						
5 7, 10 11, 2.2.58	F T	Cambridge U	96+20	6+1	6+1	8		
Forwards								
Joe Mayo*	Tipton	Dudley T						
6 2½, 13 6, 25.5.51	—	Walsall	2+5			1		
	£5000	WBA	68+5	5	7	16		1
	£60,000–player	Orient	150+5	8+1	13	35	1	3
	£90,000	Cambridge U	35+1		4	14		1
	—	Blackpool (loan)	5			1		
Graham Watson*	Doncaster	Doncaster R (A)	47+1	3	6	11		1
5 10, 11 6, 3.8.49	P E	Rotherham U	13	+1	2			2
	P E	Doncaster R	105+4	14	9	23	2	
	£4500	Cambridge U	206+3	12	11	24	1	3
	£15,000	Lincoln C	43	2	2	2		
	F T	Cambridge U	+1					
Tom Finney (NI)	Belfast	Crusaders						
5 10, 11 8, 6.11.52	£17,000	Luton T	13+1	4	2+1	5	1	
	£50,000	Sunderland	8+7		6	1		1
	£10,000	Cambridge U	237+8	14	11	56	4	
Derrick Christie	Bletchley	Northampton T (A)	116+22	11+1	4+2	18	2	1
5 8, 11 0, 15.3.57	£50,000	Cambridge U	112+3	10+1	3	16	2	
Martin Goldsmith	Carmarthen	Carmarthen T						
6 0, 10 11, 25.5.62	—	Cambridge U	15+5	1		4		
George Reilly	Bellshill	Corby T						
6 3, 13 5, 14.9.57	—	Northampton T	124+3	13	4	46	9	
	£140,000	Cambridge U	136+2	7	8	36	1	2
Steve Pyle	North Shields	Cambridge U (A)	5+1					
5 7, 10 3, 28.9.63								
Keith Lockhart	Newcastle	Cambridge U (A)	13+2	2		2		
6 0, 11 0								
Robbie Cooke	Rotherham	Mansfield T (A)	7+8		1	1		
5 9, 10 8, 16.2.57	F T	Grantham T						
	£12,000	Peterborough U	115	9	13	51	7	10
	£13,000	Cambridge U	12			2		
Kevin Smith		Cambridge U (A)	8+3			2		
Steve Clark		Cambridge U (A)						
Andy Sinton		Cambridge U (A)	13			5		

Players released since May 1982: Paul Jeffrey, (N K)

CARDIFF CITY Division 2

Back row (left to right): J. Hemmerman, R. Gibbins, P. Dwyer, J. Brown, A. Dibble, G. Bennett, R. Hatton, P. Maddy
Front row: P. Giles, D. Bennett, D. Tong, J. Lewis, J. Mullen, T. Micallef, L. Jones, P. Bodin.

Chairman: R. Grogan C ENG, MIEE, MI GAS E, AMBIM.

Vice-Chairman: J. A. Clemo, DIP PE.

Directors: G. Edwards JP, MA, J. P. Leonard.

Executive Director: J. D. Evans, MA (Cantab).

Team Manager: Len Ashurst.

Managing Director/Secretary: Ron Jones.

Year Formed: 1899. ***Turned Professional:*** 1910. Ltd Co.: 1910.

Club Nickname: 'Bluebirds'.

Previous Grounds: **Riverside, Sophia Gardens, Old Park and Fir Gardens. Moved to Ninian Park, 1910.**

Previous Name: 1899–1910, Riverside.

Previous Managers since 1946: Bill McCandless, Cyril Spiers, Trevor Morris, Bill Jones, George Swindin, Jimmy Scoular, Frank O'Farrell, Jimmy Andrews, Richie Morgan (9).

Ninian Park, Cardiff CF1 8SX. Telephone Cardiff (0222) 398636/7/8. ***Telegraphic address:*** 'Soccer Cardiff'. ***Ground capacity:*** 42,000. ***Record attendance:*** 61,566, Wales v England, 14 Oct, 1961. ***Club record:*** 57,800 v Arsenal, Division 1, 22 April, 1953. ***Record receipts:*** £31,728 v Everton, FA Cup 5th rd, 26 Feb, 1977. ***Pitch measurements:*** 114yd×78yd.

Directions to Ground: Corporation bus 2 runs past the ground; special buses run to Ninian Park from the bus station, returning after the match. Nearest railway station: Cardiff Central.

Match tickets: Bookable.

Entertainments/catering facilities: Refreshment points around the ground, 'Bluebirds Club' and 'Patrons Club'.

Club shop: Open on match days; souvenirs available during the week.

Handbook/programmes: No handbook. Back numbers of programmes available from Programme Dept, Ninian Park.

Address of Supporters Club: Bluebirds Club, Bluebirds Office, Ninian Park, Cardiff CF1 8SX.

Address of Club Shop or Boutique: Bluebirds Shop, Ninian Park, Cardiff CF1 8SX.

Note: Full club statistical records are on pages 416–455.

CARDIFF CITY 1982–83 LEAGUE RECORD

Match No.	Date	Venue	Opponents	Result	H/T Score	Lg. Pos.	Goalscorers	Attendance
1	Aug 28	H	Wrexham	L 1-2	1-1	—	Bennett D.	5018
2	Sept 5	A	Millwall	W 4-0	2-0	—	Lewis, Bennett D. 2, Gibbins	5620
3	8	A	Orient	L 0-4	0-2	—		2021
4	11	H	Wigan Ath	W 3-2	1-2	12	Lewis, Bennett G., Woof	3850
5	18	A	Walsall	W 2-1	1-1	7	Hemmerman, Dwyer	3161
6	25	H	Sheffield U	W 2-0	1-0	4	Bennett D., Hemmerman	7147
7	28	H	Exeter C	W 2-0	1-0	—	Hemmerman 2	4867
8	Oct 2	A	Oxford U	D 2-2	1-0	3	Mullen, Gibbins	6018
9	9	A	AFC Bournemouth	L 1-3	0-2	6	Hemmerman	5818
10	16	H	Gillingham	W 1-0	0-0	4	Ingram	4828
11	19	H	Bradford C	W 1-0	1-0	—	Bennett G.	5007
12	23	A	Huddersfield T	L 0-4	0-2	6		6121
13	30	H	Portsmouth	W 1-0	0-0	4	Hemmerman	7082
14	Nov 3	A	Reading	W 2-1	1-1	—	Bennett G., Dwyer	2982
15	6	H	Preston NE	W 3-1	3-0	2	Hemmerman, Bennett D., Ingram	5546
16	13	A	Lincoln C	L 1-2	1-0	3	Bennett D,	6585
17	Dec 4	A	Doncaster R	D 2-2	1-0	5	Micallef, Hemmerman	3087
18	7	H	Chesterfield	D 1-1	1-0	—	Hatton	3813
19	17	A	Southend U	W 2-1	1-0	—	Hatton, Gibbins	3476
20	27	H	Newport Co	W 3-2	1-0	2	Hemmerman 2, Hatton	15,972
21	28	A	Plymouth Arg	L 2-3	2-1	4	Hatton, Bennett G.	8631
22	Jan 1	H	Bristol R	W 3-1	2-0	4	Hemmerman 2 (1 pen), Bennett G.	11,050
23	3	A	Brentford	W 3-1	2-0	2	Gibbins, Hemmerman 2	7602
24	15	A	Wrexham	D 0-0	0-0	2		3846
25	22	H	Walsall	W 3-1	2-0	2	Bennett G., Hemmerman (pen), Bennett D.	6237
26	29	A	Exeter C	W 2-0	0-0	2	Hemmerman, Hatton	4019
27	Feb 1	H	Millwall	W 3-0	1-0	—	Bennett G., Bennett D., Hemmerman	5643
28	5	A	Sheffield U	L 0-2	0-0	1		11,641
29	12	H	Oxford U	W 3-0	1-0	1	Hemmerman (pen), Bennett D., Hatton	6970
30	16	A	Bradford C	L 2-4	0-2	—	Dwyer, Gibbins	3786
31	19	H	AFC Bournemouth	D 1-1	0-0	1	Gibbins	4878
32	26	A	Gillingham	W 3-2	2-2	2	Hemmerman 2 (1 pen), Gibbins	4587
33	Mar 1	H	Reading	D 0-0	0-0	—		6173
34	12	A	Portsmouth	D 0-0	0-0	2		24,354
35	15	H	Huddersfield T	D 1-1	1-1	—	Hatton	10,379
36	19	A	Preston NE	L 1-2	0-1	2	Hemmerman	4608
37	26	H	Lincoln C	W 1-0	0-0	3	Bennett G.	8021
38	Apr 2	H	Plymouth Arg	D 0-0	0-0	3		7226
39	4	A	Newport Co	L 0-1	0-1	—		16,052
40	9	H	Doncaster R	W 3-0	2-0	4	Tong 2, Gibbins	5456
41	16	A	Wigan Ath	D 0-0	0-0	4		4447
42	23	H	Southend U	W 4-1	3-0	3	Hatton, Lewis 2, Hemmerman	6141
43	30	A	Chesterfield	W 1-0	0-0	2	Bennett D.	2799
44	May 2	H	Brentford	W 3-1	1-0	2	McNichol (og), Hatton, Bennet D.	9112
45	7	H	Orient	W 2-0	1-0	2	Lewis, Bennett D.	11,480
46	14	A	Bristol R	D 1-1	1-0	2	Gibbins	10,731

Final League Position: 2

GOALSCORERS

League (76): Hemmerman 22 (4 pens), Bennett D. 12, Hatton 9, Gibbins 9, Bennett G. 8, Lewis 5, Dwyer 3, Ingram 2, Tong 2, Micallef 1, Mullen 1, Woof 1, own goal 1.
Milk Cup (6): Gibbins 3, Hemmerman 2, Bennett D. 1.
FA Cup (6): Hemmerman 2, Gibbins 1, Ingram 1, Jones 1, Tong 1.

Milk Cup	First Round	Hereford U (h)	2-1
		(a)	2-1
	Second Round	Arsenal (a)	1-2
		(h)	1-3
FA Cup	First Round	Wokingham (a)	1-1
		(h)	3-0
	Second Round	Weymouth (h)	2-3

Humphries	Jones	Bodin	Dwyer	Pontin	Mullen	Bennett, D.	Tong	Gibbins	Hemmerman	Maddy	Bennett, G.	Thomas (L)	Micallef	Lewis	Woof	Ingram	Dibble	Giles	Hatton	Brown	Steele (L)	Referees	Match No.
1	2	3	4*	5	6	7	8	9	10	11	12											L. Shapter	1
		3	12	5	6	7	8	9	10		2	1	4	11*								H. Taylor	2
	12	3		5	6	7	8*	9	10	11	2	1	4									M. Bodenham	3
	12	3		5*	6	7	8	9			2	1	4	11	10							T. Bune	4
	2	3	5		6	7	8	9	10			1	4	11								B. Hill	5
	2	3	5		6	7	8	9	10			1	4	11*		12						L. Burden	6
	2	3	5		6	7	8	9	10			1	4	11*		12						A. Seville	7
	2	3	5		6	7*	8	9	10			1	4	11		12						M. Dimblebee	8
	2*	3	5		6	7	8	9	10		12	1		11		4						A. Ward	9
	2	3	5			7	8	9	10		6	1		11		4						E. Crickmore	10
	2	3	5			7*	8	9	10		6	1	12	11		4						D. Lloyd	11
	2	3	5			7	8*	9	10		6	1	12	11		4						D. Owen	12
	2	3	5			7		9	10		6	1	4	11		8						J. Lovatt	13
	2	3	5			7	12	9	10		6	1	4	11		8*						D. Vickers	14
	2	3	5			7		9	10		6	1	4	11		8						R. Lewis	15
	2	3*	5		6	7	8	9	10			1	4	11		12						D. Richardson	16
	2	3	5		6		8	9	10				4*	11			1	12	7			P. Tyldesley	17
	2	3	5		6	7	4	8	10					11			1		9			M. James	18
	2		5		6	7	4	8	10		3			11			1		9			J. Deakin	19
	2		5		3	7	4	8	10		6			11			1		9			C. Thomas	20
	2		5		3*	7	4	8		12	6			11			1	10	9			T. Spencer	21
	2		5		3	7	4	8	10		6			11			1		9			R. Barratt	22
	2	12	5		3		4	8	10		6			11			1	7*	9			A. Grey	23
	2		5		3	7	4	8	10		6			11			1		9			K. Baker	24
	2		5		3	7	4	8	10		6			11			1		9			C. Downey	25
		2	5		3	7	4	8	10		6			11			1		9			Alan Robinson	26
	12	2	5		3	7	4	8	10		6*			11			1		9			M. Heath	27
	2*	11	5		3	7	4	8	10	12	6						1		9			J. Worrall	28
	2	6*	5		3	7	4	8	10	11							1	12	9			A. Glasson	29
	2	6	5*		3		4	8	10	7				11			1	12	9			G. Courtney	30
	2		5		3	7	4	8*	10		6			11					9	1		D. Hedges	31
	2		5		3	7	4	8	10		6*			11					9	1		D. Reeves	32
	2		5		3	7	4	8	10	12	6*			11					9	1		R. Milford	33
	2		5		3	7	4	8	10		6			11					9		1	L. Burden	34
	2	5			3	7	4	8	10		6			11					9		1	V. Callow	35
	2		5		3	7	4	8	10		6		11						9		1	R. Nixon	36
	2		5		3	7	4	8	10		6		11						9		1	M. Robinson	37
	2	12	5		3	7	4	8	10		6		11						9*		1	J. Holbrook	38
	2		5		3		4	8	10		6		11	9				7*	12		1	R. Lewis	39
	2	12	5		3		4	8	10		6		11	7*					9		1	E. Crickmore	40
	2		5		3	12	4*	8	10		6		11	7			1		9			G. Tyson	41
	2	5			3	7	4	8	10		6			11			1		9			D. Civil	42
		5			3	7	4	6	10	11				2			1	8	9			A. Saunders	43
	2	3	5			7	4	8	10		6			11			1		9			A. Hamil	44
	2		5		3	7	4	8	10		6			11			1		9			R. Bridges	45
	2	12	5		3	7	4	8	10*		6			11			1		9			D. Lloyd	46
1	40	27	40	4	39	40	43	46	44	5	34	15	18	39	1	7	20	4	29	3	7		
	+ 3s	+ 4s	+ 1s			+ 1s	+ 1s			+ 3s	+ 2s		+ 2s			+ 4s		+ 3s	+ 1s				

FOOTBALL LEAGUE RECORD

1920 Elected to Division 2; 1921–29 Division 1; 1929–31 Division 2; 1931–47 Division 3 (S); 1947–52 Division 2; 1952–57 Division 1; 1957–60 Division 2; 1960–62 Division 1; 1962–75 Division 2; 1975–76 Division 3; 1976–82 Division 2; 1982–83 Division 3; 1983– Division 2.

HONOURS

Football League: Division 1 – Runners-up 1923–24; Division 2 – Runners-up 1920–21, 1951–52, 1959–60; Division 3(S) – Champions 1946–47; Division 3 – Runners-up 1975–76, 1982–83. *FA Cup:* Winners 1926–27 (only occasion the Cup has been won by a club outside England); Runners-up 1925. *Football League Cup:* semi-final 1965–66. *Welsh Cup:* Winners 20 times. *Charity Shield:* 1927. **European Competitions:** *European Cup-Winners' Cup:* 1964–65, 1965–66, 1967–68, 1968–69, 1969–70, 1970–71, 1971–72, 1973–74, 1974–75, 1976–77, 1977–78.

COLOURS

Royal blue shirts and shorts, white stockings. **Change colours:** All yellow.

CARDIFF CITY

Players Names Ht, Wt, D.o.B.	Birthplace Transfer Fee	Clubs	Appearances F.L. A & S	 F.L.C. A & S	 F.A.C. A & S	Goals F.L.	 F.L.C.	 F.A.C.
Goalkeepers								
Ron Healey*	Manchester	Manchester C (A)	30	1				
5 11, 13 0, 30.8.52	—	Coventry C (loan)	3					
	—	Preston NE (loan)	6	12				
	£15,000	Cardiff C	216		9			
Andy Dibble	Cwmbran	Cardiff C (A)	21	3				
6 2½, 13 7,								
Defenders								
Phil Dwyer (W)	Cardiff	Cardiff C	392+6	20	21	36	1	
6 0, 13 0, 28.10.53								
Keith Pontin* (W)	Pontyclun	Cardiff C (A)	193	13+2	6	5		
6 1½, 12 7, 14.6.56								
Linden Jones (WU21)	Tredegar	Cardiff C (A)	137+2	10	4	2		1
5 6, 10 8, 5.3.61								
Gary Bennett	Manchester	Manchester C						
6 1, 12 1, 4.12.61	F/T	Cardiff C	53+2	3	2	9		
Jim Mullen	Jarrow	Sheffield W (A)	222+7	23	9+1	10		
5 10½, 11 12, 8.11.52	£25,000	Rotherham U	49	3	2	1		
	—	Preston NE (loan)	1					
	£10,000	Cardiff C	51	3	32	1		
Paul Bodin	Cardiff	Chelsea (N/C)						
5 10, 10 11,	—	Newport Co						
	F/T	Cardiff C	12+7	4	3	4		
Midfield								
John Lewis	Tredegar	Pontllanfraith						
5 9, 11 3, 15.10.55	—	Cardiff C	129+5	10	5	9	1	
Paul Maddy* (WU21)	Cwmcarn	Cardiff C (A)	35+8		3	3		1
5 10, 10 9, 17.8.62	—	Hereford U (loan)	9				1	
Paul Giles* (WU21)	Cardiff	Cardiff C	13+4		1+1	1		
5 10, 9 12, 21.2.61	F/T	Exeter C	9				1	
	F/T	Cardiff C	4+3					
David Tong	Blackpool	Blackpool (A)	70+8	5	1	7		
5 8, 10 1, 21.9.55	£25,000	Shrewsbury T	156+4	8	16	8		1
	F/T	Cardiff C	43+1	4	3	2		1
Forwards								
Bob Hatton*	Hull	Wolverhampton W	10	1	2	7	1	
5 11, 12 10, 10.4.47	£30,000	Bolton W	27+1			2		
	£30,000	Northampton T	29+4		3	8		1
	£15,000	Carlisle U	93	11	7	38	7	3
	£80,000	Birmingham C	170+5	12	15+1	58	5	6
	£50,000	Blackpool	75	6	3	32	2	1
	£50,000	Luton T	81+1	6	2	29	2	
	£50,000	Sheffield U	92+3	7	6	34	3	2
	F/T	Cardiff C	29+1			9		
Constantine Micallef (WU21)	Cardiff	Cardiff C (A)	67+14	5+1	2+1	11		
5 5, 11 4, 24.1.61								
Dave Bennett	Manchester	Manchester C	43+9	7	5+1	9	5	1
6 0, 11 2, 11.7.59	£120,000	Cardiff C	75+2	4	4	18	1	
Jeff Hemmerman	Hull	Hull C (A)	54+14	1	3	10		1
5 11, 11 0, 25.2.55	—	Scunthorpe U (loan)	4+1			1		
	F/T	Port Vale	13+2	3	1+1	5	1	
	F/T	Portsmouth	114+9	5	8+2	39		5
	F/T	Cardiff C	44	4	3	22	2	2
Roger Gibbins (ES)	Enfield	Tottenham H (A)						
5 11, 11 11, 6.9.55	F/T	Oxford U	16+3			2		
	F/T	Norwich C	47+1	1	2	12		1
	£60,000	New England TM						
	F/T	Cambridge U	97+3	7	2+1	12	3	1
	F/T	Cardiff C	46	4	3	9	3	1
Paul Evans		Cardiff C						
Wayne Matthews		Cardiff C						

Commercial Manager: Mrs S. Wynne (Tel. Cardiff 398636)
Club Coach:
Supporters Player of the Season 1982–83: Jeff Hemmerman
Physiotherapist: J. Goodfellow
Club Captain 1982—83: Jim Mullen
Chief Scout: Mr H. Joy.
Club Statistician:
Association of Football Statisticians Club Adviser to Yearbook: A. Jenkins.

Players released since May 1982:
Paul Davies, F. (Trowbridge); Wayne Hughes, M. (Bath C); Alan Sanders, M. (Newport YMCA); Godfrey Ingram, F. (San Jose Earthquakes); Stan Mayard, F. (Bridgend); Jim Brown, G. (N/K); Peter Francombe, D. (Bridgend T); Andy Polycarpou, M. (Greece).

CARLISLE UNITED Division 2

Back row (left to right):
Bobby Parker
Brian Hornsby
Paul Haigh
Paul Bannon
Tony Larkin
Dave Rushbury
Middle row:
Herbert Nicholson (Physio)
Bob Lee
Malcolm Poskett
Trevor Swinburne
Jon Rush
Jack Ashurst
Keith Houghton
Front row:
Russell Coughlin
Alan Shoulder
Bob Stokoe (Manager)
Gordon Staniforth
Bob Mitchell

Vice-Presidents: J. Johnstone JP, T. L. Sibson.

Chairman: J. A. Bendall.

Directors: J. C. Monkhouse, H. A. Jenkins, J. R. Sheffield, R. S. Liddell, C. Hutchinson, Dr T. Gardner MB, CHB.

Managing Director: Colin Hutchinson. ***Team Manager:*** Bob Stokoe.

Match Secretary: N. Irving.

Club Nickname: 'Cumbrians'.

Year Formed: 1904. ***Ltd Co.:*** 1921.

Previous Grounds: 1903–5, Milholme Bank; 1906–9, Devonshire Park; 1910– Brunton Park.

Previous Managers since 1946: W. Clark, Ivor Broadis, Bill Shankly, Fred Emery, Andy Beattie, Ivor Powell, Alan Ashman, Tim Ward, Bob Stokoe, Ian MacFarlane, Alan Ashman, Dick Young, Bobby Moncur, Martin Harvey (14).

Brunton Park, Carlisle CA1 1LL. Telephone Carlisle (0228) 26237. ***Record attendance:*** 27,500 v Birmingham C, FA Cup 3rd rd, 5 Jan, 1957, and v Middlesbrough, FA Cup 5th rd, 7 Feb, 1970. ***Record receipts:*** £30,616 v Newcastle U, Div 2, 20 Nov, 1982. ***Ground capacity:*** 18,000. ***Pitch measurements:*** 117yd×78yd.

Directions to Ground: City centre one mile away. Ribble buses from the Town Hall. Nearest railway station, Carlisle. By road – exit 43 from the M6, ground ¾ miles away; this avoids the town centre.

Match tickets: Bookable 1–2 weeks in advance by post or personal application.

Car parking: Car park holding 1500 vehicles adjacent to the ground. Limited street parking available.

Entertainments/catering facilities. Refreshment points around the ground.

Club shop: Brunton House open on match days and week days.

Handbooks/programmes: No handbook. Programmes available on subscription.

Note: Full club statistical records are on pages 416–455.

CARLISLE UNITED 1982–83 LEAGUE RECORD

Match No.	Date	Venue	Opponents	Result		H/T Score	Lg. Pos.	Goalscorers	Attendance
1	Aug 28	A	Derby Co	W	3-0	2-0	—	Shoulder 2, Poskett	11,206
2	Sept 4	H	Grimsby T	L	2-3	0-0	12	Shoulder, Staniforth (pen)	4683
3	7	A	Burnley	L	1-4	0-3	—	Poskett	7645
4	11	A	Leicester C	L	0-6	0-2	18		8440
5	18	H	Crystal Palace	W	4-1	2-0	14	Poskett 4	4390
6	25	A	Cambridge U	D	1-1	1-0	15	Coughlin	3051
7	28	H	Sheffield W	W	4-2	0-0	—	Bannon, Craig 2, Shoulder	6127
8	Oct 2	H	Wolverhampton W	L	0-2	0-2	13		7723
9	9	H	Charlton Ath	W	4-1	0-0	8	Poskett 2, Bannon, Larkin	4606
10	16	A	Leeds U	D	1-1	1-1	9	Shoulder	14,141
11	23	A	Oldham Ath	L	3-4	0-1	13	Larkin, Shoulder, Staniforth (pen)	4211
12	30	H	Chelsea	W	2-1	2-0	10	Poskett, Shoulder	7141
13	Nov 6	A	Blackburn R	L	2-3	1-2	13	Shoulder 2	5204
14	13	H	Rotherham U	D	2-2	1-1	14	Poskett, Bannon	5294
15	20	H	Newcastle U	W	2-0	1-0	11	Hornsby, Lee	16,276
16	27	A	QPR	L	0-1	0-1	13		9397
17	Dec 4	H	Shrewsbury T	L	2-3	2-2	15	Bannon, Poskett	4226
18	11	A	Barnsley	D	2-2	1-2	14	Craig, Lee	10,226
19	18	H	Fulham	W	3-2	0-1	13	Shoulder 2, Bannon	4859
20	27	A	Bolton W	L	0-1	0-0	15		8171
21	28	H	Middlesbrough	L	1-3	0-1	16	Shoulder (pen)	8181
22	Jan 1	A	Newcastle U	D	2-2	1-1	16	Shoulder, Bannon	29,154
23	3	A	Grimsby T	L	1-2	1-1	17	Bannon	6377
24	15	H	Derby Co	W	3-0	2-0	16	Bannon, Poskett, Shoulder	4732
25	22	A	Sheffield W	D	1-1	1-1	16	Shoulder (pen)	12,874
26	Feb 5	H	Leicester C	L	0-1	0-1	18		4402
27	12	A	Wolverhampton W	L	1-2	1-1	18	Bannon	13,171
28	19	A	Charlton Ath	D	0-0	0-0	17		4940
29	26	H	Leeds U	D	2-2	0-2	18	Bannon, Shoulder	6419
30	Mar 5	H	Oldham Ath	D	0-0	0-0	18		4054
31	12	A	Chelsea	L	2-4	1-2	18	Shoulder (pen), Haigh	6677
32	19	H	Blackburn R	W	3-1	3-1	15	Robson B., Poskett, Coughlin	4756
33	26	A	Rotherham U	W	2-1	0-0	13	Robson K., Poskett	5486
34	Apr 2	A	Middlesbrough	L	0-1	0-1	14		9965
35	5	H	Bolton W	W	5-0	3-0	—	Robson B. 2, Shoulder, Bannon, Craig	5615
36	9	A	Crystal Palace	L	1-2	1-0	14	Shoulder	5696
37	16	H	Burnley	D	1-1	0-0	14	Shoulder	5081
38	23	A	Shrewsbury T	L	1-2	0-0	14	Shoulder	3220
39	30	H	QPR	W	1-0	1-0	13	Robson K.	5724
40	May 3	H	Cambridge U	D	2-2	1-1	—	Robson B., Robson K.	4630
41	7	A	Fulham	L	0-2	0-1	13		10,045
42	14	H	Barnsley	D	1-1	0-0	14	Robson K.	5898

Final League Position: 14

GOALSCORERS

League (68): Shoulder 21 (3 pens), Poskett 14, Bannon 11, Craig 4, Robson B. 4, Robson K. 4, Coughlin 2, Larkin 2, Lee 2, Staniforth 2 (2 pens), Haigh 1, Hornsby 1.
Milk Cup (3): Ashurst 1, Coughlin 1, Staniforth 1.
FA Cup (3): Poskett 2, Bannon 1.

Milk Cup	First Round	Bolton W (h)	3-3
		(a)	0-4
FA Cup	Third Round	Burnley (h)	2-2
		(a)	1-3

Swinburne	Haigh	Rushbury	Ashurst	Houghton	Craig	Staniforth	Coughlin	Poskett	Hornsby	Shoulder	Lee	Larkin	Mitchell	Parker	Bannon	Robson K. (L)	Robson B. (L)	McCartney	Nicholson	Referees	Match No.
1	2	3	4	5	6	7	8	9	10	11										M. Dimblebee	1
1	2	3	4	5*	6	7	8	9	10	11	12									D. Richardson	2
1	2	3	4		6	7	8	9		11	12	5*	10							J. Key	3
1	2	3	4	5	6	7	8	9		11	12		10*							D. Vickers	4
1		3	4		6	7	8	9		11		5		2	10					N. Midgley	5
1		3	4		6	7	8	9		11		5		2	10					A. Ward	6
1	3		4	12	6	7*	8	9		11		5		2	10					R. Chadwick	7
1	3		4		6	7	8	9		11		5		2	10					G. Tyson	8
1	3		4		6	7	8	9		11		5		2	10					K. Walmsley	9
1	3		4	12	6	7	8*	9		11		5		2	10					P. Tydesley	10
1	3	12	4		6	7		9	8	11		5		2	10*					V. Callow	11
1	3	12	4		6*	7	8	9		11		5		2	10					R. Nixon	12
1	3	12	4		6	7	8	9*		11		5		2	10					M. Heath	13
1	3	12	4		6*	7	8	9		11		5		2	10					T. Fitzharris	14
1	3		4	6		7	8		9*	11	12	5		2	10					J. Worrall	15
1*	3	6	4	12		7	8			11	9	5		2	10					L. Shapter	16
1	3	12	4			7*	8	9	6	11		5		2	10					P. Willis	17
1	3	5	4	6	10		8*	9		11	7			2	12					D. Owen	18
1	3	5	4	6		12		9	8*	11	7			2	10					N. Wilson	19
1	3	5	4	6	10*	12		9	8	11	7			2						A. Challinor	20
1	3	5	4	6	8	7*	12	9		11				2	10					R. Guy	21
1	3	5	4	6	8		7*	9		11	12			2	10					T. Jones	22
1	3	5*	4	6	8			9	12	11	7			2	10					R. Banks	23
1	3		4	12	6	7	8*	9		11		5		2	10					A. Robinson	24
1	3		4		6	7	8	9		11		5		2	10					F. Roberts	25
1	3	12	4		6	7	8	9		11		5*		2	10					G. Courtney	26
1	3	5	4	6*	8		7	9		11				2	10					T. Bune	27
1	3	5	4	6	8		7*			11	9			2	10					A. Glasson	28
1	3	5	4	6	8		7		9	11	12			2*	10					A. Saunders	29
1	3	5	4	6	8	9	7			11	12			2*	10					N. Ashley	30
1	3	5		6*	8	7	4			11	9	12		2	10					M. James	31
1	3	5		6*		12	4	9		11				2	10	7	8			K. Redfern	32
1	3	5			12		4	9		11				2	10*	7	8	6		M. Taylor	33
1	3	5		6	10		4	9		11				2*		7	8		12	R. Chadwick	34
1	2*	5		6	12		4	9		11					10	7	8	3		G. Tyson	35
1	2	5		6	12		4	9		11					10*	7	8	3		A. Grey	36
1	2	5		6	12		4	9*		11					10	7	8	3		J. Hough	37
1	2	5		6	10*		4	9		11				12		7	8	3		G. Napthine	38
1	2	5		6	12		4	9		11*					10	7	8	3		D. Allison	39
1	2	5		6			4	9		11					10	7	8	3		N. Glover	40
1	2	5		6	12		10	9		11				4*		7	8	3		M. Bodenham	41
1	2	5		6	7		4	9		11					10*	12	8	3		D. Scott	42
42	40	29	30	25	30	23	37	36	8	42	7	17	2	31	33	10	11	9	0		
		+ 6s		+ 4s	+ 6s	+ 3s	+ 1s		+ 1s		+ 7s	+ 1s		+ 1s	+ 1s	+ 1s			+ 1s		

FOOTBALL LEAGUE RECORD

1928 Elected to Division 3(N); 1958–62 Division 4; 1962–63 Division 3; 1963–64 Division 4; 1964–65 Division 3; 1965–74 Division 2; 1974–75 Division 1; 1975–77 Division 2; 1977–82 Division 3; 1982– Division 2.

HONOURS

Football League: Division 1 best season: 22nd, 1974–75; Promoted from Division 2 (3rd) 1973–74; Division 3 – Champions 1964–65; Division 4 – Runners-up 1963–64. *FA Cup:* 6th rd 1974–75. *Football League Cup:* Semi-final 1969–70.

COLOURS

Blue shirts with red and white trim, blue shorts, white stockings with red and white trim.
Change colours: Yellow shirts, blue shorts, yellow stockings.

CARLISLE UNITED

Players Names Ht, Wt, D.o.B.	Birthplace Transfer Fee	Clubs	Appearances F.L. A & S	 F.L.C. A & S	 F.A.C. A & S	Goals F.L.	 F.L.C.	 F.A.C.
Goalkeepers								
Trevor Swinborne	East Rainton	Sunderland (A)	10		1			
6 0, 12 12, 20.6.53	F/T	Carlisle U	248	17	7			
John Rush*	Wellington, NZ	Blackpool	11					
6 0, 12 9, 13.10.61	F/T	Carlisle U						
Defenders								
Bob Parkel (EY)	Coventry	Coventry C (A)	78+3	5	6			
5 9, 10 12, 11.11.52	£55,000	Carlisle U	338+1	21+1	31	5		
Paul Haigh (EU-21)	Scarborough	Hull C (A)	179+1	13	7	8	2	1
5 10, 11 6, 4.5.58	£102,000	Carlisle U	89+2	5	12+1	1	1	
Jack Ashurst	Coatbridge	Sunderland (A)	129+11	7	8	4		
6 0, 12 4, 12.10.54	£110,000	Blackpool	53	2	4	3		1
	£40,000	Carlisle U	76	6	6	1	1	
Dave Rushbury	Wolverhampton	WBA (A)	28		3			
5 10, 11 4, 20.2.56	£60,000	Sheffield W	111+1	8	13	7		1
	£60,000	Swansea C	51+1	6	6			
	£55,000	Carlisle U	74+6	6	4			
Mike McCartney (SS)	Edinburgh	WBA (A)						
5 7, 10 12, 28.9.54	F/T	Carlisle U	148+8	11	7	17		1
	£30,000	Southampton	22	2		1		
	£50,000	Plymouth Arg	49	4	6	5		1
	P/E	Carlisle U	9					
Midfield								
Keith Houghton (ESP)	Backworth	Blyth Spartans						
6 2, 12 4, 10.3.54		Carlisle U	82+5	5	5	2		
Russell Coughlin	Swansea	Manchester C (A)						
5 8, 11 6, 15.2.60	£25,000	Blackburn R	22+2	1+1				
	£20,000	Carlisle U	92+8	3	10	10	1	
Tommy Craig (S)	Glasgow	Aberdeen						
5 8, 11 9, 21.11.50	£100,000	Sheffield W	210+4	9	9+1	38	1	1
	£120,000	Newcastle U	122+2	12	14	23	2	2
	£275,000	Aston Villa	27	4	1	2		
	£150,000	Swansea C	47+5	5	5	9	1	
	F/T	Carlisle U	48+6	2	2	7		
Brian Hornsby (EY)	Peterborough	Arsenal (A)	23+3			5		
5 8, 11 0, 10.9.54		Shrewsbury T	75	2	8	16		1
	£50,000	Sheffield W	102+4	8	10	25	1	4
	—	Chester (loan)	4					
	F/T	Edmonton Drillers						
		Carlisle U	8+1	1		1		
Forwards								
Paul Bannon	Dublin	Bridgend T						
6 2, 11 2, 15.11.56	£8500	Carlisle U	124+11	5	12+4	44	1	5
Malcolm Poskett	Middlesbrough	South Bank						
6 0, 11 7, 19.7.53		Middlesbrough	0+1					
	F/T	Whitby T						
	£25	Hartlepool U	50+1	3	3	20	1	
	£60,000	Brighton	33+12	4+1	1	16	1	
	£110,000	Watford	57+6	9	5+1	17	6	6
	£20,000	Carlisle U	36	2	2	14		1
Alan Shoulder	Bishop Auckland	Blyth Spartans						
5 5, 10 5, 4.2.53	£20,000	Newcastle U	99+8	4+2	6+1	35	2	1
	F/T	Carlisle U	42	2	2	21		1

Commercial Manager: Susan Greenall (Tel. (0228) 24014).
Player-Coach: Tommy Craig.
Supporters Player of the Season 1982–83: Alan Shoulder.
Physiotherapist: Herbert Nicholson.
Association of Football Statisticians Club Adviser to Yearbook: B. Rodgers.

Club Captain 1982–83:
Chief Scout:
Club Statistician:

Players released since May 1982: Tony Harrison, G. (North Shields); Alan Campbell, M. (Retired); Peter Nicholson, D. (Lytham St. Annes).

CHARLTON ATHLETIC Division 2

Back row (left to right): Dave Mehmet, Don McAllister, Steve White, Paul Curtis
Middle row: Charlie Hall (Physiotherapist), Lennie Lawrence (Caretaker Manager), Geoff Scott, Mark Aizlewood, Billy Lansdowne, Nicky Johns, Paul Elliott, Les Berry, Terry Naylor, Leighton Phillips (Player/Coach), Bill Gallagher (Assistant Physiotherapist)
Front row: Carl Harris, Kevin Smith, Allan Simonsen, Terry Bullivant, Derek Hales, Steve Gritt, Martin Robinson.

Chairman: M. Hulyer. ***Managing Director:*** R. D. Collins.

Director: Chief F. A. Nzeribe.

Secretary: W. J. Jenner. ***Manager:*** Lennie Lawrence.

Secretary: G. I. S. Hortop.

Year Formed: 1905. ***Turned Professional:*** 1920. ***Ltd Co.:*** 1919.

Club Nickname: 'Haddicks', 'Robins' or 'Valiants'.

Previous Grounds: 1906, Siemen's Meadow; 1907, Woolwich Common; 1909, Pound Park; 1913, Horn Lane; 1920, The Valley; 1923, Catford (The Mount); 1924, The Valley.

Previous Managers since 1946: Jimmy Seed, Jimmy Trotter, Frank Hill, Bob Stokoe, Eddie Firmani, Theo Foley, Andy Nelson, Mike Bailey, Alan Mullery, Ken Craggs (10).

The Valley, Floyd Rd, Charlton, London SE7 8AW. Telephone 01-853 0444. ***Ground capacity:*** 20,000. ***Record attendance:*** 75,031 v Aston Villa, FA Cup 5th rd, 12 Feb, 1938. ***Record receipts:*** £38,964 v Ipswich T, FA Cup 3rd rd, 3 Jan, 1983. ***Pitch measurements:*** 113yd×78yd.

Directions to Ground: Buses 53, 54, 75, 177, 180. Nearest railway station, Charlton, is on the line from London from Charing Cross and Waterloo East. The ground is 3 minutes walk from the station.

Car parking: In ground for season-ticket holders only. Off-street parking available.

Entertainments/catering facilities: The Valley Club, Harvey Gardens (01-858 1495), and Beer and Snack Bars in the ground.

Club shop: The Valley Shop in ground is open on match days.

Handbooks/programmes: Match magazine available in club shop and on subscription.

Address of Supporters Club: Same address as Club.

Address of the Club Shop or Boutique: 'The Valley Shop', The Valley, Floyd Road, London SE7 8AW. 01-858 6006.

Note: Full club statistical records are on pages 416–455.

CHARLTON ATHLETIC 1982–83 LEAGUE RECORD

Match No.	Date	Venue	Opponents	Result	H/T Score	Lg. Pos.	Goalscorers	Attendance
1	Aug 28	A	Leicester C	W 2-1	1-0	—	Walker 2	11,038
2	Sept 4	H	Sheffield W	L 0-3	0-1	14		8327
3	7	A	Wolverhampton W	L 0-5	0-2	—		13,063
4	11	A	Cambridge U	L 2-3	2-0	20	Ferns, Walker	3162
5	18	H	Grimsby T	L 0-1	0-0	21		4361
6	25	A	Oldham Ath	D 2-2	1-0	21	Bullivant, Hales	3211
7	28	H	Fulham	W 3-0	0-0	—	Mehmet, Hales, Bullivant	6790
8	Oct 2	H	Derby Co	D 1-1	0-0	17	White	4685
9	9	A	Carlisle U	L 1-4	0-0	19	Hales	4606
10	16	H	Burnley	W 2-1	1-1	16	White, Berry	5940
11	23	A	Chelsea	L 1-3	1-1	17	Hales	14,492
12	30	H	Blackburn R	W 3-0	0-0	16	White 2, Harris	5278
13	Nov 6	A	Leeds U	W 2-1	1-0	15	White, Harris	15,148
14	13	H	Middlesbrough	L 2-3	0-3	16	Hales, Simonsen	10,807
15	20	H	Rotherham U	L 1-5	0-2	18	Hales	6761
16	27	A	Shrewsbury T	D 0-0	0-0	17		4477
17	Dec 4	H	Newcastle U	W 2-0	1-0	17	McAllister, Simonsen	10,381
18	11	A	Bolton W	L 1-4	1-2	17	Simonsen	5645
19	18	H	Barnsley	W 3-2	2-1	17	Simonsen, Hales 2	4942
20	27	A	Crystal Palace	D 1-1	0-1	17	White	17,996
21	29	H	QPR	L 1-3	0-1	17	White	13,306
22	Jan 1	A	Rotherham U	L 0-1	0-0	18		8798
23	3	A	Sheffield W	L 4-5	3-1	19	Robinson 2, White, Harris	11,799
24	15	H	Leicester C	W 2-1	0-0	18	Simonsen 2	5971
25	22	A	Grimsby T	D 1-1	1-1	18	Aizlewood	5990
26	Feb 5	H	Cambridge U	W 2-1	0-0	14	Simonsen (pen), Hales	4592
27	19	H	Carlisle U	D 0-0	0-0	14		4940
28	26	A	Burnley	L 1-7	1-2	16	Hales	7022
29	Mar 5	H	Chelsea	W 5-2	2-0	13	Bullivant, Smith, Harris, Simonsen 2	11,211
30	13	A	Blackburn R	L 0-2	0-0	—		5493
31	19	H	Leeds U	L 0-1	0-0	16		8229
32	22	A	QPR	L 1-5	1-2	—	Little	10,776
33	26	A	Middlesbrough	L 0-3	0-1	18		7057
34	Apr 4	H	Crystal Palace	W 2-1	2-1	—	Harris, White	7836
35	9	A	Fulham	L 1-2	0-0	20	White	9035
36	13	A	Derby Co	D 1-1	1-1	—	McAllister	15,605
37	17	H	Oldham Ath	W 4-1	2-0	—	Hales, White, Curtis, Clements (og)	5193
38	23	A	Newcastle U	L 2-4	0-1	17	Robinson 2	20,526
39	29	H	Shrewsbury T	L 0-1	0-0	—		4838
40	May 2	H	Wolverhampton W	D 3-3	0-3	18	Smith, White, Hales	7935
41	7	A	Barnsley	D 0-0	0-0	18		6457
42	14	H	Bolton W	W 4-1	0-0	16	Hales 2 (1 pen), Gritt, Harris	8720

Final League Position: 17

GOALSCORERS

League (63): Hales 14, White 12, Simmonsen 9 (1 pen), Harris 6, Robinson 4, Bullivant 3, Walker 3, McAllister 2, Smith 2, Aizlewood 1, Berry 1, Curtis 1, Ferns 1, Gritt 1, Little 1, Mehmet 1, own goal 1.
Milk Cup (2): Hales 2 (1 pen).
FA Cup (2): Hales 1, Robinson 1.

Milk Cup	Second Round	Luton T (a)	0-3
		(h)	2-0
FA Cup	Third Round	Ipswich T (h)	2-3

Johns	McAllister	Ferns	Mehmet	Elliott	Phillips	Harris	Bullivant	White	Hales	Walker	Gritt	Berry	Lansdowne	Smith	Curtis	Scott	O'Sullivan (L)	Robinson	Aizlewood	Simonsen	Gray (L)	Dickenson	Little	McDonald (L)	*Referees*	*Match No.*
1	2	3	4	5	6	7	8	9	10	11															J. Deakin	1
1	2	3	4	5	6	7	8	9	10	11															I. Barrett	2
1	2	3	4	5	6*	7	8	9	10	11	12														N. Midgley	3
1		3	4	5		7	8	9	10	11*	2	6	12												K. Barratt	4
1	3		4	5		7	8	9	10	11	2	6													M. Bodenham	5
1		12	4	5		7	8	9	10*	11	2	6	3												M. Heath	6
1		11	4	5		7	8	9	10		2	6	3												K. Baker	7
1		11*	4	5		7	8	9		10	2	6	3	12											M. James	8
1			4	5		7	8	9*	10	11		6	3	12	2										K. Walmsley	9
1		3	4	5		7*	8	9	10	12		2				6	11								M. Taylor	10
1		3	4*	5		7	8	9	10			2				6	11	12							C. Thomas	11
1		3	4	5		7	8	9				6			2		11	10							B. Stevens	12
1				5		7	8	9				6		4	2		11	10	3						J. Lovatt	13
1				5		11	8	9	10			6			2*		4	12	3	7					A. Gunn	14
1			7	4		11	8	9	10			5			2			6	3						L. Burden	15
1	7			5		11	8	9	10			6			2			4	3						T. Jones	16
1	4			5		11	8		9			6			2			10	3	7					T. Bune	17
1	4					8			9			6		10	2			11	3	7	5				G. Napthine	18
1	4					8			9		10	6			2			11	3	7	5				D. Letts	19
1	4					8		9			10	6			2			11	3	7	5				J. Martin	20
1	4			5		8	10	9			2	6		12				11	3	7					J. Hunting	21
1	4			5		8	10	9			2	6						11	3	7					T. Holbrook	22
1	4			5		8	10	9			2	6						11	3	7					N. Wilson	23
1	4			5		8	10		9		2	6						11	3	7					A. Crickmore	24
1	4			5*		8	10		9		2	6		12				11	3	7					T. Fitzharris	25
1	4			5		8	10*		9		2	6		12				11	3	7					K. Cooper	26
1	4			5		8	10		9		2	6		12				11	3*	7					A. Glasson	27
1	4			5		8	10		9		2	6		12				11	3*	7					D. Owen	28
1						8	10		9		4	6		5	2			11	3	7					A. Grey	29
1	4					8	10			11	3	6		5	2*			9		7		12			G. Courtney	30
1	4					8	10*			11	2	6		5	12			9		7		3			E. Read	31
1	4					8					9	6		5	2			11	7			3	10		M. Dimblebee	32
1	4					8	7		9		2	6		5				11	3				10		D. Richardson	33
1	4					8		10	9		2	6		7				11				3		5	B. Daniels	34
1	4					8		10	9		2	6		7				11				3		5	T. Spencer	35
1	4					8	7	10			2	6						11	9			3		5	D. Lloyd	36
1	4					8		10	9			6		7	2			11				3		5	M. Taylor	37
1	4					8		10	9			6		7	2			11				3		5	J. Worrall	38
1	4					8		10	9			6		7	2			11				3		5	D. Hedges	39
1						8		10	9		12	6		7	2			11	4			3		5*	L. Burden	40
1	4					8		10			12	6		7*	2			11	9			3		5	G. Tyson	41
1	4					8		10	9		12	6		7*	2			11				3		5	C. Thomas	42
42	29	9	13	25	3	42	30	29	30	10	23	39	4	15	19	2	5	30	22	16	3	11	2	9		
		+ 1s								+ 1s	+ 4s		+ 1s	+ 7s	+ 1s			+ 2s				+ 1s				

FOOTBALL LEAGUE RECORD

1921 Elected to Division 3(S); 1929–33 Division 2; 1933–35 Division 3(S); 1935–36 Division 2; 1936–57 Division 1; 1957–72 Division 2; 1972–75 Division 3; 1975–80 Division 2; 1980–81 Division 3; 1981– Division 2.

HONOURS

Football League: Division 1 – Runners-up 1936–37; Division 2 – Runners-up 1935–36; Division 3(S) – Champions 1928–29, 1934–35; Promoted from Division 3 (3rd) 1974–75, 1980–81. *FA Cup:* Winners 1947; Runners-up 1946. *Football League Cup* best ever: 4th rd, 1962–63, 1964–65, 1978–79.

COLOURS

Red shirts, white shorts, red stockings.
Change colours: Yellow and blue.

CHARLTON ATHLETIC

Players Names *Ht, Wt, D.o.B.*	*Birthplace* *Transfer Fee*	*Clubs*	*Appearances* *F.L.* *A & S*	*F.L.C.* *A & S*	*F.A.C.* *A & S*	*Goals* *F.L.*	*F.L.C.*	*F.A.C.*
Goalkeepers								
Nicky Johns	Bristol	Minehead						
6 3½, 11 8, 8.6.57	£6000	Millwall	50	6	5			
	£200,000	Tampa Bay R						
	—	Sheffield U (loan)	1	1				
	£125,000	Charlton Ath	163	8	9			
Anthony Lange		Charlton Ath (A)						
10.12.64								
Defenders								
Mark Aizlewood (WU21)	Newport	Newport Co (A)	35+3		2	1		
6 0, 11 4, 1.10.59	£50,000	Luton T	90+8	7	5	3	1	
	£50,000	Charlton Ath	22		1	1		
Les Berry	Plumstead	Charlton Ath (A)	278+5	14+1	13	11		
6 2, 12 5, 4.5.56								
Kevin Dickensen	London	Tottenham H (A)						
5 5, 10 4, 24.11.61	F/T	Charlton Ath	17+3	1				
Terry Naylor*	Islington	Tottenham H	237+6	23+1	17+1		1	
5 10, 11 10, 5.12.48	£30,000	Charlton Ath	63+4	4	4			
Phil Ferns	Liverpool	Bournemouth (A)	96+1	3	4	6		
5 11, 11 4, 12.9.61	£25,000	Charlton Ath	35+3	3+1	1	1		
	—	Wimbledon (loan)	7					
Geoff Scott	Birmingham	Highgate U						
5 10½, 12 5, 31.10.56		Stoke C	76+2	7	3	3		
	£80,000	Leicester C	39	3	2			
	£50,000	Birmingham C	18+1					
	£40,000	Charlton Ath	2					
Paul Curtis	London	Charlton Ath (A)	19+1	2		1		
1.7.63								
Midfield								
Steve Gritt	Bouremouth	Bournemouth (A)	4+2	2		3		
5 10, 10 10, 31.10.57	F/T	Charlton Ath	186+19	14+1	10	17		
Kevin Smith	St Pauls Cray	Charlton Ath(A)	49+19	5	2+1	8		
5 8, 10 7, 5.12.62								
Phil Walker*	London	Epsom & Ewell						
5 9½, 12 1, 29.8.54	—	Millwall	143+3	14	5	16	2	2
	£120,000	Charlton Ath	80+9	5+2	6	15	2	
	—	Gillingham (loan)	1+1					
Barry Little	Greenwich	Charlton Ath (A)	2			1		
25.8.64								
Don McAllister	Radcliffe	Bolton W (A)	155+1	7	14	2		
5 10, 11 2, 26.5.53	£80,000	Tottenham H	168+4	13	16+1	9	1	
	£40,000	Charlton Ath	55	4	2	6		
Terry Bullivant	London	Fulham (A)	94+7	8	5	2		
5 7½, 10 11, 23.9.56	£220,000	Aston Villa	10+3		1			
	£90,000	Charlton Ath	30	2	1	3		
Forwards								
Steve Browne*	London	Charlton Ath (A)	+1					
21.6.64								
Martin Robinson	Ilford	Tottenham H (A)	5+1		1	2		1
5 8½, 11 5, 17.7.57	£15,000	Charlton Ath	188+7	14+2	8+1	48	6	2
	—	Reading (loan)	6			2		
Leroy Ambrose*	St Vincent, W.I.	Croydon						
5 9, 10 11, 22.6.60	—	Charlton Ath	28+5	1		1		
Derek Hales	Lower Halston	Dartford T						
5 9½, 11 8, 15.12.51		Luton T	5+2		+1	1		
	£4000	Charlton Ath	126+3	12	7	72	6	
	£300,000	Derby Co	22+1	1	6	4	1	2
	£110,000	West Ham U	23+1		3	10		
	£75,000	Charlton Ath	147+1	15	9	58	8	5
Carl Harris (W)	Neath	Leeds U (A)	124+30	8+6	5	26	1	1
5 9, 11 0, 3.11.56	£150,000	Charlton Ath	42	2	1	6		
Steve White	Chipping Sodbury	Mangotsfield U						
5 11, 11 10, 2.1.59		Bristol R	46+4	2	3	20	1	3
	£200,000	Luton T	63+9	3+1	2	25	1	
	£150,000	Charlton Ath	29	2		12		
	—	Lincoln C (loan)	2+1					
	—	Luton T (loan)	4					

Commercial Manager: Mr M. LaRoche (Tel. 853 0444)
Club Coach: Eddie May
Supporters Player of the Season 1982–83: Nicky Johns
Physiotherapist: Charlie Hall
Club Captain 1982–83:
Chief Scout: Les Gore
Club Statistician: Colin Cameron
Association of Football Statisticians Club Adviser to Yearbook: C. Cameron.

Players (non-appearance) granted free transfer: Mark Simpson, F.
Players released since May 1982:
Jimmy Clare, D. (N/K); Frank Clark, D. (Dulwich H); Viggo Jacobsen, M. (Denmark); Henry Laville, M. (N/K); Alan Simonsen, F. (Vejle); Mark Turkington, F. (N/K); Paul Kay, M. (Australia).

CHELSEA

Division 2

Back row (left to right): Gary Chivers, Michael Nutton, Colin Lee, Micky Droy, Colin Pates, Phil Driver, Gary Locke
Middle row: Gwyn Williams (Youth Development Officer), Ron Suart (Chief Scout), Peter Rhoades-Brown, Timmy Elmes (no longer with Club), Paul Canoville, Bob Iles, Steve Francis, Michael Fillery, Dale Jasper, Chris Hutchings, Eddie Franklin (no longer with Club), Norman Medhurst (Physiotherapist)
Front row: John Neal (Manager), Leo Donnellan, Kevin Hales, Clive Walker, Bryan Robson, David Speedie, John Bumstead, Alan Mayes, Ian McNeill (Assistant Manager).

President: The Right Hon Earl Cadogan MC, DL.

Chairman: K. W. Bates ***Vice-Chairman:*** G. Dimbleby AIED, MBIM.

Directors: Viscount Chelsea, D. Mears BSC, G. Webb, S. Tollman.

Manager: John Neal. ***Asst Manager:*** Ian McNeill.

Secretary: Sheila Marson.

Year Formed: 1905. ***Turned Professional:*** 1905. ***Ltd Co.:*** 1905.

Club Nickname: 'The Blues'.

Previous Managers since 1948: Billy Birrell, Ted Drake, Tommy Docherty, Dave Sexton, Ron Suart, Eddie McCreadie, Ken Shellito, Danny Blanchflower, Geoff Hurst (9).

Stamford Bridge, London SW6. Telephone 01-385 5546/6, (Information Service) 01-381 0111. ***Telegraphic address:*** 'Chelstam, London SW6.'

Ground capacity: 45,000 (21,500 covered). ***Record attendance:*** 82,905 v Arsenal, Division 1, 12 Oct, 1935. ***Record receipts:*** £158,227 v Tottenham H, FA Cup 6th rd, 6 March, 1982. ***Pitch measurements:*** 114yd×71yd.

Directions to Ground: Nearest station is Fulham Broadway on the Underground (District Line). London Transport regular buses to Fulham Broadway, Kings Road, Fulham Road, or Stamford Bridge.

Match tickets: Advance tickets available by postal or personal application. No telephone bookings.

Car parking: Street parking only.

Entertainments/catering facilities: Licensed bars at all points of the ground.

Club shop: Run by the Football Club; sells all types of souvenirs.

Handbooks/programmes: Programmes available on subscription.

Address of Supporters Club: Same as Football Club.

Address of the Club Shop or Boutique: Stamford Bridge, SW6.

Note: Full club statistical records are on pages 416–455.

CHELSEA 1982–83 LEAGUE RECORD

Match No.	Date	Venue	Opponents	Result		H/T Score	Lg. Pos.	Goalscorers	Attendance
1	Aug 28	A	Cambridge U	W	1-0	0-0	—	Robson	8124
2	31	H	Wolverhampton W	D	0-0	0-0	—		14,192
3	Sept 4	H	Leicester C	D	1-1	0-0	4	Droy	8075
4	8	A	Derby Co	L	0-1	0-0	—		8075
5	11	A	Newcastle U	D	1-1	1-0	11	Lee	29,084
6	18	H	Oldham Ath	W	2-0	1-0	7	Speedie 2	10,263
7	25	A	Sheffield W	L	2-3	0-1	9	Fillery (pen), Lee	18,833
8	Oct 2	H	Grimsby T	W	5-2	2-1	7	Fillery, Speedie 2, Droy, Bumstead	10,019
9	9	H	Leeds U	D	0-0	0-0	9		25,358
10	16	A	Blackburn R	L	0-3	0-1	10		6062
11	23	H	Charlton Ath	W	3-1	1-1	9	Bumstead, Pates, Robson	14,492
12	30	A	Carlisle U	L	1-2	0-2	11	Lee	7141
13	Nov 6	H	Crystal Palace	D	0-0	0-0	10		15,169
14	13	A	Barnsley	D	1-1	1-0	11	Fillery	13,286
15	20	H	Shrewsbury T	L	1-2	0-0	15	Lee	8690
16	27	A	Rotherham U	L	0-1	0-0	16		8793
17	Dec 4	H	Burnley	W	2-1	2-1	14	Speedie, Droy	8184
18	11	A	Middlesbrough	L	1-3	0-1	16	Fillery (pen)	8836
19	18	H	Bolton W	W	2-1	1-0	14	Deakin (og), Pates	6903
20	27	A	QPR	W	2-1	1-1	12	Walker, Speedie	23,744
21	28	H	Fulham	D	0-0	0-0	11		29,797
22	Jan 1	A	Shrewsbury T	L	0-2	0-0	15		7545
23	3	A	Leicester C	L	0-3	0-1	15		13,745
24	15	H	Cambridge U	W	6-0	2-0	12	Jones, Fillery 2, Bumstead, Murray (og), Mayes	7808
25	22	A	Wolverhampton W	L	1-2	1-1	14	Pates	19,533
26	Feb 5	H	Derby Co	L	1-3	1-2	14	Pates	8661
27	12	A	Grimsby T	L	1-2	1-2		Mayes	6711
28	19	A	Leeds U	D	3-3	1-1	15	Walker, Fillery (pen), Gray E. (og)	19,365
29	26	H	Blackburn R	W	2-0	1-0	13	Walker, Rhoades-Brown	6982
30	Mar 5	A	Charlton Ath	L	2-5	0-2	14	Robson, Lee	11,211
31	12	H	Carlisle U	W	4-2	2-1	13	Walker, Bumstead, Canoville 2	6677
32	19	A	Crystal Palace	D	0-0	0-0	13		13,437
33	26	H	Barnsley	L	0-3	0-1	14		7223
34	Apr 2	A	Fulham	D	1-1	1-1	13	Canoville	15,249
35	4	H	QPR	L	0-2	0-1	—		20,821
36	9	A	Oldham Ath	D	2-2	1-1	15	Fillery 2 (1 pen)	4973
37	16	H	Newcastle U	L	0-2	0-1	17		13,446
38	23	A	Burnley	L	0-3	0-1	20		7393
39	30	H	Rotherham U	D	1-1	1-1	20	Walker	8674
40	May 2	H	Sheffield W	D	1-1	1-0	19	Speedie	10,462
41	7	A	Bolton W	W	1-0	0-0	14	Walker	8687
42	14	H	Middlesbrough	D	0-0	0-0	17		19,340

Final League Position: 18

GOALSCORERS

League (51): Fillery 9 (4 pens), Speedie 7, Walker 6, Lee 5, Bumstead 4, Pates 4, Canoville 3, Droy 3, Robson 3, Mayes 2, Jones 1, Rhoades-Brown 1, own goals 3.
Milk Cup (5): Robson 2, Speedie 2, Fillery 1 (pen).
FA Cup (4): Fillery 2, Bumstead 1, Mayes 1.

Milk Cup	Second Round	Tranmere R (h)	3-1
		(a)	2-1
	Third Round	Notts Co (a)	0-2
FA Cup	Third Round	Huddersfield T (a)	1-1
		(h)	2-0
	Fourth Round	Derby Co (a)	1-2

Francis	Nutton	Hutchings	Chivers	Droy	Pates	Walker	Bumstead	Lee	Robson	Fillery	Canoville	McAndrew	Driver	Speedie	Locke	Rhoades-Brown	Mayes	Jones J.	Falco (L)	Hales	Iles	Williams	Jones K.	*Referees*	*Match No.*
1	2	3	4	5	6	7*	8	9	10	11	12													H. Taylor	1
1	2	3	4	5	6	7	8	9	10	11														M. Taylor	2
1	2	3	4	5	6		8	9	10	11		7												D. Axcell	3
1	2	3	4	5	6*		8	9	10	11	12	7												P. Tylesley	4
1	2	3	4	5			8	9	10*	11	7	6	12											D. Scott	5
1	2	3	4	5			8	9	12	11	7*	6		10										L. Shapter	6
1	2	3	4	5			8	9	12	11	7*	6		10										R. Banks	7
1		3	4	5		9	8	2		11	7	6		10										Alan Robinson	8
1		3		5	4	9	8*		12	11	7	6		10	2									T. Spencer	9
1	3			5	4		8		12	11			7	10	2	6*	9							J. Lovatt	10
1		3	6	5	4	7	8		9	11				10	2									G. Thomas	11
1		3		5	4	7	8	12	9*					10	2	11		6						R. Nixon	12
1		3	6	5	4	7	8	12	9*	11				10				2						A. Seville	13
1		3	6	5	4			9	8	11				10	2	7								P. Willis	14
1			6	5	4		8	9		11			12	10	2*	7		3						A. Crickmore	15
1		3		5		12	4	6		11			7	9*		8		2	10					R. Guy	16
1		3		5		12	4	6		11			7	9		8*		2	10					J. Martin	17
1		3		5		12	4	6		11			7	9		8*		2	10					A. Robinson	18
1		3	4	5	6	12	8						7*	9		11	10	2						R. Milford	19
1		3	4	5	6	7	8							9		11	10	2						D. Hedges	20
1		3	4	5	6	7	8			12				9		11	10*	2						B. Hill	21
1		3	4	5	6	7*	8	12		10				9		11		2						K. Cooper	22
1		3	4	5	6	7	8	12		10				9		11*		2						T. Mills	23
1			4		5	12	8*	2		7				9		11	10	3		6				B. Stevens	24
1			6		5	12	4	2		7				9*		11	10	3		8				T. Jones	25
1			6		5	10	4	2	8	7			12	9		11*		3						I. Barrett	26
1		5			6	8*		2		7			4	9		11	10	3						D. Owen	27
1*		5	12		6	8		2		7			4	9		11	10	3						K. Redfern	28
1		3	2		6	8		5		7*			4	9		11	10							K. Letts	29
1		3			6	8	12	5	10	7*	11		4	9				2						A. Grey	30
		3	5		6	8	4			7	11			9			10	2			1			M. James	31
1		3	5		6	8		4		7	11			9		10		2						L. Shapter	32
1		3	5		6	8*	4	2			11			9		10				7			12	H. King	33
		3		5	6		4	8		7	11			9		10		2			1			D. Axcell	34
		3		5	6		4	8		7	11			9		10*	12	2			1			J. Martin	35
		3			6			4		7	10			9		11	8	2			1	5		M. Robinson	36
		3		5	6		8	4		7	11*					10	9	2			1		12	E. Read	37
1			3	5	6		8	4			11		12	7		10	9*	2						M. Peck	38
1		3	4	5	6	11	10	9		7	12			8				2*						J. Bodenham	39
1		3	4	5	6	11	10	9		7				8				2						T. Glasson	40
1		3	4	5	6	11	8	9		7	10							2						T. Holbrook	41
1		3	4	5	6	11	8	9		7	10							2						K. Baker	42
37	8	36	29	31	35	23	35	31	11	36	16	7	9	34	6	25	13	28	3	3	5	1	0		
			+ 1s			+ 6s	+ 1s	+ 4s	+ 4s	+ 1s	+ 3s		+ 4s				+ 1s						+ 2s		

FOOTBALL LEAGUE RECORD

1905 Elected to Division 2; 1907–10 Division 1; 1910–12 Division 2; 1912–24 Division 1; 1924–30 Division 2; 1930–62 Division 1; 1962–63 Division 2; 1963–75 Division 1; 1975–77 Division 2; 1977–79 Division 1; 1979– Division 2.

HONOURS

Football League: Division 1 – Champions 1954–55; Division 2 – Runners-up 1906–07, 1911–12, 1929–30, 1962–63, 1976–77. *FA Cup:* Winners 1970; Runners-up 1914–15, 1966–67. *Football League Cup:* Winners 1964–65, Runners-up 1971–72. **European Competitions:** *European Fairs Cup:* 1958–60, 1965–66, 1968–69; *European Cup-Winners' Cup:* 1970–71 (winners), 1971–72.

COLOURS

All royal blue with white stripe on shorts, white stockings.
Change colours: Yellow shirts, blue shorts, yellow stockings.

CHELSEA

Players Names Ht, Wt, D.o.B.	Birthplace Transfer Fee	Clubs	Appearances F.L. A & S	 F.L.C. A & S	 F.A.C. A & S	Goals F.L.	 F.L.C.	 F.A.C.
Goalkeepers								
Bob Iles*	Leicester	Weymouth						
6 1, 12 7, 23.6.58	£10,000	Chelsea	14					
Steve Francis (EY)	Billericay	Chelsea (A)	66	5	10			
5 11, 11 5,								
Defenders								
Micky Droy	Highbury	Slough T						
6 4½, 15 5, 7.5.51	—	Chelsea	263+8	17+2	21	13	2	4
Gary Chivers*	Stockwell	Chelsea (A)	128+4	8	7	4		
5 11, 11 5, 15.5.60								
Kevin Hales	Dartford	Chelsea (A)	18+2		6	2		
5 7, 10 4, 13.1.61								
Colin Pates (EY)	Carshalton	Chelsea (A)	108	5	11	5		
6 0, 11 10, 10.8.61								
Paul Williams*	Lambeth	Chelsea (A)	1					
6 0, 11 7, 16.11.62								
Chris Hutchings	Winchester	Harrow Bor						
5 10, 11 0, 5.7.57	£10,000	Chelsea	79+4	6	7	2		
Joey Jones (W)	Llandudno	Wrexham	98	3	8	2		
5 10, 11 7, 4.3.55	£110,000	Liverpool	72	4	9	3		3
	£210,000	Wrexham	145+1	15	14	6	1	2
	£34,000	Chelsea	28		3	1		
Simon Gibson		Chelsea (A)						
Midfield								
John Bumstead	Rotherhithe	Chelsea (A)	129+5	8+1	10	13	1	2
5 7, 10 0, 27.11.58								
Mike Fillery (EY)	Mitcham	Chelsea (A)	156+5	9	11	32	6	3
5 10, 11 2, 17.9.60								
Dale Jasper	Croydon	Chelsea (A)						
5 6, 11 1, 14.1.64								
Tony McAndrew	Lanark	Middlesbrough (A)	245+2	13+2	20+1	13	1	1
5 10, 12 4, 11.4.56	£92,000	Chelsea	7	2				
Leo Donnellan	Brent	Chelsea (A)						
5 10, 11 5, 19.1.65								
Martin Nolan		Chelsea (A)						
Forwards								
Clive Walker (EY)	Oxford	Chelsea (A)	162+3	7+1	14+2	57	1	3
5 8½, 11 4, 26 5 57								
Colin Lee	Torquay	Bristol C (A)						
6 1, 11 9, 12.6.56	—	Hereford U (loan)	7+2	+1	2			
	£8000	Torquay U	35	3		14	1	
	£60,000	Tottenham H	57+5	2	6+1	18		3
	£80,000	Chelsea	109+6	6+1	10	32		2
Peter Rhoades-Brown	Hampton	Chelsea (A)	80+10	3	7+2	3		1
5 9, 11 4, 2.1.62								
Phil Driver*	Huddersfield	Bedford T						
5 10, 10 7, 10 8 59		Wimbledon	7+9			3		
	£20,000	Chelsea	25+19	+1	+1	4		
Alan Mayes*	London	QPR (A)						
5 7, 10 10, 11.12.53		Watford	110+23	11+3	5+3	31	4	1
	—	North'pton T (loan)	10			4		
	£65,000	Swindon T	89	15	8	38	9	4
	£200,000	Chelsea	61+5	1	9	18		5
Paul Canoville	Hillingdon	Hillingdon Bor						
5 10, 11 0, 4.3.62		Chelsea	16+5	2		3		
David Speedie	Glenrothes	Barnsley	10+13					
5 7, 10 4, 20.2.60		Darlington	88	4	3	21		1
	£70,000	Chelsea	34	3	3	7	2	
Bryan Robson (EU23)	Sunderland	Newcastle U	205+1	4	8	81	2	4
5 7, 11 8, 11.11.45	£125,000	West Ham U	120	13	6	47	5	1
	£145,000	Sunderland	90	5	7	34	1	4
	£80,000	West Ham U	107	2	6	47	1	3
	£40,000	Sunderland	49+3	4+1	1	23	2	
	£10,000	Carlisle U	48	2	4	21		3
	F/T	Chelsea	11+4	1+1		3	2	
	—	Carlisle U (loan)	11			4		
Apprentices								
Keith Jones	Dulwich	Chelsea (A)	+2					

Commercial Manager: (Tel.)
Club Coach: John Hollins
Club Captain 1982-83: Micky Droy
Supporters Player of the Season 1982–83: Joey Jones
Chief Scout:
Physiotherapist: Norman Medhurst
Club Statistician: Arthur Meadows
Association of Football Statisticians Club Adviser to Yearbook: D. Fletcher

Players released since May 1982: Petar Borota, G. (Benfica); Timmy Elmes, M. (N/K); Colin Viljoen, M. (Southall); Ian Britton, M. (Dundee U).

CHESTER CITY Division 4

Back row (left to right): Steve Ludham, Nigel Edwards, Gary Simpson, Trevor Storton, Phil Harrington, Grenville Millington, Peter Zelem, Paul Blackwell, John Allan, Mark Dean.
Front row: Greg Moffat, Martin Lane, Paul Johnson, Noel Bradley, Cliff Sear, John Thomas, Tom Sloan, Terry Cook, Paul Needham.

Club Patron: Duke of Westminster.

President: Reg Rowlands. ***Chairman:*** E. Barnes.

Vice-Chairman: C. Thompson.

Directors: L. Lloyd, E. J. Owen, R. S. Tresidder, D. Darlington, R. H. Croft.

Team Manager: John Sainty. ***Secretary:*** S. Gandy.

Year Formed: 1884. ***Turned Professional:*** 1902. ***Ltd Co.:*** 1909.

Club Nickname: 'The Seals'.

Previous Grounds: Faulkner Street; Old Showground; 1904, Whipcord Lane; 1906, Sealand Road.

Previous Managers since 1946: Frank Brown, Louis Page, John Harris, Stan Pearson, Bill Lambton, Peter Hauser, Ken Roberts, Alan Oakes, Cliff Sear (9).

The Stadium, Sealand Rd, Chester CH1 4LW. Telephone Chester (0244) 371376. ***Ground capacity:*** 20,000. ***Record attendance:*** 20,500 v Chelsea, FA Cup 3rd rd replay, 16 Jan, 1952. ***Record receipts:*** £15,854 v Aston Villa, FL Cup semi-final first leg, 15 Jan, 1975. ***Pitch measurements:*** 114yd×76yd.

Directions to Ground: Nearest railway station, Chester. Corporation bus to Town Hall Square, where special buses run from the Odeon Cinema to the ground.

Match tickets: No advance booking.

Car parking: Extensive parking at ground.

Entertainments/catering facilities: Catering facilities on ground.

Club shop: At ground; stocks all types of souvenirs.

Handbooks/programmes: Programmes not available on subscription.

Extra information: Additional programme shop inside the ground.

Address of the Club Shop or Boutique: 18 Grosvenor St, Chester.

Note: Full club statistical records are on pages 416–455.

CHESTER 1982–83 LEAGUE RECORD

Match No.	Date	Venue	Opponents	Result	H/T Score	Lg. Pos.	Goalscorers	Attendance
1	Aug 28	H	Crewe Alex	W 1-0	1-0	—	Edwards	3180
2	Sept 4	A	Rochdale	W 1-0	1-0	2	Thomas	1489
3	7	A	Northampton T	D 1-1	0-0	—	Thomas	2171
4	11	H	Torquay U	D 0-0	0-0	4		2370
5	18	A	Port Vale	L 1-2	1-0	6	Sproson (og)	3303
6	25	H	Hereford U	W 5-0	2-0	3	Ludlam, Thomas 2 (1 pen), Simpson, Sloan	1828
7	29	H	Blackpool	L 1-2	1-1	—	Thomas	2256
8	Oct 1	A	Halifax T	D 0-0	0-0	—		1925
9	9	A	Darlington	W 2-0	1-0	5	Thomas, Kinsey	1387
10	16	H	Mansfield T	L 1-3	0-1	10	Ludlam	1668
12	30	H	Swindon T	L 0-1	0-0	12		1544
11	30	H	Swindon T	L 0-1	0-0	12		1844
13	Nov 2	A	Bristol C	D 0-0	0-0	—		3942
14	6	H	Bury	L 0-1	0-1	15		2023
15	9	A	Colchester U	L 0-1	0-0	—		2362
16	13	A	Aldershot	W 2-1	2-1	11	Allen, Sloan	1675
17	27	A	Hull C	L 0-2	0-0	13		5047
18	Dec 4	H	Hartlepool U	W 2-1	2-1	12	Storton, Thomas	1114
19	11	H	Bristol C	W 1-0	0-0	9	Cooper (og)	1163
20	18	H	York C	L 0-1	0-1	12		1185
21	27	A	Tranmere R	W 4-2	2-1	10	Lane 2, Thomas, Ludlam	5245
22	28	H	Stockport Co	L 0-2	0-0	11		2459
23	Jan 1	A	Scunthorpe U	L 0-2	0-2	12		3639
24	3	H	Wimbledon	L 1-2	0-0	13	Thomas	1549
25	8	H	Rochdale	W 5-2	1-1	11	Thomas 3, Zelem, Wilson (pen)	1562
26	15	A	Crewe Alex	L 2-3	0-2	12	Thomas, Cooke	2895
27	22	H	Port Vale	W 1-0	0-0	11	Moss (og)	4056
28	29	A	Blackpool	D 1-1	0-0	11	Ludlam	2054
29	Feb 5	A	Hereford U	L 2-5	1-3	12	Bulmer, Williams	1961
30	12	H	Halifax T	W 2-0	1-0	11	Zelem, Williams	1907
31	16	A	Peterborough U	W 1-0	1-0	—	Wilson	1661
32	19	H	Darlington	L 2-3	2-2	10	Simpson, Thomas	1323
33	26	A	Mansfield T	L 1-2	1-0	11	Thomas	1803
34	Mar 5	H	Colchester U	D 1-1	0-0	13	Simpson	1136
35	12	A	Swindon T	W 3-2	1-1	10	Sloan, Thomas 2	3238
36	19	A	Bury	L 2-3	1-1	12	Simpson 2	2453
37	26	H	Aldershot	D 1-1	1-0	11	Manns	1197
38	Apr 2	A	Stockport Co	D 3-3	2-1	11	Thomas, Simpson, Manns	2008
39	4	H	Tranmere R	D 0-0	0-0	—		2897
40	9	A	Hartlepool U	L 0-1	0-0	12		1034
41	16	H	Northampton T	W 2-1	1-0	12	Allen, Manns	1121
42	23	A	York C	L 0-1	0-1	13		3264
43	30	H	Hull C	D 0-0	0-0	13		2281
44	May 2	A	Wimbledon	L 0-4	0-1	14		2576
45	7	A	Torquay U	W 1-0	0-0	12	Thomas	1478
46	14	H	Scunthorpe U	L 1-2	1-1	13	Thomas	2560

Final League Position: 13

GOALSCORERS

League (55): Thomas 20 (1 pen), Simpson 6, Ludlam 4, Manns 3, Sloan 3, Zelem 3, Allen 2, Lane 2, Williams 2, Wilson 2 (1 pen), Bulmer 1, Cooke 1, Edwards 1, Kinsey 1, Storton 1, own goals 3.
Milk Cup (2): Sloan 1, Thomas 1.
FA Cup (2): Lane 1, Williams 1.
Football League Trophy (8): Thomas 3 (1 pen), Sloan 2, Edwards 1, Simpson 1, own goal 1.

Milk Cup	First Round	Blackpool (h)	1-2
		(a)	1-5
FA Cup	First Round	Northwich V (h)	1-1
		(a)	1-3 (aet)
Football League Trophy		Chesterfield (a)	1-1
		Tranmere R (a)	1-2
		Shrewsbury T (h)	5-0
	Quarter-final	Newport Co (h)	0-0 (aet) (won on penalties)
	Semi-final	Lincoln C (h)	1-3 (aet)

Millington	Bradley	Edwards	Zelem	Lane	Dean	Sloan	Johnson	Simpson	Cooke	Thomas	Storton	Ludlam	Allen	Wilson (L)	Kinsey (L)	Salmon (L)	Needham	Blackwell	Williams	Moffatt	Bulmer	Workman	Harrington	Manns	Referees	Match No.
1	2	3	4	5	6	7	8	9	10	11															D. Scott	1
1	2		5	3	12	7	10*		11	8	4	6	9												K. Redfern	2
1	2		5	3		7	10		11	8	4	6	9												C. Downey	3
1	2*		5	3		7	10	12	8	11	4	6	9												A. Challinor	4
1	2*		5	3		7	10	9		11	4	12		6	8										H. Taylor	5
1		2	5	3*		7	8	9	12	10	4	6		11											J. Bray	6
1		2	5	3*		7	8	9	12	10	4	6		11											A. Hamill	7
1		2	5	3	6	7				9	4	10		11	8										R. Banks	8
1		2	5	3	6	7				9	4	10		11	8										N. Wilson	9
1		2*	5	3	6	7	8	9	11		4	10	12												R. Chadwick	10
	2		5	3	6	7		9	11	8	4	10				1									C. Seel	11
	2		5		6	7		9	11	10	4	8				1	3								K. Walmsley	12
	2		5		6	7			11	9	4	10				1	3	8							L. Shapter	13
	2*		5		6	7		12	11	9	4	10				1	3	8							G. Napthine	14
			5		2	7	8		11	9	4	10				1	3	6							A. Ward	15
		2*	5	3		7	6	11		9	4	10	8			1			12						E. Read	16
	2		5	3		7			8	9	4			10		1	11*	6		12					K. Hackett	17
	2			3		7	6		12	9	4	10	8*	11		1	5								K. Barratt	18
	5		12	3	2		6		8	9	4	10		11		1			7*						D. Allison	19
	5			3	2	7	6		8	9	4	10*		11		1					12				A. Seville	20
	5			8	2	7	6			9	4	10		3		1		11							V. Callow	21
	5			8	2	7	6		12	9	4	10		3		1		11*							G. Courtney	22
	5	6*		4	2	7				9		10		3		1	8		12		11				B. Hill	23
	5			8	2*	7			12	9		10		3		1	6*			4	11				N. Glover	24
	2*		5	3		7	12	8	6	9	4	10		11		1									G. Thomas	25
			5	3		11		10	8	9	4	7		6		1						2			J. Key	26
	2		5	3		7		8	12	9	4	10*		11								6	1		G. Tyson	27
	2		4	3		7	6	9*		10		8		11			5				12		1		A. Saunders	28
	5			4		7	6		10	8		9	12	3					2		11*		1		L. Burden	29
			5	3		7		8		9				11			2	4	6			10	1		N. Midgley	30
	4		5	3		7		8		9		6		11			2	10					1		C. Downey	31
	4		5	3		7		8		9				11			2	10	6				1		D. Civil	32
	4			3		7		8		9		11					2	10		5	6		1		E. Scales	33
	12		5*	3		7		8		9	4						2	6	10		11		1		K. Cooper	34
			5	3		7		10		9	4						2	6	11				1	8	A. Gunn	35
	2*		3	5		6		10		11	4		12				7	9					1	8	T. Mills	36
			5	3		7		8		9	4						2	6	11				1	10	M. Peck	37
			5*	3	12			8		9	4		7				2	6	11				1	10	A. Challinor	38
				3	5	7*		8		9	4						2	6	11		12		1	10	K. Walmsley	39
					3	7	11	8		9	4						2	6	5*		12		1	10	N. Wilson	40
	6		5	3	2	7				9	4		8					11					1	10	T. Holbrook	41
	6		5	3	2	7		9*			4		8					11			12		1	10	D. Richardson	42
			5	3		7				9	4		8					6		2	11		1	10	B. Newsome	43
	12		5	3*		7				9	4		8					6		2	11		1	10	S. Bates	44
	12			3		7				9	4		8				5	6		2	11		1*	10	J. Moules	45
1	12		5	3*		7				9	4		8					6		2	11			10	D. Allison	46
11	27	8	34	41	19	44	18	24	16	44	37	28	12	21	3	16	21	23	10	6	9	3	19	12		
	+ 4s		+ 1s		+ 2s		+ 1s	+ 2s	+ 6s			+ 1s	+ 3s						+ 2s	+ 1s	+ 5s					

FOOTBALL LEAGUE RECORD

1931 Elected Division 3(N); 1958–75 Division 4; 1975–82 Division 3; 1982– Division 4.

HONOURS

Football League: Division 3 best season: 5th; 1977–78; Division 3(N) – Runners-up 1935–36. *FA Cup* best season: 5th rd, 1976–77, 1979–80. *Football League Cup:* Semi-final 1974–75. *Welsh Cup:* Winners 1908, 1933, 1947. *Debenhams Cup:* Winners 1977.

COLOURS

Royal blue shirts with white stripes, royal blue shorts with red and white trim, white stockings with red and blue ringed top. **Change colours:** All yellow.

CHESTER

Players Names Ht, Wt, D.o.B.	Birthplace Transfer Fee	Clubs	Appearances F.L. A & S	 F.L.C. A & S	 F.A.C. A & S	Goals F.L.	 F.L.C.	 F.A.C.
Goalkeeper								
Phil Harrington (WY)	Bangor	Chester	29					
5 10, 11 4,								
Defenders								
Martin Lane	Altrincham	Manchester U						
5 9, 11 4, 12.4.61	F/T	Chester	41	2	2	2		1
Noel Bradley*	Manchester	Manchester C.						
5 11½, 11 4, 14.12. 57	—	Bury (loan)	9					
	F/T	Bury	15+3	1		1		
	F/T	Chester	27+4	2	2			
Trevor Storton	Keighley	Tranmere R.	111+7	5	11	9		2
6 1, 12 2, 26.11.49	£25,000	Liverpool	5	4	1			
	£20,000	Chester	378	26	23	16	1	1
Paul Needham*	Buxton	Chester (A)	55+2	2	1	1		
5 10, 11 4, 15.6.61								
Peter Zelem	Manchester	Chester (A)	67+5	2	3	4		
6 0, 11 6, 13.2. 62								
Gregory Moffatt*	Liverpool	Chester (A)	7+1					
5 11, 10 8,								
Mark Dean*	Chester	Chester (A)	23+2	1				
5 9, 11 2,								
Nigel Edwards* (WU23)	Wrexham	Blackburn R. (AM)						
5 11, 12 0, 31.12.50	—	Chester	281+9	21+1	16+2	15	1	2
	£5000	Aldershot	137	9	7+1	6		
	F/T	Chester	8	1			1	
Midfield								
Paul Blackwell	Mancot	Chester	44+2		1+1			
5 10, 11 5,								
Paul Johnson*	Stoke	Stoke C. (A)	51+5					
5 7, 11 12, 19.9.55	F/T	Chester	18+1	2	1			
Mike Williams (WY)		Chester (A)	12+2		+1	2		1
5 10								
Tom Sloan* (NI)	Ballymena	Ballymena						
5 6, 10 0, 10.7.59	£25,000	Manchester U	4+7					
	F/T	Chester	44	2	2	3	1	
Forwards								
Terry Cooke	Wrexham	Chester (A)	37+12	2+1	1	11		
5 10, 10 8, 21.2.62								
Gary Simpson*	Chesterfield	Chesterfield (A)	36+7	2	4+2	8		1
6 0, 13 2, 10.6.59	£6000	Chester	57+6	4	3	18		
John Allen	Mancot	Chester (A)	27+10		1	2		
6 0, 12 1,								
John Thomas	Wednesbury							
5 8, 11 3, 5.8.58		Everton						
	—	Tranmere R. (loan)	10+1			2		
	—	Halifax T. (loan)	5					
	F/T	Bolton W.	18+4	1	2	6	1	
	F/T	Chester	44	2		20	1	
Paul Manns	Great Haywood	Cardiff C. (N/C)						
5 6, 10 7, 15.4.61	F/T	Notts Co.	5+2			1		
	F/T	Chester	12			3		
Apprentice								
Peter Bulmer		Chester (A)	9+5			1		
5 8½								

Commercial Manager: Mr. K. Dove (Tel. 378162)
Club Coach:
Club Captain 1982–83:
Supporters Player of the Season 1982–83: John Thomas
Chief Scout:
Physiotherapist: Nil
Club Statistician:
Association of Football Statisticians Club Adviser to Yearbook: D. Orme.

Players released since May 1982:
David Burns, D. (Scarborough); Peter Henderson, F. (Telford U.); Bryn Jones, F. (Scarborough); Mike Keen, M. (retired); Alan Oakes, D. (retired); Paul Raynor, D. (Oswestry); Peter Sutcliffe, F. (Bangor C.); Jimmy Walker, D. (retired); Glen Millington, G. (retired); John Cottam, D. (Scarborough); Steve Ludlam, M. (Ilves); Ian Workman, M.. (N/C—Southport).

CHESTERFIELD Division 4

Back row (left to right): Russell Athersych, John Turner, John Partridge, Paul Gregory, Steve Robinson. *Standing:* John Short (Physio), Tony Henson, Phil Walker, Gary Bellamy, Bill Green (Player-Coach-Capt), Gary Pollard, Martin Henderson, Bill Dearden (Coach). *Seated:* John Stirk, Micky Carroll, Danny Wilson, Frank Barlow (Manager), Bob Pepper (Secretary), Andy Kowalski (Club Captain), David Windridge, Shaun O'Neill. *Front row:* Apprentices David Wood, Neil Brown, Phil Brown, Andy Higginbottom.

President: His Grace the Duke of Devonshire MC, DL, JP.

Chairman: E. I. Gaunt. ***Vice-Chairman:*** A. Bates.

Directors: F. Tuckey, E. Brocklehurst, P. C. J. T. Kirkman OBE, J. Leedham.

Team Manager: John Duncan. ***Secretary:*** R. F. Pepper.

Year Formed: 1866. ***Turned Professional:*** 1891. ***Ltd Co.:*** 1871.

Club Nickname: 'Blues' or 'Spireites'.

Previous Managers since 1946: Bob Brocklebank, Bob Marshall, Ted Davison, Duggie Livingstone, Tony McShane, Jimmy McGuigan, Joe Shaw, Arthur Cox (8).

Recreation Ground, Chesterfield S40 4SX. Telephone Chesterfield (0246) 32318. ***Ground capacity:*** 19,750 (12,000 covered). ***Record attendance:*** 30,968 v Newcastle U, Division 2, 7 April, 1939. ***Record receipts:*** £26,640 v Barnsley, Division 3, 26 Dec, 1980. ***Pitch measurements:*** 114yd×72yd.

Directions to Ground: Chesterfield railway station is one mile from the ground, via Corporation St, Holywell St, to Saltergate.

Match tickets: Seats in the Centre and Wing Stands may be booked in advance.

Car parking: Street parking permitted around the ground. Also car parks in Saltergate within ½ mile of the ground.

Entertainments/catering facilities: A social club (members only) is sited on the ground at the Saltergate entrance. Refreshment bars around the ground.

Club shop: A wide range of souvenirs available as well as programmes and handbooks.

Programme Shop: 56 St Margaret's Drive, Chesterfield.

Address of the Club Shop or Boutique: 132 Saltergate, Chesterfield.

Note: Full club statistical records are on pages 416–455.

CHESTERFIELD 1982–83 LEAGUE RECORD

Match No.	Date	Venue	Opponents	Result		H/T Score	Lg. Pos.	Goalscorers	Attendance
1	Aug 28	H	Orient	L	1-2	0-0	—	Wilson	2587
2	Sept 4	A	Newport Co	L	0-1	0-0	23		3464
3	6	A	Southend U	L	0-2	0-1	—		2836
4	11	H	Bristol R	D	0-0	0-0	24		1990
5	18	A	Reading	D	0-0	0-0	24		1927
6	25	H	Wigan Ath	W	2-0	0-0	20	Windridge, Kowalski	2825
7	28	H	Oxford U	L	1-2	1-0	—	Pollard	2618
8	Oct 2	A	Exeter C	W	3-2	0-2	19	Walker 2, Henderson	2389
9	9	A	Brentford	L	2-4	1-1	22	Wilson 2 (1 pen)	5706
10	16	H	Bradford C	W	3-0	2-0	16	Walker, Windridge 2	3850
11	19	A	Walsall	W	1-0	0-0	—	Windridge	2462
12	23	H	Plymouth Arg	L	1-2	0-2	16	Walker	3149
13	30	A	Doncaster R	D	0-0	0-0	16		4065
14	Nov 2	H	Gillingham	L	1-2	1-1	—	Windridge	2320
15	6	H	Lincoln C	L	1-2	0-1	18	Walker	4265
16	13	A	Preston NE	D	1-1	0-1	18	Wilson	3574
17	Dec 4	H	AFC Bournemouth	D	0-0	0-0	19		2226
18	7	A	Cardiff C	D	1-1	0-1	—	Henderson	3813
19	18	H	Portsmouth	L	0-1	0-0	19		2440
20	27	A	Huddersfield T	L	1-3	0-1	20	Henderson	11,603
21	28	H	Sheffield U	W	3-1	2-0	20	Henderson 2, Wilson	11,458
22	Jan 1	A	Millwall	D	1-1	1-0	19	Henderson	3215
23	3	H	Wrexham	W	5-1	3-0	18	Henderson 2, Wilson 2, Windridge	2805
24	15	A	Orient	L	0-2	0-0	19		2642
25	22	H	Reading	D	0-0	0-0	19		2703
26	29	A	Bristol R	L	0-3	0-2	22		6066
27	Feb 1	H	Newport Co	W	3-1	1-1	—	Windridge, Plummer (pen), Henderson	1645
28	5	A	Wigan Ath	D	2-2	2-1	19	Henderson L., Methven (og)	3009
29	15	A	Gillingham	L	1-3	1-1		Plummer	3187
30	19	H	Brentford	W	2-1	0-1	19	Plummer 2 (2 pens)	2291
31	26	A	Bradford C	L	0-1	0-0	21		4033
32	Mar 1	H	Walsall	D	0-0	0-0	—		2216
33	5	A	Plymouth Arg	L	0-2	0-0	21		4466
34	12	H	Doncaster R	D	3-3	0-3	21	Green, Plummer 2 (1 pen)	2875
35	15	H	Southend U	L	0-2	0-2	—		1970
36	19	A	Lincoln C	L	0-2	0-2	21		4454
37	26	H	Preston NE	D	1-1	0-0	21	Windridge	2332
38	Apr 2	A	Sheffield U	L	1-3	1-1	22	Owen	12,441
39	4	H	Huddersfield T	L	0-1	0-1	—		6729
40	9	A	AFC Bournemouth	L	1-2	1-1	24	Plummer	5227
41	16	H	Exeter C	L	1-3	0-2	24	Owen	1788
42	23	A	Portsmouth	L	0-4	0-1	24		13,003
43	30	H	Cardiff C	L	0-1	0-0	24		2799
44	May 2	A	Wrexham	D	0-0	0-0	24		2047
45	7	A	Oxford U	L	0-1	0-1	24		3363
46	14	H	Millwall	L	0-1	0-0	24		4314

Final League Position: 24

GOALSCORERS

League (43): Henderson 10, Windridge 8, Plummer 7 (4 pens), Wilson 7 (1 pen), Walker 5, Owen 2, Green 1, Kowalski 1, Pollard 1, own goal 1.
Milk Cup (2): Dawson 1, Windridge 1.
FA Cup (3): Walker 3.
Football League Trophy (3): Henson 1, Walker 1, Wilson 1 (pen).

Milk Cup	First Round	Hartlepool U (h)	2-1
		(a)	0-2 (aet)
FA Cup	First Round	Peterborough U (h)	2-2
		(a)	1-2
Football League Trophy		Chester (h)	1-1
		Shrewsbury T (h)	1-0
		Tranmere R (a)	1-1

Turner	Bellamy	Partridge	Wilson	Green	Henson	Windridge	Henderson	Dawson	Robinson	Carroll	Kowalski	O'Neill	Pollard	Walker	Stirk	Athersych	Kinsey (L)	Gregory	Plummer	Gooding	Kendall	Ivey	Thrower (L)	Ross (L)	Owen (L)	Higginbottom	Brown	*Referees*
1	2	3	4	5	6	7	8	9	10	11																		T. Holbrook
1	2	3	4	5	6	11	8	9	7		10																	M. Dimblebee
1	2	3	4	5	6	11	8	9	7*		10	12																T. Bune
1	2	3	4	5	6	11*	8	9	7		10	12																A. Robinson
1	2	3	4	5	9*	12	8			11	10		6	7														J. Deakin
1	2	3*	4	5	9	11	8	12			10		6	7														D. Brazier
1	2		4	5	9	11	8	12			10	3*	6	7														N. Ashley
1	2	3	4	5		11*	8	12			10		6	7	9													J. Martin
1	2	3*	4	5	6	11	8	12			10			9	7													D. Hedges
1	2		4	5	6	11	8				10	3		9	7													A. Seville
1	2		4	5	6	11	8				10	3		9	7													E. Scales
1	2		4	5	6	11	8	12			10	3*		9	7													R. Guy
1	2		4	5	6	11		8			10	3*	7	9		12												D. Scott
1	2		4	5	6	11	9	8			10		3*		7	12												A. Hamill
1	2		4	5	6	11		12			10	3*		9	7		8											C. Newsome
1	2		4	5	6	11					10	3		9	7		8											G. Tyson
			4	5	6	11	9		12		10	3*	2		7		8	1										J. Lovatt
	2		4	5	6	11	8		7		10		3	9				1										M. James
		3	4	5	6	11	8				10		2*	9	12			1	7									R. Bridges
	2	3	4	5			9				10		6					1	7	8	11							J. Worrall
	2	3	4	5		12	9				10		6					1	7	8*	11							T. Fitzharris
	2	3	4	5		8	9				10		6					1	7		11							A. Gunn
	2	3	4	5		8	9				10		6					1	7		11							J. Hunting
	2	3*	4	5		8	9				10		6					1	7		11	12						R. Milford
	2	3		5		8	9				10		6*					1	7	4	11	12						G. Courtney
	2	3		5		8	9				10		6					1	7	4	11							K. Salmon
	2	3		5		8	9				10		6					1	7	4*	11	12						P. Tyldesley
	2	3		5	4	8	9				10		6					1	7		11							C. Seel
	2	3		5*	4	8	9				10		6					1	7			12	11					J. Moules
	2	3		5	4	8	9				10	6						1	7*			12	11					N. Midgley
1	2	3		5*	4	8	9				10	6							7		11	12						A. Robinson
1	2	3		5		8*	9				10	6							7		11		4					M. Owen
1	5*	3				8	9				10	6			2	12			7		11		4*					B. Stevens
1	2	12		5		11	9				10*	3	6			8			7		4							M. Heath
1	2	3		5			9*			11		10	6		12	8			7		4							K. Barratt
1	2			5		11	9					3	6			8			7		4			10				A. Grey
1		3		5		11	9					2	6						7		4			10	8			G. Napthine
1		3		5		11	9				4	2	6						7					10	8			F. Roberts
1	5	3				11	9				4	2	6						7					10	8			D. Lloyd
1	6	12		5		11					4		3						7	9*	2			10	8			S. Bates
1	6			5		11					4		3*			12			7	9	2			10	8			A. Banks
1	6	12		5		11	10*				4		3						7	9	2				8			B. Daniels
1	6	8		5		11*	10				4		3			12			7	9	2							A. Saunders
1	6	8		5		11*					4		3			10			7	9	2					12		J. Deakin
1	6	8		5			11				4		3			10*			7	9	2					12		K. Cooper
1	6	8		5			11*				4		3		2				7	9						10	12	J. Bray
32	42	31	24	44	22	40	40	6	5	3	42	18	32	13	11	5	3	14	28	12	22	0	4	6	6	1	0	
		+ 3s				+ 2s		+ 6s	+ 1s			+ 2s			+ 2s	+ 5s						+ 6s				+ 2s	+ 1s	

FOOTBALL LEAGUE RECORD

1899 Elected to Division 2; 1909 failed re-election; 1921–31 Division 3(N); 1931–33 Division 2; 1933–36 Division 3(N); 1936–51 Division 2; 1951–58 Division 3(N); 1958–61 Division 3; 1961–70 Division 4; 1970–83 Division 3; 1983– Division 4.

HONOURS

Football League: Division 2 best season: 4th, 1946–47; Division 3(N) – Champions 1930–31, 1935–36; Runners-up 1933–34; Division 4 – Champions 1969–70. *FA Cup* best season: 5th rd, 1932–33, 1937–38, 1949–50. *Football League Cup* best season: 4th rd, 1964–65. *Anglo-Scottish Cup:* Winners 1980–81.

COLOURS

Royal blue shirts with white pin stripe, white shorts with blue side stripes and white stockings.
Change colours: Red shirt with white pin stripe, black shorts and stockings.

CHESTERFIELD

Players Names Ht, Wt, D.o.B.	Birthplace Transfer Fee	Clubs	Appearances F.L. A & S	 F.L.C. A & S	 F.A.C. A & S	Goals F.L.	 F.L.C.	 F.A.C.
Goalkeepers								
Paul Gregory	Sheffield	Chesterfield (A)	17		1			
5 10, 11 7, 26.7.61								
John Turner*	Peterlee	Derby Co (A)						
5 11, 12 8, 23.12.54	—	Doncaster R (loan)	4					
	—	Huddersfield T (loan)	1					
		Reading	31	5				
	£3000	Torquay U	76	6	6			
	£30,000	Chesterfield	132	8	9			
Defenders								
Shaun O'Neill*	Belfast	Leeds U (A)						
5 9, 12 2, 24.2.52	F/T	Chesterfield	319+5	22+1	17	3		
Bill Green*	Newcastle	Hartlepool U	128+3			9		
6 3, 12 8, 22.12.50	£15,000	Carlisle U	119	8	8	4		
	£90,000	West Ham U	35	3	2	1		
	£50,000	Peterborough U	30	8				
	£40,000	Chesterfield	160	11	12	5	1	2
John Stirk*	Consett	Ipswich T (A)	6	1				
5 6, 11 6, 5.9.55	£33,000	Watford	46	11	3			
	£40,000	Chesterfield	54+2		4			
Gary Bellamy	Worksop	Chesterfield (A)	67+3	4	1			
6 1¾, 11 5, 4.7.62								
John Partridge	Chesterfield	Chesterfield (a)	34+4	2				
5 11, 11 8, 14.9.62								
Gary Pollard*	Staveley	Chesterfield	83+4	4+1	9	1		
6 1, 11 10, 30.12.59								
Steve Kendal	Birtley	Nottingham F (A)	1					
	P/E	Chesterfield	22					
Midfield								
Calvin Plummer	Nottingham	Nottingham F (A)	10+2	+1		2		
0 0, 00 0, 14.2.63	P/E	Chesterfield	28			7		
Andy Higginbottom		Chesterfield (A)	1+2					
Tony Henson*	Dronfield	Alfreton T						
5 10, 11 7,	£5000	Chesterfield	26+2	2				
Andy Kowalski*	Mansfield	Worksop T						
5 10, 11 0, 26.2.53	—	Chesterfield	354+11	23+2	18+1	30	5	
Forwards								
Dave Windridge*	Atherstone	Sheffield U						
5 9, 11 0, 7.12.61	F/T	Chesterfield	66+12	1+1	3+1	14	1	
Ross Athersych*	Sheffield	Chesterfield (A)	7+7		1			
5 9, 11 4, 21.9.62								
Martin Henderson	Kirkcaldy	Glasgow R						
6 0, 12 9, 3.5.56	£30,000	Leicester C	79+12	3+1	5	12		4
	£70,000	Chesterfield	84	3	3	23		1
Steve Robinson*	Sheffield	Chesterfield (A)	8+1					
5 10, 10 10,								
Mick Gooding	Newcastle	Bishop Auckland						
5 7½, 10 7, 16.2.59	P/E	Rotherham U	90+15	9	3	9	1	
	P/E	Chesterfield	12					
Non-contract players								
Paul Ivey	Westminster	Birmingham C (A)	4+3					
5 11, 10 8, 1.4.61	F/T	Karlskrona						
	F/T	Chesterfield	+6					
Apprentices								
Philip Brown		Chesterfield (A)	+1					

Lottery Manager: Joyce Senior (Tel. Chesterfield 31535)
Advertising Executive: Jack Gee
Club Coach: Bill Dearden
Supporters Player of the Season 1982–83: Not known yet
Physiotherapist: John Short
Club Captain 1982–83: Andy Kowalski
Chief Scout: Harold Roberts
Player-Coach (Team Captain): Bill Green
Association of Football Statisticians Club Adviser to Yearbook: R. West

Players released since May 1982: Richard Denby, M. (retired); Geoff Salmons, M. (Gainsborough T); David Wood, D. (N/K); Mick Carroll, F. (N/K); Richard Dawson, F. (Scarborough).

COLCHESTER UNITED Division 4

Back row (left to right):
Kevin Beattie
Phil Coleman
Roy McDonough
Alec Chamberlain
Mike Walker
Dennis Longhorn
Steve Wignall
John Lyons
Middle row:
Allan Hunter (Player Manager)
Kevin Bremner
Ian Allinson
Andy Gooding
Tony Adcock
Cyril Lea (Coach)
Charlie Simpson (Physiotherapist)
Front row:
Mick Packer
Roger Osborne
Micky Cook
Steve Leslie
Wayne Ward
Perry Groves

Patron: A. Buck QC, MP.

Chairman: M. J. Cadman. ***Vice-Chairman:*** H. R. Piper.

Directors: N. F. Fitch, R. F. West, J. W. Rippingale.

Caretaker Manager: Cyril Lea. ***Secretary:*** Martin R. Bennet.

Year Formed: 1937. ***Turned Professional:*** 1937. ***Ltd Co.:*** 1937.

Club Nickname: 'The U's'.

Previous Managers since 1946: Ted Fenton, Jimmy Allen, Jack Butler, Benny Fenton, Neil Franklin, Dick Graham, Jim Smith, Bobby Roberts, Allan Hunter (9).

Layer Rd Ground, Colchester. Telephone (0206) 574042. ***Telegraphic address:*** 'United Colchester'. ***Ground capacity:*** 15,000. ***Record attendance:*** 19,072 v Reading, FA Cup 1st rd, 27 Nov, 1948. ***Record receipts:*** £20,265 v Manchester U, FA Cup 5th rd, 20 Feb, 1979. ***Pitch measurements:*** 110yd×71yd.

Directions to Ground: Buses from Osborne Street in Colchester, which is about 2 miles from the railway station.

Match tickets: Stand seats can be booked two weeks in advance (Ticket Office tel: Colchester 72202 or 74042.) All bookings will be accepted and held, *provided* the tickets are *paid for* and *collected* at least 48 hours before kick-off. During the 48 hours prior to the game, tickets will be available *only* to cash customers at the ground. This method should not affect people who live outside the immediate area of Layer Road, for postal applications with the appropriate remittance will still be accepted up to 72 hours before kick-off provided that such applications are accompanied by a stamped (first class) addressed envelope.

Car parking: Parking facilities in Butt Road and Layer Road, approximately 150 yards past the ground on the south side of Colchester. Free parking in Army Barracks (150 yards).

Entertainments/catering facilities: Refreshment points on the ground.

Club shop: Sells all types of souvenirs; mailing list on request.

Handbooks/programmes: Back numbers of CUFC programmes can be ordered from the club shop.

Note: Full club statistical records are on pages 416–455.

COLCHESTER UNITED 1982–83 LEAGUE RECORD

Match No.	Date	Venue	Opponents	Result		H/T Score	Lg. Pos.	Goalscorers	Attendance
1	Aug 28	H	Halifax T	W	1-0	0-0	—	McDonough	2610
2	Sept 4	A	Hereford U	D	0-0	0-0	8		2465
3	6	A	Port Vale	D	0-0	0-0	—		2877
4	10	H	Rochdale	W	4-1	2-1	—	Wignall, Allinson (pen), Lyons 2	2638
5	17	A	Crewe Alex	W	1-0	1-0	1	Lyons	2539
6	25	H	Blackpool	W	4-1	2-1	1	Lyons, Leslie, Groves, Allinson	2918
7	28	H	Hull C	D	0-0	0-0	—		2071
8	Oct 2	A	Scunthorpe U	L	1-2	0-1	5	Osborne	2616
9	10	A	Swindon T	L	0-3	0-2	—		4473
10	15	H	Darlington	D	2-2	1-0	—	Allinson, McDonough	2547
11	19	A	Northampton T	L	1-2	0-0	—	Allinson	1955
12	30	A	Bury	L	0-1	0-0	13		2653
13	Nov 2	H	Wimbledon	W	3-0	1-0	—	Allinson, McDonough 2	2219
14	5	H	Mansfield T	W	2-0	2-0	—	Lyons 2	2009
15	9	H	Chester	W	1-0	0-0	—	Wignall	2362
16	13	A	Tranmere R	W	4-2	3-1	7	McDonough, Allinson 2, Adcock	1410
17	27	A	Bristol C	W	2-0	1-0	—	Bremner, Allinson	4310
18	Dec 3	H	York C	D	0-0	0-0	—		2204
19	11	A	Hull C	L	0-3	0-0	7		4323
20	17	H	Stockport Co	W	3-0	1-0	—	Allinson 2, McDonough	1625
21	27	A	Peterborough U	L	1-2	1-1	7	Bremner	4235
22	28	H	Aldershot	D	0-0	0-0	7		2463
23	Jan 1	A	Torquay U	L	0-2	0-1	8		2758
24	3	H	Hartlepool U	W	4-1	3-1	7	Allinson, Adcock 2, Wignall	2249
25	7	H	Hereford U	W	3-2	2-1	—	Allinson 2 (1 pen), Adcock	2236
26	14	A	Halifax T	L	0-4	0-2	—		1862
27	21	H	Crewe Alex	W	4-3	3-1	—	Adcock 3, Allinson (pen)	2221
28	Feb 5	A	Blackpool	W	2-1	0-0	6	Adcock, Hull	1747
29	15	A	Wimbledon	L	1-2	1-0		Adcock	1753
30	18	H	Swindon T	W	1-0	0-0	—	Cook	2386
31	26	A	Darlington	W	3-1	2-0	5	Adcock 2, McDonough	1089
32	Mar 1	H	Northampton T	W	3-1	1-1	—	Allinson (pen), Hull, Adcock	2501
33	5	A	Chester	D	1-1	0-0	5	Adcock	1136
34	12	H	Bury	W	2-1	2-0	5	Allinson, Bowen	3357
35	19	A	Mansfield T	D	1-1	0-0	5	Hull	2371
36	25	H	Tranmere R	D	3-3	1-2	—	Osborne, Bowen, Adcock	2547
37	Apr 1	H	Peterborough U	W	1-0	1-0	—	Allinson	3759
38	2	A	Aldershot	W	1-0	1-0	—	Hull	1670
39	9	A	York C	L	0-3	0-1	5		2538
40	12	H	Port Vale	L	1-2	1-1	—	Adcock	3275
41	15	H	Scunthorpe U	W	5-1	2-1	—	Adcock 2, Allinson 2 (1 pen), Bowen	3155
42	22	A	Stockport Co	L	0-3	0-1	—		1733
43	26	A	Rochdale	L	1-2	0-2	—	Allinson	1219
44	29	H	Bristol C	W	3-1	2-1	—	Allinson (pen), Bowen, McDonough	2196
45	May 2	A	Hartlepool U	W	4-1	1-0	5	Allinson, Coleman 2, Groves	804
46	13	H	Torquay U	W	1-0	0-0	—	Wignall	2181

Final League Position: 6

GOALSCORERS

League (75): Allinson 22 (6 pens), Adcock 17, McDonough 8, Lyons 6, Bowen 4, Hull 4, Wignall 4, Bremner 2, Coleman 2, Groves 2, Osborne 2, Cook 1, Leslie 1.
Milk Cup (5): Allinson 2 (1 pen), Groves 1, Lyons 1, Wignall 1.
FA Cup (0).
Football League Trophy (6): Lyons 3, Allinson 2, Lyons 1.

Milk Cup	First Round	Aldershot (h)	2-0
		(a)	1-0
	Second Round	Southampton (h)	0-0
		(a)	2-4

FA Cup	First Round	Torquay U (h)	0-2
Football League Trophy		Southend U (h)	3-1
		Watford (a)	1-2
		Orient (a)	2-0

Walker	Cook	Coleman	Groves	Wignall	Hunter	Allinson	Osborne	Lyons	McDonough	Leslie	Bremner	Beattie	Adcock	Longhorn	Ward	Hull	Packer	Keith	Chamberlain	Linford (L)	Bowen (L)	Referees	Match No.
1	2	3	4	5	6	7	8	9	10*	11	12											R. Lewis	1
1	2	3	4	5	6	7	8	9	10	11												M. Robinson	2
1	2	3	4	5	6	7	8	9	10	11												V. Callow	3
1	2	3	4	5	6	7	8	9	10*	11	12											D. Brazier	4
1	2	3	4	5	6	7	8	9	10*	11	12											D. Allison	5
1	2	3	4	5	6*	7	8	9		11	10	12										I. Borrett	6
1	2	3	4*	5	6	7	8	9	12	11	10											C. Downey	7
1	2	3	4	5	6	7	8	9	12	11*	10											A. Robinson	8
1	2	4		5	12	7*	8	9	10	11		6	4									L. Burden	9
1	2	3		5		7	8	9	10	11		6*	4	12								D. Letts	10
1	2	3		5	4	7	8	9	10	11		6										T. Spencer	11
1	2	5		3	4	9	7	10	11	8				6								G. Tyson	12
1	2	3		5	6	7	8	9	10	11				4								H. Taylor	13
1	2	3		5	6	7	8	9	10*	11	12			4								J. Martin	14
1	2	3		5	6	7	8	9	10	11*	12			4								A. Ward	15
1	2	3		5	6	7	8		9*	11	10		12	4								D. Lloyd	16
1		3*		5	6	7	8		9	11	10		12	4	2							T. Bune	17
1	2			5	6	7	8		9	11	10			4	3							A. Gunn	18
1	2			5	6	7	8		9	11*	10		12	4	3							D. Hutchinson	19
1	2					7	8		9	11	10			4	3	6	5					A. Grey	20
1	2					7	8		9	11	10			4	3	6	5					J. Key	21
1	2			5		7	8		9		10		12	4	3	11*	6					J. Deakin	22
1	2			5		7	8		9				10		3	11	4	6				A. Glasson	23
	2		12	5		7	8		9				10	4*	3	11		6	1			M. James	24
	2			5		7	8		9				10	4	3	11		6	1			D. Reeves	25
	2	6		5		7	8						10	4	3	11			1	9		R. Guy	26
1		6		5		7	8						10	4	2	11		3		9		K. Salmon	27
1		6		5		7	8		4				10		3	11	2			9		P. Tyldesley	28
1	2	6		5		7	8*		4				11	3			9						29
1	2	6		5		7	8*		4				10	3		11				9		L. Shapter	30
1	2	6		5		7	8		4				10*	3		11				9		A. Challinor	31
1	2	6		5		7			4	8*			10	3		11				9		M. Taylor	32
1	2	6		5		7	8*		4	12			10	3	9	11						K. Cooper	33
1	2	6		5		7	8		4				10	3		11					9	M. Dimblebee	34
1	2	6	12	5		7*	8		4				10	3		11					9	R. Bridges	35
1	2	6		5		7	8*		4	12			10	3		11					9	E. Scales	36
1	2	6	12	5		7	8		4				10*	3		11					9	R. Lewis	37
1	2	6		5		7*	8		4	12			10	3		11					9	M. Robinson	38
1	2	6	12	5		7	8		4				10	3*		11					9	R. Nixon	39
1	2	6	12	5		7	8						10	3		11	4				9	D. Hedges	40
1	2	6		5		7	8			4			10			11	3				9	I. Borrett	41
1	2	6	12	5		7	8		3				10	4*		11					9	H. Wilson	42
1	2	6	12	5		7	8		4				10*			11	3				9	M. Peck	43
1	2*	6		5		7	8		12	4			10			11	3				9	T. Ward	44
1		6	12	5		7	8		2	4			10			11*	3				9	D. Shaw	45
			12	5		7	8		6	4			10		2	11*	3		1		9	A. Gunn	46
42	41	37	8	44	17	46	45	15	38	26	10	3	26	27	14	27	12	4	4	7	13		
			+ 9s		+ 1s				+ 3s	+ 3s	+ 5s	+ 1s	+ 4s	+ 1s									

FOOTBALL LEAGUE RECORD

1950 Elected to Division 3(S); 1958–61 Division 3; 1961–62 Division 4; 1962–65 Division 3; 1965–66 Division 4; 1966–68 Division 3; 1968–74 Division 4; 1974–76 Division 3; 1976–77 Division 4; 1977–81 Division 3; 1981– Division 4.

HONOURS

Football League: Division 3(S) best season: 3rd, 1956–57; Division 4 – Runners-up 1961–62. *FA Cup* best season: 1970–71, 6th rd (record for a Fourth Division club shared with Oxford United and Bradford City). *Football League Cup:* best season 5th rd 1974–75.

COLOURS

Blue and white vertical stripes, blue shorts, white stockings. **Change colours:** Red shirts, black shorts and stockings.

COLCHESTER UNITED

Players Names Ht, Wt, D.o.B.	Birthplace Transfer Fee	Clubs	Appearances F.L. A & S	 F.L.C. A & S	 F.A.C. A & S	Goals F.L.	 F.L.C.	 F.A.C.
Goalkeepers								
Mike Walker (WU23)	Colwyn Bay	Reading						
6 1, 13 2, 28.11.45	F/T	Shrewsbury T	6					
		York C	60	1	7			
		Watford	137	8	14			
		Charlton Ath (loan)	1					
	£4000	Colchester U	451	34	35			
Alec Chamberlain								
6 2, 11 11,		Ipswich T						
	F/T	Colchester U	4					
Defenders								
Mike Cook	Enfield	Orient (AM)						
5 7, 10 11, 9.4.51	—	Colchester U	573 + 4	32	43	19	1	1
Mike Packer*	London	Watford (A)	57 + 10	1	6 + 2	2		
5 10, 11 0, 20.4.50	—	Crewe Alex (loan)	12					
	F/T	Colchester U	237 + 7	21	27 + 1	20		3
Steve Wignall	Liverpool	Liverpool (AM)						
5 11, 11 11, 17.9.54	—	Doncaster R	127 + 3	6	8	1		
	£15,000	Colchester U	243 + 2	14	23	14	1	3
Phil Coleman	Woolwich	Millwall (A)	23 + 13		2	1		
5 11, 11 9, 8.9.60	£15,000	Colchester U	75 + 3	9	6	6		
Allan Hunter (NI)	Sion Mills	Coleraine						
6 0, 12 8, 30.6.46		Oldham Ath	83	5	1	1		
	£30,000	Blackburn R	84	5	2	1		
	£60,000 + player	Ipswich T	280	17	26	8	2	
	F/T	Colchester U	18 + 1	3	1			
Wayne Ward*		Colchester U (A)	17 + 2	1	1			
Midfield								
Steve Leslie (EY)	Brentwood	Colchester U	386 + 21	28 + 1	28 + 2	39	4	3
5 10, 11 0, 4.9.52								
Roger Osborne	Otley	Ipswich T	109 + 15	2 + 1	8 + 4	9		1
5 9, 10 11, 9.3.50	£25,000	Colchester U	95 + 1	8	6	7		
Perry Groves		Colchester U (A)	17 + 9	1		2	1	
Dennis Longhorn*	Southampton	Bournemouth (A)	23 + 7	1	4	1		1
5 11, 11 0, 12.9.50		Mansfield T	93 + 3	4	5	5	1	
	£49,000	Sunderland	35 + 5	1	2	3		
	£10,000 + player	Sheffield U	34 + 2		2	1		
	F/T	Aldershot	46 + 7	3 + 1	2 + 1	3		
	F/T	Colchester U	62 + 9	3 + 1	2			
John Taylor		Colchester U						
Forwards								
Ian Allinson	Hitchin	Colchester U (A)	291 + 17	22 + 1	25 + 1	69	6	5
5 10, 11 0, 1.10.57								
Roy McDonough*	Solihull	Birmingham (A)	2			1		
6 1, 11 11, 16.10.58	£15,000	Walsall	76 + 6	4	5	15	1	
	£15,000	Chelsea						
	£15,000	Colchester U	89 + 4	9	6	24	2	
Tony Adcock	Bethnal Green	Colchester U (A)	58 + 13	5 + 1	2 + 2	22		1
5 10, 10 8, 27.3.63								
Keith Bowen (WS)	Northampton	Northampton T (N/C)	61 + 4	8 + 1	2	25	1	
6 1, 11 2, 26.2.58	—	Brentford	42 + 9	+ 1	3 + 2	9		3
	£10,000	Colchester U	13			4		
Craig Oldfield		Colchester U						
Non-contract Players								
Jeff Hull	Rochford	Southend U (A)	10 + 5			1		
5 6, 9 11, 25.8.60	F/T							
	F/T	Colchester U (N/C)	27			4		

Commercial Manager: (Tel.).
Club Coach:
Supporters Player of the Season 1982–83: Mike Walker.
Physiotherapist: C. Simpson.
Club Captain 1982–83: M. Cook.
Chief Scout:
Club Statistician: Hal Mason.
Association of Football Statisticians Club Adviser to Yearbook: M. Middleton.

Players released since May 1982: Russell Cotton, M. (Tiptree); Steve Wright, D. (HJK Helsinki); John Lyons, F. (deceased); Steve Foley, F. (Braintree); Eddie Rowles, F. (Retired); Adrian Keith, D. (N/C–N/K).

COVENTRY CITY Division 1

Back row: Peter Hormantschuk, Steve Whitton, Ian Butterworth, Gary Gillespie, Paul Dyson, Les Sealey, Mark Hateley, Steve Jacobs, Gerry Daly, Derek Hall, Martin Singleton
Front row: Danny Thomas, John Hendrie, Steve Hunt, Gerry Francis, Gary Thomson, Jim Melrose, Brian Roberts, Stephen Mardenborough.

Life President: Derrick H. Robbins.

President: J. R. Mead JP. ***Chairman:*** J. W. Jamieson.

Directors: M. F. French FCA, P. D. H. Robins, T. Sergeant FRCS. ***General Secretary:*** J. D. Dent.

Team Manager: Bobby Gould ***Commercial Manager:*** George Curtis.

Year Formed: 1883. ***Turned Professional:*** 1893. ***Ltd Co.:*** 1907.

Former Names: 1883–98 Singers FC; 1898 Coventry City FC.

Club Nickname: 'Sky Blues'.

Previous Nicknames: 'Wheelmen', 'Blackbirds', 'Citizens', 'Bantams'.

Previous Grounds: Binley Rd 1883–1887, Stoke Rd 1887–1899, Highfield Rd 1899–.

Previous Managers since 1946: Dick Bayliss, Billy Frith, Harry Storer, ack Fairbrother, Charlie Elliott, Jesse Carver, George Raynor, Harry Warren, Billy Frith, Jimmy Hill, Noel Cantwell, Bob Dennison, Gordon Milne, Dave Sexton (12).

Highfield Road Stadium, King Richard Street, Coventry CV2 4FW. Telephone 0203 57171. ***Telex:*** 312132, answer back code COV AFC. ***Telegraphic address:*** 'City Football Coventry'. ***Ground capacity:*** 20,500 all-seater stadium. ***Record attendance:*** 51,455 v Wolverhampton W, Division 2, 29 April, 1967. ***Record receipts:*** £68,029.70 v West Ham U, League Cup semi-final 1st leg, 27 Jan, 1981. ***Pitch measurements:*** 110yd×75yd.

Directions to Ground: Buses from Coventry railway station to town centre (Pool Meadow bus station). Then buses 16, 17 (Hospital), 32 (Potters Green), 33 (Bell Green) to ground. Also taxis from station.

Match tickets: Stand seat tickets can be booked 21 days in advance of any home League fixture. Postal application accepted with remittance by the Ticket Office Manager at Stadium, Highfield Rd, Coventry.

Car parking: Street parking permitted all around the ground. Special coach/car park situated at Gosford Green (200 yards from stadium) on Walsgrave Road (A46).

Club shops: Sited in the main stand and Thackhall St by Pools Office.

Handbooks/programmes: Programmes available through a postal service.

Extra information: Coventry City Supporters' Club under the Sky Blue stand, Thackhall St (Tel: 26268), welcomes visiting supporters on production of the membership card of their own club. They can attend the evening entertainment if they give 48-hours' notice by post to the secretary, Frank Fountaine.

Address of London Branch of Supporters Club: 63 Lynton Ave, London W13 (01-997 4054).

Note: Full club statistical records are on pages 416–455.

COVENTRY CITY 1982–83 LEAGUE RECORD

Match No.	Date	Venue	Opponents	Result	H/T Score	Lg. Pos.	Goalscorers	Attendance
1	Aug 28	H	Southampton	W 1-0	0-0	—	Whitton	10,356
2	31	A	Swansea C	L 1-2	1-0	—	Whitton	11,712
3	Sept 4	A	Ipswich T	D 1-1	0-0	12	Thomas	16,662
4	7	H	Sunderland	W 1-0	1-0	—	Thompson G.	8190
5	11	H	Arsenal	L 0-2	0-1	12		10,245
6	18	A	Birmingham C	L 0-1	0-1	17		11,681
7	25	H	Everton	W 4-2	1-1	10	Melrose 3, Hunt	9319
8	Oct 2	A	Manchester C	L 2-3	1-1	13	Melrose, Thompson G.	25,105
9	9	A	Tottenham H	L 0-4	0-1	18		25,188
10	16	H	Notts Co	W 1-0	0-0	14	Francis	8,320
11	23	A	Watford	D 0-0	0-0	16		17,334
12	30	H	Norwich C	W 2-0	0-0	12	Hateley, Thompson G.	8305
13	Nov 6	H	Aston Villa	D 0-0	0-0	11		12,076
14	13	A	Liverpool	L 0-4	0-2	13		27,870
15	20	H	Luton T	W 4-2	0-0	11	Dyson, Whitton 2, Thompson G.	9644
16	23	H	Ipswich T	D 1-1	0-0	—	Thomas	9550
17	27	A	WBA	L 0-2	0-1	11		12,115
18	Dec 4	H	Brighton & HA	W 2-0	2-0	10	Hunt, Whitton	8054
19	11	A	West Ham U	W 3-0	3-0	8	Hateley, Roberts, Whitton	19,321
20	18	H	Stoke C	W 2-0	1-0	7	Hateley 2	10,065
21	27	A	Nottingham F	L 2-4	2-2	8	Whitton, Melrose	24,487
22	28	H	Manchester U	W 3-0	2-0	5	Hormantschuk, Hateley, Melrose	18,938
23	Jan 1	A	Luton T	W 2-1	2-0	6	Whitton, Melrose	13,072
24	15	A	Southampton	D 1-1	1-1	5	Hateley	17,145
25	22	H	Swansea C	D 0-0	0-0	5		9964
26	Feb 5	A	Sunderland	L 1-2	0-1	7	Whitton	14,356
27	12	H	Manchester C	W 4-0	2-0	5	Melrose, Hately, Gillespie, Hunt	9527
28	26	A	Notts Co	L 1-5	0-2	6	Gillespie	8689
29	Mar 5	H	Watford	L 0-1	0-1	7		11,235
30	12	H	Tottenham H	D 1-1	1-0	7	Hunt (pen)	11,004
31	19	A	Aston Villa	L 0-4	0-3	12		20,509
32	23	A	Norwich C	D 1-1	0-0	—	Whitton	13,994
33	Apr 2	A	Manchester U	L 0-3	0-2	14		36,84
34	5	H	Nottingham F	L 1-2	1-0	—	Whitton	9720
35	9	A	Arsenal	L 1-2	0-2	15	Hateley	19,152
36	12	H	Liverpool	D 0-0	0-0	—		14,821
37	16	H	Birmingham C	L 0-1	0-0	15		10,420
38	23	A	Brighton & HA	L 0-1	0-0	16		14,67
39	30	H	WBA	L 0-1	0-1	16		941
40	May 2	A	Everton	L 0-1	0-0	18		12,97
41	7	A	Stoke C	W 3-0	1-0	17	Hateley, Hendrie, Thomas	12,04
42	14	H	West Ham U	L 2-4	0-1	19	Hendrie, Whitton	10,91

Final League Position: 19

GOALSCORERS

League (48): Whitton 12, Hateley 9, Melrose 8, Hunt 4 (1 pen), Thompson G. 4, Thomas 3, Gillespie 2, Hendrie
Dyson 1, Francis 1, Hormanschuk 1, Roberts 1.
Milk Cup (3): Melrose 2, Hunt 1.
FA Cup (6): Hateley 2, Whitton 2 (1 pen), Roberts 1, Thompson G. 1.

Milk Cup	Second Round	Fulham (a)	2-2
		(h)	0-0 (aet)
	Third Round	Burnley (h)	1-2
FA Cup	Third Round	Worcester C (h)	3-1
	Fourth Round	Norwich C (h)	2-2
		(a)	1-2 (aet)

Suckling	Thomas	Roberts	Jacobs	Dyson	Gillespie	Singleton	Francis	Hateley	Thompson, G.	Whitton	Hormanschuk	Sealey	Thompson, K.	Daly	Melrose	Hall	Hunt	Butterworth	Hendrie	*Referees*	*Match No.*
1	2	3	4	5	6	7	8	9	10	11										N. Midgley	1
1	2	3	4	5	6	7*	8	9	10	11	12									D. Letts	2
	2	3	4	5	6		8	9	10	11	7	1								M. James	3
	2	3	4	5	6	12	8	9*	10	11	7	1								J. Hough	4
	2	3	4	5	6	12	8		10	11	7	1		9*						R. Nixon	5
		3	4	5	6		8			9	2	1	11		7	10				D. Richardson	6
	2	3	4	5	6		8		10	7		1	12		9		11*			J. Key	7
	2	3	4	5	6				10	7		1		8*	9		11	12		K. Hackett	8
	2	3	8	5	6				10	7		1			9		11	4		M. Taylor	9
	2	3	7	5	6		8		10			1			9		11	4		C. Downey	10
	2	3	7	5	6		8		10			1			9		11	4		D. Axcell	11
	2	3	8	5	6			9	10	12		1					11	4	7*	L. Shapter	12
	2	3	12	5	6		8*	9	10			1					11	4	7	J. Deakin	13
1	2	3	8	5	6			9	10	7							11	4		P. Tyldesley	14
	2	3	4	5	6		8*	9	10	7		1					11	12		H. King	15
	2	3	8	5	6			9	10	7		1					11	4		R. Chadwick	16
	2	3	8	5	6			9*	10	7		1			12		11	4		A. Robinson	17
	2	3	8	5	6			9	10	7		1					11	4		M. Heath	18
	2	3	8	5	6			9		7		1			10		11	4		A. Grey	19
	2	3	4	5	6		8*	9		7		1			10		11	12		B. Stevens	20
	2		3*	5	6		8	9		7		1			10		11	4	12	N. Glover	21
	2			5	6		8	9		7	3	1			10		11	4		B. Daniels	22
	2			5	6		8	9		7	3	1			10		11	4		D. Vickers	23
	2			5	6		8	9		7	3	1			10		11	4		J. Moules	24
	2	3		5	6		8	9	12	7		1			10*		11	4		Alan Robinson	25
	2	3		5	6		8	9	12	7		1			10*		11	4		N. Midgley	26
	2	3	8	5	6			9*	10	7		1			12		11	4		M. Dimblebee	27
	2	3		5	6		8	9		7*		1	12		10		11	4		J. Hough	28
	2	3	12	5	6		8	9		7		1			10		11*	4		T. Mills	29
	2	3		5	6		8	9				1	7		10		11	4		K. Cooper	30
	2	3		5	6		8	9		7		1	12		10		11	4*		T. Spencer	31
	2	3	4	5	6		8	9		7		1					10		11	J. Scales	32
	2	3	4	5	6		8	9		7*		1					10	12	11	N. Ashley	33
	2	3	4	5	6		8	9		7		1			10		11			D. Shaw	34
	2	3	4	5	6		8	9		7		1			10*		11		12	A. Glasson	35
	2	3	4	5	6		8	9		10		1					11		7	T. Ward	36
	2	3	4	5	6		8	9		10		1					11		7	J. Martin	37
	2	3	10	5	6		8	9		7*		1					11	4	12	E. Read	38
	2	3	10	5*	6		8	9		7		1			12		11	4		D. Scott	39
	2	3	6		5		8	9		7	10	1			11*			4	12	A. Challinor	40
	2	3			6		8	9		7	4	1					11	5	10	R. Chadwick	41
	2	3			6	8		9		7	4	1					11	5	10	B. Newsome	42
3	41	38	30	39	42	3	32	35	18	37	10	39	2	2	21	1	35	26	8		
			+ 2s			+ 2s			+ 2s	+ 1s	+ 1s		+ 3s		+ 3s			+ 4s	+ 4s		

FOOTBALL LEAGUE RECORD

1919 Elected to Division 2; 1925–26 Division 3(N); 1926–36 Division 3(S); 1936–52 Division 2; 1952–58 Division 3(S); 1958–59 Division 4; 1959–64 Division 3; 1964–67 Division 2; 1967 – Division 1.

HONOURS

Football League: Division 1 best season: 6th, 1969–70; Division 2 – Champions 1966–67; Division 3 – Champions 1963–64; Division 3(S) – Champions 1935–36; Runners-up 1933–34. Division 4 – Runners-up 1958–59. *FA Cup* best season: 6th rd, 1962–63, 1966–67, 1972–73, 1981–82; old 4th rd, 1909–10. *Football League Cup* best season: Semi-final 1980–81. **European Competition:** *European Fairs Cup:* 1970–71.

COLOURS

Sky blue shirts and shorts with navy and white trim, sky blue stockings.
Change colours: Red shirts and shorts with navy and white trim, red stockings.

COVENTRY CITY

Players Names Ht. Wt. D.o.B.	Birthplace Transfer Fee	Clubs	Appearances F.L. A & S	 F.L.C. A & S	 F.A.C. A & S	Goals F.L.	 F.L.C.	 F.A.C.
Goalkeepers								
Les Sealey	Bethnal Green	Coventry C (A)	158	11	9			
6 1, 11 6, 29.9.57								
Defenders								
Brian Roberts	Manchester	Coventry C (A)	179+6	16+2	9	1		1
5 8¼, 11 3, 6.11.55	—	Hereford U (loan)	5					
Paul Dyson (EU21)	Birmingham	Coventry C (A)	140	14	12	5		
6 2, 13 7, 27.12.59								
Steve Jacobs	West Ham	Coventry C (A)	76+7	4+3	2+2			
5 8, 11 0, 5.7.61								
Gary Gillespie (SU21)	Stirling	Falkirk						
6 2, 12 1, 5.7.60	£75,000	Coventry C	171+1	15	13	6		
Peter Hormantschuk	Coventry	Coventry C (A)	10+6	1	3+1	1	1	
5 10, 10 8, 11.9.62								
Danny Thomas (EU21)	Worksop	Coventry C (A)	103+5	11+1	8+1	5		
5 7, 11 0, 12.11.61								
Ian Butterworth	Crewe	Coventry C (A)	39+5	3	2+1			
6 1, 12 6, 25.1.65								
Lloyd McGrath		Coventry C (A)						
Midfield								
Gerry Daly (EI)	Dublin	Bohemians						
5 10, 10 6, 30.4.54		Manchester U	107+4	17	9	23	4	5
	£175,000	Derby Co	111+1	5	5	31	1	2
	£310,000	Coventry C	55+1	7	6	12	1	4
	—	Leicester C (loan)	17			1		
Martin Singleton (EY)	Banbury	Coventry C (A)	6+2	1		1		
5 9, 10 0, 2.8.63								
Gerry Francis (E)	Chiswick	QPR (A)	289+4	21	18	53	5	1
5 9, 12 4, 6.12.51	£465,000	Crystal Palace	59	6	1	1	1	
	£150,000	QPR	17	1	2	4		
	£165,000	Coventry C	50	1	4	2		
Derek Hall	Manchester	Coventry C (A)	1					
Forwards								
Steve Hunt	Birmingham	Aston Villa (A)	4+3			1		
5 7, 10 11, 8.7.56	£30,000	New York C						
	£40,000	Coventry C	165+5	16	10	25	3	3
Mark Hateley (EU21)	Liverpool	Coventry C (A)	86+7	8	10+1	25	3	5
6 1, 11 7, 7.11.61								
John Hendrie	Lennoxtown	Coventry C (A)	14+4	1		2		
5 8½, 10 11, 24.10.63								
Jim Melrose (SU21)	Glasgow	Partick Thistle						
5 9, 10 1, 7.10.58	£250,000	Leicester C	57+15	6	2+6	21	1	4
	P/E	Coventry City	21+3	3	1+1	8	2	
Steve Whitton	London	Coventry C (A)	64+10	2+2	3	21		
6 0, 12 7, 4.12.60								
Keith Thompson		Coventry C (A)	2+3					
Apprentices								
Perry Suckling	Leyton	Coventry C (A)	3	1				
6 0, 12.10.55								

Commercial Manager: George Curtis (Tel No:
Club Coach:
Club Captain 1982–83:
Supporters Player of the Season 1982–83: Gary Gillespie
Chief Scout:
Physiotherapist:
Club Statistician:
Association of Football Statisticians Club Adviser to Yearbook: R. Dean.

Players (non-appearance) granted free transfer: Steve Mardenborough, F.
Players released since May 1982: Russell Gordon, M. (N/K); Derek Richardson, G. (Maidstone U); Andy Willock, F. (Glasgow R); Rudi Kaiser, F. (Nice, France).

CREWE ALEXANDRA Division 4

Back row (left to right): Jim Dyer (Trainer), Mark Palios (now Tranmere R), Danny Bowers, Clive Evans, Steve Craven (now Northwich V), Steven Smith, Nick Longley, Billy Wright (now Burnley), Nigel Hart, Bernard Purdie (now Bangor), Neil Salathiel (now South Africa), Sam Chapman (Coach)
Front row: Steve Jones (no longer at club), Dave Waller, Sean Haselgrave, Peter Morris (Manager), Bob Scott, Steve Hanlon (now Finland), Tony Moore (now York C), Tony Cliss.

President: D. Godfrey.

Chairman: N. Rowlinson. ***Vice-Chairman:*** N. Hassall.

Directors: J. McHugh, K. Potts, E. Tagg, D. Rowlinson, R. Clayton, J. McMillan, J. Bowler.

Manager: Dario Gradi. ***Secretary:*** Mrs Gill Palin.

Year Formed: 1877. ***Turned Professional:*** 1893. ***Ltd Co.:*** 1892.

Club Nickname: 'Railwaymen'.

Previous Managers since 1946: George Lillycrop, Frank Hill, Arthur Turner, Harry Catterick, Ralph Ward, Maurice Lindley, Harry Ware, Jimmy McGuigan, Ernie Tagg, Dennis Viollet, Jimmy Melia, Ernie Tagg, Harry Gregg, Warwick Rimmer, Tony Waddington, Arfon Griffiths (16).

Football Ground, Gresty Rd, Crewe. Telephone Crewe (0270) 213014. ***Telegraphic address:*** 'Alex Football Crewe'. ***Ground capacity:*** 17,000. ***Record attendance:*** 20,000 v Tottenham H, FA Cup 4th rd, 30 Jan, 1960. ***Record receipts:*** £5,388 v Wigan Ath, League Cup 1st rd, 13 Aug, 1980. ***Pitch measurements:*** 112yd×74yd.

Directions to Ground: Local bus services from outlying districts. The ground is situated just five minutes' walk from Crewe railway station.

Match tickets: Advance booking for important cup ties only.

Car parking: Parking at the ground for 200 cars.

Entertainments/catering facilities: The Alexandra Club adjoining the ground is owned by the club. Refreshment points inside the ground.

Club shop: Situated at the ground; sells all types of souvenirs.

Handbooks/programmes: Handbooks on sale at matches.

Address of Supporters Club: Registered Office, Crewe Alexandra Supporters' Association, 131 Edleston Road, Crewe, Cheshire.

Address of the Club Shop or Boutique: Gresty Road, Crewe.

Note: Full club statistical records are on pages 416–455.

CREWE ALEXANDRA 1982–83 LEAGUE RECORD

Match No.	Date	Venue	Opponents	Result	H/T Score	Lg. Pos.	Goalscorers	Attendance
1	Aug 28	A	Chester	L 0-1	0-1	—		3180
2	Sept 3	H	Darlington	L 2-5	0-2	—	Craven, Evans	1739
3	7	H	Bristol C	W 4-1	1-0	—	Evans 2 (1 pen), Moore, Craven	1409
4	11	A	Bury	W 1-0	0-0	9	Jones	2164
5	17	H	Colchester U	L 0-1	0-1	—		2539
6	25	A	Swindon T	L 0-1	0-1	17		2967
7	29	A	Hartlepool U	L 0-1	0-0	—		1654
8	Oct 1	H	Mansfield T	L 1-2	1-1	—	Waddle (og)	1787
9	8	H	Rochdale	D 1-1	1-0	—	Waller	1806
10	16	A	Hereford U	L 0-1	0-0	22		2418
11	19	A	Aldershot	L 1-2	1-1	—	Evans	1574
12	22	H	Port Vale	L 1-2	1-1	24	Evans	4713
13	29	A	Halifax T	W 3-0	1-0	—	Sutton, Scott, Smith (og)	1726
14	Nov 2	H	York C	W 2-1	1-0	—	Craven, Evans	1633
15	6	A	Blackpool	L 0-2	0-2	20		3443
16	12	H	Scunthorpe U	L 0-1	0-0	—		2195
17	Dec 3	H	Torquay U	D 1-1	0-0	—	Scott	1576
18	10	A	Stockport Co	L 2-3	0-0	—	Wright, Waller	1860
19	17	H	Hull C	L 0-3	0-1	—		1404
20	27	A	Northampton T	L 0-4	0-1	24		7494
21	28	H	Peterborough U	L 0-3	0-2	24		1631
22	Jan 1	A	Tranmere R	D 1-1	0-0	24	Waller	3087
23	3	H	Stockport Co	W 3-0	1-0	24	Evans. Cliss, Moore	2508
24	8	A	Darlington	D 1-1	0-1	23	Waller	1006
25	15	H	Chester	W 3-2	2-0	22	Cliss, Waller, Bancroft	2895
26	21	A	Colchester U	L 3-4	1-3	—	Cliss 2, Bancroft	2221
27	29	H	Bury	D 3-3	3-2	22	Walker, Bancroft, Waller	2642
28	Feb 5	H	Swindon T	W 3-0	3-0	21	Lewis (og), Edwards, Waller	2536
29	15	H	Aldershot	D 0-0	0-0	—		2349
30	26	H	Hereford U	W 3-1	1-0	22	Walker 2 (1 pen), Waller	2251
31	Mar 1	A	York C	L 0-2	0-1	—		2975
32	5	A	Port Vale	D 1-1	1-0	23	Waller	8241
33	11	H	Halifax T	D 1-1	0-0	—	Waller	2518
34	15	A	Rochdale	L 0-2	0-1	—		2497
35	19	H	Blackpool	W 3-1	1-0	23	Waller, Walker 2 (1 pen)	2538
36	25	A	Scunthorpe U	L 0-2	0-0	—		2938
37	28	A	Mansfield T	L 0-1	0-0	—		2245
38	Apr 2	A	Peterborough U	L 1-2	1-0	23	Waller	2490
29	4	H	Northampton T	W 1-0	0-0	—	Waller	2197
40	9	A	Torquay U	L 1-2	0-0	23	Waller	1684
41	15	H	Hartlepool U	W 3-0	0-0	—	Waller 2, Chapman	2042
42	19	A	Wimbledon	L 2-3	1-1	—	Morris (og), Waller	2505
43	23	A	Hull C	L 0-1	0-1	22		7231
44	30	H	Wimbledon	L 0-2	0-0	23		2552
45	May 7	A	Bristol C	L 1-2	0-0	23	Chapman	4700
46	13	H	Tranmere R	L 0-1	0-0	23		2152

Final League Position: 23

GOALSCORERS

League (53): Waller 17, Evans 7 (1 pen), Walker 5 (2 pens), Cliss 4, Bancroft 3, Craven 3, Chapman 2, Moore 2, Scott 2, Edwards 1, Jones 1, Sutton 1, Wright 1, own goals 4.
Milk Cup (1): Craven 1.
FA Cup (1): Palios 1.

Milk Cup	First Round	Tranmere R (h)	1-1
		(a)	0-0
FA Cup	First Round	Boston U (a)	1-3

Smith	Moore	Bowers	Salathiel	Scott	Purdie	Haselgrave	Sutton	Brown	Craven	Goodwin	Jones	Evans	Palios	Waller	Hanlon	Hart	Wright (L)	Cliss	Metcalfe	Bancroft (L)	Walker	Brady	Edwards	Miller (L)	Chapman	Referees	Match No.
1	2	3	4	5	6	7	8	9*	10	12		11														D. Scott	1
1	2	3	4	5	6*	7	8		11	9	12	10														D. Lloyd	2
1	2	3	4	5		7	8		11	9		10	6													R. Banks	3
1	2	5	3	4	6	7			10	11*	12	9	8													T. Mills	4
1	2	3	4	5	12	7	6		11		9*	10	8													D. Allison	5
1	2	3	4	5	12	7	8*		11		9	10	6													A. Crickmore	6
1	2	3		5	6	7	4		11	12	9*	10	8													D. Hutchinson	7
1	2	3	4	5	6	7			11	9		10	8													K. Walmsley	8
1	2	3	4	5	6*	7			11	12		10	8	9												G. Napthine	8
1	2	3	4	5		7	8		11*			10	12	9	6											T. Bune	10
1	2	3	4	5		7	8				9	10		11	6											B. Stevens	11
1		3	4	5	2	7	8*		12		11	10		9	6											M. Peck	12
1		3	4	5	2	7	8		11			10		9	6											N. Glover	13
1		3	4	5	2	7	8		11			10		9	6											D. Richardson	14
1		3	4*	5	2	7	8		11		12	10		9	6											K. Redfern	15
1		3	4	5	2	7	8		11			10	6	9												H. King	16
1		3	4	5	2	7			12			10		9*		6	8	11								N. Wilson	17
1		3	2	5		7			4			10*		9	12	6	8	11								P. Willis	18
1		3	2	5		7			4			10		9		6	8	11								K. Barrett	19
1		3	2	5		7			4		9	10	12		8*	6		11								K. Cooper	20
1		3	2	5		7			4*		12	10	8	9		6		11								V. Callow	21
1	2	3		5		7*			4			10	8	9	12	6		11								A. Challinor	22
1	2	3		5	6	7			4			10	8	9				11								J. Bray	23
1	2	12		5	6	7			4			10	8*	9		3		11								T. Mills	24
1	2	3		5		7						10		9		6		11	4	8						J. Hunting	25
1	2	3		5		7			12			10		9		6*		11	4	8						K. Salmon	26
1	2*	3	6	5		7						12		9				11	4	8	10					M. Robinson	27
1		3		5		7								9		6		11		8	10	2	4			K. Hackett	28
1		3		5		7								9		6		11		8	10	2	4			T. Fitzharris	29
1		3		5					7					9		6		11		8	10	2	4			F. Roberts	30
1		3		5		12			7*					10		6		11		8	9	2	4			D. Allison	31
1		3		5					7					9		6		11		8	10	2	4			E. Read	32
1		3		5		12			7					9		6		11		8*	10	2	4			R. Chadwick	33
1		3		5		12			7*					10		6		11		8	9	2	4			R. Bridge	34
1		3		5										9		6		11		8	10	2	4	7		A. Seville	35
1		3												9		6		11		8	10	2	4	7	5	D. Hutchinson	36
1		3		5		7								9		6		11		8	10	2	4			A. Saunders	37
1		3		5		7								9		6		11		8	10		4	2		J. Moules	38
1		3		5		7								10		6		11		8	9	2	4			A. Banks	39
1		3		5		7								10		6		11		8	9	2	4			J. Martin	40
1		3		5		7								9		6		11		8*	10	2	4		12	R. Bridges	41
1		3		5		7								9		6		11		8	10	2	4*		12	K. Baker	42
1		3		5		12								9		6		11		8*	10	2	4		7	G. Courtney	43
1		3		5		7								9		6		11		8*	10	2	4		12	D. Civil	44
1		3		5		7								9		6		11			10	2	4		8	M. James	45
1		3		5		7						12		9		6		11		8*	10	2	4			G. Napthine	46
46	17	45	21	45	14	38	13	1	26	4	6	26	12	37	7	28	3	30	3	21	20	18	19	3	3		
		+ 1s			+ 2s	+ 4s			+ 3s	+ 3s	+ 4s	+ 2s	+ 2s		+ 2s										+ 3s		

FOOTBALL LEAGUE RECORD

1892 Original Member of Division 2; 1896 Failed re-election; 1921 Re-entered Division 3(N); 1958–59 Division 4; 1963–64 Division 3; 1964–68 Division 4; 1968–69 Division 3; 1969 – Division 4.

HONOURS

Football League: Division 2 best season: 10th, 1892–93. *FA Cup* best season: semi-final 1888. *Football League Cup* best season: 3rd rd, 1974–75, 1975–76, 1978–79.

COLOURS

Red shirts, white shorts, red stockings.
Change colours: Sky blue shirts and stockings, black shorts.

CREWE ALEXANDRA

Players Names Ht, Wt, D.o.B.	Birthplace Transfer Fee	Clubs	Appearances F.L. A & S	 F.L.C. A & S	 F.A.C. A & S	Goals F.L.	 F.L.C.	 F.A.C.
Goalkeepers								
Steve Smith	Lyonby	Birmingham C (A)	2		1			
6 0, 12 5, 12.6.57	F/T	Bradford C	105	8	4			
	F/T	Crewe Alex	46	2	1			
Defenders								
Steve Edwards	Birkenhead	Oldham Ath (A)	77+3	5+1	2			
5 9, 11 0, 11.1.58		Crewe Alex	19			1		
Nigel Hart	Golborne	Wigan Ath	1					
6 0, 12 13, 1.10.58	F/T	Leicester C						
	F/T	Blackpool	36+1	4+1	3			
	F/T	Crewe Alex	28					
Bob Scott	Liverpool	Wrexham	15+4					
6 2½, 13 4, 22.2.53	—	Reading (loan)	5					
	F/T	Hartlepool U	37	2	1			
	F/T	Rochdale	71	5	2	3		
	F/T	Crewe Alex	178+1	8	5	9		1
Ian Bowers	Stoke	Stoke C	35+4	2+1	4	2		
5 8¾, 10 2, 16.1.55	—	Shrewsbury T	6					
	£8000	Crewe Alex	151+3	7	5	2		
Paul Brady	Birmingham	Birmingham C (A)						
5 11, 10 8, 26.3.61	F/T	Northampton T	49+2	8	7	3		
	F/T	Crewe Alex	18					
Midfield								
Sean Haslegrave*	Stoke	Stoke C	106+7	9+2	7+1	5	1	1
5 8, 10 7, 7.6.51	£35,000	Nottingham F	5+2			1		
	£20,000	Preston NE	111+2	4	5	2		
	F/T	Crewe Alex	78+4	4	3	1		1
Forwards								
Tony Cliss	March	Peterborough U	65+20	4+1	1+2	11		
5 9, 11 0, 22.9.59	F/T	Crewe Alex	30			4		
David Waller	Winsford							
5 10, 10 0,								
		Crewe Alex	38		1	17		
Non-contract players								
Nigel Walker	Gateshead	Newcastle U	65+5	1	3	3		
5 10, 11 11, 7.4.59	F/T	San Diego						
	F/T	Sunderland						
	F/T	Crewe Alex (N/C)	20		5			
Daryl Chapman		Derby Co						
	F/T	Crewe Alex	3+3			2		

Commercial Manager: M. Challis (Tel. 0270 213014)
Club Coach: S. Chapman
Supporters Player of the Season 1982–83: Dave Waller
Physiotherapist: J. Dyer
Club Captain 1982–83: Bob Scott
Chief Scout: P. Slack
Club Statistician and Adviser to Yearbook: H. Finch

Players released since May 1982: Colin Chesters, F. (Northwich Vic); Neil Griffiths, M. (Stafford R); Duncan Heath, D. (Oswestry); Ian Howat, F. (Bangor C); Paul Keighley, F. (Bolton W N/C); Kevin Lewis, D. (Telford U); Ken Mulhearn, G. (retired); Dave Goodwin, M. (Macclesfield); Steve Jones, F. (N/K); Bernard Purdie, F. (Bangor C); Neil Salathiel, D. (South Africa); Tony Moore, D. (N/K); Mel Sutton, M. (N/K); Steve Hanlon, M. (Nantwich T); Steve Craven, M. (Northwich Victoria); Stuart Metcalfe, M. (N/K); Clive Evans, M. (N/K).

CRYSTAL PALACE Division 2

Back row (left to right): G. Smith, M. Annon, H. Hughton, F. Latty, I. Edwards, P. Wilkins, P. Barron, T. Campbell, D. Fry, G. Nebbeling, K. Oakley, T. Langley, D. Price, P. Baxter, S. Galliers, A. Mullery (Manager)
Middle row: R. Woolnough (Physio), B. Bason, K. Mabbutt, S. Brooke, P. Hinshelwood, J. Cannon, W. Gilbert, J. Murphy, S. Lovell, D. Giles, I. Salter (Coach)
Front row: M. Dodman, D. Lindsay, W. Martin, A. Leader, G. Stebbing, S. Howe, J. Carter, J. DiPalma, B. Jay.

President: S. Stephenson.

Chairman: R. G. Noades.

Directors: B. Coleman, A. De'Souza, C. D. Richards, B. Bishop, J. Rose, R. M. Marsden, A. P. Mullery MBE.

Team Manager: Alan Mullery MBE. ***Secretary:*** Alan Leather.

Year Formed: 1905. ***Turned Professional:*** 1905. ***Ltd Co.:*** 1905.

Club Nickname: 'The Eagles'.

Previous Grounds: 1905, Crystal Palace; 1915, Herne Hill; 1919, The Nest; 1924, Selhurst Park.

Previous Managers since 1946: George Irwin, Jack Butler, Ronnie Rooke, Fred Dawes, Charlie Slade, Laurie Scott, Cyril Spiers, George Smith, Arthur Rowe, Dick Graham, Bert Head, Malcolm Allison, Terry Venables, Ernie Walley, Malcolm Allison, Dario Gradi, Steve Kember (17).

Selhurst Park, London, SE25 6PU. Telephone 01-653 4462. ***Ground capacity:*** 38,500 (18,000 covered). ***Record attendance:*** 51,482 v Burnley, Division 2, 11 May, 1979. ***Record receipts:*** £74,868 v Tottenham H, Division 1, 6 Oct, 1979. ***Pitch measurements:*** 110yd×74yd.

Directions to Ground: Ground served by three stations – Selhurst (5 minutes walk), Norwood Junction (7 minutes) and Thornton Heath (10 minutes). Buses 68, 75, 154, 157, 12 (to Norwood Junction).

Match tickets: Seats bookable in advance, postal applications accepted one month in advance and personal application two weeks in advance. Postal applications must be accompanied by SAE and the correct remittance. Cheques must be made payable to Crystal Palace FC and name and address must be written on the back. Separate application must be made for each match.

Car parking: By prior arrangement only through the Secretary.

Entertainments/catering facilities: Extensive match-day catering facilities within the ground, including Strikers, a fully licensed high-class restaurant – for reservations ring 01-653 1876. Comprehensive range of non-match-day function rooms for all occasions – for details ring Tony Francis on 01-653-1876.

Club shop: Sells all types of souvenirs.

Handbooks/programmes: Programmes available on subscription.

Address of Supporters Club and Shop: Selhurst Park, SE25 6PU.

Note: Full club statistical records are on pages 416–455.

CRYSTAL PALACE 1982–83 LEAGUE RECORD

Match No.	Date	Venue	Opponents	Result	H/T Score	Lg. Pos.	Goalscorers	Attendance
1	Aug 28	H	Barnsley	D 1-1	1-1	—	Hilaire	7549
2	Sept 4	A	Rotherham U	D 2-2	0-2	15	Hinshelwood, Mabbutt	6989
3	7	H	Shrewsbury T	W 2-1	1-0	—	Mabbutt, Hilaire	6578
4	11	H	Blackburn R	W 2-0	0-0	6	Mabbutt, Hilaire	7529
5	18	A	Carlisle U	L 1-4	0-2	9	Hinshelwood	4390
6	25	H	Middlesbrough	W 3-0	2-0	6	Mabbutt 2, Edwards	7689
7	28	A	QPR	D 0-0	0-0	—		12,194
8	Oct 2	A	Bolton W	L 0-1	0-1	9		5804
9	9	A	Burnley	L 1-2	1-0	10	Hinshelwood	6429
10	16	H	Oldham Ath	W 1-0	0-0	8	Mabbutt	6643
11	23	A	Newcastle U	L 0-1	0-1	10		22,554
12	30	H	Fulham	D 1-1	0-1	12	Hilaire	14,912
13	Nov 6	A	Chelsea	D 0-0	0-0	12		15,169
14	13	H	Leeds U	D 1-1	1-1	13	Mabbutt	11,673
15	20	A	Leicester C	W 1-0	0-0	10	Mabbutt	8616
16	27	H	Wolverhampton W	L 3-4	2-3	12	Cannon, Jones, Hinshelwood	10,225
17	Dec 4	A	Grimsby T	L 1-4	1-3	16	Langley	5295
18	11	H	Sheffield W	W 2-0	2-0	11	Hinshelwood, Langley	8498
19	18	A	Derby Co	D 1-1	1-1	12	Langley	13,207
20	27	H	Charlton Ath	D 1-1	1-0	14	Jones	17,996
21	28	A	Cambridge U	L 0-1	0-0	15		4822
22	Jan 1	H	Leicester C	W 1-0	1-0	14	Langley	8801
23	3	H	Rotherham U	D 1-1	0-1	13	Hinshelwood (pen)	7704
24	15	A	Barnsley	L 1-3	0-2	15	Jones	10,120
25	22	H	QPR	L 0-3	0-1	17		14,621
26	Feb 5	A	Shrewsbury T	D 1-1	1-1	17	Hinshelwood (pen)	3716
27	22	H	Bolton W	W 3-0	2-0	—	Edwards 2, Brooks	4456
28	26	A	Oldham Ath	L 0-2	0-2	15		9780
29	Mar 5	H	Newcastle U	L 0-2	0-0	16		10,239
30	12	A	Fulham	L 0-1	0-1	17		11,234
31	19	H	Chelsea	D 0-0	0-0	17		13,437
32	26	A	Leeds U	L 1-2	1-0	19	Murphy (pen)	13,973
33	Apr 2	H	Cambridge U	D 0-0	0-0	18		5495
34	4	A	Charlton Ath	L 1-2	1-2	—	Brown	7836
35	9	H	Carlisle U	W 2-1	0-1	17	Rushbury (og), Brown	5696
36	16	A	Blackburn R	L 0-3	0-2	19		4635
37	23	H	Grimsby T	W 2-0	0-0	18	Hilaire, Brooks	5909
38	30	A	Wolverhampton W	L 0-1	0-0	19		12,523
39	May 7	H	Derby Co	W 4-1	2-0	17	Nebbeling, Mabbutt 2, Hughton	8464
40	10	A	Middlesbrough	L 0-2	0-1	—		10,014
41	14	A	Sheffield W	L 1-2	0-1	19	Murphy	11,154
42	17	H	Burnley	W 1-0	0-0	15	Edwards	22,714

Final League Position: 15

GOALSCORERS

League (43): Mabbutt 10, Hinshelwood 7 (2 pens), Hilaire 5, Edwards 4, Langley 4, Jones 3, Brooks 2, Brown 2, Murphy 2 (1 pen), Cannon 1, Hughton 1, Nebbeling 1, own goal 1.
Milk Cup (8): Edwards 2, Hinshelwood 2, Mabbutt 2, Hilaire 1, Lovell 1.
FA Cup (3): Edwards 1, Langley 1, Lovell 1.
Football League Trophy (3): Edwards 2, Brooks 1.

Milk Cup	First Round	Portsmouth (h)	2-0
		(a)	1-1
	Second Round	Peterborough U (a)	2-0
		(h)	2-1
	Third Round	Sheffield W (h)	1-2
FA Cup	Third Round	York C (h)	2-1
	Fourth Round	Birmingham C (h)	1-0
	Fifth Round	Burnley (h)	0-0
		(a)	0-1
Football		Brentford (a)	2-2
League Trophy		Wimbledon (h)	1-0
		Millwall (h)	0-3

Barron	Hinshelwood	Williams	Hughton	Cannon	Gilbert	Giles	Murphy	Langley	Mabbutt	Hilaire	Lovell	Edwards	Nebbeling	Brooks	Jones	Fry	Locke (L)	Brown	Wilkins	Referees	Match No.
1	2	3	4	5	6	7	8*	9	10	11	12									I. Borrett	1
1	2	3	4	5	6	7*	8		10	11	12	9								K. Barratt	2
1	2	3	4	5	6	7	8		10	11		9								B. Hill	3
1	2	3	4	5	6	7			10	11	8	9								I. Burden	4
1	2	3	4	5	6	7			10	11	8	9								N. Midgley	5
1	2	3	4	5	6	7			10	11	8	9								R. Milford	6
1	2	3	4	5	6	7		9	10	11	8									B. Stevens	7
1	2	3	4	5	6	7			10	11	8	9								J. Holbrook	8
1	2	3		5	6	7	4*	9	10	11	8		12							J. Lovatt	9
1	2	3	4	5	6	7			10	11	8	9								A. Grey	10
1			8	5	6	7			10	11	4	9	2	3						T. Fitzharris	11
1			8	5	6	7	3		10	11	4	9	2							B. Daniels	12
1	6		8	5		7	3		10	11	4	9	2							A. Seville	13
1	6		8	5		7	3	12	10	11	4	9*	2							M. Taylor	14
1	6		8	5*	2	7	3	9	10	11	4		12							K. Hackett	15
1	6		8	5	2	7	3		10	11	4				9					A. Robinson	16
1	6		8	5	2	7	3	10		11	4				9					T. Jones	17
	6		8	5	2	7	3	10		11			4		9	1				A. Gunn	18
	6		8	5	2	7	3	10		11			4		9	1				D. Scott	19
	6		8	5	2	7	3	10		11			4		9	1				J. Martin	20
	6		8	5	2	7	3	10		11			4		9	1				D. Hedges	21
	6		8	5	2	7*	3	10		11	12		4		9	1				T. Spencer	22
	6		8	5	2	7		10		11	3		4		9	1				J. Deakin	23
	6		8	5		7		10*		11	3	12	4		9	1	2			D. Civil	24
	6		8	5		7		10		11		12	4	3*	9	1	2			G. Napthine	25
	6		8	5	2		3	10		11		7			9	1	4			R. Banks	26
	6			5	2		3	10		11		7		8	9	1	4			A. Crickmore	27
	6		4		2	12	3	10		11		7*	5	8	9	1				R. Nixon	28
			6	5		7	3	10		11			4	8	9	1	2			M. Bodenham	29
	6		8	5			3	10		11			4		9	1	2	7		D. Letts	30
	6		8	5		10	3			11			4		9	1	2	7		L. Shapter	31
			8	5	6	10	3			11			4		9	1	2	7		D. Shaw	32
			8	5	6	10	3	12		11			4*		9	1	2	7		E. Read	33
			8	5	6	10	3	9*	12	11			4			1	2	7		B. Daniels	34
	2		4	5	6	7	10		8	11						1	3	9		A. Grey	35
	3		8	5	6	10			9	11			4*			1	2	7	12	P. Tyldesley	36
	2		8	5	6	10			9	11			4	3		1		7		S. Bates	37
	2		8	5		10	6		9	11			4	3		1		7		M. Chadwick	38
	2		4	5	6	7	10		8	11			3			1		9		A. Glasson	39
	2		4	5	6		10	7	8	11			3			1		9		G. Peck	40
	2*		4	5	6	7	10	12	8	11		9	3			1				V. Callow	41
			4	5	6	7	10*	12	8	11		9	3			1	2			D. Axcell	42
17	35	10	40	41	34	37	30	20	24	42	16	16	26	7	18	25	13	11	0		
						+ 1s		+ 4s	+ 1s		+ 3s	+ 2s	+ 2s						+ 1s		

FOOTBALL LEAGUE RECORD

1920 Original Members of Division 3; 1921–25 Division 2; 1925–58 Division 3(S); 1958–61 Division 4; 1961–64 Division 3; 1964–69 Division 2; 1969–73 Division 1; 1973–74 Division 2; 1974–77 Division 3; 1977–79 Division 2; 1979–81 Division 1; 1981– Division 2.

HONOURS

Football League: Division 1 best season: 13th, 1979–80; Division 2 – Champions 1978–79; Runners-up 1968–69; Division 3 – Runners-up 1963–64; Division 3(S) – Champions 1920–21; Runners-up 1928–29, 1930–31, 1938–39; Division 4 – Runners-up 1960–61. *FA Cup* best season: semi-final 1975–76. *Football League Cup* best season: 5th rd, 1968–69, 1970–71.

COLOURS

Red shirts with royal blue 3″ vertical stripes with plain royal blue sleeves with three red stripes. Royal blue V neck and cuffs and white numbers. Royal blue shorts and stockings with three red stripes.
Change colours: Sky blue.

CRYSTAL PALACE

Players Names Ht, Wt, D.o.B.	Birthplace Transfer Fee	Clubs	Appearances F.L. A & S	 F.L.C. A & S	 F.A.C. A & S	Goals F.L.	 F.L.C.	 F.A.C.
Goalkeepers								
David Fry	Bournemouth	Crystal Palace (A)	50		5			
Defenders								
Gary Locke (EY)	Kingsbury	Chelsea (A)	270+2	21	24	3		1
5 11, 11 5, 12.7.54	F/T	Crystal Palace	13		3			
Jim Cannon	Glasgow	Crystal Palace (A)	374+3	30+1	32	20	3	1
6 0, 13 0, 2.10.53								
Billy Gilbert (EU21)	Lewisham	Crystal Palace (A)	202+1	17	12	2		
5 11, 12 0, 10.11.59								
Paul Hinshelwood*	Bristol	Crystal Palace (A)	271+5	18	24	23	2	1
(EU21)								
6 0, 12 6, 14.5.56								
Gavin Nebbeling	South Africa	Arcadia Shepherds						
6 0, 12 4, 15.5.63	—	Crystal Palace	25+2	3	1	1		
Paul Baxter*	Hackney	Tottenham H. (A)						
5 7, 10 8, 22.4.64	F/T	Crystal Palace	1					
Midfield								
Jerry Murphy (E I)	Stepney	Crystal Palace (A)	149+12	17	13+1	14	5	
5 9, 11 0, 23.9.59								
Shaun Brooks (ES)	London	Crystal Palace (A)	44+6	4	4+2	4		
5 7, 11 0, 9.10.62								
Henry Hughton	Stratford	Orient (A)	104+7	4	9	2	1	
5 8½, 11 10, 18.11.59	F/T	Crystal Palace	40	4	2	1		
Forwards								
Ally Brown	Musselburgh	Leicester C.	93+8	11+1	7+1	32	1	2
6 0, 11 0, 12.4.51	£60,000	WBA	254+24	27	26+2	72	2	5
	F/T	Crystal Palace	11			2		
Vince Hilaire (EU21)	Forest Gate	Crystal Palace (A)	199+16	17	13	27	2	3
5 6, 10 0, 10.10.59								
Tommy Langley (EU21)	Lambeth	Chelsea (A)	129+13	4	6	40	1	2
5 11, 11 7, 8.2.58	£400,000	Q.P.R.	24+1	3		8	1	
	£200,000	Crystal Palace	54+5	5+1	5+1	9	1	1
Paul Wilkins	Hackney	Tottenham H. (A)						
6 2, 12 0 20.3.64	F/T	Crystal Palace	2+4			2		
Kevin Mabbutt (EY)	Bristol	Bristol C. (A)	112+17	11	8	28	3	7
5 7, 10 2, 5.12.58	£100,000+P/E	Crystal Palace	55+1	5	5	18	2	
David Giles (W)	Cardiff	Cardiff C. (A)	51+8	6	4	3	1	1
5 7, 10 4, 21.9.56	£30,000	Wrexham	38	3	3	2		
	£70,000	Swansea C.	49+5	2	5	13		4
	—	Orient (loan)	3			2		
	P/E	Crystal Palace	57+2	4	2+1	1		
Ian Edwards* (W)	Wrexham	Rhyl						
6 1, 12 5, 30.1.55		W.B.A	13+3	2		3		
	£20,000	Chester	104	10	6	36	3	4
	£125,000	Wrexham	71+4	6	12	20	3	1
	F/T	Crystal Palace	16+2	4	3	4	2	1
Chris Jones* (EU21)	Jersey	Tottenham H. (A)	149+15	7+1	10+2	37	1	4
5 11, 10 7, 18.4.56	F/T	Manchester C	3					
	F/T	Crystal Palace	18	4		3		

Commercial Manager: Graham Drew (Tel. 771 9502)
Club Coach: Ken Shellito
Supporters Player of the Season 1982–83: Jerry Murphy
Physiotherapist: Ron Woolnough
Club Captain 1982–83: Jim Cannon
Chief Scout:
Club Statistician: Rev. Nigel Sands
Association of Football Statisticians Club Adviser to Yearbook: M. Purkiss.

Players (non-appearance) granted free transfer: Steve Howe, M.; Keith Oakley, D.
Players released since May 1982: Graeme Smith, M. (N/K); Gary Allen, F. (N/K); Gary Williams, D. (retired); David Boulter, D. (N/K); John Phillips, G. (Hong Kong).

DARLINGTON Division 4

Back row (left to right): Alan Kamara, Harry Wilson, John Stalker, Roger Wicks, Pat Cuff, Alan Walsh, Tony McFadden, Tim Gilbert, Dave McLean.
Standing: George Herd (Coach), Bob Farrelly (Physiotherapist), Kevan Smith, Gavin Liddle, Barry Dunn, Brian Honour, Fred Barber, Tom Brady, David Wakefield, Peter May, Jeff Wilson, Bill Elliott (Manager – standing forward), David Thorne (Secretary).
Seated: Ken Warne (Director), Brian Hadley (Vice-Chairman), Leslie Moore (Chairman), Derek Mason (Director), Charles Parias (Director), Alan Moore (Director).
Seated on ground: David Young, Nigel Robson, Tony Hodgson.

President: J. L. T. Moore.

Chairman: K. W. Warne. ***Vice Chairman:*** J. B. Hadley.

Directors: D. Mason, A. Brown, A. Heaton, A. Moore, C. Parias.

Manager: Cyril Knowles. ***Secretary:*** David Thorne.

Year Formed: 1883. ***Turned Professional:*** 1908. ***Ltd Co.:*** 1891.

Club Nickname: 'The Quakers'.

Previous Managers since 1946: Bill Forrest, George Irwin, Bob Gurney, Dick Duckworth, Eddie Carr, Lol Morgan, Jimmy Greenhalgh, Ray Yeoman, Len Richley, Frank Brennan, Allan Jones, Ralph Brand, Dick Conner, Billy Horner, Peter Madden, Len Walker (16).

Feethams Ground, Darlington. Telephone Darlington (0325) 65097/67712. ***Ground capacity:*** 20,000. ***Record attendance:*** 21,023 v Bolton W, League Cup 3rd rd, 14 Nov, 1960. ***Record receipts:*** £15,059 v Sheffield U, Division 4, 15 May, 1982. ***Pitch measurements:*** 110yd×74yd.

Directions to Ground: Darlington railway station, five minutes walk.

Match tickets: Postal and telephone bookings accepted in advance of the match.

Car parking: Ample parking in surrounding side-streets.

Entertainments/catering facilities: Three nearby cafés. Three snack bars in the ground.

Address of Supporters Club: Same as Football Club.

Club shop: Shop inside the ground sells all types of souvenirs.

Handbooks/programmes: Available by postal request – individual or season subscription. Centenary Handbook available.

Extra information: The club will make every effort to cater for the disabled, the blind, or any person who has some difficulty seeking entrance because of illness.

Note: Full club statistical records are on pages 416–455.

DARLINGTON 1982–83 LEAGUE RECORD

Match No.	Date	Venue	Opponents	Result	H/T Score	Lg. Pos.	Goalscorers	Attendance
1	Aug 28	H	Rochdale	W 3-0	2-0	—	Walsh 2, Dunn	1672
2	Sept 3	A	Crewe Alex	W 5-2	2-0	—	Gilbert, McLean, Dunn, Smith, McFadden	1739
3	7	A	Halifax T	L 0-2	0-2	—		1891
4	11	H	Hereford U	W 2-1	0-0	1	Stalker 2	1818
5	18	A	Torquay U	L 0-1	0-1	4		2597
6	25	H	Port Vale	D 0-0	0-0	7		2255
7	28	H	Scunthorpe U	L 0-1	0-1	—		1574
8	Oct 2	A	Blackpool	L 0-2	0-1	16		4059
9	9	H	Chester	L 0-2	0-1	16		1387
10	15	A	Colchester U	D 2-2	0-1	—	Walsh 2	2547
11	18	A	Tranmere R	L 0-2	0-1	—		1111
12	23	H	Bury	L 1-2	1-0	16	Walsh	1240
13	30	A	Mansfield T	W 2-0	1-0	16	Walsh, McLean (pen)	1816
14	Nov 2	H	Aldershot	D 1-1	1-1	—	Smith K.	1453
15	6	H	Swindon T	W 1-0	1-0	14	Walsh	1334
16	12	A	Stockport Co	L 1-2	0-1	—	McLean	1885
17	28	A	Northampton T	D 3-3	0-0	—	Dunn 2, Walsh	2599
18	Dec 4	H	Wimbledon	L 0-2	0-2	15		1117
19	27	A	Hartlepool U	L 0-2	0-0	20		3337
20	28	H	Hull C	L 1-2	0-1	20	Walsh	2614
21	Jan 1	A	York C	L 2-5	1-2	21	McFadden 2	3679
22	3	H	Bristol C	D 2-2	2-2	21	Walsh 2	1425
23	8	H	Crewe Alex	D 1-1	1-0	21	Honour	1006
24	15	A	Rochdale	D 1-1	0-1	21	McLean	1233
25	22	H	Halifax T	L 1-2	1-1	22	McFadden	1175
26	29	A	Hereford U	D 0-0	0-0	21		2155
27	Feb 5	A	Port Vale	L 1-2	0-1	24	McFadden	4110
28	15	H	Tranmere R	W 1-0	0-0	—	Todd	1010
29	19	A	Chester	W 3-2	2-2	21	Barton, Walsh, Honour	1323
30	26	H	Colchester U	L 1-3	0-2	23	McLean (pen)	1089
31	Mar 1	A	Aldershot	W 6-1	1-0	—	Walsh, Todd 3, Barton, McFadden	1400
32	5	A	Bury	L 0-3	0-1	21		1926
33	12	H	Mansfield T	D 0-0	0-0	22		952
34	19	A	Swindon T	W 2-1	1-1	22	Allan (og), McLean	2815
35	26	H	Stockport Co	W 3-1	0-1	20	Walsh, McLean, McFadden	1012
36	Apr 2	A	Hull C	D 0-0	0-0	20		7709
37	4	H	Hartlepool U	W 2-1	0-0	—	Cartwright, McLean	3131
38	9	A	Wimbledon	L 1-3	0-2	17	Walsh	1970
39	12	H	Blackpool	L 0-1	0-1	—		1333
40	16	H	Torquay U	L 0-2	0-0	19		1122
41	23	A	Peterborough U	D 1-1	0-0	20	Walsh	2185
42	30	H	Northampton T	W 2-0	1-0	19	McLean, Honour (pen)	1042
43	May 2	A	Bristol C	D 2-2	2-1	17	Todd, Kamara	4788
44	7	A	Scunthorpe U	D 2-2	0-2	17	Todd, Smith	3305
45	14	H	York C	L 1-3	1-3	18	Todd	1668
46	17	H	Peterborough U	W 4-3	1-2	17	Todd, Walsh 2, Cartwright	1002

Final League Position: 17

GOALSCORERS

League (61): Walsh 18, Mclean 9 (2 pens), Todd 8, McFadden 7, Dunn 4, Honour 3 (1 pen), Smith K. 3, Barton 2, Cartwright 2, Stalker 2, Gilbert 1, Kamara 1, own goal 1.
Milk Cup (2): Walsh 1, own goal 1.
FA Cup (0).

Milk Cup	First Round	Peterborough U (h)	0-2
		(a)	2-4
FA Cup	First Round	Scunthorpe U (h)	0-1

Cuff	Brissett	Smith	Kamara	Wilson H.	Gilbert	Wicks	McLean	Dunn	Walsh	McFadden	Hawker	Stalker	Honour	Halliday (L)	Liddle	Rhodes (L)	McDermott	Young	Barton (L)	Todd (L)	Wilson J. H.	Wakefield	Barber	Cartwright	Referees	Match No.
1	2	3	4	5	6	7	8	9	10	11															J. Key	1
1	2	4	5	3	6*	7	8	9	10	11	12														D. Lloyd	2
1	2	4	5	3	6	7*	8	9	10	11	12														K. Baker	3
1	2	4	5	3	6		8		10	11	7	9													R. Guy	4
1	2	4	5	3			8	6	10	11	7	9*	12												E. Read	5
1	2*	4	6	3	12		8	9	10		7	11		5											N. Glover	6
1		4	6	3	2		8	9	10		7	11		5											K. Walmsley	7
1	12	4	6	3	2		8	9*	10	11	7			5											R. Nixon	8
1		4	6	3	2		8	9	10	11	7			5											N. Wilson	9
1		4	6	3			8		10		7	11	9	5	2										D. Letts	10
1	12	4	6	3			8		10		7	11*	9	5	2										A. Hamil	11
1		4	6	3			8		10		7	11	9	5	2										C. Seel	12
1	2	4	6	3	7		8	11*	10				9		12	5									N. Ashley	13
1	2	4	6	3	7		8	11	10				9			5									A. Robinson	14
1	2	4	6	3	7		8	11	10				9			5									D. Richardson	15
1	2	4	6	3	7		8	11*	10				9		12	5									V. Callow	16
1		4	6	3	7		8	11	10				9		2	5									A. Seville	17
1		4	6	3	7		8	11*	10				9		2	5	12								D. Allison	18
1		4	6	3	7		8	11*	10				9		2	5	12								K. Hackett	19
1		4	6		7		8	11	10				9		2	5		3							R. Chadwick	20
1		4	6		7		8		10	11			9		2	5		3							N. Midgley	21
1		4	6		7		8		10	11			9		2	5		3							D. Scott	22
1		4	6	3	7		8		10	11			9		2	5									T. Mills	23
1		4	6	3	7*		8		10	11			9		2	5		12							D. Owen	24
1		4	6	3	7		8		10	11			9		2	5									D. Shaw	25
1		4	6	3	7	9	8		10	11					2	5									D. Vickers	26
1		4	6	3	7		8		10	11			2*		12				5	9					H. King	27
1		4	6	3	7		8		10	11					2				5	9					D. Hutchinson	28
1		4	6	3	7		8		10	11			12		2*				5	9					D. Civil	29
1		4	6	3	7	12	8		10	11			2*						5	9					A. Challiner	30
1		4	2	3	7	6*	8		10	11			12						5	9					T. Ward	31
1		3	2	5	7	6*	8		9	11			12						4	10					J. Bray	32
1		4	2	3*	7		8		10	11			6							9	5	12			A. Banks	33
1		4	2		7		8		10	11			6					3	5	9					C. Downey	34
		4	2		7		8		10	11								3	5	9			1	6	M. Scott	35
		4	2		7		8		10	11								3	5	9			1	6	K. Walmsley	36
		4	2		7		8		10	11								3	5	9			1	6	J. Worrall	37
		4	2		7		8		10	11			12					3*	5	9			1	6	D. Axcell	38
		4	2				8		10	11			7		12			3*	5	9			1	6	J. Hough	39
		4	2			12	8		10	11			7		3				5	9*			1	6	J. Key	40
		4	2		8		7		10				11		3*			12	5	9			1	6	T. Bune	41
		4	2			6*	8		10				7		3			11	5	9		12	1		T. Fitzharris	42
		4	2				8		10				7		3			11	5	9		6	1		K. Barratt	43
		4	2		8		7*		10				11		3			12	5	9		6	1		N. Glover	44
		4	2		7		8		10				11*		3				5	9		12	1	6	N. Wilson	45
		4	2		7		8		10									3	5	9		11	1	6	T. Jones	46
34	10	46	46	30	37	7	46	16	46	27	9	7	27	7	21	14	0	12	19	20	1	3	12	9		
	+ 2s				+ 1s	+ 2s					+ 2s		+ 5s		+ 4s		+ 2s	+ 3s				+ 3s				

FOOTBALL LEAGUE RECORD

1921 Original Member Division 3(N); 1925–27 Division 2; 1927–58 Division 3(N); 1958–66 Division 4; 1966–67 Division 3; 1967– Division 4.

HONOURS

Football League: Division 2 best season: 15th, 1925–26; Division 3(N) – Champions 1924–25; Runners-up 1921–22; Division 4 – Runners-up 1965–66. *FA Cup* best season: 3rd rd, 1910–11, 5th rd, 1957–58.

COLOURS

White shirts with black collar and cuffs, black shorts, black stockings with white hoop on top.
Change colours: All royal blue or all red.

DARLINGTON

Players Names Ht, Wt, D.o.B.	Birthplace Transfer Fee	Clubs	Appearances F.L. A & S	 F.L.C. A & S	 F.A.C. A & S	Goals F.L.	 F.L.C.	 F.A.C.
Goalkeepers								
Pat Cuff* (ES)	Middlesbrough	Middlesbrough (A)	31		5			
6 0, 12 4, 19.3.52	—	Grimsby T (loan)	2					
	F/T	Millwall	42	3	1			
	F/T	Darlington	110	6	4			
Fred Barber	Ferryhill	Darlington (A)	12					
6 0, 11 10, 26.8.63								
Defenders								
Kevan Smith	Eaglescliffe	Stockton						
6 3, 11 10, 13.12.59		Darlington	162+3	4+1	7	7		1
Alan Kamara	Sheffield	Kiveton Park						
5 6, 11 2, 15.7.58		York C	10					
	F/T	Darlington	134	6	4	1		
Harry Wilson* (EY)	Hetton	Burnley (A)	10					
5 9½, 10 12, 29.11.53	£35,000	Brighton	130	9	7	4		
	P/E	Preston NE	38+4	8				
	F/T	Darlington	82+3	2	3			
David McLean (ES)	Newcastle	Newcastle U (A)	7+2	1				
5 8, 11 0, 24.11.57	£10,000	Carlisle U	9+6					
	F/T	Darlington	165+4	6	7	24		
Gavin Liddle*	Houghton-le-Spring	Hartlepool U (A)						
5 10½, 12 7, 9.5.63	F/T	Darlington	33+4					
Tim Gilbert	South Shields	Sunderland (A)	34+2	6		3		
5 9, 11 10, 28.5.58	£8,000	Cardiff C	33			1		
	F/T	Darlington	37+1	1	1	1		
Midfield								
Roger Wicks*	Darlington	Netherfield						
6 0, 11 8, 19.4.57		Darlington	31+10	1	2	4		
Brian Honour	Horden	Darlington (A)	27+7	1	1	3		
5 7, 10 7, 16.2.64								
Peter Cartwright	Newcastle	North Shields						
5 7, 10 0, 23.8.57	£5,000	Newcastle U	57+8	+3	2+1	3	1	
	—	Scunthorpe U (loan)	2+2			1		
		Darlington	9+2					
Forwards								
Alan Walsh	Hartlepool	Horden CW						
6 0, 12 8, 9.12.56		Middlesbrough	0+3					
	£15,000	Darlington	209+4	8	9+1	77	4	1
Tony McFadden*	Hexham	Reyrolles						
5 10, 12 0, 18.5.57	F/T	Darlington	44+3	2		10		
Non-contract players								
David Young	Trimdon	Darlington (A)	12+3					
5 7, 10 5, 31.1.65								
Jeff Wilson	South Shields	Darlington (A)	3					
6 3, 13 7, 7.12.64								
Dave Wakefield	South Shields	Darlington (A)	3+3					
5 8, 10 0, 15.1.65								

Commercial Manager: Alice Burton (Tel. Darlington 65097)
Club Coach:
Supporters Player of the Season 1982–83: Alan Kamara
Physiotherapist: Bob Farrelly
Club Captain 1982–83: Kevan Smith
Chief Scout:
Club Statistician: Frank Tweddle
Association of Football Statisticians Club Adviser to Yearbook: F. Tweddle

Players released since May 1982: Don Ball, D. (Bishop Auckland); Kevin Glendinning, D. (Carlisle U N/C); Ian Hamilton, F. (N/K); David Hawker, M. (Bishop Auckland); Terry Brissett, D. (N/K); Barry Dunn, F. (N/K); Steve McDermott, F. (N/K).

DERBY COUNTY — Division 2

Back row (left to right): Mick Jones (Coach), Kevin Wilson, George Foster, John McAlle, Paul Blades, Steve Cherry, Ian Dalziel, Glen Skivington, John Barton, Brian Attley, Gary Mills (now back at Seattle Sounders), Gordon Guthrie (Physio), Roy McFarland (Team Manager)
Front row: Bobby Davison, John Richards (back at Wolves), Dave Swindlehurst (now West Ham U), Archie Gemmill (Team Captain), Peter Taylor (Club Manager), Steve Powell (Club Captain), Mick Brolly, Steve Buckley. Also Paul Futcher, defender, not on picture.

Chairman: G. M. E. Watterson ***Vice-Chairman:*** J. N. Kirkland BSC, Cens, MICE.

Directors: F. W. Fern, A. S. Webb, W. Hart, T. J. East.

Club Manager: Peter Taylor.

Team Manager: Roy McFarland.

Secretary: Michael Dunford.

Year Formed: 1884. ***Turned Professional:*** 1884. ***Ltd Co.:*** 1896.

Club Nickname: 'The Rams'.

Former Grounds: 1884–95, Racecourse Ground; 1895, Baseball Ground.

Previous Managers since 1946: Stuart McMillan, Jack Barker, Harry Storer, Tim Ward, Brian Clough, Dave Mackay, Colin Murphy, Tommy Docherty, Colin Addison, John Newman (10).

Baseball Ground, Shaftesbury Crescent, Derby DE3 8NB. Telephone Derby (0332) 40105. ***Telegraphic address:*** 'Football Derby'. ***Ground capacity:*** 33,700 (16,000 seats.) ***Record attendance:*** 41,826 v Tottenham H, Division 1, 20 Sept, 1969. ***Record receipts:*** £108,000 v Manchester U, FA Cup 5th Rd, 19 Feb, 1983. ***Pitch measurements:*** 110yd×71yd.

Directions to Ground: Buses from town centre 159, 88 and 89. Nearest railway station Derby Midland.

Match tickets: Available 14 days prior to game (£4.00, £3.50, £3.00). Children £2.00. Terrace: £2.00 (home supporters).

Car parking: Eight car parks within half a mile of the ground run by the club in connection with the local corporation. Street parking half a mile from the ground.

Entertainments/catering facilities: Sportsmen's Club (members only). Licensed and refreshment bars in all parts of the ground. Executive Box complex.

Programmes: *The Ram Newspaper*, the official club programme, is available on match days priced 35p and on subscription care of the Programme Editor, Derby County Football Club.

Address of Supporters Club: Baseball Ground, Derby.

Address of the Club Shop or Boutique: The Ramtique, 57 Osmaston Road, Derby.

Note: Full club statistical records are on pages 416–455.

DERBY COUNTY 1982–83 LEAGUE RECORD

Match No.	Date	Venue	Opponents	Result		H/T Score	Lg. Pos.	Goalscorers	Attendance
1	Aug 28	H	Carlisle U	L	0-3	0-2	—		11,206
2	Sept 4	A	QPR	L	1-4	1-1	22	Gamble	10,217
3	8	H	Chelsea	W	1-0	0-0	—	Buckley (pen)	8075
4	11	H	Middlesbrough	D	1-1	1-1	16	Dalziel (pen)	9050
5	18	A	Leeds U	L	1-2	1-1	19	Brolly	16,889
6	25	H	Blackburn R	L	1-2	0-0	20	Dalziel	9361
7	Oct 2	A	Charlton Ath	D	1-1	0-0	21	Gamble	4685
8	9	H	Cambridge U	D	1-1	1-1	20	Brolly	8135
9	16	A	Grimsby T	D	1-1	1-0	21	Swindlehurst	7572
10	19	A	Barnsley	D	1-1	1-0	—	Brolly	10,343
11	23	H	Leicester C	L	0-4	0-1	21		13,191
12	30	A	Wolverhampton W	L	1-2	0-1	21	Wilson	13,804
13	Nov 6	A	Sheffield W	L	0-2	0-0	22		17,703
14	13	H	Bolton W	D	0-0	0-0	22		10,999
15	20	H	Oldham Ath	D	2-2	0-1	22	Swindlehurst, Dalziel	11,775
16	27	A	Burnley	D	1-1	0-1	22	Richards	7484
17	Dec 4	H	Rotherham U	W	3-0	1-0	21	Swindlehurst 2, Dalziel	13,149
18	11	A	Fulham	L	1-2	0-1	21	Buckley	7854
19	18	H	Crystal Palace	D	1-1	1-1	22	Richards	13,207
20	27	A	Newcastle U	L	0-1	0-0	22		30,559
21	29	H	Shrewsbury T	L	2-3	0-2	22	Davison 2	13,068
22	Jan 1	A	Oldham Ath	D	2-2	1-0	22	Swindlehurst, Gemmill (pen)	7085
23	3	H	QPR	W	2-0	1-0	22	Mills, Swindlehurst	14007
24	15	A	Carlisle U	L	0-3	0-2	22		4732
28	22	H	Leeds U	D	3-3	0-1	22	Davison, Swindlehurst, Gemmill	17,005
26	Feb 5	A	Chelsea	W	3-1	2-1	22	Francis (og), Bumstead (og), Gemmill (pen)	8661
27	26	H	Grimsby T	W	2-0	0-0	22	Moore K. (og), Davison	12,775
28	Mar 5	A	Leicester C	D	1-1	0-0	22	Barton	15,288
29	12	H	Wolverhampton W	D	1-1	1-0	22	Swindlehurst	17,644
30	15	A	Cambridge U	D	0-0	0-0	—		4476
31	19	H	Sheffield W	D	0-0	0-0	22		16,925
32	26	A	Bolton W	W	2-0	0-0	21	Brolly, Wilson	7041
33	Apr 2	A	Shrewsbury T	D	1-1	1-0	21	Hooks	7194
34	4	H	Newcastle U	W	2-1	2-0	—	Wilson, Hooks	19,779
35	9	A	Middlesbrough	W	3-2	2-0	16	Gemmil (pen), Davison 2	9078
36	13	H	Charlton Ath	D	1-1	1-1	—	Gemmill	15,605
37	16	H	Barnsley	D	1-1	1-0	15	Burns	14,861
38	23	A	Rotherham U	D	1-1	1-1	15	Gemmill (pen)	9646
39	30	H	Burnley	W	2-0	2-0	14	Wilson, Davison	14,674
40	May 2	A	Blackburn R	L	0-2	0-1	14		5619
41	7	A	Crystal Palace	L	1-4	0-2	15	Gilbert (og)	8464
42	14	H	Fulham	W	1-0	0-0	13	Davison	21,124

Final League Position: 13

GOALSCORERS

League (49): Davison 8, Swindlehurst 8, Gemmill 6 (4 pens), Brolly 4, Dalziel 4 (1 pen), Wilson 4, Buckley 2 (1 pen), Gamble 2, Hooks 2, Richards 2, Barton 1, Burns 1, Mills 1, own goals 4.
Milk Cup (11): Swindlehurst 3, Buckley 2, Wilson 2, Brolly 1, Hill 1, Skivington 1, own goal 1.
FA Cup (4): Wilson 2, Gemmill 1, Hill 1.

Milk Cup	First Round	Halifax T (a)	1-2
		(h)	5-2 (aet)
	Second Round	Hartlepool U (h)	2-0
		(a)	2-4 (aet)
	Third Round	Birmingham C (a)	1-3
FA Cup	Third Round	Nottingham F (h)	2-0
	Fourth Round	Chelsea (h)	2-1
	Fifth Round	Manchester U (h)	0-1

Commercial Manager: S. F. T. Crooks. (Tel. 40105)
Club Coach: Mick Jones
Supporters Player of the Season 1982–83: Not yet decided
Physiotherapist: Gordon Guthrie
Club Captain 1982–83: Steve Powell
Chief Scout: Ken Gutteridge
Club Statistician:
Association of Football Statisticians Club Adviser to Yearbook: S. M. McGhee.

Banovic	Barton	Attley	Powell	Foster	McAlle	Brolly	Skivington	Wilson	Swindlehurst	Reid	Emson	Hill	Gamble	Buckley	Dalziel	Blades	Mills	Cherry	Gemmill	Richards (L)	Davison	Futcher	Thomas (L)	Hooks	Burns (L)	Referees	Match No.
1	2	3	4	5	6	7	8*	9	10	11	12															M. Dimblebee	1
1	2	3	4	5	6	7	8*		10	11		12	9													E. Read	2
1	2*	8		5	6	7	4		10		12	9		3	11											P. Tyldesley	3
1		2		5	6	7	4		10	8	11	9			3											R. Banks	4
1	2	8		5*		7	4	10			12	9		3	11	6										D. Owen	5
1		2	4	5	6	7	8		10*			12	9	3	11											B. Hill	6
1	2	4	6	5		7			10		12	9	8*	3	11											M. James	7
1	2	4	6	5		7			10		12	9	8*	3	11											N. Glover	8
1	2		4	5	6	7		9	10		11				3		8									D. Hutchinson	9
1	2		4	5	6	7		9	10		11			3			8									N. Midgley	10
1	2	4		5	6	7		9	10		11			3			8									N. Wilson	11
	2		4	5	6	7	8	9				10		3	11			1								D. Vickers	12
	2		4	5		7	6	9				10		3	11		8	1								D. Allison	13
	2		4*	5	6	7	12	8	10			9		3	11			1								D. Reeves	14
	2	4		5	6	7			10					3	11			1	8	9						E. Scales	15
	2	4		5		7			10					3	11	6		1	8	9						K. Redfern	16
	2	4		5		7			10					3	11	6		1	8	9*	12					J. Moules	17
	2	4		5		7			10					3	11	6		1	8	9*	12					E. Crickmore	18
	2	4*		5		7			10					3	11	6		1	8	9	12					D. Scott	19
	2*	3		5	4	12			10						11		6	1	8	9	7					P. Tyldesley	20
	12	3		5	6	7			10						11*		2	1	4	9	8					R. Lewis	21
	2	3		5	6	7			10								11	1	4	9	8					C. Seel	22
	2	3		5	6	7			10								11	1	4	9	8					B. Newsome	23
	2	3		5	4	7	12		10							6*	11	1		9	8					A. Robinson	24
	2			5	6	7	12	9	10					3			11	1	4*		8					T. Ward	25
	2	3	5			7		9	10								11	1	4		8	6				I. Borrett	26
	2		5			7		9	10					3			11	1	4		8	6				J. Worrall	27
	2		5			7			10			9		3			11	1	4		8	6				D. Hedges	28
	2		5			7			10			9		3			11	1	4		8	6				R. Bridges	29
	2			5		7			10			9		3			11	1	4		8	6				C. Downey	30
	2		4	5		7			10		11			3				1	8		9*	6	12			B. Daniels	31
	2		5			7		9						3			11	1	4		8	6		10		A. Saunders	32
	2		5			7		9						3			11	1	4		8	6		10		R. Nixon	33
	2		5*			7		9						3			11	1	4		8	6		10	12	R. Guy	34
	2		5		12	7		9						3				1	4		8	6		10*	11	T. Mills	35
	2		5		12	7		9			11			3*				1	4		8	6			10	D. Lloyd	36
	2		5			7		9			11							1	4		8	6		10	3	A. Cooper	37
	2		5		12	7		9							11*			1	4		8	6		10	3	J. Lovatt	38
	2		5*		12	7		9			11							1	4		8	6		10	3	M. Dinblebee	39
	2	3		5	4	7		9			11	10						1			8	6				F. Roberts	40
	2	3		5	4	7	10	9			11*	12						1			8	6				A. Glasson	41
	2			5	12	7		9			11							1	4*		8	6		10	3	R. Chadwick	42
11	39	22	23	30	19	41	9	22	28	3	11	12	4	26	18	6	18	31	25	10	23	17	0	8	6		
	+ 1s				+ 5s	+ 1s	+ 3s				+ 5s	+ 3s									+ 3s		+ 1s		+ 1s		

FOOTBALL LEAGUE RECORD

1888 Founder Member of the Football League; 1907–12 Division 2; 1912–14 Division 1; 1914–15 Division 2; 1915–21 Division 1; 1921–26 Division 2; 1926–53 Division 1; 1953–55 Division 2; 1955–57 Division 3(N); 1957–69 Division 2; 1969–80 Division 1; 1980– Division 2.

HONOURS

Football League: Division 1 – Champions 1971–72, 1974–75; Runners-up 1895–96, 1929–30, 1935–36; Division 2 – Champions 1911–12, 1914–15, 1968–69; Runners-up 1925–26; Division 3(N) – Champions 1956–57; Runners-up 1955–56. *FA Cup:* Winners 1945–46; Runners-up 1897–98, 1898–99, 1902–03. *Football League Cup:* Semi-final 1967–68. *Texaco Cup:* 1971–72. *Charity Shield:* 1975. **European Competitions:** *European Cup:* 1972–73, 1975–76; *UEFA Cup:* 1974–75, 1976–77.

COLOURS

White shirts, blue shorts, white stockings.
Change colours: Orange shirts and stockings, blue shorts.

DERBY COUNTY

Players Names Ht, Wt, D.o.B.	Birthplace Transfer Fee	Clubs	Appearances F.L. A & S	 F.L.C. A & S	 F.A.C. A & S	Goals F.L.	 F.L.C.	 F.A.C.
Goalkeepers								
Steve Cherry (EY)	Nottingham	Derby Co (A)	39	2	3			
5 11, 11 0, 5.8.60	—	Port Vale (loan)	4					
Yakka Banovic (Yug)	Yugoslavia	Heidelberg U						
5 10, 11 8,	£40,000	Derby Co	32	3				
Defenders								
Paul Futcher (EU21)	Chester	Chester (a)	20		1			
6 0, 12 3, 25.9.56	£100,000	Luton T	131	4	6	1		
	£350,000	Manchester C	36+1	3+1	3			
	£150,000	Oldham Ath	98	9	4	1		
	£100,000	Derby Co	17					
Steve Buckley	Brinsley	Burton A						
5 11, 12 4, 16.10.53	£2000	Luton T	123	7	5	9		
	£165,000	Derby Co	200	12	4	13	2	
Steve Powell (EU23)	Derby	Derby Co (A)	281+9	19	25+1	18		
5 9, 12 0, 20.9.55								
Brian Attley	Cardiff	Cardiff C (A)	73+6	7+1	5	1		
5 9, 9 12, 27.8.55	£25,000	Swansea C	83+6	5	1	6		2
	£25,000	Derby Co	41	3	2	1		
	—	Oxford U (loan)	5					
John McAlle	Liverpool	Wolverh'pton W (A)	394+13	27	43+1		1	
6 0, 11 3, 31.1.50	£10,000	Sheffield U	18	4	2			
	£25,000	Derby Co	37+5	4	2+1			
John Barton	Birmingham	Worcester C						
5 10, 11 0, 24.10.53	£27,000	Everton	18+2	3				
	F/T	Derby Co	49+1	5	3	1		
George Foster	Plymouth	Plymouth Arg (A)	201+11	19	10	6		
5 10, 11 2, 26.9.56	—	Torquay U (loan)	6			3		
	—	Exeter C (loan)	28					
	£40,000	Derby Co	30	5	3			
Paul Blades		Derby Co (A)	6	1				
Midfield								
Glen Skivington	Barrow	Barrow						
5 10, 11 3, 19.1.62	£25,000	Derby Co	39+7	4		2	1	
	—	Halifax T (loan)	4					
Francis Gamble*	Liverpool	Burscough						
5 9, 11 0,		Derby Co	5+1	1	1	2		
Archie Gemmill (S)	Paisley	St Mirren						
5 5, 11 2, 24.3.47		Preston NE	93+6	5	5	13		1
	£70,000	Derby Co	261	19	28	18	1	4
	£100,000	Nottingham F	56+2	7	7	4		
	£150,000	Birmingham C	97	10	7	12	1	1
		Jacksonville TM						
	F/T	Wigan Ath (N/C)	11	2				
	—	Derby Co	25		2	6		2
Sean Lane (E.S.)	Bristol	Hereford U (A)	39+11	3+1	1+2	3		
16.1.64		Derby Co						
Forwards								
Paul Emson*	Lincoln	Briggs T						
5 11, 11 3, 22.10.58	£5000	Derby Co	112+15	4+3	1+3	13		
Paul Hooks	Wallsend	Notts Co (A)	144+29	15+1	6+3	30	5	1
5 8, 10 11, 30.5.59		Derby Co	8			2		
Kevin Wilson	Banbury	Banbury U						
5 7, 10 7, 18.4.61	£20,000	Derby Co	69+8	2+3	3	20	2	2
Andy Hill	Ilkeston	Kimberley						
6 1, 12 0,		Derby Co	18+3	3	3	2	1	1
Mike Brolly (SS)	Kilmarnock	Chelsea	7+1		1	1		
5 9, 10 4, 6.10.54	F/T	Bristol C	27+3	2	1	2		1
	£6000	Grimsby T	246+8	16	16	27	2	1
	F/T	Derby Co	41+1	5	3	4	1	
Bobby Davison	South Shields	Seaham C.W.						
5 10, 11 5, 17.7.59	£1000	Huddersfield T	1+1					
	£20,000	Halifax T	63	5	3	29	3	
	£55,000	Derby Co	23+3			8		
Paul Bancroft		Derby Co (A)						
		Crewe Alex (loan)	21			3		
Steve Devine		Wolverh'pton W (A)						
	F/T	Derby Co						

Players (non-appearance) granted free transfer: Graham Harbey, D.
Players released since May 1982: Charlie George, F. (Hong Kong); Kevin Hector, F. (Burton A); Barry Powell, M. (Hong Kong); Wayne Richards, D. (Matlock); Mark Shackleton, M. (N/K); John Clayton, F. (Hong Kong); Daryl Chapman, M. (Crewe Alex N/C); Gary Mills, F. (Seattle Sounders); David Collins. (Heanor T); Jim Collins. (N/K); John Lovatt, D. (N/K).

DONCASTER ROVERS Division 4

Back row (left to right): Billy Bremner (Manager), Carl Swan, Steve Lister, Alan Warboys, Dennis Peacock, Willie Boyd, Hugh Dowd, Ian Nimmo, Colin Douglas, Graham Cawthorne
Front row: Glenn Humphries, Alan Little, Garry Liddell, Stewart Mell, Glynn Snodin, Ian Snodin, Daral Pugh (now Huddersfield T),Billy Russell.

Doncaster Rovers Football Club Ltd.
(Founded 1879)

President: J. C. Morris. ***Vice-President:*** R. Jones.

Chairman: I. M. Jones. ***Vice Chairman:*** K. Jackson.

Directors: H. Bates, A. Phillips, K. Jackson, B. E. Boldry, J. J. Burke, G. Smith, T. C. Hamilton.

Manager: Billy Bremner.

Secretary: Sheila Louth.

Year Formed: 1879. ***Turned Professional:*** 1885. ***Ltd Co.:*** 1905 and 1920.

Club Nickname: 'Rovers'.

Previous Grounds: 1880–1916, Intake Ground: 1920–22, Benetthorpe Ground; 1922, Low Pasture, Belle Vue.

Previous Managers since 1946: Bill Marsden, Jackie Bestall, Peter Doherty, Jack Hodgson, Syd Bycroft, Jack Crayston, Jack Bestall, Norman Curtis, Danny Malloy, Oscar Hold, Bill Leivers, Keith Kettleborough, George Raynor, Lawrie McMenemy, Maurice Setters, Stan Anderson (16).

Belle Vue Ground, Doncaster. Telephone Doncaster (0302) 535281. ***Telegraphic address:*** 'Rovers Doncaster'. ***Ground capacity:*** 21,150. ***Record attendance:*** 37,149 v Hull C, Division 3(N), 2 Oct, 1948. ***Record receipts:*** £15,220.66 v Huddersfield T, Division 3, 6 Nov, 1981. ***Pitch measurements:*** 110yd×77yd.

Directions to Ground: Buses from town centre (Duke St) – Race Course, Hyde Park, and Cantley Estate services. Doncaster railway station is near the town centre.

Match tickets: No advance booking except for Cup ties.

Car parking: Very large car and coach park by ground. Entrance direct from Great North Road.

Entertainments/catering facilities: Refreshment bars in Main Stand and around the ground, including licensed bars. Social club adjoining ground.

Handbooks/programmes: Annual handbook on sale at 20p post free or at shop or Supporters Club office. Programmes on sale at shop but not on subscription.

Extra information: Development Association office on ground. Supporters Club office and shop on ground – minimum subscription 15p (Children and OAPs 10p). Handbook free to members. Phone 539679.

Address of Supporters Club: Secretary, K. J. Avis, 64 Harrowden Road, Doncaster.

Note: Full club statistical records are on pages 416–455.

DONCASTER ROVERS 1982–83 LEAGUE RECORD

Match No.	Date	Venue	Opponents	Result	H/T Score	Lg. Pos.	Goalscorers	Attendance
1	Aug 28	H	Newport Co	D 0-0	0-0	—		3471
2	Sept 4	A	Bristol R	L 0-2	0-0	20		3617
3	8	A	Oxford U	L 0-3	0-1	—		4482
4	10	H	Exeter C	W 6-1	4-0	—	Graham, Lister (pen), Liddell, Douglas, Viney (og), Snodin G.	3205
5	18	A	Southend U	L 2-3	1-1	18	Russell, Lister	2677
6	25	H	Reading	W 7-5	5-3	13	Douglas, Snodin G. 3 (2 pens), Russell, Graham, Snodin I.	3118
7	28	H	Wigan Ath	L 3-6	2-4	—	Snodin I., Douglas, Snodin G.	4457
8	Oct 2	A	Orient	L 0-1	0-0	22		1846
9	9	A	Lincoln C	L 1-5	0-1	24	Douglas	4785
10	16	H	Brentford	D 4-4	1-1	23	Snodin G., Humphries, Austin, Liddell	3265
11	19	H	Wrexham	D 1-1	0-1	—	Snodin G. (pen)	3420
12	23	A	Bradford C	L 0-1	0-1	24		5526
13	30	H	Chesterfield	D 0-0	0-0	24		4065
14	Nov 2	A	Huddersfield T	L 0-3	0-0	—		6848
15	8	H	Plymouth Arg	D 2-2	0-0	—	Russell, Austin	2942
16	13	A	Gillingham	D 1-1	0-0	24	Austin	4451
17	27	A	Portsmouth	L 1-2	1-2	24	Humphries	9474
18	Dec 4	H	Cardiff C	D 2-2	0-1	24	Douglas, Snodin G.	3087
19	18	H	Millwall	W 2-1	0-1	22	Mell, Snodin G.	2568
20	27	A	Sheffield U	L 1-3	0-1	22	Mell	16,139
21	28	H	Preston NE	W 2-0	1-0	21	Mell, Austin	3895
22	Jan 1	A	Walsall	L 0-1	0-0	23		3859
23	3	H	AFC Bournemouth	W 2-1	1-0	20	Snodin G. 2 (1 pen)	3298
24	8	H	Bristol R	L 1-2	0-1	20	Snodin G.	3234
25	15	A	Newport Co	W 2-1	2-0	20	Lister, Humphries	3482
26	22	H	Southend U	D 0-0	0-0	20		3242
27	29	A	Wigan Ath	W 3-0	2-0	19	Snodin I., Snodin G. 2 (1 pen)	4387
28	Feb 5	A	Reading	L 0-2	0-0	21		1852
29	15	A	Wrexham	L 0-5	0-1	—		1899
30	19	H	Lincoln C	D 2-2	1-1	22	Douglas, Russell	4667
31	26	A	Brentford	L 0-1	0-0	22		4413
32	Mar 1	H	Huddersfield T	L 0-4	0-2	—		6078
33	5	H	Bradford C	L 1-2	0-2	22	Walker	3473
34	12	A	Chesterfield	D 3-3	3-0	22	Walker, Austin, Russell	2875
35	19	A	Plymouth Arg	W 2-1	1-1	22	Walker 2	3406
36	25	H	Gillingham	L 0-2	0-0	—		2528
37	Apr 2	A	Preston NE	L 1-4	0-2	24	Humphries	5287
38	5	H	Sheffield U	W 2-0	0-0	—	Walker, Humphries	8446
39	9	A	Cardiff C	L 0-3	0-2	23		5456
40	12	H	Orient	L 0-3	0-1	—		2355
41	16	H	Oxford U	L 0-1	0-0	23		1592
42	23	A	Millwall	L 0-3	0-2	23		4288
43	30	H	Portsmouth	L 0-2	0-1	23		2974
44	May 2	A	AFC Bournemouth	D 2-2	0-1	23	Lister, Douglas	3995
45	7	A	Exeter C	L 0-3	0-1	23		3110
46	14	H	Walsall	L 1-3	0-0	23	Liddell	1507

Final League Position: 23

GOALSCORERS

League (57): Snodin G. 14 (5 pens), Douglas 7, Austin 5, Humphries 5, Russell 5, Walker 5, Lister 4 (1 pen), Liddell 3, Mell 3, Snodin I. 3, Graham 2, own goal 1.
Milk Cup (1): Graham 1.
FA Cup (4): Austin 1, Mell 1, Owen 1, Snodin I. 1.

Milk Cup	First Round	Huddersfield T (a)	1-1
		(h)	0-1
FA Cup	First Round	Workington (a)	2-1
	Second Round	Peterborough U (a)	2-5

Peacock	Russell	Mell	Snodin I.	Cawthorne	Humphries	Pugh	Liddell	Douglas	Graham	Lister	Little	Snodin G.	Swan	Dowd	Austin	Boyd	Wigginton	Meagan	Robertson	Watson (L)	Owen (L)	Campbell (L)	Allanson	Mann	Walker (L)	Johnson	Woods	*Referees*
1	2	3	4	5	6	7	8	9	10	11																		J. Lovatt
1	2	12	4	5	6	7	8*	9	10	11	3																	C. Callow
1	2	8	4	5	6	7	12	9	10*	11	3																	H. King
1	2	12	4	5	6	7	8	9	10*	11		3																N. Glover
1	2	8*	4	5		7	12	9	10	11		3	6															M. James
1	2	12	4	5*		7	8	9	10		11	3		6														K. Redfern
1	2		4	5*	8		12	9	10		11	3		6	7													M. Scott
	2		4		8			9	10	5	11	3		6	7	1												L. Shapter
	2		4		8		12	9	10	5	11*	3		6	7	1												I. Borrett
	2				4		8	9		11		3		6	7	1	5	10										D. Richardson
1	2			6	4		8*	9	12	11		3			7		5	10										T. Fitzharris
	2			6	4		8	9	12	11*		3			10	1	5		7									N. Midgley
1	2		4	6	12		8*	7		11		10			9		5			3								D. Scott
1	2	8	4	6				7		11		10			9		5			3								R. Bridges
1	2		4*	6	12			7		11		10			9		5			3	8							J. Hough
1	2		4	6	11*			7		12		10			9		5			3	8							A. Ward
1		12		6	2			7*		4		10			9		5		11	3	8							B. Daniels
1	2			6				7		4		10			9		5		11	3	8							P. Tyldesley
1	2	7	4		5							10			9		6		11	3	8							R. Guy
1	2	7	4		5							10			9		6		11	3	8							D. Owen
1	2	7	4		5							10			9		6		11	3	8							A. Saunders
1	2	7	4					12		11		10		6	9		5			3	8*							J. Worrall
1	2	7	4		5			12		11*		10			9		6			3	8							A. Manchester
1	2	7	4		5			8*		12		10			9		6		11	3								R. Nixon
1	2	7	4		5					8		10			9		6		11	3								E. Scales
1	2	7	4		5			12		8		3			9		6		11			10						D. Allinson
1	2	7	4		5		12	8*		6		3			9				11			10						H. Taylor
1	2	7	4		5		8*			6		3			9				11			10	12					K. Salmon
1	2*	7	4		5		12	8		6		3			9				11					10				J. Bray
1	2	7	4		5		12	8*		6		3			9				11					10				K. Barratt
1	2		4	3	5		12	8*		6					9				11					10	7			A. Gunn
1	2		4	3	5		9	8*		6					12				11					10	7			B. Hill
		8	4	3	5					6					9	1	2		11					10	7			R. Chadwick
	2	8	4		5					6		3			9	1			11					10	7			M. Heath
	2	8			5			12		6		4			9*	1			11					10	7	3		J. Deakin
1	2	8			5			12		6		4			9*				11					10	7	3		N. Wilson
1	2	8	4		5			9		6					12				11					10	7*	3		C. Newsome
1		8	4		5		11	9		6													2	10	7	3		P. Tyldesley
1		8*	4		5		12	9		6		10							11				2		7	3		E. Crickmore
1		8			5			9		6		10			12				11				2	4*	7	3		T. Jones
1	4			8	5		11	9		6		10			12								2		7*	3		K. Walmsley
1	4			8	5			9		6		10											2	11	7	3		T. Spencer
1	4	7*		8	5			9		6		10							11				2			3	12	R. Banks
1	4	7			5		12	9		6		10							11				2			3	8*	J. Moules
1		7	4		5		12	9		6		10							11				2			3	8*	D. Milford
1	5	7*	4				12			6		10			9								2	11		3	8	C. Seel
39	40	28	34	21	38	6	12	33	9	39	6	38	1	6	30	7	18	2	25	13	9	3	9	13	12	12	3	
		+ 4s			+ 2s		+ 12s	+ 5s	+ 2s	+ 2s					+ 4s								+ 1s				+ 1s	

FOOTBALL LEAGUE RECORD

1901 Elected to Division 2; 1903 Failed re-election; 1904 Re-elected; 1905 Failed re-election; 1923 Re-elected to Division 3(N); 1935–37 Division 2; 1937–47 Division 3(N); 1947–48 Division 2; 1948–50 Division 3(N); 1950–58 Division 2; 1958–59 Division 3; 1959–66 Division 4; 1966–67 Division 3; 1967–69 Division 4; 1969–71 Division 3; 1971–81 Division 4; 1981–83 Division 3; 1983– Division 4.

HONOURS

Football League: Division 2 best season: 7th, 1901–02; Division 3(N) Champions 1934–35, 1946–47, 1949–50; Runners-up 1937–38, 1938–39; Division 4 – Champions 1965–66, 1968–69; Promoted 1980–81 (3rd). *FA Cup* best season: 5th rd, 1951–52, 1953–54, 1954–55, 1955–56. *Football League Cup* best season: 5th rd, 1975–76.

DONCASTER ROVERS

Players Names Ht, Wt, D.o.B.	Birthplace Transfer Fee	Clubs	Appearances F.L. A & S	 F.L.C. A & S	 F.A.C. A & S	Goals F.L.	 F.L.C.	 F.A.C.
Goalkeepers								
Willie Boyd (SY)	Bellshill	Hull C (A)						
5 10, 11 4, 18.10.58	F/T	Doncaster R	96	3	9			
Denis Peacock	Lincoln	Nottingham F (A)	22	2				
6 2, 14 1, 19.4.53	—	Walsall (loan)	10					
	P/E	Doncaster R	199	18	8			
	£70,000	Bolton W	16	2	2			
	F/T	Doncaster R	39	2	2			
Defenders								
Peter Johnson*	Harrogate	Middlesbrough (A)	42+1		7			
5 8, 10 4, 5.10.58	£60,000	Newcastle U	16					
	—	Bristol C (loan)	20		1			1
		Doncaster R	12					
Hugh Dowd* (NI)	Lurgan	Glenavon						
6 1, 13 0, 19.5.51		Sheffield W	110+3	19	5			
	£15,000	Doncaster R	94	10	7	3		
Billy Russell (SY)	Glasgow	Everton (A)						
5 10, 11 4, 14.9.59	F/T	Celtic						
	F/T	Doncaster R	162+3	11	14	9		
Stewart Mell*	Doncaster	Appleby Frodingham						
5 10, 11 0, 15.10.57	F/T	Doncaster R	62+14	4+1	+2	14		1
Graham Cawthorne*	Doncaster	Harworth Cl						
6 3, 11 12, 30.9.58		Grimsby T	1					
	F/T	Doncaster R	33	2	2	1		
Midfield								
Steve Lister	Doncaster	Doncaster R (A)	163+7	10	10	26		
6 1, 11 10, 18.11.61								
Ian Snodin (EY)	Rotherham	Doncaster R (A)	101+7	4	6+1	8		
5 7, 8 12, 15.8.63								
Glyn Snodin	Rotherham	Doncaster R (A)	204+19	7+1	10	30		1
5 6, 9 5, 14.2.60								
Jimmy Mann*	Goole	Leeds U (A)	2	2	+1			
5 10, 11 6, 5.12.52	F/T	Bristol C	205+26	15	10+2	31	2	4
		Barnsley	14+1					
	F/T	Scunthorpe U (N/C)	2					
	F/T	Doncaster R	13					
Forwards								
Glenn Humphries (EY) 11.8.64	Hull	Doncaster R (A)	50+5	3+1	1	5		
Gary Liddell*	Bannockburn	Leeds U (A)	2+1	1				
5 9, 11 4, 27.8.54	£10,000	Grimsby T	90+15	9+3	5+1	24	2	1
	F/T	Hearts						
	F/T	Doncaster R	25+12	2			4	
Colin Douglas	Hurlford	Celtic						
6 1, 11 0,	F/T	Doncaster R	71+9	5+1	5	10	1	
Terry Austin*	Isleworth	Crystal Palace						
6 1, 12 6, 1.2.54		Ipswich T	10+9		1+1	1		
	£80,000+P/E	Plymouth Arg	58	3	5	18		
	£35,000	Walsall	44+3	3	1	19		
	P/E	Mansfield T	84	9	3	31	3	1
	£110,000	Huddersfield T	39+3	3	6	10	1	1
	P/E	Doncaster R	30+4	1	2	5		1
Non-contract Players								
Gary Allanson	Hull	Doncaster R (A)	10+1					
Apprentices								
Neil Woods		Doncaster R (A)						

Commercial Manager: N. C. Johnson (Tel.).
Assistant Manager: David Bentley.
Youth Team Coach: David Pugh.
Supporters Player of the Season 1982–83: Glyn Snodin.
Physiotherapist: Gerry Delahont.
Club Captain 1982–83:
Chief Scout:
Club Statistician: J. C. Morris.
Association of Football Statisticians Club Adviser to Yearbook: T. Wiles.

Players released since May 1982: Pat Lally, M. (Burton A); Carl Swann, D. (N/K); Ian Nimmo, F. (Retired); Alan Warboys, F. (Retired); Colin Walker, F. (Gisbourne C); Tommy Meagan, M. (N/C-USA; Clive Wigginton, D. (N/K); Stuart Robertson, M. (N/K).

COLOURS Red and white hooped shirts with a thin green hoop, white shorts with red/white/green stripe down side, white socks with red/green turnover. **Change colours:** Green shirt with white sleeves and red trim, green shorts with red/white/green stripe down side, red socks with green/white turnover.

EVERTON Division 1

Back row (left to right):
K Ratcliffe
W. Wright
M. Walsh
N. Southall
J. A. Arnold
M. N. Higgins
J. Ferguson
D. Mountfield
Middle row:
C. Harvey (2nd team trainer)
J. E. Johnson
A. Irvine
K. Richardson
G. M. Sharp
B. Borrows
A. E. King
G. Stevens
M. Heaton (1st team trainer)
J. Clinkard (Physiotherapist)
Front row:
K Sheedy
S. McMahon
A. P. Heath
H. Kendall (Manager)
T. W. Ross
J. Bailey
A. Ainscow.

Chairman: P. D. Carter CBE. ***Vice-Chairman:*** T. H. W. Scott.

Directors: A. W. Waterworth, G. A. Watts, K. M. Tamlin, J. Search, D. A. B. Newton.

Manager: Howard Kendall. ***Secretary:*** Jim Greenwood.

Year Formed: 1878. ***Turned Professional:*** 1885. ***Ltd Co.:*** 1892.

Former Grounds: 1878, Stanley Park; 1882, Priory Road; 1884, Anfield Road; 1892, Goodison Park.

Previous Managers since 1946: Theo Kelly, Cliff Britton, Ian Buchan, John Carey, Harry Catterick, Billy Bingham, Gordon Lee (7).

Goodison Park, Liverpool L4 4EL. Telephone 051-521 2020. ***Match ticket information:*** 051-523 6642 (24 hr. service). ***Ground capacity:*** 53,419 (25,000 seats). ***Record attendance:*** 78,299 v Liverpool, Division 1, 18 Sept, 1948. ***Record receipts:*** £174,945, Liverpool v Manchester U, FA Cup semi-final replay, 4 April, 1979. ***Pitch measurements:*** 112yd×78yd.

Directions to Ground: Corporation buses 19, 30A, 85, 154 from Lime St. Nearest railway station, Liverpool Lime Street.

Match tickets: Reserved stand seats are available for all home fixtures (except the match v Liverpool) at any time during the season, either by post or by personal application to the Box Office at the Goodison Rd side of the ground. The Box Office is open each weekday from 9 am to 5 pm. Postal applications should be addressed to the Box Office manager and contain the correct remittance and SAE.

Car parking: Extensive parking facilities on site at the corner of Priory and Utting Ave.

Entertainments/catering facilities: Royal Blue Restaurant open to the public for lunch on Mondays to Fridays but restricted to members on match days (051-525 7499).

Club shop: All souvenirs available from The Toffee Shop in Goodison Rd; send SAE for mail order list.

Handbooks/programmes: Match-day magazine available on seasonal subscription.

Address of Supporters Club: 38 City Road, Liverpool 4 (051-521 2020).

Note: Full club statistical records are on pages 416–455.

EVERTON 1982–83 LEAGUE RECORD

Match No.	Date	Venue	Opponents	Result		H/T Score	Lg. Pos.	Goalscorers	Attendance
1	Aug 28	A	Watford	L	0-2	0-1	—		19,630
2	31	H	Aston Villa	W	5-0	3-0	—	Heath 2, King, Sharp 2 (1 pen)	24,026
3	Sept 4	H	Tottenham H	W	3-1	3-1	5	Sheedy, Wright, McMahon	30,553
4	8	A	Manchester U	L	1-2	1-1	—	King	43,186
5	11	A	Notts Co	L	0-1	0-0	14		9197
6	18	H	Norwich C	D	1-1	0-0	13	Irvine	20,281
7	25	A	Coventry C	L	2-4	1-1	16	Heath, King	9319
8	Oct 2	H	Brighton & HA	D	2-2	1-1	17	Heath, Wright	17,539
9	9	H	Manchester C	W	2-1	1-1	13	King, McMahon	25,158
10	16	A	Swansea C	W	3-0	1-0	10	Stevenson (og), Richardson, McMahon	11,183
11	23	H	Sunderland	W	3-1	1-0	7	Johnson, Sharp, Richardson	20,360
12	30	A	Southampton	L	2-3	1-2	11	Wright, King	18,141
13	Nov 6	H	Liverpool	L	0-5	0-1	13		52,741
14	13	A	Arsenal	D	1-1	1-0	11	King	23,067
15	20	H	WBA	D	0-0	0-0	14		16,001
16	27	A	West Ham U	L	0-2	0-1	15		21,424
17	Dec 4	H	Birmingham C	D	0-0	0-0	15		13,703
18	11	A	Ipswich T	W	2-0	0-0	14	Sheedy, Richardson	17,512
19	18	H	Luton T	W	5-0	2-0	12	Bailey, Sheedy, Curran, Heath 2	14,982
20	27	A	Stoke C	L	0-1	0-0	14		25,427
21	28	H	Nottingham F	W	3-1	2-0	10	Sharp 2 (1 pen), McMahon	25,147
22	Jan 1	A	WBA	D	2-2	1-1	11	Sharp, Higgins	15,194
23	3	A	Tottenham H	L	1-2	0-1	13	Sharp	28,455
24	15	H	Watford	W	1-0	0-0	11	Johnson	19,233
25	22	A	Norwich C	W	1-0	1-0	8	Ratcliffe	14,180
26	Feb 5	H	Notts Co	W	3-0	2-0	5	King, Heath, Sheedy	14,541
27	12	A	Aston Villa	L	0-2	0-1	7		21,117
28	26	H	Swansea C	D	2-2	1-1	7	King 2	17,112
29	Mar 2	A	Manchester C	D	0-0	0-0	—		22,253
30	5	A	Sunderland	L	1-2	1-1	9	Sharp	16,051
31	15	H	Southampton	W	2-0	0-0	—	Heath, Sheedy	15,002
32	19	A	Liverpool	D	0-0	0-0	8		44,737
33	26	H	Arsenal	L	2-3	1-0	11	Ainscow, Heath	16,318
34	Apr 2	A	Nottingham F	L	0-2	0-2	13		14,815
35	4	H	Stoke C	W	3-1	0-0	—	Sheedy 2, Sharp	15,360
36	9	A	Brighton & HA	W	2-1	1-0	9	Sheedy 2	14,534
37	19	H	Manchester U	W	2-0	0-0	—	Sharp, Heath	21,707
38	23	A	Birmingham C	L	0-1	0-0	10		11,045
39	30	H	West Ham U	W	2-0	1-0	7	Sharp 2	16,355
40	May 2	H	Coventry C	W	1-0	0-0	6	Sharp (pen)	12,972
41	7	A	Luton T	W	5-1	2-1	6	Johnson, Sheedy 2, Sharp 2 (1 pen)	12,447
42	14	H	Ipswich T	D	1-1	0-0	7	Wark (og)	17,420

Final League Position: 7

GOALSCORERS

League (66): Sharp 15 (4 pens), Sheedy 11, Heath 10, King 9, McMahon 4, Johnson 3, Richardson 3, Wright 3, Ainscow 1, Bailey 1, Curran 1, Higgins 1, Irvine 1, Ratcliffe 1, own goals 2.
Milk Cup (5): King 2, Johnson 1, McMahon 1, Stevens 1.
FA Cup (7): King 2, Sharp 2, Sheedy 2, Heath 1.

Milk Cup	Second Round	Newport Co (a)	2-0
		(h)	2-2
	Third Round	Arsenal (h)	1-1
		(a)	0-3
FA Cup	Third Round	Newport Co (a)	1-1
		(h)	2-1
	Fourth Round	Shrewsbury T (h)	2-1
	Fifth Round	Tottenham H (h)	2-0
	Sixth Round	Manchester U (a)	0-1

Commercial Manager: Ralph Williams (Tel. 051-521 2020)
Club Coach: Mick Heaton
Supporters Player of the Season 1982–83:
Physiotherapist: John Clinkard
Club Captain 1982–83: Mark Higgins
Chief Scout: Harry Cooke
Club Statistician (if any):
Association of Football Statisticians Club Adviser to Yearbook: G. Smailes

Southall	Borrows	Bailey	Higgins	Wright	Heath	McMahon	Johnson	Sharp	King	Sheedy	Richardson	Irvine	Ainscow	Walsh	Ratcliffe	Ross	Keeley (L)	Arnold	Stevens	Curran (L)	Reid	Mountfield	*Referees*	*Match No.*
1	2	3	4	5	6	7*	8	9	10	11	12												K. Baker	1
1	2	3	4	5	8	6		9	10	11	12	7*											A. Challinor	2
1	2	3	4	5	8	6		9	10	11			7										D. Shaw	3
1	2	3	4	5	8	6		9	10	11	12		7*										A. Hamil	4
1	2	3	4	5	8	6		9	10	11			7										M. Dimblebee	5
1	2			5	8	6		9	10	11		7*		3	4	12							G. Newsome	6
1			4	5	8	6		9	10	11	2	12		3		7*							J. Key	7
1	2	3	4	5	7	6	8	9	10	11													C. Seel	8
1	2	3	4	5	7	6	8	9	10	11													G. Tyson	9
1	2	3	4	5		6	8	9	10	11	7												L. Barratt	10
1	2	3	4	5	7*	6	8	9	10	11	12												J. Bray	11
1	2	3	4	5		6	8*	9	10	11	7	12											A. Ward	12
1	2	3		5	7	6	8*	9	10	11	12						4						D. Civil	13
			5	4	7	6	8	9	10		11*	12			3			1	2				A. Grey	14
			4	5	7	6	8	9	10			11			3			1	2				J. Hough	15
			4	5	8*	6	12	9	10	11		7			3			1	2				V. Callow	16
		3	4	5	8	6		9	10	11								1	2	7			G. Courtney	17
		3	5		8	6	9			11	10				4			1	2	7			C. Downey	18
		3	5		8	6	9*	12		11	10				4			1	2	7			M. Peck	19
		3	5		8	6	9	12		11	10				4			1	2*	7			J. Hunting	20
		3	5		12	6	9	8*		11					4			1	2	7	10		K. Redfern	21
		3	5			6	9	8		11					4			1	2	7	10		G. Napthine	22
		3	5			6	9	8		11					4			1	2	7	10		D. Hedges	23
		3	5		7	6	12	8	9	11					4			1	2		10*		K. Hackett	24
		3	5		8	6		9	7	11					4			1	2		10		M. Taylor	25
		3	5		7*		12	8	9	11	6				4			1	2		10		T. Jones	26
		3	5		7		12	9	8	11	6				4			1	2		10*		B. Stevens	27
		3	5		10		12	9	8	11	6	7*			4			1	2				P. Tyldesley	28
		3	5		10		7	9	8	11	6				4			1	2				T. Mills	29
		3	5		10		7	9	8*	11	6	12			4			1	2				C. Seel	30
		3	5		10	8		9		11	6	7			4			1	2				D. Lloyd	31
		3	5		10	8		9		11	6	7*	12		4			1	2				N. Midgley	32
		3	5		10	8		9		11	6	12	7		4			1	2*				J. Lovatt	33
		3	5		10	8	12	9		11	6*		7		4			1	2				D. Reeves	34
		3	5		10	6	8	9		11	2		7		4			1					A. Saunders	35
		3	5		10		8	9		11	6		7		4			1	2				C. Thomas	36
		3	5		10	7	8	9		11	6				4			1	2				D. Allison	37
		3			10	7*	8	9		11	6		12		4			1	2			5	K. Cooper	38
1		3	5		10		8	9		11	6		7		4				2				K. Holbrook	39
1		3	5		10	7	8*	9		11	6	12			4				2				A. Challinor	40
1		3	5		10	7	8	9		11	6				4				2				I. Borrett	41
1		3	5		10		8	9		11	6*	12	7		4				2				G. Courtney	42
17	12	37	39	17	37	34	25	39	24	40	24	7	9	2	29	1	1	25	28	7	7	1		
					+		+	+			+	+	+			+								
					1s		6s	2s			5s	7s	2s			1s								

FOOTBALL LEAGUE RECORD

1888 Founder Member of the Football League; 1930–31 Division 2; 1931–51 Division 1; 1951–54 Division 2; 1954– Division 1.

HONOURS

Football League: Division 1 – Champions 1890–91, 1914–15, 1927–28, 1931–32, 1938–39, 1962–63, 1969–70; Runners-up 1889–90, 1894–95, 1901–02, 1904–05, 1908–09, 1911–12; Division 2 Champions 1930–31; Runners-up 1953–54. *FA Cup:* Winners 1906, 1933, 1966; Runners-up 1893, 1897, 1907, 1968. *Football League Cup:* Runners-up 1976–77. **European Competitions:** *European Cup:* 1963–64, 1970–71; *European Cup-Winners' Cup:* 1966–67. *European Fairs Cup:* 1962–63, 1964–65, 1965–66. *UEFA Cup:* 1975–76, 1978–79, 1979–80.

COLOURS

Royal blue shirts with shadow stripe and white trim, white shorts, blue and white hooped stockings.
Change colours: All Silver Grey

EVERTON

Players Names Ht. Wt. D.o.B.	Birthplace Transfer Fee	Clubs	Appearances F.L. A & S	 F.L.C. A & S	 F.A.C. A & S	Goals F.L.	 F.L.C.	 F.A.C.
Goalkeepers								
Martin Hodge	Southport	Plymouth Arg (A)	43	1	1			
6 0, 13 2, 4.2.59	£135,000	Everton	25		6			
	—	Preston NE (loan)	28					
	—	Oldham Ath (loan)	4					
	—	Gillingham (loan)	4					
	—	Preston NE (loan)	16					
Neville Southall (W)	Llandudno	Winsford U						
6 1, 12 0, 16.9.58	£6000	Bury	39		5			
	£150,000	Everton	43	2	1			
	—	Port Vale (loan)	9					
Jim Arnold (E.S.P.)	Stafford	Stafford Rgrs						
6 1, 11 5, 6.8.50	£20,000	Blackburn R	58	3	7			
	£175,000	Everton	41	6	5			
	—	Preston NE	6					
Defenders								
Billy Wright* (E.B.)	Liverpool	Everton	164+2	13	13	10		
5 11, 12 7, 28.4.58								
Mark Higgins (EY)	Buxton	Everton (A)	136+2	15	7	6		
6 1, 13 4, 29.9.58								
Kevin Ratcliffe (W)	Mancot	Everton (A)	76+1	6	2	1		
John Bailey	Liverpool	Blackburn R (A)	115+5	8	8	1		
5 8, 11 3, 1.4.57	£300,000	Everton	122	11	15	3		
Mike Walsh* (E.I.)	Manchester	Bolton W	169+8	13	10+1	4	1	
6 0, 12 1, 20.6.56	£90,000 + P/E	Everton	20	2				
	—	Norwich C (loan)	5					
	—	Burnley (loan)	3					
Gary Stevens	Barrow	Everton (A)	47	6	6	1	1	
5 11, 10 12, 27.3.63								
Derek Mountfield	Liverpool	Tranmere R (A)	26	1	1	1		
6 1, 12 7, 2.11.62	£30,000	Everton	1					
Steve Bateman		Everton (A)						
Midfield								
Kevin Richardson	Newcastle	Everton (A)	39+8	1+2	3	5		
5 7, 10 2, 4.12.62								
Trevor Ross* (SU21)	Ashton-under-Lyne	Arsenal (A)	57+1	6	3	5	3	1
5 9½, 11 10, 16.1.57	£150,000	Everton	120+6	8	13	16	3	1
	—	Portsmouth (loan)	5					
	—	Sheffield U (loan)	4					
Adrian Heath (EU21)	Stoke	Stoke C (A)	94+1	9	4	16		1
5 6, 10 1, 11.1.61	£700,000	Everton	59+1	4	5	16		1
Kevin Sheedy (NIY)	Builth Wells	Hereford U (A)	47+4	2+1	2	4		1
5 7, 9 2, 21.10.59	£80,000	Liverpool	1+2	2			2	
	£100,000	Everton	40	3	5	11		2
Peter Reid (EU21)	Huyton	Bolton W (A)	208+3	18+1	17	22	1	1
5 7, 11 5, 20.6.56	£60,000	Everton	7		3			
Jim Coyle		Everton (A)						
Forwards								
Alan Ainscow* (EY)	Bolton	Blackpool (A)	178+14	9	6+1	28		
5 6½, 9 4, 15.7.53	£40,000	Birmingham C	104+4	9	6	16	4	1
	£250,000	Everton	24+4			3		
	—	Barnsley (loan)	2					
Graeme Sharp (SU21)	Glasgow	Dumbarton						
6 1, 11 8, 16.10.60	£125,000	Everton	69+7	5	6	30		2
Alan Irvine	Glasgow	Queens Park						
5 8, 11 4,		Everton	32+7	+1	2	4		
Mick Ferguson	Newcastle	Coventry C (A)	121+6	10+2	3	51	3	
6 1, 12 8, 3.10.54	£280,000	Everton	7+1	3+1		4	2	
	—	Birmingham C (loan)	20	2		8		
Mark Leonard*	St Helens	Witton A						
5 11, 11 10,		Everton						
	—	Tranmere R (loan)	6+1					
Stuart Rimmer	Southport	Everton (A)	2					
5 7, 9 2,								
Andy King (EU21)	Luton	Luton T (A)	30+3	1	2	9		
5 9½, 10 13, 14.8.56	£35,000	Everton	150+1	21	11	38	8	2
	£425,000	QPR	28+2	1	2	9		
	£400,000	WBA	21+4	8+1		4	1	1
	P/E	Everton	24	4	4	9	2	2
Dave Johnson (E)	Liverpool	Everton (A)	47+3	2	5	11	1	2
5 10, 12 4, 23.10.51	£50,000	Ipswich T	134+3	8	15	35	5	4
	£200,000	Liverpool	128+21	15+3	17+2	55	8	6
	£100,000	Everton	25+6	4		3	1	
John Morrissey		Everton (A)						

Players (non-appearance) granted free transfer: Keith Tierney, M.; John McMahon, M.
Players released since May 1982: Simon Steele, G. (N/K).

EXETER CITY Division 3

Standing (left to right): Chris Davey (Football Secretary), Brian Godfrey (Manager), Lee Roberts, Stan McEwan, John Sparrow, Dave Pullar, Peter Shepherd (NC), Nick Marker (App), Len Bond, Graeme Kirkup (App), Keith Viney, Martin Longdon, Frank Howarth, Malcolm Musgrove (Chief Scout/Coach), Alan Beer
Seated: Aidan Gibson, David Harle, Ray Pratt, Martyn Rogers, John Delve, Tony Kellow, Peter Rogers, Perry Walters, Martin Ling, Paddy Thomas.

President: F. E. J. Dart.

Chairman: W. C. Hill. ***Executive Director:*** R. M. L. Williams MA Oxon.

Directors: F. E. J. Dart, G. Vece, S. J. West FIB, D. McCauley.

Player-Manager: Gerry Francis. ***Football Secretary:*** Chris Davey.

Commercial Manager: E. R. Ellis. ***Financial Controller:*** Carolyn Reevy.

Year Formed: 1904. ***Turned Professional:*** 1908. ***Ltd Co.:*** 1908.

Club Nickname: 'The Grecians'.

Previous Managers since 1946: George Roughton, Norman Kirkman, Norman Dodgin, Bill Thompson, Frank Broome, Glen Wilson, Cyril Spiers, Jack Edwards, Ellis Stuttard, Jock Basford, Frank Broome, John Newman, Bobby Saxton (13).

St James Park, Exeter EX4 6PX. Telephone Exeter (0392) 54073. ***Ground capacity:*** 17,500. ***Record attendance:*** 20,984 v Sunderland, FA Cup 6th rd replay, 4 March, 1931. ***Record receipts:*** £32,007 v Newcastle U, FA Cup 5th rd replay, 18 Feb, 1981. ***Pitch measurements:*** 114yd×73yd.

Directions to Ground: City buses A, D, J, K, S from city centre to The Fountain (one-minute walk to the ground). Routes G and J pass both railway stations – Exeter St David's and Exeter Central.

Match tickets: Tickets may be booked usually up to two weeks before home matches.

Car parking: No car park at the ground. Limited street parking permitted.

Entertainments/catering facilities: Members social club 'The Centre Spot', St James Park (0392 50292). Subscription £2.25; joint membership £3.50. The club is situated at the ground.

Club shop: Sells all types of souvenirs at ground.

Handbooks/programmes: Programmes can be ordered on subscription.

Extra information: Membership of the Supporters Association at 50p per year.

Address of Supporters Club: c/o St James Park, Exeter (0392 59466).

Note: Full club statistical records are on pages 416–455.

EXETER CITY 1982–83 LEAGUE RECORD

Match No.	Date	Venue	Opponents	Result		H/T Score	Lg. Pos.	Goalscorers	Attendance
1	Aug 28	A	Huddersfield T	D	1-1	0-1	—	Pullar	5168
2	Sept 4	H	Gillingham	D	2-2	1-0	17	Kellow, Pullar	2409
3	8	H	Portsmouth	D	1-1	1-0	—	Howe (og)	3146
4	10	A	Doncaster R	L	1-6	0-4	—	Rogers P.	3205
5	18	H	Preston NE	W	5-1	2-1	15	Pratt 2, Kellow, Harle, Rogers P.	2310
6	25	A	AFC Bournemouth	L	0-2	0-0	18		7547
7	28	A	Cardiff C	L	0-2	0-1	—		4867
8	Oct 2	H	Chesterfield	L	2-3	2-0	23	Rogers, Pullar	2389
9	9	A	Wrexham	W	2-1	1-0	20	Hatter, McEwan	2110
10	16	H	Millwall	W	2-1	0-1	14	Rogers, Pratt	2640
11	20	A	Lincoln C	L	1-4	0-2	—	Kellow (pen)	3699
12	23	H	Sheffield U	L	0-3	0-0	21		3858
13	30	A	Oxford U	D	1-1	0-1	19	Viney	4689
14	Nov 3	H	Wigan Ath	W	2-1	1-0	—	Rogers, Kellow	2399
15	6	H	Walsall	W	4-3	3-0	15	Kellow, Delve 2, Neville	2614
16	13	A	Bradford C	D	3-3	2-2	16	Harle, Pullar, Delve	4576
17	27	H	Orient	W	2-0	1-0	13	Kellow, Harle	2611
18	Dec 4	A	Reading	L	1-3	1-2	15	Pullar	1971
19	11	H	Reading	D	2-2	1-2	14	Kellow, Delve	2272
20	18	A	Brentford	L	0-4	0-3	14		5296
21	27	H	Plymouth Arg	W	1-0	0-0	13	Neville	9168
22	29	A	Bristol R	D	4-4	2-4	—	Rogers P. 2, Delve, McEwan	8160
23	Jan 1	H	Newport Co	L	0-1	0-0	14		3505
24	3	A	Southend U	D	1-1	1-1	14	Marker	3570
25	8	A	Gillingham	D	4-4	3-2	14	McEwan, Neville 3	2970
26	15	H	Huddersfield T	L	3-4	2-2	14	McEwan (pen), Neville, Rogers M.	2882
27	22	A	Preston NE	D	2-2	0-1	15	Pratt, Neville	3767
28	29	H	Cardiff C	L	0-2	0-0	16		4019
29	Feb 5	H	AFC Bournemouth	W	4-2	1-1	15	Viney, McEwan, Neville, Pratt	3008
30	12	A	Portsmouth	L	2-3	0-2	17	Neville 2	10,622
31	15	A	Wigan Ath	L	0-1	0-1	—		2764
32	19	H	Wrexham	D	3-3	0-0	17	Viney 2, Neville	2507
33	26	A	Millwall	L	2-5	0-3	19	Neville, Harle	2806
34	Mar 2	H	Lincoln C	W	3-1	1-0	—	McEwan, Pratt, Neville	2505
35	5	A	Sheffield U	L	0-3	0-2	19		9703
36	12	H	Oxford U	W	3-1	1-1	16	Harle 2, Kellow	2957
37	19	A	Walsall	L	2-3	0-1	19	Rogers P. 2	2669
38	26	H	Bradford C	W	2-1	1-0	18	Crown, Pratt	2639
39	Apr 1	A	Plymouth Arg	L	0-1	0-0	—		8856
40	2	H	Bristol R	L	0-1	0-1	18		5741
41	16	A	Chesterfield	W	3-1	2-0	18	Sparrow, Pratt, Crown	1788
42	23	H	Brentford	L	1-7	0-3	19	Gibson	2759
43	30	A	Orient	L	1-5	0-2	21	Neville	2407
44	May 2	H	Southend U	W	4-3	2-2	21	Neville 3, Crown	2956
45	7	H	Doncaster R	W	3-0	1-0	18	Kellow 2, Pratt	3110
46	14	A	Newport Co	D	1-1	0-1	19	Rogers P.	3520

Final League Position: 19

GOALSCORERS

League (81): Neville 17, Kellow 10 (1 pen), Rogers P. 10, Pratt 9, Harle 6, McEwan 6 (1 pen), Delve 5, Pullar 5, Viney 4, Crown 3, Gibson 1, Hatter 1, Marker 1, Rogers M. 1, Sparrow 1, own goal 1.
Milk Cup (1): Kellow 1.
FA Cup (0).
Football League Trophy (5): Pratt 2, Howarth 1, Kellow 1, Pullar 1.

Milk Cup	First Round	Newport Co (h)	1-2
		(a)	0-6
FA Cup	First Round	Plymouth Arg. (a)	0-2
Football League Trophy		Bristol C (h)	2-1
		Newport Co (a)	1-5
		Torquay U (a)	2-3

Bond	Kirkup	Viney	McEwan	Roberts	Rogers M.	Harle	Rogers P.	Kellow	Delve	Pullar	Pratt	Gibson	Hatter (L)	Neville	Howarth	Marker	Sparrow	Davies (L)	Thomas	Ling	Phillips	Burke	Shepherd	Crown (L)	*Referees*	*Match No.*
1	2	3	4	5	6	7	8	9	10	11															R. Guy	1
1	2	3	4	5	6		8	9	10	11	7														R. Milford	2
1	2	3	4	5	6	7	8	9	10	11															E. Read	3
1	2	3	4	5	6	7	8	9	10	11*		12													N. Glover	4
1		3	4	5	2	6	8	9	10		7	11													C. Downey	5
1	2	3		5		6	8	9	10	12	7*	11	4												B. Daniels	6
1	2	3		5		6	8	9	10	12	7	11*	4												A. Seville	7
1		3	4	6	2	7	8	9	10	11			5												J. Martin	8
1	2		6	5	3	7	8	9	10	11			4												D. Richardson	9
1	2	3	4		6	7	8	9	10	11*	12		5												H. King	10
1	2	3	6		4	7*	8	9	10		12		5	11											D. Scott	11
1	2*	3	6		4	7	8	9	10		11		5		12										R. Lewis	12
1		3	6			4	8	9	10		7		5	11	2										M. Taylor	13
1		3	6			4	8	9	10	11			5	7	2										D. Hedges	14
1		3	6		12	4	8	9	10	11			5	7	2*										A. Glasson	15
1		3	6		2	4	8	9	10	11			5	7											K. Redfern	16
1		3	4		2	6	8	9	10	11				7		5									T. Spencer	17
1		3	6		2	4	8	9	10	11				7		5									E. Scales	18
1		3	4		2	6	8	9*	10	11	12			7		5									B. Stevens	19
1		3	6		2	4	8		10	11	12			7		5	9*								K. Baker	20
1		3	6		2	4	8	9	10	11				7		5									D. Civil	21
1		3	6		2	4	8	9*	10	11				7		5	12								D. Reeves	22
1	12	3	6		2		8		10	11	9*			7		5	4								L. Burden	23
1		3	6		2		8		10*	11		9		7	12	5	4								B. Hill	24
1		3	6		10	4*	8			11	12	9		7		5	2								T. Bune	25
1		3	6		4		8		10	11	12	9		7		5	2*								K. Cooper	26
1		3	6		11	4	8		10		12	9		7		5	2*								R. Bridges	27
1	2	3			4	12	8		10	6	11	9		7		5*									Alan Robinson	28
1		3	4		2	6	8		10		11	9		7				5							J. Bray	29
1	12	3	6			4	8		10	9		11		7			2*	5							J. Moules	30
1	2	3*	6			4	8		10	11		9		7				5	12						J. Lovatt	31
1		3	6		2		8	9	10	4	12	11*		7				5							E. Read	32
1		3	5		2	6		10*	8	7	12	11		9				4							M. Dimblebee	33
1		3	6		2	4		9	10	11	8			7				5							J. Deakin	34
1		3			2	4	8	9*	10	6	7	11						5		12					A. Robinson	35
1		3			6	4	8	9	10	2	11			7		5									G. Napthine	36
1		3			6		8	9	10	2	12			7*		5					4	11			T. Jones	37
		3			2	4	8	9*	10		12					5					6	7	1	11	V. Callow	38
1		3			2	4	8		10*	9	12			7		5					6			11	A. Seville	39
1		3	6		2	4		12			8			7		5					10	9		11*	A. Gunn	40
1	2		6				8		10		9	5		7			3				4			11	A. Banks	41
1		2	6				8	12	10		9	5		7			3*				4			11	C. Newsome	42
1		3	6		2		8		10		12	9*		7		5					4			11	M. Taylor	43
1		3	5		2	4	7	9*	10		11			8							6			12	L. Robinson	44
1	6	3			2	4	8	9	10		11			7							5				D. Milford	45
1	11	3	6		2	4	8	9*	10		12			7							5				K. Barratt	46
45	15	44	37	9	37	36	43	31	44	30	17	17	11	33	3	18	9	7	0	0	10	3	1	6		
	+ 2s				+ 1s	+ 1s		+ 2s		+ 2s	+ 14s	+ 1s			+ 2s		+ 1s		+ 1s	+ 1s				+ 1s		

FOOTBALL LEAGUE RECORD

1920 Elected Division3; 1921–1958 Division 3(S); 1958–64 Division 4; 1964–66 Division 3; 1966–77 Division 4; 1977– Division 3.

HONOURS

Football League: Division 3 best season: 8th, 1979–80; Division 3(S) – Runners-up 1932–33; Division 4 – Runners-up 1976–77. *FA Cup* best season: 6th rd replay, 1931. *Football League Cup:* never beyond 4th rd. *Division 3(S) Cup:* Winners 1934.

COLOURS

Red and white vertical stripes, black shorts with red and white turnover.
Change colours: Light blue shirts, shorts and stockings with dark blue trim.

EXETER CITY

Players Names Ht, Wt, D.o.B.	Birthplace Transfer Fee	Clubs	Appearances F.L. A & S	 F.L.C. A & S	 F.A.C. A & S	Goals F.L.	 F.L.C.	 F.A.C.
Goalkeepers								
Len Bond	Ilminster	Bristol C (A)	30	1	4			
6 0, 12 10, 12.2.54	—	Exeter C (loan)	30		1			
	—	Torquay U (loan)	3	1				
	—	Scunthorpe U (loan)	8					
	—	Colchester U (loan)	3					
	£8000	Brentford	122	6	4			
	£10,000	Exeter C	93	3	9			
Defenders								
Martyn Rogers (EY)	Bristol	Bristol C (A)						
5 9, 11 6, 7.3.55	F/T	Bath C						
	£10,000	Exeter C	120+2	7	9	5		1
Lee Roberts*	Market Drayton	Shrewsbury (A)	9+6			1		
6 0, 12 2, 23.3.57	—	Exeter C (loan)	5+2					
	F/T	Exeter C	135+9	11	13+1	12		4
John Sparrow* (EY)	Bethnal Green	Chelsea (A)	63+6	3	2	2		
5 10, 11 12, 3.6.57	—	Millwall (loan)	7					
	£5000	Exeter C	62+1	2	4	3		
Keith Viney	Portsmouth	Portsmouth (A)	160+6	14	13	3		
5 11, 11 9, 26.10.57	F/T	Exeter C	44	2	1	4		
Nick Marker	Budleigh Salterton	Exeter C (A)	29+3		1	2		
6 0, 12 11, 3.5.65								
Midfield								
John Delve*	London	QPR (A)	9+6	+1	1			
5 7, 11 0, 27.9.53	£25,000	Plymouth Arg	127+5	8	8	6		
	£15,000	Exeter C	216	17	13	20	3	
David Pullar*	London	Portsmouth (A)	84—9	3	9	4	2	1
5 11, 11 8, 13.2.59	£12,000	Exeter C	124+6	12+1	7	22	2	3
David Harle	Denaby	Doncaster R (A)	48+13	4	1	3		
5 9, 10 7, 15.8.63	F/T	Exeter C	37+1	2	1	6		
Stan McEwan	Cambuskenneth	Blackpool (A)	204+10	16	13	24	6	2
5 11, 12 8, 8.6.57	F/T	Exeter C	36	2	1	6		
Forwards								
Peter Rogers	Bristol	Bath C						
5 9, 10 12, 22.4.53	£10,000	Exeter C	169+11	8	10+1	34	1	3
Tony Kellow	Budock Water	Falmouth T						
5 11, 12 7, 1.5.52	£13,000	Exeter C	107	12	7	40	4	4
	£105,000	Blackpool	57	4	3	23		1
	£65,000	Exeter C	133+2	20	10	61	4	6
Ray Pratt (WY)	Merthyr Tydfil	Merthyr Tydfil						
5 10, 12 4, 11.11.55	£12,000	Exeter C	53+32	2	+4	24		
Airan Gibson*	Clayton	Derby Co (A)	0+2	+1				
5 5, 10 0, 17.5.63	F/T	Exeter C	17+1			1		
Frankie Howarth	Budleigh Salterton	Exeter C (A)	4+3	1				
5 9, 10 10, 19.11.64								
Apprentices								
Martin Ling	London	Exeter C (A)	+1					
Graeme Kirkup	Cramlington	Exeter C (A)	23+2	2				
5 10, 12 2, 31.5.65								

Commercial Manager: E. R Ellis. (Tel. 59466)
Club Coach: Malcolm Musgrove
Club Captain 1982–83: John Delve
Supporters Player of the Season 1982–83: George Foster
Chief Scout:
Physiotherapist:
Club Statistician:
Association of Football Statisticians Club Adviser to Yearbook: J. Blackstone.

Players released since May 1982: Phil Fisher, F. (N/K); Peter Hatch, D. (Bideford); Ian Main, G. (Torquay U N/C); Tony Mitchell, D. (Sutton U); Phil Roberts, D. (Taunton T); Leighton Phillips, D. (N/K); John Burke, D. (N/K); Pat Thomas, (N/K); Peter Shepherd, G. (N/K).

FULHAM

Division 2

Back row (left to right): Jeff Hopkins, Dale Tempest, Sean O'Driscoll, Kevin Lock, Dean Coney
Middle row: Brian Greenaway, Steve Hatter, Gerry Peyton, Roger Brown, Jim Stannard, Tony Gale, Robert Wilson, Paul Parker
Front row: Ray Harford (Coach), Ray Lewington, Ray Houghton, Les Strong, Malcolm Macdonald (Manager), Peter O'Sullivan, John Reeves, Gordon Davies, Derek Wright (Physiotherapist).

ife-Presidents: Tommy Trinder CBE, Ted Drake, Anthony Dean.
hairman: E. Clay.
irectors: G. Clay, B. Dalton, E. Drake, M. Macdonald, G. C. Clay.
lanager: Malcolm Macdonald. ***Club Secretary:*** Mrs Y. Haines.
ear Formed: 1879. ***Turned Professional:*** 1898. ***Ltd Co.:*** 1903.
lub Nickname: 'Cottagers'.
revious Name: 1879–98, Fulham St Andrew's.
revious Grounds: Lillie Road, Fulham Cross; Barn Elms, Barnes; anelagh House; Stansfield's Field, Fulham Road; Half-Moon Cricket round, Putney; 1896, Craven Cottage.
lanagers since 1946: Jack Peart, Frank Osborne, Doug Livingstone, ill Dodgin (Snr), Bedford Jezzard, Vic Buckingham, Bobby Robson, ohnny Haynes, Bill Dodgin (Jnr), Alec Stock, Bobby Campbell (11).

raven Cottage, Stevenage Rd, Fulham, London SW6. Telephone 01-736 6561/2/3. Pools Office: 01-736 634. ***Telegraphic address:*** 'Fulhamish, London SW6'. ***Ground capacity:*** 20,000. ***Record attendance:*** 9,335 v Millwall, Division 2, 8 Oct, 1938. ***Record receipts:*** £44,763 v Manchester U, FA Cup 4th rd, 27 an, 1979. ***Pitch measurements:*** 110yd×75yd.
irections to Ground: Underground stations, Putney Bridge (District Line) and Hammersmith (District, letropolitan, Piccadilly). Then by bus – 30, 74, 85, 93, 220.
latch tickets: Computerised Box Office. Seats are bookable daily during the season 9.30–4.30.
ar parking: Parking in streets around the ground.
ntertainments/catering facilities: Social amenities available. Snack bars and licensed bars around the round. The Riverside Suite is available for conferences, weddings, parties, etc.
lub shop: Sells all types of souvenir. Open only Tuesdays and Saturdays.
landbooks/programmes: Programmes available.
xtra information: Fulham Travel Club runs trips to away matches.
ddress of Supporters Club: Fulham Travel Club, Craven Cottage, Stevenage Road, SW6.

ote: Full club statistical records are on pages 416–455.

FULHAM 1982–83 LEAGUE RECORD

Match No.	Date	Venue	Opponents	Result		H/T Score	Lg. Pos.	Goalscorers	Attendance
1	Aug 28	H	Rotherham U	D	1-1	1-1	—	Davies	7021
2	Sept 4	A	Shrewsbury T	W	1-0	0-0	10	Wilson	3525
3	7	H	QPR	D	1-1	0-0	—	Lewington	15,004
4	11	H	Bolton W	W	4-0	2-0	5	Coney 2, Lewington (pen), Houghton	5688
5	18	A	Middlesbrough	W	4-1	2-1	4	Davies 2, Lewington (pen), Houghton	6445
6	25	H	Leeds U	W	3-2	1-1	4	Davies 2, Coney	12,798
7	28	A	Charlton Ath	L	0-3	0-0	—		6790
8	Oct 2	A	Barnsley	L	3-4	3-1	5	Hopkins, Wilson, Davies	12,582
9	9	H	Blackburn R	W	3-1	2-1	5	Davies, Lewington (pen), Wilson	5698
10	16	A	Newcastle U	W	4-1	3-0	3	Davies 2, Coney, Houghton	29,490
11	23	H	Burnley	W	3-1	1-1	1	Lewington 2 (1 pen), Houghton	9040
12	30	A	Crystal Palace	D	1-1	1-0	3	O'Driscoll	14,912
13	Nov 6	H	Oldham Ath	L	0-3	0-2	4		6897
14	13	A	Grimsby T	W	4-0	2-0	3	Davies 2, Wilson, Gale	6952
15	20	A	Wolves	W	4-2	1-2	2	Lewington, Davies 2, Wilson	14,448
16	27	H	Sheffield W	W	1-0	1-0	2	Davies	13,864
17	Dec 4	A	Leicester C	L	0-2	0-0	2		9082
18	11	H	Derby Co	W	2-1	1-0	2	Thomas, Carr	7854
19	18	A	Carlisle U	L	2-3	1-0	3	Lewington (pen), O'Driscoll	4859
20	27	H	Cambridge U	D	1-1	0-1	3	Brown	9105
21	28	A	Chelsea	D	0-0	0-0	3		29,797
22	Jan 1	H	Wolverhampton W	L	1-3	1-2	3	Lewington	17,196
23	3	H	Shrewsbury T	W	2-1	0-1	3	Davies, Thomas	7786
24	15	A	Rotherham U	W	1-0	1-0	3	Brown	7667
25	22	H	Middlesbrough	W	1-0	1-0	3	Wilson	8431
26	Feb 5	A	Bolton W	W	1-0	0-0	3	O'Driscoll	6748
27	19	A	Blackburn R	D	0-0	0-0	3		6141
28	26	H	Newcastle U	D	2-2	1-2	3	Davies, Lock (pen)	14,277
29	Mar 5	A	Burnley	L	0-1	0-1	3		8828
30	12	H	Crystal Palace	W	1-0	1-0	3	Brown	11,234
31	19	A	Oldham Ath	L	0-1	0-0	3		6189
32	26	H	Grimsby T	W	4-0	2-0	3	Wilson 2, Davies, Levington	8096
33	Apr 2	H	Chelsea	D	1-1	1-1	3	Lock	15,249
34	5	A	Cambridge U	L	0-1	0-0	—		6249
35	9	H	Charlton Ath	W	2-1	0-0	3	Davies, Brown	9035
36	16	A	Leeds U	D	1-1	0-1	3	Houghton	24,328
37	19	H	Barnsley	W	1-0	0-0	—	Gale	9003
38	23	H	Leicester C	L	0-1	0-0	3		24,251
39	30	A	Sheffield W	L	1-2	0-0	3	Wilson	12,531
40	May 2	A	QPR	L	1-3	0-2	4	Davies	24,431
41	7	H	Carlisle U	W	2-0	1-0	4	Wilson 2	10,045
42	14	A	Derby Co	L	0-1	0-0	4		21,124

Final League Position: 4

GOALSCORERS

League (64): Davies 19, Wilson 11, Lewington 10 (5 pens), Houghton 5, Brown 4, Coney 4, O'Driscoll 3, Gale 2, Lock 2 (1 pen), Thomas 2, Carr 1, Hopkins 1.
Milk Cup (6): Brown 1, Coney 1, Davies 1, Gale 1, Houghton 1, own goal.
FA Cup (4): Coney 2, Houghton 1, Lewington 1.

Milk Cup	First Round	Southend U (a)	0-1
		(h)	4-2
	Second Round	Coventry C (h)	2-2
		(a)	0-0
FA Cup	Third Round	Oldham Ath (a)	2-0
	Fourth Round	Watford (a)	1-1
		(h)	1-2

Peyton	Hopkins	Strong	O'Driscoll	Brown	Gale	Davies	Wilson	Coney	Houghton	Lewington	O'Sullivan	Parker	Lock	Tempest	Carr	Thomas (L)	Rosenoir	McDermott (L)	Reeves	Referees	Match No.
1	2	3	4	5	6	7	8	9	10	11										D. Letts	1
1	2	3	4	5	6	7	8	9	10	11*	12									T. Fitzharris	2
1	2*	3	4	5	6	7	8	9	10	11		12								A. Gunn	3
1	2		4	5	6	7	8*	9	10	11		12	3							C. Thomas	4
1*	2		4	5	6	7	8	9	10	11		12	3							R. Nixon	5
1	2		4	5	6	7	8	9	10	11			3							T. Bune	6
1	2		4	5*	6	8	7	9	10	11		12	3							K. Baker	7
1	2		4	5	6	7	8	9	10	11			3							L. Robinson	8
1	2		4	5	6	7	8	9	10	11			3							A. Glasson	9
1	2		4	5	6	7	8	9	10	11			3*	12						A. Robinson	10
1	2		4	5	6	7*		9	10	11		3		8	12					E. Reed	11
1	2		4	5	6			9	10	11		8	3		7					B. Daniels	12
1	2		4	5	6		8	9	10	11		12	3		7*					D. Axcell	13
1	2		4	5	6	7	8	9	10	11			3							K. Hackett	14
1	2		4	5	6	7	8	9	10	11			3							K. Cooper	15
1	2		6	4	5	10	7	11*	8	9		12	3							D. Brazier	16
1	2		4	5	6		8		10	11			3			7	9			R. Chadwick	17
1	2		4	5	6		8		10	11*		12	3		7	9				A. Crickmore	18
1	2		4	5	6	7	8		10	11			3			9				N. Wilson	19
1	2		4	5	6	7	8	9	10	11			3							L. Burden	20
1	2		4	5	6	7	8	9	10	11			3							B. Hill	21
1	2		4	5	6	7	8	9	10	11			3							I. Borrett	22
1	2		4	5	6	7	8	9	10	11			3*			12				M. Taylor	23
1	2		4	5	6	7	8	9	10	11		3								N. Glover	24
1	2		6	4	5	7	8	9	10	11		3								K. Barrett	25
1	2		4	5	6	7	8	9	10	11		3								D. Hutchinson	26
1	2		4	5	6	7	8		10	11				9	3					T. Holbrook	27
1	2		4	5	6	7	8	9	10	11			3							L. Shapter	28
1	2		4	5	6	7	8		10	11			3	9*	12					M. Heath	29
1	2		4	5	6	7	8	9*	10	11			3					12		D. Letts	30
1	2		4	5	6	7	8*	9	10	11			3					12		G. Courtney	31
1	2		4	5	6	7	8	9	10	11			3							E. Read	32
1	2		4	5	6	7	8	9	10	11			3							D. Axcell	33
1	2		4	5	6	7*	8	9	10	11			3					12		J. Bray	34
1	2		4	5	6	7	8	9	10	11			3							T. Spencer	35
1	2*		4	5	6	7	8	9	10	11		12	3							A. Robinson	36
1	2		4	5	6	7	8	9	10	11			3							Alan Robinson	37
1	2		4	5	6	7	8	9*	10	11		12	3							H. King	38
1	2*		4	5	6	7	8	9	10	11		12	3							D. Richardson	39
1			4	5	6	7	8	9	10	11		2	3*						12	B. Hill	40
1	2		4	5	6	7	8	9	10	11			3							M. Bodenham	41
1	2		4*	5	6	7	8	9	10	11			3						12	R. Chadwick	42
42	41	3	42	42	42	38	40	37	42	42	0	6	34	3	4	3	1	0	0		
											+ 1s	+ 10s		+ 1s	+ 2s	+ 1s		+ 3s	+ 2s		

FOOTBALL LEAGUE RECORD

1907 Elected to Division 2; 1928–32 Division 3(S); 1932–49 Division 2; 1949–52 Division 1; 1952–59 Division 2; 1959–68 Division 1; 1968–69 Division 2; 1969–71 Division 3; 1971–80 Division 2; 1980–82 Division 3; 1982– Division 2.

HONOURS

Football League: Division 1 best season: 10th, 1959–60; Division 2 – Champions 1948–49; Runners-up 1958–59; Division 3(S) – Champions 1931–32; Division 3 – Runners-up 1970–71. *FA Cup:* Runners-up 1974–75. *Football League Cup* best season: 5th rd, 1967–68, 1970–71.

COLOURS

White shirts with black collar, black shorts, white stockings with three black hoops on turnover.
Change colours: Red shirts and shorts, black stockings and three red hoops on turn over.

FULHAM

Players Names Ht. Wt. D.o.B.	Birthplace Transfer Fee	Clubs	Appearances F.L. A & S	 F.L.C. A & S	 F.A.C. A & S	Goals F.L.	 F.L.C.	 F.A.C.
Goalkeepers								
Gerry Peyton (EI)	Birmingham	Atherstone U.						
6 2, 13 11, 20.5.56		Burnley	30	1	1			
	£40,000	Fulham	250	17	17			
Jim Stannard	London	Fulham	19					
6 0,13 1, 6.10.62								
Defenders								
Cliff Carr	London	Fulham (A)	4+2	1		1		
10 4, 19.6.64								
Tony Gale (EU21)	London	Fulham (A)	242	17	14	18	2	
6 1½, 12 4, 19.11.59								
Kevin Lock (EU23)	Plaistow	West Ham U.(A)	122+10	13	11+1	2		
6 0, 11 6, 27.12.53	£60,000	Fulham	165+1	11+1	9+1	20		
Roger Brown	Tamworth	AP Leamington						
6 1, 11 10, 12.12.52	£5000	Bournemouth	63	2	3	3	1	
	£85,000	Norwich C.	16	2	3			
	£100,000	Fulham	128	8	8	18	1	
Paul Parker	London	Fulham (A)	9+13	2	3			
5 7, 10 8, 4.4.64								
Jeff Hopkins (W)	Swansea	Fulham (A)	73+4	11	5	1	1	
6 0, 11 9, 14.4.64								
Steve Tapley	London	Fulham (A)						
5 11, 11 0, 3.10.63								
Midfield								
Robert Wilson	Kensington	Fulham	115+5	9+1	7+1	20	3	
5 10, 11 2, 5.6.61								
Clive Day*	Orsett	Fulham (A)	2+8					
6 0, 11 0, 27.1 61	—	Mansfield T. (loan)	10+2	2			1	
Ray Lewington	Lambeth	Chelsea (A)	80+5	3	4		4	
5 6, 10 5, 7.9.56		Vancouver W.						
	—	Wimbledon (loan)	23	2	5			
	£50,000	Fulham	102+1	13	7+1	15	1	1
Sean O'Driscoll (EI)	Wolverhampton	Alvechurch						
5 8, 10 6, 1.7.57		Fulham	131+5	11	11	13		
John Reeves	London	Fulham (A)	+2	1				
5 7, 9 10, 8.7.63								
Peter Scott	London	Fulham (A)	1	+1				
5 8, 10 7, 1.10.63								
Ray Houghton	Glasgow	West Ham U.	0+1					
5 7, 10 10, 9.1.62	F T	Fulham	42	4	3	5	1	1
Brian Cottington		Fulham (A)						
10 4								
Forwards								
Gordon Davies (W)	Merthyr Tydfil	Merthyr Tydfil						
5 7, 10 6, 3.8 55	£2000	Fulham	199+1	16	16	86	5	4
Dale Tempest	Leeds	Fulham (A)	12+7			2		
5 11, 12 0, 30.12.63								
Dean Coney	Dagenham	Fulham (A)	83	11	5	20	5	4
6 0, 12.6, 18.9.63								
Leroy Resenoir	London	Fulham	1					
6 1, 11 10, 24.3.64								
John Marshall		Fulham (A)						
11 4								

Commercial Manager: Dennis Smith (Tel. 01-736-0366)
Club Coach: Ray Harford
Supporters Player of the Season 1982–83: Ray Houghton
Physiotherapist Trainer: Derek Wright MSRG, SRRG
Club Captain 1982–83: Roger Brown
Chief Scout:
Club Statistician: Dennis Turner
Association of Football Statisticians Club Adviser to Yearbook: D. Turner.

Players (non-appearance) granted free transfer: Mike Squire; Fernando Varadi.
Players released since May 1982: Geoff Banton, D. (Kettering); Tony Finnigan, M. (N/K); Charles Johnson, M. (Wembley T); Les Strong, D. (N/K).; Peter O'Sullivan, M. (N/K); Brian Greenaway, F. (N/K).

GILLINGHAM Division 3

Top row (left to right): Colin Powell, Dean White, Ron Hillyard, Steve Bruce, Gary Sutton, John Sharpe, Mark Weatherly
Middle row: Ted Buxton (Chief Scout), Paul Taylor (Assistant Manager), Peter Shaw, Dick Tydeman (Captain), Tony Cascarino, Trevor Lee, John Sitton, Bill Collins (Trainer)
Front row: Neil Grewcock, Richie Bowman, Colin Duncan, Keith Peacock (Manager), Ken Price, Mark Miller, Micky Adams.

Chairman: Dr C. S. Grossmark. ***Vice-Chairman:*** C. A. L. Cox.

Directors: J. W. Leech, B. B. Moore.

Manager: Keith Peacock. ***Club Secretary:*** R. J. Dennison.

Assistant Manager: Paul Taylor.

Year Formed: 1893. ***Turned Professional:*** 1894. ***Ltd Co.:*** 1893.

Club Nickname: 'The Gills'.

Previous Name: New Brompton, 1893–1913.

Previous Managers since 1946: Archie Clark, Harry Barratt, Freddie Cox, Basil Hayward, Andy Nelson, Len Ashurst, Gerry Summers (7).

Priestfield Stadium, Gillingham. Telephone Medway (0634) 51854. ***Telegraphic address:*** 'Football Gillingham, Kent'. ***Ground capacity:*** 22,000. ***Record attendance:*** 23,002 v QPR, FA Cup 3rd rd, 10 Jan, 1948. ***Record receipts:*** £33,285 v WBA, FA Cup 4th rd, 23 Jan, 1982. ***Pitch measurements:*** 114yd×75yd.

GILLINGHAM F.C.

Directions to Ground: Gillingham railway station (six or seven minutes' walk). Bus services are 10 minutes from ground.

Match tickets: Can be reserved by postal application enclosing correct remittance and SAE.

Car parking: Park for 500 cars adjoining the ground, entrance in Toronto Rd.

Entertainments/catering facilities: A club house, and several bars around the ground.

Club shop: Sells all types of souvenir.

Handbooks/programmes: Programmes available on subscription. Handbooks also available.

Extra information: Enquiries about supporters association to Gillingham FC Supporters Association, Gordon Rd, Gillingham.

Address of Supporters Club: Gillingham FC Supporters' Association, Gordon Road, Gillingham.

Note: Full club statistical records are on pages 416–455.

GILLINGHAM 1982–83 LEAGUE RECORD

Match No.	Date	Venue	Opponents	Result		H/T Score	Lg. Pos.	Goalscorers	Attendance
1	Aug 28	H	Oxford U	L	0-1	0-0	—		4079
2	Sept 4	A	Exeter C	D	2-2	0-1	19	Price, Cascarino	2409
3	7	A	Bristol R	L	1-2	1-2	—	Parkin (og)	3688
4	11	H	Millwall	W	1-0	0-0	15	Cascarino	4663
5	18	A	Wrexham	L	0-1	0-1	19		2122
6	25	H	Walsall	W	3-0	1-0	14	Sinnott (og), Hart (og), Weatherly	3501
7	28	H	Reading	W	1-0	0-0	—	Cascarino	3621
8	Oct 2	A	Sheffield U	W	2-0	0-0	9	Weatherly, Bruce	12,319
9	9	H	Preston NE	W	2-1	2-0	5	Grewcock, Cascarino	4390
10	16	A	Cardiff C	L	0-1	0-0	9		4828
11	19	H	Orient	W	4-0	2-0	—	Grewcock 2, Weatherly, Tydeman	3849
12	23	A	AFC Bournemouth	W	1-0	0-0	3	Bruce (pen)	5528
13	30	H	Huddersfield T	L	1-3	1-1	6	Bruce	5919
14	Nov 2	A	Chesterfield	W	2-1	1-1	—	Weatherly, Henderson (og)	2320
15	6	A	Portsmouth	L	0-1	0-0	8		12,212
16	13	H	Doncaster R	D	1-1	0-0	8	Miller	4451
17	27	H	Wigan Ath	L	0-2	0-1	10		3952
18	Dec 4	A	Newport Co	L	1-2	0-1	12	Sitton	3727
19	18	A	Plymouth Arg	L	0-2	0-1	12		4179
20	27	H	Southend U	W	1-0	0-0	12	Weatherly	5035
21	28	A	Brentford	D	1-1	0-0	12	Bruce	7796
22	Jan 1	H	Lincoln C	L	0-2	0-1	12		5535
23	3	A	Bradford C	D	1-1	1-1	12	Weatherly	4294
24	8	H	Exeter C	D	4-4	2-3	12	Weatherly, White 3 (1 pen)	2970
25	15	A	Oxford U	D	1-1	1-0	12	Weatherly	4755
26	22	H	Wrexham	D	1-1	0-1	11	Adams	3798
27	30	A	Millwall	L	1-4	1-3	12	Cascarino	3813
28	Feb 5	A	Walsall	D	0-0	0-0	12		2608
29	15	H	Chesterfield	W	3-1	1-1	—	Handford, Bruce, Cascarino	3187
30	19	A	Preston NE	D	0-0	0-0	12		3479
31	26	H	Cardiff C	L	2-3	2-2	14	Johnson, Lansdowne	4587
32	Mar 1	A	Orient	L	0-2	0-0	—		2241
33	5	H	AFC Bournemouth	L	2-5	0-1	17	Bruce (pen), Lansdowne	3485
34	12	A	Huddersfield T	L	2-3	0-0	19	Duncan, Mehmet	8264
35	15	H	Sheffield U	L	0-2	0-2	—		3385
36	19	H	Portsmouth	W	1-0	0-0	17	Duncan	6489
37	25	A	Doncaster R	W	2-0	0-0	—	Bowman, Cascarino	2528
38	Apr 1	A	Southend U	D	1-1	0-0	—	Cascarino	4234
39	2	H	Brentford	D	2-2	1-1	15	Whitehead (og), Cascarino	4168
40	9	H	Newport Co	W	2-0	2-0	15	Weatherly, Bruce (pen)	4265
41	16	A	Reading	D	0-0	0-0	15		2566
42	23	H	Plymouth Arg	W	2-1	2-0	15	Cascarino 2	3356
43	30	A	Wigan Ath	D	2-2	2-0	14	Adams, Mehmet	3610
44	May 3	H	Bradford C	W	3-0	2-0	—	Mehmet, Cascarino, Johnson	2716
45	7	H	Bristol R	W	1-0	1-0	11	Cascarino	4024
46	14	A	Lincoln C	L	1-3	1-1	13	Cascarino	2241

Final League Position: 13

GOALSCORERS

League (58): Cascarino 14, Weatherly 9, Bruce 7 (3 pens), Grewcock 3, Mehmet 3, White 3 (1 pen), Adams 2, Duncan 2, Johnson 2, Lansdowne 2, Bowman 1, Handford 1, Miller 1, Price 1, Sitton 1, Tydeman 1, own goals 5.
Milk Cup (7): Cascarino 3, Bruce 1, Johnson 1, Price 1, Shaw 1.
FA Cup (4): Weatherly 2, Cascarino 1, Johnson 1.

Milk Cup	First Round	Orient (h)	3-0
		(a)	0-2
	Second Round	Oldham Ath (h)	2-0
		(a)	0-1
	Third Round	Tottenham H (h)	2-4
FA Cup	First Round	Dagenham (h)	1-0
	Second Round	Northampton T (h)	1-1
		(a)	2-3

Hillyard	Sharpe	Sitton	Bruce	Weatherly	Shaw	Powell	Tydeman	Grewcock	Cascarino	Price	Lee	Adams	Miller	Johnson	Sage	White	Walker (L)	Handford	Hodge (L)	Lansdowne	Foley (L)	Duncan	Horrix	Mehmet	Bowman	Stokes	*Referees*
1	2	3	4	5	6	7	8*	9	10	11	12																D. Axcell
1	2	3	4	5	6	7	8	9*	10	11		12															R. Milford
1	2	4	5	6	7	8*	9	12	10	11		3															A. Glassen
1	2	10	4	5	6	7	8		9	11		3															D. Hedges
1	2	10	4	5	6		8	11	9		7*	3	12														K. Barratt
1	2	6	4	10	5	7	8	11	9			3															M. Dimblebee
1	2	6	4	11	5	7	8*	10	9			3		12													M. James
1	2	6	4	11	5	7		10	9			3		8													D. Allison
1	2	6	4*	11		7	5	10	9	12		3		8													E. Scales
1	2		4	11	5	7	6	10*	9	12		3		8													E. Crickmore
1	2		4	11	5	7	6	10	9			3		8													J. Martin
1	2		4	11	5	7*	6	10	9	12		3		8													H. King
1	2		4	11	5	7	6	10*		9		3		8	12												C. Donney
1	2		4	11	6	7	5	10		9		3		8													A. Hamil
1	2		4	11	5	7	6	10*	9	12		3		8													K. Cooper
1			4	5			6	10	9	11		3	7*	2		12	8										A. Ward
1	2		4	5		7	6	10*	9			3		8		11	12										V. Deakin
1	2	5	4	11*			6	10	9	12		3		8		7											D. Civil
1		2		5	4	7*	6		9	11		3	12	8		10											D. Lloyd
1	2	5*	4	11			6		9	10		3	12	8		7											M. Bodenham
1	2		4	5		7	6		9	10		3		8		11											B. Stevens
1	2		4	5*	12	7	6		9	11		3		8		10											K. Salmon
1	2	12	4	10	5		6		9	11		3		8*		7											P. Tyldesley
1	2		4	10*	5	7	6		11	12		3				9		8									T. Bune
	2	12	4	10	5*		6		11	7		3				9		8	1								T. Holbrook
	2	5	4			12	6*		11	7		3				9		8	1	10							D. Vickers
		2*	4		5	7		12	11			3		6		9		8	1	10							E. Read
		2	4		5		6		11			3		7	10	9		8	1								N. Glover
1	2	5	4	10			6		11*			3		7	12	9		8									J. Moules
1	2	5	4	11			6					3		7	9			8		10							M. Peck
1	2	5	4	11			6	12				3		7				8*		10	9						D. Reeves
1	2	5	4	10			6					3		7				8*		11	9	12					J. Gray
1	2	7	4	5			6	11				3								10	9		8				T. Ward
1		2	4	5			6					3		8							9	11	7	10			D. Allinson
1		2	4	5			6					3		7	12						9*	11	8	10			A. Grey
1	2		4	9	5		6		12			3		7								11	8*	10			I. Borrett
1	2		4	9	5		7		11			3										6*	12	10	8		N. Wilson
1	2		4	9	5		7		11			3										6*	12	10	8		K. Baker
1	2		4	9	5		7		11			3			6*								12	10	8		B. Daniels
1	2		4*	9	5		6		11			3		7									12	10	8		D. Brazier
1	2	4		9	5			6*	11			3		7									12	10	8		C. Downey
1	2	4		9	5		6		11			3		7									12	10*	8		D. Letts
1	2	4		9	5		6		11			3		7									12	10	8*		J. Key
1	2	4		5					11			3		7	12			6*				8	9	10			Alan Robinson
1	2	4		9					11			3			12			6				8*	7	10		5	B. Hill
1		3		5			7		11						2			6					9	10	8	4	J. Lovatt
42	39	28	39	43	28	20	41	18	37	14	1	43	1	30	4	13	1	12	4	6	5	7	7	13	8	2	
		+ 2s			+ 1s	+ 1s		+ 3s	+ 1s	+ 6s	+ 1s	+ 1s	+ 3s	+ 1s	+ 5s	+ 1s	+ 1s					+ 1s	+ 7s				

FOOTBALL LEAGUE RECORD

1920 Original Member of Division 3; 1921 Division 3(S); 1938 Failed re-election; Southern League 1938–44; Kent League 1944–46; Southern League 1946–50; 1950 Re-elected to Division 3(S); 1958–64 Division 4; 1964–71 Division 3; 1971–74 Division 4; 1974– Division 3.

HONOURS

Football League: Division 3 best season: 4th, 1978–79; Division 4 – Champions 1963–64; Runners-up 1973–74. *FA Cup* best season: 5th rd, 1969–70. *Football League Cup* best season: 4th rd, 1964.

COLOURS

Royal blue shirts, white shorts and stockings with blue trim. **Change colours:** All red.

GILLINGHAM

Players Names Ht, Wt, D.o.B.	Birthplace Transfer Fee	Clubs	Appearances F.L. A & S	 F.L.C. A & S	 F.A.C. A & S	Goals F.L.	 F.L.C.	 F.A.C.
Goalkeepers								
Ron Hillyard	Rotherham	York C	61	2	9			
5 11, 11 4, 31.3.52	—	Hartlepool U (loan)	23					
	F/T	Gillingham	374	23	27			
Gary Sutton*	Folkestone	Gillingham (A)	11	2	2			
5 11, 11 0, 2.2.62								
Andy Poole	Chesterfield	Mansfield T (A)						
6 0, 12 2, 6.7.60	F/T	Northampton T	141	11	5			
	F/T	Wolverhampton W						
	F/T	Port Vale	2					
	F/T	Gillingham						
Defenders								
John Sharpe	Portsmouth	Southampton (A)	21		1			
5 11, 11 5, 9.10.57	£30,000	Gillingham	175+2	14	14	2		
Mark Weatherly	Canterbury	Gillingham (A)	251+23	19+3	15+4	25	1	2
6 0, 11 12, 18.1.58								
John Sitton	Hackney	Chelsea (A)	11+2					
5 11, 12 4, 21.10.59	£10,000	Millwall	43+2	2	2	1		
	£10,000	Gillingham	57+3	4	4+1	2		
Peter Shaw	Northolt	Staines T						
6 2½, 13 11, 9.1.56	£10,000	Charlton Ath	100+5	9	8	5		1
	—	Exeter C (loan)	3		1			
	F/T	Gillingham	41+1	5	1		1	
Mick Adams (EY)	Sheffield	Gillingham (A)	85+7	5	6	4		
5 6, 10 4, 8.11.61								
Steve Bruce(EY)	Corbridge	Gillingham (A)	164+1	15	8	23	6	1
6 0, 11 2, 31.12.60								
Wayne Stokes	Wolverhampton	Coventry C (A)						
	F/T	Gillingham	2					
Midfield								
Mel Sage	Gillingham	Gillingham (A)	4+6					
5 8, 10 4,								
John Overton	Rotherham	Aston Villa (A)	2+1					
5 11, 10 10, 2.5.56	—	Halifax T (loan)	14			2		
	F/T	Gillingham	177+1	15	12	10		
Colin Duncan	Plymouth	Oxford U (A)	188+1	14	6	6		
5 11, 11 0, 5.8.57	£60,000	Gillingham	82+2	6	6+1	5		
David Mehmet	London	Millwall	97+17	6+1	9+1	15		1
5 9, 11 9, 2.12.60	£120,000	Tampa Bay						
	£80,000	Charlton Ath	29	1		2		
	F/T	Gillingham	13			3		
Richie Bowman	Lewisham	Charlton Ath (A)	93+3	10+1	3	7	2	
5 6, 10 7, 25.9.54	£25,000	Reading	194	16+1	10	30	1	1
	£25,000	Gillingham	26	2	3	6		1
Dick Tydeman	Chatham	Gillingham (A)	293+2	15	14	13	1	2
6 2, 12 6, 26.5.51	£70,000	Charlton Ath	158	13	7	7		
	£30,000	Gillingham	73+1	6	8	2		
Jeff Johnson (WS)	Cardiff	Manchester C (A)	4+2					
5 8, 11 12, 26.11.53	—	Swansea C (loan)	37+2	2		4		
	£12,000	Crystal Palace	82+5	5+1	5	4	1	
	F/T	Sheffield W	177+5	17	14	6	2	1
	£60,000	Newport Co	34	3		2		
	£8000	Gillingham	30+1	3	3	2	1	1
Philip Handford	Chatham	Gillingham (A)	12			1		
Forwards								
Tony Cascarino	St Pauls Cray	Crockenhill						
6 2, 11 10,	—	Gillingham	56+6	5	2+1	19	3	1
Neil Grewcock*	Leicester	Leicester C (A)	7+1	+1		1		
5 6, 11 3, 26.4.62	F/T	Gillingham	30+4	4	2	4		
Dean Horrix	Taplow	Millwall (A)	65+7	5+1	3	19	3	
5 10, 10 8, 21.11.61	P/E	Gillingham	7+7					

Commercial Manager: Vacant.
Club Coach: Paul Taylor.
Supporters Player of the Season 1982–83: Mark Weatherly.
Physiotherapist:
Association of Football Statisticians Club Adviser to Yearbook: R. Triggs.
Club Captain 1982–83: Dick Tydeman.
Chief Scout: Ted Buxton.
Club Statistician:

Players released since May 1982:
Andy Ford, D. (Dartford); Charles Young, D. (Chatham); Mickey Harrison, D. (Gateshead); Billy Lansdowne, M. (Sweden); Tony Bottiglieri, M. (Dartford); Colin Powell, F. (Dartford); Mark Miller, F. (Whitley Bay).

GRIMSBY TOWN Division 2

Top row (left to right):
Phil Crosby
Paul Wilkinson
Nigel Batch
Kevin Moore
Peter Crotier
David Moore
Andrew Moore
Middle row:
Alan Woodward (Youth Team Coach)
John Fraser (Physio)
Tony Ford
John Stone
Dean Crombie
Gary Beacock
Neil Cooper
Kevin Kilmore
Dave Booth (Manager)
Bottom row:
Tony Thorne
Gary Hershaw
John Steeples
Andy O'Dell
Joe Waters
Kevin Drinkell
Trevor Whymark (Player Coach)
Bob Cumming
Daryl Cross
Inserts:
In shirt, Mickey Speight
In sweatshirt, Phil Bonnyman.

Chairman: R. K. Middleton. ***Vice-Chairman:*** T. J. Lindley.

Directors: T. Wilkinson, T. W. Bygott, R. Ramsden, D. W. Ramsden, P. Sheffield, D. P. Everitt FCA.

Manager: David Booth. ***Administrative Manager:*** B. J. Fleming.

Year Formed: 1878. ***Turned Professional:*** 1890. ***Ltd Co.:*** 1890.

Club Nickname: 'The Mariners'.

Previous Name: Grimsby Pelham.

Previous Grounds: Clee Park; Abbey Park.

Previous Managers since 1946: Charlie Spencer, Bill Shankly, Billy Walsh, Allenby Chilton, Bill Lambton, Tim Ward, Tom Johnston, Jimmy McGuigan, Don McEvoy, Bill Harvey, Bobby Kennedy, Lawrie McMenemy, Ron Ashman, Tommy Casey, John Newman, George Kerr (16).

Blundell Park, Cleethorpes, South Humberside DN35 7PY. Telephone Cleethorpes (0472) 697111. ***Telegraphic address:*** 'Football Grimsby'. ***Ground capacity:*** 22,146. ***Record attendance:*** 31,657 v Wolverhampton W, FA Cup 5th rd, 20 Feb, 1937. ***Record receipts:*** £29,228 v Wolverhampton W, FL Cup 5th rd, 4 Dec, 1979. ***Pitch measurements:*** 111yd×74yd.

Directions to Ground: Buses 3A, 3F, 9 run to the ground; also football specials from the town centre. Nearest railway stations are Cleethorpes and Grimsby Town.

Match tickets: Seating can be booked two weeks in advance.

Car parking: Parking permitted in all side streets around the ground.

Entertainments/catering facilities: A licensed bar and several snack bars.

Club shop: There are 5 club shops, around the ground, selling all types of souvenir.

Handbooks/programmes: Programmes on sale at matches, and souvenir shops.

Address of Supporters Club: Souvenir Shop, Blundell Park, Cleethorpes DN35 7PY.

Note: Full club statistical records are on pages 416–455.

GRIMSBY TOWN 1982–83 LEAGUE RECORD

Match No.	Date	Venue	Opponents	Result	H/T Score	Lg. Pos.	Goalscorers	Attendance
1	Aug 28	H	Leeds U	D 1-1	0-0	—	Kilmore	16,137
2	Sept 4	A	Carlisle U	W 3-2	0-0	9	Drinkell 2, Waters (pen)	4683
3	7	H	Blackburn R	W 5-0	2-0	—	Kilmore 2, Waters, Drinkell, Ford	7567
4	11	H	Shrewsbury T	W 2-0	0-0	2	Drinkell, Waters (pen)	7599
5	18	A	Charlton Ath	W 1-0	0-0	2	Kilmore	4361
6	25	H	Bolton W	W 1-0	0-0	2	Cumming	7583
7	28	A	Middlesbrough	W 4-1	1-1	—	Waters 2 (both pens), Cooper, Crombie	5927
8	Oct 2	A	Chelsea	L 2-5	1-2	2	Drinkell, Cumming	10,019
9	9	A	Leicester C	L 0-2	0-0	4		9640
10	16	H	Derby Co	D 1-1	0-1	5	Waters	7572
11	23	A	Sheffield W	L 0-2	0-1	5		17,904
12	30	H	Cambridge U	W 1-0	0-0	5	Drinkell	5738
13	Nov 6	A	Wolverhampton W	L 0-3	0-1	6		12,701
14	13	H	Fulham	L 0-4	0-2	7		6952
15	20	H	Barnsley	L 1-2	0-0	7	Whymark	7500
16	27	A	Oldham Ath	D 1-1	0-0	8	Ford	5508
17	Dec 4	H	Crystal Palace	W 4-1	3-1	5	Drinkell 3 (1 pen), Cumming	5295
18	11	A	QPR	L 0-4	0-3	8		9811
19	18	H	Burnley	W 3-2	2-2	5	Cumming, Bonnyman, Drinkell	5448
20	27	A	Rotherham U	L 0-3	0-2	8		9231
21	28	H	Newcastle U	D 2-2	1-0	7	Drinkell 2	14,983
22	Jan 1	A	Barnsley	L 0-4	0-3	10		12,318
23	3	H	Carlisle U	W 2-1	1-1	7	Drinkell, Ford	6377
24	15	A	Leeds U	L 0-1	0-0	10		13,583
25	22	H	Charlton Ath	D 1-1	0-1	8	Wilkinson	5990
26	Feb 5	A	Blackburn R	L 1-2	1-2	9	Cumming	4724
27	12	H	Chelsea	W 2-1	2-1	—	Drinkell 2	6711
28	19	H	Leicester C	W 2-0	1-0	4	Ford, Drinkell	6963
29	26	A	Derby Co	L 0-2	0-0	7		12,775
30	Mar 5	H	Sheffield W	D 1-1	0-0	9	Cumming	9472
31	12	A	Cambridge U	L 0-1	0-1	11		3337
32	19	H	Wolverhampton W	D 1-1	1-0	11	Waters (pen)	7600
33	26	A	Fulham	L 0-4	0-2	11		8096
34	Apr 2	A	Newcastle U	L 0-4	0-2	12		20,145
35	4	H	Rotherham U	L 1-2	0-0	—	Waters	7117
36	8	A	Shrewsbury T	D 0-0	0-0	—		4446
37	16	H	Middlesbrough	L 0-3	0-1	13		5985
38	23	A	Crystal Palace	L 0-2	0-0	13		5909
39	30	H	Oldham Ath	L 0-2	0-0	16		4755
40	May 2	A	Bolton W	D 0-0	0-0	15		5866
41	7	A	Burnley	D 1-1	1-1	16	Drinkell	7083
42	14	H	QPR	D 1-1	1-0	18	Cumming	9590

Final League Position: 19

GOALSCORERS

League (45): Drinkell 17 (1 pen), Waters 8 (5 pens), Cumming 7, Ford 4, Kilmore 4, Bonnyman 1, Cooper 1, Crombie 1, Whymark 1, Wilkinson 1.
Milk Cup (6): Drinkell 5, Moore K. 1.
FA Cup (2): Ford 1, Waters 1 (pen).
Football League Trophy (6): Drinkell 4, Moore K. 1, Waters 1 (pen).

Milk Cup	First Round	Scunthorpe U (a)	2-1
		(h)	0-0
	Second Round	Sheffield U (h)	3-3
		(a)	1-5
FA Cup	Third Round	Scunthorpe U (a)	0-0
		(h)	2-0
	Fourth Round	Ipswich T (a)	0-2
Football League Trophy		Sheffield U (a)	3-1
		Lincoln C (a)	1-2
		Scunthorpe U (h)	2-0

Batch	Moore D.	Crombie	Waters	Cooper	Moore K.	Ford	Kilmore	Drinkell	Bonnyman	Whymark	Speight	Cumming	Grotier	Crosby	Whitlock (L)	Stone	O'Dell	Wilkinson	Saxby (L)	Beacock	Referees	Match No.
1	2	3	4	5	6	7	8	9	10	11											J. Hunting	1
1	2	3	4	5	6	7*	8	9	10	11	12										D. Richardson	2
1		3	4	5	6	7	8	9	10	11	2										T. Mills	3
1			4	5	6	7	8	9	10	11*	2	12		3							J. Key	4
1	2	3	4	5	6		12	9	10	8*	11	7									M. Bodenham	5
1	2	3	4	5	6			9	10	8	11	7									G. Courtney	6
1	2	3	4	5	6		12	9	10	8*	11	7									N. Wilson	7
1	2*	3	4	5	6		12	9	10	8	11	7									Alan Robinson	8
1		3	4	5	6	7*	8	9	10		2	11								12	K. Salmon	9
	2		4	5	6		8	9	10	12	11*	7	1	3							D. Hutchinson	10
	2		4	5	6	12	8	9	10	11		7	1	3*							A. Hamil	11
	2					11	7	9	10	8	6	3	1		4	5					A. Robinson	12
	2					11	7*	9	10	8	6	3	1	12	4	5					H. King	13
1	2		4	7		11		9	10	8				3	6	5					K. Hackett	14
1	2		4	5		11	12	9	10*	8	7	3			6						J. Bray	15
1	2		4	5	3	7		9	10	8		11*			6	12					T. Holbrook	16
1	2		4	5	3	7		9	10	8		11			6						T. Jones	17
1	2		4	5	3	7		9	10	8					6	11					T. Spencer	18
1	2	3	4		6	7		9	10	8		11				5					I. Borrett	19
1	2	3	4		6	7		9	10	8		11				5					D. Allison	20
1	2	3	4	5	6	7		9	10	8		11*			12						M. Scott	21
1	2	3	4	5	6	7		9		8		11					10				R. Guy	22
1	2	3	4	5	6	7		9		8		11					10				R. Banks	23
1	2	3	4		6	7		9	10	8						5	11				K. Burden	24
1	2	3	4		6	7		9	11*	8						5	10	12			T. Fitzharris	25
1	2	3	4	5	6	7		9	11		10	8									R. Bridges	26
1	2	3	4	5	6	7		9	10			8					11				D. Owen	27
1	2	3	4	5	6	7		9	10			8					11				D. Scott	28
1	2	3	4	5	6	7		9	10			8					11				J. Worrall	29
1	2	3	4		6	7		9	10			8		5			11				D. Willis	30
1	2	3	4		6	7			9			8		10		12	11		5*		M. Taylor	31
1	2	3	4		6	7			8			11		5		10*	12	9			P. Tyldesley	32
1	2	12	4		6	7			8			11		3			10	9	5*		E. Read	33
1	2	3	4		6	7	12	9	8*			11		5			10				N. Glover	34
1		12	4		6	7	8	9	10			3				2*	11		5		G. Tyson	35
1	2	3	4		6	7		9	8			11					10		5		K. Barratt	36
1	2	3	4		6	7		9	8			11					10	12	5*		N. Midgley	37
1	2	3	4	7*	6	11	12	9	8								10		5		S. Bates	38
1	2	3	4		6	7	11*	9	10	8							12		5		K. Baker	39
1	2	3	4		6	7		9	10	8		11							5		B. Newsome	40
1	2	3	4		6	7		9	10	8		11							5		A. Seville	41
1	2	3	4		6	7	12	9	10	8*		11							5		D. Civil	42
38	38	30	40	24	38	36	11	39	40	27	12	32	4	9	7	10	15	2	10	0		
		+ 2s				+ 1s	+ 7s			+ 1s	+ 1s	+ 1s		+ 1s	+ 1s	+ 1s	+ 2s	+ 2s		+ 1s		

FOOTBALL LEAGUE RECORD

1892 Original Member Division 2; 1901–03 Division 1; 1903 Division 2; 1910 Failed Re-election; 1911 Re-elected Division 2; 1920–21 Division 3; 1921–26 Division 3(N); 1926–29 Division 2; 1929–32 Division 1; 1932–34 Division 2; 1934–48 Division 1; 1948–51 Division 2; 1951–56 Division 3(N); 1956–59 Division 2; 1959–62 Division 3; 1962–64 Division 2; 1964–68 Division 3; 1968–72 Division 4; 1972–77 Division 3; 1977–79 Division 4; 1979–80 Division 3; 1980– Division 2.

HONOURS

Football League: Division 1 best season: 5th, 1934–35; Division 2 – Champions 1900–01, 1933–34; Runners-up 1928–29; Division 3(N) – Champions 1925–26, 1955–56; Runners-up 1951–52; Division 3 – Champions 1979–80; Runners-up 1961–62; Division 4 – Champions 1971–72; Runners-up 1978–79. *FA Cup:* Semi-finals, 1936, 1939. *Football League Cup* best season: 5th rd, 1979–80. *League Group Cup:* 1981–82.

COLOURS

Black and white vertical striped shirts, black shorts, white stockings. **Change colours:** All red.

GRIMSBY TOWN

Players Names *Ht, Wt, D.o.B.*	*Birthplace* *Transfer Fee*	*Clubs*	*Appearances* *F.L.* *A & S*	 *F.L.C.* *A & S*	 *F.A.C.* *A & S*	*Goals* *F.L.*	 *F.L.C.*	 *F.A.C.*
Goalkeepers								
Nigel Batch	Huddersfield	Derby Co (A)	232	18	15			
Peter Grotier	Stratford	West Ham U (A)	50	4				
5 11, 12 10, 18.10.50	—	Cardiff C (loan)	2					
	£16,666	Lincoln C	233	16	14			
	£25,000	Cardiff C	38	5				
	£5000	Grimsby T	4	2				
Dave Hannay		Grimsby T						
Defenders								
Kevin Moore (ES)	Grimsby	Grimsby T	270+2	25	18	15	2	2
5 11, 11 7, 29.4.58								
David Moore	Grimsby	Grimsby T (A)	136	9	7	2		
5 10, 12 13, 17.12.59								
Dean Crombie	Lincoln	Ruston Bucyrus						
5 11, 11 7, 9.8.57	—	Lincoln C	33	1+1				
	F/T	Grimsby T	185+3	13	11	2		1
John Stone	Saltburn	South Bank						
6 0, 12 5, 3.3.53		Middlesbrough	2					
	F/T	York C	86	7	5	5		
	F/T	Darlington	120	11	10	14	1	
	£22,500	Grimsby T	89+5	11	8	2		
Phil Crosby* (EY)	Leeds	Grimsby T (A)	34+5	3	1	1		
5 9, 10 8, 9.11.62								
Neil Cooper (SS)	Aberdeen	Aberdeen						
5-10½, 11 1, 12.8.59	£35,000	Barnsley	57+3	7+1	3	6	1	1
	£35,000	Grimsby T	40	4	1	2		
Midfield								
Bob Cumming	Airdrie	Baillieston						
5 8, 11 4, 7.12.55	F/T	Grimsby T	253+15	19+1	15	48	5	2
Joe Waters (EI)	Limerick	Leicester C (A)	11+2	1	2	1		2
5 5, 10 5, 20.9.53	£8500	Grimsby T	319+1	25	18	58	5	4
Andy O'Dell	Hull	Grimsby T (A)	19+2	+2	2			
5 8, 10 8, 2.1.63								
Phil Bonnyman	Glasgow	Hamilton A						
6 0, 12 0, 6.2.54	£20,000	Carlisle U	149+3	10	14	26	2	5
	£150,000	Chesterfield	98+1	6	8	25	1	2
	£80,000	Grimsby T	40	3	1	1		
Mick Speight (EB)	Upton	Sheffield U (A)	184+15	6+1	8+2	14	1	
5 10½, 12 7, 1.11.51	£60,000	Blackburn R	50+1	6		4		
	£25,000	Grimsby T	12+1	2				
Gary Henshaw		Grimbsby T (A)						
Forwards								
Tony Ford	Grimsby	Grimsby T (A)	205+31	18+3	9+4	37	4	
5 9, 12 2, 14.5.59								
Kevin Drinkell	Grimsby	Grimsby T (A)	177+22	16+2	1+3	60	6	4
5 10, 11 10, 18.6.60								
Kevin Kilmore* (EY)	Scunthorpe	Scunthorpe U	93+9	6+2	3	28	1	
5 9 11 10, 11.11.59	£60,000	Grimsby T	70+32	4	4+2	27		2
Trevor Whymark (E)	Burston	Diss T						
6 0, 11 0, 4.5.50	—	Ipswich T	249+11	20	21	74	9	2
	£150,000	Vancouver W						
	—	Sparta Rotterdam (loan)						
	—	Derby Co (loan)	2					
	£80,000	Grimsby T	74+8	5	5	15	1	1
Paul Wilkinson	Holton-le-Clay	Grimsby T (A)	2+2		+1	1		

Commercial Manager: A. E. King (Tel. 697111)
Club Coach:
Supporters Player of the Season 1982–83: Kevin Drinkell
Physiotherapist: J. Fraser
Club Captain 1982–83: J. Waters
Chief Scout: A. Askew
Club Statistician:
Association of Football Statisticians Club Adviser to Yearbook: L. Triggs

Players released since May 1982:
Len Robinson, G. (N/K); John Steeples, F. (Scarborough); Jimmy Fell, D. (retired); Gary Beacock, F. (N/K); Tony Thorpe, D. (N/K).

HALIFAX TOWN Division 4

Back row (left to right):
Everton Carr
Keith Nobbs
Tony Smith
Malcolm Goodman
Dave Pearce
Mark Greenway
Middle row:
Alan Sutton (Physio)
Jimmy Hallybone
Dave Evans
Martin Nuttall
Lee Smelt
Mick Wood
Stephen Ward
Paul Kendall
Brian Hendy (Trainer)
Front row:
Bobby Davison
Steve Spooner
Mickey Bullock (Manager)
Dave Staniforth (Coach)
Paul Hendrie.

Chairman: J. Turner. ***Vice-Chairman:*** J. S. Crowther.

Directors: D. Sharp, M INST BM, P. Dawson, T. Dawson, J. Robinson, T. McLean, D. Wilkinson, R. Newby, C. Wood.

Manager: Mickey Bullock. ***Secretary:*** Mrs Carol Bell.

Commercial Manager: Tony Thwaites.

Year Formed: 1911. ***Turned Professional:*** 1911. ***Ltd Co.:*** 1911.

Club Nickname: 'The Shaymen'.

Previous Grounds: Sandhall and Exley.

Previous Managers since 1946: Jack Breedon, W. Wootton, Jimmy Thompson, Gerald Henry, Bobby Browne, Willie Watson, Billy Burnicle, Harry Hooper, Willie Watson, Vic Metcalfe, Alan Ball (Snr), George Kirby, Ray Henderson, George Mulhall, John Quinn, Alan Ball (Snr), Jimmy Lawson, George Kirby (18).

Shay Ground, Halifax HX1 2YS. Telephone 0422 53423. ***Ground capacity: 16,500. Record attendance:*** 36,885 v Tottenham H, FA Cup 5th rd, 14 Feb, 1953. ***Record receipts:*** £14,000 v Manchester C, FA Cup 3rd rd, 5 Jan, 1980. ***Pitch measurements:*** 110yd×70yd.

Directions to Ground: Near the town centre within a few minutes walking distance of the bus station and railway station.

Match tickets: Advance booking on application to the secretary.

Car parking: Car park is available; entrance in Shaw Hill.

Entertainments/catering facilities: Social club adjacent to club office.

Club shop: Shop on ground and also in town centre. Programmes, souvenirs, etc (wide range always available) from the Promotions Office, 11 Horton Street, Halifax. P & p must always accompany requests.

Handbooks/programmes: Handbooks and programmes available from Supporters Club, c/o Halifax Town AFC.

Address of Supporters Club: Same as Football Club.

Address of the Club Shop or Boutique: Club Shop, 11 Horton Street, Halifax, Yorks.

Note: Full club statistical records are on pages 416–455.

HALIFAX TOWN 1982–83 LEAGUE RECORD

Match No.	Date	Venue	Opponents	Result		H/T Score	Lg. Pos.	Goalscorers	Attendance
1	Aug 28	A	Colchester U	L	0-1	0-0	—		2610
2	Sept 3	H	Mansfield T	D	0-0	0-0	—		2225
3	7	H	Darlington	W	2-0	2-0	—	Hendrie, Spooner	1891
4	11	A	Swindon T	W	1-0	0-0	5	Davison	3450
5	18	H	Aldershot	L	1-3	0-1	9	Davison	2243
6	25	A	Bury	L	0-2	0-2	15		2244
7	28	A	York C	L	2-3	0-0	—	Davison 2	1772
8	Oct 1	H	Chester	D	0-0	0-0	—		1925
9	9	A	Blackpool	D	0-0	0-0	18		4150
10	15	H	Port Vale	L	0-2	0-1	—		2009
11	19	H	Bristol C	D	2-2	2-1	—	Davison 2	1465
12	23	A	Rochdale	D	2-2	2-2	17	Spooner, Keenan (og)	1765
13	29	H	Crewe Alex	L	0-3	0-1	—		1726
14	Nov 3	A	Peterborough U	L	1-2	0-1	—	Nobbs	2038
15	5	H	Hereford U	D	2-2	1-1	—	Spooner, Smith	1065
16	13	A	Wimbledon	W	4-2	1-0	20	Davison 3, Allatt	2104
17	27	A	Hartlepool U	W	2-1	0-1	18	Wood, Staniforth	1367
18	Dec 17	H	Tranmere R	L	1-2	0-1	—	Williams (og)	912
19	27	A	Hull C	D	1-1	0-0	21	Staniforth	10,042
20	28	H	Scunthorpe U	W	3-1	2-0	21	Spooner, Staniforth, Nuttall	2270
21	Jan 1	A	Stockport Co	L	2-4	0-1	20	Allatt, Spooner (pen)	2871
22	3	H	Torquay U	W	3-0	1-0	18	Spooner (pen), Nuttall, Allatt	1776
23	8	A	Mansfield T	W	2-1	1-0	14	Nuttall 2	2398
24	14	H	Colchester U	W	4-0	2-0	—	Nuttall, Staniforth 3	1863
25	22	A	Darlington	W	2-1	1-1	12	Staniforth 2	1175
26	Feb 1	H	Northampton T	W	2-0	1-0	—	Ward, Staniforth	1927
27	5	H	Bury	W	1-0	0-0	8	Evans	4021
28	12	A	Chester	L	0-2	0-1	—		1907
29	15	A	Bristol C	L	0-3	0-2	—		3169
30	18	H	Blackpool	W	2-0	0-0	—	Spooner (pen), Allatt	2366
31	26	A	Port Vale	L	1-2	1-0	9	Spooner	5163
32	Mar 1	H	Peterborough U	L	1-2	1-1	—	Staniforth	2002
33	4	H	Rochdale	D	0-0	0-0	—		2128
34	11	A	Crewe Alex	D	1-1	0-0	—	Staniforth	2518
35	15	H	Swindon T	W	1-0	0-0	—	Nuttall	1806
36	19	A	Hereford U	L	0-2	0-1	9		2006
37	Apr 1	A	Scunthorpe U	L	0-2	0-1	—		3775
38	4	H	Hull C	L	1-2	0-1	—	Nuttall	5011
39	10	A	Northampton T	L	1-3	0-0	—	Staniforth	2208
40	15	H	York C	D	2-2	1-0	—	Allatt 2	2117
41	23	A	Tranmere R	W	2-1	1-1	14	Spooner 2 (1 pen)	1401
42	29	H	Hartlepool U	D	1-1	1-0	—	Staniforth	1245
43	May 2	A	Torquay U	W	3-1	1-1	11	Wood, Allatt, Smith	1558
44	7	A	Aldershot	L	1-6	1-2	13	Staniforth	1701
45	10	H	Wimbledon	D	1-1	1-0	—	Spooner	1233
46	13	H	Stockport Co	W	1-0	1-0	—	Staniforth	1522

Final League Position: 11

GOALSCORERS

League (59): Staniforth 15, Spooner 11 (3 pens), Davison 9, Allatt 7, Nuttall 7, Smith 2, Wood 2, Evans 1, Hendrie 1, Hobbs 1, Ward 1, own goals 2.
Milk Cup (4): Davison 3, Staniforth 1.
FA Cup (0).
Football League Trophy (4): Davison 4.

Milk Cup	First Round	Derby Co (h)	2-1
		(a)	2-5 (aet)
FA Cup	First Round	North Shields (h)	0-1
Football League Trophy		Bradford C (a)	0-1
		Hull C (h)	1-0
		Hartlepool U (h)	3-0

Smelt	Nobbs	Carr	Evans	Goodman	Wood	Hallybone	Davison	Staniforth	Spooner	Ward	Smith	Hendrie	Nuttall	Butcher (L)	Kendall	Allatt	Wilkes (L)	Skivington (L)	Gallagher	*Referees*	*Match No.*
1	2	3	4	5	6	7	8	9	10	11										R. Lewis	1
1	2	3	4			7	8	10	9	11	5	6								R. Nixon	2
1	2	3	4			7	8	10	9	11	5	6								K. Baker	3
1	2	3			4	7	8	10	9	11	5	6								T. Holbrook	4
1	2	11*	4		3	7	8	10	9		5	6	12							R. Bridges	5
	2		4		5	9	11	6	7	8	3		10*	1	12					M. Peck	6
	2	3	4		6	7	8	10	9	11	5			1						A. Saunders	7
	2	3	4		6	7	8	10*	9	11	5		12	1						R. Banks	8
	2	3	4	12	6	7	8		9*	11	5		10	1						N. Ashley	9
	2	3	4	9	6*	7	8			11	5		10	1	12					N. Wilson	10
1	2		4	3	7*	12	8		9	11	5	6	10							M. Scott	11
1	2		4	3	7	12	8		9	11	5	6*	10							A. Seville	12
1	2		4	3	6	12	8	10	9	11	5		7*							N. Glover	13
1	2	12	4	3*	11		8		10	7	5	6				9				I. Borrett	14
1	2	3	4	12	11		8		10	7*	5	6				9				P. Willis	15
1	2		4	11	3		8	7	10		5	6				9				K. Barratt	16
1	2		4	11	3		8	7	10	12	5	6				9*				C. Seel	17
1	2		4	3	11			10*	8	7	5	6	12			9				G. Napthine	18
1	2		3	5*	9			12	8	6	4	7	11			10				M. Heath	19
1	2		4		3			11	8	7	5	6	10			9				J. Hough	20
1	2		4	12	3			11	8	7	5	6*	10			9				C. Newsome	21
1	2		4		3			11	8	7	5	6	10			9				G. Courtney	22
1	2		4		3			11	8	7	5	6	10			9				D. Lloyd	23
1	2		4		3			11	8	7	5	6	10			9				R. Guy	24
1	2			4	3			11	8	7	5	6	10		12	9*				D. Shaw	25
1	2			4	3			11	8	7	5	6	10		9					J. Worrall	26
1	2		4		3			11	8	7	5	6	10			9				V. Callow	27
1	2		4		3			11	8*	7	5	6	10		12	9				N. Midgley	28
1	2		4	12	3			11		7	5	6	10		8*	9				B. Daniels	29
1	2		4	12	3*			11	8	7	5	6	10			9				T. Jones	30
1	2		4	12	3*			11	8	7	5	6	10			9				K. Walmsley	31
1	2		4	12				9	10	7	5	6*	8		3	11				M. Peck	32
1	2	3		4		6			8	10	5				11	9	7			H. Taylor	33
1	2	3	4					11	8	10	5					9	7	6		R. Chadwick	34
1	2	3	4			12		11	8	10*	5		9				6	7		D. Allison	35
1	2	3	4*			12		11	8	10	5		9				6	7		B. Hill	36
1	2		4		3			11	12	10	5	6				9		8*	7	J. Lovatt	37
1	2		4		3			11	8	10	5	6*	9			12			7	A. Hamil	38
1	2		4	12				11	3	10	5	6	9			8			7*	M. James	39
1	2		4	5	3			11		10		6	8*		12	9			7	F. Roberts	40
1	2		4		3			11	8	10	5	6				9			7	T. Fitzharris	41
1	6		4	2	3			11	8	10	5					9			7	N. Ashley	42
1	2		4		3			11	8	10	5	6				9			7	D. Letts	43
1	2		4	12	3			11	8	10	5	6	9*						7	M. Taylor	44
1	2		4		3			11	8	10	5	6			9				7	K. Redfern	45
1	2		4	12	3			11	8	10*	5	6				9			7	J. Hunting	46
41	46	14	42	15	38	11	17	38	42	43	44	34	26	5	5	27	4	4	10		
		+ 1s		+ 10s		+ 5s		+ 1s	+ 1s	+ 1s			+ 3s		+ 5s	+ 1s					

FOOTBALL LEAGUE RECORD

1921 Original Member; Division 3(N); 1958–63 Division 3; 1963–69 Division 4; 1969–76 Division 3; 1976– Division 4.

HONOURS

Football League: Division 3 best season: 3rd, 1970–71; Division 3(N) – Runners-up 1934–35; Division 4 – Runners-up 1968–69. *FA Cup* best season: 5th rd, 1932–33, 1952–53. *Football League Cup* best season: 4th rd, 1964.

COLOURS

Royal blue shirts with white trim, white shorts with blue trim, blue stockings with white tops.
Change colours: Yellow shirts with blue trim, blue shorts, yellow stockings with blue tops.

HALIFAX TOWN

Players Names Ht, Wt, D.o.B.	Birthplace Transfer Fee	Clubs	Appearances F.L. A & S	 F.L.C. A & S	 F.A.C. A & S	Goals F.L.	 F.L.C.	 F.A.C.
Goalkeepers								
Lee Smelt	Edmonton	Colchester U						
6 1, 13 2, 13.3.58	F/T	Gravesend & N						
	£15,000	Nottingham F	1					
	—	Peterborough U (loan)	5	2				
	£10,000	Halifax T	75	2	1			
Defenders								
Paul Kendall 6 0, 12 6,	Halifax	Halifax T (A)	14+9					
Malcolm Goodman	Solihull	Bromsgrove R						
6 2, 12 12, 6.5.61	£2000	Halifax T	70+16	2	2	1		
Dave Evans	West Bromwich	Aston Villa (A)	2					
5 11, 12 6, 20.5.58	£25,000	Halifax T	172	6	10	7	1	
Keith Nobbs	Bishop Auckland	Middlesbrough (A)	1					
5 10, 11 10, 19.9.61	F/T	Halifax T	46	2	1	1		
Tony Smith	Sunderland	Newcastle U	1+1					
5 10, 11 11, 20.2.57	£10,000	Peterborough U	68	3	4	5		
	F/T	Halifax T	44	2	1	2		
Mick Wood	Bury	Blackburn R (A)	140+7	7+1	9	2		
5 11, 10 13, 3.7.52	£10,000	Bradford C	143+3	10+1	7	9		1
	F/T	Halifax T	38	+1	1	2		
Midfield								
Paul Hendrie (SS)	Glasgow	Rob Roy						
5 6, 10 3, 27.3.54		Birmingham C	19+4	3	3	1		
		Portland Timbers						
		Bristol R	17+13		+1	1		
	£5000	Halifax T	147	6	10	10		1
Steve Ward	Derby	Brighton (A)						
6 0, 12 12, 21.7.59	F/T	Northampton T	13+2	4		2	1	
	F/T	Halifax T	120+3	4	3+1	9		
Barry Gallagher	Bradford	Bradford C (A)	66+5	11+1	2	22	5	1
5 11, 12 3, 7.4.61	—	Mansfield T (loan)	2+1					
	F/T	Halifax T	10					
Steve Spooner	London	Derby Co (A)	7+1					
5 11, 12 10, 25.1.61	F/T	Halifax T	71+1	2	1	13		
Jim Hallybone	Leytonstone	Orient (A)	5+3		3			
5 6, 10 0, 15.5.62	F/T	Halifax T	11+5	2				
Forwards								
Dave Staniforth	Chesterfield	Sheffield U (A)	22+4	3		3		
6 2, 12 10, 6.10.50	£20,000	Bristol R	135+18	4	9+4	31	2	
	£5000	Bradford C	107+8	8	9+1	25	1	1
	F/T	Halifax T	38+1	2	1	15	1	
Martin Nuttall	Oldham	Oldham Ath (A)	8+5			1		
5 9, 11 2, 12.9.61	F/T	Halifax T	26+3			7		
Vernon Allatt	Hednesford	Hednesford T						
5 11, 11 8, 28.5.59	£2000	Halifax T	93+5	3	9	14		

Commercial Manager: Tony Thwaites (Tel. Halifax 66593)
Club Coach: David Staniforth
Supporters Player of the Season 1982–83: David Staniforth
Physiotherapist: Alan Sutton
Association of Football Statisticians Club Adviser to Yearbook: M. Belshaw

Club Captain 1982–83:
Chief Scout: Gerry Brook
Club Statistician:

Players released since May 1982: Simon Bullock, F.(retired); Glyn Chamberlain, M. (Kettering T); John Kilner, G. (South Africa); Jimmy McIlwraith, F. (N/K); Tom O'Neil, M. (N/K);Steve Walker, M. (N/K); Andy Whiteley, F. (N/K).

HARTLEPOOL UNITED Division 4

Back row (left to right): John Linacre (now Whitby), Phil Brown, Mike Fagan, Andy Linighan, John Watson, Bob Newton (now with Port Vale), Mark Lawrence, Phil Linacre, Kenny Lowe, Barrie Simpson
Front row: Trevor Hogg, Paul Staff, John Bird, George Smith (Coach), Vince Barker (Chairman), Billy Horner (Manager), Tommy Johnson (Physiotherapist), Roy Hogan, Alan Sweeney (left club), Kevin Johnson.
(Photo by courtesy Julian Gold Publishing Ltd, Hartlepool and by special arrangement with James Bond of Hartlepool.)

President: S. Spaldin. ***Chairman:*** J. V. Barker.

Vice-Chairman: B. H. Crosby.

Directors: J. S. Fullard, D. Jukes, S. I. Levinson.

Manager: Mick Docherty. ***Secretary:*** W. P. Hillan.

Year Formed: 1908. ***Turned Professional:*** 1908. Ltd Co.: 1908.

Club Nickname: 'The Pool'.

Previous Names: Hartlepools United until 1968; Hartlepool until 1977.

Previous Managers since 1946: Fred Westgarth, Ray Middleton, Bill Robinson, Allenby Chilton, Bob Gurney, Alvan Williams, Geoff Twentyman, Brian Clough, Angus McLean, John Simpson, Len Ashurst, Ken Hale, Billy Horner (13).

The Victoria Ground, 18 Scarborough Street, Hartlepool. Telephone 0429 72584; (Office) 73492. ***Ground capacity:*** 18,000. ***Record attendance:*** 17,426 v Manchester U, FA Cup 3rd rd, 5 Jan, 1957. ***Record receipts:*** £17,000 v Leeds U, FA Cup 3rd rd, 18 Jan, 1979. ***Pitch measurements:*** 113yd×77yd.

Directions to Ground: Hartlepool railway station is only a few hundred yards from the ground. Local bus services run scheduled services to Hartlepool.

Match tickets: No pre-booking of tickets.

Car parking: Ample side-street parking.

Entertainments/catering facilities: Two refreshment kiosks inside the ground.

Club shop: Open on match days; stocks all types of souvenirs on ground.

Handbooks/programmes: No handbooks. Programmes available on subscription.

Note: Full club statistical records are on pages 416–455.

HARTLEPOOL UNITED 1982–83 LEAGUE RECORD

Match No.	Date	Venue	Opponents	Result		H/T Score	Lg. Pos.	Goalscorers	Attendance
1	Aug 28	H	Scunthorpe U	D	0-0	0-0	—		1009
2	Sept 4	A	Peterborough U	L	1-2	1-1	19	Stimpson	3499
3	7	A	Rochdale	L	0-2	0-0	—		1075
4	11	H	Northampton T	W	2-1	0-1	18	Bird, Hogan	947
5	18	A	Hull C	D	1-1	0-0	18	Smith	3913
6	25	H	Tranmere R	W	4-0	2-0	14	Linacre, Linighan A. 2, Lawrence (pen)	1202
7	29	H	Crewe Alex	W	1-0	0-0	—	Higgins	1654
8	Oct 2	A	Torquay U	L	2-3	2-1	12	Brown, Hogan	2051
9	8	A	Stockport Co	D	1-1	1-0	—	Johnson	1823
10	16	H	Bristol C	W	3-1	2-1	11	Bird, Lawrence (pen), Dobson	1449
11	18	A	Port Vale	L	0-3	0-1	—		3664
12	23	H	Aldershot	D	1-1	0-0	13	Bird	1412
13	30	A	York C	L	1-5	0-2	15	Smith	1971
14	Nov 3	H	Mansfield T	L	0-4	0-2	—		1325
15	6	H	Wimbledon	W	1-0	0-0	13	Linacre	1081
16	13	A	Hereford U	L	0-1	0-1	15		2298
17	27	H	Halifax T	L	1-2	1-0	16	Linighan A.	1367
18	Dec 4	A	Chester	L	1-2	1-2	17	Lane (og)	1114
19	18	A	Swindon T	L	0-3	0-1	20		4118
20	27	H	Darlington	W	2-0	0-0	18	Lawrence 2 (1 pen)	3337
21	28	A	Bury	L	0-4	0-2	19		3275
22	Jan 1	H	Blackpool	W	2-1	1-1	18	Linacre, Smith	1569
23	3	A	Colchester U	L	1-4	1-3	19	Brown	2239
24	12	H	Peterborough U	D	0-0	0-0	—		1161
25	16	A	Scunthorpe U	L	0-3	0-1	—		4261
26	22	H	Hull C	D	0-0	0-0	19		2291
27	29	A	Northampton T	L	1-3	1-1	20	Lowe	2181
28	Feb 5	A	Tranmere R	D	1-1	0-0	20	Dobson	1545
29	12	H	Torquay U	L	0-2	0-1	20		1159
30	19	H	Stockport Co	W	3-2	1-0	19	Lawrence 2 (1 pen), Dobson	1023
31	26	A	Bristol C	L	0-2	0-1	21		4194
32	Mar 2	H	Port Vale	D	2-2	0-0	—	Staff, Linacre	1398
33	5	A	Aldershot	W	2-0	1-0	19	Staff, Robinson	1439
34	12	H	York C	W	2-0	0-0	18	Staff, Linacre	1604
35	14	A	Mansfield T	L	0-3	0-2	—		1991
36	19	A	Wimbledon	L	0-2	0-0	19		2324
37	26	H	Hereford U	L	0-1	0-0	22		1147
38	Apr 2	H	Bury	L	0-1	0-0	22		1285
39	4	A	Darlington	L	1-2	0-0	—	Robinson	3131
40	9	H	Chester	W	1-0	0-0	21	Dobson	1034
41	15	A	Crewe Alex	L	0-3	0-0	—		2042
42	23	H	Swindon T	L	1-2	1-1	23	Dobson	1126
43	29	A	Halifax T	D	1-1	0-1	—	Dobson	1245
44	May 2	H	Colchester U	L	1-4	0-1	22	Linacre	804
45	7	H	Rochdale	W	3-0	0-0	22	Hogan (pen), Staff, Dobson	1013
46	14	A	Blackpool	W	2-1	2-1	22	Linighan D., Dobson	2184

Final League Position: 22

GOALSCORERS

League (46): Dobson 8, Lawrence 6 (4 pens), Linacre 6, Staff 4, Bird 3, Hogan 3 (1 pen), Linighan A. 3, Smith 3, Brown 2, Robinson 2, Higgins 1, Johnson 1, Linighan D. 1, Lowe 1, Stimpson 1, own goal 1.
Milk Cup (7): Barker 2, Bainbridge 1, Johnson 1, Linighan A. 1, Smith 1, Staff 1.
FA Cup (4): Linacre 2, Dobson 1, Hogan 1.
Football League Trophy (1): Lawrence 1.

Milk Cup	First Round	Chesterfield (a)	1-2
		(h)	2-0 (aet)
	Second Round	Derby Co (a)	0-2
		(h)	4-2 (aet)
FA Cup	First Round	Lincoln C (h)	3-0
	Second Round	York C (h)	1-1
		(a)	0-4

Football League Trophy	Hull C (h)	1-2
	Bradford C (h)	0-4
	Halifax T (a)	0-3

Watson	Brown	Stimpson	Hogan	Bird	Linighan A.	Bainbridge	Lawrence	Smith	Staff	Johnson	Dobson	Newton	Barker	Linacre	Higgins	Lowe	Hamilton	Wright	Smithies	Borthwick	Blackburn	Stalker	Robinson	Langridge	Linighan D.	Stewart	Brown	*Referees*
1	2	3	4	5	6	7	8	9	10*	11	12																	R. Banks
1	2	3	4	5	6	7	8	10		11		9																A. Seville
1	2	3	4	5	6	7	10	8		11		9																M. Heath
1	2	3	4	5	6	7	10	8		11		9*	12															T. Fitzharris
1	6	5	8	12	2	3*	10	7		9			4	11														J. Hough
1	2	3	4		6	7	10	8		11			5	9														D. Scott
1	2	3	4	5	6	7	10	8		11					9													D. Hutchinson
1	2	3	4	5	6	7	10	8		11					9													D. Letts
1	2	3	4	5	6	7	10*		8	11	12			9														K. Baker
1	2	3		5	6	7	10				8		11	9		4												J. Key
1	2	3	4	5		6	10				8*		11	9	12	7												M. Robinson
1		3	4	5	6	12		8*	10	11			7		9													A. Challinor
1	2	3	4	5	6		9	8	7*	10			11			12												J. Worrall
1	2	3	4	5	6		9	8*	7	10			11				12											M. Peck
	2	3	4	5	6		9*		8		12		11	10		7		1										N. Midgley
	2	3	4	5	6		9		12				11	10		8*	7	1										H. Taylor
	2	3	4		6		10*		7	12	8		5	9			11	1										C. Seel
	10	3	4		6	11*	12	2	7		8		5	9				1										K. Barratt
	2		4	5	6		11	10	12	3	8*		7	10				1										B. Daniels
	2		4		6	11	10	8	7	3			5	9				1										K. Hackett
	2		7		3	5	10*	6	9	8			4	11				1	12									C. Newsome
	4	3			6		10	8	7	11			5	9				1	2									D. Hutchinson
	4	3			6		10	8*	7	11			5	9				1	2	12								M. James
	10		4	5	6		8		7	11			3						2		1	9						N. Glover
	10		4	5	6		8		7	11	12		3						2		1	9*						T. Jones
	10		4	5	6		8			11			3			7			2		1	9						A. Robinson
	2			4	5		8			11*	10		3	9		7					1	12	6					E. Scales
	2			5	6				8		9		3	11		7				10*	1		4					M. Heath
	2			5*	6		10	12	8		9		3	11		7					1		4					R. Chadwick
	2	3			6		10	12	8*		9		5	11		7					1		4					K. Walmsley
	2	3			6		10	8			9		5	11*		7					1		4	12				J. Bray
	2			5	6			8	11		9*		3	12		7					1		3	10				D. Richardson
	2	3		5	6			8	11		9			10		7					1		4					T. Glasson
	2	3		5	6			8	11		10			9		7					1		4					P. Tyldesley
	2	3		5	6			8	11		12			9		7		1					4	10*				D. Brazier
	2				6			8	11		10*		3	9		7					1		4		5			B. Stevens
	2			5	6					11			3	9		7*					1		4	10		12		J. Key
		3		5	6			8		12				10		7			2		1		4	9*		11		K. Hackett
	12			5	6			8					11	9		7			2*		1		4		2			J. Worrall
	7			5	6			4*			10		11	9					2		1		12		3	8		N. Wilson
	7			5	6			4			10		11			12			2		1			9	3*	8		R. Bridges
	7	3		5	6			4	9		10			12					2		1		11			8*		A. Challinor
	4	3	7	5	6				10		9								2		1		11			8		N. Ashley
	4	3	7*	5	6				9		10			12					2		1		11			8		D. Shaw
	12	3	4		7			2	9		10		11			8		1							6			N. Scott
	5	3	4		7			2	9		10		11			8		1							6*	12		D. Owen
14	42	31	27	33	45	14	28	30	27	22	21	3	32	27	3	20	2	12	12	1	20	3	16	5	6	6		
	+ 2s			+ 1s		+ 1s	+ 1s	+ 2s	+ 2s	+ 2s	+ 5s		+ 1s	+ 3s	+ 1s	+ 2s	+ 1s		+ 1s	+ 1s		+ 1s	+ 1s	+ 1s		+ 2s		

Also played: Fagan (no. 5*, match 45); Winn (no. 10, match 39); Boam (no. 8, match 37); McNamee (no. 12, match 36); Harding (no. 12, match 28); Taylor (no. 2, match 12).

FOOTBALL LEAGUE RECORD

1921 Original Member of Division 3(N); 1958–68 Division 4; 1968–69 Division 3; 1969– Division 4.

HONOURS

Football League: Division 3 best season: 22nd, 1968–69; Division 3(N) – Runners-up 1956–57. *FA Cup* best season: 4th rd, 1954–55, 1977–78. *Football League Cup* best season: 4th rd, 1974–75.

COLOURS

Blue and white shirts, white shorts, blue stockings. **Change colours:** All red with white stripe on shirt.

HARTLEPOOL UNITED

Players Names Ht, Wt, D.o.B.	Birthplace Transfer Fee	Clubs	Appearances F.L. A & S	 F.L.C. A & S	 F.A.C. A & S	Goals F.L.	 F.L.C.	 F.A.C.
Goalkeepers								
Eddie Blackburn	Houghton-Le-Spring	Hull C (A)	68	2	5			
5 9, 10 5, 18.4.57	£6000	York C	76	6	5			
	F/T	Hartlepool U	20					
Graham Richardson*	Sedgefield	Darlington (N/c)						
5 10, 11 4, 20.3.58	F/T	Hartlepool U	89					
Defenders								
Trevor Smith	Middlesbrough	Hartlepool U	26+6		5	1		1
6 0, 11 12, 4.4.59	F/T	Scarborough						
	—	Whitby T						
	F/T	Hartlepool U	30+2	4	2	3	1	
Alan Barker	Newcastle	Newcastle U	21+2					
5 10, 10 8, 18.12.55	£45,000	Gillingham	64			2		
	F/T	Ferryhill Ath						
	F/T	Bishop Auckland						
	F/T	Hartlepool U	32+1	2	3		2	
Mike Fagan*	Newcastle	Carlisle U (N/C)						
5 11, 12 0, 22.2.60	—	Hartlepool U	36+1	4		1		
John Bird	Doncaster	Doncaster R	48+2	3	2	3		
6 1, 13 0, 9.6.48	£5000	Preston NE	166	12	8+1	9		
	P/E	Newcastle U	84+3	4	4	5		1
	F/T	Hartlepool U	120+1	5	4	12		
Andy Linighan	Hartlepool	Hartlepool U	68	5+1	6	3	1	
6 6, 12 6, 18.6.62								
Barrie Stimpson	Billingham	Hartlepool U (A)	64+1	6	5	2		
5 10, 11 10, 8.2.64								
Phil Brown	Hartlepool	Hartlepool U	140+4	8	7	7		
5 11, 11 6, 30.5.59								
Terry Bainbridge*		Hartlepool U	23+2	3	1	1	1	
Midfield								
Mark Robinson	Middlesborough	Hull C (N/C)						
5 10, 11 8,	F/T	Hartlepool U	16+1			2		
Roy Hogan*	Hartlepool	Hartlepool U (A)	133+10	6+1	6+1	15		1
5 8, 10 6, 24.9.60								
Ken Lowe	Hartlepool	Hartlepool U (A)	23+3			1		
5 10, 11 4, 6.11.61								
Derek Loadwick*	Middlesbrough	Leeds U (A)						
5 7, 12 0, 4.10.56	F/T	Stockport Co	84					
	£8000	Hartlepool U	49+2	2	1	1		
Paul Dobson	Hartlepool	Newcastle U (N/C)						
5 11, 11 2,	F/T	Hartlepool U	23+8		3	8		1
Phil Linacre*	Middlesbrough	Coventry C (A)						
6 0, 11 0, 17.5.62	F/T	Hartlepool U	59+4	1+1	6	10		3
Mark Lawrence	Middlesbrough	Hartlepool U	149+13	7+1	5	24		
6 0, 11 2, 4.12.58	—	Port Vale (loan)	1					
David Linighan	Hartlepool	Hartlepool U	12			1		
6 2, 11 12,								
Paul Harrington		Hartlepool U						
Forwards								
Alan Harding*	Sunderland	Spennymoor						
5 9, 11 4, 14.5.48	—	Darlington	125+4	5	6	38		1
	£15,500	Lincoln C	203+6	12+1	13	38	1	3
	£3000	Hartlepool U	79+5	3	1	8	1	
Paul Staff	Hartlepool	Hartlepool U (A)	56+9	2	2	9	1	
5 9, 10 12, 30.8.62								
Kevin Johnson	Doncaster	Sheffield W (A)	0+1					
5 9, 12 10, 29.8.52	F/T	Southend U	13+4		+1	1		
	—	Gillingham (loan)	1					
		Workington	15	1	1	1		
	£3000	Hartlepool U	60+1	4	3	9		1
	£12,000	Huddersfield T	80+1	4	1+1	23		
	£25,000	Halifax T	51+6	2	1	10	1	
	P/E	Hartlepool U	59+11	5+1	3+1	3	1	
David Howard*	Hartlepool	Newcastle U						
6 0, 11 7, 3.6.62	F/T	Hartlepool U	6+3			4		
Gerry McNamee*	Consett	Hartlepool U	2+2			1		
5 11, 11 4, 16.8.60								

Commercial Manager:
Club Coach: G. Smith
Club Captain 1982–83: J Bird
Supporters Player of the Season 1982–83:
Chief Scout:
Physiotherapist: T Johnson
Club Statistician:
Association of Football Statisticians Club Adviser to Yearbook: G. Small.

Players (non-appearance) granted free transfer: Trevor Ramshaw, G.
Players released since May 1982:
Derek Hampton, F., (Whitby T); Bobby Kerr, M., (Whitby T); John Watson, G., (N/K); Martin Burleigh, G., (Bishop Auckland); Steve Winn, F., (N/C-N/K); Alan Sweeney, D., (N/K); Harry Clarke, M., (Belgium); John Linacre, F., (Whitby T); John Stalker, F., (Blue Star); Stuart Boam, D., (N/C-retired); Mark Taylor, D, (N/C-N/K); Jimmy Hamilton, M., (Gretna); Dave Stewart, F., (N/K).

HEREFORD UNITED Division 4

Back row (left to right):
Mel Pejic
John Crabbe
Derek Showers
Garry Plumley
'Dixie' McNeil
Chris Price
Ian Ross
Front row:
Winston White
Keith Hicks
Ian Bray
Sean Lane.

Chairman: P. S. Hill FRICS. ***Vice-Chairman:*** M. B. Roberts.

Directors: D. Vaughan, A. J. Phillips, G. Rivers, J. E. Jackson, G. C. E. Hales.

Manager: John Newman. ***Secretary:*** Jim Finney.

Year Formed: 1924. ***Turned Professional:*** 1924. ***Ltd Co.:*** 1939.

Club Nickname: 'United'.

Ground: Edgar Street Athletic Ground.

Previous Managers since 1946: George Tranter, Alex Massie, Joe Wade, Ray Daniel, Bob Dennison, John Charles, Colin Addison, John Sillett, Tony Ford, Mike Bailey, Frank Lord (11).

Edgar Street, Hereford. Telephone Hereford (0432) 276666. ***Ground capacity:*** 17,500. ***Record attendance:*** 18,114 v Sheffield W, FA Cup 3rd rd, 4 Jan, 1958. ***Record receipts:*** £12,666 v Bristol C, FA Cup 4th rd, 26 Jan, 1974. ***Pitch measurements:*** 111yd×80yd.

Directions to Ground: Ground very close to town centre, within five minutes walking distance from Hereford railway station and the bus station.

Match tickets: Tickets can be booked in advance.

Car parking: Parking is available around the ground for approximately 1,000 vehicles.

Entertainment/catering facilities: Canteens on the ground. A social club next to ground.

Club shop: All types of souvenirs sold on ground.

Handbooks/programmes: Programmes available on application to the club shop.

Address of Supporters Club: Edgar Street, Hereford.

Note: Full club statistical records are on pages 416–455.

HEREFORD UNITED 1982–83 LEAGUE RECORD

Match No.	Date	Venue	Opponents	Result		H/T Score	Lg. Pos.	Goalscorers	Attendance
1	Aug 28	A	Bury	L	2-3	1-1	—	Price, Crabbe	2138
2	Sept 4	H	Colchester U	D	0-0	0-0	16		2465
3	8	H	Swindon T	L	1-2	1-0	—	Harvey (pen)	2674
4	11	A	Darlington	L	1-2	0-0	24	Phillips	1818
5	18	H	Mansfield T	L	0-2	0-2	24		1960
6	25	A	Chester	L	0-5	0-2	24		1828
7	28	A	Wimbledon	L	0-1	0-1	—		1604
8	Oct 2	H	York C	D	0-0	0-0	24		2037
9	9	A	Port Vale	D	0-2	0-0	24		2875
10	16	H	Crewe Alex	W	1-0	0-0	24	Lane	2418
11	20	H	Hull C	W	2-0	1-0	—	Showers, White	2320
12	23	A	Blackpool	L	1-5	0-2	23	Phillips	3405
13	30	H	Rochdale	W	1-0	0-0	22	White	2404
14	Nov 1	A	Stockport Co	L	1-2	0-1	—	McNeil	1736
15	5	A	Halifax T	D	2-2	1-1	—	White (pen), McNeil	1065
16	13	H	Hartlepool U	W	1-0	1-0	21	Showers	2298
17	27	A	Tranmere R	L	1-2	1-0	21	Price	3194
18	Dec 4	H	Scunthorpe U	L	0-2	0-1	22		2103
19	18	H	Northampton T	D	1-1	0-0	22	Phillips	1679
20	27	A	Torquay U	L	1-2	1-1	22	Crabbe	3842
21	28	H	Bristol C	L	1-3	1-3	22	McNeil	3548
22	Jan 1	A	Peterborough U	L	0-4	0-1	23		3543
23	3	H	Aldershot	W	2-1	1-0	23	Phillips, Price	1992
24	7	A	Colchester U	L	2-3	1-2	—	Harvey, Bartley	2216
25	15	H	Bury	L	0-2	0-0	24		1920
26	22	A	Mansfield T	W	1-0	1-0	24	Lane	1655
27	29	H	Darlington	D	0-0	0-0	24		2155
28	Feb 5	H	Chester	W	5-2	3-1	22	Teasdale, Phillips 3, Price	1961
29	12	A	Swindon T	L	2-3	0-1	—	Phillips 2 (1 pen)	4042
30	15	A	Hull C	L	0-2	0-1	—		6633
31	19	H	Port Vale	L	0-2	0-1	24		3075
32	26	A	Crewe Alex	L	1-3	0-1	24	Phillips	2251
33	Mar 2	H	Stockport Co	D	0-0	0-0	—		1294
34	5	H	Blackpool	D	0-0	0-0	24		1755
35	12	A	Rochdale	L	1-4	0-1	24	Maddy	2000
36	19	H	Halifax T	W	2-0	1-0	24	Harvey, Phillips	2006
37	26	A	Hartlepool U	W	1-0	0-0	24	Phillips	1147
38	Apr 2	A	Bristol C	D	1-1	1-1	24	Phillips	6264
39	5	H	Torquay U	L	0-1	0-1	—		2533
40	8	A	Scunthorpe U	W	2-1	0-0	—	Lane, Hunter (og)	3785
41	16	H	Wimbledon	L	1-4	0-2	24	Phillips	2637
42	23	A	Northampton T	L	1-2	0-1	24	Price	2071
43	30	H	Tranmere R	W	1-0	0-0	24	Spiring	2089
44	May 2	A	Aldershot	L	1-2	1-2	24	Harvey (pen)	1653
45	7	A	York C	L	1-5	1-0	24	Pejic	2106
46	14	H	Peterborough U	L	0-1	0-0	24		2075

Final League Position: 24

GOALSCORERS

League (42): Phillips 14 (1 pen), Harvey 5 (2 pens), Price 5, Lane 3, McNeil 3, White 3 (1 pen), Crabbe 2, Showers 2, Maddy 1, Pejic 1, Spiring 1, Teasdale 1, own goal 1.
Milk Cup (2): Pejic 1, Showers 1.
FA Cup (1): Showers 1.

Milk Cup	First Round	Cardiff C (a)	1-2
		(h)	1-2
FA Cup	First Round	Portsmouth (a)	1-4

Jackson	Price	Musial	Pejic	Spiring	Bartley	Harvey	Crabbe	Showers	Phillips	White	Hicks	Gwinnett	Plumley	Bray	Lane	McNeil	Ross	Powell	Rose	Cantello	Teasdale	Maddy (L)	Carter (L)	Wilmot	Larkin	*Referees*	*Match No.*
1	2	3	4	5	6	7	8	9	10*	11					12											A. Saunders	1
1	2		4	6	3	8	7	10	9	11	5															M. Robinson	2
1	2		5	6	3	8	7	10	9	11	4															J. Lovatt	3
1	2		5	6	3	8	7	10	9	11	4															R. Guy	4
	2	7	5	6	3	8		10	9	11	4	1														K. Cooper	5
	2*	7	5	6	3	8		10	9		4		1	12	11											J. Bray	6
			5	6	3	8	7	10	9	11	4		1	2												T. Spencer	7
			5	2	6	8	7	10	9	11	4		1	3												K. Barratt	8
	2		5	7	6	8		10	9	11	4		1	3												T. Fitzharris	9
	2		5		6	8		12	9*	11	4		1	3	7	10										T. Bune	10
	2		5		6	8		9		11	4		1	3	7	10										L. Shapter	11
	2		4		6	8	12	9	10	11	5		1	3	7*											K. Hackett	12
	2		5		6			9		11	4		1	3	7	10	8									A. Crickmore	13
	2		5				8	9		11	4		1	3	7	10	6									M. Scott	14
	2		5		12		8	9*		11	4		1	3	7	10	6									P. Willis	15
	2		5				8	9		11	4		1	3	7	10	6									H. Taylor	16
	2		5		3	7		9	8	11*	4		1	6	12	10										M. Peck	17
	2		5		3	7		9	8	11	4		1	6		10										D. Hedges	18
	2	12	5			7		9	10	11	4			3	8*		6	1								E. Read	19
	2		5		8	7	6		9		4			3	11	10		1								C. Downey	20
	2	6	5			7			9	11	4			3	8	10		1								A. Seville	21
	2		5		3	7	6	12	9	11	4				8	10*		1								M. Dimblebee	22
	2		5		8	7	6		9	11	4			3		10			1							C. Thomas	23
	2*	12	5		8	7	6	10	9	11				3			4		1							D. Reeves	24
	2		5		8	7		10*	9	11	4			3	12		6		1							J. Martin	25
	2		5		12	7		10	9	11	4			3	8*		6		1							N. Midgley	26
	2		5			7			9	12	4			3	11*		6		1	8	10					D. Vickers	27
	2		5		8	7			9	11	4			3			6		1		10					L. Burden	28
	2		5		8	7			9	11	4			3	12		6		1		10*					R. Milford	29
	2		5		8	7			9	11*	4			3	12		6		1		10					R. Banks	30
	2		5		8	7			9	11	4			3	12		6		1		10*					D. Letts	31
	2		5	11*	3	7		10	9	12	4				8		6		1							F. Roberts	32
	2		5		3	7		10	9	11	4				8		6		1							J. Moules	33
	2		5		3	7		10	9	11	4				8				1			6				C. Newsome	34
			5	2	3	7			9	11	4				8				1			6	10			C. Seel	35
	2		5		3	7			9	11	4				8							6	10	1		B. Hill	36
	2		5		3	7			9	11					8							6	10	1	4	J. Key	37
	2		5		3	7			9	11					8							6	10	1	4	B. Stevens	38
	2		4	12	3	7			9	11*					8							6	10	1	5	J. Deakin	39
	2		4	11	3	7			9						8							6	10	1	5	K. Redfern	40
	2			7	3			11	9		4				8							6	10	1	5	J. Hunting	41
	2		4	8	3	7		11	9													6	10	1	5	C. Downey	42
			2	12	3	7	6*	11	9		4				8				1				10		5	A. Crickmore	43
	12		2		3	7	6	11	9		4				8								10*	1	5	M. Dimblebee	44
	2		8	6	11	7		10	9		4			3										1	5	A. Robinson	45
	2		8	6	11	7		10	9		4			3					1						5	T. Holbrook	46
4	41	4	45	16	39	41	15	30	41	35	39	1	13	26	26	12	15	4	15	1	5	9	10	9	10		
	+ 1s	+ 2s		+ 2s	+ 2s		+ 1s	+ 2s		+ 2s				+ 1s	+ 6s												

FOOTBALL LEAGUE RECORD

1972 Elected to Division 4; 1973–76 Division 3; 1976–77 Division 2; 1977–78 Division 3; 1978– Division 4.

HONOURS

Football League: Division 2 best season: 22nd, 1976–77; Division 3 – Champions 1975–76; Division 4 – Runners-up 1972–73. *FA Cup* best season: 4th rd, 1971–72, 1976–77, 1981–82. *Football League Cup* best season: 3rd rd, 1974–75. *Welsh Cup:* Finalists 3 times.

COLOURS

White shirts with red and black trim, black shorts, white stockings with red and black tops. **Change colours:** All red.

HEREFORD UNITED

Players Names Ht. Wt. D.o.B.	Birthplace Transfer Fee	Clubs	Appearances F.L. A & S	 F.L.C. A & S	 F.A.C. A & S	Goals F.L.	 F.L.C.	 F.A.C.
Goalkeepers								
Kevin Rose	Evesham	Ledbury T						
23.11.60		Lincoln C						
		Hereford U	15		1			
Defenders								
Chris Price (EY)	Hereford	Hereford U (A)	214+1	11	11	17		
5 7, 10 2, 30.3.60								
Danny Bartley* (EY)	Paulton	Bristol C (A)	92+8	4	3	7		
5 8½, 11 4, 3.10.47		Swansea C	195+4	19	8	8	1	
	F T	Hereford U	112+2	5	2	7	1	
Mel Pejic	Newcastle-u-L	Stoke C	1					
5 7½, 10 6, 27.4.59	F T	Hereford U	85	4	1	1	1	
Keith Hicks (EY)	Oldham	Oldham Ath (A)	240+2	12	15	11		
6 0, 13 2, 9.8.54	F T	Hereford U	120	3	7	1		
Tony Larkin	Wrexham	Wrexham						
6 0, 11 12, 12.1.56		Shrewsbury T	54+1	2	5			
	£7000	Carlisle U	47+2	3	4	2		
	F T	Hereford U	10					
Ian Dalziel	Sunderland	Derby Co (A)	22	3+1	1+1	4		
5 8, 11 10, 24.10.62	F T	Hereford U						
Midfield								
Jimmy Harvey (NI)	Lurgan	Glenavon						
5 9½, 11 4, 2.5.58	£30,000	Arsenal	2+1					
	F T	Hereford U	123+1	6	7+1	11		2
John Crabbe*	Weymouth	Southampton (A)	8+4		1			
5 8, 11 0, 20.10.54		Gillingham	181	10	12	12	1	
	F T	Carlisle U	26	4	3	4		
	F T	Hereford U	15+1	2	1	2		
Forwards								
Peter Spiring* (EY)	Glastonbury	Bristol C	56+5	1+1	4	16		1
5 8, 11 0, 13.12.50	£60,000	Liverpool						
	£70,000	Luton T	12+3	1		2		
	£8000	Hereford U	205+22	15+1	11	20	3	
Stuart Phillips	Halifax	Hereford U	106+6	4+1	6	29	1	2
6 0½, 11 7, 30.12.61								
Ian Bray	Neath	Hereford U (A)	42+1		3	2		
6.12.62								
Derek Showers* (W)	Merthyr	Cardiff C	76+7	9	2	10	1	1
5 11, 11 4, 28.1.53	£5000	Bournemouth	58+2	6	5	19	1	
		Portsmouth	36+3	5	1	8		
	£12,000	Hereford U	87+2	3+1	6	13	1	3
Dixie McNeil*	Melton Mowbray	Leicester C						
5 10, 11 12, 16.1.47	F T	Exeter C	31	1	1	11	1	
	F T	Corby T						
		Northampton T	85+1	4	11	33		5
	£8000	Lincoln C	96+1	2	2	53		
	£20,000	Hereford U	128+1	11	6	85	4	2
	£60,000	Wrexham	166+1	14	23	54	2	22
	F T	Hereford U	12		1	3		

Commercial Manager:
Club Coach:
Supporters Player of the Season 1982–83: Mel Pejic.
Physiotherapist: Peter Isaac.
Club Captain 1982–83: J. Harvey.
Chief Scout:
Club Statistician:
Association of Football Statisticians Club Adviser to Yearbook: L. Appleby.

Players released since May 1982:
Stuart Cornes, D. (Cheltenham T); Tommy Hughes, G. (retired); Frank McGrellis, F. (N/K); Richard Overson, D,. (Gloucester C); Drew Brand, G. (N/K); John Jackson, G. (N/K); Winston White, M. (N/K); John Teasdale, F. (N/K); Mel Gwinnett, G. (N/K); Adam Musial, D. (N/K); Andy Powell, G. (N/K).

HUDDERSFIELD TOWN Division 2

Back row (left to right): Kevin Stonehouse
Dave Sutton (Captain)
Malcolm Brown
Brian Cox
Keith Mason
Keith Hanvey
Mark Lillis
Peter Valentine (given free transfer)
Middle row: David Burke (Player of the Year)
Steve Doyle
David Cowling
Roy Greenwood
Front row: Tim Hotte (given free transfer)
Phil Wilson
Brian Stanton
Colin Russell
Daral Pugh

© 1973

Chairman: K. S. Longbottom.

Directors: J. Christie, C. Senior, E. A. Lodge, C. Hodgkinson, J. B. Buckley, F. L. Thewlis, R. E. Dobson.

Manager: Mick Buxton. ***Secretary:*** G. S. Binns.

Year Formed: 1908. ***Turned Professional:*** 1908. ***Ltd Co.:*** 1908.

Club Nickname: 'The Terriers'.

Previous Managers since 1946: David Steele, George Stephenson, Andy Beattie, Bill Shankly, Eddie Boot, Tom Johnston, Ian Greaves, Bobby Collins, Tom Johnston (9).

Leeds Rd, Huddersfield HD1 6PE. Telephone 0484 20335/6. ***Ground capacity:*** 48,000. ***Record attendance:*** 67,037 v Arsenal, FA Cup 6th rd, 27 Feb, 1932. ***Record receipts:*** £36,997 v Barnsley, Division 3, 7 Feb, 1981. ***Pitch measurements:*** 115yd×75yd.

Directions to Ground: The ground is one mile from the town centre via Corporation buses 40, 41, 42. On match days special buses run from the centre. By road, the ground can be reached along Leeds Road either from the town centre or from Leeds.

Match tickets: Admission to all parts is by payment at the turnstiles except for special matches (Tel: Huddersfield 36100).

Car parking: Ample parking accommodation on all four sides of the ground; in the region of 6000 cars can be parked within 200 yards of the turnstiles.

Entertainments/catering facilities: Licensed Presidents Club – members only. 11 unlicensed snack bars around the ground.

Club shop: Close to the ground; sells all types of souvenirs (Tel: Huddersfield 31028). Open match days.

Handbooks/programmes available on subscription from the club shop.

Address of Supporters Club: Supporters Club Offices, 286 Leeds Road, Huddersfield, Yorkshire.

Address of the Club Shop or Boutique: The Terriers Souvenir Shop, 286 Leeds Road, Huddersfield.

Note: Full club statistical records are on pages 416–455.

HUDDERSFIELD TOWN 1982–83 LEAGUE RECORD

Match No.	Date	Venue	Opponents	Result		H/T Score	Lg. Pos.	Goalscorers	Attendance
1	Aug 28	H	Exeter C	D	1-1	1-0	—	Cox M.	5168
2	Sept 4	A	Wrexham	D	1-1	0-0	18	Bater (og)	3925
3	7	A	Sheffield U	L	0-2	0-0	—		16,641
4	11	H	Walsall	D	2-2	1-1	21	Lillis, Doyle	4282
5	18	A	Newport Co	L	1-2	0-0	22	Stanton	3536
6	25	H	Oxford U	W	2-0	1-0	17	Russell 2	4958
7	28	H	Orient	W	6-0	3-0	—	Russell, Lillis, Pugh, Sutton, Stanton 2	6671
8	Oct 2	A	Millwall	L	0-3	0-1	18		3004
9	9	H	Portsmouth	D	1-1	1-1	15	Brown	6234
10	16	A	Preston NE	D	0-0	0-0	15		5570
11	19	H	Southend U	W	2-1	0-0	—	Brown (pen), Russell	4750
12	23	H	Cardiff C	W	4-0	2-0	12	Lillis 4	6121
13	30	A	Gillingham	W	3-1	1-1	8	Lillis 2, Cowling	5919
14	Nov 2	H	Doncaster R	W	3-0	0-0	—	Lillis 2, Russell	6848
15	6	A	AFC Bournemouth	W	1-0	0-0	6	Lillis	5194
16	13	H	Brentford	W	2-0	0-0	5	Russell 2	10,034
17	27	H	Bristol R	W	3-1	1-1	2	Pugh, Russell 2	8251
18	Dec 4	A	Plymouth Arg	L	1-2	0-2	4	Wilson	4227
19	18	A	Reading	D	1-1	0-0	6	Stanton	2468
20	27	H	Chesterfield	W	3-1	1-0	5	Brown (pen), Lillis, Russell	11,603
21	28	A	Lincoln C	W	2-1	0-1	3	Lillis, Hanvey	11,829
22	Jan 1	H	Bradford C	W	6-3	2-2	3	Brown (pen), Stanton 4, Wilson	18,438
23	3	A	Wigan Ath	L	0-2	0-0	4		7724
24	15	A	Exeter C	W	4-3	2-2	3	Lillis, Wilson, Stanton, Cowling	2882
25	22	H	Sheffield U	D	0-0	0-0	3		15,769
26	29	A	Walsall	L	0-2	0-2	5		3922
27	Feb 5	A	Oxford U	D	1-1	1-0	5	Brown	4975
28	12	H	Millwall	W	5-1	2-0	5	Lillis, Russell 2, Hanvey, Wilson	8111
29	14	A	Southend U	W	1-0	0-0	—	Lillis	2262
30	22	A	Portsmouth	L	2-3	0-3	—	Russell, Brown (pen)	18,615
31	26	H	Preston NE	D	1-1	0-0	4	Cowling	8562
32	Mar 1	A	Doncaster R	W	4-0	2-0	—	Cowling, Lillis, Russell, Stanton	6078
33	12	H	Gillingham	W	3-2	0-0	3	Doyle, Brown (pen), Burke	8264
34	15	A	Cardiff C	D	1-1	1-1	—	Cowling	10,379
35	19	H	AFC Bournemouth	D	0-0	0-0	3		8630
36	26	A	Brentford	L	0-1	0-1	4		6277
37	29	H	Wrexham	W	4-1	1-1	—	Lillis, Cowling, Hanvey, Stanton	9519
38	Apr 2	H	Lincoln C	D	1-1	0-1	5	Sutton	13,028
39	4	A	Chesterfield	W	1-0	1-0	—	Lillis	6729
40	9	H	Plymouth Arg	W	2-0	0-0	2	Hanvey, Brown (pen)	9277
41	16	A	Orient	W	3-1	1-0	1	Wilson, Stanton, Lillis	3498
42	23	H	Reading	W	3-1	2-1	1	Stanton, Russell, Brown (pen)	10,885
43	30	A	Bristol R	L	0-1	0-0	3		8919
44	May 7	H	Newport Co	W	1-0	0-0	3	Cowling	16,509
45	10	H	Wigan Ath	D	1-1	1-1	—	Russell	11,093
46	14	A	Bradford C	L	1-3	0-2	3	Wilson	10,375

Final League Position: 3

GOALSCORERS

League (84): Lillis 20, Russell 16, Stanton 13, Brown 9 (7 pens), Cowling 7, Wilson 6, Hanvey 4, Doyle 2, Pugh 2, Sutton 2, Burke 1, Cox M. 1, own goal 1.
Milk Cup (5): Stanton 2, Brown 1, Cowling 1, Russell 1.
FA Cup (3): Stanton 2, Brown 1.

Milk Cup	First Round	Doncaster R (h)	1-1
		(a)	1-0
	Second Round	Oxford U (h)	2-0
		(a)	0-1
	Third Round	Leeds U (a)	1-0
	Fourth Round	Arsenal (a)	0-1
FA Cup	First Round	Mossley (h)	1-0
	Second Round	Altrincham (a)	1-0
	Third Round	Chelsea (h)	1-1
		(a)	0-2

Cox B.	Brown	Valentine	Stanton	Sutton	Hanvey	Lillis	Cox M.	Greenwood	Wilson	Cowling	Hotte	Austin	Burke	Doyle	Russell	Pugh	Mason	Laverick (L)	Stonehouse	Referees	Match No.
1	2	3	4	5	6	7	8*	9	10	11	12									R. Guy	1
1	2	3	4	5	6	7	8	11	10			9								A. Hamil	2
1	2		4	5	6	7	8*	11	10			9	3	12						G. Seel	3
1	2		4	5	6	7	12	11*		10		9	3	8						P. Willis	4
1	2	6	4	5		7			10	11	9		3	8						D. Reeves	5
1	2		4	5	6	7			10	11			3	8	9					N. Wilson	6
1	2		12	5	6	7			10	11			3	8	9*	4				K. Redfern	7
1	2		12	5	6	7			10	11*			3	8	9	4				A. Grey	8
1	2			5	6	7			10	11			3	8	9	4				R. Nixon	9
1	2			5	6	7			10	11			3	8	9	4				T. Holbrook	10
1*	2		12	5	6	7			10	11			3	8	9	4				A. Saunders	11
	2		12	5	6	7			10	11			3	8	9	4*	1			D. Owen	12
1	2		4	5	6	7			10	11			3	8	9*	12				C. Downey	13
1	2		4*	5	6	7			10	11			3	8	9	12				R. Bridges	14
1	2		4	5	6	7			10	11			3	8	9					T. Bune	15
1	2		4	5	6	7			10	11			3	8	9					M. Heath	16
1	2	6	4	5		7			10				3	8	9	11				F. Roberts	17
1	2	6*	4	5		7			10	11			3	8	9	12				D. Letts	18
1	2		4	5	6	7			10	11			3	8	9*	12				M. Bodenham	19
1	2		4	5	6	7			10	11*			3	8	9	12				J. Worrall	20
1	2		4	5	6	7			10	11			3	8	9					G. Napthine	21
1	2		4	5	6	7			10	11			3	8	9					J. Hough	22
1	2		4	5	6	7			10	11			3	8*	9	12				D. Civil	23
1	2		4	5	6	7			10	11			3	8	9*	12				K. Cooper	24
1	2		4	5	6	7			10				3		9	11		8		M. Peck	25
1	2		4	5	6	7			10	11			3		9	12		8*		N. Ashley	26
1	2		4	5	6	7			10	11			3	8	9					M. James	27
1	2		4	5	6	7			10	11			3	8	9					P. Willis	28
1	2		4	5	6	7			10	11			3	8	9					D. Hedges	29
1	2		4	5	6	7			10	11			3	8	9					S. Bates	30
1	2		4	5	6	7			10*	11			3	8	9	12				J. Lovatt	31
1	2		4	5	6	7			10	11			3	8	9					B. Hill	32
1	2		4	5	6	7			10	11			3	8	9					D. Allinson	33
1	2		4	5	6	7			10	11			3	8	9					V. Callow	34
1	2		4*	5	6	7			10	11			3	8	9	12				K. Walmsley	35
1	2		4	5	6	7			10	11			3	8*	9	12				R. Milford	36
1	2		4	5	6	7			10	11			3	8	9					M. Scott	37
1	2		4	5	6	7*			10	11			3	8	9	12				N. Wilson	38
1	2		4	5	6	7			10	11			3	8	9					D. Lloyd	39
1	2		4	5*	6	7			10	11			3	8	9	12				N. Glover	40
1	2		4		6	7			10				3	8	9	5			11	L. Shapter	41
1	2		4		6	7			10	11*			3	8	9	12			5	R. Chadwick	42
1	2		4		6	7			10	11			3	8	9	12			5	R. Lewis	43
1	2		4		6	7			10	11*			3	8	9	12			5	A. Saunders	44
1	2		4		6	7			10	11			3	8	9	12			5*	K. Baker	45
1	2		4*	5	6	7			10	11			3	8	9	12				G. Tyson	46
45	46	5	40	41	43	46	3	4	45	41	1	3	44	41	41	9	1	2	5		
			+ 4s				+ 1s				+ 1s			+ 1s		+ 18s					

FOOTBALL LEAGUE RECORD

1910 Elected to Division 2; 1920–52 Division 1; 1952–53 Division 2; 1953–56 Division 1; 1956–70 Division 2; 1970–72 Division 1; 1972–73 Division 2; 1973–75 Division 3; 1975–80 Division 4; 1980–83 Division 3; 1983– Division 2.

HONOURS

Football League: Division 1 – Champions 1923–24, 1924–25, 1925–26; Runners-up 1926–27, 1927–28, 1933–34; Division 2 – Champions 1969–70; Runners-up 1919–20, 1952–53; Division 4 – Champions 1979–80. *FA Cup:* Winners 1922; Runners-up 1920, 1928, 1930, 1938. *Football League Cup:* Semi-final, 1967–68.

COLOURS

Blue and white striped shirts, white shorts, white stockings.
Change colours: All yellow.

HUDDERSFIELD TOWN

Players Names Ht, Wt, D.o.B.	Birthplace Transfer Fee	Clubs	Appearances F.L. A & S	Appearances F.L.C. A & S	Appearances F.A.C. A & S	Goals F.L.	Goals F.L.C.	Goals F.A.C.
Goalkeepers								
Alan Starling	Barking	Luton T (A)	7					
6 1, 13 4, 2.4.51	—	Torquay U (loan)	1					
	F/T	Northampton T	238	9	11	1		
	£10,000	Huddersfield T	112	10	4			
Brian Cox	Sheffield	Sheffield W (A)	22	4				
6 0, 13 3, 7.5.61	F/T	Huddersfield T	59	6	4			
Keith Mason								
		Huddersfield T	1					
Defenders								
Malcolm Brown	Salford	Bury (A)	10+1					
6 2, 13 0, 13.12.56	F/T	Huddersfield T	256	22	18	16	2	3
Dave Sutton	Tarleton	Plymouth Arg (A)	60+1	2+1	3			
6 1, 12 2, 21.1.57	—	Reading (loan)	9					
	£10,000	Huddersfield T	208	17	17	10	1	
Keith Hanvey	Manchester	Manchester C						
6 0, 12 7, 18.1.52	F/T	Swansea C	11	2				
	F/T	Rochdale	121	6	13	10		1
	£12,000	Grimsby T	54		5	2		
	F/T	Huddersfield T	196	16	12	13		1
David Burke	Liverpool	Bolton W (A)	65+4	5	1+1	1		
5 10, 10 7, 6.8.60	F/T	Huddersfield T	85	9	8	2		
Peter Valentine*	Huddersfield	Huddersfield T (A)	19	2	1	1		
5 10, 12 0, 16.4.63								
Ian Measham		Huddersfield T (A)						
5 10, 11 8,								
Midfield								
David Cowling	Doncaster	Mansfield T (A)						
5 7, 10 6, 27.11.58	F/T	Huddersfield T	184+11	12+1	16	24	1	1
Brian Stanton	Liverpool							
5 7, 10 7, 7.2.56		Bury	72+11	5	5	14		
	£12,500	Huddersfield T	156+4	8	14	37	2	6
Phil Wilson	Hemsworth	Bolton W (A)	35+4	1	2	4		
5 6, 10 4, 16.10.60	F/T	Huddersfield T	76+3	10	5	8	1	
Steve Doyle (WU21)	Neath	Preston NE (A)	178+19	16+1	15+1	8		1
5 9½, 11 1, 2.6.58	F/T	Huddersfield T	41+1	5		2		
Daral Pugh (WU21)	Sunderland	Doncaster R (A)	136+18	12	9+1	15	1	1
5 8, 10 7, 5.6.61	P/E	Huddersfield T	9+18			2		
Forwards								
Roy Greenwood	Leeds	Hull C (A)	118+6	9	11	24	4	
5 9, 10 3, 26.9.52	£140,000	Sunderland	45+11	3		9		
	£80,000	Derby Co	26+5	1	1	1		
	£25,000	Swindon T	46+4	4	2	7		
	F/T	Huddersfield T	4	2+1	+1			
Colin Russell	Liverpool	Liverpool (A)	+1					
5 7, 10 7, 21.1.61	£15,000	Huddersfield T	41	4	4	16	1	
Kevin Stonehouse	Bishop Auckland	Shildon						
5 11, 11 10, 20.9.59	—	Blackburn R	77+8	1	2	27	1	
		Huddersfield T	5					
Tim Hotte*	Bradford	Arsenal (A)						
	F/T	Huddersfield T	14+2			4		
Mark Lillis	Manchester	Huddersfield T	128+6	10	14+1	33		1
6 0, 12 12, 17.1.60								

Commercial Manager: M. Porter (Tel. Club 20335 Comm. Manager 34867)
Promotions Manager: Steve Kindon
Club Coach: John Haselden Jimmy Robson
Supporters Player of the Season 1982–83: David Burke
Physiotherapist: J. Haselden
Association of Football Statisticians Club Adviser to Yearbook: J. D. Loughrey.
Club Captain 1982–83: Dave Sutton
Chief Scout: Steve Smith
Club Statistician: Dr J. D. Loughrey

Players (non-appearance) granted free transfer: Martin Coupe, F.
Players released since May 1982:
Peter Fletcher, F. (retired); Steve Kindon, F. (retired); Bob Picton, G. (N/K); Andy Rankin, G. (retired); Ian Robins, F. (retired); Fred Robinson, D. (retired); Dick Taylor, G. (retired); Ian Thompson, F. (N/K); Maurice Cox, F. (N/C–N/K)

HULL CITY Division 3

Back row (left to right): Dale Roberts, Neil Thompson, Pete Skipper, Tony Norman, Les Mutrie, John Davies, Billy Whitehurst, Ian Davis, Steve Richards
Front row: Bobby McNeil, Brian Marwood, Steve McClaren, Garreth Roberts, Dennis Booth, Gary Swann, Andy Flounders, Billy Askew.

Chairman: D. Robinson. ***Vice-Chairman:*** T. C. Waite FIM, MIRTE.

Directors: J. Johnson MP, G. H. C. Needler BA, ACA, T. C. Cathcart. ***Team Manager:*** Colin Appleton.

Assistant Manager/Coach: Chris Chilton.

Youth Development Officer/Secretary: Bobby Brown.

Year Formed: 1904. ***Turned Professional:*** 1905. ***Ltd Co.:*** 1905.

Club Nickname: 'The Tigers'.

Previous Grounds: 1904, Boulevard Ground (Hull RFC); 1905, Anlaby Road (Hull CC); 1944/5 Boulevard Grounds; 1946, Boothferry Park.

Previous Managers since 1948: Major Frank Buckley, Raich Carter, Bob Jackson, Bob Brocklebank, Cliff Britton, Terry Neill, John Kaye, Bobby Collins, Ken Houghton, Mike Smith (10).

Boothferry Park, Hull HU4 6EU. Telephone (0482) 51119. ***Telegraphic address:*** 'Tigers Hull'. ***Ground capacity:*** 42,000. ***Record attendance: 55,019 v Manchester U, FA Cup 6th rd, 26 Feb, 1949. Record receipts:*** £22,229 v Stoke City, FA Cip 6th rd, 6 March, 1971. ***Pitch measurements:*** 112yd×75yd.

Directions to Ground: Buses 63c, 67 (Hull Corporation), 6, 155 (East Yorkshire) from coach station, Ferensway, Hull. Nearest railway stations, Hull and Boothferry Park Halt. Special trains on match days from Hull Paragon to Boothferry Park Halt; admittance to ground through turnstiles on station. Ground situated on A63 to the west of the city.

Car parking: At Kempton Road, five minutes walk from ground (opposite Three Tuns Hotel).

Entertainments/catering facilities: Catering facilities at points around the ground.

Handbooks/programmes: Programmes available on subscription.

Club shop: Club Shop, Boothferry Park, Hull. On match days, in main car park. Also in South Stand. Weekdays; articles may be purchased from the Development Association, 101 Boothferry Road, Hull. (0482) 51119.

Note: Full club statistical records are on pages 416–455.

HULL CITY 1982–83 LEAGUE RECORD

Match No.	Date	Venue	Opponents	Result		H/T Score	Lg. Pos.	Goalscorers	Attendance
1	Aug 28	A	Bristol C	L	1-2	0-1	—	Flounders	4877
2	Sept 4	H	Wimbledon	D	1-1	1-1	17	Flounders	3674
3	7	H	York C	W	4-0	1-0	—	Mutrie 2, McClaren, Flounders	3769
4	10	A	Stockport Co	D	1-1	1-1	—	Marwood	2252
5	18	H	Hartlepool U	D	1-1	0-0	11	Roberts G.	3913
6	25	A	Aldershot	W	2-1	1-0	11	Roberts G., McClaren	2345
7	28	A	Colchester U	D	0-0	0-0	—		3071
8	Oct 2	H	Swindon T	D	0-0	0-0	11		3786
9	9	H	Torquay U	W	4-1	2-1	8	Mutrie 2, Roberts D., Skipper	4128
10	15	A	Scunthorpe U	W	1-0	0-0	—	Mutrie	7483
11	20	A	Hereford U	L	0-2	0-1	—		2320
12	23	H	Northampton T	W	4-0	0-0	7	Marwood 2 (2 pens), Flounders, Whitehurst	4317
13	30	A	Tranmere R	W	1-0	0-0	7	McClaren	1548
14	Nov 2	H	Bury	W	2-1	2-0	—	Marwood, Skipper	6101
15	6	H	Peterborough U	W	4-1	2-1	3	Marwood 2, Woof, Slack (og)	5535
16	13	A	Port Vale	L	0-1	0-1	5		5298
17	27	H	Chester	W	2-0	0-0	4	Marwood, McClaren	5047
18	Dec 4	A	Blackpool	D	1-1	1-1	4	Mutrie	3395
19	11	H	Colchester U	W	3-0	0-0	4	Flounders 2, Hawley	4323
20	17	A	Crewe Alex	W	3-0	1-0	3	Marwood 2, Mutrie	1404
21	27	H	Halifax T	D	1-1	0-0	3	Skipper	10,042
22	28	A	Darlington	W	2-1	1-0	4	Askew, Marwood	2614
23	Jan 1	H	Rochdale	W	2-1	1-0	1	Roberts G., Marwood (pen)	9259
24	3	A	Mansfield T	L	1-3	0-3	1	Marwood	4560
25	8	A	Wimbledon	W	2-1	1-0	1	Roberts D., Whitehurst	2766
26	15	H	Bristol C	W	1-0	0-0	1	Mutrie	7035
27	22	A	Hartlepool U	D	0-0	0-0	1		2291
28	29	H	Stockport Co	W	7-0	4-0	1	Flounders 3, Askew, Mutrie, Roberts G., Skipper	6151
29	Feb 5	H	Aldershot	D	2-2	0-2	1	Flounders, Mutrie	6758
30	15	H	Hereford U	W	2-0	1-0	—	Woof, Whitehurst	6633
31	19	A	Torquay U	D	0-0	0-0	1		2710
32	26	H	Scunthorpe U	D	1-1	0-1	2	Marwood	14,252
33	Mar 1	A	Bury	W	3-2	1-1	—	Roberts G., Askew, Flounders	4239
34	5	A	Northampton T	W	2-1	0-0	1	Askew, Flounders	2879
35	12	H	Tranmere R	L	0-1	0-0	1		7198
36	19	A	Peterborough U	D	1-1	0-0	2	Mutrie	3805
37	26	H	Port Vale	W	1-0	0-0	1	Marwood	15,615
38	Apr 2	H	Darlington	D	0-0	0-0	1		7709
39	4	A	Halifax T	W	2-1	1-0	—	Woof, Marwood	5011
40	9	H	Blackpool	W	3-1	3-1	1	Marwood 2, Bardsley (og)	8555
41	16	A	Swindon T	W	1-0	0-0	1	Marwood	3772
42	19	A	York C	L	0-1	0-0	—		9909
43	23	H	Crewe Alex	W	1-0	1-0	1	Askew	7231
44	30	A	Chester	D	0-0	0-0	2		2281
45	May 2	H	Mansfield T	D	2-2	1-1	2	Askew, Flounders	8735
46	14	A	Rochdale	W	3-1	2-1	2	Mutrie, Roberts G., Marwood	2659

Final League Position: 2

GOALSCORERS

League (75): Marwood 19 (3 pens), Flouders 13, Mutrie 12, Askew 6, Roberts G. 6, McClaren 4, Skipper 4, Whitehurst 3, Woof 3, Roberts D. 2, Hawley 1, own goals 2.
Milk Cup (2): Flounders 1, Whitehurst 1.
FA Cup (1): own goal 1.
Football League Trophy (2): Marwood 1, Whitehurst 1.

Milk Cup	First Round	Sheffield U (a)	1-3
		(h)	1-0
FA Cup	First Round	Sheffield U (h)	1-1
		(a)	0-2

Football League Trophy	Hartlepool U (a)	2-1
	Halifax T (a)	0-1
	Bradford C (h)	0-0

Norman	Swann	Thompson	Richards	Skipper	Booth	Marwood	Askew	Whitehurst	Mutrie	Roberts G.	Flounders	McNeil	Roberts D.	McClaren	Davies	Woof	Hawley (L)	Davis	Hughes	*Referees*	*Match No.*
1	2	3	4	5	6	7	8*	9	10	11	12									K. Cooper	1
1		3		5	6	7		12	10	11	9*	2	4	8						M. Scott	2
1				5	2	9	6	11	10	7	12	3	4	8*						D. Shaw	3
1				5	6	7	3	9	10	11		2	4	8						G. Napthine	4
				5	6		3	9	10	11	7	2	4	8	1					J. Hough	5
1				5	6	7	3	9		11	10	2	4	8						E. Scales	6
1				5	6	7	3	9		11	10	2	4	8						C. Downey	7
1				5	6	7	3	9	10	11		2	4	8						T. Jones	8
1				4	6	9	5	10	11	8		2	3	7						K. Redfern	9
1				5	6	7	3	9	10	11		2	4	8						R. Guy	10
1	6			5		7	3	9	10*	11	12	2	4	8						L. Shapter	11
1	6		4	5		7	3	9		11	10*	2		8		12				G. Tyson	12
1	3		4	5		7			10	11		2		8		9		6		D. Allison	13
1				4	5	7	6*	12	10	11		2	3	8		9				J. Hunting	14
1				5	3	7		12	10*	11		2	4	8		9		6		P. Tyldesley	15
1	6			5	3	7		9	10	11		2	4	8						K. Baker	16
				5	6	7	3	9	10	11		2	4	8	1					K. Hackett	17
	12			5	6	7	3		10	11		2	4	8*	1		9			C. Seel	18
1				5	6	7	3			11	9	2	4	8			10			D. Hutchinson	19
1	2			5	6	7	3		10	11	9		4	8						K. Barratt	20
1	2			4	5		8		11	6	10		3	7			9			M. Heath	21
1	2			5	6	7	3	9	10	11			4					8		B. Chadwick	22
1	2			5	6	7	3	9	10	11			4	8						D. Civil	23
	2			5	6	7	3	9*	10	11	12		4	8	1					T. Fitzharris	24
	2			5	6	7	3*	9	10	11		12	4	8	1					A. Grey	25
	2			5	6	7	3	9*	10	11		12	4	8	1					T. Mills	26
	8	3		5	6	7			10	11	9	2	4		1					A. Robinson	27
1				5	6	7	3		10*	11	9	2	4			12		8		T. Holbrook	28
1				5	6	7	3		10	11	9	2	4	8						D. Richardson	29
1	7			5	6		3	9	10		12	2	4	8		11*				R. Banks	30
1				5	6		3	9	10			2	4	8		11		7		V. Callow	31
1				5	6	7	3	9*	10	11		2	4	8				12		N. Ashley	32
1				5	6		3		10	11	9	2	4	8				7		R. Nixon	33
1	6			5			3	12	10	11	9	2	4	8*				7		I. Borrett	34
1				5	6	7	3	12	10	11	9*	2	4	8						A. Saunders	35
1	12			5	6	7	3	8	10	11	9*	2	4							M. James	36
1				4	6	7	5	9	10	11		2	3						8	N. Glover	37
1		3		5	6	7		9	10	11			4	8					2	K. Walmsley	38
1	6	3		5		7			10	11			4	8		9			2	A. Hamil	39
1	6			4		8	5	12	11*	7			3	9		10			2	J. Bray	40
1	6	3		5		7		10		11	12		4	8		9*			2	M. Dimblebee	41
1	6	3		5		7		10		11		12	4	8		9			2*	D. Scott	42
1	3			5		7	6	12	10	11	9*		4	8					2	G. Courtney	43
	3	6		5		7		9	10	11			4	8	1				2	B. Newsome	44
	3			5		7	6	12	10*	11	9		4	8	1				2	K. Redfern	45
	3			5		7	6	9	10	11		2	4	8	1					F. Roberts	46
36	23	8	3	46	34	40	36	28	40	44	17	30	43	40	10	9	3	7	9		
	+ 2s							+ 8s			+ 6s	+ 3s				+ 2s		+ 1s			

FOOTBALL LEAGUE RECORD

1905 Elected to Division 2; 1930–33 Division 3(N); 1933–36 Division 2; 1936–49 Division 3(N); 1949–56 Division 2; 1956–58 Division 3(N); 1958–59 Division 3; 1959–60 Division 2; 1960–66 Division 3; 1966–78 Division 2; 1978–81 Division 3; 1981–83 Division 4; 1983– Division 3.

HONOURS

Football League: Division 2 best season: 3rd, 1909–10; Division 3(N) – Champions 1932–33, 1948–49; Division 3 – Champions 1965–66; Runners-up 1958–59; Division 4 – Runners-up 1982–83. *FA Cup* best season: Semi-final, 1930. *Football League Cup* best season: 4th rd, 1973–74, 1975–76, 1977–78.

COLOURS

Amber shirts with red pin stripe, black collar and cuffs, black shorts with amber and red stripe down side.
Change colours: All white.

HULL CITY

Players Names Ht, Wt, D.o.B.	Birthplace Transfer Fee	Clubs	Appearances F.L. A & S	 F.L.C. A & S	 F.A.C. A & S	Goals F.L.	 F.L.C.	 F.A.C.
Goalkeepers								
Tony Norman	Mancot	Burnley						
6 1½, 12 8, 24.2.58	£30,000	Hull C	131	5	12			
John Davies	Llandyssul	Cardiff C (A)	7					
6 3, 13 2, 18.11.59	£12,000	Hull C	24	1	2			
Defenders								
Emlyn Hughes (E)	Barrow	Blackpool	27+1	5	1			
5 10, 12 6, 28.8.47	£65,000	Liverpool	474	46	62	35	3	1
	£90,000	Wolverhampton W	56+2	12	5	2		
	F/T	Rotherham U	55+1	3	2	6		
	F/T	Hull C	9					
Dale Roberts (EY)	Newcastle	Ipswich T (A)	17+1	1	4			
5 10½, 11 5, 8.10.56	£60,000	Hull C	110+3	2	9	4		
Steve Richards*	Dundee	Hull C (A)	55+3	3	4	2		
6 0, 12 0, 24.10.61								
Bobby McNeil	Bellshill	Hull C (A)	65+3	3	12			
5 8½, 10 9, 1.11.62								
Dennis Booth	Stenley Common	Charlton Ath (A)	67+10	1	4	5		
5 7½, 10 5, 9.4.49	£7000	Blackpool	12	3				
	£7000	Southend U	77+1	3	3	1		
	£9000	Lincoln C	162	10+1	13	9		
		Watford	97+3	11	6	2		
	£40,000	Hull C	107+1	6	10	2		
Gary Swann	York	Hull C (A)	58+7	1	7	2		1
5 8½, 10 10, 11.4.62								
Peter Skipper	Hull	Hull C	22+1		1	2		
5 11, 12 6, 11.4.58	—	Scunthorpe U (loan)	0+1					
	£10,000	Darlington	91	4	5	4		
	£6000	Hull C	46	2		4		
Midfield								
Steve McClaren	Fulford	Hull C (A)	95+3	3+2	12	9		2
5 7½, 9 4, 3.5.61								
Brian Marwood	Easington	Hull C (A)	115+4	2+1	14	35		1
5 7, 9 13, 5.2.60								
Gareth Roberts	Hull	Hull C (A)	155+1	7	15	20	1	1
5 4, 10 2, 15.11.60								
Neil Thompson*	Beverley	Nottingham F (A)						
	F/T	Hull C	29+2					
Billy Askew	Lumley	Middlesbrough (A)	10+2					
5 6½, 10 2, 2.10.59	F/T	Gateshead						
	F/T	Hull C	36	1	1	6		
Ian Davis	Hull	Hull C (A)	25+3			1		
Forwards								
Billy Whitehurst	Thurnscoe	Mexborough						
6 0, 13 0, 10.6.59	£2500	Hull C	82+16	3+1	7	10	1	2
Les Mutrie (E SP)	Newcastle	Gateshead						
6 1, 11 6, 1.4.52		Carlisle U	4+1					
	F/T	Blyth Spartans						
	£30,000	Hull C	103	4	8	44		1
Andy Flounders	Hull	Hull C (A)	32+9	1+1	+2	18	1	
5 7½, 10 0, 13.12.63								
Billy Woof*	Gateshead	Middlesbrough (A)	30+16	7	+1	5	1	
5 10, 11 9, 16.8.56	—	Peterborough U (loan)	2+1					
	F/T	Blyth Spartans						
	F/T	Cardiff C	1			1		
	F/T	Hull C	9+2			3		

Commercial Manager: Tel.
Club Coach:
Club Captain 1982–83: Gareth Roberts
Supporters Player of the Season 1982–83: Peter Skipper
Chief Scout:
Physiotherapist: Jeff Radcliffe
Club Statistician:
Association of Football Statisticians Club Adviser to Yearbook: C. Elton.

Players released since May 1982: Brian Ferguson, M. (Goole T).

IPSWICH TOWN Division 1

3ack row (left to right): Tommy Parkin, Kevin O'Callaghan, Tony Kinsella, Irvin Gernon, John Linford, Kevin Steggles, Russell Osman, Trevor Putney, David Barnes
Viiddle row: Charlie Woods (First Team Coach), Bobby Ferguson (Team Manager), Mich D'Avray, Alan Brazil, Laurie Sivell, Paul Cooper, Steve McCall, John Wark, Brian Owen (Reserve Team Coach)
Front row: Terry Butcher, Paul Mariner, Frans Thijssen, Mick Mills, Robin Turner, George Burley, Eric Gates.

resident: Lady Blanche Cobbold. ***Chairman:*** P. M. Cobbold.

Directors: W. Kerr, H. R. Smith, J. M. Sangster, K. H. Brightwell, J. C. Cobbold.

Aanager: Bobby Ferguson. ***Secretary:*** D. C. Rose.

RO: Mel Henderson.

'ear Formed: 1887. ***Turned Professional:*** 1936. ***Ltd Co.:*** 1936.

lub Nickname: 'Blues' or 'Town'.

revious Managers since 1946: A. Scott Duncan, Alf Ramsey, Jackie Ailburn, Bill McGarry, Bobby Robson (5).

ortman Road, Ipswich, Suffolk IP1 2DA. Telephone 0473 219211 4 lines). ***Ground capacity:*** 37,000. ***Record attendance:*** 38,010 v Leeds U, A Cup 6th rd, 8 March, 1975. ***Record receipts:*** £105,950 v AZ 67 lkmaar, UEFA Cup final 1st leg, 6 May, 1981. ***Pitch measurements:*** 12yd×72yd.

irections to Ground: The ground is central and only two minutes walk from Ipswich railway station; he town centre is five minutes away. Local buses run past the ground.

latch tickets: On sale twelve days prior to match, price £4.00 and £4.50. Postal bookings accepted.

ar parking: Large parks in Portman Road, Portman's Walk, and off Princess Street at Greyfriars Park.

ntertainments/catering facilities: 'Centre Spot' bar and restaurant in Portman Road. Bars around the round. Executive boxes available.

lub shop: Four on the ground stock all types of souvenirs.

andbooks/programmes: Programmes available on subscription and an Annual is published.

ddress of Supporters Club: Same as Football Club.

ddress of the Club Shop or Boutique: Same as Football Club.

ote: Full club statistical records are on pages 416–455.

IPSWICH TOWN 1982–83 LEAGUE RECORD

Match No.	*Date*	*Venue*	*Opponents*	*Result*		*H/T Score*	*Lg. Pos.*	*Goalscorers*	*Attendance*
1	Aug 28	A	Brighton & HA	D	1-1	1-1	—	Gates	13,641
2	31	H	Tottenham H	L	1-2	1-0	—	Brazil	25,000
3	Sept 4	H	Coventry C	D	1-1	0-0	16	Mariner	16,662
4	7	A	West Ham U	D	1-1	1-0	—	Wark	21,963
5	11	A	Manchester U	L	1-3	1-1	21	Mariner	43,140
6	18	H	Stoke C	L	2-3	2-2	22	Brazil, Wark	19,119
7	25	A	Notts Co	W	6-0	2-0	19	Mariner 2, Brazil, Wark, Thijssen, McCall	8454
8	Oct 2	H	Liverpool	W	1-0	0-0	16	D'Avray	24,342
9	9	H	Arsenal	L	0-1	0-0	19		20,792
10	16	A	Luton T	D	1-1	1-0	20	Brazil	13,378
11	23	A	Birmingham C	D	0-0	0-0	18		12,051
12	30	H	WBA	W	6-1	4-0	15	Gates, Thijssen, Wark 4	20,011
13	Nov 6	A	Nottingham F	L	1-2	1-0	18	McCall	17,461
14	13	H	Manchester C	W	1-0	1-0	16	Wark	19,523
15	20	A	Southampton	W	1-0	0-0	12	Thijssen	18,449
16	23	A	Coventry C	D	1-1	0-0	—	Brazil	9550
17	27	H	Swansea C	W	3-1	2-0	8	Osman, Burley, Wark	17,849
18	Dec 4	A	Sunderland	W	3-2	2-1	7	Gates, Brazil 2	15,000
19	11	H	Everton	L	0-2	0-0	9		17,512
20	18	A	Watford	L	1-2	0-2	10	Mariner	18,048
21	27	H	Norwich C	L	2-3	1-1	11	Osman, Mariner	29,596
22	29	A	Aston Villa	D	1-1	1-1	13	Wark	21,912
23	Jan 1	H	Southampton	W	2-1	1-0	10	Mariner, Osman	18,866
24	15	H	Brighton & HA	W	2-0	1-0	9	Wark, Brazil	17,092
25	22	A	Stoke C	L	0-1	0-0	11		14,026
26	Feb 5	H	Manchester U	D	1-1	1-0	13	Wark	23,581
27	12	A	Liverpool	L	0-1	0-0	13		34,976
28	26	H	Luton T	W	3-0	1-0	11	Brazil, Wark, Putney	18,615
29	Mar 5	H	Birmingham C	W	3-1	0-0	8	Putney, Osman, Brazil	16,436
30	12	A	WBA	L	1-4	0-2	9	Wark	12,892
31	19	H	Nottingham F	W	2-0	1-0	10	Mariner 2	17,534
32	22	A	Arsenal	D	2-2	0-2	—	Wark, Putney	17,639
33	26	A	Manchester C	W	1-0	0-0	6	Wark	21,845
34	Apr 2	H	Aston Villa	L	1-2	1-1	8	McCall	19,912
35	4	A	Norwich C	D	0-0	0-0	—		23,476
36	9	H	Notts Co	D	0-0	0-0	11		15,924
37	16	A	Tottenham H	L	1-3	0-2	11	Mariner	30,557
38	23	H	Sunderland	W	4-1	2-0	11	Wark 2, Mariner, Turner	16,193
39	30	A	Swansea C	D	1-1	0-0	11	Mariner	8568
40	May 3	H	West Ham U	L	1-2	1-1	—	D'Avray	18,690
41	7	H	Watford	W	3-1	2-0	9	McCall, Wark 2	19,921
42	14	A	Everton	D	1-1	0-0	9	Mariner	17,420

Final League Position: 9

GOALSCORERS

League (64): Wark 20, Mariner 13, Brazil 10, McCall 4, Osman 4, Gates 3, Putney 3, Thijssen 3, D'Avray 2, Burley 1, Turner 1.
Milk Cup (1): Wark 1.
FA Cup (5): Wark 2 (1 pen), McCall 1, Osman 1, Thijssen 1.
UEFA Cup (3): Butcher 1, Gates 1, McCall 1.

Milk Cup	Second Round	Liverpool (h)	1-2
		(a)	0-2
FA Cup	Third Round	Charlton Ath (a)	3-2
	Fourth Round	Grimsby T (h)	2-0
	Fifth Round	Norwich C (a)	0-1
UEFA Cup	First Round	Roma (a)	0-3
		(h)	3-1

Cooper	Burley	Mills	Thijssen	Osman	Butcher	Wark	McCall	Mariner	O'Callaghan	Gates	Brazil	D'Avray	Sivell	Parkin	Gernon	Putney	Barnes	Steggles	Kinsella	Turner	Referees	Match No.
1	2	3	4	5	6	7	8	9	10	11											D. Hedges	1
1	2	3	4	5	6	7	8	9		11*	10			12							A. Grey	2
1	2	3	4	5	6	7	8	9	12	11*	10										M. James	3
1	2	3	4	5	6	7	8	9		11	10										K. Barratt	4
1	2	3	4	5	6	7	8*	9		11	10	12									A. Saunders	5
	2	3	4	5*	6	7	8	9		11	10		1	12							M. Taylor	6
	2	3	4	5	6	7	8	9		11	10		1								J. Lovatt	7
	2	10	4*	5	6	7	8		12	11		9	1		3						R. Lewis	8
	2	4		5	6	7	8	9	11		10		1		3*	12					J. Hunting	9
1	2	4		5	6	7	8	9		11	10				3						D. Lloyd	10
1	2	3	4	5	6	7	8	9		11	10										N. Ashley	11
1	2		4	5	6	7	8	9	12	11	10*				3						D. Reeves	12
1	2		4*	5	6	7	8		12	11	10	9			3						N. Wilson	13
1	2		4	5	6	7	8		9	11	10				3						D. Vickers	14
1	2		4	5	6	7	8	9		11	10				3						K. Salmon	15
1	2		4	5*	6	7	8	9		11	10	12			3						R. Chadwick	16
1	2		4	5	6	7	8	9		11	10						3				J. Moules	17
1	2		4	5	6	7	8	9		11	10						3				T. Fitzharris	18
1	2*		4	5	6	7	8	9	12	11	10						3				C. Donney	19
1			4	5	6	7	8	9	12	11	10					3		2*			M. Robinson	20
1			4	5	6	7	3	9	8*	11	10					12		2			A. Gunn	21
1			4	5	6	7	9		12	11	10				3	8*		2			R. Milford	22
			4	5	6	7	8	9		11	10		1		3			2			H. Taylor	23
			4	5	6	7	8	9*		11	10		1		3	12		2			J. Bray	24
			4	5	6	7	8	9	12	11*	10		1		3			2			T. Mills	25
1			4	5	6	7	8	9	11		10	12			3	2*					K. Baker	26
1			4	5	6	7	8	9	11		10	12			3	2*					G. Tyson	27
1				5	6	7	8	9	11		10			4	3	2					M. Bodenham	28
1				5	6	7	8	9	11		10			4	3	2					D. Letts	29
1				5	6	7	8	9	11		10			4	3	2					F. Roberts	30
1	2		12	5	6	7	8	9	11*			10			3	4					Alan Robinson	31
1	2		10	5	6	7	8		11			9			3	4					J. Deakin	32
1	2			5	6	7	8	9	11			10			3	4					K. Hackett	33
1	2		12	5	6	7	8	9	11			10*			3	4					E. Scales	34
1	2		4	5	6	7	8	9	11						3				10		B. Hill	35
1	2			5	6	7	8	9	11*			10				4	3		12		T. Ward	36
1	2				6	7	8	9				10				4	3*	5	11	12	T. Spencer	37
1	2				6	7	3	9	11			10				4*		5	8	12	M. Dimblebee	38
1	2				6	7	3	9	11			10			8	4		5*		12	V. Callow	39
1	2				6	7	8	9	11			10		4*	5		3			12	G. Napthine	40
1	2			5	6	7	8	9	11			10			3	4*				12	D. Axcell	41
1	2			5	6	7	8	9	11			10			3	4					G. Courtney	42
35	31	11	27	38	42	42	42	37	20	24	28	13	7	4	26	17	6	9	3	0		
			+ 2s						+ 8s			+ 4s		+ 2s		+ 3s			+ 1s	+ 5s		

FOOTBALL LEAGUE RECORD

1938 Elected to Division 3(S); 1954–55 Division 2; 1955–57 Division 3(S); 1957–61 Division 2; 1961–64 Division 1; 1964–68 Division 2; 1968– Division 1.

HONOURS

Football League: Division 1 – Champions 1961–62; Runners-up 1980–81, 1981–82; Division 2 – Champions 1960–61, 1967–68; Division 3(S) – Champions 1953–54, 1956–57. *FA Cup:* Winners 1977–78. *Football League Cup:* best season: Semi-final 1981–82. *Texaco Cup:* 1972–73. **European Competitions:** *European Cup:* 1962–63; *European Cup-Winners' Cup:* 1978–79; *UEFA Cup:* 1973–74, 1974–75, 1975–76, 1977–78, 1979–80, 1980–81 (winners), 1981–82, 1982–83.

COLOURS

Royal blue shirts with three white stripes down each arm, white shorts with three blue stripes, blue stockings with three white hoops.

Change colours: White shorts with three black stripes down each arm, black shorts with three white stripes, white stockings with three black stripes.

IPSWICH TOWN

Players Names Ht. Wt. D.o.B.	Birthplace Transfer Fee	Clubs	Appearances F.L. A & S	F.L.C. A & S	F.A.C. A & S	Goals F.L.	F.L.C.	F.A.C.
Goalkeepers								
Paul Cooper	Brierley Hill	Birmingham C (A)	17	1	4			
5 11, 12 7, 21.12.53	£27,000	Ipswich T	303	22	34			
Laurie Sivell	Lowestoft	Ipswich T (A)	135	7	18			
5 8, 11 0, 8.2.51	—	Lincoln C (loan)	2					
Gary Westwood	Barrow	Ipswich T (A)						
6 0, 13 0, 3.4.63								
Defenders								
George Burley (S)	Cumnock	Ipswich T (A)	323	22	38	5		3
5 9½, 11 0, 3.6.56								
Terry Butcher (E)	Singapore	Ipswich T	167	15	16	9		
6 4, 14 0, 28.12.58								
Ian Cranson	Easington	Ipswich T (A)						
5 11¼, 12 4, 2.7.64								
Russell Osman (E)	Ilkeston	Ipswich T (A)	228	19	26	11	2	1
6 0, 11 10, 14.2.59								
Kevin Steggles	Ditchingham	Ipswich T (A)	33	3	3	1	1	
6 0, 11 1, 19.3.61								
Irvin Gernon (EY)	Birmingham	Ipswich T (A)	30	1	3			
6 0, 11 13, 30.12.62								
Frank Yallop	Watford	Ipswich T (A)						
5 10½, 10 3, 4.4.64								
David Barnes (EY)	London	Coventry C (A)	9		4			
5 10, 10 8, 16.11.61	F T	Ipswich T	6					
Andy Lawrence		Ipswich T (A)						
Midfield								
John Wark (S)	Glasgow	Ipswich T (A)	263+1	20+1	34+1	89	6	10
5 10½, 11 12, 4.8.57								
Tommy Parkin	Gateshead	Ipswich T (A)	14+7	1				
5 7, 10 4, 1.2.56	—	Grimsby T (loan)	6	1				
	—	Peterborough U (loan)	3	2				
Bryan Klug (EY)	Coventry	Ipswich T (A)						
5 8, 10 10, 8.10.60	—	Wimbledon (loan)	10+1					
Steve McCall (EU-21)	Carlisle	Ipswich T (A)	117+8	11	10+1	6		1
5 11, 11 3, 15.10.60								
Tony Kinsella (EIU-21)	Orsett	Millwall (A)	55+6	2+1	4	1		
5 8, 10 4, 30.10.61		Tampa Bay R						
	£60,000	Ipswich T	3+1					
Trevor Putney	Harold Hill	Brentwood						
5 9½, 10 3, 11.2.61	—	Ipswich T	17+3		1	3		
Gary Davies	South Shields	Ipswich T (A)						
5 7, 9 9, 6.8.64								
Mark Brennan		Ipswich T (A)						
4.10.65								
Mike Stockwell		Ipswich T (A)						
5 6½, 10 2, 14.2.65								
Forwards								
Eric Gates (E)	Ferryhill	Ipswich T (A)	189+29	17+1	17+3	47	5	5
5 6, 10 4, 28.6.55								
Robin Turner (EY)	Carlisle	Ipswich T (A)	19+9	1+2	5+1	1	1	2
5 9, 10 8, 10.9.55								
Paul Mariner (E)	Bolton	Chorley						
6 0, 12 2, 22.5.53	£22,500	Plymouth Arg	134+1	12	11	56	2	3
	£2000,000–P E	Ipswich T	237	16	27	85	6	19
Mich D'Avray	South Africa	Ipswich T (A)	27+10	3	+1	5		1
6 1, 12 0, 19.2.62								
Kevin O'Callaghan (EI)	London	Millwall (A)	15+5	2	3+1	3	2	1
5 8½, 10 9, 29.10.61	£220,000	Ipswich T	39+28	4+3	1+5	9	1	
Russell Irving	Wallsend	Ipswich T (A)						
5 8, 11 2½, 4.1.64								
John Linford	Norwich	Gorleston						
6 2, 11 12, 6.2.57	—	Ipswich T						
	—	Colchester U (loan)	7					
	—	Southend U (loan)	6			3		

Commercial Manager: Tommy Parker (Tel. 219211)
Club Coach: Charlie Woods
Club Captain 1982–83: Paul Mariner
Supporters Player of the Season 1982–83: Paul Mariner
Chief Scout: Ron Gray
Physiotherapist: Tommy Eggleston
Club Statistician: Ron Ellis
Association of Football Statisticians Club Adviser to Yearbook: P. Voller

Players (non-appearance) granted free transfer: Ian Templeton, D.; Ian Hurrell, F.; Jim King, M.
Players released since May 1982:
George Ainsley, D. (Bury T); Dale Brooks, M. (Bishops Stortford); Ron Burns, D. (Ballymena U); Frans Thijssen, M. (Vancouver W).

LEEDS UNITED Division 2

Back row (left to right): Mark Gavin, Martin Dickinson, Neil Aspin, John Lukic, Paul Hart (now Nottingham F), David Harvey, Gary Hamson, John Donnelly, Kevin Hird
Front row: Gwyn Thomas, Aidan Butterworth, John Sheridan, Andy Ritchie, Eddie Gray, Tommy Wright, Arthur Graham, Frank Gray.

President: The Right Hon The Earl of Harewood LLD.

Vice President: S. G. Simon.

Chairman: M. Cussins. ***Vice-Chairman:*** L. Silver OBE.

Directors: R. Barker MCIT, MBIM, B. Woodward, J. W. C. Marjason, W. J. Fotherby, M. Holmes, P. Gilman.

Player Manager: Eddie Gray MBE. ***Company Secretary:*** D. J. Dowse.

Asst Manager: Jimmy Lumsden.

General Manager: Keith Archer. ***Secretary:*** David Dowse.

Year Formed: 1919, as Leeds United after disbandment (by FA order) of Leeds City (formed in 1904).

Turned Professional: 1920. Ltd Co.: 1920.

Club Nickname: 'Peacocks'.

Previous Managers since 1946: Billy Hampson, Willis Edwards, Major Frank Buckley, Raich Carter, Bill Lambton, Jack Taylor, Don Revie OBE, Brian Clough, Jimmy Armfield, Jock Stein, Jimmy Adamson, Allan Clarke (12).

Elland Road, Leeds LS11 0ES. Telephone Leeds 716037 (3 lines). ***Telegraphic address:*** 'Football Leeds'. ***Ground capacity:*** 43,900. ***Record attendance:*** 57,892 v Sunderland, FA Cup 5th rd replay, 15 March, 1967. ***Record receipts:*** £146,483, FA Cup semi-final replay, Everton v West Ham U, 16 April, 1980. ***Pitch measurements:*** 117yd×76yd.

Directions to Ground: Nearest railway station, Leeds. The city centre is within walking distance from the station and then by Corporation buses to the ground. Ground is by M6.

Match tickets: Computer installed for sale of match-by-match tickets.

Car parking: Within one minute of the ground there is a large park owned by the Leeds Greyhound Association; this holds about 1000 cars.

Entertainments /catering facilities: Supporters' social club by the ground. Snack bars around the ground.

Club shop: This operates at the ground next to the Pools Office and stocks all types of souvenirs.

Handbooks /programmes: Programmes are available from the club shop, and on subscription.

Extra information: The club have a Robotphone Answering System (Leeds 702621).

Address of Supporters Club: Leeds United Supporters Club, Fullerton Park, Elland Road, Leeds 11.

Address of the Club Shop or Boutique: Leeds United Club Shop, Elland Road, Leeds 11.

Note: Full club statistical records are on pages 416–455.

LEEDS UNITED 1982–83 LEAGUE RECORD

Match No.	Date	Venue	Opponents	Result		H/T Score	Lg. Pos.	Goalscorers	Attendance
1	Aug 28	A	Grimsby T	D	1-1	0-0	—	Connor	16,137
2	Sept 4	H	Wolverhampton W	D	0-0	0-0	17		16,462
3	8	A	Leicester C	W	1-0	0-0	—	Butterworth	12,963
4	11	A	Sheffield W	W	3-2	2-0	7	Worthington 2, Butterworth	29,050
5	18	H	Derby Co	W	2-1	1-1	5	Gray F., Worthington	16,889
6	25	A	Fulham	L	2-3	1-1	7	Thomas, Graham	12,798
7	Oct 2	H	Cambridge U	W	2-1	1-1	6	Butterworth, Hird	14,910
8	9	A	Chelsea	D	0-0	0-0	6		25,358
9	16	H	Carlisle U	D	1-1	1-1	7	Hart	14,141
10	20	H	Burnley	W	3-1	2-1	—	Worthington, Butterworth, Hird	13,827
11	23	A	Blackburn R	D	0-0	0-0	6		12,040
12	30	H	Newcastle U	W	3-1	1-0	6	Worthington, Burns, Butterworth	26,570
13	Nov 6	H	Charlton Ath	L	1-2	0-1	5	Connor	15,148
14	13	A	Crystal Palace	D	1-1	1-1	5	Connor	11,673
15	20	H	Middlesbrough	D	0-0	0-0	5		18,482
16	27	A	Barnsley	L	1-2	1-1	6	Butterworth	21,530
17	Dec 4	H	QPR	L	0-1	0-0	8		11,528
18	11	A	Rotherham U	W	1-0	0-0	6	Gavin	13,034
19	18	H	Shrewsbury T	D	1-1	1-0	8	Hird	8741
20	26	A	Oldham Ath	D	2-2	1-1	—	Burns, Sheridan	15,658
21	28	H	Bolton W	D	1-1	0-0	6	Graham	16,180
22	Jan 1	A	Middlesbrough	D	0-0	0-0	8		17,000
23	3	A	Wolverhampton W	L	0-3	0-1	9		22,567
24	15	H	Grimsby T	W	1-0	0-0	7	Butterworth	13,583
25	22	A	Derby Co	D	3-3	1-0	6	Graham 2, Hart	17,005
26	Feb 12	A	Cambridge U	D	0-0	0-0	9		6909
27	19	H	Chelsea	D	3-3	1-1	9	Butterworth, Gray F. (pen), Graham	19,365
28	26	A	Carlisle U	D	2-2	2-0	9	Connor, Butterworth	6419
29	Mar 5	H	Blackburn R	W	2-1	1-1	8	Gray F. (pen), Hird	12,280
30	12	A	Newcastle U	L	1-2	0-1	10	Connor	24,580
31	19	A	Charlton Ath	W	1-0	0-0	8	Sheridan	8229
32	26	H	Crystal Palace	W	2-1	0-1	7	Ritchie, Gray F. (pen)	13,973
33	Apr 2	A	Bolton W	W	2-1	1-0	5	Butterworth, Hart	10,784
34	5	H	Oldham Ath	D	0-0	0-0	—		18,442
35	9	A	Burnley	W	2-1	1-1	5	Ritchie, Scott (og)	12,149
36	16	H	Fulham	D	1-1	1-0	5	Wright	24,328
37	23	A	QPR	L	0-1	0-1	6		19,573
38	27	H	Sheffield W	L	1-2	1-1	—	Ritchie	16,591
39	30	H	Barnsley	D	0-0	0-0	9		15,344
40	May 2	H	Leicester C	D	2-2	1-0	8	O'Neill (og), Gray F. (pen)	14,442
41	7	A	Shrewsbury T	D	0-0	0-0	7		6052
42	14	H	Rotherham U	D	2-2	0-1	8	Butterworth, Donnelly	14,958

Final League Position: 8

GOALSCORERS

League (51): Butterworth 11, Connor 5, Graham 5, Gray F. 5 (4 pens), Worthington 5, Hird 4, Hart 3, Ritchie 3, Burns 2, Sheridan 2, Donnelly 1, Gavin 1, Thomas 1, Wright 1, own goals 2.
Milk Cup (4): Butterworth 1, Connor 1, Worthington 1, own goal 1.
FA Cup (6): Connor 2, Butterworth 1, Graham 1, Sheridan 1, own goal 1.

Milk Cup	Second Round	Newcastle U (h)	0-1
		(a)	4-1
	Third Round	Huddersfield T (h)	0-1
FA Cup	Third Round	Preston NE (h)	3-0
	Fourth Round	Arsenal (a)	1-1
		(h)	1-1 (aet)
		(a)	1-2

Lukic	Hird	Gray E.	Dickinson	Hart	Thomas	Connor	Butterworth	Worthington	Gray F.	Graham	Cherry	Burns	Gavin	Flynn	Sheridan	Aspin	McNab (L)	Donnelly	Harvey	Ritchie	Wright	Brown	Sellars	Parlane	Referees	Match No.
1	2	3	4	5	6	7	8	9	10	11															J. Hunting	1
1	2	3	4	5	6	7*	8	9	10	11	12														N. Glover	2
1	7	3	4	5	6		8	9	10	11	2														C. Thomas	3
1	7	3*	4	5	6	12	8	9	10	11	2														A. Seville	4
1	7*	3	4	5	6		8	9	10	11	2													12	D. Owen	5
1	7	3*	4	5	6		8	9	10	11	2	12													T. Bune	6
1	7		2*	5	6		8	9	10	11	3	4	12												B. Chadwick	7
1	7	3		5	6		8	9	10	11	2	4													T. Spencer	8
1	7	3		5	6	12	8	9	10*	11	2			4											P. Tyldesley	9
1	7	3		5	6		8	9	10	11	2	4													P. Willis	10
1	6	3		5	7		9	10	8	11	2	4													C. Newsome	11
1	7*	3	5		6	12	8	9	10	11	2	4													M. Heath	12
1	7	3	5		6	12	8	9	10	11	2*	4													J. Lovatt	13
1	7			5	10	8		9	3	11	2	6		4											M. Taylor	14
1	7			5	10	8	12	9*	3	11	2	6			4										M. Robinson	15
1	7			5	10	8	9		3	11	2	6			4										N. Ashley	16
1	12		2	5			9		3	11	10	6	8*		4	7									K. Walmsley	17
1	7		2	5	10		9		3	11		6	8		4										A. Hamil	18
1	7		4	5	2		9		3			6	11		8		10								G. Tyson	19
1	7		2	5	10		9		3	11		6			4		8								R. Bridges	20
1	7		2*	5	10		8		3	11		6	12		4	9									H. Taylor	21
1				5	10	8	9		3	11		6			4	2	7								D. Allison	22
1	12			5	10	8	9		3*	11		6			4	2	7								E. Scales	23
1	12	3*		5		8	9		10	11		6			4	2	7								J. Hough	24
1	12	3		5	7*	9	8		10	11		6			4	2									A. Ward	25
1	12	3	6*	5	7	8	9		10	11					4	2									R. Lewis	26
1	12	3	6	5	7*	8	9		10	11					4	2									K. Redfern	27
1	12	3	6	5	7	8	9		10	11					4*	2									A. Saunders	28
1	12		6	5	7*	8	9		3	11					4	2		10							V. Callow	29
	7		6	5		8	9		3	11		10			4	2		12	1						N. Midgley	30
	7		6	5	2	8	9		3	11					4			10	1						E. Read	31
	7		6	5	2		8		3	11					4			10	1	9					D. Shaw	32
	7		6	5	2		9		3	11					4			10	1	8					P. Scott	33
	7	12	6	5	2		8*		3	11					4			10	1	9					K. Barratt	34
	7	8	6	5	2				3	11					4			10	1	9					F. Roberts	35
	7	8	6	5	2				3	11					4	12		10	1		9*				A. Robinson	36
	7	8	6	5	2				3	11			12		4			10*	1	9					M. Crickmore	37
	7		6	5	2*		8		3	11			12		4			10	1	9					M. Peck	38
	7		6	5	2		8		3	11					4			10	1	9					J. Hunting	39
			6		7		8		3						4	2		10	1	9	11	5			P. Willis	40
			6	5	7		8*		3						4	2		10	1	9	12		11		D. Lloyd	41
	12		6	5	7		8		3	11*						2		10	1	9	4				D. Richardson	42
29	30	20	31	39	39	15	37	15	42	39	15	19	3	2	27	14	5	13	13	10	3	1	1	0		
	+ 9s	+ 1s				+ 4s	+ 1s				+ 1s	+ 1s	+ 4s			+ 1s		+ 1s			+ 1s			+ 1s		

FOOTBALL LEAGUE RECORD

1920 Elected to Division 2; 1924–27 Division 1; 1927–28 Division 2; 1928–31 Division 1; 1931–32 Division 2; 1932–47 Division 1; 1947–56 Division 2; 1956–60 Division 1; 1960–64 Division 2; 1964–82 Division 1; 1982– Division 2.

HONOURS

Football League: Division 1 – Champions 1968–69, 1973–74; Runners-up 1964–65, 1965–66, 1969–70, 1970–71, 1971–72; Division 2 – Champions 1923–24, 1963–64; Runners-up 1927–28, 1931–32, 1955–56. *FA Cup:* Winners 1972; Runners-up 1965, 1970, 1973. *Football League Cup:* Winners 1967–68. **European Competitions:** *European Cup:* 1969–70, 1974–75 (runners-up). *European Cup-Winners' Cup:* 1972–73 (runners-up). *European Fairs Cup:* 1965–66, 1966–67 (runners-up), 1967–68 (winners), 1968–69, 1970–71 (winners). *UEFA Cup:* 1971–72, 1973–74, 1979–80.

COLOURS

All white with blue and yellow stripe. **Change colours:** All yellow with blue and white trim.

LEEDS UNITED

			Appearances			Goals		
Players Names *Ht. Wt. D.o.B.*	*Birthplace* *Transfer Fee*	*Clubs*	*F.L. A & S*	*F.L.C. A & S*	*F.A.C. A & S*	*F.L.*	*F.L.C.*	*F.A.C.*
Goalkeepers								
John Lukic (EU21)	Chesterfield	Leeds U (A)	146	7	9			
6 4, 13 7, 11.12.60								
David Harvey (S)	Leeds	Leeds U	276	31	28			
5 11, 12 6, 7.2.48	£40,000	Vancouver W						
	F/T	Leeds U	13					
Philip Hughes		Manchester U (A)						
	F/T	Leeds U						
Defenders								
Kevin Hird	Colne	Blackburn R (A)	129+3	7+1	8	20	1	
5 7, 10 6, 11.2.55	£357,000	Leeds U	149+14	6+1	6+2	18		2
Tony Brown	Bradford	Thackley						
6 2½,	—	Leeds U	1					
Frank Gray (S)	Glasgow	Leeds U (A)	188+5	18+1	19+1	17	4	3
5 10, 11 10, 27.10.54	£500,000	Nottingham F	81	14	8	5	2	1
	£300,000	Leeds U	78+1	5	5	5		
Kenny Burns (S)	Glasgow	Birmingham C (A)	163+7	12+12	11	45	2	3
5 10, 11 0, 23.9.53	£150,000	Nottingham F	137	25	13	13	1	
	£400,000	Leeds U	41+2	3	3	2		
	—	Derby Co (loan)	6+1			1		
Neil Aspin	Gateshead	Leeds U (A)	15+1		4			
6 1, 12 3,								
Martin Dickinson	Leeds	Leeds U (A)	37+1		3			
5 10, 11 0, 14.3.63								
Midfield								
Eddie Gray (S)	Glasgow	Leeds U	435+13	33+2	46+1	52	6	5
5 11, 12 6, 17.1.48								
Gary Hamson	Nottingham	Sheffield U (A)	107+1	3	5	8	1	
5 8, 10 12, 24.8.59	£140,000	Leeds U	42+6	2	5+1	3		1
John Sheridan (EIY)	Stretford							
5 9, 10 8,		Leeds U	27		2	2		1
Gwyn Thomas (WU21)	Swansea	Leeds U (A)	63+9	5+1	4+1	3		
5 8, 11 0, 26.9.57								
Mark Gavin	Bailleston	Leeds U (A)	3+4			1		
5 8, 10 7,								
Forwards								
Arthur Graham (S)	Glasgow	Aberdeen						
5 8, 11 10, 26.10.52	£125,000	Leeds U	222+1	22	12	37	4	3
Derek Parlane (S)	Helensburg	Rangers						
6 0, 11 10, 5.5.53	£200,000	Leeds U	45+5	1	2	10		
Andy Ritchie (EU21)	Manchester	Manchester U (A)	26+7	3	3	13		
5 9½, 11 11, 28.11.60	£500,000	Brighton	82+7	3+1	9	23	1	2
	P/E	Leeds U	10			3		
Aiden Butterworth (ES)	Leeds	Leeds U	50+3	3	6	14	1	1
5 8, 11 0, 7.11.61								
Tommy Wright	Dunfermline	Leeds U (A)	3+1			1		
5 7, 9 9,								
John Donnelly	Glasgow	Dumbarton						
5 10, 11 0, 8.3.61	£10,000	Leeds U	13+1			1		
Apprentices								
Scott Sellars	Sheffield	Leeds U (A)	1					
5 8, 9 0,								

Commercial Manager: Bob Baldwin
Club Coach: Barry Murphy
Supporters Player of the Season 1982–83: Kenny Burns
Physiotherapist: Geoff Ladley
Club Captain 1982–83: Paul Hart
Chief Scout: Sid Owen
Club Statistician: Bob Baldwin
Association of Football Statisticians Club Adviser to Yearbook: J. Barker

Players (non-appearance) granted free transfer: Colin Thacker, D.; Tony Sharkey, D.; Wayne Roebuck, F.; Steve Taylor, F.
Players released since May 1982: Steve Balcombe, F. (Home Farm); Alan Clarke, F. (N/K); Steve Maddock, F. (N/K); David Matthews, F. (N/K); Dick Nuttall, . (N/K); Keith MacRae, G. (N/K); Peter Barnes, F. (Real Betis); Gerry Hill, M. (N/K); Mark Hinchcliffe, D. (N/K); Bob Peel, F. (N/K)

LEICESTER CITY Division 1

Back row (left to right): Keith Robson, John O'Neill, Kevin McDonald, Larry May, Nicky Walker, Mark Wallington, Tommy Williams, Norman Leet, Alan Smith, Tom English
Front row: Andy Peake, Steve Lynex, Gary Lineker, Eddie Kelly, Bobby Smith, Paul Ramsey, Paul Friar, Ian Wilson.

Chairman: T. W. Shipman. ***Vice-Chairman:*** T. E. Bloor.

Directors: W. G. Page, D. E. Sharp, W. K. Shooter FCA, T. Smeaton.

Manager: Gordon Milne. ***Gen Secretary:*** A. K. Bennett.

Assistant Manager: Gerry Summers. ***PRO:*** Graham Clark.

Year Formed: 1884.

Club Nickname: 'Filberts' or 'Foxes'.

Previous Grounds: 1884, Victoria Park; 1887, Belgrave Road; 1888, Victoria Park; 1891, Filbert Street.

Previous Name: 1884–1919, Leicester Fosse.

Previous Managers since 1946: Johnny Duncan, Norman Bullock, David Halliday, Matt Gillies, Frank O'Farrell, Jimmy Bloomfield, Frank McLintock, Jock Wallace (8).

City Stadium, Filbert St, Leicester, LE2 7FL. Telephone Leicester (0533) 555000 (Match information Leicester 551155). ***Ground capacity:*** 32,000. ***Record attendance:*** 47,298 v Tottenham H, FA Cup 5th rd, 18 Feb, 1928. ***Record receipts:*** £70,633 v Shrewsbury T, FA Cup 6th rd, 6 March, 1982. ***Pitch measurements:*** 112yd×75yd.

Directions to Ground: Corporation buses from Humberstone Gate and Waterloo St (opposite railway station) in city centre. Nearest station Leicester. Midland Red run bus services to the town centre from outlying districts.

Match tickets: Seats can be booked from two months prior to the date of match & SAE.

Car parking: Parking adjacent to the ground is for season-ticket holders only. There is nearby street parking and also a public car park about five minutes walk from the ground.

Entertainments/catering facilities: A private season-ticket members bar in the main stand, and catering bars in all sections of the ground.

Club shop: Situated under the main stand; sells all types of souvenirs.

Handbooks/programmes: Both handbooks and programmes are available from the club shop.

Address of Supporters Club: 69 Burnmoor Street, Leicester LE2 7JL.

Note: Full club statistical records are on pages 416–455.

LEICESTER CITY 1982–83 LEAGUE RECORD

Match No.	Date	Venue	Opponents	Result	H/T Score	Lg. Pos.	Goalscorers	Attendance
1	Aug 28	H	Charlton Ath	L 1-2	0-1	—	Smith B.	11,038
2	31	A	Rotherham U	W 3-1	1-1	—	Melrose, Smith A., Lineker	9254
3	Sept 4	A	Chelsea	D 1-1	0-0	8	Lineker	14,127
4	8	H	Leeds U	L 0-1	0-0	—		12,963
5	11	H	Carlisle U	W 6-0	2-0	9	Lynex 3 (2 pens), Lineker 3 (1 pen)	8440
6	18	A	Blackburn R	L 1-3	0-1	11	Smith A.	4963
7	25	H	QPR	L 0-1	0-0	13		10,647
8	Oct 2	A	Shrewsbury T	W 2-0	1-0	11	MacDonald, O'Neill	5223
9	9	H	Grimsby T	W 2-0	0-0	7	Lynex, Lineker	9640
10	16	A	Wolverhampton W	W 3-0	2-0	6	Wilson, Lineker, English	15,782
11	23	A	Derby Co	W 4-0	1-0	7	Lineker 3, Smith A.	13,191
12	30	H	Sheffield W	L 0-2	0-1	7		17,341
13	Nov 6	A	Cambridge U	L 1-3	1-3	8	Lineker	5011
14	13	H	Newcastle U	D 2-2	1-1	8	English, Lineker	15,044
15	20	H	Crystal Palace	L 0-1	0-0	12		8616
16	27	A	Bolton W	L 1-3	0-2	15	Wilson	5060
17	Dec 4	H	Fulham	W 2-0	0-0	10	Buchanan, Lineker	9082
18	11	A	Burnley	W 4-2	1-1	9	Lineker, Lynex (pen), Smith A. 2	6457
19	18	H	Oldham Ath	W 2-1	0-0	6	MacDonald (pen), Smith A.	8125
20	27	A	Middlesbrough	D 1-1	0-0	5	Lineker	12,665
21	28	H	Barnsley	W 1-0	1-0	4	Smith A.	14,838
22	Jan 1	A	Crystal Palace	L 0-1	0-1	5		8801
23	3	H	Chelsea	W 3-0	1-0	4	Lineker 2, Smith A.	13,745
24	15	A	Charlton Ath	L 1-2	0-0	5	Wilson	5971
25	22	H	Blackburn R	L 0-1	0-1	5		8361
26	Feb 5	A	Carlisle U	W 1-0	1-0	6	MacDonald	4402
27	19	A	Grimsby T	L 0-2	0-1	6		6963
28	22	H	Shrewsbury T	W 3-2	1-1	—	Lineker 2, Wilson	6155
29	26	H	Wolverhampton W	W 5-0	3-0	4	Lynex 2, Smith A., Lineker, Daly	13,530
30	Mar 5	H	Derby Co	D 1-1	0-0	4	Lynex	15,288
31	19	H	Cambridge U	W 4-0	1-0	4	Smith A. 2, Lynex (pen), Wilson	8305
32	22	A	Sheffield W	D 2-2	1-0	—	MacDonald, Smith A.	14,036
33	26	A	Newcastle U	D 2-2	1-0	4	Lineker 2	22,655
34	Apr 2	A	Barnsley	W 2-1	1-0	4	Wilson, English	13,278
35	5	H	Middlesbrough	W 1-0	0-0	—	O'Neill	12,025
36	9	A	QPR	D 2-2	0-1	4	Lineker 2	16,301
37	16	H	Rotherham U	W 3-1	1-0	4	Wilson, Lineker 2	12,978
38	23	A	Fulham	W 1-0	0-0	4	Wilson	24,251
39	30	H	Bolton W	D 0-0	0-0	4		13,959
40	May 2	A	Leeds U	D 2-2	0-1	3	Smith A., May	14,442
41	7	A	Oldham Ath	W 2-1	1-0	3	Jones, Ramsey	9088
42	14	H	Barnsley	D 0-0	0-0	3		29,376

Final League Position: 3

GOALSCORERS

League (72): Lineker 26 (1 pen), Smith A. 13, Lynex 9 (4 pens), Wilson 8, MacDonald 4 (1 pen), English 3, O'Neill 2, Buchanan 1, Daly 1, Jones 1, May 1, Melrose 1, Ramsey 1, Smith B. 1.
Milk Cup (0).
FA Cup (2): Smith A. 1, Wilson 1.

Milk Cup	Second Round	Lincoln C (a)	0-2
		(h)	0-1
FA Cup	Third Round	Notts Co (h)	2-3

Wallington	Ramsey	Friar	MacDonald	May	O'Neill	Lynex	Lineker	Smith A.	Melrose	Smith B.	Kelly	English	Wilson	Holmes	Buchanan	Leet	Williams	Robson	Daly (L)	Peake	Jones	*Referees*	*Match No.*
1	2	3	4	5	6	7	8	9	10	11												J. Deakin	1
1	2	3	4	5	6	7*	12	9	10	11	8											R. Nixon	2
1	2*	3	4	5	6	12	8	9	10	11	7											D. Axcell	3
1	2	3	4	5	6	11	8	9	10		7											C. Thomas	4
1	2	3	4	5	6	11	8	9	10		7											D. Vickers	5
1	2	3	4	5	6	7	8	9				10	11									A. Saunders	6
1	2	3	4	5	6		8	9		11		10	7									D. Lloyd	7
1	2	3	4	5	6	7	8				9	10	11									F. Roberts	8
1	2	3	4	5	6	7	8				9	10	11									K. Salmon	9
1	2	3	4	5	6	7	8	12			9*	10	11									D. Allison	10
1	2	3	4	5	6	7	8	12			9*	10	11									N. Wilson	11
1	2	12	4	5	6	7	8	9				10*	11	3								A. Grey	12
1	2	12	4	5	6	7*	8	9				10	11	3								M. James	13
1	2	3	4	5	6	7	8				9	10	11									J. Moules	14
1	2	3	4	5	6	7	8	12			9*	10	11									K. Hackett	15
1	2	3	4	5	6	7	8	12			9	10*	11									R. Bridges	16
1	2	3*	4	5	6	7	8	10			9		11		12							R. Chadwick	17
1	2		4	5	6	7	8	9			10		11		12	3*						G. Tyson	18
1	2	3	4	5	6	12	8	10			9		11		7*							K. Cooper	19
1		3	4	5	6	7	8	9			10		11				2					N. Midgley	20
1		3	4	5	6		8	9		7	10		11				2					E. Scales	21
1	2		4	5	6	12	8	10		7	9		11				3*					T. Spencer	22
1	2		4	5	6	12	8	9		7	10*		11				3					T. Mills	23
1	2		4	5	6	7	8	9		3	10*		11					12				A. Crickmore	24
1	2		4	5	6	7*	8	9		3	10	12	11									M. Dimblebee	25
1	2		4	5	6	7	8	9		3			11						10			G. Courtney	26
1	2*		4	5	6	7	8	9		3		12	11						10			D. Scott	27
1	2		4	5	6*	7	8	9		3		12	11						10			D. Reeves	28
1	2		4	5		7	8	9		3		6	11						10*	12		A. Ward	29
1	2		4		6	7	8	9		3		5	11						10			D. Hedges	30
1	2		4		6	7	8	9		3		5	11						10*	12		J. Key	31
1	2		4	12	6	7	8*	9		3		5	11						10			N. Glover	32
1	2		4		6	7	8	9		3		5	11						10			K. Walmsley	33
1	2		4		6	7	8	9		3		5	11						10			T. Fitzharris	34
1	2		4		6	7	8	9		3		5	11						10			T. Jones	35
1	2		4	12	6*	7	8	9		3		5	11						10			T. Bune	36
1	2		4		6	7	8	9		3		5	11						10			A. Grey	37
1	2		4		6	7	8	9		3		5	11						10			H. King	38
1	2		4	12	6	7*	8	9		3		5	11						10			K. Salmon	39
1	2		4	12	6		8*	9		3		5	11						10	7		P. Willis	40
1	2		4	5	6			9		3		7			12				11	8*	10	M. Peck	41
1	2		4	12	5	6		11		3		10	9						8*		7	D. Shaw	42
42	40	18	42	30	41	34	39	35	5	26	20	25	36	2	1	1	4	0	17	2	2		
		+ 2s		+ 5s		+ 4s	+ 1s	+ 4s				+ 3s			+ 3s			+ 1s		+ 2s			

FOOTBALL LEAGUE RECORD

1894 Elected to Division 2; 1908–09 Division 1; 1909–25 Division 2; 1925–35 Division 1; 1935–37 Division 2; 1937–39 Division 1; 1946–54 Division 2; 1954–55 Division 1; 1955–57 Division 2; 1957–69 Division 1; 1969–71 Division 2; 1971–78 Division 1; 1978–80 Division 2; 1980–81 Division 1; 1981–83 Division 2; 1983– Division 1.

HONOURS

Football League: Division 1 – Runners-up 1928–29; Division 2 – Champions 1924–25, 1936–37, 1953–54, 1956–57, 1970–71, 1979–80; Runners-up 1907–08. *FA Cup:* Runners-up 1949, 1961, 1963, 1969. *Football League Cup:* Winners 1964; Runners-up 1965. **European Competitions:** *European Cup-Winners' Cup:* 1961–62.

COLOURS

Royal blue shirts with white collar and cuffs, white shorts with LCFC initials on thigh, white stockings with blue tops.
Change colours:

LEICESTER CITY

Players Names *Ht, Wt, D.o.B.*	*Birthplace* *Transfer Fee*	*Clubs*	*Appearances* *F.L.* *A & S*	 *F.L.C.* *A & S*	 *F.A.C.* *A & S*	*Goals* *F.L.*	 *F.L.C.*	 *F.A.C.*
Goalkeepers								
Mark Wallington (EU-23)	Sleaford	Walsall	11		1			
6 1, 14 2½,	£35,000	Leicester C	366	19	24			
Ian Andrews		Leicester C (A)						
Defenders								
Tommy Williams	Leicester	Leicester C (A)	180 +4	8	14	10		
5 10, 10 12, 18.12.57								
Larry May	Sutton Coldfield	Leicester C (A)	180 +7	8	12	12		3
6 0, 12 6, 26.12.58								
John O'Neill (NI)	Lanark	Leicester C	170	8	13	4		1
6 0, 13 3, 11.3.58								
David Rennie (SY)	Edinburgh	Leicester C (A)						
Midfield								
Andy Peake (EU-21)	Market Harborough	Leicester C (A)	98 +4	3 +1	8	8		
5 9½, 11 2, 1.11.61								
Bobby Smith	Dalkeith	Hibernian						
5 7, 11 8, 21.12.53	£85,000	Leicester C	97 +4	5 +1	4	20		
	—	Peterborough U (loan)	5					
Ian Wilson	Aberdeen	Elgin C						
5 7, 10 11, 27.3.58	£20,000	Leicester C	129 +6	9	9	11		1
Paul Ramsey	Londonderry	Leicester C (A)	51 +2	3	1	1		
5 10, 12 0, 3.9.62								
Kevin MacDonald	Inverness	Inverness Caley						
6 0¼, 11 11, 22.12.60	£40,000	Leicester C	82 +5	6	3	7		
Keith Robson	Hetton	Newcastle U	14	1		3	2	
6 0, 11 4, 15.11.53	£25,000	West Ham U	65 +3	7	3	13	1	1
		Cardiff C	21	1		5		
	£25,000	Norwich C	61 +4	4 +1	1	13		1
	£30,000	Leicester C	8 +1	1	1 +1		1	
	—	Carlisle U (loan)	10 +1			4		
Robert Kelly		Leicester C (A)						
Forwards								
Gary Lineker	Leicester	Leicester C (A)	108 +6	5	8	49		3
5 10, 11 11, 30.11.60								
Dave Buchanan* (EY)	Newcastle	Leicester C (A)	24 +9		4 +1	7		1
5 7¼, 11 0, 23.6.62	—	Northampton T (loan)	3 +2	1				
Steve Lynex	West Bromwich	WBA (A)						
5 9, 11 5, 23.1.58	F/T	Shamrock R						
		Birmingham C	28 +18	3	1 +3	9	1	
	£60,000	Leicester C	83 +8	6	6	24	1	
Barry Cliff	Motherwell	Leicester C (A)						
5 7, 10 6,								
Tom English (EY)	Cirencester	Coventry C (A)	62 +4	7	3	17	4	1
5 9, 11 6, 18.10.61	P/E	Leicester C	25 +3	2		3		
Bobby Jones (WY)	Coventry	Manchester C (A)						
	F/T	Leicester C	2			1		
Alan Smith	Birmingham	Alvechurch						
	£22,000	Leicester C	35 +4	1	1	13		1

Commercial Manager: Peter Hill
Club Coach: Gerry Summers
Supporters Player of the Season 1982–83: Kevin McDonald
Physiotherapist: John McVey
Club Captain 1982–83: Wallington/O'Neill
Chief Scout: Gerry Summers
Club Statistician:
Association of Football Statisticians Club Adviser to Yearbook: D. Smith.

Players released since May 1982:
Paul Culpin, F. (Nuneaton Bor); Steve Saxby, F. (Shepshed Chart); Nicky Walker, G. (Motherwell); Derek Thompson, D. (Motherwell); Norman Leet, D. (Kettering); William Gibson, D. (Kettering); Peter Welsh, D. (Hibernian); Stewart Hamill, F. (Kettering); Dick Pell, F. (Enderby T); Richard Hill, F. (New Zealand); John Harland, M. (N/K); Eddie Kelly, M. (Melton T); Paul Brown, D. (N/K); Ian Sherwood, D. (N/K); Steve Humphries, G. (N/K).

LINCOLN CITY Division 3

Back row (left to right): David Beavon, Stuart Hibberd, Steve Thompson, Stuart Naylor, Tonny Cunningham (now with Barnsley), David Felgate, Trevor Peake, Glenn Cockerill, Gordon Hobson
Middle row: John Pickering (Asst Manager), George Shipley, David Carr, Colin Murphy (Manager), Phil Turner, Derek Bell, Bert Loxley (Physio)
Front row: Paul Jones, Robert Riviere, Paul Brown, Chris Moyses, Gary Strodder.

Chairman: D. W. Houston. ***Vice-Chairman:*** H. W. Dove.

Directors: D. Overton, M. Payor, J. Reames.

Manager: Colin Murphy. ***Secretary:*** Philip M. Hough.

Assistant Manager: John Pickering.

Year Formed: 1883. ***Turned Professional:*** 1892. ***Ltd Co.:*** 1892.

Club Nickname: 'The Red Imps'

Previous Grounds: 1883, John O'Gaunt's; 1894, Sincil Bank.

Previous Managers since 1946: Bill Anderson, Bob Chapman, Ron Gray, Bert Loxley, David Herd, Graham Taylor, George Kerr, Willie Bell.

Sincil Bank, Lincoln. Telephone Lincoln 22224 and Commercial Dept 42333. ***Ground capacity:*** 16,225. ***Record attendance:*** 23,196 v Derby Co, League Cup 4th rd, 15 Nov, 1967. ***Record receipts:*** £26,158.11 v West Ham Utd, Milk Cup 3rd rd, 10 Nov, 1982. ***Pitch measurements:*** 110yd×75yd.

Directions to Ground: There is a regular bus service from Lincoln Central Station to the ground, although there are no special buses. Nearest stations are Lincoln Central and Lincoln St Marks.

Car parking: Street parking only.

Entertainments/catering facilities: Social club at the ground with light catering before and after the match.

Club shop: Sited on the ground; sells all types of souvenirs.

Handbooks/programmes: Programmes available at each game or by subscription.

Address of the Club Shop or Boutique: Red Imps Shop on ground.

Note: Full club statistical records are on pages 416–455.

LINCOLN CITY 1982–83 LEAGUE RECORD

Match No.	Date	Venue	Opponents	Result	H/T Score	Lg. Pos.	Goalscorers	Attendance
1	Aug 28	H	Wigan Ath	W 2-1	2-1	—	Shipley 2 (1 pen)	3196
2	Sept 4	A	Southend U	L 0-2	0-1	14		2836
3	7	A	Wrexham	W 1-0	0-0	—	Cunningham	2971
4	11	H	Reading	W 4-0	1-0	3	Cunningham 2 (pens), Thompson S., Bell	2790
5	18	A	Bristol R	W 2-1	1-1	2	Shipley, Turner	4177
6	25	H	Orient	W 2-0	2-0	1	Bell 2	3096
7	29	H	Sheffield U	W 3-0	1-0	—	Hobson 2, Peake	8550
8	Oct 2	A	Newport Co	L 0-1	0-0	1		3749
9	9	H	Doncaster R	W 5-1	1-0	1	Shipley 2, Hobson, Humphries (og), Cockerill	4785
10	16	A	Plymouth Arg	W 2-0	1-0	1	Bell, Hobson	2921
11	20	H	Exeter C	W 4-1	2-0	—	Bell 3 (2 pens), Hobson	3699
12	23	A	Brentford	L 0-2	0-1	1		8017
13	30	H	Bradford C	W 1-0	0-0	1	Burke	5296
14	Nov 2	A	Portsmouth	L 1-4	1-2	—	Bell (pen)	12,529
15	6	A	Chesterfield	W 3-1	1-0	1	Hobson 2, Bell	4265
16	13	H	Cardiff C	W 2-1	0-1	1	Bell, Bodin (og)	6585
17	Dec 4	H	Millwall	W 3-1	2-0	1	Bell, Neale, Cockerill	4244
18	18	H	AFC Bournemouth	W 9-0	2-0	1	Hobson 3, Brignull (og), Cockerill 2, Bell 3	3597
19	27	A	Walsall	D 1-1	1-0	1	Cockerill	5284
20	28	H	Huddersfield T	L 1-2	1-0	1	Cockerill	11,829
21	Jan 1	A	Gillingham	W 2-0	1-0	1	Bell (pen), Shipley	5535
22	3	H	Preston NE	W 3-0	2-0	1	Shipley, Bell, Turner	5891
23	15	A	Wigan Ath	L 1-2	1-2	1	Burke	4731
24	22	H	Bristol R	W 2-1	1-1	1	Bell, Hobson	5342
25	29	A	Reading	D 1-1	0-1	1	Thompson S.	2453
26	Feb 5	A	Orient	D 1-1	1-1	2	Neale	2584
27	16	H	Portsmouth	L 0-3	0-1	—		6311
28	19	A	Doncaster R	D 2-2	1-1	3	Hobson, Bell (pen)	4667
29	23	H	Southend U	L 0-1	0-0	–		4000
30	26	H	Plymouth Arg	L 1-2	1-0	3	Bell (pen)	3195
31	Mar 2	A	Exeter C	L 1-3	0-1	3	Bell	2505
32	5	H	Brentford	W 2-1	1-1	—	Cockerill, Bell	3698
33	12	A	Bradford C	D 1-1	0-0	5	Burke	5026
34	16	A	Oxford U	L 0-1	0-0	—		5147
35	19	H	Chesterfield	W 2-0	2-0	4	Shipley 2	4454
36	23	H	Newport Co	L 1-4	0-3	—	Bell	4742
37	26	A	Cardiff C	L 0-1	0-0	5		8021
38	Apr 2	A	Huddersfield T	D 1-1	1-0	6	Hobson	13,028
39	4	H	Walsall	W 2-1	2-0	—	Moss, Bell (pen)	4671
40	9	A	Millwall	L 1-2	1-1	6	Hobson	3760
41	16	H	Wrexham	W 2-0	0-0	6	Turner, Moss	3505
42	23	A	AFC Bournemouth	L 0-1	0-1	6		5018
43	30	H	Oxford U	D 1-1	1-0	7	Vinter (og)	2812
44	May 2	A	Preston NE	L 0-1	0-0	7		6537
45	7	A	Sheffield U	W 1-0	1-0	7	Cockerill	11,842
46	14	H	Gillingham	W 3-1	1-1	6	Shipley, Burke 2	2241

Final League Position: 6

GOALSCORERS

League (77): Bell 23 (7 pens), Hobson 14, Shipley 10 (1 pen), Cockerill 8, Burke 5, Cunningham 3 (2 pens), Turner 3, Moss 2, Neale 2, Thompson S. 2, Peake 1, own goals 4.
Milk Cup (9): Bell 3 (1 pen), Cunningham 2, Hobson 2 (1 pen), Shipley 2.
FA Cup (0).
Football League Trophy (14): Cockerill 4, Bell 3 (1 pen), Burke 2, Cunningham 2, Peake 1, Thompson S. 1, Turner 1.

Milk Cup	First Round	York C (a)	1-2
		(h)	3-1
	Second Round	Leicester C (h)	2-0
		(a)	1-0
	Third Round	West Ham U (h)	1-1
		(a)	1-2

FA Cup	First Round	Hartlepool U (a)	0-3
Football League Trophy		Scunthorpe U (a)	1-1
		Grimsby T (h)	2-1
		Sheffield U (h)	3-1
	Quarter-final	Norwich C (h)	3-1
	Semi-final	Chester (a)	3-1
	Final	Millwall (h)	2-3

Felgate	Carr	Heath (L)	Cockerill	Peake	Strodder	Shipley	Turner	Hobson	Cunningham	Hibberd	Bell	Thompson S.	Neale	Beavon	Naylor	Burke	Gilligan (L)	Simmonite	White (L)	Kelly	Brazier	Creane	Thompson C. (L)	Moss	Referees	Match No.
1	2	3	4	5	6	7	8	9*	10	11	12														M. Robinson	1
1	2	3	4	5		11	8	9	10		12	6	7*												D. Reeves	2
1	2	3	4	5		11	8	9	10			6	7												D. Allison	3
1	2	3	4	5*		11	8	9	10	7	12	6													T. Jones	4
1	2		4	5		11	8	9	10	7		6	3												J. Moules	5
1	2	12	4	5		11	8	9		7	10	6	3*												A. Robinson	6
1	2	10	4	5		11	8	9		7		6	3												G. Tyson	7
1	2	10	4	5		11	8			7*		6	3	12	9										A. Hamil	8
1	2		4	5		11	8	9			10	6	3			7*	12								I. Borrett	9
1	2		4	5		11	8	9			10	6	3			7									D. Hedges	10
1	2		4	5		11	8	9			10	6	3			7									D. Scott	11
1	2		4	5		11	8	9			10	6	3			7*	12								Alan Robinson	12
1	2		4	5		11	8*	9			10	6	3			7	12								D. Brazier	13
1	2		4	5		11	8	9			10	6	3			7									B. Stevens	14
1	2		4	5		11	8	9			10	6	3			7									C. Newsome	15
1	2		4	5		11	8	9			10	6	3			7									D. Richardson	16
1	2		4	5			8	9		7	10	6	3					11							A. Seville	17
1	2		4	5		11	8	9			10	6*	3			7		12							N. Ashley	18
1	2		4	5		11	8	9			10	6	3			7									R. Banks	19
1	2		4	5		11	8	9			10	6	3			7									G. Napthine	20
1	12		4*	5		11	8	9			10	6	3			7		2							K. Salmon	21
1	12		4	5		11	8	9			10	6*	3			7		2							D. Lloyd	22
1			4	5		11	8	9		10		6	3			7		2							D. Hutchinson	23
1	12		4	5		11	8	9			10*	6	3			7		2							J. Hunting	25
1			4	5		11	8	9				6	3			7		2	10						A. Crickmore	25
1			4	5		11	8	9				6	3			7		2	10						Alan Robinson	26
1	6		4	5		11	8	9			10		3			7*		2	12						J. Key	27
1	6		4	5		11	8	9			10		3			7		2							K. Barratt	28
1	8		4	5		11		9*			10	6	3			7		2		12					H. Taylor	29
1			4	5		11	8	9			10	6	3			7*		2		12					D. Vickers	30
1	6		4	5		11	8			9	10		3			7		2							J. Deakin	31
1	6		4	5	12	11	8*			9	10		3			7		2							T. Holbrook	32
1			4*	5	8	11		9		12	10		3			7		2			6				R. Guy	33
1	3			5	8	11		9			10	6				7					2	4			C. Downey	34
1	2			5	12	11	8	9*			10	6	3			7							4		A. Grey	35
1				5		11	8				10	6	3			7		2					4	9	B. Hill	36
1				5		11	8	7			10	6	3					2					4	9	A. Robinson	37
1			4	5		11	8	9*			10	7	3					2			6			12	N. Wilson	38
1			4	5		11	8			12	10*		3			7		2			6			9	T. Fitzharris	39
1			4	5		11	7	9					3			10		2			6			8	D. Letts	40
1				5		11*	7	9			10		3			4		2			6		12	8	E. Scales	41
1				5	4	11		9				6	3			10					2		7	8	A. Gunn	42
1	2			5	12	11		10		4	9	6				7*		3						8	T. Jones	43
1				5	6	11		8		12	10*		3			7		2					4	9	D. Owen	44
1			4	5		11	7	9				6				10		3			2			8	M. Heath	45
1			4	5		11	7	9				6				10		3			2			8	J. Lovatt	46
46	28	6	38	46	5	45	40	41	5	11	32	36	40	0	1	35	0	24	2	0	9	1	5	10		
	+ 3s	+ 1s			+ 3s					+ 3s	+ 3s			+ 1s			+ 3s	+ 1s	+ 1s	+ 2s			+ 1s	+ 1s		

FOOTBALL LEAGUE RECORD

1892 Original Member of Division 2. Remained in Division 2 until 1920 when they failed re-election but also missed seasons 1908–09 and 1911–12, when not re-elected. 1921–32 Division 3(N); 1932–34 Division 2; 1934–48 Division 3(N); 1948–49 Division 2; 1949–52 Division 3(N); 1952–61 Division 2; 1961–62 Division 3; 1962–76 Division 4; 1976–79 Division 3; 1979–81 Division 4; 1981– Division 3.

HONOURS

Football League: Division 2 best season: 5th, 1901–02; Division 3(N) – Champions 1931–32, 1947–48, 1951–52; Runners-up 1927–28, 1930–31, 1936–37; Division 4 – Champions 1975–76; Runners-up 1980–81. *FA Cup:* best season: 1st rd of Second Series (5th rd equivalent), 1886–87, 2nd rd (5th rd equivalent), 1889–90, 1901–02. *Football League Cup:* best season: 4th rd, 1967–68.

LINCOLN CITY

Players Names / *Ht, Wt, D.o.B.*	*Birthplace* / *Transfer Fee*	*Clubs*	*Appearances* F.L. A & S	*Appearances* F.L.C. A & S	*Appearances* F.A.C. A & S	*Goals* F.L.	*Goals* F.L.C.	*Goals* F.A.C.
Goalkeepers								
David Felgate (WS)	Blaenau Festiniog	Bolton W						
6 1, 13 3, 4.3.60	—	Rochdale (Loan)	47					
	—	Crewe Alex (Loan)	14					
	£25,000	Lincoln C	131	10	5			
Stuart Naylor (EY)	Leeds	Yorkshire Amats						
6 2, 11 13, 6.12.62	—	Lincoln C	4	2	1			
	—	Peterborough U	8					
Defenders								
Gordon Simmonite (ESP)	Sheffield	Sheffield W	1					
5 10, 11 4, 25.4.57	F/T	Boston U						
	£15,000	Blackpool	63	6	4	1		
	£5000	Lincoln C	24+1					
Phil Neale	Scunthorpe	Scunthorpe U (AM)						
5 10, 11 5, 5.6.54	—	Lincoln C	264+7	8+1	11+2	21		
David Carr	Aylesham	Luton T (A)	39+4	+1	4		1	
5 11, 11 0, 31.1.57	£20,500	Lincoln C	165+2	18	7	4	1	
Trevor Peake (ESP)	Nuneaton	Nuneaton Bor						
6 0, 12 9, 10.2.57	£15,000	Lincoln C	171	16	7	7		2
Steve Thompson	Sheffield	Boston U						
5 9, 12 0, 28.7.55	£15,000	Lincoln C	96+1	12	6	6		1
Colin Brazier*	Birmingham	Alvechurch						
6 1½, 10 13, 6.6.57		Wolverhampton W	69+9	1+3	1	2		
		Jacksonville T M						
		Birmingham C	10+1	4		1		
	F/T	Lincoln C	9					
Midfield								
George Shipley	Newcastle	Southampton (A)	2+1					
5 7, 10 3, 7.3.59	—	Reading (Loan)	11+1			1		
	£45,000	Lincoln C	157	16	6	30	7	
Phil Turner	Sheffield	Lincoln C (A)	119+2	12	6	9		1
5 8, 10 7, 12.2.62								
Stuart Hibberd*	Sheffield	Lincoln C (A)	36+6	2		3		
6 0, 12 0, 11.10.61								
Glen Cockerill	Grimsby	Louth U						
6 0, 11 13, 25.8.59		Lincoln C	65+6	2	2	10		
	£110,000	Swindon T	23+3	3		1		
	£40,000	Lincoln C	81+1	13	4	19	1	
Gary Strodder		Lincoln C (A)	5+3					
Forwards								
Gordon Hobson	Sheffield	Lincoln C	189+9	15	5+1	60	3	
5 8, 10 5, 27.11.57								
Derek Bell	Wyberton	Derby Co (A)						
5 8, 10 3, 30.10.56	F/T	Halifax T	104+8	4+3	4	21	2	
	—	Sheffield W (Loan)	5			1		
		Barnsley	45+1	4	3	20	1	1
	£33,000	Lincoln C	69+14	10+2	2+1	33	4	
Marshall Burke (SY)	Glasgow	Burnley (A)	22+2	1+1	2	5		
5 7, 9 1, 26.3.59	F/T	Leeds U						
	F/T	Blackburn R	34+3	3	1	7		1
	£2500	Lincoln C	35	3	1	5		
Ernie Moss*	Chesterfield	Chesterfield	271	14+1	14	94	6	8
6 1½, 13 2, 19.10.49	£16,000	Peterborough U	34+1	5	2	9	2	1
	£20,000	Mansfield T	56+1	2		21		
	£15,000	Chesterfield	105+2	9	5	33	6	
	£16,000	Port Vale	74	4	5	23	3	2
		Lincoln C	10+1			2		

Commercial Manager: Philip Mark Hough. (Tel. 22224, Commercial Dept. 42333).
Assistant Manager: John Pickering
Supporters Player of the Season 1982–83: Glenn Cockerill
Physiotherapist: Bert Loxley
Club Captain 1982–83: Trevor Peake
Chief Scout:
Club Statistician:
Association of Football Statisticians Club Adviser to Yearbook: J. D. Holland.

Players released since May 1982:
John Ward, F., (retired); David Hughes, M., (N/K); Nolan Keeley, D., (N/K); Craig Ramsay, F., (N/K); Trevor Thompson, D., (N/K); Gerry Creane, D., (N/K); David Rodgers, D., (N/K).

COLOURS Red shirts with white sleeves, red pinstripe on sleeves and white pinstripe on main body of shirt, black collar and cuffs, white shorts and stockings. **Change colours:** Royal blue shirts with red thin stripe, black shorts, royal blue stockings.

LIVERPOOL Division 1

Back row (left to right):
A. Kennedy
P. Neal
A. Hansen
B. Grobbelaar
M. Lawrenson
I Rush
Middle row: J. Fagan (Asst to Manager)
C. Johnston
R. Whelan
S. Nicol
R. Moran (Coach)
R. Evans (Reserve Coach)
Front row:
S. Lee
P. Thompson
G. Souness
R. Paisley (Manager)
K. Dalglish
T. McDermott.

Chairman: J. W. Smith CBE, DL, JP

Directors: C. J. Hill, Coun. S. J. Moss JP, S. C. Reakes JP, H. Cartwright, J. T. Cross, W. D. Corkish FCA, R. Paisley OBE, M.SC (HON).

Team Manager: Joe Fagan.

Chief Executive/General Secretary: Peter Robinson.

Coach to Reserves: Chris Lawler.

Year Formed: 1892. ***Turned Professional:*** 1892. ***Ltd Co.:*** 1892.

Club Nickname: 'Reds' or 'Pool'.

Previous Managers since 1946: George Kay, Don Welsh, Phil Taylor, Bill Shankly, Bob Paisley (5).

Anfield Road, Liverpool 4. Telephone 051-263 2361. ***Telegraphic address:*** 'Goalkeeper Liverpool'. ***Ground capacity:*** 45,000. ***Record attendance:*** 61,905 v Wolverhampton W, FA Cup 4th rd, 2 Feb, 1952. ***Record receipts:*** £154,000 Wales v Scotland, World Cup qualifying tie, 12 Oct, 1977. ***Pitch measurements:*** 110yd×75yd.

Directions to Ground: Buses 17d from Pier Head and 26, 27 from Castle Street. Nearest stations, Bankhall and Kirkdale.

Match tickets: Postal applications nineteen days before the match.

Car parking: Limited street parking around the ground. Large privately owned car park in Priory Road within five minutes walk of the ground.

Entertainments/catering facilities: Licensed refreshment bars in all parts of the ground.

Club shop: Main shop run by the Development Association open Monday–Saturday. Small kiosks in the ground open on match days only.

Handbooks/programmes: No handbook. Programmes available on subscription from the secretary.

Address of Supporters Club: 212 Lower Breck Road.

Address of Club Shop or Boutique: Same as ground.

Note: Full club statistical records are on pages 416–455.

LIVERPOOL 1982–83 LEAGUE RECORD

Match No.	Date	Venue	Opponents	Result	H/T Score	Lg. Pos.	Goalscorers	Attendance
1	Aug 28	H	WBA	W 2-0	0-0	—	Lee, Neal (pen)	35,652
2	31	A	Birmingham C	D 0-0	0-0	—		20,176
3	Sept 4	A	Arsenal	W 2-0	1-0	3	Hodgson, Neal	36,429
4	7	H	Nottingham F	W 4-3	2-3	—	Hodgson 2, Souness, Rush	27,145
5	11	H	Luton T	D 3-3	2-1	4	Souness, Rush, Johnston	33,694
6	18	A	Swansea	W 3-0	2-0	2	Rush 2, Johnston	20,322
7	25	H	Southampton	W 5-0	3-0	1	Whelan 2, Souness, Lawrenson 2	32,996
8	Oct 2	A	Ipswich T	L 0-1	0-0	1		24,342
9	9	A	West Ham U	L 1-3	0-1	5	Souness	32,500
10	16	H	Manchester U	D 0-0	0-0	3		40,853
11	23	A	Stoke C	D 1-1	1-1	4	Lawrenson	29,411
12	30	H	Brighton & HA	W 3-1	3-1	1	Lawrenson, Dalglish 2	27,929
13	Nov 6	A	Everton	W 5-0	1-0	1	Rush 4, Lawrenson	52,741
14	13	H	Coventry C	W 4-0	2-0	1	Dalglish, Rush 3	27,870
15	20	A	Notts Co	W 2-1	0-1	1	Johnston, Dalglish	16,914
16	27	H	Tottenham H	W 3-0	1-0	1	Neal (pen), Dalglish 2	40,691
17	Dec 4	A	Norwich C	L 0-1	0-0	1		22,909
18	11	H	Watford	W 3-1	3-0	1	Rush, Neal 2 (both pens)	36,690
19	18	A	Aston Villa	W 4-2	3-2	1	Hodgson, Dalglish, Kennedy, Rush	34,568
20	27	H	Manchester C	W 5-2	3-1	1	Dalglish 3, Neal, Rush	44,664
21	28	A	Sunderland	D 0-0	0-0	1		35,041
22	Jan 1	H	Notts Co	W 5-1	2-1	1	Rush 3, Dalglish 2	33,644
23	3	H	Arsenal	W 3-1	1-0	1	Rush, Souness, Dalglish	37,713
24	15	A	WBA	W 1-0	0-0	1	Rush	24,560
25	22	H	Birmingham C	W 1-0	1-0	1	Neal	30,986
26	Feb 5	A	Luton T	W 3-1	2-1	1	Rush, Kennedy, Souness	18,434
27	12	H	Ipswich T	W 1-0	0-0	1	Dalglish	34,976
28	26	A	Manchester U	D 1-1	1-1	1	Dalglish	57,397
29	Mar 5	H	Stoke C	W 5-1	2-0	1	Dalglish 2, Neal, Johnston, Souness	30,020
30	12	H	West Ham U	W 3-0	0-0	1	Pike (og), Lee, Rush	28,511
31	19	H	Everton	D 0-0	0-0	1		44,737
32	22	A	Brighton & HA	D 2-2	0-2	1	Rush 2	25,030
33	Apr 2	H	Sunderland	W 1-0	0-0	1	Souness	35,821
34	4	A	Manchester C	W 4-0	2-0	1	Souness, Fairclough 2, Kennedy	35,647
35	9	H	Swansea C	W 3-0	0-0	1	Rush, Lee, Fairclough	30,010
36	12	A	Coventry C	D 0-0	0-0	1		14,821
37	16	A	Southampton	L 2-3	2-3	1	Dalglish, Johnston	25,578
38	23	H	Norwich C	L 0-2	0-0	1		37,022
39	30	A	Tottenham H	L 0-2	0-0	1		44,907
40	May 2	A	Nottingham F	L 0-1	0-0	1		25,107
41	7	H	Aston Villa	D 1-1	0-1	1	Johnston	39,939
42	14	A	Watford	L 1-2	0-1	1	Johnston	27,148

Final League Position: 1

GOALSCORERS

League (87): Rush 24, Dalglish 18, Souness 9, Neal 8 (4 pens), Johnston 7, Lawrenson 5, Hodgson 4, Fairclough 3, Kennedy 3, Lee 3, Whelan 2, own goal 1.
Milk Cup (14): Hodgson 2, Lawrenson 2, Rush 2, Souness 2, Whelan 2, Fairclough 1, Johnston 1, Kennedy 1, Neal 1 (pen).
FA Cup (5): Rush 2, Dalglish 1, Hodgson 1, Johnston 1.
European Cup (13): Whelan 3, Hodgson 2, Kennedy 2, Neal 2 (1 pen), Rush 2, Dalglish 1, Johnston 1.

Milk Cup	Second Round	Ipswich T (a)	2-1
		(h)	2-0
	Third Round	Rotherham U (h)	1-0
	Fourth Round	Norwich C (h)	2-0
	Fifth Round	West Ham U (h)	2-1
	Semi-final	Burnley (h)	3-0
		(a)	0-1
	Final (at Wembley)	Manchester U	2-1 (aet)
FA Cup	Third Round	Blackburn R (a)	2-1
	Fourth Round	Stoke C (h)	2-0
	Fifth Round	Brighton & HA (h)	1-2
European Cup	First Round	Dundalk (a)	4-1
		(h)	1-0
	Second Round	JK Helsinki (a)	0-1
		(h)	5-0
	Quarter-final	Widzew Lodz (a)	0-2
		(h)	3-2

Grobbelaar	Neal	Kennedy	Thompson	Lawrenson	Whelan	Dalglish	Lee	Rush	Hodgson	Souness	Johnston	Nicol	McDermott	Hansen	Fairclough	*Referees*	*Match No.*
1	2	3	4	5*	6	7	8	9	10	11	12					K. Redfern	1
1	2	3	4		6	7	8	9	10	11		5				D. Allison	2
1	2	3	4	5	6	7	8	9	10	11						J. Martin	3
1	2	3	4	5	6	7	8	9	10	11						M. Peck	4
1	2	3	4	5	6	7*	8	9	10	11	12					M. Heath	5
1	2	3	4	5		7	8	9	10*	11	6		12			A. Hamil	6
1	2	3	4	6	5	7	8	9*		11	10		12			T. Mills	7
1	2	3	4	10	5	7	8*			11	9			6	12	R. Lewis	8
1	2	3*	4	9	5	7	8	10		11	12			6		Alan Robinson	9
1	2	5	3	8	9	10	6	11		7				4		K. Walmsley	10
1	2	3	4	10	5	7	8	9		11				6		H. Taylor	11
1	2	3	4	10	5	7	8	9		11				6		M. Robinson	12
1	2	3	4	10		7*	8	9	12	11	5			6		D. Civil	13
1	2	3	4	10		7	8	9		11	5			6		R. Tyldesley	14
1	2	3	4	10		7	8	9		11	5			6		C. Thomas	15
1	2	3	4	10		7	8	9		11	5			6		G. Courtney	16
1	2	3	4	10		7	8	9		11	5			6		J. Hunting	17
1	2	3	4*		5	7	8	9		11	10			6	12	C. Newsome	18
1	2	3		4	5	7	8	9	10	11				6		M. Scott	19
1	2	3		4	5*	7	8	9	10	11				6	12	P. Willis	20
1	2	3		4		7	8	9	10	11		5		6		D. Hutchinson	21
1	2	3		4		7	8	9	10	11	5			6		A. Seville	22
1	2	3		4		7	8	9	10	11	5			6		A. Saunders	23
1	2	3		4		7	8	9	10	11	5			6		T. Bune	24
1	2	3		4	5	7	8		10	11	9			6		J. Hough	25
1	2	3		4	12	7	8	9	10	11	5*			6		B. Hill	26
1	2	3		4	12	7	8	9	10	11	5*			6		G. Tyson	27
1	2	3	4	6	5	7	8	9		11	10					K. Redfern	28
1	2	3		4	5	7	8	9		11	10			6		J. Key	29
1	2	3		4	5	7	8	9		11	10			6		K. Hackett	30
1	2	3		4	5	7	8	9	12	11*	10			6		N. Midgley	31
1	2	3	11*	4	5	7	8	9			10			6	12	K. Salmon	32
1	2	3		4	5	7	8			11	10			6	9	K. Barratt	33
1	2	3		4	5	7	8			11	10			6	9	K. Baker	34
1	2	3		4	5	7	8	9		11	10*			6	12	J. Lovatt	35
1	2	3		4	5	7	8	9		11	10			6		T. Ward	36
1	2	3		4	5	7	8		12	11	10			6	9*	B. Stevens	37
1	2	3		4	5	7	8		9	11	10			6		D. Lloyd	38
1	2	3	5	4		7		9	8	11	10			6		M. Roberts	39
1	2	3	5	4		7		9*	8	11	10	12		6		T. Mills	40
1	2	3	5	4		7	8		9	11	10			6		C. Seel	41
1	2	3	5	4*		7	8		9	11	10	12		6		A. Grey	42
42	42	42	24	40	26	42	40	34	20	41	30	2	0	34	3		
					+ 2s				+ 3s		+ 3s	+ 2s	+ 2s		+ 5s		

FOOTBALL LEAGUE RECORD

1893 Elected to Division 2; 1894–95 Division 1; 1895–96 Division 2; 1896–1904 Division 1; 1904–05 Division 2; 1905–54 Division 1; 1954–62 Division 2; 1962– Division 1.

HONOURS

Football League: Division 1 – Champions 1900–01, 1905–06, 1921–22, 1922–23, 1946–47, 1963–64, 1965–66, 1972–73, 1975–76, 1976–77, 1978–79, 1979–80, 1981–82, 1982–83 (Liverpool have a record number of 14 League Championship wins); Runners-up 1898–99, 1909–10, 1968–69, 1973–74, 1974–75, 1977–78; Division 2 – Champions 1893–94, 1895–96, 1904–05, 1961–62; *FA Cup:* Winners 1965, 1974; Runners-up 1914, 1950, 1971, 1977; *Football League Cup:* Winners 1981, 1982, 1983 (Milk Cup); Runners-up 1977–78. **European Competitions:** *European Cup:* 1964–65, 1966–67, 1973–74, 1976–77 (winners), 1977–78 (winners), 1978–79, 1979–80, 1980–81 (winners), 1981–82, 1982–83; *European Cup-Winners' Cup:* 1965–66 (runners-up), 1971–72, 1974–75; *European Fairs Cup:* 1967–68, 1968–69, 1969–70, 1970–71; *UEFA Cup:* 1972–73 (winners), 1975–76 (winners); *Super Cup:* 1977 (winners), 1978; *World Club Championship:* 1981 (runners-up).

COLOURS

All red with white trim. **Change colours:** All yellow with red trim.

LIVERPOOL

Players Names Ht. Wt. D.o.B.	Birthplace Transfer Fee	Clubs	Appearances F.L. A & S	 F.L.C. A & S	 F.A.C. A & S	Goals F.L.	 F.L.C.	 F.A.C.
Goalkeepers								
Bruce Grobbelaar	South Africa	Vancouver W						
6 1, 12 0, 6.10.57	—	Crewe Alex ( )	24			1		
	—	Vancouver W						
	£250,000	Liverpool	84	18	6			
Bob Wardle	Halifax	Bristol C (A)						
5 11, 11 2, 5.3.55	F T	Shrewsbury T	131	4	16			
		Liverpool						
Billy Stewart		Liverpool (A)						
5 11, 11 7,								
Defenders								
Phil Neal (E)	Irchester	Northampton T (A)	182+4	9	8+2	29	1	1
5 11, 12 2, 20.2.51	£65,000	Liverpool	359	49	39	35	3	2
Phil Thompson (E)	Liverpool	Liverpool (A)	337+3	42+1	36	7	1	
6 0, 11 8, 21.1.54								
Alan Hansen (S)	Alloa	Partick Thistle						
6 1, 13 0, 13.6.55	£100,000	Liverpool	195	32	20+1	6	1	2
Alan Harper	Liverpool	Liverpool (A)						
5 8, 9 7, 1.11.60								
Alan Kennedy (EB)	Sunderland	Newcastle U (A)	155+3	16	20+2	9		
5 9, 10 7, 31.8.54	£300,000	Liverpool	167+2	29	14	12	2	
Mark Lawrenson (EI)	Preston	Preston NE	73	2	5	2		1
6 0, 11 7, 2.6.57	£100,000	Brighton	152	15	7	5	1	1
	£900,000	Liverpool	77+2	18	6	7	2	1
Steve Nicol (SU-21)	Irvine	Ayr U						
5 10, 11 0,	£300,000	Liverpool	2+2					
Chris Seagraves		Liverpool (A)						
5 9, 11 0,								
John McGregor		Queens Park						
5 11, 12 0,		Liverpool						
Midfield								
Bob Savage	Liverpool	Liverpool (A)						
5 7, 11 1, 8.1.60	—	Wrexham (loan)	27		2	10		1
Howard Gayle	Liverpool	Liverpool	3+1			1		
5 10½, 10 9, 18.5.58	—	Fulham (loan)	14					
	—	Newcastle U (loan)	8			2		
	—	Birmingham C (loan)	13			1		
Graeme Souness (S)	Edinburgh	Totthenham H (A)						
5 11, 12 13, 6.5.53	£30,000	Middlesbrough	174+2	15	13	22		1
	£352,000	Liverpool	209+1	33	22	31	4	2
Ron Whelan (EI)	Dublin	Home Farm						
5 9, 10 13, 25.9.61		Liverpool	58+3	11+3	4	13	5	
Craig Johnston (EU-21)	Johannesburg, SA	Middlesbrough (A)	61+3	4+2	5+2	16		
5 9, 11 2, 8.12.60	£575,000	Liverpool	43+5	6+2	2+2	13	2	1
Sammy Lee (E)	Liverpool	Liverpool (A)	119+6	21	11	11	2	
5 7, 10 1, 7.2.59								
Darren McLean		Inverness Thistle						
5 10, 10 7,	£15,000	Liverpool						
Forwards								
Dave Fairclough* (EU-21)	Liverpool	Liverpool (A)	64+39	7+13	13+2	34	10	4
5 9, 11 0, 5.1.57								
Kenny Dalglish (S)	Glasgow	Celtic						
5 8, 11 13, 4.3.51	£440,000	Liverpool	244	42	23	96	22	12
Ian Rush (W)	St Asaph	Chester (A)	33+1		5	14		3
6 0½, 12 6, 25.10.61	£300,000	Liverpool	73	19	6	41	10	5
Steve Foley	Liverpool	Liverpool (A)						
5 7, 10 12, 4.10.62								
Dave Hodgson (EU-21)	Gateshead	Middlesbrough	116+9	6	9	16		4
5 10, 11 12, 1.11.60	£450,000	Liverpool	20+3	4+1	3	4	2	1
James Beglin		Shamrock Rov						
5.11, 11.0,		Liverpool						
Paul Jewell		Liverpool (A)						
5.8, 10.8,								
David West		Dorchester T.						
5.10, 11.0,	£20,000	Liverpool						

Coaching Staff: Moran, Bennett, Evans, Saunders *Club Captain 1982–83:* Graeme Souness
Association of Football Statisticians Club Adviser to Yearbook: B. Pead.

Players (non-appearance) granted free transfer: Tony Kelly; Ron Kilshaw; Peter King.
Players released since May 1982:

LUTON TOWN Division 1

Back row (left to right): Rob Johnson, Wayne Turner, Stacey North, Michael Small, Clive Goodyear, Frank Bunn, Billy Kellock, Paul Walsh
Middle row: John Moore, Richard Money, Mike Saxby, Andy Beasley, Jake Findlay, Alan Judge, Mark Aizlewood (now Charlton), Lil Fuccillo, Trevor Hartley
Front row: David Coates, Ricky Hill, Mal Donaghy, Kirk Stephens, Brian Horton, David Pleat (Manager), David Moss, Brian Stein, Raddy Antic, John Sheridan.

President: Tom Hodgson. ***Chairman:*** D. Mortimer.

Directors: R. J. Smith, E. S. Pearson LLM, BSC, ***R. L. Banks, D. J. Evans.***

General Secretary: G. H. Mackrell FCCA.

Club Secretary: J. S. Wilkinson. ***Executive Director:*** J. R. Smith.

Team Manager: David Pleat.

Year Formed: 1885. ***Turned Professional:*** 1890. ***Ltd Co.:*** 1897.

Club Nickname: 'The Hatters'.

Previous Grounds: 1885, Excelsior, Dallow Lane; 1897, Dunstable Road; 1905, Kenilworth Road.

Previous Managers since 1946: George Martin, Dally Duncan, Syd Owen, Sam Bartram, Bill Harvey, Allan Brown, Alec Stock, Harry Haslam (8).

70–72 Kenilworth Rd, Luton. Telephone Luton (0582) 411622. 24-hour information service: 0582-33010. ***Ticket Office:*** 0582-30748. ***Travel Club:*** 0582-412418. ***Telegraphic address:*** 'Football Luton'. ***Ground capacity: 22,601 (17,000 covered). Record attendance:*** 30,069 v Blackpool, FA Cup 6th rd replay, 4 March, 1959. ***Record receipts:*** £55,906 v Manchester U, FA Cup 4th rd, 29 Jan, 1983. ***Pitch measurements:*** 112yd×72yd.

Directions to Ground: Nearest railway station, Luton (fifteen minutes walk). There is also a frequent bus service to and from the town centre to the ground, but the ground is central.

Match tickets: Seats can be booked two weeks before the game.

Car parking: Only street parking in vicinity of ground.

Entertainments/catering facilities: Licensed bars and refreshment bars on ground.

Club shop: Sells all types of souvenirs.

Programmes: Programmes can be obtained from club shop.

Address of Supporters Club: Bobbers Club, Beech Hill Path, Luton.

Note: Full club statistical records are on pages 416–455.

LUTON TOWN 1982–83 LEAGUE RECORD

Match No.	Date	Venue	Opponents	Result	H/T Score	Lg. Pos.	Goalscorers	Attendance
1	Aug 28	A	Tottenham H	D 2-2	1-2	—	Lacy (og), Stein	39,180
2	31	H	West Ham U	L 0-2	0-0	—		13,403
3	Sept 4	H	Notts Co	W 5-3	2-2	11	Walsh 3, Hill, Moss	9071
4	8	A	Aston Villa	L 1-4	0-3	—	Moss (pen)	18,823
5	11	A	Liverpool	D 3-3	1-2	18	Stein 2, Moss	33,694
6	18	H	Brighton & HA	W 5-0	1-0	11	Stein 3, Turner, Moss	11,342
7	25	A	Stoke C	D 4-4	2-2	12	Walsh 2, Stein, Donaghy	18,475
8	Oct 2	H	Manchester U	D 1-1	0-1	12	Hill	17,009
9	9	A	Birmingham C	W 3-2	0-0	8	Stein, Walsh, Moss	13,772
10	16	H	Ipswich T	D 1-1	0-1	11	Stein (pen)	13,378
11	23	A	WBA	L 0-1	0-1	13		16,345
12	30	H	Nottingham F	L 0-2	0-1	16		12,158
13	Nov 6	H	Arsenal	D 2-2	0-0	17	Moss, Walsh	16,597
14	13	A	Sunderland	D 1-1	0-0	18	Moss	14,238
15	20	A	Coventry C	L 2-4	0-0	18	Horton, Stein	9644
16	27	H	Southampton	D 3-3	0-2	18	Hill, Stein, Goodyear	11,196
17	Dec 4	A	Swansea C	L 0-2	0-0	19		9556
18	11	H	Manchester C	W 3-1	0-0	19	Walsh, Stein 2	11,013
19	18	A	Everton	L 0-5	0-2	19		14,982
20	27	H	Watford	W 1-0	1-0	17	Goodyear	21,145
21	28	A	Norwich C	L 0-1	0-1	17		21,367
22	Jan 1	H	Coventry C	L 1-2	0-2	18	Donaghy	13,072
23	4	A	West Ham U	W 3-2	1-1	17	Walsh 3	21,435
24	15	H	Tottenham H	D 1-1	1-0	17	O'Reilly (og)	21,231
25	22	A	Brighton & HA	W 4-2	2-0	16	Hill 2, Stevens (og), Case (og)	11,705
26	Feb 5	H	Liverpool	L 1-3	1-2	17	Stein	18,434
27	26	A	Ipswich T	L 0-3	0-1	18		18,615
28	Mar 5	H	WBA	D 0-0	0-0	18		10,852
29	12	A	Nottingham F	W 1-0	1-0	19	Hill	14,387
30	19	A	Arsenal	L 1-4	0-3	18	Moss	23,987
31	26	H	Sunderland	L 1-3	1-1	19	Horton (pen)	11,221
32	Apr 2	H	Norwich C	L 0-1	0-1	21		11,211
33	4	A	Watford	L 2-5	2-2	—	Aylott, Horton	20,120
34	9	H	Aston Villa	W 2-1	1-1	19	Aylott, Moss	10,924
35	12	H	Birmingham C	W 3-1	3-0	—	Hill 2, Horton (pen)	12,868
36	16	A	Notts Co	D 1-1	0-0	19	Donaghy	8932
37	23	H	Swansea C	W 3-1	0-0	18	Walsh 3	11,561
38	30	A	Southampton	D 2-2	2-2	17	Elliott, Antic	18,237
39	May 2	H	Stoke C	D 0-0	0-0	16		11,877
40	7	H	Everton	L 1-5	1-2	21	Hill	12,447
41	9	A	Manchester U	L 0-3	0-2	—		34,213
42	14	A	Manchester C	W 1-0	0-0	18	Antic	42,843

Final League Position: 18

GOALSCORERS

League (65): Stein 14 (1 pen), Walsh 14, Hill 9, Moss 9 (1 pen), Horton 4 (2 pens), Donaghy 3, Antic 2, Aylott 2, Goodyear 2, Elliott, 1, Turner 1, own goals 4.
Milk Cup (7): Fuccillo 2, Kellock 2, Bunn 1, Moss 1, Stein 1 (pen).
FA Cup (3): Hill 1, Horton 1 (pen), Walsh 1.

Milk Cup	Second Round	Charlton Ath (h)	3-0
		(a)	0-2
	Third Round	Blackpool (h)	4-2
	Fourth Round	Tottenham H (a)	0-1
FA Cup	Third Round	Peterborough U (h)	3-0
	Fourth Round	Manchester U (h)	0-2

Findlay	Stephens	Money	Horton	Goodyear	Donaghy	Hill	Stein	Walsh	Antic	Moss	Small	Turner	Kellock	Judge	Fuccillo	Bunn	Geddis (L)	Thomas	Watts	White (L)	Elliott	Godden (L)	Aylott	Daniel	Parker	Referees	Match No.
1	2	3	4	5	6	7	8	9	10	11																T. Bune	1
1	2	3	4	5	6	7	8	9	10	11																A. Seville	2
1	2	3*	4	5	6	7	8	9	10	11	12															M. Bodenham	3
1	2		4	5	6	7	8	9	10*	11		3	12													D. Owen	4
1*	2	3	4	5	6	7	8	9	12	11		10														M. Heath	5
	2	3	4	5	6	7	8	9		11		10		1												R. Milford	6
	2	3	4	5	6	7	8	9*	12	11		10		1												G. Napthine	7
1	2	3	4	5	6	7	8	9	12	11		10*														B. Stevens	8
1	2	3	4	5	6	7	8	9		11					10											D. Scott	9
1	2	3	4	5	6	7	8	9		11					10											D. Lloyd	10
	2	3	4	5	6	7	8	9		11		12		1	10*											M. Scott	11
1		3	4	5	6	7	8	9	12	11		2	10*													J. Moules	12
1		3	4	5	6	7	8	9	12	11		2*			10											E. Reed	13
	2	3	4		6	7	8	9		11		5	10*	1		12										D. Allison	14
1	2	3	4	5		7	8	9	10	11		6														H. King	15
1	2	3*	4	5	6	7	8	9	12	11		10														K. Barratt	16
1	2	3	4	5	6	7	8	9	12	11		10*														C. Newsome	17
1	2	3	4	5	6	7	8	9		11		10														D. Axcell	18
1	2	3	4	5	6	7		9		11		10*			12		8									M. Peck	19
1	2	3	4	5	6	7		9		11					10		8									B. Daniels	20
1	2	3	4	5		7		9	12	11		6			10*		8									T. Mills	21
1	2	3	4	5	6	7		9	12	11					10*		8									D. Vickers	22
1	2		4	5	6	7		9		11		10	12			8*		3								T. Spencer	23
1	2		4	5	6	7		9				10	12			8		3	11*							M. Heath	24
1	2		4	5	6	7		9		11		10*	12			8		3								D. Letts	25
1	2	3*	4	5	6	7	8	9	12	11		10														B. Hill	26
1	2		4	5	6	7*		9		11		3	12		10					8						M. Bodenham	27
1	2		4	5	6	7		9		11		10								8	3					R. Lewis	28
1	2		4	5	6	7		9		11		10								8	3					N. Ashley	29
1	2		4	5	6	7		9		11		10								8	3					C. Thomas	30
	2		4	5	6	7		9		11		10*									3	1	8	12		A. Crickmore	31
	2		4	5	10	7		9		11								6*			3	1	8	12		M. James	32
	2	3	4		6	7		9	10	11											5	1	8			L. Shapter	33
	2	3			6	7		9	4	11		10									5	1	8			L. Burden	34
	2	3	4		6	7	12	9	10	11*											5	1	8			A. Grey	35
	2	3	4		6	7		9	10	11											5	1	8			P. Willis	36
	2	3	4		6	7		9		11		10									5	1	8			A. Hamil	37
	2	3		12	6	7		9*	4	11		10									5	1	8			J. Bray	38
	2	3	4		6	7			10	11		8									5	1	9			A. Gunn	39
	2	3	4	5	6	7		9	12	11*		10										1	8			I. Barrett	40
	2	3	4	5	6	7		9	12													1	8	11	10*	T. Holbrook	41
	2		4	3	6	7	11	9	12			10*									5	1	8			A. Challinor	42
26	40	31	40	34	40	42	20	41	11	39	0	29	2	4	8	3	4	4	1	4	13	12	12	1	1		
				+ 1s			+ 1s		+ 13s		+ 1s	+ 1s	+ 5s		+ 1s	+ 1s								+ 2s			

FOOTBALL LEAGUE RECORD

1897 Elected to Division 2; 1900 failed re-election; 1920 Division 3; 1921 Division 3(S); 1937–55 Division 2; 1955–60 Division 1; 1960–63 Division 2; 1963–65 Division 3; 1965–68 Division 4; 1968–70 Division 3; 1970–74 Division 2; 1974–75 Division 1; 1975–82 Division 2; 1982– Division 1.

HONOURS

Football League: Division 1 best season, 8th, 1957–58; Division 2 – Champions 1981–82; Runners-up 1954–55, 1973–74; Division 3 – Runners-up 1969–70; Division 4 – Champions 1967–68; Division 3(S) – Champions 1936–37; Runners-up 1935–36. *FA Cup:* Runners-up 1959. *Football League Cup:* best season: 5th rd, 1978–79.

COLOURS

White shirts with orange sleeves and shoulders with 3 white and 2 navy ½″ stripes across shoulders and sleeves, white shorts with 2 orange and 3 navy vertical stripes down sides, orange stockings with white and navy trim.

Change colours: Orange shirts with navy sleeves and shoulders with white and navy stripes across shoulder and sleeves, navy shorts with white and orange trim, orange stockings with white and navy trim.

LUTON TOWN

Players Names	*Birthplace*	*Clubs*	*Appearances* F.L.	F.L.C.	F.A.C.	*Goals* F.L.	F.L.C.	F.A.C.
Ht. Wt. D.o.B.	*Transfer Fee*		*A & S*	*A & S*	*A & S*			
Goalkeepers								
Alan Judge	Kingsbury	Luton T (A)	11	1				
5 11, 11 5, 14.5.60	—	Reading (loan)	33					
Jake Findlay	Blairgowrie	Aston Villa (A)	14	2				
6 1, 14 1, 13.7.54	£100,000	Luton T	174	11	8			
Andy Beasley	Wolverhampton	Luton T (A)						
6 1¾, 12 2, 5.2.64								
Defenders								
Mitchell Thomas	Luton	Luton T (A)	4	1	1			
6 0								
Stacey North	Luton	Luton T (A)						
6 2, 12 6, 25.11.64								
Wayne Turner	Luton	Luton T (A)	11	2		1		
5 9, 12 4, 9.3.61	—	Lincoln C (loan)	45+1	1	5	1		
Mal Donaghy (NI)	Belfast	Larne						
5 10, 12 7, 13.9.57	£20,000	Luton T	206	15	8	13		
Kirk Stephens	Coventry	Nuneaton Bor.						
5 9, 11 8, 27.2.55	£5000	Luton T	186+1	11	6	2		
Mike Saxby	Mansfield	Mansfield T (A)	76+3	2	1+1	5		
6 2, 13 10, 12.8.57	£200,000	Luton T	82	7	2	6	1	
	—	Grimsby T (loan)	10					
Richard Money	Lowestoft	Lowestoft T						
5 11½, 11 5, 13.10.55		Scunthorpe U	165+8	10	6	4		
	£30,000	Fulham	106	4	6	3		1
	£333,333	Liverpool	12+2	1	1			
	—	Derby Co (loan)	5		1			
	£100,000	Luton T	44	4	1	1		
Paul Elliott (EY)	London	Charlton Ath (A)	61+2	2	1	1		
6 1½, 12 8, 18.3.64	£145,000	Luton T	13			1		
Tim Breaker		Luton (A)						
Midfield								
Ricky Hill (E)	London	Luton T (A)	247+6	18	11	40	1	1
5 10, 11 10, 5.3.59								
Clive Goodyear	Lincoln	Luton T	72+1	5	4	4		
6 0, 12 6, 15.1.61								
Bob Johnson	Bedford	Luton T (A)						
5 6, 9 12, 22.2.62								
Raddy Antic (Yug)	Yugoslavia	Zaragoza						
22.11.49	£50,000	Luton T	49+29	4+1	+1	8	1	
Brian Horton*	Hednesford	Hednesford T						
5 9, 11 4, 4.2.49	—	Port Vale	232+4	6	16	33		3
	£30,000	Brighton	217+1	24	10	33	6	2
	£100,000	Luton T	81	6	4	5		2
Forwards								
Brian Stein	South Africa	Edgware T						
5 10, 11 8, 19.10.57	£5000	Luton T	195+10	16	7	74	5	
David Moss	Witney	Witney T						
5 10½, 11 7, 18.3.52	—	Swindon T	217+13	13	25	60	7	14
	£110,000	Luton T	185+1	14	6	77	2	3
Frankie Gunn	Birmingham	Luton T (A)	6+3	1+1	1	1	1	
5 11, 10 6, 6.11.62								
Paul Walsh (E)	Plumstead	Charlton Ath (A)	85+2	9	4	24	6	1
5 8, 10 1, 1.10.62	£400,000	Luton T	41	4	2	14		1
Trevor Aylott	London	Chelsea (A)	26+3	2	1	2		
6 1½, 14 0, 26.11.57	£60,000	Barnsley	93+3	11	9	26	7	1
	£150,000	Millwall	32		1	5		
	£55,000	Luton T	12			2		
Ray Daniel	Luton	Luton T (A)	1+2					
10 11, 10.12.64								
Mark Watts	Welham Green	Luton T (A)	1		1			
5 9½, 10 4, 24.9.65								
Gary Parker	Oxford	Luton T (A)	1					
7.9.65								

Commercial Manager: W. J. Tomlins (Tel. as main line)
Club Coach: David Coates
Supporters Player of the Season 1982–83: Paul Walsh
Physiotherapist: John Sheridan
Club Captain 1982–83: Brian Horton
Chief Scout:
Club Statistician:
Association of Football Statisticians Club Adviser to Yearbook: R. Wash.

Players released since May 1982:
Ray Brammer, F., (Reading N/C); Billy Jennings, F., (N/K); Neil Madden, M., (N/K); Mike Small, F., (Go Ahead Eagles); Pasqualle Fuccillo, M., (Tulsa Roughnecks); Seamus Heath, F., (N/K)

MANCHESTER CITY Division 2

Back row (left to right): Bobby McDonald, Chris Jones (now Crystal Palace), Aage Hareide, Alex Williams, Joe Corrigan, Tommy Caton, Kevin Bond, David Cross, Nicky Reid
Front row: Graham Baker, Kevin Reeves, Paul Power, Asa Hartford, Dennis Tueart, Ray Ranson, Phil Boyer.

Chairman: P. J. Swales.

Executive President: S. H. Cussons.

Directors: C. B. Muir, I. L. G. Niven, M. T. Horwich, W. C. Adams, F. Sellors, A. Thomas.

Secretary: J. B. Halford.

Team Manager: Billy McNeill. ***Asst Manager:*** Jimmy Frizzell.

Year Formed: 1887 as Ardwick FC; 1895 as Manchester City.

Turned Professional: 1887 as Ardwick FC. ***Ltd Co.:*** 1894.

Previous Names: 1887–94, Ardwick FC (Formed through the amalgamation of West Gorton and Gorton Athletic, the latter having been formed in 1880).

Previous Grounds: 1880–81, Clowes Street; 1881–82, Kirkmanshulme Cricket Ground; 1882–84, Queens Road; 1884–87, Pink Bank Lane; 1887–1923, Hyde Road (1894–1923, as City); 1923, Maine Road.

Previous Managers since 1946: Wilf Wild, Sam Cowan, Jock Thomson, Les McDowall, George Poyser, Joe Mercer, Malcolm Allison, John Hart, Ron Saunders, Tony Book, Malcolm Allison, John Bond, John Benson (13).

Maine Road, Moss Side, Manchester M14 7WN. Telephone 061-226 1191/2. ***Telegraphic address:*** 'Football, Manchester 14'. ***Ground capacity:*** 52,500. ***Record attendance:*** 84,569 v Stoke C, FA Cup 6th rd, 3 March, 1934 (British record for any game outside London or Glasgow). ***Record receipts:*** £165,000 Liverpool v Manchester U, FA Cup semi-final, 31 March, 1979. ***Pitch measurements:*** 119yd×79yd.

Directions to Ground: Corporation specials from Aytoun Street, Piccadilly, in centre of city. Nearest railway station, Manchester Piccadilly.

Match tickets: Advance booking 14 days prior to the match.

Car parking: Kippax Street car park holds approximately 400 cars. Also street parking.

Entertainments/catering facilities: Social club can be used by visiting supporters (contact Mr Roy Clarke). Licensed refreshment points around the ground.

Club shop: Open all week at the ground.

Handbooks/programmes: Handbook available. Programmes can be obtained on a mailing list.

Address of Manchester City Souvenir Shop: OK Souvenir Sports Ltd, Maine Road, Moss Side, Manchester M14 7WN.

Note: Full club statistical records are on pages 416–455.

MANCHESTER CITY 1982–83 LEAGUE RECORD

Match No.	Date	Venue	Opponents	Result	H/T Score	Lg. Pos.	Goalscorers	Attendance
1	Aug 28	A	Norwich C	W 2-1	2-0	—	Cross, Power	22,638
2	Sept 1	H	Stoke C	W 1-0	0-0	—	Cross	27,847
3	4	H	Watford	W 1-0	0-0	1	Tueart	29,617
4	7	A	Notts Co	L 0-1	0-1	—		9376
5	11	A	Tottenham H	W 2-1	1-0	3	Baker 2	32,483
6	18	H	Aston Villa	L 0-1	0-1	5		28,650
7	25	A	West Ham U	L 1-4	0-2	9	Boyer	23,883
8	Oct 2	H	Coventry C	W 3-2	1-1	6	Baker, Caton, Cross	25,105
9	9	A	Everton	L 1-2	1-1	7	Cross	25,158
10	16	H	Sunderland	D 2-2	0-1	6	Reeves, Cross	25,053
11	23	A	Manchester U	D 2-2	1-0	9	Tueart, Cross	57,334
12	30	H	Swansea C	W 2-1	1-0	6	Tueart, Hartford	25,021
13	Nov 6	H	Southampton	W 2-0	1-0	2	Reeves, McDonald	25,115
14	13	A	Ipswich T	L 0-1	0-1	6		19,523
15	20	H	Birmingham C	D 0-0	0-0	7		23,174
16	27	A	Nottingham F	L 0-3	0-1	9		18,184
17	Dec 4	H	Arsenal	W 2-1	0-0	9	Caton 2	23,057
18	11	A	Luton T	L 1-3	0-0	10	Cross	11,013
19	18	H	Brighton & HA	D 1-1	1-0	9	Bond	20,615
20	27	A	Liverpool	L 2-5	1-3	9	Cross, Caton	44,664
21	28	H	WBA	W 2-1	1-0	9	Kinsey, Robertson (og)	25,172
22	Jan 1	A	Birmingham C	D 2-2	1-1	9	Bond, Bodak	16,362
23	3	A	Watford	L 0-2	0-2	10		20,049
24	15	H	Norwich C	W 4-1	3-1	8	Cross 2, Bond, Hartford	22,000
25	22	A	Aston Villa	D 1-1	1-1	9	Hartford	20,415
26	Feb 5	H	Tottenham H	D 2-2	0-0	10	Tueart (pen), Cross	26,357
27	12	A	Coventry C	L 0-4	0-2	11		9527
28	19	H	Notts Co	L 0-1	0-0	12		21,199
29	26	A	Sunderland	L 2-3	0-0	15	Caton, Reeves	15,144
30	Mar 2	H	Everton	D 0-0	0-0	—		22,253
31	5	H	Manchester U	L 1-2	1-0	16	Reeves	45,400
32	12	A	Swansea C	L 1-4	0-3	17	McDonald	9884
33	19	A	Southampton	L 1-4	0-4	17	Reeves	17,201
34	26	H	Ipswich T	L 0-1	0-0	17		21,845
35	Apr 2	A	WBA	W 2-0	0-0	17	Cross, Reeves	13,654
36	4	H	Liverpool	L 0-4	0-2	—		35,647
37	9	A	Stoke C	L 0-1	0-0	17		15,372
38	16	H	West Ham U	W 2-0	2-0	17	McDonald, Tueart (pen)	23,015
39	23	A	Arsenal	L 0-3	0-1	19		16,810
40	30	H	Nottingham F	L 1-2	0-1	19	Baker	23,563
41	May 7	A	Brighton & HA	W 1-0	0-0	19	Reeves	17,794
42	14	H	Luton T	L 0-1	0-0	20		42,843

Final League Position: 20

GOALSCORERS

League (47): Cross 12, Reeves 7, Caton 5, Tueart 5 (2 pens), Baker 4, Bond 3, Hartford 3, McDonald 3, Bodak 1, Boyer 1, Kinsey 1, Power 1, own goal 1.
Milk Cup (4): Power 2, Tueart 2 (1 pen).
FA Cup (2): Cross 1, Hartford 1.

Milk Cup	Second Round	Wigan Ath (a)	1-1
		(h)	2-0
	Third Round	Southampton (h)	1-1
		(a)	0-4
FA Cup	Third Round	Sunderland (a)	0-0
		(h)	2-1
	Fourth Round	Brighton & HA (a)	0-4

Corrigan	Ranson	McDonald	Baker	Bond	Caton	Hareide	Reeves	Cross	Hartford	Power	Tueart	Williams	Jones	Boyer	Simpson	Reid	Davies	Kinsey	May	Bodak	Park (L)	Golac	Hildersley	Lomax	*Referees*	*Match No.*
1	2	3	4	5	6	7	8	9	10	11															B. Daniels	1
1	2	3	4	5	6	7	8	9	10	11															G. Courtney	2
1*	2	3	4	5	6	7	8	9	10	11	12														D. Hutchinson	3
	2	3	4	5	6	7	8	9*	10	11	12	1													L. Robinson	4
	2	6	7	4	5	3	9		8	11	12	1	10*												J. Bray	5
	2	3*	4	5	6	7	8		10	11	12	1	9												F. Roberts	6
	2	3*	4	5	6	7	8		10	11	12	1		9											D. Letts	7
	2		4	6	5		8	9	10	3	7	1			11										K. Hackett	8
	2		4		6	10	8	9		3	7	1	11*		12	5									G. Tyson	9
1	2				6		8	9	10	5	7				12	4	3	11*							A. Hamil	10
1	2	3	11	4	6		8	9	10	5	7														D. Richardson	11
1	2	3	11	4	6		8	9	10	5	7														K. Redfearn	12
1	2	3	11	4	6		8	9	10	5	7														M. Scott	13
1	2	3	11*	4	6		8	9	10	5	7					12									D. Vickers	14
1	2	3	11	4	6		8	9	10	5	7														D. Shaw	15
1	2	3		10	6		8	9		5	7					4			11						D. Hedges	16
1	2	3	11	4	6		8	9	10	5	7														D. Lloyd	17
1	2	3		11	6		8	9	10	5	7					4									D. Axcell	18
1	2	3		4	6		8	9*	10	5	7								12	11					V. Callow	19
1	2	3		4	6		8	9	10	5	7									11					P. Willis	20
1	2	3		6			8	9	10		7					4		5		11					C. Steel	21
1	2	3		6			8	9	10		7					4		5		11					H. King	22
1	2	3		6			8		10	5	7					4		9		11					J. Martin	23
1	2			3			8	9	10	5	7					4		6		11					R. Bridges	24
1	2			3	6		8	9	10	5	7					4		11							D. Reeves	25
1	2	3		5	6		8	9	10		7					4				11					C. Newsome	26
	2	3*		5	6		8	9	10			1				4			7	11	12				M. Dimblebee	27
1	2			5	6		8	9	10		7						4		3	11	12				D. Owen	28
1	2	3	9	4	6		8		10		7								5	11					J. Key	29
1	2	3	9	4	6		8		10		7					4				11					T. Mills	30
1	2	3	11*	5	6		8	9	10		7					4				12					A. Seville	31
1		3	11	5	6		8	9			7					4			12			2	10*		L. Shapter	32
			11	5	6		8	9		10	7	1				4			12			2*		3	R. Lewis	33
	2		8	3	5		7	11	9	6	12	1				4				10*					K. Hackett	34
	2		11	5	6		8	9	10	3		1				4		7							J. Deakin	35
	2		11*	5	6		8	9	10	3		1				4		7	12						K. Baker	36
	2	3		5	6		8	9	10	11		1				4		7							R. Milford	37
	2	3		5	6		8		10	11	7	1				4		9							A. Saunders	38
	5*	2	9	3	4				7	6	10	1				8		11		12					D. Brazier	39
	2	3	8	5	6				10	11	7	1				4		9							G. Courtney	40
	2	3	9	5	6		8		10	11	7	1				4									L. Burden	41
	2	3	9*	5	6		8		10	11	7	1				4		12							A. Challinor	42
25	40	32	27	40	38	8	40	31	38	33	30	17	3	1	1	24	2	12	4	12	0	2	1	1		
											+ 6s				+ 2s	+ 1s		+ 1s	+ 4s	+ 2s	+ 2s					

FOOTBALL LEAGUE RECORD

1892 Ardwick elected founder member of Division 2; 1894 Newly-formed Manchester C elected to Division 2; Division 1 1899–1902, 1903–09, 1910–26, 1928–38, 1947–50, 1951–63, 1966–83; Division 2 1902–03, 1909–10, 1926–28, 1938–47, 1950–51, 1963–66, 1983– .

HONOURS

Football League: Division 1 – Champions 1936–37, 1967–68; Runners-up 1903–04, 1920–21, 1976–77; Division 2 – Champions 1898–99, 1902–03, 1909–10, 1927–28, 1946–47, 1965–66; Runners-up 1895–96, 1950–51. *FA Cup:* Winners 1904, 1934, 1956, 1969; Runners-up 1926, 1933, 1955, 1981. *Football League Cup:* Winners 1970, 1976; Runners-up 1973–74. **European Competitions:** *European Cup:* 1968–69. *European Cup-Winners' Cup:* 1969–70 (winners), 1970–71. *UEFA Cup:* 1972–73, 1976–77, 1977–78, 1978–79.

COLOURS

Sky blue shirts with white collar and cuffs, white stripe down sleeve, sky blue shorts with white trim, sky blue stockings with white rings on top.

Change colours: White shirts with red/black diagonal stripes across chest, black shorts and stockings.

MANCHESTER CITY

Players Names *Ht. Wt. D.o.B.*	*Birthplace* *Transfer Fee*	*Clubs*	*Appearances* F.L. A & S	F.L.C. A & S	F.A.C. A & S	*Goals* F.L.	F.L.C.	F.A.C.
Goalkeepers								
John Blott	Middlesbrough	Manchester C						
5 11, 12 2,								
Alex Williams (EY)	Manchester	Manchester C (A)	22	1				
6 2½, 13 4, 13.11.61								
Defenders								
Ian Davies (WU21)	Bristol	Norwich C (A)	29+3	1	1	2		
5 9, 10 8, 29.3.57	£175,000	Newcastle U	74+1	6	1	3	1	
	F/T	Manchester C	2					
	—	Bury (loan)	14		1			
Kevin Bond (EB)	London	Bournemouth (A)						
6 1½, 13 7, 22.6.57	F/T	Norwich C	137+5	12	7	12		2
	£200,000	Seattle Sounders						
	£350,000	Manchester C	72+1	8	5	6		1
John Ryan*	Lewisham	Maidstone U						
5 11, 12 2, 20.7.47	—	Arsenal						
	F/T	Fulham	42+3	3	4	1		
	F/T	Luton T	264+2	14	17	10		
	£60,000	Norwich C	113+3	8+1	7	26	3	
	£70,000	Seattle Sounders						
		Sheffield U	56	4	6	2		
	F/T	Manchester C	19					
Ray Ranson (EU21)	St Helens	Manchester C (A)	156+1	19	12	1		
5 9½, 12 1, 12.6.60								
Nicky Reid (EU21)	Ormston	Manchester C (A)	127+3	15	10			
5 10, 11 10, 30.10.60								
Tommy Caton (EU21)	Liverpool	Manchester C (A)	148+1	18	12	6		
6 2, 12 10, 6.10.62								
Bobby McDonald	Aberdeen	Aston Villa (A)	33+6	4	3	3	1	1
5 10, 12 1, 13.4.55	£40,000	Coventry C	161	11+1	7	14		1
	£270,000	Manchester C	96	5	10+1	11	1	3
Geoff Lomax	Droylsden	Manchester C	1					
5 9, 11 8, 0.0.00								
Age Hareide* (NOR)	Norway	Molde FK						
6 2, 12 6, 0.0.00	£10,000	Manchester C	17+7	+1				
	—	Norwich C (loan)	12	2	3			1
Graham Baker (EU21)	Southampton	Southampton (A)	111+2	6+1	3	22	2	1
5 9, 10 12, 3.12.58	£225,000	Manchester C	27	4		4		
Midfield								
Paul Power (EB)	Manchester	Manchester C	247+7	26+1	22	22	2	5
5 10, 11 6, 30.10.53								
Andy May	Bury	Manchester C (A)	7+8					
5 8, 11 1, 26.2.64								
Asa Hartford (S)	Clydebank	WBA	206+7	15	19	18	2	2
5 5½, 11 2, 24.10.50	£225,000	Manchester C	184+1	21	12	22	2	1
	£450,000	Nottingham F	3					
	£400,000	Everton	81	6	11	6		1
	£350,000	Manchester C	68	8	5	6	1	1
Gary Jackson	Swinton	Manchester C (A)	6+2					
5 6½, 10 7, 0.0.00								
Forwards								
Dennis Tueart* (E)	Newcastle	Sunderland	173+5	5	17	46	2	3
5 8, 11 4, 27.11.49	£180,000	Manchester C	139+1	15	9	59	10	3
	£250,000	New York Cosmos						
	£150,000	Manchester C	77+7	12	4+2	27	8	
Kevin Reeves (E)	Burley	Bournemouth (A)	60+3	2	4	20		
5 9, 11 4, 20.10.57	£50,000	Norwich C	118+1	9	5	37	5	
	£1,250,000	Manchester C	129+1	15	13	34	1	4
Steve Kinsey	Manchester	Manchester C (A)	26+3	+1	3	1		
5 7, 10 2, 2.1.63	—	Chester (loan)	3			1		
	—	Chesterfield (loan)	3					
Clive Wilson	Manchester	Manchester C	3+1	1				
5 7, 9 10, 13.11.61	—	Chester (loan)	21			2		
Ron Hildersley	Kirkcaldy	Manchester C (A)	1					
5 4, 9 2, 6.4.65								
Peter Bodak	Birmingham	Coventry C (A)	30+2	6	6	5	1	1
5 8, 9 10, 12.8.61	F/T	Manchester U						
	F/T	Manchester C	12+2		2+1	1		

Commercial Manager: P. Critchley (Tel. 061-226 1191/2)
Club Coach:
Supporters Player of the Season 1982–83: Kevin Bond
Medical Trainer: R. Bailey
Club Captain 1982–83: P. Power
Chief Scout: K. H. Barnes
Club Statistician: W. H. Miles
Association of Football Statisticians Club Adviser to Yearbook: R. Goble.

Players (non-appearance) granted free transfer: Robin Webb, D.; Mike Queenan, D.
Players released since May 1982:
Andy Elliott, M. (N/K); Steve Evans, F. (N/K); Keith Parkinson, F. (N/K); Joe Corrigan, G. (Seattle S); Ivan Golac, D. (N/K); Tommy Hutchinson, M. (Bulova, Hong Kong); David Cross, F. (Vancouver W); Dave Wiffill, F. (Bulova, Hong Kong); Phil Boyer, F. (retired); Trevor Francis, F. (Sampadorio).

MANCHESTER UNITED Division 1

Back row (left to right): Kevin Moran, Scott McGarvey, Gordon McQueen, Gary Bailey, Stephen Pears, Paul McGrath, Ashley Grimes, Garry Birtles
Middle row: Jim McGregor (Physiotherapist), Norman Whiteside, Alan Davies, Mike Duxbury, Peter Bodak, Steve Coppell, Lou Macari, Mick Brown (Assistant Manager)
Bottom row: Remi Moses, Arnold Muhren, John Gidman, Ray Wilkins, Ron Atkinson (Manager), Martin Buchan, Arthur Albiston, Bryan Robson, Frank Stapleton.

President: Sir Matt Busby CBE, KCSG.

Chairman: C. M. Edwards. ***Vice-Chairman:*** J. A. Gibson.

Directors: W. A. Young, D. D. Haroun JP, J. G. Gulliver, R. L. Edwards, J. M. Edelson.

Chief Executive: C. Martin Edwards

Manager: Ron Atkinson. ***Secretary:*** R. L. Olive.

Year Formed: 1878 as Newton Heath; 1902, Manchester United.

Turned Professional: 1885. ***Ltd Co.:*** 1907.

Previous Name: Newton Heath, 1880–1902. ***Nickname: 'Red Devils'.***

Previous Grounds: 1880–93, North Road, Monsall Road; 1893, Bank Street; 1910, Old Trafford (Played at Maine Rd 1941–49).

Previous Managers since 1946: M. Busby, W. McGuinness, Sir M. Busby, F. O'Farrell, T. Docherty, D. Sexton (6).

Old Trafford, Manchester M16 0RA. Telephone 061-872 1661/2. ***Telegraphic address:*** 'Stadium Manchester'. ***Ground capacity:*** 58,504. ***Record attendance:*** 76, 962 Wolverhampton W v Grimsby T, FA Cup semi-final, 25 March, 1939. ***Club record:*** 70,504 v Aston Villa, Division 1, 27 Dec, 1920. ***Record receipts:*** £124,441, League Cup Final replay, Liverpool v Nottingham F, 22 March, 1978; £102,457 v Tottenham H, League Cup 2nd rd second leg, 28 Oct, 1981. ***Pitch measurements:*** 116yd×76yd.

Directions to Ground: Special buses from Aytoun Street, Cannon Street, and other special points. Frequent train service from Manchester Oxford Road station direct to the Football Ground station.

Match tickets: Seats can be booked from one calendar month before the match. Any not sold by Monday before a Saturday match can be reserved by personal application. For up-to-date ticket information, tel: 061-872 7771 (24 hour service). Tickets for over-subscribed matches are allocated by ballot.

Car parking: Large car parks within easy reach of the ground at Lancashire County Cricket Ground, Talbot Rd and Great Stone Rd (1,200). White City Stadium, Chester Rd (900).

Entertainments /catering facilities: Licensed bars around the ground. Restaurant in conference complex (not match days).

Programmes: Available on subscription and application with remittance can be sent to the ground for individual matches. The supporters' club publishes an annual handbook and newsletters.

Address of Supporters Club: Football ground, Old Trafford (sae for details). Tel: 061-872 6000.

Address of the Club Shop or Boutique: Red Devils Souvenir Shop, Old Trafford. Tel: 061-872 3398.

MANCHESTER UNITED 1982–83 LEAGUE RECORD

Match No.	Date	Venue	Opponents	Result	H/T Score	Lg. Pos.	Goalscorers	Attendance
1	Aug 28	H	Birmingham C	W 3-0	0-0	—	Moran, Stapleton, Coppell	48,673
2	Sept 1	A	Nottingham F	W 3-0	0-0	—	Wilkins, Whiteside, Robson	23,748
3	4	A	WBA	L 1-3	1-0	7	Robson	25,014
4	8	H	Everton	W 2-1	1-1	—	Whiteside, Robson	43,186
5	11	H	Ipswich T	W 3-1	1-1	2	Whiteside 2, Coppell	43,140
6	18	A	Southampton	W 1-0	0-0	1	Macari	21,700
7	25	H	Arsenal	D 0-0	0-0	2		43,198
8	Oct 2	A	Luton T	D 1-1	1-0	2	Grimes	17,009
9	19	H	Stoke C	W 1-0	0-0	1	Robson	43,132
10	16	A	Liverpool	D 0-0	0-0	1		40,853
11	23	H	Manchester C	D 2-2	0-1	1	Stapleton 2	57,334
12	30	A	West Ham U	L 1-3	0-1	3	Moran	31,684
13	Nov 6	A	Brighton & HA	L 0-1	0-0	4		18,398
14	13	H	Tottenham H	W 1-0	1-0	3	Muhren	47,869
15	20	A	Aston Villa	L 1-2	1-1	5	Stapleton	35,487
16	27	H	Norwich C	W 3-0	2-0	4	Muhren, Robson 2	34,579
17	Dec 4	A	Watford	W 1-0	0-0	2	Whiteside	25,669
18	11	H	Notts Co	W 4-0	1-0	2	Whiteside, Stapleton, Robson, Duxbury	33,618
19	18	A	Swansea C	D 0-0	0-0	2		15,748
20	27	H	Sunderland	D 0-0	0-0	3		47,783
21	28	A	Coventry C	L 0-3	0-2	3		18,938
22	Jan 1	H	Aston Villa	W 3-1	1-1	2	Stapleton 2, Coppell	41,545
23	3	H	WBA	D 0-0	0-0	3		39,123
24	15	A	Birmingham C	W 2-1	0-0	2	Whiteside, Robson	19,333
25	22	H	Nottingham F	W 2-0	0-0	2	Coppell (pen), Muhren	38,615
26	Feb 5	A	Ipswich T	D 1-1	0-1	2	Stapleton	23,531
27	26	H	Liverpool	D 1-1	1-1	3	Muhren	57,397
28	Mar 2	A	Stoke C	L 0-1	0-0	–		20,950
29	5	A	Manchester C	W 2-1	0-1	3	Stapleton 2	45,400
30	19	H	Brighton & HA	D 1-1	0-1	3	Albiston	36,700
31	22	H	West Ham U	W 2-1	0-0	—	Stapleton, McGarvey	30,227
32	Apr 2	H	Coventry C	W 3-0	2-0	2	Stapleton, Gillespie (og), Macari	36,814
33	4	A	Sunderland	D 0-0	0-0	—		31,486
34	9	H	Southampton	D 1-1	1-0	3	Robson	37,120
35	19	A	Everton	L 0-2	0-0	—		21,707
36	23	H	Watford	W 2-0	0-0	3	Cunningham, Grimes (pen)	43,048
37	30	A	Norwich C	D 1-1	0-0	3	Whiteside	22,986
38	May 2	A	Arsenal	L 0-3	0-1	4		23,602
39	7	H	Swansea C	W 2-1	1-0	3	Robson, Stapleton	35,724
40	9	H	Luton T	W 3-0	2-0	—	McGrath 2, Stapleton	34,213
41	11	A	Tottenham H	L 0-2	0-0	—		32,803
42	14	A	Notts Co	L 2-3	1-1	3	McGrath, Muhren	14,414

Final League Position: 3

GOALSCORERS

League (56): Stapleton 14, Robson 10, Whiteside 8, Muhren 5, Coppell 4 (1 pen), McGrath 3, Grimes 2 (1 pen), Macari 2, Moran 2, Albiston 1, Cunningham 1, Duxbury 1, McGarvey 1, Wilkins 1, own goal 1.
Milk Cup (21): Coppell 6 (1 pen), McQueen 3, Whiteside 3, Moran 2, Stapleton 2, Albiston 1, Moses 1, Muhren 1, Robson 1, own goal 1.
FA Cup (14): Robson 3, Stapleton 3, Whiteside 3, Coppell 1, Moran 1, Moses 1, Muhren 1 (pen), Wilkins 1.
UEFA Cup (1): Robson 1.

Milk Cup	Second Round	AFC Bournemouth (h)	2-0
		(a)	2-2
	Third Round	Bradford C (a)	0-0
		(h)	4-1
	Fourth Round	Southampton (h)	2-0
	Fifth Round	Nottingham F (h)	4-0
	Semi-final	Arsenal (a)	4-2
		(h)	2-1
	Final (at Wembley)	Liverpool	1-2 (aet)

FA Cup	Third Round	West Ham U (h)	2-0
	Fourth Round	Luton T (a)	2-0
	Fifth Round	Derby Co (a)	1-0
	Sixth Round	Everton (h)	1-0
	Semi-final (at Villa Park)	Arsenal	2-1
	Final (at Wembley)	Brighton & HA	2-2 (aet)
		Brighton & HA	4-0
UEFA Cup	First Round	Valencia (h)	0-0
		(a)	1-2

Bailey	Duxbury	Albiston	Wilkins	Moran	McQueen	Robson	Muhren	Stapleton	Whiteside	Coppell	Buchan	Grimes	Macari	Moses	McGrath	McGarvey	Gidman	Wealands (L)	Cunningham	Davies	Referees	Match No.
1	2	3	4	5	6	7	8	9	10	11											M. Peck	1
1	2	3	4	5	6	7	8	9	10	11											A. Ward	2
1	2	3	4	5	6	7	8	9	10	11											K. Salmon	3
1	2	3	4	5	6	7	8	9	10	11											A. Hamil	4
1	2	3	4	5	6	7	8	9	10	11											A. Saunders	5
1	2	3	4		5	7		9	10	11*	6	8	12								R. Lewis	6
1	2	3	4	5	6	7		9	10			8	11								P. Willis	7
1	2	3	4	5	6	7		9	10			8		11							B. Stevens	8
1	2	3	4	5	6	7		9	10			8		11							R. Bridges	9
1	2	3	4	5	6	7		9	10	11		8									K. Walmsley	10
1	2	3	4	5	6	7	8*	9	10	11			12								D. Richardson	11
1	2	3		5		7	8	9	10	11	6	4									D. Hedges	12
1	2	3		5*	6	7	8	9	10	11			12	4							T. Spencer	13
1	2	3			6	7	8	9	10	11				4	5						C. Seel	14
1	2	3		5	6	7	8	9	10	11				4		12					B. Hill	15
1	2	3		5	6	7	8	9	10*	11				4		12					J. Key	16
1	2	3			6	7	8	9	10	11	5			4							A. Glasson	17
1	2	3		5	6	7*	8	9	10	11		12		4							T. Mills	18
1	2	3		5	6	7	8	9	10	11				4							T. Bune	19
1	2	3		5	6	7	8	9	10	11				4							F. Roberts	20
1	2	3	8	5	6	7		9				11		4		10					B. Daniels	21
1	2	3		5	6	7	8	9	10	11				4							G. Tyson	22
1	2	3		5	6	7	8	9	10	11				4							D. Owen	23
1	2	3		5	6	7	8	9	10	11				4							C. Thomas	24
1	2	3		5	6	7	8	9	10	11				4							K. Hackett	25
1	2	3		5	6	7	8	9	10	11				4							K. Baker	26
1	2	3	7	5*	6		8	9	10	11			12	4							K. Redfern	27
1	2	3	7		6		8	9	10	11				4	5						K. Barrett	28
1	2	3	7		6		8	9	10	11				4	5						A. Seville	29
1	6	3	7*				8	9	10	11		4	12		5		2				R. Saunders	30
1	6	3	7				8	9*		11			12	4	5	10	2				A. Challinor	31
	2	3	7		6		8	9	10*	11			12	4	5			1			N. Ashley	32
	2	3	7		6		8	9		11			10*	4	5	12		1			J. Key	33
1	2	3	11		6	7	8	9	10					4	5						D. Hutchinson	34
	2	3	8		6	7		9	10*			11		4	5			1	12		D. Allison	35
	2	3*	8		6	7		9	10			11		4	5			1	12		D. Shaw	36
1	2		8	5	6	7		9	10			3		4					11		D. Reeves	37
1	2		8	5	6				10			3		4	7	9			11		E. Read	38
1	2		4*	5	6	7	8	9	10			3							11	12	P. Willis	39
1	2			5	6	7	8	9	10*			3			4	12				11	T. Holbrook	40
1	2	3		5		7	8	9	10			11		4	5	12					B. Hill	41
	5	4	6				7	9	10					3	8		2	1		11	R. Lewis	42
37	42	38	26	29	37	33	32	41	39	29	3	15	2	29	14	3	3	5	3	2		
												+ 1s	+ 7s			+ 5s			+ 2s	+ 1s		

FOOTBALL LEAGUE RECORD

1892 Newton Heath elected to Division 1; 1894–1906 Division 2; 1906–22 Division 1; 1922–25 Division 2; 1925–31 Division 1; 1931–36 Division 2; 1936–37 Division 1; 1937–38 Division 2; 1938–74 Division 1; 1974–75 Division 2; 1975– Division 1.

HONOURS

Football League: Division 1 – Champions 1907–08, 1910–11, 1951–52, 1955–56, 1956–57, 1964–65, 1966–67; Runners-up 1946–47, 1947–48, 1948–49, 1950–51, 1958–59, 1963–64, 1967–68, 1979–80; Division 2 – Champions 1935–36, 1974–75; Runners-up 1896–97, 1905–06, 1924–25, 1937–38. *FA Cup:* Winners 1909, 1948, 1963, 1977, 1983; Runners-up 1957, 1958, 1976, 1979. *Milk Cup:* 1982–83 (Runners-up). **European Competitions:** *European Cup:* 1956–57 (s-f), 1957–58 (s-f), 1965–66 (s-f), 1967–68 (winners), 1968–69 (s-f). *European Cup-Winners' Cup:* 1963–64, 1977–78. *European Fairs Cup:* 1964–65. *UEFA Cup:* 1976–77, 1980–81, 1982–83.

COLOURS

Red shirts with red, white and black trim, white shorts, black stockings with red tops with three white bands on top. **Change colours:** White shirts with black and red trim, black shorts with white trim, white stockings with three black hoops on top.

MANCHESTER UNITED

Players Names Ht, Wt, D.o.B.	Birthplace Transfer Fee	Clubs	Appearances F.L. A & S	F.L.C. A & S	F.A.C. A & S	Goals F.L.	F.L.C.	F.A.C.
Goalkeepers								
Gary Bailey (EB)	Ipswich	Manchester U	186	16	20			
6 1½, 12 10, 9.8.58								
Steve Pears	Brandon	Manchester U (A)						
5 11½, 11 10, 22.1.62								
Defenders								
Martin Buchan* (S)	Aberdeen	Aberdeen						
5 10, 12 2, 6.3.49	£125,000	Manchester U	376	32	39	4		
Arthur Albiston (S)	Edinburgh	Manchester U (A)	224+6	24+2	23	3	1	
5 7½, 10 13, 14.7.57								
Gordon McQueen (S)	Kilburnie	St Mirren						
6 3, 13 7, 26.6.52	£40,000	Leeds U	140	5	13	15		1
	£495,000	Manchester U	152	14	20	18	3	1
Kevin Moran (EI)	Dublin	Manchester U	101	8	9	10	2	1
5 10½, 12 8, 29.4.56								
Tony Whelan*	Dublin	Bohemians						
6 0, 12 0, 23.11.59		Manchester U	+1					
John Gidman (E)	Liverpool	Liverpool (AM)						
5 11, 12 2, 10.1.54	—	Aston Villa	196+1	21	12	9		
	£650,000	Everton	64	6	11	2	1	
	£450,000	Manchester U	39+1	2	1	1		
Paul McGrath	Ealing	St Patricks Ath						
0 0, 0 0, 0.0.00	£30,000	Manchester U	14	1	+1	3		
Mike Duxbury (EU21)	Blackburn	Manchester U (A)	88+11	9+1	+2	10		1
5 9, 10 12, 1.9.59								
William Garton		Manchester U (A)						
Andy Hill		Manchester U (A)						
Midfield								
Alan Davies (W)	Manchester	Manchester U (A)	3+1		2			
5 8, 10 4, 5.12.61								
Ray Wilkins (E)	Hillingdon	Chelsea (A)	176+3	6+1	10+1	30	2	2
5 8, 11 0, 14.9.56	£750,000	Manchester U	116+2	9+1	9	4		1
Lou Macari (S)	Aberdeen	Celtic						
5 5½, 10 13, 4.6.49	£200,000	Manchester U	311+13	23+3	31+2	78	2	8
Danny Keough	Rawtenstall	Manchester U (A)						
5 7½, 9 9, 31.1.63								
Remi Moses (EU21)	Manchester	WBA (A)	63	7	2	5	1	
5 6, 10 7, 14.11.60	£650,000	Manchester U	49+1	9	6	2	1	1
Bryan Robson (E)	Chester-Le-Street	WBA (A)	193+4	17+1	10+2	39	2	2
5 10½, 11 9, 11.1.57	£1,500,000	Manchester U	65	10	7	15	1	3
Mark Dempsey	Manchester	Manchester U (A)						
5 7, 8 9, 0.0.00								
Ashley Grimes (EI)	Dublin	Bohemians						
5 11½, 11 7, 2.8.57	£35,000	Manchester U	62+28	8	5	10		1
Arnold Muhren (HOL)	Volenram, Holland	FC Twente						
5 11, 11 1, 2.6.51	£150,000	Ipswich T	161	15	19	21	2	3
	F/T	Manchester U	32	8	6	5	1	1
Graeme Hogg		Manchester U (A)						
Forwards								
Steve Coppell (E)	Liverpool	Tranmere R	35+3	3	4	10		1
5 7, 11 11, 9.7.55	£60,000	Manchester U	320+2	27	36	53	9	4
Gary Worrall	Salford	Manchester U (A)						
5 9, 11 5, 4.11.61								
Scott McGarvey (SU21)	Glasgow	Manchester U (A)	13+10			3		
6 0, 11 5, 22.4.63								
Mark Hughes	Wrexham	Manchester U (A)						
5 9, 11 12, 1.11.63								
Frank Stapleton (EI)	Dublin	Arsenal (A)	223+2	26	32	75	14	15
5 11, 13 0, 10.7.56	£900,000	Manchester U	82	11	8	27	2	3
Norman Whiteside (NI)	Belfast	Manchester U (A)	40+1	7+2	7	9	3	3
6 0, 12 3, 0.0.00								
Lawrie Cunningham (E)	Archway	Orient (A)	72+3	5	5+1	15	1	
5 8, 10 13, 8.3.56	£110,000	WBA	81+5	6	8+1	21		3
£995,000	Real Madrid							
		Manchester U (Loan)	3+2			1		
Clayton Blackmore		Manchester U (A)						

Commercial Manager: J. Lillie (Tel. 00000)
Club Coach: M. Brown
Supporters Player of the Season 1982–83:
Physiotherapist: J. McGregor
Club Captain 1982–83: B. Robson
Chief Scout: T. Collins
Club Statistician: C. Butler
Association of Football Statisticians Club Adviser to Yearbook: J. Hewitt.

Players (non-appearance) granted free transfer: David Wynn, M.
Players released since May 1982:
David Jeffrey, D., (Linfield); Chris Lynam, F., (N/K); Kel McDermott, M., (N/K); Gareth Orritt, D., (N/K); Alan Stevenson, M., (N/K); Sean Williams, M., (N/K); Nikola Jovanovic, D., (N/K); Peter Beardsley, F., (N/K); Andy Reynolds, F., (N/K).

MANSFIELD TOWN Division 4

Back row (left to right): Geoff Allen (Trainer/Coach), Mark Reynolds, Dave Caldwell, Billy Ayre, John Dungworth, Colin Calderwood, John Matthews, Simon Woodhead, Rod Arnold
Front row: Charlie Bell, Gary Nicholson, Paul Cannell, Stuart Boam (ex-Player-Manager), Joe Laidlaw, Keith Kennedy, Kevin Bird

President: A. F. Patrick.

Chairman: R. C. Hartley. ***Vice-Chairman:*** J. B. Almond JP.

Directors: J. W. Pratt, Ian Greaves, J. N. Lea.

Manager: Ian Greaves. ***Secretary:*** J. D. Eaton.

Year Formed: 1905 ***Turned Professional:*** 1905. ***Ltd Co.:*** 1905.

Club Nickname: 'The Stags'.

Previous Managers since 1946: Roy Goodall, Freddie Steele, Stan Mercer, Charlie Mitten, Sam Weaver, Raich Carter, Tommy Cummings, Tommy Eggleston, Jock Basford, Danny Williams, David Smith, Peter Morris, Billy Bingham, Mick Jones, Stuart Boam (15).

Field Mill Ground, Quarry Lane, Mansfield. Telephone Mansfield 23567. ***Telegraphic address:*** 'Football Mansfield'. ***Ground capacity:*** 23,500. ***Record attendance:*** 24,467 v Nottingham F, FA Cup 3rd rd, 10 Jan, 1963. ***Record receipts:*** £19,227 v Sheffield W, Division 3, 15 Mar, 1980. ***Pitch measurements:*** 115yd×72yd.

Directions to Ground: Buses from town centre to within 300 yards of the ground. Nearest railway station, Alfreton and Mansfield Parkway.

Match tickets: Advance booking five days prior to match.

Car parking: Room for 500 cars at the ground and another 3,000 within 500 yards.

Entertainments/catering facilities: No club room. Licensed tea bars in the ground.

Club shop: Adjacent to the ground; sells all types of souvenirs.

Handbooks/programmes: Both on sale at the club shop.

Address of Supporters Club: Club Shop, c/o the ground.

Note: Full club statistical records are on pages 416–455.

MANSFIELD TOWN 1982–83 LEAGUE RECORD

Match No.	Date	Venue	Opponents	Result	H/T Score	Lg. Pos.	Goalscorers	Attendance
1	Aug 28	H	Blackpool	W 2-1	2-0	—	Dungworth (pen), Waddle	2627
2	Sept 3	A	Halifax T	D 0-0	0-0	—		2225
3	6	A	Tranmere R	L 0-3	0-2	—		1280
4	11	H	Port Vale	L 0-2	0-1	20		2313
5	18	A	Hereford U	W 2-0	2-0	10	Nicholson 2	1960
6	25	H	Rochdale	W 2-1	2-1	10	Waddle 2	2001
7	27	H	Peterborough U	D 0-0	0-0	—		2414
8	Oct 1	A	Crewe Alex	W 2-1	1-1	—	Waddle, Day	1787
9	9	H	Bury	L 1-4	1-1	10	Bell	2415
10	16	A	Chester	W 3-1	1-0	8	Caldwell 2, Woodhead (pen)	1668
11	18	H	Scunthorpe U	L 0-2	0-2	—		2647
12	23	A	Swindon T	L 0-4	0-2	10		3917
13	30	H	Darlington	L 0-2	0-1	11		1816
14	Nov 3	A	Hartlepool U	W 4-0	2-0	—	Caldwell, Nicholson, Woodhead (pen), Ayre	1325
15	5	A	Colchester U	L 0-2	0-2	—		2009
16	13	H	Bristol C	D 1-1	0-1	10	Newman (og)	1979
17	27	A	York C	L 1-6	1-3	12	Nicholson	2119
18	Dec 4	H	Stockport Co	W 1-0	1-0	10	Bell	1661
19	17	H	Torquay U	W 2-1	1-1	10	Dungworth, Caldwell	1293
20	27	A	Wimbledon	D 1-1	0-0	11	Nicholson	2517
21	28	H	Northampton T	W 2-0	1-0	9	Caldwell, Matthews	2841
22	Jan 1	A	Aldershot	L 1-2	0-1	10	Ayre	2235
23	3	H	Hull C	W 3-1	3-0	9	Nicholson, Dungworth 2 (1 pen)	4560
24	8	H	Halifax T	L 1-2	0-1	9	Dungworth (pen)	2398
25	15	A	Blackpool	L 1-2	0-0	11	Nicholson	2217
26	22	H	Hereford U	L 0-1	0-1	13		1655
27	29	A	Port Vale	L 1-4	0-2	14	Hutchinson	4102
28	Feb 5	A	Rochdale	D 2-2	1-1	14	Dungworth, Matthews	1028
29	19	A	Bury	L 0-1	0-0	15		2304
30	26	H	Chester	W 2-1	0-1	15	Matthews, Hutchinson	1803
31	Mar 1	A	Scunthorpe U	D 2-2	0-1	—	Bell, Bird	3562
32	5	H	Swindon T	W 1-0	0-0	14	Dungworth (pen)	2101
33	12	A	Darlington	D 0-0	0-0	14		952
34	14	H	Hartlepool U	W 3-0	2-0	—	Dungworth 3 (1 pen)	1991
35	19	H	Colchester U	D 1-1	0-0	11	Nicholson	2371
36	26	A	Bristol C	L 1-3	1-0	12	Caldwell	4919
37	28	H	Crewe Alex	W 1-0	0-0	—	Caldwell	2245
38	Apr 2	A	Northampton T	W 2-1	0-0	8	Caldwell 2	1988
39	5	H	Wimbledon	D 2-2	1-1	—	Dungworth 2 (1 pen)	3519
40	8	A	Stockport Co	D 1-1	1-1	—	Dungworth	2197
41	16	H	Tranmere R	D 1-1	0-1	8	Bell	2468
42	23	A	Torquay U	L 1-3	1-1	10	Ayre	1546
43	30	H	York C	D 2-2	1-1	10	Dungworth, Caldwell	2288
44	May 2	A	Hull C	D 2-2	1-1	10	Bell 2	8735
45	7	A	Peterborough U	L 2-3	0-1	11	Bird, Thorpe	2200
46	14	H	Aldershot	W 4-1	2-1	10	Kearney, Hutchinson, Woodhead, Bell	1786

Final League Position: 10

GOALSCORERS

League (61): Dungworth 14 (6 pens), Caldwell 10, Nicholson 8, Bell 7, Waddle 4, Ayre 3, Hutchinson 3, Matthews 3, Woodhead 3 (2 pens), Bird 2, Day 1, Kearney 1, Thorpe 1, own goal 1.
Milk Cup (0).
FA Cup (6): Dungworth 4 (1 pen), Bell 2.
Football League Trophy (3): Ayre 1, Bird 1, Dungworth 1.

Milk Cup	First Round	Bradford C (a)	0-1
		(h)	0-2
FA Cup	First Round	Stockport Co (h)	3-2
	Second Round	Bradford C (h)	1-1
		(a)	2-3
Football League Trophy		Peterborough U (h)	1-4
		Northampton T (h)	1-2
		Norwich C (h)	1-3

Arnold	Bell	Kennedy	Day (L)	Ayre	Bird	Matthews	Caldwell	Waddle	Dungworth	Laidlaw	Woodhead	Nicholson	Cannell	Boam	Hutchinson	Sindall	Blackhall	Reynolds	Calderwood	Gallagher (L)	Kearney	Rhodes (L)	Coles	Laws	Lowery (L)	Thorpe	*Referees*
1	2	3	4	5	6	7	8*	9	10	11	12																J. Hough
1	2	3	4	5	6	7	8*	9	10	11		12															R. Nixon
1	2	3	4	6	5	7	8	9	10*	11		12															D. Richardson
1		3	4	5	6	7		9	10	11	2	8															D. Hutchinson
1	12	3	4	5	6*	7		9			2	8	10	11													K. Cooper
1		3	4	5	6	7*		9	12		2	8	10	11													D. Civil
1	7	3	4	5	6			9			2	8	10	11													D. Shaw
1	7	3	4	5	6			9	10*		2	8	12	11													K. Walmsley
1	7	3	4	5	6	12		9	10		2	8		11*													T. Holbrook
1	4	3	12	5	6	7	10				2	8	9*	11													R. Chadwick
1	4	3*	12	5	6	7	10				2	8	9	11													M. Heath
1	11	3	4	5	6	7		9	8		2				10												M. James
1	4	3		5	6	7	12	9	10*		2	11				8											N. Ashley
1				5	6*	7	10	9	12		4	11				8	2	3									M. Peck
1				5		7	10	9	8		4	11				6	2	3									J. Martin
1		3		5		7	8	9	12		4*	11			10		2		6								D. Owen
1*	4	3		5		7	8		9		12	11			10			2	6								N. Wilson
1	4	3		5	2	7	10*		9		12	11			8				6								M. Dimblebee
1	4	3		5	2	7	10		9		12	11*			8				6								N. Glover
1	4	3		5	2	7	10		9			11			8				6								R. Milford
1	4	3		5	2	7	10		9			11			8				6								P. Tyldesley
1	4	3		5	2	7	10		9		12	11*			8				6								A. Crickmore
1	4	3		5		7	10*		9		12	11			8		2		6								T. Fitzharris
1	4	3		5		7	10		9		12	11			8		2*		6								D. Lloyd
1	11	3		5	6	4	10				2	9			8					7							J. Lovatt
1	11	3		5		4					2	10	9		8				6	7							N. Midgeley
1	10*	3		5	7	4			9		2	11			8				6	12							R. Guy
1	7	3		5		4	10		9		2	11			8				6								A. Hamill
1		3		5		4	10		9		7	11			8		2		6								G. Courtney
1	12	3		5		4	10		9*		7	11			8		2		6								E. Scales
1	9	3		5	12	4	10				7	11			8*		2		6								A. Challinor
1	8	3		5		4	10		9		7	11					2		6								G. Tyson
1	8	3		5		4	10		9		7	11					2		6								A. Banks
1	8	3		5		4	10		9		7	11					2		6								D. Brazier
1	4				5		10		9		7	11					2		6		3	8					R. Bridges
1	8	12			5*		10		9		7						2	11	6		3	4					T. Spencer
1					5	4	10		9		7	11					2		6		3	8					A. Saunders
1	7				5	4	10		9		2	11				12			6		3	8*					A. Ward
1	7			6	5*	4	10		9		2	11			8	12					3						D. Scott
	7			5		4	10		9		2	11			8				6		3		1				C. Seel
	7			5		4			9		2	11			8	10			6		3		1				T. Mills
1	7	12		5		4			9		2	11*			8	10			6		3						L. Burden
	7*			5	6	4	11		9		2				8	10					3		1	12			I. Barrett
1	7			5		4	10		9		2				8	11			6		3						K. Redfern
1	4			5	3		10		9		2				8	11*			6						7	12	K. Barratt
1	4			5			10		9		7				8	11*	2		6		3					12	T. Jones
43	37	32	10	42	28	39	34	14	36	4	35	37	6	7	25	9	15	4	28	2	11	4	3	0	1	0	
	+ 2s	+ 2s	+ 2s		+ 1s	+ 1s	+ 1s		+ 3s		+ 7s	+ 2s	+ 1s			+ 2s				+ 1s				+ 1s		+ 2s	

FOOTBALL LEAGUE RECORD

1931 Elected to Division 3(S); 1932–37 Division 3(N); 1937–47 Division 3(S); 1947–58 Division 3(N); 1958–60 Division 3; 1960–63 Division 4; 1963–72 Division 3; 1972–75 Division 4; 1975–77 Division 3; 1977–78 Division 2; 1978–80 Division 3; 1980– Division 4.

HONOURS

Football League: Division 2 best season: 21st, 1977–78; Division 3 – Champions 1976–77; Division 4 – Champions 1974–75; Division 3(N) – Runners-up 1950–51. *FA Cup:* best season: 6th rd, 1968–69. *Football League Cup:* best season: 5th rd, 1975–76.

COLOURS

Amber shirts, blue shorts and stockings. **Change colours:** All white with blue and amber trim.

MANSFIELD TOWN

Players Names Ht. Wt. D.o.B.	Birthplace Transfer Fee	Clubs	Appearances F.L. A & S	 F.L.C. A & S	 F.A.C. A & S	Goals F.L.	 F.L.C.	 F.A.C.
Goalkeepers								
Rod Arnold	Wolverhampton	Wolverhampton W (A)						
5 10, 11 4, 3.6.52	F/T	Mansfield T	429	27	24			
David Coles*	Wandsworth	Birmingham C (A)						
6 0, 11 0,		Mansfield T	3					
Defenders								
John Matthews	London	Arsenal (A)	38+7	6	4	2	2	1
6 0, 12 6, 1.11.55	£90,000	Sheffield U	98+5	5	5	14		1
		Mansfield T	39+1	2	3	3		
Billy Ayre	Crookhill	Scarborough						
5 11, 12 10, 7.5.52		Hartlepool U	141	6	8	27		1
		Halifax T	63	2	1	5		
		Mansfield T	42	2	3	3		
Ray Blackhall*	Ashington	Newcastle U (A)	26+11		5+2			2
5 10, 11 7, 19.2.57	£20,000	Sheffield W	115	13	13	1		
	F/T	SK Tord						
	F/T	Mansfield T	15		1			
Mark Kearney	Ormskirk	Marine						
5 10, 11 0,	£23,000	Everton						
		Mansfield T	11			1		
Colin Calderwood	Glasgow	Mansfield T	29		3			
6 0, 12 0,								
Midfield								
Charlie Bell*	Middlesbrough	Middlesbrough (A)	10			1		
5 9, 10 10, 14.11.58	F/T	Mansfield T	82+2	5	4	13		2
Jonathan Laws	Wolverhampton	Wolverhampton W (A)						
5 9, 10 7,	F/T	Mansfield T	+1					
Gary Nicholson	Newcastle	Newcastle U (A)	7+5	3				
5 7½, 9 11, 4.11.60	£10,000	Mansfield T	74+3	5	3+1	11		
Tony Lowery	Wallsend	Ashington						
5 9½, 10 6, 6.7.61	£3500	WBA	1					
	—	Walsall (loan)	4+2			1		
		Mansfield T	1					
Simon Woodhead	Dewsbury	Mansfield T	46+9	1+1	+1	3		
5 10, 11 0, 26.12.62								
Bobby Hutchinson	Glasgow	Hibernian						
5 9, 11 4, 19.6.53		Wigan Ath	34+1	4	2	3	1	
	F/T	Tranmere R	42+3	7	2	6	3	
	£12,500	Mansfield T	25		3	3		
Forwards								
Dave Caldwell	Aberdeen	Inverness Caley						
5 10, 11 6, 31.7.60		Mansfield T	89+10	9	8	28	1	2
John Dungworth	Rotherham	Huddersfield T (A)	18+5			1		
6 0, 10 7, 30.3.55	—	Barnsley (loan)	2+1			1		
	F/T	Oldham Ath	2+2					
	—	Rochdale (loan)	14			3		
		Aldershot	105	4	9	58		8
	£100,000	Shrewsbury T	81+5	2	3	17		
		Hereford U (loan)	7			3		
	F/T	Mansfield T	36+3	2	3	14		4
Alan Waddle*	Wallsend							
6 3, 12 6, 9.6.54		Halifax T	33+6	1		4		
	£40,000	Liverpool	11+5	3	2	1		
	£45,000	Leicester C	11			1		
	£22,000	Swansea C	83+7	9	8	34	4	3
	£70,000	Newport Co	19+8	1+1	1	8		
	F/T	Mansfield T	14	1		4		
Non-contract players								
Mark Sindall	Langwith	Notts Co (A)						
5 8, 10 8,	F/T	Luton T						
	F/T	Mansfield T	9+2					
Adrian Thorpe	Mansfield	Mansfield T	+2			1		
Apprentices								
Mark Reynolds	Gladwell	Mansfield T	4					
5 9, 11 0,								

Commercial Manager: Stuart Burgan (Tel. 25877)
Assistant Manager: John Jarman
Supporters Player of the Season 1982–83: Rod Arnold
Physiotherapist:
Club Captain 1982–83: K. Bird
Chief Scout:
Club Statistician:
Association of Football Statisticians Club Adviser to Yearbook: P. Stevenson

Players released since May 1982:
Barry Foster, D., (Boston U); Alex Livingstone, M., (N/K); Jim Lumby, F., (Boston U); Les McJannet, D., (Kings Lynn); Arthur Mann, M., (Boston U); Brian Thomson, F., (Kings Lynn); Joe Laidlaw, F., (N/K); Paul Cannell, F., (N/K); Kevin Bird, D., (N/K); Keith Kennedy, D., (N/K).

MIDDLESBROUGH Division 2

Back row (left to right): Terry Cochrane, Joe Bolton, Colin Ross, Irving Nattrass, David McClurg, Steve Tupling
Middle row: Stephen Bell, Mick Baxter, Tony Mowbray, Gary MacDonald, Heine Otto, David Currie, Darren Wood, Mick Angus, John Brownlie
Front row: David Shearer, Cyril Knowles (Coach), Jim Platt, Bobby Murdoch (Manager), Kelham O'Hanlon, Lew Clayton (Physio), Harold Shepherdson (Executive Officer Football), Mike Kennedy.

Chairman: M. McCullagh. ***Vice-Chairman:*** K. Varley.

Directors: E. Varley, J. D. Hatfield, G. T. Kitching, P. Cook, A. Zivanaris, G. R. Kitching.

Manager: Malcolm Allison.

Executive Officer (Football): Harold Shepherdson MBE.

Secretary: T. Edon. ***Year Formed:*** 1876.

Turned Professional: 1889; became amateur 1892, and professional again, 1899.

Ltd Co.: 1892. ***Club Nickname:*** 'The Boro'.

Previous Grounds: 1877, Old Archery Ground, Linthorpe Rd; 1903, Ayresome Park.

Previous Managers since 1946: David Jack, Walter Rowley, Bob Dennison, Raich Carter, Stan Anderson, Jack Charlton OBE, John Neal, Bobby Murdoch (8).

Ayresome Park, Middlesbrough, Cleveland TS1 4PB. Telephone 0642-819659/815996. Special Answering Service available on 0642-825383. ***Telegraphic address:*** 'Football, Middlesbrough'. ***Ground capacity:*** 42,000. ***Record attendance:*** 53,596 v Newcastle U, Division 1, 27 Dec, 1949. ***Record receipts:*** £57,710 v Barnsley, FA Cup 5th rd, 14 Feb, 1981. ***Pitch measurements:*** 115yd×75yd.

Directions to Ground: Regular buses from Newport Road bus station in Middlesbrough to the ground. By road – A1 then A19 at Dishforth roundabout.

Match tickets: By postal or personal application two weeks prior to the match.

Car parking: Off-street parking near the ground, on-street parking around the ground.

Entertainments/catering facilities: Social club (members only); refreshment bars around the ground.

Handbooks/programmes: Programmes available on subscription.

Address of the Club Shop or Boutique: Warwick Street, Middlesbrough.

Note: Full club statistical records are on pages 416–455.

MIDDLESBROUGH 1982–83 LEAGUE RECORD

Match No.	Date	Venue	Opponents	Result		H/T Score	Lg. Pos.	Goalscorers	Attendance
1	Aug 28	A	Sheffield W	L	1-3	0-0	—	Shearer	18,611
2	Sept 4	H	Burnley	L	1-4	0-3	21	Shearer	8074
3	8	A	Newcastle U	D	1-1	0-0	—	Wood	27,939
4	11	A	Derby Co	D	1-1	1-1	21	Bell	9050
5	18	H	Fulham	L	1-4	1-2	22	Shearer	6445
6	25	A	Crystal Palace	L	0-3	0-2	22		7689
7	28	H	Grimsby T	L	1-4	1-1	—	Shearer	5929
8	Oct 2	H	Oldham Ath	D	1-1	0-1	22	Otto	5635
9	9	A	Shrewsbury T	D	2-2	0-1	22	Bell, Otto	3620
10	16	H	Bolton W	W	1-0	0-0	22	MacDonald	5521
11	23	H	QPR	W	2-1	0-1	19	Nattress (pen), Otto	7892
12	30	A	Rotherham U	D	1-1	1-0	18	Otto	8135
13	Nov 6	H	Barnsley	W	2-0	1-0	18	Shearer, Wood	11,787
14	13	A	Charlton Ath	W	3-2	3-0	17	Shearer 2, Kennedy	10,807
15	20	A	Leeds U	D	0-0	0-0	17		18,482
16	27	H	Blackburn R	L	1-5	0-1	18	Cochrane	10,821
17	Dec 4	A	Wolverhampton W	L	0-4	0-3	18		11,856
18	11	H	Chelsea	W	3-1	1-0	18	Otto, Wood, Shearer	8836
19	17	A	Cambridge U	L	0-2	0-1	—		2533
20	27	H	Leicester C	D	1-1	0-0	18	Bell (pen)	12,665
21	28	A	Carlisle U	W	3-1	1-0	18	Bell 2, Sugrue	8181
22	Jan 1	H	Leeds U	D	0-0	0-0	17		17,000
23	3	A	Burnley	D	1-1	0-1	16	Shearer	9139
24	15	H	Sheffield W	D	1-1	0-0	19	Bell	11,863
25	22	A	Fulham	L	0-1	0-1	19		8431
26	Feb 5	H	Newcastle U	D	1-1	1-1	19	Baxter	25,164
27	12	A	Oldham Ath	L	0-3	0-1	19		6002
28	26	A	Bolton W	L	1-3	0-2	19	Otto	5598
29	Mar 5	A	QPR	L	1-6	1-2	21	Kennedy (pen)	9596
30	8	H	Shrewsbury T	W	2-1	1-1	—	Kennedy, Hankin	7406
31	12	H	Rotherham U	D	1-1	1-0	19	Sugrue	8875
32	19	A	Barnsley	L	0-2	0-0	20		10,681
33	26	H	Charlton Ath	W	3-0	1-0	17	Bell, Baxter 2	7057
34	Apr 2	H	Carlisle U	W	1-0	1-0	15	Bell	9965
35	5	A	Leicester C	L	0-1	0-0	—		12,025
36	9	H	Derby Co	L	2-3	0-2	19	Kennedy 2 (1 pen)	9078
37	16	A	Grimsby T	W	3-0	1-0	16	Sugrue, Hamilton, Otto	5985
38	23	H	Wolverhampton W	D	0-0	0-0	16		10,315
39	30	A	Blackburn R	D	1-1	0-1	15	Otto	4083
40	May 7	H	Cambridge U	L	0-1	0-1	21		9879
41	10	H	Crystal Palace	W	2-0	1-0	—	Hamilton, Otto (pen)	10,014
42	14	A	Chelsea	D	0-0	0-0	15		19,340

Final League Position: 16

GOALSCORERS

League (46): Otto 9 (1 pen), Shearer 9, Bell 8 (1 pen), Kennedy 5 (2 pens), Baxter 3, Sugrue 3, Wood 3, Hamilton 2, Cochrane 1, Hankin 1, MacDonald 1, Nattrass 1 (pen).
Milk Cup (3): Cochrane 1, Hankin 1, Otto 1.
FA Cup (9): Shearer 4, Bell 2, Beattie 1 (pen), Hankin 1, Otto 1.

Milk Cup	Second Round	Burnley (a)	2-3
		(h)	1-1
FA Cup	Third Round	Bishop's Stortford (h)	2-2
		(a)	2-1
	Fourth Round	Notts Co (h)	2-0
	Fifth Round	Arsenal (h)	1-1
		(a)	2-3

Platt	Ross	Bolton	Otto	Baxter	Wood	Cochrane	Currie	Shearer	Kennedy	Bell	MacDonald	Brownlie	Mowbray	Ward	Hankin	Nattrass	Roberts	Beattie	Sugrue	O'Hanlon	Hamilton	*Referees*	*Match No.*
1	2	3	4	5	6	7	8*	9	10	11	12											D. Civil	1
1	4	3	12	5	6	7*		9	8	11	10	2										C. Seel	2
1	4	3	12	5	6			9	10	11		2	7	8*								K. Walmesley	3
1	4	3	8	5	6			9*	10	11		2	7	12								R. Banks	3
1	4	3	8	5	6		12	9	10	11		2*	7									R. Nixon	5
1	4	3	8	5	6			9	10	11*		2	7	12								R. Milford	6
1	2	3	4*	5	6	12		8	10	11			7		9							N. Wilson	7
1		3	4	5	6	8			10	11	12	2*	7		9							M. Scott	8
1		3	4	5	6	8			10	11		2			9	7						H. Taylor	9
1		3	4	5	6	8				11	9	2	7			10						T. Mills	10
1		3	4	5	6	8				11	9	2	7			10						J. Key	11
1		3	4	5	6	8			10	11		2	7*		9		12					G. Napthine	12
1		3	9	4	6			11	7	10		2			8			5				N. Glover	13
1	12	3	9	4	6			11	7	10				2	8			5*				A. Gunn	14
1	5	3	9	4	6			11	7	10				2	8							L. Robinson	15
1	5*	3	9	4	6	12		11	7	10				2	8							D. Hutchinson	16
1		3	9	4	6		7	2	8	11					10	5						C. Thomas	17
1		3	9	4	6	12		7	10	11				2	8*	5						A. Robinson	18
1		3*	6	5	7	12			9	11				2	10	4			8			K. Salmon	19
1		3	6	4	7				9	11				2	10	5			8			N. Midgeley	20
1		3	6	4	9	12			8	11				2	10*	5			7			R. Guy	21
1		3	6	4	7	12		10*	9	11				2		5			8			D. Allison	22
1		3	6	4	7	12		10	9	11				2*		5			8			N. Ashley	23
		3	6*	4	7			9	10	11		2			12	5			8	1		J. Worrall	24
		3	6		7			9	10	11			2		4	5			8	1		K. Barrett	25
		3	7	5	6		12	10		11					9	2		4*	8	1		D. Shaw	26
		3	7	4	6			9	2	11			12		10	5*			8	1		C. Newsome	27
		3*	7	4	6		10		8	11			2			5			9	1	12	D. Lloyd	28
			6	4	7			10	8	11			5		9	2			3	1		D. Axcell	29
			6	4	3			10	8	11			5		9	2			7	1		P. Tyldesley	30
			6	4	3			10	8	11			5		9	2			7	1		D. Scott	31
			6	4	9			10	8	11			5			2			7	1	3	J. Lovatt	32
		3	6*	4	9		12	10	8	11			5			2			7	1		D. Richardson	33
		3	6	4	9			10	8	11			5			2			7	1		R. Chadwick	34
		3*	6	4	9				8	11			5		12	2			7	1	10	T. Jones	35
		3*	6	4	9			10	8	11			5			2		12	7	1		T. Mills	36
			6	4	9			10	8	11			5			2			7	1	3	N. Midgley	37
			6	4	9		12	10*	8	11			5			2			7	1	3	C. Seel	38
	7		6	4	9			10*	8	11	12		5			2				1	3	D. Owen	39
			6	4	9				8	11	10		5	12		2*			7	1	3	K. Walmsley	40
			6	4	9				8	11	10		5	12		2			7*	1	3	G. Peck	41
			6	4	9		8			11	10		5	7		2				1	3	K. Baker	42
23	10	32	40	41	42	7	4	29	38	42	6	12	25	11	19	29	0	3	22	19	8		
	+ 1s		+ 2s			+ 7s	+ 4s				+ 3s		+ 1s	+ 4s	+ 2s		+ 1s	+ 1s			+ 1s		

FOOTBALL LEAGUE RECORD

1899 Elected to Division 2; 1902–24 Division 1; 1924–27 Division 2; 1927–28 Division 1; 1928–29 Division 2; 1929–54 Division 1; 1954–66 Division 2; 1966–67 Division 3; 1967–74 Division 2; 1974–82 Division 1; 1982– Division 2.

HONOURS

Football League: Division 1 best season: 3rd, 1913–14. Division 2 – Champions 1926–27, 1928–29, 1973–74; Runners-up 1901–02. Division 3 – Runners-up 1966–67. *FA Cup:* best season: 6th rd, 1935–36, 1946–47, 1969–70, 1974–75, 1976–77, 1977–78; old last eight 1900–01, 1903–04. *Football League Cup:* Semi-final 1975–76. *Amateur Cup:* Winners 1895, 1898. *Anglo-Scottish Cup:* Winners 1975–76.

COLOURS

Red shirts with three narrow white stripes down the sleeves, white shorts with three white stripes on a red side panel, white stockings with three red rings at the top.

Change colours: All white.

MIDDLESBROUGH

Players Names Ht. Wt. D.o.B.	Birthplace Transfer Fee	Clubs	Appearances F.L. A & S	 F.L.C. A & S	 F.A.C. A & S	Goals F.L.	 F.L.C.	 F.A.C.
Goalkeepers								
Jim Platt (NI)	Ballymoney	Ballymena						
5 1, 12 10, 26.1.52	£27,000	Middlesbrough	401	33	32			
	—	Hartlepool U (loan)	13					
		Cardiff C (loan)	4	2				
Kel O'Hanlon	Saltburn	Middlesbrough (A)	19		3			
6 0, 12 0, 16.5.62								
Defenders								
Mike Angus*	Middlesbrough	Middlesbrough	35+2	4	1+1	1		1
5 10, 12 3, 28.10.60	—	Scunthorpe U (loan)	20		1	2		
Irving Nattrass (EU23)	Fishburn	Newcastle U (A)	226+12	21	23	16	3	1
5 11, 12 0, 12.12.52	£475,000	Middlesbrough	95+5	6+1	12	2		
Joe Bolton	Birtley	Sunderland (A)	264+9	16	22	11		1
5 11, 12 2, 2.2.55	£200,000	Middlesbrough	59	2	3	1		
Mike Baxter	Birmingham	Preston NE (A)	209+1	16	6	17	1	
6 1, 12 0, 30.12.56	£425,000	Middlesbrough	81	2	4	5		
Darren Wood (ES)	Scarborough	Middlesbrough (A)	53	2	5	4		
5 10, 11 8,								
Tony Mowbray	Saltburn	Middlesbrough (A)	25+1	2	3			
6 1, 12 2,								
John Brownlie (S)	Calder-Cruix	Hibernian						
5 11, 11 0, 11.3.52		Newcastle U	124	4	7+1	2		
	£30,000	Middlesbrough	12	2	1			
Kevin Beattie (E)	Carlisle	Ipswich T (A)	225+3	16	24+2	24		5
5 10¼, 12 4, 18.12.53	F/T	Colchester U (N/C)	3+1	1				
	F/T	Middlesbrough	3+1		1			
Midfield								
Terry Cochrane (NI)	Killyleagh	Coleraine						
5 7½, 10 8, 23.1.53		Burnley	62+5	7	4+1	13	4	
	£238,000	Middlesbrough	96+15	5	12	7	1	
Colin Ross	Dailly	Middlesbrough (A)	37+1		2			
5 7, 11 0, 29.8.62	—	Chesterfield (loan)	6					
Steve Tupling		Middlesbrough (A)						
Heine Otto (Hol)	Holland	FC Twente						
6 0, 12 0,	£125,000	Middlesbrough	80+2	5	7	13	1	1
Mick Kennedy	Salford	Halifax T (A)	74+2	2	6	4		1
5 10, 10 6, 9.4.61	£50,000	Huddersfield T	80+1	4+2	8	9		
	£100,000	Middlesbrough	38	2	4	5		
Gary Gill		Middlesbrough (A)						
Alan Roberts*		Middlesbrough (A)						
Forwards								
Paul Sugrue	Coventry	Nuneaton Bor						
5 7, 9 10, 6.11.60	£30,000	Manchester C	5+1					
	F/T	Cardiff C	2+3					
	F/T	Kansas						
	F/T	Middlesbrough	22		5	3		
Steve Bell (EY)	Middlesbrough	Middlesbrough (A)	43	1	5	8		2
5 7, 10 4,								
David Shearer*	Inverness	Inverness Clach						
5 10, 12 0,16.10.58	£5000	Middlesbrough	88+9	4+1	7+2	23		4
	—	Wigan Ath (loan)	11			9		
Bozo Jankovic (Yug)	Yugoslavia	Zeljeznicar						
6 0, 13 4, 22.5.51	£100,000	Middlesbrough	48+8	3+2	7	16	1	1
Gary MacDonald	Middlesbrough	Middlesbrough (A)	16+8	+1	1+1	2		
6 0, 12 1, 26.3.62								
David Currie	Stockton	Middlesbrough	4+5		1			
6 0, 11 13,								
Ray Hankin (EU23)	Wallsend	Burnley (A)	110+2	12	5	37	4	1
6 2, 14 0, 2.2.56	£180,000	Leeds U	82+1	15	1	32	3	
	£300,000	Vancouver W						
	£80,000	Middlesbrough	19+2	2	3	1	1	
Paul Ward	Sedgefield	Chelsea (A)						
5 11, 12 5,	F/T	Middlesbrough	11+4		1			
Apprentices								
Gary Hamilton		Middlesbrough (A)	8+1			2		

Commercial Manager: Duncan Gibson. (Tel. 0642/89785)
Club Coach: Cyril Knowles
Junior Reds Player of the Season 1982–83: Stephen Bell
Physiotherapist: Lew Clayton
Club Captain 1982–83: Jim Platt
Chief Scout:
Club Statistician: Harry Glasper
Association of Football Statisticians Club Adviser to Yearbook: I. Tewson

Players (non-appearance) granted free transfer: Frankie Harrison, F.; David McClurg, M.; Wayne Earnshaw, G.; Phil Lloyd, D.; Tony Young, D.
Players released since May 1982: Billy Ashcroft, F. (FC Twente); Neil Connell, G. (N/K); Phil McMahon, F. (N/K); Paul Robinson, D. (N/K); Bobby Thomson, M. (Hibernian); Dave McKinley, F. (N/K).

MILLWALL

Division 3

Back row (left to right): Alan McLeary, Dean Horrix, Alan West, Paul Robinson, Andy Massey
Middle row: Terry Long (Assistant Manager), Cliff Speight (Physiotherapist), David Martin, Trevor Aylott, Peter Gleasure, Paul Sansome, Keith Stevens, Lawrie Madden, Barry Kitchener (Youth Team Coach), Roger Cross (Reserve Team Coach)
Front row: Austin Hayes, Paul Roberts, Sam Allardyce, Peter Anderson (Player/Manager), Nicky Chatterton, Willie Carr, Phil Warman.

Chairman: Alan A. Thorne.

Directors: W. J. Nelan, B. A. Thorne.

Secretary: Graham Hover.

Manager: George Graham.

Assistant Manager: Theo Foley.

Year Formed: 1885. ***Turned Professional:*** 1893. ***Ltd Co.:*** 1894.

Club Nickname: 'The Lions'.

Previous Grounds: 1885, Glengall Road, Millwall; 1886, Back of 'Lord Nelson'; 1890, East Ferry Road; 1901, North Greenwich; 1910, The Den.

Previous Names: 1885, Millwall Rovers; 1889, Millwall Athletic.

Previous Managers since 1946: Jack Cock, Charlie Hewitt, Ron Gray, Jimmy Seed, Reg Smith, Ron Gray, Billy Gray, Benny Fenton, Gordon Jago, George Petchey, Peter Anderson (11).

The Den, Cold Blow Lane, London, SE14 5RH. Telephone 01-639 3143/4. ***Ground capacity:*** 32,000. ***Record attendance:*** 48,672 v Derby Co, FA Cup 5th rd, 20 Feb, 1937. ***Record receipts:*** £21,756 v Ipswich T, FA Cup 6th rd, 11 Mar, 1978. ***Pitch measurements:*** 112yd×74yd.

Directions to Ground: Buses from Central London and West End: 36, 36A, 36B, 53, 141, 171, 177, 182. From City: 21. Nearest Underground stations, New Cross or New Cross Gate (Metropolitan Line). Also New Cross Gate British Rail station.

Match tickets: Bookable 10–14 days in advance from club office.

Car parking: Car park near the ground. Also ample street parking.

Entertainments /catering facilities: Several licensed refreshment points around the ground.

Club shop: Three shops at the ground open on match days.

Programmes: Programmes available on subscription.

Address of the Club Shop or Boutique: 'The Den', Cold Blow Lane, New Cross, London, SE14.

Note: Full club statistical records are on pages 416–455.

MILLWALL 1982–83 LEAGUE RECORD

Match No.	Date	Venue	Opponents	Result	H/T Score	Lg. Pos.	Goalscorers	Attendance
1	Aug 28	A	Preston NE	L 2-3	0-2	—	Chatterton, Neal	4483
2	Sept 5	H	Cardiff C	L 0-4	0-2	—		5620
3	8	H	AFC Bournemouth	W 2-0	2-0	—	Carr, Allardyce	3012
4	11	A	Gillingham	L 0-1	0-0	22		4663
5	18	H	Bradford C	D 1-1	0-0	20	Neal	3558
6	25	A	Brentford	D 1-1	0-0	21	Aylott	6455
7	28	A	Portsmouth	L 0-2	0-0	—		7615
8	Oct 2	H	Huddersfield T	W 3-0	1-0	20	Shinton, Aylott, Massey	3004
9	9	H	Oxford U	W 2-1	1-0	13	Neal, Martin	3906
10	16	A	Exeter C	L 1-2	1-0	18	Chatterton	2840
11	19	A	Bristol R	L 0-4	0-2	—		7241
12	23	H	Walsall	D 2-2	1-1	19	Neal, Madden	3294
13	30	A	Sheffield U	D 1-1	0-1	17	Massey	13,836
14	Nov 2	H	Plymouth Arg	D 2-2	1-2	—	Chatterton (pen), Massey	3097
15	6	H	Wrexham	D 1-1	1-0	19	Neal	2943
16	13	A	Wigan Ath	L 1-3	0-2	20	Aylott	4456
17	28	H	Reading	D 1-1	0-0	—	Chatterton (pen)	3578
18	Dec 4	A	Lincoln C	L 1-3	0-2	21	Massey	4244
19	18	A	Doncaster R	L 1-2	1-0	23	Chatterton	2568
20	26	H	Orient	L 0-1	0-0	—		4740
21	28	A	Southend U	D 1-1	1-0	23	Neal	4710
22	Jan 1	H	Chesterfield	D 1-1	0-1	24	Neal	3215
23	3	A	Newport Co	D 2-2	1-2	24	Neal, Aylott	4017
24	15	H	Preston NE	W 1-0	1-0	23	O'Riordan (og)	2816
25	22	A	AFC Bournemouth	L 0-3	0-1	24		4707
26	30	H	Gillingham	W 4-1	3-1	24	Neal, Stride, Massey, Hayes	3813
27	Feb 1	A	Cardiff C	L 0-3	0-1	—		5643
28	6	H	Portsmouth	L 0-2	0-1	—		5621
29	12	A	Huddersfield T	L 1-5	0-2	23	Madden	8111
30	26	H	Exeter C	W 5-2	3-0	23	Neal 3, Aylott, Chatterton	2806
31	Mar 1	A	Plymouth Arg	L 1-3	1-0	—	Neal	4114
32	5	A	Walsall	L 0-4	0-2	24		2779
33	12	H	Sheffield U	L 1-2	0-0	24	Lovell	4055
34	19	A	Wrexham	L 3-4	2-2	24	Bremner 2, Chatterton (pen)	2668
35	27	H	Wigan Ath	W 2-0	1-0	—	Neal, Stewart	2772
36	Apr 2	H	Southend U	W 3-1	2-1	23	Otulokowski, Chatterton (pen), McLeary	3336
37	4	A	Orient	W 3-2	3-0	—	Chatterton (pen), Otulokowski, Stewart	4345
38	9	H	Lincoln C	W 2-1	1-1	22	Stewart, Neal	3760
39	12	H	Bristol R	D 1-1	0-1	—	White (pen)	4873
40	16	A	Bradford C	D 0-0	0-0	22		3953
41	23	H	Doncaster R	W 3-0	2-0	22	Neal 2, Bremner	4288
42	27	A	Oxford U	L 0-1	0-0	—		4161
43	30	A	Reading	D 3-3	1-3	21	White 2 (1 pen), Bremner	4401
44	May 2	H	Newport Co	W 3-0	0-0	22	Neal, White (pen), Bremner	5155
45	8	H	Brentford	W 1-0	1-0	22	Bremner	9097
46	14	A	Chesterfield	W 1-0	0-0	17	Cusack (pen)	4314

Final League Position: 17

GOALSCORERS

League (64): Neal 18, Chatterton 9 (5 pens), Bremner 6, Aylott 5, Massey 5, White 4 (3 pens), Stewart 3, Madden 2, Otulokowski 2, Allardyce 1, Carr 1, Cusack 1 (pen), Hayes 1, Lovell 1, Martin 1, McLeary 1, Shinton 1, Stride 1, own goal 1.
Milk Cup (2): Martin 1, Neal 1.
FA Cup (0).
Football League Trophy (13): Neal 6, Hayes 2, Aylott 1, Chatterton 1, Horrix 1, Massey 1, West 1.

Milk Cup	First Round	Northampton T (h)	0-2
		(a)	2-2
FA Cup	First Round	Slough T (a)	0-1

Football League Trophy		Wimbledon (h)	0-1
		Brentford (h)	3-0
		Crystal Palace (a)	3-0
	Quarter-final	Bradford C (h)	1-1 (aet) (won on penalties)
	Semi-final	Reading (a)	3-1
	Final	Lincoln C (a)	3-2

Gleasure	Stevens	Robinson	Chatterton	Allardyce	Madden	Massey	Carr	Aylott	Neal	West	Horrix	Sansome	Roberts	Hayes	Martin	Shinton	Anderson	McLeary	Stride	Wells (L)	Lovell	Bremner	White	Cusack	Otulakowski	Stewart (L)	Nutton	*Referees*
1	2	3	4	5	6	7*	8	9	10	11	12																	A. Hamil
	2	3	4	5				9	8*	11	12	1	6	7	10													H. Taylor
	2		6	3	5		11	9			8	1	4	7	10													I. Borrett
	2	3*	4	5	6		7	9			11	1	8		10	12												D. Hedges
	2		6	4	3		7*	11	12		9	1	5		10	8												B. Stevens
	2	5	7		3	12	8	10	6*			1	4		9	11												C. Thomas
	2	3	4		5	12	8	9	11			1	6		10	7*												A. Crickmore
	2			5	3	4		9	8	11		1	6		10	7												A. Grey
	2			5	3	4		9	8	11		1	6		10	7												J. Martin
	2		4	5	3			9	8	11		1	6		10	7		12										H. King
	2		4	5	3			9	8	11		1	6		10	7												T. Bune
	2			5	3	4		9*	8	11		1	6		10	7	12											D. Letts
	2		12	5	3	4	7		8	11	9	1	6		10*													R. Bridges
	2		11	5*	3	4	7		8		9	1	6	12	10													D. Axcell
	2	3		5		4		9	8	11	7	1	6		10													D. Brazier
	2	5		3	12	6		10	9	11*	7	1	4		8													T. Mills
	2	3	12	5		4		9	8	11*	7	1	6		10													J. Hunting
	2	3	8	5		4		9		11	7	1	6					10										A. Seville
	2		8	5		4		9		11	10	1	6	7					3									R. Guy
	2		8	5		4		9	12		10*	1	6	7	11				3									M. James
	2		7	5	10	4		9	8			1	6	11					3									M. Taylor
	2		11	5	3	4		9	8			1	6	7*		12			10									A. Gunn
	2		11	5	4			9	8			1	6		10	7			3									V. Callow
	2		11	5	4			9	8			1	6		10	7			3									L. Shapter
	2		11*	5	4			9	8			1	6	12	10	7			3									J. Martin
1			11	5	4	10		9	8*				6	7	2	12			3									E. Read
1			11	5	4*	10		9	8				6	7	2	12			3									M. Heath
1			11	5	4	10		9			8*		6	7	2	12			3									R. Milford
			11	5	12	10*		9	8				6	7	2				3	1	4							P. Willis
	12		11		4	8		10	9*				6		2				3	1	6	7						M. Dimblebee
		12	11		5	10		9	8*				6		2				3	1	4	7						A. Hamil
			11		5	10		9	8						2				3	1	4	7	6					D. Allison
			11*		3			9	8				5							1	2	7	4	6	10	12		B. Hill
			11		5			9*	12						2				3	1		7	4	6	10	8		A. Robinson
			11						8										3	1	2	7	4	6	10	9	5	A. Grey
			11						8*		12								3	1	2	9	4	6	10	7	5	A. Glasson
			11						8										3	1	2	9	4	6	10	7	5	M. Robinson
					12				8						11				3	1	2	7	4	6	10	9	5*	D. Letts
					5				8						11				3	1	2	7	4	6	10	9		K. Baker
		9			5	12			8						11*				3	1	2	7	4	6	10			M. Scott
		12			4				8						11				3*	1	2	7		6	10	9	5	T. Spencer
					9				8						11				3	1	2	7	4	6	10		5	C. Newsome
					11				8										3	1	2	7	4	6	10	9	5	M. James
					11				8										3	1	2	7	4	6	10	9	5	D. Axcell
					11				8										3	1	2	7	4	6	10	9	5	Alan Robinson
		8			11	10*												12	3	1	2	7*	4	6	9		5	J. Bray
4	25	11	30	27	34	22	8	32	37	13	12	24	31	10	33	11	0	1	27	18	17	17	14	14	14	10	10	
	+ 1s	+ 2s	+ 2s		+ 3s	+ 3s			+ 3s		+ 3s			+ 2s		+ 5s	+ 1s	+ 2s								+ 1s		

FOOTBALL LEAGUE RECORD

1920 Original Members of Division 3; 1921 Division 3(S); 1928–34 Division 2; 1934–38 Division 3(S); 1938–48 Division 2; 1948–58 Division 3(S); 1958–62 Division 4; 1962–64 Division 3; 1964–65 Division 4; 1965–66 Division 3; 1966–75 Division 2; 1975–76 Division 3; 1976–79 Division 2; 1979– Division 3.

HONOURS

Football League: Division 2 best season: 3rd, 1971–72; Division 3(S) – Champions 1927–28, 1937–38; Division 3 – Runners-up 1965–66; Division 4 – Champions 1961–62; Runners-up 1964–65. *FA Cup:* semi-final 1900, 1903, 1937 (first Division 3 side to reach semi-final). *Football League Cup:* best season: 5th rd, 1973–74, 1976–77.

COLOURS

Royal blue shirts, white shorts, blue stockings. **Change colours:** Red shirts with white trim, red shorts and stockings.

MILLWALL

Players Names Ht, Wt, D.o.B.	Birthplace Transfer Fee	Clubs	Appearances F.L. A & S	 F.L.C. A & S	 F.A.C. A & S	Goals F.L.	 F.L.C.	 F.A.C.
Goalkeepers								
Peter Gleasure	Luton	Millwall (A)	55	7	4			
5 11, 12 13, 8.10.60	—	Northampton T (loan)	11					
Paul Sansome	New Addington	Crystal Palace (A)						
5 11, 11 10, 6.10.61	F/T	Millwall	32	1	1			
Defenders								
David Stride	Lymington	Chelsea (A)	35	2				
5 9, 11 5, 14.3.58	£90,000	Memphis						
	£25,000	Millwall	27			1		
David Cusack	Rotherham	Sheffield W	92+3	7	7	1		
6 1½, 13 12, 6.6.56	£50,000	Southend U	186	13	7	17		1
	£30,000	Millwall	14			1		
Mickey Nutton	St Johns Wood	Chelsea (A)	77+2	1	3			
5 11, 10 12, 3.10.59	—	Reading (loan)	6					
	£65,000	Millwall	10					
Lawrie Madden*	London	Arsenal (AM)						
5 11, 12 6, 28.9.55	—	Mansfield (N/C)	9+1	2	2			
	—	Manchester Utd						
	—	Charlton Ath	109+4	4+2	8	7		
	£10,000	Millwall	44+3	2	1	3		
Paul Roberts	London	Millwall (A)	142+4	7+1	9			
5 10, 12 0, 27.4.62								
Paul Robinson (EY)	Hampstead	Millwall (A)	24+2	1	4			
5 10, 11 1, 5.1.63								
Keith Stevens	Wimbledon	Millwall (A)	33+1	2	1			
5 11, 11 1,								
Sam Allardyce	Dudley	Bolton W (A)	180+4	15	14+1	21	1	2
6 1½, 14 0, 19.10.54	£160,000	Sunderland	24+1	2		2		
	£95,000	Millwall	63	3	5	2		2
Steve Lovell (W)	Swansea	Crystal Palace (A)	68+6	10+1	1+1	3	1	
5 9, 11 3, 16.7.60	—	Stockport Co (loan)	12		1			1
		Millwall	17			1		
Carl Cowley		Millwall (A)						
Midfield								
Nicky Chatterton	Norwood	Crystal Palace	142+9	15	15	31	3	2
5 9, 11 0, 18.5.54	£100,000	Millwall	184+3	10	11	43	1	5
Andy Massey (EIY)	London	Millwall	65+10	2+1	6	7		
5 10, 10 9, 20.10.61								
David Martin (EY)	East Ham	Millwall (A)	103+4	7	5	3	1	
5 11, 10 11, 25.4.63								
Alan McLeary (EY)	London	Millwall (A)	1+2			1		
Anton Otulakowski	Dewsbury	Ossett Trinity						
5 7, 10 10, 29.1.56		Barnsley	42		1	2		
	£60,000	West Ham U	10+7					
	£50,000	Southend U	161+2	12	9	8		
	£30,000	Millwall	14			2		
Forwards								
Austin Hayes* (EI)	London	Southampton (A)	22+9	2+1	4	5	1	1
5 4½, 9 12, 15.7.58	£25,000	Millwall	40+7	1	2	5		1
Dean Neal	Edmonton	QPR (A)	20+3	2		8	1	
5 10½, 12 0, 5.1.61	Tulsa Roughnecks							
	£100,000	Millwall	55+7	1+1	3	18	1	1
Dean White	Hastings	Chelsea (A)						
5 10, 11 4, 4.12.58	F/T	Gillingham	108+8	+2	12+2	26		2
	P/E	Millwall	14			4		
Kevin Bremner	Banff	Keith						
5 9½, 12 3, 7.9.52	£40,000	Colchester U	89+6	5+2	10	31	3	2
	—	Birmingham C (loan)	3+1			1		
	—	Wrexham (loan)	4			1		
	—	Plymouth Arg (loan)	5			1		
	£25,000	Millwall	17			6		
John Neal		Millwall (A)						
Roger Wynter		Millwall (A)						

Commercial Manager: W. Neil (Tel. 01-639 4590)
Assistant Manager/Club Coach: Theo Foley
Supporters Player of the Season 1982–83: Dean Neal
Physiotherapist:
Club Captain 1982–83: Nicky Chatterton
Chief Scout: Bob Pearson
Club Statistician:
Association of Football Statisticians Club Adviser to Yearbook: R. Lindsey

Players released since May 1982:
Alan Slough, D. (Torquay N/C); David Rose, M. (N/K); Phil Warman, D. (retired); Willie Carr, M. (Worcester C); Alan West, M. (Hitchin T); Barry Kitchener, D. (retired); Peter Anderson, M. (N/K); Bobby Shinton, F. (N/K).

NEWCASTLE UNITED Division 2

Back row (left to right): Willie McFaul (Coach), John Trewick, Bruce Halliday, Peter Haddock, Steve Hardwick, Chris Hedworth, Jeff Clarke, Kevin Carr, Wesley Saunders, Chris Waddle, Mick Martin, Ian Liversedge (Physiotherapist)
Front row: Peter Cartwright, John Anderson, Imre Varadi, Kevin Todd, Terry McDermott, Arthur Cox (Manager), Kevin Keegan, John Craggs, Steve Carney, David McCreery, Ken Wharton.

President: F. Braithwaite OBE.

Chairman: S. Seymour. ***Vice-Chairman:*** R. Mackenzie.

Directors: F. Braithwaite OBE, J. Rush AFC, W. G. McKeag, Sir G. Bowman, W. P. Catesby, E. Dunn.

Manager: Arthur Cox.

Secretary: R. Cushing. ***Assistant Secretary:*** A. J. Garvie.

Year Formed: 1882. ***Turned Professional:*** 1889. ***Ltd Co.:*** 1890.

Club Nickname: 'Magpies'.

Previous Name: Newcastle East End until Newcastle U in 1892.

Previous Ground: Chillingham Road, Heaton, until 1892.

Previous Managers since 1946: George Martin, Duggie Livingstone, Charlie Mitten, Norman Smith, Joe Harvey, Gordon Lee, Richard Dinnis, Bill McGarry (8).

St James' Park, Newcastle-upon-Tyne NE1 4ST. Telephone Newcastle (0632) 328361. Information service 611571. ***Telegraphic address:*** 'Football, Newcastle-upon-Tyne'. ***Ground capacity:*** 37,718. ***Record attendance:*** 68,386 v Chelsea, Division 1, 3 Sept, 1930. ***Record receipts:*** £53,462 v QPR, Division 2, 28 Aug, 1982. ***Pitch measurements:*** 115yd×75yd.

Directions to Ground: The ground is central and within walking distance of the railway station and the town centre.

Match tickets: Personal applications accepted ten days before a match and postal applications accepted 14 days before a match.

Car parking: Car park on the north side of the ground. Street parking available.

Entertainments/catering facilities: Excellent facilities in the New East Stand. Refreshments available in all parts of the ground.

Club shop: Open daily (except Sunday). Open match days 9.30 am–3.00 pm.

Handbooks/programmes: Programmes if available can be ordered from the secretary price 35p.

Address of the Club Shop or Boutique: St James' Park, Newcastle-upon-Tyne NE1 4ST.

Note: Full club statistical records are on pages 416–455.

NEWCASTLE UNITED 1982–83 LEAGUE RECORD

Match No.	Date	Venue	Opponents	Result	H/T Score	Lg. Pos.	Goalscorers	Attendance
1	Aug 28	H	QPR	W 1-0	0-0	—	Keegan	36,185
2	Sept 1	A	Blackburn R	W 2-1	2-0	—	Keegan, Martin	14,421
3	4	A	Bolton W	L 1-3	0-3	3	Keegan (pen)	17,707
4	8	H	Middlesbrough	D 1-1	0-0	—	Channon	27,939
5	11	H	Chelsea	D 1-1	0-1	8	Clarke	29,084
6	18	A	Shrewsbury T	L 1-2	1-1	10	Varadi	7907
7	25	H	Barnsley	L 1-2	1-2	12	Varadi	24,511
8	Oct 2	A	Rotherham U	W 5-1	2-0	10	Keegan 4 (1 pen), Todd	12,436
9	9	A	Oldham Ath	D 2-2	2-2	12	Varadi 2	11,491
10	16	H	Fulham	L 1-4	0-3	13	Keegan (pen)	29,490
11	23	H	Crystal Palace	W 1-0	1-0	11	Waddle	22,554
12	30	A	Leeds U	L 1-3	1-1	13	Anderson	26,570
13	Nov 6	H	Burnley	W 3-0	1-0	9	Waddle, Keegan, Varadi	20,996
14	13	A	Leicester C	D 2-2	1-1	10	Keegan 2	15,044
15	20	A	Carlisle U	L 0-2	0-1	10		16,276
16	27	H	Cambridge U	W 2-0	2-0	10	Martin, McDermott	20,360
17	Dec 4	A	Charlton Ath	L 0-2	0-1	11		10,381
18	11	H	Wolverhampton W	D 1-1	1-1	12	Wharton	19,485
19	18	A	Sheffield W	D 1-1	1-0	15	Varadi	16,310
20	27	H	Derby Co	W 1-0	0-0	13	Gayle	30,559
21	28	A	Grimsby T	D 2-2	0-1	12	Varadi, Gayle	14,983
22	Jan 1	H	Carlisle U	D 2-2	1-1	13	Keegan 2	29,154
23	3	H	Bolton W	D 2-2	0-1	12	Martin, Waddle	23,455
24	15	A	QPR	L 0-2	0-0	14		13,972
25	22	H	Shrewsbury T	W 4-0	1-0	12	Wharton 2, Keegan (pen), Varadi	19,352
26	Feb 5	A	Middlesbrough	D 1-1	1-1	12	Keegan	25,164
27	19	H	Oldham Ath	W 1-0	1-0	10	McDermott	20,661
28	26	A	Fulham	D 2-2	2-1	11	Varadi, McDermott	14,277
29	Mar 5	A	Crystal Palace	W 2-0	0-0	10	Varadi, Waddle	10,239
30	12	H	Leeds U	W 2-1	1-0	6	Waddle, Keegan (pen)	24,580
31	19	A	Barnsley	L 0-1	0-0	10		13,900
32	26	H	Leicester C	D 2-2	0-1	10	Keegan, McDermott	22,655
33	Apr 2	H	Grimsby T	W 4-0	2-0	10	Keegan, Varadi 2, McDonald	20,145
34	4	A	Derby Co	L 1-2	0-2	—	Waddle	19,779
35	9	H	Blackburn R	W 3-2	2-0	9	Metcalfe (og), Varadi, Waddle	17,788
36	16	A	Chelsea	W 2-0	1-0	7	Keegan (pen), Varadi	13,446
37	20	H	Rotherham U	W 4-0	2-0	—	McDermott, Varadi, Wharton, Keegan	18,447
38	23	H	Charlton Ath	W 4-2	1-0	5	Wharton, McDermott, Varadi 2	20,526
39	30	A	Cambridge U	L 0-1	0-1	5		7591
40	May 4	A	Barnsley	W 5-0	1-0	—	McDonald 2, Keegan, Varadi 2	10,958
41	7	H	Sheffield W	W 2-1	0-0	5	Varadi, Sterland (og)	29,812
42	14	A	Wolverhampton W	D 2-2	2-2	5	McDonald, Varadi	22,446

Final League Position: 5

GOALSCORERS

League (75): Keegan 21 (6 pens), Varadi 21, Waddell 7, McDermott 6, Wharton 5, McDonald 4, Martin 3, Gayle 2, Anderson 1, Channon 1, Clarke 1, Todd 1, own goals 2.
Milk Cup (2): Clarke 1, Varadi 1.
FA Cup (1): McDermott 1.

Milk Cup	Second Round	Leeds U (a)	1-0
		(h)	1-4
FA Cup	Third Round	Brighton & HA (a)	1-1
		(h)	0-1

Hardwick	Craggs	Saunders	Trewick	Clarke	Haddock	Keegan	Martin	Varadi	Cartwright	Waddle	Wharton	Channon	Bell	Anderson	Todd	McDonald	Carr	Carney	McDermott	McCreery	Hedworth	Gayle (L)	Ferris	Thomas (L)	Referees	Match No.
1	2	3	4*	5	6	7	8	9	10	11	12														T. Mills	1
1	2	3		5	6	7	4	9	8	11*	10			12											F. Roberts	2
1	2	3		5	6	7	4	9	8	11	10														J. Lovatt	3
1	2	3		5	6	7	4	9	10	11		8													K. Walmsley	4
1	2	3		5	6	7	4	9		11*	10	8	12												D. Scott	5
1	2	3		5	6	7	4	9			10	8	11*	12											K. Baker	6
1	2	3		5	6	7	4*	9			10	8			12	11									D. Richardson	7
		3		5		7	4	9			11			2	8		1	6	10						J. Hough	8
		3		5		7	4	9			12			2	8*		1	6	10	11					D. Owen	9
		3		5		7	4	9			12			2	8*		1	6	10	11					A. Robinson	10
		3		5	6	7	4	9		11	10			2			1			8					T. Fitzharris	11
					6	7	4	9*		11	3			2			1	5	10	8	12				M. Heath	12
					6	7	4*	9		11	3			2		12	1	5	10	8					A. Challinor	13
					6	7	4	9		11	3			2			1	5	10	8					J. Moules	14
	12			5	4			9		11	3			2	7*		1	6	10	8					J. Worrall	15
	12			5			4	9*		11	3			2			1		10	8	6	7			N. Midgeley	16
				5			4			11	3			2			1	12	10	8	6	9	7*		T. Bune	17
				5			4			9	3			2		11	1		10	8	6	7			K. Hackett	18
				5	6			9		11	3			2*		4	1	12	10	8		7			T. Holbrook	19
	2			5	6	7		9		11	3						1		10	4		8			P. Tyldesley	20
				5	6	7	12	9		11	3						1	2	10	4*		8			M. Scott	21
	2			5	6	7	12	9		11	3						1		10*	4		8			T. Jones	22
				5	6	7	4			9	3			2		12	1		10	11*		8			J. Key	23
				5		7	4	9*		11	3			2		8	1	6	10				12		L. Burden	24
		3		5		7*	4	9		11	10			2		8	1	6					12		R. Chadwick	25
		3		5		7	4	9		11	10			2		8	1	6							D. Shaw	26
				5		7	4	9		11*	3			2		8	1	6	10				12		T. Mills	27
				5		7	4	9		11	3			2		8	1	6	10						L. Shapter	28
				5		7	4	9		11	3			2		8	1	6	10						M. Bodenham	29
				5		7	4	9		11	3			2		8	1	6	10						N. Midgeley	30
				5		7	4	9		11	3			2		8	1	6	10						D. Civil	31
				5		7	4	9		11	3			2		8*	1	6	10	12					K. Walmsley	32
				5		7	4	9		11	3			2		8	1	6	10*	12					N. Glover	33
				5		7	4*	9		11	3			2		8	1	6	10	12					R. Guy	34
				5		7		9*		11	3			2		8	1	6	10	4			12		A. Challinor	35
				5		7		9		11	3			2		8	1	6	10	4					E. Read	36
				5		7	12	9		11*	3			2		8	1	6	10	4					M. Wilson	37
				5		7	12	9		11	3			2*		8	1	6	10	4					J. Worrall	38
	2			5		7	12	9		11	3					8*	1	6	10	4					D. Brazier	39
				5		7		9		11	3			2		8		6	10	4				1	H. Taylor	40
				5		7		9		11	3			2		8		6	10	4				1	D. Allinson	41
				5		7	12	9		11	3			2		8*		6	10	4				1	B. Daniels	42
7	10	13	1	39	17	37	29	39	4	37	38	4	1	31	4	22	32	27	32	23	3	8	1	3		
	+ 2s						+ 6s				+ 3s		+ 1s	+ 2s	+ 1s	+ 2s		+ 2s		+ 3s	+ 1s		+ 4s			

FOOTBALL LEAGUE RECORD

93 Elected to Division 2; 1898–1934 Division 1; 1934–48 Division 2; 1948–61 Division 1; 1961–65 Division 2; 1965–78 vision 1; 1978– Division 2.

HONOURS

otball League: Division 1 – Champions 1904–05, 1906–07, 1908–09, 1926–27; Division 2 – Champions 1964–65; unners-up 1897–98, 1947–48. *FA Cup:* Winners 1910, 1924, 1932, 1951, 1952, 1955; Runners-up 1905, 1908, 1911, 74. *Football League Cup:* Runners-up 1975–76. *Texaco Cup:* Winners 1973–74, 1974–75. **European Competitions:** *uropean Fairs Cup:* 1968–69 (winners), 1969–70, 1970–71. *UEFA Cup:* 1977–78. *Anglo-Italian Cup:* Winners 1973.

COLOURS

ack and white striped shirts, black shorts, black stockings with two white hoops on the top.
ange colours: All yellow.

NEWCASTLE UNITED

Players Names Ht, Wt, D.o.B.	Birthplace Transfer Fee	Clubs	Appearances F.L. A & S	 F.L.C. A & S	 F.A.C. A & S	Goals F.L.	 F.L.C.	 F.A.C.
Goalkeeper								
Kevin Carr	Ashington	Burnley (A)						
6 2, 13 6, 6.11.58	F/T	Newcastle U	130	5	9			
Defenders								
John Anderson (EI)	Dublin	WBA (A)						
5 11, 11 6, 7.11.59	£40,000	Preston NE	47+4	2	1			
	F/T	Newcastle U	31+2	2	2	1		
John Craggs (EY)	Flint Hill	Newcastle U (A)	50+2	1	2	1		
5 8½, 12 4, 31.10.48	£60,000	Middlesbrough	408+1	31	33	12	1	
	F/T	Newcastle U	10+2	+1				
David Barton*	Bishop Auckland	Newcastle U (A)	101+1	5	2+1	5	1	
6 0, 11 7, 9.5.59	—	Blackburn R (loan)	8			1		
	—	Darlington (loan)	19			2		
Steve Carney	Wallsend	Blyth Spartans						
5 10, 11 5, 22.9.57	£3,000	Newcastle U	87+8	2	9			
Peter Haddock	Newcastle	Newcastle U (A)	45+2	1	6			
5 11, 11.5, 9.12.61								
Nick Devereaux*		Watford (A)						
	F/T	Newcastle U						
Chris Withe*	Liverpool	Newcastle U (A)	2					
5 10, 11 3, 25.9.62								
Wesley Saunders	Sunderland	Newcastle U	42	2	2			
6 0, 11 11,								
Chris Hedworth	Newcastle	Newcastle U (A)	3+1					
6 1, 10 11,								
Jeff Clarke	Pontefract	Manchester C	13	2				
6 0½, 13 8, 18.1.54	£100,000	Manchester C	178+3	14	15	6		
	F/T	Newcastle U	39	2	2	1	1	
John Carver		Newcastle U (A)						
Midfield								
Ken Wharton	Newcastle	Newcastle U	102+11	4+1	9	10		
5 8, 8 10, 28.11.60								
Mick Martin* (EI)	Dublin	Bohemians						
5 10, 10 11, 9.7.51	£30,000	Manchester U	33+7	1	2	2		
	£35,000	WBA	85+4	5+1	12	11	2	2
	£100,000	Newcastle U	139+8	6	10	5		1
John Trewick (EY)	Bedlington	WBA (A)	84+12	10+2	12	11		
5 10, 10 13, 3.6.57	£250,000	Newcastle U	62	2	7	7		
Derek Bell*	Newcastle	Newcastle U (A)	3+1					
5 8, 11 4,								
David McCreery (NI)	Belfast	Manchester U (A)	48+39	4	1	7	1	
5 6½, 10 7, 16.9.57	£200,000	QPR	54+1	8	1+1	4	1	
	£125,000	Tulsa Roughnecks						
	£80,000	Newcastle U	23+3	2				
Terry McDermott (E)	Kirkby	Bury (A)	83+7	5	5	8	1	2
5 9, 12 13, 8.12.51	£25,000	Newcastle U	55+1	4	10	6	2	2
	£166,000	Liverpool	221+11	36	23	54	5	4
	£100,000	Newcastle U	32	1	2	6		1
Paul Ferris		Newcastle U (A)	1+6					
Forwards								
Chris Waddle	Hepworth	Tow Law T						
6 0, 11 5, 14.12.60	£10,000	Newcastle U	92	3	9	15		3
Kevin Todd	Sunderland	Ryehope CA						
5 9, 12 1,	£5,000	Newcastle U	5+2	1	2+1	3		
	—	Darlington (loan)	20			8		
Imre Varadi	Paddington	Letchworth						
5 8, 11 1, 8.7.59		Sheffield U	6+4		2	4		
	£80,000	Everton	22+4		6	6		1
	£100,000	Newcastle U	81	4	5	39	1	2
Kevin Keegan (E)	Doncaster	Scunthorpe U (A)	120+4	3	14	18	1	3
5 8, 11 7, 14.2.51	£35,000	Liverpool	230	23	28	68	6	14
	£500,000	SV Hamburg						
	£400,000	Southampton	68	3	5	37	1	2
	£100,000	Newcastle U	37	2	2	21		
Neil McDonald		Newcastle U (A)	22+2		2	4		

Commercial Manager: David Hogg (Tel. 0632 328361)
Club Coach: Willie McFaul
Supporters Player of the Season 1982–83: Keevin Keegan
Physiotherapist: Ian Liversedge
Association of Football Statisticians Club Adviser to Yearbook: F. Evans.
Club Captain 1982–83: Kevin Keegan
Chief Scout: Joe Harvey
Club Statistician: Paul Joannou

Players (non-appearance) granted free transfers: Dave Willis, F.; Justin Robson, M.; Paul Malcolm, G.; Dave Thompson,
Players released since May 1982:
Phil Leaver, D. (N/K); Kevin Pugh, M. (Gateshead); Geoff Smith, M. (N/K); Simon Smith, G. (N/K); Bill Snyder, M (N/K); Gary Walton, F. (N/K).

NEWPORT COUNTY Division 3

Back row (left to right):
Vaughan Jones
Mark Kendall
Karl Elsey
Middle row:
Colin Addison (Manager)
Dave Gwyther
Jeff Johnson
John Aldridge
Neil Bailey
Nigel Vaughan
Bobby Smith (Asst Manager)
Dave Williams (Trainer/Coach)
Front row:
Ray Bishop (now at Torquay)
Steve Lowndes
Tommy Tynan
Keith Oakes (Captain)
Grant Davies
John Relish

President:* S. Jenkins.** ***Chairman: R. Ford.

Vice-Chairman: G. C. Thorneycroft.

Directors: J. Ford, A. O. Menzies, G. B. Prosser, J. P. Adams.

Manager: Colin Addison. ***Assistant Manager:*** Bobby Smith.

Secretary: Mr P. Dauncey.

Commercial Manager: P. Jones (Tel: 277472).

Youth Development Officer: G. E. A. Reynolds.

Year Formed: 1912. ***Turned Professional:*** 1912. ***Ltd Co.:*** 1912.

Club Nickname: 'The Ironsides'.

Previous Managers since 1946: Billy McCandless, Tom Bromilow, Fred Stansfield, Bill Lucas, Bobby Evans, Bill Lucas, Trevor Morris, Les Graham, Bob Ferguson, Bill Lucas, Brian Harris, Dave Elliot, Jimmy Scoular, Colin Addison, Len Ashurst (15).

Somerton Park, Newport, Gwent. Telephone 277543/277271/277472. ***Ground capacity:*** 18,000 (seating 1,200). ***Record attendance:*** 24,268 v Cardiff C, Division 3(S), 16 Oct, 1937. ***Record receipts:*** £28,050 v Carl Zeiss Jena, European Cup-Winners' Cup quarter-final 2nd leg, 18 Mar, 1981. ***Pitch measurements:*** 110yd×75yd.

Directions to Ground: Nearest railway station, Newport. By bus: the Chepstow Road bus to Beechwood and walk down over Somerton Hill; the Corporation Road bus to Cromwell Road and Somerton Park. All buses from bus centre in Dock Street.

Match tickets: Seats can be reserved from the club secretary.

Car parking: Street parking under police control.

Entertainments/catering facilities: Licensed bar in Supporters' Club. Licensed bar in the Social Club at Cromwell Road; both membership only. Licensed bars on both sides of ground.

Club shop: Sells all types of souvenirs, including 1979–80 promotion book. Souvenir list available from Commercial Department.

Handbooks/programmes: Back issues of programmes available from programme shop. Match programmes available on subscription from Commercial Department.

Address of Supporters Club: Same as Football Club.

Note: Full club statistical records are on pages 416–455.

NEWPORT COUNTY 1982–83 LEAGUE RECORD

Match No.	Date	Venue	Opponents	Result	H/T Score	Lg. Pos.	Goalscorers	Attendance
1	Aug 28	A	Doncaster R	D 0-0	0-0	—		3471
2	Sept 4	H	Chesterfield	W 1-0	0-0	5	Tynan	3464
3	7	H	Plymouth Arg	D 2-2	1-0	—	Tynan, Gwyther	3741
4	11	A	Bradford C	L 2-4	0-1	13	Aldridge, Tynan	4793
5	18	H	Huddersfield T	W 2-1	0-0	9	Aldridge 2	3536
6	25	A	Portsmouth	W 2-1	0-0	6	Vaughan, Aldridge	10,833
7	28	A	Brentford	L 0-2	0-1	—		5706
8	Oct 2	H	Lincoln C	W 1-0	0-0	8	Tynan	3749
9	9	H	Bristol R	W 2-0	1-0	4	Vaughan, Tynan	5912
10	16	A	Orient	W 5-1	1-0	3	Elsey, Tynan 2, Aldridge, Lowndes	2040
11	19	A	Preston NE	D 0-0	0-0	—		3747
12	23	H	Southend U	D 1-1	1-1	5	Oakes	4338
13	30	A	Wigan Ath	W 1-0	0-0	3	Aldridge	4108
14	Nov 2	H	Sheffield U	W 3-1	1-1	—	Aldridge, West (og), Tynan	5017
15	6	A	Reading	L 2-4	2-3	3	Bailey, Tynan (pen)	3058
16	13	H	AFC Bournemouth	W 5-1	3-0	2	Aldridge 3, Vaughan, Lowndes	4071
17	27	A	Wrexham	L 0-1	0-1	3		3246
18	Dec 4	H	Gillingham	W 2-1	1-1	3	Elsey, Lowndes	3727
19	18	H	Walsall	D 1-1	0-0	4	Vaughan	3572
20	27	A	Cardiff C	L 2-3	0-1	6	Bailey, Vaughan	15,972
21	28	H	Oxford U	L 1-2	0-1	6	Tynan	5836
22	Jan 1	A	Exeter C	W 1-0	0-0	7	Elsey	3505
23	3	H	Millwall	D 2-2	2-1	7	Gwyther, Elsey	4017
24	15	H	Doncaster R	L 1-2	0-2	7	Aldridge	3482
25	22	A	Plymouth Arg	W 4-2	2-1	7	Tynan 2, Elsey, Lowndes	4287
26	29	H	Bradford C	D 1-1	0-1	7	Bailey	3397
27	Feb 1	A	Chesterfield	L 1-3	1-1	—	Tynan	1645
28	6	H	Brentford	D 0-0	0-0	—		3401
29	15	H	Preston NE	W 3-0	0-0	—	Relish, Tynan 2 (1 pen)	2317
30	19	A	Bristol R	W 3-1	2-1	6	Aldridge, Tynan 2 (1 pen)	6812
31	26	H	Orient	W 4-1	4-0	6	Lowndes 3, Aldridge	3202
32	Mar 1	A	Sheffield U	L 0-2	0-0	—		8740
33	4	A	Southend U	W 4-1	2-0	—	Bailey, Vaughan, Lowndes, Aldridge	2476
34	12	H	Wigan Ath	W 1-0	1-0	6	Aldridge	3647
35	19	H	Reading	W 1-0	1-0	5	Tynan	3588
36	23	A	Lincoln C	W 4-1	3-0	—	Tynan 2, Lowndes 2	4742
37	26	A	AFC Bournemouth	W 1-0	1-0	2	Vaughan	9121
38	Apr 2	A	Oxford U	W 3-0	2-0	2	Tynan, Lowndes, Aldridge	6640
39	4	H	Cardiff C	W 1-0	1-0	—	Aldridge	16,052
40	9	A	Gillingham	L 0-2	0-2	1		4265
41	16	H	Portsmouth	L 0-3	0-0	3		10,419
42	23	A	Walsall	L 1-2	0-1	4	Tynan (pen)	5141
43	30	H	Wrexham	W 4-0	2-0	4	Tynan 3 (1 pen), Lowndes	4344
44	May 2	A	Millwall	L 0-3	0-0	4		5515
45	7	A	Huddersfield T	L 0-1	0-0	4		16,509
46	14	H	Exeter C	D 1-1	1-0	4	Williams	3520

Final League Position: 4

GOALSCORERS

League (76): Tynan 25 (5 pens), Aldridge 17, Lowndes 12, Vaughan 7, Elsey 5, Bailey 4, Gwyther 2, Relish 1, Oakes 1, Williams 1, own goal 1.
Milk Cup (10): Lowndes 2, Tynan 2, Vaughan 2, Aldridge 1, Elsey 1, Gwyther 1, Oakes 1.
FA Cup (7): Tynan 4 (2 pens), Aldridge 2, Gwyther 1.
Football League Trophy (9): Bailey 3, Tynan 2, Elsey 1, Gwyther 1, Lowndes 1, Williams 1.

Milk Cup	First Round	Exeter C (a)	2-1
		(h)	6-0
	Second Round	Everton (h)	0-2
		(a)	2-2
FA Cup	First Round	Enfield (a)	0-0
		(h)	4-2
	Second Round	Orient (h)	1-0
	Third Round	Everton (h)	1-1
		(a)	1-2

Football League Trophy		Torquay U (h)	0-1
		Exeter C (h)	5-1
		Bristol C (a)	4-1
	Quarter-final	Chester (a)	0-0 (lost on penalties)

Kendall	Jones	Vaughan	Bailey	Relish	Stroud	Lowndes	Gwyther	Tynan	Elsey	Moore	Davies	Aldridge	Oakes	Boyle	Plumley	Pulis	Reid	Williams	*Referees*	*Match No.*
1	2	3	4	5	6	7	8	9	10	11									J. Lovatt	1
1	2	3	6	4	5	7	9	10	8	11									M. Dimblebee	2
1	2	3	7	4	5	6	9	10	8	11									K. Salmon	3
1	2	10	12	3	6	7*		9	4	11	5	8							F. Roberts	4
1	2	10	4	3	6	7		9	11		5	8							D. Reeves	5
1	2	10	4	3	6	7	12	9	11		5	8*							M. Bodenham	6
1	2	10	4	3	6	7*	12	9	11		5	8							A. Gunn	7
1	2	10	4	3		7		9	11*	12	6	8	5						A. Hamil	8
1	2	10	4	3	6	7		9	11			8	5						M. Heath	9
1		10	4	3	6	7		9	11		2	8	5						J. Deakin	10
1	2	10	4	3	6	7		9	11			8	5						D. Shaw	11
1	2	8*	6	3	5	7		11	9	12		10	4						T. Holbrook	12
1	2	10	4	3	6	7		9	11			8	5						K. Barrett	13
1	2	10	5	3	6	7*		9	11	12		8	4						A. Glasson	14
1	2	10	4	3	6	7		9	11	12		8	5*						M. Taylor	15
1	2	10	4	3	6*	7	12	9	11			8		5					T. Jones	16
1	2	10	4	3	6	7	8	9	11					5					R. Chadwick	17
1	2	10	4	3	6	7		9	11			8		5					D. Civil	18
1	2	10	4	3	6	7		9	11*	12		8		5					L. Shapter	19
1	2	10	4	3	6	7*	12	9	11			8		5					C. Thomas	20
1	2	10	4	3*	6	7	12	9	11			8		5					A. Crickmore	21
	2	10	4	3	6		8	9	11	12		7*		5	1				L. Burden	22
	2	10	4*	3	6		8	9	7	11	12			5	1				V. Callow	23
1		10	4	3	7		12	9		11	2*	8	5	6					E. Scales	24
1		10	4	3*	6	7		9	11			8	5	2		12			J. Bray	25
1	2	10	4		6	7		9	11			8	5	3					D. Letts	26
1	2	10		3	6	7*		9	4		12	8	5	11					P. Tyldesley	27
1	2	10*		3	6	7		9	4	12		8	5	11					M. Robinson	28
1	2	10		3	6	7	12	9	11			8	5	4					T. Bune	29
1	2	10		3	6	7	12	9	11			8*	5	4					T. Ward	30
1	2	10	4	3		7	12	9	11			8	5*	6					K. Baker	31
1	2	3	4	6		7	12	9	10	11*		8		5					D. Scott	32
1	2	10	4	3	6	7		9	11			8		5					A. Gunn	33
1	2	10	4	3	6	7	12	9	11*			8		5					D. Vickers	34
1	2	10	4	3	11	7		9				8	5	6					J. Worrall	35
1	2	10	4	3	6	7		9				8	5	11					B. Hill	36
1	2	10	4*	3	6	7		9	12			8	5	11					D. Reeves	37
1	2	10		3	6	7		9	11			8	5	4					M. Dimblebee	38
1	2	10	12	3*	6	7		9	11			8	5	4					R. Lewis	39
1	2	10*	12	3	6	7		9	11			8	5	4					D. Brazier	40
1	2		10	3*	6	7		9	11			8	5	4			12		A. Seville	41
1	2	10		3*	6	7		9	11			8	5	4			12		A. Robinson	42
1	2	10	4	3	6	7		9	11			8	5						J. Martin	43
1	2	10	4	3	6	7		9*	11			8	5	12					D. Axcell	44
1	2		4		6	7	12	9	11			8	5	3			10*		A. Saunders	45
1	2		4	3	6	7	12	9				8*	5				10	11	K. Barratt	46
44	43	43	37	44	43	43	6	46	41	7	7	41	28	28	2	0	2	1		
			+ 3s				+ 13s		+ 1s	+ 7s	+ 2s			+ 1s		+ 1s	+ 2s			

FOOTBALL LEAGUE RECORD

1920 Original Member of Division 3; 1921 Division 3(S); dropped out of the Football League in 1931 but re-elected 1932; 1932–39 Division 3(S); 1946–47 Division 2; 1947–58 Division 3(S); 1958–62 Division 3; 1962–80 Division 4; 1980– Division 3.

HONOURS

Football League: Division 3 best season: 1982–83; Division 3(S) – Champions 1938–39. *FA Cup:* best season: 5th rd, 1948–49. *Football League Cup:* never past 3rd rd. *Welsh Cup:* winners 1979–80; Runners-up 1963. **European Competitions:** *European Cup-Winners' Cup:* 1980-81 (quarter-finalists).

COLOURS

Amber shirts, black shorts, amber stockings. **Change colours:** White shirts, black shorts, white stockings.

NEWPORT COUNTY

Players Names Ht, Wt, D.o.B.	Birthplace Transfer Fee	Clubs	Appearances F.L. A & S	 F.L.C. A & S	 F.A.C. A & S	Goals F.L.	 F.L.C.	 F.A.C.
Goalkeepers								
Mark Kendall (NIU21)	Blackwood	Tottenham H (A)	29	1	6			
6 0, 12 4, 20.9.58	—	Chesterfield (loan)	9					
	£45,000	Newport Co	114	8	7			
Ian Watson*	North Shields	Sunderland (A)	1		1			
5 11, 12 1, 5.2.60	—	Rochdale (loan)	33	2	5			
	F/T	Newport Co						
Gary Plumley*	Birmingham	Leicester C (A)						
6 0, 12 0, 24.3.56	F/T	Newport Co	182	12	11			
	F/T	Hereford U	13		1			
	F/T	Newport Co	2					
Defenders								
Terry Boyle (W)	Ammanford	Tottenham H (A)						
5 10, 12 4, 29.10.58	F/T	Crystal Palace	24+2		1	1		2
	—	Wimbledon (loan)	5			1		
	P/E	Bristol C	36+1	4	8		2	
	F/T	Newport Co	28+1		3			
Grant Davies*	Barrow	Preston NE (A)						
5 10, 11 4, 13.10.59	F/T	Newport Co	147+3	11	9	1		
	—	Exeter C (loan)	7					
John Relish	Liverpool	Chester (A)	10+1	3		1		
5 8, 12 0, 5.10.53	F/T	Newport Co	256+12	16	9+2	7		
Keith Oakes	Bedworth	Peterborough U (A)	48+13	7+2	4+1	2		
5 10, 12 2, 3.7.56	£15,000	Newport Co	195	12	8+1	26	1	
Vaughan Jones (WU21)	Tonyrefail	Bristol R (A)	93+8	5+3	11	3		
5 8½, 11 11, 2.9.59	F/T	Newport Co	43	4	5			
Ken Stroud	London	Swindon T (A)	302+9	30+1	31	16	2	1
5 11, 12 0, 1.12.53	F/T	Newport Co	43	3	3			
Midfield								
Nigel Vaughan (W)	Newport	Newport Co (A)	208+9	13+1	14+1	27	3	
5 5, 8 10, 20.5.59								
Neil Bailey	Billinge	Burnley (A)						
5 9, 11 0, 26.9.58	F/T	Newport Co	124+5	8	9	4		
Steve Emery	Ledbury	Hereford U (A)	203+1	17	11	10	1	
5 10, 11 10, 7.2.56	£100,000	Derby Co	73+2	2	3	4		
	F/T	Newport Co						
Carl Elsey	Swansea	Pembroke Bor						
5 10, 11 6 20.11.58	—	QPR	6+1					
	F/T	Newport Co	107+9	8+3	7	14	1	
Tony Reid	Nottingham	Derby Co (A)	27+3	2	1+1	1		
5 9, 10 10, 9.5.63	—	Scunthorpe U (loan)	6					
	F/T	Newport Co	2+2					
Forwards								
John Aldridge	Liverpool	South Liverpool						
5 11, 10 4, 18.9.58	£3500	Newport Co	131+11	9	7+1	49	4	2
Steve Lowndes (WU21)	Cwmbran	Newport Co	200+8	10+1	12	39	2	
5 7, 10 7, 17.6.60								
Kevin Moore*	Blackpool	Blackpool (A)	33+5	2	2+1	3		
5 9, 11 4, 30.1.56	—	Bury (loan)	4					
	F/T	Swansea C	51+4	4	3	6		1
	£12,000	Newport Co	140+8	10	5+1	13	1	
	—	Swindon T (loan)	1					
Tommy Tynan	Liverpool	Liverpool (A)						
5 10, 13 0, 17.11.55	—	Swansea C (loan)	6			2		
	£10,000	Sheffield W	89+2	12	4	31	5	1
	£33,000	Lincoln C	9			1		
	£25,000	Newport Co	168+15	11+1	7+1	66	5	4
Dave Gwyther* (WU21)	Birmingham	Swansea C	212+5	11	18+2	59	6	16
5 10, 13 4, 6.12.48	£12,000	Halifax T	104	8	7	26	1	2
		Rotherham U	162	16	13	45	4	6
	£40,000	Newport Co	84+21	9+1	3+2	28	2	1
	—	Crewe Alex (loan)	7			1		
Ray Pulis	Newport	Newport Co (A)	+1					
Non-contract players								
Ceri Williams		Newport Co	1	1		1		

Commercial Manager: P. Jones. (Tel. 277472)
Club Coach: R. Smith
Supporters Player of the Season 1982–83: none chosen
Physiotherapist:
Club Captain 1982–83: John Relish
Chief Scout: G. E. A. Reynolds
Club Statistician/Match Programme Editor: R. Shepherd
Association of Football Statisticians Club Adviser to Yearbook: T. Ambrosen.

Players released since May 1982:
Richard Walden, D. (Farnborough); Terry Lees, D. (Morning Star, Hong Kong); Rod Thomas, D. (retired).

NORTHAMPTON TOWN Division 4

Back row (left to right): Clive Walker (Manager), Steve Massey, David Syrett, Mark Kendall, John Buchanan, Paul Brady (transferred to Crewe), Frank Belfon, Adrian Burrows
Front row: Wakeley Gage, Peter Coffill, Adam Sandy, Paul Saunders, Ian Phillips (Captain), Gary Saxby (now Non-Contract), Mark Heeley, Peter Denyer.
(Photo courtesy Bob Thomas.)

Chairman: N. J. Ronson. ***Vice-Chairman:*** S. Wilson.

Directors: E. P. Northover, W. M. Griggs, D. Bowen.

Secretary/Director: Dave Bowen. ***Manager:*** Clive Walker.

Commercial Executive: G. Moody.

Year Formed: 1897. ***Turned Professional:*** 1901. ***Ltd Co.:*** 1901.

Club Nickname: 'The Cobblers'.

Previous Managers since 1946: T. Smith, Bob Dennison, David Smith, Dave Bowen, Jack Jennings, (caretaker) Dave Bowen, Tony Marchi, Ron Flowers, Dave Bowen, Bill Baxter, Bill Dodgin (Jnr), Pat Crerand, John Petts, Mike Keen, Clive Walker, Bill Dodgin (Jnr) (13).

County Ground, Abington Avenue, Northampton NN1 4PS. Telephone Northampton 31553. ***Ground capacity:*** 17,000 (seating 1,400). ***Record attendance:*** 24,523 v Fulham, Division 1, 23 April, 1966. ***Record receipts:*** £00,000 v Aston Villa, 3rd rd FA Cup. ***Pitch measurements:*** 120yd×75yd.

Directions to Ground: Nearest railway station, Northampton. Any bus to the town centre, then from Mercer's Row, buses 1, 21, 2 and 14, though only 2 goes right to the ground.

Match tickets: No pre-match booking.

Car parking: No car park, but ample space in nearby side-streets.

Entertainments/catering facilities: Refreshments in hotel and tea bars on ground.

Club shop: 195 Abington Ave – opposite club. Run by the Supporters Club; sells all types of souvenirs.

Handbooks/programmes: Programmes available from the Supporters Club.

Extra information: Ground is shared with Northamptonshire Cricket Club.

Address of Supporters Club: 195, Abington Avenue, Northampton.

Note: Full club statistical records are on pages 416–455.

NORTHAMPTON TOWN 1982–83 LEAGUE RECORD

Match No.	Date	Venue	Opponents	Result	H/T Score	Lg. Pos.	Goalscorers	Attendance
1	Aug 28	A	Wimbledon	D 1-1	1-1	—	Syrett	1703
2	Sept 4	H	York C	D 1-1	0-0	12	Massey	2254
3	7	H	Chester	D 1-1	0-0	—	Saxby	2171
4	11	A	Hartlepool U	L 1-2	1-0	21	Gage	947
5	19	H	Bristol C	W 7-1	3-1	22	Syrett 4, Massey 2, Denyer	3017
6	21	H	Bury	L 0-3	0-1	—		2792
7	24	A	Stockport Co	W 1-0	0-0	—	Massey	1621
8	28	H	Swindon T	L 0-1	0-1	—		2706
9	Oct 2	H	Aldershot	D 1-1	0-1	15	Massey	1706
10	10	H	Tranmere R	W 1-0	1-0	—	Massey	2433
11	16	A	Torquay U	L 1-3	1-1	13	Wilson (og)	2101
12	19	H	Colchester U	W 2-1	0-0	—	Denyer, Burrows	1955
13	23	A	Hull C	L 0-4	0-0	14		4317
14	30	H	Peterborough U	D 0-0	0-0	10		3284
15	Nov 2	A	Rochdale	L 0-2	0-1	—		1029
16	6	A	Scunthorpe U	L 1-5	0-1	16	Massey	3412
17	13	H	Blackpool	W 2-1	1-0	12	Denyer 2	1893
18	28	H	Darlington	D 3-3	1-0	—	Massey 2 (1 pen), Burrows	2599
19	Dec 18	A	Hereford U	D 1-1	0-0	14	Massey	1679
20	27	H	Crewe Alex	W 4-0	1-0	13	Burrows, Massey, Saxton, Belfon	7494
21	28	A	Mansfield T	L 0-2	0-1	15		2841
22	Jan 1	H	Port Vale	D 2-2	0-0	16	Massey, Syrett	3618
23	3	A	Bury	D 1-1	1-0	16	Syrett	3398
24	15	H	Wimbledon	D 2-2	1-2	17	Brady, Saunders	2290
25	22	A	Bristol C	W 3-1	2-1	15	Phillips, Syrett, Massey	4855
26	29	H	Hartlepool U	W 3-1	1-1	13	Syrett 2, Massey	2181
27	Feb 1	A	Halifax T	L 0-2	0-1	—		1927
28	5	H	Stockport Co	L 2-3	2-2	15	Patching, Burrows	1982
29	12	A	Aldershot	L 0-3	0-2	16		1761
30	19	A	Tranmere R	L 1-2	1-0	16	Syrett	1466
31	26	H	Torquay U	W 2-0	1-0	16	Saxby, Massey	1817
32	Mar 1	A	Colchester U	L 1-3	1-1	—	Massey	2501
33	5	H	Hull C	L 1-2	0-0	16	Gage	2879
34	12	A	Peterborough U	L 0-2	0-0	19		3778
35	15	A	York C	L 2-5	1-2	—	Massey (pen), Tucker	2811
36	20	H	Scunthorpe U	W 2-1	0-0	—	Gage, Sandy	2634
37	26	A	Blackpool	D 0-0	0-0	17		2054
38	Apr 2	H	Mansfield T	L 1-2	0-0	18	Saunders	1988
39	4	A	Crewe Alex	L 0-1	0-0	—		2197
40	10	H	Halifax T	W 3-1	0-0	—	Buchanan 2, Jeffrey	2208
41	16	A	Chester	L 1-2	0-1	18	Tucker	1121
42	19	H	Rochdale	D 1-1	0-1	—	Tucker (pen)	1728
43	23	H	Hereford U	W 2-1	1-0	16	Sandy, Massey	2071
44	30	A	Darlington	A 0-2	0-1	17		1042
45	May 8	A	Swindon T	W 5-1	2-1	—	Massey 3, Jeffrey, Syrett	3386
46	14	A	Port Vale	W 2-1	2-0	15	Coffill, Tucker (pen)	6761

Final League Position: 15

GOALSCORERS

League (65): Massey 21 (2 pens), Syrett 12, Burrows 4, Denyer 4, Tucker 4 (2 pens), Gage 3, Saxby 3, Buchanan 2, Jeffrey 2, Sandy 2, Saunders 2, Belfon 1, Brady 1, Coffill 1, Patching 1, Phillips 1, own goal 1.
Milk Cup (6): Massey 3, Syrett 2, Saxby 1.
FA Cup (8): Belfon 2, Coffill 2, Burrows 1, Denyer 1, Massey 1, Saxby 1.
Football League Trophy (4): Syrett 2, Denyer 1, Massey 1.

Milk Cup	First Round	Millwall (a)	2-0
		(h)	2-2
	Second Round	Blackpool (h)	1-1
		(a)	1-2

FA Cup	First Round	Wimbledon (h)	2-2
		(a)	2-0
	Second Round	Gillingham (a)	1-1
		(h)	3-2
	Third Round	Aston Villa (h)	0-1
Football League Trophy		Norwich C (a)	0-3
		Mansfield T (a)	2-1
		Peterborough U (a)	2-5

Freeman	Brady	Phillips	Gage	Burrows	Heeley	Coffill	Denyer	Saunders	Syrett	Perrin	Saxby	Massey	Buchanan J.	Tucker (L)	Buchanan D. (L)	Key (L)	Sandy	Muir	Belfon	Patching (L)	Kendall	Gleasure (L)	Beavon	Jeffrey	Referees	Match No.
1	2	3	4	5*	6	7	8	9	10	11	12														Alan Robinson	1
1	2	3	4	5	6		11	7	9		8	10													J. Moules	2
1	2*	3	4	5	6		11	7	9		8	10	12												C. Downey	3
	2	3	4	5	6		11	7	9		8	10									1				T. Fitzharris	4
1	2	3	4	5	6*		12	7	9		8	10	11												K. Salmon	5
1	2*	3	4	5	6		12	7	9		8	10	11												R. Lewis	6
1	2	3	4	5		6	8	7	9			10	11												C. Newsome	7
1	2*	3	4	5		6	8	7	9		12	10	11												G. Napthine	8
1		3	4	5		6	12	7	9		2	10	8						11*						D. Civil	9
1	12	3		4		6	7	5		10	9	11	8*	2											A. Grey	10
1	5	3		4	9	12	7*	6		11		10	8	2											R. Milford	11
1		3	5	4	9	12	7	6		11		10	8*	2											T. Spencer	12
1		3	5*	4	9		7	6	12			10	8	2	11										G. Tyson	13
1		3		5	6		9	4	10		7		8	2	11										D. Lloyd	14
1		3		4	6		7	5	10		11		8	2	9										N. Ashley	15
		3		5	6		7	4	9*		10	11	8	2	12	1									D. Scott	16
		3	9	5	6		7	4*			10	11	8	2	12	1									J. Martin	17
1		3	4	5		6	11				7	10	8	2			9								A. Seville	18
1		3	4	5	7	6	11*					10	8	2				9	12						E. Read	19
1		3*	4	5		7	10				6	11	8	2				9	12						K. Cooper	20
1		3*	4	5		6	11				7	10	8	2				9	12						P. Tyldesley	21
1		3	4	5		7			11		6	10	8	2				9							B. Stevens	22
1		5	4	3	12	6			10		7	9	8	2				11*							F. Roberts	23
1	5	3	4			6		7	9		11	10		2				8							V. Callow	24
1	5	3	4			6		7	10			11		2				9		8					R. Lewis	25
		3	4	5		6		7	11			10	12	2				9*		8	1				E. Scales	26
		3	4	5		6	12	7*	10			11	9	2						8	1				J. Worrall	27
		3	4	5		6		9*	11			10	8	2					12	7	1				D. Reeves	28
			4	5		6	12	3	10			11	8*	2					9	7	1				M. King	29
		3	4	5		6		9	10			11	8	2						7	1				D. Shaw	30
		3	4	5		6	7*	9	10		8	11	12	2							1				M. Scott	31
		3	4	5		6	8	10	9		7	11		2							1				M. Taylor	32
		3	4	5		6*	7	10	9		8	11		2				12			1				I. Borrett	33
		3	4				12	5	11		6	10	7	2			8	9*			1				A. Challinor	34
		3	4	5		6		9	10		8	11	7	2							1				P. Willis	35
		3	4	5		6	12		9		11	10	7	2*			8					1			T. Bune	36
			4	5		6	11	8	9		3	10		2								1	7		R. Nixon	37
			4	5		6	11	8	10		2			3			12					1	9*	7	A. Ward	38
		3	4	5		6		8	9			10	11	2								1		7	A. Banks	39
		3	5	4	12	7			10			11	9	2				6*				1		8	M. James	40
		3	5	4	6	7*	12		10			11	9	2								1		8	T. Holbrook	41
		3	4	5	6				10		8*	11	9	2			12					1		7	J. Moules	42
		3	4	5	6*		12		10			11	8	2			9					1		7	C. Downey	43
		3	4	5	6	12			11			10	8	2			9					1		7*	T. Fitzharris	44
		3		5	6	11	8	4	9			10		2								1		7	D. Letts	45
			3	5	6	11*	8	4	9			10		2					12			1		7	J. Key	46
22	11	42	40	43	20	30	25	34	37	4	26	42	32	37	3	2	5	10	2	6	11	11	2	9		
	+ 1s				+ 2s	+ 3s	+ 9s		+ 1s		+ 2s		+ 3s		+ 2s		+ 2s	+ 1s	+ 5s							

FOOTBALL LEAGUE RECORD

1920 Original Member of Division 3; 1921 Division 3(S); 1958–61 Division 4; 1961–63 Division 3; 1963–65 Division 2; 1965–66 Division 1; 1966–67 Division 2; 1967–68 Division 3; 1968–76 Division 4; 1976–77 Division 3; 1977– Division 4.

HONOURS

Football League: Division 1 best season: 21st, 1965–66; Division 2 – Runners-up 1964–65; Division 3 – Champions 1962–63; Division 3(S) – Runners-up 1927–28, 1949–50; Division 4 – Promoted 1960–61 (3rd); Runners-up 1975–76. *FA Cup:* best season: 5th rd, 1933–34, 1949–50, 1969–70. *Football League Cup:* best season: 5th rd, 1964–65, 1966–67.

COLOURS

White shirts with claret trim, claret shorts, white stockings.
Change colours: Yellow shirts with claret trim, yellow shorts and stockings.

NORTHAMPTON TOWN

Players Names Ht. Wt. D.o.B.	Birthplace Transfer Fee	Clubs	Appearances F.L. A & S	 F.L.C. A & S	 F.A.C. A & S	Goals F.L.	 F.L.C.	 F.A.C.
Goalkeepers								
Mark Kendall	Nuneaton	Aston Villa (A)						
6 0, 12 10, 10.12.61	F/T	Northampton T	11	1				
Defenders								
Paul Saunders*	Watford	Watford (A)						
5 10, 12 8, 17.12.59	F/T	Northampton T	114+12	9+1	4+1	5		
Wakeley Gage	Northampton	Desborough T						
6 4, 13 7, 5.5.58	£8000	Northampton T	133+2	8	9	7		2
Ian Phillips	Edinburgh	Ipswich T (A)						
5 8, 12 2, 23.4.59	F/T	Mansfield T	18+5		1+1	5		
	F/T	Peterborough U	97	4	12	3		
	F/T	Northampton T	42	4		1		
Billy Jeffrey	Clydebank	Oxford U (A)	311+3	25	14	24	2	
6 0, 12 0, 25.10.56	F/T	Blackpool	12+2	1	1+1	1		
	F/T	Northampton T	9			2		
Peter Denyer*	Haslemere	Portsmouth (A)	123+8	5	9	15	2	
5 11, 11 9, 26.11.57	£20,000	Northampton T	138+9	14	6	27	4	1
Adam Sandy*	Peterborough	Wolverton T						
5 10, 11 4, 22.9.58	F/T	Northampton T	88+16	5+1	3+1	7	1	1
Peter Coffill*	Romford	Watford (A)	56+7	2+2	3	6		1
5 8, 10 8, 14.2.57	£4000	Torquay U	101+21	3+1	5+1	11		
	£5000	Northampton T	64+5	6+2	5+1	3		2
Mark Heeley*	Peterborough	Peterborough U (A)	12+5			3		
5 6, 9 6, 8.9.59	£50,000	Arsenal	9+6			1		
	£33,000	Northampton T	84+8	7+1	7	5	1	
Adrian Burrows	Sutton	Mansfield T	77+1	6	1+2	6		1
5 11, 11 12, 16.1.59	F/T	Northampton T	43	4		4		
Forwards								
Steve Massey	Denton	Stockport Co (A)	87+14	8	5	20	3	1
5 11, 11 5, 28.3.58	F/T	Bournemouth	85+12	4	4+1	19	1	2
	F/T	Peterborough U	13+5		1+1	2		
	F/T	Northampton T	60	4	5	26	3	1
Frankie Belfon	Wellingborough	Northampton T	3+5		+1	1		2
5 9, 11 3,								
Dave Syrett (EY)	Salisbury	Swindon T (A)	110+12	+2	10+1	30	1	7
5 11, 11 13, 20.1.56		Mansfield T	65	4	3	20		
	£75,000	Walsall	11			3		
	£50,000	Peterborough U	75+4	7	1+1	24	2	
	F/T	Northampton T	37+1	3	1	12	2	
Non-contract players								
Gary Saxby	Mansfield	Mansfield T (A)	14+2	2		1		
5 8, 10 3, 11.12.59	F/T	Northampton T	86+10	6+1	4	11	2	
Maurice Muir (ES)	Wimbledon	Northampton T (A)	10+3		2+1			
5 9, 11 0, 19.3.63								
John Buchanan	Dingwall	Ross Co						
5 9, 10 10, 19.9.51	£2000	Northampton T	104+10	5	7	25	1	3
	P/E	Cardiff C	217+14	14+1	10+1	54	5	2
	£15,000	Northampton T	66+3	3	8	6		
Neil Freeman	Northampton	Arsenal						
6 1, 14 7, 16.2.55	F/T	Grimsby T	33	1	4			
	F/T	Southend U	69	2	5			
	£100,000	Birmingham C	31		1			
	—	Walsall (loan)	8					
	—	Huddersfield T (loan)	18					
		Peterborough U	41		3			
	F/T	Northampton T	22	3	5			

Commercial Manager: G. Moody (Tel. 712847)
Club Player Coach: John Buchanan
Club Captain 1982–83: Ian Phillips
Supporters Player of the Season 1982–83: Steve Massey
Chief Scout:
Physiotherapist:
Club Statistician:
Association of Football Statisticians Club Adviser to Yearbook: F. Grande.

Players released since May 1982:
Steve Bryant, D. (Australia); Dave Carlton, M. (retired); Kevin Farmer, F. (retired); Andy Taylor, D. (AP Leamington); David Beavons, M. (N/K); Steve Perrin, F. (N/C—Wycombe W).

NORWICH CITY Division 1

Back row (left to right): Tim Sheppard (Physio), Keith Bertschin, Dave Bennett, Aage Hareide, Chris Woods, Steve Walford, Dave Watson, Peter Mendham, Ken Brown (Manager), Mel Machin (Club Coach)
Front row: Mick McGuire, Paul Haylock, Ross Jack, Clive Baker, Denis van Wyk, John Deehan, Martin O'Neill, Mark Barham.

President: J. L. Hanly JP. ***Chairman:*** Sir A. South JP.

Vice-Chairman: G. C. Watling.

Directors: D. S. McCall, E. A. Burrell, I. D. Coutts FCA.

Manager: Ken Brown. ***Commercial Manager:*** N. S. McKay.

Secretary: N. S. Pleasants.

Year Formed: 1905. ***Turned Professional:*** 1905. Ltd Co.: 1905.

Club Nickname: 'The Canaries'.

Previous Grounds: 1905, Newmarket Road; 1908–35, The Nest, Rosary Road.

Previous Managers since 1946: Cyril Spiers, Dugald Lockhead, Norman Low, Tom Parker, Archie Macauley, Willie Reid, George Swindin, Ron Ashman, Lol Morgan, Ron Saunders, John Bond (11).

NORWICH CITY FC

Carrow Road, Norwich NR1 1JE. Telephone Norwich 612131. ***Match information:*** Norwich 612591. ***Telegraphic address:*** 'Football, Norwich'. ***Ground capacity:*** 29,000. ***Record attendance:*** 43,984 v Leicester C, FA cup 6th rd, 30 March, 1963. ***Record receipts:*** £56,894.35 v Ipswich T, League Cup 3rd rd replay, 8 Oct, 1980. ***Pitch measurements:*** 114yd×74yd.

Directions to Ground: Norwich railway station is eight minutes walk from the ground; British Rail run trains from outlying districts on match days. Coach firms also operate special services from surrounding parts. Any scheduled bus to the station and then walk.

Match tickets: Applications to the Box Office on the ground, fourteen days before matches with sae required.

Car parking: Several private car parks within walking distance of the ground. Multi-storey parks in Malt House Road and St Andrews Street. Street parking in Rouen Road, Carrow Hill, Kerrison Road, Cousins Road, and side streets off King Street. Coaches may park at Lower Clarence Road Car Park.

Entertainments/catering facilities: Norwich City have their own Public House, The Nest, in the River End Complex at Carrow road (NB: closed match days). Numerous licensed bars in the ground.

Club shop: Sells all types of souvenirs.

Programmes: Programmes available on subscription (from Carrow Road).

Address of Supporters Club: Club Canary, Norwich City Promotions, Carrow Road, Norwich.

Address of the Club Shop or Boutique: Norwich City Promotions, Carrow Road, Norwich. Telephone: Norwich 615011.

Note: Full club statistical records are on pages 416–455.

NORWICH CITY 1982–83 LEAGUE RECORD

Match No.	Date	Venue	Opponents	Result	H/T Score	Lg. Pos.	Goalscorers	Attendance
1	Aug 28	H	Manchester C	L 1-2	0-2	—	Deehan	22,638
2	31	A	Arsenal	D 1-1	0-0	—	Deehan	22,652
3	Sept 4	A	Swansea C	L 0-4	0-3	19		11,694
4	8	H	Birmingham C	W 5-1	3-1	—	Bertschin 2, O'Neill 2, Barham	13,860
5	11	H	Southampton	D 1-1	0-0	17	Deehan (pen)	16,492
6	18	A	Everton	D 1-1	0-0	19	Haylock	20,281
7	25	H	WBA	L 1-3	1-1	19	Deehan	15,130
8	Oct 2	A	Sunderland	L 1-4	0-0	21	Bennett	13,144
9	9	A	Watford	D 2-2	1-2	21	Deehan, Bertschin	18,597
10	16	H	Tottenham H	D 0-0	0-0	21		22,628
11	23	H	Aston Villa	W 1-0	0-0	19	Deehan (pen)	15,761
12	30	A	Coventry C	L 0-2	0-0	21		8305
13	Nov 6	H	Notts Co	L 1-2	0-0	21	Deehan	13,472
14	13	A	West Ham U	L 0-1	0-0	22		22,463
15	20	H	Stoke C	W 4-2	0-1	20	Deehan 2 (2 pens), Barham, Bertschin	13,658
16	27	A	Manchester U	L 0-3	0-2	21		34,579
17	Dec 4	H	Liverpool	W 1-0	0-0	20	Deehan	22,909
18	11	A	Brighton & HA	L 0-3	0-1	20		9994
19	18	H	Nottingham F	L 0-1	0-1	21		14,151
20	27	A	Ipswich T	W 3-2	1-1	20	Mendham 2, O'Neill	29,596
21	28	H	Luton T	W 1-0	1-0	20	Channon	21,367
22	Jan 1	A	Stoke C	L 0-1	0-1	19		15,669
23	3	H	Swansea C	W 1-0	0-0	17	Channon	16,296
24	15	A	Manchester C	L 1-4	1-3	20	O'Neill	22,000
25	22	H	Everton	L 0-1	0-1	20		14,180
26	Feb 5	A	Southampton	L 0-4	0-1	21		17,244
27	26	A	Tottenham H	D 0-0	0-0	21		23,342
28	Mar 2	H	Watford	W 3-0	1-0	—	Watson, Van Wyk, Deehan	16,662
29	5	A	Aston Villa	L 2-3	1-1	19	Barham, Van Wyk	18,624
30	19	A	Notts Co	D 2-2	2-1	20	Deehan (pen), Bertschin	8064
31	23	H	Coventry C	D 1-1	0-0	—	Walford	13,944
32	26	H	West Ham U	D 1-1	0-1	21	Deehan (pen)	18,582
33	Apr 2	A	Luton T	W 1-0	1-0	19	Bennett	11,211
34	4	H	Ipswich T	D 0-0	0-0	—		23,476
35	9	A	Birmingham C	W 4-0	2-0	18	Bertschin 2, Deehan 2	11,733
36	16	H	Sunderland	W 2-0	0-0	18	Deehan 2	15,883
37	20	H	Arsenal	W 3-1	1-1	—	Deehan 2, Bertschin	16,858
38	23	A	Liverpool	W 2-0	0-0	13	Lawrenson (og), O'Neill	37,022
39	30	H	Manchester U	D 1-1	0-0	14	Barham	22,986
40	May 2	A	WBA	L 0-1	0-1	14		9221
41	7	A	Nottingham F	D 2-2	2-1	14	Bennett 2	16,308
42	14	H	Brighton & HA	W 2-1	1-0	14	Channon, Deehan	20,306

Final League Position: 14

GOALSCORERS

League (52): Deehan 20 (6 pens), Bertschin 8, O'Neill 5, Barham 4, Bennett 4, Channon 3, Mendham 2, Van Wyk 2, Haylock 1, Walford 1, Watson 1, own goal 1.
Milk Cup (7): Bertschin 2, Watson 2, Bennett 1, Deehan 1, O'Neill 1.
FA Cup (7): Bertschin 4, Barham 2, Hareide 1.
Football League Trophy (13): Jack 4, Deehan 3, Downs 1, Fashanu 1, Mendham 1, O'Neill 1, Walford 1, Watson 1.

Milk Cup	Second Round	Preston NE (h)	2-1
		(a)	2-1
	Third Round	Sunderland (a)	0-0
		(h)	3-1
	Fourth Round	Liverpool (a)	0-2
FA Cup	Third Round	Swansea C (h)	2-1
	Fourth Round	Coventry C (a)	2-2
		(h)	2-1 (aet)
	Fifth Round	Ipswich T (h)	1-0
	Sixth Round	Brighton & HA (a)	0-1

Football League Trophy		Northampton T (h)	3-0
		Peterborough U (h)	6-2
		Mansfield T (a)	3-1
	Quarter-final	Lincoln C (a)	1-3

Woods	Haylock	Downs	McGuire	Walford	Watson	Barham	O'Neill	Deehan	Bertschin	Mendham	Jack	Smith	Mountford	Fashanu	Van Wyk	Alexander	Walsh (L)	Bennett	Hareide (L)	Metcalf	Crowe	Donowa	Channon	Symonds	*Referees*	*Match No.*
1	2	3	4	5	6	7	8	9	10	11*	12														B. Daniels	1
1	2		4	5	6	7	8	9	10	11*		3	12												L. Burden	2
1	2		4	5	6	7	8	9	10	11		3													B. Stevens	3
1	2	3	4	5	6	7	8	9	10*	11		12													J. Martin	4
1	2	3	4	5	6	7	8	9	10*	11		12													J. Deakin	5
1	2	3	4	5	6*	7	8	9		11				10	12										C. Newsome	6
1	2	3	4	5		7	8	6	10	11				9*		12									J. Moules	7
1	2	3	4	5		7	8	9	10								6	11							A. Challinor	8
1	2		4	5		7	8	9	10						3		6	11							D. Civil	9
1	3		4	5		7	8	9	10						2		6	11							K. Hackett	10
1	2		4	5	6		8	9	10						7		3	11							K. Salmon	11
1	2			5	6	4	8	9	10						7		3	11							L. Shapter	12
1	2		4*	5	6	7	8	9		12					10			11	3						D. Reeves	13
1	2			5	6	7*	8	9	10						4			11	3	12					B. Hill	14
1	2			5	6	7	8	9	10		12				4			11	3*						M. Dimblebee	15
1	2			5	6	7	8	9	10		12				4			11*	3						J. Key	16
1	2		4	5	6	7*	8	9	10		12				11				3						J. Hunting	17
1	2		6	5*			8	9	10		7		11		4				3		12				M. Taylor	18
1	2		4	5	6		8	9	10		7*				11				3			12			D. Vickers	19
1	2			5	6	7	8		10	4					11				3				9		A. Gunn	20
1	2	3		5	6	7	8		10	4					11								9		T. Mills	21
1	2	12		5	6	7	8	3	10	4					11*								9		K. Walmsley	22
1	2	3		5	6	7	8	11	10	4													9		C. Downey	23
1	2*	3		5		7	8	9	10	4					11				6				12		R. Bridges	24
1	2	3		5		7	8	9	12	4					11*				6				10		H. Taylor	25
1	2	12		5	6*	7		9	8	4					11				3				10		M. Bodenham	26
1	2	11		5	6	7		9	10	4					8				3						E. Read	27
1	2	3		5	6	7		9	10	4					11			8							G. Napthine	28
1	2	3			6	7		9	10	4					11			8*					12	5	J. Worrall	29
1	2	3		5	6	7		9	10	4	12				11*			8							K. Cooper	30
1	2	3		5	6	7	8*	9	10	4								11					12		J. Scales	31
1	2	3		5	6	7	8	9	10*	4	12												11		J. Bray	32
1	2	3		5	6		8	9	10	4	12							7					11*		M. James	33
1	2	3		5	6	12	8	9	10	4					11*								7		B. Hill	34
1	2	3		5	6	7		9	10	4								11					8		J. Moules	35
1	2	3		5	6	7		9	10	4								11					8		B. Daniels	36
1	2	3		5	6	7	12	9	10	4*								11					8		D. Axcell	37
1	2	3		5	6	7	4	9	10									11					8		D. Lloyd	38
1	2	3		5	6	7	4	9	10									11					8		D. Reeves	39
1	2	3		5	6*	7	4	9	10		12							11					8		A. Crickmore	40
1	2	3		5	6	7	4	9	10									11					8		A. Hamil	41
1	2	3		5	6	7	4	9	10									11					8		A. Ward	42
42	42	26	15	41	35	37	34	40	39	25	2	2	1	2	22	0	5	22	12	0	0	0	17	1		
		+ 2s				+ 1s	+ 1s		+ 1s	+ 1s	+ 8s	+ 2s	+ 1s		+ 1s	+ 1s				+ 1s	+ 1s	+ 1s	+ 3s			

FOOTBALL LEAGUE RECORD

1920 Original Member of Division 3; 1921 Division 3(S); 1934–39 Division 2; 1946–60 Division 3; 1960–72 Division 2; 1972–74 Division 1; 1974–75 Division 2; 1975–81 Division 1; 1981–82 Division 2; 1982– Division 1.

HONOURS

Football League: Division 1 best season: 10th, 1975–76; Division 2 – Champions 1971–72; Division 3(S) – Champions 1933–34; Division 3 – Runners-up 1959–60. *FA Cup:* semi-finals 1959. *Football League Cup:* Winners 1962; Runners-up 1973, 1975.

COLOURS

Yellow shirts with green pinstripe, green shorts with yellow trim, yellow stockings.
Change colours: White shirts with green pinstripe, white shorts, green stockings.

NORWICH CITY

Players Names Ht, Wt, D.o.B.	Birthplace Transfer Fee	Clubs	Appearances F.L. A & S	 F.L.C. A & S	 F.A.C. A & S	Goals F.L.	 F.L.C.	 F.A.C.
Goalkeepers								
Clive Baker	North Walsham	Norwich C	14					
5 9, 11 0, 14.2.59								
Chris Woods (EU21)	Boston	Nottingham F (A)						
6 2, 12 8, 14.11.59	£250,000	QPR	63	8	1			
	£250,000	Norwich C	94	8	8			
Greg Williams		Norwich C						
Defenders								
Greg Downs	Carlton	Norwich C (A)	101+6	5	12	3		
5 9½, 10 7, 13.12.58	—	Torquay U (loan)	1			1		
Richard Symonds*	Langham	Norwich C (A)	55+4	3+1	4			
6 1, 11 5, 21.11.59								
Dave Watson	Liverpool	Liverpool						
5 11½, 11 12, 20.11.61	£100,000	Norwich C	91	4	10	7	2	1
Paul Haylock	Lowestoft	Norwich C (A)	63	7	3+1	1		
5 8, 11 0, 24.3.63								
Steve Walford (EY)	Highgate	Tottenham H (A)	1+1					
6 1, 11 7, 5.1.58		Arsenal	64+13	5	5	3	1	
	£175,000	Norwich C	93	8	7	2		
Phil Alexander*	Reading	Wokingham T						
6 0, 12 8,		Norwich C	+1					
Daryl Godbold		Norwich C (A)						
Tony Spearing		Norwich C (A)						
Richard Sutton		Peterborough (A)						
	F/T	Norwich C						
Mark Crone		Norwich C (A)	+1					
Midfield								
Dennis Van Wijk	Holland	Ajax						
		Norwich C	22+1	4	5	2		
Peter Mountford*	Stoke	Norwich C (A)	1+3					
5 10, 10 6, 13.9.60								
Mark Barham (EY)	Folkestone	Norwich C (A)	99+5	11	8	10		1
5 7, 11 0, 12.7.62								
Peter Mendham	Kings Lynn	Norwich C (A)	85+11	4+1	12	10		
5 10, 11 6, 9.4.60								
Martin O'Neill (NI)	Kilrea	Distillery						
5 10, 11 3, 1.3.52	£15,000	Nottingham F	264+21	34	28+2	48	8	3
	£250,000	Norwich C	11			1		
	£275,000	Manchester C	12+1	3				
	£150,000	Norwich C	54+1	5	4	11	1	
Jeremy Goss		Norwich C						
Forwards								
Dave Bennett	Oldham	Manchester C (A)						
5 11, 11 7, 26.4.60	F/T	Norwich C	52+6	7	3	8	1	
Greig Shepherd	Edinburgh	Musselburgh						
6 1, 12 0, 29.9.60		Norwich C	13+3	2		2		
Ross Jack	Inverness	Everton (A)	1			1		
5 10, 11 2, 21.3.59	£20,000	Norwich C	31+25	6+1	2+1	10	2	2
John Fashanu	Kensington	Cambridge U (N/C)						
6 1, 11 12, 18.9.62	F/T	Norwich C	6+1			1		
John Deehan (EU21)	Birmingham	Aston Villa (A)	107+3	13	7+1	42	2	3
6 0, 11 3, 6.8.57	£400,000	WBA	44+3		2	5		
	£175,000	Norwich C	62	5	8	30	1	
Keith Bertschin (EU21)	Enfield	Barnet						
6 1, 11 8, 25.8.56	—	Ipswich T	19+13	1		8		
	£100,000	Birmingham C	113+5	7+1	8+1	29	1	8
	£200,000	Norwich C	74+2	5	8	20	2	4
Mick Channon (E)*	Orcheston	Southampton (A)	388+4	24	34+2	155	10	15
6 0½, 12 11, 28.11.48	£300,000	Manchester C	71+1	10+1	3+1	24	4	
	£200,000	Southampton	119	4	6	27		1
	F/T	Newcastle U	4			1		
	F/T	Bristol R	4+5	+1	1			
	F/T	Norwich C	17+2			3		
Lou Donawa		Norwich C (A)	+1	+1				
Austin O'Connor		Norwich C (A)						
Jonathan Rigby		Norwich C (A)						
Neil Riley		Norwich C (A)						
Mark Farrington		Everton (A)						
	F/T	Norwich C						
Paul Clayton		Norwich C (A)						

Commercial Manager: N. S. Mackay (Tel. Norwich 615011).
Club Coach: Mel Machin
Supporters Player of the Season 1982–83: Dave Watson
Physiotherapist: Tim Sheppard
Club Captain 1982–83: Dave Watson
Chief Scout: Ronnie Brooks, JP
Club Statistician:
Trainer: Dave Stringer
Groundsman: Russell Allison
Association of Football Statisticians Club Adviser to Yearbook: D. Pease..

Players (non-appearance) granted free transfer: David Lovett, F.
Players released since May 1982: Adrian Harris, D. (N/K); Phil Hoadley, D. (Hong Kong); Drazen Muzinic, D. (Yugoslavia); Grant Reid, M. (N/K); Colin Smith, D. (N/K); Joe Royle, F. (retired).

NOTTINGHAM FOREST Division 1

Back row (left to right): Liam O'Kane (Trainer), Calvin Plummer, Peter Davenport, Bryn Gunn, Mark Proctor, Colin Todd, Ian Wallace
Middle row: John Sheridan (Trainer), Chris Fairclough, Einar Aas, Steve Sutton, Hans Van Breukelen, Willie Young, Viv Anderson, Garry Birtles, Ron Fenton (Trainer)
Front row: Colin Walsh, Stuart Gray, Ian Bowyer, Brian Clough (Manager), John Robertson, Steve Hodge.

President: H. W. Alcock FCA.

Chairman: G. E. Macpherson JP. ***Vice-Chairman:*** F. Reacher.

Directors: G. T. Thorpe, F. T. C. Pell FCA, D. C. Pavis, M. Roworth, J. F. Hickling, F. A. Allcock, I. I. Korn.

Manager: Brian Clough. ***Sec/Treasurer:*** K. Smales.

Year Formed: 1865. ***Turned Professional:*** 1889. ***Ltd Co.:*** 1982.

Club Nickname: 'Reds'.

Previous Grounds: 1865, Forest Racecourse; 1879, The Meadows; 1880, Trent Bridge Cricket Ground; 1882, Parkside, Lenton; 1885, Gregory, Lenton; 1890, Town Grown; 1898, City Ground.

Previous Managers since 1946: Billy Walker, Andy Beattie, John Carey, Matt Gillies, Dave Mackay, Allan Brown (6).

City Ground, Nottingham NG2 5FJ. Telephone Nottingham (0602) 822202. Information Desk: 821122. ***Telegraphic address:*** 'Forestball, Nottingham'. ***Ground capacity:*** 35,000 (14,561 seats). ***Record attendance:*** 49,945 v Manchester U, Division 1, 28 Oct, 1967. ***Record receipts:*** £132,000 v Ajax, European Cup semi-final first leg, 9 April, 1980. ***Pitch measurements:*** 115yd×78yd.

Directions to Ground: From Nottingham station any bus marked 'Trent Bridge'. Corporation specials from Parliament Street.

Match tickets: Bookable fourteen days in advance of the match (personal) and twelve days (postal).

Car parking: Room for 300 cars in the East Stand car park and street parking off the Loughborough and Radcliffe Roads.

Entertainments/catering facilities: Match-day refreshment bars. Jubilee club on ground (members only).

Club shop: Three shops on the ground sell all types of souvenirs.

Handbooks/programmes: Programmes available on subscription from Carrington Publications Ltd, Wilford Crescent East, Trent Bridge, Nottingham.

Address of Supporters Club: c/o City Ground, Nottingham.

Address of the Club Shop or Boutique: Pools Office, City Ground, Nottingham NG2 5FJ.

Note: Full club statistical records are on pages 416–455.

NOTTINGHAM FOREST 1982–83 LEAGUE RECORD

Match No.	Date	Venue	Opponents	Result		H/T Score	Lg. Pos.	Goalscorers	Attendance
1	Aug 28	A	West Ham U	W	2-1	1-1	—	Walsh, Robertson (pen)	23,796
2	Sept 1	H	Manchester U	L	0-3	0-0	—		23,748
3	4	H	Brighton & HA	W	4-0	2-0	10	Wallace 2, Robertson (pen), Walsh	13,709
4	7	A	Liverpool	L	3-4	3-2	—	Hodge 2, Davenport	27,145
5	11	A	Aston Villa	L	1-4	1-2	15	Robertson (pen)	21,224
6	18	H	Watford	W	2-0	1-0	9	Walsh, Birtles	11,550
7	25	A	Tottenham H	L	1-4	1-3	13	Birtles	30,662
8	Oct 2	H	Stoke C	W	1-0	0-0	10	Birtles	17,122
9	9	A	WBA	L	1-2	1-1	10	Wallace	13,718
10	16	H	Birmingham C	D	1-1	0-1	13	Hodge	14,548
11	23	H	Arsenal	W	3-0	1-0	10	Proctor, Birtles, Wallace	17,161
12	30	A	Luton T	W	2-0	1-0	7	Wallace, Gunn	12,158
13	Nov 6	H	Ipswich T	W	2-1	0-1	5	Robertson (pen), Osman (og)	17,461
14	13	A	Southampton	D	1-1	1-0	5	Wallace	18,178
15	20	A	Sunderland	W	1-0	0-0	3	Wallace	14,716
16	27	H	Manchester C	W	3-0	1-0	3	Young, Birtles 2	18,184
17	Dec 4	A	Notts Co	L	2-3	2-2	5	Wallace, Young	23,065
18	11	H	Swansea C	W	2-1	1-0	3	Walsh, Proctor	14,585
19	18	A	Norwich C	W	1-0	1-0	3	Hodge	14,151
20	27	H	Coventry C	W	4-2	2-2	2	Young, Robertson (pen), Birtles, Proctor	24,487
21	28	A	Everton	L	1-3	0-2	2	Hodge	25,147
22	Jan 1	H	Sunderland	D	0-0	0-0	3		20,382
23	3	A	Brighton & HA	D	1-1	0-1	4	Young	10,402
24	15	H	West Ham U	W	1-0	0-0	3	Wallace	17,031
25	22	A	Manchester U	L	0-2	0-0	4		38,615
26	Feb 5	H	Aston Villa	L	1-2	1-1	4	Wilson	16,532
27	19	H	WBA	D	0-0	0-0	4		14,507
28	26	A	Birmingham C	D	1-1	0-1	4	Davenport	12,987
29	Mar 5	A	Arsenal	D	0-0	0-0	4		21,698
30	12	H	Luton T	L	0-1	0-1	4		14,387
31	16	A	Stoke C	L	0-1	0-0	—		10,877
32	19	A	Ipswich T	L	0-2	0-1	6		17,534
33	26	H	Southampton	L	1-2	1-0	10	Hodge	13,461
34	Apr 2	H	Everton	W	2-0	2-0	7	Hodge, Bowyer	14,815
35	5	A	Coventry C	W	2-1	0-1	—	Wallace, Robertson (pen)	9720
36	9	H	Tottenham H	D	2-2	2-0	6	Davenport, Bowyer	18,265
37	16	A	Watford	W	3-1	0-1	5	Bowyer, Hodge, Davenport	17,537
38	23	H	Notts Co	W	2-1	2-1	5	Swain, Proctor	25,554
39	30	A	Manchester C	W	2-1	1-0	5	Wallace, Davenport	23,563
40	May 2	H	Liverpool	W	1-0	0-0	3	Davenport	25,107
41	7	H	Norwich C	D	2-2	1-2	4	Walsh, Bowyer	16,308
42	14	A	Swansea C	W	3-0	2-0	5	Wallace 2, Anderson	9226

Final League Position: 5

GOALSCORERS

League (62): Wallace 13, Hodge 8, Birtles 7, Davenport 6, Robertson 6 (6 pens), Walsh 5, Bowyer 4, Proctor 4, Young 4, Anderson 1, Gunn 1, Swain 1, Wilson 1, own goal 1.
Milk Cup (16): Birtles 4, Wallace 4, Robertson 3 (3 pens), Proctor 2, Bowyer 1, Hodge 1, Young 1.
FA Cup (0).

Milk Cup	Second Round	WBA (h)	6-1
		(a)	1-3
	Third Round	Watford (h)	7-3
	Fourth Round	Brentford (h)	2-0
	Fifth Round	Manchester U (a)	0-4
FA Cup	Third Round	Derby Co (a)	0-2

Commercial Manager: Commercial Office (Tel. 820444).
Club Coach: Ron Fenton, Liam O'Kane John Sheridan.
Supporters Player of the Season 1982–83: Stephen Hodge.
Physiotherapist: Tony Verity.
Club Captain 1982–83: Ian Bowyer.
Chief Scout: Alan Hill.
Club Statistician: Ken Smales.
Groundsman Ted Cave.
Association of Football Statisticians Club Adviser to Yearbook: A. Johnson.

Sutton	Anderson	Bowyer	Proctor	Young	Todd	Hodge	Wallace	Plummer	Walsh	Robertson	Gunn	Van Breukelen	Birtles	Fairclough	Davenport	Gray	Ward	Swain	Wigley	Wilson	Smalley	*Referees*	*Match No.*
1	2	3	4*	5	6	7	8	9	10	11	12											A. Gunn	1
1	2	3	4	5	6	7	8	9	10	11												A. Ward	2
	2	3	4	5	6	12	8	7	10	11		1	9*									C. Thomas	3
	2	3	4		6	7	8		10	11		1		5	9							M. Peck	4
	2	3	12	5	4	7	8		10	11		1		6*	9							R. Bridges	5
	2	6	7	5		8	10		11		3	1	9	4								G. Tyson	6
	2		7	5		8	10		11		3	1	9	4		6*	12					A. Glasson	7
	2		7		4	6	10*		9	8	5	1	11	3			12					J. Deakin	8
	2	4	12		6	7	8		10	11	3	1	9	5*								E. Read	9
		12	4		6	7	8		10*	11	3	1	9	5				2				N. Midgley	10
		6	7		4		8		10*	11	3	1	9	5				2	12			G. Courtney	11
		6	7	5	4	10	8			11	3	1	9					2				J. Moules	12
		6	7	5	4	10	8			11	3	1	9					2				N. Wilson	13
		6	7	5		10	8		10*	11	3	1	9	12				2				B. Daniels	14
		3	7	5		10	8		6*	11	4	1	9	12				2				K. Walmsley	15
		6	7	5	4	10	8			11	3	1	9					2				D. Hedges	16
1		6	7*	5	4	10	8		12	11	3		9					2				D. Scott	17
1		3	7	5		10	8		6	11	4		9					2				K. Salmon	18
1		3	7	5		10	8		6	11	4		9					2				D. Vickers	19
1		6	7	5	4*	10	8		12	11	3		9					2				N. Glover	20
1		6	7	5	4*	10	8		12	11	3		9					2				K. Redfern	21
1		6	7	5	4	10	8		12	11	3		9*					2				J. Lovatt	22
1		6	7	5	4	10	8		11		3				9			2				D. Axcell	23
1		6	7	5	4	10	8			11	3		9					2				P. Tyldesley	24
1		6		5		10	8		11	7*	4			12	9	3		2				K. Hackett	25
1		6	7	5	4		8		11		3		9					2		10		D. Allison	26
1	4	5*	7	5		10	8		11		3		9					2		12		B. Hill	27
1	2	6		5	4	10	8		11				9*		12			3		7		M. Heath	28
1	2	6		5	4	10	8		11				9*		12			3		7		H. King	29
1	2	6		5	4	10	8		11*				9		12			3		7		N. Ashley	30
1	2	6		5		10	8		11*	12	4		9					3		7		A. Robinson	31
	2	6				8			10	11	4	1		5	9			3*		7	12	Alan Robinson	32
	2	3				10	8*		6	11	4	1		5	9				12	7		T. Holbrook	33
	2	6			4	10	8			11		1		5	9			3	12	7*		D. Reeves	34
	2	6		5		10	8		12	11		1		4	9			3		7*		D. Shaw	35
	2	6		5		10	8		7	11	4	1			9			3				R. Guy	36
	2	6		5		10	8		7	11	4	1			9			3				D. Letts	37
	2	6	7	5			8		10	11	4	1			9			3				A. Grey	38
	2	6		5		7	8		10	11	4	1			9			3				G. Courtney	39
	2	6		5		7	8		10	11	4	1			9			3				T. Mills	40
	2	6		5		7	8		10	11	4	1			9			3				A. Hamil	41
	2	6		5		7	8		10	11	4	1			9*			3	12			J. Martin	42
17	25	39	25	34	23	38	41	3	32	33	32	25	25	12	15	2	0	32	0	9	0		
		+ 1s	+ 2s			+ 1s			+ 5s	+ 1s	+ 1s			+ 3s	+ 3s		+ 2s		+ 4s	+ 1s	+ 1s		

FOOTBALL LEAGUE RECORD

1892 Elected to Division 1; 1906 Division 2; 1907 Division 1; 1911–22 Division 2; 1922–25 Division 1; 1925–49 Division 2; 1949–51 Division 3(S); 1951–57 Division 2; 1957–72 Division 1; 1972–77 Division 2; 1977– Division 1.

HONOURS

Football League: Division 1 – Champions 1977–78; Runners-up 1966–67, 1978–79. Division 2 – Champions 1906–07, 1921–22; Runners-up 1956–57; Division 3(S) – Champions 1950–51. *FA Cup:* Winners 1898, 1959. *Anglo-Scottish Cup:* Winners 1976–77. *Football League Cup:* Winners 1977–78, 1978–79; Runners-up 1979–80. **European Competitions:** *Fairs Cup:* 1961–62, 1967–68. *European Cup:* 1978–79 (winners), 1979–80 (winners), 1980–81. *Super Cup:* 1979–80 (winners), 1980–81 (runners-up). *World Club Championship:* 1980–81 (runners-up). *UEFA Cup:* 1983–84.

COLOURS

Red shirts with white pinstripe, white shorts, red stockings.
Change colours: All yellow.

NOTTINGHAM FOREST

Players Names Ht, Wt, D.o.B.	Birthplace Transfer Fee	Clubs	Appearances F.L. A & S	 F.L.C. A & S	 F.A.C. A & S	Goals F.L.	 F.L.C.	 F.A.C.
Goalkeepers								
Steve Sutton	Derby	Nottingham F (A)	19	2				
16.4.61	—	Mansfield T (loan)	8		1			
Hans Van Breukelen	Holland	Utrecht						
4.10.56	£200,000	Nottingham F	25	4				
Ron Sinclair	Stirling	Nottingham F (A)						
Defenders								
Kenny Swain	Birkenhead	Wycombe W						
5 11, 11 7, 28.1.52	—	Chelsea	114+5	6	7	26	1	2
	£100,000	Aston Villa	148	12	10	2	1	
	£25,000	Nottingham F	32	4	1	1		
Viv Anderson (E)	Nottingham	Nottingham F (A)	283+5	37	22+1	9	5	1
5 11, 10 4, 29.8.56								
Bryn Gunn	Kettering	Nottingham F (A)	108+2	11	7	1		
5 9, 10 5, 21.8.58								
Stuart Gray	Withernsea	Nottingham F	48+1	5+1	3	3		
5 9, 11 10, 19.4.60		Bolton W (loan)	7					
Jan Einar AAS* (Nor)	Moss, Norway	Bayern Munich						
5 9, 11 10, 12.10.55	£250,000	Nottingham F	20+1	3		1		
Willie Young (S)	Edinburgh	Aberdeen						
6 3, 12 10, 25.11.51	£100,000	Tottenham H	54	8	2	3	1	
	£80,000	Arsenal	170	20	28	11	1	3
	£170,000	Nottingham F	59	3	2	5	1	
Chris Fairclough	Nottingham	Nottingham F (A)	12+3	3				
12.4.64								
Nigel Thrower*	Nottingham	Nottingham F						
	—	Chesterfield (loan)	4					
Colin Todd (E)	Chester-Le-Street	Sunderland (A)	170+3	4	10	3		
5 9, 11 5, 12.12.48	£180,000	Derby Co	293	20	30	6		2
	£330,000	Everton	32	2	1	1		
	£300,000	Birmingham C	92+1	8	7			
	£70,000	Nottingham F	23	5				
Paul Hart	Manchester	Stockport Co	88	7	5+1	5		
6 2, 12 8, 4.5.53	£30,000	Blackpool	143	7	6	17	1	
	£300,000	Leeds U	191	17	11	16	1	1
		Nottingham F						
Mark Smalley	Newark	Nottingham F (A)	+1					
Midfield								
Mark Proctor (EU21)	Middlesbrough	Middlesbrough (A)	107+2	6	10	12	1	1
5 10, 11 9, 30.1.61	£425,000	Nottingham F	60+4	10	2	5	3	1
	—	Sunderland (loan)	5					
Jim McKechnie	Glasgow	Nottingham F (A)						
John Robertson (S)	Uddington	Nottingham F (A)	374+12	45+1	35+1	61	16	10
5 8, 10 9, 20.1.53								
Colin Walsh (SU21)	Hamiilton	Nottingham F (A)	54+14	4+2	6	12		1
5 9, 11 0, 22.7.62								
Danny Wilson	Wigan	Wigan Ath						
5 7, 10 3, 1.1.60		Bury	87+3	4	11	8		2
	£100,000	Chesterfield	100	8	9	13	1	1
	P/E	Nottingham F	9+1			1		
Ian Bowyer	Little Sutton	Manchester C (A)	42+7	6+2	4	13	2	
5 11, 11 2, 6.6.51	£25,000	Orient	75+3	5	5	18	2	2
	£40,000	Nottingham F	222+17	31+1	25	49	12	5
	£50,000	Sunderland	15	1		1		
	£50,000	Nottingham F	62+2	4	1	5	1	
David Longhurst	Northampton	Nottingham F (A)						
Forwards								
Ian Wallace (S)	Glasgow	Dumbarton						
5 7½, 10 9, 23.5.56	£75,000	Coventry C	128+2	6	4	57	2	
	£1,250,000	Nottingham F	106+1	11	7	33	8	1
Steve Wigley	Ashton-under-lyne	Curzon Ashton						
15.10.61	£2000	Nottingham F	+4	1				
Steve Hodge (EU21)	Nottingham	Nottingham F (A)	39+1	3		8	1	
5 8, 10 8, 25.10.62								
Peter Davenport	Birkenhead	Cammell Lairds						
24.3.61		Nottingham F	20+3	1	+1	6		
Gary Birtles (E)	Nottingham	Long Eaton						
5 11, 11 8, 27.7.56	£3000	Nottingham F	87	18	5	32	10	1
	£1,250,000	Manchester U	57+1	2	4	11		1
	£275,000	Nottingham F	25	4	1	7	4	

Players (non-appearance) granted free transfer: Pat Lundy, M.
Players released since May 1982: Dave Needham, D. (Toronto Buzzards); Jurgen Rober, M. (Bayer Leverkusen); Peter Ward, F. (Seattle Sounders).

NOTTS COUNTY Division 1

Back row (left to right): Pedro Richards, Trevor Christie, Mick Leonard, Raddy Avramovic, David Hunt, Tristan Benjamin, Ray O'Brien
Middle row: Jack Wheeler (Trainer), Nigel Worthington, Aki Lahtinen, Brian Kilcline, Rachid Harkouk, Gary Wood, Michael Walker (Second Team Coach), Howard Wikinson (Team Manager)
Front row: Iain McCulloch, Paul Manns, Gordon Mair, Jimmy Sirrel (General Manager), Ian McParland, John Chiedozie, Mark Goodwin.

:hairman: J. J. Dunnett MA, LLB (CANTAB), MP.

irectors: R. Sweet, J. Mounteney.

ieneral Manager: Jimmy Sirrel. ***Team Manager:*** Larry Lloyd.

:ommercial Manager: Neal Hook M INST M.

ecretary: Kenn Mott.

'ear Formed: 1872 (the oldest club in the Football League).

[urned Professional: 1885. ***Ltd Co.:*** 1888.

'revious Grounds: 1862, The Park; 1864, The Meadows; 1877, Beeston :ricket Ground; 1880, Castle Ground; 1883, Trent Bridge; 1910, /leadow Lane.

:lub Nickname: 'Magpies'.

'revious Managers since 1946: Arthur Stollery, Eric Houghton, George 'oyser, Tommy Lawton, Frank Hill, Tim Coleman, Eddie Lowe, Jack 3urkitt, Andy Beattie, Billy Gray, Jimmy Sirrel, Ron Fenton (12).

'ounty Ground, Meadow Lane, Nottingham NG2 3HJ. Telephone Nottingham (0602) 861155. ***Tele-raphic address:*** 'Notts County FC Nottingham'. ***Ground capacity:*** 23,680. ***Record attendance:*** 47,310 v 'ork C, FA Cup 6th rd, 12 Mar, 1955. ***Record receipts:*** £30,654.15 v Aston Villa, FA Cup 3rd rd, 5 Jan, 982. ***Pitch measurements:*** 117yd×76yd.

irections to Ground: Nearest railway station Nottingham from there any bus marked 'Trent Bridge'.

latch tickets: Advance bookings can be accepted by post or by personal application fourteen days efore each home game. SAE must be sent with remittance in postal applications.

'ar parking: No street parking around the ground, but ample space in the City of Nottingham Corpor-tion car park on the Cattle Market, Meadow Lane, just 400 yards from the main entrances.

ntertainments/catering facilities: Social club. Tea bars on all sides of the ground.

lub shop: Open daily; situated at the ground.

rogrammes: Back copies and subscription rates available from the club.

ddress of Suppòrters Club and Shop: c/o Club.

ote: Full club statistical records are on pages 416–455.

NOTTS COUNTY 1982–83 LEAGUE RECORD

Match No.	*Date*	*Venue*	*Opponents*	*Result*		*H/T Score*	*Lg. Pos.*	*Goalscorers*	*Attendance*
1	Aug 28	H	Swansea C	D	0-0	0-0	—		8061
2	Sept 1	A	Sunderland	D	1-1	0-0	—	Christie	18,997
3	4	A	Luton T	L	3-5	2-2	18	Kilcline, Chiedozie, Goodwin	9071
4	7	H	Manchester C	W	1-0	1-0	—	Goodwin	9376
5	11	H	Everton	W	1-0	0-0	7	Harkouk (pen)	9197
6	18	A	Arsenal	L	0-2	0-1	12		20,556
7	25	H	Ipswich	L	0-6	0-2	15		8454
8	Oct 2	A	Southampton	L	0-1	0-0	19		16,230
9	9	H	Aston Villa	W	4-1	2-0	17	Mortimer (og), Christie, Mair, McCulloch	8990
10	16	A	Coventry C	L	0-1	0-0	18		8322
11	23	A	Tottenham H	L	2-4	0-2	20	Christie, Chiedozie	25,783
12	30	H	Watford	W	3-2	1-2	18	Kilcline, McCulloch, Hooks	9171
13	Nov 6	A	Norwich C	W	2-1	0-0	15	Mair, Christie	13,472
14	13	H	Birmingham C	D	0-0	0-0	14		9118
15	20	H	Liverpool	L	1-2	1-0	16	Christie	16914
16	27	A	Brighton & HA	W	2-0	1-0	13	McCulloch 2	10,008
17	Dec 4	H	Nottingham F	W	3-2	2-2	12	McCulloch, Hooks, Christie	23,065
18	11	A	Manchester U	L	0-4	0-1	13		33,618
19	18	H	West Ham U	L	1-2	0-2	15	Worthington	8457
20	27	A	WBA	D	2-2	0-1	16	Fashanu, Goodwin	17,768
21	28	H	Stoke C	W	4-0	2-0	11	Mair, McCulloch 2, Goodwin	11,600
22	Jan 1	A	Liverpool	L	1-5	1-2	16	Fashanu	33,644
23	3	H	Sunderland	L	0-1	0-1	16		932
24	15	A	Swansea C	L	0-2	0-0	16		899
25	22	H	Arsenal	W	1-0	0-0	15	Fashanu	973
26	Feb 5	A	Everton	L	0-3	0-2	16		14,54
27	15	H	Southampton	L	1-2	1-1	—	McCulloch	585
28	19	A	Manchester C	W	1-0	0-0	16	Fashanu	21,19
29	26	H	Coventry C	W	5-1	2-0	16	Fashanu 2, Lahtinen, McCulloch, Hooks	868
30	Mar 5	H	Tottenham H	W	3-0	3-0	14	Hunt, Chiedozie 2	11,89
31	8	A	Aston Villa	L	0-2	0-1	—		17,45
32	12	A	Watford	L	3-5	1-3	14	Christie, Worthington, Fashanu	16,27
33	19	H	Norwich C	D	2-2	1-2	15	Worthington, Christie (pen)	806
34	26	A	Birmingham C	L	0-3	0-2	16		11,74
35	Apr 2	A	Stoke C	L	0-1	0-0	16		16,31
36	4	H	WBA	W	2-1	1-1	—	McCulloch, Christie (pen)	869
37	9	A	Ipswich T	D	0-0	0-0	14		15,92
38	16	H	Luton T	D	1-1	0-0	14	Chiedozie	893
39	23	A	Nottingham F	L	1-2	1-2	15	Lahtinen	25,55
40	30	H	Brighton & HA	W	1-0	0-0	15	Kilcline	734
41	May 7	A	West Ham U	L	0-2	0-1	16		17,53
42	14	H	Manchester U	W	3-2	1-1	15	Harkouk 2, McParland	14,41

Final League Position: 15

GOALSCORERS

League (55): McCulloch 10, Christie 9 (2 pens), Fashanu 7, Chiedozie 5, Goodwin 4, Harkouk 3 (1 pen), Hooks Kilcline 3, Mair 3, Worthington 3, Lahtinen 2, Hunt 1, McParland 1, own goal 1.
Milk Cup (8): Christie 2 (1 pen), Hunt 2, Chiedozie 1, Clarke 1, Hooks 1, McCulloch 1.
FA Cup (3): Fashanu 2, McCulloch 1.

Milk Cup	Second Round	Aston Villa (a)	2-1
		(h)	1-0
	Third Round	Chelsea (h)	2-0
	Fourth Round	West Ham U (h)	3-3
		(a)	0-3
FA Cup	Third Round	Leicester C (a)	3-2
	Fourth Round	Middlesbrough (a)	0-2

Avramovic	Benjamin	Worthington	Hunt	Kilcline	Richards	McParland	Harkouk	Christie	Chiedozie	Mair	Lahtinen	Goodwin	McCulloch	Hooks	Clarke	Fashanu	Leonard	O'Brien	*Referees*	*Match No.*
1	2	3	4	5	6	7*	8	9	10	11	12								B. Hill	1
1	2	3	4	5	6	12	8	9	7*	11	10								A. Robinson	2
1	2	3	4	5	6	12	8	9	7	11		10*							M. Bodenham	3
1	2	3	4	5	6		8	9	7	11		10							M. Robinson	4
1	2	3	4	5	6		8	9	7	11		10							M. Dimblebee	5
1	2	3	4	5	6		8	9	7	11*	12	10							T. Spencer	6
1	2	3	4	5	6		8	9	7			10	11						J. Lovatt	7
1	2	3	4	5	6	11	8*		7			10	9	12					A. Gunn	8
1	2	3	4*	5	6			8	7	11		12	9		10				D. Hutchinson	9
1	2*	3	4	5	6			8	7	11	12		9		10				C. Downey	10
1		3	4	5	6			8	7	11	2	12	9*		10				I. Borrett	11
1		3	4*	5	6			8	7	11		2	9	12	10				P. Willis	12
1		3		5	6			8	7	11		2	9	4	10				D. Reeves	13
1		3		5	6			8	7	11	12	2	9	4	10*				A. Saunders	14
1	2	3		5	6			8	7	11*	12	10	9	4					C. Thomas	15
1	2	3	4	5	6			8	7	11			9	10					A. Ward	16
1	2	3	4	5	6			8	7	11			9	10					D. Scott	17
1	2	3	4	5	6			8	7	11*		12	9	10					T. Mills	18
1	2	3	4	5	6			9	7	11*				10	12	8			J. Worrall	19
1	2	3	4	5	6			12	7	11		10	9			8*			N. Ashley	20
1	2	3	4	5	6				7	11		10	9*	12		8			D. Axcell	21
1	2	3	4*	5	6				7	11		10	9	12		8			A. Seville	22
1	2	3	4	5	6				7	11		10*	9	12		8			R. Bridges	23
1	2	3	4	5	6	7*		12		11		10	9			8			D. Lloyd	24
1	2	3	4	5	6			12	7*	11		10	9		12	8			R. Banks	25
1	2	3	4	5	6				7	11		10	9			8			T. Jones	26
1	2		4	5	6				7	11		10*	9	12	3	8			R. Guy	27
		3	4		6	12			7*		5	2	9	11		8	1	10	D. Owen	28
		3	4		6	12			7		5*	2	9	11		8	1	10	J. Hough	29
		3	4	5	6	12			7			2	9	11*		8	1	10	D. Brazier	30
		3	4	5	6			12	7			2*	9	11		8	1	10	R. Nixon	31
	4	3		5	6	12		10	7			2*	9		11	8	1		R. Milford	32
	2	3	4	5	6		12	10	7				9		11*	8	1		K. Cooper	33
1	2	3	4	5	6		7*	10				8	9		12			11	B. Daniels	34
1	2	11	4*	5	6		7	10			8	12	9		3				N. Midgley	35
1	2	11		5	6			8	7		10	4	9		3				K. Salmon	36
1	2	11	3	5	6	12		8	7		10	4*	9						T. Ward	37
1	2	11	3	5	6		12	8	7		10*	4	9						P. Willis	38
1	2*	11	3	5	6		12	8	7		10	4	9						A. Grey	39
1	2	11	3	5	6			8	7		10	4*	9		12				N. Wilson	40
1	2	11	3	5	6			8	7		10	4	9*		12				T. Bune	41
1	6	5	2	3	4	11	7	10	9		8								R. Lewis	42
36	34	41	37	40	42	4	11	29	39	25	12	30	34	11	11	15	6	5		
						+ 7s	+ 3s	+ 4s			+ 5s	+ 4s		+ 6s	+ 5s					

FOOTBALL LEAGUE RECORD

1888 Founder Member of the Football League; 1893–97 Division 2; 1897–1913 Division 1; 1913–14 Division 2; 1914–20 Division 1; 1920–23 Division 2; 1923–26 Division 1; 1926–30 Division 2; 1930–31 Division 3(S); 1931–35 Division 2; 1935–50 Division 3(S); 1950–58 Division 2; 1958–59 Division 3; 1959–60 Division 4; 1960–64 Division 3; 1964–71 Division 4; 1971–73 Division 3; 1973–81 Division 2; 1981– Division 1.

HONOURS

Football League: Division 1 best season: 3rd, 1890–91, 1900–01; Division 2 – Champions 1896–97, 1913–14, 1922–23; Runners-up 1894–95, 1980–81; Division 3(S) – Champions 1930–31, 1949–50; Runners-up 1936–37; Division 4 – Champions 1970–71; Runners-up 1959–60. *FA Cup:* Winners 1893–94; Runners-up 1890–91. *Football League Cup* best season: 5th rd, 1963–64, 1972–73, 1975–76.

COLOURS

Black and white striped shirts, black shorts with white stripe down the side, white stockings with black hoops at the top. **Change colours:** All yellow with blue trim or all blue.

NOTTS COUNTY

Players Names / *Ht. Wt. D.o.B.*	*Birthplace* / *Transfer Fee*	*Clubs*	*Appearances* F.L. A & S	*Appearances* F.L.C. A & S	*Appearances* F.A.C. A & S	*Goals* F.L.	*Goals* F.L.C.	*Goals* F.A.C.
Goalkeepers								
Mick Leonard	Carshalton	Epsom & Ewell						
5 11, 11 0, 9.5.59		Halifax T	69	6	1			
	£30,000	Notts Co	19	3				
Raddy Avramovic (YUG)	Yugoslavia	NK Rijeka						
6 0,12 0, 29.11.49	£200,000	Notts Co	149	15	3			
Defenders								
Pedro Richards	Edmonton	Notts Co (A)	310	26+1	11	3		
5 8, 10 8, 1.11.56								
Tristan Benjamin (EY)	St Kitts, W I	Notts Co (A)	193+15	17+1	6	4		
6 0, 11 1, 1.4.57								
Ray O'Brien (EI)	Shelbourne	Shelbourne						
5 9, 11 0, 21.5.51		Manchester U						
	£45,000	Notts Co	323	25	11	30	4	
Brian Kilcline (EU21)	Nottingham	Notts Co (A)	132+2	13	5	8		
6 2, 12 0, 7.5.62								
Nigel Worthington (NIY)	Ballymena	Ballymena U						
5 10, 12 0, 4.11.61	£10,000	Notts Co	43	5	2	3		
Aki Lahtinen (FIN)	Finland	Ops Oulu						
5 11, 11 3,	£61,000	Notts Co	17+8	2+1	1	2		
Midfield								
Gordon Mair (S.S)	Coatbridge	Notts Co (A)	108+6	9+4	4	18	2	
5 9, 10 6, 18.12.58								
David Hunt	Leicester	Derby Co (A)	5					
5 11, 11 0, 17.4.59	£30,000	Notts Co	191+5	15+1	8+1	13	3	1
Rachid Harkouk	Chelsea	Feltham						
6 0½, 12 5, 19.5.56		Crystal Palace	51+3	4+1	1+3	21	3	
	£100,000	QPR	15+5	3	1	3		
	£50,000	Notts Co	43+14	2	1+1	11		
Mark Goodwin	Sheffield	Leicester C (A)	69+22	3	4+1	8		
5 9¾, 10 9, 23.2.60	£60,000	Notts Co	76+6	5	3	10		
Forwards								
Iain M'Culloch (SU21)	Kilmarnock	Kilmarnock						
5 10, 11 0, 28.12.54	£80,000	Notts Co	192+1	17	6	51	1	1
Trevor Christie	Newcastle	Leicester C (A)	28+3	1		8		
6 2, 12 0, 28.2.59	£60,000	Notts Co	122+26	14+1	3+2	45	5	1
Ian McParland	Edinburgh	Ormiston Primrose						
5 8, 10 8, 4.10.61		Notts Co	11+14			1		
John Chiedozie (NIG)	Owerri, Nigeria	Orient (A)	131+14	8	7	20	1	2
5 7, 11 0, 18.4.60	£600,000	Notts Co	71	5	3	6	1	
Justin Fashanau (EU21)	Hackney	Norwich C (A)	84+6	8	5	34	4	1
6 1, 12 7, 18.9.62	£1,000,000	Nottingham F	31+1	4	1	3	1	
	—	Southampton (Loan)	9			3		
	£150,000	Notts Co	15	1	2	7		2
David Clarke (EY)	Nottingham	Notts Co. (A)	11+5	3+1			1	
5 10, 11 0, 3.12.64								

Commercial Manager: Neal Hook (Tel. 0602 861155).
Club Coach:
Supporters Player of the Season 1982–83: Raddy Avramovic.
Physiotherapist: Jack Wheeler.
Club Captain 1982-83: Pedro Richards.
Chief Scout:
Club Statistician: Keith Warsop.
Association of Football Statisticians Club Adviser to Yearbook: H. Worsop.

Players released since May 1982: Jim Doherty, F. (N/K) Chris Dykes, M. Worksop T.) Gary Wood, D. (Kettering).

OLDHAM ATHLETIC Division 2

Back row (left to right): Paul Futcher
Jim Steel
Andy Goram
Martin Hodge
Kenny Clements
John Bowden
Gary Hoolickin
Middle row: Billy Urmson (Coach)
Rodger Wylde
Paul Atkinson
Nick Sinclair
Dougie Anderson
Darron McDonough
John Ryan
Steve Wanless (Physiotherapist)
Front row: David Brand
John Humphreys
Steve Edwards
Joe Royle (Team Manager)
Ged Keegan (Capt)
Paul Heaton
Roger Palmer.

Chairman: H. Wilde. ***Vice-Chairman:*** R. Schofield.

Directors: J. Kershaw, I. H. Stott, G. T. Butterworth, D. A. Brierley, G. Knight.

Manager: Joe Royle. ***Secretary:*** T. Finn.

Year Formed: 1894. ***Turned Professional:*** 1899. ***Ltd Co.:*** 1906.

Club Nickname: 'The Latics'.

Previous Names: 1894, Pine Villa; 1899, Oldham Athletic.

Previous Ground: Sheepfoot Lane; 1905, Boundary Park.

Previous Managers since 1946: Bob Mellor, Frank Womack, Billy Wooton, George Hardwick, Ted Goodier, Peter McKennan, Norman Dodgin, Jack Rowley, Les McDowall, Gordon Hurst, Jimmy McIlroy, Jack Rowley, Jimmy Frizzell (13).

Boundary Park, Oldham. Telephone 061-624 4972. ***Ground capacity:*** 26,324. ***Record attendance:*** 47,671 v Sheffield W, FA Cup 4th rd, 25 Jan, 1930. ***Record receipts:*** £23,737 v Blackburn R, Division 2, 26 Dec, 1981. ***Pitch measurements:*** 110yd×74yd.

Directions to Ground: Oldham Werneth is the nearest railway station; ordinary bus routes and specials link the station to the ground at Boundary Park.

Match tickets: Tickets can be purchased in advance twelve days before the day of the match by either personal or postal application from the ticket office.

Car parking: Parking for 800 cars on site adjacent to ground.

Entertainements/catering facilities: Social club (members only); refreshment bars around the ground. Licensed bars in seated sections.

Club shop: A new shop has been opened and sells all the usual souvenirs.

Handbooks/programmes: Programmes on sale at the ground or through the post for cover price plus postage and packing.

Address of Supporters Club: Same as club.

Address of the Club Shop or Boutique: 'Latique', Boundary Park, Oldham OL1 2PA.

Note: Full club statistical records are on pages 416–455.

OLDHAM ATHLETIC 1982–83 LEAGUE RECORD

Match No.	Date	Venue	Opponents	Result	H/T Score	Lg. Pos.	Goalscorers	Attendance
1	Aug 28	H	Shrewsbury T	W 1-0	1-0	—	McLaren (og)	3731
2	Sept 4	A	Barnsley	D 1-1	0-0	11	Palmer	11,909
3	7	H	Rotherham U	D 1-1	0-0	—	Bowden	4261
4	11	H	QPR	L 0-1	0-0	13		4266
5	18	A	Chelsea	L 0-2	0-1	16		10,263
6	25	H	Charlton Ath	D 2-2	0-1	16	Palmer 2	3211
7	28	A	Bolton W	W 3-2	2-2	—	Palmer 2, Ryan	5605
8	Oct 2	A	Middlesbrough	D 1-1	1-0	12	Palmer	5635
9	9	H	Newcastle U	D 2-2	2-2	13	Heaton, Wylde	11,491
10	16	A	Crystal Palace	L 0-1	0-0	15		6643
11	23	H	Carlisle U	W 4-3	1-0	12	Ryan, Atkinson, Heaton, Palmer	4211
12	30	A	Burnley	W 2-1	0-1	9	Atkinson, Ryan	7197
13	Nov 6	A	Fulham	W 3-0	2-0	7	Wylde 2, McDonough	6897
14	13	H	Wolverhampton W	W 4-1	1-0	6	Ryan, Wylde 3	7962
15	20	A	Derby Co	D 2-2	1-0	6	Wylde, Foster (og)	11,775
16	27	H	Grimsby T	D 1-1	0-0	5	McDonough	5508
17	Dec 4	A	Sheffield W	D 1-1	0-0	7	Wylde	15,096
18	11	H	Cambridge U	W 3-0	1-0	5	Palmer, McDonough, Wylde	7127
19	18	A	Leicester C	L 1-2	0-0	7	Wylde	8125
20	26	H	Leeds U	D 2-2	1-1	—	Palmer, Ryan	15,658
21	29	A	Blackburn R	D 2-2	1-2	7	Wylde (pen), Atkinson	10,121
22	Jan 1	H	Derby Co	D 2-2	0-1	7	Bowden, Wylde	7085
23	3	H	Barnsley	D 1-1	1-0	8	Heaton	8382
24	15	A	Shrewsbury T	D 0-0	0-0	8		4630
25	22	H	Bolton W	L 2-3	1-1	9	McDonough 2	8510
26	29	A	Rotherham U	W 3-1	1-1	5	Wylde (pen), Sinclair, McDonough	6392
27	Feb 5	A	QPR	L 0-1	0-0	6		8903
28	12	H	Middlesbrough	W 3-0	1-0	4	Palmer 2, Ryan	6002
29	19	A	Newcastle U	L 0-1	0-1	5		20,661
30	26	H	Crystal Palace	W 2-0	2-0	5	Palmer, Wylde	9780
31	Mar 5	A	Carlisle U	D 0-0	0-0	5		4054
32	19	H	Fulham	W 1-0	0-0	5	Palmer	6189
33	26	A	Wolverhampton W	D 0-0	0-0	6		12,940
34	Apr 1	H	Blackburn R	D 0-0	0-0	—		7966
35	5	A	Leeds U	D 0-0	0-0	—		18,442
36	9	H	Chelsea	D 2-2	1-1	8	Wylde, Ryan	4973
37	12	H	Burnley	W 3-0	2-0	—	McDonough 2, Wylde	6126
38	17	A	Charlton Ath	L 1-4	0-2	—	Wylde	5193
39	23	H	Sheffield W	D 1-1	1-1	7	Wylde	5088
40	30	A	Grimsby T	W 2-0	0-0	7	Palmer, Ryan	4755
41	May 7	H	Leicester C	L 1-2	0-1	12	Palmer	9088
42	14	A	Cambridge U	W 4-1	0-0	7	McDonough 2, Wylde, Henry	3948

Final League Position: 7

GOALSCORERS

League (64): Wylde 19 (2 pens), Palmer 15, McDonough 10, Ryan 8, Atkinson 3, Heaton 3, Bowden 2, Henry 1, Sinclair 1, own goals 2.
Milk Cup (1): McDonough 1.
FA Cup (0).

Milk Cup	Second Round	Gillingham (a)	0-2
		(h)	1-0
FA Cup	Third Round	Fulham (h)	0-2

Hodge (L)	Sinclair	Ryan	Keegan	Clements	Futcher	Heaton	Atkinson	Humphreys	Wylde	Palmer	Steel	Bowden	Hoolickin	Goram	McDonough	Edwards	Hudson	Taylor (L)	Anderson	Henry	McMahon	Jones	Referees	Match No.
1	2	3	4	5	6	7*	8	9	10	11	12												A. Challinor	1
1	2	3	4	5	6	7	8	9	10	11													G. Napthine	2
1	2*	3	4	5	6		8		10	11	9	12	7										G. Tyson	3
1	2	3	4	5	6	7*	8		12	11	9	10											N. Ashley	4
	2	3	4	5	6		8			11	9	10	12	1	7*								L. Shapter	5
	2	3	4	5	6		8		10	11	9*	12		1	7								M. Heath	6
	2	3	4	5	6		8		10	11	9			1	7								D. Civil	7
	2	3	4	5	6		8		10	11	9*	12		1	7								M. Scott	8
	2	3	4	5	6	9	8		10	11				1	7								D. Owen	9
	2	3	4		6	9	8		10	11			5	1	7								A. Grey	10
		3	4*	5	6	9	8		10	11		12	2	1	7								V. Callow	11
		3			6	9	8		10	11		4	2	1	7	5							J. Hunting	12
		3			6	9	8		10	11		4	5	1	7	2							D. Axcell	13
		3			6	9	8		10	11		4	5	1	7	2							J. Key	14
		3		12	6	9	8		10	11		4	5	1	7	2*							E. Scales	15
		3		5	6	9	8		10	11		4		1	7	2							T. Holbrook	16
		3		5	6	9	8		10	11		4	2	1	7								J. Bray	17
		3		5	6	9	8		10	11		4	2	1	7								A. Saunders	18
		3		5	6	9	8		10	11		4	2	1	7								K. Cooper	19
		3	12	5	6	9	8*		10	11		4	2	1	7								R. Bridges	20
		3		5	6	9	8		10	11		4	2	1	7								P. Willis	21
		3		5	6	9	8		10	11		4	2	1	7								C. Seel	22
		3		5	6	9	8		10	11		4	2	1	7								M. Peck	23
		3	4	5	6	7	8		10	11			2	1	9								D. Brazier	24
	7		4	5	6		8		10	11			2	1	9	3*	12						A. Seville	25
	2		4	5			8		10	11			6	1	9	3		7					F. Roberts	26
	2	3	4	5			8			11		10	6	1	9			7					B. Daniels	27
	2	3	4	5			8			11*		10	6	1	9			7	12				C. Newsome	28
	2	3	4	5			8		12	11*		10	6	1	9			7					T. Mills	29
	2	3	4	5			8		7	11		10	6	1	9								R. Nixon	30
	2	3	4	5			8		7	11		10	6	1	9								N. Ashley	31
	2	3	4	5			8		7	11			6	1	9					10			G. Courtney	32
	2	3		5			8		7	11		4	6	1	9					10			C. Downey	33
	2	3		5			8		7	11		4	6	1	9					10			J. Hough	34
	2	3		5			8		7	11		4	6*	1	9				12	10			K. Barratt	35
	2*	3		5			8		7	11		4		1	9		12		6	10			M. Robinson	36
		3		5			8		7	11		4		1	9				6	10	2		A. Challinor	37
		3		5			8		7	11		4		1	9		12		6	10	2*		M. Taylor	38
		3		5			8	12	7	11		4*	6	1	9		2			10			K. Redfern	39
		3		5			8		7	11			6	1	9		4			10		2	K. Baker	40
	12	3		5			8		7	11			6	1	9		4			10		2*	N. Peck	41
	2	3		5*			8		7	11		12	6	1	9		4			10			T. Bune	42
4	23	40	20	37	25	19	42	2	37	42	6	26	30	38	38	7	4	4	3	11	2	2		
	+ 1s		+ 1s	+ 1s				+ 1s	+ 2s		+ 1s	+ 5s	+ 1s				+ 3s		+ 2s					

FOOTBALL LEAGUE RECORD

1907 Elected to Division 2; 1910–23 Division 1; 1923–35 Division 2; 1935–53 Division 3(N); 1953–54 Division 2; 1954–58 Division 3; 1958–63; Division 4; 1963–69 Division 3; 1969–71 Division 4; 1971–74 Division 3; 1974– Division 2.

HONOURS

Football League: Division 1 – Runners-up 1914–15; Division 2 – Runners-up 1909–10; Division 3(N) – Champions 1952–53; Division 3 – Champions 1973–74; Division 4 – Runners-up 1962–63. *FA Cup:* semi-final 1913. *Football League Cup:* never past 3rd rd.

COLOURS

Royal blue shirts with white trim on sleeves, white shorts with blue stripe down the side, white stockings.
Change colours: Tangerine shirts, blue shorts, tangerine stockings.

OLDHAM ATHLETIC

Players Names Ht, Wt, D.o.B.	Birthplace Transfer Fee	Clubs	Appearances F.L. A & S	 F.L.C. A & S	 F.A.C. A & S	Goals F.L.	 F.L.C.	 F.A.C.
Goalkeepers								
Andy Goram	Bury	WBA (A)						
5 10, 11 6,	F/T	Oldham Ath	41	2	1			
Brian Parkin		Oldham Ath						
Defenders								
Gary Hoolickin	Middleton	Oldham Ath (A)	94+2	13	3+1	1		
5 11, 11 1, 29.10.57								
Nicky Sinclair	Manchester							
5 11, 11 7, 3.1.60		Oldham Ath	54+2	3		1		
Kenny Clements	Manchester	Manchester C	116+3	18	7			
6 1, 12 6, 9.4.55	£200,000	Oldham Ath	140+1	6	6	2		
John Hudson		Manchester C						
	F/T	Oldham Ath	4+3					
Ian McMahon		Oldham Ath (A)	2					
John Ryan	Oldham	Oldham Ath (A)	77	6	2	8		
5 10, 11 7, 18.2.62								
Alex Jones		Oldham Ath (A)	2					
Midfield								
Gerard Keegan* (EU21)	Manchester	Manchester C (A)	32+5	4+1	+1	2	1	
5 6½, 10 9, 3.10.55	£25,000	Oldham Ath	139+5	10	5	5		
Darren McDonough	Antwerp, Belgium	Oldham Ath (A)	84+5	7	2	14	1	
5 11, 11 0, 7.11.62								
Paul Atkinson (EY)	Pudsey	Oldham Ath (A)	139+4	9+1	5	11		
5 10, 11 5, 14.8.61								
Tony Henry	Newcastle	Manchester C (A)	68+11	7	3+1	6	6	
5 11, 12 0, 26.11.57	£125,000	Bolton W	80	3	3	22	2	
	£21,000	Oldham Ath	11			1		
Forwards								
Paul Heaton	Hyde	Oldham Ath (A)	114+12	9+2	4	26	2	1
5 9, 10 2, 24.1.61								
Roger Wyloe	Sheffield	Sheffield W (A)	157+12	10	15	54	8	4
6 1½, 12 0, 8.3.54	£80,000	Oldham Ath	109+4	8	4	51		
Doug Anderson	Hong Kong	Port Glasgow						
5 11½, 9 5, 29.8.63		Oldham Ath	4+3					
Roger Palmer	Manchester	Manchester C (A)	22+9	3+3		9	1	
5 10, 10 10, 30.1.59	£70,000	Oldham Ath	98+2	7	4	28		
John Bowden	Stockport	Oldham Ath	29+7	2	1	4		
6 0, 11 7, 21.1.63								
John Humphreys		Oldham Ath (A)	2+1	+1				

Commercial Manager: Alan Hardy. (Tel. 061-652 0966)
Club Coach: Billy Umson
Club Captain 1982–83: Kenny Clements
Supporters Player of the Season 1982–83: Andy Goram
Chief Scout:
Physiotherapist: Steve Wanless
Club Statistician: Neil Holmes
Association of Football Statisticians Club Adviser to Yearbook: D. Williams

Players (non-appearance) granted free transfer: John Murphy, F.; Steve Millington, M.
Players released since May 1982: Andrew Birchenough, D. (N/K); Mark Cooper, D. (N/K); Derek Egan, M. (N/K); Peter McDonnell, G. (N/K); David Brand, F. (Southport).

ORIENT Division 3

Back row (left to right): Steve Parsons, David Peach, John Bolle, Bill Roffey, Robert Fisher, Barry Silkman
Middle row: Bill Songhurst (Physio), Keith Houchen, Nigel Gray, Kevin Shoemake, Mervyn Day, Stuart Hinchliffe, Colin Footer, Keith Osgood, Dario Gradi (Youth Development Officer)
Front row: Robert Vincent, Tommy Cunningham, Mark McNeil, Frank Clark (Asst Manager), Ken Knighton (Manager), Kevin Godfrey, Peter Taylor, Mark Blackhall
On ground: Jamie Mankelow, Steve Castle, Malcolm Hawkes, Peter Smith, John Cornwell, Andy Sussex, David Manning, Jeff Eyers.

Chairman: N. Ovendon. ***Managing Director:*** B. Winston.

Directors: A. Pincus, D. L. Weinrabe, A. Harding, M. Ovendon.

Manager: Frank Clark.

Secretary: Miss Carol Stokes. ***Asst Sec.:*** Mrs Sue Tilling.

Year Formed: 1881. ***Turned Professional:*** 1903. ***Ltd Co.:*** 1906.

Club Nickname: 'The O's'.

Previous Names: 1881–86, Glyn Cricket and Football Club; 1886–88, Eagle Football Club; 1888–98, Orient Football Club; 1898–1946, Clapton Orient; 1946–66, Leyton Orient.

Previous Grounds: Glyn Rd (1884–96), Whittles Athletic Ground (1896–1900), Millfields Rd (1900–30), and Lea Bridge Rd (1930–37).

Previous Managers since 1946: Charles Hewitt, Neil McBain, Alec Stock, Les Gore, Alec Stock, John Carey, Benny Fenton, Dave Sexton, Dick Graham, Jimmy Bloomfield, George Petchey, Jimmy Bloomfield, Ken Knighton (13).

Leyton Stadium, Brisbane Road, Leyton, London E10 5NE. Telephone 01-539 2223/4. ***Telegraphic address:*** 'The Orient', Leyton E10. ***Ground capacity:*** 26,500 (7,171 seats). ***Record attendance:*** 34,345 v West Ham U, FA Cup 4th rd, 25 Jan, 1964. ***Record receipts:*** £41,765.20 v West Ham U, FA Cup 4th rd, 26 Jan, 1980. ***Pitch measurements:*** 110yd×75yd.

Directions to Ground: Buses 69, 58, 278, 241 pass the ground. From the centre of London, journey by underground (Central Line) to Leyton station; the ground is a few minutes' walk. Nearest BR station is Leyton Midland Road (10 minutes' walk).

Match tickets: Can be booked at least two weeks in advance.

Car parking: Street parking around the ground. A NCP five minutes from Brisbane Road (off Oliver Road).

Entertainments/catering facilities: Supporters' Section Club and snack bar points around the ground.

Club shop: Sells all types of souvenirs and sportswear.

Handbooks/programmes: Programmes can be obtained on subscription, and back numbers can be ordered from the club shop.

Extra information: The club operates a Pools Section and Travel Service. All enquiries to 369 High Road, Leyton, E10 (01-539 4483/4). Club's official historian – Neil Kaufman – can answer queries connected with the history of the club; c/o the Secretary.

ORIENT 1982–83 LEAGUE RECORD

Match No.	Date	Venue	Opponents	Result		H/T Score	Lg. Pos.	Goalscorers	Attendance
1	Aug 28	A	Chesterfield	W	2-1	0-0	—	Taylor, Godfrey	2587
2	Sept 4	H	Bradford C	L	0-1	0-0	13		2565
3	8	H	Cardiff C	W	4-0	2-0	—	Foster, Godfrey 2, Silkman	2021
4	11	A	Plymouth Arg	L	0-2	0-1	9		3649
5	18	H	Brentford	D	3-3	1-0	10	Donn, Roffey 2	3458
6	25	A	Lincoln C	L	0-2	0-2	15		3096
7	28	A	Huddersfield T	L	0-6	0-3	—		6671
8	Oct 2	H	Doncaster R	W	1-0	0-0	14	Donn	1846
9	9	A	Reading	L	0-3	0-1	18		2539
10	16	H	Newport Co	L	1-5	0-1	21	McNeil	2040
11	19	A	Gillingham	L	0-4	0-2	—		3849
12	23	H	Bristol R	L	1-5	0-1	23	Peach	2534
13	29	A	Southend U	D	1-1	1-0	—	Cunningham	5138
14	Nov 2	H	Walsall	W	2-1	1-0	—	Hawley, Sussex	1935
15	6	H	Wigan Ath	D	1-1	1-1	21	Godfrey	2266
16	13	A	Wrexham	L	0-1	0-0	21		2333
17	27	A	Exeter C	L	0-2	0-1	21		2611
18	Dec 4	H	Oxford U	L	1-5	1-3	22	Houchen	2242
19	17	H	Preston NE	W	2-1	1-1	20	Peach (pen), Kitchen	1668
20	26	A	Millwall	W	1-0	0-0	—	Houchen	4740
21	28	H	AFC Bournemouth	W	5-0	2-0	19	Kitchen, Godfrey 2, Cornwell, Houchen	3718
22	Jan 1	A	Sheffield U	L	0-3	0-0	18		10,973
23	12	A	Bradford C	W	3-2	1-1	—	Kitchen, Gray, Peach (pen)	3315
24	15	H	Chesterfield	W	2-0	0-0	15	Peach (pen), Kitchen	2642
25	18	H	Portsmouth	W	2-1	1-1	—	Peach (pen), Sussex	3961
26	22	A	Brentford	L	2-5	1-1	13	Blackhall, Godfrey	5209
27	29	H	Plymouth Arg	L	0-2	0-2	14		2699
28	Feb 5	H	Lincoln	D	1-1	1-1	17	Peach	2584
29	15	A	Walsall	L	0-2	0-2	—		2328
30	20	H	Reading	D	3-3	1-2	—	Godfrey, Cunningham 2	2538
31	26	A	Newport Co	L	1-4	0-4	20	Silkman	3202
32	Mar 1	H	Gillingham	W	2-0	0-0	—	Gray, Houchen (pen)	2241
33	5	A	Bristol R	L	1-2	1-1	20	Godfrey	5642
34	13	H	Southend U	D	1-1	0-0	—	Houchen	3073
35	19	A	Wigan Ath	W	1-0	0-0	18	Godfrey	2954
36	25	H	Wrexham	D	0-0	0-0	—		1969
37	Apr 2	A	AFC Bournemouth	L	0-2	0-0	19		7039
38	4	H	Millwall	L	2-3	0-3	—	Cornwell, Houchen	4345
39	9	A	Oxford U	D	2-2	1-1	20	Houchen, Kitchen	4033
40	12	A	Doncaster R	W	3-0	1-0	—	Kitchen 2, Cornwell	2355
41	16	H	Huddersfield T	L	1-3	0-1	19	McNeil	3498
42	23	A	Preston NE	L	1-2	1-0	20	Foster	5628
43	30	H	Exeter C	W	5-1	2-0	18	Houchen 2, McNeil 3	2407
44	May 2	A	Portsmouth	D	2-2	0-0	19	McNeil, Kitchen	16,232
45	7	A	Cardiff C	L	0-2	0-1	20		11,480
46	14	H	Sheffield U	W	4-1	2-1	20	Houchen, Kitchen, Godfrey, Roffey	4468

Final League Position: 20

GOALSCORERS

League (64): Godfrey 11, Houchen 10, Kitchen 9, McNeil 6, Peach 6 (4 pens), Roffey 3, Cornwell 3, Cunningham 3, Donn 2, Foster 2, Gray 2, Silkman 2, Sussex 2, Blackhall 1, Hawley 1, Taylor 1.
Milk Cup (2): Cunningham 1, Osgood 1.
FA Cup (4): Godfrey 2, Foster 1, Sussex 1.
Football League Trophy (2): Taylor 1, own goal 1.

Milk Cup	First Round	Gillingham (a)	0-3
		(h)	2-0
FA Cup	First Round	Bristol C (h)	4-1
	Second Round	Newport Co (a)	0-1
Football League Trophy		Watford (a)	1-4
		Southend U (a)	1-1
		Colchester U (h)	0-2

Day	Fisher	Peach	Foster	Gray	Roffey	Godfrey	Donn	Houchen	Silkman	Taylor	Osgood	Vincent	Blackhall	Cornwell	Smith	Cunningham	McNeil	Sussex	Lee (L)	Hawley (L)	Kitchen	Mankelow	Price	*Referees*	*Match No.*
1	2	3	4	5	6	7	8	9*	10	11			12											T. Holbrook	1
1	2	3	4	5	6	7	8	9	10	11														M. Taylor	2
1		3	4	5		7	8		10	11	2	6	9											M. Bodenham	3
1		3*	4	5		7	8			11	2	6	9	12	10									E. Read	4
1			4	5	3	7	8		10	11	2		9			6								J. Hunting	5
1			4	5	3	7	8		10	11*	2		9			6	12							A. Robinson	6
1			4		3	7	8		10		2	12	9*		5	6	11							K. Redfern	7
1			4		3	7	8		10	12	2		9		5	6	11*							L. Shapter	8
1			4	6	3	7	8		10	12	2	11*	9		5									V. Callow	9
1			4	5	3	7	8		10	11	2		12		6*		9							J. Deakin	10
1			4		3	7				11	2			8	5	6	9	10						J. Martin	11
1		5	4		3	7			12	11	2*					6		10	8	9				B. Hill	12
1		3	4		2		6			11		7				5		10	8	9				D. Letts	13
1		3	4		2	12	6			11		7				5		10	8	9*				T. Bune	14
1		3	4		2	9	6			11		7				5		10	8					J. Bray	15
1		3	4		2	12	6			11*		7				5		10	8	9				N. Glover	16
1		3	4		2	8	6*	9		11	7			12		5		10						T. Spencer	17
1		3	4		2	8	6	9		11*	7		12			5		10						H. Taylor	18
1		3	4		2	8		9			7			6		5		10			11			D. Brazier	19
1		3	4		2	8		9			7			6	12	5		11*			10			M. James	20
1		3	4		2	8		9			7*			6	12	5		11			10			A. Grey	21
1		3	4		2	8		9			7			6		5		11			10			R. Banks	22
1		3	4	6	2	8		9						7		5		11			10			R. Nixon	23
1		3	4	7	2	8		9						6		5		11			10			R. Milford	24
1		3	4	7	2	8		9						6	12	5		11			10*			D. Hedges	25
1		3	4	7	2	8		9					10	6		5		11						A. Glasson	26
1		3	4		2	8		9			7		10*	6	12	5		11						I. Borrett	27
1		3	4		2	8		9			7*		10	6		5		11				12		Alan Robinson	28
1		3		7	2	8	4	9	12				10*	6		5		11						G. Napthine	29
1		3		7	2	8	4	9	12					6		5		11				10*		A. Seville	30
1		3*	4	7	2	8	12	9	10					6		5		11						K. Baker	31
1			4	7	2	8	3	9	10	12				6		5		11*						J. Gray	32
1			4	7	2	8	3	9*	10	12				6	11	5								C. Thomas	33
1		3	4	5		11	7	9						2			12	6			10		8*	B. Stevens	34
1		5	3	4		11	7	9						2			12	6*			10		8	A. Hamil	35
1			4	5	3	11	7	9						2			6				10		8	K. Barratt	36
1		7	4	5	3	11		9						2			6				10		8	M. Bodenham	37
1		7	4	5	3	11		9	12					2			6				10*		8	M. Robinson	38
1		7	4	5	3	11		9						2			6				10		8	D. Lloyd	39
1		3	4	5	2	6		9						8			11				10		7	T. Jones	40
1		3	4	5	2	7		9	12					8			11				10		6*	L. Shapter	41
1			5	4	2	8*		9	7					6	12		11				10		3	J. Key	42
1			5	4	2	8		9	7					6			11				10		3	M. Taylor	43
1		3	4	5	2	7*		9	6					8	12		11				10			T. Bune	44
1		3	4	5	2	12		9	6					8	7*		11				10			R. Bridges	45
1		3		5	2	7		9	6					8		4	11				10			H. King	46
46	2	34	43	30	42	42	23	32	17	15	18	7	11	29	8	28	15	24	5	4	20	1	10		
						+ 3s	+ 1s		+ 5s	+ 4s		+ 1s	+ 3s	+ 2s	+ 6s		+ 3s					+ 1s			

FOOTBALL LEAGUE RECORD

1905 Elected to Division 2; 1929–56 Division 3(S); 1956–62 Division 2; 1962–63 Division 1; 1963–66 Division 2; 1966–70 Division 3; 1970–82 Division 2; 1982– Division 3.

HONOURS

Football League: Division 1 best season: 22nd, 1962–63; Division 2 – Runners-up 1961–62; Division 3 – Champions 1969–70; Division 3(S) – Champions 1955–56; Runners-up 1954–55. *FA Cup:* Semi-final 1977–78. *Football League Cup* best season: 5th rd, 1963.

COLOURS

All red. **Change colours:** All blue.

ORIENT

Players Names Ht. Wt. D.o.B.	Birthplace Transfer Fee	Clubs	Appearances F.L. A & S	 F.L.C. A & S	 F.A.C. A & S	Goals F.L.	 F.L.C.	 F.A.C.
Goalkeepers								
Mervyn Day (EU23)	Chelmsford	West Ham U (A)	194	14	14			
6 2, 14 2, 26.6.55	£100,000	Orient	170	8	10			
Kevin Shoemake		Orient (A)						
Defenders								
Peter Smith	Islington	Orient (A)	8+6					
20.11.64								
Colin Foster	Rochford	Orient (A)	66	2	2	4	2	
6 4, 13 10,								
Bill Roffey	Stepney	Crystal Palace (A)	24	1				
5 11, 12 13, 6.2.54	£5000	Orient	296+3	15+1	17+1	8		1
Nigel Gray	Fulham	Orient (A)	233	8	20+1	2		
6 3, 13 4, 2.11.56	—	Charlton Ath (loan)	3					
Tommy Cunningham	London	Chelsea (A)						
6 0, 11 3, 7.12.55	F/T	QPR	27+3	1+1	3	2		
	£45,000	Wimbledon	99	11	6	12		2
	£60,000	Orient	46	1+1	2	4	1	
David Peach* (EU21)	Bedford	Gillingham (A)	186+1	9	9	30	1	
5 9, 11 6, 21.1.51	£50,000	Southampton	221+3	19	23+1	34	2	6
	£150,000	Swindon T	52+1	4	3	2		
	F/T	Orient	47	1	2	6		
Keith Osgood (EY)	Ealing	Tottenham H (A)	112+1	11	3	13	1	
5 11, 11 2, 8.5.55	£130,000	Coventry C	24+1	1		1		
	£150,000	Derby Co	61+8	4	1	10		
	£20,000	Orient	24	1	5		1	
Midfield								
Peter Taylor* (E)	Southend	Southend U (A)	57+18	1+1	1	12	1	
5 9, 11 7, 3.1.53	£120,000	Crystal Palace	122	9	11	33	1	4
	£200,000	Tottenham H	116+7	4+2	8+3	31		2
	£150,000	Orient	49+7	4	2	11		
	—	Oldham Ath (loan)	4					
Barry Silkman*	London	Barnet						
5 8, 10 13, 29.6.52		Hereford U	18+19	1	1	2		
	F/T	Crystal Palace	40+8	1	5	7		1
	£53,000	Plymouth Arg	14		1	2		
	—	Luton T (loan)	3					
	£60,000	Manchester C	19	2		3		
	£50,000	Brentford	14	2		1		
	£5000	QPR	22+1		2	2		
	£15,000	Orient	50+7	1	4+1	7		
John Cornwell		Orient (A)	29+2		1	3		
Nigel Donn*	Maidstone	Gillingham (A)	2+1	2	1			
5 10, 10 8, 2.3.62	F/T	Orient	23+1	2	1	2		
Forwards								
Kevin Godfrey	Kennington	Orient (A)	105+13	4+1	14	21		2
5 10, 11 2, 24.2.60								
Billy Hurley* (ES)	Leytonstone	Orient (A)	1+1					
5 9½, 12 6, 11.12.59								
Mark Blackhall*	Upney	Orient (A)	12+6	1	1	1		
6 0, 12 2, 17.11.60								
Mark McNeil	Bethnal Green	Orient (A)	35+7		1+1	9		
5 10, 10 5, 3.12.62								
Keith Houchen	Middlesbrough	Chesterfield (N/C)						
6 2, 11 4, 25.7.60	F/T	Hartlepool U	162+10	8	4+1	65	1	
	£25,000	Orient	46	1	2	11		
Andy Sussex	Islington	Orient (A)	32		2	3		1
Jamie Mankelow*	Higham Park	Orient (A)	1+1					
Peter Kitchen	Mexborough	Doncaster R	221+7	16	12	89	7	6
5 8, 11 1, 16.2.52	£30,000	Orient	64+1	4	11	28	1	9
	£150,000	Fulham	21+3			6		
	£100,000	Cardiff C	64+3	5	1	21	1	
	F/T	Happy Valley, HK						
	F/T	Orient	20			9		

Commercial Manager: Frank Woolf (Tel.).
Club Coach:
Club Captain 1982–83: Mervyn Day.
Supporters Player of the Season 1982–83: Bill Roffey.
Chief Scout:
Physiotherapist: Bill Songhurst.
Club Statistician:
Association of Football Statisticians Club Adviser to Yearbook: A. Higgins.

Players (non-appearance) granted free transfer: John Bolle, F.; Jeff Eyers, D.
Players released since May 1982:
Tunji Banjo, M. (AEL Limasol); Jeff Fielding, G. (Harlow T); Mark Kane, M. (Walthamstow Ave); John Margerrison, F. (Wealdstone); Bob Waterfall, D. (Clapton); Robert Vincent, M. (N/K); Stuart Hincliffe, G. (Goole T); Tommy Taylor, D. (Antwerp); David Price, M. (N/C—N/K); Steve Parson, F. (retired).

OXFORD UNITED Division 3

Back row (left to right): Gary Briggs, Roy Burton, David Fogg, John Butcher, David Grant
Middle row: Ken Fish (Trainer), Andy Thomas, Mick Vinter, Tim Smithers, Malcolm Shotton, Trevor Hebberd, Steve Biggins, Ray Graydon (Coach)
Front row: Kevin Brock, David Linney, Mark Jones, Jim Smith (Manager), Ray Train, Gary Bennett, Peter Foley.

OXFORD UNITED F.C.

President: The Duke of Marlborough.

Chairman: I. R. Maxwell MC.

Vice-Chairmen: Dr D. Morris BSC, D PHIL, W. H. Reeves, L. Town.

Directors: W. Black, G. E. Coppock, H. Kimber, P. Reeves, P. McGeough.

Manager: Jim Smith. ***Secretary:*** Jim Hunt.

Year Formed: 1896. ***Turned Professional:*** 1949. ***Ltd Co.:*** 1949.

Club Nickname: 'The U's'.

Previous Names: Headington United; 1960, Oxford United.

Previous Managers since the War: Arthur Turner, Ron Saunders, Gerry Summers, Mike Brown, Bill Asprey, Ian Greaves (6).

Manor Ground, Headington, Oxford. Telephone Oxford (0865) 61503. ***Ground capacity:*** 17,350. ***Record attendance:*** 22,730 v Preson NE, FA Cup 6th rd, 29 Feb, 1964. ***Record receipts:*** £17,740 v Portsmouth, Division 3, 18 Sept, 1982. ***Pitch measurements:*** 112yd×78yd.

Directions to Ground: Bus 2A/2B/2C from the city centre. Nearest railway station is Oxford General. From the station take Bus 501 to Queens Lane and then take Bus 2A/2B/2C. By road, take Oxford ring road to the east of the city, following the signs for Headington. Leave the ring road at Green Road roundabout into London Road; the ground is on the right after going straight across at the traffic lights.

Match tickets: Subject to availability tickets may be booked fourteen days prior to the match.

Car parking: Parking is available in certain streets around the ground.

Entertainments/catering facilities: Public houses, and cafés, all just minutes from the ground. Refreshments available inside the ground.

Club shop: Sited on the ground, open match days only selling all types of souvenirs (mail order list sent on receipt of SAE) as well as a wide range of all club programmes for both current and previous seasons.

Handbooks/programmes: Handbook on sale at £1+20p postage and packing. Programmes available on subscription. Applications to the Club office.

Address of Supporters Club: Supporters Club Offices, Manor Ground, Headington, Oxford.

Note: Full club statistical records are on pages 416–455.

OXFORD UNITED 1982–83 LEAGUE RECORD

Match No.	Date	Venue	Opponents	Result		H/T Score	Lg. Pos.	Goalscorers	Atten-dance
1	Aug 28	A	Gillingham	W	1-0	0-0	—	Barnett	4079
2	Sept 4	H	AFC Bournemouth	W	2-0	0-0	2	Vinter, Thomas	4729
3	8	H	Doncaster R	W	3-0	1-0	—	Brock, Biggins, Thomas	4482
4	11	A	Preston NE	W	2-1	1-0	1	Hebberd, Thomas	4481
5	18	H	Portsmouth	D	1-1	1-1	1	Briggs	9918
6	25	A	Huddersfield T	L	0-2	0-1	2		4958
7	28	A	Chesterfield	W	2-1	0-1	—	Brock, Hebberd	2618
8	Oct 2	H	Cardiff C	D	2-2	0-1	2	Fogg, Brock	6018
9	9	A	Millwall	L	1-2	0-1	3	Thomas	3906
10	16	H	Walsall	W	4-2	3-1	2	Shotton, Whatmore, Fogg (pen), Brock	4732
11	20	H	Brentford	D	2-2	1-1	—	Whatmore, Fogg (pen)	6113
12	23	A	Wrexham	D	1-1	1-0	4	Vinter	2491
13	30	H	Exeter C	D	1-1	1-0	5	Whatmore	4689
14	Nov 3	A	Bradford C	L	2-3	1-2	—	Whatmore 2	6171
15	6	H	Sheffield U	D	0-0	0-0	9		6201
16	13	A	Plymouth Arg	L	1-2	0-1	10	Fogg (pen)	3908
17	Dec 4	A	Orient	W	5-1	3-1	11	Lawrence, Foley 2, Vinter, Smithers	2242
18	18	A	Wigan Ath	W	1-0	1-0	9	Foley	4008
19	27	H	Bristol R	W	4-2	2-1	7	Foley 2, Grant, Lawrence	9551
20	28	A	Newport Co	W	2-1	1-0	9	Hebberd 2 (1 pen)	5836
21	Jan 1	H	Southend U	W	1-0	1-0	5	Vinter	7021
22	3	A	Reading	W	3-0	2-0	5	Vinter, Lawrence 2	6154
23	15	H	Gillingham	D	1-1	0-1	5	Lawrence	4755
24	22	A	Portsmouth	L	0-1	0-1	6		10,882
25	29	H	Preston NE	W	3-2	1-1	6	Smithers, Vinter 2	4441
26	Feb 1	A	AFC Bournemouth	L	0-2	0-0	—		3776
27	5	H	Huddersfield T	D	1-1	0-1	6	Barnett (pen)	4975
28	12	A	Cardiff C	L	0-3	0-1	6		6970
29	26	A	Walsall	L	0-1	0-0	7		3104
30	Mar 2	H	Bradford C	W	5-1	4-1	—	Thomas, Vinter, Whatmore 3	4064
31	5	H	Wrexham	W	2-0	1-0	7	Vinter, Whatmore	4811
32	12	A	Exeter C	L	1-3	1-1	7	Lawrence	2957
33	16	H	Lincoln C	W	1-0	0-0	—	Whatmore	5147
34	19	A	Sheffield U	L	2-3	1-0	7	Jones, Vinter	11,786
35	22	A	Brentford	D	1-1	0-1	—	Hebberd	5086
36	26	H	Plymouth Arg	D	1-1	1-1	7	Hebberd (pen)	4786
37	Apr 2	H	Newport Co	L	0-3	0-2	7		6640
38	5	A	Bristol R	W	1-0	0-0	—	Hebberd	8190
39	9	H	Orient	D	2-2	1-1	7	Hebberd 2	4033
40	16	A	Doncaster R	W	1-0	0-0	7	Hebberd	1592
41	23	H	Wigan Ath	W	2-0	1-0	7	Lawrence, Thomas	4596
42	27	H	Millwall	W	1-0	0-0	—	Fogg (pen)	4161
43	30	A	Lincoln C	D	1-1	0-1	6	Lawrence	2812
44	May 2	H	Reading	L	1-2	0-0	6	Whatmore	6739
45	7	H	Chesterfield	W	1-0	1-0	5	Lawrence	3363
46	13	A	Southend U	W	2-1	1-1	—	Whatmore, Thomas	1954

Final League Position: 5

GOALSCORERS

League (71): Whatmore 12, Hebberd 10 (2 pens), Vinter 10, Lawrence 9, Thomas 7, Fogg 5 (4 pens), Foley 5, Brock 4, Barnett 2 (1 pen), Smithers 2, Biggins 1, Briggs 1, Grant 1, Jones 1, Shotton 1.
Milk Cup (5): Barnett 1, Biggins 1, Fogg 1 (pen), Thomas 1, Vinter 1.
FA Cup (11): Foley 4, Vinter 3, Fogg 2 (2 pens), Hebberd 1, Shotton 1.
Football League Trophy (4): Foley 2, Hebberd 1, Thomas 1.

Milk Cup	First Round	Reading (a)	2-0
		(h)	2-0
	Second Round	Huddersfield T (a)	0-2
		(h)	1-0
FA Cup	First Round	Folkestone (h)	5-2
	Second Round	Worthing (h)	4-0
	Third Round	Torquay U (h)	1-1
		(a)	1-2

Football League Trophy	Reading (a)	1-2
	Aldershot (a)	3-1
	AFC Bournemouth (a)	0-3

Burton	Fogg	Linney	Brock	Briggs	Shotton	Barnett	Biggins	Vinter	Hebberd	Train	Thomas	Jones	Foley	Whatmore	Butcher	Grant	Lawrence	Smithers	Donovan (L)	Hardwick	Attley (L)	McIntosh	Referees	Match No.
1	2	3	4	5	6	7	8	9	10	11*	12												D. Axcell	1
1	3	2	7	5	6	8	9*	10	11	4	12												R. Lewis	2
1	3	2	7	5	6	8	10	9	11	4*	12												H. King	3
1	3	2		5	6	8	10*	9	11	4	12	7											J. Lovatt	4
1	3	2	7	5	6	8	12	9*	11	4	10												M. Robinson	5
1	3	2	7*	5	6	8	10		11	4	9	12											N. Wilson	6
1	3	2	7	5	6	8	10	9	11	4													N. Ashley	7
1	3	2	7	5	6	8	10*	9	11	4	12												M. Dimblebee	8
1	3	2	8	5	6	7			11	4	9		10										J. Martin	9
1	3	2	7	5	6	8			11	4			10	9									B. Daniels	10
1	3	2	7	5	6	8		12	11	4			10*	9									H. Taylor	11
	3	2	7*	5	6	8		10	11	4	12			9	1								R. Banks	12
	3	2	7	5	6	8*		9	11	4	12			10	1								M. Taylor	13
		2*	7	5	6			9	11		4	8	12	10	1	3							T. Fitzharris	14
	4	2	7		6			9	5		11	8		10	1	3							E. Scales	15
	4	2	7		6			9	5		11*	8	12	10	1	3							C. Thomas	16
	5	2	12		6			9*	10	4			8		1	3	7	11					H. Taylor	17
	3	2	6		4	12		11	8				10		1	5	7*	9					K. Redfern	18
	5	2	4		6			9	10				8		1	3	7	11					D. Letts	19
1	5*	2	4		6			9	10	11		12	8				7	3					A. Crickmore	20
	5	2	4		6			9	10	11			8		1		7	3					A. Hamil	21
	5	2			6	11		9	10	12		4	8*		1		7	3					D. Reeves	22
	2			5	6	12		9	10*	4			8		1	3	7	11					T. Holbrook	23
	2		10	5	6	12		9		4			8*		1	3	7	11					A. Gunn	24
	2		10	5	6			9		4		12	8		1	3	7*	11					M. Bodenham	25
	2		10		6		5	9		4		7			1	3		11	8				R. Milford	26
	2*			5	6	10		9		4		7	12		1	3		11	8				M. James	27
		2		5	6			9		4	10	12			1	3*	7	11	8				A. Glasson	28
		2		5	6			9	10	4*	12	7		8		3		11		1			R. Chadwick	29
		2	7	5	6			9	10	4	11			8		3				1			T. Spencer	30
		2	7	5	6			9	10	4	11			8		3				1			D. Civil	31
			7	5	6			9	10	4	11*	12		8		3	2			1			G. Napthine	32
				5	6			9	10	4		11		8			7	3		1	2		C. Downey	33
			12	5	6			9	10	4*		11		8			7	3		1	2		D. Richardson	34
			12	5	6			9	10			7		8		3*	4	11		1	2		D. Axcell	35
			11	5	6		12	9	10			7		8			4*	3		1	2		M. Heath	36
			4	5	6	11		9	10			12		8			7	3		1	2*		M. Dimblebee	37
			11	5	6			9	10	4		7		8		3				1		2	A. Seville	38
			11*	5	6	12		9	10	4		7		8		3				1		2	D. Lloyd	39
	2		11	5	6			9	10	4		7		8*		3		12		1			K. Walmsley	40
	2		11	5	6	4		9			8	7					10	3		1			J. Moules	41
	2		11	5	6	4		9			8	7					10	3		1			C. Newsome	42
	2*		11	5	6			9	4		8	7		12			10	3		1			T. Jones	43
	2		11	5	6			9*	4		12	7		8			10	3		1			J. Hunting	44
	2			5	6			9	4	7	11			8			10	3		1			K. Cooper	45
	2			5	6			9	10	4	11	12		8			7	3*		1			M. Taylor	46
12	33	26	34	37	46	18	8	42	39	33	15	19	12	22	16	20	22	24	3	18	5	2		
			+ 3s			+ 4s	+ 2s	+ 1s		+ 1s	+ 9s	+ 7s	+ 3s	+ 1s				+ 1s						

FOOTBALL LEAGUE RECORD

1962 Elected to Division 4; 1965–68 Division 3; 1968–76 Division 2; 1976– Division 3.

HONOURS

Football League: Division 2 best season: 8th, 1972–73; Division 3 – Champions 1967–68; Division 4 – Promoted 1964–65 (4th). *FA Cup* best season: 6th rd, 1963–64 (record for 4th Division club), 1981–82. *Football League Cup* best season: 5th rd, 1969–70.

COLOURS

Yellow shirts with blue trim, blue shorts, yellow stockings.
Change colours: All red.

OXFORD UNITED

Players Names Ht. Wt. D.o.B.	Birthplace Transfer Fee	Clubs	Appearances F.L. A & S	 F.L.C. A & S	 F.A.C. A & S	Goals F.L.	 F.L.C.	 F.A.C.
Goalkeepers								
John Butcher	Newcastle	Blackburn R	104	9	5			
6 2, 12 3, 27.5.56	F/T	Oxford U	16	1	4			
	—	Halifax T (loan)	5					
Steve Hardwick (EY)	Mansfield	Chesterfield	38	2	4			
5 11, 13 0, 6.9.56	£80,000	Newcastle U	92	3	4			
	£20,000	Oxford U	18					
Defenders								
David Fogg	Liverpool	Wrexham	159+2	4	13+1			
5 10½, 11 8, 28.5.51	F/T	Oxford U	284+4	22+1	16	16	2	2
Gary Briggs	Leeds	Middlesbrough (A)						
6 3, 12 10, 21.6.59	£12,500	Oxford U	229	18	11	6		
Tim Smithers	Ramsgate	Nuneaton Bor						
5 11, 10 4, 22.1.56	£15,000	Oxford U	95+4	9	11	6		1
Malcolm Shotton	Newcastle	Leicester C (A)						
6 3, 13 12, 16.2.57	F/T	Nuneaton Bor						
	£15,000	Oxford U	124	14	10	10	2	1
David Grant	Sheffield	Sheffield W (A)	132+1	11	4+2	4	1	
6 0, 12 8, 2.6.60	F/T	Oxford U	20		1	1		
Midfield								
Kevin Brock (ES)	Middleton Stoney	Oxford U (A)	99+11	9+1	5+1	16	1	
5 9, 10 12, 9.9.62								
Ray Train	Nuneaton	Walsall (A)	67+6		5	11		1
5 5, 10 5, 10.2.51	£15,000	Carlisle U	154+1	5	13	8		
	£80,000	Sunderland	31+1	4	1	1	2	
	£50,000	Bolton W	49+2	3	3			
	£50,000	Watford	91+1	8+1	9	3	1	
	£10,000	Oxford U	48+1	4	2+1			
Trevor Hebberd	Winchester	Southampton (A)	69+28	9+1	4+3	7	3	
5 11½, 11 4, 19.6.58	—	Bolton W (loan)	6					
	—	Leicester C (loan)	4			1		
	£80,000	Oxford U	54	4	4	12		1
Mark Jones	Berinsfield	Oxford U (A)	74+11	8	5+1	6		
5 8, 9 12, 26.9.61								
David Linney*	Birmingham	Birmingham C (A)	+1					
5.9.61	F/T	Oxford U	26	4	4			
Stuart Gibson	Nottingham	Birmingham C (A)						
5 11, 12 7, 22.7.63	F/T	Oxford U						
Steve Aries		Oxford U						
Forwards								
Peter Foley (EIY)	Bicester	Oxford U (A)	262+15	26	13	70	8	9
5 11, 11 12, 10.9.56	—	Gillingham (loan)	5					
Andy Thomas	Oxford	Oxford U (A)	53+19	4+2	6	22	2	3
6 0, 10 10, 16.12.62	—	Fulham (loan)	3+1			2		
	—	Derby Co (loan)	+1					
Steve Biggins	Walsall	Hednesford T						
6 0, 11 12, 20.6.54	£6000	Shrewsbury	140+6	7	11	41	2	3
	F/T	Oxford U	8+2	2		1	1	
Mick Vinter	Boston	Boston U						
5 9, 11 0, 23.5.54	—	Notts Co	135+31	8+2	7+1	53	2	5
	£150,000	Wrexham	90+12	9	10+1	25	5	7
	£25,000	Oxford U	42+1	4	4	10	1	3
George Lawrence	London	Southampton (A)	7+3	2+1		1		
5 10, 12 2, 14.9.62	£45,000	Oxford U	37		3	13		
Neil Whatmore	Ellesmere Port	Bolton W (A)	262+15	22+1	20	102	7	6
5 9½, 11 8, 17.5.55	£340,000	Birmingham C	24+2	1		6	1	
	—	Bolton W (loan)	10			3		
	£25,000	Oxford U	22+1			12		
Gary Barnett	Stratford	Coventry C (A)			2			
5 5, 9 4, 11.3.63	F/T	Oxford U	18+4	3		2	1	
	—	Wimbledon (loan)	5			1		
Non-Contract Player								
Malcolm McIntosh	Oxford	Oxford U (A)	53+3	4+1	2			
5 8, 11 0, 6.7.59	F/T	Kettering T						
	F/T	Oxford U	2					

Commercial Manager: Jim Hunt until new Commercial Manager is appointed (Tel. Oxford 64615).
Club Coach: Ray Graydon.
Club Captain 1982–83: Malcolm Shotton.
Supporters Player of the Season 1982–83: Trevor Hebberd.
Chief Scout:
Club Statistician: Mick Brown.
Physiotherapist: Ken Fish.
Association of Football Statisticians Club Adviser to Yearbook: M. Brown.

Players (non-appearance) granted free transfer: Paul Spittle, F.
Players released since May 1982: Paul Berry, F. (N/K); Steve Foster, G. (N/K); Jason Seacole, F. (Witney T); Roy Burton, G. (N/K); Clive Morgan, M. (Oxford C).

PETERBOROUGH UNITED Division 4

Back row (left to right):
Tony Cliss
Mike Imlach
Colin Clarke
Trevor Slack
David Seaman
Neil Firm
Ian Benjamin
Stephen Collins
Front row:
John Winters
Phillip Chard
Robbie Cooke
Billy Rodaway
Trevor Quow
Michael Gynn
Ivor Linton.

Chairman: W. O'Neill Wilde.

Vice-Chairman: C. Duddington.

Directors: S. E. Nicholas, A. Hand, G. H. Woodcock, D. E. Ringham, S. Kendrick.

Manager: John Wile.

General Manager /Secretary: A. V. Blades.

Commercial Manager: E. Stafford.

Year Formed: 1923. ***Turned Professional:*** 1934. ***Ltd Co.:*** 1934.

Club Nickname: 'The Posh'.

Previous Name: Peterborough and Fletton United until 1934.

Previous Managers since Election to Football League: Jimmy Hagan, Jack Fairbrother, Gordon Clark, Norman Rigby, Jim Iley, Noel Cantwell, John Barnwell, Billy Hails, Peter Morris, Martin Wilkinson (10).

London Road Ground, Peterborough PE2 8AL. Telephone Peterborough (0733) 63947. ***Ground capacity:*** 30,000. ***Record attendance:*** 30,096 v Swansea T, FA Cup 5th rd, 20 Feb, 1965. ***Record receipts:*** £44,157.83 v Manchester U, FA Cup 5th rd, 14 Feb, 1981. ***Pitch measurements:*** 112yd×76yd.

Directions to Ground: Peterborough Station Bus terminal (20 minutes' walking distance).

Match tickets: Bookable fourteen days in advance.

Car parking: Ample parking available at the ground.

Entertainments /catering facilities: Supporters' Club provides entertainment. Licensed refreshment kiosks in the ground.

Club shop: Sells all types of souvenirs (postal requests to General Manager).

Handbooks /programmes: Handbooks available and programmes can be ordered on subscription.

Address of Supporters Club: Same as Football Club.

Note: Full club statistical records are on pages 416–455.

PETERBOROUGH UNITED 1982–83 LEAGUE RECORD

Match No.	Date	Venue	Opponents	Result	H/T Score	Lg. Pos.	Goalscorers	Attendance
1	Aug 28	A	Stockport Co	D 1-1	0-1	—	Benjamin	2003
2	Sept 4	H	Hartlepool U	W 2-1	1-1	6	Linton, Winters	3499
3	8	H	Wimbledon	L 0-3	0-1	—		3458
4	11	A	Aldershot	L 0-2	0-1	19		1691
5	18	H	Bury	D 1-1	1-0	20	Gynn	2826
6	25	A	York C	D 1-1	0-1	19	Cooke	1872
7	27	A	Mansfield T	D 0-0	0-0	—		2414
8	Oct 2	H	Bristol C	W 3-0	2-0	17	Benjamin, Gynn 2	2739
9	9	H	Scunthorpe U	L 0-1	0-1	17		3075
10	16	A	Tranmere R	L 0-1	0-1	17		1086
11	20	A	Chester	D 1-1	0-1	—	Gynn	1401
12	23	H	Torquay U	L 1-3	0-3	18	Clarke	2869
13	30	A	Northampton T	D 0-0	0-0	17		3284
14	Nov 3	H	Halifax T	W 2-1	1-0	—	Firm, Small	2038
15	6	A	Hull C	L 1-4	1-2	19	Clarke	5535
16	13	H	Rochdale	W 1-0	1-0	18	Cooke	2245
17	27	H	Port Vale	D 0-0	0-0	15		3043
18	Dec 4	A	Swindon T	L 0-1	0-0	16		3961
19	27	H	Colchester U	W 2-1	1-1	16	Winters, Firm	4235
20	28	A	Crewe Alex	W 3-0	2-0	14	Clarke, Gynn 2	1631
21	Jan 1	H	Hereford U	W 4-0	1-0	13	Gynn 2, Cooke, Firm	3543
22	3	A	Blackpool	W 3-0	1-0	12	Gynn, Clarke, Cooke	2388
23	12	A	Hartlepool U	D 0-0	0-0	—		1161
24	15	H	Stockport Co	W 1-0	1-0	10	Benjamin	2911
25	22	A	Wimbledon	L 1-2	1-1	10	Quow	2119
26	29	H	Aldershot	D 0-0	0-0	10		2841
27	Feb 5	H	York C	D 2-2	1-1	11	Glynn, Cooke	2652
28	12	A	Bristol C	L 0-1	0-1	12		3959
29	16	H	Chester	L 0-1	0-1	—		1661
30	26	H	Tranmere R	W 3-0	1-0	13	Clarke, Ippolitto, Gynn	2045
31	Mar 1	A	Halifax T	W 2-1	1-1	—	Ippolitto 2	2002
32	5	A	Torquay U	L 1-2	0-1	12	Young (og)	1537
33	12	H	Northampton T	W 2-0	0-0	9	Gynn, Clarke	3778
34	19	H	Hull C	D 1-1	0-0	10	Gynn	3805
35	26	A	Rochdale	D 1-1	0-0	9	Chard	1560
36	Apr 1	A	Colchester U	L 0-1	0-1	—		3759
37	2	H	Crewe Alex	W 2-1	0-1	10	Chard (pen), Clarke	2490
38	9	H	Swindon T	W 4-3	4-1	10	Slack, Chard (pen), Clarke, Gynn	2522
39	16	A	Bury	L 0-1	0-1	10		2761
40	23	H	Darlington	D 1-1	0-0	11	Linton	2185
41	26	A	Scunthorpe U	L 0-3	0-0	—		3211
42	29	A	Port Vale	L 1-2	1-2	—	Gynn	5375
43	May 4	H	Blackpool	W 3-1	3-1	—	Gynn, Chard, Benjamin	1636
44	7	H	Mansfield T	W 3-2	1-0	9	Gynn, Rayment, Clarke	2200
45	14	A	Hereford U	W 1-0	0-0	9	Rayment	2075
46	17	A	Darlington	L 3-4	2-1	9	Linton, Benjamin 2	1002

Final League Position: 9

GOALSCORERS

League (58): Gynn 17, Clarke 9, Benjamin 6, Cooke 5, Chard 4 (2 pens), Firm 3, Ippolitto 3, Linton 3, Rayment 2, Winters 2, Quow 1, Slack 1, Small 1, own goal 1.
Milk Cup (7): Cooke 3, Benjamin 1, Clarke 1, Gynn 1, Imlach 1.
FA Cup (9): Gynn 3, Cooke 3, Clarke 2, Quow 1.
Football League Trophy (11): Benjamin 5, Chard 2, Clarke 1, Cooke 1, Linton 1, Slack 1.

Milk Cup	First Round	Darlington (a)	2-0
		(a)	4-2
	Second Round	Crystal Palace (h)	0-2
		(a)	1-2
FA Cup	First Round	Chesterfield (a)	2-2
		(h)	2-1
	Second Round	Doncaster R (h)	5-2
	Third Round	Luton T (a)	0-3

Football League Trophy	Mansfield T (h)	4-1
	Norwich C (a)	2-6
	Northampton T (h)	5-2

Seaman	Winters	Collins	Gynn	Firm	Rodaway	Slack	Benjamin	Cooke	Linton	Chard	Rayment	Sutton	Imlach	Clarke	Cliss	Quow	Naylor (L)	Ippolito	Carmichael	Mercer	Small (L)	*Referees*	*Match No.*
1	2	3	4	5	6	7	8	9	10	11												K. Walmsley	1
1	2	3	4	5	6	7	10	9	8	11												A. Seville	2
1		3	4	5	6	7	10	9	8	11	2*		12									D. Hedges	3
1	2	3	4		6		10	9	8	11		5*	12	7								A. Gunn	4
1	2	3	4	5	6		10	9	8	11			7									D. Axcell	5
1		3	4	5	6	7	10	9	8	11*	2				12							R. Guy	6
1		3	4	5	6	7	10	9	8	11	2											D. Shaw	7
1		3	5	4	6	7	10	9	8*	11					12	2						K. Baker	8
1	2	3	4	5	6	7*	10	9	12	11						8						J. Moules	9
1	2	3	4	5	6		10		9	11						8					7	J. Hough	10
1	2	3	4	5	6		10		9	11				7		8						C. Seel	11
1		12	4	5	6		10		9	11*			3	7	2	8						E. Scales	12
1		9	4	5		6	10*			11	2		3	7		8					12	D. Lloyd	13
1		9	4	5		6	10			11*	2		3	7		8					12	L. Borrett	14
1		12	4	5		6	10			11	2		3	7		8*					9	P. Tyldesley	15
1	2	3	4	5	8	6	10	9		11				7								M. Robinson	16
1	2	3	4*	5	8	6	10	9		11				7		12						D. Vickers	17
1	2	3	4	5	8	6	10*	9		12				7		11						H. King	18
1	2	3	4	5	7	6	10*	9		12				7		11						J. Key	19
1	2	3	4	5	8	6	10	9*		12				7		11						V. Callow	20
1	2	3	4	5	8	6	10	9						7		11						M. Dimblebee	21
1	2	3	4	5	8	6	10	9		12				7		11*						M. Heath	22
1		3	4	5		6	10	9		8	2			7		11						N. Glover	23
1		3		5		6	10	9	4	8	2		11	7								D. Letts	24
1	2	3	4		5	6	10	9		8				7		11						M. Bodenham	25
1	2	3	4		5	6	10	9		8				7		11						J. Bray	26
1	2	3	4	5	8	6	10	9		12				7		11*						J. Martin	27
1	2	3	4	5	8	6	10	9		11				7								L. Burden	28
1	2	3	4	5	8	6	10	9		11				7								C. Downey	29
	2	3	4	5	8	6	10		12	9*				7			1	11				K. Salmon	30
	2	3	4	5	8	6	10			9				7			1	11				M. Peck	31
	2	3	4	5		6	10		8	9				7			1	11				R. Milford	32
		3	4	5		6	10		8	9				7			1	11	2			A. Challinor	33
		3	4	5	12	6	10		8	9				7			1	11*	2			M. James	34
		3	4	5	8	6	10		11	9				7			1		2			B. Newsome	35
	2	3	4	5	8	6	10		11	9*				7			1		12			R. Lewis	36
	2	11	4	5	8	6	10			9				7			1		3			J. Moules	37
1	2	3	4		8	6	10			9				7				11		5		D. Reeves	38
1	2	3	4		5	8	10		6	9				7				11				D. Hutchinson	39
1	2	3	4	5	8	6	10		11	9				7								T. Bune	40
1	2	3	4	5	8	6	10			9	11			7								G. Tyson	41
1	2	3	4	5	8	6	10			9	11			7								G. Napthine	42
1	2	3	4	5	8	6	10			9	11			7								D. Brazier	43
1	2	3	4*	5	8	6	10		12	9	11			7								K. Barratt	44
1		3			8		10		9		11		4	7				6	5	2		T. Holbrook	45
1		4			8	5	10		6	9	11		3	7						2		T. Jones	46
38	31	44	43	39	38	40	46	23	21	39	14	1	8	37	1	17	8	8	5	3	2		
		+ 2s			+ 1s				+ 3s	+ 5s			+ 2s		+ 2s	+ 1s			+ 1s		+ 2s		

FOOTBALL LEAGUE RECORD

1960 Elected to Division 4; 1961–68 Division 3, when they were demoted for financial irregularities; 1968–74 Division 4; 1974–79 Division 3; 1979– Division 4.

HONOURS

Football League: Division 3 best season: 4th, 1977–78. Division 4 – Champions 1960–61, 1973–74. *FA Cup* best season: 6th rd, 1965. *Football League Cup:* semi-final 1966.

COLOURS

Royal blue shirts, white shorts, blue stockings with white tops.
Change colours: All yellow with blue trim.

PETERBOROUGH UNITED

Players Names Ht, Wt, D.o.B.	Birthplace Transfer Fee	Clubs	Appearances F.L. A & S	 F.L.C. A & S	 F.A.C. A & S	Goals F.L.	 F.L.C.	 F.A.C.
Goalkeepers								
David Seaman	Rotherham	Leeds U (A)						
6 2, 13 0, 19.9.63	£4000	Peterborough U	38	4	4			
Defenders								
Steve Mercer*	Barking	Cambridge U (N/C)						
	F/T	Peterborough U	3					
John Winters	Wisbech	Peterborough U (A)	60	4+1	4	3		
5 8, 11 8, 24.10.60								
Trevor Slack	Peterborough	Peterborough U (A)	82	9	10	7	1	1
6 1¾, 12 2, 26.9.62								
Steve Collins	Stamford	Peterborough U (A)	92+2	9	8	1		
5 8, 11 4, 21.3.62								
Billy Rodaway (ES)	Liverpool	Burnley (A)	207+2	16	11	1		
5 10, 13 2, 26.9.54	F/T	Peterborough U	80+1	6	6			
Neil Firm	Bradford	Leeds U (A)	11+1					
6 3, 13 7, 23.1.58	—	Oldham Ath (Loan)	9					
	£10,000	Peterborough U	39	3	4	3		
Mike Imlach	Croydon	Everton (A)						
5 9, 11 8, 19.9.62	F/T	Preston NE						
	F/T	Leeds U						
	F/T	Peterborough U	8+2	2			1	
Pat Rayment	Peterborough	Peterborough U (A)	16	1		2		
5 11, 12 3, 11.4.65								
Midfield								
Micky Gynn	Peterborough	Peterborough U (A)	152+4	12	13	33	1	2
5 5, 10 6, 19.8.61								
Phil Chard	Corby	Nottingham F (N/C)						
5 8, 11 3, 16.10.60	—	Peterborough U	90+19	9+2	6	10	1	1
Ian Benjamin (EY)	Nottingham	Sheffield U (A)	4+1	1+1		3		
5 11, 12 4, 11.12.61	£125,000	WBA	1+1					
	F/T	Peterborough U	46	4	4	6	1	
Trevor Quow	Peterborough	Peterborough U (A)	103+6	10+1	7+1	9		2
5 6, 10 4, 28.9.60								
Forwards								
Colin Clarke	Newry	Ispwich T (A)						
5 11, 12 10, 30.10.62	F/T	Peterborough U	59+5	3	4	13	1	2
Ivor Linton	West Bromwich	Aston Villa (A)	16+11		1			
5 10, 10 13, 20.11.59	F/T	Peterborough U	21+3	3		3		
Mario Ippolito	Peterborough	Peterborough U	8			3		
5 8, 10 6, 16.4.64								
Apprentices								
Richard Sutton	Gravesend	Peterborough U (A)	1					
6 0, 12 0, 21.8.65								

Commercial Manager: Ellis Stafford. (Tel. 0733-69760)
Club Coach: Bill Harvey
Supporters Player of the Season 1982–83: Mick Gwyn, Trevor Slack
Physiotherapist: Bill Harvey
Club Captain 1982–83: Billy Rodaway
Chief Scout:
Club Statistician: M. Robinson
Association of Football Statisticians Club Adviser to Yearbook: M. Robinson

Players released since May 1982:
Campbell Chapman, F. (Stamford); Tim Gale, F. (N/K); Gordon Hodgson, M. (Kings Lynn); Jack Carmichael, D. (N/C —retired).

PLYMOUTH ARGYLE Division 3

Back row (left to right): Tony Denis, Gordon Nisbet, Tyrone James, Mike Ham, Geoff Crudgington, Neil Hards, Forbes Phillipson-Masters, John Sims, John Uzzell, Mark Rowe
Front row: Kevin Hodges, Andy Rogers, Mike McCartney, Mike Carter, Bobby Moncur (Manager), Geoff Cook, Chris Harrison, David Phillips, Leigh Cooper.

President: G. H. Gillan. ***Chairman:*** S. W. Dawe.

Vice-Chairman: P. D. Bloom.

Directors: R. Daniel, R. Burroughs ARICS, G. E. Jasper, J. E. C. Kent. ***Team Manager:*** Bobby Moncur.

Asst Manager: Martin Harvey. ***Secretary:*** Graham Little.

Year Formed: 1886. ***Turned Professional:*** 1903. ***Ltd Co.:*** 1903.

Club Nickname: 'The Pilgrims'.

Previous Name: 1886–1903, Argyle Athletic Club.

Previous Managers since 1946: Jack Tresadern, Jimmy Rae, Jack Rowley, Neil Dougall, Ellis Stuttard, Andy Beattie, Malcolm Allison, Derek Ufton, Billy Bingham, Ellis Stuttard, Tony Waiters, Mike Kelly, Malcolm Allison, Bobby Saxton (14).

Home Park Plymouth, Devon PL2 3DQ. Telephone Plymouth (0752) 52561/2/3. Lottery Shop: 51041. ***Ground capacity:*** 38,000 (20,000 covered). ***Record attendance:*** 43,596 v Aston Villa, Division 2, 10 Oct, 1936. ***Record receipts:*** over £10,000 (official figure not disclosed by club) v Manchester C, League Cup semi-final, 23 Jan, 1974. ***Pitch measurements:*** 112yd×75yd.

Directions to Ground: Special City buses from the Plymouth bus station at Bretonside. Nearest railway station Plymouth.

Match tickets: Grand Stand and Mayflower Stand tickets are available 2–3 weeks before each first-team game.

Car parking: Car park adjoining the ground holds 2000 cars.

Entertainments/catering facilities: Eight refreshment bars around the ground.

Club shop: Situated on the ground; sells all types of souvenirs.

Handbooks/programmes: Programmes sent to all parts of the world.

Address of Supporters Club: Same as Football Club.

Address of the Club Shop or Boutique: The Pilgrim Shop, Home Park, Plymouth, Devon.

Note: Full club statistical records are on pages 416–455.

PLYMOUTH ARGYLE 1982–83 LEAGUE RECORD

Match No.	Date	Venue	Opponents	Result	H/T Score	Lg. Pos.	Goalscorers	Attendance
1	Aug 28	H	Southend U	W 1-0	0-0	—	Harrison (pen)	3850
2	Sept 4	A	Reading	L 2-3	0-2	12	Cook (pen), Uzell	2102
3	7	A	Newport Co	D 2-2	0-1	—	Cook, Hodges	3741
4	11	H	Orient	W 2-0	1-0	6	Hodges 2	3649
5	18	A	Sheffield U	L 1-3	0-0	11	Sims	13,604
6	25	H	Wrexham	W 2-0	1-0	7	Gooding, Rogers	3628
7	28	H	Bristol R	L 0-4	0-0	—		3542
8	Oct 2	A	Wigan Ath	L 0-3	0-2	15		5011
9	9	A	Bradford C	L 0-4	0-1	19		4690
10	16	H	Lincoln C	L 0-2	0-1	20		2921
11	19	H	AFC Bournemouth	W 2-0	1-0	—	Hodges, Sims	2525
12	23	A	Chesterfield	W 2-1	2-0	14	Hodges, Nisbet	3149
13	30	H	Brentford	W 2-0	0-0	14	Cook, Sims	4036
14	Nov 2	A	Millwall	D 2-2	2-1	—	Cooper, Madden (og)	3097
15	8	A	Doncaster R	D 2-2	0-0	—	McCartney, Hodges	2942
16	13	H	Oxford U	W 2-1	1-0	11	McCartney, Sims	3908
17	27	A	Preston NE	D 2-2	0-2	11	Cooper, Hodges	3633
18	Dec 4	H	Huddersfield T	W 2-1	2-0	10	Cook (pen), Hodges	4227
19	18	H	Gillingham	W 2-0	1-0	8	Sims, Rogers	4179
20	27	A	Exeter C	L 0-1	0-0	9		9168
21	28	H	Cardiff C	W 3-2	1-2	7	Sims 2, Carter	8631
22	Jan 1	A	Portsmouth	L 1-2	0-2	8	McLaughlin (og)	15,856
23	14	A	Southend U	L 1-3	0-2	—	Phillips	3082
24	22	H	Newport Co	L 2-4	1-2	12	Vaughan (og), Cook	4287
25	29	A	Orient	W 2-0	2-0	10	McCartney (pen), Hodges	2699
26	Feb 1	H	Reading	W 3-0	2-0	—	Williams (og), Bremner, McCartney (pen)	3504
27	5	A	Bristol R	L 0-2	0-0	8		6556
28	8	H	Walsall	D 0-0	0-0	—		3148
29	19	H	Bradford C	W 3-1	1-0	8	Cooper, McCartney (pen), Hodges	3644
30	26	A	Lincoln C	W 2-1	0-1	8	Hodges, Phillips	3915
31	Mar 1	H	Millwall	W 3-1	0-1	—	Phillips 2, Sims	4114
32	5	H	Chesterfield	W 2-0	0-0	8	Phillips, Rogers	4466
33	11	A	Brentford	L 0-2	0-0	—		4967
34	15	A	AFC Bournemouth	L 0-1	0-1	—		4258
35	19	H	Doncaster R	L 1-2	1-1	8	Phillips	3406
36	26	A	Oxford U	D 1-1	1-1	9	Cooper	4786
37	Apr 1	H	Exeter C	W 1-0	0-0	—	Sims	8856
38	2	A	Cardiff C	D 0-0	0-0	8		7226
39	9	A	Huddersfield T	L 0-2	0-0	9		9277
40	16	H	Sheffield U	W 3-1	0-1	8	Phillips, Nisbet, Staniforth	3665
41	19	H	Wigan Ath	L 0-2	0-0	—		3097
42	23	A	Gillingham	L 1-2	0-2	9	Phillips	3356
43	30	H	Preston NE	D 1-1	0-1	8	Smith	2912
44	May 2	A	Walsall	L 0-2	0-0	9		3473
45	7	A	Wrexham	W 3-2	1-2	8	Sims, Rogers 2	2250
46	14	H	Portsmouth	L 0-1	0-0	8		14,173

Final League Position: 8

GOALSCORERS

League (61): Hodges 11, Sims 10, Phillips 8, Cooke 5 (2 pens), McCartney 5 (3 pens), Rogers 5, Cooper 4, Nisbet 2, Bremner 1, Carter 1, Gooding 1, Harrison 1 (pen), Smith 1, Staniforth 1, Uzell 1, own goals 4.
Milk Cup (2): Sims 2.
FA Cup (5): Sims 2, Hodges 1, McCartney 1, Rogers 1.

Milk Cup	First Round	AFC Bournemouth (h)	2-0
		(a)	0-3 (aet)
FA Cup	First Round	Exeter C (h)	2-0
	Second Round	Bristol R (a)	2-2
		(h)	1-0
	Third Round	Watford (a)	0-2

Crudgington	Nisbet	Uzzell	Harrison	Phillipson-Masters	Cooper	Hodges	Phillips	Sims	Gooding	Rogers	Carter	Cook	McCartney	Rowe	Dennis	Smith (L)	Hards	Bremner (L)	Ham	Staniforth	Referees	Match No.
1	2	3	4	5	6	7	8	9	10	11											A. Glasson	1
1	2	3	4	5*	6	7		9	10	11	12	8									B. Daniels	2
1	2	3	4		6	7		10	8	11		9	5								K. Salmon	3
1	2	3	4		6	7		9	10	11	12	8*	5								E. Read	4
1	4	3			6	7	2	9	10	11	12	8*	5								R. Chadwick	5
1	2	3		4	6	7		9	10	11		8	5								J. Martin	6
1	2	3		4	6	7		9	10	11	12	8*	5								Alan Robinson	7
1	2	5	3	4	6	7		11		9*	10		8	12							A. Saunders	8
1	2	3	4	5	6	7		9			8		10		11						A. Shaw	9
1	2	3	4		6	7	12	9		11	8*		10			5					D. Hedges	10
1	2	3	4		6	7		9		11		8	10			5					K. Callow	11
1	2	3	4		6	7		9		11		8	10			5					B. Guy	12
1	2	3	4		6	7		9		11		8	10			5					R. Milford	13
1	2	3	4		6	7		9		11		8	10			5					D. Axcell	14
1	2	3	4		6	7		9		11		8	10			5					J. Hough	15
1	2	3	4		6	7		9		11		8	10			5					C. Thomas	16
1	2		4		6	7		9		11		8	10	3		5					T. Mills	17
1	2	3	4		6	7				11	9	8	10			5					D. Letts	18
1	2	3	4		6	7		9		11		8	10			5					D. Lloyd	19
	2	3	4		6	7		9		11	12	8*	10			5	1				D. Civil	20
	2	3	4		6	7		9		11	8		10			5	1				T. Spencer	21
1	2	3	4		6	7		9		11	8*	12	10			5					A. Ward	22
1	2	3			6	7	4	9		11		8	10			5					M. Dimblebee	23
1	2		4		6	7	3	9		11		8	10			5					J. Bray	24
1	2	3	4		6	7		9		11			10			5		8			I. Borrett	25
1	2	3	4		6	7		9		11			10			5		8			S. Bates	26
1	2	3	4		6	7	12	9*		11			10			5		8			E. Scales	27
1	2	3	4		6	7		9		11			10			5		8			J. Martin	28
1	2	3	4		6	7		9		11			10					8	5		T. Bune	29
1	2	3	4		6	7	12	9		11		8*	10						5		D. Vickers	30
1	2	3	4			7	8	9		11			10	6		5					A. Hamil	31
1	2	3	4		6*	7	8	9		11	12		10			5					B. Stevens	32
1	2	3	4		6	7	8	9		11			10			5					D. Brazier	33
1	2	3	4		6	7	8	9		11			10			5					M. Robinson	34
1	2	3	4		6	8	11	10		9			7			5					J. Deakin	35
1	2	3	4		6	7	8	9		11						5				10	M. Heath	36
1	2	3	4		6	7	8	9		11						5				10	A. Seville	37
1	2	3	4		6	7	8	9		11						5				10	T. Holbrook	38
1	2	3	4		6	7	8	9		11									5	10	N. Glover	39
1	2	3	4		6	7	8	9		11						5				10	Alan Robinson	40
1	2	3	4		6	7	8			11					9	5				10	C. Thomas	41
1	2	3	4		6	7	8			11				12	9*	5				10	D. Letts	42
1	2	3*	4		6	7	8	12		11				10		5				9	A. Glasson	43
1	2		4		6	7	8	9		11				3		5				10	D. Richardson	44
1	2				6	7	8	9		11				3		5			4	10	J. Hough	45
1	2	3	4		6	7	8	9						11		5				10	K. Cooper	46
44	46	42	41	6	45	46	20	42	7	44	6	19	33	6	3	34	2	5	4	11		
							+ 3s	+ 1s			+ 6s	+ 1s		+ 2s								

FOOTBALL LEAGUE RECORD

1920 Original Member of Division 3; 1921–30 Division 3(S); 1930–50 Division 2; 1950–52 Division 3(S); 1952–56 Division 2; 1956–58 Division 3(S); 1958–59 Division 3; 1959–68 Division 2; 1968–75 Division 3; 1975–77 Division 2; 1977– Division 3.

HONOURS

Football League: Division 2 best season: 4th, 1931–32, 1952–53; Division 3(S) – Champions 1929–30, 1951–52; Runners-up 1921–22, 1922–23, 1923–24, 1924–25, 1925–26, 1926–27 (record of six consecutive years); Division 3 – Champions 1958–59; Runners-up 1974–75. *FA Cup* best season: 5th rd, 1952–53. *Football League Cup:* semi-final, 1965, 1974.

COLOURS

Green shirts with black trim, white shorts, green stockings with black and white loops. **Change colours:** All yellow.

PLYMOUTH ARGYLE

Players Names *Ht, Wt, D.o.B.*	*Birthplace* *Transfer Fee*	*Clubs*	*Appearances* *F.L.* *A & S*	*F.L.C.* *A & S*	*F.A.C.* *A & S*	*Goals* *F.L.*	*F.L.C.*	*F.A.C.*
Goalkeepers								
Geoff Crudgington (ES)	Wolverhampton	Wolverhampton W (AM)						
6 0, 12 2, 14.2.52	—	Aston Villa	4					
	—	Bradford C (loan)	1					
	F/T	Crewe Alex	250	15	14			
	£20,000	Swansea C	52	9	4			
	£40,000	Plymouth Arg	173	8	11			
Neil Hards*	Portsmouth	Plymouth Arg (A)	6	3				
6 0, 12 7, 28.1.62								
Defenders								
Lindsay Smith	Enfield	Colchester U (A)	185+27	8+2	12+1	16	2	1
5 11, 12 0, 18.9.54	—	Charlton Ath (loan)	1					
	—	Millwall (loan)	4+1					
		Cambridge U	173+1	9	7+1	7		
	—	Lincoln C (loan)	5					
	£25,000	Plymouth Arg	34		4	1		
John Uzzell	Plymouth	Plymouth Arg (A)	157+2	4	3	4		
5 10, 11 3, 31.3.59								
Tyrone James*	Paddington	Fulham	18+2		+1			
6 2, 11 0, 19.9.56	£15,000	Plymouth Arg	77+4	7	2			
	—	Torquay U (loan)	13			1		
Chris Harrison	Launceston	Plymouth Arg (A)	243+4	15	13+1	6	1	
5 8, 10 6, 17.10.56								
Michael Ham	Plymouth	Plymouth Arg (A)	5					
6 1, 12 0								
Paul Chambers		Plymouth Arg (A)						
Midfield								
Kevin Hodges	Bridport	Plymouth Arg (A)	183+6	13+1	12	32		2
5 7, 10 0, 12.6.60								
Leigh Cooper	Reading	Plymouth Arg (A)	129	5	11	12		
5 8, 10 9, 7.5.61								
Gordon Nisbet	Wallsend	WBA	136	8	13			
5 10, 12 2, 18.9.51	£30,000	Hull C	190+3	11	10	1		1
	£30,000	Plymouth Arg	110	6	6	5		
David Phillips	Welberg, W.G.	Plymouth Arg (A)	26+5		2+1	9		
5 9, 10 10,								
Mark Rowe	Wadebridge	Plymouth Arg (A)	8+4		1			
5 6, 10 0,								
Ray Gooding	Hartlepool	Coventry C (A)	46+3	2	3	5		
5 8, 11 5, 16.2.59	—	Bristol C (loan)	3					
	F/T	Plymouth Arg	7	2		1		
Forwards								
Gordon Staniforth (ES)	Hull	Hull C (A)	7+5			2		
5 6, 9 12, 23.3.57	£10,000	York C	128	7	6	33	2	4
	£120,000	Carlisle U	118+8	7	17	33	2	3
		Plymouth Arg	11			1		
John Sims	Belper	Derby Co (A)	2+1					
6 0, 12 10, 14.8.52	—	Luton T (loan)	3	1		1		
	—	Oxford U (loan)	6+1			1		
	—	Colchester U (loan)	2					
	£10,000	Notts Co	48+13	4	2	13	1	
	£12,000	Exeter C	33+1	5	2	11	1	
	£22,500	Plymouth Arg	161+2	8	11	43	2	2
Andy Rogers	Chatteris	Chatteris T						
5 8, 10 0, 1.12.56		Peterborough U	25+4	3		1		
	F/T	Hampton						
		Southampton	+5					
	£50,000	Plymouth Arg	84	4	6	9		1
Jeff Cook	Hartlepool	Hellenic S.A.						
5 9, 11 3, 14.3.53	—	Stoke C	22+8	1	2+1	5		2
	—	Bradford C (loan)	8			1		
	—	Plymouth Arg (loan)	4+3			5		
	£25,000	Plymouth Arg	55+1	3	4	21		
Tony Dennis*	Taplow	Plymouth Arg (A)	7+2					
5 6, 10 2,								
Mike Carter	Warrington	Bolton W (A)	37+12	3+1	3	8		
5 9, 10 7, 18.4.60	—	Mansfield T (loan)	18			4		
	—	Swindon T (loan)	4+1					
	F/T	Plymouth Arg	6+6	+1		1		
	—	Hereford U (loan)	10					
Mike Shannon		Plymouth Arg (A)						

Commercial Manager: W. E. Pearce (Tel. 0752-51041).
Club Coach: M. Harvey.
Supporters Player of the Season 1982–83: Gordon Nisbet.
Physiotherapist: None.
Club Captain 1982–83: Geoff Crudgington.
Chief Scout: None.
Club Statistician: S. Rendell.
Association of Football Statisticians Club Adviser to Yearbook: F. Lee.

Players released since May 1982: Jeremy Collins, M. (Falmouth); Mark Graves, F. (Wealdstone); Nigel Jarvis, M. (Yeovil T); Chris Jefferis, D. (Saltash U); David Kemp, F. (San Jose E.).

PORTSMOUTH Division 2

Back row (left to right): J. McLaughlin, A. Rogers, D. Crown, N. Webb, P. Wimbledon, C. Sullivan
Middle row: M. Tait, R. Doyle, S. Aizlewood, A. Gosney, A. Knight, A. Rollings, W. Rafferty, T. Senior
Front row: R. Campbell (Manager), S. Berry, P. Ellis, A. Biley, E. Howe, D. Thomas, G. Neave (Physiotherapist).

Vice-President: Sir A. L. Blake MC, LLB, KCVO.

Chairman: B. J. Deacon. ***Vice-Chairman:*** J. R. Parkhouse.

Directors: D. K. Deacon, S. W. Sloan, G. G. Gauntlett, Mrs J. Deacon.

Manager: Bobby Campbell. ***Company Secretary:*** W. J. B. Davis.

Year Formed: 1898. ***Turned Professional:*** 1898. ***Ltd Co.:*** 1898.

Club Nickname: 'Pompey'.

Previous Managers since 1946: Jack Tinn, Bob Jackson, Eddie Lever, Freddie Cox, George Smith, John Mortimore, Ron Tindall, Ian St John, Jimmy Dickinson MBE, Frank Burrows (10).

Fratton Park, Frogmore Rd, Portsmouth PO4 8RA. Telephone Portsmouth 731204/5. ***Telegraphic address:*** 'Pompey Portsm'th'. ***Ground capacity:*** 40,000 (14,200 covered). ***Record attendance:*** 51,385 v Derby Co, FA Cup 6th rd, 26 Feb, 1949. ***Record receipts:*** £59,042.50 v Cardiff C, Div 3, 12 Mar, 1983. ***Pitch measurements:*** 116yd×73yd.

Directions to Ground: Fratton station on main line from London Waterloo is just four minutes walk from the ground. Buses 17 and 18 from Portsmouth Harbour station and Gosport Ferry Terminal to the ground. Buses also from Portsmouth station.

Match tickets: South Stand centre section (the best seats) bookable ten days in advance.

Car parking: Only side-street parking.

Entertainments/catering facilities: The Pompey public house and reception rooms adjoin the ground and are owned by the club. There are also several bars around the ground.

Club shop: 42 Frogmore Road.

Handbooks/programmes: No handbook. The match-day magazine available on subscription.

Address of Supporters Club: 57 Frogmore Road, Portsmouth.

Address of the Club Shop or Boutique: The Club Shop, Portsmouth, 42 Frogmore Road, Portsmouth.

Note: Full club statistical records are on pages 416–455.

PORTSMOUTH 1982–83 LEAGUE RECORD

Match No.	Date	Venue	Opponents	Result		H/T Score	Lg. Pos.	Goalscorers	Attendance
1	Aug 28	H	Sheffield U	W	4-1	1-1	—	Biley, Howe, Webb, Tait	13,361
2	Sept 4	A	Walsall	W	3-0	1-0	1	Rafferty, Tait, Biley	2922
3	8	A	Exeter C	D	1-1	0-1	—	Rafferty	3146
4	11	H	Wrexham	W	3-0	1-0	2	Biley 2, Tait	10,867
5	18	A	Oxford U	D	1-1	1-1	3	Doyle (pen)	9918
6	25	H	Newport Co	L	1-2	0-0	5	Biley	10,833
7	28	H	Millwall	W	2-0	0-0	—	Rafferty, Biley	7615
8	Oct 1	A	Southend U	L	0-4	0-1	—		4589
9	9	A	Huddersfield T	D	1-1	1-1	9	Biley	6239
10	16	H	AFC Bournemouth	L	0-2	0-0	11		10,961
11	19	A	Wigan Ath	W	1-0	0-0	—	Biley	4504
12	23	H	Preston NE	W	3-1	1-1	7	Rafferty 3	10,331
13	30	A	Cardiff C	L	0-1	0-0	7		7082
14	Nov 2	H	Lincoln C	W	4-1	2-1	—	Biley 3, Rafferty	12,529
15	6	H	Gillingham	W	1-0	0-0	5	Rogers	12,212
16	13	A	Bristol R	L	1-5	0-3	6	Rafferty	9389
17	27	H	Doncaster R	W	2-1	2-1	6	Aizlewood (pen), Webb	9474
18	Dec 4	A	Bradford C	D	2-2	0-1	6	Biley 2	4961
19	18	A	Chesterfield	W	1-0	0-0	5	Tait	2440
20	27	H	Brentford	W	2-1	1-1	4	Ellis, Webb	14,476
21	28	A	Reading	W	2-1	0-0	2	Biley, Aizlewood (pen)	7646
22	Jan 1	H	Plymouth Arg	W	2-1	2-0	2	Webb, Smith (og)	15,856
23	15	A	Sheffield U	L	1-2	0-0	6	Aizlewood (pen)	12,907
24	18	A	Orient	L	1-2	1-1	—	Rafferty	3961
25	22	H	Oxford U	W	1-0	1-0	4	Rafferty	10,882
26	29	A	Wrexham	W	2-0	0-0	3	Biley, Rafferty	3007
27	Feb 6	A	Millwall	W	2-0	1-0	—	Tait, Webb	5621
28	12	H	Exeter C	W	3-2	2-0	2	Biley, Tait, Howe	10,622
29	16	A	Lincoln C	W	3-0	1-0	—	Aizlewood, Rafferty 2	6311
30	22	H	Huddersfield T	W	3-2	3-0	—	Aizlewood (pen), Webb 2	18,615
31	26	A	AFC Bournemouth	W	2-0	1-0	1	Aizlewood (pen), Biley	13,406
32	Mar 1	H	Wigan Ath	D	0-0	0-0	—		16,139
33	5	A	Preston NE	D	0-0	0-0	1		5610
34	12	H	Cardiff C	D	0-0	0-0	1		24,354
35	19	A	Gillingham	L	0-1	0-0	1		6489
36	26	H	Bristol R	W	1-0	1-0	1	Tait	17,828
37	Apr 1	A	Brentford	D	1-1	0-1	—	Morgan	12,593
38	2	H	Reading	D	2-2	1-1	1	Dillon 2 (2 pens)	15,327
39	9	H	Bradford C	L	0-1	0-1	3		12,198
40	16	A	Newport Co	W	3-0	0-0	2	Rafferty 2, Biley	10,419
41	23	H	Chesterfield	W	4-0	1-0	2	Dillon 2, Rogers, Biley	13,003
42	30	A	Doncaster R	W	2-0	1-0	1	Rafferty, Webb	2974
43	May 2	H	Orient	D	2-2	0-0	1	Biley, Rafferty	16,232
44	7	H	Southend U	W	2-0	1-0	1	Dillon, Biley	17,858
45	10	H	Walsall	W	1-0	1-0	—	Aizlewood	22,244
46	14	A	Plymouth Arg	W	1-0	0-0	1	Biley	14,173

Final League Position: 1

GOALSCORERS

League (74): Biley 22, Rafferty 17, Webb 8, Aizlewood 7 (5 pens), Tait 7, Dillon 5 (2 pens), Howe 2, Rogers 2, Doyle 1 (pen), Ellis 1, Morgan 1, own goal 1.
Milk Cup (1): Biley 1.
FA Cup (5): Biley 2, Rafferty 2, Webb 1.

Milk Cup	First Round	Crystal Palace (a)	0-2	**FA Cup**	First Round	Hereford U (h)	4-1
		(h)	1-1		Second Round	Aldershot (h)	1-3

Commercial Manager: J. L. Allen (Tel. 731204).
Club Coach:
Club Captain 1982–83: Bill Rafferty.
Supporters Player of the Season 1982–83: Alan Biley.
Chief Scout: D. Healey.
Physiotherapist: G. Neave.
Club Statistician:
Association of Football Statisticians Club Adviser to Yearbook: D. Robinson.

Knight	McLaughlin	Sullivan	Doyle	Howe	Aizlewood	Webb	Tait	Rafferty	Biley	Rogers	Ellis	Thomas	Berry	Senior	Ross (L)	Rollings	Crown	Dillon	Morgan	Referees	Match No.
1	2	3	4	5	6	7	8	9*	10	11	12									D. Vickers	1
1	2	3	4	5	6	7*	8	9	10		12	11								D. Owen	2
1	2	3	4	5	6		10	9	8	12	7*	11								E. Read	3
1	2	3	4	5	6		8	9	10		7	11								E. Scales	4
1	2	3	4	5	6		8	9	10		7	11								M. Robinson	5
1	2	3	4	5	6		8	9	10	12	7	11*								M. Bodenham	6
1	2	3	4	5	6	7	8	9	10	11										A. Crickmore	7
1	2	3	4	5	6	7	8	9	10	11										C. Downey	8
1	2	3	4	5	6	7	8	9	10	11										R. Nixon	9
1	2	3	4	5	6*	7	8		10	11			12	9						K. Salmon	10
1	2	3	6	4		7	5	10	11	8		9								C. Newsome	11
1		3	4		5	8	6	9	10	11		7			2					M. Dimblebee	12
1		3	4		5	8	6	9	10	11		7			2					J. Lovatt	13
1		3	4	5	6	7	8	9	10	11					2					B. Stevens	14
1		3	4	5	6	7	8	9	10	11					2					K. Cooper	15
1		3	4	5	6	7	8	9	10	11		12			2*					D. Civil	16
1	2	3	4	6	5	7	8	9	10	11										B. Daniels	17
1	2	3	4	5		7	8	9	10	11						6				N. Glover	18
1	2	3*	4	5		7	8	9	10	11	12					6				R. Bridges	19
1	2	3	4	5	6	7		9	10	11	8									M. James	20
1	2	3	4	5	6	7		9*	10	11	8						12			D. Lloyd	21
1	2	3	4	5	6*	7	8	9	10	11	12									A. Ward	22
1		3	4	5	6	7	8	9	10	11	2									K. Redfern	23
1		3	4	5	6	7	8	9	10	11	2*	12								D. Hedges	24
1		3	4	5	6	7	8	9	10*	11	2	12								A. Gunn	25
1	2	3	4	5	6	7	8	9	10	11										K. Walmsley	26
1	2	3	4	5	6	7	8	9	10			11								R. Milford	27
1	2	3	4	5	6	7	8	9	10	11										J. Moules	28
1	2	3	4	5*	6	7	8	9	10	11	12									J. Key	29
1	2	3	4		6	7	8	9	10	1						5				S. Bates	30
1	2	3	4		6	7	8	9	10	11	12					5*				C. Downey	31
1	2	3	4			7	8		10	11	6	12		9*		5				D. Reeves	32
1		3	4		6	7	8	9	10	11	2					5				J. Hough	33
1		3	4		6	7	8	9	10	11	2					5				L. Burden	34
1	2	3	4		6	7	8	9*	10	11	12					5				I. Borrett	35
1	2	3			6	7	4		10	11						5		8	9	L. Shapter	36
1	2	3	4		6	7	5		10	11								8	9	H. Taylor	37
1	2	3			6	7	4		10	11						5		8	9	C. Thomas	38
1		3*	4		6	7	5	9	10	11	2							8	12	E. Scales	39
1	2*	3	4		6	7	5	9	10	11	12							8		A. Seville	40
1		3	4		6	7	5*	9	10	11	2							8	12	B. Daniels	41
1	2	3	4		6*	7	5	9	10	11	12							8		R. Banks	42
1	2	3	4		6	7	5	9	10*	11								8	12	T. Bune	43
1	2	3	4		6	7	5	9	10	11	12							8		E. Read	44
1		3	4		6	7	5	9	10	11	2							8		D. Axcell	45
1		3	4		6	7	5	9	10	11	2							8		K. Cooper	46
46	32	46	44	27	42	42	44	41	46	40	16	9	0	2	5	10	0	11	3		
										+ 2s	+ 10s	+ 4s	+ 1s				+ 1s		+ 3s		

FOOTBALL LEAGUE RECORD

1920 Original Member of Division 3; 1921 Division 3(S); 1924–27 Division 2; 1927–59 Division 1; 1959–61 Division 2; 1961–62 Division 3; 1962–76 Division 2; 1976–78 Division 3; 1978–80 Division 4; 1980–83 Division 3; 1983– Division 2.

HONOURS

Football League: Division 1 – Champions 1948–49, 1949–50; Division 2 – Runners-up 1926–27; Division 3(S) – Champions 1923–24; Division 3 – Champions 1961–62, 1982–83. *FA Cup:* Winners 1939; Runners-up 1929, 1934. *Football League Cup* best season: 5th rd, 1961.

COLOURS

Royal blue shirts with white collar and cuffs, white shorts, red stockings.
Change colours: Red shirts with white collar and cuffs, red shorts, white stockings.

PORTSMOUTH

			Appearances			Goals		
Players Names Ht, Wt, D.o.B.	*Birthplace Transfer Fee*	*Clubs*	*F.L. A & S*	*F.L.C. A & S*	*F.A.C. A & S*	*F.L.*	*F.L.C.*	*F.A.C.*
Goalkeepers								
Alan Knight (EY)	Balham	Portsmouth (A)	101	6	7			
6 1, 13 1, 3.7.61								
Andy Gosney (EY)	Southampton	Portsmouth (A)	1					
6 4, 13 5,								
Trevor Inch		Portsmouth (A)						
Defenders								
John Roles	London	Portsmouth (A)						
John McLaughlin (EY)	Edmonton	Colchester U (A)	66	2	4	2		
5 8, 10 10, 29.10.54		Swindon T	199+3	15	21	8		
	£45,000	Portsmouth	139	11	6	1		
Peter Ellis (EU23)	Portsmouth	Portsmouth (A)	216+19	15+2	13	1	1	
5 11, 11 6, 20.3.56								
Steve Aizlewood (WS)	Newport	Newport Co	191+6	11	9	17		
5 11, 13 11, 9.10.52	£13,500	Swindon T	111+1	13	13	10	2	
	£45,000	Portsmouth	154	12	10	13		
Andy Rollings	Portishead	Norwich C (A)	4					
6 2, 12 12, 14.12.54	£5000	Brighton	168	15	9	10	1	
	P/E	Swindon T	11+1	4		1	1	
	£5000	Portsmouth	29	3	2	1		
Colin Sullivan (EU23)	Saltash	Plymouth Arg (A)	225+5	14	12	7		
5 7, 11 3, 24.6.51	£70,000	Norwich C	154+3	16	9	3		
	£60,000	Cardiff C	61+2	4	2	1		
	F/T	Hereford U	8		4			
	F/T	Portsmouth	64	2	2			
Ernie Howe	Chiswick	Hounslow T						
6 2¾, 12 12, 15.2.53	—	Fulham	68+2	8+2	2	10	1	1
	£50,000	QPR	89	5	12	3		3
	F/T	Portsmouth	27	2	2	2		
Midfield								
Kevin Dillon (EU21)	Sunderland	Birmingham C (A)	181+5	14	9	15	3	
5 11, 10 13, 18.12.59	£200,000	Portsmouth	11			5		
Bobby Doyle	Dumbarton	Dumbarton						
6 0, 11 12, 27.12.53	F/T	Barnsley	148+1	5	6	16		
	£20,000	Peterborough U	130	18	8	10	2	
	£120,000	Blackpool	47+2	6	5	2		
	£90,000	Portsmouth	112	6	2	13	1	
Paul Wimbleton (ES)	Portsmouth	Portsmouth (A)	4+4					
5 8, 10 6,								
Steve Berry	Gosport	Portsmouth (A)	26+2	2+1		2	1	
5 7, 10 6, 4.4.63								
David Crown	Enfield	Walthamstow A						
5 10, 11 4, 16.2.58	£13,000	Brentford	44+2	4	3	8	1	1
	P/E	Portsmouth	25+3		2	2		
Neil Webb (EY)	Reading	Reading (A)	65+7	2	2	22		
5 11, 11 6, 30.7.63	£87,500	Portsmouth	42	1	2	8		1
Forwards								
Alan Biley	Leighton Buzzard	Luton T (A)						
5 8, 10 9, 26.2.57	F/T	Cambridge U	160+5	12	5	75	4	3
	£350,000	Derby Co	47	2	2	19		
	£300,000	Everton	16+3			3		
	£100,000	Portsmouth	46	2	2	23	1	2
Trevor Senior	Dorchester	Dorchester T						
6 1½, 12 8,	£20,000	Portsmouth	11	+2		2		
		Aldershot (Loan)	10			6		
Alan Rogers	Plymouth	Plymouth Arg (A)	107+10	13	7	5		
5 10, 10 7, 6.7.54	£15,000	Portsmouth	141+6	13+1	9+2	14	2	
Mick Tait	Wallsend	Oxford U (A)	61+3	2+1	2	23	1	
5 11, 12 5, 30.9.56	£65,000	Carlisle U	101+5	7	7	20		2
	£150,000	Hull C	29+4		1	3		1
	£100,000	Portsmouth	114+3	9+2	5	23		1
Billy Rafferty	Glasgow	Coventry C	27	3	1	3		1
6 0, 12 6, 30.12.50	P/E	Blackpool	35+1		1	9		
	£25,000	Plymouth Arg	89+1	5	6	35	1	4
	£19,000	Carlisle U	72	7	6	27	5	7
	£125,000	Wolverhampton W	41+3	3	3	6		2
	£175,000	Newcastle U	34+5	2	1	6	2	
	£85,000	Portsmouth	98+4	5	4	40	1	2
Dave Thomas (E)	Kirkby	Burnley (A)	153+4	16	4	19	4	
5 8, 10 8, 5.10.50	£165,000	QPR	181+1	17	14	29	3	2
	£200,000	Everton	71	7	2	4	1	
	£325,000	Wolverhampton W	10	4	1			
		Vancouver W						
		Middlesbrough	13			1		
	F/T	Portsmouth	9+4		+1			
Nicky Morgan	East Ham	West Ham (A)	14+7	1		2		
5 10, 12 8, 30.10.59	£50,000	Portsmouth	3+3			1		
Paul Wood	Newcastle	Portsmouth (A)						

Players released since May 1982: Alex Cropley, M. (N/K).

PORT VALE Division 3

Back row (left to right): Tartt, Cegielski, Harrison, Lawrence, Ridley, Sproson
Front row: Shankland, Hunter, Waddington, Chamberlain, N., Bromage, Chamberlain, M., Armstrong, Greenhoff.

PORT VALE F.C.

VALIANTS

1876

Chairman: J. D. Lloyd. ***Vice-Chairman:*** D. P. McGrath.

Directors: D. S. Jones, A. McPherson, J. Lloyd, J. Burgess (President), D. Ratcliffe JP.

Manager: John McGrath. ***Secretary:*** Andrew Waterhouse.

Chief Coach: John Rudge.

Year Formed: 1876. ***Turned Professional:*** 1885. ***Ltd Co.:*** 1911.

Club Nickname: 'Valiants'.

Previous Name: Burslem Port Vale; became Port Vale, 1913.

Previous Grounds: 1876, Limekin Lane, Longport; 1881, Westport; 1884, Moorland Road, Burslem; 1886, Athletic Ground, Cobridge; 1913, Recreation Ground, Hanley; 1950, Vale Park.

Previous Managers since 1946: Billy Frith, Gordon Hodgson, Ivor Powell, Freddie Steele, Norman Low, Freddie Steele, Jackie Mudie, Sir Stanley Matthews, Gordon Lee, Roy Sproson, Colin Harper, Bob Smith, Dennis Butler, Alan Bloor (14).

Vale Park, Burslem, Stoke-on-Trent. Telephone 0782-814134. ***Ground capacity:*** 35,000. ***Record attendance:*** 50,000 v Aston Villa, FA Cup 5th rd, 20 Feb, 1960. ***Record receipts:*** £11,991 v Burnley, FA Cup 4th rd, 29 Jan, 1977. ***Pitch measurements:*** 116yd×76yd.

Directions to Ground: Nearest railway station, Stoke-on-Trent; there are frequent bus services from the town centre to Burslem.

Match tickets: Not bookable in advance.

Car parking: Parking is available behind the Railway Stand on Hamil Road, and on the Lorne Street side of the ground.

Entertainments/catering facilities: Light refreshments served on the ground. Social club on the Hamil Road side of the ground provides entertainment on certain evenings; membership by subscription.

Club shop: Sells all types of souvenirs.

Handbooks/programmes: Programmes are available on application to the club office or to the club shop.

Address of Supporters Club: Hamil Rd, Burslem, Stoke-on-Trent ST6 1AW.

Note: Full club statistical records are on pages 416–455.

PORT VALE 1982–83 LEAGUE RECORD

Match No.	Date	Venue	Opponents	Result		H/T Score	Lg. Pos.	Goalscorers	Attendance
1	Aug 28	A	Swindon T	L	0-1	0-0	—		3602
2	Sept 4	H	Bury	D	0-0	0-0	21		2888
3	6	H	Colchester U	D	0-0	0-0	—		2877
4	11	A	Mansfield T	W	2-0	1-0	12	Ridley, Bromage	2313
5	18	H	Chester	W	2-1	0-1	5	Sproson 2	3303
6	25	A	Darlington	D	0-0	0-0	13		2255
7	28	A	Aldershot	W	4-1	2-0	—	Moss, Tartt, Earle, Newton	1781
8	Oct 2	H	Stockport Co	L	2-3	2-0	9	Newton, Armstrong	3474
9	9	H	Hereford U	W	2-0	0-0	7	Cegielski, Bright	2875
10	15	A	Halifax T	W	2-0	1-0	—	Moss, Ridley	2009
11	18	H	Hartlepool U	W	3-0	1-0	—	Moss, Armstrong, Hunter	3664
12	22	A	Crewe Alex	W	2-1	1-1	—	Cegielski, Newton	4713
13	30	H	Blackpool	W	1-0	0-0	3	Newton (pen)	5449
14	Nov 2	A	Scunthorpe U	L	0-1	0-0	—		3766
15	6	A	Rochdale	D	3-3	0-1	6	Hunter, Moss, Greenhoff	2234
16	13	H	Hull C	W	1-0	1-0	3	Sproson	5298
17	27	A	Peterborough U	D	0-0	0-0	5		3043
18	Dec 4	H	Tranmere R	L	0-1	0-1	6		3452
19	18	H	Wimbledon	W	1-0	1-0	5	Newton	2761
20	27	A	Bristol C	W	3-1	1-0	5	Armstrong, Moss, Newton	6729
21	28	H	Torquay U	W	1-0	0-0	3	Moss	4760
22	Jan 1	A	Northampton T	D	2-2	0-0	3	Moss, Newton (pen)	3618
23	3	H	York C	W	2-1	2-0	3	Greenhoff, Moss	6056
24	8	A	Bury	W	1-0	0-0	2	Hunter	4748
25	15	H	Swindon T	W	3-0	1-0	2	Moss, Newton 2	6397
26	22	A	Chester	L	0-1	0-0	3		4056
27	29	H	Mansfield T	W	4-1	2-0	2	Armstrong 2, Fox, Newton	4102
28	Feb 5	H	Darlington	W	2-1	1-0	2	Armstrong, Moss	4110
29	19	A	Hereford U	W	2-0	1-0	2	Newton, Ridley	3075
30	26	H	Halifax T	W	2-1	0-1	1	Sproson, Hunter	5163
31	Mar 2	A	Hartlepool U	D	2-2	0-0	—	Ridley, Newton	1398
32	5	H	Crewe Alex	D	1-1	0-1	2	Tartt	8241
33	12	A	Blackpool	L	0-2	0-0	3		4519
34	19	H	Rochdale	W	4-0	1-0	3	Bromage, Newton 3	5129
35	26	A	Hull C	L	0-1	0-0	3		15,615
36	Apr 2	A	Torquay U	W	1-0	0-0	4	Steel	2593
37	4	H	Bristol C	D	1-1	1-1	—	Armstrong	6573
38	8	A	Tranmere R	W	2-0	1-0	—	Newton, Fox	3251
39	12	A	Colchester U	W	2-1	1-1	—	Newton, Fox	3275
40	16	H	Aldershot	W	2-1	0-1	2	Cegielski, Newton (pen)	5624
41	23	A	Wimbledon	L	0-1	0-0	3		4061
42	29	H	Peterborough U	W	2-1	2-1	—	Cegielski, Newton	5375
43	May 2	A	York C	D	0-0	0-0	3		4814
44	6	A	Stockport Co	W	2-0	1-0	—	Steel 2	5516
45	9	H	Scunthorpe U	L	0-1	0-0	—		6212
46	14	H	Northampton T	L	1-2	0-2	3	Newton (pen)	6761

Final League Position: 3

GOALSCORERS

League (67): Newton 20 (4 pens), Moss 10, Armstrong 7, Cegielski 4, Hunter 4, Ridley 4, Sproson 4, Fox 3, Steel 3, Bromage 2, Greenhoff 2, Tartt 2, Bright 1, Earle 1.
Milk Cup (1): Moss 1.
FA Cup (0).

Milk Cup	First Round	Rochdale (h)	1-0
		(a)	0-2
FA Cup	First Round	Bradford C (h)	0-1

Siddall	Tartt	Bromage	Hunter	Sproson	Cegielski	Sheldon (L)	Moss	Greenhoff	Ridley	Earle	Armstrong	Chamberlain	Newton	Lawrence L.	Bright	Fox	Shankland	McAdam	Southall (L)	Waddington	Poole	Steel	Lawrence M.	Referees	Match No.
1	2	3	4	5	6	7	8	9	10	11														E. Scales	1
1	2	3	4	5	6	7	8		10		9	11												K. Hackett	2
1	2	3	4	5	6	11	8		10		9	7												V. Callow	3
1	2	3	4	5	6	11	8		10		9	7												D. Hutchinson	4
1	2	3	4	5		11	8		6		9	7	10											H. Taylor	5
1	2	3	4	5	6		8		10		11	7	9											N. Glover	6
1	2	3	4	5	6		8	10		7	11		9											K. Salmon	7
1	2	3	4	5	6		8*	10		7	11		9	12										K. Cooper	8
1		3	4	5	6			10*	2	7	11		9	8	12									T. Fitzharris	9
1	2	3	4	5	6		8		10	12	11		9	7*										N. Wilson	10
1	2	3	4	5	6		8		10	7*	11		9	12										M. Robinson	11
1	2	3	4	5	6		8		10	7	11		9											M. Peck	12
1	2	3	4	5	6		8		10		11		9			7								J. Key	13
1	2	3	4*	5	6		8		10		11		9	12		7								A. Saunders	14
1	2	3	4	5	6		8	12	10*		11		9			7								G. Courtney	15
1	2	3	4	5	6		8	12	10*		11		9			7								K. Baker	16
1	2	3	4	5	6		8		10		11		9			7								D. Vickers	17
1	2	3	4	5	6		8		10		11*		9			7	12							N. Midgley	18
1	2	3	4	5	6		8	10			11		9			7								F. Roberts	19
1*	2	3	4	5	6		8	10	12		11		9			7								A. Glasson	20
	2	3	4	5	6		8	11	12		10*		9			7		1						R. Nixon	21
	2	3	4	5	6		8	10	11*				9			7			1	12				B. Stevens	22
	2	3	4	5	6		8	10	11				9			7			1					R. Milford	23
	2	5	7	3	4		11	8	6				10			9			1					K. Redfern	24
	2	3	4	5	6		8	10*	12		11		9			7			1					A. Scott	25
	2	3	4	5	6		8	10*	12		11		9			7			1					G. Tyson	26
	2	3	4	5	6		8	10*	12		11		9			7			1					R. Guy	27
	2	3	4	5	6		8		10		11		9			7			1					H. King	28
	2	3	4	5	6		8		10		11		9			7			1					D. Letts	29
	2	3	4	5	6				9		11		10	8		7			1					K. Walmsley	30
	2	3	4	5	6				10		11		9	8		7		1						D. Richardson	31
	2	3	4	5	6		8		10		11		9			7					1			E. Read	32
	2	3	4	5	6		8		10*		11		9			7	12				1			T. Mills	33
1	2	3	4	5	6						11		9			7						8	10	D. Lloyd	34
1	2	5	11*	3	4				12		6			10		9						7	8	M. Glover	35
1	2	3	4		6				5		11		9			7						8	10	S. Bates	36
1	2	3	4		6				5	12	11		9			7						8	10*	A. Robinson	37
1	2	3	4		6				5		11		9			7						8	10	R. Chadwick	38
1	2	3	4		6				5		11		9			7						8	10	D. Hedges	39
1	2	3	4	12	6				5		11		9			7						8	10*	K. Barrett	40
1	2	3	4	5	6				10*		11		9			7						8	12	B. Hill	41
1	2	3*	4	5	6						11		9			7	12					8	10	G. Napthine	42
1	2	3	4*	5	6				12		11		9			7						8	10	G. Courtney	43
1	2	3	4	5	6				12		11		9			7						8	10*	D. Scott	44
1	2	3	4	5	6				10		11		9			7						8		D. Brazier	45
1	2	3	4	5	6				12		11*		9			7	10					8		J. Key	46
33	45	46	46	41	45	5	30	13	32	6	42	5	41	5	0	34	1	2	9	0	2	13	10		
				+ 1s				+ 2s	+ 9s	+ 2s				+ 3s	+ 1s		+ 3s			+ 1s			+ 1s		

FOOTBALL LEAGUE RECORD

Original Member Division 2, 1892–96; Failed re-election in 1896; Re-elected 1898; Resigned 1907; Returned in Oct. 1919, when they took over the fixtures of Leeds City; 1929–30 Division 3(N); 1930–36 Division 2; 1936–38 Division 3(N); 1938–52 Division 3(S); 1952–54 Division 3(N); 1954–57 Division 2; 1957–58 Division 3(S); 1958–59 Division 4; 1959–65 Division 3; 1965–70 Division 4; 1970–78 Division 3; 1978–83 Division 4; 1983– Division 3.

HONOURS

Football League: Division 2 best season: 5th, 1930–31; Division 3(N) – Champions 1929–30, 1953–54; Runners-up 1952–53; Division 4 – Champions 1958–59; Promoted 1969–70 (4th). *FA Cup:* semi-final 1954, when in Division 3. *Football League Cup:* never past 2nd rd.

COLOURS

White shirts with black trim, black shorts, white stockings. **Change colours:** Yellow shirts, green shorts, yellow stockings.

PORT VALE

Players Names Ht, Wt, D.o.B.	Birthplace Transfer Fee	Clubs	Appearances F.L. A & S	 F.L.C. A & S	 F.A.C. A & S	Goals F.L.	 F.L.C.	 F.A.C.
Goalkeepers								
Barry Siddall (EY)	Ellesmere Port	Bolton W (A)	137	10	11			
6 0½, 14 4, 12.9.54	£80,000	Sunderland	167	11	9			
	—	Darlington (loan)	8					
	F/T	Port Vale	33	2	1			
Neil McAdam*	East Kilbride	Northwich Vic						
	—	Port Vale	2					
Defenders								
Phil Sproson	Trent Vale	Port Vale	188+4	9	11+1	14		
6 0, 12 0, 13.10.59								
Colin Tartt*	Liverpool	Alsager T						
5 11, 11 7, 23.11.50	—	Port Vale	171+4	5	8+2	7		2
	£15,000	Chesterfield	185+1	15	12	7	2	1
	£15,000	Port Vale	83	2	6	6		
Wayne Cegielski (WU21)	Bedwelty	Tottenham H (A)						
6 0, 12 0, 11.1.56	—	Northampton T (loan)	11					
	F/T	Schalke O4						
	F/T	Wrexham	112+11	7+1	10+2			1
	F/T	Port Vale	45	2		5		
John Ridley	Consett	Port Vale	149+7	8	13	3		1
6 1½, 12 6, 27.4.52	£55,000	Leicester C	17+7		2			
	£35,000	Chesterfield	121+3	9	6	8		
	F/T	Port Vale	32+9	2	1	4		
Chris Banks		Port Vale						
Midfield								
Felix Healy (NI)	Londonderry	Finn Harps						
5 11, 12 0, 27.9.55	£9000	Port Vale	40+1	2	1	2		
Russell Bromage	Stoke	Port Vale (A)	184+7	10	11	9	1	
5 11, 11 5, 9.11.59								
Terry Armstrong	Barnsley	Huddersfield T (A)	36+4			2		
5 10, 12 2, 10.7.58	F/T	Port Vale	91+2	5	5	10		1
Geoff Hunter	Hull	Manchester U (A)						
5 9, 10 5, 27.10.59	F/T	Crewe Alex	86+1	4	2	8	1	
	£10,500	Port Vale	85+2	5	6	7		
Steve Waddington	Crewe	Stoke C (A)	49+3	1	3	5		1
5 8, 9 12, 5.2.56	£40,000	Walsall	122+8	4	7	12		1
	F/T	Port Vale	+1	1				
Forwards								
Andy Shankland	Stoke	Port Vale (A)	7+9	1		1		
5 8, 9 0,								
Mark Bright	Stoke	Leek T						
6 10, 11 0,	—	Port Vale	1+2			1		
Steve Fox	Tamworth	Birmingham C (A)	26+3			1		
5 8, 11 2, 17.2.58	£90,000	Wrexham	136+6	7+1	15	10		2
	F/T	Port Vale	34		1	3		
Les Lawrence	Wolverhampton	Stourbridge						
6 3, 11 0, 18.5.57		Shrewsbury T	10+4		1	2		
	F/T	Telford U						
		Torquay U	170+19	11+4	9+1	45	4	4
	F/T	Weymouth						
	F/T	Port Vale	5+3	+1				
Bob Newton	Chesterfield	Huddersfield T (A)	37+5	3+1	3	7	3	2
5 11, 12 6, 23.11.56	£5000	Hartlepool U	150	5	12	48	2	10
	£20,000	Port Vale	41		1	20		
Jim Steel	Dumphries	Oldham Ath (A)	101+7	8+1	6	24	1	
6 3, 11 6, 4.12.59	—	Wigan Ath (loan)	2			2		
	—	Wrexham (loan)	9			6		
	£5000	Port Vale	13			3		
Bobbie Earle		Stoke C (N/C)						
	F/T	Port Vale	6+2	1		1		

Lottery Manager: Mike Cullerton (Tel. 0782 85524).
Club Coach: John Rudge.
Supporters Player of the Season 1982–83: Wayne Cegielski.
Physiotherapist: Lol Hamlett.
Association of Football Statisticians Club Adviser to Yearbook: S. Askey.
Club Captain 1982–83: Russell Bromage.
Chief Scout: Ray Williams.
Club Statistician:

Players released since May 1982:
Paul Bennett, M. (Northwich Vic); John Miller, M. (retired); Gary Loughran, D. (N/K); Stuart Eccleston, D. (N/K).

PRESTON NORTH END Division 3

Back row (left to right): Don O'Riordan (Captain), Jonathan Clark, Steve Elliott, Peter Litchfield, Glen Campbell, Willie Naughton, Mike Farelly, Tommy Booth
Centre row: Geoff Nulty (Asst Manager), Harry Hubbick (Kit Manager), Andy McAteer, Simon Westwell, Mark Walsh, Alex Bruce, Gordon Coleman, Gary Hough, Neil Hanson, Dennis Loze (Physio), Alan Kelly (Reserve Team Manager)
Front row: Graham Houston, Chris Hunter, Gary Buckley, Gordon Lee (Manager), Peter Sayer, Graham Bell, John Kelly.

President: Tom Finney OBE, JP.

Chairman: Alan R. W. Jones JP, FRICS.

Vice-Chairman: T. J. Hemmings.

Managing Director: B. J. Campbell.

Directors: T. W. S. Croft FCIOB, K. W. Leeming, T. H. Gore, E. Griffith BVSC, MRCVS, M. H. McCann LLB, A. C. Pilkington AICS, F INST FF.

Team Manager: Gordon Lee.

Secretary: D. J. Allan. ***Asst Manager:*** Geoff Nulty.

Year Formed: 1881. ***Turned Professional:*** 1885. ***Ltd Co.:*** 1893.

Club Nickname: 'The Lilywhites' or 'North End'.

Previous Managers since 1946: W. Scott, Scot Symon, Frank Hill, Cliff Britton, Jimmy Milne, Bobby Seith, Alan Ball Snr, Bobby Charlton CBE, Harry Catterick, Nobby Stiles, Tommy Docherty (11).

Deepdale, Preston PR1 6RU. Telephone 0772-795919. ***Ansaphone:*** Preston 709170. ***Ground capacity:*** 25,000. ***Record attendance:*** 42,684 v Arsenal, Division 1, 23 Apr, 1938. ***Record receipts:*** £28,303.40 v Blackburn R, Division 2, 21 April, 1981. ***Pitch measurements:*** 112yd×78yd.

Directions to Ground: Special buses to Deepdale from outlying areas and town centre bus station. Nearest railway station: Preston.

Match tickets: Postal applications (remittance and SAE), may be made 14 days before the match.

Car parking: Club car park on the Deepdale Road (West Stand) side of the ground, holds 500 vehicles. Only limited off-street parking.

Entertainments/catering facilities: The ground is well-equipped for normal match-day refreshments.

Club shop: Open on match days only. All postal enquiries to: The Commercial Manager, Preston North End Commercial Department, Lowthorpe Road, Deepdale, Preston PR1 6RU (Tel: Preston 795465/795156).

Handbooks/programmes: No handbook. Programmes available on subscription from the Commercial Manager.

Address of Supporters Club: c/o Preston North End FC, Deepdale, Preston.

Address of the Club Shop: The Lilywhite Shop, Preston North End FC, Deepdale, Preston.

Note: Full club statistical records are on pages 416–455.

PRESTON NORTH END 1982–83 LEAGUE RECORD

Match No.	Date	Venue	Opponents	Result	H/T Score	Lg. Pos.	Goalscorers	Attendance
1	Aug 28	H	Millwall	W 3-2	2-0	—	Elliott 3 (1 pen)	4483
2	Sept 4	A	Sheffield U	L 1-2	1-1	10	Kelly	14527
3	7	A	Walsall	L 1-2	1-0	—	McAteer	2060
4	11	H	Oxford U	L 1-2	0-1	20	Elliott	4481
5	18	A	Exeter C	L 1-5	1-2	23	Elliott (pen)	2310
6	25	H	Bristol R	D 2-2	2-1	23	Bell, Elliott	3880
7	28	H	Wrexham	W 3-0	1-0	—	O'Riordan, Elliott 2	3363
8	Oct 2	A	Reading	W 3-2	1-2	13	Elliott 2, Bruce	1713
9	9	A	Gillingham	L 1-2	0-2	16	Bruce	4390
10	16	H	Huddersfield T	D 0-0	0-0	17		5570
11	19	H	Newport Co	D 0-0	0-0	—		3747
12	23	A	Portsmouth	L 1-3	1-1	17	Bruce	10,331
13	30	H	AFC Bournemouth	L 0-1	0-1	20		3589
14	Nov 2	A	Brentford	L 1-3	0-0	—	Elliott	6142
15	6	A	Cardiff C	L 1-3	0-3	22	O'Riordan	5,546
16	13	H	Chesterfield	D 1-1	1-0	23	Houston	3574
17	27	H	Plymouth Arg	D 2-2	2-0	22	McAteer, Elliott	3633
18	Dec 3	A	Southend U	W 3-2	2-2	—	Elliott, Houston, Walsh	3749
19	17	A	Orient	L 1-2	1-1	21	Coleman	1668
20	27	H	Bradford C	D 0-0	0-0	21		7238
21	28	A	Doncaster R	L 0-2	0-1	22		3895
22	Jan 1	H	Wigan Ath	W 4-1	2-1	22	Bruce 2, McAteer, Kelly (pen)	7565
23	3	A	Lincoln C	L 0-3	0-2	23		5891
24	15	A	Millwall	L 0-1	0-1	24		2816
25	22	H	Exeter C	D 2-2	1-0	21	Elliott, Bruce	3767
26	29	A	Oxford U	L 2-3	1-1	21	Gowling, Naughton	4441
27	Feb 5	A	Wrexham	L 1-3	0-2	24	Bell	1920
28	15	A	Newport Co	L 0-3	0-0	—		2317
29	19	H	Gillingham	D 0-0	0-0	24		3479
30	26	A	Huddersfield T	D 1-1	0-0	24	O'Riordan	8562
31	Mar 1	H	Brentford	W 3-0	2-0	—	Elliott, Bell, Westwell	3669
32	5	H	Portsmouth	D 0-0	0-0	23		5610
33	12	A	AFC Bournemouth	L 0-4	0-1	23		4407
34	19	H	Cardiff C	W 2-1	1-0	23	Bruce, Elliott	4608
35	26	A	Chesterfield	D 1-1	0-0	23	O'Riordan	2332
36	29	H	Walsall	W 1-0	1-0	—	Sayer	4013
37	Apr 2	H	Doncaster R	W 4-1	2-0	21	Hinnigan, McAteer, Elliott, Humphries (og)	5287
38	4	A	Bradford C	W 2-1	0-1	—	Gowling, McAteer (pen)	4357
39	8	H	Southend U	D 1-1	0-1	—	Bell	6286
40	12	H	Sheffield U	W 1-0	0-0	—	Houston S. (og)	6296
41	16	A	Bristol R	L 2-3	1-0	21	Elliott, Hinnigan	5189
42	23	H	Orient	W 2-1	0-1	18	Hinnigan, Sayer	5628
43	30	A	Plymouth Arg	D 1-1	1-0	19	Booth	2912
44	May 2	H	Lincoln C	W 1-0	0-0	17	Gowling	6537
45	7	H	Reading	W 2-0	2-0	16	Gowling, Elliott	7253
46	14	A	Wigan Ath	W 1-0	1-0	16	Gowling	7191

Final League Position: 16

GOALSCORERS

League (60): Elliott 19 (2 pens), Bruce 7, Gowling 5, McAteer 5 (1 pen), Bell 4, O'Riordan 4, Hinnigan 3, Houston 2, Kelly 2 (1 pen), Sayer 2, Booth 1, Coleman 1, Naughton 1, Walsh 1, Westwell 1, own goals 2.
Milk Cup (4): Elliott 2, Bruce 1, Naughton 1.
FA Cup (7): Coleman 2, Elliott 2, Kelly 1 (pen), McAteer 1, O'Riordan 1.

Milk Cup	First Round	Walsall (a)	1-0
		(h)	1-1
	Second Round	Norwich C (a)	1-2
		(h)	1-2
FA Cup	First Round	Shepshed (h)	5-1
	Second Round	Blackpool (h)	2-1
	Third Round	Leeds U (a)	0-3

Litchfield	Walsh	McAteer	O'Riordan	Westwell	Coleman	Kelly	Bell	Elliott	Naughton	Bruce	Houston	Gowling	Buckley	Arnold (L)	Clark	Campbell	Sayer	Booth	Farrelly	Lodge	Hunter	Hodge (L)	Hinnigan	*Referees*	*Match No.*
1	2	3	4	5	6	7*	8	9	10	11	12													A. Hamil	1
1	2	3	4	5		7	8	9	10	11*	12	6												J. Bray	2
1	2	3	4	5		7	8	9	10	11		6												K. Cooper	3
1	2	3	4	5		7	8	9	10	12	11*	6												J. Lovatt	4
1	2	3	4	5*	12	7	8	9	10		11	6												G. Downey	5
1	2	3	4	5	12	7	8	9	10*		11	6												A. Challinor	6
1	2	3	4	5		7	8	9	10		11	6												C. Seel	7
1	2	3		5	4	7	8	9	10	12	11*	6												D. Axcell	8
1	2*	3		5	4	7	8	9	10	11		6	12											E. Scales	9
	2	3		5	4*	7	8	9	10	11		6	12	1										T. Holbrook	10
	2*	3		5		7	8	9	10	11		6	12	1	4									D. Shaw	11
	2*	3		5		7	8	9	10	11		6	12	1	4									M. Dimblebee	12
	2*	3	12	5		7	8	9	10	11		6		1	4									D. Hutchinson	13
	5	3*	4	2		7	8	9		11	12	6	10	1										L. Burden	14
			4	2	5	7	8	9	3*	11	12	6	10	1										R. Lewis	15
		3	4	2	5	7		9	12		11	6	10*			1	8							G. Tyson	16
1	7	3	4	2	5			9	10		11	6					8							T. Mills	17
1	7	3	4	2	5			9	10		11	6					8							Alan Robinson	18
1	7	3	4	2	5			9	10*		11	6	12				8							D. Brazier	19
1	7	3	4	2	5*		12	9	10		11	6					8							T. Jones	20
1	7	3	4	2		10	5	9		12	11	6					8*							A. Saunders	21
1	7	3	4		5	2		9		10	11	6					8							P. Willis	22
1	7	3	4		5	2		9		10	11	6					8							D. Lloyd	23
1		3	2			7	9		10	8	11	4	6					5						L. Shapter	24
1		3	4	2		7	11	9	10	8			6					5						R. Bridges	25
1		3	4	2		7*	11	9	10	12		8	6					5						M. Bodenham	26
1		3	4	2		7*	11	9	10	8		5	6						12					A. Seville	27
1	7	3	4	5			11	9	10	8*									2	6	12			T. Bune	28
1	7*	3	4	5	12		11	9	10	8									2	6				M. G. Peck	29
1	7	3	4	5		12	11	9	10	8									2*	6				J. Lovatt	30
	7	3	4	5	2*		11	9	10	8		12								6		1		N. Ashley	31
	7*	3	4	5	2		11	9	10	8		12								6		1		J. Hough	32
	7*	3	4	5	2	12	11	9	10	8										6		1		A. Crickmore	33
		3	4	5*			11	9	10	8		12					7			6		1	2	R. Nixon	34
		3	4			12	11	9	10			8					7*	5		6		1	2	G. Napthine	35
		3	4				11	9	10			8					7	5		6		1	2	F. Roberts	36
		3	4				11	9	10			8					7	5		6		1	2	C. Newsome	37
		3	4				11	9	10			8					7	5		6		1	2	C. Seel	38
		3	4				11	9	10	12		8					7*	5		6		1	2	M. Heath	39
			4				11	9	10			8					7	5	2	6		1	3	G. Courtney	40
		3*	4			12	11	9			10	8					7	5		6		1	2	D. Hedges	41
		3	4				11	9	10		12	8*					7	5		6		1	2	J. Key	42
		3	4			12	11	9	10			8*					7	5		6		1	2	A. Glasson	43
		3	4				11	9	10			8					7	5		6		1	2	D. Owen	44
		3	4				11	9	10			8					7	5		6		1	2	K. Hackett	45
		5	3			12	8	10	11			9*					7	4		6		1	2	T. Mills	46
23	27	44	40	31	15	23	39	45	40	22	15	37	7	6	3	1	21	15	4	19	0	16	13		
			+ 1s		+ 3s	+ 6s	+ 1s		+ 1s	+ 5s	+ 5s	+ 3s	+ 5s						+ 1s		+ 1s				

FOOTBALL LEAGUE RECORD

1888 Original Member of League; 1901–04 Division 2; 1904–12 Division 1; 1912–13 Division 2; 1913–14 Division 1; 1914–15 Division 2; 1919–25 Division 1; 1925–34 Division 2; 1934–49 Division 1; 1949–51 Division 2; 1951–61 Division 1; 1961–70 Division 2; 1970–71 Division 3; 1971–74 Division 2; 1974–78 Division 3; 1978–81 Division 2; 1981– Division 3.

HONOURS

Football League: Division 1 – Champions 1888–89 (first champions), 1889–90; Runners-up 1890–91, 1891–92, 1892–93, 1905–06, 1952–53, 1957–58; Division 2 – Champions 1903–04, 1912–13, 1950–51; Runners-up 1914–15, 1933–34; Division 3 – Champions 1970–71. *FA Cup:* Winners 1889, 1938; Runners-up 1888, 1922, 1937, 1954, 1964. *Double Performed:* 1888–89. *Football League Cup* best season: 4th rd, 1963, 1966, 1972, 1981.

COLOURS White shirts with navy blue collars and cuffs, navy blue shorts with white trim, white stockings with navy blue rings. **Change colours:** Yellow shirts, royal blue shorts, yellow stockings.

PRESTON NORTH END

Players Names Ht. Wt. D.o.B.	Birthplace Transfer Fee	Clubs	Appearances F.L. A & S	 F.L.C. A & S	 F.A.C. A & S	Goals F.L.	 F.L.C.	 F.A.C.
Goalkeepers								
Peter Litchfield*	Manchester	Droylsaen						
6 1, 12 12, 27.7.56	£3000	Preston NE	44	8	4			
Glen Campbell*	Leyland	Preston NE (A)	1					
5 11, 11 7, 26.2.65								
Defenders								
Donal O'Riordan* (EIU21)	Dublin	Derby Co (A)	2–4	–1		1		
5 11, 12 0, 14.5.57	—	Doncaster R (loan)	2					
	£30,000	Tulsa Roughnecks						
	£30,000	Preston NE	153–5	10	8	8		1
Simon Westwell*	Clitheroe	Preston NE (A)	63	11	2	1		
5 9½, 9 7, 13.11.61								
Andy M'Ateer	Preston	Preston NE (A)	126	12	6	5		1
5 10, 11 3, 24.4.61								
Tommy Booth (EU23)	Manchester	Manchester C	380–2	44–2	27	25	3	5
6 2½, 13 5, 9.11.49	£30,000	Preston NE	42	1	1	1		
Mark Walsh*	Preston	Preston NE (A)	31–6	5–1	2	2		
5 10, 10 10, 7.10.62								
Mike Farrelly* (ES)	Manchester	Preston NE	7–5	2–1				
5 11½, 11 11, 1.1.62								
Joe Hinnigan	Liverpool	South Liverpool						
6 0½, 12 10, 3.12.55	£1000	Wigan Ath	66	4	7	10		
	£80,000	Sunderland	63	1	1	4		
	£15,000	Preston NE	13			3		
Midfield								
Graham Bell* (EY)	Middleton	Chadderton						
5 9, 10 6, 30.3.55	—	Oldham Ath	166–4	9	6–1	9		1
	£80,000	Preston NE	140–3	11–1	1–1	9	1	
	—	Huddersfield T (loan)	2					
Peter Sayer* (W)	Cardiff	Cardiff C	70–12	7	4	14	2	2
5 7, 11 0, 2.5.55	£100,000	Brighton	46–9	7	1–1	6		
	£80,000	Preston NE	27–3	–1		2		
	—	Cardiff C (loan)	4			1		
Paul Lodge (ES)	Liverpool	Everton (A)	20–4	5	6			
5 8½, 10 11, 13.2.61	—	Wigan Ath (loan)	5			1		
	—	Rotherham U (loan)	4					
	F T	Preston NE	19		2			
Gordon Coleman*	Nottingham	Preston NE	248–21	20	12	25	2	3
5 9, 10 12, 11.2.54								
Jonathan Clark (WU21)	Swansea	Manchester U (A)	0–1					
5 10, 11 10, 12.11.58	£50,000	Derby Co	48–5	4	4	3		
	F T	Preston NE	21	5	1		1	
Gary Buckley*	Manchester	Manchester C (A)	4–2	2				
5 5, 10 0, 3.3.61	£35,000	Preston NE	27–8	2	1	2		
John Kelly*	Bebbington	Cammell Lairds						
5 9½, 10 6, 20.10.60	—	Tranmere R	55–9	7	1	9	1	
	£35,000	Preston NE	51–8	4	2	7		1
Forwards								
Alex Bruce* (SU23)	Dundee	Preston NE (A)	55–7	1	3	22		
5 8, 11 0, 23.12.52	£150,000	Newcastle U	16–4			3		
	P E	Preston NE	288–13	23–2	16	135	7	6
Graham Houston*	Gibraltar	Preston NE	41–15	5	5	3		1
5 8, 11 4, 24.2.60								
Steve Elliott	Haltwhistle	Nottingham F (A)	4	2				
5 11½, 11 10, 15.9.58	£95,000	Preston NE	158–6	11–1	5	54	2	2
Willie Naughton*	Catrine	Preston NE (A)	82–5	6	4	6	2	
6 0, 12 8, 20.3.62								
Chris Hunter*	Hong Kong	Preston NE (A)	–1					
5 7½, 10 7, 18.1.64								
Alan Gowling* (EU23)	Stockport	Manchester Univ						
6 1, 12 0, 16.3.48	—	Manchester U	64–7	7	6	18		2
	£65,000	Huddersfield T	128	6	5	58	2	1
	F T	Newcastle U	91–1	8	14	30	7	8
	F T	Bolton W	147–2	8	8	28	2	1
	F T	Preston NE	37–3	3	4	5		

Commercial Manager: David Bradshaw (Tel. 795468)
Club Coach: Geoff Nulty
Supporters Player of the Season 1982–83: Steve Elliot
Physiotherapist: Dennis Loze
Club Captain 1982–83: Gordon Coleman
Chief Scout:
Club Statistician:
Association of Football Statisticians Club Adviser to Yearbook: C. Bland

Players (non-appearance) granted free transfer: Gary Hough, D.; Neil Hanson, D.
Players released since May 1982:
Jimmy Bell, D. (Hibernian); Brian Taylor, D. (Lytham St. Annes).

QUEEN'S PARK RANGERS Division 1

Back row (left to right): Alan Harris (Asst. Manager), Ian Dawes, Terry Fenwick, Ian Gillard (now Aldershot), Ernie How (now Portsmouth), Peter Hucker, Steve Wicks, Bob Hazell, Mike Flanagan, Tony Currie, Jock Skinner (Kit Man), Dave Butler (Physio)
Front row: Gary Micklewhite, Warren Niell, Gary Waddock, Glen Roeder, Clive Allen, John Gregory, Simon Stainrod.

President: Sir Stanley Rous CBE.

Chairman: J. A. Gregory. ***Vice-Chairman:*** J. C. Gregory.

Executive Director: A. Williamson.

Directors: C. J. Armstrong FCA, A. D. Farmer MPS, B. A. V. Henson FCA, A. Ingham, Councillor W. C. Smith JP, T. Venables.

Team Manager: Terry Venables.

Acting Secretary: A. Ingham.

Assistant Team Manager: Alan Harris.

Year Formed: 1885. ***Turned Professional:*** 1898. ***Ltd Co.:*** 1899.

Club Nickname: 'Rangers' or 'R's'.

Previous Name: 1885–7, St Jude's; 1887, became Queen's Park Rangers.

Previous Grounds: 1885, Welford's Fields; 1888, London Scottish Ground, Brondesbury; Home Farm: Kensal Rise Green: Gun Club, Wormwood Scrubs: Kilburn Cricket Ground; 1899, Kensal Rise Athletic Ground; 1901, Latimer Road, Notting Hill; 1904, Agricultural Society, Park Royal; 1907, Park Royal Ground; 1917, Loftus Road; 1931, White City; 1933, Loftus Road; 1962, White City; 1963, Loftus Road.

Previous Managers since 1946: Dave Mangnall, Jack Taylor, Alec Stock, Tommy Docherty, Les Allen, Gordon Jago, Dave Sexton, Frank Sibley, Steve Burtenshaw, Tommy Docherty (10).

South Africa Road, W12 7PA. Telephone 01-743 0262/3/4/5. ***Telegraphic address:*** 'Queu Pear'. ***Ground capacity:*** 30,000 (23,000 covered). ***Record attendance:*** 35,353 v Leeds U, Division 1, 27 April, 1974. ***Record receipts:*** £79,660 v Tottenham H, FA Cup 3rd rd, 3 Jan, 1981. ***Pitch measurements:*** 112yd×72yd.

Directions to Ground: Buses 12 and 207. Nos 11, 49, 72, 88, 105, 220 go near Shepherd's Bush (Metropolitan and Central Lines) and White City (Central Line – five to ten minutes walk).

Match tickets: Seats bookable one month in advance of the match.

Car parking: White City park, adjacent to the ground, is recommended. Limited parking in side-streets.

Entertainments/catering facilities: Various bars around the ground.

Club shop: Programme shop in South Africa Road and kiosks inside the ground.

Handbooks/programmes: Available from programme shop.

Address of Supporters Club: c/o Football Club.

Address of the Club Shop or Boutique: Supporters Club Shop, Queen's Park Rangers FC, South Africa Road, London W12.

Note: Full club statistical records are on pages 416–455.

QUEEN'S PARK RANGERS 1982–83 LEAGUE RECORD

Match No.	Date	Venue	Opponents	Result	H/T Score	Lg. Pos.	Goalscorers	Attendance
1	Aug 28	A	Newcastle U	L 0-1	0-0	—		36,185
2	31	H	Cambridge U	W 2-1	1-0	—	Sealy 2	9686
3	Sept 4	H	Derby Co	W 4-1	1-1	2	Gregory, Fenwick (pen), Stainrod 2	10,217
4	7	A	Fulham	D 1-1	0-0	—	Stainrod	15,004
5	11	A	Oldham Ath	W 1-0	0-0	3	Gregory	4266
6	18	H	Sheffield W	L 0-2	0-1	6		13,733
7	25	A	Leicester C	W 1-0	0-0	5	O'Neill (og)	10,647
8	28	H	Crystal Palace	D 0-0	0-0	—		12,194
9	Oct 2	H	Burnley	W 3-2	0-2	4	Neill, Allen, Micklewhite	9145
10	9	A	Barnsley	W 1-0	0-0	2	Allen	13,270
11	16	H	Shrewsbury T	W 4-0	3-0	1	Allen, Flanagan, Micklewhite, Gregory	9275
12	23	A	Middlesbrough	L 1-2	1-0	3	Allen	7892
13	30	H	Bolton W	W 1-0	0-0	2	Stainrod	9363
14	Nov 6	A	Rotherham U	D 0-0	0-0	3		7402
15	13	H	Blackburn R	D 2-2	1-1	2	Allen, Fenwick (pen)	9149
16	20	A	Cambridge U	W 4-1	2-0	1	Wicks, Sealy, Allen 2	5685
17	27	H	Carlisle U	W 1-0	1-0	1	Fenwick	9397
18	Dec 4	A	Leeds U	W 1-0	0-0	1	Allen	11,528
19	11	H	Grimsby T	W 4-0	3-0	1	Neill, Sealy, Gregory, Micklewhite	9811
20	18	A	Wolverhampton W	L 0-4	0-0	1		15,423
21	27	H	Chelsea	L 1-2	1-1	2	Sealy	23,744
22	29	A	Charlton Ath	W 3-1	1-0	2	Micklewhite 2, Sealy	13,306
23	Jan 3	A	Derby Co	L 0-2	0-1	2		14,007
24	15	H	Newcastle U	W 2-0	0-0	2	Gregory 2	13,972
25	22	A	Crystal Palace	W 3-0	1-0	2	Allen 2, Hazell	14,621
26	Feb 5	H	Oldham Ath	W 1-0	0-0	2	Sealy	8903
27	19	H	Barnsley	W 3-0	2-0	2	Gregory, Sealy, Flanagan	10,271
28	26	A	Shrewsbury T	D 0-0	0-0	2		4397
29	Mar 5	H	Middlesbrough	W 6-1	2-1	2	Micklewhite, Flanagan, Allen 3, Gregory	9596
30	12	A	Bolton W	L 2-3	1-2	2	Gregory (pen), Sealy	6373
31	19	H	Rotherham U	W 4-0	4-0	1	Sealy, Flanagan, Gregory 2	9541
32	22	H	Charlton Ath	W 5-1	2-1	—	Sealy 2, Hazell, Gregory, Stainrod	10,776
33	26	A	Blackburn R	W 3-1	2-1	1	Stainrod 2, Flanagan	5317
34	Apr 4	A	Chelsea	W 2-0	1-0	—	Gregory, Sealy	20,821
35	9	H	Leicester C	D 2-2	1-0	1	Gregory, Sealy	16,301
36	19	A	Sheffield W	W 1-0	0-0	—	Flanagan	11,713
37	23	H	Leeds U	W 1-0	1-0	1	Hart (og)	19,573
38	30	A	Carlisle U	L 0-1	0-1	1		5724
39	May 2	H	Fulham	W 3-1	2-0	1	Gregory, Sealy, Stainrod	24,431
40	7	H	Wolverhampton W	W 2-1	1-1	1	Flanagan, Hazell	19,854
41	10	A	Burnley	L 1-2	0-2	—	Sealy	7191
42	14	A	Grimsby T	D 1-1	0-1	1	Stainrod	9590

Final League Position: 1

GOALSCORERS

League (77): Sealy 16, Gregory 15 (1 pen), Allen 13, Stainrod 9, Flanagan 7, Micklewhite 6, Fenwick 3 (2 pens), Hazell 3, Neill 2, Wicks 1, own goals 2.
Milk Cup (1): Gregory 1.
FA Cup (2): Fenwick 1 (pen), Micklewhite 1.

Milk Cup	Second Round	Rotherham U (a)	1-2
		(h)	0-0
FA Cup	Third Round	WBA (a)	2-3

Hucker	Neill	Dawes	Waddock	Hazell	Fenwick	Micklewhite	Stewart	Sealy	Stainrod	Gregory	Burke	Wilkins	Fereday	Allen	Flanagan	Currie	O'Connor	Wicks	Roeder	Duffield	Referees	Match No.
1	2	3	4	5	6	7*	8	9	10	11	12										T. Mills	1
1	2	3	4	5	6	7	8	9	10	11											R. Milford	2
1	2	3	4	5	6	7	8*	9	10	11		12									E. Read	3
1	2	3	4	5	6	7	8	9	10	11											A. Gunn	4
1	2	3	4	5	6	7	8*	9	10	11		12									N. Ashley	5
1	2	3	4	5	6	7*	8	9	10	11	12										Alan Robinson	6
1	2	3	4	5	6	7	8*	9	10	11			12								D. Lloyd	7
1	2	3	4	5	6	7*	8	9	10	11			12								B. Stevens	8
1	2	3	4	5	6	7	8	9		11				10							H. King	9
1	2	3	4	5	6	7	8		10	11		12		9*							R. Chadwick	10
1	2	3	4	5	6	7		10		11			12	9	8*						A. Glasson	11
1	2	3	4	5	6	7	8*	10		11			12	9							J. Key	12
1	2	3	4	5	6	7	8*		10	11				9		12					J. Martin	13
1	2	3	4	5	6	7	8*	12	10	11				9							K. Baker	14
1	2	3		5	6	7*	8	4		11				9		10	12				J. Deakin	15
1	2	3		5	6	7	12	8	10	11				9				4*			I. Borrett	16
1	2	3		5	6	7		8	10	11				9					4		L. Shapter	17
1	2	3		5	6	7		8	10	11				9*					4		K. Walmsley	18
1	2	3		5	6	7		8	10*	11				9	12				4		T. Spencer	19
1	2	3		5	6	7	12	8	10	11				9					4		A. Robinson	20
1		3		5	6	7*	10	8		11	12			9			2		4		D. Hedges	21
1	2	3		5	6	7	12	8		11				9	10				4		J. Hunting	22
1	2	3		5	6	7	12	8		11*				9	10				4		C. Newsome	23
1	2	3	4	5	6	7		8		11				9	10						L. Burden	24
1	2	3	4	5	6	7		8		11				9	10						G. Napthine	25
1	2	3	4		6	7		8		11				9	10			5			B. Daniels	26
1	2	3	4		6	7		8	12	11				9*	10			5			M. Taylor	27
1	2	3	4		6	7		8	12	11				9*	10			5			R. Guy	28
1		3	4	5		7		8		11				9	10			6	2		D. Axcell	29
1		3*	4	5				8	7	11			12	9	10			6	2		K. Redfern	30
1	2	3	4	5	6	7		8	9	11					10						A. Gunn	31
1	2	3	4	5	6	7*		8	9	11				12	10						M. Dimblebee	32
1	2	3	4	5	6	7		8	9	11					10						C. Seel	33
1	2	3	4	5	6			8*	9	11				12	10			7			J. Martin	34
1	2	3	4	5	6	7		8	9	11					10						T. Bune	35
1	2	3	4	5	6			8	9	11					10			7			R. Nixon	36
1	2	3	4	5	6			8	9	11					10			7			A. Crickmore	37
1	2	3	4	5	6			8	9	11	12				10*			7			D. Allison	38
1	2	3	4	5	6			8	9	11					10			7			B. Hill	39
1	2	3	4	5	6	12		8	9	11					10*			7			A. Grey	40
1	2	3	4	5	6			8	9	11				10				7			J. Worrall	41
1	2	3	4	5				8	9	11	6				10*			7		12	D. Civil	42
42	39	42	33	39	39	33	15	39	29	42	1	0	0	23	21	1	1	14	9	0		
						+ 1s	+ 4s	+ 1s	+ 2s		+ 4s	+ 3s	+ 5s	+ 2s	+ 1s	+ 1s	+ 1s			+ 1s		

FOOTBALL LEAGUE RECORD

1920 Original Members of Division 3; 1921 Division 3(S); 1948–52 Division 2; 1952–58 Division 3(S); 1958–67 Division 3; 1967–68 Division 2; 1968–69 Division 1; 1969–73 Division 2; 1973–79 Division 1; 1979–83 Division 2; 1983– Division 1.

HONOURS

Football League: Division 1 – Runners-up 1975–76; Division 2 – Champions 1982–83; Runners-up 1967–68, 1972–73; Division 3(S) – Champions 1947–48; Runners-up 1946–47; Division 3 – Champions 1966–67. *FA Cup:* Runners-up 1982. *Football League Cup:* Winners 1966–67. (In 1966–67 won Division 3 and Football League Cup.) **European Competition:** *UEFA Cup:* 1976–77.

COLOURS

Blue and white hooped shirts, white shorts, white stockings with 3 blue bands at top.
Change colours: Red shorts, black shorts, black stockings with 4 red bands at top.

QUEENS PARK RANGERS

Players Names	*Birthplace*	*Clubs*	*Appearances*			*Goals*		
Ht, Wt, D.o.B.	*Transfer Fee*		*F.L. A & S*	*F.L.C. A & S*	*F.A.C. A & S*	*F.L.*	*F.L.C.*	*F.A.C.*
Goalkeepers								
Peter Hucker	London	QPR (A)	65	2	9			
6 4½, 13 0, 28.10.59								
Graham Benstead (EY)	Woking	QPR (A)			1			
6 2, 12 10, 20.8.63								
Defenders								
Glen Roeder (EB)	Woodford	Orient (A)	107+8	8	13	4		
6 2½, 12 8, 13.12.55	£250,000	QPR	156	13	11	17	1	
Bob Hazell (EU21)	Jamaica, WI	Wolverhampton W (A)	32+1		3	1		
6 1½, 14 1, 14.6.59	£240,000	QPR	94+6	11+1	6	8		1
Dean Wilkins*	Hillingdon	QPR (A)	1+5	1				
5 8½, 11 10, 12.7.62								
Warren Neill (ES)	Acton	QPR (A)	53+1	2+1	4+1	2		1
5 10½, 12 5, 21.11.62								
Martin Duffield (EY)		QPR (A)	+1					
5 10,								
Ian Dawes (ES)	Croydon	QPR (A)	47	2	1			
5 8, 10 12, 22.2.63								
Steve Wicks (EU21)	Reading	Chelsea (A)	117+1	3	5	5		2
6 2¼, 13 2, 3.10.56	£275,000	Derby Co	24	1				
	£300,000	QPR	73	5+1	3			
	£250,000	Crystal Palace	14		5	1		
	£250,000	QPR	23			1		
Doug McClure		QPR (A)						
5 9,								
Midfield								
Gary Waddock (EI)	Kingsbury	QPR (A)	105+12	8+1	12	4		
5 10, 11 12, 17.3.62								
Terry Fenwick (EU21)	Durham	Crystal Palace (A)	62+8	4+1	7			2
5 10, 10 11, 17.11.59	£100,000	QPR	94	6	11	10		2
John Gregory (E)	Scunthorpe	Northampton T (A)	187	8	7	8	1	1
6 1, 11 5, 11.5.54	£40,000	Aston Villa	59+6	5	2	10	1	
	£250,000	Brighton	72	6	3	7		
	£300,000	QPR	76	6	7	24	3	
Alan McDonald	Belfast	QPR (A)						
6 2½, 12 7, 12.10.63	—	Charlton Ath (loan)	9					
Mark O'Connor	Basildon	QPR (A)	2+1					
5 6, 9 10, 10.3.63								
Alan Comfort		QPR (A)						
5 8,								
Forwards								
Steve Burke (EY)	Nottingham	Nottingham F (A)						
5 10, 10 8, 29.9.60	£125,000	QPR	42+20	4+2	+3	5		
Gary Micklewhite	London	Manchester U (A)						
5 8, 9 10, 21.3.61	F/T	QPR	57+4	5+1	5+1	8	3	1
Ian Stewart (NI)	Belfast	QPR	17+6	+3	1+1			
5 6½, 11 9, 10.9.61	—	Millwall (loan)	10+1			3		
Wayne Fereday	Warley	QPR (A)	7+8	1	+1	2		
5 9½, 11 8, 16.6.63								
Tony Sealy	London	Southampton (A)	2+5					
5 8½, 10 11, 7.5.59	£50,000	Crystal Palace	16+8	+2	1	5		
	—	Port Vale (loan)	17			6		
	£75,000	QPR	51+4	3	1	18		
	—	Port Vale (loan)	6			4		
Clive Allen (EU21)	London	QPR (A)	43+6	5	1	32	2	
5 10, 11 0, 20.5.61	£1,250,000	Arsenal						
	£1,250,000	Crystal Palace	25	4		9		
	£425,000+P E	QPR	59+3	4	8	26	1	7
Ian Muir* (EY)	Coventry	QPR (A)	2			2		
5 6½, 10 9, 5.5.63	—	Burnley (loan)	1+1			1		
Mike Flanagan (EB)	Ilford	Tottenham H (Am)						
5 10½, 11 10, 9.11.52	—	Charlton Ath	241+13	23	16+1	85	7	3
	£650,000	Crystal Palace	56	7	1	8	4	
	£150,000	QPR	70+3	3	12	20	2	
Simon Stainrod (EY)	Sheffield	Sheffield U (A)	59+8	1+1	1+1	14		
6 1½, 11 11, 1.2.59	£60,000	Oldham Ath	69	3	1	21	1	
	£275,000	QPR	83+2	6	11	30	2	6

Commercial Manager: A. Ingham (Tel. 749 1890)
Club Coach: Allan Harris
Supporters Player of the Season 1982–83: John Gregory
Physiotherapist: D. Butler
Club Captain 1982–83: Terry Fenwick
Chief Scout: A. Warren
Club Statistician: Derek Buxton
Association of Football Statisticians Club Adviser to Yearbook: S. Fell

Players released since May 1982:
Tony Currie, M. (Toronto Bliz.).

READING Division 4

Back row (left to right):
Williams
Dixon
Hicks
Barnes
Sanchez
Nutton
Middle row:
Maurice Evans (Manager)
Doherty
White
Judge
Fearon
Wood
Bason
Stewart
Henderson (Coach)
Front row:
John
Earls
Beavon
Thompson
Donnellan
Richardson

Chairman: Roger Smee. ***Vice-Chairman:*** J. H. Brooks.
Directors: R. Tranter, R. Cox.

Manager: Maurice Evans. ***Secretary/Manager:*** Roy Bentley.

Year Formed: 1871. ***Turned Professional:*** 1895. ***Ltd Co.:*** 1895.

Club Nickname: 'The Royals'.

Previous Grounds: 1871, Reading Recreation; Reading Cricket Ground; 1882, Coley Park; 1889, Caversham Cricket Ground; 1896, Elm Park.

Previous Managers since the War: Joe Edelston, Ted Drake, Jack Smith, Harry Johnston, Roy Bentley, Jack Mansell, Charlie Hurley (7).

Elm Park, Norfolk Road, Reading. Telephone 0734-57878/9/0. ***Ground capacity:*** 27,200. ***Record attendance:*** 33,042 v Brentford, FA Cup 5th rd, 19 Feb, 1927. ***Record receipts:*** £25,972 v Southampton, League Cup 4th rd, 8 Nov, 1978. ***Pitch measurements:*** 112yd×77yd.

Directions to Ground: Corporation specials from St Mary's Butts (town centre) and from Northumberland Avenue. Usual buses within a few minutes of the ground. Nearest railway station, Reading.

Match tickets: Stand tickets are bookable in advance for all first-team matches 14 days before the match.

Car parking: Space is available for approximately 300 cars adjoining the ground entrance in Norfolk Road and Tilehurst Road.

Entertainments/catering facilities: Catering is available in each of the five stands and also on the terraces.

Club shop: Shops in Norfolk Road and on the West Terrace are open on match days selling all types of souvenirs.

Handbooks/programmes: The Supporters' Club produces a handbook and these are available on application to the club. Unsold programmes are available after each match at the programme shop on the West Terrace.

Address of Supporters Club: Reading Football Supporters Club, Elm Park, Norfolk Road, Reading.

Note: Full club statistical records are on pages 416–455.

READING 1982–83 LEAGUE RECORD

Match No.	Date	Venue	Opponents	Result		H/T Score	Lg. Pos.	Goalscorers	Attendance
1	Aug 28	A	Bradford C	L	2-3	2-2	—	Beavon, Dixon	5001
2	Sept 4	H	Plymouth Arg	W	3-2	2-0	9	Earles, Dixon 2	2102
3	8	H	Brentford	D	1-1	1-0	—	Dixon	3555
4	11	A	Lincoln C	L	0-4	0-1	17		2790
5	18	H	Chesterfield	D	0-0	0-0	17		1927
6	25	A	Doncaster R	L	5-7	3-5	22	Dixon 4, Robinson	3118
7	28	A	Gillingham	L	0-1	0-0	—		3621
8	Oct 2	H	Preston NE	L	2-3	2-1	24	Dixon 2	1713
9	9	H	Orient	W	3-0	1-0	23	Earles 2, Robinson	2539
10	15	A	Southend U	L	2-4	2-3	—	Dixon, Earles	3688
11	19	A	Sheffield U	D	1-1	0-0	—	Beavon	11,971
12	23	H	Wigan Ath	W	2-1	0-1	18	Dixon, Doherty	2621
13	30	A	Bristol R	L	0-3	0-1	21		7270
14	Nov 3	H	Cardiff C	L	1-2	1-1	—	Sanchez	2982
15	6	H	Newport Co	W	4-2	3-2	20	Dixon 3, Stant	3058
16	13	A	Walsall	L	1-2	0-1	19	Stant	2343
17	28	A	Millwall	D	1-1	0-0	—	Earles	3578
18	Dec 4	H	Exeter C	W	3-1	2-1	18	Dixon 2, Beavon	1971
19	11	A	Exeter C	D	2-2	2-1	18	Dixon 2	2272
20	18	H	Huddersfield T	D	1-1	0-0	17	Dixon	2468
21	27	A	AFC Bournemouth	D	1-1	0-1	18	Tutty	6118
22	28	H	Portsmouth	L	1-2	0-0	19	Dixon	7646
23	Jan 1	A	Wrexham	L	0-4	0-2	20		3390
24	3	H	Oxford U	L	0-3	0-2	22		6154
25	15	H	Bradford C	W	2-1	1-0	22	Matthews, Doherty	2050
26	22	A	Chesterfield	D	0-0	0-0	21		2703
27	29	H	Lincoln C	D	1-1	1-0	21	Barnes	2453
28	Feb 1	A	Plymouth Arg	L	0-3	0-2	—		3504
29	5	H	Doncaster R	W	2-0	0-0	20	Williams, Doherty	1852
30	12	A	Brentford	W	2-1	2-0	19	Williams, Price	6273
31	20	A	Orient	D	3-3	2-1	—	Beavon, Doherty, Richardson	2538
32	23	H	Sheffield U	W	2-0	0-0	—	King (og), Donnellan	2375
33	26	H	Southend U	D	1-1	0-0	15	Donnellan	2664
34	Mar 1	A	Cardiff C	D	0-0	0-0	—		6173
35	5	A	Wigan Ath	D	2-2	1-0	16	Doherty, Barnes	3042
36	12	H	Bristol R	L	1-2	0-0	18	Dixon	4270
37	19	A	Newport Co	L	0-1	0-1	20		3588
38	25	H	Walsall	D	1-1	1-1	—	Dixon	3107
39	Apr 2	A	Portsmouth	D	2-2	1-1	20	Price, Earles	15,327
40	4	H	AFC Bournemouth	W	2-1	1-1	—	Hicks, White	4424
41	16	H	Gillingham	D	0-0	0-0	20		2566
42	23	A	Huddersfield T	L	1-3	1-2	21	Price	10,885
43	30	H	Millwall	D	3-3	3-1	20	Earles, Price, Dixon	4401
44	May 2	A	Oxford U	W	2-1	0-0	20	Jones (og), Dixon (pen)	6739
45	7	A	Preston NE	L	0-2	0-2	21		7253
46	14	H	Wrexham	W	1-0	1-0	21	Dixon	5252

Final League Position: 21

GOALSCORERS

League (64): Dixon 26 (1 pen), Earles 7, Doherty 5, Beavon 4, Price 4, Barnes 2, Donnellan 2, Robinson 2, Stant 2, Williams 2, Hicks 1, Matthews 1, Richardson 1, Sanchez 1, Tutty 1, White 1, own goals 2.
Milk Cup (0).
FA Cup (1): Earles 1.
Football League Trophy (15): Dixon 6, Donnellan 4, Beavon 2 (2 pens), Doherty 1, Donnellan 1, O'Sullivan 1.

Milk Cup	First Round	Oxford U (h)	0-2
		(a)	0-2
FA Cup	First Round	Bishop's Stortford (h)	1-2
Football League Trophy		Oxford U (h)	2-1
		AFC Bournemouth (h)	4-2
		Aldershot (a)	3-3
	Quarter-final	Watford (h)	5-3
	Semi-final	Millwall (h)	1-3

Fearon	Williams	White	Beavon	Hicks	Wood	Earles	Kearney	Dixon	Bason	Donnellan	Judge (L)	Richardson	Sanchez	Barnes	McMahon	Robinson (L)	Dawtry	Henderson	Doherty	Stant	O'Sullivan (L)	Tutty	Matthews	Price	Nutton (L)	*Referees*	*Match No.*
1	2	3	4	5	6	7	8	9	10	11																D. Allison	1
	2*	12	4	5	6	8		9	7	11	1	3	10													B. Daniels	2
		3	4	5	6	8		9	7	11	1	2	10													J. Bray	3
		3	4	5		8		9	7*	11	1	2	10	6	12											T. Jones	4
1	2		4		6	7		9	10			3		5		8	11									J. Deakin	5
1	2	12	4			7		9	10*			3	6	5		8	11									K. Redfern	6
1	2	6	4			8		9					10	5		11	7	3								M. James	7
1	2	6	4			8		9					10	5		11	7	3								D. Axcell	8
1	2	6	4	5		8		9	7			3	10			11										V. Callow	9
1	2		4	5	6	8		9	7	12		3	10			11*										A. Gunn	10
1	2		4	5	6	8		9	7			3	10						11							N. Wilson	11
1	2	12	4	5	6	8*		9	7			3	10						11							A. Glasson	12
1	2		4	5*	6		8	9	7	12		3	10*						11							T. Spencer	13
1	2	12	4	5	6		8	9	7			3*	10						11							D. Vickers	14
1	2	3	4	5			6	9	7	11									10	8						M. Taylor	15
1	2	3	4	5			6	9	7*	11			12						10	8						A. Challinor	16
	2	3	4		6	8		9	7	11	1			5							10					J. Hunting	17
	2		4		6	8		9	7	11*	1	3	12	5							10					E. Scales	18
	2		4	5	6			9	7	11*	1	3	8						12		10					B. Stevens	19
	2		4	5	6	12		9	7	11*	1	3	8								10					M. Bodenham	20
			4	5	6	11		9	7*	12	1	3	8								10	2				Alan Robinson	21
	2		4	5	6	11		9	7	12	1	3	8*								10					D. Lloyd	22
		3	4	5	6	8			10		1	2	9						7*		11	12				D. Shaw	23
			4	5	6	8			7		1	3	10*						9	12	11	2				D. Reeves	24
	9	3	4	5	6	8			10		1	2							11				7			I. Borrett	25
	9	6	4	5		8			10		1	3							11			2	7			G. Courtney	26
	8	3	4	5*					10		1	2		6					7		11		12	9		A. Crickmore	27
	5	6	4						10		1	3			12				11	8		2	7*	9		S. Bates	28
	8	3	4						10		1	2		5					11			12	7*	9	6	K. Salmon	29
	8	3	4						10		1	2	11	5					7					9	6	J. Deakin	30
	8	3	4							10	1	2	11	5					7					9	6	A. Seville	31
	8	3*	4						10	12	1	2	11	5					7					9	6	K. Barrett	32
	6		4			8			10	2	1	3	11	5					7					9		H. King	33
	2		4					9	10	8	1	3	11	5					7						6	R. Milford	34
	2		4					9	10	8	1	3*	11	5				12	7						6	F. Roberts	35
	2	6	4	5				9	10		1	3	11						7					8		T. Holbrook	36
	2	6	4	5				9	10		1	3	11						7					8		J. Worrall	37
	2	6	4	5		7		9	10		1	3	11											8		J. Moules	38
	2	6	4	5		7		9	10		1	3	11											8		C. Thomas	39
	2	6	4	5		7		9*	10		1	3	11	12										8		B. Stevens	40
	2	6	4	5		7		9	10		1	3	11						12					8*		C. Downey	41
	2*	6	4	5		7		9	10		1	3	11	12										8		R. Chadwick	42
	2		4	5		7		9			1	3	10	6					11					8		M. James	43
	2		4	5		7		9			1	3	11	6				8	10							J. Hunting	44
	2		4	5		7		9	10		1	3	11	6										8		K. Hackett	45
	3		4	5		7		9	10		1	2	11	6*				12						8		A. Gunn	46
13	41	25	46	32	18	30	5	35	41	14	33	40	35	19	0	6	4	3	23	3	9	4	4	17	6		
		+ 4s				+ 1s				+ 5s			+ 2s	+ 2s	+ 2s			+ 2s	+ 2s	+ 1s		+ 2s	+ 1s				

FOOTBALL LEAGUE RECORD

1920 Original Member of Division 3; 1921–26 Division 3(S); 1926–31 Division 2; 1931–58 Division 3(S); 1958–71 Division 3; 1971–76 Division 4; 1976–77 Division 3; 1977–79 Division 4; 1979–83 Division 3; 1983– Division 4.

HONOURS

Football League: Division 2 best season: 14th, 1926–27; Division 3(S) – Champions 1925–26; Runners-up 1931–32, 1934–35, 1948–49, 1951–52; Division 4 – Champions 1978–79. *FA Cup:* semi-final 1927. *Football League Cup* best season: 4th rd, 1965, 1966, 1978.

COLOURS

Blue and white hooped shirts, white shorts, white stockings with two blue rings. **Change colours:** All yellow.

READING

Players Names Ht. Wt. D.o.B.	Birthplace Transfer Fee	Clubs	Appearances F.L. A & S	 F.L.C. A & S	 F.A.C. A & S	Goals F.L.	 F.L.C.	 F.A.C.
Goalkeeper								
Ron Fearon	Romford	QPR						
6 0, 12 2, 19.11.60	F/T	Reading	61	4	2			
Defenders								
Martin Hicks	Stratford-on-Avon	Stratford T						
6 3, 13 6, 27.2.57	—	Charlton Ath						
	£3000	Reading	168+1	12	7	9		
Stewart Henderson* (SS)	Bridge of Allen	Chelsea						
5 8, 11 9, 5.6.47	F/T	Brighton	198	14	14	1		
	F/T	Reading	159+5	11	4	8		
Mark White	Sheffield	Sheffield U (A)						
5 10, 11 12, 26.10.58	F/T	Reading	153+6	13	9	1		
Steve Wood	Bracknell	Reading (A)	57+1	3	2			
6 1, 12 7, 2.2.63								
Mike Barnes	Reading	Reading (A)	24+4	1		2		
6 4, 13 4, 17.9.63								
Jerry Williams	Didcot	Reading (A)	134+13	6	3	9	1	
5 11, 11 10, 24.3.60								
Steve Richardson	Slough	Southampton (A)						
5 5, 10 3, 11.2.62	F/T	Reading	40	1+1		1		
Midfield								
Stewart Beavon	Wolverhampton	Tottenham H (A)	3+1	+1				
5 6½, 10 6, 30.11.58	—	Notts Co (Loan)	6					
	£40,000	Reading	120+3	7+1	3	15		
Brian Bason* (ES)	Epsom	Chelsea (A)	18+1	2		1		
5 9½, 12 0, 3.9.55	£30,000	Plymouth Arg	127+3	11	5	10	1	
	£80,000	Crystal Palace	25+2	4				
	—	Portsmouth (Loan)	9					
	F/T	Reading	41	2	1			
Mike Doherty*		Basingstoke						
5 7, 10 0,	£3000	Reading	23+2		1	5		
Forwards								
Pat Earles* (ES)	Tichfield	Southampton (A)	4+8	1	+1	1	1	
5 7, 11 6, 22.3.55	£12,500	Reading	240+7	18	8+1	68	10	6
Mike Kearney*	Glasgow	Peterhill						
6 0, 12 0, 18.2.53		Shrewsbury T	143+6	8	9	41		2
		Chester	37+1	4	2	5	1	1
	£40,000	Reading	78+9	4	7	24	1	6
	£50,000	Chester	9					
	£50,000	Reading	57+1	3		12		
Lawrie Sanchez	Lambeth	Reading	189+13	17+1	11	16		1
6 1, 12 0, 22.10.59								
Kerry Dixon	Luton	Dunstable T						
6 0, 13 0, 24.7.61	£20,000	Reading	110+6	6+1	2+1	51		
Gary Donnellan*	London	Chelsea (A)						
5 8, 12 0, 3.7.62	F/T	Watford						
	£5000	Reading	33+8	2	1	5		
Ken Price	Dudley	Dudley T						
5 10, 11 10, 26.2.54	£1000	Southend U	1					
	F/T	Gillingham	247+3	15+2	20+1	79	7	4
	£10,000	Reading	17			4		
Non-contract players								
Wayne Tutty		Banbury T						
5 9, 10 7,	F/T	Reading	4+2			1		
Mark Matthews								
5 6, 9 0,		Reading	5+1			1		

Commercial Manager: Albert Moss (c/o Club)
Club Coach:
Supporters Player of the Season 1982–83: Steve Richardson
Physiotherapist: Glen Hunter
Association of Football Statisticians Club Adviser to Yearbook: D. Downs

Club Captain 1982–83: Martin Hicks
Chief Scout:
Club Statistician: D. Downs

Players released since May 1982:
Jon Cullen, D. (Larnaca, Cyprus); Alan Lewis, M. (Witney T); Gary Heale, F. (Sparta Rotterdam); Phil Stant, F. (N/C—Army); Des McMahon, F. (Wokingham).

ROCHDALE Division 4

Back row (left to right): J. Greenhoff (Manager), B. Greenhoff, E. Snookes, A. Higgins, C. Pearce, M. French, M. Hilditch, B. Taylor, B. Williams, S. Thompson, R. Greaves (Player/Coach)
Front row: A. Weir, P. Farrell, N. Hamilton, E. Martinez, G. Keenan, E. Carr.

Chairman: D. F. Kilpatrick.

Directors: G. Morris FCA, C. W. Walkden, W. H. C. Dronsfield.

Manager: Jimmy Greenhoff. ***Secretary:*** Bill Kenyon.

Year Formed: 1907. ***Turned Professional:*** 1907. ***Ltd Co.:*** 1910.

Club Nickname: 'The Dale'.

Previous Managers since 1946: Ted Goodier, Jack Warner, Harry Catterick, Jack Marshall, Tony Collins, Bob Stokoe, Len Richley, Dick Conner, Walter Joyce, Brian Green, Mike Ferguson, Doug Collins, Bob Stokoe, Peter Madden (14).

Spotland, Willbutts Lane, Rochdale OL11 5DR. Telephone 0706-44648/9. ***Ground capacity:*** 28,000. ***Record attendance:*** 24,231 v Notts County, FA Cup 2nd rd, 10 Dec, 1949. ***Record receipts:*** £5330 v Sheffield U, Division 4, 16 Jan, 1982. ***Pitch measurements:*** 113yd×75yd.

Directions to Ground: Bus station – Norden for Churchill Street; Greave for ground.

Match tickets: Seats can be reserved in advance.

Car parking: Car parking at the ground and in the adjacent side-streets.

Entertainments/catering facilities: A social club in the car park.

Club shop: Sells all types of souvenirs and programmes.

Handbooks/programmes: 'Forward with the Dale – A History of Rochdale AFC' £1.25 (inc P+P) from Club Shop.

Extra information: Social club.

Address of Supporters Club: Rochdale AFC Soccer Shop, Spotland, Sandy Lane, Rochdale.

Note: Full club statistical records are on pages 416–455.

ROCHDALE 1982–83 LEAGUE RECORD

Match No.	Date	Venue	Opponents	Result	H/T Score	Lg. Pos.	Goalscorers	Attendance
1	Aug 28	A	Darlington	L 0-3	0-2	—		1672
2	Sept 4	H	Chester	L 0-1	0-1	24		1489
3	7	H	Hartlepool U	W 2-0	0-0	—	Stafford, Wellings	1075
4	10	A	Colchester U	L 1-4	1-2	—	Wellings (pen)	2638
5	18	H	Swindon T	D 1-1	1-1	21	Hilditch	1292
6	25	A	Mansfield T	L 1-2	1-2	22	Comstive	2001
7	27	A	Stockport Co	D 2-2	0-1	—	Hamilton, Farrell	1873
8	Oct 2	H	Bury	D 0-0	0-0	21		3207
9	8	A	Crewe Alex	D 1-1	0-1	—	French	1806
10	16	H	Blackpool	W 3-1	1-1	18	Hilditch, Wellings, Comstive	2001
11	19	A	Wimbledon	L 0-3	0-1	—		2294
12	23	H	Halifax T	D 2-2	0-2	20	Hilditch, Thompson D.	1765
13	30	A	Hereford U	L 0-1	0-0	19		2404
14	Nov 2	H	Northampton T	W 2-0	1-0	—	Keenan, Hamilton	1029
15	6	H	Port Vale	D 3-3	1-0	17	French, Wellings 2	2234
16	13	A	Peterborough U	L 0-1	0-1	19		2245
17	27	A	Torquay U	L 2-3	1-1	20	Hilditch, Hamilton	2409
18	Dec 4	H	Bristol C	W 1-0	0-0	19	Farrell	1307
19	11	H	Wimbledon	L 0-2	0-1	20		1096
20	18	H	Aldershot	W 3-1	2-0	15	Thompson D., Martinez, French (pen)	1003
21	27	A	Scunthorpe U	D 1-1	1-0	17	French (pen)	4845
22	28	H	York C	W 1-0	0-0	18	Farrell	2127
23	Jan 1	A	Hull C	L 1-2	0-1	17	Thompson D.	9259
24	3	H	Tranmere R	W 4-2	3-1	14	Mooney (og), Hilditch, McElhinney, Martinez	1758
25	8	A	Chester	L 2-5	1-1	15	French, Zelem (og)	1562
26	15	H	Darlington	D 1-1	1-0	16	Farrell	1233
27	22	A	Swindon T	L 1-4	1-1	17	Hilditch	4425
28	Feb 5	H	Mansfield T	D 2-2	1-1	17	Thompson D., Farrell	1028
29	12	A	Bury	D 0-0	0-0	17		4376
30	26	A	Blackpool	L 0-1	0-1	20		2373
31	Mar 4	A	Halifax T	D 0-0	0-0	—		2128
32	12	H	Hereford U	W 4-1	1-0	21	French 3, Thompson S.	2000
33	15	H	Crewe Alex	W 2-0	1-0	—	Thompson S., Farrell	2497
34	19	A	Port Vale	L 0-4	0-1	18		5129
35	26	H	Peterborough U	D 1-1	0-0	21	Higgins	1560
36	Apr 2	A	York C	L 0-1	0-1	21		3357
37	4	H	Scunthorpe U	L 0-1	0-0	—		2056
38	9	A	Bristol C	D 0-0	0-0	22		4772
39	16	H	Stockport Co	W 1-0	1-0	20	French (pen)	1834
40	19	A	Northampton T	D 1-1	1-0	—	French	1728
41	23	A	Aldershot	L 4-6	1-3	21	Farrell 2, Hilditch, Thompson D.	1651
42	26	H	Colchester U	W 2-1	2-0	—	Higgins, French	1219
43	30	H	Torquay U	D 2-2	1-2	18	Farrell, Thompson S.	1382
44	May 7	A	Hartlepool U	L 0-3	0-0	20		1013
45	14	H	Hull C	L 1-3	1-2	21	Martinez	2659
46	16	A	Tranmere R	D 0-0	0-0	20		1982

Final League Position: 20

GOALSCORERS

League (55): French 11 (3 pens), Farrell 9, Hilditch 7, Thompson D. 5, Wellings 5 (1 pen), Hamilton 3, Martinez 3, Thompson S. 3, Comstive 2, Higgins 2, Keenan 1, McElhinney 1, Stafford 1, own goals 2.
Milk Cup (2): Wellings 2 (1 pen).
FA Cup (1): Wellings 1 (pen).

Milk Cup	First Round	Port Vale (a)	0-1
		(h)	2-0
	Second Round	Bradford C (h)	0-1
		(a)	0-4
FA Cup	First Round	Altrincham (a)	1-2

Pearce	Warriner	Trainer	Weir	Snookes	Blair	Thompson D.	French	Hamilton	Wellings	Farrell	Martinez	Williams	Hilditch	Keenan	Comstive (L)	Garner (L)	Taylor	Greaves	Swan (L)	McElhinney (L)	Nicholson	Thompson S.	Greenhoff J.	Greenhoff B.	Carr	Higgins	Crawford	*Referees*
1	2	3	4	5	6	7*	8	9	10	11	12																	J. Key
1		5*	6	3	2	12	9	8	10	7		4	11															K. Redfern
1	2	4		3	5	7*	12		10	8		6	9															M. Heath
1	2	5	4*	3		12	9	7	11	8		6	10															D. Brazier
1	2	5				7	9	8	10	4	12	6	11	3*														C. Seel
1		5				7		8	10	4	11	6	9	2	3													D. Civil
1		5				7		8	10	4	11	6	9	2	3													H. Taylor
1				3		7		8	10	4		6	9	2	11	5												R. Willis
1				3		7	9	8	10	4		6	11	2		5												G. Napthine
1				3		7	9		10	4		6	11	2	8	5												F. Roberts
1				3		7	9		10	4	12	6	11	2	8		5*											L. Burden
1				3		7	9*		10	4	12	6	11	2	8	5												A. Seville
1			5	3		7	9	8	10		4	6	11*	2														A. Crickmore
1				3		7	9	4	10		11	6	8	2					5									N. Ashley
1				3		7	9		10	4		6	11	2				8	5									G. Courtney
1				3		7	9		10	4	12	6	11	2*				8	5									M. Robinson
1			9	3		12		7*	10	4	8		11	2						5	6							B. Stevens
1			12	3		7		11	10	4			9	2				8		5*	6							A. Challinor
1				8		6			11*	7		5	10	2				9		4	3	12						T. Holbrook
1				3		7	9			4	11	6	10	2				8		5								D. Hutchinson
1				3		7	10			4	11	6	9	2				8		5								J. Bray
1				3		7	9		12	4	11	6	10	2*				8		5								J. Lovatt
1				3		7	10		9	4	11	6	2					8		5								D. Civil
1				3		7	9		12	4	11	6	10					8*		5	2							K. Hackett
1			8	3		7	9		12	4	11*	6	10							5	2							C. Thomas
1				3		7	9			4	11	6	10					8		5	2							D. Owen
1				3		7	9		12	4	11*	6	10					8		5	2							D. Brazier
1				3		7	9			4	11	6	10	2				8		5								A. Hamil
1				5		10	11			7			6	2	9		4	8		3								D. Allinson
1				3		7	9			4		12	10	2	11		6	8*		5								N. Glover
1				3		7	9					2	10		11		6	4		5		8						M. Taylor
1				3		7	9			4	11		12				6	2		5		8	10*					C. Seel
1				3		7	9			4	11						6	2		5		8	10					R. Bridge
1			9	3*		7				4			11				6	2		5		12	10	8				D. Lloyd
1						7				4	11			2			6			5		8	10		3	9		B. Newsome
1						7				4	11	5		2			6*	12				8	10		3	9		A. Saunders
						7				4	11	6		2						5		8	10*		3	9	1	T. Mills
						7	9			4		6	11	2									10	8	3	5	1	D. Hedges
						7	9			4		6	11	2									10	8	3	5	1	K. Redfern
						7	9	8		4		6	11										10	2	3	5	1	J. Moules
						7	9	8*		4		6	11				5	12					10	2	3		1	R. Milford
						7	9			4	11			3			6					8	10	2		5	1	M. Peck
						7	9			4	11	12		3			6					8	10*	2		5	1	D. Hedges
				3		7	9			4	11	6	10*				12					8			2	5	1	M. Scott
						7	9			4	11	6	10	2								8			3	5	1	F. Roberts
				3		7	9			4	11	12	10	2			6*	8								5	1	J. Worrall
36	4	7	7	33	3	43	35	14	20	43	24	34	38	30	9	4	13	19	3	20	7	10	12	7	9	11	10	
			+ 1s			+ 3s	+ 1s		+ 4s		+ 5s	+ 3s	+ 1s				+ 1s	+ 2s					+ 2s					

Also played: O'Connor (no. 12, match 37); Thomas (no. 12, match 13); Stafford (no. 11, match 3).

FOOTBALL LEAGUE RECORD

1921 Elected to Division 3(N); 1958–59 Division 3; 1959–60 Division 4; 1969–74 Division 3; 1974– Division 4.

HONOURS

Football League: Division 3 best season: 9th, 1969–70; Division 3(N) – Runners-up 1923–24, 1926–27. *FA Cup* best season: 4th rd, 1970–71. *Football League Cup:* Runners-up 1962 (record for 4th Division club).

COLOURS

Royal blue shirts, white shorts, blue stockings with white trim.
Change colours: White shirts, blue shorts, white stockings.

ROCHDALE

Players Names *Ht, Wt, D.o.B.*	*Birthplace* *Transfer Fee*	*Clubs*	*Appearances* *F.L.* *A & S*	*F.L.C.* *A & S*	*F.A.C.* *A & S*	*Goals* *F.L.*	*F.L.C.*	*F.A.C.*
Goalkeepers								
Chris Pearce* (WS)	Newport	Wolverhampton W (A)						
6 0, 11 4, 7.8.61	F/T	Blackburn R						
	—	Rochdale (loan)	5	2				
	F/T	Rochdale	36	4	1			
Defenders								
Gerry Keenan*	Liverpool							
5 9, 11 0, 25.7.54		Bury	69+2	10	4	3		
	£15,000	Port Vale	105+1	6	2	7		
	F/T	Rochdale	30	2	1	1		
Eric Snookes*	Birmingham	Preston NE (A)	20		1			
5 7, 10 0, 6.3.55	F/T	Crewe Alex	33+1	3	2			
	F/T	Southport	104+4	10	3	2	3	
	£1000	Rochdale	183	11	10	1		
Brian Taylor*	Hodthorpe	Middlesbrough (A)	14+4	1+1		1		
5 11, 11 9, 12.2.54		Doncaster R	118+1	9	3	12	1	
	F/T	Rochdale	152+2	5	7	10		
Alan Weir* (EY)	South Shields	Sunderland (A)	1					
5 6, 9 8, 1.9.59	£12,000	Rochdale	96+10	6	7	3		
Bill Williams	Rochdale	Rochdale	38+5	4				
5 10, 12 7,								
Everton Carr*	Antigua, W.I.	Leicester C (A)	11+1	2				
5 7, 11 6, 11.1.61	F/T	Halifax T	35+3	4	1			
	F/T	Rochdale	9					
Midfield								
Eugene Martinez*	Chelmsford							
5 8, 10 10, 6.7.57		Bradford C	38+14	1+1	4+1	5		1
	F/T	Rochdale	110+6	5+1	5	16	1	
Neville Hamilton	Leicester	Leicester C (A)	4					
5 8, 10 0, 19.4.60	£25,000	Mansfield T	84+5	5+1	5	4	1	
	F/T	Rochdale	34+1	3+2	+1	4		
Peter Farrell	Liverpool							
5 7, 10 9, 10.1.57		Bury	49+5	3+2	2	9		
	£40,000	Port Vale	85+4	2	6	10		
	F/T	Rochdale	43	3		9		
Roy Greaves*	Farnworth	Bolton W	487+7	41	39	66	9	10
5 11, 11 12, 4.4.47	F/T	Seattle Sounders						
	F/T	Rochdale	19+2		1			
Forwards								
Mark Hilditch*	Royton	Rochdale	184+13	10	11	40	1	3
5 11, 11 8, 20.8.60								
Micky French* (EY)	Eastbourne	QPR (A)						
6 0, 12 4, 7.5.55	£2000	Brentford	56+9	4	2	16		
	£7000	Swindon T	5+5	1		1		
	P/E	Doncaster R	36	3	2	5		
	F/T	Aldershot	70+4	2	4+2	16	1	1
	F/T	Rochdale	35+1	3	1	11		
Stuart Thompson (ES)		Rochdale (A)	10+2			3		
Non-contract Players								
Geoff Thomas		Rochdale	+1					
Malcolm O'Connor		Rochdale	+1					
Dave Thompson		Rochdale	44+4	3	1	5		
5 9, 11 6,								
Jimmy Greenhoff (EU21)	Barnsley	Leeds U (A)	90+6	12	9+1	19	4	1
5 9, 12 0 9.6.46	£75,000	Birmingham C	31		5	14		1
	£100,000	Stoke C	274	29	20	76	9	11
	£120,000	Manchester U	94+3	3	18	26	1	9
	F/T	Crewe Alex	11			4		
	F/T	Toronto Bliz.						
	F/T	Port Vale	44+4	2+1	4+1	5		
	F/T	Rochdale	12					
Andy Higgins	Bolsover	Chesterfield	1					
6 3, 12 4, 12.2.60	F/T	Port Vale	11+3	+1	2			
	F/T	Hartlepool U	3+1	1		1		
	F/T	Rochdale	11			2		

Commercial Manager: Brian Johnson (Tel. Rochdale 0706 44648)
Club Coach:
Club Captain 1982–83: B. Taylor
Supporters Player of the Season 1982–83: Dave Thompson
Chief Scout: T. Nichol
Physiotherapist:
Club Statistician: B. Clough
Association of Football Statisticians Club Adviser to Yearbook: S. Birch.

Players released since May 1982:
Peter Burke, D. (N/K); Terry Cooper, D. (N/K); Terry Dolan, M. (N/K); Dave Esser, F. (N/K); Darren Lambert, D. (N/K); Nigel O'Loughlin, M. (N/K); Mick Poole, G. (N/K); Jack Trainer, D. (N/K); Andy Stafford, F. (N/K); William Garner, D. (on loan—Celtic); Graeme Crawford, G. (N/C—N/K); Ron Blair, M. (N/C—N/K); Brian Greenhoff, D. (N/C—N/K).

ROTHERHAM UNITED — Division 3

Back row (left to right): Ian Alexander, Ian Vaughan, Rod Fern, Ronnie Moore, Robert Mimms, Ray Mountford, Paul Stancliffe, Nigel Johnson, Gerry Forrest, Ashley Taylor
Middle row: Barry Claxton (Asst Manager), Emlyn Hughes OBE (Manager), Tony Morton (Youth Coach), Mark Rhodes, Joe McBride, Gerry Gow, John Breckin, John Green, John Seasman, Tony Towner, Mick Gooding, Peter Carr
Front row: Mick Cronly, Neil Benton, Gary Ingham, John Durham, Gordon Brown, John McFadzean.

Chairman: Anton Johnson.

Directors: C. R. Wright, J. Layden.

Player-Manager: George Kerr. ***Secretary:*** J. E. Bennison.

Year Formed: 1884. ***Turned Professional:*** 1905. ***Ltd Co.:*** 1920.

Club Nickname: 'The Merry Millers'.

Previous Names: 1884, Thornhill United; 1905, Rotherham County; 1925, amalgamated with Rotherham Town under Rotherham United.

Previous Grounds: Red House Ground; 1907, Millmoor.

Previous Managers since 1946: Reg Freeman, Andy Smailes, Tom Johnston, Danny Williams, Jack Mansell, Tommy Docherty, Jimmy McAnearney, Jimmy McGuigan, Ian Porterfield, Emlyn Hughes (10).

Millmoor Ground, Rotherham. Telephone Rotherham (0709) 562434. ***Telegraphic address:*** 'Holmes Millmoor, Rotherham'. ***Ground capacity:*** 21,000. ***Record attendance:*** 25,000 v Sheffield U, Division 2, 13 Dec, 1952 and v Sheffield W, Division 2, 26 Jan, 1952. ***Record receipts:*** £34,217 v Sheffield W, Division 2, 4 May, 1982. ***Pitch measurements:*** 115yd×76yd.

Directions to Ground: Corporation buses from town centre. Also regular service buses from Sheffield to town centre. Nearest railway station, Rotherham on Sheffield line. Station opposite ground.

Match tickets: Seats can be reserved one month before the match.

Car parking: There are parks in Kimberworth Road and Main St (the municipal car park); both are within easy reach of the ground.

Entertainments/catering facilities: There are refreshment kiosks on all four sides of the ground and also behind the grandstand, and the Windmill where meals may be obtained if booked in advance and drinks are served during licensing hours.

Club shop: Sited on the forecourt of the ground; stocks all types of souvenirs.

Handbooks/programmes: No handbook, but programmes may be obtained from the club or the club shop.

Address of Supporters Club: Red and White Shop, c/o Millmoor, Rotherham.

Note: Full club statistical records are on pages 416–455.

ROTHERHAM UNITED 1982–83 LEAGUE RECORD

Match No.	Date	Venue	Opponents	Result		H/T Score	Lg. Pos.	Goalscorers	Attendance
1	Aug 28	A	Fulham	D	1-1	1-1	—	McBride	7021
2	31	H	Leicester C	L	1-3	1-1	—	Gow	9254
3	Sept 4	H	Crystal Palace	D	2-2	2-0	18	Seasman, Hughes (pen)	6989
4	7	A	Oldham Ath	D	1-1	0-0	—	Hughes (pen)	4261
5	11	A	Burnley	W	2-1	1-0	12	Fern 2	9099
6	18	H	Cambridge U	W	2-0	1-0	8	Fern 2	6654
7	25	A	Wolverhampton W	L	0-2	0-1	10		16,377
8	Oct 2	H	Newcastle U	L	1-5	0-2	16	McBride	12,436
9	9	A	Bolton W	D	2-2	1-2	15	Seasman, Gow	6577
10	16	H	Barnsley	W	1-0	1-0	11	Seasman	13,791
11	23	A	Shrewsbury T	L	0-2	0-0	15		3926
12	30	H	Middlesbrough	D	1-1	0-1	14	Moore	8135
13	Nov 6	H	QPR	D	0-0	0-0	17		7402
14	13	A	Carlisle U	D	2-2	1-1	18	Gooding, Green	5294
15	20	A	Charlton Ath	W	5-1	2-1	14	McBride, Moore 3 (1 pen), Towner	6761
16	27	H	Chelsea	W	1-0	0-0	11	Seasman	8793
17	Dec 4	A	Derby Co	L	0-3	0-1	13		13,149
18	11	H	Leeds U	L	1-1	0-0	15		13,034
19	18	A	Blackburn R	L	0-3	0-0	17		6333
20	27	H	Grimsby T	W	3-0	2-0	16	Bonnyman (og), Walker 2	9231
21	28	A	Sheffield W	W	1-0	0-0	13	McBride	25,024
22	Jan 1	H	Charlton Ath	W	1-0	0-0	9	Fern	8798
23	3	A	Crystal Palace	D	1-1	1-0	10	Gow	7704
24	15	H	Fulham	L	0-1	0-1	11		7667
25	22	A	Cambridge U	L	0-2	0-1	13		3090
26	29	H	Oldham Ath	L	1-3	1-1	13	Hughes (pen)	6392
27	Feb 5	H	Burnley	D	1-1	0-1	13	McBride	6079
28	19	H	Bolton W	D	1-1	1-1	13	McBride	5646
29	26	A	Barnsley	L	1-2	0-0	16	Moore	13,941
30	Mar 5	H	Shrewsbury T	L	0-3	0-1	17		4810
31	12	A	Middlesbrough	D	1-1	0-1	16	Hughes (pen)	8875
32	19	A	QPR	L	0-4	0-4	18		9541
33	26	H	Carlisle U	L	1-2	0-0	20	McBride (pen)	5486
34	Apr 2	H	Sheffield W	L	0-3	0-0	20		11,250
35	4	A	Grimsby T	W	2-1	0-0	—	Arnott, McBride	7117
36	9	H	Wolverhampton W	D	1-1	0-1	18	Seasman	7286
37	16	A	Leicester C	L	1-3	0-1	21	McBride	12,978
38	20	A	Newcastle U	L	0-4	0-2	—		18,447
39	23	H	Derby Co	D	1-1	1-1	21	Seasman (pen)	9646
40	30	A	Chelsea	D	1-1	1-1	21	Arnott	8674
41	May 7	H	Blackburn R	W	3-1	2-0	21	Seasman 3 (1 pen)	5871
42	14	A	Leeds U	D	2-2	1-0	20	McBride 2	14,958

Final League Position: 20

GOALSCORERS

League (45): McBride 11 (1 pen), Seasman 9 (2 pens), Fern 5, Moore 5 (1 pen), Hughes 4 (4 pens), Gow 3, Arnott 2, Walker 2, Gooding 1, Green 1, Towner 1, own goal 1.
Milk Cup (2): Green 1, Seasman 1.
FA Cup (1): Seasman 1.

Milk Cup	Second Round	QPR (h)	2-1
		(a)	0-0
	Third Round	Liverpool (a)	0-1
FA Cup	Third Round	Shrewsbury T (a)	1-2

Mimms	Forrest	Stancliffe	Green	Breckin	Towner	Gow	Hughes	McBride	Fern	Seasman	Moore	Gooding	McEwan	Henson	Mountford	Walker	Lodge	Friar	Johnson	Arnott (L)	Mitchell	Alexander	Conroy	*Referees*	*Match No.*
1	2	5	6	3	7	8	4	11	9	10														D. Letts	1
1	2	5	6	3	7	8	4	11		10	9													R. Nixon	2
1	2	5	6	3	7	8	4	11		10	9													K. Barrett	3
	2	5*	6	3	7	8	4	11	10		9	12			1									G. Tyson	4
	2		6	3	7	8	5	11	10		9		4		1									G. Courtney	5
	2		6	3	7*	8	5	11	10		9	12	4		1									D. Shaw	6
	2		6	3		8	5	11		10*	9	7	4	12	1									D. Hedges	7
	2		6	3		8	5	11		10	9		4	7	1									J. Hough	8
	2		6	3	7	8	5	11		10	9		4		1									M. Peck	9
	2		6	3	7	8	5	11		10	9		4		1									K. Redfern	10
	2		6	3	7	8	5	11	12	10*	9		4		1									J. Worrall	11
	2		6	3	7	8	5	11	10*		9	12	4		1									G. Napthine	12
	2		6	3	7	8	5	11		10	9			4	1									K. Baker	13
	2		6	3	7		5	11		10	9	8		4	1									T. Fitzharris	14
	2		6		7	8	5	11		10	9	4		3	1									L. Burden	15
	2		6		7	8	5	11		10	9	4		3	1									R. Guy	16
	2		6		7	8	5	11*		10	9	4	12	3	1									J. Moules	17
	2		6		7	8	5	11		10	9	4		3	1									A. Hamil	18
	2		6	3	7	8	5	11	12	10	9*			4	1									D. Civil	19
	2		6		7	8	5	11			9		4	3	1	10								D. Allison	20
	2		6		7	8	5	11		9			4	3	1	10								R. Bridges	21
	2		6		7	8	5	11	10	12	9		4*	3	1									T. Holbrook	22
	2		6		7	8	5	11	12	4	9*			3	1	10								J. Deakin	23
	2		6		7*		5	11	12	4	9			3	1	10	8							N. Glover	24
	2		6		7		5	11	9	4				3	1	10	8							D. Axcell	25
	2		6		7	8	5	11	12	9				3	1	10	4*							F. Roberts	26
	2		6		7	8	5	11			9			3	1	10	4							D. Brazier	27
1	2		6		7	8	5	11			9		4			10		3						M. Heath	28
1	2		6		7	8	5	11			9		4			10		3						A. Seville	29
1	2		6		7	8	5	11		12	9		4			10*		3						M. Scott	30
1	2		6		7	8	5	11			9			10				3	4					D. Scott	31
1	2		6		7	8	5	11		9				10				3	4					A. Gunn	32
1	2		6			4		11		8	9							3	5	7	10			M. Taylor	33
1	2*	5				4		11		8	9		12					3	6	7	10			B. Hill	34
1		5				4		11		8	9*		2					3	6	7	10	12		G. Tyson	35
1		5	4					11		9	12		2					3	6	7	10	8*		J. Worrall	36
1		5	4					11		9			2	12				3	6	7*	10	8		A. Grey	37
	2	5	6			4		11		8	9		12					3		7*	10		1	M. Wilson	38
	2	5				4		11		8	9		7					3	6		10		1	J. Lovatt	39
	2	5				4		11		8*	9		12					3	6	7	10		1	J. Bodenham	40
	2	5				4		11		8	9*		12					3	6	7	10		1	T. Jones	41
	2	5				4		11		8	9*		12					3	6	7	10		1	D. Richardson	42
13	39	13	36	15	30	37	32	42	7	31	35	6	18	18	24	10	4	15	11	9	10	2	5		
									+ 5s	+ 2s	+ 1s	+ 3s	+ 6s	+ 2s								+ 1s			

FOOTBALL LEAGUE RECORD

1893 Rotherham Town elected to Division 2; 1896 Failed re-election; 1919 Rotherham County elected to Division 2; 1923–51 Division 3(N); 1951–68 Division 2; 1968–73 Division 3; 1973–75 Division 4; 1975–81 Division 3; 1981–83 Division 2; 1983– Division 3.

HONOURS

Football League: Division 2 best season: 3rd, 1954–55 (equal points with champions and runners-up); Division 3 – Champions 1980–81; Division 3(N) – Champions 1950–51; Runners-up 1946–47, 1947–48, 1948–49. *FA Cup* best season: 5th rd, 1953, 1968. *Football League Cup:* Runners-up 1961.

COLOURS

Red shirts, white collar and sleeves, white (or black) shorts, red stockings.
Change colours: Yellow shirts with blue trim, blue shorts with yellow trim, yellow stockings.

ROTHERHAM UNITED

Players Names Ht. Wt. D.o.B.	Birthplace Transfer Fee	Clubs	Appearances F.L. A & S	F.L.C. A & S	F.A.C. A & S	Goals F.L.	F.L.C.	F.A.C.
Goalkeepers								
Ray Mountford	Mexborough	Manchester U (A)						
6 3, 12 7, 28.4.58	F/T	Rotherham U	123	11	8			
Robert Mimms	York	Halifax T (A)						
6 6, 12 4,	£15,000	Rotherham U	15					
Defenders								
Gerry Forrest	Stockton	South Bank						
5 11, 10 7, 21.1.57		Rotherham U	251	22	15	7		
John Green	Rotherham	Rotherham U (A)	246+1	20	17	8	2	2
5 10, 12 1, 7.8.58								
Paul Stancliffe	Sheffield	Rotherham U (A)	285	10	22	8		2
6 0, 11 10, 5.5.58								
Ashley Taylor*	Conisborough	Rotherham U (A)	21+1	1	3			
5 10, 10 4, 11.12.59								
Nigel Johnson		Rotherham U (A)	11					
Paul Friar	Glasgow	Leicester C (A)	56+2		6			
5 8, 10 11, 6.6.63	£10,000	Rotherham U	15					
Midfield								
Mark Rhodes	Sheffield	Rotherham U (A)	199+3	13	15	11		
5 9, 10 11, 26.8.57	—	Darlington (loan)	14		1			
	—	Mansfield T (loan)	4					
Phil Henson	Manchester	Manchester C (A)	12+5	1	+1			
5 10, 9 12, 30.3.53	—	Swansea C (loan)	1	1+1				
	£50,000	Sheffield W	65+7	5	2	9		
	£30,000	Stockport Co	65+2	4	4	13	1	
		Rotherham U	83+5	6	5	7	1	
Billy McEwan	Cleland	Hibernian						
5 10, 11 2, 20.6.51		Blackpool	4	2				
		Brighton	27	1		3		
	P E	Chesterfield	79+1	4	7	7		1
	£15,000	Mansfield T	32	2		3		
		Peterborough U	62+1	8	6	3		
	£30,000	Rotherham U	69+8	6	3+1	10		
Tony Towner	Brighton	Brighton (A)	153+9	10+2	8+1	24		1
5 6, 10 0, 2.5.55	£65,000	Millwall	68	2	6	13		1
	£185,000	Rotherham U	108	6	3	12		2
	—	Sheffield U (loan)	9+1			1		
John Seasman	Liverpool	Tranmere R (A)	15+2					
5 9, 11 3, 21.2.55	£5000	Luton T	7+1			2		
	£10,000	Millwall	157+1	16+1	11	35	5	1
	£90,000	Rotherham U	86+6	5	2	25	1	1
Gerry Gow (SU23)	Glasgow	Bristol C	368+7	24+2	17	47	3	2
5 8, 10 8, 29.5.52	£175,000	Manchester C	26		9	5		2
	£80,000	Rotherham U	58	2	1	4		
Bobby Mitchell	South Shields	Sunderland (A)	1+2					
5 10, 11 0, 4.1.55	F/T	Blackburn R	17+12		2	6		1
	F T	Grimsby T	142	16	8	6	1	
	F T	Carlisle U	2					
	F T	Rotherham U	10					
Forwards								
Phil Walker	Kirkby	Chesterfield	151+15	13	10	38	3	5
6 0, 12 1, 27.1.57	P/E	Rotherham U	10			2		
Ronnie Moore	Liverpool	Tranmere R	248+1	18	12	72	4	1
6 0, 12 13, 29.1.53	£120,000	Cardiff C	54+2	2	2	6		
	£100,000	Rotherham U	120+1	7	5	49	2	
Ian Alexander	Glasgow							
		Rotherham U	5+6					
Joe McBride (SU21)	Glasgow	Everton (A)	51+6	3	6	9	1	1
5 8, 10 8, 17.8.60	£50,000	Rotherham U	42	3	1	11		
Non-contract players								
Steve Conroy (ES)	Chesterfield	Sheffield U (A)	104	9	6			
6 0¼, 12 2, 19.12.56	F/T	Rotherham U	5					

Commercial Manager: Mr. J. W. Adams (Tel. 0709 562760).
Club Coach:
Club Captain 1982–83: John Green
Supporters Player of the Season 1982–83: Gerry Forrest
Chief Scout: A. Turner
Physiotherapist: A. B. Claxton
Club Statistician:
Association of Football Statisticians Club Adviser to Yearbook: M. Smith.

Players released since May 1982:
Chris Waller, M., (N/K); Peter Carr, M., (Gainsborough Trin); Steve Fleetwood, M., (N/K); Rod Fern, F., (N/K); Ian Vaughan, F., (Burton Alb).

SCUNTHORPE UNITED Division 3

Back row (left to right): Cowling, Boxall, Neenan, Hunter, Parkinson
Middle row: Webster, Keeley, Pointon, Johnson, Fowler, Oates, Snow
Front row: O'Berg, Clarke (Manager), Baines (Player-Coach), Cammack, McLoughlin (Coach), Leman

President: Sir Reginald Sheffield, Bt. ***Chairman:*** D. J. Wraith.

Vice-Chairman: J. T. Empson.

Directors: T. E. Belton, G. J. Alston, P. J. Cooper.

Manager: Allan Clarke. ***Secretary:*** A. D. Rowing.

Year Formed: 1904. ***Turned Professional:*** 1912. ***Ltd Co.:*** 1912.

Club Nickname: 'The Iron'.

Previous Name: Amalgamated with Lindsey United to become Scunthorpe United, 1910. (Dropped '& Lindsey' in 1958).

Previous Managers since 1946: Leslie Jones, Bill Corkhill, Ron Suart, Tony McShane, Bill Lambton (3 days, shortest ever term of office), Frank Soo, Dick Duckworth, Freddie Goodwin, Ron Ashman, Ron Bradley, Dickie Rooks, Ron Ashman, John Duncan (13).

Old Show Ground, Scunthorpe, South Humberside. Telephone Scunthorpe 842954/848077. ***Ground capacity:*** 25,000. ***Record attendance:*** 23,935 v Portsmouth, FA Cup 4th rd, 30 Jan, 1954. ***Record receipts:*** £20,562 v Grimsby T, FA Cup 3rd rd, 8 Jan, 1983. ***Pitch measurements:*** 112yd×78yd.

Directions to Ground: Several buses run near the ground. Nearest railway station is Scunthorpe. By road along M180, A18 from Doncaster via Berkeley Circle, Doncaster Road Hill, and Henderson Avenue; M180 and A18 from Grimsby; A15 from Lincoln via Queensway Circle, Ashby Road, Station Roundabout, Church Lane, Exeter Road, and Doncaster Road; via A1 on A638 to Retford, A620 to Gainsborough, A159 to Scunthorpe.

Match tickets: Tickets are bookable up to the day of the match unless advertised otherwise in the local press. No telephone bookings accepted.

Car parking: Club car park adjoining the ground holds 40–50 cars. Ample street parking.

Entertainments/catering facilities: Hot and cold refreshments served on first-team match days from various points around the ground. Sportsmans Bar and the 1500 Club enable members to watch matches in comfort.

Club shop: Sports and Leisure Shop adjoining ground sells all types of club mementoes.

Handbooks/programmes: Handbook, current and past programmes available at Sports and Leisure Shop at ground. Postal enquiries must enclose sae.

Address of Supporters Club: Scunthorpe U Official Supporters Club, c/o Old Show Ground, Scunthorpe.

Note: Full club statistical records are on pages 416–455.

SCUNTHORPE UNITED 1982–83 LEAGUE RECORD

Match No.	Date	Venue	Opponents	Result		H/T Score	Lg. Pos.	Goalscorers	Attendance
1	Aug 28	A	Hartlepool U	D	0-0	0-0	—		1009
2	Sept 4	H	Aldershot	D	1-1	1-0	15	Hunter	1309
3	7	H	Stockport Co	W	3-0	2-0	—	Telfer 2, Cowling	1335
4	19	H	Wimbledon	D	2-2	0-1	8	O'Berg 2	1611
5	19	H	York C	D	0-0	0-0	—		2436
6	25	A	Bristol C	W	2-0	0-0	6	O'Berg, Parkinson	3890
7	28	A	Darlington	W	1-0	1-0	—	Hunter	1574
8	Oct 2	H	Colchester U	W	2-1	1-0	4	O'Berg, Angus	2616
9	9	A	Peterborough U	W	1-0	1-0	3	Angus	3075
10	15	H	Hull C	L	0-1	0-0	—		7483
11	18	A	Mansfield T	W	2-0	2-0	—	Hunter, Cowling	2647
12	23	H	Tranmere R	W	2-1	0-0	3	Baines, Cowling	3052
13	30	A	Torquay U	D	1-1	0-0	4	Cammack	3005
14	Nov 2	H	Port Vale	W	1-0	0-0	—	Cammack	3766
15	6	H	Northampton T	W	5-1	1-0	1	O'Berg 2, Cammack 3	3412
16	12	A	Crewe Alex	W	1-0	0-0	—	O'Berg	2195
17	27	H	Bury	L	0-1	0-1	2		6335
18	Dec 4	A	Hereford U	W	2-0	1-0	2	Cammack, Cartwright	2103
19	18	A	Blackpool	L	1-3	0-0	4	Cammack	2860
20	27	H	Rochdale	D	1-1	0-1	4	Cammack	4845
21	28	A	Halifax T	L	1-3	0-2	5	Parkinson (pen)	2270
22	Jan 1	H	Chester	W	2-0	2-0	5	Cammack 2	3639
23	3	A	Swindon T	D	2-2	2-1	6	Parkinson, Cammack	6728
24	16	H	Hartlepool U	W	3-0	1-0	—	Hunter, Parkinson, Cowling	4261
25	23	A	York C	L	1-2	1-1	—	Cowling	7097
26	29	H	Wimbledon	D	0-0	0-0	5		3846
27	Feb 5	H	Bristol C	D	1-1	0-0	5	Parkinson	3624
28	12	A	Stockport Co	D	1-1	0-1	5	Cammack	2328
29	26	A	Hull C	D	1-1	1-0	6	Leman	14,252
30	Mar 1	H	Mansfield T	D	2-2	1-0	—	Cammack 2	3562
31	5	A	Tranmere R	W	4-0	3-0	6	Leman, Cammack 2, Parkinson	1652
32	12	H	Torquay U	W	2-0	1-0	6	Hunter 2	3342
33	15	A	Aldershot	D	1-1	1-1	—	O'Berg	1422
34	20	A	Northampton T	L	1-2	0-0	—	Cowling	2634
35	25	H	Crewe Alex	W	2-0	0-0	—	Hunter 2	2938
36	Apr 1	H	Halifax T	W	2-0	1-0	—	Lester, Cammack	3775
37	4	A	Rochdale	W	1-0	0-0	—	Graham	2056
38	8	H	Hereford U	L	1-2	0-0	—	Cammack (pen)	3785
39	15	A	Colchester U	L	1-5	1-2	—	Cammack	3155
40	23	H	Blackpool	W	4-3	1-2	7	Cowling 2, Cammack 2 (1 pen)	2791
41	26	H	Peterborough U	W	3-0	0-0	—	Lester, Cammack, Pointon	3211
42	30	A	Bury	L	0-1	0-0	6		4739
43	May 2	H	Swindon T	W	2-0	1-0	6	Cammack, Lester	3546
44	7	H	Darlington	D	2-2	2-0	6	Cammack 2	3305
45	9	A	Port Vale	W	1-0	0-0	—	Cowling	6212
46	14	A	Chester	W	2-1	1-1	4	Graham 2	2560

Final League Position: 4

GOALSCORERS

League (71): Cammack 25 (2 pens), Cowling 9, Hunter 8, O'Berg 8, Parkinson 6 (1 pen), Graham 3, Lester 3, Angus 2, Telfer 2, Leman 2, Baines 1, Cartwright 1, Pointon 1.
Milk Cup (1): Cowling 1.
FA Cup (3): Cammack 1, Cowling 1, O'Berg 1.
Football League Trophy (1): Hunter 1.

Milk Cup	First Round	Grimsby T (h)	1-2
		(a)	0-0
FA Cup	First Round	Darlington (a)	1-0
	Second Round	Northwich Vic (h)	2-1
	Third Round	Grimsby T (h)	0-0
		(a)	0-2
Football League Trophy		Lincoln C (h)	1-1
		Sheffield U (h)	0-0
		Grimsby T (a)	0-2

Neenan	Keeley	Pointon	Fowler	Boxall	Hunter	Cammack	Parkinson	Cowling	Telfer	Leman	O'Berg	Oates	Duncan	Baines	Gilbert	Angus (L)	Cartwright (L)	Mann	Reid (L)	Graham	Lester	Webster	Snow	Referees	Match No.
1	2	3	4	5	6	7	8*	9	10	11	12													R. Banks	1
1	2	11	4	5	6	7*	8	9	10		12	3												N. Midgley	2
1		3	4	5	6		8	9	10	11	7	2*	12											D. Hutchinson	3
1	2	3	4	5	6		8		10	11	7		9*	12										A. Glasson	4
1	2	3	4	5	6		8		10*	11	9		12		7									T. Fitzharris	5
1	2	3	4	5	6		12		10*	11	7		9			8								T. Holbrook	6
1	2	3	4	5	6	7	10*	9		11			12			8								K. Walmsley	7
1	2	3	4	5	6	8		9		11	7					10								A. Robinson	8
1	2	3	4		6	8		9		11	7			5		10								J. A. Moules	9
1	2	3		12	6	8	4*	9		11	7			5		10								R. Guy	10
1	2	3			6		4	9		11	7		8	5		10								M. Heath	11
1	2	5			4	11	6	10		8	9			3		7								J. Hunting	12
1	2	3	12		6	8	4	9		11	7			5		10*								J. Deakin	13
1	2	3			6	8	4	9		11	7			5		10								A. Saunders	14
1	2	5			4	11	6	10		8	9			3		7								D. Scott	15
1	2	3	12		6	8	4*	9		11	7			5		10								H. King	16
1	2	3	12		6	8	4*	9		11	7			5		10								M. Scott	17
1	2	3			6	8		9		11	7			5		10	4							D. Hedges	18
1	2	3			6	8		9		11*	7	12		5		10	4							D. Owen	19
1	2*	3	4		6	8	11	9			7			5		10	12							J. Bray	20
1		3	4		6	8	11	9			7	2		5		10								J. Hough	21
1		3	4		6	8	11	9			7*	2		5		10	12							B. Hill	22
1		3	4		6	8	11	9			7	2		5		10								A. Ward	23
1		3	4*	5	6	8	11	9	12		7	2				10								T. Jones	24
1		3		12	6	8	4	9		11		2		5		10*		7						K. Walmsley	25
1		3		4	6	8	10	9		11	7	2		5										R. Chadwick	26
1		3		4	6	8	10			11	7	2		5				9						A. Hamil	27
1		3	4	12	6*	8	10	9		11	7	2		5										A. Hamil	28
1	2	3			6	8	10	9		11	7			5					4					N. Ashley	29
1	2	3*		12	6	8	10	9		11		7		5					4					A. Challinor	30
1	2	3			6	8	10	9		11	7			5					4					N. Wilson	31
1	2	3			6	8	10	9*		11	7			5					4	12				M. Robinson	32
1	2	3			6	8	10	9		11	7			5					4					M. Bodenham	33
1	2	3			6	8	10	9		11	7*	12		5					4					T. Bune	34
1	2	3			6	8	10	9		11				5						7	4			D. Hutchinson	35
1	2	3		4	6	8		10*		11		12		5						7	9			J. Lovatt	36
1	2	3		4	6	8		9		11				5						7	10			T. Mills	37
1	2	3		4	6	8		9		11				5						7	10			K. Redfern	38
1	2	3		4	6	8		9		11				5						7	10			I. Borrett	39
1	2*	3		4	6	8		9		11		12		5						7	10			V. Callow	40
1	2	3		4	6	8		9		11				5						7	10			G. Tyson	41
1	12	3		4	6	8		9		11*		2		5						7	10			M. Peck	42
1		3		4	6	8		9			11	2		5						7	10			R. Nixon	43
1		3		4	6	8		9			11	2		5						7	10			N. Glover	44
1	12	3		4	6	8		9			11*	2		5						7	10			D. Brazier	45
1	11*	3		4	6	8		9				2		5						7		10	12	D. Allison	46
46	33	46	15	22	46	41	30	42	6	36	32	16	3	37	1	20	2	2	6	12	11	1	0		
	+ 2s		+ 3s	+ 4s			+ 1s		+ 1s		+ 2s	+ 4s	+ 3s	+ 1s			+ 2s			+ 1s			+ 1s		

FOOTBALL LEAGUE RECORD

1950 Elected to Division 3(N); 1958–64 Division 2; 1964–68 Division 3; 1968–72 Division 4; 1972–73 Division 3; 1973–83 Division 4; 1983– Division 3.

HONOURS

Football League: Division 2 best season: 4th, 1961–62; Division 3(N) – Champions 1957–58. *FA Cup* best season' 5th rd, 1957–58, 1969–70. *Football League Cup:* never past 3rd rd.

COLOURS

Sky blue shirts with claret 'V' and trim, sky blue shorts and stockings with claret trim.
Change colours: All yellow with green 'V' and trim.

SCUNTHORPE UNITED

Players Names Ht, Wt, D.o.B.	Birthplace Transfer Fee	Clubs	Appearances F.L. A & S	 F.L.C. A & S	 F.A.C. A & S	Goals F.L.	 F.L.C.	 F.A.C.
Goalkeepers								
Joe Neenan	Manchester	York C (A)	56	5	3			
6 3, 11 13, 17.3.59	P/E	Scunthorpe U	136	6	11			
Defenders								
Neil Pointon	Church Warsop	Scunthorpe U (A)	51	1	4	1		
5 10, 12 10,								
Bob Oates* (EY)	Leeds	Leeds Ashley Rd						
5 11½, 11 7, 26.7.56	—	Scunthorpe U	306+9	18+1	14	15	1	
Andy Keeley* (EY)	Basildon	Tottenham H (A)	5+1					
5 9¼, 11 4, 16.9.56		Sheffield U	28	1				
	F/T	Scunthorpe U	75+2	4	6	1		
Les Hunter	Middlesbrough	Chesterfield (A)	156+9	15+1	13+1	8	2	1
6 2, 11 10, 15.1.58	F/T	Scunthorpe U	46	2	4	8		
Steve Baines	Newark	Nottingham F (A)	2					
6 0, 12 12, 23.6.54	F/T	Huddersfield T	113+1	11	7	10	1	1
	£15,000	Bradford C	98+1	8	4	17	1	2
	£50,000	Walsall	47+1	2	1	5		
	—	Bury (loan)	7					
	£5000	Scunthorpe U	37+1		4	1		
Midfield								
Mike Lester	Manchester	Oldham Ath (A)	26+1	2		1		
5 9½, 11 8, 1.5.56	£80,000	Manchester C	1+1					
	—	Stockport Co (loan)	8+1	1		1		
	£10,000	Washington Dips						
		Grimsby T	45+3	3+1	+1	10	2	
	£20,000	Barnsley	64	6	8	11		2
		Exeter C	18+1	4	1	6		
	F/T	Bradford C	46+3	5	4	2		1
	£7000	Scunthorpe U	11			3		
Dennis Leman (ES)	Newcastle	Manchester C (A)	10+7	2+1	+1	1	1	
5 5, 11 4, 1.12.54	£9000	Sheffield W	89+15	4	9	9		1
	—	Wrexham (loan)	17			1		
	F/T	Scunthorpe U	36	2	2	2		
Noel Parkinson	Hull	Ipswich T (A)						
5 8, 10 7, 16.11.59	—	Bristol R (loan)	5			1		
	—	Brentford (loan)	9+1					
	£35,000	Mansfield T	66+4	5+1	6	13	1	3
	F/T	Scunthorpe U	30+1	2	3	6		
Forwards								
Steve Cammack (EY)	Sheffield	Sheffield U (A)	21+15	1+1		5		
5 10¼, 11 9, 20.3.54		Chesterfield	95+18	7+1	4	21	3	
	£12,500	Scunthorpe U	84	2	4	27		1
	£29,000+player	Lincoln C	18	4+1	2+1	6		1
	£3000+player	Scunthorpe U	50+1	1	4	28		1
Chris Cowling	Scunthorpe	Scunthorpe U (A)	73+11	3	9	13	1	3
6 1½, 11 0, 19.9.62								
Paul O'Berg	Hull	Bridlington Trin						
5 5, 9 4, 8.5.58	—	Scunthorpe U	95+10	3+3	10	21		2
Non-Contract Players								
Alan Boxall	Woolwich	Barton T						
6 3¾, 14 2, 11.5.53	—	Scunthorpe U	46+4	2	3	1		
Tommy Graham	Glasgow	Arthurlie						
5 9, 10 10, 31.3.58	—	Aston Villa						
	£25,000	Barnsley	36+2	2	1	13	1	
	£20,000	Halifax T	68+3	2	1	17		
	F/T	Doncaster R (N/C)	9+2	2		2	1	
	F/T	Scunthorpe U	12+1			3		
Simon Snow		Scunthorpe U (A)	+1					
Ian Webster								
		Scunthorpe U	1					

Lottery Manager: T. J. Burdass (Tel. 848077)
Player Coach: G. J. Baines
Supporters Player of the Season 1982–83: Les Hunter
Physiotherapist: P. McLoughlin
Association of Football Statisticians Club Adviser to Yearbook: M. Girdham

Club Captain 1982–83:
Chief Scout:
Club Statistician:

Players released since May 1982:
Tony Arins, D. (N/K); Gordon Boyd, M. (N/K); David Pall, D. (East Fife); Steve Davy, D. (Appleby Froddingham); Ron Goodlass, F. (Hong Kong); Paul Johnson, G. (N/K); Alan Thompson, D. (N/K); Martin Fowler, M. (Police); George Telfer, F. (Altrincham); David Gilbert, F. (Boston U); Vince Grimes, M. (N/K); Paul Moss, M. (Worcester C); John Duncan, F. (retired)

SHEFFIELD UNITED Division 3

Back row (left to right):
K. Arnott
M. Trusson
K. Waugh
J. McPhail
S. Houston
S. Conroy
R. Hatton
R. Atkins
Middle row:
M. Henderson
S. Neville
P. Garner
C. Coldwell
J. McSeveney
J. Dixon
G. Brazil
P. Richardson
S. Charles
Front row:
C. Morris
K. Edwards
E. Curran
I. Porterfield
J. King
A. Kenworthy
R. McHale.

Chairman: R. J. Brealey.

Directors: A. H. Laver, A. H. Barrington, R. Wragg M INST BM, D. Dooley (Associate). ***Manager:*** Ian Porterfield.

Secretary: Richard Chester FAAL.

Year Formed: 1889. ***Turned Professional:*** 1889. ***Ltd Co.:*** 1899.

Club Nickname: 'The Blades'.

Previous Managers since 1946: Ted Davison, Reg Freeman, Joe Mercer, John Harris, Arthur Rowley, John Harris, Ken Furphy, Jimmy Sirrel, Harry Haslam, Martin Peters (10).

Bramall Lane Ground, Sheffield, S2 4SU. Telephone Sheffield (0742) 738955/6/7. ***Telegraphic address:*** 'United, Sheffield'. ***Ground capacity:*** 49,000 (15,300 seats). ***Record attendance:*** 68,287 v Leeds U, FA Cup 5th rd, 15 Feb, 1936. ***Record receipts:*** £65,092 v Sheffield W, Division 3, 5 Apr, 1980. ***Pitch measurements:*** 117yd×75yd.

Directions to Ground: Buses 34, 35, 38, 42, 45 from the central bus station. Sheffield railway station is within walking distance of the town centre.

Match tickets: Tickets bookable fourteen days prior to match.

Car parking: The ground is five minutes from car parks in the city centre. Ample parking in side-streets around Bramall Lane.

Entertainments/catering facilities: Numerous bars and buffets in the ground. Executive Suite offers pre-match meals (Tel: 755277 for reservations). Lounge bars in Lane Social Club.

Club shop: Sells all types of souvenirs.

Handbooks/programmes: Mail order service available through the club shop.

Address of Supporters Club: Secretary, c/o SUFC, Bramall Lane, Sheffield S2 4SU.

Address of the Club Shop or Boutique: Lane Souvenir Shop, John Street, Sheffield S2 4SU.

Note: Full club statistical records are on pages 416–455.

SHEFFIELD UNITED 1982–83 LEAGUE RECORD

Match No.	Date	Venue	Opponents	Result	H/T Score	Lg. Pos.	Goalscorers	Attendance
1	Aug 28	A	Portsmouth	L 1-4	1-1	—	Edwards	13,361
2	Sept 4	H	Preston NE	W 2-1	1-1	16	Edwards, Kenworthy (pen)	14,527
3	7	H	Huddersfield T	W 2-0	0-0	—	Curran 2	16,641
4	11	A	AFC Bournemouth	D 0-0	0-0	7		6424
5	18	H	Plymouth Arg	W 3-1	0-0	5	Kenworthy, Young 2	13,604
6	25	A	Cardiff C	L 0-2	0-1	9		7147
7	29	A	Lincoln C	L 0-3	0-1	—		8550
8	Oct 2	H	Gillingham	L 0-2	0-0	16		12,319
9	9	A	Walsall	D 0-0	0-0	14		5369
10	16	H	Wrexham	W 2-0	1-0	13	Morris (pen), Edwards	11,582
11	19	H	Reading	D 1-1	0-0	—	Brazil	11,971
12	23	A	Exeter C	W 3-0	0-0	11	Morris 3 (1 pen)	3858
13	30	H	Millwall	D 1-1	1-0	13	Arnott	13,836
14	Nov 2	A	Newport Co	L 1-3	1-1	—	Hatton	5017
15	6	A	Oxford U	D 0-0	0-0	13		6201
16	13	H	Southend U	L 0-1	0-0	13		11,032
17	27	H	Brentford	L 1-2	1-2	17	Edwards	10,202
18	Dec 4	A	Wigan Ath	L 2-3	0-2	17	Morris (pen), Trusson	5050
19	27	H	Doncaster R	W 3-1	1-0	17	Morris 2 (2 pens), Edwards	16,139
20	28	A	Chesterfield	L 1-3	0-2	18	Trusson	11,458
21	Jan 1	H	Orient	W 3-0	0-0	17	King, Morris (pen), Brazil	10,973
22	15	H	Portsmouth	W 2-1	0-0	16	Morris 2	12,907
23	22	A	Huddersfield T	D 0-0	0-0	16		15,769
24	29	H	AFC Bournemouth	D 2-2	1-1	15	West, Young	11,614
25	Feb 5	H	Cardiff C	W 2-0	0-0	13	Morris (pen), Young	11,641
26	19	H	Walsall	W 3-1	2-0	15	Trusson 2, Brazil	11,070
27	23	A	Reading	L 0-2	0-0	—		2375
28	26	A	Wrexham	L 1-4	1-1	16	Trusson	3953
29	Mar 1	H	Newport Co	W 2-0	0-0	—	Curran, Edwards	8740
30	5	H	Exeter C	W 3-0	2-0	12	Edwards 2, Brazil	9703
31	12	A	Millwall	W 2-1	0-0	11	Trusson, Cusack (og)	4055
32	15	A	Gillingham	W 2-0	2-0	—	Edwards, Young	3385
33	19	H	Oxford U	W 3-2	0-1	10	Kenworthy, Edwards, Young	11,786
34	26	A	Southend U	L 1-3	1-1	10	Morris (pen)	3769
35	29	A	Bristol R	L 1-2	0-2	—	Trusson	6595
36	Apr 2	H	Chesterfield	W 3-1	1-1	10	Trusson, Brazil, Edwards	12,441
37	5	A	Doncaster R	L 0-2	0-0	—		8446
38	9	H	Wigan Ath	W 2-0	1-0	8	Richardson, Trusson	8918
39	12	A	Preston NE	L 0-1	0-0	—		6296
40	16	A	Plymouth Arg	L 1-3	1-0	10	Morris	3665
41	23	H	Bradford C	W 2-1	0-1	8	Edwards, Towner	9375
42	30	A	Brentford	L 1-2	1-0	10	Morris (pen)	4987
43	May 2	H	Bristol R	W 2-1	0-1	8	Young, Edwards	7694
44	7	H	Lincoln C	L 0-1	0-1	9		11,842
45	8	A	Bradford C	L 0-2	0-2	—		4576
46	14	A	Orient	L 1-4	1-2	11	Houston	4468

Final League Position: 11

GOALSCORERS

League (62): Morris 14 (9 pens), Edwards 13, Trusson 9, Young 7, Brazil 5, Curran 3, Kenworthy 3 (1 pen), Arnott 1, Hatton 1, Houston 1, King 1, Richardson 1, Towner 1, West 1, own goal 1.
Milk Cup (12): Edwards 5, Young 3, Morris 2 (2 pens), Charles 1, Richardson 1.
FA Cup (11): Edwards 5, Morris 3, Young 3.
Football League Trophy (2): Edwards 1, Kenworthy 1 (pen).

Cup results can be found in individual cup sections.

Marketing Executive: Andy Daykin (Tel. 738955)
Club Coach:
Supporters Player of the Season 1982–83: Mike Trusson
Physiotherapist:
Club Captain 1982–83: Stuart Houston
Chief Scout:
Club Statistician:
Association of Football Statisticians Club Adviser to Yearbook: A. Treherne.

Conroy	Henderson	Garner	McHale	McPhail	Kenworthy	Morris	Arnott	Edwards	King	Curran	Charles	Young	Houston	Trusson	Hatton	Atkins	Brazil	Richardson	West	Ross (L)	Waugh	Smith	Towner (L)	Cooper	*Referees*	*Match No.*
1	2	3	4	5	6	7	8	9	10	11															D. Vickers	1
1	12	3	4	5	2	6*	8	9	7	11		10													J. Bray	2
1	2	3	4	5	6		8	9	11	7	12	10*													C. Seel	3
1	2		4	5	6		8	9	11*	7	3	10	12												K. Cooper	4
1	2		4	5	6			9		7	11	10	3	8											R. Chadwick	5
1	2		4	5*	6			9		7	11	10	3	8	12										L. Burden	6
1	2	3	4		6			9		7*	11	10	5	8	12										G. Tyson	7
1		3	4		6	7	8*	9				10	5		12	2	11								D. Allison	8
1		3		5		7			11*	10	8	9	6			2	12	4							D. Brazier	9
1		3		5		7		12		10	8	9*	6			2	11	4							V. Callow	10
1		3		5*		7		12		10	8	9	6			2	11	4							N. Wilson	11
1		3				7				8	10	9	6			2	11	4	5						R. Lewis	12
1		3				7	4	9		10	8		6				11	2	5						R. Bridges	13
1		3				7	4	9	11*	12	8		6		10	2			5						A. Glasson	14
1		3	4		6	7		9			11		5	8	10	2									E. Scales	15
1		3*			6	7		9			11		5	8	10	2	12	4							R. Guy	16
1	2				6	7		9		11	3	12	5	8*			10	4							R. Nixon	17
1	2				6	7		9			3	10	5	8			11			4					J. Hough	18
	2		4	5	6	7		9			3	10*		8			12			11	1				D. Owen	19
	2	3	4	5	6	7		9			10*			8			12			11	1				T. Fitzharris	20
	2	3	4*		6	7		9	12				5	8			10			11	1				R. Banks	21
	2	3				7		9	11	10			6	8			4		5		1				K. Redfern	22
	2	3				7		9	11	10		8	6				4		5		1				M. Peck	23
	2	3				7		9	11	10		8	6				4		5		1				P. Willis	24
	2	3				7		9		10	11	8	6				4		5		1				J. Worrall	25
		3				7		9	11	10	2		6	8			4		5		1				J. Lovatt	26
		3			12	7		9	11*	10	2		6	8			4		5		1				K. Barrett	27
	2	3				7		9	11		10		6	8			4		5		1				C. Thomas	28
	2	3			6	7		9		10	11			8			4		5		1				D. Scott	29
	2	3			6	7		9		10	11			8			4		5		1				A. Robinson	30
	2	3			6	7		9		11	4	10		8			12		5		1*				B. Hill	31
	2	3			6	7		9		11	4	10		8					5		1				A. Grey	32
	2	3			6	7		9		11	4*	10		8			12		5		1				D. Richardson	33
	4	3			6	7		12		10		9*		8					5		1	2	11		J. Martin	34
	4	3				7			9*	11		10	6	8			12		5		1	2			B. Daniels	35
	4	3				7		9		11		10*	6	8			12		5		1	2			F. Roberts	36
	4					7		9		11	3		6	8			10		5		1	2*	12		P. Tyldesley	37
					3	11					10		6	8			9	4	5		1	2	7		B. Newsome	38
	3					10		12			11		6	8			9*	4	5		1	2	7		G. Courtney	39
	3					10		12			11		6	8			9*	4	5		1	2	7		Alan Robinson	40
		2				10		9		12	3		6	8			11	4*	5		1		7		M. Midgley	41
		2				10		9		11	3	12	6	8				4	5*		1		7		T. Bune	42
	2	3				10		9		11	5*	12	6	8				4			1		7		D. Civil	43
	2	3				10		9		11		8	6	5			12	4*			1		7		M. Heath	44
	2	3*				7		9			10		6	8			11	4	5		1			12	K. Walmsley	45
	2					10		9			3*		6	8			12	4	5		1		7	11	H. King	46
18	31	35	12	11	22	41	7	37	13	31	34	23	34	32	3	8	23	16	26	4	28	7	9	1		
	+ 1s				+ 1s			+ 5s	+ 1s	+ 2s	+ 1s	+ 3s	+ 1s		+ 3s		+ 10s						+ 1s	+ 1s		

FOOTBALL LEAGUE RECORD

1892 Elected to Division 2; 1893–1934 Division 1; 1934–39 Division 2; 1946–49 Division 1; 1949–53 Division 2; 1953–56 Division 1; 1956–61 Division 2; 1961–68 Division 1; 1968–71 Division 2; 1971–76 Division 1; 1976–79 Division 2; 1979–81 Division 3; 1981–82 Division 4; 1982– Division 3.

HONOURS

Football League: Division 1 – Champions 1897–98; Runners-up 1896–97, 1899–1900; Division 2 – Champions 1952–53; Runners-up 1892–93, 1938–39, 1960–61, 1970–71; Division 4 – Champions 1981–82. *FA Cup:* Winners 1899, 1902, 1915, 1925; Runners-up 1901, 1936. *Football League Cup* best season: 5th rd, 1961–62, 1966–67, 1971–72.

COLOURS

Red and white striped shirts, black shorts, red and white stockings.
Change colours: Yellow shirts and stockings with blue trim, white shorts.

SHEFFIELD UNITED

Players Names / Ht, Wt, D.o.B.	Birthplace / Transfer Fee	Clubs	Appearances F.L. A & S	Appearances F.L.C. A & S	Appearances F.A.C. A & S	Goals F.L.	Goals F.L.C.	Goals F.A.C.
Goalkeepers								
Keith Waugh	Sunderland	Sunderland (A)						
6 1, 12 0, 27.10.56	F/T	Peterborough U	195	22	10			
	£90,000	Sheffield U	73	4	6			
Defenders								
Mike Henderson	Gosforth	Sunderland (A)	81+3	2	6	2		
5 10, 11 6, 31.3.56	£140,000	Watford	50+1	8+1	4			
	F/T	Cardiff C	11					
	F/T	Sheffield U	31+1	2	6			
Stewart Houston* (S)	Dunoon	Port Glasgow						
5 11, 12 3, 20.8.49		Chelsea	6+3	1+1	3			
		Brentford	77	3	2	9		
	£40,000	Manchester U	204+1	17	22	13	2	1
	F/T	Sheffield U	93+1	8	10	1		
Gary West		Sheffield U (A)	26	1	1	1		
Tony Kenworthy (EY)	Leeds	Sheffield U (A)	242+4	14	15	33	1	1
5 10, 10 7, 30.10.58								
Paul Garner (EY)	Doncaster	Huddersfield T (A)	96	8	2	2		
5 9, 10 10, 1.12.55	£60,000	Sheffield U	224+3	8+1	14	6		1
Midfield								
Ray McHale	Sheffield	Chesterfield	123+1	10	8	27	2	1
5 8, 12 6, 12.8.50	P/E	Halifax T	86	6	5	21		4
		Swindon T	171+2	22	21	33	4	6
	£100,000	Brighton	9+2	2				
	£60,00	Barnsley	52+1	8	1	1		
	£20,000	Sheffield U	12	3+1	2			
	—	Bury (loan)	6					
Kevin Arnott	Bensham	Sunderland (A)	132+1	7	6	16	1	
5 10, 11 12, 28.9.58	—	Blackburn R (loan)	17			2		
	F/T	Sheffield U	7	3		1		
	—	Blackburn R (loan)	11+1			1		
	—	Rotherham U (loan)	9			2		
Gary Brazil	Tunbridge Wells	Crystal Palace (A)						
19.9.62	F/T	Sheffield U	25+12	2	2+3	5		
Steve Charles	Sheffield	Sheffield U	99+11	10	9+1	8	1	1
5 9, 10 7,								
Paul Richardson (EY)	Shirebrook	Nottingham F (A)	198+23	9+1	16	18	2	1
5 11, 12 0, 25.10.49		Chester	28		5	2		
	£30,000	Stoke C	124+3	10+1	3+1	10	1	
	£15,000	Sheffield U	35+1	4	4	2	1	
	—	Blackpool (loan)	4					
Jeff King*	Fauldhouse	Albion R						
5 8, 10 2, 9.11.53		Derby Co	13+2	1+1	1+1			
	—	Notts Co (loan	3					
	—	Portsmouth (loan)	4					
		Walsall	50+1	3	5	4		2
		Sheffield W	54+3	9	2	5	1	1
	F/T	Sheffield U	35+2	1	2	5		
Mike Trusson	Northolt	Plymouth Arg (A)	65+8	12	1+1	15	4	
5 10, 12 4, 26.5.59	£70,000	Sheffield U	114+1	8	11	28		
Forwards								
Alan Young (SS)	Kirkcaldy	Oldham Ath	107+15	3	6	30	1	4
6 0, 12 7, 26.10.55	£250,000	Leicester C	102+2	5	10	26	1	2
	£160,000	Sheffield U	23+3	4	2	7	3	3
Colin Morris	Blyth	Burnley (A)	9+1		+1			
5 7, 10 5, 22.8.53		Southend	133	11	12	25	4	1
	£111,111	Blackpool	87	6	7	27	3	3
	£100,000	Sheffield U	64	3+1	6	18	2	3
Steve Neville	Walthamstow	Southampton (A)	5		1+1	1		
5 9½, 11 0, 18.9.57		Exeter C	90+3	9	3	22	3	1
	£80,000	Sheffield U	40+9	4	5+1	6		
	—	Exeter C (loan)	33		1	17		
Terry Curran	Kinsley	Doncaster R	67+1	4	3+1	11		
5 10, 12 6, 20.3.55	£60,000	Nottingham F	46+2	2		12	1	
	—	Bury (loan)	2					
	£50,000	Derby Co	26		3	2		
	£60,000	Southampton	25+1	8	5		1	
	£100,000	Sheffield W	122+3	8	3	35	4	
	£100,000	Sheffield U	31+2	4	4	3		
	—	Everton (loan)	7			1		
Keith Edwards	Stockton							
5 10, 10 3, 16.7.57		Sheffield U	64+6	2	3	29		
	£60,000	Hull C	130+2	9	10	57	1	5
	£95,000	Sheffield U	78+5	2+2	8	48	5	6

Additional Players: Robert Atkins (D) 8 FL, 2 FLC, Paul Smith (D) 7 FL, Richard Cooper (F) 1+1 FL, Julian Broddie (F) 1 FL.
Players (non-appearance) granted free transfer: Geoff Dey, D.
Players released since May 1982: Paul Casey, D. (Boston U); Phil Jones, D. (Boston U); Peter Moore, D. (N/K); Trenton Wiggan, F. (Gainsborough Trin.); Martin Peters, M. (Retired); Les Tibbott, D. (Retired).

SHEFFIELD WEDNESDAY Division 2

Photo on the left: I. Bailey
Back row (left to right): M. Lyons, G. Oliver, J. Pearson, A. McCulloch, Peter Shirtliff, T. Matthewson
Middle row: F. Blunstone (Coach), M. Setters (Coach), R. Beaumont, M. Smith, D. Redfern, B. Bolder, M. Sterland, A. Mirocevic, A. Toms (PTI), J. Honey (Physio)
Front row: G. Owen, G. Shelton, C. Williamson, M. Pickering, J. Charlton (Manager), G. Megson, G. Bannister, Paul Shirtliff, K. Taylor.

Vice-Presidents: R. R. Gunstone, S. Ashton, C. Turner.

Chairman: H. E. McGee. ***Vice-Chairman:*** M. Sheppard JP, FCA.

Directors: S. L. Speight OBE, C. Woodward, K. T. Addy, E. Barron, G. K. Hulley. ***Manager:*** Howard Wilkinson.

Secretary: Eric England FAAL. ***Club Nickname:*** 'The Owls'.

Commercial Manager: D. Woodhead.

Year Formed: 1867 (fifth oldest League Club).

Turned Professional: 1887. ***Ltd. Co.:*** 1899.

Previous Grounds: 1867, Highfield; 1869, Myrtle Road; 1877, Sheaf House; 1887, Olive Grove; 1899, Owlerton (since 1912 known as Hillsborough). Some games were played at Endcliffe in the 1880s. Until 1895 Bramall Lane was used for some games.

Previous Managers since 1946: Secretary/Manager Eric Taylor, Harry Catterick, Vic Buckingham, Alan Brown, Jack Marshall, Danny Williams, Derek Dooley, Steve Burtenshaw, Len Ashurst, Jack Charlton OBE (10).

Hillsborough, Sheffield, S6 1SW. Telephone Sheffield (0742) 343123. Box Office: Sheffield 343122. ***Telegraphic address:*** 'Wednesday, Sheffield 6'. ***Ground capacity:*** 50,174. ***Record attendance:*** 72,841 v Manchester C, FA Cup 5th rd, 17 Feb, 1934. ***Record receipts:*** £192,162, Tottenham H v Wolverhampton W, FA Cup semi-final, 11 April, 1981 (record for FA Cup-tie other than the Final). ***Pitch measurements:*** 115yd×75yd. ***Club Restaurant:*** Adjoining South Stand.

Directions to Ground: Buses 42, 53, 81, 2 from the city centre. Sheffield station is close to the centre.

Match tickets: Seats can be booked in advance in the South and North Stands. Postal applications to the Box Office not more than three weeks before the match. Tickets are offered subject to being unsold when the application is received. Remittance and SAE must be enclosed.

Car parking: Street parking available. Also a park at the training ground in Middlewood Road.

Entertainments/catering facilities: Refreshment bars in all parts of the ground.

Club shop: Two shops in the ground sell all types of souvenirs.

Handbooks/programmes: Handbooks available from the secretary. Programmes on subscription.

'Owl' Shop and Supporters Club: Same address as Football Club.

Note: Full club statistical records are on pages 416–455.

SHEFFIELD WEDNESDAY 1982–83 LEAGUE RECORD

Match No.	Date	Venue	Opponents	Result	H/T Score	Lg. Pos.	Goalscorers	Attendance
1	Aug 28	H	Middlesbrough	W 3-1	0-0	—	Bannister (pen), Pearson 2	18,611
2	Sept 4	A	Charlton Ath	W 3-0	1-0	1	Taylor, Bannister (pen), Pearson	8327
3	7	H	Bolton W	W 3-1	1-0	—	Pearson 2, Shelton	17,307
4	11	H	Leeds U	L 2-3	0-2	4	Bannister, Megson	29,050
5	18	A	QPR	W 2-0	1-0	3	McCulloch, Bannister	13,733
6	25	H	Chelsea	W 3-2	1-0	3	Shelton, Bannister (pen), Smith	18,833
7	28	A	Carlisle U	L 2-4	0-0	3	Smith, Owen	6127
8	Oct 2	A	Blackburn R	W 3-2	1-1	—	Bannister 2 (1 pen), Megson	10,362
9	9	H	Wolverhampton W	D 0-0	0-0	3		21,519
10	16	A	Cambridge U	D 2-2	0-0	4	Bannister 2	5677
11	23	H	Grimsby T	W 2-0	1-0	2	Lyons, Shelton	17,904
12	30	A	Leicester C	W 2-0	1-0	1	Mirocevic, Shelton	17,341
13	Nov 6	H	Derby Co	W 2-0	0-0	1	Bannister 2 (1 pen)	17,703
14	13	A	Shrewsbury T	L 0-1	0-0	1		8033
15	20	H	Burnley	D 1-1	1-1	3	Taylor	16,117
16	27	A	Fulham	L 0-1	0-1	3		13,864
17	Dec 4	H	Oldham Ath	D 1-1	0-0	4	Bannister	15,096
18	11	A	Crystal Palace	L 0-2	0-2	4		8498
19	18	H	Newcastle U	D 1-1	0-1	4	Haddock (og)	16,310
20	27	A	Barnsley	D 0-0	0-0	4		23,275
21	28	H	Rotherham U	L 0-1	0-0	5		25,024
22	Jan 1	A	Burnley	L 1-4	0-2	6	McCulloch	9644
23	3	H	Charlton Ath	W 5-4	1-3	5	McCulloch 2, Bannister, Gritt (og), Lyons	11,799
24	15	A	Middlesbrough	D 1-1	0-0	4	Pearson	11,863
25	22	H	Carlisle U	D 1-1	1-1	4	Taylor	12,874
26	Feb 15	H	Blackburn R	D 0-0	0-0	—		11,648
27	26	H	Cambridge U	W 3-1	2-0	6	McCulloch 2, Mills	12,815
28	Mar 1	A	Wolverhampton W	L 0-1	0-1	—		16,656
29	5	A	Grimsby T	D 1-1	0-0	6	Pearson	9472
30	Mar 19	A	Derby Co	D 0-0	0-0	9		16,925
31	22	H	Leicester C	D 2-2	0-1	—	McCulloch, Megson	14,036
32	26	H	Shrewsbury T	D 0-0	0-0	9		14,320
33	Apr 2	A	Rotherham U	W 3-0	0-0	7	Bannister 2, Mills	11,250
34	4	H	Barnsley	L 0-1	0-0	—		22,427
35	9	A	Bolton W	W 2-0	2-0	6	Megson, Bannister	6408
36	19	H	QPR	L 0-1	0-0	—		11,713
37	23	A	Oldham Ath	D 1-1	1-1	10	Bannister	5088
38	27	A	Leeds U	W 2-1	1-1	—	Hart (og), Bannister	16,591
39	30	H	Fulham	W 2-1	0-0	6	Mills, Lyons	12,531
40	May 2	A	Chelsea	D 1-1	0-1	6	Bannister	10,462
41	7	A	Newcastle U	L 1-2	0-0	6	Heard	29,812
42	14	H	Crystal Palace	W 2-1	1-0	6	Heard, Bannister	11,154

Final League Position: 6

GOALSCORERS

League (60): Bannister 20 (5 pens), McCulloch 7, Pearson 7, Megson 4, Shelton 4, Lyons 3, Mills 3, Taylor 3, Heard 2, Smith 2, Mirocevic 1, Owen 1, own goals 3.
Milk Cup (6): Taylor 3, Bannister 1, McCulloch 1, Megson 1.
FA Cup (16): Megson 5 (1 pen), McCulloch 2, Shelton 2, Bannister 1, Lyons 1, Mirocevic 1, Smith 1, Sterland 1, Taylor 1 (pen), own goal 1.

Milk Cup	Second Round	Bristol C (a)	2-1
		(h)	1-1
	Third Round	Crystal Palace (a)	2-1
	Fourth Round	Barnsley (h)	1-0
	Fifth Round	Arsenal (a)	0-1
FA Cup	Third Round	Southend U (a)	0-0
		(h)	2-2 (aet)
		(h)	2-1
	Fourth Round	Torquay U (a)	3-2
	Fifth Round	Cambridge U (a)	2-1
	Sixth Round	Burnley (a)	1-1
		(h)	5-0
	Semi-final	Brighton & HA	1-2 (at Highbury)

Bolder	Sterland	Bailey	Smith	Lyons	Shelton	Taylor	Megson	Pearson	Bannister	Mirocevic	Simmons	Shirtliff Peter	McCulloch	Pickering	Owen	Shirtliff Paul	Williamson	Matthewson	Mills D	Heard	Oliver	Mills S.	Referees	Match No.
1	2	3	4	5	6	7	8	9	10	11*	12												D. Civil	1
1		3	4	5	6	8	7	11	9	10		2											I. Borrett	2
1		3	4	5	6	8	7	11	9	10		2											P. Willis	3
1	2	3	4	5	6	7*	8	9	10	11			12										A. Seville	4
1	2	3	4	5	6	7	8		9	11*			10	12									Alan Robinson	5
1	2	3	4	5	6	8	7	11	9						10								R. Banks	6
1	2	3	4	5	6	7*	8	11	9					12	10								R. Chadwick	7
1	2	3	4	5	6	8	7	11	9						10								N. Ashley	8
1	2	3	4	5	6	8	7	11	9						10								J. Hough	9
1	2	3	4	5	6	8	7		9				10	12	11*								D. Vickers	10
1	2	3	4	5	6	8	7	11	9				10										A. Hamill	11
1	2	3	4	5	6	8	7		9	11*			10	12									A. Grey	12
1	2	3	4	5	6	8	7		9	11			10										D. Allison	13
1	2	3	4	5	6	8	7		9	11	10*					12							J. Hunting	14
1		3	4	5	6	8	7		9	11		2	10										D. Lloyd	15
1		3	6*	4	5	8	7	12	9	11		2	10										D. Brazier	16
1	2	3	4	5		8	7	11	9	6			10										J. Bray	17
1	2	3	4	5		8	7		9				10			6	11						A. Gunn	18
1	2	3	4	5	6	8*	7	12	9	11			10										T. Holbrook	19
1	2	3	4	5	6	8	7	11	9	10													G. Courtney	20
1	2	3	4	5	6	8	7	11	9	10*			12										R. Bridges	21
1	2	6	4	5	8		7	11	9	10*			12					3					A. Saunders	22
1	2	3*	4	5	6	8	7	11	9				10									12	N. Wilson	23
1	2	3	4	5	6	8*	7	10	9						12					11			J. Worrall	24
1	2	3	4	5	6	8*		10	9	7					12					11			F. Roberts	25
1	2	3	4	5	6	8*	7	12					10						9	11			M. Scott	26
1	2	3	4	5	6		7		9				10						8	11			H. Taylor	27
1	2	3	4	5	6		7	12	9				10*						8	11			B. Stevens	28
1	2*	3	4	5	7		6	9	10		12								11	8			D. Willis	29
1	2	3	4		6	9	7	12				5	10*						8	11			B. Daniels	30
1	2	3	4	5	6	8	7	9					10							11			N. Glover	31
1	2	3		5	6*	8	7	12	9			4	10							11			N. Midgeley	32
1	2	3	4	5	6		7	12	9				10*						8	11			B. Hill	33
1		3	4	5	6		7	12	9				10*				2		8	11			M. Heath	34
1	2	3*	4	5	6	12	7		9				10						8	11			D. Owen	35
1			4		6		7	12	9			2	10				3		8*	11	5		R. Nixon	36
1			4		6		7	10	9			2					3·		8	11	5		K. Redfern	37
1	2		4	5	6		7		9				10				3		8	11			M. Peck	38
1	2		4	5	6*		7	12	9				10				3		8	11			D. Richardson	39
1	2		4	5	6		7		9				10				3		8	11			A. Glasson	40
1	2		4	5	6		7	10	9								3		8	11			D. Allinson	41
1	2		4	5	6		7		9				10				3		8	11			V. Callow	42
42	35	35	41	39	40	28	41	20	39	16	1	8	25	0	5	1	9	1	15	19	2	0		
						+ 1s		+ 10s			+ 2s		+ 3s	+ 4s	+ 2s	+ 1s						+ 1s		

FOOTBALL LEAGUE RECORD

1892 Elected to Division 1; 1899–1900 Division 2; 1900–20 Division 1; 1920–26 Division 2; 1926–37 Division 1; 1937–50 Division 2; 1950–51 Division 1; 1951–52 Division 2; 1952–55 Division 1; 1955–56 Division 2; 1956–58 Division 1; 1958–59 Division 2; 1959–70 Division 1; 1970–75 Division 2; 1975–80 Division 3; 1980– Division 2.

HONOURS

Football League: Division 1 – Champions 1902–03, 1903–04, 1928–29, 1929–30; Runners-up 1960–61; Division 2 – Champions 1899–1900, 1925–26, 1951–52, 1955–56, 1958–59; Runners-up 1949–50; Division 3 – Runners-up 1979–80. *FA Cup:* Winners 1896, 1907, 1935; Runners-up 1890, 1966. *Football League Cup* best season: 5th rd 1982–83. **European Competitions:** *Fairs Cup:* 1961–62, 1963–64.

COLOURS

Blue and white striped shirts, blue shorts, white stockings.
Change colours: Yellow shirts with blue trim, white shorts, yellow stockings with blue band.

SHEFFIELD WEDNESDAY

Players Names Ht, Wt, D.o.B.	*Birthplace Transfer Fee*	*Clubs*	*Appearances F.L. A & S*	*F.L.C. A & S*	*F.A.C. A & S*	*Goals F.L.*	*F.L.C.*	*F.A.C.*
Goalkeepers								
Bob Bolder	Dover	Dover T						
6 1, 14 8, 2.10.58		Sheffield W	196	16	12			
Dave Redfern	Sheffield	Sheffield W						
6 1, 13 8								
Defenders								
Mark Smith (EU21)	Sheffield	Sheffield W (A)	189+1	17	21	12	1	2
6 0½, 12 2, 21.3.60								
Mike Pickering	Huddersfield	Barnsley	100	6	3	1		
5 11, 12 8, 29.9.56	£35,000	Southampton	44	3	4			
	£65,000	Sheffield W	106+4	8+2	9	1		
Peter Shirtliff	Chapletown	Sheffield W (A)	96	4+2	4	3		
5 11, 12 2, 6.4.61								
Charlie Williamson	Sheffield	Sheffield W (A)	52	3	1	1		
5 10, 11 3, 16.3.62								
Gavin Oliver	Felling	Sheffield W (A)	2+2	+1				
5 11, 13 2, 6.9.62	—	Tranmere R (Loan)	17			1		
Trevor Matthewson	Sheffield	Sheffield W (A)	3		2			
6 1, 12 5, 12.2.63								
Ian Bailey	Middlesbrough	Middlesbrough (A)	140+5	10+1	13+1	1		1
5 9, 11 12, 20.10.56	—	Doncaster R (Loan)	9					
	—	Carlisle U (Loan)	7			1		
	—	Bolton W (Loan)	5					
	£80,000	Sheffield W	35	5	5			
Mick Lyons (EU23)	Liverpool	Everton (A)	364+25	37	34+2	48	5	6
6 0, 12 2, 8.12.61	£100,000	Sheffield W	39	5	7	3		1
Midfield								
Kevin Taylor	Wakefield	Sheffield W (A)	117+3	11	6	21	5	1
5 8, 11 11, 22.1.61								
Mel Sterland	Sheffield	Sheffield W (A)	84+4	6	9+1	3		1
5 11, 13 2, 1.10.61								
Paul Shirtliff	Barnsley	Sheffield W (A)	7+2	1				
5 5, 8 12, 3.11.62								
Gary Megson	Manchester	Plymouth Arg (A)	78	9	5	10		
5 10, 11 6, 2.5.59	£200,000	Everton	20+3		3	2		1
	£130,000	Sheffield W	81	7	8	8	1	5
Gary Shelton	Nottingham	Walsall (A)	12+12	+1	2+2			1
5 7, 10 0, 21.3.58	£80,000	Aston Villa	24	2+1		7	1	
	—	Notts Co (Loan)	8					
	£50,000	Sheffield W	47+2	3	8	5		2
Pat Heard (EY)	Hull	Everton (A)	10+1					
5 10, 11 0½, 17.3.60	£100,000	Aston Villa	20+4	+1		2		
	£60,000	Sheffield W	19		5	2		
Simon Mills	Sheffield	Sheffield W (A)	+1		1			
16.8.64								
Forwards								
Andy McCulloch (SU23)	Northampton	Walton & Hersham						
6 2, 13 11, 3.1.51	—	QPR	30+12	3	+1	10	1	
	£45,000	Cardiff C	58	3	5	24	3	3
	£70,000	Oxford U	41	1	1	9		
	£25,000	Brentford	115+2	2	3	48		
	£70,000	Sheffield W	122+3	14	10	44	1	4
John Pearson	Sheffield	Sheffield W (A)	40+29	3+1	5+2	18	1	1
6 1, 11 10, 1.9.63								
Gary Bannister (EU21)	Warrington	Coventry C (A)	17+5	2	2	3		
5 8½, 11 3, 22.7.60	£100,000	Sheffield W	81	7	7	41	2	1
Gordon Owen*	Barnsley	Sheffield W	33+15	7+4	1+1	5	2	
5 8, 10 9, 14.6.59	—	Rotherham U (Loan)	9					
	—	Doncaster R (Loan)	9		2			1
	—	Chesterfield (Loan)	6			2		
Chris Morris	Dronfield	Sheffield W						
Tony Simmons		Sheffield W (A)	1+3	1				
David Mills (EB)	Whitby	Middlesbrough (A)	278+17	21+1	27	76	8	10
5 8 , 11 0, 6.12.51	£500,000	WBA	44+12	6+2	2+2	5		
	—	Newcastle U (Loan)	23			4		
	£30,000	Sheffield W	15		4	3		
David Mossman		Sheffield W						

Commercial Manager: D. Woodhead (Tel. 337235).
Club Coach: M. Setters.
Club Captain 1982–83: M. Lyons.
Supporters Player of the Season 1982–83: G. Bannister.
Chief Scout: J. Harris.
Physiotherapist: J. Honey.
Club Statistician:
Association of Football Statisticians Club Adviser to Yearbook: M. Renshaw.

Players (non-appearance) granted free transfer: Bob Kenney, D.; Richard Beaumont, M.; Chris Riley, M.
Players released since May 1982:
Jim Holton, D. (Talbot F.C.); Ante Mirocevic, M. (Yugoslavia).

SHREWSBURY TOWN Division 2

Back row (left to right):
Alan Brown
Steve Perks
Nigel Pearson
Steve Ogrizovic
Gary Stevens
Middle row:
Steve Cross
Ross Maclaren
Colin Griffin
Phil Bates
Carleton Leonard
Paul Petts
Graham Turner
(Player/Manager)
Front row:
Colin Robinson
Bernard McNally
Wayne Williams
Martin Sankey
Paul Johnson.

President: L. Tudor-Owen.

Chairman: H. S. Yates. ***Vice-Chairman:*** K. R. Woodhouse.

Directors: L. Tudor-Owen, A. C. Williams, F. C. G. Fry, P. W. Newbrook. ***Player/Manager:*** Graham Turner. ***Commercial Manager:*** I. Hookway.

Secretary: M. J. Starkey. ***Club Nickname:*** 'Town'.

Year Formed: 1886. ***Turned Professional:*** 1905 (approx). ***Ltd Co.:*** 1936.

Previous Ground: Old Shrewsbury Racecourse.

Previous Managers since the War: Sam Crooks, Walter Rowley, Harry Potts, John Spuhler, Arthur Rowley, Harry Gregg, Maurice Evans, Alan Durban, Richie Barker (9).

Gay Meadow, Shrewsbury. Telephone Shrewsbury (0743) 60111. ***Match information:*** 8040. ***Ground capacity:*** 18,000. ***Record attendance:*** 18,917 v Walsall, Division 3, 26 Apr, 1961. ***Record receipts:*** £36,240 v Ipswich T, FA Cup 5th rd, 13 Feb, 1982. ***Pitch measurements:*** 116yd×76yd.

Directions to Ground: Midland Red schedule bus services from main bus station in Barker Street to the ground. Special coach facilities are arranged by local companies from neighbouring districts. Shrewsbury railway station is ten minutes walk from the ground.

Car parking: A park adjacent to the ground and a free public car park five minutes walk away.

Entertainments/catering facilities: Buffets are situated on each side of the ground.

Club shop: Sells all types of souvenirs.

Handbooks/programmes: No handbook. Programmes can be obtained through the post at 35p each plus sae to Promotions Office, Gay Meadow, Shrewsbury. Mark envelope 'Programme'.

Address of Supporters Club: c/o Football Club.

Note: Full club statistical records are on pages 416–455.

SHREWSBURY TOWN 1982–83 LEAGUE RECORD

Match No.	Date	Venue	Opponents	Result		H/T Score	Lg. Pos.	Goalscorers	Attendance
1	Aug 28	A	Oldham Ath	L	0-1	0-1	—		3731
2	Sept 4	H	Fulham	L	0-1	0-0	19		3525
3	7	A	Crystal Palace	L	1-2	0-1	—	Petts	6578
4	11	A	Grimsby T	L	0-2	0-0	22		7599
5	18	H	Newcastle U	W	2-1	1-1	20	Bates, Brown	7907
6	25	A	Burnley	W	2-1	1-1	17	MacLaren (pen), Bates	6436
7	28	H	Cambridge U	W	2-1	1-1	—	Stevens, Cross	2974
8	Oct 2	H	Leicester C	L	0-2	0-1	14		5223
9	9	H	Middlesbrough	D	2-2	1-0	16	Stevens, Petts	3620
10	16	A	QPR	L	0-4	0-3	18		9275
11	23	H	Rotherham U	W	2-0	0-0	16	Johnson, Petts	3926
12	30	A	Barnsley	D	2-2	2-2	15	MacLaren, Brown	11,150
13	Nov 6	A	Bolton W	W	4-1	1-0	14	Petts 2, Williams, Cross	4879
14	13	H	Sheffield W	W	1-0	0-0	9	Brown	8033
15	20	A	Chelsea	W	2-1	0-0	8	McNally, Cross	8690
16	27	H	Charlton Ath	D	0-0	0-0	9		4477
17	Dec 4	A	Carlisle U	W	3-2	2-2	6	Bates 2, Brown	4226
18	11	H	Blackburn R	D	0-0	0-0	7		4833
19	18	A	Leeds U	D	1-1	0-1	9	MacLaren (pen)	8741
20	27	H	Wolverhampton W	L	0-2	0-1	10		13,336
21	29	A	Derby Co	W	3-2	2-0	6	Stevens 2, Brown	13,068
22	Jan 1	H	Chelsea	W	2-0	0-0	4	Stevens, Brown	7545
23	3	A	Fulham	L	1-2	1-0	6	Cross	7786
24	15	H	Oldham Ath	D	0-0	0-0	6		4630
25	22	A	Newcastle U	L	0-4	0-1	7		19,352
26	Feb 5	H	Crystal Palace	D	1-1	1-1	8	Brown	3716
27	22	A	Leicester C	L	2-3	1-1	—	Williams, Robinson	6155
28	26	H	QPR	D	0-0	0-0	12		4397
29	Mar 5	A	Rotherham U	W	3-0	1-0	11	Williams, Bates, Brown	4810
30	8	A	Middlesbrough	L	1-2	1-1	—	MacLaren	7406
31	12	H	Barnsley	W	3-1	0-1	7	MacLaren (pen), Robinson, Pearson	4024
32	19	H	Boolton W	W	1-0	1-0	6	Brown	4163
33	26	A	Sheffield W	D	0-0	0-0	8		14,320
34	Apr 2	H	Derby Co	D	1-1	0-1	9	Robinson	7194
35	4	A	Wolverhampton W	D	2-2	1-2	—	Bates 2	17,509
36	8	H	Grimsby T	D	0-0	0-0	—		4446
37	16	A	Cambridge U	D	0-0	0-0	10		3615
38	23	H	Carlisle U	W	2-1	0-0	8	Williams, Bates	3220
39	29	A	Charlton Ath	W	1-0	0-0	—	Brown	4838
40	May 3	H	Burnley	L	1-2	0-0	—	Bates	3537
41	7	H	Leeds U	D	0-0	0-0	8		6052
42	14	A	Blackburn R	L	0-1	0-1	9		3797

Final League Position: 9

GOALSCORERS

League (48): Brown 10, Bates 9, MacLaren 5 (3 pens), Petts 5, Stevens 5, Cross 4, Williams 4, Robinson 3, Johnson 1, McNally 1, Pearson 1.
Milk Cup (4): Brown 2, Cross 2.
FA Cup (3): Brown 2, Cross 1.
Football League Trophy (1):

Milk Cup	First Round	Wrexham (a)	0-1
		(h)	2-0
	Second Round	Birmingham C (h)	1-1
		(a)	1-4
FA Cup	Third Round	Rotherham U (h)	2-1
	Fourth Round	Everton (a)	1-2
Football League Trophy		Tranmere R (h)	1-1
		Chesterfield (a)	0-1
		Chester (a)	0-5

Ogrizovic	Williams	Johnson	Turner	Pearson	Griffin	Petts	MacLaren	Brown	Cross	Bates	Sankey	Stevens	Leonard	McNally	Robinson	Foster	Nardiello	Referees	Match No.
1	2	3	4*	5	6	7	8	9	10	11	12							A. Challinor	1
1	2	3		5	6	4	8	9	7	11		10						T. Fitzharris	2
1	2	3		5	6	4	8	9	7	11		10						B. Hill	3
1	2	3		5	6	4	8	9	7	11		10						J. Key	4
1	2	3	12	5	6	4*	8	9	7	11		10						K. Baker	5
1	2	3	12	5	6	4	8	9*	7	11		10						R. Nixon	6
1	2	3	5		6	4	8		7	11		10	9					D. Scott	7
1	2	3	12		6	4	8	9	7	11		10	5*					F. Roberts	8
1	2	3	9*	5	6	4	8		7	11	12	10						M. Taylor	9
1	2	3		5	6	4	8	9	7	11	12	10*						A. Glasson	10
1	2	3		5	6	4	8	9	7	11				10				J. Worrall	11
1	2			5	6	4	8	9	7	11	12		3	10*				A. Saunders	12
1	2			5	6	4	8	9	7	11			3	10				C. Seel	13
1	2			5	6	4	8	9*	7	11		12	3	10				J. Hunting	14
1	2		12	5	6	4*	8		7	11		9	3	10				A. Crickmore	15
1	2			5	6	4	8		7	11		9	3	10				T. Jones	16
1	2			5	6	4	8	9	7	11			3	10				P. Willis	17
1	2		8	5	6	4		9	7	11			3	10				M. Robinson	18
1	2		12	5	6	4	8	9	7	11			3*	10				G. Tyson	19
1	2			5	6	4	8	9	7	11		12	3*	10				D. Shaw	20
1	2	3	12	5	6	4	8	9*	7			11		10				R. Lewis	21
1	2	3		5	6	4	8	9	7*	12		11		10				K. Cooper	22
1	2	3		5	6	4		9	7	12		11	8	10*				M. Taylor	23
1	2	3		5	6	4	8	9	7	12		11*		10				D. Brazier	24
1	2*	3		5	6	12	8	9	7	4		11		10				R. Chadwick	25
1	2	3		5	6	4	8	9	7			11		10				R. Banks	26
1	2	3	4	5		9	8		7			11	6	10*	12			D. Reeves	27
1	2	3	5			4*	8		7	10	12	11	6		9			R. Guy	28
1	2	3	4	5			8	9	7	6*		11	12		10			M. Scott	29
1	2	3	4	5		7*	8	9		6		11	12		10			P. Tyldesley	30
1	2	3	4	5		7	8	9		11		6			10			J. Hough	31
1	2	3	4	5		7	8	9		11		6			10			H. King	32
1	2	3	4	5		7	8	9		11		6			10			N. Midgeley	33
1	2	3	12	5		4*	8	9	7			6		11	10			R. Nixon	34
1	2	3	4	5	10		8	9	7*	11		6			12			D. Richardson	35
1	2	3		5	4		8	9		11		6		7	10			K. Barratt	36
1	2	3	12	5	4*		8	9		11		6		7	10			M. bodenham	37
1	2	3		5	4	12	8	9*		11		6		7	10			G. Napthine	38
1	2	3		5	4	12	8	9	10*	11		6		7				D. Hedges	39
1	2	3		5	4	12	8	9	10*	11		6		7				J. Bray	40
1	2	3		5	4	10*	8	9		11		6		7		12		D. Lloyd	41
1	2	3		5	4*		8	9		11		6		7		10	12	M. Peck	42
42	42	33	12	39	34	33	40	36	33	35	0	33	14	25	10	1	0		
			+ 8s			+ 4s				+ 3s	+ 5s	+ 2s	+ 2s		+ 2s	+ 1s	+ 1s		

FOOTBALL LEAGUE RECORD

1950 Elected to Division 3(N); 1951–58 Division 3(S); 1958–59 Division 4; 1959–74 Division 3; 1974–75 Division 4; 1975–79 Division 3; 1979– Division 2.

HONOURS

Football League: Division 2 best season: 9th, 1982–83; Division 3 – Champions 1978–79; Division 4 – Runners-up 1974–75. *FA Cup* best season: 6th rd, 1978–79, 1981–82. *Football League Cup:* semi-final 1961. *Welsh Cup:* Winners 1891, 1938, 1977, 1979. Runners-up 1931, 1948, 1980.

COLOURS

Blue and amber shirts, amber shorts and stockings.
Change colours: Red or white.

SHREWSBURY TOWN

Players Names / *Ht, Wt, D.o.B.*	*Birthplace* / *Transfer Fee*	*Clubs*	*Appearances* F.L. A & S	F.L.C. A & S	F.A.C. A & S	*Goals* F.L.	F.L.C.	F.A.C.
Goalkeepers								
Steve Perks	Shrewsbury	Shrewsbury T (A)						
6 0, 11 4, 19.4.63								
Steve Osrizovic	Mansfield	Chesterfield	16	2				
6 3, 14 7, 12.9.57	£70,000	Liverpool	4					
	P/E	Shrewsbury T	42	2	2			
Defenders								
Colin Griffin	Dudley	Derby Co (A)						
6 0, 11 7, 8.1.56	£10,000	Shrewsbury T	295+2	14	26	6		
Carleton Leonard*	Oswestry	Shrewsbury T	224+3	9	20	1		1
5 9, 10 3, 3.2.58								
Paul Johnson	Stoke	Stoke C (A)	33+1					
5 9, 11 3, 25.5.59	£20,000	Shrewsbury T	74	4	6	2		
Wayne Williams	Telford	Shrewsbury T (A)	42	2		4		
5 9, 11 10,								
Nigel Pearson	Nottingham	Heanor T						
6 1, 12 6,	£5000	Shrewsbury T	39	2		1		
Midfield								
Steve Cross	Wolverhampton	Shrewsbury T (A)	125+21	6	9	11	3	3
5 11, 10 4, 22.12.59								
Graham Turner (EY)	Ellesmere Port	Wrexham	77		3			
5 11, 11 10, 5.10.47	F/T	Chester	215+3	13	15	5		
	£30,000	Shrewsbury T	332+12	17	27	22	2	1
Ross MacLaren	Edinburgh	Rangers						
14.4.62	F/T	Shrewsbury T	76+3	4	3	5	1	
Bernard McNally	Shrewsbury	Shrewsbury T (A)	57+2	3	6	2		
5 7, 9 11, 17.2.63								
Forwards								
Paul Petts (EY)	Hackney	Bristol R (A)	12+1	+2				
5 9, 10 11, 27.9.61	£30,000	Shrewsbury T	73+9	6	3	6		
Chic Bates	West Bromwich	Stourbridge						
6 0, 12 0, 28.11.49	£5000	Shrewsbury T	160	9	14	45	2	5
	£40,000	Swindon T	50+13	5+1	4	15	1	2
	£50,000	Bristol R	26+3	5+1		4	2	
	£10,000	Shrewsbury T	84+9	4	8	15	1	3
Martin Sankey*		Shrewsbury T (A)	+5	+2				
5 8, 10 12,								
Alan Brown	Easington	Sunderland (A)	87+26	7	4	21	4	
5 11½, 12 10, 22.5.59	—	Newcastle U (loan)	5			3		
	P/E	Shrewsbury T	36	1		10	2	
Gary Stevens	Birmingham	Evesham U						
6 2, 12 0, 30.8.54	£4000	Cardiff C	138+12	9	4+2	44	3	
	£20,000	Shrewsbury T	33+2	1		5		
Colin Robinson		Mile Oak R						
5 10, 11 0,		Shrewsbury T	10+2			3		
Apprentices								
Carl Foster		Shrewsbury (A)	1+1					
Gerardo Nardiello		Shrewsbury T (A)	+1					

Commercial Manager: I. Hookway (Tel. 56316).
Club Coach:
Supporters Player of the Season 1982–83: Nigel Pearson.
Physiotherapist: Wayne Jones.
Club Captain 1982–83: Chick Bates.
Chief Scout: R. Jukes.
Club Statistician:
Association of Football Statisticians Club Adviser to Yearbook: P. Stocken

Players released since May 1982:
Tim Cook, M. (Telford U); Charles Gibson, F. (East Stirling); John McGrath, D. (Worcester C).

SOUTHAMPTON Division 1

Back row (left to right): Dennis Rofe
Mark Whitlock
Justin Fashanu
Mark Wright
George Lawrence
Keith Cassells
David Armstrong
Middle row:
Lew Chatterley (Coach)
Steve Baker
Reuben Agboola
Peter Wells
Peter Shilton
David Puckett
Danny Wallace
John Mortimer (Assistant Manager)
Front row:
Steve Moran
Steve Williams
Alan Ball
Lawrie McMenemy (Manager)
Nick Holmes
Malcolm Waldron
Chris Nicholl.

Chairman: A. A. Woodford.

Directors: J. Corbett, Lt-Col Sir George Meyrick (Bart) MC, TD, B. G. W. Bowyer JP, F. G. Askham FCA, E. T. Bates.

Manager: Lawrie McMenemy.

Assistant Manager: John Mortimore.

Secretary: Brian Truscott. ***Club Nickname:*** 'The Saints'.

Year Formed: 1885. ***Turned Professional:*** 1894. ***Ltd Co.:*** 1897.

Previous Name: Southampton St Mary's until 1885.

Previous Grounds: 1885, Antelope Ground; 1897, County Cricket Ground; 1898, The Dell.

Previous Managers since 1946: Bill Dodgin (Snr), Sid Cann, George Roughton, Ted Bates (4).

The Dell, Milton Road, Southampton SO9 4XX. Telephone Southampton (0703) 39445 and 39633. ***Ground capacity:*** 25,000 ***Record attendance:*** 31,044 v Manchester U, Division 1, 8 Oct, 1969. ***Record receipts:*** £69,690 v Liverpool, Division 1, 16 April, 1983. ***Pitch measurements:*** 110yd×72yd.

Directions to Ground: The ground is ten minutes' walk from Southampton Central station via Hill Lane. Buses 2 and 5 from the city centre pass the ground, which is only ten minutes walk from the centre.

Match tickets: No seats available, all seats being sold to season-ticket holders. Room on the terraces for 8,800 standing, and admission is by purchasing tickets in advance (none sold on day).

Car parking: Ony street parking in the vicinity of the ground. Municipal car parks in the city centre.

Entertainments /catering facilities: Licensed bars inside the ground (stands only).

Club shop: Situated in Milton Road, and at Hanover Buildings in City Centre.

Handbooks /programmes: Handbooks not published annually. Programmes available on subscription.

Address of Supporters Club: Same as Football Club.

Note: Full club statistical records are on pages 416–455.

SOUTHAMPTON 1982–83 LEAGUE RECORD

Match No.	Date	Venue	Opponents	Result	H/T Score	Lg. Pos.	Goalscorers	Attendance
1	Aug 28	A	Coventry C	L 0-1	0-0	—		10,356
2	31	H	Watford	L 1-4	1-2	—	Lawrence	19,714
3	Sept 4	H	Aston Villa	W 1-0	1-0	15	Fashanu	17,943
4	8	A	Tottenham H	L 0-6	0-2	—		26,579
5	11	A	Norwich C	D 1-1	0-0	20	Armstrong	16,492
6	18	H	Manchester U	L 0-1	0-0	20		21,700
7	25	A	Liverpool	L 0-5	0-3	22		32,996
8	Oct 2	H	Notts Co	W 1-0	0-0	20	Fashanu	16,230
9	9	A	Sunderland	D 1-1	0-0	20	Williams	15,635
10	16	H	West Ham U	W 3-0	1-0	19	Williams, Ball, Moran	19,840
11	23	A	Swansea C	L 2-3	1-0	21	Fashanu, Wallace	10,694
12	30	H	Everton	W 3-2	2-1	19	Cassells, Moran (pen), Wallace	18,141
13	Nov 6	A	Manchester C	L 0-2	0-1	19		25,115
14	13	H	Nottingham F	D 1-1	0-1	19	Moran (pen)	18,178
15	20	H	Ipswich T	L 0-1	0-0	19		18,449
16	27	A	Luton T	D 3-3	2-0	19	Wallace, Cassells, Armstrong	11,196
17	Dec 4	H	Stoke C	W 1-0	0-0	17	Wallace	17,198
18	11	A	Birmingham C	W 2-0	0-0	16	Moran, Wallace	11,199
19	18	H	WBA	W 4-1	1-1	13	Wallace, Armstrong, Moran, Puckett	16,896
20	27	A	Brighton & HA	W 1-0	0-0	10	Wallace	21,794
21	28	H	Arsenal	D 2-2	0-1	12	Holmes, Puckett	22,025
22	Jan 1	A	Ipswich T	L 1-2	0-1	15	Wright	18,866
23	3	A	Aston Villa	L 0-2	0-1	15		19,925
24	15	H	Coventry C	D 1-1	1-1	15	Armstrong	17,145
25	22	A	Watford	L 0-2	0-0	17		17,189
26	Feb 5	H	Norwich C	W 4-0	1-0	17	Williams, Holmes, Wallace, Moran	17,244
27	15	A	Notts Co	W 2-1	1-1	—	Puckett, Wallace	5856
28	19	H	Sunderland	W 2-0	1-0	10	Holmes, Mills	17,326
29	26	A	West Ham U	D 1-1	1-1	10	Wallace	19,626
30	Mar 5	H	Swansea C	W 2-1	0-0	6	Baird, Armstrong	16,842
31	15	A	Everton	L 0-2	0-0	—		15,002
32	19	H	Manchester C	W 4-1	4-0	7	Moran 3, Baird	17,201
33	26	A	Nottingham F	W 2-1	0-1	5	Armstrong, Wallace	13,461
34	Apr 2	A	Arsenal	D 0-0	0-0	6		24,911
35	5	H	Brighton & HA	D 0-0	0-0	—		18,253
36	9	A	Manchester U	D 1-1	0-1	8	Foyle	37,120
37	16	H	Liverpool	W 3-2	3-2	7	Moran (pen), Holmes 2	25,578
38	23	A	Stoke C	D 1-1	0-0	8	Wallace	14,903
39	30	H	Luton T	D 2-2	2-2	8	Wright, Armstrong	18,237
40	May 3	H	Tottenham H	L 1-2	1-1	—	Armstrong	21,602
41	7	A	WBA	L 0-1	0-1	10		11,241
42	14	H	Birmingham C	L 0-1	0-0	12		20,327

Final League Position: 12

GOALSCORERS

League (54): Wallace 12, Moran 10 (3 pens), Armstrong 8, Holmes 5, Fashanu 3, Puckett 3, Williams 3, Baird 2, Cassells 2, Wright 2, Ball 1, Foyle 1, Lawrence 1, Mills 1.
Milk Cup (9): Moran 2, Armstrong 1, Cassells 1, Holmes 1, Puckett 1, Wallace 1, Williams 1, Wright 1.
FA Cup (0).
UEFA Cup (2): Williams 1, Wright 1.

Milk Cup	Second Round	Colchester U (a)	0-0
		(h)	4-2
	Third Round	Manchester C (a)	1-1
		(h)	4-0
	Fourth Round	Manchester U (a)	0-2
FA Cup	Third Round	Tottenham H (a)	0-1
UEFA Cup		Norrköping (h)	2-2
		(a)	0-0

Shilton	Baker	Rofe	Agboola	Nicholl	Wright	Ball	Holmes	Fashanu (L)	Armstrong	Puckett	Cassells	Williams	Lawrence	Wallace	Moran	Wells	Mills	Foyle	Baird	Waldron	Referees	Match No.
1	2	3	4	5	6	7	8*	9	10	11	12										N. Midgley	1
1		3	6	5	2	7		9	10	11		4	8								L. Shapter	2
1	2	3		5	6	7		9	10	11		4	8								C. Downey	3
1	2	3*	8	5	6	7		9	10	11		4	12								B. Stevens	4
1	2	3	8	5	6	7		9	10		11	4									J. Deakin	5
1	2	3	11	5	6*	7			10		8	4		12	9						R. Lewis	6
1	2		11	5	6	7*	3		10		8	4		12	9						T. Mills	7
1		2	6	5		7	3	9	10	8		4	11								A. Gunn	8
1		2	6	5		7	3	9	10			4	11*	12	8						J. Worrall	9
		2		5	6	7	3	9	10	12		4	11*		8	1					J. Hunting	10
		2		5	6	7	3	9	10			4		11	8	1					M. Heath	11
1		2		5	6	7	3		10		9	4		11	8						A. Ward	12
1	2	3		5	6		7*		10	12	9	4		11	8						M. Scott	13
1			2	5	6		7		10	12	9*	4		11	8		3				B. Daniels	14
1			2	5	6		7		10	12	9*	4		11	8		3				K. Salmon	15
1		7	2	5	6				10		9	4		11	8		3				K. Barratt	16
1			2	5	6		7		10	8		4		11	9		3				D. Reeves	17
1			2	5	6		7		10	9		4		11	8		3				R. Nixon	18
			2	5	6		7		10	9		4		11	8	1	3				M. James	19
1		3	2	5	6		7		10	8		4		11	9						M. Dimblebee	20
1		3*	2	5	6		7		10	8	12	4		11	9						K. Baker	21
1			2	5	6		7		10	8		4		11	9		3				M. Taylor	22
1			2	5	6		7		10	8*	12	4		11	9		3				D. Shaw	23
1			2	5	6		7		10			4		11	9		3	8			J. Moules	24
1			2	5	6		7		10		8	4		11	9		3				T. Bune	25
1			2	5	6		7		10	8	12	4		11	9		3*				M. Bodenham	26
1			2	5	6		7		10	8		4		11	9		3				R. Guy	27
1			2	5	6		7		10	8*		4		11	9		3		12		D. Brazier	28
1			2	5	6		7		10			4		11	9		3		8		M. Robinson	29
1			2	5	6		7		10			4		11	9		3		8		M. Taylor	30
1		4	2	5	6		7*		10					11	9		3	12	8		D. Lloyd	31
1			2	5	6		7		10*			4		11	9		3	12	8		R. Lewis	32
1			2	5	6		7		10			4		11	9		3		8		T. Holbrook	33
1			2	5	6		7		10			4		11	9		3		8		I. Borrett	34
1			2	5	6		7		10	12		4		11	9		3		8*		D. Reeves	35
1			2	5	6		12		10			4		11	9		3	8		7*	D. Hutchinson	36
1			2	5	6		7		10			4		11	9		3	8			B. Stevens	37
1			2	5			7		10	12		4		11	9		3	8*		6	N. Glover	38
1			2	5	6		7		10	12		4		11	9		3		8*		J. Bray	39
1			2	5	6		7		10*	8		4		11	9		3	12			R. Milford	40
1		12	2	5	6		7			8				11	9		3*		10	4	R. Banks	41
1			2	5	6		7		10	8*		4		11	9		3		12		D. Hedges	42
39	7	16	37	42	39	12	35	9	41	18	9	39	5	32	36	3	27	4	9	3		
		+ 1s					+ 1s			+ 7s	+ 4s		+ 1s	+ 3s				+ 3s	+ 2s			

FOOTBALL LEAGUE RECORD

1920 Original Members of Division 3; 1921 Division 3(S); 1922–53 Division 2; 1953–58 Division 3(S); 1958–60 Division 3; 1960–66 Division 2; 1966–74 Division 1; 1974–78 Division 2; 1978– Division 1.

HONOURS

Football League: Division 1 best season: 6th, 1980–81; Division 2 – Runners-up 1965–66, 1977–78; Division 3(S) – Champions 1921–22; Runners-up 1920–21; Division 3 – Champions 1959–60. *FA Cup:* Winners 1975–76; Runners-up 1900, 1902. *Football League Cup:* Runners-up 1978–79. **European Competitions:** *European Fairs Cup:* 1969–70; *UEFA Cup:* 1971–72, 1981–82, 1982–83; *European Cup-Winners' Cup:* 1976–77.

COLOURS

Red and white striped shirts, black shorts, white stockings.
Change colours: Light and dark blue striped shirts, dark blue shorts, light blue stockings.

SOUTHAMPTON

Players Names Ht, Wt, D.o.B.	Birthplace Transfer Fee	Clubs	Appearances F.L. A & S	 F.L.C. A & S	 F.A.C. A & S	Goals F.L.	 F.L.C.	 F.A.C.
Goalkeepers								
Peter Wells*	Nottingham	Nottingham F (A)	27		2			
6 1, 13 4, 13.8.56	£16,000	Southampton	141	3	12			
	—	Millwall (loan)	18					
Ivan Katalinic (YUG)	Yugoslavia	Red Star Belgrade						
6 0½, 12 3, 17.5.51	£100,000	Southampton	48	3	1			
Peter Shilton (E)	Leicester	Leicester C (A)	286	20	30	1		
6 0, 12 10, 18.9.49	£300,000	Stoke C	110	4	7			
	£270,000	Nottingham F	202	26	18			
	£325,000	Southampton	39	5	1			
Alistair Sperring	Hayling Island	Southampton (A)						
6 2, 12 10,								
Defenders								
Malcolm Waldron	Emsworth	Southampton (A)	177+1	19	15	10		
6 0, 12 4, 6.9.56								
Chris Nicholl (NI)	Wilmslow	Burnley						
6 2, 12 13, 12.10.46	F/T	Witton A						
		Halifax T	42	2	6	3		
	£25,000	Luton T	98	4	4	6		
	£90,000	Aston Villa	210	27	12	11	5	4
	£90,000	Southampton	228	21	17	8	1	
Mark Whitlock	Portsmouth	Southampton (A)	9			1		
5 11, 12 3, 14.3.61	—	Grimsby T (loan)	7+1					
	—	Aldershot (loan)	14					
Steve Baker	Newcastle	Southampton (A)	13	2				
5 5, 10 2, 16.6.62								
Mark Wright (EU21)	Dorchester-on-	Oxford U	8+2		1			
6 3, 11 6, 1.8.63	Thames							
	£115,000	Southampton	42	4	1	2	1	
Nick Holmes	Southampton	Southampton (A)	332+6	23	31	50	5	2
5 11, 12 2, 11.11.54								
Mick Mills (E)	Godalming	Portsmouth (A)						
5 7½, 11 10, 4.1.49	F/T	Ipswich T	588+3	43+3	57	22	2	5
	£50,000	Southampton	27		1	1		
Dennis Rofe (EU23)	Fulham	Orient (A)	170+1	7	11	6		
5 7, 10 11, 1.6.50	£112,000	Leicester C	290	12	21	6		
	£80,000	Chelsea	58+1	2	1+1			
	F/T	Southampton	16+1	5				
Barry Blankley	Farnborough	Southampton (A)						
5 8½, 10 5,								
Alan Knill (WY)	Slough	Southampton (A)						
6 2½, 10 9,								
Reuben Agboola	London	Southampton (A)	47+1	5	1			
5 10, 11 7, 30.5.62								
David Armstrong (E)	Durham	Middlesbrough (A)	357+2	27	29	59	6	8
5 8, 11 3, 26.12.54	£600,000	Southampton	82	6	2	23	1	
Steve Williams (EB)	London	Southampton (A)	236+1	23+1	21	14	3	2
5 10½, 10 11, 12.7.58								
Forwards								
Danny Wallace (EU21)	London	Southampton (A)	37+7	5	1+1	12	1	
5 4½, 9 12,								
David Puckett	Southampton	Southampton (A)	26+23	1+3		6	1	
5 7, 10 2, 29.10.60								
Steve Moran (EU21)	Croydon	Southampton	84+2	5+2	5	38	3	3
5 8, 10 11, 10.1.61								
Martin Foyle	Salisbury	Southampton	4+3			1		
5 9¾, 11 2, 2.5.63								
Ian Baird	Southampton	Southampton (A)	9+2			2		
6 0, 12 7,								

Commercial Manager: Malcolm Price (Tel. 0703 36617)
Club Coach: Lew Chatterley
Supporters Player of the Season 1982–83: Mark Wright
Physiotherapist: Don Taylor
Club Captain 1982–83:
Chief Scout:
Club Statistician:
Association of Football Statisticians Club Adviser to Yearbook: D. Buckle

Players (non-appearance) granted free transfer: Jeremy Stagg, M.
Players released since May 1982:
Colin Dixon, D. (N/K); David Madden, M. (N/K); Joe Blochel, F. (R.S. Southampton); Peter Vacher, D. (N/K); Bob Lee, F. (N/K); Ian Juryeff, F. (Norway); Paul Wiltshire, F. (N/K).

SOUTHEND UNITED Division 3

Back row (left to right): Frankie Banks (Youth Team Coach)
John Keeley
Dave Cusack
Mervyn Cawston
Brian Beckett (Coach)
Middle row:
Paul Clark
Steve Yates
Keith Mercer
Garry Nelson
Tony Hadley
John Walker
Micky Stead
Front row:
Danny Greaves
Steve Phillips
Glenn Pennyfather
Dave Smith (Manager)
Ron Pountney
Phil Dudley (now with Chelmsford City)
Anton Otulakowski.

President: N. L. Mitchell. ***Chairman:*** M. D. Rubin ACIS.

Directors: J. N. Woodcock, L. H. Lesser FCA, D. A. Smith, F. Bonfield, A. R. Rubin, F. H. Walton, E. Simons FCA.

Associate Director: A. Gershlick

Manager: . ***Secretary:*** K. Holmes FAAI, F INST CM.

Club Nickname: 'The Shrimpers'.

Year Formed: 1906. ***Turned Professional:*** 1906. ***Ltd Co.:*** 1919.

Previous Grounds: 1906, Roots Hall, Prittlewell; 1920, Kursaal; 1934, Southend Stadium; 1955, Roots Hall Football Ground.

Previous Managers since 1946: Harry Warren, Eddie Perry, Frank Broome, Ted Fenton, Alvan Williams, Ernie Shepherd, Geoff Hudson, Arthur Rowley, David Smith (9).

Roots Hall Football Ground, Victoria Avenue, Southend-on-Sea. Telephone Southend (0702) 40707. ***Ground capacity:*** 32,000 (16,000 covered). ***Record attendance:*** 31,033 v Liverpool, FA Cup 3rd rd, 10 Jan, 1979. ***Record receipts:*** £36,599 v Liverpool, FA Cup 3rd rd, 10 Jan, 1979. ***Pitch measurements:*** 110yd×74yd.

Directions to Ground: Regular buses from Southend Central station in the High Street; the station is on the London line from Fenchurch Street. Prittlewell, five minutes walk from the ground, is served by trains from Liverpool Street, London.

Match tickets: Seats can be purchased fourteen days before the match.

Car parking: Two car parks at the ground hold approximately 700 cars. Ample parking in side-streets.

Entertainments/catering facilities: Tea bars all around the ground. There is a social club for members and *bona fide* visitors.

Club shop: Situated in Victoria Avenue opposite the ground; sells all types of souvenirs.

Handbooks/programmes: Programmes are available from the club shop; programmes are available on subscription.

Address of Supporters Club: 374 Victoria Ave, Southend-on-Sea, Essex.

Address of the Club Shop or Boutique: 374 Victoria Avenue, Southend-on-Sea.

Note: Full club statistical records are on pages 416–455.

SOUTHEND UNITED 1982–83 LEAGUE RECORD

Match No.	Date	Venue	Opponents	Result	H/T Score	Lg. Pos.	Goalscorers	Attendance
1	Aug 28	A	Plymouth Arg	L 0-1	0-0	—		3850
2	Sept 4	H	Lincoln C	W 2-0	1-0	8	Phillips, Nelson	2836
3	6	H	Chesterfield	W 2-0	1-0	—	Yates, Greaves	2836
4	11	A	Brentford	L 2-4	0-1	10	Nelson, Mercer	5604
5	18	H	Doncaster R	W 3-2	1-1	6	Nelson, Phillips 2	2677
6	25	A	Bradford C	L 0-1	0-1	11		5150
7	28	A	AFC Bournemouth	W 2-0	0-0	—	Phillips, Mercer	4502
8	Oct 1	H	Portsmouth	W 4-0	1-0	—	Cusack (pen), Otulokowski, Nelson, Pountney	4589
9	9	A	Wigan Ath	L 0-4	0-2	10		4705
10	15	H	Reading	W 4-2	3-2	—	Mercer2, Phillips, Otulokowski	3688
11	19	A	Huddersfield T	L 1-2	0-0	—	Yates	4750
12	23	A	Newport Co	D 1-1	1-1	10	Greaves	4338
13	29	H	Orient	D 1-1	0-1	—	Otulokowski	5138
14	Nov 2	A	Wrexham	L 2-3	1-2	—	Greaves, Pennyfather	1802
15	5	H	Bristol R	W 1-0	0-0	—	Greaves	3480
16	13	A	Sheffield U	W 1-0	0-0	9	Phillips	11,032
17	27	A	Walsall	W 3-1	1-0	7	Phillips, Cusack, Greaves	2453
18	Dec 3	H	Preston NE	L 2-3	2-2	—	Mercer, Nelson	3749
19	17	H	Cardiff C	L 1-2	0-1	10	Mercer	3476
20	27	A	Gillingham	L 0-1	0-0	11		5035
21	28	H	Millwall	D 1-1	0-1	11	Cusack	4710
22	Jan 1	A	Oxford U	L 0-1	0-1	11		7021
23	3	H	Exeter C	D 1-1	1-1	11	Phillips	3570
24	14	H	Plymouth Arg	W 3-1	2-0	—	Mercer, Yates, Phillips	3082
25	22	A	Doncaster R	D 0-0	0-0	10		3242
26	29	H	Brentford	W 4-2	2-0	8	Mercer, Greaves, Otulokowski, Cusack (pen)	3074
27	Feb 5	H	Bradford C	D 1-1	1-1	9	Phillips	2858
28	14	H	Huddersfield T	L 0-1	0-0	—		2262
29	18	H	Wigan Ath	W 2-0	2-0	—	Methven (og), Otulokowski	2277
30	23	A	Lincoln C	W 1-0	0-0	—	Phillips	4000
31	26	A	Reading	D 1-1	0-0	9	Nelson	2664
32	28	H	Wrexham	D 2-2	2-0	—	Pountney 2	2512
33	Mar 4	H	Newport Co	L 1-4	0-2	—	Pountney	2476
34	13	A	Orient	D 1-1	0-0	—	Linford	3073
35	15	A	Chesterfield	W 2-0	2-0	—	Nelson, Linford	1970
36	19	A	Bristol R	D 2-2	0-0	9	Linford, Phillips (pen)	6025
37	26	H	Sheffield U	W 3-1	1-1	8	Phillips 3 (1 pen)	3769
38	Apr 1	H	Gillingham	D 1-1	0-0	—	Moody	4234
39	2	A	Millwall	L 1-3	1-2	9	Nelson	3336
40	8	A	Preston NE	D 1-1	1-0	—	Phillips	6286
41	16	H	AFC Bournemouth	D 0-0	0-0	9		4275
42	23	A	Cardiff C	L 1-4	0-3	11	Clark	6141
43	29	H	Walsall	D 1-1	0-0	—	Greaves	1904
44	May 2	A	Exeter C	L 3-4	2-2	13	Pountney, Greaves, Phillips	2956
45	7	A	Portsmouth	L 0-2	0-1	14		17,858
46	13	H	Oxford U	L 1-2	1-1	—	May	1954

Final League Position: 15

GOALSCORERS

League (66): Phillips 17 (2 pens), Greaves 8, Mercer 8, Nelson 8, Otulokowski 5, Pountney 5, Cusack 4 (2 pens), Yates 3, Linford 3, Clark 1, May 1, Moody 1, Pennyfather 1, own goal 1.
Milk Cup (3): Nelson 1, Pennyfather 1, Yates 1.
FA Cup (8): Pountney 3, Cusack 1 (pen), Mercer 1, Phillips 1, own goals 2.
Football League Trophy (3): Cusack 1, Pennyfather 1, Phillips 1.

Milk Cup	First Round	Fulham (h)	1-0
		(a)	2-4
FA Cup	First Round	AFC Bournemouth (a)	2-0
	Second Round	Yeovil T (h)	3-0
	Third Round	Sheffield W (h)	0-0
		(a)	2-2 (aet)
		(a)	1-2

Football League Trophy	Colchester U (a)	1-3
	Orient (h)	1-1
	Watford (h)	1-4

Cawston	Stead	Pountney	Clark	Moody	Cusack	Otulokowski	Phillips	Mercer	Pennyfather	Nelson	Greaves	Yates	Hadley	Keeley	Dudley	Owers	Thomas (L)	May	Linford (L)	Delf	Walker	*Referees*	*Match No.*
1	2	3	4	5	6	7	8	9*	10	11	12											A. Glasson	1
1	2	7		5		4	8	9*	10	11	12	3	6									D. Reeves	2
1	2	7		5		4	8		10	11	9	3	6									T. Bune	3
1	2	7			6	4	8	9	10*	11	12	3	5									L. Shapter	4
	2	7		5	6	4	8	9	10	11		3		1								M. James	5
	2	7	4	5	6		8		10	11	9*		12	1	3							A. Bridges	6
	2	7	4	5*	6	12	8	9	10	11		3		1								E. Read	7
	2	7	4		6	5	8	9	10	11		3		1								C. Downey	8
1	2	7	4		3	6	9	11	8	10		5										J. Key	9
1	2	7		5	6	4	8	9	10	11		3										A. Gunn	10
1	2	7	4	5*	6	10	8	9		11	12	3										A. Saunders	11
1	2	7	4		5	9			8	11	10	3	6									T. Holbrook	12
1	2	7	4			10	6		8	11	9*	3	5			12						D. Letts	13
1	2	7	4*		6	10		8	5	11	9	3	12									D. Lloyd	14
1	2	7	4		6	5		9	10	11	8	3										A. Grey	15
	2	7	4		6	10	5	8		11	9		3	1								R. Guy	16
	2	7	4		6	5	8	9		11	10		3	1								R. Milford	17
	2*	7	4		6	5	8	9		11	10	12	3	1								Alan Robinson	18
1	2	7			6	5	8	9	10	11		3	4									J. Deakin	19
1	2	7			6	10	8	9*	4	11	12	3	5									M. Bodenham	20
1	2	7			6	5	8	9	10	11		3	4									M. Taylor	21
1	2	7	12	6		5	8	9	10	11*		3	4									A. Hamill	22
1	2	7	10	6		5	8	9		12	*11	3	4									B. Hill	23
1	2	7	4		6	10*	8	9	12	11		3	5									M. Dimblebee	24
1		7	4		6	10	8	9	2	11		3	5									D. Allison	25
1	2	7	4*	12	6	10	8	9			11	3	5									G. Napthine	26
	2*	7		4	6	10	8	9		12	11	3	5				1					A. Ward	27
	2	7	4		6	10	8	9		12*	11	3	5				1					D. Hedges	28
	2	7	4		6	10	8*	9	12	11		3	5				1					I. Borrett	29
	2	7	4		6	10	8	9		11		3	5				1					H. Taylor	30
	2	7	4		6	10	8	9	12	11*		3	5				1					H. King	31
	2	7	4		6	10	8	9		11	12	3*	5				1					R. Lewis	32
1	2	7			6		8	9*	4	11		3	5			12		10				A. Gunn	33
1	2	7	4	6			8	9*	3	11			5					12	10			B. Stevens	34
1	2	7		4			8		3	11			5			9		6	10			K. Barratt	35
1	2	7		6			8		3	11			5			9		4	10			L. Burden	36
	2	7		6			8		3	11		5				4		9	10	1		J. Martin	37
1	2	7	12	6			8		3	11		5*				10		4	9			K. Baker	38
1	2	7	5	6			8		3	11			12			9		4	10			T. Glasson	39
1	2	7	12	6			8	10	3	11		5				9*		4				M. Heath	40
1	2	7	6				8	10	12	11		5*	3			9		4				K. Salmon	41
1	2	7	6	5			8			11	10		3			9		4				D. Civil	42
1	2	7		3			8	6		11	10					9		4			5	Alan Robinson	43
1	2	7		5			8	6	12	11	9					10		4*			3	M. Robinson	44
1	3	7	6	5			8	9	2	11	10*					12		4				E. Read	45
1	3	7	4	6			8	9	2	11*						12		5			10	M. Taylor	46
32	45	46	28	23	28	30	43	36	29	42	17	32	28	7	1	10	6	13	6	1	3		
			+ 3s	+ 1s		+ 1s			+ 5s	+ 3s	+ 6s	+ 1s	+ 3s			+ 4s		+ 1s					

FOOTBALL LEAGUE RECORD

1920 Original Member of Division 3; 1921 Division 3(S); 1958–66 Division 3; 1966–72 Division 4; 1972–76 Division 3; 1976–78 Division 4; 1978–80 Division 3; 1980–81 Division 4; 1981– Division 3.

HONOURS

Football League: Division 3(S) best season: 3rd, 1931–32, 1949–50; Division 4 – Champions 1980–81; Runners-up 1971–72, 1977–78. *FA Cup* best season: old 3rd rd, 1920–21, 5th rd, 1925–26, 1951–52, 1975–76. *Football League Cup:* never past 3rd rd.

COLOURS

White shirts with blue sleeves and blue V neck and red and white cuffs, blue shorts and stockings.
Change colours: Red shirts with white pinstripe, red shorts and stockings.

SOUTHEND UNITED

Players Names Ht, Wt, D.o.B.	Birthplace Transfer Fee	Clubs	Appearances F.L. A & S	 F.L.C. A & S	 F.A.C. A & S	Goals F.L.	 F.L.C.	 F.A.C.
Goalkeepers								
John Keeley	Plaistow	Southend U (A)	38	2	3			
6 0, 12 3, 27.7.61								
Mervyn Cawston (ES)	Norwich	Norwich C (A)	4					
6 2, 13 4, 4.2.52	—	Southend U (loan)	10					
	—	Newport Co (loan)	4					
	F/T	Gillingham	19	1	1			
	£8500	Chicago Stings						
	£20,000	Southend U	178	11	12			
Defenders								
Alan Moody* (ES)	Middlesbrough	Middlesbrough (A)	44+2		2			
5 11, 11 10, 18.1.51	£15,000	Southend U	421+2	24	30+1	41		3
John Walker*	Rochford	Southend U (A)	38+13	1+1	5+1			1
5 10, 11 5, 10.12.58								
Steve Yates	Burton	Leicester C (A)	12+7	1	1			
6 0, 12 13, 8.12.53	£15,000	Southend U	212+1	13	12	8	1	
Midfield								
Glenn Pennyfather	Billericay	Southend U (A)	63+5	2	4+3	5	1	
5 8, 10 4, 11.2.63								
Ron Pountney	Bilston	Walsall	1					
5 6, 9 13, 19.3.55	F/T	Port Vale						
	F/T	Bilston						
	£12,000	Southend U	268+12	14+1	21+1	25	2	6
Warren May		Southend U (A)	13+1			1		
Mick Stead	West Ham	Tottenham H (A)	14+1					
5 8, 11 7, 28.2.57	—	Swansea C (loan)	5			1		
	£50,000	Southend U	198+1	13	13	4		
Keith Mercer	Lewisham	Watford (A)	109+25	10+4	6	46	3	4
5 9, 13 0, 14.10.56	£80,000	Southend U	132	6	7	35		1
Paul Clark (EY)	Benfleet	Southend U (A)	29+4	+1	1	1		
5 10, 12 5, 14.9.58	£55,000	Brighton	69+10	8+1	4+1	9		
	—	Reading (loan)	2					
	F/T	Southend U	28+3	1	4	1		
Forwards								
Gary Nelson	Braintree	Southend U	106+22	3+1	6+2	17	1	
5 10, 10 10, 16.1.61								
Derek Spence* (NI)	Belfast	Crusaders						
5 10, 11 3, 18.1.52		Oldham Ath	5+1					
	£2500	Bury	140	13	10	44	7	4
	£50,000	Blackpool	24+3		2	2		1
		Olympiakos						
		Blackpool	58	7	4	18	2	
	£111,111	Southend U	100+4	4	2	32	1	
Danny Greaves	Upminster	Tottenham H (N/C)						
5 7, 9 7,	—	Southend U	30+18		1+1	14		
Steve Phillips (EY)	Edmonton	Birmingham C (A)	15+5	2		1		
5 6, 10 9, 4.8.54	—	Torquay U (loan)	6					
		Northampton T	50+1	3	1	8		
	£19,000	Brentford	156+1	5	4	65	1	3
	£40,000	Northampton T	75	7	4	29	3	2
	£15,000	Southend U	61	2	5	27		1
Adrian Owers		Southend U (A)	10+4					
Non-contract players								
Barrie Delf								
		Southend U	1					

Commercial Manager: R. A. Kitson (Tel. No. Southend 611350).
Club Coach: Frankie Banks
Club Captain 1982–83: Keith Mercer
Supporters Player of the Season 1982–83: Ron Pountney
Chief Scout: Bob Walls
Physiotherapist:
Club Statistician:
Association of Football Statisticians Club Adviser to Yearbook: P. Esdale.

Players (non-appearance) granted free transfer: Steve Butler, F.; Murray Jones, F.
Players released since May 1982:
Phil Dudley, D., (Chelmsford C); Graham Franklin, F., (Basildon U); Tony Hadley, D., (Sweden).

STOCKPORT COUNTY Division 4

Back row (left to right): Howard Jones (Programme Editor), Terry McCreery (Chief Executive/Company Secretary), Andy Thorpe, Terry Park, Nigel Smith, Mickey Wardrobe, Brian Lloyd, Tommy Sword (Captain), Paul Bowles, Mike Quinn, Eric Webster (Manager), Chris Wych (Physiotherapist)
Front row: Oshor Williams, Trevor Phillips, John Rutter, Graham White (Director), Dragon Lukic (Director), Alan Kirk (President/Chairman), Josh Lewis (Director), Dean Emerson, Tony Coyle, Steve Sherlock.

President/Chairman: A. N. Kirk.

Directors: P. Lukic, A. M. Barlow, J. Lewis, J. R. G. White.

Chief Executive/Secretary: T. R. McCreery FAAI.

Manager: Eric Webster.

Assistant Secretary/Commercial Manager: Peter Lamb.

Year Formed: 1883. ***Turned Professional:*** 1891. ***Ltd Co.:*** 1908.

Club Nickname: 'County'.

Previous Names: Heaton Norris Rovers 1883–88, Heaton Norris 1888–90.

Previous Grounds: 1883 Heaton Norris Recreation Ground, 1884 Heaton Norris Wanderers Cricket Ground, 1885 Chorlton's Farm, Chorlton's Lane, 1886 Heaton Norris Cricket Ground, 1887 Wilkes' Field, Belmont Street, 1889 Nursery Inn, Green Lane, 1902 Edgeley Park.

Previous Managers since 1946: Bob Marshall, Andy Beattie, Dick Duckworth, Willie Moir, Reg Flewin, Trevor Porteous, Bert Trautmann, Eddie Quigley, Jimmy Meadows, Walter Galbraith, Matt Woods, Brian Doyle, Jimmy Meadows, Roy Chapman, Eddie Quigley, Alan Thompson, Mike Summerbee, Jimmy McGuigan (18).

Edgeley Park, Hardcastle Road, Stockport, Cheshire SK3 9DD. Telephone: 061-480 8888. ***Ground capacity:*** 16,500. ***Record attendance:*** 27,833 v Liverpool, FA Cup 5th rd, 11 Feb, 1950. ***Record receipts:*** £19,382 v Arsenal, League Cup 3rd rd, 22 Sept, 1980. ***Pitch measurements:*** 110yd×75yd.

Directions to Ground: Edgeley Park is situated within a mile of Mersey Square, the town centre; the ground is a few minutes walk via Wellington Road South and Greek Street. The main line railway station lies just off Greek Street and is only a five minute walk to the Ground.

Match tickets: Seats can be reserved in the Main Stand by post or by telephone.

Car parking: Ample street parking around the ground.

Entertainments/catering facilities: Top class cabaret club next to the ground; four refreshment bars around the ground (not licensed).

Supporters Club shop: Small kiosk situated on Popular side of ground.

Handbooks/programmes: The *Matchday Magazine* is available on match days or by subsciption to the Programme Editor: Howard Jones.

Note: Full club statistical records are on pages 416–455.

STOCKPORT COUNTY 1982–83 LEAGUE RECORD

Match No.	Date	Venue	Opponents	Result		H/T Score	Lg. Pos.	Goalscorers	Attendance
1	Aug 28	H	Peterborough U	D	1-1	1-0	—	Park	2003
2	Sept 4	A	Torquay U	L	0-3	0-1	—		2079
3	7	A	Scunthorpe U	L	0-3	0-2	—		1335
4	10	H	Hull C	D	1-1	1-1	—	Emerson	2252
5	18	A	Tranmere R	D	1-1	0-0	23	Quinn	1536
6	24	H	Northampton T	L	0-1	0-0	—		1621
7	27	H	Rochdale	D	2-2	1-0	—	Williams, Power	1873
8	Oct 2	A	Port Vale	W	3-2	0-2	19	Power 2, Phillips	3474
9	8	H	Hartlepool U	D	1-1	0-1	—	Phillips	1823
10	16	A	Aldershot	L	1-2	1-2	20	Coyle	1417
11	19	A	Bury	L	2-3	1-1	—	Quinn, Phillips	2447
12	22	H	York C	W	2-1	0-0	—	Quinn, Coyle	2014
13	30	A	Wimbledon	L	1-2	0-1	18	Quinn	2294
14	Nov 1	H	Hereford U	W	2-1	1-0	—	Price (og), Phillips	1736
15	6	A	Bristol C	D	2-2	0-0	18	Quinn, Newman (og)	4645
16	12	H	Darlington	W	2-1	1-0	—	Quinn 2	1885
17	26	H	Swindon T	L	1-2	1-1	—	Phillips	2197
18	Dec 4	A	Mansfield T	L	0-1	0-1	20		1661
19	10	H	Crewe Alex	W	3-2	0-0	—	Quinn 3 (1 pen)	1860
20	17	A	Colchester U	L	0-3	0-1	—		1625
21	27	H	Blackpool	W	3-0	2-0	14	Phillips 2, Quinn	3673
22	28	A	Chester	W	2-0	0-0	13	Power, Quinn (pen)	2459
23	Jan 1	H	Halifax T	W	4-2	1-0	11	Quinn 3, Emerson	2871
24	3	A	Crewe Alex	L	0-3	0-1	12		2508
25	15	A	Peterborough U	L	0-1	0-1	15		2911
26	21	H	Tranmere R	W	3-2	1-0	—	Power, Wardrobe 2	2198
27	29	A	Hull C	L	0-7	0-4	16		6151
28	Feb 5	A	Northampton T	W	3-2	2-2	13	Rutter, Power, Phillips	1982
29	12	H	Scunthorpe U	D	1-1	1-0	14	Coyle	2328
30	14	H	Bury	W	2-1	1-1	—	Williams, Quinn	3058
31	19	A	Hartlepool U	L	2-3	0-1	12	Quinn 2	1023
32	26	H	Aldershot	W	2-1	0-1	10	Quinn 2	1853
33	Mar 2	A	Hereford U	D	0-0	0-0	—		1294
34	5	A	York C	L	1-3	1-0	11	Power	2883
35	11	H	Wimbledon	L	1-3	0-2	—	Coyle	2260
36	18	H	Bristol C	D	2-2	1-1	—	Power, Emerson	2036
37	26	A	Darlington	L	1-3	1-0	14	Sword	1012
38	Apr 1	A	Blackpool	D	0-0	0-0	—		3126
39	2	H	Chester	D	3-3	1-2	13	Quinn 2, Phillips	2006
40	8	H	Mansfield T	D	1-1	1-1	—	Power	2197
41	16	A	Rochdale	L	0-1	0-1	15		1834
42	17	H	Torquay U	W	1-0	1-0	—	Quinn	1985
43	22	H	Colchester U	W	3-0	1-0	—	Smith, Coyle, Quinn	1733
44	30	A	Swindon T	L	0-2	0-0	12		2669
45	May 6	H	Port Vale	L	0-2	0-1	—		5516
46	13	A	Halifax T	L	0-1	0-1	—		1522

Final League Position: 16

GOALSCORERS

League (60): Quinn 24 (2 pens), Phillips 9, Power 9, Coyle 5, Emerson 3, Wardrobe 2, Williams 2, Park 1, Rutter 1, Smith 1, Sword 1, own goals 2.
Milk Cup (2): Emerson 1, Park 1.
FA Cup (2): Park 1, Williams 1.

Milk Cup	First Round	Wigan Ath (h)	1-1
		(a)	1-1 (lost on penalties)
FA Cup	First Round	Mansfield T (a)	2-3

Lloyd	Thorpe	Sherlock	Emerson	Bowles	Smith	Williams	Phillips	Quinn	Park	Coyle	Rutter	Wardrobe	Power	Leigh	Sword	Seddon	Liptrott	Referees	Match No.
1	2	3	4	5	6	7	8	9	10	11*	12							K. Walmsley	1
1	4*	3	7	5	6	9	10	11	8		2	12						L. Burden	2
1	12	3	4	5	6	7	8	9	10	11*	2							D. Hutchinson	3
1	2	11	4	5	6	7	8	9	10		3							G. Napthine	4
1	3	11	4	5	6	7	8	9	10		2							H. King	5
1	3	11	4	5	6	7	8	9	10		2							C. Newsome	6
1	5	3	4		6	7	8		10	11	2		9					H. Taylor	7
1	6	3	4*	5	11	7	8	12	10		2		9					K. Cooper	8
1	6		4	5	2	7	8		10	11	3		9					K. Baker	9
1	7	3	5	6	2	8	9			11	4		10					M. Bodenham	10
1	3	5	8	4		6	9	11	7		2		10					D. Civil	11
1	6	3	4	5		7	8	9	10	11	2							D. Allison	12
1	6	3	4	5	12	7	8	9	10		2*	11						I. Borrett	13
1	6	3	4	5	2	7	8	9	10	12		11*						M. Scott	14
1	6	3	4	5		7	8	9	10	11	2							C. Downey	15
1	6	3	4	5		7	8	9	10	11	2							V. Callow	16
1	6	3	4	5	12	7*	8	9	10	11	2							A. Saunders	17
1	6	3	4	5	7		8	9	10	11	2							M. Dimbledee	18
1	6	3	4	5	7		8	9	10	11	2							P. Willis	19
1	6	3	4	5	7		8	9		11	2	12		10*				A. Grey	20
1	6	3	4		7		8	9		11	2	12	10		5			M. Robinson	21
1	6	3	4		7		8	9		11	2		10		5			G. Courtney	22
1	6	3	4		7		8	9		11	2		10		5			C. Newsome	23
1	6	3	4	12	7		8	9		11	2		10*		5			J. Bray	24
1	2		4	6	7	11	8	9		12	3*		10		5			D. Letts	25
1	2		4	6	11	7	8				3	9	10		5			J. Key	26
1	8		4	6	3	7				11	2	9	10		5			T. Holbrook	27
1	3		6	5	11	7*	8			12	2	10	9		4			D. Reeves	28
1	6	3	4		8	7	12	9		11*	2		10		5			A. Hamil	29
1	6	3	4		8*	7	11	9			2	12	10		5			R. Bridges	30
1	6	3	4			7		9		11	2	8	10		5			K. Walmsley	31
1	6	3	4				8*	9		11	2	7	10	12	5			K. Hackett	32
1	6	3	4		7			9		11	2	8	10		5			J. Moules	33
1	6	3	4		7			9		11	2	8	10		5			M. Peck	34
1	6	3	4		12		7	9		11	2	8*	10		5			D. Richardson	35
1	6	3	4		11	7	8			9	2		10		5			F. Roberts	36
1	6	3	4		11	7	8	9			2		10		5			M. Scott	37
1	6	3	4		8	7		9		11	2		10		5			P. Willis	38
1	6	3	4		11	7	8	9			2		10		5			A. Challinor	39
1	6	3	4		8	7		9		11	2		10		5			C. Seel	40
1	3			6	8	7	4	9		11	2		10		5			K. Redfern	41
1	3		4	6	8	7		9		11	2		10		5			K. Barratt	42
1	3		4	6	8	7		9		11	2		10		5			N. Wilson	43
1	3		4	6*	8	7	12	9		11	2		10		5			B. Stevens	44
1	5		4		6	7	8	9				11	10*	2		3	12	D. Scott	45
1	3		4	6*	7		10	9		11	2	8		12	5			J. Hunting	46
46	45	35	45	28	37	34	36	38	18	31	43	12	30	2	25	1	0		
	+ 1s			+ 1s	+ 3s		+ 2s	+ 1s		+ 3s	+ 1s	+ 4s		+ 2s			+ 1s		

FOOTBALL LEAGUE RECORD

1900 Elected to Division 2; 1904 failed re-election; 1905–21 Division 2; 1921–22 Division 3(N); 1922–26 Division 2; 1926–37 Division 3(N); 1937–38 Division 2; 1938–58 Division 3(N); 1958–59 Division 3; 1959–67 Division 4; 1967–70 Division 3; 1970– Division 4.

HONOURS

Football League: Division 2 best season: 17th, 1905–06; Division 3(N) – Champions 1921–22, 1936–37; Runners-up 1928–29, 1929–30; Division 4 – Champions 1966–67. *FA Cup* best season: 5th rd, 1935, 1950. *Football League Cup* best season: 4th rd, 1972–73.

COLOURS

Royal blue and white striped shirts, blue trim and white sleeves, white shorts with blue trim, red stockings with three white bands at top. **Change colours:** Yellow shirts, green shorts and stockings with yellow bands at turn over.

STOCKPORT COUNTY

Players Names Ht, Wt, D.o.B.	Birthplace Transfer Fee	Clubs	Appearances F.L. A & S	 F.L.C. A & S	 F.A.C. A & S	Goals F.L.	 F.L.C.	 F.A.C.
Goalkeepers								
Brian Lloyd* (W)	St Asaph	Rhyl						
6 1, 13 7, 18.3.48		Stockport Co	32	3				
		Southend U	46	1	5			
		Wrexham	266	14	22			
	£6000	Chester	94	8	5			
	—	Port Vale (loan)	16					
	F/T	Stockport Co	91	4	3	1		
Defenders								
John Rutter	Warrington	Wolverhampton W (A)						
5 9, 10 10, 13.9.52		Bournemouth	2+2					
		Exeter C	31+1	2	2	1		
	F/T	Stockport Co	305+3	21	14	9		
Andy Thorpe	Stockport	Stockport Co	206+2	12	5	2		
5 11, 12 0, 15.9.60								
Steve Sherlock	Birmingham	Manchester C (A)						
5 9, 11 8, 10.5.59	F/T	Luton T	2	1				
	F/T	Stockport Co	158+3	11+1	4	7		
Paul Bowles	Manchester	Crewe Alex (A)	174+4	13	9	20	2	1
6 1, 12 11, 31.5.57		Port Vale	98	4	11	8		
	F/T	Stockport Co	30+1	2				
Midfield								
Nigel Smith	Manchester	Blackburn R (N/C)						
6 0, 11 2, 22.4.59	—	Stockport Co	70+3	2	2	1		1
Terry Park*	Liverpool	Wolverhampton W						
5 11, 11 10, 7.2.57								
		Stockport Co	87+3	5	7	8	1	5
		Minnesota Kicks						
		Stockport Co	72	7	8	7	1	2
	—	Manchester C (loan)	+2					
Dean Emerson	Salford							
5 8, 10 8,		Stockport Co	68	2	1	4	1	
Forwards								
Oshor Williams	Stockton	Middlesbrough (A)						
5 9½, 11 7, 21.4.58	F/T	Manchester U						
	F/T	Gateshead						
	£2000	Southampton	4+2					
	—	Exeter C (loan)	2+1					
	£10,000	Stockport Co	141	10	5	18		3
Tony Coyle	Glasgow	Albion R						
5 10, 11 12, 17.1.60		Stockport Co	115+3	6	5	13		
Tommy Sword	Newcastle	Bishop Auckland						
6 2, 14 0, 12.11.57	£6000	Stockport Co	108+1	6	3	17		
Mike Power	Stockport							
6 0, 12 0, 3.10.61		Stockport Co	30		2	9		
Micky Wardrobe*	Newcastle	Burnley (A)	+1		1			
5 11, 12 0, 24.3.62	F/T	Stockport Co	19+8	2		2		
Mike Quinn	Liverpool	Derby Co (A)						
5 9½, 10 0, 2.5.62	F/T	Wigan Ath	56+13	5	3	19		
	F/T	Stockport Co	38+1	2	1	24		
Trevor Phillips* (EY)	Rotherham	Rotherham U (A)	289+33	18+1	18+4	81	5	6
5 6, 11 2, 18.9.52		Hull C	22	2		3		
	£51,000	Chester	57+7		2	11		
	F/T	Stockport Co	49+2	2	1	5		
Non-Contract Players								
Mark Leigh	Manchester	Manchester C (A)						
4.10.61	F/T	Stockport Co	4+2			1		
Andy Seddon								
		Stockport Co	3					
Dave Liptrott								
		Stockport Co	+1					

Commercial Manager: Peter Lamb
Club Coach:
Supporters Player of the Season 1982–83: Dean Emerson
Physiotherapist: Chris Wych
Association of Football Statisticians Club Adviser to Yearbook: H. Jones
Club Captain 1982–83: Tommy Sword
Chief Scout:
Club Statistician: Howard Jones

Players released since May 1982:
Steve Uzelac, D. (N/K); David Sunley, F. (N/K); David Booth, M. (N/K)

STOKE CITY Division 1

Back row (left to right):
Dave McAughtrie
Stephen Ford
Brendan O'Callaghan
George Berry
Stephen Bould
Middle row:
Tony Lacey (Coach)
Loek Ursem (returned to Holland)
Mark Chamberlain
Peter Fox
Sammy McIlroy
Mark Harrison
Derek Parkin
Paul Maguire
Mike Allen (Physiotherapist)
Front row:
Peter Hampton
Peter Griffiths
Bill Asprey (Assistant Manager)
Dave Watson (Club Captain)
Richie Barker (Manager)
Mickey Thomas
Paul Bracewell.

Chairman: P. Axon. ***Directors:*** A. W. Clubb, F. Edwards.

Manager: Richie Barker. ***Assistant Manager:*** Bill Asprey.

Secretary: M. J. Potts.

Year Formed: 1863 (second oldest League Club).

Turned Professional: 1885. ***Ltd Co.:*** 1908.

Club Nickname: 'The Potters'.

Previous Grounds: 1875, Sweeting's Field; 1878, Victoria Ground (previously known as the Athletic Club Ground).

Previous Managers since 1946: Bob McGrory, Frank Taylor, Tony Waddington, George Eastham, Alan A'Court, Alan Durban (6).

Victoria Ground, Stoke-on-Trent. Telephone Stoke-on-Trent 413511. ***Telegraphic address:*** 'Football, Stoke-on-Trent'. ***Ground capacity:*** 35,000. ***Record attendance:*** 51,380 v Arsenal, Division 1, 29 Mar, 1937. ***Record receipts:*** £43,000 v Manchester C, Division 1, Sept 1981. ***Pitch measurements:*** 116yd×75yd.

Directions to Ground: Stoke-on-Trent railway station, on the main line from London, is five minutes walk from the ground. No special buses from the town centre because the ground is central. By road, Stoke is well served by the M6 which passes just two miles from the city.

Match tickets: Bookable two weeks before the match. Ticket office tel: Stoke-on-Trent 413961.

Car parking: The official car park in Wheildon Road holds 2,000 cars. Street parking permitted.

Entertainments/catering facilities: Social club. Refreshments obtainable on the ground.

Handbooks/programmes: Programmes available on subscription.

Address of Social Club: c/o Football Club.

Address of Club Shop: Boothen Old Road, Stoke-on-Trent.

Address of Supporters Club: 1 Lime Street, Stoke-on-Trent.

Note: Full club statistical records are on pages 416–455.

STOKE CITY 1982–83 LEAGUE RECORD

Match No.	Date	Venue	Opponents	Result	H/T Score	Lg. Pos.	Goalscorers	Attendance
1	Aug 28	H	Arsenal	W 2-1	1-0	—	Berry, O'Callaghan	15,504
2	Sept 1	A	Manchester C	L 0-1	0-0	—		27,847
3	4	A	Birmingham C	W 4-1	4-0	9	Hawker (og), Chamberlain M. 2, Griffiths	14,412
4	8	H	WBA	L 0-3	0-2	—		17,447
5	11	H	Swansea C	W 4-1	2-1	6	Watson, Thomas, Davies (og), Maguire (pen)	14,058
6	18	A	Ipswich T	W 3-2	2-2	4	Thomas, Maguire 2 (1 pen)	19,199
7	25	H	Luton T	D 4-4	2-2	6	Berry 2, Bracewell, O'Callaghan	18,475
8	Oct 2	A	Nottingham F	L 0-1	0-0	8		17,122
9	9	A	Manchester U	L 0-1	0-0	9		43,132
10	16	H	Brighton & HA	W 3-0	2-0	7	Thomas, Chamberlain M., McIlroy	13,936
11	23	H	Liverpool	D 1-1	1-1	8	Thomas	29,411
12	30	A	Sunderland	D 2-2	1-2	9	Maguire, Chamberlain M.	16,406
13	Nov 6	H	West Ham U	W 5-2	4-1	7	O'Callaghan, Hampton, Thomas, McIlroy 2	17,589
14	13	A	Watford	L 0-1	0-1	9		18,713
15	20	A	Norwich C	L 2-4	1-0	10	McIlroy, O'Callaghan	13,658
16	27	H	Aston Villa	L 0-3	0-1	12		18,886
17	Dec 4	A	Southampton	L 0-1	0-0	13		17,198
18	11	H	Tottenham H	W 2-0	1-0	11	Watson, McIlroy	15,849
19	18	A	Coventry C	L 0-2	0-1	14		10,065
20	27	H	Everton	W 1-0	0-0	12	Chamberlain M.	25,427
21	28	A	Notts Co	L 0-4	0-2	15		11,600
22	Jan 1	H	Norwich C	W 1-0	1-0	13	McIlroy	15,669
23	3	H	Birmingham C	D 1-1	0-1	12	Painter	15,428
24	15	A	Arsenal	L 0-3	0-2	14		19,428
25	22	H	Ipswich T	W 1-0	0-0	12	Painter	14,026
26	Feb 5	A	WBA	D 1-1	1-0	13	Berry	11,486
27	26	A	Brighton & HA	W 2-1	2-1	13	Thomas, Painter	14,937
28	Mar 2	H	Manchester U	W 1-0	0-0	—	O'Callaghan	20,950
29	5	A	Liverpool	L 1-5	0-2	12	Bracewell	30,020
30	12	H	Sunderland	L 0-1	0-0	13		12,806
31	16	H	Nottingham F	W 1-0	0-0	—	Thomas	10,877
32	19	A	West Ham U	D 1-1	0-0	9	Thomas	16,466
33	26	H	Watford	W 4-0	1-0	7	Thomas, Painter, Chamberlain M., McAughtrie	14,276
34	Apr 2	H	Notts Co	W 1-0	0-0	5	McIlroy (pen)	16,314
35	4	A	Everton	L 1-3	0-0	—	Thomas	15,360
36	9	H	Manchester C	W 1-0	0-0	5	McIlroy	15,372
37	16	A	Swansea C	D 1-1	0-1	6	Thomas	10,100
38	23	H	Southampton	D 1-1	0-0	7	Berry	14,903
39	30	A	Aston Villa	L 0-4	0-1	9		20,944
40	May 2	A	Luton T	D 0-0	0-0	9		11,877
41	7	H	Coventry C	L 0-3	0-1	11		12,048
42	14	A	Tottenham H	L 1-4	0-2	13	Maguire (pen)	33,691

Final League Position: 13

GOALSCORERS

League (53): Thomas 11, McIlroy 8 (1 pen), Chamberlain M. 6, Berry 5, Maguire 5 (3 pens), O'Callaghan 5, Painter 4, Bracewell 2, Watson 2, Griffiths 1, Hampton 1, McAughtrie 1, own goals 2.
Milk Cup (2): Thomas 1, Watson 1.
FA Cup (3): McAughtrie 1, Painter 1, own goal 1.

Milk Cup	Second Round	West Ham U (h)	1-1
		(a)	1-2
FA Cup	Third Round	Sheffield U (a)	0-0
		(h)	3-2
	Fourth Round	Liverpool (a)	0-2

Fox	Parkin D.	Hampton	Bracewell	McAughtrie	Berry	Griffiths	McIlroy	O'Callaghan	Thomas	Chamberlain M.	Maguire	Watson	Dodd	Chamberlain N.	Harrison	Maskery	Ursem	Painter	Bould	Lennox	Parkin S.	Saunders	Heath	*Referees*	*Match No.*
1	2	3	4	5	6	7	8	9	10	11														C. Thomas	1
1	2	3	4	5	6	7*	8	9	10	11	12													G. Courtney	2
1	2	3	4	5*	6	7	8	9	10	11	12													D. Allison	3
1	2		4		6	7	8	9	10	11	3	5												K. Hackett	4
1	2	3*	4		6	12	8	9	10	11	7	5												N. Wilson	5
1	2	3	4		6		8	9	10	11	7	5												M. Taylor	6
1	2	3	4	12	6		8	9	10*	11	7	5												G. Napthine	7
1	2	12	4		6		8	9		11	7	5	3	10*										J. Deakin	8
	2	3*	4		6	12	8	9	10	11	7	5			1									R. Bridges	9
	2	3	4	6			8	9	10*	11	7	5	12		1									A. Challinor	10
	2	3	4	6			8	9	10	11*	7	5			1									H. Taylor	11
	2	3	4	6			8	9	10	11	7	5			1									M. Peck	12
	2	3	4	6	12		8	9*	10	11	7	5			1									F. Roberts	13
	2	3	4	6	12		8	9	10	11	7*	5			1									D. Letts	14
	2	3	4	6	12		8	9	10	11	7*	5			1									M. Dimblebee	15
1	2	3	4	6			8	9	10	11	7	5												D. Scott	16
1	2	3	4	6	12		8	9	10	11	7*	5												D. Reeves	17
1	2	3	4		6		8	9	10	11	7	5												R. Banks	18
1	2	3			6		8	9	10	11	7*	5				4	12							B. Stevens	19
1	2*	3	4		6		8	9	10	11		5				12		7						J. Hunting	20
1	2	3	4		6		8	9	10	11		5				12		7*						D. Axcell	21
1	2	3	4		6		8	9	10*	11		5				12		7						K. Walmsley	22
1	2	3	4		6		8	9	10	11*		5				12		7						D. Hutchinson	23
1	2	3	4				8	9	10			5		6		11*	12	7						M. James	24
1	2	3	4		6		8	9	10		11	5						7*	12					T. Mills	25
1	2	3	4		6	11	8	9	10			5*						7	12					T. Spencer	26
1	2	3	4		6		8	9*	10	11		5						7		12				J. Moules	27
1	2	3	4		6		8	9	10	11		5						7						K. Barrett	28
1	2	3	4	12	6		8	9	10	11		5						7*						J. Key	29
1	2*	3	4		6		8	9	10	11		5						7	12					K. Baker	30
1		3	4		6		8	9	10	11		5						7			2			A. Robinson	31
1		3	4		6	12	8	9*	10	11		5						7	2					M. Bodenham	32
1		3	4	12	6	9	8		10	11*		5						7	2					R. Guy	33
1		3	4	6		9	8		10	11		5						7	2					N. Midgley	34
1			4	3	6	9			10		11	5						7	2	8*		12		A. Saunders	35
1		3	4	6		9	8		10	11		5						7	2					R. Milford	36
1		3	4		6		8	9	10	11		5						7	2					S. Bates	37
1		3	4		6		8	9	10	11		5						7	2					N. Glover	38
1		12	4	5		6	8	9	10	11	3*							7	2					C. Downley	39
1		3	4	6			8	5	10	11	9							7	2					A. Gunn	40
1		3	4			9	8	5*	10	11	6							7	2				12	R. Chadwick	41
1		3	4	6*		12	8		10		7			9		11			5		2			I. Borrett	42
35	30	38	41	17	27	11	41	37	41	37	22	35	1	3	7	3	0	22	11	1	2	0	0		
		+ 2s		+ 3s	+ 4s	+ 4s					+ 2s		+ 1s			+ 4s	+ 2s		+ 3s	+ 1s		+ 1s	+ 1s		

FOOTBALL LEAGUE RECORD

1888 Founder Members of Football League; 1890 Not re-elected; 1891 Re-elected; Relegated in 1907, and after one year in Division 2, resigned for financial reasons; Re-elected to Division 2 in 1919; 1922–23 Division 1; 1923–26 Division 2; 1926–27 Division 3(N); 1927–33 Division 2; 1933–53 Division 1; 1953–63 Division 2; 1963–77 Division 1; 1977–79 Division 2; 1979– Division 1.

HONOURS

Football League: Division best season: 4th, 1935–36, 1946–47; Division 2 – Champions 1932–33, 1962–63; Runners-up 1921–22; Promoted 1978–79 (3rd); Division 3(N) – Champions 1926–27. *FA Cup:* Semi-finals 1899, 1971, 1972. *Football League Cup:* Winners 1971–72. **European Competitions:** *UEFA Cup:* 1972–73, 1974–75.

COLOURS

Red and white striped shirts, white shorts and stockings.
Change colours: All sky blue.

STOKE CITY

Players Names Ht. Wt. D.o.B.	Birthplace Transfer Fee	Clubs	Appearances F.L. A & S	 F.L.C. A & S	 F.A.C. A & S	Goals F.L.	 F.L.C.	 F.A.C.
Goalkeepers								
Peter Fox	Scunthorpe	Sheffield W (A)	49		3			
5 10½, 12 4, 5.7.57	—	Barnsley (loan)	1					
	£15,000	Stoke C	139	6	7			
Mark Harrison	Spondon	Southampton (A)						
6 0½, 12 7, 11.12.60		Port Vale	70	3	5			
	£15,000	Stoke C	7	1				
Philip Pritchard	Birmingham	Stoke C (A)						
Defenders								
David McAughtrie	Cumnock	Stoke C (A)	30+3	1		1		
6 1, 12 3, 30.1.63								
Peter Hampton (EY)	Oldham	Leeds U (A)	63+5	5+1	5	2		
5 7½, 10 9, 12.9.54	£165,000	Stoke C	113+3	6	6	3		
Derek Parkin (EU23)	Newcastle	Huddersfield T	60+1	7	2	1		
5 8½, 11 0, 2.1.48	£75,000	Wolverhampton W	500+1	35	45+1	6	2	1
	F/T	Stoke C	40	1	3			
Steve Bould	Stoke	Stoke C (A)	12+4					
6 2½, 11 13, 16.11.62	—	Torquay U (loan)	9		2			
George Berry (W)	West Germany	Wolverhampton W (A)	124+4	14	21	4		2
6 0¾, 11 12, 19.11.57	F/T	Stoke C	27+4	1	2	5		
Midfield								
Paul Bracewell (EU21)	Stoke	Stoke C (A)	123+6	6	6	5		1
5 8, 10 9, 19.7.62								
Steve Lennox	Aberdeen	Stoke C (A)	1+1					
5 7½, 10 7,								
Sammy McIlroy (NI)	Belfast	Manchester U (A)	320+22	25+3	35+3	57	6	6
5 9½, 11 4, 2.8.54	£350,000	Stoke C	59	2	3	11		
Peter Griffiths	Barnstaple	Bideford						
5 6, 10 8, 14.8.57	£15,000	Stoke C	43+13	+2	1	5		
Chris Maskery	Stoke	Stoke C (A)	3+4		1			
Forwards								
Bren O'Callaghan (EI)	Bradford	Doncaster R	184+3	15	10	65	10	2
6 2½, 14 0, 23.7.55	£40,000	Stoke C	198+9	12	7	44	2	
Paul Maguire	Glasgow	Kilburnie						
5 8, 11 6, 21.8.56	—	Shrewsbury	143+8	8	18	35	1	12
	£262,000	Stoke C	69+5	5	3	15		
Ian Painter	Wombourne	Stoke C (A)	22		2+1	4		
Neville Chamberlain	Stoke	Port Vale (A)	133+8	7	10	33	3	6
5 7½, 11 5, 22.1.60	£40,000	Stoke C	3					
Mark Chamberlain (E)	Stoke	Port Vale (A)	90+6	4	10	17		2
5 8½, 9 8, 19.11.61	£135,000	Stoke C	37	2	1	6		
Micky Thomas (W)	Mochdre	Wrexham	217+13	17+1	20+4	33	2	2
5 6, 10 6, 7.7.54	£300,000	Manchester U	90	5	13	11	2	2
	£450,000	Everton	10					
	£400,000	Brighton	18+2		6			1
	£200,000	Stoke C	41	2		11	1	
Philip Heath	Stoke	Stoke C (A)	+1					
Non-contract Players								
Carl Saunders	Birmingham	Stoke C	+1					
Apprentices								
Steve Parkin		Stoke C (A)	2					

Commercial Manager: D. H. J. Kernick (Tel. 0782 45840)
Club Coach: Tony Lacey
Supporters Player of the Season 1982–83: Mickey Thomas
Physiotherapist: M. Allen
Association of Football Statisticians Club Adviser to Yearbook: W. Martin

Club Captain 1982–83: Dave Watson
Chief Scout:
Club Statistician:

Players (non-appearance) granted free transfer: Cliff Wallace, D.
Players released since May 1982:
Steve Kirk, D. (Partick Th); Colin Singer (N/K); Dennis Thorley, D. (N/K); Steve Ford, F. (Stafford R); Dave Watson, D. (Vancouver W); Loek Ursem, M. (Haarlem); John Lumsden, M. (N/K); Kevin Ronan, M. (N/K).

SUNDERLAND Division 1

Back row (left to right): P. Eustace (Coach), S. Elliott, N. Pickering, J. Hinnigan, C. West, M. Prudhoe, C. Turner, R. Hindmarch, G. Chisholm, I. Atkins, J. Cooke, M. Docherty (Coach)
Middle row: G. Rowell, M. Buckley, A. McCoist, A. Durban (Manager), I. Munro, S. Cummins, B. Venison
Front row: P. O'Donnell, B. Wardrobe, M. Whitfield.

Chairman: T. Cowie. ***Vice-Chairman:*** K. I. Collings.

Directors: E. M. Evans, F. S. Cronin, J. M. Ditchburn, I. T. S. Fraser, P. J. Heyward.

Manager: Alan Durban. ***General Manager/Secretary:*** G. Davidson.

Year Formed: 1879. ***Turned Professional:*** 1886. ***Ltd Co.:*** 1906.

Club Nickname: 'Rokerites'.

Previous Grounds: 1879, Blue House Field, Hendon; 1881, Ashbrooke; 1883, site of Cooper Street; 1884, Abbs Field, Fulwell; 1886, Newcastle Road; 1898, Roker Park.

Previous Name: 1879–81, Sunderland and District Teachers' AFC.

Previous Managers since 1946: Bill Murray, Alan Brown, George Hardwick, Ian McColl, Alan Brown, Bob Stokoe, Jimmy Adamson, Billy Elliott, Ken Knighton.

Roker Park Ground, Sunderland. Telephone 0783-40332. ***Telegraphic address:*** 'Football, Sunderland'. ***Ground capacity:*** 47,000. ***Record attendance:*** 75,118 v Derby Co, FA Cup 6th rd replay, 8 Mar, 1933. ***Record receipts:*** £63,211 v Southampton, Division 1, 23 Aug, 1980. ***Pitch measurements:*** 113yd×74yd.

Directions to Ground: From Sunderland railway station and Seaburn railway station take buses 123 and 124 to Redby Community Centre: the ground is five minutes walk away. Special buses from the town centre. By road via M1, A690 to Sunderland, and then route to Roker Park is signed.

Match tickets: Seats may be booked ten days prior to the match.

Car parking: Parking for 1500 cars, 200 yards from ground.

Entertainments/catering facilities: Hot and cold drinks, pies, sandwiches, etc. available in the ground.

Club shop: Open daily; sells all types of souvenirs.

Handbooks/programmes: Programmes are obtainable on subscription; details from the Club Shop.

Address of Supporters Club: c/o Football Club.

Note: Full club statistical records are on pages 416–455.

SUNDERLAND 1982–83 LEAGUE RECORD

Match No.	*Date*	*Venue*	*Opponents*	*Result*		*H/T Score*	*Lg. Pos.*	*Goalscorers*	*Attendance*
1	Aug 28	A	Aston Villa	W	3-1	0-1	—	West, McCoist, Pickering	22,945
2	Sept 1	H	Notts Co	D	1-1	0-0	—	Rowell	18,997
3	4	H	West Ham U	W	1-0	1-0	4	Rowell	19,239
4	7	A	Coventry C	L	0-1	0-1	—		8190
5	11	A	Brighton & HA	L	2-3	2-0	11	Cummins, McCoist	10,264
6	18	H	Tottenham H	L	0-1	0-1	14		21,137
7	25	A	Watford	L	0-8	0-4	18		16,744
8	Oct 2	H	Norwich C	W	4-1	0-0	15	Rowell 2, McCoist, Cooke	13,144
9	9	H	Southampton	D	1-1	0-0	16	McCoist	15,635
10	16	A	Manchester C	D	2-2	1-0	15	McCoist, Buckley	25,053
11	23	A	Everton	L	1-3	0-1	17	McCoist	20,360
12	30	H	Stoke C	D	2-2	2-1	20	Pickering, Rowell	16,406
13	Nov 6	A	Swansea C	L	0-3	0-2	20		10,034
14	13	H	Luton T	D	1-1	0-0	20	Atkins	14,238
15	20	H	Nottingham F	L	0-1	0-0	21		14,716
16	27	A	Birmingham C	L	1-2	0-1	22	Rowell	12,375
17	Dec 4	H	Ipswich T	L	2-3	1-2	22	Atkins, Worthington	15,000
18	11	A	WBA	L	0-3	0-2	22		11,136
19	18	H	Arsenal	W	3-0	1-0	20	Rowell 3	11,753
20	27	A	Manchester U	D	0-0	0-0	22		47,763
21	28	H	Liverpool	D	0-0	0-0	22		35,041
22	Jan 1	A	Nottingham F	D	0-0	0-0	22		20,382
23	3	A	Notts Co	W	1-0	1-0	21	Cummins	9,327
24	15	H	Aston Villa	W	2-0	1-0	19	McNaught (og), Worthington	16,052
25	22	A	Tottenham H	D	1-1	0-1	19	Cummins (pen)	25,250
26	Feb 5	H	Coventry C	W	2-1	1-0	19	Cummins, Rowell	14,356
27	19	A	Southampton	L	0-2	0-1	18		17,326
28	26	H	Manchester C	W	3-2	0-0	17	Atkins, Rowell 2 (pen)	15,144
29	Mar 5	H	Everton	W	2-1	1-1	17	Rowell 2 (1 pen)	16,051
30	12	A	Stoke C	W	1-0	0-0	15	Rowell	12,806
31	19	H	Swansea C	D	1-1	0-0	16	Rowell	17,445
32	26	A	Luton T	W	3-1	1-1	15	Pickering 2, James	11,221
33	Apr 2	A	Liverpool	;	0-1	0-0	15		35,821
34	4	H	Manchester U	D	0-0	0-0	—		31,486
35	9	A	West Ham U	L	1-2	0-0	16	Pickering	20,053
36	16	A	Norwich C	L	0-2	0-0	16		15,883
37	19	H	Brighton & HA	D	1-1	1-1	—	Pickering	13,414
38	23	A	Ipswich T	L	1-4	0-2	17	Pickering	16,193
39	30	H	Birmingham C	L	1-2	1-0	18	West	14,818
40	May 2	H	Watford	D	2-2	2-1	17	Atkins, James	13,971
41	7	A	Arsenal	W	1-0	0-0	15	West	18,053
42	14	H	WBA	D	1-1	0-1	16	Chisholm	16,376

Final League Position: 16

GOALSCORERS

League (48): Rowell 16 (2 pens), Pickering 7, McCoist 6, Atkins 4, Cummins 4 (1 pen), West 3, James 2, Worthington 2, Buckley 1, Chisholm 1, Cooke 1, own goal 1.
Milk Cup (7): Chisholm 2, Rowell 2 (1 pen), Cummins 1, Hindmarch 1, McCoist 1.
FA Cup (1): Chisholm 1.

Milk Cup	Second Round	Wolverhampton W (a)	1-1
		(h)	5-0
	Third Round	Norwich C (h)	0-0
		(a)	1-3
FA Cup	Third Round	Manchester C (h)	0-0
		(a)	1-2

Turner	Venison	Munro	Atkins	Chisholm	Elliott	Buckley	West	McCoist	Pickering	Cummins	Hindmarch	Rowell	Cooke	Hinnigan	Nicholl	Worthington	Prudhoe	James	Proctor (L)	Whitfield	Referees	Match No.
1	2	3	4	5	6	7	8	9	10	11											H. King	1
1	2	3	4		6	7	8	9	10*	11	5	12									A. Robinson	2
1	2	3	4		6	7		9	10	11	5	8									R. Chadwick	3
1	2	3	4		6*	7		9	10	11	5	8	12								J. Hough	4
1	2*	3		6		7		9	10	11	5	8	12	4							B. Daniels	5
1	2	3		6		7		9	10*	11	5	8	12	4							P. Tyldesley	6
1	2	3	4			7		9	10	11	5	8			6						V. Callow	7
1	4	3			6	7		9	10		5	8	11		2						A. Challinor	8
1		3	4		6	7		9	10		5	8	11		2						J. Worrall	9
1	11	3	4	5	6	7		9	10	12		8			2*						A. Hamil	10
1	12	3	4	5	6*	7	10	9		11		8			2						J. Bray	11
1	11	3		5		7	10	9	6		4	8			2						M. Peck	12
1	11	3	12	5		7*	10	9	6		4	8			2						R. Milford	13
1	11	3	4		5		10	9	6	7		8			2						R. Allison	14
1	11	3	4		5	10	9	12	6*	7		8			2						K. Walmsley	15
1		3	4	6	5	7	12	10		11*		8	9		2						D. Owen	16
1		3	4		5	7		10		11	6	8			2	9					T. Fitzharris	17
	2	3	4		6				10			8	11	5	7	9	1				R. Guy	18
1	7	3	4	5	6				10	11		8			2	9					K. Hackett	19
1	3		4	5	6		7		10	11		8			2	9					F. Roberts	20
1	7		4	5	6*			12	3	11		8	10		2	9					D. Hutchinson	21
1	7		4	5		6	9		3	11		8	10		2						J. Lovatt	22
1	7		4	5		8	9		3	11	6		10		2						R. Bridges	23
1	7	3	4	5			8	12	6	11					2	9*		10			N. Wilson	24
1	7	3	4	5			8	12	6	11					2	9*		10			B. Hill	25
1	7	3*	4	5		12			6	11		8			2	9		10			N. Midgley	26
1	7	3	4	5			12		6	11*		8			2	9		10			D. Brazier	27
1	7	3	4	5					6	11		8			2	9		10			J. Key	28
1	7	3	4	5			12		6	11		8			2	9		10*			C. Seel	29
1	7	3	4	5			9		6	11		8			2			10			K. Baker	30
1	7		4	5				12	3	11*		8			2	9		10	6		A. Banks	31
1	7	3	4	5					11			9			2	8		10	6		A. Crickmore	32
1	7	3	4	5			12		11			8			2	9*		10	6		K. Barratt	33
1	7	3	4	5				12	11*			8			2	9		10	6		J. Key	34
1		3		5	4			12	11	7*		8			2	9		10	6		H. Taylor	35
1*	7	3	4	5		12	9	11	6			8						10		2	B. Daniels	36
	7	3	4	5					6			8	11			9	1	10		2	D. Richardson	37
	2	3	4	6			8	12	11		5		7			9*	1	10			M. Dimblebee	38
	7	3	4	5			9		6	11		8					1	10		2	K. Walmsley	39
	7	3	4	5	2		9	12	6	11		8					1	10*			N. Midgley	40
	7	3	4	5	2		9	10	6	11			8				1				T. Spencer	41
		3	4	5	2*		9	11	8		6		7			12	1	10			P. Tyldesley	42
35	36	37	36	32	20	18	19	19	39	29	14	34	11	3	29	18	7	18	5	3		
	+ 1s		+ 1s			+ 2s	+ 4s	+ 9s		+ 1s		+ 1s	+ 3s			+ 1s						

FOOTBALL LEAGUE RECORD

1890 Elected to Divisio 1 (record run of 57 seasons); 1958–64 Division 2; 1964–70 Division 1; 1970–76 Division 2; 1976–77 Division 1; 1977–80 Division 2; 1980– Division 1.

HONOURS

Football League: Division 1 – Champions 1891–92, 1992–93, 1894–95, 1901–02, 1912–13, 1935–36; Runners-up 1893–94, 1897–98, 1900–01, 1922–23, 1934–35; Division 2 – Champions 1975–76; Runners-up 1963–64, 1979–80. *FA Cup:* Winners 1937, 1973; Runners-up 1913. *Football League Cup:* semi-finals: 1963. **European Competitions:** *European Cup-Winners' Cup:* 1973–74.

COLOURS

Red and white striped shirts, black shorts, red stockings with white top.
Change colours: Blue shirts with red trim, red shorts with white trim, blue stockings with red tops.

SUNDERLAND

Players Names Ht, Wt, D.o.B.	Birthplace Transfer Fee	Clubs	Appearances F.L. A & S	 F.L.C. A & S	 F.A.C. A & S	Goals F.L.	 F.L.C.	 F.A.C.
Goalkeepers								
Chris Turner (EY)	Sheffield	Sheffield W (A)	91	11	13			
5 10½, 11 11, 15.9.58	—	Lincoln C (loan)	5		1			
	£80,000	Sunderland	111	7	4			
Mark Prudhoe	Durham	Sunderland (A)	7					
6 1, 11 8, 11.11.63								
Defenders								
Rob Hindmarch	Stannington	Sunderland (A)	102	5+2	5	2	1	
6 1½, 13 4, 27.4.61								
Gordon Chisholm	Glasgow	Sunderland (A)	124+4	8+4	6	5	2	2
6 0¾, 12 0, 8.4.60								
Iain Munro (S)	Uddingston	St Mirren						
5 7½, 10 5, 24.8.51	£250,000	Stoke C	32		2	1		
	£150,000	Sunderland	71	7				
Nick Pickering	Newcastle	Sunderland (A)	76	6	5	10		
6 1, 11 11, 4.8.63								
Shaun Elliot	Hebden Bridge	Sunderland (A)	220+4	17	12	10		
6 0, 11 6, 26.1.58								
Midfield								
Mike Buckley* (EU23)	Manchester	Everton (A)	128+7	12	7	10	1	1
5 6, 10 7, 4.11.53	£90,000	Sunderland	117+4	8	5	7	1	1
Stan Cummins	Durham	Middlesbrough (A)	39+5	+1	7	9		1
5 6, 9 1, 6.12.58	£300,000	Sunderland	132+1	6	8	29	3	
Ally McCoist	Glasgow	St Johnstone						
5 11, 11 9, 4.8.63	£320,000	Sunderland	38+18	5	3+1	8	1	
Barry Venison (EU21)	Stanley	Sunderland (A)	53+4	5	2+1	1		
5 10½, 11 12, 16.8.64								
Gary Quinn		Wolverhampton W (A)						
	F/T	Sunderland						
Forwards								
Colin West	Wallsend	Sunderland (A)	32+9	4	1	9		
6 1½, 13 2, 13.11.62								
Gary Rowell (EU21)	Seaham	Sunderland (A)	198+22	15+2	13	80	3	3
5 10, 11 3, 6.6.57								
John Cooke	Salford	Sunderland (A)	37+8	1	3+1	4		
5 8, 11 0, 25.4.62,								
Mike Whitfield*	Sunderland	Sunderland (A)	3					
5 8½, 11 0, 17.10.62								
Ian Atkins	Birmingham	Shrewsbury T (A)	273+5	13	23	58	3	3
5 10, 11 0,, 16.1.57	P/E	Sunderland	36+1	3	2	4		
Frank Worthington (E)	Halifax	Huddersfield T (A)	166+5	9	12	42	2	5
5 10, 11 10, 23.11.48	£70,000	Leicester C	209+1	10+1	18	72	2	4
	£87,000	Bolton W	81+3	2+1	5	35	2	1
	£150,000	Birmingham C	71+4	6	7	30	2	2
	£100,000	Leeds U	32	3		14	1	
	£50,000	Sunderland	18+1		1	2		
Leighton James (W)	Llwchwyr	Burnley (A)	180+1	14	10	44	6	1
5 9½, 12 6, 16.2.53	£140,000	Derby Co	67+1	7	11	15	2	2
	£180,000	QPR	27+1		5	4		2
	£165,000	Burnley	76	3	5	9		1
	£130,000	Swansea C	88+10	6	1	27		
	F/T	Sunderland	18			2		

Commercial Manager: C. O'Donnell (0783 672275)
Club Coach: Peter Eustace
Supporters Player of the Season 1982–83: Ian Atkins
Physiotherapist:
Club Captain 1982–83: Ian Munro
Chief Scout:
Club Statistician: Club Secretary
Association of Football Statisticians Club Adviser to Yearbook: W. Simmons

Players (non-appearance) granted free transfer: Barry Wardrobe, F.; Pat O'Donnell, F.
Players released since May 1982:
Paul Brown, D. (Horden CW); John McGinley, M. (Gateshead); Jim Montgomery, G. (retired); Jimmy Nicholl, D. (Toronto Blizz.); Alan Lane, M. (N/K); Simon Tait, F. (N/K).

SWANSEA CITY Division 2

Top row (left to right): Tony Guard, Chris Marustik, Ian Walsh BobLatchford, Jeremy Charles, Max Thompson, Nigel Stevenson, Colin Irwin, Gary Stanley, Neil Robinson, Dean Saunders
Second row: Terry Medwin (left), Huw Lake, Darren Gale, Jimmy Loveridge, Chris Sander, Dai Davies, Mike Hughes, Dudley Lewis, Gary Richards, Dean Holtham, Les Chappell (Youth/Reserve Team Coach)
Third row: Phil Boersma (Assistant Manager), Alan Curtis, Robbie James, Dzemal Hadziabdic, Ante Rajkovic, John Toshack (Manager), Ray Kennedy, John Mahoney, Leighton James (left), Wyndham Evans, Doug Livermore (1st Team Coach)
Bottom row: Geoff Howells, Anthony Cottey, Lee Merrells (left), Colin Pascoe, Adrian Mills, Huw Morgan, Roger Mullen, David Hough.

Joint President: P. E. Holden, I. C. Pursey.

Chairman: M. Struel. ***Vice-Chairman:*** T. J. Phillips.

Directors: E. P. Walters, P. L. W. Owen, R. G. Jones, W. C. Floyd, D. W. A. Rees, D. G. Sharpe, P. K. Howard MPS.

Team Manager: John Toshack. ***Assistant Manager:*** Phil Boersma.

General Secretary: G. J. Daniels FAAI.

Football Secretary: T. A. Howard.

Year Formed: 1900. ***Turned Professional:*** 1912. ***Ltd Co.:*** 1912.

Club Nickname: 'The Swans'.

Previous Name: Swansea Town until Feb 1970.

Previous Managers since 1946: Bill McCandless, Ron Burgess, Trevor Morris, Glyn Davies, Bill Lucas, Roy Bentley, Harry Gregg, Harry Griffiths (8).

Vetch Field, Swansea. Telephone Swansea 474114. Ticket office: 474102. ***Ground capacity:*** 26,237. ***Record attendance:*** 32,796 v Arsenal, FA Cup 4th rd, 17 Feb, 1968. ***Record receipts:*** £33,141 v Manchester U, Division 1, 30 Jan, 1982. ***Pitch measurements:*** 110yd×70yd.

Directions to Ground: five minutes' walk from bus depot. South Wales Transport Co Ltd services from High Street General station to Lower Oxford Street. Parking facilities available at the Quadrant.

Match tickets: Tickets on sale at the ticket office, Vetch Field, Swansea approx. two weeks before the match.

Car parking: Car park 200 yards from the ground in The Kingsway. Side-street parking available.

Entertainments /catering facilities: Disc Jockey programme prior to the match. Licensed bar and refreshment kiosk inside the ground.

Club shop: Situated in William Street; sells all types of souvenirs. Tel: 462584.

Handbooks /programmes: No handbook. Programmes can be obtained from the Commercial Manager.

Address of Supporters Club: John Button, 33 William St, Swansea (0792-460958).

Note: Full club statistical records are on pages 416–455.

SWANSEA CITY 1982–83 LEAGUE RECORD

Match No.	Date	Venue	Opponents	Result	H/T Score	Lg. Pos.	Goalscorers	Attendance
1	Aug 28	A	Notts Co	D 0-0	0-0	—		8061
2	31	H	Coventry C	W 2-1	0-1	—	James R. (pen), Latchford	11,712
3	Sept 4	H	Norwich C	W 4-0	3-0	2	Latchford 3, James R.	11,694
4	7	A	Watford	L 1-2	0-1	—	Stevenson	15,535
5	11	A	Stoke C	L 1-4	1-2	10	Latchford	14,058
6	18	H	Liverpool	L 0-3	0-2	16		20,322
7	25	A	Aston Villa	L 0-2	0-2	17		21,246
8	Oct 2	H	Tottenham H	W 2-0	0-0	14	Thompson, Latchford	16,381
9	9	A	Brighton & HA	D 1-1	0-1	15	Lewis	11,050
10	16	H	Everton	L 0-3	0-1	17		11,183
11	23	H	Southampton	W 3-2	0-1	15	Rofe (og), James R., Latchford	10,694
12	30	A	Manchester C	L 1-2	0-1	17	Latchford	25,021
13	Nov 6	H	Sunderland	W 3-0	2-0	14	Curtis 2, James R.	10,034
14	13	A	WBA	D 3-3	0-2	12	James L., Charles, James R.	12,432
15	20	H	Arsenal	L 1-2	0-0	15	Latchford	12,389
16	27	A	Ipswich T	L 1-3	0-2	16	James L.	17,849
17	Dec 4	H	Luton T	W 2-0	0-0	14	Curtis, Latchford	9556
18	11	A	Nottingham F	L 1-2	0-1	17	James R.	14,585
19	18	H	Manchester U	D 0-0	0-0	17		15,748
20	27	A	West Ham U	L 2-3	2-0	18	Latchford 2	23,843
21	29	H	Birmingham C	D 0-0	0-0	17		11,840
22	Jan 1	A	Arsenal	L 1-2	0-2	17	Curtis	25,237
23	3	A	Norwich C	L 0-1	0-0	19		16,296
24	15	H	Notts Co	W 2-0	0-0	18	Gale, Latchford	8992
25	22	A	Coventry C	D 0-0	0-0	18		9964
26	Feb 6	H	Watford	L 1-3	1-0	—	Latchford	14,461
27	12	A	Tottenham H	L 0-1	0-1	19		24,632
28	26	A	Everton	D 2-2	1-1	19	James R., Gale	17,112
29	Mar 1	H	Brighton & HA	L 1-2	1-1	—	Latchford	8825
30	5	A	Southampton	L 1-2	0-0	20	Loveridge	16,842
31	12	H	Manchester C	W 4-1	3-0	18	Latchford, Walsh 2, James R. (pen)	9884
32	19	A	Sunderland	D 1-1	0-0	19	Marustik	17,445
33	26	H	WBA	W 2-1	1-0	18	James R., Latchford	11,222
34	Apr 2	A	Birmingham C	D 1-1	0-0	18	Latchford	13,591
35	5	H	West Ham U	L 1-5	1-2	—	Walsh	13,303
36	9	A	Liverpool	L 0-3	0-0	20		30,010
37	16	H	Stoke C	D 1-1	1-0	20	Charles	10,100
38	23	A	Luton T	L 1-3	0-0	22	Latchford	11,561
39	30	H	Ipswich T	D 1-1	0-0	22	Rajkovic	8568
40	May 2	H	Aston Villa	W 2-1	1-1	21	Pascoe, Gale	9173
41	7	A	Manchester U	L 1-2	0-1	21	Latchford	35,724
42	14	H	Nottingham F	L 0-3	0-2	21		9226

Final League Position: 21

GOALSCORERS

League (51): Latchford 20, James R. 9 (2 pens), Curtis 4, Gale 3, Walsh 3, Charles 2, James L. 2, Lewis 1, Loveridge 1, Marustik 1, Pascoe 1, Rajkovic 1, Stevenson 1, Thompson 1, own goal 1.
Milk Cup (5): Latchford 4, Loveridge 1.
FA Cup (1): Gale 1.
European Cup-Winners Cup (20): Charles 4, Walsh 3, Curtis 2, Gale 2, Loveridge 2, Hadziabdic 1, Irwin 1, Latchford 1, Rajkovic 1, Stevenson 1, Toshack 1, own goal 1.

Milk Cup	Second Round	Bristol R (a)	0-1
		(h)	3-0
	Third Round	Brentford (a)	1-1
		(h)	1-2
FA Cup	Third Round	Norwich C (a)	1-2
European Cup-Winners' Cup	Prel. Round	Braga (h)	3-0
		(a)	0-1
	First Round	Sliema W (h)	12-0
		(a)	5-0
	Second Round	Paris S-G (h)	0-1
		(a)	0-2

Commercial Manager: Geoff Ford (Tel. 0792 42182)
Club Coach: Doug Livermore
Supporters Player of the Season 1982–83: Bob Latchford
Physiotherapist:
Club Captain 1982–83: Robbie James
Chief Scout:
Club Statistician: Prof David Farmer
Association of Football Statisticians Club Adviser to Yearbook: D. Farmer.

Davies	Marustik	Hadziabdic	Irwin	Mahoney	Stanley	James L.	James R.	Charles	Stevenson	Latchford	Curtis	Rajkovic	Kennedy	Loveridge	Lewis	Thompson	Gale	Walsh	Evans	Robinson	Richards	Pascoe	Sander	Lake	*Referees*	*Match No.*
1	2	3	4	5	6	7	8	9	10	11															B. Hill	1
1	2*	3	4	5		7	8	9	10	11	12	6													D. Letts	2
1	2	3	4		12	9	8*	10	5	11	7	6													B. Stevens	3
1	2	3	4			7	8	9	10	11*	12	6	5												M. Taylor	4
1	2*	3	4			9	8	12	10	11	7	6	5												N. Wilson	5
1	2*	3	4			12	8	9	10	11	7	6	5												A. Hamil	6
1	12	3	4*	6	2		8	9	10	11			5	7											T. Fitzharris	7
1	2			6		9	8	4		11	7		5		3	10									A. Seville	8
1		3		11*		9	8	4	6		7		5		2	10	12								D. Vickers	9
1				3		9	8	4	10*	11	7		5		2	6		12							K. Barratt	10
1		3		11*	10		8			9	7	6	5	12	2				4						M. Heath	11
1		3		5	2	9*	8	4	10	11	12	6						7							K. Redfern	12
1	3*			5	11	12	8	4	10		7	6			2			9							R. Milford	13
1		3		9	2	7	8	4	10	11		6	5*							12					R. Nixon	14
1		3		9	2		8	4	10	11		6		7	5										G. Napthine	15
1		3		5	2	9	8	5	10	11		4		7											J. Moules	16
1		3		9	2	12	8	4	10	11	7*	6	5												C. Newsome	17
1		3		9	2	12	8	10		11	7	6	5*							4					K. Salmon	18
1		3		9	2	12	8	10		11	7*	6							5	4					T. Bune	19
1		3		9	2	7	8	10		11		6							5	4					T. Borrett	20
1		3		4		9	8	10*	12	11	7	6							5	2					A. Glasson	21
1		3		5	12	9			10	11	7*	6			8				4	2					D. Hedges	22
1		3		9	12		8		10	11	7	6			4				5	2*					C. Downey	23
1		3		9	10*		8	4	5	11	7	6					12			2					D. Lloyd	24
1	3			9	10		8	4	5	11		6					7			2					Alan Robinson	25
1	3				12		8	4*	5	11	7	6	10				9			2					N. Ashley	26
1		3		9	10		8	4		11	7	6*	5				12			2					J. Hunting	27
1		3		10			8			11			5	7	4		9			2	6				P. Tyldesley	28
1		3		7*			8			11			5	10	4		9			2	6	12			A. Crickmore	29
1	2	12					9	4				10	5*	7	6		11			8	3				M. Taylor	30
	2				10		8	4		11		6		7	5		12	9*			3		1		L. Shapter	31
	2				10		8			11		6		7	5		9			4	3		1		A. Banks	32
	2				10		8		4	11	12	6		7	5			9*			3		1		L. Burden	33
	2				10		8		4	11		6		7	5			9			3		1		R. Bridges	34
	2				10		8		4	11		6		7	5		12	9*			3		1		D. Civil	35
	2				10		8	12		9		5		7	6					4	3	11*	1		J. Lovatt	36
	2						8	4	12	11		6		7	5			9*		10	3		1		S. Bates	37
	2						8	4		11		6	10	7	5					9*	3	12	1		A. Hamil	38
	2						8	4		11		6	10	7*	5		9				3	12	1		V. Callow	39
	2				10		8	4		11			5		6		9				3	7	1		D. Hedges	40
	2				10		8	4		11			5		6		9				3	7	1		P. Willis	41
			6		8				5			4	10	7	2		9				3	11*	1	12	J. Martin	42
30	22	24	8	24	24	14	40	30	24	38	17	33	21	16	23	3	10	7	6	17	15	4	12	0		
	+ 1s	+ 1s			+ 4s	+ 5s		+ 2s	+ 2s		+ 4s			+ 1s			+ 5s	+ 1s		+ 1s		+ 3s		+ 1s		

FOOTBALL LEAGUE RECORD

1920 Original Member of Division 3; 1921–25 Division 3(S); 1925–47 Division 2; 1947–49 Division 3(S); 1949–65 Division 2; 1965–67 Division 3; 1967–70 Division 4; 1970–73 Division 3; 1973–78 Division 4; 1978–79 Division 3; 1979–81 Division 2; 1981–83 Division 1; 1983– Division 2.

HONOURS

Football League: Division 1 best season: 6th 1981–82; Division 2 – Promoted 1980–81 (3rd); Division 3(S) – Champions 1924–25, 1948–49; Division 3 – Promoted 1978–79 (3rd); Division 4 – Promoted 1969–70 (3rd), 1977–78 (3rd). *FA Cup:* semi-finals 1926, 1964. *Football League Cup* best season: 4th rd, 1964–65, 1976–77. *Welsh Cup:* Winners 8 times. Runners-up 8 times. **European Competition:** *European Cup-Winners' Cup:* 1961–62, 1966–67, 1981–82, 1982–83.

COLOURS

All white with black trim. **Change colours:** Red shirts, black shorts and stockings.

SWANSEA CITY

Players Names	*Birthplace*	*Clubs*	*Appearances*			*Goals*		
Ht, Wt, D.o.B.	*Transfer Fee*		*F.L. A & S*	*F.L.C. A & S*	*F.A.C. A & S*	*F.L.*	*F.L.C.*	*F.A.C.*
Goalkeepers								
Chris Sander	Swansea	Swansea C (A)	13					
5 11, 10 4, 11.11.62								
Dai Davies (W)	Ammanford	Ammanford T						
6 1, 13 3, 1.4.48		Swansea C	9		2			
	£15,000	Everton	82	6	5			
	—	Swansea C (loan)	6					
	£50,000	Wrexham	144	10	10			
	£35,000	Swansea C	71	6	2			
Mike Hughes	Swansea	Swansea C (A)						
5 10½, 11 3, 19.8.64								
Defenders								
Wyndham Evans*	Llanelli	Stoke C (AM)						
5 9½, 13 0, 19.3.51	—	Swansea C (A)	349+5	18	11	19		1
Nigel Stevenson (W)	Swansea	Swansea C (A)	202+9	7	7	11		
6 2, 12 10, 2.11.58								
Neil Robinson	Liverpool	Everton (A)	13+3	3	1	1		
5 8, 10 6, 20.4.57	£70,000	Swansea C	91+7	4	2	8		
Dudley Lewis (WU21)	Swansea	Swansea C (A)	36	2	1	1		
5 10¼, 10 9, 17.11.62								
Dzemal Hadziabdic	Yugoslavia	Velez Mostar						
(YUG)								
5 8¼, 10 11, 25.7.53	£160,000	Swansea C	87+1	4	1	2		
Colin Irwin	Liverpool	Liverpool	26+3	6	4	3		
6 1, 12 13, 9.2.57	£340,000	Swansea C	45	2	1		1	
Gary Richards	Swansea	Swansea C (A)	16		1			
5 8½, 11 2, 2.8.63								
Max Thomson	Liverpool	Liverpool (A)	1					
6 2½, 14 0, 31.2.56	£80,000	Blackpool	92+7	9	3	6		
	£20,000	Swansea C	25+1	2	1	2		
Chris Marustik (W)	Swansea	Swansea C (A)	56+8	5	7	2		
5 8¼, 11 5, 10.8.61								
Midfield								
John Mahoney (W)	Cardiff	Ashton U						
5 8, 11 4, 20.9.46		Crewe Alex	16+2	1	4	5		1
	£19,500	Stoke C	272+12	22+2	14+1	25	1	1
	£90,000	Middlesbrough	77	6	7	1		1
	£100,000	Swansea C	106+4	8	4+1	1	1	
Ante Rajkovic (YUG)	Yugoslavia	Sarajevo						
5 11¼, 12 13, 17.8.52	£100,000	Swansea C	75	4	1	2		
Huw Lake	Swansea	Swansea C (A)	+1					
5 9, 10 9, 20.8.63								
Tony Guard	Swansea	Swansea C (A)						
5 6½, 9 3, 19.4.64								
Gary Stanley	Burton	Chelsea (A)	105+4	5	4+1	15		
5 9, 12 6, 4.3.54	£300,000	Everton	52	7	2	1		
	£150,000	Swansea C	46+11	4	1	3		
Ray Kennedy (E)	Seaton Delavel	Arsenal (A)	156+2	11	24	53	4	6
5 11, 13 4, 28.7.51	£180,000	Liverpool	265+3	35	28	51	6	3
	£160,000	Swansea C	39	3		2		
Dean Holtham		Cardiff C (A)						
	F/T	Swansea C						
Huw Morgan		Swansea C (A)						
Forwards								
Bob Latchford (E)	Birmingham	Birmingham C (A)	157+2	15+2	11	68	6	6
6 0, 13 6, 18.1.51	£350,000	Everton	235+1	28	17	106	19	10
	£125,000	Swansea C	69	5	1	32	4	
Ian Walsh (W)	St Davids	Crystal Palace (A)	101+16	1+3	11	23	2	2
5 9½, 11 6, 4.9.58	P/E	Swansea C	10+3			5		
Robbie James (W)	Swansea	Swansea C (A)	386+8	21	19	99	6	5
5 11, 13 1, 23.3.57								
Jeremy Charles (W)	Swansea	Swansea C (A)	214+23	18	11	53	7	3
6 1¼, 13 1, 26.9.59								
John Toshack (W)	Cardiff	Cardiff C (A)	159+3	6	6	75	2	1
6 1, 12 0, 22.3.49	£110,000	Liverpool	169+3	13	23	74	3	8
	F/T	Swansea C	55+5	9	9	24	2	3
Dean Saunders	Swansea	Swansea C (A)						
5 8½, 10 0, 21.6.64								
Colin Pascoe	Aberavon	Swansea C (A)	4+3			1		
5 9½, 10 0, 9.4.65								
Jimmy Loveridge (WU21)	Swansea	Swansea C (A)	18+3	1+1		1	1	
5 8¼, 11 2, 19.10.62								
Darren Gale	Port Talbot	Swansea C (A)	10+6		1	3		1
5 10½, 12 13, 25.10.63								
Alan Curtis (W)	Rhondda	Swansea C	244+4	12	14	72	6	7
5 11, 12 8, 16.4.54	£370,000	Leeds U	28	2	1	5		
	£165,000	Swansea C	73+8	5	3	20		

Players (non-appearance) granted free transfer: Jeff Howells.
Players released since May 1982: Bryan Cokeley, (N/K); Neil Henson, M. (N/K); Pat McQuillan, F. (N/K); Dave Stewart, G. (Hong Kong).

SWINDON TOWN Division 4

Back row (left to right):
Jimmy Quinn
Russell Lewis
Charlie Henry
Jimmy Allen
Mark Stevens
Paul Rideout
Andy Rowland
Middle row:
Martin Blackler
Brian Hughes
Howard Pritchard
Ken Beamish
David Bristow
Roy Carter
Kevin Baddeley
David Round
Front row:
Mike Graham
Gary Emmanuel
Paul Batty
John Trollope (Manager)
Ray Baverstock
Leigh Barnard
Gary Williams.

President: W. H. Castle. ***Chairman:*** C. J. Green.

Directors: T. J. R. Kearsley, R. Stephenson, M. W. Earle, W. H. Dore, L. Smart, G. Whittock, G. P. Heath, N. Arkell, G. Herbert, B. Hillier, C. Howard.

Team Manager: K. Beamish.

Admin Manager /Secretary: R. Jefferies.

Finance Manager: R. A. Morse. ***Club Nickname:*** 'Robins'.

Year Formed: 1881. ***Turned Professional:*** 1894. ***Ltd Co.:*** 1894.

Previous Ground: 1881–96, The Croft.

Previous Managers since 1946: Louis Page, Maurice Lindley, Bert Head, Danny Williams, Fred Ford, Dave Mackay, Les Allen, Danny Williams, Bob Smith (9).

County Ground, Swindon, Wiltshire. Telephone Swindon (0793) 22118.

Ground capacity: 26,000 (6500 seats). ***Record attendance:*** 32,000 v Arsenal, FA Cup 3rd rd, 15 Jan, 1972. ***Record receipts:*** £56,024 v Tottenham H, FA Cup 4th rd, 26 Jan, 1980. ***Pitch measurements:*** 114yd×72yd.

Directions to Ground: Both Swindon bus and railway stations are half a mile from the ground.

Match tickets: Available 3 weeks in advance.

Car parking: Corporation car park adjacent to the west end of the ground, off County Road.

Entertainments /catering facilities: The Supporters' Club Rendezvous Club and Squash Club in the North Stand. Refreshment kiosks in all parts of the ground. No licensed bars on terraces or stands.

Club shop: Postal enquiries welcome. All types of souvenirs are stocked.

Handbooks /programmes: Programmes available by postal application, or subscription.

Address of Supporters Club: Swindon Town Supporters Club, County Ground, Swindon, Wilts.

Address of the Club Shop or Boutique: **Souvenir and Sports Shop, Swindon Town FC, County Ground, Swindon.**

Note: Full club statistical records are on pages 416–455.

SWINDON TOWN 1982–83 LEAGUE RECORD

Match No.	Date	Venue	Opponents	Result	H/T Score	Lg. Pos.	Goalscorers	Attendance
1	Aug 28	H	Port Vale	W 1-0	0-0	—	Rideout	3602
2	Sept 4	A	Blackpool	L 1-2	1-1	10	Carter	3593
3	8	A	Hereford U	W 2-1	0-1	—	Rowland, Quinn	2674
4	11	H	Halifax T	L 0-1	0-0	10		3450
5	18	A	Rochdale	D 1-1	1-1	8	Emmanuel	1292
6	25	H	Crewe Alex	W 1-0	1-0	9	Rowland	2967
7	28	A	Northampton T	W 1-0	1-0	—	Rideout (pen)	2706
8	Oct 2	A	Hull C	D 0-0	0-0	6		3786
9	10	H	Colchester U	W 3-0	2-0	—	Rideout (pen), Rowland 2	4473
10	16	A	Bury	D 0-0	0-0	6		2497
11	20	A	Torquay U	D 1-1	0-0	—	Rideout	2979
12	23	H	Mansfield T	W 4-0	2-0	6	Rideout, Barnard, Rowland, Pritchard	3917
13	30	A	Chester	W 1-0	0-0	5	Rowland	1544
14	Nov 2	H	Tranmere R	W 4-2	2-1	—	Rideout 2 (2 pens), Rowland, Barnard	4407
15	6	A	Darlington	L 0-1	0-1	7		1334
16	13	H	York C	W 3-2	2-1	4	Rowland, Rideout, Pritchard	4081
17	26	A	Stockport Co	W 2-1	1-1	—	Emmanuel, Rowland	2197
18	Dec 4	H	Peterborough U	W 1-0	0-0	3	Rideout (pen)	3961
19	18	H	Hartlepool U	W 3-0	1-0	2	Rideout (pen), Rowland 2	4118
20	27	A	Aldershot	D 1-1	0-0	2	Lewis	5087
21	28	H	Wimbledon	L 0-1	0-0	2		8164
22	Jan 1	A	Bristol C	D 1-1	0-0	4	Pritchard	9002
23	3	H	Scunthorpe U	D 2-2	1-2	5	Rowland, Rideout (pen)	6728
24	15	A	Port Vale	L 0-3	0-1	6		6397
25	22	H	Rochdale	W 4-1	1-1	6	Rideout 3 (1 pen), Pritchard	4425
26	Feb 5	A	Crewe Alex	L 0-3	0-3	7		2536
27	12	H	Hereford U	W 3-2	1-0	6	Pritchard, Rideout, Bray (og)	4042
28	18	A	Colchester U	L 0-1	0-0	—		2386
29	26	H	Bury	D 1-1	1-1	7	Pritchard	4692
30	28	A	Tranmere R	L 0-2	0-0	—		1521
31	Mar 5	A	Mansfield T	L 0-1	0-0	8		2101
32	12	H	Chester	L 2-3	1-1	8	Rowland, Rideout	3238
33	15	A	Halifax T	L 0-1	0-0	—		1806
34	19	H	Darlington	L 1-2	1-1	8	Rowland	2815
35	26	A	York C	D 0-0	0-0	8		3265
36	Apr 1	A	Wimbledon	D 0-0	0-0	—		3400
37	4	H	Aldershot	W 2-0	0-0	—	Batty, Bailie	3494
38	9	A	Peterborough U	L 3-4	1-4	8	Rideout, Barnard, Rowland	2522
39	16	H	Hull C	L 0-1	0-0	9		3772
40	19	H	Blackpool	D 3-3	2-3	—	Baddeley, Rowland, Pritchard	2408
41	23	A	Hartlepool U	W 2-1	1-1	8	Rideout 2 (1 pen)	1126
42	26	H	Torquay U	W 2-1	1-0	—	Pritchard, Rideout	2509
43	30	H	Stockport Co	W 2-0	0-0	8	Pritchard, Quinn	2669
44	May 2	A	Scunthorpe U	L 0-2	0-1	8		3546
45	8	H	Northampton T	L 1-5	1-2	—	Quinn	3386
46	14	H	Bristol C	W 2-0	1-0	8	Barnard, Pritchard	5103

Final League Position: 8

GOALSCORERS

League (61): Rideout 20 (9 pens), Rowland 16, Pritchard 10, Barnard 4, Quinn 3, Emmanuel 2, Bailie 1, Batty 1, Baddeley 1, Carter 1, Lewis 1, own goal 1.
Milk Cup (2): Rideout 2.
FA Cup (15): Pritchard 5, Rowland 4, Batty 2, Barnard 1, Henry 1, Lewis 1, Rideout 1.

Milk Cup	First Round	Bristol C (h)	2-1
		(a)	0-2
FA Cup	First Round	Wealdstone (h)	2-0
	Second Round	Brentford (h)	2-2
		(a)	3-1
	Third Round	Aldershot (h)	7-0
	Fourth Round	Burnley (a)	1-3

Allan	Henry	Baddeley	Emmanuel	Lewis	Graham	Pritchard	Hughes	Rideout	Rowland	Barnard	Baverstock	Carter	Quinn	Batty	Bailie	Blackler	Moore (L)	Stevens	Referees	Match No.
1	2	3	4	5	6	7	8	9	10	11									E. Scales	1
1		3*	4	5	6	12	8	9	10	11	2	7							P. Willis	2
1		3	4*	5	6		8	9	10	11	2	7	12						J. Lovatt	3
1		3	4*	5	6		8	9	10	11	2	7	12						T. Holbrook	4
1	2	3	4	5	6	7	8	9	10	11									C. Seel	5
1	2	3	4	5	6	7		9	10	11				8					A. Crickmore	6
1	2	3	4	5	6	7		9	10	11				8					G. Napthine	7
1	2	3	4	5	6	7		9	10	11				8					T. Jones	8
1	2	3	4	5	6	7*	12	9	10	11				8					L. Burden	9
1	2	5	8	4	3		6	10	11	9				7					D. Owen	10
1	2	3	4	5	6	7		9	10	11				8					K. Cooper	11
1	2	3	4	5	6	7		9*	10	11			12	8					M. James	12
1	2	3	4	5	6	7		9	10	11				8					K. Walmsley	13
1	2	3	4	5	6	7		9	10	11				8					M. Dimblebee	14
1		3	4	5	6		7	9	10	11	2			8					D. Richardson	15
1	2	3	4	5	6	7*		9	10	11			12	8					K. Salmon	16
1	2	3	4	5	6	7		9	10	11				8					A. Saunders	17
1	2	3	4	5	6	7		9	10	11				8					H. W. King	18
1		3	4	5	6	7		9	10	11				8	2				B. Daniels	19
1		3	4	5	6	7		9	10	11				8	2				J. Moules	20
1			4	5	6	7			10	11	3		9	8	2				J. Bray	21
1			4	5	6	7		9	10	11	2			8	3				M. Robinson	22
1		3	4	5	6	7		9	10	11				8	2				A. Ward	23
1				5	6	7	4	9	10	11	2			8	3				D. Scott	24
1				5	6	7	4	9	10	11	2			8	3				D. Brazier	25
1			4	5	6	7		9	10	11	2			8	3				K. Hackett	26
1			4	5	6	7*		9	10	11	2		12	8	3				R. Milford	27
1			4	5	6		7	9		11	2		10	8	3				M. Bodenham	28
1			4	5	6	7		9	10	11	2			8	3				A. Hamil	29
1			4	5	6	7*		9	10	11	2		12	8	3				R. Banks	30
1	2*	3	4	5	6		8	9	10	11			7			12			G. Tyson	31
1	2	3	4	5	6	7		9	10	11						8			A. Gunn	32
1		3	4	5	6	7		9	10	11				8	2				D. Allison	33
1		3	4	5	6	7		9	10	8				12	2		11*		C. Downey	34
1		3		5	6			9	10	8	7			4	2	11			R. Fitzharris	35
1		3		5	6			9	10	8	7			4	2	11			M. Taylor	36
1		3		5	6			9	10	8	7			4	2	11			V. Callow	37
1		3		5	6	12		9	10	8	7			4	2	11*			D. Reeves	38
1		3		5	6	7		9	10	8				4	2	11			M. Dimblebee	39
1		3		5	6	7	12	9	10	8				4	2	11*			R. Lewis	40
1		3		5	6	7	11	9	10	8				4	2				A. Challinor	41
1		3		5	6	7	11	9	10	8				4	2				H. Taylor	42
1		3		5*	6	7	11	9	10	8			12	4	2				B. Stevens	43
1	5	3			6	7	11*	9	10	8			12	4	2				R. Nixon	44
1*	5	3			6	7	11	9	10	8			12	4	2				D. Letts	45
	5	3			6	7			10	8			9	4	2	11		1	L. Shapter	46
45	19	37	32	43	46	35	16	44	45	46	17	3	4	38	26	8	1	1		
						+ 2s	+ 2s						+ 9s	+ 1s		+ 1s				

FOOTBALL LEAGUE RECORD

1920 Original Member of Division 3; 1921–58 Division 3(S); 1958–63 Division 3; 1963–65 Division 2; 1965–69 Division 3; 1969–74 Division 2; 1974–82 Division 3; 1982– Division 4.

HONOURS

Football League: Division 2 best season: 5th, 1969–70. Division 3 – Runners-up 1962–63, 1968–69. *FA Cup:* semi-finals 1910, 1912. *Football League Cup:* Winners 1968–69. *Anglo-Italian Cup:* Winners 1970.

COLOURS

Red shirts with white trim, white shorts, red stockings. **Change colours:** Yellow shirts and stockings, blue shorts.

SWINDON TOWN

Players Names Ht, Wt, D.o.B.	Birthplace Transfer Fee	Clubs	Appearances F.L. A & S	 F.L.C. A & S	 F.A.C. A & S	Goals F.L.	 F.L.C.	 F.A.C.
Goalkeepers								
Jim Allan	Inverness	Swindon T (A)	363	35	35			
6 0, 12 0, 10.11.53								
Mark Stevens*	Bristol	Bristol R (A)						
6 1½, 13 4, 31.1.63	F/T	Swindon T	1					
Defenders								
Russell Lewis	Neath	Everwarm						
5 10½, 13 3, 15.9.56	—	Swindon	175+6	17	16	7	1	2
Charlie Henry	Acton	Swindon T (A)	91+2	6	5	3		1
5 11, 12 8, 13.2.62								
Kevin Baddeley	Swindon	Bristol C (A)	1					
5 9½, 12 1, 12.3.62	F/T	Swindon T	65	2+1	5	2	1	
Ray Baverstock*	Southall	Swindon T (A)	17		2			
5 8, 11 4								
Colin Baillie	Belfast	Swindon T (A)	27		3	1		
5 11, 10 11,								
Midfield								
Martin Blackler*	Swindon	Swindon T (A)	8+1					
5 10, 11 6, 14.3.63								
Gary Emmanuel (WU23)	Swansea	Birmingham C (A)	61+10	1	5	6		
5 9, 11 3, 1.2.54	£50,000	Bristol R	59+6	4	3	2		
	P/E	Swindon T	68+1	4	7	4		
Paul Batty	Edlington	Swindon T (A)	38+1		5	1		2
5 7, 10 11,								
Mike Graham	Lancaster	Bolton W (A)	43+3	3	2			
5 9½, 11 7, 24.2.59	F/T	Swindon T	76	4	7	1		
Brian Hughes*	Ludgershall	Swindon T (A)	67+1	4	2+2	7		
5 11, 10 9, 20.8.62								
Leigh Barnard	Worsley	Portsmouth (A)	71+8	4	6	8		
5 7½, 9 10, 29.10.58	—	Peterboro U (loan)	1+3					
	F/t	Swindon T	46	2	5	4		1
Forwards								
Andy Rowland (EY)	Derby	Derby Co (AM)						
5 10½, 12 1, 8.9.54	—	Bury	169+5	19	10	58	8	4
	£80,000	Swindon T	186	18	15+1	69	5	8
Paul Rideout (ES)	Bournemouth	Swindon T (A)	90+5	3	7	38	2	1
5 11½, 12 1, 14.8.64								
Jimmy Quinn	Belfast	Oswestry T						
6 1, 11 2,	£10,000	Swindon T	6+11	+1	+2	1		
Ken Beamish*	Bebbington	Tranmere R	176+1	2+1	4	49	1	1
6 0, 11 11, 25.8.47		Brighton	86+10	2	1	27	1	
	£30,000	Blackburn R	86	9	3	18	5	2
	£10,000	Port Vale	84+1	5	8+1	29		7
	£30,000	Bury	49	2	4	20		1
	£30,000	Tranmere R	57+2	2	7	15		3
	F/T	Swindon T	1+1	1+1				
Howard Pritchard*	Cardiff	Bristol C (A)	31+7	1	5+1	2		2
5 10, 12 7, 18.10.58	F/T	Swindon T	59+6	2+1	8	11		8

Commercial Manager: Mike Lewis (Tel.)
Club Coach:
Club Captain (1982-83) Andy Rowland
Supporters Player of the Season 1982–83: Paul Rideout
Chief Scout:
Physiotherapist: Kevin Morris
Club Statistician:
Association of Football Statisticians Club Adviser to Yearbook: T. Angell

Players (non-appearance) granted free transfer: David Bristow; David Round, D.
Players released since May 1982: Steve Abbley, F. (Cheltenham T); Paul Short, M. (N/K); Craig Moores, F. (N/K).

TORQUAY UNITED Division 4

Back row (left to right): Jackie Gallagher, Steve Cooper, Alan Little, Graham Horn, Steve Bould (on loan from Stoke C), Graham Jones, Brian Wilson
Front row: Bruce Rioch (Manager), Colin Anderson, Ray Bishop, Brian O'Donnell, John Doyle, Steve Grapes, Willie Young, Alan Slough (Team Coach).

Chairman: A. J. Boyce. ***Vice-Chairman:*** M. C. Spedding.

Directors: D. C. Hair MRCVS, J. H. Perry, Lt-Col W. J. Elliott MBE, FCIS, L. W. Leppington ERD, L. W. Pope, W. W. Rogers, J. Farrell OBE, G. Harvey.

General Manager: Frank O'Farrell. ***Secretary:*** D. J. Easton.

Team Manager: Bruce Rioch. ***Nickname:*** 'The Gulls'.

Year Formed: 1898. ***Turned Professional:*** 1921. ***Ltd Co.:*** 1921.

Previous Name: 1910, Torquay Town; 1921, Torquay United.

Previous Grounds: 1898, Teignmouth Road; 1901, Torquay Recreation Ground; 1905, Cricket Field Road; 1907–10, Torquay Cricket Ground.

Previous Managers since 1946: Jack Butler, John McNeil, Bob John, Alex Massie, Eric Webber, Frank O'Farrell, Allan Brown, Jack Edwards, Malcolm Musgrove, Frank O'Farrell, Mike Green, Frank O'Farrell (12).

Plainmoor Ground, Torquay, Devon TQ1 3PS. Telephone Torquay (0803) 38666/7. ***Ground capacity:*** 22,000. ***Record attendance:*** 21,908 v Huddersfield T, FA Cup 4th rd, 29 Jan, 1955. ***Record receipts:*** £14,300 v Sheffield W, FA Cup 4th rd, 29 Jan, 1983. ***Pitch measurements:*** 112yd×74yd.

Directions to Ground: Train to Torquay railway station. Bus 30 runs every twelve minutes from the station.

Match tickets: Stand seats available a fortnight before the match. Postal applications accepted provided correct remittance and sae are enclosed.

Car parking: Some street parking. Coaches park at Lymington Road coach station.

Entertainments/catering facilities: 200 Club – a match day venue luxury club – membership £6 (48 hours notice required for membership). Supporters' Social Club – open all week – now completely up-dated with luxury furnishings – membership £1, OAPs 50p (48 hours notice required).

Club shop: Sells all types of souvenirs.

Handbooks/programmes: For programmes contact the club shop.

Extra information: Running commentaries of home matches to local hospitals. Twelve free seats supplied to members of the local Rehabilitation Centre of the Royal National Institute for the Blind who can listen to the hospital commentary while experiencing the match atmosphere.

Address of Supporters Association: Plainmoor, Torquay, Devon.

Address of Club Shop: The Gull Shop, Torquay U Supporters Association, Plainmoor, Torquay, Devon.

Note: Full club statistical records are on pages 416–455.

TORQUAY UNITED 1982–83 LEAGUE RECORD

Match No.	Date	Venue	Opponents	Result		H/T Score	Lg. Pos.	Goalscorers	Attendance
1	Aug 28	A	York C	D	1-1	0-1	—	Bishop	1737
2	Sept 4	H	Stockport Co	W	3-0	1-0	3	Cooper, Sheridan, Bishop	2079
3	8	H	Aldershot	W	4-2	4-1	—	Bishop 2 (1 pen), Cooper 2	2198
4	11	A	Chester	D	0-0	0-0	2		2370
5	18	H	Darlington	W	1-0	1-0	1	Cooper	2597
6	25	A	Wimbledon	L	1-4	0-3	4	Doyle	2047
7	28	A	Bristol C	W	1-0	1-0	—	Gallagher	3041
8	Oct 2	H	Hartlepool U	W	3-2	1-2	1	Cooper, Gallagher, Doyle (pen)	2051
9	9	A	Hull C	L	1-4	1-2	4	Gallagher	4128
10	16	H	Northampton T	W	3-1	1-1	3	Carter 2, Gallagher	2101
11	20	H	Swindon T	D	1-1	0-0	—	Cooper	2979
12	23	H	Peterborough U	W	3-1	3-0	5	Carter 2, Cooper	2869
13	30	H	Scunthorpe U	D	1-1	0-0	6	Carter	3005
14	Nov 2	A	Blackpool	L	0-1	0-0	—		2734
15	6	H	Tranmere R	W	3-0	1-0	5	Cooper, Rioch (pen), Anderson	2545
16	13	A	Bury	L	0-3	0-2	8		2735
17	27	H	Rochdale	W	3-2	1-1	7	Cooper 2, Wilson	2409
18	Dec 3	A	Crewe Alex	D	1-1	0-0	—	Little	1576
19	17	A	Mansfield T	L	1-2	1-1	8	Gallagher	1293
20	27	H	Hereford U	W	2-1	1-1	8	Little, Crabbe (og)	3842
21	28	A	Port Vale	L	0-1	0-0	8		4760
22	Jan 1	H	Colchester U	W	2-0	1-0	7	Cooper, Hughes	2758
23	3	A	Halifax T	L	0-3	0-1	8		1776
24	15	H	York C	L	1-3	0-2	8	Bishop	2738
25	22	A	Aldershot	L	1-2	1-0	8	Anderson	1706
26	Feb 5	H	Wimbledon	L	0-1	0-0	10		2316
27	12	A	Hartlepool U	W	2-0	1-0	8	Wilson, Anderson	1159
28	19	H	Hull C	D	0-0	0-0	11		2710
29	26	A	Northampton T	L	0-2	0-1	12		1817
30	Mar 2	H	Blackpool	L	1-3	1-3	—	Anderson	1802
31	5	H	Peterborough U	W	2-1	1-0	9	Carter, Cooper	1537
32	12	A	Scunthorpe U	L	0-2	0-1	12		3342
33	18	A	Tranmere R	L	0-2	0-2	—		1503
34	20	H	Bristol C	L	0-2	0-1	—		3094
35	26	H	Bury	L	2-3	0-1	13	Rioch, Cooper	1565
36	Apr 2	H	Port Vale	L	0-1	0-0	14		2593
37	5	A	Hereford U	W	1-0	1-0	—	Price (og)	2533
38	9	H	Crewe Alex	W	2-1	0-0	11	Carter, Cooper	1684
39	16	A	Darlington	W	2-0	0-0	11	Gallagher, Doyle	1122
40	17	A	Stockport Co	L	0-1	0-1	—		1935
41	23	H	Mansfield T	W	3-1	1-1	9	Gallagher, Bishop, Little (pen)	1546
42	26	A	Swindon T	L	1-2	0-1	—	Cooper	2509
43	30	A	Rochdale	D	2-2	2-1	9	Carter, James	1382
44	May 2	H	Halifax T	L	1-3	1-1	9	Anderson	1558
45	7	H	Chester	L	0-1	0-0	10		1478
46	13	A	Colchester U	L	0-1	0-0	—		2181

Final League Position: 12

GOALSCORERS

League (56): Cooper 15, Carter 8, Gallagher 7, Bishop 6 (1 pen), Anderson 5, Doyle 3 (1 pen), Little 3 (1 pen), Rioch 2 (1 pen), Wilson 2, Hughes 1, James 1, Sheridan 1, own goals 2.
Milk Cup (2): Cooper 2.
FA Cup (11): Bishop 3, Cooper 2, Gallagher 2, Anderson 1, Hughes 1, Little 1, Wilson 1.
Football League Trophy (4): Cooper 2, Gallagher 1 Wilson 1.

Milk Cup	First Round	Bristol R (a)	2-2
		(h)	0-4
FA Cup	First Round	Colchester U (a)	2-0
	Second Round	Carshalton (h)	4-1
	Third Round	Oxford U (a)	1-1
		(h)	2-1
	Fourth Round	Sheffield W (h)	2-3

Football League Trophy	Newport Co (a)	1-0
	Bristol C (a)	0-1
	Exeter C (h)	3-2

Horn	Doyle	Jones	Wilson	Wigginton	Sheridan	Grapes	Bishop	Cooper	Rioch	Gallagher	Smith	Steeples (L)	Brown	Anderson	Sermanni	Young	O'Donnell	Little	Carter	Bould (L)	Hughes (L)	Thompson	Holmes	James (L)	Pluckrose	Referees	Match No.
1	2	3	4	5	6*	7	8	9	10	11	12															T. Jones	1
1	8	5	6	9	4	10*	11	2		7	3		12													L. Burden	2
1	2	3	4	5	6	7	8*	9		11	10	12														D. Lloyd	3
1	2	3	4	5	6*	7		9		11	10	8	12													A. Challinor	4
1	2		4	5		7*		9	3	11	10	8	12	6												E. Read	5
1	2		3	4		6		10*	8	11	5	9		7	12											M. Taylor	6
1	2		4	5		7		9	12	11	3	8*	6	10												D. Vickers	7
1	2		4	5		7		9	12	11	3		6	10	8*											D. Letts	8
1			4	5		7		9	2	11	3		6*	10	8	12										K. Redfern	9
1	2		4			7		9	6	11				10			3	5	8							R. Milford	10
1	2		4			6		10		11				8			3	7	9	5						K. Cooper	11
1	2		4			7		9	12	11				10			3	6	8*	5						E. J. Scales	12
1	2					7*		9	4	11			12	10			3	5	8	6						J. Deakin	13
1	2					7		9	4	11				10			3	5	8	6						J. Worrall	14
1	2					7		9	4	11				10			3	5	8	6						Alan Robinson	15
1	2		5			6		10	4	11			12	9			8*	7		3						N. Ashley	16
1	2		3			7	8*	9		11			12	10			4	5		6						B. Stevens	17
1	2		3			7	8	9		11				10			4	5		6						N. Wilson	18
1	2		3			7	9			11			4*	10		12	8	5		6						N. Glover	19
1	2		3			7	9		4*	11				10		12	8	5			6					C. Downey	20
1	2		3			7		9		11			12	10		4	8*	5			6					R. Nixon	21
1	2		3		4	7		9		11				10			8	5			6					A. Glasson	22
1	2		3		4			9		11				10		7	8	5			6					G. Courtney	23
1	2		3		4*	7	12	9		11				10			8	5			6					T. Spencer	24
1	2		3		4	7	11	9		12				10			8	5*			6					B. Daniels	25
1	2*		3		4		7	9		11				10			8	5			6	12				E. Read	26
1	2		4			7	11	9						10		3		5	8		6					R. Chadwick	27
1	2		4			7	11	9		12				10		3		5*	8		6					V. Callow	28
1	2		3		4		11	9*		12				10		6	5	7	8							M. Scott	29
1	2		4		6		11	9						10		3	7	5	8							T. Bune	30
1			4		6*	7		9	12	11	2			10		3		5	8							R. Milford	31
1		7	4				12	9	6	11	2			10		3		5	8*							M. Robinson	32
1	8	7	4				9		6	11	2			10				5					3			P. Willis	33
1		7	4				9		6	11	2			10		3		5						8		C. Thomas	34
1		2	4			7		9	12	11*				10				5	8				3	6		D. Hedges	35
1	12	6	4			7		9		11				10				5*	8				3	2		S. Bates	36
1	4	2				7	11	9						10				5	8				3	6		J. Deakin	37
1	2*	6				7	11	9			12			10				5	8				3	4		J. Martin	38
1	2	6					11	9		8	7			10				5					3	4		J. Key	39
1	2	6			12		11	9		8	7*			10				5					3	4		K. Barratt	40
1	2	6					7	9		11				10				5	8				3	4		L. Burden	41
1	2	6			12		7*	9		11				10				5	8				3	4		H. Taylor	42
1	8	6			7*		12			10	2			9				5	11					4	3	D. Hedges	43
1	11	6			7*			9		12	2			10				5	8					4	3	D. Letts	44
1	11	6			7					9	2			10				5	8					4	3	J. Moules	45
1	3	6			7		11			9				10				5	8				2	4		A. Gunn	46
46	40	19	33	9	16	31	22	39	13	38	17	4	4	42	2	9	19	37	22	9	9	0	10	13	3		
	+ 1s				+ 2s		+ 3s		+ 5s	+ 4s	+ 2s	+ 1s	+ 7s		+ 1s	+ 3s						+ 1s					

FOOTBALL LEAGUE RECORD

1927 Elected to Division 3(S); 1958–60 Division 4; 1960–62 Division 3; 1962–66 Division 4; 1966–72 Division 3; 1972– Division 4.

HONOURS

Football League: Division 3 best season: 4th, 1967–68. Division 3(S) – Runners-up 1956–57; Division 4 – Promoted 1959–60 (3rd), 1965–66 (3rd). *FA Cup* best season: 4th rd, 1949, 1955, 1971, 1983. *Football League Cup:* never past 3rd rd.

COLOURS

Yellow shirts, blue shorts, yellow stockings. **Change colours:** All white.

TORQUAY UNITED

Players Names *Ht. Wt. D.o.B.*	*Birthplace* *Transfer Fee*	*Clubs*	*Appearances* F.L. A & S	F.L.C. A & S	F.A.C. A & S	*Goals* F.L.	F.L.C.	F.A.C.
Goalkeepers								
Graham Horn*	Westminster	Arsenal (A)						
6 2, 14 1, 23.8.54	—	Portsmouth (loan)	22	2	2			
		Luton T	58	3	5			
	—	Brentford (loan)	3					
		Los Angeles A						
		Charlton Ath						
	F/T	Kettering T						
		Southend U	9					
	F/T	Aldershot	9					
	F/T	Torquay U	46	2	5			
Defenders								
Brian Wilson	Newcastle	Blackpool (A)	21+10	3		6		
5 9, 10 5, 14.4.57	£6000	Torquay U	129+2	4	4+1	6		1
Frank Sheridan	London	Derby Co (A)	41+2	1		5		
6 0, 11 0, 9.12.61	F/T	Torquay U	16+2	1	3	1		
Graham Jones*	Worsley	Luton T (A)	31+8		4			
6 0, 13 0, 2.6.59	£10,000	Torquay U	114	5	6	6		
Midfield								
Bruce Rioch (S)	Aldershot	Luton T (A)	148+1	9	9	47	3	2
5 11, 12 5, 6.9.47	£100,000	Aston Villa	149+5	15	8	34	3	
	£200,000	Derby Co	106	10	9	34	5	7
	£300,000	Everton	30	2	7	3		1
	£25,000	Derby Co	40+1	1	3	4		2
	—	Birmingham C (loan)	3					
	—	Sheffield U (loan)	8			1		
	£300,000	Seatle Sounders						
	F/T	Torquay U	63+6	3+1	7	6		
Willie Young*	Glasgow	Arthurlie						
5 7, 11 7, 24.2.56		Aston Villa	3					
	£10,000	Torquay U	35+3		1			
Alan Little	Newcastle	Aston Villa (A)	2+1	2			1	
5 11½, 12 12, 5.2.55		Southend U	102+1	4	11	12	1	
		Barnsley	91	9	4	14	1	
	£30,000	Doncaster R	84+1	2	6	11		1
	P/E	Torquay U	37		5	3		1
Roy Carter	Torpoint	Falmouth T						
6 0½, 11 7, 19.2.54		Hereford U	64+7	9	4+1	9	3	1
	£22,000	Swindon T	193+7	22+1	11	34	2	2
	—	Bristol R (loan)	4			1		
	F/T	Torquay U	22			8		
Forwards								
Steve Cooper (EY)	Basingstoke	Stourbridge						
5 11, 11 0, 14.12.55	£5000	Torquay U	192+11	12	15+1	68	4	7
Ray Bishop	Hengoed	Cheltenham T						
5 10, 11 0, 24.11.55		Cardiff C	92+10	7+2	4	25	3	
	£10,000	Newport Co	8+10			2		
	£5000	Torquay U	22+3	1	1+1	6		3
Colin Anderson	Newcastle	Burnley (A)	3+3					
5 7, 10 0,26.4.62	F/T	Torquay U	42		5	5		1
Non-contract players								
Jimmy Holmes (EI)	Dublin	Coventry C (A)	122+6	9	11+1	7		
5 9, 11 7, 11.11.53	£100,000	Tottenham H	81	2	9	2		
		Vancouver W						
	F/T	Leicester C	2					
	F/T	Brentford	4					
	F/T	Torquay U	10					
Mark Smith	Torquay	Torquay U	18+6	2				
5 9, 11 0, 9.10.61								
Alan Pluckrose	Southwater	Falmouth T						
5 9, 11 0, 3.7.63	—	Torquay U	3					

Commercial Manager: M. J. Goulding. (Tel. 39349)
Club Coach: A. Slough
Supporters Player of the Season 1982–83: Colin Anderson
Physiotherapist: W. J. Wright
Association of Football Statisticians Club Adviser to Yearbook: J. Lovis

Club Captain 1982–83: B. Wilson
Chief Scout: N.A.
Club Statistician: John Lovis

Players released since May 1982:
Richard Bourne, D. (Weymouth); Albert Larmour, D. (retired); Steve Grapes, M. (Bath); Tony Brown, F. (Stafford R); Steve Thompson, M. (N/C—Falmouth); Brian O'Donnell, M. (N/C—Australia); John Doyle, D. (N/K); Tom Sermanni, M. (Australia); Jackie Gallagher, F. (N/C—N/K).

TOTTENHAM HOTSPUR Division 1

Back row (left to right): Paul Price, Gary O'Reilly, Mark Falco, Anthony Parks, Ray Clemence, John Lacy, Anthony Galvin, Paul Miller, Ken Oliver (Youth Team Manager)
Middle row: Robbie Stepney (Reserve Team Manager), Chris Hughton, Ian Cook, Patrick Corbett, Mike Varney (Physio), Steve Archibald, Garth Crooks, Graham Roberts, John Wallis (Coach)
Front row: Gary Mabbutt, Mike Hazard, Glenn Hoddle, Peter Shreeves (Assistant Manager), Keith Burkinshaw (Manager), Steve Perryman, Gary Brooke, Terry Gibson.

Chairman: D. A. Alexiou. ***Vice-Chairman:*** F. P. Sinclair.

Directors: P. Leaver, P. Bobroff.

Manager: Keith Burkinshaw. ***Assistant Manager:*** Peter Shreeves.

Financial Controller: D. Peter.

Secretary: P. Day. ***Assistant Secretary:*** Peter Barnes.

Year Formed: 1882. ***Turned Professional:*** 1895. Ltd Co.: 1898.

Club Nickname: 'Spurs'

Previous Grounds: 1882, Tottenham Marshes; 1885, Northumberland Park; 1898, White Hart Lane.

Previous Name: 1882–85, Hotspur Football Club.

Previous Managers since 1946: Joe Hulme, Arthur Rowe, Jimmy Anderson, Bill Nicholson, Terry Neill (5).

748 High Rd, Tottenham, London, N17. Telephone 01-801 3411. ***Ground capacity:*** 50,000. ***Record attendance:*** 75,038 v Sunderland, FA Cup 6th rd, 5 March, 1938. ***Record receipts:*** £136,407.70 v WBA, League Cup semi-final 2nd leg, 10 Feb, 1982. ***Pitch:*** 110yd×73yd.

Direction to Ground: Underground to Manor House (Piccadilly line), or Seven Sisters (Victoria line). From Manor House, buses 279, 259; from Seven Sisters 67, 149, 171, 243, 259, 123, 279. White Hart Lane station is three minutes' walk from the ground and is served by trains from Liverpool St.

Match tickets: For League matches, seats can be booked not earlier than three weeks before the match. At the Park Lane and Paxton Road ends, there are seats available at the turnstiles.

Car parking: No street parking wihin a ¼ mile radius of the ground.

Entertainments/catering facilities: Hot food available at snack bars in the ground.

Club shop: There are shops on the corner of Park Lane and High Rd, and Paxton Rd and High Rd.

Handbooks/programmes: Programmes available on subscription to shop.

Extra information: Supporters' Club with a present membership of over 7000 is open to new members; information from the Secretary, Mr D. Smith (Tel: 808 7430).

Address of Supporters Club: 744 High Road, N17.

Note: Full club statistical records are on pages 416–455.

TOTTENHAM HOTSPUR 1982–83 LEAGUE RECORD

Match No.	Date	Venue	Opponents	Result	H/T Score	Lg. Pos.	Goalscorers	Attendance
1	Aug 28	H	Luton T	D 2-2	2-1	—	Mabbutt, Hazard	39,180
2	31	A	Ipswich T	W 2-1	0-1	—	Archibald, Crooks	25,000
3	Sept 4	A	Everton	L 1-3	1-3	13	Archibald	30,553
4	8	H	Southampton	W 6-0	2-0	—	Galvin 2, Villa, Perryman, Crooks, Brooke (pen)	26,579
5	11	H	Manchester C	L 1-2	0-1	9	Mabbutt	32,483
6	18	A	Sunderland	W 1-0	1-0	7	Brooke	21,137
7	25	H	Nottingham F	W 4-1	3-1	5	Mabbutt 2, Crooks 2	30,662
8	Oct 2	A	Swansea C	L 0-2	0-0	7		16,381
9	9	H	Coventry C	W 4-0	1-0	6	Crooks, Brooke 3 (1 pen)	25,188
10	16	A	Norwich C	D 0-0	0-0	6		22,628
11	23	H	Notts Co	W 4-2	2-0	3	Mabbutt, Crooks 2, Brooke	25,783
12	30	A	Aston Villa	L 0-4	0-0	5		25,992
13	Nov 6	H	Watford	L 0-1	0-0	9		42,215
14	13	A	Manchester U	L 0-1	0-1	10		47,869
15	20	H	West Ham U	W 2-1	0-1	8	Archibald 2	41,960
16	27	A	Liverpool	L 0-3	0-1	10		40,691
17	Dec 4	H	WBA	D 1-1	1-0	11	Galvin	26,208
18	11	A	Stoke C	L 0-2	0-1	12		15,849
19	18	H	Birmingham C	W 2-1	0-0	11	Mabbutt 2	20,546
20	27	A	Arsenal	L 0-2	0-1	13		51,497
21	28	H	Brighton & HA	W 2-0	1-0	14	Villa, Hughton	23,994
22	Jan 1	A	West Ham U	L 0-3	0-1	12		33,383
23	3	H	Everton	W 2-1	1-0	9	Gibson 2	28,455
24	15	A	Luton T	D 1-1	0-1	10	Hoddle	21,231
25	22	H	Sunderland	D 1-1	1-0	10	Gibson	25,250
26	Feb 5	A	Manchester C	D 2-2	0-0	11	Brooke (pen), Gibson	26,357
27	12	H	Swansea C	W 1-0	1-0	8	Crooks	24,632
28	26	H	Norwich C	D 0-0	0-0	8		23,342
29	Mar 5	A	Notts Co	L 0-3	0-3	13		11,896
30	12	A	Coventry C	D 1-1	0-1	12	Miller	11,004
31	19	A	Watford	W 1-0	1-0	11	Falco	27,371
32	23	H	Aston Villa	W 2-0	1-0	—	Falco 2	22,455
33	Apr 2	A	Brighton & HA	L 1-2	1-0	10	Roberts	20,359
34	4	H	Arsenal	W 5-0	3-0	—	Hughton 2, Falco 2, Brazil	43,642
35	9	A	Nottingham F	D 2-2	0-2	10	Brazil, Mabbutt	18,265
36	16	H	Ipswich T	W 3-1	2-0	8	Brazil 2, Mabbutt	30,557
37	23	A	WBA	W 1-0	1-0	6	Archibald	14,940
38	30	H	Liverpool	W 2-0	0-0	6	Archibald 2	44,907
39	May 3	A	Southampton	W 2-1	1-1	—	Brazil, Mabbutt	21,602
40	7	A	Birmingham C	L 0-2	0-1	7		18,947
41	11	H	Manchester U	W 2-0	0-0	—	Roberts, Archibald	32,803
42	14	H	Stoke C	W 4-1	2-0	4	Brazil, Archibald 3	33,691

Final League Position: 4

GOALSCORERS

League (65): Archibald 11, Mabbutt 10, Crooks 8, Brooke 7 (3 pens), Brazil 6, Falco 5, Gibson 4, Galvin 3, Hughton 3, Roberts 2, Villa 2, Hazard 1, Hoddle 1, Miller 1, Perryman 1.
Milk Cup (8): Crooks 3, Archibald 2, Brooke 1 (pen), Gibson 1, Villa 1.
FA Cup (3): Crooks 1, Gibson 1, Hazard 1.
European Cup-Winners' Cup (9): Crooks 3, Archibald 2, Brooke 1, Gibson 1, Hughton 1, Mabbutt 1.

Milk Cup	Second Round	Brighton & HA (h)	1-1
		(a)	1-0
	Third Round	Gillingham (a)	4-2
	Fourth Round	Luton T (h)	1-0
	Fifth Round	Burnley (h)	1-4
European Cup-Winners' Cup	First Round	Coleraine (a)	3-0
		(h)	4-0
	Second Round	Bayern Munich (h)	1-1
		(a)	1-4
FA Cup	Third Round	Southampton (h)	1-0
	Fourth Round	WBA (h)	2-1
	Fifth Round	Everton (a)	0-2

Commercial Manager: Mike Lewis. (Tel. 808 0281 808 4940)
Club Coach: Peter Shreeves (Asst. Manager)
Supporters Player of the Season 1982–83:
Physiotherapist: Mike Varney
Club Captain 1982-83: Steve Perryman
Chief Scout/Consultant: W. E. Nicholson
Club Statistician: Les Yates. Programme Editor
Association of Football Statisticians Club Adviser to Yearbook: A. Porter

Clemence	Hughton	Miller	Lacy	Hazard	Perryman	Mabbutt	Archibald	Galvin	Hoddle	Crooks	Brooke	Price	Villa	Roberts	Crook	Falco	O'Reilly	Parks	Corbett	Mazzon	Webster	Gibson	Dick	Ardiles	Brazil	*Referees*	*Match No.*
1	2	3	4	5	6	7	8*	9	10	11	12															T. Bune	1
1	2	3	4		6	7	8	9	10	11	5															M. James	2
1	2	3*	4	12	6	7	8	9	10	11	5															D. Shaw	3
1	2		4	7	6		8	9	10*	11	5	3	12													B. Stevens	4
1			3	7*	2	5	9	11		10	6	4	8	12												J. Bray	5
1	2	4			6	7	8	9		11	5	3	10													P. Tyldesley	6
1	2	4		8*	6	7				11	5	3	10		12	9										A. Glasson	7
1	2		3	9	6	7	8			11	5*	4	10				12									A. Seville	8
	2	4	3	9		7	8*			11	5		10			12	6	1								M. Ta¸!or	9
1		4	3	9		7	8			11	5	2	10				6									K. Hackett	10
1		4	5	6		9				11	7	2	10*		12	8	3									I. Borrett	11
1	3	4	5	6		9				11	7	2	10			8										C. Thomas	12
1	2	3	5	12	6	7	8		10	11	4		9*													A. Gunn	13
1	2	3	5		6	7	8		10	11	9						4									C. Seel	14
1	2			5	6*	7	8		10	11	12	3	9				4									R. Lewis	15
1	2			5*	6	10	8	9		11		3	7	12			4									G. Courtney	16
1	2					7	8	9	10	11		3	5	6			4									M. Bodenham	17
1	2		4			7	8	9	10	11*		3	5	6					12							R. Banks	18
1	2		3	8	6	7		9	10	11	12		5*	4												L. Burden	19
1	2			5	6	4	8	9*	10	11	12			7			3									L. Shapter	20
1	2			5	6		8		10	11	7		9	4*	12		3									K. Barratt	21
1	2				6		8		10	11	9	4	5				7			3						M. Scott	22
1	2				6		8		10		7						3			4	5	9	11			D. Hedges	23
1	2				6	11	8		12		5		10	4			3					9*		7		M. Heath	24
1	2		3		6	11	8		10				5	4								9	7			B. Hill	25
1	2		3		6	8				11	10		5	4		12						9		7*		C. Newsome	26
1	2*		3		6	8		7		11	10	4	5			12						9				J. Hunting	27
1	2		3	5*	6	8		7		11		4	10	12								9				E. Read	28
1	2		3		6	8		7		11		4	5*	12		10						9				D. Brazier	29
1	2	5			6	8		7						4	11*	10	3				12	9				K. Cooper	30
1	2	5			6	7		8						4		9	3					11			10	K. Baker	31
1	2	5			6	7		11	10*					4		9	3					12			8	D. Axcell	32
1	2		5	12		7	8	11						4		9	3					6*			10	V. Callow	33
1	2	5				7	8	9						4		11	3					6			10	Alan Robinson	34
1	2	5			12	7	8	9						4		11	3*					6			10	R. Guy	35
1	2	5			6	7	8		12					4		11	3*					9			10	T. Spencer	36
1	2	5			6	7	8	9	10					4			3					12			11*	J. Hough	37
1	2	5			6	7	8	9	10					4			3								11	M. Roberts	38
1	2	5			6	7	8	9	10					4			3								11	R. Milford	39
1	2	5				7	8	9	10					4		12	3					6*			11	A. Challinor	40
1		5	2		6	7	8	9	10					4			3								11	B. Hill	41
1	2	5	4		6	7	8	9	10							12	3*								11	I. Borrett	42
41	38	23	22	15	32	38	31	26	22	26	19	16	22	20	1	11	25	1	0	2	1	14	2	2	12		
				+ 3s	+ 1s				+ 2s		+ 4s		+ 1s	+ 4s	+ 3s	+ 5s	+ 1s		+ 1s		+ 1s	+ 2s					

FOOTBALL LEAGUE RECORD

1908 Elected to Division 2; 1909–15 Division 1; 1919–20 Division 2; 1920–28 Division 1; 1928–33 Division 2; 1933–35 Division 1; 1935–50 Division 2; 1950–77 Division 1; 1977–78 Division 2; 1978– Division 1.

HONOURS

Football League: Division 1 – Champions 1950–51, 1960–61; Runners-up 1921–22, 1951–52, 1956–57, 1962–63; Division 2 – Champions 1919–20, 1949–50; Runners-up 1908–09, 1932–33; Promoted 1977–78 (3rd). *FA Cup:* Winners 1901 (as non-League club), 1921, 1961, 1962, 1967, 1981, 1982. *Football League Cup:* Winners 1970–71, 1972–73; Runners-up 1981–82. **European Competitions:** *European Cup:* 1961–62; *European Cup-Winners' Cup*: 1962–63 (winners), 1963–64, 1967–68, 1981–82 (runners-up), 1982–83; *EUFA Cup:* 1971–72 (winners), 1972–73, 1973–74 (runners-up), 1983–84.

COLOURS

White shirts, navy blue shorts, white stockings. **Change colours:** All sky blue.

TOTTENHAM HOTSPUR

Players Names *Ht, Wt, D.o.B.*	*Birthplace* *Transfer Fee*	*Clubs*	*Appearances* *F.L.* *A & S*	*F.L.C.* *A & S*	*F.A.C.* *A & S*	*Goals* *F.L.*	*F.L.C.*	*F.A.C.*
Goalkeepers								
Tony Parks	Hackney	Tottenham H (A)	3					
5 10½, 10 8, 26.1.63								
Ray Clemence (E)	Skegness	Notts Co (AM)						
5 11½, 12 9, 5.8.48	—	Scunthorpe U	48		2			
	£20,000	Liverpool	470	55	54			
	£300,000	Tottenham H	79	13	10			
Defenders								
Chris Hughton (EI)	Forest Gate	Tottenham H	148	20	22	7	1	1
5 7¾, 11 5, 11.12.58								
John Lacy*	Liverpool	Kingstonians						
6 1, 12 4, 14.8.51	—	Fulham	164+4	9	16	7	1	
	£200,000	Tottenham H	99+5	11	12	2	1	
Giorgio Mazzon*	Cheshunt	Waltham N T						
5 10, 11 9, 4.9.60	—	Tottenham H	3+1	+2	1			
Peter Southey	Putney	Tottenham (A)	1					
5 9, 11 0, 4.1.62								
Paul Miller	Stepney	Tottenham H (A)	116+1	13	21+1	5		1
6 1, 12 2, 11.10.59								
Graham Roberts (E)	Southampton	Weymouth						
5 10, 12 12, 3.7.59	£30,000	Tottenham H	76+9	7+1	17	8		1
Pat Corbett* (EY)	Hackney	Tottenham H	3+2			1		
6 0, 11 0, 12.2.63								
Paul Price (W)	St Albans	Luton T	206+1	13	9	8		
5 11, 12 0, 23.3.54	£200,000	Tottenham H	34+3	6	6			
Ken Dixon	Hornsey	Tottenham H (A)						
5 7, 9 0, 19.1.64								
Simon Webster	Hinckley	Tottenham H (A)	1+1					
6 0, 11 0, 20.1.64								
Ian Culverhouse	Bishops Stortford	Tottenham H (A)						
5 9, , 22.9.64								
Midfield								
Steve Perryman (E)	Ealing	Tottenham H (A)	548+1	54	57	28	3	2
5 8, 10 0, 21.12.51								
Glenn Hoddle (E)	Hayes	Tottenham H (A)	255+4	25	30+1	66	5	9
6 0, 11 6, 27.10.57								
Mike Hazard	Sunderland	Tottenham H (A)	46+7	8+1	6+1	8	3	2
5 7, 10 5, 5.2.60								
Gary O'Reilly (EIY)	Isleworth	Tottenham H	30+3	4	1			
5 11, , 21.3.61								
Osvaldo Ardiles (ARG)	Argentine	Huracan						
5 6, 9 10, 3.8.52	£325,000	Tottenham H	142	18	24	13	2	4
Ricky Villa* (ARG)	Argentine	Racing						
6 0, 12 5, 18.8.52	£375,000	Tottenham H	124+9	15+1	21	18	3	3
Ian Crook	Romford	Tottenham H (A)	4+4					
5 8, 10 6, 18.1.63								
Allan Cockram	Kensington	Tottenham H						
5 7, 10 0, 8.10.63								
Gary Brooke	Bethnal Green	Tottenham H (A)	41+16	3+1	3+8	14	1	1
5 6, 10 5, 24.11.60								
Mark Bowen (WY)	Neath	Tottenham H (A)						
5.8, , 7.12.63								
Gary Mabbutt (E)	Bristol	Bristol R (A)	122+9	10	5+1	10	1	1
5 10, 10 6, 23.8.61	£105,000	Tottenham H	38	5	2+1	10		
Forwards								
Tony Galvin (EI)	Huddersfield	Goole T						
5 9, 11 5, 12.7.56	£30,000	Tottenham H	83+3	9	16+1	10		1
Mark Falco (EY)	Hackney	Tottenham H (A)	43+7	5+2	5	14		1
6 0, 12 0, 22.10.60	—	Chelsea (loan)	3					
Terry Gibson (EY)	Walthamstow	Tottenham H (A)	16+2	1	5	4	1	1
5 5, 10 0, 23.12.62								
Steve Archibald (S)	Glasgow	Aberdeen						
5 10, 11 2, 27.9.56	£800,000	Tottenham H	97+2	15	14+1	37	6	4
Garth Crooks (EU21)	Stoke	Stoke C (A)	141+6	10+2	3+2	48	4	1
5 8, 11 6, 10.3.58	£600,000	Tottenham H	93	17	18	37	5	8
Ally Dick (SY)	Stirling	Tottenham H (A)	3		2			
5 9, 10 7, 25.4.65								
Alan Brazil (S)	Glasgow	Ipswich T (A)	143+11	14+1	18+2	70	3	6
6 0, 12 4, 15.6.59	£500,000	Tottenham H	12			6		
Mike McCabe (EIY)	Waterford	Tottenham H (A)						
5 7, , 21.8.64								
Richard Cook		Tottenham H (A)						
Robert Brace		Tottenham H(A)						

Players released since May 1982:
Milija Aleksic, G (South Africa); John Cooper, D (N/K); Mark Hughes, G (Walthamstow A).

TRANMERE ROVERS — Division 4

Back row (left to right):
John Kerr
David Burgess
John Williams
Scott Endersby
Les Parry
Bobby Hutchinson (now Mansfield T)
Mark Ferguson
Ray Mathias
Front row:
Bryan Hamilton (Player/Manager)
Neville Powell
Kevin Mooney
Steve Mungall
Ian Griffiths

Chairman: H. B. Thomas.

Directors: H. A. Bainbridge FCA, G. A. Gould FCA, G. J. H. Kemp. A. J. Adams, G. L. Baird, H. Jones, W. R. McAteer, F. J. Williams, N. J. Hulsgrove.

General Manager/Secretary: Jack Butterfield.

Team Manager: Bryan Hamilton.

Year Formed: 1883. ***Turned Professional:*** 1912. ***Ltd Co.:*** 1920.

Commercial Department: 051-608 3677/4194.

Club Nickname: 'The Rovers'.

Previous Managers since 1946: Ernie Blackburn, Noel Kelly, Peter Farrell, Walter Galbraith, Dave Russell, Jackie Wright, Ron Yeats, John King (8).

Prenton Park, Prenton Road West, Birkenhead. Telephone 051-608 3677/4194. ***Ground capacity:*** 18,000. ***Record attendance:*** 24,424 v Stoke C, FA Cup 4th rd, 5 Feb, 1972. ***Record receipts:*** £16,392.90 v Wolverhampton W, FA Cup 3rd rd, 8 Jan, 1983. ***Pitch measurements:*** 112yd×74yd.

Directions to Ground: Special buses from railway stations, Hamilton Square and Rock Ferry. Mersey Railway Liverpool, to Hamilton Square, then buses 80 to 90 or 64.

Match tickets: Not available in advance.

Car parking: Large car park at the back of the stand.

Entertainments/catering facilities: Snack bars in ground.

Club shop: Prenton Road West.

Handbooks/programmes: Programmes available on subscription.

Address of Supporters Club: Supporters Assn, Prenton Park, Birkenhead.

Note: Full club statistical records are on pages 416–455.

TRANMERE ROVERS 1982–83 LEAGUE RECORD

Match No.	Date	Venue	Opponents	Result		H/T Score	Lg. Pos.	Goalscorers	Attendance
1	Aug 28	A	Aldershot	L	0-1	0-1	—		1653
2	Sept 4	H	Bristol C	D	2-2	2-0	18	Hamilton, Kerr	1534
3	6	H	Mansfield T	W	3-0	2-0	—	Hamilton, Powell, Hutchinson	1280
4	11	A	York C	L	1-2	0-1	17	Hamilton	1632
5	18	H	Stockport Co	D	1-1	0-0	16	Griffiths	1536
6	25	A	Hartlepool	L	0-4	0-2	20		1202
7	28	A	Bury	L	0-3	0-2	—		1796
8	Oct 2	H	Wimbledon	L	0-2	0-1	22		1231
9	10	A	Northampton T	L	0-1	0-1	—		2433
10	16	H	Peterborough U	W	1-0	1-0	21	Hamilton	1086
11	18	H	Darlington	W	2-0	1-0	—	Brown, Hutchinson	1111
12	23	A	Scunthorpe U	L	1-2	0-0	21	Brown	3052
13	30	H	Hull C	L	0-1	0-0	20		1548
14	Nov 2	A	Swindon T	L	2-4	1-2	—	Brown, Kerr	4407
15	6	A	Torquay U	L	0-3	0-1	24		2545
16	13	H	Colchester U	L	2-4	1-3	24	Mungall, Kerr	1410
17	27	H	Hereford U	W	2-1	0-1	22	Ferguson, Aspinall	3194
18	Dec 4	A	Port Vale	W	1-0	1-0	21	Sproson (og)	3452
19	17	A	Halifax T	W	2-1	1-0	17	Ferguson 2	912
20	27	H	Chester	L	2-4	1-2	19	Griffiths, Powell	5245
21	28	A	Blackpool	W	2-0	1-0	17	Brown 2	3563
22	Jan 1	H	Crewe Alex	D	1-1	0-0	19	Aspinall	3087
23	3	A	Rochdale	L	2-4	1-3	20	Ferguson, Kerr	1758
24	18	A	Bristol C	L	0-1	0-0	—		3344
25	21	A	Stockport Co	L	2-3	0-1	—	Brown, Ferguson	2198
26	25	H	Aldershot	D	1-1	0-0	—	Griffiths	1509
27	29	H	York C	W	3-0	0-0	19	Oliver, Kerr, Aspinall	1802
28	Feb 5	H	Hartlepool U	D	1-1	0-0	19	Kerr	1545
29	15	A	Darlington	L	0-1	0-0	19		1010
30	19	H	Northampton T	W	2-1	0-1	17	Brown, Wellings	1466
31	26	A	Peterborough U	L	0-3	0-1	19		2045
32	28	H	Swindon T	W	2-0	0-0	—	Wellings, Aspinall	1521
33	Mar 5	H	Scunthorpe U	L	0-4	0-3	18		1652
34	12	A	Hull C	W	1-0	0-0	17	Ferguson	7198
35	15	A	Wimbledon	L	0-4	0-2	—		2113
36	18	H	Torquay U	W	2-0	2-0	—	Ferguson, Brown	1503
37	25	A	Colchester U	D	3-3	2-1	—	Griffiths, Aspinall, Brown	2547
38	Apr 2	H	Blackpool	D	1-1	1-1	16	Brown	1831
39	4	A	Chester	D	0-0	0-0	—		2897
40	8	H	Port Vale	L	0-2	0-1	—		3251
41	16	A	Mansfield T	D	1-1	1-0	17	Kerr	2468
42	23	H	Halifax T	L	1-2	1-1	19	Kerr	1401
43	30	A	Hereford U	L	0-1	0-0	21		2089
44	May 7	H	Bury	D	1-1	1-1	21	Brown	2623
45	13	A	Crewe Alex	W	1-0	0-0	20	Wellings	2152
46	16	H	Rochdale	D	0-0	0-0	19		1982

Final League Position: 19

GOALSCORERS

League (49): Brown 11, Kerr 8, Ferguson 7, Aspinall 5, Griffiths 4, Hamilton 4, Wellings 3, Hutchinson 2, Powell 2, Mungall 1, Oliver 1, own goal 1.
Milk Cup (3): Aspinall 1, Brown 1, Hutchinson 1.
FA Cup (7): Brown 4 (1 pen), Aspinall 1, Griffiths 1, Kerr 1.
Football League Trophy (4): Kerr 2, Griffiths 1, Hutchinson 1.

Milk Cup	First Round	Crewe Alex (a)	1-1
		(h)	0-0 (aet)
	Second Round	Chelsea (a)	1-3
		(h)	1-2
FA Cup	First Round	Scarborough (h)	4-2
	Second Round	Telford U (a)	1-1
		(h)	2-1
	Third Round	Wolverhampton W (h)	0-1

Football League Trophy	Shrewsbury T (a)	1-1
	Chester (h)	2-1
	Chesterfield (h)	1-1

Endersby	Mungall	Burgess	Parry	Hamilton	Williams J.	Powell	Hutchinson	Kerr	McKenna	Griffiths	Mooney	Ferguson	Mathias	Aspinall	McGuire	Prosser	Brown O.	Adkins	Brown A.	Brown D.	Wood S.	Oliver (L)	Warriner	Williams G.	Leonard (L)	Wellings	Palios	*Referees*
1	2	3	4	5	6	7	8	9	10*	11	12																	D. Brazier
1	10	2	4	5	6	7	8	9		11	3*	12																P. Tyldesley
1		2	4	5	6*	7	8	9	12	11	3	10																D. Richardson
1	4	5	3	7		6		10	11*	9	8		2	12														K. Redfern
1		2	4	5		7		9	12	11	3	6	10	8*														H. King
1		2	4	5	6	7	10	9		11	3	8		12														D. Scott
1		2	4	7	3	6	10	11		9	5			8*	12													M. Heath
1		2		5	6	7		9		11	3*	4		10	12	8												D. Hutchinson
1	4	2			6	7		9		11*	3	8		5		12	10											A. Grey
1	9	3		8	4	12		10*			5	7	2	6			11											J. Hough
1	7	4	3	5*	6		9			11		8	2	12			10											A. Hamil
1	7	2	3		6	5				11		8	4	9			10											J. Hunting
1	9	3	4*		5	6		8		10		7	2	11	12													D. Allison
1	7	2			6	5		9		11	3		4	8			10											M. Dimblebee
1	5	2			6	12		9		11	3	7	4	8*			10											Alan Robinson
	5	2			6	7		9		11		12	4	8			10*	1	3									D. Lloyd
1	2	3		5	6			9		11	4	7		8			10											M. Peck
1	2	3		5	6			9		11	4	7		8			10											M. Midgley
1	2	3		5	6			9		11	4	7		8			10											G. Napthine
1	2	3		5	6	12		9		11	4	7*		8			10											V. Callow
1	2	3		5	6*	12		9		11	4	7		8			10											T. Holbrook
1		3		5	6	2		9		11	4	7*		8	12		10											A. Challinor
1		3		5	6	12		9		11	4	7		8			10*			2								K. Hackett
1	2	3		5*		7		9		11	4			8			10				12	6						J. Martin
1		3				7		9		11	4	5	2	8			10					6						J. Key
1	2	3			6	7		9		11		12		8			10					4	5*					C. Newsome
1	2	3		5	6	7		9		11		12		8			10*					4						C. Seel
1	2	3		5	6	7		9		11		8					10*					4	12					M. Heath
1		3		5	6	7				11		8					10*					4	12	2	9			D. Hutchinson
1		2		5*	6	7				11		8					10					4	12	3		9		D. Shaw
1		2			6	7				11		12		8			10					4	5*	3		9		K. Salmon
		3			6	7		9*		11				8			12	1				4	5	2		10		R. Banks
		3			6*	7		10			11			8			12	1				4	5	2		9		N. Wilson
	5	3			6					11		7		8			9	1				4		2		10		A. Saunders
		3			6					11		7		8			10	1				4	12	2		9	5	T. Spencer
	12	3		5*	6					11		7		8			10	1				4		2		9		P. Willis
		2		5	6					11		7		8			10	1				4		3		9		E. Scales
	5	3			6	7*		12		11				8			10	1				4		2		9		A. Hamil
	5	3			6					11				8			10	1				4	7*	2		9	12	K. Walmsley
	6	3		5						11		7		8			10	1				4		2*		9	12	R. Chadwick
1	5	3		2				8		11		7	4				10								12	9*	6	T. Mills
1	4	3				12		8		11*		7	2				10								5	9	6	T. Fitzharris
1	4	3		10				8				7	2	11*			12								5	9	6	A. Crickmore
1	4	3				9		8		11		7	2				10								5		6	J. Lovatt
1	4	3				9				11		7	2	12										8*	5	10	6	G. Napthine
1	4	3				8				9		6	2	5											11	10	7	J. Worrall
36	30	46	10	27	35	28	6	32	2	43	21	32	16	33	0	1	32	10	1	1	0	17	5	13	6	16	7	
	+ 1s					+ 6s		+ 1s	+ 2s		+ 1s	+ 5s		+ 4s	+ 4s	+ 1s	+ 3s				+ 1s		+ 4s		+ 1s		+ 2s	

FOOTBALL LEAGUE RECORD

1921 Original Member of Division 3(N); 1938–39 Division 2; 1946–58 Division 3(N); 1958–61 Division 3; 1961–67 Division 4; 1967–75 Division 3; 1975–76 Division 4; 1976–79 Division 3; 1979– Division 4.

HONOURS

Football League: Division 2 best season: 22nd, 1938–39; Division 3(N) – Champions 1937–38; Promotion to 3rd Division: 1966–67, 1975–76. *FA Cup* best season: 5th rd, 1967–68. *Football League Cup* best season: 4th rd, 1961, 1982. *Welsh Cup:* Winners 1935. Runners-up 1934.

COLOURS

Blue shirts with red pinstripe, white shorts, white stockings with blue and red trim. **Change colours:** All red.

TRANMERE ROVERS

Players Names Ht, Wt, D.o.B.	Birthplace Transfer Fee	Clubs	Appearances F.L. A & S	 F.L.C. A & S	 F.A.C. A & S	Goals F.L.	 F.L.C.	 F.A.C.
Goalkeepers								
Scott Endersby*	Lewisham	Ipswich T (A)						
5 10, 12 11, 20.2.62	F/T	Tranmere R (A)	79	6	6			
Nigel Adkins		Tranmere R (A)	10					
Defenders								
Gary Williams	Nantwich	Tranmere R. (N/C)	1					
5 9½, 11 5, 14.5.59	F/T	Djugarden						
	£40,000	Blackpool	30+1	4	2	2		1
	£40,000	Swindon T	37+1	2	2	3		
	F/T	Tranmere R	13					
Ray Mathias	Liverpool	Tranmere R (A)	549+9	35	28	5		
5 9, 11 4, 13.12. 46								
Kevin Mooney*	Liverpool	Bangor						
23.8.59		Bury	1					
	F/T	Telford						
	F/T	Tranmere R	21+1	2+1	3			
Les Parry	Wallasey	Tranmere R	245+4	19	12	4		
5 11, 11 0, 13.11.53								
Steve Mungall	Bellshill	Motherwell						
5 8, 10 2, 22.5.58	F/T	Tranmere R	129+8	9+2	10+1	5		
Dave Burgess		Tranmere R	92	10	6	1		
5 10, 11 2,								
John Williams	Liverpool	Tranmere R	106+4	9	6	8		
6 2, 13 6, 3.10.60								
Midfield								
Ian Griffiths;	Birkenhead	Tranmere R	110+6	9	9	5		1
5 5, 10 7, 17.4.60								
Bryan Hamilton* (NI)	Belfast	Linfield						
5 8, 11 2, 21.12.46	£15,000	Ipswich T	142+11	11+1	11+1	43	3	5
	£40,000	Everton	38+3	7	2	5		
	£12,500	Millwall	48+1	6	5	6	1	
	£20,000	Swindon T	19+5		1	1		
	F/T	Tranmere R	89+8	6	6	6		
John Aspinall								
		Tranmere R	33+4	3	4	5	1	1
Forwards								
John Kerr*	Birkenhead	Tranmere R (A)	126+9	10	6+2	38	4	1
5 11, 12 5, 23.11.59								
Neville Powell*	Flint	Tranmere R (A)	53+7	4	1+3	3		
5 8, 10 1, 2.9.63								
Mark Ferguson		Tranmere R	36+6	2	3	8		
Owen Brown	Liverpool	Liverpool						
5 10¼, 11 10, 4.9.60	F/T	Carlisle U	4	+2	2	2	2	3
	F/T	Tranmere R	29+8	6	2	8	5	1
	F/T	Crewe Alex	1					
	F/T	Tranmere R	32+3	1	6	11	1	5
Mark Palios	Birkenhead	Tranmere R	177+13	15	8	25		
5 8, 10 13, 9.11.52	F/T	Crewe Alex	102+2	1	4	23		1
	F/T	Tranmere R	7+2					
Non-contract players								
Andy Brown								
		Tranmere R	1					
Apprentices								
Ray Woods		Tranmere R (A)	+1					

Commercial Manager: Ray Stubbs (Tel. 051-608 3677/4194)
Club Coach: Ray Mathias
Club Captain 1982–83: Les Parry
Supporters Player of the Season 1982–83: Ian Griffiths
Chief Scout:
Physiotherapist: Judith Ford
Association of Football Statisticians Club Adviser to Yearbook: B Jones

Players released since May 1982:
Dickie Johnson, G. (Altrincham); Brian Morley, D. (Northwich Vic.); Ken McKenna (N/C-N/K); Reg McGuire (N/C-N/K); Neil Prosser, F. (N/C-N/K); Dave Brown, D. (N/C-N/K); Steve Warriner, D. (N/K); Barry Wellings, F. (N/K).

WALSALL Division 3

Back row (left to right): Brian Caswell, Richard O'Kelly, Peter Hart, Steve Round, Julian Marshall, Ron Green, Kenny Mower, Duncan Ross, Ollie Kearns, Don Penn, Gary Pendrey (Player/Coach)
Seated: Craig Shakespeare, Kenny Beech, John Teasdale, Alan Buckley (Player/Manager), David Arthur, Davis Preece, Mark Rees.
Front row: Les Sinnott, Colin Caddick, Mark Bates, Paul Jones.

Chairman: K. E. Wheldon.

Directors: J. A. Harris, S. E. Boler, R. Homden, B. E. Bradnack.

Player-Manager: Alan Buckley.

Secretary: H. J. Westmancoat FAAI.

Year Formed: 1888. ***Turned Professional:*** 1888. ***Ltd Co.:*** 1921.

Club Nickname: 'The Saddlers'.

Previous Names: Walsall Swifts (Founded 1877) and Walsall Town (Founded 1879) amalgamated in 1888 and were known as Walsall Town Swifts until 1895.

Previous Managers since 1946: Harry Hibbs, Tony McPhee, Brough Fletcher, Major Buckley, John Love, Billy Moore, Alf Wood, Ray Shaw, Ron Lewin, Dick Graham, Billy Moor, John Smith, Ronnie Allen, Doug Fraser, Dave Mackay, Alan Ashman, Frank Sibley, Alan Buckley, Neil Martin (19).

Fellows Park, Walsall. Telephone 0922 22791. ***Telegraphic address:*** 'Walsall FC, Walsall'. ***Ground capacity:*** 24,100. ***Record attendance:*** 25,453 v Newcastle U, Division 2, 29 Aug, 1961. ***Record receipts:*** £33,093 v Birmingham C, FA Cup 3rd rd, 11 Jan, 1983. ***Pitch measurements:*** 113yd×73yd.

Directions to Ground: Corporation specials from Bradford Place. Buses 237 and 238 within walking distance of the ground. Nearest railway stations, Bescot (ten minutes' walk from ground) and Walsall.

Match tickets: Seats can be booked at any time by postal, personal, or telephone application to the ticket office; tel: 0922 22791.

Car parking: Car park in Hillary Street for 100 cars. Side-street parking available.

Entertainments/catering facilities: Tea bars and licensed bars inside the ground.

Club shop: The Boutique, is open on match days.

Address of Supporters Club: **Saddlers Club, Wallows Lane, Walsall, Staffs.**

Note: Full club statistical records are on pages 416–455.

WALSALL 1982–83 LEAGUE RECORD

Match No.	Date	Venue	Opponents	Result	H/T Score	Lg. Pos.	Goalscorers	Attendance
1	Aug 28	A	AFC Bournemouth	L 0-3	0-0	—		5330
2	Sept 4	H	Portsmouth	L 0-3	0-1	24		2922
3	7	H	Preston NE	W 2-1	0-1	—	Teasdale 2	2060
4	11	A	Huddersfield T	D 2-2	1-1	19	Preece, Pendrey	4282
5	18	H	Cardiff C	L 1-2	1-1	21	Buckley (pen)	3161
6	25	A	Gillingham	L 0-3	0-1	24		3501
7	29	A	Bradford C	D 1-1	0-0	—	Kearns O.	4642
8	Oct 2	H	Brentford	W 2-1	0-0	21	Kearns O., Shakespeare	2723
9	9	H	Sheffield U	D 0-0	0-0	21		5369
10	16	A	Oxford U	L 2-4	1-3	23	Beech, Buckley	4732
11	19	H	Chesterfield	L 0-1	0-0	—		2462
12	23	A	Millwall	D 2-2	1-1	22	Kearns O. 2	3294
13	30	H	Wrexham	D 1-1	1-1	22	Kearns O.	2473
14	Nov 2	A	Orient	L 1-2	0-1	—	O'Kelly	1935
15	6	A	Exeter C	L 3-4	0-3	23	Buckley 2, Round	2614
16	13	H	Reading	W 2-1	1-0	22	Kearns O., Beech	2343
17	27	H	Southend U	L 1-3	0-1	23	Buckley	2453
18	Dec 4	A	Bristol R	L 0-2	0-2	23		4822
19	18	A	Newport Co	D 1-1	0-0	24	Penn	3572
20	27	H	Lincoln C	D 1-1	0-1	24	Summerfield	5284
21	29	A	Wigan Ath	W 3-1	0-0	—	Buckley, Summerfield, Preece	4564
22	Jan 1	H	Doncaster R	W 1-0	0-0	21	Buckley	3859
23	15	H	AFC Bournemouth	W 3-1	2-1	21	Kearns O. 2 (1 pen), Buckley	2735
24	22	A	Cardiff C	L 1-3	0-2	22	Beech	6237
25	29	H	Huddersfield T	W 2-0	2-0	20	Kearns O., O'Kelly	3922
26	Feb 5	H	Gillingham	D 0-0	0-0	22		2608
27	8	A	Plymouth Arg	D 0-0	0-0	—		3148
28	15	H	Orient	W 2-0	2-0	—	Buckley, O'Kelly	2328
29	19	A	Sheffield U	L 1-3	0-2	20	Shakespeare	11,070
30	26	H	Oxford U	W 1-0	0-0	17	Summerfield	3104
31	Mar 1	A	Chesterfield	D 0-0	0-0	—		2216
32	5	H	Millwall	W 4-0	2-0	15	Kearns O., Summerfield, Lovell (og), O'Kelly	2779
33	12	A	Wrexham	L 0-4	0-0	17		2748
34	19	H	Exeter C	W 3-2	1-0	16	Kearns O., Summerfield 2	2669
35	25	A	Reading	D 1-1	1-1	—	Summerfield	3107
36	29	A	Preston NE	L 0-1	0-1	—		4013
37	Apr 2	H	Wigan Ath	W 2-0	1-0	16	O'Kelly, Summerfield	2829
38	4	A	Lincoln C	L 1-2	0-2	—	Buckley	4671
39	9	H	Bristol R	W 5-0	2-0	14	Sinnott, Mower, Summerfield, Buckley, Shakespeare	4559
40	16	A	Brentford	W 3-2	2-1	13	Rees 2, Sinnott	4868
41	23	H	Newport Co	W 2-1	1-0	12	O'Kelly, Shakespeare	5141
42	29	A	Southend U	D 1-1	0-0	—	O'Kelly	1904
43	May 2	H	Plymouth Arg	W 2-0	0-0	11	Buckley, Penn	3473
44	7	H	Bradford C	D 1-1	1-1	12	Penn	3322
45	10	A	Portsmouth	L 0-1	0-1	—		22,244
46	14	A	Doncaster R	W 3-1	0-0	10	Rees, Buckley, O'Kelly	1507

Final League Position: 10

GOALSCORERS

League (64): Buckley 13 (1 pen), Kearns O. 11 (1 pen), Summerfield 9, O'Kelly 7, Shakespeare 4, Beech 3, Rees 3, Penn 3, Preece 2, Sinnott 2, Teasdale 2, Mower 1, Pendry 1, Round 1, own goals 2.
Milk Cup (1): Preece 1.
FA Cup (6): Buckley 2, Kearns 1, Preece 1, Round 1, Shakespeare 1.

Milk Cup	First Round	Preston NE (h)	0-1
		(a)	1-1
FA Cup	First Round	Kettering (h)	3-0
	Second Round	North Shields (a)	3-0
	Third Round	Birmingham C (h)	0-0
		(a)	0-1

Green	Arthur	Mower	Beech	Marshall	Hart	Rees	O'Kelly	Kearns O.	Buckley	Preece	Round	Teasdale	Sinnott	Caswell	Shakespeare	Pendry	Bates	Kearns M.	Penn	Hawker (L)	Summerfield	Jones	*Referees*	*Match No.*
1	2	3	4	5	6	7	8*	9	10	11	12												A. Crickmore	1
1	2	3	4	5	6			9*	10	11	12	7	8										D. Owen	2
1	2	3	4		6			9	10	11*	12	7	5	8									K. Cooper	3
1		3	4		6			9	10	11		7*	5	2	12	8							P. Willis	4
1		3*	4		6	12		9	10	11		7	5	2	8								B. Hill	5
1		3	4		6			9	10	11		7	5	2	12	8*							M. Dimblebee	6
1		3	4	5	6			9	10	11				2	7	8							P. Tyldesley	7
1		3	4	5	6			9	10	11	12			2	7	8*							R. Guy	8
1	8	3	4	5	6			9	10	11				2	7								D. Brazier	9
1	8	3	4	5	6			9	10	11	12			2	7*								B. Daniels	10
1	12	3	4	5	6		7		10	11	9			2*		8							E. Scales	11
1		3	4	5	6		7	9*	10	11	12			2		8							D. Letts	12
1		3	4	5	6		7	9	10	11	12			2*		8							T. Mills	13
1		3	4	5	6		7	9	10	11	12					8*	2						T. Bune	14
1		3	4*		6		7	9	10	11	12		5	8			2						A. Glasson	15
1		3	4		6		7*	9	10	8	12		5	11			2						A. Challinor	16
		3	2		6	12	4*	9	10	8			5	11				1	7				R. Milford	17
		3	2		6	7	4	9	10	8			5	11				1					D. Vickers	18
1		3	4		6	12			10*	8				2	11				7	5	9		L. Shapter	19
1		3	4		6		8	12	10					2	11*				7	5	9		R. Banks	20
1		3	4		6	7	11		10	8				2						5	9		D. Shaw	21
1		3	4		6	7	11		10	8			5	2							9		J. Worrall	22
1		3	4		6	7		9	10	8			5	2	11								J. Deakin	23
1		3	4		6	7*	11	9	10	8			5	2	12								C. Downey	24
1		3	4		6		11	9	10	8			5	2	7								N. Ashley	25
1	2	3	4		6		11	9	10	8			5		7*							12	N. Glover	26
1		3	4		6		11	9	10*	8	12		5	2	7								J. Martin	27
1		3	4		6	7	11	12	10	8			5	2*							9		G. Napthine	28
1	2*	3	4		6	7	11	12	10				5		8						9		J. Lovatt	29
1		3	4		6	7	11	12	10*				5	2	8						9		R. Chadwick	30
1		3	4		6		11	7	10				5	2	8						9		D. Owen	31
1		3	4		6		11	7	10	8			5	2*	12						9		D. Allison	32
1		3	4		6		11	9	10*	8			5	2	12							7	D. Hutchinson	33
1	2	3	4		6		11	7	10	8*			5		12						9		T. Jones	34
1		3	4		6		11	7	10*	8			5	2	12						9		J. Moules	35
1		3	4		6		11	7	10	8			5	2							9		F. Roberts	36
1*		3	4		6		11	7	12	8			5	2	10						9		D. Hedges	37
		3	4		6		11	7	12	8			5	2	10*			1			9		T. Fitzharris	38
		3			6	7	11	12	10*	8			5	2	4			1			9		P. Tyldesley	39
		3	6			7	11	12	10*	8			5	2	4			1			9		L. Burden	40
		3			6	7	11	9	10	8			5	2	4			1					A. Robinson	41
		3			6	7	11		10	8			5	2	4			1			9		Alan Robinson	42
		3			6		11		10	8			5	2	4			1	7		9		D. Richardson	43
		3	2		6		11*	12	10	8			5		4			1	7		9		K. Salmon	44
		3			6	7	11		10	8				2	4			1		5	9		D. Axcell	45
					6	7	11		10	8				3	4		2	1		5	9		C. Seel	46
35	8	45	40	10	45	15	35	31	44	42	1	5	32	39	24	8	4	11	5	5	21	1		
	+ 1s					+ 3s		+ 7s	+ 2s		+ 11s				+ 7s							+ 1s		

FOOTBALL LEAGUE RECORD

1892 Elected to Division 2; 1895 failed re-election; 1896–1901 Division 2; 1901 failed re-election; 1921 Original Member of Division 3(N); 1927–31 Division 3(S); 1931–36 Division 3(N); 1936–58 Division 3(S); 1958–60 Division 4; 1960–61 Division 3; 1961–63 Division 2; 1963–79 Division 3; 1979–80 Division 4; 1980– Division 3.

HONOURS

Football League: Division 2 best season: 6th, 1898–99; Division 3 – Runners-up 1960–61; Division 4 – Champions 1959–60; Runners-up 1979–80. *FA Cup* best season: 5th rd, 1939, 1975, 1978, and last 16 1888–89. *Football League Cup* best season: 4th rd, 1966–67.

COLOURS

Red shirts, white shorts, red stockings. **Change colours:** All blue.

WALSALL

Players Names Ht, Wt, D.o.B.	Birthplace Transfer Fee	Clubs	Appearances F.L. A & S	F.L.C. A & S	F.A.C. A & S	Goals F.L.	F.L.C.	F.A.C.
Goalkeepers								
Ron Green	Birmingham	Alvechurch						
6 2, 14 0, 13.10.56	£2000	Walsall	146	4	11			
Martin Conneally*	Lichfield	Walsall (A)	3					
6 10, 12 0, 2.2.62								
Mike Kearns* (EI)	Banbury	Oxford U (A)	67	5	6			
6 4½, 14 0, 26.11.50	—	Plymouth Arg (loan)	1					
	—	Charlton Ath (loan)	4					
	£10,000	Walsall	249	18	22			
	F/T	Wolverhampton W	9		1			
	F/T	Walsall	11		1			
Defenders								
Lee Sinnott	Pelsall	Walsall (A)	36	2	4	2		
6 1, 11 9								
Brian Caswell	Wednesbury	Walsall (A)	322+11	18	19	17	1	1
5 10, 10 7, 14.2.56								
Kenny Mower	Walsall	Walsall (A)	156+1	6	12	4		
6 0¾, 12 4, 1.12.60								
Peter Hart	Mexborough	Huddersfield T (A)	208+2	14	5	7		1
5 11, 12 7, 14.8.57	£80,000	Walsall	135	68	6			
David Arthur*	Bushbury	WBA (A)	2+1	3				
5 8, 11 1, 9.3.60	F/T	Walsall	8+1	1				
Mark Bates	Walsall	Walsall (A)	4					
5 10, 10 6, 25.4.65								
Gary Pendrey	Birmingham	Birmingham C (A)	287+17	21+2	15+1	4	1	
5 10, 12 0, 9.2.49	£30,000	WBA	18					
	F/T	Torquay U	12	2				
	F/T	Bristol R	1					
	F/T	Walsall	8			1		
Phil Hawker	Solihull	Birmingham C (A)	34+1	2		1		
6 1, 11 6, 7.12.62	F/T	Walsall	5					
Midfield								
Ken Beech*	Stoke	Port Vale (A)	169+6	9	11+2	17	1	3
5 7, 10 2, 28.5.63	£10,000	Walsall	78+1	4	6	5		
Richard O'Kelly	West Bromwich	Alvechurch						
5 10, 11 8, 8.8.57	£5000	Walsall	91+11	1+1	5	21		
David Preece	Bridgnorth	Walsall (A)	54+4	2	4	2	1	1
5 5, 10 0, 28.5.63								
Forwards								
Don Penn*	Smethwick	Walsall	132+9	6	10+2	54	2	2
5 10, 12 0, 15.3.60								
Mark Rees (ES)	Smethwick	Walsall (A)	88+22	2	3+3	18		
5 10, 11 10, 13.10.61								
Alan Buckley	Mansfield	Nottingham F(A)	16+2	+1		1		
5 6, 10 9, 20.4.51	£20,000	Walsall	241	18	18	125	11	9
	£175,000	Birmingham C	24+4	1		8		
	£175,000	Walsall	156+7	9	10+1	47	1	5
Steve Round*	Bridgnorth	Walsall (A)	5+19	+2	1+1	3		1
6 1, 12 2, 28.2.63								
Craig Shakespeare	Birmingham	Walsall (A)	24+8	1	1	4		1
5 10, 11 5, 26.10.63								
Ollie Kearns*	Banbury	Banbury U						
6 2, 12 9, 12.6.56		Reading	75+11	4+2	6+1	40	1	2
	F/T	Oxford U	9+9	+2	+1	4		
	F/T	Walsall	31+7	2	2	11		1
Kevin Summerfield	Walsall	WBA (A)	5+4	2	1+1	4		1
6 0, 10 7, 7.1.59	F/T	Birmingham C	2+3	1		1		
	F/T	Walsall	21			9		
Apprentices								
Paul Jones		Walsall (A)	1+1					
5 9, 10 4								

Commercial Manager:
Club Coach: Gary Pendrey
Club Captain 1982–83: Peter Hart
Supporters Player of the Season 1982–83: Lee Sinnott
Chief Scout: Steve Toesbury
Physiotherapist: Fred Pedley
Club Statistician: Geoff Allman
Association of Football Statisticians Club Adviser to Yearbook: D. Glover

Players (non-appearance) granted free transfer: Duncan Ross, D.; Colin Caddick, D.
Players released since May 1982:
Colin Harrison, D. (Rushall Olympic); John Horne, D. (Kidderminster); John Loveridge, M. (Alvechurch); Tony Macken, D. (N/K); Steve Smith, F. (N/K); Julian Marshall, D. (Worcester C).

WATFORD Division 1

Back row (from left to right): Les Taylor, Martin Patching, Kenny Jackett, Steve Sherwood, Keith Pritchett, John Barnes, Wilf Rostron
Centre row: Pat Rice, David Johnson, Nigel Callaghan, Eric Steele, Jan Lohman, Gerry Armstrong, Luther Blissett
Front row: Ian Bolton, Charlie Palmer, Steve Sims, Ross Jenkins, Jimmy Gilligan, Paul Franklin, Steve Terry.

Chairman: E. John ***Vice-Chairman:*** G. A. Smith.

Directors: J. Harrowell, Bertie Mee, J. Reid, H. M. Stratford JP.

Chief Executive & Company Secretary: Eddie Plumley FAAI.

General Manager: Graham Taylor.

Marketing Manager: Caroline Gillies M INST M, MIPR.

Year Formed: 1891. ***Turned Professional:*** 1897. ***Ltd Co.: 1909.***

Nickname: 'The Hornets' ***Previous Name:*** West Herts.

Previous Grounds: 1899, Cassio Road; 1922, Vicarage Road.

Previous Managers since 1946: Jack Bray, Eddie Hapgood, Haydn Green, Ron Gray, Len Goulden, Johnny Paton, Neil McBain, Ron Burgess, Bill McGarry, Ken Furphy, George Kirby, Mike Keen (12).

Vicarage Road Stadium, Watford WD1 8ER. Telephone Watford (0923) 49747–9. Answerphone Service – Watford 44930 for information.

Ground capacity: 28,500. ***Record attendance:*** 34,099 v Manchester U, FA Cup 4th rd, 3 Feb, 1969. ***Record receipts:*** £61,684 v West Ham U, FA Cup 4th rd, 23 Jan, 1982. ***Pitch measurements:*** 113yd×73yd.

Directions to Ground: Buses 321 and 327 from Watford Junction. This and Watford High Street Station are both within walking distance from the ground. Trains from London leave Euston Station.

Match tickets: Stand seats bookable ten days before each League match. Visiting terrace supporters will be guided by Police to special visitors enclosure.

Car parking: Parking for season ticket holders only at the ground, but several multi-storey car parks a few minutes away.

Entertainments /catering facilities: Pre-match entertainment at all League and Cup games. Tea kiosks and hot dog stands inside the ground.

Club shop: 'Hornet Shop' at Club Precinct sell all types of clothing, souvenirs and programmes.

Handbooks /programmes: Programmes are available on subscription. Price 50p, plus postage. Handbook £1, will be available for season 1983–84 with full statistics and interesting information and action pictures.

Address of Supporters Club: Watford FC Supporters Club, c/o Vicarage Road, Watford.

Address of Club Shop: 85 Vicarage Road Precinct, Watford.

Note: Full club statistical records are on pages 416–455.

WATFORD 1982–83 LEAGUE RECORD

Match No.	Date	Venue	Opponents	Result	H/T Score	Lg. Pos.	Goalscorers	Attendance
1	Aug 28	H	Everton	W 2-0	1-0	—	Armstrong, Rice	19,630
2	31	A	Southampton	W 4-1	2-1	—	Callaghan 2, Armstrong, Jenkins	19,714
3	Sept 4	A	Manchester C	L 0-1	0-0	8		29,617
4	7	H	Swansea C	W 2-1	1-0	—	Blissett (pen), Callaghan	15,535
5	11	H	WBA	W 3-0	1-0	1	Blissett 2, Taylor	17,603
6	18	A	Nottingham F	L 0-2	0-1	3		11,550
7	25	H	Sunderland	W 8-0	4-0	3	Callaghan 2, Blissett 4, Jenkins 2	16,744
8	Oct 2	A	Birmingham C	D 1-1	1-0	3	Blissett	13,870
9	9	H	Norwich C	D 2-2	2-1	4	Jackett, Terry	18,597
10	16	A	Aston Villa	L 0-3	0-1	5		21,572
11	23	H	Coventry C	D 0-0	0-0	6		17,334
12	30	A	Notts Co	L 2-3	2-1	8	Barnes, Blissett	9171
13	Nov 6	A	Tottenham H	W 1-0	0-0	6	Taylor	42,215
14	13	H	Stoke C	W 1-0	1-0	4	Barnes	18,713
15	20	H	Brighton & HA	W 4-1	1-0	2	Barnes, Blissett 2 (2 pens), Taylor	16,529
16	27	A	Arsenal	W 4-2	1-1	2	Barnes 2, Jackett, Robson (og)	34,287
17	Dec 4	H	Manchester U	L 0-1	0-0	4		25,669
18	11	A	Liverpool	L 1-3	0-3	5	Rostron	36,690
19	18	H	Ipswich T	W 2-1	2-0	4	Jenkins, Taylor	18,048
20	27	A	Luton T	L 0-1	0-1	5		21,145
21	29	H	West Ham U	W 2-1	1-0	3	Jackett, Jenkins	24,870
22	Jan 1	A	Brighton & HA	D 1-1	0-0	4	Jackett	15,139
23	3	H	Manchester C	W 2-0	2-0	2	Gilligan 2	20,049
24	15	A	Everton	L 0-1	0-0	4		19,233
25	22	H	Southampton	W 2-0	0-0	3	Nicholl (og), Blissett	17,189
26	Feb 6	A	Swansea C	W 3-1	0-1	—	Blissett 2, Barnes	14,461
27	26	H	Aston Villa	W 2-1	1-1	2	Blissett, Rostron	19,318
28	Mar 2	A	Norwich C	L 0-3	0-1	—		16,662
29	5	A	Coventry C	W 1-0	1-0	3	Taylor	11,235
30	12	H	Notts Co	W 5-3	3-1	2	Blissett 3, Barnes, Callaghan	16,273
31	19	H	Tottenham H	L 0-1	0-1	2		27,371
32	22	H	Birmingham C	W 2-1	0-0	—	Blissett 2	14,229
33	26	A	Stoke C	L 0-4	0-1	2		14,276
34	Apr 2	A	West Ham U	L 1-2	1-1	3	Callaghan	22,647
35	4	H	Luton T	W 5-2	2-2	—	Blissett 2, Jobson, Callaghan, Barnes	20,120
36	9	A	WBA	W 3-1	1-0	2	Barnes, Callaghan, Lohman	11,828
37	16	H	Nottingham F	L 1-3	1-0	2	Blissett (pen)	17,537
38	23	A	Manchester U	L 0-2	0-0	2		43,048
39	30	H	Arsenal	W 2-1	0-0	2	Barnes, Blissett (pen)	20,043
40	May 2	A	Sunderland	D 2-2	1-2	2	Blissett 2	13,971
41	7	A	Ipswich T	L 1-3	0-2	2	Rostron	19,921
42	14	H	Liverpool	W 2-1	1-0	2	Patching, Blissett	27,148

Final League Position: 2

GOALSCORERS

League (74): Blissett 27 (5 pens), Barnes 10, Callaghan 9, Jenkins 5, Taylor 5, Jackett 4, Rostron 3, Armstrong 2, Gilligan 2, Jobson 1, Lohman 1, Patching 1, Rice 1, Terry 1, own goals 2.
Milk Cup (7): Jenkins 3, Armstrong 1, Blissett 1, Sims 1, Taylor 1.
FA Cup (6): Blissett 2 (1 pen), Lohman 2, Barnes 1, Rostron 1.
Football League Trophy (13): Blissett 3, Jenkins 3, Barnes 2, Armstrong 1, Gilligan 1, Lohman 1, Terry 1, own goal 1.

Milk Cup	Second Round	Bolton W (a)	2-1
		(h)	2-1 (aet)
	Third Round	Nottingham F (a)	3-7
FA Cup	Third Round	Plymouth Arg (h)	2-0
	Fourth Round	Fulham (h)	1-1
		(a)	2-1
	Fifth Round	Aston Villa (a)	1-4
Football League Trophy		Orient (h)	4-1
		Colchester U (h)	2-1
		Southend U (a)	4-1
	Quarter-final	Reading (a)	3-5

Sherwood	Rice	Rostron	Blissett	Bolton	Jackett	Callaghan	Armstrong	Jenkins	Lohman	Barnes	Taylor	Terry	Patching	Sims	Gilligan	Johnson	Jobson	Sterling	Franklin	*Referees*	*Match No.*
1	2	3	4	5	6	7*	8	9	10	11	12									K. Baker	1
1	2	3	4	5	6	7	8	9	10	11										L. Shapter	2
1	2	3	4	5	6	7	8	9	10*	11	12									D. Hutchinson	3
1	2	3	10	5	6	7	8	9*	12	11	4									H. Taylor	4
1	2	3	8	5	6	7	9		10	11	4									I. Borrett	5
1	2	3	8	5	6	7	9	12	10*	11	4									G. Tyson	6
1	2	3	8	6	10	7		9		11	4	5								V. Callow	7
1	2	3	8	6	10	7	12	9		11*	4	5								P. Tyldesley	8
1		3	8	6	10	7	12	9		11	4*	5	2							D. Civil	9
1		3	8	6	10	7	12	9*		11	4	5	2							R. Banks	10
1	2	3	8		6	7	9*	12	10	11	4			5						D. Axcell	11
1	2	3	8	6	10	7		9		11	4			5						P. Willis	12
1	2	3	8	6	10	7		9		11	4			5						A. Gunn	13
1	2	3	8	6	10	7				11	4			5	9					D. Letts	14
1	2	3	8	6	10	7				11	4			5	9*	12				A. Seville	15
1	2	3	8	6	10	7		9		11	4			5						A. Hamil	16
1	2	3	8	6	10	7		9*		11	4			5		12				A. Glasson	17
1	2	3	8	6	10	7		9		11	4			5						C. Newsome	18
1	2	3		6	10	7		9		8	4			5			11			M. Robinson	19
1	2	3	8	6	10	7		9		11	4			5						B. Daniels	20
1	2	3	8	6	10	7		9		11	4			5						C. Thomas	21
1	2	3	8	6	10	7		9*	12	11	4			5						J. Hunting	22
1	2	3	8	6	10	7				11	4			5	9					J. Martin	23
1	2	3	8	6	10	7		9*	12	11	4			5						K. Hackett	24
1	2	3	8	6	10	7				11	4			5	9					T. Bune	25
1	2	3	8	6	10	7			11	9	4			5						N. Ashley	26
1	2	3	8	6	10	7				9	4			5			11			M. James	27
1	2	3	8	6	10	7*	12			9	4			5			11			G. Napthine	28
1	2	3	8	6	10	7				9	4			5			11			T. Mills	29
1	2	3	8	6	10*	7			12	9	4			5			11			R. Milford	30
1	2	3	8	6	10	7	12			9	4			5			11*			K. Baker	31
1	2	3	8	6	10	7	12			9	4			5			11*			M. Taylor	32
1	2	3	8	6	10*	7	9		12	11	4			5						R. Guy	33
1	2	3	8	6		7	12		10*	9	4			5			11			Alan Robinson	34
1	2	3	8		6	7*	12		11	9	4	5					10			L. Shapter	35
1	2	3	8	6	10	7			11	9	4	5								T. Jones	36
1	2	3	8		6	7	12		11*	9	4	5					10			D. Letts	37
1	2	3	8	6	10					9	4			5		11*	7	12		D. Shaw	38
1	2	3	8	6	10	7				9	4			5			11			M. Scott	39
1	2	3	8	5	6	7	12		10	9	4					11*				N. Midgeley	40
1	2	3	8		6	4	12		10	9				5			11*	7		D. Axcell	41
1	2	3	8		10	7			12	9			4	5*				11	6	A. Grey	42
42	40	42	41	37	41	41	8	18	13	42	37	7	3	28	4	2	13	2	1		
							+ 11s	+ 2s	+ 6s		+ 2s					+ 2s		+ 1s			

FOOTBALL LEAGUE RECORD

1920 Original Member of Division 3; 1921–58 Division 3(S); 1958–60 Division 4; 1960–69 Division 3; 1969–72 Division 2; 1972–75 Division 3; 1976–78 Division 4; 1978–79 Division 3; 1979–82 Division 2; 1982– Division 1.

HONOURS

Football League: Best season Division 1: 1982–83 Runners-up. Division 2 Runners-up 1981–82; Division 3 – Champions 1968–69, Runners-up 1978–79; Division 4 – Champions 1977–78; Promoted 1959–60 (4th). *FA Cup:* semi-final 1970. *Football League Cup:* semi-final 1978–79. *FA Youth Cup:* Winners 1981–82. *UEFA Cup:* 1983–84.

COLOURS

Yellow shirts with black and red facings, red shorts, red stockings with black and yellow tops.
Change colours: White shirts, black shorts, black stockings with red and yellow tops.

WATFORD

Players Names Ht, Wt, D.o.B.	Birthplace Transfer Fee	Clubs	Appearances F.L. A & S	Appearances F.L.C. A & S	Appearances F.A.C. A & S	Goals F.L.	Goals F.L.C.	Goals F.A.C.
Goalkeepers								
Steve Sherwood	Selby	Chelsea (A)	16	1				
6 4, 14 7, 10.12.53	—	Millwall (loan)	1					
	—	Brentford (loan)	62	2	2			
	£4000	Watford	149	20	14			
Eric Steele	Newcastle	Newcastle U						
6 0, 12 8, 14.5.54		Peterborough U	124	11	13			
	£19,000	Brighton	87	9	2			
	£100,000	Watford	49	7	4			
	—	Cardiff C (loan)	7					
Defenders								
Steve Sims (EU21)	Lincoln	Leicester C (A)	78+1	5	3	3		
6 1½, 13 9, 2.7.57	£175,000	Watford	128+2	13	11	4	2	
Ian Bolton	Leicester	Birmingham C (A)						
6 1½, 12 7, 13.7.53	F/T	Notts Co	61+9	4+1	3	4		
	—	Lincoln C (loan)	1					
	£12,500	Watford	224	28+1	15	28	5	2
Steve Terry	Clapton	Watford (A)	40	6	3	3	1	
6 1½, 13 3, 14.6.62								
Kenny Jacket (W)	Watford	Watford (A)	102+1	15+1	7	9	1	
5 10½, 11 3 5.1.62								
Pat Rice (NI)	Belfast	Arsenal	391+6	36	67	11		1
5 9½, 12 7, 17.3.49	£20,000	Watford	106	9	10	1		
Charlie Palmer	Aylesbury	Watford (A)						
5 11, 11 9								
Paul Franklin	Ilford	Watford (A)	1					
6 0, 11 8,								
Neil Price	Hemel Hempstead	Watford (A)						
5 9, 10 10,								
Midfield								
Martin Patching (EY)	Rotherham	Wolverh'pton W (A)	78+12	3	5+3	10		1
6 0, 12 9, 1.11.58	£100,000	Watford	23+1	4	3+1	3	1	2
	—	North'pton T (loan)	6			1		
Les Taylor	North Shields	Oxford U (A)	219	16	3	15	1	
5 8, 11 7, 4.12.56	£105,000	Watford	102+3	9	9	10	3	
Richard Jobson	Hull	Burton A						
6 1, 12 2,	£15,000	Watford	13			1		
Alan Paris	Slough	Slough T						
6 0, 11 6,		Watford						
Francis Cassidy	Watford	Watford (A)						
5 9, 10 12,								
Neil Williams	Waltham Abbey	Watford (A)						
5 10, 11 0,								
Forwards								
Wilf Rostron (ES)	Sunderland	Arsenal (A)	12+5	1	1	2		
5 7, 11 1, 29.9.56	£40,000	Sunderland	75+1	4	4	17	1	
	£150,000	Watford	121+6	11+1	10+1	9	1	2
Ross Jenkins*	Kensington	Crystal Palace (A)	15	2		2		
6 2, 12 2, 4.11.51	£30,000	Watford	312+27	33+4	18+1	118	16	5
Luther Blissett (E)	Jamaica, W.I.	Watford	222+24	26+1	17	95	13	3
5 10½, 11 13,1.2.58								
Gerry Armstrong (NI)	Belfast	Bangor						
5 11¾, 13 0, 23.5.54	£25,000	Tottenham H	65+19	3+1	6+4	10	3	3
	£250,000	Watford	50+26	5+2	5+2	12	3	2
John Barnes (E)	Jamaica, W.I.	Sudbury Court						
5 11, 11 10, 7.9.63	—	Watford	77+1	8	7	23	1	1
Ian Richardson	Ely	Watford (A)						
5 8½, 10 6,	—	Blackpool (loan)	5			2		
Jimmy Gilligan	Hammersmith	Watford (A)	4+1	+1	2	2		
6 2, 11 7	—	Lincoln C (loan)	+3					
Jan Lohman (HOLU21)	Dussen, Holland	Lokeren						
5 10, 11 2,	£25,000	Watford	39+5	1	5+1	3		3
Dave Johnson	Gloucester	Redhill						
5 8, 10 10,	—	Watford	2+3	+1				
Nigel Callaghan (EU21)	Singapore	Watford (A)	94+6	10+2	8+1	16	1	1
5 9, 10 9, 12.9.62								
Apprentices								
Worrell Sterling	Bethnal Green	Watford (A)	2+1					
5 8, 10 8,								

Marketing Manager: Caroline Gillies. (Tel. as Club)
Club Coaches: John Ward, Tom Walley, Steve Harrison *Club Captain 1982–83:* Pat Rice
Supporters Player of the Season 1982–83: Wilf Rostron
Physiotherapist: Billy Hails
Association of Football Statisticians Club Adviser to Yearbook: T. G. Jones

Players released since May 1982: Colin Hull, D. (Bishops Stortford).

WEST BROMWICH ALBION Division 1

Back row (left to right): Cyrille Regis, Martin Jol, Peter Eastoe, Brendon Batson, Tony Godden, Mark Grew, Martyn Bennett, Derek Monaghan, Alistair Brown, Alistair Robertson, Richard Roberts (Physiotherapist)
Front row: Barry Cowdrill, Derek Statham, Alan Webb, Gary Owen, Steve Mackenzie, Ron Wylie (Manager), Clive Whitehead, Nicky Cross, Romeo Zondervan, David Mills (now with Sheffield Wednesday).

President: J. W. Gaunt. ***Vice-President:*** F. T. D. Hall.

Chairman: F. A. Millichip. ***Vice-Chairman:*** J. Gordon.

Directors: C. I. Edwards. D. B. Boundy, J. S. Lucas, A. Everiss JP.

Manager: Ron Wylie. ***Secretary:*** A. E. Rance.

Assistant Secretary: Ray Fairfax.

Year Formed: 1879. ***Turned Professional:*** 1885. ***Ltd Co.:*** 1892.

Club Nicknames: 'Throstles', 'Baggies', 'Albion'.

Previous Grounds: 1879, Coopers Hill; 1879. Dartmouth Park; 1881, Bunns Field, Walsall Street; 1882, Four Acres (Dartmouth Cricket Club); 1885, Stoney Lane; 1900, The Hawthornes. ***Previous Name:*** 1879–81, West Bromwich Strollers.

Previous Managers since 1946: Jack Smith, Vic Buckingham, Gordon Clark, Archie Macaulay, Jimmy Hagan, Alan Ashman, Don Howe, John Giles, Ronnie Allen, Ron Atkinson, Ronnie Allen (11).

The Hawthorns, West Bromwich B71 4LF. Telephone 021-525 8888. Box Office 021-553 5472. ***Ground capacity:*** 38,600 (seats 12,500). ***Record attendance:*** 64,815 v Arsenal, FA Cup 6th rd, 6 Mar, 1937. ***Record receipts:*** £79,494.76 v Tottenham H, League Cup semi-final, 3 Feb, 1982. ***Pitch:*** 115yd×75yd.

Directions to Ground: Buses 72, 74, 75, and 79 from outside Birmingham New Street station run directly to the ground. A special bus service from the centre of West Bromwich runs every three minutes on match days. ***Address of Supporters Club:*** Throstle Club, Birmingham Road, West Bromwich, Staffs.

Match tickets: Advance bookings for Centre and Wing Stands accepted six weeks in advance by post including remittance and sae. Telephone bookings are accepted but not before two days prior to the match; tickets reserved by telephone must be collected at least thirty minutes before kick-off. A limited number of unreserved seats in the Paddock is available at Door E1 on the day of the match.

Car parking: Street parking permitted in certain areas, all within 10 minutes' walk of the ground.

Entertainments /catering facilities: Several restaurants within walking distance of the ground. Snack bars in the ground. Excellent facilities at The Hawthorns Throstle Club include a full-course lunch.

Club shop: Situated in the Pools Office in Birmingham Rd, and open from 9–5 Mon–Sat. Stocks over 200 different articles. Excellent mailing service. Price list available on request.

Handbooks /programmes: Handbook and programmes available on subscription.

Extra information: There are three Throstle Clubs in the surrounding areas, and one for under-15s.

Note: Full club statistical records are on pages 416–455.

WEST BROMWICH ALBION 1982–83 LEAGUE RECORD

Match No.	Date	Venue	Opponents	Result	H/T Score	Lg. Pos.	Goalscorers	Attendance
1	Aug 28	A	Liverpool	L 0-2	0-0	—		35,652
2	Sept 1	H	Brighton & HA	W 5-0	0-0	—	Cross, Brown 2, Jol, Eastoe	11,546
3	4	H	Manchester U	W 3-1	0-1	6	Bennett, Eastoe, Brown	25,014
4	8	A	Stoke C	W 3-0	2-0	—	Regis, Eastoe, Brown	17,447
5	11	A	Watford	L 0-3	0-1	5		17,603
6	18	H	West Ham U	L 1-2	1-2	8	Eastoe	15,321
7	25	A	Norwich C	W 3-1	1-1	7	Regis 3	15,130
8	Oct 2	H	Aston Villa	W 1-0	0-0	5	Cross	25,300
9	9	H	Nottingham F	W 2-1	1-1	3	Regis, Owen	13,718
10	16	A	Arsenal	L 0-2	0-2	4		21,666
11	23	H	Luton T	W 1-0	1-0	2	Whitehead	16,345
12	30	A	Ipswich T	L 1-6	0-4	4	Regis	20,011
13	Nov 6	A	Birmingham C	L 1-2	1-0	8	Eastoe	18,520
14	13	H	Swansea C	D 3-3	2-0	8	Cross, Jol, Eastoe	12,432
15	20	A	Everton	D 0-0	0-0	9		16,001
16	27	H	Coventry C	W 2-0	1-0	7	Robertson, Regis	12,115
17	Dec 4	A	Tottenham H	D 1-1	0-1	8	Mills	26,208
18	11	H	Sunderland	W 3-0	2-0	6	Robertson, Owen, Zondervan	11,136
19	18	A	Southampton	L 1-4	1-1	8	Regis	16,896
20	27	H	Notts Co	D 2-2	1-0	6	Eastoe, Owen	17,768
21	28	A	Manchester C	L 1-2	0-1	8	Brown	25,172
22	Jan 1	H	Everton	D 2-2	1-1	7	Zondervan, Owen	15,194
23	3	A	Manchester U	D 0-0	0-0	8		39,123
24	15	H	Liverpool	L 0-1	0-0	12		24,560
25	22	A	West Ham U	W 1-0	1-0	13	Eastoe	19,887
26	Feb 5	H	Stoke C	D 1-1	0-1	9	Cross	11,486
27	12	A	Brighton & HA	D 0-0	0-0	9		9902
28	19	A	Nottingham F	D 0-0	0-0	9		14,507
29	26	H	Arsenal	D 0-0	0-0	9		13,923
30	Mar 5	A	Luton T	D 0-0	0-0	11		10,852
31	12	H	Ipswich T	W 4-1	2-0	6	Thompson 2, Statham, Gernon (og)	12,892
32	19	H	Birmingham C	W 2-0	1-0	5	Regis, Thompson	20,794
33	26	A	Swansea C	L 1-2	0-1	8	Thompson	11,222
34	Apr 2	H	Manchester C	L 0-2	0-0	9		13,654
35	4	A	Notts Co	L 1-2	1-1	—	Thompson	8692
36	9	H	Watford	L 1-3	0-1	13	Jol	11,828
37	19	A	Aston Villa	L 0-1	0-1	—		26,921
38	23	H	Tottenham H	L 0-1	0-1	14		14,940
39	30	A	Coventry C	W 1-0	1-0	13	Perry	9410
40	May 2	H	Norwich C	W 1-0	1-0	13	Thompson	9221
41	7	H	Southampton	W 1-0	1-0	12	Statham	11,241
42	14	A	Sunderland	D 1-1	1-0	11	Thompson	16,376

Final League Position: 11

GOALSCORERS

League (51): Regis 9, Eastoe 8, Thompson 7, Brown 5, Cross 4, Owen 4, Jol 3, Robertson 2, Statham 2, Zondervan 2, Bennett 1, Mills 1, Perry 1, Whitehead 1, own goal 1.
Milk Cup (4): Regis 2, Cross 1, Whitehead 1.
FA Cup (4): Owen 2 (1 pen), Eastoe 1, Whitehead 1.

Milk Cup	Second Round	Nottingham F (a)	1-6
		(h)	3-1
FA Cup	Third Round	QPR (h)	3-2
	Fourth Round	Tottenham H (a)	1-2

Commercial Manager: Contact Secretary
Club Coach: Mike Kelly
Supporters Player of the Season 1982–83: Romeo Zondervan
Physiotherapist: Richard Roberts
Association of Football Statisticians Club Adviser to Yearbook: Tony Matthews.

Club Captain 1982–83: Alistair Robertson
Chief Scout: Roy Horobin
Club Statistician: Tony Mathews

Grew	Batson	Cowdrill	Zondervan	Bennett	Robertson	Jol	Brown	Eastoe	Mackenzie	Whitehead	Owen	Cross	Regis	Statham	Godden	Wile	Mills	Barron	Webb	Lewis	Thompson	Perry	Luke	Robson	Referees	Match No.
1	2	3	4	5	6*	7	8	9	10	11									12						K. Redfern	1
1	2		4	5	6	7	8	9		3	10	11													N. Glover	2
1	2		4	5	6	7	8	11		3	10		9												K. Salmon	3
1	2		4	5	6	7	8	11		3	10		9												K. Hackett	4
1	2		4	5	6	7	8	11		3	10		9												I. Borrett	5
1	2		4	5	6	7	8*	11		3	10	12	9												K. Walmsley	6
1	2		4	5	6	7	8	11		3	10		9												J. Moules	7
1	2		4	5	6	7	8	11		3	10	9													T. Mills	8
1	2		4	5	6	7	8	11*		3	10	12	9												E. Read	9
1	2		4	5	6	7	8			3	10	11*	9	12											B. Hill	10
	2		4	5	6	7	8			11	10		9	3	1										M. Scott	11
	2*		4		6	7	8			11	10	12	9	3	1	5									D. Reeves	12
			2	4*	6	7		8		11	10	12	9	3	1	5									J. Worrall	13
			4		6	7		11		2	10	8	9	3	1	5									R. Nixon	14
			4		6	7		11		2	10	8	9	3	1	5									J. Hough	15
			4		6	7		11		2	10	8	9	3	1	5									A. Robinson	16
			4		6	7		11*		2	10	8	9	3	1	5	12								M. Bodenham	17
			4		6	7		11		2	10	8*	9	3	1	5	12								R. Guy	18
			4		6	7		11		2	10	8	9	3	1	5									M. James	19
			4		6	7		11		2	10	8	9	3	1	5									N. Ashley	20
			4*	12	6	7	8	11		2	10		9	3	1	5									C. Seel	21
			4		6	7		11		2	10	8*	9	3	1	5	12								G. Napthine	22
			4	8	6	7		11		2	10		9	3		5		1							D. Owen	23
			4	8	6	7		11		2	10		9	3		5		1							T. Bune	24
			4	8	6	7		11		2	10	12	9*	3		5		1							M. Taylor	25
			4	2	6	7	8	11			10	9		3		5		1							T. Spencer	26
			4	6		7	8	11				9		3		5		1	2	10					E. Scale	27
			4	6		7	8	11				9		3		5		1	2	10					B. Hill	28
			4	2*	6	7		11		12	10	8		3		5		1			9				N. Wilson	29
			6	3	5	7		11			10	8		2		4		1			9				R. Lewis	30
			4	6				12		7	10	11	9*	3		5		1	2		8				F. Roberts	31
			4	6						7	10	11	9	3		5		1	2		8				R. Chadwick	32
			4		6	7				11*	10	12	9	3		5		1	2		8				L. Burden	33
			4		6	7		11		2	10*	9		3		5		1		12	8				J. Deakin	34
					6	7		9		4		11		3		5		1	2	10	8				K. Salmon	35
		3	4		6	7		9		2	10	11				5		1				8			T. Jones	36
			4		6	7				2	10	11		3		5		1	9			8			L. Shapter	37
			4		6	7				11*	10		9	3		5		1	2		8	12			J. Hough	38
			12		6	7*				4	10	11		3		5		1	2		8	9			D. Scott	39
			4		6						10	11		3		5		1	2	7*	9	8	12		A. Crickmore	40
			4		6	7*					10	11		3		5		1	2		9	8		12	R. Banks	41
			4			7				2	10	11		3		5		1	6		9	8*		12	P. Tyldesley	42
10	12	2	40	22	37	39	16	30	1	35	38	26	26	31	12	31	0	20	12	4	12	6	0	0		
			†1s	†1s				†1s		†1s		†6s		†1s			†3s		†1s	†1s		†1s	†1s	†2s		

FOOTBALL LEAGUE RECORD

1888 Founder Member of Football League; 1901–02 Division 2; 1902–04 Division 1; 1904–11 Division 2; 1911–27 Division 1; 1927–31 Division 2; 1931–38 Division 1; 1938–49 Division 2; 1949–73 Division 1; 1973–76 Division 2; 1976– Division 1.

HONOURS

Football League: Division 1 – Champions 1919–20; Runners-up 1924–25, 1953–54. Division 2 – Champions 1901–02, 1910–11; Runners-up 1930–31, 1948–49; Promoted to Division 1 1975–76 (3rd). *FA Cup:* Winners 1888, 1892, 1931, 1954, 1968; Runners-up 1886, 1887, 1895, 1912, 1935. *Football League Cup:* Winners 1965–66; Runners-up 1966–67, 1869–70. **European Competitions:** *European Cup-Winners' Cup:* 1968–69; *European Fairs Cup:* 1966–67; *UEFA Cup:* 1978–79, 1979–80, 1981–82.

COLOURS

Navy blue and white striped shirts, white shorts and stockings.
Change colours: Yellow shirts with navy blue pinstripe hoops and trim, navy blue shorts, yellow stockings.

WEST BROMWICH ALBION

Players Names *Ht, Wt, D.o.B.*	*Birthplace* *Transfer Fee*	*Clubs*	*Appearances* *F.L.* *A & S*	 *F.L.C.* *A & S*	 *F.A.C.* *A & S*	*Goals* *F.L.*	 *F.L.C.*	 *F.A.C.*
Goalkeepers								
Tony Godden	Gillingham	Ashford T						
6 0½, 13 0, 2.8.55	£2500	WBA	205	21	16			
	—	Luton T (loan)	12					
Mark Grew	Bilston	WBA	33	8	5			
5 10, 11 3, 15.2.58	—	Wigan Ath (loan)	4					
Paul Barron	London	Slough T						
6 2, 13 5, 16.9.53	—	Plymouth Arg	44	4	4			
	£60,000	Arsenal	8					
	£400,000	Crystal Palace	90	13	5			
	£60,000	WBA	20		2			
Defenders								
Ally Robertson (SY)	Philipstoun	WBA (A)	441+2	41	32+2	8	2	
5 11, 12 2, 9.9.52								
John Wile*	Sherburn	Durham C						
6 1½, 12 0, 9.3.47	—	Sunderland						
	F/T	Peterborough U	116+2	5	1	7		
	£30,000	WBA	499+1	42	42	24	2	2
Derek Statham (EB)	Wolverhampton	WBA (A)	208+1	24	23	4	1	1
5 5½, 11 1, 24.3.59								
Brendon Batson (EB)	Grenada, WI	Arsenal (A)	6+4					
5 10, 11 7, 6.2.53	F/T	Cambridge U	162+1	9	9	6		
	£30,000	WBA	172	21	13	1		1
Martyn Bennett (ES)	Birmingham	WBA (A)	66+1	5	7	4		
6 0, 12 12, 4.8.61								
Alan Webb	Wrockwardine	WBA (A)	18+1					
5 9½, 12 0, 1.1.63								
Barry Cowdrill	Birmingham	Sutton CT						
5 11, 11 4, 3.1.57	£5000	WBA	27+2	2+1	2			1
John Smith	Northfield	WBA (A)						
5 10, 10 10, 14.6.64								
Wayne Ebanks	Birmingham	WBA						
5 10, 11 5, 2.10.64								
Midfield								
Romeo Zondervan (Hol)	Surinam	FC Twente						
5 9½, 11 2, 4.3.59	£225,000	WBA	53+2	2	3	2		
Noel Luke	Birmingham	WBA	+1					
5 11, 10 11, 28.12.64								
Gary Owen (EB)	St Helens	Manchester C (A)	101+2	8	7	19	2	2
5 9, 11 3, 7.7.58	£465,000	WBA	148	21	9+1	18	1	3
Gary Childs (EY)	Birmingham	WBA (A)	2					
5 7, 10 8, 19.4.64								
Steve MacKenzie (EU21)	Romford	Crystal Palace (A)						
5 10, 11 3, 23.11.61	£250,000	Manchester C	56+2	11	8	8		2
	£650,000	WBA	38	9	5	5	1	1
Micky Lewis	Birmingham	WBA	7+2	+1	1			
5 6, 10 6, 15.2.65								
Martin Jol (Hol)	Hague, Holland	FC Twente						
5 11, 11 2, 16.1.56	£255,000	WBA	48	9	4	4		
Clive Whitehead	Birmingham	Bristol C	209+20	17+3	10	10	2	2
5 10½, 11 4, 24.11.55	£100,000	WBA	43+1	2	4	2	1	2
Gary Robson	Durham	WBA (A)	+2					
5 5, 10 11, 6.7.65								
Forwards								
Gary Thompson (EU21)	Birmingham	Coventry C (A)	127+7	12+1	11	38	7	4
6 0, 12 9, 7.10.59	£225,000	WBA	12			7		
Derek Monaghan (EY)	Bromsgrove	WBA (A)	12+4	2+1	1	1	1	
5 10, 11 3, 20.1.59								
Cyrille Regis (E)	French Guyana	Hayes						
6 0, 13 4, 9.2.58	£5000	WBA	196+4	24+1	24	71	13	10
Nicky Cross	Birmingham	WBA (A)	37+19	2+1	3	7	2	
5 9, 11 2, 7.2.61								
Colin Jones	Birmingham	WBA (A)						
5 9, 11 0, 30.10.63								
Peter Frain	Birmingham	WBA						
5 8½, 11 2, 18.3.65								
Mick Perry	Wimbledon	WBA (A)	6+1			1		
5 10, 11 4, 4.4.64								
Peter Eastoe (EY)	Tamworth	Wolverhmptn W (A)	4+2					
5 9½, 11 0, 2.8.53	£88,000	Swindon T	91	5	12	43	2	6
	£80,000	QPR	69+3	8	3	15	5	
	P/E	Everton	88+7	7	11	26	1	5
	P/E	WBA	30+1	1	2	8		1
Kevin Kent		WBA (A)						
5 9, 11 0,								

Players (non-appearance) granted free transfer: Andy Lacey, D.; Martin Pike, M.
Players released since May 1982: David Carlisle, G. (N/K); John Snape, D. (N/K).

WEST HAM UNITED Division 1

Back row (left to right):
Paul Brush
Trevor Brooking
Tom McAlister
Billy Bonds *(capt)*
Phil Parkes
Alvin Martin
Sandy Clark
Centre row:
George Cowie
Frank Lampard
Nicky Morgan
Ray Stewart
Alan Devonshire
Pat Holland
Neil Orr
Front row:
Paul Goddard
Everald la Ronde
Jimmy Neighbour
Paul Allen
Geoff Pike
Francois van der Elst
Bobby Barnes.
(Copyright: West Ham United 1982)

President: R. H. Pratt. ***Chairman:*** L. C. Cearns.

Directors: W. F. Cearns, B. R. Cearns FCIS, J. Petchey, M. W. Cearns AIB.

Manager: John Lyall. ***PRO:*** Jack Helliar (476-1905).

Chief Executive and Secretary: Eddie Chapman FAAI.

Year Formed: 1900. ***Turned Professional:*** 1900. ***Ltd Co.:*** 1900.

Previous Grounds: Memorial Recreation Ground, Canning Town; 1904 Boleyn Ground.

Club Nickname: 'The Hammers'.

Previous Managers since 1946: Charlie Paynter, Ted Fenton, Ron Greenwood (3).

Boleyn Ground, Green Street, Upton Park, London E13. Telephone 01-472 2740. Answerphone 01-470 1325. ***Ground capacity:*** 35,500. ***Record attendance:*** 42,322 v Tottenham H, Division 1, 17 Oct, 1970. ***Record receipts:*** £71,455 v Aston Villa, FA Cup 6th rd, 8 Mar, 1980. ***Pitch measurements:*** 110yd×72yd.

Directions to Ground: Nearest station Upton Park (Underground, District Line) – five minutes' walk. Buses from Barking Road, Romford Road and Green Street.

Match tickets: Advance booking, by personal application or by post three weeks prior to League matches.

Car parking: Ample side-street parking available.

Entertainments/catering facilities: Refreshment points around the ground.

Club shop: Situated on the ground; sells all types of souvenirs.

Handbook/programmes: Programmes and handbook available by post from either Sales Service c/o West Ham United FC or from Helliar & Sons, 237 Barking Road, London E13 8EQ.

Address of Supporters Club: Castle Street, Upton Park, E13.

Address of the Club Shop or Boutique: Hammers Shop, Boleyn Ground, Green Street, Upton Park.

West Ham Statisticians Group: 7 Bells Chase, Gt Baddow (Tel. 0245-72031).

Note: Full club statistical records are on pages 416–455.

WEST HAM UNITED 1982–83 LEAGUE RECORD

Match No.	Date	Venue	Opponents	Result	H/T Score	Lg. Pos.	Goalscorers	Attendance
1	Aug 28	H	Nottingham F	L 1-2	1-1	—	Stewart (pen)	23,796
2	31	A	Luton T	W 2-0	0-0	—	Goddard, Bonds	13,403
3	Sept 4	A	Sunderland	L 0-1	0-1	14		19,239
4	7	H	Ipswich T	D 1-1	0-1	—	Lampard	21,963
5	11	H	Birmingham C	W 5-0	2-0	8	Van der Elst, Goddard, Stewart (pen), Martin, Clark	18,754
6	18	A	WBA	W 2-1	2-1	6	Clark, Van der Elst	15,321
7	25	H	Manchester C	W 4-1	2-0	4	Clark 2, Goddard, Van der Elst	23,883
8	Oct 2	A	Arsenal	W 3-2	2-1	4	Van der Elst, Goddard, Martin	30,484
9	9	H	Liverpool	W 3-1	1-0	2	Martin, Pike, Clark	32,500
10	16	A	Southampton	L 0-3	0-1	2		19,840
11	23	A	Brighton & HA	L 1-3	0-1	5	Devonshire	20,490
12	30	H	Manchester U	W 3-1	1-0	2	Goddard, Stewart (pen), Pike	31,684
13	Nov 6	A	Stoke C	L 2-5	1-4	3	Stewart (pen), Pike	17,589
14	13	H	Norwich C	W 1-0	0-0	2	Clark	22,463
15	20	A	Tottenham H	L 1-2	1-0	4	Van der Elst	41,960
16	27	H	Everton	W 2-0	1-0	5	Stevens (og), Bonds	21,424
17	Dec 4	A	Aston Villa	L 0-1	0-0	6		24,658
18	11	H	Coventry C	L 0-3	0-3	7		19,321
19	18	A	Notts Co	W 2-1	2-0	6	Dickens, Hunt (og)	8457
20	27	H	Swansea C	W 3-2	0-2	4	Stewart (pen), Van der Elst, Goddard	23,843
21	29	A	Watford	L 1-2	0-1	5	Stewart (pen)	24,870
22	Jan 1	H	Tottenham H	W 3-0	1-0	5	Cottee, Stewart (pen), Pike	33,383
23	4	H	Luton T	L 2-3	1-1	5	Cottee, Clark	21,435
24	15	A	Nottingham F	L 0-1	0-0	6		17,031
25	22	H	WBA	L 0-1	0-1	6		19,887
26	Feb 5	A	Birmingham C	L 0-3	0-1	8		12,539
27	26	H	Southampton	D 1-1	1-1	12	Lampard	19,626
28	Mar 5	H	Brighton & HA	W 2-1	0-0	10	Dickens, Cottee	16,850
29	12	A	Liverpool	L 0-3	0-0	11		28,511
30	19	H	Stoke C	D 1-1	0-0	13	Bould (og)	16,466
31	22	A	Manchester U	L 1-2	0-0	—	Devonshire	30,227
32	26	A	Norwich C	D 1-1	1-0	14	Dickens	18,582
33	Apr 2	H	Watford	W 2-1	1-1	12	Van der Elst, Swindlehurst	22,647
34	5	A	Swansea C	W 5-1	2-1	—	Pike 2, Devonshire, Dickens 2	13,303
35	9	H	Sunderland	W 2-1	0-0	7	Dickens, Goddard	20,053
36	16	A	Manchester C	L 0-2	0-2	9		23,015
37	23	H	Aston Villa	W 2-0	0-0	9	Swindlehurst, Bonds	21,822
38	30	A	Everton	L 0-2	0-1	10		16,355
39	May 3	A	Ipswich T	W 2-1	1-1	—	Goddard, Stewart (pen)	18,690
40	7	H	Notts Co	W 2-0	1-0	8	Van der Elst, Goddard	17,534
41	10	H	Arsenal	L 1-3	0-3	—	Van der Elst	28,930
42	14	A	Coventry C	W 4-2	1-0	8	Goddard, Cottee 2, Swindlehurst	10,919

Final League Position: 8

GOALSCORERS

League (68): Goddard 10, Van der Elst 9, Stewart 8 (8 pens), Clark 7, Dickens 6, Pike 6, Cottee 5, Bonds 3, Devonshire 3, Martin 3, Swindlehurst 3, Lampard 2, own goals 3.
Milk Cup (13): Clark 3, Stewart 3, Van der Elst 3, Allen 2, Goddard 2.
FA Cup (0).

Milk Cup	Second Round	Stoke C (a)	1-1
		(h)	2-1
	Third Round	Lincoln C (a)	1-1
		(h)	2-1 (aet)
	Fourth Round	Notts Co (a)	3-3
		(h)	3-0
	Fifth Round	Liverpool (a)	1-2
FA Cup	Third Round	Manchester U (a)	0-2

Parkes	Stewart	Lampard	Bonds	Martin	Devonshire	Van der Elst	Goddard	Clark	Allen	Pike	Neighbour	Morgan	Orr	Brush	Gallagher	Dickens	Cottee	Cowie	Swindlehurst	Brooking	Referees	Match No.
1	2	3	4	5	6	7	8	9	10	11											A. Gunn	1
1	2	3	4	5	6	7	8	9	10		11*	12									A. Seville	2
1	2	3	4	5	6	7	8	9	10	11											R. Chadwick	3
1	2	3	4	5	6	7	8	9	10	11											K. Barratt	4
1	2	3	4	5	6	7	8	9	10	11											M. James	5
1	2	3	4	5	6	7	8	9	10	11											K. Walmsley	6
1	2*	3	4	5	6	7	8	9	10	11			12								D. Letts	7
1	2	3	4	5	6	7*	8	9	10	11			12								T. Bune	8
1	2	3	4*	5	6		8	9	10	11	7		12								Alan Robinson	9
1	2	3	4	5	6	7	8	9	10	11											J. Hunting	10
1	2	3	4	5	6	7	8	9	10	11											L. Burden	11
1	2	3	4	5	6	7	8	9	10	11											D. Hedges	12
1	2		4	5	6	7*	8	9	10	11			12	3							F. Roberts	13
1	2	3	4	5	6	7	8	9	10	11											B. Hill	14
1	2	3	4	5		7	8	9	10	11	6										R. Lewis	15
1	2	3	4	5	6*	7	8	9	10	11		12									V. Callow	16
1	2	3		5		7	8	9	10	11			4	6							E. Read	17
1	2	3			6*	7	8		10	11		12	4	9	5						A. Grey	18
1		2				7	8	9	10	11			4	3	5	6					J. Worrall	19
1	2			5	6	7	8	9	10	11			4	3							I. Borrett	20
1	2	3		5	6	7	8	9	10	11					4						C. Thomas	21
1	2			5	6	7		9	10	11					3	4	8				M. Scott	22
1	2			5*	6	7		9	10	11		12			3	4	8				T. Spencer	23
1	2*	3	4	5	6	7	8	9	10	11					12						P. Tyldesley	24
1		2	4	5	6	7*	8	9	10	11					3			12			M. Taylor	25
1		2	4	5	6	7	8	9	10*						3	12		11			T. Fitzharris	26
1	2	3	4	5	6	7	8	9*	10	11							12				M. Robinson	27
1	2*	3		5	6	7			10	11		8			4	12	9				J. Deakin	28
1	2	3	4	5	6	7	9		10	11		8									K. Hackett	29
1	2	3	4	5	6	7	8		10	11		9									M. Bodenham	30
1	2	3	4	5	6	7	8		10	11			9*			12					A. Challinor	31
1	2	3	4	5	6		8			11			7			10			9		J. Bray	32
1	2	3	4	5	6	7	8			11						10	12		9*		Alan Robinson	33
1	2	3	4	5	6	7	8			11			9			10					D. Civil	34
1	2	3	4	5	6	7	8			11						10	12		9*		H. Taylor	35
1	2	3	4		6	7	8*		9	11			5			10	12				A. Saunders	36
1	2	3*	4	5	6	7	8			11			12			10			9		C. Thomas	37
1	2		4	5	6	7	8			11				3		10			9		K. Holbrook	38
1	2	3	4	5	6	7	8			11						10			9		G. Napthine	39
1	2	3	4	5	6	7	8			11						10			9		T. Bune	40
1	2	3	4	5	6	7	8			11									9	10	A. Gunn	41
1	2	3	4		6	7	8		10	11*			5				12		9		B. Newsome	42
42	39	37	34	38	39	40	39	26	33	40	3	3	9	6	8	12	3	1	9	1		
												+ 4s	+ 5s		+ 1s	+ 3s	+ 5s	+ 1s				

FOOTBALL LEAGUE RECORD

1919 Elected to Division 2; 1923–32 Division 1; 1932–58 Division 2; 1958–78 Division 1; 1978–81 Division 2; 1981– Division 1.

HONOURS

Football League: Division 1 best season: 6th, 1926–27, 1958–59, 1972–73. Division 2 – Champions 1957–58, 1980–81; Runners-up 1922–23. *FA Cup:* Winners 1964, 1975, 1980; Runners-up 1922–23. *Football League Cup:* Runners-up 1966, 1981. **European Competition:** *European Cup-Winners' Cup:* 1964–65 (winners), 1965–66, 1975–76 (runners-up), 1980–81.

COLOURS

Claret shirts with sky blue sleeves and trim, white shorts and stockings.
Change colours: White shirts with three claret stripes down sleeves, blue shorts with three claret stripes, blue stockings.

WEST HAM UNITED

Players Names / Ht. Wt. D.o.B.	Birthplace / Transfer Fee	Clubs	Appearances F.L. A & S	Appearances F.L.C. A & S	Appearances F.A.C. A & S	Goals F.L.	Goals F.L.C.	Goals F.A.C.
Goalkeepers								
Phil Parkes (E)	Sedgley	Walsall	52	1	7			
6 3, 14 9, 8.8.50	£15,000	QPR	344	27	27			
	£50,000	West Ham U	181	28	14			
Tom McAlister	Clydebank	Sheffield U (A)	63	6	2			
6 0, 11 1, 10.12.52		Rotherham U	159	12	14			
	£50,000	Blackpool	16	4				
	F/T	Swindon T	1					
	—	Bristol R (loan)	13					
	F/T	West Ham U	3	1				
John Vaughan	Isleworth	West Ham U (A)						
Defenders								
Frank Lampard (E)	West Ham	West Ham (A)	528+4	51	40	18	1	2
5 11, 12 9, 20.9.48								
Paul Brush	London	West Ham U (A)	116+7	12+1	8			
5 11, 11 12, 22.2.58								
Alvin Martin (E)	Bootle	West Ham U (A)	174+2	29	13	12	2	
6 1, 13 0, 29.7.58								
Ray Stewart (S)	Perth	Dundee U						
5 11, 12 0, 7.9.59	£43,000	West Ham U	160	28	14	33	9	4
Billy Bonds (EU23)	Woolwich	Charlton Ath (A)	95	3	2	1		
6 0½, 13 2, 17.9.46	£49,000	West Ham U	574+1	58	41	45	6	2
Everald Laronde	East Ham	West Ham U (A)	6+1					
5 9, 10 12, 24.1.63								
Neil Orr	Greenock	Morton						
5 10, 10 7	£400,000	West Ham U	33+5	4		1		
Joe Gallagher	Liverpool	Birmingham C (a)	281+5	16	21	17	4	3
6 1, 12 0, 11.1.55	£350,000	Wolverhampton W	31	2	1			
	F/T	West Ham U	8+1	1	1			
Gerhard Ampofo	Kilburn	West Ham U (A)						
George Parris	Ilford	West Ham						
Midfield								
Mick McGiven	Newcastle	Sunderland	107+6	3	2	9		1
6 0, 11 13, 7.2.51	£25,000	West Ham U	46+2	2	3			
Trevor Brooking (E)	Barking	West Ham (A)	486+7	50	37	84	6	3
6 0½, 13 0, 2.10 48								
Geoff Pike	Clapton	West Ham U (A)	198+14	28+1	14+2	28	2	2
5 6, 11 3, 28.9.56								
George Cowie*	Findochty	West Ham (A)	6+2	1				
5 9, 11 0, 9.5.61								
Paul Allen (EY)	Aveley	West Ham U (A)	92+3	15+4	9+1	3	2	1
5 7, 9 12, 28.8.62								
Bobby Barnes	Kingston	West Ham U (A)	2+7	1+1		1		
5 7, 10 8, 17.12.62								
Francois Van Der Elst (Bel)	Opwyk, Belgium	New York Cosmos						
	£400,000	West Ham U	61+1	5+1	2	14	3	
Alan Dickens	Plaistow	West Ham U (A)	12+3			6		
Warren Donald	Hillingdon	West Ham U (A)						
Forwards								
Alan Devonshire (E)	London	Southall						
5 10½, 11 0. 13.4.56	£5000	West Ham U	247+3	30	17	23		1
Pat Holland	Poplar	West Ham U (A)	227+18	22+3	12+4	23	3	4
5 10, 11 7, 13.9.50	—	Bournemouth (loan)	10					
Jimmy Neighbour*	Chingford	Tottenham H (A)	104+15	14+3	10+1	8	1	1
5 7½, 10 8, 15.11.50	£70,000	Norwich C	104+2	5	4	5		
	—	Bournemouth (loan)	6					
Paul Goddard (E)	Harlington	QPR (A)	63+7	4+1		23		
5 9½, 11 5, 12.10.59	£800,000	West Ham U	114+1	21	5	42	8	
Keith McPherson	Greenwich	West Ham U (A)						
Mark Schiavi	London	West Ham U (A)						
Dave Swindlehurst (EU21)	Edgware	Crystal Palace (A)	221+16	17	22	73	3	4
6 2, 13 3, 6.1.56	£41,000	Derby Co	110	9	6		29	3
	£200,000	West Ham U	9			3		
Greg Gampbell	Portsmouth	West Ham U (A)						
Tony Cottee	West Ham	West Ham U (A)	3+5	1		5		
Dave Matthews		West Ham U (A)						

Commercial Manager: B. C. Blower
Club Coach:
Supporters Player of the Season 1982–83: Alvin Martin
Physiotherapist:
Club Captain 1982–83: Billy Bonds
Chief Scout: E. Bailey
Club Statistician:
Association of Football Statisticians Club Adviser to Yearbook: J. Northcutt.

Players (non-appearance) granted free transfer: Alf Wright, F.; Glenn Burvill, M.; Chris Ampofo, M.
Players released since May 1982: Steve Milton, F. (Epsom & E); Stuart Pearson, F. (retired); Mark Smith, D. (N/K); Bobby Wall, M. (N/K); Wayne Reader (N/K); Alex Clark, F. (Glasgow R).

WIGAN ATHLETIC Division 3

Back row (left to right): Ken Banks (Trainer), Les Bradd, John Rogers, Graham Barrow, Roy Tunks, Colin Methven, Peter Houghton, Alex Cribley, Kevin Langley, Harry McNally (Chief Scout)
Middle row: John MacMahon, David Glenn, Kevin Sheldon, John Butler, Larry Lloyd (Manager), Phil Williams, Eamon O'Keefe, Jimmy Weston
Front row: Wayne Aspinall, Graeme Hatton, Andrew Phillips.

Chairman: A. Muir.

Directors: J. Bennett, B. Heathcote, T. Hitchen, A. O. Horrocks (President).

Company Secretary: Colin Burke.

Vice-Presidents: J. H. Farrimond and A. Fitch.

Asst Secretary: J. H. Farrimond. ***Manager:*** Harry McNally.

Year Formed: 1932. ***Club Nickname:*** 'The Latics'.

Previous Managers of Note: Ted Goodier, Allan Brown, Gordon Milne, Ian McNeill, Larry Lloyd, Bobby Charlton (acting) (6).

Springfield Park, Wigan. Telephone: 0942 44433. ***Telegraphic address:*** Springfield, Wigan. ***Ground capacity:*** 30,000. ***Record attendance:*** 27,500 v Hereford U, 12 Dec, 1953. ***Record receipts:*** £29,169 v Aston Villa, League Cup 4th rd, 1 Dec, 1981. ***Pitch measurements:*** 117yd×73yd.

Directions to Ground: Wigan Wallgate and Wigan North West Railway Stations. Wigan is served by three motorways, the M6, the M61 and the M62, with convenient access and exit points. Wigan also enjoys the facilities of the main London to Scotland railway line.

Match tickets: Stand – available fourteen days prior to game.

Car parking: On ground and within close proximity to ground.

Entertainments /catering facilities: Licensed bar and tea bar in Stand, tea bars and social club on ground.

Extra information: Springfield Park covers approximately nine acres and is owned by Wigan Athletic AFC Ltd. The ground will hold over 30,000 spectators with seating accommodation for 1069 and additional covered standing accommodation for 10,000 with an Executive Lounge, seating 60.

Note: Full club statistical records are on pages 416–455.

WIGAN ATHLETIC 1982–83 LEAGUE RECORD

Match No.	Date	Venue	Opponents	Result		H/T Score	Lg. Pos.	Goalscorers	Attendance
1	Aug 28	A	Lincoln C	L	1-2	1-2	—	Bradd	3196
2	Sept 4	H	Brentford	W	3-2	2-1	11	Houghton, O'Keefe (pen), Lodge (pen)	5019
3	7	H	Bradford C	W	3-2	0-0	—	Butler, Houghton, Rogers	5339
4	11	A	Cardiff C	L	2-3	2-1	11	Houghton, Rogers	3850
5	18	H	AFC Bournemouth	L	1-2	0-2	16	O'Keefe	4866
6	25	A	Chesterfield	L	0-2	0-0	19		2825
7	28	A	Doncaster R	W	6-3	4-2	—	Methven, Houghton 3, O'Keefe, Bradd	4457
8	Oct 2	H	Plymouth Arg	W	3-0	2-0	11	Bradd 2, O'Keefe	5011
9	9	H	Southend U	W	4-0	2-0	8	O'Keefe 3 (1 pen), Houghton	4705
10	16	A	Bristol R	L	0-4	0-0	12		4439
11	19	H	Portsmouth	L	0-1	0-0	—		4504
12	23	A	Reading	L	1-2	1-0	15	Bradd	2621
13	30	H	Newport Co	L	0-1	0-0	15		4108
14	Nov 3	A	Exeter C	L	1-2	0-1	—	Weston	2399
15	6	A	Orient	D	1-1	1-1	17	Houghton	2266
16	13	H	Millwall	W	3-1	2-0	17	Bradd, Houghton 2	4456
17	27	A	Gillingham	W	2-0	1-0	15	Langley, Lowe	3952
18	Dec 4	H	Sheffield U	W	3-2	2-0	13	Lowe, Steel 2	5050
19	18	H	Oxford U	L	0-1	0-1	13		4008
20	27	A	Wrexham	D	1-1	0-0	14	O'Keefe	4091
21	29	H	Walsall	L	1-3	0-0	—	Langley	4564
22	Jan 1	A	Preston NE	L	1-4	1-2	16	O'Keefe	7685
23	3	H	Huddersfield T	W	2-0	0-0	13	Lowe, Cox (og)	7724
24	8	A	Brentford	W	3-1	2-0	10	O'Keefe, McMahon, Butler	4939
25	15	H	Lincoln C	W	2-1	2-1	8	Lowe, Barrow	4731
26	22	A	Bradford C	W	1-0	1-0	8	O'Keefe (pen)	4741
27	29	H	Doncaster R	L	0-3	0-2	9		4387
28	Feb 5	H	Chesterfield	D	2-2	1-2	10	O'Keefe, Lowe	3009
29	15	H	Exeter C	W	1-0	1-0	—	O'Keefe	2764
30	18	A	Southend U	L	0-2	0-2	—		2277
31	26	H	Bristol R	L	0-5	0-2	11		3288
32	Mar 1	A	Portsmouth	D	0-0	0-0	—		16,139
33	5	H	Reading	D	2-2	0-1	11	Butler, O'Keefe (pen)	3042
34	12	A	Newport Co	L	0-1	0-1	13		3647
35	19	H	Orient	L	0-1	0-0	15		2954
36	27	A	Millwall	L	0-2	0-1	—		2772
37	Apr 2	A	Walsall	L	0-2	0-1	17		2829
38	4	H	Wrexham	W	3-1	0-1	—	Cribley, Barrow, Houghton	3377
39	9	A	Sheffield U	L	0-2	0-1	17		8918
40	16	H	Cardiff C	D	0-0	0-0	17		4447
41	19	A	Plymouth Arg	W	2-0	0-0	—	O'Keefe, Butler	3097
42	20	A	Oxford U	L	0-2	0-1	16		4596
43	30	H	Gillingham	D	2-2	0-2	16	O'Keefe (pen), Barrow	3610
44	May 7	A	AFC Bournemouth	D	2-2	0-2	17	Lowe, Houghton	4523
45	10	A	Huddersfield T	D	1-1	1-1	—	Brown (og)	11,093
46	14	H	Preston NE	L	0-1	0-1	18		7191

Final League Position: 18

GOALSCORERS

League (60): O'Keefe 16 (5 pens), Houghton 12, Bradd 6, Lowe 6, Butler 4, Barrow 3, Langley 2, Rogers 2, Steel 2, Cribley 1, Lodge 1 (pen), McMahon 1, Methven 1, Weston 1, own goals 2.
Milk Cup (3): Bradd 1, O'Keefe 1, own goal 1.
FA Cup (1): Butler 1.

Milk Cup	First Round	Stockport Co (a)	1-1
		(h)	1-1 (aet) (won on penalties)
	Second Round	Manchester C (h)	1-1
		(h)	0-2
FA Cup	First Round	Telford U (h)	0-0
		(a)	1-2

Tunks	McMahon	Glenn	O'Keefe	Cribley	Methven	Lodge (L)	Barrow	Bradd	Houghton	Rogers	Butler	Weston	Langley	Lloyd	Gemmill	Williams	Lowe	Walsh	Sheldon	Steel (L)	Shaw	Young	Referees	Match No.
1	2	3	4	5	6	7	8	9	10	11*	12												M. Robinson	1
1	2		6	3	4	7	8	9*	10	11	12	5											G. Tyson	2
1	2		4	5	6	7	8		10	11	9	3											T. Holbrook	3
1	2		4	5	6	7	8	9	10*	11	12	3											T. Bune	4
1	2		4	5	6	7		9*	10	12	11	3	8										K. Hackett	5
1	2		4	3	6			9	11	12	8*		7	5	10								D. Brazier	6
1	2		4	8	6			9	10			3	7	5	11								M. Scott	7
1	2	12	9	7	4			10	11			5	6	3*	8								A. Saunders	8
1	2	7	9	4				10	11			5	6	3	8								J. Key	9
1	2	7	4	8				9	10			3	6	5	11								K. Cooper	10
1	2		6*	8	5			9			10	3	7	4	11	12							C. Newsome	11
1	2			8	6			9	10		7	3	12	5*	11		4						A. Glasson	12
1	2	3			5			8	9		6	7	12		10		4*	11					K. Barratt	13
1		4			6			9	10		3	8	2		11			5	7				D. Hedges	14
1		3		2	6			9	10		4	8			11			5	7				J. Bray	15
1	2			3	4			10	9		6	8			7			5		11			T. Mills	16
1	2			3	6						9	11	4				10	5	7		8		J. Deakin	17
1	2			3	6						7	11	4				10	5		9	8		J. Hough	18
1	2	7	4	3	6			12			9	11	8				10*	5					K. Redfern	19
1	2	7	10	3*	6		8	12			9	11	4					5					H. King	20
1	2	7	10	3	6		8	12			9*	11	4					5					D. Shaw	21
1	2	7*	10	3	6		8				9	11	4				12	5					P. Willis	22
1	2	3	10	4	6		8				9	11					12	5	7*				D. Civil	23
1	2	3	10	4	6		8				9	11					7	5					M. Bodenham	24
1	2	6	10	5	4		8				9	11					7	3					D. Hutchinson	25
1	2	3	10	4	6		8		12		9	11					7*	5					N. Ashley	26
1	2	3	10	4	6		8		12		9	11					7*	5					M. Heath	27
1	2*	3	10	4	6		8		7		9	11					12	5					C. Seel	28
1	2	3	10	4	6		8		7		9	11						5					J. Lovatt	29
1	2		10*	3	6		8		12		9	11	4				7	5					I. Borrett	30
1	2	3	10		6		8		12		9	11	4*				7	5					G. Napthine	31
1	2	3			6		8		10		4	11					9	5	7				D. Reeves	32
1	2	3	9		6		8		10		4	11						5	7				F. Roberts	33
1	2	3	9	11	6		8		10		4						7	5					D. Vickers	34
1	2		10	3	5				12		6	11	7			8*	9	4					A. Hamil	35
1	2	11	12	3	6			5	9		4						10		7		8*		A. Grey	36
1	2	3	9	4	6		8	12	10		11*						7	5					D. Hedges	37
1		3		8	6		4		11			10	2				9	5	7				D. Owen	38
1		3	12	8	6		4		11*			10	2				9	5	7				B. Newsome	39
1			11	9	4		6				7	5	2				10	3	8				G. Tyson	40
1			10	8	6		4				11	3	2				9	5	7				C. Thomas	41
1			10	8	6		4		12		11	3	2				9	5	7*				J. Moules	42
1			10	8	6		4		12		11	3	2				9	5	7*				J. Key	43
1			10	5	6			12	11		4	3	2				9		7*			8	E. Scales	44
1			10	5	6		4		11		7	3	2				9					8	K. Baker	45
1				7	4		6	12	11		9	5*	2				10	3				8	T. Mills	46
46	35	25	34	41	44	5	28	16	27	4	37	41	26	7	11	1	25	31	14	2	3	3		
		+ 1s	+ 2s					+ 6s	+ 7s	+ 2s	+ 3s		+ 2s			+ 1s	+ 3s							

FOOTBALL LEAGUE RECORD

1978 Elected to Division 4; 1982– Division 3.

HONOURS

Best season in Division 3: 18th 1982–83, Division 4, Promoted (3rd) 1981–82. *FA Cup:* 4th rd 1979–80, *Football League Cup* best season: 4th rd 1981–82.

COLOURS

Royal blue shirts and shorts, white stockings.
Change colours: Yellow shirts and stockings, green shorts.

WIGAN ATHLETIC

Players Names Ht, Wt, D.o.B.	Birthplace Transfer Fee	Clubs	Appearances F.L. A & S	 F.L.C. A & S	 F.A.C. A & S	Goals F.L.	 F.L.C.	 F.A.C.
Goalkeepers								
Roy Tunks	W Germany	Rotherham U (A)	138	9	8			
6 1, 13 11, 21.1.51	—	York C (loan)	4					
	£7000	Preston NE	277	20	16			
	F/T	Wigan Ath	77	6	4			
Defenders								
Larry Lloyd (E)	Bristol	Bristol R	43	1	7	1		
6 2, 13 7, 6.10.48	£50,000	Liverpool	150	20	15	4		
	£240,000	Coventry C	50	1	3	5		1
	£60,000	Nottingham F	148	23	14	6	3	1
	F/T	Wigan Ath	52	5		2		
Colin Methven	India	East Fife						
6 2, 12 7, 10.12.55	£30,000	Wigan Ath	176+1	14	12	14	3	
Alex Cribley	Liverpool	Liverpool						
5 11¼, 12 9, 1.4.57	F/T	Wigan Ath	100+2	8+1	6	1		
John McMahon*	Manchester	Preston NE (A)	256+1	22	12	7		
5 9, 11 2, 7.12.49	—	Southend U (loan)	3					
	—	Chesterfield (loan)	1					
	F/T	Crewe Alex	67	2	1	2		
	F/T	Wigan Ath	71	10	3	5		
John Butler	Liverpool	Prescot Cables						
5 11, 11 7	£100	Wigan Ath	38+3	1+1	2	4		1
David Glenn*	Wigan	Wigan Ath (A)	68+4	7	+1	4		
5 10, 10 10, 30.11.62								
Steve Walsh	Preston	Wigan Ath	31	1				
6 0, 11 10								
Midfield								
Graham Barrow	Chorley	Altrincham						
6 2, 13 7,	£12,500	Wigan Ath	68+1	6	2	15	3	
Kevin Langley	St Helens	Wigan Ath (A)	27+3	3	2	2		
6 1, 9 0,								
Jimmy Weston*	Whiston	Skelmersdale						
5 9, 11 0, 16.9.55	£2500	Blackpool	97+8	7	4	8		
	£5000	Torquay U	38	3	4	1		1
	£7500	Wigan Ath	63+3	3	2	2		
Kevin Sheldon*	Stoke	Stoke C (A)	12+3					
5 5½, 9 4, 14.6.56	F/T	Wigan Ath	29	6	4	1		
	—	Port Vale (loan)	5					
Phil Williams (WS)	Swansea	Arsenal (A)						
5 7, 10 11, 5.4.58	F/T	Blackpool						
	F/T	USA						
	F/T	Crewe Alex	39	1	2	3		
	F/T	Wigan Ath	1+1	1	2			
Forwards								
Peter Houghton	Liverpool	South Liverpool						
5 11, 12 7, 30.11.54	£500	Wigan Ath	164+15	16+1	14	61	3	3
Les Bradd*	Buxton	Rotherham U	3					
6 1, 13 0, 6.11.47	£5000	Notts Co	381+17	17	22	125	7	4
	F/T	Stockport Co	116+1	9	6	31	2	3
	F/T	Wigan Ath	57+6	8	4	25	2	
	—	Bristol R (loan)	1			1		
Eamon O'Keefe (EI)	Manchester	Stalybridge C						
5 7, 11 5, 13.10.53	£6000	Plymouth Arg						
	F/T	Hyde U						
	—	Saudi Arabia						
	F/T	Mossley						
	£22,000	Everton	26+14	1	4	6	1	1
	£65,000	Wigan Ath	56+2	3		25	1	
Non-contract players								
Mark Shaw	Wigan	Wigan Ath	3					
5 9, 10 7								
David Young	Manchester	Wigan Ath	3					
5 8, 10 10								
Apprentices								
David Lowe	Liverpool	Wigan Ath (A)	25+3	1		6		
5 9, 10 6								

Commercial Manager: C. T. Burke (acting)
Club Coach: Ken Banks
Supporters Player of the Season 1982–83: Jimmy Weston
Physiotherapist:
Association of Football Statisticians Club Adviser to Yearbook: G. Lea.

Club Captain 1982–83: E. O'Keefe
Chief Scout:
Club Statistician:

Players released since May 1982: John Brown, G. (Macclesfield); Neil Davids, D. (Bromsgrove); Steve McAdam, D. (Ireland); Jeff Wright, M. (Barrow); Mark Wignall, M. (Morecambe); John Rogers, F. (Altrincham); Bob Ward, G. (retired); Les Bradd (Kettering T).

WIMBLEDON Division 3

Back row (left to right): John Leslie, Paul Fishenden, Doug Hatcher, Alan Cork, Steve Ketteridge
Middle row: Allan Gillett (Asst Manager), Mark Morris, Glyn Hodges, Tony Tagg, David Beasant, Stewart Evans, Michael Smith, Steve Jones, Derek French (Physiotherapist), David Bassett (Manager)
Front row: Chris Dibble, Wayne Entwistle, Steve Galliers, Gary Peters, Dean Thomas, Wally Downes, Kevin Gage.

President: Rt Hon Sir Michael Havers QC, MP.

Chairman: B. Reynolds. ***Vice-Chairman:*** G. M. Dell.

Directors: S. Hammam, P. Cork, G. M. Dell, E. C. Gush, Q. Spicer.

Manager: Dave Bassett. ***Secretary:*** Adrian Cook.

Year Formed: 1889. ***Turned Professional:*** 1964. ***Ltd Co.:*** 1964.

Previous Name: Wimbledon Old Centrals 1899–1905.

Club Nickname: 'The Dons'.

Previous Managers since 1955: Les Henley, Mike Everitt, Dick Graham, Allen Batsford, Dario Gradi (5).

Plough Lane Ground, Durnsford Road, Wimbledon, London SW19 (first used in 1912). Telephone: 01-946 6311. ***Ground capacity:*** 15,000. ***Record attendance:*** 18,000 v HMS Victory in FA Amateur Cup 3rd rd, 1934–35. ***Record receipts:*** £30,600 v Leeds U, FA Cup 4th rd replay at Crystal Palace, 1974–75. ***Pitch measurements:*** 110yd×73yd.

Directions to Ground: Nearest station Wimbledon or Haydons Road (SR), South Wimbledon Underground. Buses: 77a from Wimbledon, 189 from Tooting.

Match tickets: Available fourteen days prior to game for important matches.

Car parking: On ground and in streets quarter mile from ground.

Entertainment/catering facilities: Four licensed bars and two tea bars in main stand. Sportsman Public House adjacent to ground and owned by club.

Club shop: Two shops, one in Durnsford Road open weekdays, one in ground open matchdays. Sell all types of souvenirs.

Handbooks/programmes: Supporters Club Handbook published annually. Programmes available on subscription.

Address of Supporters Club and Club Shop: Plough Lane Ground, Durnsford Road.

Note: Full club statistical records are on pages 416–455.

WIMBLEDON 1982–83 LEAGUE RECORD

Match No.	Date	Venue	Opponents	Result		H/T Score	Lg. Pos.	Goalscorers	Attendance
1	Aug 28	H	Northampton T	D	1-1	1-1	—	Ketteridge	1703
2	Sept 4	A	Hull C	D	1-1	1-1	13	Thomas	3674
3	8	A	Peterborough U	W	3-0	1-0	—	Evans, Ketteridge, Thomas (pen)	3458
4	11	H	Scunthorpe U	D	2-2	1-0	7	Peters, Evans	1611
5	18	A	Blackpool	D	1-1	0-0	7	Leslie	3929
6	25	H	Torquay U	W	4-1	3-0	5	Evans 3, Ketteridge	2047
7	28	H	Hereford U	W	1-0	0-0	—	Morris	1604
8	Oct 2	A	Tranmere R	W	2-0	1-0	2	Leslie, Gage	1231
9	9	H	Aldershot	W	6-1	2-1	1	Hodges 2, Ketteridge, Gage 2, Leslie	2440
10	16	A	York C	W	4-1	0-0	1	Leslie 2, Hood (og), Entwistle	2064
11	19	H	Rochdale	W	3-0	1-0	—	Peters 2, Leslie	2294
12	23	A	Bristol C	L	2-4	0-3	2	Leslie, Thomas (pen)	4723
13	30	H	Stockport Co	W	2-1	1-0	2	Leslie, Thomas	2294
14	Nov 2	A	Colchester U	L	0-3	0-1	—		2219
15	6	A	Hartlepool U	L	0-1	0-0	4		1081
16	13	H	Halifax T	L	2-4	0-1	6	Entwistle, Thomas (pen)	2104
17	Dec 4	A	Darlington	W	2-0	2-0	8	Leslie 2	1117
18	11	A	Rochdale	W	2-0	1-0	5	Evans, Entwistle	1096
19	18	A	Port Vale	L	0-1	0-1	7		2761
20	27	H	Mansfield T	D	1-1	0-0	6	Galliers	2517
21	28	A	Swindon T	W	1-0	0-0	6	Leslie	8164
22	Jan 1	H	Bury	W	2-1	0-0	6	Brown (og), Leslie	2467
23	4	A	Chester	W	2-1	0-0	4	Evans, Smith	1549
24	8	H	Hull C	L	1-2	0-1	4	Evans	2766
25	15	A	Northampton T	D	2-2	2-1	4	Leslie 2	2290
26	22	H	Peterborough U	W	2-1	1-1	4	Evans, Leslie	2119
27	29	A	Scunthorpe U	D	0-0	0-0	4		3846
28	Feb 5	A	Torquay U	W	1-0	0-0	4	Hatter	2316
29	15	H	Colchester U	W	2-1	0-1	—	Smith, Hodges	1753
30	19	A	Aldershot	D	1-1	1-0	4	Fishenden (pen)	2720
31	26	H	York C	W	4-3	2-0	3	Evans 2, Leslie, Barnett	2168
32	Mar 5	H	Bristol C	W	2-1	2-0	3	Newman (og), Leslie	2541
33	11	A	Stockport Co	W	3-1	2-0	—	Morris, Hodges, Leslie	2260
34	15	H	Tranmere R	W	4-0	2-0	—	Peters, Leslie 2, Galliers	2113
35	19	H	Hartlepool U	W	2-0	0-0	1	Leslie, Hodges	2324
36	Apr 1	H	Swindon T	D	0-0	0-0	—		3400
37	5	A	Mansfield T	D	2-2	1-1	—	Bird (og), Evans	3519
38	9	H	Darlington	W	3-1	2-0	2	Evans, Ketteridge, Morris	1970
39	16	A	Hereford U	W	4-1	2-0	3	Cork, Ketteridge, Hodges 2	2637
40	19	H	Crewe Alex	W	3-2	1-1	—	Hodges, Cork, Leslie	2505
41	23	H	Port Vale	W	1-0	0-0	2	Ketteridge	4061
42	30	A	Crewe Alex	W	2-0	0-0	1	Downes, Smith	2552
43	May 2	H	Chester	W	4-0	1-0	1	Cork 3, Smith	2576
44	7	H	Blackpool	W	5-0	3-0	1	Leslie, Sparrow, Hodges, Fishenden, Gage	2717
45	10	A	Halifax T	D	1-1	0-1	—	Fishenden	1233
46	14	A	Bury	W	3-1	2-0	1	Evans, Downes, Fishenden	6760

Final League Position: 1

GOALSCORERS

League (96): Leslie 23, Evans 14, Hodges 9, Ketteridge 7, Cork 5, Thomas 5 (3 pens), Fishenden 4 (1 pen), Gage 4, Peters 4, Smith 4, Entwistle 3, Morris 3, Downes 2, Galliers 2, Barnett 1, Belfield 1, Hatter 1, Sparrow 1, own goals 4.
Milk Cup (1): Leslie 1.
FA Cup (2): Entwistle 1, Leslie 1.
Football League Trophy (2): Evans 2.

Milk Cup	First Round	Brentford (h)	1-1
		(a)	0-2
FA Cup	First Round	Northampton T (a)	2-2
		(h)	0-2
Football League Trophy		Millwall (a)	1-0
		Crystal Palace (a)	0-1
		Brentford (h)	1-3

Beasant	Peters	Thomas	Galliers	Tagg	Morris	Evans	Ketteridge	Leslie	Downes	Dibble	Gage	Entwistle	Hodges	Jones	Fishenden	Belfield	Ferns (L)	Smith	Hatter	Sparrow (L)	Barnett (L)	Cork	Referees	Match No.
1	2	3	4	5	6	7	8	9	10	11													Alan Robinson	1
1	2	3	4	5	6	7*	8	9	10	11	12												M. Scott	2
1	2	3	4	5	6	7	8	9	10	11													D. Hedges	3
1	2	3	4	5	6	7	8	9	10	11*		12											A. Glasson	4
1	2*	3	4	5	6	7	8	9	10		12		11										T. Jones	5
1	2	5	6	3	4	9	7	10	8		12		11*										M. Taylor	6
1	2	3	4		6	7	8	9	10		12		11	5*									T. Spencer	7
1	2	3	4		6	7*	8	9	10		12		11	5									D. Hutchinson	8
1	2	3		5	6	7	8	9	10		4		11										M. Robinson	9
1	2	3		5	6	7*	8	9	10		4	12	11										G. Courtney	10
1	2	3		5	6	7*	8	9	10		4		11		12								L. Burden	11
1	2	3	12	5*	6	7	8	9	10		4		11										D. Civil	12
1	2	3	4	5	6	7	8	9	10				11										I. Borrett	13
1	2	3	4	5	6*		8	9	10		12	7	11										H. Taylor	14
1	2	3		5	6			9	10	4			11		8	7							N. Midgley	15
1	2	3		5	6			9*	10	4	12	8	11			7							K. Barratt	16
1	2		4			7	8	9*	10		11		12				3	5	6				D. Allison	17
1	2		4			7	8		10		11	9*	12	3				5	6				T. Holbrook	18
1	2		4			7	8		10*		11	9	12				3	5	6				F. Roberts	19
1	2		4			7	8	9	10*		11		12				3	5	6				R. Milford	20
1	2		4			7	8	9	10		11						3	5	6				J. Bray	21
1	2		4			7	8	9	10		11*		12				3	5	6				Alan Robinson	22
1	2		4			7	8	9	10		11						3	5	6				N. Glover	23
1	2		4			7	8	9	10		11						3	5	6				A. Grey	24
1	2		4		3	7	8	9*	10		11	12						5	6				V. Callow	25
1	2		4			7	8	9	10		11*	12						5	6	3			M. Bodenham	26
1	2		4		6	7	8	9		10*		12	11					5		3			D. Shaw	27
1	2		4			7	8	9			11		10*			12		5	6	3			E. Read	28
1	2		4			7	8	9					10		11			5	6	3			L. Shapter	29
1	2		4			7	8	9*					10		11	12		5	6	3			L. Burden	30
1	2		4			7	8	9*					10		12			5	6	3	11		A. Crickmore	31
1	2					7		9			11		10		12	8		5	6*	3	4		M. Dimblebee	32
1	2		4		6	7		9*	12				10			8		5		3	11		D. Richardson	33
1	2		4			7	8	9	12				10					5	6*	3	11		T. Spencer	34
1	2					7	8	9					10			4		5	6	3	11		B. Stevens	35
1	2		4		5	7	8		11	12			10*			9			6	3			M. Taylor	36
1	2		4		5	7	8		11				10						6	3		9	D. Scott	37
1	2	3	4		5	7	8	12	11				10*						6			9	D. Axcell/D. King	38
1	2	3	4		5	7	8	12	11				10						6			9*	J. Hunting	39
1	2	3	4		5	7*	8	11			12		10						6			9	K. Baker	40
1	2		4				8	7	11				10					5	6	3		9	B. Hill	41
1	2	4				12	8	7	11				10					5	6	3		9*	D. Civil	42
1	2	4				12	8*	7	11				10					5	6	3		9	S. Bates	43
1	2	4				7		9	8		11		10*		12			5	6	3			B. Daniels	44
1	2	4			5	7		9	10		11*		12		8				6	3			K. Redfern	45
1	2	5			8	9		10	7				11		6			3	4				A. Saunders	46
46	46	24	33	14	26	40	39	40	36	7	18	4	31	3	5	6	7	24	28	17	5	7		
			+ 1s			+ 2s		+ 2s	+ 2s	+ 1s	+ 8s	+ 5s	+ 6s		+ 4s	+ 2s								

FOOTBALL LEAGUE RECORD

1977–79 Division 4; 1979–80 Division 3; 1980–81 Division 4; 1981–82 Division 3; 1982–83 Division 4; 1983– Division 3.

HONOURS

Best season in Division 3: 21st, 1981–82. Division 4: Champions 1982–83. *FA Cup* best season: 4th rd, 1974–75, 1980–81. *Football League Cup* best season: 4th rd, 1979–80. *League Group Cup:* Runners-up 1981–82.

COLOURS

Royal blue shirts with yellow trim, blue shorts with yellow trim, blue stockings.
Change colours: Yellow shirts with blue trim, yellow shorts with blue trim, yellow stockings.

WIMBLEDON

Players Names Ht. Wt. D.o.B.	Birthplace Transfer Fee	Clubs	Appearances F.L. A & S	 F.L.C. A & S	 F.A.C. A & S	Goals F.L.	 F.L.C.	 F.A.C.
Goalkeepers								
Dave Beasant	Willesden	Edgware T						
6 3, 13 0, 20.3.59	—	Wimbledon	128	4	4			
Defenders								
Mick Smith	Sunderland	Lincoln C	20+5	2				
6 0½, 11 9, 28.10.58	£12,500	Wimbledon	127+1	6	7	8		2
Wally Downes	London	Wimbledon A)	139+4	11+1	5+1	10		
5 10, 10 11, 9.6.61								
Dean Thomas*	Bedworth	Nuneaton Bor						
5 9, 11 8, 19.12.61	£8000	Wimbledon	42	2		5		
Mark Morris	Morden	Wimbledon	59	2	4	4		
6 0, 11 10, 26.9.62								
Gary Peters	Carshalton	Guildford C						
5 11, 11 12, 3.8.54		Reading	150+6	15	9+1	7		
	£30,000	Fulham	57+5	4	4	2		
	F T	Wimbledon	46	2		4		
Steve Hatter	London	Fulham (A)	25+1	+1	4	1		
6 2, 13 0, 21.10.58	—	Exeter C (loan)	11			1		
	£6000	Wimbledon	28			1		
Midfield								
Steve Ketteridge	Stevenage	Derby Co (A)						
5 8½, 10 7, 7.11.59	£3000	Wimbledon	158+7	11	9	22		1
Kevin Gage (E.Y.)	London	Wimbledon (A)	34+14	1+1	1+2	5		
5 9, 11 2, 21.4.64								
Glyn Hodges (WU21)	Streatham	Wimbledon (A)	90+11	3	3+2	16		
6 0, 12 3, 30.4.63								
Steve Galliers	Fulwood	Chorley						
5 6, 9 7, 21.8.57	£1,500	Wimbledon	148+7	17+1	13+1	10	2	
	£70,000	Crystal Palace	8+5					
	£15,000	Wimbledon	33+1	2	2	2		
Forwards								
Alan Cork	Derby	Derby Co						
6 0, 12 0, 8.10.59	—	Lincoln C (loan)	5					
	F T	Wimbledon	157+1	14	15	66	4	4
John Leslie	London	Dulwich H						
5 8, 11 2, 25.10.55	—	Wimbledon	242+11	20+1	14+2	86	10	5
Stewart Evans	Maltby	Rotherham U (A)						
6 3, 11 5, 15.11.60	F T	Gainsborough						
	£7000	Sheffield U						
	F T	Wimbledon	58+2	2	1	18		
Non-contract players								
Paul Fishenden	Hillingdon	Wimbledon	9+5		2	5		
6 0, 10 12, 2.8.63								

Commercial Manager: Eric Willcocks (Tel. 946-6311)
Club Coach: The Manager
Supporters Player of the Season 1982–83: John Leslie
Physiotherapist: Derek French
Association of Football Statisticians Club Adviser to Yearbook: S. King
Club Captain 1982–83: Gary Peters
Chief Scout:
Club Statistician:

Players released since May 1982:
Gary Armstrong, D. (N/K); Peter Brown, D. (Hemel Hempstead); Peter Suddaby, D. (Retired); Steve Jones, D. (N/K); Tony Tagg, D. (Carshalton); Mike Belfield, M. (N/K); Chris Dibble, F. (N/K); Wayne Entwhistle, F. (Grays Ath).

WOLVERHAMPTON WANDERERS F.C. (1982) LTD Division 1

Back row (left to right): Kenny Hibbitt, Wayne Clarke, Pete Daniel, Andy Gray, Robert Coy
Middle row: Paul Bradshaw, Geoffrey Palmer, John Humphreys, John Richards, Mike Hollifield, Hugh Atkinson, Mel Eves, John Burridge
Front row: Jim Barron (Asst Manager), John Pender, Paul Butler, Gordon Smith, Billy Livingstone, Mike Matthews, Graham Hawkins (Manager).

President: J. R. Ireland.

Chairman/Chief Executive: Derek Dougan ***Vice-Chairman:*** D. Hope.

Team Manager: Graham Hawkins. ***General Manager:*** E. Woodward. ***Company Secretary:*** R. A. Loveland.

Club Secretary: Peter Redfern. ***Club Accountant:*** K. D. Pearson ACIS

Year Formed: 1877. ***Turned Professional:*** 1888. ***Ltd Co.:*** 1982.

Previous Grounds: 1877, Goldthorn Hill; 1884, Dudley Road; 1889, Molineux.

Club Nickname: 'Wolves'.

Previous Name: 1880, St Luke's, Blakenhall combined with The Wanderers to become Wolverhampton Wanderers (1923) Ltd until 1982.

Previous Managers since 1946: Ted Vizard, Stan Cullis, Andy Beattie, Ron Allen, Bill McGarry, Sammy Chung, John Barnwell, Ian Greaves (8).

Molineux Grounds, Wolverhampton WV1 4QR. Telephone Admin office – Wolverhampton (0902) 712181; Ticket office – 711457/711432. ***Telegraphic address:*** 'Wanderers, Wolverhampton'. ***Ground capacity:*** 38,000. ***Record attendance:*** 61,315 v Liverpool, FA Cup 5th rd, 11 Feb, 1939. ***Record receipts:*** £80,839 v Swindon T, League Cup semi-final, 12 Feb, 1980. ***Pitch measurements:*** 115yd×72yd.

Directions to Ground: The ground is within easy walking distance of both Wolverhampton High Level railway station and the town centre. For this reason the local bus company does not operate special services on match days.

Match tickets: Seats are bookable by post one month before the match.

Car parking: Parking is available around 'The West Park', in various side streets, and at the Molineux Hotel.

Entertainments/catering facilities: Entertainment at the Wolves Sporting Club a few yards from the ground. Bars are provided all around the ground.

Club shop: The club shop is situated on the official car park at the ground.

Handbooks/programmes: No handbook. Programmes available on subscription.

Address of the Club Shop or Boutique: 'The Lair', Wolverhampton W FC, Molineux Grounds, Wolverhampton, West Midlands.

Note: Full club statistical records are on pages 416–455.

WOLVERHAMPTON WANDERERS 1982–83 LEAGUE RECORD

Match No.	Date	Venue	Opponents	Result	H/T Score	Lg. Pos.	Goalscorers	Attendance
1	Aug 28	H	Blackburn R	W 2-1	0-1	—	Eves 2	15,605
2	31	A	Chelsea	D 0-0	0-0	—		14,192
3	Sept 4	A	Leeds U	D 0-0	0-0	5		16,462
4	7	H	Charlton Ath	W 5-0	2-0	—	Eves, Gray, Palmer, Clarke, Matthews	13,063
5	11	H	Barnsley	W 2-0	0-0	1	Humphrey, Eves	15,065
6	18	A	Bolton W	W 1-0	0-0	1	Livingstone	9264
7	25	H	Rotherham U	W 2-0	1-0	1	Clarke, Humphrey	16,377
8	Oct 2	A	Carlisle U	W 2-0	2-0	1	Smith, Livingstone	7723
9	9	A	Sheffield W	D 0-0	0-0	1		21,519
10	16	H	Leicester C	L 0-3	0-2	2		15,782
11	30	H	Derby Co	W 2-1	1-0	4	Palmer (pen), Gray	13,804
12	Nov 2	A	Cambridge U	L 1-2	0-1	—	Eves	4571
13	6	H	Grimsby T	W 3-0	1-0	2	Gray, Eves, Clarke	12,701
14	13	A	Oldham Ath	L 1-4	0-1	4	Hibbitt	7962
15	20	H	Fulham	L 2-4	2-1	4	Clarke, Gray	14,448
16	27	A	Crystal Palace	W 4-3	3-2	4	Matthews 2, Clarke, Gray	10,225
17	Dec 4	H	Middlesbrough	W 4-0	3-0	3	Eves 2, Cartwright, Dodd	11,856
18	11	A	Newcastle U	D 1-1	1-1	3	Eves	19,485
19	18	H	QPR	W 4-0	0-0	2	Humphrey, Clarke, Palmer (pen), Dodd	15,423
20	27	A	Shrewsbury T	W 2-0	1-0	1	Clarke 2	13,336
21	28	H	Burnley	W 2-0	0-0	1	Eves, Gray	21,961
22	Jan 1	A	Fulham	W 3-1	2-1	1	Pender, Clarke, Eves	17,196
23	3	H	Leeds U	W 3-0	1-0	1	Clarke, Gray, Eves	22,567
24	15	A	Blackburn R	D 2-2	0-2	1	Matthews, Dodd	7401
25	22	H	Chelsea	W 2-1	1-1	1	Eves, Clarke	19,533
26	Feb 5	A	Barnsley	L 1-2	1-1	1	Smith	13,535
27	12	H	Carlisle U	W 2-1	1-1	1	Eves, Livingstone	13,171
28	26	A	Leicester C	L 0-5	0-3	1		13,530
29	Mar 1	H	Sheffield W	W 1-0	1-0	—	Clarke (pen)	16,656
30	5	H	Cambridge U	D 1-1	0-0	1	Eves	13,204
31	12	A	Derby Co	D 1-1	0-1	1	Kellock	17,644
32	19	A	Grimsby T	D 1-1	0-1	2	Eves	7600
33	26	H	Oldham Ath	D 0-0	0-0	2		12,940
34	Apr 2	A	Burnley	W 1-0	1-0	2	Palmer	9593
35	4	H	Shrewsbury T	D 2-2	2-1	—	Palmer (pen), Eves	17,509
36	9	A	Rotherham U	D 1-1	1-0	2	Hibbitt	7286
37	16	H	Bolton W	D 0-0	0-0	2		12,723
38	23	A	Middlesbrough	D 0-0	0-0	2		10,315
39	30	H	Crystal Palace	W 1-0	0-0	2	Gray	12,523
40	May 2	A	Charlton Ath	D 3-3	3-0	2	Kellock 2, Eves	7935
41	7	A	QPR	L 1-2	1-1	2	Gray	19,854
42	14	H	Newcastle U	D 2-2	2-2	2	Matthews, Gray	22,446

Final League Position: 2

GOALSCORERS

League (68): Eves 18, Clarke 12 (1 pen), Gray 10, Matthews 5, Palmer 5 (3 pens), Dodd 3, Humphrey 3, Kellock 3, Livingstone 3, Hibbitt 2, Smith 2, Cartwright 1, Pender 1.
Milk Cup (1): Eves 1.
FA Cup (1): Hibbitt 1.

Milk Cup	Second Round	Sunderland (h)	1-1
		(a)	0-5
FA Cup	Third Round	Tranmere R (a)	1-0
	Fourth Round	Aston Villa (a)	0-1

Burridge	Humphrey	Wintersgill	Palmer	Pender	Coy	Daniel	Clarke	Livingstone	Eves	Matthews	Butler	Smith	Gray	Hibbitt	Gallagher	Dodd	Cartwright	Rudge	Kellock	Richards	*Referees*	*Match No.*
1	2	3	4	5	6	7	8	9*	10	11	12										E. Read	1
1	2	3*	4	5	6	7	8	9	10	11		12									M. Taylor	2
1	2		3	5	6	7	8		10	11		4	9								N. Glover	3
1	2		3	5	6	7	8		10	11	12	4	9*								N. Midgley	4
1	2		3	5	6	7	8	9*	10	11	12	4									A. Ward	5
1	2		3	5	6	7	8	9	10	11		4									D. Hutchinson	6
1	2		3	5	6	7	8	9	10	11		4									D. Hedges	7
1	2		3	5	6	7	8	9	10	11		4									G. Tyson	8
1	2		3	5	6	7	8	9*	10	11		4		12							J. Hough	9
1	2		3	5	6	7	8	9	10	11		4*		12							D. Allison	10
1	2		3	5	6		8		10	4	11		9	7							D. Vickers	11
1	2		3	5	6		8	11*	10	4	12		9	7							A. Gunn	12
1	2		3*		6	7	8		10	11	12		9	4	5						H. King	13
1	2		3		6	7	8*		10	11			9	4	5		12				J. Key	14
1	2		3		6	7	8		10*	11			9	4	5		12				K. Cooper	15
1	2		3	5			8		10	11			9	4		6	7				Alan Robinson	16
1	2		3	5			8		10	11			9	4		6	7				C. Thomas	17
1	2		3	5			8		10	11			9	4		6	7				K. Hackett	18
1	2		3	5			8		10	11			9	7		6		4			A. Robinson	19
1	2		3	5	12		8		10	11*			9	4		6		7			D. Shaw	20
1	2		3	5	12		8		10			11	9	7		6		4*			K. Salmon	21
1	2		3	5			8		10	11		4	9	7		6					I. Borrett	22
1	2		3	5*	12		8		10	11		4	9	7		6					E. Scales	23
1	2		3	5			8		10	11		4	9	7		6					A. Challinor	24
1	2		3	5			8		10	11		4	9	7		6					T. Jones	25
1	2		3	5			8		10	11		4	9			6		7			N. Wilson	26
1	2		3	5			8	12	10	11*			9	7		6		4			T. Bune	27
1	2		3*	5			8		10	11		12	9	7		6		4			A. Ward	28
1	2			5			8		10	11		3	9	7		6		4			B. Stevens	29
1	2		12	5			8		10	11		3	9	7		6		4*			T. Fitzharris	30
1	2		3	5					10	11		4	9	7		6			8		R. Bridges	31
1	2		3	5			8		10	11*		4	9			6			7	12	P. Tyldesley	32
1	2		3	5			8		10	11		4	9	12		6			7*		C. Downey	33
1	2		3	5			8		10	11		4		12		6			7*	9	T. Mills	34
1	2		3	5			8		10	11		4	9			6			7		D. Richardson	35
1	2		3	5					10	11		4	9	7		6			8*	12	J. Worrall	36
1	2		3	5			8*			11	12	4	9	7		6				10	N. Ashley	37
1	2		3	5			8	10		11		12	9*	7		6	4				C. Seel	38
1	2		3	5			8		10*	11	12		9	7		6	4				M. Chadwick	39
1	2		3	5			8		10				9	7		6	4		11		L. Burden	40
1	2		3	5					10	11			9	7		6	4		8		A. Grey	41
1	2		3	5			12		10	11*		4	9	7		6			8		B. Daniels	42
42	42	2	40	39	15	13	38	10	40	40	1	24	33	27	3	27	7	8	9	2		
			+ 1s		+ 3s		+ 1s	+ 1s			+ 7s	+ 3s		+ 4s			+ 2s			+ 2s		

FOOTBALL LEAGUE RECORD

1888 Founder Members of Football League; 1906–23 Division 2; 1923–24 Division 3(N); 1924–32 Division 2; 1932–65 Division 1; 1965–67 Division 2; 1967–76 Division 1; 1976–77 Division 2; 1977–82 Division 1; 1982–83 Division 2; 1983– Division 1.

HONOURS

Football League: Division 1 – Champions 1953–54, 1957–58, 1958–59; Runners-up 1937–38, 1938–39, 1949–50, 1954–55, 1959–60; Division 2 – Champions 1931–32, 1976–77; Runners-up 1966–67, 1982–83; Division 3(N) – Champions 1923–24. *FA Cup:* Winners 1893, 1908, 1949, 1960; Runners-up 1889, 1896, 1921, 1939. *Football League Cup:* Winners 1973–74, 1979–80. *Texaco Cup:* 1970–71. **European Competitions:** *European Cup:* 1958–59, 1959–60. *European Cup-Winners' Cup:* 1960–61. *UEFA Cup:* 1971–72 (runners-up), 1973–74, 1974-75, 1980–81.

COLOURS

Old gold shirts, black collar, cuffs and shorts, old gold stockings. **Change colours:** All white.

WOLVERHAMPTON WANDERERS

Players Names Ht, Wt, D.o.B.	Birthplace Transfer Fee	Clubs	Appearances F.L. A & S	 F.L.C. A & S	 F.A.C. A & S	Goals F.L.	 F.L.C.	 F.A.C.
Goalkeepers								
Paul Bradshaw (EU21)	Altrincham	Blackburn R (A)	78	3	4			
6 2½, 12 1, 28.4.56	£150,000	Wolverhptn W	190	16	23			
John Burridge	Workington	Workington (A)	27	1	4			
5 10½, 12 3, 3.12.51	£10,000	Blackpool	134	10	4			
	£100,000	Aston Villa	65	9	6			
	—	Southend U (loan)	6					
	£50,000	Crystal Palace	88	7	7			
	£200,000	QPR	39	4	2			
	£80,000	Wolverhptn W	42	2	2			
Defenders								
Geoff Palmer (EU23)	Cannock	Wolverhptn W (A)	354+3	30	35+1	12	2	
5 10, 10 5, 11.7.54								
John Humphrey	Paddington	Wolverhptn W (A)	79	2	2	3		
5 9½, 10 13, 31.1.61								
Robert Coy	Birmingham	Wolverhptn W (A)	35+3	2				
5 11, 11 12, 30.11.61								
Mike Hollifield	Middlesbrough	Wolverhptn W (A)	21		4			
5 10½, 11 0, 2.5.61								
John Pender (EIY)	Luton	Wolverhptn W (A)	47	2	2	1		
6 0½, 12 3, 19.11.63								
Gordon Smith	Glasgow	St Johnstone						
5 9, 12 1, 3.7.54	£80,000	Aston Villa	76+3	8+1	1			
	£150,000	Tottenham H	34+4	6		1		
	F/T	Wolverhptn W	24+3	1	2	2		
Alan Dodd (EU23)	Stoke	Stoke C (A)	349+7	25	15	3	1	
5 10¼, 12 3, 20.9.53	£40,000	Wolverhptn W	27		2	3		
Midfield								
Peter Daniel (EU21)	Hull	Hull C	113	2	8	9		
5 8½, 11 3, 12.12.55	£150,000	Wolverhptn W	138	16	16	13	2	1
Kenny Hibbitt (EU23)	Bradford	Bradford PA (A)	13+2	1				
5 10, 12 0, 3.1.51	£10,000	Wolverhptn W	427+15	32+1	46	88	12	10
Hugh Atkinson (EIU21)	Dublin	Wolverhptn W (A)	38+8	1	4	3		
6 0, 11 9, 8.11.60								
Tony Kernan* (EIY)	Letterkenny	Wolverhptn W (A)	1					
5 8, 9 13, 31.8.63								
Dale Rudge	Wolverhampton	Wolverhptn W (A)	8		1			
5 8, 10 6, 9.9.63								
Billy Kellock (SS)	Glasgow	Aston Villa (A)						
5 10, 11 10, 7.2.54	F/T	Cardiff C	33+2		7	2		3
	£5000	Norwich C	1+2					
	F/T	Milwall						
	F/T	Chelmsford C						
	F/T	Kettering T						
	£30,000	Peterborough U	134	12	10	43	4	1
	£30,000	Luton T	2+5	1	+1		2	
	£20,000	Wolverhptn W	9			3		
Ian Cartwright	Birmingham	Wolverhptn W (A)	7+2			1		
5 8½, 10 12, 13.11.64								
Forwards								
Mick Matthews	Hull	Wolverhptn W (A)	70+4	4	2+1	7		
5 7½, 10 12, 25.9.60								
John Richards (E)	Warrington	Wolverhptn W	365+22	32+1	42+2	144	18	24
5 9, 11 1, 9.11.50	—	Derby Co (loan)	10			2		
Mel Eves (EB)	Wednesbury	Wolverhptn W	155+10	11+1	16	41	3	4
5 10½, 10 1, 10.9.56								
Wayne Clarke (EY)	Wolverhampton	Wolverhptn W (A)	100+17	6+2	6+2	24		
5 11¼, 10 6, 28.2.61								
Andy Gray (S)	Glasgow	Dundee U						
5 11, 11 7, 30.11.55	£110,000	Aston Villa	112+1	18	6	54	10	3
	£1,525,000	Wolverhptn W	121+3	12	13	36	3	3
Paul Butler	Stockton	Wolverhptn W (A)	1+7	+2				
5 7, 10 4, 9.6.64								
Billy Livingstone (SY)	Coventry	Wolverhptn W (A)	10+1	1		3		
5 10, 11 3, 13.8.64								
John Croke		Wolverhptn W						
5 11, 11 10,								
Apprentices								
David Wintersgill	York	Wolverhptn W (A)	2					
5 10, 11 2, 19.9.65								

General Manager: Eric Woodward (Tel. 0902 712181)
Asst Manager: Jim Barron
Supporters Player of the Season 1982–83: John Burridge
Physiotherapist: Dennis Conyerd
Club Captain 1982–83: J. Richards
Chief Scout: Frank Upton
Club Statistician: None
Association of Football Statisticians Club Adviser to Yearbook: A. Matthews

Players (non-appearance) granted free transfers: Steve Pugh, D.
Players released since May 1982: Peter Knowles, M. (retired); Steve Lowe, G. (N/K); Craig Moss, F. (Worcester C); Rafael Villazan, D. (Uruguay); Steve McLaren, F. (Hibernian); David Beattie, M. (N/K).

WREXHAM Division 4

Back row (left to right): Darren Baker, Andy Edwards, Mark Emmerson, Medwyn Evans, Shaun Cunnington, Steve Jones, John Williams
Middle row: Norman Wilson (General Secretary), Jake King, Jackie Keay, Steve Dowman, Eddie Niedzweicki, Stuart Parker, Drew Brand (returned to Hereford), Alan Hill, Gareth Davis, Phil Bater (Captain), George Showell (Physiotherapist) (now retired)
Front row: John Muldoon, Robbie Savage, Dave Gregory, Ray Bunkell (Assistant Manager), Bobby Roberts (Manager), Simon Hunt, Ian Arkwright, Steve Buxton.

President: F. Wellum. ***Chairman:*** F. J. Tomlinson.

Vice-Chairman: W. P. Griffiths.

Directors: G. Mytton, W. Jones, S. Freudmann, C. Griffiths.

Manager: Bobby Roberts.

General Secretary: C. N. Wilson FAAI.

Year Formed: 1873 (oldest Club in Wales).

Turned Professional: 1912. ***Ltd. Co.:*** 1912.

Previous Ground: Acton Park. ***Club Nickname:*** 'Robins'.

Previous Managers since 1946: Tom Williams, Les McDowell, Peter Jackson, Cliff Lloyd, John Love, Bill Morris, Ken Barnes, Bill Morris, Jack Rowley, Alvan Williams, John Neal, Arfon Griffiths MBE, Mel Sutton (13).

Racecourse Ground, Mold Road, Wrexham. Telephone Wrexham (0978) 262129. ***Telegraphic address:*** 'Football, Wrexham'. ***Ground capacity:*** 30,000 (18,000 covered). ***Record attendance:*** 34,445 v Manchester U, FA Cup 4th rd, 26 Jan, 1957. ***Record receipts:*** £25,107 v Anderlecht, European Cup-Winners' Cup quarter-final, 17 Mar, 1976. ***Pitch measurements:*** 117yd×75yd.

Directions to Ground: Wrexham General railway station is only 200 yards from the ground. Trains run from Chester and Shrewsbury. Bus services from outlying districts to town.

Match tickets: Stand tickets bookable in advance.

Car parking: Berse Field Main Car Park plus parking grounds at St Marks, Bodhyfryd Square, Eagles Meadows, Old Guild Hall, Hill Street, Holt Street, and Town Hill, Hill Street.

Entertainments/catering facilities: A social club and four catering kiosks at the ground.

Club shop: Situated on Mold Road.

Handbooks/programmes: Programmes available on subscription.

Extra information: Season tickets available for all parts of the ground and all stands.

Address of Supporters Club: Secretary, Lyn Williams, c/o Centre Spot, Mold Rd, Wrexham.

Note: Full club statistical records are on pages 416–455.

WREXHAM 1982–83 LEAGUE RECORD

Match No.	Date	Venue	Opponents	Result	H/T Score	Lg. Pos.	Goalscorers	Attendance
1	Aug 28	A	Cardiff C	W 2-1	1-1	—	Arkwright, McNeil	5018
2	Sept 4	H	Huddersfield T	D 1-1	0-0	4	Dowman	3925
3	7	H	Lincoln C	L 0-1	0-0	—		2971
4	11	A	Portsmouth	L 0-3	0-1	17		10,867
5	18	H	Gillingham	W 1-0	1-0	14	Buxton	2122
6	25	A	Plymouth Arg	L 0-2	0-1	16		3628
7	28	A	Preston NE	L 0-3	0-1	—		3363
8	Oct 2	H	AFC Bournemouth	W 1-0	1-0	17	Muldoon	2046
9	9	H	Exeter C	L 1-2	0-1	17	Buxton	2110
10	16	A	Sheffield U	L 0-2	0-1	19		11,582
11	19	A	Doncaster R	D 1-1	1-0	—	Baker	3420
12	23	H	Oxford U	D 1-1	0-1	20	Savage	2491
13	30	A	Walsall	D 1-1	1-1	18	Savage	2473
14	Nov 2	H	Southend U	W 3-2	2-1	—	Buxton 2 (1 pen), Savage	1802
15	6	A	Millwall	D 1-1	0-1	16	Muldoon	2943
16	13	H	Orient	W 1-0	0-0	15	Buxton (pen)	2333
17	27	H	Newport Co	W 1-0	1-0	14	Savage	3246
18	Dec 4	A	Brentford	L 1-4	1-1	16	King	5606
19	18	A	Bristol R	L 0-4	0-0	16		4607
20	27	H	Wigan Ath	D 1-1	0-0	16	Arkwright	4591
21	28	A	Bradford C	D 0-0	0-0	15		5542
22	Jan 1	H	Reading	W 4-0	2-0	13	Bremner, Gregory (pen), Savage, Hunt	3390
23	3	A	Chesterfield	L 1-5	0-3	15	Savage	2805
24	15	H	Cardiff C	H 0-0	0-0	17		3846
25	22	A	Gillingham	D 1-1	1-1	17	Arkwright	3798
26	29	H	Portsmouth	L 0-2	0-0	18		3007
27	Feb 5	H	Preston NE	W 3-1	2-0	18	Gregory, Buxton, Savage	1920
28	12	A	AFC Bournemouth	D 1-1	0-0	16	Hunt	3827
29	15	H	Doncaster R	W 5-0	1-0	—	Hunt 2, Savage, Steele 2	1899
30	19	A	Exeter C	D 3-3	0-0	13	Buxton, Steel 2	2507
31	26	H	Sheffield U	W 4-1	1-1	12	Hunt, Steel 2, Dowman	3953
32	28	A	Southend U	D 2-2	0-2	—	Savage, Arkwright	2512
33	Mar 5	A	Oxford U	L 0-2	0-1	13		4811
34	12	H	Walsall	W 4-0	0-0	12	Keay, Buxton, Gregory, Arkwright	2748
35	19	H	Millwall	W 4-3	2-2	11	Hunt 2, Arkwright, Buxton	2668
36	25	A	Orient	D 0-0	0-0	—		1969
37	29	A	Huddersfield T	L 1-4	1-1	—	Hill	9519
38	Apr 2	H	Bradford C	L 0-4	0-2	13		2808
39	4	A	Wigan Ath	L 1-3	1-0	—	Gregory	3377
40	8	H	Brentford	L 3-4	3-3	—	Savage, Keay, Buxton	2104
41	16	A	Lincoln C	L 0-2	0-0	16		3505
42	22	H	Bristol R	D 0-0	0-0	—		2053
43	30	A	Newport Co	L 0-4	0-2	17		4344
44	May 2	H	Chesterfield	D 0-0	0-0	18		2047
45	7	H	Plymouth Arg	L 2-3	2-1	19	Gregory, Muldoon	2250
46	14	A	Reading	L 0-1	0-1	21		5252

Final League Position: 22

GOALSCORERS

League (56): Buxton 10 (2 pens), Savage 10, Hunt 7, Arkwright 6, Steel 6, Gregory 5 (1 pen), Muldoon 3, Dowman 2, Keay 2, Baker 1, Bremner 1, Hill 1, King 1, McNeil 1.
Milk Cup (1): Hunt 1.
FA Cup (5): Gregory 1, Hunt, Keay 1, Muldoon 1, Savage 1.

Milk Cup	First Round	Shrewsbury T (h)	1-0
		(a)	0-2
FA Cup	First Round	Holbeach (a)	4-0
	Second Round	Worcester C (a)	1-2

Neidzwiecki	Jones	Bater	Arkwright	Dowman	Hill	Hunt	Gregory	Fox	McNeil	Buxton	Edwards	Keay	King	Davis	Baker	Humphries	Muldoon	Emmerson	Evans	Savage (L)	Brand (L)	Cunnington	Barker	Bremner (L)	Steele (L)	Jones S.	*Referees*
1	2	3	4	5	6	7	8	9	10	11																	L. Shapter
1	2	3	4	5	6	7	8	9	10	11																	A. Hamil
1	3		4	5	2*	7	8	9	10	11	12	6															D. Allison
1	2	4	5	3	12	7	8	9*		11		6	10														E. Scales
1	3	7	4	5	2		8	9	10	11		6															K. Barratt
1		7		5	2	4	8	9	10*	11		6		3	12												J. Martin
	3	7	9	5	2*	4	12				10	6				1	8	11									C. Seel
		3	7	5	9	4	8		10	11		6*		2		1	12										N. Midgley
1		3	7	5	9	4*	8		10	11			12	2			6										D. Richardson
1	10	3	7	5	9	4	8			11				2*			6		12								V. Callow
1		3	7	5	9	4	8			11	12				2*		6		10								T. Fitzharris
1		3	7	5	9	2	8			11					12		6		10*	4							R. Banks
1		3	7	5		2	8			11	12			9*	10		6			4							T. Mills
1		3	7	5		2	8*			11	12	9			10		6			4							D. Lloyd
1		3	7	5	10	2				11		9	8				6			4							D. Brazier
1		3	7	5		2	10			11		9	8*		12		6			4							N. Glover
1		3	7	5		2	8			11		9	10				6			4							R. Chadwick
		3	7	5	4	2	10			11		9	8		12		6*				1						B. Hill
1			7		3	2	8			11	12	9	10		6*					4		5					C. Downey
1		3	9	5	12	7*	8			10		6	2				11			4							H. King
1		3	7	5	12	2	8*			11		9	10		6					4			6				M. Peck
1		3	9	5		7	8					6	2		11					4				10			D. Shaw
1		3	7	5		9	8				12	6	2		11*					4				10			J. Hunting
1		3	7	5		9	8			11		6	2							4				10			K. Baker
1			7	5	3	9	8			11		6	2							4				10			D. Vickers
1			7	5	3	9				8		6	2		11*					4		12			10		K. Walmsley
1			7	5	3	9	11			8		6	2							4					10		A. Seville
1		3	7	5		9	11			8		6	2							4					10		D. Axcell
1		3	7	5		9	11			8		6	2							4					10		J. Bray
1		3	7	5*	12	9	11			8		6	2							4					10		E. Read
1		3	7	5		9	11			8		6	2							4					10		C. Thomas
1		3	7	5	12	9	11			8		6	2							4*					10		R. Lewis
1		3	7	5	12	9	11			8		6	2							4*					10		D. Civil
1			7	5	3	9	11			8		6	2				4								10		D. Hutchinson
1		10	7	5	3	9	11			8	12	6	2				4*										A. Robinson
1		10	7	5	12	9	11			8		6	2				4*		3								K. Barratt
1		4	7	5	10	9	11				8	6	2				12		3*								M. Scott
1			7	5*	3	9	11				8		2		10					4						6	G. Napthine
1			7		5	9	11			8			2		4*		10	12		6						3	D. Owen
1		3	7		6	9	11*			8	12	5	2				10			4							K. Hackett
1		3	7	6		9				8	11	5*	2				10			4						12	E. Scales
1		3	7	5	11	9				8	12	6	2				10		4*								H. Taylor
1		8	7	5	11	9					4*	6	2		12		10									3	J. Martin
1		3	7	5		9	11					6	2				10			8						4	J. Deakin
1		3		5		9	11			8		6	2				10			4		12				7	J. Hough
			4*	5	3	9	11			8		6	2				10		7			12					A. Gunn
42	7	37	44	43	26	45	40	6	7	39	5	37	33	5	10	2	23	1	6	27	1	1	1	4	9	5	
					+ 7s		+ 1s				+ 10s		+ 1s		+ 5s		+ 2s	+ 1s	+ 1s			+ 3s				+ 1s	

Also played: Parker (no. 1, match 46), Williams (no. 12, match 38).

FOOTBALL LEAGUE RECORD

1921 Original Members of Division 3(N); 1958–60 Division 3; 1960–62 Division 4; 1962–64 Division 3; 1964–70 Division 4; 1970–78 Division 3; 1978–82 Division 2; 1982–83 Division 3; 1983– Division 4.

HONOURS

Football League: Division 2 best season: 15th, 1978–79; Division 3 – Champions 1977–78; Division 3(N) – Runners-up 1932–33; Division 4 – Runners-up 1969–70. *FA Cup* best season: 6th rd, 1973–74, 1977–78. *Football League Cup* best season: 5th rd, 1961, 1978. *Welsh Cup:* Winners 21 times. Runners-up 18 times. Record number of victories and appearances in finals. **European Competition:** *European Cup-Winners' Cup:* 1972–73, 1975–76, 1978–79, 1979–80.

COLOURS

Red shirts with white trim, navy blue shorts, white stockings. **Change colours:** Sky blue shirts and stockings, white shorts.

WREXHAM

Players Names Ht, Wt, D.o.B.	Birthplace Transfer Fee	Clubs	*Appearances* F.L. A & S	F.L.C. A & S	F.A.C. A & S	*Goals* F.L.	F.L.C.	F.A.C.
Goalkeepers								
Eddie Niedzwiecki (WS)	Bangor	Wrexham	111	10	7			
6 0, 11 0, 3.5.59								
Stuart Parker	Winsford	Wrexham	1					
6 1, 12 9,								
Defenders								
Alan Hill*	Chester	Wrexham	173+26	18	18+4	7		
5 11, 11 4, 22.6.55								
Steve Rowman	Manor Park	Colchester U (A)	150+4	10+1	21	21	2	3
5 11, 12 4, 15.4.58	£75,000	Wrexham	87	7	6	2		1
Phil Bater (WU21)	Cardiff	Bristol R (A)	211+1	12	13	2		
5 10½, 12 12, 26.10.55	£50,000	Wrexham	73	5	6	1		
John Keay	Glasgow	Celtic						
6 0, 12 6, 14.6.60	F/T	Shrewsbury T	152+3	7	15	20		2
	£18,000	Wrexham	37	1	2	2		1
Jake King	Glasgow	Shrewsbury T (A)	304+2	14	26	20		1
5 10, 11 0, 29.1.55	F/T	Wrexham	33+1		2	1		
Midfield								
Ian Arkwright*	Shafton	Wolverha'ton W (A)	3+1					
5 8¼, 10 8, 18.9.59	£100,000	Wrexham	74+1	4	7	6		
Simon Hunt	Chester	Wrexham	60+4	4+2	3	9	2	1
5 6, 10 1,								
David Gregory	Peterborough	Chatteris T						
5 9, 11 6, 6.10.51		Peterborough U	125+17	10+1	13+1	32	2	6
	£55,000	Stoke C	22+1	1	1	3		1
	—	Blackburn R (loan)	5	1		3	1	
	£30,000	Bury	50+2	2	4	13	1	6
	£30,000	Portsmouth	64+10	7	4	18	2	1
	F/T	Wrexham	40+1	2	2	4		1
John Muldoon	Little Sutton	Wrexham	23+2		2	3		1
Forwards								
Steve Buxton	Birmingham	Wrexham	75+14	3+2	4	18		
5 5, 9 8, 13.3.60								
Non-contract players								
Andy Edwards	Wrexham	Wrexham	5+9	1				
Darren Baker	Wednesbury	Wrexham	10+5					1
Mark Emerson	Cuddington	Wrexham	1+1					
Medwyn Evans	Bryntec	Wrexham	6+1					
Shaun Cunningham	Bourne	Wrexham	1+3					
John Williams	Bala	Wrexham	+1					
Steve Jones	Wrexham	Wrexham	3+1					

Commercial Manager: S. R. Slater. (Tel. 0978 352536).
Club Coach:
Supporters Player of the Season 1982–83: Robbie Savage.
Physiotherapist: George Showell.
Association of Football Statisticians Club Adviser to Yearbook: G. Davies.
Club Captain (1982–83): Phil Bater
Chief Scout:
Club Statistician:

Players released since May 1982:
Mark Jones, F. (N/K); Gareth Davis, D. (Lex).

YORK CITY Division 4

Back row (left to right): Viv Busby, John Simpson, Tommy Stanley, Richard Dawson, Chris Evans, Roger Jones, Eddie Blackburn, Mick Astbury, Keith Walwyn, Ricky Sbragia, Mick Laverick, Denis Smith
Front row: John Bentham, John Byrne, Derek Hood, Malcolm Crosby, Brian Pollard, Steve Senior, Eddie Flood, Gary Ford.

President: F. H. Magson. ***Chairman:*** M. D. B. Sinclair.

Directors: D. M. Craig JP, BSC, FICE, FI, MUN E, FCI ARB, M CONS E, B. A. Houghton, R. B. Strachan MA, LLB, FCIS, C. Webb, E. B. Swallow.

Player-Manager: Denis Smith. ***Club Secretary:*** Tom Hughes.

Sales Executive: S. B. Winship. ***Medical Officer:*** Dr A. I. MacLeod.

Year Formed: 1922. ***Turned Professional:*** 1922. ***Ltd Co.:*** 1922.

Club Nickname: 'Minstermen'.

Previous Grounds: 1922, Fulfordgate; 1932, Bootham Crescent.

Previous Managers since 1946: Tom Mitchell, Dick Duckworth, Charlie Spencer, Jimmy McCormack, Sam Bartram, Tom Lockie, Joe Shaw, Tom Johnston, Wilf McGuiness, Charlie Wright, Barry Lyons (11).

Bootham Crescent, York. Telephone: York (0904) 24447. ***Telegraphic address:*** 'City Football, York'. ***Ground capacity:*** 13,500. ***Record attendance:*** 28,123 v Huddersfield T, FA Cup 6th rd, 5 Mar, 1938. ***Record receipts:*** £17,300 v Hull C, Div 4, 19 April, 1983. ***Pitch measurements:*** 115yd×75yd.

Directions to Ground: Buses 2, 2a, and 8 every ten minutes from York railway station to the ground.

Match tickets: On sale fourteen days prior to match.

Car parking: Ample parking in side-streets.

Entertainments/catering facilities: Licensed Social Club open to members only. Three tea bars on the ground.

Club shop: Selling all types of souvenirs.

Handbooks/programmes: Programmes available on subscription, details available from the Secretary. Programme shop at the ground stocking a wide variety of English, Scottish and non-League programmes.

Address of Supporters Club: G. J. Mortimer, Secretary, 2 Plantation Grove, Boroughbridge Road, York.

Note: Full club statistical records are on pages 416–455.

YORK CITY 1982–83 LEAGUE RECORD

Match No.	Date	Venue	Opponents	Result	H/T Score	Lg. Pos.	Goalscorers	Attendance
1	Aug 28	H	Torquay U	D 1-1	1-0	—	Hood (pen)	1737
2	Sept 4	A	Northampton T	D 1-1	0-0	14	Laverick	2254
3	7	A	Hull C	L 0-4	0-1	—		3769
4	11	H	Tranmere R	W 2-1	1-0	16	Hood (pen), Walwyn	1632
5	19	A	Scunthorpe U	D 0-0	0-0	—		.2436
6	25	H	Peterborough U	D 1-1	0-1	16	Ford	1872
7	28	H	Halifax T	W 3-2	0-0	—	Laverick, Ford, Busby	1772
8	Oct 2	A	Hereford U	D 0-0	0-0	14		2037
9	9	A	Bristol C	D 2-2	1-1	13	Byrne, Ford	3680
10	16	H	Wimbledon	L 1-4	0-0	15	Pollard	2064
11	19	A	Blackpool	D 1-1	0-1	—	Walwyn	2765
12	22	A	Stockport Co	L 1-2	0-0	—	Walwyn	2014
13	30	H	Hartlepool U	W 5-1	2-0	14	Hood, Crosby, Walwyn, Ford, Pollard	1971
14	Nov 2	A	Crewe Alex	L 1-2	0-1	—	Smith	1633
15	6	H	Aldershot	W 4-0	2-0	12	Pollard 2 (1 pen), Byrne 2	1743
16	13	A	Swindon T	L 2-3	1-2	14	Ford, Walwyn	4081
17	27	H	Mansfield T	W 6-1	3-1	11	Walwyn 3, Pollard 2, Crosby	2119
18	Dec 3	A	Colchester U	D 0-0	0-0	—		2204
19	18	A	Chester	W 1-0	1-0	11	Walwyn	1185
20	27	H	Bury	W 3-1	1-0	9	Bramhall (og), Pollard (pen), Walwyn	5174
21	28	A	Rochdale	L 0-1	0-0	10		2127
22	Jan 1	H	Darlington	W 5-2	2-1	9	Smith 2, Busby, Byrne 2	3679
23	3	A	Port Vale	L 1-2	0-2	10	Busby	6056
24	15	A	Torquay U	W 3-1	2-0	9	Byrne, Walwyn, Pollard	2738
25	23	H	Scunthorpe U	W 2-1	1-1	—	Walwyn, Ford	7097
26	29	A	Tranmere R	L 0-3	0-0	8		1802
27	Feb 5	A	Peterborough U	D 2-2	1-1	9	Hood, Pollard (pen)	2652
28	15	H	Blackpool	W 2-0	0-0	—	Ford, Byrne	2937
29	19	H	Bristol C	W 3-0	0-0	8	Byrne 2, Pollard (pen)	2879
30	26	A	Wimbledon	L 3-4	0-2	8	Smith M. (og), Walwyn, Hay	2168
31	Mar 1	H	Crewe Alex	W 2-0	1-0	—	Smith, Walwyn	2975
32	5	H	Stockport Co	W 3-1	0-1	7	Ford, Pollard 2 (1 pen)	2883
33	12	A	Hartlepool U	L 0-2	0-0	7		1604
34	15	H	Northampton T	W 5-2	2-1	—	Ford 2, Walwyn, Pollard, Hood	2802
35	19	A	Aldershot	W 3-2	2-2	7	Byrne, Walwyn 2	1528
36	26	H	Swindon T	D 0-0	0-0	7		3265
37	Apr 2	H	Rochdale	W 1-0	1-0	7	Walwyn	3357
38	4	A	Bury	L 1-2	1-0	—	Walwyn	3543
39	9	H	Colchester U	W 3-0	1-0	7	Busby, Pollard (pen), Senior	2538
40	15	A	Halifax T	D 2-2	0-1	—	Pollard (pen), Sbragia	2117
41	19	H	Hull C	W 1-0	0-0	—	Byrne	9909
42	23	H	Chester	W 1-0	1-0	6	McPhail	3264
43	30	A	Mansfield T	D 2-2	1-1	7	Ford, Walwyn	2288
44	May 2	H	Port Vale	D 0-0	0-0	7		4814
45	7	H	Hereford U	W 5-1	0-1	7	Pollard 2, Phillips (og), Hood, McPhail	2106
46	14	A	Darlington	W 3-1	3-1	7	Byrne, Hood, Walwyn	1668

Final League Position: 7

GOALSCORERS

League (88): Walwyn 21, Pollard 17 (7 pens), Byrne 12, Ford 11, Hood 7 (2 pens), Busby 4, Smith 4, Crosby 2, Laverick 2, McPhail 2, Hay 1, Sbragia 1, Senior 1, own goals 3.
Milk Cup (3): Byrne 1, Walwyn 1, own goal 1.
FA Cup (9): Ford 2, Hood 2, Pollard 2, Walwyn 2, Byrne 1.

Milk Cup	First Round	Lincoln C (h)	2-1
		(a)	1-3
FA Cup	First Round	Bury (h)	3-1
	Second Round	Hartlepool U (a)	1-1
		(h)	4-0
	Third Round	Crystal Palace (a)	1-2

Jones	Evans	Hay	Sbragia	Hood	Laverick	Pollard	Ford	Busby	Byrne	Crosby	Senior	Smith	Walwyn	Dawson	Stanley	Astbury	McPhail	King	Referees	Match No.
1	2	3	4	5	6	7	8	9*	10	11	12								T. Jones	1
1	2	3	4	6	11	7	8		10			5	9						J. Moules	2
1	2	3	4	6	11	8	7		10			5	9						D. Shaw	3
1	2	3	4	6	11	6	8		10			5	9						K. Redfern	4
1	2	3	4	6	11	7*	8		10	5	12		9						T. Fitzharris	5
1	2	3	4	6	11	7*	8		10	5	12		9						R. Guy	6
1	2	3	4	6	11	7	8	12	10*	5			9						A. Saunders	7
1	2	3	4	6	11	7	8		10	5			9						K. Barratt	8
1	2		4	6		7	8	12	10	5	11*		9	3					C. Thomas	9
1	2		4	6	11	7	8	12	10	5			9	3*					G. Courtney	10
1	2		4	3	11	7	8	10		5		6	9						M. Peck	11
1	2		4	3	11	7	8	10*	12	5		6	9						D. Allison	12
1	2	3	4	6		11	7		10	8		5	9						J. Worrall	13
1	2	3	4	6		11	7		10	8		5	9						D. Richardson	14
1	2	3	4	6		11	7		10	8		5	9						R. Banks	15
1	2	3	4	6		11	7		10	8		5	9						K. Salmon	16
1	2	3	4	6		11	7		10	8		5	9						N. Wilson	17
1	2	3	4	6		11	7		10	8		5	9						A. Gunn	18
1	2	3	4	6	7	11	10			8		5	9						A. Seville	19
1	2	3	4	6	12	11	7	10		8		5	9*						H. Taylor	20
1	2	3	4	6		11	7	10*	9	8		5			12				J. Lovatt	21
	2	3	4	6	12	11	7	9	10	8*		5				1			N. Midgley	22
	2*	3	4	6	12	11	7	9	10	8		5				1			R. Milford	23
1	2	3	4	6		11	7		10	8		5	9						T. Spencer	24
1	2	3	4	6		11	7		10	8		5	9						K. Walmsley	25
1	2	3	4*	6		11	7	12	10	8		5	9						C. Seel	26
1	2*	3	4	6		12	7		10	8		5	9				11		J. Martin	27
1	2	3	4	6		11	7		10	8		5*	9				12		G. Tyson	28
1	2	3	4	6		11	7		10	8		5	9						J. Hough	29
1	2	3	4	6		12	7		10	8		5	9				11*		E. Crickmore	30
1	2	3	4	6		11	7		10	8		5	9						D. Allison	31
1	2	3	4	6		11	7		10	8		5	9						M. Peck	32
	2	3	4	6		11	7		10	8		5	9			1			P. Tyldesley	33
	2	3	4	6		11	7		10	8		5	9			1			P. Willis	34
1	2	3	4	6		11	7		10	8		5	9						K. Salmon	35
1	2	3	4	6		11	7		10	8		5	9						R. Fitzharris	36
1	2	3	4	6		11	7	12	10	8*		5	9						A. Saunders	37
1	2	3	4	6		11	7	12	10		8*		9				5		N. Ashley	38
1	2	3	4	6		11	7	9	10		8						5		R. Nixon	39
1	2	3	4	6		11		7	10		8*		9				5	12	F. Roberts	40
1	2	3	4	6		11	7		10		8		9				5		D. Scott	41
1	2	3	4	6		11	7		10		8		9				5		D. Richardson	42
1	2	3	4	6		11	7		10	8			9				5		I. Borrett	43
1	2	3	4	6		11	7*	12	10	8			9				5		G. Courtney	44
1	2	3	4	6		11	7		10	8			9				5		A. Robinson	45
1	2	3	4	6		11	7		10*	8	12		9				5		N. Wilson	46
42	46	42	46	46	12	44	45	9	42	38	6	30	41	2	0	4	11	0		
					+ 3s	+ 2s		+ 7s	+ 1s		+ 4s				+ 1s		+ 1s	+ 1s		

FOOTBALL LEAGUE RECORD

1929 Elected to Division 3(N); 1958–59 Division 4; 1959–60 Division 3; 1960–65 Division 4; 1965–66 Division 3; 1966–71 Division 4; 1971–74 Division 3; 1974–76 Division 2; 1976–77 Division 3; 1977– Division 4.

HONOURS

Football League: Division 2 best season: 15th, 1974–75; Division 3 – Promoted 1973–74 (3rd); Division 4 – Promoted 1958–59 (3rd), 1964–65 (3rd), 1970–71 (4th). *FA Cup:* semi-finals 1955, when in Division 3. *Football League Cup* best season: 5th rd, 1962.

COLOURS

Red shirts with white trim, white shorts with red stripe, red stockings.

Change colours: White shirts with red trim, black shorts, black stockings with white and red tops.

YORK CITY

Players Names Ht, Wt, D.o.B.	Birthplace Transfer Fee	Clubs	Appearances F.L. A & S	 F.L.C. A & S	 F.A.C. A & S	Goals F.L.	 F.L.C.	 F.A.C.
Goalkeepers								
Mike Astbury	Leeds	York C (A)	20		1			
5 11, 13 0, 22.1.64								
Roger Jones (EU23)	Upton	Portsmouth (A)						
5 11, 13 0, 8.11.46	F/T	Bournemouth	160	8	8			
	£30,000	Blackburn R	242	15	15			
	£50,000	Newcastle U	5					
	F/T	Stoke C	101	8	3			
	£20,000	Derby Co	59	3	3			
	F/T	Birmingham C (loan)	4					
	F/T	York C	42	2	3			
Defenders								
Steve Senior	Sheffield	York C (A)	28+9		3	2		
5 8½, 11 4, 15.5.63								
Alan Hay	Dunfermline	Bolton W (N/C)						
5 11¾, 12 0, 28.11.58	—	Bristol C	72+2	4+2	4	1		
	F/T	York C	42	2	4	1		
Ricky Sbraggia	Lennoxtown	Birmingham C (A)	14+1			1		
6 0, 11 0, 26.5.56	£15,000	Walsall	77	2	5	4		
	£35,000	Blackpool	24+2	1		1		
	F/T	York C	46	2	4	1		
John MacPhail	Dundee	Dundee						
6 0½, 12 3, 7.12.55	£30,000	Sheffield U	135	9	8	7		1
	F/T	York C	11+1			2		
Chris Evans	Rhondda	Arsenal (A)						
5 10, 11 2, 13.10.62	F/T	Stoke C						
	F/T	York C	46	2	4			
Midfield								
Gary Ford	York	York C (A)	184+7	10	17	29	1	4
5 8, 11 10, 8.2.61								
Malcolm Crosby	South Shields	Aldershot (A)	272+22	11	18+1	23	2	2
5 9, 11 3, 4.7.54	P/E	York C	57+4		7	4		
Derek Hood	Washington	WBA (A)						
5 11, 12 8, 17.12.58	F/T	Hull C	20+4	3	4			
	£1000	York C	150	5	9	16		2
Forwards								
John Byrne	Manchester	York C (A)	111+8	4+2	7+1	26	2	2
6 0, 12 4, 1.2.61								
Keith Walwyn	Jamaica, WI	Winterton						
6 1, 13 2, 17.2.56	—	Chesterfield	3	+1	1+1	2		
	£4000	York C	85	4	7	44	1	4
Brian Pollard (EY)	York	York C	151+12	11+1	10+1	34	1	2
5 5, 10 10, 22.5.54	£33,000	Watford	68+3	8+1	4+1	8		
	£60,000	Mansfield T	45+9	4	2	5	1	1
	F/T	Blackpool	0+1					
	F/T	York C	69+3	2	7	20		4
Non-contract players								
Dennis Smith	Stoke	Stoke C	406+1	34	22	30	5	3
6 0, 12 2, 19.11.47	—	York C (loan)	7			1		
	F/T	York C	30	2	4	4		
Viv Busby	Slough	Wycombe W						
6 0, 11 12, 19.6.49	—	Luton T	64+13	3+1	1	16		
	—	Newcastle U (loan)	4	1		2		
	£35,000	Fulham	114+4	10	15	29	1	7
	£50,000	Norwich C	22		1	11		
	£50,000	Stoke C	33+17	3+4		9	1	
	—	Sheffield U (loan)	3			1		
		Tulsa R						
	£40,000+player	Blackburn R	8			1		
	F/T	York C	9+7			4		

Commercial Manager:
Club Coach: Viv Busby
Club Captain 1982–83: Roger Jones
Supporters Player of the Season 1982–83: Derek Hood
Chief Scout:
Physiotherapist: John Simpson
Club Statistician: David Batters
Association of Football Statisticians Club Adviser to Yearbook: D. Batters.

Players released since May 1982: Derek Craig, D. (N/K); Mike Czuczman, D. (Hull N/C); Robert Kay, D. (retired); Eddie Flood, D. (retired); John Bentham, D. (N/K); Mick Laverick, M. (Boston U); Tommy Stanley, M. (N/K); David King, (N/K); Richard Dawson, D. (Scarborough); Peter Aitken, D. (Hong Kong).

FOOTBALL LEAGUE FINAL TABLES

DIVISION 1

		Home					Away					
	P	W	D	L	F	A	W	D	L	F	A	Pts
1. Liverpool	42	16	4	1	55	16	8	6	7	32	21	82
2. Watford	42	16	2	3	49	20	6	3	12	25	37	71
3. Manchester U	42	14	7	0	39	10	5	6	10	17	28	70
4. Tottenham H	42	15	4	2	50	15	5	5	11	15	35	69
5. Nottingham F	42	12	5	4	34	18	8	4	9	28	32	69
6. Aston Villa	42	17	2	2	47	15	4	3	14	15	35	68
7. Everton	42	13	6	2	43	19	5	4	12	23	29	64
8. West Ham U	42	13	3	5	41	23	7	1	13	27	39	64
9. Ipswich T	42	11	3	7	39	23	4	10	7	25	27	58
10. Arsenal	42	11	6	4	36	19	5	4	12	22	37	58
11. WBA	42	11	5	5	35	20	4	7	10	16	29	57
12. Southampton	42	11	5	5	36	22	4	7	10	18	36	57
13. Stoke C	42	13	4	4	34	21	3	5	13	19	43	57
14. Norwich C	42	10	6	5	30	18	4	6	11	22	40	54
15. Notts Co	42	12	4	5	37	25	3	3	15	18	46	52
16. Sunderland	42	7	10	4	30	22	5	4	12	18	39	50
17. Birmingham C	42	9	7	5	29	24	3	7	11	11	31	50
18. Luton T	42	7	7	7	34	33	5	6	10	31	51	49
19. Coventry C	42	10	5	6	29	17	3	4	14	19	42	48
20. Manchester C	42	9	5	7	26	23	4	3	14	21	47	47
21. Swansea C	42	10	4	7	32	29	0	7	14	19	40	41
22. Brighton & HA	42	8	7	6	25	22	1	6	14	13	46	40

DIVISION 2

		Home					Away					
	P	W	D	L	F	A	W	D	L	F	A	Pts
1. QPR	42	16	3	2	51	16	10	4	7	26	20	85
2. Wolverhampton W	42	14	5	2	42	16	6	10	5	26	28	75
3. Leicester C	42	11	4	6	36	15	9	6	6	36	29	70
4. Fulham	42	13	5	3	36	20	7	4	10	28	27	69
5. Newcastle U	42	13	6	2	43	21	5	7	9	32	32	67
6. Sheffield W	42	9	8	4	33	23	7	7	7	27	24	63
7. Oldham Ath	42	8	10	3	38	24	6	9	6	26	23	61
8. Leeds U	42	7	11	3	28	22	6	10	5	23	24	60
9. Shrewsbury T	42	8	9	4	20	15	7	5	9	28	33	59
10. Barnsley	42	9	8	4	37	28	5	7	9	20	27	57
11. Blackburn R	42	11	7	3	38	21	4	5	12	20	37	57
12. Cambridge U	42	11	7	3	26	17	2	5	14	16	43	51
13. Derby Co	42	7	10	4	27	24	3	9	9	22	34	49
14. Carlisle U	42	10	6	5	44	28	2	6	13	24	42	48
15. Crystal Palace	42	11	7	3	31	17	1	5	15	12	35	48
16. Middlesbrough	42	8	7	6	27	29	3	8	10	19	38	48
18. Charlton Ath	42	11	3	7	40	31	2	6	13	23	55	48
18. Chelsea	42	8	8	5	31	22	3	6	12	20	39	47
19. Grimsby T	42	9	7	5	32	26	3	4	14	13	44	47
20. Rotherham U	42	6	7	8	22	29	4	8	9	23	39	45
21. Burnley	42	10	4	7	38	24	2	4	15	18	42	44
22. Bolton W	42	10	2	9	30	26	1	9	11	12	35	44

DIVISION 3

	Home						Away					
	P	W	D	L	F	A	W	D	L	F	A	Pts
1. Portsmouth	46	16	4	3	43	19	11	6	6	31	22	91
2. Cardiff C	46	17	5	1	45	14	8	6	9	31	36	86
3. Huddersfield T	46	15	8	0	56	18	8	5	10	28	31	82
4. Newport Co	46	13	7	3	40	20	10	2	11	36	34	78
5. Oxford U	46	12	9	2	41	23	10	3	10	30	30	78
6. Lincoln C	46	17	1	5	55	22	6	6	11	22	29	76
7. Bristol R	46	16	4	3	55	21	6	5	12	29	37	75
8. Plymouth Arg	46	15	2	6	37	23	4	6	13	24	43	65
9. Brentford	46	14	4	5	50	28	4	6	13	38	49	64
10. Walsall	46	14	5	4	38	19	3	8	12	26	44	64
11. Sheffield U	46	16	3	4	44	20	3	4	16	18	44	64
12. Bradford C	46	11	7	5	41	27	5	6	12	27	42	61
13. Gillingham	46	12	4	7	37	29	4	9	10	21	30	61
14. AFC Bournemouth	46	11	7	5	35	20	5	6	12	24	48	61
15. Southend U	46	10	8	5	41	28	5	6	12	25	37	59
16. Preston NE	46	11	10	2	35	17	4	3	16	25	52	58
17. Millwall	46	12	7	4	41	24	2	6	15	23	53	55
18. Wigan Ath	46	10	4	9	35	33	5	5	13	25	39	54
19. Exeter C	46	12	4	7	49	43	2	8	13	32	61	54
20. Orient	46	10	6	7	44	38	5	3	15	20	50	54
21. Reading	46	10	8	5	37	28	2	9	12	27	51	53
22. Wrexham	46	11	6	6	40	26	1	9	13	16	50	51
23. Doncaster R	46	6	8	9	38	44	3	3	17	19	53	38
24. Chesterfield	46	6	6	11	28	28	2	7	14	15	40	37

DIVISION 4

	Home						Away					
	P	W	D	L	F	A	W	D	L	F	A	Pts
1. Wimbledon	46	17	4	2	57	23	12	7	4	39	22	98
2. Hull C	46	14	8	1	48	14	11	7	5	27	20	90
3. Port Vale	46	15	4	4	37	16	11	6	6	30	18	88
4. Scunthorpe U	46	13	7	3	41	17	10	7	6	30	25	83
5. Bury	46	15	4	4	43	20	8	8	7	31	26	81
6. Colchester U	46	17	5	1	51	19	7	4	12	24	36	81
7. York C	46	18	4	1	59	19	4	9	10	29	39	79
8. Swindon T	46	14	3	6	45	27	5	8	10	16	27	68
9. Peterborough U	46	13	6	4	38	23	4	7	12	20	29	64
10. Mansfield T	46	11	6	6	32	26	5	7	11	29	44	61
11. Halifax T	46	9	8	6	31	23	7	4	12	28	43	60
12. Torquay U	46	12	3	8	38	30	5	4	14	18	35	58
13. Chester	46	8	6	9	28	24	7	5	11	27	36	56
14. Bristol C	46	10	8	5	32	25	3	9	11	27	45	56
15. Northampton T	46	10	8	5	43	29	4	4	15	22	46	54
16. Stockport Co	46	11	8	4	41	31	3	4	16	19	48	54
17. Darlington	46	8	5	10	27	30	5	8	10	34	41	52
18. Aldershot	46	11	5	7	40	35	1	10	12	21	47	51
19. Tranmere R	46	8	8	7	30	29	5	3	15	19	42	50
20. Rochdale	46	11	8	4	38	25	0	8	15	17	48	49
21. Blackpool	46	10	8	5	32	23	3	4	16	23	51	49
22. Hartlepool U	46	11	5	7	30	24	2	4	17	16	52	48
23. Crewe Alex	46	9	5	9	35	32	2	3	18	18	39	41
24. Hereford U	46	8	6	9	19	23	3	2	18	23	56	41

FOOTBALL LEAGUE 1888–89 to 1982–83

FOOTBALL LEAGUE

	First	*Pts*	*Second*	*Pts*	*Third*	*Pts*
1888–89*a*	Preston NE	40	Aston Villa	29	Wolverhampton W	28
1889–90*a*	Preston NE	33	Everton	31	Blackburn R	27
1890–91*a*	Everton	29	Preston NE	27	Notts Co	26
1891–92*b*	Sunderland	42	Preston NE	37	Bolton W	36

FIRST DIVISION

Maximum points:a 44; *b* 52; *c* 60; *d* 68; *e* 76; *f* 84; *g* 126.

1892–93*c*	Sunderland	48	Preston NE	37	Everton	36
1893–94*c*	Aston Villa	44	Sunderland	38	Derby Co	36
1894–95*c*	Sunderland	47	Everton	42	Aston Villa	39
1895–96*c*	Aston Villa	45	Derby Co	41	Everton	39
1896–97*c*	Aston Villa	47	Sheffield U	36	Derby Co	36
1897–98*c*	Sheffield U	42	Sunderland	37	Wolverhampton W	35
1898–99*d*	Aston Villa	45	Liverpool	43	Burnley	39
1899–1900*d*	Aston Villa	50	Sheffield U	48	Sunderland	41
1900–01*d*	Liverpool	45	Sunderland	43	Notts Co	40
1901–02*d*	Sunderland	44	Everton	41	Newcastle U	37
1902–03*d*	The Wednesday	42	Aston Villa	41	Sunderland	41
1903–04*d*	The Wednesday	47	Manchester C	44	Everton	43
1904–05*d*	Newcastle U	48	Everton	47	Manchester C	46
1905–06*e*	Liverpool	51	Preston NE	47	The Wednesday	44
1906–07*e*	Newcastle U	51	Bristol C	48	Everton	45
1907–08*e*	Manchester U	52	Aston Villa	43	Manchester C	43
1908–09*e*	Newcastle U	53	Everton	46	Sunderland	44
1909–10*e*	Aston Villa	53	Liverpool	48	Blackburn R	45
1910–11*e*	Manchester U	52	Aston Villa	51	Sunderland	45
1911–12*e*	Blackburn R	49	Everton	46	Newcastle U	44
1912–13*e*	Sunderland	54	Aston Villa	50	Sheffield W	49
1913–14*e*	Blackburn R	51	Aston Villa	44	Middlesbrough	43
1914–15*e*	Everton	46	Oldham Ath	45	Blackburn R	43
1919–20*f*	WBA	60	Burnley	51	Chelsea	49
1920–21*f*	Burnley	59	Manchester C	54	Bolton W	52
1921–22*f*	Liverpool	57	Tottenham H	51	Burnley	49
1922-23*f*	Liverpool	60	Sunderland	54	Huddersfield T	53
1923–24*f*	Huddersfield T*	57	Cardiff C	57	Sunderland	53
1924–25*f*	Huddersfield T	58	WBA	56	Bolton W	55
1925–26*f*	Huddersfield T	57	Arsenal	52	Sunderland	48
1926–27*f*	Newcastle U	56	Huddersfield T	51	Sunderland	49
1927–28*f*	Everton	53	Huddersfield T	51	Leicester C	48
1928–29*f*	Sheffield W	52	Leicester C	51	Aston Villa	50
1929–30*f*	Sheffield W	60	Derby Co	50	Manchester C	47
1930–31*f*	Arsenal	66	Aston Villa	59	Sheffield W	52
1931–32*f*	Everton	56	Arsenal	54	Sheffield W	50
1932–33*f*	Arsenal	58	Aston Villa	54	Sheffield W	51
1933–34*f*	Arsenal	59	Huddersfield T	56	Tottenham H	49
1934–35*f*	Arsenal	58	Sunderland	54	Sheffield W	49
1935–36*f*	Sunderland	56	Derby Co	48	Huddersfield T	48
1936–37*f*	Manchester C	57	Charlton Ath	54	Arsenal	52
1937–38*f*	Arsenal	52	Wolverhampton W	51	Preston NE	49
1938–39*f*	Everton	59	Wolverhampton W	55	Charlton Ath	50
1946–47*f*	Liverpool	57	Manchester U	56	Wolverhampton W	56
1947–48*f*	Arsenal	59	Manchester U	52	Burnley	52
1948–49*f*	Portsmouth	58	Manchester U	53	Derby Co	53
1949–50*f*	Portsmouth*	53	Wolverhampton W	53	Sunderland	52
1950–51*f*	Tottenham H	60	Manchester U	56	Blackpool	50
1951–52*f*	Manchester U	57	Tottenham H	53	Arsenal	53
1952–53*f*	Arsenal*	54	Preston NE	54	Wolverhampton W	51
1953–54*f*	Wolverhampton W	57	WBA	53	Huddersfield T	51
1954–55*f*	Chelsea	52	Wolverhampton W	48	Portsmouth	48
1955–56*f*	Manchester U	60	Blackpool	49	Wolverhampton W	49
1956–57*f*	Manchester U	64	Tottenham H	56	Preston NE	56
1957–58*f*	Wolverhampton W	64	Preston NE	59	Tottenham H	51
1958–59*f*	Wolverhampton W	61	Manchester U	55	Arsenal	50

* *Won on goal average.*

	First	Pts	Second	Pts	Third	Pts
1959–60*f*	Burnley	55	Wolverhampton W	54	Tottenham H	53
1960–61*f*	Tottenham H	66	Sheffield W	58	Wolverhampton W	57
1961–62*f*	Ipswich T	56	Burnley	53	Tottenham H	52
1962–63*f*	Everton	61	Tottenham H	55	Burnley	54
1963–64*f*	Liverpool	57	Manchester U	53	Everton	52
1964–65*f*	Manchester U*	61	Leeds U	61	Chelsea	56
1965–66*f*	Liverpool	61	Leeds U	55	Burnley	55
1966–67*f*	Manchester U	60	Nottingham F	56	Tottenham H	56
1967–68*f*	Manchester C	58	Manchester U	56	Liverpool	55
1968–69*f*	Leeds U	67	Liverpool	61	Everton	57
1969–70*f*	Everton	66	Leeds U	57	Chelsea	55
1970–71*f*	Arsenal	65	Leeds U	64	Tottenham H	52
1971–72*f*	Derby Co	58	Leeds U	57	Liverpool	57
1972–73*f*	Liverpool	60	Arsenal	57	Leeds U	53
1973–74*f*	Leeds U	62	Liverpool	57	Derby Co	48
1974–75*f*	Derby Co	53	Liverpool	51	Ipswich T	57
1975–76*f*	Liverpool	60	QPR	59	Manchester U	56
1976–77*f*	Liverpool	57	Manchester C	56	Ipswich T	52
1977–78*f*	Nottingham F	64	Liverpool	57	Everton	55
1978–79*f*	Liverpool	68	Nottingham F	60	WBA	59
1979–80*f*	Liverpool	60	Manchester U	58	Ipswich T	53
1980–81*f*	Aston Villa	60	Ipswich T	56	Arsenal	53
1981–82*g*	Liverpool	87	Ipswich T	83	Manchester U	78
1982–83*g*	Liverpool	82	Watford	71	Manchester U	70

No competition during 1915–19 and 1939–46.

SECOND DIVISION

Maximum points: a 44; *b* 56; *c* 60; *d* 68; *e* 76; *f* 84; *g* 126.

	First	Pts	Second	Pts	Third	Pts
1892–93*a*	Small Heath	36	Sheffield U	35	Darwen	30
1893–94*b*	Liverpool	50	Small Heath	42	Notts Co	39
1894–95*c*	Bury	48	Notts Co	39	Newton Heath	38
1895–96*c*	Liverpool*	46	Manchester C	46	Grimsby T	42
1896–97*c*	Notts Co	42	Newton Heath	39	Grimsby T	38
1897–98*c*	Burnley	48	Newcastle U	45	Manchester C	39
1898–99*d*	Manchester C	52	Glossop NE	46	Leicester Fosse	45
1899–1900*d*	The Wednesday	54	Bolton W	52	Small Heath	46
1900–01*d*	Grimsby T	49	Small Heath	48	Burnley	44
1901–02*d*	WBA	55	Middlesbrough	51	Preston NE	42
1902–03*d*	Manchester C	54	Small Heath	51	Woolwich A	48
1903–04*d*	Preston NE	50	Woolwich A	49	Manchester U	48
1904–05*d*	Liverpool	58	Bolton W	56	Manchester U	53
1905–06*e*	Bristol C	66	Manchester U	62	Chelsea	53
1906–07*e*	Nottingham F	60	Chelsea	57	Leicester Fosse	48
1907–08*e*	Bradford C	54	Leicester Fosse	52	Oldham Ath	50
1908–09*e*	Bolton W	52	Tottenham H*	51	WBA	51
1909–10*e*	Manchester C	54	Oldham Ath*	53	Hull C	53
1910–11*e*	WBA	53	Bolton W	51	Chelsea	49
1911–12*e*	Derby Co*	54	Chelsea	54	Burnley	52
1912–13*e*	Preston NE	53	Burnley	50	Birmingham	46
1913–14*e*	Notts Co	53	Bradford PA	49	Woolwich A	49
1914–15*e*	Derby Co	53	Preston NE	50	Barnsley	47
1919–20*f*	Tottenham H	70	Huddersfield T	64	Birmingham	56
1920–21*f*	Birmingham*	58	Cardiff C	58	Bristol C	51
1921–22*f*	Nottingham F	56	Stoke C	52	Barnsley	52
1922–23*f*	Notts Co	53	West Ham U*	51	Leicester C	51
1923–24*f*	Leeds U	54	Bury*	51	Derby Co	51
1924–25*f*	Leicester C	59	Manchester U	57	Derby Co	55
1925–26*f*	Sheffield W	60	Derby Co	57	Chelsea	52
1926–27*f*	Middlesbrough	62	Portsmouth*	54	Manchester C	54
1927–28*f*	Manchester C	59	Leeds U	57	Chelsea	54
1928–29*f*	Middlesbrough	55	Grimsby T	53	Bradford	48
1929–30*f*	Blackpool	58	Chelsea	55	Oldham Ath	53
1930–31*f*	Everton	61	WBA	54	Tottenham H	51
1931–32*f*	Wolverhampton W	56	Leeds U	54	Stoke C	52
1932–33*f*	Stoke C	56	Tottenham H	55	Fulham	50
1933–34*f*	Grimsby T	59	Preston NE	52	Bolton W	51
1934–35*f*	Brentford	61	Bolton W*	56	West Ham U	56
1935–36*f*	Manchester U	56	Charlton Ath	55	Sheffield U	52
1936–37*f*	Leicester C	56	Blackpool	55	Bury	52

* *Won on goal average.*

	First	Pts	Second	Pts	Third	Pts
1937–38*f*	Aston Villa	57	Manchester U*	53	Sheffield U	53
1938–39*f*	Blackburn R	55	Sheffield U	54	Sheffield W	53
1946–47*f*	Manchester C	62	Burnley	58	Birmingham C	55
1947–48*f*	Birmingham C	59	Newcastle U	56	Southampton	52
1948–49*f*	Fulham	57	WBA	56	Southampton	55
1949–50*f*	Tottenham H	61	Sheffield W*	52	Sheffield U	52
1950–51*f*	Preston NE	57	Manchester C	52	Cardiff C	50
1951–52*f*	Sheffield W	53	Cardiff C*	51	Birmingham C	51
1952–53*f*	Sheffield U	60	Huddersfield T	58	Luton T	52
1953–54*f*	Leicester C*	56	Everton	56	Blackburn R	55
1954–55*f*	Birmingham C*	54	Luton T*	54	Rotherham U	54
1955–56*f*	Sheffield W	55	Leeds U	52	Liverpool	48
1956–57*f*	Leicester C	61	Nottingham F	54	Liverpool	53
1957–58*f*	West Ham U	57	Blackburn R	56	Charlton Ath	55
1958–59*f*	Sheffield W	62	Fulham	60	Sheffield U	53
1959–60*f*	Aston Villa	59	Cardiff C	58	Liverpool	50
1960–61*f*	Ipswich T	59	Sheffield U	58	Liverpool	52
1961–62*f*	Liverpool	62	Leyton O	54	Sunderland	53
1962–63*f*	Stoke C	53	Chelsea*	52	Sunderland	52
1963–64*f*	Leeds U	63	Sunderland	61	Preston NE	56
1964–65*f*	Newcastle U	57	Northampton T	56	Bolton W	50
1965–66*f*	Manchester C	59	Southampton	54	Coventry C	53
1966–67*f*	Coventry C	59	Wolverhampton W	58	Carlisle U	52
1967–68*f*	Ipswich T	59	QPR*	58	Blackpool	58
1968–69*f*	Derby Co	63	Crystal Palace	56	Charlton Ath	50
1969–70*f*	Huddersfield T	60	Blackpool	53	Leicester C	51
1970–71*f*	Leicester C	59	Sheffield U	56	Cardiff C	53
1971–72*f*	Norwich C	57	Birmingham C	56	Millwall	55
1972–73*f*	Burnley	62	QPR	61	Aston Villa	50
1973–74*f*	Middlesbrough	65	Luton T	50	Carlisle U	49
1974–75*f*	Manchester U	61	Aston Villa	58	Norwich C	53
1975–76*f*	Sunderland	56	Bristol C	53	WBA	53
1976–77*f*	Wolverhampton W	57	Chelsea	55	Nottingham F	52
1977–78*f*	Bolton W	58	Southampton	57	Tottenham H	56
1978–79*f*	Crystal Palace	57	Brighton	56	Stoke C	56
1979–80*f*	Leicester C	55	Sunderland	54	Birmingham C	53
1980–81*f*	West Ham U	66	Notts Co	53	Swansea C*	50
1981–82*g*	Luton T	88	Watford	80	Norwich C	71
1982–83*g*	QPR	85	Wolverhampton W	75	Leicester C	70

No competition during 1915–19 and 1939–46.

THIRD DIVISION

Maximum points: 92; 138† from 1981–82

	First	Pts	Second	Pts	Third	Pts
1958–59	Plymouth Arg	62	Hull C	61	Brentford	57
1959–60	Southampton	61	Norwich C	59	Shrewsbury T	52
1960–61	Bury	68	Walsall	62	QPR	60
1961–62	Portsmouth	65	Grimsby T	62	Bournemouth	59
1962–63	Northampton T	62	Swindon T	58	Port Vale	54
1963–64	Coventry C*	60	Crystal Palace	60	Watford	58
1964–65	Carlisle U	60	Bristol C*	59	Mansfield T	59
1965–66	Hull C	69	Millwall	65	QPR	57
1966–67	QPR	67	Middlesbrough	55	Watford	54
1967–68	Oxford U	57	Bury	56	Shrewsbury T	55
1968–69	Watford*	64	Swindon T	64	Luton T	61
1969–70	Orient	62	Luton T	60	Bristol R	56
1970–71	Preston NE	61	Fulham	60	Halifax T	56
1971–72	Aston Villa	70	Brighton	65	Bournemouth	62
1972–73	Bolton W	61	Notts Co	57	Blackburn R	55
1973–74	Oldham Ath	62	Bristol R	61	York C	61
1974–75	Blackburn R	60	Plymouth Arg	59	Charlton Ath	55
1975–76	Hereford U	63	Cardiff C	57	Millwall	56
1976–77	Mansfield T	64	Brighton & HA	61	Crystal Palace	59
1977–78	Wrexham	61	Cambridge U	58	Preston NE	56
1978–79	Shrewsbury T	61	Watford	60	Swansea C	60
1979–80	Grimsby T	62	Blackburn R	59	Sheffield W	58
1980–81	Rotherham U	61	Barnsley*	59	Charlton Ath	59
1981–82†	Burnley*	80	Carlisle U	80	Fulham	78
1982–83†	Portsmouth	91	Cardiff C	86	Huddersfield T	82

**Won on goal average/goal difference.*

FOURTH DIVISION

Maximum points: 92; 138‡ from 1981–82

	First	Pts	Second	Pts	Third	Pts	Fourth	Pts
1958–59	Port Vale	64	Coventry C	60	York C	60	Shrewsbury T	58
1959–60	Walsall	65	Notts Co	60	Torquay U	60	Watford	57
1960–61	Peterborough U	66	Crystal Palace	64	Northampton T	60	Bradford PA	60
1961–62†	Millwall	56	Colchester U	55	Wrexham	53	Carlisle U	52
1962–63	Brentford	62	Oldham Ath	59	Crewe Alex	59	Mansfield T	57
1963–64	Gillingham*	60	Carlisle U	60	Workington T	59	Exeter C	58
1964–65	Brighton	63	Millwall	62	York C	62	Oxford U	61
1965–66	Doncaster R*	59	Darlington	59	Torquay U	58	Colchester U	56
1966–67	Stockport Co	64	Southport	59	Barrow	59	Tranmere R	58
1967–68	Luton T	66	Barnsley	61	Hartlepools U	60	Crewe Alex	58
1968–69	Doncaster R	59	Halifax T	57	Rochdale	56	Bradford C	56
1969–70	Chesterfield	64	Wrexham	61	Swansea C	60	Port Vale	59
1970–71	Notts Co	69	Bournemouth	60	Oldham Ath	59	York C	56
1971–72	Grimsby T	63	Southend U	60	Brentford	59	Scunthorpe U	57
1972–73	Southport	62	Hereford U	58	Cambridge U	57	Aldershot*	56
1973–74	Peterborough U	65	Gillingham	62	Colchester U	60	Bury	59
1974–75	Mansfield T	68	Shrewsbury T	62	Rotherham U	59	Chester	57
1975–76	Lincoln C	74	Northampton T	68	Reading	60	Tranmere R	58
1976–77	Cambridge U	65	Exeter C	62	Colchester U	59	Bradford C	59
1977–78	Watford	71	Southend U	60	Swansea C	56	Brentford	56
1978–79	Reading	65	Grimsby T	61	Wimbledon	61	Barnsley	61
1979–80	Huddersfield T	66	Walsall	64	Newport Co	61	Portsmouth	60
1980–81	Southend U	67	Lincoln C	65	Doncaster R	56	Wimbledon	55
1981–82‡	Sheffield U	96	Bradford C*	91	Wigan Ath	91	AFC Bournemouth	88
1982–83‡	Wimbledon	98	Hull C	90	Port Vale	88	Scunthorpe U	83

†*Maximum points:* 88 owing to Accrington Stanley's resignation.

THIRD DIVISION—SOUTH (1921–1958)

Maximum points: a 84; *b* 76; *c* 80; *d* 92.

	First	Pts	Second	Pts	Third	Pts
1920–21*a*	Crystal Palace	59	Southampton	54	QPR	53
1921–22*a*	Southampton*	61	Plymouth Arg	61	Portsmouth	53
1922–23*a*	Bristol C	59	Plymouth Arg	53	Swansea T	53
1923–24*a*	Portsmouth	59	Plymouth Arg	55	Millwall	54
1924–25*a*	Swansea T	57	Plymouth Arg	56	Bristol C	53
1925–26*a*	Reading	57	Plymouth Arg	56	Millwall	53
1926–27*a*	Bristol C	62	Plymouth Arg	60	Millwall	56
1927–28*a*	Millwall	65	Northampton T	55	Plymouth Arg	53
1928–29*a*	Charlton Ath*	54	Crystal Palace	54	Northampton T	52
1929–30*a*	Plymouth Arg	68	Brentford	61	QPR	51
1930–31*a*	Notts Co	59	Crystal Palace	51	Brentford	50
1931–32*a*	Fulham	57	Reading	55	Southend U	53
1932–33*a*	Brentford	62	Exeter C	58	Norwich C	57
1933–34*a*	Norwich C	61	Coventry C	54	Reading	54
1934–35*a*	Charlton Ath	61	Reading	53	Coventry C	51
1935–36*a*	Coventry C	57	Luton T	56	Reading	54
1936–37*a*	Luton T	58	Notts Co	56	Brighton	53
1937–38*a*	Millwall	56	Bristol C	55	QPR	53
1938–39*a*	Newport Co	55	Crystal Palace	52	Brighton	49
1939–46	Competition cancelled owing to war.					
1946–47*a*	Cardiff C	66	QPR	57	Bristol C	51
1947–48*a*	QPR	61	Bournemouth	57	Walsall	51
1948–49*a*	Swansea T	62	Reading	55	Bournemouth	52
1949–50*a*	Notts Co	58	Northampton T	51	Southend U	51
1950–51*d*	Nottingham F	70	Norwich C	64	Reading	57
1951–52*d*	Plymouth Arg	66	Reading	61	Norwich C	61
1952–53*d*	Bristol R	64	Millwall	62	Northampton T	62
1953–54*d*	Ipswich T	64	Brighton	61	Bristol C	56
1954–55*d*	Bristol C	70	Leyton O	61	Southampton	59
1955–56*d*	Leyton O	66	Brighton	65	Ipswich T	64
1956–57*d*	Ipswich T*	59	Torquay U	59	Colchester U	58
1957–58*d*	Brighton	60	Brentford	58	Plymouth Arg	58

* *Won on goal average/goal difference.*

THIRD DIVISION—NORTH (1921–1958)

Maximum points: a 84; b 76; c 80; d 92.

	First	*Pts*	*Second*	*Pts*	*Third*	*Pts*
1921–22*b*	Stockport Co	56	Darlington	50	Grimsby T	50
1922–23*b*	Nelson	51	Bradford PA	47	Walsall	46
1923–24*a*	Wolverhampton W	63	Rochdale	62	Chesterfield	54
1924–25*a*	Darlington	58	Nelson	53	New Brighton	53
1925–26*a*	Grimsby T	61	Bradford PA	60	Rochdale	59
1926–27*a*	Stoke C	63	Rochdale	58	Bradford PA	55
1927–28*a*	Bradford PA	63	Lincoln C	55	Stockport Co	54
1928–29*a*	Bradford C	63	Stockport Co	62	Wrexham	52
1929–30*a*	Port Vale	67	Stockport Co	63	Darlington	50
1930–31*a*	Chesterfield	58	Lincoln C	57	Wrexham	54
1931–32*c*	Lincoln C*	57	Gateshead	57	Chester	50
1932–33*a*	Hull C	59	Wrexham	57	Stockport Co	54
1933–34*a*	Barnsley	62	Chesterfield	61	Stockport Co	59
1934–35*a*	Doncaster R	57	Halifax T	55	Chester	54
1935–36*a*	Chesterfield	60	Chester	55	Tranmere R	55
1936–37*a*	Stockport Co	60	Lincoln C	57	Chester	53
1937–38*a*	Tranmere R	56	Doncaster R	54	Hull C	53
1938–39*a*	Barnsley	67	Doncaster R	56	Bradford C	52
1939–46	Competition cancelled owing to war.					
1946–47*a*	Doncaster R	72	Rotherham U	64	Chester	56
1947–48*a*	Lincoln C	60	Rotherham U	59	Wrexham	50
1948–49*a*	Hull C	65	Rotherham U	62	Doncaster R	50
1949–50*a*	Doncaster R	55	Gateshead	53	Rochdale	51
1950–51*d*	Rotherham U	71	Mansfield T	64	Carlisle U	62
1951–52*d*	Lincoln C	69	Grimsby T	66	Stockport Co	59
1952–53*d*	Oldham Ath	59	Port Vale	58	Wrexham	56
1953–54*d*	Port Vale	69	Barnsley	58	Scunthorpe U	57
1954–55*d*	Barnsley	65	Accrington S	61	Scunthorpe U	58
1955–56*d*	Grimsby T	68	Derby Co	63	Accrington S	59
1956–57*d*	Derby Co	63	Hartlepools U	59	Accrington S	58
1957–58*d*	Scunthorpe U	66	Accrington S	59	Bradford C	57

* *Won on goal average.*

LEAGUE TITLE WINS

LEAGUE DIVISION 1 – Liverpool 14, Arsenal 8, Manchester U 7, Everton 7, Aston Villa 7, Sunderland 6, Newcastle U 4, Sheffield W 4, Huddersfield T 3, Wolverhampton W 3, Blackburn R 2, Portsmouth 2, Preston NE 2, Burnley 2, Manchester C 2, Tottenham H 2, Leeds U 2, Derby Co 2, Chelsea 1, Sheffield U 1, WBA 1, Ipswich T 1, Nottingham F 1.

LEAGUE DIVISION 2 – Leicester C 6, Manchester C 6, Sheffield W 5, Birmingham C (one as Small Heath) 4, Liverpool 4, Notts Co 3, Preston NE 3, Derby Co 3, Middlesbrough 3, Grimsby T 2, Nottingham F 2, Tottenham H 2, WBA 2, Aston Villa 2, Stoke C 2, Leeds U 2, Ipswich T 2, Burnley 2, Manchester U 2, West Ham U 2, Wolverhampton W 2, Bolton W 2, Huddersfield T 1, Bristol C 1, Brentford 1, Bury 1, Bradford C 1, Everton 1, Fulham 1, Sheffield U 1, Newcastle U 1, Coventry C 1, Blackpool 1, Blackburn R 1, Norwich C 1, Sunderland 1, Crystal Palace 1, Luton T 1, QPR 1.

LEAGUE DIVISION 3 – Portsmouth 2, Plymouth Arg, Southampton, Bury, Northampton T, Coventry C, Carlisle U, Hull C, QPR, Oxford U, Watford, Leyton O, Preston NE, Aston Villa, Bolton W, Oldham Ath, Blackburn R, Hereford U, Mansfield T, Wrexham, Shrewsbury T, Grimsby T, Rotherham U, Burnley 1 each.

LEAGUE DIVISION 4 – Doncaster R 2, Peterborough U 2; Port Vale, Walsall, Millwall, Brentford, Gillingham, Brighton, Stockport Co, Luton T, Chesterfield, Notts Co, Grimsby T, Southport, Mansfield T, Lincoln C, Cambridge U, Watford, Reading, Huddersfield T, Southend U, Sheffield U, Wimbledon 1 each.

To 1957–58

DIVISION 3 (South) – Bristol C 3; Charlton Ath, Ipswich T, Millwall, Notts Co, Plymouth Arg, Swansea T 2; Brentford, Bristol R, Cardiff C, Crystal Palace, Coventry C, Fulham, Leyton O, Luton T, Newport Co, Nottingham F, Norwich C, Portsmouth, QPR, Reading, Southampton, Brighton 1.

DIVISION 3 (North) – Barnsley, Doncaster R, Lincoln C 3; Chesterfield, Grimsby T, Hull C, Port Vale, Stockport Co 2; Bradford PA, Bradford C, Darlington, Derby Co, Nelson, Oldham Ath, Rotherham U, Stoke C, Tranmere R, Wolverhampton W, Scunthorpe U 1.

RELEGATED CLUBS

1891–92 League extended. Newton Heath, Sheffield W and Nottingham F admitted. *Second Division formed* including Darwen.

1892–93 In Test matches, Sheffield U and Darwen won promotion in place of Notts Co and Accrington S.

1893–94 In Tests, Liverpool and Small Heath won promotion. Newton Heath and Darwen relegated.

1894–95 After Tests, Bury promoted, Liverpool relegated.

1895–96 After Tests, Liverpool promoted, Small Heath relegated.

1896–97 After Tests, Notts Co promoted, Burnley relegated.

1897–98 Test system abolished after success of Stoke C and Burnley. League extended. Blackburn R and Newcastle U elected to First Division. *Automatic promotion and relegation introduced.*

DIVISION 1 TO DIVISION 2

1898–99 Bolton W and Sheffield W
1899–1900 Burnley and Glossop
1900–01 Preston NE and WBA
1901–02 Small Heath and Manchester C
1902–03 Grimsby T and Bolton W
1903–04 Liverpool and WBA
1904–05 League extended. Bury and Notts Co, two bottom clubs in First Division, re-elected.
1905–06 Nottingham F and Wolverhampton W
1906–07 Derby Co and Stoke C
1907–08 Bolton W and Birmingham C
1908–09 Manchester C and Leicester Fosse
1909–10 Bolton W and Chelsea
1910–11 Bristol C and Nottingham F
1911–12 Preston NE and Bury
1912–13 Notts Co and Woolwich Arsenal
1913–14 Preston NE and Derby Co
1914–15 Tottenham H and Chelsea*
1919–20 Notts Co and Sheffield W
1920–21 Derby Co and Bradford
1921–22 Bradford C and Manchester U
1922–23 Stoke C and Oldham Ath
1923–24 Chelsea and Middlesbrough
1924–25 Preston NE and Nottingham F
1925–26 Manchester C and Notts Co
1926–27 Leeds U and WBA
1927–28 Tottenham H and Middlesbrough
1928–29 Bury and Cardiff C
1929–30 Burnley and Everton
1930–31 Leeds U and Manchester U
1931–32 Grimsby T and West Ham U
1932–33 Bolton W and Blackpool
1933–34 Newcastle U and Sheffield U
1934–35 Leicester C and Tottenham H
1935–36 Aston Villa and Blackburn R
1936–37 Manchester U and Sheffield W
1937–38 Manchester C and WBA
1938–39 Birmingham C and Leicester C
1946–47 Brentford and Leeds U
1947–48 Blackburn R and Grimsby T
1948–49 Preston NE and Sheffield U
1949–50 Manchester C and Birmingham C
1950–51 Sheffield W and Everton
1951–52 Huddersfield and Fulham
1952–53 Stoke C and Derby Co
1953–54 Middlesbrough and Liverpool
1954–55 Leicester C and Sheffield W
1955–56 Huddersfield and Sheffield U
1956–57 Charlton Ath and Cardiff C
1957–58 Sheffield W and Sunderland
1958–59 Portsmouth and Aston Villa
1959–60 Luton T and Leeds U
1960–61 Preston NE and Newcastle U
1961–62 Chelsea and Cardiff C
1962–63 Manchester C and Leyton O
1963–64 Bolton W and Ipswich T
1964–65 Wolverhampton W and Birmingham C
1965–66 Northampton T and Blackburn R
1966–67 Aston Villa and Blackpool
1967–68 Fulham and Sheffield U
1968–69 Leicester C and QPR
1969–70 Sunderland and Sheffield W
1970–71 Burnley and Blackpool
1971–72 Huddersfield T and Nottingham F
1972–73 Crystal Palace and WBA
1973–74 Southampton, Manchester U, Norwich C
1974–75 Luton T, Chelsea, Carlisle U
1975–76 Wolverhampton W, Burnley, Sheffield U
1976–77 Sunderland, Stoke C, Tottenham H
1977–78 West Ham U, Newcastle U, Leicester C
1978–79 QPR, Birmingham C, Chelsea
1979–80 Bristol C, Derby Co, Bolton W
1980–81 Norwich C, Leicester C, Crystal Palace
1981–82 Leeds U, Wolverhampton W, Middlesbrough
1982–83 Manchester C, Swansea C, Brighton & HA

*Subsequently re-elected to Division 1 when League was extended after the War.

DIVISION 2 TO DIVISION 3

1920–21 Stockport Co
1921–22 Bradford and Bristol C
1922–23 Rotherham C and Wolverhampton W
1923–24 Nelson and Bristol C
1924–25 Crystal Palace and Coventry C
1925–26 Stoke C and Stockport Co
1926–27 Darlington and Bradford C
1927–28 Fulham and South Shields
1928–29 Port Vale and Clapton O
1929–30 Hull C and Notts Co
1930–31 Reading and Cardiff C
1931–32 Barnsley and Bristol C
1932–33 Chesterfield and Charlton Ath
1933–34 Millwall and Lincoln C
1934–35 Oldham Ath and Notts Co
1935–36 Port Vale and Hull C
1936–37 Doncaster R and Bradford C
1937–38 Barnsley and Stockport Co
1938–39 Norwich C and Tranmere R
1946–47 Swansea T and Newport Co
1947–48 Doncaster R and Millwall
1948–49 Nottingham F and Lincoln C
1949–50 Plymouth Arg and Bradford
1950–51 Grimsby T and Chesterfield
1951–52 Coventry C and QPR
1952–53 Southampton and Barnsley
1953–54 Brentford and Oldham Ath
1954–55 Ipswich T and Derby Co
1955–56 Plymouth Arg and Hull C
1956–57 Port Vale and Bury
1957–58 Doncaster R and Notts Co
1958–59 Barnsley and Grimsby T
1959–60 Bristol C and Hull C
1960–61 Lincoln C and Portsmouth
1961–62 Brighton and Bristol R
1962–63 Walsall and Luton T
1963–64 Grimsby T and Scunthorpe U
1964–65 Swindon T and Swansea T
1965–66 Middlesbrough and Leyton O
1966–67 Northampton T and Bury
1967–68 Plymouth Arg and Rotherham U
1968–69 Fulham and Bury
1969–70 Preston NE and Aston Villa
1970–71 Blackburn R and Bolton W
1971–72 Charlton Ath and Watford
1972–73 Huddersfield T and Brighton
1973–74 Crystal Palace, Preston NE, Swindon T
1974–75 Millwall, Cardiff C, Sheffield W
1975–76 Oxford U, York C, Portsmouth
1976–77 Carlisle U, Plymouth Arg, Hereford U
1977–78 Blackpool, Mansfield T, Hull C
1978–79 Sheffield U, Millwall, Blackburn R
1979–80 Fulham, Burnley, Charlton Ath
1980–81 Preston NE, Bristol C, Bristol R
1981–82 Cardiff C, Wrexham, Orient
1982–83 Rotherham U, Burnley, Bolton W

DIVISION 3 TO DIVISION 4

1958–59 Rochdale, Notts Co, Doncaster R and Stockport Co
1959–60 Accrington S, Wrexham, Mansfield T and York C
1960–61 Chesterfield, Colchester U, Bradford C and Tranmere R
1961–62 Newport Co, Brentford, Lincoln C and Torquay U
1962–63 Bradford, Brighton, Carlisle U and Halifax T
1963–64 Millwall, Crewe Alex, Wrexham and Notts Co
1964–65 Luton T, Port Vale, Colchester U and Barnsley
1965–66 Southend U, Exeter C, Brentford and York C
1966–67 Doncaster R, Workington T, Darlington and Swansea T
1967–68 Scunthorpe U, Colchester U, Grimsby T and Peterborough U (demoted)
1968–69 Oldham Ath, Crewe Alex, Hartlepool and Northampton T
1969–70 Bournemouth, Southport, Barrow, Stockport Co
1970–71 Reading, Bury, Doncaster R, Gillingham
1971–72 Mansfield T, Barnsley, Torquay U, Bradford C
1972–73 Rotherham U, Brentford, Swansea C, Scunthorpe U
1973–74 Cambridge U, Shrewsbury T, Southport, Rochdale
1974–75 AFC Bournemouth, Tranmere R, Watford, Huddersfield T
1975–76 Aldershot, Colchester U, Southend U, Halifax T
1976–77 Reading, Northampton T, Grimsby T, York C
1977–78 Port Vale, Bradford C, Hereford U, Portsmouth
1978–79 Peterborough U, Walsall, Tranmere R, Lincoln C
1979–80 Bury, Southend U, Mansfield T, Wimbledon
1980–81 Sheffield U, Colchester U, Blackpool, Hull C
1981–82 Wimbledon, Swindon T, Bristol C, Chester
1982–83 Reading, Wrexham, Doncaster R, Chesterfield

APPLICATIONS FOR RE-ELECTION

FOURTH DIVISION

Ten: Hartlepool U.
Seven: Crewe Alex
Six: Barrow (lost League place to Hereford U 1972), Southport (lost League place to Wigan Ath 1978), York C
Five: Darlington, Lincoln C, Workington (lost League place to Wimbledon 1977), Rochdale
Four: Bradford PA (lost League place to Cambridge United 1970), Chester, Halifax T, Newport Co, Stockport Co
Three: Doncaster R, Northampton T, Hereford U
Two: Bradford C, Oldham Ath, Scunthorpe U
One: Aldershot, Colchester U, Exeter C, Gateshead (lost League place to Peterborough U 1960), Grimsby T, Swansea C, Tranmere R, Wrexham, Blackpool
Accrington S resigned and Oxford U were elected 1962.
Port Vale were forced to re-apply following expulsion in 1968.

THIRD DIVISIONS NORTH & SOUTH

Seven: Walsall.
Six: Exeter C, Halifax T, Newport Co.
Five: Accrington S, Barrow, Gillingham, New Brighton, Southport.
Four: Rochdale, Norwich C.
Three: Crystal Palace, Crewe Alex, Darlington, Hartlepool, Merthyr T, Swindon T.
Two: Aberdare Ath, Aldershot, Ashington, Bournemouth, Brentford, Chester, Colchester U, Durham C, Millwall, Nelson, QPR, Rotherham U, Southend U, Tranmere R, Watford, Workington
One: Bradford C, Bradford PA, Brighton, Bristol R, Cardiff C, Carlisle U, Charlton Ath, Gateshead, Grimsby T, Mansfield T, Shrewsbury T, Torquay U, York C.

FIRST DIVISION CLUBS RECORD VICTORIES

Only one First Division club has achieved its record victory away from home and that feat was recorded by **Nottingham Forest** when they thrashed **Clapton**, one of the famous amateur clubs of the day, 14-0 in the 1890–91 season.

When **Luton Town** recorded their famous 12-0 victory over **Bristol Rovers**, a stalwart defender, Joe Payne, had only recently been drafted into their attack to 'give a little extra punch'. He just about managed that on this occasion – by scoring 10, a record individual tally in a Football League match.

Anderlecht, who provided the opposition when the 'Busby Babes' of **Manchester United** scored a record ten goals, went on to become a European power themselves, but often senior clubs set up their records against cup opposition from inferior leagues. However, **West Ham United** certainly worked hard for their two 8-0 victories, both registered in League games, against **Rotherham United** in Division Two in 'the fifties' and ten years later against **Sunderland** in Division One.

After **Crewe Alexandra** had drawn 2-2 in the Fourth Round of the F.A. Cup in 1960 they travelled down to White Hart Lane with hopes of another close battle with **Spurs**. It certainly turned out to be a day to be remembered in both club's histories – **Tottenham** won 13-2!

Arsenal	12-0	v	Loughborough Town	Div 2	12 Mar 1900
Aston Villa	13-0	v	Wednesbury Old Athletic	F.A. Cup 1st Rd.	1886
Birmingham City	12-0	v	Walsall Town Swifts	Div 2	17 Dec 1892
	12-0	v	Doncaster Rovers	Div 2	11 Apr 1903
Coventry City	9-0	v	Bristol C	Div 3 (S)	28 Apr 1934
Everton	11-2	v	Derby County	F.A. Cup 1st Rd.	1889–90
Ipswich Town	10-0	v	Floriana (Malta)	Euro. Cup 1st Rd.	25 Sept 1962
Leicester City	10-0	v	Portsmouth	Div 1	20 Oct 1928
Liverpool	11-0	v	Stromsgodset (Norway)	E. Cup Winners' C. 1st Rd. 1st Leg	17 Sept 1974
Luton Town	12-0	v	Bristol Rovers	Div 3 (S)	13 Apr 1936
Manchester United	10-0	v	Anderlecht (Belgium) (at Maine Rd)	Euro. Cup Pre. Rd.	26 Sept 1956
Norwich City	10-2	v	Coventry City	Div 3 (S)	15 Mar 1930
Nottingham Forest	14-0	v	Clapton (A)	F.A. Cup 1st Rd.	1890–91
Notts County	15-0	v	Thornhill United*	F.A. Cup 1st Rd.	24 Oct 1885
QPR	9-2	v	Tranmere Rovers	Div 3	3 Dec 1960
Southampton	11-0	v	Northampton Town	Southern Lge	28 Dec 1901
	11-0	v	Watford	Southern Lge	13 Dec 1902
	9-3	v	Wolverhampton W.	Div 2	8 Sept 1965
Stoke City	10-3	v	WBA	Div 1	4 Feb 1937
Sunderland	11-1	v	Fairfield	F.A. Cup 1st Rd.	1894–95
Tottenham Hotspur	13-2	v	Crewe Alexandra	F.A. Cup 4th Rd. Replay	3 Feb 1960
Watford	10-1	v	Lowestoft Town	F.A. Cup 1st Rd.	27 Nov 1926
West Bromwich Albion	12-0	v	Darwen	Div 1	4 Apr 1892
West Ham United	8-0	v	Rotherham United	Div 2	8 Mar 1958
	8-0	v	Sunderland	Div 1	19 Oct 1968
Wolverhampton Wanderers	14-0	v	Crosswell's Brewery	F.A. Cup 2nd Rd.	1886–87

All victories have been achieved by clubs playing at 'home' unless otherwise stated.

* Thornhill United became Rotherham County in 1905 and amalgamated with Rotherham Town to become Rotherham United in 1925.

FIRST DIVISION CLUBS RECORD DEFEATS

Blackburn Rovers certainly feature prominently in these records as they have inflicted no less than six record defeats spread over seven decades, with the latest in 1963 against **West Ham U**. Rovers also hold the record against **Middlesbrough** of the Second Division and **Bury** of the Fourth and their victory at West Ham is the only record defeat suffered by a club playing at home.

Considering **Liverpool**'s dominance of the First Division in recent years compared with **Birmingham City**'s constant struggle, 'The Blues' record win in 1954 may cause a few eyebrows to be raised! While it is perhaps not surprising that the least emphatic beatings received by First Division clubs are those inflicted on the consistent **Manchester United** and **Tottenham Hotspur**.

Is it a coincidence that four records have been achieved at the Christmas holiday season?

Arsenal	0-8	v	Loughborough Town	Div 2	12 Dec 1896
Aston Villa	1-8	v	Blackburn Rovers	F.A. Cup 3rd Rd.	1888–89
Birmingham City	1-9	v	Sheffield Wednesday	Div 1	13 Dec 1930
	1-9	v	Blackburn Rovers	Div 1	5 Jan 1895
Coventry City	2-10	v	Norwich City	Div 3 (S)	15 Mar 1930
Everton	4-10	v	Tottenham Hotspur	Div 1	11 Oct 1958
Ipswich Town	1-10	v	Fulham	Div 1	26 Dec 1963*
Leicester City	0-12	v	Nottingham Forest	Div 1	21 Apr 1909†
Liverpool	1-9	v	Birmingham City	Div 2	11 Dec 1954
Luton Town	0-9	v	Small Heath	Div 2	12 Nov 1898
Manchester United	0-7	v	Blackburn Rovers	Div 1	10 Apr 1926
	0-7	v	Aston Villa	Div 1	27 Dec 1930*
	0-7	v	Wolverhamton Wanderers	Div 2	26 Dec 1931*
Norwich City	2-10	v	Swindon Town	Southern Lge	5 Sept 1908
Nottingham Forest	1-9	v	Blackburn Rovers	Div 2	10 Apr 1937
Notts County	1-9	v	Blackburn Rovers	Div 1	16 Nov 1889
	1-9	v	Aston Villa	Div 1	29 Sept 1888
	1-9	v	Portsmouth	Div 2	9 Apr 1927
QPR	1-8	v	Mansfield Town	Div 3	15 Mar 1965
	1-8	v	Manchester United	Div 1	19 Mar 1969
Southampton	0-8	v	Tottenham Hotspur	Div 2	28 Mar 1936
	0-8	v	Everton	Div 1	20 Nov 1971
Stoke City	0-10	v	Preston NE	Div 1	14 Sept 1889
Sunderland	0-8	v	West Ham United	Div 1	19 Oct 1968
	0-8	v	Watford	Div 1	25 Sept 1982
Tottenham Hotspur	0-7	v	Liverpool	Div 1	2 Sept 1978
Watford	0-10	v	Wolverhampton Wanderers	F.A. Cup 1st Rd.	13 Jan 1912
	0-11	v	Southampton	Southern Lge	13 Dec 1902
West Bromwich Albion	3-10	v	Stoke City	Div 1	4 Feb 1937
West Ham United	2-8	v	Blackburn Rovers	Div 1	26 Dec 1963*
Wolverhampton Wanderers	1-10	v	Newton Heath	Div 1	15 Oct 1892

All defeats have been suffered by clubs playing away from home unless otherwise stated.

* Christmas holiday match
†As Leicester Fosse

SECOND DIVISION CLUBS: RECORD VICTORIES

Despite a sad season finished off by relegation, at least **Swansea City** had the pleasure of breaking their goalscoring record last season when they hammered the Maltese Cup Winners, **Sliema**, 12-0, in their first European cup tie of the tournament. Another Maltese club provided **Ipswich Town** with a famous victory when **Floriana** were the opposition in the European Cup in 1962.

However, the most memorable of these records could well be the 13-0 victory achieved by **Newcastle United** against **Newport County** in 1946 in front of 52,137 fans. That season 'The Magpies' average attendance was 49,336 was the best in the country; and on this particular day the club gave a new signing his first match since arriving from Bradford – his name: **Len Shackleton** – and his reaction to a debut in front of so many fanatical 'Geordies' was to score six goals! The other scorers that day were Charlie Wayman 4, Jackie Milburn 2 and Roy Bentley. What careers they all had in front of them!

Barnsley	9-0	v	Loughborough Town	Div 2	28 Jan 1899
	9-0	v	Accrington Stanley (A)	Div 3 (N)	3 Feb 1934
Blackburn Rovers	11-0	v	Rossendale United	F.A. Cup 1st Rd.	1884–85
Brighton & Hove Albion	10-1	v	Wisbech	F.A. Cup 1st Rd.	13 Nov 1965
Cambridge United	6-0	v	Darlington	Div 4	18 Sept 1971
Cardiff City	9-2	v	Thames	Div 3 (S)	6th Feb 1932
Carlisle United	8-0	v	Hartlepool United	Div 3 (N)	1 Sept 1928
	8-0	v	Scunthorpe United	Div 3 (N)	25 Dec 1952*
Charlton Athletic	8-1	v	Middlesbrough	Div 1	12 Sept 1953
Chelsea	13-0	v	Jeunesse Hautcharage	E. Cup Winners' Cup Pre. Rd.	29 Sept 1971
Crystal Palace	9-0	v	Barrow	Div 4	10 Oct 1959
Derby County	12-0	v	Finn Harps	UEFA Cup 1st Rd. 1st Leg	15 Sept 1976
Fulham	10-1	v	Ipswich Town	Div 1	26 Dec 1963*
Grimsby Town	9-2	v	Darwen	Div 2	15 Apr 1899
Huddersfield Town	10-1	v	Blackpool	Div 1	13 Dec 1930
Leeds United	10-0	v	Lyn Oslo	Euro Cup 1st Rd. 1st Leg	17 Sept 1969
Manchester City	11-3	v	Lincoln City	Div 2	23 Mar 1895
Middlesbrough	9-0	v	Brighton & Hove Albion	Div 2	23 Aug 1958†
Newcastle United	13-0	v	Newport County	Div 2	5 Oct 1946
Oldham Athletic	11-0	v	Southport	Div 4	26 Dec 1962*
Portsmouth	9-1	v	Notts County	Div 2	9 Apr 1927
Sheffield Wednesday	12-0	v	Halliwell	F.A. Cup 1st Rd.	17 Jan 1891
Shrewsbury Town	7-0	v	Swindon Town	Div 3 (S)	6 May 1955
Swansea City	12-0	v	Sliema (Malta)	E. Cup Winners' Cup 1st Rd. 1st Leg	15 Sept 1982

All victories have been achieved by clubs playing at 'home' unless otherwise stated.
* Christmas holiday match
†First day of season

SECOND DIVISION CLUBS: RECORD DEFEATS

Quite remarkably many record defeats have been suffered in the opening week of the season. Having sweated through six weeks of pre-season training, the shock of such demoralising early defeats could have been disastrous and the training staff's methods must have been under review but, of the Second Division clubs, **Brighton & Hove Albion** finished the season in 12th position, and **Leeds United** in eighteenth.

Cambridge United have spaced their record defeats out evenly, having suffered one 0-6 reverse in each Division. The latest of these was at **Chelsea** last season but they finished higher in the league than the London club.

On Christmas Day 1935 **Oldham Athletic** beat **Tranmere Rovers** 4-1; they certainly must have celebrated quite well as the return game provided the highest goal aggregate in a League match and the Merseyside club gained revenge in no uncertain manner.

Barnsley	0-9	v	Notts County	Div 2	19 Nov 1927
Blackburn Rovers	0-8	v	Arsenal	Div 1	25 Feb 1933
Brighton & Hove Albion	0-9	v	Middlesbrough	Div 2	23 Aug 1958†
Cambridge United	0-6	v	Aldershot	Div 3	13 Apr 1974
	0-6	v	Darlington	Div 4	28 Sept 1974
	0-6	v	Chelsea	Div 2	15 Jan 1983
Cardiff City	2-11	v	Sheffield United	Div 1	1 Jan 1926
Carlisle United	1-11	v	Hull City	Div 3 (N)	14 Jan 1939
Charlton Athletic	1-11	v	Aston Villa	Div 2	14 Nov 1959
Chelsea	1-8	v	Wolverhampton Wanderers	Div 1	26 Sept 1953
Crystal Palace	4-11	v	Manchester City	F.A. Cup 5th Rd.	20th Feb 1926*
Derby County	2-11	v	Everton	F.A. Cup 1st Rd.	1889–90
Fulham	0-9	v	Wolverhampton Wanderers	Div 1	16 Sept 1959
Grimsby Town	1-9	v	Arsenal	Div 1	28 Jan 1931
Huddersfield Town	0-8	v	Middlesbrough	Div 1	30 Sept 1950
Leeds United	1-8	v	Stoke City	Div 1	27 Aug 1934†
Manchester City	1-9	v	Everton	Div 1	3 Sept 1906
Middlesbrough	0-9	v	Blackburn Rovers	Div 2	6 Nov 1954
Newcastle United	0-9	v	Burton Wanderers	Div 2	15 Apr 1895
Oldham Athletic	4-13	v	Tranmere Rovers	Div 3 (N)	26 Dec 1935‡
Portsmouth	0-10	v	Leicester City	Div 1	20 Oct 1928
Sheffield Wednesday	0-10	v	Aston Villa	Div 1	5 Oct 1912
Shrewsbury Town	1-8	v	Norwich City	Div 3 (S)	13 Sept 1952
	1-8	v	Coventry City	Div 3	22 Oct 1963
Swansea City	1-8	v	Fulham	Div 2	22 Jan 1938

All defeats have been suffered by clubs playing away from home unless otherwise stated.
* A record score for a Fifth Round F.A. Cup-tie
† First week of the season
‡ Christmas holiday fixture

THIRD DIVISION CLUBS: RECORD VICTORIES

The **Preston North End** victory is particularly famous as it is the largest ever recorded in the F.A. Cup but, although they reached the Cup Final that season, they lost to WBA 1-2.

Two local 'derby' cup ties produced record victories for League clubs when **Scunthorpe** United defeated **Boston United** and **Southend United** entertained **Brentwood**.

Another memorable match between local rivals took place during **Merthyr**'s short period in the Football League and it gave **Newport County** their record victory.

To lose 0-10 at home must have shaken **Port Vale** in 1892 but they didn't finish bottom that season and recovered well to finish in seventh place the following year.

Bolton Wanderers	9-0	v	Loughborough Town	Div 2	28 Jan 1899
A.F.C. Bournemouth	11-0	v	Margate	F.A. Cup 1st Rd.	20 Nov 1971
Bradford City	11-1	v	Rotherham United	Div 3 (N)	25 Aug 1928†
Brentford	9-0	v	Wrexham	Div 3	15 Oct 1963
Bristol Rovers	7-0	v	Swansea Town	Div 2	2 Oct 1954
	7-0	v	Brighton	Div 3 (S)	29 Nov 1952
	7-0	v	Shrewsbury Town	Div 3	21 Mar 1964
Burnley	9-0	v	Darwen	Div 1	9 Jan 1892
	9-0	v	Crystal Palace	F.A. Cup 2nd Rd. Replay	1908–09
	9-0	v	New Brighton	F.A. Cup 4th Rd.	26 Jan 1957
Exter City	8-1	v	Coventry City	Div 3 (S)	4 Dec 1926
	8-1	v	Aldershot	Div 3 (S)	4 May 1935
Gillingham	10-1	v	Gorleston	F.A. Cup 1st Rd.	16 Nov 1957
Hull City	11-1	v	Carlisle United	Div 3 (N)	14 Jan 1939
Lincoln City	11-1	v	Crewe Alexandra	Div 3 (N)	29 Sept 1951
Millwall	9-1	v	Torquay United	Div 3 (S)	29 Aug 1927*
	9-1	v	Coventry City	Div 3 (S)	19 Nov 1927*
Newport County	10-0	v	Merthyr Tydfil	Div 3 (S)	10 Apr 1930
Orient	9-2	v	Aldershot	Div 3 (S)	10 Feb 1934
	9-2	v	Chester (A)	League Cup 3rd Rd.	15 Oct 1962
Oxford United	7-0	v	Barrow	Div 4	19 Dec 1964
Plymouth Argyle	8-1	v	Millwall	Div 2	16 Jan 1932
Port Vale	9-1	v	Chesterfield	Div 2	24 Sept 1932
Preston North End	26-0	v	Hyde	F.A. Cup 1st Series, 1st Rd.	15 Oct 1887
Rotherham United	8-0	v	Oldham Athletic	Div 3 (N)	26 May 1947
Scunthorpe United	9-0	v	Boston United	F.A. Cup 1st Rd.	21 Nov 1953
Sheffield United	10-0	v	Port Vale (A)	Div 2	10 Dec 1892
	10-0	v	Burnley	Div 1	19 Jan 1929
Southend United	10-1	v	Golders Green	F.A. Cup 1st Rd.	24 Nov 1934
	10-1	v	Brentwood	F.A. Cup 2nd Rd.	7 Dec 1968
Walsall	10-0	v	Darwen	Div 2	4 Mar 1899
Wigan Athletic	7-2	v	Scunthorpe United (A)	Div 4	12 Mar 1982
Wimbledon	15-2	v	Polytechnic	F.A. Cup Pre. Rd.	7 Feb 1957

All victories have been achieved at 'home' unless otherwise stated.

* These two victories were recorded in the same season, with one win coming on the opening day of the campaign. **Millwall** won the championship that season with a home record of Pl 21 W 19 D 2 L 0 F 87 A 15.

† Another victory recorded on the opening day of the season.

THIRD DIVISION CLUBS: RECORD DEFEATS

When **Aston Villa** inflicted a record 0-8 defeat at **Clapton Orient** in a Fourth Round F.A. Cup replay it caused quite a surprise as they had drawn at home 0-0!

In the same season that **Notts County** crashed nine goals past **Exeter City** they also beat **Ipswich Town** 9-2 and **Newport County** 11-1 at home. Their goal record at Meadow Lane was 68-19 but they only finished in eleventh position.

What an end of season for **Blackpool** in 1948 when, after losing the Cup Final, they travelled to near neighbours **Preston North End** for the last match of the season and won 7-0. **Preston North End** still finished higher (7th) in the First Division than Stanley Matthews and company.

Bolton Wanderers	0-7	v	Manchester City	Div 1	21 Mar 1936
A.F.C. Bournemouth	0-9	v	Lincoln City	Div 3	18 Dec 1982
Bradford City	1-9	v	Colchester United	Div 4	30 Dec 1961
Brentford	0-7	v	Swansea Town	Div 3 (S)	8 Nov 1924
	0-7	v	Walsall	Div 3 (S)	19 Jan 1957
Bristol Rovers	0-12	v	Luton Town	Div 3 (S)	13 Apr 1936
Burnley	0-10	v	Aston Villa	Div 1	29 Aug 1925†
	0-10	v	Sheffield United	Div 1	19 Jan 1929
Exeter City	0-9	v	Notts County	Div 3 (S)	16 Oct 1948
	0-9	v	Northampton Town	Div 3 (S)	12 Apr 1958
Gillingham	2-9	v	Nottingham Forest	Div 3 (S)	18 Nov 1950
Hull City	0-8	v	Wolverhampton Wanderers	Div 2	4 Nov 1911
Lincoln City	3-11	v	Manchester City	Div 2	23 Mar 1895
Millwall	1-9	v	Aston Villa	F.A. Cup 4th Rd.	30 Jan 1929
Newport County	0-13	v	Newcastle United	Div 2	5 Oct 1946
Orient (as Clapton Orient)	0-8	v	Aston Villa (H)	F.A. Cup 4th Rd. Replay	30 Jan 1929
Oxford United	0-5	v	Cardiff City	Div 2	8 Feb 1969
	0-5	v	Cardiff City	Div 2	12 Sept 1973
	0-5	v	Nottingham Forest (H)	League Cup 3rd Rd.	4 Oct 1978
Plymouth Argyle	0-9	v	Stoke City	Div 2	17 Dec 1960
Port Vale	0-10	v	Sheffield United (H)	Div 2	10 Dec 1892
	0-10	v	Notts County	Div 2	26 Feb 1895
Preston North End	0-7	v	Blackpool (H)	Div 1	1 May 1948
Rotherham United	1-11	v	Bradford City	Div 3 (N)	25 Aug 1928†
Scunthorpe United	0-8	v	Carlisle United	Div 3(N)	25 Dec 1952*
Sheffield United	0-13	v	Bolton Wanderers	F.A. Cup 2nd Rd.	1 Feb 1890
Southend United	1-9	v	Brighton	Div 3	27 Nov 1965
Walsall	0-12	v	Small Heath	Div 2	17 Dec 1892
	0-12	v	Darwen	Div 2	26 Dec 1896*
Wigan Athletic	0-4	v	Huddersfield Town	Div 4	9 Oct 1979
	0-4	v	Lincoln City	Div 4	29 Feb 1980
	0-5	v	Bristol Rovers	Div 3	26 Feb 1983
Wimbledon	0-8	v	Everton	League Cup 2nd Rd.	29 Aug 1978

All defeats were suffered by clubs playing away from home unless otherwise stated.

* Christmas holiday matches. Although **Scunthorpe United** just lost at home to **Carlisle United**, 1-2, **Walsall** certainly gained revenge for their deafeat by beating **Darwen** 4-0 at home later in the season.
† Matches played on the first day of the season. Both **Burnley** and **Rotherham United** returned home to win their first games in front of their own supporters.

FOURTH DIVISION CLUBS: RECORD VICTORIES

Not surprisingly five record victories of Fourth Division clubs have been recorded in the F.A. Cup. The Third and Fourth Division clubs enter the competition in the First Round Proper along with thirty-two 'Non-League' clubs and there is always the chance of a big score against the amateurs and semi-professionals.

Blackpool's last major cup triumph was achieved when they won the Anglo-Italian Tournament in 1971 but the following year when they broke their goalscoring record they lost in the final.

Aldershot	8-1	v	Gateshead	Div 4	13 Sept 1958
Blackpool	10-0	v	Lanerossi Vincenza	Anglo-Italian Tournament	10 June 1972
Bristol City	11-0	v	Chichester	F.A. Cup 1st Rd.	5 Nov 1960
Bury	12-1	v	v Stockton (A)	F.A. Cup 1st Rd. Replay	1896–97
Chester	12-0	v	York City	Div 3 (N)	1 Feb 1936
Chesterfield	10-0	v	Glossop North End	Div 2	17 Jan 1903
Colchester United	9-1	v	Bradford City	Div 4	30 Dec 1961
Crewe Alexandra	8-0	v	Rotherham United	Div 3 (N)	1 Oct 1932
Darlington	9-2	v	Lincoln City	Div 3 (N)	7 Jan 1928
Doncaster Rovers	10-0	v	Darlington	Div 4	25 Jan 1964
Halifax Town	7-0	v	Bishop Auckland	F.A. Cup 2nd Rd. Replay	10 Jan 1967
Hartlepool United	10-1	v	Barrow	Div 4	4 Apr 1959
Hereford United	11-0	v	Thynnes	F.A. Cup	Sept 1947
Mansfield Town	9-2	v	Rotherham United	Div 3 (N)	27 Dec 1932*
	9-2	v	Hounslow Town	F.A. Cup 1st Rd. Replay	5 Nov 1962
Northampton Town	10-0	v	Walsall	Div 3 (S)	5 Nov 1927
Peterborough United	8-1	v	Oldham United	Div 4	26 Nov 1969
Reading	10-2	v	Crystal Palace	Div 3 (S)	4 Sept 1946
Rochdale	8-1	v	Chesterfield	Div 3 (N)	18 Dec 1926
Stockport County	13-0	v	Halifax Town	Div 3 (N)	6 Jan 1934
Swindon Town	10-1	v	Farnham United Breweries (A)	F.A. Cup 1st Rd.	28 Nov 1925
Torquay United	9-0	v	Swindon Town	Div 3 (S)	8 Mar 1952
Tranmere Rovers	13-4	v	Oldham Athletic	Div 3 (N)	26 Dec 1935*
Wrexham	10-1	v	Hartlepool United	Div 4	3 March 1962
York City	9-1	v	Southport	Div 3 (N)	2 Feb 1957

All victories were achieved at 'home' unless otherwise stated.

* Christmas holiday fixture

FOURTH DIVISION CLUBS: RECORD DEFEATS

The Christmas spirit didn't mean much to **Rochdale Football Club** at the end of 'The Twenties'. They lost 0-8 to **Wrexham** on 28th December 1929, lost to **Southport** 0-4 twice over the Christmas of 1930 and then equalled their worst defeat on Christmas Day 1931 when they lost 1-9.

An extraordinary sequence of results was produced by **Peterborough United** and **Northampton Town** in their 2nd Round F.A. Cup pairing in the 1946–47 season. Two 1-1 draws was followed by an 8-1 victory for 'The Cobblers' on neutral ground.

Aldershot	0-9	v	Bristol City	Div 3 (S)	28 Dec 1946
Blackpool	1-10	v	Small Heath	Div 2	2 Mar 1901
	1-10	v	Huddersfield Town	Div 1	13 Dec 1930
Bristol City	0-9	v	Coventry City	Div 3 (S)	28 Apr 1934
Bury	0-10	v	Blackburn Rovers	F.A. Cup	1887–88?
Chester	2-11	v	Oldham Athletic	Div 3 (N)	19 Jan 1952
Chesterfield	1-9	v	Port Vale	Div 2	24 Sept 1932
Colchester United	0-7	v	Leyton Orient	Div 3 (S)	5 Jan 1952
	0-7	v	Reading	Div 3 (S)	18 Sept 1957
Crewe Alexandra	2-13	v	Tottenham Hotspur	F.A. Cup 4th Rd. Replay	3 Feb 1960
Darlington	0-10	v	Doncaster Rovers	Div 4	25 Jan 1964
Halifax Town	0-13	v	Stockport County	Div 3 (N)	6 Jan 1934
Hartlepool United	1-10	v	Wrexham	Div 4	3 Mar 1962
Hereford United	0-5	v	Wrexham	Div 3	22 Dec 1973
	1-6	v	Tranmere Rovers	Div 3	29 Nov 1974
	1-6	v	Wolverhampton Wanderers (H)	Div 2	2 Oct 1976
Mansfield Town	1-8	v	Walsall	Div 3 (N)	19 Jan 1933
Northampton Town	0-10	v	Bournemouth	Div 3 (S)	2 Sept 1939‡
	0-11	v	Southampton	Southern Lge	28 Dec 1901
Peterborough United	1-8	v	Northampton Town (N)	F.A. Cup 2nd Rd. 2nd Replay	1946–47
Reading	0-18	v	Preston North End	F.A. Cup 1st Rd.	1893-94
Rochdale	1-9	v	Tranmere Rovers	Div 3 (N)	25 Dec 1931*
	0-8	v	Wrexham	Div 3 (N)	28 Dec 1929*
Stockport County	1-8	v	Chesterfield	Div 2	19 Apr 1902
Swindon Town	1-10	v	Manchester City	F.A. Cup 4th Rd. Replay	29 Jan 1930
Torquay United	2-10	v	Fulham	Div 3 (S)	7 Sept 1931
	2-10	v	Luton Town	Div 3 (S)	2 Sept 1933
Tranmere Rovers	1-9	v	Tottenham Hotspur	F.A. Cup 3rd Rd. Replay	14 Jan 1953
Wrexham	0-4	v	Everton	League Cup	29 Aug 1978
York City	0-12	v	Chester	Div 3 (N)	1 Feb 1936

All defeats were suffered by clubs playing away unless otherwise stated.
* Christmas holiday fixture
‡ This match was played on the last day of football before the Second World War

First Division Club Records: Position — Goals — Points

What a great season 1930–31 must have been for the fans! Three clubs created goalscoring records which still stand to-day but this is not surprising as all three scored over 120. Ten other records were set up in the 'fifties' which was a time when attendances were impressive and defences could be described as naive by to-day's standards. However, the outlawing of the 'professional' cheat encouraged strikers last year and one team to take advantage of this was Watford who, of course, enjoyed their best season in the Football League and also scored 74 goals in their first season in the top sphere.

	Best League Position	*Most Goals in a Season*			*Most Points (2 for a win)*			*Most Points (3 for a win)*		
Arsenal	1st	127	Div 1	1930–31	66	Div 1	1930–31	71	Div 1	1981–82
Aston Villa	1st	128	Div 1	1930–31	70	Div 3	1971–72			
Birmingham C	6th	103*	Div 2	1893–94	59	Div 2	1947–48			
Coventry C	6th	108	Div 3 (S)	1931–32	60	Div 4	1958–59			
					60	Div 3	1963–64			
Everton	1st	121	Div 2	1930–31	66	Div 1	1969–70			
Ipswich T	1st	106	Div 3 (S)	1955–56	64	Div 3 (S)	1954–55			
Leicester C	2nd	109	Div 2	1956–57	61	Div 2	1956–57	70	Div 2	1982–83
Liverpool	1st	106†	Div 2	1895–96	68	Div 1	1978–79	87‡	Div 1	1981–82
Luton T	8th	103	Div 3 (S)	1936–37	66	Div 4	1967–68	88‡	Div 2	1981–82
Manchester U	1st	103	Div 1	1956–57	64	Div 1	1956–57	78	Div 1	1981–82
		103	Div 1	1958–59						
Norwich C	10th	99	Div 3 (S)	1952–53	64	Div 3 (S)	1950–51	71	Div 2	1981–82
Nottingham F	1st	110	Div 3 (S)	1950–51	70	Div 3 (S)	1950–51			
Notts Co	3rd	107	Div 4	1959–60	69	Div 4	1970–71			
QPR	2nd	111	Div 3	1961–62	67	Div 3	1966–67	85	Div 2	1982–83
Southampton	6th	112	Div 3 (S)	1957–58	61	Div 3 (S)	1921–22	66	Div 1	1981–82
					61	Div 3	1959–60			
Stoke C	4th	92	Div 3 (N)	1926–27	63	Div 3 (N)	1926–27			
Sunderland	1st	109	Div 1	1935–36	61	Div 2	1963–64			
Tottenham H	1st	115	Div 1	1960–61	70	Div 2	1919–20	71	Div 1	1981–82
Watford	2nd	92	Div 4	1959–60	71	Div 4	1977–78	80	Div 2	1981–82
West Bromwich A	1st	105	Div 2	1929–30	60	Div 1	1919–20			
West Ham U	6th	101	Div 2	1957–58	66	Div 2	1980–81			
Wolverhampton W	1st	115	Div 2	1931–32	64	Div 1	1957–58	75	Div 2	1982–83

* Only 28 games played
† Only thirty games played
‡ Records for their divisions

Second Division Club Records: Position — Goals — Points

Despite the recession and very limited funds, one of last season's success stories must have been produced by Shrewsbury Town who enjoyed their best ever season in The Football League. Much credit should go to their directors and their hard-working manager Graham Turner, who have proved that a good youth policy and coaching plus a shrewd use of the transfer market can bring results.

	Best League Position	*Most Goals in a Season*			*Most Points (2 for a win)*			*Most Points (3 for a win)*		
Barnsley	3rd – Div 2	118	Div 3 (N)	1933–34	67	Div 3 (N)	1938–39	67	Div 2	1981–82
Blackburn R	1st	114	Div 2	1954–55	60	Div 3	1974–75			
Brighton & HA	16th	112	Div 3 (S)	1955–56	65	Div 3 (S)	1955–56			
					65	Div 3	1971–72			
Cambridge U	8th – Div 2	87	Div 4	1976–77	65	Div 4	1976–77			
Cardiff C	2nd	93	Div 3 (S)	1946–47	66	Div 3 (S)	1946–47	86	Div 3	1982–83
Carlisle U	22nd	113	Div 4	1963–64	62	Div 3 (N)	1950–51	80	Div 3	1981–82
Charlton Ath	2nd	107	Div 2	1957–58	61	Div 3 (S)	1934–35			
Chelsea	1st	98	Div 1	1960–61	57	Div 2	1906–07	57	Div 2	1981–82
Crystal Palace	13th	110	Div 4	1960–61	64	Div 4	1960–61			
Derby Co	1st	111	Div 3 (N)	1956–57	63	Div 2	1968–69			
					63	Div 3 (N)	1958–59			
					63	Div 3 (N)	1956–57			
Fulham	10th	111	Div 3 (S)	1931–32	60	Div 2	1958–59			
					60	Div 2	1970–71	78	Div 3	1981–82
Grimsby T	5th	103	Div 2	1933 34	68	Div 3 (N)	1955–56			
Huddersfield T	1st	101	Div 4	1979–80	66	Div 4	1979–80	82	Div 3	1982–83
Leeds U	1st	98	Div 2	1927–28	67	Div 1	1968–69			
Manchester C	1st	108	Div 2	1926–27	62	Div 2	1946–47			
Middlesbrough	3rd	122	Div 2	1926–27	65	Div 2	1973–74			
Newcastle U	1st	98	Div 1	1951–52	57	Div 2	1964–65	67	Div 2	1982–83
Oldham Ath	2nd	95	Div 4	1962–63	62	Div 3	1973–74			
Portsmouth	1st	91	Div 4	1979–80	65	Div 3	1961–62	91*	Div 3	1982–83
Sheffield W	1st	106	Div 2	1958–59	62	Div 2	1958–59	70	Div 2	1981–82
Shrewsbury T	9th – Div 2	101	Div 4	1958–59	62	Div 4	1974–75			
Swansea C	6th	90	Div 2	1956–57	62	Div 3 (S)	1948–49			

* Denotes a record for the Division
Club's best positions all refer to the First Division unless otherwise stated

Third Division Club Records: Position — Goals — Points

	Best League Position	*Most Goals in a Season*			*Most Points (2 for a win)*			*Most Points (3 for a win)*		
Bolton W	3rd	96	Div 2	1934–35	61	Div 3	1974–75			
AFC Bournemouth	3rd – Div 3	88	Div 3 (S)	1956–57	62	Div 3	1971–72	88	Div 4	1981–82
Bradford C	5th	128	Div 3 (N)	1928–29	63	Div 3 (N)	1928–29	91	Div 4	1981–82
Brentford	5th	98	Div 4	1962–63	62	Div 3 (S)	1932–33	68	Div 3	1981–82
					62	Div 4	1962–63			
Bristol R	6th – Div 2	92	Div 3 (S)	1952–53	64	Div 3 (S)	1952–53	75	Div 3	1982–83
Burnley	1st	102	Div 1	1960–61	62	Div 2	1972–73	80	Div 3	1981–82
Exeter C	8th – Div 3	88	Div 3 (S)	1932–33	62	Div 4	1976–77			
Gillingham	4th – Div 3	90	Div 4	1973–74	62	Div 4	1973–74			
Hull C	3rd – Div 2	109	Div 3	1965–66	69	Div 3	1965–66	90	Div 4	1982–83
Lincoln C	5th – Div 2	121	Div 3 (N)	1951–52	74	Div 4	1975–76	77	Div 3	1981–82
Millwall	3rd – Div 2	127	Div 3 (S)	1927–28	65	Div 3 (S)	1927–28	67	Div 3	1981–82
Newport Co	22nd – Div 2	85	Div 4	1964–65	61	Div 4	1979–80	78	Div 3	1982–83
Orient	22nd	106	Div 3 (S)	1955–56	66	Div 3 (S)	1955–56			
Oxford U	8th – Div 2	87	Div 4	1964–65	61	Div 4	1964–64	78	Div 3	1982–83
Plymouth Arg	4th – Div 2	107	Div 3 (S)	1925–26	68	Div 3 (S)	1929–30			
				Div 3 (S)	1951–52					
Port Vale	5th – Div 2	110	Div 4	1958–59	69	Div 3 (N)	1953–54	88	Div 4	1982–83
Rotherham U	3rd – Div 2	114	Div 3 (N)	1946–47	71	Div 3 (N)	1950–51			
Scunthorpe U	4th – Div 2	88	Div 3 (N)	1957–58	66	Div 3 (N)	1957–58	83	Div 4	1982–83
Sheffield U	1st	102	Div 1	1925–26	60	Div 2	1952–53	96	Div 4	1981–82
Southend U	3rd – Div 3 (S)	92	Div 3 (S)	1950–51	67	Div 4	1980–81	69	Div 3	1981–82
Walsall	6th – Div 2	102	Div 4	1959–60	65	Div 4	1959–60			
Wigan Ath	18th – Div 3	80	Div 4	1981–82	55	Div 4	1978–79			
					55	Div 4	1979–80	91	Div 4	1981–82
Wimbledon	21st – Div 3	96	Div 4	1982–83	61	Div 4	1978–79	98	Div 4	1982–83
Preston NE	1st	100	Div 2	1927–28	61	Div 3	1970–71	61	Div 3	1981–82
		100	Div 1	1957–58						

Fourth Division Club Records: Position — Goals — Points

	Best League Position	*Most Goals in a Season*			*Most Points (2 for a win)*			*Most Points (3 for a win)*		
Aldershot	8th – Div 3	83	Div 4	1963–64	57	Div 4	1978–79			
Blackpool	2nd	98	Div 2	1929–30	58 58	Div 2 Div 2	1929–30 1967–68	58	Div 4	1981–82
Bristol C	2nd	104	Div 3 (S)	1926–27	70	Div 3 (S)	1954–55			
Bury	4th	108	Div 3	1960–61	68	Div 3	1960–61	81	Div 4	1982–83
Chester	5th – Div 3	119	Div 4	1964–65	56 56	Div 3 (N) Div 4	1946–47 1964–65	56	Div 4	1982–83
Chesterfield	4th – Div 2	102	Div 3 (N)	1930–31	64	Div 4	1969–70	64	Div 3	1981–82
Colchester U	3rd – Div 3 (S)	104	Div 4	1961–62	60	Div 4	1973–74	81	Div 4	1982–83
Crewe Alex	10th – Div 2	95	Div 3 (N)	1931–32	59	Div 4	1962–63			
Darlington	15th – Div 2	108	Div 3 (N)	1929–30	59	Div 4	1965–66			
Doncaster R	7th – Div 2	123	Div 3 (N)	1946–47	72	Div 3 (N)	1946–47			
Halifax T	3rd – Div 3	83	Div 3 (N)	1957–58	57	Div 4	1968–69	60	Div 4	1982–83
Hartlepool U	22nd – Div 3	90	Div 3 (N)	1956–57	60	Div 4	1967–68			
Hereford U	22nd – Div 2	86	Div 3	1975–76	63	Div 3	1975–76	67	Div 4	1981–82
Mansfield T	21st – Div 2	108	Div 4	1962–63	68	Div 4	1974–75			
Northampton T	21st – Div 3 (S)	109	Div 3	1952–53	109	Div 3	1962–63			
Peterborough U	4th – Div 3	134	Div 4	1960–61	66	Div 4	1960–61	82	Div 4	1981–82
Reading	14th – Div 2	112	Div 3 (S)	1951–52	65	Div 4	1978–79			
Rochdale	9th – Div 3	105	Div 3 (N)	1926–27	62	Div 3 (N)	1923–24			
Stockport Co	17th – Div 2	115	Div 3 (N)	1957–58	64	Div 4	1966–67			
Swindon T	5th – Div 2	100	Div 3 (S)	1926–27	64	Div 3	1968–69	68	Div 4	1982–83
Torquay U	4th – Div 3	89	Div 3 (S)	1956–57	60	Div 4	1959 60			
Tranmere R	22nd – Div 2	111	Div 3 (N)	1930–31	60	Div 4	1964–65	60	Div 4	1981–82
Wrexham	15th – Div 2	106	Div 3 (N)	1932–33	61 61	Div 4 Div 3	1969–70 1977–78			
York C	15th – Div 2	92	Div 3 (N)	1954–55	62	Div 4	1964–65	79	Div 4	1982–83

Club's best positions refer to the First Division unless otherwise stated

LEADING GOALSCORERS 1982–83

Listed in order of League goals scored.

DIVISION 1

	League	*Milk Cup*	*FA Cup*	*European*	*Total*
Luther Blissett (Watford)	27	1	2	–	30
Ian Rush (Liverpool)	24	2	2	2	30
Bob Latchford (Swansea C)	20	4	–	1	25
Gary Shaw (Aston Villa)	17	–	1	5	23
John Wark (Ipswich T)	20	1	2	–	23
John Deehan (Norwich C)	20	1	–	–	21
Tony Woodcock (Arsenal)	14	3	4	–	21
Kenny Dalglish (Liverpool)	18	–	1	1	20
Peter Withe (Aston Villa)	16	1	1	2	20
Gary Rowell (Sunderland)	16	2	–	–	18
Frank Stapleton (Manchester U)	14	2	3	–	19
Ian Wallace (Nottingham F)	13	4	–	–	17
Alan Brazil (Tottenham H)	16	–	–	–	16
(includes 10 for Ipswich T)					
Graeme Sharp (Everton)	14	–	2	–	16
Steve Archibald (Tottenham H)	11	2	–	2	15
Garth Crooks (Tottenham H)	8	3	1	3	15
Brian Stein (Luton T)	14	1	–	–	15
Brian Robson (Manchester U)	10	1	3	1	15
Paul Walsh (Luton T)	14	–	1	–	15
Keith Bertschin (Norwich C)	8	2	4	–	14
David Swindlehurst (West Ham U)	11	3	–	–	14
(includes 11 for Derby Co)					
Steve Whitton (Coventry C)	12	–	2	–	14
Norman Whiteside (Manchester U)	8	3	3	–	14
David Cross (Manchester C)	12	–	1	–	13
Andy King (Everton)	9	2	2	–	13
Kevin Sheedy (Everton)	11	–	2	–	13
Danny Wallace (Southampton)	12	1	–	–	13
Paul Mariner (Ipswich T)	13	–	–	–	13
Gordon Cowans (Aston Villa)	10	–	1	1	12
Justin Fashanu (Notts Co)	10	–	2	–	12
(includes 3 for Southampton)					
Paul Goddard (West Ham U)	10	2	–	–	12
Iain McCulloch (Notts Co)	10	1	1	–	12
Kevin Moran (Southampton)	10	2	–	–	12
Alan Sunderland (Arsenal)	6	5	1	–	12
Mickey Thomas (Stoke C)	11	1	–	–	12
Garry Thompson (WBA)	11	1	–	–	12
(includes 5 for Coventry C)					
Francois Van der Elst (West Ham U)	9	3	–	–	12
John Barnes (Watford)	10	–	1	–	11
Gary Birtles (Nottingham F)	7	4	–	–	11
Trevor Christie (Notts Co)	9	2	–	–	11
Steve Coppell (Manchester U)	4	6	1	–	11
Adrian Heath (Everton)	10	–	1	–	11
Phil Neal (Liverpool)	8	1	–	2	11
Cyrille Regis (WBA)	9	2	–	–	11
Graeme Souness (Liverpool)	9	2	–	–	11
Ray Stewart (West Ham U)	8	3	–	–	11
Gary Mabbutt (Tottenham H)	10	–	–	1	11
Mark Hateley (Coventry C)	9	–	2	–	11
Jim Melrose (Coventry C)	9	2	–	–	11
(includes 1 for Leicester C)					
Sandy Clark (West Ham U)	7	3	–	–	10
Ricky Hill (Luton T)	9	–	1	–	10
Craig Johnston (Liverpool)	7	1	1	1	10
David Moss (Luton T)	9	1	–	–	10
Graham Rix (Arsenal)	6	–	4	–	10
Brian Talbot (Arsenal)	9	–	1	–	10
Mick Robinson (Brighton & HA)	7	–	3	–	10

DIVISION 2

	League	*Milk Cup*	*FA Cup*	*Total*
Gary Lineker (Leicester C)	26	–	–	26
Simon Garner (Blackburn R)	22	–	1	23
Gary Bannister (Sheffield U)	20	1	1	22
Kevin Drinkell (Grimsby T)	17	5	–	22
Imre Varadi (Newcastle U)	21	1	–0	22
Ronnie Glavin (Barnsley)	17	3	1	21
Kevin Keegan (Newcastle U)	21	–	–	21
Alan Shoulder (Carlisle U)	21	–	–	21
Gordon Davies (Fulham)	19	1	–	20
Bobby Davison (Derby Co) (includes 12 for Halifax T)	17	3	–	20
Mel Eves (Wolverhampton W)	18	1	–	19
Billy Hamilton (Burnley)	13	4	2	19
Roger Wylde (Oldham Ath)	19	–	–	19
Derek Hales (Charlton Ath)	14	2	1	17
John Gregory (QPR)	15	1	–	16
Malcolm Poskett (Carlisle U)	14	–	2	16
Tony Sealy (QPR)	16	–	–	16
Roger Palmer (Oldham Ath)	15	–	–	15
Steve Taylor (Burnley)	12	1	2	15
Alan Brown (Shrewsbury T)	10	2	2	14
Alan Smith (Leicester C)	13	–	1	14
Clive Allen (QPR)	13	0	–	13
Aiden Butterworth (Leeds)	11	1	1	13
David Shearer (Middlesbrough)	9	–	4	13
Paul Bannon (Carlisle U)	11	–	1	12
Wayne Clarke (Wolverhampton W)	12	–	–	12
Tony Cunningham (Barnsley) (includes 5 for Lincoln C)	10	2	–	12
Mike Fillery (Chelsea)	9	1	2	12
Tony Henry (Oldham Ath) (includes 11 for Bolton W)	10	2	–	12
Kevin Mabbutt (C Palace)	10	2	–	12
Steve White (Charlton Ath)	12	–	–	12
Ray Lewington (Fulham)	10	–	1	11
Joe McBride (Rotherham U)	11	–	–	11
Darren McDonough (Oldham Ath)	10	1	–	11
Gary Megson (Sheffield W)	5	1	5	11
Heine Otto (Middlesbrough)	9	1	1	11
Derrick Parker (Barnsley)	11	–	–	11
George Reilly (Cambridge U)	10	–	1	11
Trevor Steven (Burnley)	8	1	2	11
Robert Wilson (Fulham)	11	–	–	11
John Seasman (Rotherham U)	9	1	1	11
Steve Bell (Middlesbrough)	8	–	2	10
Andy Gray (Wolverhampton W)	10	–	–	10
Andy McCulloch (Sheffield W)	7	1	2	10
Phil Walker (Rotherham U) (includes 8 for Chesterfield)	7	–	3	10

Leading Career Goalscorers in The Football League/Milk Cup

29 Bob Latchford (Swansea City)

22 Kenny Dalglish (Liverpool)

20 Bob Hatton (Cardiff C)

18 John Richards (Wolverhampton W)

17 Ernie Moss (Lincoln City), Ian Bowyer (Nottingham F)

16 Ross Jenkins (Watford), Frank Stapleton (Manchester U), Alan Sunderland (Arsenal), Peter Withe (Aston Villa), John Robertson (Nottingham F)

15 Ronnie Glavin (Barnsley), Derek Hales (Charlton Ath), Peter Noble (Blackpool), David Johnson (Everton)

14 Gary Birtles (Nottingham F), Mick Channon (Norwich C), Jimmy Greenhoff (Rochdale)

13 Luther Blissett (Watford), Mike Flanagan (QPR), Jimmy Greenhoff (Rochdale), David Gwyther (Newport Co), Andy Gray (Wolverhampton W), Alan Mayes (Chelsea), Bryan 'Pop' Robson (Chelsea), Cyrille Regis (WBA), Andy Rowlands (Swindon T)

12 Alan Buckley (Walsall), Martin Dobson (Burnley), Kenny Hibbitt (Wolverhampton W), Brendan O'Callaghan (Stoke C), Dennis Tueart (Manchester C), Tony Woodcock (Arsenal)

11 Les Bradd (Wigan Ath), Pat Earles (Reading), Alan Gowling (Preston NE), Andy King (Everton), Bruce Rioch (Torquay U)

10 Stan Bowles (Brentford), Bobby Campbell (Bradford C), Joe Cooke (Bradford C), John Hollins (Chelsea), Ray Kennedy (Swansea C), John Leslie (Wimbledon), George Reilly (Cambridge U), Ian Rush (Liverpool), Tommy Tynan (Newport Co), Ian Wallace (Nottingham F)

9 Steve Coppell (Manchester U)

8 Terry McDermott (Newcastle)

DIVISION 3

	League	*Milk Cup*	*FA Cup*	*Total*
Tommy Tynan (Newport Co)	25	2	4	31
Bobby Campbell (Bradford C)	25	3	2	30
Derek Bell (Lincoln C)	23	3	–	26
Kerry Dixon (Reading)	26	–	–	26
Jeff Hemmerman (Cardiff C)	22	2	2	26
Alan Biley (Portsmouth)	22	1	2	25
Francis Joseph (Brentford)	23	1	1	25
Keith Edwards (Sheffield U)	13	5	5	23
Steve Elliott (Preston NE)	19	2	2	23
Paul Randall (Bristol R)	20	2	–	22
Mark Lillis (Huddersfield T)	19	–	–	19
Dean Neal (Millwall)	19	–	–	19
Billy Rafferty (Portsmouth)	17	–	2	19
Colin Morris (Sheffield U)	14	2	3	19
Tony Cascarino (Gillingham)	14	3	1	18
John Aldridge (Newport Co)	15	1	2	18
Trevor Morgan (AFC Bournemouth)	16	2	–	18
Steve Phillips (Southend)	17	–	1	18
Steve Neville (Exeter C)	17	–	–	17
Eamonn O'Keefe (Wigan Ath)	16	1	–	17
Gary Roberts (Brentford)	12	3	2	17
Colin Russell (Huddersfield T)	16	1	–	17
Brian Stanton (Huddersfield T)	13	2	2	17
Gordon Hobson (Lincoln C)	14	2	–	16
Neil Whatmore (Oxford U) (includes 4 for Bolton)	15	–	1	16
Alan Buckley (Walsall)	13	–	2	15
John Sims (Plymouth Arg)	10	2	2	14
Tony Mahoney (Brentford)	8	3	3	14
Glen Snodin (Doncaster R)	14	–	–	14
Mick Vinter (Oxford U)	10	1	3	14
Steve Lowndes (Newport Co)	12	2	–	14
Dave Bennett (Cardiff C)	12	1	–	13
Kevin Godfrey (Orient)	11	–	2	13
Alan Young (Sheffield U)	7	3	3	13
Ernie Moss (Lincoln C) (includes 11 for Port Vale)	12	1	–	13
Roger Gibbins (Cardiff C)	8	3	1	12
Kevin Hodges (Plymouth Arg)	11	–	1	12
Peter Houghton (Wigan Ath)	12	–	–	12
Ollie Kearns (Walsall)	11	–	1	12
David Williams (Bristol R)	9	1	2	12
George Shipley (Lincoln C)	10	2	–	12
Kevin Summerfield (Walsall) (includes 2 for Birmingham C)	10	–	1	11
Stan Bowles (Brentford)	10	1	–	11
Trevor Hebberd (Oxford U)	10	–	1	11
Chris Kamara (Brentford)	11	–	–	11
Tony Kellow (Exeter C)	10	1	–	11
? Savage (Wrexham)	10	–	1	11
Mark Weatherly (Gillingham)	9	–	2	11
Malcolm Brown (Huddersfield T)	9	1	1	11
Keith Cassells (Brentford) (includes 3 for Southampton)	10	1	–	11
Steve Buxton (Wrexham)	10	–	–	10
Kevin Dillon (Portsmouth) (includes 5 for Birmingham C)	8	2	–	10
Tom Heffernan (AFC Bournemouth)	10	–	–	10
Martin Henderson (Chesterfield)	10	–	–	10
Keith Houchen (Orient)	10	–	–	10
Peter Rogers (Exeter C)	10	–	–	10
Graham Withey (Bristol R)	10	–	–	10
George Lawrence (Oxford U) (includes 1 for Southampton)	10	–	–	10
Bob Hatton (Cardiff C) (includes 1 for Sheffield U)				

DIVISION 4

	League	Milk Cup	FA Cup	Total
Dale Banton (Aldershot)	24	–	4	28
Steve Cammack (Scunthorpe U)	25	–	1	26
Ian Allinson (Colchester U)	22	2	–	24
John Leslie (Wimbledon)	22	1	1	24
Steve Massey (Northampton T)	20	3	1	24
Mike Quinn (Stockport)	24	–	–	24
Keith Walwyn (York)	21	1	2	24
Paul Rideout (Swindon T)	20	2	1	23
Mick Gynn (Peterborough U)	17	1	3	21
John Thomas (Chester)	20	1	–	21
Craig Madden (Bury)	19	1	–	20
Bob Newton (Port Vale)	20	–	–	20
Andy Rowland (Swindon T)	16	–	4	20
Steve Cooper (Torquay U)	15	2	2	19
Brian Marwood (Hull C)	19	–	–	19
Brian Pollard (York C)	17	–	2	19
Alan Walsh (Darlington)	18	1	–	19
John Dungworth (Mansfield T)	14	–	4	18
Tony Adcock (Colchester U)	17	–	–	17
David Waller (Crewe Alex)	17	–	–	17
Owen Brown (Tranmere R)	11	1	4	16
Glynn Riley (Bristol C)	16	–	–	16
Dave Staniforth (Halifax T)	15	1	–	16
Howard Pritchard (Swindon T)	10	–	5	15
Tom Ritchie (Bristol C)	14	1	–	15
Dave Bamber (Blackpool)	9	4	1	14
Stewart Evans (Wimbledon)	14	–	–	14
Andy Flounders (Hull C)	13	1	–	14
Gary Ford (York C)	12	–	2	14
Stuart Phillips (Hereford U)	14	–	–	14
Dave Syrett (Northampton T)	12	2	–	14
John Byrne (York C)	11	1	1	13
Colin Clarke (Peterborough U)	9	1	2	12
Les Mutrie (Hull C)	12	–	–	12
Chris Cowling (Scunthorpe U)	10	1	1	12
Robbie Cooke (Peterborough U)	5	3	3	11
Mickey French (Rochdale)	11	–	–	11
Steve Spooner (Halifax T)	11	–	–	11
Dave Caldwell (Mansfield T)	10	–	–	10
Steve Johnson (Bury)	10	–	–	10
Stuart Parker (Bury)	10	–	–	10

First Division scorers shown: League – Milk Cup – FA Cup – European Comps. (Total):
All other divisions shown: League – Milk Cup – FA Cup (Total).

Leading Career Goalscorers in The FA Cup

27 'Dixie' McNeill (Hereford U)

25 David Gwyther (Newport Co)

24 John Richards (Wolverhampton W)

22 Jimmy Greenhoff (Rochdale), Kevin Keegan (Newcastle U), Paul Mariner (Ipswich T)

21 George Best (AFC Bournemouth)

18 Frank Stapleton (Manchester U)

17 David Moss (Luton T), Paul Maguire (Stoke C)

16 Mick Channon (Norwich C), Bob Latchford (Swansea C), Billy Rafferty (Portsmouth), Alan Sunderland (Arsenal)

15 Alan Ball (Bristol R), David Gregory (Wrexham), Peter Kitchen (Orient), Bryan 'Pop' Robson (Chelsea), Mick Vinter (Oxford U)

14 Ken Beamish (Swindon T), Alan Buckley (Walsall)

13 Kenny Dalglish (Liverpool), Alan Gowling (Preston NE), Jimmy Greenhoff (Rochdale), Bob Hatton (Cardiff C), Peter Withe (Aston Villa)

12 Peter Eastoe (WBE), David Johnson (Everton), David Mills (Sheffield W), Bob Newton (Port Vale), Bruce Rioch (Torquay U), Andy Rowlands (Swindon T), John Toshack (Swansea C), Frank Worthington (Sunderland)

11 Stan Bowles (Brentford), John Dungworth (Mansfield T), Keith Edwards (Sheffield U), Gerry Daley (Coventry C), Tony Kellow (Exeter C), Ray McHale (Sheffield U), Robbie Cooke (Cambridge U), Ernie Moss (Lincoln C)

10 'Chic' Bates (Shrewsbury T), Robbie Cooke (Cambridge U), Roy Greaves (Rochdale), Kenny Hibbitt (Wolverhampton W), Alan Mayes (Chelsea), Derrick Parker (Barnsley), John Robertson (Nottingham F), Ian Rush (Liverpool), Cyrille Regis (WBA), John Wark (Ipswich T), Tony Woodcock (Arsenal).

9 Terry McDermott (Newcastle)

HAT TRICK HEROES 1982–83

FOOTBALL LEAGUE

August
28 Steve Elliot 3, Preston N.E. v Millwall, Div 3

September
4 Paul Walsh 3, Luton T. v Notts Co., Div 1
Bob Latchford 3, Swansea C. v Norwich C., Div 1
7 Billy Hamilton 3, Burnley v Carlisle U., Div 2
11 Steve Lynex 3, Leicester C. v Carlisle U., Div 2
Gary Lineker 3, Leicester C. v Carlisle U., Div 2
18 Brian Stein 3, Luton T. v Brighton & H.A., Div 1
Malcolm Poskett 4, Carlisle U. v Crystal Palace, Div 2
19 Dave Syrett 4, Northampton T. v Bristol C., Div 4
25 Jim Melrose 3, Coventry C. v Everton, Div 1
Luther Blissett 4, Watford v Sunderland, Div 1
Cyrille Regis 3, W.B.A. v Norwich C., Div 1
Ian Snodin 3, Doncaster R. v Reading, Div 3
Kerry Dixon 4, Reading v Doncaster R., Div 3
Stewart Evans 3, Wimbledon v Torquay U., Div 4
28 Peter Houghton 3, Wigan Ath. v Doncaster R., Div 3

October
2 Kevin Keegan 4, Newcastle U. v Rotherham U., Div 2
9 Gary Brooke 3, Tottenham H. v Coventry C., Div 1
Eamonn O'Keefe 3, Wigan Ath. v Exeter C., Div 3
20 Derek Bell 3, Lincoln C. v Exeter C., Div 3
23 Gary Lineker 3, Leicester C. v Derby Co., Div 2
Mark Lillis 4, Huddersfield T. v Cardiff C., Div 3
Bill Rafferty 3, Portsmouth v Preston N.E., Div 3
Colin Morris 3, Sheffield U. v Exeter C., Div 3
Glyn Riley 3, Bristol C. v Wimbledon, Div 4
30 John Wark 4, Ipswich T. v W.B.A., Div 1

November
2 Alan Biley 3, Portsmouth v Lincoln C., Div 3
6 Ian Rush 4, Liverpool v Everton, Div 1
Kerry Dixon 3, Reading v Newport Co., Div 3
Steve Cammack 3, Scunthorpe U. v Northampton T., Div 4
13 Ian Rush 3, Liverpool v Coventry C., Div 1
Roger Wylde 3, Oldham Ath. v Wolverhampton W., Div 2
John Aldridge 3, Newport Co. v AFC Bournemouth, Div 3
Bobby Davison 3, Halifax T. v Wimbledon, Div 4
20 Ronnie Moore 3, Rotherham U. v Charlton Ath., Div 2
27 Keith Walwyn 3, York C. v Mansfield T., Div 4

December
4 Kevin Drinkell 3, Grimsby T. v Crystal Palace, Div 2
10 Michael Quinn 3, Stockport Co. v Crewe Alex., Div 4
18 Gary Rowell 3, Sunderland v Arsenal, Div 1
Gordon Hobson 3, Lincoln C. v AFC Bournemouth, Div 3
Derek Bell 3, Lincoln C. v AFC Bournemouth, Div 3
27 Kenny Dalglish 3, Liverpool v Manchester C., Div 1
28 Craig Madden 3, Bury v Hartlepool U., Div 4

January
1 Ian Rush 3, Liverpool v Notts Co., Div 1
Steve Taylor 3, Burnley v Sheffield W., Div 2
Brian Stanton 4, Huddersfield T. v Bradford C., Div 3
Michael Quinn 3, Stockport Co. v Halifax T., Div 4
4 Paul Walsh 3, Luton T. v West Ham U., Div 1
8 Dean White 3, Gillingham v Exeter C., Div 3
Steve Neville 3, Gillingham v Exeter C., Div 3
John Thomas 3, Chester v Rochdale, Div 4
14 Dave Staniforth 3, Halifax T. v Colchester U., Div 4
21 Tony Adcock 3, Colchester U. v Crewe Alex., Div 4
22 Tom Heffernan 3, AFC Bournemouth v Millwall, Div 3
Paul Rideout 3, Swindon T. v Rochdale, Div 4
29 Andy Flounders 3, Hull C. v Stockport Co., Div 4

February
5 Stuart Phillips 3, Hereford U. v Chester, Div 4
26 Steve Taylor 3, Burnley v Charlton Ath., Div 2
Billy Hamilton 3, Burnley v Charlton Ath., Div 2
Dean Neal 3, Millwall v Exeter C., Div 3
Steve Lowndes 3, Newport Co. v Orient, Div 3

March
1 Kevin Todd 3, Darlington v Aldershot, Div 4
2 Neil Whatmore 3, Oxford U. v Bradford C., Div 3
5 Clive Allen 3, Q.P.R. v Middlesbrough, Div 2
12 Luther Blissett 3, Watford v Notts Co., Div 1
Micky French 3, Rochdale v Hereford U., Div 4
14 John Dungworth 3, Mansfield T. v Hartlepool U., Div 4
19 Tony Woodcock 3, Arsenal v Luton T., Div 1
Steve Moran 3, Southampton v Manchester C., Div 1
Bob Newton 3, Port Vale v Rochdale, Div 4
26 Steve Phillips 3, Southend U. v Sheffield U., Div 3

April
23 Brian Talbot 3, Arsenal v Manchester C., Div 1
Paul Walsh 3, Luton T. v Swansea C., Div 1
Dale Banton 3, Aldershot v Rochdale, Div 4
Trevor Senior 3, Aldershot v Rochdale, Div 4
30 Tommy Tynan 3, Newport Co., v Wrexham, Div 3
Mark McNeil 3, Orient v Exeter C., Div 3

May
2 Steve Neville 3, Exeter C. v Southend U., Div 3
Alan Cork 3, Wimbledon v Chester, Div 4
7 John Seasman 3, Rotherham U. v Blackburn R., Div 2
Dale Banton 5, Aldershot v Halifax T., Div 4
14 Steve Archibald 3, Tottenham H. v Stoke C., Div 1

MILK CUP

October
12 Kevin Drinkell 3, Grimsby T. v Sheffield U., Rd 2
26 Bob Latchford 3, Swansea C. v Bristol R., Rd 2
Keith Edwards 3, Sheffield U. v Grimsby T., Rd 2

November
23 Alan Sunderland 3, Arsenal v Everton, Rd 3 replay

December
7 Francois Van Der Elst 3, West Ham U. v Notts Co., Rd 4

FA CUP

November
20 Tony Mahoney 3, Brentford v Windsor & Eton, Rd 1
Owen Brown 3, Tranmere R. v Scarborough, Rd 1
23 Tommy Tynan 3, Newport Co. v Enfield, Rd 1 re-play

December
14 Alan Young 3, Sheffield U. v Boston, Rd 2 re-play

January
8 Howard Pritchard 3, Swindon T. v Aldershot, Rd 3
Andy Rowland 3, Swindon T. v Aldershot, Rd 3

CAREER RECORDS OF LEADING GOALSCORERS

	FL	FLC	FAC	Total
Bryan 'Pop' Robson (Chelsea)	260	13	15	288
'Dixie' NcNeill (Hereford U)	239	3	27	269
Bob Latchford (Swansea C)	206	29	16	251
Bob Hatton (Cardiff C)	217	20	13	250
Mick Channon (Norwich C)	210	14	16	240
Frank Worthington (Sunderland)	195	9	12	216
Ernie Moss (Lincoln C)	182	17	11	210
Alan Buckley (Walsall)	181	12	14	207
Les Bradd (Wigan Ath)	182	11	7	200
David Gwyther (Newport Co)	160	13	25	198
John Toshack (Swansea C)	173	7	12	192
John Richards (Wolverhampton W)	146	18	24	188
Alan Ball (Bristol R)	161	6	15	183
Jimmy Greenoff (Rochdale)	144	14	22	180
Ken Beamish (Swindon T)	158	7	14	179
Peter Kitchen (Orient)	153	9	15	177
George Best (Bournemouth)	147	8	21	176
Kevin Keegan (Newcastle U)	144	9	22	175
Alex Bruce (Preston NE)	160	7	6	173
Paul Mariner (Ipswich T)	141	8	22	171
Derek Hales (Charlton Ath)	145	15	7	167
Peter Noble (Blackpool)	146	15	3	164
David Moss (Luton T)	137	9	17	163
Alan Gowling (Preston NE)	139	11	13	163
Andy Rowlands (Swindon T)	127	13	12	152
Keith Edwards (Sheffield U)	134	6	11	151
Billy Rafferty (Portsmouth)	126	9	16	151
Bruce Rioch (Torquay U)	127	11	12	150
Stan Bowles (Brentford)	127	10	11	148
Andy McCulloch (Sheffield W)	135	5	7	147
Tony Kellow (Exeter C)	124	8	11	143
Ross Jenkins (Watford)	120	16	5	141
Peter Withe (Aston Villa)	111	16	13	140
Steve Phillips (Southend U)	129	4	6	139
Neil Whatmore (Oxford U)	123	8	6	137
Frank Stapleton (Manchester U)	102	16	18	136
Ronnie Moore (Rotherham U)	127	6	1	134
Alan Biley (Portsmouth)	121	5	5	131
Kenny Dalglish (Liverpool)	96	22	13	131
David Johnson (Everton)	104	15	12	131
Mike Flanagan (QPR)	112	13	3	128
Ray Kennedy (Swansea C)	106	10	9	125
Brendan O'Callaghan (Stoke C)	109	12	2	123
Dennis Tueart (Manchester C)	105	12	6	123
Alan Sunderland (Arsenal)	90	16	16	122
Roger Wylde (Oldham Ath)	105	8	4	117
Ally Brown (Crystal Palace)	106	3	7	116
Bobby Campbell (Bradford C)	103	10	2	115
Leighton James (Sunderland)	101	8	6	115
Tommy Tynan (Newport Co)	100	10	5	115
David Swindlehurst (West Ham U)	105	6	4	115
Alan Mayes (Chelsea)	91	13	10	114
Peter Eastoe (WBA)	92	8	12	112
Luther Blissett (Watford)	95	13	3	111
Trevor Phillips (Stockport Co)	100	5	6	111
Mick Vinter (Oxford U)	88	8	15	111
Alan Curtis (Swansea C)	97	6	7	110
Ian Bowyer (Nottingham F)	86	17	7	110
Kenny Hibbitt (Wolverhampton W)	88	12	10	110
Robbie James (Swansea C)	99	6	5	110
Andy Gray (Wolverhampton W)	90	13	6	109
Derek Spence (Southend U)	96	8	5	109
John Dungworth (Mansfield T)	97	0	11	108
Martin Dobson (Burnley)	88	12	8	108
David Mills (Sheffield W)	89	6	12	107
Joe Cooke (Bradford C)	88	10	8	106
John Wark (Ipswich T)	89	6	10	105
Garth Crooks (Tottenham H)	85	9	9	103
Steve Taylor (Burnley)	88	8	6	102
Kevin Reeves (Manchester C)	91	6	4	101
Dave Syrett (Northampton T)	89	5	7	101
Ian Wallace (Nottingham F)	90	10	1	101
John Leslie (Wimbledon)	85	10	5	100
Ray McHale (Sheffield U)	82	6	11	99
David Armstrong (Southampton)	82	7	8	97
John Buchanan (Northampton T)	85	6	5	96
Murray Brodie (Aldershot)	86	2	7	95
Gordon Davies (Fulham)	86	5	4	95

Peter Taylor (Orient)	87	2	6	95
Chic Bates (Shrewsbury T)	79	6	10	95
David Gregory (Wrexham)	74	5	15	94
Cyrille Regis (WBA)	71	13	10	94
George Reilly (Cambridge U)	82	10	2	94
Trevor Brooking (West Ham U)	84	6	3	93
Steve Cammack (Scunthorpe U)	87	3	3	93
Derrick Parker (Barnsley)	78	5	10	93
Bob Newton (Port Vale)	75	5	12	92
Terry McDermott (Newcastle U)	74	8	9	91
Tom Ritchie (Bristol C)	85	4	2	91
Alan Harding (Hartlepool U)	84	2	4	90
Ken Price (Reading)	79	7	4	90
Terry Austin (Doncaster R)	84	3	2	89
Tony Evans (Birmingham C)	75	9	5	89
Jeff Hemmerman (Cardiff C)	77	3	8	88
Lou Macari (Manchester U)	78	2	8	88
Trevor Lee (Bournemouth)	79	3	5	87
Keith Mercer (Southend U)	81	3	5	87
John Robertson (Nottingham F)	61	16	10	87
Tommy Craig (Carlisle U)	79	4	3	86
Pat Earles (Reading)	69	11	6	86
Peter Foley (Oxford U)	70	8	8	86
Mike Kearney (Reading)	82	1	3	86
Colin Morris (Sheffield U)	70	9	7	86
Gary Rowell (Sunderland)	80	3	3	86
Alan Brazil (Tottenham H)	76	3	6	85
Nicky Phatterton (Millwall)	74	4	7	85
Gerry Daley (Coventry C)	68	6	11	85
Roy Greaves (Rochdale)	66	9	10	85
Andy King (Everton)	69	11	5	85
Craig Madden (Bury)	75	4	6	85
Trevor Whymark (Grimsby T)	74	9	2	85
Viv Busby (York City)	75	2	7	84
Brian Horton (Luton T)	71	6	7	84
Derek Bell (Lincoln C)	75	7	1	83
John Deehan (Norwich C)	77	3	3	83
Malcolm Poskett (Carlisle U)	67	8	7	82
Alan Walsh (Darlington)	77	4	1	82
Ronnie Glavin (Barnsley)	62	15	4	81
David Peach (Orient)	72	3	6	81
Ian Allinson (Colchester U)	69	6	5	80
Terry Gray (Bradford C)	72	4	4	80
Glenn Hoddle (Tottenham H)	66	5	9	80
Sammy McIlroy (Stoke C)	68	6	6	80
Gordon Staniforth (Plymouth Arg)	69	4	7	80
Brian Stein (Luton T)	74	6	0	80
Steve Cooper (Torquay U)	68	4	7	79
Ian Mellor (Bradford C)	66	7	6	79
Paul Randell (Bristol R)	75	2	2	79
Dave Staniforth (Halifax T)	74	4	1	79
Clive Allen (QPR)	67	3	7	77
Steve Coppell (Manchester U)	63	9	5	77
Ian Edwards (Crystal Palace)	63	8	6	77
Ray Hankin (Middlesbrough)	69	7	1	77
Keith Houchen (Orient)	76	1	0	77
David McNiven (Blackpool)	75	0	2	77
Steve Massey (Northampton T)	66	7	4	77
Alan Young (Sheffield U)	63	5	9	77
John Hollins (Chelsea)	61	10	5	76
Ian Rush (Liverpool)	55	10	10	75
Mick Tait (Portsmouth)	70	1	4	75
Alan Cork (Wimbledon)	66	4	4	74
Brian Pollard (York C)	67	2	5	74
Simon Stainrod (QPR)	65	3	6	74
Gerry Francis (Coventry C)	66	6	1	73
Paul Goddard (West Ham U)	65	8	0	73
Joe Mayo (Cambridge U)	67	1	5	73
John Sims (Plymouth Arg)	67	4	2	73
Keith Bertschin (Norwich C)	57	3	12	72
Phil Neal (Liverpool)	64	4	3	71
John Seasman (Rotherham U)	62	7	2	71
Robbie Cooke (Lincoln C)	53	7	10	70
Terry Curran (Sheffield U)	64	6	0	70
Kevin Drinkell (Grimsby T)	60	6	4	70
Bryan Hamilton (Tranmere R)	61	4	5	70
Colin Lee (Chelsea)	64	1	5	70
Joe Waters (Grimsby T)	59	5	6	70
Graham Watson (Cambridge U)	61	3	6	70
Ian Atkins (Sunderland)	62	3	3	68
Mick Ferguson (Everton)	63	5	0	68
Tom Finney (Cambridge U)	62	5	1	68
Paul Maguire (Stoke C)	50	1	17	68
Mick Robinson (Brighton & HA)	60	5	3	68
Kenny Burns (Leeds U)	61	3	3	67

Peter Houghton (Wigan Ath)	61	3	3	67
David Williams (Bristol R)	57	4	6	67
Gary Birtles (Nottingham F)	50	14	2	66
Alan Birch (Barnsley)	58	5	1	64
Alan Crawford (Bristol C)	49	6	9	64
Simon Garner (Blackburn R)	57	3	4	64
Jeremy Charles (Swansea C)	53	7	3	63
Eddie Gray (Leeds U)	52	6	5	63
Tommy Langley (Crystal Palace)	57	3	3	63
Mick Lyons (Sheffield W)	51	5	7	63
Martin Robinson (Charlton Ath)	53	6	4	63
Dave Thomas (Portsmouth)	53	8	2	63
Gordon Hobson (Lincoln C)	60	3	0	63
Phil Bonnyman (Grimsby T)	52	3	7	62
Gerry Gow (Rotherham U)	55	3	4	62
Bryan Robson (Manchester U)	54	3	5	62
Steve White (Charlton Ath)	57	2	3	62
Steve Johnson (Bury)	52	5	4	61
Gary Shaw (Aston Villa)	53	4	4	61
Clive Walker (Chelsea)	57	1	3	61
Tony Woodcock (Arsenal)	39	12	10	61
Roy Carter (Torquay U)	52	5	3	60
Martin O'Neill (Norwich C)	49	8	3	60
Alan Shoulder (Carlisle U)	56	2	2	60
Graeme Souness (Liverpool)	53	4	3	60
Trevor Christie (Notts Co)	53	5	1	59
Ian Moores (Bolton W)	49	6	4	59
Brian Stanton (Huddersfield T)	51	2	6	59
Alan Waddle (Newport Co)	52	4	3	59
Steve Elliott (Preston NE)	54	2	2	58
John Hawley (Arsenal)	54	3	1	58
Ollie Kearns (Walsall)	55	1	2	58
Kevin Kilmore (Grimsby T)	55	1	2	58
Kevin Mabbutt (Crystal Palace)	46	5	7	58
Ian McDonald (Aldershot)	50	5	3	58
Don Penn (Walsall)	54	2	2	58
Eric Gates (Ipswich T)	47	5	5	57
Nick Holmes (Southampton)	50	5	2	57
Derek Showers (Hereford U)	50	3	4	57
Brian Talbot (Arsenal)	49	2	5	56
Gary Thompson (WBA)	45	7	4	56
Bob Cumming (Grimsby T)	48	5	2	55
Justin Fashanu (Notts Co)	47	5	3	55
John Gregory (QPR)	49	5	1	55
Tony Morley (Aston Villa)	44	7	4	55
Billy Bonds (West Ham U)	46	6	2	54
Tony Funnell (Bournemouth)	48	2	4	54
Billy Hamilton (Burnley)	42	5	7	54
Tony Towner (Rotherham U)	50	0	4	54
John Aldridge (Newport Co)	47	4	2	53
Brian Hornsby (Carlisle U)	47	1	5	53
Billy Kellock (Wolverhampton W)	46	6	1	53
Les Lawrence (Port Vale)	45	4	4	53
Iain McCulloch (Notts Co)	51	1	1	53
Chris Turner (Cambridge U)	45	3	5	53
Imre Varadi (Newcastle U)	49	1	3	53
Alan Ainscow (Everton)	47	4	1	52
Gary Lineker (Leicester C)	49	0	3	52
Gary Stevens (Shrewsbury T)	49	3	0	52
Micky Thomas (Stoke C)	44	4	4	52
Kerry Dixon (Reading)	51	0	0	51
Micky French (Rochdale)	49	1	1	51
Chris Kamara (Brentford)	44	2	5	51
Stuart Parker (Bury)	44	0	7	51
Keith Walwyn (York C)	46	1	4	51
Peter Denyer (Northampton T)	43	6	1	50
Archie Gemmell (Derby Co)	47	1	2	50
Kevin Johnson (Hartlepool U)	47	2	1	50
Steve Neville (Sheffield U)	46	3	1	50
Eric Potts (Bury)	41	7	2	50

FIRST DIVISION CLUB GOALSCORING RECORDS

	MOST LEAGUE GOALS IN A SEASON			MOST LEAGUE GOALS IN A CAREER		
ARSENAL	Ted Drake	42	Div 1 1934–35	Cliff Bastin	150	1930–47
ASTON VILLA	'Pongo' Waring	49	Div 1 1930–31	Harry Hampton	213	1904–20
				Billy Walker	213	1919–34
BIRMINGHAM C	Joe Bradford	29	Div 1 1927–28	Joe Bradford	249	1920–35
COVENTRY C	Clarrie Bourton	49	Div 3(S) 1931–32	Clarrie Bourton	171	1931–37
EVERTON	Bill 'Dixie' Dean	*60	Div 1 1927–28	Bill 'Dixie' Dean	349	1925–37
IPSWICH T	Ted Phillips	41	Div 3(S) 1956–57	Ray Crawford	203	1958–63 & 1966–69
LEICESTER C	Arthur Rowley	44	Div 2 1956–57	Arthur Chandler	259	1923–35
LIVERPOOL	Roger Hunt	41	Div 2 1961–62	Roger Hunt	245	1959–69
LUTON T	Joe Payne	55	Div 3(S) 1936–37	Gordon Turner	243	1949–64
MANCHESTER U	Dennis Viollet	32	Div 1 1959–60	Bobby Charlton	198	1956–73
NORWICH C	Ralph Hunt	31	Div 3(S) 1955–56	Johnny Gavin	122	1945–54 & 1955–58
NOTTINGHAM F	Wally Ardron	36	Div 3(S) 1950–51	Grenville Morris	199	1898–1913
NOTTS CO	Tom Keetley	39	Div 3(S) 1930–31	Les Bradd	125	1967–78
QPR	George Goddard	37	Div 3(S) 1929–30	George Goddard	172	1926–34
SOUTHAMPTON	Derek Reeves	39	Div 3 1959–60	Mike Channon	182	1966–77 & 1979–82
STOKE C	Freddie Steele	33	Div 1 1936–37	Freddie Steele	142	1934–49
SUNDERLAND	Dave Halliday	43	Div 1 1928–29	Charlie Buchan	209	1911–25
TOTTENHAM H	Jimmy Greaves	37	Div 1 1962–63	Jimmy Greaves	220	1961–70
WATFORD	Cliff Holton	42	Div 4 1959–60	Tom Barnett	144	1928–39
WBA	William 'Ginger' Richardson	39	Div 1 1935–36	Tony Brown	218	1963–79
WEST HAM U	Vic Watson	41	Div 1 1929–30	Vic Watson	306	1920–35
WOLVERHAMPTON W	Dennis Westcott	37	Div 1 1946–47	Bill Harthill	164	1928–35

** Record for First Division*

Jimmy Greaves *Tottenham Hotspur*

Arthur Rowley *Leicester City (seen here in Fulham colours)*

SECOND DIVISION CLUB GOALSCORING RECORDS

	MOST LEAGUE GOALS IN A SEASON			MOST LEAGUE GOALS IN A CAREER		
BARNSLEY	Cecil McCormack	33	Div 2 1950–51	Ernest Hine	123	1921–26 & 1934–38
BLACKBURN R	Ted Harper	43	Div 1 1925–26	Tommy Briggs	140	1952–58
BRIGHTON & HA	Peter Ward	32	Div 3 1976–77	Tommy Cook	113	1922–29
CAMBRIDGE U	Alan Biley	21	Div 3 1977–78	Alan Biley	74	1975–80
CARDIFF C	Stan Richards	31	Div 3(S) 1946–47	Len Davies	127	1921–29
CARLISLE U	Jimmy McConnell	42	Div 3(N) 1928–29	Jimmy McConnell	126	1928–32
CHARLTON ATH	Ralph Allen	32	Div 3(S) 1934–35	Stuart Leary	153	1953–62
CHELSEA	Jimmy Greaves	41	Div 1 1960–61	Bobby Tambling	164	1958–70
CRYSTAL P	Peter Simpson	46	Div 3(S) 1930–31	Peter Simpson	154	1930–36
DERBY CO	Jack Bowers	37	Div 1 1930–31	Steve Bloomer	291	1892–1906 & 1910–1914
	Ray Straw	37	Div 3(N) 1956–57			
FULHAM	Frank Newton	41	Div 3(S) 1931–32	Bedford Jezzard	154	1948–56
GRIMSBY T	Pat Glover	42	Div 2 1933–34	Pat Glover	182	1930–39
HUDDERSFIELD T	Sam Taylor	35	Div 2 1919–20	George Brown	142	1921–29
	George Brown	35	Div 1 1925–26			
LEEDS U	John Charles	42	Div 2 1953–54	John Charles	154	1948–57 & 1962
MANCHESTER C	Tommy Johnson	38	Div 1 1928–29	Tommy Johnson	158	1919–30
MIDDLESBROUGH	George Camsell	*59	Div 2 1926–27	George Camsell	326	1925–39
NEWCASTLE U	Hughie Gallacher	36	Div 1 1926–27	Jackie Milburn	178	1946–57
OLDHAM ATH	Tom Davis	33	Div 3(N) 1936–37	Eric Gemmell	110	1947–54
PORTSMOUTH	Billy Hainey	40	Div 2 1926–27	Peter Harris	194	1946–60
SHEFFIELD WED	'Derek' Dooley	46	Div 2 1951–52	Andy Wilson	200	1900–20
SHREWSBURY T	Arthur Rowley	38	Div 4 1958–59	Arthur Rowley	152	1958–65†
SWANSEA C	Cyril Pearce	35	Div 2 1931–32	Ivor Allchurch	166	1949–58 & 1965–68

* *Record for Second Division.*

† *With Shrewsbury Town Arthur Rowley completed his Football League scoring record of 434 goals.*

'Derek' Dooley *Sheffield Wednesday*

THIRD DIVISION CLUB GOALSCORING RECORDS

	MOST LEAGUE GOALS IN A SEASON			MOST LEAGUE GOALS IN A CAREER		
BOLTON W	Joe Smith	38	Div 1 1920–21	Nat Lofthouse	255	1946–61
AFC BOURNEMOUTH	Ted MacDougall	42	Div 4 1970–71	Ron Eyre	202	1924–33
BRADFORD C	David Layne	34	Div 4 1961–62	Frank O'Rourke	88	1906–13
BRENTFORD	Jack Holliday	38	Div 3(S) 1932–33	Jim Towers	153	1954–61
BRISTOL R	Geoff Bradford	33	Div 3(S) 1952–53	Geoff Bradford	245	1949–64
BURNLEY	George Beel	35	Div 1 1927–28	George Beel	178	1923–32
EXETER C	Fred Whitlow	34	Div 3(S) 1932–33	Alan Banks	105	1963–66 & 1967–73
GILLINGHAM	Ernie Morgan	31	Div 3(S) 1954–55	Brian Yeo	135	1963–75
	Brian Yeo	31	Div 4 1973–74			
HULL C	Bill McNaughton	41	Div 3(N) 1932–33	Chris Chilton	194	1960–71
LINCOLN C	Allan Hall	42	Div 3(N) 1931–32	Andy Graver	144	1950–55 & 1958–61
MILLWALL	Richard Parker	37	Div 3(S) 1926–27	Derek Possee	79	1967–73
NEWPORT CO	Tudor Martin	34	Div 3(S) 1929–30	Reg Parker	99	1948–54
ORIENT	Tom Johnston	35	Div 2 1957–58	Tom Johnston	121	1956–58 & 1959–61
OXFORD U	Colin Booth	23	Div 4 1964–65	Graham Atkinson	73	1962–73
PLYMOUTH ARG	Jack Cock	32	Div 3(S) 1925–26	Sammy Black	180	1924–38
PORT VALE	Wilf Kirkham	38	Div 2 1926–27	Wilf Kirkham	154	1923–29 & 1931–33
PRESTON NE	Ted Harper	37	Div 2 1932–33	Tom Finney	187	1946–60
ROTHERHAM U	Wally Ardron	38	Div 3(N) 1946–47	Gladstone Guest	130	1946–56
SCUNTHORPE U	Barrie Thomas	31	Div 2 1961–62	Barrie Thomas	92	1959–62 & 1964–66
SHEFFIELD U	Jimmy Dunne	41	Div 1 1930–31	Harry Johnson	205	1919–30
SOUTHEND U	Jim Shankley	31	Div 3(S) 1928–29	Roy Hollis	122	1953–60
	Sam McCrory	31	Div 3(S) 1957–58			
WALSALL	Gilbert Alsop	40	Div 3(N) 1933–34 & 1934–35	Tony Richards	184	1954–63
				Colin Taylor	184	1958–63, 1964–68 & 1969–73
WIGAN ATH	Les Bradd	19	Div 4 1981–82	Peter Houghton	61	1978–83
WIMBLEDON	Alan Cork	23	Div 3 1980–81	John Leslie	86	1977–83

Geoff Bradford *Bristol Rovers*

FOURTH DIVISION CLUB GOALSCORING RECORDS

	MOST LEAGUE GOALS IN A SEASON			MOST LEAGUE GOALS IN A CAREER		
ALDERSHOT	John Dungworth	26	Div 4 1978–79	Jack Howarth	171	1965–71 & 1972–77
BLACKPOOL	Jimmy Hampson	45	Div 2 1929–30	Jimmy Hampson	247	1927–38
BRISTOL C	Don Clark	36	Div 3(S) 1946–47	John Atyeo	315	1951–66
BURY	Craig Madden	35	Div 4 1981–82	Norman Bullock	124	1920–35
CHESTER	Dick Yates	36	Div 3(N) 1946–47	Gary Talbot	83	1963–67 & 1968–70
CHESTERFIELD	Jimmy Gordon	44	Div 3(N) 1925–26	Ernie Moss	127	1963–67 & 1968–70
COLCHESTER U	Bobby Hunt	37	Div 4 1861–62	Martyn King	131	1959–65
CREWE ALEX	Terry Harkin	34	Div 4 1964–65	Bert Swindells	126	1928–37
DARLINGTON	David Brown	39	Div 3(N) 1924–25	David Brown	74	1923–26
DONCASTER R	Clarrie Jordan	42	Div 3(N) 1946–47	Tom Keetley	180	1923–29
HALIFAX T	Albert Valentine	34	Div 3(N) 1934–35	Ernie Dixon	129	1922–30
HARTLEPOOL U	Billy Robinson	28	Div 3(N) 1927–28	Ken Johnson	98	1949–60
HEREFORD U	'Dixie' McNeil	35	Div 3 1975–76	'Dixie' McNeil	85	1974–77
MANSFIELD T	Ted Harston	55	Div 3(N) 1936–37	Harry Johnson	104	1931–36
NORTHAMPTON T	Cliff Holton	36	Div 3 1961–62	Jack English	135	1947–60
PETERBOROUGH U	Terry Bly	52	Div 4 1960–61	Jim Hall	122	1967–75
READING	Ronnie Blackman	39	Div 3(S) 1951–52	Ronnie Blackman	156	1947–54
ROCHDALE	Albert Whitehurst	44	Div 3(N) 1926–27	Reg Jenkins	119	1964–73
STOCKPORT CO	Alf Lithgoe	46	Div 3(N) 1933–34	Jack Connor	132	1951–56
SWINDON T	Harry Morris	47	Div 3(S) 1926–27	Harry Morris	216	1926–33
TORQUAY U	Sammy Collins	40	Div 3(S) 1955–56	Sammy Collins	204	1948–58
TRANMERE R	'Bunny' Bell	35	Div 3(N) 1933–34	'Bunny' Bell	104	1931–36
WREXHAM	Tom Bamford	44	Div 3(N) 1933–34	Tom Bamford	175	1928–34
YORK C	Bill Fenton	31	Div 3(N) 1951–52	Norman Wilkinson	125	1954–66
	Arthur Bottom	31	Div 3(N) 1955–56			

Terry Bly *Peterborough United (seen here in Norwich City colours)*

RECORD INTERNATIONAL AND CLUB APPEARANCES

FIRST DIVISION CLUB RECORDS

MOST LEAGUE APPEARANCES FOR CLUB				MOST 'CAPPED' PLAYER		
Arsenal	500	George Armstrong	1960–77	Pat Rice	49	N Ireland
Aston Villa	560	Charlie Aitken	1961–76	Peter McParland	33 (34)	N Ireland
Birmingham C	486	Gil Merrick	1946 60	Malcolm Page	28	Wales
Coventry C	486	George Curtis	1956–70	Dave Clements	21 (48)	N Ireland
Everton	465	Ted Sagar	1929–53	Alan Ball	39 (72)	England
Ipswich T	591	Mick Mills	1966–82	Alan Hunter	47 (53)	N Ireland
Leicester C	528	Adam Black	1920–35	Gordon Banks	37 (73)	England
Liverpool	640	Ian Callaghan	1960–78	Emlyn Hughes	59 (62)	England
Luton Town	494	Bob Morton	1948–64	Mal Donaghy	24	N Ireland
Manchester U	606	Bobby Charlton	1956–73	Bobby Charlton	106	England
Norwich C	590	Ron Ashman	1947–64	Martin O'Neill	19 (57)	N Ireland
Nottingham F	614	Bob McKinlay	1951–70	Martin O'Neill	36 (57)	N Ireland
Notts Co	564	Albert Ironmonger	1904–26	H. A. Cursham	8	England
QPR	519	Tony Ingham	1950–63	Don Givens	26 (56)	Eire
Southampton	713	Terry Paine	1956–74	Mick Channon	45 (46)	England
Stoke C	506	Eric Skeels	1958–76	Gordon Banks	36 (73)	England
Sunderland	537	Jim Montgomery	1962–77	Billy Bingham	33 (56)	N Ireland
				Martin Harvey	33	N Ireland
Tottenham H	549	Steve Perryman	1969–	Pat Jennings	68 (99)	N Ireland
Watford	411	Duncan Welbourne	1963–74	Gerry Armstrong	21 (48)	N Ireland
WBA	574	Tony Brown	1963–80	Stuart Williams	33 (43)	Wales
West Ham U	575	Billy Bonds	1967–	Bobby Moore	108	England
Wolverhampton	501	Derek Parkin	1967–82	Billy Wright	105	England

Appearances as substitutes are included in the above totals

Mick Mills *Ipswich Town*

Martin O'Neill *Norwich City*

SECOND DIVISION CLUB RECORDS

Club	MOST LEAGUE APPEARANCES FOR CLUB			MOST 'CAPPED' PLAYER		
Barnsley	514	Barry Murphy	1962–78	Eddie McMorran	9 (15)	N Ireland
Blackburn R	580	Ronnie Clayton	1950–69	Bob Crompton	41	England
Brighton & HA	509	'Tug' Wilson	1922–36	Mick Robinson	13	Eire
				Mark Lawrenson	13 (21)	Eire
Cambridge U	338	Steve Fallon	1974–	Tom Finney	7 (14)	N Ireland
Cardiff C	445	Tom Farquarson	1922–35	Alf Sherwood	39 (41)	Wales
Carlisle U	466	Alan Ross	1963–79	Eric Welsh	4	N Ireland
Charlton Ath	582	Sam Bartram	1934–56	John Hewie	19	Scotland
Chelsea	655	Ron Harris	1962–80	Ray Wilkins	24 (54)	England
Crystal P	432	Terry Long	1956–69	Paddy Mulligan	14 (51)	Eire
Derby Co	486	Kevin Hector	1966–78, 1980–82	Roy McFarland	28	England
Fulham	594	Johnny Haynes	1952–70	Johnny Haynes	56	England
Grimsby T	448	Keith Jobling	1953–69	Pat Glover	7	Wales
Huddersfield T	520	Billy Smith	1914–34	Jimmy Nicholson	31 (41)	N Ireland
Leeds U	629	Jack Charlton	1953–73	Billy Bremner	54	Scotland
Manchester C	565	Alan Oakes	1959–76	Colin Bell	48	England
Middlesbrough	563	Tim Williamson	1902–23	Alf McMichael	40	N Ireland
Oldham Ath	525	Ian Wood	1966–80	Albert Gray	9 (24)	Wales
Portsmouth	764	Jimmy Dickinson	1946–65	Jimmy Dickinson	48	England
Sheffield W	502	Andy Wilson	1900–20	Ron Springett	33	England
Shrewsbury T	370	Ken Mulhearn	1971–80	Jimmy McLaughlin	5 (12)	N Ireland
Swansea C	585	Wilfred Milne	1919–37	Ivor Allchurch	42 (68)	Wales

Jimmy Dickinson *Portsmouth*

Ivor Allchurch *Newcastle United*

THIRD DIVISION CLUB RECORDS

MOST LEAGUE APPEARANCES FOR CLUB			MOST 'CAPPED' PLAYER		
Bournemouth	412 Ray Bumstead	1958–70	Tommy Godwin	4 (13)	Eire
Bradford C	472 'Cec' Podd	1970–	Harry Hampton	9	N Ireland
Brentford	514 Ken Coote	1949–64	Idris Hopkins	12	Wales
Bristol R	545 Stuart Taylor	1966–80	Matt O'Mahoney	6	Eire, N. I.
Burnley	530 Jerry Dawson	1906–29	Jimmy McIlroy	51 (55)	N Ireland
Bolton W	519 Eddie Hopkinson	1956–70	Nat Lofthouse	33	England
Exeter C	495 Arnold Mitchell	1952–66	Dermot Curtis	1 (17)	Eire
Gillingham	571 John Simpson	1957–72	Damien Richardson	2 (3)	Eire
Hull C	520 Andy Davison	1952–67	Terry Neill	15 (59)	N Ireland
Lincoln C	402 Tony Emery	1946–59	David Pugh	3 (7)	Wales
			George Moulson	3	Eire
Millwall	523 Barry Kitchiner	1967–82	Eamonn Dunphy	22 (23)	Eire
Newport Co	526 Len Weare	1955–70	Fred Cook	2 (8)	Wales
			Alf Sherwood	2 (41)	Wales
			Harold Williams	2	Wales
			Jack Nicholls	2 (4)	Wales
			Billy Thomas	2	Wales
			Steve Lowndes	2	Wales
Orient	431 Peter Allen	1965–78	Tony Grealish	8 (30)	Eire
Oxford U	480 John Shuker	1962–77	Dave Roberts	6 (17)	Wales
Plymouth Arg	470 Sammy Black	1924–38	Moses Russell	20 (23)	Wales
Port Vale	761 Roy Sproson	1950–72	Sammy Morgan	7 (18)	N Ireland
Preston NE	447 Alan Kelly	1961–75	Tom Finney	76	England
Rotherham U	459 Danny Williams	1946–62	Harold Millership	6	Wales
Scunthorpe U	600 Jack Brownsword	1950–65			
Sheffield U	629 Joe Shaw	1948–66	Billy Gillespie	25	N Ireland
Southend U	451 'Sandy' Anderson	1950–63	George McKenzie	9	Eire
Walsall	467 Colin Harrison	1964–82	Mick Kearns	15 (17)	Eire
Wigan Ath	173 Peter Houghton	1978–			
Wimbledon	253 John Leslie	1977–			

Roy Sproson *Port Vale*

Nat Lofthouse *Bolton*

FOURTH DIVISION CLUB RECORDS

MOST LEAGUE APPEARANCES FOR CLUB			MOST 'CAPPED' PLAYER		
Aldershot	461 Murray Brodie	1964–83	Peter Scott	1 (10)	N Ireland
Blackpool	568 Jimmy Armfield	1952–71	Jimmy Armfield	43	England
Bristol C	597 John Atyeo	1951–66	Billy Wedlock	26	England
Bury	506 Norman Bullock	1920–35	Bill Gorman	11 (13)	Eire, (4) N Ireland
Chester C	408 Ray Gill	1951–62	Bill Lewis	7 (30)	Wales
Chesterfield	613 Dave Blakey	1948–67	Walter McMillen	4 (7)	N Ireland
Colchester U	577 Micky Cook	1969–			
Crewe Alex	436 Tommy Lowrie	1966–78	Bill Lewis	12 (30)	Wales
Darlington	442 Ron Greener	1955–68			
Doncaster R	406 Fred Emery	1925–36	Len Graham	14	N Ireland
Halifax T	367 John Pickering	1965–74			
Hartlepool U	448 Wattie Moore	1948–64	Ambrose Fogarty	1 (11)	Eire
Hereford U	240 Tommy Hughes	1973–82	Brian Evans	1 (7)	Wales
Mansfield T	413 Sandy Pate	1967–78	John McClelland	6 (15)	N Ireland
Northampton T	521 Tommy Fowler	1946–61	E. Lloyd Davies	12 (16)	Wales
Peterborough U	440 Tommy Robson	1968–81	Tony Millington	8 (21)	Wales
Reading	471 Steve Death	1969–82	Pat McConnell	8	N Ireland
Rochdale	317 Graham Smith	1966–74			
Stockport Co	465 Bob Murray	1952–63	Harry Hardy	1	England
Swindon T	770 John Trollope	1960–80	Rod Thomas	30 (50)	Wales
Torquay U	443 Dennis Lewis	1947–59			
Tranmere R	595 Harold Bell	*1946–64	Albert Gray	3 (22)	Wales
Wrexham	592 Arfon Griffiths	1959–61, 1962–79	Dai Davies	18 (51)	Wales
York C	481 Barry Jackson	1958–70	Peter Scott	7 (10)	N Ireland

* *Including the League record of 401 consecutive appearances.*

Jimmy Armfield *Blackpool*

Dai Davies *Wrexham*

TRANSFERS 1982–3

* *Denotes player involved in exchange deal*

	From	*To*
August		
Ian Atkins	Shrewsbury Town	Sunderland
Trevor Aylott	Barnsley	Millwall
Billy Ayre	Halifax Town	Mansfield Town
Graham Baker	Southampton	Manchester City
Ian Bailey	Middlesbrough	Sheffield Wednesday
Steve Baines	Walsall	Scunthorpe United
Alan Biley	Everton	Portsmouth
Phil Bonnyman	Chesterfield	Grimsby Town
Ian Britton	Chelsea	Dundee United
Alan Brown	Sunderland	Shrewsbury Town
John Brownlie	Newcastle United	Middlesbrough
Willie Carr	Wolverhampton Wanderers	Millwall
Mark Chamberlain	Port Vale	Stoke City
Lee Chapman	Stoke City	Arsenal
Paul Clark	Brighton & Hove Albion	Southend United
David Cross	West Ham United	Manchester City
Terry Curran	Sheffield Wednesday	Sheffield United
Peter Eastoe	Everton	West Bromwich Albion
Neil Firm	Leeds United	Peterborough United
Mark Harrison	Port Vale	Stoke City
David Hodgson	Middlesbrough	Liverpool
David Johnson	Liverpool	Everton
Kevin Keegan	Southampton	Newcastle United
Mick Kennedy	Huddersfield Town	Middlesbrough
Mick Lyons	Everton	Sheffield Wednesday
Joe McBride	Everton	Rotherham United
Ray McHale	Barnsley	Sheffield United
Charles McManus	Stoke City	Bradford City
Gary McManus	Ipswich Town	Notts County
Gary Mabbutt	Bristol Rovers	Tottenham Hotspur
John Matthews	Sheffield United	Mansfied Town
Steve Ogrizovic	Liverpool	Shrewsbury Town
Vince O'Keefe	Torquay United	Blackburn Rovers
Malcolm Poskett	Watford	Carlisle United
Colin Randell	Plymouth Argyle	Blackburn Rovers
Bryan Robson	Carlisle United	Chelsea
Billy Ronson	Wrexham	Barnsley
David Seaman	Leeds United	Peterborough United
Kevin Sheedy	Liverpool	Everton
Peter Shilton	Nottingham Forest	Southampton
Peter Skipper	Darlington	Hull City
Micky Speight	Blackburn Rovers	Grimsby Town
Micky Thomas	Brighton & Hove Albion	Stoke City
Bobby Thomson	Middlesbrough	Hibernian
Colin Todd	Birmingham City	Nottingham Forest
Mick Vinter	Wrexham	Oxford United
Bob Wardle	Shrewsbury Town	Liverpool
Neil Webb	Reading	Portsmouth
Peter Welsh	Leicester City	Hibernian
Alex Young	Leicester City	Sheffield United
Temporary Transfers		
David Barton	Newcastle United	Blackburn Rovers
John Burridge	Queen's Park Rangers	Wolverhampton Wanderers
Clive Day	Fulham	Mansfied Town
Justin Fashanu	Nottingham Forest	Southampton
Howard Goddard	AFC Bournemouth	Aldershot
Seamus Heath	Luton Town	Lincoln City
Paul Lodge	Everton	Wigan Athletic
Billy McLaren	Wolverhampton Wanderers	Hibernian
Martin New	Barnsley	Wigan Athletic
Mike Salmon	Blackburn Rovers	Leeds United
Kevin Sheldon	Wigan Athletic	Port Vale
September		
Terry Austin	Huddersfield Town	Doncaster Rovers
Garry Birtles	Manchester United	Nottingham Forest
Noel Blake	Aston Villa	Birmingham City
John Burridge	Queen's Park Rangers	Wolverhampton Wanderers
Neville Chamberlain	Port Vale	Stoke City
Tony Cunningham	Lincoln City	Barnsley
Tom English	Coventry City	Leicester City
Alex Gibson	Birmingham City	Oxford United

	From	*To*
Howard Goddard	AFC Bournemouth	Aldershot
John Keay	Shrewsbury Town	Wrexham
Tony McAndrew	Middlesbrough	Chelsea
Terry McDermott	Liverpool	Newcastle United
Jim Melrose	Leicester City	Coventry City
Jimmy Mullen	Rotherham United	Cardiff City
Bob Newton	Hartlepool United	Port Vale
Daral Pugh	Doncaster Rovers	Huddersfield Town
Colin Russell	Liverpool	Huddersfield Town
Gary Stevens	Cardiff City	Shrewsbury Town

Temporary Transfers

Mike Angus	Middlesbrough	Scunthorpe United
John Beck	Fulham	AFC Bournemouth
John Butcher	Oxford United	Halifax Town
Paul Comstive	Blackburn Rovers	Rochdale
Bruce Halliday	Newcastle United	Darlington
Steve Hatter	Fulham	Exeter City
Martin Hodge	Oldham Athletic	Everton (Tr Back)
Jeff Johnson	Newport County	Gillingham
Peter Johnson	Newcastle United	Bristol City
Alan Judge	Luton Town	Reading
Alan Judge	Reading	Luton Town (Tr Back)
Steve Kinsey	Manchester City	Chester
David McClurg	Middlesbrough	Cliftonville
Martin Robinson	Charlton Athletic	Reading
John Steeples	Grimsby Town	Torquay United
John Steeples	Torquay United	Grimsby Town (Tr Back)
Clive Wilson	Manchester City	Chester

October

Marshall Burke	Blackburn Rovers	Lincoln City
Bobby Hutchinson	Tranmere Rovers	Mansfield Town
Joey Jones	Wrexham	Chelsea
Alan Little	Doncaster Rovers	Torquay United
Geoff Scott	Birmingham City	Charlton Athletic
Clive Wigginton	Torquay United	Doncaster Rovers

Temporary Transfers

Jim Arnold	Everton	Preston North End
Steve Bould	Stoke City	Torquay United
Kevin Bremner	Colchester United	Birmingham City
David Buchanan	Leicester City	Northampton Town
John Butcher	Halifax Town	Oxford United (Tr Back)
Roy Carter	Swindon Town	Torquay United
Bobby Cooke	Peterborough United	Luton Town
Bill Garner	Celtic	Rochdale
Jim Gilligan	Watford	Lincoln City
Nigel Gray	Orient	Blackburn Rovers
John Hawley	Arsenal	Orient
Glen Keeley	Blackburn Rovers	Everton
Trevor Lee	Gillingham	Orient
Joe Mayo	Cambridge United	Blackpool
Ian Muir	Queen's Park Rangers	Burnley
Donal Murphy	Blackburn Rovers	Drogheda
Steve Neville	Sheffield United	Exter City
Peter O'Sullivan	Fulham	Charlton Athletic
Mark Rhodes	Rotherham United	Darlington
Trevor Ross	Everton	Portsmouth
Mike Salmon	Blackburn Rovers	Chester
Bobby Savage	Liverpool	Wrexham
Mike Small	Luton Town	Peterborough United
Lindsay Smith	Cambridge United	Plymouth Argyle
Kenny Swain	Aston Villa	Nottingham Forest
Carl Swan	Doncaster Rovers	Rochdale
Billy Tucker	Brentford	Northampton Town
Mike Walsh	Everton	Norwich City
Peter Ward	Nottingham Forest	Brighton & Hove Albion
Garry Watson	Bradford City	Doncaster Rovers
Neil Whatmore	Birmingham City	Oxford United
Mark Whitlock	Southampton	Grimsby Town

November

Mark Aizlewood	Luton Town	Charlton Athletic
Alan Dodd	Stoke City	Wolverhampton Wanderers
Bobby Fisher	Orient	Cambridge United
Brian Flynn	Leeds United	Burnley
Jeff Johnson	Newport County	Gillingham
George Lawrence	Southampton	Oxford United

	From	To
Trevor Lee	Gillingham	AFC Bournemouth
Mick Mills	Ipswich Town	Southampton
Gordon Simmonite	Blackpool	Lincoln City
Lindsay Smith	Cambridge United	Plymouth Argyle

Temporary Transfers

Alan Ainscow	Everton	Barnsley
Jim Arnold	Preston North End	Everton (Tr Back)
Kevin Arnott	Sheffield United	Blackburn Rovers
Andy Brand	Hereford United	Wrexham
Kevin Bremner	Birmingham City	Colchester United (Tr Back)
Bobby Cooke	Luton Town	Peterborough United (Tr Back)
Ian Davies	Manchester City	Bury
Mark Falco	Tottenham Hotspur	Chelsea
Mick Ferguson	Everton	Birmingham City
Howard Gayle	Liverpool	Newcastle United
David Glenn	Wigan Athletic	Chelsea
Bruce Halliday	Newcastle United	Bury
Age Hareide	Manchester City	Norwich City
Nigel Hart	Blackpool	Crewe Alexandra
Steve Hatter	Fulham	Wimbledon
Alan Judge	Luton Town	Reading
Richard Key	Cambridge United	Northampton Town
Steve Kinsey	Manchester City	Chesterfield
Gerald McElhinney	Bolton Wanderers	Rochdale
Paul Maddy	Cardiff City	Stoke City
Peter O'Sullivan	Fulham	Reading
Gordon Owen	Sheffield Wednesday	Doncaster Rovers
Forbes Phillipson-Masters	Plymouth Argyle	Bristol City
John Richards	Wolverhampton Wanderers	Derby County
Micky Small	Peterborough United	Luton Town (Tr Back)
Kevin Smith	Charlton Athletic	Aston Villa
Bobby Smith	Leicester City	Hibernian
Billy Steel	Oldham Athletic	Wigan Athletic
Martin Thomas	Cardiff City	Bristol Rovers (Tr Back)
Phil Walker	Charlton Athletic	Gillingham
Clive Wilson	Manchester City	Chester
Billy Wright	Burnley	Crewe Alexandra

December

Paul Barron	Crystal Palace	West Bromwich Albion
Trevor Cherry	Leeds United	Bradford City
Tony Cliss	Peterborough United	Crewe Alexandra
Bobby Davison	Halifax Town	Derby County
Justin Fashanu	Nottingham Forest	Notts County
Mick Gooding	Rotherham United	Chesterfield
Bruce Halliday	Newcastle United	Bury
Joe Hinnigan	Sunderland	Preston North End
Peter Reid	Bolton Wanderers	Everton
Philip Walker	Chesterfield	Rotherham United
Frank Worthington	Leeds United	Sunderland

Temporary Transfers

Peter Bodak	Manchester United	Manchester City
Les Bradd	Wigan Athletic	Bristol Rovers
Kevin Bremner	Colchester United	Wrexham
Roy Carter	Swindon Town	Bristol Rovers
Peter Cartwright	Newcastle United	Scunthorpe United
Terry Curran	Sheffield United	Everton
Phil Ferns	Charlton Athletic	Wimbledon
David Geddis	Aston Villa	Luton Town
Nigel Gray	Orient	Charlton Athletic
Phil Hawker	Birmingham City	Walsall
John Hawley	Arsenal	Hull City
Mark Hughes	Bristol Rovers	Torquay United
Steve Kendal	Nottingham Forest	Chesterfield
Neil McNab	Brighton & Hove Albion	Leeds United
Calvin Plummer	Nottingham Forest	Chesterfield
Ian Richardson	Watford	Blackpool
Trevor Ross	Everton	Sheffield United
Gordon Smith	Brighton & Hove Albion	Glasgow Rangers
Kevin Smith	Aston Villa	Charlton Athletic (Tr Back)
Neville Southall	Everton	Port Vale
Les Strong	Fulham	Brentford
Kevin Summerfield	Birmingham City	Walsall
Andy Thomas	Oxford United	Fulham
Martin Thomas	Bristol Rovers	Tottenham Hotspur
Mike Walsh	Everton	Burnley
Gary Westwood	Ipswich Town	Crystal Palace
Neil Watmore	Birmingham City	Bolton Wanderers

	From	To
January		
Alan Ball	Southampton	Bristol Rovers
Peter Bodak	Manchester United	Manchester City
Paul Futcher	Oldham Athletic	Derby County
Tim Heard	Aston Villa	Sheffield Wednesday
Leighton James	Swansea City	Sunderland
Steve Kendal	Nottingham Forest	Chesterfield
David Mills	West Bromwich Albion	Sheffield Wednesday
Calvin Plummer	Nottingham Forest	Chesterfield
Ken Price	Gillingham	Reading
Kenny Swain	Aston Villa	Nottingham Forest
Joe Walker	Leicester City	Motherwell
Danny Wilson	Chesterfield	Nottingham Forest

Temporary Transfers

Paul Bancroft	Derby County	Crewe Alexandra
Eddie Blackburn	York City	Hartlepool United
Kevin Bremner	Wrexham	Colchester United (Tr Back)
Kevin Bremner	Colchester United	Plymouth Argyle
Winston Campbell	Barnsley	Doncaster Rovers
Gerard Daly	Coventry City	Leicester City
Barry Gallagher	Bradford City	Mansfield Town
Howard Gayle	Newcastle United	Liverpool (Tr Back)
Howard Gayle	Liverpool	Birmingham City
Martin Hodge	Everton	Gillingham
Micky Laverick	York City	Huddersfield Town
John Linford	Ipswich Town	Colchester United
Gary Locke	Chelsea	Crystal Palace
Paul Lodge	Everton	Rotherham United
David Madden	Southampton	AFC Bournemouth
Jimmy Neighbour	West Ham United	AFC Bournemouth
Gavin Oliver	Sheffield Wednesday	Tranmere Rovers
Terry Park	Stockport County	Manchester City
Martin Patching	Watford	Northampton Town
Paul Richardson	Sheffield United	Blackpool
Neville Southall	Port Vale	Everton (Tr Back)
Neville Southall	Everton	Port Vale
Brian Sparrow	Arsenal	Wimbledon
Billy Steel	Oldham Athletic	Wrexham
Peter Taylor	Orient	Oldham Athletic
Andy Thomas	Fulham	Oxford United (Tr Back)
Garry Watson	Doncaster Rovers	Bradford City (Tr Back)
Gary Westwood	Crystal Palace	Ipswich Town (Tr Back)
Steve White	Charlton Athletic	Lincoln City

February

Paul Brady	Northampton Town	Crewe Alexandra
Kevin Bremner	Colchester United	Millwall
Roy Carter	Swindon Town	Torquay United
Keith Cassells	Southampton	Brentford
Bobby Cooke	Peterborough United	Cambridge United
Terry Donovan	Aston Villa	Burnley
Steve Edwards	Oldham Athletic	Crewe Alexandra
John Friar	Leicester City	Rotherham United
Steve Hardwick	Newcastle United	Oxford United
Steve Hatter	Fulham	Wimbledon
Paul Lodge	Everton	Preston North End
Kevin Summerfield	Birmingham City	Walsall
Garry Thompson	Coventry City	West Bromwich Albion
Neil Whatmore	Birmingham City	Oxford United

Temporary Transfers

Gary Barnett	Oxford United	Wimbledon
David Barton	Newcastle United	Darlington
John Breckin	Rotherham United	Bury
Kevin Bremner	Plymouth Argyle	Colchester United (Tr Back)
Paul Comstive	Blackburn Rovers	Rochdale
Grant Davies	Newport County	Exeter City
Terry Donovan	Aston Villa	Oxford United
Peter Foley	Oxford United	Gillingham
Martin Hodge	Everton	Preston North End
Mark Leonard	Everton	Tranmere Rovers
Steve Lovell	Crystal Palace	Millwall
Ray McHale	Sheffield United	Bury
John McPhail	Sheffield United	York City
Ian Moores	Bolton Wanderers	Barnsley
Stuart Naylor	Lincoln City	Peterborough United
Micky Nutton	Chelsea	Reading
Tony Reid	Derby County	Scunthorpe United
John Richards	Derby County	Wolverhampton Wanderers (Tr Back)

	From	To
Martin Thomas	Bristol Rovers	Southend United
Nigel Thrower	Nottingham Forest	Chesterfield
Kevin Todd	Newcastle United	Darlington
Colin Walker	Barnsley	Doncaster Rovers
Tom Wardrobe	Sunderland	St Mirren
Jeff Wealands	Birmingham City	Manchester United
Peter Wells	Southampton	Millwall
Neil Whatmore	Bolton Wanderers	Birmingham City (Tr Back)
Steve White	Lincoln City	Charlton Athletic (Tr Back)
Steve White	Charlton Athletic	Luton Town

March

Trevor Aylott	Millwall	Luton Town
Brian Borrows	Everton	Bolton Wanderers
Alan Brazil	Ipswich Town	Tottenham Hotspur
John Breckin	Rotherham United	Bury
Peter Cartwright	Newcastle United	Darlington
Sandy Clark	West Ham United	Glasgow Rangers
David Coles	Birmingham City	Mansfield Town
Terry Connor	Leeds United	Brighton & Hove Albion
Alan Curbishley	Birmingham City	Aston Villa
David Cusack	Southend United	Millwall
Kevin Dillon	Birmingham City	Portsmouth
John Donnelly	Dumbarton	Leeds United
Paul Elliott	Charlton Athletic	Luton Town
Barry Gallagher	Bradford City	Halifax Town
Mike Halsall	Liverpool	Birmingham City
Phil Hawker	Birmingham City	Walsall
Tony Henry	Bolton Wanderers	Oldham Athletic
Paul Hooks	Notts County	Derby County
Bobby Hopkins	Aston Villa	Birmingham City
Dean Horrix	Millwall	Gillingham
Peter Johnson	Newcastle United	Doncaster Rovers
Billy Kellock	Luton Town	Wolverhampton Wanderers
Mike Lester	Bradford City	Scunthorpe United
Steve Lovell	Crystal Palace	Millwall
Mick McGuire	Norwich City	Barnsley
John MacPhail	Sheffield United	York City
Bobby Mitchell	Carlisle United	Rotherham United
Nicky Morgan	West Ham United	Portsmouth
Ernie Moss	Port Vale	Lincoln City
Micky Nutton	Chelsea	Millwall
Anton Otulakowski	Southend United	Millwall
Andy Ritchie	Brighton & Hove Albion	Leeds United
Gordon Staniforth	Carlisle United	Plymouth Argyle
Billy Steel	Oldham Athletic	Port Vale
Kevin Stonehouse	Blackburn Rovers	Huddersfield Town
David Swindlehurst	Derby County	West Ham United
Dean White	Gillingham	Millwall

Temporary Transfers

Kevin Arnott	Blackburn Rovers	Sheffield United (Tr Back)
Kevin Arnott	Sheffield United	Rotherham United
Brian Attley	Derby County	Oxford United
Keith Bowen	Brentford	Colchester United
Kenny Burns	Leeds United	Derby County
Mike Carter	Plymouth Argyle	Hereford United
Phil Cavener	Burnley	Bradford City
David Crown	Portsmouth	Exeter City
Peter Gleasure	Millwall	Northampton Town
Tony Godden	West Bromwich Albion	Luton Town
Stuart Gray	Nottingham Forest	Bolton Wanderers
Tyrone James	Plymouth Argyle	Torquay United
Mark Kearney	Everton	Mansfield Town
Mark Lawrence	Hartlepool United	Port Vale
Mark Leonard	Everton	Tranmere Rovers
John Linford	Colchester United	Ipswich Town (Tr Back)
John Linford	Ipswich Town	Southend United
Brian McDermott	Arsenal	Fulham
Alan McDonald	Queen's Park Rangers	Charlton Athletic
Paul McGee	Burnley	Dundalk
Neil McNab	Brighton & Hove Albion	Portsmouth
Paul Maddy	Cardiff City	Hereford United
David Miller	Burnley	Crewe Alexandra
Kevin Moore	Newport County	Swindon Town
Donal Murphy	Blackburn Rovers	Bohemians
Gordon Owen	Sheffield Wednesday	Chesterfield
Mark Proctor	Nottingham Forest	Sunderland
Mark Rhodes	Rotherham	Mansfield Town
Bryan Robson	Chelsea	Carlisle United
Keith Robson	Leicester City	Carlisle United
Colin Ross	Middlesbrough	Chesterfield

	From	To
Mike Saxby	Luton Town	Grimsby Town
Trevor Senior	Portsmouth	Aldershot
Glenn Skivington	Derby County	Halifax Town
Micky Speight	Grimsby Town	Bury
Billy Steel	Wrexham	Oldham Athletic (Tr Back)
Eric Steele	Watford	Cardiff City
Ian Stewart	Queen's Park Rangers	Millwall
Andy Thomas	Oxford United	Derby County
Martin Thomas	Bristol Rovers	Newcastle United
Chris Thompson	Bolton Wanderers	Lincoln City
Tony Towner	Rotherham United	Sheffield United
Steve White	Luton Town	Charlton Athletic (Tr Back)
Mark Whitlock	Southampton	Aldershot
David Wilkes	Barnsley	Halifax Town
Rhys Wilmot	Arsenal	Hereford United
April		
Keith Bowen	Brentford	Colchester United
Mark Kearney	Everton	Mansfield Town
Temporary Transfers		
Tony Lowery	West Bromwich Albion	Mansfield Town
Gerard McElhinney	Rochdale	Bolton Wanderers (Tr Back)
Neil McNab	Portsmouth	Brighton & Hove Albion (Tr Back)
May		
Joseph McLaughlin	Greenock Morton	Chelsea
Edward Niedzwiecki	Wrexham	Chelsea
June		
Kenneth Armstrong	Kilmarnock	Southampton
John Bamber	Blackpool	Coventry City
Ian Banks	Barnsley	Leicester City
Michael Bennett	Bolton Wanderers	Wolverhampton Wanderers
Michael Ferguson	Everton	Birmingham City
Howard Gayle	Liverpool	Birmingham City
Alan Harper	Liverpool	Everton
Mark Hateley	Coventry City	Portsmouth
Alistair McCoist	Sunderland	Glasgow Rangers
Paul Rideout	Swindon Town	Aston Villa
John Robertson	Nottingham Forest	Derby County
Nigel Spackman	AFC Bournemouth	Chelsea
Gary Stevens	Brighton & Hove Albion	Tottenham Hotspur
Daniel Thomas	Coventry City	Tottenham Hotspur
Andrew Watson	Aberdeen	Leeds United
Frank Worthington	Sunderland	Southampton

Everton defender Steve McMahon transferred in the close season to Aston Villa for £300,000.

TRANSFER FEES

RECORD TRANSFER FEES PAID BY FIRST DIVISION CLUBS

Arsenal	£1,250,000	to Queen's Park Rangers	for Clive Allen	June 1980
Aston Villa	500,000	to Newcastle United	for Peter Withe	May 1980
Birmingham City	350,000	to Derby County	for David Langan	June 1980
Coventry City	325,000	to Bristol City	for Gary Collier	July 1979
Everton	700,000	to Stoke City	for Adrian Heath	Jan 1982
Ipswich Town	250,000	to Millwall	for Kevin O'Callaghan	Jan 1980
Leicester City	250,000	to FC Bruges	for Roger Davies	Dec 1977
	250,000	to Oldham Athletic	for Alan Young	July 1979
	250,000	to Partick Thistle	for Jim Melrose	July 1980
Liverpool	900,000	to Brighton & Hove Albion	for Mark Lawrenson	Aug 1981
Luton Town	200,000	to Mansfield Town	for Mike Saxby	July 1979
	200,000	to Bristol Rovers	for Steve White	Dec 1980
Manchester United	1,500,000	to West Bromwich Albion	for Bryan Robson	Oct 1981
Norwich City	300,000	to Hajduk Split	for Drazen Muzinic	Sept 1980
Nottingham Forest	1,250,000	to Coventry City	for Ian Wallace	July 1980
Notts County	600,000	to Orient	for John Chiedozie	Aug 1981
Queen's Park Rangers	400,000	to Sheffield United	for Tony Currie	Aug 1979
Southampton	600,000	to Middlesbrough	for David Armstrong	Aug 1981
Stoke City	350,000	to Manchester United	for Sammy McIlroy	1982
Sunderland	320,000	to San Lorenzo	for Claudio Maranoni	Dec 1979
Tottenham Hotspur	800,000	to Aberdeen	for Steve Archibald	May 1980
Watford	250,000	to Tottenham Hotspur	for Gerry Armstrong	Nov 1980
West Bromwich Albion	748,000	to Manchester City	for Peter Barnes	July 1979
West Ham United	800,000	to Queen's Park Rangers	for Paul Goddard	July 1979
Wolverhampton Wanderers	1,175,000	to Aston Villa	for Andy Gray	Aug 1980

RECORD TRANSFER FEES RECEIVED BY FIRST DIVISION CLUBS

Arsenal	£1,250,000	from Crystal Palace	for Clive Allen	Aug 1980
Aston Villa	1,469,000	from Wolverhampton Wanderers (1,175,000 Basic Fee)	for Andy Gray	Sept 1979
Birmingham City	975,000	from Nottingham Forest	for Trevor Francis	Feb 1979
Coventry City	1,250,000	from Nottingham Forest	for Ian Wallace	July 1980
Everton	450,000	from Manchester United	for John Gidman	Aug 1981
Ipswich Town	500,000	from Tottenham Hotspur	for Alan Brazil	1983
Leicester City	325,000	from Stoke City	for Peter Shilton	Nov 1974
Liverpool	500,000	from Hamburg SV	for Kevin Keegan	June 1977
Luton Town	350,000	from Manchester City	for Paul Futcher	June 1978
Manchester United	500,000	from Brighton & Hove Albion	for Andy Ritchie	Oct 1980
Norwich City	1,000,000	from Manchester City	for Kevin Reeves	Mar 1980
	1,000,000	from Nottingham Forest	for Justin Fashanu	Aug 1981
Nottingham Forest	1,250,000	from Manchester United	for Gary Birtles	Oct 1980
Notts County	150,000	from Wrexham	for Mark Vinter	June 1979
Queen's Park Rangers	1,250,000	from Arsenal	for Clive Allen	June 1980
Southampton	300,000	from Manchester City	for Mick Channon	July 1977
Stoke City	700,000	from Everton	for Adrian Heath	Jan 1982
Sunderland	275,000	from Manchester City	for Dennis Tueart	Mar 1974
Tottenham Hotspur	250,000	from Bolton Wanderers	for Neil McNab	Nov 1978
Watford	110,000	from West Ham United	for Billy Jennings	Sept 1974
West Bromwich Albion	1,500,000	from Manchester United	for Bryan Robson	Oct 1981
West Ham United	225,000	from Birmingham City	for Alan Curbishley	June 1979
Wolverhampton Wanderers	1,000,000	from Manchester City	for Steve Daley	Sept 1979

RECORD TRANSFER FEES PAID BY SECOND DIVISION CLUBS

Barnsley	£95,000	to Crystal Palace	for Ian Evans	Mar 1980
	£95,000	to Wolverhampton Wanderers	for Alan Birch	
Blackburn Rovers	100,000	to Chelsea	for Duncan McKenzie	Mar 1979
Brighton & Hove Albion	500,000	to Manchester United	for Andy Ritchie	Oct 1980
Cambridge United	140,000	to Northampton Town	for George Reilly	Nov 1979
Cardiff City	200,000	to San Jose Earthquakes	for Godfrey Ingram	Sept 1982
Carlisle United	120,000	to York City	for Gordon Staniforth	Oct 1979
Charlton Athletic	324,000	to Barcelona	for Allan Simonson	1982
Chelsea	225,000	to Celtic	for David Hay	July 1974
Crystal Palace	800,000 (nett)	to Arsenal	for Clive Allen	Aug 1980
Derby County	410,000	to Crystal Palace	for David Swindlehurst	April 1980
Fulham	150,000	to Orient	for Peter Kitchen	Feb 1979
	150,000	to Brighton & Hove Albion	for Teddy Maybank	Dec 1979
Grimsby Town	80,000	to Vancouver Whitecaps	for Trevor Whymark	Dec 1980
Huddersfield Town	110,000	to Mansfield Town	for Terry Austin	Dec 1980
Leeds United	930,000	to West Bromwich Albion	for Peter Barnes	Aug 1981
Manchester City	1,150,000	to Wolverhampton Wanderers	for Steve Daley	Sept 1979
Middlesbrough	475,000	to Newcastle United	for Irving Nattrass	Aug 1979
Newcastle United	250,000	to West Bromwich Albion	for John Trewick	Dec 1980
Oldham Athletic	200,000	to Manchester City	for Kenny Clements	Sept 1979
Portsmouth	180,000	to Coventry City	for Mark Hateley	Mar 1983
Sheffield Wednesday	200,000	to Budocnost	for Ante Mirocevic	1980
Shrewsbury Town	100,000	to Aldershot	for John Dungworth	Nov 1979
Swansea City	340,000	to Liverpool	for Colin Irwin	Aug 1981

RECORD TRANSFER FEES RECEIVED BY SECOND DIVISION CLUBS

Barnsley	£69,000	from West Ham United	for Anton Otulakowski	Oct 1976
Blackburn Rovers	357,000	from Leeds United	for Kevin Hird	Feb 1979
Brighton & Hove Albion	900,000	from Liverpool	for Mark Lawrenson	Aug 1981
Cambridge United	350,000	from Derby County	for Alan Biley	Jan 1980
Cardiff City	110,000	from Liverpool	for John Toshack	Nov 1970
Carlisle United	275,000	from Vancouver Whitecaps	for Peter Beardsley	
Charlton Athletic	650,000	from Crystal Palace	for Mike Flanagan	Aug 1979
Chelsea	825,000	from Manchester United	for Ray Wilkins	Aug 1979
Crystal Palace	800,000 (nett)	from Arsenal	for Kenny Sansom	Aug 1980
Derby County	400,000	from Southampton	for Charlie George	Dec 1978
Fulham	333,333	from Liverpool	for Richard Money	May 1980
Grimsby Town	125,000	from Aston Villa	for Terry Donavan	July 1979
Huddersfield Town	100,000	from Leeds United	for Trevor Cherry	June 1972
Leeds United	500,000	from Nottingham Forest	for Frank Gray	July 1979
Manchester City	800,000	from Sampdoria	for Trevor Francis	July 1982
Middlesbrough	600,000	from Southampton	for David Armstrong	Aug 1981
Newcastle United	500,000	from Aston Villa	for Peter Withe	May 1980
Oldham Athletic	275,000	from Queen's Park Rangers	for Simon Stainrod	Nov 1980
Portsmouth	130,000	from Brighton & Hove Albion	for Steve Foster	June 1979
Sheffield Wednesday	120,000	from Newcastle United	for Tommy Craig	Jan 1975
Shrewsbury Town	262,000	from Stoke City	for Paul Maguire	Sept 1980
Swansea City	370,000	from Leeds United	for Alan Curtis	May 1979

RECORD TRANSFER FEES PAID BY THIRD DIVISION CLUBS

Bolton Wanderers	£350,000	to West Bromwich Albion	for Len Cantello	May 1979
AFC Bournemouth	70,000	to Cardiff City	for Brian Clark	Oct 1972
Bradford City	31,000	to Burnley	for Billy Ingham	Aug 1980
Brentford	65,000	to Bury	for Alan Whitehead	July 1981
Bristol Rovers	100,000	to Birmingham City	for Stewart Barrowclough	July 1979
Burnley	165,000	to Queen's Park Rangers	for Leighton James	Sept 1978
Exeter City	65,000	to Blackpool	for Tony Kellow	Mar 1980
Gillingham	90,000	to Colchester United	for Trevor Lee	Jan 1981
Hull City	150,000	to Carlisle United	for Mick Tait	Sept 1979
Lincoln City	45,000	to Southampton	for George Shipley	Jan 1980
Millwall	150,000	to Barnsley	for Trevor Aylott	1982
Newport County	80,000	to Swansea City	for Alan Waddle	Jan 1981
Orient	150,000	to Tottenham Hotspur	for Peter Taylor	Nov 1980
Oxford United	75,000	to Cardiff City	for Andy McCulloch	July 1974
Plymouth Argyle	75,000	to Carlisle United	for David Kemp	Sept 1979
Port Vale	40,000	to Bury	for Peter Farrell	Nov 1978
	40,000	to Wolverhampton Wanderers	for Ken Todd	Aug 1978
	40,000	to Crewe Alexandra	for Paul Bowles	Sept 1979
Preston North End	95,000	to Nottingham Forest	for Steve Elliot	Mar 1979
Rotherham United	100,000	to Cardiff City	for Ronnie Moore	Aug 1980
Sheffield United	160,000	to River Plate	for Alex Sabella	July 1978
	160,000	to Leicester City	for Alan Young	Aug 1982
Scunthorpe United	25,000	to Notts County	for Rick Green	Aug 1979
Southend United	111,111	to Blackpool	for Derek Spence	Dec 1979
Walsall	175,000	to Birmingham City	for Alan Buckley	June 1979
Wigan Athletic	65,000	to Everton	for Eamonn O'Keefe	Jan 1982
Wimbledon	45,000	to Queen's Park Rangers	for Tommy Cunningham	Mar 1979

RECORD TRANSFER FEES RECEIVED BY THIRD DIVISION CLUBS

Bolton Wanderers	£340,000	from Birmingham City	for Neil Whatmore	Aug 1974
AFC Bournemouth	195,000	from Manchester United	for Ted MacDougall	Sept 1972
Bradford City	50,000	from Walsall	for Steve Baines	July 1980
Brentford	60,000	from Sheffield Wednesday	for Andy McCulloch	June 1979
Bristol Rovers	200,000	from Luton Town	for Steve White	Dec 1979
Burnley	300,000	from Everton	for Martin Dobson	Aug 1974
	300,000	from Derby County	for Leighton James	Nov 1975
Exeter City	105,000	from Blackpool	for Tony Kellow	Nov 1978
Gillingham	70,000	from Charlton Athletic	for Dick Tydeman	Dec 1976
Hull City	200,000	from Manchester United	for Stuart Pearson	May 1974
Lincoln City	180,000	from Newcastle United	for Mick Harford	Dec 1980
Millwall	250,000	from Ipswich Town	for Kevin O'Callaghan	Jan 1980
Newport County	50,000	from Luton Town	for Mark Aizlewood	Mar 1978
Orient	600,000	from Notts County	for John Chirdozie	Aug 1981
Oxford United	100,000	from Watford	for Les Taylor	Nov 1980
Plymouth Argyle	250,000	from Everton	for Gary Megson	Feb 1980
Port Vale	135,000	from Stoke City	for Mark Chamberlain	1982
Preston North End	765,000	from Manchester City	for Mick Robinson	June 1979
Rotherham United	100,000	from Sunderland	for Dave Watson	Dec 1970
Scunthorpe United	60,000	from Grimsby Town	for Kevin Kilmore	Sept 1979
Sheffield U	£400,000	from Leeds United	for Alex Sabella	May 1980
Southend United	120,000	from Crystal Palace	for Peter Taylor	Oct 1973
Walsall	175,000	from Birmingham City	for Alan Buckley	Oct 1978
Wigan Athletic	135,000	from Sunderland	for Joe Hinnigan	Feb 1980
Wimbledon	70,000	from Crystal Palace	for Steve Galliers	Oct 1981

RECORD TRANSFER FEES PAID BY FOURTH DIVISION CLUBS

Aldershot	£54,000	to Portsmouth	for Colin Garwood	Feb 1980
Blackpool	110,000	to Peterborough United	for Bob Doyle	July 1979
Bristol City	235,000	to St Mirren	for Tony Fitzpatrick	July 1979
Bury	30,000	to Port Vale	for Ken Beamish	Sept 1978
	30,000	to Stoke City	for David Gregory	Sept 1978
Chester	45,000	to Carlisle United	for Steve Ludlam	May 1980
Chesterfield	150,000	to Carlisle United	for Phil Bonnyman	Mar 1980
Colchester United	25,000	to Ipswich Town	for Roger Osborne	Feb 1981
Crewe Alexandra	10,000	to Derby County	for Colin Chesters	Sept 1979
	10,000	to Sheffield United	for Mike Guy	Sept 1979
Darlington	17,000	to Notts County	for Eric Probert	Oct 1978
Doncaster Rovers	30,000	to Barnsley	for Alan Little	Dec 1979
Halifax Town	25,000	to Huddersfield Town	for Kevin Johnson	Aug 1978
Hartlepool United	10,000	to Sunderland	for Ambrose Fogerty	Nov 1963
Hereford United	25,000	to Aston Villa	for David Cunningham	Aug 1979
Mansfield Town	75,000	to Luton Town	for Steve Taylor	July 1979
Northampton Town	40,000	to Brentford	for Steve Phillips	Aug 1980
Peterborough United	60,000	to West Ham United	for Bill Green	July 1978
Reading	50,000	to Charlton Athletic	for Dave Shipperley	Sept 1979
Rochdale	12,000	to Sunderland	for Alan Weir	June 1979
Stockport County	25,000	to Albion Rovers	for Tony Coyle	Dec 1979
Swindon Town	150,000	to Southampton	for David Peach	Mar 1980
Torquay United	25,000	to Exeter City	for Vince O'Keefe	Mar 1980
Tranmere Rovers	20,000	to Charlton Athletic	for Hugh McAuley	Aug 1978
Wrexham	210,000	to Liverpool	for Joey Jones	Oct 1978
York City	18,000	to Bournemouth	for Micky Cave	Aug 1974

RECORD TRANSFER FEES RECEIVED BY FOURTH DIVISION CLUBS

Aldershot	£100,000	from Shrewsbury Town	for John Dungworth	Nov 1979
Blackpool	325,000	from Everton	for Mickey Walsh	Aug 1978
Bristol City	325,000	from Coventry City	for Gary Collier	July 1979
Bury	150,000	from Chesterfield	for Danny Wilson	July 1980
	150,000	from Everton	for Neville Southall	July 1981
Chester	300,000	from Liverpool	for Ian Rush	May 1980
Chesterfield	200,000	from Wolverhampton Wanderers	for Alan Birch	Aug 1981
Colchester United	90,000	from Gillingham	for Trevor Lee	Jan 1981
Crewe Alexandra	40,000	from Port Vale	for Paul Bowles	Sept 1979
Darlington	65,000	from Chelsea	for David Speedie	May 1982
Doncaster Rovers	70,000	from Preston North End	for Mike Elwiss	Feb 1974
	70,000	from Bolton Wanderers	for Dennis Peacock	Mar 1980
Halifax Town	55,000	from Huddersfield Town	for Mick Kennedy	Aug 1980
Hartlepool United	60,000	from Brighton & Hove Albion	for Malcolm Poskett	Feb 1978
Hereford United	100,000	from Derby County	for Steve Emery	Sept 1979
Mansfield Town	200,000	from Luton Town	for Mike Saxby	July 1979
Northampton Town	140,000	from Cambridge United	for George Reilly	Nov 1979
Peterborough U	110,000	from Blackpool	for Bob Doyle	July 1979
Reading	87,500	from Portsmouth	for Neil Webb	June 1982
Rochdale	40,000 +player	from Norwich City	for David Cross	Oct 1971
Stockport County	80,000	from Manchester City	for Stuart Lee	Sept 1979
Swindon Town	175,000	from Chelsea	for Alan Mayes	Dec 1980
Torquay United	80,000	from Tottenham Hotspur	for Colin Lee	Oct 1977
Tranmere Rovers	120,000	from Cardiff City	for Ronnie Moore	Feb 1979
Wrexham	300,000	from Manchester United	for Micky Thomas	Nov 1978
	300,000	from Manchester City	for Bobby Shinton	July 1979
York City	120,000	from Carlisle United	for Gordon Staniforth	Oct 1979

* *Malcolm Darling moved from Norwich in the transaction that took David Cross to Norwich City.*

THE MANAGERS

A directory of Football League managers with biographical details. In some entries information has been at the discretion of individuals.

ADDISON, Colin. *Manager:* Hereford U (player-manager), Durban C, Notts Co (assistant), Newport Co, WBA (assistant), Derby Co, Newport Co Feb 1982– . *Honours:* Promotion to Division 3 1973. *Player:* York C, Nottingham F, Arsenal, Sheffield U, Hereford U.

ALLISON, Malcolm. *Manager:* Bath City, Plymouth Arg; *Assistant Manager, Team Manager:* Manchester C; *Manager*: Crystal Palace; *Coach:* Galatasaray, Turkey; *Consultant, Assistant Manager, Team Manager:* Plymouth Arg; *Manager:* Crystal Palace; *Manager:* Sporting Lisbon, Middlesbrough Oct 1982– . *Honours:* League Champions, FA Cup Winners, League Cup Winners, European Cup Winners' Cup winners with Manchester C. *Player:* Charlton Ath, West Ham U.

APPLETON, Colin. *Manager:* Hull C June 1982– . Formerly Scarborough. *Honours:* Runners-up Division 4 1983. *Player:* Leicester C, Charlton Ath, Barrow.

ASHURST, Len. *Manager:* Hartlepool, Gillingham, Sheffield W, Newport Co, Cardiff C Mar 1982– . *Honours:* Promotion to Division 2 1983. *Player:* Sunderland 1957–1971; Hartlepool 1971–1973. *Honours:* One Under-23 cap for England. Promotion to Division 3 1980.

ATKINSON, Ron. *Manager:* Kettering T, Cambridge U, WBA, Manchester U June 1981– . *Honours:* Division 4 Champions 1977. F.A. Cup winners 1983. Milk Cup runners-up 1983. *Player:* Aston Villa, Oxford U, Kettering T. *Honours:* Promotion to Division 3 1965; Division 3 Championship medal 1968.

BARKER, Richie. *Manager:* Stoke C June 1981– . Formerly assistant-manager Wolverhampton W. *Player:* Derby Co, Notts Co, Peterborough U.

BARTON, Tony. *Manager:* Aston Villa, March 1982– . Formerly assistant manager. *Honours:* European Cup Winners 1982. *Player:* Fulham (groundstaff), Sutton U, Fulham, Nottingham Forest, Portsmouth. *Coach:* Portsmouth, Aston Villa.

BASSETT, Dave. *Manager:* Wimbledon Jan 1981– . *Honours:* Promotion to Division 3 1981, Champions Division 4 1983. *Player:* On the books of Watford and Chelsea. Walton & Hersham, Wimbledon.

BEAMISH, Ken. *Manager:* Swindon T March 1983– . Formerly club coach. *Player:* Tranmere R, Brighton & HA, Blackburn R, Port Vale, Bury. *Honours:* Promotion to 3rd Division 1966–67 (Tranmere R); Promotion to Division 2 1971–72 (Brighton & HA); Champions of Division 3 1974-75 (Blackburn R).

BOAM, Stuart. *Player-Manager:* Mansfield T July 1981– . *Player:* Mansfield T, Middlesbrough, Newcastle U. *Honours:* Division 2 championship medal 1974.

BOND, John. *Manager:* AFC Bournemouth, Norwich C, Manchester C, Burnley June 1983– . *Honours:* AFC Bournemouth, Promotion to Division 3; Norwich C, Promotion to Division 1 1975; Manchester C FA Cup runners-up 1981. *Player:* West Ham U (17 years), Torquay U (3 years). *Honours:* West Ham U Division 2 Championship medal 1958; FA Cup winners medal 1964; Torquay U, Promotion to Division 3 1966.

BOOTH, Dave. *Manager:* Grimsby T, Feb 1982– . *Player:* Barnsley, Grimsby T. *Coach:* Grimsby T.

BREMNER, Billy. *Manager:* Doncaster R, November 1978– . *Honours:* Promotion to Division 3, 1981. *Player:* Leeds U, Hull C. *Honours:* FA Cup winners medal 1972, runners-up 1965, 1970, 1973. League Cup winners medal 1968; European Cup runners-up medal 1975; UEFA Cup winners medal 1968, 1971; runners-up 1967. Footballer of the Year 1970. Fifty-four full Scottish caps.

BROWN, Ken. *Manager:* Norwich C Nov 1980– . Formerly assistant manager. *Honours:* Division 2 promotion 1982. *Player:* West Ham U, Torquay U, Hereford U. Trainer-coach Bournemouth. *Honours:* West Ham U, Division 2 Championship 1958. FA Cup winners medal 1964, European Cup-Winners' Cup winners medal 1965, League Cup runners-up medal 1966.

BUCKLEY, Alan. *Player-Manager:* Walsall July 1982– . *Player:* Walsall, Birmingham C, Walsall. *Honours:* Promotion to Division 3 1980.

BULLOCK, Mickey. *Manager:* Halifax T July 1981– (formerly Coach). *Player:* Birmingham C, Oxford U, Orient, Halifax T.

BURKINSHAW, Keith. *Manager:* Tottenham H July 1976– . *Honours:* Promotion to Division 1 1978; FA Cup winners 1981, 1982; League Cup runners-up 1982. *Coach:* Newcastle U 1968–1975; Tottenham H 1975–1976. *Honours:* FA Cup finalists 1974. *Player:* Liverpool 1954–1958; Workington 1958–1965; Scunthorpe U 1965–1968.

BUXTON, Mick. *Manager:* Huddersfield T October 1978– . *Coach:* Huddersfield T, Southend U. *Player:* Burnley, Halifax T. *Honours:* Division 4 Champions 1980. Division 3 runners-up 1983.

CALLAGHAN, Fred. *Manager:* Woking, Brentford 1980– . *Player:* Fulham. *Coach:* Brentford.

CAMPBELL, Bobby. *Manager:* Fulham, Portsmouth March 1982– . *Coach:* QPR, Arsenal, Fulham. *Assistant Manager:* Aldershot, Portsmouth. *Honours:* Division 2 Championship 1977. Division Three Championship 1983. *Player:* Liverpool, Portsmouth, Aldershot.

CHERRY, Trevor. *Player-Manager:* Bradford C November 1982– . *Player:* Huddersfield T, Leeds U. *Honours:* 27 Full England caps, FA Cup Runners-Up medal 1972–73, Championship medal 1973–1974, Second Division Championship 1969–70.

CLARK, Frank. *Assistant Manager:* Sunderland. *Assistant Manager:* Orient. *Manager:* Orient May 1982– . *Player:* Newcastle U and Nottingham F. *Honours:* Football League XI, England Amateur and Youth caps. Division 2 Championship medal 1964–65, FA Cup Runners-Up medal 1973–74, European Cup medal 1978–79, Championship medal 1977-78, League Cup Winners medals 1977–78 and 1979–80, League Cup runners-up medal 1978–79.

CLARKE, Allan. *Manager:* Barnsley, Leeds U, Scunthorpe U Feb 1983– . *Honours:* Promotion to Division 3, 1983. *Player:* Walsall, Fulham, Leicester C, Leeds U. *Honours:* Championship Medal 1974, FA Cup Winners medal 1972, FA Cup Runners-up medals 1970, 1973. European Cup Runners-Up medal 1975. UEFA Cup Winners medal 1971. Six Under 23 and 19 full England caps.

CLOUGH, Brian. *Manager:* Hartlepool, Derby Co, Brighton & HA, Leeds U, Nottingham F January 1975– . *Honours:* Division 2 Championship 1969; Division 1 Championship 1972; Promotion to Division 1 1977; Division 1 Championship 1978; League Cup winners 1978, 1979; European Cup winners 1979, 1980; Division 1 runners-up 1979. *Player:* Middlesbrough, Sunderland. *Honours:* Three Under-23 caps and two full caps for England.

COOPER, Terry. *Manager:* Bristol C May 1982– . *Player-Manager:* Bristol R. *Player:* Leeds U, Middlesbrough, Bristol C, Bristol R, Doncaster R. *Coach:* Bristol R. *Honours:* 20 full England caps.

COX, Arthur. *Manager:* Chesterfield, Newcastle U Sept 1980– . *Coach:* Youth coach Coventry C, chief coach Walsall, Aston Villa, Preston NE, Halifax T. *Assistant Manager:* Sunderland. *Honours:* Preston NE Division 3 Championship; Sunderland Division 2 Championship; FA Cup winners 1973. *Player:* Coventry C 1955–1958 (broken leg ended career at 18). Joined coaching staff.

CRAGGS, Ken. *Manager:* Charlton Ath June 1982– . *Assistant-manager:* Charlton Ath, Brighton & HA.

DOCHERTY, John. *Manager:* Brentford, Cambridge U January 1978– . *Coach:* Cambridge U. *Player:* Brentford 1959–1961; 1965–1968; 1970–1974; Sheffield U 1961–1965; Reading 1968–1970; QPR player/coach 1974–1975.

DUNCAN, John. *Player-Manager:* Scunthorpe U. *Manager:* Hartlepool U, Chesterfield June 1983– . *Player:* Dundee, Tottenham H, Derby Co.

DURBAN, William Alan. *Manager:* Shrewsbury T, Stoke C, Sunderland June 1981– . *Honours:* Division 4 runners-up 1975. *Player:* Cardiff C 1959–1963; Derby Co 1963–1973; Shrewsbury T 1973–1978. *Honours:* 27 full caps for Wales; Division 2 Championship medal 1969; Division 1 Championship medal 1972; promotion to Division 3 1975; promotion to Division 1 1979.

ELLIS, Sam. *Manager:* Blackpool June 1982– . *Coach:* Watford. *Player:* Sheffield W, Mansfield T, Lincoln C, Watford.

EVANS, Maurice. *Manager:* Shrewsbury T 1972–1974; Reading May 1977– . *Coach:* Shrewsbury T 1968–1972; Reading 1974–1977. *Honours:* Promotion to Division 3 1968. *Player:* Reading 1953–1967. *Honours:* Football Combination team 1957; Division 3 South team 1957.

FAGAN, Joe. *Player-Manager:* Nelson. *Trainer:* Rochdale, Liverpool. *Assistant Manager:* Liverpool. *Manager:* Liverpool June 1983– . *Player:* Manchester C, Bradford (Park Avenue), Altrincham, Nelson.

FERGUSON, Bobby. *Manager:* Newport Co, Ipswich T July 1982– . Formerly coach. *Player:* Newport Co, Cardiff C, Derby Co, Newcastle U.

FRANCIS, Gerry. *Manager:* Exeter C. *Player:* QPR, Crystal Palace, Coventry C. *Honours:* 12 full international caps for England.

GOULD, Bobby. *Manager:* Bristol R, Coventry C May 1983– . *Assistant Manager:* Aldershot Oct 1981. *Player:* Coventry C, Arsenal, Wolverhampton W (two spells), Bristol C, WBA, West Ham U, Bristol R, Hereford U, Wimbledon, Aldershot. *Coach:* Chelsea.

GRADI, Dario. *Manager:* Wimbledon, Crystal Palace. *Coach:* Chelsea, Derby Co, Wimbledon and Youth Team coach at Orient. *Manager:* Crewe Alexandra May 1983– .*Honours:* Promotion to Division 3 1979. *Player:* Sutton United and England Amateurs.

GRAHAM, George. *Coach:* Crystal Palace. *Manager:* Millwall Dec 1982– . *Honours:* Football League Trophy Winners 1983. *Player:* Aston Villa, Chelsea, Arsenal, Manchester U, Portsmouth, Crystal Palace. *Honours:* 12 Full Scottish caps, League Cup winners medal 1964–65, Promotion to Division 2 1976–77.

GRAY, Eddie M.B.E. *Player-Manager:* Leeds U July 1982– . *Player:* Leeds U. *Honours:* 12 full caps for Scotland. F.A. Cup winners medal 1972, F.A. Cup runners-up 1970, 1973. League Cup winners medal 1968. Division One Championship medal 1969. Fairs Cup winners medal 1968, Fairs Cup runners-up medal 1967. European Cup runners-up medal 1975.

GREAVES, Ian. *Manager:* Huddersfield T, Bolton W, Hereford U (assistant), Oxford U, Wolverhampton Wanderers, Mansfield T Jan 83– . *Honours:* Division 2 Champions 1970, 1978. *Player:* Manchester U, Lincoln C, Oldham Ath. *Honours:* Championship medal 1956, FA Cup runners-up medal 1958.

GREENHOFF, Jimmy. *Manager:* Rochdale Mar 1983– . *Player:* Leeds U, Birmingham C, Stoke C, Manchester U, Crewe Alexandra, Port Vale. *Honours:* England Under 23 (5), Football League XI. Division 2 Championship 1963–64, League Cup winners medal 1971–72, FA Cup winners medal 1977.

HAMILTON, Bryan. *Manager:* Tranmere Rovers Oct 1980– . *Player:* Linfield, Ipswich T, Everton, Millwall, Swindon T. *Honours:* 50 full Northern Ireland caps.

HAWKINS, Graham. *Manager/Assistant Manager:* Shrewsbury T, Wolverhampton W Aug 1982– . *Honours:* Runners-up Division 2 1983. *Player:* Wolverhampton W, Preston NE, Blackburn R, Port Vale.

HUGHES, Emlyn. *Player-Manager* Rotherham U July 1981– . *Player:* Blackpool, Liverpool, Wolverhampton W. *Honours:* Division 1 championship medals 1973, 1976, 1977, 1979. FA Cup winners medal 1974; runners-up medals 1971, 1977. League Cup winners medal 1980; runners-up medal 1978. UEFA Cup winners medals 1973, 1976. European Cup winners medals 1977, 1978. 62 full England caps.

HUNTER, Norman. *Manager:* Barnsley Sept 1980– . *Honours:* Promotion to Division 2 1981. *Player:* Leeds U, Bristol C, Barnsley (player-manager). *Honours:* 1972 FA Cup winners medal; 1965, 1970, 1973 FA Cup runners-up medals; 1968 League Cup winners medal; 1975 European Cup runners-up medal; 1973 European Cup-Winners' Cup runners-up medal; 1968, 1971 UEFA Cup winners medals; 1967 UEFA Cup runners-up medal. Under-23 and 28 full England caps.

ILEY, Jim. *Manager:* Peterborough U 1969; Barnsley 1973; Blackburn R, Bury 1980– . *Honours:* Watney Cup entry 1973, 1974. *Player:* Sheffield U 1953–1957; Tottenham H 1958–1959; Nottingham F 1959–1963; Newcastle U 1963–1969; Peterborough U 1969–1973. *Honours:* Football League XI with Sheffield U, Tottenham H. Under-23 cap for England and FA XI representative team.

KENDALL, Howard. *Player/Manager:* Blackburn R, Everton May 1981– . *Player:* Preston NE, Everton. While with Preston, he was the youngest player ever to appear in the FA Cup final. *Honours:* Promotion to Div 2 1980.

KERR, George. *Manager:* Lincoln C (formerly Assistant Manager), Grimsby T. *Manager:* Rotherham U April 1983– . *Player:* Barnsley, Bury, Oxford U. *Honours:* Division 3 Promotion 1980.

LAWRENCE, Len. *Assistant Manager:* Plymouth Arg. *Assistant Manager:* Lincoln C. *Reserve Team Coach:* Charlton Ath. *Manager:* Dec 1982– . Charlton Ath Nov 1983– . *Player:* Croydon, Carshalton Ath, Sutton U.

LEA, Cyril. *Coach:* Ipswich T, Hull C, Wales, Colchester U. *Manager:* Colchester U May 1983– . *Player:* Orient, Ipswich T. *Honours:* Two Full Welsh Caps. Promotion to Division 1 as Runners-Up 1961–62.

LEE, Gordon. *Manager:* Port Vale 1968–1973; Blackburn R 1973–1975; Newcastle U 1975–1977; Everton 1977–1981; Preston NE Dec 1981– . *Honours:* Port Vale Division 3 promotion 1971; Blackburn R Division 3 Champions 1975; Newcastle U League Cup runners-up 1976; Division 3 Manager of the Year 1975. *Player:* Aston Villa 1955–1966; Shrewsbury T 1966–1968. *Honours:* Aston Villa, League Cup winners medal 1961; League Cup runners-up medal 1963.

LYALL, John. *Manager:* West Ham U August 1974– . Previously Assistant Manager 1971. *Honours:* FA Cup winners 1975, 1980; Division 2 champions 1981; League Cup runners-up 1981. *Player:* West Ham U 1957. *Honours:* Youth International.

MACDONALD, Malcolm. *Manager:* Fulham Nov 1980– . *Honours:* Division 3 promotion 1982. Formerly Chief Marketing Executive. *Player:* Tonbridge, Fulham, Luton T, Newcastle U, Arsenal. *Honours:* FA Cup runners-up medal 1974, League Cup runners-up medal 1976, FA Cup runners-up medal 1978. Under-23 and 14 full England caps.

McFARLAND, Roy. *Manager:* Bradford C May 1981– . *Honours:* Division 4 promotion 1982. *Player:* Tranmere R, Derby Co. *Honours:* Division 2 Championship 1969, Division 1 Championship 1972. Under-23 and 28 full England caps.

McGOVERN, John. *Player-Manager:* Bolton W July 1982– . *Player:* Hartlepool U, Derby Co, Leeds U, Nottingham F.

McGRATH, John. *Manager:* Southampton youth side 1975–79, Port Vale Dec 1979– . *Coach:* Southampton. *Honours:* Promotion to Division 3 1983. *Player:* Bury, Newcastle U, Southampton.

McMENEMY, Lawrie. *Manager:* Bishop Auckland, Doncaster R 1968–1971; Grimsby T 1971–1973; Southampton June 1973– . *Honours:* Doncaster R, Division 4 Championship 1969; Grimsby T, Division 4 Championship 1972; Southampton, FA Cup Winners 1976. League Cup runners-up 1979. *Player:* Newcastle U, Gateshead.

McNALLY, Harry. *Coach:* Skelmersdale United. *Manager:* Altrincham, Southport. *Chief Scout:* Wigan Ath. *Assistant Manager:* Wigan Ath. *Manager:* Wigan Ath June 1983– . *Player:* Skelmersdale United.

MADDEN, Peter. *Manager:* Darlington, Rochdale 1980– . *Assistant Manager:* Rochdale. *Player:* Rotherham U 1955–66, Bradford PA 1966–67, Aldershot 1967–68, Skegness 1968–70. *Honours:* Rotherham U League Cup runners-up medal 1961. Two Lincolnshire Cup medals with Skegness.

MEGSON, Don. *Manager:* Bristol R, Portland Timbers, AFC Bournemouth March 1983– . *Player:* Sheffield W, Bristol R. *Honours:* Football League XI, FA Cup runners-up medal 1965–66, Runners-up in Division 1 1960-61.

MELIA, Jimmy. Manager: Aldershot, Crewe Alex, Brighton & HA March 1983– . *Honours:* FA Cup Runners-Up 1982–83. *Player:* Liverpool, Wolverhampton W, Southampton, Aldershot, Crewe Alex. *Honours:* Two Full England caps, Football League XI, England Youth and Schools. Second Division Championship Medal 1961–62. Runners-Up Division Two 1965–66.

MILNE, Gordon. *Manager:* Leicester C Aug 1982– . Formerly chief executive and manager: Coventry C. *Player:* Preston NE, Liverpool, Blackpool. *Honours:* 14 full caps for England; Liverpool Division 2 championship medals 1964 and 1966; FA Cup winners medal 1965. Promotion to Division 1 1983.

MONCUR, Bobby. *Manager:* Carlisle U, Hearts, Plymouth Arg June 1981– . *Honours:* Scottish Division 1 championship 1980. *Player:* Newcastle U, Sunderland. *Honours:* One Under-23 and 16 full Scottish caps; UEFA Cup winners medal 1969; FA Cup runners-up medal 1974; Division 2 championship 1965; Anglo-Italian Cup winners medal 1973; Division 2 championship 1976.

MULLERY, Alan. *Manager:* Brighton & HA, Charlton Ath, Crystal Palace June 1982– . *Honours:* Promotion to Division 2 1977; Promotion to Division 1 1979. *Player:* Fulham 1959–1964; Tottenham H 1964–1972; Fulham 1972–1976. *Honours:* 35 England caps; FA Cup winners medal 1967; FA Cup runners-up medal 1975; League Cup winners medal 1971; UEFA Cup winners medal 1972; Footballer of the Year 1975; Played for Great Britain XI.

MURDOCH, Bobby. *Manager:* Middlesbrough May 1981– . Formerly youth team coach. *Player:* Celtic, Middlesbrough. *Honours:* Regular member of Celtic first team squad during eight of their nine successive Scottish League championship successes 1966–1972. Division 2 Championship medal with Middlesbrough 1974. Scottish international 12 caps. European Cup winners medal 1967, runners-up 1970.

MURPHY, Colin. *Manager:* Derby Co, Lincoln C November 1978– . *Coach:* Derby Co (reserve team), Nottingham F (reserve team), Notts Co (assistant manager). *Player:* Cork Hibs, Wimbledon, Hastings U, Crystal Palace. *Honours:* Derby Co Central League runners-up 1974–75; Lincoln C Division 4 runners-up 1981.

NEAL, John. *Manager:* Wrexham, Middlesbrough, Chelsea May 1981– . *Honours:* Promotion to Division 3 1970; Welsh Cup winners 1972, 1975; Qualified for Cup-Winners' Cup 1973, 1976 (quarter-finalists). *Player:* Hull C 1949–1955; Swindon T 1956–1958; Aston Villa 1959–1963; Southend U 1964–1967. *Honours:* Aston Villa, Division 2 championship medal 1960; League Cup winners medal 1961.

NEILL, Terry. *Manager:* Hull C, N Ireland, Tottenham H, 1974–76; Arsenal July 1976– . *Honours:* FA Cup Winners 1979; Runners-up 1978; 1980. *Player:* Arsenal 1959–1970; Hull C 1970–1974. *Honours:* Schoolboy, Youth, Under-23, 'B' and 59 full caps for N Ireland.

NEWMAN, John. *Manager:* Exeter C, Grimsby T, Derby Co, Hereford U 19 – . Formerly assistant. *Honours:* Division 4 runners-up 1979. *Player:* Birmingham C, Leicester C, Plymouth Arg, Exeter C. *Honours:* Birmingham C Division 2 championship 1955; FA Cup runners-up 1956. Football League.

PEACOCK, Keith. *Manager:* Gillingham July 1981– . *Assistant Manager:* Tampa Bay Rowdies. *Player:* Charlton Ath.

PLEAT, David. *Manager:* Nuneaton B, Luton T January 1978– . *Honours:* Division 2 Champions 1982. *Coach:* Luton T. *Player:* Nottingham F, Luton T, Shrewsbury T, Exeter C, Peterborough U. *Honours:* England schools and youth international.

PORTERFIELD, Ian. *Player/Manager:* Rotherham U, Sheffield U June 1981– . *Honours:* Division 3 Championship 1981; Division 4 Championship 1982. *Player:* Raith R, Sunderland, Reading, Sheffield W. Scored the goal for Sunderland which beat Leeds U in the 1973 FA Cup final.

RIOCH, Bruce. *Player-Manager:* Torquay U July 1982– . Formerly player-coach. *Player:* Luton T, Aston V, Derby Co, Everton, Derby Co, Torquay U. *Honours:* 24 full caps for Scotland.

ROBERTS, Bobby. *Manager:* Colchester U, Wrexham June 1982– . Promotion to Division 3 1977. *Player:* Motherwell, Leicester C, Mansfield T. *Honours:* One Under-23 cap for Scotland; Scottish League.

ROYLE, Joe. *Manager:* Oldham Ath July 1982– . *Player:* Everton, Manchester C, Bristol C, Norwich C. *Honours:* Six full caps for England.

SAINTY, John.*Coach:* AFC Bournemouth, Norwich C, Manchester C, Chester. *Manager:* Chester April 1983– . *Player:* Tottenham H, Reading, AFC Bournemouth, Mansfield T, Aldershot. *Honours:* England Schools. Promotion to Division 3 1970–71.

SAUNDERS, Ron. *Manager:* Yeovil 1967; Oxford U 1969; Norwich C 1969; Manchester C 1973; Aston Villa June 1974–1982; Birmingham C Jan 1982– . *Honours:* Norwich C Champions Division 2 1972; League Cup runners-up 1973; Manchester C League Cup runners-up 1974; Aston Villa League Cup winners 1975 and 1977; Runners-up Division 2 1975, Division 1 Championship 1981; Manager of the Year 1975. *Player:* Everton, Tonbridge, Gillingham, Portsmouth, Watford, Charlton Ath.

SAXTON, Bobby. *Manager:* Exeter C (player-manager), Plymouth Arg, Blackburn R May 1981– . *Honours:* Promotion to Division 3 1977. *Player:* Derby Co 1962–1968; Plymouth Arg 1968–1975; Exeter C 1975– . *Honours:* Promotion to Division 2 Plymouth Arg 1975.

SIRREL, Jimmy. *General Manager/Manager:* Brentford 1965–1969; Notts Co 1969–1975; Sheffield U 1975–1977; Notts Co October 1977– . *Honours:* Notts Co, Division 4 Champions 1971; Division 3 runners-up 1973; Division 2 runners-up 1981. *Player:* Glasgow Celtic 1945–1949; Bradford PA 1949–1951; Brighton & HA 1951–1954; Aldershot 1954–1955 (later trainer).

SMITH, Denis. *Player-Manager:* York C May 1982– . *Player:* Stoke C.

SMITH, Jimmy. *Manager:* Boston U 1968–1972; Colchester U 1972–1975; Blackburn R 1975–1978; Birmingham C March 1978–1982; Oxford U March 1982– . *Honours:* Boston U Eastern Professional Floodlight Cup winners; Colchester U promoted from Division 4 1974. Promoted Div 1 1980. *Player:* Sheffield U 1957–1961; Aldershot 1961–1964; Halifax T 1964–1967; Lincoln C 1967–1968; Boston U 1968–1972.

STOKOE, Bob. *Manager:* Charlton Ath, Rochdale, Carlisle U, Blackpool, Sunderland, Bury, Blackpool, Rochdale, Carlisle U 1980– . *Honours:* Sunderland FA Cup winners 1973. Division 2 champions 1976; Division 3 promotion 1982. *Player:* Newcastle U (13 years), Bury (player-manager). *Honours:* FA Cup winners medal 1955.

TAYLOR, Graham. *Manager:* Lincoln C, Watford June 1977– . *Honours:* Division 4 Championship 1976, 1978; Division 3 runners-up 1979; Division 2 runners-up 1982; Division 1 runners-up 1983. *Player:* Grimsby T 1962–1968; Lincoln C 1968–1972.

TAYLOR, Peter. Management team with Brian Clough at Hartlepool U, Derby Co, Brighton & HA (had a spell without Clough) Nottingham F. *Club Manager:* Derby Co Nov 1982– . *Honours:* Division 2 Championship 1969, Championship 1972, Promotion to Division 1 1977, The Championship 1978, League Cup Winners 1978, 1979, Runners-Up 1980, European Cup Winners 1979, 1980. Division One Runners-Up 1979. *Player:* Coventry C, Middlesbrough, Port Vale.

TOSHACK, John. *Player-Manager:* Swansea C February 1978– . *Honours:* Promotion to Division 3 1978, Division 2 1979, Division 1 1981. *Player:* Cardiff C, Liverpool, Swansea C. *Honours:* Three Under-23 and 39 full Welsh caps.

TURNER, Graham. *Player-Manager:* Shrewsbury T December 1978– . *Player:* Wrexham, Chester, Shrewsbury T. *Honours:* Promotion 1979.

VENABLES, Terry. *Manager:* Crystal Palace June 1976– (formerly coach), QPR Oct 1980– . *Honours:* Promotion to Division 2 1976, Division 2 Championship 1979. *Player:* Chelsea, Tottenham H, QPR, Crystal Palace. *Honours:* capped at all levels by England schools, youth, Amateur, Under-23 and two full honours; Promotion to Division 1 1963 Chelsea; League Cup winners medal 1965 Chelsea; FA Cup winners medal 1967 Tottenham H.

WALKER, Clive. *Manager:* Northampton T May 1982– . *Coach:* Northampton T. *Player:* Leicester C, Northampton T, Mansfield T.

WALKER, Len. *Manager:* Darlington, Aldershot April 1981– . *Player:* Spennymoor, Middlesbrough, Newcastle U, Aldershot, Darlington (player-coach).

WEBSTER, Eric. *Manager:* Stockport Co April 1982– . Formerly assistant and groundsman.

WILE, John. *Player-Manager:* Peterborough U May 1983– . *Player:* Durham City, Sunderland, Peterborough U, WBA. *Honours:* Promotion to Division 1 1975–76.

WILKINSON, Howard. *Player-Manager:* Boston United. *Assistant Manager:* England Under 21, *Manager:* England Semi-Professional team. *Assistant Manager:* Notts Co. *Manager:* England Under 21. *Team Manager:* Notts Co. *Manager:* Sheffield W June 1983– . *Honours:* Promotion to Division 1 1980–81, Four Nations Championship Semi-Professional Winners 1979. *Player:* Sheffield W, Brighton & HA, Boston United. *Honours:* England Youth International.

WILLIAMS, David. *Player-Manager:* Bristol Rovers May 1983– . *Player:* Bristol R. *Honours:* Wales Under 23.

WYLIE, Ron. *Manager:* WBA July 1982– . *Assistant Manager:* Coventry C. *Coach:* Birmingham C, Aston V, Bulova (Hong Kong). *Player:* Birmingham C, Aston V, Notts Co.

Jimmy Melia
Brighton and Hove Albion

Terry Venables
Queens Park Rangers

FACES OF MANAGEMENT 1983–84

Keith Burkinshaw
Tottenham Hotspur

John Toshack
Swansea City

BELL'S SCOTCH WHISKY FOOTBALL MANAGERS AWARDS 1969–70 TO 1982–83

Key: d – Divisional Manager of the Month, M – Manager of the Month, D – Divisional Manager of the Season, Y – Manager of the Year, S – Special Award.

Adamson, J.	(Burnley) 72/73 d2, d2, D2; 73/74 M
Addison, C.	Hereford U) 72/73 d4, d4
Allen, R.	(WBA) 77/78 d1; 81/82 M
Allison, M.	(Manchester C) 71/72 M; (Crystal Palace) 75/76 d3
Anderson, S.	(Doncaster R) 75/76 d4
Andrews, J.	(Cardiff C) 75/76 d3, d3
Appleton, C.	(Hull C) 82/83 d4
Armfield, J.	(Bolton W) 72/73 d3, D3; (Leeds U) M
Ashman, A.	(Carlisle U) 73/74 d2; 74/75 M
Ashman, R.	(Scunthorpe U) 71/72 d4
Ashurst, L.	(Hartlepool U) 73/74 d4; (Cardiff C) 82/83 d3
Atkinson, R.	(Cambridge U) 74/75 d4; 76/77 d4, d4, D4; (WBA) 79/81 M, M; (Manchester U) 82/83 M
Bailey, M.	(Charlton Ath) 80/81 d3, d3
Ball, A.	(Halifax T) 70/71 d3, D3; 72/73 d2
Barlow, F.	(Chesterfield) 80/81 d3
Barnwell, J.	(Peterborough U) 77/78 d3; (Wolverhampton W) 79/80 M
Basford, J.	(Mansfield T) 70/71 d3
Barton, T.	(Aston Villa) 81/82 M; 82 S
Bassett, D.	(Wimbledon) 80/81 d4; 82/83 d4, D4
Bates, T.	(Southampton) 70/71 d1
Bentley, R.	(Swansea C) 69/70 d4; 71/72 d3
Bingham, B.	(Everton) 73/74 M; 82 S
Bloomfield, J.	(Orient) 69/70 d3, D3
Blunstone, F.	(Brentford) 71/72 d4, d4
Bond, J.	(Bournemouth) 70/71 d4; 71/72 d3; 72/73 d3; (Norwich C) 74/75 d2; 79/80 M; (Manchester C) 80/81 M, M
Book, T.	(Manchester C) 75/76 M, M; 76/77 M; 77/78 d1
Booth, D.	(Grimsby T) 82/83 d2
Bowen, D.	(Northampton T) 70/71 d4
Bremner, B.	(Doncaster R) 79/80 d4; 80/81 d4; 81/82 d3
Brown, A.	(Bury) 73/74 d4; (Blackpool) 77/78 d2
Brown, K.	(Norwich C) 82/83 M
Buckley, A.	(Walsall) 79/80 d4
Burkinshaw, K.	(Tottenham H) 77/78 M; 79/80 M; 81/82 M, d1
Burrows, F.	(Portsmouth) 80/81 d3
Buxton, M.	(Huddersfield T) 79/80 d4, D4
Campbell, B.	(Bristol R) 77/78 d2
Campbell, R.	(Portsmouth) 82/83 d3, D3
Cantwell, N.	(Coventry C) 69/70 d1; (Peterborough U) 73/74 d4, D4; 75/76 d3
Casper, F.	(Burnley) 82/83 d2
Catterick, H.	(Everton) 69/70 M, M; (Preston NE) 76/77 d3
Charlton, J.	(Middlesbrough) 73/74 M, M; 74 Y; 74/75 M; (Sheffield W) 79/80 d3; 81–82 d2; 82/83 M
Chung, S.	(Wolverhampton W) 76/77 d2, d2, D2
Clarke, A.	(Barnsley) 78/79 d4; 79/80 d3
Clough, B.	(Derby Co) 69/70 M, M; 72/73 M; (Nottingham F) 77/78 M, M, M, M; 78 Y; 78/79 M, M, M, M; 79 S; 79/80 M; 80 S
Connor, D.	(Rochdale) 70/71 d3
Cox, A.	(Newcastle U) 80/81 d2
Crompton, J.	(Barrow) 71/72 d4
Crowe, V.	(Aston Villa) 70/71 d3, M; 71/72 d3, D3
Dickinson, J.	(Portsmouth) 78/79 d4
Dicks, A.	(Bristol C) 70/71 d2; 71/72 d2; 73/74 d2; 75/76 d2
Docherty, J.	(Brentford) 74/75 d4
Docherty, T.	(Manchester U) 74/75 d2, d2, D2; 75/76 M, M, D1; 76/77 M
Dodgin Sr., B.	(Bristol R) 69/70 d3; 70/71 d3
Dodgin Jr., B.	(Fulham) 70/71 d3; (Northampton T) 75/76 d4; (Brentford) 78/79 d4; 79/80 d3
Doyle, B.	(Workington) 70/71 d4
Durban, A.	(Shrewsbury T) 73/74 d3; 74/75 d4; 75/76 d3; 76/77 d3; (Stoke C) 78/79 d2
Elliott, B.	(Sunderland) 78/79 d2
Evans, M.	(Reading) 78/79 d4, D4
Fenton, B.	(Millwall) 71/72 d2
Fenton, R.	(Notts Co) 76/77 d2
Ferguson, A.	(Aberdeen) 82/83 S
Fraser, D.	(Walsall) 74/75 d3
Frizzell, J.	(Oldham Ath) 70/71 d4; 72/73 d3; 73/74 d3, D3
Furphy, K.	(Watford) 69/70 M; (Blackburn R) 72/73 d3
Goodwin, F.	(Birmingham C) 70/71 d2; 71/72 d2, d2
Gradi, D.	(Wimbledon) 78/79 d4; 80/81 d4
Graham, D.	(Colchester U) 70/71 M
Graham, G.	(Millwall) 82/83 d3
Greaves, I.	(Huddersfield T) 69/70 M, D2; (Bolton W) 75/76 d2; 76/77 d2, d2; 77/78 d2, d2, D2
Greenwood, R.	(West Ham U) 71/72 M; 73/74 M
Griffiths, A.	(Wrexham) 77/78 d3, d3, M, d3, D3
Griffiths, H.	(Swansea C) 76/77 d4; 77/78 d4
Gould, B.	(Bristol R) 82/83 d3
Hamilton, B.	(Tranmere R) 82/83 d4
Harris, J.	(Sheffield U) 69/70 d2; 70/71 d2; 71/72 M
Harvey, J.	(Newcastle U) 72/73 d1
Haslam, H.	(Luton T) 72/73 d2; 73/74 d2; 74/75 d1; 76/77 d2; 79/80 d3
Hawkins, G.	(Wolverhampton W) 82/83 d2
Head, B.	(Crystal Palace) 70/71 d1
Herd, D.	(Lincoln C) 71/72 d4
Horner, B.	(Hartlepool U) 79/80 d4
Howe, D.	(WBA) 71/72 d1; 73/74 d2
Hughes, E.	(Rotherham U) 81/82 M
Hunter, A.	(Colchester U) 82/83 d4
Hunter, N.	(Barnsley) 80/81 d3, d3, d3
Hurley, C.	(Reading) 73/74 d4
Hurst, G.	(Chelsea) 79/80 M; 80/81 d2, d2
Iley, J.	(Peterborough U) 71/72 d4; (Bury) 82/83 d4
Jago, G.	(QPR) 71/72 d2; 72/73 d2; 73/74 M; (Millwall) 75/76 d3
Johnston, T.	(Huddersfield T) 73/74 d3; 76/77 d4

Kaye, J. (Hull C) 74/75 d2
Keen, M. (Northampton T) 77/78 d4
Kendall, H. (Blackburn R) 79/80 d3, d3; 80/81 d2
Kennedy, B. (Bradford C) 75/76 d4, d4; 76/77 d4
Kerr, G. (Grimsby T) 79/80 d3, d3, D3
Kirby, G. (Halifax T) 70/71 d3; 79/80 d4
Knighton, K. (Orient) 81/82 d2
Lee, G. (Port Vale) 69/70 d4; (Blackburn R) 74/75 d3, d3, D3 (Newcastle U) 75/76 M; (Everton) 77/78 M; 79/79 M; 80/81 M; (Preston NE) 81/82 d3
Leivers, B. (Cambridge U) 72/73 d4
Lloyd, L. (Wigan Ath) 81/82 d4
Lucas, B. (Newport Co) 70/71 d4; 72/73 d4
Lyall, J. (West Ham U) 74/75 M; 78/79 d2; 79/80 d2, D2; 80/81 d2, d2, D2; 81/82 d2; 82/83 d1
MacDonald, M. (Fulham) 80/81 d3; 81/82 d3; 82/83 d2
Mackay, D. (Derby Co) 74/75 d1, D1; 75/76 M; (Walsall) 77/78 d3
McAnearney, J. (Rotherham U) 71/72 d3
McAnearney, T. (Aldershot) 72/73 d4; 77/78 d4; 78/79 d4
McCreadie, E. (Chelsea) 75/76 d2; 76/77 d2, M
McFarland, R. (Bradford C) 81/82 d4
McGarry, B. (Wolverhampton W) 71/72 M; 79/80 d2
McGuigan, J. (Chesterfield) 69/70 d4, M; (Rotherham U) 74/75 d4; 76/77 d3, d3
McMenemy, L. (Grimsby T) 71/72 d4, D4; (Southampton) 75/76 d2, d2 D2; 78/79 d1; 80/81 M; 82/83 M
McNeill, I. (Wigan Ath) 78/79 d4; 79/80 d4
McGrath, J. (Port Vale) 82/83 d4
Madden, P. (Darlington) 75/76 d4
Mansell, J. (Reading) 69/70 d3
Meadows, J. (Southport) 71/72 d4; 72/73 d4
Mee, B. (Arsenal) 70/71 M, M; 71 Y; 72/73 M
Megson, D. (Bristol R) 72/73 d3; 73/74 d3, d3; 75/76 d2
Meldrum, C. (Workington T) 74/75 d4
Melia, J. (Crewe Alex) 74/75 d4
Mercer J. (Coventry C) 72/73 M
Miller, B. (Burnley) 79/80 d2; 81/82 d3, D3
Milne, G. (Coventry C) 73/74 d1; (Leicester C) 82/83 d2
Moore, B. (Walsall) 71/72 d3; 72/73 d3
Morgan, R. (Cardiff C) 78/79 d2
Morris, P. (Mansfield T) 76/77 d3, D3; (Peterborough U) 80/81 d4; 81/82 d4
Mulhall, G. (Bradford C) 79/80 d4; 80/81 d4
Mullery, A. (Brighton & HA) 76/77 M, d3; 77/78 d2; 78/79 d2
Murphy, C. (Lincoln C) 80/81 d4; 81/82 d3; 82/83 d3
Musgrove, M. (Torquay U) 73/74 d4
Neal, J. (Wrexham) 73/74 d3, d3; 76/77 d3; (Chelsea) 81/82 d2
Neill, T. Hull C) 70/71 d2; (Arsenal) 79/80 d1 M; 81/82 d1
Nelson, A. (Gillingham) 73/74 d4; (Charlton Ath) 74/75 d3; 78/79 d2
Newman, J. (Exeter C) 72/73 d4; (Derby Co) 78/79 d4, d4
Nicholson, B. (Tottenham H) 70/71 M
Oakes, A. (Chester) 76/77 d3; 77/78 d3; 78/79 d3
O'Farrell, F. (Leicester C) 70/71 d2, M, D1; (Manchester U) M; (Torquay U) 81/82 d4
Paisley, B. (Liverpool) 75/76 M, M; 76 Y; 76/77 d1, M, M; 77 Y; 77/78 d1; 78 S; 78/79 M; 79 Y; 79/80 M; 80 Y; 80/81 M; 81 S; 81/82 M, M; 82 Y; 82/83 M, M d1, Y
Peacock, K. (Gillingham) 81/82 d3
Petchey, G. (Orient) 71/72 M; 73/74 d2; 77/78 d2
Pleat, D. (Luton T) 79/80 d2; 81/82 M, D2
Potts, H. (Blackpool) 73/74 d2; (Burnley) 77/78 d2; 78/79 d2
Porterfield, I. (Rotherham U) 80/81 D3; (Sheffield U) 81/82 d4, D4
Quigley, E. (Stockport Co) 76/77 d4
Revie, D. (Leeds U) 69 Y; 69/70 M; 70 Y; 70/71 M; 72 Y; 72/73 M; 73/74 M, M, M; 74 S
Ramsey, Sir Alf (Birmingham C) 77/78 M
Roberts, B. (Colchester U) 76/77 d4, d4; 77/78 d3; 81/82 d4, d4
Roberts, K. (Chester) 73/74 d4; 74/75 M
Robson, B. (Ipswich T) 70/71 M; 72/73 M; 74/75 M; 76/77 M; 78/79 M; 80/81 M, M, M; 81 S
Rowley, A. (Southend U) 71/72 d4; 74/75 d3
Richley, L. (Darlington) 70/71 d4
Saunders, R. (Norwich C) 71/72 d2, d2, D2; 72/73 M; (Aston Villa) 74/75 d2, M, d2; 75 Y; 76/77 M, M; 80/81 M; 81 Y
Saward, P. (Brighton & HA) 70/71 d3; 71/72 d3 d3; 72/73 d2
Scoular, J. (Cardiff C) 70/71 d2
Saxton, B. (Plymouth Arg) 80/81 d3
Sexton, D. (Chelsea) 69/70 M; 71/72 M; (QPR) 74/75 d1; 75/76 M; 76/77 d1
Shankly, B. (Liverpool) 70/71 M; 71/72 M; 72/73 M, M; 73 Y; 73/74 d1; 74 Y
Shannon, L. (Blackpool) 69/70 d2
Shaw, J. (Chesterfield) 73/74 d3; 74/75 d3
Sillett, J. (Hereford U) 75/76 d3, D3
Sirrel, J. (Notts Co) 70/71 d4, d4, D4; 71/72 d3; 72/73 d3, d3; 75/76 d2
Smith, B. (Bury) 74/75 d4; 75/76 d3; 77/78 d3; 78/79 d3; 79/80 d3
Smith, D. (Mansfield T) 74/75 d4; 75/76 d3; (Southend U) 76/77 d4; 77/78 d4; 78/79 d3; 79/80 d3; 80/81 d4, d4, D4
Smith, J. (Colchester U) 72/73 d4; 73/74 d4; 74/75 d3; (Blackburn R) 77/78 d2; (Oxford U) 81/82 d3; 82/83 d3
Stiles, N. (Preston NE) 79/80 d2
Stock, A. (Luton T) 70/71 d2; (Fulham) 73/74 d2; 74/75 M; 75/76 d2
Stokoe, B. (Blackpool) 71/72 d2; (Sunderland) 72/73 M, d2; 73 S; 74/75 d2; 75/76 d2; 76 S; (Carlisle U) 81/82 d3
Stuttard, E. (Plymouth Arg) 71/72 d3
Summers, G. (Oxford U) 70/71 d2; 72/73 d2; (Gillingham) 78/79 d3
Taylor, G. (Lincoln C) 74/75 d4; 75/76 d4, d4, d4, d4, D4; 77/78 d4, d4, d4, D4; 81/82 d2; 82 S; 82/83 M
Thompson, A. (Stockport Co) 77/78 d4
Toshack, J. (Swansea C) 78/79 d3; 79/80 d2; 80/81 d2; 81 S
Turner, G. (Shrewsbury T) 78/79 M, D3; 79/80 d2
Venables, T. (Crystal Palace) 78/79 d2, d2, D2; 79/80 M; (QPR) 81/82 d2; 82/83 M, D2
Waddington, T. (Stoke C) 70/71 d1; 71/72 M; 74/75 M
Wallace, J. (Leicester C) 79/80 d2; 80 S; 81/82 d2
Waiters, T. (Plymouth Argyle) 73/74 d3; 74/75 d3
Webb, D. (AFC Bournemouth) 80/81 d4; 81/82 d4
Williams, D. (Mansfield T) 72/73 d4; (Swindon T) 74/75 d3
Yeats, R. (Tranmere R) 72/73 d3

FOOTBALL LEAGUE REFEREES 1983–84

There are four newly appointed referees to the Football League for the season 1983–84 and they are Jim Ashworth, Alf Buksh, Roger Dilkes and Ian Hendrick, and they, of course, replace various retiring referees including last season's FA Cup Final referee, Alf Grey and FA Vase Final referee, Brian Daniels. The longest serving referee on the Football League is now Clive Thomas of Porthcawl.
The full list is as follows:

Allison, D. B. (Lancaster)
Ashley N. J. (Nantwich)
Ashworth J. (Oakham, Leics)
Axcell D. J. (Southend)

Baker K. W. (Rugby)
Banks R. A. (Manchester)
Barratt K. P. (Coventry)
Bates S. G. (Bristol)
Bodenham M. J. (Brighton)
Borrett I. J. (Eye, Suffolk)
Bray J. E. (Hinckley, Leics)
Brazier D. H. (Northampton)
Bridges R. (Deeside)
Buksh A. N. (London)
Bune T. G. (Yattendon, Berks)
Burden L. F. (Poole, Dorset)

Callow V. G. (Solihull)
Challinor A. (Rotherham)
Cooper K. (Pontypridd)
Courtney G. (Spennymoor)
Crickmore E. A. (Plymouth)

Deakin J. C. (Barry, S. Glam.)
Dilkes L. R. (Mossley)
Dimblebee M. (Stevenage)
Downey C. (Hounslow)

Fitzharris T. (Bolton)

Glover N. H. (Chorley)
Gunn A. (Burgess Hill, Sussex)
Guy R. (Kirkby, Merseyside)

Hackett K. S. (Sheffield)
Heath M. J. (Stoke)
Hedges D. A. (Oxford)
Hendrick J. A. (Preston)
Hill B. (Kettering)
Holbrook T. J. (Wolverhampton)
Hough J. D. (Macclesfield)
Hunting J. (Leicester)
Hutchinson D.(Harrogate)

James M. L. (Horsham)
Jones T. A. (Macclesfield)

Key J. M. (Rotherham)
King H. W. (Merthyr Tydfil)

Letts D. (Aldershot)
Lewis R. S. (Great Bookham, Surrey)
Lovatt J. (Crewe)

Martin J. E. (Nr. Alton, Hants)
Midgley N. (Salford)
Milford R. G. (Bristol)
Mills T. (Barnsley)
Moules J. A. (Ongar, Essex)

Napthine G. J. (Loughborough)
Nixon R. F. (West Kirby, Wirral)

Owen D. (Bebington, Wirral)

Peck M. G. (Kendal)

Read E. A. (Bristol)
Redfern K. A. (Whitley Bay)
Reeves D. V. (Uxbridge)
Richardson D. (Blackburn)
Roberts F. (Prestatyn)
Robinson Alan (Portsmouth)
Robinson Arthur (Manchester)
Robinson L. M. (Sutton Coldfield)

Salmon K. G. (Cuffley, Herts)
Saunders A. (Newcastle-upon-Tyne)
Scales E. J. (Ware, Herts)
Scott D. (Burnley)
Scott M. P. (Nottingham)
Seel C. N. (Carlisle)
Seville A. (Birmingham)
Shapter L. C. (Torquay)
Shaw D. (Sandbach)
Spencer T. D. (Salisbury)
Stevens B. T. (Stonehouse)

Taylor H. (Oadby, Leics)
Taylor M. J.(Deal, Kent)
Thomas C. (Porthcawl)
Tyldesley P. A. (Stockport)
Tyson G. M. (Sunderland)

Vickers D. S. (Ilford)

Walmsley K. (Blackpool)
Ward A. W. (London)
Willis P. N. (Meadowfield, Co. Durham)
Wilson N. L. (Morecambe)
Worral J. B. (Warrington)

In the match details shown in the club section Alan Robinson is shown as 'Alan' but Arthur Robinson is shown as A. Robinson. Also because they are known as Maurice and Alan, L. M. Robinson is shown as M. Robinson and E. A. Crickmore as A. Crickmore.

ATTENDANCES AT FOOTBALL LEAGUE MATCHES

Season	*Matches*	*Total*	*Div. 1*	*Div. 2*	*Div. 3 (S)*	*Div. 3 (N)*
1946–47	1848	35,604,606	15,005,316	11,071,572	5,664,004	3,863,714
1947–48	1848	40,259,130	16,732,341	12,286,350	6,653,610	4,586,829
1948–49	1848	41,271,414	17,914,667	11,353,237	6,998,429	5,005,081
1949–50	1848	40,517,865	17,278,625	11,694,158	7,104,155	4,440,927
1950–51	2028	39,584,967	16,679,454	10,780,580	7,367,884	4,757,109
1951–52	2028	39,015,866	16,110,322	11,066,189	6,958,927	4,880,428
1952–53	2028	37,149,966	16,050,278	9,686,654	6,704,299	4,708,735
1953–54	2028	36,174,590	16,154,915	9,510,053	6,311,508	4,198,114
1954–55	2028	34,133,103	15,087,221	8,988,794	5,996,017	4,051,071
1955–56	2028	33,150,809	14,108,961	9,080,002	5,692,479	4,269,367
1956–57	2028	32,744,405	13,803,037	8,718,162	5,622,189	4,601,017
1957–58	2028	33,562,208	14,468,652	8,663,712	6,097,183	4,332,661
					Div. 3	*Div. 4*
1958–59	2028	33,610,985	14,727,691	8,641,997	5,946,600	4,276,697
1959–60	2028	32,538,611	14,391,227	8,399,627	5,739,707	4,008,050
1960–61	2028	28,619,754	12,926,948	7,033,936	4,784,256	3,874,614
1961–62	2015	27,979,902	12,061,194	7,453,089	5,199,106	3,266,513
1962–63	2028	28,885,852	12,490,239	7,792,770	5,341,362	3,261,481
1963–64	2028	28,535,022	12,486,626	7,594,158	5,419,157	3,035,081
1964–65	2028	27,641,168	12,708,752	6,984,104	4,436,245	3,512,067
1965–66	2028	27,206,980	12,480,644	6,914,757	4,779,150	3,032,429
1966–67	2028	28,902,596	14,242,957	7,253,819	4,421,172	2,984,648
1967–68	2028	30,107,298	15,289,410	7,450,410	4,013,087	3,354,391
1968–69	2028	29,382,172	14,584,851	7,382,390	4,339,656	3,075,275
1969–70	2028	29,600,972	14,868,754	7,581,728	4,223,761	2,926,729
1970–71	2028	28,194,146	13,954,337	7,098,265	4,377,213	2,764,331
1971–72	2028	28,700,729	14,484,603	6,769,308	4,697,392	2,749,426
1972–73	2028	25,448,642	13,998,154	5,631,730	3,737,252	2,081,506
1973–74	2027	24,982,203	13,070,991	6,326,108	3,421,624	2,163,480
1974–75	2028	25,577,977	12,613,178	6,955,970	4,086,145	1,992,684
1975–76	2028	24,896,053	13,089,861	5,798,405	3,948,449	2,059,338
1976–77	2028	26,182,800	13,647,585	6,250,597	4,152,218	2,132,400
1977–78	2028	25,392,872	13,255,677	6,474,763	3,332,042	2,330,390
1978–79	2028	24,540,627	12,704,549	6,153,223	3,374,558	2,308,297
1979–80	2028	24,623,975	12,163,002	6,112,025	3,999,328	2,349,620
1980–81	2028	21,907,569	11,392,894	5,175,442	3,637,854	1,701,379
1981–82	2028	20,006,961	10,420,793	4,750,463	2,836,915	1,998,790
1982–83	2028	18,788,822	9,321,018	4,979,331	2,941,516	1,546,957

DID YOU KNOW?

The first club to move up from the Third Division and win the First Division Championship was **Portsmouth**.

Charlton Athletic are the only club to have progressed from the Third Division to the First in two seasons (1934–35, 1935–36), they then finished as runners-up in the First Division.

Northampton Town were the first club to progress from the Fourth Division to the First Division (1961–1965).

When **Chester** went into the Third Division at the end of the 1974–75 season they were the last Football League club to have achieved promotion.

In **Carlisle United**'s only season in the First Division they won their first three league games to go top. But this form wasn't continued and the little Cumbrian club were relegated.

The **Ipswich Town** side that won the First Division Championship in 1962 contained five players (Bailey, Carberry, Phillips, Elsworthy and Leadbetter) who had been regulars in the Third Division side of the mid fifties.

Grimsby Town have played in all six divisions of the Football League: First, Second, Third, Third (South), Third (North) and Fourth and have played all the other clubs in the League.

Just three seasons after finishing as Runners Up in Division Three (North) (1956–57) **Hartlepool** conceded a Fourth Division record of 109 goals.

Oxford United reached the Second Division having spent three seasons in Divisions Four and three in Division Three after joining the Football League in season 1962–63.

Hereford United won promotion to the Third Division in their first season in the Football League (1972–73) and then moved up to the Second Division after three seasons in Division Three.

Lincoln City have played all 91 other League clubs and have beaten all except **Aston Villa**, **Chelsea** and **Norwich City**.

Portsmouth became the first club to win the Third Division Championship for a second time when they became champions last season.

FOOTBALL LEAGUE ATTENDANCES 1982–83

FIRST DIVISION

	1982–83 Total Gate	Average	1981–82 Total Gate	Difference
Watford	408,534	19,454	307,261	+101,273
Norwich C	371,238	17,678	297,844	+73,394
Stoke C	349,167	16,627	307,335	+41,832
Luton T	282,492	13,452	249,497	+32,995
Liverpool	731,514	34,834	736,280	−4766
Birmingham C	333,480	15,880	359,453	−25,973
Arsenal	507,192	24,152	535,370	−28,178
Notts Co	215,544	10,264	244,178	−28,634
WBA	320,355	15,255	352,499	−32,144
Ipswich T	413,196	19,676	460,435	−47,239
Nottingham F	374,346	17,826	418,686	−47,340
Sunderland	364,413	17,353	411,765	−47,352
Coventry C	220,059	10,479	275,099	−55,040
Manchester U	873,033	41,573	935,983	−62,950
Southampton	393,057	18,717	458,537	−65,480
Aston Villa	498,792	23,752	564,388	−65,596
Brighton & HA	308,364	14,684	383,132	−74,768
West Ham U	478,254	22,774	558,284	−80,030
Everton	426,510	20,310	518,147	−91,637
Tottenham H	643,545	30,654	737,096	−93,551
Swansea C	245,301	11,681	382,745	−137,144
Manchester C	562,632	26,792	715,332	−152,700

SECOND DIVISION

	1982–83 Total Gate	Average	1981–82 Total Gate	Difference
Newcastle U	507,759	24,179	362,797	+144,962
Fulham	227,556	10,836	159,572	+67,984
Derby Co	285,579	13,599	248,381	+37,269
Burnley	189,084	9,004	159,535	+29,549
Carlisle U	124,803	5943	101,418	+23,385
Shrewsbury T	110,775	5275	95,981	+14,794
Charlton Ath	151,053	7193	139,619	+11,434
Wolverhampton W	329,343	15,683	320,090	+9253
QPR	268,926	12,806	264,055	+4871
Oldham Ath	146,601	6981	147,481	−88
Bolton W	157,752	7512	159,540	−1788
Chelsea	267,288	12,728	275,770	−8482
Crystal P	206,808	9848	217,996	−11,188
Cambridge U	95,172	4532	106,536	−11,364
Grimsby T	162,645	7745	176,527	−13,882
Blackburn R	149,436	7116	176,499	−27,063
Leicester C	269,199	12,819	297,844	−28,623
Rotherham U	174,636	8316	206,992	−32,356
Sheffield W	349,797	16,657	402,571	−52,74
Barnsley	258,720	12,320	317,050	−58,330
Middlesbrough	210,231	10,011	281,668	−71,437
Leeds U	336,168	16,008	736,280	−128,123

THIRD DIVISION

	1982–83 Total Gate	Average	1981–82 Total Gate	Difference
Portsmouth	323,311	14,057	196,510	+126,801
Huddersfield T	213,049	9263	155,154	+57,895
Cardiff C	161,529	7023	117,049	+44,480
Brentford	152,145	6615	130,935	+21,210
Bristol R	142,393	6191	128,794	+13,599
Lincoln C	109,227	4749	97,113	+12,114
Newport Co	108,330	4710	102,548	+5,782
AFC Bournemouth	131,629	5723	136,468	−4839
Plymouth Arg	104,236	4532	110,219	−5983
Oxford U	125,948	5476	134,562	−8614
Exeter C	77,487	3369	88,729	−11,242
Walsall	74,566	3242	86,122	−11,556
Preston NE	113,574	4938	126,425	−12,851
Bradford C	111,136	4832	124,004	−12,868
Millwall	92,713	4031	106,387	−13,674
Reading	75,141	3267	92,403	−17,262
Gillingham	95,381	4147	120,546	−25,165
Wrexham	62,330	2710	90,390	−28,060
Orient	62,698	2726	92,805	−30,107
Wigan	102,097	4439	134,313	−32,216
Chesterfield	74,773	3251	109,304	−34,531
Doncaster R	80,868	3516	120,393	−39,525
Southend U	75,417	3279	116,901	−41,484
Sheffield U	271,538	11,806	342,505	−70,967

FOURTH DIVISION

	1982–83 Total Gate	Average	1981–82 Total Gate	Difference
Hull C	159,666	6942	91,838	+67,828
Scunthorpe U	82,202	3574	51,327	+30,875
Port Vale	110,837	4819	83,691	+27,146
York C	74,243	3243	54,283	+20,306
Northampton T	59,685	2595	53,036	+6649
Tranmere R	44,367	1929	39,916	+4451
Torquay U	53,176	2312	51,693	+1483
Crewe Alex	51,612	2244	50,517	+1095
Rochdale	38,847	1689	42,259	−3412
Aldershot	44,344	1928	49,860	−5516
Wimbledon	54,142	2354	59,702	−5560
Stockport Co	52,969	2303	58,583	−5614
Chester	43,769	1903	49,917	−6148
Colchester U	58,696	2552	65,767	−7071
Hereford U	51,382	2234	59,616	−8234
Mansfield T	53,176	2312	61,749	−8573
Bury	71,116	3092	81,830	−10,714
Halifax T	44,275	1925	55,362	−11,087
Hartlepool U	31,487	1369	47,256	−15,769
Darlington	33,442	1454	57,720	−24,278
Blackpool	69,046	3002	97,142	28,096
Bristol C	107,985	4695	149,754	−41,769
Swindon T	91,862	3994	133,972	−42,110
Peterborough U	64,285	2795	108,055	−43,770

AWARDS 1982–83

FOOTBALLER OF THE YEAR

Kenny Dalglish became only the fourth player, after Tom Finney, Danny Blanchflower and Stanley Matthews, to win the Football Writers' Association Footballer of the Year Award for a second time. During the season he played his 90th senior International for Scotland, scored his 300th goal in senior club football and after a quiet start to the season produced some of the most brilliant attacking skills seen in the Football League for a very long time.

Award Winners
1947–48 Stanley Matthews (Blackpool), 1948–49 Johnny Carey (Manchester U), 1949–50 Joe Mercer (Arsenal), 1950–51 Harry Johnston (Blackpool), 1951–52 Billy Wright (Wolverhampton W), 1952–53 Nat Lofthouse (Bolton W), 1953–54 Tom Finney (Preston NE), 1954–55 Don Revie (Manchester C), 1955–56 Bert Trautmann (Manchester C), 1956–57 Tom Finney (Preston NE), 1957–58 Danny Blanchflower (Tottenham H), 1958–59 Syd Owen (Luton T), 1959–60 Bill Slater (Wolverhampton W), 1960–61 Danny Blanchflower (Tottenham H), 1961–62 Jimmy Adamson (Burnley), 1962–63 Stanley Matthews (Stoke C), 1963–64 Bobby Moore (West Ham U), 1964–65 Bobby Collins (Leeds U), 1965–66 Bobby Charlton (Manchester U), 1966–67 Jackie Charlton (Leeds U), 1967–68 George Best (Manchester U), 1968–69 Dave Mackay (Derby Co) shared with Tony Book (Manchester C), 1969–70 Billy Bremner (Leeds U), 1970–71 Frank McLintock (Arsenal), 1971–72 Gordon Banks (Stoke C), 1972–73 Pat Jennings (Tottenham H), 1973–74 Ian Callaghan (Liverpool), 1974–75 Alan Mullery (Fulham), 1975–76 Kevin Keegan (Liverpool), 1976–77 Emlyn Hughes (Liverpool), 1977–78 Kenny Burns (Nottingham F), 1978–79 Kenny Dalglish (Liverpool), 1979–80 Terry McDermott (Liverpool), 1980–81 Frans Thijssen (Ipswich T), 1981–82 Steve Perryman (Tottenham H), 1982–83 Kenny Dalglish (Liverpool).

THE PFA AWARDS 1973–1983

Player of the Year: Kenny Dalglish (Liverpool)
Previous Winners (in order): Norman Hunter (Leeds U), Colin Todd (Derby Co), Pat Jennings (Tottenham H), Andy Gray (Aston V), Peter Shilton (Nottingham F), Liam Brady (Arsenal), Terry McDermott (Liverpool), John Wark (Ipswich T), Kevin Keegan (Southampton).
Young Player of the Year: Ian Rush (Liverpool)
Previous Winners (in order): Kevin Beattie (Ipswich T), Mervyn Day (West Ham U), Peter Barnes (Manchester C), Andy Gray (Aston Villa), Tony Woodcock (Nottingham F), Cyrille Regis (WBA), Glen Hoddle (Tottenham H), Gary Shaw (Aston V), Steve Moran (Southampton).
Merit Awards: Bob Paisley (Liverpool)
Previous Winners (in order): Bobby Charlton and Cliff Lloyd (Two awards in 1973–74), Denis Law, George Eastham, Jack Taylor, Bill Shankley, Tom Finney, Sir Matt Busby, John Trollope, Joe Mercer OBE.

The following four teams were selected by the Professional Footballers' Association as the best eleven players in their respective divisions.
Division 1: Peter Shilton (Southampton); Danny Thomas (Coventry C), Mark Lawrenson (Liverpool), Alan Hansen (Liverpool), Kenny Sansom (Arsenal), Bryan Robson (Manchester U), Graeme Souness (Liverpool), Sammy Lee (Liverpool), Ian Rush (Liverpool), Kenny Dalglish (Liverpool), Steve Coppell (Manchester U).

Division 2: John Burridge (Wolverhampton W); John Humphrey (Wolverhampton W), Mick McCarthy (Barnsley), Tony Gale (Fulham), John Ryan (Oldham), Kenny Hibbitt (Wolverhampton W), Ray Houghton (Fulham), Ronnie Glavin (Barnsley), Kevin Keegan (Newcastle U), Andy Gray (Wolverhampton W), Gordon Davies (Fulham).

Division 3: David Felgate (Lincoln C); Malcolm Brown (Huddersfield T), Trevor Peake (Linclon C), Steve Bruce (Gillingham), Mick Adams (Gillingham), Neil Webb (Portsmouth), David Williams (Bristol R), Bobby Doyle (Portsmouth), Kerry Dixon (Reading), Alan Biley (Portsmouth), Glenn Cockerill (Lincoln C).

Division 4: Iain Hesford (Blackpool); Chris Price (Hereford U), Paul Hilton (Bury), Phil Sproson (Port Vale), Russell Bromage (Port Vale), Micky Glynn (Peterborough U), Gary Emmanuel (Swindon T), Geoff Hunter (Port Vale), Les Mutrie (Hull C), Paul Rideout (Swindon T), Steve Fox (Port Vale).

To be described as a 'player's player' is considered the ultimate compliment in the game, so the honours announced by the P.F.A. every year, when a 'team' of players are selected from each division, are treasured by the professionals in the Football League.

It is interesting to see how a great many players have kept their popularity with their fellow professionals despite moving through the divisions, but Kenny Sansom must be the most consistently honoured among today's senior players, as since he established himself in the Crystal Palace side during the 1976–77 season he has featured as the best left back in whatever division he has played (one Division Three award, two Division Two, and four in Division One).

Peter Shilton hasn't quite achieved a 100% record but for the last six years he has held the First Division goalkeeping spot and the most outstanding team effort was by West Ham United who claimed eight Second Division places in 1980.

Division One Awards

1973 Pat Jennings (Tottenham H); Paul Madeley (Leeds U), Roy McFarland (Derby Co), Norman Hunter (Leeds U), Colin Todd (Derby Co); Billy Bremner (Leeds U), Tony Currie (Sheffield U), Johnny Giles (Leeds U); Mike Channon (Southampton), Malcolm MacDonald (Newcastle U), Allan Clarke (Leeds U).

1974 Peter Shilton (Stoke C); Paul Madeley (Leeds U), Kevin Beattie (Ipswich T), Billy Bonds (West Ham U), Gordon McQueen (Manchester U), Colin Todd (Derby Co), Duncan McKenzie (Leeds U), Colin Bell (Manchester C), Bob Latchford (Everton), Alan Hudson (Stoke C), Leighton James (Burnley).

1975 Pat Jennings (Tottenham H); Paul Madeley (Leeds U), Kevin Beattie (Ipswich T), Don Masson (QPR), Roy McFarland (Derby Co), Colin Todd (Derby Co), Kevin Keegan (Liverpool), Alan Hudson (Stoke C), Duncan McKenzie (Leeds U), John Toshack (Liverpool), Dennis Tueart (Manchester C).

1976 Ray Clemence (Liverpool); John Gidman (Aston V), Mick Mills (Ipswich T), Brian Talbot (Ipswich T), Roy McFarland (Derby Co), Kevin Beattie (Ipswich T), Kevin Keegan (Liverpool), Trevor Francis (Birmingham C), Andy Gray (Aston V), Trevor Brooking (West Ham U), Dennis Tueart (Manchester C).

1977 Peter Shilton (Nottingham F); John Gidman (Aston V), Derek Statham (WBA), Liam Brady (Arsenal), Gordon McQueen (Manchester U), Martin Buchan (Manchester U), Steve Coppell (Manchester U), Trevor Francis (Birmingham C), Joe Jordan (Manchester U), Trevor Brooking (West Ham U), John Robertson (Nottingham F).

1978 Peter Shilton (Nottingham F); Viv Anderson (Nottingham F), David O'Leary (Arsenal), Dave Watson (Manchester C), Derek Statham (WBA), Liam Brady (Arsenal), Tony Currie (Leeds U), Osvaldo Ardiles (Tottenham H), Cyrille Regis (WBA), Kenny Dalglish (Liverpool), Laurie Cunningham (WBA).

1979 Peter Shilton (Nottingham F); Viv Anderson (Nottingham F), Dave Watson (Southampton), David O'Leary (Arsenal), Kenny Sansom (Arsenal), Terry McDermott (Liverpool), Liam Brady (Arsenal), Glen Hoddle (Tottenham H), Kenny Dalglish (Liverpool), David Johnson (Liverpool), Garry Birtles (Nottingham F).

1980 Peter Shilton (Nottingham F); Kenny Swain (Aston V), Russell Osman (Ipswich T), Allan Evans (Aston V), Kenny Sansom (Arsenal), Frans Thijssen (Ipswich T), John Wark (Ipswich T), Graeme Souness (Liverpool), Paul Mariner (Ipswich T), Kenny Dalglish (Liverpool), Gary Shaw (Aston V).

1981 Peter Shilton (Nottingham F); Kenny Swain (Aston V), David O'Leary (Arsenal), Alan Hansen (Liverpool), Kenny Sansom (Arsenal), Graeme Souness (Liverpool), Glen Hoddle (Tottenham H), Bryan Robson (Manchester U), Trevor Francis (Manchester C), Kevin Keegan (Southampton), Cyrille Regis (WBA).

Division Two Awards

1973 Bryan King (Millwall); John Craggs (Middlesbrough), Dave Watson (Sunderland), Willie Maddren (Middlesbrough), John Gorman (Carlisle U), Bruce Rioch (Aston V), Don Masson (Notts Co), Asa Hartford (WBA), Dennis Tueart (Sunderland), Duncan McKenzie (Nottingham F), Don Rogers (Crystal P).

1974 Bryan King (Millwall); John Gidman (Aston V), Stewart Houston (Manchester U), Len Cantello (WBA), Dave Watson (Sunderland), Martin Buchan (Manchester U), Ray Graydon (Aston V), Mike Channon (Southampton), Stuart Pearson (Manchester U), Phil Boyer (Norwich C), Billy Hughes (Sunderland).

1975 Jim Montgomery (Sunderland); Gary Lock (Chelsea), John Gorman (Carlisle U), Tony Towers (Sunderland), Paul Jones (Bolton W), Geoff Merrick (Bristol C), Bobby Kerr (Sunderland), Mike Channon (Southampton), Paul Cheesley (Bristol C), Johnny Giles (WBA), Peter Thompson (Bolton W).

1976 George Wood (Blackpool); Gary Lock (Chelsea), David Peach (Southampton), Gary Stanley (Chelsea), Paul Jones (Bolton W), Paul Futcher (Luton T), George Best (Fulham), Ray Wilkins (Chelsea), John Richards (Wolverhampton W), Mike Channon (Southampton), John Robertson (Nottingham F).

1977 Barry Daines (Tottenham H); Terry Naylor (Tottenham H), Kenny Sansom (Crystal P), Glen Hoddle (Tottenham H), Paul Jones (Bolton W), Paul Futcher (Luton T), Alan Ball (Southampton), Peter Ward (Brighton & HA), John Duncan (Tottenham H), Peter Reid (Bolton W), Peter Taylor (Tottenham H).

1978 Mark Wallington (Leicester C); Kevin Hird (Leeds U), Mark Lawrenson (Brighton & HA), Mike Doyle (Stoke C), Kenny Sansom (Crystal P), Trevor Brooking (West Ham U), Howard Kendall (Stoke C), Brian Horton (Brighton & HA), Bryan Robson (West Ham U), Mike Flanagan (Charlton Ath), Peter Withe (Newcastle U).

1979 Phil Parkes (West Ham U); Kirk Stephens (Luton T), Colin Todd (Birmingham C), Billy Bonds (West Ham U), Mark Dennis (Birmingham C), Archie Gemmill (Birmingham C), Trevor Brooking (West Ham U), Alan Devonshire (West Ham U), Clive Allen (QPR), Peter Withe (Newcastle U), David Moss (Luton T).

1980 Phil Parkes (West Ham U); Ray Stewart (West Ham U), Alvin Martin (West Ham U), Billy Bonds (West Ham U), Ray O'Brien (Notts Co), Trevor Brooking (West Ham U), Tony Currie (QPR), Alan Devonshire (West Ham U), Paul Goddard (West Ham U), David Cross (West Ham U), Terry Curran (Sheffield W).

1981 Mark Wallington (Leicester C); Kirk Stephens (Luton T), Mike McCarthy (Barnsley), Glen Roeder (QPR), Steve Buckley (Derby Co), Ricky Hill (Luton T), Ian Banks (Barnsley), Brian Horton (Luton T), David Moss (Luton T), Simon Stainrod (QPR), Paul Walsh (Charlton Ath).

RECORDS

Major British Records

HIGHEST SCORES

FOOTBALL LEAGUE

Division 1	(*Home*)	WBA	12	Darwen	0	4 April 1892
		Nottingham F	12	Leicester Fosse	0	21 April 1909
	(*Away*)	Newcastle U	1	Sunderland	9	5 Dec 1908
		Cardiff C	1	Wolverhampton W	9	3 Sept 1955
Division 2	(*Home*)	Newcastle U	13	Newport Co	0	5 Oct 1946
	(*Away*)	Burslem PV	0	Sheffield U	10	10 Dec 1892
Division 3	(*Home*)	Tranmere R	9	Accrington S	0	18 April 1959
		Brentford	9	Wrexham	0	15 Oct 1963
	(*Away*)	Halifax T	0	Fulham	8	16 Sept 1969
		Brighton	2	Bristol R	8	1 Dec 1973
Division 3(S)	(*Home*)	Luton T	12	Bristol R	0	13 April 1936
	(*Away*)	Northampton T	0	Walsall	8	2 Feb 1947
Division 3(N)	(*Home*)	Stockport Co	13	Halifax T	0	6 Jan 1934
	(*Away*)	Accrington S	0	Barnsley	9	3 Feb 1934
Division 4	(*Home*)	Oldham Ath	11	Southport	0	26 Dec 1962
	(*Away*)	Crewe Alex	1	Rotherham U	8	8 Sept 1973

When **Sunderland** won 9-1 at **Newcastle United** in 1908, the score equalled the highest away win in the First Division, but even more impressive was the fact that their local rivals went on to win the Championship that season by seven points!

Tranmere Rovers' record win 13-4 v **Oldham Athletic** also produced the Football League's highest scoring game. On the day, Bunny Bell scored nine goals and missed a penalty.

When **Stockport County** beat **Halifax Town** 13-0 in a League game during the 1933–34 season they created a League record by scoring 11 goals in the second half.

MOST GOALS FOR IN A SEASON

FOOTBALL LEAGUE		*Goals*	*Games*	*Season*
Division 1	Aston V	128	42	1930–31
Division 2	Middlesbrough	122	42	1926–27
Division 3(S)	Millwall	127	42	1927–28
Division 3(N)	Bradford C	128	42	1928–29
Division 3	QPR	111	46	1961–62
Division 4	Peterborough U	134	46	1960–61

Wolves hit a century of league goals in four consecutive seasons between 1957–61.

Peterborough United set up a goalscoring record in Division Four (134 goals) in their very first season in the Football League.

Manchester City scored more goals (80) than any other First Division club in season 1937–38 but were relegated.

FEWEST GOALS FOR IN A SEASON

FOOTBALL LEAGUE	(minimum 42 games)	*Goals*	*Games*	*Season*
Division 1	Leicester C	26	42	1977–78
Division 2	Watford	24	42	1971–72
Division 3(S)	Crystal Palace	33	42	1950–51
Division 3(N)	Crewe Alex	32	42	1923–24
Division 3	Stockport Co	27	46	1969–70
Division 4	Bradford	30	46	1967–68
	Workington	30	46	1975–76
	Gillingham	30	46	1963–64

MOST GOALS AGAINST IN A SEASON

FOOTBALL LEAGUE		*Goals*	*Games*	*Season*
Division 1	Blackpool	125	42	1930-31
Division 2	Darwen	141	34	1898–99
Division 3(S)	Merthyr T	135	42	1929–30
Division 3(N)	Nelson	136	42	1927–28
Division 3	Accrington S	123	46	1959–60
Division 4	Hartlepools U	109	46	1959–60

FEWEST GOALS AGAINST IN A SEASON

FOOTBALL LEAGUE	(minimum 42 games)	*Goals*	*Games*	*Season*
Division 1	Liverpool	16	42	1978–79
Division 2	Manchester U	23	42	1924–25
Division 3(S)	Southampton	21	42	1921–22
Division 3(N)	Port Vale	21	46	1953–54
Division 3	Rotherham U	32	46	1980–81
Division 4	Lincoln C	25	46	1980–81

In the 1947–48 season **Birmingham City** only conceded 11 goals in their 21 away league matches. This is the best away record in Division Two since the Second World War.

In 1928–29 **Cardiff City** conceded the fewest number of goals in the First Division but were relegated.

MOST POINTS IN A SEASON

FOOTBALL LEAGUE	(under old system)	*Points*	*Games*	*Season*
Division 1	Liverpool	68	42	1978–79
Division 2	Tottenham H	70	42	1919–20
Division 3	Aston V	70	46	1971–72
Division 3(S)	Nottingham F	70	46	1950–51
	Bristol C	70	46	1954–55
Division 3(N)	Doncaster R	72	42	1946–47
Division 4	Lincoln C	74	46	1975–76
FOOTBALL LEAGUE	(three points for a win)			
Division 1	Liverpool	87	42	1981–82
Division 2	Luton T	88	42	1981–82
Division 3	Portsmouth	91	46	1982–83
Division 4	Wimbledon	98	46	1982–83

Liverpool won the Championship last season by 11 points. Other impressive large margins in Division One were achieved by **Preston NE** (11 pts from Aston Villa) 1888–89, **Sunderland** (11 pts from Preston NE) 1892–93, **Aston Villa** (11 pts from Sheffield United) 1896–97, **Manchester United** (11 pts from Blackpool) 1955–56 and **Sheffield Wednesday** (10 pts from Derby County) 1929–30.

The biggest Championship-winning margin for any division of the Football League is 15 points; by **Middlesbrough** in Division 2 in 1973–74.

FEWEST POINTS IN A SEASON

FOOTBALL LEAGUE	(minimum 34 games)	*Points*	*Games*	*Season*
Division 1	Leeds U	18	42	1946–47
	QPR	18	42	1968–69
	Glossop	18	34	1899–1900
	Notts Co	18	34	1904–05
	Woolwich Arsenal	18	38	1912–13
Division 2	Doncaster R	8	34	1904–05
	Loughborough T	8	34	
1899–1900				
Division 3	Rochdale	21	46	1973–74
Division 3(S)	Merthyr T	21	42	1924–25 & 1929–30
	QPR	21	42	1925–26
Division 3(N)	Rochdale	11	40	1931–32
Division 4	Bradford	20	46	1968–69

MOST WINS IN A SEASON

FOOTBALL LEAGUE		*Wins*	*Games*	*Season*
Division 1	Tottenham H	31	42	1960–61
Division 2	Tottenham H	32	42	1919–20
Division 3(S)	Millwall	30	42	1927–28
	Plymouth Arg	30	42	1929–30
	Cardiff C	30	42	1946–47
	Nottingham F	30	46	1950–51
	Bristol C	30	46	1954–55
Division 3(N)	Doncaster R	33	42	1946–47
Division 3	Aston Villa	32	46	1971–72
Division 4	Lincoln C	32	46	1975–76

Millwall have completed a season with an unbeaten home record in four Divisions: Div One – 1971–72; Div 2 – 1965–66; Div 4 – 1964–65; Div 3 (S) – 1927–28. They are the only club to have achieved this feat.

Nottingham Forest hold the Football League record of 42 successive League matches without defeat.

Leeds United created a new Football League record when they remained unbeaten for the first 29 games at the beginning of the 1973–74 season.

Millwall were unbeaten for 59 successive League matches at the Den between 24 August 1964 and 14 January 1967.

Blackburn Rovers were unbeaten for 35 consecutive League matches in season 1881–82.

Bristol Rovers played 27 games without defeat in Division Three (South) in 1952–53 (a record for the division) and also avoided defeat for 27 Division Three games from the beginning of the 1973–74 season (another record).

RECORD HOME WINS IN A SEASON

Brentford won all 21 games in Division 3(S), 1929–30

RECORD AWAY WINS IN A SEASON

Doncaster R won 18 of 21 games in Division 3(N), 1946–47

FEWEST WINS IN A SEASON

FOOTBALL LEAGUE		*Wins*	*Games*	*Season*
Division 1	Stoke	3	22	1889–90
	Woolwich Arsenal	3	38	1912–13
Division 2	Loughborough T	1	34	1899–1900
Division 3(S)	Merthyr T	6	42	1929–30
Division 3(N)	Rochdale	4	40	1931–32
Division 3	Rochdale	2	46	1973–74
Division 4	Bradford	4	46	1967–68

Crewe Alexandra played 30 consecutive League games in 1956–57 without recording a single victory.

MOST DEFEATS IN A SEASON

FOOTBALL LEAGUE		*Defeats*	*Games*	*Season*
Division 1	Leeds U	30	42	1946–47
	Blackburn R	30	42	1965–66
Division 2	Tranmere R	31	42	1938–39
Division 3	Newport Co	31	46	1961–62
Division 3(S)	Merthyr T	29	42	1924–25
Division 3(N)	Rochdale	33	40	1931–32
Division 4	Workington	32	46	1975–76

FEWEST DEFEATS IN A SEASON

FOOTBALL LEAGUE		Defeats	Games	Season
Division 1	Preston NE	0	22	1888–89
	Leeds U	2	42	1968–69
Division 2	Liverpool	0	28	1893–94
	Burnley	2	30	1897–98
	Bristol C	2	38	1905–06
	Leeds U	3	42	1963–64
Division 3	QPR	5	46	1966–67
Division 3(S)	Southampton	4	42	1921–22
	Plymouth Arg	4	42	1929–30
Division 3(N)	Port Vale	3	46	1953–54
	Doncaster R	3	42	1946–47
	Wolverhampton W	3	42	1923–24
Division 4	Lincoln C	4	46	1975–76
	Sheffield U	4	46	1981–82

In 1921–22 **Southampton** lost only four League games and conceded only 21 goals; both records for Division Three (South).

MOST DRAWN GAMES IN A SEASON

FOOTBALL LEAGUE		Draws	Games	Season
Division 1	Norwich C	23	42	1978–79

MOST GOALS IN A GAME

FOOTBALL LEAGUE		
Division 1	Ted Drake (Arsenal) 7 goals v Aston Villa	14 Dec 1935
Division 2	Tommy Briggs (Blackburn R) 7 goals v Bristol R	5 Feb 1955
	Neville Coleman (Stoke C) 7 goals v Lincoln C	23 Feb 1957
Division 3(S)	Joe Payne (Luton T) 10 goals v Bristol R	13 April 1936
Division 3(N)	Robert Bell (Tranmere R) 9 goals v Oldham Ath	26 Dec 1935
Division 3	Steve Earle (Fulham) 5 goals v Halifax T	16 Sept 1969
	Barrie Thomas (Scunthorpe U) 5 goals v Luton T	24 April 1965
	Keith East (Swindon T) 5 goals v Mansfield T	20 Nov 1965
	Alf Wood (Shrewsbury T) 5 goals v Blackburn R	2 Oct 1971
Division 4	Herbert Lister (Oldham Ath) 6 goals v Southport	26 Dec 1962

Neville Coleman of **Stoke City** scored seven goals as an orthodox winger, against **Lincoln City** in 1957. This was a record for a player in his position at the time.

FA CUP	Ted MacDougall (Bournemouth) 9 goals v Margate (*1st Round*)	20 Nov 1971

MOST LEAGUE GOALS IN A SEASON

FOOTBALL LEAGUE		Goals	Games	Season
Division 1	Dixie Dean (Everton)	60	39	1927–28
Division 2	George Camsell (Middlesbrough)	59	37	1926–27
Division 3(S)	Joe Payne (Luton T)	55	39	1936–37
Division 3(N)	Ted Harston (Mansfield T)	55	41	1936–37
Division 3	Derek Reeves (Southampton)	39	46	1959–60
Division 4	Terry Bly (Peterborough U)	52	46	1960–61

MOST LEAGUE GOALS IN A CAREER

FOOTBALL LEAGUE		Goals	Games	Season
Arthur Rowley	WBA	4	24	1946–48
	Fulham	27	56	1948–50
	Leicester C	251	303	1950–58
	Shrewsbury T	152	236	1958–65
		434	619	

FOOTBALL LEAGUE FIRSTS

The first five Football League games were played on 8 September, 1888. Bolton Wanderers were three goals up in about six minutes against Derby Co, but were eventually beaten 6-3. Cox of Aston Villa scored the first 'own goal', giving Wolverhampton W an early lead, but Villa recovered to draw 1-1.

Huddersfield T became the first team to complete a hat-trick of League Championships – 1924–25–26.

The Football League played their first representative game in April 1891. It was against the Football Alliance at Sheffield and resulted in a 1-1 draw.

Floodlit football

The first-ever game by floodlight was between two Sheffield Association teams at Bramall Lane, 14 October, 1878.

The first Football League game under floodlights was Portsmouth v Newcastle U at Fratton Park, 22 February, 1956.

Equipment, etc.

Shinguards were first introduced and registered by Sam Widdowson of Nottingham F in 1874. The cross-bar first replaced the tape in 1875, and the whistle was used by the referee for the first time in 1878. Goalnets were invented and patented by J. A. Brodie of Liverpool in 1890.

Nottingham F were the first club to use shinguards (1874), the referee's whistle (1878), three half backs (1885), the crossbar instead of tape (1891) and oval section goal posts (1921).

Substitutes

First substitute in a Football League game was Keith Peacock of Charlton Ath, at Bolton, 21 August, 1965.

The first substitute to score in a Football League game was Bobby Knox (Barrow) v Wrexham, Division 4, 21 August, 1965.

Radio and TV

The first match broadcast in England was the First Division game between Arsenal and Sheffield U at Highbury, 22 January, 1927.

The first Football League game to be televised was Blackpool v Bolton W, 10 September, 1960.

Corner kick

Billy Smith was the first player to score direct from a corner kick in a Football League game – Huddersfield T v Arsenal, 11 October, 1924.

Limited Company

The first football club to form itself into a limited liability company was Birmingham C in 1888. At that time they were known as Small Heath.

Penalty kick

The first player to score from a penalty kick in a Football League match was Heath of Wolverhampton W v Accrington, Division 1, 14 September, 1891.

Professional

The identity of the first professional footballer may never be definitely established, but it was probably J. J. Lang, a Scot who joined Sheffield Wednesday in 1876 after playing for Clydesdale and Glasgow Eastern.

Tour

Oxford University were the first to send a football team on an overseas tour when in 1875 they visited Germany.

Sunday football

The first Football League game to be played on a Sunday was between Millwall and Fulham on the morning of 20 January, 1974. Eleven other Football League games were played later the same day.

OTHER FOOTBALL LEAGUE RECORDS

The oldest player to appear in the Football League was **Neil McBain** who played in goal for New Brighton v Hartlepools U, Division 3(N), 15 March, 1947. He was then aged 52 years 4 months.

The record for most appearances in the Football League during one season by a player over 40 years of age was created by **Bob McGrory**. In his last season as a player with Stoke C (1934–35) he appeared in all 42 First Division games. Bob was then 43 years of age.

The record for most consecutive appearances in the Football League was created by **Harold Bell**, Tranmere R centre-half. From the opening game of season 1946–47 Bell did not miss a single game until August 1955 – a run of 401 consecutive Division 3(N) matches. Including FA Cup, Liverpool Senior Cup and Cheshire Bowl games, Bell enjoyed a run of 459 consecutive first team appearances.

John Trollope created a club record by making 770 League appearances for Swindon T between 1960 and 1980.

In the Scottish League the record for most appearances for a single club was created by Bob Ferrier with 626 for Motherwell between 1918 and 1937.

Since substitutes were introduced into League football in 1965, **Bristol C** is the club that has played through the longest spell without calling upon one of these players – a run of 52 League games, 4 FA Cup, and 2 League Cup ties from February 1966 to April 1967.

The shortest player to appear in the Football League is outside-right **Fred le May**, who was only 5ft tall. He played for Thames 1930–31, Watford 1931–32, and Clapton Orient 1932–33. The tallest was **Albert Iremonger**, Notts Co and Lincoln C goalkeeper 1904–27. He was 6ft 5in tall.

The longest single game on record is that between **Stockport Co** and **Doncaster R**, 30 March, 1946. In an effort to reach a decisive result, this Third Division (N) Cup tie continued for 203 minutes before bad light forced an abandonment.

Rochdale suffered 14 consecutive home defeats in Division 3(N) in 1931–32. This is a Football League record. After beating New Brighton 3-2 on 7 November, 1931, they did not get another home point until holding Barrow to a goalless draw in their second home game of season 1932–33. During that same period Rochdale suffered one run of 17 consecutive defeats (home and away) – also a Football League record.

In season 1904–05 **Manchester U** won 14 consecutive Division 2 games. This Football League record was equalled by Bristol C and Preston NE in Division 2 in 1905–06 and 1950–51 respectively.

Nottingham F were undefeated in a run of 42 First Division games, November 1977 to December 1978. This is a Football League record.

The longest run without defeat in a single season of Football League games is one of 30 matches by **Burnley** in Division 1 in 1920–21.

Six men have both played in and managed Football League Championship winning teams: **Ted Drake**, Arsenal, centre-forward, 1933–34, 1934–35, 1937–38, Chelsea, manager, 1954–55. **Bill Nicholson**, Tottenham H, right half-back, 1950–51, manager, 1960–61. **Alf Ramsey**, right-back, Tottenham H, 1950–51, Ipswich T, manager, 1961–62. **Joe Mercer**, left-half, Everton 1938–39, Arsenal, 1947–48, 1952–53, Manchester C, manager, 1967–68. **Dave Mackay**, left-half, Tottenham H, 1960–61, Derby Co, manager, 1974–75. **Bob Paisley**, Liverpool, left half-back, 1946–47, manager, 1975–76, 1976–77, 1978–79, 1979–80, 1980–81, 1981–82, 1982–83.

In 1973–74 **Leeds U** created a Football League record for the longest run without defeat from the start of a season – 29 First Division games before losing 2-3 at Stoke. It could be said that this only equalled Liverpool's run in the Second Division in 1893–94 when they were unbeaten in all 28 games. Their 29th game that season was the extra 'Test Match' to decide promotion and relegation between the First and Second Divisions.

The youngest player to appear in the Football League is **Albert Geldard** who was aged 15 years 156 days when making his début for Bradford against Millwall, Division 2, 16 September, 1929.

Dave Mackay holds aloft the Division 2 championship trophy that gave Derby County promotion in 1969.

DID YOU KNOW?

QPR have had more home grounds (12) than any other present Football League club. They have also played one 'home' game at Highbury.

In 1929 **Bob Suter** played in goal for **Halifax Town** at the age of 47.

The 1952–53 season was a disastrous one for **Barnsley** who won only five matches, conceded 108 goals and were 17 points adrift at the foot of Division Two. However, it only took them two seasons to take the Third Division North title.

When **Carlisle United** reached the First Division in 1974–75 season, it was a particularly outstanding achievement for a little club who only a few years previously had considered joining the Scottish League to better itself!

In 1976–77 season the attendance for the Third Division match at the Racecourse Ground between **Wrexham** and **Lincoln City** was 7753. In the return match at Sincil Bank later in the season the attendance was again 7753!

In 1960–61 **Shrewsbury Town** met **Swindon Town** six times; in the League, FA Cup, and League Cup and didn't lose once.

In season 1980–81, **Chesterfield** played 65 competitive games (46 League, 6 FA Cup, 4 League Cup and 9 Anglo-Scottish Cup) a record for a Third Division club.

When **Huddersfield Town** won promotion to the First Division in season 1952–53 the club fielded an unchanged defence (Nos 1–6) throughout the season.

Grimsby Town's home ground is in the neighbouring town of Cleethorpes.

The smallest number of players called upon by a club to complete a season of Football League games is 14. **Liverpool** did so when winning the Championship in 1965–66, and **Aston Villa** equalled it in 1980–81 when they too won the Championship.

Millwall played 11 games without conceding a goal in season 1925–26. This is a League record jointly held with **Reading** whose record appearance maker, goalkeeper **Steve Death**, remained unbeaten for the final eleven Football League matches of the 1978–79 season. However, in terms of minutes unbeaten (1103) he created a record.

As champions of the Southern League, **Brighton & Hove Albion** played **Aston Villa** (League Champions) in the FA Shield and won 1-0. The players were all rewarded with a £10 bonus except for Charlie Webb, an amateur, who received a gold tie pin.

GOALSCORING

Full back **Jimmy Evans** topped **Southend United**'s goalscoring list with 10 penalties.

Frank Keeting scored six times in twenty-one minutes for **Lincoln City** against **Halifax Town** on 16 January 1932.

Rotherham United full back **Irvine Rhodes** scored twice on his debut against **Hartlepools** in March 1937.

Barry Lines of **Northampton Town** was the first player to play and score in all four Divisions of the Football League for the same club.

The first ever goal scored in the Fourth Division was by **Alan Woan** of **Northampton Town** when he scored in the first minute against Port Vale on the first day of the 1958–59 season.

Arnold Birch the goalkeeper from **Chesterfield** in season 1923–24 scored five league goals, all from the penalty spot.

In 1933–34 **Oliver Brown** was **Brighton**'s leading goalscorer with 12 goals; yet he only played in 8 matches.

Aldershot held the record for the fastest league goal (until 1964), when **Albert Mundy** scored at **Hartlepools United** on 25th October 1958 after 6 seconds.

The record for scoring the fastest goal in a Football League game is claimed by **Jim Fryatt**. According to referee Mr R. J. Simon this player scored for **Bradford** v **Tranmere R** only 4 seconds after the kick-off, 25 April, 1964. Fastest own goal was in 6 seconds by **Pat Kruse** (**Torquay United**) for **Cambridge United**, 3 January, 1977.

John McIntyre scored four goals in 5 minutes for **Blackburn R** v **Everton**, Division 1, 16 September, 1922. **W. G. Richardson** also scored four goals in 5 minutes for **WBA**, Division 1, 7 November, 1931, but this was even more remarkable because the feat was achieved in an away game – against **West Ham U**.

The record number of penalties missed by one side in a Football League Division 1 game is three: by **Fletcher (2)** and **Thornley** for **Manchester C** against **Newcastle U**, 27 January, 1912.

The most penalties scored by a player in a First Division game is three – **Billy Walker** for **Aston Villa** v **Bradford C**, 12 November, 1921; **Charlie Mitten** for **Manchester U** v **Aston Villa**, 8 March, 1950; and **Ken Barnes** for **Manchester C** v **Everton**, 7 December, 1957.

Only two players have scored two goals for each side in a Football League game, **Sam Wynne** did so in a Division 2 game, 6 October, 1923, scoring twice for **Oldham Ath** as well as putting two through his own goal for **Manchester U**. **Chris Nicholl** (**Aston Villa**) scored all the goals in a 2-2 draw with **Leicester C**, Division 1, 20 March, 1976.

Jimmy Cookson reached a first century of Football League goals in the shortest time. He made his début for **Chesterfield** in 1925 and reached his century in December 1927 with **West Bromwich A**, his 87th Football League game.

The record number of goals scored by a player making his Football League début is five – by **George Hilsdon** for **Chelsea** v **Glossop**, Division 2, 1 September, 1906.

Luther Blissett *Watford*

Gary Lineker *Leicester City*

FOOTBALL LEAGUE DIVISIONAL LEADING GOALSCORERS 1982–83

Tommy Tynan *Newport County*

Dale Banton *Aldershot*

CUP HONOURS CHART

DIVISON ONE CLUBS – BEST PERFORMANCES

	FA Cup	Milk Cup	EC	ECWC	UEFAC	Misc
Arsenal	W (5)	F (2)	QF	F	W	
Aston Villa	W (7)	W (3)	W		QF	
Birmingham C	F (2)	W			F (2) *	
Coventry C	6th Rd (4)	SF			2nd Rd	
Everton	W (3)	F	QF	2nd Rd	3rd Rd	
Ipswich T	W	SF	1st Rd	QF	W	Texaco W
Leicester C	F (4)	W		2nd Rd		
Liverpool	W (2)	W (3)	W (3)	F	W (2)	Super Cup W WCC R/u
Luton T	F	5th Rd				
Man Utd	W (5)	F†	W	QF	2nd Rd	
Norwich C	SF	W				
Nottm F	W (2)	W (2)	W (2)		2nd Rd	Super Cup W WCC R/u AS W
Notts Co	W	5th Rd (3)				
QPR	F	W			QF	
Southampton	W	F		QF	3rd Rd	
Stoke C	SF (3)	W			1st Rd	
Sunderland	W (2)	SF		2nd Rd		
Tottenham H	W (7)	W (3)	SF	W	W	
Watford	SF	SF				
WBA	W (5)	W		QF	QF	
West Ham U	W (3)	F		W		
Wolverhampton W	W (4)	W (2)	2nd Rd	SF	F	Texaco W

W = Winners F = Finalists SF = Semi-Final QF = Quarter-Finalists
WCC = World Club Championship AS = Anglo-Scottish Cup
* European Fairs Cup
† Achieved last season

Brighton goalkeeper Graham Moseley saves under pressure from Manchester United's Gordon McQueen during the 1983 FA Cup final.

DIVISION TWO CLUBS

	FA Cup	Milk Cup	EC	ECWC	UEFAC	Misc
Barnsley	W	5th Rd				
Blackburn R	W (6)	SF				
Brighton & HA	F†	5th Rd				CS W
Cambridge U	6th Rd†	4th Rd				
Cardiff C	W	SF		QF (2)		WC W (20)
Carlisle U	6th Rd	SF				
Charlton A	W	4th Rd (3)				
Chelsea	W	W		W	SF	
Crystal P	SF	5th Rd (2)				
Derby Co	W	SF	SF		3rd Rd	Texaco W CS W
Fulham	F	5th Rd (2)				
Grimsby T	SF (2)	5th Rd				LGC W
Huddersfield T	W	SF				
Leeds U	W	W	F	F	W (2)*	
Man C	W (4)	W (2)	1st Rd	W	QF	
Middlesbrough	6th Rd (8)‡	SF				AS W FAAC W (2)
Newcastle U	W (6)	F			W*	Texaco W (2) AI W
Oldham Ath	SF	3rd Rd Rep				
Portsmouth	W	5th Rd				
Sheff Wed	W (3)	5th Rd†			QF	
Shrewsbury T	6th Rd (2)	SF				WC (4)
Swansea C	SF (2)	4th Rd (2)				WC (8)

CS = Charity Shield LGC = League Group Cup

AS = Anglo-Scottish Cup FAAC = FA Amateur Cup

WC = Welsh Cup AI = Anglo-Italian

* European Fairs Cup

† Achieved last season

‡ In 1900–01 and 1903–04 Middlesbrough reached the last eight but it was not known as the 6th round at that time

Goalmouth action from the 1976 FA Cup final, in which Southampton beat Manchester United 1-0.

CUP HONOURS CHART

Div 3	FA Cup	Milk Cup	Misc	Div 4	FA Cup	Milk Cup	Misc
Bolton W	W (4)	SF		Aldershot	5th Rd Rep	2nd Rd	
Bournemouth	6th Rd	4th Rd (2)		Blackpool	W	SF	AI W
Bradford C	W	5th Rd		Bristol C	F	SF	AS W WC W
Brentford	6th Rd (3)	4th Rd†		Bury	W (2)	SF	
Bristol R	6th Rd (2)	5th Rd]2)		Chester	5th Rd (2)	SF	WC (3) DC
Burnley	W	SF (3)		Chesterfield	5th Rd (3)	4th Rd	AS W
Exeter C	6th Rd Rep	4th Rd		Colchester U	6th Rd	5th Rd	
Gillingham	5th Rd	4th Rd		Crewe Alex	SF	3rd Rd (3)	WC W (2)
Hull C	SF	4th Rd (3)		Darlington	5th Rd	5th Rd	
Lincoln C	5th Rd (3)*	4th Rd		Doncaster R	5th Rd (4)	5th Rd	
Millwall	SF (3)	5th Rd (2)		Halifax T	5th Rd (2)	4th Rd	
Newport C	5th Rd	3rd Rd	ECWC QF WC W (1)	Hartlepool U	4th Rd (2)	4th Rd	
Orient	SF	5th Rd		Hereford U	4th Rd (3)	3rd Rd	WC F (3)
Oxford U	6th Rd (2)	5th Rd		Mansfield T	6th Rd	5th Rd	
Plymouth A	5th Rd	SF (2)		Northampton T	5th Rd (3)	5th Rd (2)	
Port Vale	SF	2nd Rd		Peterborough U	6th Rd	SF	
Preston NE	W (2)	4th Rd (4)		Reading	SF	4th Rd (3)	
Rotherham U	5th Rd (2)	F		Rochdale	4th Rd	F	
Scunthorpe U	5th Rd (2)	3rd Rd (2)		Stockport Co	5th Rd	4th Rd	
Sheff U	W (4)	5th Rd (3)		Swindon T	SF (2)	W	AI W
Southend U	5th Rd (4)‡	3rd Rd		Torquay U	4th Rd (3)	3rd Rd	
Walsall	5th Rd (4)‡	4th Rd		Tranmere R	5th Rd	4th Rd (2)	WC W
Wigan Ath	4th Rd	4th Rd		Wrexham	6th Rd (2)	5th Rd (2)	WC W (21)
Wimbledon	4th Rd (2)	4th Rd	LGC F	York C	SF	5th Rd	

AS = Anglo-Scottish Cup WC = Welsh Cup DC = Debenhams Cup
AI = Anglo-Italian LGC = League Group Cup
ECWC = European Cup-Winners' Cup

* Rounds reached in the Second Series of the competition in 1886–87, 1889–90 and 1901–02 were the equivalent of the present day Fifth Round.

† Achieved last season

‡ In 1920–21 Southend United reached the Third Round which was the equivalent of the present day Fifth Round and in 1888–89 Walsall reached the last sixteen

Last season saw the twenty fifth anniversary of Manchester United's tragic air crash at Munich. The next four pages are produced as a tribute to a great club and show the club's statistics as they might have been shown if the Rothmans Football Yearbook had been published at the beginning of the 1958–59 season

MANCHESTER UNITED DIV. 1

Back row (left to right):
Eddie Colman
Bill Foulkes
Ray Wood
Roger Byrne
Mark Jones
Duncan Edwards
Front row:
Dennis Viollet
Johnny Berry
Tommy Taylor
Billy Whelan
David Pegg

Chairman: H. Hardman, Esq.

Manager: Matt Busby. ***Secretary:*** R. L. Olive.

Year Formed: 1878 as Newton Heath; 1902 Manchester United.

Turned Professional: 1885. Limited Company 1907.

Previous Name: Newton Heath, 1880–1902.

Previous Grounds: 1880–93, North Road, Monsall Road; 1893, Bank Street; 1910, Old Trafford; (played at Maine Road 1941–49).

Football League Record: 1892 Newton Heath elected to Division 1; 1894–1906 Division 2; 1906–22 Division 1; 1922–25 Division 2; 1925–31 Division 1; 1931–36 Division 2; 1936–37 Division 1; 1937–38 Division 2; 1938–58 Division 1.

Honours: Football League Division 1, Champions 1907–08, 1910–11, 1951–52, 1955–56, 1956–57; Runners-up: 1946–47, 1947–48, 1948–49, 1950–51; Division 2 Champions: 1935–36; Runners-up: 1896–97, 1905–06, 1924–25, 1937–38; FA Cup Winners: 1909, 1948; Runners-up: 1957, 1958.

European Competitions: European Cup, Semi-finalists: 1956–57, 1957–58.

Record Victory: 10-0 v Anderlecht, European Cup, Preliminary Round 1956–57.

Record Defeat: 0-7 v Aston Villa, Division 1, December 27, 1930.

Most League Points: 64 Division 1, 1956–57.

Most League Goals: 103 Division 1, 1956–57.

Highest League Scorer in Season: Jack Rowley 30, 1951–52.

Most Goals in Total Aggregate: Jack Rowley 175, 1937–55.

Most Capped Player: Johnny Carey 36 (Eire 29, Northern Ireland 7).

Most League appearances: Joe Spence 481, 1919–33).

Record Transfer Fee Received: £25,000 from Derby Co for Johnny Morris, March 1949.

Record Transfer Fee Paid: £29,999 to Barnsley for Tommy Taylor, March 1953.

Managers since the war: Matt Busby.

Old Trafford, Manchester: Telephone: Trafford Park 1661.

Record Attendance: 76,962 Wolverhampton W v Grimsby T, FA Cup Semi-final, 25 March 1939.

Club Record: 70,504 v Aston Villa, Division 1, 27 December 1920.

Record Receipts: £19,000 v Real Madrid (European Cup Semi-final 2nd leg) 25 April 1957.

Pitch Measurements: 116 yds×76 yds.

1957–58 LEAGUE RECORD

Match No.	Date	Venue	Opponents	Result	H/T Score	Lg. Pos.	Goalscorers	Attendance
1	Aug 24	A	Leicester C	W 3-0			Whelan 3	40,214
2	28	H	Everton	W 3-0			Taylor T., Viollet, own goal	59,103
3	31	H	Manchester C	W 4-1			Edwards, Berry, Taylor T., Viollet	63,103
4	Sept 4	A	Everton	D 3-3			Berry, Whelan, Viollet	72,077
5	7	H	Leeds U	W 5-0			Berry 2, Taylor 2, Viollet	50,598
6	9	A	Blackpool	W 4-1			Whelan 2, Viollet 2	34,181
7	14	A	Bolton W	L 0-4				48,603
8	18	H	Blackpool	L 1-2			Edwards	40,763
9	21	H	Arsenal	W 4-2			Whelan 2, Taylor T., Pegg	47,142
10	28	A	Wolverhampton W	L 1-3			Doherty	48,825
11	Oct 5	H	Aston Villa	W 4-1			Taylor T. 2, Pegg, own goal	43,102
12	12	A	Nottingham F	W 2-1			Whelan, Viollet	47,654
13	19	H	Portsmouth	L 0-3				38,253
14	26	A	WBA	L 3-4			Whelan, Taylor T. 2	52,839
15	Nov 2	H	Burnley	W 1-0			Taylor T.	49,449
16	9	A	Preston NE	D 1-1			Whelan	39,066
17	16	H	Sheffield W	W 2-1			Webster 2	40,866
18	23	A	Newcastle U	W 2-1			Edwards, Taylor T.	53,890
19	30	H	Tottenham H	L 3-4			Whelan, Pegg 2	43,077
20	Dec 7	A	Birmingham C	D 3-3			Taylor T., Viollet 2	35,791
21	14	H	Chelsea	L 0-1				36,853
22	21	H	Leicester C	W 4-0			Viollet 2, Charlton, Scanlon	41,631
23	25	H	Luton T	W 3-0			Taylor T., Viollet, Charlton	39,444
24	26	A	Luton T	D 2-2			Taylor T., Scanlon	26,458
25	28	A	Manchester C	D 2-2			Viollet, Charlton	70,483
26	Jan 11	A	Leeds U	D 1-1			Viollet	39,400
27	18	H	Bolton W	W 7-2			Charlton 3, Viollet 2, Edwards, Scanlon	44,141
28	Feb 1	A	Arsenal	W 5-4			Taylor T. 2, Viollet, Charlton, Edwards	63,578
29	22	H	Nottingham F	D 1-1			Dawson	66,346
30	Mar 3	H	WBA	L 0-4				63,278
31	15	A	Burnley	L 0-3				37,247
32	29	A	Sheffield W	L 0-1				35,608
33	31	A	Aston Villa	L 2-3			Charlton, Webster	18,000
34	Apr 4	H	Sunderland	D 2-2			Charlton, Dawson	47,187
35	5	H	Preston NE	D 0-0				48,167
36	7	A	Sunderland	W 2-1			Webster 2	51,382
37	12	A	Tottenham H	L 0-1				59,836
38	16	A	Portsmouth	D 3-3			Dawson, Webster, Taylor E.	39,975
39	19	H	Birmingham C	L 0-2				38,991
40	21	H	Wolverhampton W	L 0-4				33,267
41	23	H	Newcastle U	D 1-1			Webster	28,393
42	26	A	Chelsea	L 1-2			Taylor E.	45,011

Final League Position: 9

GOALSCORERS

League (85): Viollet 17, Taylor T. 16, Whelan 12, Charlton 9, Webster 7, Edwards 5, Berry 4, Pegg 4, Dawson 3, Scanlon 3, Taylor E. 2, own goals 2.
FA Cup (18): Charlton 5, Dawson 5, Brennan 3, Viollet 3, Taylor E. 1, Webster 1.
European Cup (19): Viollet 4, Charlton 3, Pegg 3, Taylor T. 3, Whelan 2, Berry 1, Colman 1, Taylor E. 1, Webster 1.

Wood	Foulkes	Byrne	Colman	Blanchflower	Edwards	Berry	Whelan	Taylor T.	Viollet	Pegg	McGuinness	Doherty	Charlton	Goodwin	Jones M.	Dawson	Webster	Scanlon	Gaskell	Gregg	Morgans	Greaves	Cope	Crowther	Taylor E.	Pearson	Brennan	Harrop	Heron	Jones P.	Match No.
1	2	3	4	5	6	7	8	9	10	11																					1
1	2	3	4	5	6	7	8	9	10	11																					2
1	2	3	4	5	6	7	8	9	10	11																					3
1	2	3	4	5	6	7	8	9	10	11																					4
1	2	3	4	5	6	7	8	9	10	11																					5
1	2	3	4	5	6	7	8	9	10	11																					6
1	2	3	4	5	6	7	8	9	10	11																					7
1	2	3	4	5	6	7	8	9	10	11																					8
1	2	3	4	5	6	7	8	9	10	11																					9
1	2			5	6	7		9		11	3	8	10	4																	10
1	2	3	4			7	8	9		11	6		10		5																11
1	2	3	4	5	6	7	8	9	10	11																					12
1	2		4	5		7	8		10	11	6					9														3	13
1	2	3		5	6	7	8	9		11			10	4																	14
1	2	3		5	6	7	8	9		11				4			10														15
1	2	3		5	6	7	8	9		11				4			10														16
1	2	3	4	5	6	7	8	9		11							10														17
1	2	3	4	5	6		8	9		11							10	7													18
	2	3	4	5	6		8			11			10				9	7	1												19
1	2	3	4		6	7	8	9	10	11					5																20
1	2	3	4		6	7	8	9	10	11					5																21
	2	3	4		6			9	10				8		5			11		1	7										22
	2	3	4		6			9	10				8		5			11		1	7										23
	2	3	4		6	7		9	10				8		5			11		1											24
	2	3	4		6				10				8		5		9	11		1	7										25
	2	3	4		6			9	10				8		5			11		1	7										26
	2	3	4		6			9	10				8		5			11		1	7										27
	2	3	4		6			9	10				8		5			11		1	7										28
	2													4		9	7			1		3	5	6	8	10	11				29
	2												11	4		9	7			1		3	5		8	10		6			30
	2												11	4		9	7			1		3	5	6		10		8			31
	2												10	4		9	7			1			3	6	8		11	5			32
	2												10	4		9	7			1			3	6		8	11	5			33
	2												10	4		9	7			1		3	5	6	8		11				34
	2												10	4			9			1	7	3	5	6	8				11		35
	2										6		10	4			9			1	7	3			8	11		5			36
	2												10	4			9			1	7	3	5	6	8	11					37
	2										6					7	9		1		11	3	5	4	8	10					38
	2													4		7	9			1	11	3	5	6	8	10					39
	2								10		6			4		7	9		1		11	3	5			8					40
	2										6		10			7	9			1	11	3	5	4	8						41
	2								10				9	4		7	11			1		3	5	6	8						42
20	42	26	24	18	26	20	20	25	22	21	7	1	21	16	10	12	20	9	3	19	13	12	13	11	11	8	5	5	1	1	

Competition	Round	Opponents	Result
FA Cup	Third Round	Workington (a)	3-1
	Fourth Round	Ipswich T (h)	2-0
	Fifth Round	Sheffield W (h)	3-0
	Sixth Round	WBA (a)	2-2
		(h)	1-0
	Semi-final	Fulham	2-2 (at Villa Park)
			5-3 (at Highbury)
	Final	Bolton W	0-2 (at Wembley)
European Champions' Cup	First Round	Shamrock R (a)	6-0
		(h)	3-2
	Second Round	Dukla Prague (h)	3-0
		(a)	0-1
	Quarter-final	Red Star Belgrade (h)	2-1
		(a)	3-3
	Semi-final	AC Milan (h)	2-1
		(a)	0-4

MANCHESTER UNITED

	Ht	Wt	Birthplace	Clubs	Lge App.	Lge Gls
Goalkeepers						
Harry Gregg	6 0	12 8	Derry	Doncaster R	93	—
(N Ireland)				Manchester U	19	—
Ray Wood	5 11	11 12	Hebburn-on-Tyne	Darlington	12	—
(England)				Manchester U	186	—
David Gaskell	5 11	11 0	Wigan	Manchester U	3	—
Gordon Clayton	6 0	13 9	Wednesbury	Manchester U	2	—
Tony Hawksworth	5 9	10 12	Sheffield	Manchester U	1	—
Fullbacks						
Roger Byrne (England) (deceased)	5 9	11 11	Manchester	Manchester U	245	17
Geoff Bent (deceased)	5 11	11 11	Salford	Manchester U	14	—
Bill Foulkes (England)	5 11	12 4	St Helens	Manchester U	182	1
Ian Greaves	6 0	12 4	Oldham	Manchester U	31	—
Joe Carolan	5 10	11 4	Dublin	Manchester U	—	—
Jimmy Shiels	5 9	11 0	Derry	Manchester U	—	—
Barry Smith	5 10	10 12	Manchester	Manchester U	—	—
Halfbacks						
Jackie Blanchflower (N Ireland)	5 11	11 0	Belfast	Manchester U	104	26
Duncan Edwards (England) (deceased)	5 11	13 0	Dudley	Manchester U	151	19
Mark Jones (deceased)	6 0	13 8	Barnsley	Manchester U	104	1
Eddie Colman (deceased)	5 7	9 10	Salford	Manchester U	85	1
Stan Crowther	5 11	11 3	Bilston	Aston Villa	50	4
				Manchester U	11	—
Freddie Goodwin	6 2	13 2	Heywood	Manchester U	35	—
Ron Cope	5 11	11 10	Crewe	Manchester U	15	—
Robert English	5 11	11 7	Stockport	Manchester U	—	—
Bobby Harrop	5 10	12 4	Manchester	Manchester U	5	—
Reg Holland	5 10	11 7	Sutton-in-Ashfield	Manchester U	—	—
Peter Jones	5 10	11 5	Manchester	Manchester U	1	—
Wilf McGuinness	5 8	10 8	Manchester	Manchester U	23	—
Forwards						
David Pegg (England) (deceased)	5 9	11 11	Doncaster	Manchester U	127	24
Tommy Taylor	6 0	12 11	Barnsley	Barnsley	44	26
(England) (deceased)				Manchester U	168	112
Billy Whelan (Eire) (deceased)	5 10	11 11	Dublin	Manchester U	79	43
Johnny Berry	5 5	9 8	Aldershot	Birmingham C	103	5
(England)				Manchester U	247	37
Bobby Charlton (England)	5 8	10 13	Ashington	Manchester U	35	18
Ernie Taylor	5 5	10 6	Sunderland	Newcastle U	107	19
(England)				Blackpool	217	53
				Manchester U	11	2
Dennis Viollet	5 8	10 9	Manchester	Manchester U	149	85
Colin Webster	5 9	11 12	Cardiff	Cardiff C	—	—
(Wales)				Manchester U	58	22
Albert Scanlon	5 10	10 11	Manchester	Manchester U	34	10
Seamus Brennan	5 10	10 7	Manchester	Manchester U	5	—
Alex Dawson	5 10	12 7	Aberdeen	Manchester U	15	6
Ken Morgans	5 8	10 8	Swansea	Manchester U	13	—
Mark Pearson	5 7	10 8	Sheffield	Manchester U	8	—
Johnny Giles	5 8	11 0	Dublin	Manchester U	—	—
Jimmy Elms	5 8	10 12	Manchester	Manchester U	—	—
Tommy Heron	5 8	11 6	Irvine	Manchester U	1	—
Reg Hunter	5 7	10 7	Colwyn Bay	Manchester U	—	—

END OF SEASON FREE TRANSFERS

Arsenal: Mark Gerbaldi, John Hollins, John Devine, John Hawley, George Wood.
Aston Villa: None.
Birmingham C: Frank Carrodus, Derek McKay, Nigel Winterburn, Jeff Wealands.
Brighton & HA: Danny Deans.
Coventry C: Stephen Mardenborough.
Everton: Alan Ainscow, John McMahon, Trevor Ross, Simon Steele, Keith Tierney, Mike Walsh, Billy Wright.
Ipswich T: Jimmy King, Ian Hurrell, Declan Shearer, Ian Templeton, Grahan Bassett.
Liverpool: David Fairclough, Tony Kelly, Ronald Kilshaw, Peter King.
Luton T: Brian Horton.
Manchester C: Dennis Tueart, Robin Webb, Mick Queenan.
Manchester U: Martin Buchan, Lawrence Pearson, Anthony Whelan, David Wynn.
Norwich C: Peter Mountford, Phil Alexander, Richard Symonds.
Nottingham F: Patrick Lunday, Nigel Thrower, Einar Aas.
Notts Co: None.
Southampton: Colin Dixon, Bob Lee, David Madden, Jeremy Stagg, Peter Wells, Tommy Munday, Leslie Cleevley.
Stoke C: Kevin Ronan, Cliff Wallace.
Sunderland: Mike Buckley, Barry Wardrobe, Micky Whitfield, Patrick O'Donnell.
Swansea C: Wyndham Evans.
Tottenham H: George Mazzon, Patrick Corbett, John Lacy, Ricky Villa.
Watford: Ross Jenkins.
WBA: Martin Pike, Andrew Lacey, John Snate, David Carlisle, John Wile.
West Ham U: Not announced.

Barnsley: Stewart Barrowclough, John Bukovina, Ernie Heseltine, Paul Longdon, Gary Pierce, Don Souter, Paul Wakefield, Phil Watkin.
Blackburn R: Gary Butcher, Paul Comstive, Nicky Salmon, Paul Gooddy.
Bolton W: Chris Thompson, Mike Bennett, Mike Doyle, Neil Berry, Paul Jones, Jim McDonagh.
Burnley: Alan Stevenson, Billy Wright, Mark Allen, Steve Taylor, Tommy Cassidy, Phil Cavener, Paul Dixon, Paul McGee.
Cambridge U: Richard Key, Joe Mayo, Floyd Streete, Tommy O'Neill, Nicky Prince.
Carlisle U: None.
Charlton Ath: Phil Walker, Steve Browne, Mark Simpson.
Chelsea: Alan Mayes, Gary Chivers, Phil Driver, Bob Iles, Paul Williams.
Crystal Palace: Paul Baxter, Ian Edwards, Paul Hinshelwood, Steve Howe, Chris Jones, Keith Oakley.
Derby Co: Paul Emson, Brian Attley, Glen Skivington, Yakka Banovic, John McAlle.
Fulham: Michael Squires, Clive Day, Fernando Varadi.
Grimsby T: Phil Crosbie, Kevin Kilmore.
Leeds U: Tony Sharkey, Steve Taylor, Wayne Roebuck, Mark Hinchcliffe.
Leicester C: David Buchanan, Stever Humphreys.
Middlesbrough: Mick Angus, Alan Roberts, Wayne Earnshaw, Phil Lloyd, David Shearer, Joe Bolton, Frank Harrison, David McClurg, Tony Young.
Newcastle U: Mick Martin, David Barton, John Craggs, Chris Withe, Justin Robson, David Willis, Paul Malcolm, David Thompson, Nick Devereux.
Oldham Ath: Ged Keegan, Steve Millington, John Murphy.
QPR: Dean Wilkins, Ian Muir.
Rotherham U: Ashley Taylor.
Sheffield W: Richard Beaumont, Bob Kenny, Gordon Owen, Chris Reilly.
Shrewsbury T: Carleton Leonard, Martin Sankey.
Wolverhampton W: John Richards, Mick Hollifield.

AFC Bournemouth: Andrew Crawford, Tony Funnell, Kenny Allen, Derek Dawkins, Brian Mundee.
Bradford C: Brian Chippendale, Les Chapman, Neil Ramsbottom, John Black.
Brentford: Stan Bowles, Keith Tongue, Barry Tucker, Stephen Wolsey, Peter Caswell.
Bristol R: John McDowell, Alan Ball, Paul Wheeler.
Cardiff C: Paul Maddy, Paul Giles, Keith Pontin.
Chesterfield: Russell Athersych, Bill Green, Tony Henson, Andy Kowalski, Sean O'Neill, Gary Pollard, John Stirk, Steven Robinson, John Turner, David Windridge, Andy Higginbottom.
Doncaster R: Terry Austin, Graham Cawthorne, Hugh Dowd, Gary Liddell, Peter Johnson, Jimmy Mann, Stuart Robertson, Stewart Mell.
Exeter C: John Delve, Dave Pullar, Lee Roberts, John Sparrow, Aidan Gibson, Pete Shepherd.
Gillingham: Neil Grewcock, Gary Sutton.
Huddersfield T: Tim Hotte, Martin Coupe, Peter Valentine, Mark Ratcliffe.
Lincoln C: Colin Brazier, Ernie Moss, Stuart Hibberd.
Millwall: Austin Hayes, Sam Allardyce.
Newport Co: Grant Davies, Steve Emery, Billy Fleming, Dave Gwyther, Kevin Moore, Gary Plumley, Ian Watson.
Orient: Barry Silkman, Mark Blackhall, Jamie Mankelow, John Bolle.
Oxford U: David Linney, Paul Spittle.
Plymouth Arg: Tony Dennis, Neil Hards, Tyrone James.
Portsmouth: No frees.
PNE: Graham Bell, Alex Bruce, Gary Buckley, Glen Campbell, Gordon Coleman, Michael Farrelly, Alan Gowling, Neil Hanson, Gary Hough, Graham Houston, Chris Hunter, John Kelly, Peter Litchfield, Willie Naughton, Donald O'Riordan, Peter Sayer, Mark Walsh, Simon Westwell.
Reading: Brian Bason, Pat Earles (retiring), Mick Kearney (retiring), Gary Donnellan, Mike Doherty.
Sheffield U: Stewart Houston, Geoff Dey, Jeff King.
Southend U: Murray Jones, Steve Butler, Alan Moody, Derek Spence.
Walsall: Julian Marshal, David Arthur, Ollie Kearns, Steve Round, Duncan Ross, Colin Caddick, Don Penn, Kenny Beach.
Wigan Ath: David Glenn, Jimmy Weston, Kevin Sheldon, Les Bradd, John McMahon.
Wrexham: Ian Arkwright, Alan Hill.

Aldershot: Manny Andruszewski, Murray Brodie, Mark Sandford, Peter Scott.
Blackpool: David Hockaday, Joey Scott, Peter Noble.
Bristol C: Errington Kelly, Nyrere Kelly.
Bury: John Platt, Steve Kenworthy, Tommy Gore, Franny Firth, Stuart Barker, Paul Cruickshank, Bruce Halliday, John Breckin, Mark Hilton.
Chester: Nigel Edwards, Noel Bradley, Mark Dean, Greg Moffatt, Gary Simpson, Tom Sloan, Paul Needham, Paul Johnson.
Colchester U: Mick Packer, Wayne Ward, Dennis Longhorn.
Crewe Alex: Sean Haslegrave, Clive Evans.
Darlington: Pat Cuff, Harry Wilson, Roger Wicks, Tony McFadden, Tom Brady, Steve McDermott, Peter May, Nigel Robson.
Halifax T: Jimmy Hallybone.
Hartlepool U: Roy Hogan, Terry Bainbridge, Michael Fagan, Jed McNamee, Alan Harding, Phil Linacre, David Howard, David Stewart.
Hereford U: Danny Bartley, John Crabbe, Derek Showers, Peter Spiring.
Hull C: Steve Richards, Neil Thompson, Billy Woof.
Mansfield T: Kevin Bird, Ray Blackhall, Paul Canell, David Coles, Keith Kennedy, Charlie Bell.
Northampton T: Paul Saunders, Peter Denyer, Peter Coffil, Mark Heeley, Adam Sandy.
Peterborough U: Steve Mercer.
Port Vale: Neil McAdam.
Rochdale: Mark Hilditch, Eugene Martinez, Brian Taylor, Alan Weir, Micky French, Chris Pearce, Gerry Keenan, Roy Greaves, Everton Carr, Eric Snookes.
Scunthorpe U: Andy Keeley, Bob Oates.
Stockport: Trevor Phillips, Mike Wardrobe, Brian Lloyd.
Swindon T: Howard Pritchard, Ray Baverstock, Martin Blackler, David Bristow, Brian Hughes, David Round, Mark Stevens.
Torquay U: John Doyle, Jackie Gallagher, Steve Grapes, Graham Horn, Graham Jones, Willie Young.
Tranmere R: Ian Griffiths, John Kerr, Scott Endersby (now Swindon), Steve Warriner.
Wimbledon: No frees.
York C: Richard Dawson.

ACTION

During the 1983–1984 football season sports photographers are invited to submit their entries for the best football pictures of the season. Those considered to be outstanding will be published in next years Rothmans Football Yearbook under categories of excitement, action and comedy. In the following four pages we are showing some excellent action shots taken during the past season.

Norwich City's Keith Bertchin crashes an exciting far post header into the side netting against Tottenham in the League.
Photo: Sporting Pictures (U.K.) Ltd.

Poor Derek Scott of Burnley sees his header fly over Brian Flynn to register an 'own goal' for Leeds United.
Photo: Varley Picture Agency

Aston Villa's new International goalkeeper Nigel Spink makes a close range save from Luther Blissett of Watford.
Photo: Sporting Pictures (UK) Ltd.

A perfect flying header by Manchester United's Gordon McQueen beats the Stoke City defence but scrapes the wrong side of the bar.
Photo: County Press

FA CUP GOALMOUTH THRILLS

Gary Mabbutt sails gracefully forward to power in an effort for Spurs against WBA, but 'keeper Paul Barron (out of picture) saves. *Photo: Hailey Sports*

Just a little bit too high! Burnley's Billy Hamilton has the ball plucked off his foot by Crystal Palace 'keeper David Fry. *Photo: Press Association*

Goal! Watford's Jan Lohman takes off in a crowded goalmouth to head a brave goal against Fulham.
Photo: Sports News Agency

There must be easier ways! Sheffield Wednesday's Andy McCulloch goes close with a spectacular scissor kick against Cambridge United.
Photo: Varley Picture Agency

MILK CUP GOALS

Steve Coppell crashes in a perfect shot that beats the Arsenal defence from 25 yards.
Photo: Northwest Counties Press

Wrong way! Phil Neal does it again against Burnley and sends the 'keeper the wrong way from the penalty spot.
Photo: Northwest Counties Press

It's well worth a smile. West Ham United's Sandy Clarke slides in a goal against Stoke City.
Photo: Sporting Pictures (UK) Ltd.

YEARBOOK CLUB STATISTICIANS

The Editorial Committee of The Rothmans Football Yearbook would like to thank the following members of the Association of Football Statisticians who have agreed to act as advisers for the clubs shown:

Aldershot: P. Worrall
Arsenal: Joe Waters
Aston Villa: D. Hodges
Barnsley: Arthur Bower
Birmingham C: Dave Drage
Blackburn R: H. Berry
Bolton W: Simon Marland
AFC Bournemouth: J. Treleven
Bradford C: Terry Frost
Brentford: Graham Haynes
Brighton: T. Carder
Bristol C: D. Woods
Bristol R: M. D. Jay
Burnley: W. G. Chadwick
Bury: P. Greenlees
Cambridge U: C. Faiers
Cardiff C: A. Jenkins
Carlisle U: B. Rodgers
Charlton Ath: Colin Cameron
Chelsea: D. Fletcher
Chester: D. Orme
Chesterfield: R. West
Colchester U: M. Middleton
Coventry C: R. Dean
Crewe Alex: Mr. Finch, c/o Crewe Alexandra FC
Crystal Palace: Mike Purkiss
Darlington: F. Tweddle
Derby Co: S. McGhee
Doncaster R: Terry Wiles
Exeter C: Jim Blackstone
Everton: G. Smailes
Fulham: Mr Turner, c/o Fulham FC
Gillingham: Roger Triggs
Grimsby T: Les Triggs
Halifax T: M. Belshaw
Hartlepool U: Gordon Small
Hereford U: L. Appleby
Huddersfield T: J. D. Loughrey
Hull C: Chris Elton
Ipswich T: P. Voller
Leeds U: Julian Baker
Leicester C: Dave Smith
Lincoln C: J. D. Holland
Liverpool: Brian Pead
Luton T: R. Wash
Manchester C: Ray Goble
Manchester U: John Hewitt
Mansfield T: Pete Stevenson
Middlesbrough: I. Tewson
Millwall: R. Lindsay
Newcastle U: F. Evans
Newport Co: Tony Ambrosen
Northampton T: F. Grande
Norwich C: D. Pease
Nottingham F: Andy Johnson
Notts Co: H. Warsop
Oldham Ath: D. Williams
Orient: A. Higgins
Oxford U: Mick Brown, c/o Oxford United
Peterborough U: M. Robinson
Plymouth Arg: F. Lee
Portsmouth: Doug Robinson
Port Vale: S. Askey
Preston NE: L. Bland
QPR: Stewart Fell
Reading: David Downs
Rochdale: S. Birch
Rotherham U: M. Smith
Scunthorpe U: M. Girdham
Sheffield U: Andrew Treherne
Sheffield W: Mick Renshaw
Shrewsbury T: P. Stocken
Southampton: D. Buckle
Southend U: P. Esdale
Stockport Co: A. Jones
Stoke C: Wade Martin
Sunderland: W. Simmons
Swansea C: David Farmer
Swindon T: Tony Angell
Torquay U: J. Lovis
Tottenham H: Andy Porter
Tranmere R: Bernard Jones
Walsall: D. Glover
Watford: Trefor Jones
WBA: Tony Matthews
West Ham U: John Northcutt
Wigan Ath: G. Lea
Wimbledon: S. King
Wolverhampton W: Les Smith
Wrexham: Gareth Davies
York C: David Batters

FIRST DIVISION CLUB ENTRANCE FEES 1983–84

	Standing	Children	Cheapest Seats	Dearest Seats
Arsenal	2.20	1.10	3.50	6.50
Aston Villa	2.00	1.00	4.00	5.00
Birmingham C	2.50	1.25*	3.00	5.00
Coventry C (all seats) from 2.00 to 5.00				
Everton	2.00	—	4.00	4.00
Ipswich T	2.00	1.00	4.00	5.00
Leicester C	2.50	—	3.50	5.00
Liverpool	2.00	1.40	3.40	4.00
Luton T	2.50	1.50*	4.00	5.00
Manchester U	2.00	1.00	2,60	4.10
Norwich C	2.20	1.00	3.00	5.00
Nottingham Forest	2.00	1.00	3.00*	5.00
Notts Co	2.00	1.00*	4.00	5.00
QPR	2.50	1.50	4.00	6.00
Southampton	2.50			
Stoke C	2.00	1.00*	3.00	4.00
Sunderland	2.10	1.30	3.20	3.70
Tottenham H	2.20	1.10	4.50	9.00
Watford	2.30*	—	3.50	6.00
WBA	2.00	—	2.80	4.50
West Ham U	2.30	1.00	4.50	6.50
Wolverhampton W	2.00	1.00	4.00	5.00

* Birmingham C: only applies to Junior Blues member; Luton Town: only applies to home supporters; Nottingham Forest: only if accompanied by an adult or Junior Reds member; Notts Co: only applies to Junior Magpie members; Stoke C: only if accompanied by an adult and there are cheap seats for children; Sunderland: entrance to terracing at side of pitch costs £2.30; Watford: entrance to visitors' terracing and covered standing area costs £2.80.

A TRIBUTE TO LIVERPOOL

Above: An historic moment as Bob Paisley, on his last visit to Wembley as manager of Liverpool, holds the Milk Cup aloft, having been the first manager to climb the famous Wembley staircase.

Right: A familiar sight! A happy Kenny Dalglish, the Football Writers' Footballer of the Year and P.F.A. Player of the Year, is congratulated by two of his senior colleagues, Phil Neal and Graeme Souness.

Below: Can there be a better feeling? Another trophy has been won at Wembley, and Manchester United have been beaten in a wonderful Milk Cup Final atmosphere.

Above: A vital goal by Kenny Dalglish at Old Trafford gives Liverpool a draw and keeps United firmly behind in the league by 15 points.

Left: Milk Cup hero! Ronnie Whelan scored the vital winning goal, but here he is seen vollying over the bar early in the game.

Below: No, it's not blow football! Craig Johnston watches Ian Rush – P.F.A. and Robinsons Barley Water Young Player of the Year – crash home Liverpool's first against Arsenal at Anfield.

Right: Over the moon? Bruce Grobbelaar, Liverpool's controversial goalkeeper, celebrates Liverpool's equaliser against Brighton in the FA Cup, but on this occasion there was no happy ending.

Above: 'Octupussy' starring Barney Rubble (Alan Kennedy no. 3) who has just equalised against Manchester United in the Milk Cup final. Alan has been nicknamed Barney by the Kop who have made him one of their favourites.

Below: Power and concentration! Even when tired, Kenny Dalglish is poised beautifully to crash another shot against the Manchester United defence, in this case Remi Moses and Mike Duxbury.

LIVERPOOL'S LEAGUE CUP/MILK CUP RECORD 1980–83

Individual Records

(Minimum 5 appearances)

	Pld	*Goals*	*Winners Medals*
Phil Neal	27	2	3
Kenny Dalglish	25	12	3
Graeme Souness	25	3	2
Alan Hansen	24	1	2
Sammy Lee	22	2	3
Alan Kennedy	21	2	3
Terry McDermott	19	4	2
Ian Rush	19	10	3
Bruce Grobbelaar	18	–	2
Mark Lawrenson	18	2	2
Phil Thompson	17	–	2
Ray Kennedy	12	2	1
Ronnie Whelan	11+3	5	2
Ray Clemence	9	–	1
David Johnson	6+3	8	1
Craig Johnston	6+2	2	1
David Fairclough	3+3	3	1
David Hodgson	4+1	2	–

	Pld	*W*	*D*	*L*	*F*	*A*
1980–81	9	6	2	1	21	6
1981–82	10	7	3	0	28	5
1982–83	8	7	0	1	14	4
Total	27	20	5	2	63	15

Liverpool only used 24 players in the competition over three years but 16 of them scored during those competitions.

Liverpool 1980–81 Football League Cup	2nd Rd 1st Leg v Bradford C (A) Lost 0-1, 16,232	2nd Rd 2nd Leg v Bradford C (H) Won 4-0, 21,107	3rd Rd v Swindon T (H) Won 5-0, 16,566	4th Rd v Portsmouth (H) Won 4-1, 32,021	5th Rd v Birmingham C (H) Won 3-1, 30,236	S-Final 1st Leg v Man City (A) Won 1-0, 48,045	S-Final 2nd Leg v Man City (H) Drawn 1-1, 46,711	Final v West Ham U (N) Drawn 1-1 aet, 100,000	Final Replay v West Ham U (N) Won 2-1, 36,693	Apps	Goals
Clemence	1	1	1	1	1	1	1	1	1	9	
Neal	2	2	2	2	2	2	2	2	2	9	
Kennedy, A.	3	3		6	3	3		3^{1}	3	7	*1*
Thompson	4	4	4			4	4		4	6	
Kennedy, R.	5	5^{1}	5	5	5	5^{1}	5	5	5	9	*2*
Hansen	6	6	6	4	4		6	6	6^{1}	8	*1*
Fairclough	7	12	9^{2}			9				3+1	*2*
Case	8	8						12	11	3+1	
Johnson	9	9^{1}*		9^{2}	9^{1}		9			5	*4*
McDermott	10	10	10	10	10^{1}	10	10	10	10	9	*1*
Souness	11	11	11	11^{1}	11	11	11	11		8	*1*
Dalglish		7^{2}	7^{1}	7^{1}	7^{1}	7	7^{1}	7	7^{1}	8	*7*
Cohen			3							1	
Lee			8^{2}	8	8	8	8	8	8	7	*2*
Irwin				3	6	6		4		4	
Money							3			1	
Heighway								9*		1	
Rush									9	1	
Grobbelaar											
Whelan											
Lawrenson											
Sheedy											
Johnston											

Liverpool 1981–82 Milk Cup	2nd Rd 1st Leg	2nd Rd 2nd Leg	3rd Rd	4th Rd	5th Rd	5th Rd Rply	S-Final 1st Leg	S-Final 2nd Leg	Final			
	v Exeter C (H) Won 5-0, 11,478	v Exeter C (A) Won 6-0, 11,740	v Middlesbrough (H) Won 4-1, 16,145	v Arsenal (A) Drawn 0-0, 37,917	v Arsenal (H) Won 3-0, 21,375	v Barnsley (H) Drawn 0-0, 33,707	v Barnsley (A) Won 3-1, 29,639	v Ipswich T (A) Won 2-0, 26,690	v Ipswich T (H) Drawn 2-2, 34,933	v Tottenham H (N) Won 3-1 aet, 100,000	Apps	Goals
Grobbelaar	1	1	1	1	1	1	1	1	1	1	10	
Neal	2	2¹	2	2	2	2	2	2	2	2	10	*1*
Kennedy, A.	3				3	8		4	4	3	6	
Thompson	4	4	4	4		4	4*			4	7	
Lawrenson	5	3	3	3	4	3	3	3	3	6	10	
Whelan	6¹	8		8		5	5	5	5	5²	8	*3*
Dalglish	7¹	7¹	7	7	7¹	7	7¹	7	7¹	7	10	*5*
Lee	8				8*		8	8	8	8	6	
Rush	9²	9²	9¹	9*	9	9	9	9¹	9¹	9¹	10	*8*
McDermott	10¹	10	10*	10	10ᴾ	10	10	10¹	10	10*	10	*3*
Souness	11		11	11	11	11	11¹	11	11	11	9	*1*
Kennedy, R.		5		5	5						3	
Hansen		6	6	6	6	6	6	6	6		8	
Sheedy		11¹	5¹								2	*2*
Johnson			8²	12			12¹			12	1+3	*3*
Johnston		10[illegible]	12		12¹						0+2	*1*
												28

Liverpool 1982–83 Milk Cup	2nd Rd 1st Leg	2nd Rd 2nd Leg	3rd Rd	4th Rd	5th Rd	S-Final 1st Leg	S-Final 2nd Leg	Final		
	v Ipswich T (A) Won 2-1, 19,329	v Ipswich T (H) Won 2-0, 17,698	v Rotherham U (H) Won 1-0, 20,412	v Norwich C (H) Won 2-0, 13,235	v West Ham U (H) Won 2-1, 23,953	v Burnley (H) Won 3-0, 33,520	v Burnley (A) Lost 0-1, 22,350	v Man Utd (N) Won 2-1 aet, 100,000	Apps	Goals
Grobbelaar	1	1	1	1	1	1	1	1	8	
Neal	2	2	2	2	2	2ᴾ	2	2	8	*1*
Kennedy, A.	3	3	3	3	3	3	3	3¹	8	*1*
Thompson	4	4	4	4					4	
Whelan	5	5¹			12	12	12	5¹	3+3	*2*
Hansen	6	6	6	6	6	6	6	6	8	
Dalglish	7	7*		7	7	7	7	7	7	
Lee	8	8	8	8	8	8	8	8	8	
Rush	9²	9	9	9	9	9	9	9	8	*2*
Lawrenson	10	10¹	10	10*¹	4	4	4	4	8	*2*
Souness	11	11	11	11	11¹	11¹	11	11	8	*2*
Hodgson		12	7		10¹	10¹	10*		4+1	*2*
Johnston			5¹	5	5*	5*	5	10*	6	*1*
Fairclough				12¹				12	0+2	*1*
										14

Bob Paisley, seen here after the Investiture for his OBE from the Silver Jubilee and Birthday Honours List, announced his retirement as manager of Liverpool at the end of the 1982–83 season. Bob guided Liverpool to an incredible array of trophies:–
The Football League Championship 1976, 1977, 1979, 1980, 1982, 1983
The Football League 'Milk' Cup 1981, 1982, 1983
The European Champions Cup 1977, 1978, 1981
The U.E.F.A. Cup 1976
The Charity Shield 1974 (shared), 1976, 1977, 1979, 1980, 1982
No other manager has been as successful!

THE FOOTBALL LEAGUE CUP

1960–1982

THE MILK CUP

1982–1983

LEAGUE CUP FINALISTS 1961–82

1960–61 ROTHERHAM UNITED Ironside; Perry, Morgan; Lambert, Madden, Waterhouse; Webster, Weston, Houghton, Kirkman, Bambridge. *Scorers:* Webster, Kirkman.

2-0 ASTON VILLA Sims; Lynn, Lee; Crowe, Dugdale, Deakin; McEwan, Thomson, Brown, Wylie, McParland.

ASTON VILLA Sidebottom; Neal, Lee; Crowe, Dugdale, Deakin; McEwan, O'Neill, McParland, Thomson, Burrows. *Scorers:* O'Neill, Burrows, McParland.

3-0 aet ROTHERHAM UNITED Ironside; Perry, Morgan; Lambert, Madden, Waterhouse; Webster, Weston, Houghton, Kirkman, Bambridge.

Aston Villa won on aggregate 3–2.

1961–62 ROCHDALE Burgin; Milburn, Winton, Bodell, Aspden, Thompson; Wragg, Hepton, Bimpson, Cairns, Whitaker.

0-3 NORWICH CITY Kennon; McCrohan, Ashman; Burton, Butler, Mullett; Mannion, Lythgoe, Scott, Hill, Punton. *Scorers:* Lythgoe 2, Punton.

NORWICH CITY Kennon; McCrohan, Ashman, Burton, Butler, Mullett; Mannion, Lythgoe, Scott, Hill, Punton. *Scorer:* Hill.

1-0 ROCHDALE Burgin; Milburn, Winton; Bodell, Aspden, Thompson; Whyke, Richardson, Bimpson, Cairns, Whitaker.

Norwich City won on aggregate 4-0.

1962–63 BIRMINGHAM CITY Schofield; Lynn, Green, Hennessey, Smith, Beard; Hellawell, Bloomfield, Harris, Leek, Auld. *Scorers:* Leek 2, Bloomfield.

3-1 ASTON VILLA Sims, Fraser, Aitken; Crowe, Sleeuwenhoek, Lee; Baker, Graham, Thomson, Wylie, Burrows. Scorer: Thomson.

ASTON VILLA Chatterley took the place of Sleeuwenhoek.

0-0 BIRMINGHAM CITY No change in team.

Birmingham City won on aggregate 3-1.

1963–64 STOKE CITY Leslie; Asprey, Allen; Palmer, Kinnell, Skeels; Dobing, Viollet, Ritchie, McIlroy, Bebbington. *Scorer:* Bebbington.

1-1 LEICESTER CITY Banks; Sjoberg, Appleton; Dougan, King, Cross; Riley, Heath, Keyworth, Gibson, Stringfellow. *Scorer:* Gibson.

LEICESTER CITY Banks; Sjoberg, Norman, Cross, King, Appleton, Riley, Gibson, Keyworth, Sweenie, Stringfellow. *Scorers:* Stringfellow, Gibson, Riley.

3-2 STOKE CITY Irvine; Asprey, Allen, Palmer, Kinnell, Skeels, Dobing, Viollet, Ritchie, McIlroy, Bebbington. *Scorers:* Viollet, Kinnell.

Leicester City won on aggregate 4-3

1964–65 CHELSEA Bonetti; Hinton, Harris; Hollins, Young, Boyle; Murray, Graham, McCreadie, Venables, Tambling. *Scorers:* Tambling, Venables (pen), McCreadie.

3-2 LEICESTER CITY Banks; Sjoberg, Norman; Chalmers, King, Appleton; Hodgson, Cross, Goodfellow, Gibson, Sweenie. *Scorers:* Appleton, Goodfellow.

LEICESTER CITY Banks; Walker, Norman, Roberts, Sjoberg, Appleton, Hodgson, Cross, Goodfellow, Gibson, Stringfellow.

0-0 CHELSEA Bonetti; Hinton, McCreadie, Harris, Mortimore, Upton, Murray, Boyle, Bridges, Venables, Tambling.

Chelsea won on aggregate 3-2.

1965–66 WEST HAM UNITED Standen; Burnett, Burkett, Peters, Brown, Moore, Brabrook, Boyce, Byrne, Hurst, Dear. *Scorers:* Moore, Byrne.

2-1 WEST BROMWICH ALBION Potter; Cram, Fairfax, Fraser, Campbell, Williams, Brown, Astle, Kaye, Lovett, Clark. *Scorer:* Astle.

WEST BROMWICH ALBION Potter; Cram, Fairfax, Fraser, Campbell, Williams, Brown, Astle, Kaye, Hope, Clark.*Scorers:* Kaye, Brown, Clark, Williams.

4-1 WEST HAM UNITED Standen; Burnett, Peters, Bovington, Brown, Moore, Brabrook, Boyce, Byrne, Hurst, Sissons. *Scorer:* Peters.

West Bromwich Albion won on aggregate 5-3.

1966–67 QUEEN'S PARK RANGERS Springett; Hazell, Langley, Sibley, Hunt, Keen, Lazarus, Sanderson, Allen, Marsh, R. Morgan. *Scorers:* R. Morgan, Marsh, Lazarus.

3-2 WEST BROMWICH ALBION Sheppard; Cram, Williams, Collard, D. Clarke, Fraser, Brown, Astle, Kaye, Hope, C. Clark. *Scorer:* C. Clark 2.

1967–68 LEEDS UNITED Sprake; Reaney, Cooper; Bremner, Charlton, Hunter, Greenhoff, Lorimer, Madeley, Giles, Gray (Belfitt). *Scorer:* Cooper.

1-0 ARSENAL Furnell; Storey, McNab; McLintock, Simpson, Ure, Radford, Jenkins, Graham, Sammels, Armstrong.

1968–69 SWINDON TOWN Downsborough; Thomas, Trollope; Butler, Burrows, Harland; Heath, Smart, Smith, Noble (Penman), Rogers. *Scorers:* Smart, Rogers 2.

3-1 ARSENAL Wilson; Storey, McNab; McLintock, Ure, Simpson (Graham); Radford, Sammels, Court, Gould, Armstrong. *Scorer:* Gould.

1969–70 MANCHESTER CITY Corrigan; Book, Mann; Doyle, Booth, Oakes, Heslop, Bell, Summerbee (Bowyer), Lee, Pardoe. *Scorers:* Doyle, Pardoe.

2-1 WEST BROMWICH ALBION Osborne; Fraser, Wilson, Brown, Talbut, Kaye; Cantello, Suggett, Astle, Hartford (Krzywicki), Hope. *Scorer:* Astle.

1970–71 TOTTENHAM HOTSPUR Jennings; Kinnear, Knowles; Mullery, Collins, Beal; Gilzean, Perryman, Chivers, Peters, Neighbour. *Scorer:* Chivers 2.

2-0 ASTON VILLA Dunn; Bradley, Aitken; Godfrey, Turnbull, Tiler; McMahon, Rioch, Lochhead, Hamilton, Anderson.

1971–72 STOKE CITY Banks; Marsh, Pejic, Bernard, Smith, Bloor, Conroy, Greenhoff (Mahoney), Ritchie, Dobing, Eastham. *Scorers:* Conroy, Eastham.

2-1 CHELSEA Bonetti; Mulligan (Baldwin), Harris, Hollins, Dempsey, Webb, Cooke, Garland, Osgood, Hudson, Houseman. *Scorer:* Osgood.

1972–73 TOTTENHAM HOTSPUR Jennings; Kinnear, Knowles, Pratt (Coates), England, Beal, Gilzean, Perryman, Chivers, Peters, Pearce. *Scorer:* Coates.

1-0 NORWICH CITY Keelan; Payne, Butler, Stringer, Forbes, Briggs, Livermore, Blair (Howard), Cross, Paddon, Anderson.

1973–74 WOLVERHAMPTON WANDERERS Pierce; Palmer, Parkin, Bailey, Munro, McAlle, Sunderland, Hibbitt, Richards, Dougan, Wagstaffe (Powell). *Scorers:* Hibbitt, Richards.

2-1 MANCHESTER CITY MacRae; Pardoe, Donachie, Doyle, Booth, Towers, Summerbee, Bell, Lee, Law, Marsh. *Scorer:* Bell.

1974–75 ASTON VILLA Cumbes; Robson, Aitken, Ross, Nicholl, McDonald, Graydon, Little, Leonard, Hamilton, Carrodus. *Scorer:* Graydon.

1-0 NORWICH CITY Keelan; Machin, Sullivan, Morris, Forbes, Stringer, Miller, MacDougall, Boyer, Suggett, Powell.

1975–76 MANCHESTER CITY Corrigan; Keegan, Donachie, Doyle, Watson, Oakes, Barnes, Booth, Royle, Hartford, Tueart. *Scorers:* Barnes, Tueart.

2-1 NEWCASTLE UNITED Mahoney; Nattrass, Kennedy, Barrowclough, Keeley, Howard, Burns, Cassidy, Macdonald, Gowling, Craig. *Scorer:* Gowling.

1976–77 ASTON VILLA Burridge; Gidman, Robson, Phillips, Nicholl, Mortimer, Deehan, Little, Gray, Cropley, Carrodus.

0-0 EVERTON Lawson; Jones, Darracott, Lyons, McNaught, King, Hamilton, Dobson, Latchford, McKenzie, Goodlass.

First replay (at Hillsborough)

ASTON VILLA Burridge; Gidman, Robson, Phillips, Nicholl, Mortimer, Deehan, Little, Gray, Cowans, Carrodus. *Scorer:* Kenyon og.

***R*: 1-1 aet** EVERTON Lawson; Bernard, Darracott, Lyons, McNaught, King, Hamilton (Pearson), Kenyon, Latchford, McKenzie, Goodlass. *Scorer:* Latchford.

Second replay (at Old Trafford, Manchester)

***R*: 3-2 aet** ASTON VILLA Burridge; Gidman (Smith), Robson, Phillips, Nicholl, Mortimer, Graydon, Little, Deehan, Cropley, Cowans. *Scorers:* Little 2, Nicholl.

EVERTON Lawson; Robinson, Darracott, Lyons, McNaught, King, Hamilton, Dobson, Latchford, Pearson (Seargeant), Goodlass. *Scorers:* Latchford, Lyons.

1977–78 NOTTINGHAM FOREST Woods; Anderson, Clark, McGovern (O'Hare), Lloyd, Burns, O'Neill, Bowyer, Withe, Woodcock, Robertson.

0-0 aet LIVERPOOL Clemence; Neal, Smith, Thompson, Kennedy (Fairclough), Hughes, Dalglish, Case, Heighway, McDermott, Callaghan.

Replay (at Old Trafford, Manchester)

***R*: 1-0** NOTTINGHAM FOREST Woods; Anderson, Clark, O'Hare, Lloyd, Burns, O'Neill, Bowyer, Withe, Woodcock, Robertson. *Scorer:* Robertson (pen).

LIVERPOOL Clemence; Neal, Smith, Thompson, Kennedy, Hughes, Dalglish, Case (Fairclough), Heighway, McDermott, Callaghan.

1978–79 NOTTINGHAM FOREST Shilton; Barrett, Clark, McGovern, Lloyd, Needham, O'Neill, Gemmill, Birtles, Woodcock, Robertson. *Scorers:* Birtles 2, Woodcock.

3-2 SOUTHAMPTON Gennoe; Golac, Peach, Williams, Nicholl, Waldron, Ball, Boyer, Hayes (Sealy), Holmes, Curran. *Scorers:* Peach, Holmes.

1979–80 WOLVERHAMPTON WANDERERS Bradshaw; Palmer, Parkin, Daniel, Berry, Hughes, Carr, Hibbitt, Gray, Richards, Eves. *Scorer:* Gray.

1-0 NOTTINGHAM FOREST Shilton; Anderson, Gray, McGovern, Needham, Burnes, O'Neill, Bowyer, Birtles, Francis, Robertson.

1980–81 LIVERPOOL Clemence; Neal, A. Kennedy, Irwin, R. Kennedy, Hansen, Dalglish, Lee, Heighway (Case), McDermott, Souness. *Scorer:* A. Kennedy.

1-1 aet WEST HAM UNITED Parkes; Stewart, Lampard, Bonds, Martin, Devonshire, Neighbour, Goddard (Pearson), Cross, Brooking, Pike. *Scorer:* Stewart (pen).

Replay (at Villa Park)

***R*: 2-1** LIVERPOOL Clemence; Neal, A. Kennedy, Thompson, R. Kennedy, Hansen, Dalglish, Lee, Rush, McDermott, Case. *Scorers:* Dalglish, Hansen.

WEST HAM UNITED Parkes, Stewart, Lampard, Bonds, Martin, Devonshire, Neighbour, Goddard, Cross, Brooking, Pike (Pearson). *Scorer:* Goddard.

1981–82 LIVERPOOL Grobbelaar; Neal, Kennedy A., Thompson, Whelan, Lawrenson, Dalglish, Lee, Rush, McDermott (Johnson), Souness. *Scorers:* Whelan 2, Rush.

3-1 aet TOTTENHAM HOTSPUR Clemence; Hughton, Miller, Prize, Hazard (Villa), Perryman, Ardiles, Archibald, Galvin, Hoddle, Crooks. *Scorer:* Archibald.

MILK CUP 1982–83

Milk Cup First Round

BURNLEY START OUT ON A GREAT CUP SEASON

Little did **Burnley** know what a momentous cup season they had to look forward to when they ran out at Gigg Lane, **Bury** for their League cup tie on 31 August. They certainly started in style with a 5-3 away victory and eight different players (including an opponent) scored for them before they finished 8-4 aggregate winners!

Halifax Town raised a few hopes for a better season by beating the more famous **Derby County**, but faltered badly in the second leg to lose 4-6 overall.

The best attendances supported the Yorkshire clashes between **Sheffield United** and **Hull City** – 7036 paying at Bramall Lane and 7119 at Boothferry Park to see United win 3-2 on aggregate and the southern battle between **Crystal Palace** (6631) and **Portsmouth** (10,689) which was won by the Londoners 3-1.

In this, the first two legged round of the competition, the draw ensures that practically all games are local 'derbies' but of course in August many teams have yet to settle down so form cannot be taken as a reliable guide to the season ahead.

FIRST ROUND, FIRST LEG

30 AUG

Port Vale (0) 1 *(Moss)*

Rochdale (0) 0 2565

Port Vale: Siddall; Tartt, Bromage, Hunter, Sproson, Cegielski, Ridley, Moss, Earle (Lawrence), Armstrong, Waddington.
Rochdale: Pearce; Blair, Snookes, Williams, Trainer, Weir, Farrell, Hamilton, French, Wellings, Hilditch.
Referee: D. Owen (Wirral).

Stockport Co (1) 1 *(Emerson)*

Wigan Ath (1) 1 *(O'Keefe)* 3418

Stockport Co: Lloyd; Thorpe, Rutter, Emerson, Bowles, Smith, Williams, Phillips, Quinn, Park, Sherlock.
Wigan Ath: Tunks; McMahon, Glenn, O'Keefe, Cribley, Methven, Langley, Barrow, Bradd, Houghton, Rogers.
Referee: C. Steel (Carlisle).

Wimbledon (0) 1 *(Lesley)*

Brentford (1) 1 *(Roberts)* 3927

Wimbledon: Beasant; Peters, Thomas, Galliers, Tagg, Morris, Evans, Ketteridge, Lesley, Downs, Dibble.
Brentford: Roche, Tucker, Spencer, Booker, Whitehead, Hurlock, Kamara, Joseph, Mahoney, Bowles, Roberts.
Referee: T. Bune (Newbury).

31 AUG

Bristol R (1) 2 *(Randall, Williams, D.)*

Torquay U (0) 2 *(Cooper 2)* 3629

Bristol R: Kite; Curle, Slatter, McCaffery, Parkin, Hughes (Kelly), Williams G., Williams D., Stephens, Randall, Barrett.
Torquay U: Hern; Doyle, Smith, Wilson, Wigginton, Sheridan (Rioch), Grapes, Jones, Bishop, Cooper, Gallagher.
Referee: J. Bray (Hinckley).

Bury (2) 3 *(Cruikshank, Gore, Jakub)*

Burnley (2) 5 *(Scott, Wharton, Phelan, Steven, McGee)* 3111

Bury: Platt; Gardner, Kenworthy, Gore, Hilton P., Bramhall, Potts, Madden, Parker, Jakub, Cruikshank.
Burnley: Stevenson; Laws, Wharton, Scott (Taylor), Phelan, Holt, Dobson, Stevens, Hamilton, McGee, Young.
Referee: D. Hutchinson (Harrogate).

Cardiff C (0) 2 *(Bennett D., Gibbins)*
Hereford U (0) 1

(Showers) *1808 Cardiff C:* Thomas, Jones, Bodin, Bennett G. (Micallef), Pontin, Mullen, Bennett D., Tong, Gibbins, Hemmerman, Lewis.
Hereford U: Jackson; Price, Bartley, Pejic, Spiring, Musial, Crabbe, Harvey, Phillips, Showers, White.
Referee: S. G. Bates (Bristol).

Carlisle U (1) 3 *(Staniforth, Ashurst, Coughlin)*

Bolton W (2) 3 *(Doyle, Hoggan, Moores)* 4239

Carlisle U: Swinburne; Haigh, Rushbury, Ashurst, Houghton, Craig, Staniforth, Coughlin, Poskett, Hornsby, Shoulder.
Bolton W: McDonagh; Whitworth, Bennett, McGovern, Jones (Berry), Doyle, Chandler, Henry, Moores, Reid, Hoggan.
Referee: K. Redfern (Whitley Bay).

Chesterfield (1) 2 *(Dawson, Windridge)*

Hartlepool U) (0) 1 *(Linighan)* 1690

Chesterfield: Turner; Bellamy, Partridge, Wilson, Green, Henson, Windridge, Henderson, Dawson, Kowalski, Carroll (O'Neill).
Hartlepool U: Watson; Brown, Stimpson, Hogan, Bird, Linighan, Bainbridge, Lawrence, Newton, Smith, Johnson.
Referee: D. Civil (Birmingham).

Colchester U (2) 2 *(Wignall, Groves)*

Aldershot (0) 0 1665

Colchester: Walker; Cook, Coleman, Groves, Wignall, Hunter, Allinson, Osborne, Lyons (Bremner), McDonough, Leslie.
Aldershot: Johnson; Andruszewski, Gillard, Briley, Wood, Jopling, Shrubb, Banton, Goddard, McDonald, Brodie.
Referee: M. Dimblebee (Stevenage).

Crewe Alex (0) 1 *(Craven)*

Tranmere R (0) 1 *(Hutchinson)* 1907

Crewe Alex: Smith; Moore, Bowers, Salathiel, Scott, Purdie, Haslegrave, Sutton, Goodwin, Evans, Craven.
Tranmere R: Endersby; Mungall, Burgess, Parry, Hamiton, Williams, Powell, Hutchinson, Kerr, Mooney, Griffiths.
Referee: M. P. Scott (Nottingham).

Crystal Palace (0) 2 *(Hinshelwood 2)*

Portsmouth (0) 0 6631

Crystal Palace: Barron; Hinshelwood, Williams, Hughton, Cannon, Nebbeling, Giles, Lovell, Langley, Mabbutt (Price), Hilaire.
Portsmouth: Knight; McLaughlin, Sullivan, Doyle, Howe, Aizlewood, Ellis (Senior), Webb, Tait, Biley, Rogers.
Referee: K. W. Baker (Rugby).

Darlington (0) 0

Peterborough U (1) 2 *(Gynn, Cooke)* 2436

Darlington: Cuff; Brissett, Wilson, Smith, Kamara, Gilbert, Wicks (Stalker), McLean, Dunn, Walsh, McFadden.
Peterborough U: Seaman; Winters, Collins, Gynn, Firm, Rodaway, Slack, Linton, Cooke, Benjamin, Chard.
Referee: T. Fitzharris (Bolton).

Gillingham (2) 3 *(Bruce, Cascarino 2)*

Orient (0) (0) 2984

Gillingham: Sutton; Sharpe, Sitton, Bruce, Weatherly, Shaw, Powell, Tydeman, Cascarino, Grewcock, Lee.
Orient: Day; Fisher, Peach, Foster, Gray, Roffey, Godfrey, Donn, Houchen, Vincent, Taylor (Blackhall).
Referee: A. Gunn (Burgess Hill).

Halifax T (0) 2 *(Davison, Staniforth)*

Derby Co (0) 1 *(Swindlehurst)* 2820

Halifax T: Smelt; Nobbs, Carr, Evans (Wood), Smith, Hendrie, Hallybone, Davison, Spooner, Staniforth, Ward.
Derby Co: Banovic; Barton, Attley, Powell, Foster, McAlle, Brolly, Skivington, Wilson (Emson), Swindlehurst, Reid.
Referee: D. Shaw (Sandbach).

Huddersfield T (0) 1 *(Stanton)*
Doncaster R (1) 1

(Graham) *4430 Huddersfield T:* Cox B.; Brown, Valentine, Stanton, Sutton, Hanvey, Lillis, Cox M., Austin, Wilson, Greenwood.
Doncaster R: Peacock; Russell, Mell, Snodin I., Cawthorne, Humphries, Pugh, Liddell, Douglas, Graham, Lister.
Referee: K. Walmsley (Blackpool).

Millwall (0) 0

Northampton T (1) 2 *(Syrett, Saxby)* 2947

Millwall: Gleasure; Stevens, Robinson, Chatterton, Allardyce, Madden, Carr, Neal, Aylott, Martin, West (Horrix).
Northampton T: Freeman; Brady, Phillips, Gage, Burrows, Heeley, Saunders, Saxby, Syrett, Massey, Denyer.
Referee: M. J. Bodenham (Brighton).

Plymouth Arg (0) 2 *(Sims 2)*

AFC Bournemouth (0) 0 3103

Plymouth Arg: Crudgington; Nisbet, Uzzell, Harrison, Phillipson-Masters, Cooper, Hodges, Cook, Sims, Gooding, Rogers.
AFC Bournemouth: Allen; Heffernan, Sulley, Spackman, Brignull, Imray, Carter, Williams, Morgan, Crawford, Dawtrey.
Referee: T. Stevens (Bristol).

Scunthorpe U (0) 1 *(Cowling)*

Grimsby T (0) 2 *(Drinkell 2)* 2620

Scunthorpe U: Neenan; Keeley, Oates, Fowler, Boxall, Hunter, Cammack, Parkinson, Cowling, Telfer, Leman (O'Berg).
Grimsby T: Batch; Moore D., Crombie, Waters, Cooper, Moore K., Ford, Kilmore, Drinkell, Bonnyman, Whymark.
Referee: G. M. Tyson (Sunderland).

Sheffield U (0) 3 *(Young 2, Edwards)*

Hull C (0) 1 *(Whitehurst)* 7036

Sheffield U: Conroy; Henderson, Garner, McHale, MacPhail, Kenworthy (Morris), Curran, Arnott, Edwards, Young, King.
Hull C: Norman; Swann, McNeil, Roberts D., Skipper, Booth, Marwood, McClaren (Flounders), Whitehurst, Mutrie, Roberts G.
Referee: N. Midgley (Salford).

Swindon T (1) 2 *(Rideout 2* [1 pen]*)*

Bristol C (0) 1 *(Boyle)* 3736

Swindon T: Allan; Henry, Baddeley, Emmanuel, Lewis, Graham, Pritchard (Carter), Hughes, Rideout, Rowland, Barnard.
Bristol C: Shaw; Riley, Economou, Musker (Bray), Cooper, Ritchie, Crawford.
Referee: J. C. Deakin (Bedford).

Walsall (0) 0

Preston NE (0) 1 *(Naughton)* 2490

Walsall: Green; Arthur, Mower (Round), Beech, Marshall, Hart, Rees, Sinnot, Kearns, Buckley, Preece.
Preston NE: Litchfield: Walsh, McAteer, O'Riordan, Westwell, Farrelly, Kelly, Bell, Elliott, Naughton, Bruce.
Referee: J. M. Key (Rotherham).

Wrexham (1) 1 *(Hunt)*

Shrewsbury T (0) 0 3218

Wrexham: Niedzwiecki; Jones, Bater, Arkwright, Dowman, Hill, Hunt, Gregory, Fox, Edwards, Buxton.
Shrewsbury T: Ogrizovic; Williams, Johnson, Sankey, Griffin, Pearson, Petts, MacLaren, Brown, Cross, Pates.
Referee: P. Tyldesley (Stockport).

York C (1) 2 *(Walwyn, Byrne)*

Lincoln C (0) 1 *(Hobson)* 1982

York C: Jones; Evans, Hay, Sbragia, Smith, Hood, Pollard, Ford, Walwyn, Byrne, Loverick.
Lincoln C: Felgate; Carr, Heath, Cockerill, Peake, Thompson, Hibbert (Bell), Turner, Hobson, Cunningham, Shipley.
Referee: R. Chadwick (Darwen).

1 SEPT

Bradford C (0) 1 *(Campbell)*

Mansfield T (0) 0 3265

Bradford C: McManus; McCall, Chapman, Lester, Cooke, Jackson, Gray, Gallagher, Campbell, McNiven, Mellor.
Mansfield T: Arnold; Bell, Kennedy, Day, Ayre, Bird, Matthews, Caldwell, Waddle, Dungworth, Laidlaw.
Referee: A. Banks (Manchester).

Exeter C (0) 1 *(Kellow)*

Newport Co (1) 2 *(Lowndes, Gwyther)* 2292

Exeter C: Bond; Kirkup, Viney, McEwan, Roberts, Howarth, Harle, Rogers P., Kellow, Delve, Pullar.
Newport Co: Kendall; Jones, Vaughan, Bailey, Relish, Stroud, Lowndes, Gwyther, Tynan, Elsey, Moore.
Referee: M. James (Horsham).

Southend U: (1) 1 *(Nelson)*

Fulham (0) 0 2671

Southend U: Cawston; Stead, Yates, Clark, Moody, Cusack, Pountney, Phillips, Mercer, Pennyfather, Nelson.
Fulham: Peyton; Hopkins, Lock, O'Driscoll, Brown, Gale, Davies, Wilson, Coney, Houghton, Lewington.
Referee: D. Hedges (Oxford).

Reading (0) 0

Oxford U (2) 2 *(Fogg pen, Barnett)* 2786

Reading: Fearon; Williams, White (Richardson), Beavon, Hicks, Wood, Earles, Kearney, Dixon, Bason, Donnellan.
Oxford U: Burton; Linney, Fogg, Train, Briggs, Shotton, Brock, Barnett, Biggins, Vinter, Hebberd.
Referee: J. Moules (Ongar).

Chester (1) 1 *(Sloan)*

Blackpool (0) 2 *(Bamber, Serella)* 2557

Chester: Millington; Edwards, Bradley, Zelem, Lane, Dean, Sloan, Johnson, Simpson, Cooke, Thomas.
Blackpool: Hesford; Butler, Brockbank, Deary, Hetzke, Serella, Noble, Hockaday, Bamber, Pashley, Downes.
Referee: D. Lloyd (Fernhill Heath).

FIRST ROUND, SECOND LEG

13 SEPT

Mansfield T (0) 0

Bradford C (1) 2 *(Campbell, Ellis)* 2260

Bradford C won 3-0
Mansfield T: Arnold; Woodhead, Kennedy, Day, Ayre, Bird, Matthews, Nicholson, Cannell, Dungworth, Laidlaw.
Bradford C: McManus; Watson, Chapman, Lester, Cooke, Jackson, Gray, Gallagher, Campbell, Ellis, Mellor.
Referee: J. C. Deakin (Bedford).

Tranmere R (0) 0

Crewe Alex (0) 0 1709

Aggregate 1-1; Tranmere R won on away goals rule.
Tranmere R: Endersby; Burgess, Mooney, Parry, Hamilton, Mungall, Powell, Aspinall (McKenna), Kerr, Mathias, Griffiths.
Crewe Alex: Smith; Moore, Bowers, Salathiel, Scott, Purdie, Haslegrave, Palios, Goodwin (Jones), Evans, Craven.
Referee: A. Robinson (Radcliffe).

14 SEPT

Aldershot (0) 0

Colchester U (0) 1 *(Allinson)* 1680

Colchester won 3-0
Aldershot: Johnson; Andruszewski, Gillard, Briley (Lucas), Wood, Jopling, Shrubb, Banton, Sanford, McDonald, Brodie.
Colchester U: Walker; Cook, Coleman, Groves, Wignall, Hunter, Allinson, Osborne, Lyons, McDonough, Leslie.
Referee: M. Taylor (Deal).

Blackpool (2) 5 *(Serella, Hetzke, Deary, Stewart, Pashley* pen*)*

Chester (0) 1 *(Thomas)* 3429

Blackpool won 7-2
Blackpool: Hesford; Simmonite, Brockbank, Deary, Hetzke, Serella, Noble, Hockaday, Stewart, Pashley, Butler.
Chester: Millington; Bradley, Lane, Storton, Zelem, Ludlam, Sloan, Thomas, Simpson, Johnson, Cook.
Referee: T. Mills (Barnsley).

Bolton W (1) 4 *)Henry 2, Doyle, Moore)*

Carlisle U (0) 0 4039

Bolton W won 7-3
Bolton W: McDonagh; Whitworth, Bennett, McGovern, Jones, Doyle, Chandler, Henry, Moore, Reid, Berry.
Carlisle U: Swinburne; Haigh (Parker), Rushbury, Ashurst, Craig, Houghton, Staniforth, Coughlin, Poskett, Lee, Shoulder.
Referee: A. J. Hamil (Wolverhampton).

AFC Bournemouth (1) 3 *(Funnell, Brignull, Morgan)*

Plymouth Arg (0) 0 3353

After Extra Time. AFC Bournemouth won 3-2
AFC Bournemouth: Allen; Sulley, O'Donnell, Brignull, Compton, Carter, Williams, Morgan, Funnell, Mundee (Dawkins).
Plymouth Arg: Crudgington; Nisbet, Uzzell, Harrison, McCartney, Cooper (Carter), Hodges, Cook, Sims, Gooding, Rogers.
Referee: C. Downey (Hounslow).

Brentford (1) 2 *(Mahoney 2)*

Wimbledon (0) 0 5747

Brentford won 3-1
Brentford: Roche; Rowe, Tucker, McNicholl, Whitehead, Hurlock, Kamara, Joseph, Mahoney, Bowles, Roberts.
Wimbledon: Beasant; Peters, Thomas, Hodges (Gage), Morris, Jones, Ketteridge, Downes, Leslie, Galliers, Evans.
Referee: D. J. Axcell (Southend).

Bristol C (2) 2 *(Boyle, Ritchie)*

Swindon T (0) 0 3752

Bristol C won 3-2
Bristol C: Shaw; Stevens, Newman, Williams, Boyle, Cooper, Riley, Chandler, Bray, Ritchie, Thompson.
Swindon T: Allan; Henry (Quinn), Baddeley, Emmanuel, Lewis, Graham, Pritchard, Hughes, Rideout, Rowland, Barnard.
Referee: A. Robinson (Portsmouth).

Burnley (1) 3 *(Cruikshank og, Laws* pen*, Hamilton)*

Bury (0) 1 *(Madden)* 3548

Burnley won 8-4
Burnley: Stevenson; Laws, Wharton, Scott, Phelan, Holt, Dobson, Stevens, Hamilton, McGee (Taylor), Cassidy.
Bury: Brown; Gardner, Kenworthy, Gore, Hilton P., Cruickshank, Potts, Madden, Johnson, Parker, Firth.
Referee: N. Wilson (Morecambe).

Doncaster R (0) 0

Huddersfield T (0) 1 *(Brown)* 4690

Huddersfield T won 2-1
Doncaster R: Peacock; Russell, Snodin I., Snodin G., Cawthorne, Humphries, Pugh, Liddell (Mell), Douglas, Graham, Lister.
Huddersfield T: Cox; Brown, Burke, Stanton, Sutton, Valentine, Lillis, Doyle, Greenwood, Wilson, Cowling.
Referee: M. Robinson (Sutton Coldfield).

Fulham (1) 4 *(Yates og, Coney, Houghton, Davies)*

Southend U (0) 2 *(Pennyfather, Yates)* 4641

Fulham won 4-3
Fulham: Peyton; Hopkins, Lock, O'Driscoll, Brown, Gale, Davies, Parker, Coney, Houghton, Lewington.
Southend U: Keeley; Stead, Yates, Otulakowski (Hadley), Moody, Cusack, Pountney, Phillips, Mercer, Pennyfather, Nelson.
Referee: J. Martin (Alton).

Grimsby T (0) 0

Scunthorpe U (0) 0 3347

Grimsby T won 2-1
Grimsby T: Batch; Speight (Cumming), Crosby, Waters, Cooper, Moore K., Ford, Kilmore, Drinkell, Bonnyman, Whymark.
Scunthorpe U: Neenan; Keeley, Pointon, Fowler, Boxall, Hunter, Gilbert, Parkinson, O'Berg, Telfer (Duncan), Leman.
Referee: G. J. Napthine (Loughborough).

Hull C (1) 1 *(Flounders)*

Sheffield U (0) 0 7119

Sheffield won 3-2
Hull C: Davies; McNeil, Roberts G., Skipper, Askew, McClaren, Roberts D., Booth, Flounders, Mutrie, Whitehurst.
Sheffield U: Conroy; Henderson, Houston, MacPhail, Kenworthy (Edwards), Charles, Trusson, McHale, Arnott, Young, Curran.
Referee: A Saunders (Newcastle).

Newport Co (3) 6 *(Lowndes, Elsey, Aldridge, Vaughan 2, Tynan)*

Exeter C (0) 0 2686

Newport Co won 8-1
Newport Co: Kendall; Jones, Relish, Elsey, Davies, Stroud, Lowndes, Aldridge, Tynan, Vaughan, Williams.
Exeter C: Bond; Kirkup, Viney, McEwan, Roberts, Rogers M., Harle, Rogers P., Kellow, Delve, Pullar (Gibson).
Referee: H. Taylor (Oadby).

Northampton T (1) 2 *(Massey 2)*

Millwall (0) 2 *(Martin, Neal)* 2855

Northampton T won 4-2
Northampton T: Kendall; Brady, Phillips, Gage, Buchanan, Heeley, Saunders, Saxby (Coffill), Syrett, Massey, Denyer.
Millwall: Sansome; Stevens, Madden, Chatterton, Allardyce, Roberts, Carr, Shinton, Aylott, Martin, Horrix (Neal).
Referee: J. Lovatt (Crewe).

Orient (2) 2 *(Osgood, Cunningham)*

Gillingham (0) 0 2003

Gillingham won 3-2
Orient: Day; Osgood, Roffey, Foster, Gray, Vincent, Godfrey, Donn, Blackhall, Silkman, Taylor (Cunningham).
Gillingham: Hillyard; Sharpe, Adams, Bruce, Weatherly, Shaw, Powell, Tydeman, Cascarino, Sitton, Price.
Referee: L. E. Burden (Dorset).

Portsmouth (1) 1 *(Biley)*

Crystal Palace (1) 1 *(Lovell)* 10,689

Crystal Palace won 3-1
Portsmouth: Knight; McLaughlin, Sullivan, Doyle, Howe, Ellis, Rogers, Tait, Rafferty, Biley (Senior), Thomas.
Crystal Palace: Barron; Hinshelwood, Williams, Hughton, Cannon, Gilbert, Lovell, Murphy, Edwards, Mabbutt, Hilaire.
Referee: C. Thomas (Porthcawl).

Preston NE (0) 1 *(Elliott)*

Walsall (1) 1 *(Preece)* 3137

Preston NE won 2-1
Preston NE: Litchfield; Walsh, McAteer, O'Riordan, Westwell, Gowling, Kelly, Bell, Elliott, Naughton, Houston.
Walsall: Green; Caswell, Mower, Beech, Sinnott, Hart, Teasdale, Shakespeare (Round), Kearns, Buckley, Preece.
Referee: K. Hackett (Sheffield).

Rochdale (0) 2 *(Wellings 2* [1 pen]*)*

Port Vale (0) 0 1536

Rochdale won 2-1
Rochdale: Pearce; Warriner, Blair (Martinez), Farrell, Trainer, Williams, Thompson, Hamilton, French, Wellings, Hilditch.
Port Vale: Siddall; Tartt, Bromage, Hunter, Sproson, Cegielski, Ridley (Greenhoff), Moss, Armstrong, Chamberlain, Shankland.
Referee: R. Bridges (Teesside).

Shrewsbury T (0) 2 *(Brown, Cross)*

Wrexham (0) 0 2850

Shrewsbury T won 2-1
Shrewsbury T: Ogrizovic; Williams, Johnson, Griffin, Pearson, MacLaren, Petts, Cross, Bates, Steven, Brown.
Wrexham: Niedzwiecki; Hill, Jones, Dowman, Keay, Arkwright, Bates, McNeil, Gregory (Hunt), Fox, Buxton.
Referee: R. Milford (Bristol).

Wigan Ath (0) 1 *(Bradd)*

Stockport Co (0) 1 *(Park)* 4008

Aggregate 2-2. Wigan Ath won on penalties
Wigan Ath: Tunks; McMahon, Weston, O'Keefe, Cribley, Methven, Langley, Butler, Bradd, Williams, Rogers.
Stockport Co: Lloyd; Thorpe, Rutter, Emerson, Bowles, Smith, Williams, Phillips, Quinn, Park, Sherlock.
Referee: F. Roberts (Prestatyn).

15 SEPT

Derby Co (2) 5 *(Skivington, Hill, Buckley 2* [1 pen]*, Wilson)*

Halifax T (0) 2 *(Davison 2)* 8534

After Extra Time. Derby Co won 6-4
Derby Co: Banovic; Barton, Buckley, Skivington, Foster, McAlle, Brolly, Attley, Hill, Swindlehurst, Dalziel (Wilson).
Halifax T: Smelt; Nobbs, Carr (Wood), Evans, Smith, Hendrie, Hallybone, Davison, Spooner, Staniforth, Ward.
Referee: B. G. Callow (Solihull).

Hartlepool U (1) 2 *(Barker, Bainbridge)*

Chesterfield (0) 0 1122

After Extra Time. Hartlepool U won 3-2
Hartlepool U: Watson; Brown, Stimpson, Hogan, Barker, Linighan, Bainbridge, Smith, Linacre P., Lawrence, Johnson.
Chesterfield: Turner; Bellamy, Partridge, Wilson, Green, Pollard, Walker, Henderson, Henson (Dawson), Kowalski, Carroll.
Referee: B. Allison (Lancaster).

Hereford U (1) 1 *(Pejic)*

Cardiff C (1) 2 *(Gibbins, Hemmerman)* 3301

Cardiff C won 4-2
Hereford U: Jackson; Price, Bartley, Hicks, Pejic, Spiring (Lane), Crabbe, Harvey, Phillips, Showers, White.
Cardiff C: Thomas; Jones, Bodin, Mullen, Bennett G., Micallef, Bennett D., Tong, Gibbins, Hemmerman, Lewis.
Referee: J. Haigh (Macclesfield).

Lincoln C (0) 3 *(Cunningham 2* [1 pen]*, Hobson)*

York C (0) 1 *(Thompson og)* 2716

Lincoln C won 4-3
Lincoln C: Felgate; Carr, Neale, Cockerill, Peake, Thompson, Hibberd, Turner, Hobson, Cunningham, Shipley.
York C: Jones; Evans, Hay, Sbragia, Smith, Hood, Pollard, Ford, Walwyn, Byrne, Laverick.
Referee: M. Heath (Stoke).

Oxford U (1) 2 *(Vinter, Thomas)*

Reading (0) 0 4882

Oxford U won 4-0
Oxford U: Burton; Linney, Fogg, Train, Briggs, Shotton, Brock, Barnett, Vinter, Thomas, Hebberd.
Reading: Fearon; Richardson, White, Beavon, Barnes, Wood, Bason, Earles, Dixon, Sanchez, Donnellan.
Referee: B. Hill (Kettering).

Peterborough U (4) 4 *(Benjamin, Imlach, Cooke 2)*

Darlington (1) 2 *(Winters og, Walsh)* 2117

Peterborough U won 6-2
Peterborough U: Seaman; Winters, Collins, Gynn, Firm, Rodaway, Imlach (Cliss), Linton, Cooke, Benjamin, Chard.
Darlington: Cuff; Brissett, Wilson, Smith, Kamara, Honour, Hawker, McLean, Stalker, Walsh, McFadden.
Referee: D. Reeves (Uxbridge).

Torquay U (0) 0

Bristol R (2) 4 *(Platnauer, Barrett, Randall, Stephens)* 3204

Bristol R won 6-2
Torquay U: Horn; Doyle, Rioch, Wilson, Wiggington, Brown, Grapes, Steeples, Cooper, Smith, Gallagher.
Bristol R: Kite; Slatter, Williams B., Williams G., Parkin, McCaffery, Platnauer (Stephens), Williams D., Kelly, Randall, Barrett.
Referee: A. Seville (Birmingham).

Milk Cup Second Round

LINCOLN CITY AND LEEDS UNITED TAKE THE HONOURS

Lincoln City's comprehensive 3-0 aggregate victory over Second Division Leicester City was probably the round's most complete performance, but for excitement and spectacular goals, **Leeds United**'s sparkling 4-2 victory, clinched in extra time at Newcastle, following a 0-1 defeat at home, really hit the headlines. Terry Connor scored a superb goal after replacing player-manager Eddie Gray for the second half of extra time and made another for Aiden Butterworth.

The highest scorers were **Sheffield United** who beat Grimsby Town 8-4 (3-3, 5-1) with a hat-trick from Keith Edwards in the home tie, while **Nottingham Forest** registered 6 at home to **WBA**.

AFC Bournemouth thoroughly enjoyed their games with **Manchester United**, and indeed, only conceded an early 'own goal' from coach Harry Redknapp and a late second in the 80th minute to Stapleton; before drawing in the second leg 2-2 at home. Unfortunately Ray Wilkins lost the captaincy of both United and England through an injury in this tie, so will not have such happy memories.

Other good efforts in this round were recorded by **Brentford** who beat Blackburn Rovers (3-2, 0-0), **Newport County** whose 2-2 draw at Everton was not enough to cancel out a 0-2 home defeat, **Notts County** who beat Aston Villa twice (2-1, 1-0), **Gillingham** who beat Oldham Athletic 3-1 and plucky **Charlton Athletic** who just failed to catch Luton Town after giving them a three goal start. They beat the 'Hatters' 2-0 in the second leg.

In general, results went with the form book and **17** First Division clubs were joined by **8** from the Second and **7** from the Third Divisions in the Third Round. **Blackpool** who lost 2-4 at **Luton** were the last representatives of the Fourth Division.

SECOND ROUND, FIRST LEG

4 OCT

Bristol C (0) 1 *(Newman)*

Sheffield W (2) 2 *(Taylor 2)* 4486

Bristol C: Shaw; Newman, Williams, Nicholls, Boyles, Riley, Bray, Economou, Chandler, Thompson, Crawford.
Sheffield W: Bolder; Sterland, Bailey, Smith, Lyons, Shelton, Megson (Pickering), Taylor, Bannister, Owen, Simmons.
Referee: D. A. Hedges.

5 OCT

Arsenal (0) 2 *(Hollins, Davis)*

Cardiff C (0) 1 *(Gibbins)* 15,115

Arsenal: Wood; Hollins, Sansome, Talbot, O'Leary, Whyte, Davis, Robson, Sunderland, Woodcock, Rix.
Cardiff C: Thomas; Jones, Bodin, Micallef, Dwyer, Mullen, Bennett, Tong, Gibbins, Hemmerman, Lewis.
Referee: A. Gunn (Sussex).

Bolton W (1) 1 *(Hoggan)*

Watford (1) 2 *(Armstrong, Jenkins)* 5664

Bolton W: McDonach; Whitworth, Deakin, McGovern, Jones, McElhinney, Chandler, Henry, Rudge, Reid (Moores), Hoggan.
Watford: Sherwood; Rice (Armstrong), Rostron, Taylor, Terry, Bolton, Callaghan, Blissett, Jenkins, Jackett, Barnes.
Referee: M. J. Heath (Stoke).

Brentford (2) 3 *(Joseph, Hurlock, Bowles* pen*)*

Blackburn R (2) 2 *(Fazackerley, Stonehouse)* 6201

Brentford: Roche; Rowe, Wilkins, McNichol, Whitehead, Hurlock, Kamara, Joseph, Mahoney, Bowles, Roberts.
Blackburn R: Gennoe; Branagan, Rathbone, Randell (Miller), Mail, Fazackerley, Hamilton, Stonehouse, Bell, garner, Brotherston.
Referee: I. J. Borrett (Suffolk).

Bristol R (0) 1 *(Parkin)*

Swansea C (0) 0 9279

Bristol R: Kite; Slatter, Williams B., Williams G., Parkin, McCaffery, Holloway, Williams D., Kelly, Randall, Barrett (Stephens).
Swansea C: Davies; Marustik, Lewis, Charles, Kennedy, Mahoney, Curtis, James R., Loveridge, Thompson, Latchford.
Referee: M. James (Horsham).

Burnley (1) 3 *(Hamilton, Phelan, Young)*

Middlesbrough (1) 2 *(Otto, Cochrane)* 3926

Burnley: Stevenson; Laws, Wharton, Scott, Phelan, Holt, Dobson, Steven (Cassidy), Hamilton, Taylor, Young.
Middlesbrough: Platt; Brownlie, Bolton, Mowbray, Baxter, Wood, Cochrane, Otto (Nattrass), Hankin, Kennedy, Bell.
Referee: F. Roberts (Clwyd).

Fulham (2) 2 *(Gale, Brown)*

Coventry C (2) 2 *(Melrose 2)* 6237

Fulham: Peyton; Hopkins, Lock, O'Driscoll, Brown, Gale, Davies, Wilson, Coney, Houghton, Lewington.
Coventry C: Sealey; Thomas, Hormantschuck, Butterworth, Dyson, Gillespie, Whitton, Jacobs, Melrose, Thompson, Hunt.
Referee: M. J. Bodenham (Brighton).

Gillingham (0) 2 *(Shaw, Cascarino)*

Oldham Ath (0) 0 4070

Gillingham: Hillyard; Sharpe, Adams, Bruce, Shaw, Sitton (Price), Powell, Johnson, Cascarino, Grewcock, Weatherly.
Oldham Ath: Goram; Sinclair, Ryan, Keegan, Clements, Futcher, McDonough, Atkinson, Bowden, Wylde, Palmer.
Referee: R. Lewis (Gt Bookham).

Huddersfield T (1) 2 *(Russell, Stanton)*

Oxford U (0) 0 4362

Huddersfield T: Cox; Brown, Burke, Stanton, Sutton, Hanvey, Lillis, Doyle, Russell, Wilson, Gowling.
Oxford U: Burton; Linney, Fogg, Train (Thomas), Briggs, Shotton, Brock, Jones, Vinter, Foley, Hebberd.
Referee: G. Tyson (Sunderland).

Ipswich T (0) 1 *(Wark)*

Liverpool (1) 2 *(Rush 2)* 19,329

Ipswich T: Sivell; Burley, Gernon, Mills, Osman, Butcher, Wark, McCall, D'Avray, Brazil, O'Callaghan.
Liverpool: Grobbelaar; Neal, Kennedy, Thompson, Whelan, Hansen, Dalglish, Lee, Rush, Lawrenson, Souness.
Referee: B. Daniels (Brentwood).

Luton T (2) 3 *(Stein* pen, *Fuccillo 2)*

Charlton Ath (0) 0 7,030

Luton T: Findlay, Stephens, Money, Horton, Goodyear, Donaghy, Hill, Stein, Walsh, Fuccillo, Moss.
Charlton Ath: Johns; Curtis, Lansdowne, Mehmet, Elliott, Berry, Harris, Bullivant, White, Hales (Gritt), Walker.
Referee: A. Robinson (Waterlooville).

Newport Co (0) 0

Everton (1) 2 *(McMahon, King)* 8293

Newport Co: Kendall; Jones, Relish, Bailey (Gwyther), Oakes, Davies, Elsey, Aldridge, Tynan, Vaughan, Moore.
Everton: Southall; Borrows, Bailey, Ratcliffe, Wright, McMahon, Heath (Richardson), Johnson, Sharp, King, Sheedy.
Referee: T. Spencer (Salisbury).

Northampton T (1) 1 *(Massey)*

Blackpool (0) 1 *(Bamber)* 2490

Northampton T: Freeman; Saxby, Phillips, Gage, Burrows, Coffill (Perrin), Buchanan, Saunders, Denyer, Massey, Heeley.
Blackpool: Hesford; Simmonite, Brockbank, Jeffrey, Greenall, Hart, Hockaday, Stewart, Bamber, Pashley, Downes.
Referee: D. Letts (Basingstoke).

Rochdale (0) 0

Bradford C (1) 1 *(Gallagher)* 2196

Rochdale: Pearce; Keegan, Snookes, Farrell, Garner, Williams, Thompson, Hamilton, Hilditch, Wellings, Comstive.
Bradford C: McManus; Podd, Chapman, Lester, Cooke, McFarland, Gray, Gallagher, Campbell, Ellis, Mellor.
Referee: A. J. Hamil (Wolverhampton).

Rotherham U (1) 2 *(Green, Seasman)*

QPR (0) 1 *(Gregory)* 5603

Rotherham U: Mountford; Forrest, Breckin, McEwan, Hughes, Green, Towner, Gow, Moore, Seasman, McBride.
QPR: Hucker; Neill, Dawes, Waddock, Hazell, Fenwick, Micklewhite, Allen, Sealy, Stainrod, Gregory.
Referee: D. Richardson (Gt Harwood).

Shrewsbury T (1) 1 *(Round)*

Birmingham C (1) 1 *(Handysides)* 5003

Shrewsbury T: Ogrizovic; Williams, Johnson, Cross, Pearson, Leonard, Petts, MacLaren, Turner, Stevens (Sankey), Bates.
Birmingham C: Blyth; Langan, Van den Hauwe, Stevenson, Blake, Broadhurst, Summerfield (Carrodus), Dillon, Brazier, Curbishley, Handysides.
Referee: A. Robinson (Manchester).

Wigan Ath (0) 1 *(Caton og)*

Manchester C (0) 1 *(Tueart)* 12,194

Wigan Ath: Tunks; McMahon, Weston, O'Keefe, Lloyd, Methven, Glenn, Cribley, Bradd, Houghton, Gemmill.
Manchester C: Williams; Ransom, Power, Baker, Bond, Caton, Tueart, Reeves, Cross, Hartford, Boyer.
Referee: N. G. Peck (Kendal).

Wolverhampton W (1) 1 *(Eves)*

Sunderland (1) 1 *(Rowell* pen*)* 13,662

Wolverhampton W: Burridge; Humphrey, Palmer, Smith, Pender, Coy, Daniel, Clarke, Livingstone (Butler), Eves, Matthews.
Sunderland: Turner; Nicholl, Munro, Atkins, Hindmarch, Elliott, Buckley (Chisholm), Rowell, McCoist, Pickering, Cooke.
Referee: J. A. Moules (Ongar).

6 OCT

Aston Villa (1) 1 *(Withe)*

Notts Co (0) 2 *(Chiedozie, Clarke)* 16,312

Aston Villa: Rimmer; Jones (Heard), Williams, Ormsby, McNaught, Mortimer, Bremner, Shaw, Withe, Cowans, Morley.
Notts Co: Avramovic; Benjamin, Worthington, Hunt, Kilcline, Richards, Chiedozie, Harkouk (Clarke), Christie, McCulloch, Mair.
Referee: M. Glover (Chorley).

Chelsea (3) 3 *(Speedie 2, Fillery* pen*)*

Tranmere R (1) 1 *(Brown)* 7982

Chelsea: Francis; Lee (Driver), Hutchings, Chivers, Droy, McAndrew, Canoville, Bumstead, Walker, Speedie, Fillery.
Tranmere R: Endersby; Burgess, Aspinall, Mathias, Hamilton, Williams, Powell (McGuire), Ferguson, Kerr, Brown, Griffiths.
Referee: K. Barrett (Coventry).

Colchester U (0) 0

Southampton (0) 0 7967

Colchester U: Walker; Cook, Coleman, Adcock, Wignall, Beattie (Bremner), Allinson, Osborne, Lyons, McDonough, Leslie.
Southampton: Shilton; Baker, Rofe, Williams, Nicholls, Agboola, Ball, Cassells, Wallace, Armstrong, Lawrence.
Referee: B. Hill (Kettering).

Derby Co (1) 2 *(Watson og, Swindlehurst)*

Hartlepool U (0) 0 7656

Derby Co: Banovic; Barton, Buckley, Attley, Foster, Powell, Brolly, Gamble, Hill (Emson), Swindlehurst, Dalziel.
Hartlepool U: Watson; Brown, Stimpson, Hogan, Bird, Linighan, Bainbridge, Smith, Higgins (Linacre), Lawrence, Johnson.
Referee: J. Lovatt (Crewe).

Leeds U (0) 0

Newcastle U (1) 1 *(Varadi)* 24,012

Leeds U: Lukic; Cherry (Connor), Gray E., Burns, Hart, Thomas, Hird, Butterworth, Worthington, Gray F., Graham.
Newcastle U: Carr; Anderson, Saunders, Martin, Clarke, Carney, Keegan, Todd, Varadi, McDermott, McCreery (Wharton).
Referee: R. F. Nixon (Wirral).

Lincoln C (2) 2 *(Bell, Shipley)*

Leicester C (0) 0 6775

Lincoln C: Felgate; Carr, Neale, Cockerill, Peake, Thompson, Burke, Turner, Hobson, Bell, Shipley.
Leicester C: Wallington; Ramsey, Friar, MacDonald, May, O'Neill, Lynex, Lineker, Kelly, English, Wilson.
Referee: P. Tyldesley (Stockport).

Manchester U (1) 2 *(Redknapp og, Stapleton)*

AFC Bournemouth (0) 0 22,091

Manchester U: Bailey; Duxbury, Albiston, Wilkins, Moran, McQueen, Robson, Grimes, Stapleton, Beardsley (Whiteside), Moses.
AFC Bournemouth: Allen; Heffernan, Sulley, Spackman, Brignull, Compton, Redknapp, Williams, Morgan, Funnell, Crawford.
Referee: D. Lloyd (Fernhill Heath).

Norwich C (1) 2 *(Bertschin, O'Neill)*

Preston NE (1) 1 *(Bruce)* 7273

Norwich C: Woods: Haylock, Downs, McGuire (Mendham), Walford, Smith, Barham, O'Neill, Deehan, Bertschin, Bennett.
Preston NE: Litchfield; Walsh, McAteer, Coleman, Westwell, Gowling, Kelly, Bell, Elliott, Naughton, Bruce.
Referee: A. W. Ward (London).

Nottingham F (3) 6 *(Wallace 2, Robertson* [2 pens], *Hodge, Birtles)*

WBA (1) 1 *(Regis)* 11,969

Nottingham F: Van Breukelen; Anderson, Gunn, Proctor, Fairclough, Todd, Hodge, Wallace, Birtles, Walsh, Robertson.
WBA: Grew; Batson, Whitehead, Zondervan, Bennett, Robertson, Jol, Brown, Regis, Owen, Eastoe.
Referee: R. Banks (Manchester).

Peterborough U (0) 0

Crystal Palace (1) 2 *(Edwards 2)* 3798

Peterborough U: Seaman; Quow (Winters), Collins, Gynn, Firm, Rodaway, Slack, Linton, Cooke, Benjamin, Chard.
Crystal Palace: Barron; Hinshelwood, Williams, Murphy, Cannon, Gilbert, Giles, Lovell, Edwards, Mabbutt, Hilaire.
Referee: C. Newsome (Shropshire).

Stoke C (0) 1 *(Thomas)*

West Ham U (0) 1 *(Stewart* pen*)* 18,079

Stoke C: Fox; Parkin, Hampton, Bracewell, Watson, Berry, Maguire, McIlroy, O'Callaghan, Thomas, Chamberlain M. (Griffiths).
West Ham U: Parkes; Stewart, Lampard, Orr, Martin, Devonshire, Neighbour, Goddard, Clark, Allen, Pike.
Referee: H. King (Merthyr Tydfil).

Tottenham H (0) 1 *(Brooke* pen*)*

Brighton & HA (1) 1 *(Clemence og)* 20,416

Tottenham H: Clemence, Hughton, Lacy, Price, Brooke, O'Reilly, Mabbutt, Archibald, Hazard, Villa, Crooks (Falco).
Brighton & HA: Moseley; Stevens, Shanks, Grealish, Foster, Gatting, Case, Ritchie, Robinson, McNab, Smith.
Referee: K. W. Baker (Rugby).

12 OCT

Barnsley (1) 2 *(Glavin, McCarthy)*

Cambridge U (0) 1 *(Finney)* 8794

Barnsley: Horn; Law, Chambers, Glavin, Banks, McCarthy, Souter, Parker, Walker, Ronson, Birch.
Cambridge U: Webster; Donaldson, Murray, Turner, Fallon, Lockhart (Christie), Nicholls, O'Neill, Reilly, Streete, Finney.
Referee: J. Worrall (Warrington).

Grimsby T (0) 3 *(Drinkell 3)*

Sheffield U (2) 3 *(Richardson, Young, Morris* pen*)* 5295

Grimsby T: Grotier; Moore D., Crosby, Waters, Cooper, Moore K., Cumming, Kilmore, Drinkell, Bonnyman, Speight.
Sheffield U: Conroy; Atkins, Garner, Richardson, MacPhail, Houston, Morris, Charles, Young, Curran, Brazil (McHale).
Referee: H. Taylor (Derby).

SECOND ROUND, SECOND LEG

Hartlepool U (2) 4 *(Barker, Smith, Staff, Johnson)*

Derby Co (1) 2 *(Wilson, Brolly)* 3596

After Extra Time. Derby Co won on away goals rule
Hartlepool U: Watson; Brown, Stimpson, Hogan, Bird, Linighan, Staff, Smith, Lawrence, Johnson, Barker.
Derby Co: Cherry; Barton, Buckley, Blades, Foster, McAlle, Brolly, Mills (Dalziel), Wilson, Swindlehurst, Skivington.
Referee: T. Mills (Barnsley).

26 OCT

Birmingham C (1) 4 *(Evans, Curbishley 2, Dillon)*

Shrewsbury T (1) 1 *(Brown)* 7861

Birmingham C won 5-2
Birmingham C: Blyth; Mumford, Van den Hauwe, Stevenson, Blake, Broadhurst, Dillon, Evans, Brazier, Curbishley, Handysides.
Shrewsbury T: Ogrizovic; Williams, Johnson (Sankey), Petts, Pearson, Griffin, Cross, MacLaren, Brown, McNally, Bates.
Referee: K. Hackett (Sheffield).

Blackpool (0) 2 *(Downes* pen, *Bamber)*

Northampton T (0) 1 *(Syrett)*

After Extra Time. Blackpool won 3-2
Blackpool: Hesford; Simmonite, Hart, Deary, Hetzke, Serella, Hockaday, Stewart, Bamber, Pashley, Downes.
Northampton T: Freeman; Denyer, Phillips, Brady, Burrows, Heeley, Buchanan J., Saunders, Syrett (Coffill), Massey, Buchanan D.
Referee: R. Bridges (Deeside).

AFC Bournemouth (1) 2 *(Compton, Morgan)*

Manchester U (2) 2 *(Muhren, Coppell* pen*)* 13,226

Manchester U won 4-2
AFC Bournemouth: Leigh; Heffernan, Sulley, Spackman, Brignull, Compton, Carter, Williams, Morgan, Dawtry (Funnell), Graham.
Manchester U: Bailey; Duxbury, Albiston, Wilkins (Macari), Grimes, Buchan, Robson, Muhren, Stapleton, Whiteside, Coppell.
Referee: D. Vickers (Ilford).

Brighton & HA (0) 0

Tottenham H (0) 1 *(Crooks)* 20,763

Tottenham won 2-1
Brighton & HA: Moseley; Shanks, Pearce, Grealish (Ritchie), Foster, Gatting, Smillie, McNab, Robinson, Ward, Smith.
Tottenham H: Clemence; Price, O'Reilly, Miller, Lacy, Hazard, Brooke, Falco (Mazzon), Mabbutt, Villa, Crooks.
Referee: G. Napthine (Loughborough).

Cambridge U (1) 1 *(Christie)*

Barnsley (1) 3 *(Donaldson og, Birch, Banks)* 3717

Barnsley won 5-2
Cambridge U: Webster; Donaldson, Murray, Turner, Fallon, Lockhart, Christie, O'Neill, Reilly, Streete, Finney.
Barnsley: Horn; Joyce, Chambers, Glavin, Banks, McCarthy, Souter, Campbell, Parker, Ranson, Birch.
Referee: D. V. Reeves (Middlesex).

Cardiff C (0) 1 *(Hemmerman)*

Arsenal (2) 3 *(Sunderland, Woodcock, Davis)* 11,632

Arsenal won 5-2
Cardiff C: Thomas; Jones (Ingram), Bodin, Micallef, Dwyer, Bennett G., Bennett D., Tong, Gibbins, Hemmerman, Lewis.
Arsenal: Wood; Hollins, Sansom, Talbot, O'Leary, Whyte, Davis, Sunderland, Robson, Woodcock, Rix.
Referee: V. Callow (Solihull).

Charlton Ath (1) 2 *(Hales 2* [1 pen]*)*

Luton T (0) 0 5973

Luton won 3-2
Charlton Ath: Johns; Curtis, Walker (Ferns), Robinson, Elliott, Berry, Harris, Bullivant, White, Hales, O'Sullivan.
Luton T: Findlay; Thomas, Money, Horton, Goodyear, Donaghy, Hill, Stein, Walsh, Turner, Moss.
Referee: L. C. Shapter (Torquay).

Coventry C (0) 0

Fulham (0) 0 8217

After Extra Time. Coventry won on away goals rule
Coventry C: Sealey; Thomas, Roberts, Butterworth, Dyson, Gillespie, Jacobs, Francis (Whitton), Melrose, Thompson, Hunt.
Fulham: Peyton; Hopkins, Parker, O'Driscoll, Brown, Gale, Reeves (Scott), Carr, Coney, Houghton, Lewington.
Referee: R. Milford (Bristol).

Crystal Palace (2) 2 *(Mabbutt, Hilaire)*

Peterborough U (1) 1 *(Clarke)* 4502

Crystal Palace won 4-1
Crystal Palace: Barron; Gilbert, Lovell, Hughton, Cannon, Nebbeling, Giles, Brooks, Edwards, Mabbutt, Hilaire.
Peterborough U: Seaman; Rayment, Imlach, Gynn, Slack, Rodaway, Clarke, Quow, Collins, Benjamin, Chard.
Referee: A. R. Glasson (Salisbury).

Liverpool (2) 2 *(Whelan, Lawrenson)*

Ipswich T (0) 0 17,698

Liverpool won 4-1
Liverpool: Grobbelaar; Neal, Kennedy, Thompson, Whelan, Hansen, Dalglish (Hodgson), Lee, Rush, Lawrenson, Souness.
Ipswich T: Cooper; Burley, Mills, Thijssen, Osman, Butcher, Wark (O'Callaghan), McCall, Mariner, Brazil, Gates.
Referee: A. Challinor (Rotherham).

Middlesbrough (1) 1 *(Hankin)*

Burnley (0) 1 *(Laws* pen*)* 10,328

Burnley won 4-3
Middlesbrough: Platt; Brownlie, Bolton, Otto, Baxter, Wood, Mowbray, Cochrane, Hankin, Nattrass (MacDonald), Kennedy.
Burnley: Stevenson; Laws, Wharton, McGee, Phelan, Holt, Dobson, Stephen, Hamilton, Cavener, Young.

Notts Co (0) 1 *(Hunt)*

Aston Villa (0) 0 *6921* *Notts Co won 3-1*
Notts Co: Avramovic; Goodwin, Worthington, Hunt, Kilcline, Richards, Chiedozie, Christie, McCulloch, Clarke (Hooks), Mair.
Aston Villa: Rimmer; Jones (Deacy), Gibson, Williams, McNaught, Mortimer, Bremner, Shaw, Geddis, Cowans, Morley.
Referee: R. Chadwick (Darwen).

Oldham Ath (0) 1 *(McDonough)*

Gillingham (0) 0 3302

Gillingham won 2-1
Oldham Ath: Goram, Hoolikin, Ryan, Bowden, Edwards, Futcher, McDonough, Atkinson, Heston, Wylde (Humphries), Palmer.
Gillingham: Hillyard; Sharpe, Adams, Bruce, Shaw, Tydeman, Price, Johnson, Cascarino (Powell), Grewcock, Weatherly.
Referee: G. Courtney (Spennymoor).

Preston NE (0) 1 *(Elliott)*

Norwich C (1) 2 *(Bertschin, Bennett)* 6082

Norwich C won 4-2
Preston NE: Litchfield; Walsh, McAteer, Clark, Westwell, Gowling, Kelly, Bell, Elliott, Naughton, Bruce.
Norwich C: Woods; Haylock, Van Wyk, Mendham (Jack), Walford, Watson, Barham, O'Neill, Deehan, Bertschin, Bennett.
Referee: K. A. Redfern (Whitley Bay).

QPR (0) 0

Rotherham U (0) 0 9653

Rotherham U won 2-1
QPR: Hucker; Neill, Dawes, Waddock, Hazell, Fenwick, Micklewhite, Sealy (Stewart), Allen, Stainrod, Gregory.
Rotherham U: Mountford; Forrest, Breckin, McEwan, Hughes, Green, Henson, Gow, Gooding, Seasman, McBride.
Referee: C. Thomas (Porthcawl).

Southampton (2) 4 *(Wallace, Cassells, Armstrong, Moran)*

Colchester U (1) 2 *(Allinson* pen*, Lyons)* 9676

Southampton won 4-2
Southampton: Shilton; Rofe (Puckett), Holmes, Williams, Nicholl, Wright, Ball, Moran, Cassells, Armstrong, Wallace.
Colchester U: Walker; Cook, Coleman, Hunter, Wignall, Ward, Allinson, Osborne, Lyons, McDonough, Leslie.
Referee: E. A. Read (Bristol).

Sheffield W (0) 1 *(Taylor)*

Bristol C (0) 1 *(Chandler)* 7920

After Extra Time. Sheffield W won 3-2
Sheffield W: Bolder; Sterland, Bailey, Smith, Lyons, Shirtliff, Paul (Pickering), Megson, Taylor, Bannister, McCulloch, Owen.
Bristol C: Shaw; Newman, Thompson (Kelly), Nicholls, Boyle, Riley, Economou, Ritchie, Chandler, Cooper, Crawford.
Referee: N. Midgeley (Salford).

Sheffield U (2) 5 *(Charles, Morris* pen*, Edwards 3)*

Grimsby T (1) 1 *(Moore K.)* 13,637

Sheffield U won 8-4
Sheffield U: Conroy; Richardson, Garner, Arnott, West, Houston, Morris, Charles, Young (Edwards), Curran, Brazil.
Grimsby T: Grotier; Moore D., Crosby, Waters, Cooper (O'Dell), Moore K., Cumming, Whymark, Drinkell, Stone, Ford.
Referee: N. J. Ashley (Nantwich).

Swansea C (1) 3 *(Latchford 3)*

Bristol R (0) 0 9755

Swansea C won 3-1
Swansea C: Davies; Evans, Hadziabdic, Charles, Kennedy, Rajkovic, Curtis, James R., James L., Stanley, Latchford.
Bristol R: Kite; Slatter, Williams B., Williams G., Parkin, McCaffery, Holloway, Williams D., Withey, Randall, Barrett (Channon).
Referee: L. M. Robinson (Sutton Coldfield).

Watford 2

Bolton W 1 11,520

Watford won 4-2
Watford: Sherwood; Rice, Rostron, Taylor, Sims, Jackett, Callaghan, Blissett, Jenkins, Lohman (Bolton), Barnes.
Bolton W: McDonagh; Berry, Bennett, McGovern, Jones, McElhinney, Foster, Rudge, Reid (Thompson), Moores, Hoggan.
Referee: A. W. Grey (Gt Yarmouth).

West Ham (0) 2 *(Goddard, Clark)*

Stoke C (0) 1 *(Watson)* 18,348

West Ham U won 3-2
West Ham U: Parkes; Stewart, Lampard, Bonds, Martin, Devonshire, Van der Elst, Goddard, Clark, Allen, Pike (Neighbour).
Stoke C: Harrison; Pike, Hampton, Bracewell, Watson, McAughtrie, Maguire, McIlroy, O'Callaghan, Thomas, Chamberlain M.
Referee: J. E. Martin (Alton).

27 OCT

Blackburn R (0) 0

Brenford (0) 0 4137

Brentford won 3-2
Blackburn R: Gennoe; Brannigan, Rathbone, Randell, Mail, Fazackerley, Miller, Hamilton, Bell, Garner, Brotherston.
Brentford: Roche; Rowe, Harris, McNicholl, Whitehead, Booker, Kamara, Joseph, Mahoney, Bowles, Roberts.
Referee: A. Seville (Birmingham).

Bradford C (2) 4 *(Mellor, Cooke 2, Gallagher)*

Rochdale (0) 0 3206

Bradford C won 5-0
Bradford C: McManus; Podd, Chapman, Lester (Gallagher), Jackson, McFarland, Gray, Ellis, Cooke, McNiven, Mellor.
Rochdale: Pearce; Keenan, Snookes, Warriner (Hamilton), Taylor, Williams, Thompson, Martinez, French, Wellings, Hilditch.
Referee: A. Saunders (Newcastle).

Everton (1) 2 *(King, Johnson)*

Newport Co (1) 2 *(Tynan, Oakes)* 8941

Everton won 4-2
Everton: Southall; Borrows, Bailey, Higgins, Wright, McMahon, Heath (sub Richardson), Johnson, Sharp, King, Sheedy.
Newport Co: Kendall; Jones, Relish, Bailey, Oakes, Stroud, Lowndes, Aldridge, Tynan, Vaughan, Elsey.
Referee: P. N. Willis (Co Durham).

Leicester C (0) 0

Lincoln C (0) 1 *(Bell* pen*)* 10,000

Lincoln C won 3-0
Leicester C: Wallington; Ramsey, Friar, McDonald, May, O'Neill, Lynex, Lineker, Smith A., English, Wilson.
Lincoln C: Felgate; Carr, Neale, Cockerill, Peake, Thompson, Burke, Turner, Hobson, Bell, Shipley.
Referee: J. Worrall (Warrington).

Manchester C (2) 2 *(Power 2)*

Wigan Ath (0) 0 16,083

Manchester C won 3-1
Manchester C: Corrigan; Ranson, McDonald, Bond, Power, Caton, Tueart, Reeves, Cross, Hartford, Baker.
Wigan Ath: Tunks; McMahon, Cribley, Lowe (Butler), Walsh, Methven, Glenn, Weston, Bradd, Houghton, Gemmill.
Referee: J. Hunting (Leicester).

Newcastle U (1) 1 *(Clarke)*

Leeds U (1) 4 *)Saunders, Worthington, Butterworth, Connor)* 24,173

After Extra Time. Leeds won 4-2
Newcastle U: Carr; Anderson, Saunders, Martin, Clarke (Craggs), Haddock, Keegan, McCreery, Varadi, Wharton, Waddle.
Leeds U: Lukic; Cherry, Gray E. (Connor), Burns, Hart, Thomas, Hird, Butterworth, Worthington, Gray F., Graham.
Referee: C. N. Seel (Carlisle).

Oxford U (0) 1 *(Biggins)*

Huddersfield T (0) 0 4982

Huddersfield T won 2-1
Oxford U: Butcher; Linney, Fogg, Train (Thomas), Briggs, Shotton, Brock, Barnett, Vinter, Biggins, Hebberd.
Huddersfield T: Cox; Brown, Burke, Stanton, Sutton, Hanvey, Lillis, Doyle, Russell, Wilson, Cowling.
Referee: K. Salmon (Barnet).

Sunderland (4) 5 *(Chisholm 2, Hindmarch, Rowell, McCoist)*

Wolverhampton W (0) 0 11,901

Sunderland won 6-1
Sunderland: Turner; Nicholl, Munro, Hindmarch, Chisholm, Pickering, Buckley, Rowell, McCoist, West, Venison.
Wolverhampton W: Burridge; Humphrey, Palmer, Hibbitt, Pender, Coy, Daniel, Clarke, Gray, Eves, Matthews (Butler).
Referee: D. Scott (Burnley).

Tranmere R (1) 1 *(Aspinall)*

Chelsea (1) 2 *(Robson 2)* 4579

Chelsea won 5-2
Tranmere R: Endersby; Mathias, Burgess, Parry, Powell, Williams, Mungall, Ferguson (Moody), Kerr, Aspinall, Griffiths.
Chelsea: Francis; Locke, Hutchings, Pates, Droy, McAndrew, Walker, Bumstead, Robson, Speedie, Fillery.
Referee: D. W. Civil (Birmingham).

WBA (1) 3 *(Whitehead, Cross, Regis)*

Nottingham F (1) 1 *(Birtles)* 6536

Nottingham F won 7-4
WBA: Godden; Batson, Statham, Zondervan, Wile, Robertson, Jol, Brown, Regis (Cowdrill), Cross, Whitehead.
Nottingham F: Van Breukelan; Swain, Gunn, Todd, Fairclough, Bowyer, Proctor (Plummer), Wallace, Birtles, Wigley, Robertson.
Referee: B. Stevens (Stonehouse).

Milk Cup Third Round

BRENTFORD CREATE CLUB HISTORY

After a hard fought home draw with First Division Swansea City, **Brentford** pulled off the result of the round by scoring in the first minute and eventually clinching a 2-1 victory.

Burnley also claimed a First Division scalp by winning 2-1 at Coventry City, and **Bradford City** thrilled a home crowd of 15,568 with a 0-0 draw with Manchester United.

Free-scoring **Nottingham Forest** followed their six goals in the previous round with a storming 7-2 defeat of high-flying Watford, while two Yorkshire 'local derbies' saw **Barnsley** beat Sheffield United 3-1 in front of 25,207, at Bramall Lane, and **Huddersfield Town** achieve another away win, at Leeds, where the attendance was 24,215.

Poor Bradford City eventually enjoyed a share of a good replay crowd at Old Trafford, but lost the services of Roy McFarland who moved to Derby County before the second tie was played.

Other replay winners were **Southampton** who thrashed Manchester City 4-0, **Arsenal** who beat Everton 3-0 and **Norwich City** and **West Ham United** who put out Sunderland and Lincoln City respectively. **Lincoln City** took the 'Hammers' to extra time and once again their form suggested that they might well emulate the feats of Watford, the club managed by their 'old boy', Graham Taylor who had progressed to the First Division so quickly and successfully.

On to the Fourth Round moved **11** clubs from the First Division, **2** from the Second and **3** from the Third.

THIRD ROUND

9 NOV

Birmingham C (1) 3 *(Handysides, Dillon* pen, *Curbishley)*

Derby Co (0) 1 *(Swindlehurst)* 12,475

Birmingham C: Coton; Hagan, Van den Hauwe, Stevenson, Blake, Broadhurst, Dillon, Brazier, Ferguson, Curbishley, Handysides.
Derby Co: Cherry; Barton, Buckley, Powell, Foster, McAlle, Brolly, Mills (Wilson), Hill, Swindlehurst, Dalziel.
Referee: K. Salmon (Barnet).

Brentford (1) 1 *(Roberts)*

Swansea C (1) 1 *(Latchford)* 15,261

Brentford: Roche; Rowe (Booker), Harris, McNichol, Whitehead, Hurlock, Kamara, Joseph, Mahoney, Bowles, Roberts.
Swansea C: Davies; Stanley, Habziabdic, Charles, Kennedy, Rajkovic, Curtis, James R., Mahoney, Stevenson, Latchford.
Referee: T. D. Spencer (Salisbury).

Coventry C (1) 1 *(Hunt)*

Burnley (1) 2 *(McGee 2)* 7559

Coventry C: Suckling; Thomas, Roberts, Butterworth, Dyson, Gillespie, Hendrie (Whitton), Singleton, Melrose, Thompson, Hunt.
Burnley: Stevenson; Laws, Cassidy, Phelan, Holt, Scott, Dobson, Steven, Taylor, McGee, Young.
Referee: T. G. Bune (Cranleigh).

Crystal Palace (0) 1 *(Mabbutt)*

Sheffield W (2) 2 *(Megson, Bannister)* 8146

Crystal Palace: Barron; Hinshelwood, Murphy, Lovell (Langley), Cannon, Nebbeling, Giles, Hughton, Edwards, Mabbutt, Hilaire.
Sheffield W: Bolder; Sterland, Bailey, Pickering, Lyons, Shelton, Megson, Taylor, Bannister, McCulloch (Shirtliff, Peter), Mirocevic.
Referee: H. W. King (Merthyr Tydfil).

Everton (1) 1 *(Stevens)*

Arsenal (0) 1 *(Robson)* 13,089

Everton: Arnold; Stevens, Ratcliffe, Higgins, Wright, McMahon, Heath, Johnson (Irvine), Sharp, King, Richardson.
Arsenal: Jennings; O'Shea, Sansom, Talbot, O'Leary, Whyte, Davis, Sunderland (Chapman), Robson, Woodcock, Rix.
Referee: D. Hutchinson (Harrogate).

Gillingham (1) 2 *(Johnson, Price)*

Tottenham H (2) 4 *(Crooks 2, Archibald 2)* 14,466

Gillingham: Hillyard; Sharpe, Adams, Bruce, Shaw (Price), Tydeman, Powell, Johnson, Cascarino, Grewcock, Weatherly.
Tottenham H: Clemence; Hughton, Miller, Hazard, Lacy, Perryman, Mabbutt, Archibald, Brooke, Hoddle, Crooks.
Referee: A. Robinson (Waterlooville).

Luton T (1) 4 *(Kellock 2, Bunn, Moss)*

Blackpool (1) 2 *(Bamber, Pashley)* 6409

Luton T: Judge; Stephens, Money, Horton, Goodyear (Bunn), Donaghy, Kellock, Stein, Walsh, Fuccillo, Moss.
Blackpool: Hesford; Simmonite, Hart, Deary, Hetzke, Serella, Hockaday, Stewart, Bamber, Pashley, Downes.
Referee: A. Gunn (Sussex).

Notts Co (2) 2 *(Christie* pen, *Hooks)*

Chelsea (0) 0 8852

Notts Co: Avramovic; Goodwin, Worthington, Hooks, Kilcline (Lahtinen), Richards, Chiedozie, Christie, McCulloch, Clarke, Mair.
Chelsea: Francis; Locke, Hutchings, Pates, Droy, Chivers, Canoville, Bumstead, Lee, Speedie (Robson), Fillery.
Referee: N. Midgeley (Salford).

Sheffield U (1) 1 *(Edwards)*

Barnsley (0) 3 *(Glavin 2, Kenworthy og)* 25,207

Sheffield U: Conroy; Atkins, Garner, McHale, Houston, Kenworthy, Morris, Trusson, Edwards, Hatton, Charles.
Barnsley: Horn; Joyce, Chambers, Glavin, Banks, McCarthy, Souter, Campbell (Airey), Parker, Ronson, Birch.
Referee: P. Tyldesley (Stockport).

10 NOV

Bradford C (0) 0

Manchester U (0) 0 15,568

Bradford C: McManus; Podd, Chapman, Lester, Cooke, McFarland, Ellis, Jackson, Campbell, McNiven, Mellor.
Manchester U: Bailey; Duxbury, Albiston, Moses, McGrath, McQueen, Robson, Muhren, Stapleton, Whiteside, Coppell.
Referee: J. Hunting (Leicester).

Leeds U (0) 0

Huddersfield T (0) 1 *(Cowling)* 24,215

Leeds U: Lukic; Cherry, Gray E. (Hird), Burns, Hart, Thomas, Connor, Butterworth, Worthington, Gray F., Graham.
Huddersfield T: Cox; Brown, Burke, Stanton, Sutton, Hanvey, Lillis, Doyle, Russell, Wilson, Cowling.
Referee: G. Courtney (Spennymoor).

Lincoln C (0) 1 *(Bell)*

West Ham U (1) 1 *(Goddard)* 13,899

Lincoln C: Felgate; Carr, Neale, Cockerill, Peake, Thompson, Burke, Turner, Hobson, Bell, Shipley.
West Ham U: Parkes; Stewart, Brush, Bonds, Martin, Devonshire, Orr (Van der Elst), Goddard, Clark, Allen, Pike.
Referee: K. Baker (Rugby).

Liverpool (0) 1 *(Johnston)*

Rotherham U (0) 0 20,412

Liverpool: Grobbelaar; Neal, Kennedy, Thompson, Johnston, Hansen, Hodgson, Lee, Rush, Lawrenson, Souness.
Rotherham U: Mountford; Forrest, Breckin, Henson, Hughes, Green, Towner, Gooding, Moore, Seasman, McBride.
Referee: C. Seel (Carlisle).

Manchester C (1) 1 *(Tueart* pen*)*

Southampton (1) 1 *(Wright)* 17,463

Manchester C: Corrigan; Ranson, McDonald, Bond, Power, Caton, Tueart, Reeves, Cross, Hartford, Baker.
Southampton: Shilton; Agboola, Rofe, Williams, Nicholl, Wright, Holmes, Moran, Cassells, Armstrong, Wallace.
Referee: A. Challinor (Maltby).

Nottingham F (4) 7 *(Young, Proctor 2, Birtles 2, Bowyer, Wallace)*

Watford (2) 3 *(Jenkins 2, Taylor)* 14,873

Nottingham F: Van Breukelen; Swain, Gunn, Todd (Walsh), Young, Bowyer, Proctor, Wallace, Birtles, Hodge, Robertson.
Watford: Sherwood; Rice, Rostron, Taylor, Sims (Johnson), Bolton, Callaghan, Blissett, Jenkins, Jackett, Barnes.
Referee: R. Chadwick (Darwen).

Sunderland (0) 0

Norwich C (0) 0 10,934

Sunderland: Turner; Nicholl, Munro, Atkins Elliott, Pickering, Buckley (Chisholm), Rowell, McCoist, West, Venison.
Norwich C: Woods; Haylock, Hareide, McGuire, Walford, Watson, Barham, O'Neill, Deehan, Van Wyk, Bennett.
Referee: N. Glover (Chorley).

THIRD ROUND REPLAYS

17 NOV

Swansea C (0) 1 *)Loveridge)*

Brentford (1) 2 *(Roberts, Mahoney T.)* 6676

Swansea: Davies; Stanley, Hadziabdic, Charles, Robinson (Loveridge), Rajkovic, James L., James R., Mahoney J., Stevenson, Latchford.
Brentford: Roche, Rowe, Harris, McNichol, Whitehead, Hurlock, Kamara, Joseph, Mahoney T., Bowles, Roberts.
Referee: E. A. Read (Bristol).

23 NOV

Arsenal (2) 3 *(Sunderland 3)*

Everton (0) 0 19,547

Arsenal: Wood; O'Shea, Sansom, Talbot, O'Leary, Whyte, Davis, Sunderland, Robson, Woodcock (Chapman), Rix.
Everton: Arnold; Stevens, Ratcliffe, Wright, Higgins, McMahon, Heath, Johnson, Sharp, King, Sheedy.
Referee: M. J. Taylor (Kent).

24 NOV

Manchester U (3) 4 *(Moses, Albiston, Moran, Coppell)*

Bradford C (0) 1 *(Campbell)* 24,507

Manchester U: Bailey; Duxbury, Albiston, Moses, Moran, McQueen, Robson, Muhren, Stapleton, Macari, Coppell (Whiteside).
Bradford C: McManus, Podd, Chapman, McCall, Cooke, Jackson, Gray, Ellis, Campbell, McNiven, Mellor.
Referee: J. E. Bray (Hinckley).

Norwich (1) 3 *(Watson 2, Deehan)*

Sunderland (1) 1 *(Cummins)* 19,776

Norwich C: Woods; Haylock, Van Wyk, McGuire, Walford, Watson, Barham, O'Neill, Deehan, Bertschin (Donowa), Jack.
Sunderland: Turner; Venison, Munro, Atkins, Elliott, Nicholl, Buckley (Hindmarch), Rowell, West, McCoist, Cummins.
Referee: M. Scott (Nottingham).

Southampton (1) 4 *(Williams, Moran, Puckett, Holmes)*

Manchester C (0) 0 13,298

Southampton: Shilton; Agboola, Rofe, Williams, Nicholl, Wright, Holmes, Moran, Cassells (Puckett), Armstrong, Wallace.
Manchester C: Corrigan; Ransom, McDonald, Bond, Power, Caton, Reid, Reeves, Cross, Hartford, Baker.
Referee: C. Thomas (Porthcawl).

29 NOV

West Ham U (1) 2 *(Stewart, Clark)*

Lincoln C (0) 1 *(Clark og)* 13,686

West Ham U: Parkes; Stewart, Lampard, Bonds, Martin, Neighbour (Barnes), Van Der Elst, Goddard, Clark, Allen, Pike.
Lincoln C: Felgate; Carr, Neale, Cockerill, Peake, Thompson, Hibberd, Turner, Hobson, Bell, Shipley.
Referee: A. J. Glasson (Salisbury).

Milk Cup Fourth Round

BURNLEY MARCH ON

An 'own goal' seventeen minutes from time ruined the evening for First Division Birmingham City, having pulled two goals back against **Burnley**, while an all Second Division match, which was yet another Milk Cup Yorkshire 'Derby', produced the biggest attendance of the round at Hillsborough, where 33,354 saw **Wednesday** beat Barnsley 1-0.

The big names moved confidently forward with home victories, so **Arsenal**, **Liverpool**, **Manchester United**, **Nottingham Forest**, and **Tottenham Hotspur** were safely through and were joined by **West Ham United** who followed an exciting 3-3 draw at Meadow Lane with a conclusive 3-0 victory over Notts County at home. This meant six First Division clubs were joined by Second Division Burnley and Sheffield Wednesday, in the Quarter-Finals.

FOURTH ROUND

30 NOV

Arsenal (1) 1 *(Sunderland* pen*)*

Huddersfield T (0) 0 17,742

Arsenal: Wood; O'Shea, Sansom, Talbot, O'Leary, Whyte, Davis, Sunderland, Robson, Woodcock, Rix.
Huddersfield T: Cox; Brown, Burke, Stanton, Sutton, Hanvey, Lillis, Doyle, Russell, Wilson, Cowling.
Referee: A. Seville (Birmingham).

ACTION FROM THE MILK CUP

Above: Rotherham United 'keeper Ray Mountford makes one of many good saves from QPR's John Gregory in a 2nd round, 2nd leg match at Loftus Road.

Below: Steve Archibald in action for Tottenham Hotspur against Luton Town in a 4th round clash at White Hart Lane.

Burnley (2) 3 *(McGee, Taylor, Brazier og)*

Birmingham C (0) 2 *(Evans, Handysides)* 10,405

Burnley: Stevenson; Laws, Wharton, Cassidy, Phelan, Flynn, Dobson, Steven, Hamilton, Taylor, McGee.
Birmingham C: Coton; Hagan (Phillips), Brazier, Stevenson, Blake, Broadhurst, Dillon, Evans, Ferguson, Curbishley, Handysides.
Referee: T. Mills (Barnsley).

Liverpool (1) 2 *(Lawrenson, Fairclough)*

Norwich C (0) 0 13,235

Liverpool: Grobbelaar; Neal, Kennedy, Thompson, Johnston, Hansen, Dalglish, Lee, Rush, Lawrenson (Fairclough), Souness.
Norwich C: Woods; Haylock, Van Wyk, McGuire, Walford, Watson, Barham, O'Neill, Deehan, Bertschin, Hareide.
Referee: D. Shaw (Cheshire).

Sheffield W (1) 1 *(McCulloch)*

Barnsley (0) 0 33,354

Sheffield W: Bolder; Sterland, Bailey, Smith, Lyons, Mirocevic, Megson, Taylor, Baninister, McCulloch, Pearson.
Barnsley: Horn; Joyce, Chambers, Glavin, Banks, McCarthy, Souter, Campbell, Parker, Ronson, Barrowclough.
Referee: K. Walmsley (Blackpool).

1 DEC

Manchester U (1) 2 *(McQueen, Whiteside)*

Southampton (0) 0 28,378

Manchester U: Bailey; Duxbury, Albiston, Moses, Moran, McQueen, Robson, Muhren, Stapleton, Whiteside, Coppell.
Southampton: Shilton; Agboola, Rofe (Puckett), Williams, Nicholl, Wright, Holmes, Moran, Cassells, Armstrong, Wallace.
Referee: G. Courtney (Spennymoor).

Nottingham F (1) 2 *(Wallace, Robertson* pen*)*

Brentford (0) 0 16,479

Nottingham F: Van Breukelen; Swain, Gunn, Todd, Young, Bowyer, Proctor (Walsh), Wallace, Birtles, Hodge, Robertson.
Brentford: Roche; Rowe, Wilkins, Booker, Whitehead, Harris, Kamara, Joseph, Mahoney (Bowen), Bowles, Roberts.
Referee: J. Worrall (Warrington).

Tottenham H (0) 1 *(Villa)*

Luton T (0) 0 27,461

Tottenham H: Clemence; Hughton, Price, O'Reilly, Villa, Roberts, Mabbutt, Archibald, Galvin, Hoddle, Crooks.
Luton T: Findlay; Stephens, Money, Horton, Goodyear, Donaghy, Hill, Stein, Walsh, Turner (Antic), Moss.
Referee: J. E. Martin (Alton).

7 Dec

Notts Co (0) 3 *(McCulloch, Christie, Hunt)*

West Ham U (0) 3 *(Van der Elst 3)* 7525

Notts Co: Avramovic; Benjamin, Worthington, Hunt, Kilcline, Richards, Chiedozie, Christie, McCulloch, Hooks, Mair.
West Ham U: Parkes; Stewart, Lampard, Orr, Martin, Devonshire, Van der Elst, Goddard, Clark, Allen, Pike.
Referee:

FOURTH ROUND REPLAY

21 DEC

West Ham U (1) 3 *(Stewart* pen, *Clark, Allen)*

Notts Co (0) 0 12,906

West Ham U: Parkes; Stewart, Brush, Orr, Martin, Devonshire, Van der Elst, Goddard, Clark, Allen, Pike.
Notts Co: Avramovic; Benjamin, Worthington, Hunt, Kilcline, Richards, Chiedozie, Christie, Fashanu, Goodwin, Clarke (Mair).
Referee: L. Shapter (Torquay).

Milk Cup Quarter Finals

HERO HAMILTON

The draw suggested that all four home clubs should qualify for the Semi-Finals and in three games, despite tight battles, at Highbury and Anfield, the results went to form.

Arsenal's new signing from Yugoslavia, Petrovic, starred in their 1-0 victory over Sheffield Wednesdayin front of 30,937 and despite a late equaliser from Allen, West Ham couldn't prevent **Liverpool**'s captain, Souness from hitting a winner with just four minutes to go.

Manchester United found their tie a little easier as they beat Forest 4-0, but the 'Result of the Round' was undoubtedly produced by **Burnley**. The Lanchashire club who were struggling near the foot of Division Two and whose Manager and loyal servant, Brian Miller, had been relieved of his duties on the day of the match, took on the might of Spurs and recorded an unbelievable 4-1 victory at White Hart Lane. Their goals were shared by Billy Hamilton and Graham Roberts – of Spurs! The club had once before reached the Semi-Finals when they lost to the eventual winners Swindon Town in season 1968–69.

QUARTER-FINALS

18 JAN

Arsenal (0) 1 *(Woodcock)*

Sheffield W (0) 0 *30,937* *Arsenal:* Jennings; Hollins, Sansom, Nicholas, O'Leary, Robson, Davis, Sunderland, Petrovic, Woodcock, Rix.
Sheffield W: Bolder; Sterland, Bailey, Smith, Lyons, Shelton, Megson, Taylor, Bannister, Pearson, Mirocevic.
Referee: L. Burden (Corfe Mullen).

Liverpool (0) 2 *(Hodgson, Souness)*

West Ham U (0) 1 *(Allen)* 23,953

Liverpool: Grobbelaar; Neal, Kennedy, Lawrenson, Johnston (Whelan), Hansen, Dalglish, Lee, Rush, Hodgson, Souness.
West Ham U: Parkes; Cowie, Gallagher, Bonds, Martin, Devonshire, Van der Elst, Goddard, Clark, Allen, Pike.
Referee: M. J. Heath (Stoke).

19 JAN

Manchester U (1) 4 *(McQueen 2, Coppell, Robson)*

Nottingham F (0) 0 44,400

Manchester U: Bailey; Duxbury, Albiston, Moses, Moran, McQueen, Robson, Muhren, Stapleton, Whiteside, Coppell.
Nottingham F: Sutton; Swain, Gunn, Todd, Young, Bowyer, Proctor (Gray), Wallace, Davenport, Hodge, Robertson.
Referee: B. Newsome (Broseley).

THE MILK CUP FINAL AT WEMBLEY

Above: Norman Whiteside celebrates the opening goal for United.

Below: A victorious Liverpool team celebrate with a lap of honour after defeating Manchester United 2-1.

Tottenham H (0) 1 *(Gibson)*

Burnley (0) 4 *(Roberts 2 ogs, Hamilton 2)* 30,771

Tottenham H: Clemence; Hughton, O'Reilly, Roberts, Villa (Brooke), Perryman, Ardiles, Archibald, Gibson, Hoddle, Mabbutt.
Burnley:

Referee:

Milk Cup Semi-Finals

LIVERPOOL AND MANCHESTER UNITED IN THE FINAL

With three teams from Lancashire contesting the semi-finals it was not surprising that the North West was captivated by four intriguing ties.

Arsenal gave themselves an obscure hope of salvaging something from the round after their 2-4 defeat at home. But their two late goals, after **United** had swept them off a frozen Highbury pitch with a devastating display of aggressive football did little to compensate for the visitors' four goals.

In the second leg, it was Steve Coppell, enjoying a superb season, who scored his sixth Milk Cup goal of the campaign finally to snuff out any idea 'The Gunners' had of hauling themselves back into the reckoning. A total of 99,771 watched two tremendous semi-finals and little did they all realise that the two 'giants' would be meeting in yet another mammoth battle in the FA Cup later in the season.

At the time of their first meeting, **Liverpool** were in such devastating form as they dominated the First Division championship race, that little **Burnley** were given no chance despite their superb quarter-final victory at White Hart Lane. However, although the scoreline looked secure enough, a dazzling mid-field display by Trevor Steven and two missed chances by the hard working Derek Scott, certainly gave the home side a severe fright. A 1-0 second leg victory was little consolation for two fine performances by the Second Division side but quite amazingly at this stage they could still look forward to the FA Cup.

SEMI-FINAL, FIRST LEG

8 FEB

Liverpool (1) 3 *(Souness, Neal* pen, *Hodgson)*

Burnley (0) 0 33,520

Liverpool: Grobbelaar; Neal, Kennedy, Lawrenson, Johnston (Whelan), Hansen, Dalglish, Lee, Rush, Hodgson, Souness.
Burnley: Stevenson; Laws, Donachie, Phelan, Dobson, Flynn, Scott, Steven, Hamilton, Taylor, Young.
Referee: R. Lewis (Great Bookham).

15 FEB

Arsenal (0) 2 *(Woodcock, Nicholas)*

Manchester U (2) 4 *(Whiteside, Stapleton, Coppell 2)* 43,136

Arsenal: Jennings; Hollins, Sansom, Robson, O'Leary (Davis), Nicholas, Talbot, Meade, Petrovic, Woodcock, Rix.
Manchester U: Bailey; Duxbury, Albiston, Moses, Moran, McQueen, Robson, Muhren, Stapleton, Whiteside, Coppell.
Referee: J. Martin (Alton).

SECOND LEG

Burnley (0) 1 *(Scott)*

Liverpool (0) 0 22,350

Burnley: Stevenson; Laws, Donachie, Scott, Dobson, Phelan, Steven, Flynn, Hamilton, Taylor (Cassidy), Young.
Liverpool: Grobbelaar; Neal, Kennedy, Lawrenson, Johnston, Hansen, Dalglish, Lee, Rush, Hodgson (Whelan), Souness.
Referee: K. Walmsley (Blackpool).

22 FEB

Manchester U (0) 2 *(Coppell, Moran)*

Arsenal (0) 1 *(Meade)* 56,635

Manchester U won 6-3
Manchester U: Bailey; Duxbury, Albiston, Moses, Moran, McQueen, Robson (Wilkins), Muhren, Stapleton, Whiteside, Coppell.
Arsenal: Jennings; Hollins (Davis), Sansom, Robson, Whyte, Nicholas, Talbot, Meade, Petrovic, Woodcock, Rix.
Referee: L. Shapter (Torquay).

FINAL (at Wembley)

26 MAR

Liverpool (0) 2 *(Kennedy, Whelan) aet*

Manchester U (1) 1 *(Whiteside)* 100,000

Receipts: £730,000 90 Minutes: 1-1
Liverpool: Grobbelaar; Neal, Kennedy, Lawrenson, Whelan, Hansen, Dalglish, Lee, Rush, Johnston (Fairclough), Souness.
Manchester U: Bailey; Duxbury, Albiston, Moses, Moran (Macari), McQueen, Wilkins, Muhren, Stapleton, Whiteside, Coppell.

The holders of the Milk Cup retained the trophy deservedly after a thrilling afternoon's football. Although a goal down after only twelve minutes to a well executed piece of Whiteside virtuosity, the team never lost their composure and attacked methodically for the rest of the match against an opposition, which found itself forced by injuries and Liverpool pressure into constant defence.

The pressure eventually told and Kennedy equalised with a long shot, which bounced slightly unluckily for Bailey. Once again, Liverpool needed extra-time but by then United were crippled by a succession of injuries which made it necessary for Moran to be substituted and left McQueen limping but still making gallant attempts to contribute. With the match almost one hundred minutes old Whelan did yet another sortie down the left flank and when he saw most of his options closed he sent over a swinging shot which well beat the desperate dive of Bailey.

The worthy winners then produced a magnificent gesture when Souness, the captain, insisted that the retiring Mr Bob Paisley should accept the Cup, which he did to a great ovation. Who can say that there is no sentiment left in Football?

Liverpool and Nottingham Forest are the only two clubs to have played in three consecutive League/Milk Cup Finals and **Liverpool** achieved a record by winning the trophy on all three occasions.

FOOTBALL LEAGUE TROPHY 1982–83

13 AUG

Colchester U (0) 3 *(Coleman, Allinson, Lyons)*

Southend U (0) 1 *(Cusack)* 1622

Colchester U: Walker; Cook, Coleman, Groves, Wignall, Hunter, Allinson, Osborne, Lyons, McDonough, Adcock.
Southend U: Keeley; Stead, Yates, Pountney, Clark, Cusack (Hadley), Pennyfather, Phillips, Mercer, Nelson, Greaves.

Shrewsbury T (0) 1 *(Foster)*

Tranmere R (0) 1 *(Kerr)* 886

Shrewsbury T: Ogrizovic; Williams, Cross, Turner, Pearson, MacLaren, Sankey, Petts, Brown (Nardiello), Foster, Bates.
Tranmere R: Endersby; Muncall, Burgess, Parry, Hamilton, Williams, Powell, McKenna, Kerr, Hutchinson, Griffiths.

14 AUG

AFC Bournemouth (1) 2 *(Dantry, Spackman)*

Aldershot (1) 2 *(McDonald, Sanford)* 2412

AFC Bournemouth: Leigh; Dawkins, O'Donnell, Spackman, Brignull, Compton, Dawtry (Heffernan), Williams, Goddard, Funnell, Carter.
Aldershot: Johnson; Scott, Gillard, Briley (Lucas), Wood, Jopling, Shrubb, Banton, Sanford, McDonald, Brodie.

Bradford C (1) 1 *(Campbell)*

Halifax T (0) 0 2420

Bradford C: Burton; Podd (McCall), Watson, Lester (Chapman), Cooke, Jackson, Gray, Gallagher, Campbell, McNiven, Mellor.
Halifax T: Smelt; Nobbs, Carr, Evans, Smith, Hendrie, Hallybone, Davison, Saniforth, Spooner, Ward.

Brentford (0) 2 *(Joseph, Rogers)*

C Palace (0) 2 *(Edwards, Brooks)* 3397

Brentford: Borota; Tucker, Wilkins, McNichol, Whitehead, Hurlock, Kamara (Booker), Mahoney, Joseph, Bowles, Roberts.
C Palace: Barron; Hinshelwood, Hughton, Cannon, Nebelling, Gilbert, Langley (Brooks), Wilkins, Edwards, Murphy, Giles.

Chesterfield (1) 1 *(Henson)*

Chester (0) 1 *(Sloan)* 1149

Chesterfield: Turner; Bellamy, O'Neill, Wilson, Green, Henson, Windridge, Kowalski, Athersych, Henderson, Carroll.
Chester: Millington; Bradley, Lane, Storton, Zelem, Dean, Sloan, Allen, Simpson (Harrison), Ludlam, Cooke.

Exeter C (0) 2 *(Kellow, Pratt)*

Bristol C (0) 1 *(Economou)* 1040

Exeter C: Bond; Kirkup, Viney, McEwan (Howarth), Roberts, Rogers M., Harle, Rogers P., Kellow, Delve, Pratt.
Bristol C: Shaw; Stevens, Llewellyn, Newman, Boyle, Riley (Thompson), Economou, Musker, Chandler, Ritchie, Bray (Cooper).

Hartlepool U (1) 1 *(Lawrence)*

Hull C (2) 2 *(Whitehurst, Marwood)* 962

Hartlepool U: Watson; Lowe (Staff), Stimpson, Hogan, Fagan, Brown, Linighan (Bainbridge), Lawrence, Newton, Linacre, Johnson.
Hull C: Norman; McNeil, Thompson, Roberts J. D., Skipper, Booth (Davis), Marwood, McClaren, Whitehurst, Mutrie (Flounders), Roberts G. W.

Millwall (0) 0

Wimbledon (1) 1 *(Evans)* 2632

Millwall: Gleasure; Stevens, Madden, Chatterton, Allardyce, Roberts, Massey, Carr, Aylott, Martin, Horrix (Neal).
Wimbledon: Beasant; Peters, Thomas, Morris, Tagg, Evans (Entwistle), Dibble, Ketteridge, Leslie, Downes, Hodges (Gage).

Newport Co (0) 0

Torquay U (1) 1 *(Gallagher)* 1501

Newport Co: Kendall; Jones, Relish, Thorpe, Davies (Gwyther), Johnson, Lowndes (Williams), Aldridge, Tynan, Vaughan, Bailey.
Torquay U: Horn; Doyle, Jones, Wilson, Wigginton, Sheridan, Grapes, Brown, Cooper, Rioch, Gallagher.

Norwich C (1) 3 *(Watson, Deehan, Jack)*

Northampton T (0) 0 1801

Norwich C: Woods; Haylock, Walford, McGuire, Alexander, Watson, Barham, O'Neill, Deehan (Symonds), Jack (Mountford), Mendham.
Northampton T: Kendall; Brady, Phillips, Coffill, Burrows, Heeley, Denyer (Buchanan), Saxby, Saunders, Syrett, Massey.

Peterborough U (2) 4 *(Linton, Benjamin 2, Chard)*

Mansfield T (0) 1 *(Bird)* 1885

Peterborough U: Seaman; Winters, Collins, Gynn, Firm, Rodaway, Slack, Linton, Cooke, Benjamin, Chard.
Mansfield T: Arnold; Bird, Kennedy, Bell, Boam, Calderwood, Mathews, Cannell(Waddle), Dungworth, Laidlaw, Nicholson (Caldwell).

Reading (0) 2 *(Beavon* pen, *Bason)*

Oxford U (1) 1 *(Hebberd* pen*)* 1601

Reading: Fearon; Williams, White, Beavon, Hicks, Barnes, Earles, Kearney (Bason), Dixon, Docherty (Sanchez), Donnellan.
Oxford U: Burton; Linney, Grant (Smithers), Train, Briggs, Shotton, Brock, Vinter, Biggins (Thomas), Hebberd, Barnett.

Scunthorpe U (1) 1 *(Hunter)*

Lincoln C (1) 1 *(Cunningham)* 1022

Scunthorpe U: Neenan (Johnson); Keeley, Pointon, Fowler, Boxall, Hunter, Cammack (Cowling), Parkinson, O'Berg, Telfer, Leman.
Lincoln C: Naylor; Moyses (Brown), Carr, Cockerill, Peake, Thompson, Hibberd, Turner, Hobson, Cunningham, Shipley.

Sheffield U (0) 1 *(Kenworthy)*

Grimsby T (1) 3 *)Drinkell 3)* 5381

Sheffield U: Waugh; Atkins, Henderson, McHale, McPhail, Kenworthy, King, Arnott, Edwards, Hatton, Curran.
Grimsby T: Batch; Moore D., Crombie, Waters, Cooper, Moore K. T., Ford (Steeples), Whymark, Drinkell, Bonnyman (Beacock), Speight.

Watford (2) 4 *(Jenkins 2, Terry, Gilligan)*

Orient (1) 1 *(Rice og)* 4063

Watford: Sherwood; Rice, Pritchett, Blissett, Terry, Sims, Callaghan (Johnson), Armstrong, Jenkins (Gilligan), Jackett, Barnes.
Orient: Day; Fisher, Peach, Osgood, Foster (Silkman), Vincent, Sussex, Gray, Houchen, Blackhall, Taylor.

16 AUG

Mansfield T (1) 1 *(Ayre)*

Northampton T (1) 2 *(Massey, Syrett)* 1485

Mansfield T: Arnold; Bird, Kennedy, Bell, Boam, Ayre, Mathews, Caldwell, Waddle, Dungworth, Laidlaw.
Northampton T: Kendall; Brady, Phillips, Gage, Saunders, Heeley, Saxby, Perrin, Syrett, Massey, Buchanan.

Southend U (1) 1 *(Phillips)*

Orient (1) 1 *(Taylor)* 2025

Southend U: Cawston; Dudley, Yates, Greaves, May, Cusack, Pountney, Phillips, Mercer, Nelson, Otulakowski.
Orient: Day; Fisher, Peach, Foster, Gray (Cunningham), Sussex, Godfrey, Vincent, Houchen, Silkman (Blackhall), Taylor.

17 AUG

Aldershot (1) 1 *(McDonald)*

Oxford U (1) 3 *(Foley 2, Thomas)* 1191

Aldershot: Johnson; Scott, Gillard, Shrubb, Wood, Jopling, Lucas, Banton, Sanford, McDonald, Brodie.
Oxford U: Butcher; Fogg, Grant (Linney), Brock (Smithers), Briggs, Shotton, Jones, Vinter, Foley, Thomas, Hebberd.

Bristol C (0) 1 *(Ritchie)*

Torquay U (0) 0 1421

Bristol C: Shaw; Stevens, Newman, Nicholls, Boyle, Riley, Economou, Musker, Chandler, Ritchie, Crawford.
Torquay U: Horn; Doyle, Jones, Wilson, Wigginton, Sheridan, Grapes, Brown, Cooper, Rioch, Gallagher.

Chesterfield (0) 1 *(Walker)*

Shrewsbury T (0) 0 1177

Chesterfield: Turner; Bellamy, Partridge, Wilson, Green, Henson, Robinson, Henderson, Walker, Kowalski, Carroll (Windridge).
Shrewsbury T: Ogrizovic; Williams, Cross, Petts, Pearson, Johnson, Sankey, Nardiello, Brown, Foster, Bates

C Palace (0) 1 *(Edwards)*

Wimbledon (0) 0 2852

C Palace: Fry; Hinshelwood, Hughton, Cannon, Nebbelling, Lovell, Langley (Annon), Wilkins, Edwards, Brooks, Giles.
Wimbledon: Beasant; Peters (Gage), Thomas, Morris, Tagg, Evans, Dibble, Ketteridge, Leslie, Downes, Hodges.

Halifax T (1) 1 *(Davison)*

Hull C (0) 0 1323

Halifax T: Smelt; Nobbs, Carr, Evans, Smith, Hendrie, Hallybone, Davison, Staniforth, Spooner, Ward.
Hull C: Norman; McNeil, Thompson, Roberts J.D., Skipper, Booth, Marwood, Davis, Whitehurst, Mutrie, Roberts G. W. (McLaren).

Millwall (0) 3 *(Hayes, Aylott, Neal)*

Brentford (0) 0 2105

Millwall: Gleasure; Stevens, Robinson, Chatterton, Allardyce, Madden, Hayes, Carr, Aylott, Martin, Neal.
Brentford: Borota; Tucker, Wilkins, Spencer, Whitehead, Hurlock, Kamara, Johnson, Bowen, Booker, Roberts.

Scunthorpe U (0) 0

Sheffield U (0) 0 1874

Scunthorpe U: Johnson; Keeley, Pointon, Fowler, Boxall, Hunter, O'Berg (Gilbert), Parkinson (Duncan), Cowling, Telfer, Leman.
Sheffield U: Waugh (Conroy); Henderson, Atkin, McHale, Houston, Kenworthy, Morris (Hatton), Arnott, Edwards, King, Curran.

Watford (0) 2 *(Blissett, Jenkins)*

Colchester U (0) 1 *(Allinson)* 3837

Watford: Sherwood; Rice (Patching), Rostron, Lohman, Terry (Armstrong), Sims, Callaghan, Blissett, Jenkins, Jackett, Barnes.
Colchester U: Walker; Cook, Coleman, Groves, Wignall, Beattie (Hunter), Allinson, Osborne, Lyons (McDonough), Bremner, Leslie.

18 AUG

Hartlepool U (0) 0

Bradford C (1) 4 *(Campbell 2, Gray, Watson)* 655

Hartlepool U: Watson; Taylor, Stimpson, Hogan, Linighan, Brown, Fagan, Lawrence, Newton, Linacre (Staff), Johnson.
Bradford C: McManus; McCall, Chapman, Watson, Cooke, Jackson, Gray, Gallagher, Campbell, McNiven, Mellor.

Lincoln C (1) 2 *(Cockerill, Thompson)*

Grimsby T (0) 1 *(Drinkell)* 1430

Lincoln C: Felgate; Carr, Moyses, Cockerill, Peake, Thompson, Hibberd, Turner, Harlow, Cunningham, Shipley.
Grimsby T: Batch; Moore D., Crosby, Waters, Cooper, Moore K. T., Kilmore, Whymark (Ford), Drinkell, Bonnyman, Crombie.

Newport Co (4) 5 *(Bailey 2, Gwyther, Tynan, Elsey)*

Exeter C (1) 1 *(Howarth)* 1084

Newport Co: Kendall; Jones, Vaughan, Bailey, Relish (Thorpe), Stroud, Lowndes, Gwyther (Aldridge), Tynan, Elsey, Williams.
Exeter C: Shepherd (Bond); Howarth, Viney, McEwan, Roberts, Rogers, Pullar, Longden, Pratt, Delve, Gibson (Walter).

Norwich C (1) 6 *(Jack 3, O'Neill, Deehan, Downs)*

Peterborough U (2) 2 *(Clarke, Benjamin)* 1901

Norwich C: Woods; Haylock, Walford, McGuire, Smith, Watson, Barham, O'Neill, Deehan, Jack, Downs.
Peterborough U: Seaman; Winters, Imlach, Gynn, Firm, Rodaway (Cooke), Slack, Linton, Clarke, Benjamin, Chard.

Reading (2) 4 *(Dixon 2, Beavon* pen, *Donnellan)*

AFC Bournemouth 1 *(Graham, Dawtry)* 1136

Reading: Fearon; Williams, Richardson, Beavon, Hicks, Wood, Bason, Earles, Dixon, Doherty, Donnellan.
AFC Bournemouth: Allen; Heffernan, Mundee, Spackman, Brignull, Compton (Morgan), Dawtry, Williams, Funnell, Graham, Crawford.

Tranmere R (1) 2 *(Kerr, Griffiths)*

Chester (0) 1 *(Simpson)* 1143

Tranmere R: Endersby; Mungall, Burgess, Parry (Brown), Hamilton, Williams, Mathias, McKenna, Kerr, Hutchinson, Griffiths.
Chester: Harrington; Bradley, Lane, Storton (Edwards), Zelem, Dean (Ludlam), Sloan, Allen, Simpson, Johnson, Thomas.

21 AUG

Aldershot (2) 3 *(Banton, Shrubb, Sanford)*

Reading (1) 3 *(Dixon 3)* 1744

Aldershot: Johnson (Holmes); Andruszewski (Scott); Gillard, Briley, Wood, Jopling, Shrubb, Banton, Sanford, McDonald, Brodie.
Reading: Fearon; Williams, Richardson, Beavon, Hicks, Barnes (Doherty), Earles, Kearney, Dixon, McMahon (Sanchez), Donnellan.

AFC Bournemouth (1) 3 *(Morgan, Spackman, Dawtry)*

Oxford U (0) 0 2561

AFC Bournemouth: Allen; Heffernan, Sulley, Spackman, Brignull, Impey, Dawtry, O'Donnell, Morgan, Funnell Crawford.
Oxford U: Burton; Fogg, Grant (Linney), Brock, Briggs, Shotton, Barnett, Foley, Vinter (Biggins), Hebberd, Thomas.

Bristol C (1) 1 *(Chandler)*

Newport Co (2) 4 *(Bailey, Lowndes, Tynan, Williams)* 2252

Bristol C: Shaw; Stevens, Llewellyn, Nicholls, Newman, Riley, Economou (Cooper), Musker, Chandler (Panes), Ritchie, Crawford.
Newport Co: Kendall; Jones, Vaughan, Bailey, Thorpe, Stroud, Lowndes, Gwyther (Aldridge), Tynan, Elsey, Williams (Fleming).

Chester (2) 5 *(Edwards, Thomas 2* [1 pen], *Sloan, MacLaren og)*

Shrewsbury T (0) 0 1022

Chester: Millington; Edwards, Bradley, Zelem, Lane, Dean, Sloan, Johnson, Simpson, Cooke, Thomas.
Shrewsbury T: Ogrizovic (Perks); Williams, Cross, Griffin, Pearson, Petts, Sankey, Foster, Brown, Nardiello, MacLaren.

C Palace (0) 0

Millwall (2) 3 *(Neal 2, Chatterton)* 4844

C Palace: Barron; Hinshelwood, Hughton, Cannon, Nebbeling, Gilbert, Langley, Brooks (Annon), Edwards, Wilkins (Lovell), Giles.
Millwall: Gleasure; Stevens, Robinson, Chatterton, Allardyce, Madden, Massey, Carr (Shinton), Aylott, Neal, West.

Grimsby T (0) 2 *(Waters* pen, *Moore K.)*

Scunthorpe U (0) 0 2334

Grimsby T: Batch; Moore D., Crombie, Waters, Cooper, Moore K. T., Ford (Cumming), Whymark (Kilmore), Drinkell, Bonnyman, Speight.
Scunthorpe U: Neenan; Totty (Keely), Pointon, Fowler, Boxall, Hunter, O'Berg (Gilbert), Parkinson, Cowling, Duncan, Leman.

Halifax T (2) 3 *(Davison 3)*

Hartlepool U (0) 0 928

Halifax T: Smelt; Nobbs, Carr, Evans (Goodman), Smith, Hendrie, Hallybone, Davison, Staniforth, Spooner, Ward.
Hartlepool U: Wright; Taylor, Stimpson, Hogan (Lowe), Bird, Brown, Bainbridge, Lawrence (Gollogly), Newton, Staff, Johnson.

Hull C (0) 0

Bradford C (0) 0 3202

Hull C: Norman; Swann, Thompson, Roberts, Skipper, Booth, Marwood, Davis, Whitehurst, Mutrie, McClaren (Flounders).
Bradford C: McManus; McCall, Chapman, Watson, Cooke, Jackson, Gray, Gallagher (Ellis), Campbell, McNiven, Mellor.

Lincoln C (1) 3 *(Cockerill 2, Cunningham)*

Sheffield U (1) 1 *(Edwards)* 2820

Lincoln C: Naylor; Carr, Moyses, Cockerill, Peake, Thompson, Hibberd, Turner, Hobson, Cunningham, Shipley.
Sheffield U: Waugh (Conroy); Henderson, Kenworthy, McHale, McPhail, Houston, Morris, Arnott, Edwards, King, Curran.

Mansfield T (0) 1 *(Dungworth)*

Norwich C (1) 3 *(Mendham, Walford, Deehan)* 1985

Mansfield T: Arnold; Bell, Kennedy, Woodhead, Bird, Ayre, Mathews, Caldwell, Waddle, Dungworth, Laidlaw.
Norwich C: Woods; Mendham, Walford, McGuire, Smith, Watson, Barham (Haylock), O'Neill, Deehan, Jack, Downs.

Orient (0) 0

Colchester U (0) 2 *(Lyons 2)* 1384

Orient: Day; Fisher (McNeil), Peach, Foster, Gray, Sussex, Godfrey (Blackhall), Donn, Houchen, Silkman, Taylor.
Colchester U: Walker; Cook, Coleman, Groves, Wignall, Beattie (Hunter), Allinson, Osborne, Lyons, McDonough, Adcock (Leslie).

Peterborough U (3) 5 *(Slack, Cooke, Benjamin 2, Chard)*

Northampton T (0) 2 *(Syrett, Denyer)* 2192

Peterborough U: Seaman; Winters, Imlach, Gynn, Firm, Rodaway, Slack, Linton, Cooke, Benjamin, Chard.
Northampton T: Kendall; Brady, Phillips, Gage, Saunders (Burrows), Heeley, Saxby, Perrin, Syrett, Massey, Buchanan (Denyer).

Southend U (1) 1 *(Pennyfather)*

Watford (1) 4 *(Blissett, Armstrong, Lohman, May og)* 2447

Southend U: Cawston; Stead, Yates, Clark (Greaves), May (Hadley), Cusack, Pountney, Phillips, Mercer, Pennyfather, Otulakowski.
Watford: Sherwood; Patching, Rostron, Blissett, Sims (Pritchett), Bolton, Callaghan (Lohman), Armstrong, Jenkins, Jackett, Barnes.

Torquay U (1) 3 *(Cooper 2, Wilson)*

Exeter C (1) 2 *(Pullar, Pratt)* 2384

Torquay U: Horn; Doyle, Jones, Wilson, Wigginton, Sheridan, Grapes, Bishop, Cooper, Rioch, Gallagher.

Exeter C: Bond; Kirkup, Viney, McEwan, Howarth, Rogers M., Harle, Rogers P., Kellow, Delve, Pullar (Pratt).

Tranmere R (0) 1 *(Hutchinson)*

Chesterfield (0) 1 *(Wilson* pen*)* 949

Tranmere R: Endersby; Mungall, Burgess, Parry, Hamilton, Williams, Powell (Maguire), Hutchinson, Kerr, McKenna (Mathias), Griffiths.
Chesterfield: Turner; Bellamy, Partridge, Wilson, Green, Henson (Robinson), Dawson, Henderson, Walker, Kowalski (O'Neill), Windridge.

Wimbledon (0) 1 *(Evans)*

Brentford (1) 3 *(Johnson, Mahoney, Roberts)* 2019

Wimbledon: Beasant; Gage, Thomas (Wadley), Galliers, Morris, Jones, Entwistle, Ketteridge, Evans, Hodges (Downes), Dibble.
Brentford: Borota; Rowe, Wilkins, McNichol, Whitehead, Hurlock, Kamara, Johnson, Mahoney, Bowles (Booker), Roberts.

FINAL GROUP TABLES

	P	*W*	*D*	*L*	*F*	*A*	*Pts*
Watford	3	3	0	0	10	3	9+2=11
Colchester U	3	2	0	1	6	3	6+1= 7
Southend U	3	0	1	2	3	8	1
Orient	3	0	1	2	2	7	1
	3	1	1	1	7	3	4+1= 5
Chester							
Tranmere R	3	1	2	0	4	3	5
Chesterfield	3	1	2	0	3	2	5
Shrewsbury T	3	0	1	2	1	7	1
	3	2	1	0	9	6	7+2= 9
Reading							
Bournemouth	3	1	1	1	7	6	4+1= 5
Oxford U	3	1	0	2	4	6	3+1= 4
Aldershot	3	0	2	1	6	8	2+1= 3
	3	2	1	0	5	0	7+1= 8
Bradford C							
Halifax T	3	2	0	1	4	1	6+1= 7
Hull C	3	1	1	1	2	2	4
Hartlepool U	3	0	0	3	1	9	0
	3	2	0	1	6	1	6+2= 8
Millwall							
Brentford	3	1	1	1	5	6	4+1= 5
C Palace	3	1	1	1	3	5	4
Wimbledon	3	1	0	1	2	4	3
	3	2	0	1	9	3	6+2= 8
Newport Co							
Torquay U	3	2	0	1	4	3	6+1= 7
Exeter C	3	1	0	2	5	9	3
Bristol C	3	1	0	2	3	6	3
	3	3	0	0	12	3	9+3=12
Norwich C							
Peterborough U	3	2	0	1	11	9	6+2= 8
Northampton T	3	1	0	2	4	9	3
Mansfield T	3	0	0	3	3	9	0
	3	2	1	0	6	3	7+1= 8
Lincoln C							
Grimsby T	3	2	0	1	6	3	6+1= 7
Scunthorpe U	3	0	2	1	1	3	2
Sheffield U	3	0	1	2	2	6	1

A bonus point was awarded to each club scoring three or more goals in a match.

QUARTER-FINALS

6 DEC

Millwall (0) 1 *(West)*

Bradford C (1) 1 *(Lester)* 2081

aet. Millwall won 4-2 on penalties.
Millwall: Sansome; Stevens, Stride, Carr, Allardyce, Roberts (Madden), Hayes, McLeary, Aylott, Horrix (Shinton), West.
Bradford C: McManus; Podd, Chapman, Lester, Cooke, Jackson, Ellis (Black), Gray, Campbell McNiven (Gallagher), Mellor.

8 DEC

Lincoln C (0) 3 *(Bell 3)*

Norwich C (0) 1 *(Fashanu)* 3853

Lincoln C: Felgate; Carr, Neale (Strodder), Cockerill, Peake, Simmonite, Burke, Turner, Hobson (Hall), Bell, Shipley.
Norwich C: Woods; Haylock, Hareide, McGuire, Walford (Mountford), Donawa (Alexander), Jack, O'Neill, Deehan, Fashanu, Van Wyk.

Reading (1) 5 *(Dunnellan 3, Dixon, O'Sullivan)*

Watford (1) 3 *(Barnes 2, Blissett)* 3517

Reading: Judge; Williams, Richardson, Beavon, Hicks, Wood, Bason, Sanchez (Doherty), Dixon, O'Sullivan, Donnellan.
Watford: Steele; Palmer, Rostron (Price), Patching, Sims, Bolton, Callaghan, Blissett, Barnes, Jobson, Johnson.

26 JAN

Chester (0) 0

Newport Co (0) 0 999

aet. Chester won 5-4 on penalties.
Chester: Harrington; Bradley, Lane, Storton, Zelem, Workman (Johnson), Sloan, Simpson (Cook), Thomas, Ludlam, Wilson.
Newport Co: Kendall; Davies, Vaughan, Bailey, Oakes, Stroud, Lowndes, Aldridge, Tynan, Pulis (Fleming), Elsey.

SEMI-FINALS

26 JAN

Reading (0) 1 *(Doherty)*

Millwall (2) 3 *(Hayes, Neal, Horrix)* 2658

Reading: Judge; Tutty, Richardson, Beavon, Hicks, White, Mathews, Donnellan (Bason), Williams, Doherty, McMahon.
Millwall: Gleasure; Martin, Stride (Robinson), Madden, Allardyce, Roberts, Hayes, Neal, Aylott (Horrix), Massey, Chatterton.

8 FEB

Chester (1) 1 *(Thomas)*

Lincoln C (1) 3 *(Cockerill, Peake, Turner)* 1058

Chester: Harrington; Edwards (Cooke), Lane, Bradley, Zelem, Workman, Sloan, Simpson, Thomas, Williams, Wilson.
Lincoln C: Felgate; Simmonite, Neale, Hobson, Peake, Carr, Burke (Cockerill), White (Turner), Kelly, Bell, Shipley.

FINAL

20 APRIL

Lincoln C (1) 2 *(Burke 2)*

Milwall (0) 3 *(Martin 2, McLeary)* 3142

Lincoln C: Felgate; Carr, Simmonite, Brazier, Peake, Strodder, Burke, Turner, Hobson, Moss, Shipley.
Millwall: Sansome; Stevens, Stride, Madden, Allardyce, Roberts, Massey, Neal, Martin, Robinson, McLeary.

THE FA CUP

THE FOOTBALL ASSOCIATION OFFICIALS

Patron: HER MAJESTY THE QUEEN

President: HRH THE DUKE OF KENT

Honorary Vice-Presidents

His Grace the Duke of Marlborough; The Rt Hon The Earl of Derby MC; Air Vice-Marshal D. P. Hall CBE, AFC; Lt-General Sir Edward A. Burgess KCB, OBE; Admiral Sir Anthony Morton KCB; Right Hon Earl of Harewood LLD; Sir Stanley Rous CBE; Sir Cyril Hawker; Sir Walter Winterbottom CBE; Sir Denis Follows CBE; Rt Hon Lord Westwood FCIS, JP

Chairman of the Council

F. A. Millichip (West Bromwich Albion FC)

Vice-Chairman of the Council

A. D. McMullen MBE (Bedfordshire FA)

Life Vice-Presidents

I. Robinson (Liverpool County FA);
E. D. Smith MBE, JP (Cumberland FA);
Sir Harold Thompson CBE, FRS (Oxford University);
S. W. Jacobs (Oxfordshire FA);

Vice-Presidents

A. D. McMullen MBE (Bedfordshire FA);
W. H. Webster CBE (Cambridge University);
E. Kangley (Sheffield and Hallamshire FA);
E. A. Brown (Suffolk County FA);
R. Wragg (Football League);
R. H. Speake

Secretary

E. Croker, 16 Lancaster Gate, London W2 3LW

FA Challenge Cup Committee

L. Smart (Chairman), H. W. Alcock, W. T. Annable, E. A. Brown, R. Daniel, Dr C. Grossmark, W. S. G. Needham, G. H. C. Needler, C. H. Norsworthy, F. V. Peart, A. L. Smith, J. Smith, D. Tana

FA CUP FINALS 1872–1982

1872 and 1874–92	Kennington Oval	1911	Replay at Old Trafford
1873	Lillie Bridge	1912	Replay at Bramall Lane
1893	Fallowfield, Manchester	1915	Old Trafford, Manchester
1894	Everton	1920–22	Stamford Bridge
1895–1914	Crystal Palace	1923 to date	Wembley
1901	Replay at Bolton	1970	Replay at Old Trafford
1910	Replay at Everton	1981	Replay at Wembley

Year	*Winners*	*Runners-up*	*Score*
1872	Wanderers	Royal Engineers	1-0
1873	Wanderers	Oxford University	2-0
1874	Oxford University	Royal Engineers	2-0
1875	Royal Engineers	Old Etonians	2-0 (after 1-1 draw)
1876	Wanderers	Old Etonians	3-0 (after 1-1 draw)
1877	Wanderers	Oxford University	2-1 (aet)
1878	Wanderers*	Royal Engineers	3-1
1879	Old Etonians	Clapham R	1-0
1880	Clapham R	Oxford University	1-0
1881	Old Carthusians	Old Etonians	3-0
1882	Old Etonians	Blackburn R	1-0
1883	Blackburn Olympic	Old Etonians	2-1 (aet)
1884	Blackburn R	Queen's Park, Glasgow	2-1
1885	Blackburn R	Queen's Park, Glasgow	2-0
1886	Blackburn R†	WBA	2-0 (after 0-0 draw)
1887	Aston Villa	WBA	2-0
1888	WBA	Preston NE	2-1
1889	Preston NE	Wolverhampton W	3-0
1890	Blackburn R	Sheffield W	6-1
1891	Blackburn R	Notts Co	3-1
1892	WBA	Aston Villa	3-0
1893	Wolverhampton W	Everton	1-0
1894	Notts Co	Bolton W	4-1
1895	Aston Villa	WBA	1-0
1896	Sheffield W	Wolverhampton W	2-1
1897	Aston Villa	Everton	3-2
1898	Nottingham F	Derby Co	3-1
1899	Sheffield U	Derby Co	4-1
1900	Bury	Southampton	4-0
1901	Tottenham H	Sheffield U	3-1 (after 2-2 draw)
1902	Sheffield U	Southampton	2-1 (after 1-1 draw)
1903	Bury	Derby Co	6-0
1904	Manchester C	Bolton W	1-0
1905	Aston Villa	Newcastle U	2-0
1906	Everton	Newcastle U	1-0
1907	Sheffield W	Everton	2-1
1908	Wolverhampton W	Newcastle U	3-1
1909	Manchester U	Bristol C	1-0
1910	Newcastle U	Barnsley	2-0 (after 1-1 draw)
1911	Bradford C	Newcastle U	1-0 (after 0-0 draw)
1912	Barnsley	WBA	1-0 (aet)
1913	Aston Villa	Sunderland	1-0 (after 0-0 draw)
1914	Burnley	Liverpool	1-0
1915	Sheffield U	Chelsea	3-0
1920	Aston Villa	Huddersfield T	1-0 (aet)
1921	Tottenham H	Wolverhampton W	1-0
1922	Huddersfield T	Preston NE	1-0
1923	Bolton W	West Ham U	2-0
1924	Newcastle U	Aston Villa	2-0
1925	Sheffield U	Cardiff C	1-0
1926	Bolton W	Manchester C	1-0
1927	Cardiff C	Arsenal	1-0
1928	Blackburn R	Huddersfield T	3-1
1929	Bolton W	Portsmouth	2-0
1930	Arsenal	Huddersfield T	2-0
1931	WBA	Birmingham	2-1
1932	Newcastle U	Arsenal	2-1
1933	Everton	Manchester C	3-0
1934	Manchester C	Portsmouth	2-1
1935	Sheffield W	WBA	4-2
1936	Arsenal	Sheffield U	1-0
1937	Sunderland	Preston NE	3-1
1938	Preston NE	Huddersfield T	1-0 (aet)
1939	Portsmouth	Wolverhampton W	4-1
1946	Derby Co	Charlton Ath	4-1 (aet)
1947	Charlton Ath	Burnley	1-0 (aet)
1948	Manchester U	Blackpool	4-2
1949	Wolverhampton W	Leicester C	3-1
1950	Arsenal	Liverpool	2-0
1951	Newcastle U	Blackpool	2-0
1952	Newcastle U	Arsenal	1-0

What a comeback! In one of the most thrilling of post-war FA Cup finals, Stanley Mortensen scores the second of his two goals as Blackpool battled back from 1-3 to a 4-3 victory.

Year	*Winners*	*Runners-up*	*Score*
1953	Blackpool	Bolton W	4-3
1954	WBA	Preston NE	3-2
1955	Newcastle U	Manchester C	3-1
1956	Manchester C	Birmingham C	3-1
1957	Aston Villa	Manchester U	2-1
1958	Bolton W	Manchester U	2-0
1959	Nottingham F	Luton T	2-1
1960	Wolverhampton W	Blackburn R	3-0
1961	Tottenham H	Leicester C	2-0
1962	Tottenham H	Burnley	3-1
1963	Manchester U	Leicester C	3-1
1964	West Ham U	Preston NE	3-2
1965	Liverpool	Leeds U	2-1 (aet)
1966	Everton	Sheffield W	3-2
1967	Tottenham H	Chelsea	2-1
1968	WBA	Everton	1-0 (aet)
1969	Manchester C	Leicester C	1-0
1970	Chelsea	Leeds U	2-1 (aet)
	(after 2-2 draw, after extra time, at Wembley)		
1971	Arsenal	Liverpool	2-1 (aet)
1972	Leeds U	Arsenal	1-0
1973	Sunderland	Leeds U	1-0
1974	Liverpool	Newcastle U	3-0
1975	West Ham U	Fulham	2-0
1976	Southampton	Manchester U	1-0
1977	Manchester U	Liverpool	2-1
1978	Ipswich T	Arsenal	1-0
1979	Arsenal	Manchester U	3-2
1980	West Ham U	Arsenal	1-0
1981	Tottenham H	Manchester C	3-2
	(after 1-1 draw, after extra time, at Wembley)		
1982	Tottenham H	QPR	1-0
	(after 1-1 draw, after extra time, at Wembley)		

* *Won outright, but restored to the Football Association.*

† *A special trophy was awarded for third consecutive win.*

The 1927 FA Cup final, and Cardiff's Ferguson raises his arms in joy because Arsenal goalkeeper Lewis has just let what looked like an easy save slip through his arms and over the line. Cardiff held the 1-0 scoreline to become the first and only team to take the Cup out of England.

FA CUP WINS

Aston Villa 7, Tottenham H 7, Blackburn R 6, Newcastle U 6, Arsenal 5, The Wanderers 5, WBA 5, Manchester U 5, Sheffield U 4, Bolton W 4, Wolverhampton W 4, Manchester C 4, Sheffield W 3, Everton 3, West Ham U 3, Bury 2, Old Etonians 2, Preston NE 2, Nottingham F 2, Sunderland 2, Liverpool 2, Barnsley 1, Blackburn Olympic 1, Blackpool 1, Bradford C 1, Burnley 1, Cardiff C 1, Charlton Ath 1, Chelsea 1, Clapham R 1, Derby Co 1, Huddersfield T 1, Notts Co 1, Old Carthusians 1, Oxford University 1, Portsmouth 1, Royal Engineers 1, Leeds U 1, Southampton 1, Ipswich T 1.

APPEARANCES IN FINALS

Arsenal 11, Newcastle U 11, WBA 10, Aston Villa 9, Blackburn R 8, Manchester U 9, Manchester C 8, Wolverhampton W 8, Bolton W 7, Preston NE 7, Everton 7, *Tottenham H 7, Liverpool 6, Old Etonians 6, Sheffield U 6, Huddersfield T 5, *The Wanderers 5, Sheffield W 5, Derby Co 4, Oxford University 4, Royal Engineers 4, Leeds U 4, Leicester C 4, West Ham U 4, Blackpool 3, Burnley 3, Chelsea 3, Portsmouth 3, Sunderland 3, Southampton 3, Barnsley 2, Birmingham C 2, *Bury 2, Cardiff C 2, Charlton Ath 2, Clapham R 2, Notts Co 2, Queen's Park (Glasgow) 2, *Nottingham F 2, *Blackburn Olympic 1, *Bradford C 1, Bristol C 1, *Old Carthusians 1, Luton T 1, Fulham 1, *Ipswich T 1, QPR 1, Brighton & HA 1.

* *Denotes undefeated.*

APPEARANCES IN SEMI-FINALS

WBA 19, Everton 18, Aston Villa 17, Blackburn R 16, Arsenal 16, Manchester U 16, Sheffield W 14, Derby Co 13, Liverpool 13, Newcastle U 13, Wolverhampton W 13, Bolton W 12, Tottenham H 11, Sunderland 10, Preston NE 10, Manchester C 10, Sheffield U 10, Chelsea 10, Nottingham F 9, Birmingham C 9, Burnley 8, Southampton 8, Huddersfield T 7, Leeds U 7, Leicester C 7, Old Etonians 6, Oxford University 6, The Wanderers 5, Notts Co 5, Fulham 5, West Ham U 5, Portsmouth 4, Queen's Park (Glasgow) 4, Royal Engineers 4, Blackpool 3, Cardiff C 3, Clapham R 3, Millwall 3, Old Carthusians 3, The Swifts 3, Stoke C 3, Ipswich T 3, Barnsley 2, Blackburn Olympic 2, Bristol C 2, Bury 2, Charlton Ath 2, Grimsby T 2, Swansea T 2, Swindon T 2, Crystal Palace 2, Bradford C 1, Cambridge University 1, Crewe Alex 1, Darwen 1, Derby Junction 1, Glasgow R 1, Hull C 1, Marlow 1, Old Harrovians 1, Oldham Ath 1, Port Vale 1, Reading 1, Shropshire W 1, York C 1, Luton T 1, Norwich C 1, Watford 1, Orient 1, QPR 1, Brighton & HA 1.

FA CUP FINALISTS 1872–1982

Some goalscorers in the early years are not available.
R: replay; aet: after extra time.

1871–72 THE WANDERERS R. de C. Welch; C. W. Alcock, M. P. Betts, A. G. Bonsor, E. E. Bowen, W. P. Crake, T. C. Hooman, E. Lubbock, A. C. Thompson, R. W. S. Vidal, C. H. R. Wollaston. (In alphabetical order.) *Scorer:* 'A. H. Chequer' (M. P. Betts).
1-0 ROYAL ENGINEERS Capt. Marindin; Capt. Merriman, Lieut. Addison; Lieut. Creswell, Lieut. Mitchell, Lieut. Renny-Tailyour; Lieut. Rich, Lieut. Goodwyn, Lieut. Muirhead, Lieut. Cotter, Lieut. Bogle.

1872–73 THE WANDERERS E. E. Bowen; C. M. Thompson, R. de C. Welch; Hon. A. F. Kinnaird, L. S. Howell, C. H. R. Wollaston; J. R. Sturgiss, Rev. H. H. Stewart, W. S. Kenyon-Slaney, R. K. Kingsford, A. G. Bonsor. *Scorers:* Wollaston, Kinnaird.
2-0 OXFORD UNIVERSITY A. Kirke-Smith; A. J. Leach, C. C. Mackarness; F. H. Birley, C. J. Longman, F. B. Chappell-Maddison; H. B. Cixon, W. B. Paton, R. W. S. Vidal, W. E. Sumner, C. J. Ottaway.

1873–74 OXFORD UNIVERSITY C. E. B. Neapean; C. C. Mackarness, F. H. Birley; F. T. Green, R. W. S. Vidal, C. J. Ottaway; R. H. Benson, F. J. Patton, W. S. Rawson, F. B. Chappell-Maddison, Rev. A. H. Johnson. *Scorers:* Mackarness, Patton.
2-0 ROYAL ENGINEERS Capt. Merriman; Major Marindin, Lieut. G. W. Addison; Lieut. G. C. Onslow, Lieut. H. G. Oliver, Lieut. T. Digby; Lieut. H. W. Renny-Tailyour, Lieut. H. E. Rawson, Lieut. J. E. Blackman, Lieut. A. K. Wood, Lieut. P. G. von Donop.

1874–75 ROYAL ENGINEERS Capt. Merriman; Lieut. G. H. Sim, Lieut. G. Onslow; Lieut. R. M. Ruck, Lieut. P. G. von Donop, Lieut. C. K. Wood; Lieut. H. E. Rawson, Lieut. R. H. Stafford, Capt. H. W. Renny-Tailyour, Lieut. Mein, Lieut. C. Wingfield Stratford. *Scorer:* (First match) Not known; (Second match) Renny-Tailyour, Stafford.
1-1 OLD ETONIANS Capt. E. H. Drummond-Moray; M. Farrer, E. Lubbock; F. H. Wilson, Hon. A. F. Kinnaird, J. H. Stronge; F. J. Patton, C. E. Farmer, A. G. Bonsor, A. Lubbock, T.
***R*:2-0** Hammond. (C. J. Ottaway, W. S. Kenyon-Slaney, R. H. Benson and A. G. Thompson took part in the first match in place of A. Lubbock, T. Hammond, M. Farrer and Capt. E. H. Drummond-Moray.) *Scorer:* Bonsor.

1875–76 THE WANDERERS W. D. O. Greig; A. Stratford, W. Lindsay; F. B. C. Maddison, F. H. Birley, C. H. R. Wollaston; H. Heron, F. Heron, J. H. Edwards, J. Kenrick, T. Hughes. *Scorers:* (First match) Edwards; (Second match) Wollaston, Hughes 2.
1-1 OLD ETONIANS Q. Hogg; E. Lubbock, Hon. E. Lyttelton; M. G. Faner, Hon. A. F. Kinnaird, J. H. Stronge; W. S. Kenyon-Slaney, Hon. A. Lyttelton, J. R. Sturgis, A. G. Bonsor, H. P.
***R*:3-0** Allene. (C. Meysey, A. C. Thompson and J. E. C. Welldon took part in the first match in place of J. H. Stronge, M. G. Faner and E. Lubbock.) *Scorer:* Bonsor.

1876–77 THE WANDERERS F. H. Bitley; C. A. Denton, F. T. Green; H. Heron, T. Hughes, J. Kenrick; Hon. A. F. Kinnaird, W. Lindsay, A. Stratford, H. Wace, C. H. R. Wollaston. (In
2-1 alphabetical order.) *Scorers:* Heron, Kenrick.
aet OXFORD UNIVERSITY E. H. Allington; J. Bain, O. R. Dunnell; J. H. Savory, A. H. Todd, E. W. Waddington; P. H. Fernandez, A. F. Hills, H. S. Otter, E. H. Parry, W. S. Rawson. *Scorer:* Kinnaird og.

1877–78 THE WANDERERS J. Kirkpatrick; A. Stratford, W. Lindsay; Hon. A. F. Kinnaird, F. T. Green, C. H. R. Wollaston; H. Heron, J. G. Wylie, H. Wace, C. A. Denton, J. Kenrick.
3-1 ROYAL ENGINEERS L. B. Friend; J. H. Cowan, W. J. Morris; C. B. Mayne, F. C. Heath, C. E. Haynes; M. Lindsay, R. B. Hedley, F. G. Bond, H. H. Barnet, O. E. Ruck.

1878–79 OLD ETONIANS J. P. Hawtrey; E. Christian, L. Bury; Hon. A. F. Kinnaird, E. Lubbock, C. J. Clerke; N. Pares, H. C. Goodhart, H. Whitfield, J. B. T. Chevallier, H. Beaufoy.
1-0 CLAPHAM ROVERS R. H. Birkett; R. A. Ogilvie, E. Field; N. C. Bailey, J. F. M. Prinsep, F. L. Rawson; A. J. Stanley, S. W. Scott, H. S. Bevington, E. F. Growse, C. Keith-Falconer.

1879–80 CLAPHAM ROVERS R. H. Birkett; R. A. Ogilvie, E. Field; A. Weston, N. C. Bailey, H. Brougham; A. J. Stanley, F. Barry, F. J. Sparks, C. A. Lloyd-Jones, E. A. Ram. *Scorer:* Lloyd-Jones.
1-0 OXFORD UNIVERSITY P. C. Parr; C. W. Wilson, C. J. S. King; F. A. H. Phillips, B. Rogers, R. T. Heygate; G. B. Childs, J. Eyre, F. D. Crowdy, E. H. Hill, J. B. Lubbock.

1880–81 OLD CARTHUSIANS L. F. Gillett; W. H. Norris, E. G. Colvin; J. F. M. Prinsep, A. J. Vintcent, W. E. Hansell; L. M. Richards, W. R. Page, E. G. Wynyard, E. H. Parry, A. H. Todd.
3-0 OLD ETONIANS J. F. P. Rawlinson; C. W. Foley, C. H. French; Hon. A. F. Kinnaird, R. B. Farrer, J. B. T. Chevallier; W. J. Anderson, H. C. Goodhart, R. H. Macaulay, H. Whitfield, P. C. Novelli.

1881–82 OLD ETONIANS J. F. P. Rawlinson; T. H. French, P. J. de Paravicini; Hon. A. F. Kinnaird, C. W. Foley, P. C. Novelli; A. T. R. Dunn, R. H. Macaulay, H. C. Goodhart, W. J. Anderson, J. B. T. Chevallier. *Scorer:* Anderson.
1-0 BLACKBURN ROVERS R. Howarth; H. McIntyre, F. Suter; H. Sharples, F. W. Hargreaves, J. Duckworth; J. Douglas, T. Strachan, J. Brown, G. Avery, J. Hargreaves.

1882–83 BLACKBURN OLYMPIC T. Hacking; J. T. Ward, S. A. Warburton; T. Gibson, W. Astley, J. Hunter; T. Dewhurst, A. Matthews, G. Wilson, J. Costley, J. Yates. *Scorers:* Costley, Matthews.
2-1 OLD ETONIANS J. F. P. Rawlinson, T. H. French, P. J. de Paravicini, Hon. A. F. Kinnaird,
aet C. W. Foley, J. B. T. Chevallier, W. J. Anderson, R. H. Macaulay, H. C. Goodhart, A. T. B. Dunn, H. W. Bainbridge. *Scorer:* Goodhart.

1883–84 BLACKBURN ROVERS H. J. Arthur; J. Beverley, F. Suter; H. McIntyre, J. Hargreaves, J. H. Forrest; J. M. Lofthouse, J. Douglas, J. Sowerbutts, J. Inglis, J. Brown. *Scorers:* Brown, Forrest.
2-1 QUEEN'S PARK G. Gillespie; W. Arnott, J. MacDonald; C. Campbell, J. J. Gow, W. Anderson; W. W. Watt, Dr Smith, W. Harrower, D. S. Allan, R. M. Christie. *Scorer:* Christie.

1884–85 BLACKBURN ROVERS H. J. Arthur; R. G. Turner, F. Suter; H. McIntyre, G. Haworth, J. H. Forrest; J. M. Lofthouse, J. Douglas, J. Brown, H. E. Fecitt, J. Sowerbutts. *Scorers:* Forrest, Brown.
2-0 QUEEN'S PARK G. Gillespie; W. Arnott, W. Macleod; C. Campbell, J. MacDonald, A. Hamilton; W. Anderson, W. Sellar, W. Gray, N. McWhannel, D. S. Allan.

1885–86 BLACKBURN ROVERS H. J. Arthur; Turner, Suter; Douglas, Forrest, McIntyre; Walton, Strachan, Brown, Fecitt, J. Sowerbutts. (Heyes played in the first match at the Oval, but Walton
0-0 took his place in the replay.) *Scorers:* Sowerbutts, Brown.
***R*:2-0** WEST BROMWICH ALBION Roberts; H. Green, H. Bell; Horton, Perry, Timmins; Woodhall, T. Green, Bayliss, Loach, G. Bell.

1886–87 ASTON VILLA Warner; Coulton, Simmonds; Yates, Dawson, Burton; Davis, Brown, Hunter, Vaughton, Hodgetts. *Scorers:* Hodgetts, Hunter.
2-0 WEST BROMWICH ALBION Roberts; H. Green, Aldridge; Horton, Perry, Timmins; Woodhall, T. Green, Bayliss, Paddock, Pearson.

1887–88 WEST BROMWICH ALBION Roberts; Aldridge, Green; Horton, Perry, Timmins; Bassett, Woodhall, Bayliss, Wilson, Pearson. *Scorers:* Bayliss, Woodhall.
2-1 PRESTON NORTH END Dr R. H. Mills-Roberts; Howarth, N. J. Ross; Holmes, Russell, Graham; Gordon, J. Ross, J. Goodall, F. Dewhurst, Drummond. *Scorer:* Goodall.

1888–89 PRESTON NORTH END Dr R. H. Mills-Roberts; Howarth, Holmes; Drummond, Russell, Graham; Gordon, Ross, J. Goodall, F. Dewhurst, Thompson. *Scorers:* Dewhurst, Ross, Thompson.
3-0 WOLVERHAMPTON WANDERERS Baynton; Baugh, Mason; Fletcher, Allen, Lowder; Hunter, Wykes, Broodie, Wood, Knight.

1889–90 BLACKBURN ROVERS J. K. Horne; Southworth (Jas.), Forbes; Barton, Dewar, Forrest; Lofthouse, Campbell, Southworth (John), Walton, Townley. *Scorer:* Dewar, Southworth (John), Lofthouse, Townley 3.
6-1 SHEFFIELD WEDNESDAY Smith (J.); Brayshaw, H. Morley; Dungworth, Betts, Waller; Ingram, Woodhouse, Bennett, Mumford, Cawley. *Scorer:* Bennett.

1890–91 BLACKBURN ROVERS Pennington; Brandon, J. Forbes; Barton, Dewar, Forrest; Lofthouse, Walton, Southworth (John), Hall, Townley. *Scorers:* Dewar, Southworth, Townley.
3-1 NOTTS COUNTY Thraves; Ferguson, Hendry; H. Osborne, Calderhead, Shelton; A. McGregor, McInnes, Oswald, Locker, H. B. Daft. *Scorer:* Oswald.

1891–92 WEST BROMWICH ALBION Reader; Nicholson, McCulloch, Reynolds, Perry, Groves; Bassett, McLeod, Nicholls, Pearson, Geddes. *Scorers:* Geddes, Nicholls, Reynolds.
3-0 ASTON VILLA Warner; Evans, Cox; H. Devey, Cowan, Baird; Athersmith, J. Devey, Dickson, Campbell, Hodgetts.

1892–93 WOLVERHAMPTON WANDERERS Rose; Baugh, Swift; Malpass, Allen, Kinsey; R. Topham, Wykes, Butcher, Wood, Griffin. *Scorer:* Allen.
1-0 EVERTON Williams; Howarth, Kelso; Stewart, Holt, Boyle; Latta, Gordon, Maxwell, Chadwick, Milward.

1893–94 NOTTS COUNTY Toone; Harper, Hendry; Bramley, Calderhead, A. Shelton; Watson, Donnelly, Logan, Bruce, H. B. Daft. *Scorers:* Watson, Logan 3.
4-1 BOLTON WANDERERS Sutcliffe; Somerville, Jones; Gardiner, Paton, Hughes; Dickinson, Wilson, Tannahill, Bentley, Cassidy. *Scorer:* Cassidy.

1894–95 ASTON VILLA Wilkes; Spencer, Welford; Reynolds, Cowan (Jas.), Russell; Athersmith, Chatt, J. Devey, Hodgetts, S. Smith. *Scorer:* Chatt.
1-0 WEST BROMWICH ALBION Reader; Williams, Horton; Taggart, Higgins, T. Perry; Bassett, McLeod, Richards, Hutchinson, Banks.

1895–96 SHEFFIELD WEDNESDAY Massey; Earp, Langley; H. Brandon, Crawshaw, Petrie; Brash, Brady, L. Bell, Davis, Spiksley. *Scorer:* Spiksley 2.
2-1 WOLVERHAMPTON WANDERERS Tennant; Baugh, Dunn; Owen, Malpass, Griffiths; Tonks, Henderson, Beats, Wood, Black. *Scorer:* Black.

1896–97 ASTON VILLA Whitehouse; Spencer, Evans; Reynolds, Cowan (Jas.), Crabtree; Athersmith, J. Devey, Campbell, Wheldon, Cowan (John). *Scorers:* Campbell, Wheldon, Crabtree.
3-2 EVERTON Menham; Meecham, Storrier; Boyle, Holt, Stewart; Taylor, Bell, Hartley, Chadwick, Milward. *Scorers:* Bell, Boyle.

1897–98 NOTTINGHAM FOREST Allsop; Richie, Scott; Forman (Frank), McPherson, Wragg; McInnes, Richards, Benbow, Capes, Spouncer. *Scorers:* Capes 2, McPherson.
3-1 DERBY COUNTY Fryer; Methven, Leiper; Cox, A. Goodall, Turner; J. Goodall, Bloomer, Boag, Stevenson, McQueen. *Scorer:* Bloomer.

1898–99 SHEFFIELD UNITED Foulke; Thickett, Boyle; Johnson, Morren, Needham; Bennett, Beers, Hedley, Almond, Priest. *Scorers:* Bennett, Beers, Almond, Priest.
4-1 DERBY COUNTY Fryer; Methven, Staley; Cox, Paterson, May; Arkesden, Bloomer, Boag, McDonald, Allen. *Scorer:* Boag.

1899– BURY Thompson; Darrock, Davidson; Pray, Leeming, Ross; Richards, Wood, McLuckie, Sagar, Plant.
1900 *Scorers:* McLuckie 2, Wood, Plant.
4-0 SOUTHAMPTON Robinson; Meehan, Durber; Meston, Chadwick, Petrie; Turner, Yates, Farrell, Wood, Milward.

1900–01 TOTTENHAM HOTSPUR Clawley; Erentz, Tait; Norris, Hughes, Jones; Smith, Cameron, Brown, Copeland, Kirwan. *Scorers:* (First match) Brown 2; (Second match), Cameron, Smith, Brown.
2-2 SHEFFIELD UNITED Foulke; Thickett, Boyle; Johnson, Morren, Needham; Bennett, Field,
***R*:3-1** Hedley, Priest, Lipsham. *Scorers:* (First match) Bennett, Priest; (Second match) Priest.

1901–02 SHEFFIELD UNITED Foulke; Thickett, Boyle; Needham, Wilkinson, Johnson; Barnes, Common, Hedley, Priest, Lipsham. (Bennett was injured in the first match and Barnes took his place in the replay.) *Scorers:* (First match) Common; (Second match) Hedley, Barnes.
1-1 SOUTHAMPTON Robinson; C. B. Fry, Molyneux; Meston, Bowman, Lee; A. Turner, Wood,
***R*:2-1** Brown, Chadwick, J. Turner. *Scorers:* (First match) Wood; (Second match) Brown.

1902–03 BURY Monteith; Lindsey, McEwen; Johnson, Thorpe, Ross; Richards, Wood, Sagar, Leeming, Plant. *Scorers:* Ross, Sagar, Leeming 2, Wood, Plant.
6-0 DERBY COUNTY Fryer; Methven, Morris; Warren, A. Goodall, May; Warrington, York, Boag, Richards, Davis.

1903–04 MANCHESTER CITY Hillman; McMahon, Burgess; Frost, Hynds, S. B. Ashworth; Meredith, Livingstone, Gillespie, A. Turnbull, Booth. *Scorer:* Meredith.
1-0 BOLTON WANDERERS D. Davies; Brown, Struthers; Clifford, Greenhaigh, Freebairn; Stokes, Marsh, Yenson, White, Taylor.

1904–05 ASTON VILLA George; Spencer, Miles; Pearson, Leake, Windmill; Brawn, Garratty, Hampton, Bache, Hall. *Scorer:* Hampton 2.

2-0 NEWCASTLE UNITED Lawrence; McCombie, Carr; Gardner, Aitken, McWilliam; Rutherford, Howie, Appleyard, Veitch, Gosnell.

1905–06 EVERTON Scott; W. Balmer, Crelly; Makepeace, Taylor, Abbott; Sharp, Bolton, Young, Settle, H. P. Hardman. *Scorer:* Young.

1-0 NEWCASTLE UNITED Lawrence; McCombie, Carr; Gardner, Aitken, McWilliam; Rutherford, Howie, Veitch, Orr, Gosnell.

1906–07 SHEFFIELD WEDNESDAY Lyall; Layton, Burton; Brittleton, Crawshaw, Bartlett; Chapman, Bradshaw, Wilson, Stewart, Simpson. *Scorers:* Stewart, Simpson.

2-1 EVERTON Scott; W. Balmer, R. Balmer; Makepeace, Taylor, Abbott; Sharp, Bolton, Young, Settle, H. P. Hardman. *Scorer:* Sharp.

1907–08 WOLVERHAMPTON WANDERERS Lunn; Jones, Collins; Rev. K. R. G. Hunt, Wooldridge, Bishop; Harrison, Shelton, Hedley, Radford, Pedley. *Scorers:* Hunt, Hedley, Harrison.

3-1 NEWCASTLE UNITED Lawrence; McCracken, Pudan; Gardner, Veitch, McWilliam; Rutherford, Howie, Appleyard, Speedie, Wilson. *Scorer:* Howie.

1908–09 MANCHESTER UNITED Moger; Stacey, Hayes; Duckworth, Roberts, Bell; Meredith, Halse, J. Turnbull, A. Turnbull, Wall. *Scorer:* A. Turnbull.

1-0 BRISTOL CITY Clay; Annan, Cottle; Hanlin, Wedlock, Spear; Staniforth, Hardy, Gilligan, Burton, Hilton.

1909–10 NEWCASTLE UNITED Lawrence; McCracken, Carr; Veitch, Low, McWilliam; Rutherford, Howie, Shepherd, Higgins, Wilson. (Whitson was injured in first match and Carr took his place in the replay.) *Scorers:* (First match) Rutherford; (Second match) Shepherd 2 (1 pen).

1-1 BARNSLEY Mearns; Downs, Ness; Glendinning, Boyle, Utley; Bartrop, Gadsby, Lillycrop,
***R:*2-0** Tuffnell, Forman. *Scorer:* (First match) Tuffnell.

1910–11 BRADFORD CITY Mellors; Campbell, Taylor; Robinson, Torrance, McDonald; Logan, Spiers, O'Rourke, Devine, Thompson. (Gildea played centre-half in the first match.) *Scorer:* Spiers.

0-0 NEWCASTLE UNITED Lawrence; McCracken, Whitson; Veitch, Low, Willis; Rutherford,
***R:*1-0** Jobey, Stewart, Higgins, Wilson.

1911–12 BARNSLEY Cooper; Downs, Taylor; Glendinning, Bratley, Utley; Bartrop, Tuffnell,
0-0 Lillycrop, Travers, Moore. *Scorer:* Tuffnell.
***R:*2-0** WEST BROMWICH ALBION Pearson; Cook, Pennington; Baddeley, Buck, McNeal;
aet Jephcott, Wright, Pailor, Bowser, Shearman.

1912–13 ASTON VILLA Hardy; Lyons, Weston; Barber, Harrop, Leach; Wallace, Halse, Hampton, C. Stephenson, Bache. *Scorer:* Barber.

1-0 SUNDERLAND Butler; Gladwin, Ness; Cuggy, Thompson, Low; Mordue, Buchan, Richardson, Holley, Martin.

1913–14 BURNLEY Sewell; Bamford, Taylor; Halley, Boyle, Watson; Nesbit, Lindley, Freeman, Hodgson, Mosscrop. *Scorer:* Freeman.

1-0 LIVERPOOL Campbell; Longworth, Pursell; Fairfoul, Ferguson, McKinlay; Sheldon, Metcalf, Miller, Lacey, Nicholl.

1914–15 SHEFFIELD UNITED Gough; Cook, English; Sturgess, Brelsford, Utley; Simmons, Fazackerley, Kitchen, Masterman, Evans. *Scorers:* Simmons, Fazackerley, Kitchen.

3-0 CHELSEA Molyneux; Bettridge, Harrow; Taylor, Logan, Walker; Ford, Halse, Thompson, Croal, McNeil.

1919–20 ASTON VILLA Hardy; Smart, Weston; Ducat, Barson, Moss; Wallace, Kirton, Walker, C. Stephenson, Dorrell. *Scorer:* Kirton.

1-0 HUDDERSFIELD TOWN Mutch; Wood, Bullock; Slade, Wilson, Watson; Richardson,
aet Mann, Taylor, Swan, Islip.

1920–21 TOTTENHAM HOTSPUR Hunter; Clay, McDonald; Smith, Walters, Grimsdell; Banks, Seed, Cantrell, Bliss, Dimmock. *Scorer:* Dimmock.

1-0 WOLVERHAMPTON WANDERERS George; Woodward, Marshall; Gregory, Hodnet, Riley; Lea, Burrill, Edmonds, Potts, Brooks.

1921–22 HUDDERSFIELD TOWN Mutch; Wood, Wadsworth; Slade, Wilson, Watson; Richardson, Mann, Islip, Stephenson, W. H. Smith. *Scorer:* Smith (pen).

1-0 PRESTON NORTH END J. F. Mitchell; Hamilton, Doolan; Duxbury, McCall, Williamson; Rawlings, Jefferis, Roberts, Woodhouse, Quinn.

1922–23 BOLTON WANDERERS Pym; Haworth, Finney; Nuttall, Seddon, Jennings; Butler, Jack, J. R. Smith, J. Smith, Vizard. *Scorers:* Jack, J. R. Smith.

2-0 WEST HAM UNITED Hufton; Henderson, Young; Bishop, Kay, Tresadern, Richards, Brown, V. Watson, Moore, Ruffell.

1923–24 NEWCASTLE UNITED Bradley; Hampson, Hudspeth; Mooney, Spencer, Gibson; Low, Cowan, Harris, McDonald, Seymour. *Scorers:* Harris, Seymour.

2-0 ASTON VILLA Jackson; Smart, Mort; Moss, Dr V. E. Milne, Blackburn; York, Kirton, Capewell, Walker, Dorrell.

1924–25 SHEFFIELD UNITED Sutcliffe; Cook, Milton; Pantling, King, Green; Mercer, Boyle, Johnson, Gillespie, Tunstall. *Scorer:* Tunstall.

1-0 CARDIFF CITY Farquharson; Nelson, Blair; Wake, Keenor, Hardy; W. Davies; Gill, Nicholson, Beadles, J. Evans.

1925–26 BOLTON WANDERERS Pym; Haworth, Greenhalgh; Nuttall, Seddon, Jennings; Butler, Jack, J. R. Smith, J. Smith, Vizard. *Scorer:* Jack.

1-0 MANCHESTER CITY Goodchild; Cookson, McCloy; Pringle, Cowan, McMullan; Austin, Browell, Roberts, Johnson, Hicks.

1926–27 CARDIFF CITY Farquharson; Nelson, Watson; Keenor, Sloan, Hardy; Curtis, Irving, Ferguson, L. Davies, McLachlan. *Scorer:* Ferguson.

1-0 ARSENAL Lewis; Parker, Kennedy; Baker, Butler, John; Hulme, Buchan, Brain, Blyth, Hoar.

1927–28 BLACKBURN ROVERS Crawford; Hutton, Jones; Healless, Rankin, Campbell; Thornewell, Puddefoot, Roscamp, McLean, Rigby. *Scorers:* Roscamp 2, McLean.

3-1 HUDDERSFIELD TOWN Mercer; Goodall, Barkas; Redfern, Wilson, Steele; A. Jackson, Kelly, Brown, Stephenson, W. H. Smith. *Scorer:* Jackson.

Alex James (far left) scores Arsenal's first goal in their first FA Cup victory – a 2-0 defeat of Huddersfield Town in 1930.

1928–29 BOLTON WANDERERS Pym; Haworth, Finney; Kean, Seddon, Nuttall; Butler, McClelland, Blackmore, Gibson, W. Cook. *Scorers:* Butler, Blackmore.

2-0 PORTSMOUTH Gilfillan; Mackie, Bell; Nichol, McIlwaine, Thackeray; Forward, J. Smith, Weddle, Watson, F. Cook.

1929–30 ARSENAL Preedy; Parker, Hapgood; Baker, Seddon, John; Hulme, Jack, Lambert, James, Bastin. *Scorers:* James, Lambert.

2-0 HUDDERSFIELD TOWN Turner; Goodall, Spence; Naylor, Wilson, Campbell; A. Jackson, Kelly, Davies, Raw, W. H. Smith.

1930–31 WEST BROMWICH ALBION Pearson; Shaw, Trentham; Magee, W. Richardson, Edwards; Glidden, Carter, W. G. Richardson, Sandford, Wood. *Scorer:* W. G. Richardson 2.

2-1 BIRMINGHAM Hibbs; Liddell, Barkas; Cringan, Morrall, Leslie; Briggs, Crosbie, Bradford, Gregg, Curtis. *Scorer:* Bradford.

1931–32 NEWCASTLE UNITED McInroy; Nelson, Fairhurst; McKenzie, Davidson, Weaver; Boyd, Richardson, Allen, McMenemy, Lang. *Scorer:* Allen 2.

2-1 ARSENAL Moss; Parker, Hapgood; C. Jones, Roberts, Male; Hulme, Jack, Lambert, Bastin, John. *Scorer:* John.

1932–33 EVERTON Sagar; Cook, Cresswell; Britton, White, Thomson; Geldard, Dunn, Dean, Johnson, Stein. *Scorers:* Stein, Dean, Dunn.

3-0 MANCHESTER CITY Langford; Cann, Dale; Busby, Cowan, Bray; Toseland, Marshall, Herd, McMullan, Brook.

1933–34 MANCHESTER CITY Swift; Barnett, Dale; Busby, Cowan, Bray; Toseland, Marshall, Tilson, Herd, Brook. *Scorer:* Tilson 2.

2-1 PORTSMOUTH Gilfillan; Mackie, W. Smith; Nichol, Allen, Thackeray; Worrall, J. Smith, Weddle, Easson, Rutherford. *Scorer:* Rutherford.

1934–35 SHEFFIELD WEDNESDAY Brown; Nibloe, Catlin; Sharp, Millership, Burrows; Hooper, Surtees, Palethorpe, Starling, Rimmer. *Scorers:* Rimmer 2, Palethorpe, Hooper.

4-2 WEST BROMWICH ALBION Pearson; Shaw, Trentham; Murphy, W. Richardson, Edwards; Glidden, Carter, W. G. Richardson, Sandford, Boyes. *Scorers:* Boyes, Sandford.

1935–36 ARSENAL Wilson; Male, Hapgood; Crayston, Robertson, Copping; Hulme, Bowden, Drake, James, Bastin. *Scorer:* Drake.

1-0 SHEFFIELD UNITED Smith; Hooper, Wilkinson; Jackson, Johnson, McPherson; Barton, Barclay, Dodds, Pickering, Williams.

1936–37 SUNDERLAND Mapson; Gorman, Hall; Thomson, Johnson, McNab; Duns, Carter, Gurney, Gallacher, Burbanks. *Scorers:* Gurney, Carter, Burbanks.

3-1 PRESTON NORTH END Burns; Gallimore, A. Beattie; Shankly, Tremelling, Milne; Dougal, Beresford, F. O'Donnell, Fagan, H. O'Donnell. *Scorer:* F. O'Donnell.

1937–38 PRESTON NORTH END Holdcroft; Gallimore, A. Beattie; Shankly, Smith, Batey; Watmough, Mutch, Maxwell, R. Beattie, H. O'Donnell. *Scorer:* Mutch (pen).

1-0 aet HUDDERSFIELD TOWN Hesford; Craig, Mountford; Willingham, Young, Boot; Hulme, Isaac, McFadyen, Barclay, Beasley.

1938–39 PORTSMOUTH Walker; Morgan, Rochford; Guthrie, Rowe, Wharton; Worrall, McAlinden, Anderson, Barlow, Parker. *Scorers:* Parker 2, Barlow, Anderson.

4-1 WOLVERHAMPTON WANDERERS Scott; Morris, Taylor; Galley, Cullis, Gardiner; Burton, McIntosh, Westcott, Dorsett, Maguire. *Scorer:* Dorsett.

1945–46 DERBY COUNTY Woodley; Nicholas, Howe; Bullions, Leuty, Musson; Harrison, Carter, Stamps, Doherty, Duncan. *Scorers:* H. Turner og, Doherty, Stamps 2.

4-1 aet CHARLTON ATHLETIC Bartram; Phipps, Shreeve; H. Turner, Oakes, Johnson; Fell, Brown, A. A. Turner, Welsh, Duffy. *Scorer:* H. Turner.

1946–47 CHARLTON ATHLETIC Bartram; Crocker, Shreeve; Johnson, Phipps, Whittaker; Hurst, Dawson, W. Robinson, Welsh, Duffy. *Scorer:* Duffy.

1-0 aet BURNLEY Strong; Woodruff, Mather; Attwell, Brown, Bray; Chew, Morris, Harrison, Potts, F. P. Kippax.

1947–48 MANCHESTER UNITED Crompton; Carey, Aston; Anderson, Chilton, Cockburn; Delaney, Morris, Rowley, Pearson, Mitten. *Scorers:* Rowley 2, Pearson, Anderson.

4-2 BLACKPOOL Robinson; Shimwell, Crosland; Johnston, Hayward, Kelly; Matthews, Munro, Mortensen, Dick, Rickett. *Scorers:* Shimwell (pen), Mortensen.

1948–49 WOLVERHAMPTON WANDERERS Williams; Pritchard, Springthorpe; W. Crook, Shorthouse, Wright; Hancock, Smyth, Pye, Dunn, Mullen. *Scorers:* Pye 2, Smyth.

3-1 LEICESTER CITY Bradley; Jelly, Scott; W. Harrison, Plummer, King; Griffiths, Lee, J. Harrison, Chisholm, Adam. *Scorer:* Griffiths.

1949–50 ARSENAL Swindin; Scott, Barnes; Forbes, L. Compton, Mercer; Cox, Logie, Goring, Lewis, D. Compton. *Scorer:* Lewis 2.

2-0 LIVERPOOL Sidlow; Lambert, Spicer; Taylor, Hughes, Jones; Payne, Baron, Stubbins, Fagan, Liddell.

1950–51 NEWCASTLE UNITED Fairbrother; Cowell, Corbett; Harvey, Brennan, Crowe; Walker, Taylor, Milburn, G. Robledo, Mitchell. *Scorer:* Milburn 2.

2-0 BLACKPOOL Farm; Shimwell, Garrett; Johnston, Hayward, Kelly; Matthews, Mudie, Mortensen; W. J. Slater, Perry.

1951–52 NEWCASTLE UNITED Simpson; Cowell, McMichael; Harvey, Brennan, E. Robledo, Walker, Foulkes, Milburn, G. Robledo, Mitchell. *Scorer:* G. Robledo.

1-0 ARSENAL Swindin; Barnes, L. Smith; Forbes, Daniel, Mercer; Cox, Logie, Holton, Lishman, Roper.

1952–53 BLACKPOOL Farm; Shimwell, Garrett; Fenton, Johnston, Robinson; Matthews, Taylor, Mortensen, Mudie, Perry. *Scorers:* Mortensen 3, Perry.

4-3 BOLTON WANDERERS Hanson; Ball, R. Banks; Wheeler, Barass, Bell; Holden, Moir, Lofthouse, Hassall, Langton. *Scorers:* Lofthouse, Moir, Bell.

1953–54 WEST BROMWICH ALBION Sanders; Kennedy, Millard; Dudley, Dugdale, Barlow; Griffin, Ryan, Allen, Nicholls, Lee. *Scorers:* Allen 2 (1 pen), Griffin.

3-2 PRESTON NORTH END Thompson; Cunningham, Walton; Docherty, Marston, Forbes; Finney, Foster, Wayman, Baxter, Morrison. *Scorers:* Morrison, Wayman.

Nat Lofthouse of Bolton Wanderers turns in triumph after scoring the first goal of Bolton's 2-0 victory over a Manchester United side still reeling in the aftermath of the Munich air disaster.

1954–55 NEWCASTLE UNITED Simpson; Cowell, Batty; Scoular, Stokoe, Casey; White, Milburn, Keeble, Hannah, Mitchell. *Scorers:* Milburn, Mitchell, Hannah.
3-1 MANCHESTER CITY Trautmann; Meadows, Little; Barnes, Ewing, Paul; Spurdle, Hayes, Revie, Johnstone, Fagan. *Scorer:* Johnstone.

1955–56 MANCHESTER CITY Trautmann; Leivers, Little; Barnes, Ewing, Paul; Johnstone, Hayes, Revie, Dyson, Clarke. *Scorers:* Hayes, Dyson, Johnstone.
3-1 BIRMINGHAM CITY Merrick; Hall, Green; Newman, Smith, Boyd; Astall, Kinsey, Brown, Murphy, Govan. *Scorer:* Kinsey.

1956–57 ASTON VILLA Sims; Lynn, Aldis; Crowther, Dugdale, Saward; Smith, Sewell, Myerscough, Dixon, McParland. *Scorer:* McParland 2.
2-1 MANCHESTER UNITED Wood; Foulkes, Byrne; Colman, J. Blanchflower, Edwards; Berry, Whelan, T. Taylor, R. Charlton, Pegg. *Scorer:* Taylor.

1957–58 BOLTON WANDERERS Hopkinson; Hartle, Banks; Hennin, Higgins, Edwards; Birch, Stevens, Lofthouse, Parry, Holden. *Scorer:* Lofthouse 2.
2-0 MANCHESTER UNITED Gregg; Foulkes, Greaves; Goodwin, Cope, Crowther; Dawson, E. Taylor; R. Charlton, Viollet, Webster.

1958–59 NOTTINGHAM FOREST Thomson; Whare, McDonald; Whitefoot, McKinlay, Burkitt; Dwight, Quigley, Wilson, Gray, Imlach. *Scorers:* Dwight, Wilson.
2-1 LUTON TOWN Baynham; McNally, Hawkes; Groves, Owen, Pacey; Bingham, Brown, Morton, Cummins, Gregory. *Scorer:* Pacey.

1959–60 WOLVERHAMPTON WANDERERS Finlayson; Showell, Harris; Clamp, Slater, Flowers; Deeley, Stobart, Murray, Broadbent, Horne. *Scorers:* McGrath og, Deeley 2.
3-0 BLACKBURN ROVERS Leyland; Bray, Whelan; Clayton, Woods, McGrath; Bimpson, Dobing, Dougan, Douglas, McLeod.

1960–61 TOTTENHAM HOTSPUR Brown; Baker, Henry; D. Blanchflower, Norman, Mackay; Jones, White, Smith, Allen, Dyson. *Scorers:* Smith, Dyson.
2-0 LEICESTER CITY Banks; Chalmers, Norman; McLintock, King, Appleton; Riley, Walsh, McIlmoyle, Keyworth, Cheesebrough.

1961–62 TOTTENHAM HOTSPUR Brown; Baker, Henry; D. Blanchflower, Norman, Mackay; Medwin, White, Smith, Greaves, Jones. *Scorers:* Greaves, Smith, Blanchflower (pen).
3-1 BURNLEY Blacklaw; Angus, Elder; Adamson, Cummings, Miller; Connelly, McIlroy, Pointer, Robson, Harris. *Scorer:* Robson.

1962–63 MANCHESTER UNITED Gaskell; Dunne, Cantwell; Crerand, Foulkes, Setters; Giles, Quixall, Herd, Law, R. Charlton. *Scorers:* Law, Herd 2.
3-1 LEICESTER CITY Banks; Sjoberg, Norman; McLintock, King, Appleton; Riley, Cross, Keyworth, Gibson, Stringfellow. *Scorer:* Keyworth.

1963–64 WEST HAM UNITED Standen; Bond, Burkett; Bovington, Brown, Moore; Brabrook, Boyce, Byrne, Hurst, Sissons. *Scorers:* Sissons, Hurst, Boyce.
3-2 PRESTON NORTH END Kelly; Ross, Smith; Lawton, Singleton, Kendall; Wilson, Ashworth, Dawson, Spavin, Holden. *Scorers:* Holden, Dawson.

1964–65 LIVERPOOL Lawrence; Lawler, Byrne; Strong, Yeats, Stevenson; Callaghan, Hunt, St John, Smith, Thompson. *Scorers:* Hunt, St John.
2-1 aet LEEDS UNITED Sprake; Reaney, Bell; Bremner, J. Charlton, Hunter; Giles, Storrie, Peacock, Collins, Johanneson. *Scorer:* Bremner.

Chelsea goalkeeper Peter Bonetti dives in vain as a shot from Tottenham's Saul (not in picture) finds the net for Spurs' second goal in their 2-1 FA Cup final victory in 1967.

Ian Porterfield (far left) drives home the goal that gave underdogs Sunderland a famous FA Cup final victory against Leeds United in 1973.

1965–66 EVERTON West; Wright, Wilson; Gabriel, Labone, Harris; Scott, Trebilcock, Young, Harvey, Temple. *Scorers:* Trebilcock 2, Temple.

3-2 SHEFFIELD WEDNESDAY Springett; Smith, Megson; Eustace, Ellis, Young; Pugh, Fantham, McCalliog, Ford, Quinn. *Scorers:* McCalliog, Ford.

1966–67 TOTTENHAM HOTSPUR Jennings; Kinnear, Knowles; Mullery, England, Mackay; Robertson, Greaves, Gilzean, Venables, Saul. *Scorers:* Robertson, Saul.

2-1 CHELSEA Bonetti; A. Harris, McCreadie; Hollins, Hinton, R. Harris; Cooke, Baldwin, Hateley, Tambling, Boyle. *Scorer:* Tambling.

1967–68 WEST BROMWICH ALBION Osborne; Fraser, Williams; Brown, Talbut, Kaye (Clarke); Lovett, Collard, Astle, Hope, Clark. *Scorer:* Astle.

1-0 aet EVERTON West; Wright, Wilson; Kendall, Labone, Harvey; Husband, Ball, Royle, Hurst, Morrisey.

1968–69 MANCHESTER CITY Dowd; Book, Pardoe; Doyle, Booth, Oakes; Summerbee, Bell, Lee, Young, Coleman. *Scorer:* Young.

1-0 LEICESTER CITY Shilton; Rodrigues, Nish; Roberts, Woollett, Cross; Fern, Gibson, Lochhead, Clarke, Glover (Manley).

1969–70 CHELSEA Bonetti; Webb, McCreadie; Hollins, Dempsey, R. Harris (Hinton); Baldwin, Houseman, Osgood, Hutchinson, Cooke. *Scorers:* Houseman, Hutchinson.

2-2 aet LEEDS UNITED Sprake; Madeley, Cooper; Bremner, J. Charlton, Hunter; Lorimer, Clarke, Jones, Giles, E. Gray. *Scorers:* Charlton, Jones.

Replay (at Old Trafford, Manchester)

***R:*2-1 aet** CHELSEA Bonetti; R. Harris, McCreadie; Hollins, Dempsey, Webb; Baldwin, Cooke, Osgood (Hinton), Hutchinson, Houseman. *Scorers:* Osgood, Webb.

LEEDS UNITED Harvey; Madeley, Cooper; Bremner, J. Charlton, Hunter; Lorimer, Clarke, Jones, Giles, E. Gray. *Scorer:* Jones.

1970–71 ARSENAL Wilson; Rice, McNab; Storey (Kelly), McLintock, Simpson; Armstrong, Graham, Radford, Kennedy, George. *Scorers:* Kelly, George.

2-1 aet LIVERPOOL Clemence; Lawler, Lindsay; Smith, Lloyd, Hughes; Callaghan, Evans (Thompson), Heighway, Toshack, Hall. *Scorer:* Heighway.

1971–72 LEEDS UNITED Harvey; Reaney, Madeley; Bremner, J. Charlton, Hunter; Lorimer, Clarke, Jones, Giles, E. Gray. *Scorer:* Clarke.

1-0 ARSENAL Barnett; Rice, McNab; Storey, McLintock, Simpson; Armstrong, Ball, George, Radford (Kennedy), Graham.

1972–73 SUNDERLAND Montgomery; Malone, Guthrie; Horswill, Watson, Pitt; Kerr, Hughes, Halom, Porterfield, Tueart. *Scorer:* Porterfield.

1-0 LEEDS UNITED Harvey; Reaney, Cherry; Bremner, Madeley, Hunter; Lorimer, Clarke, Jones, Giles, E. Gray (Yorath).

1973–74 LIVERPOOL Clemence; Smith, Lindsay, Thompson, Cormack, Hughes, Keegan, Hall, Heighway, Toshack, Callaghan. *Scorers:* Keegan 2, Heighway.

3-0 NEWCASTLE UNITED McFaul; Clark, Kennedy, McDermott, Howard, Moncur, Smith (Gibb), Cassidy, Macdonald, Tudor, Hibbitt.

1974–75 WEST HAM UNITED Day; McDowell, T. Taylor, Lock, Lampard, Bonds, Paddon, Brooking, Jennings, A. Taylor, Holland. *Scorer:* A. Taylor 2.

2-0 FULHAM Mellor; Cutbush, Lacy, Moore, Fraser, Mullery, Conway, Slough, Mitchell, Busby, Barrett.

1975–76 SOUTHAMPTON Turner; Rodrigues, Peach; Holmes, Blyth, Steele; Gilchrist, Channon, Osgood, McCalliog, Stokes. *Scorer:* Stokes.

1-0 MANCHESTER UNITED Stepney; Forsyth, Houston; Daly, Greenhoff, Buchan; Coppell, McIlroy, Pearson, Macari, Hill (McCreery).

1976–77 MANCHESTER UNITED Stepney; Nicholl, Albiston; McIlroy, B. Greenhoff, Buchan; Coppell, J. Greenhoff, Pearson, Macari, Hill (McCreery). *Scorers:* Pearson, J. Greenhoff.

2-1 LIVERPOOL Clemence; Neal, Jones; Smith, Kennedy, Hughes; Keegan, Case, Heighway, Johnson (Callaghan), McDermott. *Scorer:* Case.

1977–78 IPSWICH TOWN Cooper; Burley, Mills; Osborne (Lambert), Hunter, Beattie, Talbot, Wark, Mariner, Geddis, Woods. *Scorer:* Osborne.

1-0 ARSENAL Jennings; Rice, Nelson, Price, Young, O'Leary, Brady (Rix), Hudson, Macdonald, Stapleton, Sunderland.

1978–79 ARSENAL Jennings; Rice, Nelson, Talbot, O'Leary, Young, Brady, Sunderland, Stapleton, Price (Walford), Rix. *Scorers:* Talbot, Stapleton, Sunderland.

3-2 MANCHESTER UNITED Bailey; Nicholl, Albiston, McIlroy, McQueen, Buchan, Coppell, J. Greenhoff, Jordan, Macari, Thomas. *Scorers:* McQueen, McIlroy.

1979–80 WEST HAM UNITED Parkes; Stewart, Lampard, Bonds, Martin, Devonshire, Allen, Pearson, Cross, Brooking, Pike. *Scorer:* Brooking.

1-0 ARSENAL Jennings; Rice, Devine (Nelson), Talbot, O'Leary, Young, Brady, Sunderland, Stapleton, Price, Rix

1980–81 TOTTENHAM HOTSPUR Aleksic; Hughton, Miller, Roberts, Perryman, Villa (Brooke), Ardiles, Archibald, Galvin, Hoddle, Crooks. *Scorer:* Hutchison og.

1-1 aet MANCHESTER CITY Corrigan; Ranson, McDonald, Reid, Power, Caton, Bennett, Gow, MacKenzie, Hutchison (Henry), Reeves. *Scorer:* Hutchison.

***R*:3-2** TOTTENHAM HOTSPUR Aleksic; Hughton, Miller, Roberts, Perryman, Villa, Ardiles, Archibald, Galvin, Hoddle, Crooks. *Scorers:* Villa 2, Crooks.

MANCHESTER CITY Corrigan; Ranson, McDonald (Tueart), Caton, Reid, Gow, Power, MacKenzie, Reeves, Bennett, Hutchison. *Scorers:* MacKenzie, Reeves (pen).

1981–82 QPR Hucker; Fenwick, Gillard, Waddock, Hazell, Roeder, Currie, Flanagan, Allen (Micklewhite), Stainrod, Gregory. *Scorer:* Fenwick.

1-1 aet TOTTENHAM HOTSPUR Clemence; Hughton, Miller, Price, Hazard (Brooke), Perryman, Roberts, Archibald, Galvin, Hoddle, Crooks. *Scorer:* Hoddle.

***R*:0-1** QPR Hucker; Fenwick, Gillard, Waddock, Hazell, Neill, Currie, Flanagan, Micklewhite (Burke), Stainrod, Gregory.

TOTTENHAM HOTSPUR Clemence; Hughton, Miller, Price, Hazard (Brooke), Perryman, Roberts, Archibald, Galvin, Hoddle, Crooks. *Scorer:* Hoddle (pen).

Brian Talbot scores Arsenal's first goal in their 3-2 FA Cup final win against Manchester United in 1979. Talbot thus earned the distinction of successive cup-winners' medals with different teams, having been in Ipswich's winning side against Arsenal the year before.

FA CUP 1982–83

QUALIFYING ROUNDS

Preliminary Round

Barrow v Crook Town	2-0
Consett v Lancaster City	0-3
Bridlington Trinity v Whitley Bay	3-1
Gateshead v Durham City	1-1
Morecambe v Whitby Town	2-0
Ashington v Chester-le-Street	2-2
Harrogate Town v West Auckland Town	3-0
Frickley Athletic v Shildon	5-3
Stalybridge Celtic v Burscough	1-1
South Liverpool v Horwich RMI	1-4
Lytham v Southport	1-2
Chorley v Formby	5-0
Bootle v Droylesden	3-0
Clitheroe v Leyland Motors	0-1
Skelmersdale United v Prestwich Heys	0-4
Gresley Rovers v Worksop Town	2-4
Winsford United v Blakenall	1-2
Witton Albion v Ilkeston Town	2-0
Denaby United v Shepshed Charterhouse	1-3
Goole Town v North Ferriby United	1-0
Arnold v Hinckley Athletic	0-1
Boston v Bourne Town	1-3
Matlock Town v Dudley Town	0-2
Long Eaton United v Wednesfield Social	1-0
Sutton Town v Heanor Town	2-1
Malvern Town v Racing Club Warwick	0-0
Friar Lane OB v Milton Keynes City	1-1
Lye Town v Bridgnorth Town	0-2
Highgate United v Chipping Norton Town	3-0
Sutton Coldfield Town v Walsall Borough	4-2
Kidderminster Harriers v Redditch United	0-0
Buckingham Town v Desborough Town	1-0
Spalding United v Irthlingboro' Diamonds	0-1
Cambridge City v March Town United	0-0
Wellingborough Town v Basildon United	5-2
Great Yarmouth Town v Ampthill Town	2-0
Wootton Blue Cross v Kempston Rovers	2-0
Haverhill Rovers v Epping Town	3-0
Heybridge Swifts v Thetford Town	1-0
Saffron Walden Town v Ruislip Manor	5-2
Barton Rovers v Cheshunt	2-0
Chelmsford City v Finchley	3-1
Chalfont St Peter v Rainham Town	2-1
Hounslow v Cray Wanderers	2-5
Berkhamsted Town v Dulwich Hamlet	3-3
Hemel Hempstead v Hillingdon Borough	0-0
Harefield United v Croydon	0-4
Abingdon Town v Aylesbury United	3-2
Wokingham Town v Andover	6-1
Dorking Town v Arundel	2-1
Woking v Chatham Town	0-0
Metropolitan Police v Sittingbourne	1-2
Ashford Town v Sheppey United	0-2
Faversham Town v Peacehaven & Tels C	2-0
Tunbridge Wells v Canterbury City	0-3
Totting & Mitcham United v Molesey	3-1
Herne Bay v Bognor Regis Town	0-1
Chertsey Town v Bromley	1-12
Dartford v Whitehawk	5-2
Epsom & Ewell v Walton & Hersham	1-2
Littlehampton Town v Newport IOW	0-3
Worthing v Fleet Town	7-1
AFC Totton v Marlow	1-0
Waterlooville v Bracknell Town	1-2
Salisbury v Calne Town	3-2
Poole Town v Basingstoke Town	0-0
Paulton Rovers v Bristol Manor Farm	0-2
Moreton Town v Ton Pentre	2-2
Mangotsfield United v Newbury Town	3-2
Cinderford Town v Melksham Town	3-0
Barry Town v Haverfordwest County	2-0
St Blazey v Clandown	3-1
Bridport v Wimborne Town	2-3
Penzance v Wellington Town	2-1
Liskeard Athletic v Ottery St Mary	1-0

Replays

Durham City v Gateshead	2-2
Chester-le-Street v Ashington	2-1
Burscough v Stalybridge Celtic	4-1
Racing Club Warwick v Malvern Town	4-3
Milton Keynes City v Friar Lane OB	aet 1-4
Redditch United v Kidderminster Harriers	2-3
March Town United v Cambridge City	3-2
Dulwich Hamlet v Berkhamsted Town	6-0
Hillingdon Borough v Hemel Hempstead	0-1
Chatham Town v Woking	2-1
Basingstoke Town v Poole Town	2-0
Ton Pentre v Moreton Town	4-1

Second Replay

Gateshead v Durham City (*at Blyth Spartans FC*)	2-1

First Round Qualifying

Yorkshire Amateur v Bishop Auckland	0-1
Blue Star v Lancaster City	1-2
Ferryhill Athletic v Barrow	0-1
Wingate v Annfield Plain	1-3
Evenwood Town v Horden CW	1-3
Peterlee Newtown v Gateshead	1-2
Farsley Celtic v Bridlington Trinity	3-0
North Shields v Eppleton CW	6-0
Emley v South Bank	3-6
Guisborough Town v Chester-le-Street	0-0
Tow Law Town v Morecambe	3-5
Willington v Brandon United	0-5
Fleetwood Town v Spennymoor United	1-2
Netherfield v Frickley Athletic	0-2
Accrington Stanley v Harrogate Town	1-1
Billingham Synthonia v Seaham CW Red Star	0-1
Colwyn Bay v Caernarfon Town	0-3
New Mills v Horwich RMI	0-3
Oswestry Town v Burscough	2-1
Prescot Cables v Marine	2-1
Thackley v Runcorn	0-0
Rossendale United v Chorley	0-3
Darwen v Southport	2-0
Curzon Ashton v Rhyl	4-1
Ossett Albion v Hyde United	1-2
Ashton United v Leyland Motors	6-2
St Helens Town v Bootle	0-4
Macclesfield Town v Bangor City	3-1
Telford United v Buxton	3-0
Glossop v Worksop Town	2-5
Eastwood Town v Prestwich Heys	4-2
Hednesford Town v Congleton Town	1-2
Oldbury United v Burton Albion	0-0
Nantwich Town v Witton Albion	0-3
Bilston v Blakenall	2-2
Shifnal Town v Leek Town	1-0
Stamford v Nuneaton Borough	1-1
Brigg Town v Goole Town	1-1
Alfreton Town v Shepshed Charterhouse	0-4
Gainsborough Trinity v Appleby Frod'ham	2-2
Armitage v Willenhall Town	3-2
Winterton Rangers v Bourne Town	4-3
Grantham v Hinckley Athletic	2-0
Belper Town v Mexboro' Town Athletic	1-1
Tividale v Bromsgrove Rovers	0-1
Holbeach United v Long Eaton United	3-1
Rushall Olympic v Dudley Town	1-1
Moor Green v Sutton Town	4-0
Coventry Sporting v AP Leamington	0-4
Stourbridge v Friar Lane OB	3-0
Tamworth v Racing Club Warwick	2-1
Rushden Town v Bridgnorth Town	0-2
Alvechurch v Worcester City	2-4
Enderby Town v Sutton Coldfield Town	1-4
VS Rugby v Highgate United	3-1

Rothwell Town v Darlaston	3-0
Halesowen Town v Corby Town	1-2
Mile Oak Rovers & Y v Buckingham Town	2-0
Banbury United v Kidderminster Harriers	0-2
Flackwell Heath v Bedworth United	0-1
Gorleston v King's Lynn	2-3
Skegness Town v March Town United	3-0
Felixstowe Town v Irthlingboro' Dia.	1-1
Ely City v Lowestoft Town	1-3
Billericay Town v Wisbech Town	3-1
Chatteris Town v Gt Yarmouth Town	1-6
Hitchin Town v Wellingborough Town	0-4
Ware v Soham Town Rangers	1-1
Edgware v Bedford Town – w.o. for Edgware	
Aveley v Haverhill Rovers	5-0
Walthamstow Avenue v Wootton Blue Cross	2-0
Woodford Town v Heybridge Swifts	3-1
Tring Town v Dunstable	1-0
Newmarket Town v Boreham Wood	0-3
Hayes v Saffron Walden Town	2-1
Hornchurch v Harwich & Parkston	1-0
Royston Town v Leytonstone & Ilford	0-5
Sudbury Town v Chelmsford City	1-1
Grays Athletic v Barton Rovers	1-0
Tilbury v Stowmarket	3-2
Letchworth GC v Harrow Borough	0-6
Chesham United v Cray Wanderers	3-2
Clapton v Chalfont St Peter	3-1
Feltham v Tiptree United	3-0
Merstham v Hendon	0-2
Haringey Borough v Hemel Hempstead	0-3
Leyton-Wingate v Dulwich Hamlet	2-2
Wealdstone v Hertford Town	5-0
Erith & Belvedere v Wembley	1-2
St Albans City v Abington Town	4-1
Hampton v Croydon	2-0
Hoddesdon Town v Windsor & Eton	0-2
Horsham v Kingstonian	0-3
Staines Town v Dorking Town (*at Dorking Town FC*)	5-0
Whyteleafe v Wokingham Town	0-0
Three Bridges v Uxbridge	0-0
Ringmer v Addlestone & Weybridge Town	2-1
Southall v Sittingbourne Town	1-1
Hastings Town v Chatham Town	2-7
Folkestone v Burnham	2-0
Horley Town v Carshalton Athletic	1-2
Egham Town v Faversham Town	0-0
Welling United v Sheppey United	2-0
Southwick v Banstead Athletic	2-2
Steyning Town v Dover	3-4
Lewes v Tooting & Mitcham United	2-3
Burgess Hill Town v Canterbury City	2-2
Deal Town v Redhill	3-1
Pagham v Hastings United	1-3
Whitstable Town v Bromley	1-0
Eastbourne Town v Bognor Regis Town	1-3
Hailsham Town v Thanet United	0-3
Wick v Corinthian-Casuals	1-2
Tonbridge AFC v Walton & Hersham	2-0
Haywards Heath v Dartford	1-6
Horsham YMCA v Ramsgate	1-1
Fareham Town v Farnborough Town	2-3
Crawley Town v Worthing	1-2
Eastleigh v Newport IOW	2-2
Horndean v Eastbourne United	1-1
Oxford City v Dorchester Town	2-2
Gosport Borough v Bracknell	1-0
Brockenhurst v AFC Totton	1-2
Maidenhead United v Chichester City	4-2
Frome Town v Witney Town	1-1
Chippenham Town v Basingstoke Town	1-1
Slough Town v Salisbury	2-0
Devizes Town v Camberley Town	1-0
Thames United v Cheltenham Town	2-3
Trowbridge Town v Ton Pentre	2-0
Welton Rovers v Bristol Manor Farm	0-0
Gloucester City v Llanelli	1-0
Hungerford Town v Merthyr Tydfil	0-3
Bridgend Town v Cinderford Town	2-1
Bridgwater Town v Mangotsfield United	1-1
Forest Green Rovers v Barry Town	2-3
Bath City v Taunton Town	2-2
Falmouth Town v Wimborne Town	1-2
Clevedon Town v St Blazey	0-2
Glastonbury v Barnstable Town	1-1
Weston-super-Mare v Bideford	1-4
Tiverton Town v Liskeard Athletic	2-2
Chard Town v Penzance	2-1
Shepton Mallet Town v Torrington	3-0

Replays

Chester-le-Street v Guisborough Town	3-0
Harrogate Town v Accrington Stanley	3-1
Runcorn v Thackley	2-1
Burton Albion v Oldbury United	1-0
Blakenall v Bilston	aet 1-2
Nuneaton Borough v Stamford	5-0
Goole Town v Brigg Town	7-2
Appleby Frod'ham v Gainsborough Trinity	0-0
Mexboro' Town Athletic v Belper Town	0-3
Dudley Town v Rushall Olympic	0-1
Irthlingboro' Dia. v Felixstowe Town	3-1
Soham Town Rangers v Ware	4-2
Chelmsford City v Sudbury Town	3-1
Dulwich Hamlet v Leyton-Wingate	2-0
Wokingham Town v Whyteleafe	aet 1-0
Uxbridge v Three Bridges	aet 1-2
Sittingbourne v Southall	1-3
Faversham Town v Egham Town	1-3
Banstead Athletic v Southwick	0-1
Canterbury City v Burgess Hill Town	aet 2-1
Ramsgate v Horsham YMCA	2-1
Newport IOW v Eastleigh	aet 1-3
Eastbourne United v Horndean	3-2
Dorchester Town v Oxford City	1-0
Witney Town v Frome Town	2-2
Basingstoke Town v Chippenham Town	3-2
Bristol Manor Farm v Welton Rovers	1-0
Mangotsfield United v Bridgwater Town	1-2
Taunton Town v Bath City	aet 2-4
Barnstable Town v Glastonbury	4-1
Liskeard Athletic v Tiverton Town	2-1

Second Replays

Gainsborough Trinity v Appleby Frod'm	2-1
Frome Town v Witney Town	2-1

Second Round Qualifying

Bishop Auckland v Annfield Plain	2-3
Lancaster City v Barrow	0-0
Horden CW v North Shields	0-1
Gateshead v Farsley Celtic	5-1
South Bank v Brandon United	2-1
Chester-le-Street v Morecambe	1-5
Spennymoor United v Seaham CW Red Star	2-1
Frickley Athletic v Harrogate Town	3-1
Caernarfon Town v Prescot Cables	4-1
Horwich RMI v Oswestry Town	5-1
Runcorn v Curzon Ashton	3-0
Chorley v Darwen	0-0
Hyde United v Macclesfield Town	2-5
Ashton United v Bootle	0-0
Telford United v Congleton Town	3-2
Worksop Town v Eastwood Town	1-1
Burton Albion v Shifnal Town	2-4
Witton Albion v Bilston	4-2
Nuneaton Boro' v Gainsboro' Trinity	3-3
Goole Town v Shepshed Charterhouse	0-2
Armitage v Belper Town	1-1
Winterton Rangers v Grantham	0-0
Bromsgrove Rovers v Moor Green	2-2
Holbeach United v Rushall Olympic	1-0
AP Leamington v Bridgnorth Town	6-1
Stourbridge v Tamworth	3-2
Worcester City v Rothwell Town	3-1
Sutton Coldfield Town v VS Rugby	2-1
Corby Town v Bedworth United	1-0
Mile Oak Rovers & Y v Kidderminster H	2-7
King's Lynn v Lowestoft Town	2-1
Skegness Town v Irthlingboro' Diamonds	0-0
Billericay Town v Soham Town Rangers	5-3
Gt Yarmouth Town v Wellingboro' Town	1-1
Edgware v Woodford Town	0-1
Aveley v Walthamstow Avenue	1-3
Tring Town v Hornchurch	2-2
Boreham Wood v Hayes	3-0

Leytonstone & Ilford v Tilbury	1-1
Chelmsford City v Grays Athletic	3-2
Harrow Borough v Feltham	2-3
Chesham United v Clapton	3-1
Hendon v Wealdstone	1-1
Hemel Hempstead v Dulwich Hamlet	1-2
Wembley v Windsor & Eton	1-3
St Albans City v Hampton	1-3
Kingstonian v Three Bridges	4-3
Staines Town v Wokingham Town 0-2 (*at Wokingham Town FC*)	
Ringmer v Folkestone	0-2
Southall v Chatham Town	2-2
Carshalton Athletic v Southwick	3-1
Egham Town v Welling United	2-0
Dover v Deal Town	0-3
Tooting & Mitcham Utd v Canterbury City	2-0
Hastings United v Thanet United	1-2
Whitstable Town v Bognor Regis Town	0-3
Corinthian-Casuals v Ramsgate (*at Dulwich Hamlet FC*)	1-0
Tonbridge AFC v Dartford	2-3
Farnborough Town v Eastbourne United	2-1
Worthing v Eastleigh	3-1
Dorchester Town v Maidenhead United	1-1
Gosport Borough v AFC Totton	2-2
Frome Town v Devizes Town	4-2
Basingstoke Town v Slough Town	2-2
Cheltenham Town v Gloucester City	5-1
Trowbridge Town v Bristol Manor Farm	3-0
Merthyr Tydfil v Barry Town	3-1
Bridgend Town v Bridgwater Town	1-0
Bath City v Barnstaple Town	4-2
Wimborne Town v St Blazey	3-2
Bideford v Shepton Mallet Town	3-1
Liskeard Athletic v Chard Town	3-0

Replays

Barrow v Lancaster City	1-0
Darwen v Chorley	0-3
Bootle v Ashton United	0-1
Eastwood Town v Worksop Town	3-1
Gainsboro' Trinity v Nuneaton Boro'	2-0
Belper Town v Armitage	0-1
Grantham v Winterton Rangers	4-0
Moor Green v Bromsgrove Rovers	1-0
Irthlingboro' Diamonds v Skegness Town	1-0
Wellingboro' Town v Gt Yarmouth Town	2-0
Hornchurch v Tring Town	0-0
Tilbury v Leytonstone & Ilford	2-2
Wealdstone v Hendon	aet 3-2
Chatham Town v Southall	aet 4-2
Maidenhead United v Dorchester Town	0-2
AFC Totton v Gosport Borough	2-1
Slough Town v Basingstoke Town	2-0

Second Replays

Hornchurch v Tring Town	0-3
Leytonstone & Ilford v Tilbury	2-1

Third Round Qualifying

Barrow v Annfield Plain	8-0
Gateshead v North Shields	2-4
Morecambe v South Bank	1-1
Frickley Athletic v Spennymoor United	1-1
Horwich RMI v Caernarfon Town	2-2
Chorley v Runcorn	2-2
Ashton United v Macclesfield Town	0-2
Eastwood Town v Telford United	2-2
Witton Albion v Shifnal Town	0-2
Shepshed Charterhouse v Gainsboro' Trin	3-0
Grantham v Armitage	3-1
Holbeach United v Moor Green	2-1
Stourbridge v AP Leamington	1-1
Sutton Coldfield Town v Worcester City	2-4
Kidderminster Harriers v Corby Town	1-3
Irthlingboro' Diamonds v Kings Lynn	1-2
Wellingborough Town v Billericay Town	1-1
Walthamstow Avenue v Woodford Town	2-0
Boreham Wood v Tring Town	3-0
Chelmsford City v Leytonstone & Ilford	0-0
Chesham United v Feltham	1-0
Dulwich Hamlet v Wealdstone	0-0
Hampton v Windsor & Eton	1-2
Wokingham Town v Kingstonian	2-2
Chatham Town v Folkestone	1-1
Egham Town v Carshalton Athletic	0-2
Tooting & Mitcham United v Deal Town	8-1
Bognor Regis Town v Thanet United	3-0
Dartford v Corinthian-Casuals	2-1
Worthing v Farnborough Town	1-0
AFC Totton v Dorchester Town	1-0
Slough Town v Frome Town	3-0
Trowbridge Town v Cheltenham Town	1-1
Bridgend Town v Merthyr Tydfil	1-3
Wimborne Town v Bath City	1-0
Liskeard Athletic v Bideford	1-2

Replays

South Bank v Morecambe	1-0
Spennymoor United v Frickley Athletic	1-1
Caernarfon Town v Horwich RMI	0-2
Runcorn v Chorley	4-0
Telford United v Eastwood Town	4-0
AP Leamington v Stourbridge	2-0
Billericay Town v Wellingoborough Town	1-2
Leytonstone & Ilford v Chelmsford City	0-0
Wealdstone v Dulwich Hamlet	2-1
Kingstonian v Wokingham Town	1-1
Folkestone v Chatham Town	5-0
Cheltenham Town v Trowbridge Town	1-0

Second Replays

Frickley Athletic v Spennymoor United	2-3
Chelmsford City v Leytonstone & Ilford	2-1
Wokingham Town v Kingstonian	2-0

Fourth Round Qualifying

Mossley v South Bank	1-0
North Shields v Barrow	2-1
Macclesfield Town v Stafford Rangers	3-1
Scarborough v Spennymoor United	4-2
Horwich RMI v Runcorn	2-2
Northwich Victoria v Blyth Spartans	3-0
Workington v Penrith	2-2
Corby Town v Holbeach United	0-1
Kettering Town v AP Leamington	3-1
Harlow Town v Bishop's Stortford	1-1
Telford United v Grantham	3-0
Worcester City v Wellingborough Town	2-1
Boston United v Shifnal Town	4-1
Shepshed Charterhouse v Kings Lynn	2-1
Gravesend & N'fleet v Maidstone United	1-2
Dagenham v Tooting & Mitcham United	2-0
Chelmsford City v Chesham United	1-3
Boreham Wood v Dartford	1-1
Wealdstone v Sutton United	3-1
Walthamstow Ave v Carshalton Ath	1-1
Barking v Folkestone	0-2
Cheltenham Town v Weymouth	0-0
Yeovil Town v Bognor Regis Town	4-2
Worthing v Minehead	2-2
Wimborne Town v Merthyr Tydfil	1-0
Wokingham Town v Leatherhead	1-0
AFC Totton v Windsor & Eton	0-0
Slough Town v Bideford	7-1

Replays

Runcorn v Horwich RMI	0-1
Penrith v Workington	0-2
Bishop's Stortford v Harlow Town	4-0
Dartford v Boreham Wood	aet 2-1
Carshalton Ath v Walthamstow Ave	aet 2-1
Weymouth v Cheltenham Town	4-0
Minehead v Worthing	0-3
Windsor & Eton v AFC Totton	1-0

FA CUP 1982–83

FA Cup First Round

ELEVEN 'NON-LEAGUE' CLUBS MOVE ON

It is no longer a surprise if **Altrincham** beat a League club, so their progress into the Second Round at the expense of lowly **Rochdale** didn't hit the headlines. Unfortunately both sides had two players sent off and this sad feature dominated the round as a total of twelve players failed to hear the final whistle. A very unwelcome record!

The scourge of the Football League, the visiting hooligan, ruined the big day for two 'non league' clubs, **Wokingham** and **Slough Town**. However, their results proved some sort of compensation as **Cardiff** were held at Wokingham and **Millwall** were beaten at Slough.

Great results were achieved by **Bishop's Stortford** at **Reading** and **Northwich Victoria** who beat Chester in a home replay. While probably the only player/groundsman in the cup, **Chris Cook**, scored two match winning goals for **Boston United** in their 3-1 win over **Crewe**.

Little **Wimborne** from the Western League's lower division were the real minnows and they enjoyed their day out at Aldershot, while 'non-League' giants **Wycombe Wanderers** were given a standing ovation at Eastville where Bristol Rovers just scraped in 1-0.

Tranmere Rovers, in desperate financial trouble, achieved an all important victory over **Scarborough** and little **Shepshed Charterhouse** from the new Northern Counties (East) created club history with a visit to famous **Preston North End**.

Two local 'derbies' attracted good attendances, 9,152 at Hull for the visit of **Sheffield United** and 10,202 at **Plymouth** to watch the home side's 2-0 victory over **Exeter City**, while **Portsmouth** also had over 10,000 at Fratton Park to see Billy Rafferty score a hat trick in their 4-1 defeat of **Hereford United**.

Eighty clubs took part in this round, 24 from the Third Division, 24 from the Fourth Division, 14 Alliance, 8 Isthmian, 3 Northern Premier League, 2 Southern League, and one each from the Northern, Western, United Counties, Northern Counties (East) and the North West Counties Leagues.

20 NOV

Aldershot (2) 4 *(Banton 2 [1 pen], Sanford, Brodie)*

Wimborne (0) 0 2630

Aldershot: Johnson, Scott, Wooler, Briley, Wood, Jopling, Shrubb (Lucas), Banton, Sanford, McDonald, Brodie.
Wimborne: Manuel; Logan, Loveridge, Cannie N., Collie, Burns, Tucker, Coombes, Cannie B., Bridle, Stroud (Beardsley).
Referee: J. Moules (Ongar).

Altrincham (1) 2 *(Davison, Howard)*

Rochdale (0) 1 *(Wellings pen)* 3053

Altrincham: Johnson D., Allan, Davison, Kenyon, Cuddy, Anderson, Bailey, Heathcote, Johnson J., Rogers, Howard.
Rochdale: Pearce, Kee an (Hamilton), Snookes, Martinez, Swan, Weir, Thompson, Greaves, French, Wellings, Hilditch.
Referee: V. Callow (Solihull).

Blackpool (0) 3 *(Pashley, Bamber, Deary pen)*

Horwich RMI (0) 0 5280

Blackpool: Hesford, Bardsley, Hart, Deary, Hetzke, Serella, Hockaday, Noble, Bamber, Pashley, Downes (Jeffrey).
Horwich RMI: McMahon; Griffiths, Parry, Waywell, Filous (Brown), Kilgannon, Garrett, Haslem, Lang, Caldwell, MacLachlan.
Referee: J. Lovatt (Crewe).

Boston United (0) 3 *(Lumby, Cook 2)*

Crewe Alex (1) 1 *(Palios)* 3311

Boston: Blackwell, Lyon, Mann, Tiler, Jones, Allen, Cox (Casey), Cook, Lumby, Mallender, Gilbert.
Crewe Alex: Smith; Purdie, Bowers, Salathiel, Scott, Palios, Haslegrave, Sutton (Hanlon), Waller, Evans, Craven.
Referee: J. Deakin (Bedford).

AFC Bournemouth (0) 0

Southend U (2) 2 *(Spackman og, Morgan og)* 4835

AFC Bournemouth: Allen, Golac, Sulley (Graham), Spackman, Brignull, Dawkins, Carter, Williams, Morgan, Funnell, Dawtry.
Southend U: Keeley; Stead, Hadley, Clark, Otulakowski, Cusack, Pountney, Phillips, Mercer, Greaves (Pennyfather), Nelson.
Referee: T. Ward (London).

Bristol R (0) 1 *(Stephens)*

Wycombe Wanderers (0) 0 6420

Bristol R: Kite; Slatter, Williams B., Williams G., Parkin, McCaffery, Holloway, Williams D., Stephens, Randall, Barrett.
Wycombe Wanderers: Lester; Norman, Hill, Toll, Vircavs, Dell, Borg, Jacobs, Glynn, Long, Wilson.
Referee: R. Glasson (Salisbury).

Carshalton Ath (1) 4 *(Dark, Levington 2, Tuite)*

Barnet (0) 0 1100

Carshalton Ath: Collier; Maurice, Akers, Raffington, Coghill, Fraser, Parsons, Levington, Tuite, Friend, Dark.
Barnet: Phillips; Garner, Sargent, Chivers, Kruse (Gallagher), Pittaway, Millett, Ragan, Stein, Barnes, Mahoney.
Referee: T. G. Bune (Newbury).

Chesham U (0) 0

Yeovil (1) 1 *(Bell)* 1332

Chesham U: Allies; Cerasale, McGonagle (Greenhalgh), Morrissey, Holmes, Jones, Brown, Adams, Woodstock, Huxley, Nash.
Yeovil: Langley; Giles, Gold (Williams), Payne, Andrews, Beck, Platt, James, Bell, Ritchie, Brown.
Referee: D. H. Nevin (Woking).

Chester (0) 1 *(Lane)*

Northwich Victoria (1) 1 *(Wilson)* 4400

Chester: Salmon; Bradley, Lane, Storton, Zelem, Johnson (Blackwell), Sloan, Allen, Simpson, Ludlam, Thomas.
Northwich Victoria: Ryan; Fretwell, Murphy, Jones, Forshaw, Ward, Anderson, Bradley, Reid (Bennett), Chesters, Wilson.
Referee: A. Hamil (Wolverhampton).

Chesterfield (1) 2 *(Walker 2)*

Peterborough U (1) 2 *(Clarke, Glynn)* 2965

Chesterfield: Turner; Stirk, O'Neill, Wilson, Green, Bellamy, Windridge, Athersych, Walker, Kowalski, Carroll (Dawson).
Peterborough U: Seaman; Winters, Collins, Glynn, Firm, Slack, Clarke, Rodaway, Cooke, Benjamin, Chard.
Referee: R. Nixon (Wirral).

Colchester U (0) 0

Torquay U (1) 2 *Little, Cooper)* 2913

Colchester U: Walker; Ward, Coleman (Adcock), Hunter, Longhorn, Wignall, Allinson, Osborne, McDonough, Bremner, Leslie.
Torquay U: Horn; Doyle, Wilson, Rioch, Little, Bould, Grapes, O'Donnell, Cooper, Anderson, Gallagher.
Referee: D. L. Reeves (Uxbridge).

Darlington (0) 0

Scunthorpe U (0) 1 *(Cammack)* 2540

Darlington: Cuff; Brisset, Wilson, Smith, Rhodes, Kamara, Gilbert, McLean, Honour, Walsh, Dunn.
Scunthorpe U: Neenan; Keeley, Pointon, Parkinson, Baines, Hunter, O'Berg, Cammack, Cowling (Fowler), Angus, Leman.
Referee: C. Seel (Carlisle).

Enfield (0) 0

Newport Co (0) 0 2541

Enfield: Jacobs: Savage, Tone, Barrett, Waite, Ironton, Oliver, Taylor, Ashford, Turner, King.
Newport Co: Kendall; Jones, Vaughan, Bailey, Gwyther, Relish, Lowndes, Aldridge, Tynan, Elsey, Moore.
Referee: J. Martin (Alton).

Gillingham (0) 1 *(Cascarino)*

Dagenham (0) 0 3889

Gillingham: Hillyard; Sharpe, Adams, Bruce, Weatherly, Tydeman, Miller (White), Johnson, Cascarino, Grewcock, Price.
Dagenham: Hutley; Boyce, Knapman, Dunwell, Campbell, Wade, Francis, Stewart, Reeves, Wilson, Armstrong.
Referee: A. Gunn (Burgess Hill).

Halifax T (0) 0

North Shields (0) 1 *(McCaffery)* 2277

Halifax T: Smelt; Nobbs (Ward), Wood, Evans, Smith, Hendrie, Staniforth, Davison, Allatt, Spooner, Goodman.
North Shields: Harrison; Waterson, Dickson, Varty (Cassidy), Harmison, Young, Smith, Doig, Ross, Donaldson, McCaffery.
Referee: T. Fitzharris (Bolton).

Hartlepool U (1) 3 *(Linacre 2, Hogan)*

Lincoln C (0) 0 2204

Hartlepool U: Wright; Brown, Stimpson, Hogan, Linacre, Linighan, Staff, Hamilton, Dobson, Lawrence, Barker.
Lincoln C: Felgate; Carr, Neale, Cockerill, Peake, Thompson, Burke, Turner, Hobson, Bell, Shipley.
Referee: N. Glover (Chorley).

Holbeach U (0) 0

Wrexham (2) 4 *(Keay, Gregory, Savage, Muldoon)* 3143

Holbeach U: Secker; Kwiatkowski, Gosling, Hudson, Day, Delahoy, Maltby, Bemrose, Merchant (Langford), Ransome, Lowery.
Wrexham: Niedzwiecki; Hunt, Bater, Savage, Dowman, Muldoon, Arkwright, King, Keay, Gregory, Buxton.
Referee: K. Baker (Rugby).

Huddersfield T (0) 1 *(Brown)*

Mossley (0) 0 7599

Huddersfield T: Cox; Brown, Burke, Stanton, Sutton, Hanvey (Greenwood), Lillis, Doyle, Russell, Wilson, Cowling.
Mossley: Sherlock; Phillips, Gorman, Derbyshire, Duff, Roberts, Szarbo, Young, Tate (Gallagher), O'Connor, Wagstaffe.
Referee: D. Scott (Burnley).

Hull C (0) 1 *(Kenworthy og)*

Sheffield U (1) 1 *(Edwards)* 9152

Hull C: Norman; McNeil, Skipper, Roberts D., Booth, Swan, Roberts G., Marwood, McClaren, Whitehurst, Mutrie.
Sheffield U: Conroy; Henderson, Houston, Kenworthy, Charles, Morris, Richardson, Curran, Trusson, Edwards, Hatton (Brazil).
Rferee: M. Scott (Nottingham).

Macclesfield (0) 1 *(Long)*

Worcester C (1) 5 *(Moss 2, Tuohy 3)* 2143

Macclesfield: Eales; Elsby, Fairclough, Wardle (Walker), Seddon, Marsden, Long, Gay, Griffin, Keelan, Kersley.
Worcester C: Carter; Selby, McGrath, Phelps, Tudor, Williams J., Williams B. (Stanton), Hughes, Tuohy, Crompton, Moss.
Referee: K. P. Barrett (Coventry).

Mansfield T (1) 3 *(Bell, Dungworth 2)*

***Stockport Co* (1) 2** *(Williams, Park)* 2215

Mansfield T: Arnold; Blackhall (Woodhead), Kennedy, Bell, Ayre, Calderwood, Matthews, Hutchinson, Dungworth, Nicholson.
Stockport Co: Lloyd; Smith, Rutter, Emmerson, Bowles, Thorpe, Williams, Phillips, Quinn, Park, Coyle.
Referee: M. J. Heath (Stoke).

Northampton T (1) 2 *(Burrows, Denyer)*

Wimbledon (0) 2 *(Leslie, Entwistle)* 2832

Northampton T: Freeman; Brady, Phillips, Gage, Burrows, Heeley, Saxby, Buchanan (Coffill), Saunders, Denyer, Massey.
Wimbledon: Beasant; Leslie, Jones, Galliers, Smith, Morris, Entwistle, Ketteridge, Fishenden (Gage), Downes, Dibble.
Referee: D. J. Axcell (Southend).

Orient (3) 4 *(Foster, Godfrey 2, Sussex)*

Bristol C (1) 1 *(Johnson)* 2772

Orient: Day; Roffey, Peach, Foster, Cunningham, Donn, Osgood, Godfrey, Houchen, Sussex, Taylor.
Bristol C: Shaw; Stevens, Johnson, Nicholl, Newman, Riley, Economou, Ritchie (Thompson), Williams, Cooper, Crawford.
Referee: M. L. Jones (Sussex).

Oxford U (3) 5 *(Shotton, Fogg* pen*, Vinter, Foley 2)*

Folkestone (1) 2 *(Fusco N.* pen*, Plews)* 4138

Oxford U: Butcher; Linney, Grant, Train, Fogg, Shotton, Brock (Jones), Foley, Vinter, Hebberd, Smithers.
Folkestone: Munden; Wiltshire, Christie, Fusco R., Brooks, Fusco N., Richardson, Plews, Cugley, Hilton, Allen (Bartlett).
Referee: B. H. Daniels (Brentwood).

Mossley's Mal Wagstaffe beats Huddersfield 'keeper Brian Cox in their FA Cup first round clash at Leeds Road, but the goal was disallowed for off-side, and Huddersfield went on to win 1-0.

Plymouth (0) 2 *(Hodges, Sims)*

Exeter C (0) 0 10,202

Plymouth: Crudgington; Nisbet, Rowe, Harrison, Smith, Cooper, Hodges, Cook, Sims, McCartney, Rogers.
Exeter C: Bond; Rogers M., Viney, Harle, Marker, McEwan, Neville, Rogers P., Kellow, Delve, Pullar.
Referee: E. Read (Bristol).

Portsmouth (2) 4 *(Biley 2, Rafferty 2)*

Hereford U (0) 1 *(Showers)* 10,005

Portsmouth: Knight; McLaughlin, Sullivan, Doyle, Howe, Aizlewood, Webb, Tait, Rafferty, Biley, Rogers.
Hereford U: Plumley; Price, Bray, Hicks, Pejic, Ross, Lane, Crabbe (Harvey), Showers, McNeil, White.
Referee: D. Vickers (Ilford).

Port Vale (0) 0

Bradford C (0) 1 *(Campbell)* 6151

Port Vale: Siddall; Tartt, Bromage, Hunter, Sproson, Cegielski, Fox, Moss, Newton, Ridley (Greenhoff), Armstrong.
Bradford C: McManus; Podd, Chapman, Lester, Cooke, Jackson, McFarland, Ellis, Campbell, McNiven, Mellor.
Referee: C. Newsome (Shropshire).

Preston NE (3) 5 *(Elliott 2, Kelly, Coleman, McAteer)*

Shepshed Charterhouse (0) 1 *(Jeans)* 6200

Preston NE: Litchfield; Westwell, McAteer, O'Riordan, Coleman, Gowling, Kelly, Sayer, Elliott, Naughton, Houston.
Shepshed Charterhouse: King; Black (Chamberlain), Mitchell, Chapman, Hendrick, Matthams, Lissanan, Fearn, Jenas, Gould, Kirk.
Referee: A. Challinor (Maltby).

Reading (0) 1 *(Earles)*

Bishops Stortford (0) 2 *(Sullivan, Worrell)* 2931

Reading: Fearon; Williams, White, Beavon, Hicks, Wood, Bason, Stant, Dixon, Doherty (Earles), Donnellan.
Bishops Stortford: Welsh; Wickenden, Brown, Smith, Elley, Hull, Avery, Bradford, Worrell, Simmonds, Sullivan.
Referee: R. Milford (Bristol).

Slough T (0) 1 *(Attrell)*

Millwall (0) 0 5000

Slough T: Parsons; Yerby, Hutchinson, Maloney, Webster, Evans, Powell, White (Petty), Attrell, Russell, Dodds.
Millwall: Sansome; Stevens, Robinson, Massey, Allardyce, Roberts, Horrix, Neal, Aylott, Martin, Madden.
Referee: M. Taylor (Deal).

Swindon T (0) 2 *Henry, Rideout)*

Wealdstone (0) 0 4035

Swindon T: Allan; Henry, Baddeley, Emmanuel, Lewis, Graham, Pritchard, Batty, Rideout, Rowland, Barnard.
Wealdstone: Goddard; Perkins, Pearce, Byatt, Bogart, Barwick, Davies, Wainwright, Cordice A., Graves, Cordice N.
Referee: B. T. Stevens (Stonehouse).

Tranmere R (2) 4 *(Kerr, Brown O. 3)*

Scarborough (1) 2 *(Hamson 2)* 2836

Tranmere R: Endersby; Mungall, Burgess, Brown A., Hamilton, Williams, Powell, Aspinall, Kerr, Brown O., Griffiths.
Scarborough: Letheran; Parker (Howey), Bunns, Magee, Cottam, Cook, Sellers, Jones, Hanson, Bowman, Olney.
Referee: P. Tyldesley (Stockport).

Walsall (1) 3 *(Kearns, Preece, Buckley)*

Kettering (0) 0 3471

Walsall: Green; Bates (Penn), Mower, Beech, Sinnott, Hart, O'Kelly, Preece, Kearns, Buckley, Caswell.
Kettering: Tingay; McGoldrick, Forster, Chamberlain, Palmer, Banton, Hamill, Goode (Hosbauer), Duggan, Murphy, Pownall.
Referee: D. Hedges (Oxford).

Weymouth (0) 4 *(Morrell, Peter 2, Bourne, Pearson)*

Maidstone (2) 3 *(Hill, Bartley 2)* 2003

Weymouth: Baker; Morrell, Peter, Morrell, Paul, Elliott, Arnold, Finnigan (Bourne), Baber, Pearson, Iannonie, Barthwick, Banjafield.
Maidstone: Richardson; Thompson, Moore, Hill, Newson, Watson, Hughes, Penfold, Green, Bartley, Ovard.
Referee: A. Robinson (Waterlooville).

Windsor and Eton (0) 0

Brentford (3) 7 *(Mahoney 3, McNichol, Joseph, Hurlock 2)* 6309

Windsor and Eton: Wills; Mitchell, Briggs, King, Smith, Baron, Butler, White, Edwards (Woodcraft), McCulloch, Yates.
Brentford: Roche; Rowe, Harris (Booker), McNichol, Whitehead, Hurlock, Kamara, Bowles, Joseph, Mahoney, Roberts.
Referee: D. W. Civil (Bormingham).

Wokingham T (1) 1 *(Torrance)*

Cardiff C (0) 1 *(Tong)* 3000

Wokingham T: Hatcher; Steer, Ryan, Wilks, Purser, Cox, Cotterell, Torrance, Morton, Brown (Gane), Stanley.
Cardiff C: Dibble; Jones, Bodin (Ingram), Micallef, Dwyer, Mullen, Bennett, Tong, Gibbins, Hemmerman, Lewis.
Referee: C. Downey (Hounslow).

Workington T (0) 1 *(Gill)*

Doncaster R (1) 2 *(Owen, Austin)* 1336

Workington T: Fisher; McDonald (Harris), Kent, Benfold, Johnston, Williams, Carruthers, Smith, Gill, Wann, Harrison.
Doncaster R: Peacock; Russell, Snodin G., Humphreys, Wigginton, Cawthorne, Robertson, Owen, Douglas (Mell), Austin, Lister.
Referee: D. B. Allinson (Lancaster).

Worthing (0) 2 *(Lelliot, Cornwell)*

Dartford (1) 1 *(Lazarus)* 2042

Worthing: Dovey; Flood, Cox, Aitken, Raynsford, Lelliott, Gill, Dove, Cornwell, Edmonds, Foreman.
Dartford: Moseley; Dixon, Tunbridge, O'Sullivan A., Coupland, Robinson, Brown, O'Sullivan W., Lazarus, Burman, Myers.
Referee: D. Letts (Aldershot).

York C (0) 3 *(Hood, Ford, Walwyn)*

Bury (1) 1 *(Hilton)* 3057

York C: Jones; Evans, Hay, Sbragia, Smith, Hood, Ford, Crosby, Walwyn, Byrne, Pollard.
Bury: Brown; Gardner, Davies, Gore, Hilton, Bramhall, Firth, Madden, Parker, Jakub, Potts.
Referee: M. G. Peck (Kendal).

21 NOV

Wigan Ath (0) 0

Telford U (0) 0 4805

Wigan Ath: Tunks; McMahon, Weston, Cribley, Methven, Butler, Langley, Williams, Houghton, Bradd, Sheldon.
Telford: Charlton; Lewis, Walker, Martin, Turner, Joseph, Barnett, Hogan, Neale, Mather, Alcock.
Referee: N. Ashley (Nantwich).

22 NOV

FIRST ROUND REPLAYS

Northwich Victoria (0) 3 *(Chesters, Ward 2)*

Chester (0) 1 *(Williams)* *aet* 4014

Northwich Victoria: Ryan; Fretwell, Murphy, Jones, Forshaw, Bennett, Anderson (Morley), Bradley, Ward, Chesters, Wilson.
Chester: Salmon; Bradley, Lane, Storton, Zelem, Blackwell, Sloan, Cooke, Thomas, Ludlam (Williams), Simpson.
Referee: A. Hamill (Wolverhampton).

23 NOV

Cardiff C (1) 3 *(Jones, Hemmerman, Ingram)*

Wokingham T (0) 0 3755

Cardiff C: Dibble; Jones, Bodin, Ingram, Dwyer, Mullen, Bennett D. (Micallef), Tong, Gibbins, Hemmerman, Lewis.
Wokingham T: Hatcher; Steer, Ryan, Wilkes, Purser, Cox, Cottrell, Torrance, Morton, Brown, Stanley (Gane).
Referee: C. Downey (Middlesex).

Newport Co (0) 4 *(Tynan 3* [1 pen]*, Aldridge)*

Enfield (2) 2 *(Taylor, Turner* pen*)* 4014

Newport Co: Kendall; Jones, Vaughan, Bailey, Gwyther, Relish, Lowndes, Aldridge, Tynan, Elsey, Moore (Davies).
Enfield: Jacobs; Savage, Tone, Barrett, Waite, Ironton (Holmes), Oliver, Taylor, Ashford, Turner, King.
Referee: J. Martin (Alton).

Sheffield U (1) 2 *Morris, Edwards)*

Hull C (0) 0 12,232

Sheffield U: Conroy; Henderson, Garner, Richardson, Houston, Kenworthy, Morris, Charles, Edwards, Brazil, Curran.
Hull C: Norman; McNeil, Askew, Roberts D., Skipper, Booth, Marwood, McClaren, Whitehurst, Mutrie, Roberts G.
Referee: M. P. Scott (Nottingham).

Telford U (0) 2 *(Walker, Neale)*

Wigan Ath (0) 1 *(Butler)* 5097

Telford: Charlton; Eaton, Turner, Joseph, Walker, Martin, Barnett, Neale, Mather, Hogan, Alcock.
Wigan Ath: Tunks; McMahon, Weston, Butler, Cribley, Methven, Sheldon, Langley, Bradd, Houghton, Williams.
Referee: N. Ashley (Nantwich).

Wimbledon (0) 0

Northampton T (1) 2 *(Coffill 2)* 2097

Wimbledon: Beasant; Leslie, Jones, Galliers, Smith, Morris, Dibble, Ketteridge, Entwistle (Gage), Downes, Evans.
Northampton T: Freeman; Brady, Phillips, Gage, Burrows, Heeley, Saxby, Buchanan, Coffill, Denyer, Massey.
Referee: D. Axcell (Southend).

24 NOV

Peterborough U (1) 2 *(Gynn, Cooke* pen*)*

Chesterfield (1) 1 *(Walker)* 3185

Peterborough U: Seaman; Winters, Collins, Gynn, Firm, Slack, Clarke, Rodaway, Cooke, Benjamin (Quow), Chard.
Chesterfield: Gregory; Pollard, O'Neill, Wilson, Green, Henson (Windridge), Stirk, Henderson, Walker, Kowalski, Carroll.
Referee: R. Nixon (Wirral).

FA Cup Second Round

WEYMOUTH WIN AT CARDIFF

The forty clubs competing in this round were made up of **17** Third Division clubs, **12** from the Fourth Division, **6** Alliance clubs, **4** Isthmians and **North Shields** from The Northern League.

The heroes of the day were undoubtedly **Weymouth** who trailed **Cardiff City** by two goals at half time but came back to win 3-2, a great effort in any game, but against a team confidently placed near the top of Division Three; it really was a bit special!

Lyndon Lynch, a Marvin Hagler 'look alike', scored three at Slough to give **Bishop's Stortford** a place in the Third Round draw and **Worcester City** came from behind to beat **Wrexham** with two goals from **Paul Moss**.

Memories of the Tom Finney and Stanley Matthews era were rekindled as **Preston** beat **Blackpool** 2-1 in front of 14,008 and despite another good attendance at Portsmouth (13,250), visiting **Aldershot** achieved a surprise 3-1 victory.

Tranmere Rovers beat Telford in a replay and grabbed themselves a possible lifeline, if the draw proved kind to them, while **Boston United** qualified for a replay at Bramall Lane, which was lucrative but not productive and **Altrincham** failed to reach the Third Round for the first time in five years when they lost 0-1 to a very good **Huddersfield** side.

11 Dec 1982

Altrincham (0) 0

Huddersfield (1) 1 *(Stanton)* 5800

Altrincham: Johnson D.; Allan, Davison, Bailey, Cuddy, Gardner, Bennett (Constantine), Heathcote, Johnson J., Rogers, Howard.
Huddersfield T: Cox; Brown, Burke, Stanton, Sutton, Valentine, Lillis, Doyle, Russell, Wilson, Cowling.
Referee: P. Chadwick (Darwen).

Boston (1) 1 *(Lumby)*

Sheffield U (0) 1 *(Edwards)* 5729

Boston: Blackwell; Lyon, Mann, Tiles, Jones, Allen, Casey, Cook, Lumby, Mallender, Gilbert.
Sheffield U: Waugh; Henderson, Kenworthy, McHale, MacPhail, Houston, Morris, Trusson, Edwards, Young, Charles.
Referee: I. J. Borrett (Eye).

Bristol R (1) 2 *(Williams D. 2)*

Plymouth Arg (1) 2 *(Rogers, Sims)* 9018

Bristol R: Kite; Slatter, Williams B., Williams G., Parkin, McCaffery, Holloway, Williams D., Stephens (Withey), Randell, Barrett.
Plymouth Arg: Crudgington; Nisbet, Uzzell, Harrison, Smith, Cooper, Hodges, Cook, Sims, McCartney, Rogers.
Referee: L. Burden (Poole).

Cardiff C (2) 2 *(Gibbins, Hemmerman)*

Weymouth (0) 3 *(Iannone, Finnegan, Pearson)* 4446

Cardiff C: Dibble, Jones, Bodin, Tong (Giles), Dwyer, Mullen, Bennett D., Bennett G., Gibbins, Hemmerman, Lewis.
Weymouth: Baker; Morrell Peter, Morrell Paul, Elliott, Arnold, Finnegan, Baber, Pearson, Iannone, Borthwick, Benjafield.
Referee: B. Hill (Kettering).

Gillingham (0) 1 *(Johnson)*

Northampton T (1) 1 *(Saxby)* 4054

Gillingham: Sutton; Sharpe, Adams, Bruce (Price), Sitton, Tydeman, Powell, Johnson, Cascarino, White, Weatherly.
Northampton T: Freeman; Brady, Phillips, Gage, Burrows, Coffill, Saxby, Buchanan, Muir, Massey, Denyer.
Referee: J. Moules (Ongar).

Hartlepool U (0) 1 *(Dobson)*

York C (0) 1 *(Pollard)* 3344

Hartlepool U: Watson, Smith, Stimpson, Hogan, Baker, Linighan, Staff, Dobson, Linacre, Brown, Lawrence.
York C: Jones; Evans, Hay, Sbragia, Smith, Hood, Ford, Crosby, Walwyn, Byrne, Pollard.
Referee: K. Walmsley (Blackpool).

Mansfield T (1) 1 *(Dungworth* pen*)*

Bradford C (1) 1 *(Gray)* 2962

Mansfield T: Arnold; Bird, Kennedy, Bell, Ayre, Calderwood, Matthews, Hutchinson, Dungworth, Caldwell, Nicholson.
Bradford C: McManus; Podd, Chapman, Lester, Cooke, Jackson, Ellis, Gray, Campbell, McNiven, Mellor.
Referee: N. Midgeley (Salford).

Newport Co (0) 1 *(Tynan* pen*)*

Orient (0) 0 4013

Newport Co: Kendall; Jones, Relish, Bailey, Boyle, Stroud, Lowndes, Aldridge, Tynan, Vaughan, Elsey (Moore).
Orient: Day; Roffey, Peach, Foster, Cunningham, Cornwell, Osgood, Godfrey, Houchen, Sussex, Blackhall.
Referee: K. Baker (Rugby).

North Shields (0) 0

Walsall (0) 3 *(Round, Buckley, Caswell)* 3200

North Shields: Harrison; Waterson, Dickson, Varty, Harriston, Young, Smith, Doig, Ross, Donaldson, McCaffery (Armstrong).
Walsall: Kearns; Caswell, Mower, Beech, Sinnott, Hart, Penn, Preece, Round, Buckley, Shakespeare.
Referee: M. D. Peck (Kendall).

Oxford U (0) 4 *(Hebberd, Foley, Vinter)*

Worthing (0) 0 5430

Oxford U: Butcher; Linney, Fogg, Train, Briggs, Shotton, Lawrence, Foley, Vinter, Hebberd, Smithers.
Worthing: Dovey; Flood, Cox, Aitken, Raynsford, Elliott, Gill (Bernard), Dove, Cornwell, Edmonds, Foreman.
Referee: M. Dimblebee (Stevenage).

Peterborough U (2) 5 *(Cooke 2, Clarke, Quow, Gynn)*

Doncaster R (1) 2 *(Snodin, Mell)* 4012

Peterborough U: Seaman; Winters, Collins, Gynn, Firm, Slack, Clarke, Rodaway, Cooke, Benjamin, Quow.
Doncaster R: Peacock; Russell, Snodin G., Snodin I., Wigginton, Cawthorne, Douglas (Mell), Owen, Austin, Lister, Robertson.
Referee: J. Bray (Hinckley).

Portsmouth (1) 1 *(Webb)*

Aldershot (2) 3 *(Briley, Banton 2)* 13,250

Portsmouth: Knight; McLaughlin, Sullivan (Thomas), Doyle, Howe, Ellis, Webb, Tait, Rafferty, Biley, Rogers.
Aldershot: Johnson; Scott, Gillard, Briley (Goddard), Wooler, Jopling, Shrubb, Banton, Sanford, McDonald, Brodie.
Referee: M. Bodenham (Brighton).

Jeff Johnson of Altrincham (right) gets in a cross despite the attentions of a Huddersfield Town defender in their second round FA Cup tie.

Preston NE (0) 2 *(Coleman, O'Riordan)*

Blackpool (0) 1 *(Brockbank)* 14,008

Preston NE: Litchfield; Westwell, McAteer, O'Riordan, Coleman, Gowling, Walsh, Sayer, Elliott, Naughton, Houston.
Blackpool: Hesford; Bardsley, Butler, Noble, Hetzke, Serella, Hockaday (Brockbank), Jeffrey, Bamber, Pashley, Downes.
Referee: J. B. Worrall (Warrington).

Scunthorpe U (1) 2 *(Cowling, O'Berg)*

Northwich Vic (1) 1 *(Chesters)* 5457

Scunthorpe U: Neenan; Keeley, Pointon, Fowler, Baines, Hunter, O'Berg, Cammack, Cowling, Angus, Leman.
Northwich Vic: Ryan; Fretwell, Murphy, Jones K., Oakes, Bennett, Morley (Jones P.), Abel, Ward, Chesters, Wilson.
Referee: J. Hunting (Leicester).

Slough (0) 1 *(Evans)*

Bishops Stortford (0) 4 *(Lynch 3, Simmonds)* 3000

Slough: Mitchell; Yerby, Maloney, Hutchinson, Araguez, Evans, Powell (Petty), White, Attrell, Russell, Dodds.
Bishops Stortford: Welsh; Wickenden, Smith, Elley, Brown, Hull, Avery, Lynch, Worrell, Simmonds, Sullivan.
Referee: A. R. Robinson (Waterlooville).

Southend U (1) 3 *(Phillips, Pountney 2)*

Yeovil (0) 0 4544

Southend U: Cawston; Stead, Hadley, Yates, Otulakowski, Cusack, Pountney, Phillips, Mercer, Pennyfather, Nelson.
Yeovil: Langley; Giles, Gold, Paine, Andrews, Beck, Platt, James, Bell, Ritchie, Brown.
Referee: T. G. Bune (Yattendon).

Swindon T (2) 2 *(Lewis, Barnard)*

Brentford (0) 2 *(Bowen, Roberts)* 7176

Swindon T: Allan; Henry (Quinn), Baddeley, Emmanuel, Lewis, Graham, Pritchard, Batty, Rideout, Rowland, Barnard.
Brentford: Roche; Rowe (Bowen), Wilkins, Booker, Whitehead, Hurlock, Kamara, Joseph, Mahoney, Bowles, Roberts.
Referee: J. E. Martin (Alton).

Telford U (0) 1 *(Mather* pen*)*

Tranmere R (1) 1 *(Brown* pen*)* 4010

Telford U: Charlton; Lewis, Eaton, Mayman, Walker, Martin (Gardner), Joseph, Neale, Mather, Hogan, Alcock.
Tranmere R: Endersby; Mungall, Burgess, Mooney, Hamilton (Powell), Williams, Ferguson, Aspinall, Kerr, Brown, Griffiths.
Referee: F. Roberts (Prestatyn).

Torquay U (1) 4 *(Anderson, Bishop 2, Wilson)*

Carshalton Ath (0) 1 *(Lewington)* 3409

Torquay U: Horn; Doyle, Wilson, Rioch, Little, Bould, Brown, O'Donnell, Bishop, Anderson, Gallagher.
Carshalton Ath: Collier; Maurice, Akers, Raffington, Coghill, Fraser (Bangs), Parsons, Lewington, Tuite, Friend, Dark.
Referee: E. Read (Bristol).

Worcester C (0) 2 *(Moss P. 2)*

Wrexham (0) 1 *(Hunt)* 5500

Worcester C: Parkes; Hunt, McGrath, Phelps, Tudor, Hughes, Williams J., Williams B., Tuohy, Crompton, Moss P.
Wrexham: Niedzwiecki; Hunt, Bater, Savage, Dowman, Muldoon, Arkwright, Gregory, Keay, King, Buxton.
Referee: A. Seville (Birmingham).

SECOND ROUND REPLAYS

14 DEC

Brentford (0) 1 *(Roberts)*

Swindon T (0) 3 *aet (Rowland, Pritchard, Batty)* 7383

Brentford: Roche; Rowe, Wilkins, Booker, Whitehead, Hurlock, Kamara, Joseph, Mahoney (Bowen), Bowles, Roberts.
Swindon T: Allan; Bailey, Baddeley, Emmanuel, Lewis, Graham, Pritchard, Batty, Rideout, Rowland, Barnard (Hughes).
Referee: J. E. Martin (Alton).

Northampton T (0) 3 *(Belfon 2, Massey)*

Gillingham (1) 2 *(Weatherly 2)* 4290

Northampton T: Freeman; Brady (Belfon), Phillips, Gage, Burrows, Coffil, Saxby, Buchanan, Muir, Denyer, Massey.
Gillingham: Sutton; Sharpe, Adams, Shaw, Sitton, Tydeman, Powell (Cascarino), Johnson, Price, Grewcock, Weatherly.
Referee: J. A. Moules (Ongar).

Sheffield U (2) 5 *(Young 3, Morris, Edwards)*

Boston U (1) 1 *Henderson og)* 11,045

Sheffield U: Waugh; Henderson, Kenworthy, McHale, MacPhail, Houston, Morris, Trusson, Edwards, Young, Charles (Brazil).
Boston U: Blackwell; Lyon, Mann, Tiler, Jones, Allen, Casey, Cook (Cox), Lumby, Mallender, Gilbert.
Referee: I. J. Borrett (Suffolk).

Tranmere R (0) 2 *(Aspinall, Griffiths)*

Telford U (1) 1 *(Mather)* 4087

Tranmere R: Endersby; Mungall, Burgess, Mooney, Hamilton, Williams, Ferguson (Powell), Aspinall, Kerr, Brown, Griffiths.
Telford U: Charlton; Lewis, Eaton, Mayman, Walker, Barnett (Gardner), Joseph, Neale, Mather, Hogan, Alcock.
Referee: F. Roberts (Prestatyn).

York C (1) 4 *(Hood, Pollard, Byrne, Ford)*

Hartlepool U (0) 0 *4206* *York C:* Jones; Evans, Hay, Sbragia, Smith, Hood, Ford, Crosby, Walwyn, Byrne, Pollard.
Hartlepool U: Watson; Smith, Stimpson (Johnson), Hogan, Barker, Linighan, Bird, Dobson, Linacre, Brown, Lawrence.
Referee: K. Walmsley (Blackpool).

SECOND ROUND REPLAY

15 DEC

Bradford C (2) 3 *(Campbell, Lester, McNiven)*

Mansfield T (1) 2 *(Dungworth, Bell)* 3081

Bradford C: McManus; Podd, Chapman, Lester, Cooke, Jackson, Ellis, Gray, Campbell, McNiven, Mellor.
Mansfield T: Arnold; Bird, Kennedy, Bell, Ayre, Calderwood, Matthews, Hutchinson, Dungworth, Caldwell, Nicholson.
Referee: N. Midgley (Salford).

SECOND ROUND REPLAY

20 DEC

Plymouth Arg (0) 1 *(McCartney)*

Bristol R (0) 0 9130

Plymouth Arg: Crudgington; Nisbet, Uzzell, Harrison, Smith, Cooper, Hodges, Cook, Sims, McCartney, Rogers.
Bristol R: Kite; Slatter, Williams B., Williams G., Parkin, McCaffery, Channon, Williams D. (Platnaeur), Stephens, Withey, Barrett.
Referee: K. L. Burden (Dorset).

FA Cup Third Round

TAYLOR'S DERBY BEAT CLOUGH'S FOREST

The First and Second Division clubs joined by **9** Third Division clubs, **8** the Fourth and **3** Non-League clubs, set out on the road to Wembley.

Very few surprises hit the headlines although Isthmian Leaguers **Bishop's Stortford** pulled back two goals to draw at **Middlesbrough** with reserve midfield player **Richard Bradford** scoring them both. Six thousand packed into Stortford's ground to see **Lyndon Lynch** give the home side an interval replay lead but there was no fairy tale ending, as **Malcolm Allison's** side scored twice through **Shearer**.

Favourites **Liverpool** allowed **Blackburn** to score first but they like **Manchester United, Spurs, Arsenal, Aston Villa** and **Manchester City** all moved into the second round without too much fuss.

Little **Newport County**, having played **Everton** twice in the Milk Cup already, gained a creditable home draw before losing 1-2 at Goodison Park, and both Alliance clubs fought hard before going out – **Worcester City** after holding a lead at **Coventry City** and **Weymouth** to a late goal at **Cambridge United**.

The tie that really caught the imagination of the media, however, was **Nottingham Forest's** visit to **Derby County**, where Peter Taylor played host to Brian Clough. Derby in dire financial troubles and perilously near the foot of Division Two showed far too much determination and will to win for the Forest lads and **Archie Gemmell** emerged as the day's hero.

One result which gave a lot of satisfaction in the Midlands was **WBA's** 3-2 victory over **QPR**, as the Londoners had beaten Albion at the semi-final stage last season and despite a support of over 32,000 at St James Park, **Newcastle** couldn't improve on their draw at **Brighton**, and lost 0-1.

The best attendances of the round were at:

Manchester United v West Ham United	44,143
Tottenham Hotspur v Southampton	38,040
Newcastle United v Brighton & Hove Albion	32,134
Derby County v Nottingham Forest	28,494

495,178 people attended the cup ties on Saturday 8 January giving an average of 15,474 per match, this compared with an average of 15,997 in the previous season.

8 JAN

Arsenal (1) 2 *(Davis, Rix)*

Bolton W (0) 1 *(Whatmore)* 22,576

Arsenal: Jennings; Hollins, Sansom, Talbot, O'Leary, Robson, Davis, Sunderland, Nicholas, Woodcock, Rix.
Bolton W: McDonagh; Whitworth, Bennett, Henry, Jones, Deakin, Chandler, Whatmore, Foster, Hoggan, Thompson.
Referee: B. L. Newsome (Shropshire).

Blackburn R (1) 1 *(Garner)*

Liverpool (2) 2 *(Hodgson, Rush)* 21,966

Blackburn R: Gennoe; Branagan, Rathbone, Randell, Mail, Fazackerley, Miller, Arnott, Bell, Garner, Brotherston.
Liverpool: Grobbelaar; Neal, Kennedy, Lawrenson, Johnston, Hansen, Dalglish, Lee, Rush, Hodgson, Souness.
Referee: K. Hackett (Sheffield).

Bradford C (0) 0

Barnsley (0) 1 *(Glavin)* 11,012

Bradford C: McManus; Podd, Chapman, Lester, Cooke, Cherry, Ellis (Jackson), Gray, Campbell, McNiven, Yorath.
Barnsley: Pierce; Joyce, Chambers, Glavin, McCarthy, Banks, Law, Parker, Ronson, Cunningham, Birch.
Referee: A. Banks (Manchester).

Brighton & HA (0) 1 *(Ritchie)*

Newcastle U (0) 1 *(McDermott)* 17,711

Brighton: Moseley; Ramsey, Pearce, Grealish, Foster, Stevens, Case, Ward, Robinson, Ritchie, Stille.
Newcastle U: Carr; Anderson, Wharton, Martin, Clarke, Carney, Keegan, McDonald, Varadi, McDermott, Waddle.
Referee: T. Glasson (Salisbury).

Cambridge U (0) 1 *(Reilly)*

Weymouth (0) 0 5019

Cambridge U: Webster; Fisher, Murray, Turner, Fallon, O'Neill, Cartwright, Spriggs, Reilly, Mayo, Finney.
Weymouth: Baker; Morrell Peter, Morrell Paul, Elliott, Arnold, Finnigan, Baber, Pearson, Iannone, Borthwick, Benjafield.
Referee: A. Gunn (Burgess Hill).

Carlisle U (1) 2 *(Bannon, Poskett)*

Burnley (1) 2 *(Taylor, Wharton)* 6998

Carlisle U: Swinburne, Parker, Haigh, Ashurst, Rushbury, Houghton, Staniforth (Lee), Craig, Poskett, Bannon, Shoulder.
Burnley: O'Rourke; Laws, Donachie, Phelan, Holt, Flynn (Wharton), Scott, Steven, Hamilton, Taylor, Young.
Referee: R. Bridges (Deeside).

Charlton Ath (2) 2 *(Robinson, Hales)*

Ipswich T (2) 3 *(Thijssen, Wark 2* [1 pen]*)* 16,699

Charlton Ath: Johns; Gritt, Aizlewood, McAllister, Elliott, Berry, Simonsen, Harris, Hales, Bullivant, Robinson.
Ipswich T: Sivell; Steggles, Gernon, Thijssen, Osman, Butcher, Wark, McCall, Mariner, Brazil, Gates.
Referee: A. Robinson (Hampshire).

Coventry C (2) 3 *(Whitton 2* [1 pen], *Hateley)*

Worcester C (1) 1 *(Moss pen)* 11,843

Coventry C: Sealey; Thomas, Hormantschuk, Butterworth, Dyson, Gillespie, Whitton, Francis, Hateley, Melrose, Hunt.
Worcester C: Parkes; Selby, Hunt, Phelps, Tudor, Hughes, Williams B., Williams J., Tuohy, Crompton, Moss.
Referee: C. Downey (Hounslow).

Crystal Palace (1) 2 *(Lovell, Langley)*

York C (1) 1 *(Walwyn)* 7837

Crystal Palace: Fry; Gilbert, Lovell, Nebbeling, Cannon, Hinshelwood, Giles, Hughton, Jones, Langley, Hilaire.
York C: Astbury; Evans, Hay, Sbragia, Smith, Hood, Ford, Crosby, Walwyn, Byrne, Pollard.
Referee: D. A. Hedges (Oxford).

Derby Co (0) 2 *(Gemmill, Hill)*

Nottingham F (0) 0 28,494

Derby Co: Cherry; Barton, Attley, Gemmill (Dalziel), Foster, McAlle, Brolly, Wilson, Hill, Swindlehurst, Mills.
Nottingham F: Sutton; Swain, Bowyer, Gunn, Young, Walsh, Proctor, Wallace, Birtles, Hodge, Robertson (Davenport).
Referee: G. Courtney (Co Durham).

Huddersfield T (1) 1 *(Stanton)*

Chelsea (0) 1 *(Mayes)* 17,004

Huddersfield T: Cox; Brown, Burke, Stanton, Sutton, Hanvey, Lillis, Doyle, Russell, Wilson, Cowling.
Chelsea: Francis; Lee, Jones, Chivers, Droy, Pates, Fillery, Bumstead, Speedie (Walker), Mayes, Rhoades-Brown.
Referee: N. Midgley (Salford).

Leeds U (1) 3 *(Sheridan, Connor, Graham)*

Preston NE (0) 0 16,816

Leeds U: Lukic; Aspin, Gray E., Sheridan (Hird), Hart, Burns, McNab, Connor, Butterworth, Thomas, Graham.
Preston NE: Litchfield; O'Riordan, McAteer, Kelly, Booth, Gowling, Walsh, Bruce, Elliott, Naughton, Houston (Bell).
Referee: N. J. Ashley (Nantwich).

Worcester City goalkeeper Phil Parks collects the ball during the FA Cup third round tie against Coventry City.

Leicester C (0) 2 *(Smith A., Wilson)*

Notts Co (2) 3 *(Fashanu 2, McCulloch)* 18,384

Leicester C: Wallington; Ramsey, Rowell, MacDonald, May, O'Neill, Lynex, Lineker (Robson), Smith A., Buchanan, Wilson.
Notts Co: Avramovic; Benjamin, Worthington, Hunt, Kilcline, Richards, Chiedozie, Fashanu, McCulloch, Goodwin, Mair.
Referee: A. J. Hamil (Wolverhampton).

Luton T (2) 3 *(Horton* pen, *Hill, Walsh)*

Peterborough U (0) 0 11,151

Luton T: Findlay; Stephens, Thomas, Horton, Goodyear, Donaghy, Hill, Bunn, Walsh, Turner, Watts.
Peterborough U: Seaman; Winters, Collins, Gynn, Firm, Slack, Clarke, Rodaway, Cooke, Benjamin, Quow.
Referee: J. E. Martin (Alton).

Manchester U (1) 2 *(Coppell, Stapleton)*

West Ham U (0) 0 44,143

Manchester U: Bailey; Duxbury, Albiston, Moses, Moran, McQueen, Robson, Muhren, Stapleton, Whiteside, Coppell.
West Ham U: Parkes; Stewart, Lampard, Bonds, Gallagher, Devonshire, Van der Elst, Cottee, Clark, Allen, Pike.
Referee: D. Hutchinson (Harrogate).

Middlesbrough (2) 2 *(Bell 2)*

Bishop's Stortford (0) 2 *(Bradford 2)* 13,207

Middlesbrough: Platt; Kennedy, Bolton, Baxter, Nattrass, Otto, Wood, Sugrue, Shearer, Hankin, Bell.
Bishop's Stortford: Welsh; Wickenden, Brown, Bradford, Elley, Hull, Avery, Lynch, Worrell, Simmonds, Sullivan.
Referee: R. Chadwick (Darwen).

Newport Co (0) 1 *(Gwyther)*

Everton (0) 1 *(Sheedy)* 9527

Newport Co: Kendall; Jones, Stroud, Bailey, Boyle (Gwyther), Davies, Moore, Aldridge, Tynan, Vaughan, Elsey.
Everton: Arnold; Stevens, Bailey, Ratcliffe, Higgins, McMahon, Heath, Sharp, King, Reid, Sheedy.
Referee: B. Stevens (Stonehouse).

Northampton T (0) 0

Aston Villa (1) 1 *(Walters)* 14,529

Northampton T: Freeman; Tucker, Phillips, Gage, Burrows, Coffill, Saxby, Buchanan, Syrett, Massey, Heeley (Muir).
Aston Villa: Spink; Jones, Williams, Evans, McNaught, Mortimer, Bremner, Walters, Withe, Cowans, Morley.
Referee: A. Ward (London).

Norwich C (2) 2 *(Bertschin 2)*

Swansea C (1) 1 *(Gale)* 13,222

Norwich C: Woods; Haylock, Downs, Mendham, Walford, Watson, Barham, O'Neill, Deehan, Bertschin, Van Wyk.
Swansea C: Davies; Richards, Hadziabdic, Rajkovic, Charles, Lewis, Curtis, James (Mahoney), Gale, Marustik, Latchford.
Referee: L. Robinson (Sutton Coldfield).

Oldham Ath (0) 0

Fulham (0) 2 *(Coney, Houghton)* 8087

Oldham Ath: Goram; Hoolickin, Ryan, Bowden, Clements, Futcher, McDonough, Atkinson, Heaton, Wylde, Palmer.
Fulham: Peyton; Hopkins, Parker, O'Driscoll, Brown, Gale, Davies, Wilson, Coney, Houghton, Lewington.
Referee: D. Civil (Birmingham).

Oxford U (1) 1 *(Foley)*

Torquay U (1) 1 *Gallagher)* 6880

Oxford U: Butcher; Linney, Smithers, Brock, Fogg, Shotton, Lawrence, Foley, Vinter, Hebberd, Barnett.
Torquay U: Horn; Doyle, Wilson, Sheridan, Little, Hughes, Young, O'Donnell, Cooper, Anderson, Gallagher.
Referee: M. J. Taylor (Deal).

Scunthorpe U (0) 0

Grimsby T (0) 0 11,010

Scunthorpe U: Neenan; Oates, Pointon, Fowler, Baines, Hunter, O'Berg, Cammack, Cowling, Angus, Parkinson.
Grimsby T: Batch; Moore D., Crombie, Waters, Cooper, Moore K., Ford, Whymark, Drinkell, O'Dell, Cumming.
Referee: A. Challinor (Rotherham).

Sheffield U (0) 0

Stoke C (0) 0 23,239

Sheffield U: Waugh; Henderson, Garner, Brazil, Houston, Kenworthy, Morris, Trusson, Edwards, Curran, King.
Stoke C: Fox; Parkin, Hampton, Bracewell, Watson, Berry, Painter, McIlroy, O'Callaghan, Thomas, Maskery.
Referee: B. Hill (Kettering).

Shrewsbury T (0) 2 *(Brown 2)*

Rotherham U (0) 1 *(Seasman)* 6027

Shrewsbury T: Ogrizovic; Williams, Johnson, Petts, Pearson, Griffin, Cross, Leonard, Brown, McNally, Stevens.
Rotherham U: Mountford; Forrest, Henson, Seasman, Hughes, Green, Towner, Gow, Moore, Fern, McBride.
Referee: G. Napthine (Leicester).

Southend U (0) 0

Sheffield W (0) 0 6973

Southend U: Cawston; Stead, Yates, Clark, Hadley, Cusack (Pennyfather), Pountney, Phillips, Mercer, Otulakowski, Nelson.
Sheffield W: Bolder; Sterland, Matthewson, Smith, Lyons, Shelton, Megson, Taylor, Bannister, McCulloch, Pearson.
Referee: K. G. Salmon (Barnet).

Sunderland (0) 0

Manchester C (0) 0 21,518

Sunderland: Turner; Nicholl, Pickering, Atkins, Elliott, Chisholm, Venison, Rowell, West, Cooke, Cummings.
Manchester C: Corrigan; Ranson, Bond, Reid, Power, Caton, Bodak, Reeves, Cross (Tueart), Hartford, Kinsey.
Referee: J. Worrall (Warrington).

Swindon T (2) 7 *(Pritchard 3, Rowland 3, Batty)*

Aldershot (0) 0 7187

Swindon T: Allan; Bailie, Baverstock, Emmanuel, Lewis, Graham, Pritchard, Batty, Rideout, Rowland, Barnard (Quinn).
Aldershot: Johnson; Shrubb, Gillard (Scott), Biley, Wooler, Jopling, Lucas, Banton, Goddard, McDonald, Robinson.
Referee: D. S. Vickers (Ilford).

Lyndon Lynch scores Bishops Stortford's goal during their 2-1 defeat by Middlesbrough in the third round of the FA Cup.

Tottenham H (0) 1 *(Hazard)*

Southampton (0) 0 38,040

Tottenham H: Clemence; Hughton, O'Reilly, Roberts, Hazard, Perryman, Brooke, Archibald, Gibson (Mabbutt), Villa, Dick.
Southampton: Shilton; Agboola, Mills, Williams, Nicholl, Wright, Holmes, Cassells, Moran, Armstrong, Wallace.
Referee: J. Hunting (Leicester).

Tranmere R (0) 0

Wolverhampton W (0) 1 *(Hibbitt)* 10,803

Tranmere R: Endersby; Mungall, Burgess, Mooney, Hamilton, Williams, Ferguson, Aspinall, Kerr, Brown (Powell), Griffiths.
Wolverhampton W: Burridge; Humphrey, Palmer, Smith, Pender, Dodd, Hibbitt, Clarke, Gray, Eves, Matthews.
Referee: J. D. Hough (Macclesfield).

Walsall (0) 0

Birmingham C (0) 0 12,967

Walsall: Green; Caswell, Mower, Beech, Sinnott, Hart, Rees, Preece, Penn, Buckley, O'Kelly.
Birmingham C: Coton; Hagan, Dennis, Stevenson, Blake, Broadhurst, Dillon, Phillips, Harford (Brazier), Curbishley, Handysides.
Referee: B. Daniels (Brentwood).

Watford (1) 2 *(Rostron, Blissett)*

Plymouth Arg (0) 0 17,630

Watford: Sherwood; Rice, Rostron, Taylor, Sims, Bolton, Callaghan, Blissett, Gilligan, Jackett, Barnes.
Plymouth Arg: Crudgington; Nisbet, Uzzell, Phillips, Smith, Cooper, Hodges, Cook, Sims, McCartney, Rogers.
Referee: R. S. Lewis (Gt. Bookham).

WBA (1) 3 *(Owen 2* [1 pen]*, Eastoe)*

QPR (1) 2 *(Fenwick pen, Micklewhite)* 16,528

WBA: Barron; Whitehead, Statham, Zondervan, Wile, Robertson, Jol, Bennett, Regis, Owen, Eastoe.
QPR: Benstead; Neill, Dawes, Roeder, Hazell (Burke), Fenwick, Micklewhite, Sealy, Allen, Flanagan, Waddock.
Referee: P. Willis (Meadowfield).

THIRD ROUND REPLAYS

11 JAN

Birmingham C (0) 1 *aet (Summerfield)*

Walsall (0) 0 14,774

Birmingham C: Coton; Hagan, Dennis, Stevenson, Blake, Broadhurst, Dillon, Brazier (Summerfield), Ferguson, Curbishley, Handysides.
Walsall: Green; Caswell, Mower, Beech, Sinnott, Hart, Rees, Preece, Kearns (Round), Buckley, O'Kelly.
Referee: B. H. Daniels (Brentwood).

Bishop's Stortford (1) 1 *(Lynch)*

Middlesbrough (0) 2 *(Shearer 2)* 6000

Bishop's Stortford: Welsh; Wickenden, Brown, Bradford, Elley, Hull, Avery, Lynch, Worrell (Levey), Simmonds, Sullivan.
Middlesbrough: Platt; Brownie, Ward, Baxter, Nattrass, Otto, Wood, Sugrue, Shearer, Kennedy, Bell.
Referee: R. Chadwick (Darwen).

Burnley (1) 3 *(Flynn, Steven, Laws* pen*)*

Carlisle U (0) 1 *(Poskett)* 9439

Burnley: O'Rourke; Laws, Donachie, Holt, Phelan, Flynn, Scott (Wharton), Steven, Hamilton, Taylor, Young.
Carlisle U: Swinburne; Parker, Haigh, Ashurst, Rushbury, Houghton (Lee), Coughlin, Craig, Poskett, Bannon, Shoulder.
Referee: R. Bridges (Deeside).

Everton (1) 2 *(Sharp, King)*

Newport Co (0) 1 *(Aldridge)* 18,565

Everton: Arnold; Stevens, Bailey, Ratcliffe, Higgins, McMahon, Heath, Sharp, King, Reid, Sheedy.
Newport Co: Kendall; Jones, Stroud, Bailey, Oakes, Boyle, Moore (Gwyther), Aldridge, Tynan, Vaughan, Elsey.
Referee: B. Stevens (Stonehouse).

Grimsby T (1) 2 *(Ford, Waters* pen*)*

Scunthorpe U (0) 0 9509

Grimsby T: Batch; Moore D., Crombie, Waters, Stone, Moore K., Ford, Whymark, Drinkell (Wilkinson), O'Dell, Bonnyman.
Scunthorpe U: Neenan; Oates, Pointon, Fowler (Telfer), Baines, Hunter, O'Berg, Cammack, Cowling, Angus, Parkinson.
Referee: A. Challinor (Rotherham).

Sheffield W (1) 2 *aet (Smith, Megson)*

Southend U (1) 2 *(Mercer, Pountney)* 11,093

Sheffield W: Bolder; Shirtliff, Peter, Matthewson, Smith, Lyons, Shelton, Megson, Taylor, Bannister, McCulloch (Mirocevic), Pearson.
Southend U: Cawston; Stead, Yates, Clark, Hadley, Cusack, Pountney, Phillips, Mercer, Otulakowski (Pennyfather), Nelson.
Referee: K. G. Salmon (Barnet).

THIRD ROUND REPLAYS

12 JAN

Chelsea (0) 2 *(Bumstead, Fillery)*

Huddersfield T (0) 0 14,417

Chelsea: Francis; Lee, Jones, Chivers, Droy, Pates, Fillery, Bumstead, Speedie, Mayes, Rhoades-Brown.
Huddersfield T: Cox; Brown, Burke, Stanton, Sutton, Hanvey, Lillis, Doyle (Pugh), Russell, Wilson, Cowling.
Referee: N. Midgley (Salford).

Manchester C (2) 2 *(Hartford, Cross)*

Sunderland (0) 1 *(Chisholm)* 22,356

Manchester C: Corrigan; Ranson, Bond, Reid, Power, Kinsey, Tueart, Reeves, Cross, Hartford, Bodak (McDonald).
Sunderland: Turner; Nicholl, Pickering, Atkins, Chisholm, Elliott, Venison, Rowell, Worthington, Cooke (McCoist), Cummins.
Referee: J. Worrall (Warrington).

Newcastle U (0) 0

Brighton & HA (0) 1 *(Ward)* 32,134

Newcastle U: Carr; Anderson, Wharton, Martin, Clarke, Carney, Keegan, McDonald, Varadi, McDermott, Waddle.
Brighton & HA: Moseley; Ramsey, Pearce, Grealish, Gatting, Stevens, Case, Ward, Robinson, Ritchie, Stille (Smillie).
Referee: T. Mills (Barnsley).

Stoke C (1) 3 *(McAughtrie, Painter, Henderson og)*

Sheffield U (2) 2 *(Edwards, Morris* pen*)* 18,515

Stoke C: Fox; Parkin, Hampton, Bracewell, Watson, McAughtrie, Maguire, McIlroy, O'Callaghan, Thomas, Chamberlain (Painter).
Sheffield U: Waugh; Henderson, Garner, Charles, West (Brazil), Houston, Morris, Trusson, Edwards, Curran, King.
Referee: B. Hill (Kettering).

Torquay U (1) 2 *(Cooper, Gallagher)*

Oxford U (0) 1 *(Fogg* pen*)* 6402

Toruay U: Horn; Doyle, Wilson, Sheridan, Little, Hughes, Grapes, O'Donnell, Cooper, Anderson, Gallagher.
Oxford U: Butcher; Linney (Train), Smithers, Barnett, Fogg, Shotton, Lawrence, Foley, Vinter, Hebberd, Brock.
Referee: R. Lewis (Gt. Bookham).

THIRD ROUND, SECOND REPLAY

24 JAN

Sheffield W (1) 2 *(Keeley og, Taylor* pen*)*

Southend U (0) 1 *(Cusack* pen*)* 10,767

Sheffield W: Bolder; Sterland, Bailey, Smith, Lyons, Shelton, Mills, Taylor, Bannister, Pearson, Mirocevic.
Southend U: Keeley; Pennyfather (Moody), Yates, Clark, Hadley, Cusack, Pountney, Phillips, Mercer, Otulakowski, Nelson.
Referee: D. Shaw (Sandbach).

FA Cup Fourth Round

SECOND DIVISION'S BOTTOM FOUR QUALIFY FOR FIFTH ROUND

Thirty-two clubs went into the hat for this round but only two, **Swindon Town** of the Third and **Torquay** of the Fourth, could be described as potential 'giantkillers'.

However, the draw paired these two with Second Division opposition and **Sheffield Wednesday** at Torquay and **Burnley** eliminated the last two 'minnows'. This left the seniors to sort each other out and once again there were very few surprises.

Home wins for **Everton, Liverpool, Aston Villa, Spurs, Ipswich Town** and **Watford** presented a very powerful squad from the First Division and they were joined by colleagues **Norwich City** and **Brighton**, whose emphatic 4-0 victory over **Manchester City** probably convinced **John Bond** that it was time to move on.

Manchester United pulled off an excellent away win at **Luton Town** but **Arsenal** took three games to eliminate **Leeds United**. This meant that **10** First Division clubs and **6** from the Second Division went into the bag for the Fifth Round, but the Second Division qualifiers included the bottom four clubs in the Division, **Middlesbrough, Cambridge United, Burnley** and **Derby County**!

Poor Derby, having suffered at the hands of the Leeds louts one week, had to face the renowned Chelsea mob the next, but at least they won!

What a great Cup season Burnley were enjoying. They had already reached the Milk Cup Semi-Final, but no doubt they, like their colleagues in distress, would willingly have swapped Cup glory for league points.

Sheffield Wednesday had also enjoyed a good Milk Cup run but their promotion challenge had faltered, while **Crystal Palace** who had beaten Birmingham City with surprising ease were the only club from the Second Division with no league tension.

FOURTH ROUND

29 JAN

Arsenal (0) 1 *(Sunderland)*

Leeds U (0) 1 *(Nicholas og)* 33,930

Arsenal: Jennings; Hollins, Sansom, Robson, O'Leary, Nicholas, Talbot, Sunderland, Petrovic, Woodcock, Rix.
Leeds U: Lukic; Aspin, Gray E., Thomas, Hart, Dickinson, Hamson (Hird), Connor, Butterworth, Gray F., Graham.
Referee: M. J. Taylor (Herts).

Aston Villa (1) 1 *(Withe)*

Wolverhampton W (0) 0 43,121

Aston Villa: Spink; Williams, Gibson, Evans, McNaught, Blair, Bremner, Shaw, Withe, Cowans, Morley.
Wolverhampton W: Burridge; Humphrey, Palmer, Smith, Pender, Dodd, Hibbitt, Rudge, Gray, Eves, Matthews.
Referee: K. Hackett (Sheffield).

Brighton & HA (2) 4 *(Case, Smillie, Robinson 2)*

Manchester C (0) 0 16,804

Brighton & HA: Moseley; Ramsey, Gatting, Grealish, Foster, Stevens, Case, Ritchie, Robinson, Smith, Smillie.
Manchester C: Corrigan; Ranson, Bond, Reid, Power (Bodak), Caton, Tueart, Reeves, Cross, Hartford, Kinsey.
Referee: C. Downey (Hounslow).

Burnley (2) 3 *(Hamilton 2, Steven)*

Swindon T (0) 1 *(Pritchard)* 9786

Burnley: Stevenson; Scott, Donachie, Phelan, Dobson, Flynn, Cavener (Cassidy), Steven, Hamilton, Taylor, Young.
Swindon T: Allan; Baverstock (Quinn), Bailie, Emmanuel, Lewis, Graham, Pritchard, Batty, Rideout, Rowland, Barnard.
Referee: K. Redfern (Whitley Bay).

Cambridge U (0) 1 *(Mayo)*

Barnsley (0) 0 6612

Cambridge U: Webster; Donaldson, Murray, Turner, Fallon, O'Neill, Cartwright, Spriggs (Streete), Reilly, Mayo, Fisher.
Barnsley: Pierce; Joyce, Chambers, Glavin, Banks, McCarthy, Law, Parker, Ronson, Walker (Barrowclough), Birch.
Referee: B. H. Daniels (Brentwood).

Coventry C (1) 2 *(Thompson, Roberts)*

Norwich C (0) 2 *(Hareide, Barham)* 13,073

Coventry C: Sealey; Thomas, Roberts, Hormantschuck, Dyson, Gillespie, Whitton, Francis, Hateley, Thompson, Hunt.
Norwich C: Woods; Hareide, Downs, Mendham, Walford, Watson, Barham, O'Neill, Deehan, Bertschin, Van Wyk.
Referee: B. Hill (Kettering).

Crystal Palace (0) 1 *(Edwards)*

Birmingham C (0) 0 12,327

Crystal Palace: Fry; Gilbert, Murphy, Locke, Cannon, Hinshelwood, Edwards, Hughton, Jones, Langley, Hilaire.
Birmingham C: Coton; Hagan, Dennis, Brazier, Blake, Broadhurst, Dillon, Gayle, Harford, Curbishley, Summerfield (Handysides).
Referee: L. C. Shapter (Torquay).

Derby Co (1) 2 *(Wilson 2)*

Chelsea (0) 1 *(Fillery)* 23,383

Derby Co: Cherry; Barton, Attley, Powell, Foster, McAlle, Brolly, Wilson, Hill, Swindlehurst, Mills.
Chelsea: Francis; Lee, Jones, Bumstead, Droy (Walker), Pates, Fillery, Hales, Speedie, Mayes, Rhoades-Brown.
Referee: A. W. Grey (Gt. Yarmouth).

Ipswich T (1) 2 *(Osman, McCall)*

Grimsby T (0) 0 21,455

Ipswich T: Cooper; Steggles, Gernon, Thijssen, Osman, Butcher, Wark, McCall, Mariner, Brazil, O'Callaghan.
Grimsby T: Batch; Moore D., Crombie, Waters, Cooper, Moore K., Ford, Whymark (Wilkinson), Drinkell, Bonnyman, Speight.
Referee: M. Heath (Stoke).

Liverpool (1) 2 *(Dalglish, Rush)*

Stoke C (0) 0 36,666

Liverpool: Grobbelaar; Neal, Kennedy, Lawrenson, Johnston, Hansen, Dalglish, Lee, Rush, Hodgson, Souness.
Stoke C: Fox; Parkin, Hampton, Bracewell, Watson, Berry, Painter, McIlroy, O'Callaghan, Thomas, Maguire.
Referee: G. Courtney (Co. Durham).

Luton T (0) 0

Manchester U (0) 2 *(Moses, Moran)* 20,516

Luton T: Findlay; Stephens, Money, Horton, Goodyear, Donaghy, Hill, Stein, Walsh, Turner (Kellock), Moss.
Manchester U: Bailey; Duxbury, Albiston, Moses, Moran, McQueen, Robson, Muhren, Stapleton, Whiteside, Coppell.
Referee: R. Lewis (Gt. Bookham).

Middlesbrough (1) 2 *(Hankin, Beattie* pen*)*

Notts Co (0) 0 17,114

Middlesbrough: O'Hanlon; Mowbray, Bolton, Nattrass, Beattie, Otto, Wood, Sugrue, Hankin, Shearer, Bell.
Notts Co: Avramovic; Benjamin, Worthington, Hunt, Kilcline, Richards, Chiedozie, Fashanu, McCulloch, Goodwin, Mair (Christie).
Referee: D. Hutchinson (Harrogate).

Torquay U (1) 2 *(Hughes, Bishop)*

Sheffield W (1) 3 *(Lyons, Sterland, Megson)* 7823

Torquay U: Horn; Doyle, Wilson, Sheridan, Little, Hughes, Grapes (Bishop), O'Donnell, Cooper, Anderson, Gallagher.
Sheffield W: Bolder; Sterland, Bailey, Smith, Lyons, Shelton, Megson, Taylor (Pearson), Bannister, McCulloch, Heard.
Referee: J. Hunting (Leicester).

Tottenham H (0) 2 *(Crooks, Gibson)*

WBA (0) 1 *(Whitehead)* 38,208

Tottenham H: Clemence; Hughton, Lacy, Roberts, Villa, Perryman, Ardiles, Mabbutt, Gibson, Dick (Brooke), Crooks.
WBA: Barron; Whitehead (Brown), Statham, Zondervan, Wile, Robertson, Jol, Bennett, Cross, Owen, Eastoe.
Referee: N. Midgley (Salford).

Watford (0) 1 *(Lohman)*

Fulham (0) 1 *(Coney)* 24,574

Watford: Sherwood; Rice, Rostron, Taylor, Sims, Bolton, Callaghan, Blissett, Gilligan (Lohman), Jackett, Barnes.
Fulham: Peyton; Hopkins, Parker, O'Driscoll, Brown, Gale, Davies, Wilson, Coney, Houghton, Lewington.
Referee: A. Gunn (Burgess Hill).

FOURTH ROUND

30 JAN

Everton (1) 2 *(Sheedy, Heath)*

Shrewsbury T (0) 1 *(Cross)* 35,188

Everton: Arnold; Stevens, Bailey, Ratcliffe, Higgins, McMahon, Heath, Sharp, King, Reid, Sheedy.
Shrewsbury T: Ogrizovic; Cross, Johnson, Bates, Pearson, Griffin, Petts, McLaren, Brown, McNally, Stevens.
Referee: K. Barrett (Coventry).

FOURTH ROUND REPLAY

1 FEB

Fulham (0) 1 *(Lewington)*

Watford (1) 2 *(Lohman, Barnes)* 22,206

Fulham: Peyton; Hopkins, Parker, O'Driscoll, Brown, Gale, Davies, Wilson, Coney, Houghton, Lewington.
Watford: Sherwood; Rice, Rostron, Taylor, Sims, Bolton, Callaghan, Blissett, Barnes, Jackett, Lohman.
Referee: A. Gunn (Sussex).

FOURTH ROUND REPLAY

2 FEB

Leeds U (0) 1 *aet (Butterworth)*

Arsenal (0) 1 *(Rix)* 24,410

Leeds U: Lukic; Aspin, Gray E., Thomas, Hart, Dickinson, Hird, Butterworth, Connor, Gray F., Graham.
Arsenal: Jennings; Hollins, Sansom, Robson, O'Leary, Nicholas, Talbot, Sunderland (Davis), Petrovic, Woodcock, Rix.
Referee: J. Hunting (Leicester).

Norwich C (0) 2 *aet (Bertschin, Roberts og)*

Coventry C (1) 1 *(Hateley)* 18,625

Norwich C: Woods; Hareide, Downs, Mendham, Walford, Watson, Barham, O'Neill (Haylock), Deehan, Bertschin, Van Wyk.
Coventry C: Sealey; Thomas, Roberts, Butterworth, Dyson, Gillespie, Whitton, Jacobs, Hateley, Thompson, Hunt (Melrose).
Referee: B. Hill (Kettering).

FOURTH ROUND, SECOND REPLAY

9 FEB

Arsenal (0) 2 *(Woodcock, Rix)*

Leeds U (0) 1 *(Connor)* 26,802

Arsenal: Jennings; Hollins, Sansom, Robson, O'Leary, Nicholas, Talbot, Meade, Petrovic, Woodcock, Rix.
Leeds U: Lukic; Aspin, Gray E., Sheridan, Hart, Dickinson, Thomas, Connor, Butterworth, Gray F., Graham.
Referee: J. Hunting (Leicester).

Fifth Round FA Cup

BRIGHTON ROCK THE FAVOURITES

With everyone talking of a **Liverpool** 'clean sweep' of the honours, little **Brighton** probably benefitted from their tie being held back to the Sunday, thus avoiding clash with the **Everton** v **Spurs** match.

All eyes were on them, caretaker manager **Jimmy Melia** enjoyed the publicity of returning to Anfield and **Jimmy Case** could not wait to prove a few points to the club that had sold him in his prime. Add to this an evening together in Liverpool before the match and the support of 5000 fans who had made the game an excuse for a great weekend away and you had the ideal stage for a shock result.

So was it a surprise? A number of people had felt it in their bones and, when **Phil Neal** missed a chance from the penalty spot to equalise **Jimmy Case's** late goal, it turned out to be just one of those days when Football's special fates had taken a hand with proceedings.

No credit should be taken from **Brighton**, however, and they added their name to the previous day's heroes who included **Everton**, who had finally halted **Spurs'** great FA Cup run which had covered three seasons, and **Norwich City** who had beaten local rivals **Ipswich Town** in a pulsating cup tie.

Poor **Watford**, who could have easily been three up at Villa Park, were punished for sloppy finishing when the European Champions turned on the style to score four times.

Cambridge United made club history by reaching the Fifth Round but **Sheffield Wednesday** curbed the threat of United's giant strikers and won through two goals from Gary Megson.

Late goals gave **Middlesbrough** a replay at **Arsenal**, where an early deficit of two put them out of the game, and **Manchester United** a victory at **Derby County**, while an all Second Division battle went to a replay at **Crystal Palace** and saw **Burnley** go through on a penalty.

FIFTH ROUND

19 FEB

Aston Villa (2) 4 *(Shaw, Morley, Gibson, Cowans)*

Watford (0) 1 *(Blissett pen)* 34,330

Aston Villa: Spink; Williams, Gibson, Evans, McNaught, Mortimer, Blair, Shaw, Walters, Cowans, Morley.
Watford: Sherwood; Rice, Rostron, Taylor, Sims, Bolton, Callaghan, Blissett, Barnes, Jackett, Lohman (Armstrong).
Referee: C. Seel (Carlisle).

Cambridge U (0) 1 *(Turner)*

Sheffield W (1) 2 *(Megson 2)* 10,834

Cambridge U: Webster; Donaldson, Murray, Turner, Fallon, O'Neill, Cartwright, Finney, Reilly, Mayo, Fisher.
Sheffield W: Bolder; Sterland, Bailey, Smith, Lyons, Shelton, Megson, Mills, Pearson, McCulloch, Heard.
Referee: J. E. Martin (Alton).

Crystal Palace (0) 0

Burnley (0) 0 14,949

Crystal Palace: Fry; Gilbert, Murphy, Locke, Cannon, Hinshelwood, Edwards, Brooks, Jones (Giles), Langley, Hilaire.
Burnley: Stevenson; Laws, Donachie, Phelan, Dobson, Flynn, Scott, Steven, Hamilton, Taylor, Young.
Referee: M. P. Scott (Nottingham).

Derby Co (0) 0

Manchester U (0) 1 *(Whiteside)* 33,022

Derby Co: Cherry; Barton, Buckley, Powell, Foster, Gemmill, Brolly, Wilson (McAlle), Hill, Swindlehurst, Mills.
Manchester U: Bailey; Duxbury, Albiston, Moses, Moran, McQueen, Robson, Muhren, Stapleton, Whiteside, Coppell.
Referee: B. Daniels (Brentwood).

Everton (0) 2 *(King, Sharp)*

Tottenham H (0) 0 42,995

Everton: Arnold; Stevens, Bailey, Ratcliffe, Higgins, Richardson, Irvine, King, Sharp, Heath, Sheedy.
Tottenham H: Clemence; Hughton, Lacy, Price, Villa (Hoddle), Perryman, Galvin, Mabbutt, Gibson, Hazard, Crooks.
Referee: P. Willis (Co. Durham).

Norwich City forward Keith Bertschin climbs high over Brighton's Gary Stevens during their FA Cup quarter-final clash at Brighton's Goldstone ground.

Liverpool's Craig Johnston lands on his back after scoring with a spectacular overhead kick, but goals from Ryan and Case at the other end saw Brighton go through to the 6th round.

Middlesbrough (0) 1 *(Otto)*

Arsenal (0) 1 *(Rix)* 20,580

Middlesbrough: O'Hanlon; Nattrass, Mowbray, Baxter, Bolton (MacDonald), Otto, Wood, Kennedy, Sugrue, Currie, Bell.
Arsenal: Jennings; Hollins, Sansom, Robson, Whyte, Nicholas, Talbot, Davis, Petrovic, Woodcock, Rix.
Referee: D. Richardson (Gt. Harwood).

Norwich C (1) 1 *(Bertschin)*

Ipswich T (0) 0 28,001

Norwich C: Woods; Haylock, Hareide, Mendham, Walford, Watson, Barham, Van Wyk, Deehan, Bertschin, Downs.
Ipswich T: Cooper; Putney, Gernon, Thijssen, Osman, Butcher, Wark, McCall (Turner), Mariner, Brazil, O'Callaghan.
Referee: R. Lewis (Gt. Bookham).

20 FEB

Liverpool (0) 1 *(Johnston)*

Brighton & HA (1) 2 *(Ryan, Case)* 44,868

Liverpool: Grobbelaar; Neal, Kennedy, Lawrenson, Whelan, Hansen, Dalglish, Lee, Rush, Hodgson (Johnston), Souness.
Brighton & HA: Digweed; Ramsey, Gatting, Grealish, Foster, Stevens, Case, Ward, Robinson, Ryan, Smillie.
Referee: A. W. Grey (Great Yarmouth).

FIFTH ROUND REPLAYS

28 FEB

Arsenal (2) 3 *(Woodcock, Davis, Talbot)*

Middlesbrough (1) 2 *(Shearer 2)* 26,689

Arsenal: Jennings; Hollins, Sansom, Robson, Whyte, Nicholas, Talbot, Davis, Sunderland, Woodcock, Rix.
Middlesbrough: O'Hanlon; Kennedy, Mowbray, Baxter, Nattrass, Otto, Wood, Sugrue, Hankin, Shearer, Bell.
Referee: D. Richardson (Gt. Harwood).

Burnley (0) 1 *(Taylor* pen*)*

Crystal Palace (0) 0 16,150

Burnley: Stevenson; Laws, Donachie, Scott, Phelan, Flynn, Dobson, Steven, Hamilton, Taylor, Young.
Crystal Palace: Fry; Locke, Hinshelwood, Brooks, Gilbert, Cannon, Edwards, Murphy, Jones, Langley, Hilaire.
Referee: M. Scott (Nottingham).

Sixth Round FA Cup

GARY MEGSON KEEPS HIS RECORD

Two meetings of the giants left the way clear for a cup fairy story to be enjoyed by one of the competition's rank outsiders, so when **Arsenal** eliminated **Aston Villa** with surprising ease in a cup tie that seemed to lack the usual commitment and atmosphere and another late goal saw **Manchester United** through, the Semi-Final draw was all important.

There they were again, having contested the Milk Cup two legged semi-final, **United** and **Arsenal** were paired together in the 'red corner' while out of the 'blue corner' **Brighton** and **Sheffield Wednesday** prepared for the fight of their lives.

Manchester United's quite brilliant winning goal from a limping **Frank Stapleton**, made by substitute **Lou Macari** during the minute he was on the field, was a quite undeserved disappointment for **Everton** and in particular **Jim Arnold**, their goalkeeper, who certainly had earned a replay. But that is Cup Football!

On the south coast, the cup tie between two First Division clubs with relegation problems produced an exciting spectacle but 'some terrible football', in the words of an exultant **Jimmy Melia**. His match winner with a controversial goal was of course – **Jimmy Case**.

One Second Division club was guaranteed a place in the Semi-Finals, but after an excellent, evenly fought tie at Turf Moor, **Wednesday** enjoyed 'one of those nights' when everything went right and in front of 41,731 spectators, reminding Hillsborough of the good old days, **Burnley** were swamped by five goals. **Gary Megson**, son of Don, who had captained **Wednesday** at Wembley in 1966, kept his record of scoring in each round, and manager **Jackie Charlton's** smile covered the Pennines!

SIXTH ROUND

12 MAR

Arsenal (2) 2 *(Woodcock, Petrovic)*

Aston Villa (0) 0 41,774

Arsenal: Jennings; Hollins, Sansom, Robson, Whyte, Nicholas, Petrovic, Davis, Sunderland, Woodcock, Rix.
Aston Villa: Spink; Deacy, Gibson, Evans, Williams, Mortimer, Bremner, Shaw, Withe, Cowans, Morley.
Referee: K. Walmsley.

Brighton & HA (0) 1 *(Case)*

Norwich C (0) 0 28,800

Brighton & HA: Moseley; Ramsey, Gatting, Grealish, Foster, Stevens, Case, Ritchie, Robinson, Ryan, Smillie.
Norwich C: Woods; Haylock, Downs, Mendham, Symonds, Watson, Barham, Bennett, Deehan, Bertschin, Van Wyk (McGuire).
Referee: A. Robinson.

Burnley (0) 1 *(Cassidy)*

Sheffield W (1) 1 *(Bannister)* 23,134

Burnley: Stevenson; Laws, Donachie, Phelan, Dobson, Flynn, Cassidy, Steven, Hamilton, Taylor, Young.
Sheffield W: Bolder; Sterland, Bailey, Smith, Lyons, Shelton, Megson, Mills, Bannister (Pearson), McCulloch, Heard.
Referee: G. Tyson.

Manchester U (0) 1 *(Stapleton)*

Everton (0) 0 58,198

Manchester U: Bailey; Duxbury (Macari), Albiston, Moses, Moran, McQueen, Wilkins, Muhren, Stapleton, Whiteside, Coppell.
Everton: Arnold; Stevens, Bailey, Ratcliffe, Higgins, Richardson, Irvine, McMahon, Sharp, Heath, Sheedy.
Referee: J. B. Worrall.

SIXTH ROUND REPLAY

16 MAR

Sheffield W (3) 5 *(Shelton 2, Megson* pen*, McCulloch 2)*

Burnley (0) 0 41,731

Sheffield W: Bolder; Sterland, Bailey, Smith, Shirtliff, Shelton, Megson, Mills, Taylor, McCulloch, Heard.
Burnley: Stevenson; Laws, Donachie, Phelan, Dobson (Donovan), Flynn, Scott, Steven, Hamilton, Taylor, Young.
Referee: G. Tyson.

Manchester United 'keeper Gary Bailey dives bravely to foil Everton's Adrian Heath (centre) during United's 1-0 win.

Woodcock shows his delight after scoring in Arsenal's 2-0 quarter-final victory over Aston Villa.

SEMI-FINALS – 16 APRIL

Manchester U (0) 2 *(Robson, Whiteside)*
Arsenal (1) 1 *(Woodcock)*
At Villa Park 46,535

Having beaten Arsenal in The Milk Cup Semi-Finals already, Manchester United dominated the first half of this very competitive and entertaining game but trailed by a single goal at half time. Tony Woodcock punished the United defence for failing to clear a harmless looking attack and tapped in a simple goal after 35 minutes. The mid-field was well contested with Talbot and Stewart Robson presenting a strong physical challenge to Bryan Robson before Talbot's booking and injury to the Arsenal youngster reduced their effectiveness.

United's all round dominance was finally rewarded with an excellent goal after just five minutes of the second half. McQueen, quite outstanding in the air, powered a clearance to Ashley Grimes on the left wing, whose early centre was met superbly by Bryan Robson. A quick turn away from Talbot and a crisp angled shot across Wood was too good for the Arsenal defence.

Lifted by this success it was all United and it came as no surprise when Norman Whiteside volleyed home an Albiston cross in the 70th minute in superb fashion. Arsenal battled bravely to the end of an excellent Semi-Final but United deservedly qualified for their second Wembley Cup Final of the season.

Manchester U: Bailey; Duxbury, Albiston, Moses, Moran (McGrath), McQueen, Robson B., Grimes, Stapleton, Whiteside, Wilkins.
Arsenal: Wood; Robson S. (Chapman), Sansom, Whyte, O'Leary, Hollins, Talbot, Davis, Petrovic, Woodcock, Rix.
Referee: K. Hackett (Sheffield).

Brighton & HA (1) 2 *(Case, Robinson)*
Sheffield W (0) 1 *(Mirosevic)*
At Highbury 54,000

In another excellent cup tie which had none of the defensive tactics usually associated with semi-finals, Brighton & Hove Albion made a dream come true thanks to two flashes of brilliance from Jimmy Case.

After 14 minutes the experienced ex-Liverpool mid-field player crashed home a backheeled pass from a free kick by Grealish and this lead gave 'The Seagulls' the confidence to control mid-field and hold the initiative until half time.

Wednesday came back well after the interval and the speedy Bannister caused problems before Ante Mirocevic knocked in a rebound following a Megson free kick in the 56th minute.

Northern hopes were soon shattered however as, with 12 minutes to go Case sent Smith away and after a goalmouth scramble, Mike Robinson scored the vital match winner. Before the final whistle, the Brighton defence performed heroics as Foster cleared off the line with an overhead kick and Graham Moseley made two excellent saves.

The pure joy expressed by Jimmy Melia at the end must have warmed the hearts of all who had worried about the game losing its romance. Second Division Sheffield Wednesday had battled well but relegation candidates Brighton had qualified to play in an FA Cup Final at Wembley for the first time in their history.

Brighton & HA: Moseley; Stevens, Pearce, Grealish, Foster, Gatting, Case, Howlett, Robinson, Smith G., Smillie.
Sheffield W: Bolder; Sterland, Heard, Smith M., Lyons, Shelton, Megson, Mills, Bannister, McCulloch, Mirocevic.
Referee: G. Courtney (Spennymoor, Co Durham).

Gary Stevens celebrates with Gerry Ryan (No. 12) after scoring Brighton's equaliser, forcing the final into extra time.

FA CUP FINAL – 21 MAY 1983

Brighton & HA (1) 2 *(Smith, Stevens)*
Manchester U (0) 2 *(Stapleton, Wilkins)*
At Wembley 100,000

As complete outsiders, Brighton & Hove Albion took the field without Foster their suspended captain, in very relaxed mood. They knew they had nothing to lose and indeed in the early exchanges they looked more direct, as Robinson rampaged and the ball was swung across the United defence. So after 14 minutes a Brighton goal through Gordon Smith was well deserved as he headed in a flighted centre from Howlett.

Slowly but surely United played themselves back into the game and both Ramsey and Robinson cleared off the line. Brighton also had their chances but just ten minutes after half time, Whiteside touched on a Duxbury cross and there was Stapleton to score at the far post. It was sad that Ramsey, who had just received a bad knock from Whiteside was not fit enough to cover correctly during this attack and subsequently left the field to be substituted by Ryan.

It looked as if the Seasiders' chance had gone and when Ray Wilkins curled in a superb goal to give United the lead after 73 minutes no one gave Jimmy Melia's men much chance of coming back. But with just three minutes to go a Jimmy Case corner was pulled back to Grealish and the skipper's stab into the box was pounced upon by Brighton's hero, Stevens, and suddenly Brighton had been reprieved.

With both sides tired after a gruelling but exciting match it was not surprising that no goals came in extra time. Brighton did have the last chance however as Mick Robinson, battling to the last, forced his way through to set up a great chance for Smith. The world seemed to stand still as the hero of the first half saw Bailey save his shot bravely and we all looked forward to Thursday's replay.

Brighton & HA: Moseley; Ramsey (Ryan), Stevens, Gatting, Pearce, Smillie, Case, Grealish, Howlett, Robinson, Smith.
Manchester U: Bailey; Duxbury, Moran, McQueen, Albiston, Davies, Wilkins, Robson, Muhren, Stapleton, Whiteside.
Referee: A. W. Grey (Great Yarmouth).

FINAL REPLAY – 26 MAY 1983

Manchester U (3) 4 *(Robson 2, Whiteside, Muhren* pen*)*
Brighton & HA (0) 0
At Wembley 100,000

The return of skipper Foster should have helped Brighton and Hove Albion in this replay but perhaps the splitting of the successful Stevens-Gatting partnership unsettled the defence. Whatever the cause, however, it was clear to see that an inspired United were in no mood to give the opposition a second chance.

On Sir Matt Busby's 74th birthday, in a carnival atmosphere where everyone seemed to be enjoying themselves, the red shirts of Manchester were everywhere. Their least experienced player, Davies, again shone and Bryan Robson once more proved to be his side's inspiration.

Mid-way through the first half, two goals in four minutes ensured the cup would be on its way to Lancashire. Firstly Albiston and Davies combined to give Robson a straightforward goal and then Muhren's corner kick was touched on by Davies for Whiteside to power in the second. The young Irishman had now scored at Wembley in both The Milk Cup and FA Cup Finals in his first full season!

Jimmy Case saw his deflected shot well saved under the crossbar by Bailey as the first half came to a close but it was skipper Robson again who virtually had the game sewn up as he pounced on a Stapleton header to score from close range and send his side in with a three-goal advantage.

The second half saw a more relaxed game as Brighton realized their chances had gone and United were happy with their lead. However, a penalty after 62 minutes by Muhren after Stevens had held Robson, gave United the biggest Cup Final victory at Wembley but Brighton were not disgraced. Indeed they received a well deserved ovation following their fine contribution to two excellent cup ties, for which both clubs deserve credit for the quality, excitement and sportsmanship shown.

Brighton & HA: Moseley; Gatting, Pearce, Grealish, Foster, Stevens, Case, Howlett, Robinson, Smith, Smillie.
Manchester U: Bailey; Duxbury, Albiston, Wilkins, Moran, McQueen, Robson, Muhren, Stapleton, Whiteside, Davies.
Referee: A. W. Grey (Great Yarmouth).

Manchester United captain Bryan Robson receives the FA Cup from HRH Princess Michael of Kent.

FA CUP FACTS AND FIGURES

Blackburn Rovers hold the record for the longest run of consecutive FA Cup ties without defeat. From December 1883 to December 1886 they were unbeaten in 24 Cup ties and won the trophy three times during this period.

The longest FA Cup tie was played between **Alvechurch** and **Oxford City** in 1971. This Fourth Qualifying Round match was won 1-0 by **Alvechurch** after 11 hours play (six games).

The fastest goals scored in an FA Cup Final at Wembley were obtained in the first minute. In 1928, **John Roscamp** put **Blackburn Rovers** ahead when he charged both the **Huddersfield Town** goalkeeper and the ball into the net and in 1955 **Jackie Milburn** headed **Newcastle United** into the lead against **Manchester City**.

The youngest player to take part in an FA Cup Final is **Paul Allen** who was selected for **West Ham United** to play against **Arsenal** on 10 May 1980 when he was 17 years 256 days old.

Twelve players were sent off in First Round cup ties on Saturday last season. This broke the previous record for one day, of eight, recorded in 1915.

Tottenham Hotspur were the first Southern club to win the Cup. Spurs were then members of The Southern League and so, were the first and only 'Non Football League' club to carry off the trophy.

King George V was the first reigning monarch to attend a Cup Final. He saw **Burnley** beat **Liverpool** at the Crystal Palace in 1914.

David Jack (**Bolton Wanderers**) scored the first goal in a Wembley Cup Final. This was in 1923 when an estimated 123,000 people broke the barriers to watch the Wanderers beat **West Ham United** 2-0.

Extra time was first played in a Cup Final in 1877. **Wanderers** and **Oxford University** were drawing 1-1 at full time, and Wanderers finished as 2-1 winners.

The first cup tie played under floodlights was a replay between **Kidderminster Harriers** and **Brierley Hill Alliance**, 14 September, 1955.

The first hat trick in an FA Cup Final was scored by **William Townley** for **Blackburn Rovers** v **Sheffield Wednesday** in 1890.

Shinguards were first used in the FA Cup Final in 1892.

The first FA Cup tie to be televised, other than the final, was **Charlton Athletic** v **Blackburn Rovers**, 5th Rd on 8 February, 1947.

As a 'Non League' club **Hereford United** reached the First Round of the FA Cup on 21 consecutive seasons.

A Bradford firm designed the present FA Cup, the third actual trophy, in 1910. The first club to win it was **Bradford City** in 1911.

When **Barnsley** won the FA Cup in season 1911–12 they played a total of 20 hours of football involving 12 games, half of which were goalless draws, and they conceded only three goals.

When **Notts County** won the FA Cup in 1893–94 they became the first Second Division club to win the competition.

Only five clubs from the Third Division have reached the Semi-Final stage of the FA Cup. They were **Millwall**, **York City**, **Port Vale**, **Norwich City** and **Crystal Palace**.

Having been officially formed into a Limited Company in 1939 and having been accepted by the Southern League, **Hereford United** played an FA Cup tie in only their second senior competitive game.

The only club to have played against clubs from all four 'home' countries in the FA Cup is **Nottingham Forest**.

Harry Brooks scored five goals for **Aldershot** in each of two successive FA Cup ties in the 1945–46 season.

Reading first appeared in the FA Cup 1st Round in 1877, only **Notts County** of the present Football League clubs have played in the competition so long ago.

Colchester United reached the 5th Round of the FA Cup in 1947–48 as a Non League club. Their best season in the competition since joining the League was in 1970–71 when they reached the 6th Round as a Fourth Division club. Only **Oxford United** and **Bradford City** have equalled that feat from the Fourth Division.

FA CHARITY SHIELD WINNERS 1908–82

Year	*Winners*	*Runners-up*	*Score*
1908	Manchester U	QPR	4-0 after 1-1 draw
1909	Newcastle U	Northampton T	2-0
1910	Brighton	Aston Villa	1-0
1911	Manchester U	Swindon T	8-4
1912	Blackburn R	QPR	2-1
1913	Professionals	Amateurs	7-2
1919	WBA	Tottenham H	2-0
1920	Tottenham H	Burnley	2-0
1921	Huddersfield	Liverpool	1-0
1922	Not played		
1923	Professionals	Amateurs	2-0
1924	Professionals	Amateurs	3-1
1925	Amateurs	Professionals	6-1
1926	Amateurs	Professionals	6-3
1927	Cardiff C	Corinthians	2-1
1928	Everton	Blackburn R	2-1
1929	Professionals	Amateurs	3-0
1930	Arsenal	Sheffield W	2-1
1931	Arsenal	WBA	1-0
1932	Everton	Newcastle U	5-3
1933	Arsenal	Everton	3-0
1934	Arsenal	Manchester C	4-0
1935	Sheffield W	Arsenal	1-0
1936	Sunderland	Arsenal	2-1
1937	Manchester C	Sunderland	2-0
1938	Arsenal	Preston NE	2-1
1948	Arsenal	Manchester U	4-3
1949	Portsmouth	Wolverhampton W	1-1*
1950	World Cup Team	Canadian Touring Team	4-2
1951	Tottenham H	Newcastle U	2-1
1952	Manchester U	Newcastle U	4-2
1953	Arsenal	Blackpool	3-1
1954	Wolverhampton W	WBA	4-4*
1955	Chelsea	Newcastle U	3-0
1956	Manchester U	Manchester C	1-0
1957	Manchester U	Aston Villa	4-0
1958	Bolton W	Wolverhampton W	4-1
1959	Wolverhampton W	Nottingham F	3-1
1960	Burnley	Wolverhampton W	2-2*
1961	Tottenham H	FA XI	3-2
1962	Tottenham H	Ipswich T	5-1
1963	Everton	Manchester U	4-0
1964	Liverpool	West Ham U	2-2*
1965	Manchester U	Liverpool	2-2*
1966	Liverpool	Everton	1-0
1967	Manchester U	Tottenham H	3-3*
1968	Manchester C	WBA	6-1
1969	Leeds U	Manchester C	2-1
1970	Everton	Chelsea	2-1
1971	Leicester C	Liverpool	1-0
1972	Manchester C	Aston Villa	1-0
1973	Burnley	Manchester C	1-0
1974	Liverpool†	Leeds	1-1
1975	Derby Co	West Ham U	2-0
1976	Liverpool	Southampton	1-0
1977	Liverpool	Manchester U	0-0*
1978	Nottingham F	Ipswich T	5-0
1979	Liverpool	Arsenal	3-1
1980	Liverpool	West Ham U	1-0
1981	Aston Villa	Tottenham H	2-2*

* *Each club retained shield for six months.* † *Won on penalties.*

FA CHARITY SHIELD 1982

Liverpool (0) 1 Tottenham H (0) 0

At Wembley, 21 August, 1982. Attendance 82,000. Receipts £410,000

Liverpool: Grobbelaar; Neal, Thompson, Hansen, Kennedy, Lee, Lawrenson, Souness, Whelan, Dalglish (Hodgson 77 mins), Rush.

Tottenham H: Clemence; O'Reilly (Perryman 65 mins), Miller, Lacy, Hughton, Hoddle, Hazard (Falco 78 mins). Mabbutt, Galvin, Archibald, Crooks. *Scorer:* Liverpool – Rush.

SCOTTISH FOOTBALL ASSOCIATION OFFICIALS

Patron: Her Majesty the Queen
Hon. President: The Right Hon., The Lord Ross of Marnock
President: Tommy Younger (Hibs)
Vice-President: David H. Will (Brechin City)
2nd Vice-President: David Letham (Queen's Park)
Treasurer: Peter Gardiner (Stirling Albion)
Secretary: Ernie Walker

Council

E. Houston (Threave Rovers)
D. Faulds (Kilmarnock)
J. Y. Craig (St Mirren)
J. M. Farrell (Celtic)
J. F. McBeth (Clyde)
A. C. Dick (Hamilton Accademicals)
A. M. Jackson (Dumbarton)
E. Moffat (Falkirk)
A. W. Mercer (Hearts)
M. Scott (Coldstream United)
J. Urquhart (Raith Rovers)
M. Speedie (Dundee)
A. G. Webster (Forfar Athletic)
C. Anderson (Aberdeen)
J. S. McDonald (Inverness Thistle)
J. S. Brown (Stranraer)
T. A. Shand (Partick Thistle)
C. A. Steedman (Clydebank)
J. Watters (Dunfermline)
J. M. Grant (Dundee United)
J. G. Rattray (Keith)
R. R. McDonald (Brora Rangers)
Dr J. Crorie (Clyde)
J. W. Baxter (East Fife)
T. L. Devlin (Celtic)
W. H. Dickie (Motherwell)
M. Foy (Dumbarton)
I. R. G. Gellatly (Dundee)
J. Jenkins (Stenhousmuir)
A. McNab (Berwick Rangers)
J. L. McPherson (Morton)
R. H. Simpson (Rangers)
J. S. Steedman (Clydebank)
R. Hay (Scottish Amateur FA)
T. A. Wilkie (Scottish Amateur FA)
R. F. McDonald (Scottish Juvenile FA)
J. Leitch (Scottish Schools FA)
Major H. J. Smith (Army FA)

THE SCOTTISH SEASON 1982–83

If the form of the National team is the main criterion by which a season is judged then 1982–83 must be cited as a disaster. In seven outings Scotland only managed to win twice – once at Hampden against East Germany and once in Cardiff against Wales in the British Championship; two opponents (Switzerland and Northern Ireland) came to Hampden and left without losing, and before the end of April it was known that Scotland could not qualify for the final stages of the European Championships. Finally, the visit to Wembley, was another horror story with a very disappointing Scottish outfit surrendering to a respectable but by no means great England team, which was allowed to stroll through the game with scarcely a challenge from its guests.

However, even at a National level all was not a picture of gloom with the Under-21 side remaining unbeaten and likely to progress far, whilst the Youths again reached the final stages of their European competition before falling to a very good (on the night) England team. But there was another disappointment at Semi-Professional level when a squad drawn from the Scottish First Division came second to an English selection from outside the Football League. This is a tournament held annually involving the 'Auld Enemy', Italy, Holland and Scotland and there really should be no good reason why Scotland should not win more often without any difficulty.

Having given the gloomy part of the picture it must now be time to list the plus marks gained and – thanks to two excellent North-East teams – there were several. Pride of place must go to Aberdeen, who became the third team of Scots to win a European competition; I choose my words carefully, because in general it is cosmopolitan selections which carry off such honours, but each time a trophy has come to Scotland the winners have been represented exclusively by Scots and that is some cause for considerable pride. Aberdeen joined Celtic (European Cup in 1967) and Rangers (Cup Winners Cup in 1972) in the Hall of Fame and their victory in the Cup Winners Cup was gained most impressively with only one defeat in any leg of any round and only one yellow card in the whole competition. In the Quarter Finals Bayern Munich were beaten with a late rally at Pittodrie, Waterschei of Belgium were heavily defeated in the Semi-Finals and in a Final played in very wet conditions in Gothenburg Real Madrid were fortunate to take the match into extra-time before John Hewitt's brave header clinched victory seven minutes before the second hour elapsed; Eric Black had put Aberdeen ahead early on only for the defence to slip up and concede a penalty from which the Spanish side equallised. Perhaps, Real Madrid are not like their famous forerunners, but even so it was a formidable achievement. In keeping with the generally improved behaviour of Scottish supporters Aberdeen's following gained nothing but praise from the Swedish authorities. Altogether it was a good night for Scotland. Here at least good management, discipline and organisation prevailed.

Other good marks were earned from the domestic competitions with Glasgow's only success coming in the League Cup where Celtic beat Rangers more comfortably than the score (2-1) might suggest. The latter were also to be victims of Aberdeen's second triumph of the season, when Eric Black scored the only goal of a 'dour' final four minutes from the end of extra-time. The Dons were not at their best against a plucky Light Blues outfit, but as McCloy had been the busier of two good goalkeepers no-one could really say that on pressure alone Aberdeen should not have won.

The League for once provided a story-book ending with a first-ever success for Dundee United, who only took the lead from the long-term front-runners (Celtic – who else?) during the last month of the season. Even so, the last day was decisive with Dundee United needing victory in their local Derby at Dens Park to be sure of taking the Flag and this they did by a very narrow margin of the odd goal in three. Meanwhile, both Celtic and Aberdeen (again) were in hot pursuit and ready to punish any slips. Celtic could not be said to have been given an easy final game against Rangers at Ibrox and they had to recover from a two goal half-time deficit to win once again against their traditional rivals; the final score was 4-2. This left Aberdeen's last match as something of an irrelevance, but the Dons still managed a resounding victory over Hibernian and some would say that it was only the pressure of trying to win too many competitions that prevented them from being Champions as well. Even so their record speaks for itself.

Further down the scale it was good to see St Johnstone and Hearts, both former European campaigners, promoted to the Premier Division and it must be said that in neither case did it seem that failure was likely. Down to the First Division went Morton and Kilmarnock, the latter after yet another single season 'upstairs', whilst Morton have been in danger for several seasons. In the Second Division Meadowbank Thistle lifted them-

selves off their usual basement seat and won promotion thanks largely to a very good start to the campaign, in which they were eventually pushed into second place by a buoyant Brechin City, which has been threatening better things for itself for some few seasons. Hats off to Iain Fleming and his small squad for bringing another honour to the North-East. It is good to see the honours go round. Back to Division Two go Queen's Park and Dunfermline Athletic – not altogether good news for those who have a soft spot for amateurs.

So another season passes and we look forward to 1983–84. What is in store for us? Can we hope that our National team will respond to the wonderful loyalty of its fans by giving us all something to cheer? The British Championship and a victory at Hampden over England will do for a start. With five teams in Europe we have a strong hand; can even more success be achieved? We shall see, but let us hope for an enjoyable and peaceful season for all fans. We might even see Dundee United's great Jim McLean smile more!

SCOTTISH LEAGUE REFEREES, 1982–83

H. Alexander (Irvine)
E. K. Brollis (Bishopbriggs)
I. R. Cathcart (Bridge of Allan)
R. R. Cuthill (Winchburgh)
M. Delaney (Cleland)
D. S. Downie (Edinburgh)
J. Duncan (Gorebridge)
A. Ferguson (Giffnock)
D. M. Galloway (Pitlessie)
D. D. Hope (Erskine)
K. J. Hope (Clarkston)
A. N. Huett (Edinburgh)
W. P. Knowles (Inverurie)
B. R. McGinlay (Balfron)
A. McGunnigle (Glasgow)
W. McLeish (Stonehouse)
T. Muirhead (Stenhousemuir)
E. H. Pringle (Edinburgh)
D. Ramsay (Edinburgh)
J. R. S. Renton (Cowdenbeath)
B. Robertson (East Kilbride)
A. M. Roy (Elgin)
C. C. Sinclair (Forfar)
G. B. Smith (Edinburgh)
D. F. T. Syme (Glasgow)
L. B. Thow (Ayr)
J. J. Timmons (Kilwinning)
R. B. Valentine (Dundee)
A. W. Waddell (Edinburgh)
C. J. White (Clarkston)
H. F. Williamson (Renfrew)
H. Young (Larkhall)

SCOTTISH REFEREES IN EUROPE, 1982–83

European Cup

1st Round	Hvidovre v Juventus	G. Smith
2nd Round	Olympiakos v SV Hamburg	B. R. McGinlay
Quarter Final	Sporting Lisbon v Real San Sebastion	R. B. Valentine

Cup Winners' Cup

2nd Round	Red Star Belgrade v Barcelona	R. B. Valentine

UEFA Cup

1st Round	Dynamo Tblisi v Napoli	R. B. Valentine
	Tatabanya v St Etienne	D. Syme
	Athletico Bilbao v Ferencvaros	B. R. McGinlay
	Lokeren v Stal Mielic	K. J. Hope
2nd Round	Norrkoping v AS Roma	D. Syme
3rd Round	Seville v Kaiserslautern	R. B. Valentine
Quarter Final	Valencia v Anderlecht	B. R. McGinlay
Semi-Final	University Craivo v Benfica	R. B. Valentine

RECORDS

Major Scottish Records

HIGHEST SCORES

Arbroath 36 Bon Accord 0. *First Round, Scottish FA Cup* 5 Sept 1885
(This is a British Record for a first class match.)

SCOTTISH LEAGUE

Premier Division	(*Home*)	Aberdeen	8	Motherwell	0	26 Mar 1979
	(*Away*)	Kilmarnock	1	Rangers	8	20 Sept 1980
Division 1	(*Home*)	Celtic	11	Dundee	0	26 Oct 1895
	(*Away*)	Airdrieonians	1	Hibernian	11	24 Oct 1959
Division 2	(*Home*)	East Fife	13	Edinburgh C	2	11 Dec 1937
	(*Away*)	Alloa Ath	0	Dundee	10	8 Mar 1947

MOST GOALS 'FOR' IN A SEASON

		Goals	*Games*	*Season*
Premier Division	Celtic	79	36	1976–77
Division 1	Hearts	132	34	1957–58
Division 2	Raith R	142	34	1937–38

FEWEST GOALS 'FOR' IN A SEASON

	(minimum 42 games)	*Goals*	*Games*	*Season*
Premier Division	Clydebank	23	36	1977–78
	Kilmarnock	23	36	1980–81
Division 1	Stirling Alb	18	39	1980–81
Division 2	Lochgelly U	20	38	1923–24

MOST GOALS 'AGAINST' IN A SEASON

		Goals	*Games*	*Season*
Premier Division	Motherwell	86	36	1978–79
Division 1	Leith Ath	137	38	1931–32
Division 2	Edinburgh C	146	38	1931–32

FEWEST GOALS 'AGAINST' IN A SEASON

		Goals	*Games*	*Season*
Premier Division	Rangers	24	36	1975–76
Division 1	Celtic	14	38	1913–14
Division 2	Morton	20	38	1966–67

MOST POINTS IN A SEASON

		Points	*Games*	*Season*
Premier Division	Celtic	56	36	1980–81
Division 1	Rangers	76	42	1920–21
Division 2	Morton	69	38	1966–67

FEWEST POINTS IN A SEASON

		Points	*Games*	*Season*
(minimum 30 games)				
Premier Division	St Johnstone	11	36	1975–76
Division 1	Stirling Alb	6	30	1954–55

MOST WINS IN A SEASON

		Wins	Games	Season
Premier Division	Celtic	26	36	1980–81
Division 1	Rangers	35	42	1920–21
Division 2	Morton	33	38	1966–67

FEWEST WINS IN A SEASON

		Wins	Games	Season
Premier Division	St Johnstone	3	36	1975–76
Division 1	Vale of Leven	0	22	1891–92
Division 2	East Stirlingshire	1	22	1905–06
	Forfar Ath	1	38	1974–75

MOST DEFEATS IN A SEASON

		Defeats	Games	Season
Premier Division	St Johnstone	28	36	1975–76
Division 1	St Mirren	31	42	1920–21
Division 2	Lochgelly U	30	38	1923–24
	Brechin C	30	36	1962–63
	Forfar Ath	30	38	1974–75

FEWEST DEFEATS IN A SEASON

		Defeats	Games	Season
Premier Division	Celtic	4	36	1976–77
Division 1	Celtic	0	18	1897–98
	Rangers	0	18	1898–99
	Rangers	1	42	1920–21
	Hearts	1	34	1957–58
	Celtic	1	34	1967–68
	Rangers	1	34	1967–68
Division 2	Kilmarnock	0	18	1898–99
	Clyde	1	36	1956–57
	Morton	1	36	1963–64

MOST DRAWN GAMES IN A SEASON

		Draws	Games	Season
Premier Division	Hibernian	18	36	1976–77

MOST GOALS IN A GAME

Division 1	Jimmy McGrory (Celtic) 8 goals v Dunfermline Ath	14 Sept 1928
Division 2	Owen McNally (Arthurlie) 8 goals v Armadale	1 Oct 1927
	Jim Dyet (King's Park) 8 goals v Forfar Ath	2 Jan 1930
	John Calder (Morton) 8 goals v Raith R	18 Apr 1936
	John Petrie (Arbroath) 13 goals v Bon Accord (*SFA Cup 1st Round*)	5 Sept 1885

MOST LEAGUE GOALS IN A SEASON

		Goals	Games	Season
Division 1	William McFadyen (Motherwell)	52	34	1931–32
Division 2	Jim Smith (Ayr)	66	38	1927–28

MOST LEAGUE GOALS IN A CAREER

		Goals	Games	Season
Jimmy McGrory	Celtic	1	3	1922–23
	Clydebank	13	30	1923–24
	Celtic	396	375	1924–38
		410	408	1922–38

ABERDEEN Premier Division

Year Formed: 1903
Ground: Pittodrie Stadium. *Size:* 110yd×71yd. *Capacity:* 24,000 (all seated and all covered).
Telephone: Aberdeen 632328, 633497.
Manager: Alec Ferguson. *Assistant-Manager:* Archie Knox.
Secretary: I. J. Taggart. *Trainer:* Teddy Scott. *Physiotherapist:* Roland Arnott.
Club Colours: Red shirts, red shorts, red stockings.
Club Nickname: The Dons.
Record Attendance: 45,061 v Hearts, Scottish Cup 4th rd, 13 March, 1954.
(Present Aberdeen FC have had no other ground but Pittodrie.)
Record Transfer Fee Received: £800,000 from Tottenham H for Steve Archibald, May 1980.
European Competitions: *Fairs Cup* 1968–69; *European Cup-Winners Cup* 1967–68, 1970–71, 1978–79, 1982–83 (Winners); *UEFA Cup* 1971–72, 1972–73, 1973–74, 1977–78, 1979–80, 1981–82; *European Cup* 1980–81.

1982-83 LEAGUE RECORD

Match No.	Date	Venue	Opponents	Result		H/T Score	League Pos'n	Goalscorers	Attendance
1	Sept 4	A	Dundee U	L	0-2	0-2	—		11,683
2	11	H	Morton	W	4-1	2-1	3	Strachan (pen), Black, Simpson, Hewitt	8000
3	18	A	St Mirren	D	1-1	0-0	5	McGhee	4800
4	25	H	Rangers	L	1-2	0-0	5	Strachan	22,000
5	Oct 2	H	Motherwell	W	2-1	0-1	5	Cowan, Miller	8000
6	9	A	Celtic	W	3-1	0-0	5	Strachan (pen), Simpson, McGhee	29,733
7	16	H	Dundee	W	1-0	1-0	4	Weir	9000
8	23	A	Kilmarnock	W	2-0	1-0	4	Black, Hewitt	3400
9	30	A	Hibs	D	1-1	0-0	3	Weir	6000
10	Nov 6	H	Dundee U	W	5-1	3-1	2	Rougvie 2, Cooper, Black, Strachan	10,000
11	13	A	Morton	D	1-1	0-0	3	Black	3000
12	20	H	St Mirren	W	4-0	1-0	3	Strachan (pen), Black, McGhee, Hewitt	10,000
13	27	A	Rangers	W	1-0	0-0	3	Black	24,000
14	Dec 4	A	Motherwell	W	2-0	0-0	3	Strachan (pen), Weir	4929
15	11	H	Celtic	L	1-2	1-1	3	McGhee	25,000
16	18	A	Dundee	W	2-0	1-0	3	McGhee 2	6528
17	27	H	Kilmarnock	W	2-0	1-0	3	Weir, McGhee	14,500
18	Jan 1	H	Hibs	W	2-0	2-0	3	McGhee 2	14,000
19	3	A	Dundee U	W	3-0	2-0	2	Simpson, Weir, McGhee	17,851
20	8	H	Morton	W	2-0	0-0	2	Simpson, McGhee	14,000
21	15	A	St Mirren	D	1-1	0-1	2	Black	4530
22	22	H	Rangers	W	2-0	1-0	2	Rougvie, McGhee	22,000
23	Feb 8	H	Motherwell	W	5-1	2-1	2	McLeish, McMaster, Black, McGhee, Cooper	13,000
24	12	A	Celtic	W	3-1	2-1	1	Black 3	42,831
25	26	H	Dundee	W	3-1	0-1	1	Weir, Black, Bell	11,450
26	Mar 5	A	Kilmarnock	W	2-1	2-0	1	Watson, McGhee	2400
27	19	H	Dundee U	L	1-2	0-2	1	Strachan (pen)	22,800
28	26	A	Morton	W	2-1	0-1	1	Watson, Black	4000
29	Apr 2	H	St Mirren	L	0-1	0-0	3		12,000
30	9	A	Rangers	L	1-2	1-1	3	McLeish	19,800
31	23	H	Celtic	W	1-0	1-0	3	McGhee	24,500
32	27	A	Motherwell	W	3-0	1-0	3	McGhee, Strachan, Hewitt	6715
33	30	A	Dundee	W	2-0	2-0	3	Hewitt, Strachan	10,076
34	May 2	A	Hibs	D	0-0	0-0	3		8000
35	4	H	Kilmarnock	W	5-0	2-0	3	Angus 2, Strachan 2, McMaster	12,500
36	14	H	Hibs	W	5-0	2-0	3	Brazil (og), McGhee, Strachan (pen), Cowan, Angus	24,000

Final League Position: 3

Goalscorers

League: McGhee 17, Strachan 12, Black 12, Weir 6, Simpson 5, Hewitt 5, Rougvie 3, Angus 3, McMasters 2, Cowan 2, McLeish 2, Watson 1, Miller 1, Bell 1, opponent 1.
League Cup: Strachan 7, Bell 3, McGhee 4, Black 3, Hewitt 1, Rougvie 1.
Scottish Cup: Weir 4, Simpson 2, Watson 1, McGhee 1, Cooper 1, Black 1.
European Cup Winners Cup: McGhee 6, Hewitt 5, Black 3, Simpson 3, Weir 2, Strachan 1, Kennedy 1, Bell 1, Miller 1, McLeish 1, opponent 1.

Honours

Scottish League – Division 1 Champions 1954–55; Runners-up 1910–11, 1936–37, 1955–56, 1970–71, 1971–72; Premier Division Champions 1979–80; Runners-up 1977–78; 1980–81, 1981–82.
Scottish Cup – Winners 1947, 1970, 1982, 1983; Runners-up 1937, 1953, 1954, 1959, 1967, 1978.
Scottish League Cup – Winners 1955–56, 1976–77; Runners-up 1946–47, 1978–79, 1979–80.
Drybrough Cup – Winners 1971.
Record Victory: 13–0 v Peterhead, Scottish Cup, 9 Feb, 1923.
Record Defeat: 0–8 v Celtic, Division 1, 30 Jan, 1965.
Most League Points: 61, Division 1, 1935–36.
Most Individual League Goals in Season: 38, Benny Yorston, Division 1, 1929–30.
Most Capped Player: Willie Miller, 19, Scotland.

Leighton	Gunn	Kennedy	McMaster	Cooper	McLeish	Miller	Strachan	Simpson	McGhee	Bell	Black	Rougvie	Weir	Hewitt	Watson	Cowan	McCall	Falconer	Angus	Hamilton	Mitchell	Porteous	*Match No.*
1		2	3	4	5	6	7	8	9	10*	11†		12	14									1
1		2	3	4*		6	7	10	9	12	8†	5	11	14									2
1		2	3	4	5	6	7	8*	14		9	12	11	10†									3
1		2		4	5	6	7	8	9	10	11*	3	12										4
1		2	4		5	6	7	8	9			3*	11	10†	12	14							5
1			4	2	5	6	7	8	9	10*		3	11		12								6
1			4	2	5	6	7*	8†	9	10	12	3	11		14								7
1			4	2	5	6	7*	8		10	9	3	11	12									8
	1		4	2	5	6	7	8*		10†	9	3	11	14	12								9
1		2		4	5	6	7	8	9		10	3	11										10
1		2		4	5	6	7	8	9*	12	10	3	11										11
1		2		4	5	6	7	8*	9	10	11	3	11	12									12
1		2		4*	5	6	7	8	9	10	12	3	11										13
1		2		4	5	6	7	8	9	10	9*	3	11	12†	14								14
1		2		4	5	6	7	8	9	10†	14	3*	11	12									15
1		2		4	5	6	7	8	9		10	3	11										16
1		2		4	5	6	7	8	9*		10	3	11				12						17
1		2			5	6	7*	8	9	4	10†	3	11		12		14						18
1		2	14	4	5	6	7*	8†	9	10	12	3	11										19
1		2	14	4*	5	6		8	9	10	7†	3	11		12								20
1		2	14		5	6	7	8†	9	10	12	3	11		4*								21
1		2	12	4*	5	6	7†	14	9	10	8	3	11										22
1		2	4	12	5	6		8	9	10	7*	3	11†		14								23
1		2		4	5	6		8	9	10	7	3	11										24
1		2	4	14	5	6		12	9	10	7	3*	11		8†								25
1		2	12	4	5	6	7	8	9		11	3*			10								26
1			4	2	5	6	7	12	9	8*	14	3	11†	10									27
1		2	3	4*	14	6	7	8	9		10	5†	11		12								28
1		2	3*	4†	5	6	7	8	9		10	12	11		14								29
1		2	14	4	5	6	7	8	9	10	12	3†	11*										30
1			4	2	5	6	7	14	9*			3	11†	10*	8			12					31
1			4	2*	5	6	7	8	9†			3		11	10				12	14			32
1			4	2†	5	6	7	8	9		12	3		11	10†				14				33
1			3	2	5	6	7		9			12	11	8	4				10*				34
1			3			6	7			12	14	5	11	9	4*				10		2	8†	35
1			3		5*	6	7		9		8†	2		11	4	14			10	12			36
35	1	25	19	29	33	36	32	29	31	20	23	32	29	9	8	–	–	–	3	–	1	1	
			+ 6s	+ 2s	+ 1s			+ 4s	+ 1s	+ 3s	+ 9s	+ 3s	+ 2s	+ 7s	+ 10s	+ 2s	+ 2s	+ 1s	+ 2s	+ 2s			

The Dons looked Championship material all through the season and only when their rash of committments in the closing weeks of a tremendous campaign stretched resources to the limit did their bid falter.
Highlight of their league season was two winning performances at Parkhead and a 5–1 defeat of Champions Dundee United at Pittodrie.
Ever present skipper Willie Miller has never played better, within a side that is certain to be involved with the chase for all the silverware again this season.

AIRDRIE Division 1

Year Formed: 1878
Ground: Broomfield Park. *Size:* 112yd×68yd. *Capacity:* 20,000 (2000 seats).
Telephone: Airdrie 62067.
Manager: William Munro. *Coach:* Billy Reid. *Second Team:* R. Morrison.
Secretary: George W. Peat CA.
Club Colours: White shirt with red diamond, white shorts, red stockings and white diamond tops.
Club Nickname: Diamonds or Waysiders.
Record Attendance: 24,000 v Hearts, Scottish Cup, 8 March, 1952.

1982-83 LEAGUE RECORD

Match No.	Date	Venue	Opponents	Result	H/T Score	League Pos'n	Goalscorers	Attendance
1	Sept 4	H	Dumbarton	L 1-2	0-2	10	Coyle o.g.	1200
2	8	A	Alloa	W 2-1	1-1	6	B. Miller, Garner o.g.	800
3	11	A	Raith Rovers	W 3-0	2-0	3	B. Miller 2, McKeown	800
4	15	H	Hamilton	W 2-0	0-0	2	G. Anderson P, McDonagh	1200
5	18	H	Partick Th.	L 1-3	1-2	2	McGuire	2500
6	22	A	Clydebank	W 4-0	1-0	2	March, Rodger, McGuire, McKeown	800
7	25	A	Falkirk	W 3-1	1-0	2	McKeown, Flood, McGuire	2500
8	Oct 2	H	Dunfermline	D 1-1	1-0	3	Rodger	1100
9	9	A	St. Johnstone	L 0-1	0-1	4		2590
10	16	H	Clyde	L 3-4	1-2	6	B. Miller, Weir, Rodger	1000
11	23	H	Ayr United	W 3-1	0-0	4	Gordon, McGuire, McLauchlan	1100
12	30	A	Queen's Park	D 1-1	1-1	5	B. Miller	882
13	Nov 6	A	Hearts	W 4-2	3-1	5	Flood 2, Faulds, Miller	5656
14	13	H	Alloa	W 2-1	1-1	3	Flood 2	900
15	20	A	Partick Th.	L 0-1	0-0	4		3192
16	27	H	Clydebank	D 2-2	1-0	4	Flood 2	1200
17	Dec 4	A	Dunfermline	L 0-1	0-1	5		1038
18	11	H	Falkirk	W 3-1	1-0	3	McDonagh, B. Miller, Jarvie	1000
19	27	H	Raith Rovers	L 1-2	1-1	5	Rodger	1200
20	Jan 1	A	Hamilton	W 4-0	2-0	5	Gordon, Flood, McDonagh, McGuire	1586
21	3	H	Hearts	L 0-1	0-0	5		4500
22	8	A	Clyde	L 1-2	1-1	5	Dempsey o.g.	781
23	15	H	St. Johnstone	W 2-0	1-0	5	Martin, Jarvie	1500
24	22	H	Queen's Park	L 0-1	0-0	5		1200
25	Feb 5	A	Ayr United	L 0-1	0-1	5		924
26	23	A	Dumbarton	D 0-0	0-0	5		800
27	26	A	Falkirk	L 0-2	0-0	5		1100
28	Mar 5	A	Hamilton	W 3-0	2-0	5	Jarvie, B. Miller 2	1000
29	15	H	Clyde	W 1-0	0-0	5	Jarvie	900
30	19	A	Ayr United	D 1-1	0-1	5	Rodger	939
31	26	A	Dumbarton	D 1-1	1-1	5	Flood	450
32	Apr 2	H	Hearts	L 0-2	0-1	5		3000
33	5	A	Dunfermline	W 4-0	1-0	5	B. Miller, S. Miller, Coyle, McCafferty	1000
34	9	A	Queen's Park	L 3-4	2-1	5	McLauchlan, (P), McCafferty, Nicholson o.g.	648
35	16	H	Raith Rovers	W 4-2	2-1	5	B. Miller, 2, Anderson, Walker	600
36	23	A	Clydebank	L 0-2	0-0	5		657
37	30	H	St. Johnstone	D 1-1	0-0	5	Gordon	2000
38	May 7	A	Partick Th.	W 1-0	0-0	5	Walker	1600
39	14	H	Alloa	L 0-1	0-1	5		1000

Final League Position: 5

Goalscorers

League: B. Miller 12, Flood 9, Rodger 5, Jarvie 4, opponents 4, McKeown 3, McDonagh 3, Gordon 3, G. Anderson 2, McLaughlan 2, McCafferty 2, Walker 2, March 1, Weir 1, Faulds 1, Martin 1, S. Miller, Coyle 1.
League Cup: Miller 4, Flood 2, Campbell 1, Faulds 1, opponent 1.
Scottish Cup: Flood 2, Miller, Gordon 1.

Honours
Scottish League – Division 1 Runners-up 1922–23, 1923–24, 1924–25, 1925–26, 1979–80; Division 2 Champions 1902–03, 1954–55, 1973–74; Runners-up 1900–01, 1946–47, 1949-50, 1965–66.
Scottish Cup – Winners 1924; Runners-up 1975.
Scottish League Cup – None.
Spring Cup – Winners 1975–76.
Record Victory: 15-1 v Dundee Wanderers, Division 2, 1 Dec, 1894.
Record Defeat: 1-11 v Hibernian, Division 1, 24 Oct, 1959.
Most League Points: 60, Division 2, 1973–74.
Most Individual League Goals in Season: 45, H. G. Yarnall, Division 1, 1916–17.
Most Capped Player: Jimmy Crapnell, 9, Scotland.
Highest goalscorers in British league football 1973–74 with 102 goals.

Martin	Anderson, G.	Rodger	McLaughlin	March	Campbell	Faulds	McKeown	Miller, B.	Flood	Coyle	Gordon	McGuire	McCafferty	Cairney	Anderson, N.	Weir	Jarvie	Yule	Campbell	McDonagh	Black	Walker	Stewart	Miller, S.	Stevens	*Match No.*
1	2	3	4	5	6	7	8	9	10	11																1
1		3	4	5		11†	7	9	10	6*		14	12	2	8											2
1	2	3	4	5			8	9	10		6	7	11													3
1	2	3	4	5			8	9	10	12	6*	7	11†									14				4
1	2	3	4	5			8	9	10		6	7	11													5
1	2	3	4	5			8	9	10		6	7	11													*6
1	14	3	4	5			7*	9†	10	6		11		2	8							12				7
1		3	4	5			7	9	10	6		11*		2	8					12						8
1		3	4	5		12	7	9*	10					2		6	8	11								9
1	2	3	4	5			7	9	10			11		12		6*	8									10
1		3	4	5		12	8	9			6	7			2		10	11*								11
1	2	3	4	5*	12		8	9	7		6	11					10									12
1	5	3	4		12	11	7	9	10		6			2			8*									13
1	5	3	4		12	11	7	9†	10		6	14		2			8*									14
1	5	3	4		14	11	7	9	10†		6	12		2			8*									15
1	5	3	4		12	11†	7	9	10		6	14		2			8*									16
1	5	3				12	7	9	10*		6	11		2	4				8							17
1	5	3	4					9			6	11		2	8		7			10						18
*1	5	3	4					9			6	11		2	8		7			10						19
1	5	3	4				12		9†		6	11		2	8		7*	14		10						20
1	5	3	4						9		6	11		2	8		7			10						21
1	5	3	4*	14				12	9		6†	11		2	8		7			10						22
1	4	5						9						2	6		7	11	8		3	10				23
1	4	5						9*			6			2	10			11	8	12	3	7				24
1	5	3	4					9	10		6			2		8*	12	11	7							25
1	5	3	4					9	10		6			2		8		11	7							26
1	6	14	4	5				9*	10		11†	12		2			8				3	7				27
1	2		4	5				9			6				8		10	11			3	7				28
1	5	3	4				7	9		10	6	11			2		8									29
1	5	3	4				7	9*	12	10	6	11			2		8									30
1	2	3	4	5			7*		9	10	6	11					8					12				31
1	5	3	4	12			8		9*	11	6	10			2							7				32
1	5	3	4					9			6	11	10		8								2	7		*33
1		3	4	5				9		12	6*		11		8							7	2	10		34
1		3	4	5			12	9			6		10*		8							11	2	7		35
1		3	4	5				9			6		10		8							11	2	7		36
1		3	4	5			2	9*			6		10		8		12					11		7		37
1		3	4	5			2	9			6		10		8							11		7		38
1		3		5			2	9		12	6	8	10*									11		7	4	39
39	28	37	35	21	1	6	24	34	24	8	32	21	11	19	22	4	19	7	5	5	4	11	4	7	1	
	+ 1s	+ 1s		+ 2s	+ 5s	+ 3s	+ 2s	+ 1s	+ 1s	+ 3s		+ 5s	+ 1s	+ 1s			+ 2s	+ 1s		+ 2s		+ 3s				

No quick return to the Premier League for Airdrie, who can reflect on their indifferent home form, when analysing a season when they ended 15 points short of promotion. Only three goals in a seven game spell at the start of the year ended any hope they had of recapturing the form that earned a top three place for the opening month of the season.

ALBION ROVERS Division 2

Year Formed: 1882. *Ground:* Cliftonhill Park. *Capacity:* 10,000 (580 seats). *Size:* 110yd×74yd.
Telephone: Coatbridge 32350.
Manager: Martin Ferguson. *Secretary:* David Forrester CA.
Club Colours: Primrose shirts with red trim and number, red shorts, primrose stockings.
Record Attendance: 27,381 v Rangers, Scottish Cup 2nd rd, 8 Feb, 1936
Previous Grounds: Meadow Park, Whifflet, 1881–1919.
Club Nickname: The Wee Rovers.

1982-83 LEAGUE RECORD

Match No.	Date	Venue	Opponents	Result		H/T Score	League Pos'n	Goalscorers	Atten-dance
1	Sept 4	A	Arbroath	L	1-3	1-1	10	Jenkins	541
2	8	H	Stirling Alb	W	3-0	1-0	9	Ferrie, Evans, Main	400
3	11	H	East Fife	W	1-0	0-0	3	Leishman	150
4	14	A	Stenhousemuir	L	0-1	0-1	7		350
5	18	A	Montrose	D	3-3	2-0	7	Dow 2, Sheran o.g.	250
6	22	H	Q.O.S.	W	3-1	2-1	4	Ferrie, Dow, Evans	250
7	25	H	Cowdenbeath	L	0-2	0-0	6		400
8	Oct 2	A	East Stirling	D	1-1	0-1	9	Gibson P.	250
9	9	H	Brechin City	D	0-0	0-0	8		600
10	16	A	Meadowbank	L	3-4	2-1	8	Conn 2, Dow	300
11	23	A	Berwick	L	0-4	0-2	11		665
12	Nov 2	H	Forfar	L	0-1	0-0	11		250
13	9	H	Stranraer	L	2-3	0-1	12	Conn, Burgess	200
14	13	A	Stirling A	D	2-2	1-1	12	Evans, Burgess	563
15	20	H	Montrose	W	2-1	2-0	12	Mathieson o.g., Houston	200
16	27	A	Q.O.S.	L	0-5	0-3	12		750
17	Dec 4	H	East Stirling	W	3-1	1-1	12	Gibson 2 (1 pen), Livingstone	400
18	27	A	East Fife	L	3-4	1-1	12	Evans, Conn, Burgess	530
19	Jan 1	H	Stenhousemuir	W	2-1	0-0	12	Conn 2	300
20	3	A	Stranraer	W	5-1	4-1	10	Evans, Gibson 2, Conn 2	650
21	15	H	Arbroath	L	1-3	1-0	10	Evans	300
22	22	A	Forfar	L	0-2	0-1	11		900
23	Feb 23	A	Brechin	L	0-3	0-1	12		550
24	26	A	Montrose	W	2-1	0-0	11	Evans, Livingstone	150
25	Mar 2	H	Berwick	L	0-1	0-0	9		200
26	5	H	Stranraer	L	1-2	1-1	11	Woods	150
27	9	A	Cowdenbeath	D	1-1	0-1	11	Gray	300
28	12	A	Stirling Alb	W	2-1	0-0	10	Evans, Main	650
29	19	H	Forfar	W	1-0	0-0	10	Evans	250
30	26	H	East Fife	D	1-1	0-1	10	Main	300
31	Apr 2	A	Stenhousemuir	L	0-1	0-0	10		300
32	5	H	Meadowbank	W	4-0	2-0	10	Gallagher 2, Newman, Evans	1100
33	9	A	Brechin City	L	0-3	0-2	10		500
34	13	H	Cowdenbeath	W	2-0	0-0	10	Burgess, Kasule	350
35	16	H	Meadowbank	L	1-3	1-2	10	Gray P.	300
36	23	H	Arbroath	L	0-2	0-2	10		300
37	30	A	East Stirling	W	3-1	1-1	10	Boyle, Evans 2	250
38	May 7	A	Q.O.S.	L	0-2	0-1	10		350
39	14	H	Berwick	W	2-1	2-1	10	McGorm 2	300

Final League Position: 10

Goalscorers

League: Evans 12, Conn 8, Gibson 5, Dow 4, Burgess 4, Main 3, Ferrie 2, Livingstone 2, Gray 2, Gallagher 2, McGorm 2, opponents 2, Jenkins 1, Houston 1, Woods 1, Kasule 1, Boyle 1, Newman 1, Leishman 1.
League Cup: Evans 3, Burgess 1, Dow 1, Houston 1.
Scottish Cup: Livingstone 2, Evans.

Honours

Scottish League – Division 2 Champions 1933–34; Runners-up 1913–14, 1937–37, 1947–48.
Scottish Cup – Runners-up 1920.
Record Victory: 12-0 v Airdriehill, Scottish Cup, 3 Sept, 1887.
Record Defeat: 1-9 v Motherwell, Division 1, 2 Jan, 1937.
Most League Points: 54, Division 2, 1929–30.
Most Individual League Goals in Season: 41, Jim Renwick, 1932–33.
Most Capped Player: Jock White, 1(2), Scotland.

Purdie	Allan	Lapsley	Leishman	Collins	Main	Dow	Burgess	Houston	Evans	Conn	Ferrie	Balavage	Gibson	Murray	Livingstone	McQueen	Gray	Newman	Woods	Greene	Newman	O'Hagan	Trialist	Kasule	Boyle	Grant	Ross	McGorm	*Match No.*
1	2	3	4	5	6	7	8	9	10	11*			12																1
1	2	3	4	8	11	10*	5		7	9	6																12		2
1	2	3	4	8	11	10	5		7	9	6*		12																3
1	2	3*	4	8	11	10	5	12	7	9	6																		4
1	2*	3	4	8	6	7	5	9	10	14	11†				12														5
	2	3	4	8	11	7	5	9*	10	12	6	1																	6
	2	3*	4	8	11	7	5	9	10	12	6	1																	7
	2	3	4	6	11	7	5	9	10*			1	8														12		8
1*	2	12	4	8	6	7		9	10	3				5	11†	14													9
	2			6	11	7	5	9	10	3		1		4	8														10
1	2		4	6	11	7	5	9	10	3					12	8*													11
1	7	3	5		11	6		9	10	8				4		2													12
1	2	3	5	6	8	7*	12	9†	10	11				4				14											13
1	2	6	4		11	12	9*	8	10	3			7	5															14
	2	6	4	12	11*		9	8	10	3		1	7	5															15
1	2†	6*	4	8		10	9	11		3			7	5	12	14													16
	2	3	3	10		7	5	6	9	11		1	8*			12													17
	2	3		8		7	5		9	11		1	10*			4	6				12								18
	2	3				7*	5		9	6		1	12	4	8		10	11											19
	2	3		6†		12	5		9	11		1	10	4*	7	14	8												20
		3	2	4	12	7	5		9	11		1	10*		8		6												21
	2		4*			7	5		9	11		1	10		8	12	6	3											22
	10			4	9	7	5			11		1	12		8	2	6									3*			23
	10		2	4	3	7	5		9	11		1			8		6												24
1	8		2	4	3	7	5			11							6				9		10						25
1	8*		2	4		12	5		9	3							6		7	10	11								26
	8		2	4			5		9	3		1	12				6	7	10	11*									27
	8		2	4	12		5		9	3		1					6		7	11		10*							28
	8		2	4	10†		5*		9	3		1		14			6		7	11		12							29
1	8		2	4	11*		5		9	3							6		7	10		12							30
	10	3		4			5		9*			1		14		2		12	7	11		6†	8						31
1		3		4			5		9	6						2			7	11	10		8						32
1	8†	3*		4	11		5		9					14		2	6		7	10		12							33
1				4			5		9							2	10		7	6	11*		3	8	12				34
1	12			4			5		9	6						2	8		7	10		3		11*					35
				4	11		5*		9	10		1		6		2	12		7	8		3†		14					36
				4	11		5		8	3		1		12		2*	6		7	10				14	9†				37
		12		4	11		5		9	3		1		6		2*	8		7	10									38
				4	11		5			3		1		2		14	6		7	10				12	9*			8†	39
18	31	21	25	34	20	27	36	14	35	32	6	21	9	12	8	12	19	2	14	14	5	5	4	1	2	1	0	1	
	+ 1s	+ 2s		+ 1s	+ 2s	+ 3s	+ 1s	+ 1s		+ 3s			+ 5s	+ 4s	+ 2s	+ 7s	+ 1s	+ 2s			+ 1s	+ 3s		+ 4s			+ 2s		

No significant change in the club's fortunes but the transfer of Peter Houston to Alloa in December would not help them lose their mid-table tag. However striker Steve Evans responded well to the challenge, and he scored a dozen times for Rovers who were able to improve their league position by one place from last season.

ALLOA Division 1

Year Formed: 1883. *Ground:* Recreation Ground. *Size:* 110yd×75yd. *Capacity:* 9000.
Telephone: Alloa 722695.
Manager: Willie Garner. *Secretary:* George Ormiston. *Coach:* Martin Boyle.
Club Colours: Gold with black trim, black shorts, gold socks with black tops.
Club Nickname: The Wasps.
Record Attendance: 13,000 v Dunfermline Ath, Scottish Cup 3rd replay, 26 Feb, 1939.

1982-83 LEAGUE RECORD

Match No.	Date	Venue	Opponents	Result		H/T Score	League Pos'n	Goalscorers	Attendance
1	Sept 4	A	Ayr United	L	1-2	1-1	11	Lloyd	1228
2	8	H	Airdrie	L	1-2	1-1	14	Munro	800
3	11	H	Clydebank	W	2-0	0-0	8	Purdie, Wilson	683
4	15	A	Falkirk	W	1-0	0-0	6	Murray	1000
5	18	A	St. Johnstone	L	1-3	1-2	8	McComb	2106
6	22	H	Raith Rovers	W	3-0	2-0	3	Garner, McComb, Houston	600
7	25	H	Hamilton	W	4-2	2-2	3	Houston, Murray, Grant, McComb	727
8	Oct 2	A	Queen's Park	W	2-1	1-1	4	Purdie, Woods (og)	800
9	9	A	Hearts	L	0-3	0-0	6		4382
10	16	H	Partick Th.	W	2-1	1-1	3	McComb, Lloyd	1094
11	23	A	Clyde	L	0-2	0-0	7		670
12	30	H	Dumbarton	W	2-0	0-0	6	Purdie, Holt	557
13	Nov 6	H	Dunfermline	D	2-2	2-1	6	Holt, Grant	1518
14	13	A	Airdrie	L	1-2	1-1	8	Campbell	900
15	20	H	St. Johnstone	L	0-2	0-1	8		1772
16	27	A	Raith Rovers	W	1-0	1-0	8	Campbell	1200
17	Dec 4	H	Queen's Park	W	4-1	2-0	6	Lloyd 2, Thomson, Campbell	719
18	11	A	Hamilton	D	1-1	1-1	6	Smith	703
19	27	A	Clydebank	D	2-2	1-0	6	Purdie, McComb	700
20	Jan 1	H	Falkirk	L	0-2	0-1	7		1758
21	3	A	Dunfermline	L	0-2	0-1	7		1400
22	8	A	Partick Th.	D	1-1	1-1	7	Lloyd	1900
23	15	H	Hearts	D	0-0	0-0	7		2591
24	22	A	Dumbarton	W	2-1	0-1	6	Houston, Campbell	450
25	Feb 8	H	Clyde	L	1-3	0-1	7	McComb	900
26	12	H	Clydebank	L	1-2	0-1	7	Garner (pen)	811
27	19	H	Ayr United	D	0-0	0-0	5		606
28	26	A	Raith Rovers	L	1-3	1-0	8	McComb	900
29	Mar 5	H	Queen's Park	W	3-1	2-1	6	McComb 2, Grant	626
30	15	A	Partick Th.	W	2-1	0-0	6	McComb, Munro	1600
31	19	H	Dumbarton	D	0-0	0-0	6		647
32	26	H	Dunfermline	D	1-1	0-0	6	McComb	1063
33	Apr 2	A	Hamilton	L	0-2	0-0	6		839
34	9	A	Clyde	D	3-3	1-2	6	Munro, Garner (pen), Campbell	575
35	16	H	Ayr United	W	3-0	0-0	6	Grant 2, Munro	514
36	23	H	Hearts	D	1-1	0-1	6	Garner (pen)	2395
37	30	H	Falkirk	L	1-2	0-0	6	Campbell	2000
38	May 7	H	St. Johnstone	D	1-1	0-0	6	Garner	2985
39	14	A	Airdrie	W	1-0	1-0	6	McComb	1000

Final League Position: 6

Goalscorers

League: McComb 12, Campbell 6, Lloyd 5, Garner 5, Grant 5, Munro 4, Purdie 4, Houston 3, Murray 2, Holt 2, Wilson 1, Thomson 1, Smith 1, opponent 1.
League Cup: Gray 2, Garner 1, Murray 1, Houston 1, Munro 1, Grant 1.
Scottish Cup: McComb 1.

Honours

Scottish League – Division 2 Champions 1921–22; Runners-up 1938–39, 1976–77, 1981–82.
Record Victory: 9–2 v Forfar, Division 2, 18 March, 1933.
Record Defeat: 0–10 v Dundee, Division 2, 8 March, 1947. 0–10 v Third Lanark (H), 8 August, 1953 (LG Cup).
Most League Points: 60, 1921–22.
Most Individual League Goals in Season: 49, Wee Crilley, Division 2, 1931–32.
Most Capped Player: Jock Hepburn, 1, Scotland.

Hunter	Thomson	McKenzie	Purdie	Garner	Houston	Grant	Wilson	Lloyd	McComb	Munro	Murray	Holt	Haggart	Gray	Campbell	Smith	Martin	Stewart	*Match No.*
1	2	3	4	5	6*	7	8	9	10	11	12								1
*1	2	3	4	5	6	7	8*	9		11	10		12						2
1	2	3	4	5	6	7	12	9	8*	11	10								3
*1	2	3	4	5	6	7		9	8	11	10								4
1	2	3	4	5	6	7		9	8	11	10*	12							5
*1	2	3*	4	5	6	7	8	9†		11	10	14	12						6
1	2	3	4	5	6	7		9	8	11	10								7
1	2	3	4		6	7	12	9	8*	11	10	5							8
1	2		4		6	7		9*	8	11	10	5	3	12					9
1	2		4		6	7		9	8	11	10	5	3						10
1	2		4		6	7		9*	8	11	10	5	3				12		11
1	2		4	5	8	7		9*		11	10	6	3	12					12
1	2			5	8	7		9	12	11	10†	6*	3	4	12				13
1	2		4	5	6	7		14	8	11	9†	12	3*		10				14
1	2		4	5	6	7*		12		11	9	14	3		10	8†			15
1	2		4	5	6	7				11	10*	12	3		9	8			16
1	2		4	5	6	7		10		11			3		9	8			17
1	2		4	5	6	7		10	12	11			3		9*	8			18
*1	2		4	5	6	7		9		11			3		10	8			19
1	2		4	5	6	7*		10†	9	11		12	3		14	8			20
*1	2		4	5	6	7		10	9	11			3			8			21
1	2		4	5	6	7		10		11		9	3			8			22
1	2		4	5	10	7		9		11		6	3			8			23
1	2	3		5	4	9		10	8	11		6			7				24
1	4	3		5	6	9		12	10	11			2		8*	7			25
1	4	3		5	6	7	8*		10	11	12		2		9†	14			26
1	2		4*	5	6	7	8	10†		11	9		3		14	12			27
1	2			5	6	7	8*		10	11	9		3		12	4			28
1	2			5	6	7		12	9	11	10*		3			8	4		29
*1	2			5	6	7		10	9	11	8		3			4			30
1	2	3		5	6	7		12	9	11	10*					8	4		31
1	2	3		5	6	7	14	12	9	11†	10*					8	4		32
1	4	3		5	6	7			9	11		10				8	2		33
1	8	10†		5	6	7		9		11		12	3		14	2*	4		34
1	4	3		5	6	7		10		11	9†	14			12	8	2		35
1	4			5	6	7		10*		11	12	2			9	8	3		36
1	2			5	6	7		14	9	11†		10*	3		12	8	4		37
1	4			5	6	7		10	9	11			3			8	2		38
1	4			8	6	7*		10	9	11		12	3			8	2		39
39	39	16	23	35	39	39	6	28	24	39	22	12	25	1	9	22	10	0	
							+	+	+		+	+	+	+	+	+		+	
							3s	7s	2s		3s	9s	2s	2s	8s	2s		1s	

Alloa's sixth place in their return season to Division One rates as one of the success stories of the year. Not even the waygoing of their very impressive manager Alec Totten to Falkirk in mid season could halt their momentum and Willie Garner certainly kept up the good work. Hard graft is the hallmark of their side and no one did more than defender Kenny Thomson and winger Arthur Grant.

ARBROATH Division 2

Year Formed: 1878. *Ground:* Gayfield Park. *Size:* 115ydx73yd. *Capacity:* 10,000. *Telephone:* Arbroath 72157.
Manager: Ian J. Stewart. *Trainer:* John Smith. *Coach:* Frank Koper.
Club Colours: Maroon shirts, white shorts, maroon stockings.
Club Nichname Red Lichties.
Record Attendance: 13,510 v Rangers, Scottish Cup 3rd rd, 23 Feb, 1952.
Record Transfer Fee Received: £50,000 from Motherwell for Joe Carson, Jan 1980 and £50,000 from Motherwell for Albert Kidd, Jan 1980.

1982-83 LEAGUE RECORD

Match No.	Date	Venue	Opponents	Result	H/T Score	League Pos'n	Goalscorers	Atten-dance
1	Sept 4	H	Albion Rovers	W 3-1	1-1	2	Shaw, Steele, H. Hill	541
2	8	A	Berwick	L 1-2	0-1	8	Shaw	558
3	11	A	Q.O.S.	L 1-2	1-0	10	Steele	750
4	15	H	Forfar	W 2-1	2-0	6	Robb 2	700
5	18	H	East Stirling	W 4-1	1-0	4	Robb 2, Shaw, H. Hill	574
6	22	A	Stenhousemuir	W 6-1	4-0	2	Robb 2, Kopel, Gavine, Shaw, McKenzie	500
7	25	A	East Fife	D 2-2	2-2	3	Steele, Gavine	530
8	Oct 2	H	Stirling Albion	W 1-0	0-0	2	Steele	695
9	9	A	Stranraer	W 1-0	1-0	2	Burke	250
10	16	H	Montrose	W 3-1	1-1	2	Steele, Powell, Gavine	772
11	23	A	Meadowbank	L 1-2	0-0	2	Robb	900
12	30	H	Cowdenbeath	W 1-0	0-0	2	Shaw	573
13	Nov 6	A	Brechin	L 1-3	0-2	2	Gavine	600
14	13	H	Berwick	L 0-2	0-1	3		645
15	20	A	East Stirling	W 3-1	2-1	2	Gavine, Robb P, Lees	250
16	27	H	Stenhousemuir	D 0-0	0-0	2		598
17	Dec 4	A	Stirling Albion	L 0-1	0-1	4		650
18	18	H	East Fife	W 3-1	1-0	2	Docherty, Robb, Gavine	498
19	27	H	Q.O.S.	W 3-2	2-1	2	Gavine, Robb, Steele	765
20	Jan 1	A	Forfar	D 1-1	1-1	3	Steele	1708
21	3	H	Brechin	L 0-3	0-2	3		1400
22	15	A	Albion Rovers	W 3-1	0-1	3	Steele, Robb, Gavine	300
23	22	A	Cowdenbeath	L 1-2	0-0	3	Shaw	350
24	29	H	Meadowbank	D 2-2	0-2	3	Steele, Gavine	691
25	Feb 5	H	Stranraer	W 3-0	1-0	3	Shaw 2, Docherty	449
26	16	A	Montrose	L 1-2	0-1	3	Docherty	450
27	23	H	Forfar	D 3-3	3-1	3	Robb, Gavine 2	818
28	26	A	Cowdenbeath	L 2-3	1-2	3	Gavine 2	350
29	Mar 5	A	Stirling Albion	W 1-0	0-0	4	Shaw	454
30	12	A	Montrose	W 3-0	0-0	4	Harley 2, Lees	400
31	19	H	Berwick	W 3-1	0-1	3	Steele, Harley, Lees	502
32	26	A	Meadowbank	W 3-0	2-0	3	Gavine, Lees, Shaw	500
33	April 2	A	Q.O.S.	D 1-1	1-1	3	Shaw	50
34	9	H	East Stirling	W 4-0	1-0	3	McKenzie, H. Hill 2, Harley	482
35	16	H	Brechin City	D 1-1	1-1	3	Lees	1324
36	23	A	Albion Rovers	W 2-0	2-0	3	Harley, Steele	300
37	30	H	Stranraer	W 3-2	2-0	3	McKenzie, Harley, Steele	417
38	May 7	H	Stenhousemuir	W 5-2	3-2	3	Steele 3 (1 pen), Shaw, Lees	957
39	14	A	East Fife	L 0-4	0-0	3		481

Final League Position: 3

Goalscorers

League: Steele 15, Gavine 14, Shaw 12, Robb 12, Lees 6, Harley 6, H. Hill 4, McKenzie 3, Docherty 3, Kopel 1, Burke 1, Powell 1
League Cup: Steele 1, Yule 1, Hill 1, Shaw 1.

Honours
Scottish League – Division 2 Runners-up 1934–35, 1958–59, 1967–68, 1971–72.
Record Victory: 36-0 v Bon Accord, Scottish Cup 1st rd, 12 Sept, 1885.
Record Defeat: 0-8 v Kilmarnock, Division 2, 3 Jan, 1949.
Most League Points: 57, Division 2, 1966–67.
Most League Goals: 87, Division 2,1967–68.
Most Individual League Goals in Season: 45, Dave Easson, Division 2, 1958–59.
Most League Goals in Aggregate: Jimmy Jack, 120, 1966–71.
Most Capped Player: Ned Doig, 2(5), Scotland.

Robertson	Larter	Forsyth	Kopel	McKenzie	Young	Burke	Steele	Hill H.	Robb	Shaw	Yule	Docherty	Powell	Gavine	Lees	Newman	Harley	Cavellini	Taylor	Casey	Durno	Davie	Hill T.	Grant	Rendall	*Match No.*
1		2	3	4	5	6*	7	8	9†	10	11	12			14											1
1		2	3	4	5		7	8*	9	10	11	6		12												2
1		2	3	4	5		9	8		10	11	6†	7*	14			12									3
1		2	3	4	5		7†	8	9*	10	11	14		6			12									4
1		2	3	4	5		7*	8	9	10†	11	14		6			12									5
1		2	3	4	5	14	7	8	9†	10*	11	12		6												6
1		2	3	4	5		7	8	9*	10	11	12		6												7
1		2	3	4	5	6	7*	8	9	10	11†		12		14											8
1		2	3	4	5	6	7	8	9*	10				12	11											9
1		2		4	5	3	7	8	9	10			11*	6	12											10
1		2		4	5	3	7	8*	9	10		12	11†	6	14											11
1		2		4	5	3	7	8	9	10			11*	6			12									12
1		5		2	3	14	7	8	9			4		10	12	6*	11†									13
1		2	3	4	5	12	7	8	9	10				6*	11											14
	1	2	3	4	5		12	8	9	10				6	11			7*								15
	1	2	3	4	5		14	8	9	10				6	11†		12	7*								16
	1		3	4		14	7†	8	12	10		2		6	11*		9		5							17
	1		3	4		8	11*		9	10		2		6	14		7†		5		12					18
	1		3	4		12	11*		9†	10				6	14		7		5	2	8					19
	1		3	4			11†	8*	9	10		12		6	14		7		5	2						20
	1		3	4		12		8*	9	10				6	11		7		5	2						21
	1	11	3	4	5		7	8	9	10		2		6												22
	1	2	3	4	5	12	7	8†	9	10				6			14			11*						23
1		2	3	4		12	7*	8	9	10				6						11		5				24
1		2	3	4			11†	8	9	10		7*		6	14		12					5				25
1		2	3	4		10*		8	9	12		7		6	11†		14					5				26
1		2	3	4					9	10		7		6	12			11*		8		5				27
1		2	4	5				12	9	10		7		6	14			11†		8*			3			28
1		2	4	8	5			7*	9†	10				6	14		11			12			3			29
1		2	4	11	5				9*	10				6	12		7			8			3			30
	1	2	4	11*	5		9	12		10				6	14		7			8†			3			31
	1	2	4	8	5		9†	12		10			14	6*	11		7						3			32
	1	2	4	8	5		9*			10			12	6	11		7						3			33
	1		4	2	5	6	9*	8	14	10			12		11		7†						3			34
	1	2	4	6	5		9†	8		10			12		11*		7		14				3			35
	1	2	4	6	5		9*	8†		10			12		11		7		14				3			36
	1	2	4†	6	5		9	8		10				14	11*		7						3	12		37
	1	2	4	11	5		9	8*		10				6	12		7†						3	14		38
	1	2	4	11	5*		9	8		10			12	6	7								3†		12	39
21	18	33	35	39	29	9	31	31	28	37	8	10	4	30	14	1	16	4	5	9	1	4	12	0	0	
						+ 8s	+ 2s	+ 3s	+ 2s	+ 1s		+ 7s	+ 7s	+ 4s	+ 15s		+ 8s		+ 2s	+ 1s	+ 1s			+ 2s	+ 1s	

Another near miss for Arbroath who have finished in third place for the second successive season, and manager Ian Stewart will look at the 'goals against' column for the reason.
The 51 they conceded was higher than any other team in the top six, undoing all the good work that his front players had put in—scoring 78—the highest in the division.

AYR UNITED Division 1

Year Formed: 1910
Ground: Somerset Park. *Size:* 111ydx75yd. *Capacity:* 18,500 (1500 seats).
Telephone: Ayr (0292) 263 435.
Manager: George Caldwell. *Asst. Manager:* Derek Whiteford.
Secretary: R. A. G. Loudon.
Club Colours: White shirts with black facings, black shorts, white stockings.
Club Nickname: The Honest Men.
Record Attendance: 25,225 v Rangers, Division 1, 13 Sept, 1969.

1982-83 LEAGUE RECORD

Match No.	Date	Venue	Opponents	Result		H/T Score	League Pos'n	Goalscorers	Atten-dance
1	Sept 4	H	Alloa	W	2-1	1-1	2	Larnach, Frye	1228
2	11	A	Hearts	D	1-1	0-0	4	Larnach	5601
3	15	H	Partick T	W	2-1	1-1	3	Ahern (2 pen)	1500
4	18	H	Hamilton	D	1-1	0-1	3	McNaughton	1470
5	22	A	Queen's Park	L	1-3	1-2	4	Larnach	650
6	25	A	Dunfermline	L	0-1	0-1	7		1800
7	29	A	Dumbarton	L	0-1	0-0	8		500
8	Oct 2	H	Clydebank	L	1-3	1-0	11	McInally	1213
9	9	A	Falkirk	W	3-1	2-1	10	McAllister, McNaughton, A. Oliver (o.g.)	800
10	16	H	St Johnstone	D	1-1	0-1	9	McAllister	1439
11	23	A	Airdrie	L	1-3	0-0	9	Larnach	1100
12	30	H	Raith Rovers	L	0-4	0-1	10		1007
13	Nov 6	A	Clyde	L	1-3	1-2	11	Larnach	580
14	13	H	Dumbarton	L	0-1	0-0	13		938
15	20	A	Hamilton	D	1-1	1-0	12	Kean	783
16	27	H	Queen's Park	D	2-2	0-1	12	Kean, McAllister	1048
17	Dec 4	A	Clydebank	W	1-0	1-0	11	Larnach	463
18	11	H	Dunfermline	W	1-0	1-0	10	Ahern	1105
19	27	H	Hearts	L	0-3	0-3	10		2500
20	Jan 1	A	Partick T	D	2-2	1-1	10	Kean, McInally	2000
21	3	H	Clyde	W	2-0	0-0	9	Dempsey (o.g.), McInally	1700
22	8	A	St Johnstone	L	0-2	0-1	10		2430
23	15	H	Falkirk	W	4-0	1-0	9	Frye 2, McAllister, Christie	1107
24	22	A	Raith Rovers	W	1-0	0-0	9	Larnach	970
25	Feb 5	H	Airdrie	W	1-0	1-0	8	Cleland	924
26	12	A	Hearts	L	1-5	1-2	9	McNaughton	4294
27	19	A	Alloa	D	0-0	0-0	8		606
28	26	H	St Johnstone	L	0-1	0-0	9		1062
29	Mar 5	H	Clydebank	W	1-0	0-0	7	Ahern	778
30	12	A	Falkirk	L	0-2	0-1	8		1200
31	19	H	Airdrie	D	1-1	1-0	9	Frye	939
32	26	A	Partick T	L	1-3	1-2	11	Ahern (pen)	2035
33	April 2	H	Dumbarton	L	1-2	0-1	11	Ward	900
34	9	H	Dunfermline	L	2-3	1-1	12	Frye, McInally	700
35	16	A	Alloa	L	0-3	0-0	12		514
36	23	A	Hamilton	L	0-1	0-1	13		852
37	30	H	Queen's Park	W	4-0	1-0	12	McInally 3, Connor	929
38	May 7	H	Raith Rovers	W	3-2	1-0	12	Connor 3	1142
39	14	A	Clyde	L	2-3	0-1	12	Frye 2 (1 pen)	1050

Final League Position: 12

Goalscorers

League: Larnach 7, Frye 7, McInally 7, Ahern 5, McAllister 4, Connor 4, McNaughton 3, Kean 3, opponents 2, Christie 1, Clelland 1, Ward 1.
League Cup: Larnach 3, McInally 3, Shanks 1, opponent 1.
Cup: Larnach 1.

Honours
Scottish League – Division 2 Champions 1911-12, 1912-13, 1927-28, 1936-37, 1958-59, 1965-66; Runners-up 1910-11, 1955-56, 1968-69.
Scottish Cup: None.
Scottish League Cup: None.
Record Victory: 11-1 v Dumbarton, League Cup, 13 Aug, 1952.
Record Defeat: 0-9 v Rangers, Division 1, 16 Nov, 1929; 0-9 v Hearts, Division 1, 28 Feb, 1931; 0-9 v Third Lanark Dec 4, 1954 (Division 2).
Most League Points: 60, Division 2, 1958-59.
Most Individual League Goals in Season: 66, Jimmy Smith, 1927-28.
Most Capped Player: Jim Nisbet, 3, Scotland.

Rennie	Shanks	Hetherington	Ahern	McAllister	Fleeting	Frye	McInally	Larnach	Connor	Ward	Armour	McGee	McNaughton	Hendry	Lapsley	Christie	Hume	Brown	Morris	Kean	MacKay	Cleland	Buchanan	Hunter	Spiers	Newman	*Match No.*
1	2	3*	4	5	6	7	8	9	10	11	12																1
1	2		3	5	6	7*	8	9	10	11	4*		14												12		2
*1	2		3	5	6	7*	8	9	10	11	4																3
1	2		4	5	6*	7†	8	9	10	14	12	3	11														4
*1	2		4	5	6	7	8	9	10			3	11														5
1	2		6			12	8	9	10	11*	4	3	7	5													6
*1	2		6			11	8	9	10		4	3	7	5													7
1	2		6			11†	8	9	10	14	4*	3	7	5			12										8
1	2		6	5			7	9	10		8	3	11	4													9
1	2		6	5			11	9	10†		12	3*	7	4	8	12											10
1	2		6	5			8	9	3		14	12	7*	4	10†	11											11
1	2		6	5			8	9	3	14			7†	4*	12	11	10										12
	2	4	6	14			8	9	3					5	10	11†	7*	1	12								13
1	2		8	5	6	9*	11		10				7		3				4	12							14
1	2		10	5	6	12	11	9	3				7*						4	8							15
	2		10	5	6	9†	11		3	14			7*			12			4	8	1						16
	2		10	5	6	12	7*	9	3							11			4	8	1						17
	2		10	5	6	14	7*		3			12	9			11†			4	8	1						18
*	2		10	5	6		11	9	3				7						4	8	1						19
	2*		10	5	6	14	11	9	3					7		12			4	8†	1						20
*			10	5	6	14	7	9	3	12				2		11†	8*		4		1						21
	12		10	5	6		7	9	3					2		11†	14		4	8*	1						22
	2		10	5	6	7	11	9*	3							12	8		4		1						23
	2		10	5	6	7	11	9	3							12	8*		4		1						24
		12		5	6			8*	3		4		7	2					11		1	9	10				25
	12	8		5	6	14			3		4		7	2*					11		1	9	10†				26
	2			5	6				3	8	12	10*	7	4					11		1	9					27
			10	5	6	7			3	8			9			11			2	4	1						28
		2	10	5		7†			3	8			9			11			4	6*	1		12	14			29
		2	10	5			14		3	8			7*			11†			6	4	1		12	9			30
		2	10	5		7	8		3	4*						11			6		1		12	9			31
		2	10	5		7	8*		3	4						11			6	12	1		14	9†			32
	14	2	10	5		7	9		3	8			12			11†			6	4*	1						33
	4	2*	10†	5		9	14		3	11	8						7		6		1		12				34
	2					9	8		3	12	4		14				7†		6	10	1				5	11*	35
1	2		8			12	7*		10	11	4	3					14		6	9†					5		36
1	2			5		9	7		8	10	4*	3				11			6							12	37
1	2		12	5		9	7		8	10	4*	3				11			6								38
1	2			5		9	7		8	10	4*	3	14			11†			6						12		39
18	29	9	32	33	20	22	32	22	39	16	14	12	20	14	4	16	7	1	26	13	20	3	2	3	2	1	
	+ 3s	+ 1s	+ 1s	+ 1s		+ 7s	+ 2s			+ 6s	+ 5s	+ 2s	+ 4s		+ 1s	+ 4s	+ 3s		+ 1s	+ 2s			+ 5s	+ 1s	+ 2s	+ 1s	

A disappointing period for Ayr, who were expected to build on their sixth placing last season, and launch a real effort for promotion.
However, a stream of indifferent displays soon had them in the grip of relegation nerves and it took three successive victories in the closing three weeks to win a reprieve.

BERWICK RANGERS Division 2

Year Formed: 1881. *Ground:* Shielfield Park. *Size:* 112yd×76yd. *Capacity:* 10,673 (1473 seats).
Telephone: Berwick (0289) 307424
Player Manager: Eric Tait. *Commercial Manager:* Ian Davison.
Secretary: Dennis McCleary. *Limited Company:* 1952.
Club Colurs: Gold shirts with black vertical stripes, black shorts, gold stockings.
Record Attendance: 13,365 v Rangers, Scottish Cup 1st rd, 28 Jan, 1967.
Club Nickname: The Borderers.

1982-83 LEAGUE RECORD

Match No.	Date	Venue	Opponents	Result		H/T Score	League Pos'n	Goalscorers	Atten-dance
1	Sept 4	A	Stenhousemuir	D	0-0	0-0	7		350
2	8	H	Arbroath	W	2-1	1-0	8	Romaines, Tait	550
3	11	H	Stranraer	D	2-2	1-0	4	Cameron, Romaines	598
4	15	A	Meadowbank	L	2-4	1-1	9	Davidson, Marshall	475
5	18	H	Stirling Albion	D	2-2	0-0	9	Cashmore, Armstrong	601
6	22	A	Forfar	D	2-2	1-2	7	Davidson, Romaines	867
7	25	H	Montrose	D	1-1	0-1	7	Cashmore	564
8	Oct 2	A	Q.O.S.	W	2-1	2-0	7	Davidson, McSherry	700
9	9	H	Cowdenbeath	W	2-1	0-0	3	Cashmore, Tracey	570
10	16	A	East Stirling	W	4-0	2-0	3	Cashmore 4 (1 pen)	250
11	23	H	Albion Rovers	W	4-0	2-0	3	Davidson, Romaines, Cashmore, Tracey	665
12	30	A	Brechin	L	0-2	0-0	3		350
13	Nov 6	H	East Fife	W	1-0	1-0	3	Hamilton 1 (og)	606
14	13	A	Arbroath	W	2-0	1-0	2	Romaines, Armstrong	645
15	20	A	Stirling Albion	L	1-3	1-1	3	Romaines	686
16	27	H	Forfar	L	1-2	0-1	3	Tait	200
17	Dec 4	H	Q.O.S.	L	0-4	0-2	5		661
18	18	A	Montrose	L	0-1	0-0	5		150
19	27	A	Stranraer	L	0-1	0-0	8		650
20	Jan 1	H	Meadowbank	D	0-0	0-0	8		770
21	3	A	East Fife	W	1-0	0-0	7	Porter	850
22	15	H	Stenhousemuir	L	2-4	0-3	8	Porter, Grady	553
23	22	H	Brechin	D	1-1	0-0	9	Armstrong (pen).	575
24	Feb 5	A	Cowdenbeath	L	0-2	0-1			350
25	12	H	East Stirling	L	0-3	0-2	9		448
26	19	A	Meadowbank	L	0-5	0-3	9		400
27	26	H	Q.O.S.	W	1-0	1-0	9	Armstrong (pen).	574
28	Mar 2	A	Albion Rovers	W	1-0	0-0	9	McGlynn	200
29	5	A	Stenhousemuir	W	1-0	0-0	9	Porter	300
30	12	H	Brechin	D	1-1	0-0	9	Romaines	621
31	19	A	Arbroath	L	1-3	1-0	9	Moyes	502
32	26	H	Montrose	W	3-1	1-1	8	Armstrong 2 (1 pen), Grady	526
33	Apr 2	A	East Fife	L	0-3	0-2	9		472
34	9	H	Stirling Albion	L	0-3	0-2	9		676
35	16	A	Stranraer	W	3-0	1-0	9	Grady 3	200
36	23	H	East Stirling	L	1-3	0-2	9	Grady	497
37	30	H	Cowdenbeath	D	1-1	1-1	9	Romaines	471
38	May 7	A	Forfar	D	1-1	0-1	9	Millar	614
39	14	A	Albion Rovers	L	1-2	1-2	9	McCann (pen)	300

Final League Position: 9

Goalscorers

League: Romaines 8, Cashmore 8, Armstrong 6, Grady 5, Davidson 4, Porter 3, Tracy 2, Tait 2, Cameron 1, Marshall 1, McSherry 1, McGlynn 1, Moyes 1, Millar 1, McCann 1, opponent 1
League Cup: Armstrong 2, Tait 1, Romaines 1, Lawson 1
Scottish Cup: Tait 1, McSherry 1, Romaines 1

Honours

Scottish League – Division 2 Champions 1978–79.
East of Scotland FA Shield – Winners 1981.
Record Victory: 8-1 v Forfar Athletic, Division 2, 25 Dec, 1965, 8-1 v Vale of Leithin, Scottish Cup, Dec, 1966.
Record Defeat: 1-9 v Hamilton A, Division 2, 9 Aug, 1980.
Most League Points: 54, Division 2, 1978–79.
Most Individual League Goals in Season: 38, Ken Bowron, Division 2, 1963–64.
Most League Goals: 83, Division 2, 1961–62.
Most League Appearances: Eric Tait, 334, 1970–82.
Best Cup Run: 1963 League Cup semi-final, 1-3, v Rangers (Hampden Park).
Extra Information: Only Scottish League club with home ground in England.
Previous Grounds: Bull Stob Close, Pier Field, Meadow Field, Union Park and Old Shielfield.

Millar	McDermott	McCann	McLennan	McSherry	Jeffries	Muir	Lawson	Romaines	Tait	Armstrong	Docherty	Moyes	Cameron	Clark	Cashmore	Davidson	McGlynn	Tracey	McCoy	Wilson	Porter	Glynn	Clelland	Grady	Purves	Cordery	Connor	Redpath	Spence	Marshall	Newman	Hibbert	*Match No.*
	1	2	3	4	5	6	7	8	9	10	11																						1
	1	11		4	5	6*		8	9	10	3		2	7		12																	2
	1		2	4	5			8	9	10	6†	3	7	11*		12														14			3
	1		14	4	5			8	9	10	6†	3	2	7*		11														12			4
	1			4	5			8	9*	10	3	2	6		7	11				12													5
	1	11		4	5	6		8		10	3	2			9	7																	6
	1	11		4	5	6		8		10	3*	2		14	9	7†				12													7
	1		2*	4	5	6		8		10	3			14	9	7†	11			12													8
	1		3	4	5	6			8	10		2			9†	7*	11	12		14													9
	1		3	4	5	6		7	8	10†		2			9	14	11*	12															10
	1	12	3	4	5	6		7	8*	10		2			9	11†		14															11
	1	11	3	4	5	6		7	8	10*		2			9	12																	12
	1	2	3	4	5	6		7	8	10				12	9			11*															13
	1	2	3	4	5	6		7	8	10					9			11*									12						14
	1	2	3	4	5	6		7	8	10				11				9															15
	1	2	3	4	5	6		9	8	10							12		7	11*							12						16
	1	2†	3	4	5	6			8	10		11		9					7*	14	12												17
	1	3	11	4	5	6			8	10		2							9*		7		12										18
		3	2	4	5	6		7	10	11												1	9							8			19
		3		4	5	6		7	10	11		2									12	1	9*							8			20
		3		4		6		7	10	11		2					8				12	1	9*							5			21
		3		4	5	6		7	10*	11		2					8				12	1	9*	14									22
		3	14		5	6		7	10	11		2	4	12†							8	1		9*									23
	1	3	2		5	6			10	11	8*		7					9			14				4†	12							24
	1	3	2	8	5	6		7	10*	11								9†			12		14			4							25
		3		4*	5	6		7		11							12				8				10	2†	14	1	9				26
		3			4	6		7*		11			2				12				10	1	14						9†	5	8		27
		3			4	6		7		11			2				8				10	1	12						9*	5			28
		3			4	6		7		11			2				8				10	1							9	5			29
		3	14		4	6		7		11			2†				8				10	1		9*					12	5			30
	1	3			4	6		7		11		2	12				8*				10			9						5			31
	1	3			4	6		7	12	11		2					8				10*			9						5			32
10	1				4	6		7		11		2	12				3				8*			9						5			33
	1	3			4	6			8	11		2	10*				7†	12						9						5	14		34
		3			4	6			8	11		7	2								10	1		9						5			35
		3			4	6			8	11		7	2								10	1		9						5			36
		3			4	6				11	12	7	2					8			9	1							5		10*		37
10		3			6	5		7		11		2						8			9	1								4			38
		3			6*	4		8		11	12	2	5			7		10			9	1											39
2	24	31	16	24	38	36	1	31	25	39	9	24	15	5	10	8	12	8	3	1	15	14	4	7	2	2	0	1	4	15	1	1	
		1s	3s						1s		2s		2s	4s		4s	3s	4s		5s	6s		4s	1s		1s	3s		1s	2s	1s		

Another club with managerial changes and, after being considered amongst the favourites for promotion, perhaps their 9th place was the most disappointing performance in Division Two. An alarming slump in the scoring rate during the second half of the season, just 18 from their final 23 games, was the main reason for the slide down the table.

BRECHIN CITY Division 1

Year Formed: 1906. *Ground:* Glebe Park. *Size:* 110yd×67yd. *Capacity:* 7500.
Telephone: Brechin 2856.
Manager: Iain Fleming. *Secretary:* George Johnston.
Club Colours: Red shirts, shorts and stockings.
Club Nickname: City.
Record Attendance: 8123 v Aberdeen, Scottish Cup 3rd rd, 3 Feb, 1973.

1982-83 LEAGUE RECORD

Match No.	Date	Venue	Opponents	Result		H/T Score	League Pos'n	Goalscorers	Attendance
1	Sept 4	A	Stranraer	W	2-1	1-0	6	Mackie, I. Campbell	200
2	8	H	East Fife	D	0-0	0-0	4		600
3	11	H	Stirling Alb.	L	1-2	1-1	8	I. Campbell	400
4	15	A	Montrose	W	2-1	1-1	5	Cormack, Paterson	650
5	18	A	Meadowbank	L	1-2	0-1	8	I. Campbell	400
6	22	H	Cowdenbeath	D	1-1	0-1	7	Elvin (pen)	500
7	25	H	East Stirling	W	3-0	2-0	4	Cord, Lesslie, I. Campbell	300
8	Oct 2	A	Stenhousemuir	D	2-2	1-1	6	I. Campbell 2	350
9	9	A	Albion Rovers	D	0-0	0-0	5		600
10	16	H	Forfar	D	1-1	0-0	6	Elvin (pen)	800
11	23	A	Q.O.S.	L	1-3	0-2	6	I. Campbell	600
12	30	H	Berwick	W	2-1	0-0	4	I. Campbell (2 pen)	350
13	Nov 6	H	Arbroath	W	3-1	2-0	4	Fleming, Henderson, I. Campbell	600
14	13	A	East Fife	W	2-1	0-0	4	I. Campbell, Malone	645
15	20	H	Meadowbank	D	1-1	1-0	4	Malone	600
16	Dec 1	A	Cowdenbeath	W	3-1	2-1	3	Stewart 2, Mackie	350
17	4	H	Stenhousemuir	W	5-2	1-0	2	Paterson 3, Lesslie 2	300
18	27	A	Stirling Alb.	D	1-1	1-1	3	Paterson	650
19	Jan 1	H	Montrose	W	4-1	1-0	2	Elvin, I. Campbell, Lesslie, Malone	900
20	3	A	Arbroath	W	3-0	2-0	2	I. Campbell, Fleming, Elvin	1400
21	15	H	Stranraer	W	4-2	3-0	2	Elvin 3 (2 pen), Mackie	300
22	22	A	Berwick	D	1-1	0-0	2	Graham	575
23	Feb 19	H	Stirling Alb.	W	3-1	1-0	2	Lesslie, I. Campbell, Paterson	480
24	22	H	Albion Rovers	W	3-0	1-0	2	I. Campbell, Simpson, Mackie	550
25	26	A	Stranraer	W	3-1	0-1	2	Stewart, Malone 2	360
26	Mar 2	A	Forfar	L	1-2	0-2	2	Elvin (pen)	1503
27	5	H	Montrose	W	3-1	0-0	1	Simpson, Hay, Malone	500
28	9	H	Q.O.S.	L	2-3	1-1	1	I. Campbell, Fleming	650
29	12	A	Berwick	D	1-1	0-0	2	Paterson	621
30	15	A	East Stirling	W	3-0	2-0	1	Fleming, Graham, I. Campbell	450
31	19	H	Cowdenbeath	W	4-1	1-0	1	Campbell 3, Paterson	500
32	26	H	Q.O.S.	W	1-0	0-0	1	Paterson	500
33	Apr 2	A	East Stirling	D	2-2	0-0	1	Graham (pen), Paterson	250
34	9	H	Albion Rovers	W	3-0	2-0	1	Paterson, I. Campbell 2	500
35	16	A	Arbroath	D	1-1	1-1	2	Campbell	1324
36	23	A	East Fife	W	2-1	0-0	1	Campbell, Paterson	665
37	30	H	Forfar	W	1-0	0-0	1	Lesslie	1217
38	May 7	H	Meadowbank	D	1-1	1-0	1	Lesslie	1600
39	14	A	Stenhousemuir	D	0-0	0-0	1		350

Final League Position: 1

Goalscorers

League: I. Campbell 24, Paterson 12, Elvin 8, Lesslie 7, Malone 6, Mackie 4, Fleming 4, Stewart 3, Graham 3, Simpson 2, Cormack 1, Cord 1, Henderson 1, May 1.
League Cup: McWalter 2, Graham 2, Peterson 2, Stewart 1, Campbell 1, Mackay 1, Millican 1.
Scottish Cup: I. Campbell 2

Honours
Record Victory: 12-1 v Thornhill, Scottish Cup 1st rd, 28 Jan, 1926.
Record Defeat: 0-10 v Aidrie, Albion R. and Cowdenbeath all in Division 2, 1937–38
Most League Points: 55, Division 2, 1982-83.
Most Individual Goals in Season: 51, Dave Paris, 1948–49.
Highest League Placing: 1st, Division 2, 1982–83.
Honours: Division 2 Champions 1982–83.

Neilson	Watt	McWalter	Lesslie	Reid	Hay	Campbell, I.	Mackie	Paterson	Elvin	Cormack	Millican	Campbell, R.	Newman	Stewart	Cord	Mackay	Henderson	Graham	Jack	Fleming	Malone	Simpson	Wilson	Cramond	Hegarty	McBride	*Match No.*
1	2	3	4	5	6	7	8*	9†	10	11	14	12															1
1	2	3	4	5	6	7	8*	12	10		9			11†													2
1	2	11	4	3	5	7		9	10	14		6*	8†			12											3
1	2		4	5*		7		14	12	11	10†	8			3	6	9										4
1	2		4		5	7		9†	8	11		6		14	3	12	10*										5
1	2		4	3	5	7		11	10		12	8		6		9*											6
1	2		4	3		7		11	8		14	5		6*	10	9†	12										7
1	2		4	3	5	7		11	8		14	6			10*	9†	12										8
1	2	8	4	3	5	10		11	7		9†	6*		12		14											9
1	2	10	4	3	5	7		11	8			6†		14		12		9*									10
1	2	10	4	5		9		11*	6			8		3		12			7								11
1	2	10	4	3	5	7		9				12		6*			11			8							12
1	2	10	4	3	5	7		8						6			11*		12	9							13
1	2	10	4	3	5	7		8						6			11*			9	12						14
1	2	10	4	3	5	7	12	8†						6*						9	11		14				15
1	2	12	4	3	5	7	8	9						6						10	11*						16
1	2	12	4	3	5	7	6	8						10						9†	11*		14				17
1	2		4	3	5	7	8	11	10					12						9	6*						18
1	2	9*	4	3	5	7		11	10†					8							6	14	12				19
1	2		4	3	5	7	12	11	10†					8						9*	6		14				20
1	2		4	3	5	7	6	8	10					12						9	11*						21
1	2*		4	3	5	7	6	10	8					11				12		9							22
1	2		4	3	5	7	6	9	10					11							8						23
1	2		4	3	5	7	6	9	10*					11								8	12				24
1	2		4	3	5	7	6	10						8						9*	12	14	11†				25
1	2		4	3	5	7	6	9	11†									14		10	8*	12					26
1	2	11	4	3	5	7		9†	10					6*				14			8	12					27
1	2		4	3	5	7	6	8	10											9		11					28
1	2		4	3	5	7	6	12	8					11†				10*		9		14					29
1	2		4	3	5	7	6	11	10									8*		9			12				30
1	2		4	3	5	7	6	10	8											9		12	11*				31
1	2		4	3	5	7	6	8	10											9				11			32
1	2		4	3	5	7	6	8	10†									14		9			11*		12		33
1	2		4	3	5	7	6	11	8											9					10		34
1	2		4	3	5	7	6	11	8*											9	12				10		35
1	2			3	5	7	4*	11	14					6				8*		9		12			10		36
1	2		4	3	5	7		11	8					6						9		10					37
1	2		4	3	5*	7	12	11	8					10				14		9†		6					38
1	2		4		5	7	6	11	8											10*	9†	14	12			3	39
39	39	12	38	37	36	39	21	36	20	3	3	9	1	21	4	4	5	4	1	24	11	4	3	1	3	1	
		+					+	+	+	+	+	+		+		+	+	+	+		+	+	+		+		
		2s					3s	3s	2s	1s	4s	2s		5s		5s	2s	5s	1s		3s	8s	7s		1s		

A marvellous season for a team that were bottom of the table just five years ago. Brechin started the season under Doug Houston before he left and was replaced by Iain Fleming.
Under Fleming they clinched their first ever Championship by including just two defeats in his 28 games in charge, with Ian Campbell's 27 goals equalling his best ever effort.

CELTIC Premier Division

Year Formed: 1888. *Ground:* Celtic Park. *Size:* 115yd×75yd. *Capacity:* 67,500 (9000 seats). *Telephone:* 041-554 2710. *Manager:* Billy McNeill. *Secretary:* Desmond White CA. *Asst Manager:* John Clark. *Commercial Manager:* Jack McGinn. *Club Colours:* Green and white hooped shirts, white shorts. *Club Nickname:* The Bhoys. *Record Attendance:* 92,000 v Rangers, Division 1, 1 Jan, 1938.
European Competitions: *European Cup* 1966–67 (winners), 1967–68, 1968–69, 1969–70 (finalists), 1970–71, 1971–72, 1972–73, 1973–74, 1974–75, 1977–78, 1979–80, 1981–82, 1982–83; *European Cup-Winners' Cup* 1963–64, 1965–66, 1975–76, 1980–81; *Fairs Cup* 1962–63, 1964–65; *UEFA Cup* 1976–77. *Coronation Cup:* 1953. *Empire Exhibition Cup:* 1938.

1982-83 LEAGUE RECORD

Match No.	Date	Venue	Opponents	Result		H/T Score	League Pos'n	Goalscorers	Attendance
1	Sept 4	H	Dundee	W	2-0	2-0	—	Provan, Aitken	19,122
2	11	A	St. Mirren	W	2-1	0-1	1	Nicholas (2 pens)	15,000
3	18	A	Motherwell	W	7-0	3-0	1	Nicholas 3, Aitken 2, McGarvey, MacLeod	17,092
4	25	H	Hibs	W	2-0	1-0	1	MacLeod, McStay	16,371
5	Oct 2	A	Dundee United	D	2-2	1-0	1	McStay, Aitken	20,009
6	9	H	Aberdeen	L	1-3	0-0	1	Nicholas	29,733
7	16	H	Kilmarnock	W	2-1	0-0	1	Nicholas 2	11,063
8	23	A	Morton	W	2-1	2-0	1	McGarvey, Nicholas	12,000
9	30	H	Rangers	W	3-2	1-2	1	McStay, McGarvey, MacLeod	60,408
10	Nov 6	A	Dundee	W	3-2	3-0	1	Nicholas (pen) Burns, McGarvey	11,681
11	13	H	St. Mirren	W	5-0	4-0	1	Nicholas 3 (1 pen) Aitken, Burns	15,044
12	20	H	Motherwell	W	3-1	0-0	1	McStay, Nicholas, Burns	14,963
13	27	A	Hibs	W	3-2	1-0	1	McGarvey 2, McStay	17,121
14	Dec 11	A	Aberdeen	W	2-1	1-1	1	MacLeod, Provan	25,000
15	18	A	Kilmarnock	W	4-0	1-0	1	Provan, McAdam, McGarvey, Burns	9000
16	27	H	Morton	W	5-1	1-1	1	Nicholas (pen), Reid, MacLeod, McGarvey 2	19,953
17	Jan 1	A	Rangers	W	2-1	1-1	1	McStay, Nicholas	44,000
18	3	H	Dundee	D	2-2	1-0	1	Burns, Nicholas	16,615
19	8	A	St. Mirren	W	1-0	1-0	1	MacLeod	14,748
20	15	A	Motherwell	L	1-2	1-0	1	MacLeod	15,290
21	22	H	Hibs	W	4-1	1-1	1	Nicholas, McCluskey, McGarvey 2	17,106
22	Feb 5	A	Dundee United	D	1-1	1-1	1	Nicholas	17,289
23	12	H	Aberdeen	L	1-3	1-2	2	Nicholas	42,831
24	26	H	Kilmarnock	W	4-0	1-0	2	McGarvey 2, Nicholas (pen) MacLeod	10,691
25	Mar 5	A	Morton	W	3-0	1-0	2	Sullivan, MacLeod, McCluskey	10,000
26	19	A	Dundee	L	1-2	1-2	3	McGarvey	11,196
27	23	H	Rangers	D	0-0	0-0	2		51,062
28	26	H	St. Mirren	D	1-1	0-0	2	Provan	15,935
29	Apr 2	H	Motherwell	W	3-0	2-0	1	McGarvey, McAdam, Harrow o.g.	15,454
30	6	H	Dundee United	W	2-0	0-0	1	McGarvey, Nicholas	34,508
31	9	A	Hibs	W	3-0	2-0	1	Nicholas 2, Provan	15,500
32	20	H	Dundee United	L	2-3	1-1	1	Nicholas (pen), Burns	23,965
33	23	A	Aberdeen	L	0-1	0-1	2		24,500
34	30	A	Kilmarnock	W	5-0	2-0	2	McGrain, MacLeod 2, Burns, Nicholas	7900
35	May 7	H	Morton	W	2-0	2-0	2	Aitken, Nicholas (pen)	12,610
36	14	A	Rangers	W	4-2	0-2	2	Nicholas (2 pens), McAdam, McGarvey	40,000

Final League Position: 2

Goalscorers

League: Nicholas 29, McGarvey 17, MacLeod 11, Burns 7, Aitken 6, McStay 6, Provan 5, McAdam 3, McCluskey 2, Reid 1, Sullivan 1, McGrain 1, opponent 1.
League Cup: Nicholas 13, McCluskey 6, MacLeod 5, Burns 3, McGarvey 3, Provan 3, Reid 2, Dobbin 1, McGrain 1, McStay 1, Crainie 1, Aitken 1, Opponent 1.
Scottish Cup: Nicholas 4, McGarvey 3, McCluskey 2, MacLeod 1.
European Cup: Nicholas 2, MacLeod 2, McGarvey 1, McCluskey 1.

Honours

Scottish League: Division 1 Champions 1892–93, 1893–94, 1895–96, 1897–98, 1904–05, 1905–06, 1906–07, 1907–08, 1908–09, 1909–10, 1913–14, 1914–15, 1915–16, 1916-17, 1918–19, 1921–22, 1925–26, 1935–36, 1937–38, 1953–54, 1965–66, 1966–67, 1967–68, 1968–69, 1969–70, 1970–71, 1971–72, 1972–73, 1973–74; Runners-up 16 times; Premier Division Champions 1977, 1979, 1981, 1982; Runners-up 1976, 1980. *Scottish Cup:* Winners 1892, 1899, 1900, 1904, 1907, 1908, 1911, 1912, 1914, 1923, 1925, 1927, 1931, 1933, 1937, 1951, 1954, 1965, 1967, 1969, 1971, 1972, 1974, 1975, 1977, 1980; Runners-up 14 times. *Scottish League Cup:* Winners 1956–57, 1957–58, 1965–66, 1966–67, 1967–68, 1968–69, 1969–70, 1974–75, 1982–83; Runners-up 7 times. *Record Victory:* 11-0 v Dundee, Division 1, 26 Oct, 1895. *Record Defeat:* 0-8 v Motherwell, Division 1, 30 Apr, 1937. *Most League Points:* 67, 1915–16, 1921–22. *Most Individual League Goals in Season:* 50, James McGrory, 1935–36. *Most Goals in Total Aggregate:* 397, James McGrory, 1922–39. *Most Capped Player:* Danny McGrain, 62, Scotland.

Bonner	McGrain	Reid	Aitken	McAdam	MacLeod	Provan	McStay, P	McCluskey	Burns	Nicholas	Crainie	Moyes	McGarvey	Sullivan	Sinclair	McInally	McStay, W	*Match No.*
1	2	3	4	5	6	7	8	9	10	11								1
1	2	3	4	5	6		8	9*	10	11	7		12					2
1	2	3	4	5	10	7	8	14		11†	12	6	9*					3
1	2	3	4	5	6	7	8	12		11			9*	10				4
1	2	3	4	5	10	7	8	12		11			9*		6			5
1	2	3	4	5	10*	7	8			11	12		9		6			6
1		3	4	5	10	7	8			11	9	6	12		2*			7
1	2	3	4	5	10	7	8			11	12		9*		6			8
1	2	3	4	5	10	7	8			11			9		6			9
1	2		4	5	10	7	8		6	11			9		3			10
1	2		4	5	10	7	8	12	6	11			9*		3			11
1	2		4	5	10	7	8	12	6	11			9*		3			12
1	2		4	5		7	8		10	11		6	9		3			13
1	2		4	5	6	7	8		10	11					9			14
1	2		4	5	6	7*	8	12	10	11			9		3			15
1	2	14		5	6	7	8	12	10	11		4†	9*		3			16
1	2	3		5	6	7	8		10	11			9		4			17
1	2	3		5	6	7	8		10	11			9		4			18
1	2	3	7	5	8	9†	6	14		11*			10	12	4			19
1	2	3	4		10	7	8	11					9	6	5			20
1	2	3	4	5	6	7	8	11		10			9					21
1	2	3	4	5	10	7	8	11		9					6			22
1	2	3*	4	5	10	7	8	12		11			9		6			23
1	2		4	5	10	7†	8	14		9*			11	6	3	12		24
1	2		4	5	10		8	7		9			11	6	3			25
1	2	14	4	5	10	7	8	12		9			11	6†	3*			26
1	2	3	4	5	10	7†	8	12		11			9	6				27
1	2	3	4	5	10	7	8			11			9	6				28
1	2	3	4	5	6	7	8			9	10		11*				14	29
1	2	3	4	5	6	7	8		10	9			11					30
1	2	3	4	5	6	7	8		10	9			11					31
1		3	4	5	6	7	8	12	10	9			11		2*			32
1	2	3*	4	5	6	7	8		10	9		12	11					33
1	2		4	5	6	7	8		10	9			11		3			34
1	2	3	4	5	10		8	7		9	12		11*		6			35
1	2		4	5	6	7	8		10	9			11		3			36
36	34	24	33	36	35	33	36	7	17	35	3	4	32	7	25	0	0	
		+ 2s						+ 3s			+ 4s	+ 1s	+ 2s	+ 1s		+ 1s	+ 1s	

Despite having more depth of striking talent than their close rivals, Celtic relinquished their grasp on the Championship, when their form deserted them in a three day spell in April.
Successive defeats by Dundee United and Aberdeen tore the initiative from Parkhead and although eleven goals were scored in their final three matches there was no slip from Dundee United.
In a season that most Celtic fans will remember for the incredible scoring exploits of Charlie Nicholas, it would be unfair to forget the formidable contribution made by Paul McStay, Roy Aitken and Frank McGarvey.

CLYDE Division 1

Year Formed: 1878
Ground: Shawfield Stadium, Glasgow C5. *Size:* 1110yd×70yd. *Capacity:* 25,000 (2000 seats).
Telephone: 041-647 6329.
Manager: Craig Brown BA, DPE. *Coach:* Rab Thorburn BSC. *Commercial Manager:* John Donnelly.
Secretary: John F. McBeth ARICS.
Club Colours: White shirts with red facings, black shorts, red stockings.
Club Nickname: The Bully Wee.
Record Attendance: 52,000 v Rangers, Division 1, 21 Nov, 1908.

1982-83 LEAGUE RECORD

Match No.	Date	Venue	Opponents	Result	H/T Score	League Pos'n	Goalscorers	Attendance
1	Sept 4	H	Falkirk	L 0-1	0-1	13		630
2	8	A	Dunfermline	D 1-1	0-0	11	McCutcheon	1200
3	11	H	St Johnstone	L 1-3	1-1	13	Reilly	780
4	14	A	Queen's Park	D 0-0	0-0	14		1000
5	18	H	Clydebank	L 3-5	2-4	14	McCutcheon 2, Reilly	600
6	25	A	Hearts	L 0-1	0-0	14		4734
7	Oct 2	H	Dumbarton	L 0-4	0-3	14		607
8	5	A	Partick Th	L 1-2	0-1	14	Masterton	1800
9	9	H	Raith Rovers	L 0-2	0-0	14		550
10	16	A	Airdrie	W 4-3	2-1	14	Masterton 3, O'Neill	1000
11	23	H	Alloa	W 2-0	0-0	14	Masterton 2	670
12	30	A	Hamilton	L 0-1	0-0	14		843
13	Nov 6	H	Ayr United	W 3-1	2-1	13	O'Neill 2, Reilly	580
14	13	A	Falkirk	W 1-0	0-0	10	O'Neill	2000
15	20	A	Clydebank	D 2-2	1-1	10	McLaren, Nevin	815
16	27	H	Partick Th	L 1-3	0-1	11	O'Neill	1700
17	Dec 4	A	Dumbarton	W 3-1	2-0	10	Masterton 2, Reilly	500
18	11	H	Hearts	L 2-3	0-1	11	Reilly 2	2300
19	27	A	St Johnstone	L 1-2	1-0	11	Masterton	1800
20	Jan 1	H	Queen's Park	L 0-1	0-1	13		908
21	3	A	Ayr United	L 0-2	0-0	14		1700
22	8	H	Airdrie	W 2-1	1-1	13	Flexney, Doherty	781
23	15	A	Raith Rovers	L 1-2	0-1	11	O'Neill, Reilly	1100
24	22	H	Hamilton	W 5-2	1-1	11	Doherty, Evans, O'Neill, Sinclair, Dempsey	833
25	Feb 8	A	Alloa	W 3-1	1-0		O'Neill, Doherty, Nevin	900
26	26	H	Partick Th	L 0-2	0-1	12		1434
27	Mar 5	H	Dumbarton	W 1-0	0-0	11	Dempsey	480
28	9	H	Dunfermline	W 1-0	0-0		Nevin	550
29	15	A	Airdrie	L 0-1	0-0		Nevin	900
30	19	H	Queen's Park	W 2-1	1-1	10	McVeigh P (pen) Reilly	750
31	23	A	Falkirk	W 2-1	1-1		Nevin, O'Neill	1200
32	26	A	Hearts	L 1-3	0-1	7	O'Neill	4647
33	Apr 2	A	Clydebank	L 1-2	0-0	10	McVeigh P (pen)	925
34	9	H	Alloa	D 3-3	2-1	10	Masteton 2, Doherty	575
35	16	H	St Johnstone	L 0-1	0-0	10		777
36	23	A	Dunfermline	D 0-0	0-0	10		1420
37	30	H	Raith Rovers	D 3-3	0-0	10	Sinclair, O'Neill, Masterton	713
38	May 7	A	Hamilton	L 1-4	0-0	11	Masterton	1233
39	14	H	Ayr United	W 3-2	1-0	10	Masterton, Nevin, Doherty	1050

Final League Position: 10

Goalscorers

League: Masterton 14, O'Neill 10, Reilly 8, Nevin 5, Doherty 5, McCutcheon 3, Sinclair 2, Dempsey 2, McVeigh 2, McClaren 1, Flexney 1, Evans 1.
League Cup: Masterton 1, Reilly 1, Flexney 1, O'Neill 1, McCutcheon 1.
Scottish Cup: Nevin 1, Dempsey 1, Evans 1, Masterton 1, Flexney 1, Sinclair 1, opponent 1.

Honours
Scottish League – Division 2 Champions 1904–05, 1951–52, 1956–57, 1961–62, 1972–73, 1977–78, 1981–82; Runners-up 1903–04, 1905–06, 1925–26, 1963–64.
Scottish FA Cup: Winners 1939, 1955, 1958; Runners-up 1910, 1912, 1949.
Record Victory: 11-1 v Cowdenbeath, Division 2, 6 Oct, 1951.
Record Defeat: 0-11 v Dumbarton, Scottish Cup 4th rd, 22 Nov, 1879; 0-11 v Rangers, Scottish Cup 4th rd, 13 Nov, 1980.
Most League Points: 64, Division 2, 1956–57
Most Individual League Goals in Season: 32, Bill Boyd, 1932–33.
Most Capped Player: Tommy Ring, 12, Scotland.

Young	Rae	McQueen	McLaren	Dempsey	Reilley	Nevin	Sinclair	Masterton	O'Neill	McCutcheon	Brogan	Clark	Flexney	Doherty	Rae	Evans	Wood	McVeigh	McColl	Howie	Coutts	*Match No.*
1	2	3	4	5	6	7	8	9	10*	11†	12										14	1
1	2	3	4	5	7	11	8		10	9	6											2
1	2	3	4	5	7	11	8		10	9	6											3
	4	3	2	5	9	11	8		7	10	6	1										4
	2	3	4		7	11		14	10	9	6	1	5*	8†							12	5
		3	5		9	11	8	14	10†		2	1		7*	4	6	12					6
		3	5		7†	11	8	14	10	9	2	1		12	4*	6						7
*1		3	5		9	11		12	10	7*	2		4	8		6						8
1		3		5	7	11	8	9	12		2		4			6*	10					9
1		3	14	5	7	11	8	9	12		2		4			6		10†				10
1		3		5	7†	11	8	9	6*		2		4	14		12		10				11
1		3	12	5	7	11	8	9	6*		2		4					10				12
1		3	8*	5	7	11	14		9	12	2		4			6		10†				13
1		3	8	5	7	11*	12		9		2				4	6		10				14
1		3	8		7	11	12		9		2		5		4	6		10*				15
1		3	8		7†	11	12	14	9		2		5			6*		10	4			16
1		3	8*	4	7	14	12	11	9		2					6		10†	5			17
1		3	8*	5	7	12		11	9		2					6		10	4			18
*1		3	8	4		7		11	9		2					6*	12	10	5			19
1		3		5		7*	8	11	9		2					6	12	10	4			20
*1		3	12	5		14	8	11		9	2*		10	7†		6			4			21
1		3		5		7	8	11†	9*	12			10	14		6		2	4			22
1		3		5	12	7*	8		9	14			10	11†		6		2	4			23
1		3		5	7	14	8		9	12			10	11		6†		2	4*			24
*1		3		5	7*	11	8		9				10	8		6		2	4	12		25
1		3		5*	7†	11	8	14	9				12	10		6		2	4			26
1		3		5	9	11	8						10	7	4	6		2				27
*1		3		5	9*	11	8	12					10	7	4	6		2				28
*1		3		5	9	11		8	10					7	4	6		2				29
1		3		5†	14	11	8	12	9				10	7	4	6		2*				30
*1		3			10	11	8		9				5	7	4	6		2				31
1		3			10†	11	8		9	14	12		5*	7	4	6		2				32
1		3			10	11	8		9				5	7	4	6		2				33
1		3				11	8	10*	9				5	7	4	6		2		12		34
1		3*		4	14	11	8†	10	9	12			5	7		6		2				35
1		3		4	12	11	8	10*	9				5	7		6		2				36
1				4	12	11	8	10	9†		3*		5	7	12	6		2				37
1				4	12	11	8	10	9				5	7*	3	6		2				38
1	3			4	7*	11	8	10	9				5	12		6		2				39
35	6	36	15	29	28	35	29	18	34	8	21	4	26	20	13	32	1	29	11	0	0	
			+ 3s		+ 6s	+ 4s	+ 5s	+ 8s	+ 2s	+ 6s	+ 2s		+ 1s	+ 4s	+ 1s	+ 1s	+ 3s			+ 2s	+ 2s	

Found life in Division One far more demanding than did their partners in promotion from last season Alloa but showed great spirit in the tense closing weeks of the season. Striker Danny Masterton retains his nose for goals and claimed 14, while tiny winger Pat Nevin continued to display the fine form that earned him inclusion in the Scotland Youth Team.

CLYDEBANK Division 1

Year Formed: 1965. *Ground:* Kilbowie Park. *Size:* 110yd×68yd. *Capacity:* 9900 (all seated).
Telephone: 041-952 2887.
Secretary: I. C. Steedman. *Coach:* Sam Henderson.
Club Colours: White shirts with red and black vertical stripes on the left breast and red stripe on sleeves, white shorts with red and black vertical stripe and white stockings with red and black tops.
Club Nickname: The Bankies.
Record Attendance: 14,900 v Hibernian, Scottish Cup 1st rd, 10 Feb, 1965.

1982-83 LEAGUE RECORD

Match No.	Date	Venue	Opponents	Result		H/T Score	League Pos'n	Goalscorers	Attendance
1	Sept 4	A	Raith Rovers	D	1-1	1-0	6	Hughes	531
2	11	A	Alloa	L	0-2	0-0	12		683
3	15	H	Dumbarton	W	5-1	1-1	5	Coyne 2, Ronald, Williamson, Given	789
4	18	A	Clyde	W	5-3	4-2	4	Williamson 2, Coyne, Hughes, Ronald	600
5	22	H	Airdrie	L	0-4	0-1	9		800
6	25	H	Queen's Park	W	2-0	1-0	5	Williamson 2	778
7	29	A	Hearts	L	1-4	0-2		Ronald	5500
8	Oct 2	A	Ayr United	W	3-1	0-1	6	Coyne 2, Treanor (pen)	1213
9	9	A	Partick Th.	W	1-0	1-0	5	Treanor	4382
10	16	H	Dunfermline	D	1-1	1-0	5	Robertson (og)	440
11	23	A	Falkirk	W	2-0	0-0	3	Ronald, Williamson	1500
12	30	H	St. Johnstone	W	1-0	1-0	3	Caldwell (og)	897
13	Nov 6	A	Hamilton	W	2-0	1-0	2	Ronald, Coyne	887
14	13	H	Hearts	L	0-3	0-1	4		2116
15	20	H	Clyde	D	2-2	1-1	3	Coyne, Given	815
16	27	A	Airdrie	D	2-2	0-1	3	McGhie, Given (pen)	1200
17	Dec 4	H	Ayr United	L	0-1	0-1	4		463
18	11	A	Queen's Park	D	2-2	0-0	5	Williamson, Coyne	756
19	18	A	Raith Rovers	W	3-0	1-0	3	Given, Coyne, Ronald	1050
20	27	H	Alloa	D	2-2	0-1	3	Coyne, Williamson	700
21	Jan 1	A	Dumbarton	W	4-0	1-0	3	Williamson 2, Hughes, Coyne	1000
22	3	H	Hamilton	W	2-1	0-0	3	McGhie, Williamson	650
23	15	H	Partick Th.	L	1-3	0-1	3	Coyne	1750
24	22	A	St. Johnstone	W	1-0	0-0	3	McGhie	2415
25	Feb 5	H	Falkirk	L	0-2	0-2	4		542
26	12	A	Alloa	W	2-1	1-0	3	McCabe, Coyne	811
27	23	A	Dunfermline	D	1-1	0-0	3	Williamson	1500
28	26	H	Dumbarton	W	3-1	1-1	3	Williamson, Given, Coyne	656
29	Mar 5	A	Ayr United	L	0-1	0-0	4		778
30	12	H	St. Johnstone	W	6-1	2-1	3	Coyne 3, Given (pen), McGhie, Williamson	837
31	19	A	Dunfermline	D	1-1	0-0	3	Williamson	1100
32	26	A	Raith Rovers	W	3-1	1-1	3	Coyne 2, Williamson	1000
33	Apr 2	H	Clyde	W	2-1	0-0	3	McKeown, Williamson	925
34	9	A	Falkirk	W	2-0	2-0	3	Hughes, Treanor (pen)	1300
35	16	A	Hearts	D	2-2	1-1	4	McCabe 2	6432
36	23	H	Airdrie	W	2-0	0-0	3	Murray, McKeown	657
37	30	H	Hamilton	D	1-1	1-1	3	Williamson	576
38	May 7	A	Queen's Park	W	3-1	3-0	3	Williamson 3	665
39	14	H	Partick Th.	L	1-2	0-2	3	Hughes	1429

Final League Position: 3

Goalscorers

League: Williamson 21, Coyne 19, Ronald 6, Given 6, Hughes 5, McGhie 4, Treanor 3, McCabe 3, McKeown 2, opponents 2, Murray 1.
League Cup: Williamson 3, Coyne 2, Given 1, Treanor 1, Ronald 1.

Honours
Scottish League – Division 1 Runners-up 1976–77; Division 2 Champions 1975–76.
Spring Cup– Runners-up 1975–76.
Record Victory: 8-1 v Arbroath, Division 1, 3 Jan, 1977.
Record Defeat: 1-9 v Gala Fairydean, Scottish Cup qualifying rd, 15 Sept, 1965.
Most League Points: 58, Division 1, 1976–77.
Most Individual League Goals in Season: 28, Blair Miller, Division 1, 1978–79.

Gallacher	Treanor	Gervaise	Fallon	McGhie	Given	Ronald	Hughes	Williamson	Murray	McCabe	Coyne	Cameron	McKeown	Brodie	McLaughlan	Dickson	Sinclair	*Match No.*
1	2	3	4	5	6	7	8	9	10	11								1
1	2	3	4	5	6*	7	8	10		11	9						12	2
*1	2	3	4	5	6	7	8	10		11	9							3
1	2	3	4	5	6	7	8	9		11	10							4
*1	2	3	4	5	6	7	8	9		11	10							5
1	2	3	4		6	7	8	9		11	10*	5					12	6
*1	2	3	4	5	6	7	8	9		11	10							7
1	2	3	4	5	6*	7	8	9		11	10		12					8
1	2	3	4	5	6	7	8	9		11	10							9
1	2	3	4	5	6	7	8	9		11	10							10
1	2	3	4	5	6	7	8	9		11	10							11
1	2	3	4	5		7*	8	9		11	10		6				12	12
1	2	3	4	5	6*	7	8	9		11	10		12					13
1	2	3	4	5	6	7	8	9		11	10*		12					14
1	2	3	4	5	6	7	8	9		11	10							15
1	2	3	4	5	6	7	8*	9		11	10		12					16
1	2	3	4	5	6	7*	8†	9		11	10		12				14	17
	2	3	4	5	6	7	8	9		11	10			1				18
1	2		4	5	6	7	8	9		11	10				3			19
*1	2		4	5	6	7	8	9		11	10				3			20
1	2		4	5	6	7	8	9		11	10				3			21
*1	2	3	4	5	6	7	8	9		11	10							22
1	2	3	4	5	6	7	8*	9		11	10		12					23
1	2	3	4	5	6	7	8	9		11	10							24
1	2	3	4	5	6	7	8	9		11*	10		12					25
1	2	3	4	5	6		8	9		11	10		7					26
*1	2	3	4	5	6		8	9		11	10		7					27
1	2	3	4	5	6		8	9		11	10*		7				12	28
1	2	3	4	5	6		8	9		11	10		7					29
1	2	3	4*	5	6	7	8	9		11	10					12		30
1	2	3	4	5	6*	7	8	9		11	10		12					31
1	2	3	4	5	6*	7	8	9			10		11			12		32
1	2	3*	4	5		7	8	9	6		10		11			12		33
1	2	6	4	5		7	8	9		11	10	3						34
	2		4	5		7	8	9		11	10	3	6	1				35
	2		4	5		7		9	12	11	10	3	6†	1		14	8*	36
			4	5	6		8	9		11*	10	3	7	1		2	12	37
1		2	4	5	6	12	8†	9		11	10	3*	7			14		38
1		2	4	5	3	7	8	9		11	10		6					39
35	36	33	39	38	34	33	38	39	2	37	38	6	12	4	3	1	1	
						+ 1s			+- 1s				+ 8s			+ 5s	+ 7s	

No shortage of talent at Kilbowie Park, where they continually produce good young players, and all that halted their Premier League ambitions was uncharacteristic home lapses. Strikers Bobby Williamson and Tommy Coyne – 21 and 20 respectively – grabbed forty-one of their league goals between them and captured the attention of scouts on both sides of the border.

COWDENBEATH Division 2

Year Formed: 1881. *Ground:* Central Park. *Size:* 110yd×70yd. *Capacity:* 10,000.
Telephone: Cowdenbeath 511205
Manager: Hugh Wilson. *Secretary:* W. Foster.
Club Colours: Royal blue shirt, white shorts, white stockings with blue and white tops.
Club Nickname: Cowden.
Record Attendance: 25,586 v Rangers, League Cup quarter-final, 21 Sept, 1949.
Previous Grounds: North End Park, 1881–1917.

1982-83 LEAGUE RECORD

Match No.	Date	Venue	Opponents	Result		H/T Score	League Pos'n	Goalscorers	Attendance
1	Sept 4	A	Meadowbank	L	0-2	0-2	12		200
2	11	H	Montrose	L	2-3	0-1	14	Miller, Liddle	250
3	15	A	East Fife	D	1-1	1-0	8	Miller	400
4	18	H	Stenhousemuir	W	2-0	0-0	11	Forrest 2	250
5	22	H	Brechin City	D	1-1	1-0	12	Miller	500
6	25	A	Albion Rovers	W	2-0	0-0	9	Forrest 2	400
7	29	H	Stranraer	W	2-1	2-0	5	Ferguson, McIntosh	260
8	Oct 2	H	Forfar	W	2-0	2-0	3	Liddle, Miller (pen)	450
9	9	A	Berwick	L	1-2	0-0	6	Rose	570
10	16	H	Q.O.S.	W	2-1	1-1	4	Miller (pen), McIntosh	350
11	23	H	East Stirling	D	1-1	0-1	4	McIntosh	400
12	30	A	Arbroath	L	0-1	0-0	5		573
13	Nov 6	H	Stirling Albion	D	0-0	0-0	5		400
14	13	A	Stranraer	L	0-2	0-2	7		360
15	20	A	Stenhousemuir	D	2-2	0-0	7	Ferguson, Christie	350
16	Dec 1	H	Brechin	L	1-3	1-2	8	McIntosh	350
17	4	A	Forfar	D	0-0	0-0	9		770
18	27	A	Montrose	W	4-0		9	Liddle 2, Mitchell, McIntosh	350
19	Jan 1	H	East Fife	L	2-4	1-3	9	Gibson 2	600
20	3	A	Stirling Albion	D	2-2	1-0	9	Ferguson, McIntosh	525
21	15	H	Meadowbank	W	3-1	2-0	9	Liddle, Gibson 2	350
22	22	H	Arbroath	W	2-1	0-0	8	Liddle, McIntosh	350
23	Feb 5	H	Berwick	W	2-0	1-0	7	Gibson, McIntosh	350
24	16	A	Q.O.S.	D	0-0	0-0	7		575
25	26	H	Arbroath	W	3-2	2-1	7	McIntosh 2 (1 pen), Hyslop	350
26	Mar 1	A	East Stirling	L	0-2	0-1	7		300
27	5	A	East Fife	W	2-0	1-0	6	McIntosh, Gibson	612
28	9	H	Albion Rovers	D	1-1	1-0	6	McIntosh	300
29	12	H	East Stirling	W	3-1	2-1	5	Oliver, Scott, Gibson	300
30	19	A	Brechin City	L	1-4	0-1	5	Tierney	500
31	26	H	Stenhousemuir	D	1-1	0-1	5	Henderson	300
32	Apr 2	A	Stirling Albion	L	1-3	0-2	7	Shanks	550
33	9	H	Q.O.S.	L	2-3	2-2	8	Robertson, Tierney	200
34	13	A	Albion Rovers	L	0-2	0-0	8		350
35	16	A	Forfar	L	0-2	0-1	8		788
36	27	H	Stranraer	W	4-0	1-0	8	Gibson 4	300
37	30	A	Berwick	D	1-1	1-1	8	Gibson	471
38	May 7	A	Montrose	D	1-1	1-0	8	Gibson	150
39	14	H	Meadowbank	L	0-1	0-1	8		250

Final League Position: 8

Goalscorers

League: Gibson 13, McIntosh 12, Liddle 6, Miller 5, Forrest 4, Ferguson 3, Tierney 2, Rose 1, Christie 1, Mitchell 1, Hyslop 1, Oliver 1, Scott 1, Henderson 1, Shanks 1, Robertson 1.
League Cup: Marshall 3, McIntosh 2, Liddle 2, Ferguson 1, McFarlane 1, opponent 1.

Honours

Scottish League – Division 2 Champions 1913–14, 1914–15, 1938–39; Runners-up 1921–22, 1923–24, 1969–70.
Record Victory: 12-0 v St Johnstone, Scottish Cup 1st rd, 21 Jan, 1928.
Record Defeat: 1-11 v Clyde, Division 2, 6 Oct, 1951.
Most League Points: 60, Division 2, 1938–39.
Most Individual League Goals in Season: 40, Willie Devlin, Division 1, 1925–26.
Most Capped Player: Jim Paterson, 3, Scotland.

Allan	Campbell	Rose	Tierney	Russell	McFarlane	Marshall	Ferguson	Liddle	Forrest	Hyslop	McIntosh	Leven	Miller	Fairley	Henderson	Park	Scott	Morris	Ballantyne	Gilchrist	Oliver	Gibson	Mitchell	Dunlop	Trialist	Grant	Robertson	Shanks	Williamson	Christie	Burt	Hird	*Match No.*
1	2	3	4	5	6	7	8	9	10*	11			12																				1
1	2	3	4	5†	6*	7	8	9	14	11	10		12																				2
*1	2	3	5		6*	7	8	9	12	10		4	11																				3
1	2	3	5			8	6*	9	11	10	12	4	7																				4
1	2*	3	5				8		9	11	10	4	7	6		12																	5
1		3	5		8	11	2		9			4	7	6	10																		6
*1	2	3	5				8	9*	7		10†	4	11	6	12	14																	7
1		3	2	5			8	9†	10	11	14	4	7*	6	12																		8
1	2	3	6	5			8†	9	11		14	4	7*	10		12																	9
1	2*	3	5			6†	8	9	11		10	4	7		14	12																	10
1		3	5				2	9	11		10	4	7*	6	12	8																	11
1	12	3	5				2	9	7*	8	10	4		11	14		6*																12
1	2	3	5				8		9†	11	7*	4		10	14	12	6																13
1	2*	3	5				8			11	7	4		10			6	9		14													14
1		3	5				7	9	11†	8	10			6*					2	4										14	12		15
*1		3	5				8	9	12	11	10	4	14	6					2*											7†			16
1	2	3	5					9	11		10		7	6			8			4													17
*1		3	5					9			10*	4		8	12				2		6	7	11										18
*1		3	5†				12	9			10	4		8*	14				2		6	7	11										19
*1		3	5				2	9		7	10*		12						1	4	6	8	11										20
1							2	9		8	10*	5					3			6	5	7	11								12		21
1		3	4				8	9			10						6			2	5	7	11										22
1			2				8			11	9	4					6			3	5	7	10										23
*1			2				8†			11*	9	4					6			3	5	7	10	14	12								24
1			5				2			9	10	4*					8			3	6	7	11	12									25
*1		2	5				4			9*	10					14	8			3†	6	7	11	14									26
1		2	5								10	4					6			3	8	7	11	9									27
*1		3*	5				12				9	4				14	10			2	6	7	11†	8									28
1			2								9	4	11				6			3	5	7	10	8									29
1			2				12				9	4	11			14	6			3	5	7	10†	8*									30
1			5				8				9	4	11*			12	6			2†	14	7	10		3								31
1			5				2									12	6			3	4	7	11*			8	9†	10		14			32
1			5				2*					4			11		6					7	10	8*		12	9		3	14			33
*1											10	4		14	9†		3				5	7	11				12	6	2		8*		34
1		3	5								10	4		14	12		6			2		7	11				9*			8†			35
1		3									10	4			9†		6			5		7	11				12		2	14		8*	36
1		3									9*	4			8†		6			5		10	11				14		2		12	7	37
1		3									9*		12		8		6			4	5	10†	11				14		2			7	38
1		3					14				8*		11				6			4	5	9	10						2†	12		7	39
39	11	29	33	4	4	6	26	18	13	17	31	29	14	14	6	1	23	1	4	20	17	22	22	5	1	1	3	2	16	2	1	4	
	+ 1s						+ 4s		+ 3s		+ 3s		+ 5s	+ 2s	+ 9s	+ 10s				+ 1s	+ 1s			+ 3s	+ 1s	+ 1s	+ 4s			+ 5s	+ 3s		

A mixed season when the Fife team gave themselves an outside chance of promotion in March but slipped in the end with only one victory in their last ten games. Willie Gibson's move from neighbours Raith Rovers in December saw the ex-Hearts player score 13 times in the second half of the season – including his 100th league goal at Berwick in February.

DUMBARTON Premier Division

Year Formed: 1872. *Ground:* Boghead Park. *Size:* 112yd×74yd. *Capacity:* 18,000. *Telephone:* Dumbarton 62569.
Manager: Billy Lamont. *Assistant Manager:* Billy Simpson.
Club Colours: White with gold horizontal band between two black bands, white shorts and stockings.
Club Nickname: Sons.
Record Attendance: 18,000 v Raith Rovers, Scottish Cup 7th rd, 2 Mar, 1957.
Previous Name: Dumbarton Athletic.

1982-83 LEAGUE RECORD

Match No.	Date	Venue	Opponents	Result		H/T Score	League Pos'n	Goalscorers	Attendance
1	Sept 4	A	Airdrie	W	2-1	1-0	3	Stevenson, Blair	1200
2	11	H	Falkirk	W	5-1	4-0	2	Craig 3, Donnelly, Stevenson	550
3	15	A	Clydebank	L	1-5	1-1	4	Dunlop	789
4	18	H	Dunfermline	D	1-1	0-0	5	Donnelly (pen)	450
5	25	H	St. Johnstone	W	4-1	2-0	4	Blair 2, Dunlop, Stevenson	1000
6	29	H	Ayr United	W	1-0	0-0	3	Donnelly	1500
7	Oct 2	A	Clyde	W	4-0	3-0	2	Donnelly 3 (1 pen), Blair	607
8	6	A	Hearts	D	1-1	0-0	2	Donnelly	5000
9	9	H	Hamilton	L	1-5	0-1	3	Brown	700
10	16	A	Raith Rovers	L	0-3	0-1	4		500
11	23	H	Partick Th.	D	1-1	0-0	5	Stevenson	1500
12	30	A	Alloa	L	0-2	0-0	6		557
13	Nov 6	H	Queen's Park	D	1-1	1-1	7	Stevenson	600
14	13	A	Ayr United	W	1-0	0-0	6	Stevenson	938
15	20	A	Dunfermline	W	3-0	2-0	6	Blair 2, Stevenson	1200
16	27	H	Hearts	D	1-1	0-0	6	Blair	3000
17	Dec 4	H	Clyde	L	1-3	0-2	7	Craig	500
18	11	A	St. Johnstone	L	0-1	0-1	8		2042
19	27	A	Falkirk	L	1-2	0-0	8	Dunlop	1400
20	Jan 1	H	Clydebank	L	0-4	0-1	8		1000
21	3	A	Queen's Park	L	1-2	1-0	8	Montgomerie	700
22	8	H	Raith Rovers	W	2-1	1-1	8	Stevenson, Close	500
23	15	A	Hamilton	W	3-0	0-0	8	Blair 2, Donnelly	724
24	22	H	Alloa	L	1-2	1-0	8	Craig	450
25	Feb 5	A	Partick Th.	L	2-3	1-1	9	Craig, McGowan	1789
26	12	H	Queen's Park	W	2-1	1-0	6	Coyle, Blair	600
27	23	H	Airdrie	D	0-0	0-0	6		800
28	26	A	Clydebank	L	1-3	1-1	7	McGowan M.	656
29	Mar 5	A	Clyde	L	0-1	0-0	9		490
30	12	H	Dunfermline	L	1-3	0-1	10	Close	500
31	19	A	Alloa	D	0-0	0-0	11		647
32	26	H	Airdrie	D	1-1	1-1	10	Rodger o.g.	450
33	Apr 2	A	Ayr United	W	2-1	1-0	8	Stevenson, McGowan	900
34	9	A	Raith Rovers	D	0-0	0-0	8		600
35	16	H	Hamilton	D	1-1	1-0	8	Montgomerie	400
36	23	A	St. Johnstone	L	0-1	0-0	9		2317
37	30	H	Partick Th.	W	2-1	1-0	8	McCaig, McGowan P.	1500
38	May 7	H	Hearts	L	0-4	0-2	9		4000
39	14	A	Falkirk	W	2-1	1-0	7	Craig, McGrogan	1800

Final League Position: 7

Goalscorers

League: Blair 10, Stevenson 9, Donnelly 8, Craig 7, Dunlop 3, McGowan P. 3, Montgomerie 2, Close 2, Brown 1, McGowan M. 1, Coyle 1, McCaig 1, McGrogan 1, opponent 1.
League Cup: Donnelly 5, Stevenson 1, Rankin 1.

Honours
Original members of Scottish League 1890.
Scottish League: Division 1 Champions 1890–91 (shared with Rangers), 1891–92; Division 2 Champions 1910–11, 1971–72; Runners-up 1907–08.
Scottish Cup: Winners 1883; Runners-up 1881, 1882, 1187, 1891, 1897.
Record Victory: 13-1 v Kirkintilloch Central, Scottish Cup 1st rd, 1 Sept, 1888.
Record Defeat: 1-11 v Albion Rovers, Division 2, 30 Jan, 1926; 1-11 v Ayr United, League Cup, 13 August, 1952:
Most League Points: 52, Division 2, 1971–72.
Most Individual League Goals in Season: 38, Kenny Wilson, Division 2, 1971–72.
Most Capped Player: John Lindsay, 8 Scotland; James McAulay, 8, Scotland.

Carson	Brown	McGowan, M	Burnett	McNeill	Coyle	Craig	Clougherty	Stevenson	Donnelly	Blair	McGowan, P	Dunlop	McCulley	Close	McGrogan	Montgomerie	Bowman	Newman	McCaig	Bourke	Hughes	McAteer	McKenzie	*Match No.*
1	2*	3	4	5	6	7	8	9	10	11		12												1
1	2	3	12	5	6	7	4	14	10	11†	8*	9												2
*1	2	3		5	6	7	4		10	11	8	9												3
1	2	3		5	6	7	4	12	10	11	8	9*												4
1	8	3	2	5			6	7	10	11	4	9												5
*1	2	3	5		6		8	7	10	11	4	9												6
1	2	3	5		6	14	8	7*	10	11	4	9†			12									7
*1	2		3	5	6		4*	12	10	11	8	9	7											8
1	2	3	12	5	6	7	4*	9†	10	11		14	8											9
1	2	12	3	5	6		4	7	10	11		9†	8*		14									10
1	2	3	5	12	6	8		7	10	11	4	9*												11
1	12	3	2	5	6	14		11	10†	7	8	9*		4										12
1		3*	2		6	12	4	9	10	7	8			5	11									13
1			3		6	14	4	12	10	7	8	9*		5	11†	2								14
1			3		6	12	4	7	10	11	8*	9		5		2								15
1		3		4	8	9	6	7*	10	11				5	12	2								16
1		12	3		6	9	4	7	10†	11	8			5*	12	2								17
1	12		3		4	9†	6	7*	10	11	8	14		5		2								18
*1		3		4	8		6	7	10	11		9		5		2								19
1	2*			5	4	14	6	7	10	11	8	9†		12		3								20
*1			3		4	9	6	7	10	11	8			5		2								21
1			3		6	9	4	7*	10	11	8			5	12	2								22
1			3		6	9	4	7	10	11	8			5		2								23
1			3	4	6	9		7	10	11	8			5		2								24
1		11	3		6	7	4	12	10*	9	8			5		2								25
1		11	3	5	6	7*	4	12	10	9	8					2								26
*1		11	3	5	6	7	4		10	9	8					2								27
		11	3	5	6	7*	4	9	10		8				12	2	1							28
		10	3	5*	8	14	6	7		11	4			12	9†	2	1							29
1		10	3	5†	8	11	6	12			7	9		4	14			2*						*30
1		14	3	5	10		6	11				12		4†	9	2			7*	8				31
1			3	5	8		6	11			12			4*	10	2			7	9				32
1	12			5	8	10	6	11			4	9*				3			7		2			33
1	12			5	8	10	6	11†			4	14				3			7*	9	2			34
1		3		5	8	10	6	11			4					2			12	9		7*		35
1		3		5	8		6	11			4				10	2			7	9				36
1		3	5		8	12	6	11			4	10*				2			7	9				37
1		14	3	5	4	11	6	9*			10†	8				2			7	12				38
1			3	5	8	7	6	12			10				11	2				9			4*	39
37	12	22	28	26	38	23	36	29	28	28	32	18	3	16	7	25	2	1	7	7	2	1	1	
	+ 4s	+ 4s	+ 2s	+ 1s		+ 8s		+ 8s			+ 1s	+ 5s		+ 2s	+ 7s				+ 1s	+ 1s				

Started and finished the season well but periods out of touch on either side of New Year turned a third position in October into tenth place by March.
Always capable of troubling the best—as in 4-1 defeat of St. Johnstone; but they lack the consistency and grit that would make them candidates for honours.

DUNDEE Premier Division

Year Formed: 1893
Ground: Dens Park. *Size:* 113yd×73yd. *Capacity:* 22,381 (12,130 seats).
Telephone: Dundee 826104.
Manager: Donald MacKay. *Coach:* Jocky Scott.
Secretary: Ian Gellatly. *Physiotherapist:* Eric Ferguson.
Club Colours: Dark blue shirts with blue, red and white trim, white shorts, red stockings.
Club Nickname: Dark Blues of The Dee.
Record Attendance: 43,024 v Rangers, Scottish Cup, 1953.
Previous Name: East End and Our Boys amalgamated to become Dundee in 1893.
Previous Ground: Carolina Port, 1893–98.
Record Transfer Fee Received: £210,000 from Rangers for Ian Redford, Feb 1980.
European Competitions: *European Cup* 1962–63 (semi-final); *European Cup-Winners' Cup* 1964–65; *Fairs Cup* 1967–68 (semi-final); *UEFA Cup* 1971–72, 1974–75.

1982-83 LEAGUE RECORD

Match No.	Date	Venue	Opponents	Result		H/T Score	League Pos'n	Goalscorers	Atten-dance
1	Sept 4	A	Celtic	L	0-2	0-2			19,122
2	11	H	Motherwell	W	3-1	2-1	4	Ferguson (2 pens), Stephen	4621
3	18	H	Morton	W	2-0	1-0	4	Sinclair 2	3979
4	25	A	Kilmarnock	D	0-0	0-0	4		2000
5	Oct 2	A	Rangers	D	1-1	0-0	4	Fraser	16,000
6	9	H	Hibs	W	2-1	1-1	4	Smith, Ferguson	5287
7	16	H	Aberdeen	L	0-1	0-1	5		9000
8	23	H	St.Mirren	D	1-1	1-0	5	Stephen	4831
9	30	A	Dundee United	L	0-1	0-0	5		14,959
10	Nov 6	H	Celtic	L	2-3	0-3	5	Fraser 2	11,681
11	13	A	Motherwell	L	0-1	0-0	5		3295
12	20	A	Morton	W	2-1	0-1	5	Bell, Mackie	2500
13	27	H	Kilmarnock	W	5-2	3-0	5	Murphy 2, Bell, Mackie, Fraser	4311
14	Dec 11	A	Hibs	D	1-1	1-0	5	Mackie	5350
15	18	H	Aberdeen	L	0-2	0-1	5		6528
16	27	A	St. Mirren	D	0-0	0-0	5		4412
17	Jan 1	H	Dundee United	L	0-2	0-1	5		18,109
18	3	A	Celtic	D	2-2	0-1	5	Sinclair 2	16,615
19	8	H	Motherwell	W	3-1	0-1	5	Ferguson, Mackie, Stephen	5131
20	15	H	Morton	D	3-3	3-1	5	Ferguson, Sinclair, Stephen	4557
21	22	A	Kilmarnock	L	0-2	0-1	5		1900
22	Feb 5	A	Rangers	D	1-1	0-0	5	Bell	7000
23	22	H	Hibs	L	0-1	0-1	5		4363
24	26	A	Aberdeen	L	1-3	0-1	6	Stephen	11,450
25	Mar 2	H	Rangers	W	1-0	0-0	5	Kidd	6624
26	5	H	St. Mirren	L	2-5	1-2	5	Scrimgeour, Kidd	4161
27	12	A	Dundee United	L	3-5	0-1	5	Ferguson (pen), Kidd, Fraser	13,443
28	19	H	Celtic	W	2-1	2-1	6	Kidd, Scrimgeour	11,196
29	26	A	Motherwell	D	1-1	0-1	6	Ferguson	3222
30	Apr 2	A	Morton	L	0-1	0-1	7		3000
31	9	H	Kilmarnock	D	0-0	0-0	6		3376
32	23	A	Hibs	D	0-0	0-0	7		4000
33	30	H	Aberdeen	L	0-2	0-2	7		10,076
34	May 3	H	Rangers	W	2-1	1-1	6	Ferguson, Sinclair	4788
35	9	A	St. Mirren	L	1-2	0-1	6	Mackie	6000
36	14	A	Dundee United	L	1-2	1-2	6	Ferguson	25,000

Final League Position: 6

Goalscorers

League: Ferguson 9, Sinclair 6, Stephen 5, Fraser 5, Mackie 5, Kidd 4, Bell 3, Murphy 2, Scrimgeour 2, Smith 1.
League Cup: Ferguson 6, Stephen 2, Mackie 2, Kidd 1, Sinclair 1, Fraser 1, Davidson 1.
Scottish Cup: Ferguson 1, Sinclair 1.

Honours

Scottish League – Division 1 Champions 1961–62, 1978–79; Runners-up 1902–03, 1906–07, 1908–09, 1948–49, 1980–81; Division 2 Champions 1946–47.
Scottish Cup – Winners 1910; Runners-up 1925, 1952, 1964.
Scottish League Cup – Winners 1951–52, 1952–53, 1973–74; Runners-up 1967–68, 1980–81.
Record Victory: 10–0 v Alloa, Division 2, 8 Mar, 1947, 10–0 v Dunfermline Ath, Division 2, 22 Mar, 1947.
Record Defeat: 0–11 v Celtic, Division 1, 26 Oct, 1895.
Most League Points: 55, Division 1, 1978–79.
Most Individual League Goals in Season: 38, Dave Halliday, 1923–24.
Most Capped Player: Alex Hamilton, 24, Scotland.

Kelly	McGeachie	McKimmie	Fraser	Smith	Glennie	Mackie	Bell	Davidson	Kidd	Fleming	MacDonald	Ferguson	Stephen	Sinclair	Scrimgeour	Murphy	McGlashan	Geddes	McLelland	McKinlay	*Match No.*
1	2	3	4	5	6	7	8	9	10*	11				12							1
1	2*	3	4	5		10		9†	14	8	6	7	11	12							2
1		3	4	5*	2	10	12			8	6	7	11	9							3
1		3	4	5	2	10				8	6	7	11	9							4
1		3	4	5	2	10		9*		8	6	7	11	12							5
1		3	4	5	2	10				8	6	7	11	9							6
1		3	4	5	2	10	9†			8	6*	7	11	14	12						7
1		3*	4	5	2	10	12	14		8	6	7†	11	9							8
1		3	4	5	2	10	12	9	14		6	7	11†		8*						9
1		3*	4	5	2	10	12	9	14		6	7†	11		8						10
1			4	5	2	10	8		7*		6		11	9	3	12					11
1		12	4	5	2	10	8†		7*		6		11	9	3	14					12
1			4	5	2	10	8				6		11	9	3	7					13
1		12	4	5	2	10	8				6		11	9	3*	7					14
1	14	3	4	5	2*	10	8				6		11†	9		7	12				15
1	11	3	4	5	2	10	8				6	12		9		7*					16
1	8	3	4	5	2*	10	4†				6	9	11	14	12	7					17
1				5	2	10	4				6	7	8	9	3	11					18
1		12	4	5	2	10	8				6	7	11	9	3*						19
1	2*	3	4	5†		10	8				6	7	11	9	12	14					20
1	12		4	5	2	10	8				6*	7	11	9	3						21
1	2	3	4	5		10	8				6	7	11	9							22
1	2	3	4	5		10	8				6	7	11	9*		12					23
1	2	3	4	5	14	10	12		9†		6	7	11		8*						24
1	2*	3	4	5	14	10	12		11		6	7		9†	8						25
1	2	3	4	5		10	9		11		6	7*			8		14				26
	2	3	4	5		12	8†		11		6	7		9	10			1*	14		27
1	2	3	4	5		7	8		11*		6	12		9	10						28
1	2	3	4	5		7	8		11		6			9	10						29
1	2	3	4	5		7	8*		11†		6	12	14	9	10						30
1	2*	3	4	5		7	8		10		6	9†	11	12	14						31
1	2	3	4	5		7	12		11*		6		10	9	8						32
1	2*	3	4	5	8	7		9	12		6	11	14		10†						33
1	8	3	4	5	2	12			10		6	7	11	9*							34
1	8	6	4	5	2	12			10*			7	11	9						3	35
1	8	3	4	5	2*	12			11		6	7	10	9							36
35	20	29	35	36	23	32	21	6	15	8	34	25	27	25	18	6	0	1	0	1	
	+ 2s	+ 3s			+ 2s	+ 4s	+ 7s	+ 1s	+ 4s			+ 3s	+ 2s	+ 6s	+ 4s	+ 4s	+ 2s		+ 1s		

Although having to perform in the shadow of close neighbours United for the season, Dundee's campaign must go down as one of slight improvement.
They rarely indicated that they are likely to become involved in the late stages of any of the tournaments, but succeeded in consolidating in the Premier Division they rejoined two years ago.
Difficult to see any major progression, with a squad limited in numbers by financial restrictions but avoiding relegation seems well within the scope of the current side.

DUNDEE UNITED Premier Division

Year Formed: 1909 as Dundee Hibernians, became Dundee U in 1923.
Ground: Tannadice Park. *Size:* 110yd×74yd. *Capacity:* 22,250 (2,250 seats).
Telephone: Dundee 86289.
Manager: Jim McLean. *Asst. Manager:* Walter Smith.
Secretary: Mrs Helen Lindsay. *Physiotherapist:* Andy Dickson.
Club colours: Tangerine shirts with black trim, black shorts with tangerine trim.
Club Nickname: Terrors.
Record Attendance: 28,000 v Barcelona, Fairs Cup, 1966.
Record Transfer Fee Received: £400,000 from West Ham for Ray Stewart, Sept 1979.
Record Transfer Fee Paid: £165,000 to Chelsea for Eammon Bannon, Oct 1979.
European Competitions: *Fairs Cup* 1966–67, 1969–70, 1970–71; *European Cup-Winners' Cup* 1974–75; *UEFA Cup* 1975–76, 1977–78, 1978-79, 1980–81, 1981–82, 1982–83.

1982-83 LEAGUE RECORD

Match No.	Date	Venue	Opponents	Result	H/T Score	League Pos'n	Goalscorers	Attendance
1	Sept 4	H	Aberdeen	W 2-0	2-0	–	Malpas, Dodds	11,683
2	11	A	Rangers	D 0-0	0-0	2		25,000
3	18	A	Hibs	D 0-0	0-0	4		5562
4	25	H	St Mirren	W 3-0	1-0	3	Milne, Sturrock 2	6832
5	Oct 2	H	Celtic	D 2-2	0-1	3	Dodds, Milne	20,009
6	9	A	Kilmarnock	D 1-1	0-1	3	Milne (pen)	2500
7	16	H	Morton	W 6-0	5-0	2	Dodds 3, Narey 2, Kirkwood	5986
8	23	A	Motherwell	W 2-0	0-0	2	Narey, Kirkwood	4555
9	30	H	Dundee	W 1-0	0-0	2	Dodds	14,959
10	Nov 6	A	Aberdeen	L 1-5	1-3	3	Gough	14,000
11	13	H	Rangers	W 4-2	1-1	2	Milne 2, Gough, Dodds	16,470
12	20	H	Hibs	W 3-0	1-0	2	Bannon, Reilly, Dodds	7374
13	27	A	St Mirren	W 2-0	0-0	2	Bannon, Dodds	3823
14	Dec 11	H	Kilmarnock	W 7-0	1-0	2	Reilly 2, Dodds 2, Bannon, Milne, Narey	7259
15	18	A	Morton	W 2-1	1-1	2	Reilly, Sturrock	2000
16	27	H	Motherwell	W 5-0	2-0	2	Milne, Bannon (pen), Reilly, Hegarty, Sturrock	7682
17	Jan 1	A	Dundee	W 2-0	1-0	2	Milne 2	18,109
18	3	H	Aberdeen	L 0-3	0-2	3		17,852
19	8	A	Rangers	L 1-2	1-1	3	Reilly	15,500
20	15	A	Hibs	D 0-0	0-0	3		5000
21	22	H	St Mirren	W 3-2	3-1	3	Kirkwood, Dodds 2	6714
22	Feb 5	H	Celtic	D 1-1	1-1	3	Dodds	17,289
23	12	A	Kilmarnock	W 5-0	2-0	3	Holt 3, Kirkwood, Dodds	1850
24	26	H	Morton	D 1-1	0-0	3	Gough	5986
25	Mar 5	A	Motherwell	W 4-1	2-1	3	Gough 2, Milne, Dodds	3589
26	12	H	Dundee	W 5-3	1-0	3	Gough 2, Reilly, Hegarty, Dodds	13,443
27	19	A	Aberdeen	W 2-1	2-0	3	Milne 2	22,800
28	26	H	Hibs	D 3-3	3-1	3	Dodds, Britton, Gough	7279
29	Apr 4	H	Rangers	W 3-1	1-0	2	Milne, Sturrock 2	14,142
30	6	A	Celtic	L 0-2	0-0	2		34,508
31	9	A	St Mirren	W 2-1	2-1	2	Bannon (pen), Sturrock	4617
32	20	A	Celtic	W 3-2	1-1	2	Hegarty, Bannon (pen), Milne	23,965
33	23	H	Kilmarnock	W 4-0	4-0	1	Stark 2, Holt, Sturrock	7516
34	30	A	Morton	W 4-0	1-0	1	Dodds 2, Milne, Narey	6800
35	Apr 7	H	Motherwell	W 4-0	1-0	1	Bannon 2 (1 pen), Dodds 2	11,993
36	14	A	Dundee	W 2-1	2-1	1	Milne, Bannon	25,000

Final League Position: 1

Goalscorers

League: Dodds 22, Milne 16, Bannon 9, Sturrock 8, Gough 8, Reilly 7, Narey 5, Kirkwood 4, Holt 4, Hegarty 3, Stark 2, Malpas 1, Britton 1.
League Cup: Sturrock 7, Dodds 5, Bannon 3, Narey 3, Payne 2, Milne 2, Gough 1, Malpas 1.
UEFA Cup: Milne 3, Hegarty 2, Dodds 1, Kirkwood 1, Narey 1, Sturrock 1, Britton 1.

Honours

Scottish League: Scottish League Champions 1982–83. Division 2 Champions 1924–25, 1928–29; Runners-up 1930–31, 1959–60.
Scottish Cup: Runners-up 1973–74, 1980–81.
Scottish League Cup: Winners 1979–80, 1980–81; Runners-up 1981–82.
Summer Cup: Runners-up 1964–65.
Scottish Wartime Cup: Runners-up 1939–40.
Record Victory: 14-0 v Nithsdale Wanderers, Scottish Cup 1st rd, 17 Jan, 1931.
Record Defeat: 1-12 v Motherwell, Division 2, 23 Jan, 1954.
Most League Points: 51, Division 2, 1928–29.
Most Individual League Goals in Season: 41, John Coyle, Division 2, 1955–56.
Most Capped Player: David Narey, 16, Scotland.
Most League Goals: 108, Division 2, 1935–36.
Highest Scorer in Total Aggregate: Peter McKay, 202.
Most Appearances: Doug Smith, 587, 1959–76.

McAlpine	Malpas	Stark	Gough	Hegarty	Narey	Britton	Milne	Kirkwood	Sturrock	Dodds	Bannon	Payne	Phillip	Holt	Taylor	Reilly	Clark	McNeil	Murray	*Match No.*
1	2	3*	4	5	6	7	8	9	10	11	12									1
1	3		4	5	6	7	12	2	10	11	8	9*								2
1	2	3	4	5	6	7*	14	12	10	11	8	9†								3
1	14	3	4	5	6	12	8†	9	10	11	7		2*							4
1	2	3	4	5	6	14	8	9	10	11	7*			12†						5
1	2	3	4	5	6	7*	8	9	10	11				12						6
1	12	3	4	5	6		8	9†	10	11	7*	14		2						7
1	7	3	4	5	6	10*	8	9		11				2		12				8
1		3	4	5	6		8	9		11			2	10	7*	12				9
1	2	3	4	5	6		8	9		11*	7			10		12				10
1	3	2	4	5	6		8	9	10	11	7									11
1	3	2	4	5	6		8*	9†	10	11	7				14	12				12
1	3		4	5	6		8	9	10*	12	7			2		11				13
1	3	2	4	5	6		8	9*	10	12	7			14		11†				14
1	3	2	4	5	6		8		10	11	7			12		9*				15
1	3	2	4	5	6		8	12	10	11	7					9*				16
1	3	2	4	5	6		8	12	10	11	7					9*				17
1	3*	2	4	5	6		8	9†	10	11	7			12		14				18
1	3	2	4	5	6		8*	10		11	7					9		12		19
1		14	4	5	6	8†	12		10	11	7		3	2		9*				20
1	3	2	4	5	6		8	9		11				10			7			21
1	3	2	4	5	6			9	10	11	7			8						22
1	3		4	5	6		12	9*	10	11	7		2	8						23
1	3	2	4	5	6		8	12	10	11	7*			9†		14				24
1	12	2	4	5	6		8	9*		11	7			10					3	25
1	3	2	4	5	6		8*	9	10	11†	7			12		14				26
1	3	2	4	5	6		8	9		11	7		10							27
1	3	2	4	5	6	8		9		11	7*				12	10				28
1	3	2	4	5	6		8		10	11	7			9						29
1	3	2	4	5	6*		8		10	11	7			9		12				30
1	3		4	5	6		8	9	10	11	7			2						31
1	3	2	4	5	6		8		10	11	7			9						32
1	3	2		5	6	12	8	4	10	11	7			9*						33
1*	3	2	4	5	6		8	12	10	11	7			9						34
1	3	2		5	6		8	4	10	11	7			9						35
1	3	2	4	5	6		8	9	10*	11	7			12						36
36	31	31	34	36	36	7	30	26	28	34	31	2	5	18	1	8	1	0	1	
	+ 3s	+ 1s				+ 3s	+ 4s	+ 5s		+ 2s	+ 1s	+ 1s		+ 7s	+ 2s	+ 8s		+ 1s		

A historic first ever Championship made this a best ever season for the country's most improved side. United's breathtaking last day win at Dens Park ended a record equalling campaign when they stayed the course better than any.
90 league goals gave them the record since the inception of the Premier league – with Celtic – and their 56 points equalled the best, again by Celtic, in 1980/81.
In a 36 game programme that included ony four defeats theirs' was truly a team performance but perhaps the solidarity of Paul Hegarty at the back and the goals of Dave Dodds were influential elements.

DUNFERMLINE ATHLETIC Division 2

Year Formed: 1885.
Ground: East End Park. *Size:* 114yd×72yd. *Capacity:* 27,500 (3000 seats).
Telephone: Dunfermline 724295.
Manager: Tom Forsyth. *Physiotherapist:* Phillip Yeates.
Secretary: Jim McColville JP.
Club Colours: White and black vertical pinstripe shirts, black shorts.
Club Nickname: The Pars.
Record Attendance: 27,816 v Celtic, Division 1, 1968.
European Competitions: *European Cup-Winners' Cup* 1961–62, 1968–69; *Fairs Cup* 1962–63, 1964–65, 1965–66. 1966–67, 1969–70.

1982-83 LEAGUE RECORD

Match No.	Date	Venue	Opponents	Result	H/T Score	League Pos'n	Goalscorers	Attendance
1	Sept 4	A	Partick Th.	D 1-1	0-0	7	Jenkins	2500
2	8	H	Clyde	D 1-1	0-0	7	Rae (og)	1200
3	11	A	Hamilton	L 1-4	1-2	9	Morrison (pen)	800
4	14	H	Raith Rovers	L 1-2	1-1	11	Urquhart o.g.	1900
5	18	A	Dumbarton	D 1-1	0-0	12	Jenkins	450
6	22	H	St. Johnstone	L 2-4	0-3	13	Hegarty, Forrest	2100
7	25	H	Ayr United	W 1-0	1-0	11	Forrest	1800
8	Oct 2	A	Airdrie	D 1-1	0-1	11	Blackie	1100
9	9	H	Queen's Park	D 1-1	1-0	11	Tait	1500
10	16	A	Clydebank	D 1-1	0-1	10	Considine	440
11	23	A	Hearts	L 1-4	1-1	10	Hamill	5997
12	30	H	Falkirk	D 0-0	0-0	10		1250
13	Nov 6	A	Alloa	D 2-2	1-2	9	Forrest, Morrison	1518
14	13	H	Partick Th.	L 0-4	0-1	10		1950
15	20	H	Dumbarton	L 0-3	0-2	13		1200
16	27	A	St. Johnstone	L 0-2	0-0	14		2442
17	Dec 4	H	Airdrie	W 1-0	1-0	12	Forrest	1039
18	11	A	Ayr United	L 0-1	0-1	13		1105
19	27	H	Hamilton	D 1-1	1-0	12	Wilcox	1500
20	Jan 1	A	Raith Rovers	L 0-6	0-3	14		2500
21	3	H	Alloa	W 2-0	1-0	13	Morrison 2	1400
22	15	A	Queen's Park	D 2-2	1-1	14	Rodier, Forrest	644
23	22	A	Falkirk	L 0-1	0-1	14		2500
24	Feb 9	H	Hearts	W 2-1	0-1	14	Jenkins, Forrest (pen)	3500
25	23	H	Clydebank	D 1-1	0-0	14	Morrison	1500
26	26	A	Hamilton	L 0-4	0-0	14		943
27	Mar 5	H	Partick Th.	L 0-3	0-2	14		1480
28	9	A	Clyde	L 0-1	0-0	14		550
29	12	A	Dumbarton	W 3-1	1-0	13	McCathie, Forrest, Hamill	500
30	19	H	Clydebank	D 1-1	0-0	13	Stewart	1100
31	26	A	Alloa	D 1-1	0-0	13	Stewart	1063
32	Apr 2	H	Raith Rovers	D 2-2	0-1	13	Morrison 2 (1 pen)	2100
33	5	H	Airdrie	L 0-4	0-1	13		1000
34	9	A	Ayr United	W 3-2	1-1	13	Stewart 2, Forrest	700
35	16	H	Queen's Park	W 1-0	1-0	13	Stewart	1250
36	23	H	Clyde	D 0-0	0-0	12		1420
37	30	A	Hearts	D 3-3	0-2	13	McCathie, Morrison, Gauld (og)	6427
38	May 10	H	Falkirk	D 2-2	0-1	13	McCathie, Stewart	1200
39	14	A	St. Johnstone	L 0-1	0-1	13		4932

Final League Position: 13

Goalscorers

League: Morrison 8, Forrest 8, Stewart 6, Jenkins 3, McCathie 3, opponents 3, Hamill 2, Hegarty 1, Blackie 1, Tait 1, Considine 1, Wilcox 1, Rodier 1.
League Cup: Morrison 3.
Scottish Cup: Jenkins 2, Tait 2, Rodier 1.

Honours

Scottish League – Division 2 Champions 1925–26; Runners-up 1912–13, 1933–34, 1954–55, 1957–58, 1972–73, 1978–79.
Scottish Cup: Winners 1961, 1968; Runners-up 1965.
Scottish League Cup: Runners-up 1949–50.
Record Victory: 11-2 v Stenhousemuir, Division 2, 27 Sept, 1930.
Record Defeat: 0-10 v Dundee, Division 2, 22 Mar, 1947.
Most League Points: 59, Division 2, 1925–26.
Most Individual League Goals in Season: 55, Bobby Skinner, Division 2, 1925–26.
Most Capped Player: Andy Wilson, 6(12), Scotland.

Young	Whyte	Robertson	Grant	Wilcox	Dall R.	Hegarty	Jenkins	Hamill	Morrison	McCathie	Forrest	Considine	Tait	Stewart	Dall S.	Bowie	Donnelly	Ford	Wildridge	Sermanni	Smith	Moffat	Crawford	Rodier	McGovern	Wilson	Blackie	Nicol	*Match No.*
1		2	3	4	5	6	7	8*	9‡	10	11		12		14														1
*1		2	3	4	5	10	11	8	9	6	7																		2
1		2	3	4	5	10	11†	8	9	6	7*		12		14														3
*1		2	3		5	6	11	8	9			4	7	10															4
1		2	3		5	8	11	6			14	4	7*	9	10†	12													5
*1		2	3		5	6	11	8				4	7	9	10														6
	1	2	3	5		6		8			11	4	7	10		9													7
	1	2	3	5		6*		8			11†	4	7	10		9	12										14		8
	1	2	3	5				6	9		11*	4	8			7	10										12		9
	1	2	3	5				8†	9		11	4	6			7*	10										12	14	10
	1	2	3	5			10	8	9		7*	4		11				6									12		11
	1	2		5			10*	6	9		7	4		11				8	3		12								12
	1			5			10*	6*	9		7	4		11*		14	12	2	3	8*									13
	1	2					10	6*	9*	5	7	4				14		12	3	8	11								14
		2*					8		10	5	9	4				11	12	6	3	7†	14	1							15
		2	3*				6		9†	5	11	4	12			7	8			10		1					14		16
		3		5						6	11	4				7	8	10				1	2	9					17
		3		5					12	8	11*	4		7			6	10				1	2	9					18
*		3		5			10				11	4		9			8	6				1	2	7					19
		3		5			10*	7	8		11	4					6				12	1	2	9					20
*	1			5			8	7	10		11						6		3		4		2	9					21
	1	10		5			11†		9		7			14			6*	12	3		4		2	8					22
	1	7		5					10		11	3		12			8	6*			4		2	9					23
*	1	2	3	5			10			8	11		9			6					4			7					24
*	1	2		5			10			8			9			6					4		3	7		11			25
	1	3		5			10†		14	8	11		9			6*	12				4		2	7					26
	1			5			12	6	10	9	11						7				4		2	8*	3				27
*	1	6		5			10			8	11		9	12							4		2*		14	3	7†		28
	1	2		5				8	12	10	11			9		7					4*				6	3			29
	1	2	3	5				6		10	11			9		7					8*			12	4				30
	1	2		5				8		10*	11			9		7							12	6	4	3			31
	1			5				8	12	10	11	*		9		7							2	6	4	3			32
*	1	2		5				8	11	10				9		7								6	4	3			33
	1			5					8	10	11			9		7							2	6	4	3			34
	1			5					10	8	11		2	9		7	12				4*			6		3			35
	1	8		5					10	4	11		2	9		7								6		3			36
	1	8		5					7	10	11		2	9							4			6		3			37
	1	2		5					7	8	11		3	9			10				4			6					38
	1	2		5			10		8	10*	11†		14	9		7					4			6		3			39
6	27	33	14	33	6	8	21	22	24	24	34	18	15	21	2	19	12	8	6	4	15	6	13	20	7	11	1	0	
							+1s		+4s		+1s		+4s	+3s	+2s	+3s	+5s	+2s			+3s		+1s	+1s	+1s		+5s	+1s	

A difficult first season for manager Tom Forsyth who found a shortage of goals the most pressing problem in an unsuccessful effort to avoid relegation.
Twelve blank days in their 39 game card tells it all, but with promising front players Robert Stewart and Steve Morrison now operating in a lower league they will be amongst the front runners in Division Two.

EAST FIFE — Division 2

Year Formed: 1903
Ground: Bayview Park, Methil, Fife KY8 3AG, Scotland. *Size:* 110yd×71yd. *Capacity:* 15,000.
Telephone: Leven 26323.
General Manager: Jimmy Bonthrone.
Secretary: Mrs. I. McCammon.
Club Colours: Black and white striped shirts, white shorts, black stockings.
Record Attendance: 22,515 v Raith R, Division 1, 2 Jan, 1950.
Club Nickname: The Fifers.

1982-83 LEAGUE RECORD

Match No.	Date	Venue	Opponents	Result		H/T Score	League Pos'n	Goalscorers	Attendance
1	Sept 4	H	East Stirling	W	3-1	0-1	3	O'Brien 2, Hutt.	500
2	8	A	Brechin	D	0-0	0-0	6		300
3	11	A	Albion Rovers	L	0-1	0-0	7		150
4	15	H	Cowdenbeath	D	1-1	0-1	8	Halley	400
5	18	A	Q.O.S.	W	5-1	1-1	3	Scott, Caithness, O'Brien 2, Hutt	860
6	22	H	Montrose	L	0-1	0-1	5		450
7	25	H	Arbroath	D	2-2	2-2	5	Scott 2	530
8	Oct 2	A	Meadowbank	W	2-0	0-0	5	Scott 2	500
9	9	H	Stenhousemuir	D	1-1	0-0	4	Pryde	544
10	16	A	Stirling Albion	L	0-1	0-0	7		350
11	23	A	Forfar	L	1-4	1-1	8	Thomson P (pen)	908
12	30	H	Stranrear	D	2-2	2-2	8	Durie, Hutt	340
13	Nov 6	A	Berwick	D	0-1	0-1	10		606
14	13	H	Brechin	L	1-2	0-0	11	Hutt	455
15	20	H	Q.O.S.	D	0-0	0-0	11		412
16	27	A	Montrose	W	2-0	1-0	10	Caithness 2	200
17	Dec 4	H	Meadowbank	W	5-0	4-0	8	Burt 3, Scott, Thomson P (pen)	770
18	11	A	Q.O.S.	W	2-1	0-0	7	Thomson 2	750
19	18	A	Arbroath	L	1-3	0-1	7	Thomson	498
20	27	H	Albion Rovers	W	4-3	1-1	5	Caithness 2, Kirk, Hutt	530
21	Jan 1	A	Cowdenbeath	W	4-2	3-1	5	Hutt 2, Thomson, Caithness	600
22	3	H	Berwick	L	0-1	0-0	6		850
23	15	A	East Stirling	W	3-0	2-0	4	Kirk, Caithness, Scott	300
24	22	A	Stranraer	D	2-2	2-0	4	Kirk, Thomson	350
25	Feb 9	A	Stenhousemuir	L	2-3	0-3	6	Kirk, Scott	300
26	12	H	Stirling Albion	W	1-0	1-0	6	Thomson	651
27	23	H	Stranraer	W	3-0	1-0	4	Thomson, Scott, Caithness	400
28	26	A	Forfar	D	0-0	0-0	4		900
29	Mar 3	H	Cowdenbeath	L	0-2	0-2	5		612
30	9	H	Forfar	L	0-2	0-1	8		700
31	19	H	Montrose	W	4-0	4-0	7	Halley, Thomson P (pen) Caithness 2	2,450
32	26	A	Albion Rovers	D	1-1	1-0	6	Thomson P (pen)	300
33	Apr 2	H	Berwick	W	3-0	2-0	5	Thomson 2 (1P pen), Kirk	472
34	9	A	Stenhousemuir	W	2-0	0-0	5	Hamilton, Rae	250
35	16	A	Stirling Albion	D	2-2	1-1	5	Kirk 2	660
36	23	H	Brechin City	L	1-2	0-0	6	Kirk	665
37	30	A	Meadowbank	W	3-0	2-0	6	Scott, Hutt 2	900
38	May 7	A	East Stirling	D	1-1	0-0	6	Durie	500
39	14	H	Arbroath	W	4-0	0-0	6	Scott, Pryde, Caithness, Kopel O.G.	481

Final League Position: 6

Goalscorers

League: Thomson 13, Scott 11, Caithness 11, Hutt 9, Kirk 8, O'Brien 4, Burt 3, Halley 2, Durie 2, Pryde 2, Hamilton 1, Rae 1, opponents 1.
Scottish Cup: Scott 1, Thomson 1, Caithness 1

Honours
Scottish League – Division 2 Champions 1947–48; Runners-up 1929–30, 1970–71.
Scottish Cup – Winners 1938 (only Second Division winners); Runners-up 1927, 1950
Scottish League Cup – Winners 1947–48 (only Second Division winners), 1949–50, 1953–54.
Record Victory: 13-2 v Edinburgh City, Division 2, 11 Dec. 1937.
Record Defeat: 0-9 v Hearts, Division 1, 5 Oct, 1957.
Most League Points: 57, Division 2, 1929–30.
Most Individual League Goals in a Season: 41, Henry Morris, Division 2, 1947–48.
Most Capped Player: George Aitken, 5 (8), Scotland.

Gorman	Marshall	Muirhead	Thomson	McLaren	Halley	Durie	O'Brien	Hamilton	Scott	Hutt	Caithness	Clarke	Pryde	Kirk	Beveridge	Wedderburn	Burt	Markey	Wilson	Meakin	Sokoluk	Rae	*Match No.*
1		2	3	4	5	6	7	8	9	10	11*		12										1
*1		2	6	4	5	7†	11*	8	9	10		3	12		14								2
1		2	6	4	5	11*		8	9	10		3	7†			12			14				3
*1		2	2	3	4	5	6	12	8	9*	10	11		7									4
1		2		4	5	6*	7	8	9	10	11†	3	12			14							5
*1		2	6	4	5		7	8	9	10	11	†3†	12			14							6
1		2	6	4†	5		7*	8	9	10	12	3	11			14							7
1		2	6	4	5		11	8	9	10		3	7										8
1		2	6	4	5		11	8	9	10		3	7										9
1		2	6	4	5	12	11	8	9	10		3	7*										10
1		2	6	4	5	7	9	8		10	11	3*					12						11
1		4	6		5	8*	7	2	9	10	11	3								12			12
1			3		5	6*		8	9	7	10	4	11	2		12							13
1		2	6*		5	12†		8	9	7	11		14	3	4	10							14
1		14	6	4	5			8	9*	10	7	3		2		12	11†						15
1			6	4	5			8	9	10	11	3		2			7						16
1			6	4	5			8	9	10	11	3		2			7						17
1			6	4	5	12		8	9	10	11†	3		2		14	7*						18
1		14	6	4	5	7		8	9	10	11*	2†						3			12		19
*1			6	4	5			8		10	11	3	7	2					9				20
*1			6	4	5			8		10	11	3	7	2			9*		12				21
*1			6	4	5	12		8		10	11	3	7	2			9*						22
1			6	4	5			8	9	10	11	2	7	3									23
1			6	4	5	12		8	9	10	11	3	7*	2									24
*1			6	4	5	12		8	9	10	11*	3†	7	2			14						25
1			6	4	5	11*		8	9	10		3	7	2			12						26
*1			6	4	5	12		8	9	10	11	3*	7	2									27
1			6	4	5			8	9	10	11	3	7	2									28
1			6	4	5	12		8	9†	10	11	3*	7	2	14								29
*	1		6	4	5	7*		8	9	10	11	3	12	2									30
	1		3	4	5	6		8	9	10	11		7*	2								12	31
	1		3	4†	5	6		8	9	10	11*	14	7	2								12	32
	1		3	4	5	6*		8	9	10	11		7	2								12	33
	1		3	4	5	6*		8	9	10	11		7	2								12	34
	1		6	4	5			8	9	10	11	3	7*	2								12	35
	1	4	6	3	5			8	9	10	11		7	2									36
	1	12	3	4	5			8	9*	7	10	6	11	2									37
	1		6	4	5	8		2	9	10	11	3*	7									12	38
	1		6	3	5	4		8	9	7	10		11	2									39
29	10	14	38	36	39	17	10	39	35	39	32	30	26	25	1	1	6	1	1	0	0	0	
		+				+	+				+	+	+		+	+	+		+	+	+	+	
		3s				8s	1s				1s	1s	6s		2s	7s	3s		2s	1s	1s	6s	

A season of improvement when East Fife secured 43 points, the best for four years. With 68 goals to their credit, they stepped up on that score also, that number representing their best total since the leagues were reconstructed eight years ago.

EAST STIRLING Division 2

Year Formed: 1881. *Ground:*Firs Park. *Size:* 112yd×72yd. *Capacity:* 12,000.
Telephone: Falkirk 23583. *Secretary:* P. I. McKay. *Manager:* Billy Little.
Club Colours: Black and white 1-inch hoops, black shorts, red stockings.
Club Nickname: The Shire.
Record Attendance: 11,500 v Hibernian, Scottish Cup, 10 Feb, 1969.

1982-83 LEAGUE RECORD

Match No.	*Date*	*Venue*	*Opponents*	*Result*		*H/T Score*	*League Pos'n*	*Goalscorers*	*Attendance*
1	Sept 4	A	East Fife.	L	1-3	1-0	11	Renwick	500
2	8	H	Montrose	D	0-0	0-0	10		200
3	11	H	Meadowbank	L	1-3	0-1	13	Ross	500
4	15	A	Stirling Alb.	L	0-2	0-1	14		600
5	18	A	Arbroath	L	1-3	0-1	14	Trialist P.	574
6	22	H	Stranraer	L	1-2	1-1	14	McCaig	150
7	25	A	Brechin	L	0-3	0-2	14		300
8	Oct 2	H	Albion Rovers	D	1-1	1-0	14	McCaig	250
9	9	A	Forfar	L	1-5	10-	14	McCaig	982
10	16	H	Berwick	L	0-4	0-3	14		250
11	23	A	Cowdenbeath	D	1-1	1-0	14	Grant	400
12	Nov 3	H	Q.O.S.	L	1-2	1-0	14	Gibson	150
13	6	H	Stenhousemuir	W	2-1	1-0	14	Gibson, Rennie O.G.	350
14	13	A	Montrose	W	2-1	0-1	14	Ashwood, Gibson	250
15	20	H	Arbroath	L	1-3	1-2	14	Grant	250
16	27	A	Stranraer	L	1-2	0-1	14	Hughes	375
17	Dec 4	A	Albion Rovers	L	1-3	1-1	14	Campbell P.	400
18	27	A	Meadowbank	D	0-0	0-0	14		450
19	Jan 1	H	Stirling Alb.	W	2-1	1-1	14	Watt, Gibson	350
20	3	A	Stenhousemuir	D	2-2	1-0	14	Rennie, Grant	300
21	15	H	East Fife	L	0-3	0-1	14		300
22	22	A	Q.O.S.	D	2-2	1-1	14	Ashwood, Watt	800
23	Feb 5	H	Forfar	L	1-4	1-0	14	Campbell P.	350
24	12	A	Berwick	W	3-0	2-0	14	Ballantyne, Jack 2	488
25	19	H	Montrose	W	3-1	1-1	14	Campbell, Watt, Ballantyne	300
26	26	A	Stenhousemuir	D	1-1	1-1	14	Ashwood	350
27	Mar 1	H	Cowdenbeath	W	2-0	1-0	13	Meakin, Ballantyne	300
28	5	H	Forfar	L	0-1	0-1	13		250
29	12	A	Cowdenbeath	L	1-3	1-2	13	Jack	300
30	15	A	Brechin City	L	0-3	0-2	13		450
31	19	H	Meadowbank	L	1-2	1-2	13	Meakin P.	500
32	26	A	Stranraer	L	0-1	0-1	13	Sweeney	250
33	Apr 2	H	Brechin City	D	2-2	0-0	14	Ballantyne, Renwick	250
34	9	A	Arbroath	L	0-4	0-1	14		482
35	16	H	Q.O.S.	L	0-1	0-0	14		250
36	23	A	Berwick	W	3-1	2-0	13	Gibson 2, Steen	497
37	30	H	Albion Rovers	L	1-3	1-1	13	Steel	250
38	May 7	H	East Fife	D	1-1	0-0	13	Meakin	500
39	14	A	Stirling Alb.	L	1-3	0-1	13	Grant	1050

Final League Position: 13

Goalscorers

League: Gibson 6, Grant 4, Ballantyne 4, McCaig 3, Ashwood 3, Campbell 3, Meakin 3, Watts 3, Jack 3, Renwick 2, Ross 1, Hughes 1, Rennie 1, Steen 1, Steel 1, Trialist 1, opponent 1.
League Cup: Gibson 2, Watt, Gray.

Honours
Scottish League – Division 2 Champions 1931–32; Runners-up 1962–63, 1979–80.
Record Victory: 10-1 v Stenhousemuir, Scottish 1st rd, 1 Sept, 1888.
Record Defeat: 1-12 v Dundee U, Division 2, 13 Apr, 1936.
Most League Points: 55, Division 2, 1931–32.
Most Individual League Goals in a Season: 36, Malcolm Morrison, Division 2, 1938–39.
Most Capped Player: Humphrey Jones, 5, Wales.

Marshall	Young	Renwick	Kettings	Caldwell	Rennie	Edgar	Watt	Gibson	Gray	Ross	Blair	Tierney	Trialist	McCaig	Ashwood	Grant	Newman	McShane	Meakin	Campbell	Tempany	Leetion	Trialist	Hughes	Jack	Wood	Strickland	Ballantyne	Lapsley	Steen	*Match No.*
1		2	3	4	5	7	8	9	10	11†			14																		1
*1		2	10	4	5	12	8	9	6†	11	3	7*																			2
1		2	10†	4	5	12	8*	9	6	11	3	7																			3
*1		4	3	5		7		9	11	6	*2			8			10	12													4
1		4	3	12		7		9†	10	11*	5	2	6	8				14													5
*1		4	3	12		7*	10	8	11		5	2	6	9																	6
1		4	3	12		7*	8	9†	6		5	2		10	11			14													7
1		5	6	7			10	4			3	2		8	11	9*		12													8
1		5	6	7			12	10			3*	2		8	11	9															9
1		5	3	7			10*	11	6			2		8		9		12													10
1		4			5			12	6		3	2		8*	11	9	7									10					11
*1		2			6	*	14	9	12		3	4	5		10		7				11†	8									12
1		3	12				10*	9				2			11				4	5	6	8									13
1		3						9				2		7*	11	12			6	5	8	10	4								14
1		3	14				4*	9	7			2		12	11				6	5	8†	10									15
	1	3						9			5	2		8†	11	10			6	4		7*		14	12						16
	1	2			5			9*			3			10	11	12			6	4		14		7†	11						17
*	1				5		10	14			3	2		9†	11	7*			6	4	12				8						18
*					5		10	9			3	2	1	12	11	7*			6	4					8						19
*		12			5		10	9			3	2	1	14	11	7†			6	4*					8						20
	1	3			5			9				2		11	10	12			6	4					8*	7					21
	1	3					12	8			5	2		10	9				4	7					6*	11					22
	1	3			5		8	9				2		7*	10	14			6	4						11†			12		23
	1	3			5		7					2			11				6	4					10		8	9			24
	1	3			5		7	12				2			11				6	4*				10		8	9				25
	1	3			5		7	14				2			11				6	4*				10†		8	9		12		26
*		4			5		7				3	2	1		11				6								10	9		8	27
	1	4					7*	12			5	2			11					6							10	9	3	8	28
	1	4					7†	14			5	2			11					6*					12		10	9	3	8	29
*		8			5*		12†	14			6	2			11								10		7			9	3	4	30
	1	4					12	8			5	2			11					6					7		10	9			31
	1	4			5		12	8			3	2							6	14					10†		7*	9			32
	1	3						7			4	2							6				10		8*		9		11		33
	1	8			5†		14	10			3	2							6								12	9		7	34
	1	3					12	9			2	4							6								10			8	35
	1	3					10	9			2					12			6	5*							8			7	36
	1	3			5		10	8			2								6								8			7	37
	1				5		10*	9			3	2							6								8			7	38
	1	12			5*		10	9†			3	2							6								11			8	39
15	20	34	10	7	21	5	23	30	10	5	29	34	6	15	24	8	3	0	23	18	4	5	3	1	12	3	13	11	3	12	
		+ 2s	+ 2s	+ 3s		+ 2s	+ 8s	+ 7s	+ 1s			+ 1s		+ 3s		+ 5s		+ 5s		+ 1s	+ 1s	+ 1s		+ 1s	+ 2s	+ 1s	+ 2s			+ 2s	

Despite using an incredible 47 players during the season, the Falkirk team got no nearer to finding a settled selection. Manager Billy Little, appointed midway through the season, will make that his first priority after the club has slipped from the First Division to second bottom place in Division Two in two seasons.

FALKIRK — Division 1

Year Formed: 1876.
Ground: Brockville Park. *Size:* 100yd×70yd. *Capacity:* 22,550 (2750 seats).
Telephone: Falkirk 24121
Manager: Alex Totten. Asst Manager: Gregor Abel. *Physiotherapist/Trainer:* Tom Logan.
Secretary: W. Barrie Scott, C.A. *PRO:* William McFarlane.
Club Colours: Navy blue shirts with white trimmings and white motif, white shorts, red stockings.
Club Nickname: The Bairns.
Record Attendance: 23,100 v. Celtic, Scottish Cup 3rd rd, 21 Feb, 1953.

1982-83 LEAGUE RECORD

Match No.	Date	Venue	Opponents	Result	H/T Score	League Pos'n	Goalscorers	Attendance
1	Sept 4	A	Clyde	W 1-0	1-0	5	Smith	630
2	11	A	Dumbarton	L 1-5	0-4	10	Ward	550
3	15	H	Alloa	L 0-1	0-0	6		1000
4	18	H	Hearts	D 1-1	1-1	13	Thomson	3500
5	22	A	Hamilton	L 1-2		12	Oliver M.	800
6	25	H	Airdrie	L 1-3	0-1	13	Brown	2500
7	29	H	Partick Th	W 2-1	1-1	12	Perry, Herd	1400
8	Oct 2	A	St Johnstone	L 0-4	0-1	13		2047
9	9	H	Ayr United	L 1-3	1-2	13	Oliver A.	800
10	16	A	Queen's Park	W 2-0	2-0	13.	Smith, Perry	681
11	23	H	Clydebank	L 0-2	0-0	13		1250
12	30	A	Dunfermline	D 0-0	0-0	13.		1250
13	Nov 6	A	Raith Rovers	L 1-2	0-1	14	Oliver M.	1500
14	13	H	Clyde	L 0-1	0-0	14		2000
15	20	A	Hearts	L 1-3	0-3	14	Ward	4847
16	27	H	Hamilton	W 1-0	0-0	13	Hoggan (pen)	1000
17	Dec 4	H	St. Johnstone	L 0-1	0-0	14		1500
18	11	A	Airdrie	L 1-3	0-1	14	Forrest	1000
19	27	H	Dumbarton	W 2-1	0-0	14	Mackin, Jobson	1400
20	Jan 1	A	Alloa	W 2-0	1-0	12	Houston 2	1758
21	3	H	Raith Rovers	W 2-0	0-0	11	Houston, Herd	1500
22	8	H	Queen's Park	W 2-0	2-0	9	Brown, Hoggan	2500
23	15	A	Ayr United	L 0-4	0-1	10		1107
24	22	H	Dunfermline	W 1-0	1-0	10	Hoggan (pen)	2500
25	Feb 5	A	Clydebank	W 2-0	2-0	10	Hoggan (pen), Brown	542
26	26	A	Airdrie	W 2-0	0-0	10	Forrest, Houston	1100
27	Mar 5	A	Hearts	W 2-1	0-1	10	McCulley, Mackin	5500
28	12	H	Ayr United	W 2-0	1-0	7	Mackin, Houston	1200
29	19	A	St Johnstone	L 0-1	0-0	8		2295
30	23	H	Clyde	L 1-2	1-1	9	Jobson	1200
31	26	H	Hamilton	D 1-1	1-1	8	McCulley (pen).	1100
32	Apr 2	A	Queen's Park	D 1-1	1-1	9	Houston	711
33	6	A	Partick Th	D 1-1	0-1	8	Herd	1500
34	9	H	Clydebank	L 0-2	0-2	9		1300
35	16	A	Partick Th	L 2-4	0-1	9	Kemp, Brown	1534
36	23	A	Raith Rovers	W 3-0	2-0	7	Herd, Jobson, Forrest	800
37	30	H	Alloa	W 2-1	0-0	7	Houston, Jobson	2000
38	May 9	A	Dunfermline	D 2-2	1-0	8	Houston, Mackin	1200
39	14	H	Dumbarton	L 1-2	0-1	8	McCulley	1800

Final League Position: 8

Goalscorers

League: Houston 8, Herd 4, Hoggan 4, Mackin 4, Jobson 4, Brown 4, Forrest 3, McCulley 3, Smith 2, Ward 2, M. Oliver 2, Perry 2, Thomson I, A. Oliver 1, Kemp 1
League Cup: Herd 2, Wilson 1.

Honours
Scottish League: Division 2 Champions 1931–32; Runners-up 1962–63, 1979–80.
Record Victory: 10-1 v Stenhousemuir, Scottish Cup 1st rd, 1 Sept, 1888.
Record Defeat: 1-12 v Dundee U, Division 2, 13 Apr, 1936.
Most League Points: 55, Division 2, 1931–32.
Most Individual League Goals in a Season: 36, Malcolm Morrison, Division 2, 1938–39.
Most Capped Player: Humphrey-Jones, 5, Wales.

Watson	Hoggan	Nicol	Brown	Mackin	Wilson	Perry	Oliver M.	Smith	Ward	Thomson	Herd	Fowler	Masterton	Carroll	Oliver A.	McKenna	Ashwood	Love	McCulley	Forrest	Stevenson	Houston	Jobson	Kemp	Lapsley	Irvine	*Match No.*
1	2	3	4	5	6	7	8	9	10*	11		12															1
1	2	3*	4	5	6†	7	10	14	9	11	8	12															2
*1	2	3	4	5	6	7		9	10	11	8																3
1		2	4	5	14	7	12		9†	11	8	3	6*	10													4
*1		2	4	5		7			9	11	8	3	6	10													5
1	3	2	4		12			9‡	14	11	8		6*	10	5	7											6
*1	3	2	4	5		7		14	12	11*	8			10	6	*9											7
1	3	2	4	5		7		14	12	11†	8			10	6*	9											8
1	11	2	4	5		7	3	8†	14				12	10	6	9*											9
1	3	2	4	5		7		9		11	8			10				6									10
1	3	2	4	5	14	7*	12	9†		11	8			10				6									11
1	3	2	4	5			6			11	10			9	8			7									12
1	3*	2	4	5		12	6			11	8	14		10	9†			7									13
1		2	4	5		9				11	8	3		10	7			6									14
1		2	4	5		10	6		12		8	3*		11	9			7									15
1	3	2	4	5		7		9	10*	12	11				6			8									16
1	3	2	4	5		7	6		11	10	9							8									17
1	3	2	4	5		7		9	*	6	8								10	11	12						18
*1	3	2	4	5							8								6	7	11	9	10				19
1	3	2	14	5		7									12			6	8*	11	4†	9	10				20
*1	3	2	4	5							8								6	7	11	9	10				21
1	3	2	4	5		7					14				8				12	11†	6*	9	10				22
1	3	2	4	5		7					8*							6	14	12	11†	9	10				23
1	3	2	4	5		12									8			6	7	11		9	10*				24
1	3	2	4	5							14				8			6*	7	11†	12	9	10				25
1	3	2	4	5							7				6*			10	8†	11		9					26
1	3*	2	4	5						12	7				6			10†	8	11		9	12				27
1	3	2	4	5							7*				6				8	11	10	9	12				28
1	3	2	4	5						14	12				6				8*	11†	10	9	7				29
*1	3	2	4	5											6	11	10	7			9	8					30
1		2	4	5		12			14						6		11†	10	7		3	9	8*				31
1		2	4	5		7*						11				6		12	10	8		3	9				32
*1		2	4	5		7					8				6	11	10			3	9						33
1		2	4	5		7					8				6*		11†	10	14			9	12	3			34
1		2	4	6		7				14					6*		11†			8	3	10	9	12			35
1	3	2	4	5		12				6	7								8*	14	11	9	10†				36
1		2	4	5		14				6*	7								8†		11	9	10	12	3		37
1		2	4	5						6	7								8		11	9	10		3		38
1		2	4	5						6	7*								8		3	9	12	10		11	39
39	27	39	38	38	3	22	8	8	7	18	29	4	3	12	22	4	5	19	17	12	15	21	14	2	2	1	
			+ 1s		+ 3s	+ 5s	+ 2s	+ 2s	+ 5s	+ 4s	+ 3s	+ 3s	+ 1s		+ 1s		+ 1s		+ 3s	+ 2s	+ 2s		+ 4s	+ 2s			

Bottom of the table when Alex Totten replaced John Haggart in December, Falkirk quickly embarked on a sequence of nine games with just one defeat to turn certain relegation into a position of security in mid table. The eight goals scored by Peter Houston after his move from Albion Rovers emphasised the wisdom of that transfer activity and Falkirk look to have the scope to build and improve again.

FORFAR ATHLETIC Division 2

Year Formed: 1884. *Ground:* Station Park. *Size:* 115yd×69yd. *Capacity:* 9300 (800 seated).
Telephone: Forfar 63576 and 62817.
Manager: Doug Howton. *Secretary:* James Robertson.
Assistant Manager: Henry Hall.
Club Colours: Sky blue shirts with white facings, white shorts, white stockings.
Club Nickname: Loons and Sky Blues.
Record Attendance: 10,780 v Rangers, Scottish Cup 2nd rd, 2 Feb, 1970.

1982-83 LEAGUE RECORD

Match No.	Date	Venue	Opponents	Result	H/T Score	League Pos'n	Goalscorers	Attendance
1	Sept 4	A	Stirling Albion	L 0-2	0-0	13		450
2	8	H	Meadowbank	L 0-1	0-0	14		867
3	11	H	Stenhousemuir	D 0-0	0-0	12		760
4	15	A	Arbroath	L 1-2	0-2	13	Hancock	700
5	18	A	Stranraer	L 1-2	1-1	13	Allan	375
6	22	H	Berwick	D 2-2	1-2	13	Alexander, Clark	867
7	25	H	Q.O.S.	W 1-0	1-0	13	Gallacher	869
8	Oct 2	A	Cowdenbeath	L 1-2	0-2	13	Clark	450
9	9	H	East Stirling	W 5-1	0-1	12	Gallacher 4, Caldwell o.g.	982
10	16	A	Brechin	D 1-1	0-0	12	McPhee P.	800
11	23	H	East Fife	W 4-1	1-1	10	Clark 2, Downie, McPhee (pen)	908
12	Nov 2	A	Albion Rovers	W 1-0	0-0	8	Allan	250
13	6	H	Montrose	D 2-2	0-1	9	Gallacher, Allan	982
14	13	A	Meadowbank	L 0-1	0-0	10		700
15	20	H	Stranraer	W 5-1	5-1	8	McPhee, Clark, Gallacher, Leitch, McDonald	823
16	27	A	Berwick	W 2-1	1-0	7	Clark, McDonald	200
17	Dec 4	H	Cowdenbeath	D 0-0	0-0	7		770
18	27	A	Stenhousemuir	W 1-0	1-0	7	Lorimer	300
19	Jan 1	H	Arbroath	D 1-1	1-1	5	McDonald	1712
20	3	A	Montrose	W 2-1	1-1	5	Clark, McDonald	650
21	15	H	Stirling Albion	D 0-0	0-0	5		930
22	22	H	Albion Rovers	W 2-0	1-0	5	Farningham, McDonald	900
23	Feb 5	A	East Stirling	W 4-1	0-1	5	McDonald 2, McPhee (pen), Clark	350
24	23	A	Arbroath	D 3-3	1-3	5	McDonald 3	818
25	26	H	East Fife	D 0-0	0-0	6		900
26	Mar 2	H	Brechin	W 2-1	2-0	3	Gallacher, Farningham	1503
27	5	A	East Stirling	W 1-1	1-0	3	McDonald	250
28	9	A	East Fife	W 2-0	1-0	3	McDonald, Bennett	700
29	12	H	Stenhousemuir	D 2-2	1-0	3	McDonald, McPhee	945
30	19	A	Albion Rovers	L 0-1	0-1	4		250
31	26	H	Stirling Albion	W 2-0	1-0	4	Liddle, McDonald	825
32	29	A	Q.O.S.	D 1-1	1-0	4	Alexander	500
33	Apr 2	H	Meadowbank	L 0-3	0-0	4		1104
34	9	A	Stranraer	W 2-1	1-1	4	Liddle, McDonald (pen)	200
35	16	H	Cowdenbeath	W 2-1	1-0	4	Cormack, Turnbull	788
36	23	A	Q.O.S.	W 2-1	1-0	4	Turnbull, McDonald	500
37	30	A	Brechin	L 0-1	0-0	4		1217
38	May 7	H	Berwick	D 1-1	1-0	4	Farningham	614
39	13	A	Montrose	W 2-1	1-0	4	McPhee, Gallacher	350

Final League Position: 4

Goalscorers

League: McDonald 16, Gallacher 9, Clark 8, McPhee 6, Allan 3, Farningham 3, Alexander 2, Turnbull 2, Liddle 2, Hancock 1, Downie 1, Leitch 1, Lorimer 1, Bennett 1, Cormack 1, opponents 1.
League Cup: Clark 2, Allan 1, Alexander 1, Porter 1.
Scottish Cup: McDonald 5, Gallacher 2, Lorimer 2, Clark 1, McPhee 1.

Honours
Scottish League Cup – Semi-Finalists 1977–78.
Scottish Cup – Semi-Finalists 1981–82.
Forfarshire Cup – Winners 9 times.
Record Victory - 14-1 v Lindertis, Scottish Cup 1st rd, 1 Sept, 1888.
Record Defeat: 2-12 v King's Park, Division 2, 2 Jan, 1930.
Most League Points: 48, Division 2, 1982–83.
Most Individual League Goals in Season: 45, Dave Kilgour, Division 2, 1929–30.

Kennedy	Graham	Bennett	Lorimer	Brown	Brash	McPhee	Alexander	Morris	Hancock	Leitch	Clark	Allan	Gallacher	Martin	Porter	Newman	Craig	Weir	Downie	McDonald	Farningham	Smith	Turnbull	Cormack	Liddle	Bell	*Match No.*
1		3	2	4*	5	6	7†	8	9	10	11	14	12														1
1		3	2	4		6	12	8	9*	10	11	5	7														2
1		3	2	4	5	6		8		7	12	14	9	10*	11†												3
1		3	2	4†	5	6		8	12	14	11	10	7			9*											4
1		3	2		5	10		4	9*	8	11	6	7		12												5
1			2	4	5	3	12		9*	8	11	6	7		10												6
1		2	3	4	5	8		6		10	11		7		9*		12										7
1		2	3	4	5	11		6*		8	9	12	10				7										8
1		2	3	4	5	8				10	9		11				7	6									9
1		2	3	4	5	8				10	9		11		12		7*	6									10
1		2	10*		5	3		4		7	9		8	14	11†			6	12								11
1		2	10		5	3	14	4			9	12	8†	7*				6	11								12
1		2	10		5	3	9*	4				8	11		12			6	7								13
1		2	12		5*	3		4		7	9	10	11					6	7								14
1			2	14		3	12	4		10	8†	5	11					6	9*	7							15
1			2	6		3		4		7	9	5	11					8		10							16
1				4	5	3		2		8	9	12	7					10	6*	11†				14			17
1		2	8		5	3		6		12	10		11*					4		9	7						18
1		2	8†		5	3		6		14	10	*	11					4		9	7			12			19
1		2				3		4		8	7		9*					6	12	11	10	5					20
1		2			5	3		4		8			9					6		11	10		7*	12			21
1		2	12	4	5	3				14			9					6		11	8		10*	7†			22
1		2	10	4	5	3				7*	12		9					6		11	8						23
1		2	10†	4	5	3		6		14	7		9*							11	8			12			24
1		2		4	5	3		6		10			12							11	8			7*	9		25
1		2	7	4	5	3	12						9					6		11	8				10*		26
1		2	7	4	5	3	10						9					6		11	8						27
1		2	7	4	5	3							9					6		11	8				10		28
	1	2*		4	5	3				7		12	9					6		11	8				10		29
	1	2		4	5	3		14		7			9*					6†		11	8			12	10		30
1		2		4	5	3	7	6			14		9							11	8*		12		10†		31
1				4	5	3	7	2			12		9*							11	8				10		32
1		2*			5	3	7	6			14		9†							11	8	4	12		10		33
1		2	10	4		3						5						6		11	8			7	9		34
1		2	10*	4		3						5						6		11	8		12	7	9		35
1		2		4		3	6	5												11	8		10	7	9		36
*1		2		4		3	6	5		14	12									11	8		10*	7†	9		37
1		2*			5	6		4		7	9		12					14		11†	8		10			3	38
1			3	4	5	10		2		7	9*		8					6		11†			12	14			39
37	2	33	25	27	31	39	8	27	4	22	21	10	32	2	4	1	3	24	5	25	21	2	5	6	12	1	
			+ 2s	+ 1s			+ 5s	+ 1s	+ 1s	+ 6s	+ 6s	+ 6s	+ 3s	+ 1s	+ 3s		+ 1s	+ 1s	+ 2s				+ 4s	+ 6s			

The opening weeks of the season presented Forfar with a leeway so great that even a consistent run of form from the end of September could not overcome.
Their 46 points from 30 games after taking six outings to gain a first success would have been enough to win a place in Division One if extended through the whole season and Forfar are likely to go close again.

HAMILTON ACADEMICAL Division 1

Year Formed: 1875.
Ground: Douglas Park (since 1888). *Size:* 104yd×72yd. *Capacity:* 14,065 (1065 seated).
Telephone: Hamilton 286103.
Manager: Bertie Auld. *Commercial Manager:* David S. Morrison.
Secretary: Joseph Friel. *PRO:* Alan Dick. *Physiotherapist:* R. Reid. *Coach:* P. Barkey.
Club Colours: Red and white hooped shirts, white shorts with white stockings.
Club Nickname: The Accies.
Record attendance: 28,690 v Hearts, Scottish Cup 3rd rd, 3 Mar, 1937.
Previous Grounds: Bent Farm, South Avenue, South Haugh.
Record Transfer Fee Received: £27,500 from Dundee United for Paul Hegarty, Nov 1974.
Record Transfer Fee Paid: £15,000 to Motherwell for Bobby Graham, July 1977.

1982-83 LEAGUE RECORD

Match No.	Date	Venue	Opponents	Result		H/T Score	League Pos'n	Goalscorers	Attendance
1	Sept 4	A	St Johnstone	L	0-3	0-0	14		1519
2	8	H	Queen's Park	D	2-2	0-1	12	Craig, McDowall	750
3	11	H	Dunfermline	W	4-1	2-1	6	Wilson, Fairlie 3 (2 pens)	800
4	15	A	Airdrie	L	0-2	0-0	9		1200
5	18	A	Ayr United	D	1-1	1-0	9	Fairlie P.	1470
6	22	H	Falkirk	W	2-1	0-1	6	Oliver A. (og), Wilson	800
7	25	A	Alloa	L	2-4	2-2	9	Fairlie, Wright	727
8	Oct 2	H	Partick Th	L	1-2	0-0	10	McDowall	1663
9	9	A	Dumbarton	W	5-1	1-0	9	Donnelly, McNaught, Craig, Fairlie, Murphy	700
10	16	H	Hearts	L	1-3	1-0	10	Donnelly	2204
11	23	A	Raith Rovers	L	1-4	1-1	10	Wright	1000
12	30	H	Clyde	W	1-0	0-0	9	Donnelly	843
13	Nov 6	H	Clydebank	L	0-2	0-1	9		887
14	13	A	Queen's Park	W	3-1	2-1	9	Fairlie 2, Mitchell	844
15	20	H	Ayr United	D	1-1	0-1	9	Wright	783
16	27	A	Falkirk	L	0-1	0-0	9		1000
17	Dec 4	A	Partick Th	D	1-1	1-0	9	Phillips	1892
18	11	H	Alloa	D	1-1	1-1	9	Gorman	703
19	18	H	St Johnstone	D	1-1	1-0	9	Fairlie	1213
20	27	A	Dunfermline	D	1-1	0-1	9	Fairlie P.	1500
21	Jan 1	H	Airdrie	L	0-4	0-2	9		1586
22	3	A	Clydebank	L	1-2	0-0	10	Treanor (og)	650
23	8	A	Hearts	L	1-2	1-1	11	Donnelly	5081
24	15	H	Dumbarton	L	0-3	0-0	12		724
25	22	A	Clyde	L	2-5	1-1	13	Wright, Fairlie P.	833
26	Feb 5	H	Raith Rovers	D	2-2	2-0	13	McLaughlin, Phillips	724
27	12	A	St Johnstone	W	2-0	2-0	12	McLaughlin, McDowall	2321
28	26	H	Dunfermline	W	4-0	0-0	11	Fairlie 2, Phillips, McLaughlin	943
29	Mar 5	H	Airdrie	L	0-3	0-2	12		1000
30	15	A	Queen's Park	W	4-1	1-0	12	Wright, McLaughlin 2, Phillips	693
31	19	H	Raith Rovers	L	0-5	0-0	12		824
32	26	A	Falkirk	D	1-1	1-1	12	McLaughlin	1100
33	Apr 2	H	Alloa	W	2-0	0-0	12	McDowall, Wright	839
34	9	H	Partick Th	D	0-0	0-0	11		1493
35	16	A	Dumbarton	D	1-1	0-1	11	Hamill	400
36	23	A	Ayr United	W	1-0	1-0	11	McLaughlin	852
37	30	A	Clydebank	D	1-1	1-1	11	Fairlie P.	576
38	May 7	H	Clyde	W	4-1	0-0	8	Fairlie, McDowall, Hamill, McLaughlin	1233
39	14	A	Hearts	L	0-2	0-1	11		9136

Final League Position: 11

Goalscorers

League: Fairlie 15, McLaughlin 8, Wright 6, McDowall 5, Donnelly 4, Phillips 4, Craig 2, Wilson 2, Hamill 2, opponents 2, McNaught 1, Murphy 1, Mitchell 1, Gorman 1.
League Cup: Fairlie 2, McDowall 1.

Honours
Scottish League: Division 2 Champions 1903–04; Runners-up 1952–53, 1964–65.
Scottish Cup: Runners-up 1911, 1935. *Lanarkshire Cup:* 9 times winners
Best Season: 4th in Division 1, 1934–35.
Record Victory: 10-2 v Cowdenbeath, Division 1, 15 Oct, 1932.
Record Defeat: 1-11 v Hibernian, Division 1, 6 Nov, 1965.
Most League Points: 55, Division 2, 1973–74.
Most League Goals: 92, Division 1, 1932–33.
Most Individual League Goals in a Season: 34, David Wilson, 1936–37.
Highest Scorer in Total Aggregate: 246, David Wilson, 1928–39.
Most Capped Players: Jimmy King, 2, Bobby Howe, 2, Scotland.
Extra Information: The hat-trick by John Brown v Berwick R, 9 Aug, 1980, is the only one (without the aid of a penalty) by a full-back in Scottish League history.

Howie	Ferguson	McNaught	Coglan	Wright	McDougall	Blackley	Fairlie	McDowall	Craig	Marshall	Mitchell	Hamill	Wilson	Donnelly	Brown	Murphy	McAdam	MacLeod	Moffat	Marshall	Paton	Gorman	Hackett	Frew	Phillips	Sammeroff	McLelland	McLaughlin	Lapsley	Spiers	Callan	*Match No.*
	1	2	3	4	5	6	7	8	9	10*	11†	12										14											1
	1	2	3	4	5	6	7		8	10	11		9																				2
	1	2		4		6	7	10	8		5	3	9	11*																		12	3
	1	2		4		6	7	10	8		5	3	9	11																			4
	1	2			5		7	10	9		6	4	8		3	11																5
*	1	2			5		7	10	9		6	4	8		3	11																6
	1	2		4	5		7	10	9†	14	6	12	8		3*	11																7
14	1	2		4	5		7	10	9†		6	12	8		3*	11																8
	1	2		4	5		7	10	14		6	3	12	9†		11	8*															9
	1	2		4	5		7	8	12		6*	3	14	9		11	10†															10
	1	2		4	5		7	8	11	12		3	14	9	6*		10†															11
		2		4	5		7	6	9*			3	14	12			11		1	8	10†											12
		2		4	5			8	9			3	7	12			11		1	6	10*											13
	1	2		4	5		7				8	3	11				10			6		9										14
	1	2		4	5		7	8			10	3	11*							6	12	9										15
	1	2		4	5		7	8	14	12	6*	3					10					11	9†									16
	1			4	5		7	8		12	6	3		10								11*		2	9							17
	1			4	5		7	8			6	3		10*			12					11		2	9							18
	1			4	5		7	8			6	3					10					11		2	9							19
*	1			4	5		7	8			6	3					11					10		2	9							20
	1	12		4	5		7			8	6	3		10							14	11†		2*	9							21
*	1			4	5		7	8			6		3				10					11		2	9							22
12	1	2		4	5	11	7				6	3		10*										8	9							23
12		2		4	5	6	7	8			3	11		10*											9	1						24
	1	2		4			7	8			6	3		11*								12			9		5	10				25
	1	2		4	5		7	8			3									10		11			9			6				26
	1	2		10	5	4	7	8			3														9		6	11				27
	1	2		10	5	6	7	8			3*	12													9		4	11				28
1	2*		10	5	6	7	8			3							14				12			9			4†	11				29
*	1	2		10	5	6	7	8			3														9		4	11				30
	1	14		2	5	6*	7	8			3							12				11†			9		4	10				31
	1			2	5	4	7	8			3	12		10*											9		6	11				32
	1			2	5	6	7	8			12	3		11*											9		4	10				33
	1			2	5	6	7	8				3		11											9		4	10*		12		34
	1			2	5	6	7	8			12	14		10													4	11†	3	9*		35
1			2	5	6	7	8				3		4														9	11	10			36
	1			2	5	6	7	8				11		12	3										9*		4	10				37
	1			2	5	6	7	8				11			3										9		4	10				38
	1	12		2	5	6	7	8				11		14	3										9		4*	10†				39
0	36	24	3	37	36	19	38	35	11	3	29	26	11	16	8	6	10	0	2	5	2	11	1	7	21	1	14	15	2	1	0	
+3s		+3s							+3s	+4s	+2s	+6s	+4s	+4s			+1s	+2s			+3s	+2s								+1s	+1s	

Unreliable in a season when Bertie Auld was their third manager, but there are talented players in the side with free scoring midfield player Jamie Fairlie the pick. Only four wins away from home reveals their difficulty but under Auld they are likely to be nearer the top than the bottom this season.

HEART OF MIDLOTHIAN Premier Division

Year Formed: 1874.
Ground: Tyneside Park, Gorgie Road, Edinburgh EH11 2NL. *Size:* 110yd×76yd. *Capacity:* 23,450 (7000 seats).
Telephone: 031-337 6132.
Manager: Alex MacDonald. *Asst. Manager:* Sandy Jardine.
Secretary: L. W. Porteous. *Trainer:* Andy Stevenson.
Club Colours: Maroon shirts, white collar and cuffs, white shorts, maroon stockings with white tops.
Club Nickname: Jam Tarts.
Record Attendance: 53,496 v Rangers, Scottish Cup 3rd rd, 13 Feb, 1932.
Previous Grounds: The Meadows, 1873–78; Powderhall, 1878–81; Tynecastle, 1881–86; Tyneside Park, 1886–
Record Transfer Fee Received: £200,000 from Chelsea for Eamonn Bannon, Jan 1979.
Record Transfer Fee Paid: £100,000 to Dundee U for Willie Pettigrew, Sept 1981.
European Competitions: *European Cup* 1958–59, 1960–61; *Fairs Cup* 1961–62, 1963–64, 1965–66; *European Cup-Winners' Cup* 1976–77.

1982-83 LEAGUE RECORD

Match No.	Date	Venue	Opponents	Result	H/T Score	League Pos'n	Goalscorers	Attendance
1	Sept 4	A	Queen's Park	W 2-1	0-1	4	Marinello, Bowman	1817
2	11	H	Ayr United	D 1-1	0-0	5	O'Connor	5601
3	15	A	St. Johnstone	D 1-1	0-0	1	Pettigrew	3900
4	18	A	Falkirk	D 1-1	1-1	6	O'Connor	3500
5	25	H	Clyde	W 1-0	0-0	6	Bowman	4734
6	29	H	Clydebank	W 4-1	2-0	4	Pettigrew, O'Connor, Jardine (pen), Byrne	5500
7	Oct 2	A	Raith Rovers	L 0-1	0-0	5		3000
8	6	H	Dumbarton	D 1-1	0-0	5	O'Connor	5000
9	9	H	Alloa	W 3-0	0-0	2	R. MacDonald, Robertson, Holt o.g.	4382
10	16	A	Hamilton	W 3-1	0-1	2	A. MacDonald, Byrne, O'Connor	2204
11	23	A	Dunfermline	W 4-1	0-1	2	O'Connor, Bowman, Johnstone, A. MacDonald	5997
12	30	A	Partick Th.	D 1-1	0-1	2	Robertson	3045
13	Nov 6	H	Airdrie	L 2-4	1-3	3	O'Connor, Jardine (pen)	5656
14	13	A	Clydebank	W 3-0	1-0	2	Mackay, O'Connor, Robertson	2116
15	20	H	Falkirk	W 3-1	3-0	2	Johnstone, Robertson 2	4847
16	27	A	Dumbarton	D 1-1	0-0	2	O'Connor	3000
17	Dec 4	H	Raith Rovers	W 2-0	1-0	2	Mackay, Johnstone (pen)	4190
18	11	A	Clyde	W 3-2	1-0	2	A. MacDonald, Pettigrew 2	2300
19	27	A	Ayr United	W 3-0	3-0	2	Pettigrew, O'Connor, A. MacDonald	2500
20	Jan 1	H	St. Johnstone	W 1-0	1-0	2	Pettigrew	14,554
21	3	A	Airdrie	W 1-0	0-0	2	Pettigrew	4500
22	8	H	Hamilton	W 2-1	1-1	2	Pettigrew, O'Connor	5081
23	15	A	Alloa	D 0-0	0-0	1		2591
24	22	H	Partick Th.	L 0-1	0-0	1		7061
25	Feb 9	A	Dunfermline	L 1-2	0-1	2	R. MacDonald	3500
26	12	H	Ayr United	W 5-1	2-1	1	O'Connor, Pettigrew, Mackay, Bowman, Byrne	4294
27	26	A	Queen's Park	W 3-0	1-0	1	Robertson	1468
28	Mar 5	H	Falkirk	L 1-2	1-0	2	O'Connor	5500
29	19	H	Partick Th.	W 4-0	1-0	2	Robertson 3, Pettigrew	7000
30	26	H	Clyde	W 3-1	1-0	2	Robertson, Mackay, R. MacDonald	4647
31	29	A	Raith Rovers	L 2-4	1-1	2	Johnstone 2 (1 pen)	2100
32	Apr 2	A	Airdrie	W 2-0	1-0	1	Mackay (pen), Robertson	3000
33	6	H	Queen's Park	W 2-0	1-0	1	Robertson, O'Connor	5500
34	9	A	St. Johnstone	L 1-2	0-1	1	Bowman	7501
35	16	H	Clydebank	D 2-2	1-1	2	Robertson 2	6432
36	23	A	Alloa	D 1-1	1-0	2	A. MacDonald	2395
37	30	H	Dunfermline	D 3-3	2-0	2	Robertson 3	6427
38	May 7	A	Dumbarton	W 4-0	2-0	2	Robertson 2, O'Connor, Mackay	4000
39	14	H	Hamilton	W 2-0	1-0	2	Johnston, O'Connor	9136

Final League Position: 2

Goalscorers

League: Robertson 21, O'Connor 17, Pettigrew 9, Johnston 6, MacKay 6, Bowman 5, A. MacDonald 5, Byrne 3, R. MacDonald 3, Jardin 2, Marinello 1, Opponent 1.
League Cup: Pettigrew 7, O'Connor 4, A. MacDonald 3, Shields 2, Bowman 2, Marinello 1, Opponent 1.
Scottish Cup: O'Connor 2, Shields 1, A. MacDonald 1, R. MacDonald 1.

Honours

Scottish League – Division 1 Champions 1894–95, 1896–97, 1957–58, 1959–60, 1979–80; Runners-up 1893–94, 1898–99, 1903–04, 1905–06, 1914–15, 1937–38, 1953–54, 1956–57, 1958–59, 1964–65, 1977–78, 1982–83.
Scottish Cup – Winners 1891, 1896, 1901, 1906, 1956; Runners-up 1903, 1907, 1968, 1976.
Scottish League Cup – Winners 1954–55, 1958–59, 1959–60, 1962–63; Runners-up 1961–62.
Record Victory: 15-0 v King's Park, Scottish Cup 2nd rd, 13 Feb, 1937.
Record Defeat: 0-7 v Hibernian, Division 1, 1 Jan, 1973.
Most League Points: 62, Division 1, 1957–58.
Most League Goals: 132, Division 1, 1957–58. (Record for Division 1.)
Most Individual Goals in Season: 44, Barney Battles, 1930–31.
Highest Scorer in Total Aggregate: Jimmy Wardhaugh, 206, 1946–59.
Most Capped Player: Bobby Walker, 29, Scotland.

Smith	Kidd	Shields	Byrne	MacDonald, R.	Jardine	Bowman	Pettigrew	O'Connor	MacDonald, A.	McCoy	Marinello	MacLaren	Mackay	Johnston	Robertson	Gauld	*Match No.*
1	2	3	4	5	6	7	8	9	10*	11†	14	12					1
1	2	3	4	5	6	7	8	9	10	12	11*						2
1	2	3	4	5	6	7	8	9	11			10					3
1	2	3	4*	5	6	7	8†	9	10		11	12	14				4
1	2	3	4	5	6	7	8	9					10	11			5
1	2	3	4	5	6	7	8	9	10					11			6
1		2	3*	4	5	6	7	8	9†		14		12	10	11		7
1	2	3	4	5	6	7	8	9					10	11			8
1	2	3	4	5	6	7	8*	9	14				10	11†	12		9
1	2	3	4	5	6	7	8*	9	10					11	12		10
1	2	3	4	5	6	7	8	9*	10			14		11†	12		11
1	2	3	4*	5	6	7	8*	9	10				12	11	12		12
1	2	3	4*	5	6	7		9		14		10	12	11†	8		13
1	2	3		5	6	7		9	10				4	11	8		14
1	2	3	12	5	6	7	14	9	10*				4	11†	8		15
1	2		14	5	6	7	12	9	10*				4	11†	8	3	16
1	2			5	6	7	12	9	10				4	11	8*	3	17
1	2		4	5	6	7	8	9	11				10			3	18
1	2		4	5	6	7	8	9	11				10			3	19
1	2		4	5	6	7	8	9				11	10			3	20
1	2		4	5	6	7	8	9	11			10				3	21
1	2	3	4	5	6	7	8	9	11				10*	12			22
1	2	3	4	5	6	7	8	9	10				12	11*			23
1	2	3	4*	5	6	7	8†	9	10				11	12	14		24
1	2	3	7	5	6	4	8	9					10		11		25
1	2	3	7	5	6	4	8	9					10	11			26
1		3	7	5	6	4	8	9*	12				10		11	2	27
1		3	7*	5	6	4	8†	9	10	14			12		11	2	28
1	2			5	6	4	8	9	10				7		11	3	29
1	2			5	6	4	12	9*	10				7	11	8	3	30
1	2			5	6*	4	9		10			12	7	11	8	3	31
1	2			5	6	4		9				10	7	11	8	3	32
1	2			5	6	4		9	10				7	11	8	3	33
1	2			5	6	4	12	9	10				7	11*	8	3	34
1	2			5	6	4	12	9*	10			3	7	11	8		35
1	2		7*	5	6	4	9†	14	10			3	11	12	8		36
1	2			5	6	4		9*	10	12			7	11	8	3	37
1	2			5	6	4		9	10				7	11	8	3	38
1	2		12	5	6	4	14	9†	10				7	11	8	3*	39
39	37	22	25	39	39	39	26	37	29	1	2	8	26	24	19	17	
			+				+	+	+	+	+	+	+	+	+		
			3s				7s	1s	2s	5s	1s	5s	6s	3s	4s		

Big financial gamble by the Edinburgh club to win promotion paid off but their very experienced side may find the task of staying up rather demanding.
Never out of the first two since early October, Hearts had not only to thank player manager Alex MacDonald for plotting their way to the Premier League but also for his strong influence from midfield.

HIBERNIAN Premier Division

Year Formed: 1875. *Ground:* Easter Road Park. *Size:* 112yd×74yd. *Capacity:* 29,464 (6636 seats).
Telephone: 031-661 2159.
Manager: Pat Stanton. *Secetary:* C. F. Graham.
Club Colours: Green shirts with white collars and sleeves, white shorts, green and white stockings.
Club Nickname: Hi-Bees.
Record Attendance: 66,840 v Hearts, Division 1, 2 Jan, 1950.
Previous Name: Edinburgh Hibernians. *Previous Ground:* Mayfield 1875–80.
Record Transfer Fee Received: £275,000 from Aston Villa for Des Bremner, Sept 1979.
Record Transfer Fee Paid: £120,000 to Everton for Joe Harper, Feb 1974.
European Competitions: *European Cup* 1955–56; *European Cup-Winners' Cup* 1972–73; *Fairs Cup* 1960–61,1961–62, 1962–63, 1965–66, 1967–68, 1968–69; *UEFA Cup* 1973–74, 1974–75, 1976–77, 1978–79.

1982-83 LEAGUE RECORD

Match No.	Date	Venue	Opponents	Result		H/T Score	League Pos'n	Goalscorers	Attendance
1	Sept 4	H	St Mirren	D	0-0	0-0	—		5471
2	11	A	Kilmarnock	D	1-1	1-0	7	Jamieson	2800
3	18	H	Dundee United	D	0-0	0-0	6		5350
4	25	A	Celtic	L	0-2	0-1	6		16,371
5	Oct 2	H	Morton	L	1-2	1-0	8	Thomson	4000
6	9	A	Dundee	L	1-2	1-1	10	Rae	5287
7	16	H	Motherwell	W	1-0	0-0	7	Rae	4000
8	23	A	Rangers	L	2-3	1-2	8	Murray 2	17,000
9	30	H	Aberdeen	D	1-1	0-0	8	Murray	6000
10	Nov 6	A	St Mirren	L	0-3	0-3	8		3660
11	13	H	Kilmarnock	D	2-2	1-1	8	Thomson, Jamieson	4132
12	20	A	Dundee United	L	0-3	0-1	9		7374
13	27	H	Celtic	L	2-3	0-1	10	Murray 2	17,121
14	Dec 4	A	Morton	D	0-0	0-0	10		1800
15	11	H	Dundee	D	1-1	0-1	8	Rae	5350
16	18	A	Motherwell	W	1-0	1-0	7	Murray	3815
17	27	H	Rangers	D	0-0	0-0	7		16,000
18	Jan 1	A	Aberdeen	L	0-2	0-2	7		14,000
19	3	H	St Mirren	D	1-1	1-0	8	Duncan	6080
20	8	A	Kilmarnock	W	2-0	2-0	6	Conroy, Jamieson	2100
21	15	H	Dundee United	D	0-0	0-0	7		5000
22	22	A	Celtic	L	1-4	1-1	7	MacLeod o.g.	17,106
23	Feb 5	H	Morton	W	2-0	1-0	6	Harvey, Rae	4736
24	22	A	Dundee	W	1-0	1-0	6	Rice	4363
25	26	H	Motherwell	D	1-1	1-1	5	Irvine	4300
26	Mar 5	A	Rangers	D	1-1	0-0	7	Jamieson	10,975
27	19	A	St Mirren	L	0-3	0-0	7		4215
28	26	A	Dundee United	D	3-3	1-3	7	Rae, Irvine, Rice	7279
29	Apr 2	H	Kilmarnock	W	8-1	2-1	6	Duncan, Thomson 2, Irvine 2 McNamara, Rae, McCurdy	4000
30	9	H	Celtic	L	0-3	0-2	7		15,500
31	16	A	Morton	W	1-0	0-0	6	Thomson	2400
32	23	H	Dundee	D	0-0	0-0	6		4000
33	30	A	Motherwell	L	0-2	0-1	6		3532
34	May 2	H	Aberdeen	D	0-0	0-0	6		8000
35	7	H	Rangers	L	1-2	0-2	7	Callachan	10,500
36	14	A	Aberdeen	L	0-5	0-2	7		24,000

Final League Position: 7

Goalscorers

League: Rae 6, Murray 6, Thomson 5, Jamieson 4, Irvine 4, Duncan 2, Rice 2, Conroy 1 Harvey 1, McNamara 1, McCurdy 1, Callachan 1, opponent 1.
League Cup: Rae 3, Rodier 1, Murray 1, Welsh 1.
Scottish Cup: Rae 1

Honours
Scottish League – Division 1 Champions 1902–03, 1947–48, 1950–51, 1951–52, 1980–81; Runners-up 1896–97, 1946–47, 1949–50, 1952–53, 1973–74; Division 2 Champions 1893–94, 1894–95, 1932–33.
Scottish Cup – Winners 1887, 1902; Runners-up 1896, 1914, 1923, 1924, 1947, 1958, 1972, 1979.
Scottish League Cup – Winners 1972–73; Runners-up 1950–51, 1968–69, 1974–75.
Drybrough Cup – Winners 1972–73, 1973–74.
Record Victory: 15-1 v Peebles Rovers, Scottish Cup 2nd rd, 11 Feb, 1961.
Record Defeat: 0-10 v Rangers, Division 1, 4 Dec, 1898.
Most League Points: 57, Division 1, 1980–81.
Most Individual League Goals in Season: 42, Joe Baker, Division 1, 1959–60.
Most Capped Player: Lawrie Reilly, 38, Scotland.

McArthur	Rough	Sneddon	Schaedler	McNamara	Welsh	Brazil	Callachan	Flavell	Rae	Murray	Duncan	Jamieson	Thomson	Turnbull	Irvine	Rice	Conroy	Robertson	Smith	Harvey	Rodier	Byrne	McCurdy	McKee	*Match No.*
1		2	3	4	5	6	7	8	9	10*	11										12				1
1		2	3	4		6	7	8*	5	11	12	9†	10	14											2
1		2	3	4	8	6*	7	12	5	11	14	9†	10												3
1		2	3*	4		6	7	11	5	10		8	9	12											4
1		2		4			7		5	11	3	9	10	6	8	11									5
1		2		4			7		5		3	9	10	6	8										6
1		2		4			7		5	12	3	9*		6	10		8	11							7
1*		2		4			7		5	11	3		10	6	9		8				12				8
1		2		4			7*		5	11	3		10	6	9		8	12							9
1		2		4			7		5	11	3		10*	6	9		8		12						10
1		2					7		5	11	3		10*	6	9		4	12	8						11
1		2					7		5	11	3	12	10	6	9*		4		8						12
	1	2			12		7*		5	11	3	9	10	6			4		8						13
	1	2					7		5	11	9	4	10	3			8		6						14
	1	2		6			7		9	10	3	5		4			8	11							15
	1	2		6			7		4	11	9	5		3		10	8								16
	1	2		6			7		4	11	9	5		3		10	8								17
	1	2		6			7†		4	11	9	5	12	3*		10	8					14			18
	1	2		6					4	11	9	5	8	3		10*	7	12							19
	1	2		6					4	11	9	5	8	3†	12	10	7								20
	1	2		6	4				5	11	9		10*	3	12	8	7								21
	1	2		6	4				5	11*	9	12		3	10	8	7								22
	1	2	3	6	10*				5	12	7		9	4	14	8				11†					23
	1	2*	3	6					5		14		10	4	9	8	7			11					24
	1	2		6	12				5		3*		10	4	9	8	7			11					25
	1	2		6					5		12	4	10	3	9	8*	7			11†				14	26
	1	2		6			4		5	12	3		10		9	8	7			11*					27
	1	2		6			12		5		3		10	4	9	8	7*			11					28
	1	2		6			7		5		3		10	4	9	8				11*			14		29
	1	2		6		12	7		5	14	3		10	4	9*	8				11†					30
	1	2	14			6	7*		5		3		10	4	9	8				11†			12		31
	1	2			5	4	7				3	14	10	6	9†	8				11*			12		32
	1	2			4	6	7				3	5	9	10		8*				11			12		33
	1	3			5	4	7			9	11		10		8	6								2	34
	1	3		12	5	4	7			8*	11		10		9	6				14				2†	35
	1	3		6	5†	4	7				11		10		9	8	2*			14				12	36
12	24	36	6	27	10	10	27	3	31	22	31	16	29	28	21	22	22	2	4	11	0	0	0	2	
			+ 1s	+ 1s	+ 2s	+ 1s	+ 1s	+ 1s		+ 4s	+ 4s	+ 3s	+ 1s	+ 2s	+ 3s			+ 3s	+ 1s	+ 2s	+ 2s	+ 1s	+ 4s	+ 2s	

Treble chance experts with 15 draws and that statistic indicates their state of development. Another season of turmoil behind the scenes that leaves stability the most needed quality. Some promising youngsters have made the breakthrough, notably Youth cap Brian Rice, but a few more needed if real progress is to be achieved.

KILMARNOCK Division 1

Year Formed: 1869
Ground: Rugby Park. *Size:* 115yd×75yd. *Capacity:* 18,500 (4200 seats).
Telephone: Kilmarnock 25184
Manager: Jim Clunie. *Asst. Manager:* Davy Wilson. *Secretary/General Manager:* Walter W. McCrae.
Trainer/Physiotherapist: Hugh Allan.
Club Colours: Blue and white hoops, blue shorts.
Club Nickname: Killie
Record Attendance: 34,246 v Rangers, League Cup, Aug 1963.
Record Transfer Fee Received: £120,000 from Celtic for David Provan, Sept 1978
European Competitions: *European Cup* 1965–66; *Fairs Cup* 1964–65, 1966–67, 1969–70.

1982-83 LEAGUE RECORD

Match No.	Date	Venue	Opponents	Result		H/T Score	League Pos'n	Goalscorers	Attendance
1	Sept 4	A	Morton	D	0-0	0-0	—		2300
2	11	H	Hibernian	D	1-1	0-1	6	Clarke	2800
3	18	A	Rangers	L	0-5	0-2	8		17,000
4	25	H	Dundee	D	0-0	0-0	8		2000
5	Oct 2	A	St Mirren	L	2-3	2-2	9	McLean, Mauchlen	3568
6	9	H	Dundee United	D	1-1	1-0	8	Gallagher	2500
7	16	A	Celtic	L	1-2	0-0	9	Clarke	11,063
8	23	H	Aberdeen	L	0-2	0-1	9		3400
9	30	A	Motherwell	L	1-4	1-1	10	McLean	3016
10	Nov 6	H	Morton	W	3-1	1-0	9	J. Clark, Gallagher, Bourke	1850
11	13	A	Hibernian	D	2-2	1-1	9	Bryson, McDicken	4132
12	20	H	Rangers	D	0-0	0-0	7		9500
13	27	A	Dundee	L	2-5	0-3	8	J. Clark, MacLeod	4311
14	Dec 4	H	St Mirren	D	2-2	1-0	7	Clarke, Bourke	2200
15	11	A	Dundee United	L	0-7	0-1	10		7259
16	18	H	Celtic	L	0-4	0-1	10		9000
17	27	A	Aberdeen	L	0-2	0-1	10		14,500
18	Jan 1	H	Motherwell	L	0-2	0-1	10		3300
19	3	A	Morton	L	0-3	0-1	10		3500
20	8	H	Hibernian	L	0-2	0-2	10		2100
21	15	A	Rangers	D	1-1	0-0	10	McGivern	7000
22	22	H	Dundee	W	2-0	1-0	10	Gallagher, J. Clark (pen)	1900
23	Feb 5	A	St Mirren	L	0-2	0-1	10		3303
24	12	H	Dundee United	L	0-5	0-2	10		1850
25	26	A	Celtic	L	0-4	0-1	10		10,691
26	Mar 5	H	Aberdeen	L	1-2	0-2	10	Gallagher	2400
27	12	A	Motherwell	L	1-3	0-2	10	McGivern	2895
28	19	H	Morton	W	4-0	2-0	10	Gallagher 2, McGivern, J. Clark	1200
29	26	H	Rangers	L	0-1	0-1	10		6500
30	Apr 2	A	Hibernian	L	1-8	1-2	10	Gallagher	4000
31	9	A	Dundee	D	0-0	0-0	10		3376
32	23	A	Dundee United	L	0-4	0-4	10		7516
33	27	H	St Mirren	D	2-2	0-2	10	Gallagher 2	1000
34	30	H	Celtic	L	0-5	0-2	10		7900
35	May 4	A	Aberdeen	L	0-5	0-2	10		12,500
36	14	H	Motherwell	D	1-1	1-1	10	Simpson	1203

Final League Position: 10

Goalscorers

League: Gallagher 9, J. Clark 4, Clarke 3, McGivern 3, McLean 2, Bourke 2, Mauchlen 1, Bryson 1, McDicken 1, MacLeod 1, Simpson 1
League Cup: McLean 6, Bourke 3, Mauchlen 2, Gallagher 1, Clarke 1, McCann 1, McGivern 1
Scottish Cup: Bryson 1, Gallagher 1, McGivern 1

Honours
Scottish League – Division 1 Champions 1964–65; Runners-up 1959–60, 1960–61, 1962–63, 1963–64, 1975–76, 1978–79, 1981–82; Division 2 Champions 1897–98, 1898–99; Runners-up 1953–54, 1973–74.
Scottish Cup – Winners 1920, 1929; Runners-up 1898, 1932, 1938, 1957, 1960.
Scottish League Cup – Runners-up 1953, 1961, 1963.
Record Victory: 13-2 v Saltcoats Victoria, Scottish Cup 2nd rd, 12 Sept 1896. 12-0 v Girvan Amateurs, Ayrshire Cup Final, 8 Dec 1982
Record Defeat: 0-8 v Hibernian, Division 1, 22 Aug, 1925; 0-8 v Rangers, Division 1, 27 Feb 1937. 0-8 v Queens Park 1892-93 (Div 2)
Most League Points: 58, Division 2, 1973–74
Most Individual League Goals in Season: 35, Peerie Cunningham, Division 1, 1927–28.
Most Capped Player: Joe Nibloe, 11, Scotland.

McCulloch	Wilson	McDicken	Robertson	Clark J.	Armstrong	McClurg	Bryson	MacLeod	Bourke	McLean	Gallagher	Clarke P.	Eadie	Clarke R.	McGivern	Cockburn	Simpson	Clinging	Muir	McKinna	Cuthbertson	*Match No.*
1		2	3	4	5	6	7	8	9	10	11											1
1		2		4	5	3	7	8*			11	6	9	10						12		2
1		2		4	5	3	12	8			11	6	9	10†	7*	14						3
1		2		4	5		7	3		8	11	6	9*	10	12							4
1		2		4	5		7	3	9	8	11*	6		10	12							5
1		2		4	5	10	14	3	12	8*	9	6		11†	7							6
1		2		4	5	10*	11	3	12	8	9	6			7							7
1		5	2	4		10	11	3	12	8*	9	6			7							8
1		5	2	4			12	10	9	8	11	6			7*	3						9
1		5*	2	4		12	11	10	14	8	9	6			7†	3						10
1		5	2	4			11	10*	12	8	9	6			7	3						11
1		5	2	4			11†	10	14	8	9	6*		12	7	3						12
1		5	2	4			11*	10	12	8	9	6			7	3						13
1		5	2	4				10	9	8	11	6			7	3						14
1		5	2	4				10	9	8	11	6			7	3						15
1		5	2	4		8*	11†	10			9	6		12	7	3				14		16
1		5	3	4			12	8	9	2	11*	6			7	10						17
1		5	3	4			14	8	9	2	11†	6			7	10*	12					18
1			3	4	5		11*		12	2	9	8		6	7		10					19
1				4	5		12	8		2*	9	6		3	7		10	11				20
1		2		4	5			8			9	6		3	7		10	11				21
1		2		4	5		12	8			9	6		3	7		10	11*				22
1		2		4	5		11	8*	12		9	6		3	7		10					23
	1	2		4	5	14	11	8			9	6		3	7*		10†		11	12		24
1		5		4		14		8	11		9	6		3	7*	2	10					25
1		5		4		2		8†	9	14	11			6	7*	3	10		12			26
1		5*		4				8	9	12	11	6		3	7	2	10					27
1				4	5		11*	8			9	6		3	7	2	10				12	28
1				4	5	8	11	10			9	6		3	7	2						29
1		14		4	5	11*	12				9	6		3	7	2	10				8*	30
1				4	5			8		2		6	9	3	7		10		11			31
1		12		4	5*			8		2	14	6	9	3	7		10		11†			32
1		5		4			12	8			11	6	9*	3	7	2	10					33
1		5		4			9	8			11	6		3	7*	2	10		12			34
1		5		4			9	8			11	6		3	7*	2	10		12			35
1		12		4	5		9†	8				6*	14	3	7	2	10		11			36
35	1	28	13	36	19	10	19	34	10	19	33	34	6	23	32	20	17	3	4	0	1	
		+ 3s				+ 3s	+ 9s		+ 9s	+ 2s	+ 1s		+ 1s	+ 2s	+ 2s	+ 1s	+ 1s		+ 3s	+ 3s	+ 1s	

A dismal season for the Ayrshire team who were to find just how arduous is the transition from Division One to the Premier League. A record 91 goals conceded in a programme that included 8-1 and 7-0 defeats, and only twice during the 36 games were they able to score more than two goals.

MEADOWBANK THISTLE Division 1

Year Formed: 1974. (Previously called Ferranti Thistle, founded 1943.) *Ground:* Meadowbank Stadium.
Size: 105yd×72yd. *Capacity:* 16,000 (at present only main stand, 7500 seats, is used for football).
Telephone: (Secretary's office) 031-337 2442, ext 3666.
Manager: Terry Christie. *Secretary:* William L. Mill.
Club Colours: Amber with black trim shirts, black shorts, amber stockings.
Record Attendance: 4000 v Albion Rovers, Scottish League Cup, 9 Aug, 1974.
Club Nickname: The Jags.

1982-83 LEAGUE RECORD

Match No.	*Date*	*Venue*	*Opponents*	*Result*		*H/T Score*	*League Pos'n*	*Goalscorers*	*Attendance*
1	Sept 4	H	Cowdenbeath	W	2-0	2-0	4	Hendrie 2	200
2	8	A	Forfar	W	1-0	0-0	1	Sprott	876
3	11	A	East Stirling	W	3-1	1-0	1	Robertson 2, Hendrie	500
4	15	H	Berwick	W	4-2	1-1	1	Boyd 2, Hendrie, Lawson	475
5	18	H	Brechin City	W	2-1	1-0	1	Robertson 2	400
6	22	A	Stirling Alb.	D	1-1	1-0	1	Conroy	750
7	25	A	Stranraer	W	2-1	1-0	1	Sprott, Jobson	462
8	Oct 2	H	East Fife	L	0-2	0-0	1		500
9	9	A	Montrose	W	1-0	0-0	1	Hendrie	350
10	16	H	Albion Rovers	W	4-3	1-2	1	Conroy, Hendrie, Sprott, Lawson	300
11	23	H	Arbroath	W	2-1	0-0	1	Sprott, Boyd	900
12	30	A	Stenhousemuir	W	2-1	1-0	1	Boyd, Jobson	400
13	Nov 6	A	Q.O.S.	D	1-1	1-1	1	Lawson	750
14	13	H	Forfar	W	1-0	0-0	1	Sprott	700
15	20	A	Brechin City	D	1-1	0-1	1	Georgeson	600
16	27	H	Stirling Albion	W	3-1	1-1	1	Dawson (og), Sprott, Jobson	500
17	Dec 4	A	East Fife	L	0-5	0-4	1		492
18	27	H	East Stirling	D	0-0	0-0	1		450
19	Jan 1	A	Berwick	D	0-0	0-0	1		770
20	4	H	Q.O.S.	W	1-0	1-0	1	Smith	1100
21	15	A	Cowdenbeath	L	1-3	0-2	1	Smith	350
22	22	H	Stenhousemuir	W	3-1	2-0	1	Hendrie 3	400
23	29	A	Arbroath	D	2-2	2-0	1	Hendrie, Conroy	691
24	Feb 5	H	Montrose	W	5-0	0-0	1	Boyd, Hendrie 2, Smith, Stewart	260
25	19	H	Berwick	W	5-0	3-0	1	Boyd, Godfrey, Lawson 2, Sprott (pen)	400
26	26	A	Stirling Albion	L	0-2	0-1	1		800
27	Mar 5	H	Q.O.S.	L	1-2	0-0	2	Smith	400
28	12	A	Stranraer	W	2-0	0-0	1	Smith, Sprott (pen)	350
29	19	A	East Stirling	W	2-1	2-1	2	Stewart, Young (og)	500
30	26	H	Arbroath	L	0-3	0-2	2		500
31	Apr 2	A	Forfar	W	3-0	0-0	2	Sprott, Lawson 2	1104
32	5	A	Albion Rovers	L	0-4	0-2	2		1100
33	9	H	Montrose	W	2-0	1-0	2	Smith, Lawson	300
34	13	H	Stranraer	W	1-0	1-0	2	Hendrie	450
35	16	A	Albion Rovers	W	3-1	2-1	1	Boyd, Sprott 2 (1 pen)	250
36	23	H	Stenhousemuir	D	1-1	0-0	2	Godfrey	915
37	30	H	East Fife	L	0-3	0-2	2		900
38	May 7	A	Brechin	D	1-1	0-1	2	Lawson	1600
39	14	A	Cowdenbeath	W	1-0	1-0	2	Godfrey	250

Final League Position: 2

Goalscorers

League: Hendrie 13, Sprott 11, Lawson 9, Boyd 7, Smith 6, Robertson 4, Conroy 3, Jobson 3, Godfrey 3, Stewart 2, opponents 2, Georgeson 1.
League Cup: Jobson 3, Sprott 3, Boyd.
Scottish Cup: Boyd.

Honours
Scottish League – Division 2 Runners-up 1982–83.
East of Scotland Qualifying Cup – Winners 1963–64.
Scottish Qualifying Cup (South) – Winners 1973–74.
Record Victory: 6-1 v Stenhousemuir, Division 2, 6 Feb, 1982, 5-0 v Montrose, 5 Feb, 1983, 5-0 v Berwick, 19 Feb, 1983.
Record Defeat: 0-8 v Hamilton A, Division 2, 14 Dec, 1974.
Most League Points: 54, Division 2, 1982–83.
Most Individual League Goals in a Season: 17, John Jobson, Division 2, 1979–80.

McQueen	Burrell	Conroy	Godfrey	Salton	Dunn	Hendrie	Robertson	Jobson	Boyd	Sprott	Lawson	Fraser	Korotkich	Stewart	Georgeson	Dall	Smith	Ford	McArthur	Scott	Neilson	*Match No.*
1	2	3	4	5	6	7	8	9*	10	11			12									1
*1	2	3	4	5	6	7	8	9	10	11												2
1	2	3*	4	5	6	7	9		10	11	8	12										3
*1	2*	3	4	5	6	7	9		10	11	8	12										4
1	2	3	4*	5	6	7	9		10	11	8	12										5
*1	2†	3	4		6	7	9*	12	10	11	8	5	14									6
1	2	3	4		6	7	9*	12	10	11	8	5										7
1		3	4	5*	2	7	10	8	6	11†	9	12	14									8
1		3	4		2	7		9	10	11	8	5	6*		12							9
1		3	4*	5	2	7		9	10	11	8	6			12							10
1		3	4	5	2	7		9	10	11	8	6										11
1		3	4	5	2	7		9	10	11	8	6										12
1		6	4		2	7*		9	10	11	8	3		5	12							13
1		6	4		2			9	10	11	8	3		5	7*					12		14
1	14	6	4		2	7†		9*	10	11	8	3		5	12							15
1		6	4		2	7		9	10	11	8	3		5								16
1	12	6	4		2	7		9	10	11	8†	3*		5	12							17
*1	3	6	4		2	7			10	11	8*			5	12		9					18
*1	3*	6	4		2	7			10	11	8			5		12	9					19
*1		6	4		2	7			10	11	8	3		5*		12	9					20
1		6			2	7*			10	11	8	3		5	12	4†	9				14	21
1	3	6	4		2	7			10	11	8			5	12		9*					22
1	3	6	4		2	7			10	11	8*			5	12		9					23
1	3†	6	4		2	7			10*	11	8	14		5	12		9					24
1	3†	6	4		2	7			10	11	8	14		5	12		9*					25
1		6	4		2	7			10	11	8	3		5	9*						12	26
1		6	4		2				10	11	8	3		5			9	7				27
1		6	4		2				10	11	8*	3		5	12		9	7				28
1		6	4		2				10	11	8*	3		5	12		9	7				29
1	14	6	5		2	7			10	11	8	3			12		9*	4†				30
1	3		4		2	7			5	11	9	6			8*		12	10				31
*1	3†	10	4		2	7			5	11	9	6			8*		12	14				32
1			4		2	7			10	11	8*	3		5	12		9	6				33
*1			4		2	7			10	11	8	3		5	12		9*	6				34
1			4		2	7			10	11	8	3		5	12		9*	6				35
1			4		2	7			10	11	8	3†	14	5	12		9*	6				36
		6	4		2	7			10†	11*	8	3		5	9		12	14	1			37
1		6	4		2	7			10	11	8*			5	12		9	3				38
1		3†	4		2	7			10		8	14	6*	5	11		9	12				39
38	15	34	38	9	39	35	8	12	39	38	37	25	2	24	6	1	18	10	1	0	0	
	+ 3s							+ 2s				+ 7s	+ 4s		+ 19s	+ 2s	+ 3s	+ 3s		+ 1s	+ 2s	

A historic season for Scotland's youngest senior club. Admitted to the league just eight years ago their promotion is the perfect answer to those who criticised that decision.
They added 22 points to their previous best and, although the chasing group came close at times, their 27 points from 16 opening games earned a cushion that could not be overhauled.

MONTROSE Division 2

Year Formed: 1879. *Ground:* Links Park. *Size:* 114yd×66yd. *Capacity:* 9000. *Telephone:* Montrose 3200.
Manager: Dennis D'Arcy.
Secretary: William Coull.
Club Colours: Royal blue shirts, white shorts, red stockings.
Club Nickname: Gable Endies.
Record Attendance: 8983 v Dundee, Scottish Cup 3rd rd, 17 Mar, 1973.
Record Transfer Fee Received: £50,000 from Hibernian for Gary Murray, Dec 1980.

1982-83 LEAGUE RECORD

Match No.	Date	Venue	Opponents	Result		H/T Score	League Pos'n	Goalscorers	Attendance
1	Sept 4	H	Q.O.S.	L	1-5	0-1	14	McManus	250
2	8	A	East Stirling	D	0-0	0-0	11		200
3	11	A	Cowdenbeath	W	3-2	1-0	9	Barr (pen), Campbell, Copeland	250
4	15	H	Brechin	L	1-2	1-1	10	Fletcher	650
5	18	H	Albion Rovers	D	3-3	0-2	10	Turnbull, Copeland, Taylor	250
6	22	A	East Fife	W	1-0	1-0	9	Fletcher	450
7	25	A	Berwick	D	1-1	1-0	8	Fletcher	564
8	Oct 2	H	Stranraer	W	3-1	2-1	8	Barr, Fletcher, Copeland	270
9	9	H	Meadowbank	L	0-1	0-0	9		350
10	16	A	Arbroath	L	1-3	1-1	9	Oliver	772
11	23	H	Stenhousemuir	W	1-0	1-0	7	Craig	250
12	30	A	Stirling Albion	W	3-2	1-0	7	Copeland 3	530
13	Nov 6	A	Forfar	D	2-2	1-0	7	Copeland, McManus	982
14	13	H	East Stirling	L	1-2	1-0	8	McManus	250
15	20	A	Albion Rovers	L	1-2	0-2	9	Oliver	200
16	27	H	East Fife	L	0-2	0-1	11		200
17	Dec 4	A	Stranraer	D	3-3	1-3	11	Copeland, Turnbull, Matheson	319
18	18	H	Berwick	W	1-0	0-0	9	Copeland	150
19	27	H	Cowdenbeath	L	0-4	0-1	11		350
20	Jan 1	A	Brechin	L	0-4	0-1	11		900
21	3	H	Forfar	L	1-2	1-1	12	Turnbull	650
22	22	H	Stirling Albion	L	0-1	0-0	12		200
23	Feb 5	A	Meadowbank	L	0-5	0-0	12		260
24	16	H	Arbroath	W	2-1	1-0	11	Copeland, Barr	450
25	19	A	East Stirling	L	1-3	1-1	11	McManus	300
26	23	A	Stenhousemuir	L	1-3	0-1	11	Copeland	300
27	26	H	Albion Rovers	L	1-2	0-0	13	Barr	150
28	Mar 2	A	Q.O.S.	L	0-4	0-3	14		400
29	5	A	Brechin	L	1-3	0-0	14	Duffy	500
30	12	H	Arbroath	L	0-3	0-0	14		400
31	19	A	East Fife	L	0-4	0-4	14		450
32	26	A	Berwick	L	1-3	1-1	14	McManus	526
33	Apr 2	H	Stranraer	W	1-0	0-0	13	McManus	100
34	9	A	Meadowbank	L	0-2	0-1	13		300
35	16	H	Stenhousemuir	L	0-1	0-0	13		150
36	23	A	Stirling Albion	L	0-1	0-1	14		630
37	30	A	Q.O.S.	L	0-6	0-3	14		400
38	May 7	H	Cowdenbeath	D	1-1	0-1	14	Duffy	150
39	13	H	Forfar	L	1-2	0-1	14	Copeland	350

Final League Position: 14

Goalscorers

League: Copeland 12, McManus 6, Barr 4, Fletcher 4, Turnbull 3, Duffy 2, Oliver 2, Campbell 1, Taylor 1, Craig 1, Matheson 1.
League Cup: Turnbull 1, Copeland 1, Nicol 1, Taylor 1, Cooper 1, Oliver 1.
Scottish Cup: Nicol 1, Copeland 1, McManus 1.

Honours
Record Victory: 12-0 v Vale of Leithen, Scottish Cup 2nd rd, 4 Jan, 1975.
Record Defeat: 0-13 v Aberdeen, 17 Mar, 1951.
Most League Points: 53, Division 2, 1974–75.
Most Capped Player: Alexander Keillor, 2 (6), Scotland.

Charles	Barr	Forbes	Fletcher	Sheran	Mathieson	McDonald	Cooper	Copeland	Turnbull	McManus	Nicol	Campbell	Cormack	Oliver	Craig	Taylor	Neil	Adam	Bennett	Newman	Newman	Dufy	McLaren	Downie	Forrest	Bain	Middleton	D'Arcy	Cullerton	Loch	Franklin	*Match No.*
1	2		7	5	6		10	9	3	11*	8†	14	4			12																1
1	2	3	4	5	6	7†	8*	9	10	11	12					14																2
1	2*	3	4	5	6		8	14	10	11†	7	9				12																3
1	2	3	4	5	6		8	9	10	11*	7†	12				14																4
1	2	3	7	5	6		8	9†	10			12	4	11*		14																5
1	2	3	7	5	6		8		10			9	4	11																		6
1	2	3	7	5	6		8	11	10			9	4																			7
1	2	3	7	5	6		8†	9		12		11*	4		10	14																8
1	2	3	7	5	6			9	12	11			4*		10	8																9
1	3		7	5	6	4	12	9		11	8			10*			2															10
1	2	3	7*		6	14	8†	9		11	12		4		10		5															11
1		2	7		6			9	3	11			4	12	10*	8	5															12
1		2	7		6	12		9	3	11			4	10*		8	5															13
1	2	3	14		6		8*	9		11	7†		4	10		12	5															14
1	10	2	7		6			9	3	11	8						5															15
1	2	3	12	5	6				10	11	7*		14	9†				4	8													16
1		2	7	10	6			9	3		12		14				5	4†		8	11*											17
1	2	3	7	5	10			9		11			12							8		6										18
1	2	3	7	5	10			9	12	11								4*				6	8									19
1	7	3	4	5	10			9		11							2					6	8									20
1	4	2	7†	5	10			9	3	11	14						12					6*	8									21
1	2	3	12	5			7	9		11	8*						4					6		10								22
1	2	3	10	5	7			9			8*						4					6			11		12					23
1	2	3	12	5	8		6*	9		11									10			4		7								24
1	2	3		5	8		6	9		11*												4		7		10	12					25
1		3	11		8			9			7*				12		5					4		6		10	2					26
1		3	9		8		6	10		11							5							7			2	4	3			27
1		2			8†		6	9		11	12						5					4		7*	14	10			3			28
1		3						9		11	6						5					7		8*	12	10	2	4				29
1		3		12	7		6*	9		11	8						5					4			10		2					30
1		3			7		9†	8*		11	6				14		5					4			10		2	12				31
1	2			5				9		11					8			6*				12		7			3	4		10		32
1	6	3		5				9		11					8								12	7*			2	4		10		33
1		3		5				9		11					8							6		7			2	4		10		34
1		3		5				9							7							6		12	11		2	4		10	8*	35
1		4		5			6	9							7			8				3			11		2			10		36
*1		4		5			6	9							14			11†				3			8*		2		12	10		37
1		4					6	9										8				3			11		2	5		10	7	38
1		4					6	9									12	8			11	3					2*	5		10	7	39
39	24	36	22	26	29	1	21	36	13	27	13	4	9	6	9	3	16	8	2	2	2	19	3	10	7	4	13	8	2	8	3	
			+ 4s	+ 1s		+ 2s	+ 1s	+ 1s	+ 2s	+ 1s	+ 5s	+ 2s	+ 3s	+ 1s	+ 3s	+ 7s	+ 2s					+ 1s	+ 1s	+ 1s	+ 2s		+ 2s	+ 1s	+ 1s			

A dreadful spell for the Angus club, who have slipped from a challenging position in Division One eight years ago, to the foot of Division Two. Only Kilmarnock can top the 86 goals they conceded and, with just five goals to show for their closing 12 games, that leaves a massive re-building operation for former player Dennis D'Arcy.

MORTON Division 1

Year Formed: 1874. *Limited Company:* 1896.
Ground: Cappielow Park, Greenock PA15 2TY. *Size:* 110yd×71yd. *Capacity:* 16,400 (6400 seats).
Telephone: Greenock 25594.
Player/Coach: Alex Miller
Secretaries: T. Robertson & Co. CA, Greenock.
Club Colours: Blue and white hooped shirts, white shorts and stockings.
Club Nickname: Ton.
Record Attendance: 23,500 v Celtic, Division 1, 1922.
Record Transfer Fee Received: £300,000 from West Ham U for Neil Orr, Dec 1981.
European Competitions: Fairs Cup 1968–69.

1982-83 LEAGUE RECORD

Match No.	Date	Venue	Opponents	Result		H/T Score	League Pos'n	Goalscorers	Atten-dance
1	Sept 4	H	Kilmarnock	D	0-0	0-0	—		2300
2	11	A	Aberdeen	L	1-4	1-2	10	McNeil	8000
3	18	A	Dundee	L	0-2	0-1	9		3979
4	25	H	Motherwell	W	3-1	1-0	7	Ritchie, McNab, Rooney	1600
5	Oct 2	A	Hibernian	W	2-1	0-1	6	Ritchie, McNab	4000
6	9	H	Rangers	D	0-0	0-0	6		15,000
7	16	A	Dundee United	L	0-6	0-5	6		5986
8	23	H	Celtic	L	1-2	0-2	7	Rooney	12,000
9	30	A	St. Mirren	D	1-1	1-0	7	Cochrane	3346
10	Nov 6	A	Kilmarnock	L	1-3	0-1	7	McNeil	1850
11	13	H	Aberdeen	W	1-1	1-0	7	McNab	3000
12	20	H	Dundee	L	1-2	1-0	8	Docherty	2500
13	27	A	Motherwell	L	1-3	0-3	9	Hutchinson	3134
14	Dec 4	H	Hibernian	D	0-0	0-0	8		1800
15	11	A	Rangers	D	1-1	1-0	7	Rooney	9500
16	18	H	Dundee United	L	1-2	1-0	8	McNab	2000
17	27	A	Celtic	L	1-5	1-1	8	MacLeod (og)	19,953
18	Jan 1	H	St. Mirren	W	2-0	1-0	8	Gibson, Hutchinson	2200
19	3	H	Kilmarnock	W	3-0	1-0	7	Rooney, McNab, Hutchinson	3500
20	8	A	Aberdeen	L	0-2	0-0	8		14,000
21	15	A	Dundee	D	3-3	1-3	9	Payne, Rooney 2	4557
22	22	H	Motherwell	L	0-1	0-0	9		3500
23	Feb 5	A	Hibernian	L	0-2	0-1	9		4736
24	12	H	Rangers	L	0-5	0-1	9		6900
25	26	A	Dundee United	D	1-1	0-0	9	Hutchinson	5986
26	Mar 5	H	Celtic	L	0-3	0-1	9		10,000
27	16	A	St. Mirren	W	3-2	2-1	9	Gavigan, Houston, Fulton (og)	3344
28	19	A	Kilmarnock	L	0-4	0-2	9		1200
29	26	H	Aberdeen	L	1-2	1-0	9	Ritchie	4000
30	Apr 2	H	Dundee	W	1-0	1-0	9	McNeil	3000
31	9	A	Motherwell	L	1-4	0-0	9	Payne P.	3764
32	16	H	Hibernian	L	0-1	0-0	9		2400
33	23	A	Rangers	L	0-2	0-1	9		9500
34	30	H	Dundee United	L	0-4	0-1	9		6800
35	May 7	A	Celtic	L	0-2	0-2	9		12,610
36	14	H	St. Mirren	L	0-2	0-1	9		2000

Final League Position: 9

Goalscorers

League: Rooney 6, McNab 5, Hutchinson 4, McNeil 3, Ritchie 3, Payne 2, opponents 2, Cochrane 1, Docherty 1, Gibson 1, Gavigan 1, Houston 1.
League Cup: Rooney 5, Docherty 3, Ritchie 3, Hutchinson 2, McNab 1, McNeil 1, Cochrane 1.
Scottish Cup: Hutchinson 1, McNab 1.

Honours
Scottish League – Division 1 Champions 1977–78; Runners-up 1916–17; Division 2 Champions 1949–50, 1963–64, 1966–67; Runners-up 1899–1900, 1928–29, 1936–37.
Scottish Cup – Winners 1922; Runners-up 1948.
Scottish League Cup – Runners-up 1964.
Southern League Cup – Runners-up 1941–42.
Renfrewshire Cup: 39 times winners.
War Shield winners: 1914.
Record Victory: 11-0 v Carfin Shamrock, Scottish Cup 1st rd, 13 Nov, 1886.
Record Defeat: 1-10 v Port Glasgow Ath, Division 2, 5 May, 1894. 1-10 v St Bernards, Division 2, 14 Oct, 1933.
Most League Points: 69, Division 2, 1966–67.
Most League Goals: 135, Division 2, 1963–64.
Most Individual League Goals in Season: 41, Allan McGraw, Division 2, 1963–64.
Most Capped Player: Jimmy Cowan, 25, Scotland.

Baines	Houston	Holmes	Rooney	McLaughlin	Duffy	McNeil	Docherty	Hutchinson	Cochrane	Ritchie	Gavigan	Jackson	McNab	Kyle	Higgins	Slaven	Hayes	Payne	Gibson	Doak	McCallum	*Match No.*
1	2	3	4	5	6	7	8	9	10	11												1
1	2		4	5	6	8*	3	9	10	14	7	12	11†									2
1	2	3	4	5		10	8	9	14	11†	12	6	7*									3
1	2	3	10	5	4		8†	9	14	11	12	6	7*									4
1	2	3	10	5	4		8	9*	12	11		6	7									5
1	2	3	10	5	4	12	8	9†	14	11		6	7*									6
1	2	3	10	5	4		8*	9	12	11		6	7									7
1	2	3	4	5	6	14	8*	9	10	11†	12		7									8
1	2	3	6	5	4	7	14	9*	8	12	10		11†									9
	2	3	6	5	4*	7	12	9	8		10†		11	1	14							10
1	2	3	4			8	6	5	10		9		7		11							11
1	2	3	4			7*	6	5	8	11			10		9	12						12
1	2	3	4	5		7	9	6	8	11						10*				12		13
1	2	3	4	5	6		8	9	10	11*			7		12							14
1	2	3	4	5	6	7*	8		9	12			10		11							15
1	10†	3	4	5	6	7*	8		9	12			11				2			14		16
1	2	3	4	5	6	7*	14	9†	10	12			11			8						17
1	2	3	4	5	6		12	9	10				11					7*	8			18
1	2	3	4	5	6			9	10				11					7	8			19
1	2	3	4	5	6			9	10				11*			12		7	8			20
1	2	3	4*	5	6			9	10				11			12		7	8			21
1	2	3	4	5	6		14	9*	10†				11			12		7	8			22
1	2	3	4	5	6			9	10	12			11					7	8*			23
1	2	3	4	5	6		8	9*		11			10†			12		7	14			24
1	11*	3	4	5	6	10	9	8			12							7		2		25
1	14	3	4	5		8	10	9*			12		11†				2	7		6		26
1	11	3	4	5	6		8		9		10						2	7				27
1	11	3	4	5	6†	14	8		9		10						2*	7		12		28
	2	3	4	5		7	6	9	10	11			8	1								29
1	2	3	4	5		7		9	10	11†	14		8*					12		6		30
1	2	3	4	5		7		9	10	11†			8				14	12		6*		31
1	11†	3	4	5		10*		6	9		12		8				2	7		14		32
1	11	3	4	5	6	14		9	10*		12		8†				2	7				33
1	11	3	4*	5	6			9	8	12	14					10†	2	7				34
	9	3	4	5	6				10	11	8			1			2	7				35
	9	3	4	5	6	10				11			8†	1			2	7*		12	14	36
33	35	35	36	34	27	18	20	30	27	16	7	5	29	3	3	3	9	16	6	4	0	
	+ 1s					+ 4s	+ 5s		+ 5s	+ 7s	+ 9s	+ 1s			+ 2s	+ 5s	+ 1s	+ 2s	+ 1s	+ 5s	+ 1s	

The Premier League's "survival experts" finally came unstuck and Morton's gloom was underlined when dramatic cutbacks meant that the club could no longer afford to keep manager Benny Rooney.
Difficult to see them making any real impact on the game in such circumstances. Ever presents Jim Holmes and Jim Rooney did most to try to avoid the drop.

MOTHERWELL Premier Division

Year Formed: 1886.
Ground: Fir Park. *Size:* 110yd×72yd. *Capacity:* 22,600 (3200 seats).
Telephone: Motherwell 61437.
Manager: Jock Wallace. *Assistant Manager:* Frank Connor.
Secretary: Jack McGraw.
Club Colours: Amber with claret.
Club Nickname: Well.
Record Attendance: 35,632 v Rangers, Scottish Cup 4th rd replay, 12 Mar, 1952.
Previous Names: Club formed following the amalgamation of Alpha and Glencairn, known as Wee Alpha for a year before becoming Motherwell in 1886.
Previous Grounds: Roman Park, Dalziel Park.

1982-83 LEAGUE RECORD

Match No.	Date	Venue	Opponents	Result		H/T Score	League Pos'n	Goalscorers	Atten-dance
1	Sept 4	H	Rangers	D	2-2	0-1	—	Clelland, Carson	19,159
2	11	A	Dundee	L	1-3	1-2	9	Rafferty	4621
3	18	H	Celtic	L	0-7	0-3	10		17,092
4	25	A	Morton	L	1-3	0-1	10	Conn	1600
5	Oct 2	A	Aberdeen	L	1-2	1-0	10	Edvaldsson	8000
6	9	H	St Mirren	W	2-0	0-0	9	McLeod, Flavell	4292
7	16	A	Hibernians	L	0-1	0-1	10		4000
8	23	H	Dundee United	L	0-2	0-0	10		4555
9	30	H	Kilmarnock	W	4-1	1-1	9	McLaughlin, McClair, Flavell 2	3016
10	Nov 6	A	Rangers	L	0-4	0-1	10		17,000
11	13	H	Dundee	W	1-0	0-0	10	Flavell	3295
12	20	A	Celtic	L	1-3	0-0	10	Flavell	14,963
13	27	H	Morton	W	3-1	3-0	6	McLelland, Mauchlen, Rafferty	3134
14	Dec 4	H	Aberdeen	L	0-2	0-0	9		4929
15	11	A	St Mirren	L	0-3	0-1	9		3563
16	18	H	Hibernians	L	0-1	0-1	9		3815
17	27	A	Dundee United	L	0-5	0-2	9		7682
18	Jan 1	A	Kilmarnock	W	2-0	1-0	9	Flavell, Mauchlen	3300
19	3	H	Rangers	W	3-0	1-0	9	McClair 3	11,383
20	8	A	Dundee	L	1-3	1-0	9	Edvaldsson	5131
21	15	H	Celtic	W	2-1	0-1	6	McClair 2 (1 pen)	15,290
22	22	A	Morton	W	1-0	0-0	6	McClair	3500
23	Feb 5	A	Aberdeen	L	1-5	1-2	8	Rafferty	13,000
24	26	A	Hibernians	D	1-1	1-1	8	Harrow	4300
25	Mar 1	H	St Mirren	D	0-0	0-0	8		4029
26	5	H	Dundee United	L	1-4	1-2	8	Gahagan	3589
27	12	H	Kilmarnock	W	3-1	2-0	8	Rafferty, McClair, Mauchlen	2895
28	19	A	Rangers	L	0-1	0-1	8		17,000
29	26	H	Dundee	D	1-1	1-0	8	Forbes	3222
30	Apr 2	A	Celtic	L	0-3	0-2	8		15,454
31	9	H	Morton	W	4-1	0-0	8	Gahagan 2, Harrow, McClair	3764
32	23	A	St Mirren	L	0-4	0-1	8		3257
33	27	H	Aberdeen	L	0-3	0-1	8		6715
34	30	H	Hibernians	W	2-0	1-0	8	McClair, Gahagan	3532
35	May 7	A	Dundee United	L	0-4	0-1	8		11,993
36	14	A	Kilmarnock	D	1-1	1-1	8	McClair	1203

Final League Position: 8

Goalscorers

League: McClair 11, Flavell 6, Rafferty 4, Gahagan 4, Mauchlen 3, Edvaldsson 2, Harrow 2, Clelland 1, Carson 1, Conn 1, McLeod 1, McLaughlin 1, McLelland 1, Forbes 1.
League Cup: McClair 4, Conn 2, O'Hara 1, Coyne 1, McLelland 1 Forbes 1.
Scottish Cup: Harrow 1, McClair 1, Forbes 1.

Honours

Scottish League – Division 1 Champions 1931–32, 1981–82; Runners-up 1926–27, 1929–30, 1932–33, 1933–34; Division 2 Champions 1953–54, 1968–69; Runners-up 1894–95, 1902–03.
Scottish Cup – Winners 1952; Runners-up 1931, 1933, 1939, 1951.
Scottish League Cup – Winners 1950–51; Runners-up 1954–55.
Record Victory: 12-1 v Dundee U, Division 2, 23 Jan, 1954.
Record Defeat: 0-8 v Aberdeen, Premier Division, 26 March, 1979.
Most League Points: 66, Division 1, 1931–32.
Most Individual League Goals in Season: 52, Willie McFadyen, 1931–32.
Highest Scorer in Total Aggragate: Hugh Ferguson, 283, 1916–25.
Most Capped Player: George Stevenson, 12, Scotland.

Sproat	McLeod	Forsyth	McLelland	Carson	Forbes	Gahagen	Rafferty	Irvine	Edvaldsson	McLaughlin	McClair	Coyne	Clelland	Wark	Conn	O'Hara	Clinging	Flavell	Mauchlen	Burns	Dornan	Harrow	Walker	Cormack	Graham	McAllister	*Match No.*
1	2	3	4	5	6	7	8	9*	10	11†			12				14										1
1	2	3	4		5	6	7	11		10	6*	8	9	9†		14		12									2
1	2		4	5		8	7		9		6			3	10	11											3
1	2	3			4	11	6		5	12	7*	8†	9		10	14											4
1	2	3	9	4			6		5			12	14		10†	11	7*	8									5
1	2	3	9	4			14		5						10†	11	7*	8	6	12							6
1	2	3	9	4		14	10†		5			12				11		8	6	7*							7
1	2	3	9†	4		12	14		5	10						11		8	6	7*							8
1	2	3	9	4		7			5	10*	12					11		8	6								9
1	2	3	9	4	12	7			5		10					11		8*	6								10
1	2	3	9	4	14	7	6		5		10*		12			11†		8									11
1	2	3	9*	4	14	7	6		5		10					11†	12	8									12
1	2	3	9	4	12	7	10		5							11		8*	6								13
1	2	3	9		4	7	10		5							11		8	6								14
1	2	3	9		4	7	10*		5		12					11		8	6								15
1	2	3			4	7	10*		5	9	14					11†		8	6					12			16
1	2	3	12		4	7†			5	9*	10					11	14	8	6								17
1	3			4	12		8*		5	14	10†					11		7	6		2	9					18
1		3		4			8		5		10					11		7	6		2	9					19
1		3		4	12		8		5	14	10†					11		7*	6		2	9					20
	3*			4	10		8		5		7	12				11			6		2	9	1				21
1	3			4	12		10		5		7					11		8*	6		2	9					22
				4	6		8		5		7					11		2	10		3	9	1				23
	3				4	7*	8		5		10†	14				11	12		6		2	9	1				24
	3				4	7	8		5		10	6				11					2	9	1				25
	3				4	7	8		5		10					11			6		2	9	1				26
	3				4	7	8*			5	10	12				11†	14		6		2	9	1				27
	3				4	7	8*		5		10	12				11†		14	6		2	9	1				28
	3				4	7	8		5		10	11							6		2	9	1				29
	3					7	12				8	10		4		11*		9	6		2	5	1				30
						7	8		5		10			4		11*		3	6		2	9	12				31
		14				7	8		5		10	6†		4		11		3			2	9*	12	1			32
	3					7	8		5		10			4		11		6			2	9*	1	12			33
	3			5	12	7	6		4		10			14		11†		8			2	9*	1				34
	3			5	4	7	6*		9		10					12		8	11*		2		1		14		35
	3			5	4	11†	8		9*		10					14		7	6		2		1		12		36
21	31	18	14	20	17	26	30	1	35	6	26	6	2	5	4	30	2	25	25	2	19	17	15	0	0	0	
		+ 1s	+ 1s		+ 8s	+ 2s	+ 3s			+ 3s	+ 3s	+ 6s	+ 3s	+ 1s	+ 1s	+ 3	+ 6s	+ 1s		+ 1s				+ 4s	+ 1s	+ 1s	

Survival was the name of the game for Jock Wallace and they preserved Premier League status with some ease in the end after a worrying time in the spring. Youth player Brian McClair emerged as a youngster capable of further development while the recruitment of Ally Mauchlen from Kilmarnock added vital experience and steel.

PARTICK THISTLE Division 1

Year Formed: 1876. *Address:* Firhill Park, Glasgow, N.W. *Size:* 110yd×71yd. *Capacity:* 22,000 (3500 seated).
Telephone: 041-946 2673
Team Manager: Peter Cormack. *Admin. Manager:* Scot Symon. *Secretary:* L. J. McIntyre, CA.
Previous Grounds: Kelvingrove, 1876–81; Jordanvale Park, 1881–83; Muirpark, 1883–85; Meadowside Park, 1891–1908; Firhill Park, 1909 (1908–9, Ibrox was used by Partick T when they had no ground of their own, but some 'home games' still had to be played away).
Nickname: The Jags.
Colours: Red and yellow shirts with broad vertical stripes, red shorts, red stockings with black and yellow tops.
Record Attendance: 49,838 v Rangers, Division 1, 18 Feb, 1922.
European Competitions: *Fairs Cup* 1963–64; *UEFA Cup* 1973–74.

1982-83 LEAGUE RECORD

Match No.	Date	Venue	Opponents	Result		H/T Score	League Pos'n	Goalscorers	Attendance
1	Sept 4	H	Dunfermline	D	1-1	0-0	8	Wilcox (og)	2500
2	11	H	Queen's Park	L	2-3	0-0	11	Park, Watson	1738
3	15	A	Ayr United	L	1-2	1-1	13	O'Hara	1500
4	18	A	Airdrie	W	3-1	2-1	11	Johnston, J. Doyle, McDowall	2500
5	25	H	Raith Rovers	W	2-1	0-0	10	Jardine, O'Hara	1800
6	29	A	Falkirk	L	1-2	1-1	5	Johnston	1400
7	Oct 2	A	Hamilton	W	2-1	0-0	7	Johnston 2	1663
8	5	H	Clydebank	W	2-1	1-0	7	Johnston, McDowall	1880
9	9	H	Clydebank	L	0-1	0-1	7		2080
10	16	A	Alloa	L	1-2	1-1	8	O'Hara	1094
11	23	A	Dumbarton	D	1-1	0-0	8	Watson (pen)	1500
12	30	H	Hearts	D	1-1	1-0	8	O'Hara	3045
13	Nov 6	H	St Johnstone	W	3-1	0-0	8	O'Hara, Rutherford (og), Johnston	3160
14	13	A	Dunfermline	W	4-0	1-0	7	Johnston 2, Considine (og), Park	1950
15	20	H	Airdrie	W	1-0	0-0	7	Jardine	3192
16	27	A	Clyde	W	3-1	1-0	5	Park 2, Brogan (og)	1700
17	Dec 4	H	Hamilton	D	1-1	0-1	3	Park	1892
18	11	A	Raith Rovers	D	2-2	0-1	4	Johnston, Jardine	1600
19	27	A	Queen's Park	W	4-1	1-0	4	Jardine, Johnston, Watson, Park	2300
20	Jan 1	H	Ayr United	D	2-2	1-1	4	Johnston, Park	2000
21	3	A	St Johnstone	L	0-1	0-1	4		4700
22	8	H	Alloa	D	1-1	1-1	4	Johnston	1900
23	15	A	Clydebank	W	3-1	1-0	4	Whittaker, Park, Johnston	1750
24	22	A	Hearts	W	1-0	0-0	4	Park	7061
25	Feb 5	H	Dumbarton	W	3-2	1-1	3	Park 2, McDonald	1789
26	26	A	Clyde	W	2-0	1-0	4	Johnston, Park	1434
27	Mar 5	A	Dunfermline	W	3-0	2-0	3	J. Doyle 2, Watson	1480
28	15	H	Alloa	L	1-2	0-0	4	Watson	1600
29	19	A	Hearts	L	0-4	0-1	4		7000
30	22	H	Raith Rovers	W	1-0	1-0	4	McDowall	1600
31	26	H	Ayr United	W	3-1	2-1	4	Watson 2 (1 pen), McDowall	2035
32	Apr 2	H	St Johnstone	W	2-1	1-1	4	Buckley, Kenny	4193
33	6	H	Falkirk	D	1-1	1-0	3	Johnston	1500
34	9	A	Hamilton	D	0-0	0-0	4		1493
35	16	H	Falkirk	W	4-2	1-0	3	Johnston 3 (2 pens), Watson	1534
36	23	A	Queen's Park	W	1-0	1-0	4	Johnston	1667
37	30	A	Dumbarton	L	1-2	0-1	4	Johnston	1500
38	May 7	H	Airdrie	L	0-1	0-0	4		1600
39	14	A	Clydebank	W	2-1	2-0	4	Johnston, McDowall	1420

Final League Position: 4

Goalscorers

League: Johnston 21, Park 12, Watson 8, O'Hara 5, McDowall 5, Jardine 4, opponents 4, J. Doyle 3, Whittaker 1, McDonald 1, Buckley 1, Kenny 1.
League Cup: Johnston 5, Watson 3, Park 1, Jardine 1, Whittaker 1, Kenny 1.
Scottish Cup: Johnston 6, Park 2, Doyle 1, Watson 1, McDonald 1, opponents 1.

Honours

Scottish League: Division 1 Champions 1975–76; Division 2 Champions 1896–97, 1899–1900, 1970–71; Runners-up 1901–02.
Scottish Cup: Winners 1921; Runners-up 1930.
Scottish League Cup: Winners 1971–72; Runners-up 1953–54, 1956–57, 1958–59.
Glasgow Cup: 1980–81.
Most Capped Player: Alan Rough, 51, Scotland.
Most League Points: 56, Division 2, 1970–71.
Record Victory: 16–0 v Royal Albert, Scottish Cup 1st rd, 17 Jan, 1931.
Record Defeat: 0–10 v Queen's Park, Scottish Cup 6th rd, 3 Dec, 1881.
Most Individual League Goals in Season: 41, Alec Hair, Division 1, 1926–27.

Rough	Murray	Kay	Whittaker	Dunlop	Watson	Park	McDonald	Johnston	Doyle, J.	Clark	Smith	Jardine	O'Hara	Docherty, G.	Doyle, G.	Kenny	McDowall	Docherty, J.	Jackson	McNab	Welsh	Buckley	Lapsley	Scott	*Match No.*
1	2	3	4	5	6*	7	8	9	10	11†						14							12		1
1	2	3	4		6	7		9		11†	5	8*	10			14	12								2
1	2	3	4		6	7		9		11	5	8	10												3
1	2	4	3		5		11	9	8			6	10*	7			12								4
1		4	3		5	7	11	9	6			8	10		2*	12									5
1	2	4	3		5	7	11	9	6			8	10												6
1	4		3		5	10	12	9				8	6	7	2	11*									7
1	4		3		5	10		9				8	6	7	2	11*	12								8
1	4	2	3		5	10	12	9	8				6	7*		11†	14								9
1	4	2	3		5	7	11	9	8				6*			12	10								10
1	4	2	3		5	7	11	9	8*				6	14				10*						12	11
1	4	2	3		6	7*		11	10			8	9					12	5						12
1	4	2	3		6	7*		9	10			8	11					12	5						13
1	4	2	3		10	7*	12	9	6*			8	11					12	5						14
1	4	2	3		6	7*	12	9	10			8	11				14		5*						15
	4	2	3	12	6	7		9	10†			8	11				14		5*	1					16
		2	3	4*	6	7	12	9	10			8	11†				14		5	1					17
	4	2	3		6	7	11*	9	10			8	12						5	1					18
	4	2	3		6	7		9	10			8	11						5	1					19
	4		3		6	7	12	9	10*			8	11						5	1	2				20
	4		3	12		7	6	9	10			8†	11			14			5*	1	2				21
	4		3	5	6*	7	11	9	10				14		8†	12				1	2				22
	4		3	5	6	7	8	9	10				11		2					1					23
	4		3	5	6	7	8	9	10				11		2					1					24
	4	2	3	5	6	7	8	9	10				11							1					25
	4	2*	3		6	7†	8	9	10				11		12		14		5	1					26
	4	2	3		6		8	9	10				11				7		5	1					27
	4	2	3		6	7	8	9	10*				11				12		5	1					28
	4	2	3		6	7	8	9*	10				11†	12			12		5	1					29
	2		3	5	6		7	9	10				11				8		4	1					30
	8	2*	3	5	6		7	9						12	10		11		4	1					31
	2	12	3	5	6		8	9								7*	10		4	1		11			32
	2		3	5	6		8	9					11		10				4	1		7			33
	4	2	3	5	6	7	8	9					11				10*			1		12			34
	4	2	3	5	6		8	9					11				10			1		7			35
	4	3		5†	6	7		9	10				11		2*		8			1	12	14			36
	4	3			6	7	8†	9	10				12				14		5*	1	2	11			37
	5	3			6*	7	8†	9	10						2	12	14			1	4	11			38
	4	2	3		5	7	6	9					10				8			1		11			39
15	37	29	36	13	38	33	25	39	29	3	2	17	32	4	10	4	9	1	19	23	5	6	0	0	
		+ 1s		+ 2s			+ 6s						+ 3s	+ 3s	+ 1s	+ 7s	+ 12s	+ 3s			+ 1s	+ 2s	+ 1s	+ 1s	

Dreadful start to the league campaign, which produced only three victories in their opening twelve games, always had Partick struggling to catch up.
Striker Maurice Johnston with 21 league goals emerged as their best contributor as Partick must avoid the prospect of becoming permanent inhabitants of Division One.

QUEEN OF THE SOUTH Division 2

Year Formed: 1919. *Ground:* Palmerston Park. *Size:* 111yd×73yd. *Capacity:* 20,000.
Telephone: Dumfries 54853.
Manager: Drew Busby. *Secretary:* J. K. Parrell.
Club Colours: Royal blue shirts with white facings, white shorts, royal blue stockings with two white hoops on top.
Club Nickname: Queens or The Doonhamers.
Record Attendance: 24,500 v Hearts, Scottish Cup 3rd rd, 23 Feb, 1952.

1982-83 LEAGUE RECORD

Match No.	Date	Venue	Opponents	Result		H/T Score	League Pos'n	Goalscorers	Attendance
1	Sept 4	A	Montrose	W	5-1	1-0	1	Cloy (2 pen), Gordon 2, Alexander	250
2	8	H	Stenhousemuir	L	1-2	0-2	2	Clark	900
3	11	H	Arbroath	W	2-1	0-1	2	Cloy, Robertson J.	750
4	15	A	Stranraer	W	3-0	0-0	2	Busby, Alexander, Kennedy	850
5	18	H	East Fife	L	1-5	1-1	5	Robertson J.	860
6	22	A	Albion Rovers	L	1-3	1-2	6	Robertson J.	350
7	25	A	Forfar	L	0-1	0-1	10		869
8	Oct. 2	H	Berwick	L	1-2	0-2	11	Busby	700
9	9	H	Stirling Alb	W	1-0	0-0	10	Alexander	600
10	16	A	Cowdenbeath	L	1-2	1-1	10	Alexander	350
11	23	H	Brechin	W	3-1	2-0	9	Robertson J. 2, Alexander	600
12	Nov 3	A	East Stirling	W	2-1	0-1	8	Coughlin, Alexander	150
13	6	H	Meadowbank	D	1-1	1-1	8	Gordon	750
14	13	A	Stenhousemuir	W	3-2	1-2	5	McMinn, Alexander, Coughlin	400
15	20	A	East Fife	D	0-0	0-0	6		412
16	27	H	Albion Rovers	W	5-0	3-0	4	Gordon, Alexander, Coughlin, Robertson J. 2	750
17	Dec 4	A	Berwick	W	4-0	2-0	3	Gordon, Alexander, Robertson J., Busby	661
18	11	H	East Fife	L	1-2	0-0	3	Robertson J.	750
19	27	A	Arbroath	L	2-3	1-1	4	Cloy, Wilkie	765
20	Jan 1	H	Stranraer	W	6-3	2-1	4	Alexander, Coughlin, Cloy, Cochrane 2, Newman	800
21	3	A	Meadowbank	L	0-1	0-1	4		1100
22	22	H	East Stirling	D	2-2	1-1	7	Alexander, Cloy (pen)	800
23	Feb 5	A	Stirling Alb	D	1-1	1-4	8	Alexander	700
24	16	H	Cowdenbeath	D	0-0	0-0	7		575
25	19	H	Stenhousemuir	D	2-2	1-1	8	Cochrane, Robertson J.	600
26	26	A	Berwick	L	0-1	0-1	8		574
27	Mar 2	H	Montrose	W	4-0	2-0	8	Gordon 2, Cloy, Busby	400
28	5	A	Meadowbank	W	2-1	0-0	8	Alexander, Robertson J.	400
29	9	A	Brechin City	W	3-2	1-1	6	Alexander, Busby, McCann	650
30	19	H	Stirling Alb.	L	3-5	2-0	8	Cloy (pen), Busby, Gordon	600
31	26	A	Brechin City	L	0-1	0-0	9		500
32	29	H	Forfar	D	1-1	0-1	8	Steedman	400
33	Apr 2	H	Arbroath	D	1-1	1-1	8	Busby	500
34	9	A	Cowdenbeath	W	3-2	2-2	7	Alexander 3	200
35	16	A	East Stirling	W	1-0	0-0	7	Alexander	250
36	23	H	Forfar	L	1-2	0-1	7	Alexander	500
37	30	H	Montrose	W	6-0	3-0	7	Robertson G., Alexander 3, Gordon, Steedman	400
38	May 7	H	Albion Rovers	W	2-0	1-0	7	Alexander, Cloy	350
39	14	A	Stranraer	D	0-0	0-0	7		350

Final League Position: 7

Goalscorers

League: Alexander 23, Robertson J. 11, Cloy 9, Gordon 9, Busby 7, Coughlin 4, Cochrane 3, Steedman 2, Clark 1, Kennedy 1, McMinn 1, Wilkie 1, McCann 1, Robertson G. 1 Newman 1.
League Cup: Robertson G. 1, McLeod 1, Alexander 1.
Scottish Cup: McCann 2, Alexander 1, Robertson J. 1

Honours

Scottish League: Division 2 Champions 1950–51; Runners-up 1932–33, 1961–62,1974–75, 1980–81.
Record Victory: 11-1 v Stranraer, Scottish Cup 1st rd, 16 Jan, 1932.
Record Defeat: 2–10 v Dundee, Division 1, 1 Dec, 1962.
Most League Points: 53, Division 2, 1961-62.
Most Individual League Goals in Season: 33, Jimmy Gray, Division 2, 1927–28.
Most Capped Player: Billy Houliston, 3, Scotland.

Davidson	Wilkie	Gray	Maxwell	Clark	Gordon	Robertson G.	Busby	Alexander	Cloy	Robertson J.	Kennedy	Elder	Walker	Young J.	McCann	Miller	Newman	Coughlin	McMinn	Cochrane	Evans	Gardner	Beckett	McLaren	Young W.	Steedman	Trialist	*Match No.*
1	2	3	4	5	6	7	8*	9	10†	11	14				12													1
*1	2	3	4	5	6*	7†	8	9	10	11	12				14													2
1	2	3	4	5		7*	8	9	10	11	6					12												3
*1	2	3	4	6	12		8	9	7*	11	10	5																4
1	2	3	4	6	12		8	9*	7	11	10	5†				14												5
*1	7	3		4		12	8*	9	10	11	6	5				2												6
1		3	4†	5	8	7*	14	9	10	11			2			12									6			7
1	2	3		5	8		12	9	6	11					7	10*									4			8
1	2	3		5	10		9	8	6	11					7										4			9
1	2	3	14	5	7			8	6	9					11*		10	12†							4			10
1	2	3	4	5	7			8	6	9								11							10			11
*1		3		5	7			8	14	11*					12	2	10†	6	9						4			12
1		3		5	7			8	2	11								6	9	10					4			13
1	2	3*		5	7†	10		8	6	11					14			12	9						4			14
1	2	3	12			7*		8	6	11					14				9	10†	5				4			15
1	2	3	14			7		10	6	9					11			12	8*		5†				4			16
1	2	3				7	9*	8	6	11					10			12			5				4			17
1	2	3				7	9*	8	6	11					10			12			5				4			18
*1	2	3					9	8	6	11					7		10				5				4			19
*1	2	3						8	6	11							10		9	7	5				4			20
*1	2	3				9	14	8	6	11							10*	12		7	5†				4			21
1	2	3			7	9†	12	8	6	11						14		10*			5				4			22
1	2	3			7			9	6	11				4						10	5	8						23
*1					7		8	9	6	11				4		2			10		5		3					24
1	7							9		11				4		2			8	10	5		3	6				25
1	6			5	12		8	9		11									10*	7				3	4			26
*1	2	3			7		9	8	6	11									10					5	4			27
1	2	3			7		9*	8	6	11					12				10					5	4			28
*1	2	3			7		9	8	6	11									10					5	4			29
1	2	3		5	7		9*	8	6†	11					12				10	14					4			30
1	2	3			7		9*	8	6	11					12				10						4	5		31
*1	2	3			7*		9	8	6	11					12				10						4	5		32
1	2	3			7		9		6	11					8				10						4	5		33
1	2	3			7		9	8	6	11						4			10							5		34
1	2	3			7			8	6	11					9				10						4	5		35
1		3				7	9	8	6	11						2			10						4	5		36
*1	2	3			10	7	9*	8	6†	11									14						4	5	12	37
1	2	3			6	7	9	8	11										10						4	5		38
1	2	3		14	6	7	9*	8†	11										10						4	5	12	39
39	34	36	7	16	25	15	24	38	36	37	4	3	1	3	9	7	5	4	21	7	11	1	2	5	29	9	0	
			+ 3s	+ 1s	+ 3s	+ 1s	+ 4s		+ 1s		+ 2s				+ 9s	+ 4s	+ 6s	+ 1s	+ 1s								+ 2s	

More was seen of Queens this season, but they emerged as one of the most unpredictable teams in Scotland with no real form pattern being produced. They started the season with a 5-1 win at Montrose but have conceded five twice at home, including an incredible 5-3 defeat by Stirling Albion, when they led 3-0 after 63 minutes—then lost five goals in the next 17.

QUEEN'S PARK Division 2

Year Formed: 1867 *Ground:* Hampden Park, Glasgow G42. *Size:* 115yd×75yd. *Capacity:* 75,800.
Telephone: 041-632 1275 (ground). (under construction).
Coach: Eddie Hunter.
Secetary: James C. Rutherford.
Club Colours: Black and white hooped shirts, white shorts, white stockings with two black hoops on top.
Club Nickname: Spiders.
Only amateur club in British senior football.
Record Attendance: 97,000 v Rangers, Scottish Cup 2nd rd, 18 Feb, 1933. (Record for ground – 149,547, Scotland v England, 1937).
Previous Grounds: Queen's Park Recreation Ground 1867–73; 'First' Hampden (site: approx Florida Ave) 1873–83; 'Second' Hampden (renamed Cathkin Park and used by Third Lanark FC until 1967) 1883–1903.

1982-83 LEAGUE RECORD

Match No.	Date	Venue	Opponents	Result		H/T Score	League Pos'n	Goalscorers	Attendance
1	Sept 4	H	Hearts	L	1-2	1-0	12	Cook	1817
2	8	A	Hamilton	D	2-2	1-0	10	Grant, Nicholson	750
3	11	A	Partick Thistle	W	3-2	0-0	7	Gilmour 2, Grant	1738
4	14	H	Clyde	D	0-0	0-0	5		1000
5	18	A	Raith Rovers	L	1-3	0-2	10	Gilmour	500
6	22	H	Ayr United	W	3-1	2-1	5	Gilmour 2, Quinn	650
7	25	A	Clydebank	L	0-2	0-1	8		778
8	Oct 2	H	Alloa	L	1-2	1-1	9	McFarlane	800
9	9	A	Dunfermiline	D	1-1	0-1	12	Quinn	1500
10	16	H	Falkirk	L	0-2	0-2	12		681
11	23	A	St Johnstone	L	1-4	0-2	12	McFarlane	2321
12	30	H	Airdrie	D	1-1	1-1	12	Crawley	882
13	Nov 6	A	Dumbarton	D	1-1	1-1	11	Grant	600
14	13	H	Hamilton	L	1-3	1-2	12	Grant (pen)	844
15	20	H	Raith Rovers	D	2-2	0-1	11	Grant, Houston o.g.	753
16	27	A	Ayr United	D	2-2	1-0	10	Graham, Quinn	1048
17	Dec 4	A	Alloa	L	1-4	0-2	13	McFarlane	719
18	11	H	Clydebank	D	2-2	0-0	12	Quinn, Grant	756
19	27	H	Partick Thistle	L	1-4	0-1	13	Quinn	2300
20	Jan 1	A	Clyde	W	1-0	1-0	11	Gilmour	908
21	3	H	Dumbarton	W	2-1	0-1	12	Crawley 2	700
22	8	A	Falkirk	L	0-2	0-2	12		2500
23	15	H	Dunfermiline	D	2-2	1-1	13	Nicholson, Quinn	644
24	22	A	Airdrie	W	1-0	1-0	12	Grant	1200
25	Feb 5	H	St Johnstone	L	1-2	1-1	12	Gilmour	974
26	12	A	Dumbarton	L	1-2	0-1	13	McNiven	600
27	26	H	Hearts	L	0-3	0-1	13		1468
28	Mar 5	A	Alloa	L	1-3	1-2	13	Nicholson	626
29	15	H	Hamilton	L	1-4	0-1	14	Gilmour (pen)	693
30	19	A	Clyde	L	1-2	1-1	14	Nicholson	750
31	26	A	St Johnstone	L	1-2	1-2	14	Crawley	1924
32	Apr 2	H	Falkirk	D	1-1	1-1	14	McNiven	711
33	6	A	Hearts	L	0-2	0-1	14		5500
34	9	H	Airdrie	W	4-3	1-2	14	Quinn 2, Gilmour, Nicholson	648
35	16	A	Dunfermiline	L	0-1	0-1	14		1250
36	23	H	Partick Thistle	L	0-1	0-1	14		1667
37	30	A	Ayr United	L	0-4	0-1	14		929
38	May 7	H	Clydebank	L	1-3	0-1	14	Gilmour	665
39	14	A	Raith Rovers	D	2-2	1-0	14	Quinn, Grant	800

Final League Position: 14

Goalscorers

League: Gilmour 10, Quinn 9, Graw 8, Nicholson 5, Crawley 4, Grant 3, McNiven 2, Cook 1, Graham 1, opponent 1.
League Cup: Gilmour 3, Verrachia 1, McNiven 1, Grawley 1.
Scottish Cup: Gilmour 2, Crawley 2, Brannigan 1, Robertson 1.

Honours
Scottish League – Division 2 Champions 1922–23, 1955–56, 1980–81
Scottish Cup – Winners 1874, 1875, 1876, 1880, 1881, 18782, 1884, 1886, 1890, 1893; Runners-up 1892, 1900.
FA Cup – Runners-up 1884, 1885.
Record Victory: 16-0 v St Peters, Scottish Cup 1st rd, Sept 1885.
Record Defeat: 0-9 v Motherwell, Division 1, 26 Apr, 1930.
Most League Points: 57, Division 2, 1922–23.
Most Individual league Goals in Season: 32, Peter Buchan, Division 2, 1962–63.
Most Capped Player: Watty Arnott, 14, Scotland.

Atkins	McFarlane	Dickson	Rennie	Woods	McNiven	Cook	Crawley	Nicholson	Grant	Gilmour	Graham	Caven	Cairns	Quinn	Robertson	Hunter	Verrechia	Storrie	Brannigan	Chalmers	Shearer	Walker	*Match No.*
1	2	3	4	5	6	7	8	9	10*	11				12									1
1	2	3	4	5	6	7	8	9	10	11													2
1	2	3	4	5	6		7	9	10	11	8												3
1	2	3	4	5	6		7	9	10	11	8*			12									4
1	2	3	4	5	6		7	9	10	11	8												5
1	2	3	4	5	6		7	9	10	11				8									6
1	6	3	4			7		9		11†	8	2*	5	10			12			12			7
1	2	3	4	5	6	7		9		11				10*	8		12						8
1	2	3	4	5	6*	7		9	10	11	8				12								9
1	2	3	4	5	6	7*	8	9†	10	11				12	14								10
1	6	3	2	5	7*	4	8	9†	10	11	14			12									11
1	2		4		6	5	7		9	11	8			10		3							12
1	2		4	12	6	5	7*		9	11†	8			10		3	14						13
1	2		4	5	6		7		10*	11	8			9		3	12						14
1	2	3	4		6*	5	7		10	11	8				12		9†				14		15
1	2	3	4	5		7	6		10	11	8			9									16
1	2	3	4	5		7	6		10	11	8*			9	12								17
	8	3	4	5	6		7		10	11*	12			9		2		1					18
*	7	3	4	5	6		8		10	11				9		2		1					19
1	2	3	4	5	6		7		10	11	8			9									20
*		3	4	5	6		7		10	11	9			8		2		1					21
1	2	3	4	5	6		7	12	10*	11	8			9									22
1		3	4	5	6		7	10		11	8			9		2							23
1		3	4		6	2	7	10	9	11	8*				12				5				24
1	2	3	4		6		7	10	9	11					8				5				25
1	2	3	4*		6		7	10†	9	11	8			14	12				5				26
1	2	3		5	6	4	7		10	11	8			9									27
1	2*	3	12	5	7	4	6	11†	10	14	8			9									28
*1	2	3		5	6	4	7	9	10	11	8												29
1	2	3	4*	5	6		7	10		11	8			9					12				30
1	2	3		6	6	4	7	9*	10	11	8						12						31
1	2	3		7	6	4			10*	11	8			9			12		5				32
*1	7	3		5	6	4		10		11	8			9		2							33
1	7	3		5	6	4		12	10*	11	8			9		2							34
1	7	3		5	6	4		10		11*	8					2	9			12			35
1	7	3		4	9	12	6	10			8*		2				11†		5	14			36
1	2	3		10	6*	4	7		9		8			11†		12			5		14		37
1	2	3		4	6		7	10		11	8			9					5*			12	38
1	2	3		4			6		10	11	8			9	7				5				39
36	36	36	27	32	35	22	32	25	31	36	30	1	2	23	3	10	3	3	8	0	0	0	
			+ 1s	+ 1s		+ 1s		+ 2s		+ 1s	+ 2s			+ 5s	+ 6s	+ 1s	+ 6s		+ 1s	+ 3s	+ 2s	+ 1s	

The loss of several fine players to the professional scene finally caught up with Queen's, but they fought hard against the odds to stay up. Defender Joe Woods and striker Jimmy Quinn took the chance to break into the first team and they will find the Second Division considerable less exacting.

RAITH ROVERS Division 1

Year Formed: 1883. *Limited Company:* 1907. *Ground:* Stark's Park. *Size:* 113yd×67yd.
Capacity: 22,150 (3150 seats). *Telephone:* Kirkcaldy 263514.
Manager: Gordon Wallace. *Club Secretary:* Mrs M. B. Watters.
Club Colours: Royal blue, white.
Record Attendance: 31,306 v Hearts, Scottish Cup 2nd rd, 7 Feb, 1953.
Previous Grounds: Robbie's Park 1883–89.
Managers since the War: Bert Herdman, Hugh Shaw, Doug Cowie, George Farm, Tommy Walker, Jimmy Millar, Bill Baxter, George Farm, Bert Paton, Andy Matthew, Willie McLean.

1982-83 LEAGUE RECORD

Match No.	Date	Venue	Opponents	Result		H/T Score	League Pos'n	Goalscorers	Attendance
1	Sept 4	A	Clydebank	D	1-1	0-1	9	More	531
2	8	H	St Johnstone	L	0-3	0-1	13		1100
3	11	H	Airdrie	L	0-3	0-2	14		800
4	14	A	Dunfermline	W	2-1	1-1	10	Harris 2	1900
5	18	H	Queen's Park	W	3-1	2-0	7	Russell, Harris (pen), Ballantyne	500
6	22	A	Alloa	L	0-3	0-2	10		600
7	25	A	Partick Thistle	L	1-2	0-0	12	Harris	1800
8	Oct 2	H	Hearts	W	1-0	0-0	8	Harris	3000
9	9	A	Clyde	W	2-0	0-0	8	Harris, Russell	550
10	16	H	Dumbarton	W	3-0	1-0	7	Russell, Spence, Harris	500
11	23	H	Hamilton	W	4-1	1-1	6	Robinson, Harris, Russell, Kerr	1000
12	30	A	Ayr United	W	4-0	1-0	4	Russell 2, Harris, Spence	1007
13	Nov 6	H	Falkirk	W	2-1	1-0	4	Harris (pen) Spence	1500
14	13	A	St Johnstone	L	1-2	0-1	5	Harris	3123
15	20	A	Queen's Park	D	2-2	1-0	5	More, Ballantyne	753
16	27	H	Alloa	L	0-1	0-1	7		1200
17	Dec 4	A	Hearts	L	0-2	0-1	8		4190
18	11	H	Partick Thistle	D	2-2	1-0	7	Russell 2	1600
19	18	H	Clydebank	L	0-3	0-1	8		1050
20	27	A	Airdrie	W	2-1	1-1	7	Harris, Spence	1200
21	Jan 1	H	Dunfermline	W	6-0	3-0	5	Russell 2, Thomson, Spence, Harris, Ballantyne	2500
22	3	A	Falkirk	L	0-2	0-0	6		2000
23	8	A	Dumbarton	L	1-2	1-1	6	Russell	500
24	15	H	Clyde	L	1-3	0-1	6	Smith	1100
25	22	H	Ayr United	L	0-1	0-0	7		970
26	Feb 2	A	Hamilton	D	2-2	0-2	7	Thomson, Candlish	724
27	26	H	Alloa	W	3-1	0-1	6	Smith, Russell, Thomson (og)	900
28	Mar 5	A	St Johnstone	L	0-1	0-0	8		2174
29	19	A	Hamilton	W	5-0	0-0	7	Marshall 2, Harris, Kerr (pen), Russell (pen)	824
30	22	A	Partick Thistle	L	0-1	0-1	7		1600
31	26	H	Clydebank	L	1-3	1-1	9	Kerr (pen).	1000
32	29	H	Hearts	W	4-2	1-1	7	Harris, Kerr (pen), Marshall, More	2100
33	Apr 2	A	Dunfermline	D	2-2	1-0	7	McCathie (og), Crawford (og)	2100
34	9	H	Dumbarton	D	0-0	0-0	7		600
35	16	A	Airdrie	L	2-4	1-2	7	Harris, More	600
36	23	H	Falkirk	L	0-3	0-2	8		700
37	30	A	Clyde	D	3-3	0-0	9	Kerr (pen), Marshall 2	713
38	May 7	A	Ayr United	L	2-3	0-1	10	Harris, Thomson	1142
39	14	H	Queen's Park	D	2-2	0-1	9	Marshall, Harris	800

Final League Position: 9

Goalscorers

League: Harris 18, Russell 13, Marshall 6, Spence 5, Kerr 5, More 4, Ballantyne 3, Thomson 3, opponents 3, Smith 2, Candlish 1, Robinson 1.
League Cup: Harris 2, Ballantyne 1, Russell 1, Gibson 1.
Scottish Cup:

Honours
Scottish League – Division 2 Champions 1907–08, 1909–10 (shared), 1937–38, 1948–49; Runners-up 1908-09, 1926–27, 1966–67, 1975–76, 1977–78.
Scottish Cup – Runners-up 1913.
Scottish League Cup – Runners-up 1948–49
Record Victory: 10-1 v Coldstream, Scottish Cup 2 rd, 13 Feb 1954.
Record Defeat: 2-11 v Morton, Division 2, 18 March 1936.
Most League points: 59, Division 2, 1937–38.
Most Individual League Goals in Season: 38, Norman Haywood, Divison 2, 1937–38.
Most Capped Player: Dave Morris, 6, Scotland.
Most League Goals: 142, Division 2, 1937–38.
British Record Goalscorers: 142 goals in 34 Division 2 matches, 1937–38.

Walker	Cramb	Robertson	Candlish	Thomson	Forsyth	More	Robinson	Gibson	Harris	McCulloch	Mitchell	Sweeney	Houston	McDonough	Urquhart	Ballantyne	Steen	Russell	McCulloch	Spence	Kerr	Steel	Gillespie	Marshall	Smith	*Match No.*
1		2*	3	4	5	6	7	8	9	10	11				12											1
1		2	3	4	5*	6	7	8	9	10	11				12											2
1		2		4		6	7	8	9	10*	11†	3	5		12	14										3
1				6		5	7	8	11				2	3	4	9	10									4
1				6		5	7		11				2	3	4	9	10	8								5
1				6	5		7		11				2	3	4	9		8	10							6
1				6		5	7		11				2	3	4	9*	10	8		12						7
1				6		5	7		9				2	3	4	12	10	8*		11						8
1				6		5	7		9*				2	3	4	12	10†	8		11	14					9
1				6		5	7		9				2	3	4			8		11	10					10
1				6		5	7		9				2	3	4			8		11	10					11
1				6		5	7		9*				2	3	4	12		8		11	10					12
1				6		5	7		9				2	3	4			8		11	10					13
1				6		5	7		9				2	3	4	12		8*		11	10					14
1				6		5	7		9				2	3	4	12		8*		11	10					15
1				6		5*	7	14	11				2	3	4	9	12	8†			10					16
1		2	12	6	5*		4	14	9					3		8†	7			11	10					17
1		2	14	6			4		9*					3		12	7	8		11†	10	5				18
1			12	6			4*		9				2	3		14	7†	8		11	10	5				19
1			3			5			9				4	2				8		11	10		6	7		20
1			3	5					9				4	2		12		8		11*	10		6	7		21
1			3	5					9				4	2		14	12	8		11†	10		6*	7		22
1			3	5					9				4	2				8		11	10		6	7		23
1		2	3	6		5							4					8		11	10			7	12	24
	1	2	3	6		5							4					8		11	10			7	9	25
1		2	3	6		5							4		7			8			10			11	9	26
1		2	3		6	5			7						4			9			10			11	8	27
1		2	3		6*	5			7				12		4			9			10			11	8	28
1		2	3		6	5			7						4			9		12	10*			11	8	29
1		2	3		6	5			7						4			9			10			11	8	30
1		2	3		6	5			7				12		4			9*			10			11	8	31
1		2	3		6	5			7				4		8						10			11	9	32
1		2		12	6	5			7					3	4			9*			10			11	8	33
1		4	3		6	5			7					2	8			12			10			11*	9	34
	1	4	3		6	5			11						8			9			10		2		7	35
	1	2		3	6	5			7						4			9		12	10			11*	8	36
1		2			6	5	7*		9						4	12			10		3			11	8	37
1		2		3	6	5	12		7						4	14		9	10*					11†	8	38
1		2		3	6	5			7						4			9	10					11	8	39
36	3	21	17	28	17	32	20	4	36	3	3	1	23	22	27	7	8	31	4	17	28	2	5	19	15	
			+ 3s	+ 1s			+ 1s	+ 2s					+ 2s		+ 3s	+ 12s	+ 2s	+ 1s		+ 3s	+ 1s				+ 1s	

A shattering series of injuries made it very difficult for the Fifers to find a settled team and pattern during an unsteady season when manager Gordon Wallace can reflect on one startling step forward.
64 League goals compared with 31 last season was enough to earn a league placing three steps up the table, leaving defensive leaks the priority for the coming campaign.

RANGERS Premier Division

Year Formed: 1873. *Turned Professional:* 1893. *Limited Company:* 1899.
*Ground:*Ibrox Stadium, Glasgow G5I 2XD. *Size:* 115yd×75yd. *Capacity:* 44,000 (19,000 seated).
Telephone: 041-427 0159. *Manager:* John Greig MBE. *Asst. Manager:* Tommy McLean. *Secretary:* R. C. Ogilvie.
Club Colours: Royal blue shirts with white shorts, royal blue stockings.
Club Nickname: Blues or Gers.
Record Attendance: 118,567 v Celtic, Division 1, 2 Jan, 1939.
Previous Grounds: Flesher's Haugh on Glasgow Green was shared with Great Eastern FC; Kinning Park, Burnbank; Ibrox Park since 1887.
Record Transfer Fee Received: £140,000, from Coventry C for Colin Stein, Oct 1972.
Record Transfer Fee Paid: £225,000 to Hibernian for Craig Paterson, July 1982.
European Competitions: *European Cup* 1956–57, 1957–58, 1959–60, 1961–62, 1963–64, 1964–65, 1975–76, 1976–77; 1978–79; *European Cup-Winners' Cup* 1960–61 (finalists), 1962–63, 1966–67 (finalists), 1969–70, 1971–72 (winners), 1973–74, 1977–78, 1979–80, 1981–82. *Fairs Cup* 1967–68, 1968–69, 1970–71. *UEFA Cup* 1982–83.

1982-83 LEAGUE RECORD

Match No.	Date	Venue	Opponents	Result		H/T Score	League Pos'n	Goalscorers	Attendance
1	Sept 4	A	Motherwell	D	2-2	1-0	—	Prytz (pen), Redford	19,159
2	11	H	Dundee United	D	0-0	0-0	5		25,000
3	18	H	Kilmarnock	W	5-0	2-0	2	MacDonald 2, Russell, Johnstone, McClelland	17,000
4	25	A	Aberdeen	W	2-1	0-0	2	Johnstone, Prytz	22,000
5	Oct 2	H	Dundee	D	1-1	0-0	2	Johnstone	16,000
6	9	A	Morton	D	0-0	0-0	2		15,000
7	16	A	St Mirren	D	2-2	1-1	3	Bett, McKinnon	12,121
8	23	H	Hibernian	W	3-2	2-1	3	Johnstone 2, McNamara o.g.	17,000
9	30	A	Celtic	L	2-3	2-1	4	Prytz, Cooper	60,408
10	Nov 6	H	Motherwell	W	4-0	1-0	4	Dalziel 2, MacDonald 2	17,000
11	13	A	Dundee United	L	2-4	1-1	4	Johnstone, Cooper	16,470
12	20	A	Kilmarnock	D	0-0	0-0	4		9500
13	27	H	Aberdeen	L	0-1	0-0	4		24,000
14	Dec 11	H	Morton	D	1-1	0-1	4	Prytz (pen)	9500
15	18	H	St Mirren	W	1-0	1-0	4	MacDonald	10,500
16	27	A	Hibernian	D	0-0	0-0	4		16,000
17	Jan 1	H	Celtic	L	1-2	1-1	4	Black	44,000
18	3	A	Motherwell	L	0-3	0-1	4		11,383
19	8	H	Dundee United	W	2-1	1-1	4	Prytz, Kennedy	15,500
20	15	H	Kilmarnock	D	1-1	0-0	4	MacDonald	7000
21	22	A	Aberdeen	L	0-2	0-1	4		22,000
22	Feb 5	H	Dundee	D	1-1	0-0	4	McPherson	7000
23	12	A	Morton	W	5-0	1-0	4	Bett 2, Kennedy 2, MacDonald	6900
24	26	A	St Mirren	L	0-1	0-1	4		11,484
25	Mar 2	A	Dundee	L	0-1	0-0	4		6624
26	5	H	Hibernian	D	1-1	0-0	4	Dalziel	10,975
27	19	H	Motherwell	W	1-0	1-0	4	McClelland	17,000
28	23	A	Celtic	D	0-0	0-0	4		51,062
29	26	A	Kilmarnock	W	1-0	1-0	4	MacDonald	6500
30	Apr 2	A	Dundee United	L	1-3	0-1	4	Clark	14,142
31	9	H	Aberdeen	W	2-1	1-1	4	Redford, Bett	19,800
32	23	H	Morton	W	2-0	1-0	4	MacDonald, Redford	9500
33	30	H	St Mirren	W	4-0	1-0	4	Bett 2 (1 pen), MacDonald, Clark	9000
34	May 3	A	Dundee	L	1-2	1-1	4	Clark	4788
35	7	A	Hibernian	W	2-1	2-0	4	Cooper 2	10,500
36	14	H	Celtic	L	2-4	2-0	4	Cooper, Clark	40,000

Final League Position: 4

Goalscorers

League: MacDonald 10, Johnstone 6, Bett 6, Prytz 5, Cooper 5, Clark 4, Redford 3, Dalziel 3, Kennedy 3, McClelland 2, Russell 1, McKinnon 1, Black 1, McPherson 1, opponent 1.
League Cup: MacDonald 8, Bett 5, Cooper 5, Johnstone 3, Paterson 2, Prytz 2, Dalziel 1, Redford 1, McPherson 1, Black 1, McClelland 1.
Scottish Cup: MacDonald 2, Clark 2, Kennedy 1, Dalziel 1, Cooper 1, opponent 1.
UEFA Cup: Johnstone 2, Cooper 1, McClelland 1.

Honours

Scottish League: Division 1 Champions 1890–91 (shared with Dumbarton), 1898–99, 1899–1900, 1900–01, 1901–02, 1910–11, 1911–12, 1912–13, 1917–18, 1919–20, 1920–21, 1922–23, 1923–24, 1924–25, 1926–27, 1927–28, 1928–29, 1929–30, 1930–31, 1932–33, 1933–34, 1934–35, 1936–37, 1938–39, 1946–47, 1948–49, 1949–50, 1952–53, 1955–56, 1956–57, 1958–59, 1960–61, 1962–63, 1963–64, 1974–75; Runners-up 21 times; Premier Division Champions 1975–76, 1977–78; Runners-up 1976–77, 1978–79.
Scottish Cup: Winners 1894, 1897, 1898, 1903, 1928, 1930, 1932, 1934, 1935, 1936, 1948, 1949, 1950, 1953, 1960, 1962, 1963, 1964, 1966, 1973, 1976, 1978, 1979, 1981; Runners-up 14 times.
Scottish League Cup: Winners 1946–47, 1948–49, 1960–61, 1961–62, 1963–64, 1964–65, 1970–71, 1975–76, 1977–78, 1978–79, 1981–82; Runners-up 6 times.
Record Victory: 14-2 v Blairgowrie, Scottish Cup 1st rd, 20 Jan, 1934. *Record Defeat:* 2-10 v Airdrieonians, 1886.
Most League Points: 76, Division 1, 1920–21. *Most Individual League Goals in Season:* 44, Sam English, Division 1, 1931–32. *Highest Scorer in Total Aggregate:* Bob McPhail, 233, 1927–39. *Most Capped Player:* George Young, 53, Scotland. *Most League Appearances:* John Greig, 496, 1962–78.

Stewart	McCloy	McKinnon	Dawson	McClelland	Paterson	Bett	Cooper	Prytz	McAdam	Redford	MacDonald	Johnstone	Russell	Stevens	Dalziel	McPherson	Smith	Mackay	Kennedy	Black	Robertson	Davies	Lyall	Clark	Bruce	*Match No.*
1		2	3	4	5	6	7	8	9	10	11															1
1		2	3	4	5	6	7*	8		10	11	9	12													2
1		2	3	4	5*	6	7	8		12	11†	9	10					14								3
1		2	3	4	5	6	7	8*	12	11		9	10													4
1		2	3*	4		6	7	8	5	14	11	9	10†							12						5
1		2		4	5	6	11	8*		3	7	9	10			12										6
1		2		4	5	6	7	8		3	11	9	10													7
1		2	12	4		6	7	8*		3	11†	9	10	5							14					8
1		2	3	4		6	7	8*	14	11	12	9	10†	5												9
1		2	3	4		6	7*	8			11		10†	5	9	14			12							10
1		2	3	4		6	7			10	11*	9		5	12	8										11
1		2	3	4		6	7†	8		10	11	9		5*		12					14					12
1		2	3*	4		6	7	8		10	11	9†			14	5		12								13
1		2		4	5	6	7*	8		3	9		10†		12		11			14						14
1		2*		4	5	6		14		3	11†		8				12	7	9	10						15
1		2		4	5	6		12		3	11		8					7*	9	10						16
1		2		3	5	6	7			12	11		8	4					9	10*						17
1		2		3	5	6	7				11		8	4					9	10						18
	1	2		5		6	12	7		3		11	8*	4					9	10						19
	1	2*		5		6	7	8†		3	14	11		4		12			9	10						20
	1	2	10	5		6	7*	8†		3	12	11		4					9	14						21
	1		2	4		6		8		10		11			7	5			9	3						22
	1		2	4		6		8		10		11			7	5			9	3						23
	1		2	4		6	12	8		10					7	5			9*	3	11					24
	1		2	4		6		12		10†					7	5			9*	3	11	8	14			25
	1	2		4		6	12	8		10		11†			7	5			9	3*		14				26
	1	12	2	3	5	6	7*	8†		10	11				14	4								9		27
	1	8	2	3	5	6	7	12		10*	11†				14	4								9		28
	1	8	2	3	5	6	7			10	11					4								9		29
	1	8	2	4	5	6	7	10*		3	11												14	9		30
	1	8	2	3	5	6	12			10	11†		7*		14	4								9		31
	1	8	2	3	5	6		10†		12	11		7*		14	4								9		32
	1	8	2	3	5	6	7	12		10*	11†		12			4								9		33
	1	2		3		6	7	12		10	11		8*			5						14	4†	9		34
			2		5		7	6				4	8*		11	12				14		10†	3	9	1	35
	1	8*	2	3	5	6	7			10	11†		12		14	4								9		36
18	17	30	24	35	20	35	26	24	2	29	25	18	18	10	7	15	1	2	12	11	2	2	2	10	1	
		+ 1s	+ 1s				+ 5s	+ 6s	+ 2s	+ 4s	+ 3s		+ 3s		+ 7s	+ 5s	+ 1s	+ 2s	+ 1s	+ 4s	+ 2s	+ 2s	+ 2s			

Another season of frustration and disappointment for the Ibrox club, reflected in their finishing fourth in the table, some 18 points behind Champions Dundee United. Injury kept record purchase Craig Paterson out of the team for 15 games and effected stability in defence but, even with him in the team, Rangers rarely looked consistent enough to sustain a lasting league challenge. Some promising young players were introduced by John Greig who will glean most satisfaction from the rapid improvement made by defender Davie McPherson and an impressive late show by the unfortunate Bobby Russell.

ST JOHNSTONE Division 1

Year Formed: 1884
Ground: Muirton Park. *Size:* 109yd×74yd. *Capacity:* 24,950 (2415 seats).
Telephone: Perth 26961.
Manager: Alec Rennie.
Secretary: George Bell. *Coach:* T. G. Fleming.
Club Colours: Royal blue with white pinstripe, white shorts and white stockings with royal blue tops.
Club Nickname: Saints.
Record Attendance: 29,972 v Dundee, Scottish Cup 2nd rd, 10 Feb, 1952.
Previous Ground: Recreation Ground.
European Competition: *UEFA Cup* 1971–72.

1982-83 LEAGUE RECORD

Match No.	Date	Venue	Opponents	Result		H/T Score	League Pos'n	Goalscorers	Attendance
1	Sept 4	H	Hamilton	W	3-0	0-0	1	Brogan 2, Rutherford	1519
2	8	A	Raith Rovers	W	3-0	1-0	1	Brogan 2, Morton	1100
3	11	A	Clyde	W	3-0	1-1	1	Brogan 2, Caldwell	780
4	15	H	Hearts	D	1-1	0-0	1	Addison	3900
5	18	H	Alloa	W	3-1	2-1	1	Brannigan 2, Pelosi	2106
6	22	A	Dunfermline	W	4-2	3-0	1	Pelosi, Brannigan, Brogan, Beedie,	2100
7	25	A	Dumbarton	L	1-4	0-2	1	Brogan	1000
8	Oct 2	H	Falkirk	W	4-0	1-0	1	Pelosi, Brogan, Brannigan, McNeil	2047
9	9	H	Airdrie	W	1-0	1-0	1	Addison	2590
10	16	A	Ayr United	D	1-1	0-1	1	Brogan	1439
11	23	H	Queen's Park	W	4-1	2-0	1	Brogan 2, Morton (pen), Pelosi	2321
12	30	A	Clydebank	L	0-1	0-0	1		897
13	Nov 6	A	Partick Thistle	L	1-3	0-0	1	Brogan	3160
14	13	H	Raith Rovers	W	2-1	1-0	1	Brogan, Morton	3123
15	20	A	Alloa	W	2-0	1-0	1	Brogan, Beedie	1772
16	27	H	Dunfermline	W	2-0	0-0	1	Caldwell, Rutherford	2442
17	Dec 4	A	Falkirk	W	1-0	0-0	1	Brannigan	1500
18	11	H	Dumbarton	W	1-0	1-0	1	Brogan	2042
19	18	A	Hamilton	D	1-1	0-1	1	Pelosi	1213
20	27	H	Clyde	W	2-1	0-1	1	Morton 2 (1 pen)	1800
21	Jan 1	A	Hearts	L	0-1	0-1	1		14,554
22	3	H	Partick Thistle	W	1-0	1-0	1	Brogan	4700
23	8	H	Ayr United	W	2-0	1-0	1	Brannigan, Brogan	2430
24	15	A	Airdrie	L	0-2	0-1	2		1500
25	22	H	Clydebank	L	0-1	0-0	2		2415
26	Feb 5	A	Queen's Park	W	2-1	1-1	1	Barron, Brannigan	974
27	12	H	Hamilton	L	0-2	0-2	2		2321
28	26	A	Ayr United	W	1-0	0-0	2	Brogan	1062
29	Mar 5	H	Raith Rovers	W	1-0	0-0	1	Brogan	2174
30	12	A	Clydebank	L	1-6	1-2	1	Morton (pen)	837
31	19	H	Falkirk	W	1-0	0-0	1	Brannigan	2295
32	26	H	Queen's Park	W	2-1	2-1	1	Brogan 2	1924
33	Apr 2	A	Partick Thistle	L	1-2	1-1	2	Brogan	4193
34	9	H	Hearts	W	2-1	1-0	2	Morton, Blair	7501
35	16	A	Clyde	W	1-0	0-0	1	Brogan	777
36	23	H	Dumbarton	W	1-0	0-0	1	Gibson	2317
37	30	A	Airdrie	D	1-1	0-0	1	Brogan	2000
38	May 7	A	Alloa	D	1-1	0-0	1	Brannigan	2985
39	14	H	Dunfermline	W	1-0	1-0	1	Brogan	4932

Final League Position: 1

Goalscorers

League: Brogan 26, Brannigan 9, Morton 7, Pelosi 5, Rutherford 2, Caldwell 2, Addison 2, Beedie 2, McNeil 1, Barron 1, Blair 1, Gibson 1.
League Cup: Brogan 10, Morton 3, Beedie 1, Addison 1.
Scottish Cup: Barron

Honours
Scottish League – Division 1 Champions 1982–83. Division 2 Champions 1923–24, 1959–60, 1962–63; Runners-up 1931–32.
Scottish League Cup – Runners-up 1969–70.
Record Victory: 8-1 v Partick T, League Cup, 16 Aug, 1969.
Record Defeat: 1-10 v Third Lanark, Scottish Cup 1st rd, 24 Jan, 1903.
Most League Points: 56, Division 2, 1923–24.
Most Individual League Goals in Season: 36, Jimmy Benson, Division 2, 1931–32.
Most Capped Player: Sandy McLaren, 5, Scotland.

Tulloch	Drummond	McDonald	Caldwell	McNeil	Fleming	Mackay	Rutherford	Addison	Brogan	Pelosi	Morton	Brannigan	Breedie	Kennedy	McVicar	Kilgour	Barron	O'Brien	McCafferty	Blair	Gibson	McDonald	Day	Reid	*Match No.*
1			2	3	4	5	6	7	8	9*	10	11						12							1
1			2	3			6	7	8	9	10	11	4	5											2
1			2	3			6	7	8	9	10	11	4	5											3
1			2	3			6	7	8	9	10	11	4	5											4
1			2	3			6	7*	8†	9	10	11	4	5		12		14							5
1			2	3			6	7	8	9	10	11	4	5											6
1			2	3	12		6	7	8	9†	10	11	4*	5				14							7
	1		5	3	2		6	7	8	9	10	11	4												8
		1	5	3	2		6	7	8	9	10	11	4												9
		1	5	3	2		6	7	8	9	10	11*	4									12			10
		1	5	3	2		6	7	8	9	10	11	4												11
		1	5	3	2		6	7	8	9	10	11	4												12
		1	5	3	2*		6	7	8	9	10	11	4		12										13
		1	5	3			6	7	8	9	10	11	4		2										14
		1	5	3			6	7	8	9	10	11	4		2										15
		1	5	3	10		6	7	8	9		11	4		2										16
		1		3*	12	5	6†	7	8	9	10	11	4		2		14								17
		1				3	6	7	8	9	10	11	4	5	2										18
		1			12	3*	6	7	8	9	10	11	4	5	2										19
		1	2				6	7	8	9	10	11	4	5	3										20
		1	2				6	7	8	9*	10	11	4	5	3			12							21
		1	2		9		6	7	8		10	11	4	5	3										22
		1	2		9		6	7	8		10	11	4	5	3										23
		1	2				6	7*	8		10	11		5	9	3	4		12						24
		1	3		2*		6	7	8		10	11		5			4	9†	14				12		25
		1	2		9		6	7	8			11		5	3		4		10						26
		1	2		9		6	7	8	14		11	12	5	3		4*		10†						27
		1	5				6	7	8	9	10	11	4		3	2									28
		1	5				6	7	8	9*	10	11	4		3	2								12	29
		1	5		7*		6		8		10	11	4		3	2				9				12	30
		1	5				6	7	8		10	11	4		3	2				9					31
		1	5				6	7	8		10	11	4		3	2				9					32
		1	5		12		6		8	14	10	11†	4		3	2				9*	7				33
		1	5				6		8	14	10	11†	4		3	2				9	7				34
		1	5				6	10	8			11	4		3	2				9	7				35
		1	5		4*		6	10	8	12		11			3	2				9	7				36
		1	5				6	10	8			11	4		3	2				9	7				37
		1	5				6	10	8	12	14	11	4		3	2				9†	7*				38
		1	5				6	10	8		9*	11	4		3	2				12	7				39
7	1	31	36	17	15	4	39	36	39	23	32	39	33	16	25	13	4	1	2	9	7	0	0	0	
					+ 4s					+ 5s	+ 1s		+ 1s		+ 1s	+ 1s	+ 1s	+ 4s	+ 2s	+ 1s		+ 1s	+ 1s	+ 2s	

Led by the prodigious scorer John Brogan, the Perth club emerged as Champions, by virtue of the consistency with which they sought the prize.
25 wins, bettered only by Motherwell last season, indicate that Alec Rennie's team are promoted on merit although several of his players will face the prospect of tackling the Premier Division for the first time.

ST MIRREN Premier Division

Year Formed: 1876. *Ground:* St Mirren Park (also known as Love Street). *Size:* 115yd×74yd. *Capacity:* 25,800.
Telephone: 041-889 2558 and 840 1337.
Manager: Ricky McFarlane. *Asst. Manager:* Erik Sorenson. *Secetary:* A. W. Marshall.
Club Colours: Black and white stripes, black shorts and black stockings with three white bands.
Club Nickname: The Buddies.
Record Attendance: 47,428 v Celtic, Scottish Cup 4th rd, 7 Mar, 1925.
European Competition: *UEFA Cup:* 1980–81.

1982-83 LEAGUE RECORD

Match No.	Date	Venue	Opponents	Result		H/T Score	League Pos'n	Goalscorers	Attendance
1	Sept 4	A	Hibernian	D	0-0	0-0	—		5471
2	11	H	Celtic	L	1-2	1-0	8	Richardson	15,000
3	18	H	Aberdeen	D	1-1	0-0	7	Scanlon	4800
4	25	A	Dundee United	L	0-3	0-1	9		6832
5	Oct 2	H	Kilmarnock	W	3-2	2-2	7	McDougall, Stark, McAvennie	3568
6	9	A	Motherwell	L	0-2	0-0	7		4292
7	16	H	Rangers	D	2-2	1-1	8	Scanlon, McDougall	12,121
8	23	A	Dundee	D	1-1	0-1	6	McAvennie	4831
9	30	H	Morton	D	1-1	0-1	6	Baines o.g.	3346
10	Nov 6	H	Hibernian	W	3-0	3-0	6	Fulton, McAvennie, Somner	3660
11	13	A	Celtic	L	0-5	0-4	6		15,044
12	20	A	Aberdeen	L	0-4	0-1	6		10,000
13	27	H	Dundee United	L	0-2	0-0	7		3823
14	Dec 4	A	Kilmarnock	D	2-2	0-1	6	McAvennie, Somner	2200
15	11	H	Motherwell	W	3-0	1-0	6	Scanlon 2, Abercromby	3563
16	18	A	Rangers	L	0-1	0-1	6		10,500
17	27	H	Dundee	D	0-0	0-0	6		4412
18	Jan 1	A	Morton	L	0-2	0-1	6		2200
19	3	A	Hibernian	D	1-1	0-1	6	Sneddon o.g.	6080
20	8	H	Celtic	L	0-1	0-1	7		14,748
21	15	H	Aberdeen	D	1-1	1-0	8	Scanlon	4530
22	22	A	Dundee United	L	2-3	1-3	8	McDougall, Somner	6714
23	Feb 5	H	Kilmarnock	W	2-0	1-0	7	Stark, McDougall	3303
24	26	H	Rangers	W	1-0	1-0	7	Fitzpatrick	11,484
25	Mar 1	A	Motherwell	D	0-0	0-0	7		4029
26	5	A	Dundee	W	5-2	2-1	6	Scanlon 2, Fitzpatrick, Wardrope, Logan	4161
27	16	H	Morton	L	2-3	1-2	5	Stark 2	3344
28	19	H	Hibernian	W	3-0	0-0	5	Fulton, Somner, Logan	4215
29	26	A	Celtic	D	1-1	0-0	5	Fulton	15,935
30	Apr 2	A	Aberdeen	W	1-0	0-0	5	McEachran	12,000
31	9	H	Dundee United	L	1-2	1-2	5	Somner	4617
32	23	H	Motherwell	W	4-0	1-0	5	McAvennie 3 (1 pen), McDougall	3257
33	27	A	Kilmarnock	D	2-2	2-0	5	McAvennie, McDougall	1000
34	30	A	Rangers	L	0-4	0-1	5		9000
35	May 9	H	Dundee	W	2-1	1-0	5	Logan, McDougall	6000
36	14	H	Morton	W	2-0	1-0	5	McDougall 2	2000

Final League Position: 5

Goalscorers

League: McDougall 9, McAvennie 7, Scanlon 7, Somner 5, Stark 4, Logan 3, Fulton 3, Fitzpatrick 2, opponents 2, Richardson 1, Abercromby 1, Wardrope 1, McEachran.
League Cup: McAvennie 4, Stark 4, McDougall 4, Richardson 3, Logan 1.
Scottish Cup: Stark 3, McDougall 2, Somner 1, McAvennie 1, Scanlon 1, opponent 1.

Honours
Scottish League – Division 1 Champions 1976–77; Division 2 Champions 1967–68; Runners-up 1935–36.
Scottish Cup – Winners 1926, 1959; Runners-up 1908, 1934, 1962.
Victory Cup: 1919–20.
Scottish Summer Cup: 1943–44.
Scottish League Cup: Runners-up 1955–56.
Anglo-Scottish Cup: Winners 1979–80.
Record Victory: 15-0 v Glasgow University, Scottish Cup 1st rd, 30 Jan, 1960.
Record Defeat: 0-9 v Rangers, Division 1, 4 Dec, 1897.
Most League Points: 62, Division 2, 1967–68; Division 1, 1976–77.
Most Individual League Goals in Season: 45, Dunky Walker, Division 1, 1921–22.
Most Capped Player: Iain Munro, 7, Scotland.

Thomson	Wilson	Clarke	Fitzpatrick	McCormack	Copland	McDougall	Stark	McAvennie	Richardson	Abercromby	Scanlon	McAveety	Fulton	Somner	Walker	Logan	Charnley	Wardrope	Money	McEachran	Speirs	Campbell	*Match No.*
1	2	3	4	5	6	7	8	9	10	11													1
1	2	3	4	5	6	7*	8	9	10		11					12							2
1	2		4	5	6	9*	8	7	10		11	3				12							3
1	2		4	5	6	12	7	9	8	10	11*	5											4
1	2		4	3	6	7	8	9	10		11	5											5
1	2	3	4		6	7*	8	9	10		11	5				12							6
1	2	3	4		6	7	8	9		10	11		5										7
1	2	3	4		6	7*	8	9	14	10	11†		5	12									8
1	2	3	4		6	7*	14	9	8	10	11†		5	12									9
1	2	3	4		6	12	7	10	8*	11			5	9									10
1	2	3	4		6	12	7*	10	8	11			5	9									11
1	2	3	4		6	12	7*	10	8	11			5	9									12
1	2	3			6	8	7	10*	4	11	12		5	9									13
1	2	10	4		6	14	9	7	8		11†		5	12	3*								14
1	2	3			4		7	10	8	6	11		5	9									15
1	2	3	4		6		7	10*	8		11		5	9		12							16
1	2	6	4				7	10	8	3	11		5	9									17
1	2	3*	4†		6	14	12	7	8	10	11		5	9		11							18
1	2					9	7	10	8	3	12		5		4	11	6*						19
1	2	3				9	7	10	8	6			5	12	4	11*							20
1	2	3				9	7	10	8	6	11		5		4								21
1	2	3				9	7	10	8	6	11*		5	12	4								22
1	2	3		4		9	7	10	8	6			5	11									23
1	2	3	4	6		9	7	10	8		11*		5					12					24
	2	3	4	6		9	7	10	8				5	11					1				25
1	2	3	4	6				10	8		11		5	9		12		7*					26
1	2	3	4	6		9	7	10	8		11*		5	12									27
1	2	3		4		8	7	10		6			5	9		11							28
1	2	3	4	6			7	8		10			5	9		11							29
1	2	3*		4	6	12		10	8	11			5			7		9†		14			30
1	2	3	4	6				10	8*	11			5	9		7				14			31
1	2	3		6		9		8	4	10			5					11		7			32
1	2	3	4	6		9		8		10	11*		5	12				7					33
1	2	3	4	6		9*	7	8	10				5	11†							12	14	34
1	2	3	4	6		9	7	8	10				5			11							35
1	2		4	6		9*	7	10	8	3			5		14	12						11†	36
35	36	31	26	19	18	23	29	36	31	24	19	4	30	15	5	8	1	4	1	1	0	1	
						+ 7s	+ 2s		+ 1s		+ 2s			+ 7s	+ 1s	+ 6s		+ 1s		+ 2s	+ 1s	+ 1s	

Distinctly out of touch in the opening half of the season, St Mirren were at one stage entitled to be considered relegation candidates. However the return after injury of defender John McCormack in February injected much needed vision and leadership into the team, who benefited by breaking from the bottom reaches of the table to finish a creditable fifth.

STENHOUSEMUIR Division 2

Year Formed: 1884. *Ground:* Ochilview Park. *Size:* 112yd×78yd. *Capacity:* 10,450 (450 seated).
Telephone: Larbert (0324) 562992.
Team Manager: Jim Black. *Secretary:* Jim Richardson. *Trainer:* W. Williamson.
Club Colours: Maroon shirts with white trimmings, white shorts and stockings.
Change Colours: Sky blue shirts with white trimmings, white shorts and stockings.
Club Nickname: The Warriors.
Previous Grounds: Tryst Ground until 1886, Goschen Park 1886–1890, Ochilview Park from 1890.
Record Attendance: 12,500 v East Fife, Scottish Cup 4th rd, 11 Mar, 1950.
Record Receipts: £2,800 v Celtic, Scottish League Cup quarter-final 1st leg, 10 Sept, 1975.

1982-83 LEAGUE RECORD

Match No.	Date	Venue	Opponents	Result		H/T Score	League Pos'n	Goalscorers	Attendance
1	Sept 4	H	Berwick	D	0-0	0-0	8		350
2	8	A	Q. O. S.	W	2-1	2-0	4	Strain, Munn	900
3	11	A	Forfar	D	0-0	0-0	5		760
4	14	H	Albion Rovers	W	1-0	1-0	4	Thompson	350
5	18	A	Cowdenbeath	L	0-2	0-0	6		250
6	22	H	Arbroath	L	1-6	0-4	10	Murray	500
7	25	A	Stirling Albion	L	0-1	0-1	11		600
8	Oct 2	H	Brechin City	D	2-2	1-1	10	Murray, Munn	350
9	9	A	East Fife	D	1-1	0-0	11	Munn	544
10	16	H	Stranraer	L	2-3	0-3	11	Quinn 2	350
11	23	A	Montrose	L	0-1	0-1	13		250
12	30	H	Meadowbank	L	1-2	0-1	13	Quinn	400
13	Nov 6	A	East Stirling	L	1-2	0-1	13	Thompson	350
14	13	H	Q. O. S.	L	2-3	2-1	13	Gordon (og), Murray	400
15	20	H	Cowdenbeath	D	2-2	0-0	13	Quinn, Thompson	350
16	27	A	Arbroath	D	0-0	0-0	13		598
17	Dec 4	A	Brechin City	L	2-5	0-1	13	Thompson 2	300
18	27	H	Forfar	L	0-1	0-1	13		300
19	Jan 1	A	Albion Rovers	L	1-2	0-0	13	Jenkins	300
20	3	H	East Stirling	D	2-2	0-1	13	Murray, Munn	300
21	15	A	Berwick	W	4-2	3-0	13	Caldwell, McCann (og), Murray 2	553
22	22	A	Meadowbank	L	1-3	0-2	13	Murray	400
23	Feb 9	H	East Fife	W	3-2	3-0	13	Gillen 2, Murray	300
24	12	A	Stranraer	L	0-2	0-1	13		360
25	19	A	Q. O. S.	D	2-2	1-1	13	Johnston, Murray	600
26	23	H	Montrose	W	3-1	1-0	13	Thompson, Murray, Newman	300
27	26	H	East Stirling	D	1-1	1-1	12	Buchanan	350
28	Mar 5	H	Berwick	L	0-1	0-0	12		300
29	9	H	Stirling Albion	D	0-0	0-0	13		450
30	12	A	Forfar	D	2-2	0-1	12	Buchanan, Murray	945
31	19	H	Stranraer	D	1-1	1-1	12	Murray	250
32	26	A	Cowdenbeath	D	1-1	1-0	12	Murray	300
33	Apr 4	H	Albion Rovers	W	1-0	0-0	12	Thompson	300
34	9	H	East Fife	L	0-2	0-0	12		250
35	16	A	Montrose	W	1-0	0-0	11	McRoberts	150
36	23	A	Meadowbank	D	1-1	0-0	11	Murray	915
37	30	H	Stirling Albion	L	0-4	0-2	11		300
38	May 7	A	Arbroath	L	2-5	2-3	11	Thompson, Murray (pen)	957
39	14	H	Brechin City	D	0-0	0-0	11		350

Final League Position: 11

Goalscorers

League: Murray 15, Thompson 8, Munn 4, Quinn 4, Gillen 2, Buchanan 2, opponents 2, Strain 1, Jenkins 1, Caldwell 1, Johnston 1, McRoberts 1, Newman 1.
League Cup: Murray 2, Erwin 1, Buchanan 1.
Scottish Cup: Murray 1, Erwin 1.

Honours
Scottish Cup – 1902–03 (semi-finalists).
Stirlingshire Cup – Winners 8 times.
Scottish Qualifying Cup – Winners 1900–01, 1901–02.
Record Victory: 9-2 v Dundee U, Division 2, 16 Apr, 1937.
Record Defeat: 2-11 v Dunfermline Ath, Division 2, 27 Sept, 1930.
Most League Points: 50, Division 2, 1960–61.
Most League Goals: 99, Division 2, 1960–61.
Most Individual Goals in Season: 31, Evelyn Morrison, Division 2, 1927–28 and Robert Murray, Division 2, 1936–37.
Record Transfer Fee Received: £11,000 from Forfar Athletic for Stephen Hancock, Aug 1981.

Howie	Rennie	Mullen	Strain	Evans	Buchanan	Thompson	Erwin	Murray	Johnston	Gillen	McCusker	Munn	Spence	Quinn	Gillespie	Kennedy	Newman	Caldwell	Jenkins	Trialist	McLeod	Larsley	McRoberts	Stirling	Hamilton	Beattie	Meakin	*Match No.*
1	2	3	4	5*	6	7	8	9	10	11			12															1
*1	3	6	2		5	7	8*		10	11	12	9	4															2
1	3	6	2		5	4		9	10	11	7	8																3
*1	3	6	2		5	9		12	11		8	10*	4	7														4
1	3	6	2		5	7			10	11	8	9	4															5
*1	3*		2	5	6	7	8	10	12	11		9	4															6
1	2*		4	5	6	7	8	9	10	3		11	12															7
1	2	6			5	9	8	11*	10	3		4		7										12				8
1		6			5	9	2	11	10	3		4		7*	8									12				9
1		6	12	2†	5	9		11	10*	3	14	4		7		8												10
1	2	6			5	9	4	12		3	14	11†		7	10*	8												11
1	2	6			5	9	4	14	12	3		11†		7	8	10*												12
1	2	6			5	9	4	11*		3	14	12		7	8	10†												13
1	2		4		6	9	5	11	10	3		12		7*	8													14
1	2				6	9	4		10	3		11		7*	8			5						12				15
1	2	6*	12		8	7	4	9	11	3					10			5										16
1	2		12		6	9		11	10	3*	4	7			8			5										17
*	2				6	9		10	11	3		7*		12	4			5	8	1								18
*	2				6	9	4*	11†		3	12	14		7	8			5	10	1								19
*1	2				8	4	6	9		3		12		7	10*			5	11									20
1	2	6			10	7	4	9		3				8				5	11									21
1	2	6			10†	7	4	9		3	14	12		8*				5	11									22
*1	2					7	6	9		3	4	10			8			5	11									23
	2†	14				7	6	9		3	4	10			8*			5	11	1				12				24
1			2		8	7	6	10	4	3		12						5	11		9*							25
*1			2		5	7	6	10	4	3							8		11		9							26
1			2		8	7	6	10	4	3								5	11		9							27
1			2		8	7	6	9	4	3		10						5	11									28
*1	3		2		8	7	6	9	4			10						5	11									29
1	3*		2		8	7	6	9	4	12		10†						5	11					14				30
1			2		8	7	6	9	4			10*						5	11			3		12				31
1			2		8	7	6	9*	4	3		12		10	11			5										32
1			2		8	7	6	9	11	3				10*	12			5					4					33
1			2		8	7	6	9	11	3		12		10*				5					4					34
1			2		8	7	6	9	4	3					11			5					10					35
1			2		8	7	6	9	4	3					11			5					10					36
1			2		8	7	6	9	4	3	12				11*			5					10					37
1	3		2		8*	7	6	9	11	14		10		12				5					4†					38
			2		5	7	6	9		3		4		10											1	8	11	39
35	26	14	23	4	37	39	33	33	28	34	6	22	4	17	17	4	1	23	14	3	3	1	6	0	1	1	1	
		+ 1s	+ 3s					+ 3s	+ 2s	+ 2s	+ 7s	+ 8s	+ 2s	+ 2s	+ 1s									+ 6s				

Gavin Murray's 15 goal's were the feature of an indistinguished season when the Larbert side spent most of the nine months lodged in the bottom two places of the table.
However just three defeats in their final eleven games hinted that a tightening up exercise had been successful and that some optimism could be permitted.

STIRLING ALBION Division 2

Year Formed: 1945. *Ground:* Annfield Park. *Size:* 110yd×74yd. *Capacity:* 20,000 (900 seated).
Telephone: Stirling 3584.
Manager: Alex Smith. *Secretary:* Duncan McCallum.
Club Colours: Red shirts, socks and shorts.
Record Attendance: 26,400 v Celtic, Scottish Cup 4th rd, 14 Mar, 1959.

1982-83 LEAGUE RECORD

Match No.	Date	Venue	Opponents	Result		H/T Score	League Pos'n	Goalscorers	Attendance
1	Sept 4	H	Forfar	W	2-0	0-0	5	Colquhoun, Leetion	450
2	8	A	Albion Rovers	L	0-3	0-1	6		400
3	11	A	Brechin	W	2-1	1-1	6	Colquhoun 2	400
4	15	H	East Stirling	W	2-0	1-0	3	Torrance, Leetion	600
5	18	A	Berwick	D	2-2	0-0	2	Cavanagh, Colquhoun	601
6	22	H	Meadowbank	D	1-1	0-1	3	Conroy o.g.	800
7	25	H	Stenhousemuir	W	1-0	1-0	3	Colquhoun (pen)	600
8	Nov 2	A	Arbroath	L	0-1	0-0	4		695
9	9	A	Q.O.S.	L	0-1	0-0	7		600
10	16	H	East Fife	W	1-0	0-0	5	McNeil	350
11	23	A	Stranraer	D	1-1	0-0	5	Steele	350
12	30	H	Montrose	L	2-3	0-1	6	Steedman, Leetion	530
13	Nov 6	A	Cowdenbeath	D	0-0	0-0	6		400
14	13	H	Albion Rovers	D	2-2	1-1	6	Torrance, Colquhoun	563
15	20	H	Berwick	W	3-1	1-1	5	Colquhoun, Steele 2	686
16	27	A	Meadowbank	L	1-3	1-1	6	Steedman	500
17	Dec 4	H	Arbroath	W	1-0	1-0	6	Moffat	650
18	27	H	Brechin City	D	1-1	1-1	6	Torrance	650
19	Jan 1	A	East Stirling	L	1-2	1-1	8	Torrance	350
20	3	H	Cowdenbeath	D	2-2	0-1	8	Colquhoun, Torrance	525
21	15	A	Forfar	D	0-0	0-0	7		930
22	22	A	Montrose	W	1-0	0-0	6	Colquhoun	200
23	29	H	Stranraer	W	1-0	0-0	4	Torrance	600
24	Feb 5	H	Q.O.S.	W	4-1	1-1	4	Colquhoun 2, Steele 2	700
25	12	A	East Fife	L	0-1	0-1	4		651
26	19	A	Brechin City	L	1-3	0-1	4	McRoberts	480
27	26	H	Meadowbank	W	2-0	1-0	5	Torrance, Colquhoun	800
28	Mar 5	A	Arbroath	L	0-1	0-0	7		454
29	9	A	Stenhousemuir	D	0-0	0-0	7		450
30	12	H	Albion Rovers	L	1-2	0-0	7	Steedman	650
31	19	A	Q.O.S.	W	5-3	0-2	6	Colquhoun 2, Torrance 3	600
32	26	A	Forfar	L	0-2	0-1	7		825
33	Apr 2	H	Cowdenbeath	W	3-1	2-0	6	Colquhoun 2, Walker	550
34	9	A	Berwick	W	3-0	2-0	6	Colquhoun (pen), Torrance 2	676
35	16	H	East Fife	D	2-2	1-1	6	Torrance, Cavanagh	660
36	23	H	Montrose	W	1-0	1-0	5	Irvine	630
37	30	A	Stenhousemuir	W	4-0	2-0	5	Colquhoun 3, Cavanagh	300
38	May 10	A	Stranraer	W	1-0	0-0	5	Torrance	600
39	14	H	East Stirling	W	3-1	1-0	5	Irvine, Colquhoun, McNeil	1050

Final League Position: 5

Goalscorers

League: Colquhoun 21, Torrance 14, Steele 5, Leetion 3, Cavanagh 3, Steedman 3, Irvine 2, McNeil 2, Moffat 1, McRoberts 1, Walker 1, opponent 1.
League Cup: Colquhoun 3, Dawson 1, McNeil 1.
Scottish Cup: Colquhoun 1.

Honours

Scottish League: Division 2 Champions 1952–53, 1957–58m 1960–61, 1964–65, 1976–77; Runners-up 1948–49, 1950–51.
Record Victory: 7-0 v Albion R, Division 2, 19 Nov, 1947; v Montrose, Division 2, 28 Sept, 1957; v St Mirren, Division 1, 5 March, 1960; v Arbroath, Division 2, 11 Mar, 1961.
Record Defeat: 0-9 v Dundee United, Division 1, 30 Dec, 1967.
Most League Points: 59, Division 2, 1964–65.
Most Individual League Goals in Season: 29, Joe Hughes, 1969–70.

Arthur	Walker	Dawson	McSherry	Steedman	McRoberts	Philliben	Moffat	Colquhoun	Torrance	Steele	McNeil	Cavanagh	Leetion	Aitchison	Spence	Grant	Graham	Irvine	Crolla	Fryer	Curran	Maxwell	*Match No.*
1		2		3	4†	5	6	7	8	9	10*	11	12	14									1
*1		2		3	4	5	6	7	8†	9	10*	11	12	14									2
1		2		3†	4	5	6	7	8	9*	12	11	10	14									3
*1		2		3	4	5	6	7	8	9	12	11†	10*	14									4
1		2		3	4	5	6	7	8	9		11	10*	12									5
*1		2		3	4	5	6	7	8	9		11	10										6
1				3	4†	5	6	7	8*	9	12	11	10	2						14			7
1		8		3	4	5	6	7		9	12	11	10	2*									8
1		2		3	4*	5	6	7		8	9	11	10	12									9
1		2		5	12	4	6	7*	8	9	14	11†	10		3								10
1		2		5	9†	4	6	7		12	14	11	10		3	8*							11
1		2†		5	12	4	6	7	8*	9	14	11	10		3								12
1				5	12	4	6	7	8	9		11*	10	2	3								13
	8	2		5	10	4	6	7	9†	14		11	12	3*			1						14
	8	2		5		4	6	7	9			11	10		3		1						15
	8	2		5		4	6	7	9		12	11*	10		3		1						16
	10	2		5		4	6	7	8	9		11*	12		3		1						17
*1	10	2		5		4	6	7	8	9	12	11*			3								18
*1	10			5		4	6	7	8	9	14	11†	12	2	3*								19
*1	4†	3		5			6	7	8	12	14	11*	10	2				9					20
1	2	3			4	14	6	7		12	8†	11	10	5				9*					21
1	2	3			4		6	7		12	8	11	10	5				9*					22
1	2	3			4*	5	6	7	9	12	8†	11	10		14								23
1	2	3				4	6	7	8	9	12	11†	12	5	10*								24
1	2*	12		3		4	6	7	8	9		11†	14	5	10								25
1	2†	12		3	4		6	7	8	9*		14	11	5	10								26
1	8	2		5	4		10	7	9					6	3				11				27
1	8	2		5	3†	4		7		12	9	14	10*	6					11				28
*1	8	2		5		4	10	7	9			12		6	3				11*				29
1	8	2		5		4	10	7	9			12	14	6*	3				11†				30
1	8	2				4	6	7	9			11	10*	5	3				12				31
1	8	2				4	6	7	9		12	11†		5*	3			14	10				32
1	4	3	8			5	6	7			9		10	2				11					33
1	2	3	4			5	6	7	8*		9	12	10					11*			14		34
1	2	3	4			5	6	7	8		9*	12	10					11					35
1	2	3	4			5	6	7	8			11	10					9*				12	36
1	2	3	4			5	6	7	8		12	11†	10					9*				14	37
1	2	3	4			5	6	7	8			11	10					9					38
1	2	3	4			5	6	7	8		12	11	10*					9†				14	39
35	26	34	7	26	17	34	38	39	32	18	10	31	27	18	17	1	4	10	5	0	0	0	
		+ 2s			+ 3s	+ 1s				+ 7s	+ 15s	+ 6s	+ 8s	+ 6s	+ 1s			+ 1s	+ 1s	+ 1s	+ 1s	+ 3s	

A solid season's work that suggests Albion will be a real force in the coming season. Manager Alex Smith has an abundance of talented front players, notably John Colquhoun. His 21 league goals soon brought him to the attention of several Premier League and English clubs and only the depressed state of the transfer market has averted a move.

STRANRAER Division 2

Year Formed: 1870. *Ground:* Stair Park. *Size:* 110yd×70yd. *Capacity:* 5500.
Telephone: Stranraer 3271.
Manager: Dave Sneddon. *Secretary:* Graham Rodgers.
Club Colours: Royal blue shirts, white shorts, blue stockings with red tops.
Record Attendance: 6500 v Rangers, Scottish Cup 1st rd, 24 Jan, 1948.

1982-83 LEAGUE RECORD

Match No.	Date	Venue	Opponents	Result		H/T Score	League Pos'n	Goalscorers	Attendance
1	Sept 4	H	Brechin City	L	1-2	0-1	9	McDonald	200
2	11	A	Berwick	D	2-2	0-1	10	McBride, Sweeney	598
3	15	H	Q.O.S	L	0-3	0-0	12		850
4	18	H	Forfar	W	2-1	1-1	11	Sweeney, Knox	375
5	22	A	East Stirling	W	2-1	1-1	11	McBride 2	150
6	25	H	Meadowbank	L	1-2	0-1	12	Hay (pen)	462
7	29	A	Cowdenbeath	L	1-2	0-2	12	Hay	260
8	Oct 2	A	Montrose	L	1-3	1-2	12	Sweeney	270
9	9	H	Arbroath	L	0-1	0-1	13		250
10	16	A	Stenhousemuir	W	3-2	2-0	13.	Knox, Bryce, McBride	350
11	23	H	Stirling Albion	D	1-1	0-0	12	McDonald	350
12	30	A	East Fife	D	2-2	2-2	12	Sweeney 2	340
13	Nov 9	A	Albion Rovers	W	3-2	1-0	11	Taylor 2, Newman	200
14	13	H	Cowdenbeath	W	2-0	2-0	9	McBride, Hay (pen)	360
15	20	A	Forfar	L	1-5	1-5	10	Hay	823
16	27	H	East Stirling	W	2-1	1-0	9	Neil, McBride	375
17	Dec 4	H	Montrose	D	3-3	3-1	10	McBride, Sweeney, Hay	319
18	27	H	Berwick	W	1-0	0-0	10	McBride	650
19	Jan 1	A	Q.O.S.	L	3-6	1-2	10	Murdoch, Bryce, Knox	800
20	3	H	Albion Rovers	L	1-5	1-4	11	Neil	650
21	15	A	Brechin City	L	2-4	0-3	11	Sweeney, McDonald	300
22	22	H	East Fife	D	2-2	0-2	10	Sweeney 2	350
23	29	A	Stirling Albion	L	0-1	0-0	10		600
24	Feb 5	A	Arbroath	L	0-3	0-1	10		449
25	12	H	Stenhousemuir	W	2-0	1-0	10	Knox, McBride	360
26	23	A	East Fife	L	0-3	0-1	10		400
27	26	H	Brechin City	L	1-3	1-0	10	Neil	360
28	Mar 5	A	Albion Rovers	W	2-1	1-1	10	Hay (pen), Sweeney	150
29	12	H	Meadowbank	L	0-2	0-0	11		350
30	19	A	Stenhousemuir	D	1-1	1-1	11	Murdoch	250
31	26	H	East Stirling	W	1-0	1-0	11	Sweeney	250
32	Apr 2	A	Montrose	L	0-1	0-0	11		100
33	9	H	Forfar	L	1-2	1-1	11	Quinn	200
34	13	A	Meadowbank	L	0-1	0-1	11		450
35	16	H	Berwick	L	0-3	0-1	12		200
36	27	A	Cowdenbeath	L	0-4	0-1	12		000
37	30	A	Arbroath	L	2-3	0-2	12	Dolan, Neil	417
38	May 10	H	Stirling Albion	L	0-1	0-0	12		600
39	14	H	Q.O.S.	D	0-0	0-0	12		350

Final League Position: 12

Goalscorers

League: Sweeney 11, McBride 9, Hay 6, Neil 4, Knox 4, Mcdonald 3, Bryce 2, Taylor 2, Murdoch 2, Quinn 1, Dolan 1, Newman 1.
League Cup: Neil 2, Taylor 2, Dolan 2, Hay 1.
Scottish Cup: Bryce 1, Sweeney 1.

Honours
Record Victory: 7–0 v Brechin C, Division 2, 6 Feb, 1965.
Record Defeat: 1-11 v Queen of the South, Scottish Cup 1st rd, 16 Jan, 1932.
Most League Points: 44, Division 2, 1960–61, 1971–72.
Most Individual Goals in Season: Derek Frye, 27, Division 2, 1977–78.

Strachan	McDonald	Hay	McCaig	Filson	Quinn	Neil	Knox	McBride	Taylor	Bryce	Murdoch	Sweeney	Kirkland	Maxwell	Trialist	Docherty	Parker	Dolan	McKie	Newman	Murphy	*Match No.*
1	2	3	4	5	6	7	8	9	10	11												1
1	2	3	4	5	6	7	11†	10	9*		8	12							14			2
*1	2	3	5	6	4	7*	12	9	10	11	8											3
1	2	3	5	6	4	7	12	9		10*	8†	11							12			4
*1	2	3	5	6	4	7	10†	9		14	12				11				8*			5
1	2	3	5	6	4*	7	14	9		10†	8	11							12			6
*1	2	3	5	6	4	7	8	9		10					11*				12			7
1	2	3		6	4	7	8	9		10*	5	11	12									8
1	2	3	5	6	4	7	8	9				11	10*						12			9
1	2	3	5	6	4*	7†	8	9		10		11						12	14			10
1	2	3	5	6	4	7	8	9		10		11*						12				11
1	2	3	5	6	4	7	8	9		10		11										12
*1	2	3	5	6	8	7		9	11	10					4							13
1	2	3	5	6	4	7	8	9		10		11										14
1	2	3	5	6	4	7	8	9		10		11										15
1	2	3	5	6	4	7	8	9*		10		11								12		16
1	2*	3	5	6	4	7	8	9		10	12	11										17
*1		3	5	6	4	7	8	9		10	2	11										18
*1		3	5	6	4	7	8	9		10	2	11*						12				19
*1		3	5	6	4	7	8	9†		10	2	11*						12	14			20
1	2	3	5	6	4	7	8	9		10		11										21
1	2	3	5	6	4	12	8	9		10*		11		7								22
1	2	3	5	6	4	12	8	9		10*		11		7								23
1	2	3	5	6	4*	12	8	9		10†		11		7				14				24
1	2	3	5	6	4	10	8	9				11		7								25
*1	2	3	5	6	4*		10	9		11†	12			8		7		14				26
1	2	3	5	6		7	10	12			4	11		8	9*							27
1	2	3	5	6†	10	7			12		4	11*		8		9		14				28
1	2	3	5		6	7*	10	9	11	12	4			8								29
1	2	3	5	6		7	10	9	11*	14	4†	12		8								30
1	2		5	6	4		10	9	12	7	3	11*		8								31
1	2		5†	6	4	12	10	9	14	7*	3	11		8								32
1	3		5	6	4	7*	8	9				11		14		12	2	10†				33
*1	3		5	6			10	9						8	4	11*	2	12		7		34
1	3		5	6	4		8	7	11		12	9		8†			2*	14				35
*1	3		5	6	4	7†	8	9*	12	10	2	11						14				36
1	3		5	6		14	4	12	9*	10†	2	11		8				7				37
1	3		5	6	4	7	8		9	10	2							11*			12	38
1	3		5	6		7	4	8	9	10*	2	11									12	39
39	36	30	38	38	34	35	37	37	9	28	18	28	1	14	5	3	3	3	1	1	0	
									+ 4s	+ 3s	+ 4s	+ 2s	+ 1s	+ 1s		+ 1s		+ 10s	+ 7s	+ 1s	+ 2s	

It has been some time since Stranraer showed any indication that they would be involved in the top half of the league, but perhaps their lowly league position is slightly unflattering.
Manager Dave Sneddon has attempted to bring some regularity to his team and most of their programme was completed by 14 players.

SCOTTISH LEAGUE FINAL TABLES

PREMIER DIVISION

		Home					Away					
	P	W	D	L	F	A	W	D	L	F	A	Pts
1. Dundee U	36	13	4	1	57	18	11	4	3	33	17	56
2. Celtic	36	12	3	3	44	18	13	2	3	46	18	55
3. Aberdeen	36	14	0	4	46	12	11	5	2	30	12	55
4. Rangers	36	9	6	3	32	16	4	6	8	20	25	38
5. St Mirren	36	8	5	5	30	18	3	7	8	17	33	34
6. Dundee	36	8	3	7	29	28	1	8	9	13	25	29
7. Hibernian	36	3	11	4	21	17	4	4	10	14	34	29
8. Motherwell	36	9	3	6	28	27	2	2	14	11	46	27
9. Morton	36	4	4	10	14	26	2	4	12	16	48	20
10. Kilmarnock	36	3	7	8	17	31	0	4	14	11	60	17

FIRST DIVISION

		Home					Away					
	P	W	D	L	F	A	W	D	L	F	A	Pts
1. St Johnstone	39	17	1	2	34	10	8	4	7	25	27	55
2. Hearts	39	13	4	3	46	20	9	6	4	33	18	45
3. Clydebank	39	8	5	6	32	27	12	5	3	40	22	50
4. Partick T	39	9	6	4	31	23	11	3	6	35	22	49
5. Airdrieonians	39	7	3	9	27	27	9	4	7	35	19	39
6. Alloa Ath	39	8	7	5	31	21	6	4	9	21	31	39
7. Dumbarton	39	6	7	6	26	32	7	3	10	24	27	36
8. Falkirk	39	8	2	9	20	22	7	4	9	25	33	36
9. Raith R	39	8	3	8	32	29	5	5	10	32	34	34
10. Clyde	39	8	2	10	32	38	6	4	9	23	28	34
11. Hamilton A	39	7	6	7	27	32	4	6	9	27	34	34
12. Ayr U	39	9	4	7	29	26	3	4	12	16	35	32
13. Dunfermline Ath	39	5	9	6	19	30	2	8	9	20	39	31
14. Queen's Park	39	3	6	10	24	39	3	5	12	20	41	23

SECOND DIVISION

		Home					Away					
	P	W	D	L	F	A	W	D	L	F	A	Pts
1. Brechin C	39	13	5	2	46	17	8	8	3	31	21	55
2. Meadowbank T	39	13	2	4	37	20	10	6	4	27	25	54
3. Arbroath	39	14	4	2	45	23	7	3	9	33	28	49
4. Forfar Ath	39	8	9	2	31	16	10	3	7	27	22	48
5. Stirling A	39	12	5	2	35	17	6	5	9	22	24	46
6. East Fife	39	8	5	6	35	20	8	6	6	33	23	43
7. Queen of the S	39	8	6	6	44	30	9	2	8	31	35	42
8. Cowdenbeath	39	10	4	5	35	25	3	8	9	19	28	38
9. Berwick R	39	6	7	6	25	30	7	3	10	22	30	36
10. Albion R	39	10	2	8	29	23	4	4	11	26	43	34
11. Stenhousemuir	39	4	8	8	22	33	3	7	9	21	33	29
12. Stranraer	39	6	4	10	21	32	4	3	12	25	47	27
13. East Stirling	39	4	4	12	20	38	3	5	11	21	41	23
14. Montrose	39	5	2	12	18	33	3	4	13	19	53	22

SCOTTISH LEAGUE 1890–91 to 1982–83

*On goal average/difference. †Held jointly after indecisive play-off. ‡Won on deciding match.
††Held jointly. ¶Two points deducted for fielding ineligible player.
Competition suspended 1940–45 during war. ‡‡Two points deducted for registration irregularities.

PREMIER DIVISION

Maximum points: 72

	First	*Pts*	*Second*	*Pts*	*Third*	*Pts*
1975–76	Rangers	54	Celtic	48	Hibernian	43
1976–77	Celtic	55	Rangers	46	Aberdeen	43
1977–78	Rangers	55	Aberdeen	53	Dundee U	40
1978–79	Celtic	48	Rangers	45	Dundee U	44
1979–80	Aberdeen	48	Celtic	47	St Mirren	42
1980–81	Celtic	56	Aberdeen	49	Rangers*	44
1981–82	Celtic	55	Aberdeen	53	Rangers	43
1982–83	Dundee U	56	Celtic*	55	Aberdeen	55

FIRST DIVISION

Maximum points: 52

1975–76	Partick T	41	Kilmarnock	35	Montrose	30
			Maximum points: 78			
1976–77	St Mirren	62	Clydebank	58	Dundee	51
1977–78	Morton*	58	Hearts	58	Dundee	57
1978–79	Dundee	55	Kilmarnock*	54	Clydebank	54
1979–80	Hearts	53	Airdrieonians	51	Ayr U	44
1980–81	Hibernian	57	Dundee	52	St Johnstone	51
1981–82	Motherwell	61	Kilmarnock	51	Hearts	50
1982–83	St Johnstone	55	Hearts	54	Clydebank	50

SECOND DIVISION

Maximum points: 52

1975–76	Clydebank*	40	Raith R	40	Alloa	35
			Maximum points: 78			
1976–77	Stirling A	55	Alloa	51	Dunfermline Ath	50
1977–78	Clyde*	53	Raith R	53	Dunfermline Ath	48
1978–79	Berwick R	54	Dunfermline Ath	52	Falkirk	50
1979–80	Falkirk	50	East Stirling	49	Forfar Ath	46
1980–81	Queen's Park	50	Queen of the S	46	Cowdenbeath	45
1981–82	Clyde	59	Alloa*	50	Arbroath	50
1982–83	Brechin C	55	Meadowbank T	54	Arbroath	49

FIRST DIVISION to 1974–75

Maximum points: a 36; *b* 44; *c* 40; *d* 52; *e* 60; *f* 68; *g* 76; *h* 84.

1890–91*a*††	Dumbarton	29	Rangers	29	Celtic	24
1891–92*b*	Dumbarton	37	Celtic	35	Hearts	30
1892–93*a*	Celtic	29	Rangers	28	St Mirren	23
1893–94*a*	Celtic	29	Hearts	26	St Bernard's	22
1894–95*a*	Hearts	31	Celtic	26	Rangers	21
1895–96*a*	Celtic	30	Rangers	26	Hibernian	24
1896–97*a*	Hearts	28	Hibernian	26	Rangers	25
1897–98*a*	Celtic	33	Rangers	29	Hibernian	22
1898–99*a*	Rangers	36	Hearts	26	Celtic	24
1899–1900*a*	Rangers	32	Celtic	25	Hibernian	24
1900–01*c*	Rangers	35	Celtic	29	Hibernian	25
1901–02*a*	Rangers	28	Celtic	26	Hearts	22
1902–03*b*	Hibernian	37	Dundee	31	Rangers	29
1903–04*d*	Third Lanark	43	Hearts	39	Rangers*	38
1904–05*d*	Celtic‡	41	Rangers	41	Third Lanark	35
1905–06*e*	Celtic	49	Hearts	43	Airdrieonians	38
1906–07*f*	Celtic	55	Dundee	48	Rangers	45
1907–08*f*	Celtic	55	Falkirk	51	Rangers	50
1908–09*f*	Celtic	51	Dundee	50	Clyde	48
1909–10*f*	Celtic	54	Falkirk	52	Rangers	46
1910–11*f*	Rangers	52	Aberdeen	48	Falkirk	44
1911–12*f*	Rangers	51	Celtic	45	Clyde	42
1912–13*f*	Rangers	53	Celtic	49	Hearts*	41

	First	Pts	Second	Pts	Third	Pts
1913–14*g*	Celtic	65	Rangers	59	Hearts*	54
1914–15*g*	Celtic	65	Hearts	61	Rangers	50
1915–16*g*	Celtic	67	Rangers	56	Morton	51
1916–17*g*	Celtic	64	Morton	54	Rangers	53
1917–18*f*	Rangers	56	Celtic	55	Kilmarnock	43
1918–19*f*	Celtic	58	Rangers	57	Morton	47
1919–20*h*	Rangers	71	Celtic	68	Motherwell	57
1920–21*h*	Rangers	76	Celtic	66	Hearts	56
1921–22*h*	Celtic	67	Rangers	66	Raith R	56
1922–23*g*	Rangers	55	Airdrieonians	50	Celtic	46
1923–24*g*	Rangers	59	Airdrieonians	50	Celtic	41
1924–25*g*	Rangers	60	Airdrieonians	57	Hibernian	52
1925–26*g*	Celtic	58	Airdrieonians*	50	Hearts	50
1926–27*g*	Rangers	56	Motherwell	51	Celtic	49
1927–28*g*	Rangers	60	Celtic*	55	Motherwell	55
1928–29*g*	Rangers	67	Celtic	51	Motherwell	50
1929–30*g*	Rangers	60	Motherwell	55	Aberdeen	53
1930–31*g*	Rangers	60	Celtic	58	Motherwell	56
1931–32*g*	Motherwell	66	Rangers	61	Celtic	48
1932–33*g*	Rangers	62	Motherwell	59	Hearts	50
1933–34*g*	Rangers	66	Motherwell	62	Celtic	47
1934–35*g*	Rangers	55	Celtic	52	Hearts	50
1935–36*g*	Celtic	66	Rangers*	61	Aberdeen	61
1936–37*g*	Rangers	61	Aberdeen	54	Celtic	52
1937–38*g*	Celtic	61	Hearts	58	Rangers	49
1938–39*g*	Rangers	59	Celtic	48	Aberdeen	46
1946–47*e*	Rangers	46	Hibernian	44	Aberdeen	39
1947–48*e*	Hibernian	48	Rangers	46	Partick T	36
1948–49*e*	Rangers	46	Dundee	45	Hibernian	39
1949–50*e*	Rangers	50	Hibernian	49	Hearts	43
1950–51*e*	Hibernian	48	Rangers*	38	Dundee	38
1951–52*e*	Hibernian	45	Rangers	41	East Fife	37
1952–53*e*	Rangers*	43	Hibernian	43	East Fife	39
1953–54*e*	Celtic	43	Hearts	38	Partick T	35
1954–55*e*	Aberdeen	49	Celtic	46	Rangers	41
1955–56*f*	Rangers	52	Aberdeen	46	Hearts*	45
1956–57*f*	Rangers	55	Hearts	53	Kilmarnock	42
1957–58*f*	Hearts	62	Rangers	49	Celtic	46
1958–59*f*	Rangers	50	Hearts	48	Motherwell	44
1959–60*f*	Hearts	54	Kilmarnock	50	Rangers*	42
1960–61*f*	Rangers	51	Kilmarnock	50	Third Lanark	42
1961–62*f*	Dundee	54	Rangers	51	Celtic	46
1962–63*f*	Rangers	57	Kilmarnock	48	Partick T	46
1963–64*f*	Rangers	55	Kilmarnock	49	Celtic*	47
1964–65*f*	Kilmarnock*	50	Hearts	50	Dunfermline Ath	49
1965–66*f*	Celtic	57	Rangers	55	Kilmarnock	45
1966–67*f*	Celtic	58	Rangers	55	Clyde	46
1967–68*f*	Celtic	63	Rangers	61	Hibernian	45
1968–69*f*	Celtic	54	Rangers	49	Dunfermline Ath	45
1969–70*f*	Celtic	57	Rangers	45	Hibernian	44
1970–71*f*	Celtic	56	Aberdeen	54	St Johnstone	44
1971–72*f*	Celtic	60	Aberdeen	50	Rangers	44
1972–73*f*	Celtic	57	Rangers	56	Hibernian	45
1973–74*f*	Celtic	53	Hibernian	49	Rangers	48
1974–75*f*	Rangers	56	Hibernian	49	Celtic	45

SECOND DIVISION to 1974–75

Maximum points: a 76; *b* 72; *c* 68; *d* 52; *e* 60; *f* 36; *g* 44; *h* 52.

1893–94*f*	Hibernian	29	Cowlairs	27	Clyde	24
1894–95*f*	Hibernian	30	Motherwell	22	Port Glasgow	20
1895–96*f*	Abercorn	27	Leith Ath	23	Renton	21
1896–97*f*	Partick T	31	Leith Ath	27	Kilmarnock	21
1897–98*f*	Kilmarnock	29	Port Glasgow	25	Morton	22
1898–99*f*	Kilmarnock	32	Leith Ath	27	Port Glasgow	25
1899–1900*f*	Partick T	29	Morton	26	Port Glasgow	20
1900–01*f*	St Bernard's	26	Airdrieonians	23	Abercorn	21
1901–02*g*	Port Glasgow	32	Partick T	31	Motherwell	26
1902–03*g*	Airdrieonians	35	Motherwell	28	Ayr U	27
1903–04*g*	Hamilton A	37	Clyde	29	Ayr U	28
1904–05*g*	Clyde	32	Falkirk	28	Hamilton A	27

	First	Pts	Second	Pts	Third	Pts
1905–06*g*	Leith Ath	34	Clyde	31	Albion R	27
1906–07*g*	St Bernard's	32	Vale of Leven*	27	Arthurlie	27
1907–08*g*	Raith R	30	Dumbarton	‡‡27	Ayr U	27
1908–09*g*	Abercorn	31	Raith R*	28	Vale of Leven	28
1909–10*g*‡	Leith Ath	33	Raith R	33	St Bernard's	27
1910–11*g*	Dumbarton	31	Ayr U	27	Albion R	25
1911–12*g*	Ayr U	35	Abercorn	30	Dumbarton	27
1912–13*h*	Ayr U	34	Dunfermline Ath	33	East Stirling	32
1913–14*g*	Cowdenbeath	31	Albion R	27	Dunfermline Ath	26
1914–15*h*	Cowdenbeath*	37	St Bernard's*	37	Leith Ath	37
1921–22*a*	Alloa	60	Cowdenbeath	47	Armadale	45
1922–23*a*	Queen's Park	57	Clydebank	¶50	St Johnstone	¶45
1923–24*a*	St Johnstone	56	Cowdenbeath	55	Bathgate	44
1924–25*a*	Dundee U	50	Clydebank	48	Clyde	47
1925–26*a*	Dunfermline Ath	59	Clyde	53	Ayr U	52
1926–27*a*	Bo'ness	56	Raith R	49	Clydebank	45
1927–28*a*	Ayr U	54	Third Lanark	45	King's Park	44
1928–29*b*	Dundee U	51	Morton	50	Arbroath	47
1929–30*a*	Leith Ath*	57	East Fife	57	Albion R	54
1930–31*a*	Third Lanark	61	Dundee U	50	Dunfermline Ath	47
1931–32*a*	East Stirling*	55	St Johnstone	55	Raith Rovers*	46
1932–33*c*	Hibernian	54	Queen of the S	49	Dunfermline Ath	47
1933–34*c*	Albion R	45	Dunfermline Ath*	44	Arbroath	44
1934–35*c*	Third Lanark	52	Arbroath	50	St Bernard's	47
1935–36*c*	Falkirk	59	St Mirren	52	Morton	48
1936–37*c*	Ayr U	54	Morton	51	St Bernard's	48
1937–38*c*	Raith R	59	Albion R	48	Airdrieonians	47
1938–39*c*	Cowdenbeath	60	Alloa*	48	East Fife	48
1946–47*d*	Dundee	45	Airdrieonians	42	East Fife	31
1947–48*e*	East Fife	53	Albion R	42	Hamilton A	40
1948–49*e*	Raith R*	42	Stirling Albion	42	Airdrieonians*	41
1949–50*e*	Morton	47	Airdrieonians	44	St Johnstone*	36
1950–51*e*	Queen of the S*	45	Stirling Albion	45	Ayr U*	36
1951–52*e*	Clyde	44	Falkirk	43	Ayr U	39
1952–53*e*	Stirling Albion	44	Hamilton A	43	Queen's Park	37
1953–54*e*	Motherwell	45	Kilmarnock	42	Third Lanark*	36
1954–55*e*	Airdrieonians	46	Dunfermline Ath	42	Hamilton A	39
1955–56*b*	Queen's Park	54	Ayr U	51	St Johnstone	49
1956–57*b*	Clyde	64	Third Lanark	51	Cowdenbeath	45
1957–58*b*	Stirling Albion	55	Dunfermline Ath	53	Arbroath	47
1958–59*b*	Ayr U	60	Arbroath	51	Stenhousemuir	40
1959–60*b*	St Johnstone	53	Dundee U	50	Queen of the S	49
1960–61*b*	Stirling Albion	55	Falkirk	54	Stenhousemuir	50
1961–62*b*	Clyde	54	Queen of the S	53	Morton	44
1962–63*b*	St Johnstone	55	East Stirling	49	Morton	48
1963–64*b*	Morton	67	Clyde	53	Arbroath	46
1964–65*b*	Stirling Albion	59	Hamilton A	50	Queen of the S	45
1965–66*b*	Ayr U	53	Airdrieonians	50	Queen of the S	49
1966–67*b*	Morton	69	Raith R	58	Arbroath	57
1967–68*b*	St Mirren	62	Arbroath	53	East Fife	40
1968–69*b*	Motherwell	64	Ayr U	53	East Fife*	47
1969–70*b*	Falkirk	56	Cowdenbeath	55	Queen of the S	50
1970–71*b*	Partick T	56	East Fife	51	Arbroath	46
1971–72*b*	Dumbarton*	52	Arbroath	52	Stirling Albion	50
1972–73*b*	Clyde	56	Dunfermline Ath	52	Raith R*	47
1973–74*b*	Airdrieonians	60	Kilmarnock	58	Hamilton A	55
1974–75*a*	Falkirk	54	Queen of the S	53	Montrose	53

Elected to First Division: 1894 Clyde; 1897 Partick T; 1899 Kilmarnock; 1900 Partick T; 1902 Partick T; 1903 Airdrieonians; 1905 Falkirk, Aberdeen and Hamilton A; 1906 Clyde; 1910 Raith R; 1913 Ayr U.

RELEGATED FROM PREMIER DIVISION

1975–76 Dundee, St Johnstone
1976–77 Hearts, Kilmarnock
1977–78 Ayr U, Clydebank
1978–79 Hearts, Motherwell
1979–80 Dundee, Hibernian
1980–81 Kilmarnock, Hearts
1981–82 Partick T, Airdrieonians
1982–83 Morton, Kilmarnock

RELEGATED FROM DIVISION 1

1975–76 Dunfermline Ath, Clyde
1976–77 Raith R, Falkirk
1977–78 Alloa Ath, East Fife
1978–79 Montrose, Queen of the S
1979–80 Arbroath, Clyde
1980–81 Stirling A, Berwick R
1981–82 East Stirling, Queen of the S
1982–83 Dunfermline Ath, Queen's Park

RELEGATED FROM DIVISION 1 (to 1973–74)

1921–22*Queen's Park, Dumbarton, Clydebank
1922–23 Albion R, Alloa Ath
1923–24 Clyde, Clydebank
1924–25 Third Lanark, Ayr U
1925–26 Raith R, Clydebank
1926–27 Morton, Dundee U
1927–28 Dunfermline Ath, Bo'ness
1928–29 Third Lanark, Raith R
1929–30 St Johnstone, Dundee U
1930–31 Hibernian, East Fife
1931–32 Dundee U, Leith Ath
1932–33 Morton, East Stirling
1933–34 Third Lanark, Cowdenbeath
1934–35 St Mirren, Falkirk
1935–36 Aidrieonians, Ayr U
1936–37 Dunfermline Ath, Albion R
1937–38 Dundee, Morton
1938–39 Queen's Park, Raith R
1946–47 Kilmarnock, Hamilton A
1947–48 Airdrieonians, Queen's Park
1948–49 Morton, Albion R
1949–50 Queen of the S, Stirling Albion
1950–51 Clyde, Falkirk
1951–52 Morton, Stirling Albion
1952–53 Motherwell, Third Lanark
1953–54 Airdrieonians, Hamilton A
1954–55 No clubs relegated
1955–56 Stirling Albion, Clyde
1956–57 Dunfermline Ath, Ayr U
1957–58 East Fife, Queen's Park
1958–59 Queen of the S, Falkirk
1959–60 Arbroath, Stirling Albion
1960–61 Ayr U, Clyde
1961–62 St Johnstone, Stirling Albion
1962–63 Clyde, Raith R
1963–64 Queen of the S, East Stirling
1964–65 Airdrieonians, Third Lanark
1965–66 Morton, Hamilton A
1966–67 St Mirren, Ayr U
1967–68 Motherwell, Stirling Albion
1968–69 Falkirk, Arbroath
1969–70 Raith R, Partick T
1970–71 St Mirren, Cowdenbeath
1971–72 Clyde, Dunfermline Ath
1972–73 Kilmarnock, Airdrieonians
1973–74 East Fife, Falkirk

*Season 1921–22 – only 1 club promoted, 3 clubs relegated.

The Scottish Football League was reconstructed into three divisions at the end of the 1974–75 season, so the usual relegation statistics do not apply.

SCOTTISH RECORDS

Celtic created a Scottish League record when they remained unbeaten in 62 games between November 1915 to April 1917.

The Scottish League record for the longest run of consecutive victories was created by **Morton** in Division Two during the 1963–64 season when they won 23 games in a row.

Dundee only called upon 15 players when they won The Scottish League Championship in season 1961–62.

Last season saw **Rangers** make their eighth consecutive Scottish Cup Final appearance since 1976.

SCOTTISH CUP FINALS 1874–1983

Year	*Winners*	*Runners-up*	*Score*
1874	Queen's Park	Clydesdale	2-0
1875	Queen's Park	Renton	3-0
1876	Queen's Park	Third Lanark	2-0 after 1-1 draw
1877	Vale of Leven	Rangers	3-2 after 0-0 and 1-1 draws
1878	Vale of Leven	Third Lanark	1-0
1879	Vale of Leven*	Rangers	
1880	Queen's Park	Thornlibank	3-0
1881	Queen's Park†	Dumbarton	3-1
1882	Queen's Park	Dumbarton	4-1 after 2-2 draw
1883	Dumbarton	Vale of Leven	2-1 after 2-2 draw
1884	Queen's Park‡	Vale of Leven	
1885	Renton	Vale of Leven	3-1 after 0-0 draw
1886	Queen's Park	Renton	3-1
1887	Hibernian	Dumbarton	2-1
1888	Renton	Cambuslang	6-1
1889	Third Lanark§	Celtic	2-1
1890	Queen's Park	Vale of Leven	2-1 after 1-1 draw
1891	Hearts	Dumbarton	1-0
1892	Celtic¶	Queen's Park	5-1
1893	Queen's Park	Celtic	2-1
1894	Rangers	Celtic	3-1
1895	St Bernard's	Renton	2-1
1896	Hearts	Hibernian	3-1
1897	Rangers	Dumbarton	5-1
1898	Rangers	Kilmarnock	2-0
1899	Celtic	Rangers	2-0
1900	Celtic	Queen's Park	4-3
1901	Hearts	Celtic	4-3
1902	Hibernian	Celtic	1-0
1903	Rangers	Hearts	2-0 after 1-1 and 0-0 draws
1904	Celtic	Rangers	3-2
1905	Third Lanark	Rangers	3-1 after 0-0 draw
1906	Hearts	Third Lanark	1-0
1907	Celtic	Hearts	3-0
1908	Celtic	St Mirren	5-1
1909	••		
1910	Dundee	Clyde	2-1 after 2-2 and 0-0 draws
1911	Celtic	Hamilton A	2-0 after 0-0 draw
1912	Celtic	Clyde	2-0
1913	Falkirk	Raith R	2-0
1914	Celtic	Hibernian	4-1 after 0-0 draw
1920	Kilmarnock	Albion R	3-2
1921	Partick T	Rangers	1-0
1922	Morton	Rangers	1-0
1923	Celtic	Hibernian	1-0
1924	Airdrieonians	Hibernian	2-0
1925	Celtic	Dundee	2-1
1926	St Mirren	Celtic	2-0
1927	Celtic	East Fife	3-1
1928	Rangers	Celtic	4-0
1929	Kilmarnock	Rangers	2-0
1930	Rangers	Partick T	2-1 after 0-0 draw
1931	Celtic	Motherwell	4-2 after 2-2 draw
1932	Rangers	Kilmarnock	3-0 after 1-1 draw
1933	Celtic	Motherwell	1-0
1934	Rangers	St Mirren	5-0
1935	Rangers	Hamilton A	2-1
1936	Rangers	Third Lanark	1-0
1937	Celtic	Aberdeen	2-1
1938	East Fife	Kilmarnock	4-2 after 1-1 draw
1939	Clyde	Motherwell	4-0
1947	Aberdeen	Hibernian	2-1
1948	Rangers	Morton	1-0 after 1-1 draw
1949	Rangers	Clyde	4-1
1950	Rangers	East Fife	3-0
1951	Celtic	Motherwell	1-0
1952	Motherwell	Dundee	4-0

Eric Black (no. 10) scores the extra-time winner for Aberdeen against Rangers in the 1983 Scottish Cup final.

Year	*Winners*	*Runners-up*	*Score*
1953	Rangers	Aberdeen	1-0 after 1-1 draw
1954	Celtic	Aberdeen	2-1
1955	Clyde	Celtic	1-0 after 1-1 draw
1956	Hearts	Celtic	3-1
1957	Falkirk	Kilmarnock	2-1 after 1-1 draw
1958	Clyde	Hibernian	1-0
1959	St Mirren	Aberdeen	3-1
1960	Rangers	Kilmarnock	2-0
1961	Dunfermline Ath	Celtic	2-0 after 0-0 draw
1962	Rangers	St Mirren	2-0
1963	Rangers	Celtic	3-0 after 1-1 draw
1964	Rangers	Dundee	3-1
1965	Celtic	Dunfermline Ath	3-2
1966	Rangers	Celtic	1-0 after 0-0 draw
1967	Celtic	Aberdeen	2-0
1968	Dunfermline Ath	Hearts	3-1
1969	Celtic	Rangers	4-0
1970	Aberdeen	Celtic	3-1
1971	Celtic	Rangers	2-1 after 1-1 draw
1972	Celtic	Hibernian	6-1
1973	Rangers	Celtic	3-2
1974	Celtic	Dundee U	3-0
1975	Celtic	Airdrieonians	3-1
1976	Rangers	Hearts	3-1
1977	Celtic	Rangers	1-0
1978	Rangers	Aberdeen	2-1
1979	Rangers	Hibernian	3-2 after 0-0 and 0-0 draws
1980	Celtic	Rangers	1-0
1981	Rangers	Dundee U	4-1 after 0-0 draw
1982	Aberdeen	Rangers	4-1 (aet)
1983	Aberdeen	Rangers	1-0 (aet)

*Vale of Leven awarded cup, Rangers failed to appear for replay after 1-1 draw.
†After Dumbarton protested the first game, which Queen's Park won 2-1.
‡Queen's Park awarded cup, Vale of Leven failing to appear.
§Replay by order of Scottish FA because of playing conditions in first match, won 3-0 by Third Lanark.
¶After mutual protested game which Celtic won 1-0.
•• Owing to riot, the cup was withheld after two drawn games – Celtic 2-1, Rangers 2-1.

SCOTTISH CUP 1982–83

ELGIN CITY – THE GIANT KILLERS

Second Division Forfar, who were eliminated by Rangers in the semi-final of the Cup last season – but only after a replay, stole the First Round headlines when their five goals at Highland League Peterhead earned them £500 for each goal. In a scheme to add goals to the country's Premier knockout competition, the S.F.A. ploughed much of the money into making the tournament a spectacle.

Elsewhere, non league Brora Rangers forged a little bit of Cup history by achieving their first ever Scottish Cup victory. In two previous ventures they had failed at the first hurdle.

But their victory was against lowly Selkirk leaving their Highland neighbours Elgin to claim the shock of the initial round by travelling to Edinburgh and ousting Meadowbank, who at the time enjoyed a five point lead at the top of Division Two. Meadowbank's Walter Boyd scored the quickest goal of the round when he opened the scoring after only 51 seconds.

FIRST ROUND

11 DEC

Brechin C (0) 2 *(Campbell 2)*

Cowdenbeath (0) 0 400

Brechin C: Neilson; Watt, Reid, McWalter (Wilson), Lesslie, Mackie, Campbell, Paterson, Fleming, Stewart, Malone.
Cowdenbeath: Allan; Ballantyne (McCulloch), Rose, Gilchrist, Tierney, Fairley, Christie (Henderson), Scott, Liddle, McIntosh, Miller.

Meadowbank T (1) 1 *(Boyd)*

Elgin City (1) 2 *(S. Kellas, Bremner)* 650

Meadowbank T: McQueen; Dunn, Burrell, Dall (Georgeson), Stewart, Conroy, Neilson (Hendrie), Lawson, Jobson, Boyd, Sprott.
Elgin City: McHattie; Brown, Massie; McAndrew, Bremner, McHardy, S. Kellas, Drews, Dunbar (Armstrong), Blacklaw, Ironside.

Selkirk (0) 0

Brora Rangers (1) 2 *(Hamilton, McAskill)* 300

Selkirk: Anderson; Brownlie, Ferguson, Bell, Laurie, Hendry, Muir (Purves), Austin, Whitehead, McLaren (Lochrie), MacDonald.
Brora Rangers: Suttar; Mulholland, Allan R., Norris, Allan D., McAskill D., Maxwell (Gunn), McAskill B., Jackson, Hamilton, McKay.

18 DEC

Peterhead (0) 0

Forfar Ath (2) 5 *(Gallacher, McDonald 2, Clark, Lorimer)* 1000

Peterhead: Clark; Rennie, David Smith, Sievwright, Lawson, Proud, McCallan, Barbour, Donald Smith, Donald, Allan, Taylor G. (Porter).
Forfar Ath: Kennedy; Bennett, McPhee, Morris, Brash, Farningham, Leitch, Lorimer, McDonald, Clark, Gallacher.

Stirling Albion (0) 1 *(Colquhoun)*

East Stirling (0) 0 588

Stirling Albion: Arthur; Dawson, Spence, McRoberts, Steedman, Moffat, Colquhoun, Torrance, Steele, Walker, Cavanagh.
East Stirling: Young; Tierney, Blair, Tempany, Rennie, Meakin, Grant, Jack, Gibson, Watt, Ashwood.

Vale of Leithen (0) 0

Stranraer (0) 0 150

Vale of Leithen: Arnot; Darling, Ross, Reid, Bird, Turnbull, Lamont, Cormack, Hogarth, Forsyth (Tulloch), McGauran.
Stranraer: Strachan; Murdoch, Hay, Quinn, McCaig, Filson, Neil, Knox, McBride, Bryce, Sweeney.

FIRST ROUND REPLAY

20 DEC

Stranraer (0) 2 *(Bryce, Sweeney)*

Vale of Leithen (0) 0 250

Stranraer: Strachan; Murdoch, Hay; Quinn, McCaig, Filson, Reid, Knox, McBride, Bryce, Sweeney.
Vale of Leithen: Arnot; Darling, Ross, Reid, Bird, Turnbull (Graham), Lamont, Cormack, Hogarth, Forsyth (Tulloch), McGauran.

THREE GOALS FOR FORFAR IN FOUR MINUTES

Giant killers Brora Rangers proved that they had stamina as well as Cup potential, when enduring a five and a half hour marathon, against Second Division Montrose, before winning a second replay 5-2. Scotland's most northerly club possessed resilience too, for in that third game in Inverness, referee Colin Sinclair collapsed with hypathermia five minutes from the end.

The scoring highlight of the round again came from Cup specialists Forfar, who knocked in three inside four first half minutes to dispose of their Highland League opponents Inverness Caley.

However Brora will not be alone in the third round, for Elgin City joined them by virtue of a fine second half showing against East of Scotland League side Gala Fairydean. The men from the north scuttled their far travelled opponents 5-2, their goals coming in a 29 minute second half spell.

SECOND ROUND
8 JAN

Albion Rovers (0) 1

(Evans) *Stranraer (0) 0*

300 Albion Rovers: Balavage; Allan, Lapsley, Collins, Burgess, Leishman, Dow, Livingstone, Evans, Gibson, Conn.
Stranraer: Strachan; McDonald, Hay, Quinn, McCaig, Gilson, Neill, Knox, McBride, Bryce (Sweeney), Dolan.

Berwick R (2) 1 *(Tait, McSherry)*

Stirling Albion (0) 0 700

Berwick R: Glynn; Moyes, McCann, McSherry, Jeffries, Muir, Romaines, McGlynn (Porter), Clelland, Tait, Armstrong.
Stirling Albion: Arthur; Aitchison, Dawson, Philliben, Steedman, Moffat; Colquhoun, Torrance, Steele, Walker (Leetion), McNeill.

Brora Rangers (0) 0

Montrose (0) 0 860

Brora Rangers: Suttar; Mulholland, Allan R., Norris, Allan D., Hamilton, McAskill B., McAskill D., Jackson, Murray, Mackay.
Montrose: Charles; Barr, Forbes, Mathieson, Sheran, Duffy, Fletcher (Craig), McLaren (Nicol), Copeland, Fullerton, McManus.

East Fife (1) 1 *(Scott)*

Brechin C (0) 0 940

East Fife: Gorman; Kirk, Clarke, McLaren, Halley, Thomson, Durie, Hamilton, Scott, Hutt, Caithness.
Brechin C: Neilson; Watt, Reid, Lesslie, Hay, Malone, Campbell, Stewart, Fleming, Elvin, Paterson.

Elgin City (0) 5 *(Armstrong 2, McHardy, Kellas F., Drews)*

Gala Fairydean (0) 2 *(Thomson A., Lothian)* 1180

Elgin City: McHattie; Brown (Bruce), Masson, McAndrew, Bremner, McHardy, Kellas F., Drews, Blacklaw, Armstrong, Ironside (Kellas S.).
Gala Fairydean: Frame; Mann, Nicol, Frizzel, Stewart, Thomson M. (Thomson A.); Anderson, Dick, Lothian, Renton, Norman.

Forfar Ath (3) 3 *(McDonald 2, Gallacher)*

Inverness Caley (0) 0 1202

Forfar Ath: Kennedy; Bennett, McPhee, Morris, Brash, Weir, Clark (Cormack), Leitch, Gallacher, Farningham, McDonald.
Inverness Caley: MacDonald W.; Davidson, Mann, Dewar, Summers, Corbett, Docherty, Lisle, Urquhart, MackIntosh R., Robertson.

Queen of the South (1) 3 *(McCann 2, Alexander)*

Hawick Royal Albert (0) 0 992

Queen of the South: Davidson; Wilkie, Busby, Young, Evans, Cloy, Gordon, Alexander, Robertson G., McCann, Robertson J.
Hawick Royal Albert: McConnell; McLean, Frizzel, Colville, Rutherford, Loughran, Brown, Noble (Hedley), McConnell, Watson, Ritchie.

Stenhousemuir (0) 1 *(Murray)*

Arbroath (0) 0 350

Stenhousemuir: Howie; Rennie, Gillon, Erwin, Caldwell, Mullen, Thomson, Quinn, Buchanan, Murray, Jenkins.
Arbroath: Larter; Casey, Kopel, McKenzie, Taylor, Gavine, Harley, Docherty, Robb, Shaw, Steele (Hill).

SECOND ROUND REPLAY

16 JAN

Montrose (1) 1 *(Nicol)*

Brora Rangers (0) 1 *(McAskill B.)* 400

Montrose: Charles; Barr, Forbes, Mathieson, Sheran, Duffy (Neil), Fletcher, Nicol, Oliver (Forrest), Cullerton, McManus.
Brora Rangers: Suttar; Mulholland, Hamilton, Christie, Allan (Duffy), Gair (Gunn), McAskill B., Maxwell, Jackson, McAskill D., Mackay.

SECOND ROUND, SECOND REPLAY

18 JAN

Brora Rangers (1) 5 *(Gunn 2, McAskill B, Allan, Mackay)*

Montrose (1) 2 *(Copeland, McManus)* 1150

after extra time. At Inverness.
Brora Rangers: Suttar; Mulholland, Hamilton, Norris, Christie (Allan), Gair (Gunn), McAskill B., Maxwell, Jackson, McAskill D., Mackay.
Montrose: Charles; Barr, Forbes, Mathieson, Sheran, Duffy, Cooper (Nicol), Copeland (Forrest), Cullerton, McManus.

ST MIRREN KNOCK OUT DUNDEE UNITED AGAIN

First Division Partick Thistle required seven hours of action, before they could make Premier League strugglers Kilmarnock concede defeat, with 20 year old Maurice Johnston breaking the dealock in the third replay. Cup holders Aberdeen gave notice that they were not to surrender the trophy, without a struggle, when having four individual scorers in an emphatic win at Easter Road. It was disappointing to note that the game produced the biggest crowd of the round – only 14,289.

Perhaps the fact that Rangers, Celtic and Dundee were, like Aberdeen, away from home contributed and it was United's trip to Love Street that was to see the first of the big guns depart.

Doug Somner snatched the vital goal that meant the Tannadice team were out on the same venue as last year, although on that occasion it was in the quarter final stage.

The financial well being of the competition was still assured however, when Celtic were comfortable winners at Clydebank and their Old Firm rivals Rangers overcame the stuffy challenge of Falkirk at Brockville.

THIRD ROUND

28 JAN

Alloa (0) 1 *(McComb)*

Morton (1) 2 *(Hutchison, McNab)* 2034

Alloa: Hunter; Thomson, Haggart, Holt, Garner, Campbell (McComb), Smith, Grant, Lloyd, Houston, Munro.
Morton: Baines; Houston, Holmes, Rooney, McLaughlin, Duffy, Payne, Gibson (Docherty), Hutchison, Cochrane, McNab.

Ayr United (0) 1 *(Larnach)*

Albion Rovers (0) 2 *(Livingstone 2)* 1372

Ayr United: MacKay; Shanks, Connor, Morris, McAllister, Fleeting, Frye, McInally, Larnach, Ahern, Christie.
Albion Rovers: Balavage; Allan, Grant, Leishman, Burgess, Collins, Dow, Gray, Evans, Livingstone, Conn.

Clyde (0) 0

Motherwell (0) 0 3831

Clyde: Young; McVeigh, McQueen, McColl, Dempsey, Evans, Reilly, Sinclair, Nevin, Flexney, Docherty.
Motherwell: Walker; Dornan, McLeod, Carson, Edvaldsson, Rafferty (Gahagan), McClair, Flavell, Harrow (Forsyth), Forbes, O'Hara.

Clydebank (0) 0

Celtic (1) 3 *(Nicholas 2, McCluskey)* 9500

Clydebank: Gallacher; Treanor, Gervaise, Fallon, McGhie, Given, Ronald, Hughes, Williamson, Coyne, McCabe.
Celtic: Bonner; McGrain, Reid, Aitken, McAdam, MacLeod, Provan, McStay (Sullivan), Nicholas, McCluskey, McGarvey.

Dumbarton (0) 0

Aidrieonians (1) 1 *(Flood)* 957

Dumbarton: Carson; Montgomerie, Burnett, Close (McGowan P.), McNeill, Coyle, Brown, Craig, Dunlop (Stevenson), Donnelly, Blair.
Airdrieonians: Martin; Cairney, Rodger, McLaughlin, Anderson G., Gordon, Campbell (Weir), Flood, Miller, Anderson N., Yule.

Dundee (1) 2 *(Ferguson, Sinclair)*

Brora Rangers (1) 1 *(Maxwell)* 5823

Dundee: Kelly; Glennie, McKimmie; Fraser, Smith, McGeachie, Ferguson, Bell, Sinclair, Mackie (Murphy), Stephen.
Brora Rangers: Suttar; Mulholland, Hamilton, Norris (Allan), Christie, Gair (Gunn), McAskill B., McAskill D., Jackson, Maxwell, Mackay.

Dunfermline Ath (2) 5 *(Jenkins 2, Tait 2, Rodier)*

Elgin City (0) 0 2500

Dunfermline Ath: Whyte; Robertson, Grant (Crawford), Smith, Wilcox, Bowie (Stewart), Rodier, McCathie, Tait, Jenkins, Forrest.
Elgin City: McHattie; Brown, Masson, McAndrews, Bremner, McHardy, Kellas F. (Bruce), Drews, Blacklaw, Armstrong, Kellas N.

East Fife (1) 1 *(Thomson)*

Raith Rovers (0) 0 5760

East Fife: Gorman; Kirk, Clarke, McLaren, Halley, Thomson, Pryde (Durie), Hamilton, Scott, Hutt, Caithness.
Raith Rovers: Walker; Robertson, Candlish, Houston, More, Thomson, Marshall (Robinson), Russell, Smith, Kerr, Spence.

Falkirk (0) 0

Rangers (0) 2 *(liver og, Kennedy)* 15,000

Falkirk: Watson; Nicol, Hoggan, Brown, Mackin, Love, Perry, Oliver, Houston, McCullie (Stevenson), Forrest.
Rangers: McCloy; Dawson, Black, Stevens, McClelland, Bett, Cooper, Prytz, Kennedy, Redford, Johnstone (Dalziel).

Forfar Ath (1) 2 *(McPhee, Lorimer)*

Berwick R (1) 1 *(Romaines)* 1108

Forfar Ath: Kennedy; Bennett, McPhee, Brown, Brash, Weir, Leitch, Farningham, Gallacher, Lorimer, McDonald.
Berwick R: McDermott; Moyes, McCann (McLellan), Cameron (Marshall), Jeffries, Muir, Romaines, Porter, Tracey, Docherty, Armstrong.

Hibernian (0) 1 *(Rae)*

Aberdeen (2) 4 *(Weir, Simpson, Watson, McGhee)* 14,289

Hibernian: Rough; Sneddon, Schaedler, Rice, Rae, McNamara, Callachan (Irvine), Conroy (Welsh), Duncan, Thomson, Murray.
Aberdeen: Leighton; Kennedy, Rougvie, McMaster, McLeish, Miller, Black (Watson), Simpson, McGhee, Bell (Cooper), Weir.

Partick T (0) 1 *(Johnston)*

Kilmarnock (0) 1 *(Bryson)* 4398

Partick T: McNab; Doyle G. (Kay), Whittaker, Murray, Dunlop, Watson, Park, McDonald, Johnston, Doyle J., O'Hara.
Kilmarnock: McCulloch; McDicken, Clark R., Clark J., Armstrong, Clarke, McGivern, MacLeod, Gallagher, Simpson, Clinging (Bryson).

St Mirren (1) 1 *(Somner)*

Dundee U (0) 0 7020

St Mirren: Thomson; Wilson, Clarke, McCormack, Fulton, Abercromby, Stark, Richardson, McDougall, McAvennie, Somner.
Dundee U: McAlpine; Stark, Malpas, Gough, Hegarty, Narey, Holt, Milne, Kirkwood (Clark), Sturrock, Dodds.

Queen's Park (1) 4 *(Brannigan, Robertson, Gilmour, Crawley)*

Stenhousemuir (0) 1 *(Erwin)* 800

Queen's Park: Atkins; Cook, Dickson, Rennie, Brannigan, McNiven, Crawley, Graham (Robertson), Grant, Nicholson, Gilmour.
Stenhousemuir: Howie; Rennie, Gillen, Erwin, Caldwell, Thompson, Buchanan, Mullen, Gillespie, Murray (Johnston), Jenkins (Munn).

Queen of the South (0) 1 *(Robertson J.)*

Hearts (0) 1 *(Shields)* 3800

Queen of the South: Davidson; Wilkie, Grant, Young, Evans, Cloy (McCann), Gordon, Busby, Alexander, Miller, Robertson J.
Hearts: Smith; Kidd (Byrne), Shields, Bowman, MacDonald R., Jardine, MacKay, Pettigrew, Robertson, MacDonald A., Johnston.

29 JAN

Hamilton A (0) 0

St Johnstone (1) 1 *(Barron)* 2693

Hamilton A: Ferguson; Wright, Hamill; Blackley (Paton), McDougall, Mitchell, Fairlie, McDowall, Phillips, Gorman (Hackett), Donnelly.

THIRD ROUND REPLAYS

2 FEB

Motherwell (3) 3 *(Harrow, McClair, Forbes)*

Clyde (1) 4 *(Nevin, Dempsey, Evans, Flavell og)* 4656

After extra time.
Motherwell: Walker; Dornan, Mauchlen, Carson, Edvaldsson, Rafferty, McClair, Flavell (Forsyth), Harrow, Forbes, O'Hara (Gahagan).
Clyde: Young; McVeigh, McQueen, McColl, Dempsey, Evans, Reilly, Sinclair (O'Neill), Nevin, Flexney, Doherty (Brogan).

Hearts (1) 1 *(O'Connor)*

Queen of the South (0) 0 5609

Hearts: Smith; Kidd, Shields, Bowman, MacDonald R., Jardine, Mackay (Byrne), Pettigrew (McCoy), O'Connor, MacDonald A., Johnston.
Queen of the South: Davidson; Miller, Gray, Young, Evans, Cloy, Gordon (Coughlin), Busby (McCann), Alexander, Cochrane, Robertson J.

Kilmarnock (0) 0

Partick T (0) 0 3900

After extra time.
Kilmarnock: McCulloch; McDicken, Clark R., Clark J., Armstrong, Clarke, McGivern, MacLeod, Gallagher, Simpson, Bryson (Bourke).
Partick T: McNab; Kay, Whittaker, Murray, Dunlop, Watson, Park, McDonald, Johnston, Doyle J., O'Hara.

THIRD ROUND, SECOND REPLAY

7 FEB

Partick T (1) 2 *(Johnston, McDowall)*

Kilmarnock (0) 2 *(Gallagher, McGivern)* 5141

After extra time.
Partick T: McNab: Kay, Whittaker, Murray, Dunlop (Doherty), Watson, Park, McDonald, Johnston, Doyle J., O'Hara (McDowall).
Kilmarnock: Wilson; McDicken, Clark R., Clark J., Armstrong, Clarke, McGivern, MacLeod, Gallagher, Simpson, Bryson.

THIRD ROUND, THIRD REPLAY

9 FEB

Kilmarnock (0) 0

Partick T (0) 1 *(Johnston)* 3800

Kilmarnock: Wilson; McDicken, Clark R., Clark J., Armstrong, Clarke, McGivern, MacLeod, Gallagher, Simpson, Bryson (Bourke).
Partick T: McNab; Kay, Whittaker, Murray, Jackson, Watson, Park, McDonald, Johnston, Doyle J., McDowall.

ELEVEN HOURS, FORTY THREE MINUTES FOR TWO VICTORIES

Once again Partick Thistle emerged as the marathon men of the round, when it needed two replays and a lights failure to see them into the last eight. In all the Firhill side had played 11 hours and forty three minutes – just to get through two rounds.

As expected, Celtic were too strong for Dunfermline, and Aberdeen had enough to end Dundee's hopes of Cup glory, but Rangers had their usual trouble with Second Division Forfar.

Indeed the Angus part-timers took the lead through young Kenny McDonald three minutes before half time and it took all Rangers determination in front of an impatient Ibrox crowd finally to wear them down with two John MacDonald goals.

Airdrie, Queen's Park, Hearts and Partick meant that the First Division made up half the teams in the draw, and significantly St Mirren demonstrated their return to form with a 2-0 victory over Morton at Cappielow.

FOURTH ROUND

19 FEB

Aberdeen (0) 1 *(Simpson)*

Dundee (0) 0 16,000

Aberdeen: Leighton, Kennedy, Rougvie, Cooper, McLeish, Miller, Black, Simpson, McGhee, Bell, Weir.
Dundee: Kelly, McGeachie, McKimmie, Fraser, Smith, MacDonald, Ferguson, Bell (Glennie), Sinclair, Mackie, Stephen (Murphy).

Albion R (0) 0

Aidrieonians (2) 3 *(Millar, Gordon, Flood)* 3395

Albion R: Balavage; Allan, Grant, Leishman, Burgess, Collins, Dow (Gibson), Livingstone, Evans, Gray, Conn.
Airdrieonians: Martin; Cairney, Black, McLaughlin, March, Anderson, Walker, Jarvie, Millar (McGuire), Flood, Gordon.

Celtic (0) 3 *(McGarvey 2, McCluskey)*

Dunfermline Ath (0) 0 12,374

Celtic: Bonner; McGrain, McInally, Aitken, McAdam, Sinclair (McCluskey), Provan, McStay, McGarvey, MacLeod, Nicholas.
Dunfermline Ath: Whyte; Robertson, Crawford, Smith, Wilcox, Bowie, Rodier, McCathie, Tait, Jenkins (Stewart), Forrest.

Morton (0) 0

St Mirren (1) 2 *(McDougall 2)* 6500

Morton: Baines; Houston, Holmes, Rooney, McLaughlin, Duffy, Payne, Gibson, Hutchison, Docherty, Slaven (Ritchie).
St Mirren: Thomson; Wilson, Clark, Fitzpatrick, Fulton, McCormack, Stark, Richardson, McDougall, McAvennie, Scanlon (Wardrope).

Partick T (0) 2 *(Flexney og, Johnston)*

Clyde (0) 2 *(Masterton, Flexney)* 5274

Partick T: McNab; Kay, Whittaker, Murray, Jackson, Watson, Park, McDonald, Johnston (Doyle G.), O'Hara (McDowall).
Clyde: Young; McVeigh, McQueen, McColl, Dempsey, Evans, Reilly (Masterton), Sinclair, O'Neill (Flexney), Docherty, Nevin.

Queen's Park (1) 1 *(Crawley)*

St Johnstone (0) 0 1448

Queen's Park: Atkins; McFarlane, Dickson, Cook, Woods, McNiven, Crawley, Graham, Quinn (Nicholson), Grant, Gilmour.
St Johnstone: McDonald; Caldwell, McVicar; Beedie, Kennedy, Rutherford, Addison, Brogan, Pelosi (McCafferty), Barron, Fleming.

Rangers (0) 2 *(MacDonald 2)*

Forfar Ath (1) 1 *(McDonald)* 12,500

Rangers: McCloy; Dawson, Black, McClelland, McPherson, Bett, Dalziel, Prytz (Robertson), Kennedy, Redford, MacDonald.
Forfar Ath: Kennedy; Bennett, McPhee, Brown, Brash, Weir (Leitch), Cormack (Clark), Farningham, Gallacher, Lorimer, McDonald.

20 FEB

Hearts (1) 2 *(MacDonald R, O'Connor)*

East Fife (1) 1 *(Caithness)* 9336

Hearts: Smith; Gauld, Shields, Bowman, MacDonald (McCoy), Jardine, Byrne, Pettigrew, O'Connor, Mackay, Robertson.
East Fife: Gorman; Kirk, Clarke, McLaren, Halley, Thomson, Pryde, Hamilton, Scott, Hutt, Caithness.

FOURTH ROUND REPLAY

23 FEB

Clyde (1) 1 *(Sinclair)*

Partick T (1) 1 *(Doyle J.)* 5135

Abandoned after 103 minutes because of lights failure.
Clyde: Young; McVeigh, McQueen, McColl, Dempsey, Evans, Reilly, Sinclair, O'Neill, Docherty, Nevin.
Partick T: McNab; Kay, Whittaker, Murray, Jackson, Watson, Park (McDowall), McDonald, Johnston, Doyle J., O'Hara.

FOURTH ROUND, SECOND REPLAY

28 FEB

Clyde (0) 0

Partick T (4) 6 *(Johnston 3, Park 2* [1 pen], *Watson)* 3818

Clyde: Young; McVeigh, McQueen, McColl, Dempsey, Evans, Masterton, Sinclair (Reilly), O'Neill, Docherty, Nevin (Flexney).
Partick T: McNab; Kay, Whittaker, Murray, Welsh, Watson, Park, McDonald, Johnston, Doyle G., O'Hara.

No shocks at the Quarter Final stage, although both Queen's Park and Partick Thistle gave Rangers and Aberdeen something to think about on their way to the last four.

The big talking point of course was the controversial sending off of Hearts winger Willie Johnston at Parkhead. The former Rangers and West Brom player was shown the red card by referee Brian McGinlay after a clash with Davie Provan – the 20th time he has been sent off in a stormy career.

St Mirren's Billy Stark grabbed the first hattrick of the Cup at Airdrie, and as the Paisley side scored five there were those who saw them going into the semis with a real chance of lifting the trophy.

QUARTER FINALS

12 MAR

Airdrieonians (0) 0

St Mirren (2) 5 *(Stark 3, McAvennie, Scanlon)* 8500

Airdrieonians: Martin; Anderson G., Rodger, McLaughlin, March, Gordon, McKeown (Flood), Anderson N., Miller, Jarvie, Yule (McGuire).
St Mirren: Thomson; Wilson, Clarke, Fitzpatrick, Fulton, McCormack; Stark, Richardson, Somner, McAvennie (Abercromby), Scanlon.

Celtic (1) 4 *(Nicholas 2, MacLeod, McGarvey)*

Hearts (0) 1 *(MacDonald A.)* 25,458

Celtic: Bonner; McGrain, Sinclair, Aitken, McAdam, Sullivan, Provan, McStay, Nicholas, MacLeod, McGarvey.
Hearts: Smith; Kidd, Shields (McLaren), Bowman, MacDonald R., Jardine, MacKay, Robertson, O'Connor (Pettigrew), MacDonald A., Johnston.

Partick T (0) 1 *(McDonald)*

Aberdeen (1) 2 *(Cooper, Weir)* 12,092

Partick T: McNab; Doyle G., Whittaker, Murray, Jackson, Watson, Park, McDonald (McDowall), Johnston, Doyle J., O'Hara.
Aberdeen: Leighton; Kennedy, Rougvie, Cooper, McLeish, Miller, Strachan, Simpson, McGhee, Bell (Black), Weir.

Queen's Park (0) 1 *(Gilmour)*

Rangers (2) 2 *(Dalziel, Cooper)* 13,716

Queen's Park: Atkins; Cairns, Dickson, Cook, Woods, McNiven, Crawley, Graham, Nicholson (Quinn), Grant, Gilmour.
Rangers: McCloy; McKinnon, McClelland, McPherson, Paterson (Lyall), Bett, Dalziel, Prytz, Kennedy (McAdam), Redford, Cooper.

SCOTTISH FA CUP, SEMI-FINALS

Aberdeen reached the first of two finals, when they made a third successful journey to meet Celtic in Glasgow during the season. In a game heavily criticised for the over use of the respective physical attributes of the teams it was ironic that the winning goal should come from a substitution following one of many injuries. Peter Weir replaced the concussed Neale Cooper in the 42nd minute, and made his introduction decisive when heading the winner 23 minutes later. Across the city, Rangers met in a repeat of a clash at the same stage two seasons ago. Sandy Clark had Rangers in front in the first game, until a tragic late own goal by Craig Paterson, preserved St Mirren's link with the competition. The tie switched from Parkhead to Hampden for the replay, and after both sides can claim they had chances to win the right to meet Aberdeen, Clark popped up one minute from the end of extra time, to more than justify the £165,000 it cost to bring him back to Scotland from West Ham United.

16 APRIL

Aberdeen (0) 1 *(Weir)*

Celtic (0) 0 51,152

(At Hampden Park)

Aberdeen: Leighton; Kennedy, Rougvie, Cooper (Weir), McLeish, Miller, Strachan, Simpson, McGhee, Bell, Black (Watson).
Celtic: Bonner; Sinclair, Reid, Aitken, McAdam, MacLeod, Provan, McStay, McCluskey (Crainie), Burns, McGarvey.

Rangers (0) 1 *(Clark)*

St Mirren (0) 1 *(Paterson og)* 31,102

(At Celtic Park)

Rangers: McCloy; Dawson, McClelland, McPherson, Paterson, Bett, Russell, McKinnon, Clark, Redford, Cooper.
St Mirren: Thomson; Wilson, Clarke (Fitzpatrick); Richardson, Fulton, McCormack, McDougall, McAvennie, Somner, Abercromby, Scanlon (Logan).

19 APRIL

SEMI-FINAL REPLAY

Rangers (0)1 *(Clark)*

St Mirren (0) 0 25,125

(At Hampden Park). aet.

Rangers: McCloy; Dawson, McClelland; McPherson, Paterson, Bett, Russell, McKinnon, Clark, Redford (Macdonald), Cooper (Prytz).
St Mirren: Thomson; Wilson, Clarke (Fitzpatrick); Richardson, Fulton, McCormack, McDougall, McAvennie, Somner, Abercromby, Scanlon (Logan).

Aberdeen's inspirational captain Willie Miller, seen here winning a tackle in the Cup-Winners Cup Final, led his club through their best ever season.

Aberdeen became the first club outside the Old Firm this century to win the Scottish Cup in successive years, but only after one of the least interesting Finals that Hampden has staged. Both sides seemed to be suffering the effects of a long hard season and with only four minutes of extra time remaining both teams would have been happy to accept a draw, and the chance to put on a spectacular in the replay. Alec Ferguson's men dragged up one last push and when Mark McGhee's cross from the right took an unkind deflection off Craig Paterson, Eric Black who had been involved in the build up outside the box, finished his run by placing the decisive header wide of Peter McCloy. Although the partially refurbished stadium had only 62,979 fans in its 75,800 places, that represented an increase of 9191, when the same two teams met twelve months earlier. Further evidence that the Scottish game is pushing back what had earlier seemed to be an unstoppable slide in appeal.

FINAL *(At Hampden Park)*

21 MAY

Aberdeen (0) 1 *(Black) aet*

Rangers (0) 0 62,979

Aberdeen: Leighton: Rougvie (Watson), Cooper, McLeish, Miller, Strachan, Simpson, McGhee, Black, Weir (Hewitt).
Rangers: McCloy; Dawson, McClelland, McPherson, Paterson, Bett, Cooper (Davies), McKinnon, Clark, Russell, MacDonald (Dalziel).

Aberdeen 'keeper Jim Leighton punches clear as David McPherson and Sandy Clarke challenge. Willie Miller is the Aberdeen player reluctantly providing support for McPherson.

DUNDEE UNITED F.C. winners of the Premier League title 1983

Back row (left to right): Hamish McAlpine, David Dodds, Ian Phillip, David Narey, Richard Gough, Derek Stark, John Holt, Eamonn Bannon, Walter Smith (coach)
Front row: Andy Dickson (physio), John Reilly, Ralph Milne, Paul Sturrock, Paul Hegarty (captain), Billy Kirkwood, Maurice Malpas, Jim McLean (manager)

Charlie Nicholas, Celtic's star forward, shows some of the skill that brought him the title of Scotland's 'Player of the Year'

SCOTTISH LEAGUE CUP FINALS 1946–83

Season	*Winners*	*Runners-up*	*Score*
1946–47	Rangers	Aberdeen	4-0
1947–48	East Fife	Falkirk	4-1 after 0-0 draw
1948–49	Rangers	Raith R	2-0
1949–50	East Fife	Dunfermline Ath	3-0
1950–51	Motherwell	Hibernian	3-0
1951–52	Dundee	Rangers	3-2
1952–53	Dundee	Kilmarnock	2-0
1953–54	East Fife	Partick T	3-2
1954–55	Hearts	Motherwell	4-2
1955–56	Aberdeen	St Mirren	2-1
1956–57	Celtic	Partick T	3-0 after 0-0 draw
1957–58	Celtic	Rangers	7-1
1958–59	Hearts	Partick T	5-1
1959–60	Hearts	Third Lanark	2-1
1960–61	Rangers	Kilmarnock	2-0
1961–62	Rangers	Hearts	3-1 after 1-1 draw
1962–63	Hearts	Kilmarnock	1-0
1963–64	Rangers	Morton	5-0
1964–65	Rangers	Celtic	2-1
1965–66	Celtic	Rangers	2-1
1966–67	Celtic	Rangers	1-0
1967–68	Celtic	Dundee	5-3
1968–69	Celtic	Hibernian	6-2
1969–70	Celtic	St Johnstone	1-0
1970–71	Rangers	Celtic	1-0
1971–72	Partick T	Celtic	4-1
1972–73	Hibernian	Celtic	2-1
1973–74	Dundee	Celtic	1-0
1974–75	Celtic	Hibernian	6-3
1975–76	Rangers	Celtic	1-0
1976–77	Aberdeen	Celtic	2-1
1977–78	Rangers	Celtic	2-1
1978–79	Rangers	Aberdeen	2-1
1979–80	Dundee U	Aberdeen	3-0 after 0-0 draw
1980–81	Dundee U	Dundee	3-0
1981–82	Rangers	Dundee U	2-1
1982–83	Celtic	Rangers	2-1

Jubilant Celtic players parade the Scottish League Cup they have just won by beating Rangers 2-1 in December 1982.

SCOTTISH LEAGUE CUP 1982–83

11 AUG SECTION 2

Morton 2 *(Hutchison, Ritchie* pen*)*

Aberdeen 2 *(Strachan* pen, *McGhee)* 3000

Morton: Baines; Houston (Higgins), Holmes, Rooney, McLaughlin, Duffy, McNeil, Docherty, Hutchison, Cochrane, Ritchie.
Aberdeen: Leighton; Kennedy, Rougvie, Cooper, McLeish, Miller, Strachan, Black (Cowan), McGhee, Angus, Weir (Simpson).

14 AUG SECTION 1

Arbroath 1 *(Hill)*

Alloa 2 *(Munro* pen, *Gray)* 800

Arbroath: Robertson; Docherty, Kopel, Glover, McKenzie, Burke, Steele, Hill, Robb (Lees), Shaw, Yule.
Alloa: Hunter; Thomson, Haggart, Purdie, Gray, Munro, Paterson, Smith, McComb (Murray), Houston, Grant.
Dunfermline Ath: Whyte; Ford, Hegarty, Wilcox, Dall R., Considine, Robertson (McNaughton), McCathie, Morrison, Jenkins (Nicol), Forrest.

Celtic 6 *(Reid* pen, *Provan 2, McCluskey 2, McGarvey)*

Dunfermline Ath 0 14,500

Celtic: Bonner; McGrain, Reid, Aitken, Moyes, McLeod, Provan, McStay, McCluskey (Crainie), Burns, McGarvey (Nicholas).

SECTION 2

Aberdeen 3 *(Black 3)*

Dundee 3 *(Ferguson 2* [1 pen], *Stephen)* 9000

Aberdeen: Leighton; Kennedy, Rougvie, Cooper, McLeish, Miller, Strachan, Black (Cowan), McGhee, Simpson, Angus (Hewitt).
Dundee: Blair; McKimmie, McLelland, Fraser, MacDonald, Glennie, Ferguson, McGeachie, Sinclair (Davidson), Mackie, Stephen.

Dumbarton 1 *(Rankin)*

Morton 3 *(Ritchie, McNeil, Docherty)* 1000

Dumbarton: Carson; Close, McGowan M., Clougherty, McNeil, Coyle, Rankin (Brown), McGowan P. (Craig), Dunlop, Donnelly, Blair.
Morton: Baines; Houston, Holmes, Rooney, McLaughlin, Hutchison, McNeil, Docherty, Higgins (McNab), Cochrane, Ritchie.

SECTION 3

Airdrieonians 1 *(Flood)*

Clydebank 3 *(Williamson, Coyne 2)* 2000

Airdrieonians: Martin; Anderson N., Rodger, Anderson G., March, Gordon, Faulds, Kerr (Walker), Millar, Flood, Coyle.
Clydebank: Gallacher; Treanor, Gervaise, Fallon, McGhie, Given, Ronald (McKeown), Hughes, Williamson, Coyne, McCabe.

Hibernian 1 *(Rae)*

Rangers 1 *(Macdonald)* 14,900

Hibernian: McArthur; Sneddon, Schaedler, Brazil, Welsh, McNamara, Callachan, Rae, Rodier, Turnbull, Thomson.
Rangers: Stewart, MacKinnon, Dawson (Davies), McClelland, Paterson, Miller, Prytz (MacKay), Bett, McAdam, Redford, MacDonald.

SECTION 4

Dundee U 3 *(Kirkwood, Dodds, Sturrock)*

St Johnstone 0 7001

Dundee U: McAlpine; Phillip, Stark, Gough, Hegarty (Kirkwood), Narey, Britton, Malpas, Payne (Taylor), Sturrock, Dodds.
St Johnstone: Tulloch; Mackay (Rutherford), McNeil, Beedie, Kennedy, Caldwell, Addison, Brogan, Pelosi, Morton, Brannigan.

Raith R 0

Falkirk 0 1000

Raith R: Walker; Houston, Candlish, Robinson, Forsyth, More, Harris (Thomson), Urquhart, Ballantyne, Gibson, Mitchell (Spence).
Falkirk: Watson; Hoggan, Nicol, Brown, Oliver M., Wilson, Oliver A., Herd (Thomson), Ward, Smith, Perry.

SECTION 5

Forfar Ath 2 *(Allan, Alexander)*

Clyde 0 899

Forfar Ath: Kennedy; Lorimer, McPhee, Brown, Allan, Morris, Alexander, Farningham, Clark, Leitch, Porter.
Clyde: Young; Brogan, Flexney, McColl (Rae), Dempsey, McCutcheon, Doherty (Wood), Sinclair, Masterton, McQueen, Nevin.

Motherwell 2 *(Coyne, Conn)*

Hearts 1 *(O'Connor)* 5105

Motherwell: Sproat; MacLeod, Forsyth, McLelland, Carson, Forbes, McClair (Rafferty), Coyne, Irvine, Conn (Gahagan), O'Hara.
Hearts: Smith; Kidd, Shields, Byrne, MacDonald R., Jardine, MacLaren, Pettigrew, Mackay (O'Connor), MacDonald A., Marinello (McCoy).

SECTION 6

Stirling Alb 2 *(Colquhoun* pen, *Dawson)*

Queen of the S 0 800

Stirling Alb: Arthur; Dawson, Steedman, Crolla (Torrance), Philliben, Moffat, Colquhoun, McRoberts, Steele (McNeill), Leetion, Cavanagh.
Queen of the S: Davidson; Miller (Coughlin), Gray, Maxwell, Clark, Wilkie, Gordon, Busby (G. Robertson), Alexander, Cloy, Robertson J.

St Mirren 3 *(Richardson 3)*

Ayr U 1 *(McInally)* 3462

St Mirren: Thomson; Wilson, Clarke, Fitzpatrick, Fulton, McCormack, Logan, Stark, Somner, Richardson, Scanlon.
Ayr U: Rennie; Shanks, Connor, Hetherington, McAllister, Fleeting, Frye, Love (McCulley), McInally, Ahern (Hume), Ward.

SECTION 7

East Fife 0

Brechin C 0 420

East Fife: Gorman; Hamilton, Clarke, Halley, Dall, Thomson, O'Brien (Wilson), Durie, Hutt, Meakin, Scott.
Brechin C: Neilson; Watt, Cord, Lesslie, Reid, Hay, Campbell I., Stewart, McKay, Elvin, Milligan.

East Stirling 0

Partick T 4 *(Johnston 2, Kenny, Watson)* 800

East Stirling: Kelly (Watt D.); Cairney, Kettings, Renwick, Blair, Gray, Edgar, Watt N., Gibson, Melrose, Ross.
Partick T: Rough; Murray, Kay, Whittaker, Dunlop, Watson, Park, McDonald (Docherty, Doyle G.), Johnston, Doyle J., Kenny.

SECTION 8

Kilmarnock 4 *(McLean* pen, *Clarke, Mauchlen, McCann og)*

Berwick R 0 1000

Kilmarnock: McCulloch; McDicken, Robertson, Clark J., Armstrong, Clarke, McGivern (Bryson), McLean (MacLeod), Bourke, Mauchlen, Gallacher.
Berwick R: McDermott; Moyes, McCann, McSherry, Jefferies, Muir, Armstrong (McLennan), Marshall, Tait, Romaines, Lawson.

Queens Park 1 *(Crawley)*

Hamilton A 1 *(McDowall)* 740

Queens Park: Atkins; Cook, Dickson, Rennie, Woods, McFarlane, Crawley, McNiven, Nicholson (Verrachia), Grant, Gilmour.
Hamilton: Ferguson; McNaught, Colgan, Wright, McDougall, Blackley, Fairlie, McDowall, Paton, Craig (Gorman), Mitchell.

SECTION 9

Albion R 2 *(Burgess, Evans)*

Stranraer 2 *(Dolan, Hay* pen*)* 300

Albion R: Balavage; Allan, Lapsley, Leishman, Burgess, McGrath, Gibson, Houston, Conn, Evans, Dow.
Stranraer: Strachan; Parker, Hay, Knox, McCaig, Filson, Neil, Dolan, McBride, Bryce, Sweeney (Murdoch).

Cowdenbeath 0

Montrose 1 *(Nicol)* 550

Cowdenbeath: Allan; Campbell, Rose, Levein, Tierney, Fairley, Miller (Forrest), Hyslop, Liddle, Marshall (McFarlane), McIntosh.
Montrose: Charles; Barr, Forbes, Taylor, Shernan, Mathieson, Oliver (Campbell), Nicol, Copeland, Cooper, McManus (Turnbull).

Stenhousemuir 1 *(Erwin)*

Meadowbank T 1 *(Sprott)* 350

Stenhousemuir: Howie; Strain, Mullen, McCusker, Evans, Buchanan, Thomson (Smith), Murray, Spence, Erwin, Gillon (Stirling).
Meadowbank T: McQueen; Burrell (Johnstone), Conroy, Godfrey, Salton, Boyd, Hendrie, Dunn, Jobson, Neilson (Scott), Sprott.

18 AUG SECTION 1

Alloa 0 3850

Celtic 5 *(Reid* pen, *McGrain, Burns, McStay, McCluskey)*

Alloa: Hunter; Thomson, Haggart, Purdie, Gray, Munro, Paterson, Smith, McComb, Houston, Grant.
Celtic: Bonner; McGrain, Reid, Aitken, Moyes, MacLeod, Provan, McStay, McCluskey, Burns, McGarvey.

Dunfermline Ath 0

Arbroath 0 1500

Dunfermline Ath: Whyte; Ford, Hegarty, Considine, Dall R., McCathie, McNaughton, Bowie, Morrison, Jenkins, Forrest.
Arbroath: Robertson; McKenzie, Kopel, Glover, Young, Burke, Steele, Hill, Robb, Shaw, Lees.

SECTION 2

Dundee 3 *(Ferguson 2, Mackie)*

Dumbarton 2 *(Donnelly* [2 pens]*)* 3400

Dundee: Blair; McKimmie, McLelland, Fraser, MacDonald, Glennie, Ferguson (Fleming), McGeachie, Sinclair (Davidson), Mackie, Stephen.
Dumbarton: Carson; Brown. McGowan M., Craig, Close, Coyle, Blair, Burnett, Dunlop, Donnelly, McGrogan (Montgomery).

SECTION 3

Clydebank 0

Hibernian 2 *(Murray, Rae)* 800

Clydebank: Gallacher; Treanor, Gervaise, Fallon, McGhie, McKeown, Ronald, Hughes, Williamson, Coyne, McCabe.
Hibernian: McArthur; Sneddon, Schaedler, Brazil, Welsh, McNamara, Callachan, Rae, Murray, Turnbull, Thomson.

Rangers 3 *(Bett, Paterson, Black)*

Airdrieonians 1 *(Flood)* 9500

Rangers: Stewart; MacKinnon, Black, McClelland, Paterson, Bett, Prytz, Kennedy, McAdam, Redford, MacDonald.
Airdrieonians: Martin; Anderson N., Rodger, McLaughlin, March, Gordon, Walker, McKeown, Millar, Flood, Coyle.

SECTION 4

Falkirk 0

Dundee U 4 *(Narey, Sturrock, Malpas, Milne)* 3200

Falkirk: Watson; Hoggan, Nicol, Brown, Oliver M., Wilson, Oliver A., Herd, Ward, Smith, Perry.
Dundee U: McAlpine; Phillip, Stark, Gough, Hegarty, Narey, Britton, Malpas, Payne, Sturrock (Milne), Dodds.

St Johnstone 5 *(Addison, Morton, Brogan 3)*

Raith R 0 2000

St Johnstone: Tulloch; Caldwell, McNeil, Beedie, Kennedy, Rutherford, Addison, Brogan, Pelosi, Morton, Fleming.
Raith R: Walker; Houston, Candlish, Robinson, Forsyth, More, Harris, Urquhart, Ballantyne, Gibson, Mitchell.

SECTION 5

Clyde 3 *(Reilly, Flexney, O'Neill)*

Motherwell 3 *(Conn, McClair, McLelland)* 1300

Clyde: Young; Brogan, Flexney, McColl, Dempsey, McQueen, Reilly, Sinclair, McCutcheon, O'Neill, Nevin.
Motherwell: Sproat; MacLeod, Forsyth, McLelland, Carson, Forbes, McClair, Coyne, Irvine, Conn, O'Hara.

Hearts 2 *(O'Connor 2)*

Forfar Ath 1 *(Porter)* 4100

Hearts: Smith; Kidd, Shields, Byrne, MacDonald R., Jardine, Bowman, Pettigrew, O'Connor, MacDonald A., Marinello.
Forfar: Kennedy; Lorimer, McPhee, Brown, Allan, Morris, Alexander, Farningham, Clark, Leitch, Porter.

SECTION 6

Ayr U 0

Stirling Albion 0 900

Ayr U: Rennie; Shanks, Ahern, Hetherington, McAllister, Love, Frye, Hume, McInally, Connor, Ward.
Stirling Albion: Arthur; Dawson, Steedman, Grant, Philliben, Moffat, Colquhoun, McRoberts, Steele, Leetion, Cavanagh.

Queen of the S 0

St Mirren 1 *(McDougall)* 800

Queen of the S: Davidson; Miller, Gray, Maxwell, Clark, Wilkie, Gordon, Busby, Alexander, Cloy, Robertson J.
St Mirren: Thomson; Wilson, Clarke, Fitzpatrick, Fulton, McCormack, Logan, Stark, Somner (McDougall), Richardson, Scanlon.

SECTION 7

Brechin C 4 *(Campbell I.* pen, *McKay, Paterson, Millican)*

East Stirling 0 350

Brechin C: Neilson; Watt, Cord, Lesslie, Reid, Hay, Campbell I. (Cormack), Stewart, McKay (Paterson), Elvin, Millican.
East Stirling: Marshall; Blair, Kettings, Caldwell, Rennie I., Rennie C., Edgar, Watt N., Melrose, Gibson (Ross), Gray (Wilkie).

Partick T 0

East Fife 0 1500

Partick T: Rough; Murray, Kay, Whittaker, Dunlop, Watson, Park, McDonald, Johnston, Doyle J., Kenny.
East Fife: Gorman; McLaren, Clarke, Hutt, Dall, Halley, Meakin, Hamilton, Scott, Thomson, Caithness.

SECTION 8

Berwick R 1 *(Lawson)*

Queen's Park 0 500

Berwick R: McDermott; Moyes, McCann, McSherry, Jefferies, Muir, Armstrong, Marshall, Tait, Romaines, Lawson.
Queen's Park: Atkins; Cook, Dickson, Rennie, Woods, McFarlane, Crawley, McNiven, Nicholson, Grant, Gilmour.

Hamilton A 0

Kilmarnock 0 1000

Hamilton: Ferguson; McNaught, Colgan, Wright, McDougall, Blackley, Fairlie, McDowall, Paton, Craig, Mitchell.
Kilmarnock: McCulloch; McDicken, Robertson, Clark J., Armstrong, Clarke, McGivern, McLean, Bourke, Mauchlen, Gallacher.

SECTION 9

Meadowbank T 3 *(Sprott, Jobson, Boyd)*

Albion R 2 *(Evans, Dow)* 250

Meadowbank T: McQueen; Burrell, Conroy, Godfrey, Salton, Boyd, Hendrie, Dunn, Jobson, Neilson, Sprott.
Albion R: Balavage; Allan, Lapsley, Leishman, Burgess, McGrath, Gibson, Houston, Conn, Evans, Dow.

Stenhousemuir 2 *(Murray, Buchanan)*

Montrose 2 *(Taylor, Cooper)* 346

Stenhousemuir: Howie; Strain, Rennie, Thomson, Evans, Buchanan, McCusker, Munn, Murray, Erwin, Gillon.
Montrose: Charles; Barr, Forbes, Taylor, Shernan, Mathieson, Oliver, Nicol, Copeland, Cooper, McDonald.

Stranraer 1 *(Dolan)*

Cowdenbeath 3 *(Liddle, McIntosh, Marshall)* 300

Stranraer: Strachan; McDonald, Hay, Knox, McCaig, Filson, Neil, Dolan, McBride, Bryce, Sweeney.
Cowdenbeath: Allan; Campbell, Rose, Tierney, Russell, McCulloch, Marshall, Ferguson, Liddle, Fairley, McIntosh.

21 AUG SECTION 1

Arbroath 0

Celtic 3 *(McCluskey, Nicholas, Crainie)* 5275

Arbroath: Robertson; McKenzie, Kopel, Glover, Young, Burke, Steele, Hill, Robb (Yule), Shaw, Lees.
Celtic: Bonner; McGrain, Reid, Aitken, Moyes, MacLeod, Provan, McStay, McCluskey (Nicholas), Burns, McGarvey.

Dunfermline Ath 2 *(Morrison 2)*

Alloa 1 *(Grant)* 1200

Dunfermline Ath: Whyte; Ford, Hegarty, Considine, Dall R., McCathie, McNaughton, Bowie, Morrison, Jenkins, Forrest.
Alloa: Hunter; Thomson, Haggart (Ballantyne), Purdie, Gray, Munro, Paterson, Smith, McComb (Houston), Murray, Grant.

SECTION 2

Aberdeen 3 (McGhee, Strachan 2)

Dumbarton 0 8000

Aberdeen: Leighton; Kennedy, McMaster, Simpson, McLeish, Miller, Strachan, Black, McGhee (Hewitt), Bell (Rougvie), Weir.
Dumbarton: Carson; Walker (Stevenson), McGowan M., Clougherty, Close, Coyle, Blair (Burnett), Brown, Dunlop, Donnelly, McGrogan.

Morton 4 *(Rooney, Cochrane, Ritchie, Docherty)*

Dundee 1 *(Davidson)* 2500

Morton: Baines; Houston, Holmes, Rooney, McLaughlin, Duffy, McNeil (Higgins), Docherty, Hutchison, Cochrane, Ritchie (Gavigan).
Dundee: Blair; McKimmie, McLelland (Davidson), Fraser, Scrimgeour, Glennie, Ferguson, McGeachie (Fleming), Sinclair, Mackie, Stephen.

SECTION 3

Clydebank 1 *(Ronald)*

Rangers 4 *(Prytz, MacDonald 2, McClelland)* 7000

Clydebank: Gallacher; Treanor, Gervaise, Fallon, McGhie, Given, Ronald, Hughes (McKeown), Williamson (Sinclair), Coyne, McCabe.
Rangers: Stewart; MacKinnon, Black (Kennedy), McClelland, Paterson, Bett, Cooper, Prytz, McAdam (Dawson), Redford, MacDonald.

Hibernian 1 *(Welsh)*

Airdrieonians 1 *(Schnedler og)* 3500

Hibernian: McArthur; Sneddon, Schaedler (Duncan), Brazil, Welsh, McNamara, Callachan, Rae, Rodier (Murray), Turnbull, Thomson.
Airdrieonians: Martin; Anderson N., Rodger, McLaughlin, March, Gordon, Walker, McKeown, Millar, Flood, Coyle.

SECTION 4

Dundee U 5 *(Narey 2, Payne, Britton, Milne)*

Raith R 1 *(Harris)* 5000

Dundee U: McAlpine; Phillip, Stark, Gough, Hegarty, Narey, Britton (Kirkwood), Malpas (Milne), Payne, Sturrock, Dodds.
Raith R: Walker; Houston, Candlish, Robinson, Forsyth, More, Steen, Thomson, Ballantyne, Gibson (Russell), Harris.

Falkirk 1 *(Wilson* pen*)*

St Johnstone 6 *(Brogan 5, Morton)* 2000

Falkirk: Watson; Hoggan, Nicol, Brown, Oliver M., Wilson, Oliver A., Herd, Smith, Thomson, Perry.
St Johnstone: Tulloch; Caldwell, McNeil, Beedie, Kennedy, Rutherford, Addison, Brogan, Pelosi, Morton, Fleming.

SECTION 5

Clyde 1 *(McCutcheon)* 2900

Hearts 7 *(Pettigrew 4, Bowman, Shields, Brogan og)*

Clyde: Young; Brogan, Flexney, McColl, Dempsey, McQueen, Reilly, Sinclair, McCutcheon, O'Neill, Nevin.
Hearts: Smith; Kidd, Shields, Byrne, MacDonald R., Jardine. Bowman, Pettigrew, O'Connor, MacDonald A. (Mackay), Marinello.

Motherwell 1 *(Forbes)*

Forfar Ath 1 *(Clark)* 4000

Motherwell: Sproat; MacLeod, Forsyth (Gahagan), McLelland, Carson, Forbes, McClair, Coyne, Irvine, Conn, O'Hara.
Forfar Ath: Kennedy; Lorimer, McPhee, Brown, Allan, Morris, Alexander, Farningham, Clark, Leitch, Porter.

SECTION 6

Ayr U 0

Queen of the S 2 *(McLeod, Alexander)* 1000

Ayr U: Rennie; Shanks, McGhee, Hetherington, McAllister, Love, Frye, Hume, McInally, Connor, Christie.
Queen of the S: Davidson; Wilkie, Gray, Maxwell, Clark, Cloy, McLeod, Gordon (McCann), Alexander, Kennedy, Robertson J.

Stirling Albion 0

St Mirren 3 *(McAvennie 2, Stark)* 800

Stirling Albion: Arthur; Dawson, Steedman, Grant (Torrance), Philliben, Moffat, Colquhoun (McNeill), McRoberts, Steele, Leetion, Cavanagh.
St Mirren: Thomson; Wilson, Clarke, Fitzpatrick, Fulton, McCormack, Richardson, Stark, McAvennie, Abercromby (McDougall), Scanlon.

SECTION 7

East Fife 0

East Stirling 1 *(Gibson)* 200

East Fife: Gorman; McLaren, Thomson, Halley, Dall, Meakin, O'Brien, Hamilton, Scott, Hutt, Caithness (Wilson).
East Stirling: Marshall; Renwick, Kettings, Caldwell, Rennie I., Wilkie, Tierney, Melrose (Watt N.), Gibson (Edgar), Gray, Ross.

Partick T 0

Brechin C 0 1500

Partick T: Rough; Murray, Kay, Whittaker, Dunlop, Watson, Park, Jardine, Johnston, Doyle J., McDowall.
Brechin C: Neilson; Watt, Cord, Lesslie, Reid, Hay, Campbell I., Stewart, McKay, Elvin, Milligan.

SECTION 8

Berwick R 0

Hamilton A 1 *(Fairlie* pen*)* 585

Berwick R: McDermott; Moyes, McLennan, McSherry, Jefferies, Muir, McKenna, Romaines, Tait, McCann, Clark.
Hamilton: Ferguson; McNaught, Mitchell, Hamill, McDougall, Blackley, Fairlie, McDowall, Craig, Gorman, Donnelly.

Queen's Park 0

Kilmarnock 2 *(McLean* pen, *McGivern)* 600

Queen's Park: Atkins; McFarlane, Dickson, Rennie, Woods, McNiven, Crawley, Graham, Nicholson (Chalmers), Grant, Gilmour.
Kilmarnock: McCulloch; McDicken, Robertson, Clark J., Armstrong, Clarke, McGivern (MacLeod), McLean, Bourke, Mauchlen (Bryson), Gallacher.

SECTION 9

Albion R 0

Stenhousemuir 0 250

Albion R: Balavage; McQueen, Main, Leishman, Burgess, Ferrie, Dow, Collins, Houston, Evans, Conn (Ross).
Stenhousemuir: Howie; Strain, Rennie, McCusker, Evans, Buchanan, Stirling, Thomson, Murray, Erwin, Gillon.

Meadowbank T 0

Cowdenbeath 1 *(Marshall)* 250

Meadowbank T: McQueen; Dunn, Fraser, Godfrey, Salton, Conroy, Hendrie (Korotkich), Georgeson (Scott), Jobson, Boyd, Sprott.
Cowdenbeath: Allan; Campbell, Rose, Tierney, Russell, McCulloch, Marshall, Ferguson, Liddle, Fairley (Miller), McIntosh (Hyslop).

Montrose 1 *(Oliver)*

Stranraer 0 250

Montrose: Charles; Barr, Forbes, Taylor, Shernan, Mathieson, Oliver, Nicol, Copeland, Cooper, McDonald.
Stranraer: Strachan; McDonald, Hay, Quinn, McCaig, Filson, McBride, Dolan, Taylor, Bryce, Sweeney (Neil).

25 AUG SECTION 1

Arbroath 1 *(Shaw)*

Dunfermline Ath 0 490

Arbroath: Robertson; McKenzie, Kopel, Glover, Young, Burke, Steele, Hill, Robb, Shaw, Lees (Yule).
Dunfermline Ath: Whyte; Ford, Grant, Considine, Dall R., Hegarty, Bowie, Jenkins, Morrison, Dall S., Forrest.

Celtic 4 *(Nicholas, MacLeod, Aitken, Burns)*

Alloa 1 *(Gray* pen*)* 6500

Celtic: Bonner; McGrain, Reid, Aitken, Moyes, MacLeod, Provan, McStay, Nicholas, Burns, McGarvey.
Alloa: Hunter; Thomson, McKenzie, Purdie, Gray, Munro, Paterson (Haggart), Smith (Murray), McComb, Houston, Grant.

SECTION 2

Aberdeen 3 *(Bell 2, Rougvie)*

Morton 0 11,000

Aberdeen: Leighton; Rougvie, McMaster, Cooper, McLeish, Miller, Strachan (Hewitt), Black, McGhee, Bell, Simpson (Angus).
Morton: Baines; Houston, Holmes, Rooney, McLaughlin, Duffy, McNeil, Docherty, Hutchison, Cochrane, Ritchie (Gavigan).

Dumbarton 2 *(Donnelly* [2 pens]*)*

Dundee 3 *(Ferguson* pen, *Fraser, Sinclair)* 400

Dumbarton: Carson; Brown, McGowan M., Walker, Burnett, Coyle, Blair, Clougherty, Dunlop, Donnelly, Stevenson.
Dundee: R. Geddes; McKimmie, McLelland, Fraser, Glennie, McGeachie, Ferguson. Geddes A. (Fleming), Sinclair, Mackie, Stephen.

SECTION 3

Airdrieonians 1 *(Millar)*

Rangers 2 *(Dalziel, Paterson)* 6000

Airdrieonians: Martin; N. Anderson, Rodger, McLaughlin, March, Gordon, Faulds, McKeown, Millar, Flood, Coyle.
Rangers: Stewart; MacKinnon, Black, McClelland, Paterson, Bett, Cooper, Prytz, Dalziel, Redford, MacDonald.

Hibernian 1 *(Rodier)*

Clydebank 1 *(Given)* 2300

Hibernian: McArthur; Sneddon, Turnbull, Brazil, Welsh, McNamara, Callachan, Rae, Rodier, Murray, Thomson.
Clydebank: Gallacher; Treanor, Gervaise, Fallon, McGie, Given, Ronald, Hughes, Williamson, Coyne, McCabe.

SECTION 4

Dundee U 4 *(Dodds 2, Payne, Sturrock)*

Falkirk 0 4300

Dundee U: Gardiner; Phillip (Bannon), Stark, Gough, Hegarty, Narey, Britton, Malpas (Holt), Payne, Sturrock, Dodds.
Falkirk: Watson; Hoggan, Nicol, Brown, Fowler, Wilson, A. Oliver (Hendrie), Herd, Smith, Ward, Thomson.

Raith R 3 *(Ballantyne, Russell, Gibson)*

St Johnstone 3 *(Brogan 2, Beedie)* 2350

Raith R: Walker; Robertson, Candlish, Robinson, More, Thomson, Steen, Russell, Ballantyne, McCullough, Harris (Gibson).
St Johnstone: Tulloch; Caldwell, McNeil, Beedie, Kennedy, Rutherford, Addison, Brogan, Pelosi, Morton, Fleming (Brannigan).

SECTION 5

Forfar Ath 0

Hearts 2 *(A. MacDonald, Marinello)* 1900

Forfar Ath: Kennedy; Lorimer, McPhee, Morris, Brash, Allan, Alexander, Farningham, Clark, Leitch (Hancock), Porter (Tennant).
Hearts: Smith; Kidd, Shields, Byrne, R. MacDonald, Jardine, Bowman, Pettigrew, O'Connor, A. MacDonald, Marinello (MacLaren).

Motherwell 3 *(McClair 3,* [1 pen]*)*

Clyde 1 *(Masterton)* 3200

Motherwell: Sproat; MacLeod, Wark, McLelland, Carson, Forbes, Gahagan, Clinging (McClair), Clelland, Conn (Coyne), O'Hara.
Clyde: Young; Coutts, McQueen, Rae, McLaren, Flexney, Reilly, Sinclair, McCutcheon, O'Neill, Nevin (Masterton).

SECTION 6

Stirling Albion 1 *(McNeill)*

Ayr U 1 *(Larnach)* 400

Stirling Albion: Arthur; Dawson, Steedman, Grant (Torrance), Philliben, Moffat, Colquhoun (McNeill), McRoberts, Steele, Leetion, Cavanagh.
Ayr U: Rennie; Shanks, McGhee, Ahern, McAllister, Fleeting, Frye, McCulley (Armour), Larnach, Connor, Ward.

St Mirren 6 *(McAvennie 2, Stark 2, McDougall 2)*

Queen of the S 0 1500

St Mirren: Thomson; Walker, Clarke, Fitzpatrick, McCormack, Copland, McDougall, Stark, McAvennie, Abercromby, Richardson.
Queen of the S: Davidson; Wilkie, Gray, Maxwell, Clark, Cloy, McLeod, G. Robertson, Alexander, Miller, J. Robertson.

SECTION 7

East Fife 0

Partick T 3 *(Johnston, Park, Jardine)* 450

East Fife: Gorman; McLaren, Clarke, Halley, Dall, Thomson, Durie, Hamilton, Scott, Hutt, O'Brien.
Partick T: Rough; G. Doyle, Kay, Whittaker, Dunlop, Watson, Park, Jardine, Johnston, J. Doyle, McDowall.

East Stirling 1 *(Gibson)*

Brechin 1 *(Stewart)* 250

East Stirling: Marshall; Renwick, Kettings, Caldwall, I. Rennie, Wilkie, Cairnie, Edgar, Gibson, Gray, Ross.
Brechin C: Neilson; Watt, Cord, Lesslie, Reid, Hay, Campbell I., Stewart, McKay, Elvin, Milligan.

SECTION 8

Kilmarnock 1 *(Bourke)*

Hamilton A 0 1400

Kilmarnock: McCulloch; McDicken, Robertson, Clark J., Clarke, McClurg, McGivern, MacLeod, Bourke, Mauchlen, Gallacher.
Hamilton A: Ferguson; McNaught, Colgan, Fairlie, McDowall, Blackley, Wright, McDougall, Donnelly, Mitchell, Wilson.

Queen's Park 2 *(Verrachie, McNiven)*

Berwick R 1 *(Armstrong)* 479

Queen's Park: Atkins; McFarlane, Dickson, Rennie, Woods, McNiven, Crawley, Graham, Verrachia, Grant, Gilmour.
Berwick R: McDermott; McCann, McLennan, McSherry, Jefferies, Muir, McKenna, Romaines, Tait, Armstrong, Clark.

SECTION 9

Cowdenbeath 2 *(Ferguson, Burgess og)*

Albion R 1 *(Houston)* 250

Cowdenbeath: Allan; Campbell, Rose, Tierney, Russell, McCulloch, Marshall, Ferguson, Liddle, McIntosh, Hyslop.
Albion R: Purdie; McQueen, Lapsley, Leishman, Burgess, Collins, Ferrie, Dow, Houston, Evans, Gibson.

Montrose 0

Meadowbank T 1 *(Jobson)* 250

Montrose: Charles; Barr, Forbes, Taylor, Shernan, Mathieson, Oliver, Nicol, Copeland, Cooper, McManus.
Meadowbank T: McQueen; Dunn, Conroy, Gorfrey, Salton, Korotkich, Hendrie, Georgeson, Jobson, Boyd, Sprott.

Stenhousemuir 0

Stranraer 4 *(Neil 2, Taylor 2)* 300

Stenhousemuir: Howie; Strain, Rennie, McCusker, Evans, Buchanan, Stirling, Thomson, Murray, Erwin, Gillon.
Stranraer: Strachan; McDonald, Hay, Quinn, McCaig, Filson, McBride, Dolan, Taylor, Bryce, Sweeney.

28 AUG SECTION 1

Alloa 0

Arbroath 1 *(Steele)* 500

Alloa: Hunter; Thomson, McKenzie, Purdie, Garner, Houston, Murray (Gray), Wilson, McComb, Munro, Grant.
Arbroath: Robertson; McKenzie, Kopel, Durno, Young, Burke (Yule), Steele, Hill, Robb (Docherty), Shaw, Lees.

Dunfermline Ath 1 *(Morrison)*

Celtic 7 *(Nicholas 4, Burns, McCluskey, R. Dall og)* 8000

Dunfermline Ath: Whyte; Ford, Hegarty, Considine, Dall R., Hepburn (Robertson), Bowie, Hamill, Morrison, Jenkins (Dall S.), Forrest.
Celtic: Bonner; McGrain (Sinclair), McInally, Aitken, McAdam, MacLeod, Provan (Halpin), Conroy, McCluskey, Burns, Nicholas.

SECTION 2

Dundee 1 *(Stephen)*

Aberdeen 5 *(Strachan 4* [1 pen], *McGhee)* 6900

Dundee: Geddes R.; McKimmie, McLelland, Fraser, Glennie, McGeachie, Ferguson, Geddes A. (Kidd), Sinclair (Davidson), Mackie, Stephen.
Aberdeen: Leighton; Kennedy, McMaster, Cooper, Rougvie (Black, Angus), Miller, Stachan, Simpson, McGhee, Bell, Hewitt.

Morton 4 *(Rooney 2, Docherty, McNab)*

Dumbarton 1 *(Stevenson)* 2310

Morton: Baines; Houston, Holmes, Rooney, McLaughlin, Duffy, McNeil (McNab), Docherty, Hutchison, Cochrane, Ritchie (Gavigan).
Dumbarton: Carson; Brown, Bennett, Montgomery (McGrogan), Clougherty, Coyle, Craig, Walker (Dunlop), Stevenson, Donnelly, Blair.

SECTION 3

Clydebank 1 *(Williamson)*

Airdrieonians 2 *(Millar 2)* 1000

Clydebank: Gallacher; Treanor, Gervaise, Fallon, McGhie, Given, Ronald, Hughes, Williamson, Coyne, McKeown.
Airdrieonians: Martin; Anderson N., Rodger, McLaughlin, March, Gordon (McGuire), Faulds, McKeown, Millar, Flood, Coyle.

Rangers 0

Hibernian 0 17,600

Rangers: Stewart; MacKinnon, Black, McClelland, Paterson, Bett, Cooper, Prytz, McAdam, Redford, MacDonald.
Hibernian: McArthur; Sneddon, Turnbull, McNamara, Jamieson, Duncan, Callachan, Rae (Murray), Rodier (McWilliam), Flavell, Thomson.

SECTION 4

Falkirk 2 *(Herd 2)*

Raith R 0 1500

Falkirk: Watson, Hoggan, Nicol, Brown, Mackin, Wilson, Perry, Herd (Fowler), Smith, Ward (Hendrie), Thomson.
Raith R: Walker; Robertson, Candlish, Robinson, More, Thomson, Steen, Russell, Ballantyne, McCulloch, Harris (Gibson).

St Johnstone 0

Dundee U 3 *(Dodds, Bannon, Kirkwood)* 4092

St Johnstone: Tulloch; Caldwell, McNeil, Beedie, Mackay, Rutherford, Addison, Brogan, Pelosi, Morton, Fleming.
Dundee U: McAlpine; Holt (Kirkwood), Stark, Gough, Hegarty, Narey, Britton, Malpas, Bannon, Sturrock, Dodds.

SECTION 5

Clyde 0

Forfar Ath 1 *(Clarke)* 750

Clyde: Young; Coutts, McQueen, Rae, McLaren, Wood, Reilly, Sinclair, Masterton, O'Neill, Nevin.
Forfar Ath: Kennedy; Lorimer, Bennett, Brown, Brash, McPhee, Craig, Farningham, Hancock, Leitch, Clark.

Hearts 1 *(McDonald A.)*

Motherwell 0 9000

Hearts: Smith; Kidd, Shields, Byrne, MacDonald, Jardine, Bowman, Pettigrew, O'Connor, MacDonald A., McCoy.
Motherwell: Sproat; MacLeod, Forsyth, McLelland, Carson, McClair, Gahagan (Clinging), Coyne, Clelland, Conn, O'Hara (Rafferty).

SECTION 6

Ayr U 2 *(Larnach, Thomson og)*

St Mirren 1 *(McDougall)* 1800

Ayr U: Rennie; Shanks, McGhee, Ahern, McAllister (Armour), Fleeting, Frye, McInally, Larnach, Connor, Ward.
St Mirren: Thomson; Walker, Fulton (Abercromby), Fitzpatrick, McCormack, Copland, McDougall, Stark, McAvennie, Richardson (Logan), Scanlon.

Queen of the S 0

Stirling Albion 2 *(Colquhoun 2* [1 pen]*)* 640

Queen of the S: Davidson; Wilkie, Gray, Maxwell, Clark, Cloy, McLeod, Robertson G., Alexander, Miller, Robertson J.
Stirling Albion: Arthur; Davidson, Steedman, Grant, Philliben, Moffat, ColOquhoun, McRoberts, Steele, Leetion, Cavanagh.

SECTION 7

Brechin C 4 *(McWalter, Graham 2, Paterson)*

East Fife 0 400

Brechin C: Neilson; Watt, Mackie, Lesslie, Reid, Hay, Paterson, Stewart, McKay (McWalter), Elvin, Cormack (Graham).
East Fife: Gorman; Clarke, McLaren, Halley, Dall, Thomson, O'Brien, Hamilton, Scott, Hutt, Caithness.

Partick T 4 *(Watson 2* [1 pen], *Johnston 2)*

East Stirling 2 *(Watt, Gray)* 2000

Partick T: Rough; Murray, Kay, Whittaker, Dunlop, Watson, Park (McDowall), Jardine, Johnston, Doyle J. (Docherty), McDonald.
East Stirling: Marshall; Renwick, Kettings, Caldwell (Edgar), Rennie I., Wilkie, Gray, Tinney, Gibson, Watt (N), Ross (Melrose).

SECTION 8

Berwick R 2 *(Armstrong, Tait)*

Kilmarnock 1 *(McLean* pen*)* 670

Berwick R: McDermott; McCann, McLennan, McSherry, Jefferies, Muir, Lawson, Romaines (McKenna), Tait, Armstrong, Clark (Davidson).
Kilmarnock: McCulloch; McDicken, Robertson, J. Clark, McClurg, McGivern (McLean), MacLeod, Bourke, Mauchlen (Bryson), Gallacher.

Hamilton A 1 *(Fairlie* pen*)*

Queen's Park 2 *(Gilmour 2)* 600

Hamilton A: Ferguson; McNaught, Colgan, Wright, McDougall, Blackley, Fairlie, McDowall, Paton (Gorman), Mitchell, Barkley.
Queen's Park: Atkins; McFarlane, Dickson, Rennie, Woods, McNiven, Crawley, Graham, Verrachia (Chalmers), Grant, Gilmour.

SECTION 9

Albion R 1 *(Evans)*

Montrose 2 *(Turnbull, Copeland)* 250

Albion R: Purdie; Main, Lapsley, Leishman, Burgess, Houston, Gibson, Collins, Dow, Evans, Conn.
Montrose: Charles; Barr, Nicholson, Taylor, Shernan, Mathieson, Oliver, Nicol, Copeland, Cooper, Turnbull (McManus).

Cowdenbeath 1 *(McIntosh)*

Stenhousemuir 1 *(Murray)* 300

Cowdenbeath: Allan; Campbell, Rose, Tierney, Russell, McCulloch, Marshall, Ferguson, Liddle, McIntosh, Hyslop.
Stenhousemuir: Howie; Strain, Rennie, McCusker, Evans, Buchanan, Stirling, Thomson, Murray, Erwin, Gillon.

Stranraer 0

Meadowbank T 2 *(Jobson, Sprott* pen*)* 200

Stranraer: Stachan; McDonald, Hay, Quinn, McCaig, Filson, McBride, Dolan, Taylor, Bryce, Sweeney.
Meadowbank T: McQueen; Dunn, Conroy, Godfrey, Salton, Korotkich, Hendrie, Georgeson, Jobson, Boyd, Sprott.

1 SEPT SECTION 1

Alloa 3 *(Garner, Murray, Houston)*

Dunfermline Ath 0 650

Alloa: Hunter; Thomson, McKenzie, Purdie, Garner, Houston, Gray (Murray), Wilson, McComb, Munro, Grant.
Dunfermline Ath: Whyte; Ford, Hegarty, Considine, Dall R., Hepburn, Bowie, Hamill, Morrison, Jenkins, Forrest.

Celtic 4 *(MacLeod, McCluskey, Nicholas, Dobbin)*

Arbroath 1 *(Yule)* 5200

Celtic: Bonner; McGrain, Reid, Aitken, McAdam, MacLeod, Buckley, Dobbin, McCluskey (McGarvey), Burns, Nicholas (Crainie).
Arbroath: Robertson; McKenzie, Kopel, Durno (Hill T.), Young (Davey), Gavine, Harley, Docherty, Powell, Hill H., Yule.

SECTION 2

Dundee 3 *(Ferguson, Kidd, Mackie)*

Morton 3 *(Rooney 2, Hutchison)* 1900

Dundee: Kelly; McGeachie, McKimmie, Fraser, Smith, Glennie, Ferguson (Sinclair), Kidd, Davidson, Mackie, Stephen (Fleming).
Morton: Baines; Houston, Holmes, Rooney, McLaughlin, Duffy, McNeil (NcNab), Docherty, Hutchison, Cochrane, Ritchie.

SECTION 3

Airdrieonians 3 *(Millar, Campbell, Faulds)*

Hibernian 1 *(Rae)* 2000

Airdrieonians: Martin; Anderson, Rodger, McLaughlin, March, Campbell, Faulds, McKeown, Millar, Flood, Coyle.
Hibernian: McArthur; Sneddon, Turnbull, McNamara, Jamieson, Duncan, Flavell, Welsh, Rae, Callachan, Thomson.

Rangers 3 *(MacDonald, Redford, Prytz* pen*)*

Clydebank 2 *(Williamson, Treanor)* 6300

Rangers: Stewart; MacKinnon, Black, McClelland, Paterson, Bett, Cooper, Prytz, Dalziel (Mackay), Redford, MacDonald.
Clydebank: Gallacher; Treanor, Gervaise, Fallon, McGhie, Given, Ronald, Hughes, W—lliamson, Coyne, McCabe.

SECTION 4

Raith R 1 *(Harris)*

Dundee U 3 *(Dodds, Sturrock, Bannon* pen*)* 3000

Raith R: Walker; Robertson, Candlish, Thomson, Forsyth, More, Robinson, Gibson, Harris, McCulloch, Mitchell.
Dundee U: McAlpine; Phillip, Stark, Holt, Hegarty, Narey, Britton, Payne, Sturrock, Dodds.

St Johnstone 1 *(Morton* pen*)*

Falkirk 0 2000

St Johnstone: Tulloch; Caldwell, McNeil, Beedie, Mackay, Rutherford, Addison, Brogan, Pelosi, Morton, Fleming (Brannigan).
Falkirk: Watson; Hoggan, Nicol, Brown, Mackin, Wilson, Perry, Herd, Smith (Oliver A.), Ward, Thomson.

SECTION 5

Forfar Ath 0

Motherwell 1 *(O'Hara)* 900

Forfar Ath: Kennedy; Lorimer, Bennett, Brown, Brash, McPhee, Porter, Farningham, Hancock (Alexander), Leitch, Clark.
Motherwell: Sproat; MacLeod, Forsyth, McLelland, Edvaldsson, McLaughlin, Gahagan, Rafferty, Clelland, McClair, O'Hara (Coyne).

Hearts 3 *(Shields, Bowman, Pettigrew)*

Clyde 0 5000

Hearts: Smith; Kidd, Shields, Byrne, MacDonald R., Jardine, Bowman, Pettigrew (Robertson), O'Connor, MacDonald A. (MacLaren), McCoy.
Clyde: Young; Coutts, McQueen, Rae, Dempsey, McLaren, Sinclair, Reilly (Nevin), Masterton, O'Neill, McCutcheon.

SECTION 6

Queen of the S 1 *(Robertson G.)*

Ayr U 4 *(Shanks, Larnach, McInally 2)* 550

Queen of the S: Davidson; Wilkie, Gray, Maxwell, Clark, Cloy, McLeod, G. Robertson, Alexander, Miller, Robertson J.
Ayr U: Rennie; Shanks, McGhee, Ahern, McAllister, Fleeting, Frye, McInally, Larnach, Connor, Ward.

St Mirren 0

Stirling A 0 1500

St Mirren: Thomson; Wilson, Clarke, Fitzpatrick, McCormack, Copland, McDougall, Stark, Somner, McAvennie, Abercromby.
Stirling A: Arthur; Dawson, Steedman, McRoberts, Philliben, Moffat, Colquhoun, Torrance, Steele, McNeill, Cavanagh.

SECTION 7

Brechin C 1 *(McWalter)*

Partick T 1 *(Whittaker)* 746

Brechin C: Neilson; Watt, McWalter, Lesslie, Reid, Hay, Paterson, Campbell R., McKay, Elvin, Graham (Campbell I.).
Partick T: Rough; Murray, Kay (Lapsley), Whittaker, Dunlop, Watson, Park, Docherty, Johnston, Doyle J., McDonald.

East Stirling 0

East Fife 0 200

East Stirling: marshall; Renwick, Kettings, Caldwell, Rennie I., Wilkie, Gray, Tinney, Gibson, Watt N., Ross.
East Fife: Gorman; Clarke, McLaren, Halley, Dall, Thomson, O'Brien, Hamilton, Scott, Hutt, Caithness.

SECTION 8

Hamilton A 0

Berwick R 1 *(Romaines pen)* 450

Hamilton A: Ferguson; McNaught, Colgan, Wright, McDougall, Blackley, Fairlie, McDowall, Paton, Mitchell, Barkley.
Berwick R: McDermott; McCann, McLennan, McSherry, Jefferies, Muir, Lawson, Romaines, Tait, Armstrong, Clark.

Kilmarnock 5 *(Bourke 2, McLean, Gallacher, Mauchlen)*

Queen's Park 1 *(Gilmour)* 1000

Kilmarnock: McCulloch; McDicken, Robertson, Clark J., Clarke, McClurg, McGivern (McLean), MacLeod, Bourke, Mauchlen, Gallacher.
Queen's Park: Atkins; McFarlane, Dickson, Rennie, Woods, McNiven, Crawley, Graham, Grant, Verrachia, Gilmour.

SECTION 9

Play Off

Cowdenbeath 3 *(McFarlane, Liddle, Hyslop)*

Meadowbank T 0 600

Cowdenbeath: Allan; Campbell, Rose, Tierney, Russell, McCulloch (McFarlane), Marshall, Ferguson, Liddle, McIntosh, Hyslop.
Meadowbank T.: McQueen; Dunn, Conroy, Godfrey, Salton, Korotkich, Hendrie, Georgeson, Jobson, Boyd, Sprott.

		Home			Away					
	P	*W*	*D*	*L*	*W*	*D*	*L*	*F*	*A*	*Pts*
				Section 1						
Celtic	6	3	0	0	3	0	0	29	3	12
Arbroath	6	1	0	2	1	1	1	4	9	5
Alloa Ath	6	1	0	2	1	0	2	7	13	4
Dunfermline	6	1	1	1	0	0	3	3	18	3
				Section 2						
Aberdeen	6	2	1	0	2	1	0	18	7	10
Morton	6	2	1	0	1	1	1	16	11	8
Dundee	6	1	1	1	1	1	1	14	19	6
Dumbarton	6	0	0	3	0	0	3	7	18	0
				Section 3						
Rangers	6	2	1	0	2	1	0	13	6	10
Hibernian	6	0	3	0	1	1	1	6	6	6
Airdrie	6	1	0	2	1	1	1	9	11	5
Clydebank	6	0	0	3	1	1	1	8	13	3
				Section 3						
Dundee U	6	3	0	0	3	0	0	22	2	12
St Johnstone	6	2	0	1	1	1	1	15	10	7
Falkirk	6	1	0	2	0	1	2	3	15	3
Raith R	6	0	2	1	0	0	3	5	18	2
				Section 5						
Hearts	6	3	0	0	2	0	1	16	4	10
Motherwell	6	2	1	0	1	1	1	10	7	8
Forfar A	6	1	0	2	1	1	1	5	6	5
Clyde	6	0	1	2	0	0	3	5	19	1
				Section 6						
St Mirren	6	2	1	0	2	0	1	14	3	9
Stirling A	6	1	1	1	1	2	0	5	4	7
Ayr U	6	1	1	1	1	1	1	8	8	6
Q.O.S.	6	0	0	3	1	0	2	3	15	2
				Section 7						
Partick T	6	1	2	0	2	1	0	12	3	9
Brechin C	6	2	1	0	0	3	0	10	12	8
E Stirling	6	0	2	1	1	0	2	4	13	4
East Fife	6	0	1	2	0	2	1	0	8	3
				Section 8						
Kilmarnock	6	3	0	0	1	1	1	13	3	9
Berwick R	6	2	0	1	1	0	2	5	8	6
Queen's P	6	1	1	1	1	0	2	6	11	5
Hamilton	6	0	1	2	1	1	1	3	5	4
				Section 9						
Cowdenbth	5	1	1	1	2	0	0	7	4	7
Meadowbnk	5	1	0	1	2	1	0	7	4	7
Montrose	5	1	0	1	2	1	0	6	4	7
Stenhousemuir	5	0	2	1	0	2	0	4	8	4
Stranraer	5	0	0	2	1	1	1	7	8	3
Albion R	5	0	2	1	0	0	2	6	9	2

Cowdenbeath won play-off.

6 SEPT SECTIONAL PLAY-OFF. FIRST LEG

Kilmarnock 1 *(McLean pen)*

Cowdenbeath 0 850

Kilmarnock: McCulloch; McDicken, Robertson, Clark J., Clarke, McClurg, McLean, MacLeod, Bourke, Mauchlen, Gallacher.
Cowdenbeath: Allan; Campbell, Rose, Tierney, Russell, McFarlane, Marshall, Ferguson, Liddle, McIntosh, Hyslop.

8 SEPT SECTIONAL PLAY-OFF, SECOND LEG

Cowdenbeath 1 *(Marshall)*

Kilmarnock 0 800

Aggregate 1-1. Kilmarnock won after extra-time and penalties.

Cowdenbeath: Allan; Campbell, Rose, Tierney, Russell, McFarlane, Marshall, Ferguson (Forrest), Liddle, McIntosh (Miller), Hyslop.
Kilmarnock: McCulloch; McDicken, Robertson, Clark J., Clarke, McClurg, McGivern, MacLeod, Bourke, Mauchlen (Bryson), Gallacher (McLean).

SECTION 2

Dumbarton 1 *(Donnelly pen)*

Aberdeen 2 *(Bell, Hewitt)* 750

Dumbarton: Carson; Brown, McNeill (McGowan M.), McGowan P., Close, Coyle, Craig, Burnett, Dunlop, Donnelly, Stevenson.
Aberdeen: Leighton; Mitchell, McMaster, Cooper, McLeish (Cowan), Miller, Black, Watson, Hewitt, Simpson (Bell), Weir.

15 SEPT QUARTER-FINAL, FIRST LEG

Celtic 4 *(Provan, Nicholas, MacLeod, McGarvey)*

Partick T 0 9250

Celtic: Bonner; McGrain, Reid, Aitken, McAdam, MacLeod, Provan, McStay, McCluskey (McGarvey), Burns, Nicholas.
Partick T: Rough; Murray, Kay, Doyle G. (McDonald), Whittaker, Lapsley, Park, Clark, Johnston, Doyle J., Kenny.

St Mirren 1 *(Logan)*

Hearts 1 *(Pettigrew)* 5500

St Mirren: Thomson; Wilson, Clarke, Fitzpatrick, Copland, McDougall, Stark, McAvennie, Richardson, Abercromby (Logan).
Hearts: Smith; Kidd, Shields, Byrne, MacDonald R., Jardine, Bowman, Pettigrew, O'Connor, MacLaren, MacDonald A.

22 SEPT QUARTER-FINAL, FIRST LEG

Aberdeen 1 *(McGhee)*

Dundee U 3 *(Kirkwood, Bannon, Gough)* 13,000

Aberdeen: Leighton; Rougvie (Kennedy), McMaster, Cooper, McLeish, Miller, Stachan, Watson (Black), McGhee, Hewitt, Weir.
Dundee U: McAlpine; Phillip (Malpas), Stark, Gough, Hegarty, Narey, Bannon, Milne, Kirkwood, Sturrock, Dodds.

Kilmarnock 1 *(McLean)*

Rangers 6 *(Cooper 4, MacDonald 2)* 5500

Kilmarnock: McCulloch; McLean, Cockburn, Clark J., Armstrong, McDicken, Bryson, MacLeod, Eadie, Mauchlen, Gallacher.
Rangers: Stewart; MacKinnon, Dawson, McClelland, paterson, Bett, Cooper, Prytz, Johnstone, Russell, MacDonald.

SECOND LEG

Hearts 2 *(MacDonald A., Pettigrew)*

St Mirren 1 *(Stark)* 12,000 (Aggregate 3-2)

Hearts: Smith; Kidd, Shields, Byrne, MacDonald R., Jardine, Bowman, Pettigrew, MacLaren (Johnston), MacDonald A.
St Mirren: Thomson; Wilson, McAveety, Fitzpatrick, McCormack, Copland, McAvennie, Stark, Logan, Richardson, Scanlon.

Partick T 0

Celtic 3 *(Nicholas 2, MacLeod)* 8000 (Aggregate 0-7)

Partick T: Rough; Murray, Whittaker, Kay, Scott, Jardine, Docherty, McDowall, Johnston, Doyle J., McDonald.
Celtic: Latchford; Sinclair, Reid, Aitken, McAdam, Moyes (Sullivan), Provan, McStay, McGarvey, MacLeod, Nicholas.

6 OCT SECOND LEG

Dundee U 1 *(Sturrock* pen*)*

Aberdeen 0 11,700 (Aggregate 4-1)

Dundee U: McAlpine; Phillip, Stark, Gough, Hegarty, Narey, Malpas, Milne, Kirkwood, Sturrock, Dodds.
Aberdeen: Leighton; Cooper, Rougvie, McMaster, McLeish, Miller, Stachan, Simpson, McGhee (Black), Hewitt, Weir.

Rangers 6 *(MacDonald 2, Johnstone 2, McPherson, Bett* pen*)*

Kilmarnock 0 5000 (Aggregate 12-1)

Rangers: Stewart; MacKinnon, Redford, McClelland, Paterson, Bett (Black), Cooper (Davies), McPherson, Johnstone, Russell, MacDonald.
Kilmarnock: McCulloch; McLean, MacLeod, Clark J., Clarke, McDicken, McGivern, McClurg, Bourke (Bryson), Mauchlen, Gallacher.

SEMI-FINALS

27 OCT SEMI-FINAL, FIRST LEG

Celtic 2 *(Nicholas* pen, *McGarvey)*

Dundee U 0 19,100

Celtic: Bonner; McGrain, Reid, Aitken, McAdam, Sinclair, Provan, McStay, McGarvey (Crainie), MacLeod, Nicholas.
Dundee U: McAlpine; Phillip, Stark, Gough, Hegarty, Narey, Holt, Milne, Kirkwood, Payne (Reilly), Dodds.

Rangers 2 *(Cooper, Bett)*

Hearts 0 25,000

Rangers: Stewart; MacKinnon, Redford, McClelland, Stevens, Bett, Cooper, Prytz, Johnstone, Russell, McAdam (MacDonald).
Hearts: Smith; Kidd, Shields, Byrne, MacDonald R., Jardine, Bowman, Pettigrew, O'Connor, MacLaren, Macdonald A.

10 NOV SECOND LEG

Dundee U 2 *(Sturrock 2)*

Celtic 1 *(Nicholas)* 15,400 (Aggregate 2-3)

Dundee U: McAlpine; Holt, Malpas, Gough, Hegarty, Narey, Bannon, Milne, Kirkwood, Sturrock, Dodds.
Celtic: Bonner; McGrain, Sinclair, Aitken, McAdam, Burns, Provan (McCluskey), McStay, McGarvey, MacLeod, Nicholas.

Hearts 1 *(O'Connor)*

Rangers 2 *(Bett* pen, *Johnstone)* 19,000 (Aggregate 1-4)

Hearts: Smith; Kidd, Shields, Byrne, MacDonald R., Jardine, Bowman, Robertson (Pettigrew), O'Connor, Mackay, Johnston.
Rangers: Stewart; MacKinnon, Dawson, McClelland, Stevens, Bett, Cooper (Dalziel), Redford, Johnstone, Russell (McPherson), MacDonald.

4 DEC FINAL (Hampden Park)

Celtic 2 *(Nicholas, MacLeod)*

Rangers 1 *(Bett)* 55,372

Celtic: Bonner; McGrain, Sinclair, Aitken, McAdam, MacLeod, Provan, McStay (Reid), McGarvey, Burns, Nicholas.
Rangers: Stewart; MacKinnon, Redford, McClelland, Paterson, Bett, Cooper, Prytz (Dawson), Johnstone, Russell (MacDonald), Smith.

REVIEW OF SCOTTISH PREMIER LEAGUE ATTENDANCES 1982–83

In a season when the Premier League induced three teams to contest its conclusion – for the first time – many may greet the news of an upturn in attendances with little surprise.

That however, would be to diminish the achievement, and to ignore the many innovative schemes that contributed, together with the many external factors that may have contrived to mirror the downward spiral being experienced across Europe.

The first and perhaps most important step, was the initiative of the Scottish League that allowed clubs to retain the proceeds of their own league attendances, which gave birth to a concerted effort to compete vigorously with football's many counter attractions.

Almost every club has made special arrangements for various minority groups within the community, particularly the unemployed, and clubs were soon to learn that this did not only swell numbers, but portrayed the game in a much more caring and positive way, to the general public. There were several spectacular examples that projected just such an image. Perhaps the one that captured the most telling headlines was the scheme devised by Dundee United, when they undertook to pay the admission of their fans on Morton's ground, for the third last Saturday of the season. Of course, the eventual Champions were keen to muster as much sympathetic support for a game of such importance, but it was a public relations exercise of some excellence.

Even in the lower Divisions, enterprise was not ignored. Hearts and St Johnstone – two welcome returning teams to the Premier League – both subsidised travel for the supporters during the season and Stirling Albion invited their supporters to pay just 10p for their final home game. These are just a few examples however, that reflect the constructive way which clubs are now tackling the game's biggest challenges and they are entitled to congratulations.

However, the final note of optimism on the subject is not a reflective one but an exciting look forward. The two clubs joining the Premier Division, Hearts and St Johnstone, are both sufficiently well supported as to ensure the trend will continue.

Their introduction, together with the excellent standards achieved on the pitch by our top clubs will combine to make further gains and dispel the voices of gloom and doom that have created such a dismal outlook for so long.

AVERAGE ATTENDANCES – PREMIER LEAGUE

	1980–81	*1981–82*	*1982–83*
Aberdeen	12,315	11,360	15,534
Celtic	22,862	22,718	23,740
Dundee	—	7570	7929
Dundee U	7716	9416	11,133
Hibernian	—	7445	7109
Kilmarnock	4506	—	3463
Motherwell	—	—	6509
Morton	6003	3871	4237
Rangers	18,328	16,399	17,681
St Mirren	7859	6954	5990
Aidrie	4964	3820	—
Hearts	7758	—	—
Partick T	5481	5117	—
Overall Average	9779	9467	10,332
Overall Totals	1,760,220	1,704,060	1,859,856

EUROPEAN FOOTBALL CHAMPIONSHIP

(formerly EUROPEAN NATIONS' CUP)

Year	*Winners*		*Runners-up*		*Venue*
1960	USSR	2	Yugoslavia	1	Paris
1964	Spain	2	USSR	1	Madrid
1968	Italy	2	Yugoslavia	0	Rome
			After 1-1 draw		
1972	West Germany	3	USSR	0	Brussels
1976	Czechoslovakia	2	West Germany	2	Belgrade
	Czechoslovakia won on penalties				
1980	West Germany	2	Belgium	1	Rome

1958–60

Semi-Finals

Yugoslavia 5, France 4 (in Paris)
USSR 3, Czechoslovakia 0 (in Marseilles)

Third Place Match (Marseilles)

Czechoslovakia 2, France 0

Final (Paris, 10 July, 1960)

USSR (0) 2, Yugoslavia (1) 1 after extra time
USSR: Yachin; Tchekeli, Kroutikov; Voinov, Maslenkin, Netto; Metreveli, Ivanov, Ponedelnik, Bubukin, Meshki.
Yugoslavia: Vidinic; Durkovic, Jusufi; Zanetic, Miladinovic, Perusic; Sekularac, Jerkovic, Galic, Matus, Kostic.
Scorers: Metreveli, Ponedelnik for USSR; Netto og for Yugoslavia.

1962–64

Semi-Finals

USSR 3, Denmark 0 (in Barcelona)
Spain 2, Hungary 1 (in Madrid)

Third Place Match (Barcelona)

Hungary 3, Denmark 1 after extra time

Final (Madrid, 21 June, 1964)

Spain (1) 2, USSR (1) 1

Spain: Iribar; Rivilla, Calleja; Fuste, Olivella, Zoco; Amancio, Pereda, Marcellino, Suarez, Lapetra.
USSR: Yachin; Chustikov, Mudrik, Voronin, Shesternjev, Anitchkin; Chislenko, Ivanov, Ponedelnik, Kornaev, Khusainov.
Scorers: Pereda, Marcellino for Spain; Khusainov for USSR.

1966–68

Semi-Finals

Yugoslavia 1, England 0 (in Florence)
Italy 0, USSR 0 (Italy won toss) (in Naples)

Third Place Match (Rome)

England 2, USSR 0

Final (Rome, 8 June, 1968)

Italy (0) 1, Yugoslavia (1) 1

Italy: Zoff; Burgnich, Facchetti; Ferrini, Guarneri, Castano; Domenghini, Juliano, Anastasi, Lodetti, Prati.
Yugoslavia: Pantelic; Fazlagic, Damjanovic; Pavlovic, Paunovic, Holcer; Petkovic, Acimovic, Musemic, Trivic, Dzajic.
Scorers: Domenghini for Italy; Dzajic for Yugoslavia.

Replayed Final (Rome, 10 June, 1968)

Italy (2) 2, Yugoslavia (0) 0

Italy: Zoff; Burgnich, Facchetti; Rosato, Guarneri, Salvadore; Domenghini, Mazzola, Anastasi, De Sisti, Riva.
Yugoslavia: Pantelic; Fazlagic, Damjanovic, Pavlovic, Paunovic, Holcer; Hosic, Acimovic, Musemic, Trivic, Dzajic.
Scorers: Riva, Anastasi for Italy.

1970–72

Semi-Finals

USSR 1, Hungary 0 (in Brussels)
West Germany 2, Belgium 1 (in Antwerp)

Third Place Match (Liège)

Belgium 2, Hungary 1

Final (Brussels, 18 June, 1972)

West Germany (1) 3, USSR (0) 0

West Germany: Maier, Hottges, Schwarzenbeck, Beckenbauer, Breitner, Hoeness, Wimmer, Netzer, Heynkes, Müller, Kremers.
USSR: Rudakov, Dzodzuashvili, Khurtsilava, Kaplichny, Istomin, Troshkin, Kolotov, Baidachni, Konkov (Dolmatov), Banishevski (Kozinkievits), Onishenko.
Scorers: Müller 2, Wimmer for West Germany.

1974–76

Semi-Finals

Czechoslovakia 3, Holland 1 after extra time (in Zagreb)
West Germany 4, Yugoslavia 2 after extra time (in Belgrade)

Third Place Match (Zagreb)

Holland 3, Yugoslavia 2 after extra time

Final (Belgrade, 20 June, 1976)

Czechoslovakia (2) 2, West Germany (1) 2 (aet)
(*Czechoslovakia won 5-3 on penalties*)

Czechoslovakia: Viktor; Dobias (Vesely F.), Pivarnik, Ondrus, Capkovic, Gogh, Moder, Panenka, Svehlic (Jurkemik), Masny, Nehoda.
West Germany: Maier; Vogts, Beckenbauer, Schwarzenbeck, Dietz, Bonhof, Wimmer (Flohe), Müller D., Beer (Bongartz), Hoeness, Holzenbein.
Scorers: Svehlic, Dobias for Czechoslovakia; Müller, Holzenbein for West Germany.

1978–80

Third Place Match (Naples)

Italy 1, Czechoslovakia 1
(*Czechoslovakia won 9-8 on penalties*)

Final (Rome, 22 June, 1980)

West Germany (1) 2, Belgium (0) 1

West Germany: Schumacher; Briegel, Forster K., Dietz, Schuster, Rummenigge, Hrubesch, Müller, Aloffs, Stielike, Kaltz.
Belgium: Pfaff; Gerets, Millecamps, Meeuws, Renquin, Cools, Van der Eycken, Van Moer, Mommens, Van der Elst, Ceulemans.
Scorers: Hrubesch 2 for West Germany; Van der Eychen for Belgium.

EUROPEAN FOOTBALL CHAMPIONSHIP 1982–83

(Hosts and automatic qualifiers – France)

QUALIFYING MATCHES

GROUP 1

Belgium (1) **3** *(Egli og, Coeck, Vandenbergh)*

Switzerland (0) **0** Brussels 20,000

Referee: Bergamo.

Scotland (0) **2** *(Wark, Sturrock)*

E Germany (0) **0** Glasgow 50,000

Scotland: Leighton; Narey, Hansen, Miller, Gray F., Souness, Strachan, Wark, Archibald, Brazil (Sturrock), Robertson.
E Germany: Rudwaleit; Kreer, Stahmann, Trieloff, Baum, Schnuphase, Pilz, Dorner (Pommerenke), Hafner (Liebers), Streich, Riediger.
Referee: Konrath.

Switzerland (0) **2** *(Sulser, Egli)*

Scotland (0) **0** Berne 26,500

Switzerland: Burgener; Egli, Geiger, Ludi, Wehrli, Decastel (Barberis), Favre, Heinz Hermann, Ponte, Sulser, Elsener (Zwicker).
Scotland: Leighton; Narey, Hansen, Miller, Gray F., Strachan, Souness, Wark, Robertson, Sturrock (Archibald), Brazil.
Referee: Christov.

Belgium (2) **3** *(Vandenbergh, Van Der Elst 2)*

Scotland (2) **2** *(Dalglish 2)* Brussels 49,000

Belgium: Pfaff; Gerets, Daerden, Meeuws, Baecke, Vandermissen, Coeck, Ceulemans, Vercauteren (Verheyen), Vandenbergh (De Schrijver), Van Der Elst.
Scotland: Leighton: Narey, McLeish, Hansen, Gray F., Strachan (Sturrock), Aitken, Souness, Bett (Burns), Archibald, Dalglish.
Referee: Garrido.

Scotland (0) **2** *(Wark, Nicholas)*

Switzerland (1) **2** *(Egli, Heinz Hermann)* Glasgow 40,000

Scotland: Leighton; Gough, Miller, Hansen (McLeish), Gray F., Strachan, Souness, Wark, Dalglish, Nicholas, Weir.
Switzerland: Burgener; Geiger, Wehrli, Ludi, Egli, Decastel, Favre, Heinz Hermann (Zwicker), Sulser (In-Albon), Ponte, Elsener.
Referee: Corver.

E Germany (0) **1** *(Streich)*

Belgium (1) **2** *(Van Der Elst, Vandenbergh)* Leipzig 75,000

Referee: Carpenter.

Belgium (2) **2** *(Ceulemans, Coeck)*

E Germany (1) **1** *(Streich)* Brussels 44,000

Referee: Guruceta Muro.

Switzerland (0) **0**

E Germany (0) **0** Berne 32,000

Referee: Ericsson.

	P	*W*	*D*	*L*	*F*	*A*	*Pts*
Belgium	4	4	0	0	10	4	8
Switzerland	4	1	2	1	4	5	4
Scotland	4	1	1	2	6	7	3
E Germany	4	0	1	3	2	6	1

Remaining Fixtures: Oct 12 Scotland v Belgium; Oct 12 E Germany v Switzerland; Nov 9 Switzerland v Belgium; Nov 16 E Germany v Scotland.

GROUP 2

Finland (0) **2** *(Valvee, Kousa)*

Poland (2) **3** *(Smolarek* pen, *Dziekanowski, Kupcewicz)* Kuopio 3600

Referee: Van Langenhove.

Finland (0) **0**

Portugal (1) **2** *(Nene, Oliveira)* Helsinki 3200

Referee: Scheurell.

Portugal (1) **2** *(Nene, Gomes)*

Poland (0) **1** *(Janas)* Lisbon 70,000

Referee: Wohrer.

USSR (1) **2** *(Baltacha, Nadreev)*

Finland (0) **0** Moscow 18,000

Referee: Baumann.

Poland (1) **1** *(Smolarek* pen*)*

Finland (1) **1** *(Janas og)* Warsaw 8000

Referee: Bjornestad.

USSR (2) **5** *(Tsernenkov 2, Rodionov, Demjanenko, Larionov)*

Portugal (0) **0** Moscow 90,000

Referee: Hunting.

Poland (1) **1** *(Boniek)*

USSR (0) **1** *(Wojcicki og)* Chorzow 80,000

Referee: Agnolin

Finland (0) **0**

USSR (0) **1** *(Blochin)* Helsinki 17,000

Referee: Krchnak.

	P	*W*	*D*	*L*	*F*	*A*	*Pts*
USSR	4	3	1	0	9	1	7
Poland	4	1	2	1	6	6	4
Portugal	3	2	0	1	4	6	4
Finland	5	0	1	4	3	9	1

Remaining Fixtures: Sept 21 Portugal v Finland; Oct 9 USSR v Poland; Oct 28 Poland v Portugal; Nov 13 Portugal v USSR.

GROUP 3

Denmark (0) **2** *(Hansen* pen, *Olsen)*

England (1) **2** *(Francis 2)* Copenhagen 44,300

Denmark: Rasmussen T.; Rasmussen O., Rontved, Busk, Nielsen, Lerby, Bertelsen, Olsen, Hansen, Elkjaer, Larsen, Bastrup.
England: Shilton; Neal, Osman, Butcher, Sansom, Wilkins, Robson, Rix, Morley (Hill), Francis, Mariner.
Referee: Corver.

Luxembourg (0) 0

Greece (2) 2 *(Dimopoulos, Anastopoulos)* Luxembourg 3500

Referee: Tritschier.

Luxembourg (0) 1 *(Di Domenico)*

Denmark (1) 2 *(Lerby* pen, *Berggren)* Luxembourg 2500

Referee: Biquet.

Greece (0) 0

England (1) 3 *(Woodcock 2, Lee)* Salonika 45,000

Greece: Sarganis; Gounaris, Iossifidis, Firos, Kapsis, Livathinos, Mihos, Mitropoulos, Anastopoulos, Ardizoglou (Kostikos), Mavros.
England: Shilton; Neal, Martin, Thompson, Sansom, Mabbutt, Lee, Robson, Mariner, Woodcock, Morley.
Referee: Prokov.

England (4) 9 *(Bossi og, Coppell, Woodcock, Blissett 3, Chamberlain, Hoddle, Neal)*

Luxembourg (0) 0 Wembley 35,000

England: Clemence; Neal, Martin, Butcher, Sansom, Robson, Lee, Mabbutt (Hoddle), Coppell (Chamberlain), Blissett, Woodcock.
Luxembourg: Moes; Girres, Meunier, Bossi, Rohmann, Clemens, Hellers, Weis, Dresch, Reiter, Di Domenico (Nurenberg).
Referee: Jonsson.

Luxembourg (1) 2 *(Reiter, Schreiner R.)*
Hungary (2) 6

(Poczik 3, Nyilasi, Poloskei, Hannich pen*) Luxembourg 3000*
Referee: Geurds.

England (0) 0

Greece (0) 0 Wembley 48,500

England: Shilton; Neal, Martin, Butcher, Sanson, Lee, Coppell, Mabbutt, Francis, Woodcock (Blissett), Devonshire (Rix).
Greece: Serganis; Gounaris, Xanthopoulos, Mitropoulos (Dontas), Kousoulakis, Kouis, Anastopoulos, Karoulias, Michos, Galitzis, Kostikos.
Referee: M. Krchnak.

Hungary (3) 6 *(Nyilasi 2, Hajszan, Kiss, Sventes, Burcsa)*

Luxembourg (0) 2 *(Reiter, Meauier)* Budapest 8000

Referee: Azzopardi.

England (1) 2 *(Francis, Withe)*

Hungary (0) 0 Wembley 55,000

England: Shilton; Neal, Martin, Butcher, Sansom, Lee, Mabbutt, Cowans, Francis, Withe, Blissett.
Hungary: Katzirz; Martos (Peter), Locsis, Garaba, Toth, Hannich, Nyilasi, Varga, Kardos, Kiss (Torocsik), Hajszan.
Referee: D'elia.

Denmark (0) 1 *(Busk)*

Greece (0) 0 Copenhagen 34,500

Referee: Corver.

Hungary (1) 2 *(Nyilasi, Hajszan)*

Greece (2) 3 *(Anastopoulos, Kostikos, Papaioannu)* Budapest 15,000

Referee: Sostaric.

Denmark (1) 3 *(Elkjaer, Olsen J., Simonsen* pen*)*

Hungary (1) 1 *(Nyilasi)* Copenhagen 50,000

Referee: Fahnler.

	P	*W*	*D*	*L*	*F*	*A*	*Pts*
England	5	3	2	0	16	2	8
Denmark	4	3	1	0	8	4	7
Greece	5	2	1	2	5	6	5
Hungary	5	2	0	3	15	12	4
Luxembourg	5	0	0	5	5	25	0

Remaining Fixtures: Sept 21 England v Denmark; Oct 12 Hungary v England; Oct 12 Denmark v Luxembourg; Oct 26 Hungary v Denmark; Nov 16 Greece v Denmark; Nov 16 Luxembourg v England; Dec 3 Greece v Hungary; Dec 14 Greece v Luxembourg.

GROUP 4

Wales (1) 1 *(Rush)*

Norway (0) 0 Swansea 5000

Wales: Southall; Marustick, Price, Stevenson, Jones, James, Flynn, Jackett, Thomas, Rush, Curtis (Charles).
Norway: Nygaard; Berntsen, Kojedahl, Hareide, Grondalen, Albertsen, Erlandsen (Kolishaugen), Soler, Lund, Larsen, Okland, Thoresen.
Referee: Quiniou.

Norway (1) 3 *(Lund, Okland, Hareide)*

Yugoslavia (0) 1 *(Savic)* Oslo 8000

Referee: Jargus.

Bulgaria (1) 2 *(Velitchkov, Nikolov)*

Norway (1) 2 *(Thoresen* pen, *Okland L.)* Sofia 55,000

Referee: Vassaras.

Bulgaria (0) 0

Yugoslavia (1) 1 *(Stojkovic)* Sofia 25,000

Referee: Casarin.

Yugoslavia (3) 4 *(Cvetkovic, Zivkovic, Kranjear, Jesic)*

Wales (2) 4 *(Flynn, Rush, John, James)* Titograd 20,000

Yugoslavia: Svilar; Stojkovic, Cvetkovic, Trifunovic, Ferhatovic (Djurovic), Hadzibegic, Deveric (Jesic), Nilolic, Kranjcar, Gudelj, Zivkovic.
Wales: Davies; Jones, Ratcliff, Nicholas (John), Jackett, Price, Flynn, James, Rush, Thomas (Charles), Mahoney.
Referee: Ponnet.

Wales (0) 1 *(Charles)*

Bulgaria (0) 0 Wrexham 9000

Wales: Southall; Jones, Jackett, Nicholas, Price, Ratcliffe, James, Flynn, Rush (Charles), Thomas, Davies.
Bulgaria: Velinov, Nikolov, Arabov, Petrov, Borisov, Zdravkov, Yontschev, Yordanov, Djevizov, Sadakov, Mladenov.
Referee: Kirschen.

	P	*W*	*D*	*L*	*F*	*A*	*Pts*
Wales	3	2	1	0	6	4	5
Norway	3	1	1	1	5	4	3
Yugoslavia	3	1	1	1	6	7	3
Bulgaria	3	0	1	2	2	4	1

Remaining Fixtures: Sept 7 Norway v Bulgaria; Sept 21 Norway v Wales; Oct 12 Yugoslavia v Norway; Nov 16 Bulgaria v Wales; Dec 14 Wales v Yugoslavia; Dec 21 Yugoslavia v Bulgaria.

GROUP 5

Rumania (2) 3 *(Vaetus, Camataru, Boloni)*
Cyprus (1) 1 *(Vrachimis)* Hunedsara 20,000
Referee: Hoxha.

Rumania (1) 2 *(Andone, Klein)*
Sweden (0) 0 Bucharest 50,000
Referee: Sostaric.

Czechoslovakia (0) 2 *(Janecka 2)*
Sweden (0) 2 *(Jingblad, Eriksson)* Bratislava 15,000
Referee: Valentine.

Cyprus (0) 0
Sweden (1) 1 *(Corneliusson)* Nicosia 8000
Referee: Midgley.

Italy (1) 2 *(Altobelli, Kapko og)*
Czechoslovakia (1) 2 *(Sloup, Chaloupka)* Milan 72,400
Referee: Corver.

Italy (0) 0
Rumania (0) 0 Florence 60,000
Referee: Konrath.

Cyprus (0) 1 *(Mavris)*
Italy (0) 1 *(Graziani)* Limassol 25,000
Referee: Dotchev.

Cyprus (1) 1 *(Teofanis)*
Czechoslovakia (0) 1 *(Bicovsky)* Nicosia 15,000
Referee: Glavina.

Rumania (1) 1 *(Boloni)*
Italy (0) 0 Bucharest 80,000
Referee: Vautrot.

Czechoslovakia (3) 6 *(Danek 2, Vizek 2, Prokes, Jurkemik)*
Cyprus (0) 0 Prague 7000
Referee: Rolles.

Sweden (0) 5 *(Prytz 2, Corneliusson, Hysen, Ravelli)*
Cyprus (0) 0 Malmoe 19,800
Referee: Smolander.

Rumania (0) 0
Czechoslovakia (1) 1 *(Vizek* pen*)* Bucharest 60,000
Referee: Ponnet.

Sweden (1) 2 *(Sandberg, Stromberg)*
Italy (0) 0 Gothenburg 35,000
Referee: Eschweiler.

	P	*W*	*D*	*L*	*F*	*A*	*Pts*
Czechoslovakia	5	2	3	0	12	5	7
Sweden	5	3	1	1	10	4	7
Rumania	5	3	1	1	6	2	7
Italy	5	0	3	2	3	6	3
Cyprus	6	0	2	4	3	17	2

Remaining Fixtures: June 9 Sweden v Rumania; Sept 21 Sweden v Czechoslovakia; Oct 15 Italy v Sweden; Nov 12 Cyprus v Rumania; Nov 16 Czechoslovakia v Rumania; Dec 22 Italy v Cyprus.

GROUP 6

Austria (2) 5 *(Hagmayr, Gasselich, Kola og, Weber, Brauneder)*
Albania (0) 0 Vienna 6000
Referee: Zetschov.

Austria (2) 2 *(Schachner 2)*
N Ireland (0) 0 Vienna 11,500
Austria: Koncilia; Krauss, Pezzey, Obermayer, Degeogi, Prohaska, Weber, Gasselich, Schachmer, Hagmayr (Pacult), Jurtin (Baumeister).
N Ireland: Platt; O'Neill J., Nicholl, McClelland, Donaghy, O'Neill M., McIlroy (Brotherston), McCreery, Armstrong, Hamilton, Stewart (Healy).
Referee: Butenko.

Turkey (0) 1 *(Arif)*
Albania (0) 0 Izmir 25,000
Referee: Igna.

N Ireland (1) 1 *(Stewart)*
W Germany (0) 0 Belfast 15,000
N Ireland: Platt; McClelland, Nicholl, O'Neill J., Donaghy, O'Neill M., Brotherston, McIlroy, Whiteside, Hamilton, Stewart.
W Germany: Schumacher; Kaltz, Stielike, Strack, Forster B., Matthous (Voller), Schuster (Engels), Briegel, Rummenigge, Allofs K., Littbarski.
Referee: Nyhus.

Austria (3) 4 *(Polster, Pezzey, Prohaska, Schachner)*
Turkey (0) 0 Vienna 8700
Referee: Suchanek.

Albania (0) 0
N Ireland (0) 0 Tirana 30,000
Albania: Musta; Targaj, Ruchi, Ragani, Ahmetani, Miuga, Kola, Vakatana, Luchi (Mucha), Bimo (Omuri), Ballgjani.
N Ireland: Platt; Nicholl, Donaghy, O'Neill J., McClelland, Stewart, Brotherston, O'Neill M., Hamilton, Whiteside, McIlroy.
Referee: Daina.

Albania (0) 1 *(Targaj* pen*)*
W Germany (0) 2 *(Voeller, Rummenigge* pen*)* Tirana 35,000
Referee: Menegali.

N Ireland (2) 2 *(O'Neill, McClelland)*
Turkey (0) 1 *(Metin)* Belfast 20,000
N Ireland: Platt; Nicholl J., McClelland, O'Neill J., Donaghy, O'Neill M., McIlroy, Stewart, Brotherston, Armstrong, Whiteside.
Turkey: Eser; Erdogan, Fatih, Yusuf, Hakan, Eren, Metin, Rasit, Hesegin, Hasan, Selcuk.
Referee: M. Delmer.

Turkey (0) 0
W Germany (2) 3 *(Rummenigge 2* [1 pen], *Dremmler)* Izmir 73,000
Referee: Christov.

Austria (0) 0
W Germany (0) 0 Vienna 60,000
Referee: McGinley.

N Ireland (0) 1 *(Stewart)*

Albania (0) 0 Belfast 14,000

N Ireland: Jennings; Nicholl J., McClelland, O'Neill J., Donaghy, O'Neill M., McIlroy, Hamilton, Armstrong, Stewart, Brotherston (Mullan).
Albania: Musta; Ruci, Ahmetagi, Eksarko (Mema), Targaj, Lame, Vukatana, Demollari, Minga, Omuri, Muca.
Referee: Nielsen.

Albania (0) 1 *(Rashid og)*

Turkey (1) 1 *(Metin)* Tirana 30,000

Referee: Salomir.

	P	*W*	*D*	*L*	*F*	*A*	*Pts*
Austria	4	3	1	0	11	0	7
N Ireland	5	3	1	1	4	3	7
W Germany	4	2	1	1	5	2	5
Turkey	5	1	1	3	3	10	3
Albania	6	0	2	4	2	10	2

Remaining Fixtures: June 8 Albania v Austria; Sept 21 N Ireland v Austria; Oct 5 W Germany v Austria; Oct 12 Turkey v N Ireland; Oct 26 W Germany v Turkey; Nov 16 W Germany v N Ireland; Nov 16 Turkey v Austria; Nov 20 W Germany v Albania.

GROUP 7

Malta (1) 2 *(Spiteri Gonzi 2)*

Iceland (0) 1 *(Geirsson M.* pen*)* Messina 1500

Referee: A. D'Elia.

Iceland (0) 1 *(Edvaldsson A.)*

Netherlands (0) 1 *(Schoenaker)* Reykjavik 3150

Referee: McGinlay.

Netherlands (1) 2 *(Schoenaker, Gullitt)*

Eire (0) 1 *(Daly)* Rotterdam 15,000

Referee: Gregr.

Eire (1) 2 *(Stapleton, Grealish)*

Iceland (0) 0 Dublin 20,000

Referee: Rion.

Spain (0) 1 *(Pedraza)*

Iceland (0) 0 Malaga 12,000

Referee: Silva.

Eire (1) 3 *(Grimes, Stapleton 2)*

Spain (1) 3 *(Macedo, Martin og, Victor)* Dublin 39,000

Referee: Redelfs.

Malta (0) 0

Netherlands (4) 6 *(Ophof* pen*, Van Kooten 2, Hovenkamp, Schoenaker 2)* Aix-la-Chapelle 13,000

Referee: Pauly.

Spain (1) 1 *(Senor* pen*)*

Netherlands (0) 0 Sevilla 65,000

Referee: Bergamo.

Malta (0) 0

Eire (0) 1 *(Stapleton)* Valetta 6000

Referee: Matthias.

Spain (0) 2 *(Santillana, Rincon)*

Eire (0) 0 Zaragoza 45,000

Referee: Butenko.

Malta (1) 2 *(Sutil 2)*

Spain (1) 3 *(Senor, Carrasco, Gordillo)* La Valetta 11,080

Referee: Giannakoudakis.

Iceland (0) 0

Spain (1) 1 *(Maceda)* Reyjkavik 4000

Referee: Bridges.

	P	*W*	*D*	*L*	*F*	*A*	*Pts*
Spain	6	5	1	0	11	5	11
Netherlands	4	2	1	1	9	3	5
Rep of Ireland	5	2	1	2	7	7	5
Malta	4	1	0	3	4	11	2
Iceland	5	0	1	4	2	7	1

Remaining Fixtures: June 5 Iceland v Malta; Sept 7 Netherlands v Iceland; Sept 21 Iceland v Rep of Ireland; Oct 12 Rep of Ireland v Netherlands; Nov 16 Netherlands v Spain; Nov 16 Rep of Ireland v Malta; Dec 17 Netherlands v Malta; Dec 21 Spain v Malta.

BLUEPRINT OF THE EUROPEAN CHAMPIONSHIP FINALS 1984

Date	*Match Order*	*Venue*	*Kick-off Time*	*Playing Teams*	
Tues 12 June	1	Paris	8.30	1–2	**Group I**
Wed 13 June	2	Lens	8.30	3–4	**Group I**
Thurs 14 June	3	Strasbourg	5.15	5–6	**Group II**
Thurs 14 June	4	St Etienne	8.30	7–8	**Group 11**
Sat 16 June	5	Nantes	5.15	1–3	**Group I**
Sat 16 June	6	Lyon	8.30	2–4	**Group I**
Sun 17 June	7	Lens	5.15	5–7	**Group II**
Sun 17 June	8	Marseille	8.30	6–8	**Group II**
Tues 19 June	9	St Etienne	8.30	1–4	**Group I**
Tues 19 June	10	Strasbourg	8.30	2–3	**Group I**
Wed 20 June	11	Paris	8.30	5–8	**Group II**
Wed 20 June	12	Nantes	8.30	6–7	**Group II**
Semi-finals					
Sat 23 June	13	Marseille	8.00	Winner Group I v Runner-up Group II	
Sun 24 June	14	Lyon	8.00	Winner Group II v Runner-up Group I	
Wed 27 June	15	Paris	8.00		**FINAL**

BRITISH HOME INTERNATIONALS

ENGLAND

Back row (left to right):
Kenny Sansom
Gary Mabbutt
Mike Duxbury
Mark Chamberlain
Alan Devonshire
Gordon Cowans
Middle row:
Ricky Hill
Luther Blissett
Peter Shilton
Ray Clemence
Peter Withe
Alvin Martin
Front row:
Phil Neal
Terry Butcher
Ray Wilkins
Trevor Francis
Sammy Lee

INTERNATIONAL CHAMPIONSHIP 1883–1983

Year	*Champions*	*Pts*
1883–84	Scotland	6
1884–85	Scotland	5
1885–86	England	5
	Scotland	5
1886–87	Scotland	6
1887–88	England	6
1888–89	Scotland	5
1889–90	Scotland	5
	England	5
1890–91	England	6
1891–92	England	6
1892–93	England	6
1893–94	Scotland	5
1894–95	England	5
1895–96	Scotland	5
1896–97	Scotland	5
1897–98	England	6
1898–99	England	6
1899–1900	Scotland	6
1900–01	England	5
1901–02	Scotland	5
1902–03	England	4
	Ireland	4
	Scotland	4
1903–04	England	5
1904–05	England	5
1905–06	England	4
	Scotland	4
1906–07	Wales	5
1907–08	Scotland	5
	England	5
1908–09	England	6
1909–10	Scotland	4
1910–11	England	5
1911–12	England	5
	Scotland	5
1912–13	England	4
1913–14	Ireland	5
1919–20	Wales	4
1920–21	Scotland	6
1921–22	Scotland	4
1922–23	Scotland	5
1923–24	Wales	6
1924–25	Scotland	6
1925–26	Scotland	6
1926–27	Scotland	4
	England	4
1927–28	Wales	5
1928–29	Scotland	6
1929–30	England	6
1930–31	Scotland	4
	England	4
1931–32	England	6
1932–33	Wales	5
1933–34	Wales	5
1934–35	England	4
	Scotland	4
1935–36	Scotland	4
1936–37	Wales	6
1937–38	England	4
1938–39	England	4
	Scotland	4
	Wales	4
1946–47	England	5
1947–48	England	5
1948–49	Scotland	6
1949–50	England	6
1950–51	Scotland	6
1951–52	Wales	5
	England	5
1952–53	England	4
	Scotland	4
1953–54	England	6
1954–55	England	6
1955–56	England	3
	Scotland	3
	Wales	3
	Ireland	3
1956–57	England	5
1957–58	England	4
	Ireland	4
1958–59	Ireland	4
	England	4
1959–60	England	4
	Scotland	4
	Wales	4
1960–61	England	6
1961–62	Scotland	6
1962–63	Scotland	6
1963–64	Scotland	4
	England	4
	Ireland	4
1964–65	England	5
1965–66	England	5
1966–67	Scotland	5
1967–68	England	5
1968–69	England	6
1969–70	England	4
	Scotland	4
	Wales	4
1970–71	England	5
1971–72	England	4
	Scotland	4
1972–73	England	6
1973–74	England	4
	Scotland	4
1974–75	England	4
1975–76	Scotland	6
1976–77	Scotland	5
1977–78	England	6
1978–79	England	5
1979–80	Ireland	5
1980–81	*Not completed*	
1981–82	England	6
1982–83	England	5

Note: In the results that follow, WC = World Cup, EC = European Championship.

Steve Coppell raises his arm in triumph after scoring England's second goal in their 3-1 victory over Scotland at Wembley in May 1979.

ENGLAND v SCOTLAND

Played: 101; England won 40, Scotland won 39, Drawn 22. *Goals:* England 182, Scotland 165.

	E	*S*
1872 Glasgow	0	0
1873 Kennington Oval	4	2
1874 Glasgow	1	2
1875 Kennington Oval	2	2
1876 Glasgow	0	3
1877 Kennington Oval	1	3
1878 Glasgow	2	7
1879 Kennington Oval	5	4
1880 Glasgow	4	5
1881 Kennington Oval	1	6
1882 Glasgow	1	5
1883 Sheffield	2	3
1884 Glasgow	0	1
1885 Kennington Oval	1	1
1886 Glasgow	1	1
1887 Blackburn	2	3
1888 Glasgow	5	0
1889 Kennington Oval	2	3
1890 Glasgow	1	1
1891 Blackburn	2	1
1892 Glasgow	4	1
1893 Richmond	5	2
1894 Glasgow	2	2
1895 Everton	3	0
1896 Glasgow	1	2
1897 Crystal Palace	1	2
1898 Glasgow	3	1
1899 Birmingham	2	1
1900 Glasgow	1	4
1901 Crystal Palace	2	2
1902 Birmingham	2	2
1903 Sheffield	1	2
1904 Glasgow	1	0
1905 Crystal Palace	1	0
1906 Glasgow	1	2
1907 Newcastle	1	1
1908 Glasgow	1	1
1909 Crystal Palace	2	0
1910 Glasgow	0	2
1911 Everton	1	1
1912 Glasgow	1	1
1913 Chelsea	1	0
1914 Glasgow	1	3
1920 Sheffield	5	4
1921 Glasgow	0	3
1922 Aston Villa	0	1
1923 Glasgow	2	2
1924 Wembley	1	1
1925 Glasgow	0	2
1926 Manchester	0	1
1927 Glasgow	2	1
1928 Wembley	1	5
1929 Glasgow	0	1
1930 Wembley	5	2
1931 Glasgow	0	2
1932 Wembley	3	0
1933 Glasgow	1	2
1934 Wembley	3	0
1935 Glasgow	0	2
1936 Wembley	1	1
1937 Glasgow	1	3
1938 Wembley	0	1
1939 Glasgow	2	1
1947 Wembley	1	1
1948 Glasgow	2	0
1949 Wembley	1	3
wc1950 Glasgow	1	0
1951 Wembley	2	3
1952 Glasgow	2	1
1953 Wembley	2	2
wc1954 Glasgow	4	2
1955 Wembley	7	2
1956 Glasgow	1	1
1957 Wembley	2	1
1958 Glasgow	4	0
1959 Wembley	1	0
1960 Glasgow	1	1
1961 Wembley	9	3
1962 Glasgow	0	2
1963 Wembley	1	2
1964 Glasgow	0	1
1965 Wembley	2	2
1966 Glasgow	4	3
EC1967 Wembley	2	3
EC1968 Glasgow	1	1
1969 Wembley	4	1
1970 Glasgow	0	0
1971 Wembley	3	1
1972 Glasgow	1	0
1973 Glasgow	5	0
1973 Wembley	1	0
1974 Glasgow	0	2
1975 Wembley	5	1
1976 Glasgow	1	2
1977 Wembley	1	2
1978 Glasgow	1	0
1979 Wembley	3	1
1980 Glasgow	2	0
1981 Wembley	0	1
1982 Glasgow	1	0
1983 Wembley	2	0

Flanked by Trevor Cherry (left) and Dave Watson, John Toshack heads for the England goal during the England v Wales fixture in May 1979.

ENGLAND v WALES

Played: 96; England won 62, Wales won 13, Drawn 21. *Goals:* England 239, Wales 89.

	E	W
1879 Kennington Oval	2	1
1880 Wrexham	3	2
1881 Blackburn	0	1
1882 Wrexham	3	5
1883 Kennington Oval	5	0
1884 Wrexham	4	0
1885 Blackburn	1	1
1886 Wrexham	3	1
1887 Kennington Oval	4	0
1888 Crewe	5	1
1889 Stoke	4	1
1890 Wrexham	3	1
1891 Sunderland	4	1
1892 Wrexham	2	0
1893 Stoke	6	0
1894 Wrexham	5	1
1894 Queen's Club, Kensington	1	1
1896 Cardiff	9	1
1897 Sheffield	4	0
1898 Wrexham	3	0
1899 Bristol	4	0
1900 Cardiff	1	1
1901 Newcastle	6	0
1902 Wrexham	0	0
1903 Portsmouth	2	1
1904 Wrexham	2	2
1905 Liverpool	3	1
1906 Cardiff	1	0
1907 Fulham	1	1
1908 Wrexham	7	1
1909 Nottingham	2	0
1910 Cardiff	1	0
1911 Millwall	3	0
1912 Wrexham	2	0
1913 Bristol	4	3
1914 Cardiff	2	0
1920 Highbury	1	2
1921 Cardiff	0	0
1922 Liverpool	1	0
1923 Cardiff	2	2
1924 Blackburn	1	2
1925 Swansea	2	1
1926 Crystal Palace	1	3
1927 Wrexham	3	3
1927 Burnley	1	2
1928 Swansea	3	2
1929 Chelsea	6	0
1930 Wrexham	4	0
1931 Liverpool	3	1
1932 Wrexham	0	0
1933 Newcastle	1	2
1934 Cardiff	4	0
1935 Wolverhampton	1	2
1936 Cardiff	1	2
1937 Middlesbrough	2	1
1938 Cardiff	2	4
1946 Manchester	3	0
1947 Cardiff	3	0
1948 Aston Villa	1	0
wc1949 Cardiff	4	1
1950 Sunderland	4	2
1951 Cardiff	1	1
1952 Wembley	5	2
wc1953 Cardiff	4	1
1954 Wembley	3	2
1955 Cardiff	1	2
1956 Wembley	3	1
1957 Cardiff	4	0
1958 Aston Villa	2	2
1959 Cardiff	1	1
1960 Wembley	5	1
1961 Cardiff	1	1
1962 Wembley	4	0
1963 Cardiff	4	0
1964 Wembley	2	1
1965 Cardiff	0	0
EC1966 Wembley	5	1
EC1967 Cardiff	3	0
1969 Wembley	2	1
1970 Cardiff	1	1
1971 Wembley	0	0
1972 Cardiff	3	0
wc1972 Cardiff	1	0
wc1973 Wembley	1	1
1973 Wembley	3	0
1974 Cardiff	2	0
1975 Wembley	2	2
1976 Wrexham	2	1
1976 Cardiff	1	0
1977 Wembley	0	1
1978 Cardiff	3	1
1979 Wembley	0	0
1980 Wrexham	1	4
1981 Wembley	0	0
1982 Cardiff	1	0
1983 Wembley	2	1

ENGLAND v IRELAND

Played: 91; England won 70, Ireland won 6, Drawn 15. *Goals:* England 312, Ireland 80.

	E	I
1882 Belfast	13	0
1883 Liverpool	7	0
1884 Belfast	8	1
1885 Manchester	4	0
1886 Belfast	6	1
1887 Sheffield	7	0
1888 Belfast	5	1
1889 Everton	6	1
1890 Belfast	9	1
1891 Wolverhampton	6	1
1892 Belfast	2	0
1893 Birmingham	6	1
1894 Belfast	2	2
1895 Derby	9	0
1896 Belfast	2	0
1897 Nottingham	6	0
1898 Belfast	3	2
1899 Sunderland	13	2
1900 Dublin	2	0
1901 Southampton	3	0
1902 Belfast	1	0
1903 Wolverhampton	4	0
1904 Belfast	3	1
1905 Middlesbrough	1	1
1906 Belfast	5	0
1907 Everton	1	0
1908 Belfast	3	1
1909 Bradford	4	0
1910 Belfast	1	1
1911 Derby	2	1
1912 Dublin	6	1
1913 Belfast	1	2
1914 Middlesbrough	0	3
1919 Belfast	1	1
1920 Sunderland	2	0
1921 Belfast	1	1
1922 West Bromwich	2	0
1923 Belfast	1	2
1924 Everton	3	1

	E	I
1925 Belfast	0	0
1926 Liverpool	3	3
1927 Belfast	0	2
1928 Everton	2	1
1929 Belfast	3	0
1930 Sheffield	5	1
1931 Belfast	6	2
1932 Blackpool	1	0
1933 Belfast	3	0
1935 Everton	2	1
1935 Belfast	3	1
1936 Stoke	3	1
1937 Belfast	5	1
1938 Manchester	7	0
1946 Belfast	7	2
1947 Everton	2	2
1948 Belfast	6	2
wc1949 Manchester	9	2
1950 Belfast	4	1
1951 Aston Villa	2	0
1952 Belfast	2	2
wc1953 Everton	3	1
1954 Belfast	2	0
1955 Wembley	3	0
1956 Belfast	1	1
1957 Wembley	2	3
1958 Belfast	3	3
1959 Wembley	2	1
1960 Belfast	5	2
1961 Wembley	1	1
1962 Belfast	3	1
1963 Wembley	8	3
1964 Belfast	4	3
1965 Wembley	2	1
EC1966 Belfast	2	0
EC1967 Wembley	2	0
1969 Belfast	3	1
1970 Wembley	3	1
1971 Belfast	1	0
1972 Wembley	0	1
1973 Everton	2	1
1974 Wembley	1	0
1975 Belfast	0	0
1976 Wembley	4	0
1977 Belfast	2	1
1978 Wembley	1	0
EC1979 Wembley	4	0
1979 Belfast	2	0
EC1979 Belfast	5	1
1980 Wembley	1	1
1982 Wembley	4	0
1983 Belfast	0	0

SCOTLAND v WALES

Played: 98; Scotland won 59, Wales won 17, Drawn 22. *Goals:* Scotland 235, Wales 108.

	S	W
1876 Glasgow	4	0
1877 Wrexham	2	0
1878 Glasgow	9	0
1879 Wrexham	3	0
1880 Glasgow	5	1
1881 Wrexham	5	1
1882 Glasgow	5	0
1883 Wrexham	4	1
1884 Glasgow	4	1
1885 Wrexham	8	1
1886 Glasgow	4	1
1887 Wrexham	2	0
1888 Edinburgh	5	1
1889 Wrexham	0	0
1890 Paisley	5	0
1891 Wrexham	4	3
1892 Edinburgh	6	1
1893 Wrexham	8	0
1894 Kilmarnock	5	2
1895 Wrexham	2	2
1896 Dundee	4	0
1897 Wrexham	2	2
1898 Motherwell	5	2
1899 Wrexham	6	0
1900 Aberdeen	5	2
1901 Wrexham	1	1
1902 Greenock	5	1
1903 Cardiff	1	0
1904 Dundee	1	1
1905 Wrexham	1	3
1906 Edinburgh	0	2
1907 Wrexham	0	1
1908 Dundee	2	1
1909 Wrexham	2	3
1910 Kilmarnock	1	0
1911 Cardiff	2	2
1912 Tynecastle	1	0
1913 Wrexham	0	0
1914 Glasgow	0	0
1920 Cardiff	1	1
1921 Aberdeen	2	1
1922 Wrexham	1	2
1923 Paisley	2	0
1924 Cardiff	0	2
1925 Tynecastle	3	1
1926 Cardiff	3	0
1927 Glasgow	3	0
1928 Wrexham	2	2
1929 Glasgow	4	2
1930 Cardiff	4	2
1931 Glasgow	1	1
1932 Wrexham	3	2
1933 Edinburgh	2	5
1934 Cardiff	2	3
1935 Aberdeen	3	2
1936 Cardiff	1	1
1937 Dundee	1	2
1938 Cardiff	1	2
1939 Edinburgh	3	2
1946 Wrexham	1	3
1947 Glasgow	1	2
wc1948 Cardiff	3	1
1949 Glasgow	2	0
1950 Cardiff	3	1
1951 Glasgow	0	1
wc1952 Cardiff	2	1
1953 Glasgow	3	3
1954 Cardiff	1	0
1955 Glasgow	2	0
1956 Cardiff	2	2
1957 Glasgow	1	1
1958 Cardiff	3	0
1959 Glasgow	1	1
1960 Cardiff	0	2
1961 Glasgow	2	0
1962 Cardiff	3	2
1963 Glasgow	2	1
1964 Cardiff	2	3
EC1965 Glasgow	4	1
EC1966 Cardiff	1	1
1967 Glasgow	3	2
1969 Wrexham	5	3
1970 Glasgow	0	0
1971 Cardiff	0	0
1972 Glasgow	1	0
1973 Wrexham	2	0
1974 Glasgow	2	0
1975 Cardiff	2	2
1976 Glasgow	3	1
wc1977 Glasgow	1	0
1977 Wrexham	0	0
wc1977 Liverpool	2	0
1978 Glasgow	1	1
1979 Cardiff	0	3
1980 Glasgow	1	0
1981 Swansea	0	2
1982 Glasgow	1	0
1983 Cardiff	2	0

SCOTLAND v IRELAND

Played: 90; Scotland won 60, Ireland won 14, Drawn 16. *Goals:* Scotland 253, Ireland 79.

	S	I
1884 Belfast	5	0
1885 Glasgow	8	2
1886 Belfast	7	2
1887 Glasgow	4	1
1888 Belfast	10	2
1889 Glasgow	7	0
1890 Belfast	4	1
1891 Glasgow	2	1
1892 Belfast	3	2
1893 Glasgow	6	1
1894 Belfast	2	1
1895 Glasgow	3	1
1896 Belfast	3	3
1897 Glasgow	5	1
1898 Belfast	3	0
1899 Glasgow	9	1
1900 Belfast	3	0
1901 Glasgow	11	0
1902 Belfast	5	1
1903 Glasgow	0	2
1904 Dublin	1	1
1905 Glasgow	4	0
1906 Dublin	1	0
1907 Glasgow	3	0
1908 Dublin	5	0
1909 Glasgow	5	0
1910 Belfast	0	1
1911 Glasgow	2	0
1912 Belfast	4	1
1913 Dublin	2	1
1914 Belfast	1	1
1920 Glasgow	3	0
1921 Belfast	2	0

		S	I
1922	Glasgow	2	1
1923	Belfast	1	0
1924	Glasgow	2	0
1925	Belfast	3	0
1926	Glasgow	4	0
1927	Belfast	2	0
1928	Glasgow	0	1
1929	Belfast	7	3
1930	Glasgow	3	1
1931	Belfast	0	0
1932	Glasgow	3	1
1933	Belfast	4	0
1934	Glasgow	1	2
1935	Belfast	1	2
1936	Edinburgh	2	1
1937	Belfast	3	1
1938	Aberdeen	1	1
1939	Belfast	2	0
1946	Glasgow	0	0
1947	Belfast	0	2
1948	Glasgow	3	2
1949	Belfast	8	2
1950	Glasgow	6	1
1951	Belfast	3	0
1952	Glasgow	1	1
1953	Belfast	3	1
1954	Glasgow	2	2
1955	Belfast	1	2
1956	Glasgow	1	0
1957	Belfast	1	1
1958	Glasgow	2	2
1959	Belfast	4	0
1960	Glasgow	5	2
1961	Belfast	6	1
1962	Glasgow	5	1
1963	Belfast	1	2
1964	Glasgow	3	2
1965	Belfast	2	3
1966	Glasgow	2	1
1967	Belfast	0	1
1969	Glasgow	1	1
1970	Belfast	1	0
1971	Glasgow	0	1
1972	Glasgow	2	0
1973	Glasgow	1	2
1974	Glasgow	0	1
1975	Glasgow	3	0
1976	Glasgow	3	0
1977	Glasgow	3	0
1978	Glasgow	1	1
1979	Glasgow	1	0
1980	Belfast	0	1
wc1981	Glasgow	1	1
1981	Glasgow	2	0
wc1981	Belfast	0	0
1982	Belfast	1	1
1983	Glasgow	0	0

WALES v IRELAND

Played: 89; Wales won 42, Ireland won 27, Drawn 20. *Goals:* Wales 180, Ireland 125.

		W	I
1882	Wrexham	7	1
1883	Belfast	1	1
1884	Wrexham	6	0
1885	Belfast	8	2
1886	Wrexham	5	0
1887	Belfast	1	4
1888	Wrexham	11	0
1889	Belfast	3	1
1890	Shrewsbury	5	2
1891	Belfast	2	7
1892	Bangor	1	1
1893	Belfast	3	4
1894	Swansea	4	1
1895	Belfast	2	2
1896	Wrexham	6	1
1897	Belfast	3	4
1898	Llandudno	0	1
1899	Belfast	0	1
1900	Llandudno	2	0
1901	Belfast	1	0
1902	Cardiff	0	3
1903	Belfast	0	2
1904	Bangor	0	1
1905	Belfast	2	2
1906	Wrexham	4	4
1907	Belfast	3	2
1908	Aberdare	0	1
1909	Belfast	3	2
1910	Wrexham	4	1
1911	Belfast	2	1
1912	Cardiff	2	3
1913	Belfast	1	0
1914	Wrexham	1	2
1920	Belfast	2	2
1921	Swansea	2	1
1922	Belfast	1	1
1923	Wrexham	0	3
1924	Belfast	1	0
1925	Wrexham	0	0
1926	Belfast	0	3
1927	Cardiff	2	2
1928	Belfast	2	1
1929	Wrexham	2	2
1930	Belfast	0	7
1931	Wrexham	3	2
1932	Belfast	0	4
1933	Wrexham	4	1
1934	Belfast	1	1
1935	Wrexham	3	1
1936	Belfast	2	3
1937	Wrexham	4	1
1938	Belfast	0	1
1939	Wrexham	3	1
1947	Belfast	1	2
1948	Wrexham	2	0
1949	Belfast	2	0
wc1950	Wrexham	0	0
1951	Belfast	2	1
1952	Swansea	3	0
1953	Belfast	3	2
wc1954	Wrexham	1	2
1955	Belfast	3	2
1956	Cardiff	1	1
1957	Belfast	0	0
1958	Cardiff	1	1
1959	Belfast	1	4
1960	Wrexham	3	2
1961	Belfast	5	1
1962	Cardiff	4	0
1963	Belfast	4	1
1964	Cardiff	2	3
1965	Belfast	5	0
1966	Cardiff	1	4
EC1967	Belfast	0	0
EC1968	Wrexham	2	0
1969	Belfast	0	0
1970	Swansea	1	0
1971	Belfast	0	1
1972	Wrexham	0	0
1973	Everton	0	1
1974	Wrexham	1	0
1975	Belfast	0	1
1976	Swansea	1	0
1977	Belfast	1	1
1978	Wrexham	1	0
1979	Belfast	1	1
1980	Cardiff	0	1
1982	Wrexham	3	0
1983	Belfast	1	0

OTHER BRITISH INTERNATIONAL RESULTS 1908–1983

ENGLAND

v ARGENTINA

			E	A
1951	9 May	Wembley	2	1
1953	17 May	Buenos Aires	0	0
		(*abandoned after 21 mins*)		
wc1962	2 June	Rancagua	3	1
1964	6 June	Rio de Janeiro	0	1
wc1966	23 July	Wembley	1	0
1974	22 May	Wembley	2	2
1977	12 June	Buenos Aires	1	1
1980	13 May	Wembley	3	1

v AUSTRALIA

			E	A
1980	31 May	Sydney	2	1
1983	11 June	Sydney	0	0
1983	15 June	Brisbane	1	0
1983	18 June	Melbourne	1	1

v AUSTRIA

			E	A
1908	6 June	Vienna	6	1
1908	8 June	Vienna	11	1
1909	1 June	Vienna	8	1
1930	14 May	Vienna	0	0
1932	7 Dec	Chelsea	4	3
1936	6 May	Vienna	1	2
1951	28 Nov	Wembley	2	2
1952	25 May	Vienna	3	2
wc1958	15 June	Boras	2	2
1961	27 May	Vienna	1	3

			E	A
1962	4 Apr	Wembley	3	1
1965	20 Oct	Wembley	2	3
1967	27 May	Vienna	1	0
1973	26 Sept	Wembley	7	0
1979	13 June	Vienna	3	4

v BELGIUM

			E	B
1921	21 May	Brussels	2	0
1923	19 Mar	Highbury	6	1
1923	1 Nov	Antwerp	2	2
1924	8 Dec	West Bromwich	4	0
1926	24 May	Antwerp	5	3
1927	11 May	Brussels	9	1
1928	19 May	Antwerp	3	1
1929	11 May	Brussels	5	1
1931	16 May	Brussels	4	1
1936	9 May	Brussels	2	3
1947	21 Sept	Brussels	5	2
1950	18 May	Brussels	4	1
1952	26 Nov	Wembley	5	0
WC1954	17 June	Basle	4	4*
1964	21 Oct	Wembley	2	2
1970	25 Feb	Brussels	3	1
EC1980	12 June	Turin	1	1

**After extra time.*

v BOHEMIA

			E	B
1908	13 June	Prague	4	0

v BRAZIL

			E	B
1956	9 May	Wembley	4	2
WC1958	11 June	Gothenburg	0	0
1959	13 May	Rio de Janeiro	0	2
WC1962	10 June	Vina del Mar	1	3
1963	8 May	Wembley	1	1
1964	30 May	Rio de Janeiro	1	5
1969	12 June	Rio de Janeiro	1	2
WC1970	7 June	Guadalajara	0	1
1976	23 May	Los Angeles	0	1
1977	8 June	Rio de Janeiro	0	0
1978	19 Apr	Wembley	1	1
1981	12 May	Wembley	0	1

v BULGARIA

			E	B
WC1962	7 June	Rancagua	0	0
1968	11 Dec	Wembley	1	1
1974	1 June	Sofia	1	0
EC1979	6 June	Sofia	3	0
EC1979	22 Nov	Wembley	2	0

v CHILE

			E	C
WC1950	25 June	Rio de Janeiro	2	0
1953	24 May	Santiago	2	1

v COLOMBIA

			E	C
1970	20 May	Bogota	4	0

v CYPRUS

			E	C
EC1975	16 Apr	Wembley	5	0
EC1975	11 May	Limassol	1	0

v CZECHOSLOVAKIA

			E	C
1934	16 May	Prague	1	2
1937	1 Dec	Tottenham	5	4
1963	29 May	Bratislava	4	2
1966	2 Nov	Wembley	0	0
WC1970	11 June	Guadalajara	1	0
1973	27 May	Prague	1	1
EC1974	30 Oct	Wembley	3	0
EC1975	30 Oct	Bratislava	1	2
1978	29 Nov	Wembley	1	0
WC1982	20 June	Bilbao	2	0

v DENMARK

			E	D
1948	26 Sept	Copenhagen	0	0
1955	2 Oct	Copenhagen	5	1
WC1956	5 Dec	Wolverhampton	5	2
WC1957	15 May	Copenhagen	4	1
1966	3 July	Copenhagen	2	0
EC1978	20 Sept	Copenhagen	4	3
EC1979	12 Sept	Wembley	1	0
EC1982	22 Sept	Copenhagen	2	2

v ECUADOR

			E	Ec
1970	24 May	Quito	2	0

v FIFA

			E	FIFA
1938	26 Oct	Highbury	3	0
1953	21 Oct	Wembley	4	4
1963	23 Oct	Wembley	2	1

England centre-forward Tommy Taylor puts England's first goal past Brazilian goalkeeper Gilmar at Wembley in May 1956.

Tony Woodcock scores in the first minute of the Greece v England European Championship match in November 1982.

v FINLAND

			E	F
1937	20 May	Helsinki	8	0
1956	20 May	Helsinki	5	1
1966	26 June	Helsinki	3	0
WC1976	13 June	Helsinki	4	1
WC1976	13 Oct	Wembley	2	1
1982	3 June	Helsinki	4	1

v FRANCE

			E	F
1923	10 May	Paris	4	1
1924	17 May	Paris	3	1
1925	21 May	Paris	3	2
1927	26 May	Paris	6	0
1928	17 May	Paris	5	1
1929	9 May	Paris	4	1
1931	14 May	Paris	2	5
1933	6 Dec	Tottenham	4	1
1938	26 May	Paris	4	2
1947	3 May	Highbury	3	0
1949	22 May	Paris	3	1
1951	3 Oct	Highbury	2	2
1955	15 May	Paris	0	1
1957	27 Nov	Wembley	4	0
EC1962	3 Oct	Sheffield	1	1
EC1963	27 Feb	Paris	2	5
WC1966	20 July	Wembley	2	0
1969	12 Mar	Wembley	5	0
WC1982	16 June	Bilbao	3	1

v GERMANY

			E	G
1930	10 May	Berlin	3	3
1935	4 Dec	Tottenham	3	0
1938	14 May	Berlin	6	3

v EAST GERMANY

			E	EG
1963	2 June	Leipzig	2	1
1970	25 Nov	Wembley	3	1
1974	29 May	Leipzig	1	1

WEST GERMANY

			E	WG
1954	1 Dec	Wembley	3	1
1956	26 May	Berlin	3	1
1965	12 May	Nuremberg	1	0
1966	23 Feb	Wembley	1	0
WC1966	30 July	Wembley	4	2*
1968	1 June	Hanover	0	1
WC1970	14 June	Leon	2	3*
EC1972	29 Apr	Wembley	1	3
EC1972	13 May	Berlin	0	0
1975	12 Mar	Wembley	2	0
1978	22 Feb	Munich	1	2
WC1982	29 June	Madrid	0	0
1982	13 Oct	Wembley	1	2

**After extra time.*

v GREECE

			E	G
EC1971	21 Apr	Wembley	3	0
EC1971	1 Dec	Athens	2	0
EC1982	17 Nov	Athens	3	0
EC1983	30 Mar	Wembley	0	0

v HUNGARY

			E	H
1908	10 June	Budapest	7	0
1909	29 May	Budapest	4	2
1909	31 May	Budapest	8	2
1934	10 May	Budapest	1	2
1936	2 Dec	Highbury	6	2
1953	25 Nov	Wembley	3	6
1954	23 May	Budapest	1	7
1960	22 May	Budapest	0	2
WC1962	31 May	Rancagua	1	2

1965	5 May	Wembley	1	0
1978	24 May	Wembley	4	1
wc1981	6 June	Budapest	3	1
wc1982	18 Nov	Wembley	1	0
EC1983	27 Apr	Wembley	2	0

v ICELAND

			E	I
1982	2 June	Reykjavik	1	1

v REPUBLIC OF IRELAND

			E	RI
1946	30 Sept	Dublin	1	0
1949	21 Sept	Everton	0	2
wc1957	8 May	Wembley	5	1
wc1957	19 May	Dublin	1	1
1964	24 May	Dublin	3	1
1976	8 Sept	Wembley	1	1
EC1978	25 Oct	Dublin	1	1
EC1980	6 Feb	Wembley	2	0

v ITALY

			E	I
1933	13 May	Rome	1	1
1934	14 Nov	Highbury	3	2
1939	13 May	Milan	2	2
1948	16 May	Turin	4	0
1949	30 Nov	Tottenham	2	0
1952	18 May	Florence	1	1
1959	6 May	Wembley	2	2
1961	24 May	Rome	3	2
1973	14 June	Turin	0	2
1973	14 Nov	Wembley	0	1
1976	28 May	New York	3	2
wc1976	17 Nov	Rome	0	2
wc1977	16 Nov	Wembley	2	0
EC1980	15 June	Turin	0	1

v KUWAIT

			E	K
wc1982	25 June	Bilbao	1	0

v LUXEMBOURG

			E	L
1927	21 May	Luxembourg	5	2
wc1960	19 Oct	Luxembourg	9	0
wc1961	28 Sept	Highbury	4	1
wc1977	30 Mar	Wembley	5	0
wc1977	12 Oct	Luxembourg	2	0
EC1982	15 Dec	Wembley	9	0

v MALTA

			E	M
EC1971	3 Feb	Valletta	1	0
EC1971	12 May	Wembley	5	0

v MEXICO

			E	M
1959	24 May	Mexico City	1	2
1961	10 May	Wembley	8	0
wc1966	16 July	Wembley	2	0
1969	1 June	Mexico City	0	0

v NETHERLANDS

			E	N
1935	18 May	Amsterdam	1	0
1946	27 Nov	Huddersfield	8	2
1964	9 Dec	Amsterdam	1	1
1969	5 Nov	Amsterdam	1	0
1970	14 Jan	Wembley	0	0
1977	9 Feb	Wembley	0	2
1982	25 May	Wembley	2	0

v NORWAY

			E	N
1937	14 May	Oslo	6	0
1938	9 Nov	Newcastle	4	0
1949	18 May	Oslo	4	1
1966	29 June	Oslo	6	1
wc1980	10 Sept	Wembley	4	0
wc1981	9 Sept	Oslo	1	2

v PERU

			E	P
1959	17 May	Lima	1	4
1962	20 May	Lima	4	0

v POLAND

			E	P
1966	5 Jan	Everton	1	1
1966	5 July	Chorzow	1	0
wc1973	6 June	Chorzow	0	2
wc1973	17 Oct	Wembley	1	1

v PORTUGAL

			E	P
1947	25 May	Lisbon	10	0
1950	14 May	Lisbon	5	3
1951	19 May	Everton	5	2
1955	22 May	Oporto	1	3
1958	7 May	Wembley	2	1
wc1961	21 May	Lisbon	1	1
wc1961	25 Oct	Wembley	2	0
1964	17 May	Lisbon	4	3
1964	4 June	São Paulo	1	1
wc1966	26 July	Wembley	2	1
1969	10 Dec	Wembley	1	0
1974	3 Apr	Lisbon	0	0
EC1974	20 Nov	Wembley	0	0
EC1975	19 Nov	Lisbon	1	1

v RUMANIA

			E	R
1939	24 May	Bucharest	2	0
1968	6 Nov	Bucharest	0	0
1969	15 Jan	Wembley	1	1
wc1970	2 June	Guadalajara	1	0
wc1980	15 Oct	Bucharest	1	2
wc1981	29 April	Wembley	0	0

v SPAIN

			E	S
1929	15 May	Madrid	3	4
1931	9 Dec	Highbury	7	1
wc1950	2 July	Rio de Janeiro	0	1
1955	18 May	Madrid	1	1
1955	30 Nov	Wembley	4	1
1960	15 May	Madrid	0	3
1960	26 Oct	Wembley	4	2
1965	8 Dec	Madrid	2	0
1967	24 May	Wembley	2	0
EC1968	3 Apr	Wembley	1	0
EC1968	8 May	Madrid	2	1
1980	26 Mar	Barcelona	2	0
EC1980	18 June	Naples	2	1
1981	25 Mar	Wembley	1	2
wc1982	5 July	Madrid	0	0

v SWEDEN

			E	S
1923	21 May	Stockholm	4	2
1923	24 May	Stockholm	3	1
1937	17 May	Stockholm	4	0
1947	19 Nov	Highbury	4	2
1949	13 May	Stockholm	1	3
1956	16 May	Stockholm	0	0
1959	28 Oct	Wembley	2	3
1965	16 May	Gothenburg	2	1
1968	22 May	Wembley	3	1
1979	10 June	Stockholm	0	0

v SWITZERLAND

			E	S
1933	20 May	Berne	4	0
1938	21 May	Zurich	1	2
1947	18 May	Zurich	0	1
1948	2 Dec	Highbury	6	0
1952	28 May	Zurich	3	0
wc1954	20 June	Berne	2	0
1962	9 May	Wembley	3	1
1963	5 June	Basle	8	1
EC1971	13 Oct	Basle	3	2
EC1971	10 Nov	Wembley	1	1

1975	3 Sept	Basle	2	1
1977	7 Sept	Wembley	0	0
wc1980	19 Nov	Wembley	2	1
wc1981	30 May	Basle	1	2

v USA

			E	*USA*
wc1950	29 June	Belo Horizonte	0	1
1953	8 June	New York	6	3
1959	28 May	Los Angeles	8	1
1964	27 May	New York	10	0

v URUGUAY

			E	*U*
1953	31 May	Montevideo	1	2
wc1954	26 June	Basle	2	4
1964	6 May	Wembley	2	1
wc1966	11 July	Wembley	0	0
1969	8 June	Montevideo	2	1
1977	15 June	Montevideo	0	0

v USSR

			E	*USSR*
1958	18 May	Moscow	1	1
wc1958	8 June	Gothenburg	2	2
wc1958	17 June	Gothenburg	0	1
1958	22 Oct	Wembley	5	0
1967	6 Dec	Wembley	2	2
EC1968	8 June	Rome	2	0
1973	10 June	Moscow	2	1

v YUGOSLAVIA

			E	*Y*
1939	18 May	Belgrade	1	2
1950	22 Nov	Highbury	2	2
1954	16 May	Belgrade	0	1
1956	28 Nov	Wembley	3	0
1958	11 May	Belgrade	0	5
1960	11 May	Wembley	3	3
1965	9 May	Belgrade	1	1
1966	4 May	Wembley	2	0
EC1968	5 June	Florence	0	1
1972	11 Oct	Wembley	1	1
1974	5 June	Belgrade	2	2

England versus The Rest of the World (FIFA) team at Wembley in 1953, and England's centre-forward Nat Lofthouse puts the FIFA goalkeeper under pressure.

The Scotland team line up prior to their European Championship game against Switzerland in March 1983 at Hampden Park.

SCOTLAND

v ARGENTINA

			S	A
1977	18 June	Buenos Aires	1	1
1979	2 June	Glasgow	1	3

v AUSTRIA

			S	A
1931	16 May	Vienna	0	5
1933	29 Nov	Glasgow	2	2
1937	9 May	Vienna	1	1
1950	13 Dec	Glasgow	0	1
1951	27 May	Vienna	0	4
wc1954	16 June	Zurich	0	1
1955	19 May	Vienna	4	1
1956	2 May	Glasgow	1	1
1960	29 May	Vienna	1	4
1963	8 May	Glasgow	4	1
		(abandoned after 79 mins)		
wc1968	6 Nov	Glasgow	2	1
wc1969	5 Nov	Vienna	0	2
EC1978	20 Sept	Vienna	2	3
EC1979	17 Oct	Glasgow	1	1

v BELGIUM

			S	B
1947	18 May	Brussels	1	2
1948	28 Apr	Glasgow	2	0
1951	20 May	Brussels	5	0
EC1971	3 Feb	Liège	0	3
EC1971	10 Nov	Aberdeen	1	0
1974	2 June	Brussels	1	2
EC1979	21 Nov	Brussels	0	2
EC1979	19 Dec	Glasgow	1	3
EC1982	15 Dec	Brussels	2	3

v BRAZIL

			S	B
1966	25 June	Glasgow	1	1
1972	5 July	Rio de Janeiro	0	1
1973	30 June	Glasgow	0	1
wc1974	18 June	Frankfurt	0	0
1977	23 June	Rio de Janeiro	0	2
wc1982	18 June	Seville	1	4

v BULGARIA

			S	B
1978	22 Feb	Glasgow	2	1

v CHILE

			S	C
1977	15 June	Santiago	4	2

v CYPRUS

			S	C
wc1968	17 Dec	Nicosia	5	0
wc1969	11 May	Glasgow	8	0

v CZECHOSLOVAKIA

			S	C
1937	22 May	Prague	3	1
1937	8 Dec	Glasgow	5	0
wc1961	14 May	Bratislava	0	4
wc1961	26 Sept	Glasgow	3	2
wc1961	29 Nov	Brussels	2	4*
1972	2 July	Porto Alegre	0	0
wc1973	26 Sept	Glasgow	2	1
wc1973	17 Oct	Prague	0	1
wc1976	13 Oct	Prague	0	2
wc1977	21 Sept	Glasgow	3	1

**After extra time.*

v DENMARK

			S	D
1951	12 May	Glasgow	3	1
1952	25 May	Copenhagen	2	1
1968	16 Oct	Copenhagen	1	0
EC1970	11 Nov	Glasgow	1	0
EC1971	9 June	Copenhagen	0	1
wc1972	18 Oct	Copenhagen	4	1
wc1972	15 Nov	Glasgow	2	0
EC1975	3 Sept	Copenhagen	1	0
EC1975	29 Oct	Glasgow	3	1

v FINLAND

			S	F
1954	25 May	Helsinki	2	1
wc1964	21 Oct	Glasgow	3	1
wc1965	27 May	Helsinki	2	1
1976	8 Sept	Glasgow	6	0

v FRANCE

			S	F
1930	18 May	Paris	2	0
1932	8 May	Paris	3	1
1948	23 May	Paris	0	3
1949	27 Apr	Glasgow	2	0
1950	27 May	Paris	1	0
1951	16 May	Glasgow	1	0
wc1958	15 June	Orebro	1	2

v GERMANY

			S	G
1929	1 June	Berlin	1	1
1936	14 Oct	Glasgow	2	0

v EAST GERMANY

			S	EG
1974	30 Oct	Glasgow	3	0
1977	7 Sept	East Berlin	0	1
EC1982	13 Oct	Glasgow	2	0

v WEST GERMANY

			S	WG
1957	22 May	Stuttgart	3	1
1959	6 May	Glasgow	3	2
1964	12 May	Hanover	2	2
wc1969	16 Apr	Glasgow	1	1
wc1969	22 Oct	Hamburg	2	3
1973	14 Nov	Glasgow	1	1
1974	27 Mar	Frankfurt	1	2

v HUNGARY

			S	H
1938	7 Dec	Glasgow	3	1
1954	8 Dec	Glasgow	2	4
1955	29 May	Budapest	1	3
1958	7 May	Glasgow	1	1
1960	5 June	Budapest	3	3
1980	31 May	Budapest	1	3

v IRAN

			S	I
wc1978	7 June	Cordoba	1	1

v REPUBLIC OF IRELAND

			S	RI
wc1961	3 May	Glasgow	4	1
wc1961	7 May	Dublin	3	0
1963	9 June	Dublin	0	1
1969	21 Sept	Dublin	1	1

v ISRAEL

			S	I
wc1981	25 Feb	Tel Aviv	1	0
wc1981	28 Apr	Glasgow	3	1

v ITALY

			S	I
1931	20 May	Rome	0	3
wc1965	9 Nov	Glasgow	1	0
wc1965	7 Dec	Naples	0	3

v LUXEMBOURG

			S	L
1947	24 May	Luxembourg	6	0

v NETHERLANDS

			S	N
1929	4 June	Amsterdam	2	0
1938	21 May	Amsterdam	3	1
1959	27 May	Amsterdam	2	1
1966	11 May	Glasgow	0	3
1968	30 May	Amsterdam	0	0
1971	1 Dec	Rotterdam	1	2
wc1978	11 June	Mendoza	3	2
1982	23 Mar	Glasgow	2	1

v NEW ZEALAND

			S	NZ
wc1982	15 June	Malaga	5	2

v NORWAY

			S	N
1929	28 May	Oslo	7	3
1954	5 May	Glasgow	1	0
1954	19 May	Oslo	1	1
1963	4 June	Bergen	3	4
1963	7 Nov	Glasgow	6	1
1974	6 June	Oslo	2	1
EC1978	25 Oct	Glasgow	3	2
EC1979	7 June	Oslo	4	0

v PARAGUAY

			S	P
wc1958	11 June	Norrkoping	2	3

v PERU

			S	P
1972	26 Apr	Glasgow	2	0
wc1978	3 June	Cordoba	1	3
1979	12 Sept	Glasgow	1	1

v POLAND

			S	P
1958	1 June	Warsaw	2	1
1960	4 May	Glasgow	2	3
wc1965	23 May	Chorzow	1	1
wc1965	13 Oct	Glasgow	1	2
1980	28 May	Poznan	0	1

v PORTUGAL

			S	P
1950	21 May	Lisbon	2	2
1955	4 May	Glasgow	3	0
1959	3 June	Lisbon	0	1
1966	18 June	Glasgow	0	1
EC1971	21 Apr	Lisbon	0	2
EC1971	13 Oct	Glasgow	2	1
1975	13 May	Glasgow	1	0
EC1978	29 Nov	Lisbon	0	1
EC1980	26 Mar	Glasgow	4	1
wc1980	15 Oct	Glasgow	0	0
wc1981	18 Nov	Lisbon	1	2

v RUMANIA

			S	R
EC1975	1 June	Bucharest	1	1
EC1975	17 Dec	Glasgow	1	1

v SPAIN

			S	Sp
wc1957	8 May	Glasgow	4	2
wc1957	26 May	Madrid	1	4
1963	13 June	Madrid	6	2
1965	8 May	Glasgow	0	0
EC1974	20 Nov	Glasgow	1	2
EC1975	5 Feb	Valencia	1	1
1982	24 Feb	Valencia	0	3

v SWEDEN

			S	Sw
1952	30 May	Stockholm	1	3
1953	6 May	Glasgow	1	2
1975	16 Apr	Gothenburg	1	1
1977	27 Apr	Glasgow	3	1
wc1980	10 Sept	Stockholm	1	0
wc1981	9 Sept	Glasgow	2	0

v SWITZERLAND

			S	Sw
1931	24 May	Geneva	3	2
1948	17 May	Berne	1	2
1950	26 Apr	Glasgow	3	1
wc1957	19 May	Basle	2	1
wc1957	6 Nov	Glasgow	3	2
1973	22 June	Berne	0	1
1976	7 Apr	Glasgow	1	0
EC1982	17 Nov	Berne	0	2
EC1983	30 May	Glasgow	2	2

v TURKEY

			S	T
1960	8 June	Ankara	2	4

v URUGUAY

			S	U
wc1954	19 June	Basle	0	7
1962	2 May	Glasgow	2	3

v USA

			S	USA
1952	30 Apr	Glasgow	6	0

v USSR

			S	USSR
1967	10 May	Glasgow	0	2
1971	14 June	Moscow	0	1
wc1982	22 June	Malaga	2	2

v YUGOSLAVIA

			S	Y
1955	15 May	Belgrade	2	2
1956	21 Nov	Glasgow	2	0
wc1958	8 June	Vasteras	1	1
1972	29 June	Belo Horizonte	2	2
wc1974	22 June	Frankfurt	1	1

v ZAIRE

			S	Z
wc1974	14 June	Dortmund	2	0

WALES

v AUSTRIA

			W	A
1954	9 May	Vienna	0	2
EC1955	23 Nov	Wrexham	1	2
EC1974	4 Sept	Vienna	1	2
1975	19 Nov	Wrexham	1	0

v BELGIUM

			W	B
1949	22 May	Liège	1	3
1949	23 Nov	Cardiff	5	1

v BULGARIA

			W	B
EC1983	27 Apr	Wrexham	1	0

v BRAZIL

			W	B
WC1958	19 June	Gothenburg	0	1
1962	12 May	Rio de Janeiro	1	3
1962	16 May	São Paulo	1	3
1966	14 May	Rio de Janeiro	1	3
1966	18 May	Belo Horizonte	0	1
1983	12 June	Cardiff	1	1

v CHILE

			W	C
1966	22 May	Santiago	0	2

v CZECHOSLOVAKIA

			W	C
WC1957	1 May	Cardiff	1	0
WC1957	26 May	Prague	0	2
EC1971	21 Apr	Swansea	1	3
EC1971	27 Oct	Prague	0	1
WC1977	30 Mar	Wrexham	3	0
WC1977	16 Nov	Prague	0	1
WC1980	19 Nov	Cardiff	1	0
WC1981	9 Sept	Prague	0	2

v DENMARK

			W	D
WC1964	21 Oct	Copenhagen	0	1
WC1965	1 Dec	Wrexham	4	2

v FINLAND

			W	F
EC1971	26 May	Helsinki	1	0
EC1971	13 Oct	Swansea	3	0

v FRANCE

			W	F
1933	25 May	Paris	1	1
1939	20 May	Paris	1	2
1953	14 May	Paris	1	6
1982	2 June	Toulouse	1	0

v EAST GERMANY

			W	EG
WC1957	19 May	Leipzig	1	2
WC1957	25 Sept	Cardiff	4	1
WC1969	16 Apr	Dresden	1	2
WC1969	22 Oct	Cardiff	1	3

v WEST GERMANY

			W	WG
1968	8 May	Cardiff	1	1
1969	26 Mar	Frankfurt	1	1
1976	6 Oct	Cardiff	0	2
1977	14 Dec	Dortmund	1	1
EC1979	2 May	Wrexham	0	2
EC1979	17 Oct	Cologne	1	5

v GREECE

			W	G
WC1964	9 Dec	Athens	0	2
WC1965	17 Mar	Cardiff	4	1

v HUNGARY

			W	H
WC1958	8 June	Sanviken	1	1
WC1958	17 June	Stockholm	2	1
1961	28 May	Budapest	2	3
EC1962	7 Nov	Budapest	1	3
EC1963	20 Mar	Cardiff	1	1
EC1974	30 Oct	Cardiff	2	0
EC1975	16 Apr	Budapest	2	1

v ICELAND

			W	I
WC1980	2 June	Reykjavik	4	0
WC1981	14 Oct	Swansea	2	2

v IRAN

			W	I
1978	18 Apr	Teheran	1	0

v REPUBLIC OF IRELAND

			W	RI
1960	28 Sept	Dublin	3	2
1979	11 Sept	Swansea	2	1
1981	24 Feb	Dublin	3	1

v ISRAEL

			W	I
WC1958	15 Jan	Tel Aviv	2	0
WC1958	5 Feb	Cardiff	2	0

v ITALY

			W	I
1965	1 May	Florence	1	4
WC1968	23 Oct	Cardiff	0	1
WC1969	4 Nov	Rome	1	4

v KUWAIT

			W	K
1977	6 Sept	Wrexham	0	0
1977	20 Sept	Kuwait	0	0

v LUXEMBOURG

			W	L
EC1974	20 Nov	Swansea	5	0
EC1975	1 May	Luxembourg	3	1

v MALTA

			W	M
EC1978	25 Oct	Wrexham	7	0
EC1979	2 June	Valletta	2	0

v MEXICO

			W	M
WC1958	11 June	Stockholm	1	1
1962	22 May	Mexico City	1	2

v NORWAY

			W	N
EC1982	22 Sept	Swansea	1	0

v POLAND

			W	P
WC1973	28 Mar	Cardiff	2	0
WC1973	26 Sept	Katowice	0	3

v PORTUGAL

			W	P
1949	15 May	Lisbon	2	3
1951	12 May	Cardiff	2	1

v RUMANIA

			W	R
EC1970	11 Nov	Cardiff	0	0
EC1971	24 Nov	Bucharest	0	2

v SPAIN

			W	S
WC1961	19 Apr	Cardiff	1	2
WC1961	18 May	Madrid	1	1
1982	24 Mar	Valencia	1	1

v SWEDEN

			W	S
WC1958	15 June	Stockholm	0	0

v SWITZERLAND

			W	S
1949	26 May	Berne	0	4
1951	16 May	Wrexham	3	2

v TURKEY

			W	T
EC1978	29 Nov	Wrexham	1	0
EC1979	21 Nov	Izmir	0	1
WC1980	15 Oct	Cardiff	4	0
WC1981	25 Mar	Ankara	1	0

v REST OF UNITED KINGDOM

			W	UK
1951	5 Dec	Cardiff	3	2
1969	28 July	Cardiff	0	1

v USSR

			W	USSR
WC1965	30 May	Moscow	1	2
WC1965	27 Oct	Cardiff	2	1
WC1981	30 May	Wrexham	0	0
WC1981	18 Nov	Tbilisi	0	3

v YUGOSLAVIA

			W	Y
1953	21 May	Belgrade	2	5
1954	22 Nov	Cardiff	1	3
EC1976	24 Apr	Zagreb	0	2
EC1976	22 May	Cardiff	1	1
EC1982	15 Dec	Titograd	4	4

The Albanian goalkeeper turns too late to stop Ian Stewart's goal for Northern Ireland in their recent European Championship clash at Windsor Park.

NORTHERN IRELAND

v ALBANIA

			NI	A
WC1965	7 May	Belfast	4	1
WC1965	24 Nov	Tirana	1	1
EC1982	15 Dec	Tirana	0	0
EC1983	27 Apr	Belfast	1	0

v ARGENTINA

			NI	A
WC1958	11 June	Halmstad	1	3

v AUSTRIA

			NI	A
WC1982	1 July	Madrid	2	2
EC1982	13 Oct	Vienna	0	2

v AUSTRALIA

			NI	A
1980	11 June	Sydney	2	1
1980	15 June	Melbourne	1	1
1980	18 June	Adelaide	2	1

v BELGIUM

			NI	B
WC1976	10 Nov	Liège	0	2
WC1977	16 Nov	Belfast	3	0

v BULGARIA

			NI	B
WC1972	18 Oct	Sofia	0	3
WC1973	26 Sept	Sheffield	0	0
EC1978	29 Nov	Sofia	2	0
EC1979	2 May	Belfast	2	0

v CYPRUS

			NI	C
EC1971	3 Feb	Nicosia	3	0
EC1971	21 Apr	Belfast	5	0
WC1973	14 Feb	Nicosia	0	1
WC1973	8 May	London	3	0

v CZECHOSLOVAKIA

			NI	C
WC1958	8 June	Halmstad	1	0
WC1958	17 June	Malmo	2	1*

*After extra time

v DENMARK

			NI	D
EC1978	25 Oct	Belfast	2	1
EC1979	6 June	Copenhagen	0	4

v FRANCE

			NI	F
1951	12 May	Belfast	2	2
1952	11 Nov	Paris	1	3
WC1958	19 June	Norrkoping	0	4
1982	24 Mar	Paris	0	4
WC1982	4 July	Madrid	1	4

West German goalkeeper Schumacher looks on in anguish as Ian Stewart scores the only goal of this European Championship clash at Windsor Park.

v WEST GERMANY

			NI	WG
wc1958	15 June	Malmo	2	2
wc1960	26 Oct	Belfast	3	4
wc1961	10 May	Hamburg	1	2
1966	7 May	Belfast	0	2
1977	27 Apr	Cologne	0	5
1982	17 Nov	Belfast	1	0

v GREECE

			NI	G
wc1961	3 May	Athens	1	2
wc1961	17 Oct	Belfast	2	0

v HONDURAS

			NI	H
wc1982	21 June	Zaragoza	1	1

v ICELAND

			NI	I
wc1977	11 June	Reykjavik	0	1
wc1977	21 Sept	Belfast	2	0

v REPUBLIC OF IRELAND

			NI	RI
EC1978	20 Sept	Dublin	0	0
EC1979	21 Nov	Belfast	1	0

v ISRAEL

			NI	I
1968	10 Sept	Jaffa	3	2
1976	3 Mar	Tel Aviv	1	1
wc1980	26 Mar	Tel Aviv	0	0
wc1981	18 Nov	Belfast	1	0

v ITALY

			NI	I
wc1957	25 Apr	Rome	0	1
1957	4 Dec	Belfast	2	2
wc1958	15 Jan	Belfast	2	1
1961	25 Apr	Bologna	2	3

v MEXICO

			NI	M
1966	22 June	Belfast	4	1

v NETHERLANDS

			NI	N
1962	9 May	Rotterdam	0	4
wc1965	17 Mar	Belfast	2	1
wc1965	7 Apr	Rotterdam	0	0
wc1976	13 Oct	Rotterdam	2	2
wc1977	12 Oct	Belfast	0	1

v NORWAY

			NI	N
EC1974	4 Sept	Oslo	1	2
EC1975	29 Oct	Belfast	3	0

v POLAND

			NI	P
EC1962	10 Oct	Katowice	2	0
EC1962	28 Nov	Belfast	2	0

v PORTUGAL

			NI	P
wc1957	16 Jan	Lisbon	1	1
wc1957	1 May	Belfast	3	0
wc1973	28 Mar	Coventry	1	1
wc1973	14 Nov	Lisbon	1	1
wc1980	19 Nov	Lisbon	0	1
wc1981	29 Apr	Belfast	1	0

v SPAIN

			NI	S
1958	15 Oct	Madrid	2	6
1963	30 May	Bilbao	1	1
1963	30 Oct	Belfast	0	1
EC1970	11 Nov	Seville	0	3
EC1972	16 Feb	Hull	1	1
wc1982	25 June	Valencia	1	0

v SWEDEN

			NI	S
EC1974	30 Oct	Solna	2	0
EC1975	3 Sept	Belfast	1	2
wc1980	15 Oct	Belfast	3	0
wc1981	3 June	Solna	0	1

v SWITZERLAND

			NI	S
wc1964	14 Oct	Belfast	1	0
wc1964	14 Nov	Lausanne	1	2

v TURKEY

			NI	T
wc1968	23 Oct	Belfast	4	1
wc1968	11 Dec	Istanbul	3	0
EC1983	30 Mar	Belfast	2	1

v URUGUAY

			NI	U
1964	29 Apr	Belfast	3	0

v USSR

			NI	USSR
wc1969	10 Sept	Belfast	0	0
wc1969	22 Oct	Moscow	0	2
EC1971	22 Sept	Moscow	0	1
EC1971	13 Oct	Belfast	1	1

v YUGOSLAVIA

			NI	Y
EC1975	16 Mar	Belfast	1	0
EC1975	19 Nov	Belgrade	0	1
wc1982	17 June	Zaragoza	0	0

REPUBLIC OF IRELAND

v ALGERIA

			RI	A
1982	28 Apr	Algiers	0	2

v ARGENTINA

			RI	A
1951	13 May	Dublin	0	1
1979	29 May	Dublin	0	0
1980	16 May	Dublin	0	1

v AUSTRIA

			RI	A
1952	7 May	Vienna	0	6
1953	25 Mar	Dublin	4	0
1958	14 Mar	Vienna	1	3
1962	8 Apr	Dublin	2	3
EC1963	25 Sept	Vienna	0	0
EC1963	13 Oct	Dublin	3	2
1966	22 May	Vienna	0	1
1968	10 Nov	Dublin	2	2
EC1971	30 May	Dublin	1	4
EC1971	10 Oct	Linz	0	6

v BELGIUM

			RI	B
1928	12 Feb	Liège	4	2
1929	30 Apr	Dublin	4	0
1930	11 May	Brussels	3	1
WC1934	25 Feb	Dublin	4	4
1949	24 Apr	Dublin	0	2
1950	10 May	Brussels	1	5
1965	24 Mar	Dublin	0	2
1966	25 May	Liège	3	2
WC1980	15 Oct	Dublin	1	1
WC1981	25 Mar	Brussels	0	1

v BRAZIL

			RI	B
1974	5 May	Rio de Janeiro	1	2
1982	27 May	Uberlandia	0	7

v BULGARIA

			RI	B
WC1977	1 June	Sofia	1	2
WC1977	12 Oct	Dublin	0	0
EC1979	19 May	Sofia	0	1
EC1979	17 Oct	Dublin	3	0

v CHILE

			RI	C
1960	30 Mar	Dublin	2	0
1972	21 June	Recife	1	2
1974	12 May	Santiago	2	1
1982	22 May	Santiago	0	1

v CYPRUS

			RI	C
WC1980	26 Mar	Nicosia	3	2
WC1980	19 Nov	Dublin	6	0

v CZECHOSLOVAKIA

			RI	C
1938	18 May	Prague	2	2
EC1959	5 Apr	Dublin	2	0
EC1959	10 May	Bratislava	0	4
WC1961	8 Oct	Dublin	1	3
1979	26 Sept	Prague	1	4
WC1961	29 Oct	Prague	1	7
EC1967	21 May	Dublin	0	2
EC1967	22 Nov	Prague	2	1
WC1969	4 May	Dublin	1	2
WC1969	7 Oct	Prague	0	3
1981	29 Apr	Dublin	3	1

v DENMARK

			RI	D
WC1956	3 Oct	Dublin	2	1
WC1957	2 Oct	Copenhagen	2	0
WC1968	4 Dec	Dublin	1	1
		(abandoned after 51 mins)		
WC1969	27 May	Copenhagen	0	2
WC1969	15 Oct	Dublin	1	1
EC1978	24 May	Copenhagen	3	3
EC1979	2 May	Dublin	2	0

Eire's Liam Brady in action against England at Wembley in February 1980, with Tony Woodcock in close attendance.

v ECUADOR

			RI	E
1972	19 June	Natal	3	2

v FINLAND

			RI	F
WC1949	8 Sept	Dublin	3	0
WC1949	9 Oct	Helsinki	1	1

v FRANCE

			RI	F
1937	23 May	Paris	2	0
1952	16 Nov	Dublin	1	1
WC1953	4 Oct	Dublin	3	5
WC1953	25 Nov	Paris	0	1
WC1972	15 Nov	Dublin	2	1
WC1973	19 May	Paris	1	1
WC1976	17 Nov	Paris	0	2
WC1977	30 Mar	Dublin	1	0
WC1980	28 Oct	Paris	0	2
WC1981	14 Oct	Dublin	3	2

v GERMANY

			RI	G
1935	8 May	Dortmund	1	3
1936	17 Oct	Dublin	5	2
1939	23 May	Bremen	1	1

v WEST GERMANY

			RI	WG
1951	17 Oct	Dublin	3	2
1952	4 May	Cologne	0	3
1955	28 May	Hamburg	1	2
1956	25 Nov	Dublin	3	0
1960	11 May	Dusseldorf	1	0
1966	4 May	Dublin	0	4
1970	9 May	Berlin	1	2
1979	22 May	Dublin	1	3
1981	21 May	Bremen	0	3†

†*v West Germany 'B'*

v HUNGARY

			RI	H
1934	15 Dec	Dublin	2	4
1936	3 May	Budapest	3	3
1936	6 Dec	Dublin	2	3
1939	19 Mar	Cork	2	2
1939	18 May	Budapest	2	2
WC1969	8 June	Dublin	1	2
WC1969	5 Nov	Budapest	0	4

v ICELAND

			RI	I
EC1962	12 Aug	Dublin	4	2
EC1962	2 Sept	Reykjavik	1	1
EC1982	13 Oct	Dublin	2	0

v LUXEMBOURG

			RI	L
1936	9 May	Luxembourg	5	1
WC1953	28 Oct	Dublin	4	0
WC1954	7 Mar	Luxembourg	1	0

v IRAN

			RI	I
1972	18 June	Recife	2	1

v N IRELAND

			RI	NI
EC1978	20 Sept	Dublin	0	0
EC1979	21 Nov	Belfast	0	1

v ITALY

			RI	I
1926	21 Mar	Turin	0	3
1927	23 Apr	Dublin	1	2
EC1970	8 Dec	Rome	0	3
EC1971	10 May	Dublin	1	2

v MALTA

			RI	M
EC1983	30 Mar	Valetta	1	0

v NETHERLANDS

			RI	N
1932	8 May	Amsterdam	2	0
1934	8 Apr	Amsterdam	2	5
1935	8 Dec	Dublin	3	5
1955	1 May	Dublin	1	0
1956	10 May	Rotterdam	4	1
WC1980	10 Sept	Dublin	2	1
WC1981	9 Sept	Rotterdam	2	2
EC1982	22 Sept	Rotterdam	1	2

v NORWAY

			RI	N
WC1937	10 Oct	Oslo	2	3
WC1937	7 Nov	Dublin	3	3
1950	26 Nov	Dublin	2	2
1951	30 May	Oslo	3	2
1954	8 Nov	Dublin	2	1
1955	25 May	Oslo	3	1
1960	6 Nov	Dublin	3	1
1964	13 May	Oslo	4	1
1973	6 June	Oslo	1	1
1976	24 Mar	Dublin	3	0
1978	21 May	Oslo	0	0

v POLAND

			RI	P
1938	22 May	Warsaw	0	6
1938	13 Nov	Dublin	3	2
1958	11 May	Katowice	2	2
1958	5 Oct	Dublin	2	2
1964	10 May	Cracow	1	3
1964	25 Oct	Dublin	3	2
1968	15 May	Dublin	2	2
1968	30 Oct	Katowice	0	1
1970	6 May	Dublin	1	2
1970	23 Sept	Dublin	0	2
1973	16 May	Wroclaw	0	2
1973	21 Oct	Dublin	1	0
1976	26 May	Posnan	2	0
1977	24 Apr	Dublin	0	0
1978	12 Apr	Lodz	0	3
1981	23 May	Bydgoszcz	0	3

v PORTUGAL

			RI	P
1946	16 June	Lisbon	1	3
1947	4 May	Dublin	0	2
1948	23 May	Lisbon	0	2
1949	22 May	Dublin	1	0
1972	25 June	Recife	1	2

v SCOTLAND

			RI	S
WC1961	3 May	Glasgow	1	4
WC1961	7 May	Dublin	0	3
1963	9 June	Dublin	1	0
1969	21 Sept	Dublin	1	1

v SPAIN

			RI	S
1931	26 Apr	Barcelona	1	1
1931	13 Dec	Dublin	0	5
1946	23 June	Madrid	1	0
1947	2 Mar	Dublin	3	2
1948	30 May	Barcelona	1	2
1949	12 June	Dublin	1	4
1952	1 June	Madrid	0	6
1955	27 Nov	Dublin	2	2
EC1964	11 Mar	Seville	1	5
EC1964	8 Apr	Dublin	0	2
WC1965	5 May	Dublin	1	0
WC1965	27 Oct	Seville	1	4
WC1965	10 Nov	Paris	0	1
EC1966	23 Oct	Dublin	0	0
EC1966	7 Dec	Valencia	0	2
1977	9 Feb	Dublin	0	1
EC1982	17 Nov	Dublin	3	3
EC1983	27 Apr	Zaragosa	0	2

v SWEDEN

			RI	S
WC1949	2 June	Stockholm	1	3
WC1949	13 Nov	Dublin	1	3
1959	1 Nov	Dublin	3	2
1960	18 May	Malmo	1	4
EC1970	14 Oct	Dublin	1	1
EC1970	28 Oct	Malmo	0	1

v SWITZERLAND

			RI	S
1935	5 May	Basle	0	1
1936	17 Mar	Dublin	1	0
1937	17 May	Berne	1	0
1938	18 Sept	Dublin	4	0
1948	5 Dec	Dublin	0	1
EC1975	11 May	Dublin	2	1
EC1975	21 May	Berne	0	1
1980	30 Apr	Dublin	2	0

v TURKEY

			RI	T
EC1966	16 Nov	Dublin	2	1
EC1967	22 Feb	Ankara	1	2
EC1974	20 Nov	Izmir	1	1
EC1975	29 Oct	Dublin	4	0
1976	13 Oct	Ankara	3	3
1978	5 Apr	Dublin	4	2

v TRINIDAD & TOBAGO

			RI	TT
1982	30 May	Port of Spain	1	2

v URUGUAY

			RI	U
1974	8 May	Montevideo	0	2

v USA

			RI	USA
1979	29 Oct	Dublin	3	2

v USSR

			RI	USSR
WC1972	18 Oct	Dublin	1	2
WC1973	13 May	Moscow	0	1
EC1974	30 Oct	Dublin	3	0
EC1975	18 May	Kiev	1	2

v WALES

			RI	W
1960	28 Sept	Dublin	2	3
1979	11 Sept	Swansea	1	2
1981	24 Feb	Dublin	1	3

v YUGOSLAVIA

			RI	Y
1955	19 Sept	Dublin	1	4

ENGLAND v YOUNG ENGLAND

			E	YE
1954	30 April	Highbury	2	1
1955	6 May	Highbury	5	0
1957	3 May	Highbury	1	2
1958	2 May	Stamford Bridge	4	1
1959	1 May	Highbury	3	3
1960	6 May	Highbury	2	1
1961	5 May	Stamford Bridge	1	1
1962	4 May	Highbury	3	2
1963	24 May	Highbury	3	2
1964	1 May	Stamford Bridge	3	0
1965	30 April	Highbury	2	2
1966	13 May	Stamford Bridge	1	1
1967	19 May	Highbury	0	5
1968	17 May	Highbury	1	4
1969	25 April	Stamford Bridge	0	0

INTERNATIONAL APPEARANCES

This is a list of full international appearances by Englishmen, Irishmen, Scotsmen and Welshmen in matches against the Home Countries and against foreign nations. It does not include unofficial matches against Commonwealth and Empire countries. The year indicated refers to the season; ie 1982 is the 1981-82 season.

Explanatory code for matches played by all five countries: A represents Austria; Alb, Albania; Alg, Algeria; Arg, Argentina; Aus, Australia; B, Bohemia; Bel, Belgium; Br, Brazil; Bul, Bulgaria; Ca, Canada; Ch, Chile; Co, Colombia; Cy, Cyprus; Cz, Czechoslovakia; D, Denmark; Ec, Ecuador; Ei, Eire; EG, East Germany; F, France; Fi, Finland; G, Germany (pre-war); Gr, Greece; H, Hungary; Ho, Holland; Hon, Honduras; I, Italy; Ic, Iceland; Ir, Iran; Is, Israel; K, Kuwait; L, Luxembourg; M, Mexico; Ma, Malta; N, Norway; Ni, Northern Ireland; Nz, New Zealand; P, Portugal; Par, Paraguay; Pe, Peru; Pol, Poland; R, Rumania; R of E, Rest of Europe; R of W, Rest of World; S, Scotland; Se, Sweden; Sp, Spain; Sw, Switzerland; T, Turkey; Tr, Trinidad & Tobago; U, Uruguay; UK, Rest of United Kingdom; US, United States of America; USSR; W, Wales; WG, West Germany; Y, Yugoslavia.

(Note: For purposes of this code, and in order to distinguish from Eire, Northern Ireland is given throughout the series as Ni).

ENGLAND

Abbott, W. (Everton), 1902 v W (1)
A'Court, A. (Liverpool), 1958 v Ni, Br, A, USSR; 1959 v W (5)
Adcock, H. (Leicester C), 1929 v F, Bel, Sp; 1930 v Ni, W (5)
Alcock, C. W. (Wanderers), 1875 v S (1)
Alderson, J. T. (C Palace), 1923 v F (1)
Aldridge, A. (WBA), 1888 v Ni; (with Walsall Town Swifts), 1889 v Ni (2)
Allen, A. (Stoke C) 1960 v Se, W, Ni (3)
Allen, A. (Aston Villa), 1888 v Ni (1)
Allen, H. (Wolverhampton W), 1888 v S, W, Ni; 1889 v S; 1890 v S (5)
Allen, J. P. (Portsmouth), 1934 v Ni, W (2)
Allen, R. (WBA), 1952 v Sw; 1954 v Y, S; 1955 v WG, W (5)
Alsford, W. J. (Tottenham H), 1935 v S (1)
Amos, A. (Old Carthusians), 1885 v S; 1886 v W (2)
Anderson, R. D. (Old Etonians), 1879 v W (1)
Anderson, S. (Sunderland), 1962, v A, S (2)
Anderson, V. (Nottingham F), 1979 v Cz, Se; 1980 v Bul, Sp; 1981 v N, R, W, S; 1982 v Ni, Ic (10)
Angus, J. (Burnley), 1961 v A (1)
Armfield, J. C. (Blackpool), 1959 v Br, Pe, M, US; 1960 v Y, Sp, H, S; 1961 v L, P, Sp, M, L, A, W, Ni, S; 1962 v A, Sw, Pe, W, Ni, S, L, P, H, Arg, Bul, Br; 1963 v F (2), Br, EG, Sw, Ni, W, S; 1964 v R of W, W, Ni, S; 1966 v Y, Fi (43)
Armitage, G. H. (Charlton Ath), 1926 v Ni (1)
Armstrong, D. (Middlesbrough), 1980 v Aus; (with Southampton), 1983 v WG (2)
Armstrong, K. (Chelsea), 1955 v S (1)
Arnold, J. (Fulham), 1933 v S (1)
Arthur, J. W. H. (Blackburn R), 1885 v S, W, Ni; 1886 v S, W; 1887 v W, Ni (7)
Ashcroft, J. (Woolwich Arsenal), 1906 v Ni, W, S (3)
Ashmore, G. S. (WBA), 1926 v Bel (1)
Ashton, C. T. (Corinthians), 1926 v Ni (1)
Ashurst, W. (Notts Co), 1923 v Se (2); 1925 v S, W, Bel (5)
Astall, G. (Birmingham C), 1956 v Fi, WG (2)
Astle, J. (WBA), 1969 v W; 1970 v S, P, Br (sub), Cz (5)
Aston, J. (Manchester U), 1949 v S, W, D, Sw, Se, N, F; 1950 v S, W, Ni, Ei, I, P, Bel, Ch, US; 1951 v Ni (17)
Athersmith, W. C. (Aston Villa), 1892 v Ni, 1897 v S, W, Ni; 1898 v S, W, Ni; 1899 v S, W, Ni; 1900 v S, W (12)
Atyeo, P. J. W. (Bristol C), 1956 v Br, Se, Sp; 1957 v D, Ei (2) (6)
Austin, S. W. (Manchester C), 1926 v Ni (1)

Bach, P. (Sunderland), 1899 v Ni (1)
Bache, J. W. (Aston Villa), 1903 v W; 1904 v W, Ni; 1905 v S; 1907 v Ni; 1910 v Ni; 1911 v S (7)
Baddeley, T. (Wolverhampton W), 1903 v S, Ni; 1904 v S, W, Ni (5)
Bagshaw, J. J. (Derby Co), 1920 v Ni (1)
Bailey, H. P. (Leicester Fosse), 1908 v W, A (2), H, B (5)
Bailey, M. A. (Charlton Ath), 1964 v US; 1965 v W (2)
Bailey, N. C. (Clapham Rovers), 1878 v S; 1879 v S, W; 1880 v S; 1881 v S; 1882 v S, W; 1883 v S, W; 1884 v S, W, Ni; 1885 v S, W, Ni; 1886 v S, W; 1887 v S, W (19)
Baily, E. F. (Tottenham H), 1950 v Sp; 1951 v Y, Ni, W; 1952 v A (2), Sw, W; 1953 v Ni (9)
Bain, J. (Oxford University), 1887 v S (1)
Baker, A. (Arsenal), 1928 v W (1)
Baker, B. H. (Everton), 1921 v Bel; (with Chelsea), 1926 v Ni (2)
Baker, J. H. (Hibernian), 1960 v Y, Sp, H, Ni, S; (with Arsenal) 1966 v Sp, Pol, Ni (8)
Ball, A. J. (Blackpool), 1965 v Y, WG, Se; 1966 v S, Sp, Fi, D, U, Arg, P, WG (2), Pol (2); (with Everton), 1967 v W, S, Ni, A, Cz, Sp; 1968 v W, S, USSR, Sp (2), Y, WG; 1969 v Ni, W, S, R (2), M, Br, U; 1970 v P, Co, Ec, R, Br, Cz (sub), WG, W, S, Bel; 1971 v Ma, EG, Gr, Ma (sub), Ni, S; 1972 v Sw, Gr; (with Arsenal) WG (2), S; 1973 v W (3), Y, S (2), Cz, Ni, Pol; 1974 v P (sub); 1975 v WG, Cy (2), Ni, W, S (72)
Ball, J. (Bury), 1928 v Ni (1)
Balmer, W. (Everton), 1905 v Ni (1)
Bamber, J. (Liverpool), 1921 v W (1)
Bambridge, A. L. (Swifts), 1881 v W; 1883 v W; 1884 v Ni (3)
Bambridge, E. C. (Swifts), 1879 v S; 1880 v S; 1881 v S; 1882 v S, W, Ni; 1883 v W; 1884 v S, W, Ni; 1885 v S, W, Ni; 1886 v S, W; 1887 v S, W, Ni (18)
Bambridge, E. H. (Swifts), 1876 v S (1)
Banks, G. (Leicester C), 1963 v S, Br, Cz, EG; 1964 v W, Ni, S, R of W, U, P (2), US, Arg; 1965 v Ni, S, H, Y, WG, Se; 1966 v Ni, S, Sp, Pol (2), WG (2), Y, Fi, U, M, F, Arg, P; 1967 v Ni, W, S, Cz; (with Stoke C), 1968 v W, Ni, S, USSR (2), Sp, WG, Y; 1969 v Ni, S, R (2), F, U, Br; 1970 v W, Ni, S, Ho, Bel, Co, Ec, R, Br, Cz; 1971 v Gr, Ma (2), Ni, S; 1972 v Sw, Gr, WG (2), W, S (73)
Banks, H. E. (Millwall), 1901 v Ni (1)
Banks, T. (Bolton W), 1958 v USSR (3), Br, A; 1959 v Ni (6)
Bannister, W. (Burnley), 1901 v W; (with Bolton W), 1902 v Ni (2)
Barclay, R. (Sheffield W), 1932 v S; 1933 v Ni; 1936 v S (3)
Barham, M. (Norwich C), 1983 v Aus (2) (2)
Barkas, S. (Manchester C), 1936 v Bel; 1937 v S; 1938 v W, Ni, Cz (5)
Barker, J. (Derby Co), 1935 v I, Ho, S, W, Ni; 1936 v G, A, S, W, Ni; 1937 v W (11)
Barker, R. (Herts Rangers), 1872 v S (1)
Barker, R. R. (Casuals), 1895 v W (1)

John Atyeo *Bristol City* and *England*

England mid-field dynamo Alan Ball

Gordon Banks *Stoke City* and *England*

Colin Bell *Manchester City* and *England*

Peter Broadbent in action for England

Barlow, R. J. (WBA), 1955 v Ni (1)
Barnes, J. (Watford), v Ni (sub), Aus (sub), Aus (2) (4)
Barnes, P. S. (Manchester C), 1978 v I, WG, Br, W, S, H; 1979 v D, Ei, Cz, Ni (2), S, Bul, A; (with WBA), 1980 v D, W; 1981 v Sp (sub), Br, W, Sw (sub); (with Leeds U), 1982 v N (sub), Ho (sub) (22)
Barnet, H. H. (Royal Engineers), 1882 v Ni (1)
Barrass, M. W. (Bolton W), 1952 v W, Ni; 1953 v S (3)
Barrett, A. F. (Fulham), 1930 v Ni (1)
Barrett, J. W. (West Ham U), 1929 v Ni (1)
Barry, L. (Leicester C), 1928 v F, Bel; 1929 v F, Bel, Sp (5)
Barson, F. (Aston Villa), 1920 v W (1)
Barton, J. (Blackburn R), 1890 v Ni (1)
Barton, P. H. (Birmingham), 1921 v Bel; 1922 v Ni; 1923 v F; 1924 v Bel, S, W; 1925 v Ni (7)
Bassett, W. I. (WBA), 1888 v Ni, 1889 v S, W; 1890 v S, W; 1891 v S, Ni; 1892 v S; 1893 v S, W; 1894 v S; 1895 v S, Ni; 1896 v S, W, Ni (16)
Bastard, S. R. (Upton Park), 1880 v S (1)
Bastin, C. S. (Arsenal), 1932 v W; 1933 v I, Sw; 1934 v S, Ni, W, H, Cz; 1935 v S, Ni, I; 1936 v S, W, G, A; 1937 v W, Ni; 1938 v S, G, Sw, F (21)
Baugh, R. (Stafford Road), 1886 v Ni; (with Wolverhampton W) 1890 v Ni (2)
Bayliss, A. E. J. M. (WBA), 1891 v Ni (1)
Baynham, R. L. (Luton T), 1956 v Ni, D, Sp (3)
Beasley, A. (Huddersfield T), 1939 v S (1)
Beats, W. E. (Wolverhampton W), 1901 v W; 1902 v S (2)
Beattie, T. K. (Ipswich T), 1975 v Cy (2), S; 1976 v Sw, P; 1977 v Fi, I (sub), Ho; 1978 v L (sub) (9)
Becton, F. (Preston NE), 1895 v Ni; (with Liverpool), 1897 v W (2)
Bedford, H. (Blackpool), 1923 v Se; 1925 v Ni (2)
Bell, C. (Manchester C), 1968 v Se, WG; 1969 v W, Bul, F, U, Br; 1970 v Ni (sub), Ho (2), P, Br (sub), Cz, WG (sub); 1972 v Gr, WG (2), W, Ni, S; 1973 v W (3), Y, S (2), Ni, Cz, Pol; 1974 v A, Pol, I, W, Ni, S, Arg, EG, Bul, Y; 1975 v Cz, P, WG, Cy (2), Ni, S; 1976 v Sw, Cy (48)
Bennett, W. (Sheffield U), 1901 v S, W (2)
Benson, R. W. (Sheffield U), 1913 v Ni (1)
Bentley, R. T. F. (Chelsea), 1949 v Se; 1950 v S, P, Bel, Ch, USA; 1953 v W, Bel; 1955 v W, WG, Sp, P (12)
Beresford, J. (Aston Villa), 1934 v Cz (1)
Berry, A. (Oxford University), 1909 v Ni (1)
Berry, J. J. (Manchester U), 1953 v Arg, Ch, U; 1956 v Se (4)
Bestall, J. G. (Grimsby T), 1935 v Ni (1)
Betmead, H. A. (Grimsby T), 1937 v Fi (1)
Betts, M. P. (Old Harrovians), 1877 v S (1)
Betts, W. (Sheffield W), 1889 v W (1)
Beverley, J. (Blackburn R), 1884 v S, W, Ni (3)
Birkett, R. H. (Clapham Rovers), 1879 v S (1)
Birkett, R. J. E. (Middlesbrough), 1936 v Ni (1)
Birley, F. H. (Oxford University), 1874 v S; (with Wanderers), 1875 v S (2)
Birtles, G. (Nottingham F), 1980 v Arg (sub), I; 1981 v R (3)
Bishop, S. M. (Leicester C), 1927 v S, Bel, L, F (4)
Blackburn, F. (Blackburn R), 1901 v S; 1902 v Ni; 1904 v S (3)
Blackburn, G. F. (Aston Villa), 1924 v F (1)
Blenkinsop, E. (Sheffield W), 1928 v F, Bel; 1929 v S, W, Ni, F, Bel, Sp; 1930 v S, W, Ni, G, A; 1931 v S, W, Ni, F, Bel; 1932 v S, W, Ni, Sp; 1933 v S, W, Ni, A (26)
Bliss, H. (Tottenham H), 1921 v S (1)
L. Blissett (Watford), 1983 v WG (sub), L, W, Gr, H, Ni, S (sub), Aus (8)
Blockley, J. P. (Arsenal), 1973 v Y (1)
Bloomer, S. (Derby Co), 1895 v S, Ni; 1896 v W, Ni; 1897 v S, W, Ni; 1898 v S; 1899 v S, W, Ni; 1900 v S; 1901 v S, W; 1902 v S, W, Ni; 1904 v S; 1905 v S, W, Ni; (with Middlesbrough), 1907 v S, W (23)
Blunstone, F. (Chelsea), 1955 v W, S, F, P; 1957 v Y (5)
Bond, R. (Preston NE), 1905 v Ni, W; 1906 v S, W, Ni; (with Bradford C), 1910 v S, W, Ni (8)
Bonetti, P. P. (Chelsea), 1966 v D; 1967 v Sp, A; 1968 v Sp; 1970 v Ho, P, WG (7)
Bonsor, A. G. (Wanderers), 1873 v S; 1875 v S (2)
Booth, F. (Manchester C), 1905 v Ni (1)
Booth, T. (Blackburn R.), 1898 v W; (with Everton), 1903 v S (2)
Bowden, E. R. (Arsenal), 1935 v W, I; 1936 v W, Ni, A; 1937 v H (6)
Bower, A. G. (Corinthians), 1924 v Ni, Bel; 1925 v W, Bel; 1927 v W (5)
Bowers, J. W. (Derby Co), 1934 v S, Ni, W (3)
Bowles, S. (QPR), 1974 v P, W, Ni; 1977 v I, Ho (5)
Bowser, S. (WBA), 1920 v Ni (1)
Boyer, P. J. (Norwich C), 1976 v W (1)
Boyes, W. (WBA), 1935 v Ho; (with Everton), 1939 v W, R of E (3)
Boyle, T. W. (Burnley), 1913 v Ni (1)
Brabrook, P. (Chelsea), 1958 v USSR; 1959 v Ni; 1960 v Sp (3)
Bradford, G. R. W. (Bristol R), 1956 v D (1)
Bradford, J. (Birmingham), 1924 v Ni; 1925 v Bel; 1928 v S; 1929 v Ni, W, F, Sp; 1930 v S, Ni, G, A; 1931 v W (12)
Bradley, W. (Manchester U), 1959 v I, US, M (sub) (3)
Bradshaw, F. (Sheffield W), 1908 v A (1)
Bradshaw, T. H. (Liverpool), 1897 v Ni (1)
Bradshaw, W. (Blackburn R), 1910 v W, Ni; 1912 v Ni; 1913 v W (4)
Brann, G. (Swifts), 1886 v S, W; 1891 v W (3)
Brawn, W. F. (Aston Villa), 1904 v W, Ni (2)
Bray, J. (Manchester C), 1935 v W; 1936 v S, W, Ni, G; 1937 v S (6)
Brayshaw, E. (Sheffield W), 1887 v Ni (1)
Bridges, B. J. (Chelsea), 1965 v S, H, Y; 1966 v A (4)
Bridgett, A. (Sunderland), 1905 v S; 1908 v S, A (2), H, B; 1909 v Ni, W, H (2), A (11)
Brindle, T. (Darwen), 1880 v S, W (2)
Brittleton, J. T. (Sheffield W), 1912 v S, W, Ni; 1913 v S; 1914 v W (5)
Britton, C. S. (Everton), 1935 v S, W, Ni, I; 1937 v S, Ni, H, N, Se (9)
Broadbent, P. F. (Wolverhampton W), 1958 v USSR; 1959 v S, W, Ni, I, Br; 1960 v S (7)
Broadis, I. A. (Manchester C), 1952 v S, A, I; 1953 v S, Arg, Ch, U, US; (with Newcastle U), 1954 v S, H, Y, Bel, Sw, U (14)
Brockbank, J. (Cambridge University), 1872 v S (1)
Brodie, J. B. (Wolverhampton W), 1889 v S, Ni; 1891 v Ni (3)
Bromilow, T. G. (Liverpool), 1921 v W; 1922 v S, W; 1923 v Bel; 1926 v Ni (5)
Bromley-Davenport, W. E. (Oxford University), 1884 v S, W (2)
Brook, E. F. (Manchester C), 1930 v Ni; 1933 v Sw: 1934 v S, W, Ni, F, H, Cz; 1935 v S, W, Ni, I; 1936 v S, W, Ni; 1937 v H; 1938 v W, Ni (18)
Brooking, T. D. (West Ham U), 1974 v P, Arg, EG, Bul, Y; 1975 v Cz (sub), P; 1976 v P, W, Br, I, Fi; 1977 v Ei, Fi, I, Ho, Ni, W; 1978 v I, WG, W, S (sub), H; 1979 v D, Ei, Ni, W (sub), S, Bul, Se (sub), A; 1980 v D, Ni, Arg (sub), W, Ni, S, Bel, Sp; 1981 v Sw, Sp, R, H; 1982 v H, S, Fi, Sp (sub) (47)
Brooks, J. (Tottenham H), 1957 v W, Y, D (3)
Broome, F. H. (Aston Villa), 1938 v G, Sw, F; 1939 v N, I, R, Y (7)
Brown, A. (Aston Villa), 1882 v S, W, Ni (3)
Brown, A. S. (Sheffield U), 1904 v W; 1906 v Ni (2)

Brown, A. (WBA), 1971 v W (1)
Brown, G. (Huddersfield T), 1927 v S, W, Ni, Bel, L, F; 1928 v W; 1929 v S; (with Aston Villa), 1933 v W (9)
Brown, J. (Blackburn R), 1881 v W; 1882 v Ni; 1885 v S, W, Ni (5)
Brown, J. H. (Sheffield W), 1927 v S, W, Bel, L, F; 1930 v Ni (6)
Brown, K. (West Ham U), 1960 v Ni (1)
Brown, W. (West Ham U), 1924 v Bel (1)
Bruton, J. (Burnley), 1928 v F, Bel; 1929 v S (3)
Bryant, W. I. (Clapton), 1925 v F (1)
Buchan, C. M. (Sunderland), 1913 v Ni; 1920 v W; 1921 v W, Bel; 1923 v F; 1924 v S (6)
Buchanan, W. S. (Clapham R), 1876 v S (1)
Buckley, F. C. (Derby Co), 1914 v Ni (1)
Bullock, F. E. (Huddersfield T), 1921 v Ni (1)
Bullock, N. (Bury), 1923 v Bel; 1926 v W; 1927 v Ni (3)
Burgess, H. (Manchester C), 1904 v S, W, Ni; 1906 v S (4)
Burgess, H. (Sheffield W), 1931 v S, Ni, F, Bel (4)
Burnup, C. J. (Cambridge University), 1896 v S (1)
Burrows, H. (Sheffield W), 1934 v H, Cz; 1935 v Ho (3)
Burton, F. E. (Nottingham F), 1889 v Ni (1)
Bury, L. (Cambridge University), 1877 v S; (with Old Etonians), 1879 v W (2)
Butcher, T. (Ipswich T), 1980 v Aus; 1981 v Sp; 1982 v W, S, F, Cz, WG, Sp; 1983 v D, WG, L, W, Gr, H, Ni, S, Aus (3) (19)
Butler, J. D. (Arsenal), 1925 v Bel (1)
Butler, W. (Bolton W), 1924 v S (1)
Byrne, G. (Liverpool), 1963 v S; 1966 v N (2)
Byrne, J. J. (C Palace), 1962 v Ni; (with West Ham U), 1963 v Sw; 1964 v S, U, P (2), Ei, Br, Arg; 1965 v W, S (11)
Byrne, R. W. (Manchester U), 1954 v S, H, Y, Bel, Sw, U; 1955 v S, W, Ni, WG, F, Sp, P; 1956 v S, W, Ni, Br, Se, Fi, WG, D, Sp; 1957 v S, W, Ni, Y, D (2), Ei (2); 1958 v W, Ni, F (33)

Callaghan, I. R. (Liverpool), 1966 v Fi, F; 1978 v Sw, L (4)
Calvey, J. (Nottingham F), 1902 v Ni (1)
Campbell, A. F. (Blackburn R), 1929 v W, Ni; (with Huddersfield T), 1931 v W, S, Ni; 1932 v W, Ni, Sp (8)
Camsell, G. H. (Middlesbrough), 1929 v F, Bel; 1930 v Ni, W; 1934 v F; 1936 v S, G, A, Bel (9)
Capes, A. J. (Stoke C), 1903 v S (1)
Carr, J. (Middlesbrough), 1920 v Ni; 1923 v W (2)
Carr, J. (Newcastle U), 1905 v Ni; 1907 v Ni (2)
Carr, W. H. (Owlerton, Sheffield), 1875 v S (1)
Carter, H. S. (Sunderland), 1934 v S, H; 1936 v G; 1937 v S, Ni, H; (with Derby Co), 1947 v S, W, Ni, Ei, Ho, F, Sw (13)
Carter, J. H. (WBA), 1926 v Bel; 1929 v Bel, Sp (3)
Catlin, A. E. (Sheffield W), 1937 v W, Ni, H, N, Se (5)
Chadwick, A. (Southampton), 1900 v S, W (2)
Chadwick, E. (Everton), 1891 v S, W; 1892 v S; 1893 v S; 1894 v S; 1896 v Ni; 1897 v S (7)
Chamberlain, M (Stoke C), 1983 v L (sub) (1)
Chambers, H. (Liverpool), 1921 v S, W, Bel; 1923 v S, W, Ni, Bel; 1924 v Ni (8)
Channon, M. R. (Southampton), 1973 v Y, S (2), Ni, W, Cz, USSR, I; 1974 v A, Pol, I, P, W, Ni, S, Arg, EG, Bul, Y; 1975 v Cz, P, WG, Cy (2), Ni (sub), W, S; 1976 v Sw, Cz, P, W, Ni, S, Br, I, Fi; 1977 v Fi, I, L, Ni, W, S, Br (sub), Arg, U; (with Manchester C), 1978 v Sw (46)
Charlton, J. (Leeds U), 1965 v S, H, Y, WG, Se; 1966 v W, Ni, S, A, Sp, Pol (2), WG (2), Y, Fi, D, U, M, F, Arg, P; 1967 v W, S, Ni, Cz; 1968 v W, Sp; 1969 v W, R, F; 1970 v Ho (2), P, Cz (35)
Charlton, R. (Manchester U), 1958 v S, P, Y; 1959 v S, W, Ni, USSR, I, Br, Pe, M, US; 1960 v W, S, Se, Y, Sp, H; 1961 v Ni, W, S, L, P, Sp, M, I, A; 1962 v W, Ni, S, A, Sw, Pe, L, P, H, Arg, Bul, Br; 1963 v S, F, Br, Cz, EG, Sw; 1964 v S, W, Ni, R of W, U, P, Ei, Br, Arg, US (sub); 1965 v Ni, S, Ho; 1966 v W, Ni, S, A, Sp, WG (2), Y, Fi, N, Pol, U, M, F, Arg, P; 1967 v Ni, W, S, Cz; 1968 v W, Ni, S, USSR (2), Sp (2), Se, Y; 1969 v S, W, Ni, R (2), Bul, M, Br; 1970 v W, Ni, Ho (2), P, Co, Ec, Cz, R, Br, WG (106)
Charnley, R. O. (Blackpool), 1963 v F (1)
Charsley, C. C. (Small Heath), 1893 v Ni (1)
Chedgzoy, S. (Everton), 1920 v W; 1921 v W, S, Ni; 1922 v Ni; 1923 v S; 1924 v W; 1925 v Ni (8)
Chenery, C. J. (C Palace), 1872 v S; 1873 v S; 1874 v S (3)
Cherry, T. J. (Leeds U), 1976 v W, S (sub), Br, Fi; 1977 v Ei, I, L, Ni, S (sub), Br, Arg, U; 1978 v Sw, L, I, Br, W; 1979 v Cz, W, Se; 1980 v Ei, Arg (sub), W, Ni, S, Aus, Sp (sub) (27)
Chilton, A. (Manchester U), 1951 v Ni; 1952 v F (2)
Chippendale, H. (Blackburn R), 1894 v Ni (1)
Chivers, M. (Tottenham H), 1971 v Ma (2), Gr, Ni, S; 1972 v Sw (1+1 sub), Gr, WG (2), Ni (sub), S; 1973 v W (3), S (2), Ni, Cz, Pol, USSR, I; 1974 v A, Pol (24)
Christian, E. (Old Etonians), 1879 v S (1)
Clamp, E. (Wolverhampton W), 1958 v USSR (2), Br, A (4)
Clapton, D. R. (Arsenal), 1959 v W (1)
Clare, T. (Stoke C), 1889 v Ni; 1892 v Ni; 1893 v W; 1894 v S (4)
Clarke, A. J. (Leeds U), 1970 v Cz; 1971 v EG, Ma, Ni, W (sub), S (sub); 1973 v S (2), W, Cz, Pol, USSR, I; 1974 v A, Pol, I; 1975 v P; 1976 v Cz, P (sub) (19)
Clarke, H. A. (Tottenham H), 1954 v S (1)
Clay, T. (Tottenham H), 1920 v W; 1922 v W, S, Ni (4)
Clayton, R. (Blackburn R), 1956 v Ni, Br, Se, Fi, WG, Sp; 1957 v S, W, Ni, Y, D (2), Ei (2); 1958 v S, W, Ni, F, P, Y, USSR; 1959 v S, W, Ni, USSR, I, Br, Pe, M, US; 1960 v W, Ni, S, Se, Y (35)
Clegg, J. C. (Sheffield W), 1872 v S (1)
Clegg, W. E. (Sheffield W), 1873 v S; (with Sheffield Albion), 1879 v W (2)
Clemence, R. N. (Liverpool), 1973 v W (2); 1974 v EG, Bul, Y; 1975 v Cz, P, WG, Cy, Ni, W, S; 1976 v Sw, Cz, P, W (2), Ni, S, Br, Fi; 1977 v Ei, Fi, I, Ho, L, S, Br, Arg, U; 1978 v Sw, L, I, WG, Ni, S; 1979 v D, Ei, Ni (2), S, Bul, A (sub); 1980 v D, Bul, Ei, Arg, W, S, Bel, Sp; 1981 v R, Sp, Br, Sw, H; (with Tottenham H), 1982 v N, Ni, Fi; 1983 v L (60)
Clement, D. T. (QPR), 1976 v W (sub), W, I; 1977 v I, Ho (5)
Clough, B. H. (Middlesbrough), 1960 v W, Se (2)
Coates, R. (Burnley), 1970 v Ni; 1971 v Gr (sub); (with Tottenham H), Ma, W (4)
Cobbold, W. N. (Cambridge University), 1883 v S, Ni; 1885 v S, Ni; 1886 v S, W; (with Old Carthusians), 1887 v S, W, Ni (9)
Cock, J. G. (Huddersfield T), 1920 v Ni; (with Chelsea), v S (2)
Cockburn, H. (Manchester U), 1947 v W, Ni, Ei; 1948 v S, I; 1949 v S, Ni, D, Sw, Se; 1951 v Arg, P; 1952 v F (13)
Cohen, G. R. (Fulham), 1964 v U, P, Ei, US, Br; 1965 v W, S, Ni, Bel, H, Ho, Y, WG, Se; 1966 v W, S, Ni, A, Sp, Pol (2), WG (2), N, D, U, M, F, Arg, P; 1967 v W, S, Ni, Cz, Sp; 1968 v W, Ni (37)
Coleclough, H. (C Palace), 1914 v W (1)
Coleman, E. H. (Dulwich Hamlet), 1921 v W (1)
Coleman, J. (Woolwich Arsenal), 1907 v Ni (1)
Common, A. (Sheffield U), 1904 v W, Ni; (with Middlesbrough), 1906 v W (3)
Compton, L. H. (Arsenal), 1951 v W, Y (2)
Conlin, J. (Bradford C), 1906 v S (1)
Connelly, J. M. (Burnley), 1960 v W, N, S, Se; 1962 v W,

Norwich and *England* striker Mick Channon

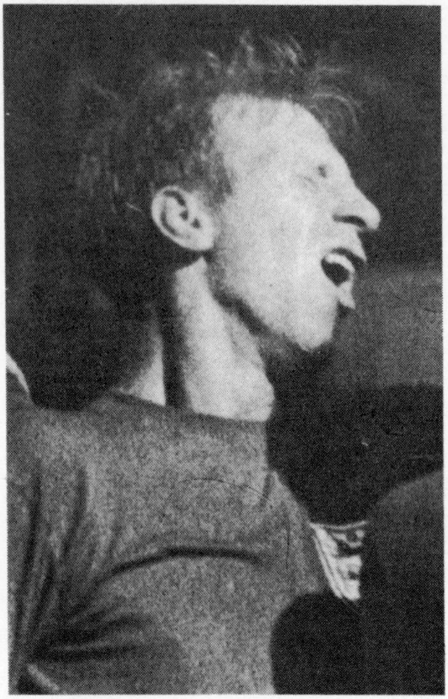

Jack Charlton *Leeds United* and *England*

'Dixie' Dean *Everton* and *England*

Tom Finney *Preston North End* and *England*

A, Sw, P; 1963 v W, F; (with Manchester U), 1965 v H, Y, Se; 1966 v W, Ni, S, A, N, D, U (20)
Cook, T. E. R. (Brighton), 1925 v W (1)
Cooper, N. C. (Cambridge University), 1893 v Ni (1)
Cooper, T. (Derby Co), 1928 v Ni; 1929 v W, Ni, S, F, Bel, Sp; 1931 v F; 1932 v W, Sp; 1933 v S; 1934 v S, H, Cz; 1935 v W (15)
Cooper, T. (Leeds U), 1969 v W, S, F, M; 1970 v Ho, Bel, Co, Ec, R, Cz, Br, WG; 1971 v EG, Ma, Ni, W, S; 1972 v Sw (2); 1975 v P (20)
Coppell, S. J. (Manchester U), 1978 v I, WG, Br, W, Ni, S, H; 1979 v D, Ei, Cz, Ni (2), W (sub), S, Bul, A; 1980 v D, Ni, Ei (sub), Sp, Arg, W, S, Bel, I; 1981 v R (sub), Sw, R, Br, W, S, Sw, H; 1982 v H, S, Fi, F, Cz, K, WG; 1983 v L, Gr (42)
Copping, W. (Leeds U), 1933 v I, Sw; 1934 v S, Ni, W, F; (with Arsenal), 1935 v Ni, I; 1936 v A, Bel; 1937 v N, Se, Fi; 1938 v S, W, Ni, Cz; 1939 v W, R of E; (with Leeds U), R (20)
Corbett, B. O. (Corinthians), 1901 v W (1)
Corbett, R. (Old Malvernians), 1903 v W (1)
Corbett, W. S. (Birmingham), 1908 v A, H, B (3)
Corrigan, J. T. (Manchester C), 1976 v I (sub), Br; 1979 v W; 1980 v Ni, Aus; 1981 v W, S; 1982 v W, Ic (9)
Cotterill, G. H. (Cambridge University), 1891 v Ni; (with Old Brightonians), 1892 v W; 1893 v S, Ni (4)
Cottle, J. R. (Bristol C), 1909 v Ni (1)
Cowan, S. (Manchester C), 1926 v Bel; 1930 v A; 1931 v Bel (3)
Cowans, G. (Aston Villa), 1983 v W, H, Ni, S, Aus (3) (7)
Cowell, A. (Blackburn R), 1910 v Ni (1)
Cox, J. (Liverpool), 1901 v Ni; 1902 v S; 1903 v S (3)
Cox, J. D. (Derby Co), 1892 v Ni (1)
Crabtree, J. W. (Burnley), 1894 v Ni; 1895 v Ni, S; (with Aston Villa), 1896 v W, S, Ni; 1899 v S, W, Ni; 1900 v S, W, Ni; 1901 v W; 1902 v W (14)
Crawford, J. F. (Chelsea), 1931 v S (1)
Crawford, R. (Ipswich T), 1962 v Ni, A (2)
Crawshaw, T. H. (Sheffield W), 1895 v Ni; 1896 v S, W, Ni; 1897 v S, W, Ni; 1901 v Ni; 1904 v W, Ni (10)
Crayston, W. J. (Arsenal), 1936 v S, W, G, A, Bel; 1938 v W, Ni, Cz (8)
Creek, F. N. S. (Corinthians), 1923 v F (1)
Cresswell, W. (South Shields), 1921 v W; (with Sunderland), 1923 v F; 1924 v Bel; 1925 v Ni; 1926 v W; 1927 v Ni; (with Everton), 1930 v Ni (7)
Crompton, R. (Blackburn R), 1902 v S, W, Ni; 1903 v S, W; 1904 v S, W, Ni; 1906 v S, W, Ni; 1907 v S, W, Ni; 1908 v S, W, Ni, A (2), H, B; 1909 v S, W, Ni, H (2), A; 1910 v S, W; 1911 v S, W, Ni; 1912 v S, W, Ni; 1913 v S, W, Ni; 1914 v S, W, Ni (41)
Crooks, S. D. (Derby Co), 1930 v S, G, A; 1931 v S, W, Ni, F, Bel; 1932 v S, W, Ni, Sp; 1933 v Ni, W, A; 1934 v S, Ni, W, F, H, Cz; 1935 v Ni; 1936 v S, W; 1937 v W, H (26)
Crowe, C. (Wolverhampton W), 1963 v F (1)
Cuggy, F. (Sunderland), 1913 v Ni; 1914 v Ni (2)
Cullis, S. (Wolverhampton W), 1938 v S, W, Ni, F, Cz; 1939 v S, Ni, R of E, N, I, R, Y (12)
Cunliffe, A. (Blackburn R), 1933 v Ni, W (2)
Cunliffe, D. (Portsmouth), 1900 v Ni (1)
Cunliffe, J. N. (Everton), 1936 v Bel (1)
Cunningham, L. (WBA), 1979 v W, Se, A (sub); (with Real Madrid), 1980 v Ei, Sp (sub); 1981 v R (sub) (6)
Currey, E. S. (Oxford University), 1890 v S, W (2)
Currie, A. W. (Sheffield U), 1972 v Ni; 1973 v USSR, I; 1974 v A, Pol, I; 1976 v Sw; (with Leeds U), 1978 v Br, W (sub), Ni, S, H (sub); 1979 v Cz, Ni (2), W, Se (17)
Cursham, A. W. (Notts Co), 1876 v S; 1877 v S; 1878 v S; 1879 v W; 1883 v S, W (6)
Cursham, H. A. (Notts Co), 1880 v W; 1882 v S, W, Ni; 1883 v S, W, Ni; 1884 v Ni (8)

Daft, H. B. (Notts Co), 1889 v Ni; 1890 v S, W; 1891 v Ni; 1892 v Ni (5)
Danks, T. (Nottingham F), 1885 v S (1)
Davenport, J. K. (Bolton W), 1885 v W; 1890 v Ni (2)
Davis, G. (Derby Co), 1904 v W, Ni (2)
Davis, H. (Sheffield W), 1903 v S, W, Ni (3)
Davison, J. E. (Sheffield W), 1922 v W (1)
Dawson, J. (Burnley), 1922 v S, Ni (2)
Day, S. H. (Old Malvernians), 1906 v Ni, W, S (3)
Dean, W. R. (Everton), 1927 v S, W, F, Bel, L; 1928 v S, W, Ni, F, Bel; 1929 v S, W, Ni; 1931 v S; 1932 v Sp; 1933 v Ni (16)
Deeley, N. V. (Wolverhampton W), 1959 v Br, Pe (2)
Devey, J. H. G. (Aston Villa), 1892 v Ni; 1894 v Ni (2)
Devonshire, A. (West Ham U), 1980 v Aus (sub), Ni; 1982 v Ho, Ic; 1983 v WG, W, Gr (7)
Dewhurst, F. (Preston NE), 1886 v W, Ni; 1887 v S, W, Ni; 1888 v S, W, Ni; 1889 v W (9)
Dewhurst, G. P. (Liverpool Ramblers), 1895 v W (1)
Dickinson, J. W. (Portsmouth), 1949 v N, F; 1950 v S, W, Ei, P, Bel, Ch, US, Sp; 1951 v Ni, W, Y; 1952 v W, Ni, S, A (2), I, Sw; 1953 v W, Ni, S, Bel, Arg, Ch, U, US; 1954 v W, Ni, S, R of E, H (2), Y, Bel, Sw, U; 1955 v Sp, P; 1956 v W, Ni, S, D, Sp; 1957 v W, Y, D (48)
Dimmock, J. H. (Tottenham H), 1921 v S; 1926 v W, Bel (3)
Ditchburn, E. G. (Tottenham H), 1949 v Sw, Se; 1953 v US; 1957 v W, Y, D (6)
Dix, R. W. (Derby Co), 1939 v N (1)
Dixon, J. A. (Notts Co), 1885 v W (1)
Dobson, A. T. C. (Notts Co), 1882 v Ni; 1884 v S, W, Ni (4)
Dobson, C. F. (Notts Co), 1886 v Ni (1)
Dobson, J. M. (Burnley), 1974 v P, EG, Bul, Y; (with Everton), 1975 v Cz (5)
Doggart, A. G. (Corinthians), 1924 v Bel (1)
Dorrell, A. R. (Aston Villa), 1925 v W, Bel, F; 1926 v Ni (4)
Douglas, B. (Blackburn R), 1958 v S, W, Ni, F, P, Y, USSR (2), Br, A; 1959 v S, USSR; 1960 v Y, H; 1961 v Ni, W, S, L, P, Sp, M, I, A; 1962 v W, Ni, S, Pe, L, P, H, Arg, Bul, Br; 1963 v S, Br, Sw (36)
Downs, R. W. (Everton), 1921 v Ni (1)
Doyle, M. (Manchester C), 1976 v W, S (sub), Br, I; 1977 v Ho (5)
Drake, E. J. (Arsenal), 1935 v Ni, I; 1936 v W; 1937 v H; 1938 v F (5)
Ducat, A. (Woolwich Arsenal), 1910 v S, W, Ni; (with Aston Villa), 1920 v S, W; 1921 v Ni (6)
Dunn, A. T. B. (Cambridge University), 1883 v Ni; 1884 v Ni; (with Old Etonians), 1892 v S, W (4)

Earle, S. G. J. (Clapton), 1924 v F; (with West Ham U), 1928 v Ni (2)
Eastham, G. (Arsenal), 1963 v Br, Cz, EG; 1964 v W, Ni, S, R of W, U, P, Ei, US, Br, Arg; 1965 v H, WG, Se; 1966 v Sp, Pol, D (19)
Eastham, G. R. (Bolton W), 1935 v Ho (1)
Eckersley, W. (Blackburn R), 1950 v Sp; 1951 v S, Y, Arg, P; 1952 v A (2), Sw; 1953 v Ni, Arg, Ch, U, US; 1954 v W, Ni, R of E, H (17)
Edwards, D. (Manchester U), 1955 v S, F, Sp, P; 1956 v S, Br, Se, Fi, WG; 1957 v S, Ni, Ei (2), D (2); 1958 v W, Ni, F (18)
Edwards, J. H. (Shropshire Wanderers), 1874 v S (1)
Edwards, W. (Leeds U), 1926 v S, W; 1927 v W, Ni, S, F, Bel, L; 1928 v S, F, Bel; 1929 v S, W, Ni; 1930 v W, Ni (16)
Ellerington, W. (Southampton), 1949 v N, F (2)
Elliott, G. W. (Middlesbrough), 1913 v Ni; 1914 v Ni; 1920 v W (3)

Elliott, W. H. (Burnley), 1952 v I, A; 1953 v Ni, W, Bel (5)
Evans, R. E. (Sheffield U), 1911 v S, W, Ni; 1912 v W (4)
Ewer, F. H. (Casuals), 1924 v F; 1925 v Bel (2)

Fairclough, P. (Old Foresters), 1878 v S (1)
Fairhurst, D. (Newcastle U), 1934 v F (1)
Fantham, J. (Sheffield W), 1962 v L (1)
Felton, W. (Sheffield W), 1925 v F (1)
Fenton, M. (Middlesbrough), 1938 v S (1)
Field, E. (Clapham Rovers), 1876 v S; 1881 v S (2)
Finney, T. (Preston NE), 1947 v W, Ni, Ei, Ho, F, P; 1948 v S, W, Ni, Bel, Se, I; 1949 v S, W, Ni, Se, N, F; 1950 v S, W, Ni, Ei, I, P, Bel, Ch, US, Sp; 1951 v W, S, Arg, P; 1952 v W, Ni, S, F, I, Sw, A; 1953 v W, Ni, S, Bel, Arg, Ch, U, US; 1954 v W, S, Bel, Sw, U, H, Y; 1955 v WG; 1956 v S, W, Ni, D, Sp; 1957 v S, W, Y, D (2), Ei (2); 1958 v W, S, F, P, Y, USSR (2); 1959 v Ni, USSR (76)
Fleming, H. J. (Swindon T), 1909 v S, H (2); 1910 v W, Ni; 1911 v W, Ni; 1912 v Ni; 1913 v S, W; 1914 v S (11)
Fletcher, A. (Wolverhampton W), 1889 v W; 1890 v W (2)
Flowers, R. (Wolverhampton W), 1955 v F; 1959 v S, W, I, Br, Pe, US, M (sub); 1960 v W, Ni, S, Se, Y, Sp, H; 1961 v Ni, W, S, L, P, Sp, M, I, A; 1962 v W, Ni, S, A, Sw, Pe, L, P, H, Arg, Bul, Br; 1963 v Ni, W, S, F (2), Sw; 1964 v Ei, US, P; 1965 v W, Ho, WG; 1966 v N (49)
Forman, Frank (Nottingham F), 1898 v S, Ni; 1899 v S, W, Ni; 1901 v S; 1902 v S, Ni; 1903 v W (9)
Forman, F. R. (Nottingham F), 1899 v S, W, Ni (3)
Forrest, J. H. (Blackburn R), 1884 v W; 1885 v S, W, Ni; 1886 v S, W; 1887 v S, W, Ni; 1889 v S; 1890 v Ni (11)
Fort, J. (Millwall), 1921 v Bel (1)
Foster, R. E. (Oxford University), 1900 v W; (with Corinthians), 1901 v W, Ni, S; 1902 v W (5)
Foster, S. (Brighton & HA), 1982 v Ni, Ho, K (3)
Foulke, W. J. (Sheffield U), 1897 v W (1)
Foulkes, W. A. (Manchester U), 1955 v Ni (1)
Fox, F. S. (Gillingham), 1925 v F (1)
Francis, G. C. J. (QPR), 1975 v Cz, P, W, S; 1976 v Sw, Cz, P, W, Ni, S, Br, Fi (12)
Francis, T. (Birmingham C), 1977 v Ho, L, S, Br; 1978 v Sw, L, I (sub), WG (sub), Br, W, S, H; (with Nottingham F), 1979 v Bul (sub), Se, A (sub); 1980 v Ni, Bul, Sp; 1981 v Sp, R, S (sub), Sw; (with Manchester C), 1982 v N, Ni, W, S (sub), Fi (sub), F, Cz, K, WG, Sp; (with Samporia), 1983 v D, Gr, H, Ni, S, Aus (3) (40)
Franklin, C. F. (Stoke C), 1947 v S, W, Ni, Ei, Ho, F, Sw, P; 1948 v S, W, Ni, Bel, Se, I; 1949 v S, W, Ni, D, Sw, N, F, Se; 1950 v W, S, Ni, Ei, I (27)
Freeman, B. C. (Everton), 1909 v S, W; (with Burnley), 1912 v S, W, Ni (5)
Froggatt, J. (Portsmouth), 1950 v Ni, I; 1951 v S; 1952 v S, A (2), I, Sw; 1953 v Ni, W, S, Bel, US (13)
Froggatt, R. (Sheffield W), 1953 v W, S, Bel, US (4)
Fry, C. B. (Corinthians), 1901 v Ni (1)
Furness, W. I. (Leeds U), 1933 v I (1)

Galley, T. (Wolverhampton W), 1937 v N, Se (2)
Gardner, T. (Aston Villa), 1934 v Cz; 1935 v Ho (2)
Garfield, B. (WBA), 1898 v Ni (1)
Garratty, W. (Aston Villa), 1903 v W (1)
Garrett, T. (Blackpool), 1952 v S, I; 1954 v W (3)
Gates, E. (Ipswich T), 1981 v N, R (2)
Gay, L. H. (Cambridge University), 1893 v S; (with Old Brightonians), 1894 v S, W (3)
Geary, F. (Everton), 1890 v Ni; 1891 v S (2)
Geaves, R. L. (Clapham Rovers), 1875 v S (1)
Gee, C. W. (Everton), 1932 v W, Sp; 1937 v Ni (3)
Geldard, A. (Everton), 1933 v I, Sw; 1935 v S; 1938 v Ni (4)
George, C. (Derby Co), 1977 v Ei (1)
George, W. (Aston Villa), 1902 v S, W, Ni (3)
Gibbins, W. V. T. (Clapton), 1924 v F; 1925 v F (2)
Gidman, J. (Aston Villa), 1977 v L (1)
Gillard, I. T. (QPR), 1975 v WG, W; 1976 v Cz (3)
Gilliat, W. E. (Old Carthusians), 1893 v Ni (1)
Goddard, P. (West Ham U), 1982 v Ic (sub) (1)
Goodall, F. R. (Huddersfield T), 1926 v S; 1927 v S, F, Bel, L; 1928 v S, W, F, Bel; 1930 v S, G, A; 1931 v S, W, Ni, Bel; 1932 v Ni; 1933 v W, Ni, A, I, Sw; 1934 v W, Ni, F (25)
Goodall, J. (Preston NE), 1888 v S, W; 1889 v S, W; (with Derby Co), 1891 v S, W; 1892 v S; 1893 v W; 1894 v S; 1895 v S, Ni; 1896 v S, W; 1898 v W (14)
Goodhart, H. C. (Old Etonians), 1883 v S, W, Ni (3)
Goodwyn, A. G. (Royal Engineers), 1873 v S (1)
Goodyer, A. C.(Nottingham F), 1879 v S (1)
Gosling, R. C. (Old Etonians), 1892 v W; 1893 v S; 1894 v W; 1895 v W, S (5)
Gosnell, A. A. (Newcastle U), 1906 v Ni (1)
Gough, H. C. (Sheffield U), 1921 v S (1)
Goulden, L. A. (West Ham U), 1937 v Se, N; 1938 v W, Ni, Cz, G, Sw, F; 1939 v S, W, R of E, I, R, Y (14)
Graham, L. (Millwall), 1925 v S, W (2)
Graham, T. (Nottingham F), 1931 v F; 1932 v Ni (2)
Grainger, C. (Sheffield U), 1956 v Br, Se, Fi, WG; 1957 v W, Ni; (with Sunderland), 1957 v S (7)
Greaves, J. (Chelsea), 1959 v Pe, M, US; 1960 v W, Se, Y, Sp; 1961 v Ni, W, S, L, P, Sp, I, A; (with Tottenham H), 1962 v S, Sw, Pe, H, Arg, Bul, Br; 1963 v Ni, W, S, F (2), Br, Cz, Sw; 1964 v W, Ni, R of W, P (2), Ei, Br, U, Arg; 1965 v Ni, S, Bel, Ho, H, Y; 1966 v W, A, Y, N, D, Pol, U, M, F; 1967 v S, Sp, A (57)
Green, F. T. (Wanderers), 1876 v S (1)
Green, G. H. (Sheffield U), 1925 v F; 1926 v S, Bel, W; 1927 v W, Ni; 1928 v F, Bel (8)
Greenhalgh, E. H. (Notts Co), 1872 v S; 1873 v S (2)
Greenhoff, B. (Manchester U), 1976 v W, Ni; 1977 v Ei, Fi, I, Ho, Ni, W, S, Br, Arg, U; 1978 v Br, W, Ni, S (sub), H (sub); (with Leeds U), 1980 v Aus (sub) (18)
Greenwood, D. H. (Blackburn R), 1882 v S, Ni (2)
Gregory, J. (QPR), 1983 v Aus (3) (3)
Grimsdell, A. (Tottenham H), 1920 v S, W; 1921 v S, Ni; 1923 v W, Ni (6)
Grosvenor, A. T. (Birmingham), 1934 v Ni, W, F (3)
Gunn, W. (Notts Co), 1884 v S, W (2)
Gurney, R. (Sunderland), 1935 v S (1)

Hacking, J. (Oldham Ath), 1929 v S, W, Ni (3)
Hadley, N. (WBA), 1903 v Ni (1)
Hagan, J. (Sheffield U), 1949 v D (1)
Haines, J. T. W. (WBA), 1949 v Sw (1)
Hall, A. E. (Aston Villa), 1910 v Ni (1)
Hall, G. W. (Tottenham H), 1934 v F; 1938 v S, W, Ni, Cz; 1939 v S, Ni, R of E, I, Y (10)
Hall, J. (Birmingham C), 1956 v S, W, Ni, Br, Se, Fi, WG, D, Sp; 1957 v S, W, Ni, Y, D (2), Ei (2) (17)
Halse, H. J. (Manchester U), 1909 v A (1)
Hammond, H. E. D. (Oxford University), 1889 v S (1)
Hampson, J. (Blackpool), 1931 v Ni, W; 1933 v A (3)
Hampton, H. (Aston Villa), 1913 v S, W; 1914 v S, W (4)
Hancocks, J. Wolverhampton W), 1949 v Sw; 1950 v W; 1951 v Y (3)
Hapgood, E. (Arsenal), 1933 v I, Sw; 1934 v S, Ni, W, H, Cz; 1935 v S, Ni, W, I, Ho; 1936 v S, Ni, W, G, A, Bel; 1937 v Fi; 1938 v S, G, Sw, F; 1939 v S, W, Ni, R of E, N, I, Y (30)
Hardinge, H. T. W. (Sheffield U), 1910 v S (1)
Hardman, H. P. (Everton), 1905 v W; 1907 v S, Ni; 1908 v W (4)
Hardwick, G. F. M. (Middlesbrough), 1947 v S, W, Ni, Ei, Ho, F, Sw, P; 1948 v S, W, Ni, Bel, Se (13)
Hardy, H. (Stockport Co), 1925 v Bel (1)
Hardy, S. (Liverpool), 1907 v S, W, Ni; 1908 v S; 1909 v

Trevor Francis on the ball for England

Jimmy Greaves *Tottenham Hotspur* and *England*

S, W, Ni, H (2), A; 1910 v S, W, Ni; 1912 v Ni; (with Aston Villa), 1913 v S; 1914 v Ni, W, S; 1920 v S, W, Ni (21)
Hargreaves, F. W. (Blackburn R), 1880 v W; 1881 v W; 1882 v Ni (3)
Hargreaves, J. (Blackburn R), 1881 v S, W (2)
Harper, E. C. (Blackburn R), 1926 v S (1)
Harris, G. (Burnley), 1966 v Pol (1)
Harris, P. P. (Portsmouth), 1950 v Ei; 1954 v H (2)
Harris, S. S. (Cambridge University), 1904 v S; (with Old Westminsters), 1905 v Ni, W; 1906 v S, W, Ni (6)
Harrison, A. H. (Old Westminsters), 1893 v S, Ni (2)
Harrison, G. (Everton), 1921 v Bel; 1922 v Ni (2)
Harrow, J. H. (Chelsea), 1923 v Ni, Se (2)
Hart, E. (Leeds U), 1929 v W; 1930 v W, Ni; 1933 v S, A; 1934 v S, H, Cz (8)
Hartley, F. (Oxford C), 1923 v F (1)
Harvey, A. (Wednesbury Strollers), 1881 v W (1)
Harvey, J. C. (Everton), 1971 v Ma (1)
Hassall, H. W. (Huddersfield T), 1951 v S, Arg, P; 1952 v F; (with Bolton W), 1954 v Ni (5)
Haworth, G. (Accrington), 1887 v Ni, W, S; 1888 v S; 1890 v S (5)
Hawtrey, J. P. (Old Etonians), 1881 v S, W (2)
Hawkes, R. M. (Luton T), 1907 v Ni; 1908 v A (2), H, B (5)
Haygarth, E. B. (Swifts), 1875 v S (1)
Haynes, J. N. (Fulham), 1955 v Ni; 1956 v S, Ni, Br, Se, Fi, WG, Sp; 1957 v W, Y, D, Ei (2); 1958 v W, Ni, S, F, P, Y, USSR (3), Br, A; 1959 v S, Ni, USSR, I, Br, Pe, M, US; 1960 v Ni, Y, Sp, H; 1961 v Ni, W, S, L, P, Sp, M, I, A; 1962 v W, Ni, S, A, Sw, Pe, P, H, Arg, Bul, Br (56)
Healless, H. (Blackburn R), 1925 v Ni; 1928 v S (2)
Hector, K. J. (Derby Co), 1974 v Pol (sub), I (sub), (2)
Hedley, G. A. (Sheffield U), 1901 v Ni (1)
Hegan, K. E. (Corinthians), 1923 v Bel, F; 1924 v Ni, Bel (4)
Hellawell, M. S. (Birmingham C), 1963 v Ni, F (2)
Henfrey, A. G. (Cambridge University), 1891 v Ni; (with Corinthians), 1892 v W; 1895 v W; 1896 v S, W (5)
Henry, R. P. (Tottenham H), 1963 v F (1)
Heron, F. (Wanderers), 1876 v S (1)
Heron, G. H. H. (Uxbridge), 1873 v S; 1874 v S; (with Wanderers), 1875 v S; 1876 v S; 1878 v S (5)
Hibbert, W. (Bury), 1910 v S (1)
Hibbs, H. E. (Birmingham), 1930 v S, W, A, G; 1931 v S, W, Ni; 1932 v W, Ni, Sp; 1933 v S, W, Ni, A, I, Sw; 1934 v Ni, W, F; 1935 v S, W, Ni, Ho; 1936 v G, W (25)
Hill, F. (Bolton W), 1963 v Ni, W (2)
Hill, J. H. (Burnley), 1925 v W; 1926 v S; 1927 v S, Ni, Bel, F; 1928 v Ni, W; 1929 v F, Bel, Sp (11)
Hill, G. A. (Manchester U), 1976 v I; 1977 v Ei (sub), Fi (sub), L; 1978 v Sw (sub), L (6)
Hill, R. (Luton T), 1983 v D (sub), WG (2)
Hill, R. H. (Millwall), 1926 v Bel (1)
Hillman, J. (Burnley), 1899 v Ni (1)
Hills, A. F. (Old Harrovians), 1879 v S (1)
Hilsdon, G. R. (Chelsea), 1907 v Ni; 1908 v S, W, Ni, A, H, B; 1909 v Ni (8)
Hine, E. W. (Leicester C), 1929 v W, Ni; 1930 v W, Ni; 1932 v W, Ni (6)
Hinton, A. T. (Wolverhampton W), 1963 v F; (with Nottingham F), 1965 v W, Bel (3)
Hitchens, G. A. (Aston Villa), 1961 v M, I, A; (with Inter-Milan), 1962 v Sw, Pe, H, Br (7)
Hobbis, H. H. F. (Charlton Ath), 1936 v A, Bel (2)
Hoddle, G. (Tottenham H), 1980 v Bul, W, Aus, Sp; 1981 v Sp, W, S; 1982 v N, Ni, W, Ic, Cz (sub), K; 1983 v L (sub), Ni, S (16)
Hodgetts, D. (Aston Villa), 1888 v S, W, Ni; 1892 v S, Ni; 1894 v Ni (6)
Hodgkinson, A. (Sheffield U), 1957 v S, Ei (2), D; 1961 v W (5)
Hodgson, G. (Liverpool), 1931 v S, Ni, W (3)
Hodkinson, J. (Blackburn R), 1913 v W, S; 1920 v Ni (3)
Hogg, W. (Sunderland), 1902 v S, W, Ni (3)
Holdcroft, G. H. (Preston NE), 1937 v W, Ni (2)
Holden, A. D. (Bolton W), 1959 v S, I, Br, Pe, M (5)
Holden, G. H. (Wednesday OA), 1881 v S; 1884 v S, W, Ni (4)
Holden-White, C. (Corinthians), 1888 v W, S (2)
Holford, T. (Stoke), 1903 v Ni (1)
Holley, G. H. (Sunderland), 1909 v S, W, H (2), A; 1910 v W; 1912 v S, W, NI; 1913 v S (10)
Holliday, E. (Middlesbrough), 1960 v W, Ni, Se (3)
Hollins, J. W. (Chelsea), 1967 v Sp (1)
Holmes, R. (Preston NE), 1888 v Ni; 1891 v S; 1892 v S; 1893 v S, W; 1894 v Ni; 1895 v Ni (7)
Holt, J. (Everton), 1890 v W; 1891 v S, W; 1892 v S, Ni; 1893 v S; 1894 v S, Ni; 1895 v S; (with Reading), 1900 v Ni (10)
Hopkinson, E. (Bolton W), 1958 v W, Ni, S, F, P, Y; 1959 v S, I, Br, Pe, M, US; 1960 v W, Se (14)
Hossack, A. H. (Corinthians), 1892 v W; 1894 v W (2)
Houghton, W. E. (Aston Villa), 1931 v Ni, W, F, Bel; 1932 v S, Ni; 1933 v A (7)
Houlker, A. E. (Blackburn R), 1902 v S; (with Portsmouth), 1903 v S, W; (with Southampton), 1906 v W, Ni (5)
Howarth, R. H. (Preston NE), 1887 v Ni; 1888 v S, W; 1891 v S; (with Everton), 1894 v Ni (5)
Howe, D. (WBA), 1958 v S, W, Ni, F, P, Y, USSR (3), Br, A; 1959 v S, W, Ni, USSR, I, Br, Pe, M, US; 1960 v W, Ni, Se (23)
Howe, J. R. (Derby Co), 1948 v I; 1949 v S, Ni (3)
Howell, L. S. (Wanderers), 1873 v S (1)
Howell, R. (Sheffield U), 1895 v Ni; (with Liverpool) 1899 v S (2)
Hudson, A. A. (Stoke C), 1975 v WG, Cy (2)
Hudson, J. (Sheffield), 1883 v Ni (1)
Hudspeth, F. C. (Newcastle U), 1926 v Ni (1)
Hufton, A. E. (West Ham U), 1924 v Bel; 1928 v S, Ni; 1929 v F, Bel, Sp (6)
Hughes, E. W. (Liverpool), 1970 v W, Ni, S, Ho, P, Bel; 1971 v EG, Ma (2), Gr, W; 1972 v Sw, Gr, Wg (2), W, Ni, S; 1973 v W (3), S (2), Pol, USSR, I; 1974 v A, Pol, I, W, Ni, S, Arg, EG, Bul, Y; 1975 v Cz, P, Cy (sub), Ni; 1977 v I, L, W, S, Br, Arg, U; 1978 v Sw, L, I, WG, Ni, S, H; 1979 v D, Ei, Ni, W, Se; (with Wolverhampton W), 1980 v Sp (sub), Ni, S (sub) (62)
Hughes, L. (Liverpool), 1950 v Ch, US, Sp (3)
Hulme, J. H. A. (Arsenal), 1927 v S, Bel, F; 1928 v S, Ni, W; 1929 v Ni, W; 1933 v S (9)
Humphreys, P. (Notts Co), 1903 v S (1)
Hunt, G. S. (Tottenham H), 1933 v I, Sw, S (3)
Hunt, Rev K. R. G. (Leyton), 1911 v S, W (2)
Hunt, R. (Liverpool), 1962 v A; 1963 v EG; 1964 v S, US, P; 1965 v W; 1966 v S, Sp, Pol (2), WG (2), Fi, N, U, M, F, Arg, P; 1967 v Ni, W, Cz, Sp, A; 1968 v W, Ni, USSR (2), Sp (2), Se, Y; 1969 v R (2) (34)
Hunter, J. (Sheffield Heeley), 1878 v S; 1880 v S, W; 1881 v S, W; 1882 v S, W (7)
Hunter, N. (Leeds U), 1966 v WG, Y, Fi, Sp (sub); 1967 v A; 1968 v Sp, Se, Y, WG, USSR; 1969 v R, W; 1970 v Ho, WG (sub); 1971 v Ma; 1972 v WG (2), W, Ni, S; 1973 v W (2) USSR (sub); 1974 v A, Pol, Ni (sub), S; 1975 v Cz (28)
Hurst, G. C. (West Ham U), 1966 v S, WG (2), Y, Fi, D, Arg, P; 1967 v Ni, W, S, Cz, Sp, A; 1968 v W, Ni, S, Se (sub), WG, USSR (2); 1969 v Ni, S, R (2), Bul, F, M, U, Br; 1970 v W, Ni, S, Ho (1 + 1 sub), Bel, Co, Ec, R, Br, WG; 1971 v EG, Gr, W, S; 1972 v Sw (2), Gr, WG (49)

England first team coach Don Howe *West Brom* and *England*

Emlyn Hughes *Liverpool* and *England*

Iremonger, J. (Nottingham F), 1901 v S; 1902 v Ni (2)

Jack, D. N. B. (Bolton W), 1924 v S, W; 1928 v F, Bel; (with Arsenal), 1930 v S, G, A; 1933 v W, A (9)
Jackson, E. (Oxford University), 1891 v W (1)
Jarrett, B. G. (Cambridge University), 1876 v S; 1877 v S; 1878 v S (3)
Jefferis, F. (Everton), 1912 v S, W (2)
Jezzard, B. A. G. (Fulham), 1954 v H; 1956 v Ni (2)
Johnson, D. E. (Ipswich T), 1975 v W, S; 1976 v Sw; (with Liverpool), 1980 v Ei, Arg, Ni, S, Bel (8)
Johnson, E. (Saltley College), 1880 v W; (with Stoke C), 1884 v Ni (2)
Johnson, J. A. (Stoke C), 1937 v N, Se, Fi, S, Ni (5)
Johnson, T. C. F. (Manchester C), 1926 v Bel; 1930 v W; (with Everton), 1932 v S, Sp; 1933 v Ni (5)
Johnson, W. H. (Sheffield U), 1900 v S, W, Ni; 1903 v S, W, Ni (6)
Johnston, H. (Blackpool), 1947 v S, Ho; 1951 v S; 1953 v Arg, Ch, U, US; 1954 v W, Ni, H (10)
Jones, A. (Walsall Town Swifts), 1882 v S, W; (with Great Lever), 1883 v S (3)
Jones, H. (Blackburn R), 1927 v S, Bel, L, F; 1928 v S, Ni (6)
Jones, H. (Nottingham F), 1923 v F (1)
Jones, M. D. (Sheffield U), 1965 v WG, Se; (with Leeds U), 1970 v Ho (3)
Jones, W. (Bristol C), 1901 v Ni (1)
Jones, W. H. (Liverpool), 1950 v P, Bel (2)
Joy, B. (Casuals), 1936 v Bel (1)

Kail, E. I. L. (Dulwich Hamlet), 1929 v F, Bel, Sp (3)
Kay, A. H. (Everton), 1963 v Sw (1)
Kean, F. W. (Sheffield W), 1923 v S, Bel; 1924 v W; 1925 v Ni; 1926 v Ni, Bel; 1927 v L; (with Bolton W), 1929 v F, Sp (9)
Keegan, J. K. (Liverpool), 1973 v W (2); 1974 v W, Ni, Arg, EG, Bul, Y; 1975 v Cz, WG, Cy (2), Ni, S; 1976 v Sw, Cz, P, W (2), Ni, S, Br, Fi; 1977 v Ei, Fi, I, Ho, L; (with SV Hamburg), W, Br, Arg, U; 1978 v Sw, I, WG, Br, H; 1979 v D, Ei, Cz, Ni, W, S, Bul, Se, A; 1980 v D, Ni, Ei, Sp (2), Arg, Bel, I; (with Southampton), 1981 v Sp, Sw, H; 1982 v N, H, Ni, S, Fi, Sp (sub) (63)
Keen, E. R. L. (Derby Co), 1933 v A; 1937 v W, Ni, H (4)
Kelly, R. (Burnley), 1920 v S; 1921 v S, W, Ni; 1922 v S, W; 1923 v S; 1924 v Ni; 1925 v W, Ni, S; (with Sunderland), 1926 v W; (with Huddersfield T), 1927 v L; 1928 v S (14)
Kennedy, R. (Liverpool), 1976 v W (2), Ni, S; 1977 v L, W, S, Br (sub), Arg (sub); 1978 v Sw, L; 1980 v Bul, Sp, Arg, W, Bel (sub), I (17)
Kenyon-Slaney, W. S. (Wanderers), 1873 v S (1)
Kevan, D. T. (WBA), 1957 v S; 1958 v W, Ni, S, P. Y, USSR (3), Br, A; 1959 v M, US; 1961 v M (14)
Kidd, B. (Manchester U), 1970 v Ni, Ec (sub) (2)
King, R. S. (Oxford University), 1882 v Ni (1)
Kingsford, R. K. (Wanderers), 1874 v S (1)
Kingsley, M. (Newcastle U), 1901 v W (1)
Kinsey, G. (Wolverhampton W), 1892 v W; 1893 v S; (with Derby Co), 1896 v W, Ni (4)
Kirchen, A. J. (Arsenal), 1937 v N, Se, Fi (3)
Kirton, W. J. (Aston Villa), 1922 v Ni (1)
Knight, A. E. (Portsmouth), 1920 v Ni (1)
Knowles, C. (Tottenham H), 1968 v USSR, Sp, Se, WG (4)

Labone, B. L. (Everton), 1963 v Ni, W, F; 1967 v Sp, A; 1968 v S, Sp, Se, Y, USSR, Wg; 1969 v Ni, S, R, Bul, M, U, Br; 1970 v S, W, Bel, Co, Ec, R, Br, WG (26)
Lampard, F. R. G. (West Ham U), 1973 v Y; 1980 v Aus (2)
Langley, E. J. (Fulham), 1958 v S, P, Y (3)
Langton, R. (Blackburn R), 1947 v W, Ni, Ei, Ho, F, Sw; 1948 v Se; (with Preston NE), 1949 v D, Se; (with Bolton W), 1950 v S; 1951 v Ni (11)
Latchford, R. D. (Everton), 1978 v I, Br, W; 1979 v D, Ei, Cz (sub), Ni (2), W, S, Bul, A (12)
Latheron, E. G. (Blackburn R), 1913 v W; 1914 v Ni (2)
Lawler, C. (Liverpool), 1971 v Ma, W, S; 1972 v Sw (4)
Lawton, T. (Everton), 1939 v S, W, Ni, R of E, N, I, R, Y; (with Chelsea), 1947 v S, W, Ni, Ei, Ho, F, Sw, P; 1948 v W, Ni, Bel; (with Notts Co), 1948 v S, Se, I; 1949 v D (23)
Leach, T. (Sheffield W), 1931 v W, Ni (2)
Leake, A. (Aston Villa), 1904 v S, Ni; 1905 v S, W, Ni (5)
Lee, E. A. (Southampton), 1904 v W (1)
Lee, F. H. (Manchester C), 1969 v Ni, W, S, Bul, F, M, U; 1970 v W, Ho (2), P, Bel, Co, Ec, R, Br, WG; 1971 v EG, Gr, Ma, Ni, W, S; 1972 v Sw (2), Gr, WG (27)
Lee, J. (Derby Co), 1951 v Ni (1)
Lee, S. (Liverpool), 1983 v Gr, L, W, Gr, H, S, Aus (7)
Leighton, J. E. (Nottingham F), 1886 v Ni (1)
Lilley, H. E. (Sheffield U), 1892 v W (1)
Linacre, H. J. (Nottingham F), 1905 v W, S (2)
Lindley, T. (Cambridge University), 1886 v S, W, Ni, 1887 v S, W, Ni; 1888 v S, W, Ni; (with Nottingham F), 1889 v S; 1890 v S, W; 1891 v Ni (13)
Lindsay, A. (Liverpool), 1974 v Arg, EG, Bul, Y (4)
Lindsay, W. (Wanderers), 1877 v S (1)
Lintott, E. H. (QPR), 1908 v S, W, Ni; (with Bradford C), 1909 v S, Ni, H (2) (7)
Lipsham, H. B. (Sheffield U), 1902 v W (1)
Little, B. (Aston Villa), 1975 v W (sub) (1)
Lloyd, L. V. (Liverpool), 1971 v W; 1972 v Sw, Ni; (with Nottingham F), 1980 v W (4)
Lockett, A. (Stoke C), 1903 v Ni (1)
Lodge, L. V. (Cambridge University), 1894 v W; 1895 v S, W; (with Corinthians), 1896 v S, Ni (5)
Lofthouse, J. M. (Blackburn R), 1885 v S, W, Ni; 1887 v S, W; (with Accrington), 1889 v Ni; (with Blackburn R), 1890 v Ni (7)
Lofthouse, N. (Bolton W), 1951 v Y; 1952 v W, Ni, S, A (2), I, Sw; 1953 v W, Ni, S, Bel, Arg, Ch, U, US; 1954 v W, Ni, R of E, Bel, U; 1955 v Ni, S, F, Sp, P; 1956 v W, S, Sp, D, Fi (sub); 1959 v W, USSR (33)
Longworth, E. (Liverpool), 1920 v S; 1921 v Bel; 1923 v S, W, Bel (5)
Lowder, A. (Wolverhampton W), 1889 v W (1)
Lowe, E. (Aston Villa), 1947 v F, Sw, P (3)
Lucas, T. (Liverpool), 1922 v Ni; 1924 v F; 1926 v Bel (3)
Luntley, E. (Nottingham F), 1880 v S, W (2)
Lyttelton, Hon. A. (Cambridge University), 1877 v S (1)
Lyttelton, Hon. E. (Cambridge University), 1878 v S (1)

McCall, J. (Preston NE), 1913 v S, W; 1914 v S; 1920 v S; 1921 v Ni (5)
McDermott, T. (Liverpool), 1978 v Sw, L; 1979 v Ni, W, Se; 1980 v D, Ni (sub), Ei, Ni, S, Bel (sub), Sp; 1981 v N, R, Sw, R (sub), Br, Sw (sub), H; 1982 v N, H, W (sub), Ho, S (sub), Ic (25)
McDonald, C. A. (Burnley), 1958 v USSR (3), Br, A; 1959 v W, Ni, USSR (8)
McFarland, R. L. (Derby Co), 1971 v Gr, Ma (2), Ni, S; 1972 v Sw, Gr, WG, W, S; 1973 v W (3), Ni, S, Cz, Pol, USSR, I; 1974 v A, Pol, I, W, Ni; 1976 v Cz, S; 1977 v Ei, I (28)
McGarry, W. H. (Huddersfield T), 1954 v Sw, U; 1956 v W, D (4)
McGuinness, W. (Manchester U), 1959 v Ni, M (2)
McInroy, A. (Sunderland), 1927 v Ni (1)
McNab, R. (Arsenal), 1969 v Ni, Bul, R (1 + 1 sub) (4)
McNeal, R. (WBA), 1914 v S, W (2)

Tottenham Hotspur and *England* newcomer Gary Mabbutt

England international Terry McDermott flanked by Phil Thompson and Emlyn Hughes

England striker Malcolm Macdonald

The legendary Stanley Matthews *England*

McNeil, M. (Middlesbrough), 1961 v W, Ni, S, L, P, Sp, M, I; 1962 v L (9)
Mabbutt, G. (Tottenham H), 1983 v WG, Gr, L, W, Gr, H, Ni, S (sub) (8)
Macaulay, R. H. (Cambridge University), 1881 v S (1)
Macdonald, M. (Newcastle U), 1972 v W, Ni, S (sub); 1973 v USSR (sub); 1974 v P, S (sub), Y (sub); 1975 v WG, Cy (2), Ni; 1976 v Sw (sub), Cz, P (14)
Macrae, S. (Notts Co), 1883 v S, W, Ni; 1884 v S, W, Ni (6)
Maddison, F. B. (Oxford University), 1872 v S (1)
Madeley, P. E. (Leeds U), 1971 v Ni; 1972 v Sw (2), Gr, WG (2), W, S; 1973 v S, Cz, Pol, USSR, I; 1974 v A, Pol, I; 1975 v Cz, P, Cy; 1976 v Cz, P, Fi; 1977 v Ei, Ho (24)
Magee, T. P. (WBA), 1923 v W, Se; 1925 v S, Bel, F (5)
Makepeace, H. (Everton), 1906 v S; 1910 v S; 1912 v S, W (4)
Male, C. G. (Arsenal), 1935 v S, Ni, I, Ho; 1936 v S, W, Ni, G, A, Bel; 1937 v S, Ni, H, N, Se, Fi; 1939 v I, R, Y (19)
Mannion, W. J. (Middlesbrough), 1947 v S, W, Ni, Ei, Ho, F, Sw, P; 1948 v W, Ni, Bel, Se, I; 1949 v N, F; 1950 v S, Ei, P, Bel, Ch, US; 1951 v Ni, W, S, Y; 1952 v F (26)
Mariner, P. (Ipswich T), 1977 v L (sub), Ni; 1978 v L, W (sub), S; 1980 v W, Ni (sub), S, Aus, I (sub), Sp (sub); 1981 v N, Sw, Sp, Sw, H; 1982 v N, H, Ho, S, Fi, F, Cz, K, WG, Sp; 1983 v d, WG, Gr, W (30)
Marsden, J. T. (Darwen), 1891 v Ni (1)
Marsden, W. (Sheffield W), 1930 v W, S, G (3)
Marsh, R. W. (QPR), 1972 v Sw (sub); (with Manchester C), WG (sub + 1), W, Ni, S; 1973 v W (2), Y (9)
Marshall, T. (Darwen), 1880 v W; 1881 v W (2)
Martin, A. (West Ham U), 1981 v Br, S (sub); 1982 v H, Fi; 1983 v Gr, L, W, Gr, H (9)
Martin, H. (Sunderland), 1914 v Ni (1)
Maskrey, H. M. (Derby Co), 1908 v Ni (1)
Mason, C. (Wolverhampton W), 1887 v Ni; 1888 v W; 1890 v Ni (3)
Matthews, R. D. (Coventry C), 1956 v S, Br, Se, WG; 1957 v Ni (5)
Matthews, S. (Stoke C), 1935 v W, I; 1936 v G; 1937 v S; 1938 v S, W, Cz, G, Sw, F; 1939 v S, W, Ni, R of E, N, I, Y; 1947 v S; (with Blackpool), 1947 v Sw, P; 1948 v S, W, Ni, Bel, I; 1949 v S, W, Ni, D, Sw; 1950 v Sp; 1951 v Ni, S; 1954 v Ni, R of E, H, Bel, U; 1955 v Ni, W, S, F, WG, Sp, P; 1956 v W, Br; 1957 v S, W, Ni, Y, D (2) Ei (54)
Matthews, V. (Sheffield U), 1928 v F, Bel (2)
Maynard, W. J. (1st Surrey Rifles), 1872 v S; 1876 v S (2)
Meadows, J. (Manchester C), 1955 v S (1)
Medley, L. D. (Tottenham H), 1951 v Y, W; 1952 v F, A, W, Ni (6)
Meehan, T. (Chelsea), 1924 v Ni (1)
Melia, J. (Liverpool), 1963 v S, Sw (2)
Mercer, D. W. (Sheffield U), 1923 v Ni, Bel (2)
Mercer, J. (Everton), 1939 v S, Ni, I, R, Y (5)
Merrick, G. H. (Birmingham C), 1952 v Ni, S, A (2), I, Sw; 1953 v Ni, W, S, Bel, Arg, Ch, U; 1954 v W, Ni, S, R of E, H (2), Y, Bel, Sw, U (23)
Metcalfe V. (Huddersfield T), 1951 v Arg, P (2)
Mew, J. W. (Manchester U), 1921 v Ni (1)
Middleditch, B. (Corinthians), 1897 v Ni (1)
Milburn, J. E. T. (Newcastle U), 1949 v S, W, Ni, Sw; 1950 v W, P, Bel, Sp; 1951 v W, Arg, P; 1952 v F; 1956 v D (13)
Miller, B. G. (Burnley), 1961 v A (1)
Miller, H. S. (Charlton Ath), 1923 v Se (1)
Mills, G. R. (Chelsea), 1938 v W, Ni, Cz (3)
Mills, M. D. (Ipswich T), 1973 v Y; 1976 v W (2), Ni, S, Br, I (sub), Fi; 1977 v Fi (sub), I, Ni, W, S; 1978 v WG, Br, W, Ni, S, H; 1979 v D, Ei, Ni (2), S, Bul, A; 1980 v D, Ni, Sp (2); 1981 v Sw (2), H; 1982 v N, H, S, Fi, F, Cz, K, WG, Sp (42)
Milne, G. (Liverpool), 1963 v Br, Cz, EG; 1964 v W, Ni, S, R of W, U, P, Ei, Br, Arg; 1965 v Ni, Bel (14)
Milton, C. A. (Arsenal), 1952 v A (1)
Milward, A. (Everton), 1891 v S, W; 1897 v S, W (4)
Mitchell, C. (Upton Park), 1880 v W; 1881 v S; 1883 v S, W; 1885 v W (5)
Mitchell, J. F. (Manchester C), 1925 v Ni (1)
Moffat, H. (Oldham Ath), 1913 v W (1)
Molyneux, G. (Southampton), 1902 v S; 1903 v S, W, Ni (4)
Moon, W. R. (Old Westminsters), 1888 v S, W; 1889 v S, W; 1890 v S, W; 1891 v S (7)
Moore, H. T. (Notts Co), 1883 v Ni; 1885 v W (2)
Moore, J. (Derby Co), 1923 v Se (1)
Moore, R. F. (West Ham U), 1962 v Pe, H, Arg, Bul, Br; 1963 v W, Ni, S, F (2), Br, Cz, EG, Sw; 1964 v W, Ni, S, R of W, U, P (2), Ei, Br, Arg; 1965 v Ni, S, Bel, H, Y, WG, Se; 1966 v W, Ni, S, A, Sp, Pol (2), WG (2), N, D, U, M, F, Arg, P; 1967 v W, Ni, S, Cz, Sp, A; 1968 v W, Ni, S, USSR (2), Sp (2), Se, Y, WG; 1969 v Ni, W, S, R, Bul, F, M, U, Br; 1970 v W, Ni, S, Ho, P, Bel, Co, Ec, R, Br, Cz, WG; 1971 v EG, Gr, Ma, Ni, S; 1972 v Sw (2), Gr, WG (2), W, S; 1973 v W (3), Y, S (2), Ni, Cz, Pol, USSR, I; 1974 v I (108)
Moore, W. G. B. (West Ham U), 1923 v Se (1)
Mordue, J. (Sunderland), 1912 v Ni; 1913 v Ni (2)
Morice, C. J. (Barnes), 1872 v S (1)
Morley, A. (Aston Villa), 1982 v H (sub), Ni, W, Ic; 1983 v D, Gr (6)
Morley, H. (Notts Co), 1910 v Ni (1)
Morren, T. (Sheffield U), 1898 v Ni (1)
Morris, F. (WBA), 1920 v S; 1921 v Ni (2)
Morris, J. (Derby Co), 1949 v N, F; 1950 v Ei (3)
Morris, W. W. (Wolverhampton W), 1939 v S, Ni, R (3)
Morse, H. (Notts Co), 1879 v S (1)
Mort, T. (Aston Villa), 1924 v W, F; 1926 v S (3)
Morten, A. (C Palace), 1873 v S (1)
Mortensen, S. H. (Blackpool), 1947 v P; 1948 v W, S, Ni, Bel, Se, I; 1949 v S, W, Ni, Se, N; 1950 v S, W, Ni, I, P, Bel, Ch, US, Sp; 1951 v S, Arg; 1954 v R of E, H (25)
Morton, J. R. (West Ham U), 1938 v Cz (1)
Mosforth, W. (Sheffield W), 1877 v S; (with Sheffield Albion), 1878 v S; 1879 v S, W; 1880 v S, W; (with Sheffield W), 1881 v W; 1882 v S, W (9)
Moss, F. (Arsenal), 1934 v S, H, Cz; 1935 v I (4)
Moss, F. (Aston Villa), 1922 v S, Ni; 1923 v Ni; 1924 v S, Bel (5)
Mosscrop, E. (Burnley), 1914 v S, W (2)
Mozley, B. (Derby Co), 1950 v W, Ni, Ei (3)
Mullen, J. (Wolverhampton W), 1947 v S; 1949 v N, F; 1950 v Bel (sub), Ch, US; 1954 v W, Ni, S, R of E, Y, Sw (12)
Mullery, A. P. (Tottenham H), 1965 v Ho; 1967 v Sp, A; 1968 v W, Ni, S, USSR, Sp (2), Se, Y; 1969 v Ni, S, R, Bul, F, M, U, Br; 1970 v W, Ni, S (sub), Ho (sub), Bel, P, Co, Ec, R, Cz, WG, Br; 1971 v Ma, EG, Gr; 1972 v Sw (35)

Neal, P. G. (Liverpool), 1976 v W, I; 1977 v W, S, Br, Arg, U; 1978 v Sw, I, WG, Ni, S, H; 1979 v D, Ei, Ni (2), S, Bul, A; 1980 v D, Ni, Sp, Arg, W, Bel, I; 1981 v R, Sw, Sp, Br, H; 1982 v N, H, W, Ho, Ic, F (sub), K; 1983 v D, Gr, L, W, Gr, H, Ni, S, Aus (2) (49)
Needham, E. (Sheffield U), 1894 v S; 1895 v S; 1897 v S, W, Ni; 1898 v S, W; 1899 v S, W, Ni; 1900 v S, Ni; 1901 v S, W, Ni; 1902 v W (16)
Newton, K. R. (Blackburn R), 1966 v S, WG; 1967 v Sp, A; 1968 v W, S, Sp, Se, Y, WG; 1969 v Ni, W, S, R,

Bul, M, U, Br, F; (with Everton), 1970 v Ni, S, Ho, Co, Ec, R, Cz, WG (27)
Nicholls, J. (WBA), 1954 v S, Y (2)
Nicholson, W. E. (Tottenham H), 1951 v P (1)
Nish, D. J. (Derby Co), 1973 v Ni; 1974 v P, W, Ni, S (5)
Norman, M. (Tottenham H), 1962 v Pe, H, Arg, Bul, Br; 1963 v S, F, Br, Cz, EG; 1964 v W, Ni, S, R of W, U, P (2), US, Br, Arg; 1965 v Ni, Bel, Ho (23)
Nuttall, H. (Bolton W), 1928 v W, Ni; 1929 v S (3)

Oakley, W. J. (Oxford University), 1895 v W; 1896 v S, W, Ni; (with Corinthians), 1897 v S, W, Ni; 1898 v S, W, Ni; 1900 v S, W, Ni; 1901 v S, W, Ni (16)
O'Dowd, J. P. (Chelsea), 1932 v S; 1933 v Ni, Sw (3)
O'Grady, M. (Huddersfield T), 1963 v Ni; (with Leeds U), 1969 v F (2)
Ogilvie, R. A. M. M. (Clapham R), 1874 v S (1)
Oliver, L. F. (Fulham), 1929 v Bel (1)
Olney, B. A. (Aston Villa), 1928 v F, Bel (2)
Osborne, F. R. (Fulham), 1923 v Ni, F; (with Tottenham H), 1925 v Bel; 1926 v Bel (4)
Osborne, R. (Leicester C), 1928 v W (1)
Osgood, P. L. (Chelsea), 1970 v Bel, R (sub), Cz (sub), 1974 v I (4)
Osman, R. (Ipswich T), 1980 v Aus; 1981 v Sp, R, Sw; 1982 v N, Ic; 1983 v D, Aus (3) (10)
Ottaway, C. J. (Oxford University), 1872 v S; 1874 v S (2)
Owen, J. R. B. (Sheffield), 1874 v S (1)
Owen, S. W. (Luton T), 1954 v H, Y, Bel (3)

Page, L. A. (Burnley), 1927 v S, W, Bel, L, F; 1928 v W, Ni (7)
Paine, T. L. (Southampton), 1963 v Cz, EG; 1964 v W, Ni, S, R of W, U, US, P; 1965 v Ni, H, Y, WG, Se; 1966 v W, A, Y, N, M (19)
Pantling, H. H. (Sheffield U), 1924 v Ni (1)
Paravacini, P. J. de (Cambridge University), 1883 v S, W, Ni (3)
Parker, T. R. (Southampton), 1925 v F (1)
Parkes, P. B. (QPR), 1974 v P (1)
Parkinson, J. (Liverpool), 1910 v S, W (2)
Parr, P. C. (Oxford University), 1882 v W (1)
Parry, E. H. (Old Carthusians), 1879 v W; 1882 v W, S (3)
Parry, R. A. (Bolton W), 1960 v Ni, S (2)
Patchitt, B. C. A. (Corinthians), 1923 v Se (2)
Pawson, F. W. (Cambridge University), 1883 v Ni; (with Swifts), 1885 v Ni (2)
Payne, J. (Luton T), 1937 v Fi (1)
Peacock, A. (Middlesbrough), 1962 v Arg, Bul; 1963 v Ni, W; (with Leeds U), 1966 v W, Ni (6)
Peacock, J. (Middlesbrough), 1929 v F, Bel, Sp (3)
Pearson, H. F. (WBA), 1932 v S (1)
Pearson, J. H. (Crewe Alex), 1892 v Ni (1)
Pearson, J. S. (Manchester U), 1976 v W, Ni, S, Br, Fi; 1977 v Ei, Ho (sub), W, S, Br, Arg, U; 1978 v I (sub), WG, Ni (15)
Pearson, S. C. (Manchester U), 1948 v S; 1949 v S, Ni; 1950 v Ni, I; 1951 v P; 1952 v S, I (8)
Pease, W. H. (Middlesbrough), 1927 v W (1)
Pegg, D. (Manchester U), 1957 v Ei (1)
Pejic, M. (Stoke C), 1974 v P, W, Ni, S (4)
Pelly, F. R. (Old Foresters), 1893 v Ni; 1894 v S, W (3)
Pennington, J. (WBA), 1907 v S, W; 1908 v S, W, Ni, A; 1909 v S, W, H (2), A; 1910 v S, W; 1911 v S, W, Ni; 1912 v S, W, Ni; 1913 v S, W; 1914 v S, Ni; 1920 v S, W (25)
Pentland, F. B. (Middlesbrough), 1909 v S, W, H (2), A (5)
Perry, C. (WBA), 1890 v Ni; 1891 v Ni; 1893 v W (3)
Perry, T. (WBA), 1898 v W (1)
Perry, W. (Blackpool), 1956 v Ni, S, Sp (3)
Perryman, S. (Tottenham H), 1982 v Ic (sub) (1)
Peters, M. (West Ham U), 1966 v Y, Fi, Pol, M, F, Arg, P, WG; 1967 v Ni, W, S, Cz; 1968 v W, Ni, S, USSR (2), Sp (2), Se, Y; 1969 v Ni, S, R, Bul, F, M, U, Br; 1970 v Ho (2), P (sub), Bel; (with Tottenham H), W, Ni, S, Co, Ec, R, Br, Cz, WG; 1971 v EG, Gr, Ma (2), Ni, W, S; 1972 v Sw, Gr, WG (1 + 1 sub) Ni (sub) 1973 v S (2), Ni, W, Cz, Pol, USSR, I; 1974 v A, Pol, I, P, S (67)
Phillips, L. H. (Portsmouth), 1952 v Ni; 1955 v W, WG (3)
Pickering, F. (Everton), 1964 v US; 1965 v Ni, Bel (3)
Pickering, W. (Sunderland), 1983 v Aus (1)
Pickering, J. (Sheffield U), 1933 v S (1)
Pike, T. M. (Cambridge University), 1886 v Ni (1)
Pilkington, B. (Burnley), 1955 v Ni (1)
Plant, J. (Bury), 1900 v S (1)
Plum, S. L. (Charlton Ath), 1923 v F (1)
Pointer, R. (Burnley), 1962 v W, L, P (3)
Porteous, T. S. (Sunderland), 1891 v W (1)
Priest, A. E. (Sheffield U), 1900 v Ni (1)
Prinsep, J. F. M. (Clapham Rovers), 1879 v S (1)
Puddefoot, S. C. (Blackburn R), 1926 v S, Ni (2)
Pye, J. (Wolverhampton W), 1950 v Ei (1)
Pym, R. H. (Bolton W), 1925 v S, W; 1926 v W (3)

Quantrill, A. (Derby Co), 1920 v S, W; 1921 v W, Ni (4)
Quixall, A. (Sheffield W), 1954 v W, Ni, R of E; 1955 v Sp, P (sub) (5)

Radford, J. (Arsenal), 1969 v R; 1972 v Sw (sub) (2)
Raikes, G. B. (Oxford University), 1895 v W; 1896 v W, Ni, S (4)
Ramsey, A. E. (Southampton), 1949 v Sw; (with Tottenham H), 1950 v S, I, P, Bel, Ch, US, Sp; 1951 v S, Ni, W, Y, Arg, P; 1952 v S, W, Ni, F, A (2), I, Sw; 1953 v Ni, W, S, Bel, Arg, Ch, U, US; 1954 v R of E, H (32)
Rawlings, A. (Preston NE), 1921 v Bel (1)
Rawlings, W. E. (Southampton), 1922 v S, W (2)
Rawlinson, J. F. P. (Cambridge University), 1882 v Ni (1)
Rawson, H. E. (Royal Engineers), 1875 v S (1)
Rawson, W. S. (Oxford University), 1875 v S; 1877 v S (2)
Read, A. (Tufnell Park), 1921 v Bel (1)
Reader, J. (WBA), 1894 v Ni (1)
Reaney, P. (Leeds U), 1969 v Bul (sub); 1970 v P; 1971 v Ma (3)
Reeves, K. (Norwich C), 1980 v Bul; (with Manchester C), Ni (2)
Regis, C. (WBA), 1982 v Ni (sub), W (sub), Ic; 1983 v WG (4)
Revie, D. G. (Manchester C), 1955 v Ni, S, F; 1956 v W, D; 1957 v Ni (6)
Reynolds, J. (WBA), 1892 v S; 1893 v S, W; (with Aston Villa), 1894 v S, Ni; 1895 v S; 1897 v S, W (8)
Richards, C. H. (Nottingham F), 1898 v Ni (1)
Richards, G. H. (Derby Co), 1909 v A (1)
Richards, J. P. (Wolverhampton W), 1973 v Ni (1)
Richardson, J. R. (Newcastle U), 1933 v I, Sw (2)
Richardson, W. G. (WBA), 1935 v Ho (1)
Rickaby, S, (WBA), 1954 v Ni (1)
Rigby, A. (Blackburn R), 1927 v S, Bel, L, F; 1928 v W (5)
Rimmer, E. J. (Sheffield W), 1930 v S, G, A; 1932 v Sp (4)
Rimmer, J. J. (Arsenal), 1976 v I (1)
Rix, G. (Arsenal), 1981 v N, R, Sw (sub), Br, W, S; 1982 v Ho (sub), Fi (sub), F, Cz, K, WG, Sp; 1983 v D, WG (sub) (15)
Robb, G. (Tottenham H), 1954 v H (1)
Roberts, C. (Manchester U), 1905 v Ni, W, S (3)
Roberts, F. (Manchester C), 1925 v S, W, Bel, F (4)
Roberts, G. (Tottenham Hotspur), 1983 v Ni, S (2)

Martin Peters, one of England's 1966 World Cup heroes

Cyrille Regis *West Brom* and *England* centre-forward

Tottenham Hotspur and *England*'s Graham Roberts

Roberts, H. (Arsenal), 1931 v S (1)
Roberts, H. (Millwall), 1931 v Bel (1)
Roberts, R. (WBA), 1887 v S; 1888 v Ni; 1890 v Ni (3)
Roberts, W. T. (Preston NE), 1924 v W, Bel (2)
Robinson, J. (Sheffield W), 1937 v Fi; 1938 v G, Sw; 1939 v W (4)
Robinson, J. W. (Derby Co), 1897 v S, Ni; (with New Brighton Tower), 1898 v S, W, Ni; (with Southampton), 1899 v W, S; 1900 v S, W, Ni; 1901 v Ni (11)
Robson, B. (WBA), 1980 v Ei, Aus; 1981 v N, R, Sw, Sp, R, Br, W, S, Sw, H; 1982 v N (with Manchester U), H, Ni, W, Ho, S, Fi, F, Cz, WG, Sp; 1983 v D, Gr, L, S (27)
Robson, R. (WBA), 1958 v F, USSR (2), Br, A; 1960 v Sp, H; 1961 v Ni, W, S, L, P, Sp, M, I; 1962 v W, Ni, Sw, L, P (20)
Rose, W. C. (Wolverhampton W), 1884 v S, W, Ni; (with Preston NE), 1886 v Ni; (with Wolverhampton W), 1891 v Ni (5)
Rostron, T. (Darwen), 1881 v S, W (2)
Rowe, A. (Tottenham H), 1934 v F (1)
Rowley, J. F. (Manchester U), 1949 v Sw, Se, F; 1950 v Ni, I; 1952 v S (6)
Rowley, W. (Stoke C), 1889 v Ni; 1892 v Ni (2)
Royle, J. (Everton), 1971 v Ma; 1973 v Y; (with Manchester C), 1976 v Ni (sub), I; 1977 v Fi, L (6)
Ruddlesdin, H. (Sheffield W), 1904 v W, Ni; 1905 v S (3)
Ruffell, J. W. (West Ham U), 1926 v S; 1927 v Ni; 1929 v S, W, Ni; 1930 v W (6)
Russell, B. B. (Royal Engineers), 1883 v W (1)
Rutherford, J. (Newcastle U), 1904 v S; 1907 v S, Ni, W; 1908 v S, Ni, W, A (2), H, B (11)

Sadler, D. (Manchester U), 1968 v Ni, USSR; 1970 v Ec (sub); 1971 v EG (4)
Sagar, C. (Bury), 1900 v Ni; 1902 v W (2)
Sagar, E. (Everton), 1936 v S, Ni, A, Bel (4)
Sandford, E. A. (WBA), 1933 v W (1)
Sandilands, R. R. (Old Westminsters), 1892 v W; 1893 v Ni; 1894 v W; 1895 v W; 1896 v W (5)
Sands, J. (Nottingham F), 1880 v W (1)
Sansom, K. (C Palace), 1979 v W; 1980 v Bul, Ei, Arg, W (sub), Ni, S, Bel, I; (with Arsenal), 1981 v N, R, Sw, Sp, R, Br, W, S, Sw; 1982 v Ni, W, Ho, S, Fi, F, Cz, WG, Sp; 1983 v D, WG, Gr, L, Gr, H, Ni, S (35)
Saunders, F. E. (Swifts), 1888 v W (1)
Savage, A. H. (C Palace), 1876 v S (1)
Sayer, J. (Stoke C), 1887 v Ni (1)
Scattergood, E. (Derby Co), 1913 v W (1)
Schofield, J. (Stoke C), 1892 v W; 1893 v W; 1895 v Ni (3)
Scott, L. (Arsenal), 1947 v S, W, Ni, Ei, Ho, F, Sw, P; 1948 v S, W, Ni, Bel, Se, I; 1949 v W, Ni, D (17)
Scott, W. R. (Brentford), 1937 v W (1)
Seddon, J. (Bolton W), 1923 v F, Se (2); 1924 v Bel; 1927 v W; 1929 v S (6)
Seed, J. M. (Tottenham H), 1921 v Bel: 1923 v W, Ni, Bel; 1925 v S (5)
Settle, J. (Bury), 1899 v S, W, Ni; (with Everton), 1902 v S, Ni; 1903 v Ni (6)
Sewell, J. (Sheffield W), 1952 v Ni, A, Sw; 1953 v Ni; 1954 v H (2) (6)
Sewell, W. R. (Blackburn R), 1924 v W (1)
Shackleton, L. F. (Sunderland), 1949 v W, D; 1950 v W; 1955 v W, WG (5)
Sharp, J. (Everton), 1903 v Ni; 1905 v S (2)
Shaw, G. E. (WBA), 1932 v S (1)
Shaw, G. L. (Sheffield U), 1959 v S, W, USSR, I; 1963 v W (5)
Shea, D. (Blackburn R), 1914 v W, Ni (2)
Shellito, K. J. (Chelsea), 1963 v Cz (1)
Shelton A. (Notts Co), 1889 v Ni; 1890 v S, W; 1891 v S, W; 1892 v S (6)
Shelton, C. (Notts Rangers), 1888 v Ni (1)
Shepherd, A. (Bolton W), 1906 v S; (with Newcastle U), 1911 v Ni (2)
Shilton, P. L. (Leicester C), 1971 v EG, W; 1972 v Sw, Ni; 1973 v Y, S (2), Ni, W, Cz, Pol, USSR, I; 1974 v A, Pol, I, W, Ni, S, Arg; (with Stoke C), 1975 v Cy; 1977 v Ni, W; (with Nottingham F), 1978 v W, H; 1979 v Cz, Se, A; 1980 v Ni, Sp, I; 1981 v N, Sw, R; 1982 v H, Ho, S, F, Cz, K, WG, Sp; (with Southampton), 1983 v D, WG, Gr, H, Ni, S, Aus (3) (53)
Shimwell, E. (Blackpool), 1949 v Se (1)
Shutt, G. (Stoke C), 1886 v Ni (1)
Silcock, J. (Manchester U), 1921 v S, W; 1923 v Se (3)
Sillett, R. P. (Chelsea), 1955 v F, Sp, P (3)
Simms, E. (Luton T), 1922 v Ni (1)
Simpson, J. (Blackburn R), 1911 v S, W, Ni; 1912 v S, W, Ni; 1913 v S; 1914 v W (8)
Slater, W. J. (Wolverhampton W), 1955 v W, WG; 1958 v S, P, Y, USSR (3), Br, A; 1959 v USSR; 1960 v S (12)
Smalley, T. (Wolverhampton W), 1937 v W (1)
Smart, T. (Aston Villa), 1921 v S; 1924 v S, W; 1926 v Ni; 1930 v W (5)
Smith, A. (Nottingham F), 1891 v S, W; 1893 v Ni (3)
Smith, A. K. (Oxford University), 1872 v S (1)
Smith, B. (Tottenham H), 1921 v S; 1922 v W (2)
Smith, C. E. (C Palace), 1876 v S (1)
Smith, G. O. (Oxford University), 1893 v Ni; 1894 v W, S; 1895 v W; 1896 v Ni, W, S; (with Old Carthusians), 1897 v Ni, W, S; 1898 v Ni, W, S; (with Corinthians), 1899 v Ni, W, S; 1899 v Ni, W, S; 1901 v S (20)
Smith, H. (Reading), 1905 v W, S; 1906 v W, Ni (4)
Smith, J. (WBA), 1920 v Ni; 1923 v Ni (2)
Smith, Joe (Bolton W), 1913 v Ni; 1914 v S, W; 1920 v W, Ni (5)
Smith, J. C. R. (Millwall), 1939 v Ni, N (2)
Smith, J. W. (Portsmouth), 1932 v Ni, W, Sp (3)
Smith, Leslie (Brentford), 1939 v R (1)
Smith, Lionel (Arsenal), 1951 v W; 1952 v W, Ni; 1953 v W, S, Bel (6)
Smith, R. A. (Tottenham H), 1961 v Ni, W, S, L, P, Sp; 1962 v S; 1963 v S, F, Br, Cz, EG; 1964 v W, Ni, R of W (15)
Smith, S. (Aston Villa), 1895 v S (1)
Smith, S. C. (Leicester C), 1936 v Ni (1)
Smith, T. (Birmingham C), 1960 v W, Se (2)
Smith, T. (Liverpool), 1971 v W (1)
Smith, W. H. (Huddersfield T), 1922 v W, S; 1928 v S (3)
Sorby, T. H. (Thursday Wanderers, Sheffield), 1879 v W (1)
Southworth, J. (Blackburn R), 1889 v W; 1891 v W; 1892 v S (3)
Sparks, F. J. (Herts Rangers), 1879 v S; (with Clapham Rovers), 1880 v S, W (3)
Spence, J. W. (Manchester U), 1926 v Bel; 1927 v Ni (2)
Spence, R. (Chelsea), 1936 v A, Bel (2)
Spencer, C. W. (Newcastle U), 1924 v S; 1925 v W (2)
Spencer, H. (Aston Villa), 1897 v S, W; 1900 v W; 1903 v Ni; 1905 v W, S (6)
Spiksley, F. (Sheffield W), 1893 v S, W; 1894 v S, Ni; 1896 v Ni; 1898 v S, W (7)
Spilsbury, B. W. (Cambridge University), 1885 v Ni; 1886 v Ni, S (3)
Spink, N. (Aston Villa), 1983 v Aus (sub) (1)
Spouncer, W. A. (Nottingham F), 1900 v W (1)
Springett, R. D. G. (Sheffield W), 1960 v Ni, S, Y, Sp, H; 1961 v Ni, S, L, P, Sp, M, I, A; 1962 v W, Ni, S, A, Sw, Pe, L, P, H, Arg, Bul, Br; 1963 v Ni, W, F (2), Sw; 1966 v W, A, N (33)
Sproston, B. (Leeds U), 1937 v W; 1938 v S, W, Ni, Cz, G, Sw, F; (with Tottenham H), 1939 v W, R of E; (with Manchester C), N (11)
Squire, R. T. (Cambridge University), 1886 v S, W, Ni (3)

Kenny Sansom *Arsenal* and *England*

Derek Statham *West Brom* and *England*

Frank Swift *Manchester City* and *England*

Stanbrough, M. H. (Old Carthusians), 1895 v W (1)
Staniforth, R. (Huddersfield T), 1954 v S, H, Y, Bel, Sw, U; 1955 v W, WG (8)
Starling, R. W. (Sheffield W), 1933 v S; (with Aston Villa), 1937 v S (2)
Statham, D. (WBA), 1983 v W, Aus (2) (3)
Steele, F. C. (Stoke C), 1937 v S, W, Ni, N, Se, Fi (6)
Stephenson, C. (Huddersfield T), 1924 v W (1)
Stephenson, G. T. (Derby Co), 1928 v F, Bel; (with Sheffield W), 1931 v F (3)
Stephenson, J. E. (Leeds U), 1938 v S; 1939 v Ni (2)
Stepney, A. C. (Manchester U), 1968 v Se (1)
Stewart, J. (Sheffield W), 1907 v S, W; (with Newcastle U), 1911 v S (3)
Stiles, N. P. (Manchester U), 1965 v S, H, Y, Se; 1966 v W, Ni, S, A, Sp, Pol (2), WG (2), N, D, U, M, F, Arg, P; 1967 v Ni, W, S, Cz; 1968 v USSR; 1969 v R; 1970 v Ni, S (28)
Stoker, J. (Birmingham), 1933 v W; 1934 v S, H (3)
Storer, H. (Derby Co), 1924 v F; 1928 v Ni (2)
Storey, P. E. (Arsenal), 1971 v Gr, Ni, S; 1972 v Sw, WG, W, Ni, S; 1973 v W (3), Y, S (2), Ni, Cz, Pol, USSR, I (19)
Storey-Moore, I. (Nottingham F), 1970 v Ho (1)
Strange, A. H. (Sheffield W), 1930 v S, A, G; 1931 v S, W, Ni, F, Bel; 1932 v S, W, Ni, Sp; 1933 v S, Ni, A, I, Sw; 1934 v Ni, W, F (20)
Stratford, A. H. (Wanderers), 1874 v S (1)
Streten, B. (Luton T), 1950 v Ni (1)
Sturgess, A. (Sheffield U), 1911 v Ni; 1914 v S (2)
Summerbee, M. G. (Manchester C), 1968 v S, Sp, WG; 1972 v Sw, WG (sub), W, Ni; 1973 v USSR (sub) (8)
Sunderland, A. (Arsenal), 1980 v Aus (1)
Sutcliffe, J. W. (Bolton W), 1893 v W; 1895 v S, Ni; 1901 v S; (with Millwall), 1903 v W (5)
Swan, P. (Sheffield W), 1960 v Y, Sp, H; 1961 v Ni, W, S, L, P, Sp, M, I, A; 1962 v W, Ni, S, A, Sw, L, P (19)
Swepstone, H. A. (Pilgrims), 1880 v S; 1882 v S, W; 1883 v S, W, Ni (6)
Swift, F. V. (Manchester C), 1947, v S, W, Ni, Ei, Ho, F, Sw, P; 1948 v S, W, Ni, Bel, Se, I; 1949 v S, W, Ni, D, N (19)

Tait, G. (Birmingham Excelsior), 1881 v W (1)
Talbot, B. (Ipswich T), 1977 v Ni (sub), S, Br, Arg, U; (with Arsenal), 1980 v Aus (6)
Tambling, R. V. (Chelsea), 1963 v W, F; 1966 v Y (3)
Tate, J. T. (Aston Villa), 1931 v F, Bel; 1933 v W (3)
Taylor, E. (Blackpool), 1954 v H (1)
Taylor, E. H. (Huddersfield T), 1923 v S, W, Ni, Bel; 1924 v S, Ni, F; 1926 v S (8)
Taylor, J. G. (Fulham), 1951 v Arg, P (2)
Taylor, P. J. (C Palace), 1976 v W (sub), W, Ni, S (4)
Taylor, P. H. (Liverpool), 1948 v W, Ni, Se (3)
Taylor, T. (Manchester U), 1953 v Arg, Ch, U; 1954 v Bel, Sw; 1956 v S, Br, Se, Fi, WG; 1957 v Ni, Y (sub), D (2), Ei (2); 1958 v W, Ni, F (19)
Temple, D. W. (Everton), 1965 v WG (1)
Thickett, H. (Sheffield U), 1899 v S, W (2)
Thomas, D. (Coventry C), 1983 v Aus (1+1 sub) (2)
Thomas, D. (QPR), 1975 v Cz (sub), P, Cy (sub + 1), W, S (sub); 1976 v Cz (sub), P (sub) (8)
Thompson, P. (Liverpool), 1964 v P (2), Ei, US, Br, Arg; 1965 v Ni, W, S, Bel, Ho; 1966 v Ni; 1968 v Ni, WG; 1970 v S, Ho (sub) (16)
Thompson, P. B. (Liverpool), 1976 v W (2), Ni, S, Br, I, Fi; 1977 v Fi; 1979 v Ei (sub), Cz, Ni, S, Bul, Se (sub), A; 1980 v D, Ni, Bul, Ei, Sp (2), Arg, W, S, Bel, I; 1981 v N, R, H; 1982 v N, H, W, Ho, S, Fi, F, Cz, K, WG, Sp; 1983 v WG, Gr (42)
Thompson, T. (Aston Villa), 1952 v W; (with Preston NE), 1957 v S (2)
Thomson, R. A. (Wolverhampton W), 1964 v Ni, US, P, Arg; 1965 v Bel, Ho, Ni, W (8)
Thornewell, G. (Derby Co), 1923 v Se (2); 1924 v F; 1925 v F (4)
Thornley, I. (Manchester C), 1907 v W (1)
Tilson, S. F. (Manchester C), 1934 v H, Cz; 1935 v W; 1936 v Ni (4)
Titmuss, F. (Southampton), 1922 v W; 1923 v W (2)
Todd, C. (Derby Co), 1972 v Ni; 1974 v P, W, Ni, S, Arg, EG, Bul, Y; 1975 v P (sub), WG, Cy (2), Ni, W, S; 1976 v Sw, Cz, P, Ni, S, Br, Fi; 1977 v Ei, Fi, Ho (sub), Ni (27)
Toone, G. (Notts Co), 1892 v S, W (2)
Topham, A. G. (Casuals), 1894 v W (1)
Topham, R. (Wolverhampton W), 1893 v Ni; (with Casuals) 1894 v W (2)
Towers, M. A. (Sunderland), 1976 v W, Ni (sub), I (3)
Townley, W. J. (Blackburn R), 1889 v W; 1890 v Ni (2)
Townrow, J. E. (Clapton Orient), 1925 v S; 1926 v W (2)
Tremelling, D. R. (Birmingham), 1928 v W (1)
Tresadern, J. (West Ham U), 1923 v S, Se (2)
Tueart, D. (Manchester C), 1975 v Cy (sub), Ni; 1977 v Fi, Ni, W (sub), S (sub) (6)
Tunstall, F. E. (Sheffield U), 1923 v S; 1924 v S, W, Ni, F; 1925 v Ni, S (7)
Turnbull, R. J. (Bradford), 1920 v Ni (1)
Turner, A. (Southampton), 1900 v Ni; 1901 v Ni (2)
Turner, H. (Huddersfield T), 1931 v F, Bel (2)
Turner, J. A. (Bolton W), 1893 v W; (with Stoke C) 1895 v Ni; (with Derby Co) 1898 v Ni (3)
Tweedy, G. J. (Grimsby T), 1937 v H (1)

Ufton, D. G. (Charlton Ath), 1954 v R of E (1)
Underwood A. (Stoke C), 1891 v Ni; 1892 v Ni (2)
Urwin, T. (Middlesbrough), 1923 v Se (2); (with Newcastle U) 1924 v Bel; 1926 v W (4)
Utley, G. (Barnsley), 1913 v Ni (1)

Vaughton, O. H. (Aston Villa), 1882 v S, W, Ni; 1884 v S, W (5)
Veitch, C. C. M. (Newcastle U), 1906 v S, W, Ni; 1907 v S, W; 1909 v W (6)
Veitch, J. G. (Old Westminsters), 1894 v W (1)
Venables, T. F. (Chelsea), 1965 v Ho, Bel (2)
Vidal, R. W. S. (Oxford University), 1873 v S (1)
Viljoen, C. (Ipswich T), 1975 v Ni, W (2)
Viollet, D. S. (Manchester U), 1960 v H; 1962 v L (2)
Von Donop (Royal Engineers), 1873 v S; 1875 v S (2)

Wace, H. (Wanderers), 1878 v S; 1879 v S, W (3)
Wadsworth, S. J. (Huddersfield T), 1922 v S; 1923 v S, Bel; 1924 v S, Ni; 1925 v S, Ni; 1926 v W; 1927 v Ni (9)
Wainscoat, W. R. (Leeds U), 1929 v S (1)
Waiters, A. K. (Blackpool), 1964 v Ei, Br; 1965 v W, Bel, Ho (5)
Walden, F. I. (Tottenham H), 1914 v S; 1922 v W (2)
Walker, W. H. (Aston Villa), 1921 v Ni; 1922 v Ni, W, S; 1923 v Se (2); 1924 v S; 1925 v Ni, W, S, Bel, F; 1926 v Ni, W, S; 1927 v Ni, W; 1933 v A (18)
Wall, G. (Manchester U), 1907 v W; 1908 v Ni; 1909 v S; 1910 v W, S; 1912 v S; 1913 v Ni (7)
Wallace, C. W. (Aston Villa), 1913 v W; 1914 v Ni; 1920 v S (3)
Walsh, P. (Luton T), 1983 v Aus (2+1 sub) (3)
Walters, A. M. (Cambridge University), 1885 v S, N; 1886 v S; 1887 v S, W; (with Old Carthusians) 1889 v S, W; 1890 v S, W (9)
Walters, P. M. (Oxford University), 1885 v S, Ni; (with Old Carthusians), 1886 v S, W, Ni; 1887 v S, W; 1888 v S, Ni; 1889 v S, W; 1890 v S, W (13)
Walton, N. (Blackburn R) 1890 v Ni (1)
Ward, J. T. (Blackburn Olympic), 1885 v W (1)

Ward, P. (Brighton & HA), 1980 v Aus (sub) (1)
Ward, T. V. (Derby Co), 1948 v Bel; 1949 v W (2)
Waring, T. (Aston Villa), 1931 v F, Bel; 1932 v S, W, Ni (5)
Warner, C. (Upton Park), 1878 v S (1)
Warren, B. (Derby Co), 1906 v S, W, Ni; 1907 v S, W, Ni; 1908 v S, W, Ni, A (2), H, B; 1909 v S, Ni, W, H (2), A; 1911 v S, Ni, W (22)
Waterfield, G. S. (Burnley), 1927 v W (1)
Watson, D. V. (Sunderland), 1974 v P, S (sub), Arg, EG, Bul, Y; 1975 v Cz, P, WG, Cy (2), Ni, W, S; (with Manchester C) 1976 v Sw, Cz (sub), P; 1977 v Ho, L, Ni, W, S, Br, Arg, U; 1978 v Sw, L, I, WG, Br, W, Ni, S, H; 1979 v D, Ei, Cz, Ni (2), W, S, Bul, Se, A; (with Werder Bremen), 1980 v D; (with Southampton) Ni, Bul, Ei, Sp (2), Arg, Ni, S, Bel, I; 1981 v N, R, Sw, R, W, S, Sw, H; (with Stoke C), 1982 v Ni, Ic (65)
Watson, V. M. (West Ham U), 1923 v W, S; 1930 v S, G, A (5)
Watson, W. (Burnley), 1913 v S; 1914 v Ni; 1920 v Ni (3)
Watson, W. (Sunderland), 1950 v Ni, I; 1951 v W, Y (4)
Weaver, S. (Newcastle U), 1932 v S, 1933 v S, Ni (3)
Webb, G. W. (West Ham U), 1911 v S, W (2)
Webster, M. (Middlesbrough), 1930 v S, A, G (3)
Wedlock, W. J. (Bristol C), 1907 v S, Ni, W; 1908 v S, Ni, W, A (2), H, B; 1909 v S, W, Ni, H (2), A; 1910 v S, W, Ni; 1911 v S, W, Ni; 1912 v S, W, Ni; 1914 v W (26)
Weir, D. (Bolton W), 1889 v S, Ni (2)
Welch, R. de C. (Wanderers), 1872 v S; (with Harrow Chequers) 1874 v S (2)
Weller, K. (Leicester C), 1974 v W, Ni, S, Arg (4)
Welsh, D. (Charlton Ath), 1938 v G, Sw; 1939 v R (3)
West, G. (Everton), 1969 v W, Bul, M (3)
Westwood, R. W. (Bolton W), 1935 v S, W, Ho; 1936 v Ni, G; 1937 v W (6)
Whateley, O. (Aston Villa), 1883 v S, Ni (2)
Wheeler, J. E. (Bolton W), 1955 v Ni (1)
Wheldon, G. F. (Aston Villa), 1897 v Ni; 1898 v S, W, Ni (4)
White, T. A. (Everton), 1933 v I (1)
Whitehead, J. (Accrington), 1893 v W; (with Blackburn R) 1894 v Ni (2)
Whitfeld, H. (Old Etonians), 1879 v W (1)
Whitham, M. (Sheffield U), 1892 v Ni (1)
Whitworth, S. (Leicester C), 1975 v WG, Cy, Ni, W, S; 1976 v Sw, P (7)
Whymark, T. J. (Ipswich T), 1978 v L (sub) (1)
Widdowson, S. W. (Nottingham F), 1880 v S (1)
Wignall, F. (Nottingham F), 1965 v W, Ho (2)
Wilkes, A. (Aston Villa), 1901 v S, W; 1902 v S, W, Ni (5)
Wilkins, R. G. (Chelsea), 1976 v I; 1977 v Ei, Fi, Ni, Br, Arg, U; 1978 v Sw (sub), L, I, WG, W, Ni, S, H; 1979 v D, Ei, Cz, Ni, W, S, Bul, Se (sub), A; (with Manchester U) 1980 v D, Ni, Bul, Sp (2), Arg, W (sub), Ni, S, Bel, I; 1981 v Sp (sub), R, Br, W, S, Sw, H (sub); 1982 v Ni, W, Ho, S, Fi, F, Cz, K, WG, Sp; 1983 v D, WG (54)
Wilkinson, B. (Sheffield U), 1904 v S (1)
Wilkinson, L. R. (Oxford University), 1891 v W (1)
Williams, B. F. (Wolverhampton W), 1949 v F; 1950 v S, W, Ei, I, P, Bel, Ch, US, Sp; 1951 v Ni, W, S, Y, Arg, P; 1952 v W, F; 1955 v S, WG, F, Sp, P; 1956 v W (24)
Williams, O. (Clapton Orient), 1923 v W, Ni (2)
Williams, S. (Southampton), 1983 v Aus (1+1 sub) (2)
Williams, W. (WBA), 1897 v Ni; 1898 v W, Ni, S; 1899 v W, Ni (6)
Williamson, E. C. (Arsenal), 1923 v Se (2) (2)
Williamson, R. G. (Middlesbrough), 1905 v Ni; 1911 v Ni, S, W; 1912 v S, W; 1913 v Ni (7)
Willingham, C. K. (Huddersfield T), 1937 v Fi; 1938 v S, G, Sw, F; 1939 v S, W, Ni, R of E, N, I, Y (12)
Willis, A. (Tottenham H), 1952 v F (1)
Wilshaw, D. J. (Wolverhampton W), 1954 v W, Sw, U; 1955 v S, F, Sp, P; 1956 v W, Ni, Fi, WG; 1957 v Ni (12)
Wilson, C. P. (Hendon), 1884 v S, W (2)
Wilson, C. W. (Oxford University), 1879 v W; 1881 v S (2)
Wilson, G. (Sheffield W), 1921 v S, W, Bel; 1922 v S, Ni; 1923 v S, W, Ni, Bel; 1924 v W, Ni, F (12)
Wilson, G. P. (Corinthians), 1900 v S, W (2)
Wilson, R. (Huddersfield T), 1960 v S, Y, Sp, H; 1962 v W, Ni, S, A, Sw, Pe, P, H, Arg, Bul, Br; 1963 v Ni, F, Br, Cz, EG, Sw; 1964 v W, S, R of W, U, P (2), Ei, Br, Arg; (with Everton), 1965 v S, H, Y, WG, Se; 1966 v WG (sub), W, Ni, A, Sp, Pol (2), Y, Fi, D, U, M, F, Arg, P, WG; 1967 v Ni, W, S, Cz, A; 1968 v Ni, S, USSR (2), Sp (2), Y (63)
Wilson, T. (Huddersfield T), 1928 v S (1)
Winckworth, W. N. (Old Westminsters), 1892 v W; 1893 v Ni (2)
Windridge, J. E. (Chelsea), 1908 v S, W, Ni, A (2), H, B; 1909 v Ni (8)
Wingfield-Stratford, C. V. (Royal Engineers), 1877 v S (1)
Withe, P. (Aston Villa), 1981 v Br, W, S; 1982 v N (sub), W, Ic; 1983 v H, Ni, S (9)
Wollaston, C. H. R. (Wanderers), 1874 v S; 1875 v S; 1877 v S; 1880 v S (4)
Wolstenholme, S. (Everton), 1904 v S; (with Blackburn R), 1905 v W, Ni (3)
Wood, H. (Wolverhampton W), 1890 v S, W; 1896 v S (3)
Wood, R. E. (Manchester U), 1955 v Ni, W; 1956 v Fi (3)
Woodcock, T. (Nottingham F), 1978 v Ni; 1979 v Ei (sub), Cz, Bul (sub), Se; 1980 v Ni; (with Cologne), Bul, Ei, Sp (2), Arg, Bel, I; 1981 v N, R, Sw, R, W (sub), S; 1982 v Ni (sub), Ho, Fi (sub), WG (sub), Sp; 1983 v WG (sub), Gr, L, Gr (28)
Woodger, G. (Oldham Ath), 1911 v Ni (1)
Woodhall, G. (WBA), 1888 v S, W (2)
Woodley, V. R. (Chelsea), 1937 v S, N, Se, Fi; 1938 v S, W, Ni, Cz, G, Sw, F; 1939 v S, W, Ni, R of E, N, I, R, Y (19)
Woodward, V. J. (Tottenham H), 1903 v S, W, Ni; 1904 v S, Ni; 1905 v S, W, Ni; 1907 v S; 1908 v S, W, Ni, A (2), H, B; 1909 v W, Ni, H (2), A; (with Chelsea), 1910 v Ni; 1911 v W (23)
Woosnam, M. (Manchester C), 1922 v W (1)
Worrall, F. (Portsmouth), 1935 v Ho; 1937 v Ni (2)
Worthington, F. S. (Leicester C), 1974 v Ni (sub), S, Arg, EG, Bul, Y; 1975 v Cz, P (sub) (8)
Wreford-Brown, C. (Oxford University), 1889 v Ni; (with Old Carthusians), 1894 v W; 1895 v W; 1898 v S (4)
Wright, E, G. D. (Cambridge University), 1906 v W (1)
Wright, J. D. (Newcastle U), 1939 v N (1)
Wright, T. J. (Everton), 1968 v USSR; 1969 v R (2), M (sub), U, Br; 1970 v W, Ho, Bel, R (sub), Br (11)
Wright, W. A. (Wolverhampton W), 1947 v S, W, Ni, Ei, Ho, F, Sw, P; 1948 v S, W, Ni, Bel, Se, I; 1949 v S, W, Ni, D, Sw, Se, N, F; 1950 v S, W, Ni, Ei, I, P, Bel, Ch, US, Sp; 1951 v Ni, S, Arg; 1952 v W, Ni, S, F, A (2), I, Sw; 1953 v Ni, W, S, Bel, Arg, Ch, U, US; 1954 v W, Ni, S, R of E, H (2), Y, Bel, Sw, U; 1955 v W, Ni, S, WG, F, Sp, P; 1956 v Ni, W, S, Br, Se, Fi, WG, D, Sp; 1957 v S, W, Ni, Y, D (2), Ei (2); 1958 v W, Ni, S, P, Y, USSR (3), Br, A, F; 1959 v W, Ni, S, USSR, I, Br, Pe, M, US (105)
Wylie, J. G. (Wanderers), 1878 v S (1)

Yates, J. (Burnley), 1889 v Ni (1)
York, R. E. (Aston Villa), 1922 v S; 1926 v S (2)
Young, A. (Huddersfield T), 1933 v W; 1937 v S, H, N, Se; 1938 v G, Sw, F; 1939 v W (9)
Young, G. M. (Sheffield W), 1965 v W (1)

R. E. Evans also played for Wales against E, Ni, S; J. Reynolds also played for Ireland against E, W, S.

NORTHERN IRELAND

Aherne, T. (Belfast C), 1947 v E; 1948 v S; 1949 v W; (with Luton T), 1950 v W (4)
Alexander, A. (Cliftonville), 1895 v S (1)
Allen, C. A. (Cliftonville), 1936 v E (1)
Allen, J. (Limavady), 1887 v E (1)
Anderson, T. (Manchester U), 1973 v Cy, E, S, W; 1974 v Bul, P; (with Swindon T), 1975 v S (sub); 1976 v Is; 1977 v Ho, Bel, WG, E, S, W, Ic; 1978 v Ic, Ho, Bel; (with Peterborough U), S, E, W; 1979 v D (22)
Anderson, W. (Linfield), 1898 v W, E, S; 1899 v S (4)
Andrews, W. (Glentoran), 1908 v S; (with Grimsby T), 1913 v E, S (3)
Armstrong, G. (Tottenham H), 1977 v WG, E, W (sub), Ic (sub); 1978 v Bel, S, E, W; 1979 v Ei, D, Bul, E, Bul, E, S, W, D; 1980 v E, Ei, Is, S, E, W, Aus (3); 1981 v Se; (with Watford), P, S, P, S, Se; 1982 v S, Is, E, F, W, Y, Hon, Sp, A, F; 1983 v A, T, Alb, S, E, W (48)

Baird, G. (Distillery), 1896 v S, E, W (3)
Baird, H. (Huddersfield T), 1939 v E (1)
Balfe, J. (Shelbourne), 1909 v E; 1910 v W (2)
Bambrick, J. (Linfield), 1929 v W, S, E; 1930 v W, S, E; 1932 v W; (with Chelsea), 1935 v W; 1936 v E, S; 1938 v W (11)
Banks, S. J. (Cliftonville), 1937 v W (1)
Barr, H. H. (Linfield), 1962 v E; (with Coventry C), 1963 v E, Pol (3)
Barron, H. (Cliftonville), 1894 v E, W, S; 1895 v S; 1896 v S; 1897 v E, W (7)
Barry, H. (Bohemians), 1900 v S (1)
Baxter, R. A. (Cliftonville), 1887 v S, W (2)
Bennett, L. V. (Dublin University), 1889 v W (1)
Berry, J. (Cliftonville), 1888 v S, W; 1889 v E (3)
Best, G. (Manchester U), 1964 v W, U; 1965 v E, Ho (2), S, Sw (2), Alb; 1966 v S, E, Alb; 1967 v E; 1968 v S; 1969 v E, S, W, T; 1970 v S, E, W, USSR; 1971 v Cy (2), Sp, E, S, W; 1972 v USSR, Sp; 1973 v Bul; 1974 v P; (with Fulham), 1977 v Ho, Bel, WG; 1978 v Ic, Ho (37)
Bingham, W. L. (Sunderland), 1951 v F; 1952 v E, S, W; 1953 v E, S, F, W; 1954 v E, S, W; 1955 v E, S, W; 1956 v E, S, W; 1957 v E, S, W, P (2), I; 1958 v S, E, W, I (2), Arg, Cz (2), WG, F; (with Luton T), 1959 v E, S, W, Sp; 1960 v S, E, W; (with Everton), 1961 v E, S, WG (2), Gr, I; 1962 v E, Gr; 1963 v E, S, Pol (2), Sp; (with Port Vale), 1964 v S, E, Sp (56)
Black, J. (Glentoran), 1901 v E (1)
Blair, H. (Portadown), 1931 v S; 1932 v S; (with Swansea), 1934 v S (3)
Blair, J. (Cliftonville), 1907 v W, E, S; 1908 v E, S (5)
Blair, R. V. (Oldham Ath), 1975 v Se (sub), S (sub), W; 1976 v Se, Is (5)
Blanchflower, R. D. (Barnsley), 1950 v S, W; 1951 v E, S; (with Aston Villa), F; 1952 v W; 1953 v E, S, W, F; 1954 v E, S, W; (with Tottenham H), 1955 v E, S, W; 1956 v E, S, W; 1957 v E, S, W, I, P (2); 1958 v E, S, W, I (2), Cz (2), Arg, F, WG; 1959 v E, S, W, Sp; 1960 v E, S, W; 1961 v E, S, W, WG (2); 1962 v E, S, W, Gr, Ho; 1963 v E, S, Pol (2) (56)
Blanchflower, J. (Manchester U), 1954 v W; 1955 v E, S; 1956 v S, W; 1957 v S, E, P; 1958 v S, E, I (2) (12)
Bookman, L. O. (Bradford C), 1914 v W; (with Luton T), 1921 v S, W; 1922 v E (4)
Bothwell, A. W. (Ards), 1926 v S, E, W; 1927 v E, W (5)
Bowler, G. C. (Hull C), 1950 v E, S, W (3)
Boyle, P. (Sheffield U), 1901 v E; 1902 v E; 1903 v S, W; 1904 v E (5)
Braithwaite, R. S. (Linfield), 1962 v W; 1963 v P, Sp; (with Middlesbrough), 1964 v W, U; 1965 v E, S, Sw (2), Ho (10)
Breen, T. (Belfast C), 1935 v E, W; 1937 v E, S; (with Manchester U), 1937 v W; 1938 v E, S; 1939 v W, S (9)
Brennan, B. (Bohemians), 1912 v W (1)
Brennan, R. A. (Luton T), 1949 v W; (with Birmingham C), 1950 v E, S, W; (with Fulham), 1951 v E (5)
Briggs, W. R. (Manchester U), 1962 v W; (with Swansea T), 1965 v Ho (2)
Brisby, D. (Distillery), 1891 v S (1)
Brolly, T. (Millwall), 1937 v W; 1938 v W; 1939 v E, W (4)
Brookes, E. A. (Shelbourne), 1920 v S (1)
Brotherston, N. (Blackburn R), 1980 v S, E, W, Aus (3); 1981 v Se, P; 1982 v S, Is, E, F, S, W, Hon (sub), A (sub); 1983 v A (sub), WG, Alb, T, Alb, S (sub), E (sub), W (24)
Brown, J. (Glenavon), 1921 v W; (with Tranmere R), 1924 v E, W (3)
Brown, J. (Wolverhampton W), 1935 v E, W; 1936 v E; (with Coventry C), 1937 v E, W; 1938 v S, W; (with Birmingham C), 1939 v E, S, W (10)
Brown, W. G. (Glenavon), 1926 v W (1)
Brown, W. M. (Limavady), 1887 v E (1)
Browne, F. (Cliftonville), 1887 v E, S, W; 1888 v E, S (5)
Browne, R. J. (Leeds U), 1936 v E, W; 1938 v E, W; 1939 v E, S (6)
Bruce, W. (Glentoran), 1961 v S; 1967 v W (2)
Buckle, H. (Cliftonville), 1882 v E (1)
Buckle, H. R. (Sunderland), 1904 v E; (with Bristol R), 1908 v W (2)
Burnett, J. (Distillery), 1894 v E, W, S; (with Glentoran), 1895 v E, W (5)
Burnison, J. (Distillery), 1901 v E, W (2)
Burnison, S. (Distillery), 1908 v E; 1910 v E, S; (with Bradford), 1911 v E, S, W; (with Distillery), 1912 v E; 1913 v W (8)
Burns, J. (Glenavon), 1923 v E (1)
Butler, M. P. (Blackpool), 1939 v W (1)

Campbell, A. C. (Crusaders), 1963 v W; 1965 v Sw (2)
Campbell, J. (Cliftonville), 1896 v W; 1897 v E, S, W; (with Distillery), 1898 v E, S, W; (with Cliftonville), 1899 v E; 1900 v E, S; 1901 v S, W; 1902 v S; 1903 v E; 1904 v S (15)
Campbell, J. P. (Fulham), 1951 v E, S (2)
Campbell, R. (Bradford C), 1982 v S, W (sub) (2)
Campbell, W. G. (Dundee), 1968 v S, E; 1969 v T; 1970 v S, W, USSR (6)
Carey, J. J. (Manchester U), 1947 v E, S, W; 1948 v E; 1949 v E, S, W (7)
Carroll, E. (Glenavon), 1925 v S (1)
Casey, T. (Newcastle U), 1955 v W; 1956 v W; 1957 v E, S, W, I, P (2); 1958 v WG, F; (with Portsmouth), 1959 v E, Sp (12)
Cashin, M. (Cliftonville), 1898 v S (1)
Caskey, W. (Derby Co), 1979 v Bul, E, Bul, E, D (sub); 1980 v E (sub); (with Tulsa R), 1982 v F (sub) (7)
Cassidy, T. (Newcastle U), 1971 v E (sub); 1972 v USSR (sub); 1974 v Bul (sub), S, E, W; 1975 v N; 1976 v S, E, W; 1977 v WG (sub); 1980 v E, Ei (sub), Is, S, E, W, Aus (3); (with Burnley), 1981 v Se, P; 1982 v Is, Sp (sub) (24)
Chambers, J. (Distillery), 1921 v W; (with Bury), 1928 v E, S, W; 1929 v E, S, W; 1930 v S, W; (with Nottingham F), 1932 v E, S, W (12)
Chatton, H. A. (Partick T), 1925 v E, S; 1926 v E (3)
Christian, J. (Linfield), 1889 v S (1)
Clarke, R. (Belfast C), 1901 v E, S (2)

Northern Ireland's Trevor Anderson

Gerry Armstrong scores for Northern Ireland

Cleary, J. (Glentoran), 1982 v S, W; 1983 v W (sub) (3)
Clements, D. (Coventry C), 1965 v W, Ho; 1966 v M; 1967 v S, W; 1968 v S, E; 1969 v T (2), S, W; 1970 v S, E, W, USSR (2); 1971 v Sp, E, S, W, Cy; (with Sheffield W), 1972 v USSR (2), Sp, E, S, W; 1973 v Bul, Cy (2), P, E, S, W; (with Everton), 1974 v Bul, P, S, E, W; 1975 v N, Y, E, S, W; 1976 v Se, Y; (with New York Cosmos), E, W (48)
Clugston, J. (Cliftonville), 1888 v W; 1889 v W, S, E; 1890 v E, S; 1891 v E, W; 1892 v E, S, W; 1893 v E, S, W (14)
Cochrane, D. (Leeds U), 1939 v E, W; 1947 v E, S, W; 1948 v E, S, W; 1949 v S, W; 1950 v S, E (12)
Cochrane, M. (Distillery), 1898 v S, W, E; 1899 v E; 1900 v E, S, W; (with Leicester Fosse), 1901 v S (8)
Cochrane, T. (Coleraine), 1976 v N; (with Burnley), 1978 v S (sub), E (sub), W (sub); 1979 v Ei (sub); (with Middlesbrough), D, Bul, E, Bul, E; 1980 v Is, E (sub), W (sub), Aus (1+2 sub); 1981 v Se (sub), P (sub), S, P, S, Se; 1982 v E (sub), F (24)
Collins, F. (Glasgow C), 1922 v S (1)
Condy, J. (Distillery), 1882 v W; 1886 v E, S (3)
Connell, T. (Coleraine), 1978 v W (sub) (1)
Connor, J. (Glentoran), 1901 v S, E; (with Belfast C), 1905 v E, S, W; 1907 v E, S; 1908 v E, S; 1909 v W; 1911 v S, E, W (13)
Connor, M. J. (Brentford), 1903 v S, W; (with Fulham), 1904 v E (3)
Cook, W. (Celtic), 1933 v E, W, S; (with Everton), 1935 v E; 1936 v S, W; 1937 v E, S, W; 1938 v E, S, W; 1939 v E, S, W (15)
Cooke, S. (Belfast YMCA), 1889 v E; (with Cliftonville), 1890 v E, S (3)
Coulter, J. (Belfast C), 1934 v E, S, W; (with Everton), 1935 v E, S, W; 1937 v S, W; (with Grimsby T), 1938 v S, W; (with Chelmsford C), 1939 v S (11)
Cowan, J. (Newcastle U), 1970 v E (sub) (1)
Cowan, T. S. (Queen's Island), 1925 v W (1)
Coyle, F. (Coleraine), 1956 v E, S; 1957 v P (with Nottingham F), 1958 v Arg (4)
Coyle, R. I. (Sheffield W), 1973 v P, Cy (sub), W (sub); 1974 v Bul (sub), P (sub) (5)
Craig, A. B. (Rangers), 1908 v E, S, W; 1909 v S; (with Morton), 1912 v S, W; 1914 v E, S, W (9)
Craig, D. J. (Newcastle U), 1967 v W; 1968 v W; 1969 v T (2), E, S, W; 1970 v E, S, W, USSR; 1971 v Cy (2), S, S (sub); 1972 v USSR, S (sub); 1973 v Cy (2), E, S, W; 1974 v Bul, P; 1975 v N (25)
Crawford, S. (Distillery), 1889 v E, W; (with Cliftonville), 1891 v E, S, W; 1893 v E, W (7)
Croft, T. (Queen's Island), 1924 v E (1)
Crone, R. (Distillery), 1889 v S; 1890 v E, S, W (4)
Crone, W. (Distillery), 1882 v W; 1884 v E, S, W; 1886 v E, S, W; 1887 v E; 1888 v E, W; 1889 v S; 1890 v W (12)
Crooks, W. (Manchester U), 1922 v W (1)
Crossan, E. (Blackburn R), 1950 v S; 1951 v E; 1955 v W (3)
Crossan, J. A. (Sparta-Rotterdam), 1960 v E; (with Sunderland), 1963 v W, P, Sp; 1964 v E, S, W, U, Sp; 1965 v E, S, Sw (2); (with Manchester C), W, Ho (2), Alb; 1966 v S, E, Alb, WG; 1967 v E, S; (with Middlesbrough), 1968 v S (24)
Crothers, C. (Distillery), 1907 v W (1)
Cumming, L. (Huddersfield T), 1929 v W, S; (with Oldham Ath), 1930 v E (3)
Cunningham, R. (Ulster), 1892 v S, E, W; 1893 v E (4)
Cunningham, W. E. (St Mirren), 1951 v W; 1953 v E; 1954 v S; 1955 v S; (with Leicester C), 1956 v E, S, W; 1957 v E, S, W, I, P (2); 1958 v S, W, I, Cz (2), Arg, WG, F; 1959 v E, S, W; 1960 v E, S, W; (with Dunfermline Ath), 1961 v W; 1962 v W, Ho (30)
Curran, S. (Belfast C), 1926 v S, W; 1928 v S (3)
Curran, J. J. (Glenavon), 1922 v W; (with Pontypridd), 1923 v E, S; (with Glenavon), 1924 v E (4)
Cush, W. W. (Glenavon), 1951 v E, S; 1954 v S, E; 1957 v W, I, P (2); (with Leeds U), 1958 v I (2), W, Cz (2), Arg, WG, F; 1959 v E, S, W, Sp; 1960 v E, S, W; (with Portadown), 1961 v WG, Gr; 1962 v Gr (26)

Dalton, W. (YMCA), 1888 v S; (with Linfield), 1890 v S, W; 1891 v S, W; 1892 v E, S, W; 1894 v E, S, W (11)
D'Arcy, S. D. (Chelsea), 1952 v W; 1953 v E; (with Brentford), 1953 v S, W, F (5)
Darling, J. (Linfield), 1897 v E, S; 1900 v S; 1902 v E, S, W; 1903 v E, S, W; 1905 v E, S, W; 1906 v E, S, W; 1908 v W; 1909 v E; 1910 v E, S, W; 1912 v S (21)
Davey, H. H. (Reading), 1926 v E; 1927 v E, S; 1928 v E; (with Portsmouth), 1928 v W (5)
Davis, T. L. (Oldham Ath), 1937 v E (1)
Davison, J. R. (Cliftonville), 1882 v E, W; 1883 v E, W; 1884 v E, W, S; 1885 v E (8)
Devine, W. (Limavady), 1886 v E, W; 1887 v W; 1888 v W (4)
Dickson, D. (Coleraine), 1970 v S (sub), W; 1973 v Cy, P (4)
Dickson, T. A. (Linfield), 1957 v S (1)
Dickson, W. (Chelsea), 1951 v W, F; 1952 v E, S, W; 1953 v E, S, W, F; (with Arsenal), 1954 v E, W; 1955 v E (12)
Diffin, W. (Belfast C), 1931 v W (1)
Dill, A. H. (Knock and Down Ath), 1882 v E, W; (with Cliftonville), 1883 v W; 1884 v E, S, W; 1885 v E, S, W (9)
Doherty, I. (Belfast C), 1901 v E (1)
Doherty, J. (Cliftonville), 1933 v E, W (2)
Doherty, M. (Derry C), 1938 v S (1)
Doherty, P. D. (Blackpool), 1935 v E, W; 1936 v E, S; (with Manchester C), 1937 v E, W; 1938 v E, S; 1939 v E, W; (with Derby Co), 1947 v E; (with Huddersfield T), 1947 v W; 1948 v E, W; 1949 v S; (with Doncaster R), 1951 v S (16)
Donaghy, M. (Luton T), 1980 v S, E, W; 1981 v Se, P, S (sub); 1982 v S, Is, E, F, S, W, Y, Hon, Sp, F; 1983 v A, WG, Alb, T, Alb, S, E, W (24)
Donnelly, L. (Distillery), 1913 v W (1)
Doran, J. F. (Brighton), 1921 v E; 1922 v E, W (3)
Dougan, A. D. (Portsmouth), 1958 v Cz; (with Blackburn R), 1960 v S; 1961 v E, W, I, Gr; (with Aston Villa), 1963 v S, P (2); (with Leicester C), 1966 v S, E, W, M, Alb, WG; 1967 v E, S; (with Wolverhampton W), 1967 v W; 1968 v S, W, Is; 1969 v T (2), E, S, W; 1970 v S, E, USSR (2); 1971 v Cy (2), Sp, E, S, W; 1972 v USSR (2), E, S, W; 1973 v Bul, Cy (43)
Douglas, J. P. (Belfast C), 1947 v E (1)
Dowd, H. O. (Glenavon), 1974 v W; 1975 v N (sub), Se (3)
Duggan, H. A. (Leeds U), 1930 v E; 1931 v E, W; 1933 v E; 1934 v E; 1935 v S, W; 1936 v S (8)
Dunne, J. (Sheffield U), 1928 v W; 1931 v W, E; 1932 v E, S; 1933 v E, W (7)

Eames, W. L. E. (Dublin U), 1885 v E, S, W (3)
Eglington, T. J. (Everton), 1947 v S, W; 1948 v E, S, W; 1949 v E (6)
Elder, A. R. (Burnley), 1960 v W; 1961 v S, E, W, WG (2), Gr; 1962 v E, S, Gr; 1963 v E, S, W, P (2), Sp; 1964 v W, U; 1965 v E, S, W, Sw (2), Ho (2), Alb; 1966 v E, S, W, M, Alb; 1967 v E, S, W; (with Stoke C), 1968 v E, W; 1969 v E (sub), S, W; 1970 v USSR (40)
Elleman, A. R. (Cliftonville), 1889 v W; 1890 v E (2)
Elwood, J. H. (Bradford), 1929 v W; 1930 v E (2)
Emerson, W. (Glentoran), 1920 v E, S, W; 1921 v E; 1922

v E, S; (with Burnley), 1922 v W; 1923 v E, S, W; 1924 v E (11)
English, S. (Glasgow R), 1933 v W, S (2)
Enright, J. (Leeds C), 1912 v S (1)

Falloon, E. (Aberdeen), 1931 v S; 1933 v S (2)
Farquharson, T. G. (Cardiff C), 1923 v S, W; 1924 v E, S, W; 1925 v E, S (7)
Farrell, P. (Distillery), 1901 v S, W (2)
Farrell, P. (Hibernian), 1938 v W (1)
Farrell, P. D. (Everton), 1947 v S, W; 1948 v E, S, W; 1949 v E, W (7)
Feeney, J. M. (Linfield), 1947 v S; (with Swansea T), 1950 v E (2)
Feeney, W. (Glentoran), 1976 v Is (1)
Ferguson, W. (Linfield), 1966 v M; 1967 v E (2)
Ferris, J. (Belfast Celtic), 1920 v E, W; (with Chelsea), 1921 v S, E; (with Belfast C), 1928 v S (5)
Ferris, R. O. (Birmingham), 1950 v S; 1951 v F; 1952 v S (3)
Finney, T. (Sunderland), 1975 v N, E (sub), S, W; 1976 v N, Y, S; (with Cambridge U), 1980 v E, Is, S, E, W, Aus (2) (14)
Fitzpatrick, J. C. (Bohemians), 1896 v E, S (2)
Flack, H. (Burnley), 1929 v S (1)
Forbes, G. (Limavady), 1888 v W; (with Distillery), 1891 v E, S (3)
Forde, J. T. (Ards), 1959 v Sp; 1961 v E, S, WG (4)
Foreman, T. A. (Cliftonville), 1899 v S (1)
Forsyth, J. (YMCA), 1888 v E, S (2)
Fox, W. (Ulster), 1887 v E, S (2)
Fulton, R. P. (Belfast C), 1930 v W; 1931 v E, S, W; 1932 v W, E; 1933 v E, S; 1934 v E, W, S; 1935 v E, W, S; 1936 v S, W; 1937 v E, S, W; 1938 v W (20)

Gaffikin, J. (Linfield Ath), 1890 v S, W; 1891 v S, W; 1892 v E, S, W; 1893 v E, S, W; 1894 v E, S, W; 1895 v E, W (15)
Galbraith, W. (Distillery), 1890 v W (1)
Gallagher, P. (Celtic), 1920 v E, S; 1922 v S; 1923 v S, W; 1924 v S, W; 1925 v S, W, E; (with Falkirk), 1927 v S (11)
Gallogly, C. (Huddersfield T), 1951 v E, S (2)
Gara, A. (Preston NE), 1902 v E, S, W (3)
Gardiner, A. (Cliftonville), 1930 v S, W; 1931 v S; 1932 v E, S (5)
Garrett, J. (Distillery), 1925 v W (1)
Gaston, R. (Oxford U), 1969 v Is (sub) (1)
Gaukrodger, G. (Linfield), 1895 v W (1)
Gaussen, A. W. (Moyola Park), 1884 v E, S; 1888 v E, W; 1889 v E, W (6)
Geary, J. (Glentoran), 1931 v S; 1932 v S (2)
Gibb, J. T. (Wellington Park) 1884 v S, W; 1885 v S, E, W; 1886 v S; 1887 v S, E, W; 1889 v S (10)
Gibb, T. J. (Cliftonville), 1936 v W (1)
Gibson W. K. (Cliftonville), 1894 v S, W, E; 1895 v S; 1897 v W; 1898 v S, W, E; 1901 v S, W, E; 1902 v S, W (13)
Gillespie, R. (Hertford), 1886 v E, S, W; 1887 v E, S, W (6)
Gillespie, W. (Sheffield U), 1913 v E, S; 1914 v E, W; 1920 v S, W; 1921 v E; 1922 v E, S, W; 1923 v E, S, W; 1924 v E, S, W; 1925 v E, S; 1926 v S, W; 1927 v E, W; 1928 v E; 1929 v E; 1931 v E (25)
Gillespie, W. (West Down), 1889 v W (1)
Goodall, A. L. (Derby Co), 1899 v S, W; 1900 v E, W; 1901 v E; 1902 v S; 1903 v E, W; (with Glossop), 1904 v E, W (10)
Goodbody, M. F. (Dublin University), 1889 v E; 1891 v W (2)
Gordon, H. (Linfield), 1891 v S; 1892 v E, S, W; 1893 v E, S, W; 1895 v E, W; 1896 v E, S (11)
Gordon, T. (Linfield), 1894 v W; 1895 v E (2)
Gorman, W. C. (Brentford), 1947 v E, S, W; 1948 v W (4)
Gowdy, J. (Glentoran), 1920 v E; (with Queen's Island), 1924 v W; (with Falkirk), 1926 v E, S; 1927 v E, S (6)
Gowdy, W. A. (Hull C), 1932 v S; (with Sheffield W), 1933 v S; (with Linfield), 1935 v E, S, W; (with Hibernian), 1936 v W (6)
Graham, W. G. L. (Doncaster R), 1951 v W, F; 1952 v E, S, W; 1953 v S, F; 1954 v E, W; 1955 v S, W; 1956 v E, S; 1959 v E (14)
Greer, W. (QPR), 1909 v E, S, W (3)
Gregg, H. (Doncaster R), 1954 v W; 1957 v E, S, W, I, P (2); 1958 v E, I; (with Manchester U), 1958 v Cz, Arg, WG, F, W; 1959 v E, W; 1960 v S, E, W; 1961 v E, S; 1962 v S, Gr; 1964 v S, E (25)

Hall, G. (Distillery), 1897 v E (1)
Halligan, W. (Derby Co), 1911 v W; (with Wolverhampton W), 1912 v E (2)
Hamill, M. (Manchester U), 1912 v E; 1914 v E, S; (with Belfast C), 1920 v E, S, W; (with Manchester C), 1921 v S (7)
Hamilton, B. (Linfield), 1969 v T; 1971 v Cy (2), E, S, W; (with Ipswich T), 1972 v USSR (1+1 sub), Sp; 1973 v Bul, Cy (2), P, E, S, W; 1974 v Bul, S, E, W; 1975 v N, Se, Y, E; 1976 v Se, N, Y; (with Everton), Is, S, E, W; 1977 v Ho, Bel, WG, E, S, W, Ic; (with Millwall), 1978 v S, E, W; 1979 v Ei (sub); (with Swindon T), Bul (2), E, S, W, D; 1980 v Aus (2 sub) (50)
Hamilton, J. (Knock), 1882 v E, W (2)
Hamilton, R. (Distillery), 1908 v W (1)
Hamilton, R. (Glasgow R), 1928 v S; 1929 v E; 1930 v S, E; 1932 v S (5)
Hamilton, W. (QPR), 1978 v S (sub); (with Burnley), 1980 v S, E, W, Aus (2); 1981 v Se, P, S, P, S, Se; 1982 v S, Is, E, W, Y, Hon, Sp, A, F; 1983 v A, WG, Alb, Alb, S, E, W (28)
Hamilton, W. D. (Dublin Association), 1885 v W (1)
Hamilton, W. J. (Dublin Association), 1885 v W (1)
Hampton, H. (Bradford C), 1911 v E, S, W; 1912 v E, W; 1913 v E, S, W; 1914 v E (9)
Hanna, D. R. A. (Portsmouth), 1899 v W (1)
Hanna, J. (Nottingham F), 1912 v S, W (2)
Hannon, D. J. (Bohemian), 1908 v E, S; 1911 v E, S; 1912 v W; 1913 v E (6)
Harkin, J. T. (Southport), 1968 v W; 1969 v T; (with Shrewsbury T), W (sub); 1970 v USSR; 1971 v Sp (5)
Harland, A. I. (Linfield), 1923 v E (1)
Harris, J. (Cliftonville), 1921 v W (1)
Harris, V. (Shelbourne), 1906 v E; 1907 v E, W; 1908 v E, W, S; (with Everton), 1909 v E, W, S; 1910 v E, S, W; 1911 v E, S, W; 1912 v E; 1913 v E, S; 1914 v S, W (20)
Harvey, M. (Sunderland), 1961 v I; 1962 v Ho; 1963 v W, Sp; 1964 v S, E, W, U, Sp; 1965 v E, S, W, Sw (2), Ho (2), Alb; 1966 v S, E, W, M, Alb, WG; 1967 v E, S; 1968 v E, W; 1969 v Is, T (2), E; 1970 v USSR; 1971 v Cy, W (sub) (33)
Hastings, J. (Knock), 1882 v E, W; (with Ulster), 1883 v W; 1884 v E, S; 1886 v E, S (7)
Hatton, S. (Linfield), 1963 v S, Pol (2)
Hayes, W. E. (Huddersfield T), 1938 v E, S; 1939 v E, S (4)
Healy, F. (Coleraine), 1982 v S, W, Hon (sub); (with Glentoran), 1983 v A (sub) (4)
Hegan, D. (WBA), 1970 v USSR; (with Wolverhampton W), 1972 v USSR, E, S, W; 1973 v Bul, Cy (7)
Henderson, A. W. (Ulster), 1885 v E, S, W (3)
Hewison, G. (Moyola Park), 1885 v E, S (2)
Hill, M. J. (Norwich C), 1959 v W; 1960 v W; 1961 v WG; 1962 v S; (with Everton), 1964 v S, E, Sp (7)

George Best *Manchester United* and *N. Ireland*

Derek Dougan *Wolves* and *N. Ireland*

N. Kernaghan *Belfast Celtic* and *N. Ireland*

Sammy McIlroy *Manchester United* and *N. Ireland*

Hinton, E. (Fulham), 1947 v S, W; 1948 v S, E, W; (with Millwall), 1951 v W, F (7)
Hopkins, J. (Brighton), 1926 v E (1)
Houston, J. (Linfield), 1912 v S, W; 1913 v W; (with Everton), 1913 v E, S; 1914 v S (6)
Houston, W. (Linfield), 1933 v W (1)
Houston, W. G. (Moyola Park), 1885 v E, S (2)
Hughes, W. (Bolton W), 1951 v W (1)
Humphries, W. (Ards), 1962 v W; (with Coventry C), 1962 v Ho; 1963 v E, S, W, Pol, Sp; 1964 v S, E, Sp; 1965 v S; (with Swansea T), 1965 v W, Ho, Alb (14)
Hunter, A. (Blackburn R), 1970 v USSR; 1971 v Cy (2), E, S, W; (with Ipswich T), 1972 v USSR (2), Sp, E, S, W; 1973 v Bul, Cy (2), P, E, S, W; 1974 v Bul, S, E, W; 1975 v N, Se, Y, E, S, W; 1976 v Se, N, Y, Is, S, E, W; 1977 v Ho, Bel, WG, E, S, W, Ic; 1978 v Ic, Ho, Bel; 1979 v Ei, D, S, W, D; 1980 v E, Ei (53)
Hunter, A. (Distillery), 1905 v W; 1906 v W, E, S; (with Belfast C), 1908 v W; 1909 v W, E, S (8)
Hunter, R. J. (Cliftonville), 1884 v E, S, W (3)
Hunter, V. (Coleraine), 1962 v E; 1964 v Sp (2)

Irvine, R. W. (Everton), 1922 v S; 1923 v E, W; 1924 v E, S; 1925 v E; 1926 v E; 1927 v E, W; 1928 v E, S; (with Portsmouth), 1929 v E; 1930 v S; (with Connah's Quay), 1931 v E; (with Derry C), 1932 v W (15)
Irvine, R. J. (Linfield), 1962 v Ho; 1963 v E, S, W, Pol (2), Sp; (with Stoke C), 1965 v W (8)
Irvine, W. J. (Burnley), 1963 v W, Sp; 1965 v S, W, Sw, Ho (2), Alb; 1966 v S, E, W, M, Alb; 1967 v E, S; 1968 v E, W; (with Preston NE), 1969 v Is, T, E; (with Brighton), 1972 v E, S, W (23)
Irving, S. J. (Dundee), 1923 v S, W; 1924 v S, E, W; 1925 v S, E, W; 1926 v S, W; (with Cardiff C), 1927 v S, E, W; 1928 v S, E, W; (with Chelsea), 1929 v E; 1931 v W (18)

Jackson, T. (Everton), 1969 v Is, E, S, W; 1970 v USSR (1+1 sub); (with Nottingham F), 1971 v Sp; 1972 v E, S, W; 1973 v Cy, E, S, W; 1974 v Bul, P, S (sub), E (sub), W (sub); 1975 v N (sub), Se, Y, E, S, W; (with Manchester U); 1976 v Se, N, Y; 1977 v Ho, Bel, WG, E, S, W, Ic (35)
Jamison, J. (Glentoran), 1976 v N (1)
Jennings, P. A. (Watford), 1964 v W, U; (with Tottenham H), 1965 v E, S, Sw (2), Ho, Alb; 1966 v S, E, W, Alb, WG; 1967 v E, S; 1968 v S, E, W; 1969 v Is, T (2), E, S, W; 1970 v S, E, USSR (2); 1971 v Cy (2), E, S, W; 1972 v USSR, Sp, S, E, W; 1973 v Bul, Cy, P, E, S, W; 1974 v P, S, E, W; 1975 v N, Se, Y, E, S, W; 1976 v Se, N, Y, Is, S, E, W; 1977 v Ho, Bel, WG, E, S, W, Ic; (with Arsenal), 1978 v Ic, Ho, Bel; 1979 v Ei, D, Bul, E, Bul, E, S, W, D; 1980 v E, Ei, Is; 1981 v S, P, S, Se; 1982 v S, Is, E, W, Y, Hon, Sp, F; 1983 v Alb, S, E, W (99)
Johnston, H. (Portadown), 1927 v W (1)
Johnston, R. (Old Park), 1885 v S, W (2)
Johnston, S. (Distillery), 1882 v W; 1884 v E; 1886 v E, S (4)
Johnston, S. (Linfield), 1890 v W; 1893 v S, W; 1894 v E (4)
Johnston, S. (Distillery), 1905 v W (1)
Johnston, W. C. (Glenavon), 1962 v W; (with Oldham Ath), 1966 v M (sub) (2)
Jones, J. (Linfield), 1930 v S, W; 1931 v S, W, E; 1932 v S, E; 1933 v S, E, W; 1934 v S, E, W; 1935 v S, E, W; 1936 v E, S; (with Hibernian), 1936 v W; 1937 v E, W, S; (with Glenavon), 1938 v E (23)
Jones, J. (Glenavon), 1956 v W; 1957 v E, W (3)
Jones, S. (Distillery), 1934 v E; (with Blackpool), 1934 v W (2)
Jordan, T. (Linfield), 1895 v E, W (2)

Kavanagh, P. J. (Glasgow C), 1930 v E (1)
Keane, T. R. (Swansea T), 1949 v S (1)
Kearns, A. (Distillery), 1900 v E, S, W; 1902 v E, S, W (6)
Keith, R, M. (Newcastle U), 1958 v E, W, Cz (2), Arg, I, WG, F; 1959 v E, S, W, Sp; 1960 v S, E; 1961 v S, E, W, I, WG (2), Gr; 1962 v W, Ho (23)
Kelly, H. R. (Fulham), 1950 v E, W; (with Southampton), 1951 v E, S (4)
Kelly, J. (Glentoran), 1896 v E (1)
Kelly, J. (Derry C), 1932 v E, W; 1933 v E, W, S; 1934 v W; 1936 v E, S, W; 1937 v S, E (11)
Kelly, P. (Manchester C), 1921 v E (1)
Kelly, P. M. (Barnsley), 1950 v S (1)
Kennedy, A. L. (Arsenal), 1923 v W; 1925 v E (2)
Kernaghan, N. (Belfast C), 1936 v W; 1937 v S; 1938 v E (3)
Kirkwood, H. (Cliftonville), 1904 v W (1)
Kirwan, J. (Tottenham H), 1900 v W; 1902 v E, W; 1903 v E, S, W; 1904 v E, S, W; 1905 v E, S, W; (with Chelsea), 1906 v E, S, W; 1907 v W; (with Clyde), 1909 v S (17)

Lacey, W. (Everton), 1909 v E, S, W; 1910 v E, S, W; 1911 v E, S, W; 1912 v E; (with Liverpool), 1913 v W; 1914 v E, S, W; 1920 v E, S, W; 1921 v E, S, W; 1922 v E, S; (with New Brighton), 1925 v E (23)
Lawther, W. I. (Sunderland), 1960 v W; 1961 v I; (with Blackburn R), 1962 v S, Ho (4)
Leatham, J. (Belfast C), 1939 v W (1)
Ledwidge, J. J. (Shelbourne), 1906 v S, W (2)
Lemon, J. (Glentoran), 1886 v W; 1888 v S; (with Belfast YMCA), 1889 v W (3)
Leslie, W. (YMCA), 1887 v E (1)
Lewis, J. (Glentoran), 1899 v S, E, W; (with Distillery), 1900 v S (4)
Little, J. (Glentoran), 1898 v W (1)
Lockhart, H. (Rossall School), 1884 v W (1)
Lockhart, N. (Linfield), 1947 v E; (with Coventry C), 1950 v W; 1951 v W; 1952 v W; (with Aston Villa), 1954 v S, E; 1955 v W; 1956 v W (8)
Lowther, R. (Glentoran), 1888 v E, S (2)
Loyal, J. (Clarence), 1891 v S (1)
Lutton, R. J. (Wolverhampton W), 1970 v S, E; (with West Ham U), 1973 v Cy (sub), S (sub), W (sub); 1974 v P (6)
Lyner, D. (Glentoran), 1920 v E, W; 1922 v S, W; (with Manchester U), 1923 v E; (with Kilmarnock), 1923 v W (6)

McAdams, W. J. (Manchester C), 1954 v W; 1955 v S; 1957 v E; 1958 v S, I; (with Bolton W), 1961 v E, S, W, I, WG (2), Gr; 1962 v E, Gr; (with Leeds U), Ho (15)
McAlery, J. M. (Cliftonville), 1882 v E, W (2)
McAlinden, J. (Belfast C), 1938 v S; 1939 v S; (with Portsmouth), 1947 v E; (with Southend U), 1949 v E (4)
McAllen, J. (Linfield), 1898 v E; 1899 v E, S, W; 1900 v E, S, W; 1901 v W; 1902 v S (9)
McAlpine, W. J. (Cliftonville), 1901 v S (1)
McArthur, A. (Distillery), 1886 v W (1)
McAuley, J. L. (Huddersfield T), 1911 v E, W; 1912 v E, S; 1913 v E, S (6)
McAuley, P. (Belfast C), 1900 v S (1)
McCabe, J. J. (Leeds U), 1949 v S, W; 1950 v E; 1951 v W; 1953 v W; 1954 v S (6)
McCabe, W. (Ulster), 1891 v E (1)
McCambridge, J. (Ballymena), 1930 v S, W; (with Cardiff C), 1931 v W; 1932 v E (4)
McCandless, J. (Bradford), 1912 v W; 1913 v W; 1920 v W, S; 1921 v E (5)
McCandless, W. (Linfield), 1920 v E, W; 1921 v E; (with

Rangers), 1921 v W; 1922 v S; 1924 v W, S; 1925 v S; 1929 v W (9)
McCann, P. (Belfast C), 1910 v E, S, W; 1911 v E; (with Glentoran), 1911 v S; 1912 v E; 1913 v W (7)
McCashin, J. (Cliftonville), 1896 v W; 1898 v S, W; 1899 v S (4)
McCavana, W. T. (Coleraine), 1955 v S; 1956 v E, S (3)
McCaw, D. (Distillery), 1882 v E (1)
McCaw, J. H. (Linfield), 1927 v W; 1930 v S; 1931 v E, S, W (5)
McClatchey, J. (Distillery), 1886 v E, S, W (3)
McClatchey, R. (Distillery), 1895 v S (1)
McCleary, J. W. (Cliftonville), 1955 v W (1)
McCleery, W. (Cliftonville), 1922 v N; 1930 v E, W; 1931 v E, S, W; 1932 v S, W; 1933 v E, W (10)
McClelland, J. (Arsenal), 1961 v W, I, WG (2), Gr; (with Fulham), 1967 v M (6)
McClelland, J. (Mansfield T), 1980 v S (sub), Aus (3); 1981 v Se, S (with Rangers), S, Se; 1982 v S, W, Y, Hon, Sp, A, F; 1983 v A, WG, Alb, T, Alb, S, E, W (23)
McCluggage, A. (Bradford), 1924 v E; (with Burnley), 1927 v S, W; 1928 v S, E, W; 1929 v S, E, W; 1930 v W; 1931 v E, W (14)
McClure, G. (Cliftonville), 1907 v S, W; 1908 v E; (with Distillery), 1909 v E (4)
McConnell, E. (Cliftonville), 1904 v S, W; (with Glentoran), 1905 v S; (with Sunderland), 1906 v E; 1907 v E; 1908 v S, W; (with Sheffield W), 1909 v S, W; 1910 v S, W, E (12)
McConnell, P. (Doncaster R), 1928 v W; (with Southport), 1932 v E (2)
McConnell, W. G. (Bohemians), 1912 v W; 1913 v E, S; 1914 v E, S, W (6)
McConnell, W. H. (Reading), 1925 v W; 1926 v E, W; 1927 v E, S, W; 1928 v E, W (8)
McCourt, F. J. (Manchester C), 1952 v E, W; 1953 v E, S, W, F (6)
McCoy, J. (Distillery), 1896 v W (1)
McCracken, R. (C Palace), 1921 v E; 1922 v E, S, W (4)
McCracken, W. (Distillery), 1902 v E, W; 1903 v E; 1904 v E, S, W; (with Newcastle U), 1905 v E, S, W; 1907 v E; 1920 v E; 1922 v E, S, W; (with Hull C), 1923 v S (15)
McCreery, D. (Manchester U), 1976 v S (sub), E, W; 1977 v Ho, Bel, WG, E, S, W, Ic; 1978 v Ic, Ho, Bel, S, E, W; 1979 v Ei, D, Bul, E, Bul, W, D; (with QPR), 1980 v E, Ei, S (sub), E (sub), W (sub), Aus (1+ sub); 1981 v Se (sub), P (sub); (with Tulsa R), S, P, Se; 1982 v S, Is, E (sub), F, Y, Hon, Sp, A, F; (with Newcastle U), v A (45)
McCrory, S. (Southend U), 1958 v E (1)
McCullough, K. (Belfast C), 1935 v W; 1936 v E; (with Manchester C), 1936 v S; 1937 v E, S (5)
McCullough, W. J. (Arsenal), 1961 v I; 1963 v Sp; 1964 v S, E, W, U, Sp; 1965 v E, Sw; (with Millwall), 1967 v E (10)
McCurdy, C. (Linfield), 1980 v Aus (sub) (1)
McDonald, R. (Glasgow R), 1930 v S; 1932 v E (2)
McDonnell, J. (Bohemians), 1911 v E, S; 1912 v W; 1913 v W (4)
McFaul, W. S. (Linfield), 1967 v E (sub); (with Newcastle U), 1970 v W; 1971 v Sp; 1972 v USSR; 1973 v Cy; 1974 v Bul (6)
McGarry, J. K. (Cliftonville), 1951 v W, F, S (3)
McGee, G. (Wellington Park), 1885 v E, S, W (3)
McGrath, R. C. (Tottenham H), 1974 v S, E, W; 1975 v N; 1976 v Is (sub); 1977 v Ho (with Manchester U), Bel, WG, E, S, W, Ic; 1978 v Ic, Ho, Bel, S, E, W; 1979 v Bul (sub), E (sub), E (sub) (21)
McGregor, S. (Glentoran), 1921 v S (1)
McGrillen, J. (Clyde), 1924 v S; (with Belfast C), 1927 v S (2)
McGuire, E. (Distillery), 1907 v S (1)
McIlroy, H. (Cliftonville), 1906 v E (1)
McIlroy, J. (Burnley), 1952 v E, S, W; 1953 v E, S, W; 1954 v E, S, W; 1955 v E, S, W; 1956 v E, S, W; 1957 v E, S, W, I, P (2); 1958 v E, S, W, I (2), Cz (2), Arg, WG, F; 1959 v E, S, W, Sp; 1960 v E, S, W; 1961 v E, W, WG (2), Gr; 1962 v E, S, Gr, Ho; 1963 v E, S, Pol (2); (with Stoke C), 1963 v W; 1966 v S, E, Alb (55)
McIlroy, S. B. (Manchester U), 1972 v Sp, S (sub); 1974 v S, E, W; 1975 v N, Se, Y, E, S, W; 1976 v Se, N, Y, S, E, W; 1977 v Ho, Bel, E, S, W, Ic; 1978 v Ic, Ho, Bel, S, E, W; 1979 v Ei, D, Bul, E, Bul, E, S, W, D; 1980 v E, Ei, Is, S, E, W; 1981 v Se, P, S, P, S, Se; 1982 v S, Is; (with Stoke C), E, F, S, W, Y, Hon, Sp, A, F; 1983 v A, WG, Alb, T, Alb, S, E, W (69)
McIlvenny, J. (Distillery), 1890 v E; 1891 v E (2)
McIlvenny, P. (Distillery), 1924 v W (1)
McKeag, W. (Glentoran), 1968 v S, W (2)
McKee, F. W. (Cliftonville), 1906 v S, W; (with Belfast C), 1914 v E, S, W (5)
McKelvie, H. (Glentoran), 1901 v W (1)
McKenna, J. (Huddersfield), 1950 v E, S, W; 1951 v E, S, F; 1952 v E (7)
McKenzie, H. (Distillery), 1923 v S (1)
McKenzie, R. (Airdrie), 1967 v W (1)
McKeown, H. (Linfield), 1892 v E, S, W; 1893 v S, W; 1894 v S, W (7)
McKie, H. (Cliftonville), 1895 v E, S, W (3)
McKinney, D. (Hull C), 1921 v S; (with Bradford C), 1924 v S (2)
McKinney, V. J. (Falkirk), 1966 v WG (1)
McKnight, J. (Preston NE), 1912 v S; (with Glentoran), 1913 v S (2)
McLaughlin, J. C. (Shrewsbury T), 1962 v E, S, W, Gr; 1963 v W; (with Swansea T), 1964 v W, U; 1965 v E, W, Sw (2); 1966 v W (12)
McLean, T. (Limavady), 1885 v S (1)
McMahon, J. (Bohemians), 1934 v S (1)
McMaster, G. (Glentoran), 1897 v E, S, W (3)
McMichael, A. (Newcastle U), 1950 v E, S; 1951 v E, S, F; 1952 v E, S, W; 1953 v E, S, W, F; 1954 v E, S, W; 1955 v E, W; 1956 v W; 1957 v E, S, W, I, P (2); 1958 v E, S, W, I (2), Cz (2), Arg, WG, F; 1959 v S, W, Sp; 1960 v E, S, W (40)
McMillan, G. (Distillery), 1903 v E; 1905 v W (2)
McMillan, S. (Manchester U), 1963 v E, S (2)
McMillen, W. S. (Manchester U), 1934 v E; 1935 v S; 1937 v S; (with Chesterfield), 1938 v S, W; 1939 v E, S (7)
McMordie, A. S. (Middlesbrough), 1969 v Is, T (2), E, S, W; 1970 v E, S, W, USSR; 1971 v Cy (2), E, S, W; 1972 v USSR, Sp, E, S, W; 1973 v Bul (21)
McMorran, E. J. (Belfast C), 1947 v E; (with Barnsley), 1951 v E, S, W; 1952 v E, S, W; 1953 v E, S, F; (with Doncaster R), 1953 v W; 1954 v E; 1956 v W; 1957 v I, P (15)
McMullan, D. (Liverpool), 1926 v E, W; 1927 v S (3)
McNinch, J. (Ballymena), 1931 v S; 1932 v S, W (3)
McParland, P. J. (Aston Villa), 1954 v W; 1955 v E, S; 1956 v E, S; 1957 v E, S, W, P; 1958 v E, S, W, I (2), Cz (2), Arg, WG, F; 1959 v E, S, W, Sp; 1960 v E, S, W; 1961 v E, S, W, I, WG (2), Gr; (with Wolverhampton W), 1962 v Ho (34)
McShane, J. (Cliftonville), 1899 v S; 1900 v E, S, W (4)
McVickers, J. (Glentoran), 1888 v E; 1889 v S (2)
McWha, W. B. R. (Knock), 1882 v E, W; (with Cliftonville), 1883 v E, W; 1884 v E; 1885 v E, W (7)
Macartney, A. (Ulster), 1903 v S, W; (with Linfield), 1904 v S, W; (with Everton), 1905 v E, S; (with Belfast C), 1907 v E, S, W; 1908 v E, S, W; (with Glentoran), 1909 v E, S, W (15)

Mackie, J. (Arsenal), 1923 v W; (with Portsmouth), 1935 v S, W (3)
Madden, O. (Norwich C), 1938 v E (1)
Magill, E. J. (Arsenal), 1962 v E, S, Gr; 1963 v E, S, W, Pol (2), Sp; 1964 v E, S, W, U, Sp; 1965 v E, S, Sw (2), Ho, Alb; 1966 v S, E; (with Brighton), 1966 v Alb, W, WG, M (26)
Maginnis, H. (Linfield), 1900 v E, S, W; 1903 v S, W; 1904 v E, S, W (8)
Maguire, E. (Distillery), 1907 v S (1)
Mahood, J. (Belfast C), 1926 v S; 1928 v E, S, W; 1929 v E, S, W; 1930 v W; (with Ballymena), 1934 v S (9)
Manderson, R. (Glasgow R), 1920 v W, S; 1925 v S, E; 1926 v S (5)
Mansfield, J. (Dublin Freebooters), 1901 v E (1)
Martin, C. J. (Glentoran), 1947 v S; (with Leeds U), 1948 v E, S, W; (with Aston Villa), 1949 v E; 1950 v W (6)
Martin, D. (Bo'ness), 1925 v S (1)
Martin, D. C. (Cliftonville), 1882 v E, W; 1883 v E (3)
Martin, D. K. (Belfast C), 1934 v E, S, W; 1935 v S; (with Wolverhampton W), 1935 v E; 1936 v W; (with Nottingham F), 1937 v S; 1938 v E, S; 1939 v S (10)
Mathieson, A. (Luton T), 1921 v W; 1922 v E (2)
Maxwell, J. (Linfield), 1902 v W; 1903 v W, E; (with Glentoran), 1905 v W, S; (with Belfast C), 1906 v W; 1907 v S (7)
Meek, H. L. (Glentoran), 1925 v W (1)
Mehaffy, J. A. C. (Queen's Island), 1922 v W (1)
Meldon, J. (Dublin Freebooters), 1899 v S, W (2)
Mercer, H. V. A. (Linfield), 1908 v E (1)
Mercer, J. T. (Distillery), 1898 v E, S, W; 1899 v E; (with Linfield), 1902 v E, W; (with Distillery), 1903 v S, W; (with Derby Co), 1904 v E, W; 1905 v S (11)
Millar, W. (Barrow), 1932 v W; 1933 v S (2)
Miller, J. (Middlesbrough), 1929 v W, S; 1930 v E (3)
Milligan, D. (Chesterfield), 1939 v W (1)
Milne, R. G. (Linfield), 1894 v E, S, W; 1895 v E, W; 1896 v E, S, W; 1897 v E, S; 1898 v E, S, W; 1899 v E, W; 1901 v W; 1902 v E, S, W; 1903 v E, S; 1904 v E, S, W; 1906 v E, S, W (27)
Mitchell, C. (Glentoran), 1934 v W (1)
Mitchell, E. J. (Cliftonville), 1933 v S (1)
Mitchell, W. (Distillery), 1932 v E, W; 1933 v E, W; (with Chelsea), 1934 v W, S; 1935 v S, E; 1936 v S, E; 1937 v E, S, W; 1938 v E, S (15)
Molyneux, T. B. (Ligoniel), 1883 v E, W; (with Cliftonville), 1884 v E, W, S; 1885 v E, W; 1886 v E, W, S; 1888 v S (11)
Montgomery, F. J. (Coleraine), 1955 v E (1)
Moore, C. (Glentoran), 1949 v W (1)
Moore, J. (Linfield Ath), 1891 v E, S, W (3)
Moore, P. (Aberdeen), 1933 v E (1)
Moore, T. (Ulster), 1887 v S, W (2)
Moore, W. (Falkirk), 1923 v S (1)
Moorhead, F. W. (Dublin University), 1885 v E (1)
Moorhead, G. (Linfield), 1923 v S; 1928 v S; 1929 v S (3)
Moran, J. (Leeds C), 1912 v S (1)
Moreland, V. (Derby Co), 1979 v Bul (sub), Bul (sub), E, S; 1980 v E, Ei (6)
Morgan, F. G. (Linfield), 1923 v E; (with Nottingham F), 1924 v S; 1927 v E; 1928 v E, S, W; 1929 v E (7)
Morgan, S. (Port Vale), 1972 v Sp; 1973 v Bul (sub), P, Cy, E, S, W; (with Aston Villa), 1974 v Bul, P, S, E; 1975 v Se; 1976 v Se (sub), N, Y; (with Brighton & HA), S, W (sub); (with Sparta Rotterdam), 1979 v D (18)
Morrison, J. (Linfield Ath), 1891 v E, W (2)
Morrison, T. (Glentoran), 1895 v E, S, W; (with Burnley), 1899 v W; 1900 v W; 1902 v E, S (7)
Morrogh, E. (Bohemians), 1896 v S (1)
Morrow, W. J. (Moyola Park), 1883 v E, W; 1884 v S (3)
Muir, R. (Oldpark), 1885 v S, W (2)
Mullan, P. (Glentoran), 1983 v S, E, W (3)
Mulholland, S. (Celtic), 1906 v S, E (2)
Mulligan, J. (Manchester C), 1921 v S (1)
Murphy, J. (Bradford C), 1910 v E, S, W (3)
Murphy, N. (QPR), 1905 v E, S, W (3)
Murray, J. M. (Motherwell), 1910 v E, S; (with Sheffield W), 1910 v W (3)

Napier, R. J. (Bolton W), 1966 v WG (1)
Neill, W. J. T. (Arsenal), 1961 v I, Gr, WG; 1962 v E, S, W, Gr; 1963 v E, W, Pol, Sp; 1964 v S, E, W, U, Sp; 1965 v E, S, W, Sw, Ho (2), Alb; 1966 v S, E, W, Alb, WG, M; 1967 v S, W; 1968 v S, E; 1969 v E, S, W, Is, T (2); 1970 v S, E, W, USSR (2); (with Hull C), 1971 v Cy, Sp; 1972 v USSR (2), Sp, S, E, W; 1973 v Bul, Cy (2), P, E, S, W (59)
Nelis, P. (Nottingham F), 1923 v E (1)
Nelson, S. (Arsenal), 1970 v W, E (sub); 1971 v Cy, Sp, E, S, W; 1972 v USSR (2), Sp, E, S, W; 1973 v Bul, Cy, P; 1974 v S, E; 1975 v Se, Y; 1976 v Se, N, Is, E; 1977 v Bel (sub), WG, W, Ic; 1978 v Ic, Ho, Bel; 1979 v Ei, D, Bul, E, Bul, E, S, W, D; 1980 v E, Ei, Is; 1981 v S, P, S, Se; (with Brighton & HA), 1982 v E, S, Sp (sub), A (51)
Nicholl, C. J. (Aston Villa), 1975 v Se, Y, E, S, W; 1976 v Se, N, Y, S, E, W; 1977 v W; (with Southampton), 1978 v Bel (sub), S, E, W; 1979 v Ei, Bul, E, Bul, E, W; 1980 v Ei, Is, S, E, W, Aus (3); 1981 v Se, P, S, P, S, Se; 1982 v S, Is, E, F, W, Y, Hon, Sp, A, F; 1983 v S (sub), E, W (49)
Nicholl, H. (Belfast C), 1902 v E, W; 1905 v E (3)
Nicholl, J. M. (Manchester U), 1976 v Is, W (sub); 1977 v Ho, Bel, E, S, W, Ic; 1978 v Ic, Ho, Bel, S, E, W; 1979 v Ei, D, Bul, E, Bul, E, S, W, D; 1980 v E, Ei, Is, S, E, W, Aus (3); 1981 v Se, P, S, P, S, Se; 1982 v S, Is, E; (with Toronto B), F, W, Y, Hon, Sp, A, F; (with Sunderland), 1983 v A, WG, Alb, T, Alb, (with Toronto), S, E, W (56)
Nicholson, J. J. (Manchester U), 1961 v S, W; 1962 v E, W, Gr, Ho; 1963 v E, S, Pol (2); (with Huddersfield T), 1965 v W, Ho (2), Alb; 1966 v S, E, W, Alb, M; 1967 v S, W; 1968 v S, E, W; 1969 v S, E, W, T (2); 1970 v S, E, W, USSR (2); 1971 v Cy (2), E, S, W; 1972 v USSR (2) (41)
Nixon, R. (Linfield), 1914 v S (1)
Nolan-Whelan, J. V. (Dublin Freebooters), 1901 v E, W; 1902 v S, W (4)

O'Brien, M. T. (QPR), 1921 v S; (with Leicester C), 1922 v S, W; 1924 v S, W; (with Hull C), 1925 v S, E, W; 1926 v W; (with Derby Co), 1927 v W (10)
O'Connell, P. (Sheffield W), 1912 v E, S; (with Hull C), 1914 v E, S, W (5)
O'Doherty, A. (Coleraine), 1970 v E, W (sub) (2)
O'Driscoll, J. F. (Swansea T), 1949 v E, S, W (3)
O'Hagan, C. (Tottenham H), 1905 v S, W; 1906 v S, W, E; (with Aberdeen), 1907 v E, S, W; 1908 v S, W; 1909 v E (11)
O'Hagan, W. (St Mirren), 1920 v E, W (2)
O'Hehir, J. C. (Bohemians), 1910 v W (1)
O'Kane, W. J. (Nottingham F), 1970 v E, W, S (sub); 1971 v Sp, E, S, W; 1972 v USSR (2); 1973 v P, Cy; 1974 v Bul, P, S, E, W; 1975 v N, Se, E, S (20)
O'Mahoney, M. T. (Bristol R), 1939 v S (1)
O'Neill, J. (Leicester C), 1980 v Is, S, E, W, Aus (3); 1981 v P, S, P, S, Se; 1982 v S, Is, E, F, S, F (sub); 1983 v A, WG, Alb, T, Alb, S (24)
O'Neill, J. (Sunderland), 1962 v W (1)
O'Neill, M. H. (Distillery), 1972 v USSR (sub), (with Nottingham F), Sp (sub), W (sub); 1973 v P, Cy, E, S, W; 1974 v Bul, P, E (sub), W; 1975 v Se, Y, E, S; 1976 v Y; 1977 v E (sub), S; 1978 v Ic, Ho, S, E, W; 1979 v Ei, D, Bul, E, Bul, D; 1980 v Ei, Is, Aus (3); 1981 v Se,

P (with Norwich C), P, S, Se; (with Manchester C), 1982 v S (with Norwich C), E, F, S, Y, Hon, Sp, A, F; 1983 v A, WG, Alb, T, Alb, S, E, W (57)

O'Reilly, H. (Dublin Freebooters), 1901 v S, W; 1904 v S (3)

Parke, J. (Linfield), 1964 v S; (with Hibernian), 1964 v E, Sp; (with Sunderland), 1965 v Sw, S, W, Ho (2), Alb; 1966 v WG; 1967 v E, S; 1968 v S, E (14)

Peacock, R. (Celtic), 1952 v S; 1953 v F; 1954 v W; 1955 v E, S; 1956 v E, S; 1957 v W, I, P; 1958 v S, E, W, I (2), Arg, Cz (2), WG; 1959 v E, S, W; 1960 v S, E; 1961 v E, S, I, WG (2), Gr; (with Coleraine), 1962 v S (31)

Peden, J. (Linfield), 1887 v S, W; 1888 v W, E; 1889 v S, E; 1890 v W, S; 1891 v W, E; 1892 v W, E; 1893 v E, S, W; (with Distillery), 1896 v W, E, S; 1897 v W, S; 1898 v W, E, S; (with Linfield), 1899 v W (24)

Percy, J. C. (Belfast YMCA), 1889 v W (1)

Platt, J. A. (Middlesbrough), 1976 v Is (sub); 1978 v S, E, W; 1980 v S, E, W, Aus (3); 1981 v Se, P; 1982 v F, S, W (sub), A; 1983 v A, WG, Alb, T (20)

Ponsonby, J. (Distillery), 1895 v S; 1896 v E, S, W; 1897 v E, S, W; 1899 v E (8)

Potts, R. M. C. (Cliftonville), 1883 v E, W (2)

Priestley, T. J. (Coleraine), 1933 v S; (with Chelsea), 1934 v E (2)

Pyper, Jas. (Cliftonville), 1897 v S, W; 1898 v S, E, W; 1899 v S; 1900 v E (7)

Pyper, John (Cliftonville), 1897 v E, S, W; 1899 v E, W; 1900 v E, W, S; 1902 v S (9)

Pyper, M. (Linfield), 1932 v W (1)

Rafferty, P. (Linfield), 1980 v E (sub) (1)

Rankine, J. (Alexander), 1883 v E, W (2)

Raper, E. O. (Dublin University), 1886 v W (1)

Rattray, D. (Avoniel), 1882 v E; 1883 v E, W (3)

Rea, B. (Glentoran), 1901 v E (1)

Redmond, J. (Cliftonville), 1884 v W (1)

Reid, G. H. (Cardiff C), 1923 v S (1)

Reid, J. (Ulster), 1883 v E; 1884 v W; 1887 v S; 1889 v W; 1890 v S, W (6)

Reid, S. E. (Derby Co), 1934 v E, W; 1936 v E (3)

Reid, W. (Hearts), 1931 v E (1)

Reilly, J. (Portsmouth), 1900 v E; 1902 v E (2)

Renneville, W. T. (Leyton), 1910 v S, E, W; (with Aston Villa), 1911 v W (4)

Reynolds, J. (Distillery), 1890 v E, W; (with Ulster), 1891 v E, S, W (5)

Reynolds, R. (Bohemians), 1905 v W (1)

Rice, P. J. (Arsenal), 1969 v Is; 1970 v USSR; 1971 v E, S, W; 1972 v USSR, Sp, E, S, W; 1973 v Bul, Cy, E, S, W; 1974 v Bul, P, S, E, W; 1975 v N, Y, E, S, W; 1976 v Se, N, Y, Is, S, E, W; 1977 v Ho, Bel, WG, E, S, Ic; 1978 v Ic, Ho, Bel; 1979 v Ei, D, E (2), S, W, D; 1980 v E (49)

Roberts, F. C. (Glentoran), 1931 v S (1)

Robinson, P. (Distillery), 1920 v S; (with Blackburn R), 1921 v W (2)

Rollo, D. (Linfield), 1912 v W; 1913 v W; 1914 v W, E; (with Blackburn R), 1920 v S, W; 1921 v E, S, W; 1922 v E; 1923 v E; 1924 v S, W; 1925 v W; 1926 v E; 1927 v E (16)

Rosbotham, A. (Cliftonville), 1887 v E, S, W; 1888 v E, S, W; 1889 v E (7)

Ross, W. E. (Newcastle U), 1969 v Is (1)

Rowley, R. W. M. (Southampton), 1929 v S, W; 1930 v W, E; (with Tottenham H), 1931 v W; 1932 v S (6)

Russell, A. (Linfield), 1947 v E (1)

Russell, S. R. (Bradford C), 1930 v E, S; (with Derry C), 1932 v E (3)

Ryan, R. A. (WBA), 1950 v W (1)

Scott, E. (Liverpool), 1920 v S; 1921 v E, S, W; 1922 v E; 1925 v W; 1926 v E, S, W; 1927 v E, S, W; 1928 v E, S, W; 1929 v E, S, W; 1930 v E; 1931 v E; 1932 v W; 1933 v E, S, W; 1934 v E, S, W; (with Belfast C), 1935 v S; 1936 v E, S, W (30)

Scott, J. (Grimsby), 1958 v Cz, F (2)

Scott, J. E. (Cliftonville), 1901 v S (1)

Scott, L. J. (Dublin University), 1895 v S, W (2)

Scott, P. W. (Everton), 1975 v W; 1976 v Y; (with York C), Is, S, E (sub), W; 1978 v S, E, W; (with Aldershot), 1979 v S (sub) (10)

Scott, T. (Cliftonville), 1894 v E, S; 1895 v S, W; 1896 v S, E, W; 1897 v E, W; 1898 v E, S, W; 1900 v W (13)

Scott, W. (Linfield), 1903 v E, S, W; 1904 v E, S, W; (with Everton), 1905 v E, S; 1907 v E, S; 1908 v E, S, W; 1909 v E, S, W; 1910 v E, S; 1911 v E, S, W; 1912 v E; (with Leeds City), 1913 v E, S, W (25)

Scraggs, M. J. (Glentoran), 1921 v W; 1922 v E (2)

Seymour, H. C. (Bohemians), 1914 v W (1)

Seymour, J. (Cliftonville), 1907 v W; 1909 v W (2)

Shanks, T. (Woolwich Arsenal), 1903 v S; 1904 v W; (with Brentford), 1905 v E (3)

Sharkey, P. (Ipswich T), 1976 v S (1)

Sheehan, Dr G. (Bohemians), 1899 v S; 1900 v E, W (3)

Sheridan, J. (Everton), 1903 v W, E, S; 1904 v E, S; (with Stoke C), 1905 v E (6)

Sherrard, J. (Limavady), 1885 v S; 1887 v W; 1888 v W (3)

Sherrard, W. (Cliftonville), 1895 v E, W, S (3)

Sherry, J. J. (Bohemians), 1906 v E; 1907 v W (2)

Shields, J. (Southampton), 1957 v S (1)

Silo, M. (Belfast YMCA), 1888 v E (1)

Simpson, W. J. (Glasgow R), 1951 v W, F; 1954 v E, S; 1955 v E; 1957 v I, P; 1958 v S, E, W, I; 1959 v S (12)

Sinclair, J. (Knock), 1882 v E, W (2)

Slemin, J. C. (Bohemians), 1909 v W (1)

Sloan, A. S. (London Caledonians), 1925 v W (1)

Sloan, D. (Oxford U), 1969 v Is; 1971 v Sp (2)

Sloan, H. A. de B. (Bohemians), 1903 v E; 1904 v S; 1905 v E; 1906 v W; 1907 v E, W; 1908 v W; 1909 v S (8)

Sloan, J. W. (Arsenal), 1947 v W (1)

Sloan, T. (Cardiff C), 1926 v S, W, E; 1927 v W, S; 1928 v E, W; 1929 v E; (with Linfield), 1930 v W, S; 1931 v S (11)

Sloan, T. (Manchester U), 1979 v S, W (sub), D (sub) (3)

Small, J. (Clarence), 1887 v E (1)

Small, J. M. (Cliftonville), 1893 v E, S, W (3)

Smith, E. E. (Cardiff C), 1921 v S; 1923 v W, E; 1924 v E (4)

Smith, J. (Distillery), 1901 v S, W (2)

Smyth, R. H. (Dublin University), 1886 v W (1)

Smyth, S. (Wolverhampton W), 1948 v E, S, W; 1949 v S, W; 1950 v E, S, W; (with Stoke C), 1952 v E (9)

Smyth, W. (Distillery), 1949 v E, S; 1954 v S, E (4)

Snape, A. (Airdrie), 1920 v E (1)

Spence, D. W. (Bury), 1975 v Y, E, S, W; 1976 v Se, Is, E, W, S (sub); (with Blackpool), 1977 v Ho (sub), WG (sub), E (sub), S (sub), W (sub), Ic (sub); 1979 v Ei, D (sub), E (sub), Bul (sub), E (sub), S, W, D; 1980 v Ei; (with Southend U), Is (sub), Aus (sub); 1981 v S (sub), Se (sub); 1982 v F (sub) (29)

Spencer, S. (Distillery), 1890 v E, S; 1892 v E, S, W; 1893 v E (6)

Spiller, E. A. (Cliftonville), 1883 v E, W; 1884 v E, W, S (5)

Stanfield, O. M. (Distillery), 1887 v E, S, W; 1888 v E, S, W; 1889 v E, S, W; 1890 v E, S; 1891 v E, S, W; 1892 v E, S, W; 1893 v E, W; 1894 v E, S, W; 1895 v E, S; 1896 v E, S, W; 1897 v E, S, W (30)

Steele, A. (Charlton Ath), 1926 v W, S; (with Fulham), 1929 v W, S (4)

Stevenson, A. E. (Rangers), 1934 v E, S, W; (with

Everton), 1935 v E, S; 1936 v S, W; 1937 v E, W; 1938 v E, W; 1939 v E, S, W; 1947 v S, W; 1948 v S (17)
Stewart, A. (Glentoran), 1967 v W; 1968 v S, E; (with Derby Co), 1968 v W; 1969 v Is, T (1+1 sub) (7)
Stewart, D. C. (Hull C), 1978 v Bel (1)
Stewart, I. (QPR), 1982 v F (sub); 1983 v A, WG, Alb, T, Alb, S, E, W (9)
Stewart, R. H. (St Columb's Court), 1890 v E, S, W; (with Cliftonville), 1892 v E, S, W; 1893 v E, W; 1894 v E, S, W (11)
Stewart, T. C. (Linfield), 1961 v W (1)
Swan, S. (Linfield), 1899 v S (1)

Taggart, J. (Walsall), 1899 v W (1)
Thompson, F. W. (Cliftonville), 1910 v E, S, W; (with Bradford C), 1911 v E; (with Linfield), v W; 1912 v E, W; 1913 v E, S, W; (with Clyde), 1914 v E, S (12)
Thompson, J. (Distillery), 1897 v S (1)
Thompson, J. (Belfast Ath), 1889 v S (1)
Thunder, P. J. (Bohemians), 1911 v W (1)
Todd, S. J. (Burnley), 1966 v M (sub); 1967 v E; 1968 v W; 1969 v E, S, W; 1970 v S, USSR; (with Sheffield W), 1971 v Cy (2), Sp (sub) (11)
Toner, J. (Arsenal), 1922 v W; 1923 v W; 1924 v W, E; 1925 v E, S; (with St Johnstone), 1927 v E, S (8)
Torrans, R. (Linfield), 1893 v S (1)
Torrans, S. (Linfield), 1889 v S; 1890 v S, W; 1891 v S, W; 1892 v E, S, W; 1893 v E, S; 1894 v E, S, W; 1895 v E; 1896 v E, S, W; 1897 v E, S, W; 1898 v E, S; 1899 v E, W; 1901 v S, W (26)
Trainor, D. (Crusaders), 1967 v W (1)
Tully, C. P. (Glasgow C), 1949 v E; 1950 v E; 1952 v S; 1953 v E, S, W, F; 1954 v S; 1956 v E; 1959 v Sp (10)
Turner, E. (Cliftonville), 1896 v E, W (2)
Turner, W. (Cliftonville), 1886 v E; 1886 v S; 1888 v S (3)
Twoomey, J. F. (Leeds U), 1938 v W; 1939 v E (2)

Uprichard, W. N. M. C. (Swindon T), 1952 v E, S, W; 1953 v E, S; (with Portsmouth), 1953 v W, F; 1955 v E, S, W; 1956 v E, S, W; 1958 v S, I, Cz; 1959 v S, Sp (18)

Vernon, J. (Belfast C), 1947 v E, S; (with WBA), 1947 v W; 1948 v E, S, W; 1949 v E, S, W; 1950 v E, S; 1951 v E, S, W, F; 1952 v S, E (17)

Waddell, T. M. R. (Cliftonville), 1906 v S (1)
Walker, J. (Doncaster R), 1955 v W (1)
Walker, T. (Bury), 1911 v S (1)
Walsh, D. J. (WBA), 1947 v S, W; 1948 v E, S, W; 1949 v E, S, W; 1950 v W (9)
Walsh, W. (Manchester C), 1948 v E, S, W; 1949 v E, S (5)
Waring, R. (Distillery), 1899 v E (1)
Warren, P. (Shelbourne), 1913 v E, S (2)
Watson, J. (Ulster), 1883 v E, W; 1886 v E, S, W; 1887 v S, W; 1889 v E, W (9)
Watson, P. (Distillery), 1971 v Cy (sub) (1)
Watson, T. (Cardiff C), 1926 v S (1)
Wattle, J. (Distillery), 1899 v E (1)
Webb, C. G. (Brighton), 1909 v S, W; 1911 v S (3)
Weir, E. (Clyde), 1939 v W (1)
Welsh, E. (Carlisle U), 1966 v W, WG, M; 1967 v W (4)
Whiteside, N. (Manchester U), 1982 v Y, Hon, Sp, A, F; 1983 v WG, Alb, T (8)
Whiteside, T. (Distillery), 1891 v E (1)
Whitfield, E. R. (Dublin University), 1886 v W (1)
Williams, J. R. (Ulster), 1886 v E, S (2)
Williamson, J. (Cliftonville), 1890 v E; 1892 v S; 1893 v S (3)
Willigham, T. (Burnley), 1933 v W; 1934 v S (2)
Willis, G. (Linfield), 1906 v S, W; 1907 v S; 1912 v S (4)
Wilson, H. (Linfield), 1925 v W (1)
Wilson, M. (Distillery), 1884 v E, S, W (3)
Wilson, R. (Cliftonville), 1888 v S (1)
Wilson, S. J. (Glenavon), 1962 v S; 1964 v S; (with Falkirk), 1964 v E, W, U, Sp; 1965 v E, Sw; (with Dundee), 1966 v W, WG; 1967 v S; 1968 v E (12)
Wilton, J. M. (St Columb's Court), 1888 v E, W; 1889 v S, E; (with Cliftonville), 1890 v E; (with St Columb's Court), 1892 v W; 1893 v S (7)
Wright, J. (Cliftonville), 1906 v E, S, W; 1907 v E, S, W (6)

Young, S. (Linfield), 1907 v E, S; 1908 v E, S; (with Airdrie), 1909 v E; 1912 v S; (with Linfield), 1914 v E, S, W (9)

SCOTLAND

Adams, J. (Hearts), 1889 v Ni; 1892 v W; 1893 v Ni (3)
Agnew, W. B. (Kilmarnock), 1907 v Ni; 1908 v W, Ni (3)
Aird, J. (Burnley), 1954 v N (2), A, U (4)
Aitken, A. (Newcastle U), 1901 v E; 1902 v E; 1903 v E, W; 1904 v E; 1905 v E, W; 1906 v E; (with Middlesbrough), 1907 v E, W; 1908 v E; (with Leicester Fosse), 1910 v E; 1911 v E, Ni (14)
Aitken, G. G. (East Fife), 1949 v E, F; 1950 v W, Ni, Sw; (with Sunderland), 1953 v W, Ni; 1954 v E (8)
Aitken, R. (Dumbarton), 1886 v E; 1888 v Ni (2)
Aitken, R. (Celtic), 1980 v Pe (sub), Bel, W (sub), E, Pol; 1983 v Bel, Ca (1+1 sub) (8)
Aitkenhead, W. A. C. (Blackburn R), 1912 v Ni (1)
Albiston, A. (Manchester U), 1982 v Ni (1)
Alexander, D. (East Stirlingshire), 1894 v W, Ni (2)
Allan, D. S. (Queen's Park), 1885 v E, W; 1886 v W (3)
Allan, G. (Liverpool), 1897 v E (1)
Allan, H. (Hearts), 1902 v W (1)
Allan, J. (Queen's Park), 1887 v E, W (2)
Allan, T. (Dundee), 1974 v WG, N (2)
Ancell, R. F. D. (Newcastle U), 1937 v W, Ni (2)
Anderson, A. (Hearts), 1933 v E; 1934 v A, E, W, Ni; 1935 v E, W, Ni; 1936 v E, W, Ni; 1937 v G, E, W, Ni, A; 1938 v E, W, Ni, Cz, Ho; 1939 v W, H (23)
Anderson, F. (Clydesdale), 1874 v E (1)
Anderson, G. (Kilmarnock), 1901 v Ni (1)
Anderson, H. A. (Raith R), 1914 v W (1)
Anderson, J. (Leicester C), 1954 v Fi (1)
Anderson, K. (Queen's Park), 1896 v Ni; 1898 v E, Ni (3)
Anderson, W. (Queen's Park), 1882 v E; 1883 v E, W; 1884 v E; 1885 v E, W (6)
Andrews, P. (Eastern), 1875 v E (1)
Archibald, A. (Rangers), 1921 v W; 1922 v W, E; 1923 v Ni; 1924 v E, W; 1931 v E; 1932 v E (8)
Archibald, S. (Aberdeen), 1980 v P (sub); (with Tottenham H), Ni, Pol, H; 1981 v Se (sub), Is, Ni, Is, Ni, E; 1982 v Ni, P, Sp (sub), Ho, Nz (sub), Br, USSR; 1983 v EG, Sw (sub), Bel (20)
Armstrong, M. W. (Aberdeen), 1936 v W, Ni; 1937 v G (3)
Arnott, W. (Queen's Park), 1883 v W; 1884 v E, Ni; 1885 v E, W; 1886 v E; 1887 v E, W; 1888 v E; 1889 v E; 1890 v E; 1891 v E; 1892 v E; 1893 v E (14)
Auld, J. R. (Third Lanark), 1887 v E, W; 1889 v W (3)
Auld, R. (Celtic), 1959 v H, P; 1960 v W (3)

Baird, A. (Queen's Park), 1892 v Ni; 1894 v W (2)
Baird, D. (Hearts), 1890 v Ni; 1891 v E; 1892 v W (3)
Baird, H. (Airdrie), 1956 v A (1)
Baird, J. C. (Vale of Leven), 1876 v E; 1878 v W; 1880 v E (3)
Baird, S. (Rangers), 1957 v Y, Sp (2), Sw, WG; 1958 v F, Ni (7)

Baird, W. U. (St Bernard), 1897 v Ni (1)
Bannon, E. (Dundee U), 1980 v Bel; 1983 v Ni, W, E, Ca (5)
Barbour, A. (Renton), 1885 v Ni (1)
Barker, J. B. (Rangers), 1893 v W; 1894 v W (2)
Barrett, F. (Dundee), 1894 v Ni; 1895 v W (2)
Battles, B. (Celtic), 1901 v E, W, Ni (3)
Battles, B. jun. (Hearts), 1931 v W (1)
Bauld, W. (Hearts), 1950 v E, Sw, P (3)
Baxter, J. C. (Rangers), 1961 v Ni, Ei (2), Cz; 1962 v Ni, W, E, Cz (2), U; 1963 v W, Ni, E, A, N, Ei, Sp; 1964 v W, E, N, WG; 1965 v W, Ni, Fi; (with Sunderland), 1966 v P, Br, Ni, W, E, I; 1967 v W, E, USSR; 1968 v W (34)
Baxter, R. D. (Middlesbrough), 1939 v E, W, H (3)
Beattie, A. (Preston NE), 1937 v E, A, Cz; 1938 v E; 1939 v W, Ni, H (7)
Beattie, R. (Preston NE), 1939 v W (1)
Begbie, I. (Hearts), 1890 v Ni; 1891 v E; 1892 v W; 1894 v E (4)
Bell, A. (Manchester U), 1912 v Ni (1)
Bell, J. (Dumbarton), 1890 v Ni; 1892 v E; (with Everton), 1896 v E; 1897 v E; 1898 v E; (with Celtic), 1899 v E, W, Ni; 1900 v E, W (10)
Bell, M. (Hearts), 1901 v W (1)
Bell, W. J. (Leeds U), 1966 v P, Br (2)
Bennett, A. (Celtic), 1904 v W; 1907 v Ni; 1908 v W; (with Rangers), 1909 v W, Ni, E; 1910 v E, W; 1911 v E, W; 1913 v Ni (11)
Bennie, R. (Airdrieonians), 1925 v W, Ni; 1926 v Ni (3)
Berry, D. (Queen's Park), 1894 v W; 1899 v W, Ni (3)
Berry, W. H. (Queen's Park), 1888 v E; 1889 v E; 1890 v E; 1891 v E (4)
Bett, J. (Rangers), 1982 v Ho; 1983 v Bel (2)
Beveridge, W. W. (Glasgow University), 1879 v E, W; 1880 v W (3)
Black, A. (Hearts), 1938 v Cz, Ho; 1939 v H (3)
Black, D. (Hurlford), 1889 v Ni (1)
Black, I. H. (Southampton), 1948 v E (1)
Blackburn, J. E. (Royal Engineers), 1873 v E (1)
Blacklaw, A. S. (Burnley), 1963 v N, Sp; 1966 v I (3)
Blackley, J. (Hibernian), 1974 v Cz, E, Bel, Z; 1976 v Sw; 1977 v W, Se (7)
Blair, D. (Clyde), 1929 v W, Ni; 1931 v E, A, I; 1932 v W, Ni; (with Aston Villa), 1933 v W (8)
Blair, J. (Sheffield W), 1920 v E, Ni; (with Cardiff C), 1921 v E; 1922 v E; 1923 v E, W, Ni; 1924 v W (8)
Blair, J. (Motherwell), 1934 v W (1)
Blair, J. A. (Blackpool), 1947 v W (1)
Blair, W. (Third Lanark), 1896 v W (1)
Blessington J. (Celtic), 1894 v E, Ni; 1896 v E, Ni (4)
Blyth, J. A. (Coventry C), 1978 v Bul, W (2)
Bone, J. (Norwich C), 1972 v Y (sub); 1973 v D (2)
Bowie, J. (Rangers), 1920 v E, Ni (2)
Bowie, W. (Linthouse), 1891 v Ni (1)
Bowman, G. A. (Montrose), 1892 v Ni (1)
Boyd, J. M. (Newcastle U), 1934 v Ni (1)
Boyd, R. (Mossend Swifts), 1889 v Ni; 1891 v W (2)
Boyd, W. G. (Clyde), 1931 v I, Sw (2)
Brackenbridge, T. (Hearts), 1888 v Ni (1)
Bradshaw, T. (Bury), 1928 v E (1)
Brand, R. (Rangers), 1961 v Ni, Cz, Ei (2); 1962 v Ni, W, Cz, U (8)
Branden, T. (Blackburn R), 1896 v E (1)
Brazil, A. (Ipswich T), 1980 v Pol (sub), H; 1982 v Sp, Ho (sub), Ni, W, E, Nz, USSR (sub); 1983 v EG, Sw, W, E (sub) (13)
Bremner, D. (Hibernian), 1976 v Sw (sub) (1)
Bremner, W. J. (Leeds U), 1965 v Sp; 1966 v E, Pol, P, Br, I (2); 1967 v W, Ni, E; 1968 v W, E; 1969 v W, E, Ni, D, A, WG, Cy (2); 1970 v Ei, WG, A; 1971 v W, E; 1972 v P, Bel, Ho, Ni, W, E, Y, Cz, Br; 1973 v D (2), E (2), Ni (sub), Sw, Br; 1974 v Cz, WG, Ni, W, E, Bel, N, Z, Br, Y; 1975 v Sp (2); 1976 v D (54)
Brennan, F. (Newcastle U), 1947 v W, Ni; 1953 v W, Ni, E; 1954 v Ni, E (7)
Breslin, B. (Hibernian), 1897 v W (1)
Brewster, G. (Everton), 1921 v E (1)
Brogan, J. (Celtic), 1971 v W, Ni, P, E (4)
Brown, A. (Middlesbrough), 1904 v E (1)
Brown, A. (St Mirren), 1890 v W; 1891 v W (2)
Brown, A. D. (East Fife), 1950 v Sw, P, F; (with Blackpool), 1952 v USA, D, Se; 1953 v W; 1954 v W, E, N (2), Fi, A, U (14)
Brown, G. C. P. (Rangers), 1931 v W; 1932 v E, W, Ni; 1933 v E; 1935 v A, E, W; 1936 v E, W; 1937 v G, E, W, Ni, Cz; 1938 v E, W, Cz, Ho (19)
Brown, H. (Partick T), 1947 v W, Bel, L (3)
Brown, J. (Cambuslang), 1890 v W (1)
Brown, J. B. (Clyde), 1939 v W (1)
Brown, J. G. (Sheffield U), 1975 v R (1)
Brown, R. (Dumbarton), 1884 v W, Ni (2)
Brown, R. (Rangers), 1947 v Ni; 1949 v Ni; 1952 v E (3)
Brown, R. jun. (Dumbarton), 1885 v W (1)
Brown, W. D. F. (Dundee), 1958 v F; 1959 v E, W, Ni; (with Tottenham H), 1960 v W, Ni, Pol, A, H, T; 1962 v Ni, W, E, Cz; 1963 v W, Ni, E, A; 1964 v Ni, W, N; 1965 v E, Fi, Pol, Sp; 1966 v Ni, Pol, I (28)
Browning, J. (Celtic), 1914 v W (1)
Brownie, J. (Hibernian), 1971 v USSR; 1972 v Pe, Ni, E; 1973 v D (2); 1976 v R (7)
Brownlie, J. (Third Lanark), 1909 v E, Ni; 1910 v E, W, Ni; 1911 v W, Ni; 1912 v W, Ni, E; 1913 v W, Ni, E; 1914 v W, Ni, E (16)
Bruce, D. (Vale of Leven), 1890 v W (1)
Bruce, R. F. (Middlesbrough), 1934 v A (1)
Buchan, M. M. (Aberdeen), 1972 v P (sub), Bel; (with Manchester U), W, Y, Cz, Br; 1973 v D (2), E; 1974 v WG, Ni, W, N, Br, Y; 1975 v EG, Sp, P; 1976 v D, R; 1977 v Fi, Cz, Ch, Arg, Br; 1978 v EG, W (sub), Ni, Pe, Ir, Ho; 1979 v A, N, P (34)
Buchanan, J. (Cambuslang), 1889 v Ni (1)
Buchanan, J. (Rangers), 1929 v E; 1930 v E (2)
Buchanan, P. S. (Chelsea), 1938 v Cz (1)
Buchanan, R. (Abercorn), 1891 v W (1)
Buckley, P. (Aberdeen), 1954 v N; 1955 v W, Ni (3)
Buick, A. (Hearts), 1902 v W, Ni (2)
Burley, G. (Ipswich T), 1979 v W, Ni, E, Arg, N; 1980 v P, Ni, E (sub), Pol; 1982 v W (sub), E (11)
Burns, F. (Manchester U), 1970 v A (1)
Burns, K. (Birmingham C), 1974 v WG; 1975 v EG (sub), Sp (2); 1977 v Cz (sub), W, Se, W (sub); (with Nottingham F), 1978 v Ni (sub), W, E, Pe, Ir; 1979 v N; 1980 v Pe, A, Bel; 1981 v Is, Ni, W (20)
Burns, T. (Celtic), 1981 v Ni; 1982 v Ho (sub), W; 1983 v Bel (sub), Ni, Ca (1 +1 sub) (7)
Busby, M. W. (Manchester C), 1934 v W (1)

Cairns, T. (Rangers), 1920 v W; 1922 v E; 1923 v E, W; 1924 v Ni; 1925 v W, E, Ni (8)
Calderhead, D. (Queen of the South), 1889 v Ni (1)
Calderwood, R. (Cartvale), 1885 v Ni, E, W (3)
Caldow, E. (Rangers), 1957 v Sp (2), Sw, WG, E; 1958 v Ni, W, Sw, Par, H, Pol, Y, F; 1959 v E, W, Ni, WG, Ho, P; 1960 v E, W, Ni, A, H, T; 1961 v E, W, Ni, Ei (2), Cz; 1962 v Ni, W, E, Cz (2), U; 1963 v W, Ni, E (40)
Callaghan, P. (Hibernian), 1900 v Ni (1)
Callaghan, W. (Dunfermline Ath), 1970 v Ei (sub), W (2)
Cameron, J. (St Mirren), 1904 v Ni; (with Chelsea), 190 v E (2)
Cameron, J. (Queen's Park), 1896 v Ni (1)
Cameron, J. (Rangers), 1886 v Ni (1)
Campbell, C. (Queen's Park), 1874 v E; 1876 v W; 187

v E, W; 1878 v E; 1879 v E; 1880 v E; 1881 v E; 1882 v E, W; 1884 v E; 1885 v E; 1886 v E (13)
Campbell, H. (Renton), 1889 v W (1)
Campbell, Jas. (Sheffield W), 1913 v W (1)
Campbell, J. (South Western), 1880 v W (1)
Campbell, J. (Kilmarnock), 1891 v Ni; 1892 v W (2)
Campbell, John (Celtic), 1893 v E, Ni; 1898 v E, Ni; 1900 v E, Ni; 1901 v E, W, Ni; 1902 v W, Ni; 1903 v W (12)
Campbell, John (Rangers), 1899 v E, W, Ni; 1901 v Ni (4)
Campbell, K. (Liverpool), 1920 v E, W, Ni; (with Partick T), 1921 v W, Ni; 1922 v W, Ni, E (8)
Campbell, P. (Rangers), 1878 v W; 1879 v W (2)
Campbell, P. (Morton), 1898 v W (1)
Campbell, R. (Falkirk), 1947 v Bel, L; (with Chelsea), 1950 v Sw, P, F (5)
Campbell, W. (Morton), 1947 v Ni; 1948 v E, Bel, Sw, F (5)
Carabine, J. (Third Lanark), 1938 v Ho; 1939 v E, Ni (3)
Carr, W. M. (Coventry C), 1970 v Ni, W, E; 1971 v D; 1972 v Pe; 1973 v D (sub) (6)
Cassidy, J. (Celtic), 1921 v W, Ni; 1923 v Ni; 1924 v W (4)
Chalmers, S. (Celtic), 1965 v W, Fi; 1966 v P (sub), Br; 1967 v Ni (5)
Chalmers, W. (Rangers), 1885 v Ni (1)
Chalmers, W. S. (Queen's Park), 1929 v Ni (1)
Chambers, T. (Hearts), 1894 v W (1)
Chaplin, G. D. (Dundee), 1908 v W (1)
Cheyne, A. G. (Aberdeen), 1929 v E, N, G, Ho; 1930 v F (5)
Christie, A. J. (Queen's Park), 1898 v W; 1899 v E, Ni (3)
Christie, R. M. (Queen's Park), 1884 v E (1)
Clark, J. (Celtic), 1966 v Br; 1967 v W, Ni, USSR (4)
Clark, R. B. (Aberdeen), 1968 v W, Ho; 1970 v Ni; 1971 v W, Ni, E, D, P, USSR; 1972 v Bel, Ni, W, E, Cz, Br; 1973 v D, E (17)
Cleland, J. (Royal Albert), 1891 v Ni (1)
Clements, R. (Leith Ath), 1891 v Ni (1)
Clunas, W. L. (Sunderland), 1924 v E; 1926 v W (2)
Collier, W. (Raith R), 1922 v W (1)
Collins, R. Y. (Celtic), 1951 v W, Ni, A; 1955 v Y, A, H; 1956 v Ni, W; 1957 v E, W, Sp (2), Sw, WG; 1958 v Ni, W, Sw, H, Pol, Y, F, Par; (with Everton), 1959 v E, W, Ni, WG, Ho, P; (with Leeds U), 1965 v E, Pol, Sp (31)
Collins, T. (Hearts), 1909 v W (1)
Colman, D. (Aberdeen), 1911 v E, W, Ni; 1913 v Ni (4)
Colquhoun, E. P. (Sheffield U), 1972 v P, Ho, Pe, Y, Cz, Br; 1973 v D (2), E (9)
Combe, J. R. (Hibernian), 1948 v E, Bel, Sw (3)
Conn, A. (Hearts), 1956 v A (1)
Conn, A. (Tottenham H), 1975 v Ni (sub), E (2)
Connachan, E. D. (Dunfermline Ath), 1962 v Cz, U (2)
Connelly, G. (Celtic), 1974 v Cz, WG (2)
Connolly, J. (Everton), 1973 v Sw (1)
Connor, J. (Airdrieonians), 1886 v Ni (1)
Connor, J. (Sunderland), 1930 v F; 1932 v Ni; 1934 v E; 1935 v Ni (4)
Cook, W. L. (Bolton W), 1934 v E; 1935 v W, Ni (3)
Cooke, C. (Dundee), 1966 v W, I; (with Chelsea), P, Br; 1968 v E, Ho; 1969 v W, Ni, A, WG (sub), Cy (2); 1970 v A; 1971 v Bel; 1975 v Sp, P (16)
Cooper, D. (Rangers), 1980 v Pe, A (sub) (2)
Cormack, P. B. (Hibernian), 1966 v Br; 1969 v D (sub); 1970 v Ei, WG; (with Nottingham F), 1971 v D (sub), W, P, E; 1972 v Ho (sub) (9)
Cowan, J. (Aston Villa), 1896 v E; 1897 v E; 1898 v E (3)
Cowan, J. (Morton), 1948 v Bel, Sw; F; 1949 v E, W, F; 1950 v E, W, Ni, Sw, P, F; 1951 v E, W, Ni, A (2), D, F, Bel; 1952 v Ni, W, USA, D, Se (25)
Cowan, W, D. (Newcastle U), 1924 v E (1)
Cowie, D. (Dundee), 1953 v E, Se; 1954 v Ni, W, Fi, N, A, U; 1955 v W, Ni, A, H; 1956 v W, A; 1957 v Ni, W; 1958 v H, Pol, Y, Par (20)
Cox, S. (Rangers), 1948 v F; 1949 v E, F; 1950 v E, F, W, Ni, Sw, P; 1951 v E, D, F, Bel, A; 1952 v Ni, W, USA, D, Se; 1953 v W, Ni, E; 1954 v W, Ni, E (25)
Craig, A. (Motherwell), 1929 v N, Ho; 1932 v E (3)
Craig, J. (Celtic), 1977 v Se (sub) (1)
Craig, J. P. (Celtic), 1968 v W (1)
Craig, T. (Rangers), 1927 v Ni; 1928 v Ni; 1929 v N, G, Ho; 1930 v Ni, E, W (8)
Craig, T. B. (Newcastle U), 1976 v Sw (1)
Crapnell, J. (Airdrieonians), 1929 v E, N, G; 1930 v F; 1931 v Ni, Sw; 1932 v E, F; 1933 v Ni (9)
Crawford, D. (St Mirren), 1894 v W, Ni; 1900 v W (3)
Crawford, J. (Queen's Park), 1932 v F, Ni; 1933 v E, W, Ni (5)
Crerand, P. T. (Celtic), 1961 v Ei (2), Cz; 1962 v Ni, W, E, Cz (2), U; 1963 v W, Ni; (with Manchester U), 1964 v Ni; 1965 v E, Pol, Fi; 1966 v Pol (16)
Cringan, W. (Celtic), 1920 v W; 1922 v E, Ni; 1923 v W, E (5)
Crosbie, J. A. (Ayr U), 1920 v W; (with Birmingham), 1922 v E (2)
Croal, J. A. (Falkirk), 1913 v Ni; 1914 v E, W (3)
Cropley, A. J. (Hibernian), 1972 v P, Bel (2)
Cross, J. H. (Third Lanark), 1903 v Ni (1)
Cruickshank, J. (Hearts), 1964 v WG; 1970 v W, E; 1971 v D, Bel; 1976 v R (6)
Crum, J. (Celtic), 1936 v E; 1939 v Ni (2)
Cullen, M. J. (Luton T), 1956 v A (1)
Cumming, D. S. (Middlesbrough), 1938 v E (1)
Cumming, J. (Hearts), 1955 v E, H, P, Y; 1960 v E, Pol, A, H, T (9)
Cummings, G. (Partick T), 1935 v E; 1936 v W, Ni; (with Aston Villa), E; 1937 v G; 1938 v W, Ni, Cz; 1939 v E (9)
Cunningham, A. N. (Rangers), 1920 v Ni; 1921 v W, E; 1922 v Ni; 1923 v E, W; 1924 v E, Ni; 1926 v E, Ni; 1927 v E, W (12)
Cunningham, W. C. (Preston NE), 1954 v N (2), U, Fi, A; 1955 v W, E, H (8)
Curran, H. P. (Wolverhampton W), 1970 v A; 1971 v Ni, E, D, USSR (sub) (5)

Dalglish, K. (Celtic), 1972 v Bel (sub), Ho; 1973 v D (1+1 sub), E (2), W, Ni, Sw, Br; 1974 v Cz (2), WG (2), Ni, W, E, Bel, N (sub), Z, Br, Y; 1975 v EG, Sp (sub+1), Se, P, W, Ni, E, R; 1976 v D (2), R, Sw, Ni, E; 1977 v Fi, Cz, W (2), Se, Ni, E, Ch, Arg, Br; (with Liverpool), 1978 v EG, Cz, W, Bul, Ni (sub), W, E, Pe, Ir, Ho; 1979 v A, N, P, W, Ni, E, Arg, N; 1980 v Pe, A, Bel (2), P, Ni, W, E, Pol, H; 1981 v Se, P, Is; 1982 v Se, Ni, P (sub), Sp, Ho, Ni, W, E, Nz, Br (sub); 1983 v Bel, Sw (90)
Davidson, D. (Queen's Park), 1878 v W; 1879 v W; 1880 v W; 1881 v E, W (5)
Davidson, J. A. (Partick T), 1954 v N (2), A, U; 1955 v W, Ni, E, H (8)
Davidson, S. (Middlesbrough), 1921 v E (1)
Dawson, A. (Rangers), 1980 v Pol (sub), H; 1983 v Ni, Ca (2) (5)
Dawson, J. (Rangers), 1935 v Ni; 1936 v E; 1937 v G, E, W, Ni, A, Cz; 1938 v W, Ho, Ni; 1939 v E, Ni, H (14)
Deans, J. (Celtic), 1975 v EG, Sp (2)
Delaney, J. (Celtic), 1936 v W, Ni; 1937 v G, E, A, Cz; 1938 v Ni; 1939 v W, Ni; (with Manchester U), 1947 v E; 1948 v E, W, Ni (13)
Devine, A. (Falkirk), 1910 v W (1)
Dewar, G. (Dumbarton), 1888 v Ni; 1889 v E (2)
Dewar, N. (Third Lanark), 1932 v E, F; 1933 v W (3)
Dick, J. (West Ham U), 1959 v E (1)
Dickie, M. (Rangers), 1897 v Ni; 1899 v Ni; 1900 v W (3)

Bill Brown *Tottenham Hotspur* and *Scotland*

Archie Gemmill *Derby County* and *Scotland*

Jimmy Gibson *Aston Villa* and *Scotland*

Dickson, W. (Kilmarnock), 1970 v Ni, W, E; 1971 v D, USSR (5)
Dickson, W. (Dumbarton), 1888 v Ni (1)
Divers, J. (Celtic), 1895 v W (1)
Divers, J. (Celtic), 1939 v Ni (1)
Docherty, T. H, (Preston NE), 1952 v W; 1953 v E, Se; 1954 v N (2), A, U; 1955 v W, E, H (2), A; 1957 v E, Y, Sp (2), Sw, WG; 1958 v Ni, W, E, Sw; (with Arsenal), 1959 v W, E, Ni (25)
Dodds, J. (Celtic), 1914 v E, W, Ni (3)
Doig, J. E. (Arbroath), 1887 v Ni; 1889 v Ni; (with Sunderland), 1896 v E; 1899 v E; 1903 v E (5)
Donachie, W. (Manchester C), 1972 v Pe, Ni, E, Y, Cz, Br; 1973 v D, E, W, Ni; 1974 v Ni; 1976 v R, Ni, W, E; 1977 v Fi, Cz, W (2), Se, Ni, E, Ch, Arg, Br; 1978 v EG, W, Bul, W, E, Ir, Ho; 1979 v A, N, P (sub) (35)
Donaldson, A. (Bolton W), 1914 v E, Ni, W; 1920 v E, Ni; 1922 v Ni (6)
Donnachie, J. (Oldham Ath), 1913 v E; 1914 v E, Ni (3)
Dougall, C. (Birmingham C), 1947 v W (1)
Dougall, J. (Preston NE), 1939 v E (1)
Dougan, R. (Hearts), 1950 v Sw (1)
Douglas, A. (Chelsea), 1911 v Ni (1)
Douglas, J. (Renfrew), 1880 v W (1)
Dowds, P. (Celtic), 1892 v Ni (1)
Downie, R. (Third Lanark), 1892 v W (1)
Doyle, D. (Celtic), 1892 v E; 1893 v W; 1894 v E; 1895 v E, Ni; 1897 v E; 1898 v E, Ni (8)
Doyle, J. (Ayr U), 1976 v R (1)
Drummond, J. (Falkirk), 1892 v Ni; (with Rangers), 1894 v Ni; 1895 v Ni, E; 1896 v E, Ni; 1897 v Ni; 1898 v E; 1900 v E; 1901 v E; 1902 v E, W, Ni; 1903 v Ni (14)
Dunbar, M. (Cartvale), 1886 v Ni (1)
Duncan, A. (Hibernian), 1975 v P (sub), W, Ni, E, R; 1976 v D (6)
Duncan, D. (Derby Co), 1933 v E, W; 1934 v A, W; 1935 v E, W; 1936 v E, W, Ni; 1937 v G, E, W, Ni; 1938 v W (14)
Duncan, D. M. (East Fife), 1948 v Bel, Sw, F (3)
Duncan, J. (Alexandra Ath), 1878 v W; 1882 v W (2)
Duncan, J. (Leicester C), 1926 v W (1)
Duncanson, J. (Rangers), 1947 v Ni (1)
Dunlop, J. (St Mirren), 1890 v W (1)
Dunlop, W. (Liverpool), 1906 v E (1)
Dunn, J. (Hibernian), 1925 v W, Ni; 1927 v Ni; 1928 v Ni, E; (with Everton), 1929 v W (6)
Dykes, J. (Hearts), 1938 v Ho; 1939 v Ni (2)

Easson, J. F. (Portsmouth), 1931 v A, Sw; 1934 v W (3)
Ellis, J. (Mossend Swifts), 1892 v Ni (1)
Evans, A. (Aston Villa), 1982 v Ho, Ni, E, Nz (4)
Evans, R. (Celtic), 1949 v E, W, Ni, F; 1950 v W, Ni, Sw, P; 1951 v E, A; 1952 v Ni; 1953 v Se; 1954 v Ni, W, E, N, Fi; 1955 v Ni, P, Y, A, H; 1956 v E, Ni, W, A; 1957 v WG, Sp; 1958 v Ni, W, E, Sw, H, Pol, Y, Par, F; 1959 v E, WG, Ho, P; 1960 v E, Ni, W, Pol; (with Chelsea), 1960 v A, H, T (48)
Ewart, J. (Bradford C), 1921 v E (1)
Ewing, T. (Partick T), 1958 v W, E (2)

Farm, G. N. (Blackpool), 1953 v W, Ni, E, Se; 1954 v Ni, W, E; 1959 v WG, Ho, P (10)
Ferguson, J. (Vale of Leven), 1874 v E; 1876 v E, W; 1877 v E, W; 1878 v W (6)
Ferguson, R. (Kilmarnock), 1966 v W, E, Ho, P, Br; 1967 v W, Ni (7)
Fernie, W. (Celtic), 1954 v Fi, A, U; 1955 v W, Ni; 1957 v E, Ni, W, Y; 1958 v W, Sw, Par (12)
Findlay, R. (Kilmarnock), 1898 v W (1)
Fitchie, T. T. (Woolwich Arsenal), 1905 v W; 1906 v W, Ni; (with Queen's Park), 1907 v W (4)
Flavell, R. (Airdrieonians), 1947 v Bel, L (2)
Fleming, C. (East Fife), 1954 v Ni (1)
Fleming, J. W. (Rangers), 1929 v G, Ho; 1930 v E (3)
Fleming, R. (Morton), 1886 v Ni (1)
Forbes, A. R. (Sheffield U), 1947 v Bel, L, E; 1948 v W, Ni; (with Arsenal), 1950 v E, P, F; 1951 v W, Ni, A; 1952 v W, D, Se (14)
Forbes, J. (Vale of Leven), 1884 v E, W, Ni; 1887 v W, E (5)
Ford, D. (Hearts), 1974 v Cz (sub), WG (sub), W (3)
Forrest, J. (Rangers), 1966 v W, I; (with Aberdeen), 1971 v Bel (sub), D, USSR (5)
Forrest, J. (Motherwell), 1958 v E (1)
Forsyth, A. (Partick T), 1972 v Y, Cz, Br; 1973 v D; (with Manchester U), E; 1975 v Sp, Ni (sub), R, EG; 1976 v D (10)
Forsyth, C. (Kilmarnock), 1964 v E; 1965 v W, Ni, Fi (4)
Forsyth, T. (Motherwell), 1971 v D; (with Rangers), 1974 v Cz; 1976 v Sw, Ni, W, E; 1977 v Fi, Se, W, Ni, E, Ch, Arg, Br; 1978 v Cz, W, Ni, W (sub), E, Pe, Ir (sub), Ho (22)
Foyers, R. (St Bernards), 1893 v W; 1894 v W (2)
Fraser, D. M. (WBA), 1968 v Ho; 1969 v Cy (2)
Fraser, J. (Moffat), 1891 v Ni (1)
Fraser, M. J. E. (Queen's Park), 1880 v W; 1882 v W, E; 1883 v W, E (5)
Fraser, J. (Dundee), 1907 v Ni (1)
Fraser, W. (Sunderland), 1955 v W, Ni (2)
Fulton, W. (Abercorn), 1884 v Ni (1)
Fyfe, J. H. (Third Lanark), 1895 v W (1)

Gabriel, J. (Everton), 1961 v W; 1964 v N (sub) (2)
Gallacher, H. K. (Airdrieonians), 1924 v Ni; 1925 v E, W, Ni; 1926 v W; (with Newcastle U), 1926 v E, Ni; 1927 v E, W, Ni; 1928 v E, W; 1929 v E, W, Ni; 1930 v W, Ni, F; (with Chelsea), 1934 v E; (with Derby Co), 1935 v E (20)
Gallacher, P. (Sunderland), 1935 v Ni (1)
Galt, J. H. (Rangers), 1908 v W, Ni (2)
Gardiner, I. (Motherwell), 1958 v W (1)
Gardner, D. R. (Third Lanark), 1897 v W (1)
Gardner, R. (Queen's Park), 1872 v E; 1873 v E; (with Clydesdale), 1874 v E; 1875 v E; 1878 v E (5)
Gemmell, T. (St Mirren), 1955 v P, Y (2)
Gemmell, T. (Celtic), 1966 v E; 1967 v W, Ni, E, USSR; 1968 v Ni, E; 1969 v W, Ni, E, D, A, WG, Cy; 1970 v E, Ei, WG; 1971 v Bel (18)
Gemmill, A. (Derby Co), 1971 v Bel; 1972 v P, Ho, Pe, Ni, W, E; 1976 v D, R, Ni, W, E; 1977 v Fi, Cz, W (2), Ni (sub), E (sub), Ch (sub), Arg, Br; 1978 v EG (sub); (with Nottingham F), Bul, Ni, W, E (sub), Pe (sub), Ir, Ho; 1979 v A, N, P, N; (with Birmingham C), 1980 v A, P, Ni, W, E, H; 1981 v Se, P, Is, Ni (43)
Gibb, W. (Clydesdale), 1873 v E (1)
Gibson, D. W. (Leicester C), 1963 v A, N, Ei, Sp; 1964 v Ni; 1965 v W, Fi (7)
Gibson, J. D. (Partick T), 1926 v E; 1927 v E, W, Ni; (with Aston Villa), 1928 v E, W; 1930 v W, Ni (8)
Gibson, N. (Rangers), 1895 v E, Ni; 1896 v E, Ni; 1897 v E, Ni; 1898 v E; 1899 v E, W, Ni; 1900 v E, Ni; 1901 v W; (with Partick T), 1905 v Ni (14)
Gilchrist, J. E. (Celtic), 1922 v E (1)
Gilhooley, M. (Hull C), 1922 v W (1)
Gillespie, G. (Rangers), 1880 v W; 1881 v E, W; 1882 v E; (with Queen's Park), 1886 v W; 1890 v W; 1891 v Ni (7)
Gillespie, Jas. (Third Lanark), 1898 v W (1)
Gillespie, John. (Queen's Park), 1896 v W (1)
Gillespie, R. (Queen's Park), 1927 v W; 1931 v W; 1932 v F; 1933 v E (4)
Gillick, T. (Everton), 1937 v A, Cz; 1939 v W, Ni, H (5)
Gilmour, J. (Dundee), 1931 v W (1)
Gilzean, A. J. (Dundee), 1964 v W, E, N, WG; 1965 v Ni,

(with Tottenham H), Sp; 1966 v Ni, W, Pol, I; 1968 v W; 1969 v W, E, WG, Cy (2), A (sub); 1970 v Ni, E (sub), WG, A; 1971 v P (22)
Glavin, R. (Celtic), 1977 v Se (1)
Glen, A. (Aberdeen), 1956 v E, Ni (2)
Glen, R. (Renton), 1895 v W; 1896 v W; (with Hibernian), 1900 v Ni (3)
Gordon, J. E. (Rangers), 1912 v E, Ni; 1913 v E, Ni, W; 1914 v E, Ni; 1920 v W, E, Ni (10)
Gossland, J. (Rangers), 1884 v Ni (1)
Goudle, J. (Abercorn), 1884 v Ni (1)
Gough, C. R. (Dundee U), 1983 v Sw, Ni, W, E, Ca (3) (7)
Gourlay, J. (Cambuslang), 1886 v Ni; 1888 v W (2)
Govan, J. (Hibernian), 1948 v E, W, Bel, Sw, F; 1949 v Ni (6)
Gow, D. R. (Rangers), 1888 v E (1)
Gow, J. J. (Queen's Park), 1885 v E (1)
Gow, J. R. (Rangers), 1888 v Ni (1)
Graham, A. (Leeds U), 1978 v EG (sub); 1979 v A (sub), N, W, Ni, E, Arg, N; 1980 v A; 1981 v W (10)
Graham, G. (Arsenal), 1972 v P, Ho, Ni, Y, Cz, Br; 1973 v D (2); (with Manchester U), E, W, Ni, Br (sub) (12)
Graham, J. (Annbank), 1884 v Ni (1)
Graham, J. A. (Arsenal), 1921 v Ni (1)
Grant, J. (Hibernian), 1959 v W, Ni (2)
Gray, A. (Hibernian), 1903 v Ni (1)
Gray, A. M. (Aston Villa), 1976 v R, Sw; 1977 v Fi, Cz; 1979 v A, N; (with Wolverhampton W), 1980 v P, E (sub); 1981 v Se, P, Is (sub), Ni; 1982 v Se (sub), Ni (sub); 1983 v Ni, W, E, Ca (1+1) (19)
Gray, D. (Rangers), 1929 v W, Ni, G, Ho; 1930 v W, E, Ni; 1931 v W; 1933 v W, Ni (10)
Gray, E. (Leeds U), 1969 v E, Cy; 1970 v WG, A; 1971 v W, Ni; 1972 v Bel, Ho; 1976 v W, E; 1977 v Fi, W (12)
Gray, F. T. (Leeds U), 1976 v Sw; 1979 v N, P, W, Ni, E, Arg (sub); (with Nottingham F) 1980 v Bel (sub); 1981 v Se, P, Is, Ni, Is, W, (with Leeds U) Ni, E; 1982 v Se, Ni, P, Sp, Ho, W, Nz, Br, USSR; 1983 v EG, Sw, Bel, Sw, W, E, Ca (32)
Gray, W. (Pollokshields Ath), 1886 v E (1)
Green, A. (Blackpool), 1971 v Bel (sub), P (sub), Ni, E; 1972 v W, E (sub) (6)
Greig, J. (Rangers), 1964 v E, WG; 1965 v W, Ni, E, Fi (2), Sp, Pol; 1966 v Ni, W, E, Pol, I (2), P, Ho, Br; 1967 v W, Ni, E; 1968 v Ni, W, E, Ho; 1969 v W, Ni, E, D, A, WG, Cy (2); 1970 v W, E, Ei, WG, A; 1971 v D, Bel, W (sub), Ni, E; 1976 v D (44)
Groves, W. (Hibernian), 1888 v W; (with Celtic), 1889 v Ni; 1890 v E (3)
Guilliland, W. (Queen's Park), 1891 v W; 1892 v Ni; 1894 v E; 1895 v E (4)

Haddock, H. (Clyde), 1955 v E, H (2), P, Y; 1958 v E (6)
Haddow, D. (Rangers), 1894 v E (1)
Haffey, F. (Celtic), 1960 v E; 1961 v E (2)
Hamilton, A. (Queen's Park), 1885 v E, W; 1886 v E; 1888 v E (4)
Hamilton, A. W. (Dundee), 1962 v Cz, U, W, E; 1963 v W, Ni, E, A, N, Ei; 1964 v Ni, W, E, N, WG; 1965 v Ni, W, E, Fi (2), Pol, Sp; 1966 v Pol, Ni (24)
Hamilton, G. (Aberdeen), 1947 v Ni; 1951 v Bel, A; 1954 v N (2) (5)
Hamilton, G. (Port Glasgow Ath), 1906 v Ni (1)
Hamilton, J. (Queen's Park), 1892 v W; 1893 v E, Ni (3)
Hamilton, J. (St Mirren), 1924 v Ni (1)
Hamilton, R. C. (Rangers), 1899 v E, W, Ni; 1900 v W; 1901 v E, Ni; 1902 v W, Ni; 1903 v E; 1904 v Ni; (with Dundee), 1911 v W (11)
Hamilton, T. (Hurlford), 1891 v Ni (1)
Hamilton, T. (Rangers), 1932 v E (1)
Hamilton, W. M. (Hibernian), 1965 v Fi (1)
Hannah, A. B. (Renton), 1888 v W (1)
Hannah, J. (Third Lanark), 1889 v W (1)
Hansen, A. D. (Liverpool), 1979 v W, Arg; 1980 v Bel, P; 1981 v Se, P, Is; 1982 v Se, Ni, P, Sp, Ni (sub), W, E, Nz, Br, USSR; 1983 v EG, Sw, Bel, Sw (21)
Hansen, J. (Partick T), 1972 v Bel (sub), Y (sub) (2)
Harkness, J. D. (Queen's Park), 1927 v E, Ni; 1928 v E; (with Hearts), 1929 v W, E, Ni; 1930 v E, W; 1932 v W, F; 1934 v Ni (11)
Harper, J. M. (Aberdeen), 1973 v D (1+1 sub); (with Hibernian), 1976 v D; (with Aberdeen), 1978 v Ir (sub) (4)
Harper, W. (Hibernian), 1923 v E, Ni, W; 1924 v E, Ni, W; 1925 v E, Ni, W; (with Arsenal), 1926 v E, Ni (11)
Harris, J. (Partick T), 1921 v W, Ni (2)
Harris, N. (Newcastle U), 1924 v E (1)
Harrower, W. (Queen's Park), 1882 v E; 1884 v Ni; 1886 v W (3)
Hartford, R. A. (WBA), 1972 v Pe, W (sub), E, Y, Cz, Br; (with Manchester C), 1976 v D, R, Ni (sub); 1977 v Cz (sub), W (sub), Se, W, Ni, E, Ch, Arg, Br; 1978 v EG, Cz, W, Bul, W, E, Pe, Ir, Ho; 1979 v A, N, P, W, Ni, E, Arg, N; (with Everton), 1980 v Pe, Bel; 1981 v Ni (sub), Is, W, Ni, E; 1982 v Se; (with Manchester C), Ni, P, Sp, Ni, W, E, Br (50)
OHarvey, D. (Leeds U), 1973 v D; 1974 v Cz, WG, Ni, W, E, Bel, Z, Br, Y; 1975 v EG, Sp (2); 1976 v D (2); 1977 v Fi (sub) (16)
Hastings, A. C. (Sunderland), 1936 v Ni; 1938 v Ni (2)
Haughney, M. (Celtic), 1954 v E (1)
Hay, D. (Celtic), 1970 v Ni, W, E; 1971 v D, Bel, W, P, Ni; 1972 v P, Bel, Ho; 1973 v W, Ni, E, Sw, Br; 1974 v Cz (2), WG, Ni, W, E, Bel, N, Z, Br, Y (27)
Hay, J. (Celtic), 1905 v Ni; 1909 v Ni; 1910 v W, Ni, E; 1911 v Ni, E; (with Newcastle U), 1912 v E, W; 1914 v E, Ni (11)
Hegarty, P. (Dundee U), 1979 v W, Ni, E, Arg, N (sub); 1980 v W, E; 1983 v Ni (8)
Heggie, C. (Rangers), 1886 v Ni (1)
Henderson, G. H. (Rangers), 1904 v Ni (1)
Henderson, J. G. (Portsmouth), 1953 v Se; 1954 v Ni, E, N; 1956 v W; (with Arsenal), 1959 v W, Ni (7)
Henderson, W. (Rangers), 1963 v W, Ni, E, A, N, Ei, Sp; 1964 v W, Ni, E, N, WG; 1965 v Fi, Pol, E, Sp; 1966 v Ni, W, Pol, I, Ho; 1967 v W, Ni; 1968 v Ho; 1969 v Ni, E, Cy; 1970 v Ei; 1971 v P (29)
Hepburn, J. (Alloa Ath), 1891 v W (1)
Hepburn, R. (Ayr U), 1932 v Ni (1)
Herd, A. C. (Hearts), 1935 v Ni (1)
Herd, D. G. (Arsenal), 1959 v E, W, Ni; 1961 v E, Cz (5)
Herd, G. (Clyde), 1958 v E; 1960 v H, T; 1961 v W, Ni (5)
Herriot, J. (Birmingham C), 1969 v Ni, E, D, Cy (2), W (sub); 1970 v Ei (sub), WG (8)
Hewie, J. D. (Charlton Ath), 1956 v E, A; 1957 v E, Ni, W, Y, Sp (2), Sw, WG; 1958 v H, Pol, Y, F; 1959 v Ho, P; 1960 v Ni, W, Pol (19)
Higgins, A. (Kilmarnock), 1885 v Ni (1)
Higgins, A. (Newcastle U), 1910 v E, Ni; 1911 v E, Ni (4)
Highet, T. C. (Queen's Park), 1875 v E; 1876 v E, W; 1878 v E (4)
Hill, D. (Rangers), 1881 v E, W; 1882 v W (3)
Hill, D. A. (Third Lanark), 1906 v Ni (1)
Hill, F. R. (Aberdeen), 1930 v F; 1931 v W, Ni (3)
Hill, J. (Hearts), 1891 v E; 1892 v W (2)
Hogg, G (Hearts), 1896 v E, Ni (2)
Hogg, J. (Ayr U), 1922 v Ni (1)
Hogg, R. M. (Celtic), 1937 v Cz (1)
Holm, A. H. (Queen's Park), 1882 v W; 1883 v E, W (3)
Holt, D. D. (Hearts), 1963 v A, N, Ei, Sp; 1964 v WG (sub) (5)

Holton, J. A. (Manchester U), 1973 v W, Ni, E, Sw, Br; 1974 v Cz, WG, Ni, W, E, N, Z, Br, Y; 1975 v EG (15)
Hope, R. (WBA), 1968 v Ho; 1969 v D (2)
Houliston, W. (Queen of the South), 1949 v E, Ni, F (3)
Houston, S. M. (Manchester U), 1976 v D (1)
Howden, W. (Partick T), 1905 v Ni (1)
Howe, R. (Hamilton A), 1929 v N, Ho (2)
Howie, J. (Newcastle U), 1905 v E; 1906 v E; 1908 v E (3)
Howie, H. (Hibernian), 1949 v W (1)
Howieson, J. (St Mirren), 1927 v Ni (1)
Hughes, J. (Celtic), 1965 v Pol, Sp; 1966 v Ni, I (2); 1968 v E; 1969 v A; 1970 v Ei (8)
Hughes, W. (Sunderland), 1975 v Se (sub) (1)
Humphries, W. (Motherwell), 1952 v Se (1)
Hunter, A. (Kilmarnock), 1972 v Pe, Y; (with Celtic), 1973 v E; 1974 v Cz (4)
Hunter, J. (Dundee), 1909 v W (1)
Hunter, J. (Third Lanark), 1874 v E; (with Eastern), 1875 v E; (with Third Lanark), 1876 v E; 1877 v W (4)
Hunter, R. (St Mirren), 1890 v Ni (1)
Hunter, W. (Motherwell), 1960 v H, T; 1961 v W (3)
Husband, J. (Partick T), 1947 v W (1)
Hutchison, T. (Coventry C), 1974 v Cz (2), WG (2), Ni, W, Bel (sub), N, Z (sub), Y (sub); 1975 v EG, Sp (2), P, E (sub), R (sub); 1976 v D (17)
Hutton, J. (Aberdeen), 1923 v E, W, Ni; 1924 v Ni; 1926 v W, E, Ni; (with Blackburn R), 1927 v Ni; 1928 v W, Ni (10)
Hutton, J. (St Bernards), 1887 v Ni (1)
Hyslop, T. (Stoke C), 1896 v E; (with Rangers), 1897 v E (2)

Imlach, J. J. S. (Nottingham F), 1958 v H, Pol, Y, F (4)
Imrie, W. N. (St Johnstone), 1929 v N, G (2)
Inglis, J. (Kilmarnock Ath), 1884 v Ni (1)
Inglis, J. (Rangers), 1883 v E, W (2)
Irons, J. H. (Queen's Park), 1900 v W (1)

Jackson, A. (Cambuslang), 1886 v W; 1888 v Ni (2)
Jackson, A. (Aberdeen), 1925 v E, W, Ni; (with Huddersfield T), 1926 v E, W, Ni; 1927 v W, Ni; 1928 v E, W; 1929 v E, W, Ni; 1930 v E, W, Ni, F (17)
Jackson, C. (Rangers), 1975 v Se, P (sub), W; 1976 v D, R, Ni, W, E (8)
Jackson, J. (Partick T), 1931 v A, I, Sw; 1933 v E; (with Chelsea), 1934 v E; 1935 v E; 1936 v W, Ni (8)
Jackson, T. A. (St Mirren), 1904 v W, E, Ni; 1905 v W; 1907 v W, Ni (6)
McGhee (   ), 1983 v Ca (1+1 sub) (2)
James, A. W. (Preston NE), 1926 v W; 1928 v E; 1929 v E, Ni; (with Arsenal), 1930 v E, W, Ni; 1933 v W (8)
Jardine, A. (Rangers), 1971 v D (sub); 1972 v P, Bel, Ho; 1973 v E, Sw, Br; 1974 v Cz (2), WG (2), Ni, W, E, Bel, N, Z, Br, Y; 1975 v EG, Sp (2), Se, P, W, Ni, E; 1977 v Se (sub), Ch (sub), Br (sub); 1978 v Cz, W, Ni, Ir; 1980 v Pe, A, Bel (2) (38)
Jarvie, A. (Airdrieonians), 1971 v P (sub), Ni (sub), E (sub) (3)
Jenkinson, T. (Hearts), 1887 v Ni (1)
Johnston, L. H. (Clyde), 1948 v Bel, Sw (2)
Johnston, R. (Sunderland), 1938 v Cz (1)
Johnston, W. (Rangers), 1966 v W, E, Pol, Ho; 1968 v W, E; 1969 v Ni (sub); 1970 v Ni; 1971 v D; (with WBA), 1977 v Se, W (sub), Ni, E, Ch, Arg, Br; 1978 v EG, Cz, W, W, E, Pe (22)
Johnstone, D. (Rangers), 1973 v W, Ni, E, Sw, Br; 1975 v EG (sub), Se (sub); 1976 v Sw, Ni (sub), E (sub); 1978 v Bul (sub), Ni, W; 1980 v Bel (14)
Johnstone, J. (Abercorn), 1888 v W (1)
Johnstone, J. (Celtic), 1965 v W, Fi; 1966 v E; 1967 v W, USSR; 1968 v W; 1969 v A, WG; 1970 v E, WG; 1971 v D, E; 1972 v P, Bel, Ho, Ni, E (sub); 1974 v W, E, Bel, N; 1975 v EG, Sp (23)
Johnstone, Jas (Kilmarnock), 1894 v W (1)
Johnstone, J. A. (Hearts), 1930 v W; 1933 v W, Ni (3)
Johnstone, R. (Hibernian), 1951 v E, D, F; 1952 v Ni, E; 1953 v E, Se; 1954 v W, E, N, Fi; 1955 v Ni, H; (with Manchester C), 1955 v E; 1956 v E, Ni, W (17)
Johnstone, W. (Third Lanark), 1887 v Ni; 1889 v W; 1890 v E (3)
Jordan, J. (Leeds U), 1973 v E (sub), Sw (sub), Br; 1974 v Cz (sub+1), WG (sub), Ni (sub), W, E, Bel, N, Z, Br, Y; 1975 v EG, Sp (2); 1976 v Ni, W, E; 1977 v Cz, W, Ni, E; 1978 v EG, Cz, W; (with Manchester U), Bul, Ni, E, Pe, Ir, Ho; 1979 v A, P, W (sub), Ni, E, N; 1980 v Bel, Ni (sub), W, E, Pol; 1981 v Is, W, E; (with AC Milan), 1982 v Se, Ho, W, E, USSR (52)

Kay, J. L. (Queen's Park), 1880 v E; 1882 v E, W; 1883 v E, W; 1884 v W (6)
Keillor, A. (Montrose), 1891 v W; 1892 v Ni; (with Dundee), 1894 v Ni; 1895 v W; 1896 v W; 1897 v W (6)
Keir, L. (Dumbarton), 1885 v W; 1886 v Ni; 1887 v E, W; 1888 v E (5)
Kelly, H. T. (Blackpool), 1952 v USA (1)
Kelly, J. (Renton), 1888 v E; (with Celtic), 1889 v E; 1890 v E; 1892 v E; 1893 v E, Ni; 1894 v W; 1896 v Ni (8)
Kelly, J. C. (Barnsley), 1949 v W, Ni (2)
Kelso, R. (Renton), 1885 v W, Ni; 1886 v W; 1887 v E, W; 1888 v E, Ni; (with Dundee), 1898 v Ni (8)
Kelso, T. (Dundee), 1914 v W (1)
Kennaway, J. (Celtic), 1934 v A, W (2)
Kennedy, A. (Eastern), 1875 v E; 1876 v E, W; (with Third Lanark), 1878 v E; 1882 v W; 1884 v W (6)
Kennedy, J. (Celtic), 1964 v W, E, WG; 1965 v W, Ni, Fi (6)
Kennedy, J. (Hibernian), 1897 v W (1)
Kennedy, S. (Aberdeen), 1978 v Bul, W, E, Pe, Ho; 1979 v A, P; 1982 v P (sub) (8)
Kennedy, S. (Partick T), 1905 v W (1)
Kennedy, S. (Rangers), 1975 v Se, P, W, Ni, E (5)
Ker, G. (Queen's Park), 1880 v E; 1881 v E, W; 1882 v W, E (5)
Ker, W. (Granville), 1872 v E; (with Queen's Park), 1873 v E (2)
Kerr, A. (Partick T), 1955 v A, H (2)
Kerr, P. (Hibernian), 1924 v Ni (1)
Key, G. (Hearts), 1902 v Ni (1)
Key, W. (Queen's Park), 1907 v Ni (1)
King, A. (Hearts), 1896 v E, W; (with Celtic), 1897 v Ni; 1898 v Ni; 1899 v Ni, W (6)
King, J. (Hamilton A), 1933 v Ni; 1934 v Ni (2)
King, W. S. (Queen's Park), 1929 v W (1)
Kinloch, J. D. (Partick T), 1922 v Ni (1)
Kinnaird, A. F. (Wanderers), 1873 v E (1)
Kinnear, D. (Rangers), 1938 v Cz (1)

Lambie, J. A. (Queen's Park), 1886 v Ni; 1887 v Ni; 1888 v E (3)
Lambie, W. A. (Queen's Park), 1892 v Ni; 1893 v W; 1894 v E; 1895 v E, Ni; 1896 v E, Ni; 1897 v E, Ni (9)
Lamont, D. (Pilgrims), 1885 v Ni (1)
Lang, A. (Dumbarton), 1880 v W (1)
Lang, J. J. (Clydesdale), 1876 v W; (with Third Lanark), 1878 v W (2)
Latta, A. (Dumbarton), 1888 v W; 1889 v E (2)
Law, D. (Huddersfield T), 1959 v W, Ni, Ho, P; 1960 v Ni, W; (with Manchester C), 1960 v E, Pol, A; 1961 v E, Ni; (with Torino), 1962 v Cz (2) E; (with Manchester U), 1963 v W, Ni, E, A, N, Ei, Sp; 1964 v W, E, N, WG; 1965 v W, Ni, E, Fi (2), Pol, Sp; 1966 v Ni, E, Pol; 1967 v W, E, USSR; 1968 v Ni; 1969 v Ni, A, WG; 1972

Willie Johnston *Glasgow Rangers* and *Scotland*

Derek Johnstone *Glasgow Rangers* and *Scotland*

Joe Jordan, has made 52 appearances for Scotland

Scotland striker Dennis Law

v Pe, Ni, W, E, Y, Cz, Br; (with Manchester C), 1974 v Cz (2), WG (2), Ni, Z (55)
Law, G. (Rangers), 1910 v E, Ni, W (3)
Law, T. (Chelsea), 1928 v E; 1930 v E (2)
Lawrence, J. (Newcastle U), 1911 v E (1)
Lawrence, T. (Liverpool), 1963 v Ei; 1969 v W, WG (3)
Lawson, D. (St Mirren), 1923 v E (1)
Leckie, R. (Queen's Park), 1872 v E (1)
Leggat, G. (Aberdeen), 1956 v E; 1957 v W; 1958 v Ni, H, Pol, Y, Par; (with Fulham), 1959 v E, W, Ni, WG, Ho; 1960 v E, Ni, W, Pol, A, H (18)
Leighton, J. (Aberdeen), 1983 v EG, Sw, Bel, Sw, W, E, Ca (2) (8)
Lennie, W. (Aberdeen), 1908 v W, Ni (2)
Lennox, R. (Celtic), 1967 v Ni, E, USSR; 1968 v W, L; 1969 v D, A, WG, Cy (sub); 1970 v W (sub) (10)
Leslie, L. G. (Airdrieonians), 1961 v W, Ni, Ei (2), Cz (5)
Liddell, W. (Liverpool), 1947 v W, Ni; 1948 v E, W, Ni; 1950 v E, W, P, F; 1951 v W, Ni, E, A; 1952 v W, Ni, E, USA, D, Se; 1953 v W, Ni, E; 1954 v W; 1955 v P, Y, A, H; 1956 v Ni (28)
Liddle, D. (East Fife), 1931 v A, I, Sw (3)
Lindsay, D. (St Mirren), 1903 v Ni (1)
Lindsay, J. (Dumbarton), 1880 v W; 1881 v W, E; 1884 v W, E; 1885 v W, E; 1886 v E (8)
Lindsay, J. (Renton), 1888 v E; 1893 v E, Ni (3)
Linwood, A. B. (Clyde), 1950 v W (1)
Little, R. J. (Rangers), 1953 v Se (1)
Livingstone, G. T. (Manchester C), 1906 v E; (with Rangers), 1907 v W (2)
Lochhead, A. (Third Lanark), 1889 v W (1)
Logan, J. (Ayr U), 1891 v W (1)
Logan, T. (Falkirk), 1913 v Ni (1)
Logie, J. T. (Arsenal), 1953 v Ni (1)
Loney, W. (Celtic), 1910 v W, Ni (2)
Long, H. (Clyde), 1947 v Ni (1)
Longair, W. (Dundee), 1894 v Ni (1)
Lorimer, P. (Leeds U), 1970 v A (sub); 1971 v W, Ni; 1972 v Ni (sub), W, E; 1973 v D (2), E (2); 1974 v WG (sub), E, Bel, N, Z, Br, Y; 1975 v Sp (sub); 1976 v D (2), R (sub) (21)
Love, A. (Aberdeen), 1931 v A, I, Sw (3)
Low, A. (Falkirk), 1934 v Ni (1)
Low, T. P. (Rangers), 1897 v Ni (1)
Low, W. L. (Newcastle U), 1911 v E, W; 1912 v Ni; 1920 v E, Ni (5)
Lowe, J. (Cambuslang), 1891 v Ni (1)
Lowe, J. (St Bernards), 1887 v Ni (1)
Lundie, J. (Hibernian), 1886 v W (1)
Lyall, J. (Sheffield W), 1905 v E (1)

McAdam, J. (Third Lanark), 1880 v W (1)
McArthur, D. (Celtic), 1895 v E, Ni; 1899 v W (3)
McAtee, A. (Celtic), 1913 v W (1)
McAulay, J. (Dumbarton), 1882 v W; (with Arthurlie), 1884 v Ni (2)
McAulay, J. (Dumbarton), 1883 v E, W; 1884 v E; 1885 v E, W; 1886 v E; 1887 v E, W (8)
McAuley, R. (Rangers), 1932 v Ni, W (2)
McBain, E. (St Mirren), 1894 v W (1)
McBain, N. (Manchester U), 1922 v E; (with Everton), 1923 v Ni; 1924 v W (3)
McBride, J. (Celtic), 1967 v W, Ni (2)
McBride, P. (Preston NE), 1904 v E; 1906 v E; 1907 v E, W; 1908 v E; 1909 v W (6)
McCall, J. (Renton), 1886 v W; 1887 v E, W; 1888 v E; 1890 v E (5)
McCalliog, J. (Sheffield W), 1967 v E, USSR; 1968 v Ni; 1969 v D; (with Wolverhampton W), 1971 v P (5)
McCallum, N. (Renton), 1888 v Ni (1)
McCann, R. J. (Motherwell), 1959 v WG; 1960 v E, Ni, W; 1961 v E (5)
McCartney, W. (Hibernian), 1902 v Ni (1)
McClory, A. (Motherwell), 1927 v W; 1928 v Ni; 1935 v W (3)
McCloy, P. (Ayr U), 1924 v E; 1925 v E (2)
McCloy, P. (Rangers), 1973 v W, Ni, Sw, Br (4)
McColl, A. (Renton), 1888 v Ni (1)
McColl, I. M. (Rangers), 1950 v E, F; 1951 v W, Ni, Bel; 1957 v E, Ni, W, Y, Sp, Sw, WG; 1958 v Ni, E (14)
McColl, R. S. (Queen's Park), 1896 v W, Ni; 1897 v Ni; 1898 v Ni; 1899 v Ni, E, W; 1900 v E, W; 1901 v E, W; (with Newcastle U), 1902 v E; (with Queen's Park), 1908 v Ni (13)
McColl, W. (Renton), 1895 v W (1)
McCombie, A. (Sunderland), 1903 v E, W; (with Newcastle U), 1905 v E, W (4)
McCorkindale, J. (Partick T), 1891 v W (1)
McCormick, R. (Abercorn), 1886 v W (1)
McCrae, D. (St Mirren), 1929 v N, G (2)
McCreadie, A. (Rangers), 1893 v W; 1894 v E (2)
McCreadie, E. G. (Chelsea), 1965 v E, Sp, Fi, Pol; 1966 v P, Ni, W, Pol, I; 1967 v E, USSR; 1968 v Ni, W, E, Ho; 1969 v W, Ni, E, D, A, WG, Cy (2) (23)
McCulloch, D. (Hearts), 1935 v W; (with Brentford), 1936 v E; 1937 v W, Ni; 1938 v Cz; (with Derby Co), 1939 v H, W (7)
MacDonald, A. (Rangers), 1976 v Sw (1)
McDonald, J. (Edinburgh University), 1886 v E (1)
McDonald, J. (Sunderland), 1956 v W, Ni (2)
MacDougall, E. J. (Norwich C) 1975 v Se, P, W, Ni, E; 1976 v D, R (7)
McDougall, J. (Liverpool), 1931 v I, A (2)
McDougall, J. (Airdrieonians), 1926 v Ni (1)
McDougall, J. (Vale of Leven), 1877 v E, W; 1878 v E; 1879 v E, W (5)
McFadyen, W. (Motherwell), 1934 v A, W (2)
Macfarlane, A. (Dundee), 1904 v W; 1906 v W; 1908 v W; 1909 v Ni; 1911 v W (5)
McFarlane, R. (Greenock Morton), 1896 v W (1)
Macfarlane, W. (Hearts), 1947 v L (1)
McGarr, E. (Aberdeen), 1970 v Ei, A (2)
McGarvey, F. P. (Liverpool), 1979 v Ni (sub), Arg (2)
McGeoch, A. (Dumbreck), 1876 v E, W; 1877 v E, W (4)
McGhee, J. (Hibernian), 1886 v W (1)
McGonagle, W. (Celtic), 1933 v E; 1934 v A, E, Ni; 1935 v Ni, W (6)
McGrain, D. (Celtic), 1973 v W, Ni, E, Sw, Br; 1974 v Cz (2), WG, W (sub), E, Bel, N, Z, Br, Y; 1975 v Sp, Se, P, W, Ni, E, R; 1976 v D (2), Sw, Ni, W, E; 1977 v Fi, Cz, W (2), Se, Ni, E, Ch, Arg, Br; 1978 v EG, Cz; 1980 v Bel, P, Ni, W, E, Pol, H; 1981 v Se, P, Is, Ni, Is, W (sub), Ni, E; 1982 v Se, Sp, Ho, Ni, E, Nz, USSR (sub) (62)
McGregor, J. C. (Vale of Leven), 1877 v E, W; 1878 v E; 1880 v E (4)
McGrory, J. E. (Kilmarnock), 1965 v Ni, Fi; 1966 v P (3)
McGrory, J. (Celtic), 1928 v Ni; 1931 v E; 1932 v Ni, W; 1933 v E, Ni; 1934 v Ni (7)
McGuire, W. (Beith), 1881 v E, W (2)
McGurk, F. (Birmingham), 1934 v W (1)
McHardy, H. (Rangers), 1885 v Ni (1)
McInally, T. B. (Celtic), 1926 v Ni; 1927 v W (2)
McInnes, T. (Cowlairs), 1889 v Ni (1)
McIntosh, W. (Third Lanark), 1905 v Ni (1)
McIntyre, A. (Vale of Leven), 1878 v E; 1882 v E (2)
McIntyre, H. (Rangers), 1880 v W (1)
McIntyre, J. (Rangers), 1884 v W (1)
McKay, D. (Celtic), 1959 v E, WG, Ho, P; 1960 v E, Pol, A, H, T; 1961 v W, Ni; 1962 v Ni, Cz, U (sub) (14)
Mackay, D. C. (Hearts), 1957 v Sp; 1958 v F; 1959 v W, Ni; (with Tottenham H), 1959 v WG, E; 1960 v W, Ni, A, Pol, H, T; 1961 v W, Ni, E; 1963 v E, A, N; 1964 v Ni, W, N; 1966 v Ni (22)

McKay, J. (Blackburn R), 1924 v W (1)
McKay, R. (Newcastle U), 1928 v W (1)
McKean, R. (Rangers), 1976 v Sw (1)
McKenzie, D. (Brentford), 1938 v Ni (1)
Mackenzie, J. A. (Partick T), 1954 v W, E, N, Fi, A, U; 1955 v E, H; 1956 v A (9)
McKeown, M. (Celtic), 1889 v Ni; 1890 v E (2)
McKie, J. (East Stirling), 1898 v W (1)
McKillop, T. R. (Rangers), 1938 v Ho (1)
McKinlay, D. (Liverpool), 1922 v W, Ni (2)
McKinnon, A. (Queen's Park), 1874 v E (1)
McKinnon, R. (Rangers), 1966 v W, E, I (2), Ho, Br; 1967 v W, Ni, E; 1968 v Ni, W, E, Ho; 1969 v D, A, WG, Cy; 1970 v Ni, W, E, Ei, WG, A; 1971 v D, Bel, P, USSR, D (28)
MacKinnon, W. (Dumbarton), 1883 v E, W; 1884 v E, W (4)
McKinnon, W. W. (Queen's Park), 1872 v E; 1873 v E; 1874 v E; 1875 v E; 1876 v E, W; 1877 v E; 1878 v E; 1879 v E (9)
McLaren, A. (St Johnstone), 1929 v N, G, Ho; 1933 v W, Ni (5)
McLaren, A. (Preston NE), 1947 v E, Bel, L; 1948 v W (4)
McLaren, J. (Hibernian), 1888 v W; (with Celtic), 1889 v E; 1890 v E (3)
McLean, A. (Celtic), 1926 v W, Ni; 1927 v W, E (4)
McLean, D. (St Bernards), 1896 v W; 1897 v Ni (2)
McLean, D. (Sheffield W), 1912 v E (1)
McLean, G. (Dundee), 1968 v Ho (1)
McLean, T. (Kilmarnock), 1969 v D, Cy, W; 1970 v Ni, W; 1971 v D (6)
McLeish, A. (Aberdeen), 1980 v F, Ni, W, E, Pol, H; 1981 v Se, Is, Ni, Is, Ni, E; 1982 v Se, Sp, Ni, Br (sub); 1983 v Bel, Sw, W, E, Ca (3) (23)
McLeod, D. (Celtic), 1905 v Ni; 1906 v E, W, Ni (4)
McLeod, J. (Dumbarton), 1888 v Ni; 1889 v W; 1890 v Ni; 1892 v E; 1893 v W (5)
MacLeod, J. M. (Hibernian), 1961 v E, Ei (2), Cz (4)
McLeod, W. (Cowlairs), 1886 v Ni (1)
McLintock, A. (Vale of Leven), 1875 v E; 1876 v E; 1880 v E (3)
McLintock, F. (Leicester C), 1963 v N (sub), Ei, Sp; (with Arsenal), 1965 v Ni; 1967 v USSR; 1970 v Ni; 1971 v W, Ni, E (9)
McLuckie, J. S. (Manchester C), 1934 v W (1)
McMahon, A. (Celtic), 1892 v E; 1893 v E, Ni; 1894 v E; 1901 v Ni; 1902 v W (6)
McMenemy, J. (Celtic), 1905 v Ni; 1909 v Ni; 1910 v E, W; 1911 v Ni, W, E; 1912 v W; 1914 v W, Ni, E; 1920 v Ni (12)
McMenemy, J. (Motherwell), 1934 v W (1)
McMillan, J. (St Bernards), 1897 v W (1)
McMillan, I. L. (Airdrieonians), 1952 v E, USA, D; 1955 v E; 1956 v E; (with Rangers), 1961 v Cz (6)
McMillan, T. (Dumbarton), 1887 v Ni (1)
McMullan, J. (Partick T), 1920 v W; 1921 v W, Ni, E; 1924 v E, Ni; 1925 v E; 1926 v W; (with Manchester C), 1926 v E; 1927 v E, W; 1928 v E, W; 1929 v W, E, Ni (16)
McNab, A. (Morton), 1921 v E, Ni (2)
McNab, A. (Sunderland), 1937 v A; (with WBA), 1939 v E (2)
McNab, C. D. (Dundee), 1931 v E, W, A, I, Sw; 1932 v E (6)
McNab, J. S. (Liverpool), 1923 v W (1)
McNair, A. (Celtic), 1906 v W; 1907 v Ni; 1908 v E, W; 1909 v E; 1910 v W; 1912 v E, W, Ni; 1913 v E; 1914 v E, Ni; 1920 v E, W, Ni (15)
McNaught, W. (Raith R), 1951 v A, W, Ni; 1952 v E; 1955 v Ni (5)
McNeil, H. (Queen's Park), 1874 v E; 1875 v E; 1876 v E, W; 1877 v W; 1878 v E; 1879 v E, W; 1881 v E, W (10)
McNeil, M. (Rangers), 1876 v W; 1880 v E (2)
McNeill, W. (Celtic), 1961 v E, Ei (2), Cz; 1962 v Ni, E, Cz, U; 1963 v Ei, Sp; 1964 v W, E, WG; 1965 v E, Fi, Pol, Sp; 1966 v Ni, Pol; 1967 v USSR; 1968 v E; 1969 v Cy, W, E, Cy (sub); 1970 v WG; 1972 v Ni, W, E (29)
McPhail, J. (Celtic), 1950 v W; 1951 v W, Ni, A; 1954 v Ni (5)
McPhail, R. (Airdrieonians), 1927 v E; (with Rangers), 1929 v W; 1931 v E, Ni; 1932 v W, Ni, F; 1933 v E, Ni; 1934 v A, Ni; 1935 v E; 1937 v G, E, Cz; 1938 v W, Ni (17)
McPherson, D. (Kilmarnock), 1892 v Ni (1)
McPherson, J. (Kilmarnock), 1888 v W; (with Cowlairs), 1889 v E; 1890 v Ni, E; (with Rangers), 1892 v W; 1894 v E; 1895 v E, Ni; 1897 v Ni (9)
McPherson, J. (Clydesdale), 1875 v E (1)
McPherson, J. (Vale of Leven), 1879 v E, W; 1880 v E; 1881 v W; 1883 v E, W; 1884 v E; 1885 v N (8)
McPherson, J. (Hearts), 1891 v E (1)
McPherson, R. (Arthurlie), 1882 v E (1)
McQueen, G. (Leeds U), 1974 v Bel; 1975 v Sp (2), P, W, Ni, E, R; 1976 v D; 1977 v Cz, W (2), Ni, E; 1978 v EG, Cz, W; (with Manchester U), Bul, Ni, W; 1979 v A, N, P, Ni, E, N; 1980 v Pe, A, Bel; 1981 v W (30)
McQueen, M. (Leith Ath), 1890 v W; 1891 v W (2)
McRorie, D. M. (Morton), 1931 v W (1)
McSpadyen, A. (Partick T), 1939 v E, H (2)
McStay, W. (Celtic), 1921 v W, Ni; 1925 v E, Ni, W; 1926 v E, Ni, W; 1927 v E, Ni, W; 1928 v W, Ni (13)
McTavish, J. (Falkirk), 1910 v Ni (1)
McWhattie, G. C. (Queen's Park), 1901 v W, Ni (2)
McWilliam, P. (Newcastle U) 1905 v E; 1906 v E; 1907 v E, W; 1909 v E, W; 1910 v E; 1911 v W (8)
Macari, L. (Celtic), 1972 v W (sub), E, Y, Cz, Br; 1973 v D; (with Manchester U), E (2), W (sub), Ni (sub); 1975 v Se, P (sub), W, E (sub), R; 1977 v Ni (sub), E (sub), Ch, Arg; 1978 v EG, W, Bul, Pe (sub), Ir (24)
Macauley, A. R. (Brentford), 1947 v E; (with Arsenal), 1948 v E, W, Ni, Bel, Sw, F (7)
Madden, J. (Celtic), 1893 v W; 1895 v W (2)
Main, F. R. (Rangers), 1938 v W (1)
Main, J. (Hibernian), 1909 v Ni (1)
Maley, W. (Celtic), 1893 v E, Ni (2)
Marshall, H. (Celtic), 1899 v W; 1900 v Ni (2)
Marshall, J. (Rangers), 1932 v E; 1933 v E; 1934 v E (3)
Marshall, J. (Middlesbrough), 1921 v E, W, Ni; 1922 v E, W, Ni; (with Llanelly), 1924 v W (7)
Marshall, J. (Third Lanark), 1885 v Ni; 1886 v W; 1887 v E, W (4)
Marshall, R. W. (Rangers), 1892 v Ni; 1894 v Ni (2)
Martin, F. (Aberdeen), 1954 v N (2), A, U; 1955 v E, H (6)
Martin, N. (Hibernian), 1965 v Fi, Pol; (with Sunderland), 1966 v I (3)
Martis, J. (Motherwell), 1961 v W (1)
Mason, J. (Third Lanark), 1949 v E, W, Ni; 1950 v Ni; 1951 v Ni, Bel, A (7)
Massie, A. (Hearts), 1932 v Ni, W, F; 1933 v Ni; 1934 v E, Ni; 1935 v E, Ni, W; 1936 v W, Ni; (with Aston Villa), 1936 v E; 1937 v G, E, W, Ni, A; 1938 v W (18)
Masson, D. S. (QPR), 1976 v Ni, W, E; 1977 v Fi, Cz, W, Ni, E, Ch, Arg, Br; 1978 v EG, Cz, W; (with Derby Co), Ni, E, Pe (17)
Mathers, D. (Partick T), 1954 v Fi (1)
Maxwell, W. S. (Stoke C), 1898 v E (1)
May, J. (Rangers), 1906 v W, Ni; 1908 v E, Ni; 1909 v W (5)
Meechan, P. (Celtic), 1896 v Ni (1)
Meiklejohn, D. D. (Rangers), 1922 v W; 1924 v W; 1925

Scotland and *Celtic* captain Danny McGrain

James McGrory *Celtic* and *Scotland*

Bobby Moncur *Newcastle* and *Scotland*

v W, Ni, E; 1928 v W, Ni; 1929 v E, Ni; 1930 v E, Ni; 1931 v E; 1932 v W, Ni; 1934 v A (15)
Menzies, A. (Hearts), 1906 v E (1)
Mercer, R. (Hearts), 1912 v W; 1913 v Ni (2)
Middleton, R. (Cowdenbeath), 1930 v Ni (1)
Millar, J. (Rangers), 1897 v E; 1898 v E, W (3)
Millar, J. (Rangers), 1963 v A, Ei (2)
Millar, A. (Hearts), 1939 v W (1)
Miller, J. (St Mirren), 1931 v E, I, Sw; 1932 v F; 1934 v E (5)
Miller, P. (Dumbarton), 1882 v E; 1883 v E, W (3)
Miller, T. (Liverpool), 1920 v E; (with Manchester U), 1921 v E, Ni (3)
Miller, W. (Third Lanark), 1876 v E (1)
Miller, W. (Celtic), 1947 v E, W, Bel, L; 1948 v W, Ni (6)
Miller, W. (Aberdeen), 1975 v R; 1978 v Bul; 1980 v Bel, W, E, Pol, H; 1981 v Se, P, Is (sub), Ni, W, Ni, E; 1982 v Ni, P, Ho, Br, USSR; 1983 v EG, Sw, Sw, W, E, Ca (3) (27)
Mills, W. (Aberdeen), 1936 v W, Ni; 1937 v W (3)
Milne, J. V. (Middlesbrough), 1938 v E; 1939 v E (2)
Mitchell, D. (Rangers), 1890 v Ni; 1892 v E; 1893 v E, Ni; 1894 v E (5)
Mitchell, J. (Kilmarnock), 1908 v Ni; 1910 v Ni, W (3)
Mitchell, R. C. (Newcastle U), 1951 v D, F (2)
Mochan, N. (Celtic), 1954 v N, A, U (3)
Moir, W. (Bolton W), 1950 v E (1)
Moncur, R. (Newcastle U), 1968 v Ho; 1970 v Ni, W, E, Ei; 1971 v D, Bel, W, P, Ni, E, D; 1972 v Pe, Ni, W, E (16)
Morgan, H. (St Mirren), 1898 v W; (with Liverpool), 1899 v E (2)
Morgan, W. (Burnley), 1968 v Ni; (with Manchester U) 1972 v Pe, Y, Cz, Br; 1973 v D (2), E (2), W, Ni, Sw, Br; 1974 v Cz (2), WG (2), Ni, Bel (sub), Br, Y (21)
Morris, D. (Raith R), 1923 v Ni; 1924 v E, Ni; 1925 v E, W, Ni (6)
Morris, H. (East Fife), 1950 v Ni (1)
Morrison, T. (St Mirren), 1927 v E (1)
Morton, A. L. (Queen's Park), 1920 v W, Ni; (with Rangers), 1921 v E; 1922 v E, W; 1923 v E, W, Ni; 1924 v E, W, Ni; 1925 v E, W, Ni; 1927 v E, Ni; 1928 v E, W, Ni; 1929 v E, W, Ni; 1930 v E, W, Ni; 1931 v E, W, Ni; 1932 v E, W, F (31)
Morton, H. A. (Kilmarnock), 1929 v G, Ho (2)
Mudie, J. K. (Blackpool), 1957 v W, Ni, E, Y, Sw, Sp (2), WG; 1958 v Ni, E, W, Sw, H, Pol, Y, Par, F (17)
Muir, W. (Dundee), 1907 v Ni (1)
Muirhead, T. A. (Rangers), 1922 v Ni; 1923 v E; 1924 v W; 1927 v Ni; 1928 v Ni; 1929 v W, Ni; 1930 v W (8)
Mulhall, G. (Aberdeen), 1960 v Ni; (with Sunderland), 1963 v Ni; 1964 v Ni (3)
Munro, A. D. (Hearts), 1937 v W, Ni; (with Blackpool), 1938 v Ho (3)
Munro, F. M. (Wolverhampton W), 1971 v Ni (sub), E (sub), D, USSR; 1975 v Se, W (sub), Ni, E, R (9)
Munro, I. (St Mirren), 1979 v Arg, N; 1980 v Pe, A, Bel, W, E (7)
Munro, N. (Abercorn), 1888 v W; 1889 v E (2)
Murdoch, J. (Motherwell), 1931 v Ni (1)
Murdoch, R. (Celtic), 1966 v W, E, I (2); 1967 v Ni; 1968 v Ni; 1969 v W, Ni, E, WG, Cy; 1970 v A (12)
Murphy, F. (Celtic), 1938 v Ho (1)
Murray, J. (Renton), 1895 v W (1)
Murray, J. (Hearts), 1958 v E, H, Pol, Y, F (5)
Murray, J. W. (Vale of Leven), 1890 v W (1)
Murray, P. (Hibernian), 1896 v Ni; 1897 v W (2)
Murray, S. (Aberdeen), 1972 v Bel (1)
Mutch, G. (Preston NE), 1938 v E (1)

Napier, C. E. (Celtic), 1932 v E; 1935 v E, W; (with Derby Co), 1937 v Ni, A (5)
Narey, D. (Dundee U), 1977 v Se (sub); 1979 v P, Ni (sub), Arg; 1980 v P, Ni, Pol, H; 1981 v W, E (sub); 1982 v Ho, W, E, Nz (sub), Br, USSR; 1983 v EG, Sw, Bel, Ni, W, E, Ca (3) (25)
Neil, R. G. (Hibernian), 1896 v W; (with Rangers), 1900 v W (2)
Neill, R. W. (Queen's Park), 1876 v W; 1877 v E, W; 1878 v W; 1880 v E (5)
Neilles, P. (Hearts), 1914 v W, Ni (2)
Nelson, J. (Cardiff C), 1925 v W, Ni; 1928 v E; 1930 v F (4)
Niblo, T. D. (Aston Villa), 1904 v E (1)
Nibloe, J. (Kilmarnock), 1929 v E, N, Ho; 1930 v W; 1931 v E, Ni, A, I, Sw; 1932 v E, F (11)
Nicholas, C. (Celtic), 1983 v Sw, Ni, E, Ca (3) (6)
Nisbet, J. (Ayr U), 1929 v N, G, Ho (3)
Niven, J. B. (Moffatt), 1885 v Ni (1)

O'Donnell, F. (Preston NE), 1937 v E, A, Cz; 1938 v E, W; (with Blackpool), Ho (6)
Ogilvie, D. H. (Motherwell), 1934 v A (1)
O'Hare, J. (Derby Co), 1970 v W, Ni, E; 1971 v D, Bel, W, Ni; 1972 v P, Bel, Ho (sub), Pe, Ni, W (13)
Ormond, W. E. (Hibernian), 1954 v E, N, Fi, A, U; 1959 v E (6)
O'Rourke, F. (Airdrieonians), 1907 v Ni (1)
Orr, J. (Kilmarnock), 1892 v W (1)
Orr, R. (Newcastle U), 1902 v E; 1904 v E (2)
Orr, T. (Morton), 1952 v Ni, W (2)
Orr, W. (Celtic), 1900 v Ni; 1903 v Ni; 1904 v W (3)
Orrock, R. (Falkirk), 1913 v W (1)
Oswald, J. (Third Lanark), 1889 v E; (with St Bernards), 1895 v E; (with Rangers), 1897 v W (3)

Parker, A. H. (Falkirk), 1955 v P, Y, A; 1956 v E, Ni, W, A; 1957 v Ni, W, Y; 1958 v Ni, W, E, Sw; (with Everton), Par (15)
Parlane, D. (Rangers), 1973 v W, Sw, Br; 1975 v Sp (sub), Se, P, W, Ni, E, R; 1976 v D (sub); 1977 v W (12)
Parlane, R. (Vale of Leven), 1878 v W; 1879 v E, W (3)
Paterson, G. D. (Celtic), 1939 v Ni (1)
Paterson, J. (Leicester C), 1920 v E (1)
Paterson, J. (Cowdenbeath), 1931 v A, I, Sw (3)
Paton, A. (Motherwell), 1952 v D, Se (2)
Paton, D. (St Bernards), 1896 v W (1)
Paton, M. (Dumbarton), 1883 v E; 1884 v W; 1885 v W, E; 1886 v E (5)
Paton, R. (Vale of Leven), 1879 v E, W (2)
Patrick, J. (St Mirren), 1897 v E, W (2)
Paul, H. McD. (Queen's Park), 1909 v E, W, Ni (3)
Paul, W. (Partick T), 1888 v W; 1889 v W; 1890 v W (3)
Paul, W. (Dykebar), 1891 v Ni (1)
Pearson, T. (Newcastle U), 1947 v E, Bel (2)
Penman, A. (Dundee), 1966 v Ho (1)
Pettigrew, W. (Motherwell), 1976 v Sw, Ni, W; 1977 v W (sub), Se (5)
Phillips, J. (Queen's Park), 1877 v E, W; 1878 v W (3)
Plenderleith, J. B. (Manchester C), 1961 v Ni (1)
Porteous, W. (Hearts), 1903 v Ni (1)
Pringle, C. (St Mirren), 1921 v W (1)
Provan, D. (Rangers), 1964 v Ni, N; 1966 v I (2), Ho (5)
Provan, D. (Celtic), 1980 v Bel (2 sub), P (sub), Ni (sub); 1981 v Is, W, E; 1982 v Se, P, Ni (10)
Pursell, P. (Queen's Park), 1914 v W (1)

Quinn, J. (Celtic), 1905 v Ni; 1906 v Ni, W; 1908 v Ni, E; 1909 v E; 1910 v E, Ni, W; 1912 v E, W (11)
Quinn, P. (Motherwell), 1961 v E, Ei (2); 1962 v U (4)

Rae, J. (Third Lanark), 1889 v W; 1890 v Ni (2)
Raeside, J. S. (Third Lanark), 1906 v W (1)

Raisbeck, A. G. (Liverpool), 1900 v E; 1901 v E; 1902 v E; 1903 v E, W; 1904 v E; 1906 v E; 1907 v E (8)
Rankin, G. (Vale of Leven), 1890 v Ni; 1891 v E (2)
Rankin, R. (St Mirren), 1929 v N, G, Ho (3)
Redpath, W. (Motherwell), 1949 v W, Ni; 1951 v E, D, F, Bel, A; 1952 v Ni, E (9)
Reid, J. G. (Airdrieonians), 1914 v W; 1920 v W; 1924 v Ni (3)
Reid, R. (Brentford), 1938 v E, Ni (2)
Reid, W. (Rangers), 1911 v E, W, Ni; 1912 v Ni; 1913 v E, W, Ni; 1914 v E, Ni (9)
Reilly, L. (Hibernian), 1949 v E, W, F; 1950 v W, Ni, Sw, F; 1951 v W, E, D, F, Bel, A; 1952 v Ni, W, E, USA, D, Se; 1953 v Ni, W, E, Se; 1954 v W; 1955 v H (2), P, Y, A, E; 1956 v E, W, Ni, A; 1957 v E, Ni, W, Y (38)
Rennie, H. G. (Hearts), 1900 v E, Ni; (with Hibernian), 1901 v E; 1902 v E, Ni, W; 1903 v Ni, W; 1904 v Ni; 1905 v W; 1906 v Ni; 1908 v Ni, W (13)
Renny-Tailyour, H. W. (Royal Engineers), 1873 v E (1)
Rhind, A. (Queen's Park), 1872 v E (1)
Richmond, A. (Queen's Park), 1906 v W (1)
Richmond, J. T. (Clydesdale), 1877 v E; (with Queen's Park), 1878 v E; 1882 v W (3)
Ring, T. (Clyde), 1953 v Se; 1955 v W, Ni, E, H; 1957 v E, Sp (2), Sw, WG; 1958 v Ni, Sw (12)
Rioch, B. D. (Derby Co), 1975 v P, W, Ni, E, R; 1976 v D (2), R, Ni, W, E; 1977 v Fi, Cz, W; (with Everton), W, Ni, E, Ch, Br; 1978 v Cz; (with Derby Co), Ni, E, Pe, Ho (24)
Ritchie, A. (East Stirlingshire), 1891 v W (1)
Ritchie, H. (Hibernian), 1923 v W; 1928 v Ni (2)
Ritchie, J. (Queen's Park), 1897 v W (1)
Ritchie, W. (Rangers), 1962 v U (sub) (1)
Robb, D. T. (Aberdeen), 1971 v W, E, P, D (sub), USSR (5)
Robb, W. (Rangers), 1926 v W; (with Hibernian), 1928 v W (2)
Robertson, A. (Clyde), 1955 v P, A, H; 1958 v Sw, Par (5)
Robertson, G. (Motherwell), 1910 v W; (with Sheffield W), 1912 v W; 1913 v E, Ni (4)
Robertson, G. (Kilmarnock), 1938 v Cz (1)
Robertson, H. (Dundee), 1962 v Cz (1)
Robertson, J. (Dundee), 1931 v A, I (2)
Robertson, J. (Nottingham F), 1978 v Ni, Ir; 1979 v P, N; 1980 v Pe, A, Bel (2), P; 1981 v Se, P, Is, Ni, Is, Ni, E; 1982 v Se, Ni (2), E (sub), Nz, Br, USSR; 1983 v EG, Sw (25)
Robertson, J. G. (Tottenham H), 1965 v W (1)
Robertson, J. T. (Everton), 1898 v E; (with Southampton), 1899 v E; (with Rangers), 1900 v E, W; 1901 v W, Ni, E; 1902 v W, Ni, E; 1903 v E, W; 1904 v E, W, Ni; 1905 v W (16)
Robertson, P. (Dundee), 1903 v Ni (1)
Robertson, T. (Queen's Park), 1889 v Ni; 1890 v E; 1891 v W; 1892 v Ni (4)
Robertson, T. (Hearts), 1898 v Ni (1)
Robertson, W. (Dumbarton), 1887 v E, W (2)
Robinson, R. (Dundee), 1974 v WG (sub); 1975 v Se, Ni, R (sub) (4)
Rough, A. (Partick T), 1976 v Sw, Ni, W, E; 1977 v Fi, Cz, W (2), Se, Ni, E, Ch, Arg, Br; 1978 v Cz, W, Ni, E, Pe, Ir, Ho; 1979 v A, P, W, Arg, N; 1980 v Pe, A, Bel (2), P, W, E, Pol, H; 1981 v Se, P, Is, Ni, Is, W, E; 1982 v Se, Ni, Sp, Ho, W, E, Nz, Br, USSR (51)
Rowan, A. (Caledonian), 1880 v E; (with Queen's Park), 1882 v W (2)
Russell, D. (Hearts), 1895 v E, Ni; (with Celtic), 1897 v W; 1898 v Ni; 1901 v W, Ni (6)
Russell, J. (Cambuslang), 1890 v Ni (1)
Russell, W. F. (Airdrieonians), 1924 v W; 1925 v E (2)
Rutherford, E. (Rangers), 1948 v F (1)

St John, I. (Motherwell), 1959 v WG; 1960 v E, Ni, W, Pol, A; 1961 v E; (with Liverpool), 1962 v Ni, W, E, Cz (2), U; 1963 v W, Ni, E, N, Ei (sub), Sp; 1964 v Ni; 1965 v E (21)
Sawers, W. (Dundee), 1895 v W (1)
Scarff, P. (Celtic), 1931 v Ni (1)
Schaedler, E. (Hibernian), 1974 v WG (1)
Scott, A. S. (Rangers), 1957 v Ni, Y, WG; 1958 v W, Sw; 1959 v P; 1962 v Ni, W, E, Cz, U; (with Everton), 1964 v W, N; 1965 v Fi; 1966 v P, Br (16)
Scott, J. (Hibernian), 1966 v Ho (1)
Scott, J. (Dundee), 1971 v D (sub), USSR (2)
Scott, M. (Airdrieonians), 1898 v W (1)
Scott, R. (Airdrieonians), 1894 v Ni (1)
Scoular, J. (Portsmouth), 1951 v D, F, A; 1952 v E, USA, D, Se; 1953 v W, Ni (9)
Sellar, W. (Battlefield), 1885 v E; 1886 v E; 1887 v E, W; 1888 v E; (with Queen's Park), 1891 v E; 1892 v E; 1893 v E, Ni (9)
Semple, W. (Cambuslang), 1886 v W (1)
Shankly, W. (Preston NE), 1938 v E; 1939 v E, W, Ni, H (5)
Sharp, J. (Dundee), 1904 v W; (with Woolwich Arsenal), 1907 v W, E; 1908 v E; (with Fulham), 1909 v W (5)
Shaw, D. (Hibernian), 1947 v W, Ni; 1948 v E, Bel, Sw, F; 1949 v W, Ni (8)
Shaw, F. W. (Pollokshields Ath), 1884 v E, W (2)
Shaw, J. (Rangers), 1947 v E, Bel, L; 1948 v Ni (4)
Shearer, R. (Rangers), 1961 v E, Ei (2), Cz (4)
Sillars, D. C. (Queen's Park), 1891 v Ni; 1892 v E; 1893 v W; 1894 v E; 1895 v W (5)
Simpson, J. (Third Lanark), 1895 v E, W, Ni (3)
Simpson, J. (Rangers), 1935 v E, W, Ni; 1936 v E, W, Ni; 1937 v G, E, W, Ni, A, Cz; 1938 v W, Ni (14)
Simpson, N. (Aberdeen), 1983 v Ni (1)
Simpson, R. C. (Celtic), 1967 v E, USSR; 1968 v Ni, E; 1969 v A (5)
Sinclair, G. L. (Hearts), 1910 v Ni; 1912 v W, Ni (3)
Sinclair, J. W. E. (Leicester C), 1966 v P (1)
Skene, L. H. (Queen's Park), 1904 v W (1)
Sloan, T. (Third Lanark), 1904 v W (1)
Smellie, R. (Queen's Park), 1887 v Ni; 1888 v W; 1889 v E; 1891 v E; 1893 v E, Ni (6)
Smith, A. (Rangers), 1898 v E; 1900 v E, Ni, W; 1901 v E, Ni, W; 1902 v E, Ni, W; 1903 v E, Ni, W; 1904 v Ni; 1905 v W; 1906 v E, Ni; 1907 v W; 1911 v E, Ni (20)
Smith, D. (Aberdeen), 1966 v Ho; (with Rangers), 1968 v Ho (2)
Smith, G. (Hibernian), 1947 v E, Ni; 1948 v W, Bel, Sw, F; 1952 v E, USA; 1955 v P, Y, A, H; 1956 v E, Ni, W; 1957 v Sp (2), Sw (18)
Smith, J. (Rangers), 1935 v Ni; 1938 v Ni (2)
Smith, J. (Ayr U), 1924 v E (1)
Smith, J. (Aberdeen), 1968 v Ho (sub); (with Newcastle U), 1974 v WG, Ni (sub), W (sub) (4)
Smith, J. E. (Celtic), 1959 v H, P (2)
Smith, Jas. (Queen's Park), 1872 v E (1)
Smith, John. (Mauchline), 1877 v E, W; 1879 v E, W; (with Edinburgh University), 1880 v E; (with Queen's Park), 1881 v W, E; 1883 v E, W; 1884 v E (10)
Smith, N. (Rangers), 1897 v E; 1898 v W; 1899 v E, W, Ni; 1900 v E, W, Ni; 1901 v Ni, W; 1902 v E, Ni (12)
Smith, R. (Queen's Park), 1872 v E; 1873 v E (2)
Smith, T. M. (Kilmarnock), 1934 v E; (with Preston NE), 1938 v E (2)
Somers, P. (Celtic), 1905 v E, Ni; 1907 v Ni; 1909 v W (4)
Somers, W. S. (Third Lanark), 1879 v E, W; (with Queen's Park), 1880 v W (3)
Somerville, G. (Queen's Park), 1886 v E (1)
Souness, G. J. (Middlesbrough), 1975 v EG, Sp, Se; (with Liverpool), 1978 v Bul, W, E (sub), Ho; 1979 v A, N, W, Ni, E; 1980 v Pe, A, Bel, P, Ni; 1981 v P, Is (2);

Reilly scores for Scotland against England

Ian St John *Scotland*

1982 v Ni, P, Sp, W, E, Nz, Br, USSR; 1983 v EG, Sw, Bel, W, E, Ca (2+1 sub) (35)
Speedie, F. (Rangers), 1903 v E, W, Ni (3)
Speirs, J. H. (Rangers), 1908 v W (1)
Stanton, P. (Hibernian), 1966 v Ho; 1969 v Ni; 1970 v Ei, A; 1971 v D, Bel, P, USSR, D; 1972 v P, Bel, Ho, W; 1973 v W, Ni; 1974 v WG (16)
Stark, J. (Rangers), 1909 v E, Ni (2)
Steel, W. (Morton), 1947 v E, Bel, L; (with Derby Co), 1948 v F, E, W, Ni; 1949 v E, W, Ni, F; 1950 v E, W, Ni, Sw, P, F; (with Dundee), 1951 v W, Ni, E, A (2), D, F, Bel; 1952 v W; 1953 v W, E, Ni, Se (30)
Steele, D. M. (Huddersfield), 1923 v E, W, Ni (3)
Stein, C. (Rangers), 1969 v W, Ni, D, E, Cy (2); 1970 v A (sub), Ni (sub), W, E, Ei, WG; 1971 v D, USSR, Bel, D; 1972 v Cz (sub); (with Coventry C), 1973 v E (2 sub), W (sub), Ni (21)
Stephen, J. F. (Bradford), 1947 v W; 1948 v W (2)
Stevenson, G. (Motherwell), 1928 v W, Ni; 1930 v Ni, E, F; 1931 v E, W; 1932 v W, Ni; 1933 v Ni; 1934 v E; 1935 v Ni (12)
Stewart, A. (Queen's Park), 1888 v Ni; 1889 v W (2)
Stewart, A. (Third Lanark), 1894 v W (1)
Stewart, D. (Dumbarton), 1888 v Ni (1)
Stewart, D. (Queen's Park), 1893 v W; 1894 v Ni; 1897 v Ni (3)
Stewart, D. S. (Leeds U), 1978 v EG (1)
Stewart, G. (Hibernian), 1906 v W, E; (with Manchester C), 1907 v E, W (4)
Stewart, J. (Kilmarnock), 1977 v Ch (sub); (with Middlesbrough), 1979 v N (2)
Stewart, R. (West Ham U), 1981 v W, Ni, E; 1982 v Ni, P, W (6)
Stewart, W. E. (Queen's Park), 1898 v Ni; 1900 v Ni (2)
Storrier, D. (Celtic), 1899 v E, W, Ni (3)
Strachan, G. (Aberdeen), 1980 v Ni, W, E, Pol, H (sub); 1981 v Se, P; 1982 v Ni, P, Sp, Ho (sub), Nz, Br, USSR; 1983 v EG, Sw, Bel, Sw, W, E, Ca (2+1 sub) (23)
Sturrock, P. (Dundee U), 1981 v W (sub), Ni, E (sub); 1982 v P, Ni (sub), W (sub), E (sub); 1983 v EG (sub), Sw, Bel (sub), Ca (3) (13)
Summers, W. (St Mirren), 1926 v E (1)
Symon, J. S. (Rangers), 1939 v H (1)

Tait, T. S. (Sunderland), 1911 v W (1)
Taylor, J. (Queen's Park), 1872 v E; 1873 v E; 1874 v E; 1875 v E; 1876 v E, W (6)
Taylor, J. D. (Dumbarton), 1892 v W; 1893 v W; 1894 v Ni; (with St Mirren), 1895 v Ni (4)
Taylor, W. (Hearts), 1892 v E (1)
Telfer, W. (Motherwell), 1933 v Ni; 1934 v Ni (2)
Telfer, W. D. (St Mirren), 1954 v W (1)
Templeton, R. (Aston Villa), 1902 v E; (with Newcastle U), 1903 v E, W; 1904 v E; (with Woolwich Arsenal), 1905 v W; (with Kilmarnock), 1908 v Ni; 1910 v E, Ni; 1912 v E, Ni; 1913 v W (11)
Thomson, A. (Arthurlie), 1886 v Ni (1)
Thomson, A. (Airdrieonians), 1909 v Ni (1)
Thomson, A. (Celtic), 1926 v E; 1932 v F; 1933 v W (3)
Thomson, A. (Third Lanark), 1889 v W (1)
Thomson, C. (Hearts), 1904 v Ni; 1905 v E, Ni, W; 1906 v W, Ni; 1907 v E, W, Ni; 1908 v E, W, Ni; (with Sunderland), 1909 v W; 1910 v E; 1911 v Ni; 1912 v E, W; 1913 v E, W; 1914 v E, Ni (21)
Thomson, C. (Sunderland), 1937 v Cz (1)
Thomson, D. (Dundee), 1920 v W (1)
Thomson, J. (Celtic), 1930 v F; 1931 v E, W, Ni (4)
Thomson, J. J. (Queen's Park), 1872 v E; 1873 v E; 1874 v E (3)
Thomson, J. R. (Everton), 1933 v W (1)
Thomson, R. (Celtic), 1932 v W (1)
Thomson, R. W. (Falkirk), 1927 v E (1)
Thomson, S. (Rangers), 1884 v W, Ni (2)
Thomson, W. (Dumbarton), 1892 v W; 1893 v W; 1898 v Ni, W (4)
Thomson, W. (Dundee), 1896 v W (1)
Thornton, W. (Rangers), 1947 v W, Ni; 1948 v E, Ni; 1949 v F; 1952 v D, Se (7)
Thomson, W. (St Mirren), 1980 v Ni; 1981 v Ni (sub), Ni; 1982 v P; 1983 v Ni, Ca (6)
Toner, W. (Kilmarnock), 1959 v W, Ni (2)
Townsley, T. (Falkirk), 1926 v W (1)
Troup, A. (Dundee), 1920 v E; 1921 v W, Ni; 1922 v Ni; (with Everton), 1926 v E (5)
Turnbull, E. (Hibernian), 1948 v Bel, Sw; 1951 v A; 1958 v H, Pol, Y, Par, F (8)
Turner, T. (Arthurlie), 1884 v W (1)
Turner, W. (Pollokshields), 1885 v Ni; 1886 v Ni (2)

Ure, J. F. (Dundee), 1962 v W, Cz; 1963 v W, Ni, E, A, N, Sp; (with Arsenal), 1964 v Ni, N; 1968 v Ni (11)
Urquhart, D. (Hibernian), 1934 v W (1)

Vallance, T. (Rangers), 1877 v E, W; 1878 v E; 1879 v E, W; 1881 v E, W (7)
Venters, A. (Cowdenbeath), 1934 v Ni; (with Rangers), 1936 v E; 1939 v E (3)

Waddell, T. S. (Queen's Park), 1891 v Ni; 1892 v E; 1893 v E, Ni; 1895 v E, Ni (6)
Waddell, W. (Rangers), 1947 v W; 1949 v E, W, Ni, F; 1950 v E, Ni; 1951 v E, D, F, Bel, A; 1952 v Ni, W; 1954 v Ni; 1955 v W, Ni (17)
Wales, H. M. (Motherwell), 1933 v W (1)
Walker, F. (Third Lanark), 1922 v W (1)
Walker, G. (St Mirren), 1930 v F; 1931 v Ni, A, Sw (4)
Walker, J. (Hearts), 1895 v Ni; 1897 v W; 1898 v Ni; (with Rangers), 1904 v W, Ni (5)
Walker, J. (Swindon T), 1911 v E, W, Ni; 1912 v E, W, Ni; 1913 v E, W, Ni (9)
Walker, R. (Hearts), 1900 v E, Ni; 1901 v E, W; 1902 v E, W, Ni; 1903 v E, W, Ni; 1904 v E, W, Ni; 1905 v E, W, Ni; 1906 v Ni; 1907 v E, Ni; 1908 v E, W, Ni; 1909 v E, W; 1912 v E, W, Ni; 1913 v E, W (29)
Walker, T. (Hearts), 1935 v E, W; 1936 v E, W, Ni; 1937 v G, E, W, Ni, A, Cz; 1938 v E, W, Ni, Cz, Ho; 1939 v E, W, Ni, H (20)
Walker, W. (Clyde), 1909 v Ni; 1910 v Ni (2)
Wallace, I. A. (Coventry C), 1978 v Bul (sub); 1979 v P (sub), W (3)
Wallace, W. S. B. (Hearts), 1965 v Ni; 1966 v E, Ho; (with Celtic), 1967 v E, USSR (sub); 1968 v Ni; 1969 v E (sub) (7)
Wardhaugh, J. (Hearts), 1955 v H; 1957 v Ni (2)
Wark, J. (Ipswich T), 1979 v W, Ni, E, Arg, N (sub); 1980 v Pe, A, Bel (2); 1981 v Is, Ni; 1982 v Se, Sp, Ho, Ni, Nz, Br, USSR; 1983 v EG, Sw, Sw, Ni, E (sub) (23)
Watson, A. (Queen's Park), 1881 v E, W; 1882 v E (3)
Watson, J. (Sunderland), 1903 v E, W; 1904 v E; 1905 v E; (with Middlesbrough), 1909 v E, Ni (6)
Watson, J. (Motherwell), 1948 v Ni; (with Huddersfield T), 1954 v Ni (2)
Watson, J. A. K. (Rangers), 1878 v W (1)
Watson, P. R. (Blackpool), 1934 v A (1)
Watson, R. (Motherwell), 1971 v USSR (1)
Watson, W. (Falkirk), 1898 v W (1)
Watt, F. (Kilbirnie), 1889 v W, Ni; 1890 v W; 1891 v E (4)
Watt, W. W. (Queen's Park), 1887 v Ni (1)
Waugh, W. (Hearts), 1938 v Cz (1)
Weir, A. (Motherwell), 1959 v WG; 1960 v E, P, A, H, T (6)
Weir, J. (Third Lanark), 1887 v Ni (1)
Weir, J. B. (Queen's Park), 1872 v E; 1874 v E; 1875 v E; 1878 v W (4)

Weir, P. (St Mirren), 1980 v N (sub), W, Pol (sub), H; (with Aberdeen), 1983 v Sw (5)
White, John (Albion R), 1922 v W; (with Hearts), 1923 v Ni (2)
White, J. A. (Falkirk), 1959 v WG, Ho, P; 1960 v Ni; (with Tottenham H), 1960 v W, Pol, A, T; 1961 v W; 1962 v Ni, W, E, Cz (2); 1963 v W, Ni, E; 1964 v Ni, W, E, N, WG (22)
White, W. (Bolton W), 1907 v E; 1908 v E (2)
Whitelaw, A. (Vale of Leven), 1887 v Ni; 1890 v W (2)
Wilson, A. (Sheffield W), 1907 v E; 1908 v E; 1912 v E; 1913 v E, W; 1914 v Ni (6)
Wilson, A. (Portsmouth), 1954 v Fi (1)
Wilson, A. N. (Dunfermline), 1920 v E, W, Ni; 1921 v E, W, Ni; (with Middlesbrough), 1922 v E, W, Ni; 1923 v E, W, Ni (12)
Wilson, D. (Queen's Park), 1900 v W (1)
Wilson, D. (Oldham Ath), 1913 v E (1)
Wilson, D. (Rangers), 1961 v E, W, Ni, Ei (2), Cz; 1962 v Ni, W, E, Cz, U; 1963 v W, E, A, N, Ei, Sp; 1964 v E, WG; 1965 v Ni, E, Fi (22)
Wilson, G. W. (Hearts), 1904 v W; 1905 v E, Ni; 1906 v W; (with Everton), 1907 v E; (with Newcastle U), 1909 v E (6)
Wilson, Hugh, (Newmilns), 1890 v W; (with Sunderland), 1897 v E; (with Third Lanark), 1902 v W; 1904 v Ni (4)
Wilson, J. (Vale of Leven), 1888 v W; 1889 v E; 1890 v E; 1891 v E (4)
Wilson, P. (Celtic), 1926 v Ni; 1930 v F; 1931 v Ni; 1933 v E (4)
Wilson, P. (Celtic), 1975 v Sp (sub) (1)
Wilson, R. P. (Arsenal), 1972 v P, Ho (2)
Wiseman, W. (Queen's Park), 1927 v W; 1930 v Ni (2)
Wood, G. (Everton), 1979 v Ni, E, Arg (sub); (with Arsenal), 1982 v Ni (4)
Woodburn, W. A. (Rangers), 1947 v E, Bel, L; 1948 v W, Ni; 1949 v E, F; 1950 v E, W, Ni, P, F; 1951 v E, W, Ni, A (2), D, F, Bel; 1952 v E, W, Ni, USA (24)
Wotherspoon, D. N. (Queen's Park), 1872 v E; 1873 v E (2)
Wright, T. (Sunderland), 1953 v W, Ni, E (3)
Wylie, T. G. (Rangers), 1890 v Ni (1)

Yeats, R. (Liverpool), 1965 v W; 1966 v I (2)
Yorston, B. C. (Aberdeen), 1931 v Ni (1)
Yorston, H. (Aberdeen), 1955 v W (1)
Young, A. (Hearts), 1960 v E, A (sub), H, T; 1961 v W, Ni; (with Everton), Ei; 1966 v P (8)
Young, A. (Everton), 1905 v E; 1907 v W (2)
Young, G. L. (Rangers), 1947 v E, Ni, Bel, L; 1948 v E, Ni, Bel, Sw, F; 1949 v E, W, Ni, F; 1950 v E, W, Ni, Sw, P, F; 1951 v E, W, Ni, A (2), D, F, Bel; 1952 v E, W, Ni, USA, D, Se; 1953 v W, E, Ni, Se; 1954 v Ni, W; 1955 v W, Ni, P, Y; 1956 v Ni, W, E, A; 1957 v E, Ni, W, Y, Sp, Sw (53)
Young, J. (Celtic), 1906 v Ni (1)
Younger, T. (Hibernian), 1955 v P, Y, A, H; 1956 v E, Ni, W, A; (with Liverpool), 1957 v E, Ni, W, Y, Sp (2), Sw, WG; 1958 v Ni, W, E, Sw, H, Pol, Y, Par (24)

WALES

Adams, H. (Berwyn R), 1882 v Ni, E; (with Druids), 1883 v Ni, E (4)
Allchurch, I. J. (Swansea T), 1951 v E, Ni, P, Sw; 1952 v E, S, Ni, R of UK; 1953 v S, E, Ni, F, Y; 1954 v S, E, Ni, A; 1955 v S, E, Ni, Y; 1956 v E, S, Ni, A; 1957 v E, S; 1958 v Ni, Is (2), H (2), M, Sw, Br; (with Newcastle U), 1959 v E, S, Ni; 1960 v E, S; 1961 v Ni, H, Sp (2); 1962 v E, S, Br (2), M; (with Cardiff C), 1963 v S, E, Ni, H (2); 1964 v E; 1965 v S, E, Ni, Gr, I, USSR; 1966 (with Swansea T), v USSR, E, S, D, Br (2), Ch (68)
Allchurch, L. (Swansea T), 1955 v Ni; 1956 v A; 1958 v S, Ni, EG, Is; 1959 v S; (with Sheffield U), 1962 v S, Ni, Br; 1964 v E (11)
Allen, B. W. (Coventry C), 1951 v S, E (2)
Arridge, S. (Bootle), 1892 v S, Ni; (with Everton), 1894 v Ni; 1895 v Ni; 1896 v E; (with New Brighton Tower), 1898 v E, Ni; 1899 v E (8)
Astley, D. J. (Charlton Ath), 1931 v Ni; (with Aston Villa), 1932 v E; 1933 v E, S, Ni; 1934 v E, S; 1935 v S; 1936 v E, Ni; (with Derby Co), 1939 v E, S; (with Blackpool), F (13)
Atherton, R. W. (Hibernian), 1899 v E, Ni; 1903 v E, S, Ni; (with Middlesbrough), 1904 v E, S, Ni; 1905 v Ni (9)

Bailiff, W. E. (Llanelly), 1913 v E, S, Ni; 1920 v Ni (4)
Baker, C. W. (Cardiff C), 1958 v M; 1960 v S, Ni; 1961 v S, E, Ei; 1962 v S (7)
Baker, W. G. (Cardiff C), 1948 v Ni (1)
Bamford, T. (Wrexham), 1931 v E, S, Ni; 1932 v Ni; 1933 v F (5)
Barnes, W. (Arsenal), 1948 v E, S, Ni; 1949 v E, S, Ni; 1950 v E, S, Ni, Bel; 1951 v E, S, Ni, P; 1952 v E, S, Ni, R of UK; 1954 v E, S; 1955 v S, Y (22)
Bartley, T. (Glossop NE), 1898 v E (1)
Beadles, G. H. (Cardiff C), 1925 v E, S (2)
Bell, W. S. (Shrewsbury Engineers), 1881 v E, S; (with Crewe Alex), 1886 v E, S, Ni (5)
Bennion, S. R. (Manchester U), 1926 v S; 1927 v S; 1928 v S, E, Ni; 1929 v S, E, Ni; 1930 v S; 1932 v Ni (10)
Berry, G. F. (Wolverhampton W), 1979 v WG; 1980 v Ei, WG (sub), T; (with Stoke C), 1983 v E (sub) (5)
Blew, H. (Wrexham), 1899 v E, S, Ni; 1902 v S, Ni; 1903 v E, S; 1904 v E, S, Ni; 1905 v S, Ni; 1906 v E, S, Ni; 1907 v S; 1908 v E, S, Ni; 1909 v E, S; 1910 v E (22)
Boden, T. (Wrexham), 1880 v E (1)
Bostock, A. M. (Shrewsbury), 1892 v Ni (1)
Boulter, L. M. (Brentford), 1939 v Ni (1)
Bowdler, H. E. (Shrewsbury), 1893 v S (1)
Bowdler, J. C. H. (Shrewsbury), 1890 v Ni; (with Wolverhampton W), 1891 v S; 1892 v Ni; (with Shrewsbury), 1894 v E (4)
Bowen, D. L. (Arsenal), 1955 v S, Y; 1957 v Ni, Cz, EG; 1958 v E, S, Ni, EG, Is (2), H (2), M, Se, Br; 1959 v E, S, Ni (19)
Bowen, E. (Druids), 1880 v S; 1883 v S (2)
Bowsher, S. J. (Burnley), 1929 v Ni (1)
Boyle, T. (C Palace), 1981 v Ei, S (sub) (2)
Britten, T. J. (Parkgrove), 1878 v S; (with Presteigne), 1880 v S (2)
Brookes, S. J. (Llandudno), 1900 v E, Ni (2)
Brown, A. I. (Aberdare Ath), 1926 v Ni (1)
Bryan, T. (Oswestry), 1886 v E, Ni (2)
Buckland, T. (Bangor), 1899 v E (1)
Burgess, W. A. R. (Tottenham H), 1947 v E, S, Ni; 1948 v E, S; 1949 v E, S, Ni, P, Bel, Sw; 1950 v E, S, Ni, Bel; 1951 v S, Ni, P, Sw; 1952 v E, S, Ni, R of UK; 1953 v S, E, Ni, F, Y; 1954 v S, E, Ni, A (32)
Burke, T. (Wrexham), 1883 v E; 1884 v S; 1885 v E, S, Ni; (with Newton Heath), 1887 v E, S; 1888 v S (8)
Burnett, T. B. (Ruabon), 1877 v S (1)
Burton, A. D. (Norwich C), 1963 v Ni, H; (with Newcastle U), 1964 v E; 1969 v S, E, Ni, I, EG; 1972 v Cz (9)
Butler, A. (Druids), 1900 v S, Ni (2)
Butler, J. (Chirk), 1893 v E, S, Ni (3)

Cartwright, L. (Coventry C), 1974 v E (sub), S, Ni; 1976 v S (sub); 1977 v WG (sub); (with Wrexham), 1978 v Ir (sub); 1979 v Ma (7)
Carty, T. (Wrexham), 1889 v Ni (1)

Challen, J. B. (Corinthians), 1887 v E, S; 1888 v E; (with Wellingborough GS), 1890 v E (4)
Chapman, T. (Newtown), 1894 v E, S, Ni; 1895 v S, Ni; (with Manchester C), 1896 v E; 1897 v E (7)
Charles, J. (Swansea C), 1981 v Cz, T (sub), S (sub), USSR (sub); 1982 v Ic; 1983 v N (sub), T (sub), Bul (sub), S, Ni, Br (11
Charles, M. (Swansea T), 1955 v Ni; 1956 v E, S, A; 1957 v E, Ni, Cz (2), EG; 1958 v E, S, EG, Is (2), H (2), M, Se, Br; 1959 v E, S; (with Arsenal), 1961 v Ni, H, Sp (2); 1962 v E, S; (with Cardiff C), 1962 v Br, Ni; 1963 v S, H (31)
Charles, W. J. (Leeds U), 1950 v Ni; 1951 v Sw; 1953 v Ni, F, Y; 1954 v E, S, Ni, A; 1955 v S, E, Ni, Y; 1956 v E, S, A, Ni; 1957 v E, S, Ni, Cz (2), EG; (with Juventus), 1958 v Is (2), H (2) M, Se; 1960 v S; 1962 v E, Br (2), M; (with Leeds U), 1963 v S; (with Cardiff C), 1964 v S; 1965 v S, USSR (38)
Clarke, R. J. (Manchester C), 1949 v E; 1950 v S, Ni, Bel; 1951 v E, S, Ni, P, Sw; 1952 v S, E, Ni, R of UK; 1953 v S, E; 1954 v E, S, Ni; 1955 v Y, S, E; 1956 v Ni (22)
Collier, D. J. (Grimsby T), 1921 v S (1)
Collins, W. S. (Llanelly), 1931 v S (1)
Conde, C. (Chirk), 1884 v E, S, Ni (3)
Cook, F. C. (Newport Co), 1925 v E, S; (with Portsmouth), 1928 v E, S; 1930 v E, S, Ni; 1932 v E (8)
Crompton, W. (Wrexham), 1931 v E, S, Ni (3)
Cross, E. A. (Wrexham), 1876 v S; 1877 v S (2)
Cross, K. (Druids), 1879 v S; 1881 v E, S (3)
Crowe, V. H. (Aston Villa), 1959 v E, Ni; 1960 v E, Ni; 1961 v S, E, Ni, Ei, H, Sp (2); 1962 v E, S, Br, M; 1963 v H (16)
Cumner, R. H. (Arsenal), 1939 v E, S, Ni (3)
Curtis, A. (Swansea C), 1976 v E, Y (sub), S, Ni, Y (sub), E; 1977 v WG, S (sub), Ni (sub); 1978 v WG, E, S; 1979 v WG, S; (with Leeds U), E, Ni, Ma; 1980 v Ei, WG, T; (with Swansea C), 1982 v Cz, Ic, USSR, Sp, E, S, Ni; 1983 v N (28)
Curtis, E. R. (Cardiff C), 1928 v S; (with Birmingham), 1932 v S; 1934 v Ni (3)

Daniel, R. W. (Arsenal), 1951 v E, Ni, P; 1952 v E, S, Ni, R of UK; 1953 v S, E, Ni, F, Y; (with Sunderland), 1954 v E, S, Ni; 1955 v E, Ni; 1957 v S, E, Ni, Cz (21)
Darvell, S. (Oxford University), 1897 v S, Ni (2)
Davies, A. (Manchester U), 1983 v Ni, Br (2)
Davies, A. (Wrexham), 1876 v S; 1877 v S (2)
Davies, A. (Shrewsbury), 1891 v Ni (1)
Davies, A. (Druids), 1904 v S; (with Middlesbrough), 1905 v S (2)
Davies, A. O. (Barmouth), 1885 v Ni; 1886 v E, S; (with Swifts), 1887 v E, S; 1888 v E, Ni; (with Wrexham), 1889 v S; (with Crewe Alex), 1890 v E (9)
Davies, C. (Brecon), 1899 v Ni; (with Hereford), 1900 v Ni (2)
Davies, C. (Charlton Ath), 1972 v R (sub) (1)
Davies, D. (Bolton W), 1904 v S, Ni; 1908 v E (sub) (3)
Davies, D. W. (Treharris), 1912 v Ni; (with Oldham Ath), 1913 v Ni (2)
Davies, E. Lloyd, (Stoke C), 1904 v E; 1907 v E, S, Ni; (with Northampton T), 1908 v S; 1909 v Ni; 1910 v Ni; 1911 v E, S; 1912 v E, S; 1913 v E, S; 1914 v Ni, E, S (16)
Davies, E. R. (Newcastle U), 1953 v S, E; 1954 v E, S; 1958 v E, EG (6)
Davies, G. (Fulham), 1980 v T, Ic; 1982 v Sp (sub), F (sub); 1983 v E, Bul, S, Ni, Br (9)
Davies, Rev. H. (Wrexham), 1928 v Ni (1)
Davies, Idwal (Liverpool Marine), 1923 v S (1)
Davies, J. E. (Oswestry), 1885 v E (1)
Davies, Jas. (Wrexham), 1878 v S (1)
Davies, John. (Wrexham), 1879 v S (1)
Davies, Jos. (Everton), 1889 v S, Ni; (with Chirk), 1891 v Ni; (with Ardwick), v E, S; (with Sheffield U), 1895 v E, S, Ni; (with Manchester C), 1896 v E; (with Millwall), 1897 v E; (with Reading), 1900 v E (11)
Davies, Jos. (Newton Heath), 1888 v E, S, Ni; 1889 v S; 1890 v E; (with Wolverhampton W), 1892 v E; 1893 v E (7)
Davies, J. P. (Druids), 1883 v E, Ni (2)
Davies, Ll. (Wrexham), 1907 v Ni; 1910 v Ni, S, E; (with Everton), 1911 v S, Ni; 1912 v Ni, S, E; 1913 v Ni, S, E; 1914 v Ni (13)
Davies, L. S. (Cardiff C), 1922 v E, S, Ni; 1923 v E, S, Ni; 1924 v E, S, Ni; 1925 v S, Ni; 1926 v E, Ni; 1927 v E, Ni; 1928 v S, Ni, E; 1929 v S, Ni, E; 1930 v E, S (23)
Davies, O. (Wrexham), 1890 v S (1)
Davies, R. (Wrexham), 1883 v Ni; 1884 v Ni; 1885 v Ni (3)
Davies, R. (Druids), 1885 v E (1)
Davies, R. L. (Wrexham), 1892 v Ni (1)
Davies, R. O. (Wrexham), 1892 v Ni, E (2)
Davies, R. T. (Norwich C), 1964 v Ni; 1965 v E; 1966 v Br (2), Ch; (with Southampton), 1967 v S, E, Ni; 1968 v S, Ni, WG; 1969 v S, E, Ni, I, WG, R of UK; 1970 v E, S, Ni; 1971 v Cz, S, E, Ni; 1972 v R, E, S, N; (with Portsmouth), 1974 v E (29)
Davies, R. W. (Bolton W), 1964 v E; 1965 v E, S, Ni, D, Gr, USSR; 1966 v E, S, Ni, USSR, D, Br (2), Ch (sub); 1967 v S; (with Newcastle U), E; 1968 v S, Ni, WG; 1969 v S, E, Ni, I; 1970 v EG; 1971 v R, Cz; (with Manchester C), 1972 v E, S, Ni; (with Manchester U), 1973 v E, S (sub), Ni; (with Blackpool), 1974 v Pol (34)
Davies, Stanley (Preston NE), 1920 v E, S, Ni; (with Everton), 1921 v E, S, Ni; (with WBA), 1922 v E, S, Ni; 1923 v S; 1925 v S, Ni; 1926 v S, E, Ni; 1927 v S; 1928 v S; (with Rotherham U), 1930 v Ni (18)
Davies, T. (Oswestry), 1886 v E (1)
Davies, T. (Druids), 1903 v E, Ni, S; 1904 v S (4)
Davies, W. (Swansea T), 1924 v E, S, Ni; (with Cardiff C), 1925 v E, S, Ni; 1926 v E, S, Ni; 1927 v S; 1928 v Ni; (with Notts Co), 1929 v E, S, Ni; 1930 v E, S, Ni (17)
Davies, W. (Wrexham), 1884 v Ni (1)
Davies, William (Wrexham), 1903 v Ni; 1905 v Ni; (with Blackburn R), 1908 v E, S; 1909 v E, S, Ni; 1911 v E, S, Ni; 1912 v Ni (11)
Davies, W. C. (C Palace), 1908 v S; (with WBA), 1909 v E; 1910 v S; (with C Palace), 1914 v E (4)
Davies, W. D. (Everton), 1975 v H, L, S, E, Ni; 1976 v Y (2), E, Ni; 1977 v WG, S (2), Cz, E, Ni; 1978 v K; (with Wrexham), S, Cz, WG, Ir, E, S, Ni; 1979 v Ma, T, WG S, E, Ni, Ma; 1980 v Ei, WG, T, E, S, Ni, Ic; 1981 v T, Cz, Ei, T, S, E, USSR; (with Swansea C), 1982 v Cz, Ic, USSR, Sp, E, S, F; 1983 v Y (52)
Davies, W. H. (Oswestry), 1876 v S; 1877 v S; 1879 v E; 1880 v E (4)
Davies, W. O. (Millwall Ath), 1913 v E, S, Ni; 1914 v S, Ni (5)
Davis, G. (Wrexham), 1978 v Ir, E (sub), Ni (3)
Day, A. (Tottenham H), 1934 v Ni (1)
Deacy, N. (PSV Eindhoven), 1977 v Cz, S, E, Ni; 1978 v K (sub), S (sub), Cz (sub), WG, Ir, S (sub), Ni; (with Beringen), 1979 v T (12)
Dearson, D. J. (Birmingham), 1939 v S, Ni, F (3)
Derrett, S. C. (Cardiff C), 1969 v S, WG; 1970 v I; 1971 v Fi (4)
Dewey, F. T. (Cardiff Corinthians), 1931 v E, S (2)
Doughty, J. (Druids), 1886 v S; (with Newton Heath), 1887 v S, Ni; 1888 v E, S, Ni; 1889 v S; 1890 v E (8)
Doughty, R. (Newton Heath and Druids), 1888 v S, Ni; 1890 v E (3)
Durban, A. (Derby Co), 1966 v Br (sub); 1967 v Ni; 1968 v E, S, Ni, WG; 1969 v EG, S, E, Ni, WG; 1970 v E, S,

Alan Davies *Manchester United* and *Wales*

Player and now manager of Wales – Mike England

Arfon Griffiths *Wrexham* and *Wales*

Ni, EG, I; 1971 v R, S, E, Ni, Cz, Fi; 1972 v Fi, Cz, E, S, Ni (27)
Dwyer, P. (Cardiff C), 1978 v Ir, E, S, Ni; 1979 v T, S, E, Ni, Ma (sub); 1980 v WG (10)

Edwards, C. (Wrexham), 1878 v S (1)
Edwards, G. (Birmingham C), 1947 v E, S, Ni; 1948 v E, S, Ni; (with Cardiff C), 1949 v Ni, P, Bel, Sw; 1950 v E, S (12)
Edwards, H. (Wrexham Civil Service), 1878 v S; 1880 v E; 1882 v E, S; 1883 v S; 1884 v Ni; 1887 v Ni (7)
Edwards, R. I. (Chester), 1978 v K (sub); 1979 v Ma, WG; (with Wrexham), 1980 v T (sub) (4)
Edwards, J. H. (Oswestry), 1895 v Ni; 1897 v E, Ni; (with Aberystwyth), 1898 v Ni (4)
Edwards, J. H. (Wanderers), 1876 v S (1)
Edwards, L. T. (Charlton Ath), 1957 v Ni, EG (2)
Edwards, T. (Linfield), 1932 v S (1)
Egan, W. (Chirk), 1892 v S (1)
Ellis, B. (Motherwell), 1932 v E; 1933 v E, S; 1934 v S; 1936 v E; 1937 v S (6)
Ellis, E. (Nunhead), 1931 v E; (with Oswestry), S; 1932 v Ni (3)
Emanuel, W. J. (Bristol C), 1973 v E (sub), Ni (sub) (2)
England, H. M. (Blackburn R), 1962 v Ni, Br, M; 1963 v Ni, H; 1964 v E, S, Ni; 1965 v E, D, Gr (2), USSR, Ni, I; 1966 v E, S, Ni, USSR, D; (with Tottenham H), 1967 v S, E; 1968 v E, Ni, WG; 1969 v EG; 1970 v R of UK, EG, E, S, Ni, I; 1971 v R; 1972 v Fi, E, S, Ni; 1973 v E (3), S; 1974 v Pol; 1975 v H, L (44)
Evans, B. C. (Swansea C), 1972 v Fi, Cz; 1973 v E (2), Pol, S; (with Hereford U), 1974 v Pol (7)
Evans, D. G. (Reading), 1926 v Ni; 1927 v Ni, E; (with Huddersfield T), 1929 v S (4)
Evans, H. P. (Cardiff C), 1922 v E, S, Ni; 1924 v E, S, Ni (6)
Evans, I. (Crystal Palace), 1976 v A, E, Y (2), E, Ni; 1977 v WG, S (2), Cz, E, Ni; 1978 v K (13)
Evans, J. (Cardiff C), 1912 v Ni; 1913 v Ni; 1914 v S; 1920 v S, Ni; 1922 v Ni; 1923 v E, Ni (8)
Evans, J. (Oswestry), 1893 v Ni; 1894 v E, Ni (3)
Evans, J. H. (Southend U), 1922 v E, S, Ni; 1923 v S (4)
Evans, Len (Cardiff C), 1931 v E, S; (with Birmingham), 1934 v Ni (3)
Evans, L. H. (Aberdare Ath), 1927 v Ni (1)
Evans, M. (Oswestry), 1884 v E (1)
Evans, R. (Clapton), 1902 v Ni (1)
Evans, R. E. (Wrexham), 1906 v E, S; (with Aston Villa), Ni; 1907 v E; 1908 v E, S; (with Sheffield U), 1909 v S; 1910 v E, S, Ni (10)
Evans, R. O. (Wrexham), 1902 v Ni; 1903 v E, S, Ni; (with Blackburn R), 1908 v Ni; (with Coventry C), 1911 v E, Ni; 1912 v E, S, Ni (10)
Evans, R. S. (Swansea T), 1964 v Ni (1)
Evans T. J. (Clapton Orient), 1927 v S; 1928 v E, S; (with Newcastle U), Ni (4)
Evans, W. (Tottenham H), 1933 v Ni; 1934 v E, S; 1935 v E; 1936 v E, Ni (6)
Evans, W. A. W. (Oxford University), 1876 v S; 1877 v S (2)
Evans, W. G. (Bootle), 1890 v E; 1891 v E; (with Aston Villa), 1892 v E (3)
Evelyn, E. C. (Crusaders), 1887 v E (1)
Eyton-Jones, J. A. (Wrexham), 1883 v Ni; 1884 v Ni, E, S (4)

Farmer, G. (Oswestry), 1885 v E, S (2)
Finnigan, R. J. (Wrexham), 1930 v Ni (1)
Flynn, B. (Burnley), 1975 v L (2 sub), H (sub), S, E, Ni; 1976 v A, E, Y (2), E, Ni; 1977 v WG (sub), S (2), Cz, E, Ni; 1978 v K (2), S; (with Leeds U), Cz, WG, Ir (sub), E, S, Ni; 1979 v Ma, T, S, E, Ni, Ma; 1980 v Ei, WG, E, S, Ni, Ic; 1981 v T, Cz, Ei, T, S, E, USSR; 1982 v Cz, USSR, E, S, Ni, F; 1983 v N, (with Burnley), v Y, E, Bul, S, Ni, Br (60)
Ford, T. (Swansea T), 1947 v S; (with Aston Villa), 1947 v Ni; 1948 v S, Ni; 1949 v E, S, Ni, P, Bel, Sw; 1950 v E, S, Ni, Bel; 1951 v S; (with Sunderland), 1951 v E, Ni, P, Sw; 1952 v E, S, Ni, R of UK; 1953 v S, E, Ni, F, Y; (with Cardiff C), 1954 v A; 1955 v S, E, Ni, Y; 1956 v S, Ni, E, A; 1957 v S (38)
Foulkes, H. E. (WBA), 1932 v Ni (1)
Foulkes, W. I. (Newcastle U), 1952 v E, S, Ni, R of UK; 1953 v E, S, F, Y; 1954 v E, S, Ni (11)
Foulkes, W. T. (Oswestry), 1884 v Ni; 1885 v S (2)
Fowler, J. (Swansea T), 1925 v E; 1926 v E, Ni; 1927 v S; 1928 v S; 1929 v E (6)

Garner, J. (Aberystwyth), 1896 v S (1)
Giles, D. (Swansea C), 1980 v E, S, Ni, Ic; 1981 v T, Cz, T (sub), E (sub), USSR (sub); (with C Palace), 1982 v Sp (sub); 1983 v Ni (sub), Br (12)
Gillam, S. G. (Wrexham), 1889 v S, Ni; (with Shrewsbury), 1890 v E, Ni; (with Clapton), 1894 v S (5)
Glascodine, G. (Wrexham), 1879 v E (1)
Glover, E. M. (Grimsby T), 1932 v S; 1934 v Ni; 1936 v S; 1937 v E, S, Ni; 1939 v Ni (7)
Godding, G. (Wrexham), 1923 v S, Ni (2)
Godfrey, B. C. (Preston NE), 1964 v Ni; 1965 v D, I (3)
Goodwin, U. (Ruthin), 1881 v E (1)
Gough, R. T. (Oswestry White Star), 1883 v S (1)
Gray, A. (Oldham Ath), 1924 v E, S, Ni; 1925 v E, S, Ni; 1926 v E, S; 1927 v S; (with Manchester C), 1928 v E, S; 1929 v E, S, Ni; (with Manchester Central), 1930 v S; (with Tranmere R), 1932 v E, S, Ni; (with Chester), 1937 v E, S, Ni; 1938 v E, S, Ni (24)
Green, A. W. (Aston Villa), 1901 v Ni; (with Notts Co), 1903 v E; 1904 v S, Ni; 1906 v Ni, E; (with Nottingham F), 1907 v E; 1908 v S (8)
Green, C. R. (Birmingham C), 1965 v USSR, I; 1966 v E, S, USSR, Br (2); 1967 v E; 1968 v E, S, Ni, WG; 1969 v S, I, Ni (sub) (15)
Green, G. H. (Charlton Ath), 1938 v Ni; 1939 v E, Ni, F (4)
Grey, Dr W. (Druids), 1876 v S; 1878 v S (2)
Griffiths, A. T. (Wrexham), 1971 v Cz (sub); 1975 v A, H (2), L (2), E, Ni; 1976 v A, E, S, E (sub), Ni, Y (2); 1977 v WG, S (17)
Griffiths, F. J. (Blackpool), 1900 v E, S (2)
Griffiths, G. (Chirk), 1887 v Ni (1)
Griffiths, J. H. (Swansea T), 1953 v Ni (1)
Griffiths, M. W. (Leicester C), 1947 v Ni; 1949 v P, Bel; 1950 v E, S, Bel; 1951 v E, Ni, P, Sw; 1954 v A (11)
Griffiths, P. (Chirk), 1884 v E, Ni; 1888 v E; 1890 v S, Ni; 1891 v Ni (6)
Griffiths, S. (Wrexham), 1902 v S (1)
Griffiths, T. P. (Everton), 1927 v E, Ni; 1929 v E; 1930 v E; 1931 v Ni; 1932 v Ni, S, E; (with Bolton W), 1933 v F, E, S, Ni; (with Middlesbrough), 1934 v E, S; 1935 v E, Ni; 1936 v S; (with Aston Villa), Ni; 1937 v E, S, Ni (21)

Hallam, J. (Oswestry), 1889 v E (1)
Hanford, H. (Swansea T), 1934 v Ni; 1935 v S; 1936 v E; (with Sheffield W), 1936 v Ni; 1938 v E, S; 1939 v F (7)
Harrington, A. C. (Cardiff C), 1956 v Ni; 1957 v E, S; 1958 v S, Ni, Is (2); 1961 v S, E; 1962 v E, S (11)
Harris, C. S. (Leeds U), 1976 v E, S; 1978 v WG, Ir, E, S, Ni; 1979 v Ma, T, WG, E (sub), Ma; 1980 v Ni (sub), Ic (sub); 1981 v T, Cz (sub), Ei, T, S, E, USSR; 1982 v Cz, Ic, E (sub) (24)
Harris, W. C. (Middlesbrough), 1954 v A; 1957 v EG, Cz; 1958 v E, S, EG (6)

Harrison, W. C. (Wrexham), 1899 v E; 1900 v E, S, Ni; 1901 v Ni (5)
Hayes, A. (Wrexham), 1890 v Ni; 1894 v Ni (2)
Hennessey, W. T. (Birmingham C), 1962 v Ni, Br (2); 1963 v S, E, H (2); 1964 v E, S; 1965 v S, E, D, Gr, USSR; 1966 v E, USSR; (with Nottingham F), 1966 v S, Ni, D, Br (2), Ch; 1967 v S, E; 1968 v E, S, Ni; 1969 v WG, EG, R of UK, EG; (with Derby Co), 1970 v E, S, Ni; 1972 v Fi, Cz, E, S; 1973 v E (39)
Hersee, A. M. (Bangor), 1886 v S, Ni (2)
Hersee, R. (Llandudno), 1886 v Ni (1)
Hewitt, R. (Cardiff C), 1958 v Ni, Is, Se, H, Br (5)
Hewitt, T. J. (Wrexham), 1911 v E, S, Ni; (with Chelsea), 1913 v E, S, Ni; (with South Liverpool), 1914 v E, S (8)
Heywood, D. (Druids), 1879 v E (1)
Hibbott, H. (Newtown Excelsior), 1880 v E, S (2)
Hibbott, R. (Newtown), 1885 v S (1)
Higham, G. G. (Oswestry), 1878 v S; 1879 v E (2)
Hill, M. R. (Ipswich T), 1972 v Cz, R (2)
Hockey, T. (Sheffield U), 1972 v Fi, R; 1973 v E (2); (with Norwich C), Pol, S, E, Ni; (with Aston Villa), 1974 v Pol (9)
Hoddinott, T. F. (Watford), 1921 v E, S (2)
Hodgkinson, A. V. (Southampton), 1908 v Ni (1)
Hole, B. G. (Cardiff C), 1963 v Ni; 1964 v Ni; 1965 v S, E, Ni, D, Gr (2), USSR, I; 1966 v E, S, Ni, USSR, D, Br (2), Ch; (with Blackburn R), 1967 v S, E, Ni; 1968 v E, S, Ni, WG; (with Aston Villa), 1969 v I, WG, EG; 1970 v I; (with Swansea C), 1971 v R (30)
Hole, W. J. (Swansea T), 1921 v Ni; 1922 v E; 1923 v E, Ni; 1928 v E, S, Ni; 1929 v E, S (9)
Hollins, D. M. (Newcastle U), 1962 v Br (sub), M; 1963 v Ni, H; 1964 v E; 1965 v Ni, Gr, I; 1966 v S, D, Br (11)
Hopkins, I. J. (Brentford), 1935 v S, Ni; 1936 v E, Ni; 1937 v E, S, Ni; 1938 v E, Ni; 1939 v E, S, Ni (12)
Hopkins, J. (Fulham), 1983 v Ni, Br (2)
Hopkins, M. (Tottenham H), 1956 v Ni; 1957 v Ni, S, E, Cz (2), EG; 1958 v E, S, Ni, EG, Is (2), H (2), M, Se, Br; 1959 v E, S, Ni; 1960 v E, S; 1961 v Ni, H, Sp (2); 1962 v Ni, Br (2), M; 1963 v S, Ni, H (34)
Howell, E. G. (Builth), 1888 v Ni; 1890 v E; 1891 v E (3)
Howells, R. G. (Cardiff C), 1954 v E, S (2)
Hugh, A. R. (Newport Co), 1930 v Ni (1)
Hughes, A. (Rhos), 1894 v E, S (2)
Hughes, A. (Chirk), 1907 v Ni (1)
Hughes, A. J. (Aberystwyth), 1879 v S (1)
Hughes, E. (Everton), 1899 v S, Ni; (with Tottenham H), 1901 v E, S; 1902 v Ni; 1904 v E, Ni, S; 1905 v E, Ni, S; 1906 v E, Ni; 1907 v E (14)
Hughes, E. (Wrexham), 1906 v S; (with Nottingham F), 1906 v Ni; 1908 v S, E; 1910 v Ni, E, S; 1911 v Ni, E, S; (with Wrexham), 1912 v Ni, E, S; (with Manchester C), 1913 v E, S; 1914 v N (16)
Hughes, F. W. (Northwich Victoria), 1882 v E, Ni; 1883 v E, Ni, S; 1884 v S (6)
Hughes, I. (Luton T), 1951 v E, Ni, P, Sw (4)
Hughes, J. (Cambridge University), 1877 v S (1)
Hughes, J. (Liverpool), 1905 v E, S, Ni (3)
Hughes, J. I. (Blackburn R), 1935 v Ni (1)
Hughes, P. W. (Bangor), 1887 v Ni; 1889 v Ni, E (3)
Hughes, W. (Bootle), 1891 v E; 1892 v S, Ni (3)
Hughes, W. A. (Blackburn R), 1949 v E, Ni, P, Bel, Sw (5)
Hughes, W. M. (Birmingham), 1938 v E, Ni, S; 1939 v E, Ni, S, F; 1947 v E, S, Ni (10)
Humphreys, J. V. (Everton), 1947 v Ni (1)
Humphreys, R. (Druids), 1888 v Ni (1)
Hunter, W. H. (North End, Belfast), 1887 v Ni (1)

Jackett, K. (Watford), 1983 v N, Y, E, Bul, S, Ni (7)
Jackson, W. (St Helens Rec), 1899 v Ni (1)
James, E. (Chirk), 1893 v E, Ni; 1894 v E, S, Ni; 1898 v E; 1899 v Ni (7)
James, E. G. (Blackpool), 1966 v Br (2), Ch; 1967 v Ni; 1968 v S; 1971 v Cz, S, E, Ni (9)
James, L. (Burnley), 1972 v Cz, R, S (sub); 1973 v E (3), Pol, S, Ni; 1974 v Pol, E, S, Ni; 1975 v A, H (2), L (2), S, E, Ni; 1976 v A; (with Derby Co), S, E, Y (2), Ni; 1977 v WG, S (2), Cz, E, Ni; 1978 v K (2); (with QPR), WG; (with Burnley) 1979 v T; 1980 (with Swansea C), v E, S, Ni, Ic; 1981 v T, Ei, T, S, E; 1982 v Cz, Ic, USSR, E (sub), S, Ni, F; (with Sunderland), 1983 v E (sub) (54)
James, R. (Swansea C), 1979 v Ma, WG (sub), S, E, Ni, Ma; 1980 v WG; 1982 v Cz (sub), Ic, Sp, E, S, Ni, F; 1983 v N, Y, E, Bul (18)
James, W. (West Ham U), 1931 v Ni; 1932 v Ni (2)
Jarrett, R. H. (Ruthin), 1889 v Ni; 1890 v S (2)
Jarvis, A. L. (Hull C), 1967 v S, E, Ni (3)
Jenkins, E. (Lovell's Ath), 1925 v E (1)
Jenkins, J. (Brighton), 1924 v Ni, E, S; 1925 v S, Ni; 1926 v E, S; 1927 v S (8)
Jenkins, R. W. (Rhyl), 1902 v Ni (1)
Jenkyns, C. A. L. (Small Heath), 1892 v E, S, Ni; 1895 v E; (with Woolwich Arsenal), 1896 v S; (with Newton Heath), 1897 v Ni; (with Walsall), 1898 v S, E (8)
Jennings, W. (Bolton W), 1914 v E, S; 1920 v S; 1923 v Ni, E; 1924 v E, S, Ni; 1927 v S, Ni; 1929 v S (11)
John, R. F. (Arsenal), 1923 v S, Ni; 1925 v Ni; 1926 v E; 1927 v E; 1928 v E, Ni; 1930 v E, S; 1932 v E; 1933 v F, Ni; 1935 v Ni; 1936 v S; 1937 v E (15)
John, W. R. (Walsall), 1931 v Ni; (with Stoke C), 1933 v E, S, Ni, F; 1934 v E, S; (with Preston NE), 1935 v E, S; (with Sheffield U), 1936 v E, S, Ni; (with Swansea T), 1939 v E, S (14)
Johnson, M. G. (Swansea T), 1964 v Ni (1)
Jones, A. F. (Oxford University), 1877 v S (1)
Jones, A. T. (Nottingham F), 1905 v E; (with Notts Co), 1906 v E (2)
Jones, Bryn (Wolverhampton W), 1935 v Ni; 1936 v E, S, Ni; 1937 v E, S, Ni; 1938 v E, S, Ni; (with Arsenal), 1939 v E, S, Ni; 1947 v S, Ni; 1948 v E; 1949 v S (17)
Jones, B. S. (Swansea T), 1963 v S, E, Ni, H (2); 1964 v S, Ni; (with Plymouth Arg), 1965 v D; (with Cardiff C), 1969 v S, E, Ni, I (sub), WG, EG, R of UK (15)
Jones, Charlie (Nottingham F), 1926 v E; 1927 v S, Ni; 1928 v E; (with Arsenal), 1930 v E, S; 1932 v E; 1933 v F (7)
Jones, Cliff (Swansea T), 1954 v A; 1956 v E, Ni, S, A; 1957 v E, S, Ni, Cz (2), EG; 1958 v EG, E, S, Is (2); (with Tottenham H), 1958 v Ni, H (2), M, Se, Br; 1959 v Ni; 1960 v E, S, Ni; 1961 v S, E, Ni, Sp, H, Ei; 1962 v E, Ni, S, Br (2), M; 1963 v S, Ni, H; 1964 v E, S, Ni; 1965 v E, S, Ni, D, Gr (2), USSR, I; 1967 v S, E; 1968 v E, S, WG; (with Fulham), 1969 v I, R of UK (59)
Jones, C. W. (Birmingham), 1935 v Ni; 1939 v F (2)
Jones, D. (Chirk), 1888 v S, Ni; (with Bolton W), 1889 v E, S, Ni; 1890 v E, Ni; 1891 v S; 1892 v Ni; 1893 v E; 1894 v E; 1895 v E; 1898 v S; (with Manchester C), 1900 v E, Ni (15)
Jones, D. E. (Norwich C), 1976 v S, E (sub); 1978 v S, Cz, WG, Ir, E; 1980 v E (8)
Jones, D. O. (Leicester C), 1934 v E, Ni; 1935 v E, S; 1936 v E, Ni; 1937 v Ni (7)
Jones, Evan (Chelsea), 1910 v S, Ni; (with Oldham Ath), 1911 v E, S; 1912 v E, S; (with Bolton W), 1914 v Ni (7)
Jones, F. R. (Bangor), 1885 v E, Ni; 1886 v S (3)
Jones, F. W. (Small Heath), 1893 v S (1)
Jones, G. P. (Wrexham), 1907 v S, Ni (2)
Jones, H. (Aberaman), 1902 v Ni (1)
Jones, Humphrey (Bangor), 1885 v E, Ni, S; 1886 v E, Ni, S; (with Queen's Park), 1887 v E; (with East Stirling-

shire), 1889 v E, Ni; 1890 v E, S, Ni; (with Queen's Park), 1891 v E, S (14)
Jones, Ivor (Swansea T), 1920 v S, Ni; 1921 v Ni, E; 1922 v S, Ni; (with WBA), 1923 v E, Ni; 1924 v S; 1926 v Ni (10)
Jones, J. (Druids), 1876 v S (1)
Jones, J. (Berwyn Rangers), 1883 v S, Ni; 1884 v S (3)
Jones, J. (Wrexham), 1925 v Ni (1)
Jones, Jeffrey (Llandrindod Wells), 1908 v Ni; 1909 v Ni; 1910 v S (3)
Jones, J. L. (Sheffield U), 1895 v E, S, Ni; 1896 v Ni, S, E; 1897 v Ni, S, E; (with Tottenham H), 1898 v Ni, E, S; 1899 v S, Ni; 1900 v S; 1902 v E, S, Ni; 1904 v E, S, Ni (21)
Jones, J. Love (Stoke C), 1906 v S; (with Middlesbrough), 1910 v Ni (2)
Jones, J. O. (Bangor), 1901 v S, Ni (2)
Jones, J. P. (Liverpool), 1976 v A, E, S; 1977 v WG, S (2), Cz, E, Ni; 1978 v K (2), S, Cz, WG, Ir, E, S, Ni; (with Wrexham), 1979 v Ma, T, WG, S, E, Ni, Ma; 1980 v Ei, WG, T, E, S, Ni, Ic; 1981 v T, Ei, T, S, E, USSR; 1982 v Cz, Ic, USSR, Sp, E, S, Ni, F; 1983 v N, (with Chelsea), v Y, E, Bul, S, Ni, Br (53)
Jones, J. T. (Stoke C), 1912 v E, S, Ni; 1913 v E, Ni; 1914 v S, Ni; 1920 v E, S, Ni; (with C Palace), 1921 v E, S; 1922 v E, S, Ni (15)
Jones, K. (Aston Villa), 1950 v S (1)
Jones, Leslie J. (Cardiff C), 1933 v F; (with Coventry C), 1935 v Ni; 1936 v S; 1937 v E, S, Ni; (with Arsenal), 1938 v E, S, Ni; 1939 v E, S (11)
Jones, P. W. (Bristol R), 1971 v Fi (1)
Jones, R. (Bangor), 1887 v S; 1889 v E; (with Crewe Alex), 1890 v E (3)
Jones, R. (Bangor), 1900 v S, Ni (2)
Jones, R. (Druids), 1899 v S; (with Millwall), 1906 v S, Ni (3)
Jones, R. A. (Druids), 1884 v E, Ni, S; 1885 v S (4)
Jones, R. S. (Everton), 1894 v Ni; (with Leicester Fosse), 1898 v S (2)
Jones, S. (Wrexham), 1887 v Ni; (with Chester), 1890 v S (2)
Jones, S. (Wrexham), 1893 v S, Ni; (with Burton Swifts), 1895 v S; 1896 v E, Ni (5)
Jones, T. (Manchester U), 1926 v Ni; 1927 v E, Ni; 1930 v Ni (4)
Jones, T. D. (Aberdare), 1908 v Ni (1)
Jones, T. G. (Everton), 1938 v Ni; 1939 v E, S, Ni; 1947 v E, S; 1948 v E, S, Ni; 1949 v E, Ni, P, Bel, Sw; 1950 v E, S, Bel (17)
Jones, T. J. Sheffield W), 1932 v Ni; 1933 v F (2)
Jones, W. (Druids), 1899 v E (1)
Jones, W. E. A. (Swansea T), 1947 v E, S; (with Tottenham H), 1949 v E, S (4)
Jones, W. J. (Aberdare), 1901 v E, S; (with West Ham U), 1902 v E, S (4)
Jones, W. Lot (Manchester C), 1905 v E, Ni; 1906 v E, S, Ni; 1907 v E, S, Ni; 1908 v S; 1909 v E, S, Ni; 1910 v E; 1911 v E; 1913 v E, S; 1914 v S, Ni; (with Southend U), 1920 v E, Ni (20)
Jones, W. P. (Druids), 1889 v E, Ni; (with Wynstay), 1890 v S, Ni (4)
Jones, W. R. (Aberystwyth), 1897 v S (1)

Keenor, F. C. (Cardiff C), 1920 v E, Ni; 1921 v E, Ni, S; 1922 v Ni; 1923 v E, Ni, S; 1924 v E, Ni, S; 1925 v E, Ni, S; 1926 v S; 1927 v E, Ni, S; 1928 v E, Ni, S; 1929 v E, Ni, S; 1930 v E, Ni, S; 1931 v E, Ni, S; (with Crewe Alex), 1933 v S (32)
Kelly, F. C. (Wrexham), 1899 v S, Ni; (with Druids), 1902 v Ni (3)
Kelsey, A. J. (Arsenal), 1954 v Ni, A; 1955 v S, Ni, Y; 1956 v E, Ni, S, A; 1957 v E, Ni, S, Cz (2), EG; 1958 v E, S, Ni, Is (2), H (2), M, Se, Br; 1959 v E, S; 1960 v E, Ni, S; 1961 v E, Ni, S, H, Sp (2); 1962 v E, S, Ni, Br (2) (41)
Kenrick, S. L. (Druids), 1876 v S; 1877 v S; (with Oswestry), 1879 v E, S; (with Shropshire Wanderers), 1881 v E (5)
Ketley, C. F. (Druids), 1882 v Ni (1)
King, J. (Swansea T), 1955 v E (1)
Kinsey, N. (Norwich C), 1951 v Ni, P, Sw; 1952 v E; (with Birmingham C), 1954 v Ni; 1956 v E, S (7)
Krzywicki, R. L. (Huddersfield T), 1970 v E, S; (with WBA), Ni, EG, I; 1971 v R, Fi; 1972 v Cz (sub) (8)

Lambert, R. (Liverpool), 1947 v S; 1948 v E; 1949 v P, Bel, Sw (5)
Lathom, G. (Liverpool), 1905 v E, S; 1906 v S; 1907 v E, S, Ni; 1908 v E; 1909 v Ni; (with Southport Central), 1910 v E; (with Cardiff C), 1913 v Ni (10)
Lawrence, E. (Clapton Orient), 1930 v Ni; (with Notts Co), 1932 v S (2)
Lawrence, S. (Swansea T), 1932 v Ni; 1933 v F; 1934 v S, E, Ni; 1935 v E, S; 1936 v S (8)
Lea, A. (Wrexham), 1889 v E; 1891 v S, Ni; 1893 v Ni (4)
Lea, C. (Ipswich T), 1965 v Ni, I (2)
Leary, P. (Bangor), 1889 v Ni (1)
Leek, K. (Leicester C), 1961 v S, E, Ni, H, Sp (2); (with Newcastle U), 1962 v S; (with Birmingham C), v Br (sub), M; 1963 v E; 1965 v S, Gr; (with Northampton T), 1965 v Gr (13)
Lever, A. R. (Leicester C), 1953 v S (1)
Lewis, B. (Wrexham), 1891 v Ni; 1892 v S, E, Ni; (with Middlesbrough), 1893 v S, E; (with Wrexham), 1894 v S, E, Ni; 1895 v S (10)
Lewis, D. (Arsenal), 1927 v E; 1928 v Ni; 1930 v E (3)
Lewis, D. J. (Swansea T), 1933 v E, S (2)
Lewis, J. (Bristol R), 1906 v E (1)
Lewis, J. (Cardiff C), 1926 v S (1)
Lewis, T. (Wrexham), 1881 v E, S (2)
Lewis, W. L. (Swansea T), 1927 v E, Ni; 1928 v E, Ni; 1929 v S; (with Huddersfield T), 1930 v E (6)
Lewis, W. (Bangor), 1885 v E; 1886 v E, S; 1887 v E, S; 1888 v E; 1889 v E, Ni, S; (with Crewe Alex), 1890 v E, Ni, S; 1891 v E, Ni, S; 1892 v E, S, Ni; 1894 v E, S, Ni; (with Chester), 1895 v S, Ni, E; 1896 v E, S, Ni; (with Manchester C), 1897 v E, S; (with Chester), 1898 v Ni (30)
Lloyd, B. W. (Wrexham), 1976 v A, E, S (3)
Lloyd, J. W. (Wrexham), 1879 v S; (with Newtown), 1885 v S (2)
Lloyd, R. A. (Ruthin), 1891 v Ni; 1895 v S (2)
Lockley, A. (Chirk), 1898 v Ni (1)
Lovell, S. (C Palace), 1982 v USSR (sub) (1)
Lowrie, G. (Coventry C), 1948 v E, S, Ni; (with Newcastle U), 1949 v P (4)
Lowndes, N. (Newport Co), 1983 v S, Br (2)
Lucas, P. M. (Leyton Orient), 1962 v Ni, M; 1963 v S, E (4)
Lucas, W. H. (Swansea T), 1949 v S, Ni, P, Bel, Sw; 1950 v E; 1951 v E (7)
Lumberg, A. (Wrexham), 1929 v Ni; 1930 v E, S; (with Wolverhampton W), 1932 v S (4)

McMillan, R. (Shrewsbury Engineers), 1881 v E, S (2)
Mahoney, J. F. (Stoke C), 1968 v E; 1969 v EG; 1971 v Cz; 1973 v E (3), Pol, S, Ni; 1974 v Pol, E, S, Ni; 1975 v A, H (2), L (2), S, E, Ni; 1976 v A, Y (2), E, Ni; 1977 v WG, Cz, S, E, Ni; (with Middlesbrough), 1978 v K (2), S, Cz, Ir, E (sub), S, Ni; 1979 v WG, S, E, Ni, Ma; (with Swansea C), 1980 v Ei, WG, T (sub); 1982 v Ic, USSR; 1983 v Y, E (51)
Martin, T. J. (Newport Co), 1930 v Ni (1)

Marustik, C. (Swansea C), 1982 v Sp, E, S, Ni, F; 1983 v N (6)
Mates, J. (Chirk), 1891 v Ni; 1897 v E, S (3)
Mathews, R. W. (Liverpool), 1921 v Ni; (with Bristol C), 1923 v E; (with Bradford), 1926 v Ni (3)
Matthews, W. (Chester), 1905 v Ni; 1908 v E (2)
Matthias, J. S. (Brymbo), 1896 v S, Ni; (with Shrewsbury), 1897 v E, S; (with Wolverhampton W), 1899 v S (5)
Matthias, T. J. (Wrexham), 1914 v S, E; 1920 v Ni, S, E; 1921 v S, E, Ni; 1922 v S, E, Ni; 1923 v S (12)
Mays, A. W. (Wrexham), 1929 v Ni (1)
Medwin, T. C. (Swansea T), 1953 v Ni, F, Y; (with Tottenham H), 1957 v E, S, Ni, Cz (2), EG; 1958 v E, S, Ni, Is (2), H (2), M, Br; 1959 v E, S, Ni; 1960 v E, S, Ni; 1961 v S, Ei, Sp; 1963 v E, H (30)
Meredith, S. (Chirk), 1900 v S; 1901 v S, E, Ni; (with Stoke C), 1902 v E; 1903 v Ni; 1904 v E; (with Leyton), 1907 v E (8)
Meredith, W. H. (Manchester C), 1895 v E, Ni; 1896 v E, Ni; 1897 v E, Ni, S; 1898 v E, Ni; 1899 v E; 1900 v E, Ni; 1901 v E, Ni; 1902 v E, S; 1903 v E, S, Ni; 1904 v E; 1905 v E, S; (with Manchester U), 1907 v E, S, Ni; 1908 v E, Ni; 1909 v E, S, Ni; 1910 v E, S, Ni; 1911 v E, S, Ni; 1912 v E, S, Ni; 1913 v E, S, Ni; 1914 v E, S, Ni; 1920 v E, S, Ni (48)
Mielczarek, R. (Rotherham U), 1971 v Fi (1)
Millership, H. (Rotherham Co), 1920 v E, S, Ni; 1921 v E, S, Ni (6)
Millington, A. H. (WBA), 1963 v S, E, H; (with C Palace), 1965 v E, USSR; (with Peterborough U), 1966 v Ch, Br; 1967 v E, Ni; 1968 v Ni, WG; 1969 v I, EG; (with Swansea) 1970 v E, S, Ni; 1971 v Cz, Fi; 1972 v Fi (sub), Cz, R (21)
Mills, T. J. (Clapton Orient), 1934 v E, Ni; (with Leicester C), 1935 v E, S (4)
Mills-Roberts, R. H. (St Thomas' Hospital), 1885 v E, S, Ni; 1886 v E; 1887 v E; (with Preston NE), 1888 v E, Ni; (with Llanberis), 1892 v E (8)
Moore, G. (Cardiff C), 1960 v E, S, Ni; 1961 v Ei, Sp; (with Chelsea), 1962 v Br; 1963 v Ni, H; (with Manchester U), 1964 v S, Ni; (with Northampton T), 1966 v Ni, Ch; (with Charlton Ath), 1969 v S, E, Ni, R of UK; 1970 v E, S, Ni, I; 1971 v R (21)
Morgan, J. R. (Cambridge University), 1877 v S; (with Swansea), 1879 v S; (with Derby School Staff), 1880 v E, S; 1881 v E, S; 1882 v E, S, Ni; (with Swansea), 1883 v E (10)
Morgan, J. T. (Wrexham), 1905 v Ni (1)
Morgan-Owen, H. (Oxford University), 1901 v E, S; 1902 v S; 1906 v E, Ni; (with Welshpool), 1907 v S (6)
Morgan-Owen, M. M. (Oxford University), 1897 v S, Ni; 1898 v E, S; 1899 v S; 1900 v E; (with Corinthians), 1903 v S; 1906 v S, E, Ni; 1907 v E (11)
Morley, E. J. (Swansea T), 1925 v E; (with Clapton Orient), 1929 v E, S, Ni (4)
Morris, A. G. (Aberystwyth), 1896 v E, Ni, S; (with Swindon T), 1897 v E; 1898 v S; (with Nottingham F), 1899 v E, S; 1903 v E, S; 1905 v E, S; 1907 v E, S; 1908 v E; 1910 v E, S, Ni; 1911 v E, S, Ni; 1912 v E (21)
Morris, C. (Chirk), 1900 v E, S, Ni; (with Derby Co), 1901 v E, S, Ni; 1902 v E, S; 1903 v E, S, Ni; 1904 v Ni; 1905 v E, S, NI; 1906 v S; 1907 v S; 1908 v E, S; 1909 v E, S, Ni; 1910 v E, S, Ni; (with Huddersfield T), 1911 v E, S, Ni (28)
Morris, E. (Chirk), 1893 v E, S, Ni (3)
Morris, H. (Sheffield U), 1894 v S; (with Manchester C), 1896 v E; (with Grimsby T), 1897 v E (3)
Morris, J. (Oswestry), 1887 v S (1)
Morris, J. (Chirk), 1898 v Ni (1)
Morris, R. (Chirk), 1900 v E, Ni; 1901 v Ni; 1902 v S; (with Shrewsbury T), 1903 v E, Ni (6)
Morris, R. (Druids), 1902 v E, S; (with Newtown), 1902 v Ni; (with Liverpool), 1903 v S, Ni; 1904 v E, S, Ni; (with Leeds C), 1906 v S; (with Grimsby T), 1907 v Ni; (with Plymouth Arg), 1908 v Ni (11)
Morris, S. (Birmingham), 1937 v E, S; 1938 v E, S; 1939 v F (5)
Morris, W. (Burnley), 1947 v Ni; 1949 v E; 1952 v S, Ni, R of UK (5)
Moulsdale, J. R. B. (Corinthians), 1925 v Ni (1)
Murphy, J. P. (WBA), 1933 v F, E, Ni; 1934 v E, S; 1935 v E, S, Ni; 1936 v E, S, Ni; 1937 v S, Ni; 1938 v E, S (15)

Nardiello, D. (Coventry C), 1978 v Cz, WG (sub) (2)
Neal, J. E. (Colwyn Bay), 1931 v E, S (2)
Newnes, J. (Nelson), 1926 v Ni (1)
Newton, L. F. (Cardiff Corinthians), 1912 v Ni (1)
Nicholas, D. S. (Stoke C), 1923 v S; (with Swansea T), 1927 v E, Ni (3)
Nicholas, P. (C Palace), 1979 v S (sub), Ni (sub), Ma; 1980 v Ei, WG, T, E, S, Ni, Ic; 1981 v T, Cz, E; (with Arsenal), T, S, E, USSR; 1982 v Cz, Ic, USSR, Sp, E, S, Ni, F; 1983 v Y, Bul, S (sub), Ni (29)
Nicholls, J. (Newport Co), 1924 v E, Ni; (with Cardiff C), 1925 v E, S (4)
Nock, W. (Newtown), 1897 v Ni (1)
Nurse, M. T. G. (Swansea T), 1960 v E, Ni; 1961 v S, E, H, Ni, Ei, Sp (2); (with Middlesbrough), 1963 v E, H; 1964 v S (12)
O'Callaghan, E. (Tottenham H), 1929 v Ni; 1930 v S; 1932 v S, E; 1933 v Ni, S, E; 1934 v Ni, S, E; 1935 v E (11)
Oliver, A. (Blackburn R), 1905 v E; (with Bangor), S (2)
O'Sullivan, P. A. (Brighton), 1973 v S (sub); 1976 v S; 1979 v Ma (sub) (3)
Owen, D. (Oswestry), 1879 v E (1)
Owen, E. (Ruthin Grammar School), 1884 v E, Ni, S (3)
Owen, G. (Chirk), 1888 v S; (with Newton Heath), 1889 v S, Ni; 1892 v E; 1893 v Ni (5)
Owen, T (Oswestry), 1879 v E (1)
Owen, Trevor (Crewe Alex), 1899 v E, S (2)
Owen, W. (Chirk), 1884 v E; 1885 v Ni; 1887 v E; 1888 v E; 1889 v E, Ni, S; 1890 v S, Ni; 1891 v E, S, Ni; 1892 v E, S; 1893 v S, Ni (16)
Owen, W. P. (Ruthin), 1880 v E, S; 1881 v E, S; 1882 v E, S, Ni; 1883 v E, S; 1884 v E, S, Ni (12)
Owens, J. (Wrexham), 1902 v S (1)

Page, M. E. (Birmingham C), 1971 v Fi; 1972 v S, Ni; 1973 v E (1 + 1 sub), Ni; 1974 v S, Ni; 1975 v H, L, S, E, Ni; 1976 v E, Y (2), E, Ni; 1977 v WG, S; 1978 v K (sub + 1), WG, Ir, E, S; 1979 v Ma, WG (28)
Palmer, D. (Swansea T), 1957 v Cz; 1958 v E, EG (3)
Parris, J. E. (Bradford), 1932 v Ni (1)
Parry, B. J. (Swansea T), 1951 v S (1)
Parry, C. (Everton), 1891 v E, S; 1893 v E; 1894 v E; 1895 v E, S; (with Newtown), 1896 v E, S, Ni; 1897 v Ni; 1898 v E, S, Ni (13)
Parry, E. (Liverpool), 1922 v S; 1923 v E, Ni; 1925 v Ni; 1926 v Ni (5)
Parry, H. (Newtown), 1895 v Ni (1)
Parry, M. (Liverpool), 1901 v E, S, Ni; 1902 v E, S, Ni; 1903 v E, S; 1904 v E, Ni; 1906 v E; 1908 v E, S, Ni; 1909 v E, S (16)
Parry, T. D. (Oswestry), 1900 v E, S, Ni; 1901 v E, S, Ni; 1902 v E (7)
Paul, R. (Swansea T), 1949 v E, S, Ni, P, Sw; 1950 v E, S, Ni, Bel; (with Manchester C), 1951 v S, E, Ni, P, Sw; 1952 v E, S, Ni, R of UK; 1953 v S, E, Ni, F, Y; 1954 v E, S, Ni; 1955 v S, E, Y; 1956 v E, Ni, S, A (33)
Peake, E. (Aberystwyth), 1908 v Ni; (with Liverpool), 1909 v Ni, S, E; 1910 v S, Ni; 1911 v Ni; 1912 v E; 1913 v E, Ni; 1914 v Ni (11)

Peers, E. J. (Wolverhampton W), 1914 v Ni, S, E; 1920 v E, S; 1921 v S, Ni, E; (with Port Vale), 1922 v E, S, Ni; 1923 v E (12)
Perry, E. (Doncaster R), 1938 v E, S, Ni (3)
Phennah, E. (Civil Service), 1878 v S (1)
Phillips, C. (Wolverhampton W), 1931 v Ni; 1932 v E; 1933 v S; 1934 v E, S, Ni; 1935 v E, S, Ni; 1936 v S; (with Aston Villa), 1936 v E, Ni; 1938 v S (13)
Phillips, L. (Cardiff C), 1971 v Cz, S, E, Ni; 1972 v Cz, R, S, Ni; 1973 v E; 1974 v Pol (sub), Ni; 1975 v A; (with Aston Villa), H (2), L (2), S, E, Ni; 1976 v A, E, Y (2), E, Ni; 1977 v WG, S (2), Cz, E; 1978 v K (2), S, Cz, WG, E, S; 1979 v Ma; (Swansea C), T, WG, S, E, Ni, Ma; 1980 v Ei, WG, T, S (sub), Ni, Ic; 1981 v T, Cz, T, S, E, USSR; (with Charlton Ath), 1982 v Cz, USSR (58)
Phillips, T. J. S. (Chelsea), 1973 v E; 1974 v E; 1975 v H (sub); 1978 v K (4)
Phoenix, H. (Wrexham), 1882 v S (1)
Poland, G. (Wrexham), 1939 v Ni, F (2)
Pontin, K. (Cardiff C), 1980 v E (sub), S (2)
Powell, A. (Leeds U), 1947 v E, S; 1948 v E, S, Ni; (with Everton), 1949 v E; 1950 v Bel; (with Birmingham C), 1951 v S (8)
Powell, D. (Wrexham), 1968 v WG; (with Sheffield U), 1969 v S, E, Ni, I, WG; 1970 v E, S, Ni, EG; 1971 v R (11)
Powell, I. V. (QPR), 1947 v E; 1948 v E, S, Ni; (with Aston Villa), 1949 v Bel; 1950 v S, Bel; 1951 v S (8)
Powell, J. (Druids), 1878 v S; 1880 v E, S; 1882 v E, S, Ni; 1883 v E, S, Ni; (with Bolton W), 1884 v E; (with Newton Heath), 1887 v E, S; 1888 v E, S, Ni (15)
Powell, Seth (WBA), 1885 v S; 1886 v E, Ni; 1891 v E, S; 1892 v E, S (7)
Price, H. (Aston Villa), 1907 v S; (with Burton U), 1908 v Ni; (with Wrexham), 1909 v S, E, Ni (5)
Price, J. (Wrexham), 1877 v S; 1878 v S; 1879 v E; 1880 v E, S; 1881 v E, S; (with Druids), 1882 v S, E, Ni; 1883 v S, Ni (12)
Price, P. (Luton T), 1980 v E, S, Ni, Ic; 1981 v T, Cz, Ei, T, S, E, USSR; (with Tottenham H), 1982 v USSR, Sp, F; 1983 v N, Y, E, Bul, S, Ni (20)
Pring, K. D. (Rotherham U), 1966 v Ch, D; 1967 v Ni (3)
Pryce-Jones, A. W. (Newtown), 1895 v E (1)
Pryce-Jones, W. E. (Cambridge University), 1887 v S; 1888 v S, E, Ni; 1890 v Ni (5)
Pugh, A. (Rhostyllen), 1889 v S (sub) (1)
Pugh, D. H. (Wrexham), 1896 v S, Ni; 1897 v S, Ni; (with Lincoln C), 1900 v S; 1901 v S, E (7)
Pugsley, J. (Charlton Ath), 1930 v Ni (1)
Pullen, W. J. (Plymouth Arg), 1926 v E (1)

Rankmore, F. E. J. (Peterborough), 1966 v Ch (sub) (1)
Ratcliffe, K. (Everton), 1981 v Cz, Ei, T, S, E, USSR; 1982 v Cz, Ic, USSR, Sp, E; 1983 v Y, E, Bul, S, Ni, Br (17)
Rea, J. C. (Aberystwyth), 1894 v Ni, S, E; 1895 v S; 1896 v S, Ni; 1897 v S, Ni; 1898 v Ni (9)
Reece, G. I. (Sheffield U), 1966 v E, S, Ni, USSR; 1967 v S; 1969 v R of UK (sub); 1970 v I (sub); 1971 v S, E, Ni, Fi; 1972 v Fi, R, E (sub), S, Ni; (with Cardiff C), 1973 v E (sub), Ni; 1974 v Pol (sub), E, S, Ni; 1975 v A, H (2), L (2), S, Ni (29)
Reed, W. G. (Ipswich T), 1955 v S, Y (2)
Rees, R. R. (Coventry C), 1965 v S, E, Ni, D, Gr (2), I, R; 1966 v E, S, Ni, R, D, Br (2), Ch; 1967 v E, Ni; 1968 v E, S, Ni; (with WBA), WG; 1969 v I; (with Nottingham F), 1969 v WG, EG, S (sub), R of UK; 1970 v E, S, Ni, EG, I; 1971 v Cz, R, E (sub), Ni (sub), Fi; 1972 v Cz (sub), R (39)
Rees, W. (Cardiff C), 1949 v Ni, Bel, Sw; (with Tottenham H), 1950 v Ni (4)
Richards, A. (Barnsley), 1932 v S (1)
Richards, D. (Wolverhampton W), 1931 v Ni; 1933 v E, S, Ni; 1934 v E, S, Ni; 1935 v E, S, Ni; 1936 v S; (with Brentford), 1936 v E, Ni; 1937 v S, E; (with Birmingham), 1937 v Ni; 1938 v E, S, Ni; 1939 v E, S (21)
Richards, G. (Druids), 1899 v E, S, Ni; (with Oswestry), 1903 v Ni; (with Shrewsbury), 1904 v S; 1905 v Ni (6)
Richards, R. W. (Wolverhampton W), 1920 v E, S; 1921 v Ni; 1922 v E, S; (with West Ham U), 1924 v E, S, Ni; (with Mold), 1926 v S (9)
Richards, S. V. (Cardiff C), 1947 v E (1)
Richards, W. E. (Fulham), 1933 v Ni (1)
Roach, J. (Oswestry), 1885 v Ni (1)
Robbins, W. W. (Cardiff C), 1931 v E, S; 1932 v Ni, E, S; (with WBA), 1933 v F, E, S, Ni; 1934 v S; 1936 v S (11)
Roberts, D. F. (Oxford U), 1973 v Pol, E (sub), Ni; 1974 v E, S; 1975 v A; (with Hull C), L, Ni; 1976 v S, Ni, Y; 1977 v E (sub), Ni; 1978 v K (1 + sub), S, Ni (17)
Roberts, J. G. (Arsenal), 1971 v S, E, Ni, Fi; 1972 v Fi, E, Ni; (with Birmingham C), 1973 v E (2), Pol, S, Ni; 1974 v Pol, E, S, Ni; 1975 v A, H, S, E; 1976 v E, S (22)
Roberts, J. H. (Bolton), 1949 v Bel (1)
Roberts, J. (Corwen), 1879 v S; 1880 v E, S; 1882 v E, S, Ni; (with Berwyn R), 1883 v E (7)
Roberts, J. (Ruthin), 1881 v S; 1882 v S (2)
Roberts, J. (Bradford C), 1906 v Ni; 1907 v Ni (2)
Roberts, Jas. (Chirk), 1898 v S (1)
Roberts, Jas (Wrexham), 1913 v S, Ni (2)
Roberts, P. S. (Portsmouth), 1974 v E; 1975 v A, H, L (4)
Roberts, R. (Rhos), 1891 v Ni; (with Crewe Alex), 1893 v E (2)
Roberts, R. (Druids), 1884 v S; (with Bolton W), 1887 v S; 1888 v S, E; 1889 v S, E; 1890 v S; 1892 v Ni; (with PNE), S (9)
Roberts, R. (Wrexham), 1886 v Ni; 1887 v Ni; 1891 v Ni (3)
Roberts, W. (Llangollen), 1879 v E, S; 1880 v E, S; (with Berwyn R), 1881 v S; 1883 v E, S (7)
Roberts, W. (Wrexham), 1886 v E, S, Ni; 1887 v Ni (4)
Roberts, W. H. (Ruthin), 1882 v E, S; 1883 v E, S, Ni; (with Rhyl), 1884 v S (6)
Rodrigues, P. J. (Cardiff C), 1965 v Ni, Gr (2); 1966 v USSR, E, S, D; (with Leicester C), v Ni, Br (2), Ch; 1967 v S; 1968 v E, S, Ni; 1969 v E, Ni, EG, R of UK; 1970 v E, S, Ni, EG; (with Sheffield W), 1971 v R, E, S, Cz, Ni; 1972 v Fi, Cz, R, E, Ni (sub); 1973 v E (3), Pol, S, Ni; 1974 v Pol (40)
Rogers, J. P. (Wrexham), 1896 v E, S, Ni (3)
Rogers, W. (Wrexham), 1931 v E, S (2)
Roose, L. R. (Aberystwyth), 1900 v Ni; (with London Welsh), 1901 v E, S, Ni; (with Stoke C), 1902 v E, S; 1904 v E; (with Everton), 1905 v S, E; (with Stoke C), 1906 v E, S, Ni; 1907 v E, S, Ni; (with Sunderland), 1908 v E, S; 1909 v E, S, Ni; 1910 v E, S, Ni; 1911 v S (24)
Rouse, R. V. (C Palace), 1959 v Ni (1)
Rowlands, A. C. (Tranmere R), 1914 v E (1)
Rowley, T. (Tranmere R), 1959 v Ni (1)
Rush, I. (Liverpool), 1980 v S (sub), Ni; 1981 v E (sub); 1982 v Ic (sub), USSR, E, S, Ni, F; 1983 v N, Y, E, Bul (13)
Russell, M. R. (Merthyr T), 1912 v S, Ni; 1914 v E; (with Plymouth Arg), 1920 v E, S, Ni; 1921 v E, S, Ni; 1922 v E, Ni; 1923 v E, S, Ni; 1924 v E, S, Ni; 1925 v E, S; 1926 v E, S; 1928 v S; 1929 v E (23)

Sabine, H. W. (Oswestry), 1887 v Ni (1)
Savin, G. (Oswestry), 1878 v S (1)
Sayer, P. (Cardiff C), 1977 v Cz, S, E, Ni; 1978 v K (2), S (7)
Scrine, F. H. (Swansea T), 1950 v E, Ni (2)
Sear, C. R. (Manchester C), 1963 v E (1)

Ronnie Rees *Wales*

Welsh wizard Mickey Thomas

Shaw, E. G. (Oswestry), 1882 v Ni; 1884 v S, Ni (3)
Sherwood, A. T. (Cardiff C), 1947 v E, Ni; 1948 v S, Ni; 1949 v E, S, Ni, P, Sw; 1950 v E, S, Ni, Bel; 1951 v E, S, Ni, P, Sw; 1952 v E, S, Ni, R of UK; 1953 v S, E, Ni, F, Y; 1954 v E, S, Ni, A; 1955 v S, E, Y, Ni; 1956 v E, S, Ni, A; (with Newport Co), 1957 v E, S (41)
Shone, W. W. (Oswestry), 1879 v E (1)
Shortt, W. W. (Plymouth Arg), 1947 v Ni; 1950 v Ni, Bel; 1952 v E, S, Ni, R of UK; 1953 v S, E, Ni, F, Y (12)
Showers, D. (Cardiff C), 1975 v E (sub), Ni (2)
Sidlow, C. (Liverpool), 1947 v E, S; 1948 v E, S, Ni; 1949 v S; 1950 v E (7)
Sisson, H. (Wrexham Olympic), 1885 v Ni; 1886 v S, Ni (3)
Slatter, N. (Bristol R), 1983 v S (1)
Smallman, D. P. (Wrexham), 1974 v E (sub), S (sub), Ni; (with Everton), 1975 v H (sub), E, Ni (sub); 1976 v A (7)
Southall, N. (Everton), 1982 v Ni; 1983 v N, E, Bul, S, Ni, Br (7)
Sprake, G. (Leeds U), 1964 v S, Ni; 1965 v S, D, Gr; 1966 v E, Ni, USSR; 1967 v S; 1968 v E, S; 1969 v S, E, Ni, WG, R of UK; 1970 v EG, I; 1971 v R, S, E, Ni; 1972 v Fi, E, S, Ni; 1973 v E (2), Pol, S, Ni; 1974 v Pol; (with Birmingham C), S, Ni; 1975 v A, H, L (37)
Stansfield, F. (Cardiff C), 1949 v S (1)
Stevenson, B. (Leeds U), 1978 v Ni; 1979 v Ma, T, S, E, Ni, Ma; 1980 v WG, T, Ic (sub); 1982 v Cz; (with Birmingham C), Sp, S, Ni, F (15)
Stevenson, N. (Swansea C), 1982 v E, S, Ni; 1983 v N (4)
Stitfall, R. F. (Cardiff C), 1953 v E; 1957 v Cz(2)
Sullivan, D. (Cardiff C), 1953 v Ni, F, Y; 1954 v Ni; 1955 v E, Ni; 1957 v E, S; 1958 v Ni, H (2), Se, Br; 1959 v S, Ni; 1960 v E, S (17)

Tapscott, D. R. (Arsenal), 1954 v A; 1955 v S, E, Ni, Y; 1956 v E, Ni, S, A; 1957 v Ni, Cz, EG; (with Cardiff C), 1959 v E, Ni (14)
Taylor, J. (Wrexham), 1898 v E (1)
Taylor, O. D. S. (Newtown), 1893 v S, Ni; 1894 v S, Ni (4)
Thomas, C. (Druids), 1899 v Ni; 1900 v S (2)
Thomas, D. A. (Swansea T), 1957 v Cz; 1958 v EG (2)
Thomas, D. S. (Fulham), 1948 v E, S, Ni; 1949 v S (4)
Thomas, E. (Cardiff Corinthians), 1925 v E (1)
Thomas, G. (Wrexham), 1885 v E, S (2)
Thomas, H. (Manchester U), 1927 v E (1)
Thomas, M. (Wrexham), 1977 v WG, S (1 + 1 sub), Ni (sub); 1978 v K (sub), S, Cz, Ir, E, Ni (sub); 1979 v Ma; (with Manchester U), T, WG, Ma (sub); 1980 v Ei, WG (sub), T, E, S, Ni; 1981 v Cz, S, E, USSR; (with Everton), 1982 v Cz; (with Brighton & HA), USSR (sub), Sp, E, S (sub), Ni (sub); 1983 (with Stoke C), v N, Y, E, Bul, S, Ni, Br (37)
Thomas, R. J. (Swindon T), 1967 v Ni; 1968 v WG; 1969 v E, Ni, I, WG, R of UK; 1970 v E, S, Ni, EG, I; 1971 v S, E, Ni, R, Cz; 1972 v Fi, Cz, R, E, S, Ni; 1973 v E (3), Pol, S, Ni; 1974 v Pol; (with Derby Co), E, S, Ni; 1975 v H (2), L (2), S, E, Ni; 1976 v A, Y, E; 1977 v Cz, S, E, Ni; 1978 v K, S; (with Cardiff C), Cz (50)
Thomas, T. (Bangor), 1898 v S, Ni (2)
Thomas, W. R. (Newport Co), 1931 v E, S (2)
Thomson, D. (Druids), 1876 v S (1)
Thomson, G. F. (Druids), 1876 v S; 1877 v S (2)
Toshack, J. B. (Cardiff C), 1969 v S, E, Ni, WG, EG, R of UK; 1970 v EG, I; (with Liverpool), 1971 v S, E, Ni, Fi; 1972 v Fi, E; 1973 v E (3), Pol, S; 1975 v A, H (2), L (2), S, E; 1976 v Y (2), E; 1977 v S; 1978 v K (2), S, Cz; (Swansea C), 1979 v WG (sub), S, E, Ni, Ma; 1980 v WG (40)
Townsend, W. (Newtown), 1887 v Ni; 1893 v Ni (2)
Trainer, H. (Wrexham), 1895 v E, S, Ni (3)
Trainer, J. (Bolton W), 1887 v S; (with Preston NE), 1888 v S; 1889 v E; 1890 v S; 1891 v S; 1892 v Ni, S; 1893 v E; 1894 v Ni, E; 1895 v Ni, E; 1896 v S; 1897 v Ni, S, E; 1898 v S, E; 1899 v Ni, S (20)
Turner, H. G. (Charlton Ath), 1937 v E, S, Ni; 1938 v E, S, Ni; 1939 v Ni, F (8)
Turner, J. (Wrexham), 1892 v E (1)
Turner, R. E. (Wrexham), 1891 v E, Ni (2)
Turner, W. H. (Wrexham), 1887 v E, Ni; 1890 v S; 1891 v E, S (5)

Vaughan, Jas (Druids), 1893 v E, S, Ni; 1899 v E (4)
Vaughan, John (Oswestry), 1879 v S; 1880 v S; 1881 v E, S; 1882 v E, S, Ni; 1883 v E, S, Ni; (with Bolton W), 1884 v E (11)
Vaughan, J. O. (Rhyl), 1885 v Ni; 1886 v Ni, E, S (4)
Vaughan N. (Newport Co), 1983 v Y (sub), Br (2)
Vaughan, T. (Rhyl), 1885 v E (1)
Vearncombe, G. (Cardiff C), 1958 v EG; 1961 v Ei (2)
Vernon, T. R. (Blackburn R), 1957 v Ni, Cz (2), EG; 1958 v E, S, EG, Se; 1959 v S; (with Everton), 1960 v Ni; 1961 v S, E, Ei; 1962 v Ni, Br (2), M; 1963 v S, E, H; 1964 v E, S; (with Stoke C), 1965 v Ni, Gr, I; 1966 v E, S, Ni, USSR, D; 1967 v Ni; 1968 v E (32)
Villars, A. K. (Cardiff C), 1974 v E, S, Ni (sub) (3)
Vizard, E. T. (Bolton W), 1911 v E, S, Ni; 1912 v E, S; 1913 v S; 1914 v E, Ni; 1920 v E; 1921 v E, S, Ni; 1922 v E, S; 1923 v E, Ni; 1924 v E, S, Ni; 1926 v E, S; 1927 v S (22)

Walley, J. T. (Watford), 1971 v Cz (1)
Walsh, I. (C Palace), 1980 v Ei, T, E, S, Ic; 1981 v T, Cz, Ei, T, S, E, USSR; 1982 v Cz (sub), Ic; (with Swansea C), Sp, S (sub), Ni (sub), F (18)
Ward, D. (Bristol R), 1959 v E; (with Cardiff C), 1962 v E (2)
Warner, J. (Swansea T), 1937 v E; (with Manchester U), 1939 v F (2)
Warren, F. W. (Cardiff C), 1929 v Ni; (with Middlesbrough), 1931 v Ni; 1933 v F, E; (with Hearts), 1937 v Ni; 1938 v Ni (6)
Watkins, A. E. (Leicester Fosse), 1898 v E, S; (with Aston Villa), 1900 v E, S; (with Millwall), 1904 v Ni (5)
Watkins, W. M. (Stoke C), 1902 v E; 1903 v E, S; (with Aston Villa); 1904 v E, S, Ni; (with Sunderland), 1905 v E, S, Ni; (with Stoke C), 1908 v Ni (10)
Webster, C (Manchester U), 1957 v Cz; 1958 v H, M, Br (4)
Whatley, W. J. (Tottenham H), 1939 v E, S (2)
White, P. F. (London Welsh), 1896 v Ni (1)
Wilcocks, A. R. (Oswestry), 1890 v Ni (1)
Wilding, J. (Wrexham O), 1885 v E, S, Ni; 1886 v E, Ni; (with Bootle), 1887 v E; 1888 v S, Ni; (with Wrexham), 1892 v S (9)
Williams, A. L. (Wrexham), 1931 v E (1)
Williams, B. D. (Swansea T), 1928 v Ni, E; 1930 v E, S; (with Everton), 1931 v Ni; 1932 v E; 1933 v E, S, Ni; 1935 v Ni (10)
Williams, B. (Bristol C), 1930 v Ni (1)
Williams, D. R. (Merthyr T), 1921 v E, S; (with Sheffield W), 1923 v S; 1926 v S; 1927 v E, Ni; (with Manchester U), 1929 v E, S (8)
Williams, E. (Crewe Alex), 1893 v E, S (2)
Williams, E. (Druids), 1901 v E, Ni, S; 1902 v E, Ni (5)
Williams, G. (Chirk), 1893 v S; 1894 v S; 1895 v E, S, Ni; 1898 v Ni (6)
Williams, G. E. (WBA), 1960 v Ni; 1961 v S, E, Ei; 1963 v Ni, H; 1964 v E, S, Ni; 1965 v S, E, Ni, D, Gr (2), USSR, I; 1966 v Ni, Br (2), Ch; 1967 v S, E, Ni; 1968 v Ni; 1969 v I (26)
Williams, G. G. (Swansea T), 1961 v Ni, H, Sp (2); 1962 v E (5)
Williams, G. J. J. (Cardiff C), 1951 v Sw (1)

Rod Thomas *Swindon Town* and *Wales*

John Toshack *Liverpool* and *Wales*

Williams, G. O. (Wrexham), 1907 v Ni (1)
Williams, H. J. (Swansea), 1965 v Gr (2); 1972 v R (3)
Williams, H. T. (Newport Co), 1949 v Ni, Sw; (with Leeds U), 1950 v Ni; 1951 v S (4)
Williams, J. H. (Oswestry), 1884 v E (1)
Williams, J. T. (Wrexham), 1939 v F (1)
Williams J. T. (Middlesbrough), 1925 v Ni (1)
Williams, J. W. (C Palace), 1912 v S, Ni (2)
Williams, R. (Newcastle U), 1935 v S, E (2)
Williams, R. P. (Caernarvon), 1886 v S (1)
Williams, S. G. (WBA), 1954 v A; 1955 v E, Ni; 1956 v E, S, A; 1958 v E, S, Ni, Is (2), H (2), M, Se, Br; 1959 v E, S, Ni; 1960 v E, S, Ni; 1961 v Ni, Ei, H, Sp (2); 1962 v E, S, Ni, Br (2), M; (with Southampton), 1963 v S, E, H (2); 1964 v E, S; 1965 v S, E, D; 1966 v D (43)
Williams, W. (Druids), 1876 v S; 1878 v S; (with Oswestry), 1879 v E, S; (with Druids), 1880 v E, S; 1881 v E, S; 1882 v E, S, Ni; 1883 v Ni (12)
Williams, W. (Northampton T), 1925 v S (1)
Witcomb, D. F. (WBA), 1947 v E, S; (with Sheffield W), 1947 v Ni (3)
Woosnam, A. P. (Leyton Orient), 1959 v S; (with West Ham U), v E; 1960 v E, S, Ni; 1961 v S, E, Ni, Ei, Sp, H; 1962 v E, S, Ni, Br; (with Aston Villa), 1963 v Ni, H (17)
Woosnam, G. (Newton White Star), 1879 v S (1)
Worthington, T. (Newtown), 1894 v S (1)
Wynn, G. A. (Chirk), 1903 v Ni; (with Wrexham), 1909 v E, S, Ni; (with Manchester C), 1910 v E; 1911 v Ni; 1912 v E, S; 1913 v E, S; 1914 v E, S (12)

Yorath, T. C. (Leeds U), 1970 v I; 1971 v S, E, Ni; 1972 v Cz, E, S, Ni; 1973 v E, Pol, S; 1974 v Pol, E, S, Ni; 1975 v A, H (2), L (2), S; 1976 v A, E, S, Y (2), E, Ni; (with Coventry C), 1977 v WG, S (2), Cz, E, Ni; 1978 v K (2), S, Cz, WG, Ir, E, S, Ni; 1979 v T, WG, S, E, Ni; (with Tottenham H), 1980 v Ei, T, E, S, Ni, Ic; 1981 v T, Cz; (with Vancouver W), Ei, T, USSR (59)

REPUBLIC OF IRELAND

Aherne, T. (Belfast Celtic), 1946 v P, Sp; (with Luton T), 1950 v Fi, E, Fi, Se, Bel; 1951 v N, Arg, N; 1952 v WG (2), A, Sp; 1953 v F; 1954 v F (16)
Ambrose, P. (Shamrock R), 1955 v N, Ho; 1964 v Pol, N, E (5)
Anderson, J. (Preston NE), 1980 v Cz (sub), US (sub); 1982 v Ch, Br, Tr (5)
Andrews, P. (Bohemians), 1936 v Ho (1)
Arrigan, T. (Waterford), 1938 v N (1)

Bailham, E. (Shamrock R), 1964 v E (1)
Barber, E. (Shelbourne), 1966 v Sp; (with Birmingham C), 1966 v Bel (2)
Barry, P. (Fordsons), 1928 v Bel; 1929 v Bel (2)
Bermingham, J. (Bohemians), 1929 v Bel (1)
Bermingham, P. (St James' Gate), 1935 v H (1)
Braddish, S. (Dundalk), 1978 v Pol (1)
Bonner, P. (Celtic), 1981 v Pol; 1982 v Alg (2)
Bradshaw, P. (St James' Gate), 1939 v Sw, Pol, H (2), G (5)
Brady, F. (Fordsons), 1926 v I; 1927 v I (2)
Brady, T. R. (QPR), 1964 v A (2), Sp (2), Pol, N (6)
Brady, W. L. (Arsenal), 1975 v USSR, T, Sw, USSR, Sw; 1976 v T, N, Pol; 1977 v E, T, F (2), Sp, Bul; 1978 v Bul, N; 1979 v Ni, E, D, Bul, WG, Arg; 1980 v W, Bul, E, Cy; (with Juventus), 1981 v Ho, Bel, F, Cy, Bel; 1982 v Ho, F, Ch, Br, Tr; 1983 (with Sampdoria), v Ho, Sp, Ic, Ma (40)
Breen, T. (Manchester U), 1937 v Sw, F; (with Shamrock R), 1947 v E, Sp, P (5)
Brennan, F. (Drumcondra), 1965 v Bel (1)
Brennan, S. A. (Manchester U), 1965 v Sp; 1966 v Sp, A, Bel; 1967 v Sp, T, Sp; 1969 v Cz, D, H; 1970 v S, Cz, D, H, Pol (sub), WG; (with Waterford), 1971 v Pol, Se, I (19)
Brown, J. (Coventry C), 1937 v Sw, F (2)
Browne, W. (Bohemians), 1964 v A, Sp, E (3)
Burke, F. (Cork), 1934 v Bel (1)
Burke, F. (Cork Ath), 1952 v WG (1)
Burke, J. (Shamrock R), 1929 v Bel (1)
Byrne, A. B. (Southampton), 1970 v D, Pol, WG; 1971 v Pol, Se (2), I (2), A; 1973 v F, USSR (sub), F, N; 1974 v Pol (14)
Byrne, D. (Shelbourne), 1929 v Bel; (with Shamrock R), 1932 v Sp; (with Coleraine), 1934 v Bel (3)
Byrne, J. (Bray Unknowns), 1928 v Bel (1)
Byrne, P. (Shelbourne), 1931 v Sp; 1932 v Ho; (with Drumcondra), 1934 v Ho (3)
Byrne, S. (Bohemians), 1931 v Sp (1)

Campbell, N. (St Patrick's Ath), 1971 v A (sub); (with Fortuna, Cologne), 1972 v Ir, Ec, Ch, P; 1973 v USSR, F (sub); 1976 v N; 1977 v Sp, Bul (sub) (10)
Cannon, H. (Bohemians), 1926 v I; 1928 v Bel (2)
Cantwell, N. (West Ham U), 1954 v L; 1956 v Sp, Ho; 1957 v D, WG, E (2); 1958 v D, Pol, A; 1959 v Pol, Cz (2); 1960 v Se, Ch, Se; 1961 v N; (with Manchester U), 1961 v S (2); 1962 v Cz (2), A; 1963 v Ic (2), S; 1964 v A, Sp, E; 1965 v Pol, Sp; 1966 v Sp (2), A, Bel; 1967 v Sp, T (36)
Carey, J. J. (Manchester U), 1938 v N, Cz, Pol; 1939 v Sw, Pol, H (2), G; 1946 v P, Sp; 1947 v E, Sp, P; 1948 v P, Sp; 1949 v Sw, Bel, P, Se, Sp; 1950 v Fi, E, Fi, Se; 1951 v N, Arg, N; 1953 v F, A (29)
Carolan, J. (Manchester U), 1960 v Se, Ch (2)
Carroll, B. (Shelbourne), 1949 v Bel; 1950 v Fi (2)
Carroll, T. R. (Ipswich T), 1968 v Pol; 1969 v Pol, A, D; 1970 v Cz, Pol, WG; 1971 v Se; (with Birmingham C), 1972 v Ir, Ec, Ch, P; 1973 v USSR (2), Pol, F, N (17)
Chandler, J. (Leeds U), 1980 v Cz (sub), US (2)
Chatton, H. A. (Shelbourne), 1931 v Sp; (with Dumbarton), 1932 v Sp; (with Cork), 1934 v Ho (3)
Clarke, J. (Drogheda U), 1978 v Pol (sub) (1)
Clarke, K. (Drumcondra), 1948 v P, Sp (2)
Clarke, M. (Shamrock R), 1950 v Bel (1)
Clinton, T. J. (Everton), 1951 v N; 1954 v F, L (3)
Coad, P. (Shamrock R), 1947 v E, Sp, P; 1948 v P, Sp; 1949 v Sw, Bel, P, Se; 1951 v N (sub); 1952 v Sp (11)
Coffey, T. (Drumcondra), 1950 v Fi (1)
Colfer, M. D. (Shelbourne), 1950 v Bel; 1951 v N (2)
Collins, F. (Jacobs), 1927 v I (1)
Conmy, O. M. (Peterborough U), 1965 v Bel; 1967 v Cz; 1968 v Cz, Pol; 1970 v Cz (5)
Connolly, J. (Fordsons), 1926 v I (1)
Connolly, N. (Cork), 1937 v G (1)
Conroy, G. A. (Stoke C), 1970 v Cz, D, H, Pol, WG; 1971 v Pol, Se (2), I; 1973 v USSR, F, USSR, N; 1974 v Pol, Br, U, Ch; 1975 v T, Sw, USSR, Sw; 1976 v T (sub), Pol; 1977 v E, T, Pol (26)
Conway, J. P. (Fulham), 1967 v Sp, T, Sp; 1968 v Cz; 1969 v A (sub), H; 1970 v S, Cz, D, H, Pol, WG; 1971 v I, A; 1974 v U, Ch; 1976 v N, Pol; (with Manchester C), 1977 v Pol (19)
Corr, P. J. (Everton), 1949 v P, Sp; 1950 v E, Se (4)
Courtney, E. (Cork U), 1946 v P (1)
Cummins, G. P. (Luton T), 1954 v L (2); 1955 v N (2), WG; 1956 v Y, Sp; 1958 v D, Pol, A; 1959 v Pol, Cz (2); 1960 v Se, Ch, WG, Se; 1961 v S (2) (19)
Cuneen, T. (Limerick), 1951 v N (1)
Curtis, D. P. (Shelbourne), 1957 v D, WG; (with Bristol

C), 1957 v E (2); 1958 v D, Pol, A; (with Ipswich T), 1959 v Pol; 1960 v Se, Ch, WG, Se; 1961 v N, S; 1962 v A; 1963 v Ic (with Exeter C), 1964 v A (17)
Cusack, S. (Limerick), 1953 v F (1)

Daly, G. A. (Manchester U), 1973 v Pol (sub), N; 1974 v Br (sub), U (sub); 1975 v Sw (sub); 1977 v E, T, F; (with Derby Co), F, Bul; 1978 v Bul, T, D; 1979 v Ni, E, D, Bul; 1980 v Ni, E, Cy, Sw, Arg; (with Coventry C), 1981 v Ho, Bel, Cy, W, Bel, Cz, WG 'B', Pol (sub); 1982 v Alg, Ch, Br, Tr (1983 v Ho (35)
Daly, J. (Shamrock R), 1932 v Ho; 1935 v Sw (2)
Daly, M. (Wolverhampton W), 1978 v T, Pol (2)
Daly, P. Shamrock R), 1950 v Fi (sub) (1)
Davis, T. L. (Oldham Ath), 1937 v G, H; (with Tranmere R), 1938 v Cz, Pol (4)
Deacy, E. (Aston Villa), 1982 v Alg (sub), Ch, Br, Tr (4)
Dempsey, J. T. (Fulham), 1967 v Sp, Cz; 1968 v Cz, Pol; 1969 v Pol, A, D; (with Chelsea), 1969 v Cz, D; 1970 v H, WG; 1971 v Pol, Se (2), I; 1972 v Ir, Ec, Ch, P (19)
Dennehy, J. (Cork Hibernians), 1972 v Ec (sub), Ch; (with Nottingham F), 1973 v USSR (sub), Pol, F, N; 1974 v Pol (sub); 1975 v T (sub); (with Walsall), 1976 v Pol (sub); 1977 v Pol (sub) (10)
Desmond, P. (Middlesbrough), 1950 v Fi, E, Fi, Se (4)
Devine, J. (Arsenal), 1980 v Cz, Ni; 1981 v Cz, WG 'B'; 1982 v Ho, Alg; 1983 v Sp, Ma(8)
Donnelly, J. (Dundalk), 1935 v H, Sw, G; 1936 v Ho, Sw, H, L; 1937 v G, H; 1938 v N (10)
Donnelly, T. (Drumcondra), 1938 v N; (Shamrock R), 1939 v Sw (2)
Donovan, D. C. (Everton), 1955 v N, Ho, N, WG; 1957 v E (5)
Donovan, T. (Aston Villa), 1980 v Cz; 1981 v WG 'B' (sub) (2)
Dowdall, C. (Fordsons), 1928 v Bel; (with Barnsley), 1929 v Bel; (with Cork), 1931 v Sp (3)
Doyle, C. (Shelbourne), 1959 v Cz (1)
Doyle, D. (Shamrock R), 1926 v I (1)
Doyle, L. (Dolphin), 1932 v Sp (1)
Duffy, B. (Shamrock R), 1950 v Bel (1)
Duggan, H. A. (Leeds U), 1927 v I; 1930 v Bel; 1936 v H, L; (with Newport Co), 1938 v N (5)
Dunne, A. P. (Manchester U), 1962 v A; 1963 v Ic, S; 1964 v A, Sp, Pol, N, E; 1965 v Pol, Sp; 1966 v Sp (2), A, Bel; 1967 v Sp, T, Sp; 1969 v Pol, D, H; 1970 v H; 1971 v Se, I, A; (with Bolton W), 1974 v Br (sub), U, Ch; 1975 v T, Sw, USSR, Sw; 1976 v T (32)
Dunne, J. (Sheffield U), 1930 v Bel; (with Arsenal), 1936 v Sw, H, L; (with Southampton), 1937 v Sw, F; (with Shamrock R), 1938 v N (2), Cz, Pol; 1939 v Sw, Pol, H (2), G (15)
Dunne, J. C. (Fulham), 1971 v A (1)
Dunne, L. (Manchester C), 1935 v Sw, G (2)
Dunne, P. A. J. (Manchester U), 1965 v Sp; 1966 v Sp (2), WG; 1967 v T (5)
Dunne, S. (Luton T), 1953 v F, A; 1954 v F, L; 1956 v Sp, Ho; 1957 v D, WG, E; 1958 v D, Pol, A; 1959 v Pol; 1960 v WG, Se (15)
Dunne, T. (St Patrick's Ath), 1956 v Ho; 1957 v D, WG (3)
Dunning, P. (Shelbourne), 1971 v Se, I (2)
Dunphy, E. M. (York C), 1966 v Sp; (with Millwall), 1966 v WG; 1967 v T, Sp, T, Cz; 1968 v Cz, Pol; 1969 v Pol, A, D (2), H; 1970 v D, H, Pol, WG (sub); 1971 v Pol, Se (2), I (2), A (23)
Dwyer, N. M. (West Ham U), 1960 v Se, Ch, WG, Se; (with Swansea T), 1961 v W, N, S (2); 1962 v Cz (2); 1964 v Pol (sub), N, E; 1965 v Pol (14)

Egan, R. (Dundalk), 1929 v Bel (1)
Eglington, T. J. (Shamrock R), 1946 v P, Sp; (with Everton), 1947 v E, Sp, P; 1948 v P; 1949 v Sw, P, Se; 1951 v N, Arg; 1952 v WG (2), A, Sp; 1953 v F, A; 1954 v F, L, F; 1955 v N, Ho, WG; 1956 v Sp (24)
Ellis, P. (Bohemians), 1935 v Sw, G; 1936 v Ho, Sw, L; 1937 v G, H (7)

Fagan, E. (Shamrock R), 1973 v N (sub) (1)
Fagan, F. (Manchester C), 1955 v N; 1960 v Se; (with Derby Co), 1960 v Ch, WG, Se; 1961 v W, N, S (8)
Fagan, K. (Shamrock R), 1926 v I (1)
Fairclough, M. (Dundalk), 1982 v Ch (sub), Tr (sub) (2)
Fallon, S. (Celtic), 1951 v N; 1952 v WG (2), A, Sp; 1953 v F; 1955 v N, WG (8)
Fallon, W. J. (Notts Co), 1935 v H; 1936 v H; 1937 v H, Sw, F; 1939 v Sw, Pol; (with Sheffield W), 1939 v H, G (9)
Farquharson, T. G. (Cardiff C), 1929 v Bel; 1930 v Bel; 1931 v Sp; 1932 v Sp (4)
Farrell, P. (Hibernian), 1937 v Sw, F (2)
Farrell, P. D. (Shamrock R), 1946 v P, Sp; (with Everton), 1947 v Sp, P; 1948 v P, Sp; 1949 v Sw, P (sub), Sp; 1950 v E, Fi, Se; 1951 v Arg, N; 1952 v WG (2), A, Sp; 1953 v F, A; 1954 v F (2); 1955 v N, Ho, WG; 1956 v Y, Sp; 1957 v E (28)
Feenan, J. J. (Sunderland), 1937 v Sw, F (2)
Finucane, A. (Limerick), 1967 v T, Cz; 1969 v Cz, D, H; 1970 v S, Cz; 1971 v Se, I, I (sub); 1972 v A (11)
Fitzgerald, F. J. (Waterford), 1955 v Ho; 1956 v Ho (2)
Fitzgerald, P. J. (Leeds U), 1961 v W, N, S; 1962 v Cz (2) (5)
Fitzpatrick, K. (Limerick), 1970 v Cz (1)
Fitzsimons, A. G. (Middlesbrough), 1950 v Fi, Bel; 1952 v WG (2), A, Sp; 1953 v F, A; 1954 v F, L, F; 1955 v Ho, N, WG; 1956 v Y, Sp, Ho; 1957 v D, WG, E (2); 1958 v D, Pol, A; 1959 v Pol; (with Lincoln C), 1959 v Cz (26)
Flood, J. J. (Shamrock R), 1926 v I; 1929 v Bel; 1930 v Bel; 1931 v Sp; 1932 v Sp (5)
Fogarty, A. (Sunderland), 1960 v WG, Se; 1961 v S; 1962 v Cz (2); 1963 v Ic (2), S (sub); 1964 v A (2); (with Hartlepools U), Sp (11)
Foley, J. (Cork), 1934 v Bel, Ho; (with Celtic), 1935 v H, Sw, G; 1937 v G, H (7)
Foley, M. (Shelbourne), 1926 v I (1)
Foley, T. C. (Northampton T), 1964 v Sp, Pol, N; 1965 v Pol, Bel; 1966 v Sp (2), WG; 1967 v Cz (9)
Foy, T. (Shamrock R), 1938 v N; 1939 v H (2)
Fullam, J. (Preston NE), 1961 v N; (with Shamrock R), 1964 v Sp, Pol, N; 1966 v A, Bel; 1968 v Pol; 1969 v Pol, A, D; 1970 v Cz (sub) (11)
Fullam, R. (Shamrock R), 1926 v I; 1927 v I (2)

Gallagher, C. (Celtic), 1967 v T, Cz (2)
Gallagher, M. (Hibernian), 1954 v L (1)
Gallagher, P. (Falkirk), 1932 v Sp (1)
Galvin, A. (Tottenham H), 1983 v Ho, Ma (2)
Gannon, E. (Notts Co), 1949 v Sw; (with Sheffield W), 1949 v Bel, P, Se, Sp; 1950 v Fi; 1951 v N; 1952 v G, A; 1954 v L, F; 1955 v N; (with Shelbourne), 1955 v N, WG (14)
Gannon, M. (Shelbourne), 1972 v A (1)
Gaskins, P. (Shamrock R), 1934 v Bel, Ho; 1935 v H, Sw, G; (with St James' Gate), 1938 v Cz, Pol (7)
Gavin, J. T. (Norwich C), 1950 v Fi (2); 1953 v F; 1954 v L; (with Tottenham H), 1955 v Ho, WG; (with Norwich C), 1957 v D (7)
Geoghegan, M. (St James' Gate), 1937 v G; 1938 v N (2)
Gibbons, A. (St Patrick's Ath), 1952 v WG; 1954 v L; 1956 v Y, Sp (4)
Gilbert, R. (Shamrock R), 1966 v WG (1)
Giles, C. (Doncaster R), 1951 v N (1)
Giles, M. J. (Manchester U), 1960 v Se, Ch; 1961 v W, N,

S (2); 1962 v Cz (2), A; 1963 v Ic, S; (with Leeds U), 1964 v A (2), Sp (2), Pol, N, E; 1965 v Sp; 1966 v Sp (2), A, Bel; 1967 v Sp, T (2); 1969 v A, D, Cz; 1970 v S, Pol, WG; 1971 v I; 1973 v F, USSR; 1974 v Br, U, Ch; 1975 v USSR, T, Sw, USSR, Sw; (with WBA), 1976 v T; 1977 v E, T, F (2), Pol, Bul; (with Shamrock R), 1978 v Bul, T, Pol, N, D; 1979 v Ni, D, Bul, WG, Arg (60)

Givens, D. J. (Manchester U), 1969 v D, H; 1970 v S, Cz, D, H; (with Luton T), 1970 v Pol, WG; 1971 v Se, I (2), A; 1972 v Ir, Ec, P; (with QPR), 1973 v F, USSR, Pol, F, N; 1974 v Pol, Br, U, Ch; 1975 v USSR, T, Sw, USSR, Sw; 1976 v T, N, Pol; 1977 v E, T, F (2), Sp, Bul; 1978 v Bul, N, D; (with Birmingham C), 1979 v Ni (sub), E, D, Bul, WG, Arg; 1980 v US (sub), Ni (sub), Sw, Arg; 1981 v Ho, Bel, Cy (sub), W; (with Neuchatel X), 1982 v F (sub) (56)

Glen, W. (Shamrock R), 1927 v I; 1929 v Bel; 1930 v Bel; 1932 v Sp; 1936 v Ho, Sw, H, L (8)

Glynn, D. (Drumcondra), 1952 v WG; 1955 v N (2)

Godwin, T. F. (Shamrock R), 1949 v P, Se, Sp; 1950 v Fi, E; (with Leicester C), 1950 v Fi, Se, Bel; 1951 v N; (with Bournemouth & Boscombe Ath), 1956 v Ho; 1957 v E; 1958 v D, Pol (13)

Golding, L. (Shamrock R), 1928 v Bel; 1930 v Bel (2)

Gorman, W. C. (Bury), 1936 v Sw, H, L; 1937 v G, H; 1938 v N, Cz, Pol; 1939 v Sw, Pol, H; (with Brentford), 1947 v E, P (13)

Grace, J. (Drumcondra), 1926 v I (1)

Grealish, A. (Orient), 1976 v N, Pol, N, D; 1979 v Ni, E, WG, Arg; (with Luton T), 1980 v W, Cz, Bul, US, Ni, E, Cy, Sw, Arg; 1981 v Ho, Bel, F, Cy, W, Bel, WG 'B', Pol; (with Brighton & HA), 1982 v Ho, Alg, Ch, Br, Tr; 1983 v Ho, Sp, Ic, Sp (34)

Gregg, E. (Bohemians), 1978 v Pol, D (sub); 1979 v E (sub), D, Bul, WG, Arg; 1980 v W, Cz (9)

Griffith, R. (Walsall), 1935 v H (1)

Grimes, A. A. (Manchester U), 1978 v T, Pol, N (sub); 1980 v Bul, US, Ni, E, Cy; 1981 v Cz, WG 'B' (sub), Pol; 1982 v Alg; 1983 v Sp, Sp (14)

Hale, A. (Aston Villa), 1962 v A; (with Doncaster R), 1963 v Ic; 1964 v Sp (2); (with Waterford), 1967 v Sp; 1968 v Pol (sub); 1969 v Pol, A, D; 1970 v S, Cz; 1971 v Pol (sub); 1972 v A (sub) (13)

Hamilton, T. (Shamrock R), 1959 v Cz (2) (2)

Hand, E. K. (Portsmouth), 1969 v Cz (sub); 1970 v Pol, WG; 1971 v Pol, A; 1973 v USSR, F, USSR, Pol, F; 1974 v Pol, Br, U, Ch; 1975 v T, Sw, USSR, Sw; 1976 v T (19)

Harrington, W. (Cork), 1936 v Ho, Sw, H, L (4)

Hartnett, J. B. (Middlesbrough), 1949 v Sp; 1954 v L (2)

Haverty, J. (Arsenal), 1956 v Ho; 1957 v D, WG, E (2); 1958 v D, Pol, A; 1959 v Pol; 1960 v Se, Ch; 1961 v W, N, S (2); (with Blackburn R), 1962 v Cz (2); (with Millwall), 1963 v S; 1964 v A, Sp, Pol, N, E; (with Celtic), 1965 v Pol; (with Bristol R), 1965 v Sp; (with Shelbourne), 1966 v Sp (2), WG, A, Bel; 1967 v T, Sp (32)

Hayes, A. W. P. (Southampton), 1979 v D (1)

Hayes, W. E. (Huddersfield T), 1947 v E, P (2)

Hayes, W. J. (Limerick), 1949 v Bel (1)

Healey, R. (Cardiff C), 1977 v Pol; 1980 v E (sub) (2)

Heighway, S. D. (Liverpool), 1971 v Pol, Se (2), I, A; 1973 v USSR; 1975 v USSR, T, USSR; 1976 v T, N; 1977 v E, F (2), Sp, Bul; 1978 v Bul, N, D; 1979 v Ni, Bul; 1980 v Bul, US, Ni, E, Cy, Arg; 1981 v Bel, F, Cy, W, Bel; (with Minnesota K), 1982 v Ho (33)

Henderson, B. (Drumcondra), 1948 v P, Sp (2)

Hennessy, J. (Shelbourne), 1956 v Pol, B, Sp; 1966 v WG; (with St Patrick's Ath), 1969 v A (5)

Herrick, J. (Cork Hibernians), 1972 v A, Ch (sub); (with Shamrock R), 1973 v F (sub) (3)

Higgins, J. (Birmingham C), 1951 v Arg (1)

Holmes, J. (Coventry C), 1971 v A (sub); 1973 v F, USSR, Pol, F, N; 1974 v Pol, Br; 1975 v USSR, Sw; 1976 v T, N, Pol; 1977 v E, T, F, Sp; (with Tottenham H), F, Pol, Bul; 1978 v Bul, T, Pol, N, D; 1979 v Ni, E, D, Bul; 1981 (with Vancouver W), v W (30)

Horlecher, A. F. (Bohemians), 1930 v Bel; 1932 v Sp, Ho; 1935 v H; 1936 v Ho, Sw (6)

Hoy, M. (Dundalk), 1938 v N; 1939 v Sw, Pol, H (2), G (6)

Hughton, C. (Tottenham H), 1980 v US, E, Sw, Arg; 1981 v Ho, Bel, F, Cy, W, Bel, Pol; 1982 v F; 1983 v Ho, Sp, Ma, Sp (16)

Hurley, C. J. (Millwall), 1957 v E; 1958 v D, Pol, A; (with Sunderland), 1959 v Cz (2); 1960 v Se, Ch,WG, Se; 1961 v W, N, S (2); 1962 v Cz (2), A; 1963 v Ic (2), S; 1964 v A (2), Sp (2), Pol, N; 1965 v Sp; 1966 v WG, A, Bel; 1967 v T, Sp, T, Cz; 1968 v Cz, Pol (2); (with Bolton W), 1969 v D, Cz, H (40)

Hutchinson, F. (Drumcondra), 1935 v Sw, G (2)

Jordan, D. (Wolverhampton W), 1937 v Sw, F (2)

Jordan, W. (Bohemians), 1934 v Ho; 1938 v N (2)

Kavanagh, P. J. (Celtic), 1931 v Sp; 1932 v Sp (2)

Keane, T. R. (Swansea T), 1949 v Sw, P, Se, Sp (4)

Kearin, M. (Shamrock R), 1972 v A (1)

Kearns, F. T. (West Ham U), 1954 v L (1)

Kearns, M. (Oxford U), 1970 v Pol (sub); (with Walsall), 1974 v Pol (sub), U, Ch; 1976 v N, Pol; 1977 v E, T, F (2), Sp, Bul; 1978 v N, D; 1979 v Ni, E; (with Wolverhampton W), 1980 v US, Ni (18)

Kelly, J. (Derry C), 1932 v Ho; 1934 v Bel; 1936 v Sw, L (4)

Kelly, J. A. (Drumcondra), 1957 v WG, E; (with Preston NE), 1962 v A; 1963 v Ic (2), S; 1964 v A (2), Sp (2), Pol; 1965 v Bel; 1966 v A, Bel; 1967 v Sp (2), T, Cz (2), Pol; 1968 v Pol, A, D, Cz, D, H; 1970 v S, D, H, Pol, WG; 1971 v Pol, Se (2), I (2), A; 1972 v Ir, Ec, Ch, P; 1973 v USSR, F, USSR, Pol, F, N (47)

Kelly, J. P. V. (Wolverhampton W), 1961 v W, N, S; 1962 v Cz (2) (5)

Kelly, N. (Nottingham F), 1954 v L (1)

Kendrick, J. (Everton), 1927 v I; 1934 v Bel, Ho; 1936 v Ho (4)

Kennedy, W. (St James' Gate), 1932 v Ho; 1934 v Bel, Ho (3)

Keogh, J. (Shamrock R), 1966 v WG (sub) (1)

Keogh, S. (Shamrock R), 1959 v Pol (1)

Kiernan, F. W. (Shamrock R), 1951 v Arg, N; (with Southampton), 1952 v WG (2), A (5)

Kinnear, J. P. (Tottenham H), 1967 v T; 1968 v Cz, Pol; 1969 v A; 1970 v Cz, D, H, Pol; 1971 v Se (sub), I; 1972 v Ir, Ec, Ch, P; 1973 v USSR, F; 1974 v Pol, Br, U, Ch; 1975 v USSR, T, Sw, USSR; (with Brighton), 1976 v T (sub) (25)

Kinsella, J. (Shelbourne), 1928 v Bel (1)

Kinsella, P. (Shamrock R), 1932 v Ho; 1938 v N (2)

Kirkland, A. (Shamrock R), 1927 v I (1)

Lacey, W. (Shelbourne), 1927 v I; 1928 v Bel; 1930 v Bel (3)

Langan, D. (Derby Co), 1978 v T, N; 1980 v Sw, Arg; (with Birmingham C), 1981 v Ho, Bel, F, Cy, W, Bel, Cz, WG 'B', Pol; 1982 v Ho, F (15)

Lawler, J. F. (Fulham), 1953 v A; 1954 v L, F; 1955 v N, H, N, WG; 1956 v Y (8)

Lawlor, J. C. (Drumcondra), 1949 v Bel; (with Doncaster R), 1951 v N, Arg (3)

Lawlor, M. (Shamrock R), 1971 v Pol, Se (2), I (sub); 1973 v Pol (5)
Lawrenson, M. (Preston NE), 1977 v Pol; (with Brighton), 1978 v Bul, Pol, N (sub); 1979 v Ni, E; 1980 v E, Cy, Sw; 1981 v Ho, Bel, F, Cy, Pol; (with Liverpool), 1982 v Ho, F; 1983 v Ho, Sp, Ic, Ma, Sp (21)
Leech, M. (Shamrock R), 1969 v Cz, D, H; 1972 v A, Ir, Ec, P; 1973 v USSR (sub) (8)
Lennon, C. (St James' Gate), 1935 v H, Sw, G (3)
Lennox, G. (Dolphin), 1931 v Sp; 1932 v Sp (2)
Lowry, D. (St Patrick's Ath), 1962 v A (sub) (1)
Lunn, R. (Dundalk), 1939 v Sw, Pol (2)
Lynch, J. (Cork Bohemians), 1934 v Bel (1)

McAlinden, J. (Portsmouth), 1946 v P, Sp (2)
McCann, J. (Shamrock R), 1957 v WG (1)
McCarthy, J. (Bohemians), 1926 v I; 1928 v Bel; 1930 v Bel (3)
McCarthy, M. (Shamrock R), 1932 v Ho (1)
McConville, T. (Dundalk), 1972 v A; (with Waterford), 1973 v USSR, F, USSR, Pol, F (6)
McDonagh, J. (Everton), 1981 v W, Bel, Cz, WG 'B'; (with Bolton W), 1982 v Ho, F, Ch, Br; 1983 v Ho, Sp, Ic, Ma, Sp (13)
McEvoy, M. A. (Blackburn R), 1961 v S (2); 1963 v S; 1964 v A, Sp (2), Pol, N, E; 1965 v Pol, Bel, Sp; 1966 v Sp (2); 1967 v Sp, T, Cz (17)
McGee, P. (QPR), 1978 v T, N (sub), D (sub); 1979 v Ni, E, D (sub), Bul (sub), Arg (sub); 1980 v Cz, Bul; (with Preston NE), US, Ni, Cy, Sw, Arg; 1981 v Bel (sub) (16)
McGowan, D. (West Ham U), 1949 v P, Se, Sp (3)
McGowan, J. (Cork U), 1947 v Sp (1)
McGrath, M. (Blackburn R), 1958 v A; 1959 v Pol, Cz (2); 1960 v Se, WG, Se; 1961 v W; 1962 v C (2); 1963 v S; 1964 v A (2), E; 1965 v Pol, Bel, Sp; 1966 v Sp; (with Bradford), 1966 v WG, A, Bel; 1967 v T (22)
McGuire, W. (Bohemians), 1936 v Ho (1)
McKenzie, G. (Southend U), 1938 v N (2), Cz, Pol; 1939 v Sw, Pol, H (2), G (9)
Mackey, G. (Shamrock R), 1957 v D, WG, E (3)
McLoughlin, F. (Fordsons), 1930 v Bel; (with Cork), 1932 v Sp (2)
McMillan, W. (Belfast Celtic), 1946 v P, Sp (2)
McNally, J. B. (Luton T), 1959 v Cz; 1961 v Sp; 1963 v Ic (3)
Macken, A. (Derby Co), 1977 v Sp (1)
Madden, O. (Cork), 1936 v H (1)
Maguire, J. (Shamrock R), 1929 v Bel (1)
Malone, G. (Shelbourne), 1949 v Bel (1)
Mancini, T. J. (QPR), 1974 v Pol, Br, U, Ch; (with Arsenal), 1975 v USSR (5)
Martin, C. (Bo'ness), 1927 v I (1)
Martin, C. J. (Glentoran), 1946 v P (sub), Sp; 1947 v E; (with Leeds U), 1947 v Sp; 1948 v P, Sp; (with Aston Villa), 1949 v Sw, Bel, P, Se, Sp; 1950 v Fi, E, Fi, Se, Bel; 1951 v Arg; 1952 v WG, A, Sp; 1954 v F (2), L; 1955 v N, Ho, N, WG; 1956 v Y, Sp, Ho (30)
Martin, M. P. (Bohemians), 1972 v A, Ir, Ec, Ch, P; 1973 v USSR; (with Manchester U), 1973 v USSR, Pol, F, N; 1974 v Pol, Br, U, Ch; 1975 v USSR, T, Sw, USSR, Sw; (with WBA), 1976 v T, N, Pol; 1977 v E, T, F (2), Sp, Pol, Bul; (with Newcastle U), 1979 v D, Bul, WG, Arg; 1980 v W, Cz, Bul, US, Ni; 1981 v F, Bel, Cz, WG 'B'; 1982 v Ho, F, Alg, Ch, Br, Tr; 1983 v Ho, Sp, Ma, Sp (52)
Meagan, M. K. (Everton), 1961 v S; 1962 v A; 1963 v Ic; 1964 v Sp; (with Huddersfield T), 1965 v Bel; 1966 v Sp (2), A, Bel; 1967 v Sp, T, Sp, T, Cz; 1968 v Cz, Pol; (with Drogheda), 1970 v S (17)
Meehan, P. (Drumcondra), 1934 v Ho (1)
Monahan, P. (Sligo R), 1935 v Sw, G (2)
Mooney, J. (Shamrock R), 1965 v Pol, Bel (2)
Moore, P. (Shamrock R), 1931 v Sp; 1932 v Ho; (with Aberdeen), 1934 v Bel, Ho; 1935 v H, G; (with Shamrock R), 1936 v Ho; 1937 v G, H (9)
Moran, K. (Manchester U), 1980 v Sw, Arg; 1981 v Bel, F, Cy, W (sub), Bel, Cz, WG 'B', Pol; 1982 v F, Alg; 1983 v Ic (13)
Moroney, T. (West Ham U), 1948 v Sp; 1949 v P, Se, Sp; 1950 v Fi, E, Fi, Bel; 1951 v N (2); 1952 v WG; 1954 v F (12)
Moulson, C. (Lincoln C), 1936 v H, L; (with Notts Co), 1937 v H, Sw, F (5)
Moulson, G. B. (Lincoln C), 1948 v P, Sp; 1949 v Sw (3)
Mucklan, C. (Drogheda U), 1978 v Pol (1)
Muldoon, T. (Aston Villa), 1927 v I (1)
Mulligan, P. M. (Shamrock R), 1969 v Cz, D, H; 1970 v S, Cz, D; (with Chelsea), 1970 v H, Pol, WG; 1971 v Pol, Se, I; 1972 v A, Ir, Ec, Ch, P; (with Crystal Palace), 1973 v F, USSR, Pol, F, N; 1974 v Pol, Br, U, Ch; 1975 v USSR, T, Sw, USSR, Sw; (with WBA), 1976 v T, Pol; 1977 v E, T, F (2), Pol, Bul; 1978 v Bul, N, D; 1979 v E, D, Bul (sub), WG, Arg; (with Shamrock R) 1980 v W, Cz, Bul, US (sub) (51)
Munroe, L. (Shamrock R), 1954 v L (1)
Murphy, A. (Clyde), 1956 v Y (1)
Murphy, J. (C. Palace), 1980 v W, US, Cy (3)
Murray, T. (Dundalk), 1950 v Bel (1)

Newman, W. (Shelbourne), 1969 v D (1)
Nolan, R. (Shamrock R), 1957 v D, WG, E; 1958 v Pol; 1960 v Ch, WG, Se; 1962 v Cz (2); 1963 v Ic (10)

O'Brien, F. (Philadelphia F), 1980 v Cz, E, Cy (sub), Arg (4)
O'Brien, M. T. (Derby Co), 1927 v I; (with Walsall), 1929 v Bel; (with Norwich C), 1930 v Bel; (with Watford), 1932 v Ho (4)
O'Brien, R. (Notts Co), 1976 v N, Pol; 1977 v Sp, Pol (4)
O'Byrne, L. B. (Shamrock R), 1949 v Bel (1)
O'Callaghan, B. R. (Stoke C), 1979 v WG (sub), Arg (sub); 1980 v W, US; 1981 v W; 1982 v Br, Tr (7)
O'Callaghan, K. (Ipswich T), 1981 v Cz, WG 'B', Pol; 1982 v Alg, Ch, Br, Tr (sub); 1983 v Sp, Ic (sub), Ma (sub), Sp (sub) (11)
O'Connell, A. (Dundalk), 1967 v Sp; (with Bohemians), 1971 v Pol (sub) (2)
O'Connor, T. (Shamrock R), 1950 v Fi, E, Fi, Se (4)
O'Connor, T. (Fulham), 1968 v Cz; (with Dundalk), 1972 v A, Ir (sub), Ec (sub), Ch; (with Bohemians), 1973 v F (sub), Pol (sub) (7)
O'Driscoll, J. F. (Swansea T), 1949 v Sw, Bel, Se (3)
O'Driscoll, S. (Fulham), 1982 v Ch, Br, Tr (sub) (3)
O'Farrell, F. (West Ham U), 1952 v A; 1953 v A; 1954 v F; 1955 v Ho, N; 1956 v Y, Ho; (with Preston NE), 1958 v D; 1959 v Cz (9)
O'Flanagan, K. P. (Bohemians), 1938 v N, Cz, Pol, H (2), G; (with Arsenal), 1947 v E, Sp, P (10)
O'Flanagan, M. (Bohemians), 1947 v E (1)
O'Kane, P. (Bohemians), 1935 v H, Sw, G (3)
O'Keefe, E. (Everton), 1981 v W (1)
O'Keefe, T. (Cork), 1934 v Bel; (with Waterford), 1938 v Cz, Pol (3)
O'Leary, D. (Arsenal), 1977 v E, F (2), Sp, Bul; 1978 v Bul, N, D; 1979 v E, Bul, WG, Arg; 1980 v W, Bul, Ni, E, Cy; 1981 v Ho, Cz, WG 'B', Pol; 1982 v Ho, F; 1983 v Ho, Ic, Sp (26)
O'Leary, P. (Shamrock R), 1980 v Bul, US, NI, E (sub), Cz, Arg; 1981 v Ho (7)
O'Mahoney, M. T. (Bristol R), 1938 v Cz, Pol; 1939 v Sw, Pol, H, G (6)
O'Neill, F. S. (Shamrock R), 1962 v Cz (2); 1965 v Pol,

Bel, Sp; 1966 v Sp (2), WG, A; 1967 v Sp, T, Sp, T; 1969 v Pol, A, D, Cz, D (sub), H (sub); 1972 v A (20)
O'Neill, J. (Everton), 1952 v Sp; 1953 v F, A; 1954 v F, L, F; 1955 v N, Ho, N, WG; 1956 v Y, Sp; 1957 v D; 1958 v M; 1959 v Pol, Cz (2) (17)
O'Neill, J. (Preston NE), 1961 v W (1)
O'Neill, W. (Dundalk), 1936 v Ho, Sw, H, L; 1937 v G, H, Sw, F; 1938 v N; 1939 v H, G (11)
O'Reilly, J. (Brideville), 1932 v Ho; (with Aberdeen), 1934 v Bel, Ho; (with Brideville), 1936 v Ho; Sw, H, L; (with St James' Gate), 1937 v G, H, Sw, F; 1938 v N (2), Cz, Pol; 1939 v Sw, Pol, H (2), G (20)
O'Reilly, J. (Cork U), 1946 v P, Sp (2)

Peyton, G. (Fulham), 1977 v Sp (sub); 1978 v Bul, T, Pol; 1979 v D, Bul, WG, Arg; 1980 v W, Cz, Bul, E, Cy, Sw, Arg; 1981 v Ho, Bel, F, Cy; 1982 v Tr (20)
Peyton, N. (Shamrock R), 1957 v WG; (with Leeds U), 1960 v WG, Se (sub); 1961 v W; 1963 v Ic, S (6)

Reid, C. (Brideville), 1931 v Sp (1)
Richardson, D. J. (Shamrock R), 1972 v A (sub); (with Gillingham), 1973 v N (sub); 1980 v Cz (3)
Rigby, A. (St James' Gate), 1935 v H, Sw, G (3)
Ringstead, A. (Sheffield U), 1951 v Arg, N; 1952 v WG (2), A, Sp; 1953 v A; 1954 v F; 1955 v N; 1956 v Y, Sp, Ho; 1957 v E (2); 1958 v D, Pol, A; 1959 v Pol, Cz (2) (20)
Robinson, J. (Bohemians), 1928 v Bel; (with Dolphin), 1931 v Sp (2)
Robinson, M. (Brighton), 1981 v F, Cy, Bel, WG 'B', Pol; 1982 v Ho, F, Alg, Ch; 1983 v Ho, Sp, Ic, Ma (13)
Roche, P. J. (Shelbourne), 1972 v A; (with Manchester U), 1975 v USSR, T, Sw, USSR, Sw; 1976 v T (7)
Rogers, E. (Blackburn R), 1968 v Cz, Pol; 1969 v Pol, A, D, Cz, D, H; 1970 v S, D, H; 1971 v I (2), A; (with Charlton Ath), 1972 v Ir, Ec, Ch, P; 1973 v USSR (19)
Ryan, G. (Derby Co), 1978 v T; (with Brighton), 1979 v E, WG; 1980 v W, Cy (sub), Sw, Arg (sub); 1981 v F (sub), WG 'B' (sub), Pol (sub); 1982 v Ho (sub), Alg (sub), Ch (sub) Tr (14)
Ryan, R. A. (WBA), 1950 v Se, Bel; 1951 v N, Arg, N; 1952 v WG (2), A, Sp; 1953 v F, A; 1954 v F, L, F; 1955 v N; (with Derby Co), 1956 v Sp (16)

Saward, P. (Millwall), 1954 v L; (with Aston Villa), 1957 v E (2); 1958 v D, Pol, A; 1959 v Pol, Cz; 1960 v Se, Ch, WG, Se; 1961 v W, N; (with Huddersfield T), 1961 v S; 1962 v A; 1963 v Ic (2) (18)
Scannell, T. (Southend U), 1954 v L (1)
Sloan, J. W. (Arsenal), 1946 v P, Sp (2)
Smyth, M. (Shamrock R), 1969 v Pol (sub) (1)
Squires, J. (Shelbourne), 1934 v Ho (1)
Stapleton, F. (Arsenal), 1977 v T, F, Sp, Bul; 1978 v Bul, N, D; 1979 v Ni, E (sub), D, WG, Arg; 1980 v W, Bul, Ni, E, Cy; 1981 v Ho, Bel, F, Cy, Bel, Cz, WG 'B', Pol; (with Manchester U), 1982 v Ho, F, Alg; 1983 v Ho, Sp, Ic, Ma, Sp (33)
Stevenson, A. E. (Dolphin), 1932 v Ho; (with Everton), 1947 v E, Sp, P; 1948 v P, Sp; 1949 v Sw (7)
Strahan, F. (Shelbourne), 1964 v Pol, N, E; 1965 v Pol; 1966 v WG (5)
Sullivan, J. (Fordsons), 1928 v Bel (1)
Swan, M. M. G. (Drumcondra), 1960 v Se (sub) (1)
Synnott, N. (Shamrock R), 1978 v T, Pol; 1979 v Ni (3)

Thomas, P. (Waterford), 1974 v Pol, Br (2)
Traynor, T. J. (Southampton), 1954 v L; 1962 v A; 1963 v Ic (2), S; 1964 v A (2), Sp (8)
Treacy, R. C. P. (WBA), 1966 v WG; 1967 v Sp, Cz; 1968 v Cz; (with Charlton Ath), 1968 v Pol; 1969 v Pol, Cz, D; 1970 v S, D, H (sub), Pol (sub), WG (sub); 1971 v Pol, Se (sub), Se, I, A; (with Swindon T), 1972 v Ir, Ec, Ch, P; 1973 v USSR, F, USSR, Pol, F, N; 1974 v Pol; (with Preston NE), 1974 v Br; 1975 v USSR, Sw (2); 1976 v T, N (sub), Pol (sub); (with WBA), 1977 v F, Pol; 1978 (with Shamrock R), v T, Pol (2); 1980 v Cz (sub) (42)
Tuohy, L. (Shamrock R), 1956 v Y; 1959 v Cz (2); (with Newcastle U), 1962 v A; 1963 v Ic (2); (with Shamrock R), 1964 v A; 1965 v Bel (8)
Turner, A. (Celtic), 1963 v S; 1964 v Sp (2)
Turner, C. J. (Southend U), 1936 v Sw; 1937 v G, H, Sw, F; (with West Ham U), 1938 v N (2), Cz, Pol; 1939 v H (10)

Vernon, J. (Belfast Celtic), 1946 v P, Sp (2)

Waddock, G. (QPR), 1980 v Sw, Arg; 1981 v W, Pol (sub); 1982 v Alg; 1983 v Ic, Ma, Sp (8)
Walsh, D. J. (WBA), 1946 v P, Sp; 1947 v Sp, P; 1948 v P, Sp; 1949 v Sw, P, Se, Sp; 1950 v E, Fi, Se; 1951 v N; (with Aston Villa), v Arg, N; 1952 v Sp; 1953 v A; 1954 v F (2) (20)
Walsh, J. (Limerick), 1982 v Tr (1)
Walsh, M. (Blackpool), 1976 v N, Pol; 1977 v F (sub), Pol; (with Everton), 1979 v Ni (sub); (with QPR), D (sub), Bul, WG (sub), Arg; (with Porto), 1981 v Bel (sub), Cz; 1982 v Alg (sub); 1983 v Sp (13)
Walsh, M. (Everton), 1982 v Ch, Br, Tr; 1983 v Sp, (with Norwich C), Ic (5)
Walsh, W. (Manchester C), 1947 v E, Sp, P; 1948 v P, Sp; 1949 v Bel; 1950 v E, Se, Bel (9)
Waters, J. (Grimsby T), 1977 v T; 1980 v Ni (sub) (2)
Watters, F. (Shelbourne), 1926 v I (1)
Weir, E. (Clyde), 1939 v H (2), G (3)
Whelan, R. (St Patrick's Ath), 1964 v A, E (sub) (2)
Whelan, R. (Liverpool), 1981 v Cz (sub); 1982 v Ho (sub), F; 19832 v Ic, Ma, Sp (6)
Whelan, W. (Manchester U), 1956 v Ho; 1957 v D, E (2) (4)
White, J. J. (Bohemians), 1928 v Bel (1)
Whittaker, R. (Chelsea), 1959 v Cz (1)
Williams, J. (Shamrock R), 1938 v N (1)

BRITISH CHAMPIONSHIP 1982–83

Wembley Stadium, Wednesday, 23 February 1983

England (1) 2 *Butcher, Neal pen.* **Wales (1) 1** *Rush* 24,000

England: Shilton (Southampton); Neal (Liverpool), Statham (West Bromwich A), Lee (Liverpool), Martin (West Ham U), Butcher (Ipswich T), Mabbutt (Tottenham H), Blissett (Watford), Mariner (Ipswich T), Cowans (Aston Villa), Devonshire (West Ham U).
Wales: Southall (Everton)*; Jones (Chelsea), Ratcliffe (Everton), Mahoney (Swansea C), Price (Tottenham H), Jackett (Watford), Davies (Fulham), Flynn (Burnley), Rush (Liverpool), Thomas (Stoke C), R. James (Swansea C). *Substitutes:* Berry (Stoke C) for Jones, L. James (Sunderland) for Mahoney. **Southall was on loan from Everton to Port Vale at time of match.*

Hampden Park, Tuesday, 24 May 1983

Scotland (0) 0 Northern Ireland (0) 0 16,238

Scotland: Thomson (St Mirren); Dawson (Rangers), Gough (Dundee U), Simpson (Aberdeen), Hegarty (Dundee U) (Captain), Narey (Dundee U), Wark (Ipswich T), Bannon (Dundee U), Gray A. (Wolverhampton W), Burns (Celtic), Nicholas (Celtic). *Substitute:* Strachan (Aberdeen) for Simpson.
Northern Ireland: Jennings (Arsenal); Nicholl J. (Toronto Blizzards), Donaghy (Luton T), O'Neill J. (Leicester C), McClelland (Rangers), O'Neill (Norwich C) (Captain), Mullan (Glentoran), McIlroy (Stoke C), Armstrong (Watford), Hamilton (Burnley), Stewart (Queen's Park R). *Substitutes:* Nicholl C. (Southampton) for O'Neill J., and Brotherston (Blackburn R) for Hamilton.

Cardiff, Saturday, 28 May 1983

Wales (0) 0 Scotland (1) 2 *Gray A., Brazil* 14,000

Wales: Southall (Everton); Jones (Chelsea), Price (Tottenham H) (Captain), Ratcliffe (Everton), Slatter (Bristol R), Flynn (Burnley), Lowndes (Newport Co), Jackett (Watford), Thomas (Stoke C), Davies (Fulham), Charles (Swansea). *Substitute:* Nicholas (Arsenal) for Lowndes.
Scotland: Leighton (Aberdeen); Gough (Dundee U), Gray F. (Leeds U), Souness (Liverpool) (Captain), McLeish (Aberdeen), Miller (Aberdeen), Strachan (Aberdeen), Narey (Dundee U), Gray A. (Wolverhampton W), Brazil (Tottenham H), Bannon (Dundee U).

Belfast, Saturday, 28 May 1983

Northern Ireland (0) 0 England (0) 0 22,000

Northern Ireland: Jennings (Arsenal); Nicholl J. (Toronto Blizzards), Nicholl C. (Southampton), Donaghy (Luton T), McClelland (Rangers), O'Neill M. (Norwich C) (Captain), McIlroy (Stoke C), Armstrong (Watford), Hamilton (Burnley), Mullan (Glentoran), Stewart (Queen's Park R). *Substitute:* Brotherston (Blackburn R) for Mullan.
England: Shilton (Southampton) (Captain); Neal (Liverpool), Butcher (Ipswich T), Roberts (Tottenham H), Sansom (Arsenal), Mabbutt (Tottenham H), Hoddle (Tottenham H), Cowans (Aston Villa), Blissett (Watford), Withe (Aston Villa), Francis (Sampdoria). *Substitute:* Barnes (Watford) for Blissett.

Belfast, Tuesday, 31 May 1983

Northern Ireland (0) 0 Wales (0) 1 *Davies G.* 8,000

Northern Ireland: Jennings (Arsenal), Nicholl J. (Toronto Blizzards), McClelland (Rangers), Nicholl C. (Southampton), Donaghy (Luton T), McIlroy (Stoke C), Brotherston (Blackburn R), Armstrong (Watford), Hamilton (Burnley), Mullan (Glentoran), Stewart (Queen's Park R). *Substitute:* Cleary (Glentoran) for Stewart.
Wales: Southall (Everton); Hopkins (Fulham), Price (Tottenham H), Ratcliffe (Everton), Jones (Chelsea), Davies A. (Manchester U), Flynn (Burnley), Nicholas (Arsenal), Thomas (Stoke C), Davies G. (Fulham), Charles (Swansea C). *Substitute:* Giles (Crystal Palace) for Price.

Wembley, Wednesday, 1 June 1983

England (1) 2 *Robson, Cowans* **Scotland (0) (0)** 84,000

England: Shilton (Southampton) (Captain); Neal (Liverpool), Sansom (Arsenal), Lee (Liverpool), Roberts (Tottenham H), Butcher (Ipswich T), Robson (Manchester U), Francis (Sampdoria), Withe (Aston Villa), Hoddle (Tottenham H), Cowans (Aston Villa). *Substitutes:* Mabbutt (Tottenham H) for Robson, Blissett (Watford) for Withe.
Scotland: Leighton (Aberdeen); Gough (Dundee U), McLeish (Aberdeen), Miller (Aberdeen), Gray F. (Leeds U), Narey (Dundee U), Strachan (Aberdeen), Souness (Liverpool) (Captain), Gray A. (Wolverhampton W), Nicholas (Celtic), Bannon (Dundee U). *Substitutes:* Brazil (Tottenham H) for Bannon, Wark (Ipswich T) for Nicholas.

FINAL TABLE

	P	*W*	*D*	*L*	*F*	*A*	*Pts*
England	3	2	1	0	4	1	5
Scotland	3	1	1	1	2	2	3
N. Ireland	3	0	2	1	0	1	2
Wales	3	1	0	2	2	4	2

OTHER BRITISH INTERNATIONAL MATCHES 1982–83

Wembley, Wednesday, 13 Oct, 1983

England (0) 1 *(Woodcock)*

West Germany (0) 2 *(Rummenigge 2)* 68,000

England: Shilton (Southampton); Mabbutt (Tottenham H), Sansom (Arsenal), Thompson (Liverpool), Butcher (Ipswich T), Wilkins (Manchester U), Hill (Luton T), Regis (WBA), Mariner (Ipswich T), Armstrong (Southampton), Devonshire (West Ham U). *Subs:* Woodcock (Arsenal) for Mariner, Blissett (Watford) for Regis, Rix (Arsenal) for Armstrong.
West Germany: Schumacher; Kaltz, Strack, Forster K-H., Forster B., Dremmler, Briegel, Meier, Allofs, Matthaus, Rummenigge. *Subs:* Littbarski for Meier, Hieronymus for Forster K-H., Milewski for Allofs.

Cardiff, Sunday, 12 June, 1983

Wales (1) 1 *(Flynn)*

Brazil (0) 1 *(Isidoro)*

Wales: Southall (Everton); Hopkins (Fulham), Jones (Chelsea), Vaughan (Newport Co), Charles (Swansea C), Ratcliffe (Everton), Davies G. (Fulham), Flynn (Burnley), Giles (Crystal P), Thomas (Stoke C), Davies A. (Manchester U). *Subs:* Lewis (Swansea C) for Charles, Lowndes (Newport Co) for Giles.
Brazil: Leao, Betao, Marcio, Luizinho, Bordinho, Batista, Carlos Alberto Borges, Pita, Socrates, Careca, Eder. *Subs:* Jonghinho for Carlos Alberto Borges, Paulo Isidoro for Pita.

Sydney, Sunday 11 June, 1983

Australia (0) 0

England (0) 0

England: Shilton (Southampton); Thomas (Coventry C), Statham (WBA), Williams (Southampton), Osman, Butcher (Ipswich T), Barham (Norwich C), Gregory (QPR), Blissett (Watford), Francis (Sampdoria), Cowans (Aston Villa). *Subs:* Barnes (Watford) for Statham, Walsh (Luton T) for Blissett.
Australia: Greedy; Davidson, Jennings, Yankos, Ratcliffe, O'Connor S., Watson, Cant, Kosmina, Katholos, O'Connor P. *Subs:* Stone for Watson, Mitchell for O'Connor P.

Brisbane, Wednesday 15 June, 1983

Australia (0) 0

England (0) 1 *(Walsh)*

Australia: Greedy; Davidson, Jennings, Yankos, Ratcliffe, O'Connor S., Watson, Cant, Kosmina, Katholos, O'Connor P. *Subs:* Murphy, Mitchell.
England: Shilton (Southampton); Neal (Liverpool), Statham (WBA), Barham (Norwich C), Osman, Butcher (Ipswich T), Gregory (QPR), Francis (Sampdoria), Walsh (Luton T), Cowans (Aston Villa), Barnes (Watford). *Sub:* Williams (Southampton) for Statham.

Melbourne, Sunday, 19 June, 1983

Australia (1) 1 *(Neal og)*

England (1) 1 *(Francis)*

Australia: Greedy; Davidson, Jennings, Yankos, Ratcliffe, O'Connor S., Watson, Cant, Kosmina, O'Connor P., Murphy.
England: Shilton (Southampton); Neal (Liverpool), Pickering (Sunderland), Lee (Liverpool), Osman, Butcher (Ipswich T), Gregory (QPR), Francis (Sampdoria), Walsh (Luton T), Cowans (Aston Villa), Barnes (Watford). *Subs:* Spink (Aston Villa) for Shilton, Thomas (Coventry C) for Neal.

Vancouver, Sunday, 12 June, 1983

Canada (0) 0

Scotland (1) 2 *(Strachan* pen, *McGhee)*

Canada: Not available.
Scotland: Thomson (St Mirren); Gough (Dundee U), Dawson (Rangers), Aitken (Celtic), McLeish (Aberdeen), Miller (Aberdeen) (capt), Strachan (Aberdeen), Narey (Dundee U), Nicholas (Celtic), Sturrock (Dundee U), Bannon (Dundee U). *Subs:* McGhee (Aberdeen) for Nicholas, Souness (Liverpool) for Strachan.

Edmonton, Thursday, 16 June, 1983

Canada (0) 0

Scotland (1) 3 *(Nicholas, Gough, Souness)*

Canada: Not available.
Scotland: Leighton (Aberdeen); Gough (Dundee U), Gray F. (Leeds U), Narey (Dundee U), McLeish (Aberdeen), Miller (Aberdeen), Strachan (Aberdeen), Souness (Liverpool) (capt), Nicholas (Celtic), McGhee (Aberdeen), Sturrock (Dundee U). *Subs:* Aitken (Celtic) for Strachan, Gray A. (Wolverhampton W) for McGhee.

Toronto, Sunday, 19 June, 1983

Canada (0)

Scotland (2) 2 *(Gray A. 2)*

Canada: Turner; Wilson, Bridge, Moore, Lee, Gray, Miller, Connor, Felix, Mitchell, Roe.
Scotland: Leighton (Aberdeen); Gough (Dundee U), Dawson (Rangers), Narey (Dundee U), McLeish (Aberdeen), Miller (Aberdeen), Aitken (Celtic), Souness (Liverpool) (capt), Gray A. (Wolverhampton W), Sturrock (Dundee U), Nicholas (Celtic). *Sub:* Strachan (Aberdeen) for Gray A.

INTERNATIONAL

The oldest player to appear for any of the 'home' countries in a full International match was **Billy Meredith**, who was nearly 46 years of age when he played for Wales v England on 15 March, 1920.

Billy Wright of Wolverhampton Wanderers, set up a world record by playing in 70 consecutive internationals for England, from 1951 and 1959.

The record number of players from the same club in an England team is seven: Frank Moss, George Male, Eddie Hapgood, Wilf Copping, Raymond Bowden, Ted Drake and Cliff Bastin, all of **Arsenal**, played against Italy at Highbury on 14 November, 1934.

The England team twice included all **Corinthian** players in the 1890s, but this cannot be considered because the Corinthians were a combined eleven, most of their players also playing with other clubs.

The England team that won the World Cup in 1966 created a record for the country by remaining unchanged in six consecutive Internationals. The Quarter-Final, Semi-Final, Final and the next three matches.

England's longest run without defeat is one of **20 games** between 1889 and 1896.

The first representative game was played at Battersea Park, 31 March, 1866. **London** beating **Sheffield** by two goals and four 'touch downs' to nil.

The first official **England v Scotland** International match was played at the West of Scotland cricket ground, Partick on 30 November, 1872 and resulted in a 0-0 draw.

Wales played their first International in 1876, losing 0-4 to Scotland in Glasgow. Ireland's first International match was against England at Bloomfield, Belfast, when the visitors won 13-0.

Caps were first awarded for International matches in 1886.

England's first defeat on foreign soil in a full International was 3-4 by **Spain** in Madrid in 1929.

England's first defeat by a continental country at Wembley was in 1953 when **Hungary** won 6-3, and Scotland's first home defeat by a foreign team was at Hampden Park in 1950 when **Austria** won 1-0.

Billy Wright became the first International in Britain to gain 100 caps when he captained England against Scotland at Wembley in April 1959.

Terry Venables was the first player to win England International honours at Five levels: Schools, Youth, Amateur, Under 23, and Full.

The first full International to be played entirely under **floodlights** in Britain took place at Wembley in 1963 when England beat Northern Ireland 8-3.

The first instance of a **substitute** in a Home International Championship game was at Wrexham in 1889 when Pugh of Rhostyllen took over from the injured S. G. Gillam in the Welsh goal against Scotland.

England's first Substitute in a full International was **Jimmy Mullen (Wolves)** who took over from the injured **Jackie Milburn** after 10 minutes of the game against Belgium in Brussels, 18th May, 1950.

Floodlights were first switched on during an International match in England in November 1955 at Wembley when England beat Spain.

The first Fourth Division player to be capped by his country in a full international was **Vic Rouse** of **Crystal Palace** who played in goal for Wales against Northern Ireland in 1959.

Harold Fleming played eleven times for England before World War One while playing for **Swindon Town** who were competing in the Southern League.

When England lost to overseas opposition in this country for the first time, Hungary beat them at Wembley 6-3 in November 1953, and **Blackpool** had four players in the side: **Stanley Matthews**, **Stan Mortensen**, **Harry Johnstone** and **Ernie Taylor**.

In 1950–51 Second Division **Barnsley** had five Internationals on their books: **Tim Ward (England)**, **John Kelly (Scotland)**, **Eddie McMorran**, **Danny Blanchflower** and **Pat Kelly (N. Ireland)**.

HAT TRICKS (OR BETTER) - ENGLAND 1946–83

		Match result
5	M. Macdonald v Cyprus, Wembley, April 16, 1975	5-0
4	T. Lawton v Holland, Huddersfield, Nov 27, 1946	8-2
	v Portugal, Lisbon, May 27, 1947	10-0
	S. Mortensen v Portugal, Lisbon, May 27, 1947	10-0
	J. Rowley v N Ireland, Maine Road, Nov 16, 1949	9-2
	T. Finney v Portugal, Lisbon, May 14, 1950 (2 penalties)	5-2
	D. Wilshaw v Scotland, Wembley, April 2, 1955*	7-2
	J. Greaves v N Ireland, Wembley, Nov 20, 1963	8-3
	v Norway, Oslo, June 29, 1966	6-1
	R. Hunt v USA, New York, May 27, 1964	10-0
3	W. Mannion v N Ireland, Belfast, Sept 28, 1946	7-2
	S. Mortensen v Sweden, Highbury, Nov 19, 1947	4-2
	v N Ireland, Belfast, Oct 19, 1948	6-2
	J. Milburn v Wales, Cardiff, Oct 15, 1949	4-1
	R. Bentley v Wales, Wembley, Nov 10, 1954	3-2
	T. Taylor v Denmark, Wolverhampton, Dec 5, 1956	5-2
	v Eire, Wembley, May 8, 1957	5-1
	J. Haynes v Russia, Wembley, Oct 22, 1958	5-0
	R. Charlton v USA, Los Angeles, May 28, 1959	8-1
	v Mexico, Wembley, May 10, 1961	8-0
	v Switzerland, Basle, June 5, 1963	8-1
	v Luxembourg, Luxembourg, Oct 19, 1960	9-0
	J. Greaves v Luxembourg, Luxembourg, Oct 19, 1960	9-0
	v Scotland, Wembley, April 15, 1961	9-3
	v Peru, Lima, May 20, 1962	4-0
	v N Ireland, Belfast, Oct 3, 1964	4-3
	T. Paine v N Ireland, Wembley, Nov 20, 1963	8-3
	J. Byrne v Portugal, Wembley, May 17, 1964	4-3
	F. Pickering v USA, New York, May 27, 1964	10-0
	G. Hurst v West Germany, Wembley, July 30, 1966 (World Cup Final)	4-2
	v France, Wembley, March 12, 1969	5-0

* Record against Scotland.

LEADING INTERNATIONAL GOALSCORERS

(Career Goals per match)

The most successful goalscorers in terms of goals per game in International matches:

		Goals per game	*Goals*	*Caps*
1	Ernst Willimowski (Poland & Germany)	1·43	43	30
2	Hughie Gallagher (Scotland)	1·33	24	18
3	Gunnar Nordahl (Sweden)	1·30	43	33
4	Sven Rydell (Sweden)	1·13	49	43
5	Sandor Kocsis (Hungary)	1·10	75	68
	Erich Probst (Austria)	1·10	22	20
7	Gerd Müller (West Germany)	1·09	68	62
8	Pelé (Brazil)	1·3	96	93
	Just Fontaine (France)	1·03	30	29
10	Ferenc Puskas (Hungary & Spain)	0·96	85	88
11	Luigi Riva (Italy)	0·88	35	39
12	Silvio Piola (Italy)	0·88	30	34
13	Ernst Pol (Poland)	0·82	40	49
14	Alfredo Di Stefano (Argentina & Spain)	0·78	29	37
15	Jimmy Greaves (England)	0·77	44	57
	Erich Hof (Austria)	0·77	28	36
17	Wlodzimierz Lubanski (Poland)	0·62	46	67
	Giuseppe Meazza (Italy)	0·62	33	53
19	Hans-Jurgen Kreische (East Germany)	0·60	24	40
20	Uwe Seeler (West Germany)	0·59	43	72

THE WORLD CUP 1930–1982

URUGUAY 1930

Pool 1

France 4, Mexico 1
Argentina 1, France 0
Chile 3, Mexico 0
Chile 1, France 0
Argentina 6, Mexico 3
Argentina 3, Chile 1

	P	*W*	*D*	*L*	*F*	*A*	*Pts*
Argentina	3	3	0	0	10	4	6
Chile	3	2	0	1	5	3	4
France	3	1	0	2	4	3	2
Mexico	3	0	0	3	4	13	0

Pool 2

Yugoslavia 2, Brazil 1
Yugoslavia 4, Bolivia 0
Brazil 4, Bolivia 0

	P	*W*	*D*	*L*	*F*	*A*	*Pts*
Yugoslavia	2	2	0	0	6	1	4
Brazil	2	1	0	1	5	2	2
Bolivia	2	0	0	2	0	8	0

Pool 3

Rumania 3, Peru 1
Uruguay 1, Peru 0
Uruguay 4, Rumania 0

	P	*W*	*D*	*L*	*F*	*A*	*Pts*
Uruguay	2	2	0	0	5	0	4
Rumania	2	1	0	1	3	5	2
Peru	2	0	0	2	1	4	0

Pool 4

United States 3, Belgium 0
United States 3, Paraguay 0
Paraguay 1, Belgium 0

	P	*W*	*D*	*L*	*F*	*A*	*Pts*
United States	2	2	0	0	6	0	4
Paraguay	2	1	0	1	1	3	2
Belgium	2	0	0	2	0	4	0

Semi-Finals

Argentina 6, United States 1
Uruguay 6, Yugoslavia 1

Final (Montevideo, 30 July, 1930)

Uruguay (1) 4, Argentina (2) 2

Uruguay: Ballesteros; Nasazzi (capt), Mascheroni, Andrade, Fernandez, Gestido, Dorado, Scarone, Castro, Cea, Iriarte.

Argentina: Botasso; Della Torre, Paternoster, Evaristo J., Monti, Suarez, Peucelle, Varallo, Stabile, Ferreira (capt), Evaristo M.

Scorers: Dorado, Cea, Iriarte, Castro for Uruguay; Peucelle, Stabile for Argentina.

Leading scorer: Stabile (Argentina) 8.

ITALY 1934

First Round

Italy 7, United States 1
Czechoslovakia 2, Rumania 1
Germany 5, Belgium 2
Austria 3, France 2
Spain 3, Brazil 1
Switzerland 3, Holland 2
Sweden 3, Argentina 2
Hungary 4, Egypt 2

Second Round

Germany 2, Sweden 1
Austria 2, Hungary 1
Italy 1, Spain 1
Italy 1, Spain 0 *replay*
Czechoslovakia 3, Switzerland 2

Semi-Finals

Czechoslovakia 3, Germany 1 (in Rome)
Italy 1, Austria 0 (in Milan)

Third Place Match (Naples)

Germany 3, Austria 2

Final (Rome, 10 June, 1934)

Italy (0) (1) 2, Czechoslovakia (0) (1) 1 aet

Italy: Combi (capt); Monzeglio, Allemandi; Ferraris IV, Monti, Bertolini, Guaita, Meazza, Schiavio, Ferrari, Orsi.

Czechoslovakia: Planicka (capt); Zenisek, Ctyroky, Kostalek, Cambal, Krcil; Junek, Švoboda, Sobotka, Nejedly, Puc.

Scorers: Orsi, Schiavio for Italy; Puc for Czechoslovakia.

Leading scorers: Schiavio (Italy), Nejedly (Czechoslovakia), Conen (Germany) 4 each.

FRANCE 1938

First Round

Switzerland 1, Germany 1
Switzerland 4, Germany 2 *replay*
Cuba 3, Rumania 3
Cuba 2, Rumania 1 *replay*
Hungary 6, Dutch East Indies 0
France 3, Belgium 1
Czechoslovakia 3, Holland 0
Brazil 6, Poland 5
Italy 2, Norway 1

Second Round

Sweden 8, Cuba 0
Hungary 2, Switzerland 0
Italy 3, France 1
Brazil 1, Czechoslovakia 1
Brazil 2, Czechoslovakia 1 *replay*

Semi-Finals

Italy 2, Brazil 1 (in Marseilles)
Hungary 5, Sweden 1 (in Paris)

Third Place Match (Bordeaux)

Brazil 4, Sweden 2

Final (Paris, 19 June, 1938)

Italy (3) 4, Hungary (1) 2
Italy: Olivieri; Foni, Rava; Serantoni, Andreolo, Locatelli; Biavati, Meazza (capt), Piola, Ferrari, Colaussi.

Hungary: Szabo; Polgar, Biro; Szalay, Szucs, Lazar; Sas, Vincze, Sarosi (capt), Szengeller, Titkos.

Scorers: Colaussi 2, Piola 2 for Italy; Titkos, Sarosi for Hungary.

Leading Scorer: Leonidas (Brazil) 8.

BRAZIL 1950

Pool 1

Brazil 4, Mexico 0
Yugoslavia 3, Switzerland 0
Yugoslavia 4, Mexico 1
Brazil 2, Switzerland 2
Brazil 2, Yugoslavia 0
Switzerland 2, Mexico 1

	P	*W*	*D*	*L*	*F*	*A*	*Pts*
Brazil	3	2	1	0	8	2	5
Yugoslavia	3	2	0	1	7	3	4
Switzerland	3	1	1	1	4	6	3
Mexico	3	0	0	3	2	10	0

Pool 2

Spain 3, United States 1
England 2, Chile 0
United States 1, England 0
Spain 2, Chile 0
Spain 1, England 0
Chile 5, United States 2

	P	*W*	*D*	*L*	*F*	*A*	*Pts*
Spain	3	3	0	0	6	1	6
England	3	1	0	2	2	2	2
Chile	3	1	0	2	5	6	2
United States	3	1	0	2	4	8	2

Pool 3

Sweden 3, Italy 2
Sweden 2, Paraguay 2
Italy 2, Paraguay 0

	P	*W*	*D*	*L*	*F*	*A*	*Pts*
Sweden	2	1	1	0	5	4	3
Italy	2	1	0	1	4	3	2
Paraguay	2	0	1	1	2	4	1

Pool 4

Uruguay 8, Bolivia 0

	P	*W*	*D*	*L*	*F*	*A*	*Pts*
Uruguay	1	1	0	0	8	0	2
Bolivia	1	0	0	1	0	8	0

Final Pool

Final pool replaced knockout system.

Uruguay 2, Spain 2
Brazil 7, Sweden 1
Uruguay 3, Sweden 2
Brazil 6, Spain 1
Sweden 3, Spain 1

Uruguay (0) 2, Brazil (0) 1 (Rio de Janeiro, 16 July, 1950)

Uruguay: Maspoli; Matthias, Gonzales, Tejera; Gambetta, Varela (capt), Andrade; Ghiggia, Perez, Miguez, Schiaffino, Moran.

Brazil: Barbosa; Augusto (capt), Juvenal; Bauer, Danilo, Bigode; Friaça, Zizinho, Ademir, Jair, Chico.

Scorers: Schiffino, Ghiggia for Uruguay; Friaça for Brazil.

	P	*W*	*D*	*L*	*F*	*A*	*Pts*
Uruguay	3	2	1	0	7	5	5
Brazil	3	2	0	1	14	4	4
Sweden	3	1	0	2	6	11	2
Spain	3	0	1	2	4	11	1

Leading Scorer: Ademir (Brazil) 7

SWITZERLAND 1954

Group 1

Yugoslavia 1, France 0
Brazil 5, Mexico 0
France 3, Mexico 2
Brazil 1, Yugoslavia 1

	P	*W*	*D*	*L*	*F*	*A*	*Pts*
Brazil	2	1	1	0	6	1	3
Yugoslavia	2	1	1	0	2	1	3
France	2	1	0	1	3	3	2
Mexico	2	0	0	2	2	8	0

Group 2

Hungary 9, Korea 0
West Germany 4, Turkey 1
Hungary 8, West Germany 3
Turkey 7, Korea 0

	P	*W*	*D*	*L*	*F*	*A*	*Pts*
Hungary	2	2	0	0	17	3	4
West Germany	2	1	0	1	7	9	2
Turkey	2	1	0	1	8	4	2
Korea	2	0	0	2	0	16	0

Play-off: West Germany 7, Turkey 2

Group 3

Austria 1, Scotland 0
Uruguay 2, Czechoslovakia 0
Austria 5, Czechoslovakia 0
Uruguay 7, Scotland 0

	P	*W*	*D*	*L*	*F*	*A*	*Pts*
Uruguay	2	2	0	0	9	0	4
Austria	2	2	0	0	6	0	4
Czechoslovakia	2	0	0	2	0	7	0
Scotland	2	0	0	2	0	8	0

Group 4

England 4, Belgium 4
England 2, Switzerland 0
Switzerland 2, Italy 1
Italy 4, Belgium 1

	P	*W*	*D*	*L*	*F*	*A*	*Pts*
England	2	1	1	0	6	4	3
Italy	2	1	0	1	5	3	2
Switzerland	2	1	0	1	2	3	2
Belgium	2	0	1	1	5	8	1

Play-off: Switzerland 4, Italy 1

Quarter-Finals

West Germany 2, Yugoslavia 0
Hungary 4, Brazil 2
Austria 7, Switzerland 5
Uruguay 4, England 2

Semi-Finals

West Germany 6, Austria 1 (in Basle)
Hungary 4, Uruguay 2 (in Lausanne)

Third Place Match (Zurich)

Austria 3, Uruguay 1

Final (Berne, 4 July, 1954)

West Germany (2) 3, Hungary (2) 2

West Germany: Turek; Posipal, Kohlmeyer; Eckel, Liebrich, Mai; Rahn, Morlock, Walter O., Walter F. (capt), Schaefer.

Hungary: Grosics; Buzansky, Lantos; Bozsik, Lorant, Zakarias; Czibor, Kocsis, Hidegkuti, Puskas (capt), Toth J.

Scorers: Morlock, Rahn 2 for West Germany; Puskas, Czibor for Hungary.

Leading Scorer: Kocsis (Hungary) 11.

SWEDEN 1958

Group 1

West Germany 3, Argentina 1
Northern Ireland 1, Czechoslovakia 0
West Germany 2, Czechoslovakia 2
Argentina 3, Northern Ireland 1
West Germany 2, Northern Ireland 2
Czechoslovakia 6, Argentina 1

	P	*W*	*D*	*L*	*F*	*A*	*Pts*
West Germany	3	1	2	0	7	5	4
Czechoslovakia	3	1	1	1	8	4	3
Ireland	3	1	1	1	4	5	3
Argentina	3	1	0	2	5	10	2

Play-off: Northern Ireland 2, Czechoslovakia 1

Group 2

France 7, Paraguay 3
Yugoslavia 1, Scotland 1
Yugoslavia 3, France 2
Paraguay 3, Scotland 2
France 2, Scotland 1
Yugoslavia 3, Paraguay 3

	P	*W*	*D*	*L*	*F*	*A*	*Pts*
France	3	2	0	1	11	7	4
Yugoslavia	3	1	2	0	7	6	4
Paraguay	3	1	1	1	9	12	3
Scotland	3	0	1	2	4	6	1

Group 3

Sweden 3, Mexico 0
Hungary 1, Wales 1
Wales 1, Mexico 1
Sweden 2, Hungary 1
Sweden 0, Wales 0
Hungary 4, Mexico 0

	P	*W*	*D*	*L*	*F*	*A*	*Pts*
Sweden	3	2	1	0	5	1	5
Hungary	3	1	1	1	6	3	3
Wales	3	0	3	0	2	2	3
Mexico	3	0	1	2	1	8	1

Play-off: Wales 2, Hungary 1

Group 4

England 2, USSR 2
Brazil 3, Austria 0
England 0, Brazil 0
USSR 2, Austria 0
Brazil 2, USSR 0
England 2, Austria 2

	P	*W*	*D*	*L*	*F*	*A*	*Pts*
Brazil	3	2	1	0	5	0	5
England	3	0	3	0	4	4	3
USSR	3	1	1	1	4	4	3
Austria	3	0	1	2	2	7	1

Play-off: USSR 1, England 0

Quarter-Finals

France 4, Ireland 0
West Germany 1, Yugoslavia 0
Sweden 2, USSR 0
Brazil 1, Wales 0

Semi-Finals

Brazil 5, France 2 (in Stockholm)
Sweden 3, West Germany 1 (in Gothenburg)

Third Place Match (Gothenburg)

France 6, West Germany 3

Final (Stockholm, 29 June, 1958)

Brazil (2) 5, Sweden (1) 2

Brazil: Gilmar; Santos D., Santos N.; Zito, Bellini, Orlando, Garrincha, Didi, Vavà, Pelé, Zagalo.

Sweden: Svensson; Bergmark, Axbom; Boerjesson, Gustavsson, Parliag, Hamrin, Gren, Simonsson, Liedholm, Skoglund.

Scorers: Vavà 2, Pelé 2, Zagalo for Brazil; Liedholm, Simonsson for Sweden.

Leading Scorer: Fontaine (France) 13 (present record total).

CHILE 1962

Group 1

Uruguay 2, Colombia 1
USSR 2, Yugoslavia 0
Yugoslavia 3, Uruguay 1
USSR 4, Colombia 4
USSR 2, Uruguay 1
Yugoslavia 5, Colombia 0

	P	*W*	*D*	*L*	*F*	*A*	*Pts*
USSR	3	2	1	0	8	5	5
Yugoslavia	3	2	0	1	8	3	4
Uruguay	3	1	0	2	4	6	2
Colombia	3	0	1	2	5	11	1

Group 2

Chile 3, Switzerland 1
West Germany 0, Italy 0
Chile 2, Italy 0
West Germany 2, Switzerland 1
West Germany 2, Chile 0
Italy 3, Switzerland 0

	P	*W*	*D*	*L*	*F*	*A*	*Pts*
West Germany	3	2	1	0	4	1	5
Chile	3	2	0	1	5	3	4
Italy	3	1	1	1	3	2	3
Switzerland	3	0	0	3	2	8	0

Group 3

Brazil 2, Mexico 0
Czechoslovakia 1, Spain 0
Brazil 0, Czechoslovakia 0
Spain 1, Mexico 0
Brazil 2, Spain 1
Mexico 3, Czechoslovakia 1

	P	*W*	*D*	*L*	*F*	*A*	*Pts*
Brazil	3	2	1	0	4	1	5
Czechoslovakia	3	1	1	1	2	3	3
Mexico	3	1	0	2	3	4	2
Spain	3	1	0	2	2	3	2

Group 4

Argentina 1, Bulgaria 0
Hungary 2, England 1
England 3, Argentina 1
Hungary 6, Bulgaria 1
Argentina 0, Hungary 0
England 0, Bulgaria 0

	P	*W*	*D*	*L*	*F*	*A*	*Pts*
Hungary	3	2	1	0	8	2	5
England	3	1	1	1	4	3	3
Argentina	3	1	1	1	2	3	3
Bulgaria	3	0	1	2	1	7	1

Quarter-Finals

Yugoslavia 1, West Germany 0
Brazil 3, England 1
Chile 2, USSR 1
Czechoslovakia 1, Hungary 0

Semi-Finals

Brazil 4, Chile 2 (in Santiago)
Czechoslovakia 3, Yugoslavia 1 (in Viña del Mar)

Third Place Match (Santiago)

Chile 1, Yugoslavia 0

Final (Santiago, 17 June, 1962)

Brazil (1) 3, Czechoslovakia (1) 1

Brazil: Gilmar; Santos D., Mauro, Zozimo, Santos N.; Zito, Didi; Garrincha, Vavà, Amarildo, Zagalo.

Czechoslovakia: Schroiff; Tichy, Novak; Pluskal, Popluhar, Masopust, Pospichal, Scherer, Kvasniak, Kadraba, Jelinek.

Scorers: Amarildo, Zito, Vavà for Brazil; Masopust for Czechoslovakia.

Leading Scorer: Jerkovic (Yugoslavia) 5.

ENGLAND 1966

Group 1

England 0, Uruguay 0
France 1, Mexico 1
Uruguay 2, France 1
England 2, Mexico 0
Uruguay 0, Mexico 0
England 2, France 0

	P	*W*	*D*	*L*	*F*	*A*	*Pts*
England	3	2	1	0	4	0	5
Uruguay	3	1	2	0	2	1	4
Mexico	3	0	2	1	1	3	2
France	3	0	1	2	2	5	1

Group 2

West Germany 5, Switzerland 0
Argentina 2, Spain 1
Spain 2, Switzerland 1
Argentina 0, West Germany 0
Argentina 2, Switzerland 0
West Germany 2, Spain 1

	P	*W*	*D*	*L*	*F*	*A*	*Pts*
West Germany	3	2	1	0	7	1	5
Argentina	3	2	1	0	4	1	5
Spain	3	1	0	2	4	5	2
Switzerland	3	0	0	3	1	9	0

Group 3

Brazil 2, Bulgaria 0
Portugal 3, Hungary 1
Hungary 3, Brazil 1
Portugal 3, Bulgaria 0
Portugal 3, Brazil 1
Hungary 3, Bulgaria 1

	P	*W*	*D*	*L*	*F*	*A*	*Pts*
Portugal	3	3	0	0	9	2	6
Hungary	3	2	0	1	7	5	4
Brazil	3	1	0	2	4	6	2
Bulgaria	3	0	0	3	1	8	0

Group 4

USSR 3, North Korea 0
Italy 2, Chile 0
Chile 1, North Korea 1
USSR 1, Italy 0
North Korea 1, Italy 0
USSR 2, Chile 1

	P	*W*	*D*	*L*	*F*	*A*	*Pts*
USSR	3	3	0	0	6	1	6
North Korea	3	1	1	1	2	4	3
Italy	3	1	0	2	2	2	2
Chile	3	0	1	2	2	5	1

Quarter-Finals

England 1, Argentina 0
West Germany 4, Uruguay 0
Portugal 5, North Korea 3
USSR 2, Hungary 1

Semi-Finals

West Germany 2, USSR 1 (at Goodison Park)
England 2, Portugal 1 (at Wembley)

Third Place Match (Wembley)

Portugal 2, USSR 1

Final (Wembley, 30 July, 1966)

England (1) (2) 4, West Germany (1) (2) 2 aet

England: Banks; Cohen, Wilson; Stiles, Charlton J., Moore; Ball, Hurst, Hunt, Charlton R., Peters.

West Germany: Tilkowski; Hottges, Schulz, Weber, Schnellinger; Haller, Beckenbauer; Overath, Seeler, Held, Emmerich.

Scorers: Hurst 3, Peters for England; Haller, Weber for West Germany.

Leading Scorer: Eusebio (Portugal) 9.

MEXICO 1970

Group A

Mexico 0, USSR 0
Belgium 3, El Salvador 0
USSR 4, Belgium 1
Mexico 4, El Salvador 0
USSR 2, El Salvador 0
Belgium 0, Mexico 1

	P	*W*	*D*	*L*	*F*	*A*	*Pts*
USSR	3	2	1	0	6	1	5
Mexico	3	2	1	0	5	0	5
Belgium	3	1	0	2	4	5	2
El Salvador	3	0	0	3	0	9	0

Group B

Uruguay 2, Israel 0
Italy 1, Sweden 0
Uruguay 0, Italy 0
Israel 1, Sweden 1
Sweden 1, Uruguay 0
Israel 0, Italy 0

	P	*W*	*D*	*L*	*F*	*A*	*Pts*
Italy	3	1	2	0	1	0	4
Uruguay	3	1	1	1	2	1	3
Sweden	3	1	1	1	2	2	3
Israel	3	0	2	1	1	3	2

Group C

England 1, Rumania 0
Brazil 4, Czechoslovakia 1
Rumania 2, Czechoslovakia 1
Brazil 1, England 0
Brazil 3, Rumania 2
England 1, Czechoslovakia 0

	P	*W*	*D*	*L*	*F*	*A*	*Pts*
Brazil	3	3	0	0	8	3	6
England	3	2	0	1	2	1	4
Rumania	3	1	0	2	4	5	2
Czechoslovakia	3	0	0	3	2	7	0

Group D

Peru 3, Bulgaria 2
West Germany 2, Morocco 1
Peru 3, Morocco 0
West Germany 5, Bulgaria 2
West Germany 3, Peru 1
Bulgaria 1, Morocco 1

	P	*W*	*D*	*L*	*F*	*A*	*Pts*
West Germany	3	3	0	0	10	4	6
Peru	3	2	0	1	7	5	4
Bulgaria	3	0	1	2	5	9	1
Morocco	3	0	1	2	2	6	1

Quarter-Finals

Uruguay 1, USSR 0
Italy 4, Mexico 1
Brazil 4, Peru 2
West Germany 3, England 2

Semi-Finals

Italy 4, West Germany 3 (in Mexico City)
Brazil 3, Uruguay 1 (in Guadalajara)

Third Place Match (Mexico City)

West Germany 1, Uruguay 0

Final (Mexico City, 21 June, 1970)

Brazil (1) 4, Italy (1) 1

Brazil: Felix; Carlos Alberto, Brito, Piazza, Everaldo; Gerson, Clodoaldo; Jairzinho, Pelé, Tostão, Rivelino.

Italy: Albertosi; Burgnich, Cera, Rosato, Facchetti; Bertini (Juliano), Riva; Domenghini, Mazzola, De Sisti, Boninsegna (Rivera).

Scorers: Pelé, Gerson, Jairzinho, Carlos Alberto for Brazil; Boninsegna for Italy.

Leading Scorer: Müller (West Germany) 10.

WEST GERMANY 1974

Group 1

West Germany 1, Chile 0
East Germany 2, Australia 0
West Germany 3, Australia 0
East Germany 1, Chile 1
East Germany 1, West Germany 0
Chile 0, Australia 0

	P	*W*	*D*	*L*	*F*	*A*	*Pts*
East Germany	3	2	1	0	4	1	5
West Germany	3	2	0	1	4	1	4
Chile	3	0	2	1	1	2	2
Australia	3	0	1	2	0	5	1

Group 2

Brazil 0, Yugoslavia 0
Scotland 2, Zaire 0
Brazil 0, Scotland 0
Yugoslavia 9, Zaire 0
Scotland 1, Yugoslavia 1
Brazil 3, Zaire 0

	P	*W*	*D*	*L*	*F*	*A*	*Pts*
Yugoslavia	3	1	2	0	10	1	4
Brazil	3	1	2	0	3	0	4
Scotland	3	1	2	0	3	1	4
Zaire	3	0	0	3	0	14	0

Group 3

Holland 2, Uruguay 0
Sweden 0, Bulgaria 0
Holland 0, Sweden 0
Bulgaria 1, Uruguay 1
Holland 4, Bulgaria 1
Sweden 3, Uruguay 0

	P	*W*	*D*	*L*	*F*	*A*	*Pts*
Holland	3	2	1	0	6	1	5
Sweden	3	1	2	0	3	0	4
Bulgaria	3	0	2	1	2	5	2
Uruguay	3	0	1	2	1	6	1

Group 4

Italy 3, Haiti 1
Poland 3, Argentina 2
Argentina 1, Italy 1
Poland 7, Haiti 0
Argentina 4, Haiti 1
Poland 2, Italy 1

	P	*W*	*D*	*L*	*F*	*A*	*Pts*
Poland	3	3	0	0	12	3	6
Argentina	3	1	1	1	7	5	3
Italy	3	1	1	1	5	4	3
Haiti	3	0	0	3	2	14	0

Group A

Brazil 1, East Germany 0
Holland 4, Argentina 0
Holland 2, East Germany 0
Brazil 2, Argentina 1
Holland 2, Brazil 0
Argentina 1, East Germany 1

	P	*W*	*D*	*L*	*F*	*A*	*Pts*
Holland	3	3	0	0	8	0	6
Brazil	3	2	0	1	3	3	4
East Germany	3	0	1	2	1	4	1
Argentina	3	0	1	2	2	7	1

Group B

Poland 1, Sweden 0
West Germany 2, Yugoslavia 0
Poland 2, Yugoslavia 1
West Germany 4, Sweden 2
Sweden 2, Yugoslavia 1
West Germany 1, Poland 0

	P	*W*	*D*	*L*	*F*	*A*	*Pts*
West Germany	3	3	0	0	7	2	6
Poland	3	2	0	1	3	2	4
Sweden	3	1	0	2	4	6	2
Yugoslavia	3	0	0	3	2	6	0

Third Place Match (Munich)

Poland 1, Brazil 0

Final (Munich, 7 July, 1974)

West Germany (2) 2, Holland (1) 1

West Germany: Maier; Vogts, Schwarzenbeck, Beckenbauer, Breitner, Bonhof, Hoeness, Overath, Grabowski, Müller, Holzenbein.

Holland: Jongbloed; Suurbier, Rijsbergen (De Jong), Haan, Krol, Jansen, Van Hanegem, Neeskens, Rep, Cruyff, Rensenbrink (Van der Kerkhof R).

Scorers: Breitner (*pen*), Müller for West Germany; Neeskens (*pen*) for Holland.

Leading Scorer: Lato (Poland) 7.

ARGENTINA 1978

Group 1

Italy 2, France 1
Argentina 2, Hungary 1
Italy 3, Hungary 1
Argentina 2, France 1
France 3, Hungary 1
Italy 1, Argentina 0

	P	*W*	*D*	*L*	*F*	*A*	*Pts*
Italy	3	3	0	0	6	2	6
Argentina	3	2	0	1	4	3	4
France	3	1	0	2	5	5	2
Hungary	3	0	0	3	3	8	0

Group 2

West Germany 0, Poland 0
Tunisia 3, Mexico 1
Poland 1, Tunisia 0
West Germany 6, Mexico 0
Poland 3, Mexico 1
West Germany 0, Tunisia 0

	P	*W*	*D*	*L*	*F*	*A*	*Pts*
Poland	3	2	1	0	4	1	5
West Germany	3	1	2	0	6	0	4
Tunisia	3	1	1	1	3	2	3
Mexico	3	0	0	3	2	12	0

Group 3

Austria 2, Spain 1
Brazil 1, Sweden 1
Austria 1, Sweden 0
Brazil 0, Spain 0
Spain 1, Sweden 0
Brazil 1, Austria 0

	P	*W*	*D*	*L*	*F*	*A*	*Pts*
Austria	3	2	0	1	3	2	4
Brazil	3	1	2	0	2	1	4
Spain	3	1	1	1	2	2	3
Sweden	3	0	1	2	1	3	1

Group 4

Peru 3, Scotland 1
Holland 3, Iran 0
Scotland 1, Iran 1
Holland 0, Peru 0
Peru 4, Iran 1
Scotland 3, Holland 2

	P	*W*	*D*	*L*	*F*	*A*	*Pts*
Peru	3	2	1	0	7	2	5
Holland	3	1	1	1	5	3	3
Scotland	3	1	1	1	5	6	3
Iran	3	0	1	2	2	8	1

Group A

West Germany 0, Italy 0
Holland 5, Austria 1
Italy 1, Austria 0
Holland 2, West Germany 2
Holland 2, Italy 1
Austria 3, West Germany 2

	P	*W*	*D*	*L*	*F*	*A*	*Pts*
Holland	3	2	1	0	9	4	5
Italy	3	1	1	1	2	2	3
West Germany	3	0	2	1	4	5	2
Austria	3	1	0	2	4	8	2

Group B

Brazil 3, Peru 0
Argentina 2, Poland 0
Poland 1, Peru 0
Argentina 0, Brazil 0
Brazil 3, Poland 1
Argentina 6, Peru 0

	P	*W*	*D*	*L*	*F*	*A*	*Pts*
Argentina	3	2	1	0	8	0	5
Brazil	3	2	1	0	6	1	5
Poland	3	1	0	2	2	5	2
Peru	3	0	0	3	0	10	0

Third Place Match(Buenos Aires)

Brazil 2, Italy 1

Final (Buenos Aires, 25 June, 1978)

Argentina (1) (1) 3, Holland (0) (1) 1 aet

Argentina: Fillol; Passarella, Olquin, Galvan L., Tarantini, Ardiles (Larrosa), Gallego, Ortiz (Houseman), Bertoni, Luque, Kempes.

Holland: Jongbloed; Krol, Poortvliet, Brandts, Jansen (Suurbier), Haan, Neeskens, Van der Kerkhof W., Rep (Nanninga), Van der Kerkhof R., Resenbrink.

Scorers: Kempes 2, Bertoni for Argentina; Nanninga for Holland.

Leading Scorer: Kempes (Argentina) 6.

SPAIN 1982

Group 1

Italy 0, Poland o
Peru 0, Cameroon 0
Italy 1, Peru 1
Poland 0, Cameroon 0
Poland 5, Peru 1
Italy 1, Cameroon 1

	P	*W*	*D*	*L*	*F*	*A*	*Pts*
Poland	3	1	2	0	5	1	4
Italy	3	0	3	0	2	2	3
Cameroon	3	0	3	0	1	1	3
Peru	3	0	2	1	2	6	2

Group 2

Algeria 2, West Germany 1
Austria 1, Chile 0
West Germany 4, Chile 1
Austria 2, Algeria 0
Algeria 3, Chile 2
West Germany 1, Austria

	P	*W*	*D*	*L*	*F*	*A*	*Pts*
West Germany	3	2	0	1	6	3	4
Austria	3	2	0	1	3	1	4
Algeria	3	2	0	1	5	5	4
Chile	3	0	0	3	3	8	0

Group 3

Belgium 1, Argentina 0
Hungary 10, El Salvador 1
Argentina 4, Hungary 1
Belgium 1, El Salvador 0
Belgium 1, Hungary 1
Argentina 2, El Salvador 0

	P	*W*	*D*	*L*	*F*	*A*	*Pts*
Belgium	3	2	1	0	3	1	5
Argentina	3	2	0	1	6	2	4
Hungary	3	1	1	1	12	6	3
El Salvador	3	0	0	3	1	13	0

Group 4

England 3, France 1
Czechoslovakia 1, Kuwait 1
England 2, Czechoslovakia 0
France 4, Kuwait 1
France 1, Czechoslovakia 1
England 1 Kuwait 0

	P	*W*	*D*	*L*	*F*	*A*	*Pts*
England	3	3	0	0	6	1	6
France	3	1	1	1	6	5	3
Czechoslovakia	3	0	2	1	2	4	2
Kuwait	3	0	1	2	2	6	1

Group 5

Spain 1, Honduras 1
Northern Ireland 0, Yugoslavia 0
Spain 2, Yugoslavia 1
Honduras 1, Northern Ireland 1
Yugoslavia 1, Honduras 0
Northern Ireland 1, Spain 0

	P	*W*	*D*	*L*	*F*	*A*	*Pts*
Northern Ireland	3	1	2	0	2	1	4
Spain	3	1	1	1	3	3	3
Yugoslavia	3	1	1	1	2	2	3
Honduras	3	0	2	1	2	3	2

Group 6

Brazil 2, USSR 1
Scotland 5, New Zealand 2
Brazil 4, Scotland 1
USSR 3, New Zealand 0
Scotland 2, USSR 2
Brazil 4, New Zealand 0

	P	*W*	*D*	*L*	*F*	*A*	*Pts*
Brazil	3	3	0	0	10	2	6
USSR	3	1	1	1	6	4	3
Scotland	3	1	1	1	8	8	3
New Zealand	3	0	0	3	2	12	0

SECOND STAGE

Group A

Poland 3, Belgium 0
USSR 1, Belgium 0
Poland 0, USSR 0

	P	*W*	*D*	*L*	*F*	*A*	*Pts*
Poland	2	1	1	0	3	0	3
USSR	2	1	1	0	1	0	3
Belgium	2	0	0	2	0	4	0

Group B

West Germany 0, England 0
West Germany 2, Spain 1
Spain 0, England 0

	P	*W*	*D*	*L*	*F*	*A*	*Pts*
West Germany	2	1	1	0	2	1	3
England	2	0	2	0	0	0	2
Spain	2	0	1	1	1	2	1

Group C

Italy 2, Argentina 1
Brazil 3, Argentina 1
Italy 3, Brazil 2

	P	*W*	*D*	*L*	*F*	*A*	*Pts*
Italy	2	2	0	0	5	3	4
Brazil	2	1	0	1	5	4	2
Argentina	2	0	0	2	2	5	0

Group D

France 1, Austria 0
Northern Ireland 2, Austria 2
France 4, Northern Ireland 1

	P	*W*	*D*	*L*	*F*	*A*	*Pts*
France	2	2	0	0	5	1	4
Austria	2	0	1	1	2	3	1
Northern Ireland	2	0	1	1	3	6	1

Semi-Finals

Italy 2, Poland 0 (in Barcelona)
West Germany 3, France 3 (in Seville)
(*West Germany won on penalties 5-4*)

Third Place Match (Alicante)

Poland 3, France 2

Final (Madrid, 11 July, 1982)

Italy (0) 3, West Germany (0) 1

Italy: Zoff; Bergomi, Cabrini, Collovati, Scirea, Gentile, Oriali, Tardelli, Conti, Graziani (Altobelli) (Causio), Rossi.

West Germany: Schumacher; Kaltz, Forster K. H., Stielike, Forster B., Breitner, Dremmler (Hrubesch), Littbarski, Briegel, Rummenigge (Muller), Fischer.

Scorers: Rossi, Tardelli, Altobelli for Italy, Breitner for West Germany.

Leading Scorer: Rossi (Italy) 6.

GOALSCORING AND ATTENDANCES IN WORLD CUP FINAL ROUNDS

	Matches	*Goals (avge)*	*Attendance (avge)*
1930, Uruguay	18	70 (3.8)	434,500 (24,138)
1934, Italy	17	70 (4.1)	395,000 (23,235)
1938, France	18	84 (4.6)	483,000 (26,833)
1950, Brazil	22	88 (4.0)	1,337,000 (60,772)
1954, Switzerland	26	140 (5.3)	943,000 (36,270)
1958, Sweden	35	126 (3.6)	868,000 (24,800)
1962, Chile	32	89 (2.7)	776,000 (24,250)
1966, England	32	89 (2.7)	1,614,677 (50,458)
1970, Mexico	32	95 (2.9)	1,673,975 (52,311)
1974, West Germany	38	97 (2.5)	1,774,022 (46,684)
1978, Argentina	38	102 (2.6)	1,610,215 (42,374)
1982, Spain	52	146 (2.8)	1,766,277 (33,967)

WORLD CUP (1930–1982)

LEADING GOALSCORERS

1930	Stabile (Argentina)	8
1934	Schiavio (Italy)	4
	Nejedly (Czechoslovakia)	4
	Conen (Germany)	4
1938	Leonidas (Brazil)	8
1950	Ademir (Brazil)	7
1954	Kocsis (Hungary)	11
1958	Fontaine (France)	13
1962	Albert (Hungary)	4
	Garrincha (Brazil)	4
	Ivanov (Russia)	4
	Jerkovic (Yugoslavia)	4
	L. Sanchez (Chile)	4
	Vava (Brazil)	4
1966	Eusebio (Portugal)	9
1970	Müller (West Germany)	10
1974	Lato (Poland)	7
1978	Kempes (Argentina)	6
1982	Rossi (Italy)	6

OVERALL TOP SCORERS IN WORLD CUP FINAL STAGES

Müller (West Germany)	14
Fontaine (France)	13
Pelé (Brazil)	12
Kocsis (Hungary)	11
Rahn (West Germany)	10
Lato (Poland)	10
Seeler (West Germany)	10
Ademir (Brazil)	9
Cubillas (Peru)	9
Eusebio (Portugal)	9
Jairzinho (Brazil)	9
Rossi (Italy)	9
Vava (Brazil)	9
Leonidas (Brazil)	8
Morlock (West Germany)	8
Rummenigge (West Germany)	8
Schiaffino (Uruguay)	8
Stabile (Argentina)	8
Rep (Holland)	7
Tichy (Hungary)	7
Zsengeller (Hungary)	7

1982 WORLD CUP – GOALSCORERS

6 ROSSI (Italy).

5 Rummenigge (West Germany).

4 Boniek (Poland), Zico (Brazil).

3 Kiss (Hungary), Armstrong (N Ireland), Falcao (Brazil), Giresse (France).

2 Six, Genghini, Rocheteau, Platini (all France); Socrates, Serginho, Eder (all Brazil); Maradona, Bertoni, Passarella (all Argentina); Nyilasi, Poloskei, Fazekas (all Hungary); Robson, Francis (both England); Littbarski, Fischer (both West Germany); Wark (Scotland), Schachner (Austria), Assad (Algeria), Hamilton (N Ireland), Panenka (Czechoslovakia).

1 Oscar (Brazil), Tresor, Girard, Bossis, Soler, Couriol (all France); Altobelli, Tardelli, Conti, Graziani (all Italy); Breitner, Hrubesch, Reinders (all West Germany); Lato, Szarmach, Smolarek, Ciolek, Buncol, Majewski, Kupcewicz (all Poland); Krankl, Pezzey, Hintermaier (all Austria); Ufarte, Juanito, Zamora, Saura (all Spain); Blokhin, Shengelia, Chivadze, Gavrilov, Bal, Baltacha (all Russia); Varga, Toth, Szentes (all Hungary); Dalglish, Robertson, Narey, Jordan, Souness, Archibald (all Scotland); Belloumi, Bensaoula, Madjer (all Algeria); Coeck, Van den Bergh, Czerniatynski (all Belgium); Letelier, Moscoso, Neira (all Chile); Petrovic, Gudelj (both Yugoslavia); Woodin, Sumner (both New Zealand); Al-Dakheel, Al-Buloushi (both Kuwait); Zelaya, Laing (both Honduras); Diaz, Ardiles (both Argentina); La Rosa (Peru), M'Bida (Cameroon), Mariner (England), Zapata (El Salvador).

OWN GOALS

Barmos (Czechoslovakia), Collovati (Italy).

ENGLAND 'B' INTERNATIONAL MATCHES

v AUSTRALIA

			E	A
1980	17 Nov	Birmingham	1	0

v AUSTRIA

			E	A
*1979	12 June	Klagenfurt	1	0

**Abandoned after an hour's play.*

v CZECHOSLOVAKIA

			E	C
1978	28 Nov	Prague	1	0

v FINLAND

			E	F
1949	15 May	Helsinki	4	0

v FRANCE

			E	F
1952	22 May	Le Havre	1	7

v WEST GERMANY

			E	WG
1954	24 Mar	Gelsenkirchen	4	0
1955	23 Mar	Sheffield	1	1
1978	21 Feb	Augsburg	1	2

v ITALY

			E	I
1950	11 May	Milan	0	5

v LUXEMBOURG

			E	L
1950	21 May	Luxembourg	2	1

v MALAYSIA

			E	M
1978	30 May	Kuala Lumpur	1	1

v THE NETHERLANDS

			E	N
1949	18 May	Amsterdam	4	0
1950	22 Feb	Newcastle	1	0
1950	17 Mar	Amsterdam	0	3
1952	26 Mar	Amsterdam	1	0

v NEW ZEALAND

			E	NZ
1978	7 June	Christchurch	4	0
1978	11 June	Wellington	3	1
1978	14 June	Auckland	4	0
1979	17 Oct	Auckland	4	1

v SCOTLAND

			E	S
1953	11 Mar	Edinburgh	2	2
1954	3 Mar	Sunderland	1	1
1956	29 Feb	Dundee	2	2
1957	6 Feb	Birmingham	4	1

v SPAIN

			E	S
1980	26 Mar	Sunderland	1	0
1981	25 Mar	Granada	2	3

v SWITZERLAND

			E	S
1950	18 Jan	Sheffield	5	0
1954	22 May	Basle	0	2
1956	21 Mar	Southampton	4	1

v USA

			E	USA
1980	14 Oct	Manchester	1	0

v YUGOSLAVIA

			E	Y
1954	16 May	Lubljana	1	2
1955	19 Oct	Manchester	5	1

ENGLAND UNOFFICIAL INTERNATIONAL MATCHES

v SCOTLAND

			E	S
D1902	5 Apr	Glasgow	1	1
†1919	26 Apr	Everton	2	2
†1919	3 May	Glasgow	4	3
J1935	21 Aug	Glasgow	2	4
*1939	2 Dec	Newcastle	2	1
*1940	11 May	Glasgow	1	1
*1941	8 Feb	Newcastle	2	3
*1941	3 May	Glasgow	3	1
*1941	4 Oct	Wembley	2	0
*1942	17 Jan	Wembley	3	0
*1942	18 Apr	Glasgow	4	5
*1942	10 Oct	Wembley	0	0
*1943	17 Apr	Glasgow	4	0
*1943	16 Oct	Manchester	8	0
*1944	19 Feb	Wembley	6	2
*1944	22 Apr	Glasgow	3	2
*1944	14 Oct	Wembley	6	2
*1945	3 Feb	Aston Villa	3	2
*1945	14 April	Glasgow	6	1
†1946	13 Apr	Glasgow	0	1

v SWITZERLAND

			E	S
†1946	11 May	Chelsea	4	1

v FRANCE

			E	F
*1945	26 May	Wembley	2	2

v WALES

			E	W
†1919	11 Oct	Cardiff	1	2
†1919	18 Oct	Stoke	2	0
*1939	11 Nov	Cardiff	1	1
*1939	18 Nov	Wrexham	3	2
*1940	13 Apr	Wembley	0	1
*1941	26 Apr	Nottingham	4	1
*1941	7 June	Cardiff	3	2
*1941	25 Oct	Birmingham	2	1
*1942	9 May	Cardiff	0	1
*1942	24 Oct	Wolverhampton	1	2
*1943	27 Feb	Wembley	5	3
*1943	8 May	Cardiff	1	1
*1943	25 Sept	Wembley	8	3
*1944	6 May	Cardiff	2	0
*1944	16 Sept	Liverpool	2	2
*1945	5 May	Cardiff	3	2
†1945	20 Oct	West Bromwich	0	1

v IRELAND

			E	I
†1945	15 Sept	Belfast	1	0

v BELGIUM

			E	B
†1946	19 Jan	Wembley	2	0

v TEAM AMERICA

			E	TA
B1976	30 May	Philadelphia	3	1

D*Declared unofficial owing to disaster at ground.* †*Victory matches.* J*Jubilee match.* **War-time matches.* B*American Bicentennial Tournament.*

ENGLAND 'B' CAPS

Key:
A – *Austria*; Aus – *Australia*; Cz – *Czechoslovakia*; Fi – *Finland*; F – *France*; Ho – *Holland*; I – *Italy*; L – *Luxembourg*; m – *Malaysia*; Nz – *New Zealand*; Sp – *Spain*; Si – *Singapore*; Sw – *Switzerland*; S – *Scotland*; US – *United States of America*; WG – *West Germany*; Y – *Yugoslavia*.

Adamson, J. (Burnley), 1953 v S (1)
Allen, R. (WBA), 1954 v S, Sw (2)
Anderson, S. (Sunderland), 1957 v S (1)
Anderson, V. (Nottingham F), 1978 v m, Nz (3), Si; 1979 v A; 1980 v Sp (7)
Armstrong, D. (Middlesbrough), 1980 v Sp; 1981 v US (2)
Armstrong, K. (Chelsea), 1954 v S, WG, Y (3)
Ashcroft, C. T. (Liverpool), 1952 v Ho (1)
Astall, G. (Plymouth Arg), 1952 v F (1)
Atyeo, J. (Bristol C), 1955 v WG; 1956 v Y, S (3)

Bailey, G. (Manchester U), 1981 v US, Aus (2)
Baily, E. (Tottenham H), 1950 v Sw, I, Ho (3)
Barlow, R. (WBA), 1952 v F; 1953 v S (2)
Barnes, P. (WBA), 1981 v US (1)
Baynham, R. (Luton T), 1956 v Y (1)
Bell, E. (Bolton W), 1954 v S, Y (2)
Bentley, R. (Chelsea), 1949 v Ho (1)
Berry, J. (Manchester U), 1952 v Ho (1)
Birtles, G. (Nottingham F), 1980 v Sp (1)
Bond, K. (Norwich C), 1979 v Nz (Manchester C); 1981 v Aus (sub) (2)
Boyd, L. (Birmingham C), 1952 v Ho (1)
Briggs, T. (Grimsby T), 1950 v Sw (1)
Broadbent, P. (Wolverhampton W), 1956 v S (1)
Burgin, E. (Sheffield U), 1954 v WG, Y (2)
Butcher, T. (Ipswich T), 1979 v A (1)
Byrne, R. (Manchester U), 1953 v S; 1954 v S, WG (3)

Clarke, H. (Tottenham H), 1954 v WG (1)
Clayton, R. (Blackburn R), 1956 v Y (1)
Clough, B. (Middlesbrough), 1957 v S (1)
Cockburn, H. (Manchester U), 1949 v Ho (1)
Corrigan, J. (Manchester C), 1978 v WG, m, Nz (3), Si; 1979 v Cz, A; 1980 v Sp; 1981 v Sp (10)
Cowans, G. (Aston Villa), 1981 v Aus (1)
Crosland, J. (Blackpool), 1950 v I, L (2)
Cummings, T. (Burnley), 1953 v S; 1956 v S, Sw (3)
Cunningham, L. (WBA), 1979 v Cz (1)

Daley, S. (Wolverhampton W), 1978 v m, Nz (2 plus 1 sub), Si; 1979 v Cz (6)
Devonshire, A. (West Ham U), 1980 v Nz (sub) (1)
Dickinson, J. (Portsmouth), 1949 v Fi; 1950 v Sw, Ho (3)
Ditchburn, E. (Tottenham H), 1949 v Ho; 1959 v Sw (2)
Douglas, B. (Blackburn R), 1956 v Sw (1)
Dugdale, J. (WBA), 1954 v S, Y, Sw (3)

Eckersley, W. (Blackburn R), 1950 v Ho (2), I (3)
Edwards, D. (Manchester U), 1954 v Sw, WG; 1955 v WG; 1956 v Sw (4)
Ellerington, W. (Southampton), 1949 v Fi (1)
Elliott, S. (Sunderland), 1980 v Sp; 1981 v US, Sp (3)
Else, F. (Preston NE), 1957 v S (1)
Eves, M. (Wolverhampton W), 1978 v Nz (2 sub), Si (sub) (3)

Fairclough, D. (Liverpool), 1978 v WG (1)
Fashanu, J. (Nottingham F), 1980 v Nz (sub) (1)
Finney, A. (Sheffield W), 1956 v S (1)
Flanagan, M. (Charlton Ath), 1978 v WG; 1979 v Cz (2) (C Palace); 1980 v Nz (3)
Foster, R. (Preston NE), 1952 v F (1)
Froggatt, R. (Sheffield W), 1950 v Sw (1)

Gallagher, J. (Birmingham C), 1981 v Aus (1)
Geddis, D. (Ipswich T), 1978 v m (sub) (1)
Gibson, C. (Aston Villa), 1949 v Ho (1)
Gidman, J. (Aston Villa), 1978 v WG; 1979 v Cz (2)
Grainger, J. (Rotherham U), 1953 v S (1)
Grant, W. (Cardiff C), 1952 v F (1)
Gratrix, R. (Blackpool), 1956 v Sw (1)
Gray, W. (Chelsea), 1950 v Sw (1)
Green, K. (Birmingham C), 1954 v Sw, Y (2)
Greenhoff, B. (Manchester U), 1979 v Cz (1)
Greenwood, R. (Brentford), 1952 v Ho (1)
Gregory, E. (West Ham U), 1952 v F (1)
Groves, V. (Orient), 1956 v Y (1)
Gunter, P. (Portsmouth), 1952 v F (1)

Hall, J. (Birmingham C), 1955 v WG (1)
Harmer, T. (Tottenham H), 1952 v Ho (1)
Harrison, W. (Leicester C), 1949 v Fi, Ho (2)
Hawksworth, D. (Sheffield U), 1952 v F (1)
Haynes, W. (Fulham), 1954 v S, WG (2), Y, Sw (5)
Hazell, R. (Wolverhampton W), 1979 v Cz (sub) (1)
Hilaire, V. (C Palace), 1980 v Nz (1)
Hill, G. (Manchester U/Derby Co), 1978 v WG, m, Nz (3), Si (6)
Hoddle, G. (Tottenham H), 1979 v A, 1980 v Nz (2)
Holden, W. (Burnley), 1953 v S (1)
Hollins, J. (QPR), 1978 v m, Nz (3), Si (5)
Hooper, H. (West Ham U), 1954 v S, WG, Y, Sw; 1955 v WG; 1957 v S (6)
Howe, D. (WBA), 1957 v S (1)
Hughes, L. (Liverpool), 1950 v Sw (1)

Jezzard, B. (Fulham), 1954 v WG, Y; 1956 v Y (3)
Jones, W. (Liverpool), 1949 v Ho (1)

Kennedy, A. (Newcastle U), 1978 v WG, m, Nz (3), Si; 1980 v Sp (7)
Kennedy, J. (WBA), 1952 v F; 1956 v Y, S (3)
Kiernan, W. (Charlton Ath), 1955 v WG (1)
King, R. (Port Vale), 1954 v Sw (1)

Langley, J. (Brighton & HA), 1955 v WG; 1956 v S, Y (3)
Langley, T. (Chelsea), 1978 v Nz (2 subs), Si (sub) (3)
Langton, R. (Preston NE), 1949 v Ho; 1950 v I, Ho (3)
Leuty, L. (Derby Co), 1949 v Fi, Ho; 1950 v Ho (3)
Lewis, R. (Arsenal), 1950 v I, L (2)
Lishman, D. (Arsenal), 1953 v S (1)
Lofthouse, N. (Bolton W), 1950 v Ho (1)
Lyons, M. (Everton), 1979 v Cz (1)

McDermott, T. (Liverpool), 1978 v WG (1)
McGarry, W. (Huddersfield T), 1954 v Sw (1)
McGhee, T. (Portsmouth), 1956 v Y (1)
Mackenzie, S. (Manchester C), 1981 v Sp (1)
Mannion, W. (Midd esbrough), 1949 v Fi; 1950 v Ho (2)
Mansell, J. (Portsmouth), 1954 v Y; 1956 v Sw (2)
Marchi, A. (Tottenham H), 1957 v S (1)
Mariner, P. (Ipswich T), 1978 v WG, m, Nz (2 plus 1 sub), Si; 1980 v Sp (7)
Martin, A. (West Ham U), 1981 v Sp (1)
Matthews, R. (Coventry C), 1955 v WG; 1956 v S, Sw (3)
Middleton, R. (Chesterfield), 1950 v Ho (2), I, L (4)
Milburn, S. (Chesterfield), 1950 v Ho (1)
Mitchell, A. (Luton T), 1952 v Ho (1)
Money, R. (Liverpool), 1980 v Nz (sub) (1)
Morley, A. (Aston Villa), 1981 v Sp, Aus (sub) (2)
Morris, J. (Derby Co), 1949 v Fi (1)
Mortimer, D. (Coventry C), 1978 v WG; 1979 v Cz; (Aston Villa); 1981 v Aus (3)
Morton, R. (Luton T), 1956 v Sw (1)
Mullen, J. (Wolverhampton W), 1949 v Fi; 1950 v Ho, L (3)

Needham, D. (Nottingham F), 1978 v WG, m, Nz (3), Si (6)
Nevercott, K. (Norwich C), 1953 v S (1)
Nicholson, W. (Tottenham H), 1950 v Sw, I, Ho (3)

Osman, R. (Ipswich T), 1980 v Sp; 1981 v US (2)
Owen, G. (Manchester C), 1978 v WG (sub), m (sub), Nz (3), Si (sub); 1979 v Cz (sub) (7)

Parkes, P. (West Ham U), 1980 v Nz (1)
Parsons, E. (West Ham U), 1949 v Fi, Ho (2)
Payne, J. (Liverpool), 1950 v I, Ho, L (3)
Peach, D. (Southampton), 1980 v Nz (1)
Pegg, D. (Manchester U), 1956 v Sw (1)
Perry, W. (Blackpool), 1956 v S, Y (2)
Pilkington, B. (Burnley), 1954 v S; 1957 v S (2).
Power, P. (Manchester C), 1981 v Sp (sub) (1)
Pye, J. (Wolverhampton W), 1950 v I, Ho, L (3)

Quested, L. (Fulham), 1950 v Ho (1)
Quigley, E. (Preston NE), 1950 v Ho, L (2)
Quixley, A. (Sheffield W), 1953 v S; 1954 v Y, Sw (3)

Reeves, K. (Manchester C), 1979 v A; 1981 v US (sub), Sp (3)
Regis, C. (WBA), 1979 v Cz (sub); 1981 v US, Aus (3)
Revie, D. (Manchester C), 1954 v S (1)
Richards, J. (Wolverhampton W), 1978 v m, Nz, Si (3)
Rickett, W. (Sheffield W), 1950 v Sw (1)
Rix, G. (Arsenal), 1979 v A, 1980 v Nz; 1981 v Sp (3)
Robb, G. (Tottenham H), 1954 v WG, Y, Sw (3)
Robson, B. (WBA), 1979 v A, 1980 v Sp (2)
Roeder, G. (Orient), 1978 v m (sub), Nz (3), Si, (QPR); 1980 v Nz (6)
Roper, D. (Arsenal), 1963 v S (1)
Rowley, A. (Leicester C), 1956 v Sw (1)
Rowley, J. (Manchester U), 1949 v Ho (1)
Rutter, C. (Cardiff C), 1952 v Ho (1)

Sanson, K. (C. Palace), 1979 v Cz, A (2)
Scott, L. (Arsenal), 1950 v Ho; 1950 v I, Ho, L (4)
Shackleton, L. (Sunderland), 1950 v Ho (1)
Shannon, L. (Burnley), 1952 v F; 1954 v WG; 1956 v S (3)
Sillett, P. (Chelsea), 1957 v S (1)
Sims, S. (Leicester C), 1978 v m (1)
Smith, T. (Birmingham C), 1955 v WG; 1957 v S (2)
Speight, M. (Sheffield U), 1978 v Nz (1 plus 2 subs), Si (sub) (4)
Staniforth, R. (Huddersfield T), 1953 v S; 1954 v S, WG (3)
Statham, D. (WBA), 1981 v US, Sp (2)
Stokes, A. (Tottenham H), 1957 v S (1)
Sunderland, A. (Arsenal), 1978 v WG (sub); 1979 v Cz; 1980 v Nz, Sp; 1981 v US, Aus, Sp (7)
Swift, H. (Sheffield W), 1950 v Sw (1)
Swinbourne, R. (Wolverhampton W), 1955 v WG (1)

Talbot, B. (Ipswich T), 1978 v m, Nz (3), Si; 1979 v Cz (Arsenal); 1980 v Nz; 1981 v US (8)
Taylor, E. (Blackpool), 1956 v Sw (1)
Taylor, J. (Luton T), 1952 v Ho (1)
Taylor, P. (Liverpool), 1950 v Ho, L (2)
Taylor, T. (Manchester U), 1956 v S, Sw (2)
Thompson, P. (Liverpool), 1978 v WG (1)
Thompson, T. (Preston NE), 1957 v S (1)

Vaughan, C. (Charlton Ath), 1952 v Ho (1)

Waldron, M. (Southampton), 1980 v Nz (1)
Walters, S. (Tottenham H), 1950 v Ho (1)
Ward, P. (Nottingham F), 1981 v US (sub), Aus (2)
Watson, W. (Sunderland), 1950 v I, Ho, L (3)
Westwood, E. (Manchester C), 1949 v Fi, Ho (2)
Wheeler, J. (Bolton W), 1952 v Ho, F; 1955 v WG; 1956 v S (4)
Wicks, S. (Reading), 1952 v F (1)
Willemse, S. (Chelsea), 1954 v Sw (1)
Williams, B. (Wolverhampton W), 1949 v Fi (1)
Williams, S. (Southampton), 1979 v A; 1981 v US, Aus, Sp (4)
Wilshaw, D. (Wolverhampton W), 1949 v Fi; 1954 v Sw (2)
Withers, C. (Tottenham H), 1952 v Ho (1)
Wood, R. (Manchester U), 1954 v S (1)
Woodcock, A. (Cologne), 1979 v A (1)
Wright, J. (Blackpool), 1950 v L (1)
Wright, W. (Everton), 1979 v A; 1981 v Aus (2)

England winger Tony Woodcock receives close attention from two Greek defenders

Victory and Wartime Internationals

1919 and 1946 Victory Internationals. 1940–45 Wartime Internationals. (No caps were awarded for these games.) Abbreviations, E, England; S, Scotland; W, Wales; I, Ireland; B, Belgium; F, France; Sw, Switzerland.

ENGLAND

Bacuzzi, J. (Fulham), 1940 v S (2), W (2); 1942 v S (3), W (1); 1943 v S (1), W (1)
Bagshaw, J. (Derby Co.), 1920 v W (1)
Ball, W. (Birmingham), 1920 v W (1)
Balmer, J. (Everton), 1940 v W (1)
Barnes, H. (Manchester C.), 1920 v W (1)
Barrass, M. (Bolton W.), 1946 v W (1)
Bartram, S. (Charlton Ath.), 1941 v S (1), W (1)
Birkett, R. (Newcastle U.), 1941 v S (1)
Britton, C. (Everton), 1941 v W (2); 1942 v W (1); 1943 v S (2), v W (3); 1944 v S (2), W (2)
Brook, E. (Manchester C.), 1940 v W (1)
Brooks, S. (Wolverhampton W.), 1920 v W (1)
Broome, F. (Aston Villa), 1940 v S (1), W (1)
Brown, R. (Charlton Ath.), 1945 v W (1), S (2); 1946 v Bel. F, Sw
Buchan, C. (Sunderland), 1920 v W (1)
Buckingham, V. (Tottenham H.), 1941 v W (2)

Carter, H. (Sunderland), 1940 v S (1); 1943 v S (1), W (2); 1944 v S (3), W (2); 1945 v W (2), S (2); 1946 v I, F, Sw
Clifton, H. (Newcastle U.), 1940 v S (1)
Cock, J. (Huddersfield T.), 1920 v W (1)
Compton, D. (Arsenal), 1941 v S (1); 1942 v S (2), W (1); 1943 v S (2), W (2); 1944 v S (1), W (1); 1945 v W (1); 1946 v S
Compton, L. (Arsenal), 1940 v W (1); 1943 v S (1), W (1); 1944 v S (1), W (1)
Crayston, J. (Arsenal), 1940 v W (1)
Crook, H. (Blackburn R.), 1940 v W (1)
Cullis, S. (Wolverhampton W.), 1941 v S (2), W (2); 1942 v S (2), W (1); 1943 v S (2), W (3); 1944 v S (3), W (2); 1945 v W (2)

Ditchburn, E. (Tottenham H.), 1944 v S (1), W (1)
Duckworth, F. (Blackburn R.), 1919 v S (2)

Edelston, M. (Reading), 1941 v W (1); 1942 v S (1), W (2); 1943 v S (1)
Elliott, W. (W.B.A.), 1944 v W (1); 1946 v S

Fenton, E. (West Ham U.), 1940 v W (1)
Fenton, M. (Middlesborough), 1946 v W
Finch, L. C. (Barnet), 1941 v W (1)
Fisher, F. (Millwall), 1941 v W (1)
Fleetwood, T. (Everton), 1919 v S (2)
Flewin, R. (Portsmouth), 1945 v W (1)
Franklin, N. (Stoke C.), 1945 v W (1), S (2); 1946 v I, B, F, Sw, S, W

Gibbons, A. H. (Tottenham H.), 1943 v W (1)
Goslin, H. (Bolton W.), 1940 v S (1); 1941 v S (1); 1942 v S (1), W (1)
Goulden, L. (West Ham U.), 1940 v W (1); 1941 v S (2), W (1); 1945 v S (1)
Greenhalgh, N. (Everton), 1940 v S (1)
Grenyer, A. (Everton), 1920 v W (1)
Grimsdell, A. (Tottenham H.), 1919 v S (2)

Hagan, J. (Sheffield U.), 1941 v W (2); 1942 v S (3), W (1); 1943 v S (2), W (2); 1944 v S (3); W (1); 1946 v S
Hall, G. W. (Tottenham H.), 1940 v W (1); 1942 v W (1)
Hanson, J. (Chelsea), 1941 v S (1)
Hapgood, E. (Arsenal), 1940 v S (1), W (2); 1941 v S (1), W (1); 1942 v S (3), W (2); 1943 v S (1), W (2)
Hardy, S. (Aston Villa), 1919 v S (2), W (1)
Harper, B. (Barnsley), 1940 v S (1)
Hardwick, G. (Middlesbrough), 1941 v W (1); 1943 v S (1), W (2); 1944 v S (2), W (1); 1945 v W (2), S (3); 1946 v B, F, Sw, S.

Hendren, E. (Brentford), 1920 v W (1)
Hilditch, C. (Manchester U.), 1920 v W (1)
Hodkinson, J. (Blackburn R.), 1920 v W (1)
Hudspeth, F. (Newcastle U.), 1920 v W (1)

Johnson, W. H. (Charlton Ath), 1946 v Sw
Joy, B. (Arsenal), 1945 v S (1)

Kinsell, H. (W.B.A.), 1946 v I, W.
Kirchen, A. (Arsenal), 1941 v W (1); 1942 v S (1), W (1)
Knight, A. E. (Portsmouth), 1920 v W (1)

Lawton, T. (Everton), 1940 v S (1); 1942 v S (2), W (1); 1943 v S (1), W (1); 1944 v S (3), W (1); 1945 v W (2), S (3); 1946 v I, B, F, Sw, S
Longworth, E. (Liverpool), 1919 v S (2)

McCall, J. (Preston N.E.), 1919 v S (2)
Mannion, W. (Middlesbrough), 1941 v S (2); 1942 v S (2)
Mapson, J. (Sunderland), 1941 v W (1)
Marks, G. (Arsenal), 1942 v S (3), W (2); 1943 v S (1), W (2)
Martin, H. (Sunderland), 1919 v S (2)
Martin, J. (Aston Villa), 1940 v S (1), W (2)
Mason, G. (Coventry C.), 1942 v S (1), W (1)
Matthews, S. (Stoke C.), 1940 v S (2), W (2); 1941 v S (1); 1942 v S (3), W (1); 1943 v S (2), W (3); 1944 v S (3), W (1); 1945 v S (3); 1946 v I, B, F, Sw, W
Mercer, J. (Everton), 1940 v S (2), W (2); 1941 v S (2); 1942 v S (2), W (1); 1943 v S (2), W (3); 1944 v S (3), W (1); 1945 v S (3); 1946 v I, B, Sw, S, W
Mortensen, S. (Blackpool), 1945 v W (1); 1946 v I
Mountford, R. (Huddersfield T.), 1941 v S (1)
Mullen, J. (Wolverhampton W.), 1943 v W (1); 1945 v W (1); 1946 v B

Oakes, R. J. (Charlton Ath.), 1940 v W (1)

Parker, C. (Stoke C.), 1920 v W (1)
Pearson, T. (Newcastle U.), 1940 v S (1)
Puddefoot, S. (West Ham U.), 1919 v W (2); 1920 v W (1)
Pye, J. (Notts. Co.), 1946 v B

Richardson, J. (Newcastle U.), 1940 v S (1)
Rooke, R. (Fulham), 1943 v W (1)
Rowley, J. (Manchester U.), 1944 v W (1)
Roxburgh, A. (Blackpool), 1944 v W (1)

Scott, L. (Arsenal), 1942 v W (1); 1944 v S (2), W (2); 1945 v W (2), S (3); 1946 v I, B, F, Sw, S, W
Shackleton, L. (Bradford), 1946 v S
Shea, D. (Blackburn R.), 1919 v S (2)
Smith, G. (Charlton Ath.), 1945 v W (1)
Smith J. (Bolton W.), 1919 v S (2)
Smith J. (W.B.A.), 1920 v W (1)
Smith, J. R. (Millwall), 1940 v S (1), W (2); 1941 v W (1)
Smith, L. (Brentford), 1940 v W (1); 1942 v W (1); 1944 v S (2), W (1); 1945 v W (1), S (3); 1946 v I, F, Sw
Soo, F. (Stoke C.), 1942 v W (1); 1944 v S (1); 1945 v S (3); 1946 v I, F, W
Sproston, B. (Manchester C.), 1940 v W (2), S (1)
Stubbins, A. (Newcastle U.), 1946 v W
Swift, F. (Manchester C.), 1940 v W (1); 1941 v S (1); 1943 v S (1), W (1); 1944 v S (2); 1945 v W (1), S (3); 1946 v I, B, Sw, S
Swinburne, T. (Newcastle U.), 1920 v S (1)

Taylor, F. (Wolverhampton W.), 1944 v S (1)
Turnbull, R. (Newcastle U.), 1919 v S (2); 1920 v W (1)

Voysey, W. (Millwall), 1920 v W (1)

Watson, W. (Burnley), 1920 v W (1)
Watson, W. (Huddersfield T.), 1946 v W
Welsh, D. (Charlton Ath.), 1940 v S (1), W (1); 1941 v S (1), W (2); 1942 v W (2), W (1); 1944 v W (1); 1945 v W (2)
Westcott, D. (Wolverhampton W.), 1943 v S (1), W (2)
Whittingham, R. (Stoke), 1920 v W (1)
Williams, B. (Walsall), 1945 v W (1); (with Wolverhampton W.); 1946 v F, W
Williamson, E. G. (Arsenal), 1920 v W (1)
Willingham, K. (Huddersfield T.), 1940 v W (2), S (1); 1941 v S (1); 1942 v S (2)
Woodley, V. (Chelsea), 1940 v W (1), S (1)
Wright, W. (Wolverhampton W.), 1946 v B, Sw, S

SCOTLAND

Ancell, R. (Newcastle U.), 1940 v E (1)

Baird, A. (Aberdeen), 1946 v B
Baxter, W. (Hearts), 1940 v E (2); (with Middlesbrough), 1944 v E (1); 1945 v E (1)
Beattie, A. (Preston N.E.), 1941 v E (1); 1942 v E (3); 1943 v E (1)
Black, A. (Hearts), 1942 v E (1)
Blair, J. (Rangers), 1919 v E (2)
Bogan, S. (Hibernian), 1944 v E (1)* (injured and substituted, See Johnstone)
Bowie, J. (Rangers), 1919 v E (2)
Bremner, G. (Arsenal), 1942 v E (1); 1943 v E (1)
Brennan, F. (Airdrieonians), 1946 v E, Sw
Brown, G. (Rangers), 1941 v E (2)
Brown, J. (Morton), 1919 v E (2)
Brown, R. (Queen's Park), 1945 v E (2); 1946 v W, I, E, B; (with Rangers), Sw
Brown, T. (Hearts), 1940 v E (1)
Buchan, W. (Blackpool), 1943 v E (1)
Busby, M. (Liverpool), 1942 v E (2); 1943 v E (1); 1944 v E (2); 1945 v E (2)

Campbell, J. (Clyde), 1946 v B
Campbell, W. (Morton), 1944 v E (1); 1946 v W, I, E, Sw
Carabine, J. (Third Lanark), 1940 v E (2); 1941 v E (1); 1942 v E (3); 1943 v E (3); 1944 v E (1)
Caskie, J. (Everton), 1940 v E (2); 1941 v E (2); 1942 v E (2); 1944 v E (2); 1945 v E (1)
Chisholm K. (Queen's Park), 1946 v I
Corbett, W. (Celtic), 1943 v E (1)
Crozier, J. (Brentford), 1944 v E (3)
Cumming, D. (Middlesbrough), 1945 v E (1)
Cummings, G. (Aston Villa), 1945 v E (1)

Dawson, J. (Rangers), 1940 v E (2); 1941 v E (2); 1942 v E (3); 1943 v E (2)
Deakin, J. (St. Mirren), 1944 v E (1); 1946 v W.B.
Delaney, J. (Celtic), 1944 v E (1); 1945 v E (1); 1946 v E, B, Sw
Dodds, J. (Blackpool), 1940 v E (1); 1942 v E (1); 1943 v E (1); 1944 v E (2); 1945 v E (1); 1946 v W, I
Donaldson, A. (Bolton W.), 1919 v E (1)
Dougal, J. (Preston N.E.), 1940 v E (1)
Dougall, N. (Birmingham C.), 1946 v E
Duncanson, J. (Rangers), 1944) v E (2)
Dykes, J. (Hearts), 1941 v E (2); 1942 v E (2)

Fagan, W. (Liverpool), 1945 v E (1)
Finan, R. (Blackpool), 1940 v E (1)
Flavell, R. (Airdrieonians), 1944 v E (1)

Gillick, T. (Everton), 1941 v E (1); 1942 v E (1); 1944 v E (1)
Gordon, J. E. (Rangers), 1919 v E (2)

Hamilton, G. (Aberdeen), 1946 v I, E
Harley, J. (Liverpool), 1945 v E (2)
Harris, J. (Wolverhampton W.), 1945 v E (1)
Harris, J. R. (Queen's Park), 1945 v E (1)
Hogg, R. (Celtic), 1941 v E (1)
Herd, A. (Manchester C.), 1942 v E (1)
Husband, J. (Partick T.), 1946 v E, Sw

Johnston, R. (Rangers), 1942 v E (1)
Johnstone, L. (Clyde), 1945 v E (1) (sub for Bogan)

Kean, S. (Hibernian), 1943 v E (1)
Kelly, W. (Morton), 1945 v E (1)
Kilmarnock, W. (Motherwell), 1944 v E (1)
Kirton, J. (Stoke C.), 1944 v E (1)

Liddell, W. (Liverpool), 1942 v E (1); 1943 v E (2); 1945 v E (1); 1946 v W, I, E, Sw
Linwood, A. (St. Mirren), 1944 v E (1)
Little, A. (Rangers), 1944 v E (1)

Macaulay, A. (West Ham U.), 1944 v E (2); 1945 v E (3)
McClure, D. (Hearts), 1940 v E (1)
McCullough, D. (Falkirk), 1940 v E (1)
McDonald, P. (Celtic), 1941 v E (1); 1942 v E (1); 1944 v E (1)
McGowan, J. (Partick T.), 1946 v I, B
McMenemey, J. (Celtic), 1919 v E (2)
McMullen, J. (Partick T.), 1919 v E (2)
McNair, A. (Celtic), 1919 v E (2)
McPhee, J. (Falkirk), 1946 v W
Morton, A. (Queen's Park), 1919 v E (2)
Milne, J. (Middlesbrough), 1941 v E (1)
Miller, A. (Hearts), 1944 v E (1)

Napier, C. (Falkirk), 1940 v E (1)

Paterson, G. (Celtic), 1946 v W, I, B
Paton, J. (Motherwell), 1946 v W, I, B
Pinkerton, H. (Falkirk), 1940 v E (1)

Reid, J. (Airdrieonians), 1919 v E (1)
Richardson, B. (Ayr U.), 1919 v E (1)

Shankly, W. (Preston N.E.), 1940 v E (1); 1941 v E (1); 1942 v E (3); 1943 v E (2)
Shaw, D. (Hibernian), 1946 v E, Sw
Shaw, J. (Rangers), 1941 v E (1); 1943 v E (1); 1946 v W, I, E, B, Sw
Smith, G. (Hibernian), 1945 v E (1); 1946 v W, B
Smith, J. (Rangers), 1941 v E (2); 1942 v E (1)
Smith, T. (Preston N.E.), 1942 v E (1)
Stenhouse, J. (St. Mirren), 1944 v E (1)
Stephen, J. (Bradford), 1944 v E (2); 1945 v E (3)

Thornton, W. (Rangers), 1946 v Sw
Thyne, R. (Darlington), 1945 v E (2)

Venters, A. (Rangers), 1940 v E (1); 1941 v E (1); 1943 v E (1)

Waddell, W. (Rangers), 1942 v E (1); 1943 v E (2); 1944 v E (1); 1945 v E (1); 1946 v W, I, E, Sw
Walker, T. (Hearts), 1940 v E (2); 1941 v E (2); 1942 v E (2); 1943 v E (1); 1944 v E (2); 1945 v E (1); 1946 v B, Sw
Wallace, W. (Clyde), 1941 v E (1); 1942 v E (1); 1943 v E (1)
Williams, D. (Clyde), 1942 v E (1)
Wilson, A. (Hearts), 1919 v E (1)
Wright, A. (Morton), 1919 v E (2)

WALES

Astbury, D. (Chester), 1945–46 v E
Astley, D. (Blackpool), 1940 v E (3); 1941 v E

Barnes, W. (Arsenal), 1942 v E; 1945 v E
Burgess, R. (Tottenham H.), 1940 v E (2); 1941 v E; 1942 v E (2); 1945 v E (2); 1946 v E, S, I

Clarke, N. (Cardiff C.), 1946 v I
Cummer, H. (Arsenal), 1940 v E (2); 1942 v E; 1943 v E (3); 1944 v E; 1945 v E (2); 1946 v E, S

Davies, LL. (Northampton), 1920 v E
Davies, R. (Nottingham F.), 1940 v E; 1944 v E; 1945 v E; 1946 v E, S
Davies, S. (Preston N.E.), 1920 v E
Davies, W. (Watford), 1944 v E
Dearson, D. (Birmingham), 1940 v E (2); 1941 v E (2); 1942 v E (2); 1943 v E (3); 1944 v E (2); 1945 v E (2); 1946 v E, S

Edwards, G. (Coventry C.), 1945 v E; (with Birmingham C.), 1946 v E, S
Evans, J. (Cardiff C.), 1920 v E

Ford, T. (Swansea T.), 1946 v I

Glover, E. (Plymouth Arg.), 1946 v E
Goodwin, A. (Oldham Ath.), 1920 v E (2)
Green, G. (Charlton Ath.), 1940 v E; 1942 v E

Hopkins, I. (Brentford), 1940 v E (3); 1941 v E; 1942 v E (2); 1943 v E (2); 1944 v E
Hughes, A. (Manchester C.), 1920 v E
Hughes, W. (Birmingham), 1940 v E; 1941 v E (2); 1943 v E (3); 1944 v E; 1945 v E (2); 1946 v E, S, I

James, J. (Cardiff C.), 1941 v E; 1942 v E
John, W. R. (Swansea T.), 1940 v E
Jones, B. (Arsenal), 1940 v E (3); 1941 v E (2); 1943 v E (3)
Jones, J. T. (Stoke C.), 1920 v E (2)
Jones, L. (Arsenal), 1940–41 v E; 1942 v E (2); 1945 v E; (with Swansea T.), 1946 v S
Jones, T. G. (Everton), 1940 v E (2); 1941 v E; 1942 v E (2); 1943 v E (3); 1944 v E; 1946 v I
Jones, W. L. (Southend U.), 1920 v E (2)

Keenor, S. (Cardiff C.), 1920 v E (2)

Lambert, R. (Liverpool), 1943 v E; 1944 v E (2); 1945 v E
Lowrie, G. (Northampton), 1942 v E; 1943 v E (3); 1944 v E (2); (with Coventry C.), 1945 v E; 1946 v E, S
Lucas, W. (Swindon T.), 1942 v E, 1943 v E (2); 1944 v E; 1945 v E (2); 1946 v E, I

Matthews, R. (Liverpool), 1920 v E (2)
Meredith, W. (Manchester C.), 1920 v E (2)
Morris, W. (Burnley), 1946 v I
Morris, W. (Birmingham), 1944 v E
Mortensen, S. (Blackpool), 1944 v E (sub)
Murphy, E. (Bradford C.), 1943 v E; 1944 v E

Peers, E. (Wolverhampton W.), 1920 v E (2)
Perry, E. (Fulham), 1941 v E
Poland, G. (Liverpool), 1942 v E (2); 1943 v E (2)
Powell, A. (Leeds U.), 1943 v E; 1944 v E; 1940, I
Powell, I. (Q.P.R.), 1943 v E (3); 1944 v E*

Redfern, W. (Derby Co.), 1940 v E
Rees, W. (Cardiff C.), 1945 v E
Rogers, W. (Wrexham), 1941 v E; (with Swansea T.), 1945 v E
Russell, M. (Plymouth Arg.), 1920 v E

Sherwood, A. (Cardiff C.), 1946 v I
Shortt, W. (Plymouth Arg.), 1946 v I
Sidlow, C. (Wolverhampton W.), 1940 v E (2); 1941 v E (2); 1943 v E; 1944 v E (2); 1945 v E (2); 1946 v E, S
Smith, A. J. (Chelsea), 1940 v E
Squires, C. (Swansea T.), 1942 v E; 1946 v S

Turner, H. (Charlton Ath.), 1940 v E (2); 1941 v E (2); 1942 v E (2); 1943 v E (2)

Vizard, E. (Bolton W.), 1920 v E

Warner, J. (Manchester U.), 1946 v I
Whatley, W. (Tottenham H.), 1940 v E
Williams, G. (Millwall), 1940 v E; 1941 v E
Winter, F. (Bolton W.), 1945 v E; 1946 v E (*Injured at Wembley 1944, Mortensen, S. came on as sub)
Witcomb, D. (W.B.A.), 1940 v E (2); 1941 v E (2); 1942 v E (2); 1946 v S
Woodward, V. (Fulham), 1941 v E
Wynn, G. (Manchester C.), 1920 v E

N. IRELAND

Ahearne, B. (Belfast Celtic), 1946 v S, W

Breen, C. (Linfield), 1946 v E, S, W
Bonnar, P. (Belfast Celtic), 1946 v E, S

Carey, T. (Manchester U.), 1946 v S, W.

Doherty, P. (Manchester C.), 1946 v E; (with Derby Co.), v W

Feeney, J. (Linfield), 1946 v E, S

Jones, S. (Blackpool), 1946 v E

McCarthy, J. (Belfast Celtic), 1946 v E
McKenna, J. (Linfield), 1946 v E, W
McMillan, W. (Belfast Celtic), 1946 v E, S, W

O'Flanagan, Dr. K. (Arsenal), 1946 v S, W

Sloan, P. (Tranmere R.), 1946 v E, W
Stevenson, A. (Everton), 1946 v S

Todd, J. (Blackpool), 1946 v E, S

Vernon, J. (Belfast Celtic), 1946 v E, S, W

Walsh, D. (Linfield), 1946 v S, W
Waters, P. (Glentoran), 1946 v W

INTER-LEAGUE 1892–1976

FOOTBALL LEAGUE v SCOTTISH LEAGUE

Played 69. England won 38; Scotland 18; drawn 13.

Year Venue	*Goals* FL	SL
1892 Bolton	2	2
1893 Glasgow	4	3
1894 Liverpool	1	1
1895 Glasgow	4	1
1896 Liverpool	5	1
1897 Glasgow	0	3
1898 Birmingham	1	2
1899 Glasgow	4	1
1900 London	2	2
1901 Glasgow	2	6
1902 Newcastle	6	3
1903 Glasgow	3	0
1904 Manchester	2	1
1905 Glasgow	3	2
1906 London	6	2
1907 Glasgow	0	0
1908 Birmingham	2	0
1909 Glasgow	1	3
1910 Blackburn	2	3
1911 Glasgow	1	1
1912 Middlesbrough	2	0
1913 Glasgow	1	4
1914 Burnley	2	3
1915 Glasgow	4	1
1916–18 Not played		
1920 Glasgow	4	0
1921 Highbury	1	0
1922 Glasgow	3	0
1923 Newcastle	2	1
1924 Glasgow	1	1
1925 Everton	4	3
1926 Glasgow	2	0
1927 Leicester	2	2
1928 Glasgow	6	2
1929 Birmingham	2	1
1930 Glasgow	1	2
1931 Tottenham	7	3
1932 Glasgow	3	4
1933 Manchester	0	3
1934 Glasgow	2	2
1935 Stamford Bdge	2	1
1936 Glasgow	2	2
1937 Everton	2	1
1938 Glasgow	0	1
1939 Wolverh'ton	3	0
1940–46 Not played		
1947 Glasgow	3	1
1948 Newcastle	1	1
1949 Glasgow	3	0
1950 Middlesbrough	3	1
1951 Glasgow	0	1
1952 Sheffield	2	1
1953 Glasgow	0	1
1954 Stamford Bdge	4	0
1955 Glasgow	2	3
1956 Sheffield	4	2
1957 Glasgow	2	3
1958 Newcastle	4	1
1959 Glasgow	1	1
1960 Highbury	1	0
1961 Glasgow	2	3
1962 Birmingham	3	4
1963 Not played		
1964 Sunderland	2	2
1965 Glasgow	2	2
1966 Newcastle	1	3
1967 Glasgow	3	0
1968 Middlesbrough	2	0
1969 Glasgow	3	1
1970 Coventry	3	2
1971 Glasgow	1	0
1972 Middlesbrough	3	2
1973 Glasgow	2	2
1974 Maine Road	5	0
1976 Glasgow	1	0

FOOTBALL LEAGUE v IRISH LEAGUE

Played 61. England won 54; Ireland 3; drawn 4.

Year Venue	*Goals* FL	IL
1894 Belfast	4	2
1895 Not played		
1896 Stoke	2	2
1897 Belfast	2	0
1898 Manchester	8	1
1899 Belfast	5	1
1900 Bolton	3	1
1901 Belfast	4	2
1902 Woolwich	9	0
1903 Belfast	3	2
1904 Bradford	2	1
1905 Belfast	2	0
1906 Manchester	4	0
1970 Belfast	6	0
1908 Sunderland	6	3
1909 Belfast	5	0
1910 Oldham	8	1
1911 Belfast	6	2
1912 Liverpool	4	0
1913 Belfast	0	0
1914 Belfast	2	0
1915 West Bromwich	2	1
1916–19 Not played		
1920 Liverpool	2	2
1921 Not played		
1922 Belfast	1	0
1923 Bolton	5	1
1924 Belfast	9	2
1925 Belfast	5	0
1926 Liverpool	5	1
1927 Belfast	6	1
1928 Newcastle	9	1
1929 Belfast	5	0
1930 Everton	5	2
1931 Belfast	2	2
1932 Blackpool	4	0
1933 Belfast	5	2
1934 Preston	4	0
1935 Belfast	6	1
1936 Blackpool	1	2
1937 Belfast	2	3
1938 Blackpool	3	0
1939 Belfast	8	2
1940–46 Not played		
1947 Everton	4	2
1948 Belfast	4	3
1949 Liverpool	5	1
1950 Belfast	3	1
1951 Blackpool	6	3
1952 Belfast	9	0
1953 Wolverh'ton	7	1
1954 Belfast	5	0
1955 Liverpool	4	2
1956 Belfast	2	5
1957 Newcastle	3	2
1958 Belfast	4	2
1959 Liverpool	5	2
1960 Belfast	5	0
1961 Blackpool	5	2
1962 Belfast	6	1
1963 Norwich	3	1
1964 Belfast	4	0
1966 Plymouth	12	0
1968 Belfast	1	0
1970 Norwich	5	0

SCOTTISH LEAGUE v IRISH LEAGUE

Played 62. Scotland won 56, Ireland 5, drawn 1.

Year Venue	*Goals* SL	IL
1893 Belfast	2	3
1894 Glasgow	6	2
1895 Belfast	4	1
1896 Glasgow	3	2
1897 Belfast	2	0
1898 Dundee	5	0
1899 Belfast	1	3
1900 Edinburgh	6	0
1901 Belfast	2	1
1902 Dundee	3	0
1903 Belfast	0	1
1904 Paisley	3	1
1905–8 Not played		
1909 Belfast	2	1
1910 Glasgow	2	0
1911 Belfast	3	1
1912 Glasgow	3	0
1913 Belfast	3	1
1914 Belfast	2	1
1915 Belfast	2	1
1916–19 Not played		
1920 Belfast	2	0
1921 Glasgow	3	0
1922 Glasgow	3	0
1923 Glasgow	3	0
1924 Belfast	1	0
1925 Edinburgh	3	0
1926 Belfast	7	3
1927 Edinburgh	5	2
1928 Belfast	2	1
1929 Glasgow	8	2
1930 Belfast	4	1
1931 Glasgow	5	0
1932 Belfast	2	3
1933 Glasgow	4	1
1934 Belfast	0	3

Year Venue	Goals SL	IL	Year Venue	Goals SL	IL	Year Venue	Goals SL	IL
1935 Glasgow	3	2	1950 Glasgow	8	1	1960 Glasgow	7	1
1936 Belfast	3	2	1951 Belfast	4	0	1961 Belfast	2	1
1937 Glasgow	5	2	1952 Glasgow	3	0	1962 Glasgow	7	0
1938 Belfast	3	2	1953 Belfast	5	1	1946 Belfast	4	1
1939 Glasgow	6	1	1954 Glasgow	4	0	1966 Glasgow	6	2
1939† Belfast	3	2	1955 Belfast	5	1	1968 Belfast	2	0
1940–46 Not played			1956 Glasgow	3	0	1970 Glasgow	5	3
1947 Belfast	7	4	1957 Belfast	7	1	1978 Motherwell	1	1
1948 Glasgow	3	0	1958 Glasgow	7	0	1980 Belfast	4	2
1949 Belfast	1	0	1959 Belfast	5	0			

† Played in season 1939–40 prior to the outbreak of war.

SCOTTISH LEAGUE v LEAGUE OF IRELAND

Year Venue	Goals SL	LoI	Year Venue	Goals SL	LoI	Year Venue	Goals	
						1962 Dublin	1	1
1938 Dublin	1	2	1955 Glasgow	5	0	1963 Glasgow	11	0
1948 Dublin	2	0	1956 Dublin	4	2	1965 Dublin	2	2
1949 Glasgow	5	1	1957 Glasgow	3	1	1967 Glasgow	6	0
1950 Dublin	1	0	1958 Dublin	5	1	1969 Dublin	0	0
1951 Glasgow	7	0	1959 Glasgow	1	0	1970 Glasgow	1	0
1952 Dublin	2	0	1960 Dublin	4	1	1971 Glasgow	1	0
1953 Glasgow	5	1	1961 Glasgow	5	1	1980 Dublin	1	2
1954 Dublin	3	1						

FOOTBALL LEAGUE v LEAGUE OF IRELAND

Year Venue	Goals FL	LoI	Year Venue	Goals FL	LoI	Year Venue	Goals FL	LoI
1947 Dublin	3	1	1954 Manchester	9	1	1961 Dublin	4	0
1948 Preston	4	0	1955 Dublin	6	0	1962 Bristol	5	2
1949 Dublin	5	0	1956 Everton	5	1	1963 Dublin	1	2
1950 Wolverh'ton	7	0	1957 Dublin	3	3	1965 Hull	5	0
1951 Dublin	1	0	1958 Leeds	3	1	1967 Dublin	7	2
1952 Liverpool	9	1	1959 Dublin	0	0	1969 Barnsley	3	0
1953 Dublin	2	0	1960 Blackburn	2	0	1972 Dublin	2	1

THE LEAGUE v SOUTHERN LEAGUE

Year Venue	Goals TL	SL	Year Venue	Goals TL	SL	Year Venue	Goals TL	SL
1909–10 Chelsea	2	3	1911–12 Stoke	2	1	1913–14 Millwall	3	1
1910–11 Tottenham	2	3	1912–13 Manchester	2	1	1914–15 Highbury	2	1

FOOTBALL LEAGUE v INTERNATIONAL FOOTBALL COMBINATION OF DENMARK

Year Venue	Goals FL	IL	Year Venue	Goals FL	IL	Year Venue	Goals FL	IL
1961 Milan	2	4	1962 Old Trafford	0	2	1963 Highbury	3	2
						1964 Milan	0	1

FOOTBALL LEAGUE v BELGIAN LEAGUE

Year Venue	Goals FL	BL
1967 Brussels	2	2

UNDER-23 INTERNATIONAL MATCHES 1954–76

ENGLAND v AUSTRIA

				England	Austria
1965	June	2	Vienna	0	0
1967	May	10	Hull	3	0

ENGLAND v BELGIUM

				England	Belgium
1962	Nov	7	Plymouth	6	1
1969	May	25	Ostend	1	0

ENGLAND v BULGARIA

				England	Bulgaria
1957	May	19	Sofia	1	2
1957	Sept	25	Chelsea	6	2
1967	June	3	Sofia	1	1
1970	Apr	8	Plymouth	4	1

ENGLAND v CZECHOSLOVAKIA

				England	Czecho.
1957	May	30	Bratislava	2	0
1958	Oct	15	Norwich	3	0
1965	April	7	Leeds	0	0
1965	May	29	Liberec	0	0
1973	Mar	7	Villa Park	1	0
1973	June	1	Bratislava	0	3
1974	Oct	29	Selhurst Park	3	1
1975	Oct	28	Trnava	1	1

ENGLAND v DENMARK

				England	Denmark
1955	Sept	28	Portsmouth	5	1
1956	Sept	26	Copenhagen	3	0
1973	May	24	Naestved	1	1
1973	Nov	13	Portsmouth	1	1

ENGLAND v FRANCE

				England	France
1956	Oct	17	Bristol	0	0
1959	Mar	18	Lyons	1	1
1959	Nov	11	Sunderland	2	0
1964	April	8	Rouen	2	2
1965	Nov	3	Norwich	3	0
1974	May	19	Valence	2	2

ENGLAND v EAST GERMANY

				England	East Germany
1960	May	15	Berlin	4	1
1972	Mar	22	Bristol	0	1
1972	June	1	Leipzig	2	2

ENGLAND v WEST GERMANY

				England	West Germany
1959	May	10	Bochum	2	2
1961	Mar	15	Tottenham	4	1
1963	Nov	27	Liverpool	4	1
1965	May	25	Frieberg	0	1
1968	June	3	Kassel	1	0
1970	Oct	14	Leicester	3	1

ENGLAND v GREECE

				England	Greece
1962	Nov	28	Birmingham	5	0
1967	May	31	Athens	0	0

ENGLAND v HUNGARY

				England	Hungary
1959	Sept	23	Liverpool	0	1
1964	May	13	Budapest	1	2
1968	May	1	Everton	4	0
1968	May	30	Budapest	0	1
1976	Mar	10	Budapest	0	3
1976	Mar	23	Old Trafford	3	1

ENGLAND v ISRAEL

				England	Israel
1960	May	22	Tel Aviv	0	4
1961	Nov	9	Leeds	7	1
1964	May	17	Tel Aviv	4	0

ENGLAND v ITALY

				England	Italy
1954	Jan	20	Bologna	0	3
1955	Jan	19	Chelsea	5	1
1959	May	7	Milan	3	0
1960	Nov	2	Newcastle	1	1
1967	Dec	20	Nottingham	1	0
1968	May	25	Trieste	1	1

ENGLAND v NETHERLANDS

				England	Netherlands
1960	Mar	16	Sheffield	5	2
1961	Nov	29	Rotterdam	5	2
1968	Nov	13	Birmingham	2	2
1969	May	22	Deventer	1	2
1973	Jan	2	Highbury	3	1
1973	May	29	Maastricht	0	1

ENGLAND v POLAND

				England	Poland
1958	Sept	24	Sheffield	4	1
1960	May	18	Warsaw	3	2
1972	June	4	Warsaw	3	0

ENGLAND v PORTUGAL

				England	Portugal
1969	April	16	Coventry	4	0
1969	May	28	Funchal	1	1
1973	Oct	16	Plymouth	0	0
1974	Nov	19	Lisbon	3	2
1975	Nov	18	Selhurst Park	2	0

ENGLAND v RUMANIA

				England	Rumania
1957	May	26	Bucharest	1	0
1957	Oct	16	Wembley	3	2
1963	June	2	Bucharest	0	1
1964	Nov	25	Coventry	5	0

ENGLAND v SCOTLAND

				England	Scotland
1955	Feb	8	Glasgow	6	0
1956	Feb	8	Sheffield	3	1
1957	Feb	26	Glasgow	1	1
1958	Jan	15	Everton	3	1
1960	Mar	2	Glasgow	4	4
1961	Mar	1	Middlesbrough	0	1
1962	Feb	28	Aberdeen	4	2
1964	Feb	5	Newcastle	3	2
1965	Feb	24	Aberdeen	0	0
1967	Mar	1	Newcastle	1	3
1968	Feb	7	Glasgow	2	1
1970	Mar	4	Sunderland	3	1*
1971	Feb	24	Glasgow	2	2
1972	Feb	16	Derby	2	2
1973	Feb	13	Kilmarnock	2	1
1974	Mar	13	Newcastle	2	0
1974	Dec	18	Aberdeen	3	0

* Abandoned, snow, after 62 minutes.

ENGLAND v SWEDEN

				England	Sweden
1970	Nov	11	Hull	2	0

ENGLAND v SWITZERLAND

				England	Switzerland
1971	Nov	24	Ipswich	1	1

ENGLAND v TURKEY

				England	Turkey
1962	Mar	22	Southampton	4	1
1964	May	20	Istanbul	0	3
1966	April	20	Blackburn	2	0
1967	June	7	Ankara	3	0
1974	May	11	Ankara	0	0†

ENGLAND v USSR

				England	USSR
1969	Oct	22	Manchester	2	0
1972	June	7	Kiev	0	0

ENGLAND v WALES

				England	Wales
1958	April	23	Wrexham	1	2
1961	Feb	8	Everton	2	0
1963	Nov	13	Bristol	1	1
1964	Nov	4	Wrexham	3	2
1966	Oct	12	Wolverhampton	8	0
1967	Nov	1	Swansea	2	1
1968	Oct	2	Wrexham	3	1
1969	Oct	1	Bristol	2	0
1970	Dec	2	Wrexham	0	0
1972	Jan	5	Swindon	2	0
1972	Nov	29	Wrexham	3	0
1974	Jan	16	Bristol	0	0
1975	Jan	21	Wrexham	2	0

ENGLAND v YUGOSLAVIA

				England	Yugoslavia
1963	Mar	21	Manchester	0	0
1963	May	29	Belgrade	4	2
1965	Nov	24	Southampton	2	1
1974	May	15	Zrenjanin	0	1

SCOTLAND v WALES

				Scotland	Wales
1959	Nov	25	Wrexham	1	1
1962	Dec	5	Aberdeen	2	0
1966	Nov	30	Wrexham	6	0
1968	Dec	10	Edinburgh	0	1
1970	Jan	14	Aberdeen	1	1
1971	Jan	13	Swansea	0	1
1972	Jan	26	Aberdeen	2	0
1973	Mar	14	Swansea	2	1
1974	Feb	27	Aberdeen	3	0
1975	Feb	25	Swansea	0	2
1976	Feb	4	Wrexham	3	2

SCOTLAND v BRITISH ARMY

				Scotland	Army
1961	Feb	13	Motherwell	3	2

SCOTLAND v BELGIUM

				Scotland	Belgium
1960	April	20	Ghent	1	1

SCOTLAND v DENMARK

				Scotland	Denmark
1975	Oct	28	Edinburgh	4	1

SCOTLAND v FRANCE

				Scotland	France
1964	May	24	Nantes	0	0
1969	Dec	3	Glasgow	4	0

SCOTLAND v HOLLAND

				Scotland	Holland
1957	Oct	24	Edinburgh	4	1
1958	Oct	30	Amsterdam	2	1
1976	Feb	18	Breda	0	2
1976	Mar	24	Edinburgh	2	0

SCOTLAND v SWEDEN

				Scotland	Sweden
1975	Apr	16	Gothenburg	2	1

SCOTLAND v RUMANIA

				Scotland	Rumania
1975	May	31	Bucharest	2	1
1975	Dec	16	Falkirk	4	0

WALES v NORTHERN IRELAND

				Wales	N. Ireland
1962	Feb	7	Belfast	0	0
1963	Feb	27	Swansea	5	1
1964	Feb	5	Belfast	3	3
1965	Feb	10	Cardiff	2	2
1967	Feb	22	Belfast	1	2*
1968	Mar	20	Cardiff	0	1
1969	Mar	3	Wrexham (post. through snow)	–	–

* Abandoned 73 minutes, waterlogged.
† Abandoned half-time, rain.

ENGLISH UNDER-23 GOALSCORERS

13 Greaves; 11 Tambling; 8 Haynes; 7 Chivers, Clarke; 6 Byrne (J.), Hill (F.), Hinton (A.); 5 Charlton, Edwards (D.), Kidd; 4 Baker, Currie, Farmer, Jones (M.), Macdonald, Osgood, Pickering, Royle; 3 Blunstone, Channon, Eastham, Hollins, Johnson, Mills (D.), Paine, Pointer, Taylor; 2 Armstrong, Atyeo, Ball, Chisnall, Coates, Clough, Crowe, Greenhoff, Harrison, Holliday, Hooper, Latchford (R.), Marsh, Morgan, Mortimer, Murray (J.), Peters, Radford, Smith (T.), Stokes (A.), Stokes (D.), Tueart, Whymark; 1 A'Court, Ayre, Barrowclough, Beattie, Bell, Birchenall, Blockley, Bloomfield, Brabrook, Brooking, Case, Cross, Curry, Dobing, Dyson, Fletcher, George, Gillard, Harris (G.), Harris (J.), Hayes, Hill (G.), Hill (S.), Hitchens, Hurst (G.), Hurst (J.), Husband, Kay, Keegan, Kendall, Knowles (C.), Knowles (P.), Lloyd, Mannion, Moore, Murray (A.), Newton (H.), Nish, O'Grady, O'Rourke, Opponents, Paddon, Parry, Richards, Robson (B.), Robson (J.), (Burnley), Robson (J.), (Derby Co), Robson (R.), Rodgers, Sammels, Setters, Shawcross, Sissons, Suddick, Whitworth, Worthington.

UNDER-23 APPEARANCES 1954–76

ENGLAND

A'Court, A. (Liverpool): 1957 v F, Bul, Cz; 1958 v Bul, R, S, W. (7)
Allen, A. (Stoke C): 1959 v P, Cz, F, It, WG; 1960 v Hun, S. (7)
Allen, L. (Tottenham H): 1961 v W. (1)
Anderson, S. (Sunderland): 1955 v S (sub); 1956 v D; 1957 v F, Bul. (4)
Angus, J. (Burnley): 1959 v WG; 1960 v EG, P, Is; 1961 v It, W; 1962 v S. (7)
Armfield, J. (Blackpool): 1957 v D, Bul, R, Cz; 1958 v R; 1959 v P, Cz, F, It. (9)
Armstrong, D. (Middlesbrough): 1975 v P, W; 1976 v Cz, P (4)
Armstrong, G. (Arsenal): 1965 v Cz, WG, A; 1966 v Y, T. (5)
Ashurst, L. (Sunderland): 1961 v WG (1)
Aston, J. (Manchester U): 1970 v W. (1)
Atyeo, R. (Bristol C): 1955 v It, S. (2)
Ayre, R. (Charlton Ath): 1955 v It, S. (2)

Badger, L. (Sheffield U): 1964 v S, Hun, Is, T; 1965 v W, R, S, Cz, A; 1966 v T; 1968 v W, Hun (sub), WG. (13)
Bailey, M. (Charlton Ath): 1964 v S, F, Hun, Is, T. (5)
Baker, J. (Hibernian): 1959 v P, Cz; 1960 v F, Ho; 1961 v It; (Arsenal) 1963 v Y. (6)
Baldwin, T. (Chelsea): 1968 v It, WG. (2)
Ball, A. (Blackpool): 1965 v W, R, S, Cz, WG, Cz, A; 1966 v F. (8)
Banks, G. (Leicester C): 1961 v W, S. (2)
Barnwell, J. (Arsenal): 1961 v WG. (1)
Barrett, L. (Fulham): 1967 v G. (1)
Barrowclough, S. (Newcastle U): 1973 v W, S, Cz, D, Ho. (5)
Beattie, K. (Ipswich T): 1973 v W, Ho, S; 1974 v Pol, W, T, Y, F; 1975 v W (9)
Bell, C. (Manchester C): 1968 v S, Hun. (2)
Bennett, A. (Rotherham U): 1965 v W. (1)
Bernard, M. (Stoke C): 1971 v WG (sub), Se (sub), W. (3)
Birchenall, A. (Sheffield U): 1966 v T; 1968 v W, (Chelsea) It, WG. (4)
Blockley, J. (Coventry C): 1972 v Sw, W, S, EG, USSR, Pol; (Arsenal) 1973 v S, D, Ho, Cz. (10)
Bloomfield, J. (Arsenal): 1957 v D, Bul. (2)
Blunstone, F. (Chelsea): 1954 v It; 1955 v It, S; 1956 v D; 1957 v D. (5)
Bonds, W. (West Ham U): 1969 v W, Ho. (2)
Bonetti, P. (Chelsea): 1962 v S, T; 1963 v Bel, G, Y, Y, R; 1964 v F, Hun, Is, T; 1965 v A. (12)
Booth, C. (Wolverhampton W): 1957 v F (sub). (1)
Booth, T. (Manchester C): 1969 v Pt; 1972 v Sw, W, S. (4)
Boyer, P. (Norwich C): 1975 v S; 1976 v Cz. (2)
Brabrook, P. (Chelsea): 1958 v Bul, R, S; 1959 v P, Cz, It, WG; 1960 v Hun; 1961 v S. (9)
Broadbent, P. (Wolverhampton W): 1954 v It. (1)
Brooking, T. (West Ham U): 1972 v Sw. (1)
Buckley, M. (Everton): 1975 v P; 1976 v Cz. (2)
Burnside, D. (WBA): 1962 v T. (1)
Burrows, H. (Aston Villa): 1963 v G. (1)
Byrne, G. (Liverpool): 1961 v W. (1)
Byrne, J. (C. Palace): 1961 v W, S, WG; 1962 v Is, Ho, S, (West Ham U) T. (7)

Callaghan, I. (Liverpool): 1963 v G, Y, Y, R. (4)
Cantello, L. (WBA): 1972 v EG; 1973 v W, Ho (2), D, Cz; 1974 v Pol, D. (8)
Case, J. (Liverpool): 1976 v H. (1)
Cattlin, C. (Coventry C): 1969 v W, Ho. (2)
Channon, M. (Southampton): 1971 v Se, W, S; 1972 v Sw, W, S, EG (2) USSR (sub). (9)
Charlton, R. (Manchester U): 1959 v P, Cz, F; 1960 v Hun, S; 1961 v It. (6)
Cheesebrough, A. (Burnley): 1957 v F. (1)
Chisnall, P. (Manchesrer U): 1964 v W, WG, S, F. (4)
Chivers, M. (Southampton): 1964 v F (sub), Hun; 1965 v W, R (sub), S, Cz, WG, Cz, A (sub); 1966 v F, Y; 1968 v It, (Tottenham H) S, Hun, It, Hun, WG. (17)
Clark, C. (WBA): 1961 v W. (1)
Clarke, A. (Fulham): 1967 v W, A, G, Bul, T; (Leicester C) 1969 v Pt. (6)
Clayton, R. (Blackburn R): 1956 v D, S; 1957 v D, S, R, Cz. (6)
Clemence, R. (Liverpool): 1968 v W; 1971 v Se, W, S. (4)
Clough, B. (Middlesbrough): 1957 v S, Bul; 1958 v W. (3)
Coates, R. (Burnley): 1967 v W, G, Bul, T; 1969 v Ho, Pt, N, Bel. (8)
Cohen, G. (Fulham): 1960 v Hun, F, S, Ho; 1961 v S, WG; 1963 v Y, R. (8)
Connelly, J. (Burnley): 1961 v It. (1)
Coppell, S. (Manchester U): 1976 v H. (1)
Corrigan, J. (Manchester C): 1970 v USSR. (1)
Crawford, B. (Blackpool): 1962 v S. (1)
Cross, G. (Leicester C): 1963 v Y, Y, R; 1964 v W, WG, S, F, Hun, Is, T; 1966 v T. (11)
Crowe, C. (Leeds U): 1960 v F, S; (Blackburn R) 1961 v W, S. (4)
Crowther, S. (Aston Villa): 1958 v Bul, R, S. (3)
Currie, A. (Sheffield U): 1970 v W, Bul; 1971 v WG, S; 1972 v W, S, EG, Pol, USSR; 1973 v W, Ho, S, Cz (13)
Curry, W. (Newcastle U): 1958 v R. (1)

Davies, R. (Derby Co): 1974 v S (sub). (1)
Day, M. (West Ham U): 1974 v Y, F (sub); 1975 v S, W; 1976 v P (5)
Deakin, A. (Aston Villa): 1962 v Is, T; 1963 v Y (2), R; 1964 v T (sub). (6)
Dobing, P. (Blackburn R): 1959 v WG; 1960 v F, EG, P, Is; 1961 v It, S. (7)
Dobson, C. (Sheffield W): 1963 v Y (sub), R. (2)
Dobson, A. (Stoke C): 1975 v Cz, P, S; 1976 v Cz, P, H. (6)
Dodgin, W. (Arsenal): 1954 v It. (1)
Douglas, B. (Blackburn R): 1957 v D, F, Bul, R, Cz. (5)
Doyle, M. (Manchester C): 1968 v Hun, It, Hun, WG; 1969 v Pt, Ho, Bel, Pt. (8)
Dyson, J. (Manchester C): 1957 v S. (1)
Dyson, K. (Newcastle U): 1970 v Bul. (1)

Eastham, G. (Newcastle U): 1960 v F, S, Ho, EG, P, Is. (6)
Edwards, D. (Manchester U): 1954 v It; 1955 v It, S; 1956 v S; 1957 v R, Cz. (6)
Edwards, P. (Manchester U): 1970 v Bul (sub); 1971 v WG, Se. (3)
Ellis, Sam (Sheffield W): 1969 v W; 1970 v W, USSR. (3)
Ellis, Sidney (Charlton Ath): 1954 v It. (1)
Evans, A. (Liverpool): 1969 v Ho, Pt, Bel, Pt. (4)

Fantham, J. (Sheffield W): 1961 v It. (1)
Farmer, E. (Wolverhampton W): 1962 v Is, Ho. (2)
Farmer, J. (Stoke C): 1967 v W. (1)
Finney, A. (Sheffield W): 1954 v It; 1956 v S; 1957 v S. (3)
Fletcher, P. (Burnley): 1974 v D (sub), W, Y, F (sub). (4)
Flowers, R. (Wolverhampton W): 1955 v It, S. (2)
Ford, D. (Sheffield W): 1967 v W, S. (2)
Foulkes, W. (Manchester U): 1955 v It, S. (2)
Francis, G. (QPR): 1974 v D, S, T, Y (sub), F; 1976 v H. (6)
Francis, T. (Birmingham C): 1974 v Pol, D, W; 1976 v P, H. (5)

Garland, C. (Bristol C): 1970 v Bul (sub). (1)
George, C. (Arsenal): 1973 v W, Ho, Cz; 1974 v Pol, D. (5)
Gidman, J. (Aston Villa): 1975 v Cz; 1976 v Cz, P, H. (4)
Gillard, I. (QPR): 1974 v S, T, Y, F: 1975 v S/ (5)
Glazier, W. (Coventry C): 1965 v R, S, Cz. (3)
Gowling, A. (Manchester U): 1972 v Sw. (1)
Greaves, J. (Chelsea): 1958 v Bul, R, S, W; 1959 v P, Cz, F, It; 1960 v Hun, S, Ho; (Tottenham H) 1962 v S. (12)
Greenhoff, B. (Manchester U): 1974 v Y, F (sub); 1975 v Cz; 1976 v H. (4)
Greenhoff, J. (Birmingham C): 1969 v W, Ho, Ho (sub), Bel; 1976 v H. (5)
Groves, V. (Arsenal): 1957 v F. (1)
Grummitt, P. (Nottingham F): 1962 v Ho; 1964 v W, WG. (3)
Gunter, P. (Portsmouth): 1954 v It. (1)

Hankin, R. (Burnley): 1975 v Cz (sub), S, W. (3)
Harris, Gordon (Burnley): 1962 v Is; 1963 v Y. (2)
Harris, Gerry (Wolverhampton W): 1958 v Bul, R, S, W. (4)
Harris, J. (Everton): 1956 v S. (1)

Harris, R. (Chelsea): 1967 v W; 1968 v It, Hun, WG. (4)
Harrison, M. (Chelsea): 1961 v WG; 1962 v S, T. (3)
Harvey, J. (Everton): 1967 v S, A, G, Bul, T. (5)
Hayes, J. (Manchester C): 1958 v S, W. (2)
Haynes, J. (Fulham): 1955 v It, S; 1956 v D, S; 1957 v S, R, Cz; 1958 v Bul. (8)
Hibbitt, K. (Wolverhampton W): 1971 v W (sub) (1)
Hill, F. (Bolton W): 1961 v WG; 1962 v Is, Ho, S, T; 1963 v Bel, G, Y, Y, R. (10)
Hill, G. (Manchester U): 1976 v H. (1)
Hill, S. (Blackpool): 1962 v Is, Bel, S, T. (4)
Hindley, P. (Nottingham F): 1967 v G. (1)
Hinton, A. (Wolverhampton W): 1963 v Y, R; 1964 v W, (Nottingham F) Hun, Is, T; 1965 v R. (7)
Hinton, M. (Charlton Ath): 1962 v S, T; 1963 v Bel. (3)
Hitchens, G. (Cardiff C): 1957 v D. (1)
Hodgkinson, A. (Sheffield U): 1957 v D, F, S; 1958 v R, W; 1959 v P, Cz. (7)
Holiday, E. (Middlesbrough): 1960 v Hun, Ho, EG, P, Is (5)
Hollins, J. (Chelsea): 1965 v W, Cz, A; 1966 v F, Y; 1967 v W, S, A; 1968 v W, It, S, Hun. (12)
Hooper, H. (West Ham U): 1955 v It, S. (2)
Hopkinson, E. (Bolton W): 1957 v Bul, R, Cz; 1958 v Bul, S; 1959 v F. (6)
Howe, D. (WBA): 1956 v S; 1957 v F, S; 1958 v Bul, S, W. (6)
Hudson, A. (Chelsea): 1970 v S; 1971 v W, S; 1972 v S, EG; (with Stoke C), 1974 v S, T, Y, F; 1976 v H. (10)
Hughes, E. (Liverpool): 1968 v W, It, S; 1969 v Ho, Bel, Pt (sub); 1970 v R, Bul. (8)
Hunt, R. P. (Swindon T): 1963 v R; (Wolverhampton W) 1966 v Y, T. (3)
Hunter, N. (Leeds U): 1965 v W, R, S. (3)
Hurst, G. (West Ham U): 1964 v W, F, Is, T. (4)
Hurst, J. (Everton): 1967 v G, Bul, T; 1969 v W, Ho (2), Bel, Pt; 1970 v USSR. (9)
Husband, J. (Everton): 1967 v A (sub), G, Bul; 1970 v USSR, S. (5)
Hutchinson, I. (Chelsea): 1971 v W, S. (2)

Iley, J. (Tottenham H): 1958 v W. (1)

Jeffrey, A. (Doncaster R): 1957 v D, F. (2)
Jeffries, D. (Manchester C): 1972 v EG. (1)
Johnson, D. (Ipswich T): 1973 v Cz (2), Ho; 1974 v Pol; 1975 v Cz, P, W; 1976 v P, H. (9)
Jones, G. (Middlesbrough): 1962 v Is, Ho, S, T; 1963 v Bel, G. Y; 1974 v W, WG. (9)
Jones, M. (Sheffield U): 1965 v R, S, Cz, WG, A; 1966 v F, Y, T; 1967 v A. (9)
Jones, R. (Bournemouth): 1968 v Hun. (1)

Kay, A. (Sheffield W): 1959 v It, WG; 1960 v S, Ho, EG, P, Is. (7)
Kaye, A. (Barnsley): 1956 v D. (1)
Keegan, K. (Liverpool): 1972 v S, EG (2), Pol, USSR. (5)
Kember, S. (C Palace): 1971 v WG; (Chelsea) 1972 v Sw, EG. (3)
Kendall, H. (Everton): 1968 v W, It (2), Hun; 1969 v W, Ho. (6)
Kennedy, A. (Newcastle U): 1975 v Cz, P; 1976 v Cz, P, H. (2) (6)
Kennedy, R. (Arsenal): 1972 v W; 1973 v Ho, (1+1 sub), D, Cz (sub); 1974 v Pol (6)
Kevan, D. (WBA): 1957 v Bul, R, Cz; 1958 v Bul. (4)
Kidd, B. (Manchester U): 1968 v W, It, S; 1969 v Ho, Bel (sub); 1970 v W, USSR, S; 1971 v WG, Se. (10)
Kirkham, J. (Wolverhampton W): 1961 v W, S. (2)
Kirkup, J. (West Ham U): 1962 v Is, Ho, T. (3)
Knowles, C. (Tottenham H): 1965 v W; 1967 v W, S, G, Bul, T. (6)
Knowles, P. (Wolverhampton W): 1968 v W, It; 1969 v W, Ho. (4)

Labone, B. (Everton): 1961 v It, W, S; 1962 v Is, Ho; 1963 v Y, R. (7)
Lampard, F. (West Ham U): 1972 v Sw, EG, Pol, USSR. (4)
Latchford, P. (WBA): 1974 v Pol, W. (2)
Latchford, R. (Birmingham C): 1974 v D, W; (Everton) S, T, Y, F. (6)
Lawler, C. (Liverpool): 1966 v F, Y; 1967 v S, A. (4)
Leary, S. (Charlton Ath): 1954 v It. (1)
Le Flem, R. (Nottingham F): 1962 v Ho. (1)
Lloyd, L. (Liverpool): 1971 v WG, Se, W, S; 1972 v EG (2), Pol, USSR. (8)
Lock, K. (West Ham U): 1973 v D, Ho, Cz; 1976 v H. (4)
Lyons, M. (Everton): 1975 v Cz, P, S, W (sub); 1976 v Cz (5)

Maddren, W. (Middlesbrough): 1973 v Cz; 1974 v D, S, Y (sub), F. (5)
Macedo, E. (Fulham): 1959 v It, WG; 1960 v Hun, F, Ho, EG, P, Is; 1961 v It, WG. (10)
Mannion, G. (Wolverhampton W): 1960 v P, Is. (2)
Marsh, R. (QPR): 1968 v S, Hun. (2)
Marshall, G. (Hearts): 1960 v S. (1)
Matthews, R. (Coventry C): 1955 v It, S; 1965 v D, S. (4)
McDermott, T. (Newcastle U): 1974 v W. (1)
Macdonald, M. (Newcastle U): 1972 v W, S, EG; 1973 v W. (4)
McDowell, J. (West Ham U): 1973 v W, Ho (2), S, Cz (2), D; 1974 v Pol, D, S, T, Y (sub), F. (13)
McFarland, R. (Derby Co): 1969 v Ho (2), Bel, Pt; 1970 v S. (5)
McGrath, J. (Newcastle U): 1961 v WG. (1)
McGuinness, W. (Manchester U): 1959 v P, Cz, F; 1960 v Hun. (4)
McNeil, M. (Middlesbrough): 1960 v F, Ho, EG, P, Is; 1961 v It, S; 1963 v Bel, G. (9)
Miller, B. (Burnley): 1960 v EG, P, Is. (3)
Mills, D. (Middlesbrough): 1974 v S, T, Y, F; 1975 v Cz; 1976 v Cz, P (sub), H (sub). (8)
Mills, M. (Ipswich T): 1971 v W; 1972 v S, EG, Pol, USSR. (5)
Mills, S. J. (Southampton): 1974 v W. (1)
Mobley, V. (Sheffield W): 1965 v W, R, S, Cz, WG, Cz, A; 1966 v F, Y; 1967 v A, G, Bul, T. (13)
Montgomery, J. (Sunderland): 1964 v S; 1967 v S, A, G, Bul, T. (6)
Moore, I. (Nottingham F): 1967 v S, A. (2)
Moore, R. (West Ham U): 1961 v It, W, S, WG, 1962 v Is, Ho, S, T. (8)
Moores, I. (Stoke C): 1975 v W; 1976 v Cz. (2)
Morgan, R. (Tottenham H): 1970 v Bul. (1)
Morley, M. (Preston NE): 1975 v W (sub). (1)
Mortimer, D. (Coventry C): 1973 v W, Ho (2), S, Cz (2). (6)
Mullery, A. (Fulham): 1961 v It; 1962 v Ho; 1963 v Bel. (3)
Murray, A. (Chelsea): 1965 v R, S, Cz, WG, Cz, A. (6)
Murray, J. (Wolverhampton W): 1958 v S; 1959 v F. (2)

Nattrass, I. (Newcastle U): 1976 v H. (1)
Neal, R. (Lincoln C): 1957 v D, F, S, (Birmingham C) Bul. (4)
Newton, H. (Nottingham F): 1965 v R, Cz; 1967 v Bul, T. (4)
Newton, K. (Blackburn R): 1964 v S, Hun, Is, T. (4)
Nicholls, J. (WBA): 1954 v It. (1)
Nisbet, G. (WBA): 1972 v EG. (1)
Nish, D. (Leicester C): 1969 v Pt (sub), Bel, Pt; 1970 v W, USSR, S, Bul; 1971 v Se, W, S. (10)
Norman, M. (Tottenham H): 1956 v S; 1957 v R, Cz. (3)

O'Grady, M. (Huddersfield T): 1961 v S; 1963 v Bel; (Leeds U) 1966 v F. (3)
O'Neil, B. (Burnley): 1966 v T. (1)
O'Rourke, J. (Middlesbrough): 1967 v T. (1)
Osgood, P. (Chelsea): 1968 v W, S, Hun; 1970 v W, USSR, S. (6)

Pacey, D. (Luton T): 1959 v WG. (1)
Paine, T. (Southampton): 1960 v Ho, EG; 1961 v WG; 1962 v T (sub). (4)
Paddon, G. (West Ham U): 1976 v H. (1)
Palmer, G. (Wolverhampton W.): 1974 v W; 1975 v P. (2)
Pardoe, G. (Manchester C): 1968 v Hun; 1969 Pt, Bel, Pt. (4)
Parkes, P. (QPR): 1972 v W, S, EG; 1973 v D, Cz; 1976 v Cz. (6)
Parkin, D. (Wolverhampton W): 1970 v W, USSR, Bul, S; 1971 v S. (5)
Parry, R. (Bolton W): 1958 v R; 1959 v F, It, WG. (4)
Payne, D. (C Palace): 1968 v W (sub). (1)
Pearson, S. (Manchester U): 1976 v H. (1)
Pegg, D. (Manchester U): 1956 v S; 1957 v S, R. (3)
Pejic, M. (Stoke C): 1972 v Pol, USSR; 1973 v W, Ho (2), S, D, Cz. (8)

Perryman, S. (Tottenham H): 1972 v EG, Pol, USSR; 1973 v S, D Ho, Cz; 1974 v Pol, D, W, S, T, Y; 1975 v Cz, P, S, W. (17)
Peters, M. (West Ham U): 1963 v Bel, G; 1964 v W, WG; 1966 v T. (5)
Pickering, F. (Blackburn R): 1964 v W, WG, S. (3)
Piper, N. (Plymouth Arg): 1970 v Bul; (Portsmouth) 1971 v WG, Se, S. (4)
Pointer, R. (Burnley): 1959 v It; 1960 v Hun, EG, P, Is. (5)
Powell, B. (Wolverhampton W): 1974 v S; 1975 v Cz, P (sub), S. (4)
Powell, S. (Derby Co): 1975 v S. (1)
Pugh, J. (Sheffield W): 1970 v W. (1)

Quixall, A. (Sheffield W): 1956 v S. (1)

Radford, J. (Arsenal): 1969 v W, Ho (2), Pt. (4)
Rankin, A. (Everton): 1965 v W. (1)
Reaney, P. (Leeds U): 1964 v F; 1965 v S, WG, Cz; 1967 v S. (5)
Richards, J. (Wolverhampton W): 1972 v EG, Pol, USSR; 1973 v S; 1974 v Pol (sub), W. (6)
Riley, H. (Leicester C): 1958 v W; 1961 v W. (2)
Robson, B. (Newcastle U): 1967 v S; 1969 v Pt. (2)
Robson, Jimmy (Burnley): 1959 v WG. (1)
Robson, John (Derby Co): 1971 v WG, Se, S; 1972 v W, S, EG; (Aston Villa) 1973 v Cz. (7)
Robson, R. (Fulham): 1956 v D. (1)
Rofe, D. (Leicester C): 1973 v Cz (sub). (1)
Rogers, D. (Swindon T): 1966 v Y; 1968 v W. (2)
Royle, J. (Everton): 1968 v Hun (sub), Hun; 1969 Ho, Bel (sub), Pt; 1970 v USSR, S (sub); 1971 v WG, Se; 1972 v Sw. (10)

Sadler, D. (Manchester U): 1967 v S; 1968 v W; 1969 v Pt. (3)
Sammels, J. (Arsenal): 1967 v W, A, G, Bul, T; 1968 v It (2), Hun, WG. (9)
Scanlon, A. (Manchester U): 1959 v P, Cz, F, It, WG. (5)
Scott, M. (Chelsea): 1959 v P, Cz, F; 1960 v Hun. (4)
Setters, M. (WBA): 1958 v Bul, R, S, W; 1959 v P, Cz, F, It, WG; 1960 v Hun, F, (Manchester U) S, Ho, EG, P, Is. (16)
Shaw, B. (Sheffield U): 1968 v It, Hun. (2)
Shaw, G. (Sheffield U): 1956 v D; 1957 v D, F, S, Bul. (5)
Shawcross, D. (Manchester C): 1961 v WG. (1)
Shellito, K. (Chelsea): 1963 v Y. (1)
Shilton, P. (Leicester C): 1969 v W, Ho (2), Pt (2); 1970 v W, Bul, S; 1971 v WG; 1972 v Sw, EG, Pol, USSR. (13)
Sillett, P. (Chelsea): 1955 v It, S; 1956 v D. (3)
Sissons, J. (West Ham U): 1965 v W, S; 1967 v W; 1968 v Hun, WG; 1969 v W, Pt (2), Ho, Bel. (10)
Sleeuwenhoek, J. (Aston Villa): 1963 v G, Y. (2)
Smith, J. (West Ham U): 1960 v F. (1)
Smith, Tommy (Liverpool): 1965 v Cz (2), WG, A; 1966 v F, Y; 1967 v S, A; 1968 v It, S. (10)
Smith, Trevor (Birmingham C): 1955 v It, S; 1956 v D, S; 1957 v D, F, S, Bul, R, Cz; 1958, v Bul, R, S, W; 1959 v It. (15)
Smith, W. (Sheffield W): 1969 v Pt (2), Ho; 1970 v W, Bul, S. (6)

Springett, P. (Sheffield W): 1968 v It (2), S, Hun, WG; 1968 v Bel. (6)
Stephenson, A. (C Palace): 1967 v W; 1968 v It, S, (West Ham U) Hun (2), It, WG. (7)
Stepney, A. (Millwall): 1966 v F, Y, T. (3)
Stevens, D. (Bolton W): 1957 v R, Cz. (2)
Stevenson, A. (Burnley): 1973 v W, Ho (2), S, Cz; 1974 v D, S, T, F; 1975 v Cz, P. (11)
Stiles, N. (Manchester U): 1965 v S, WG, Cz. (3)
Stokes, A. (Tottenham H): 1956 v D. (1)
Stokes, D. (Huddersfield T): 1963 v Bel, G, Y, R (sub). (4)
Suddick, A. (Newcastle U): 1963 v Bel, Y. (2)
Sullivan, C. (Plymouth Arg): 1974 v Pol, D. (2)
Summerbee, M. (Manchester C): 1966 v T. (1)
Sunderland, A. (Wolverhampton W): 1974 v S (sub). (1)
Swan, P. (Sheffield W): 1960 v F, S, Ho. (3)
Sydenham, J. (Southampton): 1960 v F, S. (2)

Talbut, J. (Burnley): 1964 v W, WG, S, F, Hun, Is, T. (7)
Tambling, R. (Chelsea): 1963 v Bel, G, Y; 1964 v WG, S, F, Hun, Is, T; 1965 v W (sub), R, Cz, A. (13)
Taylor, P. (C Palace): 1975 v Cz, P; 1976 v Cz (sub), P. (4)
Taylor, T. (West Ham U): 1972 v EG (sub); 1973 v W, Ho, Cz; 1974 v Pol, D, W, S, T, Y; 1976 v P. (11)
Thomas, D. (Burnley): 1970 v Bul, S; 1971 v WG, Se, W; 1972 v Sw, S, EG; (QPR) 1974 v D (sub), T, F. (11)
Thompson, P. (Liverpool): 1964 v WG, S, F; 1966 v F. (4)
Thompson, P. B. (Liverpool): 1975 v W; 1976 v H. (2)
Thomson, R. (Wolverhampton W): 1963 v Y, R; 1964 v W, WG, F; 1965 v R, Cz, WG, Cz, A: 1966 v F, Y, T; 1967 v W, A. (15)
Todd, C. (Sunderland): 1968 v Hun, Hun (sub), WG; 1969 v W, Ho (sub); 1970 v W, USSR, S; 1971 v WG, Se, W (Derby Co) S; 1972 v W; 1975 v W. (14)
Towers, A. (Manchester C): 1972 v USSR, R (sub); 1973 v D, Cz (Sunderland); 1975 v W; 1976 v Cz, P, H. (8)
Tueart, D. (Manchester C): 1975 v S. (1)

Usher, B. (Sunderland): 1964 v F. (1)

Venables, T. (Chelsea): 1963 v G; 1964 v Hun, Is, T. (4)

Wallington, M. (Leicester C): 1976 v H (2). (2)
West, A. (Burnley): 1972 v W. (1)
West, G. (Blackpool): 1962 v Is; (Everton) 1965 v WG, Cz. (3)
Whitefoot, G. (Manchester U): 1954 v It. (1)
Whitham, J. (Sheffield W): 1969 v W (sub). (1)
Whittle, A. (Everton): 1971 v W. (1)
Whitworth, S. (Leicester C): 1972 v Sw; W; 1974 v Y, F; 1975 v S (2), W. (6)
Whymark, T. (Ipswich T): 1973 v Ho (2), S, Cz (2), D; 1975 v P. (7)
Wilkins, R. (Chelsea): v P, H. (2)
Wilson, D. (Preston NE): 1964 v W, WG, S, Hun, Is, T; 1965 v W. (7)
Wood, R. (Manchester U): 1954 v It. (1)
Worthington, F. (Huddersfield T): 1972 v Pol, USSR. (2)
Wright, T. (Everton): 1967 v Bul, T; 1968 v It (2), S, Hun (2). (7)

NORTHERN IRELAND
(all matches against Wales)

Briggs, R. (Manchester U): 1962; (Swansea T), 1965. (2)
Burke, (Portadown): 1963. (1)

Campbell, W. (Distillery): 1964; (Sunderland) 1965 (Dundee): 1967. (3)
Clarke, F. (Arsenal): 1962, 1963, 1964, 1965. (4)
Clarke, N. (Ballymena): 1962; (Sunderland) 1963. (2)
Clements, D. (Coventry C): 1965, 1967, 1968. (3)
Craig, D. (Newcastle U): 1965, 1967. (2)
Craig, W. (Linfield): 1965. (1)

Dunlop, J. (Coleraine): 1965, 1968. (2)

Elder, A. (Burnley): 1964. (1)
Elwood, J. (L. Orient): 1962. (1)

Hamilton, B. (Linfield): 1968. (1)

Harkin, T. (Port Vale): 1963. (1)
Harvey, M. (Sunderland): 1962, 1963, 1964. (3)

Irvine, R. (Linfield): 1963. (1)
Irvine, W. (Burnley): 1963, 1964, 1965. (3)

Jackson, T. (Everton): 1968. (1)
Jennings, P. (Watford): 1964. (1)
Johnston, W. (Glenavon): 1962. (1)

Magill, J. (Arsenal): 1962. (1)
McAvoy, W. (Ards): 1968. (1)
McCaffrey, W. (Leicester C): 1963 (1)
McIlroy (Burnley): 1968. (1)
McKeag, W. (Glentoran): 1967, 1968. (2)
McKenzie, R. (Airdrieonians): 1967, 1968. (2)
McKinney (Falkirk): 1967. (1)

McLaughlin, J. (Shrewsbury T): 1963 (Swansea T), 1964. (2)
McMillan, S. (Wrexham): 1964. (1)
McMordie, E. (Middlesbrough): 1967. (1)
McNeill, M. (Middlesbrough): 1968. (1)
Morrow (Glentoran): 1968. (1)

Napier, J. (Bolton W): 1967; (Brighton) 1968. (2)
Neill, T. (Arsenal): 1962, 1963, 1964, 1965, (4)
Nicholson, J. (Manchester U): 1962, 1963, 1964, (Huddersfield T), 1965. (4)

O'Neill, J. (Sunderland): 1962. (1)

Rice, P. (Arsenal): 1968. (1)
Ross, E. (Glentoran): 1967. (1)

Sloan, D. (Scunthorpe U): 1964. (1)

Todd, S. (Burnley): 1965, 1967, 1968. (3)
Trainor, D. (Crusaders): 1967. (1)

Welsh, E. (Distillery): 1962. (1)

Ireland also played an under 23 international v Italy on 26 March, 1969 at Brescia losing 1-2.

Team:—

Gaston, R. (Oxford United)
Hamilton, B. (Linfield)
Hunter, A. (Oldham Athletic)
Johnston, J. (Blackpool)
McKenzie, R. (Airdrieonians)
Morrow, T. (Glentoran)
Mullan, B. (Fulham)
Nelson, S. (Arsenal)
O'Doherty, A. (Coleraine)
Rice, P. (Arsenal)
Todd, S. (Burnley)

SCOTLAND

Aitken, C. (Aston Villa): 1962 v E, W; 1963 v W. (3)
Alderson, B. (Coventry C): 1973 v E. (1)
Allan, W. (Aberdeen): 1963 v W. (1)
Anderson, G. (Morton): 1973 v W. (1)

Baillie, D. (Airdrieonians): 1955 v E; 1959 v W. (2)
Baird, D. (Partick T): 1959 v W. (1)
Baxter, James (Raith R): 1959 v W. (1)
Baxter, John (Hibernian): 1959 v W. (1)
Baxter, T. (Queen of the South): 1956 v E. (1)
Beattie, R. (Celtic): 1958 v Ho (2), E. (3)
Blacklaw, J. (Hibernian): 1970 v F, E, W; 1971 v E. (4)
Bone, J. (Norwich C): 1972 v E, W; 1973 v E. (3)
Brand, W. (Rangers): 1958 v E. (1)
Bremner, D. (Hibernian): 1975 v E, W, Se; 1976 v D (2), R, W, Ho (2). (9)
Bremner, W. (Leeds U): 1964 v E, F; 1965 v W, E. (4)
Brown, H. (Kilmarnock): 1963 v W. (1)
Brown, J. (Chesterfield): 1974 v W (sub), E (sub) (Sheffield U); 1975 v E (sub), Se (sub). (4)
Brownlie, J. (Hibernian): 1972 v 1, W; 1976 v W, Ho (2). (5)
Bruce, A. (Newcastle U): 1974 v E. (1)
Buchan, M. (Aberdeen): 1971 v W; 1972 v W, E. (3)
Burley, G. (Ipswich T): 1975 v E, Se (2).
Burns, F. (Manchester U): 1968 v E. (1)
Burns, K. (Birmingham C): 1974 v W; 1976 v Ho. (2)

Calderwood, R. (Birmingham C): 1974 v E. (1)
Caldow, E. (Rangers): 1955 v E; 1957 v E. (2)
Campbell, A. (Charlton Ath): 1970 v W. (1)
Carr, W. (Coventry C): 1970 v F, W; 1971 v W; 1972 v E. (4)
Clark, R. (Aberdeen): 1967 v W, E. (2)
Clunie (Hearts): 1970 v E, W. (2)
Colquhoun (WBA): 1968 v E. (1)
Colrain (Celtic): 1958 v Ho. (1)
Conn, A. (Tottenham H): 1975 v R; 1976 v D, R. (3)
Connelly, G. (Celtic): 1970 v E; 1971 v E; 1972 v E. (3)
Connolly, J. (Everton): 1971 v W; 1973 v W. (2)
Cooke, C. (Aberdeen): 1963 v W; 1964 v W; 1965 v W; (Dundee) 1965 v E. (4)
Cormack, P. (Hibernian): 1965 v W, E; 1967 v W, E; 1968 v E. (5)
Cousin, A. (Dundee): 1958 v Ho; 1960 v E, Bel. (3)
Craig, J. (Partick T): 1976 v D, R, W, Ho. (4)
Craig, T. (Sheffield W): 1974 v E (Newcastle U): 1975 v W, Se, R; 1976 v D (2), R, W, Ho. (9)
Crawford, I. (Hearts): 1957 v E. (1)
Crerand, P. (Celtic): 1961 v E. (1)
Cropley, A. (Hibernian): 1972 v W; 1973 v E; 1974 v W. (3)
Cruickshank, J. (Queen's Park): 1960 v Bel; (Hearts): 1964 v W, E. (3)
Currie, D. (Clyde): 1958 v Ho (2), E; 1959 v W. (4)
Dalglish, K. (Celtic): 1972 v W, E; 1973 v W; 1976 v H. (4)
Davie, A. (Dundee U): 1964 v F. (1)
Dickson, P. (Queen of the South): 1976 v H (sub). (1)
Dickson, W. (Kilmarnock): 1970 v E. (1)
Donachie, W. (Manchester C): 1972 v W, E. (2)
Donaldson, A. (Dundee): 1965 v W, E. (2)
Doyle, J. (Ayr U): 1973 v E, W; 1974 v W (sub). (3)
Duff, W. (Hearts): 1955 v E. (1)
Duncan, A. (Hibernian): 1971 v E. (1)

Eston, J. (Hibernian): 1964 v W. (1)
Edwards, A. (Dunfermline Ath): 1976 v W. (1)
Ewen, R. (Aberdeen): 1959 v W. (1)

Ferguson, R. (West Ham U): 1968 v E. (1)
Forrest, J. (Rangers): 1964 v W; 1965 v E. (2)
Forsyth, A. (Manchester U): 1974 v W. (1)
Forsyth, C. (St Mirren): 1957 v E. (1)
Forsyth, T. (Motherwell): 1971 v E. (1)
Fraser, C. (Dunfermline Ath): 1962 v W; (Aston Villa) 1963 v W. (2)

Gabriel, J. (Dundee): 1960 v W (Everton), E, Bel; 1962 v W; 1963 v W, E. (6)
Gemmill, A. (Preston NE): 1970 v E. (1)
Gibb, T. (Partick T): 1968 v E (sub). (1)
Gibson, I. (Middlesbrough): 1964 v W, F. (2)
Gillies, D. (Bristol C): 1974 v E. (1)
Gilzean, A. (Dundee): 1961 v E; 1962 v W, E. (3)
Glen, A. (Queen's Park): 1957 v E. (1)
Gow, G. (Bristol C): 1974 v E (sub). (1)
Graham, A. (Aberdeen): 1975 v E, Se, R (sub). (3)
Graham, G. (Chelsea): 1965 v W, E. (2)
Gray, A. (Dundee): 1975 v E, W, R; (Aston Villa), 1976 v D. (4)
Gray, E. (Leeds U): 1976 v W, E. (2)
Gray, F. (Leeds U): 1974 v E; 1976 v D (2), R, Ho. (5)
Greig, J. (Rangers): 1964 v W, E. (2)

Hamilton, J. (Hearts): 1956 v E; 1957 v E. (2)
Hamilton, R. (Kilmarnock): 1965 v W. (1)
Hansen, A. (Partick T): 1975 v Se; 1976 v R, W. (sub). (3)
Harper, J. (Aberdeen): 1970 v W (sub); 1971 v W. (2)
Harrower, J. (Hibernian): 1958 v Ho. (1)
Hartford, A. (WBA): 1970 v W; 1971 v W; 1972 v E; 1973 v E, W. (5)
Hay, D. (Celtic): 1970 v F; 1971 v E, W. (3)
Henderson, W. (Rangers): 1962 v W, E. (2)
Herd, G. (Clyde): 1958 v Ho. (2)
Hermiston, J. (Aberdeen): 1971 v W. (1)
Hewie, J. (Charlton Ath): 1957 v E. (1)
Higgins, W. (Hearts): 1960 v E, W, Bel; 1962 v E. (4)
Hill, A. (Clyde): 1955 v E. (1)
Hilley, D. (Third Lanark): 1961 v E. (1)
Hogan, J. (Partick T): 1961 v E. (1)
Hollywood, D. (Southampton): 1965 v E. (1)
Holmes, R. (St Mirren): 1955 v E. (1)
Holt, D. (Queen's Park): 1958 v Ho; (Hearts). (1)
Holton, J. (Manchester U): 1973 v W (1)
Hood, H. (Clyde): 1968 v E. (1)
Hope, R. (WBA): 1967 v W. (1)
Houston, S. (Manchester U): 1975 v Se, R. (2)
Hughes, J. (Celtic): 1961 v E; 1962 v W, E; 1964 v E. (4)

Hughes, T. (Chelsea): 1970 v F, E. (2)
Hunter, A. (Kilmarnock): 1971 v E (sub); 1972 v W, E. (3)
Hunter, W. (Motherwell): 1960 v W, E, Bel; 1962 v E. (4)
Hutchison, T. (Blackpool): 1971 v W. (1)

Jackson, C. (Rangers): 1976 v Ho. (1)
Jardine, S. (Rangers): 1971 v E, W (sub); 1972 v W, E. (4)
Jarvie, A. (Airdrieonians): 1971 v E. (1)
Jeffrey, R. (Celtic): 1963 v W. (1)
Jordan, J. (Leeds U): 1976 v Ho. (1)
Johnston, W. (Rangers): 1970 v F, E. (2)
Johnstone, D, (Rangers): 1974 v W, E; 1975 v E; 1976 v W, Ho (2). (6)
Johnstone, J. (Celtic): 1964 v F, E. (2)

Kelly, E. (Arsenal): 1971 v E, W; 1974 v W. (3)
Kennedy, J. (Kilmarnock): 1958 v N. (1)
Kennedy, S. (Falkirk): 1973 v E, W; 1975 v W. (3)
Kennedy, S. (Rangers): 1975 v W. (1)
King, A. (Kilmarnock): 1964 v W, F; 1965 v W. (3)

Lamb, A. (Preston NE): 1974 v E (sub). (1)
Law, D. (Huddersfield T): 1960 v W, E; 1961 v E. (3)
Lawrence, T. (Liverpool): 1963 v W. (1)
Leggat, G. (Aberdeen): 1955 v E. (1)
Lochhead, A. (Burnley): 1963 v W. (1)
Lorimer, P. (Leeds U): 1970 v W, F. (2)

Macari, L. (Celtic): 1972 v W, E. (2)
Mackay, D. (Hearts): 1955 v E; 1957 v E; 1958 v Ho, E. (4)
Mackay, D. (Celtic): 1959 v W; 1960 v E, W, Bel. (4)
Malone, D. (Ayr U): 1970 v F. (1)
Martin, N. (Hibernian): 1964 v F. (1)
Martis, J. (Motherwell): 1960 v E. (1)
Marinello, P. (Hibernian): 1970 v F (sub), (Arsenal) v E (sub). (2)
McCalliog, J. (Sheffield W): 1967 v W, E. (2)
McCluskey, P. (Celtic): 1973 v E, W (sub); 1975 v E, W, R; 1976 v D. (6)
McCulloch, W. (Cardiff C): 1973 v W (sub). (1)
McDonald, I. (St Johnstone): 1974 v E. (1)
McDonald, R. (Celtic).
MacDonald, A. (Rangers): 1975 v E. (1)
McDougall, I. (Rangers): 1975 v W. (1)
McGillivray, A. (Third Lanark): 1962 v E. (1)
McGovern (Derby Co): 1972 v W; 1973 v W. (2)
McGrain, D. (Celtic): 1973 v W, E. (2)
McGrory, J. (Kilmarnock): 1964 v F, E; 1965 v W. (3)
McIntosh, J. (Falkirk): 1956 v E; 1958 v E, Ho. (3)
McLelland, C. (Aberdeen): 1976 v W, Ho. (2)
McLeod, J. M. (Hibernian): 1961 v E. (1)
McLintock, F. (Leicester C): 1962 v E. (1)
McMillan, T. (Aberdeen): 1967 v W, E. (2)
McNeill, W. (Celtic): 1960 v Bel; 1961 v E; 1962 v W, E; 1963 v W. (5)
McParland, D. (Partick T): 1955 v E. (1)
McQuade, D. (Partick T): 1972 v W (sub). (1)
MacRae, K. (Motherwell): 1971 v E, W. (2)
McVie, W. (Motherwell): 1976 v W, Ho. (2)
Milne, A. (Cardiff C): 1960 v W. (1)
Mitchell, I. (Dundee U): 1967 v W, E. (2)
Morgan, W. (Burnley): 1968 v E. (1)
Miller, W. (Aberdeen): 1974 v E; 1975 v E, W, Se; 1976 v D, R, W, Ho (2). (9)
Morrison, R. (Aberdeen): 1956 v E. (1)
Moncur, R. (Newcastle U): 1968 v E. (1)
Munro, F. (Wolverhampton W): 1970 v F, E, W (sub); 1971 v W. (4)
Murdoch, R. (Celtic): 1964 v E. (1)
Murray, D. (Cardiff C): 1965 v E. (1)
Murray, G. (Motherwell): 1964 v F; 1965 v W, E. (3)
Murray, M. (Rangers): 1965 v E; 1957 v E.(2)
Murray, S. (Dundee): 1968 v E. (1)

Narey, D. (Dundee U): 1975 v R; 1976 v D (2). (3)
Nicol, R. (Hibernian): 1956 v E; 1958 v Ho. (2)

Ogston, J. (Aberdeen): 1961 v E; 1962 v W, E. (3)
O'Hara, E. (Falkirk): 1958 v Ho (2), E. (3)
O'Hare, J. (Derby Co): 1970 v F, E, W. (3)
Oliver, J. (Hearts): 1971 v W (sub). (1)

Parker, A. (Falkirk): 1955 v E; 1956 v E; 1957 v E; 1958 v Ho (2), E. (6)
Parlane, D. (Rangers): 1973 v E (sub), W; 1974 v W; 1975 v E, W. (5)
Pearson, J. (St Johnstone): 1974 v W, E; 1975 (Everton) v W (sub), Se, R; 1976 v D. (6)
Penman, A. (Dundee): 1960 v Bel: 1962 v W; 1964 v W; 1965 v E. (4)
Pettigrew, W. (Aberdeen): 1975 v Se, R; 1976 v D (2), R, W, Ho. (7)
Phillip, I. (Crystal Palace): 1973 v E. (1)
Plenderleith, J. (Hibernian): 1957 v E; 1958 v Ho (2), E; 1960 v W. (5)
Prentice, R. (Hearts): 1974 v W; 1976 v D (sub), R. (3)
Price, W. (Airdrieonians): 1956 v E; 1958 v Ho. (2)
Provan, D. (Rangers): 1964 v E. (1)
Purdie, I. (Aberdeen): 1975 v E (sub). (1)

Rae, I. (Falkirk): 1956 v E. (1)
Reilly, F. (Dunfermline Ath): 1957 v E. (1)
Riddell, I. (St Mirren): 1960 v E; 1961 v E. (2)
Robb, D. (Aberdeen): 1970 v F, W; 1971 v E. (3)
Roberts, R. (Motherwell): 1962 v W. (1)
Robertson, H. (Dundee): 1962 v W. (1)
Robertson, J. (St Mirren): 1964 v W; (Tottenham H) 1964 v F; 1965 v W; 1968 v E. (4)
Robinson, R. (Dundee): 1974 v W. (1)
Rough, A. (Partick T): 1973 v E; 1975 v Se, R; 1976 v D (2), R, W, Ho (2). (9)

St John, I. (Motherwell): 1960 v E, Bel. (2)
Scott, A. (Rangers): 1958 v E. (1)
Sharkey, D. (Sunderland): 1964 v F, E. (2)
Shevlane, C. (Hearts): 1964 v W, F, E; 1965 v W. (4)
Slater, R. (Falkirk): 1959 v W. (1)
Smith, D. (Aberdeen): 1963 v W; 1964 v W. (2)
Smith, G. (Kilmarnock): 1975 v W, Se, R (sub); 1976 v W (sub). (4)
Smith, G. (St Johnstone): 1975 v R; 1976 v D (2), R. (4)
Smith, J. (Aberdeen): 1967 v E. (1)
Smith, J. (Aberdeen): 1976 v Ho. (1)
Sneddon, D. (Dundee): 1959 v W. (1)
Souness, G. (Middlesbrough): 1974 v E; 1976 v Ho. (2)
Stanton, P. (Hibernian): 1967 v W, E; 1968 v E. (3)
Stein, C. (Hibernian): 1968 v E. (1)
Stewart, D. (Ayr U): 1970 v W. (1)
Stewart, J. (Kilmarnock): 1973 v W; 1974 v W, E; 1975 v E; 1976 v W (sub). (5)
Sullivan, D. (Clyde): 1975 v E, W (sub). (2)

Thomson, A. (Hearts): 1970 v F, E, W. (3)
Thomson, J. (Hearts): 1958 v E; 1960 v Bel. (2)
Tinney, H. (Partick T): 1967 v W, E. (2)

Ure, I. (Dundee): 1961 v E. (1)

Wallace, J. (Dunfermline Ath): 1974 v W. (1)
Walsh, J. (Celtic): 1955 v E. (1)
Weir, A. (Motherwell): 1960 v E, Bel, W. (3)
White, J. (Tottenham H): 1960 v W. (1)
Whyte, J. (Aberdeen): 1967 v W, E. (2)
Wilson, R. (WBA): 1970 v W. (1)
Wilson, D. (Rangers): 1959 v W. (1)
Wishart, R. (Aberdeen): 1955 v E; 1956 v E. (2)

Young, A. (Hearts): 1956 v E; 1957 v E; 1958 v E, Ho; 1959 v W; 1960 v W. (6)
Young, I. (Celtic): 1965 v E. (1)
Young, Q. (Ayr U): 1971 v E. (1)
Young, W. (Aberdeen): 1972 v W; 1973 v E; 1975 v W, R; 1976 v D. (5)

WALES

Aitken, P. (Bristol R): 1975 v E, S; 1976 v S (sub). (3)
Aizlewood, S. (Newport Co): 1972 v E, S; 1973 v S; 1974 v E; 1976 v S. (5)

Baker, C. (Cardiff C): 1958. (1)
Baker, T. (Plymouth Arg): 1958 v E; 1959 v S. (2)
Barry, M. (Carlisle U): 1975 v E (sub). (1)
Blore, R. (Southport): 1962 v S; (Blackburn R) 1965 v E, D, Ni. (4)
Burton, O. (Newport Co): 1961 v E; (Norwich C), 1963 v S, Ni; (Newcastle U) 1965 v E, S. (5)

Cartwright, L. (Coventry C): 1974 v S; 1975 v E, S; 1976 v S. (4)
Charles, M. (Swansea T): 1958 v E. (1)
Coldrick, G. (Cardiff C): 1967 v S; 1968 v E. (2)
Collins, J. (Portsmouth): 1967 v E, Ni; (Tottenham H) 1968 v E, Ni; 1969 v E; (Portsmouth) 1972 v E, S. (7)
Curtis, A. (Swansea C): 1976 v S (sub). (1)

Davies, C. (Charlton Ath): 1971 v E, S; 1972 v E, S (sub). (4)
Davies, D. (Swansea C): 1971 v E, (Everton) S; 1975 v E. (3)
Davies, D. L. (Cardiff C): 1967 v E. (1)
Davies, R. (Norwich C): 1964 v S, Ni; 1965 v S. (3)
Davies, W. (Bolton W): 1963 v S; 1964 v E; 1965 v S, Ni. (4)
Davis, G. (Wrexham): 1970 v E, S; 1971 v E, S. (4)
Deacy, N. (PSV Eindhoven): 1976 v S. (1)
Derrett, S. (Cardiff C): 1970 v E; 1971 v E, S. (3)
Draper, D. (Swansea T): 1965 v E. (1)
Durban, A. (Cardiff C): 1963 v Ni; (Derby Co) 1964 v E, S, Ni. (4)
Dwyer, P. (Cardiff C): 1974 v E, S; 1975 v E, S; 1976 v S. (5)

Edwards, M. (Bolton W): 1958 v E; 1959 v S. (2)
Edwards, N. (Chester): 1973 v E, S; 1974 v E. (3)
Edwards, T. (Charlton Ath): 1958 v E; 1959 v S, Ni. (2)
Emmanuel, G. (Birmingham C): 1975 v S. (1)
England, M. (Blackburn R): 1960 v S; 1961 v E; 1962 v S, Ni; 1963 v Ni; 1964 v E, S, Ni; 1965 v E, S, Ni. (11)
Evans, B. C. (Swansea T): 1965 v E, S. (2)
Evans, I. (QPR): 1973 v E; 1974 v S. (2)
Evans, M. (Wrexham): 1967 v Ni; 1970 v E. (2)
Evans, R. (Swansea T): 1963 v Ni; 1964 v E, Ni. (3)

Flynn, B. (Burnley): 1975 v E, S. (2)
Fox, A. (Wrexham): 1959 v S. (1)

Gammon, S. (Cardiff C): 1960 v S; 1962 v Ni. (2)
Green, C. (Everton): 1962 v S, Ni; 1963 v S (Birmingham C) Ni; 1964 v E, S; 1965 v Ni. (7)
Griffiths, A. (Arsenal): 1961 v E (sub); 1962 v Ni; 1963 v S; (Wrexham) 1964
Griffiths, C. (Manchester U): 1974 v E, S. (2)
Godfrey, B. (Scunthorpe U): 1962 v Ni. (1)
Gwyther, D. (Swansea C): 1972 v E, S. (2)

Harris, C. (Leeds U): 1976 v S. (1)
Hawkins, D. (Leeds U): 1967 v S, Ni; 1968 v E, Ni; 1969 v E; (Shrewsbury T) 1970 v S. (6)
Hennessey, T. (Birmingham C): 1962 v Ni; 1963 v Ni; 1964 v S, Ni; 1965 v E, S. (6)
Hole, B. (Cardiff C): 1961 v S; 1962 v S; 1963 v S; 1965 v S, Ni. (5)
Hollins, D. (Brighton & HA): 1960 v S; 1961 v E. (2)
Hopkins, M. (Tottenham H): 1958 v E. (1)
Hubbard, T. (Swindon T): 1973 v S (sub); 1974 v E. (2)
Hughes, B. (Swansea T): 1960 v S; 1961 v E. (2)
Hughes, J. (Blackpool): 1971 v E (sub) S. (2)
Humphreys, G. (Everton): 1965 v Ni; 1967 v E, S, Ni; 1969 v E. (5)

James, G. (Blackpool): 1965 v E, Ni. (2)
James, L. (Burnley): 1972 v E, S; 1973 v E, S; 1974 v E; 1975 v E, S. (7)
John, D. (Cardiff C): 1965 v S. (1)
Johnson, J. (C Palace): 1974 v S; 1976 v S. (2)
Johnson, M. (Swansea T): 1963 v S; 1964 v E. (2)
Jones, A. (Swansea T): 1967 v E. (1)
Jones, B. (Bristol R): 1971 v E. (1)
Jones, B. (Swansea T): 1961 v E; 1962 v S, Ni; 1963 v S, Ni; 1964 v E, Ni; (Plymouth Arg) 1965 v S. (8)
Jones, C. (Tottenham H): 1958 v E. (1)
Jones, D. (Bournemouth): 1973 v S; 1974 v E, S. (4)
Jones, F. (Brighton & HA): 1959 v S; (Swindon) 1961 v E. (2)
Jones, J. (Wrexham): 1974 v S; 1975 v E, S (Liverpool); 1976 v S. (4)
Jones, K. (Cardiff C): 1958 v E. (1)
Jones, T. L. (Wrexham), 1963 v S. (1)
Jones, W. (Bristol R): 1968 v E, Ni; 1969 v E; 1970 v S; 1971 v E, S. (6)

Krzywicki, R. (WBA): 1967 v E, S; 1970 v S. (3)

Leek, K. (Northampton T): 1958 v E. (1)
Letheran, G. (Leeds U): 1976 v S. (1)
Lewis, B. (Cardiff C): 1965 v Ni; 1967 v E, S; 1968 v E; (Watford) 1968 v Ni. (5)
Lewis, J. (Grimsby T): 1976 v S. (1)
Llewellyn, D. (West Ham U): 1972 v S. (1)
Lloyd, B. (Southend U): 1970 v E, S. (2)
Lucas, A. (Wrexham): 1967 v S. (1)
Lucas, M. (Leyton O): 1962 v S. (1)

Mahoney, J. (Crewe Alex): 1967 v Ni; (Stoke C) 1969 v E; 1970 v E. (3)
Mielczarek, R. (Huddersfield T): 1968 v E, Ni. (2)
Millington, T. (WBA): 1962 v S, Ni; 1963 v S, Ni. (4)
Moore, G. (Cardiff C): 1960 v S; 1961 v E; 1962 v S; (Chelsea) 1962 v Ni; 1963 v S, Ni; (Manchester U) 1964 v E, S, Ni. (9)
Morgan, R. (Cardiff C): 1970 v S. (1)
Morgans, K. (Manchester U): 1959 v S; 1960 v S. (2)

Nurse, M. (Swansea T): 1960 v S; 1961 v E. (2)

Orritt, B. (Birmingham C): 1958 v E; 1939 v S; 1960 v S. (3)
O'Sullivan, P. (Brighton & HA): 1971 v S (sub), 1972 v E, S; 1973 v E, S; 1976 v S. (6)

Page, M. (Birmingham C): 1967 v E, S; 1968 v Ni; 1969 v E; 1970 v E, S. (6)
Parton, J. (Burnley): 1972 v E, S; 1974 v E. (3)
Pearson, D.; 1970 v S. (1)
Phillips, J. (Chelsea): 1973 v E, S; 1974 v S; 1975 v S. (4)
Phillips, L. (Cardiff C): 1971 v S; 1972 v S; 1973 v E, S (Aston Villa). (4)
Powell, D. (Wrexham): 1967 v E, Ni; 1968 v E, Ni. (4)
Price, P. (Peterborough U): 1970 v E, S; 1971 v E, S. (4)
Prince, F. (Bristol R): 1971 v S; 1972 v E, S; 1973 v E. (4)
Pugh, D. (Newport Co): 1967 v E, S. (2)

Randell, C. (Plymouth Arg): 1975 v E. (1)
Rankmore, F. (Cardiff C): 1962 v S, Ni. (2)
Rees, R. (Coventry C): 1963 v S, Ni; 1964 v E, S, Ni; 1965 v E, Ni. (7)
Rodrigues, P. (Cardiff C): 1964 v S, Ni; 1965 v E, S, Ni. (5)
Roberts, D. (Oxford U): 1973 v E, S; 1975 v E, (Hull C) S. (4)
Roberts, J. (Swansea T): 1967 v Ni; 1968 v E; (Northampton T) 1968 v Ni (sub); 1969 v E; 1970 v E. (5)
Roberts, P. (Bristol R): 1971 v E, S; 1972 v E, S; 1973 v E, S. (6)
Roberts, R. (Wrexham): 1962 v S, Ni. (2)
Rouse, V. (C Palace): 1959 v S. (1)
Rowland, J. (Newport Co): 1959 v S. (1)
Ryan, J. (Charlton Ath): 1965 v E. (1)

Screen, A. L. (Swansea C); 1971 v S (sub). (1)
Screen, W. (Swansea T): 1968 v Ni; 1969 v E. (2)
Sear, C. (Manchester C): 1959 v S; 1960 v S. (2)
Showers, J. (Cardiff C): 1973 v E, S; 1974 v E, S; 1975 v E, S. (6)
Simpkins, K. (Hartlepool U): 1967 v S. (1)
Smallman, D. (Wrexham): 1973 v S; 1974 v E, S; 1975 v E, (Everton) S. (5)
Sprake, G. (Leeds U): 1964 v E, S, Ni; 1965 v E, Ni. (5)
Stephens, J. (Hull C): 1958 v E. (1)
Summerhayes, D. (Cardiff C): 1967 v S. (1)

Thomas, G. (Swansea T): 1968 v E; 1971 v E, S. (3)
Thomas, M. (Wrexham): 1876 v S (sub). (1)
Thomas, J. (Newport Co): 1967 v Ni. (1)
Thomas, R. (Swindon T): 1967 v S, Ni; 1968 v Ni; 1969 v E; 1970 v E, S. (6)
Todd, K. H. (Swansea T): 1963 v Ni. (1)
Toshack, J. (Cardiff C): 1967 v E, (Liverpool) 1971 v E; 1972 v E. (3)

Vernon, R. (Blackburn R): 1959 v S. (1)
Villars, A. (Cardiff C): 1974 v E, S. (2)

Walker, M. (York C): 1967 v Ni; 1968 v E, Ni; (Watford) 1969 v E. (4)
Walley, T. (Arsenal): 1967 v E; Ni; (Watford) 1968 v E, Ni. (4)
Williams, D. (Bristol R): 1976 v S. (1)
Williams, G. (Swansea T): 1960 v S. (1)
Williams, G. E. (WBA): 1960 v S; 1961 v E. (2)
Williams, H. (Swansea T): 1961 v E; 1962 v S; 1964 v S, E, Ni. (5)

Yorath, T. (Leeds U): 1969 v E; 1970 v E, S; 1971 v E; 1972 v E, S; 1973 v E. (7)
Young, G. (Newport Co): 1970 v E. (1)

European Under-21 Championship 1980–82

Group 1	*P*	*W*	*D*	*L*	*F*	*A*	*Pts*
West Germany	6	5	0	1	15	5	10
Bulgaria	6	5	0	1	7	5	10
Austria	6	1	1	4	3	9	3
Finland	6	0	1	5	4	10	1

Group 2	*P*	*W*	*D*	*L*	*F*	*A*	*Pts*
France	4	3	0	1	7	4	6
Belgium	4	2	0	2	4	4	4
Cyprus	4	1	0	3	4	7	2

Group 3	*P*	*W*	*D*	*L*	*F*	*A*	*Pts*
USSR	4	1	3	0	1	0	5
Czechoslovakia	4	1	2	1	4	2	4
Turkey	4	1	1	2	2	5	3

Group 4	*P*	*W*	*D*	*L*	*F*	*A*	*Pts*
England	6	4	1	1	12	5	9
Hungary	6	3	0	3	12	9	6
Rumania	6	2	1	3	9	12	5
Switzerland	6	1	2	3	5	12	4

Group 5	*P*	*W*	*D*	*L*	*F*	*A*	*Pts*
Italy	4	3	0	1	5	2	6
Yugoslavia	4	2	1	1	4	2	5
Greece	4	0	1	3	2	7	1

Group 6	*P*	*W*	*D*	*L*	*F*	*A*	*Pts*
Scotland	4	2	1	1	7	4	5
Denmark	4	1	2	1	4	4	4
Sweden	4	1	1	2	3	6	3

Group 7	*P*	*W*	*D*	*L*	*F*	*A*	*Pts*
Poland	4	4	0	0	11	3	8
Norway	4	1	1	2	5	6	3
East Germany	4	0	1	3	4	11	1

Group 8	*P*	*W*	*D*	*L*	*F*	*A*	*Pts*
Spain	4	4	0	0	13	3	8
Netherlands	4	2	0	2	4	4	4
Luxembourg	4	0	0	4	2	12	0

Quarter-Finals
France 0, USSR 0; USSR 4, France 2; Spain 1, West Germany 0; West Germany 2, Spain 0; Poland 1, England 2; England 2, Poland 2; Italy 0, Scotland 1; Scotland 0, Italy 0.

Semi-Finals
Scotland 0, England 1; England 1, Scotland 1; USSR 3, West Germany 4; West Germany 5, USSR 0.

Final

Sheffield United Ground – First Leg
England 3 (*Owen 2, Fashanu*)
West Germany 1 (*Voeller*)
England: Hesford; D. Thomas, Caton, Fenwick, Duxbury, Lee, Owen, Hodgson (Fashanu), McCall, Goddard, Shaw.
West Germany: Immel; Gells, Otten, Strack, Wuttke (Reichart), Reinhardt, Rolff, Allofs T., Engels, Kempe (Kroth), Voeller.

Bremen – Second Leg
West Germany 3 (*Littbarski 3*)
England 2 (Duxbury, Goddard)
West Germany: Immel; Reinhardt, Gells, Otten, Moehlmann, Geiger, Engels, Kroth, Littbarski, Allofs T., Reichert.
England: Hesford; Thomas D., Duxbury, Caton, Fenwick, McCall, Owen, Lee, Goddard, Heath, Shaw.

England win on 5-4 aggregate.

Previous Under-21 Champions: 1978 Yugoslavia, 1980 Soviet Union.

EUROPEAN UNDER 21 CHAMPIONSHIP 1982–84
(GROUP POSITIONS AT 1.6.83)

GROUP 1

Edinburgh, 12 Oct, 1982

Scotland (1) 2 *(Walsh, Simpson)*

E Germany (0) 0 5000

Scotland: McAlpine; Gough, Nicol, Simpson, McLaughlin, Cooper, Black, McStay (Doyle), Nicholas (Ferguson), Walsh, Hewitt.
E Germany: Muller; Sanger, Alms, Utess, Schossier, Backs, Ernst, Leiberam, Meixner, Schulbe, Halata.
Referee: Lund Sorensen.

Berne, 16 Nov, 1982

Switzerland (0) 3 *(Zaugg, Koller, Sutter)*

Scotland (2) 4 *(McStay, Nicholas, Hewitt, Gough)* 1900

Switzerland: Brunner; Andermatt, Schallibaum, Rietmann, Tanner, Kundert (Zaugg), Sutter, Perret, Jeitziner, Koller, Bernaschina.
Scotland: McAlpine; Gough, Nicol, McStay, McLaughlin, Cooper (Crainie), Simpson, Nicholas, Walsh, Hewitt, Black.
Referee: Nagy.

Ghent, 14 Dec, 1982

Belgium (1) 1 *(Goossens)*

Scotland (1) 2 *(Nicholas, McGarvey)* 1500

Belgium: Verlinden; Van Walleghem, Cossey, De Wolff, Delangre, Sanders, Van Der Elst, Creve, Van Der Linden, Goossens, Claesen.
Scotland: McAlpine; Malpas, Nicol, Cooper, McLaughlin, Gough, Black, Stephen, Walsh, Simpson, McGarvey (Nicholas).
Referee: Dielia.

Dundee, 29 March, 1983

Scotland (0) 2 *(Black 2* [1 pen]*)*

Switzerland (0) 1 *(Koller* pen*)* 11,000

Scotland: McAlpine; Nicol, Malpas, McStay, McLaughlin, Cooper, Black, Simpson, McGarvey, Walsh, Hewitt.
Switzerland: Brunner; Andermatt, Rietman, Kundert, Tanner, Perret, Ledmer, Jaitziner, Sutter, Koller, Cina.
Referee: Bjornestad.

Other Group 1 Results
Belgium 0, Switzerland 0
E Germany 2, Belgium 1
Belgium 4, E Germany 2

	P	*W*	*D*	*L*	*F*	*A*	*Pts*
Scotland	4	4	0	0	10	5	8
Belgium	4	1	1	2	6	6	3
E Germany	3	1	0	2	4	7	2
Switzerland	3	0	1	2	4	6	1

Group 2
USSR 1, Poland 1
Finland 0, Poland 0
Finland 1, Portugal 1
Portugal 1, Poland 0
USSR 2, Finland 2
Poland 4, Finland 0
USSR 1, Portugal 1
Finland 0, USSR 1

	P	*W*	*D*	*L*	*F*	*A*	*Pts*
USSR	4	1	3	0	5	4	5
Portugal	3	1	2	0	3	2	4
Poland	4	1	2	1	5	2	4
Finland	5	0	3	2	3	8	3

GROUP 3

Hvivodre, 22 Sept, 1982

Denmark (1) 1 *(Christensen)*

England (1) 4 *(Mabbutt 2, Regis, Davis)* 500

Denmark: Jorgensen; Larsen H. (Larsen S.), Sorensen, Larson J., Hansen, Steffensen (Kjeldsen), Helt, Christensen, Heintze, Frimann, Vilfort.
England: Bailey; Venison, Mabbutt, McMahon, Kilkline, Whyte, Callaghan, Bracewell (Walsh), Regis, Davis (Pickering), Barnes.
Referee: Herrmann.

Athens, 16 Nov, 1982

Greece (0) 1 *(Georgamilis)*

England (0) 0 10,000

Greece: Kitsfoudis; Manolas, Georgamilis, Alvazides, Karaglozopoulos, Voutiritsas, Saravakos, Antoniou, Batsinilas (Madridis), Vlachos (Patrinos), Papadopoulos.
England: Bailey; Venison, Statham, McMahon (Bracewell), Kilkline, Whyte, Barnes (Hodge), Walsh, Hateley, Davis, Chamberlain.
Referee: Salomir.

Portsmouth, 29 March, 1983

England (1) 2 *(Wallace, Mpontzos og)*

Greece (0) 1 *(Voutirinsas)* 8499

England: Knight; Thomas, Gernon, Bracewell, Wright, Caton, McMahon, Walsh (Callaghan), Hately, Pickering (Davis), Wallace.
Greece: Gitsioudis; Manolas, Georgamalis, Vitsibons, Mpontzos, Aijavidis, Dimopoulos, Patronis, Voutirinsas, Valchos, Mavridid.
Referee: Viriato.

Newcastle, 26 April, 1983

England (0) 1 *(Walsh)*

Hungary (0) 0 7000

England: Knight; Thomas, Ryan, Bracewell, Wright, Stevens, Wallace, Walsh (Callaghan), Hateley (Davis), Pickering, Barnes.
Hungary: Disztl P.; Disztl L., Grosz, Szabo, Gere, Horvath, Kiprich (Teodoru), Csongradi, Kurucz, Detari, Boda.
Referee: Daina.

Other Group 3 Results
Hungary 1, Greece 1
Denmark 2, Hungary 1

	P	*W*	*D*	*L*	*F*	*A*	*Pts*
England	4	3	0	1	7	3	6
Greece	4	1	2	1	4	4	4
Denmark	3	1	1	1	4	6	3
Hungary	3	0	1	2	2	4	1

GROUP 4

Cardiff, 22 Sept, 1982

Wales (0) 0

Norway (0) 0 870

Wales: Wilmott; Hopkins, Lewis D., Slatter, Lewis J., Davies, Phillips, Bowen (Maddy), Loveridge, Hughes, Micaleff.
Norway: Thorstudt; Sorlie, Beunk, Halvor, Madsen, Sanderud, Fjelstad (Andersen J.), Brandhaug, Granstein, Andersen, C., Bergmolde.
Referee: Delacour.

Niksic, 14 Dec, 1982

Yugoslavia (0) 2 *(Mance 2)*

Wales (0) 0 7000

Yugoslavia: Pudar; Brnovic, Rac, Milosevic, Elzner, Radanovic (Caplik), Kajtaz, Bozovic, Cvetkovic, Gracan (Mance), Dinovic.
Wales: Wilmot; Hopkins, Lewis, Slatter, Bodin, Davies, Williams G., Williams D., Marustik, Giles, Hughes (Hodges).
Referee: Ture

Bangor, 26 April, 1983

Wales (0) 0

Bulgaria (1) 1 *(Valtchev)* 2403

Wales: Dibble; Hopkins, Marustik, Williams G. (Hodges), Slatter, Lewis, Davies, Loveridge, Gale (Pascoe), Walsh, Roberts.
Bulgaria: Valov; Koev, Mladenov D., Markov, Nikoltchev, Yanchev, Sirakov, Bakalov, Valtchev, Bakardjiev, Pachev.

Other Group 4 Results
Norway 2, Yugoslavia 2
Bulgaria 2, Norway 0
Bulgaria 0, Yugoslavia 2

	P	*W*	*D*	*L*	*F*	*A*	*Pts*
Yugoslavia	3	2	1	0	6	2	5
Bulgaria	3	2	0	1	3	2	4
Norway	3	0	2	1	2	4	2
Wales	3	0	1	2	0	3	1

GROUP 5
Cyprus 1, Rumania 2
Italy 2, Rumania 0
Czechoslovakia 2, Italy 1
Cyprus 0, Italy 1
Czechoslovakia 2, Cyprus 0
Cyprus 1, Czechoslovakia 4
Italy 2, Czechoslovakia 1

	P	*W*	*D*	*L*	*F*	*A*	*Pts*
Czechoslovakia	4	3	0	1	9	4	6
Italy	4	3	0	1	6	3	6
Rumania	2	1	0	1	2	3	2
Cyprus	4	0	0	4	2	9	0

GROUP 6
Austria 1, Albania 2
Turkey 0, Albania 1
Austria 1, Turkey 1
Albania 1, W Germany 1
Turkey 0, W Germany 1
Austria 1, W Germany 1
Albania 1, Turkey 0

	P	*W*	*D*	*L*	*F*	*A*	*Pts*
Albania	4	3	1	0	5	2	7
W Germany	3	1	2	0	3	2	4
Austria	3	0	2	1	3	4	2
Turkey	4	0	1	3	1	4	1

GROUP 7
Iceland 1, Netherlands 1
Spain 1, Iceland 0
Netherlands 5, Spain 0
Iceland 0, Spain 0

	P	*W*	*D*	*L*	*F*	*A*	*Pts*
Netherlands	2	1	1	0	6	1	3
Spain	3	1	1	1	1	5	3
Iceland	3	0	2	1	1	2	2

GROUP 8
Luxembourg 0, Sweden 4
France 1, Sweden 0
Luxembourg 0, France 5
Sweden 4, Luxembourg 1

	P	*W*	*D*	*L*	*F*	*A*	*Pts*
Sweden	3	2	0	1	8	2	4
France	2	2	0	0	6	0	4
Luxembourg	3	0	0	3	1	13	0

UNDER-21 APPEARANCES 1976–1983

ENGLAND

Allen, C. (QPR) 1980 v EG (sub); 1981 (C Palace) v N, R (3)
Anderson, V. A. (Nottingham F), 1978 v I (1)
Bailey, G. R. (Manchester U), 1979 v W, Bul; 1980 v D, S (2), EG; 1982 v N; 1983 v D, Gr (11)
Baker, G. E. (Southampton), 1981 v N, R (2)
Bannister, G. (Sheffield W), 1982 v Pol (1)
Barnes, J. (Watford), 1983 v D, Gr (2)
Bertschin, K. E. (Birmingham C), 1977 v S; 1978 v Y (2) (3)
Birtles, G. (Nottingham F), 1980 v Bul, EG (sub) (2)
Blissett, L. L. (Watford), 1979 v W, Bul (sub), Se; 1980 v D (4)
Bracewell, P. (Stoke C), 1983 v D, Gr (2, one sub), H (4)
Bradshaw, P. W. (Wolverhampton W), 1977 v W, S; 1978 v Fi, Y (4)
Butcher, T. I. (Ipswich T), 1979 v Se; 1980 v D, Bul, S (2), EG (2) (7)
Callaghan, N. (Watford), 1983 v D, Gr (sub), H (sub) (3)
Caton, T. (Manchester C), 1982 v N, H (sub), Pol (2), S; 1983 v WG (2), Gr (8)
Chamberlain, M. (Stoke C), 1983 v Gr (1)
Chapman, L. (Stoke C), 1981 v Ei (1)
Corrigan, J. T. (Manchester C), 1978 v I (2), Y (3)
Cowans, G. S. (Aston Villa), 1979 v W, Se; 1980 v Bul, EG; 1981 v R (5)
Crooks, G. (Stoke C), 1980 v Bul, S (2), EG (sub) (4)
Cunningham, L. (WBA), 1977 v S, Fi, N (sub); 1978 v N, Fi, I (6)

Curbishley, L. C. (Birmingham C), 1981 v Sw (1)
Davis, P. (Arsenal), 1982 v Pol, S; 1983 v D, Gr (2, one sub), H (sub) (6)
Deehan, J. M. (Aston Villa), 1977 v N; 1978 v N, Fi, I; 1979 v Bul Se (sub); 1980 v D (7)
Dennis, M. E. (Birmingham C), 1980 v Bul; 1981 v N, R (3)
Dillon, K. P. (Birmingham C), 1981 v R (1)
Duxbury, M. (Manchester U), 1981 v Sw (sub), Ei (sub), R (sub); Sw; 1982 v N; 1983 v WG (2) (7)
Dyson, P. I. (Coventry C), 1981 v N, R, Sw, Ei (4)

Fairclough, D. (Liverpool), 1977 v W (1)
Fashanu, J. (Norwich C), 1980 v EG; 1981 v N (sub), R, Sw, Ei (sub), H; (Nottingham F), 1982 v N, H, Pol, S; 1983 v WG (sub) (11)
Fenwick, T. W. (C Palace), 1981 v N, R, Sw, Ei, (QPR), R; 1982 v N, H, S (2); 1983 v WG (2) (11)
Foster, S. (Brighton & HA), 1980 v EG (sub) (1)
Futcher, P. (Luton T), 1977 v W, S, Fi, N; (Manchester C), 1978 v N, Fi, I (2), Y (2); 1979 v D (11)

Gale, A. (Fulham), 1982 v Pol (1)
Gernon, T. (Ipswich T), 1983 v Gr (1)
Gibson, C. (Aston Villa), 1982 v N (1)
Gilbert, W. A. (C Palace), 1979 v W, Bul; 1980 v Bul; 1981 v N, R, Sw, R, Sw, H; 1982 v N (sub), H (11)
Goddard, P. (West Ham U), 1981 v N, Sw, Ei (sub); 1982 v N (sub), Pol, S; 1983 v WG (2) (8)

Haigh, P. (Hull C), 1977 v N (sub) (1)
Hateley, M. (Coventry C), 1982 v Pol, S; 1983 v Gr (2), H (5)
Hazell, R. J. (Wolverhampton W), 1979 v D (1)
Heath, A. (Stoke C), 1981 v R, Sw, H; 1982 v N, H, (Everton), Pol, S; 1983 v WG (8)
Hesford, I. (Blackpool), 1981 v Ei (sub), Pol (2), S (2); 1983 v WG (2) (7)
Hilaire, V. (C Palace), 1980 v Bul, S (2, one sub), EG (2); 1981 v N, R, Sw (sub); 1982 v Pol (sub) (9)
Hinshelwood, P. A. (C Palace), 1978 v N; 1980 v EG (2)
Hoddle, G. (Tottenham H), 1977 v W (sub); 1978 v Fi (sub), I (2), Y; 1979 v D, W, Bul; 1980 v S (2), EG (2) (12)
Hodge, S. (Nottingham F), 1983 v Gr (sub) (1)
Hodgson, D. J. (Middlesbrough), 1981 v N, R (sub), Sw, Ei; 1982 v Pol; 1983 v WG (6)

Johnston, C. P. (Middlesbrough), 1981 v N, Ei (2)
Jones, D. R. (Everton), 1977 v W (1)
Jones, C. H. (Tottenham H), 1978 v Y (sub) (1)

Keegan, G. A. (Manchester C), 1977 v W (1)
Kilcline, B. (Notts C), 1983 v D, Gr (2)
King, A. E. (Everton), 1977 v W; 1978 v Y (2)
Knight, A. (Portsmouth), 1983 v Gr, H (2)

Langley, T. W. (Chelsea), 1978 v I (sub) (1)
Lee, S. (Liverpool), 1981 v R, Sw, H; 1982 v S; 1983 v WG (2) (6)
Lukic, J. (Leeds U), 1981 v N, R, Ei, R, Sw, H; 1982 v H (7)

Mabbutt, G. (Bristol R), 1982 v Pol (2), S; 1983 v D (3)
McCall, S. H. (Ipswich T), 1981 v Sw, H; 1982 v H, S; 1983 v WG (2) (6)
MacKenzie, S. (WBA), 1982 v N, S (2) (3)
McMahon, S. (Everton), 1981 v Ei; 1982 v Pol; 1983 v D, Gr (2) (5)
Middleton, J. (Nottingham F), 1977 v Fi, N; (with Derby Co), 1978 v N (3)
Mills, G. R. (Nottingham F), 1981 v R; 1982 v N (2)
Moran, S. (Southampton), 1982 v N (sub) (1)
Moses, R. M. (WBA), 1981 v N (sub), Sw, Ei, R, Sw, H; 1982 v N (sub), (Manchester U), H (8)

Osman, R. C. (Ipswich T), 1979 v W (sub), Se; 1980 v D, S (2), EG (2) (7)
Owen, G. A. (Manchester C), 1977 v S, Fi, N; 1978 v N, Fi, I (2), Y; 1979 v D, W; (WBA), Bul, Se (sub); 1980 v D, S (2), EG; 1981 v Sw, R; 1982 v N (sub), H; 1983 v WG (2) (22)

Parkes, P. B. F. (QPR), 1979 v D (1)
Peach, D. S. (Southampton), 1977 v S, Fi, N; 1978 v N, I (2) (8)
Peake, A. (Leicester C), 1982 v Pol (1)
Pickering, N. (Sunderland), 1983 v D (sub), Gr, H (3)

Ranson, R. (Manchester C), 1980 v Bul, EG; 1981 v R (sub), R, Sw, Sw (sub), H, Pol (2), S (10)
Reeves, K. P. (Norwich C), 1978 v I, Y (2); 1979 v N, W, Bul, Sw; 1980, v D, S; (Manchester C), EG (10)
Regis, C. (WBA), 1979 v D, Bul, Se; 1980 v S, EG, 1983 v D (6)
Reid, N. S. (Manchester C), 1981 v H (sub); 1982 v H, Pol (2), S (2) (6)
Reid, P. (Bolton W), 1977 v S, Fi, N; 1978 v Fi, I, Y (6)
Richards, J. P. (Wolverhampton W), 1977 v Fi, N (2)
Ritchie, A. (Brighton & HA), 1982 v Pol (1)
Rix, G. (Arsenal), 1978 v Fi (sub), Y; 1979 v D, Se; 1980 v D (sub), Bul, S (7)
Robson, B. (WBA), 1979 v W, Bul (sub), Se; 1980 v D, Bul, S (2) (7)
Rowell, G. (Sunderland), 1977 v Fi (1)
Ryan, J. (Oldham Ath), 1983 v H (1)

Sansom, K. G. (C Palace), 1979 v D, W, Bul, Se; 1980 v S (2), EG (2) (8)
Shaw, G. R. (Aston Villa), 1981 v Ei, Sw, H; 1982 v H, S; 1983 v WG (2) (7)
Sims, S. (Leicester C), 1977 v W, S, Fi, N; 1978 v N, Fi, I (2) Y (2) (10)
Smith, M. (Sheffield W), 1981 v Ei, R, Sw, H; 1982 v Pol (sub) (5)
Statham, D. J. (WBA), 1978 v Fi, 1979 v W, Bul, Se; 1980 v D; 1983 v D (6)
Sunderland, A. (Wolverhampton W), 1977 v W (1)
Swindlehurst, D. (C Palace), 1977 v W (1)
Stevens, G. (Brighton & HA), 1983 v H (1)

Talbot, B. (Ipswich T), 1977 v W (1)
Thomas, D. (Coventry C), 1981 v Ei; 1983 v WG (2), Gr, H (5)
Thompson, G. L. (Coventry C), 1981 v R, Sw, H; 1982 v N, H, S (6)

Venison, B. (Sunderland), 1983 v D, Gr (2)

Wallace, D. (Southampton), 1983 v Gr, H (2)
Walsh, P. (Luton T), 1983 v D (sub), Gr (2), H (4)
Ward, P. D. (Brighton & HA), 1978 v N; 1980 v EG (2)
Whyte, C. (Arsenal), 1982 v S (2, one sub); 1983 v D, Gr (4)
Wicks, S. (QPR), 1982 v S (1)
Wilkins, R. C. (Chelsea), 1977 v W (1)
Williams, S. C. (Southampton), 1977 v S, Fi, N; 1978 v NI (sub), I, Y (2); 1979 v D, Bul, Se (sub); 1980 v D, EG (2) (14)
Woodcock, A. S. (Nottingham F), 1978 v Fi, I (2)
Woods, C. C. E. (Nottingham F), 1979 v W (sub), Se; (QPR), 1980 v Bul, EG; 1981 v Sw (5)
Wright, M. (Southampton), 1983 v Gr, H (2)
Wright, W. (Everton), 1979 v D, W, Bul; 1980 v D, S (2) (6)

SCOTLAND

Aitken, R. (Celtic), 1977 v Cz, W, Sw; 1978 v Cz, W; 1979 v P, N (2); 1980 v B, E (10)
Albiston A. (Manchester U), 1977 v Cz, W, Sw; 1978 v Sw, Cz (5)
Archibald, S. (Aberdeen), 1980 v B, E (2), WG; (with Tottenham H), 1981 v D (5)

Bannon, E. J. P. (Hearts), 1979 v US, (with Chelsea), P, N (2); (with Dundee U), 1980 v B, WG, E (7)
Bell, D. (Aberdeen), 1981 v D (1)
Bett, J. (Rangers), 1981 v Se, D; 1982 v Se, D, I, E (2) (7)
Blair, A. (Coventry C), 1980 v E; 1981 v Se, (with Aston Villa), 1982 v Se, D, I (5)
Brazil, A. (Hibernian), 1978 v W (1)
Brazil, A. (Ipswich T), 1979 v N; 1980 v B (2), E (2), WG; 1981 v Se; 1982 v Se (8)
Brough, J. (Hearts), 1981 v D (1)
Burley, G. E. (Ipswich T), 1977 v Cz, W, Sw; 1978 v Sw, Cz (5)
Burns, T. (Celtic), 1977 v Cz, W, E; 1978 v Sw; 1982 v E (5)

Casey, J. (Celtic), 1978 v W (1)
Clark, R. (Aberdeen), 1977 v Cz, W, Sw (3)
Connor, R. (Ayr U), 1981 v Se; 1982 v Se (2)
Cooper, D. (Clyde), 1977 v Cz, W, Sw, E; (with Rangers), 1978 v Sw, Cz (6)
Cooper, N. (Aberdeen), 1982 v D, E (2) (3)
Craig, T. (Newcastle U), 1977 v E (1)

Dawson, A. (Rangers), 1979 v P, N (2); 1980 v B (2), E (2) WG (8)
Dodds, D. (Dundee U), 1978 v W (1)
Doyle, J. (Partick T), 1981 v D, I (sub) (2)

Ferguson, R. (Hamilton A), 1977 v E (1)
Fitzpatrick, A. (St Mirren), 1977 v W (sub), Sw (sub), E; 1978 v Sw, Cz (5)
Fulton, M. (St Mirren), 1980 v B, WG, E; 1981 v Se, D (sub) (5)

Geddes, R. (Dundee), 1982 v Se, D, E (2) (4)
Gillespie, G. (Coventry C), 1979 v US; 1980 v E; 1981 v D; 1982 v Se, D, I (2), E (8)

Hartford, R. A. (Manchester C), 1977 v Sw (1)
Hewitt, J. (Aberdeen), 1982 v I (1)

Jardine, I. (Kilmarnock), 1979 v US (1)

Leighton, J. (Aberdeen), 1982 v I (1)
Lindsey, J. (Motherwell), 1979 v US (1)

McAvennie, F. (St Mirren), 1982 v I, E (2)
McBride, J. (Everton), 1981 v D (1)
McCluskey, G. (Celtic), 1979 v US, P; 1980 v B (2); 1982 v D, I (6)
McCulloch, A. (Kilmarnock), 1981 v Se (1)
McCulloch, I. (Notts Co), 1982 v E (2)
MacDonald, J. (Rangers), 1980 v WG (sub); 1981 v Se; 1982 v Se (sub), L, I (2), E (2 sub) (7)
McGarvey, F. (St Mirren), 1977 v E; 1978 v Cz; (with Celtic), 1982 v D (3)
McGarvey, S. (Manchester U), 1982 v E (sub) (1)
McGhee, M. (Aberdeen), 1981 v D (1)
McLaughlin, J. (Morton), 1981 v D; 1982 v Se, D, I, E (2) (6)
McLeish, A. (Aberdeen), 1978 v W; 1979 v US; 1980 v B, E (2) (5)
MacLeod, A. (Hibernian), 1979 v P, N (2) (3)
MacLeod, M. (Dumbarton), 1979 v US; (with Celtic), P (sub), N (2); 1980 v B (5)
McNab, N. (Tottenham H), 1978 v W (1)
McNichol, J. (Brentford), 1979 v P, N (2); 1980 v B (2), WG, E (7)
McNiven, D. (Leeds U), 1977 v Cz, W (sub), Sw (sub) (3)
Melrose, J. (Partick T), 1977 v Sw; 1979 v US, P, N (2); 1980 v B (sub), WG, E (8)
Miller, W. (Aberdeen), 1978 v Sw, Cz (2)
Milne, R. (Dundee U), 1982 v Se (sub) (1)
Muir, L. (Hibernian), 1977 v Cz (sub) (1)

Narey, D. (Dundee U), 1977 v Cz, Sw; 1978 v Sw, Cz (4)
Nicholas, C. (Celtic), 1981 v Se; 1982 v Se (2)
Nicol, S. (Ayr U), 1981 v Se; 1982 v Se, D; (with Liverpool), 1982 v I (2), E (2) (7)

Orr, N. (Morton), 1978 v W (sub); 1979 v US, P, N (2); 1980 v B, E (7)

Parlane, D. (Rangers), 1977 v W (1)
Paterson, C. (Hibernian), 1981 v Se; 1982 v I (2)
Payne, G. (Dundee U), 1978 v Sw, Cz, W (3)
Provan, D. (Kilmarnock), 1977 v Cz (sub) (1)

Redford, I. (Rangers), 1981 v Se (sub); 1982 v Se, D, I (2), E (6)
Reid, M. (Celtic), 1982 v E (1)
Reid, R. (St Mirren), 1977 v W, Sw, E (3)
Richardson, L. (St Mirren), 1980 v WG, E (sub) (2)
Ritchie, A. (Morton), 1980 v B (1)
Robertson, C. (Rangers), 1977 v E (sub) (1)
Ross, T. W. (Arsenal), 1977 v W (1)
Russell, R. (Rangers), 1978 v W; 1980 v B (2)

Sharp, G. (Everton), 1982 v E (1)
Simpson, N. (Aberdeen), 1982 v I (2), E (3)
Sinclair, G. (Dumbarton), 1977 v E (1)
Smith, G. (Rangers), 1978 v W (1)
Sneddon, A. (Celtic), 1979 v US (1)
Stanton, P. (Hibernian), 1977 v Cz (1)
Stevens, G. (Motherwell), 1977 v E (1)
Stewart, J. (Kilmarnock), 1978 v Sw, Cz; (with Middlesbrough), 1979 v P (3)
Stewart, R. (Dundee U), 1979 v P, N (2); (with West Ham U), 1980 v B (2), E (2), WG; 1981 v D; 1982 v I (2), E (12)
Strachan, G. (Aberdeen), 1980 v B (1)
Sturrock, P. (Dundee U), 1977 v Cz, W, Sw, E; 1978 v Sw, Cz; 1982 v Se, I, E (9)

Thomson, W. (Partick T), 1977 v E (sub); 1978 v W; (with St Mirren), 1979 v US, N (2); 1980 v B (2), E (2), WG (10)
Tolmie, J. (Morton), 1980 v B (sub) (1)

Wallace, I. (Coventry C), 1978 v Sw (1)
Wark, J. (Ipswich T), 1977 v Cz, W, Sw; 1978 v W; 1979 v P; 1980 v E (2), WG (8)
Watson, A. (Aberdeen), 1981 v Se, D; 1982 v D, I (sub) (4)
Watson, K. (Rangers), 1977 v E; 1978 v Sw (sub) (2)

WALES

Aizlewood, M. (Luton T), 1979 v E; 1981 v Ho (2)

Balcombe, S. (Leeds U), 1982 v F (sub) (1)
Bater, P. T. (Bristol R), 1977 v E, S (2)
Boyle, T. (Crystal Palace), 1982 v F (1)

Cegielski, W. (Wrexham), 1977 v E (sub), S (2)
Charles, J. M. (Swansea C), 1979 v E; 1981 v Ho (2)
Clark, J. (Manchester U), 1978 v S; (with Derby Co), 1979 v E (2)
Curtis, A. T. (Swansea C), 1977 v E (1)

Davies, A. (Manchester U), 1982 v F, Ho (3)
Davies, I. C. (Norwich C), 1978 v S (sub) (1)
Deacy, N. (PSV Eindhoven), 1977 v S (1)
Doyle, S. C. (Preston NE), 1979 v E (sub) (1)
Dwyer, P. J. (Cardiff C), 1979 v E (1)

Edwards, R. I. (Chester), 1977 v S; 1978 v W (2)
Evans, A. (Bristol R), 1977 v E (1)

Giles, D. C. (Cardiff C), 1977 v S; 1978 v S; 1981 (with Swansea C), v Ho (3)
Giles, P. (Cardiff C), 1982 v F, Ho (3)

Hopkins, J. (Fulham), 1982 v F (sub), Ho (2)
Hughes, W. (WBA), 1977 v E, S; 1978 v S (3)

Jackett, K. (Watford), 1981 v Ho; 1982 v F (2)
James, R. M. (Swansea C), 1977 v E, S; 1978 v S (3)
Jones, F. (Wrexham), 1981 v Ho (1)
Jones, L. (Cardiff C), 1982 v F, Ho (3)
Jones, V. (Bristol R), 1979 v E; 1981 v Ho (2)

Kendall, M. (Tottenham H), 1978 v S (1)

Letheran, G. (Leeds U), 1977 v E, S (2)
Lewis, D. (Swansea C), 1982 v F, Ho (3)
Loveridge, J. (Swansea C), 1982 v Ho (1)
Lowndes, S. R. (Newport Co), 1979 v E; 1981 v Ho (2)

Maddy, P. (Cardiff C), 1982 v Ho (1)
Marustik, C. (Swansea C), 1982 v F (2) (2)
Micallef, C. (Cardiff C), 1982 v F, Ho (2)

Nardiello, D. (Coventry C), 1978 v S (1)
Nicholas, P. (C Palace), 1978 v S; 1979 v E; (with Arsenal), 1982 v F (3)

Phillips, L. (Swansea C), 1979 v E (1)
Pontin, K. (Cardiff C), 1978 v S (1)
Price, P. (Luton T), 1981 v Ho (1)
Pugh, D. (Doncaster R), 1982 v F (2) (2)

Ratcliffe, K. (Everton), 1981 v Ho; 1982 v F (2)
Roberts, J. G. (Wrexham), 1977 v E (1)
Rush, I. (Liverpool), 1981 v Ho; 1982 v F (2)

Sayer, P. A. (Cardiff C), 1977 v E, S (2)
Stevenson, N. (Swansea C), 1982 v F, Ho (2)
Stevenson, W. B. (Leeds U), 1977 v E, S; 1978 v S (3)

Thomas, Martin R. (Bristol R), 1979 v E; 1981 v Ho (2)
Thomas, Mickey R. (Wrexham), 1977 v E; 1978 v S (2)
Thomas, D. G. (Leeds U), 1977 v E; 1979 v E (2)
Tibbott, L. (Ipswich T), 1977 v E, S (2)

Vaughan, N. (Newport Co), 1982 v F, Ho (2)

Walsh, I. P. (C Palace), 1979 v E (1)
Wilmot, R. (Arsenal), 1982 v F, Ho (3)

NORTHERN IRELAND

Team v Republic of Ireland 1978: Johnston; Nicholl, Hayes, Moreland, O'Neill, Donaghy, Sloan (sub), Harley, Brotherston, Blackledge, Hamilton, McCreery.

SEMI-PROFESSIONAL TOURNAMENT

THE VICTORIOUS ENGLAND TEAM

Left to right: Davison, Sellers, Barrett, Thompson, Watson, Richardson, Johnson and Robinson

Semi-Professional Four Nations Tournament

Previous Winners: 1979 England; 1980 Scotland; 1981 Scotland; 1982 Scotland; 1983 England.

Scotland (2) 3 *(Nijholt o.g., Beedie, Johnston)*

Holland (2) 3 *(De Jonge, Vincent, Van der Akker)*

Scotland: Gallagher (Clydebank), Nicoll (Falkirk), Conner (Ayr United), Beedie (St Johnstone), Mackin (Falkirk), Morris (Ayr United), McCabe (Clydebank), Brogan (St Johnstone), Johnston (Partick Thistle), Morton (St Johnstone), Gilmour (Queens Park).
Subs: Fallow (Clydebank) for Nicoll and Doyle (Partick Thistle) for Beedie.

England (0) 2 *(Sellers, Cordice)*

Italy (0) 0

England: Richardson (Maidstone), Thompson (Maidstone), Davison (Altrincham), Robinson (Blyth Spartans), Barrett (Enfield), Sellers (Scarborough), Watson (Maidstone), Johnson (Altrincham), Cordice (Wealdstone), Williams (Telford), Ashford (Enfield).

Scotland (1) 3 *(Gilmour 2(pen) Morton pen)*

Italy (0) 1 *(Cipriani)*

Scotland changes: Doyle for Nicoll and Colquhoun (Stirling Albion) for Brogan

England (2) 6 *(Williams, Johnson, Davison pen, Cordice, Watson, Ashford)*

Holland (0) 0

England changes: Clarke (Blythe Spartans) for Richardson. *Subs:* Ironton (Enfield) for Johnson and Derbyshire (Mossley) for Watson

Holland (2) 3 *(Oosterhaven, De Jonge, Van de Akker)*

Italy (1) 2 *(Pelorado, Attrice)*

England (0) 2 *(Davison pen, Williams)*

Scotland (1) 1 *(Harris)*

England: No changes from second match. *Subs:* Derbyshire for Johnson and Ward (Northwich Victoria) for Sellers.
Scotland: Changes from second game: Nicoll for Doyle, Brogan for Colquhoun and Harris (Raith Rovers) for Gilmour. *Subs:* Gilmour for Brogan and Colquhoun for Harris.

Final Table

	P	*W*	*D*	*L*	*F*	*A*	*Pts*
England	3	3	0	0	10	1	6
Scotland	3	1	1	1	7	6	3
Holland	3	1	1	1	6	11	3
Italy	3	0	0	0	3	8	0

YOUTH TOURNAMENT, NORWAY

13 JULY 1982

England 1 *(Simmonds)*

Norway 4

England: Andrews (Leicester C); Brown (Aston Villa), McClure (QPR), Robson (Arsenal), Culverhouse (Tottenham H) (Mitchell (Luton T)),Kerslake (QPR), Little (Charlton Ath), Venison (Sunderland), Comfort (QPR) (Davis (Ipswich T)), Rideout (Swindon T), Rimmer (Everton) (Simmonds (Sheffield W)).

15 JULY, 1982

England 5 *(Davis 2, Venison 2, Thomas)*

Denmark 2

England: Greygoose (Cambridge U); Thomas (Luton T), Robson (Arsenal), McLeary (Millwall), McClure (QPR), Kerslake (QPR), Little (Charlton Ath), Davis (Ipswich T), Rimmer (Everton (Ian Andrews (Leicester C)), Venison (Sunderland), Simmonds (Sheffield W).

17 JULY 1982

England 3 *(Venison 2, Kerslake)*

Poland 2

England: Greygoose (Cambridge U) (Ian Culverhouse (Tottenham H)); Thomas (Luton T), Robson (Arsenal), McLeary (Millwall), McClure (QPR), Kerslake (QPR), Little (Charlton Ath), Davis (Ipswich T), Rimmer (Everton) (Ian Andrews (Leicester C)), Venison (Sunderland), Simmons (Sheffield W).

YOUTH TOURNAMENT, YUGOSLAVIA

2 SEPT, 1982

England 3 *(Coffee 3)*

R.I. Istra 1

England: Andrews (Leicester C); McGrath (Coventry C), McClure (QPR), McLeary (Millwall), West (Sheffield U), Dickens (West Ham U), Lewis (WBA), Little (Charlton Ath), Cottee (West Ham U), Davies (Ipswich T) (Kerslake (QPR)).

4 SEPT, 1982

England 1 *(Simmons)*

USSR 0

England: Andrews (Leicester C); McGrath (Coventry C), McClure (QPR), McLeary (Millwall), West (Sheffield U), Dickens (West Ham U), Kerslake (QPR), Little (Charlton Ath), Simmons (Sheffield W), Cottee (West Ham U), Lewis (WBA).

6 SEPT, 1982

England 2 *(Cottee, Kerslake)*

Switzerland 0

England: Andrews (Leicester C) (Greygoose (Cambridge U)); McGrath (Coventry C), McClure (QPR) (Davis (Stoke C)), McLeary (Millwall), West (Sheffield U) (Sutton (Peterborough U)), Dickens (West Ham U), Kerslake (QPR), Little (Charlton Ath), Simmons (Sheffield W), Cottee (West Ham U), Davies (Ipswich T) (Cook (Tottenham H)).

9 SEPT, 1982

England 1 *(Simmons)*

Yugoslavia 0

England: Andrews (Leicester C); McGrath (Coventry C), McClure (QPR), McLeary (Millwall), West (Sheffield U), Dickens (West Ham U), Kerslake (QPR), Little (Charlton Ath), Simmons (Sheffield W), Cottee (West Ham U), Lewis (WBA).

UNDER-17 YOUTH TOURNAMENT

England 0

USSR 0

England: Williams (Watford); Parkin (Stoke C), Aldrige (Manchester C), Keown (Manchester U), Adams (Arsenal), Metcalf (Norwich C), Porter (Watford), Jones (Chelsea) (Cooke (Tottenham H)), Atkinson (Sunderland), Wood (Manchester U), Lambert (Brighton & HA).

England 5 *(Lambert 2, Porter 2, Cooke)*

China 1

England: Williams (Watford); Parkin (Stoke C), Aldridge (Manchester C), Keown (Manchester U), Adams (Arsenal), Metcalf (Norwich C), Porter (Watford), Cooke (Tottenham H), Atkinson (Sunderland, Wood (Manchester U) (Sherringham (Millwall)), Lambert (Brighton & HA).

England 0

France 2

England: Williams (Watford); Parkin (Stoke C), Aldridge (Manchester C), Keown (Arsenal), Adams (Arsenal), Metcalf (Norwich C) (Stebbings (Crystal P)), Porter (Watford), Cooke (Tottenham H), Atkinson (Sunderland), Wood (Manchester U), Lambert (Brighton & HA) (E. Sherringham (Millwall)).

England 1 *(Atkinson)*

Qatar 1 *(5th/6th place match)*

England: Digby (Manchester U); Parkin (Stoke C), Aldridge (Manchester C), Cooper (QPR), Jeffels (Barnsley), Adams (Arsenal), Stebbings (Crystal P), Jones (Chelsea) (Cooke (Tottenham H)), Atkinson (Sunderland), Wood (Manchester U) (Lambert (Brighton & HA)), Sheringham (Millwall).

OTHER YOUTH INTERNATIONALS

21 FEB, 1983

Israel U21 XI 1

England U18 Youth XI 4 *(Simmons 2, Rideout, Thompson)*

England: Suckling (Coventry C); Little (Charlton Ath), Spearing (Norwich C), Mills (Sheffield W (Norton (Aston Villa)), Hill (Manchester U), Blades (Derby Co), Kerslake (QPR), Simmons (Sheffield W), Rideout (Swindon T), Clarke (Notts Co) (McDonald (Newcastle U)), Thompson (Coventry C) (Bell, (Middlesbrough)).

23 FEB, 1983

Israel Olympic XI 2

England Under 18 XI 4 *(Simmons 2, Kerslake 2)*

England: Suckling (Coventry C); Little (Charlton Ath), Spearing (Norwich C) (McDonald (Newcastle U)), Mills (Sheffield W), Hill (Manchester U) (Norton (Aston Villa)), Blades (Derby Co), Kerslake (QPR), Simmons (Sheffield W), Rideout (Swindon T) (Stewart (Blackpool)), Clarke (Notts Co), Bell (Middlesbrough).

13 APRIL, 1983

England 1 *(Simmons)*

Belgium 1 (Friendly)

England: Suckling (Coventry C); Venison (Sunderland), Spearing (Norwich C), Mills (Sheffield W) (Smalley (Nottingham F)), Humphries (Doncaster R), Blades (Derby Co), Kerslake (QPR), Simmons (Sheffield W), Rideout (Swindon T) (Painter (Stoke C)), Dickens (West Ham U), Atkinson (Sunderland) (Morrison (Everton)).

ENGLAND YOUTH INTERNATIONAL MATCHES 1947–83

** Professionals. † Abandoned.* UYT *UEFA Youth Tournament.* WYT *World Youth Tournament.*

v SCOTLAND

			E	S
1947	25 Oct	Doncaster	4	2
1948	30 Oct	Aberdeen	1	3
UYT1949	21 Apr	Utrecht	0	1
1950	4 Feb	Carlisle	7	1
1951	3 Feb	Kilmarnock	6	1
1952	15 Mar	Sunderland	3	1
1953	7 Feb	Glasgow	4	3
1954	6 Feb	Middlesbrough	2	1
1955	5 Mar	Kilmarnock	3	4
1956	3 Mar	Preston	2	2
1957	9 Mar	Aberdeen	3	1
1958	1 Mar	Hull	2	0
1959	28 Feb	Aberdeen	1	1
1960	27 Feb	Newcastle	1	1
1961	25 Feb	Elgin	3	2
1962	24 Feb	Peterborough	4	2
*UYT1963	19 Apr	White City	1	0
1963	18 May	Dumfries	3	1
1964	22 Feb	Middlesbrough	1	1
1965	27 Feb	Inverness	1	2
1966	5 Feb	Hereford	5	3
1967	4 Feb	Aberdeen	0	1
*UYT1967	1 Mar	Southampton	1	0
*UYT1967	15 Mar	Dundee	0	0
1968	3 Feb	Walsall	0	5
1969	1 Feb	Stranraer	1	1
1970	31 Jan	Derby	1	2
1971	30 Jan	Greenock	1	2
1972	30 Jan	Bournemouth	2	0
1973	20 Jan	Kilmarnock	3	2
1974	26 Jan	Brighton	2	2
*UYT 1981	27 May	Aachen	0	1
*UYT 1982	23 Feb	Glasgow	0	1
*UYT 1982	23 Mar	Coventry	2	2
*UYT1983	15 May	Birmingham	4	2

v WALES

			E	W
1948	28 Feb	High Wycombe	4	2
UYT1948	15 Apr	Shepherds Bush	4	0
1949	26 Feb	Swansea	0	0
1950	25 Feb	Worcester	1	0
1951	17 Feb	Wrexham	1	1
1952	23 Feb	Plymouth	6	0
1953	21 Feb	Swansea	4	2
1954	20 Feb	Derby	2	1
1955	19 Feb	Milford Haven	7	2
1956	18 Feb	Shrewsbury	5	1
1957	9 Feb	Cardiff	7	1
1958	15 Feb	Reading	8	2
1959	14 Feb	Portmadoc	3	0
1960	19 Mar	Canterbury	1	1
1961	18 Mar	Newtown	4	0
1962	17 Mar	Swindon	4	0
1963	16 Mar	Haverfordwest	1	0
1964	15 Mar	Leeds	2	1
1965	20 Mar	Newport	2	2
1966	19 Mar	Northampton	4	1
1967	18 Mar	Cwmbran	3	3
1968	16 Mar	Watford	2	3
1969	15 Mar	Haverfordwest	3	1
*UYT1970	25 Feb	Newport	0	0
*UYT1970	18 Mar	Leyton	1	2
1970	20 Apr	Reading	0	0
1971	20 Feb	Aberystwyth	1	2
1972	19 Feb	Swindon	4	0
1973	24 Feb	Portmadoc	4	1
*UYT1974	9 Jan	West Bromwich	1	0
1974	2 Mar	Shrewsbury	2	1
*UYT1974	13 Mar	Cardiff	0	1
*UYT1976	11 Feb	Cardiff	1	0
*UYT1976	3 Mar	Maine Rd	2	3
*UYT1977	9 Mar	West Bromwich	1	0
*UYT1977	23 Mar	Cardiff	1	1

v NORTHERN IRELAND

			E	NI
1948	15 May	Belfast	2	2
UYT1949	18 Apr	Haarlem	3	3
1949	14 May	Hull	4	2
1950	6 May	Belfast	0	1
1951	5 May	Liverpool	5	2
1952	19 Apr	Belfast	0	2
1953	11 Apr	Wolverhampton	0	0
UYT1954	10 Apr	Bruehl	5	0
1954	8 May	Newtownards	2	2
1955	14 May	Watford	3	0
1956	12 May	Belfast	0	1
1957	11 May	Leyton	6	2
1958	10 May	Bangor	2	4
1959	9 May	Liverpool	5	0
1960	14 May	Portadown	5	2
1961	13 May	Manchester	2	0
1962	12 May	Londonderry	1	2
*UYT1963	23 Apr	Wembley	4	0
1963	11 May	Oldham	1	1
1964	25 Jan	Belfast	3	1
1965	22 Jan	Birkenhead	2	3
1966	26 Feb	Belfast	4	0
1967	25 Feb	Stockport	3	0
1968	23 Feb	Belfast	0	2
1969	28 Feb	Birkenhead	0	2
1970	28 Feb	Lurgan	1	3
1971	6 Mar	Blackpool	1	1
1972	11 Mar	Chester	1	1
*UYT1972	17 May	Sabadell	4	0
1973	24 Mar	Telford	3	0
1974	19 Apr	Birkenhead	1	2
*UYT1975	13 May	Kriens	3	0
*UYT1980	16 May	Arnstadt	1	0

v ARGENTINA

			E	A
*WYT1981	5 Oct	Sydney	1	1

v AUSTRIA

			E	A
UYT1949	19 Apr	Zeist	4	2
UYT1952	17 Apr	Barcelona	5	5
UYT1957	16 Apr	Barcelona	0	3
1958	4 Mar	Highbury	3	2
1958	1 June	Graz	4	3
UYT1960	20 Apr	Vienna	0	1
*UYT1964	1 Apr	Rotterdam	2	1
1980	6 Sept	Pazin	0	1
*UYT1981	29 May	Bonn	7	0
1981	3 Sept	Umag	3	0

v AUSTRALIA

			E	A
*WYT1981	8 Oct	Sydney	1	1

v BELGIUM

			E	B
UYT1948	16 Apr	West Ham	3	1
UYT1951	22 Mar	Cannes	1	1
UYT1953	31 Mar	Brussels	2	0
†1956	7 Nov	Brussels	3	2
1957	13 Nov	Sheffield	2	0
*UYT1965	15 Apr	Ludwigshafen	3	0
*UYT1969	11 Mar	West Ham	1	0
*UYT1969	26 Mar	Waregem	2	0
UYT1972	13 May	Palma	0	0
UYT1973	4 June	Viareggio	0	0
*UYT1977	19 May	Lokeren	1	0
1979	17 Jan	Brussels	4	0
1980	8 Sept	Labia	6	1
1983	13 Apr	Birmingham	1	1

v BULGARIA

			E	B
UYT1956	28 Mar	Salgotarjan	1	2
UYT1960	16 Apr	Graz	0	1
UYT1962	24 Apr	Ploesti	0	0
*UYT1968	7 Apr	Nimes	0	0
*UYT1979	31 May	Vienna	0	1

v CAMEROON

			E	C
*WYT1981	3 Oct	Sydney	2	0

v CHINA

			E	C
1983	31 Mar	Cannes	5	1

v CZECHOSLOVAKIA

			E	C
UYT1955	7 Apr	Lucca	0	1
*UYT1966	21 May	Rijeka	2	3
*UYT1969	20 May	Leipzig	3	1
*UYT1979	24 May	Bischofshofen	3	0
1979	8 Sept	Pula	1	2
1982	11 Apr	Cannes	0	1

v DENMARK

			E	D
*1955	1 Oct	Plymouth	9	2
1956	20 May	Esbjerg	2	1
*UYT1979	31 Oct	Esbjerg	3	1
*UYT1980	26 Mar	Coventry	4	0
*1982	15 July	Stjordal	5	2

v EGYPT

			E	Eg
*WYT1981	11 Oct	Sydney	4	2

v FINLAND

			E	F
*UYT1975	19 May	Berne	1	1

v FRANCE

			E	F
1957	24 Mar	Fontainebleau	1	0
1958	22 Mar	Eastbourne	0	1
*UYT1966	23 May	Rijeka	1	2
*UYT1967	11 May	Istanbul	2	0
*1968	25 Jan	Paris	0	1
*UYT1978	8 Feb	Selhurst Park	3	1
*UYT1978	1 Mar	Paris	0	0
*UYT1979	2 June	Vienna	0	0
1982	12 Apr	Cannes	0	1
1983	2 Apr	Cannes	0	2

v EAST GERMANY

			E	EG
UYT1958	7 Apr	Neunkirchen	1	0
1959	8 Mar	Zwickau	3	4
1960	2 Apr	Portsmouth	1	1
*UYT1965	25 Apr	Essen	2	3
*UYT1969	22 May	Magdeburg	0	4
*UYT1973	10 June	Florence	3	2

v WEST GERMANY

			E	WG
UYT1953	4 Apr	Boom	3	1
UYT1954	15 Apr	Gelsenkirchen	2	2
UYT1956	1 Apr	Sztalinvaros	2	1
1957	31 Mar	Oberhausen	4	1
1958	12 Mar	Bolton	1	2
1961	12 Mar	Flensberg	0	2
*1962	31 Mar	Northampton	1	0
*1967	14 Feb	Moenchengladbach	1	0
UYT1972	22 May	Barcelona	2	0
1975	25 Jan	Las Palmas	4	2
1976	14 Nov	Monte Carlo	1	1
*UYT1979	28 May	Salzburg	2	0
1979	1 Sept	Pula	1	1

v GREECE

			E	G
UYT1957	18 Apr	Barcelona	2	3
UYT1959	2 Apr	Dimitrovo	4	0
UYT1977	23 May	Beveren	1	1

v HUNGARY

			E	H
UYT1954	11 Apr	Dusseldorf	1	3
UYT1956	31 Mar	Tatabanya	2	4
*1956	23 Oct	Tottenham	2	1
*1956	25 Oct	Sunderland	2	1
*UYT1965	21 Apr	Wuppertal	5	0
*UYT1975	16 May	Olten	3	1
*UYT1977	10 Oct	Las Palmas	3	0
1979	5 Sept	Pula	2	0
1980	11 Sept	Pula	1	2
1981	7 Sept	Porec	4	0

v ICELAND

			E	I
*UYT1973	31 May	Viareggio	2	0
*UYT1977	21 May	Turnhout	0	0

v REPUBLIC OF IRELAND

			E	RI
UYT1953	5 Apr	Leuven	2	0
*UYT1964	30 Mar	Middleburg	6	0
*UYT1968	7 Feb	Dublin	0	0
*UYT1968	28 Feb	Portsmouth	4	1
*UYT1970	14 Jan	Dublin	4	1
*UYT1970	4 Feb	Luton	10	0
*UYT1975	9 May	Brunnen	1	0
*UYT1981	11 Feb	Walsall	1	0
*UYT1981	11 Mar	Belfast	3	0

v ISRAEL

			E	I
*1962	20 May	Tel Aviv	3	1
*1962	22 May	Haifa	1	2

v ITALY

			E	I
UYT1958	13 Apr	Luxembourg	0	1
UYT1959	25 Mar	Sofia	0	3
UYT1961	4 Apr	Braga	2	3
*UYT1965	23 Apr	Marl-Huels	3	1
*UYT1966	25 May	Rijeka	1	1
*UYT1967	5 May	Izmir	1	0
1973	14 Feb	Cava dei Tirreni	0	1
1973	14 Mar	Highbury	1	0
*UYT1973	6 June	Viareggio	1	0
1978	19 Nov	Monte Carlo	1	2
*UYT1979	28 Feb	Rome	1	0
*UYT1979	4 Apr	Villa Park	2	0
*UYT1983	22 May	Watford	1	1

v LUXEMBOURG

			E	L
UYT1950	25 May	Vienna	1	2
UYT1954	17 Apr	Bad Neuenahr	0	2
1957	2 Feb	West Ham	7	1
1957	17 Nov	Luxembourg	3	0
UYT1958	9 Apr	Eschsalzette	5	0

v MALTA

			E	M
*UYT1969	18 May	Wolfen	6	0
*UYT1979	26 May	Salzburg	3	0

v NETHERLANDS

			E	N
UYT1948	17 Apr	Tottenham	3	2
UYT1951	26 Mar	Cannes	2	1
*1954	21 Nov	Arnhem	2	3
*1955	5 Nov	Norwich	3	1
1957	2 Mar	Brentford	5	5
UYT1957	14 Apr	Barcelona	1	2
1957	2 Oct	Amsterdam	3	2
1961	9 Mar	Utrecht	0	1
*1962	31 Jan	Brighton	4	0
UYT1962	22 Apr	Ploesti	0	3
*UYT1963	13 Apr	Wimbledon	5	0
*UYT1968	9 Apr	Nimes	1	0
*UYT1974	13 Feb	West Bromwich	1	1
*UYT1974	27 Feb	The Hague	1	0
*UYT1979	23 May	Halle	1	0
1982	9 Apr	Cannes	1	0

v NORWAY

			E	N
*1982	13 July	Levanger	1	4

v POLAND

			E	P
UYT1960	18 Apr	Graz	4	2
*UYT1964	26 Mar	Breda	1	1
*UYT1971	26 May	Presov	0	0
UYT1972	20 May	Valencia	1	0
1975	21 Jan	Las Palmas	1	1
*UYT1978	9 May	Chorzow	0	2
1979	3 Sept	Porac	0	1
*UYT1980	25 May	Leipzig	2	1
*1982	17 July	Steinkver	3	2

v PORTUGAL

			E	P
UYT1954	18 Apr	Bonn	0	2
UYT1961	2 Apr	Lisbon	0	4
*UYT1964	3 Apr	The Hague	4	0
*UYT1971	30 May	Prague	3	0
1978	13 Nov	Monte Carlo	2	0
*UYT1980	18 May	Rosslau	1	1
1982	7Apr	Cannes	3	0

v QATAR

			E	Q
*WYT1981	14 Oct	Sydney	1	2
1983	4 Apr	Cannes	1	1

v RUMANIA

			E	R
1957	15 Oct	Tottenham	4	2
UYT1958	11 Apr	Luxembourg	1	0
UYT1959	31 Mar	Pazardjic	1	2
*UYT1963	15 Apr	Highbury	3	0
*WYT1981	17 Oct	Adelaide	0	1

v SAAR

			E	S
UYT1954	13 Apr	Dortmund	1	1
UYT1955	9 Apr	Prato	3	1

v SPAIN

			E	S
UYT1952	15 Apr	Barcelona	1	4
1957	26 Sept	Birmingham	4	4
UYT1958	5 Apr	Saarbrucken	2	2
*1958	8 Oct	Madrid	4	2
UYT1961	30 Mar	Lisbon	0	0
*1964	27 Feb	Murcia	2	1
*UYT1964	5 Apr	Amsterdam	4	0
*UYT1965	17 Apr	Heilbronn	0	0
*1966	30 Mar	Swindon	3	0
*UYT1967	7 May	Manisa	2	1
*1971	31 Mar	Pamplona	2	3
*1971	20 Apr	Luton	1	1
1972	9 Feb	Alicante	0	0
1972	15 Mar	Sheffield	4	1
*UYT1975	25 Feb	Bristol	1	1
*UYT1975	18 Mar	Madrid	1	0
1976	12 Nov	Monte Carlo	3	0
*UYT1978	7 May	Bukowno	1	0
1978	17 Nov	Monte Carlo	1	1
*UYT1981	25 May	Siegen	1	2
*UYT1983	13 May	Stoke	1	0

v SWEDEN

			E	S
*UYT1971	24 May	Poprad	1	0
1981	5 Sept	Pazin	3	2

v SWITZERLAND

			E	S
UYT1950	26 May	Stockerau	2	1
UYT1951	27 Mar	Nice	3	1
UYT1952	13 Apr	Barcelona	4	0
UYT1955	11 Apr	Florence	0	0
1956	11 Mar	Schaffhausen	2	0
1956	13 Oct	Brighton	2	2
1958	26 May	Zurich	3	0
*1960	8 Oct	Leyton	4	3
*†1962	22 Nov	Coventry	1	0
*1963	21 Mar	Bienne	7	1
*UYT1973	2 June	Forte dei Marim	2	0
*UYT1975	11 May	Buochs	4	0
1980	4 Sept	Rovinj	3	0
*1982	6 Sept	Porec	2	0

v TURKEY

			E	T
UYT1959	29 Mar	Dimitrovo	1	1
*UYT1978	5 May	Wodzislaw	1	1

v URUGUAY

			E	U
1977	9 Oct	Las Palmas	1	1

v USSR

			E	USSR
*UYT1963	17 Apr	Tottenham	2	0
*UYT1967	13 May	Istanbul	0	1
*UYT1968	11 Apr	Nimes	1	1
*UYT1971	28 May	Prague	1	1
1978	10 Oct	Las Palmas	1	0

*1982	4 Sept	Umag	1	0
1983	29 Mar	Cannes	0	0
*UYT1983	17 May	Aston Villa	0	2

v YUGOSLAVIA

			E	Y
UYT1953	2 April	Liège	1	1
1958	4 Feb	Chelsea	2	2
UYT1962	20 Apr	Ploesti	0	5
*UYT1967	9 May	Izmir	1	1
*UYT1971	22 May	Bardejor	1	0
UYT1972	18 May	Barcelona	1	0
1976	16 Nov	Monte Carlo	0	3
1978	15 Nov	Monte Carlo	1	1
*UYT1980	20 May	Altenburg	2	0
1981	10 Sept	Pula	5	0
*1982	9 Sept	Pula	1	0

UEFA YOUTH TOURNAMENT FINALS 1948–82

Year	*Winners*		*Runners-up*		*Venue*
1948	England	3	Netherlands	2	London
1949	France	4	Netherlands	1	Rotterdam
1950	Austria	3	France	2	Vienna
1951	Yugoslavia	3	Austria	2	Cannes
1952	Spain*	0	Belgium	0	Barcelona
1953	Hungary	2	Yugoslavia	0	Brussels
1954	Spain*	2	West Germany	2	Cologne
1955–56	Played in groups only				
1957	Austria	3	Spain	2	Madrid
1958	Italy	1	England	0	Luxembourg
1959	Bulgaria	1	Italy	0	Sofia
1960	Hungary	2	Rumania	1	Vienna
1961	Portugal	4	Poland	0	Lisbon
1962	Rumania	4	Yugoslavia	1	Bucharest
1963	England	4	Northern Ireland	0	London
1964	England	4	Spain	0	Amsterdam
1965	East Germany	3	England	2	Essen
1966	Italy†	0	USSR	0	Belgrade
1967	USSR	1	England	0	Istanbul
1968	Czechoslovakia	2	France	1	Cannes
1969	Bulgaria*	1	East Germany	1	Leipzig
1970	East Germany*	1	Netherlands	1	Glasgow
1971	England	3	Portugal	0	Prague
1972	England	2	West Germany	0	Barcelona
1973	England	3	East Germany	2	Florence
1974	Bulgaria	1	Yugoslavia	0	Malmo
1975	England	1	Finland	0	Berne
1976	USSR	1	Hungary	0	Budapest
1977	Belgium	2	Bulgaria	1	Brussels
1978	USSR	3	Yugoslavia	0	Krakow
1979	Yugoslavia	1	Bulgaria	0	Vienna
1980	England	2	Poland	1	Leipzig
1981	West Germany	1	Poland	0	Dusseldorf
1982	Scotland	3	Czechoslovakia	1	Helsinki
1983	France	1	Czechoslovakia	0	London

* *Won on toss of a coin.* † *Joint holders.*

ENGLISH YOUTH CAPS 1947–1983

(Due to lack of space the number of caps won, and the opponents, are not included)

Abrahams, R. (Essex) 1952
Adlard, S. (Lincoln C) 1968, 1969
Adams, M. (Gillingham) 1980
Adlem, R. (Dorset FA) 1965
Aitken, G. (Chelsea)
Albert, T. (Middlesex) 1949
Albeson, B. (Bury) 1965
Allen, A. (Stoke C) 1958
Allen, C. (QPR), 1978, 1979
Allen, G. (Newcastle U) 1965
Allen, P. (West Ham U) 1979, 1980, 1981, 1982
Allder, D. (Millwall) 1970
Allner, G. (Walsall) 1968
Amphlett, A. (Worcestershire) 1950
Anderson, T. (Arsenal) 1961
Andrews, I. (Leicester C) 1982
Angus, J. (Burnley) 1957, 1958
Armour, D. (Northumberland) 1953
Armstrong, G. (Arsenal) 1962
Armstrong, G. (Fulham) 1973
Arnold, G. (Aston Villa) 1963
Ash, M. (Sheffield U) 1961
Ashe, N. (Aston Villa) 1960
Ashurst, L. (Liverpool Co) 1957
Aslett, G. W. (Ipswich T) 1967
Atkins, G. (Berks & Bucks) 1951, 1952
Atkinson, P. (Sunderland) 1983
Atyeo P. J. (Wiltshire) 1950
Ayris, J. D. (West Ham U) 1971

Bacuzzi, D. (Arsenal) 1959
Badger, L. (Sheffield U) 1963
Bailey, J. (Hampshire) 1956
Baker, A. (Aston Villa) 1960, 1961, 1962
Baker, G. (Worcestershire) 1970
Baker, J. (Kingstonian) 1968
Banfield, N. A. (Crystal Palace) 1979, 1980, 1982
Bannister, K. (Sheffield & Hallam) 1948
Barber, D. (Barnsley) 1958
Barham, M. (Norwich C) 1980
Barham, R. (West Ham U) 1968
Barley, D. (Berks & Bucks) 1950
Barnes, D. (Coventry C) 1980, 1981
Barnes, P. (London FA) 1953
Barnes, P. S. (Manchester C) 1975
Barnett, G. (Everton) 1965
Barnwell, J. (Northumberland) 1956, (Middlesex) 1957
Barrett, J. (Birmingham Co) 1949
Barrett, S. T. (Winsford U) 1972
Bartley, D. R. (Bristol C) 1966
Barton, D. R. (Bristol C) 1966
Barton, A. (Middlesex) 1954, (Fulham) 1955
Barton, F. (Scunthorpe U) 1966
Batchelor, C. (West Ham U) 1973
Bates, P. (Berks & Bucks) 1953
Beal, P. (Tottenham H) 1963
Beard, M. (Birmingham C) 1959
Beattie, T. K. (Ipswich T) 1972
Beaumont, F. (Barnsley) 1958
Beavon, C. (Wolves) 1957
Beeby, O. (Leicestershire) 1953
Belger, W. (Barnet) 1961
Bell, G. (Oldham Ath), 1973
Bell, S. (Middlesbrough) 1982
Bellett, W. (Essex) 1952
Benjamin, I. (WBA) 1980
Bennett, A. (Staffs) 1949
Bennett, A. (Rotherham U) 1962
Bennett, D. (Middlesex 1951, 1952
Bennett, D. (London) 1956
Bennett, M. (Bolton W) 1980, 1981
Bennett, R. (Northampton T) 1963
Benstead, G. (QPR) 1982
Bentley, W. (Stoke C) 1966
Berick, R. (Manchester Co) 1949
Bernard, M. (Stoke C) 1966
Bertschin, K. E. (Ipswich T) 1975
Betts, A. T. (Aston Villa) 1972
Bickles, D. (West Ham U) 1961
Bidois, D. (Oxfordshire) 1951, 1952
Bielby, P. A. (Manchester U) 1975
Billington, S. (Liverpool Co) 1955
Birch, B. (Manchester Co) 1949
Birch, M. (Lancashire) 1955
Bird, R. (Birmingham C) 1958
Birtles, B. (Sheffield U) 1966
Bishop, P. (Sheffield) 1963
Black, S. (Fulham) 1973
Blades, P. (Derby Co) 1983
Block, M. (Chelsea) 1958
Bloomfield, R. (Arsenal) 1961, 1963
Bloor, A. (Stoke C) 1960
Blunstone, F. (Cheshire) 1951
Bond, D. J. (Watford) 1965
Boorn, A. (Folkestone) 1971
Boseley, G. (Gloucestershire) 1951, 1952
Bowtell, S. J. (Orient) 1969
Boyce, R. (West Ham U) 1960, 1961
Brabrook, P. (Middlesex) 1955, (Chelsea) 1957
Bradley, R. (WBA) 1956
Bradshaw, P. (Burnley) 1971, 1972
Bradshaw, P. W. (Blackburn R) 1974
Bragger, P. (West Ham U) 1967
Bramhall, J. (Hillsborough B.C.) 1958
Brennan, D. (Cheshire) 1950
Brickley, D. (West Riding) 1948
Bridges, B. (Chelsea) 1957, 1958
Brindley, J. C. (Nottingham F) 1964, 1965
Britt, M. (West Ham U) 1963
Broad, W. (Crystal Palace) 1968
Brookes, E. (Barnsley) 1961, 1962
Brooking, T. D. (West Ham U) 1967
S. Brooks (Crystal Palace) 1980, 1981
Bromilow, G. J. (Liverpool Co) 1949
Bromley, B. (Bolton W) 1964
Brown, G. (Staffs) 1951, 1952
P. Brown (Aston Villa) 1982
Brown, R. (Derbyshire) 1950
Brown, T. (Liverpool Co) 1948
Bruce, S. L. (Gillingham) 1979
Bruntlett, G. (Newcastle U) 1963
Bryant, J. (Fulham) 1973
Buchanan, D. (Leicester C) 1979
Buckley, D. W. (Stoke C) 1971
Buckley, I. (Oldham Ath) 1972
Buckley, M. J. (Everton) 1972
Bullock, P. (Stoke C) 1958, 1959
Bulmer, J. (Leyton O) 1964
Bunce, F. (Watford) 1956, 1957
Bunch, P. (WBA) 1957
Bunkell, R. K. (Tottenham H) 1968
Burbeck, R. (Leicestershire) 1952
Burke, S. J. (Nottingham F) 1978, 1979
Burke, D. I. (Bolton W) 1979
Burckitt, J. (Coventry C) 1965
Burgess, G. (Gloucestershire) 1954
Burkhill, K. (Liverpool Co) 1948
Burnside, D. (Staffs) 1957, (WBA) 1958
Burton, K. O. (Sheffield W) 1968
Busby, M. G. (QPR) 1971
Butler, I. (Rotherham U), 1962
Butterfield, G. (Southend U) 1966
Byford, G. J. (Southend U) 1974
Byrom, J. (Blackburn R) 1962
Byrne, J. (Surrey) 1956

Cahill, P. G. (Coventry C) 1974
Cakebread, G. (Middlesex) 1954
Caldwell, T. (Huddersfield T), 1957, 1958
Calvert, C. A. (York C) 1972
Canavan P. (Ipswich T) 1979
Campbell, D. (Liverpool Co) 1950
Campbell, J. (Bedford T) 1973
Campbell, R. (Liverpool) 1954
Cammack, S. R. (Sheffield U) 1972
Cantello, L. (WBA) 1970
Capewell, M. C. (Leicester C) 1974
Carlin, W. (Liverpool) 1959

Carr, G. (Northampton) 1962
Carter, L. (Crystal Palace) 1979
Cartwright, J. (West Ham U) 1957
Carley, S. W. (Bristol R) 1970
Caton, T. (Manchester C) 1980
Cavell, C. (Kent) 1951, 1952
Chadburn, A. (Quorn) 1957
Challis, R. (Gillingham) 1961
Chamberlain, T. (Middlesex) 1950
Charles, C. (West Ham U) 1970
Charles, J. (West Ham U) 1962, 1963
Charles, R. (Southampton) 1959
Charlton, M. (Hampshire) 1952
Charlton, R. (Manchester Co) 1954
Chatterley, L. C. (Aston Villa) 1963
Cheeswright, A. (Leyton O) 1964
Cherry, S. R. (Derby Co) 1979
Child, P. G. (Aston Villa) 1971
Childs, G. (WBA) 1982
Church, D. (Gloucestershire) 1950
Clapton, D. (Arsenal) 1958
Clark, F. A. (Crook Town) 1962
Clark, P. P. (Southend U)
Clark, J. L. (Northampton T) 1965
Clarke, N. (Birmingham Co) 1952, 1953
Clark, R. C. (Tottenham H) 1971
Clarke, W. (Wolverhampton W) 1979
Clayton, G. (Manchester U) 1955
Clement, D. T. (QPR) 1966
Cliss, D. (Chelsea) 1957
Close, D. B. (West Riding) 1949
Cocker, L. (Wolverhampton W) 1958
Cockcroft, V. (Wolverhampton W) 1959
Collier, A. (Bedfordshire), 1955 (Luton T) 1956, 1957
Collinson, R. (Doncaster R) 1958
Colton, E. (Sheffield W) 1957
Comford, A. (QPR) 1982
Connaughton, J. P. (Manchester U) 1968
Connelly, T. (Barnsley) 1960
Connelly, M. (Sheffield & Hallam) 1957
Connor, T. (Leeds U) 1980, 1981
Conroy, M. (Middlesex) 1952
Cooke, B. (Staffordshire) 1955, (WBA) 1956, 1957
Cooke, J. (Sunderland) 1982
Cooper, L. (Staffordshire) 1953
Cooper, S. (Worcs FA) 1974
Cotton, R. W. L. (Brentford) 1974
Corbett, A. (Wolverhampton W) 1959
Corbett, P. (Tottenham H) 1981
Cowans, G. (Aston Villa) 1977
Cowen, J. (Chelsea) 1963
Cox, C. V. (Oxford U) 1968
Craddock, T. (Herts) 1954
Craggs, J. E. (Newcastle U) 1966, 1967
Craven, T. (Barnsley) 1963
Crickson, C. (Kent) 1951
Crosby, J. (WBA) 1959
Crosby, P. (Grimsby T) 1982
Cross, G. S. (Leicester C) 1962
Crossman, D. (Tottenham H) 1964
Crowe, C. (West Riding) 1956
Cruickshank, R. (Vauxhall Motors) 1968
Culverhouse, L. (Tottenham H) 1982
Cunningham, R. (Manchester C) 1981
Curbishley, L. C. (West Ham U) 1975, 1976
Currie, A. W. (Watford/Sheffield U) 1968
Curtis, G. (Birmingham Co) 1956, (Coventry C) 1957, 1958

Dagless, M. N. (Peterborough U) 1966
Daines, B. (Tottenham H) 1970
Dale, M. A. (Hull C) 1969
Daley, S. (Wolverhampton W) 1971
Dalrymple, M. (Luton T) 1970
Dangerfield, C. G. (Wolverhampton W) 1974
Darwin, N. (Durham) 1948
Davey, S. (Plymouth Arg) 1967
Davids, N. G. (Leeds U) 1974
Dawkins, T. (West Ham U) 1964
Dawson, O. (Portsmouth) 1960
Day, M. R. (West Ham U) 1971
Dean, D. (Aston Villa) 1962
Dean, J. (Manchester Co) 1956, (Bolton W) 1957, 1958
Deehan, J. (Aston Villa) 1976
Deeman, S. (Thornycroft Ath) 1965
Dellar, B. (London) 1957
Dennis, A. (Tottenham H) 1957
Dennis, M. (Birmingham C) 1979
DePlacido, N. S. (York C) 1972
Detchon, J. (Derbyshire) 1956
Dey, G. (Sheffield U) 1982
Dickens, A. (West Ham U) 1983
Dickson, J. (Liverpool Co) 1952
Dillon, K. P. (Birmingham C) 1978
Dillon, M. L. (Tottenham H) 1971
Dillon, T. (Orient) 1972
Dilworth, J. R. (Middlesex) 1966
Docherty, M. (Burnley) 1969
Dodson, D. (Middlesex) 1956, 1957
Dodkins, H. (Essex) 1948
Donaghy, B. (WBA) 1973, 1974
Donaghy, R. (Liverpool Co) 1950
Donaldson, D. J. (Arsenal) 1972
Doyle, J. (Manchester Co) 1955
Draper, J. (Northamptonshire) 1953
Drury, C. (Staffs) 1955
Duce N. (Birmingham C) 1982
Duffield M. (QPR) 1982
Duffy, A. (Newcastle U) 1968
Dugdale, A. (Coventry C) 1971
Durrant, A. (Orient) 1970
Dyer, J. (Alvechurch) 1967

Eastoe, P. R. (Wolverhampton W) 1971, 1972
Eccleshare, K. (Bury) 1969
Edmonds, D. J. (Leeds U), 1968
Edmondson, S. J. (Lincolnshire FA) 1968
Edwards, D. (Manchester U) 1955
Ellery, L. (Cornwall County FA) 1970
Elliott, P. (Charlton Ath) 1982
Ellis, R. W. (Bolton W) 1970
Elms, J. (Manchester U) 1958
Endersby, S. (Ipswich T) 1980
English, T. (Coventry C) 1980
Entwhistle, W. P. (Bury) 1977
Etheridge, B. (Northampton T) 1962
Evans, A. (Manchester Co) 1950
Evans, A. W. (Wolverhampton W) 1967, 1968
Evans, D. (Middlesex) 1953
Evans, M. (Middlesex) 1954
Evans, R. (Chelsea) 1965
Evans, R. L. (Tottenham H) 1968

Fairclough, P. (Liverpool Co) 1952
Falco, M. (Tottenham H) 1979
Farrimond, S. (Bolton W) 1958
Fashanu, J. (Norwich C) 1979
Favager, A. (Cheshire) 1953
Feely, P. (Ipswich T) 1968
Feist, R. (Middlesex) 1957
Felton, G. M. (Northampton T) 1967
Fenton, S. J. Middlesbrough) 1969
Fenwick, T. W. (Crysal Palace) 1978
Fergey, R. (Middlesex) 1954
Fidler, M. (Barnsley) 1964
Field, J. (Tottenham H) 1972
Fillery, M. (Chelsea) 1979
Finney, R. J. (Rotherham U) 1973, 1974
Finnigan, A. (Fulham) 1981, 1982
Fisher, A. R. (Hull C) 1969
Fisher, S. (Portsmouth) 1973
Flanagan, M. A. (Tottenham H) 1971
Fletcher, M. (Derby Co) 1970
Foggon, A. (Newcastle U) 1968
Ford. A. (Bristol C) 1962
Foster, B. (Mansfield T) 1970
Foster, W. (Bolton W) 1982
Fox, J. (West Riding) 1952
Frain, P. (WBA) 1982
France, K. (Bolton W) 1959
Francis, S. (Chelsea) 1982
Francis, T. J. (Birmingham C) 1971, 1972
French, G. E. (Shrewsbury T) 1963
French, M. J. (Eastbourne U) 1971

Gaddes, R. (Portsmouth) 1960
Gage, K. (Wimbledon) 1982
Gale, A. (Fulham) 1978
Galvin, C. (Leeds U) 1970
Gaddes, R. (Portsmouth) 1960

Galvin, C. (Leeds U) 1970
Gardner, T. K. (Liverpool Co) 1948
Garner, P. (Huddersfield T) 1974
Garrett, L. (London) 1954
Garwood, C. (Peterborough U) 1967
Gaskell, D. (Manchester U) 1957, 1958, 1959
Gates, W. (Spennymoor G/T School) 1961
Geddis, D. (Ipswich T) 1976
Gernon, F. (Ipswich T) 1981
Gibson, M. (Derbyshire) 1957
Gibson, S. (Birmingham C) 1981
Gibson, T. (Tottenham H) 1979, 1980, 1981
Gidman, J. (Aston Villa) 1972
Gilbert, W. A. (Crystal Palace) 1978
Giles, P. (Staffs) 1948
Gilligan, J. (Watford) 1982
Gillingwater, D. (Gillingham) 1961
Gillott, P. (Sheffield & Hallam) 1953
Glover, G. (Everton) 1965
Gonzalez, R. (Crystl Palace) 1969
Goodwin, R. (East Riding) 1953
Gorney A. (Portsmouth) 1982
Gould, T. R. (Coventry C) 1968
Gould, W. T. (Gloucestershire) 1949
Gover, P. J. (Bristol C) 1972
Gray, T. I. (Leeds Ashley Road) 1972
Graydon, R. (Bristol R) 1965
Greaves, J. (Chelsea) 1957
Greaves, T. (Birmingham Co) 1956
Green, A. P. (Coventry C) 1972
Greenall C. (Blackpool) 1982
Greendale, M. (Hull C) 1970
Gregory, H. (Leyton Orient) 1961
Gregory, A. (Bedfordshire) 1954
Greygoose D. (Cambridge C) 1982
Groves, V. (Essex) 1951, 1952
Grummett, J. (Lincoln C) 1963
Grzadkowski, M. (Bristol R) 1967
Guest, B. J. (Lincoln C) 1977

Hagger, D. R. (Luton T) 1969
Hague, N. (Rotherham U) 1968
Haines, K. (Leicestershire & Rutland) 1956
Hall, A. (Manchester Co) 1955
Hall, C. (Nottingham F) 1966
Hall, I. (Wolverhampton W) 1958
Hall, J. (Northampton T) 1963
Hames, B. (Crystal Palace) 1962
Hamilton, D. (Sunderland) 1979
Hamilton, I. (Crysal Palace) 1962
Hamilton, I. (Chelsea) 1968, (Southend U) 1969
Hammon, K. L. (Hawick & P) 1967
Hampton, P. J. (Leeds U) 1973
Handysides, I. (Birmingham C) 1981
Hankin, R. (Burnley) 1973
Harding, D. (Sussex County FA) 1973
Hardwick, S. (Chesterfield) 1974
Harfield, I. (Southampton) 1971
Harle, D. (Doncaster R) 1982
Harper, A. (Liverpool) 1979
Harper, D. (Millwall) 1957
Harper, R. (Woodside/Wealdstone) 1967
Harris, A. (Chelsea) 1961
Harris, B. (Cheshire) 1953
Harris, R. E. (Chelsea) 1961, 1962, 1963
Harrison, F. (East Riding) 1949
Hart, V. (Cambridge U) 1959
Haslam, I. (Lancs County FA) 1970
Hateley, M. (Coventry C) 1980
Havenhand, K. (Chesterfield) 1957
Hawker, P. (Birmingham C) 1981
Hawksby, J. (Leeds U) 1959
Hawksworth, A. (Manchester Co) 1955
Haynes, J. (Middlesex) 1952
Hayzelden, G. (Tottenham H) 1973
Hazel, R. (Wiltshire) 1949
Hazell, A. P. (QPR) 1965, 1966
Hazell, R. (Wolverhampton W) 1977
Hazelden, W. (Aston Villa) 1958
Healey, G. (Hull C) 1963
Heaney, A. (Southampton) 1958
Heard, D. (Arsenal) 1959
Heard, T. (Everton) 1978
Hennin, D. (Liverpool Co) 1949
Hesford, I. (Blackpool) 1978
Hewitt, C. (Dorset) 1952
Hewitt, R. (Manchester U) 1961
Heyes, K. (Liverpool Co) 1953
Heys, G. (Macclesfield) 1974
Hicks, K. (Oldham Ath) 1973
Higgins, M. (Everton) 1977
Higgs, K. (Staffs) 1954
High, D. (Reading) 1958
Hilaire, V. (Crystal Palace) 1977, 1978
Hill, G. A. (Southend U) 1972
Hill, R. (Luton T) 1977
Hillsden, I. (Liverpool) 1954, (Everton) 1955
Hincks, K. (Leicestershire) 1949
Hindmarsh, R. (Sunderland) 1979
Hines, D. (Leicestershire) 1948
HInton, A. (Wolverhampton W) 1959
Hoddle, G. (Tottenham H) 1975, 1976
Hoadley, P. (Crystal Palace) 1970
Hodgson, G. H. (Newcastle U) 1971
Holden, D. (Lancashire) 1949
Holder, P. (Tottenham H) 1970
Holland, R. (Manchester U) 1957, 1958
Hollins, J. (Chelsea) 1964
Holmes, C. (Southampton) 1957
Holsgrove, J. (Crystal Palace) 1964
Horn, R. (Crystal Palace) 1980
Hornsby, B. G. (Arsenal) 1973
Horsfield, A. (Middlesbrough) 1964
Houghton, W. (Barnsley) 1957, 1958
Howlett, M. G. (West Ham U) 1971
Hoy, R. (Huddersfield T) 1968
Hughes, L. J. (WBA) 1969
Hulse, R. (Nantwich T) 1967
Humphries (Doncaster R) 1983
Hunt, H. (Cheshire) 1949
Hunt, P. (Southend U), 1970
Hunt, R. L. (Hull C) 1971
Hurrell, R. (Middlesex) 1953
Hurst, G. (West Ham U) 1959
Husband, J. (Everton) 1966
Hutchins, R. (Redhill) 1964
Huxford, C. (Chelsea) 1962
Huxley, G. (Brentford) 1973

Impey, J. E. (Cardiff C) 1973
Ingram, G. (Luton T) 1978
Irving, D. (Workington T) 1970
Irwin, C. (Sunderland) 1959

Jackson, D. (Liverpool Co) 1955
Jackson, J. (St Clement Danes School) 1961
Jacobs, D. (Alleyns School) 1957
Jago, G. (London) 1951, 1952
James, K. A. (Portsmouth) 1979, 1980
James, R. S. (Manchester U) 1968
James, T. P. W. (Cambridge U) 1967
Jarrold, B. (Kent) 1954
Jeffrey, A. (Sheffield & Hallam) 1955
Jenkins, L. (Aston Villa) 1979
Jennings, R. L. (Wiltshire) 1950
Jennings, W. (Watford) 1970
Jewkes, T. (Wolverhampton W) 1965
Johnson, D. (Durham Co FA) 1974
Johnson, G. (Arsenal) 1970
Johnson, R. (Leeds U) 1962
Jolley, G. (Cheshire) 1953
Jones, A. (WBA) 1961
Jones, D. (Birmingham C) 1958
Jones, D. K. (Bolton W) 1973
Jones, D. R. (Everton) 1975
Jones, G. (Bury) 1962, 1963
Jones, G. (Middlesbrough) 1961
Jones, G. A. (Birmingham Co) 1948
Jones, Glyn (Sheffield & Hallam) 1953, 1954
Jones, M. C. (Hereford U) 1974
Jones, P. (Manchester U) 1956
Jones, P. (Burnley) 1968
Jones, T. E. (Liverpool Co) 1948
Joy, D. (Durham Johnston HS) 1962

Keeley, A. J. (Tottenham H) 1975
Keeley, G. M. (Ipswich T) 1973
Keeley, J. (Liverpool Co) 1954
Kellard, R. (Southend U) 1960
Kelly, B. J. (Liverpool Co) 1951

Kelly, J. J. (Doncaster R) 1964
Kember, S. D. (Crystal Palace) 1967
Kendall, H. (Preston NE) 1964
Kendall, M. (Aston Villa) 1980, 1982
Kenworthy, A. (Sheffield U) 1977
Keown, M. (Arsenal) 1983
Kerry, D. (Derbyshire) 1955
Kerslake, D. (QPR) 1982, 1983
Kerslake, M. (Fulham) 1976
Kettle, B. (Liverpool) 1974
Kidd, B. (Manchester U) 1967
Kilmore, K. (Scunthorpe U) 1978
Kindon, S. M. (Burnley) 1968, 1969
Kingston, A. K. (Oxford U) 1977
Kinsey, S. (Manchester C) 1981, 1982
Kirkham, J. (Wolverhampton W) 1959
Kirkup, J. (West Ham U) 1957
Kite, P. (Bristol R) 1981
Klug, B. P. (Ipswich T) 1978, 1979
Knapman, J. (Torquay U) 1968, 1969
Knight, A. (Portsmouth) 1979
Knight, J. (Gloucestershire) 1953
Knott, W. (West Riding) 1951, 1952
Knowles, P. (Wolverhampton W) 1964

Lackenby, A. (North Shields Cors) 1959
Lakin, J. (Grimsby T) 1964
Lampard, F. (West Ham U) 1966, 1967
Lampe, D. (Middlesex) 1954, (Fulham) 1957
Langley, T. W. (Chelsea) 1975, 1976
Laraman, P. (Charlton Ath) 1958
Latchford, R. D. (Birmingham C) 1969
Laurel, J. (Middlesex) 1952
Laverick, R. (Chelsea) 1955
Lawler, C. (Liverpool) 1961
Lawson, I. (Burnley) 1958
Leach, M. (QPR) 1963, 1965
Leadbeater, P. (Sheffield FA) 1962
Leake, A. G. (Staffs) 1948
Leather, D. (Southampton) 1960
Leather, M. P. (Hampshire) 1948
Lee, F. (Bolton W) 1961
Lee, G. (Sheffield U) 1962
Lee, S. (Liverpool) 1977
Lee, T. (Arsenal) 1982
Leeke, A. (Worcestershire) 1954
Leslie, S. R. (Colchester U) 1971
Lewington, G. (Middlesex) 1949
Lewis, A. T. (Derby Co) 1972, 1973
Lewis, J. (Orient) 1972
Lewis, K. (Sheffield U) 1958
Lewis, M. (WBA) 1982
Lill, M. (Essex) 1954
Lindsay, A. (Bury) 1966
Little, B. (Charlton Ath) 1982
Llewellyn, H. (Liverpool Co) 1956, (Everton) 1957
Lloyd, B. (Chelsea) 1967
Lloyd, L. (Bristol R) 1967
Lock, K. J. (West Ham U) 1971, 1972
Locke, G. R. (Chelsea) 1972
Lockwood, R. (Leicestershire) 1951, 1952
Love, J. (Oxfordshire) 1955
Lukik, G. (Leeds U) 1979
Lyall, J. (West Ham U) 1957

Mabbutt, G. (Bristol R) 1980
Mabbutt, K. (Bristol C) 1977
McCabe, K. (Liverpool) 1959
McCaffery, A. (Newcastle U) 1976
McCaffrey, J. (Nottingham F) 1970
McCall, S. (Ipswich T) 1979
McCarthy, K. Coventry C) 1958
McClute, D. (QPR) 1982
McDermott, B. (Arsenal) 1979
McDonagh, J. M. (Rotherham U) 1971
McDonald, S. (Chelsea) 1974
McDonald, T. (Essex) 1956
McDowell, J. (West Ham U) 1970
McGonagle, I. (Charlton Ath) 1971
McGowan, A. (Northamptonshire FA) 1974
McGowan, G. Liverpool) 1970
McGuinness, W. (Manchester Co) 1954, (Manchester U) 1956, 1957, 1958
McGuire, M. (Coventry C) 1971
McHale, K. (West Riding) 1957, (Huddersfield T)
McLaughlin, J. (Colchester U) 1973
McPartland, D. (Middlesbrough) 1966
MacDonald, J. (Wiltshire) 1948
MacKenzie, S. (Crystal Palace) 1980
Madeley, P. (Leeds Un) 1962
Malcolm, A. (Essex) 1950
Manley, K. (Plymouth Arg) 1967
Mann, M. (Fulham) 1974
Mannion, G. (Wolverhampton W) 1958
Mansfield, P. (Derby Co) 1963
Marchi, A. (London) 1950
Marriott, T. (Bedford T) 1966
Martin, A. (West Ham U) 1976
Martin, D. (Northampton T) 1962
Martin, D. (Millwall) 1981
Martin, E. (Port Vale) 1965
Mason, S. J. (Wrexham) 1966
Massey, R. (St Paul's Coll, Cheltenham) 1963
Maxwell, D. (Carlisle U) 1965
Mayhew, B. Ipswich T) 1974
Melia, J. (Liverpool) 1956, 1958
Mellor, P. (Manchester C) 1966
Mellows, M. (Sutton U) 1966
Melville, L. (Liverpool Co) 1949
Merrick, A. R. (WBA) 1968
Metcalfe, S. M. (Blackburn R) 1969
Metchick, D. (Fulham) 1961
Middleton, H. (Wolverhampton W) 1955
Middleton, J. Nottingham F) 1975
Milkins, J. (Portsmouth) 1961
Mills, G. R. (Nottingham F) 1979
Mills, M. (Ipswich T) 1967
Mills, R. (Northamptonshire) 1951, 1952
Mills, S. (Sheffield W) 1983
Minton, A. (Staffs) 1954
Mitchell, R. D. (Cornwall) 1949
Mitten, J. (Mansfield T) 1958, (Newcastle U) 1959
Moffitt, D. (Swindon T) 1970
Mogg, D. (Bristol C) 1980
Mole, L. (Middlesbrough) 1964
Molyneux, J. A. (Cheshire) 1949
Monaghan, D. (WBA) 1977
Montgomery, J. (Sunderland) 1962
Moorcroft, M. (Sheffield & Hallam) 1948
Moore, R. (West Ham U) 1958, 1959
Morgan, R. (QPR) 1965
Morley, W. A. (Preston NE) 1973
Morris, D. J. (Westbury U) 1963
Morris, E. (Cheshire) 1948
Mortimer, D. (Coventry C) 1970
Mortimore, J. (Hampshire) 1952
Morton, R. S. (Manchester U) 1972
Moseley, G. (Derby Co) 1972
Moss, C. (Wolverhampton W) 1979
Muir, I. (QPR) 1982
Munday, B. (Gloucestershire) 1955
Munks, D. (Sheffield U), 1965
Munro, M. G. (Leicester C) 1971
Murray, A. (Chelsea) 1961
Mustill, P. R. (Huddersfield T) 1064

Naylor, S. (Lincoln C) 1981
Nicholas, A. (Chelsea) 1956, 1957
Nicholas, K. (Middlesex) 1955, (Arsenal) 1956
Nichols, A. (Ipswich T) 1981
Nightingale, M. B. (Bournemouth) 1975
Nish, D. J. (Leicester C) 1965, 1966
Noble, R. (Manchester U) 1964
Norman, D. (Alvechurch) 1964
Norman, G. D. (Essex) 1949
Norris, R. (Nottingham F) 1965
North, R. G. (West Ham U) 1972
North, S. (Luton T) 1982
Northcott, T. (Decvon) 1949
Novaki Y. (Bolton W) 1977

Oakes, M. (Leicester C) 1962
Oakley, H. (Chesterfield) 1962
Oakley, T. (St Neots T) 1970
Oates, R. A. (Leeds Ashley Road) 1974
Oliver, J. (Tottenham H) 1970
Ormsby, B. T. (Aston Villa) 1979
O'Rourke, J. (Arsenal) 1961, 1962
Osgood, K. (Tottenham H) 1973
Osgood, P. (Chelsea) 1965

Osman, R. (Derbyshire) 1949
Osman, R. (Ipswich T) 1977
Osmond, C. (Hampshire) 1954
Owen, D. (Helsoy GC) 1957
Owen, G. A. (Manchester C) 1976
Owens, M. (Newcastle U) 1976
Oxford, K. (Manchester Co) 1948

Packham, M. (Sheffield & Hallam) 1955
Pamment, M. I. (Bradford C) 1963
Parker, P. (Fulham) 1982
Parker, R. (Coventry C) 1971
Parkinson, N. D. (Ipswich T) 1978
Parnell, D. (Aldershot) 1958
Parry, R. (Lancashire) 1952
Passey, P. (Birmingham C) 1970
Patching, M. (Wolverhampton W) 1967, 1977
Pates, C. (Chelsea) 1980
Paul, A. G. (Crystal Palace) 1979
Pawley, J. (Leicester C) 1970
Peacock, A. (Middlesbrough) 1956
Peake, A. (Leicester C) 1980, 1982
Peaper, G. L. (Oxford U) 1968
Pearson, J. (Sheffield W) 1981, 1982
Pearson, M. (Manchester U) 1957
Peddlety, J. (Ipswich T) 1973
Pegram, S. F. (Enfield) 1965
Perry, R. (Wolverhampton W) 1958
Perryman, S. (Tottenham H) 1970
Peters, M. (West Ham U) 1960, 1961, 1962
Petts, J. (Middlesex) 1955, 1956, (Arsenal) 1957
Petts, P. (Bristol R) 1980
Phelan, M. (Burnley) 1981
Phillipson, F. (Durham) 1963
Phillips, S. E. (Birmingham C) 1973
Phillips, T. (Rotherham U) 1970, 1971
Phythian, E. (Bolton W) 1959
Pickering, N. (Sunderland) 1982
Piekainietis, J. (Nottingham F) 1969
Pimlott, C. (Lancs Co FA) 1970
Piper, N. J. (Plymouth Arg) 1966
Platts, C. (Leicestershire & Rutland) 1954
Pleat, D. (Nottingham F) 1961, 1962, 1963
Pollard, B. (York C) 1971, 1972
Pollard, C. J. (Birmingham Co) 1948
Pople, S. (Fulham) 1973
Powell, S. (Derby Co) 1973, 1974
Pountain, M. J. (Pershore U) 1965
Powling, R. (Arsenal) 1974
Price, A. J. (Leicester C) 1974
Price, D. J. (Arsenal) 1973
Prince, G. (Louth U) 1972
Probert, E. (Burnley) 1970
Procter, M. (Middlesbrough)
Purchase, P. (Somerset) 1952
Punter, B. (Staffs) 1953

Rankin, G. (Liverpool Co) 1948
Rands, L. (West Ham U) 1971
Ransom, R. (Manchester C) 1978
Rathbone, M. J. (Birmingham C) 1977
Reader, P. (West Ham U) 1958, 1959
Redknapp, H. (West Ham U) 1964
Redmond, P. (Liverpool Co) 1957
Redrobe, E. (Bolton W) 1961
Reeves, P. J. (Charlton Ath) 1967
Reeves, K. (Bournemouth) 1976
Reeves, R. (Berks & Bucks) 1949
Reynolds, R. (Plymouth Arg) 1966
Richardson, P. (Nottingham F) 1968
Riches, K. (North Shields) 1968
Richardson, G. C. (Hartlepool) 1976
Ricketts, G. (Gloucestershire) 1956
Rideout, P. (Swindon T) 1983
Ridler, E. (Somerset) 1949
Ridley, D. (Arsenal) 1982
Rioch, N. G. (Luton T) 1969
Riley, E. B. (Manchester U) 1971
Riley, H. (Leicestershire & Rutland) 1955
Riordan, J. (Huddersfield T) 1970
Ritchie, A. T. (Manchester U) 1978
Roach, J. (Birmingham C) 1955
Roberts, J. D. (Ipswich T) 1975
Roberts, R. (Bristol C) 1967
Roberts, T. (Scunthorpe U) 1964

Robinson, B. (Bolton W) 1961
Robinson, M. (Middlesex) 1980
Robinson, P. (Millwall) 1980
Robinson, W. (Surrey) 1952
Robson, B. (WBA) 1975
Robson, S. (Arsenal) 1981, 1982
Robson, T. H. (Northampton T) 1962
Rogers, D. (Swindon T) 1964
Rogers, M. (Bristol C) 1973
Rogers, M. (Manchester U) 1978
Roost, G. (Gloucestershire FA) 1969
Roper, D. (Bradford C) 1963
Rose, F. (Huddersfield T) 1972
Rossiter, D. (London) 1952
Rowland, A. (Derby Co) 1973
Rowlands, J. (Nottingham F) 1959
Royle, J. (Everton) 1967
Rucker, N. (Manchester Co) 1954
Rumjahn, J. R. (WBA) 1974

Sackling (Coventry C) 1983
Sadler, D. (Manchester U) 1963, 1964
Saile, M. A. (Bury) 1969
Salkeld, E. W. (Sheffield U) 1969
Salmon, D. (Brentford) 1978
Sammels, J. (Arsenal) 1963
Sanchez, J. (Arsenal) 1957
Sansom, K. (Crystal Palace) 1977
Saul, F. (Tottenham H) 1960
Saunders, R. (East Riding) 1948
Saunders, R. (Liverpool Co) 1951
Saxby, B. (Arsenal) 1956, 1957
Seaborne, K. (Essex) 1950
Seacole, J. P. (Oxford U) 1978
Sellens, C. N. (Charlton Ath) 1966
Setters, M. (WBA) 1957
Schiavi, M. (West Ham U) 1981, 1982
Scott, A. (West Ham U) 1958, 1959
Scott, M. (Middlesex 1957, (Chelsea) 1958
Scott, P. (Prescot T) 1967
Shanks, D. (Luton T) 1971
Sharp, C. (Northampton T) 1961
Sharples, S. (Everton) 1961
Shaw, B. (Sheffield U) 1963
Shaw, C. (Chelsea) 1961
Shaw, G. (Aston Villa) 1979
Shaw, N. (Middlesex) 1951, 1952
Shawcross, D. (Manchester C) 1959
Shilton, P. (Leicester C) 1967, 1968
Shreeve, D. (Middlesex) 1950
Shrewsbury, P. (Notts Co) 1965
Sibley, F. (QPR) 1966
Siddall, B. (Bolton W) 1973
Sidney, W. (Durham Co) 1949
Sillett, P. (Hampshire) 1950
Simmons, T. (Sheffield U) 1983
Simons, G. (Brentford) 1964
Sisman, G. (Luton T) 1979
Sissons, J. (West Ham U) 1963, 1964
Skull, J. (Wiltshire) 1949
Slack, P. (Peterborough U) 1981
Slackman, M. (Coventry C) 1982
Slieuwenhoek, J. (Aston Villa) 1960, 1962
Smailes, J. (Essex) 1950
Small, M. (Luton T) 1982
Smart, B. (Chelsea) 1958
Smillie, A. (West Ham U) 1958, 1959
Smith, B. (Manchester U) 1958, 1959
Smith, B. (Bolton W) 1973, 1974
Smith, D. (Gloucestershire) 1953
Smith, I. R. (Tottenham H) 1975
Smith, J. (Essex) 1953
Smith, J. (West Ham U) 1957
Smith, M. (Orient) 1980
Smith, P. (Sheffield & Hallam) 1956
Smith, R. (Manchester U) 1961
Smith, S. J. (Birmingham C) 1975
Smith, T. (Liverpool) 1963
Smith, W. (Sheffield W) 1965
Smithson, R. (Arsenal) 1962
Snodin, I. (Doncaster R) 1981, 1982
Southey, P. (Tottenham H) 1982
Spearing (Norwich C) 1983
Spence, A. (Sunderland) 1958
Spector, M. (Middlesex) 1952

Spencer, J. R. (Sheffield & Hallam) 1952, 1953
Spencer, M. (Staffs) 1951, 1952
Spencer-Smith, D. (Penzance) 1974
Spilsbury, J. (Worcestershire) 1952
Spiring, P. J. (Bristol C) 1968
Spratt, T. (Manchester U) 1959
Springett, P. (QPR) 1964
Stainrod, S. A. (Sheffield U) 1977
Starks, B. (Southampton) 1962
Statham, D. (WBA) 1977
Staton, B. (Sheffield & Hallam) 1956, (Doncaster R) 1957
Stenson, J. A. (Charlton Ath) 1968
Steven, T. (Burnley) 1982
Stewart, P. (Blackpool) 1982
Stiles, N. (Manchester U) 1959
Stirk, J. (Ipswich T) 1974
Stringer, J. (Norwich C) 1963
Stokes, R. W. (Southampton) 1969
Stonehouse, D. (North Riding) 1951, 1952
Storton, B. (Huddersfield T) 1957
Stratton, R. (Woking) 1957
Styles, A. (Everton) 1968
Suddick, A. (Newcastle U) 1962
Surgett, C. (Durham FA) 1965
Sullivan, B. (Fulham) 1959
Sullivan, C. (Plymouth Arg) 1969
Summerfield, K. (WBA) 1977
Summerill, P. E. (Birmingham C) 1966
Sutcliffe, P. D. (Manchester U) 1975
Swain, D. (Liverpool) 1970
Swan, P. (Sheffield W) 1955
Swindells, J. (Manchester Co) 1955
Swindlehurst, D. (Crystal Palace) 1974
Sydenham, J. (Southampton) 1957, 1958
Sykes, F. (West Riding) 1956
Sykes, N. (Gloucestershire) 1953
Syrett, D. K. (Swindon T) 1974
Sutton, R. (Winsford U) 1969

Tait, A. (Northumberland) 1952
Tate, G. (Leicestershire & Rutland) 1955
Taylor, R. H. (Huddersfield T) 1974, 1975
Taylor, T. (Orient) 1969, 1970
Temple, D. (Everton) 1958
Templeton, I. (Ipswich T) 1982
Templeton, S. J. (Scunthorpe U) 1972
Tether, C. (Staffs) 1955
Thomas, B. (Leicester C) 1955
Thomas, D. (Burnley) 1968, 1969
Thomas, E. (Wiltshire) 1951, 1952
Thompson, C. D. (Bolton W) 1978
Thompson, P. B. (Liverpool) 1972
Thursby, R. (Durham) 1956
Thwaites, D. (Birmingham C) 1961, 1963
Tilsed, R. (Bournemouth) 1970, 1971
Tindall, M. (Aston Villa) 1958
Tinnion, B. (Workington) 1966
Toase, D. (Durham) 1948
Todd, C. (Sunderland) 1967
Tomkins, L. (Crystal Palace) 1967
Tomlinson, J. (Liverpool) 1952
Tomkys, M. (Middlesex) 1951
Towers, M. A. (Manchester C) 1969, 1970
Townsend, N. R. (Northampton T) 1968
Trenchard, C. (Widemarsh U) 1962
Trewick, J. (WBA) 1975
Trigg, G. (Chesterfield) 1959
Trunkfield, M. (Manchester C) 1970
Turbitt, P. (Bradford C) 1969
Turner, M. (Bridport) 1957
Turner, C. R. (Sheffield W) 1977
Turner, R. D. (Ipswich T), 1974
Twist, F. (Liverpool) 1958, 1959
Twitchin, I. (Torquay U) 1969
Tynan, R. (Tranmere R) 1973, 1974

Valentine, J. (Lancashire) 1955
Venables, T. (Chelsea) 1960
Venison (Sunderland) 1983
Vickets, P. (West Riding) 1951
Vincent, J. (Birmingham C) 1965
Vine, P. (Southampton) 1958

Wagstaffe, D. (Manchester C) 1960
Wainman, W. H. (Grimsby T) 1964
Waite, J. (Grimsby T)
Wales, A. (Doncaster R) 1960
Walford, S. J. (Tottenham H) 1976
Walker, R. (Aston Villa) 1981, 1982
Walker, R. (West Ham U) 1957
Wallace, D. (Southampton) 1982
Wallington, F. M. (Lincolnshire) 1971
Walsh, P. (Charlton Ath) 1980, 1981
Walters, M. (Aston Villa) 1981, 1982
Wanklin, J. (Portsmouth) 1962
Want, A. G. (Tottenham H) 1967
Ward, G. (London & Essex) 1953
Ward, M. B. (Shrewsbury T) 1971
Ware, N. G. (Tranmere R) 1970, 1971
Warman, P. (Charlton Ath) 1968
Warner, R. (Leicester) 1949
Warnes, R. (Tooting & Mitcham) 1962
Watkins, J. (Gloucestershire) 1951, 1952
Watson, G. (Oxford U) 1979
Watts, G. (Chesterfield) 1962
Watts, R. (Essex) 1952
Webb, D. (St Albans C) 1973
Webb, N. (Reading) 1981, 1982
Webster, M. W. (Arsenal) 1969
Weir, A. (Sunderland) 1978
Welch, R. G. (Sheffield U) 1969
Went, P. F. (Leyton Orient) 1967, (Charlton Ath) 1968
West, G. (Blackpool) 1960, 1961
Westburgh, M. (West Ham U) 1968
Westwood, G. (Ipswich T) 1981
White, J. (Portsmouth) 1959
Whitear, J. (Surrey) 1953
Whitehead, C. (Bristol C) 1973
Whitington, E. (Chelsea) 1964
Whittaker, R. (Arsenal) 1962, 1963
Whittle, A. (Everton) 1968
Whitworth, S. (Leicester C) 1970
Wicks, P. (Sheffield W) 1966
Wicks, S. J. (Chelsea) 1975
Wilcox, R. J. (Leicestershire) 1975
Wileman, A. (Measham Imperial) 1958
Wilkins, R. C. (Chelsea) 1975
Wilkinson, G. (Durham) 1953
Wilkinson, H. (Sheffield W) 1962
Willder, F. (Blackpool) 1962
Williams, A. (Bristol C) 1960
Williams, A. (Manchester C) 1980
Williams E. (Canterbury C) 1974
Williams, J. (Manchester Co) 1950
Williams, W. (Watford) 1982
Williams, W. (Portsmouth) 1960
Willis, R. G. (Chelsea) 1965
Wilson, H. (Burnley) 1971
Winterburn, N. (Birmingham C) 1982
Winstanley, E. (Barnsley) 1962
Wojciechowicz (Blackpool) 1970
Wood, A. E. (Manchester C) 1964
Woods, A. (Tottenham H) 1955
Woods, C. (Nottingham F) 1977, 1978
Woodley, D. (West Ham U) 1959
Woods, B. (Manchester C) 1968
Woods, J. (Gillingham) 1966
Woolley, P. D. (Chesterfield) 1968
Woodward, A. (Sheffield U) 1965
Wootton, R. (Essex) 1954
Worley, L. (Berks & Bucks)
Wright, B. (Leicester C) 1955
Wright, B. (Leeds U) 1964
Wright, D. (Barnsley GS) 1957, 1958
Wright, J. M. (Aston Villa) 1964, 1965
Wright, V. (Lancashire) 1949
Wynn, D. (Manchester U) 1981

Yallop, F. (Ipswich T) 1982
Young, E. (Manchester U) 1971
Young, N. (Manchester C) 1962

REAL MADRID

When Liverpool, Nottingham Forest and Aston Villa provided Britain with six consecutive European Champions Cup triumphs we were justifiably proud, but for one club to hold the trophy for five years is a quite outstanding feat.

This is what the famous Real Madrid club achieved when the competition was first launched and these charts show their consistency, goalscoring, flair and tremendous support during their record-breaking years.

European Champions Cup 1955–1960

Real Madrid Statistics

	Pld	*W*	*D*	*L*	*F*	*A*
1955–56	7	5	0	2	20	10
1956–57	8	6	1	1	20	10
1957–58	7	5	1	1	25	7
1958–59	8	5	2	1	16	5
1959–60	7	6	0	1	31	10
Total	37	27	4	6	112	42

Individual Records

	Pld	*Goals*	*Winners Medals*
Di Stefano	35	36	5
Gento	35	8	5
Zarraga	31	–	5
Marquitos	28	1	4
Lesmes	28	–	3
Rial	23	14	4
Alonso	22	–	3
Kopa	22	6	3
Santamaria	21	–	3
Santisteban	16	2	2
Mateos	15	8	2
Munoz	15	1	2
Puskas	12	14	1
Atienza	11	–	2
Joseito	11	6	2
Marsal	9	5	1
Ruiz A.	9	–	1

REAL MADRID

EUROPEAN CHAMPIONS CUP 1955–56	1st Rd 1st Leg v Servette (A) Won 2-0 25,000	1st Rd 2nd Leg v Servette (H) Won 5-0 60,000	2nd Rd 1st Leg v Partizan (H) Won 4-0 100,000	2nd Rd 2nd Leg v Partizan (A) Lost 0-3 65000	S-Final 1st Leg v Milan (H) Won 4-2 116,000	S-Final 2nd Leg v Milan (A) Lost 1-2 25,000	Final v Reims (Paris) Won 4-3 38,238	APPS	GOALS
Alonso	1	1	1	1	1	1	1	7	
Navarro	2	2			2	2		4	
Lesmes	3		3	3	3	3	3	6	
Munoz	4^{1}	4	4	4	4	4	4	7	*1*
Oliva	5							1	
Zarraga	6	6	6	6	6	6	6	7	
Molowny	7	7*						2	*1*
Marsal							8	1	
Perez-Paya	8							1	
Di Stefano	9	9^{2}	9^{1}	9	9^{1}	9	9^{1}	7	*5*
Rial	10^{1}	10^{1}	10	10	10^{1}	10	10^{2}	7	*5*
Gento	11	11	11^{1}	11	11	11	11	7	*1*
Atienza		3					2	2	
Marquitos		5	5	5	5	5	5^{1}	6	*1*
Joseito		8^{1}			7^{1}	7^{1}	7	4	*3*
Becerril			2	2				2	
Castanos			7^{2}	7				2	*2*
Olsen			8	8	8^{1}			3	*1*
									20

Coach: Jose Villalonga

REAL MADRID

EUROPEAN CHAMPIONS CUP 1956–57	1st Rd 1st Leg v Rapid Vienna (H) Won 4-2 110,000	1st Rd 2nd Leg v Rapid Vienna (A) Lost 1-3 55,000	1st Rd Play-off v Rapid Vienna (H) Won 2-0 100,000	2nd Rd 1st Leg v OGC Nice (H) Won 3-0 84,000	2nd Rd 2nd Leg v OGC Nice (A) Won 3-2 24,500	S-Final 1st Leg v Man Utd (H) Won 3-1 135,000	S-Final 2nd Leg v Man Utd (A) Drawn 2-2 65,000	Final v Fiorentina (Madrid) Won 2-0 124,000	Apps	Goals
Alonso	1	1		1	1	1	1	1	7	
Atienza	2	2	2	2					4	
Lesmes	3	3	3	3	3	3	3	3	8	
Santisteban	4		4						2	
Marquitos	5	5	5	5	5	5	5	5	8	
Zarraga	6	6	6	6	6	6	6	6	8	
Kopa	7	10	8^{1}	8	8	7	7^{1}	7	8	*2*
Marsel	8^{2}	8	10						3	*2*
Di Stefano	9^{2}	9^{1}	9	9	9^{2}	9^{1}	9	9P	8	*7*
Mateos	10			10^{2}	10	8^{1}	8	8	6	*3*
Gento	11	11	11	11	11	11	11	11^{1}	8	*1*
Munoz		4		4	4	4	4	4	6	
Voseito		7	7^{1}	7^{1}	7^{1}				4	*3*
Berasaluce			1						1	
Becerril					2	2			2	
Rial						10^{1}	10^{1}	10	3	*2*
Torres							2	2	2	
										20

Coach: Jose Villalonga

REAL MADRID

EUROPEAN CHAMPIONS CUP 1957–58	1st Rd 1st Leg v Antwerp (A) Won 2-1 35,000	1st Rd 2nd Leg v Antwerp (H) Won 6-0 80,000	2nd Rd 1st Leg v Sevilla (H) Won 8-0 95,000	2nd Rd 2nd Leg v Sevilla (A) Drawn 2-2 45,000	S-Final 1st Leg v Vasas (H) Won 4-0 122,000	S-Final 2nd Leg v Vasas (A) Lost 0-2 118,000	Final v Milan (Brussels) Won 3-2 72,000	Apps	Goals
Dominguez	1	1		1				3	
Atienza	2	3		2			2	4	
Lesmes	3		3	3	3	3	3	6	
Santisteban	4	4	4		4		4	5	
Santamaria	5	5	5	5	5	5	5	7	
Zarraga	6	6	6	6	6	6	6	7	
Kopa	7	7^{1}	7^{2}	8	7	7	7	7	*3*
Marsal	8	8^{1}	8^{*1}		8^{1}	8		5	*3*
Di Stefano	9^{1}	9	9^{4}P	9	9^{3}	9	9^{1}	7	*10*
Rial	10	10^{3}	10		10	10	10^{1}	6	*4*
Gento	11	11^{1}	11^{1}		11	11	11^{1}	6	*3*
Becerril		2						1	
Alonso			1		1	1	1	4	
Marquitos			2		2	2		3	
Munoz				4		4		2	
Joseito				7			8	2	
Mateos				10				1	
Pareda				11^{2}				1	*2*
									25

* Player sent off

Coach: Luis Carniglia

REAL MADRID

EUROPEAN CHAMPIONS CUP 1958–59	1st Rd 1st Leg v Besiktas (H) Won 2-0 80,000	1st Rd 2nd Leg v Besiktas (A) Drawn 1-1 45,000	2nd rd 1st Leg v Weiner Sportklub (A) Drawn 0-0 78,652	2nd Rd 2nd Leg v Wiener Sportklub (H) Won 7-1 110,000	S-Final 1st Leg v Atletico Madrid (H) Won 2-1 114,600	S-Final 2nd Leg v Atletico Madrid (A) Lost 0-1 65,000	S-Final Play-off v Atletico Madrid (Zarragoza) Won 2-1 33,000	Final v Reims (Stuttgart) Won 2-0 72,000	Apps	Goals
Alonso	1	1	1	1					4	
Marquitos	2	2	2	2				2	5	
Lesmes	3	3	3	3	3	3	3		7	
Santisteban	4^{1}	8^{1}	4	4	4	4		4	7	*2*
Santamaria	5	5	5	5	5	5	5	5	8	
Zarraga	6	6	6	6			6	3	6	
Kopa	7^{1}	9	7	7		7	7	7	7	*1*
Rial	8		8	10^{1}	8	10		10	6	*2*
Di Stefano	9*		9	9^{4}	9	9	9^{1}	9^{1}	7	*6*
Puskas	10	10	10*		10P		10^{1}		5	*2*
Gento	11	11	11	11^{1}	11	11	11	11	8	*1*
Ruiz A.		4			6	6	4	6	5	
Joseito		7							1	
Mateos				8^{1}	7	8	8	$8†^{1}$	5	*2*
Dominguez					1	1	1	1	4	
Miche					2	2	2		3	
	* Player sent off			† Missed a penalty						*16*

Coach: Luis Carniglia

REAL MADRID

EUROPEAN CHAMPIONS CUP 1959–60	1st Rd 1st Leg Jeunesse d'esch (H) Won 7-0 70,000	1st Rd 2nd Leg v Jeunesse d'esch (A) Won 5-2 20,000	2nd Rd 1st Leg v OGC Nice (A) Lost 2-3 21,422	2nd Rd 2nd Leg v OGC Nice (H) Won 4-0 85,000	S-Final 1st Leg v Barcelona (H) Won 3-1 125,000	S-Final 2nd Leg v Barcelona (A) Won 3-1 100,000	Final v Eintracht Frankfurt (Glasgow) Won 7-3 127,621	Apps	Goals
Dominguez	1	1	1	1	1	1	1	7	
Marquitos	2		2	2	2	5	2	6	
Lesmes	3							1	
Santisteban	4		6					2	
Santamaria	5	5	5	5	5		5	6	
Zarraga	6	3					6	3	
Herrera	7^{2}	7	7^{1}	7	7			5	*3*
Mateos	8^{1}	8^{2}	9					3	*3*
Di Stefano	9^{1}	9^{1}		9^{1}	9^{2}	9	9^{3}	6	*8*
Puskas	10^{3}	10^{1}	10	10^{1}	10^{1}	10^{2}	10^{4}	7	*12*
Gento	11		11	11^{1}	11	11^{1}	11	6	*2*
Pantaleon		2						1	
Vidal		4^{1}	4	4	4	6	4	6	*1*
Ruiz A.		6		6	6	4		4	
Canario		11				7	7	3	
Miche			3	3		2		3	
Rial			8^{1}					1	*1*
Pepillo				8^{1}				1	*1*
Pachin					3	3	3	3	
Del Sol					8	8	8	3	
									31

Coach: Miguel Munoz

THE CUP LEAVES ENGLAND AFTER SIX YEARS

England's hopes were the highest in the European Cup, since in the previous six years English clubs carried off this top prize, and in this instance, we had a powerful duo in Liverpool and Aston Villa in the field. Liverpool's defeat was particularly painful, because they were in top form during the season, and their commanding lead in the First Division gave them the opportunity to concentrate on the European competition. They took their opening hurdle easily enough with a 5-1 aggregate win against the Republic of Ireland champions, Dundalk. In the second round, they were paired with the Finnish title holders, HJK Helsinki, and after a shock narrow defeat in Finland, they won the return leg 5-0, to run out once again 5-1 aggregate winners.

The draw for the quarter-finals was on paper a good one – Widzew Lodz of Poland, a team short of star player Boniek. But in the first leg in Lodz, Grobbelaar made a fatal mistake in goal, and later the Poles managed to score one more goal for a 2-0 victory. Bob Paisley remained optimistic that this score was not too big a target for the second match, and indeed Liverpool took the lead early in the game. But an uncharacteristic mistake by Graeme Souness led to a penalty, and with an away goal in their pocket, the Poles were in the driving seat. With all the Liverpool players in the opposition's half, another counter-attack resulted in another Lodz goal, and the tie was beyond redemption. Liverpool did score two late goals, the second from a blatantly off-side position, but the 3-2 victory was scant consolation for an astonishing overall defeat.

Aston Villa beat the Turkish Besiktas behind closed doors 3-1 in the first round, and in the second, they faced Dinamo Bucharest. A 2-0 victory in Rumania was an excellent result, and at home, with the help of a Gary Shaw hat-trick, the Midlanders won 4-2 for an easy 6-2 aggregate. But in the quarter-finals they were drawn against the powerful Italians, Juventus. The Fiat sponsored club spent heavily before the season started on two foreign imports, Boniek and Platini. Together with the bulk of the Italian World Cup winning side, they looked a formidable combination, and indeed, in the match at Villa Park, they took the lead in the first minute through a Paolo Rossi header. Cowans equalised in brilliant fashion, but one more imaginative attack brought a goal for Boniek – 2-1 to Juventus. The second leg seemed a formality, and sadly it was – the Italians won 3-1 – England's hopeful representatives were out of the European Cup.

Celtic also failed to make an impression, somewhat unluckily they went out against Real Sociedad of Spain in the second round. Hamburg, in the meantime, made majestic progress, studded with good away performances. Their 3-0 win at Kiev against the local team Dynamo, was one of the shock results of the tournament. Juventus were slight favourites in the Athens final, but Hamburg surprised them with their clever, imaginative football. Magath scored an early goal when his deceptive shot completely bamboozled the veteran Dino Zoff. The Juventus machine didn't function at all smoothly, Bettega was off form, and Rossi played so ineffectively, that he had to be substituted in the middle of the second half. There were no further goals – 1-0 yet again in the European Cup Final, and Hamburg's victory was the fourth for a West German club, following Bayern Munich's hat-trick in the seventies.

EUROPEAN CHAMPIONS' CUP FINALS 1956–83

Year	*Winners*		*Runners-up*		*Venue*
1956	Real Madrid	4	Stade de Reims	3	Paris
1957	Real Madrid	2	AC Fiorentina	0	Madrid
1958	Real Madrid	3	AC Milan	2	Brussels
1959	Real Madrid	2	Stade de Reims	0	Stuttgart
1960	Real Madrid	7	Eintracht Frankfurt	3	Glasgow
1961	Benfica	3	Barcelona	2	Berne
1962	Benfica	5	Real Madrid	3	Amsterdam
1963	AC Milan	2	Benfica	1	London
1964	Inter-Milan	3	Real Madrid	1	Vienna
1965	Inter-Milan	1	Benfica	0	Milan
1966	Real Madrid	2	Partizan Belgrade	1	Brussels
1967	Celtic	2	Inter-Milan	1	Lisbon
1968	Manchester U	4	Benfica	1	London
1969	AC Milan	4	Ajax Amsterdam	1	Madrid
1970	Feyenoord	2	Celtic	1	Milan
1971	Ajax Amsterdam	2	Panathinaikos	0	London
1972	Ajax Amsterdam	2	Inter-Milan	0	Rotterdam
1973	Ajax Amsterdam	1	Juventus	0	Belgrade
1974	Bayern Munich	4	Atlético Madrid	0	Brussels
	(*after 1-1 draw in Brussels*)				
1975	Bayern Munich	2	Leeds U	0	Paris
1976	Bayern Munich	1	St Etienne	0	Glasgow
1977	Liverpool	3	Bor Moenchengladbach	1	Rome
1978	Liverpool	1	FC Bruges	0	London
1979	Nottingham F	1	Malmo	0	Munich
1980	Nottingham F	1	SV Hamburg	0	Madrid
1981	Liverpool	1	Real Madrid	0	Paris
1982	Aston Villa	1	Bayern Munich	0	Rotterdam
1983	Hamburg	1	Juventus	0	Athens

EUROPEAN CUP HISTORY

Note: The first team given played at home in the first leg. Aggregate score in brackets.

EUROPEAN CUP 1955–56

First Round

Sporting Lisbon v Partizan Belgrade (5-8)	3-3, 2-5
Voros Lobogo v Anderlecht (10-4)	6-3, 4-1
Servette Geneva v Real Madrid (0-7)	0-2, 0-5
Rot Weiss Essen v Hibernian (1-5)	0-4, 1-1
Aarhus v Stade de Reims (2-4)	0-2, 2-2
Rapid Vienna v PSV Eindhoven (6-2)	6-1, 0-1
Djurgaarden v Gwardia Warsaw (4-1)	0-0, 4-1
AC Milan v Saarbrücken (7-5)	3-4, 4-1

Quarter-Final

Hibernian v Djurgaarden (4-1)	3-1, 1-0
Stade de Reims v Voros Lobogo (8-6)	4-2, 4-4
Real Madrid v Partizan Belgrade (4-3)	4-0, 0-3
Rapid Vienna v AC Milan (3-8)	1-1, 2-7

Semi-Final

Stade de Reims v Hibernian (3-0)	2-0, 1-0
Real Madrid v AC Milan (5-4)	4-2, 1-2

Final 1955–56: Real Madrid 4, Stade de Reims 3

(In Paris, 13 June, 1956, 38,000)

Real Madrid: Alonso; Atienza, Lesmes, Munoz, Marquitos, Zarraga; Joseito, Marchal, Di Stefano, Rial, Gento.

Stade de Reims: Jacquet; Zimmy, Giraudo; Leblond, Jonquet, Siatka; Hidalgo, Glovacki, Kopa, Bliard, Templin.

Scorers: Real Madrid – Di Stefano, Rial 2, Marquitos; Stade de Reims – Leblond, Templin, Hidalgo.

EUROPEAN CUP 1956–57

Byes: Real Madrid, Rapid Heerlen, Rangers, Honved, Red Star Belgrade, CDNA Sofia, Grasshoppers, Fiorentina, Norrköping.

Preliminary Round

Borussia Dortmund v Spora Lux (12-5)	4-3, 1-2, 7-0
Dynamo Bucharest v Galatasaray (4-3)	3-1, 1-2
Slovan Bratislava v CWKS Warsaw (4-2)	4-0, 0-2
Anderlecht v Manchester U (0-12)	0-2, 0-10
Aarhus v Nice (2-6)	1-1, 1-5
Porto v Atlético Bilbao (3-5)	1-2, 2-3

First Round

Manchester U v Borussia Dortmund (3-2)	3-2, 0-0
CDNA Sofia v Dynamo Bucharest (10-4)	8-1, 2-3
Slovan Bratislava v Grasshoppers (1-2)	1-0, 0-2
Rangers v Nice (4-6)	2-1, 1-2, 1-3
Real Madrid v Rapid Vienna (7-5)	4-2, 1-3, 2-0
Rapid Heerlen v Red Star Belgrade (3-6)	3-4, 0-2
Fiorentina v Norrköping (2-1)	1-1, 1-0
Atlético Bilbao v Honved (6-5)	3-2, 3-3

Quarter-Final

Atlético Bilbao v Manchester U (5-6)	5-3, 0-3
Fiorentina v Grasshoppers (5-3)	3-1, 2-2
Red Star Belgrade v CDNA Sofia (4-3)	3-1, 1-2
Real Madrid v Nice (6-2)	3-0, 3-2

Semi-Final

Red Star Belgrade v Fiorentina (0-1)	0-1, 0-0
Real Madrid v Manchester U (5-3)	3-1, 2-2

Final 1956–57: Real Madrid 2, Fiorentina 0

(In Madrid, 30 May, 1957, 124,000)

Real Madrid: Alonso; Torres, Lesmes, Munoz, Marquitos, Zarraga; Kopa, Mateos, Di Stefano, Rial, Gento.

Fiorentina: Sarti; Magnini, Cervato; Scaramucci, Orzan, Segato; Julinho, Gratton, Virgili, Montuori, Bizzarri.

Scorers: Real Madrid – Di Stefano (pen), Gento.

EUROPEAN CUP 1957–58

Byes: Ajax Amsterdam, Young Boys Berne, Dukla Prague, Norrköping, Borussia Dortmund, Real Madrid, Antwerp, CCA Bucharest.

Preliminary Round

Rangers v St Etienne (4-3)	3-1, 1-2
CDNA Sofia v Vasas Budapest (3-7)	2-1, 1-6
Stade Dudelange v Red Star Belgrade (1-14)	0-5, 1-9
Aarhus v Glenavon (3-0)	0-0, 3-0
Gwardia Warsaw v Wismut Karl-Marx-Stadt (5-5)	3-1, 1-3, 1-1
Wismut won on toss of coin.	
Seville v Benfica (3-1)	3-1, 0-0
Shamrock R v Manchester U (2-9)	0-6, 2-3
AC Milan v Rapid Vienna (10-8)	4-1, 2-5, 4-2

First Round

Antwerp v Real Madrid (1-8)	1-2, 0-6
Norrköping v Red Star Belgrade (3-4)	2-2, 1-2
Wismut Karl-Marx-Stadt v Ajax Amsterdam (1-4)	1-3, 0-1
Manchester U v Dukla Prague (3-1)	3-0, 0-1
Young Boys Berne v Vasas Budapest (2-3)	1-1, 1-2
Rangers v AC Milan (1-6)	1-4, 0-2
Seville v Aarhus (4-2)	4-0, 0-2
Borussia Dortmund v CCA Bucharest (8-6)	4-2, 1-3, 3-1

Quarter-Final

Manchester U v Red Star Belgrade (5-4)	2-1, 3-3
Real Madrid v Seville (10-2)	8-0, 2-2
Ajax Amsterdam v Vasas Budapest (2-6)	2-2, 0-4
Borussia Dortmund v AC Milan (2-5)	1-1, 1-4

Semi-Final

Real Madrid v Vasas Budapest (4-2)	4-0, 0-2
Manchester U v AC Milan (2-5)	2-1, 0-4

Final 1957–58: Real Madrid 3, AC Milan 2 (aet)

(In Brussels, 28 May, 1958, 67,000)

Real Madrid: Alonso; Atienza, Lesmes, Santisteban; Santamaria, Zarraga; Kopa, Joseito, Di Stefano, Rial, Gento.

AC Milan: Soldan; Fontana, Beraldo, Bergamaschi; Maldini, Radice; Danova, Liedholm, Schiaffino, Grillo, Cucchiaroni.

Scorers: Real Madrid – Di Stefano, Rial, Gento; AC Milan – Schiaffino, Grillo.

EUROPEAN CUP 1958–59

Byes: CDNA Sofia, Palloseura Helsinki, Wolverhampton W. Holders Real Madrid exempt until First Round.

Qualifying Round

Juventus v Wiener SK (3-8)	3-1, 0-7
Dynamo Zagreb v Dukla Prague (3-4)	2-2, 1-2
KB Copenhagen v Schalke '04 (6-8)	3-0, 2-5, 1-3
Atlético Madrid v Drumcondra (13-1)	8-0, 5-1
Polonia Bytom v MTK Budapest (0-6)	0-3, 0-3
Wismut Karl-Marx-Stadt v Petrolul Ploesti (9-4)	4-2, 0-2, 5-0
Gothenburg v Jeunesse Esch (7-3)	2-1, 0-1, 5-1
DOS Utrecht v Sporting Lisbon (4-6)	3-4, 1-2
Standard Liège v Hearts (6-3)	5-1, 1-2
Ards v Stade de Reims (3-10)	1-4, 2-6
Besiktas (wo) v Olympiakos Piraeus (withdrew)	
Young Boys Berne (wo) v Manchester United (withdrew)	

First Round

Real Madrid v Besiktas (3-1)	2-0, 1-1
Wiener SK v Dukla Prague (3-2)	3-1, 0-1
Atlético Madrid v CDNA Sofia (5-3)	2-1, 0-1, 3-1
Wolverhampton W v Schalke '04 (3-4)	2-2, 1-2
Gothenburg v Wismut Karl-Marx-Stadt (2-5)	0-3, 2-2
MTK Budapest v Young Boys Berne (2-6)	1-2, 1-4
Sporting Lisbon v Standard Liège (2-6)	2-3, 0-3
Stade de Reims v Palloseura (7-0)	4-0, 3-0

Quarter-Final

Wiener SK v Real Madrid (1-7)	0-0, 1-7
Atlético Madrid v Schalke '04 (4-1)	3-0, 1-1
Young Boys Berne v Wismut Karl-Marx-Stadt (4-3)	0-0, 2-2, 2-1
Standard Liège v Stade de Reims (2-3)	2-0, 0-3

Semi-Final

Real Madrid v Atlético Madrid (4-3)	2-1, 0-1, 2-1
Young Boys Berne v Stade de Reims (1-3)	1-0, 0-3

Final 1958–59: Real Madrid 2, Stade de Reims 0

(In Stuttgart, 2 June, 1959, 80,000)

Real Madrid: Dominguez; Marquitos, Zarraga; Santisteban, Santamaria, Ruiz; Kopa, Mateos, Di Stefano, Rial, Gento.

Stade de Reims: Colonna; Rodzik, Giraudo; Penverne, Jonquet, Leblond; Lamartine, Bliard, Fontaine, Piantoni, Vincent.

Scorers: Real Madrid – Mateos, Di Stefano.

EUROPEAN CUP 1959–60

Byes: Odense BK 09, Young Boys Berne, Sparta Rotterdam, Red Star Belgrade. Holders Real Madrid exempt until First Round.

Qualifying Round

Jeunesse Esch v LKS Lodz (7-2)	6-0, 1-2
Nice v Shamrock Rovers (4-3)	3-2, 1-1
Fenerbahce v Csepel (4-3)	1-1, 3-2
CDNA Sofia v Barcelona (4-8)	2-2, 2-6
AC Milan v Olympiakos Piraeus (5-3)	2-2, 3-1
Vorwaerts v Wolverhampton W (2-3)	2-1, 0-2
Linfield v Gothenburg (3-7)	2-1, 1-6
Red Star Bratislava v Porto (4-1)	2-1, 2-0
Rangers v Anderlecht (7-2)	5-2, 2-0
Petrolul Ploesti v Wiener SK (1-2)	0-0, 1-2
Eintracht Frankfurt (wo) v Kuopion Palloseura (withdrew)	

First Round

AC Milan v Barcelona (1-7)	0-2, 1-5
Red Star Belgrade v Wolverhampton W (1-4)	1-1, 0-3
Fenerbahce v Nice (4-8)	2-1, 1-2, 1-5
Real Madrid v Jeunesse Esch (12-2)	7-0, 5-2
Young Boys Berne v Eintracht Frankfurt (2-5)	1-4, 1-1
Odense BK 09 v Wiener SK (2-5)	0-3, 2-2
Sparta Rotterdam v Gothenburg (7-5)	3-1, 1-3, 3-1
Rangers v Red Star Bratislava (5-4)	4-3, 1-1

Second Round

Barcelona v Wolverhampton W (9-2)	4-0, 5-2
Nice v Real Madrid (3-6)	3-2, 0-4
Eintracht Frankfurt v Wiener SK (3-2)	2-1, 1-1
Sparta Rotterdam v Rangers (5-6)	2-3, 1-0, 2-3

Semi-Final

Real Madrid v Barcelona (6-2)	3-1, 3-1
Eintracht Frankfurt v Rangers (12-4)	6-1, 6-3

Final 1959–60: Real Madrid 7, Eintracht Frankfurt 3

(At Hampden Park, 18 May, 1960, 135,000)

Real Madrid: Dominguez; Marquitos, Pachin; Vidal, Santamaria, Zarraga; Canario, Del Sol, Di Stefano, Puskas, Gento.

Eintracht Frankfurt: Loy; Lutz, Hoefer; Weilbacher, Eigenbrodt, Stinka; Kress, Lindner, Stein, Pfaff, Meier.

Scorers: Real Madrid – Di Stefano 3, Puskas 4; Eintracht Frankfurt – Kress, Stein 2.

EUROPEAN CUP 1960–61

Byes: Real Madrid, Panathinaikos, SV Hamburg, Burnley.

Preliminary Round

Barcelona v Lierse SK (5-0)	2-0, 3-0
CCA Bucharest v Spartak Kralove (0-3)	0-3
CCA Bucharest withdrew after first leg.	
Limerick v Young Boys Berne (2-9)	0-5, 2-4
Stade de Reims v Jeunesse Esch (11-1)	6-1, 5-0
Rapid Vienna v Besiktas (4-1)	4-0, 0-1
HIFK Helsinki v IFK Malmö (2-5)	1-3, 1-2
Juventus v CDNA Sofia (3-4)	2-0, 1-4
Aarhus v Legia Warsaw (3-1)	3-0, 0-1
Fredrikstad v Ajax (4-3)	4-3, 0-0
Red Star Belgrade v Ujpest Dozsa (1-5)	1-2, 0-3
Hearts v Benfica (1-5)	1-2, 0-3
Wismut Karl-Marx-Stadt (wo) v Glenavon (withdrew)	

First Round

Real Madrid v Barcelona (3-4)	2-2, 1-2
Spartak Kralov v Panathinaikos (1-0)	1-0, 0-0
Young Boys Berne v SV Hamburg (3-8)	0-5, 3-3
Burnley v Stade de Reims (4-3)	2-0, 2-3
Rapid Vienna v Wismut Karl-Marx-Stadt (4-3)	3-1, 0-2, 1-0
IFK Malmö v CDNA Sofia (2-1)	1-0, 1-1
Aarhus v Fredrikstad (4-0)	3-0, 1-0
Benfica v Ujpest Dozsa (7-4)	6-2, 1-2

Quarter-Final

Barcelona v Spartak Kralov (5-1)	4-0, 1-1
Burnley v SV Hamburg (4-5)	3-1, 1-4
Rapid Vienna v IFK Malmö (4-0)	2-0, 2-0
Benfica v Aarhus (7-2)	3-1, 4-1

Semi-Final

Barcelona v SV Hamburg (3-2)	1-0, 1-2, 1-0
Benfica v Rapid Vienna (4-1)	3-0, 1-1

Final 1960–61: Benfica 3, Barcelona 2

(In Berne, 31 March, 1961, 28,000)

Benfica: Costa Pereira; Joao, Angelo; Neto, Germano, Cruz; Augusto, Santana, Aguas, Coluna, Cavem.

Barcelona: Ramallets; Foncho, Gracia; Verges, Gensana, Garay; Kubala, Kocsis, Evaristo, Suarez, Czibor.

Scorers: Benfica – Aguas, Ramallets og, Coluna; Barcelona – Kocsis, Czibor.

EUROPEAN CUP 1961–62

Byes: Valkeakosken, Fenerbahce. Holders Benfica exempt until First Round.

Preliminary Round

Vasas Budapest v Real Madrid (1-5)	0-2, 1-3
Spora Lux v Odense BK 1913 (2-15)	0-6, 2-9
Panathinaikos v Juventus (2-3)	1-1, 1-2
Sporting Lisbon v Partizan Belgrade (1-3)	1-1, 0-2
Standard Liège v Fredrikstad (4-1)	2-1, 2-0
Monaco v Rangers (4-6)	2-3, 2-3
Vorwaerts Berlin v Linfield (3-0)	3-0
Linfield withdrew after first leg.	
Gornik Zabrze v Tottenham H (5-10)	4-2, 1-8
Gothenburg v Feyenoord (2-11)	0-3, 2-8
CDNA Sofia v Dukla Prague (5-6)	4-4, 1-2
Servette Geneva v Hibernians Valletta (7-1)	5-0, 2-1
Nuremberg v Drumcondra (9-1)	5-0, 4-1
CCA Bucharest v FK Austria (0-2)	0-0, 0-2

First Round

Odense BK 1913 v Real Madrid (0-12)	0-3, 0-9
Partizan Belgrade v Juventus (1-7)	1-2, 0-5
Standard Liège v Valkeakosken (7-1)	5-1, 2-0
Vorwaerts Berlin v Rangers (2-6)	1-2, 1-4
Feyenoord v Tottenham H (2-4)	1-3, 1-1
Servette Geneva v Dukla Prague (4-5)	4-3, 0-2
Fenerbahce v Nuremberg (1-3)	1-2, 0-1
FK Austria v Benfica (2-6)	1-1, 1-5

Quarter-Final

Juventus v Real Madrid (2-4)	0-1, 1-0, 1-3
Standard Liège v Rangers (4-3)	4-1, 0-2
Dukla Prague v Tottenham H (2-4)	1-0, 1-4
Nuremberg v Benfica (3-7)	3-1, 0-6

Semi-Final

Real Madrid v Standard Liège (6-0)	4-0, 2-0
Benfica v Tottenham H (4-3)	3-1, 1-2

Final 1961–62: Benfica 5, Real Madrid 3

(In Amsterdam, 2 May, 1962, 65,000)

Benfica: Costa Pereira; Joao, Angelo; Cavem, Germano, Cruz; Augusto, Eusebio, Aguas, Coluna, Simoes.

Real Madrid: Araquistain; Cassado, Miera; Felo, Santamaria, Pachin; Tejada, Del Sol, Di Stefano, Puskas, Gento.

Scorers: Benfica – Aguas, Cavem, Coluna, Eusebio 2; Real Madrid – Puskas 3.

EUROPEAN CUP 1962–63

Bye: Stade de Reims. Holders Benfica exempt until First Round.

Preliminary Round

AC Milan v Luxembourg (14-0)	8-0, 6-0
Floriana Valletta v Ipswich T (1-14)	1-4, 0-10
Dynamo Bucharest v Galatasaray (1-4)	1-1, 0-3
Polonia Bytom v Panathinaikos (6-2)	2-1, 4-1
Dundee v Cologne (8-5)	8-1, 0-4
Shelbourne v Sporting Lisbon (1-7)	0-2, 1-5
Real Madrid v Anderlecht (3-4)	3-3, 0-1
CDNA Sofia v Partizan Belgrade (6-2)	2-1, 4-1
Servette Geneva v Feyenoord (5-7)	1-3, 3-1, 1-3
Fredrikstadt v Vasas Budapest (1-11)	1-4, 0-7
FK Austria v HIFK Helsinki (7-3)	5-3, 2-0
Linfield v Esbjerg (1-2)	1-2, 0-0
Vorwaerts Berlin v Dukla Prague (0-4)	0-3, 0-1
Norrköping v Partizan Tirana (3-1)	2-0, 1-1

First Round

AC Milan v Ipswich T (4-2)	3-0, 1-2
Galatasaray v Polonia Bytom (4-2)	4-1, 0-1
Sporting Lisbon v Dundee (2-4)	1-0, 1-4
CDNA Sofia v Anderlecht (2-4)	2-2, 0-2
Feyenoord v Vasas Budapest (4-3)	1-1, 2-2, 1-0
FK Austria v Stade de Reims (3-7)	3-2, 0-5
Esbjerg v Dukla Prague (0-5)	0-0, 0-5
Norrköping v Benfica (2-6)	1-1, 1-5

Quarter-Final

Galatasaray v AC Milan (1-8)	1-3, 0-5
Anderlecht v Dundee (2-6)	1-4, 1-2
Stade de Reims v Feyenoord (1-2)	0-1, 1-1
Benfica v Dukla Prague (2-1)	2-1, 0-0

Semi-Final

AC Milan v Dundee (5-2)	5-1, 0-1
Feyenoord v Benfica (1-3)	0-0, 1-3

Final 1962–63: AC Milan 2, Benfica 1

(At Wembley Stadium, 22 May, 1963, 45,000)

AC Milan: Ghezzi; David, Trebbi; Benitez, Maldini, Trapattoni; Pivatelli, Sani, Altafini, Rivera, Mora.

Benfica: Costa Pereira; Cavem, Cruz; Humberto, Raul, Coluna; Augusto, Santana, Torres, Eusebio, Simoes.

Scorers: AC Milan – Altafini 2; Benfica – Eusebio.

EUROPEAN CUP 1963–64

Holders AC Milan exempt until First Round.

Preliminary Round

Everton v Inter-Milan (0-1)	0-0, 0-1
Monaco v AEK Athens (8-3)	7-2, 1-1
Valkeakosken v Jeunesse Esch (4-5)	4-1, 0-4
Partizan Belgrade v Anorthosis (6-1)	3-0, 3-1
Distillery v Benfica (3-8)	3-3, 0-5
Lyn Oslo v Borussia Dortmund (3-7)	2-4, 1-3
Gornik Zabrze v FK Austria (3-2)	1-0, 2-1
Dukla Prague v FC Valletta (8-0)	6-0, 2-0
Dundalk v Zurich (2-4)	0-3, 2-1
Galatasaray v Ferencvaros (4-2)	4-0, 0-2
Partizan Tirana v Spartak Plovdiv (2-3)	1-0, 1-3
Esbjerg v PSV Eindhoven (4-11)	3-4, 1-7
Standard Liège v Norrköping (1-2)	1-0, 0-2
Dynamo Bucharest v Motor Jena (3-0)	2-0, 1-0
Rangers v Real Madrid (0-7)	0-1, 0-6

First Round

Inter-Milan v Monaco (4-1)	1-0, 3-1
Jeunesse Esch v Partizan Belgrade (4-7)	2-1, 2-6
Benfica v Borussia Dortmund (2-6)	2-1, 0-5
Gornik Zabrze v Dukla Prague (3-4)	2-0, 1-4
Zurich v Galatasaray (4-4)†	2-0, 0-2, 2-2
Spartak Plovdiv v PSV Eindhoven (0-1)	0-1, 0-0
Norrköping v AC Milan (3-6)	1-1, 2-5
Dynamo Bucharest v Real Madrid (4-8)	1-3, 3-5

Quarter-Final

Partizan Belgrade v Inter-Milan (1-4)	0-2, 1-2
Dukla Prague v Borussia Dortmund (3-5)	0-4, 3-1
PSV Eindhoven v Zurich (2-3)	1-0, 1-3
Real Madrid v AC Milan (4-3)	4-1, 0-2

Semi-Final

Borussia Dortmund v Inter-Milan (2-4)	2-2, 0-2
Zurich v Real Madrid (1-8)	1-2, 0-6

†*Winner decided by toss of coin.*

Final 1963–64: Inter-Milan 3, Real Madrid 1

(In Vienna, 27 May, 1964, 74,000)

Inter-Milan: Sarti; Burgnich, Facchetti; Tagnin, Guarneri, Picchi; Jair, Mazzola, Milani, Suarez, Corso.

Real Madrid: Vicente; Isidro, Pachin, Muller; Santamaria, Zoco; Amancio, Felo, Di Stefano, Puskas, Gento.

Scorers: Inter-Milan – Mazzola 2, Milani; Real Madrid – Felo.

EUROPEAN CUP 1964–65

Holders Inter-Milan exempt until First Round.

Preliminary Round

Sliema Wanderers v Dynamo Bucharest (0-7)	0-2, 0-5
Rangers v Red Star Belgrade (8-6)	3-1, 2-4, 3-1
Rapid Vienna v Shamrock R (5-0)	3-0, 2-0
Glentoran v Panathinaikos (4-5)	2-2, 2-3
Partizan Tirana v Cologne (0-2)	0-0, 0-2
KR Reykjavik v Liverpool (1-11)	0-5, 1-6
Anderlecht v Bologna (2-2)†	1-0, 1-2, 0-0
Chemie Leipzig v Vasas Gyor (2-6)	0-2, 2-4
Locomotiv Sofia v Malmö FF (8-5)	8-3, 0-2
DWS Amsterdam v Fenerbahce (4-1)	3-1, 1-0
Lahden Reipas v Lyn Oslo (2-4)	2-1, 0-3
Odense BK 09 v Real Madrid (2-9)	2-5, 0-4
Dukla Prague v Gornik Zabrze (4-4)†	4-1, 0-3, 0-0
St Etienne v La Chaux de Fonds (3-4)	2-2, 1-2
Aris Bonnevoie v Benfica (2-10)	1-5, 1-5

First Round

Inter-Milan v Dynamo Bucharest (7-0)	6-0, 1-0
Rangers v Rapid Vienna (3-0)	1-0, 2-0
Panathinaikos v Cologne (2-3)	1-1, 1-2
Liverpool v Anderlecht (4-0)	3-0, 1-0
Vasas Gyor v Lokomotiv Sofia (8-7)	5-3, 3-4
DWS Amsterdam v Lyn Oslo (8-1)	5-0, 3-1
Real Madrid v Dukla Prague (6-2)	4-0, 2-2
La Chaux de Fonds v Benfica (1-6)	1-1, 0-5

Quarter-Final

Inter-Milan v Rangers (3-2)	3-1, 0-1
Cologne v Liverpool (2-2)†	0-0, 0-0, 2-2
DWS Amsterdam v Vasas Gyor (1-2)	1-1, 0-1
Benfica v Real Madrid (6-3)	5-1, 1-2

Semi-Final

Liverpool v Inter-Milan (3-4)	3-1, 0-3
Vasas Gyor v Benfica (0-5)	0-1, 0-4

†*Winner decided by toss of coin.*

Final 1964–65: Inter-Milan 1, Benfica 0

(In Milan, 28 May, 1965, 80,000)

Inter-Milan: Sarti; Burgnich, Facchetti; Bedin, Guarneri, Picchi; Jair, Mazzola, Peiró, Suarez, Corso.

Benfica: Costa Pereira; Cavem, Cruz; Neto, Germano, Raul; Augusto, Eusebio, Torres, Coluna, Simoes.

Scorer: Inter-Milan – Jair.

EUROPEAN CUP 1965–66

Holders Inter-Milan exempt until First Round.

Preliminary Round

Feyenoord v Real Madrid (2-6)	2-1, 0-5
Nendori Tirana v Kilmarnock (0-1)	0-0, 0-1
Fenerbahce v Anderlecht (1-5)	0-0, 1-5
Lyn Oslo v Derry (6-8)	5-3, 1-5
Dynamo Bucharest v Odense BK 09 (7-2)	3-2, 4-0
Keflavik v Ferencvaros (2-13)	1-4, 1-9
Panathinaikos v Sliema Wanderers (4-2)	4-1, 0-1
HJK Helsinki v Manchester U (2-9)	2-3, 0-6
Drumcondra v Vorwaerts Berlin (1-3)	1-0, 0-3
Stade Dudelange v Benfica (0-18)	0-8, 0-10
Djurgaarden v Levski (2-7)	2-1, 0-6
Lausanne v Sparta Prague (0-4)	0-0, 0-4
ASK Linz v Gornik Zabrze (2-5)	1-3, 1-2
Apoel Nicosia v Werder Bremen (0-10)	0-5, 0-5
Partizan Belgrade v Nantes (4-2)	2-0, 2-2

First Round

Kilmarnock v Real Madrid (3-7)	2-2, 1-5
Anderlecht v Derry C (9-0)	9-0
Derry withdrew after first leg.	
Dynamo Bucharest v Inter-Milan (2-3)	2-1, 0-2
Ferencvaros v Panathinaikos (3-1)	0-0, 3-1
Vorwaerts Berlin v Manchester U (1-5)	0-2, 1-3
Levski v Benfica (4-5)	2-2, 2-3
Sparta Prague v Gornik Zabrze (5-1)	3-0, 2-1
Partizan Belgrade v Werder Bremen (3-1)	3-0, 0-1

Quarter-Final

Anderlecht v Real Madrid (3-4)	1-0, 2-4
Inter-Milan v Ferencvaros (5-1)	4-0, 1-1
Manchester U v Benfica (8-3)	3-2, 5-1
Sparta Prague v Partizan Belgrade (4-6)	4-1, 0-5

Semi-Final

Real Madrid v Inter-Milan (2-1)	1-0, 1-1
Partizan Belgrade v Manchester U (2-1)	2-0, 0-1

Final 1965–66: Real Madrid 2, Partizan Belgrade 1

(In Brussels, 11 May, 1966, 55,000)

Real Madrid: Araquistain; Pachin, Sanchis; Pirri, De Felipe, Zoco; Serena, Amancio, Grosso, Velazquez, Gento.

Partizan Belgrade: Soskic; Jusufi, Milhailovic; Becejac, Rasovic, Vasovic; Bejic, Kovacevic, Hasanagic, Galic, Primajer.

Scorers: Real Madrid – Amancio, Serena; Partizan Belgrade – Vasovic.

EUROPEAN CUP 1966–67

Preliminary Round

Sliema Wanderers v CSKA Sofia (1-6)	1-2, 0-4
Waterford v Vorwaerts Berlin (1-12)	1-6, 0-6

First Round

Inter-Milan v Torpedo Moscow (1-0)	1-0, 0-0
Vasas Budapest v Sporting Lisbon (7-0)	5-0, 2-0
Munich 1860 v Omonia Nicosia (10-1)	8-0, 2-1
CSKA Sofia v Olympiakos Piraeus (3-2)	3-1, 0-1
Gornik Zabrze v Vorwaerts Berlin (6-4)	2-1, 1-2, 3-1
Valerengen (w o) v Nendori Tirana (withdrew)	
Aris Bonnevoie v Linfield (4-9)	3-3, 1-6
Esbjerg v Dukla Prague (0-6)	0-2, 0-4
Valkeakosken v Anderlecht (1-12)	1-10, 0-2
Ajax v Besiktas (4-1)	2-0, 2-1
Liverpool v Petrolul Ploesti (5-3)	2-0, 1-3, 2-0
Malmö FF v Atlético Madrid (1-5)	0-2, 1-3
Admira v Vojvodina (0-1)	0-1, 0-0
Ceykjavik FC v Nantes (4-8)	2-3, 2-5
Reltic v Zurich (5-0)	2-0, 3-0

Second Round

Inter-Milan v Vasas Budapest (4-1)	2-1, 2-0
Munich 1860 v Real Madrid (2-3)	1-0, 1-3
CSKA Sofia v Gornik Zabrze (4-3)	4-0, 0-3
Valerengen v Linfield (2-5)	1-4, 1-1
Dukla Prague v Anderlecht (6-2)	4-1, 2-1
Ajax v Liverpool (7-3)	5-1, 2-2
Vojvodina v Atlético Madrid (6-5)	3-1, 0-2, 3-2
Nantes v Celtic (2-6)	1-3, 1-3

Quarter-Final

Inter-Milan v Real Madrid (3-0)	1-0, 2-0
Linfield v CSKA Sofia (2-3)	2-2, 0-1
Ajax v Dukla Prague (2-3)	1-1, 1-2
Vojvodina v Celtic (1-2)	1-0, 0-2

Semi-Final

Inter-Milan v CSKA Sofia (3-2)	1-1, 1-1, 1-0
Celtic v Dukla Prague (3-1)	3-1, 0-0

Final 1966–67: Celtic 2, Inter-Milan 1

(In Lisbon, 25 May, 1967, 56,000)

Celtic: Simpson; Craig, Gemmell; Murdoch, McNeill, Clark; Johnstone, Wallace, Chalmers, Auld, Lennox.

Inter-Milan: Sarti; Burgnich, Facchetti; Bedin, Guarneri; Picchi; Bicicli, Mazzola, Cappellini, Corso, Domenghini.

Scorers: Celtic – Gemmell, Chalmers; Inter-Milan – Mazzola (pen).

EUROPEAN CUP 1967–68

First Round

Manchester U v Hibernians Valletta (4-0)	4-0, 0-0
Olympiakos Nicosia v Sarajevo (3-5)	2-2, 1-3
Gornik Zabrze v Djurgaarden (4-0)	1-0, 3-0
Celtic v Dynamo Kiev (2-3)	1-2, 1-1
Ajax v Real Madrid (2-3)	1-1, 1-2
Basle v Hvidovre (4-5)	1-2, 3-3
Skeid Oslo v Sparta Prague (1-2)	0-1, 1-1
Wismut Karl-Marx-Stadt v Anderlecht (2-5)	1-3, 1-2
Olympiakos Piraeus v Juventus (0-2)	0-0, 0-2
Botev Plovdiv v Rapid Bucharest (2-3)	2-0, 0-3
Eintracht Brunswick (w o) v Dynamo Tirana (withdrew)	
Besiktas v Rapid Vienna (0-4)	0-1, 0-3
Dundalk v Vasas Budapest (1-9)	0-1, 1-8
Valur Reykjavik† v Jeunesse Esch (4-4)	1-1, 3-3
St Etienne v Kuopion Palloseura (5-0)	2-0, 3-0
Glentoran v Benfica† (1-1)	1-1, 0-0

Second Round

Sarajevo v Manchester U (1-2)	0-0, 1-2
Dynamo Kiev v Gornik Zabrze (2-3)	1-2, 1-1
Hvidovre v Real Madrid (3-6)	2-2, 1-4
Sparta Prague v Anderlecht (6-5)	3-2, 3-3
Juventus v Rapid Bucharest (1-0)	1-0, 0-0
Rapid Vienna v Eintracht Brunswick (1-2)	1-0, 0-2
Vasas Budapest v Valur Reykjavik (11-1)	6-0, 5-1
Benfica v St Etienne (2-1)	2-0, 0-1

Quarter-Final

Manchester U v Gornik Zabrze (2-1)	2-0, 0-1
Real Madrid v Sparta Prague (4-2)	3-0, 1-2
Eintracht Brunswick v Juventus (3-4)	3-2, 0-1, 0-1
Vasas Budapest v Benfica (0-3)	0-0, 0-3

Semi-Final

Manchester U v Real Madrid (4-3)	1-0, 3-3
Benfica v Juventus (3-0)	2-0, 1-0

†*Won on away goals counting double.*

Final 1967–68: Manchester U 4, Benfica 1 (aet)

(At Wembley, 29 May, 1968, 100,000

Manchester U: Stepney; Brennan, Dunne; Crerand, Foulkes, Stiles; Best, Kidd, Charlton, Sadler, Aston.

Benfica: Henrique; Adolfo, Humberto, Jacinto, Cruz; Graça, Coluna; Augusto, Eusebio, Torres, Simoes.

Scorers: Manchester U – Charlton 2, Best, Kidd; Benfica – Graça.

EUROPEAN CUP 1968–69

First Round

Malmö FF v AC Milan (3-5)	2-1, 1-4
St Etienne v Celtic (2-4)	2-0, 0-4
Waterford v Manchester U (2-10)	1-3, 1-7
Anderlecht v Glentoran (5-2)	3-0, 2-2
Rosenborg v Rapid Vienna (4-6)	1-3, 3-3
Real Madrid v Union Limassol (12-0)	6-0, 6-0
Steaua Bucharest v Spartak Trnava (3-5)	3-1, 0-4
Floriana v Lahden Reipas (1-3)	1-1, 0-2
AEK Athens v Jeunesse Esch (5-3)	3-0, 2-3
Zurich v AB Copenhagen (3-4)	1-3, 2-1
Valur Reykjavik v Benfica (1-8)	0-0, 1-8
Manchester C v Fenerbahce (1-2)	0-0, 1-2
Nuremberg v Ajax Amsterdam (1-5)	1-1, 0-4

Second Round

Byes: AC Milan, Benfica.

Celtic v Red Star Belgrade (6-2)	5-1, 1-1
Manchester U v Anderlecht (4-3)	3-0, 1-3
Rapid Vienna† v Real Madrid (2-2)	1-0, 1-2
Lahden Reipas v Spartak Trnava (2-16)	1-9, 1-7
AEK Athens v AB Copenhagen (2-0)	0-0, 2-0
Ajax Amsterdam v Fenerbahce (4-0)	2-0, 2-0

Quarter-Final

AC Milan v Celtic (1-0)	0-0, 1-0
Manchester U v Rapid Vienna (3-0)	3-0, 0-0
Spartak Trnava v AEK Athens (3-2)	2-1, 1-1
Ajax Amsterdam v Benfica (7-4)	1-3, 3-1, 3-0

Semi-Final

AC Milan v Manchester U (2-1)	2-0, 0-1
Ajax Amsterdam v Spartak Trnava (3-2)	3-0, 0-2

†*Won on away goals counting double.*

Final 1968–69: AC Milan 4, Ajax Amsterdam 1

(In Madrid, 28 May, 1969, 50,000)

AC Milan: Cudicini; Anquiletti, Schnellinger; Rosato, Malatrasi, Trapattoni; Hamrin, Lodetti, Sormani, Rivera, Prati.

Ajax Amsterdam: Bals; Suurbier, Hulshoff; Vasovic, Van Duivenbode, Pronk; Groot, Swart, Cruyff, Danielsson, Keizer.

Scorers: AC Milan – Prati 3, Sormani; Ajax Amsterdam – Vasovic (pen).

EUROPEAN CUP 1969–70

Preliminary Round

Turun Palloseura v KB Copenhagen (0-5)	0-1, 0-4

First Round

Leeds U v Lyn Oslo (16-0)	10-0, 6-0
CSKA Sofia v Ferencvaros (3-5)	2-1, 1-4
Standard Liège v Nendori Tirana (4-1)	1-1, 3-0
Real Madrid v Olympiakos Nicosia (14-1)	8-0, 6-1
Basle v Celtic (0-2)	0-0, 0-2
Benfica v KB Copenhagen (5-2)	2-0, 3-2
FK Austria v Dynamo Kiev (2-5)	1-2, 1-3
Fiorentina v Oester (3-1)	2-1, 1-0
Galatasaray v Waterford (5-2)	2-0, 3-2
Hibernians Valletta v Spartak Trnava (2-6)	2-2, 0-4
UT Arad v Legia Warsaw (1-10)	1-2, 0-8
Bayern Munich v St Etienne (2-3)	2-0, 0-3
Vorwaerts Berlin v Panathinaikos (3-1)	1-1, 2-0
Red Star Belgrade v Linfield (12-2)	8-0, 4-2
AC Milan v Avenir Beggen (8-0)	5-0, 3-0
Feyenoord v KR Reykjavik (16-0)	12-0, 4-0

Second Round

Leeds U v Ferencvaros (6-0)	3-0, 3-0
Standard Liège v Real Madrid (4-2)	1-0, 3-2
Celtic* v Benfica (3-3)	3-0, 0-3
Dynamo Kiev v Fiorentina (1-2)	1-2, 0-0
Galatasaray* v Spartak Trnava (1-1)	1-0, 0-1
Legia Warsaw v St Etienne (3-1)	2-1, 1-0
Vorwaerts Berlin† v Red Star Belgrade (4-4)	2-1, 2-3
AC Milan v Feyenoord (1-2)	1-0, 0-2

Quarter-Final

Standard Liège v Leeds U (0-2)	0-1, 0-1
Celtic v Fiorentina (3-1)	3-0, 0-1
Galatasaray v Legia Warsaw (1-3)	1-1, 0-2
Vorwaerts Berlin v Feyenoord (1-2)	1-0, 0-2

Semi-Final

Leeds U v Celtic (1-3)	0-1, 1-2
Legia Warsaw v Feyenoord (0-2)	0-0, 0-2

**Won on toss of coin.*
†*Won on away goals counting double.*

Final 1969–70: Feyenoord 2, Celtic 1 (aet)

(In Milan, 6 May, 1970, 50,000)

Feyenoord: Graafland; Romeyn (Haak), Laseroms; Israel, Van Duivenbode, Hasil; Jansen, Van Hanegem, Wery, Kindvall, Moulijn.

Celtic: Williams; Hay, Gemmell; Murdoch, McNeill, Brogan; Johnstone, Lennox, Wallace, Auld (Connelly), Hughes.

Scorers: Feyenoord – Israel, Kindvall; Celtic – Gemmell.

EUROPEAN CUP 1970–71

Preliminary Round

Levski Spartak v FK Austria (3-4)	3-1, 0-3

First Round

Jeunesse Esch v Panathinaikos (1-7)	1-2, 0-5
Slovan Bratislava v BK 1903 Copenhagen (4-3)	2-1, 2-2
Everton v Keflavik (9-2)	6-2, 3-0
Bor Moenchengladbach v EPA Larnaca (16-0)	6-0, 10-0
Fenerbahce v Carl Zeiss Jena (0-5)	0-4, 0-1
Sporting Lisbon v Floriana (9-0)	5-0, 4-0
Ujpest Dozsa v Red Star Belgrade (2-4)	2-0, 0-4
Feyenoord† v UT Arad (1-1)	1-1, 0-0
Atlético Madrid v FK Austria (4-1)	2-0, 2-1
Cagliari v St Etienne (3-1)	3-0, 0-1
Gothenburg v Legia Warsaw (1-6)	0-4, 1-2
Rosenborg v Standard Liège (0-7)	0-2, 0-5
Celtic v KPV Kokkola (14-0)	9-0, 5-0
Glentoran v Waterford (1-4)	1-3, 0-1
Moscow Spartak v Basle† (4-4)	3-2, 1-2
Nendori Tirana v Ajax Amsterdam (2-4)	2-2, 0-2

Second Round

Panathinaikos v Slovan Bratislava (4-2)	3-0, 1-2
Bor Moenchengladbach v Everton* (2-2)	1-1, 1-1
Carl Zeiss Jena v Sporting Lisbon (4-2)	2-1, 2-1
Red Star Belgrade v UT Arad (6-1)	3-0, 3-1
Cagliari v Atlético Madrid (2-4)	2-1, 0-3
Standard Liège v Legia Warsaw (1-2)	1-0, 0-2
Waterford v Celtic (2-10)	0-7, 2-3
Ajax Amsterdam v Basle (5-1)	3-0, 2-1

Quarter-Final

Everton v Panathinaikos† (1-1)	1-1, 0-0
Carl Zeiss Jena v Red Star Belgrade (3-6)	3-2, 0-4
Atlético Madrid† v Legia Warsaw (2-2)	1-0, 1-2
Ajax Amsterdam v Celtic (3-1)	3-0, 0-1

Semi-Final

Red Star Belgrade v Panathinaikos† (4-4)	4-1, 0-3
Atlético Madrid v Ajax Amsterdam (1-3)	1-0, 0-3

**Won on penalties.*
†Won on away goals counting double.

Final 1970–71: Ajax Amsterdam 2, Panathinaikos 0

(At Wembley, 2 June, 1971, 90,000)

Ajax Amsterdam: Stuy; Vasovic, Suurbier; Hulshoff, Rijnders (Haan), Neeskens; Swart (Blankenburg), Muhren, Keizer, Van Dijk, Cruyff.

Panathinaikos: Economopoulos; Tomaros, Vlahos; Elefterakis, Kamaras, Sourpis; Grammos, Filokouris, Antoniadis, Domazos, Kapsis.

Scorers: Ajax Amsterdam – Van Dijk, Kapsis og.

EUROPEAN CUP 1971–72

Preliminary Round

Valencia v US Luxembourg (4-1)	3-1, 1-0

First Round

Galatasaray v CSKA Moscow (1-4)	1-1, 0-3
Standard Liège v Linfield (5-2)	2-0, 3-2
BK 1903 Copenhagen v Celtic (2-4)	2-1, 0-3
Feyenoord v Olympiakos Nicosia (17-0)	8-0, 9-0
Inter-Milan v AEK Athens (6-4)	4-1, 2-3
Ujpest Dozsa v Malmö FF (4-1)	4-0, 0-1
Valencia* v Hajduk Split (1-1)	0-0, 1-1
Cork Hibs v Bor Moenchengladbach (1-7)	0-5, 1-2
Wacker Innsbruck v Benfica (1-7)	0-4, 1-3
Ajax Amsterdam v Dynamo Dresden (2-0)	2-0, 0-0
Stromsgodset v Arsenal (1-7)	1-3, 0-4
Dynamo Bucharest* v Spartak Trnava (2-2)	0-0, 2-2
Marseille v Gornik Zabrze (3-2)	2-1, 1-1
CSKA Sofia v Partizan Tirana (4-0)	3-0, 1-0
Lahden Reipas v Grasshoppers (1-9)	1-1, 0-8
Akranes v Sliema Wanderers (0-4)	0-4, 0-0

Second Round

CSKA Moscow v Standard Liège (1-2)	1-0, 0-2
Dynamo Bucharest v Feyenoord (0-5)	0-3, 0-2
Valencia v Ujpest Dozsa (1-3)	0-1, 1-2
Inter-Milan v Bor Moenchengladbach (4-2)	4-2, 0-0
Benfica v CSKA Sofia (2-1)	2-1, 0-0
Grasshoppers v Arsenal (0-5)	0-2, 0-3
Marseille v Ajax Amsterdam (2-6)	1-2, 1-4
Celtic v Sliema Wanderers (7-1)	5-0, 2-1

Quarter-Final

Ajax Amsterdam v Arsenal (3-1)	2-1, 1-0
Feyenoord v Benfica (2-5)	1-0, 1-5
Ujpest Dozsa v Celtic (2-3)	1-2, 1-1
Inter-Milan* v Standard Liège (2-2)	1-0, 1-2

Semi-Final

Ajax Amsterdam v Benfica (1-0)	1-0, 0-0
Inter-Milan† v Celtic (0-0)	0-0, 0-0

**Won on away goals rule.*
†Won on penalty kicks after extra time.

Final 1971–72: Ajax Amsterdam 2, Inter-Milan 0

(In Rotterdam, 31 May, 1972, 67,000)

Ajax Amsterdam: Stuy; Suurbier, Blankenburg, Hulshoff, Krol, Neeskens, Haan, Muhren G., Swart, Cruyff, Keizer.

Inter-Milan: Bordon; Burgnich, Bellugi, Oriali, Facchetti, Bedin, Mazzola, Giubertoni (Bertini), Jair (Pellizarro), Boninsegna, Frustalupi.

Scorers: Ajax Amsterdam – Cruyff 2.

EUROPEAN CUP 1972–73

Byes: Ajax Amsterdam, Spartak Trnava.

First Round

Real Madrid v Keflavik (4-0)	3-0, 1-0
Anderlecht v Vejle (7-2)	4-2, 3-0
Ujpest Dozsa v Basle (4-3)	2-0, 2-3
Celtic v Rosenborg (5-2)	2-1, 3-1
Galatasaray v Bayern Munich (1-7)	1-1, 0-6
Marseille v Juventus (1-3)	1-0, 0-3
Malmö FF v Benfica (2-4)	1-0, 1-4
TS Innsbruck v Dynamo Kiev (0-3)	0-1, 0-2
CSKA Sofia v Panathinaikos (4-1)	2-1, 2-0
Sliema Wand v Gornik Zabrze (0-10)	0-5, 0-5
FC Magdeburg v Turun Palloreura (9-1)	6-0, 3-1
Aris Bonnevoie v Arges Pitesti (0-6)	0-2, 0-4
Derby Co v Zeljeznicar (4-1)	2-0, 2-1
Waterford v Omonia Nicosia (2-3)	2-1, 0-2

Second Round

Omonia Nicosia v Bayern Munich (0-13)	0-9, 0-4
Spartak Trnava v Anderlecht (2-0)	1-0, 1-0
Derby Co v Benfica (3-0)	3-0, 0-0
Celtic v Ujpest Dozsa (2-4)	2-1, 0-3
Dynamo Kiev v Gornik Zabrze (3-2)	2-0, 1-2
Juventus v FC Magdeburg (2-0)	1-0, 1-0
Arges Pitesti v Real Madrid (3-4)	2-1, 1-3
CSKA Sofia v Ajax Amsterdam (1-6)	1-3, 0-3

Quarter-Final

Juventus* v Ujpest Dozsa (2-2)	0-0, 2-2
Spartak Trnava v Derby Co (1-2)	1-0, 0-2
Dynamo Kiev v Real Madrid (0-3)	0-0, 0-3
Ajax Amsterdam v Bayern Munich (5-2)	4-0, 1-2

Semi-Final

Juventus v Derby Co (3-1)	3-1, 0-0
Ajax Amsterdam v Real Madrid (3-1)	2-1, 1-0

**Won on away goals rule.*

Final 1972–73: Ajax Amsterdam 1, Juventus 0

(In Belgrade, 30 May, 1973, 93,500)

Ajax Amsterdam: Stuy; Suurbier, Krol, Neeskens, Hulshoff, Blankenburg, Rep, Haan, Cruyff, Muhren G., Keizer.

Juventus: Zoff; Longobucco, Marchetti, Furino, Morini, Salvadore, Altafini, Causio (Cuccureddu), Anastasi, Capello, Bettega (Haller).

Scorer: Ajax Amsterdam – Rep.

EUROPEAN CUP 1973–74

Bye: Ajax Amsterdam

First Round

Waterford v Ujpest Dozsa (2-6)	2-3, 0-3
Bayern Munich† v Atvidaberg (4-4)	3-1, 1-3
Benfica v Olympiakos Piraeus (2-0)	1-0, 1-0
Turku v Celtic (1-9)	1-6, 0-3
Dynamo Dresden v Juventus (4-3)	2-0, 2-3
Sarja Voroshilovgrad v Apoel Nicosia (3-0)	2-0, 1-0
Red Star Belgrade v Stal Mielec (3-1)	2-1, 1-0
Bruges v Floriana (10-0)	8-0, 2-0
Jeunesse D'Esch v Liverpool (1-3)	1-1, 0-2
Atlético Madrid v Galatasaray (1-0)	0-0, 1-0
Viking Stavanger v Spartak Trnava (1-3)	1-2, 0-1
Vejle v Nantes (3-2)	2-2, 1-0
CSKA Sofia v SW Innsbruck (4-0)	3-0, 1-0
Frem Reykjavik v Basle (2-11)	0-5, 2-6
Crusaders v Dinamo Bucharest (0-12)	0-1, 0-11

Second Round

Benfica v Ujpest Dozsa (1-3)	1-1, 0-2
Celtic v Vejle (1-0)	0-0, 1-0
Spartak Trnava v Sarja Voroshilovgrad (1-0)	0-0, 1-0
Red Star Belgrade v Liverpool (4-2)	2-1, 2-1
Bruges v Basle (6-7)	2-1, 4-6
Dinamo Bucharest v Atlético Madrid (2-4)	0-2, 2-2
Ajax Amsterdam v CSKA Sofia (1-2)	1-0, 0-2
Bayern Munich v Dynamo Dresden (7-6)	4-3, 3-3

Quarter-Final

Spartak Trnava† v Ujpest Dozsa (2-2)	1-1, 1-1
Bayern Munich v CSKA Sofia (5-3)	4-1, 1-2
Red Star Belgrade v Atlético Madrid (0-2)	0-2, 0-0
Basle v Celtic (5-6)	3-2, 2-4

Semi-Final

Ujpest Dozsa v Bayern Munich (1-4)	1-1, 0-3
Celtic v Atlético Madrid (0-2)	0-0, 0-2

†*Won on penalty kicks.*

Final 1973–74: Bayern Munich 1, Atlético Madrid 1

(In Brussels, 15 May, 1974, 65,000)

Bayern Munich: Maier; Hansen, Breitner, Schwarzenbeck, Beckenbauer, Roth, Torstensson (Durnberger), Zobel, Müller, Hoeness, Kappelmann.

Atlético Madrid: Reina; Melo, Capon, Adelardo, Heredia, Eusebio, Ufarte (Becerra), Luis, Garate, Irureta, Salcedo (Alberto).

Scorers: Bayern Munich – Schwarzenbech; Atlético Madrid – Luis.

Replay: Bayern Munich 4, Atlético Madrid 0

(In Brussels, 17 May, 1974, 65,000)

Bayern Munich: Maier; Hansen, Breitner; Schwarzenbeck, Beckenbauer, Roth, Torstensson, Zobel, Müller, Hoeness, Kappelmann.

Atlético Madrid: Reina; Melo, Capon, Adelardo (Benegas), Heredia, Eusebio, Luis, Garate, Salcedo, Alberto, Ufarte (Becerra).

Scorers: Bayern Munich – Müller 2, Hoeness 2.

EUROPEAN CUP 1974–75

First Round, First Leg

Leeds U 4 (*Lorimer pen, Clarke 2, Jordan*), Zurich 1 (*Katic*)
Celtic 1 (*Wilson*), Olympiakos Piraeus 1 (*Viera*)
Uni Craiova 2 (*Oblemenco 2*), Atvidaberg 1 (*Bo Augustsson*)
Valletta 1 (*Magro*), HJK Helsinki 0
Levski Spartak 0, Ujpest Dozsa 3 (*Horvath, Bene, Antal Dunai*)
Jeunesse D'Esch 2 (*Mond, Guiliani*), Fenerbahce 3 (*Osman, Cemel, Ender*)
Viking Stavanger 0, Ararat Erevan 2 (*Markarov 2*)
Hvidovre 0, Ruch Chorzow 0
Slovan Bratislava 4 (*Novotny, Masny 2, Svehlik*), Anderlecht 2 (*Coeck, Van Himst*)
Feyenoord 7 (*Schoenmaker, Kreuz 3, Van Hanegem 2, Ressel*), Coleraine 0
St Etienne 2 (*Herve Revelli, Bereta*), Sporting Lisbon 0
VOEST Linz 0, Barcelona 0
Hajduk Split 7 (*Zungul 2, Surjak 2, Jerkovic, Buljan, Boljat*), Keflavik 1 (*Jonsson*)

First Round, Second Leg

Zurich 2 (*Katic, Rutschmann pen*), Leeds U 1 (*Clarke*)
Olympiakos Piraeus 2 (*Kritikopoulos, Stravropoulos*), Celtic 0
Atvidaberg 3 (*Andersson, Almqvist 2*), Uni Craiova 1 (*Badin*)
HJK Helsinki 4 (*Rahja, Peltonen, Hamalainen, Forsell*), Valletta 1 (*Gigilo*)
Ujpest Dozsa 4 (*Bene 2, Antal Dunai 2*), Levski Spartak 1 (*Voinov*)
Fenerbahce 2 (*Cemil, Yilmaz*), Jeunesse D'Esch 0
Ararat Erevan 4 (*Markarov 3, Bondarenko*), Viking Stavanger 2
Ruch Chorzow 2 (*Bula 2*), Hvidovre 1 (*Pedersen B.*)
Anderlecht 3 (*Van Himst, Coeck, Thijssen*), Slovan Bratislava 1(*Masny*)
Coleraine 1 (*Simpson*), Feyenoord 4 (*Schoenmaker 3, Kreuz*)
Sporting Lisbon 1 (*Yazalde*), St Etienne 1 (*Herve Revelli*)
Barcelona 5 (*Clares 2, Asensi, Juan Carlos, Cruyff*), VOEST Linz 0
Keflavik 0, Hajduk Split 2 (*Dzoni, Mijac*)
Bayern Munich and Magdeburg received byes; Cork Celtic had a walkover when Omonia Nicosia withdrew.

Second Round, First Leg

Ujpest Dozsa 1 (*Fazekas pen*), Leeds U 2 (*Lorimer, McQueen*)
Bayern Munich 3 (*Müller 2, Wunder*), Magdeburg 2 (*Hoffmann, Sparwasser*)
Hajduk Split 4 (*Jerkovic 2, Zungul, Mijac*), St Etienne 1 (*Herve Revelli*)
Feyenoord 0, Barcelona 0
Cork Celtic 1 (*Tambling*), Ararat Erevan 2 (*Zanazanyan, Kazaryan*)
Ruch Chorzow 2 (*Kopicera, Beniger*), Fenerbahce 1 (*Niazi*)
HJK Helsinki 0, Atvidaberg 3 (*Almqvist 2, Hasselberg*)
Anderlecht 5 (*Rensenbrink 3 [2 pens], Ladinszky, Van der Elst*), Olympiakos Piraeus 1 (*Persides pen*)

Second Round, Second Leg

Leeds U 3 (*McQueen, Yorath, Bremner*), Ujpest Dozsa 0
Magdeburg 1 (*Sparwasser*), Bayern Munich 2 (*Müller 2*)
St Etienne 5 (*Triantafilos 2, Bathenay, Synaeghel, Larque*), Hajduk Split 1 (*Jovanic*)
Barcelona 3 (*Rexach 3*), Feyenoord 0
Ararat Erevan 5 (*Markarov 2, Andriassian, Kazaryan 2*), Cork Celtic 0
Fenerbahce 0, Ruch Chorzow 2 (*Kopicera, Chojnacki*)
Atvidaberg 1 (*Almqvist*), HJK Helsinki 0
Olympiakos Piraeus 3 (*Galakos 3*), Anderlecht 0

Quarter-Final, First Leg

Bayern Munich (0) 2 (*Hoeness, Torstensson*), Ararat Erevan (0) 0
Leeds U (2) 3 (*Jordan, McQueen, Lorimer*), Anderlecht (0) 0
Ruch Chorzow (2) 3 (*Maszczyk, Beniger, Bula pen*), St Etienne (0) 2 (*Larque, Triantafilos*)
Barcelona (1) 2 (*Mario Marinho, Clares*), Atvidaberg (0) 0

Quarter-Final, Second Leg

Atvidaberg (0) 0, Barcelona (1) 3 (*Gallego, Asensi, Neeskens*)
St Etienne (1) 2 (*Janvion, Herve, Revelli pen*), Ruch Chorzow (0) 0
Ararat Erevan (1) 1 (*Andriassian*), Bayern Munich (0) 0
Anderlecht (0) 0, Leeds U (0) 1 (*Bremner*)

Semi-Final, First Leg

St Etienne (0) 0, Bayern Munich (0) 0
Leeds U (1) 2 (*Bremner, Clarke*), Barcelona (0) 1 (*Asensi*)

Semi-Final, Second Leg

Bayern Munich (1) 2 (*Beckenbauer, Durnberger*), St Etienne (0) 0
Barcelona (0) 1 (*Clares*), Leeds U (1) 1 (*Lorimer*)

Final 1974–75: Bayern Munich 2, Leeds U 0

(In Paris, 28 May, 1975, 50,000)

Bayern Munich: Maier; Durnberger, Andersson (Weiss), Schwarzenbeck, Beckenbauer, Roth, Torstensson, Zobel, Müller, Hoeness (Wunder), Kapellmann.

Leeds U: Stewart; Reaney, Gray F., Bremner, Madeley, Hunter, Lorimer, Clarke, Jordan, Giles, Yorath (Gray E.).

Scorers: Bayern Munich – Roth, Müller.

EUROPEAN CUP 1975–76

First Round, First Leg
Benfica 7 (*Sheu, Nene 3, Jordao 3*), Fenerbahce 0
Borussia Moenchengladbach 1 (*Simonsen pen*), Swarowski Innsbruck 1 (*Welzl*)
KB Copenhagen 0, St Etienne 2 (*P. Revelli, Larque*)
CSKA Sofia 2 (*Denev, Marashliev*), Juventus 1 (*Anastasi*)
Floriana 0, Hajduk Split 5 (Zungul 3, Buljan, Surjak)
Jeunesse D'Esch 0, Bayern Munich 5 (*Wunder, Schuster 2, Rummenigge 2*)
Linfield 1 (*P. Malone*), PSV Eindhoven 2 (*Rene Van der Kerkhof, Edstrom*)
Malmö 2 (*Cervin, Bo Larsson*), Magdeburg 1 (*Hoffmann*)
Olympiakos 2 (*Kritikopoulos, Aidiniou*), Dynamo Kiev 2 (*Kolotov, Burjak*)
Rangers 4 (*Fyfe, Burge og, O'Hara, Johnstone*), Bohemians 1 (*Flanagan*)
Real Madrid 4 (*Santillana 2, Roberto Martinez, Netzer*), Dinamo Bucharest 1 (*Lucescu*)
Ruch Chorzow 5 (*Marx 2, Bula, Beniger, Kopicera*), Kuopion Palloseura 0
Slovan Bratislava 1 (*Masny*), Derby Co 0
Ujpest Dozsa 4 (*Fazekas, Dunai, Toth pen, Keleman*), Zurich 0
RWD Molenbeek 3 (*Boskamp, Teugals, Wellens*), Viking Stavanger 2 (*Johansson, Kvia*)
Omonia Nicosia 2 (*Philippou 2*), Akranes 1 (*Alfredsson*)

First Round, Second Leg
Akranes 4 (*M. Hallgrimsson 2, T. Thordarson, K. Thordarson*), Omonia Nicosia 0
Viking Stavanger 0, RWD Molenbeek 1 (*Neilsen*)
Bayern Munich 3 (*Schuster 3*), Jeunesse D'Esch 1 (*Zwally*)
Bohemians 1 (*T. O'Connor*), Rangers 1 (*Johnstone*)
Derby Co 3 (*Bourne, Lee 2*), Slovan Bratislava 0
Dinamo Bucharest 1 (*Satmareanu*), Real Madrid 0
Dynamo Kiev 1 (*Onischenko*), Olympiakos 0
Fenerbahce 1 (*Engin*), Benfica 0
Hajduk Split 3 (*Buljan, Djordjevic, Salvov*), Floriana 0
Juventus 2 (*Furino, Anastasi*), CSKA Sofia 0
Kuopion Palloseura 2 (*Toernroos, Heiskanen*), Ruch Chorzow 2 (*Chojnacki, Faber*)
Magdeburg 2 (*Hoffmann, Streich*), Malmö 1 (*Andersson*)
PSV Eindhoven 8 (*Lubse 2, Dahlqvist, Willy Van der Kerkhof, Van der Kuylen, Edstrom, Deacy 2*), Linfield 0
St Etienne 3 (*Rocheteau, Patrick Revelli, Larque*), KB Copenhagen 1 (*Petersen*)
Swarowski Innsbruck 1 (*Flindt*), Borussia Moenchengladbach 6 (*Stielike, Simonsen, Heynckes 4*)
Zurich 5 (*Katic, Risi 3, Kuhn*), Ujpest Dozsa 1 (*Nagy*)

Second Round, First Leg
Benfica 5 (*Moinhos, Sheu, Vitor Baptista 2, Toni*), Ujpest Dozsa 2 (*Dunai A., Fazekas*)
Borussia Moenchengladbach 2 (*Heynckes, Simonsen*), Juventus 0
Derby Co 4 (*George 3 [2 pens], Nish*), Real Madrid 1 (*Pirri*)
Dynamo Kiev 3 (*Burjak 2, Blokhin*), Akranes 0
Hajduk Split 4 (*Zungul, Rozic, Surjak, Mijac*), RWD Molenbeek 0
Malmö 1 (*Andersson T.*), Bayern Munich 0
Ruch Chorzow 1 (*Bula*), PSV Eindhoven 3 (*Lubse, Edstrom, Rene Van der Kerkhof*)
St Etienne 2 (*Patrick Revelli, Bathenay*), Rangers 0

Second Round, Second Leg
Akranes 0, Dynamo Kiev 2 (*Onischenko, Gunnlaugsson og*)
Bayern Munich 2 (*Durnberger pen, Torstensson*), Malmö 0
Juventus 2 (*Gori, Bettega*), Borussia Moenchengladbach 2 (*Danner, Simonsen*)
PSV Eindhoven 4 (*Rene Van der Kerkhof, Van der Kuylen 2, Lubse*), Ruch Chorzow 0
Rangers 1 (*MacDonald*), St Etienne 2 (*Rocheteau, Herve Revelli*)
Real Madrid 5 (*Roberto Martinez 2, Santillana 2, Pirri pen*), Derby Co 1 (*George*)
RWD Molenbeek 2 (*Teugels, Nielsen pen*), Hajduk Split 3 (*Surjak, Zungul, Jovanic*)
Ujpest Dozsa 3 (*Bene 2, Nagy L.*), Benfica 1 (*Nene*)

Quarter-Final, First Leg
Benfica 0, Bayern Munich 0
Borussia Moenchengladbach 2 (*Jensen, Wittkamp*), Real Madrid 2 (*Roberto Martinez, Pirri*)
Dynamo Kiev 2 (*Konkov, Blokhin*), St Etienne 0
Hajduk Split 2 (*Mijac, Surjak*), PSV Eindhoven 0

Quarter-Final, Second Leg
Bayern Munich 5 (*Durnberger 2, Rummenigge, Müller 2*), Benfica 1 (*Barros*)
PSV Eindhoven 3 (*Dahlqvist, Lubse, Van der Kuylen*), Hajduk Split 0
Real Madrid 1 (*Santillana*), Borussia Moenchengladbach 1 (*Heynckes*)
St Etienne 3 (*Herve Revelli, Larque, Rocheteau*), Dynamo Kiev 0 (*after extra time*)

Semi-Final, First Leg
Real Madrid 1 (*Roberto Martinez*), Bayern Munich 1 (*Müller*)
St Etienne 1 (*Larque*), PSV Eindhoven 0

Semi-Final, Second Leg
Bayern Munich 2 (*Müller 2*), Real Madrid 0
PSV Eindhoven 0, St Etienne 0

Final 1975–76: Bayern Munich 1, St Etienne 0

(At Hampden Park, 12 May, 1976, 54,864)

Bayern Munich: Maier; Hansen, Schwarzenbeck, Beckenbauer, Horsmann, Roth, Durnberger, Kapellmann, Rummenigge, Müller, Hoeness.

St Etienne: Curkovic; Repellini, Piazza, Lopez, Janvion, Bathenay, Santini, Larque, Patrick Revelli, Herve Revelli, Sarramagna (Rocheteau).

Scorer: Bayern Munich – Roth.

EUROPEAN CUP 1976–77

First Round, First Leg
Akranes 1 (*Sveinsson*), Trabzonspor 3 (*Perikli, Ali Kemal 2*)
Austria/WAC 1 (*Daxbacher*), Borussia Moenchengladbach 0
FC Bruges 2 (*Davies pen, Verbeeke*), Steaua Bucharest 1 (*Troi*)
CSKA Sofia 0, St Etienne 0
Dynamo Dresden 2 (*Kotte pen, Riedel*), Benfica 0
Dundalk 1 (*McDowell*), PSV Eindhoven 1 (*Van der Kuylen*)
Ferencvaros 5 (*Nyilasi 2, Magyar, Onhaus, Ebedli*), Jeunesse D'Esch 1 (*Giuliani*)
Dynamo Kiev 3 (Onischenko, Troshkin, Blokhin pen), Partizan Belgrade 0
Omonia Nicosia 0, PAOK Salonika 2 (*Koudas, Sarafis*)
Rangers 1 (*Parlane*), Zurich 1 (*Cucinotta*)
Stal Mielec 1 (*Sekulski*), Real Madrid 2 (*Santillani, Del Bosque*)
Viking Stavanger 2 (*Valen, Johanessen*), Banik Ostrava 1 (*Slany*)
Torino 2 (*Mozzini, Graziani*), Malmö 1 (*Jonsson*)
Liverpool 2 (*Neal pen, Toshack*), Crusaders 0
Koge 0, Bayern Munich 5 (*Torstensson 2, Müller 2, Durnberger*)
Sliema Wanderers 2 (*E. Aquilina 2*), Turun Palloseura 1 (*Mannien*)

First Round, Second Leg
Turun Palloseura 1 (*Suhonen*), Sliema Wanderers 0
Crusaders 0, Liverpool 5 (*Keegan, Johnson 2, McDermott, Heighway*)
Banik Ostrava 2 (*Vojacek 2*), Viking Stavanger 0
Bayern Munich 2 (*Beckenbauer, Torstensson*), Koge 1 (*Poulsen*)
Borussia Moenchengladbach 3 (*Stielike, Bonhof pen, Heynckes*), Austria/WAC 0
Jeunesse D'Esch 2 (*Zwallay 2*), Ferencvaros 6 (*Nyilasi 2 [1 pen], Pusztai 2, Szabo 2 [1 pen]*)
Malmö 1 (*Ljungberg pen*), Torino 1 (*Claudio Sala*)
PAOK Salonika 1 (*Sarafis*), Omonia Nicosia 1 (*Philippos pen*)
Partizan Belgrade 0, Dynamo Kiev 2 (*Muntian pen, Slobodan*)
PSV Eindhoven 6 (*Van der Kuylen, Postuma, Rene Van der Kerkhof 4*), Dundalk 0
St Etienne 1 (*Piazza*), CSKA Sofia 0
Steaua Bucharest 1 (*Vigu*), FC Bruges 1 (*Lambert*)
Trabzonspor 3 (*Huseyin 2, Engin*), Akranes 2 (*Pogarson 2 [1 pen]*)
Zurich 1 (*Martinelli*), Rangers 0
Real Madrid 1 (*Pirri*), Stal Mielec 0
Benfica 0, Dynamo Dresden 0

Second Round, First Leg
Dynamo Kiev 4 (*Burjak 2, Kolotov, Slobodan*), PAOK Salonika 0
Ferencvaros 1 (*Onhaus*), Dynamo Dresden 0
Real Madrid 0, FC Bruges 0
St Etienne 1 (*Piazza*), PSV Eindhoven 0
Torino 1 (*Wittkamp og*), Borussia Moenchengladbach 2 (*Vogts, Klinkhammer*)
Trabzonspor 1 (*Cemil pen*), Liverpool 0
Zurich 2 (*Cucinotta, Scheiwiler*), Turun Palloseura 0
Banik Ostrava 2 (*Lorenc, Licka*), Bayern Munich 1 (*Müller*)

Second Round, Second Leg
Bayern Munich 5 (*Müller 2, Rummenigge, Kapellmann, Torstensson*), Banik Ostrava 0
Borussia Moenchengladbach 0, Torino 0
FC Bruges 2 (*Le Fevre, Camacho og*), Real Madrid 0
Dynamo Dresden 4 (*Heidler, Schmuck, Riedel, Kotte*), Ferencvaros 0
Liverpool 3 (*Heighway, Johnson, Keegan*), Trabzonspor 0
Turun Palloseura 0, Zurich 1 (*Cucinotta*)
PAOK Salonika 0, Dynamo Kiev 2 (*Kolotov, Blokhin*)
PSV Eindhoven 0, St Etienne 0

Quarter-Final, First Leg
Bayern Munich 1 (*Kunkel*), Dynamo Kiev 0
Borussia Moenchengladbach 2 (*Kulik, Simonsen*), FC Bruges 2 (*Cools, Courant*)
St Etienne 1 (*Bathenay*), Liverpool 0
Zurich 2 (*Cucinotta, Risi*), Dynamo Dresden 1 (*Kreische*)

Quarter-Final, Second Leg
FC Bruges 0, Borussia Moenchengladbach 1 (*Hannes*)
Dynamo Dresden 3 (*Schade pen, Kreische 2*), Zurich 2 (*Cucinotta, Risi*)
Dynamo Kiev 2 (*Burjak pen, Slobodan*), Bayern Munich 0
Liverpool 3 (*Keegan, Kennedy, Fairclough*), St Etienne 1 (*Bathenay*)

Semi-Final, First Leg
Dynamo Kiev 1 (*Onischenko*), Borussia Moenchengladbach 0
Zurich 1 (*Risi pen*), Liverpool 3 (*Neal 2 [1 pen], Heighway*)

Semi-Final, Second Leg
Borussia Moenchengladbach 2 (*Bonhof pen, Wittkamp*), Dynamo Kiev 0
Liverpool 3 (*Case 2, Keegan*), Zurich 0

Final 1976–77: Liverpool 3, Borussia Moenchengladbach 1

(In Rome, 25 May, 1977, 57,000)

Liverpool: Clemence; Neal, Jones, Smith, Kennedy, Hughes, Keegan, Case, Heighway, Callaghan, McDermott.

Borussia Moenchengladbach: Kneib; Vogts, Klinkhammer, Wittkamp, Bonhof, Wohlers (Hannes), Simonsen, Wimmer (Kulik), Stielike, Schaffer, Heynckes.

Scorers: Liverpool – McDermott, Smith, Neal (pen); Borussia Moenchengladbach – Simonsen.

EUROPEAN CUP 1977–78

First Round, First Leg
Basle 1 (*Von Wartburg*), SW Innsbruck 3 (*Welzl 2 [1 pen], Constantini*)
Celtic 5 (*McDonald, Wilson, Craig 2, McLaughlin*), Jeunesse Esch 0
Benfica 0, Moscow Torpedo 0
Dynamo Dresden 2 (*Heidler, Schade*), Halmstad 0
Dukla Prague 1 (*Vizek*), Nantes 1 (*Amisse*)
Floriana 1 (*George Xuereb*), Panathinaikos 1 (*Aslanidis*)
Kuopion Palloseura 0, FC Bruges 4 (*Van der Eycken, Cools, Lambert, Davies*)
Levsky Spartak 3 (*Panov, Milanov 2*), Slask Wroclaw 0
Lillestrom 2 (*Lonsdal, Johansen*), Ajax Amsterdam 0
Omonia 0 Juventus 3 (*Bettega, Fanna, Virdis*)
Red Star Belgrade 3 (*Dzajic 2, Filipovic*), Sligo Rovers 0
Trabzonspor 1 (*Necdet*), BK 03 Copenhagen 0
Vasas 0, Borussia Moenchengladbach 3 (*Schaefer, Simonsen, Wohlers*)
Valur 1 (*Magnus Bergs*), Glentoran 0
Dinamo Bucharest 2 (*Vrinceanu, Georgescu*), Atlético Madrid 1 (*Luis Pereira*)

First Round, Second Leg
Ajax Amsterdam 4 (*Birkelund og, Geels, La Ling 2*), Lillestrom 0
Atlético Madrid 2 (*Benegas, Ruben Cano*), Dinamo Bucharest 0
BK 03 Copenhagen 2 (*Francker 2*), Trabzonspor 0
Borussia Moenchengladbach 1 (*Simonsen*), Vasas 1 (*Izso*)
FC Bruges 5 (*Davies 2, Van der Eycken, Simoen, Maes*), Kuopion Palloseura 2 (*Rissanen, Laikonen*)
Halmstad 2 (Johansson, Larsson), Dynamo Dresden 1 (Heidler)
Jeunesse Esch 1 (*Giuliano*), Celtic 6 (*Lennox 2, Glavin, McLaughlin, Edvaldsson 2*)
Juventus 2 (Boninsegna, Virdis), Omonia 0
Nantes 0, Dukla Prague 0
Panathinaikos 4 (*Alvarez, Antoniadis 2 [1 pen], Gonios*), Floriana 0
Slask Wroclaw 2 (*Pawlowsky, Kopycky*), Levski Spartak 2 (*Panov 2*)
Sligo Rovers 0, Red Star Belgrade 3 (*Filipovic 2, Jovanovic*)
SW Innsbruck 0, Basle 1 (*Miessen*)
Moscow Torpedo 0, Benfica 0
Benfica won 4-1 on penalties.
Glentoran 2 (*Robson, Jamison*), Valur 0

Second Round, First Leg
Benfica 1 (*Pietra pen*), BK 03 Copenhagen 0
FC Bruges 2 (*Davies pen, Cools*), Panathinaikos 0
Celtic 2 (*Craig, Burns*), SW Innsbruck 1 (*Kriess*)
Glentoran 0, Juventus 1 (*Causio*)
Levski Spartak 1 (*Voinov pen*), Ajax Amsterdam 2 (*Geels, Erkens*)
Liverpool 5 (*Hansen, Case 2, Neal pen, Kennedy*), Dynamo Dresden 1 (*Hafner*)
Nantes 1 (*Lacombe*), Atlético Madrid 1 (*Marcial*)
Red Star Belgrade 0, Borussia Moenchengladbach 3 (*Schaffer, Heynckes, Simonsen*)

Second Round, Second Leg
Ajax Amsterdam 2 (*Lerby, Geels*), Levski Spartak 1 (*Milanov*)
Atlético Madrid 2 (*Ruben Cano, Luis Pereira*), Nantes 1 (*Lacombe*)
Borussia Moenchengladbach 5 (*Simonsen 2, Heynckes, Nikolic og, Wittkamp*), Red Star Belgrade 1 (*Susic*)
BK 03 Copenhagen 0, Benfica 1 (*Pietra*)
Dynamo Dresden 2 (*Kotte, Sachse*), Liverpool 1 (*Heighway*)
SW Innsbruck 3 (*Welzl, Stering, Oberacher*), Celtic 0
Juventus 5 (Virdis 2, Boninsegna, Fanna, Benetti), Glentoran 0
Panathinaikos 1 (*Gonios*), FC Bruges 0

Quarter-Final, First Leg
Benfica 1 (*Nene*), Liverpool 2 (*Case, Hughes*)
Ajax Amsterdam 1 (*Van Dord*), Juventus 1 (*Causio*)
FC Bruges 2 (*Courant, De Cubber*), Atlético Madrid 0
SW Innsbruck 3 (*Peter Koncilia, Kriess, Werner Schwarz*), Borussia Moenchengladbach 1 (*Heynckes*)

Quarter-Final, Second Leg
Juventus 1 (*Tardelli*), Ajax Amsterdam 1 (*La Ling*)
Juventus won 3-0 on penalties.
Atlético Madrid 3 (*Benegas, Marcial 2*), FC Bruges 2 (*Cools, Lambert*)
Liverpool 4 (*Callaghan, Dalglish, McDermott, Neal*), Benfica 1 (*Nene*)
Borussia Moenchengladbach 2 (*Bonhof pen, Heynckes*), SW Innsbruck 0

Semi-Final, First Leg
Borussia Moenchengladbach 2 (*Hannes, Bonhof*), Liverpool 1 (*Johnson*)
Juventus 1 (*Bettega*), FC Bruges 0

Semi-Final, Second Leg
Liverpool 3 (*Kennedy, Dalglish, Case*), Borussia Moenchengladbach 0
FC Bruges 2 (*Bastijns, Van der Eycken*), Juventus 0

Final 1977–78: Liverpool 1, FC Bruges 0

(At Wembley, 10 May, 1978, 92,000)

Liverpool: Clemence; Neal, Thompson, Hansen, Hughes, McDermott, Kennedy, Souness, Case (Heighway), Fairclough, Dalglish.

FC Bruges: Jensen; Bastijns, Krieger, Leekens, Maes (Volders), Cools, De Cubber, Van der Eycken, Ku (Sanders), Simoen, Sorensen.

Scorer: Liverpool – Dalglish.

EUROPEAN CUP 1978–79

Preliminary Round, First Leg
Monaco 3 (Onnis, Zorzetto, Nogues), Steaua 0

Preliminary Round, Second Leg
Steaua 2 (*Troi 2*), Monaco 0

First Round, First Leg
Juventus 1 (*Virdis*), Rangers 0
Real Madrid 5 (*Jensen, Juanito 2, Del Bosque, Wolff*), Progress Niedercorn 0
AEK Athens 6 (*Bajevic 2, Ardizoglou, Tassos, Nikolau, Mavros*), Porto 1 (*Oliveira*)
Fenerbahce 2 (*Rasit, Cemil*), PSV Eindhoven 1 (*Brandts*)
Nottingham F 2 (*Birtles, Barrett*), Liverpool 0
Vllaznia 2 (*Zhega, Ballgijni*), Austria/WAC 0
Malmö 0, Monaco 0
Linfield 0, Lillestrom 0
Cologne 4 (*Littbarski, Neumann 2, Konopka*), Akranes 1 (*Hallgrimsson*)
Zbrojovka Brno 2 (*Kroupa, Janecka*), Ujpest Dozsa 2 (*Fekete, Torocsik*)
Partizan Belgrade 2 (*Prekazi, Djurovic*), Dynamo Dresden 0
Grasshoppers 8 (*Sulser 5, Ponte 2, Wehrli*), Valletta 0
Bruges 2 (*Cuelemans, Cools*), Wisla Krakow 1 (*Kapka*)
Odense 2 (Jensen M. 2), Lokomotiv Sofia 2 (*Kolev, Veliotzkov*)
Valkeakosken 0, Dynamo Kiev 1 (*Boltatsha*)
Omonia 2 (*Kanaris, Gootkrtou*), Bohemians 1 (*O'Connor*)

First Round, Second Leg
Rangers 2 (*MacDonald, Smith*), Juventus 0
Progress Niedercorn 0, Real Madrid 7 (*Pirri, Jensen, Stielike, Santillana 2, Hernandez, Bossi og*)
Porto 4 (*Vital 2, Teixeira, Gomes*), AEK Athens 1 (*Bajevic*)
PSV Eindhoven 6 (*Van der Kuylen 4, Deykers 2*), Fenerbahce 1 (*Rasit*)
Liverpool 0, Nottingham F 0
Austria/WAC 4 (*Parits, Schachner 2, Robert Sara*), Vllaznia 1 (*Hafizi*)
Monaco 0, Malmö 1 (*Kinnvall*)
Lillestrom 1 (*Lonstad*), Linfield 0
Akranes 1 (*Hein og*), Cologne 1 (*Van Gool*)
Ujpest Dozsa 0, Zbrojovka Brno 2 (*Dosek, Kroupa*)
Dynamo Dresden 2 (*Dorner, Weber*), Partizan Belgrade 0
Valletta 3 (*Seychell, Agius, Farrugia*), Grasshoppers 5 (*Sulser, Ponte, Heinz Hermann, Traber 2*)
Wisla Krakow 3 (*Kmiecik, Lipka, Krupinski*), Bruges 1 (*Van der Eycken*)
Lokomotiv Sofia 2 (*Mihailov, Kostov*), Odense 1 (*Erikson*)
Dynamo Kiev 3 (*Veremeev, Khapsalis, Buriak*), Valkeakosken 1 (*Ronkainen*)
Bohemians 1 (*Joyce*), Omonia 0

Second Round, First Leg
Real Madrid 3 (*Juanito, Garcia, Santillana*), Grasshoppers 1 (*Sulser*)
AEK Athens 1 (*Mavros*), Nottingham F 2 (*McGovern, Birtles*)
Dynamo Kiev 0, Malmö 0
Lokomotiv Sofia 0, Cologne 1 (*Zimmermann*)
Bohemians 0, Dynamo Dresden 0
Austria/WAC 4 (*Gasselich 2, Robert Sara, Schachner*), Lillestrom 1 (*Dokker*)
Rangers 0, PSV Eindhoven 0
Zbrojovka Brno 2 (*Pesice, Kroupa*), Wisla Krakow 2 (*Kmiecik, Maculewicz*)

Second Round, Second Leg
Grasshoppers 2 (*Sulser 2*), Real Madrid 0
Nottingham F 5 (*Needham, Woodcock, Anderson, Birtles 2*), AEK Athens 1 (*Bajevic*)
Malmö 2 (*Kinnvall, Cervin*), Dynamo Kiev 0
Cologne 4 (*Dieter Muller 2, Van Gool, Glowacz*), Lokomotiv Sofia 0
Dynamo Dresden 6 (*Trautmann 2, Dorner, Schmuch, Riedl, Kotte*), Bohemians 0
Lillestrom 0, Austria/WAC 0
PSV Eindhoven 2 (*Lubse, Deykers*), Rangers 3 (*MacDonald, Watson, Johnstone*)
Wisla Krakow 1 (*Kapka*), Zbrojovka Brno 1 (*Dosek*)

Quarter-Final, First Leg
Nottingham F 4 (*Birtles, Robertson pen, Gemmill, Lloyd*), Grasshoppers 1 (*Sulser*)
Cologne 1 (*Dieter Muller*), Rangers 0
Wisla Krakow 2 (*Nawalka, Kmiecik*), Malmö 1 (*Hansson*)
Austria/WAC 3 (*Schachner 2, Zach*), Dynamo Dresden 1 (*Weber*)

Quarter-Final, Second Leg
Grasshoppers 1 (*Sulser pen*), Nottingham F 1 (*O'Neill*)
Rangers 1 (*McLean*), Cologne 1 (*Dieter Muller*)
Malmö 4 (*Ljungberg 3 [2 pens], Cervin*), Wisla Krakow 1 (*Kmiecik*)
Dynamo 1 (*Riedl pen*), Austria/WAC 0

Semi-Final, First Leg
Nottingham F 3 (*Birtles, Bowyer, Robertson*), Cologne 3 (*Van Gool, Dieter Muller, Okudera*)
Austria/WAC 0, Malmö 0

Semi-Final, Second Leg
Cologne 0, Nottingham F 1 (*Bowyer*)
Malmö 1 (*Hansson*), Austria/WAC 0

Final 1978–79: Nottingham F 1, Malmö 0

(In Munich, 30 May, 1979, 57,500)

Nottingham F: Shilton; Anderson, Lloyd, Burns, Clark, Francis, McGovern, Bowyer, Robertson, Woodcock, Birtles.

Malmö: Moller; Roland Andersson, Jonsson, Magnus Andersson, Erlandsson, Tapper (Malmberg), Ljungberg, Prytz, Kinnvall, Hansson (Tommy Andersson), Cervin.

Scorer: Nottingham F – Francis.

EUROPEAN CUP 1979–80

Preliminary Round, First Leg
Dundalk 1 (*Devine*), Linfield 1 (*Feeney*)

Preliminary Round, Second Leg
Linfield 0, Dundalk 2 (*Muckian 2*)

First Round, First Leg
AC Milan 0, Porto 0
Liverpool 2 (*Johnson, Case*), Dinamo Tbilisi 1 (*Chivadze*)
Arges Pitesti 3 (*Nicolae 2, Radu*), AEK Athens 0
Partizan Tirana 1 (*Murati*), Celtic 0
Levski Spartak 0, Real Madrid 1 (*Martinez*)
Ujpest Dozsa 3 (*Sarlos, Nagy, Fazekas pen*), Dukla Prague 2 (*Gajdusek, Nehoda*)
Start Kristiansand 1 (*Ervik*), Strasbourg 2 (*Piasecki 2*)
HJK Helsinki 1 (*Rautiainen pen*), Ajax Amsterdam 8 (*Lerby 2, Tahamata 2, Arnesen 2, Krol pen, La Ling*)
Valur Reykjavik 0, SV Hamburg 3 (*Hrubesch 2, Buljan*)
Nottingham F 2 (*Bowyer 2*), Oester Vaxjo 0
Hajduk Split 1 (*Primorac*), Trabzonspor 0
Dinamo Berlin 4 (*Netz, Pelka 2, Riediger*), Ruch Chorzow 1 (*Wycislik*)
Vejle BK 3 (*Andersen, Rasmussen, Sorensen pen*), Austria Vienna 2 (*Baumeister, Schachner*)
Dundalk 2 (*Carlisle, Devine*), Hibernian Malta 0
Red Boys Differdange 2 (*Di Domenico pen, Wagner*), Omonia Nicosia 1 (*Patikis*)
Servette Geneva 3 (*Van Genechtem og, Koutas, Hamberg*), Beveren 1 (*Janssens*)

First Round, Second Leg
Porto 1 (*Duda*), AC Milan 0
Dinamo Tbilisi 3 (*Gutsayev, Shengelya, Chivadze pen*), Liverpool 0
AEK Athens 2 (*Ivan og, Vladic*), Arges Pitesti 0
Celtic 4 (*McDonald, Aitken, Davidson, McCluskey*), Partizan Tirana 1 (*Sneddon og*)
Real Madrid 2 (*Del Bosque, Cunningham pen*), Levski Spartak 0
Dukla Prague 2 (*Vizek, Nehoda*), Ujpest Dozsa 0
Strasbourg 4 (*Bianchi 3, Decastel*), Start Kristiansand 0
Ajax Amsterdam 8 (*Blanker 4, Krol 2, Everse, Lerby*), HJK Helsinki 1 (*Toivola*)
SV Hamburg 2 (Hrubesch, Wehmeyer), Valur Reykjavik 1 (*Edvaldsson*)
Oester Vaxjo 1 (*Nordgren*), Nottingham F 1 (*Woodcock*)
Trabzonspor 0, Hajduk Split 1 (*Djordjevic*)
Ruch Chorzow 0, Dinamo Berlin 0
Austria Vienna 1 (*Gasselich*), Vejle BK 1 (*Brylle*)
Hibernian Malta 1 (*Vella*), Dundalk 0
Omonia Nicosia 6 (*Kaiafas 4, Kanaris, Filippos*), Red Boys Differdange 1 (*Muller*)
Beveren 1 (*Albert pen*), Servette Geneva 1 (*Barberis*)

Second Round, First Leg
Nottingham F 2 (*Woodcock, Birtles*), Arges Pitesti 0
Vejle BK 0, Hajduk Split 3 (*Surjak, Jujowicz, Salov*)
SV Hamburg 3 (*Muchiri og, Keegan, Hartwig*), Dinamo Tbilisi 1 (*Kipiani*)
Celtic 3 (*McDonald, McCluskey, Burns*), Dundalk 2 (*Muckian, Lawlor*)
Ajax 10 (*Lerby 5, Krol pen, Arnesen, Blanker 3*), Omonia Nicosia 0
Dinamo Berlin 2 (*Pelka, Netz*), Servette Geneva 1 (*Cucinotta*)
Dukla Prague 1 (*Vizek pen*), Strasbourg 0
Porto 2 (*Gomes 2* [*1 pen*]), Real Madrid 1 (*Cunningham*)

Second Round, Second Leg
Arges Pitesti 1 (*Barbulescu pen*), Nottingham F 2 (*Bowyer, Birtles*)
Hajduk Split 1 (*Vujovic*), Vejle BK 2 (*Brille, Ostersen*)
Dinamo Tbilisi 2 (*Gutsayev, Kipiani*), SV Hamburg 3 (*Keegan, Hrubesch, Buljan*)
Dundalk 0, Celtic 0
Omonia Nicosia 4 (*Tsikkos, Demetrios, Kaiafas 2*), Ajax Amsterdam 0
Servette Geneva 2 (*Hamberg, Barberis*), Dinamo Berlin 2 (*Noak, Terletzki*)
Strasbourg 2 (*Piasecki, Decastel*), Dukla Prague 0
Real Madrid 1 (*Benito*), Porto 0

Quarter-Final, First Leg
Nottingham F 0, Dinamo Berlin 1 (*Riediger*)
SV Hamburg 1 (*Reimann*), Hajduk Split 0
Celtic 2 (*McCluskey, Doyle*), Real Madrid 0
Strasbourg 0, Ajax Amsterdam 0

Quarter-Final, Second Leg
Dinamo Berlin 1 (*Terletzki pen*), Nottingham F 3 (*Francis 2, Robertson pen*)
Hajduk Split 3 (*Vujovic 2, Primorac*), SV Hamburg 2 (*Hrubesch, Hieronymus*)
Real Madrid 3 (*Santillana, Stielike, Juanito*), Celtic 0
Ajax Amsterdam 4 (*Schoenmaker, Arnesen, Lerby, La Ling*), Strasbourg 0

Semi-Final, First Leg
Nottingham F 2 (*Francis, Robertson pen*), Ajax Amsterdam 0
Real Madrid 2 (*Santillana 2*), SV Hamburg 0

Semi-Final, Second Leg
Ajax Amsterdam 1 (*Lerby*), Nottingham F 0
SV Hamburg 5 (*Kaltz 2* [*1 pen*], *Hrubesch 2, Memering*), Real Madrid 1 (*Cunningham*)

Final 1979–80: Nottingham F 1, SV Hamburg 0

(In Madrid, 28 May, 1980, 50,000)

Nottingham F: Shilton; Anderson, Gray (Gunn), McGovern, Lloyd, Burns, O'Neill, Bowyer, Birtles, Mills (O'Hare), Robertson.

SV Hamburg: Kargus; Kaltz, Nogly, Jakobs, Buljan, Hieronymus (Hrubesch), Keegan, Memering, Milewski, Magath, Reimann.

Scorer: Nottingham F – Robertson.

EUROPEAN CUP 1980–81

Preliminary Round
Honved 8 (*Bodonyi, Garaba, Esterhazy, Kocsis, Dajka 2, Varga 2* [*1 pen*]), Valletta 0
Valletta 0, Honved 3 (*Esterhazy 2, Bodonyi*)

First Round, First Leg
Linfield 0, Nantes 1 (*Amisse*)
Aberdeen 1 (*McGhee*), Austria Vienna 0
FC Bruges 0, Basle 1 (*Maissen*)
CSKA Sofia 1 (*Yonchev*), Nottingham F 0
Dynamo Berlin 3 (*Terletzki, Trieloff, Schulz*), Apoel 0
Dynamo Tirana 0, Ajax 2 (*Arnesen 2*)
Inter-Milan 2 (*Altobelli 2* [*1 pen*]), Uni Craiova 0
Jeunesse Esch 0, Moscow Spartak 5 (*Gavrilov 3, Khidiatulin, Yartsev*)
Limerick 1 (*Kennedy*), Real Madrid 2 (*Juanito pen, Pineda*)
Olympiakos 2 (*Galakos, Ahlstrom*), Bayern Munich 4 (*Dremmler 2, Rummenigge, Kraus*)
OPS Oulu 1 (*Puotiniemi*), Liverpool 1 (*McDermott*)
Sporting Club 0, Honved 2 (*Bodonyi, Nagy*)
Trabzonspor 2 (*Sinan, Tuncay*), Szombierki Bytom 1 (*Wazniewsky*)
Viking Stavanger 2 (*Svendsen, Sabo*), Red Star Belgrade 3 (*Petrovic, Brekke og, Repcic*)
IBV Vestmannayjar 1 (*Thorleifsson*), Banik Ostrava 1 (*Danek*)
Halmstad 0, Esbjerg 0

First Round, Second Leg
Nantes 2 (*Rampillon, Trossero E.*), Linfield 0
Honved 1 (*Dajka*), Sporting Club 0
Red Star Belgrade 4 (*Djurovski, Janjanin, Petrovic, Stamenkovic*), Viking Stavanger 1 (Brekke)
Uni Craiova 1 (*Beldeanu*), Inter-Milan 1 (*Muraro*)
Szombierki Bytom 3 (*Bys, Ogaza, Srodka pen*), Tranzonspor 0
Banik Ostrava 1 (*Vojacek*), IBV Vestmannayjar 0
Real Madrid 5 (*Santillana, Juanito 2, Cunningham, Pineda*), Limerick 1 (*Kennedy*)
Moscow Spartak 4 (*Pigat og, Rodionov, Gavrilov, Yartsev*), Jeunesse Esch 0
Nottingham Forest 0, CSKA Sofia 1 (*Kerimov*)
Bayern Munich 3 (*Hoeness, Rummenigge, Janzon pen*), Olympiakos 0
Basle 4 (*Tanner, Stohler pen, Von Wartburg, Gaisser*), FC Bruges 1 (*Ceulemans*)
Esbjerg 3 (*Iversen, Lauridsen, Nielsen*), Halmstad 2 (*Johansson, Larsson*)
Ajax 1 (*Lerby pen*), Dynamo Tirana 0
Austria Vienna 0, Aberdeen 0
Apoel 2 (*Hailis, Petrou*), Dynamo Berlin 1 (*Schnuphase*)
Liverpool 10 (*Souness 3, McDermott 2, Dalglish, Lee, Kennedy R., Fairclough 2*), OPS Oulu 1 (*Armstrong*)

Second Round, First Leg
Nantes 1 (*Rio pen*), Inter-Milan 2 (*Altobelli, Prohaska*)
Real Madrid 1 (*Santillana*), Honved 0
Bayern Munich 5 (*Durnberger, Rummenigge 2, Hoeness 2*), Ajax 1 (*Arnesen*)
Aberdeen 0, Liverpool 1 (*McDermott*)
CSKA Sofia 4 (*Yonchev 3, Zdranov*), Szombierki Bytom 0
Banik Ostrava 0, Dynamo Berlin 0
Moscow Spartak 3 (*Khidiatulin 2, Shavio*), Esbjerg 0
Basle 1 (*Lauscher*), Red Star Belgrade 0

Second Round, Second Leg
Honved 0, Real Madrid 2 (*Cunningham, Garcia Hernandez*)
Inter-Milan 1 (*Altobelli*), Nantes 1 (*Amisse*)
Ajax 2 (*Wiggemansen, Rijkaart*), Bayern Munich 1 (*Rummenigge*)
Red Star Belgrade 2 (*Repcic, Janjanin*), Basle 0
Liverpool 4 (*Miller og, Neal, Dalglish, Hansen*), Aberdeen 0
Dynamo Berlin 1 (*Troppa pen*), Banik Ostrava 1 (*Knapp pen*)
Esbjerg 2 (*Lauridsen, Iversen*), Moscow Spartak 0
Szombierki Bytom 0, CSKA Sofia 1 (*Djevisov*)

Quarter-Final, First Leg
Liverpool 5 (*Souness 3, Lee, McDermott*), CSKA Sofia (*Yonchev*)
Bayern Munich 2 (*Janzon, Breitner pen*), Banik Ostrava 0
Inter-Milan 1 (*Caso*), Red Star Belgrade 1 (*Repcic*)
Moscow Spartak 0, Real Madrid 0

Quarter-Final, Second Leg
CSKA Sofia 0, Liverpool 1 (*Johnson*)
Banik Ostrava 2 (*Nemec, Licka*), Bayern Munich (*Hoeness, Kraus, Rober, Durnberger*)
Red Star Belgrade 0, Inter-Milan 1 (*Muraro*)
Real Madrid 2 (*Isidro 2*), Moscow Spartak 0

Semi-Final, First Leg
Liverpool 0, Bayern Munich 0
Real Madrid 2 (*Santillana, Juanito*), Inter-Milan 0

Semi-Final, Second Leg
Bayern Munich 1 (*Rummenigge*), Liverpool 1 (*Kennedy R.*)
Inter-Milan 1 (*Bini*), Real Madrid 0

Final 1980–81: Liverpool (0) 1, Real Madrid (0) 0
(In Paris, 27 May 1981, 48,360)

Liverpool: Clemence; Neal, Kennedy A., Thompson, Kennedy R., Hansen, Dalglish (Case), Lee, Johnson, McDermott, Souness.

Real Madrid: Rodriguez; Garcia Cortes, Camacho, Stielike, Sabido (Pineda), Del Bosque, Juanito, De Los Santos, Santillana, Navajas, Cunningham.

Scorer: Liverpool – Kennedy A.

Only four times has one player scored three goals or more in a European Cup Final:

Ferenc Puskas (Real Madrid)	4 goals in the 1959–60 Final
Ferenc Puskas (Real Madrid)	3 goals in the 1961–62 Final
Alfredo Di Stefano (Real Madrid)	3 goals in the 1959–60 Final
Pierino Prati (AC Milan)	3 goals in the 1968–69 Final

EUROPEAN CUP 1981–82

Preliminary Round
St Etienne 1 (*Lopez*), Dynamo Berlin 1 (*Lopez og*)
Dynamo Berlin 2 (*Neta, Riediger*), St Etienne 0

First Round, First Leg
Widzew Lodz 1 (*Smolarek*), Anderlecht 4 (*Lozano 2, Hansen, Petursson*)
Dynamo Berlin 2 (*Schulz, Riediger*), Zurich 0
Ferencvaros 3 (*Pogany 2, Szokolai*), Banik Ostrava 2 (*Licka, Knapp*)
Celtic 1 (*MacLeod*), Juventus 0
Hibernians 1 (*Spiteri-Gonzi*), Red Star Belgrade 2 (*Jurisic, Savic*)
OPS Oulu 0, Liverpool 1 (*Dalglish*)
Oster 0, Bayern Munich 1 (*Rummenigge*)
Benfica 3 (*Nenè, Filipovic, Mansel*), Omonia 0
Austria Vienna 3 (*Steinkogler, Gasselich 2*), Partizani 1 (*Tomori*)
Dynamo Kiev 1 (*Blokhin*), Trabzonspor 0
Start 1 (*Haugen*), AZ 67 3 (*Peters 2, Kist*)
Aston Villa 5 (*Morley, Withe 2, Donovan 2*), Valur 0
Niedercorn 1 (*Meunier*), Glentoran 1 (*Cleary*)
KB Copenhagen 1 (*Tune*), Athlone Town 1 (*O'Connor*)
CSKA Sofia 1 (*Yonchev*), Real Sociedad 0
Uni Craiova 3 (*Cirtu, Irmescu, Ticleanu*), Olympiakos 0

First Round, Second Leg
Anderlecht 2 (*Brylle, Geurts*), Widzew Lodz (*Smolarek*)
Zurich 3 (*Jerkovic 3*), Dynamo Berlin 1 (*Ullrich*)
Banik Ostrava 3 (*Sreiner, Knapp 2*), Ferencvaros 0
Juventus 2 (*Virdis, Bettega*), Celtic 0
Red Star Belgrade 8 (*Goracinov, Petrovic 2, Sestic, Savic D. 2, Savic R. 2*), Hibernians 1 (*Spiteri-Gonzi*)
Liverpool 7 (*Dalglish, McDermott 2, Kennedy R., Johnson, Rush, Lawrenson*), OPS Oulu 0
Bayern Munich 5 (*Hoeness 2, Rummenigge 2, Niedermayer*), Oster 0
Omonia 0, Benfica 1 (*Chalana*)
Partizani 1 (*Ballgjini*), Austria Vienna 0
Trabzonspor 1 (*Metin*), Dynamo Kiev 1 (*Bessonov*)
AZ 67 1 (*Metgod*), Start 0
Valur 0, Aston Villa 2 (*Shaw 2*)
Glentoran 4 (*Blackledge 2, Jameson, Manley*), Niedercorn 0
Athlone Town 2 (*Davis 2*), KB Copenhagen 2 (*Larsen, Andersen*)
Real Sociedad 0, CSKA Sofia 0
Olympiakos 2 (*Mitropoulos, Anastopoulos*), Uni Craiova 0

Second Round, First Leg
Banik 3 (*Licka 2, Knapp*), Red Star Belgrade 1 (*Krmpotic*)
Anderlecht 3 (*Geurts 2, Vercauteren*), Juventus 1 (*Marocchino*)
AZ 67 2 (*Kist, Tol*), Liverpool 2 (*Johnson, Lee*)
CSKA Sofia 2 (*Dimitrov A., Zdravkov pen*), Glentoran 0
KB Copenhagen 1 (*Foosgard*), Uni Craiova 0
Benfica 0, Bayern 0
Austria Vienna 0, Dynamo Kiev 1 (*Bal*)
Dynamo Berlin 1 (*Riediger*), Aston Villa 2 (*Morley 2*)

Second Round, Second Leg
Red Star Belgrade 3 (*Djurovski B., Savic D., Petrovic*), Banik 0
Juventus 1 (*Brio*), Anderlecht 1 (*Geurts*)
Liverpool 3 (*McDermott pen, Rush, Hansen*), AZ 67 2 (*Kist, Thompson og*)
Glentoran 2 (*Cleary, Manley*), CSKA Sofia 1 (*Dimitrov A.*)
Uni Craiova 4 (*Crisan, Balaci, Beldeanu, Camataru*), KB Copenhagen 1 (*Andersen*)
Bayern Munich 4 (*Hoeness 3, Breitner*), Benfica 1 (*Nenè pen*)
Dynamo Kiev 1 (*Buryak pen*), Austria Vienna 1 (*Petkov*)
Aston Villa 0, Dynamo Berlin 1 (*Terletzki*)

Quarter-Finals, First Leg
Anderlecht 2 (*Geurts, Lozano*), Red Star Belgrade 1 (*Djurovski B.*)
Dynamo Kiev 0, Aston Villa 0
Liverpool 1 (*Whelan*), CSKA Sofia 0
Uni Craiova 0, Bayern Munich 2 (*Breitner, Rummenigge*)

Quarter-Finals, Second Leg
Red Star Belgrade 1 (*Savic D. pen*), Anderlecht 2 (*Hofkens, Vercauteren*)
Aston Villa 2 (*Shaw, McNaught*), Dynamo Kiev 0
CSKA Sofia 2 (*Mladenov 2*), Liverpool 0
Bayern Munich 1 (*Hoeness*), Uni Craiova 1 (*Geolgau*)

Semi-Finals, First Leg
CSKA Sofia 4 (*Dimitrov G., Yonchev 2, Zdravkov pen*), Bayern Munich 3 (*Durnberger, Hoeness, Breitner*)
Aston Villa 1 (*Morley*), Anderlecht 0

Semi-Finals, Second Leg
Bayern Munich 4 (*Breitner 2 [1 pen], Rummenigge 2*), CSKA Sofia 0
Anderlecht 0, Aston Villa 0

Final 1981–82: Aston Villa (0) 1, Bayern Munich (0) 0

(In Rotterdam, 26 May, 1982, 46,000)

Aston Villa: Rimmer (Spink); Swain, Williams, Evans, McNaught, Mortimer, Bremner, Shaw, Withe, Cowans, Morley.

Bayern Munich: Muller; Dremmler, Horsmann, Weiner, Augenthaler, Kraus (Niedermayer), Durnberger, Breitner, Hoeness, Mathy (Guttler), Rummenigge.

Scorer: Aston Villa – Withe.

In European Cup Finals, Ferenc Puskas stands supreme as the leading goalscorer. The leading goalscorers in finals are as follows, with a minimum of two final goals being the qualification:

	Goals	*Pld*		*Goals*	*Pld*
Puskas (Real Madrid)	7	3	Altafini (AC Milan and Juventus)	2	2
Di Stefano (Real Madrid)	7	7	Gemmell (Celtic)	2	2
Prati (AC Milan)	3	1	Roth (Bayern Munich)	2	2
Mazzola (Inter-Milan)	3	3	Cruyff (Ajax)	2	3
Müller (Bayern Munich)	3	3	Hoeness (U) (Bayern Munich)	2	3
Eusebio (Benfica)	3	4	Vasovic (Partizan and Ajax)	2	3
Rial (Real Madrid)	3	4	Coluna (Benfica)	2	5
Charlton (Manchester U)	2	1	Gento (Real Madrid)	2	8
Aguas (Benfica)	2	2			

NB. Alfredo Di Stefano holds an all-time record of having scored at least one goal in five consecutive European Cup Finals.

EUROPEAN CUP 1982–83

Preliminary Round, First Leg
Dinamo Bucharest 3 (*Augustin, Georgescu 2*), Valerengen 1 (*Grahn*)

Preliminary Round, Second Leg
Valerengen 2 (*Jacobsen P., Davidsen*), Dinamo Bucharest 1 (*Custov*)

First Round, First Leg
Dundalk 1 (*Flanagan*), Liverpool 4 (*Whelan 2, Rush, Hodgson*)
Aston Villa 3 (*Withe, Morley, Mortimer*), Besiktas 1 (*Eksi*)
Avenir Beggen O, Rapid Vienna 5 (*Krankl 3, Panenka, Willfurth*)
Celtic 2 (*Nicholas, McGarvey*), Ajax 2 (*Olsen, Lerby*)
Dinamo Bucharest 2 (*Multescu, Georgescu*), Dukla Prague 0
Dynamo Zagreb 1 (*Cerin*), Sportin Lisbon 0
Grasshoppers Zurich 0, Dynamo Kiev 1 (*Heinz Hermann og*)
Hibernians Malta 1 (*Xuereb*), Widzew Lodz 4 (*Gloginski, Wilpstak 3*)
Hvidovre 1 (*Jensen E.*), Juventus 4 (*Platini, Rossi, Brio, Cabrini*)
Monaco 0, CSKA Sofia 0
Nendori Tirana 1 (*Kola*), Linfield 0
Omonia Nicosia 2 (*Demetriou, Kantylos*), HJK Helsinki 0
Vikingur 0, Real Sociedad 1 (*Satrustegui*)
Standard Liege 5 (*Tamahata, Daerden, Wendt, Haan, Gerets*), Raba Gyor 0
Dynamo Berlin (*Riediger*), Hamburg 1 (*Milewski*)
Olympiakos Piraeus 2 (*Anastopoulos, Kokolakis*), Oster Vaxjo 0

First Round, Second Leg
Liverpool 1 (*Whelan*), Dundalk 0
Besiktas 0, Aston Villa 0
Rapid Vienna 8 (*Weber, Krankl, Willfurth 2, Keglevits 2, Garger, Thill og*), Avenir Beggen 0
Ajax (*Vanenburg*), Celtic 2 (*Nicholas, McCluskey*)
Dukla Prague 2 (*Nehoda 2*), Dinamo Bucharest (*Talner*)
Sporting Lisbon 3 (*Oliveira 3*), Dynamo Zagreb 0
Dynamo Kiev 3 (*Burjak 2, Demyanenko*), Grasshoppers Zurich 0
Widzew Lodz 3 (*Grebosz, Matusiak 2*), Hibernians Malta 1 (*Xuereb*)
Juventus 3 (*Boniek, Platini, Rossi*), Hvidovre 3 (*Petersen 2, Hansen*)
CSKA Sofia 2 (*Zdravkov, Mladenov*), Monaco 0
Linfield 2 (*Anderson, Gibson*), Nendori Tirana 1 (*Minga*)
HJK Helsinki 3 (*Ismail 2, Rasimus*), Omonia Nicosia 0
Real Sociedad 3 (*Uralde 2, Satrustegui*), Vikingur 2 (*Thordarsson, Herbertson*)
Raba Gyor 3 (*Sventes, Hajszan, Burcsa*), Standard Liege 0
Hamburg 2 (*Hartwig, Hrubesch*), Dynamo Berlin 0
Oesters Vaxjo 1 (*Hallen*), Olympiakos Pireaus 0

Second Round, First Leg
HJK Helsinki 1 (*Ismail*), Liverpool 0
CSKA Sofia 2 (*Djevizov, Mladenov*), Sporting Lisbon 2 (*Fernandes, Xavier*)
Dinamo Bucharest 0, Aston Villa 2 (*Shaw 2*)
Hamburg 1 (*Von Heesen*), Olympiakos Pireaus 0
Rapid Vienna 2 (*Keglevits, Kienanst*), Widzew Lodz 1 (*Tlokinski*)
Real Sociedad 2 (*Satrustegui, Uralde*), Celtic 0
Standard Liege 1 (*Tamahata*), Juventus 1 (*Tardelli*)
Dynamo Kiev w.o. – Nendori Tirana withdrew

Second Round, Second Leg
Liverpool 5 (*Dalglish, Johnston, Neal, Kennedy 2*), HJK Helsinki 0
Sporting Lisbon 0, CSKA Sofia 0
Aston Villa 4 (*Shaw 3, Walters*), Dinamo Bucharest 2 (*Multescu, Iordache*)
Olympiakos Pireaus 0, Hamburg 4 (*Magath, Hrubesch, Rolff, Bastrup*)
Widzew Lodz 5 (*Wozniak 2, Rizborszki, Surlit, Wraga*), Rapid Vienna 3 (*Panenka, Leiner, Grebosz og*)
Celtic 2 (*MacLeod 2*), Real Sociedad 1 (*Uralde*)
Juventus 2 (*Rossi 2*), Standard Liege 0

Quarter-Final, First Leg
Aston Villa 1 (*Cowans*), Juventus 2 (*Rossi, Boniek*)
Sporting Lisbon 1 (*Manuel Fernandez*), Real Sociedad 0
Widzew Lodz 2 (*Tlokinski, Wraga*), Liverpool 0
Dynamo Kiev 0, Hamburg 3 (*Bastrup 3*)

Quarter-Final, Second Leg
Juventus 3 (*Platini 2, Tardelli*), Aston Villa 1 (*Withe*)
Real Sociedad 2 (*Larranaga, Basquero*), Sporting Lisbon 0
Liverpool 3 (*Neal* pen, *Rush, Hodgson*), Widzew Lodz 2 (*Tlokinski* pen, *Smolarek*)
Hamburg 1 (*Hartwig*), Dynamo Kiev 2 (*Bessonov, Jevtushenko*)

Semi-Final, First Leg
Juventus 2 (*Tardelli, Bettega*), Widzew Lodz 0
Real Sociedad 1 (*Gajate*), Hamburg 1 (*Rolff*)

Semi-Final, Second Leg
Widzew Lodz 2 (*Surlit 2*), Juventus 2 (*Rossi, Platini*)
Hamburg 2 (*Jakobs, Von Heessen*), Real Sociedad 1 (*Diego*)

Final: Hamburg (1) 1, Juventus (0) 0
Athens 80,000

Hamburg: Stein; Kaltz, Wehmeyer, Jakobs, Hieronymus, Rolff, Milewski, Groh, Hrubesch, Magath, Bastrup (Van Heessen).

Juventus: Zoff; Gentile, Cabrini, Bonini, Brio, Scirea, Bettega, Tardelli, Rossi (Marocchino), Platini, Boniek.

Scorer: Magath.

Referee: Rainea.

The Brazilian centre forward, Jose Altafini scored 14 goals in the European Cup of season 1962–63. That total included two in the 2-1 final win over Benfica at Wembley, and stands as the all-time record total. Altafini also played – for Juventus – in the 1972–73 final against Ajax, but failed to score.

Tony Morley, Aston Villa's talented winger, takes on two Juventus defenders in the European Cup quarter-final at Villa Park.

EUROPEAN CUP 1982–83

FIRST ROUND, FIRST LEG

15 SEPT

Dundalk (0) 1 *(Flanagan)*

Liverpool (3) 4 *(Whelan 2, Rush, Hodgson)* 16,500

Dundalk: Blackmore; Gregg M., Lawlor T., McConville, Dunning, Flanagan, Byrne S. (Archbold), Kehoe, Fairclough, Crawley (Ralph), King.
Liverpool: Grobbelaar; Neal, Kennedy A., Thompson, Whelan, Hansen, Dalglish, Lee, Rush, Hodgson, Souness.

Aston Villa (3) 3 *(Withe, Morley, Mortimer)*

Besiktas (0) 1 *(Eksi)* (Behind closed doors)

Aston Villa: Rimmer; Williams, Heard, Bremner, McNaught, Mortimer, Blair, Shaw, Withe, Cowans, Morley.
Besiktas: Rasim; Samet, Kadir, Ulvi, Eksi, Haluk, Ergun, Riza, Ali Kemal, Bora (Cemal), Fikret (Ziya).

Celtic (2) 2 *(Nicholas* pen, *McGarvey)*

Ajax (2) 2 *(Olsen, Lerby)* 56,299

Celtic: Bonner; McGrain, McAdam, Moyes, Reid, McStay, Burns (Sullivan), MacLeod, Provan, Nicholas, McGarvey.
Ajax: Galje; Molenaar, Van Veen, Molby, Boeve, Schoenaker, Ophof, Cruyff, Lerby, Olsen, Vanenburg.

17 Sept

Nendori Tirana (0) 1 *(Kola)*

Linfield (0) 0 25,000

Nendori Tirana: Sharra; Baci, Vladi, Bimo, Naci, Muca, Mema, Omuri, Vila, Minga, Kola.
Linfield: Dunlop; Mooney, McCartney, Walsh, Gibson, Dorman, McKee, McKeown, McGaughey, Murray, Anderson.

FIRST ROUND, SECOND LEG

29 SEPT

Ajax (0) 1 *(Vanenburg)*

Celtic (1) 2 *(Nicholas, McCluskey)* 65,000

Ajax: Schrijvers; Ophof, Van Veen, Molby, Boeve, Schoenaker, Vanenburg, Cruyff (Molenaar), Lerby, Olsen, Kieft.
Celtic: Bonner; McGrain, Aitken, McAdam, Reid, Provan (McCluskey), Sinclair, McStay (Moyes), MacLeod, McGarvey, Nicholas.

Besiktas (0) 0

Aston Villa (0) 0 45,000

Besiktas: Adem; Samet, Ulvi, Mehmet Eksi, Kadir, Ziya, Halul B., Fikret (Bora), Necdet, Ali Kemal, Halul K. (Riza).
Aston Villa: Rimmer; Jones, Evans, McNaught, Williams, Bremner, Mortimer, Cowans, Withe, Shaw, Morley.

Linfield (0) 2 *(Anderson, Gibson)*

Nendori Tirana (1) 1 *(Minga)* 5000

Linfield: Dunlop; Mooney, McCartney, Walsh, Gibson, Dornan (Hayes), McKee, McKeown, McGaughey, Murray, Anderson.
Nendori Tirana: Sharra; Baci, Vladi, Bimo, Naci, Muca (Gezdari), Mema, Omuri, Vila (Josa), Minga, Kola.

Liverpool (0) 1 *(Whelan)*

Dundalk (0) 0 12,021

Liverpool: Grobbelaar; Neal, Kennedy, Thompson, Whelan, Hansen, Dalglish, Lee, McDermott, Johnston, Souness.
Dundalk: Blackmore; Gregg, Lawlor M., McConville, Dunning, Flanagan, Byrne S., King, Fairclough, Crawley, Archbold.

SECOND ROUND, FIRST LEG

20 OCT

HJK Helsinki (1) 1 *(Ismail)*
Liverpool (0) 0 5722

HJK Helsinki: Wood; Soini, Niemi, Holopeinen, Wright, Europaeus, Bostrom, Dahlund (Rantanen), Rasimus, Ismail, Parikka (Linna).
Liverpool: Grobbelaar; Neal, Thompson, Hansen, Kennedy, Whelan, Lee, Hodgson, Souness, Dalglish, Rush.

Dinamo Bucharest (0) 0
Aston Villa (1) 2 *(Shaw 2)* 70,000

Dinamo Bucharest: Moraru; Ion, Stredie, Organin, Nicolae, Dinu, Talnar, Multescu, Vaetus (Iordache), Custov, Orac (Dragnea).
Aston Villa: Rimmer; Jones, Gibson, Evans, McNaught, Mortimer, Bremner, Shaw, Withe, Cowans, Morley.

Real Sociedad (0) 2 *(Satrustegui, Uralde)*
Celtic (0) 0 31,000

Real Sociedad: Arconada; Celayeta, Gorriz, Cortabarria, Olaizola, Diego, Zubillaga, Zamora, Uralde, Satrustegui, Lopez Ufarte.
Celtic: Bonner; McGrain, Aitken, McAdam, Reid, Sinclair, Provan, McStay, MacLeod, Nicholas, McGarvey.

SECOND ROUND, SECOND LEG

3 NOV

Liverpool (3) 5 *(Dalglish, Johnston, Neal, Kennedy 2)*
HJK Helsinki (0) 0 16,434

Liverpool: Grobbelaar; Neal, Thompson, Hansen, Kennedy, Lee, Johnston, Lawrenson, Souness, Dalglish (Hodgson), Rush.
HJK Helsinki: Wood; Soini, Niemi, Wright, Europaeus, Rantanen (Parikka), Bostrom, Dahlund (Murtonen), Rasimus, Ismail, Holopainen.

Aston Villa (1) 4 *(Shaw3, Walters)*
Dinamo Bucharest (1) 2 *(Multescu, Iordache)* 22,244

Aston Villa: Rimmer; Williams, McNaught, Evans, Gibson, Bremner, Mortimer, Cowans, Shaw (Walters), Withe, Morley.
Dinamo Bucharest: Moraru; Marin, Stredie, Dragnea, Nicolae, Dinu, Tainar, Multescu (Vaetus), Iordache, Custov, Orac (Augustin).

Celtic (1) 2 *(MacLeod 2)*
Real Sociedad (1) 1 *(Uralde)* 54,874

Celtic: Bonner; McGrain, Reid (Burns), Aitken, McAdam, MacLeod, Provan (McCluskey), McStay, McGarvey, Sinclair, Nicholas.
Real Sociedad: Arconada; Celayeta, Olaizola, Zubillaga, Gorriz, Cortabarria, Uralde, Diego (Larranaga), Satrustegui, Zamora, Lopex Ufarte.

David Hodgson in action for Liverpool against Widzew Lodz in the quarter-final 2nd leg at Anfield.

DRAW FOR EUROPEAN COMPETITIONS 1983–84

CHAMPIONS' CUP (First Round)

Roma (Italy) v IFK Gothenburg (Sweden); Athlone (Eire) v Standard Liege (Belgium); Ajax (Holland) v Olympiakos (Greece); Fenerbahce (Turkey) v Bohemians Praha (Czechoslavakia); Rapid Vienna (Austria) v Nantes (France); CSKA Sofia (Bulgaria) v Omonia Nicosia (Cyprus); BK Odense (Denmark) v **Liverpool (England)**; Benfica (Portugal) v **Linfield (N Ireland)**; Dynamo Berlin (East Germany) v Jeunesse (Luxembourg); Partizan Belgrade (Yugloslavia) v Viking Stavanger (Norway); Kuusysi Lahti (Finland) v Dinamo Bucharest (Romania); **Dundee U (Scotland)** v Hamrun Spartans (Malta); Dynamo Minsk (Russia) v Grasshoppers (Switzerland); Gyor (Hungary) v Vikingur (Iceland); Lech Poznan (Poland) v Bilbao (Spain); Bye Hamburg (West Germany).

CUP WINNERS' CUP (Preliminary Round)

Swansea City (Wales) v Magdeburg (East Germany).

FIRST ROUND

Aberdeen (Scotland) v IA Akranes (Iceland); Innsbruck (Austria) v Koln (West Germany); **Swansea C (Wales)** or Magdeburg (East Germany) v Barcelona (Spain); Juventus (Italy) v Lechia Gdansk (Poland); Paralimni Famagusta (Cyprus) v Beveren (Belgium); Dinamo Zagreb (Yugoslavia) v FC Porto (Portugal); Mersin IY (Turkey) v Spartak Varna (Bulgaria); **Manchester U (England)** v Dukla Prague (Czechoslovakia); Serviette (Switzerland) v Avenir Beggen (Luxembourg); NEC Nijmegen (Holland) v Brann Bergeb (Norway); **Rangers (Scotland)** v Valletta (Malta); AEK Athens (Greece) v Ujpest Dozsa (Hungary); Sligo Rovers (Eire) v Haka Valkeakosken (Finland); B 1901 Nykobing (Denmark) v Shakhtyor Donetsk (Russia); Hammarby (Sweden) v Nendori (Albania); Paris St Germain (France) v **Glentoran (N Ireland)**.

UEFA CUP (First Round)

Aston Villa (England) v Vitoria Guimares (Portugal); Sparta Praha (Czechoslovakia) v Real Madrid (Spain); Royal FC Antwerp (Belgium) v FC Zurich (Switzerland); Sparta Rotterdam (Holland) v **Coleraine (N Ireland)**; Banik Ostrava (Czechoslovakia) v B 1903 Copenhagen (Denmark); FK Austria (Austria) v Aris Bonnevoie (Luxembourg); Sporting Lisbon (Portugal) v Seville (Spain); PSV Eindhoven (Holland) v Ferencvaros (Hungary); Kaiserslautern (West Germany) v **Watford (England)**; Red Star Belgrade (Yugoslavia) v Verona (Italy); Groningen (Holland) v Atletico Madrid (Spain); Larissa (Greece v Honved (Hungary); Widzew Lodz (Poland) v Elfsborg Boras (Sweden); Carl Zeiss Jena (East Germany) v IBV Vestmann (Iceland); Moscow Spartak (Russia) v HJK Helsinki (Finland); Lens (France) v La Gantoise (Belgium); Anderlecht (Belgium) v Bryne IL (Norway); **Nottingham F (England)** v Vorwarts ander Oder (East Germany); **Celtic (Scotland)** v Aarhus GF (Denmark); Dynamo Kiev (Russia) v Laval (France); Werder Bremen (West Germany) v Malmo (Sweden); Drogheda (Eire) v **Tottenham H (England)**; Feyenoord (Holland) v **St Mirren (Scotland)**; Bordeaux (France) v Lokomotiv Leipzig (East Germany); Radnicki Nis (Yugoslavia) v St Gallen (Switzerland); Bayern Munich (West Germany) v Anorthosis Larnaca (Cyprus); Sportul Bucharest (Romania) v Sturm Graz (Austria); Lokomotiv Plovdiv (Bulgaria) v PAOK Salonika (Greece); Stuttgart (West Germany) v Levski Spartak (Bulgaria); Universitated Craiova (Romania) v Hajduk Split (Yugoslavia); Trabzonspor (Turkey) v Internazionale (Italy); Inter Bratislava (Czechoslovakia) v Rabat Ajaz (Malta).

WORLD SUPERCLUB CUP

Promoted by Channel Five (*Milan TV Company*)
(Milan, June–July)

Inter 1 (*Juary* 9), Flamengo 2 (*Robertinho* 26, *Baltazar* 60); Penarol 1 (*morena* 43 pen), Milan 0; Milan 2 (*Cuoghi* 51, *Serena* 64), Juventus 2 (*Platini* 39, *Rossi* 87); Inter 1 (*Bergomi* 17), Penarol 2 (*Morena* 31 pen, *Silve* 74); Juventus 0, Penarol 0; Milan 1 (*Serena* 34), Flamengo 1 (*Marinho* 79); Penarol 0, Flamengo 2 (*Junior* 21, *Baltazar* 76); Inter 0, Juventus 1 (*Storgato* 27); Juventus 2 (*Platini* 12, *Boniek* 62), Flamengo 1 (*Adilio* 18); Milan 2 (*Serena* 38, 63), Inter 1 (*Altobelli* 60).

Final Table

	P	*W*	*D*	*L*	*F*	*A*	*Pts*
Juventus (Italy)	4	2	2	0	5	3	6
Flamengo (Brazil)	4	2	1	1	6	4	5
Penarol (Uruguay)	4	2	1	1	3	3	5
Milan (Italy)	4	1	2	1	5	5	4
Inter (Italy)	4	0	0	4	3	7	0

Michel Platini won the player of the tournament award.

EUROPEAN TOP LEAGUE GOALSCORERS 1982–83

Albania: Bajaziti (Besa)	16
Austria: Krankl (Rapid)	23
Belgium: Vandenbergh (Anderlecht)	21
Bulgaria: Pechlivanov (Trakia)	20
Cyprus: Chatziliosu (Aris)	17
Czechoslovakia: Chaloupka (Bohemians)	17
Denmark: Jacquet (Vejle)	20
East Germany: Streich (Magdeburg)	19
England: Blissett (Watford)	27
Finland: Atik Ismail (HJK Helsinki)	19
France: Halilhodzic (Nantes)	27
Greece: Anastopoulos (Olympiakos)	29
Holland: Houtman (Feyenoord)	30
Hungary: Dobany (Pecs)	23
Iceland: Karlsson (Vikingur)	10
Thorleifsson (B. Vestmannaeyer	10
Italy: Platini (Juventus)	18
Luxembourg: Simon (Jeunesse)	23
Malta: Refalo (Hamrun)	7
N Ireland: Campbell (Ards)	15
Norway: Johannesen (Viking)	11
Aranerud (Hamarkameratene)	11
Poland: Okonski (Lech)	15
Tiokinski (Widzew)	15
Portugal: Gomes (Porto)	36
Republic of Ireland: Larkin (Athlone)	19
Rumania: Grosv (Bihor)	20
Scotland: Nicholas (Celtic)	27
Soviet Union: Yakubik (Paktakor Tashkent)	23
Spain: Rincon (Betis)	20
Sweden: Corneliusson (IFK)	12
Switzerland: Brigger (Servette)	23
Turkey: Selcuk (Fernerbahce)	18
West Germany: Voller (Werder Bremen)	23
Yugoslavia: Halilovic (Vinkovice)	18

EUROPEAN LEADING GOALSCORERS 1982–83

The leading British players in the Adidas Golden Boot award to Europe's top League goalscorers were Charlie Nicholas and Luther Blissett. The winner was Fernando Gomes of Porto in the Portugese football league who recorded an impressive 36 goals in 30 matches. The leaders were: Final placings: Fernando Gomes (Porto) 36 goals; Peter Houtman (Feyenoord) 30; Nikos Anastopoulos (Olympiakos) 29; Charlie Nicholas (Celtic) 27; Vadid Halilhodzic (Nantes) 27; Luther Blissett (Watford) 26; Andrzej Szarmach (Auxerre) 24; Ian Rush (Liverpool) 24; Krimau (Wetz).

ALL-TIME GOLDEN BOOT TOP THREE

Year	*Top Scorer*	*Runner-up*	*Third*
1968	Eusebio (Benfica) 42	Dunai (Ujpest) 36	Lennox (Celtic) 32
1969	Zhekov (CSKA) 36	Sideris (Olym.) 35	Dunai (Ujpest) 31 Kogelberger (FKA) 31
1970	G. Müller (Bayern) 38	Devillet (Sp. Lux) 31	Zhekov (CSKA) 31
1971	Skoblar (Marseille) 44	Keita (St.-Et.) 42	Dedes (Panionios) 28
1972	Müller (Bayern) 40	Antoniadis (Pnks) 39	Harper (Aberdeen) 33 Lee (Man City) 33 Santrac (OFK) 33
1973	Eusebio (Benfica) 40	Müller (Bayern) 36	Zhekov (CSKA) 29
1974	Yazalde (Sporting) 46	Krankl (Rapid) 36	Bianchi (Reims) 30 Heynckes (B Mg) 30 Müller (Bayern) 30
1975	Georgescu (Din. Buch) 33	Geels (Ajax) 30 Yazalde (Sptng) 30 Onnis (Monaco) 30	Riel (Antwerp) 28 V. der Kuylen (PSV) 28
1976	Kaiafas (Ominia) 39	Bianchi (Reims) 34	Risi (Zurich) 33
1977	Georgescu (D. Buch) 47	Varadi (Vasas) 36	Geels (Ajax) 34 D. Müller (Köln) 34
1978	Krankl (Rapid) 41	Bianchi (PSG) 37	Geels (Ajax) 32
1979	Kist (Alkmaar) 34	Fekete (Ujpest) 31 Mavros (AEK) 31	Krankl (Barce.) 29
1980	Vandenbergh (Lierse) 39	Fazekas (Ujpest) 36	Schachner (FK Aus.) 34
1981	Slavkov (Trakia) 31	Nyilasi (Fervrs) 30	Rummenigge (Byn) 29
1982	Kieft (Ajax) 32	Kist (Alkmaar) 29 Onnis (Tours) 29	Hansen (Odense) 28
1983	Gomes (Porto) 36	Houtman (Feyenoord) 30	Anastopoulos (Ol.) 29

Real Madrid have set all the records in the European Cup. They pulled in the two biggest crowds in Finals; forced the rules to be changed, and in left winger Francisco Gento have a man who appeared in 9 Finals. In 1956 125,000 saw Real beat Eintracht Frankfurt 7–3 in Glasgow, and in 1957 another 128,000 watched them when they beat Fiorentina 2-0 in Madrid. They were so successful that they forced the organisers to change the initial rules. It had been set out that the European Cup winners would earn the right to stage the final the following year. Thus, winners in 1956 they were at home in the 1957 final, but winning again they should have been at home at the Estadio Chamartin in 1958, but the rules were changed so that Real beat AC Milan 3-2 in the 1958 Final at the Heysel Stadium in Brussels.

ABERDEEN TRIUMPHANT

It was a foggy night in Munich town, when Tottenham were the visitors in the European Cup-Winners' Cup, second round. Their match in London ended in a 1-1 draw, so there was everything to play for, but the conditions were against good football. Indeed, a league game would have been postponed, but the referee decided that it was playable for a European tie. Bayern were the far better team, and shrouded in fog, they were 4-1 winners – the London club was out of the competition, having beaten Coleraine 7-0 aggregate in the first round.

Swansea had to play a preliminary match in this tourney, and beat Braga of Portugal 3-1. In the first round proper, they really enjoyed themselves against Sliema Wanderers, and the Maltese team were thrashed 17-0 (!), 12-0 in the home leg. But Swansea's trouble began to mount up in the second round, when they lost at home to the French Paris St Germain 1-0. They couldn't retrieve the deficit in the French capital, where they lost 0-2. So it was left to the Scottish Cup holders, Aberdeen, to carry the British flag, and they did that in glorious fashion. In the preliminary round, they beat the Swiss Cup holders, Sion, 11-1 (!) on aggregate, but in the first round they had a surprisingly difficult job against Dinamo Tirana. The home leg ended in a narrow 1-0 win, and in hostile Albania, they could only draw 0-0. Still, it was good enough, and a double against Lech Poznan of Poland carried them into the quarter-finals, where the formidable Bayern Munich were waiting for them. A heroic defensive display gave the Scottish team a 0-0 draw in West Germany, and the return leg was a classic. In a highly exciting match, Aberdeen won 3-2 with the substitute Hewitt getting the winning goal minutes before the final whistle. In the semi-final, they beat Waterschei 5-1 at home, and a narrow defeat in Belgium was not important, Aberdeen were in the final!

Real Madrid were also there thanks to impressive victories against such teams as Inter Milan and Austria Vienna, conquerors of holders Barcelona. Before the Gothenburg final, the Aberdeen manager, Alex Ferguson, made this tongue-in-cheek forecast: 'It will be a great British victory or a Scottish defeat'. He was right, we in England shouldn't claim any part of Aberdeen's victory, since we didn't share the credits with them for our triumphs in the European Cup. The final was an excellent match, worthy of the high stakes. Black gave Aberdeen the lead early in the first half, but Santillana equalised from a well-deserved penalty. At times, the Spaniards dominated play, but the Aberdeen defence was rock solid, and the final went into extra time. When everybody was ready for a penalty-kicks decider, Aberdeen led a last charge and scored a stunning goal for a 2-1 victory. A sensational match and a great triumph over one of Europe's most famous clubs for the Scottish team.

EUROPEAN CUP-WINNERS' CUP FINALS 1961–83

Year	*Winners*		*Runners-up*		*Venue*
1961	AC Fiorentina	4	Rangers	1*	
1962	Atlético Madrid	3	AC Fiorentina	0	Stuttgart
	(*after 1-1 draw in Glasgow*)				
1963	Tottenham H	5	Atlético Madrid	1	Rotterdam
1964	Sporting Club Lisbon	1	MTK Budapest	0	Antwerp
	(*after 3-3 draw in Brussels*)				
1965	West Ham U	2	TSV Munich 1860	0	London
1966	Borussia Dortmund	2	Liverpool	1	Glasgow
1967	Bayern Munich	1	Rangers	0	Nuremberg
1968	AC Milan	2	SV Hamburg	0	Rotterdam
1969	Slovan Bratislava	3	Barcelona	2	Basle
1970	Manchester C	2	Gornik Zabrze	1	Vienna
1971	Chelsea	2	Real Madrid	1	Athens
	(*after 1-1 draw in Athens*)				
1972	Rangers	3	Dynamo Moscow	2	Barcelona
1973	AC Milan	1	Leeds U	0	Salonika
1974	FC Magdeburg	2	AC Milan	0	Rotterdam
1975	Dynamo Kiev	3	Ferencvaros	0	Basle
1976	Anderlecht	4	West Ham U	2	Brussels
1977	SV Hamburg	2	Anderlecht	0	Amsterdam
1978	Anderlecht	4	Austria/WAC	0	Paris
1979	Barcelona	4	Fortuna Dusseldorf	3	Basle
1980	Valencia	0	Arsenal	0	Brussels
	(*Valencia won 5-4 on penalties*)				
1981	Dynamo Tbilisi	2	Carl Zeiss Jena	1	Dusseldorf
1982	Barcelona	2	Standard Liège	1	Barcelona
1983	Aberdeen	2	Real Madrid	1	Gothenburg

* *Aggregate scores*

CUP-WINNERS' CUP HISTORY

EUROPEAN CUP-WINNERS' CUP 1960–61

Qualifying Round
Vorwaerts Berlin v Red Brno (2-3) 2-1, 0-2
Rangers v Ferencvaros (5-4) 4-2, 1-2

Quarter-Final
Red Star Brno v Dynamo Zagreb (0-2) 0-0, 0-2
FK Austria v Wolverhampton W (2-5) 2-0, 0-5
Borussia Moenchengladbach v Rangers (0-11) 0-3, 0-8
Lucerne v Fiorentina (2-9) 0-3, 2-6

Semi-Final
Fiorentina v Dynamo Zagreb (4-2) 3-0. 1-2
Rangers v Wolverhampton W (3-1) 2-0, 1-1

Final 1960–61: Rangers 0, Fiorentina 2
(First leg, Glasgow, 17 May, 1961)
Rangers: Ritchie; Shearer, Caldow; Davis, Paterson, Baxter, Wilson, McMillan, Scott, Brand, Hume.
Fiorentina: Albertosi; Robotti, Castelletti; Gonfiantini, Orzan, Rimbaldo; Hamrin, Micheli, Da Costa, Milan, Petris.
Scorer: Fiorentina – Milan 2.

Fiorentina 2, Rangers 1
(Second leg, Florence, 27 May, 1961)
Fiorentina: Albertosi; Robotti, Castelletti; Gonfiantini, Orzan, Rimbaldo; Hamrin, Micheli, Da Costa, Milan, Petris.
Rangers: Ritchie; Shearer, Caldow; Davis, Paterson, Baxter; Scott, McMillan, Millar, Brand, Wilson.
Scorers: Fiorentina – Milan, Hamrin; Rangers – Scott.

EUROPEAN CUP-WINNERS' CUP 1961–62

Byes: Ajax Amsterdam, Werder, Aarhus, Dudelange, Progresul, Vardar, Zilina, Olympiakos. Holders Fiorentina exempt until Second Round.

First Round
Glenavon v Leicester C (2-7) 1-4, 1-3
Dunfermline Ath v St Patrick's Ath (8-1) 4-1, 4-0
Swansea T v Motor Jena (3-7) 2-2, 1-5
La Chaux de Fonds v Leixoes (6-7) 6-2, 0-5
Sedan v Atlético Madrid (3-7) 2-3, 1-4
Rapid Vienna v Spartak Varna (5-2) 0-0, 5-2
Floriana v Ujpest (4-15) 2-5, 2-10

Second Round
Fiorentina v Rapid Vienna (9-3) 3-1, 6-2
Leicester C v Atlético Madrid (1-3) 1-1, 0-2
Dunfermline Ath v Vardar Skoplje (5-2) 5-0, 0-2
Werder Bremen v Aarhus (5-2) 2-0, 3-2
Ajax Amsterdam v Ujpest (3-4) 2-1, 1-3
Olympiakos Piraeus v Dynamo Zilina (2-4) 2-3, 0-1
Leixos v Progresul (2-1) 1-1, 1-0
Motor Jena v Alliance Dudelange (9-2) 7-0, 2-2

Quarter-Final
Werder Bremen v Atlético Madrid (2-4) 1-3, 1-1
Ujpest v Dunfermline Ath (5-3) 4-3, 1-0
Dynamo Zilina v Fiorentina (3-4) 3-2, 0-2
Motor Jena v Leixoes (4-2) 1-1, 3-1

Semi-Final
Fiorentina v Ujpest (3-0) 2-0, 1-0
Motor Jena v Atlético Madrid (0-5) 0-1, 0-4

Final 1961–62: Fiorentina 1, Atlético Madrid 1
(In Glasgow, 10 May, 1962)
Fiorentina: Albertosi; Robotti, Castelletti; Malatrasi, Orzan, Marchesi; Hamrin, Ferretti, Milan, Dell'Angelo, Petris.
Atlético Madrid: Madinabeytia; Rivilla, Calleja, Ramirez, Griffa, Glaria; Jones, Adelardo, Mendonça, Peirò, Collar.
Scorers: Fiorentina – Hamrin; Atlético Madrid – Peirò.

Replay: Atlético Madrid 3, Fiorentina 0
(In Stuttgart, 5 September, 1962)
No change in teams. *Scorers:* Atlético Madrid – Jones, Mendonça, Peirò

EUROPEAN CUP-WINNERS' CUP 1962–63

Byes: Graz, Nuremberg, Portadown, Shamrock R, Slovan, Tottenham H. Holders Atlético Madrid exempt until Second Round.

First Round
Lausanne v Sparta Rotterdam (5-4) 3-0, 2-4
St Etienne v Vitoria Setubal (4-1) 1-1, 3-0
Alliance Dudelange v Odense BK 09 (2-9) 1-1, 1-8
Rangers v Seville (4-2) 4-0, 0-2
OFK Belgrade v Chemie Halle (5-3) 2-0, 3-3
Steaua Bucharest v Botev Plovdiv (4-7) 3-2, 1-5
Ujpest v Zaglebie Sosnowiec (5-0) 5-0, 0-0
Bangor C v Napoli (4-5) 2-0, 1-3, 1-2

Second Round
St Etienne v Nuremberg (0-3) 0-0, 0-3
Atlético Madrid v Hibernians Valletta (5-0) 4-0, 1-0
Shamrock R v Botev Plovdiv (0-5) 0-4, 0-1
Sturm Graz v Odense BK 09 (4-6) 1-1, 3-5
Tottenham H v Rangers (8-4) 5-2, 3-2
OFK Belgrade v Portadown (7-4) 5-1, 2-3
Lausanne v Slovan Bratislava (1-2) 1-1, 0-1
Ujpest v Napoli (3-5) 1-1, 1-1, 1-3

Quarter-Final
Slovan Bratislava v Tottenham H (2-6) 2-0, 0-6
Odense BK 09 v Nuremberg (0-7) 0-1, 0-6
Botev Plovdiv v Atlético Madrid (1-5) 1-1, 0-4
OFK Belgrade v Napoli (6-4) 2-0, 1-3, 3-1

Semi-Final
OFK Belgrade v Tottenham H (2-5) 1-2, 1-3
Nuremberg v Atlético Madrid (2-3) 2-1, 0-2

Final 1962–63: Tottenham H 5, Atlético Madrid 1
(In Rotterdam, 15 May, 1963)
Tottenham H: Brown; Baker, Henry, Blanchflower, Norman, Marchi; Jones, White, Smith, Greaves, Dyson.
Atlético Madrid: Madinabeytia; Rivilla, Rodrigues; Ramiro, Griffa, Glaria; Jones, Adelardo, Chuzo, Mendonça, Collar.
Scorers: Tottenham H – Greaves 2, White, Dyson 2; Atlético Madrid – Collar (pen).

EUROPEAN CUP-WINNERS' CUP 1963–64

Byes: Linfield, Zwickau. Holders Tottenham H exempt until Second Round.

First Round

Fenerbahce v Petrolul Ploesti (4-2)	4-1, 0-1
Basle v Celtic (1-10)	1-5, 0-5
Tilburg Willem II v Manchester U (2-7)	1-1, 1-6
SV Hamburg v US Luxembourg (7-2)	4-0, 3-2
Olympiakos Piraeus v Zaglebie Sosnowiec (4-2)	2-1, 0-1, 2-0
Shelbourne v Barcelona (1-5)	0-2, 1-3
Lyon v Odense BK 09 (6-2)	3-1, 3-1
MTK Budapest v Slavia Sofia (2-1)	1-0, 1-1
ASK Linz v Dynamo Zagreb (2-2)	1-0, 0-1, 1-1
Linz lost on toss of coin.	
Sliema Wanderers v Borough U (0-2)	0-0, 0-2
Atlanta v Sporting Lisbon (4-6)	2-0, 1-3, 1-3
Apoel Nicosia v Gjoevik Lyn (6-1)	6-0, 0-1
Helsinki Palloseura v Slovan Bratislava (2-12)	1-4, 1-8

Second Round

Tottenham H v Manchester U (3-4)	2-0, 1-4
Fenerbahce v Linfield (4-3)	4-1, 0-2
Barcelona v SV Hamburg (6-7)	4-4, 0-0, 2-3
Sporting Lisbon v Apoel Nicosia (18-1)	16-1, 2-0
Lyon v Olympiakos Piraeus (5-3)	4-1, 1-2
Motor Zwickau v MTK Budapest (1-2)	1-0, 0-2
Celtic v Dynamo Zagreb (4-2)	3-0, 1-2
Borough U v Slovan Bratislava (0-4)	0-1, 0-3

Quarter-Final

Manchester U v Sporting Lisbon (4-6)	4-1, 0-5
SV Hamburg v Lyon (1-3)	1-1, 0-2
Celtic v Slovan Bratislava (2-0)	1-0, 1-0
MTK Budapest v Fenerbahce (4-3)	2-0, 1-3, 1-0

Semi-Final

Celtic v MTK Budapest (3-4)	3-0, 0-4
Lyon v Sporting Lisbon (1-2)	0-0, 1-1, 0-1

Final 1963–64: MTK Budapest 3, Sporting Lisbon 3 (aet)
(In Brussels, 13 May, 1964)

MTK Budapest: Kovalik; Keszei, Dansky, Jenei, Nagy, Kovacs; Sandor, Vasas, Kuti, Bodor, Halapi.

Sporting Lisbon: Carvalho; Gomez, Perdis; Battista, Carlos, Geo; Mendes, Oswaldo, Mascarenhas, Figueiredo, Morais.

Scorers: MTK Budapest – Sandor 2, Kuti; Sporting Lisbon – Figueiredo 2, Dansky og.

Replay 1963–64: Sporting Lisbon 1, MTK Budapest 0
(In Antwerp, 15 May, 1964)

Teams unchanged. *Scorer:* Sporting Lisbon – Mendes.

EUROPEAN CUP-WINNERS' CUP 1964–65

Bye: Dundee. Holders Sporting Lisbon exempt until Second Round.

First Round

Admira Vienna v Legia Warsaw (1-4)	1-3, 0-1
Lausanne v Honved (2-1)	2-0, 0-1
US Luxembourg v Munich 1860 (0-10)	0-4, 0-6
Valletta v Real Zaragoza (1-8)	0-3, 1-5
AEK Athens v Dynamo Zagreb (2-3)	2-0, 0-3
Steaua Bucharest v Derry C (5-0)	3-0, 2-0
Magdeburg v Galatasaray (3-3)	1-1, 1-1, 1-1
Galatasaray won on toss of coin.	
Esbjerg v Cardiff C (0-1)	0-0, 0-1
Skeid Oslo v Valkeakosken (1-2)	1-0, 0-2
Porto v Lyon (4-0)	3-0, 1-0
Sparta Prague v Anorthosis (16-0)	10-0, 6-0
La Gantoise v West Ham U (1-2)	0-1, 1-1
Torino v Fortuna Geelen (5-3)	3-1, 2-2
Slavia Sofia v Cork Celtic (3-1)	1-1, 2-0

Second Round

Dundee v Real Zaragoza (3-4)	2-2, 1-2
Slavia Sofia v Lausanne (4-5)	1-0, 1-2, 2-3
Legia Warsaw v Galatasaray (3-2)	2-1, 0-1, 1-0
West Ham U v Sparta Prague (3-2)	2-0, 1-2
Porto v Munich 1860 (1-2)	0-1, 1-1
Steaua Bucharest v Dynamo Zagreb (1-5)	1-3, 0-2
Sporting Lisbon v Cardiff C (1-2)	1-2, 0-0
Torino v Valkeakosken (6-0)	5-0, 1-0

Quarter-Final

Real Zaragoza v Cardiff C (3-2)	2-2, 1-0
Legia Warsaw v Munich 1860 (0-4)	0-4, 0-0
Torino v Dynamo Zagreb (3-2)	1-1, 2-1
Lausanne v West Ham U (4-6)	1-2, 3-4

Semi-Final

West Ham U v Real Zaragoza (3-2)	2-1, 1-1
Torino v Munich 1860 (3-5)	2-0, 1-3, 0-2

Final 1964–65: West Ham U 2, Munich 1860 0
(At Wembley, 19 May, 1965)

West Ham U: Standen; Kirkup, Burkett; Peters, Brown, Moore; Sealey, Boyce, Hurst, Dear, Sissons.

Munich 1860: Radenkovic; Wagner, Kohlars; Bena, Reich, Luttrop; Heiss, Kuppers, Brunnenmeier, Grosser, Rebele.

Scorer: West Ham U – Sealey 2.

EUROPEAN CUP-WINNERS' CUP 1965–66

Holders West Ham U exempt until Second Round.

First Round

Juventus v Liverpool (1-2)	1-0, 0-2
Cardiff C v Standard Liège (1-3)	1-2, 0-1
Lahden Reipas v Honved (2-16)	2-10, 0-6
Dukla Prague v Stade Rennes (2-0)	2-0, 0-0
Go Ahead Deventer v Celtic (0-7)	0-6, 0-1
Aarhus v Vitoria Setubal (4-2)	2-1, 2-1
Coleraine v Dynamo Kiev (1-10)	1-6, 0-4
KR Rekyjavik v Rosenborg (2-6)	1-3, 1-3
Omonia Nicosia v Olympiakos Piraeus (1-2)	0-1, 1-1
Magdeburg v Spora Luxembourg (3-0)	1-0, 2-0
Sion v Galatasaray (6-3)	5-1, 1-2
Atlético Madrid v Dynamo Zagreb (5-0)	1-0, 4-0
Wiener Neustadt v Stinta Cluj (0-3)	0-1, 0-2
Limerick v CSKA Sofia (1-4)	1-2, 0-2
Fioriana v Borussia Dortmund (1-13)	1-5, 0-8

Second Round

Liverpool v Standard Liège (5-2)	3-1, 2-1
Dukla Prague v Honved (4-4)	3-2, 1-2
Honved won on away goals rule.	
Aarhus v Celtic (0-3)	0-1, 0-2
Rosenborg v Dynamo Kiev (1-6)	1-4, 0-2
West Ham U v Olympiakos Piraeus (6-2)	4-0, 2-2
Magdeburg v Sion (10-3)	8-1, 2-2
Stinta Cluj v Atlético Madrid (0-6)	0-2, 0-4
Borussia Dortmund v CSKA Sofia (5-4)	3-0, 2-4

Quarter-Final

Honved v Liverpool (0-2)	0-0, 0-2
Celtic v Dynamo Kiev (4-1)	3-0, 1-1
West Ham U v Magdeburg (2-1)	1-0, 1-1
Atlético Madrid v Borussia Dortmund (1-2)	1-1, 0-1

Semi-Final

Celtic v Liverpool (1-2)	1-0, 0-2
West Ham U v Borussia Dortmund (2-5)	1-2, 1-3

Final 1965–66: Borussia Dortmund 2, Liverpool 1 (aet)
(In Glasgow, 5 May, 1966)

Borussia Dortmund: Tilkowski; Cyliax, Redder; Kurrat, Paul, Assauer; Libuda, Schmidt, Held, Sturm, Emmerich.
Liverpool: Lawrence; Lawler, Byrne; Milne, Yeats, Stevenson; Callaghan, Hunt, St John, Smith, Thompson.
Scorers: Borussia Dortmund – Held, Yeats og; Liverpool – Hunt.

EUROPEAN CUP-WINNERS' CUP 1966–67

Holders Borussia Dortmund exempt until Second Round.

Preliminary Round

Valur Reykjavik v Standard Liège (2-9)	1-1, 1-8

First Round

Tatran Presov v Bayern Munich (3-4)	1-1, 2-3
Shamrock R v Spora Luxembourg (8-2)	4-1, 4-1
OFK Belgrade v Spartak Moscow (1-6)	1-3, 0-3
Rapid Vienna v Galatasaray (9-3)	4-0, 5-3
Fiorentina v Vasas Gyor (3-4)	1-0, 2-4
AEK Athens v Sporting Braga (2-4)	0-1, 2-3
Chemie Leipzig v Legia Warsaw (5-2)	3-0, 2-2
Standard Liège v Apollon Limassol (6-1)	5-1, 1-0
Servette Geneva v Kamraterna (3-2)	1-1, 2-1
Floriana v Sparta Rotterdam (1-7)	1-1, 0-6
Swansea T v Slavia Sofia (1-5)	1-1, 0-4
Strasbourg v Steaua Bucharest (2-1)	1-0, 1-1
Skeid Oslo v Real Zaragoza (4-5)	3-2, 1-3
Aalborg v Everton (1-2)	0-0, 1-2
Glentoran v Rangers (1-5)	1-1, 0-4

Second Round

Shamrock R v Bayern Munich (3-4)	1-1, 2-3
Spartak Moscow v Rapid Vienna (1-2)	1-1, 0-1
Vasas Gyor v Sporting Braga (3-2)	3-0, 0-2
Chemie Leipzig v Standard Liège† (2-2)	2-1, 0-1
Servette Geneva v Sparta Rotterdam (2-1)	2-0, 0-1
Strasbourg v Slavia Sofia (1-2)	1-0, 0-2
Real Zaragoza v Everton (2-1)	2-0, 0-1
Rangers v Borussia Dortmund (2-1)	2-1, 0-0

Quarter-Final

Rapid Vienna v Bayern Munich (1-2)	1-0, 0-2
Vasas Gyor v Standard Liège (2-3)	2-1, 0-2
Servette Geneva v Slavia Sofia (1-3)	1-0, 0-3
Rangers* v Real Zaragoza (2-2)	2-0, 0-2

Semi-Final

Bayern Munich v Standard Liège (5-1)	2-0, 3-1
Slavia Sofia v Rangers (0-2)	0-1, 0-1

**Won on toss of a disc.* †*Won on away goals counting double.*

Final 1966–67: Bayern Munich 1, Rangers 0 (aet)
(At Nuremberg, 31 May, 1967)

Bayern Munich: Maier; Nowak, Kupferschmidt; Roth, Beckenbauer, Olk; Nafziger, Ohlhauser, Müller, Koulmann, Brenninger.
Rangers: Martin; Johansen, Provan; Jardine, McKinnon, Greig; Henderson, Smith A., Hynd, Smith D., Johnston.
Scorer: Bayern Munich – Roth.

EUROPEAN CUP-WINNERS' CUP 1967–68

First Round

AC Milan v Levski Sofia (6-2)	5-1, 1-1
Vasas Gyor v Apollon Limassol (9-0)	5-0, 4-0
Altay Izmir v Standard Liège (2-3)	2-3, 0-0
Aberdeen v KR Reykjavik (14-1)	10-0, 4-1
Bayern Munich v Panathinaikos (7-1)	5-0, 2-1
Frederikstad v Vitoria Setubal (2-7)	1-5, 1-2
Valencia v Crusaders (8-2)	4-0, 4-2
FK Austria v Steaua Bucharest (1-4)	0-2, 1-2
Shamrock R v Cardiff C (1-3)	1-1, 0-2
Floriana v NAC Breda (1-3)	1-2, 0-1
Moscow Torpedo v Motor Zwickau (1-0)	0-0, 1-0
Lausanne v Spartak Trnava (3-4)	3-2, 0-2
Aris Bonneweg v Lyon (1-5)	0-3, 1-2
Hajduk Split v Tottenham H (3-6)	0-2, 3-4
HJK Helsinki v Wisla Krakow (1-8)	1-4, 0-4
SV Hamburg v Randers Freja (7-3)	5-3, 2-0

Second Round

Vasas Gyor v AC Milan* (3-3)	2-2, 1-1
Standard Liège v Aberdeen (3-2)	3-0, 0-2
Bayern Munich v Vitoria Setubal (7-3)	6-2, 1-1
Valencia v Steaua Bucharest (3-1)	3-0, 0-1
NAC Breda v Cardiff C (2-5)	1-1, 1-4
Moscow Torpedo v Spartak Trnava (6-1)	3-0, 3-1
Lyon* v Tottenham H (4-4)	1-0, 3-4
Wisla Krakow v SV Hamburg (0-5)	0-1, 0-4

Quarter-Final

Standard Liège v AC Milan (2-4)	1-1, 1-1, 0-2
Valencia v Bayern Munich (1-2)	1-1, 0-1
Cardiff C v Moscow Torpedo (2-1)	1-0, 0-1, 1-0
SV Hamburg v Lyon (4-2)	2-0, 0-2, 2-0

Semi-Final

AC Milan v Bayern Munich (2-0)	2-0, 0-0
SV Hamburg v Cardiff C (4-3)	1-1, 3-2

**Won on away goals counting double.*

Final 1967–68: AC Milan 2, SV Hamburg 0
(In Rotterdam, 23 May, 1968)

AC Milan: Cudicini; Anquilletti, Schnellinger; Trappatoni, Rosato, Scala; Hamrin, Lodetti, Sormani, Rivera, Prati.
SV Hamburg: Ozcan; Sondemann, Kurbjohn; Dieckemann, Horst, Schulz H., Dorfel II, Kramer, Seeler, Hornig, Dorfel
Scorer: AC Milan – Hamrin 2.

EUROPEAN CUP-WINNERS' CUP 1968–69

First Round

Slovan Bratislava v Bor (3-2)	3-0, 0-2
Cardiff C v Porto (3-4)	2-2, 1-2
Partizan Tirana v Torino (2-3)	1-3, 1-0
Dunfermline Ath v Apoel Nicosia (12-1)	10-1, 2-0
Olympiakos Piraeus v Fram Reykjavik (4-0)	2-0, 2-0
Bruges v WBA* (3-3)	3-1, 0-2
Bordeaux v Cologne (2-4)	2-1, 0-3
AK Graz v ADO The Hague (1-6)	1-4, 0-2
Randers Freja v Shamrock R (3-1)	1-0, 2-1
Rumelange v Sliema Wanderers* (2-2)	2-1, 0-1
Altay Izmir v Lyn Oslo (4-5)	3-1, 1-4
Crusaders v Norrköping (3-6)	2-2, 1-4
Lugano v Barcelona (0-4)	0-1, 0-3

Second Round

Byes: Torino, Barcelona

Porto v Slovan Bratislava (1-4)	1-0, 0-4
Dunfermline Ath v Olympiakos Piraeus (4-3)	4-0, 0-3
Dynamo Bucharest v WBA (1-5)	1-1, 0-4
ADO The Hague v Cologne (0-4)	0-1, 0-3
Randers Freja v Sliema Wanderers (8-0)	6-0, 2-0
Lyn Oslo v Norrköping (4-3)	2-0, 2-3

Quarter-Final

Torino v Slovan Bratislava (1-3)	0-1, 1-2
Dunfermline Ath v WBA (1-0)	0-0, 1-0
Cologne v Randers Freja (5-1)	2-1, 3-0
Barcelona v Lyn Oslo (5-4)	3-2, 2-2

Semi-Final

Dunfermline Ath v Slovan Bratislava (1-2)	1-1, 0-1
Cologne v Barcelona (3-6)	2-2, 1-4

**Won on away goals counting double.*

Final 1968–69: Slovan Bratislava 3, Barcelona 2

(In Basle, 21 May, 1969, 40,000)

Slovan Bratislava: Vencel; Filo, Hrivnak; Jan Zlocha, Horvath, Hrdlicka, Cvetler; Moder, Josef Capkovic, Jokl, Jan Capkovic.

Barcelona: Sadurni; Franch (Pereda), Eladio; Rife, Olivella, Zabalza; Pellicer, Castro (Mendoca), Zaluda, Fuste, Rexach.

Scorers: Slovan Bratislava – Cvetler, Hrivnak, Jan Capkovic; Barcelona – Zaluda, Rexach.

EUROPEAN CUP-WINNERS' CUP 1969–70

Preliminary Round

Rapid Vienna* v Moscow Torpedo (1-1)	0-0, 1-1

First Round

Olympiakos Piraeus v Gornik Zabrze (2-7)	2-2, 0-5
Rangers v Steaua Bucharest (2-0)	2-0, 0-0
IBV Reykjavik v Levski Sofia (0-8)	0-4, 0-4
Frem Copenhagen v St Gallen* (2-2)	2-1, 0-1
Ards v AS Roma (1-3)	0-0, 1-3
Rapid Vienna v PSV Eindhoven (3-6)	2-4, 1-2
Goztepe Izmir v US Luxembourg (6-2)	3-0, 3-2
Mjoendalen v Cardiff C (2-12)	1-7, 1-5
Shamrock R v Schalke 04 (2-4)	2-1, 0-3
Norrköping v Sliema Wanderers (5-2)	5-1, 0-1
Dukla Prague v Marseille (1-2)	1-0, 0-2
Dynamo Zagreb v Slovan Bratislava (3-0)	3-0, 0-0
Magdeburg v MTK Budapest (2-1)	1-1, 1-0
Academica Coimbra v Kuopion Pallo (1-0)	0-0, 1-0
Lierse v Apoel Nicosia (11-1)	10-1, 1-0
Atlético Bilbao v Manchester C (3-6)	3-3, 0-3

**Won on away goals counting double.*

Second Round

Gornik Zabrze v Rangers (6-2)	3-1, 3-1
Levski Sofia v St Gallen (4-0)	4-0, 0-0
AS Roma† v PSV Eindhoven (1-1)	1-0, 0-1
Goztepe Izmir v Cardiff C (3-1)	3-0, 0-1
Norrköping v Schalke 04 (0-1)	0-0, 0-1
Marseille v Dynamo Zagreb (1-3)	1-1, 0-2
Magdeburg v Academica Coimbra (1-2)	1-0, 0-2
Lierse v Manchester C (0-8)	0-3, 0-5

Quarter-Final

Levski Sofia v Gornik Zabrze* (4-4)	3-2, 1-2
AS Roma v Goztepe Izmir (2-0)	2-0, 0-0
Dynamo Zagreb v Schalke 04 (1-4)	1-3, 0-1
Academica Coimbra v Manchester C (0-1)	0-0, 0-1

Semi-Final

AS Roma v Gornik Zabrze† (4-4)	1-1, 2-2, 1-1
Schalke 04 v Manchester C (2-5)	1-0, 1-5

†Won on toss of coin after extra time.

Final 1969–70: Manchester C 2, Gornik Zabrze 1

(In Vienna, 20 April, 1970, 10,000)

Manchester C: Corrigan; Book, Pardoe; Doyle (Bowyer), Booth, Oakes, Heslop, Bell, Lee, Young, Towers.

Gornik Zabrze: Kostka; Gorgan, Ozlizlo; Latogha, Forenski, Szoltysik; Wilczek, Olek, Banas, Lubanski, Szaryniski.

Scorers: Manchester C – Young, Lee (pen); Gornik Zabrze – Ozlizlo.

EUROPEAN CUP-WINNERS' CUP 1970–71

Preliminary Round

Atvidaberg v Partizan Tirana (1-3)	0-2, 1-1
Bohemians v Gottwaldov (3-4)	1-2, 2-2

First Round

Manchester C* v Linfield (2-2)	1-0, 1-2
Olympija Ljubljana v Benfica (2-9)	1-1, 1-8
Akureyri v Zurich (1-14)	1-7, 0-7
Cardiff C v Pezoporikos (8-0)	8-0, 0-0
Offenbach Kickers v Bruges (2-3)	2-1, 0-2
Hibernians Valletta v Real Madrid (0-5)	0-0, 0-5
Vorwaerts Berlin* v Bologna (1-1)	0-0, 1-1
Steaua Bucharest v Karpaty Lvov (4-3)	3-3, 1-0
CSKA Sofia v Valkeakosken (11-1)	9-0, 2-1
Aberdeen v Honved† (4-4)	1-3, 3-1
Stromsgodset v Nantes (3-7)	0-5, 3-2
Aalborg v Gornik Zabrze (1-9)	0-1, 1-8
Goztepe Izmir v US Luxembourg (5-1)	5-0, 0-1
Wacker Innsbruck v Partizan Tirana (5-3)	3-2, 2-1
Gottwaldov v PSV Eindhoven* (2-2)	2-1, 0-1
Aris Salonika v Chelsea (2-6)	1-1, 1-5

Second Round

CSKA Sofia v Chelsea (0-2)	0-1, 0-1
Honved v Manchester C (0-3)	0-1, 0-2
Cardiff C v Nantes (7-2)	5-1, 2-1
Bruges v Zurich (4-3)	2-0, 2-3
PSV Eindhoven v Steaua Bucharest (7-0)	4-0, 3-0
Goztepe Izmir v Gornik Zabrze (0-4)	0-1, 0-3
Real Madrid v Wacker Innsbruck (2-1)	0-1, 2-0
Benfica v Vorwaerts Berlin† (2-2)	2-0, 0-2

Quarter-Final

Manchester C v Gornik Zabrze (5-3)	2-0, 0-2, 3-1
PSV Eindhoven v Vorwaerts Berlin (2-1)	2-0, 0-1
Cardiff C v Real Madrid (1-2)	1-0, 0-2
Bruges v Chelsea (2-4)	2-0, 0-4

Semi-Final

Chelsea v Manchester C (2-0)	1-0, 1-0
PSV Eindhoven v Real Madrid (1-2)	0-0, 1-2

**Won on away goals counting double.* *†Won on penalty kicks.*

Final 1970–71: Chelsea 2, Real Madrid 1

(after 1-1 draw aet, both games in Athens)
(First game, 19 May, 1971, 42,000)

Chelsea: Bonetti; Boyle, Harris; Hollins, Dempsey, Webb; Weller, Hudson, Osgood, Cooke, Houseman.

Real Madrid: Borja; Luis, Zunzunegui; Pirri, Benito, Zoco; Perez, Amancio, Grosso, Velazquez, Gento.

Scorers: Chelsea – Osgood; Real Madrid – Zoco.

(Second game, 21 May, 1971, 24,000)

Chelsea: Bonetti; Boyle, Harris; Cooke, Dempsey, Webb, Weller, Baldwin, Osgood (Smethurst), Hudson, Houseman.

Real Madrid: Borja; Luis, Zunzunegui; Pirri, Benito, Zoco; Fleitas, Amancio, Grosso, Velazquez (Gento), Bueno (Grande).

Scorers: Chelsea – Dempsey, Osgood; Real Madrid – Fleitas.

EUROPEAN CUP-WINNERS' CUP 1971–72

Preliminary Round

Odense BK 09 v FK Austria* (4-4)	4-2, 0-2
Hibernians Valletta v Fram Reykjavik (3-2)	3-0, 0-2

First Round

Servette Geneva v Liverpool (2-3)	2-1, 0-2
Distillery v Barcelona (1-7)	1-3, 0-4
Dynamo Berlin† v Cardiff C (2-2)	1-1, 1-1
Jeunesse Hautcharage v Chelsea (0-21)	0-8, 0-13
Limerick v Torino (0-5)	0-1, 0-4
Dynamo Tirana v FK Austria (1-2)	1-1, 0-1
Rennes v Rangers (1-2)	1-1, 0-1
Hibernians Valletta v Steaua Bucharest (0-1)	0-0, 0-1
Sporting Lisbon v Lyn Oslo (7-0)	3-0, 4-0
Skoda Pilzen v Bayern Munich (1-7)	0-1, 1-6
Komlo Banyasi v Red Star Belgrade (4-8)	2-7, 2-1
Olympiakos Piraeus v Dynamo Moscow (2-3)	0-2, 2-1
Levski Sofia v Sparta Rotterdam (1-3)	1-1, 0-2
Zaglebie Sosnowiec v Atvidaberg (4-5)	3-4, 1-1
Mikkeli v Eskisehirspor (0-4)	0-0, 0-4
Beerschot v Famagusta (8-0)	7-0, 1-0

Second Round

Liverpool v Bayern Munich (1-3)	0-0, 1-3
Atvidaberg* v Chelsea (1-1)	0-0, 1-1
Torino v FK Austria (1-0)	1-0, 0-0
Rangers† v Sporting Lisbon (6-6)	3-2, 3-4
Beerschot v Dynamo Berlin (2-6)	1-3, 1-3
Sparta Rotterdam v Red Star Belgrade (2-3)	1-1, 1-2
Barcelona v Steaua Bucharest (1-3)	0-1, 1-2
Eskisehirspor v Dynamo Moscow (0-2)	0-1, 0-1

Quarter-Final

Torino v Rangers (1-2)	1-1, 0-1
Steaua Bucharest v Bayern Munich* (1-1)	1-1, 0-0
Atvidaberg v Dynamo Berlin (2-4)	0-2, 2-2
Red Star Belgrade v Dynamo Moscow (2-3)	1-2, 1-1

Semi-Final

Bayern Munich v Rangers (1-3)	1-1, 0-2
Dynamo Berlin v Dynamo Moscow† (2-2)	1-1, 1-1

**Won on away goals rule.* *†Won on penalty kicks.*

Final 1971-72: Rangers 3, Dynamo Moscow 2

(In Barcelona, 24 May, 1972, 35,000)

Rangers: McCloy; Jardine, Mathieson, Greig, Johnstone, Smith, McLean, Conn, Stein, MacDonald, Johnston.

Dynamo Moscow: Pilgui; Basalev, Dolmatov, Zykov, Dobbonosov (Gerschkovitch), Zhukov, Baidatchini, Jakubik (Estrekov), Sabo, Makovikov, Evryuzhikhin.

Scorers: Rangers – Stein, Johnston 2; Dynamo Moscow – Estrekov, Makovikov.

EUROPEAN CUP-WINNERS' CUP 1972–73

First Round

Bastia v Atlético Madrid (1-2)	0-0, 1-2
Floriana Valletta v Ferencvaros (1-6)	1-0, 0-6
Schalke 04 v Slavia Sofia (5-2)	2-1, 3-1
Standard Liège v Sparta Prague (3-4)	1-0, 2-4
Spartak Moscow v FC Den Haag (1-0)	1-0, 0-0
Vikingur Reykjavik v Legia Warsaw (0-11)	0-2, 0-9
Ankaragucu v Leeds U (1-2)	1-1, 0-1
Hajduk Split v Fredrikstad (2-0)	1-0, 1-0
Rapid Vienna* v PAOK Saloniki (2-2)	0-0, 2-2
Zurich v Wrexham (2-3)	1-1, 1-2
Sporting Lisbon v Hibernian (3-7)	2-1, 1-6
Rapid Bucharest v Landskrona (3-1)	3-0, 0-1
Pezoporikos v Cork Hibs (2-6)	1-2, 1-4
Fremad Amager v Besa* (1-1)	1-1, 0-0
Carl Zeiss Jena v Mikkeli (8-4)	6-1, 2-3
Red Boys Differdingen v AC Milan (1-7)	1-4, 0-3

Second Round

Rapid Vienna v Rapid Bucharest (2-4)	1-1, 1-3
Carl Zeiss Jena v Leeds U (0-2)	0-0, 0-2
Wrexham v Hajduk Split* (3-3)	3-1, 0-2
Cork Hibs v Schalke 04 (0-3)	0-0, 0-3
Atlético Madrid v Spartak Moscow* (5-5)	3-4, 2-1
Hibernian v Besa (8-2)	7-1, 1-1
Ferencvaros v Sparta Prague (3-4)	2-0, 1-4
Legia Warsaw v AC Milan (2-3)	1-1, 1-2

Quarter-Final

Leeds U v Rapid Bucharest (8-1)	5-0, 3-1
Hibernian v Hajduk Split (4-5)	4-2, 0-3
Schalke 04 v Sparta Prague (2-4)	2-1, 0-3
Spartak Moscow v AC Milan (1-2)	0-1, 1-1

Semi-Final

Leeds U v Hajduk Split (1-0)	1-0, 0-0
AC Milan v Sparta Prague (2-0)	1-0, 1-0

**Won on away goals rule.*

Final 1972–73: AC Milan 1, Leeds U 0

(In Salonika, 16 May, 1973, 45,000)

AC Milan: Vecchi; Sabadini, Zigno, Anquilletti, Turone, Rosato (Dolci), Sogliano, Benetti, Bigon, Rivera, Chiarugi.

Leeds U: Harvey; Reaney, Cherry, Bates, Madeley, Hunter, Lorimer, Jordan, Jones, Gray E., Yorath (McQueen).

Scorer: AC Milan – Chiarugi.

EUROPEAN CUP-WINNERS' CUP 1973–74

First Round

Legia Warsaw v PAOK Salonika (1-2)	1-1, 0-1
Anderlecht v Zurich* (3-3)	3-2, 0-1
Vestmannajar v Bor Moenchengladbach (1-16)	0-7, 1-9
Vasas Budapest v Sunderland (0-3)	0-2, 0-1
Ankaragucu v Rangers (0-6)	0-2, 0-4
AC Milan v Dynamo Zagreb (4-1)	3-1, 1-0
Torpedo Moscow v Atlético Bilbao (0-2)	0-0, 0-2
Gzira v Brann Bergen (0-9)	0-2, 0-7
NAC v Magdeburg (0-2)	0-0, 0-2
Randers Freja v Rapid Vienna (1-2)	0-0, 1-2
Chimia Ramnicu v Glentoran (2-4)	2-2, 0-2
Larnaca v Malmo (0-11)	0-0, 0-11
Fola Esch v Beroe Stara (1-11)	0-7, 1-4
Banik Ostrava v Cork Hibs (3-1)	1-0, 2-1
Reipas Lahti v Lyon (0-2)	0-0, 0-2
Cardiff C v Sporting Lisbon (1-2)	0-0, 1-2

Second Round

Lyon v PAOK Salonika (3-7)	3-3, 0-4
Bor Moenchengladbach v Rangers (5-3)	3-0, 2-3
Brann Bergen v Glentoran (2-4)	1-1, 1-3
Banik Ostrava v Magdeburg (2-3)	2-0, 0-3
Zurich* v Malmo (1-1)	0-0, 1-1
Beroe Stara v Atlético Bilbao (3-1)	3-0, 0-1
Sunderland v Sporting Lisbon (2-3)	2-1, 0-2
AC Milan v Rapid Vienna (2-0)	0-0, 2-0

Quarter Final

Magdeburg v Beroe Stara (3-1)	2-0, 1-1
Glentoran v Bor Moenchengladbach (0-7)	0-2, 0-5
Sporting Lisbon v Zurich (4-1)	3-0, 1-1
AC Milan v PAOK Salonika (5-2)	3-0, 2-2

Semi-Final

AC Milan v Bor Moenchengladbach (2-1)	2-0, 0-1
Sporting Lisbon v Magdeburg (2-3)	1-1, 1-2

**Won on away goals rule.*

Final 1973–74: FC Magdeburg 2, AC Milan 0

(In Rotterdam, 8 May, 1974, 5000)

FC Magdeburg: Schultz; Enge, Zapf, Gaube, Abraham, Tyll, Pommerenke, Seguin, Raugust, Sparwasser, Hoffman.

AC Milan: Pizzaballa; Anquilletti, Sabadini, Lanzi, Schnellinger, Maldera, Tresoldi, Benetti, Bigon, Rivera, Bergamaschi.

Scorers: FC Magdeburg – Lanzi og, Seguin.

EUROPEAN CUP-WINNERS' CUP 1974–75

First Round, First Leg
Liverpool 11 (*Lindsay pen, Boersma 2, Thompson 2, Heighway, Cormack, Hughes, Callaghan, Smith, Kennedy*), Stromsgodset 0
Dundee United 3 (*Narey, Copland, Gardener*), Jiul Petrosani 0
Ferencvaros 2 (*Nyilasi, Szabo*), Cardiff City 0
Bursapor 4 (*Turan 2, Ali, Sinan pen*), Finn Harps 2 (*Ferry, Bradley*)
Sliema Wanderers 2 (*Camilleri 2*), Reipas Lahti 0
Dynamo Kiev 1 (*Blokhin*), CSKA Sofia 0
Malmö 1 (*Cervin*), Sion 0
Gwardia Warsaw 2 (*Sroka, Kraska*), Bologna 1 (*Savoldi*)
Slavia Prague 1 (*Herda*), Carl Zeiss Jena 0
Waregem 2 (*Delesie 2*), Austria/WAC 1 (*Pirkner*)
PAOK Salonika 1 (*Terzanides*), Red Star Belgrade 0
PSV Eindhoven 10 (*Van der Kuylen 3, Lubse 3, Kemper, Deykers, Edstrom, Van Kraay*), Ards 0
Fram Reykjavik 0, Real Madrid 2 (*Roberto Martinez 2*)
Benfica 4 (*Jordao 2, Humberto, Nene*), Vanlose 0
Eintracht Frankfurt 3 (*Holzenbein 2, Rohrbach*), Monaco 0

First Round, Second Leg
Stromsgodset 0, Liverpool 1 (*Kennedy*)
Jiul Petrosani 2 (*Rosnai, Tonca*), Dundee United 0
Cardiff City 1 (*Dwyer*), Ferencvaros 4 (*Takacs, Szabo, Pusztai, Mate*)
Finn Harps 0, Bursaspor 0
Reipas Lahti 4 (*Salonen, Lahtanen, Sandberg 2*), Sliema Wanderers 1 (*Aquilina*)
CSKA Sofia 0, Dynamo Kiev 1 (*Blokhin*)
Sion 1 (*Suiza*), Malmö 0
Bologna 2 (*Savoldi 2*),Gwardia Warsaw 1 (*Terlecki*)
Carl Zeiss Jena 1 (*Stein*), Slavia Prague 0
Austria/WAC 4 (*Pirkner 2, Weigel, Fiala*), Waregem 1 (*Koudijzer*)
Red Star Belgrade 2 (*Petrovic V., Savic*), PAOK Salonika 0
Ards 1 (*Guy*), PSV Eindhoven 4 (*Van der Kuylen, Edstrom, Dahlqvist 2*)
Real Madrid 6 (*Pirri 2, Santillana, Netzer, Macanas, Aguilar*), Fram Reykjavik 0
Vanlose 1 (*Petersen*), Benfica 4 (*Nene, Jordao 2, Barros*)
Monaco 2 (*Onnis, Petit*), Eintracht Frankfurt 2 (*Beverungen, Nickel*)
Avenir Beggen had a walkover when Paralimni withdrew.

Second Round, First Leg
Liverpool 1 (*Keegan*), Ferencvaros 1 (*Mate*)
Dundee United 0, Bursaspor 0
Real Madrid 3 (*Krieger og, Santillana, Roberto Martinez*), Austria/WAC 0
Gwardia Warsaw 1 (*Malkiewicz*), PSV Eindhoven 5 (*Willy Van der Kerkhof, Kialak og, Deykers, Lubse, Van der Kuylen*)
Carl Zeiss Jena 1 (*Vogel*), Benfica 1 (*Nene*)
Red Star Belgrade 6 (*Sestic 3, Filipovic 2, Rajkovic*), Avenir Beggen 1 (*Sinner*)
Malmö 3 (*Larsson 2, Sjoberg*), Reipas Lahti 1 (*Kautonen*)
Eintracht Frankfurt 2 (*Nickel, Koerbel*), Dynamo Kiev 3 (*Kolotov, Blokhin, Muntian*)

Second Round, Second Leg
Ferencvaros 0, Liverpool 0
Bursaspor 1 (*Vahit*), Dundee United 0
Austria/WAC 2 (*Pirkner, Fiala*), Real Madrid 2 (*Roberto Martinez, Netzer*)
PSV Eindhoven 3 (*Van der Kuylen 2 [1 pen], Lubse*), Gwardia Warsaw 0
Benfica 0, Carl Zeiss Jena 0
Avenir Beggen 1 (*Dresch*), Red Star Belgrade 5 (*Rajkovic 2, Filipovic, Sestic, Savic*)
Reipas Lahti 0, Malmö 0
Dynamo Kiev 2 (*Onischenko 2*), Eintracht Frankfurt 1 (*Rohrbach*)

Quarter-Finals, First Leg
Real Madrid 2 (*Santillana, Netzer pen*), Red Star Belgrade 0
PSV Eindhoven 0, Benfica 0
Malmö 1 (*Sjoberg*), Ferencvaros 3 (*Nyilasi, Magyar, Mate*)
Bursaspor 0, Dynamo Kiev 1 (*Onischenko*)

Quarter-Finals, Second Leg
Benfica 1 (*Humberto*), PSV Eindhoven 2 (*Willy Van der Kerkhof, Quaars*)
Ferencvaros 1 (*Mate*), Malmö 1 (*Sjoberg*)
Dynamo Kiev 2 (*Kolotov pen, Muntian*), Bursaspor 0
Red Star Belgrade 2 (*Dzajic, Petrovic O. pen*), Real Madrid 0
Red Star Belgrade won on penalties.

Semi-Finals, First Leg
Ferencvaros 2 (*Branikovits, Magyar*), Red Star Belgrade 1 (*Savic*)
Dynamo Kiev 3 (*Kolotov, Onischenko, Blokhin*), PSV Eindhoven 0

Semi-Finals, Second Leg
Red Star Belgrade 2 (*Keri, Filipovic*), Ferencvaros 2 (*Pusztai, Megyesi pen*)
PSV Eindhoven 2 (*Edstrom 2*), Dynamo Kiev 1 (*Burjak*)

Final 1974–75: Dynamo Kiev 3, Ferencvaros 0

(at Basle, 14 May, 1975, 13,000)

Dynamo Kiev: Rudakov; Fomenko, Troshkin, Reshko, Matvienko, Muntian, Konkov, Burjak, Kolotov, Onischenko, Blokhin.

Ferencvaros: Geczi; Pataki, Martos, Rab, Megyesi, Nyilasi (Onhaus), Juhasz, Mucha, Szabo, Mate, Magyar.

Scorers: Dynamo Kiev – Onischenko 2, Blokhin.

EUROPEAN CUP-WINNERS' CUP 1975–76

First Round, First Leg
Ararat Erevan 9 (*Markarov 5 [1 pen], Oganiesian 2, Petrosian S., Bondarenko*), Anorthosis 0
Basle 1 (*Schoenberger*), Atlético Madrid 2 (*Garate, Ayala*)
Besiktas 0, Fiorentina 3 (*Caso 2, Casarsa*)
Borac Banja Luka 9 (*Cetina 3, Ibrahimbegovic 5, Jurkovic*), US Rumelange 0
Eintracht Frankfurt 5 (*Korbel, Beverungen, Holzenbein, Nickel 2*), Coleraine 1 (*Cochrane*)
Haladas Szombathely 7 (*Fedor 2, Horath 2, Frakas og, Halmosi*), Valletta 0
Home Farm 1 (*Brophy*), Lens 1 (*Hopquin*)
Lahden Reipas 2 (*Lindholm, Tupasela*), West Ham U 2 (*Brooking, Bonds*)
Panathinaikos 0, Sachsenring Zwickau 0
Rapid Bucharest 1 (*Thissen og*), Anderlecht 0
Spartak Trnava 0, Boavista 0
Skeid Oslo 1 (*Skjoensberg B.*), Stal Rzeszow 4 (*Kozierski 2, Curylo, Krawczyk*)
Sturm Graz 3 (*Stendal 2 pens, Kulmer*), Slavia Sofia 1 (*Kostov*)
Valur Reykjavik 0, Celtic 2 (*Dalglish, McDonald*)
Vejle 0, Den Haag 2 (*Jol, Van Leeuwen*)
Wrexham 2 (*Griffiths, Davis*), Djurgaardens 1 (*Krantz*)

First Round, Second Leg
Anderlecht 2 (*Van Binst, Rensenbrink*), Rapid Bucharest 0
Anorthosis 1 (*Fivos pen*), Ararat Erevan 1 (*Bondarenko*)
Atlético Madrid 1 (*Becerra*), Basle 1 (*Demarmels*)
Boavista 3 (*Mane, Celse, Salvador*), Spartak Trnava 0
Celtic 7 (*Edvaldsson, Dalglish, McCluskey pen, Hood 2, Deans, Callaghan*), Valur 0
Den Haag 2 (*Perazic, Mansveld*), Vejle 0
Djurgaarden 1 (*Lovfors*), Wrexham 1 (*Whittle*)
Lens 6 (*Northeaux, Mujica pen, Kaiser 3, Llorens*), Home Farm 0
Sachsenring Zwickau 2 (*Schykowski, Dietzsch pen*), Panathinaikos 0
Slavia Sofia 1 (*Kostov*), Sturm Graz 0
West Ham U 3 (*Robson 2, Jennings*), Reipas Landen 0
US Rumelange 1 (*Rohmann*), Borac Banja Luka 5 (*Smilevski, Reso, Kovahevic, Vidacek, Marjonaovic*)
Coleraine 2 (*McCurdy, Cochrane*), Eintracht Frankfurt 6 (*Grabowski 3, Nickel, Lorenz, Holzenbein*)
Valletta 1 (*Giglio*), Haladas Szombathely 1 (*Karaci*)
Fiorentina 3 (*Caso 2, Casarsa*), Besiktas 0
Stal Rzeszow 4 (*Kozierski, Miler, Krawczyk, Napieracz*), Skeid Oslo 0

Second Round, First Leg
Anderlecht 3 (*Rensenbrink 2, Coeck*), Borac Banja Luka 0
Ararat Erevan 1 (*Petrosian S.*), West Ham U 1 (*Taylor A.*)
Atlético Madrid 1 (*Bacerra*), Eintracht Frankfurt 2 (*Holzenbein 2*)
Boavista 0, Celtic 0
Den Haag 3 (*Schoenmaker, Van Vliet, Van Leeawen*), Lens 2 (*Zuraszek, Janovic*)
Fiorentina 1 (*Speggiorin*), Sachsenring Zwickau 0
Sturm Graz 2 (*Stendal, Stenier pen*), Haladas Szombathely 0
Wrexham 2 (*Ashcroft 2*), Stal Rzeszow 0

Second Round, Second Leg
Borac Banja Luka 1 (*Ibrahimbegovic*), Anderlecht 0
Celtic 3, (*Dalglish, Edvaldsson, Deans*), Boavista 1 (*Mane*)
Eintracht Frankfurt 1 (*Reichel*), Atlético Madrid 0
Haladas Szombathely 1 (*Horvath*), Sturm Graz 1 (*Jurtin*)
Lens 1 (*Mujica pen*), Den Haag 3 (*Shoenmaker 2, Van Leeuwen*)
Sachsenring Zwickau 1 (*Schykowski J.*), Fiorentina 0
Stal Rzeszow 1 (*Kozierski*), Wrexham 1 (*Sutton*)
West Ham U 3 (*Paddon, Robson, Taylor A.*), Ararat Erevan 1 (*Petrosian N.*)

Quarter-Finals, First Leg
Anderlecht 1 (*Van Binst*), Wrexham 0
Celtic 1 (*Dalglish*), Sachsenring Zwickau 1 (*Blank*)
Den Haag 4 (*Mansveld 3 [2 pens], Schoenmaker*), West Ham U 2 (*Jennings 2*)
Sturm Graz 0, Eintracht Frankfurt 2 (*Holzenbein, Wenzel*)

Quarter-Finals, Second Leg
Eintracht Frankfurt 1 (*Holzenbein*), Sturm Graz 0
Sachsenring Zwickau 1 (*Blank*), Celtic 0
West Ham U 3 (*Taylor A., Lampard, Bonds pen*), Den Haag 1 (*Schoenmaker*)
Wrexham 1 (*Lee*), Anderlecht 1 (*Rensenbrink*)

Semi-Finals, First Leg
Eintracht Frankfurt 2 (*Neuberger, Kraus*), West Ham U 1 (*Paddon*)
Sachsenring Zwickau 0, Anderlecht 3 (*Van der Elst 2, Rensenbrink*)

Semi-Finals, Second Leg
Anderlecht 2 (*Rensenbrink, Van der Elst*), Sachsenring Zwickau 0
West Ham U 3 (*Brooking 2, Robson*), Eintracht Frankfurt 1 (*Beverungen*)

Final 1976–76: Anderlecht 4, West Ham U 2

(At Heysel Stadium, Brussels, 5 May, 1976, 58,000)

Anderlecht: Ruiter; Lomme, Broos, Van Binst, Thissen, Dockx, Coeck (Vercauteren), Van der Elst, Ressel, Haan, Rensenbrink.

West Ham U: Day; Coleman, Bonds, Taylor T., Lampard (Taylor A.), McDowell, Brooking, Paddon, Holland, Jennings, Robson.

Scorers: Anderlecht – Rensenbrink 2 (1 pen), Van der Elst 2; West Ham U – Holland, Robson.

EUROPEAN CUP-WINNERS' CUP 1976–77

Preliminary Round, First Leg
Cardiff City 1 (*Evans*), Servette 0

Preliminary Round, Second Leg
Servette 2 (*Bizzini, Pfister*), Cardiff City 1 (*Showers*)

First Round, First Leg
Lierse 1 (*Ceulemans*), Hajduk Split 0
MTK Budapest 3 (*Kunszt, Kovacs, Borso*), Sparta Prague 1 (*Cermak*)
AIK Stockholm 1 (*Wallgren*), Galatasaray 2 (*Gokmen, Nehmet*)
Anderlecht 2 (*Van der Elst, Rensenbrink*), Roda JC 1 (*Toonstra*)
Bodo Glimt 0, Napoli 2 (*Speggiorin 2*)
Bohemians 2 (*Ryan, Hansen B. og*), Esbjerg 1 (*Nielsen H.*)
Cardiff City 1 (*Alston*), Dynamo Tbilisi 0
Carrick Rangers 3 (*Prenter 2, Connor*), Aris Bonnevoie 1 (*Pissinger*)
Hamburg 3 (*Zaczyk, Reimann, Hidien*), Keflavik 0
Iraklis 0, Apoel Nicosia 0
Lokomotive Leipzig 2 (*Sekora, Fritsche*), Hearts 0
Southampton 4 (*Waldron, Channon 2* [*1 pen*], *Osgood*), Marseille 0
Levski Spartak 12 (*Yordanov 2, Milanov 6, Panov 2, Spassov 2*), Reipas Lahden 2 (*Sandberg, Tupasela*)
Floriana 1 (*Vassallo*), Slask Wroclaw 4 (*Gavslovski 2, Kwiatkowski, Farrugia og*)
Rapid Vienna 1 (*Krankl*), Atlético Madrid 2 (*Cano, Ayala*)
CSU Galati 2 (*Simionescu, Holzer*), Boavista 3 (*Mane 2, Salvador*)

First Round, Second Leg
Apoel Nicosia 2 (*Marcou 2*), Iraklis 0
Atlético Madrid 1 (*Leivinha*), Rapid Vienna 1 (*Krejcirik*)
Boavista 2 (*Mane 2*), CSU Galati 0
Esbjerg 0, Bohemians 1 (*Mitten*)
Galatasaray 1 (*Gokmen*), AIK Stockholm 1 (*Wallgren*)
Hajduk Split 3 (*Zungul 2, Jerkovic*), Lierse 0
Hearts 5 (*Kay, Gibson 2, Brown, Busby*), Lokomotive Leipzig 1 (*Fritsche*)
Keflavik 1 (*Johansson S.*), Hamburg 1 (*Hidien*)
Reipas Lahden 1 (*Sandberg*), Levski Spartak 7 (*Panov, Milanov 4* [*2 pens*], *Spassov, Krastanov*)
Marseille 2 (*Nogues, Emon*), Southampton 1 (*Peach*)
Napoli 1 (*Massa*), Bodo Glimt 0
Roda JC 2 (*Vermeulen, Van der Lem pen*), Anderlecht 3 (*Rensenbrink, Van der Elst 2*)
Slask Wroclaw 2 (*Pawlowski, Ehrlich*), Floriana 0
Sparta Prague 1 (*Urban*), MTK Budapest 1 (*Kunszt*)

Dynamo Tbilisi 3 (*Gutsaev, Kipiani, Kandeladze pen*
Cardiff City 0
Aris Bonnevoie 2 (*Werner, Langers*), Carrick Rangers (*Irwin*)

Second Round, First Leg
Anderlecht 5 (*Coeck, Vercauteren, Rensenbrink 2* [*pen*]), Galatasaray 1 (*Ozdewak*)
Apoel Nicosia 1 (*Leonidas*), Napoli 1 (*Savoldi pen*)
Atlético Madrid 1 (*Cano*), Hajduk Split 0
Boavista 3 (*Celso 2, Mane*), Levski Spartak 1 (*Milanov*)
Carrick Rangers 2 (*Irwin, Prenter*), Southampton (*Channon 2, Stokes, McCalliog, Osgood*)
Hamburg 4 (*Bjornmose, Eigl, Reimann, Gallacher og*
Hearts 2 (*Busby, Park*)
Dynamo Tbilisi 1 (*Macheidze*), MTK Budapest 4 (*Shy*
loshi, Takach 2, Kish)
Slask Wroclaw 3 (*Kwiatkowski, Sybis 2*), Bohemians 0

Second Round, Second Leg
Bohemians 0, Slask Wroclaw 1 (*Pawlowski*)
Galatasaray 1 (*Gokmen*), Anderlecht 5 (*Rensenbrink*
Haan, Ressel, Coeck)
Hearts 1 (*Gibson*), Hamburg 4 (*Eigl 2, Magath 2*)
Levski Spartak 2 (*Panov, Milanov*), Boavista 0
MTK Budapest 1 (*Koritar*), Dynamo Tbilisi 0
Southampton 4 (*Williams, Hayes 2, Stokes*), Carric
Rangers 1 (*Reid*)
Napoli 2 (*Speggiorin, Massa*), Apoel Nicosia 0
Hajduk Split 1 (*Zungul*), Atlético Madrid 2 (*Ayala, Lea*

Quarter-Finals, First Leg
Anderlecht 2 (*Ressel, Rensenbrink*), Southampton 0
Levski Spartak 2 (*Tsvetkov, Milanov*), Atlético Madrid (*Ayala*)
MTK Budapest 1 (*Borso*), Hamburg 1 (*Volkert*)
Slask Wroclaw 0, Napoli 0

Quarter-Finals, Second Leg
Atlético Madrid 2 (*Ayala 2 pens*), Levski Spartak 0
Hamburg 4 (*Reimann 2, Kaltz pen, Zaczyk*), MTK Buda
pest 1 (*Siklosi*)
Napoli 2 (*Massa, Chiarugi*), Slask Wroclaw 0
Southampton 2 (*Peach pen, MacDougall*), Anderlecht (*Van der Elst*)

Semi-Finals, First Leg
Napoli 1 (*Bruscolotti*), Anderlecht 0
Atlético Madrid 3 (*Cano 2, Leal*), Hamburg 1 (*Magath*)

Semi-Finals, Second Leg
Hamburg 3 (*Capon og, Reimann, Keller*), Atlético Ma
rid 0
Anderlecht 2 (*Thissen, Van der Elst*), Napoli 0

Final 1976–77: Hamburg 2, Anderlecht 0

(In Amsterdam, 11 May, 1977, 65,000)

Hamburg: Kargus; Kaltz, Ripp, Nogly, Hidien, Steffenhagen, Keller, Reimann, Memering, Magath, Volkert.

Anderlecht: Ruiter; Van Binst, Van den Daele, Broos, Thissen, Van der Elst, Coeck, Haan, Dockx (Van Poucke Ressel, Rensenbrink.

Scorers: Hamburg – Volkert (pen), Magath.

EUROPEAN CUP-WINNERS' CUP 1977–78

Preliminary Round, First Leg
Rangers 1 (*Greig*), Young Boys 0

Preliminary Round, Second Leg
Young Boys 2 (*Jackson og, Leuzinger*), Rangers 2 (*Johnstone, Smith*)

First Round, First Leg
Lokomotiv Sofia 1 (*Kolev*), Anderlecht 6 (*Van der Elst 4 [1 pen], Nielsen, Van Poucke*)
Besiktas 2 (*Zeferiya Burth, Paunovic*), Diosgyor 0
Betis 2 (*Garcia Soriano, Eulate*), AC Milan 0
Brann Bergen 1 (*Aase*), IA Akranes 0
Cardiff City 0, Austria/WAC 0
Coleraine 1 (*Tweed*), Lokomotiv Leipzig 4 (*Eichhorn, Kuhn, Lowe 2*)
Dundalk 1 (*Flanagan*), Hajduk Split 0
Hamburg 8 (*Keller 4, Volkert pen, Buljan, Steffenhagen, Reimann*), Lahden Reipas 1 (*Riotto*)
FC Cologne 2 (*Lohr, Muller*), Porto 2 (*Gabriel, Octavio*)
Lokomotiv Kosice 0, Oster Vaxjo 0
PAOK Salonika 2 (*Pelios, Anastasiadis*), Zaglebie Sosnowiec 0
Progres Niedercorn 0, Vejle 1 (*Steen Tychosen*)
Rangers 0, Twente 0
St Etienne 1 (*Synaeghel*), Manchester U 1 (*Hill*)
Olympiakos Nicosia 1 (*Aristidou*), Uni Craiova 6 (*Balaci 2, Girtsu, Marcu, Crisan, Irinescu*)
Valletta 0, Moscow Dynamo 2 (*Kazachenok, Maximenkov*)

First Round, Second Leg
IA Akranes 0, Brann Bergen 4 (*Aase 2, Dahlhaug, Tronstad*)
Anderlecht 2 (*Van der Elst, Bouvy*), Lokomotiv Sofia 0
Austria/WAC 1 (*Baumeister*), Cardiff City 0
Diosgyor 5 (*Fuko, Olah 2 [1 pen], Fekete 2*), *Besiktas 0*
Hajduk Split 4 (Vujovic, McManus og, Rukljac, McConville og), Dundalk 0
Lahden Reipas 2 (*Riotto 2*), Hamburg 5 (*Volkert pen, Keegan, Magath, Keller, Steffenhagen*)
Lokomotiv Leipzig 2 (*Altmann, Fritschepen*), Coleraine 2 (*Guy 2*)
AC Milan 2 (*Tosetto, Capello*), Betis 1 (*Lopez*)
Oster Vaxjo 2 (*Bild, Evesson*), Lokomotiv Kosice 2 (*Jozsa, Dobrovic*)
Porto 1 (*Murca*), FC Cologne 0
Twente 3 (*Gritter, Arnold Muhren, Van der Vall*), Rangers 0
Uni Craiova 2 (*Marcu, Cirtu*), Olympiakos Nicosia 0
Vejle 9 (*Sorensen, Ostergaard 2, Eg, Norgaard 3, Schacke, Tychosen*), Progres Niedercorn 0
Zaglebie Sosnowiec 0, PAOK Salonika 2 (*Kermanidis, Damanikis*)
Moscow Dynamo 5 (*Kolyesov 3, Jakubik, Kazachenkov*), Valletta 0
Manchester U 2 (*Pearson, Coppell*), St Etienne 0

Second Round, First Leg
Austria/WAC 0, Lokomotiv Kosice 0
Diosgyor 2 (*Tatar, Varadi*), Hajduk Split 1 (*Muzinic*)
Hamburg 1 (*Keller*), Anderlecht 2 (*Coeck, Rensenbrink*)
Lokomotiv Leipzig 1 (*Grobner*), Betis 1 (*Lopez*)
Moscow Dynamo 2 (*Kazachenov, Minaev*), Uni Craiova 0
Twente 2 (*Gritter 2*), Brann Bergen 0
Vejle 3 (*Eg, Jaquet, Ostergaard*), PAOK Salonika 0
Porto 4 (*Duda 3, Oliveira*), Manchester U 0

Second Round, Second Leg
Anderlecht 1 (*Van der Elst*), Hamburg 1 (*Keegan*)
Betis 2 (*Garcia Soriano 2*), Lokomotiv Leipzig 1 (*Liebers*)
Brann Bergen 1 (*Tronstad*), Twente 2 (*Gritter, Thoresen*)
Uni Craiova 2 (*Cirtu, Beideanu*), Moscow Dynamo 0
Dynamo won 3-0 on penalties
Hajduk Split 2 (*Vujovic, Rukljac pen*) Diosgyor 1 (*Tatar*)
Hajduk Split won 4-3 on penalties
Lokomotiv Kosice 1 (*Farkas pen*), Austria/WAC 1 (*Morales*)
Manchester U 5 (*Coppell 2, Murca 2 og, Nicholl*), Porto 2 (*Seninho 2*)
PAOK Salonika 2 (*Orfanos, Kermanides*), Vejle 1 (*Jaquet*)

Quarter-Finals, First Leg
Vejle 0, Twente 3 (*Arnold Muhren, Gritter, Thijssen*)
Austria/WAC 1 (*Parits*), Hajduk Split 1 (*Surjak*)
Betis 0, Moscow Dynamo 0
Porto 1 (*Gomes*), Anderlecht 0

Quarter-Finals, Second Leg
Hajduk Split 1 (*Cop*), Austria/WAC 1 (*Daxbacher*)
Austria/WAC won 3-0 on penalties.
Moscow Dynamo 3 (*Gershkovich, Kazachenov, Maximenkov*), Betis 0
Anderlecht 3 (*Rensenbrink pen, Nielsen, Vercauteren*), Porto 0
Twente 4 (*Thijssen, Overweg, Gritter, Van der Vall*), Vejle 0

Semi-Finals, First Leg
Moscow Dynamo 2 (*Tseretli, Gershkovich*), Austria/WAC 1 (*Baumeister*)
Twente 0, Anderlecht 1 (*Nielsen*)

Semi-Finals, Second Leg
Anderlecht 2 (*Haan, Rensenbrink pen*), Twente 0
Austria/WAC 2 (*Pirkner pen, Morales*), Moscow Dynamo 1 (*Yakubik*)

Final 1977–78: Anderlecht 4, Austria/WAC 0
(In Paris, 3 May, 1978, 48,679)

Anderlecht: De Bree; Van Binst, Broos, Dusbaba, Thissen, Van der Elst, Haan, Nielsen, Coeck, Vercauteren (Dockx), Rensenbrink.

Austria/WAC: Baumgartner; Robert Sara, Josef Sara, Obermayer, Baumeister, Prohaska, Daxbacher (Martinez), Gasselich, Morales (Drazen), Pirkner, Parits.

Scorers: Anderlecht – Rensenbrink 2, Van Binst 2.

EUROPEAN CUP-WINNERS' CUP 1978–79

First Round, First Leg
Floriana 1 (*Xuereb R.*), Inter-Milan 3 (*Altobelli 3*)
Valur 1 (*Albertsson*), Magdeburg 1 (*Steinbach*)
Sporting Lisbon 0, Banik Ostrava 1 (*Antalik*)
Beveren 3 (*Albert, Stevens, Schonberger*), Ballymena 0
Ferencvaros 2 (*Nyilasi, Major*), Kalmar 0
Marek Stanke Dimitrov 3 (*Petrov V., Petrov I. 2*), Aberdeen 2 (*Jarvie, Harper*)
Barcelona 3 (*Krankl 2, Sanchez*), Shakhtor 0
PAOK Salonika 2 (*Karmanides, Sarafis*), Servette 0
Uni Craiova 3 (*Camataru 2, Crisan*), Fortuna Dusseldorf 4 (*Fanz 2, Allofs, Zimmermann*)
Zaglebie Sosnowiec 2 (*Zarichta, Starinskj*), SW Innsbruck 3 (*Peter Koncilia, Oberacher, Brasoler*)
AZ 67 0, Ipswich T 0
Apoel 0
Shamrock Rovers 2 (*Giles, Lynex*)
Rijeka 3 (*Tomic, Durkalic, Curkov*), Wrexham 0
Bodo Glimt 4 (*Solhang 2, Berg, Hanssen*), Union Luxembourg 1 (*Teitgen*)
Frem 2 (*Jacobsen, Hansen*), Nancy 0

First Round, Second Leg
Inter-Milan 5 (*Muraro 2, Fedele 2, Chierico*), Floriana 0
Magdeburg 4 (*Seguin, Steinbach, Hoffmann, Streich*), Valur 0
Banik Ostrava 1 (*Licka*), Sporting Lisbon 0
Ballymena 0, Beveren 3 (*Jansen 2, Wissmann*)
Kalmar 2 (*Magnusson, Nyberg*), Ferencvaros 2 (*Ebedli, Szokolai*)
Aberdeen 3 (*Strachan, Jarvie, Harper*), Marek Stanke Dimitrov 0
Shakhtor 1 (*Resnik*), Barcelona 1 (*Krankl*)
Servette 4 (*Pfister, Hamberg, Elia 2*), PAOK Salonika 0
Fortuna Dusseldorf 1 (*Bommer*), Uni Craiova 1 (*Marcu*)
SW Innsbruck 1 (*Koterva og*), Zaglebie Sosnowiec 1 (*Dvorczik*)
Ipswich T 2 (*Mariner, Wark*), AZ 67 0
Shamrock Rovers 1 (*Lynex*), Apoel 0
Wrexham 2 (*McNeil, Cartwright*), Rijeka 0
Union Luxembourg 1 (*Teitgen*), Bodo Glimt 0
Nancy 4 (*Curbelo, Jeannol 2, Zenier*), Frem 0

Second Round, First Leg
Servette 2 (*Hamberg, Barberis*), Nancy 1 (*Robio*)
Banik Ostrava 3 (*Knapp, Radimec, Rygel*), Shamrock Rovers 0
Ipswich T 1 (*Wark*), SW Innsbruck 0
Anderlecht 3 (*Van der Elst 2, Coeck*), Barcelona 0
Inter-Milan 5 (*Beccalossi, Altobelli 3, Muraro*), Bodo Glimt 0
Fortuna Dusseldorf 3 (*Gunther 2, Zimmermann*), Aberdeen 0
Rijeka 0, Beveren 0
Magdeburg 1 (*Streich*), Ferencvaros 0

Second Round, Second Leg
Nancy 2 (*Zenier, Umpierrez*), Servette 2 (*Elia, Schnyder*)
Shamrock Rovers 1 (*Giles*), Banik Ostrava 3 (*Licka 2, Albrecht*)
SW Innsbruck 1 (*Oberacher*), Ipswich T 1 (*Burley*)
Barcelona 3 (*Krankl, Heredia, Zuviria*), Anderlecht 0
Bodo Glimt 1 (*Hansen*), Inter-Milan 2 (*Altobelli, Scanziani*)
Aberdeen 2 (*McLelland, Jarvie*), Fortuna Dusseldorf 0
Beveren 2 (*Baecke 2*), Rijeka 0
Ferencvaros 2 (*Pusztai, Szokolai*), Magdeburg 1 (*Stachmann*)

Quarter-Finals, First Leg
Inter-Milan 0, Beveren 0
Fortuna Dusseldorf 0, Servette 0
Ipswich T 2 (*Gates 2*), Barcelona 1 (*Esteban*)
Magdeburg 2 (*Streich 2*), Banik Ostrava 1 (*Antalik*)

Quarter-Finals, Second Leg
Beveren 1 (*Stevens*), Inter-Milan 0
Servette 1 (*Andrey*), Fortuna Dusseldorf 1 (*Bommer*)
Barcelona 1 (*Migueli*), Ipswich T 0
Banik Ostrava 4 (*Rygel 2, Albrecht, Nemec*), Magdeburg 2 (*Sparwasser, Pommerenke*)

Semi-Finals, First Leg
Fortuna Dusseldorf 3 (*Klaus Allofs 2, Thomas Allofs*), Banik Ostrava 1 (*Nemec*)
Barcelona 1 (*Rexach pen*), Beveren 0

Semi-Finals, Second Leg
Banik Ostrava 2 (*Licka, Antalik*), Fortuna Dusseldorf 1 (*Zewe*)
Beveren 0, Barcelona 1 (*Krankl pen*)

Final 1978–79: Barcelona 4, Fortuna Dusseldorf 3 aet

(In Basle, 16 May, 1979)

Barcelona: Artola; Zuviria, Migueli, Costas (Martinez), Albaladejo (De la Cruz), Sanchez, Neeskens, Asensi, Rexach, Krankl, Carrasco.

Fortuna Dusseldorf: Daniel; Baltes, Zewe, Zimmermann (Lund), Brei (Weikl), Kohnen, Bommer, Schmitz, Thomas Allofs, Klaus Allofs, Seel.

Scorers: Barcelona – Sanchez, Asensi, Rexach, Krankl; Fortuna Dusseldorf – Klaus Allofs, Seel 2.

EUROPEAN CUP-WINNERS' CUP 1979–80

Preliminary Round, First Leg
Rangers 1 (*Smith*), Lillestrom 0
B 1903 6 (*Haarby, Larsen, Kristiansen 2, Thygesen 2*), Apoel 0

Preliminary Round, Second Leg
Lillestrom 0, Rangers 2 (*MacDonald A., Johnstone*)
Apoel 0, B 1903 1 (*Larsen*)

First Round, First Leg
Juventus 2 (*Pozsgai og, Cabrini*), Raba Gyor 0
Reipas Lahti 0, Aris Bonnevoi 1 (*Schlitz*)
Arka Gdynia 3 (*Kwiatkovski, Kornynt 2*), Stara Zagora 2 (*Petkov, Lipenski*)
Panionios 4 (*Liolios 2, Pafiakakis, Anastopoulos*), Twente Enschede 0
Innsbruck 1 (*Poell pen*), Lokomotiv Kosice 2 (*Strapek, Jacko*)
Rangers 2 (*MacDonald, McLean*), Fortuna Dusseldorf 1 (*Wenzel*)
Arsenal 2 (*Sunderland, Young*), Fenerbahce 0
B 1903 2 (*Thycosen, Hansen*), Valencia 2 (*Arias, Castellanos*)
Wrexham 3 (*McNeil, Fox, Buxton*), Magdeburg 2 (*Streich, Steinbach*)
IFK Gothenburg 1 (*Holmgren*), Waterford 0
Beerschot 0, Rijeka Fiume 0
Young Boys Berne 2 (*Zwygart, Schoenenberger*), Steaua Bucharest 2 (*Soica, Jordanescu*)
Sliema Wanderers 2 (*Tortell 2 pens*), Boavista 1 (*Eliseu*)
Cliftonville 0, Nantes 1 (*Rampillon*)
IA Akranes 0, Barcelona 1 (*Rexach*)

First Round, Second Leg
Raba Gyor 2 (*Furino og, Poczik*), Juventus 1 (*Causio*)
Aris Bonnevoi 1 (*Colling*), Reipas Lahti 0
Stara Zagora 2 (*Stoyanov, Petkov*), Arka Gdynia 0
Twente Enschede 3 (*Bos pen, Linstadt, Otto*), Panionios 1 (*Anastopoulos*)
Lokomotiv Kosice 1 (*Kozak*), Innsbruck 0
Fortuna Dusseldorf 0, Rangers 0
Fenerbahce 0, Arsenal 0
Valencia 4 (*Felman, Kempes 2, Saura*), B 1903 0
Magdeburg 5 (*Hoffman 2, Newes, Steinbach pen, Streich*), Wrexham 2 (*Vinter, Hill*)
Waterford 1 (*Keane*), IFK Gothenburg 1 (*Holmgren*)
Rijeka Fiume 2 (*Radovic 2*), Beerschot 1 (*Demushel*)
Steaua Bucharest 6 (*Mitu, Sames 2, Aelenei, Raducanu, Zahlu*), Young Boys Berne 0
Boavista 8 (*Ailten, Julio 3, Moinhos, Salvador, Folha, Oscar*), Sliema Wanderers 0
Nantes 7 (*Pecout 3, Trossero 2, Rampillon, Rio*), Cliftonville 0
Barcelona 5 (*Krankl, Simonsen, Rexach, Carrasco, Asensi*), IA Akranes 0

Second Round, First Leg
Stara Zagora 1 (*Stojanov pen*), Juventus 0
Panionios 1 (*Anastopoulos*), IFK Gothenburg 0
Lokomotiv Kosice 2 (*Kozak 2*), Rijeka Fiume 0
Valencia 1 (*Kempes*), Rangers 1 (*McLean*)
Nantes 3 (*Pecout 2, Toure*), Steaua Bucharest 2 (*Raducanu 2 [1 pen]*)
Arsenal 2 (*Young, Sunderland*), Magdeburg 1 (*Pommerenke*)
Aris Bonnevoi 1 (*Mattes*), Barcelona 4 (*Simonsen 3, Rexach*)
Dynamo Moscow 0, Boavista 0

Second Round, Second Leg
Juventus 3 (*Scirea, Causio, Verza*), Stara Zagora 0
IFK Gothenburg 2 (*Nordin, Holmgren*), Panionios 0
Rijeka Fiume 3 (*Desnica 3*), Lokomotiv Kosice 0
Rangers 1 (*Johnstone*), Valencia 3 (*Bonhof, Kempes2*)
Steaua Bucharest 1 (*Jordanescu*), Nantes 2 (*Pecout, Amisse*)
Magdeburg 2 (*Streich, Stahmann*), Arsenal 2 (*Rice, Brady*)
Barcelona 7 (*Krankl 3, Heredia 2, Carrasco, Canito*), Aris Bonnevoi 1 (*Tuliuv*)
Boavista 1 (*Moinhos*), Dynamo Moscow 1 (*Minaev*)

Quarter-Finals, First Leg
Rijeka Fiume 0, Juventus 0
Arsenal 5 (*Sunderland 2, Price, Brady, Young*), IFK Gothenburg 1 (*Nilsson*)
Barcelona 0, Valencia 1 (*Pablo*)
Dynamo Moscow 0, Nantes 2 (*Tusseau, Pecout*)

Quarter-Finals, Second Leg
Juventus 2 (*Causio, Bettega*), Rijeka Fiume 0
IFK Gothenburg 0, Arsenal 0
Valencia 4 (*Saura 2, Bonhof, Kempes pen*), Barcelona 3 (*Canito 2, Landaburu*)
Nantes 2 (*Michel, Toure*), Dynamo Moscow 3 (*Minaev, Gatzaiev, Kolessov*)

Semi-Finals, First Leg
Arsenal 1 (*Bettega og*), Juventus 1 (*Cabrini*)
Nantes 2 (*Baronchelli 2*), Valencia 1 (*Kempes*)

Semi-Finals, Second Leg
Juventus 0, Arsenal 1 (*Vaessen*)
Valencia 4 (*Bonhof, Michel og, Kempes 2 [1 pen]*), Nantes 0

Final 1979–80: Valencia 0, Arsenal 0 (aet)
Valencia won 5-4 on penalties.
(In Brussels, 14 May, 1980, 40,000)

Valencia: Pereira; Carrette, Botubot, Arias, Tendillo, Solsona, Saura, Bonhof, Kempes, Subirates (Castellanos), Pablo.
Arsenal: Jennings; Rice, Nelson, Talbot, O'Leary, Young, Brady, Sunderland, Stapleton, Price (Hollins), Rix.

EUROPEAN CUP-WINNERS' CUP 1980–81

Preliminary Round
Celtic 6 (*McGarvey 2, McCluskey 2, Nedder og, Sullivan*), Diosgyor 0
Diosgyor 2 (*Gorgey 2*), Celtic 1 (*Nicholas*)
Altay Izmir 0, Benfica 0
Benfica 4 (*Chalana, Humberto, Nene, Cesar*), Altay Izmir 0

First Round, First Leg
Newport Co 4 (*Gwyther, Moore, Aldridge, Bruton*), Crusaders 0
Spora Luxembourg 0, Sparta Prague 6 (*Berger 2, Kotek, Chalana, Chaloupka 2*)
Slavia Sofia 3 (*Tsvetkov pen, Velichkov 2*), Legia Warsaw 1 (*Miloszewisz*)
Castilla 3 (*Paco, Balin, Cidon*), West Ham U 1 (*Cross*)
Celtic 2 (*Nicholas 2*), Poli Timisoara 1 (*Adrian*)
Dynamo Zagreb 0, Benfica 0
Fortuna Dusseldorf 5 (*Kohnen 2, Wenzel, Klaus Allofs, Theis*), Austria Salzburg 0
Hibernians Malta 1 (*Xuereb P.*), Waterford 0
Ilves Tampere 1 (*Uimonen*), Feyenoord 3 (*Notten pen, Van Deinsen, Troost*)
Hvidovre 1 (*Steen Hansen pen*), Fram Reykjavik 0
Kastoria 0, Dynamo Tbilisi 0
Malmö 1 (*McKinnon*), Partizan Tirana 0
Omonia Nicosia 1 (*Kanaris*), Waterschei 3 (*Van Pouche, Janssen, Meds*)
Roma 3 (*Pruzzo, Ancelotti, Falcao*), Carl Zeiss Jena 0
Sion 1 (*Brigger*), Haugar 1 (*Osborne*)
Valencia 2 (*Kempes, Morena pen*), Monaco 0

First Round, Second Leg
Monaco 3 (*Petit 2, Barberis*), Valencia 3 (*Morena, Kempes, Felman*)
Benfica 2 (*Nene, Cesar*), Dynamo Zagreb 0
Haugar 2 (*Nilsen, Kristophersen pen*), Sion 0
Partizan Tirana 0, Malmö 0
Poli Timisoara 1 (*Paltinisan*), Celtic 0
Waterford 4 (*Kirk 2, Finucane, Fitzpatrick*), Hibernians Malta 0
Sparta Prague 6 (*Pospisil, Slany, Jarohm 2, Berger, Horvath*), Spora Luxembourg 0
Dynamo Tbilisi 2 (*Shengelia, Gutsayev*), Kastoria 0
Legia Warsaw 1 (*Okonski pen*), Slavia Sofia 0
Austria Salzburg 0, Fortuna Dusseldorf 3 (*Thomas Allofs, Dusend 2*)
West Ham U 5 (*Pike, Cross 3, Goddard*), Castilla 1 (*Bernal*)
Feyenoord 4 (*Vermaulen, Nielsen, Troost, Notten*), Ilves Tampere 2 (Prinen pen, Wacklin)
Waterschei 4 (*Janssen, Plessers pen, Van Poucke, Grundel*), Omonia Nicosia 0
Fram Reykjavik 0, Hvidovre 2 (*Ambrose, Hansen*)
Crusaders 0, Newport Co 0
Carl Zeiss Jena 4 (*Krause, Lindeman, Bielau 2*) Roma 0

Second Round, First Leg
Carl Zeiss Jena 3 (*Sengewald, Schnuphase pen, Trocha*), Valencia 1 (*Morena*)
Malmö 1 (*Andersson M.*), Benfica 0
Waterschei 0, Fortuna Dusseldorf 0
Feyenoord 2 (*Wijnstekers, Bouwens*), Hvidovre 1 (*Mannicke*)
Sparta Prague 2 (*Vkovjak 2*), Slavia Sofia 0
Waterford 0, Dynamo Tbilisi 1 (*Shengelia*)
Haugar 0, Newport Co 0
West Ham U 4 (*Bonds, Goddard, Stewart pen, Cross*), Poli Timisoara 0

Second Round, Second Leg
Newport Co 6 (*Gwyther, Lowndes, Aldridge, Tynan 2, Moore*), Haugar 0
Valencia 1 (*Botubot*), Carl Zeiss Jena 0
Poli Timisoara 1 (*Paltinisan*), West Ham U 0
Dynamo Tbilisi 4 (*Daraselia 2, Chivadze, Chilaia*), Waterford 0
Fortuna Dusseldorf 1 (*Bansemer*), Waterschei 0
Feyenoord 1 (*Nielsen*), Hvidovre 0
Slavia Sofia 3 (*Velitchkov, Jeliazkov, Tsvetkov*), Sparta Prague 0
Benfica 2 (*Nene 2*), Malmö 0

Quarter-Final, First Leg
West Ham U 1 (*Cross*), Dynamo Tbilisi 4 (*Chivadze, Gutsayev, Shengelia 2*)
Carl Zeiss Jena 2 (*Raab 2*), Newport Co 2 (*Tynan 2*)
Slavia Sofia 3 (*Tsvetkov 2 [1 pen], Aliev*), Feyenoord 2 (*Nielsen, Vermeulen pen*)
Fortuna Dusseldorf 2 (*Wenzel, Dusend*), Benfica 2 (*Carlos Manuel, Humberto*)

Quarter-Final, Second Leg
Feyenoord 4 (*Notten, Van Deinsen, Vermeulen, Bouwens*), Slavia Sofia 0
Benfica 1 (*Chalana*), Fortuna Dusseldorf 0
Dynamo Tbilisi 0, West Ham U 1 (*Pearson*)
Newport Co 0, Carl Zeiss Jena 1 (*Kurbjuweit*)

Semi-Final, First Leg
Carl Zeiss Jena 2 (*Bielau, Raab*), Benfica 0
Dynamo Tbilisi 3 (*Sulakvelidze 2, Gutsayev*), Feyenoord 0

Semi-Final, Second Leg
Benfica 1 (*Reinaldo*), Carl Zeiss Jena 0
Feyenoord 2 (*Bouwens, Notten pen*), Dynamo Tbilisi 0

Final 1980–81: Dynamo Tbilisi (0) 2, Carl Zeiss Jena (0) 1

(In Dusseldorf, 13 May, 1981, 9000)

Dynamo Tbilisi: Gabelia; Kostava, Chivadze, Khisanishvili, Tavadze, Svanadze (Kakilashvili), Sulakvelidze, Daraselia, Gutsayev, Kipiani, Shengelia.

Carl Zeiss Jena: Grapenthin; Brauer, Kurbjuweit, Schnuphase, Schilling, Hoppe (Overmann), Krause, Lindemann, Bielau (Topfer), Raab, Vogel.

Scorers: Dynamo Tbilisi – Gutsayev, Daraselia; Carl Zeiss Jena – Hoppe.

EUROPEAN CUP-WINNERS' CUP 1981–82

Preliminary Round
Poli Timisoara 2 (*Anghel, Nedelcu*), Lok Leipzig 0
Lok Leipzig 5 (*Baum, Moldt, Zoetzsche, Kuhn 2*), Poli Timisoara 0

First Round, First Leg
Ajax 1 (*Lerby*), Tottenham H 3 (*Falco 2, Villa*)
KTP 0, Bastia 0
Eintracht Frankfurt 2 (*Pezzey, Koerbel*), PAOK Salonika 0
Dynamo Tbilisi 2 (*Zhvania, Shengelia*), Grazer AK 0
Barcelona 4 (*Quini, Simonsen 2, Schuster*), Trakia Plovdiv 1 (*Slavkov*)
Swansea C 0, Lok Leipzig 1 (*Kinne*)
Valerengen 2 (*Jacobsen 2*), Legia Warsaw 2 (*Majevsky, Okonski*)
SKA Rostov 3 (*Varov 2, Andreyev*), Ankaragucu 0
Paralimni 1 (*Goumenos*), Vasas 0
Ballymena U 0, AS Roma 2 (*Chierico, Ancelotti*)
Lausanne 2 (*Parietti, Kok*), Kalmar 1 (*Magnusson*)
Jeunesse Esch 1 (*Scheichlev*), Velez 1 (*Mueahasanovic*)
Floriana 1 (*Aquilina*), Standard Liège 3 (*Meeuws, Voordeckers, Vandermissen*)
Fram 2 (*Torfarsson, Sveinjonsson*), Dundalk 1 (*Fairclough*)
Dukla Prague 3 (*Rada, Stambachr, Nehoda*), Glasgow Rangers 0
Vejle 2 (*Andersen, Gert*), Porto 1 (*Romero*)

First Round, Second Leg
Tottenham 3 (*Galvin, Falco, Ardiles*), Ajax 0
Bastia 5 (*Cazes, Ihily 2, Ponte, Milla*), KTP 0
PAOK Salonika 2 (*Kostikos 2*), Eintracht Frankfurt 0
Grazer AK 2 (*Riedl, Schicker*), Dynamo Tbilisi 2 (*Shengelia 2*)
Trakia Plovdiv 1 (*Slavkov*), Barcelona 0
Lok Leipzig 2 (*Kinne, Moldt*), Swansea C 1 (*Charles*)
Legia Warsaw 4 (*Baran, Adamczyk, Topoiskim, Milosevic*), Valerengen 1 (*Moen*)
Ankaragucu 0, SKA Rostov 2 (*Andreyev, Vanadiev*)
Vasas 8 (*Varadi 3, Kiss 2, Szebergyinszky, Iszo 2*), Paralimni 0
AS Roma 4 (*Spinosi, Pruzzo 2, Giovanelli*), Ballymena U 0
Kalmar 3 (*Ohllson 2, Persson*), Lausanne 2 (*Parietti, Kok*)
Velez 6 (*Okuka 2, Skocajic, Natijevic 2, Bajevic*), Jeunesse Esch 1 (*Scheitler*)
Standard Liège 9 (*Voordeckers 3, Plessers 2, Vandermissen, Tahamata, Haan, Meeuws*), Floriana 0
Dundalk 4 (*Flanagan pen, Fairclough, Lawlor, Dubb*), Fram 0
Glasgow Rangers 2 (*Bett, MacDonald*), Dukla Prague 1 (*Stambachr*)
Porto 3 (*Jaime 2, Sousa*), Vejle 0

Second Round, First Leg
Legia Warsaw 2 (*Adamczyk, Baran*), Lausanne 1 (*Kok*)
SKA Rostov 1 (*Yashin*), Eintracht Frankfurt 0
Dukla Prague 1 (*Kozak*), Barcelona 0
Porto 2 (*Walsh, Costa*), AS Roma 0
Dundalk 1 (*Fairclough*), Tottenham H 1 (*Crooks*)
Vasas 0, Standard Liège 2 (*Tahamata 2*)
Lok Leipzig 1 (*Zoetzsche*), Velez 1 (*Vukoje*)
Bastia 1 (*Milla*), Dynamo Tbilisi 1 (*Gutsayev*)

Second Round, Second Leg
Lausanne 1 (*Ley-Ravello*), Legia Warsaw 1 (*Baran*)
Eintracht Frankfurt 2 (*Pezzey, Lorant pen*), SKA Rostov 0
Barcelona 4 (*Moran, Sanchez, Alesanco, Schuster*), Dukla Prague 0
AS Roma 0, Porto 0
Tottenham H 1 (*Crooks*), Dundalk 0
Standard Liège 2 (*Voordeckers 2*), Vasas 0
Velez 1 (*Bajevic*), Lok Leipzig 1 (*Zotzsche pen*)
Dynamo Tbilisi 3 (*Shengelia 2, Sulakvelidze*), Bastia 1 (*Milla*)

Quarter-Finals, First Leg
Legia Warsaw 0, Dynamo Tbilisi 1 (*Sulakvelidze*)
Lok Leipzig 0, Barcelona 3 (*Quini, Moran, Simonsen*)
Standard Liège 2 (*Englebert, Gabriel og*), Porto 0
Tottenham H 2 (*Miller, Hazard*), Eintracht Frankfurt 0

Quarter-Finals, Second Leg
Barcelona 1 (*Moran*), Lok Leipzig 2 (*Schone, Bernschein*)
Dynamo Tbilisi 1 (*Shengelia*), Legia Warsaw 0
Eintract Frankfurt 2 (*Borchers, Cha Bum Kun*), Tottenham H 1 (*Hoddle*)
Porto 2 (*Jacques, Walsh*), Standard Liège 2 (*Lecloux, Vandermissen*)

Semi-Finals, First Leg
Tottenham H 1 (*Roberts*), Barcelona 1 (*Olmo*)
Dynamo Tbilisi 0, Standard Liège 1 (*Daerden*)

Semi-Finals, Second Leg
Barcelona 1 (*Simonsen*), Tottenham H 0
Standard Liège 1 (*Daerden*), Dynamo Tbilisi 0

Final 1981–82: Barcelona (1) 2, Standard Liège (1) 1
(In Barcelona, 12 May, 1982, 100,000)

Barcelona: Urruti; Gerardo, Migueli, Alescanco, Manolo, Sanchez, Moratalla, Esteban, Simonsen, Quini, Carrasco.

Standard Liège: Preud'homme; Gerets, Poel, Meeuws, Plessers, Vandermissen, Daerden, Haan, Botteron, Tahamata, Wendt.

Scorers: Barcelona – Simonsen, Quini; Standard Liège – Vandermissen.

EUROPEAN CUP-WINNERS' CUP 1982–83

Preliminary Round, First Leg
Aberdeen 7 (*Black 2, Strachan, Hewitt, Simpson, McGhee, Kennedy*), Sion 0
Swansea C 3 (*Charles 2, Cardoso og*), Braga 0

Preliminary Round, Second Leg
Sion 1 (*Bregy*), Aberdeen 4 (*Hewitt, Miller, McGhee 2*)
Braga 1 (*Marustik og*), Swansea C 0

First Round, First Leg
IBV Vestmannaeyjar 0, Lech Poznan 1 (*Partunski*)
Aberdeen 1 (*Hewitt*), Dinamo Tirana 0
Baia Mare 0, Real Madrid 0
Barcelona 8 (*Maradona 3, Schuster 2, Victor, Urbano, Alesanco*), Apollon Limassol 0
Coleraine 0, Tottenham H 3 (*Crooks 2, Archibald*)
Dynamo Dresden 3 (*Trautmann 2, Pilz*), BK Copenhagen 2 (*Francker, Madsen*)
Austria Vienna 2 (*Polster, Steinkogler*), Panathinaikos 0
Galataseray 2 (*Faith Rasit, Mustafa*), Kuuysi-69 1 (*Annunen*)
IFK Gothenburg 1 (*Stromberg*), Ujpest Dozsa 1 (*Kovacs J.*)
Inter-Milan 2 (*Altobelli, Sabato*), Slovan Bratislava 0
Lillestroem 0, Red Star Belgrade 4 (*Savic 2, Janjanin, Jovin*)
Limerick 1 (*Nolan*), AZ 67 Alkmaar 1 (*Jonker*)
Lokomotiv Sofia 1 (*Milanov*), Paris St Germain 0
Swansea C 12 (*Charles 2, Loveridge 2, Walsh 3, Irwin, Latchford, Hadziabdic, Rajkovic, Stevenson*), Sliema Wanderers 0
Torpedo Moscow 1 (*Petrakov*), Bayern Munich 1 (*Breitner*)
Waterschei 7 (*Gudmundsson 2, Berger 2, Pier Janssen, Vliegen, Copinx*), Red Boys Differdange 1 (*Di Domenico*)

First Round, Second Leg
Lech Poznan 3 (*Okonski 2, Niewiadowski*), IBV Vestmannaeyjar 0
Dinamo Tirana 0, Aberdeen 0
Real Madrid 5 (*Juanita, Isidro, Garcia Hernandez, Santillana, Metgod*), Baia Mare 2 (*Koller, Buzgau*)
Apollon Limassol 1 (*Christodoniou*), Barcelona 1 (*Moratalla*)
Tottenham H 4 (*Crooks, Mabbutt, Brooks, Gibson*), Coleraine 0
BK Copenhagen 2 (*Larsen, Madsen*), Dynamo Dresden 1 (*Pilz*)
Panathinaikos 2 (*Anastiasadis, Charalambidis*), Austria Vienna 1 (*Polster*)
Kuuysi-69 1 (*Kallio*), Galataseray 1 (*Hosic*)
Ujpest Dozsa 3 (*Kiss S. 2, Tirocsik*), IFK Gothenburg 1 (*Szendrei og*)
Slovan Bratislava 2 (*Takacs, Bobek*), Inter-Milan 1 (*Muller*)
Red Star Belgrade 3 (*Djurovski 2, Djuric*), Lillestroem 0
AZ 67 Alkmaar 1 (*Jonker*), Limerick 0
Paris St Germain 5 (*Toko 2, Bathenai, N'Gom, Lemouft*), Lokomotiv Sofia 1 (*Bogdanov*)
Sliema Wanderers 0, Swansea C 5 (*Curtis 2, Gale 2, Toshack*)
Bayern Munich 0, Torpedo Moscow 0
Red Boys Differdange 0, Waterschei 1 (*Janssen*)

Second Round, First Leg
Aberdeen 2 (*McGhee, Weir*), Lech Poznan 0
AZ 67 Alkmaar 1 (*Tiktak*), Inter-Milan 0
BK Copenhagen 0, Waterschei 2 (*Janssen R., Gudmundsson*)
Galataseray 2 (*Sejdic 2*), Austria Vienna 4 (*Polster 2, Steinkogler, Gasselich*)
Real Madrid 3 (*Santillana 2, Juanito*), Ujpest Dozsa 1 (*Kiss S.*)
Red Star Belgrade 2 (*Janjanin 2*), Barcelona 4 (*Maradona 2, Schuster 2*)
Swansea C 0, Paris St Germain 1 (*Toko*)
Tottenham H 1 (*Archibald*), Bayern Munich 1 (*Breitner*)

Second Round, Second Leg
Lech Poznan 0, Aberdeen 1 (*Bell*)
Inter-Milan 2 (*Juary, Altobelli*), AZ 67 Alkmaar 0
Waterschei 4 (*Janssen P., Plessers P., Gudmondsson, Vliegen*), BK Copenhagen 1 (*Dalsborg*)
Austria Vienna 0, Galataseray 1 (*Mustafa*)
Ujpest Dozsa 0, Real Madrid 1 (*Santillana*)
Barcelona 2 (*Schuster, Alesanco*), Red Star Belgrade 1 (*Djurovski*)
Paris St Germain 2 (*Kist, Fernandez*), Swansea C 0
Bayern Munich 4 (*Hoeness, Horsmann, Breitner, Rummenigge*), Tottenham H 1 (*Hughton*)

Quarter-Finals, First Leg
Bayern Munich 0, Aberdeen 0
Inter-Milan 1 (*Oriali*), Real Madrid 1 (*Gallego*)
Austria Vienna 0, Barcelona 0
Paris St Germain 2 (*Fernandez, Pilorget*), Waterschei 0

Quarter-Finals, Second Leg
Aberdeen 3 (*Simpson, McLeish, Hewitt*), Bayern Munich 2 (*Augenthaler, Pflugler*)
Real Madrid 3 (*Santillana 2, Juanito*), Austria Vienna 1 (*Juan Jose og*)
Barcelona 1 (*Alexanco*), Austria Vienna 1 (*Steinkogler*)
Waterschei 3 (*Gudmundsson, Janssen R., Janssen P.*), Paris St Germain 0

Semi-Final, First Leg
Austria Vienna 2 (*Polster, Magyar*), Real Madrid 2 (*Santillana, San Jose*)
Aberdeen 5 (*Black, Simpson, Weir, McGhee 2*), Waterschei 1 (*Gudmundsson*)

Semi-Final, Second Leg
Real Madrid 3 (*Santillana 3, Juanito*), Austria Vienna 1 (*Juan Jose og*)
Waterschei 1 (*Voordeckers*), Aberdeen 0

Final: Aberdeen (1) 2, Real Madrid (1) 1
Gothenburg 17,804

Aberdeen: Leighton; Rougvie, Miller, McLeish, McMaster, Cooper, Strachan, Simpson, Weir, McGhee, Black (Hewitt).

Real Madrid: Augustin; Metgod, Bonet, Camacho (San Jose), Juan Jose, Angel, Gallego, Stielike, Juanito, Santillana, Isidro (Salguero).

Scorers: Aberdeen – Black, Hewitt; Real Madrid: Juanito (pen).

Referee: Menegali.

EUROPEAN CUP-WINNERS' CUP 1982–83

PRELIMINARY ROUND, FIRST LEG

17 AUG

Swansea C (1) 3 *(Charles 2, Cardoso og)*

Sporting Braga (0) 0 10,641

Swansea C: Davies; Marustik, Hadziabdic, Irwin, Kennedy, Rajkovic, James R., James L., Charles, Stevenson (Thompson), Latchford (Walsh).
Sporting Braga: Helder; Artur, Cardoso, Nelito, Guedes, Serra, Oliveira, Paris, Gomes (Malheiro), Manoel, Santos.

18 AUG

Aberdeen (4) 7 *(Black 2, Stachan, Hewitt, Simpson, McGhee, Kennedy)*

Sion (0) 0 10,000

Aberdeen: Leighton; McMaster, Kennedy, Simpson, McLeish, Miller, Strachan, Black (Weir), McGhee, Bell (Rougvie), Hewitt.
Sion: Pittier; Valentini J. Y., Richard, Balet, Valentini P. A., Lopez, Bregy, Bernhard Karlen, Cernicky, Luisier (Cucinotta), Cina.

PRELIMINARY ROUND, SECOND LEG

25 AUG

Sporting Braga (0) 1 *(Marustik og)*

Swansea C (0) 0 18,000

Sporting Braga: Helder; Artur, Cardoso, Paris, Guedes, Serra, Oliveira, Spencer (Fontes), Manoel (Malheiro), Gomes, Santos.
Swansea C: Davies; Marustik, Hadziabdic, Irwin, Mahoney, Rajkovic, James L., James R., Charles, Stanley, Latchford.

1 SEPT

Sion (1) 1 *(Bregy)*

Aberdeen (1) 4 *(Hewitt, Miller, McGhee 2)* 2400

Sion: Pittier; Valentini J. Y., Richard, Moulin, Karlen L., Cernicky, Lopez, Luisier (Karlen B.), Bregy, Cucinotta, Cina (Tachet).
Aberdeen: Leighton; Cooper, Miller, Kennedy, McMaster, Stachan (Black), Bell (McLeish), Simpson, Hewitt, McGhee, Weir.

FIRST ROUND, FIRST LEG

15 SEPT

Aberdeen (1) 1 *(Hewitt)*

Dinamo Tirana (0) 0 14,000

Aberdeen: Leighton; Kennedy, McMaster, Bell (Cooper), Rougvie, Miller, Stachan, Simpson, McGhee, Hewitt, Weir.
Dinamo Tirana: Luarasi; Kugi, Bragu, Targei, Ruci, Xhafa, Gega, Canai, Zeri, Fagekugi, Dermorraii.

Coleraine (0) 0

Tottenham H (1) 3 *(Archibald, Crooks 2)* 12,000

Coleraine: Magee; McDowell, McNutt, O'Kane, Shannon, Mullan, Henry, Healy, McCoy, Dickson, McManus.
Tottenham H: Clemence; Hughton, Price, Lacy, Brooke, Perryman, Mabbutt, Archibald, Galvin, Villa, Crooks.

Swansea C (4) 12 *(Charles 2, Loveridge 2, Irwin, Latchford, Hadziabdic, Walsh 3, Rajkovic, Stevenson)*

Sliema Wanderers (0) 0 5130

Swansea C: Davies; Marustik, Hadziabdic, Irwin, Kennedy, Rajkovic, Loveridge (James L.), James R., Charles, Stevenson, Latchford (Walsh).
Sliema Wanderers: Zammit; Losco, Camilleri, Torrell, Schembri, Portelli, Caruana, Fabri, Tabone, Buttigieg, Aquilina.

FIRST ROUND, SECOND LEG

29 SEPT

Tottenham H (1) 4 *(Crookes, Mabbutt, Brooke, Gibson)*

Coleraine (0) 0 20,925

Tottenham H: Clemence (Parks); Hughton, Price, Lacy, Brooke, Perryman, Mabbutt, Hazard, Archibald, Villa, Crooks (Gibson).
Coleraine: Magee; McDowell, McNutt (McCready), O'Kane, Shannon, Mullan, Henry, Healy, McCoy, Dickson (Allun), McManus.

Dinamo Tirana (0) 0

Aberdeen (0) 0 25,000

Dinamo Tirana: Luarasi; Dautaj, Pargaj, Gegaj, Kuqi, Petoruci, Dalia, Marko, Zeri, Canaj, Demelari.
Aberdeen: Leighton; Kennedy, Cooper, Rougvie, McLeish, Miller, Strachan, Simpson, McGhee, Bell, Weir.

Sliema Wanderers (0) 0

Swansea C (3) 5 *(Curtis 2, Gale 2, Toshack)* 2000

Sliema Wanderers: Zammit; Theuma, Cancelleri, Losco, Schembri, Portelli, Buttigieg, Fabri, Tortell, Aquilina, Onemo.
Swansea C: Sander; Lewis, Hadziabdic, Charles, Kennedy, Thompson, Curtis (Toshack), Stanley, Gale, Marustik, Loveridge.

SECOND ROUND, FIRST LEG

20 OCT

Aberdeen (0) 2 *(McGhee, Weir)*

Lech Poznan (0) 0 18,000

Aberdeen: Leighton; Cooper, McMaster, Bell, McLeish, Miller, Strachan, Simpson, McGhee, Black, Weir.
Lech Poznan: Płesnierowicz; Pawlik, Szewczyk, Adamiec, Barczak, Strugarek, Kupcewicz, Oblewski, Malek, Okonski, Bukowski.

Swansea C (0) 0

Paris Saint-Germain (0) 1 *(Toko)* 9505

Swansea C: Davies; Hadziabdic, Kennedy R., Stevenson, Marustik (James L.), Lewis, Mahoney, James R., Curtis, Latchford (Walsh), Stanley.
Paris St Germain: Baratelli; Fernandez, Pilorget, Bathenay, Guillochon, Lemoult, Zaremba, Ardiles, Dahleb, Toko, Kist.

Tottenham H (1) 1 *(Archibald)*

Bayern Munich (0) 1 *(Breitner)* 36,488

Tottenham H: Clemence; Price, Miller, Lacy, O'Reilly (Gibson), Hazard, Brooke, Villa, Mabbutt, Archibald (Falco), Crooks.
Bayern Munich: Pfaff; Martin, Augenthaler, Grobe, Horsmann, Dremmler, Kraus, Breitner, Dürnberger, Hoeness, Rummenigge.

SECOND ROUND, SECOND LEG

3 NOV

Bayern Munich (1) 4 *(Hoeness, Horsmann, Breitner, Rummenigge)*

Tottenham H (0) 1 *(Hughton)* 50,000

Bayern Munich: Pfaff; Augenthaler, Dremmler, Grobe, Horsmann, Kraus, Breitner, Dürnberger, Del'Haye, Hoeness, Rummenigge.
Tottenham H: Clemence; Hughton, Price, Miller (Perryman), Lacy, Hazard, Mabbutt, Brooke (Hoddle), Villa, Archibald, Crooks.

Lech Poznan (0) 0

Aberdeen (0) 1 *(Bell)* 33,000

Lech Poznan: Plesnierowicz; Barczak, Szewczyk (Krzyzanowski), Adamiec, Pawlak, Malek, Oblewski (Stroinski), Kupcewicz, Okonski, Bak, Niewiadomski.
Aberdeen: Leighton; Kennedy, Rougvie, McMaster (Cooper), McLeish, Miller, Strachan, Simpson, McGhee, Weir, Bell.

Paris St Germain (1) 2 *(Kist, Fernandez)*

Swansea C (0) 0 50,000

Paris St Germain: Baratelli; Col, Piloret, Bathenay, Guillochon, Lemoult, Zaremba, Fernandez, Dahleb, Toko, Kist (N'Gom).
Swansea C: Davies; Hadziabdic (Lewis), Stevenson, Rajkovic, Stanley, James R., Charles, Mahoney, James L., Latchford (Walsh), Curtis.

Mark McGhee scores Aberdeen's fifth goal in their European Cup-Winners' Cup semi-final first leg rout of Waterschei.

ENGLISH CLUBS ECLIPSED

The UEFA Cup is a colourful, interesting competition, but our foursome received humiliating defeats in the very first round. I cannot use a kinder word, after all it is quite unusual that such a formidable foursome as Arsenal, Manchester United, Ipswich and Southampton should be beaten by Russian, Spanish, Italian and Swedish opposition at the very first hurdle. Arsenal were actually leading 2-0 in the first leg of their match against Spartak Moscow, but lost 3-2. With two away goals in the bag, it seemed an easy task to equalise that deficit, but in the return leg at Highbury, the Russians scored first. Arsenal foolishly threw caution to the wind, and began to attack with ten men. The Russians defended well, their counter-attacks were deadly, and finally won 5-2 for a devastating 8-4 aggregate. Manchester United faced a ruthless Valencia side at Old Trafford. The Spaniards anti-football antics were not controlled or punished sufficiently by an ineffective referee – they got away with more than just a 0-0 scoreline. In Valencia, United took the lead, but they didn't defend very well and eventually lost 2-1. Ipswich had a miserable night in Rome and they lost 3-0 against the local team in the first leg. In the return match, they played much better, scored three times, which is not a mean achievement against any Italian team, but conceded an all-important 'away goal', and AS Roma were through to the next round. Southampton played very poorly at home against the modest Norrkopping, and couldn't do better than draw 2-2. At home, the Swedes were defending manfully, and a 0-0 draw meant that no English teams were left in this competition.

Once again it was left to a Scottish club to carry the British flag, and Dundee United travelled as far as the quarter-finals. Their victims were the good class PSV Eindhoven (3-1), Viking Stavangar (3-1) and Werder Bremen (3-2). Eventually they failed against Bohemians Prague by a solitary goal conceded in Czechoslovakia. In the meantime, Benfica and Anderlecht were making their way to the final. Benfica, the eventual Portuguese champions, didn't lose a single match in their quest for a place, and Anderlecht accounted for PS Kuopio, Porto, Sarajevo, Valencia and Bohemians Prague.

The two-legged final was a closely fought affair, the Belgians managed to win the first match at home 1-0, and with some clever football, they fought to a 1-1 draw in Lisbon. So, the previous winners of the Cup-Winners' Cup are able to house the UEFA Cup in their boardroom for a year as well.

EUROPEAN FAIRS CUP FINALS 1958–71

1958 Barcelona 8, London 2*
1960 Barcelona 4, Birmingham C 1*
1961 AS Roma 4, Birmingham C 2*
1962 Valencia 7, Barcelona 3*
1963 Valencia 4, Dynamo Zagreb 1*
1964 Real Zaragoza 2, Valencia 1
1965 Ferencvaros 1, Juventus 0
1966 Barcelona 4, Real Zaragoza 3*
1967 Dynamo Zagreb 2, Leeds U 0*
1968 Leeds U 1, Ferencvaros 0*
1969 Newcastle U 6, Ujpest Dozsa 2*
1970 Arsenal 4, Anderlecht 3*
1971 Leeds U 3, Juventus 3*
(*Leeds won on away goals*)

UEFA CUP FINALS 1972–83

1972 Tottenham H 3, Wolverhampton W 2*
1973 Liverpool 3, Bor Moenchengladbach 2*
1974 Feyenoord 4, Tottenham H 2*
1975 Bor Moenchengladbach 5, Twente Enschede 1*
1976 Liverpool 4, FC Bruges 3*
1977 Juventus 2, Athletic Bilbao 2*
(*Juventus won on away goals*)
1978 PSV Eindhoven 3, Bastia 0*
1979 Bor Moenchengladbach 2, Red Star Belgrade 1*
1980 Eintracht Frankfurt 3, Bor Moenchengladbach 3*
(*Eintracht Frankfurt won on away goals*)
1981 Ipswich T 5, AZ 67 Alkmaar 4*
1982 IFK Gothenburg 4, SV Hamburg 0*
1983 Anderlecht 2, Benfica 1*

**Aggregate scores*

FAIRS & UEFA CUP HISTORY

FAIRS CUP 1955–58

Group A
Barcelona 6, Copenhagen 2
Copenhagen 1, Barcelona 1
Vienna withdrew

	P	W	D	L	F	A	Pts
Barcelona	2	1	1	0	7	3	3
Copenhagen	2	0	1	1	3	7	1

Group B
Inter-Milan 0, Birmingham C 0
Zagreb 0, Birmingham C 1
Zagreb 0, Inter-Milan 1
Birmingham C 3, Zagreb 0
Inter-Milan 4, Zagreb 0
Birmingham C 2, Inter-Milan 1

	P	W	D	L	F	A	Pts
Birmingham C	4	3	1	0	6	1	7
Inter-Milan	4	2	1	1	6	2	5
Zagreb	4	0	0	4	0	9	0

Group C
Leipzig 6, Lausanne 3
Lausanne 7, Leipzig 3
Cologne withdrew

	P	W	D	L	F	A	Pts
Lausanne	2	1	0	1	10	9	2
Leipzig	2	1	0	1	9	10	2

Group D
Basle 0, London 5
London 3, Frankfurt 2
London 1, Basle 0
Frankfurt 5, Basle 1
Frankfurt 1, London 0
Basle 6, Frankfurt 2

	P	W	D	L	F	A	Pts
London	4	3	0	1	9	3	6
Frankfurt	4	2	0	2	10	10	4
Basle	4	1	0	3	7	13	2

Semi-Final

Birmingham C v Barcelona (5-6)	4-3, 0-1, 1-2
Lausanne v London (2-3)	2-1, 0-2

Final

London v Barcelona (2-8)	**2-2, 0-6**

FAIRS CUP 1958–60

First Round

Basle v Barcelona (3-7)	1-2, 2-5
Inter-Milan v Lyon (8-1)	7-0, 1-1
Belgrade v Lausanne (11-4)	6-1, 5-3
Frem Copenhagen v Chelsea (2-7)	1-3, 1-4
Union St Gilloise v Leipzig (6-1)	6-0, 0-1
Hanover 96 v AS Roma (2-4)	1-3, 1-1
Zagreb v Ujpest Dozsa (4-3)	4-2, 0-1
Cologne v Birmingham C (2-4)	2-2, 0-2

Quarter-Final

Barcelona v Inter-Milan (8-2)	4-0, 4-2
Chelsea v Belgrade (2-4)	1-0, 1-4
Union St Gilloise v AS Roma (3-1)	2-0, 1-1
Birmingham C v Zagreb (4-3)	1-0, 3-3

Semi-Final

Belgrade v Barcelona (2-4)	1-1, 1-3
Union St Gilloise v Birmingham C (4-8)	2-4, 2-4

Final

Birmingham C v Barcelona (1-4)	**0-0, 1-4**

FAIRS CUP 1960–61

First Round

Union St Gilloise v AS Roma (1-4)	0-0, 1-4
Lyon v Cologne (3-4)	1-3, 2-1
Lausanne v Hibernian (0-2)	0-2
Lausanne withdrew after first leg.	
Zagreb v Barcelona (4-5)	1-1, 3-4
Leipzig v Belgrade (6-8)	5-2, 1-4, 0-2
Inter-Milan v Hanover 96 (14-3)	8-2, 6-1
Copenhagen v Basle (11-4)	8-1, 3-3
Birmingham C v Ujpest Dozsa (5-3)	3-2, 2-1

Quarter-Final

Cologne v AS Roma (3-6)	0-2, 2-0, 1-4
Barcelona v Hibernian (6-7)	4-4, 2-3
Inter-Milan v Belgrade (5-1)	5-0, 0-1
Copenhagen v Birmingham C (4-9)	4-4, 0-5

Semi-Final

Hibernian v AS Roma (5-11)	2-2, 3-3, 0-6
Inter-Milan v Birmingham C (2-4)	1-2, 1-2

Final

Birmingham C v AS Roma (2-4)	**2-2, 0-2**

FAIRS CUP 1961–62

First Round

Valencia v Nottingham F (7-1)	2-0, 5-1
Lausanne	bye
Cologne v Inter-Milan (7-9)	4-2, 0-2, 3-5
Union St Gilloise v Hearts (1-5)	1-3, 0-2
Spartak Brno v Leipzig (3-6)	2-2, 1-4
Strasbourg v MTK Budapest (3-13)	1-3, 2-10
AC Milan v Novisad (0-2)	0-0, 0-2
Iraklis Salonika	bye
Basle v Red Star Belgrade (2-5)	1-1, 1-4
Hibernian v Belenenses (6-4)	3-3, 3-1
Hanover 96 v Espanol (0-3)	0-1, 0-2
Birmingham C	bye
Lyon v Sheffield W (6-7)	4-2, 2-5
AS Roma	bye
Copenhagen v Dynamo Zagreb (4-9)	2-7, 2-2
West Berlin v Barcelona (1-3)	1-0, 0-3

Second Round

Lausanne v Valencia (3-4)	3-4
Second leg not played.	
Hearts v Inter-Milan (0-5)	0-1, 0-4
MTK Budapest v Leipzig (5-3)	3-0, 0-3, 2-0
Iraklis Salonika v Novisad (3-10)	2-1, 1-9
Red Star Belgrade v Hibernian (5-0)	4-0, 1-0
Espanol v Birmingham C (5-3)	5-2, 0-1
Sheffield W v AS Roma (4-1)	4-0, 0-1
Barcelona v Dynamo Zagreb (7-3)	5-1, 2-2

Quarter-Final

Valencia v Inter-Milan (5-3)	2-0, 3-3
Novisad v MTK Budapest (2-6)	1-4, 1-2
Espanol v Red Star Belgrade (2-6)	2-1, 0-5
Sheffield W v Barcelona (3-4)	3-2, 0-2

Semi-Final

Valencia v MTK Budapest (10-3)	3-0, 7-3
Red Star Belgrade v Barcelona (1-6)	0-2, 1-4

Final

Valencia v Barcelona (7-3)	**6-2, 1-1**

FAIRS CUP 1962–63

First Round

Valencia v Celtic (6-4)	4-2, 2-2
Everton v Dunfermline Ath (1-2)	1-0, 0-2
Hibernian v Copenhagen (7-2)	4-0, 3-2
DOS Utrecht v Tasmania Berlin (5-3)	3-2, 2-1
Altay Izmir v AS Roma (3-13)	2-3, 1-10
Glentoran v Real Zaragoza (2-8)	0-2, 2-6
Rapid Vienna v Red Star Belgrade (1-2)	1-1, 0-1
Barcelona v Belenenses (5-4)	1-1, 1-1, 3-2
Viktoria Cologne v Ferencvaros (5-7)	4-3, 1-4
Sampdoria v Aris Luxembourg (3-0)	1-0, 2-0
Petrolul Ploesti v Spartak Brno (4-3)	4-2, 0-1
Vojvodina v Leipzig (1-2)	1-0, 0-2
Basle v Bayern Munich (0-3)	0-3
Second leg not played.	
Drumcondra v Odense BK 09 (6-5)	4-1, 2-4
Marseille v Union St Gilloise (3-4)	1-0, 2-4
Porto v Dynamo Zagreb (1-2)	1-2, 0-0

Second Round

Valencia v Dunfermline Ath (7-6)	4-0, 2-6, 1-0
DOS Utrecht v Hibernian (1-3)	0-1, 1-2
Real Zaragoza v AS Roma (3-6)	2-4, 1-2
Red Star Belgrade v Barcelona (4-3)	3-2, 0-1, 1-0
Sampdoria v Ferencvaros (1-6)	1-0, 0-6
Petrolul Ploesti v Leipzig (2-1)	1-0, 0-1, 1-0
Bayern Munich v Drumcondra (6-1)	6-0, 0-1
Dynamo Zagreb v Union St Gilloise (5-4)	2-1, 0-1, 3-2

Quarter-Final

Valencia v Hibernian (6-2)	5-0, 1-2
AS Roma v Red Star Belgrade (3-2)	3-0, 0-2
Ferencvaros v Petrolul Ploesti (2-1)	2-0, 0-1
Bayern Munich v Dynamo Zagreb (1-4)	1-4, 0-0

Semi-Final

Valencia v AS Roma (3-1)	3-0, 0-1
Ferencvaros v Dynamo Zagreb (1-3)	0-1, 1-2

Final

Dynamo Zagreb v Valencia (1-4)	**1-2, 0-2**

FAIRS CUP 1963–64

First Round

Real Zaragoza v Iraklis Salonika (9-1)	3-0, 6-1
Lausanne v Hearts (9-8)	2-2, 4-4, 3-2
Atlético Madrid v Porto (2-1)	2-1, 0-0
Juventus v OFK Belgrade (4-3)	2-1, 1-2, 1-0
Aris Luxembourg v Liège (0-2)	0-2, 0-0
Staevnet Copenhagen v Arsenal (4-9)	1-7, 3-2
Glentoran v Partick T (1-7)	1-4, 0-3
Spartak Brno v Servette Geneva (7-1)	5-0, 2-1
Cologne v La Gantoise (4-2)	3-1, 1-1
DOS Utrecht v Sheffield W (2-8)	1-4, 1-4
Hertha Berlin v AS Roma (1-5)	1-3, 0-2
Tresnjevka Zagreb v Belenenses (1-4)	0-2, 1-2
Ujpest Dozsa v Lokomotiv Leipzig (3-2)	0-0, 3-2
Red Flag Brasov v Lokomotiv Plovdiv (2-5)	1-3, 1-2
Rapid Vienna v Racing Club de Paris (4-2)	1-0, 3-2
Shamrock Rovers v Valencia (2-3)	0-1, 2-2

Second Round

Lausanne v Real Zaragoza (1-5)	1-2, 0-3
Juventus v Atlético Madrid (3-1)	1-0, 2-1
Arsenal v Liège (2-4)	1-1, 1-3
Partick T v Spartak Brno (3-6)	3-2, 0-4
Cologne v Sheffield W (5-3)	3-2, 2-1
AS Roma v Belenenses (3-1)	2-1, 1-0
Ujpest Dozsa v Lokomotiv Plovdiv (3-1)	0-0, 3-1
Rapid Vienna v Valencia (2-3)	0-0, 2-3

Quarter-Final

Real Zaragoza v Juventus (3-2)	3-2, 0-0
Liège v Spartak Brno (3-2)	2-0, 0-2, 1-0
AS Roma v Cologne (3-5)	3-1, 0-4
Valencia v Ujpest Dozsa (6-5)	5-2, 1-3

Semi-Final

Liège v Real Zaragoza (2-4)	1-0, 1-2, 0-2
Valencia v Cologne (4-3)	4-1, 0-2

Final (at Barcelona)

Real Zaragoza v Valencia	**2-1**

FAIRS CUP 1964–65

First Round

Union St Gilloise v Juventus (0-2)	0-1, 0-1
Betis v Stade Français (1-3)	1-1, 0-2
Goztepe Izmir v Petrolul Ploesti (1-3)	1-2, 0-1
Vojvodina v Lokomotiv Plovdiv (2-4)	1-1, 1-1, 0-2
KB Copenhagen v DOS Utrecht (4-6)	3-4, 1-2
Valencia v Liège (2-4)	1-1, 1-3
Belenenses v Shelbourne (2-3)	1-1, 0-0, 1-2
Servette Geneva v Atlético Madrid (3-8)	2-2, 1-6
Basle v Spora Luxembourg (2-1)	2-0, 0-1
Strasbourg v AC Milan (2-1)	2-0, 0-1
Barcelona v Fiorentina (2-1)	0-1, 2-0
Leixoes v Celtic (1-4)	1-1, 0-3
Borussia Dortmund v Bordeaux (4-3)	4-1, 0-2
Manchester U v Djurgaarden (7-2)	1-1, 6-1
Eintracht Frankfurt v Kilmarnock (4-5)	3-0, 1-5
Valerengen v Everton (4-9)	2-5, 2-4
Atlético Bilbao v OFK Belgrade (4-2)	2-2, 2-0
Hertha Berlin v Antwerp (2-3)	2-1, 0-2
Odense BK 13 v Stuttgart (1-4)	1-3, 0-1
Dunfermline Ath v Oergryte (4-2)	4-2, 0-0
Dynamo Zagreb v Graz (9-2)	3-2, 6-0
Aris Salonika v AS Roma (0-3)	0-0, 0-3
Wiener SK v Lokomotiv Leipzig (3-1)	2-1, 1-0
Ferencvaros v Spartak Brno (2-1)	2-0, 0-1

Second Round

Stade Français v Juventus (0-1)	0-0, 0-1
Petrolul Ploesti v Lokomotiv Plovdiv (1-2)	1-0, 0-2
DOS Utrecht v Liège (0-4)	0-2, 0-2
Shelbourne v Atlético Madrid (0-2)	0-1, 0-1
Basle v Strasbourg (2-6)	0-1, 2-5
Barcelona v Celtic (3-1)	3-1, 0-0
Borussia Dortmund v Manchester U (1-10)	1-6, 0-4
Kilmarnock v Everton (1-6)	0-2, 1-4
Atlético Bilbao v Antwerp (3-0)	2-0, 1-0
Dunfermline Ath v Stuttgart (1-0)	1-0, 0-0
Dynamo Zagreb v AS Roma (1-2)	1-1, 0-1
Ferencvaros v Wiener SK (4-2)	0-1, 2-1, 2-0

Third Round

Juventus v Lokomotiv Plovdiv (4-3)	1-1, 1-1, 2-1
Liège v Atlético Madrid (1-2)	1-0, 0-2
Strasbourg v Barcelona (2-2)	0-0, 2-2, 0-0
Strasbourg won on toss of coin.	
Manchester U v Everton (3-2)	1-1, 2-1
Atlético Bilbao v Dunfermline Ath (3-2)	1-0, 0-1, 2-1
AS Roma v Ferencvaros (1-3)	1-2, 0-1

Quarter-Final

Byes: Juventus, Atlético Madrid

Strasbourg v Manchester U (0-5)	0-5, 0-0
Ferencvaros v Atlético Bilbao (5-2)	1-0, 1-2, 3-0

Semi-Final

Atlético Madrid v Juventus (5-7)	3-1, 1-3, 1-3
Manchester U v Ferencvaros (4-5)	3-2, 0-1, 1-2

Final (in Turin)

Juventus v Ferencvaros	**0-1**

FAIRS CUP 1965–66

First Round

Byes: Hanover 96, Espanol, Red Flag Brasov, Goztepe Izmir, Servette Geneva, CUF, Lokomotiv Leipzig, Basle, Aris Salonika, Ujpest Dozsa, Dunfermline Ath, KB Copenhagen, Hearts, Valerengen, Shamrock Rovers, Real Zaragoza.

DOS Utrecht v Barcelona (1-7)	0-0, 1-7
Antwerp v Glentoran (4-3)	1-0, 3-3
Stade Français v Porto (0-1)	0-0, 0-1
Bordeaux v Sporting Lisbon (1-10)	0-4, 1-6
Liège v Dynamo Zagreb (1-2)	1-0, 0-2
Munich 1860 v Malmö FF (7-1)	4-1, 3-0
AIK Stockholm v Daring (3-1)	3-1, 0-0
AC Milan* v Strasbourg (3-3)	1-0, 1-2, 1-1
Wiener SK v PAOK Salonika (7-2)	6-0, 1-2
Chelsea v AS Roma (4-1)	4-1, 0-0
Leeds U v Torino (2-1)	2-1, 0-0
Hibernian v Valencia (2-5)	2-0, 0-2, 0-3
US Luxembourg v Cologne (0-17)	0-4, 0-13
Nuremberg v Everton (1-2)	1-1, 0-1
Red Star Belgrade v Fiorentina (1-7)	0-4, 1-3
Spartak Brno v Lokomotiv Plovdiv (2-1)	2-0, 0-1

Second Round

Antwerp v Barcelona (2-3)	2-1, 0-2
Hanover 96 v Porto (6-2)	5-0, 1-2
Sporting Lisbon v Espanol (6-7)	2-1, 3-4, 1-2
Dynamo Zagreb v Red Flag Brasov (2-3)	2-2, 0-1
Goztepe Izmir v Munich 1860 (3-10)	2-1, 1-9
AIK Stockholm v Servette Geneva (3-5)	2-1, 1-4
CUF v AC Milan (2-3)	2-0, 0-2, 0-1
Wiener SK v Chelsea (1-2)	1-0, 0-2
Lokomotiv Leipzig v Leeds U (1-2)	1-2, 0-0
Basle v Valencia (2-8)	1-3, 1-5
Aris Salonika v Cologne (2-3)	2-1, 0-2
Ujpest Dozsa v Everton (4-2)	3-0, 1-2
Dunfermline Ath v KB Copenhagen (9-2)	5-0, 4-2
Fiorentina v Spartak Brno (2-4)	2-0, 0-4
Hearts v Valerengen (4-1)	1-0, 3-1
Shamrock Rovers v Real Zaragoza (2-3)	1-1, 1-2

Third Round

Hanover 96 v Barcelona* (3-3)	2-1, 0-1, 1-1
Espanol v Red Flag Brasov (6-5)	3-1, 2-4, 1-0
Servette Geneva v Munich 1860 (2-5)	1-1, 1-4
AC Milan v Chelsea* (4-4)	2-1, 1-2, 1-1
Leeds U v Valencia (2-1)	1-1, 1-0
Cologne v Ujpest Dozsa (3-6)	3-2, 0-4
Dunfermline Ath v Spartak Brno (2-0)	2-0, 0-0
Hearts v Real Zaragoza (5-6)	3-3, 2-2, 0-1

Quarter-Final

Barcelona v Espanol (2-0)	1-0, 1-0
Munich 1860 v Chelsea (2-3)	2-2, 0-1
Leeds U v Ujpest Dozsa (5-2)	4-1, 1-1
Dunfermline Ath v Real Zaragoza (3-4)	1-0, 2-4

Semi-Final

Barcelona v Chelsea (7-2)	2-0, 0-2, 5-0
Real Zaragoza v Leeds U (5-3)	1-0, 1-2, 3-1

Final

Barcelona v Real Zaragoza (4-3)	**0-1, 4-2**

**Won on toss after extra time.*

EUROPEAN FAIRS CUP 1966–67

First Round

Byes: Leeds U, DWS Amsterdam, WBA, Sparta Prague, Liège, Benfica, Spartak Plovdiv, Kilmarnock, La Gantoise, Hvidovre, Lausanne, Odense BK 09, Vitoria Setubal, Dundee U, Barcelona, Toulouse.

Nuremberg v Valencia (1-4)	1-2, 0-2
Red Star Belgrade v Atlético Bilbao (5-2)	5-0, 0-2
DOS Utrecht v Basle (4-3)	2-1, 2-2
Bologna v Goztepe Izmir (5-2)	2-1, 3-1
Djurgaarden v Lokomotiv Leipzig (2-5)	1-3, 1-2
US Luxembourg v Antwerp (0-2)	0-1, 0-1
Porto v Bordeaux* (3-3)	2-1, 1-2
Drumcondra v Eintracht Frankfurt (1-8)	0-2, 1-6
Nice v Oergryte (3-4)	2-2, 1-2
Olympia Ljubljana v Ferencvaros (3-6)	3-3, 0-3
Stuttgart v Burnley (1-3)	1-1, 0-2
Wiener SK v Napoli (2-5)	1-2, 1-3
Juventus v Aris Salonika (7-0)	5-0, 2-0
Dynamo Pitesti v Seville (4-2)	2-0, 2-2
Frigg Oslo v Dunfermline Ath (2-6)	1-3, 1-3
Spartak Brno v Dynamo Zagreb* (2-2)	0-2, 2-0

Second Round

DWS Amsterdam v Leeds U (2-8)	1-3, 1-5
Valencia v Red Star Belgrade (3-1)	1-0, 2-1
WBA v DOS Utrecht (6-3)	5-2, 1-1
Sparta Prague v Bologna (3-4)	2-2, 1-2
Liège v Lokomotiv Leipzig (1-2)	0-0, 1-2
Spartak Plovdiv v Benfica (1-4)	1-1, 0-3
Antwerp v Kilmarnock (2-8)	0-1, 2-7
La Gantoise v Bordeaux (1-0)	1-0, 0-0
Eintracht Frankfurt v Hvidovre (7-3)	5-1, 2-2
Oergryte v Ferencvaros (1-7)	0-0, 1-7
Lausanne v Burnley (1-8)	1-3, 0-5
Odense BK 09 v Napoli (2-6)	1-4, 1-2
Juventus v Vitoria Setubal (5-1)	3-1, 2-0
Barcelona v Dundee U (1-4)	1-2, 0-2
Toulouse v Dynamo Pitesti (4-5)	3-0, 1-5
Dunfermline Ath v Dynamo Zagreb† (4-4)	4-2, 0-2

Third Round

Leeds U v Valencia (3-1)	1-1, 2-0
Bologna v WBA (6-1)	3-0, 3-1
Lokomotiv Leipzig v Benfica (4-3)	3-1, 1-2
Kilmarnock v La Gantoise (3-1)	1-0, 2-1
Eintracht Frankfurt v Ferencvaros (5-3)	4-1, 1-2
Burnley v Naples (3-0)	3-0, 0-0
Juventus v Dundee U (3-1)	3-0, 0-1
Dynamo Pitesti v Dynamo Zagreb (0-1)	0-1, 0-0

Quarter-Final

Bologna v Leeds U* (1-1)	1-0, 0-1
Lokomotiv Leipzig v Kilmarnock (1-2)	1-0, 0-2
Eintracht Frankfurt v Burnley (3-2)	1-1, 2-1
Juventus v Dynamo Zagreb (2-5)	2-2, 0-3

Semi-Final

Leeds U v Kilmarnock (4-2)	4-2, 0-0
Eintracht Frankfurt v Dynamo Zagreb (3-4)	3-0, 0-4

Final

Dynamo Zagreb v Leeds U (2-0) — 2-0, 0-0

**Won on toss of coin.* †*Won on away goals rule.*

EUROPEAN FAIRS CUP 1967–68

First Round

Spora Luxembourg v Leeds U (0-16)	0-9, 0-7
PAOK Salonika v Liège (2-5)	0-2, 2-3
Wiener SK v Atlético Madrid (3-7)	2-5, 1-2
St Patrick's Athletic v Bordeaux (4-9)	1-3, 3-6
DOS Utrecht v Real Zaragoza (4-5)	3-2, 1-3
Napoli v Hanover 96 (5-1)	4-0, 1-1
Bologna v Lyn Oslo (2-0)	2-0, 0-0
Nice v Fiorentina (0-5)	0-1, 0-4
Dynamo Dresden v Rangers (2-3)	1-1, 1-2
Servette Geneva v Munich 1860 (2-6)	2-2, 0-4
Argesul Pitesti v Ferencvaros (3-5)	3-1, 0-4
Malmö FF v Liverpool (1-4)	0-2, 1-2
Hibernian v Porto (4-3)	3-0, 1-3
Eintracht Frankfurt v Nottingham F (0-5)	0-1, 0-4
Dynamo Zagreb v Petrolul Ploesti (5-2)	5-0, 0-2
Bruges v Sporting Lisbon (1-2)	0-0, 1-2
Frem Copenhagen v Atlético Bilbao (2-4)	0-1, 2-3
Zurich v Barcelona (3-2)	3-1, 0-1
Lokomotiv Leipzig v Linfield (5-2)	5-1, 0-1
DWS Amsterdam v Dundee (2-4)	2-1, 0-3
Partizan Belgrade v Lokomotiv Plovdiv (6-2)	5-1, 1-1
Vojvodina v CUF (4-1)	1-0, 3-1
Cologne v Slavia Prague (4-2)	2-0, 2-2
Antwerp v Goztepe Izmir (1-2)	1-2, 0-0

Second Round

Nottingham F v Zurich (2-2)	2-1, 0-1
Zurich won on away goals rule.	
Bordeaux v Atlético Bilbao (1-4)	1-3, 0-1
Dundee v Liège (7-2)	3-1, 4-1
Vojvodina v Lokomotiv Leipzig (2-0)	0-0, 2-0
Real Zaragoza v Ferencvaros (2-4)	2-1, 0-3
Liverpool v Munich 1860 (9-2)	8-0, 1-2
Rangers v Cologne (4-3)	3-0, 1-3
Bologna v Dynamo Zagreb (2-1)	0-0, 2-1
Napoli v Hibernian (4-6)	4-1, 0-5
Partizan Belgrade v Leeds U (2-3)	1-2, 1-1
Fiorentina v Sporting Lisbon (2-3)	1-1, 1-2
Atlético Madrid v Goztepe Izmir (2-3)	2-0, 0-3

Third Round

Byes: Atlético Bilbao, Bologna, Dundee, Rangers

Ferencvaros v Liverpool (2-0)	1-0, 1-0
Leeds U v Hibernian (2-1)	1-0, 1-1
Vojvodina v Goztepe Izmir (2-0)	1-0, 1-0
Zurich v Sporting Lisbon (3-1)	3-0, 0-1

Quarter-Final

Ferencvaros v Atlético Bilbao (4-2)	2-1, 2-1
Rangers v Leeds U (0-2)	0-0, 0-2
Dundee v Zurich (2-0)	1-0, 1-0
Bologna v Vojvodina (2-0)	0-0, 2-0

Semi-Final

Dundee v Leeds U (1-2)	1-1, 0-1
Ferencvaros v Bologna (5-4)	3-2, 2-2

Final

Leeds U v Ferencvaros (1-0) — 1-0, 0-0

EUROPEAN FAIRS CUP 1968–69

First Round

Byes: Argesul, Leipzig, Ujpest

Chelsea v Morton (9-3)	5-0, 4-3
Newcastle U v Feyenoord (4-2)	4-0, 0-2
Atlético Bilbao* v Liverpool (3-3)	2-1, 1-2
Rangers v Vojvodina (2-1)	2-0, 0-1
Ljubljana v Hibernian (1-5)	0-3, 1-2
Rapid Bucharest v OFK Belgrade (4-7)	3-1, 1-6
Wiener SK v Slavia Prague (1-5)	1-0, 0-5
Skeid Oslo v AIK Stockholm (2-3)	1-1, 1-2
Trakia Plovdiv v Real Zaragoza† (3-3)	3-1, 0-2
Dynamo Zagreb v Fiorentina (2-3)	1-1, 1-2
Legia Warsaw v Munich 1860 (9-2)	6-0, 3-2
Daring v Panathinaikos (2-3)	2-1, 0-2
Wacker Innsbruck v Eintracht Frankfurt (2-5)	2-2, 0-3
Sporting Lisbon v Valencia (5-4)	4-0, 1-4
Bologna v Basle (6-2)	4-1, 2-1
Aris Salonika v Hibernians Valletta (7-0)	1-0, 6-0
DOS Utrecht v Dundalk (2-3)	1-1, 1-2
Atlético Madrid v Waregem* (2-2)	2-1, 0-1
Hansa Rostock v Nice (4-2)	3-0, 1-2
Goztepe Izmir* v Marseille (2-2)	2-0, 0-2
Metz v SV Hamburg (3-7)	1-4, 2-3
Lyon* v Academica Coimbra (1-1)	1-0, 0-1
Lausanne v Juventus (0-4)	0-2, 0-2
Beerschot v DWS Amsterdam (2-3)	1-1, 1-2
Hanover 96 v Odense BK 09 (4-2)	3-2, 1-0
Vitoria Setubal v Linfield (6-1)	3-0, 3-1
Standard Liège v Leeds U (2-3)	0-0, 2-3
Napoli v Grasshoppers (3-2)	3-1, 0-1
Slavia Sofia v Aberdeen (0-2)	0-0, 0-2

Second Round

Hibernian v Lokomotiv Leipzig (4-1)	3-1, 1-0
Leeds U* v Napoli (2-2)	2-0, 0-2
Rangers v Dundalk (9-1)	6-1, 3-0
Aberdeen v Real Zaragoza (2-4)	2-1, 0-3
Chelsea v DWS Amsterdam* (0-0)	0-0, 0-0
Sporting Lisbon v Newcastle U (1-2)	1-1, 0-1
Vitoria Setubal v Lyon (7-1)	5-0, 2-1
Goztepe Izmir v Argesul Pitesti (5-3)	3-0, 2-3
Hansa Rostock v Fiorentina† (4-4)	3-2, 1-2
SV Hamburg v Slavia Prague (5-4)	4-1, 1-3
Panathinaikos v Atlético Bilbao (0-1)	0-0, 0-1
OFK Belgrade v Bologna (2-1)	1-0, 1-1
Aris Salonika v Ujpest Dozsa (2-11)	1-2, 1-9
AIK Stockholm v Hanover 96 (6-7)	4-2, 2-5
Waregem v Legia Warsaw (1-2)	1-0, 0-2
Juventus v Eintracht Frankfurt (0-1)	0-0, 0-1

Third Round

Leeds U v Hanover 96 (7-2)	5-1, 2-1
SV Hamburg† v Hibernian (2-2)	1-0, 1-2
Legia Warsaw v Ujpest Dozsa (2-3)	0-1, 2-2
Real Zaragoza v Newcastle U† (4-4)	3-2, 1-2
OFK Belgrade v Goztepe Izmir† (3-3)	3-1, 0-2
Eintracht Frankfurt v Atlético Bilbao (1-2)	1-1, 0-1
DWS Amsterdam v Rangers (1-4)	0-2, 1-2
Vitoria Setubal v Fiorentina (4-2)	3-0, 1-2

Quarter-Final

Newcastle U v Vitoria Setubal (6-4)	5-1, 1-3
Rangers v Atlético Bilbao (4-3)	4-1, 0-2
Leeds U v Ujpest Dozsa (0-3)	0-1, 0-2
Goztepe Izmir v SV Hamburg	

Hamburg withdrew

Semi-Final

Goztepe Izmir v Ujpest Dozsa (1-8)	1-4, 0-4
Rangers v Newcastle U (0-2)	0-0, 0-2

Final

Newcastle U v Ujpest Dozsa (6-2)	**3-0, 3-2**

**Won on toss of coin.*

†Won on away goals rule

EUROPEAN FAIRS CUP 1969–70

First Round

Arsenal v Glentoran (3-1)	3-0, 0-1
Dundee U v Newcastle U (1-3)	1-2, 0-1
Liverpool v Dundalk (14-0)	10-0, 4-0
Partizan Belgrade v Ujpest Dozsa (2-3)	2-1, 0-2
Sabadell v Bruges (3-5)	2-0, 1-5
Las Palmas v Hertha Berlin (0-1)	0-0, 0-1
Wiener SK v Ruch Chorzow (5-6)	4-2, 1-4
Rouen v Twente (2-1)	2-0, 0-1
Vitoria Guimaraes v Banik Ostrava (2-1)	1-0, 1-1
Sporting Lisbon v ASK Linz (6-2)	4-0, 2-2
Carl Zeiss Jena v Altay Izmir (1-0)	1-0, 0-0
Lausanne v Vasas Gyor (2-4)	1-2, 1-2
Rosenborg v Southampton (1-2)	1-0, 0-2
Hansa Rostock v Panionios (3-2)	3-0, 0-2
Dynamo Bacau v Floriana (7-0)	6-0, 1-0
Slavia Sofia v Valencia (3-1)	2-0, 1-1
Inter-Milan v Sparta Prague (4-0)	3-0, 1-0
Juventus v Lokomotiv Plovdiv (5-2)	3-1, 2-1
Stuttgart v Malmö FF (4-1)	3-0, 1-1
Hanover 96 v Ajax (2-4)	2-1, 0-3
Aris Salonika v Cagliari (1-4)	1-1, 0-3
Metz v Napoli (2-3)	1-1, 1-2
Barcelona v Odense BK 09 (6-0)	4-0, 2-0
Gwardia Warsaw v Vojvodina (2-1)	1-0, 1-1
Dunfermline Ath v Bordeaux (4-2)	4-0, 0-2
Zurich v Kilmarnock (4-5)	3-2, 1-3
Munich 1860 v Skeid Oslo (3-4)	2-2, 1-2
Valur Reykjavik v Anderlecht (0-8)	0-6, 0-2
SC Charleroi v ZNK Zagreb (5-2)	2-1, 3-1
Hvidovre v Porto (1-4)	1-2, 0-2
Jeunesse Esch v Coleraine (3-6)	3-2, 0-4
Vitoria Setubal v Rapid Bucharest (7-2)	3-1, 4-1

Second Round

Sporting Lisbon v Arsenal (0-3)	0-0, 0-3
SC Charleroi v Rouen† (3-3)	3-1, 0-2
Skeid Oslo v Dynamo Bacau (0-2)	0-0, 0-2
Kilmarnock v Slavia Sofia (4-3)	4-1, 0-2
Ajax v Ruch Chorzow (9-1)	7-0, 2-1
Stuttgart v Napoli (0-1)	0-0, 0-1
Carl Zeiss Jena v Cagliari (3-0)	2-0, 1-0
Bruges v Ujpest Dozsa† (5-5)	5-2, 0-3
Hansa Rostock v Inter-Milan (2-4)	2-1, 0-3
Vasas Gyor v Barcelona (2-5)	2-3, 0-2
Hertha Berlin v Juventus (3-1)	3-1, 0-0
Vitoria Setubal† v Liverpool (3-3)	1-0, 2-3
Porto v Newcastle U (0-1)	0-0, 0-1
Vitoria Guimaraes v Southampton (4-8)	3-3, 1-5
Dunfermline Ath v Gwardia Warsaw (3-1)	2-1, 1-0
Anderlecht v Coleraine (13-4)	6-1, 7-3

Third Round

Rouen v Arsenal (0-1)	0-0, 0-1
Kilmarnock v Dynamo Bacau (1-3)	1-1, 0-2
Napoli v Ajax (1-4)	1-0, 0-4
Carl Zeiss Jena v Ujpest Dozsa (4-0)	1-0, 3-0
Barcelona v Inter-Milan (2-3)	1-2, 1-1
Vitoria Setubal v Hertha Berlin (1-2)	1-1, 0-1
Newcastle U† v Southampton (1-1)	0-0, 1-1
Anderlecht† v Dunfermline Ath (3-3)	1-0, 2-3

Quarter-Final

Dynamo Bacau v Arsenal (1-9)	0-2, 1-7
Carl Zeiss Jena v Ajax (4-6)	3-1, 1-5
Hertha Berlin v Inter-Milan (1-2)	1-0, 0-2
Anderlecht† v Newcastle U (3-3)	2-0, 1-3

Semi-Final

Arsenal v Ajax (3-1)	3-0, 0-1
Anderlecht v Inter-Milan (2-1)	0-1, 2-0

† Won on away goals counting double.

Final 1969–70: Anderlecht 3, Arsenal 1

(At Brussels, 22 April, 1970, 37,000)

Anderlecht: Trappeniers; Heylens, Velkeneers; Nordahl, Kialunda, Cornelis (Peeters); Desanghere, Devrindt, Mulder, Van Himst, Puis.

Arsenal: Wilson; Storey, McNab; Kelly, McLintock, Simpson; Armstrong, Sammels, Radford, George (Kennedy), Graham.

Scorers: Anderlecht – Devrindt, Mulder 2; Arsenal – Kennedy.

Arsenal 3, Anderlecht 0

(At Highbury, 28 April, 1970, 51,612)

Arsenal: Wilson; Storey, McNab; Kelly, McLintock, Simpson; Armstrong, Sammels, Radford, George, Graham.

Anderlecht: Trappeniers; Heylens, Maartens; Nordahl, Velkeneers, Kialunda; Desanghere, Devrindt, Mulder, Van Himst, Puis.

Scorers: Arsenal – Kelly, Radford, Sammels.

EUROPEAN FAIRS CUP 1970–71

First Round

AEK Athens v Twente (0-4)	0-1, 0-3
Zeljeznicar v Anderlecht (7-9)	4-5, 3-4
La Gantoise v SV Hamburg (1-8)	0-1, 1-7
Seville v Eskisehirspor (2-3)	1-0, 1-3
Coleraine v Kilmarnock (4-3)	1-1, 3-2
Dundee U v Grasshoppers (3-2)	3-2, 0-0
Sarpsborg v Leeds U (0-6)	0-1, 0-5
Spartak Trnava* v Marseille (2-2)	2-0, 0-2
Cologne v Sedan (5-2)	5-1, 0-1
Lausanne v Vitoria Setubal (1-4)	0-2, 1-2
Hibernian v Malmo FF (9-2)	6-0, 3-2
Liverpool v Ferencvaros (2-1)	1-0, 1-1
Trakia Plovdiv v Coventry C (1-6)	1-4, 0-2
Lazio v Arsenal (2-4)	2-2, 0-2
Bayern Munich v Rangers (2-1)	1-0, 1-1
Dynamo Bucharest v PAOK Salonika (5-1)	5-0, 0-1
Uni Craiova v Pecs Dozsa (2-4)	2-1, 0-3
Katowice v Barcelona (2-4)	0-1, 2-3
Wiener SK v Beveren (0-5)	0-2, 0-3
Ilves Kissat v Sturm Graz (4-5)	4-2, 0-3
Barreirense v Dynamo Zagreb (3-6)	2-0, 1-6
Hajduk Split v Slavia Sofia (3-1)	3-0, 0-1
Cork Hibs v Valencia (1-6)	0-3, 1-3
Sparta Prague v Atletico Bilbao (3-1)	2-0, 1-1
Partizan Belgrade v Dynamo Dresden (0-6)	0-0, 0-6
AB Copenhagen v Sliema Wanderers (10-2)	7-0, 3-2
Juventus v Rumelange (11-0)	7-0, 4-0
Nykoping v Hertha Berlin (3-8)	2-4, 1-4
Ruch Chorzow v Fiorentina (1-3)	1-1, 0-2
Inter-Milan v Newcastle U (1-3)	1-1, 0-2
Sparta Rotterdam v Akranes (15-0)	6-0, 9-0
Vitoria Guimaraes v Angouleme (4-3)	3-0, 1-3

Second Round

Hibernian v Vitoria Guimaraes (3-2)	2-0, 1-2
Sparta Rotterdam v Coleraine (4-1)	2-0, 2-1
Bayern Munich v Coventry C (7-3)	6-1, 1-2
Barcelona v Juventus (2-4)	1-2, 1-2
Fiorentina v Cologne (1-3)	1-2, 0-1
Sturm Graz v Arsenal (1-2)	1-0, 0-2
Leeds U† v Dynamo Dresden (2-2)	1-0, 1-2
Liverpool v Dynamo Bucharest (4-1)	3-0, 1-1
AB Copenhagen v Anderlecht (1-7)	1-3, 0-4
Newcastle U v Pecs Dozsa* (2-2)	2-0, 0-2
Sparta Prague v Dundee U (3-2)	3-1, 0-1
Hertha Berlin v Spartak Trnava (2-3)	1-0, 1-3
Dynamo Zagreb v Hamburg (4-1)	4-0, 0-1
Vitoria Setubal v Hajduk Split (3-2)	2-0, 1-2
Valencia v Beveren (1-2)	0-1, 1-1
Eskisehir v Twente (4-8)	3-2, 1-6

Third Round

Spartak Trnava v Cologne (0-4)	0-1, 0-3
Bayern Munich v Sparta Rotterdam (5-2)	2-1, 3-1
Leeds U v Sparta Prague (9-2)	6-0, 3-2
Arsenal v Beveren (4-0)	4-0, 0-0
Pecs Dozsa v Juventus (0-3)	0-1, 0-2
Dynamo Zagreb v Twente (2-3)	2-2, 0-1
Anderlecht v Vitoria Setubal (3-4)	2-1, 1-3
Hibernian v Liverpool (0-3)	0-1, 0-2

Quarter-Final

Juventus v Twente (4-2)	2-0, 2-2
Arsenal v Cologne†(2-2)	2-1, 0-1
Leeds U v Setubal (3-2)	2-1, 1-1
Liverpool v Bayern Munich (4-1)	3-0, 1-1

Semi-Final

Liverpool v Leeds U (0-1)	0-1, 0-0
Cologne v Juventus (1-3)	1-1, 0-2

* *Won on penalty kicks.* † *Won on away goals rule.*

Final 1970–71: Juventus 2, Leeds U 2

(In Turin, 29 May, 1971, 45,000)

Juventus: Piloni; Spinosi, Marchetti, Furino, Morini, Salvadore, Haller, Causio, Anastasi (Novellini), Capello, Bettega.

Leeds U: Sprake; Reaney, Cooper, Bremner, Charlton, Hunter, Lorimer, Clarke, Jones (Bates), Giles, Madeley.

Scorers: Juventus – Bettega, Capello; Leeds U – Madeley, Bates.

Leeds U 1, Juventus 1

(At Leeds, 2 June, 1971, 42,483)

Leeds U: Sprake; Reaney, Cooper, Bremner, Charlton, Hunter, Lorimer, Clarke, Jones, Giles, Madeley (Bates).

Juventus: Tancredi; Spinosi, Marchetti, Furino, Morini, Salvadore, Haller, Causio, Anastasi, Capello, Bettega.

Scorers: Leeds U – Clarke; Juventus – Anastasi.

Leeds U won on away goals rule.

UEFA CUP 1971–72

First Round

Hertha Berlin v Elfsborg (7-2)	4-1, 3-1
Dundee v Akademisk Copenhagen (5-2)	4-2, 1-0
Rosenborg v IFK Helsinki (4-0)	3-0, 1-0
Vasas Budapest v Shelbourne (2-1)	1-0, 1-1
Glentoran v Eintracht Brunswick (1-7)	0-1, 1-6
Keflavik v Tottenham H (1-15)	1-6, 0-9
Celta Vigo v Aberdeen (0-3)	0-2, 0-1
FC Den Haag v Aris Luxembourg (6-1)	5-0, 1-1
Wolverhampton W v Academica Coimbra (7-1)	4-1, 3-0
St Etienne v Cologne (2-3)	1-1, 1-2
Lugano v Legia Warsaw (1-3)	1-3, 0-0
Porto v Nantes (1-3)	0-2, 1-1
SV Hamburg v St Johnstone (2-4)	2-1, 0-3
Southampton v Atlético Bilbao (2-3)	2-1, 0-2
Bologna v Anderlecht (3-1)	2-0, 1-1
Napoli v Rapid Bucharest (1-2)	1-0, 0-2
Vitoria Setubal* v Nimes (2-2)	1-0, 1-2
Atlético Madrid v Panionios* (2-2)	2-1, 0-1
Carl Zeiss Jena v Lokomotiv Plovdiv (4-3)	3-0, 1-3
Basle v Real Madrid (2-4)	1-2, 1-2
Marsa v Juventus (0-11)	0-6, 0-5
Dynamo Zagreb v Botev Vratza (8-2)	6-1, 2-1
UT Arad v Austria Salzburg (5-4)	4-1, 1-3
Fenerbahce v Ferencvaros (2-4)	1-1, 1-3
AC Milan v Dighenis (7-0)	4-0, 3-0
Spartak Moscow v VSS Kosice (3-2)	1-2, 2-0
OFK Belgrade v Djurgaarden (6-3)	2-2, 4-1
Rapid Vienna	Bye
Zeljeznicar v Bruges (4-3)	3-0, 1-3
Chemie Halle (withdrew) v PSV Eindhoven (0-0)	0-0, –
Zaglebie Walbrzych v Union Teplice (4-2)	1-0, 3-2
Lierse v Leeds U (4-2)	0-2, 4-0

Second Round

Rosenborg v Lierse* (4-4)	4-1, 0-3
Rapid Bucharest v Legia Warsaw (4-2)	4-0, 0-2
Cologne v Dundee (4-5)	2-1, 2-4
FC Den Haag v Wolverhampton W (1-7)	1-3, 0-4
Zeljeznicar* v Bologna (3-3)	1-1, 2-2
Nantes v Tottenham H (0-1)	0-0, 0-1
Eintracht Brunswick v Atlético Bilbao (4-3)	2-1, 2-2
St Johnstone v Vasas Budapest (2-1)	2-0, 0-1
Spartak Moscow v Vitoria Setubal (0-4)	0-0, 0-4
Hertha Berlin v AC Milan (4-5)	2-1, 2-4
OFK Belgrade v Carl Zeiss Jena (1-5)	1-1, 0-4
Zaglebie Walbrzych v UT Arad (2-3)	1-1, 1-2
Dynamo Zagreb v Rapid Vienna* (2-2)	2-2, 0-0
Real Madrid v PSV Eindhoven* (3-3)	3-1, 0-2
Juventus v Aberdeen (3-1)	2-0, 1-1
Ferencvaros v Panionios (6-0)	6-0, –

Panionios disqualified

Third Round

AC Milan v Dundee (3-2)	3-0, 0-2
Carl Zeiss Jena v Wolverhampton W (0-4)	0-1, 0-3
Eintracht Brunswick v Ferencvaros (3-6)	1-1, 2-5
PSV Eindhoven v Lierse (1-4)	1-0, 0-4
Rapid Vienna v Juventus (1-5)	0-1, 1-4
St Johnstone v Zeljeznicar (2-5)	1-0, 1-5
Tottenham H v Rapid Bucharest (5-0)	3-0, 2-0
UT Arad v Vitoria Setubal (3-1)	3-0, 0-1

Quarter-Final

AC Milan v Lierse (3-1)	2-0, 1-1
UT Arad v Tottenham H (1-3)	0-2, 1-1
Ferencvaros† v Zeljeznicar (3-3)	1-2, 2-1
Juventus v Wolverhampton W (2-3)	1-1, 1-2

Semi-Final

Tottenham H v AC Milan (3-2)	2-1, 1-1
Ferencvaros v Wolverhampton W (3-4)	2-2, 1-2

* *Won on away goals rule.* † *Won on penalty kicks.*

Final 1971–72: Wolverhampton W 1, Tottenham H 2

(At Wolverhampton, 3 May, 1972, 45,000)

Wolverhampton W: Parkes; Shaw, Taylor, Hegan, Munro, McAlle, McCalliog, Hibbitt, Richards, Dougan, Wagstaffe.

Tottenham H: Jennings; Kinnear, Knowles, Mullery, England, Beal, Coates (Pratt), Perryman, Chivers, Peters, Gilzean.

Scorers: Wolverhampton W – McCalliog; Tottenham H – Chivers 2.

Tottenham H 1, Wolverhampton W 1

(At White Hart Lane, 17 May, 1972)

Tottenham H: Jennings; Kinnear, Knowles, Mullery, England, Beal, Coates, Perryman, Chivers, Peters, Gilzean.

Wolverhampton W: Parkes; Shaw, Taylor, Hegan, Munro, McAlle, McCalliog, Hibbitt (Bailey), Richards, Dougan (Curran), Wagstaffe.

Scorers: Tottenham H – Mullery; Wolverhampton W – Wagstaffe.

UEFA CUP 1972–73

First Round

Aberdeen v Bor Moenchengladbach (5-9)	2-3, 3-6
Atvidaberg v Bruges (5-6)	3-5, 2-1
Manchester C v Valencia (3-4)	2-2, 1-2
Lyn Oslo v Tottenham H (3-12)	3-6, 0-6
Cologne v Bohemians (5-1)	2-1, 3-0
Honved v Partick T (4-0)	1-0, 3-0
Viking Stavanger v IBV Vastmannejar (1-0)	1-0, 0-0
Feyenoord v US Rumelange (21-0)	9-0, 12-0
Liverpool v Eintracht Frankfurt (2-0)	2-0, 0-0
Grasshoppers v Nimes (4-2)	2-1, 2-1
Vitoria Setubal v Zaglebie Sosnowiec (6-2)	6-1, 0-1
Stoke C v Kaiserslautern (3-5)	3-1, 0-4
Racing White v CUF Barrierense (0-3)	0-1, 0-2
Torino v Las Palmas (2-4)	2-0, 0-4
Sochaux v Frem Copenhagen (2-5)	1-3, 1-2
Olympiakos Piraeus v Cagliari (3-1)	2-1, 1-0
Angers v Dynamo Berlin (2-3)	1-1, 1-2
Porto v Barcelona (4-1)	3-1, 1-0
Univ Cluj v Levski Sofia (5-6)	4-1, 1-5
Red Star Belgrade v Lausanne (7-4)	5-1, 2-3
Inter-Milan v FC Valetta (7-1)	6-1, 1-0
Beroe Stara v FK Austria (10-1)	7-0, 3-1
UT Arad v Norrköping (1-4)	1-2, 0-2
EPA Larna v Ararat Erevan (0-2)	0-1, 0-1
AEK Athens v Salgotarjan (4-2)	3-1, 1-1
Eskisehirspor v Fiorentina (1-5)	1-2, 0-3
Dukla Prague v OFK Belgrade (3-5)	2-2, 1-3
Slovan Bratislava v Vojvodina (8-1)	6-0, 2-1
Dynamo Tbilisi v FC Twente (3-4)	3-2, 0-2
Ruch Chorzow v Fenerbahce (3-1)	3-0, 0-1
Dynamo Dresden v Voest Linz (4-2)	2-0, 2-2
Hvidovre Copenhagen	bye

Second Round

Dynamo Berlin v Levski Sofia (3-2)	3-0, 0-2
Bor Moenchengladbach v Hvidovre Copenhagen (6-1)	3-0, 3-1
Porto v Bruges (5-3)	3-0, 2-3
Tottenham H v Olympiakos Piraeus (4-1)	4-0, 0-1
Red Star Belgrade v Valencia (4-1)	3-1, 1-0
Inter-Milan v Norrköping (4-2)	2-2, 2-0
Viking Stavanger v Cologne (2-9)	1-0, 1-9
Beroe Stara v Honved (3-1)	3-0, 0-1
Feyenoord v OFK Belgrade* (5-5)	4-3, 1-2
Liverpool v AEK Athens (6-1)	3-0, 3-1

Vitoria Setubal* v Fiorentina (2-2)	1-0, 1-2
Grasshoppers v Ararat Erevan (3-7)	1-3, 2-4
CUF Barreirense v Kaiserslautern (2-3)	1-3, 1-0
Las Palmas v Slovan Bratislava (3-2)	2-2, 1-0
Ruch Chorzow v Dynamo Dresden (0-4)	0-1, 0-3
Frem Copenhagen v FC Twente (0-9)	0-5, 0-4

Third Round

Ararat Erevan v Kaiserslautern† (2-2)	2-0, 0-2
Cologne v Bor Moenchengladbach (0-5)	0-0, 0-5
Tottenham H v Red Star Belgrade (2-1)	2-0, 0-1
FC Twente v Las Palmas (4-2)	3-0, 1-2
OFK Belgrade v Beroe Stara (3-1)	0-0, 3-1
Vitoria Setubal v Inter-Milan (2-1)	2-0, 0-1
Dynamo Berlin v Liverpool (1-3)	0-0, 1-3
Porto v Dynamo Dresden (1-3)	1-2, 0-1

Quarter-Final

Kaiserslautern v Bor Moenchengladbach (2-9)	1-2, 1-7
OFK Belgrade v FC Twente (3-4)	3-2, 0-2
Tottenham H* v Vitoria Setubal (2-2)	1-0, 1-2
Liverpool v Dynamo Dresden (3-0)	2-0, 1-0

Semi-Final

Liverpool* v Tottenham H (2-2)	1-0, 1-2
Bor Moenchengladbach v FC Twente (5-1)	3-0, 2-1

** Won on away goals rule. † Won on penalty kicks.*

Final 1972–73: Liverpool 3, Borussia Moenchengladbach 0
(At Liverpool, 10 May, 1973, 41,169)

Liverpool: Clemence; Lawler, Lindsay, Smith, Lloyd, Hughes, Keegan, Cormack, Toshack, Heighway (Hall), Callaghan.
Borussia Moenchengladbach: Kleff; Danner, Michallik, Vogts, Bonhof, Kulik, Jensen, Wimmer, Rupp (Simonsen), Netzer, Heynckes.
Scorers: Liverpool – Keegan 2, Lloyd.

Borussia Moenchengladbach 2, Liverpool 0
(At Moenchengladbach, 23 May, 1973, 35,000)

Borussia Moenchengladbach: Kleff; Vogts, Surau, Netzer, Bonhof, Danner, Wimmer, Kulik, Jensen, Rupp, Heynckes.
Liverpool: Clemence; Lawler, Lindsay, Smith, Lloyd, Hughes, Keegan, Cormack, Heighway (Boersma), Toshack, Callaghan.
Scorer: Bor Moenchengladbach – Heynckes 2.

UEFA CUP 1973–74

First Round

Fredrikstad v Dynamo Kiev (0-5)	0-1, 0-4
Ruch Chorzow v Wuppertal (8-6)	4-1, 4-5
BK 1903 Copenhagen v AIK (3-2)	2-1, 1-1
Carl Zeiss Jena v Mikkelin (6-0)	3-0, 3-0
Stroemgodset v Leeds U (2-7)	1-1, 1-6
Oesters v Feyenoord (2-5)	1-3, 1-2
Hibernian v Keflavik (3-1)	2-0, 1-1
Nice v Barcelona (3-2)	3-0, 0-2
Fortuna Dusseldorf v Naestved (3-2)	1-0, 2-2
Grasshoppers v Tottenham H (2-9)	1-5, 1-4
Aberdeen v Finn Harps (7-2)	4-1, 3-1
Dundee v FC Twente (3-7)	1-3, 2-4
Espanol v RWD Molenbeek (2-4)	0-3, 2-1
Belenenses v Wolverhampton W (1-4)	0-2, 1-2
US Luxembourg v Marseille (1-12)	0-5, 1-7
Setubal v Beerschot (4-0)	2-0, 2-0
Ipswich T v Real Madrid (1-0)	1-0, 0-0
Lazio v Sion (4-3)	3-0, 1-3
Sliema Wanderers v Lokomotiv Plovdiv (0-3)	0-2, 0-1
Fiorentina v Univ Craiova (0-1)	0-0, 0-1
Ferencvaros v Gwardia Warsaw (1-3)	0-1, 1-2
Stuttgart v Olympiakos Nicosia (13-0)	9-0, 4-0
Tatran Presov v Velez (5-3)	4-2, 1-1
Dynamo Tbilisi v Slavia Sofia (4-3)	4-1, 0-2
Panathinaikos v OFK Belgrade* (2-2)	1-2, 1-0
Admira-Wacker* v Inter-Milan (2-2)	1-0, 1-2
Fenerbahce v Agres Pitesti (6-2)	5-1, 1-1
VSS Kosice v Honved (3-5)	1-0, 2-5
Torino v Lokomotiv Leipzig (2-4)	1-2, 1-2
Eskisehirspor v Cologne (0-2)	0-0, 0-2
Panachaiki v AK Graz (3-1)	2-1, 1-0
Ards v Standard Liège (4-8)	3-2, 1-6

Second Round

Admira-Wacker v Fortuna Dusseldorf (2-4)	2-1, 0-3
Aberdeen v Tottenham H (2-5)	1-1, 1-4
Dynamo Tbilisi v OFK Belgrade (8-1)	3-0, 5-1
Nice v Fenerbahce (4-2)	4-0, 0-2
Lokomotiv Leipzig* v Wolverhampton W (4-4)	3-0, 1-4
Panachaiki v FC Twente (1-8)	1-1, 0-7
Setubal* v RWD Molenbeek (2-2)	1-0, 1-2
Marseille v Cologne (2-6)	2-0, 0-6
Ipswich T v Lazio (6-4)	4-0, 2-4
Dynamo Kiev v BK 1903 Copenhagen (3-1)	1-0, 2-1
Lokomotiv Plovdiv v Honved (5-7)	3-4, 2-3
Ruch Chorzow v Carl Zeiss Jena (3-1)	3-0, 0-1
Stuttgart v Tatran Presov (8-4)	3-1, 5-3
Leeds U† v Hibernian (0-0)	0-0, 0-0
Feyenoord v Gwardia Warsaw (3-2)	3-1, 0-1
Standard Liège v Univ Craiova (3-1)	2-0, 1-1

Third Round

Dynamo Kiev v Stuttgart (2-3)	2-0, 0-3
Dynamo Tbilisi v Tottenham H (2-6)	1-1, 1-5
Ipswich T v FC Twente (3-1)	1-0, 2-1
Honved v Ruch Chorzow (2-5)	2-0, 0-5
Leeds U v Setubal (2-3)	1-0, 1-3
Fortuna Dusseldorf v Lokomotiv Leipzig (2-4)	2-1, 0-3
Nice v Cologne (1-4)	1-0, 0-4
Standard Liège v Feyenoord* (3-3)	3-1, 0-2

Quarter-Final

Ipswich T v Lokomotiv Leipzig† (1-1)	1-0, 0-1
Cologne v Tottenham H (1-5)	1-2, 0-3
Stuttgart v Setubal (3-2)	1-0, 2-2
Ruch Chorzow v Feyenoord (2-4)	1-1, 1-3

Semi-Final

Lokomotiv Leipzig v Tottenham H (1-4)	1-2, 0-2
Feyenoord v Stuttgart (4-3)	2-1, 2-2

** Won on away goals. † Won on penalties.*

Final 1973–74: Tottenham Hotspur 2, Feyenoord 2
(At White Hart Lane, 21 May, 1974, 46,281)

Tottenham: Jennings; Evans, Naylor, Pratt, England, Beal, McGrath, Perryman, Chivers, Peters, Coates.
Feyenoord: Treytel; Rijsbergen, Van Daele, Israel, Vos, De Jong, Jansen, Van Hanegem, Ressel, Schoenmaker, Kristensen.
Scorers: Tottenham – England, Van Daele og; Feyenoord – Van Hanegem, De Jong.

Feyenoord 2, Tottenham Hotspur 0
(At Rotterdam, 29 May, 1974, 68,000)

Feyenoord: Treytel; Rijsbergen, Van Daele, Israel, Vos, Ramljak, Jansen, De Jong, Ressel, Schoenmaker, Kristensen (Boskamp) (Wery).
Tottenham: Jennings; Evans, Naylor, Pratt (Holder), England, Beal, McGrath, Perryman, Chivers, Peters, Coates.
Scorers: Feyenoord – Rijsbergen, Ressel.

UEFA CUP 1974–75

First Round, First Leg

Lyon 7 (*Lacombe 3, Maillard 3, Maniero*), Red Boys 0
Valur 0, Portadown 0
Derby Co 4 (*Hector 2, Daniel, Lee*), Servette 1 (*Petrovic*)
Ipswich T 2 (*Talbot, Hamilton*), Twente 2 (*Zuidema, Pahlplatz*)
Stoke C 1 (*Smith*), Ajax 1 (*Krol*)
RWD Molenbeek 1 (*Wellens*), Dundee 0
Rosenborg 2 (*Iversen 2*), Hibernian 3 (*Stanton, Gordon, Cropley*)
Porto 4 (*McAlle og, Cubillas, Flavio, Gomes*), Wolverhampton W 1 (*Bailey*)
Etar 0, Inter-Milan 0
Gornik Zabrze 2 (*Kurzeja, Kwasny*), Partizan Belgrade 2 (*Zavitic, Vukotic*)
Start 1 (*Mathiesen M.*), Djurgaarden 2 (*Svensson M., Skotte*)
Boluspor 0, Dynamo Bucharest 1 (*Deleanu*)
Spartak Moscow 3 (*Piscarov, Gladulin, Lovchev*), Velez Mostar 1 (*Bajevic*)
Besiktas 2 (*Sinan, Tezcan*), Steagul Brasov 0
SW Innsbruck 2 (*Flindt 2*), Borussia Moenchengladbach 1 (*Heynckes*)
Sturm Graz 2 (*Stendal, Kulmer*), Antwerp 1 (*Heyligen*)
Randers Freja 1 (*Nielsen*), Dynamo Dresden 1 (*Dorner*)
Hamburg 3 (*Volkert 2, Kaltz*), Bohemians 0
Rapid Vienna 3 (*Pajenk, Ritter, Krankl*), Aris Salonika 1 (*Alexiadis*)
Real Sociedad 0, Banik Ostrava 1 (*Micka*)
Lokomotiv Plovdiv 3 (*Kourbanov, Bonev, Stamboliev*), Raba ETO 1 (*Glazer*)
Oesters 3 (*Mattsson 2, Nordenberg pen*), Dynamo Moscow 2 (*Koslov, Pavlenkov*)
Nantes 2 (*Rampillon, Michel*), Legia Warsaw 2 (*Bialad 2*)
Napoli 2 (*Massa, Pogliana*), Videoton 0
Vorwaerts 2 (*Schutz, Krautzk*), Juventus 1 (*Capello*)
Grasshoppers 2 (*Elsener, Grahn*), Panathinaikos 0
Torino 1 (*Pulici*), Fortuna Dusseldorf 1 (*Zewe*)
Cologne 5 (*Muller 2, Flohe 2, Lohr*), Kokkolan 1 (*Makela*)
FC Amsterdam 5 (*Jansen 2, Otto, Koopman, Husers*), Hibernian Malta 0
KB Copenhagen 3 (*Sorensen, Holstrom, Bernborg*), Atlético Madrid 2 (*Ayala, Salcedo*)
Vitoria Setubal 1 (*Vicente*), Real Zaragoza 1 (*Arrua*)

First Round, Second Leg

Red Boys 1 (*Cristophe*), Lyon 4 (*Domenech 2, Mariot, Bernard*)
Portadown 2 (*McFaul, Morrison pen*), Valur 1 (*Albertson*)
Servette 1 (*Martin*), Derby Co 2 (*Lee, Hector*)
Twente 1 (*Bos*), Ipswich T 1 (*Hamilton*)
Ajax 0, Stoke C 0
Dundee 2 (*Duncan, Jocky Scott*), RWD Molenbeek 4 (*Teugels, Boskamp, Wellens 2*)
Hibernian 9 (*Harper 2, Munro 2, Stanton 2, Cropley 2, Gordon*), Rosenborg 1 (*Iversen*)
Wolverhampton W 3 (*Richards, Dougan, Daley*), Porto 1 (*Cubillas*)
Inter-Milan 3 (*Oriali, Boninsegna 2*), Etar 0
Partizan Belgrade 3 (*Dordevic, Vukotic, Todozevic*), Gornik Zabrze 0
Djurgaarden 5 (*Skotte, Stenbach, Karlsson 2, Samuelsson*) Start 1 (*Mathiesen*)
Dynamo Bucharest 3 (*Dinu, Dumitrache, Lucescu*), Boluspor 0
Velez Mostar 2 (*Colic, Popic*), Spartak Moscow 0
Steagul Brasov 3 (*Serbaniou 3*), Besiktas 0
Borussia Moenchengladbach 3 (*Heynckes, Jensen, Vogts*), SW Innsbruck 0
Antwerp 1 (*Kodat*), Sturm Graz 0
Dynamo Dresden 0, Randers Freja 0
Bohemians 0, Hamburg 1 (*Bertl*)
Aris Salonika 1 (*Alexiadis*), Rapid Vienna 0
Banik Ostrava 4 (*Vojacek, Slany, Albrecht, Kolecko*), Real Sociedad 0
Raba ETO 3 (*Sebo, Penzes, Proczik*), Lokomotiv Plovdiv 1 (*Kichekov*)
Dynamo Moscow 2 (*Evryuzhikhin, Petrushin*), Oesters 1 (*Svensson*)
Legia Warsaw 0, Nantes 1 (*Merigot*)
Videoton 1 (*Wollek*), Napoli 1 (*Braglia*)
Juventus 3 (*Anastasi, Altafini, Hause og*), Vorwaerts 0
Panathinaikos 2 (*Antoniadis 2*), Grasshoppers 1 (*Santrac*)
Fortuna Dusseldorf 3 (*Zimmerman, Seel, Geye pen*), Torino 1 (*Agroppi*)
Kokkolan 1 (*Lamberg*), Cologne 4 (*Neumann, Lohr, Simmet 2*)
Hibernian Malta 0, FC Amsterdam 7 (*Karte 2, Jansen 2, Franz, Husers, Dekkers*)
Atlético Madrid 4 (*Leal, Garate, Irureta 2*), KB Copenhagen 0
Real Zaragoza 4 (*Arrua, Diarte, Castany, Leiros*), Vitoria Setubal 0
Dukla Prague had a walkover when Pezoporikos withdrew

Second Round, First Leg

Derby Co 2 (*Nish, Rioch pen*), Atlético Madrid 2 (*Luis pen, Ayala*)
Hibernian 2 (*Stanton, Cropley*), Juventus 4 (*Gentile, Altafini 2, Cuccurredu*)
Partizan Belgrade 5 (*Kosic 2, Zavajic, Nikolic, Vukotic*), Portadown 0
Nantes 1 (*Bossis*), Banik Ostrava 0
Dynamo Bucharest 1 (*Dinu*), Cologne 1 (*Luscher*)
Raba ETO 2 (*Varsanyi, Stolz*), Fortuna Dusseldorf 0
Rapid Vienna 1 (*Ritter*), Velez Mostar 1 (*Halaldiz*)
Dynamo Dresden 1 (*Sasche*), Dynamo Moscow 0
Grasshoppers 2 (*Grahn, Santrac*), Real Zaragoza 1 (*Arrua*)
Borussia Moenchengladbach 1 (*Simonsen*), Lyon 0
Hamburg 8 (*Volkert 2, Bertl, Zaczyk, Memering, Nogly, Ripp, Krobach*), Steagul Brasov 0
Twente 2 (*Thijseen, Van der Vall*), RWD Molenbeek 1 (*Koens*)
Djurgaarden 0, Dukla Prague 2 (*Nehoda, Gajdusek*)
Inter-Milan 1 (*Boninsegna*), FC Amsterdam 2 (*Jansen 2*)
Napoli 1 (*Orlandini*), Porto 0
Ajax 1 (*Gerrie Muhren*), Antwerp 0

Second Round, Second Leg

Atlético Madrid 2 (*Luis 2*), Derby Co 2 (*Rioch, Hector*)
Derby won 7-6 on penalties
Juventus 4 (*Bettega, Anastasi 2, Altafini*), Hibernian 0
Portadown 1 (*Malcolmson*), Partizan Belgrade 1 (*Tordevic*)
Banik Ostrava (*Klement 2*), Nantes 0
Cologne 3 (*Overath, Muller, Neumann*), Dynamo Bucharest 2 (*Custov, Georgescu*)
Fortuna Dusseldorf 3 (*Herzog, Szernotzky, Brucken*), Raba ETO 0
Velez Mostar 1 (*Halaldiz*), Rapid Vienna 0
Dynamo Moscow 1 (*Korneev*), Dynamo Dresden 0
Real Zaragoza 5 (*Rubial 2, Soto, Oldhauser og, Niggl og*), Grasshoppers 0
Lyon 2 (*Valette, Domenech R.*), Borussia Moenchengladbach 5 (*Bonhof 2, Simonsen 2, Kulik*)
Steagul Brasov 1 (*Curbaniou*), Hamburg 2 (*Kaltz, Bjornmose*)
RWD Molenbeek 0, Twente 1 (*Zuidema*)
Dukla Prague 3 (*Nehoda 2, Macela*), Djurgaarden 1 (*Svensson*)
FC Amsterdam 0, Inter-Milan 0
Porto 0, Napoli 1 (*Juliano*)
Antwerp 2 (*Kodat, Riedl pen*), Ajax 1 (*Geels*)

Third Round, First Leg

Napoli 0, Banik Ostrava 2 (*Albrecht, Kolecko*)
Hamburg 4 (*Bjornmose 2, Volkert, Nogly*), Dynamo Dresden 1 (*Schmuck*)
Dukla Prague 3 (*Dvorak, Krumich, Nehoda*), Twente 1 (*Jeuring*)
Partizan Belgrade 1 (*Vukotic*), Cologne 0
Borussia Moenchengladbach 5 (*Heynckes 2, Simonsen 2, Bonhof*), Real Zaragoza 0
FC Amsterdam 3 (*Husers 2, Kriegler og*), Fortuna Dusseldorf 0

Juventus 1 (*Damiani*), Ajax 0
Derby Co 3 (*Bourne 2, Hinton*), Velez Mostar 1 (*Vladic*)

Third Round, Second Leg
Banik Ostrava 1 (*Slany*), Napoli 1 (*Ferrandini*)
Dynamo Dresden 2 (*Dorner, Hafner*), Hamburg 2 (*Bertl 2*)
Twente 5 (*Zuidema 3, Notten 2*), Dukla Prague 0
Cologne 5 (*Overath, Lohr, Muller, Glowacz, Flohe*), Partizan Belgrade 1 (*Pavlovic*)
Real Zaragoza 2 (*Vileta, Galdos*), Borussia Moenchengladbach 4 (*Simonsen, Heynckes 2, Stielike*)
Fortuna Dusseldorf 1 (*Seel*), FC Amsterdam 2 (*Husers, Jansen*)
Ajax 2 (*Blankenburg, Gerrie Muhren*), Juventus 1 (*Damiani pen*)
Velez Mostar 4 (*Bajevic pen, Pecelj, Vladic, Primorac pen*), Derby Co 1 (*Hector*)

Quarter-Finals, First Leg
Juventus 2 (*Capello, Viola*), Hamburg 0
Cologne 5 (*Flohe 2 [1 pen], Muller 3*), FC Amsterdam 1 (*Visser*)
Velez Mostar 1 (*Kvesic*), Twente 0
Banik Ostrava 0, Borussia Moenchengladbach 1 (*Heynckes*)

Quarter-Finals, Second Leg
Hamburg 0, Juventus 0
Borussia Moenchengladbach 3 (*Micka og, Heynckes, Vogts*), Banik Ostrava 1 (*Hudecek*)
FC Amsterdam 2 (*Jansen 2*), Cologne 3 (*Strack, Muller, Lohr*)
Twente 2 (*Zuidema, Overweg*), Velez Mostar 0

Semi-Finals, First Leg
Twente 3 (*Jeuring, Zuidema 2*), Juventus 1 (*Altafini*)
Cologne 1 (*Lohr*), Borussia Moenchengladbach 3 (*Simonsen 2, Danner*)

Semi-Finals, Second Leg
Juventus 0, Twente 1 (*Zuidema*)
Borussia Moenchengladbach 1 (*Danner*), Cologne 0

Final 1974–75: Borussia Moenchengladbach 0, Twente Enschede 0
(At Dusseldorf, 7 May, 1975, 45,000)

Borussia Moenchengladbach: Kleff; Wittkamp, Stielike, Vogts, Surau, Bonhof, Wimmer, Danner (Del Haye), Kulik (Schaffer), Simonsen, Jensen.

Twente Enschede: Gross; Drost, Van Ierssel, Overweg, Oranen, Thijssen, Pahlplatz, Van der Vall, Bos, Jeuring (Achterberg), Zuidema.

Twente Enschede 1, Borussia Moenchengladbach 5
(At Enschede, 21 May, 1975, 24,500)

Twente Enschede: Gross; Drost, Van Ierssel, Overweg, Oranen, Bos (Muhren), Thijssen, Pahlplatz (Achterberg), Van der Vall, Jeuring, Zuidema.

Borussia Moenchengladbach: Kleff; Wittkamp, Vogts, Surau (Schafer), Klinkhammer, Bonhof, Wimmer (Koppel), Danner, Simonsen, Jensen, Heynckes.

Scorers: Borussia Moenchengladbach – Heynckes 3, Simonsen 2 (1 pen); Twente Enschede – Drost.

UEFA CUP 1975–76

First Round, First Leg

Duisburg 7 (*Mertakas og, Lehmann 3, Worm 2, Thies*), Paralimni 1 (*Chatzyannis*)
Glentoran 1 (*Jamieson*), Ajax 6 (*Geels 4, Meyer, Notten*)
Grasshoppers 3 (*Elsener, Santrac, Bosco*), Real Sociedad 3(*Satrustegui 2, Murillo*)
PAOK Salonika 1 (*Koudas*), Barcelona 0
AIK Stockholm 1 (*Leback pen*), Spartak Moscow 1 (*Lovchev*)
Antwerp 4 (*Heylingen, Kodat 3*), Aston Villa 1 (*Graydon*)
Bohemians Prague 1 (*Masnik*), Honved 2 (*Pinter, Toth*)
Carl Zeiss Jena 3 (*Sengewald 2, Kurbjuweit*), Marseille 0
Uni Craiova 1 (*Oblemenco*), Red Star Belgrade 3 (*Filipovic 2, Savic*)
Everton 0, AC Milan 0
Feyenoord 1 (*De Jong*), Ipswich T 2 (*Whymark, Johnson*)
GAIS Gothenburg 2 (*Palsson 2 [1 pen]*) Slask Wroclaw 1 (*Kwaitkowski*)
Hertha Berlin 4 (*Kostedde 2, Hoor 2*), HJK Helsinki 1 (*Kangaslorpi*)
Hibernian 1 (*Harper*), Liverpool 0
Holbaek 0, Stal Mielec 1 (*Domarski*)
Cologne 2 (*Glowacz, Lohr*), B 1903 Copenhagen 0
Lyon 4 (*Jodar, Millard 2, Mihajlovic*), Bruges 3 (*Van der Eycken 3 [1 pen]*)
Molde 1 (*Wetterdahl*), Oesters Vaxjo 0
Tirgu Mures 2 (*Muresan, Faxekas*), Dynamo Dresden 2 (*Schade, Heidler*)
Chernomonretz Odessa 1 (*Doroschenko*), Lazio 0
Porto 7 (*Julio, Cubillas 3 [1 pen], Oliveira, Octavio, Gomes*), Avenir Beggen 0
Rapid Vienna 1 (*Widmann*), Galatasaray 0
Roma 2 (*Pellegrini, Petrini*), Dounav Russe 0
Moscow Torpedo 4 (*Grishken 2, Sakharov pen, Belenkov*), Napoli 1 (*Savoldi*)
VOEST Linz 2 (*Scharmann, Stering*), Vasas Budapest 0
Vojvodina 0, AEK Athens 0
Young Boys 0, Hamburg 0
Athlone T 3 (*Martin, Davis 2*), Valerengen 1 (*Olsen*)
Inter Bratislava 5 (*Levicky, Luprich, Petras, Jurkemik, Sajanek*), Zaragoza 0
Keflavik 0, Dundee U 2 (*Narey 2*)
Levski Spartak 3 (*Spassov 2, Panov*), Eskisehirspor 0
Sliema Wanderers 1 (*Azzopardi*), Sporting Lisbon 2 (*Marinho, Fernandez*)

First Round, Second Leg

Paralimni 2 (*Konstantinou A., Mertakas*), Duisburg 3 (*Dietz, Krause, Seliger*)
Dundee U 4 (*Hall 2, Hegarty pen, Sturrock*), Keflavik 0
Liverpool 3 (*Toshack 3*), Hibernian 1 (*Edwards*)
AEK Athens 3 (*Papaioannou, Papadopoulos, Wagner*), Vojvodina 1 (*Buikov*)
Ajax 8 (*Notten, Van Dord, Geels 3, Gerrie Muhren, Brokamp 2*), Glentoran 0
Aston Villa 0, Antwerp 1 (*Kodat*)
Barcelona 6 (*Neeskens 2 pens, Rexach 2, Cruyff*), PAOK Salonika 1 (*Anastasiadis*)
Bruges 3 (*Van der Eycken, Valette og, Chnier og*), Lyon 0
Avenir Beggen 0, Porto 3 (*Julio, Grilli og, Seninho*)
Marseille 0, Carl Zeiss Jena 1 (*Irmscher*)
B 1903 Copenhagen 2 (*Christiansen 2*), Cologne 3 (*Brucken 3*)
Dounav Russe 1 (*Ivanov*), Roma 0
Dynamo Dresden 4 (*Heidler 3, Kreische*), Tirgu Mures 1 (*Muresan*)
Eskisehirspor 1 (*Mehmet*), Levski Spartak 4 (*Spassov 2, Panov, Milanov*)
Galatasaray 3 (*Sevki, Gokmen 2*), Rapid Vienna 1 (*Krankl*)
Hamburg 4 (*Reimann, Bertl 2, Bjornmose*), Young Boys 2 (*Siegenthaler 2*)
HJK Helsinki 1 (*Salo*), Hertha Berlin 2 (*Sidka, Grau*)
Honved 1 (*Kocsis pen*), Bohemians Prague 1 (*Panenka*)
Ipswich T 2 (*Woods, Whymark*), Feyenoord 0
Lazio 3 (*Chinaglia 3 [1 pen]*), Chernomoretz Odessa 0
AC Milan 1 (*Calloni pen*), Everton 0
Napoli 1 (*Braglia*), Moscow Torpedo 1 (*Filatov*)
Oesters Vaxjo 6 (*Svensson, Matsson 2, Evesson, Ejderstedt, Isaxsson*), Molde 0
Red Star Belgrade 1 (*Filipovic pen*), Uni Craiova 1 (*Krizan*)
Real Sociedad 1 (*Urreisti*), Grasshoppers 1 (*Santrac*)
Slask Wroclaw 4 (*Sybis 3, Pawlowski*), GAIS Gothenburg 2 (*Hans Johanson 2*)
Moscow Spartak 1 (*Andreyev*), AIK Stockholm 0
Sporting Lisbon 3 (*Baltazar, Da Costa, Manuel Fernandes pen*), Sliema Wanderers 1 (*Loporto*)
Stal Mielec 2 (*Karas, Krawczyk*), Holbaek 1 (*Torben Hansen*)
Valerengen 1 (*Dag Olvavason*), Athlone T 1 (*Martin*)
Vasas Budapest 4 (*Varadi 2, Kovacs, Izso*), VOEST Linz 0
Zaragoza 2 (*Pepe Gonzalez pen, Arrua*), Inter Bratislava 3 (*Jurkemik, Petras, Mraz*)

Second Round, First Leg

Duisburg 3 (*Schneider W., Worm, Krause*), Levski Spartak 2 (*Panov 2*)
Athlone 0, AC Milan 0
Carl Zeiss Jena 1 (*Kurbjuweit*), Stal Mielec 0
Dundee U 1 (*Rennie*), Porto 2 (*Oliveira, Seninho*)
Galatasaray 2 (*Sevki, Gokmen*), Moscow Torpedo 4 (*Enver og, Hrobroskin, Sakharov pen, Maksimenkov*)
Hertha Berlin 1 (*Kostedde*), Ajax 0
Honved 2 (*Weimper 2*), Dynamo Dresden 2 (*Heidler 2*)
Inter Bratislava 2 (*Luprich pen, Mraz*), AEK Athens 0
Ipswich T 3 (*Gates, Peddelty, Austin*), Bruges 0
Spartak Moscow 2 (*Lovchev 2*), Cologne 0
Oesters Vaxjo 1 (*Evansson*), Roma 0
Real Sociedad 1 (*Amas*), Liverpool 3 (*Heighway, Callaghan, Thompson*)
Red Star Belgrade 1 (*Susic*), Hamburg 1 (*Bjornmose*)
Slask Wroclaw 1 (*Pawlowski*), Antwerp 1 (*Houwaart*)
Vasas Budapest 3 (*Kovacs 2, Varad pen*), Sporting Lisbon 1 (*Chico*)
Lazio 0, Barcelona 3 (*Lazio refused to play because of possible political demonstrations against the Spaniards. FIFA thus awarded the game to Barcelona 3-0*).

Second Round, Second Leg

Levski Spartak 2 (*Ivkov, Panov pen*), Duisburg 1 (*Worm*)
Liverpool 6 (*Toshack, Kennedy 2, Fairclough, Heighway, Neal*), Real Sociedad 0
Ajax 4 (Brokamp, Geels 2 [1 pen], Meyer), Hertha Berlin 1 (*Kostedde*)
Antwerp 1 (*De Schrijver*), Slask Wroclaw 2 (*Sybis, Pawlowski*)
AEK Athens 3 (*Tassos 2 [1 pen], Wagner*), Inter Bratislava 1 (*Novotny*)
Barcelona 4 (*Sotil, Cruyff, Neeskens, Fortes*), Lazio 0
Bruges 4 (*Lambert 1 pen, De Cubber, Le Fevre, Van der Eycken*), Ipswich T 0
Dynamo Dresden 1 (*Dorner pen*), Honved 0
Hamburg 4 (*Reimann 2, Ettmayer, Memering*), Red Star Belgrade 0
Cologne 0, Moscow Spartak 1 (*Andreyev*)
AC Milan 3 (*Vincenzi, Benetti 2 [1 pen]*), Athlone T 0
Moscow Torpedo 3 (*Degtyarev, Sahkarov pen, Budulakin*), Galatasaray 0
Porto 1 (*Seninho*), Dundee U 1 (*Hegarty*)
Roma 2 (*Pellegrini, Boni*), Oesters Vaxjo 0
Sporting Lisbon 2 (*Manuel Fernandes 2*), Vasas Budapest 1 (*Grass*)
Stal Mielec 1 (*Karas*), Carl Zeiss Jena 0

Third Round, First Leg

Ajax 2 (*Geels, Steffenhagen*), Levski Spartak 1 (*Voinov*)
Barcelona 3 (*Migueli, Rexach, Neeskens*), Vasas Budapest 1 (*Muller*)
Bruges 1 (*Cools*), Roma 0
Dynamo Dresden 3 (*Riedel 2, Kreische*), Moscow Torpedo 0
Hamburg 2 (*Zaczyk, Volkert pen*), Porto 0
Inter Bratislava 1 (*Saljanek*), Stal Mielec 0
Slask Wroclaw 1 (*Pawlowski*), Liverpool 2 (*Faber og, Toshack*)

AC Milan 4 (*Calloni 2, Bigon, Maldera*), Moscow Spartak 0

Dynamo Dresden 0, Liverpool 0
Hamburg 1 (*Bertl*), Stal Mielec 1 (*Oratowski*)

Third Round, Second Leg
Levski Spartak 2 (*Panov 2*), Ajax 1 (*Geels*)
Liverpool 3 (*Case 3*), Slask Wroclaw 0
Moscow Spartak 2 (*Papayev, Ovchev*), AC Milan 0
Moscow Torpedo 3 (*Dedtyaryov 2, Petrenko*), Dynamo Dresden 1 (*Heidler*)
Porto 2 (*Julio, Cubillas*), Hamburg 1 (*Reimann*)
Roma 0, Bruges 1 (*Lambert*)
Stal Mielec 2 (*Sekulski, Karas*), Inter Bratislava 0
Vasas Budapest 0, Barcelona 1 (*Fortes*)

Quarter-Finals, First Leg
Barcelona 4 (*Neeskens pen, Marcial, Asensi, Heredia*), Levski Spartak 0
Bruges 2 (*Le Fevre, Krieger*), AC Milan 0

Quarter-Finals, Second Leg
Levski Spartak 5 (*Panov 2 [1 pen], Yordanov 2, Spassov*), Barcelona 4 (*Marcial, Asensi, Heredia, Neeskens pen*)
Liverpool 2 (*Case, Keegan*), Dynamo Dresden 1 (*Heidler*)
AC Milan 2 (*Chiarugi 2*), Bruges 1 (*Sanders*)
Stal Mielec 0, Hamburg 1 (*Nogly*)

Semi-Finals, First Leg
Barcelona 0, Liverpool 1 (*Toshack*)
Hamburg 1 (*Reimann*), Bruges 1 (*Lambert*)

Semi-Finals, Second Leg
Bruges 1 (*Kaltz og*), Hamburg 0
Liverpool 1 (*Thompson*), Barcelona 1 (*Rexach*)

Final 1975-76: Liverpool 3, Bruges 2

(At Anfield, 28 April, 1976, 56,000)

Liverpool: Clemence; Smith, Neal, Thompson, Kennedy, Hughes, Keegan, Fairclough, Heighway, Toshack (Case), Callaghan.

Bruges: Jensen; Bastyns, Krieger, Leekens, Volders, Cools, Van der Eycken, De Cubber, Van Gool, Lambert, Le Fevre.

Scorers: Liverpool – Kennedy, Case, Keegan (pen); Bruges – Lambert, Cools.

Bruges 1, Liverpool 1

(At Olympia Stadium, Bruges, 19 May, 1976, 32,000)

Bruges: Jensen; Bastyns, Krieger, Leekens, Volders, Cools, Van der Eycken, Van Gool, Lambert (Sanders), De Cubber (Hinderyckx), Le Fevre.

Liverpool: Clemence; Smith, Neal, Thompson, Kennedy, Hughes, Keegan, Case, Heighway, Toshack (Fairclough), Callaghan.

Scorers: Bruges – Lambert (pen); Liverpool – Keegan.

UEFA CUP 1976–77

First Round, First Leg

Porto 2 (*Rodolfo, Cubillas*), Schalke 04 2 (*Erwin Kremers, Fischer*)
Fram Reykjavik 0, Slovan Bratislava 3 (*Haraslin 2, Mrva*)
Glentoran 3 (*Feeney 2, Dickinson*), Basle 2 (*Maissen, Ramseier*)
Paralimni 1 (*Mertakas*), Kaiserslautern 3 (*Rinderl, Meier, Spiergeri*)
AEK Athens 2 (*Nikoloudis, Papaioannou*), Moscow Dynamo 0
Ajax 1 (*Krol*), Manchester U 0
Austria Salzburg 5 (*Schwarz 3 [1 pen], Haider 2*), Adanaspor 0
Belenenses 2 (*Quaresma, Horta*), Barcelona 2 (*Heredia 2*)
Celtic 2 (*McDonald, Dalglish*), Wisla Krakow 2 (*Kmiecik, Wrobel*)
Derby Co 12 (*Hector 5, Rioch, James 3, George 3*), Finn Harps 0
Dinamo Bucharest 0, AC Milan 0
Eintracht Brunswick 7 (*Hollmann, Stoltenburg 2, Frank 3, Gersdorff*), Holbaek 0
Espanol 3 (*Cuesta, Maranon, Caszely*), Nice 1 (*Toko*)
Feyenoord 3 (*Schneider pen, Kreuz, Vreysen*), Djurgaarden 0
Fenerbahce 2 (*Cemil 2*), Videoton 1 (*Nagy*)
Grasshoppers 7 (*Bosco, Ponte, Seller 2, Bauer, Cornioley 2 [1 pen]*), Hibernian Malta 0
Hibernian 1 (*Brownlie*), Sochaux 0
Internazionale 0, Honved 1 (*Kozma*)
Cologne 2 (*Flohe pen, Van Gool*), GKS Tychy 0
Kuopion Palloseura 3 (*Toernroos, Rissanen 2*), Oester Vaxjo 2 (*Stromberg, Ejderstedt*)
Magdeburg 3 (*Steinbach, Streich 2 [1 pen]*), Cesena 0
Manchester C 1 (*Kidd*), Juventus 0
Naestved 0, RWD Molenbeek 3 (*Boskamp, Wellens 2*)
QPR 4 (*Bowles 3, Masson*), Brann Bergen 0
Red Boys Differdange 0, Lokeren 3 (*Verheyen 2, Dalving*)
Slavia Prague 2 (*Herda, Radolsky*), Akademik Sofia 0
Schachtjor Donetzk 3 (*Rogovsky, Sokolvsky, Starukhin*), Dynamo Berlin 0
Sportul Studentesc 3 (*Grosu, Ionescu 2*), Olympiakos 0
SW Innsbruck 2 (*Sterig, Pezzey*), Start Kristiansand 1 (*Mathiesen pen*)
ASA Tirgu Mures 0, Dynamo Zagreb 1 (*Jurisic*)
Ujpest Dozsa 1 (*Dunai I.*), Atlético Bilbao 0
Lokomotiv Plovdiv 2 (*Fidanov, Bonev*), Red Star Belgrade 1 (*Filipovic*)

First Round, Second Leg

Adanaspor 2 (*Isa, Sener*), Austria Salzburg 0
Akademik Sofia 3 (*Dimitrov 2, Yankov*), Slavia Prague 0
Barcelona 3 (*Rexach, Asensi, Clares*), Belenenses 2 (*Vasques, Rocha*)
Basle 3 (*Nielsen, Mundschin, Demarmels*), Glentoran 0
Dynamo Berlin 1 (*Noak*), Schachtjor Donetzk 1 (*Rogowski*)
Atlético Bilbao 5 (*Rojo 2, Dani 3*), Ujpest Dozsa 0
Brann Bergen 0, QPR 7 (*Webb, Givens 2, Bowles 3, Thomas*)
Cesena 3 (*Mariani, Pepe, Macchi*), Magdeburg 1 (*Sparwasser*)
Djurgaarden 2 (*Karlsson K., Stenbaek*), Feyenoord 1 (*Nico Jansen*)
Dynamo Zagreb 3 (*Sensen 2, Bogdan*), ASA Tirgu Mures 0
Finn Harps 1 (*McFarland og*), Derby Co 4 (*Hector 2, George 2*)
Hibernian Malta 0, Grasshoppers 2 (*Sieler, Cornioley pen*)
Holbaek 1 (*Tofte*), Eintracht Brunswick 0
Honved 1 (*Poczik*), Internazionale 1 (*Mariani*)
Juventus 2 (*Scirea, Boninsegna*), Manchester C 0
Lokeren 3 (*Mommens, Hansen, Lubanski*), Red Boys Differdange 1 (*Flenghi pen*)
Manchester U 2 (*Macari, McIlroy*), Ajax 0
Moscow Dynamo 2 (*Bubnov, Yukubik pen*), AEK Athens 1 (*Tassos pen*)
Nice 2 (*Toko, Bjekovic*), Espanol 1 (*Aquino pen*)
Oester Vaxjo 2 (*Stromberg, Svensson*), Kuopion Palloseura 0
Olympiakos 2 (*Galakos, Karavitis pen*), Sportul Studentesc 1 (*Radacanu*)
RWD Molenbeek 4 (*Koons, Boskamp 2 [1 pen], Cordier*), Naestved 0
Schalke 04 3 (*Fichtel, Abramczik, Fischer*), Porto 2 (*Oliveira 2*)
Slovan Bratislava 5 (*Pekarik, Ondrus, Barto, Capkovic, Atlasson og*), Fram Reykjavik 0
Sochaux 0, Hibernian 0
Start Kristiansand 0, SW Innsbruck 5 (*Koncilia 2, Sterling 2 [1 pen], Witzl*)
GKS Tychy 1 (*Ogaza*), Cologne 1 (*Muller*)
Videoton 4 (*Wollek, Kovacs J., Szalmasy 2*), Fenerbahce 0
Wisla Krakow 2 (*Kmiecik 2*), Celtic 0
Kaiserslautern 8 (*Toppmuller 4, Pirrung 2, Meier, Riedl*), Paralimni 0
AC Milan 2 (*Calloni, Silva*), Dinamo Bucharest 1 (*Satmareanu*)
Red Star Belgrade 4 (*Bolicevic, Filipovic 2, Stamenkovic*), Lokomotiv Plovdiv 1 (*Bonev*)

Second Round, First Leg

AEK Athens 2 (*Wagner 2*), Derby Co 0
Akademik Sofia 4 (*Paunov 2, Manolov, Dimitrov*), AC Milan 3 (*Capello 2, Colovatti*)
Austria Salzburg 2 (*Schwarz P., Schwarz W. pen*), Red Star Belgrade 1 (*Filipovic*)
Barcelona 2 (*Cruyff, Clares*), Lokeren 0
Basle 1 (*Marti*), Atlético Bilbao 1 (*Madariaga*)
Eintracht Brunswick 2 (*Frank, Stolzenburg*), Espanol 1 (*Maranon*)
Hibernian 2 (*Blackley, Brownlie*), Oester Vaxjo 0
SW Innsbruck 1 (*Sterling*), Videoton 1 (*Czeczeli pen*)
Kaiserslautern 2 (*Briegel 2*), Feyenoord 2 (*De Jong, Nico Jansen*)
Cologne 2 (*Konopka, Muller*), Grasshoppers 0
Magdeburg 2 (*Steinbach, Zapf*), Dynamo Zagreb 0
Manchester U 1 (*Hill*), Juventus 0
Schachtjor Donetzk 3 (*Shevluch, Starukhin, Vasin*), Honved 0
Slovan Bratislava 3 (*Novotny, Haraslin, Ondrus*), QPR 3 (*Bowles 2, Givens*)
Sportul Studentesc 0, Schalke 04 1 (*Fischer*)
Wisla Krakow 1 (*Kapka*), RWD Molenbeek 1 (*Olsen*)

Second Round, Second Leg

Atlético Bilbao 3 (*Villar, Carlos, Rojo I*), Basle 1 (*Marti*)
Derby Co 2 (*George, Rioch*), AEK Athens 3 (*Nikoloudis, Tassos, Wagner*)
Dynamo Zagreb 2 (*Kranjcar 2*), Magdeburg 2 (*Streich, Pommerenke*)
Espanol 2 (*Jeremias, Ortiz Aquino pen*), Eintracht Brunswick 0
Feyenoord 5 (*Wim Jansen, Nico Jansen, De Jong, Van Deinsen, Schneider pen*), Kaiserslautern 0
Grasshoppers 2 (*Bauer pen, Bosco*), FC Cologne 3 (*Muller, Larsen 2*)
Honved 2 (*Kozma 2 [1 pen]*), Schachtjor Donetzk 3 (*Shevluik, Reznik 2*)
Juventus 3 (*Boninsegna 2, Benetti*), Manchester U 0
AC Milan 2 (*Calloni, Morini*), Akademik Sofia 0
Oester Vaxjo 4 (*Linderoth 2, Ejderstedt 2*), Hibernian 1 (*Smith*)
QPR 5 (*Givens 3 [1 pen], Bowles, Clement*), Slovan Bratislava 2 (*Ondrus, Jan Capkovic*)
Red Star Belgrade 1 (*Filipovic*), Austria Salzburg 0
RWD Molenbeek 1 (*Nielsen*), Wisla Krakow 1 (*Maculewicz*)
Schalke 04 4 (*Bongartz 2, Fischer 2*), Sportul Studentesc 0
Videoton 1 (*Nagy*), SW Innsbruck 0
Lokeren 2 (*Verheyen, Dalving*), Barcelona 1 (*Cruyff*)

Third Round, First Leg

AEK Athens 2 (*Papaioannou, Mavros*), Red Star Belgrade 0
Atlético Bilbao 4 (*Dani 2 [1 pen], Carlos 2*), AC Milan 1 (*Capello*)

Espanol 0, Feyenoord 1 (*De Felipe og*)
Juventus 3 (*Bettega, Tardelli, Boninsegna*), Schachtjor Donetzk 0
Magdeburg 5 (*Streich, Tyll 2, Mewes, Pommerenke*), Videoton 0
Oester Vaxjo 0, Barcelona 3 (*Clares 2, Neeskens*)
QPR 3 (*Givens, Webb, Bowles*), Cologne 0
RWD Molenbeek 1 (*Lafont*), Schalke 04 0

Third Round, Second Leg
Cologne 4 (*Muller 2, Lohr, Weber*), QPR 1 (*Masson*)
Barcelona 5 (*Clares, Cruyff, Asensi 2, Heredia*), Oester Vaxjo 1 (*Everson*)
Feyenoord 2 (*Krauz, Nico Jansen*), Espanol 0
AC Milan 3 (*Calloni 2 [1 pen], Biasiolo*), Atlético Bilbao 1 (*Madariaga pen*)
Red Star Belgrade 3 (*Baralic, Filipovic, Savic*), AEK Athens 1 (*Wagner*)
Schalke 04 1 (Abramczik), RWD Molenbeek 1 (*Teugels*)
Schachtjor Donetsk 1 (*Shevluk*), Juventus 0
Videoton 1 (*Nagy J.*), Magdeburg 0

Quarter-Final, First Leg
Atlético Bilbao 2 (*Churruca, Dani pen*), Barcelona 1 (*Asensi*)
Feyenoord 0, RWD Molenbeek 0
Magdeburg 1 (*Streich*), Juventus 3 (*Cuccureddu, Benetti, Boninsegna*)
QPR 3 (*Francis 2 pens, Bowles*), AEK Athens 0

Quarter-Final, Second Leg
AEK Athens 3 (*Mavros 2, Papaioannou*), QPR 0
Barcelona 2 (*Cruyff 2*), Atlético Bilbao 2 (*Irureta 2*)
Juventus 1 (*Cuccureddu*), Magdeburg 0
RWD Molenbeek 2 (*Wellens, Teugels pen*), Feyenoord 1 (*De Jong*)

Semi-Final, First Leg
RWD Molenbeek 1 (*Teugels*), Atlético Bilbao 1 (*Churruca*)
Juventus 4 (*Cuccureddu, Bettega 2, Causio*), AEK Athens 1 (*Papadopoulos*)

Semi-Final, Second Leg
AEK Athens 0, Juventus 1 (*Bettega*)
Atlético Bilbao 0, RWD Molenbeek 0

Final 1976–77: Juventus 1, Atlético Bilbao 0
(In Turin, 4 May, 1977, 75,000)

Juventus: Zoff; Cuccureddu, Gentile, Scirea, Morini, Tardelli, Furino, Benetti, Causio, Boninsegna (Gori), Bettega.
Atlético Bilbao: Iribar; Villar, Escalza, Guoicoechea, Guisasola, Quaderra, Irureta, Rojo II, Dani, Churruca, Rojo I.
Scorer: Juventus – Tardelli.

Atlético Bilbao 2, Juventus 1
(In Bilbao, 18 May, 1977, 43,000)

Atlético Bilbao: Iribar; Lasa (Carlos), Guisasola, Alesanco, Escalza, Villar, Churruca, Irureta, Amarrortu, Dani, Rojo I.
Juventus: Zoff; Cuccureddu, Morini, Scirea, Gentile, Causio, Tardelli, Furino, Benetti, Boninsegna (Spinosi), Bettega.
Scorers: Atlético Bilbao – Irureta, Carlos; Juventus – Bettega.
Juventus won on away goals rule.

UEFA CUP 1977–78

First Round, First Leg

Eintracht Frankfurt 5 (*Nickel 2, Wenzel, Kraus, Grabowski*), Sliema Wanderers 0
AZ 67 11 (*Van Hanegem, Arntz, Nygaard 3, Peters 4, Kist 2*), Red Boys 1 (*Christoph pen*)
Aston Villa 4 (*Gray, Deehan 2, Little*), Fenerbahce 0
Barcelona 5 (*Heredia 2, Cruyff pen, Clares, Zuviria*), Steaua 1 (*Nastase*)
Bastia 3 (*Felix 3*), Sporting Lisbon 2 (*Jordao pen, Fraguito*)
Bayern Munich 8 (*Oblak, Rummenigge 3, Hoeness, Müller 3*), Mjondalen 0
Boavista 1 (*Jorge Gomes*), Lazio 0
Bohemians 0, Newcastle U 0
Carl Zeiss Jena 5 (*Trocha 2, Vogel 2 [1 pen], Topfer*), Altay Izmir 1 (*Mustafa pen*)
Dundee U 1 (*Sturrock*), KB Copenhagen 0
Fiorentina 0, Schalke 04 0
Frem Copenhagen 0, Grasshoppers 2 (*Elsener, Becker*)
Glenavon 2 (*Malone pen, McDonald*), PSV Eindhoven 6 (*Van der Kuylen 2, Van Kraay, Deijkers, Deacy, Lubse*)
Gornik Zabrze 5 (*Gizil 3, Radecki, Wasilewski*), Haka Valkeakosken 3 (*Jarzyna og, Vimomen, Pivinen*)
Internazionale 0, Dynamo Tbilisi 1 (*Kipiani*)
Dynamo Kiev 1 (*Vermeeyev*), Eintracht Brunswick 1 (*Frank*)
Landskrona 0, Ipswich T 1 (*Whymark*)
Las Palmas 5 (*Maciel 2 [1 pen], Juani, Morete 2*), Sloboda Tuzla 0
Lens 4 (*Bosudira, Francoise, Djeballi, Elie*), Malmö FF 1 (*Sjoberg*)
Linz ASK 3 (*Koegelberger 2, Vokovic*), Ujpest Dozsa 2 (*Torocsik 2*)
Odra Opole 1 (*Decker*), Magdeburg 2 (*Sparwasser 2*)
Olympiakos Piraeus 3 (*Karavisis, Losanda, Galakos*), Dynamo Zagreb 1 (*Zedec*)
Manchester C 2 (*Barnes, Channon*), Widzew Lodz 2 (*Boniek 2 [1 pen]*)
Marek Stanke Dimitrov 3 (*Pargov, Petrov 2*), Ferencvaros 0
Rapid Vienna 1 (*Walzer*), Inter Bratislava 0
RWD Molenbeek 0, Aberdeen 0
Servette 1 (*Barberis*), Atlético Bilbao 0
Standard Liège 1 (*Nickel*), Slavia Prague 0
Start Kristiansand 6 (*Myhre, Skuse, Haugen 2, Mathisen 2 [1 pen]*), Fram Reykjavik 0
ASA Tirgu Mures 1 (*Fanici*), AEK Athens 0
Torino 3 (*Pulici 2, Claudio Sala*), Apoel 0
Zurich 1 (*Risi*), CSKA Sofia 0

First Round, Second Leg

Aberdeen 1 (*Jarvie*), RWD Molenbeek 2 (*Gores, Wellens*)
AEK Athens 3 (*Papaioannou, Viera, Moussouris*), ASA Tirgu Mures 0
Altay Izmir 4 (*Mustafa 2, Murat 2*), Carl Zeiss Jena 1 (*Lindemann*)
Apoel 1 (*Marcou*), Torino 1 (*Garritano*)
Atlético Bilbao 2 (*Dani, Amorrortu*), Servette 0
CSKA Sofia 1 (*Markov*), Zurich 1 (*Cuccinotta*)
Eintracht Brunswick 0, Dynamo Kiev 0
Fenebahce 0, Aston Villa 2 (*Deehan, Little*)
Ferencvaros 2 (*Pusztai, Ebedli pen*), Marek Stanke 0
Grasshoppers 6 (*Meyer 2, Becker, Elsener, Ponte 2*), Frem Copenhagen 1 (*Mikkelsen*)
Inter Bratislava 3 (*Novotny 2, Levicky 2*), Rapid Vienna 0
Ipswich T 5 (*Whymark 4 [1 pen], Mariner*), Landskrona 0
Lazio 5 (*Garlaschelli 2, Giordano 3*), Boavista 0
Magdeburg 1 (*Streich*), Odra Opole 1 (*Kiose*)
Malmö FF 2 (*Cervin, Ljungberg*), Lens 0
Mjondalen 0, Bayern Munich 4 (*Rausch, Gruber, Kunkel, Niedermaier*)
Newcastle U 4 (*Gowling 2, Craig T. 2*), Bohemians 0
PSV Eindhoven 5 (*Rene Van der Kerkhof, Lubse 2, Deijkers 2*), Glenavon 0
Schalke 04 2 (*Abramczik, Helmut Kremers*), Fiorentina 1 (*Desolati*)
Slavia Prague 3 (*Vesely, Notovy, Nachtman*), Standard Liège 2 (*Nickel, Sigurvinsson*)
Sliema Wanderers 0, Eintracht Frankfurt 0
Sloboda Tuzla 4 (*Gec, Kovacevic 2, Mulahasonovic*), Las Palmas 3 (*Morete 2, Maciel*)
Sporting Lisbon 1 (*Manuel Fernandes*), Bastia 2 (*Rep, Desvignes*)
Steaua 1 (*Dumitru pen*), Barcelona 3 (*Cruyff, Asensi, Sanchez*)
Dynamo Tbilisi 0, Internazionale 0
Ujpest Dozsa 7 (*Fazekas 2, Toth 2, Torocsik, Sarlos, Fekete*), Linz ASK 0
Valkeakosken 0, Gornik Zabrze 0
Widzew Lodz 0, Manchester C 0
Dynamo Zagreb 5 (*Cerin 2, Senzen, Zajec pen, Bonic*), Olympiakos Piraeus 1 (*Caravitis pen*)
Start Kristiansand 2 (*Skuseth, Ole Olsen*), Fram Reykjavik 0
Red Boys 0, AZ 67 5 (*Kist 3, Van Hanegem, Van Rijnsoer*)
KB Copenhagen 3 (*Andersen 3*), Dundee U 0

Second Round, First Leg

AEK Athens 2 (*Mavros, Nikoloudis*), Standard Liège 2 (*Sigurvinsson, Poul*)
AZ 67 1 (*Nygaard*), Barcelona 1 (*Neeskens*)
Aston Villa 2 (*McNaught 2*), Gornik Zabrze 0
Bastia 2 (*Papi 2*), Newcastle U 1 (*Cannell*)
Bayern Munich 3 (*Müller, Rummenigge 2*), Marek Stanke 0
Inter Bratislava 1 (*Sajanek*), Grasshoppers 0
Ipswich T 1 (*Gates*), Las Palmas 0
KB Copenhagen 1 (*Laudrup*), Dynamo Tbilisi 4 (*Chivadze, Kipiani, Chelebadze, Shengekiya*)
Lazio 2 (*Wilson, Giordano*), Lens 0
Magdeburg 4 (*Sparwasser 3, Steinbach*), Schalke 04 2 (*Demange, Abramczik*)
RWD Molenbeek 1 (*Wellens*), Carl Zeiss Jena 1 (*Lindemann*)
Start Kristiansand 1 (*Helge Haugen*), Eintracht Brunswick 0
Torino 3 (*Pulici, Patrizio Sala, Pecci*), Dynamo Zagreb 1 (*Cerin*)
Ujpest Dozsa 2 (*Torocsik, Viczko*), Atlético Bilbao 0
Widzew Lodz 3 (*Rozborsky, Kowenicki, Boniek*), PSV Eindhoven 5 (*Deijkers 2, Deacy, Van der Kuylen, Francois*)
Zurich 0, Eintracht Frankfurt 3 (*Holzenbein, Wenzel 2*)

Second Round, Second Leg

Barcelona 1 (*Rexach pen*), AZ 67 1 (*Kist*)
Barcelona won on penalties 5-4.
Atlético Bilbao 3 (*Dani 2, Tirapu*), Ujpest Dozsa 0
Eintracht Brunswick 4 (*Breitner, Handschuh, Hollman 2*), Start Kristiansand 0
Carl Zeiss Jena 1 (*Lindemann pen*), RWD Molenbeek 1 (*Alhino*)
Carl Zeiss Jena won on penalties 6-5.
Dynamo Zagreb 1 (*Senzen*), Torino 0
Eintracht Frankfurt 4 (*Kraus, Grabowski, Stepanovic, Krobach*), Zurich 3 (*Risi 2 [1 pen], Torstensson*)
Gornik Zabrze 1 (*Marcinkowski*), Aston Villa 1 (*Gray*)
Grasshoppers 5 (*Elsener 2, Ponte, Sulser, Hey*), Inter Bratislava 1 (*Jurkemik*)
Marek Stanke 2 (*Petrov, Pargov*), Bayern Munich 0
Las Palmas 3 (*Morete 2, Felix*), Ipswich T 3 (*Mariner 2, Tibbott*)
Lens 6 (*Six 3, Bousdira, Djebali 2*), Lazio 0
Newcastle U 1 (*Gowling*), Bastia 3 (*De Zerbi, Rep 2*)
PSV Eindhoven 1 (*Deijkers*), Widzew Lodz 0
Schalke 04 1 (*Kremers*), Magdeburg 3 (*Pommerenke 2, Steinbach*)
Standard Liège 4 (*Labarbe, Riedl, Nickel, Gorez*), AEK Athens 1 (*Ardizoglou*)
Dynamo Tbilisi 2 (*Kipiani, Chelebadze*), KB Copenhagen 1 (*Andersen*)

Third Round, First Leg

Aston Villa 2 (*Iribar og, Deehan*), Atlético Bilbao 0
Bastia 2 (*Papi, Rep*), Torino 1 (*Pulici*)
Carl Zeiss Jena 2 (*Schnuphase, Lindemann*), Standard Liège 0

Eintracht Frankfurt 4 (*Grabowski, Holzenbein, Kraus, Skala*), Bayern Munich 0
Ipswich T 3 (*Gates, Whymark, Talbot*), Barcelona 0
Magdeburg 4 (*Zapf, Pommerenke pen, Mewes, Steinbach*), Lens 0
PSV Eindhoven 2 (*Lubse, Van der Kuylen*), Eintracht Brunswick 0
Dynamo Tbilisi 1 (*Shengelia*), Grasshoppers 0

Third Round, Second Leg
Atlético Bilbao 1 (*Dani*), Aston Villa 1 (*Mortimer*)
Barcelona 3 (*Cruyff 2, Rexach pen*), Ipswich T 0
Barcelona won on penalties 3-1.
Bayern Munich 1 (*Rummenigge*), Eintracht Frankfurt 2 (*Wenzel, Holzenbein*)
Eintracht Brunswick 1 (*Bruns*), PSV Eindhoven 2 (*Van Kraay, Deijkers*)
Grasshoppers 4 (*Sulser, Ponte 2 [1 pen], Elsener*), Dynamo Tbilisi 0
Lens 2 (*Bousdira 2*), Magdeburg 0
Standard Liège 1 (*Nickel*), Carl Zeiss Jena 2 (*Szengewald, Weise pen*)
Torino 2 (*Graziani 2*), Bastia 3 (*Larios, Krimau 2*)

Quarter-Final, First Leg
Aston Villa 2 (*McNaught, Deehan*), Barcelona 2 (*Cruyff, Zuviria*)
Bastia 7 (*Larios, Papi, Mariot, Felix 2, Cazes, Franceschetti*), Carl Zeiss Jena 2 (*Raab 2*)
Magdeburg 1 (Streich), PSV Eindhoven 0
Eintracht Frankfurt 3 (*Kraus, Holzenbein 2 [1 pen]*), Grasshoppers 2 (*Bosco, Ponte pen*)

Quarter-Final, Second Leg
Grasshoppers 1 (*Ponte pen*), Eintracht Frankfurt 0
Carl Zeiss Jena 4 (*Raab, Lindemann, Vogel, Topfer pen*), Bastia 2 (*Papi, Krimau*)
PSV Eindhoven 4 (*Brandst 2, Seguin og, Lubse*), Magdeburg 2 (*Hoffman, Pommerenke*)
Barcelona 2 (*Migueli, Asensi*), Aston Villa 1 (*Little*)

Semi-Final, First Leg
Grasshoppers 3 (*Hermann, Ponte pen, Montandon*), Bastia 2 (*Krimau, Papi pen*)
PSV Eindhoven 3 (*Olmo og, Lubse, Postuma*), Barcelona 0

Semi-Final, Second Leg
Barcelona 3 (*Rexach 2 pens, Fortes*), PSV Eindhoven 1 (*Deacy*)
Bastia 1 (*Papi*), Grasshoppers 0

Final 1977–78: Bastia 0, PSV Eindhoven 0

(In Corsica, 26 April, 1978, 15,000)

Bastia: Hiard; Burkhard, Guesdon, Orlanducci, Cazes, Papi, Lacuseta (Felix), Larios, Rep, Krimau, Mariot.

PSV Eindhoven: Van Beveren; Van Kraay, Krijgh, Stevens, Brandts, Poortvliet, Van der Kuylen, Willy Van der Kerkhof, Deijkers, Rene Van der Kerkhof, Lubse.

PSV Eindhoven 3, Bastia 0

(In Eindhoven, 9 May, 1978, 27,000)

PSV Eindhoven: Van Beveren; Krijgh, Stevens, Van Kraay (Deacy), Brandts, Willy Van der Kerkhof, Poortvliet, Van der Kuylen, Lubse, Deijkers, Rene Van der Kerkhof.

Bastia: Hiard (Weller); Marchioni, Orlanducci, Guesdon, Cazes, Lacuesta, Larios, Papi, Rep, Krimau, Mariot (De Zerbi).

Scorers: PSV Eindhoven – Willy Van der Kerkhof, Deijkers, Van der Kuylen.

UEFA CUP 1978–79

First Round, First Leg
Dukla Prague 1 (*Nehoda*), Lanerossi Vicenza 0
AC Milan 1 (*Novellino*), Lokomotiv Kosice 0
CSKA Sofia 2 (*Djevizov, Christov*), Valencia 1 (*Solsona*)
Borussia Moenchengladbach 5 (*Bruns 2, Gores, Nielsen, Simonsen*), Sturm Graz 1 (*Jurtin*)
Arges Pitesti 3 (*Toma, Moiceanu 2*), Panathinaikos 0
Atlético Bilbao 2 (*Van Dord og, Vidal*), Ajax 0
Everton 5 (*King 2, Thomas, Walsh, Latchford*), Finn Harps 0
Jeunesse Esch 0, Lausanne 0
Nantes 0, Benfica 2 (*Chalana, Nene*)
Gijon 3 (*Ferrero, Moran 2*), Torino 0
Sporting Braga 5 (*Chico Gordo 4, Lito*), Hibernians 0
Galatasaray 1 (*Fatih*), WBA 3 (*Robson, Regis, Cunningham*)
Dynamo Berlin 5 (*Riediger 3, Netz, Brillat*), Red Star Belgrade 2 (*Sestic, Savic*)
Palloseura 2 (*Monkkanen, Eiskanen*), 1903 Copenhagen 1 (*Haarby*)
Basle 2 (*Tanner, Stohler*), Stuttgart 3 (*Ohlicher 2, Dieter Hoeness*)
Torpedo Moscow 4 (*Vassilev, Mironov, Grijsin, Sutsijlin*), Molde 0
Elfsborg 2 (*Svensson, Magnusson*), Strasbourg 0
Duisburg 5 (*Jara, Alhaus, Bussers, Worm 2*), Lech Poznan 0
Standard Liège 1 (*Denier*), Dundee U 0
Start Kristiansand 0, Esbjerg 0
Arsenal 3 (*Stapleton 2, Sunderland*), Lokomotiv Leipzig 0
Carl Zeiss Jena 1 (*Topfer*), Lierse 0
Glentoran 0, IBV Vestmann 0
Twente 1 (*Thorsen*), Manchester C 1 (*Watson*)
Hibernian 3 (*Higgins 2, Temperley*), IFK Norrköping 2 (*Ohlsson, Andersson*)
Timisoara 2 (*Cotec, Paltinisan*), MTK Budapest 0
Pezoporikos 2 (*Teofonu 2*), Slask Wroclaw 2 (*Pawlowski, Sybis*)
Olympiakos 2 (Kritikopoulos, Kaltzas), Levski Spartak 1 (*Panov*)
Dynamo Tbilisi 2 (*Kipiani, Shengelja*), Napoli 0
Hajduk Split 2 (*Kop, Luchetin*), Rapid Vienna 0
Hertha Berlin 0, Trakia Plovdiv 0
Honved 6 (*Lukacs, Weimper 2, Gijmesi, Bodoyni, Nagy*), Adanaspor 0

First Round, Second Leg
Lanerossi Vicenza 1 (*Briaschi*), Dukla Prague 1 (*Roselli og*)
Lokomotiv Kosice 1 (*Kozak*), AC Milan 0
Valencia 4 (*Saura 2, Kempes, Felman*), CSKA Sofia 1 (*Christov*)
Sturm Graz 1 (*Schilcher*), Borussia Moenchengladbach 2 (*Simonsen, Bruns*)
Panathinaikos 1 (*Gonios*), Arges Pitesti 2 (*Duru, Radu*)
Ajax 3 (*Clarke 2, Lerby*), Atlético Bilbao 0
Finn Harps 0, Everton 5 (*King, Latchford, Walsh, Ross, Dobson*)
Lausanne 2 (*Dizerens, Sanpedro*), Jeunesse Esch 0
Benfica 0, Nantes 0
Torino 1 (*Graziani*), Gijon 0
Hibernians 3 (*Spiteri Gonzi, Mizzi 2*), Sporting Braga 2 (*Chico Gordo, Reinaldo*)
WBA 3 (*Robson, Cunningham, Trewick*), Galatasaray 1 (*Turgay*)
Red Star Belgrade 4 (*Borovnicka 2, Savic, Sestic*), Dynamo Berlin 1 (*Riediger*)
1903 Copenhagen 4 (*Christensen, Smidt, Larsen, Dam*), Palloseura 4 (*Eiskanen 2, Heinalainen, Rautio*)
Stuttgart 4 (*Kelsch 3, Hansi Muller*), Basle 1 (*Schonberger*)
Molde 3 (*Brakstad, Bjoraa, Fuglseth*), Torpedo Moscow 3 (*Vassilev 2, Zotijlin*)
Strasbourg 4 (*Piasecki, Tanter, Marx, Wagner*), Elfsborg 1 (*Ahlstrom*)
Lech Poznan 2 (*Kasalik, Okonski*), Duisburg 5 (*Bussers, Worm 2, Wenten, Buttgereit*)
Dundee U 0, Standard Liège 0
Esbjerg 1 (*Iversen*), Start Kristiansand 0
Lokomotiv Leipzig 1 (*Stapleton og*), Arsenal 4 (*Price, Sunderland, Stapleton 2*)
Lierse 2 (*Bosche, Van den Bergh*), Carl Zeiss Jena 2 (*Schupase, Topfer*)
IBV Westmann 1 (*Oskarsson*), Glentoran 1 (*McFall*)
Manchester C 3 (*Kidd, Bell, Overweg og*), Twente 2 (*Wildschut, Gritter*)
IFK Norrköping 0, Hibernian 0
MTK Budapest 2 (Koritar, Nadu og), Timisoara 1 (*Petrescu*)
Slask Wroclaw 5 (*Garlowski, Faber, Olesiak, Kwiatkowski, Sybis*), Pezoporikos 1 (*Lambrou*)
Levski Spartak 3 (*Milkov, Panov, Voinov*), Olympiakos 1 (*Kaltzas*)
Napoli 1 (*Savoldi*), Dynamo Tbilisi 1 (*Daraselia*)
Rapid Vienna 2 (*Krejcirik, Francker*), Hajduk Split 1 (*Zungul*)
Trakia Plovdiv 1 (*Argirov*), Hertha Berlin 2 (*Granitza 2*)
Adanaspor 2 (*Irfan, Necip*), Honved 2 (*Sener og, Pinter*)

Second Round, First Leg
Ajax 1 (*Lerby*), Lausanne 0
Benfica 0, Borussia Moenchengladbach 0
Everton 2 (*Latchford, King*), Dukla Prague 1 (*Macela*)
Arges Pitesti 2 (*Dobrin, Moiceanu*), Valencia 1 (*Felman*)
Sporting Braga 0, WBA 2 (*Regis 2*)
Torpedo Moscow 2 (*Vassilev, Sakharov*), Stuttgart 1 (*Dieter Hoeness*)
Strasbourg 2 (*Gemmrich, Piasecki*), Hibernian 0
Gijon 0, Red Star Belgrade 1 (*Misa og*)
Carl Zeiss Jena 0, Duisburg 0
Palloseura 0, Esbjerg 2 (*Bach, Nielsen*)
IBV Westmann 0, Slask Wroclaw 2 (*Kwiatkowski, Halgrimsson og*)
Manchester C 4 (*Hartford, Palmer, Kidd 2*), Standard Liège 0
Honved 4 (*Weimper 2, Gijmesi, Pinter*), Timisoara 0
Hertha Berlin 2 (*Nussing, Granitza*), Dynamo Tbilisi 0
Hajduk Split 2 (*Kop, Djordjevic*), Arsenal 1 (*Brady*)
Levski Spartak 1 (*Milkov*), AC Milan 1 (*Chiodi*)

Second Round, Second Leg
WBA 1 (*Brown A.*), Sporting Braga 0
Stuttgart 2 (*Hansi Muller, Volkert*), Torpedo Moscow 0
Hibernian 1 (*MacLeod*), Strasbourg 0
Red Star Belgrade 1 (*Petrovic*), Gijon 1 (*Borovnika og*)
Duisburg 3 (*Dietz, Jara, Fruck*), Carl Zeiss Jena 0
Esbjerg 4 (*Berthelsen, Thoresen, Stergaard, Bach*), Palloseura 1 (*Loikkanen*)
Slask Wroclaw 2 (*Nocko, Kwiatkowski*), IBV Westmann 1 (*Halgrimsson*)
Standard Liège 2 (*Sigurvinsson 2*), Manchester C 0
Timisoara 2 (*Rosca, Paltinislan*), Honved 0
Dynamo Tbilisi 1 (*Shengelia*), Hertha Berlin 0
Arsenal 1 (*Young*), Hajduk Split 0
AC Milan 3 (*Maldera, Bigon, Chiodi*), Levski Spartak 0
Dukla Prague 1 (*Gajdusek*), Everton 0
Lausanne 0, Ajax 4 (*Erkens, Clarke 2, Arnesen*)
Valencia 5 (*Kempes 2, Bonhof, Saura, Solsona*), Arges Pitesti 2 (*Moiceanu, Doru Nicolae*)
Borussia Moenchengladbach 2 (*Bruns pen, Klinkhammer*), Benfica 0

Third Round, First Leg
Stuttgart 4 (*Volkert 2 [1 pen], Kelsch, Ohlicher*), Dukla Prague 1 (*Gajdusek*)
Honved 4 (*Nagy 2, Lukacs, Weimper pen*), Ajax 1 (*Clarke pen*)
Red Star Belgrade 1 (*Blagojevic*), Arsenal 0
Esbjerg 2 (Hansen pen, Jaspersen), Hertha Berlin 1 (*Milewski*)
Borussia Moenchengladbach 1 (*Kulik pen*), Slask Wroclaw 1 (*Olesiak*)
Valencia 1 (*Felman*), WBA 1 (*Cunningham*)
Strasbourg 0, Duisburg 0
AC Milan 2 (*Bigon 2*), Manchester C 2 (*Kidd, Power*)

Third Round, Second Leg
Dukla Prague 4 (*Dieter Hoeness og, Vizek, Pelc pen, Gajdusek*), Stuttgart 0

Ajax 2 (*Clarke pen, Tahamata*), Honved 0
Arsenal 1 (*Sunderland*), Red Star Belgrade 1 (*Savic*)
Hertha Berlin 4 (*Milewski 4*), Esbjerg 0
Slask Wroclaw 2 (*Pawlowski 2 [1 pen]*), Borussia Moenchengladbach 4 (*Simonsen 3, Nielsen*)
WBA 2 (*Brown T. 2*), Valencia 0
Duisburg 4 (*Worm, Weber 2, Fruck*), Strasbourg 0
Manchester C 3 (*Booth, Hartford, Kidd*), AC Milan 0

Quarter-Finals, First Leg
Honved 2 (*Varga II, Weimper pen*), Duisburg 3 (*Worm 2, Seliger*)
Red Star Belgrade 1 (*Savic*), WBA 0
Manchester C 1 (*Channon*), Borussia Moenchengladbach 1 (*Lienen*)
Hertha Berlin 1 (*Nussing*), Dukla Prague 1 (*Pelc*)

Quarter-Finals, Second Leg
Duisburg 1 (*Bussers*), Honved 2 (*Karalyos, Pal*)
WBA 1 (*Regis*), Red Star Belgrade 1 (*Sestic*)
Borussia Moenchengladbach 3 (*Kulik, Bruns, Del Haye*), Manchester C 1 (*Deyna*)
Dukla Prague 1 (*Nehoda*), Hertha Berlin 2 (*Agerbeck, Milewski*)

Semi-Finals, First Leg
Red Star Belgrade 1 (*Savic*), Hertha Berlin 0
Duisburg 2 (*Worm, Fruck*), Borussia Moenchengladbach 2 (*Simonsen, Lausen*)

Semi-Finals, Second Leg
Hertha Berlin 2 (*Beer, Sidka*), Red Star Belgrade 1 (*Milosavljevic*)
Borussia Moenchengladbach 4 (*Simonsen 2, Kulik, Lienen*), Duisburg 1 (*Bussers*)

Final 1978–79: Red Star Belgrade 1, Borussia Moenchengladbach 1
(In Belgrade, 9 May, 1979, 87,500)

Red Star Belgrade: Stojanovic; Jovanovic, Miletovic, Jurisic, Jovin, Muslin (Krmpotic), Petrovic, Blagojevic, Milosavljevic (Milovanovic), Savic, Sestic.

Borussia Moenchengladbach: Kneib; Vogts, Hannes, Schaffer, Ringles, Schafer, Kulik, Nielsen (Danner), Wohlers (Gores), Simonsen, Lienen.

Scorers: Red Star Belgrade – Sestic; Borussia Moenchengladbach – Juristic og.

Borussia Moenchengladbach 1, Red Star Belgrade 0
(In Dusseldorf, 23 May, 1979, 45,000)

Borussia Moenchengladbach: Kneib; Vogts, Hannes, Schaffer, Ringles, Schafer, Kulik (Koppel), Gores, Wohlers, Simonsen, Lienen.

Red Star Belgrade: Stojanovic; Jovanovic, Miletovic, Jurisic, Jovin, Muslin, Petrovic, Blagojevic, Milovanovic (Sestic), Savic, Milosavljevic.

Scorer: Borussia Moenchengladbach – Simonsen (pen).

UEFA CUP 1979–80

First Round, First Leg
Perugia 1 (*Vujadinovic og*), Dinamo Zagreb 0
Inter-Milan 3 (*Muraro, Baresi, Marini*), Real Sociedad 0
Napoli 2 (*Damiani, Agostinelli*), Olympiakos 0
Stuttgart 1 (*Danova og*), Torino 0
Dundee U 0, Anderlecht 0
Glenavon 0, Standard Liège 1 (*Edstroem*)
Dinamo Kiev 2 (*Bessonov, Demianenko*), CSKA Sofia 1 (*Metodiev*)
Lokomotiv Sofia 3 (*Stankov, Velickov, Szokolov*), Ferencvaros 0
Kalmar 2 (*Sunesson, Sandberg*), IBK Keflavik 1 (*Mergeisson*)
KPT Kuopio 1 (*Pirinen*), Malmö 2 (*Andersson, Prytz pen*)
Dinamo Bucharest 3 (*Multescu, Georgescu, Vrinceanu*), Alki Larnaca 0
Bohemians Prague 0, Bayern Munich 2 (*Kraus, Rummenigge*)
Zbrojovka Brno 6 (*Mazura, Janecka 2, Kroupa, Jarusek 2*), Esbjerg 0
Valletta 0, Leeds U 4 (*Graham 3, Hart*)
Orduspor 2 (*Cihan, Arif*), Banik Ostrava 0
Wiener SK 0, Uni Craiova 0
Widzew Lodz 2 (*Boniek, Kowienicki*), St Etienne 1 (*Platini*)
Aris Salonika 3 (*Cuis, Pallas pen, Zindros*), Benfica 1 (*Reinaldo*)
Carl Zeiss Jena 2 (*Schnuphase, Lindemann*), WBA 0
Atlético Madrid 1 (*Ruben Cano*), Dinamo Dresden 2 (*Hafner, Weber*)
Aarhus 1 (*Olesen*), Stal Mielec 1 (*Karas*)
Feyenoord 1 (*Notten*), Everton 0
Skeid Oslo 1 (*Rein*), Ipswich T 3 (*Mills, Turner, Mariner*)
Gijon 0, PSV Eindhoven 0
Galatasaray 0, Red Star Belgrade 0
Aberdeen 1 (*Harper*), Eintracht Frankfurt 1 (*Bum Kun Cha*)
Rapid Vienna 0, Diosgyor 1 (*Fuko*)
Borussia Moenchengladbach 3 (*Lienen, Nickel pen, Kulik*), Viking 0
Sporting Lisbon 2 (*Fernandes 2*), Bohemians 0
Zurich 1 (*Zwicher*), Kaiserslautern 3 (*Neues, Bongartz, Wolff*)
Shakhtjor 2 (*Sokolovsky 2*), Monaco 1 (*Petit*)
Progres Niedercorn 0, Grasshoppers 2 (*Herbert Hermann, Egli*)

First Round, Second Leg
Dinamo Zagreb 0, Perugia 0
Real Sociedad 2 (*Satrustegui 2*), Inter-Milan 0
Olympiakos 1 (*Karavitis*), Napoli 0
Torino 2 (*Sala, Graziani*), Stuttgart 1 (*Ohlicher*)
Anderlecht 1 (*Nielsen*), Dundee U 1 (*Kopel*)
Standard Liège 1 (*Edstrom*), Glenavon 0
CSKA Sofia 1 (*Metodiev pen*), Dinamo Kiev 1 (*Buryak*)
Ferencvaros 2 (*Pusztai, Pogany*), Lokomotiv Sofia 0
IBK Keflavik 1 (*Andreasson og*), Kalmar 0
Malmö 2 (*Arvidsson 2*), KPT Kuopio 0
Alki Larnaca 0, Dinamo Bucharest 9 (*Georgescu 3, Vrinceanu 2, Augustin, Talanar, Multescu, Moldovan*)
Bayern Munich 2 (*Rummenigge, Breitner pen*), Bohemians Prague 2 (*Ondrus, Prokas pen*)
Esbjerg 1 (*Bach*), Zbrojovka Brno 1 (*Jarusek*)
Leeds U 3 (*Curtis, Hankin, Hart*), Valletta 0
Banik Ostrava 6 (*Knapp, Vojacek, Nemec, Licka 2, Danek*), Orduspor 0
Uni Craiova 3 (*Camataru 2, Geolganu*), Wiener SK 1 (*Drabits*)
St Etienne 3 (*Rep 3* [*1 pen*]), Widzew Lodz 0
Benfica 2 (*Reinaldo, Gomes*), Aris Salonika 1 (*Semertzidis*)
WBA 1 (*Wile*), Carl Zeiss Jena 2 (*Lindemann, Raab pen*)
Dinamo Dresden 3 (*Riedl, Ruiz og, Weber*), Atlético Madrid 0
Stal Mielec 0, Aarhus 1 (*Jensen*)
Everton 0, Feyenoord 1 (*Budding*)
Ipswich T 7 (*Wark, Muhren 2, McCall 2, Mariner, Thijssen*), Skeid Oslo 0
PSV Eindhoven 1 (*Van der Kerkhof W.*), Gijon 0
Red Star Belgrade 3 (*Savic 2, Milovanovic*), Galatasaray 1 (*Gungor*)
Eintracht Frankfurt 1 (*Holzenbein*), Aberdeen 0
Diosgyor 3 (*Szalai, Fekete, Tatar*), Rapid Vienna 2 (*Keglevits, Sallmayer*)
Viking 1 (*Bjensen*), Borussia Moenchengladbach 1 (*Kulik*)
Bohemians 0, Sporting Lisbon 0
Kaiserslautern 5 (*Melzer 2, Kaminke, Wendt, Geye*), Zurich 1 (*Zappa*)
Monaco 2 (*Onnis, Dalger*), Shakhtjor 0
Grasshoppers 4 (*Ponte, Pfister, Egli, Heinz Hermann*), Progres Niedercorn 0

Second Round, First Leg
Aris Salonika 1 (*Semertzidis*), Perugia 1 (*Rossi*)
Standard Liège 2 (*Riedl, Sigurvinsson pen*), Napoli 1 (*Capone*)
Borussia Moenchengladbach 1 (*Hannes*), Inter-Milan 1 (*Altobelli*)
Dinamo Bucharest 2 (*Multescu pen, Augustin*), Eintracht Frankfurt 0
Uni Craiova 2 (*Balaci, Irimescu*), Leeds U 0
Zbrojovka Brno 3 (*Kotasek 2, Janecka*), IBK Keflavik 1 (*Georgsson*)
Red Star Belgrade 3 (*Savic pen, Muslin, Sestic*), Carl Zeiss Jena 2 (*Raab 2* [*1 pen*])
Lokomotiv Sofia 4 (*Mihailov 4* [*2 pens*]), Monaco 2 (*Onnis 2* [*1 pen*])
Dundee U 0, Diosgyor 1 (*Fekete*)
Aarhus 1 (*Sander*), Bayern Munich 2 (*Rummenigge 2*)
Grasshoppers 0, Ipswich T 0
Feyenoord 4 (*Petursson 3* [*1 pen*], *Van Diesen*), Malmö 0
PSV Eindhoven 2 (*Van der Kerkhof R., Moster*), St Etienne 0
Sporting Lisbon 1 (*Fernandes*), Kaiserslautern 1 (*Bongartz*)
Dinamo Dresden 1 (*Weber pen*), Stuttgart 1 (*Forster*)
Banik Ostrava 1 (*Nemec*), Dinamo Kiev 0

Second Round, Second Leg
Perugia 0, Aris Salonika 3 (*Cuis, Semcrtzidis, Zindros*)
Napoli 1 (*Damiani*), Standard Liège 1 (*Riedl*)
Inter-Milan 2 (*Altobelli 2*), Borussia Moenchengladbach 3 (*Nickel 2* [*1 pen*], *Ringells*)
Eintracht Frankfurt 3 (*Bum Kun Cha, Holzenbein, Nickel*), Dinamo Bucharest 0
Leeds U 0, Uni Craiova 2 (*Ciriu, Beldeanu*)
IBK Keflavik 1 (*Olafsson*), Zbrojovka Brno 2 (*Kroupa, Kotasek*)
Carl Zeiss Jena 2 (*Trocha, Topfer*), Red Star Belgrade 3 (*Kurbjuweit og, Filipovic, Blagojevic*)
Monaco 2 (*Christophe, Onnis*), Lokomotiv Sofia 1 (*Mihailov*)
Diosgyor 3 (*Borostyan, Tatar 2* [*1 pen*]), Dundee U 1 (*Kopel*)
Bayern Munich 3 (*Hoeness D. 2, Breitner*), Aarhus 1 (*Mickelsen*)
Ipswich T 1 (*Beattie*), Grasshoppers 1 (*Sulser*)
Malmö 1 (*Arvidsson*), Feyenoord 1 (*Petursson*)
St Etienne 6 (*Larios, Santini, Platini 2, Roussey, Rep pen*), PSV Eindhoven 0
Kaiserslautern 2 (*Bongartz, Neues pen*), Sporting Lisbon 0
Stuttgart 0, Dinamo Dresden 0
Dinamo Kiev 2 (*Demianenko, Kapsalis*), Banik Ostrava 0

Third Round, First Leg
Bayern Munich 2 (*Rummenigge, Janzon*), Red Star Belgrade 0
Grasshoppers 0, Stuttgart 2 (*Klotz, Hadewicz*)
Borussia Moenchengladbach 2 (*Nickel 2*), Uni Craiova 0
Diosgyor 0, Kaiserslautern 2 (*Wendt, Bongartz*)
Eintracht Frankfurt 4 (*Bum Kun Cha, Nickel, Muller, Lotterman*), Feyenoord 1 (*Stafleu*)
Standard Liège 1 (*Voordeckers*), Zbrojovka Brno 2 (*Svoboda, Dosek*)
St Etienne 4 (*Platini, Larios, Firos og, Roussey*), Aris Salonika 1 (*Semertzidis*)
Lokomotiv Sofia 1 (*Mihailov*), Dinamo Kiev 0

Third Round, Second Leg

Red Star Belgrade 3 (*Savic, Petrovic, Repcic*), Bayern Munich 2 (*Hoeness 2*)
Stuttgart 3 (*Muller, Martin, Kelsh*), Grasshoppers 0
Uni Craiova 1 (*Irimescu*), Borussia Moenchengladbach 0
Kaiserslautern 6 (*Neues, Melzer, Brummer, Kaminke, Bongartz, Stabel pen*), Diosgyor 1 (*Borostyan*)
Feyenoord 1 (*Peters*), Eintracht Frankfurt 0
Zbrojovka Brno 3 (*Jarusel, Kroupa, Janecka*), Standard Liège 2 (*Edstrom, De Matos*)
Aris Salonika 3 (*Larios og, Pallas pen, Venos*), St Etienne 3 (*Larios, Zimako, Rep*)
Dinamo Kiev 2 (*Blochin, Kapsalis*), Lokomotiv Sofia 1 (*Doychev*)

Quarter-Final, First Leg

St Etienne 1 (*Platini*), Borussia Moenchengladbach 4 (*Nielsen 2, Nickel, Lienen*)
Kaiserslautern 1 (*Brummer*), Bayern Munich 0
Eintracht Frankfurt 4 (*Nachtweih, Lorant pen, Nickel, Karger*), Zbrojovka Brno 1 (*Horny*)
Stuttgart 3 (*Muller, Volkert 2 [1 pen]*), Lokomotiv Sofia 1 (*Kolev*)

Quarter-Final, Second Leg

Borussia Moenchengladbach 2 (*Thychosen, Hannes*), St Etienne 0
Bayern Munich 4 (*Hoeness 2, Janzon, Breitner pen*), Kaiserslautern 1 (*Wendt*)
Zbrojovka Brno 3 (*Horny, Kotasek, Kopenec*), Eintracht Frankfurt 2 (*Karger, Neuberger*)
Lokomotiv Sofia 0, Stuttgart 1 (*Ohlicher*)

Semi-Final, First Leg

Stuttgart 2 (*Ohlicher, Volkert pen*), Borussia Moenchengladbach 1 (*Nickel*)
Bayern Munich 2 (*Hoeness, Breitner pen*), Eintracht Frankfurt 0

Semi-Final, Second Leg

Borussia Moenchengladbach 2 (*Matthaus, Schaefer*), Stuttgart 0
Eintracht Frankfurt 5 (*Pezzey 2, Karger 2, Lorant pen*), Bayern Munich 1 (*Dremmler*)

Final 1979–80: Borussia Moenchengladbach 3, Eintracht Frankfurt 2

(In Moenchengladbach, 7 May, 1980, 25,000)

Borussia Moenchengladbach: Kneib; Hannes, Schaefer, Schaeffer, Ringels, Matthaus, Kulik, Nielsen (Thychosen), Del'Haye (Boedeker), Harald Nickel, Lienen.

Eintracht Frankfurt: Pahl; Pezzey, Neuberger, Koerbel, Ehrmanntraut, Lorant, Holzenbein (Nachtweih), Borchers, Bernd Nickel, Tscha, Karger (Trapp).

Scorers: Borussia Moenchengladbach – Kulik 2, Matthaus; Eintracht Frankfurt – Karger, Holzenbein.

Eintracht Frankfurt 1, Borussia Moenchengladbach 0

(In Frankfurt, 21 May, 1980, 60,000)

Eintracht Frankfurt: Pahl; Pezzey, Neuberger, Koerbel, Ehrmanntraut, Lorant, Holzenbein, Borchers, Bernd Nickel, Tscha, Nachtweih (Schaub).

Borussia Moenchengladbach: Kneib; Hannes, Fleer, Schaefer, Ringels, Matthaus (Thychosen), Boedeker, Kulik, Nielsen (Del'Haye), Harald Nickel, Lienen.

Scorer: Eintracht Frankfurt – Schaub.

Eintracht Frankfurt won on away goals.

UEFA CUP 1980–81

First Round, First Leg

AZ 67 Alkmaar 6 (*Hovenkamp, Nygaard, Peters 2, Welzl, Tol*), Red Boys 0
IA Akranes 0, Cologne 4 (*Kroth, Littbarski, Muller, Strack*)
Sliema Wanderers 0, Barcelona 2 (*Canito, Landaburu*)
Ujpest Dozsa 1 (*Kardos*), Real Sociedad 1 (*Alonso*)
Arges Pitesti 0, Utrecht 0
Ballymena U 2 (*McQuiston, Sloan*), Vorwaerts Frankfurt 1 (*Geyer*)
Bohemians Prague 3 (*Bicovsky 2, Levy*), Gijon 1 (*Ferrero*)
Dynamo Dresden 1 (*Weber*), Napredak 0
Elfsborg 1 (*Nilsson*), St Mirren 2 (*Somner, Abercromby*)
Grasshoppers 3 (*Meyer 3* [*2 pens*]), KB Copenhagen 1 (*Eigenbrod*)
Hamburg 4 (*Kaltz, Hrubesch 2, Hartwig*), Sarajevo 2 (*Susic 2*)
Ipswich T 5 (*Wark 4* [*3 pens*], *Mariner*), Aris Salonika 1 (*Pallas pen*)
Juventus 4 (*Scirea, Verza, Bettega, Cabrini pen*), Panathinaikos 0
Kaiserslautern 1 (*Funkel*), Anderlecht 0
Dynamo Kiev 1 (*Buryak pen*), Levski Spartak 1 (*Spassov*)
PSV Eindhoven 3 (*Brandts, Van Kraay, Van der Koylen pen*), Wolverhampton W 1 (*Gray*)
Kuopion Palloseura 0, St Etienne 7 (*Paganelli 2, Hyvarinen og, Platini 2, Roussey, Janvion*)
Linz ASK 1 (*Krieger*), Radnicki Nis 2 (*Stojlkovic, Pantelic pen*)
Lokeren 1 (*Verheyen pen*), Moscow Dynamo 1 (*Gassayev*)
Magdeburg 2 (*Hoffman, Pommerenke pen*), Moss 1 (*Henriksen*)
Manchester U 1 (*McIlroy*), Widzew Lodz 1 (*Surlit*)
Porto 1 (*Souza*), Dundalk 0
RWD Molenbeek 1 (*De Wolf*), Torino 2 (*Mariani, Graziani*)
Shakhtor Donetsk 1 (*Starukhin*), Eintracht Frankfurt 0
Slask Wroclaw 0, Dundee U 0
Sochaux 2 (*Jeskowiak, Ivezic pen*), Servette 0
Standard Liège 1 (*Dardenne*), Steaua Bucharest 1 (*Raducanu*)
Stuttgart 6 (*Klotz 3, Allgower 2, Kelsch*), Pezoporikos 0
Twente 5 (*Bos, Carlsson og, Kila 2, Jol*), IFK Gothenburg 1 (*Nilsson*)
Vasas 0, Boavista 2 (*Eliseu, Julio*)
Zbrojovka Brno 3 (*Kroupa, Mikulicka, Mazura*), Voest Linz 1 (*Haider*)
Fenerbahce 0, Beroe Stara Zagora 1 (*Peyev*)

First Round, Second Leg

St Etienne 7 (*Rep 4* [*1 pen*], *Lestage, Paganelli, Lopez*), Kuopion Palloseura 0
Servette 2 (*Cuccinotta, Bizzini*), Sochaux 1 (*Genghini*)
Red Boys 0, AZ 67 Alkmaar 4 (*Kist 3* [*1 pen*], *Welzl*)
Steaua Bucharest 1 (*Raducanu*), Standard Liège 2 (*Voordeckers, Edstrom*)
Aris Salonika 3 (*Tsirmokos, Drambis, Zeleidis*), Ipswich T 1 (*Gates*)
Radnicki Nis 4 (*Mitosevic, Stolijovic 2, Panajotovic*), Linz ASK 1 (*Siegl*)
Napredak 0, Dynamo Dresden 1 (*Muller pen*)
Moscow Dynamo 0, Lokeren 1 (*Verheyen*)
Vorwaerts Frankfurt 3 (*Conrad, Jarmuskiewicz, Krautzig*), Ballymena U 0
Boavista 0, Vasas 1 (*Kiss*)
IFK Gothenburg 2 (*Nilsson 2*), Twente 0
Sarajevo 3 (*Lukic, Pasic 2*), Hamburg 3 (*Hrubesch 3*)
Voest Linz 0, Zbrojovka Brno 2 (*Janecka, Kroupa*)
St Mirren 0, Elfsborg
Dundee U 7 (*Dodds 2, Hegarty, Pettigrew 2, Stark, Payne pen*), Slask Wroclaw 2 (*Pawlowski 2*)
Widzew Lodz 0, Manchester U 0
KB Copenhagen 2 (*Fossgaard, Hansen pen*), Grasshoppers 5 (*Heinz Hermann 3, Zanetti, Sulser*)
Moss 2 (*Kollshaugen 2*), Magdeburg 3 (*Streich, Mewes, Wildebrand*)
Levski Spartak 0, Kiev Dynamo 0
Beroe Stara Zagora 2 (*Petkov, Dragolov*), Fenerbahce 1 (*Selcuk*)
Anderlecht 3 (*Nielsen 3,* [*1 pen*]), Kaiserslautern 2 (*Gaye, Wendt*)
Real Sociedad 1 (*Satrustegui*), Ujpest Dozsa 0
Barcelona 1 (*Rexach pen*), Sliema Wanderers 0
Eintracht Frankfurt 3 (*Holzenbein, Cha Kun Bum 2*), Shakhtor Donetsk 0
Utrecht 2 (*Van der Lem, Carbo*), Arges Pitesti 0
Dundalk 0, Porto 0
Cologne 6 (*Engels, Muller 4, Okudera*), IA Akranes 0
Wolverhampton W 1 (*Eves*), PSV Eindhoven 0
Gijon 2 (*Ferrero, Jimenez*), Bohemians 1 (*Nemec*)
Panathinaikos 4 (*Gentile og, Andreucchi, Luvanthinos, Delikaris*), Juventus 2 (*Bettega, Fanna*)
Torino 2 (*D'Amico, Graziani*), RWD Molenbeek 2 (*De Bolle, Van de Korput og*)
Pezoporikos 1 (*Theophanous P.*), Stuttgart 4 (*Tuefekci 2, Klotz, Allgower*)

Second Round, First Leg

Sochaux 2 (*Genghini, Ravelli*), Boavista 2 (*Julio, Eliseu*)
St Mirren 0, St Etienne 0
Torino 3 (*Sala P., Pecci, Mewes og*), Magdeburg 1 (*Steinbach*)
Twente 1 (*Rohde*), Dynamo Dresden 1 (*Heidler*)
Widzew Lodz 3 (*Grebosz, Pieta, Smolarek*), Juventus 1 (Bettega)
Dundee U 1 (*Pettigrew*), Lokeren 1 (*Mommens*)
Utrecht 2 (*Carbo, Dr Kruyk pen*), Eintracht Frankfurt 1 (*Borchers*)
Ipswich T 3 (*Wark 2, Beattie*), Bohemians Prague 0
Levski Spartak 1 (*Spassov*), AZ 67 Alkmaar 1 (*Kist*)
PSV Eindhoven 1 (*Van der Kuylen*), Hamburg 1 (*Hrubesch*)
Cologne 0, Barcelona 1 (*Quini*)
Stuttgart 5 (*Tuefekci, Martin pen, Scuth og, Allgower, Klotz*), Vorwaerts Frankfurt 1 (*Krautzig*)
Kaiserslautern 1 (*Wendt*), Standard Liège 2 (*Wellens, Plessers*)
Beroe Stara Zagora 0, Radnicki Nis 1 (*Halilovic*)
Zbrojovka Brno 1 (*Murillo og*), Real Sociedad 1 (*Uraide*)
Porto 2 (*Teixeira, Albertino*), Grasshoppers 0

Second Round, Second Leg

AZ 67 Alkmaar 5 (*Tol 2, Nygaard pen, Kist, Peters*), Levski Spartak 0
Radnicki Nis 2 (*Stojikovic, Mitosevic*), Beroe Stara Zagora 1 (*Stojanov*)
Dynamo Dresden 0, Twente 0
St Etienne 2 (*Larios 2*), St Mirren 0
Boavista 0, Sochaux 1 (*Durkalic*)
Magdeburg 1 (*Tyll*), Torino 0
Juventus 3 (*Tardelli, Furino, Brady*), Widzew Lodz 1 (*Pieta*)
Eintracht Frankfurt 3 (*Karger, Nachtweih, Pezzey*), Utrecht 1 (*Neuberger og*)
Hamburg 2 (*Groh, Hrubesch*), PSV Eindhoven 1 (*Van der Kuylen*)
Standard Liège 2 (*Edström, Graf*), Kaiserslautern 1 (*Briegel*)
Barcelona 0, Cologne 4 (*Strack, Engels, Littbarski, Muller*)
Vorwaerts Frankfurt 1 (*Lindemann*), Stuttgart 2 (*Allgower, Hansi Muller pen*)
Real Sociedad 2 (*Satrustegui 2*), Zbrojovka Brno 1 (*Kotasek*)
Grasshoppers 3 (*Sulser, Koller, Pfister pen*), Porto 0
Lokeren 0, Dundee U 0
Bohemians 2 (*Micinec, Panenka*), Ipswich T 0

Third Round, First Leg

Eintracht Frankfurt 4 (*Neuberger, Borchers, Holzenbein, Nachtweih*), Sochaux 2 (*Genghini, Pezzey og*)
Hamburg 0, St Etienne 5 (*Hartwig og, Platini 2, Larios, Zimako*)
Stuttgart 3 (*Hansi Muller 2* [*1 pen*], *Karl-Heinz Forster*), Cologne 1 (*Konopka*)

Lokeren 1 (*Lato*), Real Sociedad 0
Grasshoppers 2 (*Heinz Hermann, Koller*), Torino 1 (*Sclosa*)
Radnicki Nis 2 (*Pantelic pen, Panajotovic*), AZ 67 Alkmaar 2 (*Tol, Kist*)
Standard Liège 1 (*Plessers*), Dynamo Dresden 1 (*Heidler*)
Ipswich T 5 (*Wark 3, Brazil, Mariner*), Widzew Lodz 0

Third Round, Second Leg
Sochaux 2 (*Patrick Revelli 2*), Eintracht Frankfurt 0
St Etienne 1 (Paganelli), Hamburg 0
Cologne 4 (*Dieter Muller, Strack 2, Woodcock*), Stuttgart 1 (*Konopka og*)
Widzew Lodz 1 (*Pieta*), Ipswich T 0
Dynamo Dresden 1 (*Dorner*), Standard Liège 4 (*Sigurvinsson 3, Tahamata*)
Torino 2 (*Graziani, Pulici*), Grasshoppers 1 (*Terraneo og*)
Real Sociedad 2 (*Lopez Ufarte pen, Zamora*), Lokeren 2 (*Larsen 2*)
AZ 67 Alkmaar 5 (*Kist 3, Nygaard, Welzl*), Radnicki Nis 0

Quarter-Final, First Leg
Standard Liège 0, Cologne 0
AZ 67 Alkmaar 2 (*Tol, Welzl*), Lokeren 0
St Etienne 1 (*Rep*), Ipswich T 4 (*Mariner 2, Muhren, Wark*)
Grasshoppers 0, Sochaux 0

Quarter-Final, Second Leg
Ipswich T 3 (*Butcher, Wark pen, Mariner*), St Etienne 1 (*Zimako*)
Cologne 3 (*Dieter Muller, Bonhof pen, Littbarski*), Standard Liège 2 (*Graf, Vandersmissen*)
Sochaux 2 (*Durkalic, Genghini*), Grasshoppers 1 (*Koller*)
Lokeren 1 (*Verheyen*), AZ 67 Alkmaar 0

Semi-Final, First Leg
Ipswich T 1 (*Wark*), Cologne 0
Sochaux 1 (*Genghini*), AZ 67 Alkmaar 1 (*Arntz*)

Semi-Final, Second Leg
Cologne 0, Ipswich T 1 (*Butcher*)
AZ 67 Alkmaar 3 (*Metgod, Jonker, Peters*), Sochaux 2 (*Genghini, Meyer*)

Final 1980–81: Ipswich T (1) 3, AZ 67 Alkmaar (0) 0

(At Ipswich, 6 May, 1981, 27,532)

Ipswich T: Cooper; Mills, McCall, Thijssen, Osman, Butcher, Wark, Muhren, Mariner, Brazil, Gates.

AZ 67 Alkmaar: Treytel; Van der Meer, Spelbos, Metgod, Hovenkamp, Peters, Jonker, Arntz, Nygaard (Welzl), Kist, Tol.

Scorers: Ipswich T – Wark pen, Thijssen, Mariner.

AZ 67 Alkmaar (3) 4, Ipswich T (2) 2

(In Amsterdam, 20 May, 1981, 28,500)

AZ 67 Alkmaar: Treytel; Reynders, Spelbos, Metgod, Hovenkamp, Peters, Welzl (Kist), Arntz, Jonker, Nygaard, Tol.

Ipswich T: Cooper; Mills, McCall, Thijssen, Osman, Butcher, Wark, Muhren, Mariner, Brazil, Gates.

Scorers: AZ 67 Alkmaar – Welzl, Metgod, Tol, Jonker; Ipswich T – Thijssen, Wark.

UEFA CUP 1981–82

First Round, First Leg

Adanaspor 1 (*Ozer*), Inter-Milan 3 (*Serena, Bini, Altobelli*)
Napoli 2 (*Damiani, Musella*), Radnicki 2 (*Stojanovic, Aleksic*)
Bohemians 0, Valencia 1 (*Saura*)
Nantes 1 (*Halilodzic*), Lokeren 1 (*Dobias*)
Limerick 0, Southampton 3 (*Moran 2, Armstrong*)
Sporting Lisbon 4 (*Oliveira, Carlos, Manuel, Jordao*), Red Boys 0
PSV Eindhoven 7 (*Van de Kerkof R., Van de Kerkof W., Thoresen, Geels 3, Young Mo Hooa*), Naestved 0
Boavista 4 (*Vital, Jorge Silva, Coelho, Palhares*), Atlético Madrid 1 (*Pablo*)
Rapid 2 (*Weber, Panenka*), Videoton 2 (*Szabo, Vegh*)
Neuchatel Xamax 4 (*Luthi 2, Pellegrini, Trinchero*), Sparta Prague 0
Dynamo Tirana 1 (*Zeri*), Carl Zeiss Jena 0
Tatabanya 2 (*Weimper, Csapo*), Real Madrid 1 (*Santillana*)
Aris Salonika 4 (*Panos, Kouis 3*), Sliema Wanderers 0
Malmo 2 (*Nillsson, Kinnvall*), Wisla Krakow 0
SV Hamburg 0, Utrecht 1 (*Carbo*)
Grasshoppers 1 (*Fimian*), WBA 0
Vikingur 0, Bordeaux 4 (*Fernandez, Trésor, Gemmrich, Lacombe*)
Feyenoord 2 (*Bouwens, Nielsen*), Szombierki 0
Ipswich T 1 (*Thijssen*), Aberdeen 1 (*Hewitt*)
Bryne 0, Winterslag 2 (*Berger, Weiss*)
Zenit Leningrad 1 (*Zheludkov*), Dynamo Dresden 2 (*Dorner, Heidler*)
Magdeburg 3 (*Hoffmann, Streich, Mathaus og*), Borussia Moenchengladbach 1 (*Mill*)
Haka 2 (*Kujanpas 2*), IFK Gothenburg 3 (*Fredriksson, Corneliusson, Karlsson*)
Beveren 3 (*Shoenberger, Albert, Martens*), Linfield 0
Monaco 2 (*Edstrom, Bellone*), Dundee U 5 (*Kirkwood, Dodds 2, Bannon 2 [1 pen]*)
Panathinaikos 0, Arsenal 2 (*McDermott, Meade*)
Spartak Moscow 3 (*Svetsov 2, Gavrilov*), FC Bruges 1 (*Sorensen*)
Kaiserslautern 1 (*Brehme*), Akademik 0
Apoel 1 (*Andronicou*), Arges Pitesti 1 (*Ignat*)
Hajduk 3 (*Zoran Vujovic, Zlatko Vujovic 2*), Stuttgart 1 (*Rozic og*)
Dynamo Bucarest 3 (*Georgescu 2, Dragonea*), Levski Spartak 0
Sturm Graz 1 (*Schauss*), CSKA Moscow 0

First Round, Second Leg

Inter-Milan 4 (*Beccalossi, Bagni, Serena, Altobelli*), Adanaspor 1 (*Ahmet*)
Radnicki 0, Napoli 0
Valencia 1 (*Solsona*), Bohemians 0
Lokeren 4 (*Larsen 2, Snelders, Verheyen*), Nantes 2 (*Baronchelli, Bibard*)
Southampton 1 (*Keegan*), Limerick 1 (*Morris*)
Red Boys 0, Sporting Lisbon 7 (*Oliveira 2, Inacio, Jordao, Jorge 2, Freire*)
Naestved 2 (*Hansen 2*), PSV Eindhoven 1 (*Thoresen*)
Atlético Madrid 3 (*Dirceu 2, Cano*), Boavista 1 (*Dianmantino*)
Videoton 0, Rapid 2 (*Krankl 2*)
Sparta Prague 3 (*Griga 2, Jarolim*), Neuchatel Xamax 2 (*Trinchero, Pellegrini*)
Carl Zeiss Jena 4 (*Raab, Schnuphase, Bielau, Trocha*), Dynamo Tirana 0
Real Madrid 1 (*Isidro*), Tatabanya 0
Sliema Wanderers 2 (*Tortell, Losco*), Aris Salonika 4 (*Semertzidis, Kouis, Zelidis, Panov*)
Wisla Krakow 1 (*Kapka*), Malmo 3 (*Palmer, Prytz, Nilsson*)
Utrecht 3 (*Carbo, Kruyk, Van Veen*), Hamburg 6 (*Milewski 2, Wehmeyer, Hartwig, Bastrup, Groh*)
WBA 1 (*Robertson*), Grasshoppers 3 (*Fimian, Koller, Jara*)
Bordeaux 4 (*Fernandez, Martinez, Relmy, Trésor*), Vikingur 0
Szombierki 1 (*Ogaza*), Feyenoord 1 (*Bouwens*)
Aberdeen 3 (*Strachan pen, Weir 2*), Ipswich T 1 (*Wark pen*)
Winterslag 1 (*Billen*), Bryne 2 (*Mailand, Hellvich*)
Dynamo Dresden 4 (*Trauttman, Schmuck, Ming, Heidler*), Zenit Leningrad 1 (*Kasashchen*)
Borussia Moenchengladbach 2 (*Pinkall, Matthaus*), Magdeburg 0
IFK Gothenburg 4 (*Schiller, Nilsson, Karlsson, Holmgren*), Haka 0
Linfield 0, Beveren 5 (*Martens 4, Pfaff D.*)
Dundee U 1 (*Milne*), Monaco 2 (*Edstrom, Bellone*)
Arsenal 1 (*Talbot*), Panathinaikos 0
FC Bruges 1 (*Wellens*), Spartak Moscow 3 (*Radionou, Schaavlov, Gavrilov*)
Akademik 1 (*Gorev*), Kaiserslautern 2 (*Metzgerin, Briegel*)
Arges Pitesti 4 (*Turcu, Banta, Cirstea, Callo*), Apoel 0
Stuttgart 2 (*Schaffer, Muller D.*), Hajduk 2 (*Bogdanovic, Jelinik*)
Levski Spartak 2 (*Kurdon 2*), Dynamo Bucarest 1 (*Augustin*)
CSKA Moscow 2 (*Chesnokov, Tarkhanov*), Sturm Graz 1 (*Bakota*)

Second Round, First Leg

Southampton 2 (*Keegan pen, Channon*), Sporting Lisbon 4 (*Jordao, Holmes og, Fernandes 2*)
Real Madrid 3 (*Garcia Cortes, Gallego, Isidro*), Carl Zeiss Jena 2 (*Bielau, Kurbjuweit*)
Grasshoppers 2 (*Jara, Sulser*), Radnicki 0
Aris Salonika 1 (*Kollis*), Lokeren 1 (*Larsen*)
Rapid Vienna 1 (*Panenka*), PSV Eindhoven 0
Valencia 2 (*Roberto, Welzl*), Boavista 0
Malmo 0, Neuchatel Xamax 1 (*Pellegrini*)
Bordeaux 2 (*Genimerick, Soler*), SV Hamburg 1 (*Kaltz*)
Spartak Moscow 2 (*Rolgnov, Gavrilov*), Kaiserslautern 1 (*Funkel*)
Winterslag 1 (*Berger*), Arsenal 0
Aberdeen 3 (*Strachan, Weir, Hewitt*), Arges Pitesti 0
Feyenoord 2 (*Kaczor, Vermeulen*), Dynamo Dresden 1 (*Heidler*)
Inter-Milan 1 (*Pasinato*), Dynamo Bucarest 1 (*Custov*)
Sturm Graz 2 (*Breber, Niederbacher*), IFK Gothenburg 2 (*Nilsson 2*)
Borussia Moenchengladbach 2 (*Schaffer, Hannes*), Dundee U 0
Beveren 2 (*Theunis, Van Moer*), Hajduk 3 (*Gudelj, Vujovic, Sliskovic*)

Second Round, Second Leg

Sporting Lisbon 0, Southampton 0
Carl Zeiss Jena 0, Real Madrid 0
Radnicki 2 (*Djordjevic, Savic*), Grasshoppers 0
Lokeren 4 (*Gudjohnsen, Lato, Larsen, Mommens*), Aris Salonika 0
PSV Eindhoven 2 (*Poortvliet 2*), Rapid Vienna 1 (*Krankl*)
Boavista 1 (*Diamantino*), Valencia 0
Neuchatel Xamax 1 (*Pellegrini*), Malmo 0
SV Hamburg 2 (*Hrubesch 2*), Bordeaux 0
Kaiserslautern 4 (*Funkel, Briegel 2, Geye*), Spartak Moscow 0
Arsenal 2 (*Hollins, Rix*), Winterslag 1 (*Billen*)
Arges Pitesti 2 (*Radu, Barbulescu*), Aberdeen 2 (*Strachan pen, Hewitt*)
Dynamo Dresden 1 (*Lippman*), Feyenoord 1 (*Van Deinsen*)
Dynamo Bucarest 3 (*Georgescu, Augustin, Orac*), Inter-Milan 2 (*Altobelli, Prohaska*)
IFK Gothenburg 3 (*Olgren, Nilsson, Fredriksson*), Sturm Graz 2 (*Stendarl, Bakota*)
Dundee U 5 (*Milne, Kirkwood, Sturrock, Hegarty, Bannon*) Borussia Moenchengladbach 0
Hajduk 1 (*Pasic*), Beveren 2 (*Krowe, Anters*)

Third Round, First Leg

Lokeren 1 (*Lato*), Kaiserslautern 0
Rapid Vienna 0, Real Madrid 1 (*Santillana*)
Aberdeen 3 (*Black, Watson, Hewitt*), SV Hamburg 2 (*Hrubesch 2*)
Sporting Lisbon 0, Neuchatel Xamax 0
IFK Gothenburg 3 (*Holmgren, Nilsson 2*), Dynamo Bucarest 1 (*Muttescu*)
Winterslag 0, Dundee U 0
Radnicki 2 (*Radoslajevec, Savic*), Feyenoord 0

Valencia 5 (*Tendillo, Rodriguez 2, Welzl, Arnesen*), Hajduk 1 (*Todac*)

Third Round, Second Leg
Kaiserslautern 4 (*Hofeditz, Briegel, Funkel, Eilenfeldt*), Lokeren 1 (*Gudjohnson*)
Real Madrid 0, Rapid Vienna 0
SV Hamburg 3 (*Hrubesch, Memering pen, Jakobs*), Aberdeen 1 (*McGhee*)
Neuchatel Xamax 1 (*Andrey*), Sporting Lisbon 0
Dynamo Bucarest 0, IFK Gothenburg 1 (*Nilsson*)
Dundee U 5 (*Bannon, Narey, Hegarty, Milne 2*), Winterslag 0
Feyenoord 1 (*Nielsen*), Radnicki 0
Hajduk 4 (*Gudelj 3, Primorac*), Valencia 1 (*Saura*)

Quarter-Finals, First Leg
SV Hamburg 3 (*Bastrup, Memering, Von Heesen*), Neuchatel Xamax 2 (*Givens, Luthi*)
Real Madrid 3 (*Cunningham, Garcia Hernandez, Juanito*), Kaiserslautern 1 (*Eilenfeldt pen*)
Dundee U 2 (*Narey, Dodds*), Radnicki 0
Valencia 2 (*Arnesen 2* [*1 pen*]), IFK Gothenburg 2 (*Corneliusson, Nilsson T.*)

Quarter-Finals, Second Leg
Neuchatel Xamax 0, SV Hamburg 0
Kaiserslautern 5 (*Funkel 2, Eilenfeldt, Bongartz, Geye*), Real Madrid 0
Radnicki 3 (*Panajotovic 2, Djordjevic pen*), Dundee U 0
IFK Gothenburg 2 (*Tommy Holmgren, Fredriksson pen*), Valencia 0

Semi-Finals, First Leg
Kaiserslautern 1 (*Hofeditz*), IFK Gothenburg 1 (*Corneliusson*)
Radnicki 2 (*Beganovic, Obradovic*), SV Hamburg 1 (*Von Heesen*)

Semi-Finals, Second Leg
IFK Gothenburg 2 (*Tommy Holmgren, Fredriksson pen*), Kaiserslautern 1 (*Geye*) aet
SV Hamburg 5 (*Hartwig 2, Von Heesen 2, Magath*), Radnicki 1 (*Panajotovic*)

Final 1981–82: IFK Gothenburg (0) 1, SV Hamburg (0) 0

(In Gothenburg, 5 May, 1982, 42,548)

IFK Gothenburg: Wernersson; Svensson, Hysen, Karlsson C., Fredriksson, Tord Holmgren, Karlsson J., Stromberg, Corneliusson, Nilsson (Sanberg), Tommy Holmgren (Schiller).

SV Hamburg: Stein; Kaltz, Jakobs, Hieronymus, Groh, Hartwig, Wehmeyer, Magath, Von Heesen (Memering), Bastrup, Hrubesch.

Scorer: IFK Gothenburg – Tord Holmgren.

SV Hamburg (0) 0, IFK Gothenburg (1) 3

(In Hamburg, 19 May, 1982, 60,000)

SV Hamburg: Stein; Kaltz (Hidien), Hieronymus, Groh, Wehmeyer, Hartwig, Memering, Magath, Von Heesen, Hrubesch, Bastrup.

IFK Gothenburg: Wernersson; Svensson, Hysen (Schiller), Karlsson C., Fredriksson, Tord Holmgren, Stromberg, Karlsson J., Corneliusson (Sandberg), Nilsson, Tommy Holmgren.

Scorers: IFK Gothenburg – Corneliusson, Nilsson, Fredriksson pen.

UEFA CUP 1982–83

First Round, First Leg
Spartak Moscow 3 (*Shvetsov, Gavrilov 2*), Arsenal 2 (*Robson, Chapman*)
Slavia Sofia 2 (*Radkov 2*), Sarajevo 2 (*Pasic 2*)
Anderlecht 3 (*Vercauteren, Vandenbergh, Brylle*), Kuopion 0
Benfica 2 (*Nene, Padinha*), Betis 1 (*Biosca*)
Bohemians Prague 5 (*Prylozny 3, Cermak, Hruska V.*), Admira-Wacker 0
Borussia Dortmund 0, Rangers 0
Carl Zeiss Jena 3 (*Schnuphause 2, Topfer*), Bordeaux 1 (*Giresse*)
Dundee U 1 (*Dodds*), PSV Eindhoven 1 (*Van Der Kerkhoff W.*)
Dynamo Tbilisi 2 (*Khizanishvili, Shengelia*), Naples 1 (*Diaz*)
Ferencvaros 2 (*Szabadi, Poloskei*), Atletico Bilbao 1 (*Sola*)
Glentoran 1 (*Bowers*), Banik Ostrava 3 (*Sreiner, Denek, Antalik*)
Graz AK 1 (*Schwicker*), Corvinul 1 (*Gabor*)
Haarlem 2 (*Kleton, Haar*), La Gantoise 1 (*Tokodie*)
Kaiserslautern 3 (*Nilsson, Briegel 2*), Trabzonspor 0
Manchester U 0, Valencia 0
PAOK Salonika 1 (*Dimopoulos*), Sochaux 0
Pezoporikos 2 (*Theophanos, Vernon*), FC Zurich (*Seiler, Jerkovic*)
Roma 3 (*Pruzzo 2, Osman og*), Ipswich T 0
Saint Etienne 4 (*Rep, Daniel, Roussey, Genghini*), Tatabanya 1 (*Weimper*)
Sevilla 3 (*Santi, Montero, Magdaleno*), Levsky-Spartak 1 (*Spassov*)
Slask Wroclaw 2 (*Sybis, Socha*), Dynamo Moscow 2 (*Mentyukow, Dzhavadov*)
Southampton 2 (*Williams, Wright*), Norrkoeping 2 (*Pettersson S. 2*)
Stal Mielec 1 (*Buda*), Lokeren 1 (*Van Der Gijp*)
Uni Craiova 3 (*Ungureanu, Cirtu, Balaci*), Fiorentina 1 (*Graziani*)
Utrecht 0, Porto 1 (*Sousa*)
Viking Stravanger 1 (*Refvic*), Lokomotiv Leipzig 0
Vorvaerts Frankfurt 1 (*Kautzig*), Weder Bremen 3 (*Meier, Reinders, Voeller*)
Progres Niedercorn 0, Servette 1 (*Brigger*)
Lyngsby 1 (*Klaus Jensen*), Brage 2 (*Gylienvag, Lars Sorensen og*)
Zurrieq 1 (*Farrugia*), Hajduk Split 4 (*Pesic, Adamovic, Gudelj, Deronimov*)
Fram Reykjavik 0, Shamrock Rovers 3 (*Murphy, Campbell, Gaynor*)
AEK Athens 0, Cologne 1 (*Allofs*)

First Round, Second Leg
Porto 2 (*Costa, Gomez*), Utrecht 0
Admira-Wacker 1 (*Binder*), Bohemians Prague 2 (*Zelenski, Sloup*)
Lokeren 0, Stal Mielec 0
Shamrock Rovers 4 (*O:Carroll, Buckley, Beglin, Gaynor*), Fram Reykjavik 0
Levszky-Spartak 0, Sevilla 3 (*Magdaleno, Santi, Juan Carlos*)
PSV Eindhoven 0, Dundee U 2 (*Kirkwood, Hegarty*)
La Gantoise 3 (*Koudijzerz, Shapendonk 2*), Haarlem 3 (*Bockling, Kleton, Keur*)
Valencia 2 (*Solsona, Roberto*), Manchester U 1 (*Robson*)
Ipswich T 3 (*Gates, Buthcer, Vierchowod og*), Roma 1 (*Maldera*)
Rangers 2 (*Cooper, Johnstone*), Borussia Dortmund 0
Werder Bremen 0, Vorwarts Frankfurt 2 (*Conrad, Andrich*)
Trabzonspor 0, Kaiserslautern 3 (*Eilenfeldt, Briegel 2*)
Corvinul 3 (*Andone, Klein, Dumitrache*), Graz AK 0
Sochaux 2 (*Anziani 2*), PAOK Salonika 1 (*Dimopoulos*)
Kuopio 1 (*Jukka Turunen*), Anderlecht 3 (*Vandenbergh, Coeck, Czerniatynski*)
Bordeaux 5 (*Muller 3, Giresse 2*), Carl Zeiss Jena 0
Tatabanya 0, Saint Etienne 0
Betis 1, (*Rincon*), Benfica 2 (*Carlos, Nene*)
Fiorentina 1 (*Antognoni*), Uni Craiova 0
Dynamo Moscow 0, Slask Wroclaw 1 (*Tarashevits*)
Norrkoeping 0, Southampton 0
FC Zurich 1 (*Ludi*), Pezoporikos 0
Atletico Bilbao 1 (*Dani*), Ferencvaros 1 (*Szokolai*)
Lokomotiv Leipzig 3 (*Liebers, Kuhn, Zotsche*), Viking Stavanger 2 (*Refvik, Brekke*)
Banik Ostrava 1 (*Valek*), Glentoran 0
Sarajevo 4 (*Muzemic 3, Susic*), Slavia Sofia 2 (*Velickov 2*)
Brage 2 (*Willson R., Larson og*), Lyngby 2 (*Sorensen, Schaeffer og*)
Servette 3 (*Brigger, Decastel, Saramondi*), Progres Niedecorn 0
Hajduk Split 4 (*Jerolomov 2, Cukrov 2*), Zurrieq 0
Arsenal 2 (*McDermott, Chapman*), Spartak Moscow 5 (*Svetsov, Rodinov, Shavio, Cherenkov, Gess*)
Naples 1 (*Dal Flume*), Dynamo Tbilisi 0
Cologne 5 (*Fischer 2, Slijvo 2, Engels*), AEK Athens 0

Second Round, First Leg
Anderlecht 4 (*Lozano 2, Czerniatynski, Olsen*), Porto 0
Benfica 2 (*Nene, Humberto Coelho*), Lokeren 0
Corvinul 4 (*Dumitrache, Andone, Petcu, Mateut*), Sarajevo 5 (*Lukic 3, Pask, Hadzialagic*)
Ferencvaros 1 (*Szokolai*), FC Zurich 1 (*Seiler*)
Hajduk Split 4 (*Bogdanovic, Jerolimov, Salov, Cukrov*), Bordeaux 1 (*Bracci*)
Naples 1 (*Diaz*), Kaiserslautern 2 (*Nilsson, Allofs*)
PAOK Salonika 2 (*Dimopoulos, Kostikos*), Sevilla 0
Rangers 2 (*Johnstone, McClelland*), Cologne 1 (*Allofs*)
Roma 1 (*Pruzzo*), Norrkoeping 0
Shamrock Rovers 0, Uni Craiova 2 (*Irimescu, Balaci*)
Sainte Etienne 0, Bohemians Prague 0
Slask Wroclaw 0, Servette 2 (*Decastel, Favre*)
Spartak Moscow 2 (*Gess, Shvetsov*), Haarlem 0
Valencia 1 (*Welzl*), Banik Ostrava 0
Viking Stavanger 1 (*Henriksen*), Dundee U 3 (*Milne 2, Sturrock*)
Werder Bremen 2 (*Meier, Okudera*), Brage 0

Second Round, Second Leg
Banik Ostrava 0, Valencia 0
Bohemians Prague 4 (*Nemec, Prilozny, Prokes, Micinek*), Saint Etienne 0
Bordeaux 4 (*Giresse 2, Rohr, Thouvenel*), Hajduk Split 0
Brage 2 (*Waahlstroem, Amberg*), Werder Bremen 6 (*Voeller 3, Meier 2, Gruber*)
Dundee U 0, Viking Stavanger 0
Haarlem 1 (*Huyg*), Spartak Moscow 3 (*Shetsov, Shavio, Gabrilov*)
Kaiserslautern 2 (*Nillson, Briegel*), Naples 0
Cologne 5 (*Littbarski, Engels 2, Fischer, Allofs*), Rangers 0
Lokeren 1 (*Van Der Gijp*), Benfica 2 (*Humberto Coelho, Nene*)
Norrkoeping 1 (*Bergman*), Roma 0
Porto 3 (*Costa, Walsh 2*), Anderlecht 2 (*Coeck, Vandenbergh*)
Sarajevo 4 (*Musemic, Jozic, Susic, Pasic*), Corvinul 0
Sevilla 4 (*Santi, Lopez, Magdaleno, Pintinho*), PAOK Salonika 0
Uni Craiova 3 (*Cirtu 2, Campbell og*), Shamrock Rovers 0
FC Zurich 1 (*Seiler*), Ferencvaros 0
Servette 5 (*Faure 2, Decastel 2, Brigger*), Slask Wroclaw 1 (*Dutoit og*)

Third Round, First Leg
Anderlecht 6 (*Lozano 2, Vandenbergh 2, Vercauteren, Ferhatovic og*), Sarajevo 1 (*Susic*)
Bordeaux 1 (*Giresse*), Uni Craiova 0
Dundee U 2 (*Milne, Narey*), Werder Bremen 1 (*Meier*)
Cologne 1 (*Allofs*), Roma 0
Servette 2 (*Schnyder, Elia*), Bohemians Prague 2 (*Sloup, Chaloupka*)
Sevilla 1 (*Francisco*), Kaisenslautern 0
Spartak Moscow 0, Valencia 0
FC Zurich 1 (*Rufer*), Benfica 1 (*Filipovic*)

Third Round, Second Leg
Sarajevo 1 (*Musemic*), Anderlecht 0
Uni Craiova 2 (*Ticleanu, Geolgau*), Bordeaux 0

Werder Bremen 1 (*Voeller*), Dundee U 1 (*Hegarty*)
Roma 2 (*Iorio, Falcao*), Cologne 0
Bohemians Prague 2 (*Cermak, Prilozny*), Servette 1 (*Decastel*)
Kaiserslautern 4 (*Nillson, Geye, Brehme, Eilenfeldt*), Sevilla 0
Valencia 2 (*Solsona, Moreno*), Spartak Moscow 0
Benfica 4 (*Filipovic, Dimantino, Nene 2*), FC Zurich 0

Quarter-Finals, First Leg
Bohemians Prague 1 (*Chaloupka*), Dundee U 0
Kaiserslautern 3 (*Brehme 2, Irismescu og*), Uni Craiova 2 (*Geolgari, Crisan*)
Roma 1 (*Di Bartolomei*), Benfica 2 (*Filipovic 2*)
Valencia 1 (*Solsona*), Anderlecht 2 (*Vercauteren, Coeck*)

Quarter-Finals, Second Leg
Dundee U 0, Bohemians Prague 0
Uni Craiova 1 (*Negrila*), Kaiserslautern 0
Benfica 1 (*Filipovic*), Roma 1 (*Falcao*)
Anderlecht 3 (*Brylle 2, De Groote*), Valencia 1 (*Ribes*)

Semi-Finals, First Leg
Benfica 0, Uni Craiova 0
Bohemians Prague 0, Anderlecht 1 (*Vandenbergh*)

Semi-Finals, Second Leg
Uni Craiova 1 (*Balaci*), Benfica 1 (*Filipovic*)
Anderlecht 3 (*Vandenbergh, Brylle, Czerniatynski*), Bohemians Prague 1 (*Jakubec*)

Final – First Leg, May 4: Anderlecht (1) 1, Benfica (0) 0

Brussels 60,000

Anderlecht: Munaron; Olsen, Hofkens, Peruzovic, De Groote, Frimann, Lozano, Coeck, Vercauteren, Vandenbergh (Czniatynski), Brylle.

Benfica: Bento; Humberto, Pietra, Frederico (Lopes), Alvaro, Sheu, Carlos, Manuel, Jose, Luis, Chalana, Diamantino, Filipovic (Nene).

Scorer: Anderlecht: Brylle.

Referee: Dotschev.

Final – Second Leg, May 18: Benfica (1) 1, Anderlecht (1) 1

Lisbon 80,000

Benfica: Bento; Humberto, Pietra, Lopes, Veloso, Carlos Manuel, Sheu (Filipovic), Stromberg, Chalana, Nene, Diamantino (Alves).

Anderlecht: Munaron; Olsen, De Greef, Peruzovic, De Groote, Broos, Frimann, Coeck, Vercauteren, Vandenbergh (Brylle), Lozano.

Scorers: Benfica: Sheu; Anderlecht: Lozano.

Referee: Corver.

(Anderlecht win on 2-1 aggregate).

Cologne defender Harald Konopka heads off the line from Rangers striker Derek Johnstone during their UEFA Cup second round match at Ibrox in October 1982.

UEFA CUP 1982–83

FIRST ROUND, FIRST LEG

15 SEPT

Spartak Moscow (1) 3 *(Shvetsov, Gavrilov 2* [1 pen]*)*
Arsenal (2) 2 *(Robson, Chapman)* 68,500

Spartak Moscow: Dasayev; Sochnov, Pozdnyakov, Sher bak, Romantsev, Shavlo, Shvetsov, Gess (Kalashnikov), Gavrilov, Cherenkov, Rodionov.
Arsenal: Wood; Hollins, Sansom, Talbot, O'Leary, Whyte, Davis, Robson, Chapman, Woodcock, Rix.

Borussia Dortmund (0) 0
Rangers (0) 0 54,000

Borussia Dortmund: Immel; Huber, Loose, Russmann, Bognihausen, Tenhagen, Zorc, Burgsmuller, Radacanu, Klotz, Keser (Koch).
Rangers: Stewart; McKinnon, Dawson, McClelland, Patterson, Bett, Cooper, Prytz (Miller), Johnstone, Russell, Redford.

Dundee U (1) 1 *(Dodds)*
PSV Eindhoven (0) 1 *(Van der Kerkhof W.)* 13,223

Dundee U: McAlpine; Malpass (Milner), Stark, Gough, Hegarty, Narey, Britton, Kirkwood (Phillip), Bannon, Sturrock, Dodds.
PSV Eindhoven: Doesburg; Van Aerle, Stevens, Brandts, Wildschut, Van der Kerkhof W., Lokhoff, Poortvliet, Van der Kerkhof R., Koolhof (Landsbergen), Thoresen.

Glentoran (0) 1 *(Bowers)*
Banik Ostrava (1) 3 *(Sreiner, Denek, Antalik)* 4000

Glentoran: Paterson; Neill, Connell, Keely, McCreary, Cleary, Jameson, Bowers, Manley, Mullan, Troughton (Morrison).
Banik Ostrava: Michaelik; Pechacek, Sramek, Danek, Rygel, Valek, Antalik, Namec (Radimec), Knapp, Sreiner, Licka.

Manchester U (0) 0
Valencia (0) 0 46,599

Manchester U: Bailey; Duxbury, Albiston, Wilkins, Buchan, McQueen, Robson, Grimes, Stapleton, Whiteside, Coppell.
Valencia: Sempere; Carrete, Botubot, Arias, Tendillo, Moreno (Solsona), Saura, Castellanos, Roberto, Kempes, Pablo (Subirats).

Roma (2) 3 *(Osman og, Pruzzo 2)*
Ipswich T (0) 0 60,000

Roma: Tancredi; Nappi, Nella, Vierchowod, Falcao, Maldera, Iorio, Prohaska, Pruzzo, Di Bartolomei, Valigi.
Ipswich T: Cooper; Burley, Mills, Thijssen, Osman, Butcher, Wark, McCall (O'Callaghan), Mariner, Brazil, Gates.

Southampton (0) 2 *(Williams, Wright)*
Norrkoeping (0) 2 *(Pettersson S. 2)* 10,155

Southampton: Shilton; Baker, Rofe, Williams, Nicholl, Wright, Ball, Cassells, Moran, Armstrong, Agboola.
Norrkoeping: Jonsson; Granskog, Lundstroem, Bergman, Mansson, Liljedahl, Fredriksson, Pettersson H., Svensson, Pettersson S., Hellstroem.

FIRST ROUND, SECOND LEG

29 SEPT

PSV Eindhoven (0) 0
Dundee U (2) 2 *(Kirkwood, Hegarty)* 12,000

PSV Eindhoven: Doesburg; Van Aerle (Hugh), Stevens, Brandts, Wildschut, Kokhoff (Landsbergen), Van der Kerkhof W., Poortvliet, Van der Kerkhof R., Koolhof, Thoresen.
Dundee U: McAlpine; Phillip (Malpas), Stark, Gough, Hegarty, Narey, Bannon, Milne, Kirkwood, Sturrock, Dodds.

Valencia (0) 2 *(Solsona* pen, *Roberto)*
Manchester U (1) 1 *(Robson)* 47,000

Valencia: Sempere; Carrete, Tendillo (Ribes), Arias, Botubot, Castellanos, Solsona, Roberto, Saura, Kempes, Pablo.
Manchester U: Bailey; Duxbury, Albiston, Wilkins, Moran, Buchan (Macari), Robson, Grimes, Stapleton, Whiteside, Moses (Coppell).

Ipswich T (1) 3 *(Gates, Vierchowod og, Butcher)*
Roma (0) 1 *(Maldera)* 17,751

Ipswich T: Sivell; Burley, Mills, Thijssen, Osman, Butcher, Wark, McCall, D'Avray (Linford), Brazil, Gates.
Roma: Tancredi; Nappi, Nella, Vierchowod, Falcao, Maldera, Valigi, Prohaska, Pruzzo, Di Bartolomei, Conti (Chierico).

Rangers (1) 2 *(Cooper, Johnstone)*
Borussia Dortmund (0) 0 40,000

Rangers: Stewart; McKinnon, McClelland, Peterson, Dawson, Russell (Redford), Bett, Prytz, Cooper, Johnstone, MacDonald.
Borussia Dortmund: Immel; Huber, Loose, Koch, Bonighausen, Tenhagen, Zorc, Radacanu (Abramczik), Burgsmuller, Eggeling (Klotz), Keser.

Norrkoeping (0) 0
Southampton (0) 0 10,252

Norrkoeping: Jonsson; Liljedahl, Maansson, Granskog, Lundstroem, Pettersson H., Nilsson S., Bergman, Pettersson S. (Lundqvist), Hemstroem, Svensson.
Southampton: Shilton; Baker, Nicholl, Holmes, Wright, Williams, Ball, Armstrong, Agboola, Moran, Cassells.

Banik Ostrava (0) 1 *(Valek)*
Glentoran (0) 0 15,000

Banik Ostrava: Michaelik; Pechacek, Sramek, Danek, Rygel, Valer, Antalik, Nemic, Knapp, Sreiner, Licka.
Glentoran: Paterson; McCreery, Neill, Keely, Connell, Jameson, Bowers, Morrison, Cleary, Manley, Munnan.

Arsenal (0) 2 *(McDermott, Chapman)*
Spartak Moscow (1) 5 *(Shvetsov, Rodionov, Cherenkov, Shavlo, Gess)* 28,455

Arsenal: Wood; Hollins (Sunderland), Sansom, Talbot, O'Leary, Whyte, Davis (McDermott), Robson, Chapman, Woodcock, Rix.
Spartak Moscow: Dasayev (Prudnikov); Sochnow, Pozdnyakov, Sherbak, Romantsez, Shavlo, Shvetsov, Gess (Kuznetsov), Gavrilov, Cherenkov, Rodionov.

SECOND ROUND, FIRST LEG

20 OCT

Rangers (1) 2 *)Johnstone, McClelland)*

Cologne (0) 1 *(Allofs K.)* 35,000

Rangers: Stewart; McKinnon, McClelland, Paterson (Stevens), Dawson (McDonald), Bett, Prytz, Russell, Cooper, Johnstone, Redford.
Cologne: Schumacher; Konopka (Zimmermann), Strack, Steiner, Prestin, Bonhof, Slijvo, Cullmann, Engels, Littbarski, Allofs K. (Willmer).

Viking Stavanger (0) 1 *(Henriksen)*

Dundee U (0) 3 *(Milne 2 [1 pen], Sturrock)* 8890

Viking Stavanger: Haugvaldstad; Fjetland (Johannessen), Henriksen, Svensson, Solbert, Brekke, Hammer, Goodchild, Berntsen, Refvik (Risanger), Andersen.
Dundee U: McAlpine; Holt, Stark, Gough, Hegarty, Narey, Malpas, Milne, Kirkwood, Sturrock, Dodds.

SECOND ROUND, SECOND LEG

3 NOV

Dundee U (0) 0

Viking Stavanger (0) 0 10,611

Dundee U: McAlpine; Phillip, Stark, Gough, Hegarty, Narey, Reilly, Milne, Kirkwood, Holt, Dodds.
Viking Stavanger: Johannesen E.; Fjetland, Henriksen, Svendsen, Fjelberg, Brekke, Hammer, Goodchild, Berntsen, Refvik, Andersen.

Cologne (4) 5 *(Littbarski* pen, *Engels 2* [1 pen], *Fischer, Allofs K.)*

Rangers (0) 0 61,000

Cologne: Schumacher; Prestin, Strack, Steiner, Willmer, Konopka, Slijvo, Engels, Littbarski, Fischer, Allofs K. (Cullman).
Rangers: Stewart; McKinnon, McClelland, Stevens, Dawson, Russell, Prytz, Bett, Redford (McAdam), Çooper (MacDonald), Johnstone.

THIRD ROUND, FIRST LEG

24 NOV

Dundee U (1) 2 *(Milne, Narey)*

Werder Bremen (0) 1 *(Meier)* 15,000

Dundee U: McAlpine; Gough, Hegarty, Narey, Malpas, Kirkwood, Stark (Holt), Bannon (Reilly), Milne, Sturrock, Dodds.
Werder Bremen: Burdenski; Kamp, Fichtel, Siegmann, Otten, Sidka, Gruber, Mohimann, Okudera, Voller, Meier (Bracht).

THIRD ROUND, SECOND LEG

8 DEC

Werder Bremen (0) 1 *(Voller)*

Dundee U (1) 1 *(Hegarty)* 20,000

Werder Bremen: Burdenski; Kemp (Bohnke), Otten, Gruber, (Schaaf), Fichtel, Moehimann, Sidka, Siegmann, Voller, Okudera, Meier.
Dundee U: McAlpine; Stark, Malpas, Gough, Hegarty, Narey, Bannon, Milne, Kirkwood, Sturrock, Dodds (Holt).

Dundee United and Rangers, seen here in a Premier Division clash at Tannadice Park, were the last two British clubs to survive in the UEFA Cup last season.

A TRIBUTE TO SCOTTISH CHAMPIONS DUNDEE UNITED WHO ALSO REACHED THE UEFA CUP QUARTER-FINALS

Above: A jubilant Paul Hegarty with the Scottish Championship Trophy.

Right: Midfield dynamo Paul Sturrock.

Below: Defensive action against St Mirren.

GREAT EUROPEAN CUP FINAL MOMENTS FOR BRITAIN

Above: Trevor Francis heads home the winner against Swedish Champions Malmo to give Nottingham Forest their first European Cup success in 1979.

Right: Bobby Charlton scores his second goal against Benfica in Manchester United's 4-1 victory at Wembley in 1968.

ABERDEEN MARCH ON IN THE EUROPEAN CUP-WINNERS' CUP

Above: Bayern Munich goalkeeper Manfred Müller foils another Aberdeen attack in the Quarter-final 2nd leg at Pittodrie Stadium.

Below: Aberdeen central defender Alex McLeish finds the net for Aberdeen's second goal in their 3-2 victory over Bayern.

European Footballer of the Year 1982

In a World Cup year, it is almost inevitable that one of the heroes of the global competition is elected as the outstanding player of the year. Paolo Rossi improved in the later stages of the tournament, scored six goals, and became everybody's choice for the title. He collected 115 points, well ahead of the little French general, Alain Giresse, who did a better job in Spain than his illustrious colleague, Platini. Zbigniev Boniek came third, he had only one outstanding match, but generally speaking, he is an excellent footballer. Apart from the World Cup participants, Bernd Schuster managed to collect a few votes, which is surprising, because he was injured during the second half of the year, and during the first six months, refused to play for W. Germany. This is the second time that an Italian player has won the 'Golden Ball' trophy, Gianni Rivera was the other one in 1969.

Paolo Rossi (Juventus and Italy)

1982 Poll
Points
115 **Paolo Rossi** (Juventus)
68 **Alain Giresse** (Bordeaux)
53 **Zbigniev Boniek** (Juventus)
48 **Bruno Conti** (A.S. Roma)
47 **Karl-Heinz Rummenigge** (Bayern Munich)
17 **Rinat Dasaev** (Spartak Moscow)
10 **Pierre Littbarski** (Cologne)
9 **Dino Zoff** (Juventus)
5 **Michel Platini** (Juventus)
4 **Bernd Schuster** (Barcelona)
3 **Giancarlo Antognoni** (Fiorentina)
2 **Eric Gerets** (Standard Liege), **Bruno Pezzey** (Eintract Franfurt), **Gaetano Scirea** (Juventus)
1 **Paul Breitner** (Bayern Munich), **Thomas Nillson** (Kaiserslautern), **Walter Schachner** (Cesena), **Marco Tardelli** (Juventus), **Marius Tresor** (Bordeaux).

Past Winners
1956
Stanley Matthews (Blackpool)
Alfredo di Stefano (Real Madrid)
1958
Raymond Kopa (Real Madrid)
1959
Alfredo di Stefano (Real Madrid)
1960
Luis Suarez (Barcelona)
1961
Omar Sivori (Juventus)
1962
Josef Masopust (Dukla Prague)
1963
Lev Yashin (Dynamo Moscow)
1964
Denis Law (Manchester U)
1965
Eusebio (Benfica)
1966
Bobby Charlton (Manchester U)
1967
Florian Albert (Ferencvaros)
1968
George Best (Manchester U)
1969
Gianni Rivera (Milan)
1970
Gerd Muller (Bayern Munich)
1971
Johan Cruyff (Ajax)
1972
Franz Beckenbauer (Bayern Munich)
1973
Johan Cruyff (Barcelona)
1974
Johan Cruyff (Barcelona)
1975
Oleg Blokhin (Dynamo Kiev)
1976
Franz Beckenbauer (Bayern Munich)
1977
Allan Simonsen (B. Moenchengladbach)
1978
Kevin Keegan (Hamburg)
1979
Kevin Keegan (Hamburg)
1980
Karl-Heinz Rummenigge (Bayern Munich)
1981
Karl-Heinz Rummenigge (Bayern Munich).

BRITISH AND IRISH CLUBS IN EUROPE

1955–56
EUROPEAN CUP
Hibernian (Semi-Final)

1955–58
EUROPEAN INTER-CITIES FAIRS CUP
London beat Basle, Frankfurt and Lausanne before losing to Barcelona 2-2, 2-6 in the Final.
Birmingham C knocked out Inter and Zagreb before losing to Barcelona 4-3, 0-1 and 1-2 at Basle.

1956–57
EUROPEAN CUP
Manchester U (Semi-Final)
Rangers (First Round Proper)

1957–58
EUROPEAN CUP
Manchester U (Semi-Final)
Rangers (First Round Proper)
Glenavon (Preliminary Round)
Shamrock R (Preliminary Round)

1958–60
FAIRS CUP
Birmingham C (Runners-Up)
Chelsea (Second Round)

1958–59
EUROPEAN CUP
Wolverhampton W (First Round)
Ards (Preliminary Round)
Drumcondra (Preliminary Round)
Hearts (Preliminary Round)
Manchester U were invited to compete, but were withdrawn by the Football League.

1959–60
EUROPEAN CUP
Rangers (Semi-Final)
Wolverhampton W (Quarter-Final)
Linfield (Preliminary Round)
Shamrock R (Preliminary Round)

1960–61
EUROPEAN CUP
Burnley (Quarter-Final)
Hearts (Preliminary Round)
Limerick (Preliminary Round)
Glenavon – Withdrew

EUROPEAN CUP-WINNERS' CUP
Rangers (Runners-Up)
Wolverhampton W (Semi-Final)

FAIRS CUP
Birmingham C (Runners-Up)
Hibernian (Semi-Final)

1961–62
EUROPEAN CUP
Tottenham H (Semi-Final)
Rangers (Quarter-Final)
Drumcondra (Preliminary Round)
Linfield (Preliminary Round)

EUROPEAN CUP-WINNERS' CUP
Dunfermline Ath (Quarter-Final)
Leicester C (Second Round)
Swansea T (First Round)
Glenavon (First Round)
St Patrick's Ath (Preliminary Round)

FAIRS CUP
Sheffield W (Quarter-Final)
Hearts (Second Round)
Nottingham F (First Round)
Birmingham C (Second Round)
Hibernian (Second Round)

1962–63
EUROPEAN CUP
Dundee (Semi-Final)
Ipswich T (First Round)
Shelbourne (Preliminary Round)
Linfield (Preliminary Round)

EUROPEAN CUP-WINNERS' CUP
Tottenham H(Winners)
Rangers (Second Round)
Shamrock R (Second Round)
Bangor C (First Round)
Portadown (First Round)

FAIRS CUP
Hibernian (Quarter-Final)
Dunfermline Ath (Second Round)
Glentoran (First Round)
Everton (First Round)
Celtic (First Round)
Drumcondra (Second Round)

1963–64
EUROPEAN CUP
Rangers (Preliminary Round)
Everton (Preliminary Round)
Dundalk (Preliminary Round)
Distillery (Preliminary Round)

EUROPEAN CUP-WINNERS' CUP
Celtic (Semi-Final)
Manchester U (Quarter-Final)
Linfield (Second Round)
Borough U (Second Round)
Tottenham H (Second Round)
Shelbourne (First Round)

FAIRS CUP
Partick T (Second Round)
Arsenal (Second Round)
Sheffield W (Second Round)
Hearts (First Round)
Glentoran (First Round)
Shamrock R (First Round)

1964–65		
EUROPEAN CUP	**Liverpool** (Semi-Final)	**Shamrock R** (Preliminary Round)
	Rangers (Quarter-Final)	**Glentoran** (Preliminary Round)
EUROPEAN CUP-WINNERS' CUP	**West Ham U** (Winners)	**Cork Celtic** (First Round)
	Cardiff C (Quarter-Final)	**Derry C** (First Round)
	Dundee (Second Round)	
FAIRS CUP	**Manchester U** (Semi-Final)	**Celtic** (Second Round)
	Dunfermline Ath (Third Round)	**Shelbourne** (Second Round)
	Everton (Third Round)	**Kilmarnock** (Second Round)
1965–66		
EUROPEAN CUP	**Manchester U** (Semi-Final)	**Kilmarnock** (First Round)
	Derry C (First Round)	**Drumcondra** (Preliminary Round)
EUROPEAN CUP-WINNERS' CUP	**Liverpool** (Runners-Up)	**Limerick** (First Round)
	Celtic (Semi-Final)	**Cardiff C** (First Round)
	West Ham U (Semi-Final)	**Coleraine** (First Round)
FAIRS CUP	**Leeds U** (Semi-Final)	**Everton** (Second Round)
	Chelsea (Semi-Final)	**Glentoran** (First Round)
	Dunfermline Ath (Quarter-Final)	**Hibernian** (First Round)
	Hearts (Third Round)	**Shamrock R** (Second Round)
1966–67		
EUROPEAN CUP	**Celtic** (Winners)	**Liverpool** (First Round)
	Linfield (Quarter-Final)	**Waterford** (Preliminary Round)
EUROPEAN CUP-WINNERS' CUP	**Rangers** (Runners-Up)	**Glentoran** (First Round)
	Everton (Second Round)	**Swansea T** (First Round)
	Shamrock R (Second Round)	
FAIRS CUP	**Leeds U** (Runners-Up)	**WBA** (Third Round)
	Kilmarnock (Semi-Final)	**Dunfermline Ath** (Second Round)
	Burnley (Quarter-Final)	**Drumcondra** (First Round)
	Dundee U (Third Round)	
1967–68		
EUROPEAN CUP	**Manchester U** (Winners)	**Celtic** (First Round)
	Dundalk (First Round)	**Glentoran** (First Round)
EUROPEAN CUP-WINNERS' CUP	**Cardiff C** (Semi-Final)	**Crusaders** (First Round)
	Aberdeen (Second Round)	**Shamrock R** (First Round)
	Tottenham H (Second Round)	
FAIRS CUP	**Leeds U** (Winners)	**Liverpool** (Third Round)
	Dundee (Semi-Final)	**Nottingham F** (Second Round)
	Rangers (Quarter-Final)	**Linfield** (First Round)
	Hibernian (Third Round)	**St Patrick's Ath** (First Round)
1968–69		
EUROPEAN CUP	**Manchester U** (Semi-Final)	**Glentoran** (First Round)
	Celtic (Quarter-Final)	**Waterford** (First Round)
	Manchester C (First Round)	
EUROPEAN CUP-WINNERS' CUP	**Dunfermline Ath** (Semi-Final)	**Cardiff C** (First Round)
	WBA (Quarter-Final)	**Shamrock R** (First Round)
	Crusaders (First Round)	
FAIRS CUP	**Newcastle U** (Winners)	**Chelsea** (Second Round)
	Rangers (Semi-Final)	**Dundalk** (Second Round)
	Leeds U (Quarter-Final)	**Liverpool** (First Round)
	Hibernian (Third Round)	**Linfield** (First Round)
	Aberdeen (Second Round)	**Morton** (First Round)
1969–70		
EUROPEAN CUP	**Celtic** (Runners-Up)	**Waterford** (First Round)
	Leeds U (Semi-Final)	**Linfield** (First Round)
EUROPEAN CUP-WINNERS' CUP	**Manchester C** (Winners)	**Ards** (First Round)
	Rangers (Second Round)	**Shamrock R** (First Round)
	Cardiff C (Second Round)	
EUROPEAN FAIRS CUP	**Arsenal** (Winners)	**Kilmarnock** (Third Round)
	Newcastle U (Quarter-Final)	**Dundee U** (First Round)
	Dunfermline Ath (Third Round)	**Coleraine** (Second Round)
	Southampton (Third Round)	**Dundalk** (First Round)
	Liverpool (Second Round)	**Glentoran** (First Round)

1970–71

EUROPEAN CUP	**Celtic** (Quarter-Final) **Everton** (Quarter-Final)	**Waterford** (Second Round) **Glentoran** (First Round)
EUROPEAN CUP-WINNERS' CUP	**Chelsea** (Winners) **Manchester C** (Semi-Final) **Cardiff C** (Quarter-Final)	**Linfield** (First Round) **Aberdeen** (First Round) **Bohemians** (Preliminary Round)
EUROPEAN FAIRS CUP	**Leeds U** (Winners) **Arsenal** (Quarter-Final) **Liverpool** (Semi-Final) **Newcastle U** (Second Round) **Coleraine** (Second Round)	**Dundee U** (Second Round) **Coventry C** (Second Round) **Cork Hibs** (First Round) **Rangers** (First Round) **Kilmarnock** (First Round) **Hibernian** (Third Round)

1971–72

EUROPEAN CUP	**Arsenal** (Quarter-Final) **Celtic** (Semi-Final)	**Linfield** (First Round) **Cork Hibs** (First Round)
EUROPEAN CUP-WINNERS' CUP	**Liverpool** (Second Round) **Chelsea** (Second Round) **Cardiff C** (First Round)	**Rangers** (Winners) **Distillery** (First Round) **Limerick** (First Round)
UEFA CUP	**Tottenham H** (Winners) **Wolverhampton W** (Runners-Up) **Leeds U** (First Round) **Southampton** (First Round) **Shelbourne** (First Round) **Glentoran** (First Round)	**Dundee** (Third Round) **Aberdeen** (Second Round) **St Johnstone** (Third Round)

1972–73

EUROPEAN CUP	**Derby Co** (Semi-Final) **Celtic** (Second Round)	**Waterford** (First Round)
EUROPEAN CUP-WINNERS' CUP	**Leeds U** (Runners-Up) **Hibernian** (Quarter-Final)	**Wrexham** (Second Round) **Cork Hibs** (Second Round)
UEFA CUP	**Liverpool** (Winners) **Tottenham H** (Semi-Final) **Stoke C** (First Round) **Manchester C** (First Round)	**Aberdeen** (First Round) **Partick T** (First Round) **Bohemians** (First Round)

1973–74

EUROPEAN CUP	**Liverpool** (Second Round) **Celtic** (Semi-Final)	**Waterford** (First Round) **Crusaders** (First Round)
EUROPEAN CUP-WINNERS' CUP	**Sunderland** (Second Round) **Rangers** (Second Round) **Cardiff C** (First Round)	**Glentoran** (Quarter-Final) **Cork Hibs** (First Round)
UEFA CUP	**Tottenham H** (Runners-Up) **Ipswich T** (Quarter-Final) **Leeds U** (Third Round) **Wolverhampton W** (Second Round)	**Aberdeen**(Second Round) **Hibernian** (Second Round) **Finn Harps** (First Round) **Ards** (First Round)

1974–75

EUROPEAN CUP	**Leeds U** (Runners-Up) **Celtic** (First Round)	**Coleraine** (First Round) **Cork Celtic** (Second Round)
EUROPEAN CUP-WINNERS' CUP	**Liverpool** (Second Round) **Ards** (First Round) **Cardiff C** (First Round)	**Finn Harps** (First Round) **Dundee U** (Second Round)
UEFA CUP	**Derby Co** (Third Round) **Ipswich T** (First Round) **Stoke C** (First Round) **Wolverhampton W** (First Round)	**Bohemians** (First Round) **Dundee** (First Round) **Portadown** (Second Round) **Hibernian** (Second Round)

1975–76

EUROPEAN CUP	**Derby Co** (Second Round) **Linfield** (First Round)	**Rangers** (Second Round) **Bohemians** (First Round)
EUROPEAN CUP-WINNERS' CUP	**West Ham U** (Runners-Up) **Celtic** (Quarter-Final) **Home Farm** (First Round)	**Wrexham** (Quarter-Final) **Coleraine** (First Round)
UEFA CUP	**Liverpool** (Winners) **Aston Villa** (First Round) **Glentoran** (First Round) **Athlone T** (Second Round)	**Ipswich T** (Second Round) **Everton** (First Round) **Hibernian** (First Round) **Dundee U** (Second Round)

1976–77

EUROPEAN CUP	**Liverpool** (Winners) **Crusaders** (First Round)	**Dundalk** (First Round) **Rangers** (First Round)
EUROPEAN CUP-WINNERS' CUP	**Southampton** (Quarter-Final) **Cardiff C** (First Round) **Hearts** (Second Round)	**Bohemians** (Second Round) **Carrick R** (Second Round)
UEFA CUP	**Manchester C** (First Round) **Derby Co** (Second Round) **Manchester U** (Second Round) **QPR** (Quarter-Final)	**Hibernian** (Second Round) **Glentoran** (First Round) **Celtic** (First Round) **Finn Harps** (First Round)

1977–78

EUROPEAN CUP	**Liverpool** (Winners) **Sligo Rovers** (First Round)	**Celtic** (Second Round) **Glentoran** (Second Round)
EUROPEAN CUP-WINNERS' CUP	**Rangers** (First Round) **Dundalk** (First Round) **Coleraine** (First Round)	**Cardiff C** (First Round) **Manchester U** (Second Round)
UEFA CUP	**Aston Villa** (Quarter-Final) **Manchester C** (First Round) **Bohemians** (First Round) **Glenavon** (First Round)	**Ipswich T** (Third Round) **Newcastle U** (Second Round) **Dundee U** (First Round) **Aberdeen** (First Round)

1978–79

EUROPEAN CUP	**Nottingham F** (Winners) **Liverpool** (First Round) **Linfield** (First Round)	**Rangers** (Quarter-Final) **Bohemians** (Second Round)
EUROPEAN CUP-WINNERS' CUP	**Ipswich T** (Quarter-Final) **Ballymena U** (First Round) **Wrexham** (First Round)	**Aberdeen** (Second Round) **Shamrock R** (Second Round)
UEFA CUP	**Manchester C** (Quarter-Final) **Arsenal** (Third Round) **Dundee U** (First Round) **Finn Harps** (First Round)	**WBA** (Quarter-Final) **Everton** (Second Round) **Hibernian** (Second Round) **Glentoran** (First Round)

1979–80

EUROPEAN CUP	**Nottingham F** (Winners) **Liverpool** (First Round) **Celtic** (Quarter-Final)	**Dundalk** (Second Round) **Linfield** (Preliminary Round)
EUROPEAN CUP-WINNERS' CUP	**Arsenal** (Runners-Up) **Rangers** (Second Round) **Wrexham** (First Round)	**Waterford** (First Round) **Cliftonville** (First Round)
UEFA CUP	**Leeds U** (Second Round) **Ipswich T** (Second Round) **Dundee U** (Second Round) **Aberdeen** (First Round)	**Glenavon** (First Round) **Bohemians** (First Round) **WBA** (First Round) **Everton** (First Round)

1980–81

EUROPEAN CUP	**Liverpool** (Winners) **Nottingham F** (First Round) **Aberdeen** (Second Round)	**Linfield** (First Round) **Limerick** (First Round)
EUROPEAN CUP-WINNERS' CUP	**West Ham U** (Quarter-Final) **Celtic** (First Round) **Newport Co** (Quarter-Final)	**Crusaders** (First Round) **Waterford** (Second Round)
UEFA CUP	**Ipswich T** (Winners) **Manchester U** (First Round) **Wolverhampton W** (First Round) **Dundee U** (Second Round)	**St Mirren** (Second Round) **Ballymena U** (First Round) **Dundalk** (First Round)

1981–82

EUROPEAN CUP	**Aston Villa** (Winners) **Liverpool** (Quarter-Final) **Celtic** (First Round)	**Glentoran** (Second Round) **Athlone T** (First Round)
EUROPEAN CUP-WINNERS' CUP	**Tottenham H** (Semi-Final) **Rangers** (First Round) **Swansea C** (First Round)	**Dundalk** (Second Round) **Ballymena U** (First Round)
UEFA CUP	**Arsenal** (Second Round) **Southampton** (Second Round) **Ipswich T** (First Round) **WBA** (First Round)	**Dundee U** (Quarter-Final) **Aberdeen** (Third Round) **Linfield** (First Round) **Limerick** (First Round)

Summary of Appearances

EUROPEAN CUP (1955–83)

English clubs
10 Liverpool
5 Manchester U
3 Nottingham Forest
2 Derby Co, Wolverhampton W, Everton, Leeds U, Aston Villa
1 Burnley, Tottenham H, Ipswich T, Manchester C, Arsenal, Aston Villa

Scottish clubs
13 Celtic
9 Rangers
2 Hearts
1 Dundee, Kilmarnock, Hibernian, Aberdeen

Clubs from Northern Ireland
11 Linfield
6 Glentoran
2 Crusaders
1 Glenavon, Ards, Distillery, Derry C, Coleraine

Clubs from Eire
6 Waterford
5 Dundalk
3 Drumcondra, Shamrock R
2 Bohemians, Limerick
1 Shelbourne, Cork Hibs, Cork Celtic, Sligo Rovers, Athlone T

Winners: Celtic 1966–67; Manchester U 1967–68; Liverpool 1976–77, 1977–78, 1980–81; Nottingham F 1978–79, 1979–80; Aston Villa 1981–82

Finalists: Celtic 1969–70; Leeds U 1974–75

EUROPEAN CUP-WINNERS' CUP (1960–83)

English clubs
5 Tottenham H
4 West Ham U
3 Liverpool
2 Chelsea, Manchester C, Manchester U
1 Wolverhampton W, Leicester C, Everton, WBA, Leeds U, Sunderland, Southampton, Ipswich T, Arsenal

Scottish clubs
9 Rangers
4 Celtic, Aberdeen
2 Dunfermline Ath
1 Dundee, Dundee U, Hibernian, Hearts

Welsh clubs
11 Cardiff C
4 Wrexham Swansea C
1 Bangor C, Borough U, Newport Co

Clubs from Northern Ireland
4 Coleraine
3 Crusaders
2 Glentoran, Ards, Linfield, Ballymena U
1 Glenavon, Derry C, Distillery, Portadown, Carrick Rangers, Cliftonville

Clubs from Eire
6 Shamrock R
3 Limerick
2 Cork Hibs, Bohemians, Waterford, Dundalk
1 Shelbourne, Cork Celtic, St Patrick's Ath, Finn Harps, Home Farm

Winners: Tottenham H 1962–63; West Ham U 1964–65; Manchester C 1969–70; Chelsea 1970–71; Rangers 1971–72

Finalists: Liverpool 1965–66; Rangers 1960–61, 1966–67; Leeds U 1972–73; West Ham U 1975–76; Arsenal 1979–80

EUROPEAN FAIRS CUP & UEFA CUP (1955–83)

English clubs
8 Leeds U, Ipswich T
6 Liverpool, Everton, Arsenal
4 Manchester C, Birmingham C, Newcastle U, Wolverhampton W, WBA, Manchester U, Southampton
3 Chelsea, Tottenham H
2 Sheffield W, Nottingham F, Stoke C, Derby Co, Aston Villa
1 Burnley, Coventry C, London Rep XI, QPR

Scottish clubs
12 Hibernian
10 Dundee U
7 Aberdeen
5 Dunfermline Ath
4 Kilmarnock, Rangers, Dundee
3 Hearts, Celtic
2 Partick T
1 Morton, St Johnstone, St Mirren

Clubs from Northern Ireland
9 Glentoran
3 Linfield
2 Coleraine, Glenavon
1 Ards, Portadown, Ballymena U

Clubs from Eire
4 Bohemians
3 Finn Harps, Dundalk, Shamrock R
2 Shelbourne, Drumcondra
1 St Patrick's Ath, Cork Hibs, Athlone T, Limerick

Winners: Leeds U 1967–68, 1970–71; Newcastle U 1968–69; Arsenal 1969–70; Tottenham H 1971–72; Liverpool 1972–73, 1975–76; Ipswich T 1980–81

Finalists: Birmingham C 1958–60, 1960–61; Leeds U 1966–67; Wolverhampton W 1971–72; Tottenham H 1973–74

BRITISH AND IRISH CLUBS IN EUROPE

1982–83

EUROPEAN CUP
Aston Villa (Quarter-Final)
Liverpool (Quarter-Final)
Celtic (Second Round)
Linfield (First Round)
Dundalk (First Round)

EUROPEAN CUP-WINNERS' CUP
Tottenham H (Second Round)
Aberdeen (Winners)
Swansea C (Second Round)
Coleraine (First Round)
Limerick (First Round)

UEFA CUP
Manchester U (First Round)
Arsenal (First Round)
Southampton (First Round)
Ipswich T (First Round)
Rangers (Second Round)
Dundee U (Quarter-Finals)
Glentoran (First Round)
Shamrock R (Second Round)

EUROPEAN NATIONS SECTION

Details have been listed for all European footballing nations but unfortunately owing to some countries' seasons finishing at different times from the British season, not all league champions and cup winners are known for the current season. Total number of championship and cup wins is given with winners' present names, with previous names in brackets. In the tables of league champions and cup winners, contemporary names are used.

ALBANIA

President: Zyber Konci.
Secretary: Skender Begeja.
Address of Association: Federation Albanaise de Football, Rruga, Kongresi I Permetit, 41 Tirana.
Telephone: 7256, 7984.
Cable: Albsport Tirana.
Telex: 2142.
Area: 11,100 square miles.
Population: 2,671,300. *Number of Clubs:* 42.
Teams: 219.
Number of Players: 5,038.
Year of Formation: 1932.
National Colours: Red shirts, black shorts, red stockings.
Second Choice of Colours: White shirts, white shorts, white stockings.
Name, Address and Capacity of National Stadium: Qemal Stafa, Tirana, 30,000.
Names and Capacity of Other Principal Football Grounds: Dinamo, 15,000; Shkodra, 13,000; Durresi, 15,000; Korca, 13,000; Fier, 10,000; Vlora, 13,000.
Season: September–May.

International matches 1982

22 Sept, Vienna: v Austria (a) lost 0-5
27 Oct, Ismir: v Turkey (a) lost 0-1
15 Dec, Tirana: v Northern Ireland (h) drew 0-0

League Championship wins (1945–83)

Dinamo Tirana 15; Partizan Tirana 12; 17 Nendori 6; Vlaznia 5.

Cup wins (1948–83)

Dinamo Tirana 13; Partizan Tirana 9; 17 Nendori 5; Vlaznia 3; Besa 1; Labinoti 1.

	League Champions	**Cup Winners**
1945	Vlaznia	
1946	Vlaznia	
1947	Partizan Tirana	
1948	Partizan Tirana	Partizan Tirana
1949	Partizan Tirana	Partizan Tirana
1950	Dinamo Tirana	Dinamo Tirana
1951	Dinamo Tirana	Dinamo Tirana
1952	Dinamo Tirana	Dinamo Tirana
1953	Dinamo Tirana	Dinamo Tirana
1954	Partizan Tirana	Dinamo Tirana
1955	Dinamo Tirana	*No competition*
1956	Dinamo Tirana	*No competition*
1957	Partizan Tirana	Partizan Tirana
1958	Partizan Tirana	Partizan Tirana
1959	Partizan Tirana	*No competition*
1960	Dinamo Tirana	Dinamo Tirana
1961	Partizan Tirana	Partizan Tirana
1963*	Dinamo Tirana	17 Nendori
1964	Partizan Tirana	Partizan Tirana
1965	17 Nendori	Dinamo Tirana
1966	17 Nendori	Dinamo Tirana
1967	Dinamo Tirana	Vlaznia
1968	17 Nendori	Dinamo Tirana
1969	17 Nendori	17 Nendori
1970	17 Nendori	Partizan Tirana
1971	Partizan Tirana	Dinamo Tirana
1972	Vlaznia	Besa
1973	Dinamo Tirana	Partizan Tirana
1974	Vlaznia	Dinamo Tirana
1975	Dinamo Tirana	Labinoti
1976	Dinamo Tirana	17 Nendori
1977	Dinamo Tirana	17 Nendori
1978	Dinamo Tirana	Dinamo Tirana
1979	Partizan Tirana	Vlaznia
1980	Dinamo Tirana	Partizan Tirana
1981	Partizan Tirana	Vlaznia
1982	17 Nendori	Dinamo Tirana
1983	Vlaznia	17 Nendori

* *Changed from calendar season to overlapping season from autumn to spring.*

Final League Table 1982–83

	P	*W*	*D*	*L*	*F*	*A*	*Pts*
Vlaznia	26	12	10	4	39	19	34
Partizani	26	13	8	5	32	17	34
17 Nendori	26	12	8	6	38	26	32
Flamurtari	26	11	8	7	28	23	30
Luftëtari	26	11	7	8	25	21	29
Lokomotiva	26	10	8	8	27	24	28
Skënderbeu	26	8	9	9	24	21	25
Dinamo Tirana	26	8	9	9	29	30	25
Labinoti	26	7	10	9	19	28	24
Tomori	26	6	10	10	15	24	22
Besa	26	6	9	11	28	35	21
Traktori	26	6	9	11	23	38	21
Naftëtari	26	6	8	12	23	38	20
Besëlidhja	26	5	9	12	16	22	19

AUSTRIA

President: Karl Sekanina.
Secretary: Otto Demuth.
Address of Association: Oesterreichischer Fussball-Bund, Mariahilferstrasse 99, Postfach 161, Wien A-1061.
Telephone: 57-15-36.
Cable: Football Wien.
Telex: 11919oèfb a.
Area: 32,374 square miles.
Population: 7,457,000.
Number of Clubs: 1,971. *Teams:* 8,223.
Number of Players: 287,000.
Year of Formation: 1904.
National Colours: White shirt, black shorts, black stockings.
Second Choice of Colours: Red shirts, white shorts, red stockings.
Name, Address and Capacity of National Stadium: Wiener Stadion, Prater, Vienna, 70,714.
Names, Addresses and Capacities of Other Principal Football Grounds: Linzer Stadion, Linz, 22,000; Stadion Salzburger, Bundesstadion Liebenau, Graz, 19,000; Tivoli Stadion, Innsbruck, 14,400; Stadion, Wiener Neustadt, 12,600; Bodenseestadion, Bregenz, 12,000; Stadion Klagenfurt, Klagenfurt, 11,000; Hohe Warte, Vienna Weststadion, Vienna, 20,000; Bundesstadion Sudstadt, Maria Enzersdort, 15,600.
Season: August–December; February–June.

Principal Honours

Olympic Games: *runners-up* 1936.
European Cup-Winners' Cup: *runners-up* Austria/WAC (1978).

International matches 1982

24 March, Budapest: v Hungary (a) won 3-2 (*Krankl, Schachner, Hattenberger*)
28 April, Vienna: v Czechoslovakia (h) won 2-1 (*Schachner 2*)
19 May, Vienna: v Denmark (h) won 1-0 (*Degeorgi*)
17 June, Oviedo: v Chile (W.C.) won 1-0 (*Schachner*)
21 June, Oviedo: v Algeria (W.C.) won 2-0 (*Schachner, Krankl*)
25 June, Gijon: v West Germany (W.C.) lost 0-1
28 June, Madrid: v France (W.C.) lost 0-1
1 July, Madrid: v Northern Ireland (W.C.) drew 2-2 (*Pezzey, Hintermaier*)
22 Sept, Vienna: v Albania (h) won 5-0 (*Hagmayr, Gasselich, Kola og, Weber, Brauneder*)
13 Oct, Vienna: v Northern Ireland (h) won 2-0 (*Schachner 2*)
17 Nov, Vienna: v Turkey (h) won 4-0 (*Polster, Pezzey, Prohaska, Schachner*)

Most Capped Player: Gerhardt Hanappi 93

League Championship wins (1912–83)

Rapid Vienna 27; Austria/Vienna (prev. Austria/WAC, FK Austria and WAC) 16; Admira-Energie-Wacker (prev. Sportklub Admira & Admira-Energie) 8; First Vienna 6; Tirol-Svarowski-Innsbruck (prev. Wacker Innsbruck) 5; Wiener Sportklub 3; FAC 1; Hakoah 1; Linz ASK 1; Wacker Vienna 1; WAF 1; Voest Linz 1.

Cup wins (1919–83)

Austria/WAC 21; Rapid Vienna 10; Admira-Energie-Wacker (prev. Sportklub Admira & Admira-Energie) 5; TS Innsbruck (prev. Wacker Innsbruck) 5; First Vienna 3; Linz ASK 1; Wacker Vienna 1; WAF 1; Wiener Sportklub 1, Graz AK 1.

	League Champions	Cup Winners
1954	Rapid Vienna	*No competition*
1955	First Vienna	*No competition*
1956	Rapid Vienna	*No competition*
1957	Rapid Vienna	*No competition*
1958	Wiener Sportklub	*No competition*
1959	Wiener Sportklub	Wiener AC
1960	Rapid Vienna	FK Austria
1961	FK Austria	Rapid Vienna
1962	FK Austria	FK Austria
1963	FK Austria	FK Austria
1964	Rapid Vienna	Admira-Energie
1965	Linz ASK	Linz ASK
1966	Admira-Energie	Admira-Energie
1967	Rapid Vienna	FK Austria
1968	Rapid Vienna	Rapid Vienna
1969	FK Austria	Rapid Vienna
1970	FK Austria	Wacker Innsbruck
1971	Wacker Innsbruck	FK Austria
1972	TS Innsbruck	Rapid Vienna
1973	TS Innsbruck	TS Innsbruck
1974	Voest Linz	Austria/WAC
1975	TS Innsbruck	TS Innsbruck
1976	Austria/WAC	Rapid Vienna
1977	TS Innsbruck	Austria/WAC
1978	Austria/WAC	TS Innsbruck
1979	Austria/WAC	TS Innsbruck
1980	Austria/WAC	Austria/WAC
1981	Austria/Vienna	Graz AK
1982	Rapid Vienna	Austria/Vienna
1983	Rapid Vienna	Rapid Vienna

Final League Table 1982–83

	P	*W*	*D*	*L*	*F*	*A*	*Pts*
Rapid Vienna	30	20	8	2	72	18	48
Austria/Vienna	30	22	4	4	76	27	48
SW Innsbruck	30	13	12	5	5	36	38
Sturm Graz	30	16	5	9	50	33	37
Austria Salzburg	30	14	6	10	45	34	34
Klagenfurt	30	13	6	11	52	49	32
Graz AK	30	12	8	10	40	40	32
Voest Linz	30	12	8	10	41	42	32
Eisenstadt	30	8	13	9	41	48	29
Admira Wacker	30	9	9	12	42	47	27
Wiener SK	30	10	7	13	44	60	27
Linz ASK	30	9	7	14	42	49	25
Neusiedl	30	7	7	16	29	49	21
Wels	30	6	8	16	27	46	20
Vienna	30	7	5	18	25	61	19
Simmering	30	2	7	21	20	62	11

BELGIUM

President: M. Louis Wouters.
Secretary: Albert Roosens.
Address of Association: Union Royale Belge des Sociétés de Football Association, Rue de la Loi 43, B-1040 Bruxelles.
Telephone: 02/230.07.30.
Telex: 23257 bvbfbfb.
Cable: UBSFA Bruxelles.
Area: 11,779 square miles.
Population: 9,863,374.
Number of Clubs: 3,320. *Teams:* 14,400.
Number of Players: 283,960.
Year of Formation: 1895.
National Colours: Red shirts with tricoloured (black-yellow-red) collar and cuffs, red shorts, red stockings with tricoloured (black-yellow-red) tops.
Second Choice of Colours: All white.
Name, Address and Capacity of National Stadium: Centenary Stadium, Marathon Avenue, Brussels (Heysel), 70,000.
Names, Addresses and Capacities of Other Principal Football Grounds: R. Antwerp FC-Bosuilbaan, at Deurne (Antwerp), 62,000; RFC Liégeois-Chaussée de Tongres, at Rocourt (Liège), 43,000; R. Standard C. Liégeois-2, rue de la Centrale at Sclessin (Liège), 43,000; RSC Anderlechtois-2, avenue Théo Verbeeck, Anderlecht (Brussels), 38,000.
Season: September–May.

Principal Honours

Olympic Games: *winners* 1920
European Championship: *runners-up* 1980
European Champions Cup: *runners-up* FC Bruges (1978)
European Cup-Winners' Cup: *winners* Anderlecht (1976, 1978); *runners-up* Anderlecht (1977), Standard Liège (1982)
Fairs Cup: *runners-up* Anderlecht (1970)
UEFA Cup: *runners-up* FC Bruges (1976)
Super Cup: Anderlecht (1978); *winners* Anderlecht (1983)

International matches 1982

24 March, Brussels: v Rumania (h) won 4-1 (*Verheyan 2, Czerniatynski 2*)
28 April, Brussels: v Bulgaria (h) won 2-1 (*Vandenbergh, Van Moer*)
27 May, Copenhagen: v Denmark (a) lost 0-1
13 June, Barcelona: v Argentina (W.C.) won 1-0 (*Vandenbergh*)
19 June, Elche: v El Salvador (W.C.) won 1-0 (*Coeck*)
22 June, Elche: v Hungary (W.C.) drew 1-1 (*Czerniatynski*)
28 June, Barcelona: v Poland (W.C.) lost 0-3
1 July, Barcelona: v USSR (W.C.) lost 0-1
22 Sept, Munich: v West Germany (a) drew 0-0
6 Oct, Brussels: v Switzerland (h) won 3-0 (*Coeck, Vandenbergh, Egli og*)

Most Capped Player: Paul Van Himst 81

League Championship wins (1896–1983)

Anderlecht 17; Union St Gilloise 11; Standard Liège 8; Beerschot 7; FC Bruges 6; RC Brussels 6; FC Liège 5; Daring Brussels 5; Antwerp 4; Lierse SK 3; Malines 3; CS Bruges 3; RWD Molenbeek 1, Beveren 1.

Cup wins (1954–83)

Anderlecht 5; Standard Liège 4; FC Bruges 3; Beerschot 2; Waterschei 2; Beveren 2; Antwerp 1; La Gantoise 1; Lierse SK 1; Tournai 1; Waregem 1.

	League Champions	Cup Winners
1952	FC Liège	
1953	FC Liège	
1954	Anderlecht	Standard Liège
1955	Anderlecht	Antwerp
1956	Anderlecht	Tournai
1957	Antwerp	*No competition*
1958	Standard Liège	*No competition*
1959	Anderlecht	*No competition*
1960	Lierse SK	*No competition*
1961	Standard Liège	*No competition*
1962	Anderlecht	*No competition*
1963	Standard Liège	*No competition*
1964	Anderlecht	La Gantoise
1965	Anderlecht	Anderlecht
1966	Anderlecht	Standard Liège
1967	Anderlecht	Standard Liège
1968	Anderlecht	FC Bruges
1969	Standard Liège	Lierse SK
1970	Standard Liège	FC Bruges
1971	Standard Liège	Beerschot
1972	Anderlecht	Anderlecht
1973	FC Bruges	Anderlecht
1974	Anderlecht	Waregem
1975	RWD Molenbeek	Anderlecht
1976	FC Bruges	Anderlecht
1977	FC Bruges	FC Bruges
1978	FC Bruges	Beveren
1979	Beveren	Beerschot
1980	FC Bruges	Waterschei
1981	Anderlecht	Standard Liège
1982	Standard Liège	Waterschei
1983	Standard Liège	Beveren

Final League Table 1982–83

	P	*W*	*D*	*L*	*F*	*A*	*Pts*
Standard Liège	34	22	6	6	78	34	50
Anderlecht	34	20	9	5	74	33	49
Antwerp	34	20	6	8	56	30	46
La Gantoise	34	18	10	6	60	42	46
FC Bruges	34	17	9	8	58	49	43
Beveren	34	15	10	9	68	38	40
Waterschei	34	14	9	11	48	49	37
Lokeren	34	13	9	12	42	38	35
FC Luttich	34	11	10	13	37	54	32
RWD Molenbeek	34	9	13	12	32	38	31
CS Bruges	34	7	15	12	38	49	29
Kortryk	34	10	9	15	41	55	29
Seraing	34	8	12	14	41	62	28
Lierse	34	10	7	17	34	52	27
Beerschot	34	8	9	17	43	61	25
Waregem	34	7	10	17	36	51	24
Tongeren	34	7	7	20	39	64	21
Winterslag	34	5	10	19	36	62	20

BULGARIA

President: Kroum Vassiltchev.
Secretary: Kostadin Stoytcheyski.
Address of Association: Federation Bulgare de Football, Boul. Tolboukhin 18, Sofia.
Telephone: 877490, 874725.
Cable: Besefese Sofia.
Telex: 22723, 22724 csbsfs bg.
Area: 42,830 square miles.
Population: 9,000,000.
Number of Clubs: 4,336. *Teams:* 5,781.
Number of Players: 117,940.
Year of Formation: 1923.
National Colours: White shirts, green shorts, red stockings.
Second Choice of Colours: Red shirts, green shorts, white stockings.
Name, Address and Capacity of National Stadium: 'Vassil Levski', Sofia, 55,000.
Names, Addresses and Capacities of Other Principal Football Grounds: Stade Narodna Armia, Parc de la Liberté, Sofia, 43,000; Levski-Gerena, Sofia, 40,000; Stade Slavia, Ovtcha Koupel, Sofia, 35,000; Stade Rakovski, quartier Ivan Vasoc, Sofia, 29,000; Stade Guerena, quartier Podouene, Sofia, 33,000; Stade 9 Septembre, Plovdiv, 40,000; Stade Christo Botev, Plovdiv, 30,000; Stade Yuri Gagarine, Varna, 40,000; Stade de la ville de Rousse, 20,000; Stade 9 Septembre, Bourgass, 15,000.
Season: August–December; March–June.

Principal Honours

Olympic Games: *runners-up* 1968

International matches 1982

14 April, Russe: v Rumania (h) drew 1-1 (*Lovtshev*)
28 April, Brussels: v Belgium (a) lost 1-2 (*Mladenov*)
5 May, Buenos Aires: v Argentina (a) lost 1-2 (*Mladenov*)
14 May, Lyon: v France (a) drew 0-0
8 Sept, St Gallon: v Switzerland (a) lost 2-3 (*Iontshev, Zdravkov*)
22 Sept, Burgas: v East Germany (h) drew 2-2 (*Zdravkov 2*)
14 Oct, Sofia: v Malta (h) won 7-0 (*Kerimov, Blangev, Velitchkov, Dimitrov G., Slavkov 3*)
27 Oct, Sofia: v Norway (h) drew 2-2 (*Velitchkov, Nikolov*)
17 Nov, Sofia: v Yugoslavia (h) lost 0-1

Most Capped Player: Hristo Bonev 96

League Championship wins (1925–83)

CSKA Sofia (prev. CDNA) 23; Levski Spartak(prev. Levski Sofia) 13; Slavia Sofia 6; Vladislav Varna 3; Lokomotiv Sofia 3; AS 23 Sofia 1; Botev Plovdiv 1; SC Sofia 1; Sokol Varna 1; Spartak Plovdiv 1; Tichka Varan 1; Trakia Plovdiv 1; ZSK Sofia 1.

Cup wins (1946–83)

Levski Spartak (prev. Levski Sofia) 13; CSKA Sofia (prev. CDNA) 10; Slavia Sofia 6; Lokomotiv Sofia 3; Botev Plovdiv 1; SpartakPlovdiv 1; Spartak Sofia 1; Marek Stanke 1; Trakia Plovdiv 1; Lokomotiv Plovdiv 1.

	League Champions	Cup Winners
1946	Levski Sofia	Levski Sofia
1947	Levski Sofia	Levski Sofia
1948	CDNA Sofia	Lokomotiv Sofia
1949	Levski Sofia	Levski Sofia
1950	Levski Sofia	Levski Sofia
1951	CDNA Sofia	CDNA Sofia
1952	CDNA Sofia	Slavia Sofia
1953	Levski Sofia	Lokomotiv Sofia
1954	CDNA Sofia	CDNA Sofia
1955	CDNA Sofia	CDNA Sofia
1956	CDNA Sofia	Levski Sofia
1957	CDNA Sofia	Levski Sofia
1958	CDNA Sofi:	Spartak Plovdiv
1959	CDNA Sofia	Levski Sofia
1960	CDNA Sofia	CDNA Sofia
1961	CDNA Sofia	CDNA Sofia
1962	CDNA Sofia	Botev Plovdiv
1963	Spartak Plovdiv	Slavia Sofia
1964	Lokomotiv Sofia	Slavia Sofia
1965	Levski Sofia	CSKA Sofia
1966	CSKA Sofia	Slavia Sofia
1967	Trakia Plovdiv	Levski Sofia
1968	Levski Sofia	Spartak Sofia
1969	CSKA Sofia	CSKA Sofia
1970	Levski Spartak	Levski Spartak
1971	CSKA Sofia	Levski Spartak
1972	CSKA Sofia	CSKA Sofia
1973	CSKA Sofia	CSKA Sofia
1974	Levski Spartak	CSKA Sofia
1975	CSKA Sofia	Slavia Sofia
1976	CSKA Sofia	Levski Spartak
1977	Levski Spartak	Levski Spartak
1978	Lokomotiv Sofia	Marek Stanke
1979	Levski Spartak	Levski Spartak
1980	CSKA Sofia	Slavia Sofia
1981	CSKA Sofia	Trakia Plovdiv
1982	CSKA Sofia	Lokomotiv Sofia
1983	CSKA Sofia	Lokomotiv Plovdiv

Final League Table 1982–83

	P	*W*	*D*	*L*	*F*	*A*	*Pts*
CSKA Sofia	30	18	9	3	53	20	45
Levski Spartak	30	18	6	6	50	21	42
Trakia Plovdiv	30	15	6	9	59	42	36
Lokomotiv Sofia	30	12	8	10	38	39	32
Etar Tirnovo	30	14	3	13	40	37	31
Pleven	30	13	5	12	46	40	31
Sliven	30	13	4	13	45	45	30
Botev Vratza	30	13	4	13	38	35	30
Spartak Pleven	30	12	5	13	36	38	29
Belasitsa	30	12	5	13	43	54	29
TM Varna	30	10	9	11	23	27	29
Bourgas	30	12	4	14	41	47	28
Slavia Sofia	30	11	6	13	35	37	28
Haskovo	30	9	4	17	34	40	22
Pirine	30	7	5	18	26	54	20
Kazaniak	30	7	5	18	30	53	19

CYPRUS

President: Michalakis Kyprianou.
General Secretary: Demetrakis Stephanides.
Address of Association: Cyprus Football Association, Stasinos Street 1, Engomi 114, PO Box 5071, Nicosia.
Telephone: 45341, 45342.
Telex: 3880 football cy.
Cable: Football Nicosia.
Area: 3,572 square miles.
Population: 630,000.
Number of Clubs: 42. *Teams:* 56.
Number of Players: 16,000.
Year of Formation: 1934.
National Colours: Sky blue shirts, white shorts, blue and white stockings.
Second Choice of Colours: White shirts, blue shorts, white stockings.
Name, Address and Capacity of National Stadium: GSP, Nicosia, 12,000.
Names, Addresses and Capacities of Other Principal Football Grounds: Tsition, Limassol, 20,000; GSE, Famagusta, 10,000; GSO Limassol, 10,000; GSj, Larnaca, 8,000.
Season: October–June.
All players are amateurs.

International matches 1982

14 April, Damas: v Syria (a) won 1-0 (*Vrachimis*)
1 May, Hunedsara: v Rumania (a) lost 1-3 (*Vrachimis*)
27 Oct, Nicosia: v Greece (h) drew 1-1 (*Yankoudakis*)
13 Nov, Nicosia: v Sweden (h) lost 0-1

Most Capped Player: Andreas Stylianou 43

League Championship wins (1935–83)

Apoel 12; Omonia 12; Anorthosis 6; AEL 5; EPA 3; Olympiakos 3; Chetin Kayal 1; Pezoporikos 1; Trast 1.

Cup wins (1935–83)

Apoel 10; Omonia 6; EPA 5; AEL 3; Trast 3; Chetin Kaya 2; Apollon 2; Pezoporikos 2; Anorthosis 2; Paralimni 1; Olympiakos 1.

	League Champions	Cup Winners
1946	EPA	EPA
1947	Apoel	Apoel
1948	Apoel	AEL
1949	Apoel	Anorthosis
1950	Anorthosis	EPA
1951	Chetin Kaya	Apoel
1952	Apoel	Chetin Kaya
1953	AEL	EPA
1954	Pezoporikos	Chetin Kaya
1955	AEL	EPA
1956	AEL	*No competition*
1957	Anorthosis	*No competition*
1958	Anorthosis	*No competition*
1959	*No competition*	*No competition*
1960	Anorthosis	*No competition*
1961	Omonia	*No competition*
1962	Anorthosis	Anorthosis
1963	Anorthosis	Apoel
1964	*No competition*	*No competition*
1965	Apoel	Omonia
1966	Omonia	Apollon
1967	Olympiakos	Apollon
1968	AEL	Apoel
1969	Olympiakos	Apoel
1970	EPA	Pezoporikos
1971	Olympiakos	Anorthosis
1972	Omonia	Omonia
1973	Apoel	Pezoporikos
1974	Omonia	Paralimni
1975	Omonia	Anorthosis
1976	Omonia	Apoel
1977	Omonia	Olympiakos
1978	Omonia	Apoel
1979	Omonia	Apoel
1980	Apoel	Omonia
1981	Omonia	Omonia
1982	Omonia	Omonia
1983	Omonia	Omonia

Final League Table 1982–83

	P	*W*	*D*	*L*	*F*	*A*	*Pts*
Omonia Nicosia	26	15	6	4	50	17	36
Anorthosis	26	13	9	4	46	22	35
Apoel	26	11	10	5	33	20	32
AEL	26	12	7	7	29	21	31
Pezoporikos	26	9	10	7	26	20	28
Omonia Aradippou	26	11	6	9	34	34	28
Alki	26	8	11	7	32	35	27
Athletic Union of Paralimni	26	5	13	8	35	40	23
EPA	26	8	6	12	22	33	22
Apollon	26	6	9	11	24	38	21
Olympiakos	26	5	10	10	26	43	20
Salamina	26	6	8	12	28	39	20
APOP	26	5	4	17	19	41	14

CZECHOSLOVAKIA

President: Jaromir Tomanek.
Secretary: Ing. Rudolf Bata.
Address of Association: Czechoslovak Football, 12, Na Porící, 11530 Prague, 1.
Telephone: 24 98 41, 22 58 36.
Cable: Sportsvaz Praha.
Telex: 122650 cstv c.
Area: 49,370 square miles.
Population: 16,000,000.
Number of Clubs: 5,919. *Teams:* 5,366.
Number of Players: 541,379.
Year of Formation: 1906.
National Colours: Red shirts, white shorts, blue stockings.
Second Choice of Colours: White shirts, white shorts, white stockings.
Name, Address and Capacity of National Stadium: Stadion Ceskoslovenské Armády, Praha-Strahov, 60,000.
Names, Addresses and Capacities of Other Principal Football Grounds: Slovan Bratislava, Bratislava-Tehelné Pole, 63,000; Zbrojovka Brno, Brno, 70,000; Slavia Prague, Prague, 43,000; International, Bratislava, 40,000; Sparta Praha, Prague, 38,000.
Season: August–November; February–June.

Principal Honours

World Cup: *runners-up* 1934, 1962
European Championship: *winners* 1976
Olympic Games: *runners-up* 1964
European Cup-Winners' Cup: *winners* Slovan Bratislava (1969)

International matches 1982

3 March, Sao Paul: v Brazil (a) drew 1-1 (*Janecka*)
9 March, Mar Del Plata: v Argentina (a) drew 0-0
24 March, Prague: v Greece (h) won 2-1 (*Radimec, Jarolim*)
14 April, Cologne: v West Germany (a) lost 1-2 (*Bichovsky*)
28 April, Vienna: v Austria (a) lost 1-2 (*Jakubec*)
17 June, Valladolid: v Kuwait (W.C.) drew 1-1 (*Panenka*)
20 June, Bilbao: v England (W.C.) lost 0-2
24 June, Valladolid: v France (W.C.) drew 1-1 (*Panenka*)
6 Oct, Bratislava: v Sweden (h) drew 2-2 (*Janecka 2*)
27 Oct, Copenhagen: v Denmark (a) won 3-1 (*Cermak, Fiala, Chaloupka*)
13 Nov, Milan: v Italy (a) drew 2-2 (*Sloup, Chaloupka*)

Most Capped Player: Zdenek Nehoda 88

League Championship wins (1926–83)

Sparta Prague 13; Slavia Prague 12; Dukla Prague (prev. UDA) 11; Slovan Bratislava 6; Spartak Trnava 5; Banik Ostrava 3; Inter-Bratislava 1; Spartak Hradec Kralove 1; Viktoria Zizkov 1; Zbrojovka Brno 1; Bohemians 1.

Cup wins (1961–83)

Dukla Prague 6; Slovan Bratislava 5; Sparta Prague 4; Spartak Trnava 3; Banik Ostrava 2; Lokomotiv Kosice 2; TJ Gottwaldov 1.

	League Champions	Cup Winners
1946	Sparta Prague	
1947	Slavia Prague	
1948	Sparta Prague	
1949	Slovan Bratislava	
1950	Slovan Bratislava	
1951	Slovan Bratislava	
1952	Sparta Prague	
1953	Dukla Prague	
1954	Sparta Prague	
1955	Slovan Bratislava	
1956	Dukla Prague	
1957	*No competition*	
1958	Dukla Prague	
1959	Inter-Bratislava	
1960	Hradec Kralove	
1961	Dukla Prague	Dukla Prague
1962	Dukla Prague	Slovan Bratislava
1963	Dukla Prague	Slovan Bratislava
1964	Dukla Prague	Sparta Prague
1965	Sparta Prague	Dukla Prague
1966	Dukla Prague	Dukla Prague
1967	Sparta Prague	Sparta Trnava
1968	Spartak Trnava	Slovan Bratislava
1969	Spartak Trnava	Dukla Prague
1970	Slovan Bratislava	TJ Gottwaldov
1971	Spartak Trnava	Spartak Trnava
1972	Spartak Trnava	Sparta Prague
1973	Spartak Trnava	Banik Ostrava
1974	Slovan Bratislava	Slovan Bratislava
1975	Slovan Bratislava	Spartak Trnava
1976	Banik Ostrava	Sparta Prague
1977	Dukla Prague	Lokomotiv Kosice
1978	Zbrojovka Brno	Banik Ostrava
1979	Dukla Prague	Lokomotiv Kosice
1980	Banik Ostrava	Sparta Prague
1981	Banik Ostrava	Dukla Prague
1982	Dukla Prague	Slovan Bratislava
1983	Bohemians	Dukla Prague

Final League Table 1982–83

	P	*W*	*D*	*L*	*F*	*A*	*Pts*
Bohemians	30	18	6	6	69	31	42
Banik Ostrava	30	16	8	6	48	31	40
Sparta Prague	30	14	8	8	50	35	36
Inter Bratislava	30	11	11	8	35	24	33
Dukla Prague	30	11	10	9	44	35	32
Slavia Prague	30	12	8	10	56	53	32
Vitkovice	30	13	5	12	40	39	31
Spartak Trnava	30	12	6	12	29	39	30
RH Cheb	30	9	11	10	44	38	29
Lokomotiv Kosice	30	11	7	12	41	50	29
Zilina	30	11	6	13	41	43	28
Tatran Presov	30	10	7	13	43	53	27
Slovan Bratislava	30	8	10	12	34	51	26
Nitra	30	10	6	14	41	60	26
Zbrojovka Brno	30	8	7	15	43	52	23
Olomouc	30	5	6	19	32	56	16

DENMARK

President: Carl Nielsen.
Secretary: Erik Hyldstrup.
Address of Association: Dansk Boldspil – Union PW Ligns Alle 4, Copenhagen, 2100.
Telephone: 424540.
Cable: Danksboldspil.
Telex: 15545 dbu dk.
Area: 17,159 square miles.
Population: 4,750,000.
Number of Clubs: 1,479. *Teams:* 7,400.
Number of Players: 208,350.
Year of Formation: 1889.
National Colours: Red shirts, white shorts, red stockings.
Second Choice of Colours: White shirts, red shorts, white stockings.
Name, Address and Capacity of National Stadium: Kobenhavns Idraetspark, PH-Lings-Alle 2, 50,000.
Names, Addresses and Capacities of Other Principal Football Grounds: Odense stadium, Odense, 20,000; Aarhus stadium, Aarhus, 24,000; Aalborg stadium, Aalborg, 22,000; Esbjerg stadium, Esbjerg, 18,000; Vejle stadium, Vejle, 18,000.
Season: April–November.

Principal Honours

Olympic Games: *runners-up* 1908, 1912, 1960

International matches 1982

5 May, Copenhagen: v Sweden (h) drew 1-1 (*Arnesen*)
27 May, Copenhagen: v Belgium (h) won 1-0 (*E. Larsen*)
15 June, Oslo: v Norway (a) lost 1-2 (*M. Laudrup*)
8 Aug, Copenhagen: v Finland (h) won 3-2 (*Bastrup, Lerby, Busk*)
1 Sept, Bucharest: v Rumania (a) lost 0-1
22 Sept, Copenhagen: v England (h) drew 2-2 (*Hansen, Olsen*)
27 Oct, Copenhagen: v Czechoslovakia (h) lost 1-3 (*Laudrup*)
10 Nov, Luxembourg: v Luxembourg (a) won 2-1 (*Lerby, Bergren*)

Most Capped Player: *Per Rontved 75*

League Championship wins (1913–82)

KB Copenhagen 15; B 93 Copenhagen 9; AB (Akademisk) 9; B 1903 Copenhagen 7; Frem 6; Esbjergs BK 5; AGF Aarhus 4; Vejle BK 4; Hvidovre 3; B 1909 Odense 2; Koge BK 2; Odense BK 2.

Cup wins (1955–82)

Vejle BK 6; Aarhus GF 5; BK 09 Odense 3; Randers Freja 3; Aalborg BK 2; Esbjerg BK 2; Frem 2; KB Copenhagen 1; Vanlose 1; B 1903 Copenhagen 1; Hvidovre 1; B93 Copenhagen 1.

	League Champions	Cup Winners
1946	BK 93	
1947	Akademisk	
1948	KB Copenhagen	
1949	KB Copenhagen	
1950	KB Copenhagen	
1951	Akademisk	
1952	Akademisk	
1953	KB Copenhagen	
1954	Koge BK	
1955	Aarhus GF	Aarhus GF
1956	Aarhus GF	Frem
1957	Aarhus GF	Aarhus GF
1958	Vejle	Vejle
1959	BK 09 Odense	Vejle
1960	Aarhus GF	Aarhus GF
1961	Esbjerg BK	Aarhus GF
1962	Esbjerg BK	BK Odense 09
1963	Esbjerg BK	BK Odense 09
1964	BK 09 Odense	Esbjerg
1965	Esbjerg BK	Aarhus GF
1966	Hvidovre	Aalborg BK
1967	Akademisk	Randers Freja
1968	KB Copenhagen	Randers Freja
1969	BK 03 Copenhagen	KB Copenhagen
1970	BK 03 Copenhagen	Aalborg BK
1971	Vejle	BK 09 Odense
1972	Vejle	Vejle
1973	Hvidovre	Randers Freja
1974	KB Copenhagen	Vanlose
1975	Koge BK	Vejle
1976	BK 03 Copenhagen	Esbjerg
1977	Odense BK	Vejle
1978	Vejle	Frem
1979	Esbjerg BK	B 1903 Copenhagen
1980	KB Copenhagen	Hvidovre
1981	Hvidovre	Vejle
1982	Odense BK	B 93 Copenhagen

Final League Table 1982

	P	W	D	L	F	A	Pts
Odense	30	18	5	7	51	28	41
Aarhus	30	16	8	6	61	37	40
B 1903	30	14	7	9	41	29	35
Brondbyernes	30	14	6	10	57	36	34
Lyngby	30	14	6	10	45	36	34
Hvidovre	30	12	9	9	35	30	33
Vejle	30	14	5	11	44	41	33
Naestved	30	12	8	10	36	36	32
Kolding Idraets Forening	30	8	14	8	34	38	30
Koge	30	11	7	12	47	42	29
Esbjerg	30	12	4	14	40	50	28
B 93	30	7	13	10	45	44	27
Ikast	30	9	7	14	34	45	25
B 1901	30	7	9	14	28	54	23
KB Copenhagen	30	6	6	18	44	66	18
B 1909	30	5	8	17	36	66	18

FINLAND

President: Jouko Loikkanen.
Secretary: Karl Salonen.
Address of Association: Suomen Palloliitto – Finlands Bollförbund, Stadion, 00250 Helsinki 25.
Telephone: 44 12 81.
Cable: Suomifotboll.
Telex: 123186 spl sf.
Area: 130,119 square miles.
Population: 4,792,000.
Number of Clubs: 987. *Teams:* 2,325.
Number of Players: 49,662.
Year of Formation: 1907.
National Colours: White shirts, blue shorts, white stockings.
Second Choice of Colours: Blue shirts, white shorts, blue stockings.
Name, Address and Capacity of National Stadium: Olympiastadion, Helsinki, 50,000.
Names, Addresses and Capacities of Other Principal Football Grounds: Ratina, Tampere, 25,000; Urhei Lukeskus Kotka, 14,500; Kupittaa, Turku, 11,000; Vaino Lanniemi, Kuopio, 10,100.
All amateur players.
Season: April–October.

International matches 1982

20 Feb, Lahti: v Sweden (h) drew 2-2 (*Jaankonsaari*)
21 Feb, Lahti: v Sweden (h) won 2-1 (*Jaankonsaari, Ikalainen*)
28 April, Stavanger: v Norway (a) drew 1-1 (*Ikalainen*)
3 June, Helsinki: v England (h) lost 1-4 (*Haaskivi*)
11 July, Helsinki: v Iceland (h) won 3-2 (*Ismail, Himanka, Kousa*)
11 Aug, Copenhagen: v Denmark (a) lost 2-3 (*Valvec, Turunen*)
8 Sept, Kuopio: v Poland (h) lost 2-3 (*Valvec, Kousa*)
22 Sept, Helsinki: v Portugal (h) lost 0-2
13 Oct, Moscow: v USSR (a) lost 0-2

Most Capped Player: *Arto Tolsa 76*

Championship wins (1949–82)

Turun Palloseura 5; Kupion Palloseura 5; Helsinki JK 4; Valkeakosken Haka 4; Lahden Reipas 3; IF Kamraterna 2; Kotkan TP 2; OPS Oulu 2; Turun Pyrkivä 1; IF Kronohagens 1; Helsinki PS 1; Ilves-Kissat 1; Kokkolan PV 1; IF Kamraterna I Vasa 1; Kuuysi 1.

Cup wins (1955–82)

Lahden Reipas 7; Valkeakosken Haka 7; Kotkan TP 4; Mikkelin 2; Helsinki JK 2; IFK Abo 1; Drott 1; Helsinki PS 1; Kuopion Palloseura 1; Pallo-Peikot 1; Ilves Tampere 1.

	League Champions	**Cup Winners**
1949	Turun Palloseura	
1950	Ilves-Kissat	
1951	Kotkan TP	
1952	Kotkan TP	
1953	IF Kamraterna I	
1954	Turun Pyrkivä	
1955	IF Kronohagens	Valkaekosken Haka
1956	Kuopion Palloseura	Pallo-Peikot
1957	Helsinki PS	Drott
1958	Kuopion Palloseura	Kotkan TP
1959	IF Kamraterna	Valkeakosken Haka
1960	Valkeakosken Haka	Valkeakosken Haka
1961	IF Kamraterna	Kotkan TP
1962	Valkeakosken Haka	Helsinki PS
1963	Lahden Reipas	Valkeakosken Haka
1964	Helsinki JK	Lahden Reipas
1965	Valkeakosken Haka	IFK Abo
1966	Kuopion Palloseura	Helsinki JK
1967	Lahden Reipas	Kotkan TP
1968	Turun Palloseura	Kuopion Palloseura
1969	Kokkolan PV	Valkeakosken Haka
1970	Lahden Reipas	Mikkelin
1971	Turun Palloseura	Mikkelin
1972	Turun Palloseura	Lahden Reipas
1973	Helsinki JK	Lahden Reipas
1974	Kuopion Palloseura	Lahden Reipas
1975	Turun Palloseura	Lahden Reipas
1976	Kuopion Palloseura	Lahden Reipas
1977	Valkeakosken Haka	Valkeakosken Haka
1978	Helsinki JK	Lahden Reipas
1979	OPS Oulu	Ilves
1980	OPS Oulu	Kotkan TP
1981	Helsinki JK	Helsinki JK
1982	Kuuysi	Valkaekoskan Haka

Qualifying series	P	W	D	L	F	A	Pts
TPS Turun	22	11	7	4	48	20	29
KPT Kuopion	22	11	7	4	41	22	29
Haka Valkeakosken	22	9	10	3	45	31	28
Ilves	22	10	6	6	46	38	26
HJK Helsinki	22	11	3	8	53	39	25
Kuusysi	22	11	3	8	36	26	25
KPV	22	11	3	8	38	29	25
KuPS	22	8	5	9	24	41	21
Oulun Palloseura	22	7	4	11	24	43	18
Sepsi-78	22	6	5	11	33	44	17
KTP Kotkan	22	4	3	15	29	55	11
Kuopion Elo	22	3	4	15	28	57	10

Championship	*P*	*W*	*D*	*L*	*F*	*A*	*Group Pts*		*Total*
Kuusysi	7	5	1	1	49	30	13	+11	24
HJK Helsinki	7	4	1	2	62	47	13	+ 9	22
Haka Valkeakosken	7	3	2	2	54	40	14	+ 8	22
TPS Turun	7	3	0	4	64	32	15	+ 6	21
KPT Kuopion	7	2	2	3	51	30	15	+ 6	21
KPV	7	3	0	4	49	44	13	+ 6	19
Ilves	7	2	1	4	56	57	13	+ 5	18
KuPS	7	1	3	3	31	51	11	+ 5	16

Promotion/Relegation series	*P*	*W*	*D*	*L*	*F*	*A*	*Group Pts*		*Total*
RoPS	7	6	0	1	12	4	3	+12	15
Lahden Reipas	7	5	0	2	10	11	4	+10	14
KTP Kotkan	7	5	1	1	16	6	2	+11	13
OPS	7	3	3	1	13	5	4	+ 9	13
MP	7	2	2	3	11	9	2	+ 6	8
Sepsi-78	7	2	2	4	10	14	3	+ 4	7
Elo	7	1	1	5	11	21	1	+ 3	4
FinnPa	7	0	1	6	3	16	1	+ 1	2
Moenchengladbach									
VfL Bochum	34	8	12	14	43	49			28

FRANCE

President: Fernand Sastre.
Secretary: Michel Cagnion (Dir Gen).
Address of Association: Fédération Française de Football, 60 bis, Avenue d'Iena, Paris 16e.
Telephone: 720 65–40.
Cable: Cefi Paris 034.
Telex: Fedfoot 620837 f.
Area: 209,454 square miles.
Population: 52,000,000.
Number of Clubs: 20,938. *Teams:* 52,000.
Number of Players: 1,430,679.
Year of Formation: 1919.
National Colours: Blue shirts, white shorts, red stockings.
Second Choice of Colours: White shirts, blue shorts, red stockings.
Name, Address and Capacity of National Stadium: Stade du Parc des Princes, 24 rue du Commandant Guilbaud, 75, Paris 16ème, 50,000.
Names, Addresses and Capacities of Other Principal Football Grounds: Stade Vélodrome Jean Bouin, Marseilles, 45,000; Stade Municipal de Bordeaux, Avenue de la Côte d'Argent, 33, Bordeaux, 30,000; Stade Municipal de Gerland, Lyon, 45,000; Stade Geoffroy Guichard Saint Etienne, 42,000; Stade Marcel Saupin, Nantes, 33,000; Stade de la Meinau, Strasbourg, 30,000; Stadium Municipal de Toulouse, Parc des Sports, 31 Toulouse, 30,000.
Season: August–June.

Principal Honours

European Champions Cup: *runners-up* Stade de Reims (1956, 1959); St Etienne (1976)
UEFA Cup: *runners-up* Bastia (1978)

International matches 1982

23 Feb, Paris: v Italy (h) won 2-0 (*Platini, Bravo*)
24 March, Paris: v Northern Ireland (h) won 4-0 (Zenier, Couriol, Larios, Genghini)
28 April, Paris: v Peru (h) lost 0-1
14 May, Lyon: v Bulgaria (h) drew 0-0
2 June, Toulouse: v Wales (h) lost 0-1
16 June, Bilbao: v England (W.C.) lost 1-3 (*Soler*)
21 June, Valladolid: v Kuwait (W.C.) won 4-1 (*Genghini, Platini, Six, Bossis*)
22 June, Valladolid: v Czechoslovakia (W.C.) drew 1-1 (*Six*)
28 June, Madrid: v Austria (W.C.) won 1-0 (*Genghini*)
4 July, Madrid: v Northern Ireland (W.C.) won 4-1 (*Giresse 2, Rocheteau 2*)
8 July, Seville: v West Germany (W.C.) drew 3-3 (*Platini, Tresor, Giresse*)
10 July, Alicante: v Poland (W.C.) lost 2-3 (*Girard, Couriol*)
31 Aug, Paris: v Poland (h) lost 0-4
6 Oct, Paris: v Hungary (h) won 1-0 (*Roussey*)
10 Nov, Rotterdam: v Netherlands (a) won 2-1 (*Battiston, Platini*)

Most Capped Player: Marius Tresor 64

League Championship wins (1933–83)

Saint Etienne 10; Stade de Reims 6; Nantes 6; AS Monaco 4; OGC Nice 4; Olympique Marseilles 4; Lille OSC 3; FC Sete 2; Sochaux 2; Racing Club Paris 1; Roubaix-Tourcoing 1; Girondins Bordeaux 1; Strasbourg 1.

Cup wins (1918–83)

Olympique Marseilles 9; Saint Etienne 6; Lille OSC 5; Racing Club Paris 5; Red Star 5; AS Monaco 3; Olympique Lyon 3; CAS Genereaux 2; Nancy 2; OGC Nice 2; Racing Club Strasbourg 2; Sedan 2; FC Sete 2; Stade de Reims 2; Stade Rennes 2; Paris St Germain 2; AS Cannes 1; Club Français 1; Excelsior Roubaix 1; Girondins Bordeaux 1; Le Havre 1; SO Montpelier 1; Olympique de Pantin 1; CA Paris 1; Sochaux 1; Toulouse 1; Bastia 1; Nantes 1.

	League Champions	Cup Winners
1958	Stade de Reims	Stade de Reims
1959	OGC Nice	Le Havre
1960	Stade de Reims	AS Monaco
1961	AS Monaco	Sedan
1962	Stade de Reims	Saint Etienne
1963	AS Monaco	AS Monaco
1964	Saint Etienne	Ol Lyon
1965	Nantes	Stade Rennes
1966	Nantes	Racing Club Strasbourg
1967	Saint Etienne	Ol Lyon
1968	Saint Etienne	Saint Etienne
1969	Saint Etienne	Ol Marseilles
1970	Saint Etienne	Saint Etienne
1971	Ol Marseilles	Stade Rennes
1972	Ol Marseilles	Ol Marseilles
1973	Nantes	Ol Lyon
1974	Saint Etienne	Saint Etienne
1975	Saint Etienne	Saint Etienne
1976	Saint Etienne	Ol Marseilles
1977	Nantes	Saint Etienne
1978	Monaco	Nancy
1979	Strasbourg	Nantes
1980	Nantes	Monaco
1981	Saint Etienne	Bastia
1982	Monaco	Paris St Germain
1983	Nantes	Paris St Germain

Final League Table 1982–83

	P	*W*	*D*	*L*	*F*	*A*	*Pts*
Nantes	38	24	10	4	77	29	58
Bordeaux	38	20	8	10	67	48	48
Paris SG	38	20	7	11	66	49	47
Lens	38	18	8	12	64	55	44
Laval	38	15	14	9	42	41	44
Monaco	38	14	15	9	55	35	43
Nancy	38	17	7	14	74	61	41
Auxerre	38	12	14	12	56	48	38
Metz	38	13	11	14	66	67	37
Brest	38	11	15	12	53	63	37
Toulouse	38	15	6	17	52	66	36
Sochaux	38	9	17	12	52	53	35
Lille	38	13	8	17	38	45	34
St Etienne	38	11	12	15	41	52	34
Strasbourg	38	11	11	16	40	51	33
Rouen	38	11	10	17	45	54	32
Bastia	38	9	14	15	41	52	32
Tours	38	12	7	19	58	68	31
Lyon	38	11	6	21	57	77	28
Mulhouse	38	10	8	20	46	76	28

EAST GERMANY

President: Prof. Dr Gunter Erbach.
Secretary: Karl Zimmerman.
Address of Association: Deutscher Fussball-Verband, Storkower Strasse 118, 1055 Berlin.
Telephone: 438 43 88/91, 438 44 75.
Cable: Fussball Verband Berlin.
Telex: 114919. *Area:* 41,802 square miles.
Population: 17,000,000.
Number of Clubs: 5,488. *Teams:* 28,025.
Number of Players: 557,106.
Year of Formation: 1948.
National Colours: White shirts, blue shorts, white stockings.
Second Choice of Colours: Blue shirts, white shorts, blue stockings.
Name, Address and Capacity of National Stadium: Sportforum-Leipzig, 95,000.
Names, Addresses and Capacities of Other Principal Football Grounds: Festival Stadion, Berlin; Dynamo-Stadion, Dresden, 37,000; Ernst-Thälmann-Stadion, Karl-Marx-Stadt, 45,000; Georg-Dimitroff-Stadion, Erfurt, 50,000; Kurt-Wabbel-Stadion, Halle, 32,000; Ernest-Abbe-Stadion, Jena, 25,000; Ostsee-Stadion, Rostock, 30,000; Friedrich-Ludwig-Jahn-Sportpark, Berlin, 25,000; Ernest-Grube-Stadion, Magdeburg, 45,000.
Season: August–June (with winter break).

Principal Honours

Olympic Games: *winners* 1976
European Cup-Winners' Cup: *winners* FC Magdeburg (1974); *runners-up* Carl Zeiss Jena (1981)

International matches 1982

26 Jan, Natal: v Brazil (a) lost 1-3 (*Dorner*)
10 Feb, Athens: v Greece (a) win 1-0 (*Liebers*)
2 March, Bagdad: v Iraq (a) drew 0-0
14 April, Leipzig: v Italy (h) won 1-0 (*Hause*)
5 May, Moscow: v USSR (a) lost 0-1
19 May, Halmstadt: v Sweden (a) drew 2-2 (*Jarosin, Dorner*)
8 Sept, Reykjavik: v Iceland (a) won 1-0 (*Streich*)
22 Sept, Burgas: v Bulgaria (a) drew 2-2 (*Dorner, Riediger*)
13 Oct, Glasgow: v Scotland (a) lost 0-2
17 Nov, Karl Marx Stadt: v Rumania (h) won 4-1 (*Kuhn 2, Schnuphase, Heun*)

Most Capped Player: Jurgen Croy 94

League Championship wins (1950–83)

ASK Vorwaerts 6; Dynamo Dresden 5; Dynamo Berlin 5; Wismut Karl-Marx-Stadt 4; FC Magdeburg 4; Carl Zeiss Jena (prev. Motor Jena) 3; Chemie Leipzig 2; Turbine Erfurt 2; Turbine Halle 1; Zwickau Horch 1; Empor Rostock 1.

Cup wins (1949–83)

Carl Zeiss Jena (prev. Motor Jena) 5; Dynamo Dresden 4; FC Magdeburg 4; Lokomotiv Leipzig 3; Chemie Leipzig 2; Magdeburg Aufbau 2; Motor Zwickau 2; ASK Vorwaerts 2; Dresden Einheit SC 1; Dresden VP 1; Dynamo Berlin 1; Halle Chemie SC 1; North Dessau Waggonworks 1; Thale EHW 1; Union East Berlin 1; Wismut Karl-Marx-Stadt 1; Sachsenring Zwickau 1.

	League Champions	**Cup Winners**
1949		North Dessau Waggonworks
1950	Zwickau Horch	Thale EHW
1951	Chemie Leipzig	*No competition*
1952	Halle Turbine	Dresden VP
1953	Dynamo Dresden	*No competition*
1954	Turbine Erfurt	ASK Vorwaerts
1955	Turbine Erfurt	Wismut Karl-Marx-Stadt
1956	Wismut Karl-Marx-Stadt	Chemie Leipzig
1957	Wismut Karl-Marx-Stadt	Lokomotiv Leipzig
1958	ASK Vorwaerts	Dresden Einheit SC
1959	Wismut Karl-Marx-Stadt	Dynamo Berlin
1960	ASK Vorwaerts	Motor Jena
1961	Empor Rostock	Motor Jena
1962	ASK Vorwaerts	Halle Chemie SC
1963	Motor Jena	Motor Zwickau
1964	Leipzig Chemie	Magdeburg Aufbau
1965	ASK Vorwaerts	Magdeburg Aufbau
1966	ASK Vorwaerts	Chemie Leipzig
1967	Wismut Karl-Marx-Stadt	Motor Zwickau
1968	Carl Zeiss Jena	Union East Berlin
1969	ASK Vorwaerts	FC Magdeburg
1970	Carl Zeiss Jena	ASK Vorwaerts
1971	Dynamo Dresden	Dynamo Dresden
1972	FC Magdeburg	Carl Zeiss Jena
1973	Dynamo Dresden	FC Magdeburg
1974	FC Magdeburg	Carl Zeiss Jena
1975	FC Magdeburg	Sachsenring Zwickau
1976	Dynamo Dresden	Lokomotiv Leipzig
1977	Dynamo Dresden	Dynamo Dresden
1978	FC Magdeburg	Dynamo Dresden
1979	Dynamo Berlin	FC Magdeburg
1980	Dynamo Berlin	Carl Zeiss Jena
1981	Dynamo Berlin	Lokomotiv Leipzig
1982	Dynamo Berlin	Dynamo Dresden
1983	Dynamo Berlin	Magdeburg

Final League Table 1982–83

	P	*W*	*D*	*L*	*F*	*A*	*Pts*
Dynamo Berlin	26	20	6	0	72	22	46
Vorwaerts Frankfurt	26	13	8	5	56	29	34
Carl Zeiss Jena	26	15	4	7	46	29	34
Lokomotiv Leipzig	26	12	7	7	44	27	31
Rot-Weiss Erfurt	26	11	9	6	45	37	31
Magdeburg	26	10	9	7	52	32	29
Dynamo Dresden	26	12	5	9	51	43	29
Rostock	26	11	6	9	38	40	28
Karl-Marx-Stadt	26	10	6	10	41	41	26
Aue	26	6	8	12	30	45	20
Halle	26	5	7	14	41	53	17
Union Berlin	26	5	7	14	23	50	17
Bohlen	26	4	5	17	31	79	13
Zwickau	26	2	5	19	21	64	9

WEST GERMANY

President: Hermann Neuberger.
Secretary: Hans Passlack.
Address of Association: Deutscher Fussball-Bund, Otto-Fleck-Schneise 6, Frankfurt (Main) 71.
Telephone: (0611) 67881.
Cable: Fussball, Frankfurt.
Telex: 41 6815 dfb d.
Area: 95,097 square miles.
Population: 63,300,000.
Number of Clubs: 18,957. *Teams:* 122,345.
Number of Players: 4,020,240.
Year of Formation: 1900.
National Colours: White shirts, black shorts, white stockings.
Second Choice of Colours: Green shirts, white shorts, white stockings.
Name, Address and Capacity of National Stadium: There is no stadium which could be considered as the National Stadium.
Names, Addresses and Capacities of Principal Football Grounds: Olympiastadion Berlin, 80,000 (61,800 seats); Olympiastadion München, 75,600 (44,200 seats); Neckarstadion Stuttgart, 72,200 (34,400 seats); Parkstadion Gelsenkirchen, 70,000 (36,000 seats); Rheinstadion Düsseldorf, 69,600 (31,800 seats); Waldstadion Frankfurt 61,000 (29,900 seats); Volksparkstadion Hamburg, 61,400 (27,800 seats); Niedersachsenstadion Hannover, 60,500 (39,000 seats); Westfalen Stadion Dortmund, 53,600 (16,600 seats), Müngersdorfer Stadion, Cologne 60,000 (28,000 seats).
Season: August–June.

Principal Honours

World Cup: *winners* 1954, 1974; *runners-up* 1966, 1982
European Championship: *winners* 1972, 1980; *runners-up* (1976)
World Club Champions: Bayern Munich (1976)
European Champions Cup: *winners* Bayern Munich (1974, 1975, 1976), Hamburg (1983); *runners-up* Eintracht Frankfurt (1960), Borussia Moenchengladbach (1977), SV Hamburg (1980), Bayern Munich (1982)
European Cup-Winners' Cup: *winners* Borussia Dortmund (1966), Bayern Munich (1967), SV Hamburg (1977); *runners-up* Munich 1860 (1965), SV Hamburg (1968), Fortuna Düsseldorf (1979)
UEFA Cup: *winners* Borussia Moenchengladbach (1975, 1979), Eintracht Frankfurt (1980); *runners-up* Borussia Moenchengladbach (1973, 1980), SV Hamburg (1982)

International matches 1982

17 Feb, Hanover: v Portugal (h) won 3-1 (*Fischer 2, Humberto og*)
21 March, Rio de Janeiro: v Brazil (a) lost 0-1
24 March, Buenos Aires: v Argentina (a) drew 1-1 (*Dremmler*)
14 April, Cologne: v Czechoslovakia (h) won 2-1 (*Littbarski, Breitner*)
12 May, Oslo: v Norway (a) won 4-2 (*Rummenigge 2, Littbarski 2*)
16 June, Gijon: v Algeria (W.C.) lost 1-2 (*Rummenigge*)
20 June, Gijon: v Chile (W.C.) won 4-1 (*Rummenigge 3, Reinders*)
25 June, Gijon: v Austria (W.C.) won 1-0 (*Hrubesch*)
29 June, Madrid: v England (W.C.) drew 0-0
2 July, Madrid: v Spain (W.C.) won 2-1 (*Littbarski, Fischer*)
8 July, Seville: v France (W.C.) drew 3-3 (*Littbarski, Rummenigge, Fischer*)
11 July, Madrid: v Italy (W.C.) lost 1-3 (*Breitner*)
22 Sept, Munich: v Belgium (h) drew 0-0
13 Oct, London: v England (a) won 2-1 (*Rummenigge 2*)
17 Nov, Belfast: v Northern Ireland (a) lost 0-1

Most Capped Player: Franz Beckenbauer 103

League Championship wins (1903–83)

IFC Nuremberg 9; Schalke 04 7; Bayern Munich 7; SV Hamburg 6; Borussia Moenchengladbach 5; VfB Leipzig 3; Sp Vgg Fürth 3; BorussiaDortmund 3; IFC Cologne 3; Viktoria Berlin 2; Hertha Berlin 2; Hanover 96 2; Dresden SC 2; VfB Stuttgart 2; IFC Kaiserslautern 2; Munich 1860 1; SV Werder Bremen 1; Union Berlin 1; FC Freibourg 1; Phoenix Karlsruhe 1; Karlsruher FV 1; Holstein Kiel 1; Fortuna Düsseldorf 1; Rapid Vienna 1; VfR Mannheim 1; Rot-Weiss Essen 1; Eintracht Frankfurt 1; Eintracht Brunswick 1.

Cup wins (1935–83)

Bayern Munich 6; IFC Cologne 4; IFC Nuremberg 3; Eintracht Frankfurt 3; Dresden SC 2; Fortuna Düsseldorf 2; Karlsruhe SC 2; Munich 1860 2; Schalke 04 2; VfB Stuttgart 2; Borussia Moenchengladbach 2; SV Hamburg 2; Borussia Dortmund 1; First Vienna 1; VfB Leipzig 1; Kickers Offenbach 1; Rapid Vienna 1; Rot-Weiss Essen 1; SW Essen 1; Werder Bremen 1.

	League Champions	Cup Winners
1948	IFC Nuremberg	
1949	VfR Mannheim	
1950	VfB Stuttgart	
1951	IFC Kaiserslautern	
1952	VfB Stuttgart	
1953	IFC Kaiserslautern	Rot-Weiss Essen
1954	Hanover 96	VfB Stuttgart
1955	Rot-Weiss Essen	Karlsruhe SC
1956	Borussia Dortmund	Karlsruhe SC
1957	Borussia Dortmund	Bayern Munich
1958	Schalke 04	VfB Stuttgart
1959	Eintracht Frankfurt	SW Essen

1960	SV Hamburg	Borussia Moenchengladbach
1961	IFC Nuremberg	Werder Bremen
1962	IFC Cologne	IFC Nuremberg
1963	Borussia Dortmund	SV Hamburg
1964	IFC Cologne	Munich 1860
1965	Werder Bremen	Borussia Dortmund
1966	Munich 1860	Bayern Munich
1967	Eintracht Brunswick	Bayern Munich
1968	IFC Nuremberg	IFC Cologne
1969	Bayern Munich	Bayern Munich
1970	Borussia Moenchengladbach	Kickers Offenbach
1971	Borussia Moenchengladbach	Bayern Munich
1972	Bayern Munich	Schalke 04
1973	Bayern Munich	Borussia Moenchengladbach
1974	Bayern Munich	Eintracht Frankfurt
1975	Borussia Moenchengladbach	Eintracht Frankfurt
1976	Borussia Moenchengladbach	SV Hamburg
1977	Borussia Moenchengladbach	IFC Cologne
1978	Cologne	Cologne
1979	SV Hamburg	Fortuna Düsseldorf
1980	Bayern Munich	Fortuna Düsseldorf
1981	Bayern Munich	Eintracht Frankfurt
1982	SV Hamburg	Bayern Munich
1983	SV Hamburg	Cologne

Final League Table 1982–83

	P	*W*	*D*	*L*	*F*	*A*	*Pts*
SV Hamburg	34	20	12	2	79	33	52
Werder Bremen	34	23	6	5	76	38	52
VfB Stuttgart	34	20	8	6	80	47	48
Bayern Munich	34	17	10	7	74	33	44
IFC Cologne	34	17	9	8	69	42	43
IFC Kaiserslautern	34	14	13	7	57	44	41
Borussia Dortmund	34	16	7	11	78	62	39
Arminia Bielefeld	34	12	7	15	46	71	31
Fortuna Dusseldorf	34	11	8	15	63	75	30
Eintracht Frankfurt	34	12	5	17	48	57	29
Bayer Leverkusen	34	10	9	15	43	66	29
Borussia Moenchengladbach	34	12	4	18	64	63	28
VfL Bochum	34	8	12	14	43	49	28
IFC Nuremberg	34	11	6	17	44	70	28
Braunschweig	34	8	11	15	42	65	27
Schalke	34	8	6	20	48	68	22
Karlsruhe	34	7	7	20	39	86	21
Hertha Berlin	34	5	10	19	43	67	20

GREECE

President: Dr Basile Hadzijannis.
Secretary: Charalambos David.
Address of Association: Federation Hellenique de Football Association, Singrou Avenue 137, Athenes.
Telephone: 933 4922.
Cable: Football Athenes.
Telex: 215328.
Area: 50,547 square miles.
Population: 9,850,000.
Number of Clubs: 2,624.
Teams: 1,936.
Number of Players: 163,470.
Year of Formation: 1926.
National Colours: White shirts, blue shorts, white stockings.
Second Choice of Colours: Blue shirts, white shorts, blue stockings.
Name, Address and Capacity of National Stadium: Karaïskaki, Neon Faliron, 42,000.
Names, Addresses and Capacities of Other Principal Football Grounds: Kaftatzoglion, Salonika, 47,000; AEK, Athens, 35,000; Panathinaikos, Athenes, 25,000; PAOK, Salonika, 40,000; Aris, Salonika, 30,000.

Principal Honours

European Champions Cup: *runners-up* Panathinaikos (1971)

International matches 1982

20 Jan, Athens: v Portugal (h) lost 1-2 (*Anastopoulos*)
10 Feb, Athens: v East Germany (h) lost 0-1
10 March, Athens: v USSR (h) lost 0-2
24 March, Prague: v Czechoslovakia (a) lost 1-2 (*Kouis*)
14 April, Eindhoven: v Netherlands (a) lost 0-1
9 Oct, Luxembourg: v Luxembourg (a) won 2-0 (*Dimopoulos, Anastopoulos*)
27 Oct, Nicosia: v Cyprus (a) drew 1-1 (*Mavros*)
17 Nov, Salonika: v England (h) lost 0-3
1 Dec, Athens: v Switzerland (h) lost 1-3 (*Anastopoulos*)

Most Capped Player: Mimis Papaionnou 61

League Championship wins (1928–83)

Olympiakos 24; Panathinaikos 12; AEK Athens 7; Aris Salonika 3; PAOK Salonika 1.

Cup wins (1932–83)

Olympiakos 18; AEK Athens 9; Panathinaikos 7; PAOK Salonika 2; Aris Salonika 1; Ethnikos 1; Iraklis 1; Panionios 1; Kastoria 1.

	League Champions	Cup Winners
1946	Aris Salonika	
1947	Olympiakos	Olympiakos
1948	Olympiakos	Panathinaikos
1949	*No competition*	AEK Athens
1950	Panathinaikos	AEK Athens
1951	Olympiakos	Olympiakos
1952	*No competition*	Olympiakos
1953	Panathinaikos	Olympiakos
1954	Olympiakos	Olympiakos
1955	Olympiakos	Panathinaikos
1956	Olympiakos	AEK Athens
1957	Olympiakos	Olympiakos
1958	Olympiakos	Olympiakos
1959	Olympiakos	Olympiakos
1960	Panathinaikos	Olympiakos
1961	Panathinaikos	Olympiakos
1962	Panathinaikos	Olympiakos
1963	AEK Athens	Olympiakos
1964	Panathinaikos	AEK Athens
1965	Panathinaikos	Olympiakos
1966	Olympiakos	AEK Athens
1967	Olympiakos	Panathinaikos
1968	AEK Athens	Olympiakos
1969	Panathinaikos	Panathinaikos
1970	Panathinaikos	Aris Salonika
1971	AEK Athens	Olympiakos
1972	Panathinaikos	PAOK Salonika
1973	Olympiakos	Olympiakos
1974	Olympiakos	PAOK Salonika
1975	Olympiakos	Olympiakos
1976	PAOK Salonika	Iraklis
1977	Panathinaikos	Panathinaikos
1978	AEK Athens	AEK Athens
1979	AEK Athens	Panionios
1980	Olympiakos	Kastoria
1981	Olympiakos	Olympiakos
1982	Olympiakos	Panathinaikos
1983	Olympiakos	AEK Athens

Final League Table 1982–83

	P	*W*	*D*	*L*	*F*	*A*	*Pts*
Olympiakos	34	20	10	4	50	22	50
Larissa	34	18	9	7	54	27	45
AEK Athens	34	19	7	8	54	39	45
PAOK Salonika	34	18	6	10	49	28	42
Aris Salonika	34	15	11	8	35	23	41
Panathinaikos	34	14	9	11	49	42	37
Ofi	34	14	9	11	53	48	37
Hiraklis	34	12	10	12	54	43	34
Yannina	34	10	13	11	35	34	33
Doxa	34	12	7	15	43	56	31
Ethnikos	34	11	9	14	39	38	31
Apollon	34	11	9	14	40	36	31
Serres	34	10	12	12	28	37	30
Panionios	34	11	7	16	31	44	29
Makedonikos	34	11	7	16	30	52	29
Panahaiki	34	11	4	19	34	49	26
Rhodes	34	7	7	20	25	58	21
Kastoria	34	8	4	22	31	58	20

HUNGARY

President: Gyorgy Szepesi.
Secretary: Dr Miklos Panesics.
Address of Association: Fédération Hongroise de Football, Népköztársaság utja 47, 1061 Budapest VI.
Telephone: 22 58 17, 42 13 16.
Cable: Misz-Budapest.
Telex: 225782 misz h.
Area: 35,919 square miles.
Population: 10,713,000.
Year of Formation: 1901.
Number of Clubs: 2,503. *Teams:* 5,424.
Number of Players: 143,675.
National Colours: Red shirts, white shorts, green stockings.
Second Choice of Colours: All white.
Name, Address and Capacity of National Stadium: Népstadion Budapest XIV, István Mezei ut 3/5, 80,000.
Names, Addresses and Capacities of Other Principal Football Grounds: Ferencvaros, Budapest IX Ullöi-ut, 30,000; Bp Vasas SC Budapest XIII, Fay-u 58, 20,000; Ujpesti Dozsa SE Budapest IV, Mergyeri ut 13, 25,000; MTK-VM Budapest VIII, Hungaria krt 6, 20,000; Csepel SE Budapest XXI, Béke tér, 22,000; Györi Raba ETO Györ, 28,000; Pécs MSC, Pécs, 25,000; Szegedi Egyetemi OL Szeged, 25,000; Diösgyöri VTK, Diösgyör, 25,000; Bp Honved, Budapest, 30,000.
Season: September–December; March–June.

Principal Honours

World Cup: *runners-up* 1938, 1954
Olympic Games: *winners* 1952, 1964, 1968; *runners-up* 1972
European Cup-Winners' Cup: *runners-up* MTK Budapest (1964); Ferencvaros (1975)
Fairs Cup: *winners* Ferencvaros (1965); *runners-up* Ferencvaros (1968), Ujpest Dozsa (1969)

International matches 1982

11 Feb, Auckland: v New Zealand (a) won 2-1 (*Izso, Bodonyi*)
14 Feb, Christchurch: v New Zealand (a) won 2-1 (*Poloskei, Izso*)
24 March, Budapest: v Austria (h) lost 2-3 (*Varadi, Nyilasi*)
18 April, Budapest: v Peru (h) lost 1-2 (*Szentes*)
15 June, Elche: v El Salvador (W.C.) won 10-1 (*Nyilasi 2, Poloskei, Fazekas 2, Toth, Szentes, Kiss 3*)
18 June, Alicante: v Argentina (W.C.) lost 1-4 (*Poloskei*)
22 June, Elche: v Belgium (W.C.) drew 1-1 (*Varga*)
22 Sept, Gyor: v Turkey (h) won 5-0 (*Garaba, Burcsa, Budavari, Kiss S., Poczik*)
6 Oct, Paris: v France (a) lost 0-1

Most Capped Player: Jozsef Bozsik 100

League Championship wins (1901–83)

Ferencvaros (prev. FTC) 23; MTK-VM Budapest (prev. Hungaria, Bastay and Vörös Lobogo) 18; Ujpest Dozsa 18; Vasas Budapest 6; Honved 6; Csepel 4; Raba Györ (prev. Vasas Györ) 3; BTC 2; Nagyvarad 1.

Cup wins (1910–83)*

Ferencvaros (prev. FTC) 14; MTK-VM Budapest (prev. Hungaria, Bastya and Vörös Lobogo) 9; Ujpest Dozsa 6; Raba Györ (prev.Vasas Györ) 4; Diösgyör 2; Vasas Budapest 2; Bocskai 1; Honved 1; III Ker 1; Kispesti AC 1; Soroksar 1; Szolnoki MAV 1.

* *Cup not held regularly until 1964*

	League Champions	Cup Winners
1953	Vörös Lobogo	
1954	Honved	
1955	Honved	Vasas Budapest
1956	Champ. abandoned	
1957	Vasas Budapest	
1958	MTK Budapest	Ferencvaros
1959	Vasas Csepel	
1960	Ujpest Dozsa	
1961	Vasas Budapest	
1962	Vasas Budapest	
1963	Ferencvaros	
1963*	Vasas Györ	
1964	Ferencvaros	Honved
1965	Vasas Budapest	Vasas Györ
1966	Vasas Budapest	Vasas Györ
1967	Ferencvaros	Vasas Györ
1968	Ferencvaros	MTK Budapest
1969	Ujpest Dozsa	Ujpest Dozsa
1970	Ujpest Dozsa	Ujpest Dozsa
1971	Ujpest Dozsa	Ujpest Dozsa
1972	Ujpest Dozsa	Ferencvaros
1973	Ujpest Dozsa	Vasas Budapest
1974	Ujpest Dozsa	Ferencvaros
1975	Ujpest Dozsa	Ujpest Dozsa
1976	Ferencvaros	Ferencvaros
1977	Vasas Budapest	Diösgyör
1978	Ujpest Dozsa	Ferencvaros
1979	Ujpest Dozsa	Raba Györ
1980	Honved	Diösgyör
1981	Ferencvaros	Vasas Budapest
1982	Raba Györ	Ujpest Dozsa
1983	Raba Györ	Ujpest Dozsa

* *Short season.*

Final League Table 1982–83

	P	*W*	*D*	*L*	*F*	*A*	*Pts*
Raba Györ	30	19	6	5	82	37	44
Ferencvaros	30	19	5	6	73	46	43
Honved	30	17	8	5	57	33	42
Csepel	30	13	11	6	52	46	37
Ujpest Dozsa	30	12	8	10	45	47	32
Tatabanya	30	9	11	10	42	40	29
Vasas	30	11	6	13	56	52	28
Haladas	30	10	8	12	33	40	28
Diosgyor	30	8	11	11	36	44	27
Nyiregyhaza	30	9	8	13	29	37	26
Zalaegerszeg	30	8	10	12	37	46	26
MTK Budapest	30	9	8	13	40	58	26
Videoton	30	11	3	16	48	47	25
Pecs	30	9	7	14	45	52	25
Debrecen	30	8	9	13	35	51	25
Bekscsaba	30	5	7	18	41	75	17

ICELAND

President: Ellert B. Schram.
Secretary: K. T. Sigurdsson.
Address of Association: Football Association of Iceland, PO Box 1011, Reykjavik.
Telephone: 84 44. *Cable:* KSI Reykjavik.
Telex: 2314 isi is, or 2110 (att. E. Schram).
Area: 39,768 square miles.
Population: 229,187. *Number of Clubs:* 67.
Teams: 460. *Number of Players:* 17,534.
Year of Formation: 1929.
National Colours: Blue shirts, white shorts and blue stockings.
Second Choice of Colours: White shirts, blue shorts, white stockings.
Name, Address and Capacity of National Stadium: Laugardalsvöllur, Reykjavik, 14,800.
Names and Addresses of Other Principal Football Grounds: Melavöllur, Reykjavik; Ibróttavöllurinn, Akureyri; Ibróttavöllurinn, Akranesi; Ibróttavöllurinn, Keflavik, 10,000.
Season: April–October.

International matches 1982

3 June, Reykjavik: v England (h) drew 1-1 (*Gudjohnsen*)
5 June, Messina: v Malta (a) lost 1-2 (*Geirsson*)
11 July, Helsinki: v Finland (a) lost 2-3 (*Geirsson, Edvaldsson*)
1 Sept, Reykjavik: v Holland (h) drew 1-1 (*Edvaldsson*)
8 Sept, Reykjavik: v East Germany (h) lost 0-1
13 Oct, Dublin: v Rep of Ireland (a) lost 0-2
27 Oct, Malaga: v Spain (a) lost 1-0

Most Capped Player: *Martti Geirsson 65*

League Championship wins (1912–82)

KR 20; Valur 17; Fram 15; IA Akranes 10; Vikingur 4; IBK Keflavik 3; IBV Vestmann 2.

Cup wins (1960–82)

KR 7; Valur 4; Fram 4; IBV Vestmann 3; IBA Akureyri 1; Vikingur 1; IBK Keflavik 1; IA Akranes 1; IB Akranes 1.

	League Champions	Cup Winners
1946	Fram	
1947	Fram	
1948	KR	
1949	KR	
1950	KR	
1951	IA Akranes	
1952	KR	
1953	IA Akranes	
1954	IA Akranes	
1955	KR	
1956	Valur	
1957	IA Akranes	
1958	IA Akranes	
1959	KR	
1960	IA Akranes	KR
1961	KR	KR
1962	Fram	KR
1963	KR	KR
1964	IBK Keflavik	KR
1965	KR	Valur
1966	Valur	KR
1967	Valur	KR
1968	KR	IBV Vestmann
1969	IBK Keflavik	IBV Akureyri
1970	IA Akranes	Fram
1971	IBV Vestmann	Vikingur
1972	Fram	IBV Vestmann
1973	IBK Keflavik	Fram
1974	IA Akranes	Valur
1975	IA Akranes	IBV Keflavik
1976	Valur	Valur
1977	IA Akranes	Valur
1978	Valur	IA Akranes
1979	IBV Vestmann	Fram
1980	Valur	Fram
1981	Vikingur	IBV Vestmann
1982	Vikingur	IB Akranes

Final League Table 1982

	P	*W*	*D*	*L*	*F*	*A*	*Pts*
Vikingur	18	7	9	2	25	17	23
IBV Vestmann	18	9	4	5	23	16	22
KR	18	5	11	2	14	12	21
IB Akranes	18	6	6	6	22	20	18
Valur	18	6	5	7	18	15	17
IB Isafjardar	18	6	5	7	27	29	17
UBK	18	6	5	7	18	22	17
IB Keflavikur	18	5	6	7	14	19	16
Fram	18	4	7	7	17	23	15
KA	18	4	6	8	17	22	14

REPUBLIC OF IRELAND

President: Dr B. Menton.
Secretary: P. J. O'Driscoll PC.
Address of Association: The Football Association of Ireland, 80 Merrion Square, Dublin 2.
Telephone: 76 68 64.
Cable: Soccer Dublin.
Telex: 30498.
Population: 4,000,000.
Year of Formation: 1921.
Number of Clubs: 3,503. *Teams:* 3,028.
Number of Players: 62,701.
National Colours: Green shirts, white shorts, green stockings.
Second Choice of Colours: White.
Name, Address and Capacity of National Stadium: Dalymount Park, Dublin, 45,000; and Lansdowne Road, Dublin, 48,000.
Names, Addresses and Capacities of Other Principal Football Grounds: Glenmalure Park, Milltown, Dublin, 25,000; Flower Lodge, Cork, 25,000; Lourdes Stadium, Drogheda, 25,000; Tolka Park, Dublin, 20,000; Oriel Park, Dundalk, 15,000; Richmond Park, Dublin, 10,000; Markeis Field, Limerick, 10,000; Kilcohan Park, Waterford, 15,000.
Season: August–May.

International matches 1982

28 April, Algiers: v Algeria (a) lost 0-2
21 May, Santiago: v Chile (a) lost 0-1
27 May, Uberlandis: v Brazil (a) lost 0-7
30 May, Port of Spain: v Trinidad/Tobago (a) lost 1-2 (*Brady*)
27 Sept, Rotterdam: v Netherlands (a) lost 1-2 (*Daly*)
13 Oct, Dublin: v Iceland (h) won 2-0 (*Stapleton, Grealish*)
17 Nov, Dublin: v Spain (h) drew 3-3 (*Grimes, Stapleton 2*)

Most Capped Player: Johnny Giles 60

League Championship wins (1922–83)

Shamrock Rovers 10; Shelbourne 7; Bohemians 7; Dundalk 6; Waterford 6; Cork United 5; Drumcondra 5; St Patrick's Athletic 3; St James's Gate 2; Cork Athletic 2; Sligo Rovers 2; Limerick 2; Athlone Town 2; Dolphin 1; Cork Hibernians 1; Cork Celtic 1.

Cup wins (1922–83)

Shamrock Rovers 21; Dundalk 7; Drumcondra 5; Bohemians 4; Shelbourne 3; Cork Athletic 2; Cork United 2; St James's Gate 2; St Patrick's Athletic 2; Cork Hibernians 2; Limerick 2; Waterford 2; Alton United 1; Athlone Town 1; Cork 1; Fordsons 1; Transport 1; Finn Harps 1; Home Farm 1; Sligo 1.

	League Champions	Cup Winners
1946	Cork United	Drumcondra
1947	Shelbourne	Cork United
1948	Drumcondra	Shamrock Rovers
1949	Drumcondra	Dundalk
1950	Cork Athletic	Transport
1951	Cork Athletic	Cork Athletic
1952	St Patrick's Ath	Dundalk
1953	Shelbourne	Cork Athletic
1954	Shamrock Rovers	Drumcondra
1955	St Patrick's Ath	Shamrock Rovers
1956	St Patrick's Ath	Shamrock Rovers
1957	Shamrock Rovers	Drumcondra
1958	Drumcondra	Dundalk
1959	Shamrock Rovers	St Patrick's Ath
1960	Limerick	Shelbourne
1961	Drumcondra	St Patrick's Ath
1962	Shelbourne	Shamrock Rovers
1963	Dundalk	Shelbourne
1964	Shamrock Rovers	Shamrock Rovers
1965	Drumcondra	Shamrock Rovers
1966	Waterford	Shamrock Rovers
1967	Dundalk	Shamrock Rovers
1968	Waterford	Shamrock Rovers
1969	Waterford	Shamrock Rovers
1970	Waterford	Bohemians
1971	Cork Hibernians	Limerick
1972	Waterford	Cork Hibernians
1973	Waterford	Cork Hibernians
1974	Cork Celtic	Finn Harps
1975	Bohemians	Home Farm
1976	Dundalk	Bohemians
1977	Sligo Rovers	Dundalk
1978	Bohemians	Shamrock Rovers
1979	Dundalk	Dundalk
1980	Limerick	Waterford
1981	Athlone Town	Dundalk
1982	Dundalk	Limerick
1983	Atholone Town	Sligo

Final League Table 1982–83

	P	*W*	*D*	*L*	*F*	*A*	*Pts*
Athlone Town	26	20	5	1	61	24	65
Drogheda United	26	14	7	5	43	18	49
Dundalk	26	14	6	6	32	17	48
Bohemians	26	13	7	6	42	26	46
Shelbourne	26	13	5	8	50	45	44
Shamrock Rovers	26	10	8	8	39	25	38
St Patrick's Athletic	26	10	7	9	38	38	37
Limerick United	26	10	5	11	43	35	35
Finn Harps	26	9	8	9	36	33	35
Waterford	26	8	8	10	31	24	32
Galway United	26	6	8	12	33	44	26
Sligo Rovers	26	4	9	13	27	48	21
UCD	26	4	4	18	29	63	16
Home Farm	26	2	3	20	23	65	10

ITALY

President d'honneur: Dr Artemio Franchi.
President: Avv. Federico Sordillo.
Secretary: Dr Dario Borgogno.
Address of Association: Federazione Italiana Giuoco Calcio, via Gregorio Allegri 14, CP 2450, 00198 Rome.
Telephone: 84 911.
Cable: Federcalcio Roma.
Telex: 611483 calcio.
Area: 97,068 square miles.
Population: 54,134,846.
Number of Clubs: 19,084. *Teams:* 30,618.
Number of Players: 1,022,030.
Year of Formation: 1898.
National Colours: Blue shirts, white shorts, blue stockings with white tops.
Second Choice of Colours: White shirts with light blue stripe, blue shorts and blue stockings.
Name, Address and Capacity of National Stadium: Stadio Olimpico, Roma, 90,000.
Names, Addresses and Capacities of Other Principal Football Grounds: Bologna, Stadio Comunale, Via A. Costa 176, 50,000; Firenze, Stadio Comunale, Viale M. Fanti 4/6, 67,000; Milano, Stadio Comunale San Siro, Via Fetonte, 85,000; Torino, Stadio Comunale, Corso Sebatopoli 123, 71,000; Napoli, Stadio S. Paolo, Fuorigrotta, 82,000; Genova, Stadio Luigi, Ferraris, Via del Piano, 64,000.
Season: September–June.

Principal Honours

World Cup: *winners* 1934, 1938, 1982; *runners-up* 1970
European Championship: *winners* 1968
Olympic Games: *winners* 1936
World Club Champions: Inter-Milan (1964, 1965), AC Milan (1969)
European Champions Cup: *winners* AC Milan (1963, 1969), Inter-Milan (1964, 1965); *runners-up* Fiorentina (1957), AC Milan (1958), Inter-Milan (1967, 1972), Juventus (1973, 1983)
European Cup-Winners' Cup: *winners* Fiorentina (1961), AC Milan (1968, 1973); *runners-up* Fiorentina (1962), AC Milan (1974)
Fairs Cup: *winners* AS Roma (1961); *runners-up* Juventus (1965, 1971)
UEFA Cup: *winners* Juventus (1977)

International matches 1982

23 Feb, Paris: v France (a) lost 0-2
14 April, Leipzig: v East Germany (a) lost 0-1
28 May, Geneva: v Switzerland (a) drew 1-1 (*Cabrini*)
14 June, Vigo: v Poland (W.C.) drew 0-0
18 June, Vigo: v Peru (W.C.) drew 1-1 (*Conti*)
23 June, Vigo: v Cameroon (W.C.) drew 1-1 (*Graziani*)
29 June, Barcelona: v Argentina (W.C.) won 2-1 (*Tardelli, Cabrini*)
5 July, Barcelona: v Brazil (W.C.) won 3-2 (*Rossi 3*)
8 July, Barcelona: v Poland (W.C.) won 2-0 (*Rossi 2*)
11 July, Madrid: v West Germany (W.C.) won 3-1 (*Rossi, Tardelli, Altobelli*)
27 Oct, Roma: v Switzerland (h) lost 0-1
13 Nov, Milan: v Czechoslovakia (h) drew 2-2 (*Altobelli, Kapko og*)
4 Dec, Florence: v Rumania (h) drew 0-0

Most Capped Player: Dino Zoff 112

League Championship wins (1898–1983)

Juventus 20; Inter-Milan 12; AC Milan 10; Genoa 9; Torino 8; Pro Vercelli 7; Bologna 7; Fiorentina 2; AS Roma 2; Casale 1; Novese 1; Cagliari 1; Lazio 1.

Cup wins (1922–83)

Juventus 7; Torino 4; Fiorentina 4; AC Milan 4; AS Roma 4; Inter-Milan 3; Napoli 2; Bologna 2; Atalanta 1; Genoa 1; Lazio 1; Vado 1; Venezia 1.

	League Champions	Cup Winners
1959	AC Milan	Juventus
1960	Juventus	Juventus
1961	Juventus	Fiorentina
1962	AC Milan	Napoli
1963	Inter-Milan	Atalanta
1964	Bologna	AS Roma
1965	Inter-Milan	Juventus
1966	Inter-Milan	Fiorentina
1967	Juventus	AC Milan
1968	AC Milan	Torino
1969	Fiorentina	AS Roma
1970	Cagliari	Bologna
1971	Inter-Milan	Torino
1972	Juventus	AC Milan
1973	Juventus	AC Milan
1974	Lazio	Bologna
1975	Juventus	Fiorentina
1976	Torino	Napoli
1977	Juventus	AC Milan
1978	Juventus	Inter-Milan
1979	AC Milan	Juventus
1980	Inter-Milan	AS Roma
1981	Juventus	AS Roma
1982	Juventus	Inter-Milan
1983	AS Roma	Juventus

Final League Table 1982–83

	P	*W*	*D*	*L*	*F*	*A*	*Pts*
AS Roma	30	16	11	3	47	24	43
Juventus	30	15	9	6	49	26	39
Internazionale	30	12	14	4	40	26	38
Verona	30	11	13	6	37	31	35
Fiorentina	30	12	10	8	36	25	34
Udinese	30	6	20	4	25	29	32
Sampdoria	30	8	15	7	31	30	31
Torino	30	9	12	9	30	28	30
Avellino	30	8	12	10	29	34	28
Napoli	30	7	14	9	22	29	28
Visa	30	8	11	11	27	27	27
Genoa	30	6	15	9	34	38	27
Ascoli	30	9	9	12	32	37	27
Cagliari	30	6	14	10	23	33	26
Cesena	30	4	14	12	22	35	22
Catanzaro	30	2	9	19	21	56	13

LIECHTENSTEIN

President: David Vogt.
Secretary: Dr Werner Ospelt.
Address of Association: Liechtensteiner Fussball-Verband, Postfach 165, 9490 Vaduz.
Telephone: 27128, 66251.
Year of Formation: 1933.
National Colours: Blue/red shirts, red shorts, blue stockings.
Second Choice of Colours: Yellow/red shirts, red shorts, yellow stockings.
Name, Address and Capacity of National Stadium: Landessportplatz, Vaduz, 10,000.
Population: 25,000.
Number of Clubs: 7. *Teams:* 64.
Number of Players: 1,200.
Liechtenstein has no national league. Teams compete in Swiss regional leagues.
Season: August–July.

International matches 1982

9 March, Balzers: v Switzerland (h) lost 0-1
6 June, Vaduz: v China (h) won 2-0 (*Moser M. 2*)

LUXEMBOURG

President: M. Remy Wagner.
Secretary: Mlle Eliane Cremona.
Address of Association: Fédération Luxembourgeoise de Football, 50 Rue de Strasbourg, L-2560 Luxembourg.
Telephone: 48–86–65.
Area: 999 square miles.
Population: 350,000.
Number of Clubs: 216. *Teams:* 646.
Number of Players: 22,029.
Year of Formation: 1908.
National Colours: Red shirts, white shorts, blue stockings.
Second Choice of Colours: Blue/white shirts, white shorts, blue/white stockings.
Name, Address and Capacity of National Stadium: City Stadium Luxembourg, 15,100.
Names, Addresses and Capacities of Other Principal Football Grounds: Stade Emile Mayrisch, Esch-sur-Alzette, 11,000; Stade Municipal, Differdange, 10,000.
Season: August–June.

International matches 1982

9 Oct, Luxembourg: v Greece (h) lost 0-2
10 Nov, Luxembourg: v Denmark (h) lost 1-2 (*Di Domenico*)
15 Dec, London: v England (a) lost 0-9

Most Capped Player: Francois Konter 71

League Championship wins (1910–83)

Jeunesse Esch 18; Spora Luxembourg 10; Stade Dudelange 10; Red Boys Differdange 6; US Hollerich-Bonnevoie 5; Fola Esch 5; US Luxembourg 3; Aris Bonnevoie 3; Progres Niedercorn 3; Avenir Beggen 2; Sporting Luxembourg 2; Racing Luxembourg 1; National Schiffige 1.

Cup wins (1922–83)

Red Boys Differdange 15; Spora Luxembourg 8; Jeunesse Esch 8; US Luxembourg 6; Stade Dudelange 4; Progres Niedercorn 4; Fola Esch 3; Alliance Dudelange 2; US Rumelange 2; Aris Bonnevoie 1; US Dudelange 1; Jeunesse Hautcharage 1; National Schiffige 1; Racing Luxembourg 1; SC Tetange 1; Avenir Beggen 1.

	League Champions	Cup Winners
1950	Stade Dudelange	Spora Luxembourg
1951	Jeunesse Esch	SC Tetange
1952	National Schiffige	Red Boys Differdange
1953	Progres Niedercorn	Red Boys Differdange
1954	Jeunesse Esch	Jeunesse Esch
1955	Stade Dudelange	Fola Esch
1956	Spora Luxembourg	Stade Dudelange
1957	Stade Dudelange	Spora Luxembourg
1958	Jeunesse Esch	Red Boys Differdange
1959	Jeunesse Esch	US Luxembourg
1960	Jeunesse Esch	National Schiffige
1961	Spora Luxembourg	Alliance Dudelange
1962	US Luxembourg	Alliance Dudelange
1963	Jeunesse Esch	US Luxembourg
1964	Aris Bonnevoie	US Luxembourg
1965	Stade Dudelange	Spora Luxembourg
1966	Aris Bonnevoie	Spora Luxembourg
1967	Jeunesse Esch	Aris Bonnevoie
1968	Jeunesse Esch	US Rumelange
1969	Avenir Beggen	US Luxembourg
1970	Jeunesse Esch	US Luxembourg
1971	US Luxembourg	Jeunesse Hautcharage
1972	Aris Bonnevoie	Red Boys Differdange
1973	Jeunesse Esch	Jeunesse Esch
1974	Jeunesse Esch	Jeunesse Esch
1975	Jeunesse Esch	US Rumelange
1976	Jeunesse Esch	Jeunesse Esch
1977	Jeunesse Esch	Progres Niedercorn
1978	Progres Niedercorn	Progres Niedercorn
1979	Red Boys Differdange	Red Boys Differdange
1980	Jeunesse Esch	Spora Luxembourg
1981	Progres Niedercorn	Jeunesse Esch
1982	Avenir Beggen	Red Boys Differdange
1983	Jeunesse Esch	Avenir Beggen

Final League Table 1982–83

	P	*W*	*D*	*L*	*F*	*A*	*Pts*
Jeunesse Esch	22	16	2	4	69	29	34
Avenir Beggen	22	12	5	5	39	23	29
Aris Bonnevoie	22	10	8	4	43	27	28
Progres Niedercorn	22	10	8	4	43	31	28
Grevenmacher	22	8	7	7	31	34	23
Rumelingen	22	7	7	8	33	33	21
Red Boys Differdange	22	7	6	9	36	35	20
Stade	22	5	9	8	31	44	19
Union	22	8	2	12	43	37	18
Wiltz	22	6	5	11	31	42	17
Eischen	22	6	5	11	16	38	17
Alliance	22	2	6	14	15	57	10

MALTA

President: Dr Giuseppe Mifsud Bonnici LLD.
Secretary: Frank Attard.
Address of Association: Malta Football Association, 84 Old Mint Street, Valletta, Malta.
Telephone: 22697, 67 43 72.
Cable: Football Malta Valletta.
Telex: 673 Merlin MW or 477 Madafa MW. Attn. MFA.
Area: 122 square miles.
Population: 300,000.
Number of Clubs: 157.
Number of Players: 7,644. *Teams:* 320.
Year of Formation: 1900.
National Colours: Red shirts, white shorts, red stockings.
Second Choice of Colours: White shirts, white shorts, red stockings.
Name, Address and Capacity of National Stadium: The Stadium, Gzira, 30,000.
Name, Address and Capacity of Other Principal Football Grounds: Schreiber Sports Ground, Paola, 8,000; Manoel Island Upper Ground, 10,000.
Season: September–May.

International matches 1982

5 June, Messina: v Iceland (h) won 2-1 (*Spiteri Gonzi 2*)
14 Sept, Sofia: v Bulgaria (a) lost 0-7
19 Dec, Aix-la-Chapelle: v Netherlands (h) lost 0-6

Most Capped Player: John Holland 33

League Championship wins (1910–83)

Floriana 24; Sliema Wanderers 21; Valletta 11; Hibernians 6; Hamrun Spartans 4; St George's 1; KOMR 1.

Cup wins (1935–83)

Sliema Wanderers 16; Floriana 15; Valletta 5; Hibernians 5; Gzira United 1; Melita 1; Hamrun Spartans 1.

	League Champions	Cup Winners
1946	Valletta	Sliema W
1947	Hamrun Spart	Floriana
1948	Valletta	Sliema W
1949	Sliema W	Floriana
1950	Floriana	Floriana
1951	Floriana	Sliema W
1952	Floriana	Sliema W
1953	Floriana	Floriana
1954	Sliema W	Floriana
1955	Floriana	Floriana
1956	Sliema W	Sliema W
1957	Sliema W	Floriana
1958	Floriana	Floriana
1959	Valletta	Sliema W
1960	Valletta	Valletta
1961	Hibernians	Floriana
1962	Floriana	Hibernians
1963	Valletta	Sliema W
1964	Sliema W	Valletta
1965	Sliema W	Sliema W
1966	Sliema W	Floriana
1967	Hibernians	Floriana
1968	Floriana	Sliema W
1969	Hibernians	Sliema W
1970	Floriana	Hibernians
1971	Sliema W	Hibernians
1972	Sliema W	Floriana
1973	Floriana	Gzira
1974	Valletta	Sliema W
1975	Floriana	Valletta
1976	Sliema W	Floriana
1977	Floriana	Valletta
1978	Valletta	Valletta
1979	Hibernians	Sliema W
1980	Valletta	Hibernians
1981	Hibernians	Floriana
1982	Hibernians	Hibernians
1983	Hamrun S	Hamrun S

Final League Table 1982–83

	P	*W*	*D*	*L*	*F*	*A*	*Pts*
Hamrun	14	10	4	0	24	4	24
Valletta	14	7	2	5	15	13	16
Rabat Ajax	14	6	4	4	20	19	16
Hibernians	14	4	7	3	16	14	15
Zurrieq	14	4	6	7	7	8	14
Floriana	14	3	7	4	8	7	13
Sliema	14	4	4	6	14	11	12
Zebbug Rangers	14	0	2	12	5	33	2

NETHERLANDS

President: J. W. van Marle.
Secretary/Treasurer: Drs E. J. van Eijk.
Address of Association: Koninklijke Nederlandsche Voetbalbond, (KNVB) Woudenbergseweg 56–58, Postbus 615, 3700 Am., Zeist, Netherlands.
Telephone: (0031) 3439 1922.
Cable: Voetbal Zeist.
Telex: 40497.
Area: 12,616 square miles.
Population: 14,000,000.
Number of Clubs: 7,866. *Teams:* 57,222.
Number of Players: 1,112,616.
Year of Formation: 1889.
National Colours: Orange shirts, white shorts, orange stockings.
Second Choice of Colours: All white.
Name, Address and Capacity of National Stadium: Olympisch Stadion, Stadionplein, 20, Amsterdam, 67,000.
Names, Addresses and Capacities of Other Principal Football Grounds: Stadion Feijenoord,

Olympiaweg 50, Rotterdam, 67,000; Ground of Sparta, Spartastraat 5, Rotterdam, 30,000; Stadium De Goffert, Nijmegen, 30,000; Sportpark Diekman, J. J. van Deinselaan 30, Enschede, 27,564; PSV Eindhoven, Eindhoven, 27,500; Ajax Middemweg, Amsterdam, 29,000; AZ Alkmaar Dehout, 23,000.
Season: August–June.

Principal Honours

World Cup: *runners-up* 1974, 1978
World Club Champions: Feyenoord (1970), Ajax Amsterdam (1972)
European Champions Cup: *winners* Feyenoord (1970), Ajax Amsterdam (1971, 1972, 1973); *runners-up* Ajax Amsterdam (1969)
UEFA Cup: *winners* Feyenoord (1974), PSV Eindhoven (1978); *runners-up* Twente Enschede (1975); AZ 67 Alkmaar (1981)
Super Cup: Ajax Amsterdam (1972, 1973)

International matches 1982

23 March, Glasgow: v Scotland (a) lost 1-2 (*Kieft*)
14 April, Eindhoven: v Greece (h) won 1-0 (*Ophof*)
1 Sept, Reykjavik: v Iceland (a) drew 1-1 (*Schoenaker*)
27 Sept, Rotterdam: v Rep. of Ireland (h) won 2-1 (*Schoenaker, Gullitt*)
10 Nov, Rotterdam: v France (h) lost 1-2 (*Tahamata*)
19 Dec, Aix-la-Chapelle: v Malta (a) won 6-0 (*Ophof, Van Kooten 2, Hovenkamp, Schoenaker 2*)

Most Capped Player: Rudi Krol 82

League Championship wins (1898–1983)

Ajax Amsterdam 21; Feyenoord 12; HVV The Hague 8; PSV Eindhoven 7; Sparta Rotterdam 6; Go Ahead Deventer 4; HBS The Hague 3; Willem II Tilburg 3; RCH Haarlem 2; RAP 2; Heracles 2; ADO The Hague 2; Quick The Hague 1; BVV Scheidam 1; NAC Breda 1; Eindhoven 1; Enschede 1; Volewijckers Amsterdam 1; Limburgia 1; Rapid JC Haarlem 1; DOS Utrecht 1; DWS Amsterdam 1; Haarlem 1; Be Quick Groningen 1; SVV Scheidam 1; AZ 67 Alkmaar 1.

Cup wins (1899–1983)

Ajax Amsterdam 9; Feyenoord 5; Quick The Hague 4; PSV Eindhoven 4; AZ 67 Alkmaar 3; HEC 3; Sparta Rotterdam 3; DFC 2; Fortuna Geleen 2; Haarlem 2; HBS The Hague 2; RCH 2; VOC 2; Wageningen 2; Willem II Tilburg 2; FC Den Haag 2; Concordia Rotterdam 1; CVV 1; Eindhoven 1; HVV The Hague 1; Longa 1; Quick Njimegen 1; RAP 1; Roermond 1; Schoten 1; Velocitas Breda 1; Velocitas Groningen 1; VSV 1; VUC 1; VVV Groningen 1; ZFC 1; NAC Breda 1; Twente Enschede 1.

	League Champions	Cup Winners
1946	Haarlem	
1947	Ajax Amsterdam	
1948	BVV Scheidam	Wageningen
1949	SVV Scheidam	Quick Njimegen
1950	Limburgia	PSV Eindhoven
1951	PSV Eindhoven	*No competition*
1952	Willem II Tilburg	*No competition*
1953	RCH Haarlem	*No competition*
1954	Eindhoven	*No competition*
1955	Willem II Tilburg	*No competition*
1956	Rapid JC Haarlem	*No competition*
1957	Ajax Amsterdam	Fortuna Geleen
1958	DOS Utrecht	Sparta Rotterdam
1959	Sparta Rotterdam	VVV Groningen
1960	Ajax Amsterdam	*No competition*
1961	Feyenoord	Ajax Amsterdam
1962	Feyenoord	Sparta Rotterdam
1963	PSV Eindhoven	Willem II Tilburg
1964	DWS Amsterdam	Fortuna Geleen
1965	Feyenoord	Feyenoord
1966	Ajax Amsterdam	Sparta Rotterdam
1967	Ajax Amsterdam	Ajax Amsterdam
1968	Ajax Amsterdam	ADO The Hague
1969	Feyenoord	Feyenoord
1970	Ajax Amsterdam	Ajax Amsterdam
1971	Feyenoord	Ajax Amsterdam
1972	Ajax Amsterdam	Ajax Amsterdam
1973	Ajax Amsterdam	NAC Breda
1974	Feyenoord	PSV Eindhoven
1975	PSV Eindhoven	FC Den Haag
1976	PSV Eindhoven	PSV Eindhoven
1977	Ajax Amsterdam	Twente Enschede
1978	PSV Eindhoven	AZ 67 Alkmaar
1979	Ajax Amsterdam	Ajax Amsterdam
1980	Ajax Amsterdam	Feyenoord
1981	AZ 67 Alkmaar	AZ 67 Alkmaar
1982	Ajax Amsterdam	AZ 67 Alkmaar
1983	Ajax Amsterdam	Ajax Amsterdam

Final League Table 1982–83

	P	*W*	*D*	*L*	*F*	*A*	*Pts*
Ajax Amsterdam	34	26	6	2	106	41	58
Feyenoord	34	22	10	2	72	39	54
PSV Eindhoven	34	21	9	4	80	34	51
Sparta	34	12	13	9	64	52	37
Groningen	34	11	15	8	67	57	37
Roda	34	13	9	12	56	52	35
Haarlem	34	13	9	12	49	53	35
Sittard	34	11	11	12	41	48	33
Excelsior	34	13	6	15	44	47	32
Utrecht	34	11	9	14	51	57	31
AZ 67 Alkmaar	34	11	8	15	49	40	30
Deventer	34	9	11	14	44	59	29
PEC Zwolle	34	10	7	17	40	58	27
Willem II	34	9	8	17	49	62	26
Helmond	34	8	10	16	44	70	26
Twente	34	7	11	16	36	60	25
NAC Breda	34	6	12	16	39	75	24
NEC Nijmegen	34	4	14	16	34	61	22

NORWAY

President: Eldar Hansen.
Secretary: Nicolai Johansen.
Address of Association: Norges Fotballforbunc Ullevaal Stadium, Postboks 3823, Ullevål Hag eby, Oslo 8.
Telephone: 46.98.30. *Telex:* 71722 nff n.
Cable: Fotballforbund Oslo.
Area: 125,064 square miles.
Population: 4,000,000.
Number of Clubs: 3,400. *Teams:* 9,700.
Number of Players: 177,000.
Year of Formation: 1902.
National Colours: Red shirts, white shorts, blue and white stockings.
Second Choice of Colours: Blue shirts, white shorts, blue stockings.
Name, Address and Capacity of National Stadium: Ulleval Stadium, Sognsveien 75, Oslo, 24,500.
Names, Addresses and Capacities of Other Principal Football Grounds: Bislet Stadium, Oslo, 24,000; Brann Stadium, Bergen, 26,000; Lerkendal Stadium, Trondheim, 30,000; Stavanger Stadium, Stavanger, 19,800.
Season: April–November.

International matches 1982

28 April, Stavanger: v Finland (h) drew 1-1 (*Thoresen*)
12 May, Oslo: v West Germany (h) lost 2-4 (*Okland, Albertssen*)
15 June, Oslo: v Denmark (h) won 2-1)*Hareida, V. Hansen*)
11 Aug, Oslo: v Sweden (h) won 1-0 (*Lund*)
22 Sept, Swansea: v Wales (a) lost 1-0
13 Oct, Oslo: v Yugoslavia (h) won 3-1 (*Lund, Okland, Hareida*)
27 Oct, Sofia: v Bulgaria (a) drew 2-2 (*Okland, Thoresen*)
13 Nov, Kuwait: v Kuwait (a) lost 0-1
Most Capped Player: *Torbjorn Svensson 104*

League Championship wins (1938–82)

Fredrikstad 9; Viking Stavanger 7; Rosenborg Trondheim 3; Larvik Turn 3; Lillestroem 3; Brann Bergen 2; Lyn Oslo 2; IK Start 2; Valerengen 2; Friedig 1; Fram 1; Skeid Oslo 1§römgodset Drammen 1.

Cup wins (1902–82)

Odds Bk, Skien 11; Fredrikstads 9; Lyn Oslo 8; Skeid Oslo 8; Sarpsborg FK 6; Brann Bergen 5; Orn F Horten 4; Mjondalens F 4; Lillestroem 3; Rosenborg Trondheim 3; Strömgodset Drammen 3; Viking Stavanger 3; Mercantile 2; Grane Nordstrand 1; Kvik Halden 1; Sparta 1; Gjovik 1; Bodo-Glimt 1; Valerengen 1.
(*Until* 1937 *the cup-winners were regarded as champions.*)

	League Champions	Cup Winners
1946		Lyn Oslo
1947		Skeid Oslo
1948	Freidig	Sarpsborg FK
1949	Fredrikstad	Sarpsborg FK
1950	Fram	Fredrikstad
1951	Fredrikstad	Sarpsborg FK
1952	Fredrikstad	Sparta Sarpsborg
1953	Larvik Turn	Viking Stav
1954	Fredrikstad	Skeid Oslo
1955	Larvik Turn	Skeid Oslo
1956	Larvik Turn	Skeid Oslo
1957	Fredrikstad	Fredrikstad
1958	Viking Stav	Skeid Oslo
1959	Lillestroem	Viking Stav
1960	Fredrikstad	Rosenborg Tr
1961	Fredrikstad	Fredrikstad
1962	Brann Bergen	Gjovik Lyn
1963	Brann Bergen	Skeid Oslo
1964	Lyn Oslo	Rosenborg Tr
1965	Valerengen	Skeid Oslo
1966	Skeid Oslo	Fredrikstad
1967	Rosenborg Tr	Lyn Oslo
1968	Lyn Oslo	Lyn Oslo
1969	Rosenborg Tr	Strömgodset Dr
1970	Strömgodset Dr	Strömgodset Dr
1971	Rosenborg Tr	Rosenborg Tr
1972	Viking Stav	Brann Bergen
1973	Viking Stav	Strömgodset Dr
1974	Viking Stav	Skeid Oslo
1975	Viking Stav	Bodo-Glim
1976	Lillestroem	Brann Bergen
1977	Lillestroem	Lillestroem
1978	IK Start	Lillestroem
1979	Viking Stav	Viking Stav
1980	IK Start	Valerengen
1981	Valerengen	Lillestroem
1982	Viking Stav	Brann Bergen

Final League Table 1982

	P	*W*	*D*	*L*	*F*	*A*	*Pts*
Viking Stavanger	22	11	7	4	39	24	29
Bryne	22	10	6	6	25	25	26
Lillestroem	22	11	3	8	35	26	25
Valerengen	22	10	4	8	35	21	24
Hamarkameratene	22	11	2	9	33	35	24
Rosenborg Trondheim	22	7	9	6	32	29	23
Mjondalen	22	9	5	8	28	32	23
Moss	22	6	8	8	27	26	20
IK Start	22	7	6	9	28	32	20
Fredrikstad	22	5	8	9	22	31	18
Sogndal	22	5	6	11	25	33	16
Molde	22	4	8	10	26	41	16

POLAND

President: Dr Wlodzimierz Reczek.
General-Secretary: Zbigniew Kalinski.
Address of Association: Polish Football Association, Al. Ujazdowskie 22, 00-478 Warszawa.
Telephone: 28-93-44, 29-24-89, 21-91-75.
Area: 120,359 square miles.
Population: 36,000,000.
Number of Clubs: 5,334. *Teams:* 11,343.
Number of Players: 234,052.
Year of Formation: 1923.
National Colours: White shirts, red shorts, white and red stockings.
Second Choice of Colours: Red shirts, white shorts, red stockings.
Name, Address and Capacity of National Stadium: Stadium of the X Anniversary, Warszawa, 87,000.
Names, Addresses and Capacities of Other Principal Football Grounds: Stadium Slaski, Chorzów, 93,000; Stadium Warta, Poznan, 45,000; Stadium Olimpijski, Wroclaw, 72,000; Stadium Wisla Kraków, 45,000; Stadium Ruch, Chorzów, 40,000; Stadium Legia, Warszawa, 35,000; Stadium Piast, Gliwice, 55,000; Stadium Pgoon, Szczecin, 36,000; Stadium Polonia, Bytom, 35,000; Stade KS Zawisza, Bydgoszcz, 55,000.
Season: August–November; March–June.

Principal Honours

Olympic Games: *winners* 1972; *runners-up* 1976
European Cup-Winners' Cup: *runners-up* Gornik Zabrze (1970)

International matches 1982

14 June, Vigo: v Italy (W.C.) drew 0-0
19 June, Corogne: v Cameroons (W.C.) drew 0-0
22 June, Corogne: v Peru (W.C.) won 5-1 (*Smolarek, Lato, Boniek, Buncol, Ciolek*)
28 June, Barcelona: v Belgium (W.C.) won 3-0 (*Boniek 3*)
4 July, Barcelona: v USSR (W.C.) drew 0-0
8 July, Barcelona: v Italy (W.C.) lost 0-2
10 July, Alicante: v France (W.C.) won 3-2 (*Szarmach, Majewski, Kupcewicz*)
31 Aug, Paris: v France (a) won 4-0 (*Jalocha, Kupcewicz 2, Buncol*)
8 Sept, Kuopio: v Finland (a) won 3-2 (*Smolarek, Kupcewicz, Dziekanowski*)
9 Oct, Lisbon: v Portugal (a) lost 1-2 (*Janas*)

Most Capped Player: Gregorz Lato 103

League Championship wins (1921–83)

Ruch Chorzow 12; Gornik Zabrze 10; Wisla Krakow 6; Cracovia 5; Pogon Lwow 4; Legia Warsaw 4; Warta Poznan 2; Polonia Bytom 2; Stal Mielec 2; Widzew Lodz 2; Garbarnia Krakow 1; Polonia Warsaw 1; LKS Lodz 1; Slask Wroclaw 1; Szombierki Bytom 1; Lech Poznan 1.

Cup wins (1951–83)

Legia Warsaw 7; Gornik Zabrze 6; Zaglebie Sosnowiec 4; Ruch Chorzow 2; Gwardia Warsaw 1; LKS Lodz 1; Polonia Warsaw 1; Wisla Krakow 1; Stal Rzeszow 1; Slask Wroclaw 1; Arka Gdynia 1; Lech Poznan 1; Lechia Gdansk 1.

	League Champions	Cup Winners
1946	Polonia Warsaw	
1947	Warta Poznan	
1948	Cracovia	
1949	Wisla Krakow	
1950	Wisla Krakow	
1951	Wisla Krakow	Ruch Chorzow
1952	Ruch Chorzow	Polonia Warsaw
1953	Ruch Chorzow	*No competition*
1954	Polonia Bytom	Gwardia Warsaw
1955	Legia Warsaw	Legia Warsaw
1956	Legia Warsaw	Legia Warsaw
1957	Gornik Zabrze	LKS Lodz
1958	LKS Lodz	*No competition*
1959	Gornik Zabrze	*No competition*
1960	Ruch Chorzow	*No competition*
1961	Gornik Zabrze	*No competition*
1962	Polonia Bytom	Zaglebie Sosnowiec
1963	Gornik Zabrze	Zaglebie Sosnowiec
1964	Gornik Zabrze	Legia Warsaw
1965	Gornik Zabrze	Gornik Zabrze
1966	Gornik Zabrze	Legia Warsaw
1967	Gornik Zabrze	Wisla Krakow
1968	Ruch Chorzow	Gornik Zabrze
1969	Legia Warsaw	Gornik Zabrze
1970	Legia Warsaw	Gornik Zabrze
1971	Gornik Zabrze	Gornik Zabrze
1972	Gornik Zabrze	Gornik Zabrze
1973	Stal Mielec	Legia Warsaw
1974	Ruch Chorzow	Ruch Chorzow
1975	Ruch Chorzow	Stal Rzeszow
1976	Stal Mielec	Slask Wroclaw
1977	Slask Wroclaw	Zaglebie Sosnowiec
1979	Ruch Chorzow	Arka Gdynia
1980	Szombierki Bytom	Legia Warsaw
1981	Widzew Lodz	Legia Warsaw
1982	Widzew Lodz	Lech Poznan
1983	Lech Poznan	Lechia Gdansk

Final League Table 1982–83

	P	*W*	*D*	*L*	*F*	*A*	*Pts*
Lech Poznan	30	17	5	8	42	31	39
Widzew Lodz	30	13	12	5	49	30	38
Ruch Chorzow	30	11	13	6	34	22	35
Pogon Stettin	30	12	9	9	44	25	33
Wisla Krakow	30	13	6	11	44	36	32
Slask Wroclaw	30	12	6	12	35	34	30
LKS Lodz	30	10	10	10	36	38	30
Legia Warsaw	30	11	7	12	43	39	29
Szombierki	30	8	13	9	34	37	29
Baltyk	30	9	11	10	28	31	29
Zaglebie	30	10	9	11	29	37	29
Gornik Zabrze	30	10	8	12	30	38	28
GKS Kattowice	30	10	7	13	28	34	27
Cracovia	30	5	15	10	17	33	25
Stal Mielec	30	7	10	13	27	36	24
Gwardia Warsaw	30	7	7	16	26	45	21

PORTUGAL

President: Romao Martins.
Secretary: Cesar Gracio.
Address of Association: Federação Portuguesa de Futebol, Praça de Alegria 25, Apartado 21.000, 1128 Lisboa Codex.
Telephone: 32 82 07/08/09, 32 82 00.
Cable: Futebol Lisboa.
Telex: 13 489 fpfp.
Area: 34,139 square miles.
Population: 10,000,000.
Number of Clubs: 1,251. *Teams:* 224.
Number of Players: 60,056.
Year of Formation: 1914.
National Colours: Red shirts, white shorts, red stockings.
Second Choice of Colours: All white.
Name, Address and Capacity of National Stadium: National Stadium, Lisbon, 51,000.
Names, Addresses and Capacities of Other Principal Football Grounds: Estadio de Luz, Lisbon, 69,000; Estadio Jose Alvalade, Lisbon, 47,000; Estadio do Restelo, Lisbon, 35,000; Estadio das Antas, Porto, 40,000; Estadio 28 de Maio, Braga, 30,000; Estadio Bonfim, Setubal, 20,000; Estadio Alfredo da Silva, 23,000; Estadio Municipal, Coimbra, 25,000; Estadio Municipal, Guimaraes, 25,000.
Season: September–July.

Principal Honours

European Champions Cup: *winners* Benfica (1961, 1962); *runners-up* Benfica (1963, 1965, 1968)
European Cup-Winners' Cup: *winners* Sporting Lisbon (1964)
UEFA Cup: *runners-up* Benfica (1983)

International matches 1982

20 Jan, Athens: v Greece (a) won 2-1 (*Oliveira 2*)
17 Feb, Hanover: v West Germany (a) lost 1-3 (*De Matos*)
24 March, Lugano: v Switzerland (a) lost 1-2 (*Nene*)
5 May, Sao Luiz: v Brazil (a) lost 1-3 (*Nene*)
22 Sept, Helsinki: v Finland (a) won 2-0 (*Nene, Oliveira*)
9 Oct, Lisbon: v Poland (h) won 2-1 (*Nene, Gomez*)

Most Capped Player: Mario Coluna 76

League Championship wins (1935–83)

Benfica 25; Sporting Lisbon 16; FC Porto 7; Belenenses 1.

Cup wins (1939–82)

Benfica 17; Sporting Lisbon 10; FC Porto 4 ☆avista 3; Belenenses 2; Vitoria Setubal 2; Academica Coimbra 1; Leixoes Porto 1; Sporting Braga 1.

	League Champions	**Cup Winners**
1946	Belenenses	Sporting Lisbon
1947	Sporting Lisbon	*No competition*
1948	Sporting Lisbon	Sporting Lisbon
1949	Sporting Lisbon	Benfica
1950	Benfica	*No competition*
1951	Sporting Lisbon	Benfica
1952	Sporting Lisbon	Benfica
1953	Sporting Lisbon	Benfica
1954	Sporting Lisbon	Sporting Lisbon
1955	Benfica	Benfica
1956	FC Porto	FC Porto
1957	Benfica	Benfica
1958	Sporting Lisbon	FC Porto
1959	FC Porto	Benfica
1960	Benfica	Belenenses
1961	Benfica	Leixoes
1962	Sporting Lisbon	Benfica
1963	Benfica	Sporting Lisbon
1964	Benfica	Benfica
1965	Benfica	Vitoria Setubal
1966	Sporting Lisbon	Sporting Braga
1967	Benfica	Vitoria Setubal
1968	Benfica	FC Porto
1969	Benfica	Benfica
1970	Sporting Lisbon	Benfica
1971	Benfica	Sporting Lisbon
1972	Benfica	Benfica
1973	Benfica	Sporting Lisbon
1974	Sporting Lisbon	Sporting Lisbon
1975	Benfica	Boavista
1976	Benfica	Boavista
1977	Benfica	FC Porto
1978	FC Porto	Sporting Lisbon
1979	FC Porto	Boavista
1980	Sporting Lisbon	Benfica
1981	Benfica	Benfica
1982	Sporting Lisbon	Sporting Lisbon
1983	Benfica	Benfica v Porto final

Final League Table 1982–83

	P	*W*	*D*	*L*	*F*	*A*	*Pts*
Benfica	30	22	7	1	67	13	51
Porto	30	20	7	3	73	18	47
Sporting Lisbon	30	18	6	6	48	25	42
Guimaraes	30	11	10	9	35	24	32
Boavista	30	12	6	12	29	37	30
Braga	30	13	3	14	41	43	29
Rio Ave	30	13	3	14	43	45	29
Portimonense	30	11	7	12	35	31	29
Setubal	30	12	5	13	29	33	29
Salgueiros	30	9	9	12	25	33	27
Varzim	30	8	10	12	23	39	26
Estoril	30	9	8	13	26	39	26
Espinho	30	9	7	14	23	37	25
Maritimo	30	8	9	13	26	38	25
Amora	30	6	6	18	23	55	18
Alcobaca	30	4	7	19	20	56	15

RUMANIA

President: Ing. Andrei Radulescu.
Secretary: Florian Dumitrescu.
Address of Association: Federatia Romana de Fotbal, Vasile Conta 16, Bucharest 6.
Telephone: 12–10–60, 11–97–87. *Cable:* Sportrom Bucaresti. *Telex:* 11180 Bucaresti.
Area: 91,699 square miles. *Population:* 23,000,000. *Number of Clubs:* 5,453. *Teams:* 5,777. *Number of Players:* 179,987.
Year of Formation: 1908.
National Colours: Yellow shirts, blue shorts, red stockings.
Second Choice of Colours: Blue shirts, yellow shorts, red stockings.
Name, Address and Capacity of National Stadium: 23 August, Bucharest, 95,000.
Names, Addresses and Capacities of Other Principal Football Grounds: Republicii, Bucharest, 37,000; Giulesti, Bucharest, 20,000; Municipal, Cluj, 40,000; 1 Mai, Timisoara, 30,000; 23 August, Iasi, 20,000; 1 Mai, Constanta, 20,000; Petrolul, Ploiesti, 20,000; 1 Mai, Pitesti, 20,000; Stade Central Craiova, 40,000.
Season: August–July (with winter break).

International matches 1982

24 March, Brussels: v Belgium (a) lost 1-4 (*Ticleanu*)
14 April, Russe: v Bulgaria (a) drew 1-1 (*Camataru*)
1 May, Hunedsara: v Cyprus (h) won 3-1 (*Vaetus, Camataru, Boloni*)
12 May, Rosario: v Argentina (a) lost 0-1
16 May, Lima: v Peru (a) lost 0-2
18 May, Santiago: v Chile (a) won 3-2 (*Klein 2, Augustin*)
15 July, Suceava: v Japan (h) won 4-0 (*Klein, Turcu, Boloni, Georgescu*)
18 July, Bucharest: v Japan (h) won 3-1 (*Boloni, Georgescu 2*)
1 Sept, Bucharest: v Denmark (h) won 1-0 (*Balaci*)
8 Sept, Bucharest: v Sweden (h) won 2-0 (*Andone, Klein*)
17 Nov, Karl Marx Stadt: v East Germany (a) lost 1-4 (*Boloni*)
4 Dec, Florence: v Italy (a) drew 0-0

Most Capped Player: Cornel Dini 80

League Championship wins (1910–83)

Dynamo Bucharest 11; Steaua Bucharest (prev.CCA) 9; Venus Bucharest 7; CSC Temesvar 6; UT Arad 6; Rapid Bucharest 4; Uni Craiova 3; Ripensia Temesvar 3; Petrolul Ploesti 3; Olimpia Bucharest 2; CAC Bucharest 2; Arges Pitesti 2; Soc RA Bucharest 1; Prahova Ploesti 1; CSC Brasov 1; Juventius Bucharest 1; SSUD Reita 1; Craiova Bucharest 1; Progresul 1; Ploesti United 1.

Cup wins (1934–83)

Steaua Bucharest (prev. CCA) 13; Rapid Bucharest 7; Dynamo Bucharest 4; Uni Craiova 4; UT Arad 2; CFR Bucharest 2; Progresul 2; RIP Timisoara 2; ICO Oradeo 1; Metal Ochimia Resita 1; Petrolul Ploesti 1; Stinta Cluj 1; Stinta Timisoara 1; Turnu Severin 1; Chimia Ramnicu 1; Jiul Petroseni 1; Poli Timisoara 1.

	League Champions	Cup Winners
1947	UT Arad	*No competition*
1948	UT Arad	UT Arad
1949	Progresul	CCA Bucharest
1950	UT Arad	CCA Bucharest
1951	CCA Bucharest	CCA Bucharest
1952	CCA Bucharest	CCA Bucharest
1953	CCA Bucharest	UT Arad
1954	UT Arad	Metal Och, Resitta
1955	Dynamo Bucharest	CCA Bucharest
1956	CCA Bucharest	ICO Oradea
1957	*No competition*	*No competition*
1958	Petrolul Ploesti	Stinta Timisoara
1959	Petrolul Ploesti	Dynamo Bucharest
1960	CCA Bucharest	Progresul
1961	CCA Bucharest	Progresul
1962	Dynamo Bucharest	Steaua Bucharest
1963	Dynamo Bucharest	Petrolul Ploesti
1964	Dynamo Bucharest	Dynamo Bucharest
1965	Dynamo Bucharest	Stinta Cluj
1966	Petrolul Ploesti	Steaua Bucharest
1967	Rapid Bucharest	Steaua Bucharest
1968	Steaua Bucharest	Dynamo Bucharest
1969	UT Arad	Steaua Bucharest
1970	UT Arad	Steaua Bucharest
1971	Dynamo Bucharest	Steaua Bucharest
1972	Arges Pitesti	Rapid Bucharest
1973	Dynamo Bucharest	Chimia Ramnicu
1974	Uni Craiova	Jiul Petroseni
1975	Dynamo Bucharest	Rapid Bucharest
1976	Steaua Bucharest	Steaua Bucharest
1977	Dynamo Bucharest	Uni Craiova
1978	Steaua Bucharest	Uni Craiova
1979	Arges Pitesti	Steaua Bucharest
1980	Uni Craiova	Poli Timisoara
1981	Uni Craiova	Uni Craiova
1982	Dynamo Bucharest	Dynamo Bucharest
1983	Dynamo Bucharest	Uni Craiova

Final League Table 1982–83

	P	*W*	*D*	*L*	*F*	*A*	*Pts*
Dynamo Bucharest	34	17	15	2	62	25	49
Craiova	34	20	6	8	66	29	46
Sportul	34	18	8	8	48	29	44
Arges Pitesti	34	17	6	11	50	37	40
Steaua Bucharest	34	14	10	10	47	41	38
Corvinul	34	13	8	13	46	38	34
Olt	34	14	5	15	47	36	33
Tirgu M	34	13	7	14	41	42	33
Juil Petroseni	34	12	9	13	35	43	33
Iasi	34	11	10	13	37	40	32
Bihor	34	12	8	14	56	62	32
Petrolul	34	14	4	16	38	55	32
SC Bacau	34	12	7	15	43	47	31
Tirgoviste	34	10	11	13	36	44	31
Chimia RM Valcea	34	12	7	15	33	43	31
Brasov	34	11	7	16	41	51	29
Poli Timisoara	34	9	6	19	35	64	24
Constanta	34	7	6	21	30	65	20

SPAIN

President: Pablo Porta Bussoms.
Secretary: Augustin Dominguez.
Address of Association: Real Federación Española de Futbol, Calle Alberto Bosch 13, Apartado Postal 347, Madrid 14.
Telephone: 2391000, 2391008, 2391009.
Cable: Futbol.
Telex: 42420 rfgf.*Area:* 190,115 square miles.
Population: 35,400,000.
Number of Clubs: 7,581. *Teams:* 7,581.
Number of Players: 318,392.
Year of Formation: 1913.
National Colours: Red shirts, dark blue shorts, black with yellow border stockings.
Second Choice of Colours: Blue shirts, dark blue shorts, black stockings.
No National Stadium.
Names, Addresses and Capacities of Principal Football Grounds: Santiago Bernabeu, Madrid, 101,663; Campo Nuevo, Barcelona, 120,000; Manzanares, Madrid, 70,000; Luis Casanova, Valencia, 53,436; Sánchez Pizjuan, Sevilla, 68,110; San Mamés, Bilbao, 46,273; Sarriá, Barcelona, 40,400; Riazor, La Coruña, 35,860; La Romareda, Zaragoza, 32,416.
Season: September–June.

Principal Honours

European Nations Cup: *winners* 1964
Olympic Games: *runners-up* 1920
European Champions Cup: *winners* Real Madrid (1956, 1957, 1958, 1959, 1960, 1966); *runners-up* Real Madrid (1962, 1964, 1981), Barcelona (1961), Atlético Madrid (1974)
World Club Champions: Real Madrid (1960), Atlético Madrid (1975)
European Cup-Winners' Cup: *winners* Atlético Madrid (1962), Barcelona (1979, 1982), Valencia(1980); *runners-up* Atlético Madrid (1963), Barcelona (1969), Real Madrid (1971, 1983)
Fairs Cup: *winners* Barcelona (1958, 1960, 1966), Valencia (1962, 1963), Zaragoza (1964); *runners-up* Barcelona (1962), Valencia (1964), Zaragoza (1966)
UEFA Cup: *runners-up* Athletic Bilbao (1977)
Super Cup: *winners* Valencia (1981)

International matches 1982

24 Feb, Valencia: v Scotland (h) won 3-0 (*Victor, Quini, Gallego*)
24 March, Valencia: v Wales (h) drew 1-1 (*Satrustegui*)
28 April, Valencia: v Switzerland (h) won 2-0 (*Tendillo, Alesanco*)
16 June, Valencia: v Honduras (W.C.) drew 1-1 (*Lopez, Ufarte*)
20 June, Valencia: v Yugoslavia (W.C.) won 2-1 (*Juanito, Saura*)
25 June, Valencia: v Northern Ireland (W.C.) lost 0-1
2 July, Madrid: v West Germany (W.C.) lost 1-2 (*Zamora*)
5 July, Madrid: v England (W.C.) drew 0-0
27 Oct, Malaga: v Iceland (h) won 1-0 (*Pedraza*)
17 Nov, Dublin: v Rep. of Ireland (a) drew 3-3 (*Macedo, Martin og, Victor*)

Most Capped Player: Jose Iribar 49

League Championship wins (1929–83)

Real Madrid 20; Barcelona 9; Atlético Madrid 8; Atlético Bilbao 7; Valencia 4; Real Sociedad 2; Real Betis 1; Seville 1.

Cup wins (1902–83)

Atlético Bilbao 22; Barcelona 20; Real Madrid 15; Atlético Madrid 5; Valencia 5; Real Union de Irun 3; Seville 3; Espanol 2; Real Zaragoza 2; Arenas 1; Ciclista Sebastian 1; Racing de Irun 1; Vizcaya Bilbao 1; Real Betis 1.

	League Champions	Cup Winners
1956	Atlético Bilbao	Atlético Bilbao
1957	Real Madrid	Barcelona
1958	Real Madrid	Atlético Bilbao
1959	Barcelona	Barcelona
1960	Barcelona	Atlético Madrid
1961	Real Madrid	Atlético Madrid
1962	Real Madrid	Real Madrid
1963	Real Madrid	Barcelona
1964	Real Madrid	Real Zaragoza
1965	Real Madrid	Atlético Madrid
1966	Atlético Madrid	Real Zaragoza
1967	Real Madrid	Valencia
1968	Real Madrid	Barcelona
1969	Real Madrid	Atlético Bilbao
1970	Atlético Madrid	Real Madrid
1971	Valencia	Barcelona
1972	Real Madrid	Atlético Madrid
1973	Atlético Madrid	Atlético Bilbao
1974	Barcelona	Real Madrid
1975	Real Madrid	Real Madrid
1976	Real Madrid	Atlético Madrid
1977	Atlético Madrid	Real Betis
1978	Real Madrid	Barcelona
1979	Real Madrid	Valencia
1980	Real Madrid	Real Madrid
1981	Real Sociedad	Barcelona
1982	Real Sociedad	Real Madrid
1983	Atlético Bilbao	Barcelona

Final League Table 1982–83

	P	*W*	*D*	*L*	*F*	*A*	*Pts*
Atlético Bilbao	34	22	6	6	71	36	50
Real Madrid	34	20	9	5	57	25	49
Atletico Madrid	34	20	6	8	56	38	46
Barcelona	34	17	10	7	60	29	44
Seville	34	15	12	7	44	31	42
Real Zaragoza	34	17	6	11	59	39	40
Real Sociedad	34	12	12	10	29	27	36
Gijon	34	9	15	10	32	32	33
Espanol	34	13	6	15	45	47	32
Malaga	34	10	10	14	37	48	30
Betis	34	9	12	13	42	45	30
Valladolid	34	9	11	14	34	91	29
Salamanca	34	10	6	18	31	47	28
Osasuna	34	10	6	18	39	54	26
Valencia	34	9	7	18	42	56	25
Las Palmas	34	7	11	16	32	55	25
Celta	34	9	6	19	27	56	24
Santander	34	9	5	20	44	63	23

SWEDEN

President: Tore Brodd.
Secretary: Robert Hernadi.
Address of Association: Svenska Fotbollförbundet, Box 1216 S-171 23, Solna.
Telephone: 08/27 25 00..
Cable: Fotball, Solna. *Telex:* 17711 fotball s.
Area: 173,665 square miles.
Population: 8,323,765.
Number of Clubs: 3,346. *Teams:* 8,082.
Number of Players: 170,821.
Year of Formation: 1904.
National Colours: Yellow shirts, blue shorts, yellow and blue stockings.
Second Choice of Colours: Blue shirts, white shorts, yellow stockings.
Name, Address and Capacity of National Stadium: Fotbollstadion, Solna, 52,000.
Names, Addresses and Capacities of Other Principal Football Grounds: Nya Ullevi, Göteborg, 52,000; Malmö Stadion, Malmö, 35,000; Idrottsparken, Norrköping, 35,000; Olympia, Helsingborg, 25,000; Stadion, Stockholm, 25,000.
Season: April–October.

Principal Honours

Olympic Games: *winners* 1948
World Cup: *runners-up* 1958
European Champions Cup: *runners-up* Malmö FF (1979)
UEFA Cup: *winners* IFK Gothenburg (1982)

International matches 1982

20 Feb, Lahti: v Finland (a) drew 2-2 (*Ahlstroem 2*)
21 Feb, Lahti: v Finland (a) lost 2-1 (*Dahlquist*)
5 May, Copenhagen: v Denmark (a) drew 1-1 (*Larsson T.*)
19 May, Halmstad: v East Germany (h) drew 2-2 (*Persson, Larsson*)
3 June, Stockholm: v USSR (h) drew 1-1 (*Nillsson B.*)
11 Aug, Oslo: v Norway (a) lost 0-1
8 Sept, Bucharest: v Rumania (a) lost 0-2
6 Oct, Bratislava: v Czechoslovakia (a) drew 2-2 (*Jingblad, Ericson*)
13 Sept, Nicosia: v Cyprus (a) won 1-0 (*Corneliusson*)

Most Capped Player: *Bjorn Nordquist 115*

League Championship wins (1896–1982)

Oergryte 15; Gothenburg 14; Malmö FF 12; IFK Norrköping 11; Djurgaarden 8; IFK Gothenburg 8; AIK Stockholm 8; GAIS Gothenburg 4; Boras IF Elfsborg 4; Oster Vaxjo 4; IF Halsingborg 3; Halmstad 2; Atvidaberg 2; IFK Ekilstune 1; IF Gavle Brynas 1; IF Gothenburg 1; Fassbergs 1; Norrköping IK Sleipner 1.

Cup wins (1941–82)

Malmö FF 11; IFK Norrköping 3; AIK Stockholm 3; Atvidaberg 2; IFK Gothenburg 2; GAIS Gothenburg 1; IFK Halsingborg 1; Raa 1; Landskrona 1; Kalmar 1; Oster Vaxjo 1.

	League Champions	Cup Winners
1946	IFK Norrköping	Malmö FF
1947	IFK Norrköping	Malmö FF
1948	IFK Norrköping	Raa
1949	Malmö FF	AIK Stockholm
1950	Malmö FF	AIK Stockholm
1951	Malmö FF	Malmö FF
1952	IFK Norrköping	*No competition*
1953	Malmö FF	Malmö FF
1954	GAIS Gothenburg	*No competition*
1955	Djurgaarden	*No competition*
1956	IFK Norrköping	*No competition*
1957	IFK Norrköping	*No competition*
1958	IFK Gothenburg	*No competition*
1959	Djurgaarden	*No competition*
1960	IFK Norrköping	*No competition*
1961	Boras Elfsborg	*No competition*
1962	IFK Norrköping	*No competition*
1963	IFK Norrköping	*No competition*
1964	Djurgaarden	*No competition*
1965	Malmö FF	*No competition*
1966	Djurgaarden	*No competition*
1967	Malmö FF	Malmö FF
1968	Oster Vaxjo	*No competition*
1969	IFK Gothenburg	IFK Norrköping
1970	Malmö FF	Atvidaberg
1971	Malmö FF	Atvidaberg
1972	Atvidaberg	Landskrona
1973	Atvidaberg	Malmö FF
1974	Malmö FF	Malmö FF
1975	Malmö FF	Malmö FF
1976	Halmstad BK	AIK Stockholm
1977	Malmö FF	Malmö FF
1978	Oster Vaxjo	Oster Vaxjo
1979	Halmstad BK	IFK Gothenburg
1980	Oster Vaxjo	Malmö FF
1981	Oster Vaxjo	Kalmar
1982	IFK Gothenburg	IFK Gothenburg

Final League Table 1982

	P	*W*	*D*	*L*	*F*	*A*	*Pts*
IFK Gothenburg	22	11	7	4	45	22	29
Hammarby	22	12	4	6	42	27	28
Elfborg Boras	22	9	8	5	31	21	26
Malmo	22	7	11	4	23	15	25
Oster Vaxjo	22	10	4	8	28	20	24
Brage	22	9	6	7	24	27	24
Orgryte	22	7	7	8	27	28	21
Halmstad	22	7	7	8	39	45	21
Kalmar	22	6	7	9	21	27	19
IFK Norrkoping	22	5	9	8	28	38	19
AIK	22	4	10	8	21	31	18
Atvidaberg	22	4	2	16	17	45	10

SWITZERLAND

President: Walter Baumann.
Secretary: Edgar Obertufer.
Address of Association: Schweizerischer Fussballverband, Laubeggstrasse 70 BP 24, 3000 Berne 32.
Telephone: (031) 44–62–23.
Cable: Fussballverband Berne.
Telex: 33582 sfv ch.
Area: 15,941 square miles.
Population: 6,000,000.
Number of Clubs: 1,419. *Teams:* 8,174.
Number of Players: 163,477.
Year of Formation: 1895.
National Colours: Red jersey, white shorts, red stockings.
Second Choice of Colours: White jersey, white shorts, red stockings.
Name, Address and Capacity of National Stadium: Wankdorf Stadium, Berne, 60,000.
Names, Addresses and Capacities of Other Principal Football Grounds: St Jakob Stadium, Basle, 60,000; Stade Olympique, Lausanne, 45,000; Parc des Sports des Charmilles, Genève, 38,800; Sportplatz Hardturm, Zurich, 37,200.
Season: September–May.

Principal Honours

Olympic Games: *runners-up* 1924

International matches 1982

9 March, Balzers: v Lichtenstein (a) won 1-0 (*Brigger*)
24 March, Lugano: v Portugal (h) won 2-1 (*Zappa, Egli*)
28 April, Valencia: v Spain (a) lost 0-2
19 May, Recife: v Brazil (a) drew 1-1 (*Sulser*)
28 May, Geneva: v Italy (h) drew 1-1 (*Barberis*)
8 Sept, St Gall: v Bulgaria (h) won 3-2 (*Sulser, Iliev og, Elsener*)
6 Oct, Brussels: v Belgium (a) lost 0-3
27 Oct, Rome: v Italy (a) won 1-0 (*Ewener*)
17 Nov, Berne: v Scotland (h) won 2-0 (*Sulser, Egli*)
1 Dec, Athens: v Greece (a) won 3-1 (*Egli, Sulser 2*)

Most Capped Player: Severino Minelli 79

League Championship wins (1898–1983)

Grasshoppers 19; Servette 14; Young Boys Berne 10; FC Zurich 9; FC Basle 8; Lausanne 7; La Chaux-de-Fonds 3; FC Lugano 3; Winterthur 3; FC Aarau 2; FC Anglo-Americans 1; St Gallen 1; FC Brühl 1; Cantonal-Neuchatel 1; Biel 1; Bellinzona 1; FC Etoile La Chaux-de-Fonds 1.

Cup wins (1926–83)

Grasshoppers 14; Lausanne 7; La Chaux-de-Fonds 6; FC Basle 5; FC Zurich 5; Young Boys Berne 5; Servette 5; FC Sion 4; FC Lugano 2; FC Granges 1; Lucerne 1; St Gallen 1; Urania Geneva 1; Young Fellows Zurich 1.

	League Champions	**Cup Winners**
1946	Servette	Grasshoppers
1947	Biel	FC Basle
1948	Bellinzona	La Chaux-de-Fonds
1949	FC Lugano	Servette
1950	Servette	Lausanne
1951	Lausanne	La Chaux-de-Fonds
1952	Grasshoppers	Grasshoppers
1953	FC Basle	Young Boys
1954	La Chaux-de-Fonds	La Chaux-de-Fonds
1955	La Chaux-de-Fonds	La Chaux-de-Fonds
1956	Grasshoppers	Grasshoppers
1957	Young Boys	La Chaux-de-Fonds
1958	Young Boys	Young Boys
1959	Young Boys	FC Granges
1960	Young Boys	Lucerne
1961	Servette	La Chaux-de-Fonds
1962	Servette	Lausanne
1963	FC Zurich	FC Basle
1964	La Chaux-de-Fonds	Lausanne
1965	Lausanne	FC Sion
1966	FC Zurich	FC Zurich
1967	FC Basle	FC Basle
1968	FC Zurich	FC Lugano
1969	FC Basle	St Gallen
1970	FC Basle	FC Zurich
1971	Grasshoppers	Servette
1972	FC Basle	FC Zurich
1973	FC Basle	FC Zurich
1974	FC Zurich	FC Sion
1975	FC Zurich	FC Basle
1976	FC Zurich	FC Zurich
1977	FC Basle	Young Boys
1978	Grasshoppers	Servette
1979	Servette	Servette
1980	FC Basle	FC Sion
1981	FC Zurich	Lausanne
1982	Grasshoppers	FC Sion
1983	Grasshoppers	Grasshoppers

Final League Table 1982–83

	P	*W*	*D*	*L*	*F*	*A*	*Pts*
Grasshoppers	30	24	1	5	86	29	49
Servette	30	22	4	4	65	24	48
St Gallen	30	17	6	7	61	31	40
Zurich	30	17	4	9	55	39	38
Lausanne	30	15	7	8	51	28	37
Neuchatel Xamax	30	15	7	8	61	40	37
Sion	30	12	11	7	51	36	35
Lucerne	30	14	3	13	57	56	31
Young Boys	30	11	8	11	35	42	30
Wettingen	30	8	9	13	40	47	25
Basle	30	10	5	15	47	56	25
Vevey	30	9	4	17	42	61	22
Bellinzona	30	8	5	17	36	74	21
Aurau	30	8	4	18	32	52	20
Bulle	30	4	4	22	27	87	12
Winterthur	30	2	6	22	30	74	10

TURKEY

President: Yilmaz Tokatli.
Secretary General: Ayhan Sarman.
Address of Association: Federation Turque de Football, Ulus 15 Hani, A Blok Kat 4, Ankara.
Telephone: 24 39 34/5.
Cable: Futbolspor Ankara.
Telex: 42251 tff tr.
Area: 296,185 square miles.
Population: 45,000,000.
Number of Clubs: 1,793. *Teams:* 3,586.
Number of Players: 71,273.
Year of Formation: 1923.
National Colours: White shirts with white crescent and star on red hoop, white shorts, red and white stockings.
Second Choice of Colours: Red shirts, white shorts, red and white stockings.
Name, Address and Capacity of National Stadium: Stade 19, Mayis, Ankara, 35,000.
Names, Addresses and Capacities of Other Principal Football Grounds: Stade Ali Sam, Yen Istanbul, 40,000; Stade Mithatpasat, Istanbul, 45,000; Stade Alsancak, Izmiri, 30,000; Stade d'Ataturk, Eskisehir, 35,000; Stade d'Ataturk, Adana, 30,000; Stade de Ville, Kayseri, 25,000; Stade d'Ataturk, Izmir, 70,000.
Season: September–June.

International matches 1982

22 Sept, Gyor: v Hungary (a) lost 0-5
27 Oct, Izmir: v Albania (h) won 1-0 (*Arif*)
17 Nov, Vienna: v Austria (a) lost 0-4

Most Capped Player: Seren Turgay 51

League Championship wins (1960–1983)

Fenerbahce 9; Galatasaray 5; Trabzonspor 5; Besiktas 4.

Cup wins (1963–83)

Galatasaray 7; Fenerbahce 4; Trabzonspor 2; Goztepe Izmir 2; Altay Izmir 2; Ankaragücü 2; Eskisehirspor 1; Besiktas 1.

	League Champions	Cup Winners
1960	Besiktas	
1961	*No competition*	
1962	Fenerbahce	
1963	Galatasaray	Galatasaray
1964	Fenerbahce	Galatasaray
1965	Fenerbahce	Galatasaray
1966	Besiktas	Galatasaray
1967	Besiktas	Altay Izmir
1968	Fenerbahce	Fenerbahce
1969	Galatasaray	Goztepe Izmir
1970	Fenerbahce	Goztepe Izmir
1971	Galatasaray	Eskisehirspor
1972	Galatasaray	Ankaragücü
1973	Galatasaray	Galatasaray
1974	Fenerbahce	Fenerbahce
1975	Fenerbahce	Besiktas
1976	Trabzonspor	Galatasaray
1977	Trabzonspor	Trabzonspor
1978	Fenerbahce	Trabzonspor
1979	Trabzonspor	Fenerbahce
1980	Trabzonspor	Altay Izmir
1981	Trabzonspor	Ankaragücü
1982	Besiktas	Galatasaray
1983	Fenerbahce	Fenerbahce

Final League Table 1982–83

	P	*W*	*D*	*L*	*F*	*A*	*Pts*
Fenerbahce	34	18	13	3	43	20	49
Trabzonspor	34	17	13	4	40	19	47
Galatasaray	34	17	10	7	50	33	44
Boluspor	34	16	9	9	39	23	41
Besiktas	34	16	7	11	49	30	39
Ankaragucu	34	8	18	8	38	37	34
Adana Demirspor	34	13	7	14	39	36	33
Bursaspor	34	11	11	12	36	34	33
Kecaelisper	34	10	13	11	34	37	33
Adanaspor	34	11	10	13	32	35	32
Sakaryaspor	34	13	6	15	37	43	32
Sariyer	34	8	15	11	35	43	31
Zoguidak	34	9	12	13	31	35	30
Antalyaspor	34	9	11	14	27	40	29
Mersin IY	34	10	9	15	19	32	29
Samsunspor	34	10	8	16	37	49	28
Gaziantepspor	34	9	9	16	23	35	27
Altay Izmir	34	7	7	20	27	55	21

USSR

President: Dr Boris Topornin.
Secretary: Anatoly Chetirko.
Address of Association: USSR Football Federation, Luzhnetskaya Naberezhnaja 8, 119270 Moscow.
Telephone: 201 0834.
Cable: Sportkomitet SSSR Moscow.
Area: 8,598,678 square miles.
Population: 266,560,000.
Number of Clubs: 51,299. *Teams:* 199 (teams in national championship).
Number of Players: 4,372,000. *Year of Formation:* 1912. *National Colours:* Red shirts, white shorts, red stockings.
Second Choice of Colours: White.
Name, Address and Capacity of National Stadium: Lenin Stadium, Moscow, 102,000.
Names, Addresses and Capacities of Other Principal Football Grounds: Kirov Stadium, Victory Park, Leningrad, 84,000; Pakhtakov Central Stadium, Tashkent, Socialism Street 23, 60,000; Ukraine Republic Stadium, Kiev, Krasnoarmeiskaya Street 51, 100,000; Dynamo Stadium, Moscow, Leningrad Prospect 36, 54,000; Dynamo Stadium, Tbilisi, Tseretely Street 2, 75,000.
Season: South: March–December;
Central: April–October;
North: May–September.

Principal Honours

Olympic Games: *winners* 1956
European Nations Cup: *winners* 1960; *runners-up* 1964
European Championship: *runners-up* 1972
European Cup-Winners' Cup: *winners* Dynamo Kiev (1975), Dynamo Tbilisi (1981); *runners-up* Dynamo Moscow (1972)
Super Cup: Dynamo Kiev (1975)

International matches 1982

10 Mar, Athens: v Greece (a) won 2-0 (*Tserenkov, Burjak*)
14 April, Buenos Aires: v Argentina (a) drew 1-1 (*Oganesian*)
5 May, Moscow: v East Germany (h) won 1-0 (*Shengelia*)
3 June, Stockholm: v Sweden (a) drew 1-1 (*Blokhin*)
14 June, Sevilla: v Brazil (W.C) lost 1-2 (*Bal*)
19 June, Malaga: v New Zealand (W.C.) won 3-1 (*Gavrilov, Blokhin, Baltacha*)
22 June, Malaga: v Scotland (W.C.) drew 2-2 (*Chivadze, Shengelia*)
1 July, Barcelona: v Belgium (W.C.) won 1-0 (*Oganesian*)
4 July, Barcelona: v Poland (W.C.) drew 0-0
13 Oct, Moscow: v Finland (h) won 2-0 (*Baltacha, Nadreev*)

Most Capped Player: *Lev Yashin 78*

League Championship wins (1936–82)

Dynamo Moscow 11; Dynamo Kiev 10; Spartak Moscow 10; CSKA Moscow 6; Torpedo Moscow 3; Dynamo Tbilisi 2; Saria Voroshilovgrad 1; Ararat Erevan 1; Dynamo Minsk 1.

Cup wins (1936–82)

Spartak Moscow 9; Torpedo Moscow 6; Dynamo Moscow 5; Dynamo Kiev 5; CSKA Moscow 4; Donets Shaktyor 3; Lokomotiv Moscow 2; Dynamo Tbilisi 2; Ararat Erevan 2; Karpaty Lvov 1; SKA Rostov 1; Zenit Leningrad 1.

	League Champions	Cup Winners
1954	Dynamo Moscow	Dynamo Kiev
1955	Dynamo Moscow	CSKA Moscow
1956	Spartak Moscow	*No competition*
1957	Dynamo Moscow	Lokomotiv Moscow
1958	Spartak Moscow	Spartak Moscow
1959	Dynamo Moscow	*No competition*
1960	Torpedo Moscow	Torpedo Moscow
1961	Dynamo Kiev	Donets Shaktyor
1962	Spartak Moscow	Donets Shaktyor
1963	Dynamo Moscow	Spartak Moscow
1964	Dynamo Tbilisi	Dynamo Kiev
1965	Torpedo Moscow	Spartak Moscow
1966	Dynamo Kiev	Dynamo Kiev
1967	Dynamo Kiev	Dynamo Moscow
1968	Dynamo Kiev	Torpedo Moscow
1969	Spartak Moscow	Karpaty Lvov
1970	CSKA Moscow	Dynamo Moscow
1971	Dynamo Kiev	Spartak Moscow
1972	Saria Voroshilovgrad	Torpedo Moscow
1973	Ararat Erevan	Ararat Erevan
1974	Dynamo Kiev	Dynamo Kiev
1975	Dynamo Kiev	Ararat Erevan
1976	Dynamo Moscow Torpedo Moscow	Dynamo Tbilisi
1977	Dynamo Kiev	Dynamo Moscow
1978	Dynamo Tbilisi	Dynamo Kiev
1979	Spartak Moscow	Dynamo Tbilisi
1980	Dynamo Kiev	Donets Shaktyor
1981	Dynamo Kiev	SKA Rostov
1982	Dynamo Minsk	Torpedo Moscow

* *Short league season*

Final League Table 1982

	P	*W*	*D*	*L*	*F*	*A*	*Pts*
Dynamo Minsk	34	19	9	6	63	35	47
Dynamo Kiev	34	18	10	6	58	25	46
Spartak Moscow	34	16	9	9	59	35	41
Dynamo Tbilisi	34	16	9	9	51	47	41
Ararat Erevan	34	14	10	10	50	47	38
Pachtakor Tashkent	34	13	11	10	42	38	36
Zenit Leningrad	34	12	9	13	44	41	33
Torpedo Moscow	34	11	12	11	36	33	32
Dnepr Dnepropetrovsk	34	11	12	11	34	38	32
Chernomorets Odessa	34	11	11	12	30	36	32
Dynamo Moscow	34	13	5	16	42	52	31
Metallist Charkow	34	10	11	13	32	34	30
Torpedo Kutaisi	34	10	10	14	39	45	30
CSKA Moscow	34	10	9	15	41	46	29
Shakhtyor Donetsk	34	10	9	15	42	57	29
Neftchi Baku	34	10	7	17	42	63	27
Kuban Krasnodar	34	9	9	16	37	48	27
Kairat Alma Ata	34	7	10	17	34	56	24

(*NB: clubs are allowed points for only ten drawn matches a season*)

YUGOSLAVIA

President: Drasko Popovic.
General Secretary: Banko Pejovic.
Address of Association: Yugoslav Football Association, BP 263, Terazije No 35, 11000 BP 263, Belgrade.
Telephone: 33 34 33, 33 34 47, 34 62 08.
Cable: Jugofudbal Beograd.
Telex: 11666 yu fsj.
Area: 98,766 square miles.
Population: 22,352,000.
Number of Clubs: 4,289. *Teams:* 10,755.
Number of Players: 230,405.
Year of Formation: 1919.
National Colours: Blue shirts, white shorts, red stockings.
Second Choice of Colours: White shirts, white shorts, white stockings.
No National Stadium.
Names, Addresses and Capacities of Principal Football Grounds: Red Star Stadium, Belgrade, 95,000; Yugoslav National Army, Belgrade, 55,000; Yuth Stadium, Belgrade, 25,000; Dynamo, Zagreb, 55,000; Kosevo, Sarajevo, 40,000.

Principal Honours

Olympic Games: *winners* 1960; *runners-up* 1948, 1952, 1956
European Nations Cup: *runners-up* 1960
European Championship: *runners-up* 1968
European Champions Cup: *runners-up* Partizan Belgrade (1966)
Fairs Cup: *winners* Dynamo Zagreb (1967); *runners-up* Dynamo Zagreb (1963)
UEFA Cup: *runners-up* Red Star Belgrade (1979)

International matches 1982

17 June, Zaragoza: v Northern Ireland (W.C.) drew 0-0
20 June, Valencia: v Spain (W.C.) lost 1-2 (*Gudelj*)
24 June, Zaragoza: v Honduras (W.C.) won 1-0 (*Petrovic*)
13 Oct, Oslo: v Norway (a) lost 1-3 (*Savic*)
17 Nov, Sofia: v Bulgaria (a) won 1-0 (*Stojkovic*)
15 Dec, Titograd: v Wales (h) drew 4-4 (*Cvetkovic, Zivkovic, Kranjear, Jesic*)

Most Capped Player: Dragan Dzajic 82

League Championship wins (1923–83)

Red Star Belgrade 14; Hajduk Split 9; Partizan Belgrade 9; Gradjanski Zagreb 5; BSK Belgrade 5; Dynamo Zagreb 4; Jugoslavija Belgrade 2%ncordia Zagreb 2; HASK Zagreb 1; Vojvodina Novi Sad 1; FC Sarajevo 1; Zeljeznicar 1.

Cup wins (1947–83)

Red Star Belgrade 10; Dynamo Zagreb 8; Hajduk Split 6; Partizan Belgrade 4; BSK Belgrade 2; OFK Belgrade 2; Rijeka 2; Vardar Skopje 1; Velez Mostar 1.

	League Champions	Cup Winners
1947	Partizan Belgrade	Partizan Belgrade
1948	Dynamo Zagreb	Red Star Belgrade
1949	Partizan Belgrade	Red Star Belgrade
1950	Hajduk Split	Red Star Belgrade
1951	Red Star Belgrade	Dynamo Zagreb
1952	Hajduk Split	Partizan Belgrade
1953	Red Star Belgrade	BSK Belgrade
1954	Dynamo Zagreb	Partizan Belgrade
1955	Hajduk Split	BSK Belgrade
1956	Red Star Belgrade	*No competition*
1957	Red Star Belgrade	Partizan Belgrade
1958	Dynamo Zagreb	Red Star Belgrade
1959	Red Star Belgrade	Red Star Belgrade
1960	Red Star Belgrade	Dynamo Zagreb
1961	Partizan Belgrade	Vardar Skopje
1962	Partizan Belgrade	OFK Belgrade
1963	Partizan Belgrade	Dynamo Zagreb
1964	Red Star Belgrade	Red Star Belgrade
1965	Partizan Belgrade	Dynamo Zagreb
1966	Vojvodina Novi Sad	OFK Belgrade
1967	FC Sarajevo	Hajduk Split
1968	Red Star Belgrade	Red Star Belgrade
1969	Red Star Belgrade	Dynamo Zagreb
1970	Red Star Belgrade	Red Star Belgrade
1971	Hajduk Split	Red Star Belgrade
1972	Zeljeznicar	Hajduk Split
1973	Red Star Belgrade	Dynamo Zagreb
1974	Hajduk Split	Hajduk Split
1975	Hajduk Split	Hajduk Split
1976	Partizan Belgrade	Hajduk Split
1977	Red Star Belgrade	Hajduk Split
1978	Partizan Belgrade	Rijeka
1979	Hajduk Split	Rijeka
1980	Red Star Belgrade	Dynamo Zagreb
1981	Red Star Belgrade	Velez Mostar
1982	Dynamo Zagreb	Red Star Belgrade
1983	Partizan Belgrade	Dynamo Zagreb

Final League Table 1982–83

	P	*W*	*D*	*L*	*F*	*A*	*Pts*
Partizan Belgrade	34	17	11	6	58	37	45
Dynamo Zagreb	34	14	15	5	56	40	43
Hajduk Split	34	14	15	5	51	33	43
Radnicki Nis	34	15	10	9	45	39	40
Red Star Belgrade	34	13	11	10	55	50	37
Varder Skopje	34	13	9	12	43	47	35
Sloboda	34	12	11	11	44	33	35
Olimpija	34	11	13	10	33	31	35
Vojvodina Novi Sad	34	12	10	12	38	60	34
Zeljeznicar	34	11	11	12	41	40	33
Sarajevo	34	10	12	12	45	44	32
Velez Mostar	34	11	9	14	54	57	31
Buducnost	34	11	9	14	39	52	31
Dynami Vinkovci	34	12	11	15	56	59	31
Rijeka	34	11	8	15	51	52	30
Osijek	34	11	7	16	48	51	29
OFK Belgrade	34	9	10	15	38	45	28
Galenika	34	4	12	18	31	56	20

CLUB PARTICIPATION IN EUROPEAN COMPETITIONS COUNTRY BY COUNTRY

(*Key:* CC=Champions' Cup; CWC=Cup Winner's Cup; UEFA=UEFA Cup; Fairs=Fairs Cup).

ALBANIA

Bese Kavaje – CWC *73*
Dinamo Tirana – CC*68 (w), 81*. CWC *72, 83*. UEFA *82*
17 Nendori Tirana – CC *66, 67 (w), 70, 71, 83*. UEFA *81 (w)*
Partizan Tirana – CC *63, 64, 65, 72, 80, 82*. CWC *69, 71, 81*. UEFA *81 (w)*
Vllaznia Shkodra – CC *79*. CWC *80 (w)*

AUSTRIA

Ammira Energie Wacker – CC *67*. CWC *65*. UEFA *74, 83*
Austria Salzburg – CWC *81*. UEFA *72, 77*
FK Austria – CC *62, 63, 64, 70, 71, 77, 79, 80, 81, 82*. CWC *61, 68, 72, 75, 78, 82, 83*. UEFA *73*
Grazer AK – CWC *63, 69, 82*. UEFA *74, 83*. Fairs *65*
Linzer Athletic Sportklub (Lask) – CC *66*. CWC *64*. UEFA *78, 81*
Rapid Vienna – CC *56, 57, 58, 61, 65, 68, 69, 83*. CWC *62, 67, 70, 73, 74, 77*. UEFA *72, 75, 76, 78, 79, 80, 82*. Fairs *63, 64*
Sturm Graz – CWC *76*. UEFA *75, 79, 82*. Fairs *71*
SSW Innsbruck – CC *72, 73, 74, 76, 78*. CWC *71, 79, 80*. UEFA *75, 77*. Fairs *69*
Voest – CC *75*. UEFA *73, 76, 81*
Vienna City XI – Fairs *58 (w)*
Vienna Neustadt – CWC *66*
Vienna Sportklub – CC *59, 61*. UEFA *80*. Fairs *65, 66, 67, 68, 69, 70, 71*

BELGIUM

Anderlecht – CC *56, 57, 60, 63, 65, 66, 67, 68, 69, 73, 75, 82*. CWC *74, 76, 77, 78, 79*. UEFA *72, 80, 81, 83*. Fairs *70, 71*
Antwerp – CC *58*. UEFA *75, 76*. Fairs *65, 66, 67, 68*
Beerschot – CWC *72, 80*. UEFA *74*. Fairs *69*
Beveren-Waas – CC *80*. CWC *79*. UEFA *82*. Fairs *71*
FC Bruge – CC *74, 77, 78, 79, 81*. CWC *69, 71*. UEFA *72, 73, 76, 82*. Fairs *68, 70*
Charleroi Olympique — Fairs *70*
La Gantoise – CWC *65*. UEFA *83*. Fairs *64, 67, 71*
Liege FC – Fairs *64, 65, 66, 67, 68*
Lierse – CC *61*. CWC *70, 77*. UEFA *72, 79*
Lokeren – UEFA *77, 81, 82, 83*
RWD Molenbeek – CC *76*. UEFA *73, 74, 75, 77, 78, 81*. Fairs *66, 69*
Standard Liege – CC *59, 62, 64, 70, 71, 72, 83*. CWC *66, 67, 68, 73, 82*. UEFA *74, 78, 79, 80, 81*. Fairs *69*
Union Saint-Gilloise – Fairs *60, 61, 62, 63, 65*
Waregem – CWC *75*. Fairs *69*
Waterschei – CWC *81, 83*
Winterslag – UEFA *82*

BULGARIA

Akademik Sofia – UEFA *77, 82*
Beroe Stara Zagora – CWC *74, 80*. UEFA *73, 81*
Botev Vraza – UEFA *72*
CSKA Sofia – CC *57, 58, 59, 60, 61, 62, 63, 67, 70, 72, 73, 74, 76, 77, 81, 82, 83*. CWC *66, 71, 75*. UEFA *78, 79, 80*
Dunav Rousse – UEFA *76*
Etar Tirnovo – UEFA *75*
Levsky Spartak (formerly split as Levsky and Spartak) – CC *66, 71, 75, 78, 80*. CWC *68, 69 (w), 70, 72, 77*. UEFA *73, 76, 79, 81, 82, 83*
Lokomotiv Plovdiv – UEFA *72, 74, 75, 77*. Fairs *64, 65, 66, 68, 70*
Lokomotiv Sofia – CC *65, 69 (w), 79*. CWC *78, 83*. UEFA *80*
Marek Stanke Dimitrov – CWC *79*. UEFA *78*
Slavia Sofia – CWC *64, 65, 67, 73, 76, 81*. UEFA *74, 83*. Fairs *69, 70, 71*
Spartak Plovdiv – CC *64*. Fairs *67*
Spartak Vrana – CWC *62*
Trakia Plovdiv – CC *68*. CWC *63, 82*. UEFA *79*. Fairs *69, 71*

CYPRUS

Alki Larnaca – UEFA *80*
Anorthosis Famagusta – CC *64*. CWC *65, 72, 76*
Apoel Nicosia – CC *66, 74, 81*. CWC *64, 69, 70, 77, 79, 80*. UEFA *78, 82*
Apollon Limassol – CC *69*. CWC *67, 68, 83*
Dighenis Akritas – UEFA *72*
EPA Larnaca – CC *71*. UEFA *73*
Olympiakos Nicosia – CC *68, 70, 72*. CWC *78*. UEFA *74*
Paralimni Famagusta – CWC *75 (w), 82*. UEFA *76, 77*
Omonia Nicosia – CC *67, 73, 75 (w), 76, 77, 78, 79, 80, 82, 83*. CWC *66, 81*
Pezoporikos Larnaca – CC *71, 73, 74*. CWC *75 (w)*. UEFA *79, 81, 83*

CZECHOSLOVAKIA

Banik Ostrava – CC *77, 81, 82*. CWC *74, 79*. UEFA *75, 80, 83*. Fairs *70*
Bohemians Prague – CWC *82*. UEFA *76, 80, 81, 82, 83*
Dukla Prague (previously UDA) – CC *58, 59, 62, 63, 64, 65, 67, 78, 80, 83*. CWC *66, 70, 82*. UEFA *73, 75, 79*
Dynamo Zilina – CWC *62*
Gottwaldov TJ – CWC *71*
Internacional Bratislava (formerly Ruda Hvezda/Red Star and Slovnaft) – CC *60*. CWC *76, 78*
Kosice VSS – UEFA *72, 74*
Lokomotiv Kosice – CWC *78, 80*. UEFA *79*
Ruda Hvezda (Red Star) Brno – CWC *61*
Skoda Plzen – CWC *72*
Slavia Prague – CWC *75*. UEFA *77, 78*. Fairs *68, 69*
Slovan Bratislava – CC *57, 71, 75, 76*. CWC *63, 64, 69, 70, 83*. UEFA *73, 77*
Sparta Prague (formerly Spartak Sokolovo) – CC *66, 68*. CWC *65, 73, 77, 81*. UEFA *82*. Fairs *67, 70, 71*
Spartak Hradec Kralove – CC *61*
Spartak Trnava – CC *69, 70, 72, 73, 74*. CWC *68, 76*. Fairs *71*
Tatran Presov – CWC *67*. UEFA *74*
Union Teplice – UEFA *72*
Zbrojovka Brna (formerly Spartak) – CC *79*. UEFA *80, 81*. Fairs *62, 63, 64, 65, 66, 67*

DENMARK

Aalborg – CWC *67, 71*
Aarhus – CC *56, 57, 58, 61*. CWC *62, 66*. UEFA *80*

Akademisk BK – CC *69*. UEFA *72*. Fairs *71*
B93 Copenhagen – CWC *83*
Copenhagen (City Select XI) – Fairs *58, 62, 63, 64*
Esbjerg – CC *63, 64, 67, 81*. CWC *65, 77*. UEFA *79, 80*
Falster BK 1901 Nykobing – Fairs *71*
Frem Copenhagen – CWC *70, 79*. UEFA *73, 78*. Fairs *60, 68*
Fremad Amager (Copenhagen) – CWC *73*
Holbaek Bif – UEFA *76, 77*
Hvidovre – CC *68, 75, 83*. CWC *81*. UEFA *73*. Fairs *67, 70*
KB Copenhagen – CC *59, 70, 76, 82*. UEFA *75, 78, 81*. Fairs *61, 65, 69 (w)*
BK 1903 – CC *71, 72, 78*. CWC *80*. UEFA *74, 76, 79*. Fairs *66*
Koge BK – CC *77*
Lyngby – UEFA *83*
Naestved – UEFA *74, 77, 82*
Odense (City Select XI) – Fairs *63*
Odense BK 1909 – CC *60, 65, 66, 79*. CWC *63, 72*. Fairs *67*
Odense BK 1913 – CC *62*. CWC *64*. Fairs *65, 69, 70*
Randers Freja – CWC *68, 69, 74*. UEFA *75*
Vanlose IF – CWC *75*
Vejle – CC *73, 74, 80*. CWC *76, 78, 82*

EAST GERMANY

Carl Zeiss Jena (formerly Motor and FC Jena) – CC *64, 69 (w), 71*. CWC *62, 73, 75, 81*. UEFA *72, 74, 76, 78, 79, 80, 82, 83*. Fairs *70*
Chemie Halle – CWC *63*. UEFA *72*
Chemie Leipzig (formerly Industrie and Rot) – CC *65*. CWC *67*
Dynamo Dresden (formerly Polizei and Eintracht) – CC *72, 74, 77, 78, 79*. CWC *83*. UEFA *73, 75, 76, 80, 81, 82*. Fairs *68, 71*
Dynamo (E) Berlin – CC *80, 81, 82, 83*. CWC *72*. UEFA *73, 77, 79*
Hansa Rostock (formerly Empor and FC Rostock) – Fairs *69, 70*
FC Karl-Marx-Stadt – CC *68*
Leipzig (City Select XI) – Fairs *58, 60, 61, 62, 63*
Lokomotiv Leipzig (formerly Vorwarts, Ost and SC Leipzig) – CWC *77, 78, 82*. UEFA *74, 79, 83*. Fairs *64, 65, 66, 67, 68, 69*
Magdeburg (formerly SC Aufbau) CC *73, 75, 76*. CWC *65, 66, 70, 74, 79, 80*. UEFA *77, 78, 81, 82*
Sachsenring Zwickau (formerly Horch and Motor) – CWC *64, 68, 76*
Vorwarts Frankfurt An Der Oder (formerly Vrwrts Berlin) – CC *60, 62, 63, 66, 67, 70*. CWC *61, 69 (w), 71*. UEFA *75, 81, 83*
Wismut Aue – CC *58, 59, 61*

FINLAND

HJK Helsinki – CC *66, 75, 80, 83*. CWC *68*. UEFA *76*
IFK Helsingfors – CC *61, 63*. CWC *67*. UEFA *72, 73 (w)*
Helsingin Palloseura – CC *59*. CWC *64*
Ilves Kisat (Tampere) – CWC *81*. Fairs *71*
KTP Kotko – CWC *82*
Kokkolan Pallo Veikot (Kokkola) – CC *71*. UEFA *75*
Kuopion Palloseura (Kuopio) – CC *60 (w), 68, 76, 78*. CWC *70*. UEFA *77, 79, 81*
Kuopion Palloverit (Kuopio) – UEFA *80, 83*
Kuuysi Lahti – CWC *83*
Lahden Reipas (Lahti) – CC *65, 69, 72*. CWC *66, 74, 75, 76, 77, 78, 80*
Mikkelin Palloilijat (Mikkeli) – CWC *72, 73*. UEFA *74*
Oulun Palloseura (Oulu) – CC *81, 82*
Sejnejoen Keskuskent – CWC *79*
Turun Palloseura (TPS) (Turku) – CC *70, 73, 74, 77*
Valkeakosken Haka – CC *62, 64, 67, 79*. CWC *65, 71*. UEFA *78, 82*

FRANCE

Angers – UEFA *73*
Bastia – CWC *73, 82*. UEFA *78*
Angouleme – Fairs *71*
Bordeaux – CWC *69*. UEFA *82, 83*. Fairs *65, 66, 67, 68, 70*
Lens – CWC *76*. UEFA *78*
Lyon – CWC *64, 65, 68, 74*. UEFA *75, 76*. Fairs *60, 61, 62, 69*
Marseille – CC *72, 73*. CWC *70, 77*. UEFA *74, 76*. Fairs *63, 69, 71*
Monaco – CC *62, 64, 79, 83*. CWC *75, 81*. UEFA *80, 82*
Metz – Fairs *69, 70*
Nancy-Lorraine – CWC *79*
Nantes – CC *66, 67, 74, 78, 81*. CWC *71, 80*. UEFA *72, 75, 79, 82*
Nice – CC *57, 60*. UEFA *74, 77*. Fairs *67, 68, 69*
Nimes – UEFA *72, 73*
Paris St Germain – CWC *83*
Racing Club de Paris – Fairs *64*
Reims – CC *56, 59, 61, 63*
Rennes – CWC *66, 72*
Rouen – Fairs *70*
St Etienne – CC *58, 65, 68, 69, 70, 71, 75, 76, 77, 82*. CWC *63, 78*. UEFA *72, 80, 81, 83*
Sedan – CWC *62*. Fairs *71*
Sochaux – UEFA *73, 77, 81, 83*
Stade Francais – Fairs *65, 66*
Toulouse – Fairs *67*

GREECE

AEK Athens – CC *64, 69, 72, 79, 80*. CWC *65, 67*. UEFA *73, 76, 77, 78, 83*. Fairs *71*
Aris Salonika – CWC *71*. UEFA *75, 80, 81, 82*. Fairs *66, 67, 69, 70*
Iraklis Salonika – CWC *77*. Fairs *62, 64, 65*
Kastoria – CWC *81*
Olympiakos Piraeus – CC *59 (w), 60, 67, 68, 74, 75, 76, 81, 82, 83*. CWC *62, 63 (w), 64, 66, 69, 70, 72*. UEFA *73, 77, 78, 79, 80*
Panahaiki – UEFA *74*
Panathinaikos – CC *61, 62, 63, 65, 66, 70, 71, 73, 78*. CWC *68, 76, 83*. UEFA *74, 75, 79, 81, 82*. Fairs *69*
Panionios – CWC *80*. UEFA *72*. Fairs *70*
Paok Salonika – CC *77*. CWC *73, 74, 75, 78, 79, 82*. UEFA *76, 83*. Fairs *66, 68, 71*

HOLLAND

Ajax Amsterdam – CC *58, 61, 67, 68, 69, 71, 72, 73, 74, 78, 80, 81, 83*. CWC *62, 82*. UEFA *75, 76, 77, 79*. Fairs *70*
AZ'67 Alkmaar – CC *82*. CWC *79, 83*. UEFA *78, 81*
FC Amsterdam (formerly DWS) – CC *65*. UEFA *75*. Fairs *67, 68, 69*
Feyenoord – CC *62, 63, 66, 70, 71, 72, 75*. CWC *81*. UEFA *73, 74, 76, 77, 80, 82*. Fairs *69*
Fortuna Geelen – CWC *65*
Go-Ahead Eagles (Deventer) – CWC *66*
Haarlem – UEFA *83*
Den Haag (formerly Ado) – CWC *69, 73, 76*. UEFA *72*
Nac Breda – CWC *68, 74*
PSV Eindhoven – CC *56, 64, 76, 77, 79*. CWC *70, 71, 75*. UEFA *72, 78, 80, 81, 82, 83*
Rapid Heerlen – CC *57*
Roda Kerkrade – CWC *77*
Sparta Rotterdam – CC *60*. CWC *63, 67, 72*. Fairs *71*

Twente Enschede – CWC *78, 80*. UEFA *73, 74, 75, 79, 81*. Fairs *70, 71*
Utrecht (City Select XI) – Fairs *63*
FC Utrecht (formerly Dos) – CC *59*. UEFA *82, 83*. Fairs *64, 65, 66, 67, 68, 69*
Willem II (Tilburg) – CWC *64*

HUNGARY

Budapest (City Select XI) – Fairs *61*
Csepel – CC *60*
Diosgyor – CWC *78, 81*. UEFA *80*
Dozsa Pecs – Fairs *71*
Ferencvaros – CC *64, 66, 69 (w), 70, 77, 82*. CWC *61, 73, 75, 79*. UEFA *72, 74, 78, 80, 83*. Fairs *63, 65, 67, 68, 71*
Haladas – CWC *76*
Honved – CC *57, 81*. CWC *65, 66, 71*. UEFA *73, 74, 76, 77, 79*
Komlo – CWC *72*
MTK/VM – CC *56, 59*. CWC *64, 70, 77*. UEFA *79*. Fairs *62*
Raba Eto – CC *65, 83*. CWC *67, 68, 69 (w), 80*. UEFA *75*. Fairs *70*
Salgotarjan – UEFA *73*
Tatabanya – UEFA *82, 83*
Ujpest Dozsa – CC *61, 71, 72, 73, 74, 75, 76, 79, 80*. CWC *62, 63, 83*. UEFA *77, 78, 81*. Fairs *60, 64, 66, 69, 70*
Vasas Budapest – CC *58, 62, 63, 67, 68, 78*. CWC *74, 82*. UEFA *72, 76, 81*
Videoton – UEFA *75, 77, 82*

ICELAND

Akranes – CC *72, 76, 77, 79*. CWC *78, 80*. UEFA *81*. Fairs *71*
Iba Akureyri – CWC *71*
Fram Reykjavik – CC *74*. CWC *72, 75, 81, 82*. UEFA *77, 78, 83*
Keflavik FC (IBK) – CC *66, 71, 73, 75*. CWC *77*. UEFA *72, 74, 76, 80*
KR Reykjavik – CC *65, 67, 70*. CWC *66, 68, 69*
Valur Reykjavik – CC *68, 69, 78, 80, 82*. CWC *67, 76, 79*. UEFA *75*. Fairs *70*
IBV Vestmannaeyjar – CC *81*. CWC *70, 74, 83*. UEFA *73, 79*
Vikingur – CC *83*. CWC *70, 74, 83*. UEFA *82*

ITALY

Atalanta – CWC *64*
Bologna – CC *65*. CWC *71, 75*. UEFA *72*. Fairs *67, 68, 69*
Cagliari – CC *71*. UEFA *73*. Fairs *70*
Cesena – UEFA *77*
Fiorentina – CC *57, 70*. CWC *61, 62, 67, 76*. UEFA *73, 74, 78, 83*. Fairs *65, 66, 68, 69, 71*
Internazionale – CC *64, 65, 66, 67, 72, 81*
Juventus – CC *59, 61, 62, 68, 73, 74, 76, 78, 79, 82, 83*. CWC *66, 80*. UEFA *72, 75, 77, 81*. Fairs *64, 65, 67, 69, 70, 71*
Lanerossi Vicenza – UEFA *79*
Lazio – CC *75*. UEFA *74, 76, 78*. Fairs *71*
Milan – CC *56, 58, 60, 63, 64, 69, 70, 80*. CWC *68, 73, 74, 78*. UEFA *72, 76, 77, 79*. Fairs *62, 65, 66*
Napoli – CWC *63, 77*. UEFA *72, 75, 76, 79, 80, 82, 83*. Fairs *67, 68, 69, 70*
Perugia – UEFA *80*
Roma – CWC *70, 81, 82*. UEFA *76, 83*. Fairs *60, 61, 62, 63, 64, 65, 66*
Sampdoria – Fairs *63*
Torino – CC *77*. CWC *65, 69, 72*. UEFA *73, 74, 75, 78, 79, 80, 81*. Fairs *66*

LUXEMBOURG

Alliance Dudelange – CWC *62, 63*
Aris Bonneweg – CC *65, 67, 73*. CWC *68, 77, 80*. UEFA *72*. Fairs *63, 64*
Avenir Beggen – CC *70, 83*. CWC *75*. UEFA *76*
Fola Esch – CWC *74*
Jeunesse D'Esch – CC *59, 60, 61, 64, 68, 69, 71, 74, 75, 76, 77, 78, 81, 82*. UEFA *79*. Fairs *70*
Jeunesse Hautcharage – CWC *72*
Progres Niedercorn – CC *79, 82*. CWC *78*. UEFA *80, 83*
Red Boys Differdange – CC *80*. CWC *73, 83*. UEFA *75, 77, 78, 81, 82*
Spora – CC *57, 62*. CWC *66, 67, 81*. Fairs *65, 68*
Stade Dudelange – CC *58, 66*
Union Sportive – CC *63, 72*. CWC *64, 65, 70, 71, 79*. UEFA *74*. Fairs *66, 67, 69 (w)*
Union Sportive Rumelingen – CWC *69, 76*. UEFA *73*. Fairs *71*

MALTA

Floriana – CC *63, 69, 71, 74, 76, 78, 81*. CWC *62, 66, 67, 68, 73, 77, 79, 82*. Fairs *70*
Gzira United – CWC *74*
Hibernians – CC *62, 68, 70, 80, 82, 83*. CWC *63, 71, 72, 81*. UEFA *75, 77, 79*. Fairs *69*
Marsa – UEFA *72*
Sliema Wanderers – CC *65, 66, 67, 72, 73, 77*. CWC *64, 69, 70, 75, 80, 83*. UEFA *74, 76, 78, 81, 82*. Fairs *71*
Valletta FC – CC *64, 75, 79*. CWC *65, 76, 78*. UEFA *73, 80*
Zurrieq BV – UEFA *83*

NORWAY

Bodo Glimt – CWC *77, 79*
Brann Bergen – CWC *74, 78*. UEFA *77*
Bryne – UEFA *82*
Fredrikstad – CC *61, 62, 63*. CWC *68, 73*. UEFA *74*
Frigg Oslo – Fairs *67*
Gjovik Lin – CWC *74*
Haugar – CWC *81*
Lillestroem – CC *78, 79*. CWC *80, 83*
Lyn Ski-Og – CC *64, 65, 66, 70*. CWC *69, 72*. UEFA *73*. Fairs *68*
Mjoendalen – CWC *70*. UEFA *78*
Molde – UEFA *76, 79*
Moss – UEFA *81*
Rosenberg Trondheim – CC *69, 71, 73*. CWC *66*. UEFA *72, 75*. Fairs *70*
Sarpsborg – Fairs *71*
Skeid Oslo – CC *68*. CWC *65, 67, 76*. UEFA *80*. Fairs *69, 70*
Start Kristiansand – CC *82*. UEFA *75, 77, 78, 79*
Stromgodset – CC *72*. CWC *71, 75*. UEFA *74*
Valerengens – CC *67, 83*. CWC *82*. UEFA *76*. Fairs *65, 66*
Viking Stavanger – CC *74, 75, 76, 77, 81*. UEFA *73, 83*

POLAND

Arka Gdynia – CWC *80*
Gornik Zabrze – CC *62, 64, 65, 66, 67, 68, 72, 73*. CWC *69 (w), 70, 71*. UEFA *75, 78*
Gwardia Warsaw – CC *56, 68*. CWC *75*. UEFA *74*. Fairs *70*
GKS Katowice – Fairs *71*
Lech Poznan – UEFA *79*. CWC *83*
Legia Warsaw (formerly CWKS) – CC *57, 61, 70, 71*. CWC *65, 67, 73, 74, 81, 82*. UEFA *72, 75*. Fairs *69*
LKS Lodz – CC *60*

Odra Opole – UEFA *78*
Polonia Bytom – CC *59, 63*
Ruch Chorzow – CC *69 (w), 75, 76, 80*. UEFA *73, 74*. Fairs *70, 71*
Slask Wroclaw – CC *78*. CWC *77*. UEFA *76, 79, 81, 83*
Stal Mielec – CC *74, 77*. UEFA *76, 80, 83*
Stal Rzeszaw – CWC *76*
Szombierki Bytom – CC *81*. UEFA *82*
Tychy Katowice – UEFA *77*
Widzew Lodz – CC *82, 83*. UEFA *78, 80, 81*
Wisla Krakow – CC *79*. CWC *68*. UEFA *77, 82*
Zaglebie Sosnowiecz – CWC *63, 64, 72, 78, 79*. UEFA *73*
Zaglebie Walbrzych – UEFA *72*

PORTUGAL

Academico Coimbra – CWC *70*. UEFA *72*. Fairs *69*
Barreirense – Fairs *71*
Braga – CWC *67, 83*. UEFA *79*
Cuf Barreiro – UEFA *73*. Fairs *65, 68*
Belenenses – UEFA *74, 77*. Fairs *62, 63, 64, 65*
Benfica – CC *58, 61, 62, 63, 64, 65, 66, 68, 69, 70, 72, 73, 74, 76, 77, 78, 82*. CWC *71, 75, 81*. UEFA *79, 80, 83*. Fairs *67*
Boavista – CWC *76, 77, 80*. UEFA *78, 81, 82*
Leixoes – CWC *62*. Fairs *65, 69*
Porto – CC *57, 60, 79, 80*. CWC *65, 69, 78, 82*. UEFA *72, 73, 75, 76, 77, 81, 83*. Fairs *63, 64, 66, 67, 68, 70*
Sporting Club – CC *56, 59, 62, 63, 67, 71, 75, 81, 83*. CWC *64, 65, 72, 73, 74, 79*. UEFA *76, 78, 80, 82*. Fairs *66, 68, 69, 70*
Vitoria Guimaraes – Fairs *70, 71*
Vitoria Setubal – CWC *63, 66, 68*. UEFA *72, 73, 74, 75*. Fairs *67, 69, 70, 71*

REPUBLIC OF IRELAND

Athlone – CC *82*. UEFA *76*
Bohemians – CC *76, 79*. CWC *71, 77*. UEFA *73, 75, 78, 80*
Cork Celtic – CC *75*. CWC *65*
Cork Hibernians – CC *72*. CWC *73, 74*. Fairs *71*
Dundalk – CC *64, 68, 77, 80, 83*. CWC *78, 82*. Fairs *69, 70, 81*
Finn Harps – CWC *75*. UEFA *74, 77, 79*
Home Farm (formerly Drumcondra) – CC *59, 62, 66*. CWC *76*. Fairs *63, 67*
Limerick – CC *61, 81*. CWC *66, 72, 83*. UEFA *82*
St Patrick's Ath – CWC *62*. Fairs *68*
Shamrock R – CC *58, 60, 65*. CWC *63, 67, 68, 69, 70, 79*. UEFA *83*. Fairs *64, 66*
Shelbourne – CC *63*. CWC *64*. UEFA *72*. Fairs *65*
Sligo R – CC *78*
Waterford – CC *67, 69, 70, 71, 73, 74*. CWC *80, 81*

RUMANIA

Arges Pitesti – CC *73, 80*. UEFA *74, 79, 81, 82*. Fairs *67, 68, 69*
Asa Tirgu Mures – UEFA *76, 77, 78*
SC Bacau (formerly Dinamo) – Fairs *70*
Baia Mare – CWC *83*
Chimia Ramnicul Valcea – CWC *74*
Corvinul Hunedoara – UEFA *83*
CSU Galata – CWC *77*
Dinamo Bucharest – CC *57, 63, 64, 65, 66, 72, 74, 76, 83*. CWC *69*. UEFA *75, 77, 80, 82*. Fairs *71*
Jiul Petrosani – CWC *75*
Petrolul Ploesti – CC *59, 60, 67*. CWC *64*. Fairs *63, 65, 68*
Politechnica Timisoara – CWC *81, 82*. UEFA *79*
Progresul Bucharest – CWC *62*
Rapid Bucharest – CC *68*. CWC *73, 76*. UEFA *72*. Fairs *69, 70*
Sportul Studentesc – UEFA *77*
Steagul Rosu Brasov – UEFA *75*. Fairs 64, 66
Steaua Bucharest (formerly CCA) – CC *58, 61 (w), 62, 69, 77, 79*. CWC *63, 65, 67, 68, 70, 71, 80*. UEFA *78, 81*
Uni Craiova (formerly Stiinta Cluj) – CC *75, 81, 82*. CWC *66, 78, 79*. UEFA *73, 74, 76, 80, 83*. Fairs *71*
Uta Arad – CC *70, 71*. UEFA *72, 73*

SAARLAND

FC Saarbrucken – CC *56*

SPAIN

Atletico Madrid – CC *59, 67, 71, 74, 78*. CWC *62, 63, 66, 73, 76, 77*. UEFA *72, 75, 78, 82*. Fairs *64, 65, 68, 69*
Athletic Bilbao – CC *57*. CWC *70, 74*. UEFA *72, 77, 78, 79, 83*. Fairs *65, 67, 68, 69, 71*
Barcelona – CC *60, 61, 75*. CWC *64, 69, 72, 79, 80, 82, 83*. UEFA *73, 74, 76, 77, 78, 81*. Fairs *58, 60, 61, 62, 63, 65, 66, 67, 68, 70, 71*
Betis (Seville) – CWC *78*. UEFA *83*. Fairs *65*
Castilla – CWC *81*
Celta de Vigo – UEFA *72*
Espanol (Barcelona) – UEFA *74, 77*. Fairs *62, 66*
Gijon – UEFA *79, 80, 81*
Las Palmas – UEFA *72, 78*. Fairs *70*
Real Madrid – CC *56, 57, 58, 59, 60, 61, 62, 63, 64, 65, 66, 67, 68, 69, 70, 73, 76, 77, 79, 80, 81*. CWC 71, 75, 76. UEFA *72, 74, 82*
Real Sociedad (San Sebastian) – CC *82, 83*. UEFA *75, 76, 80, 81*
Sabadell – Fairs *70*
Sevilla – CC *58*. CWC *63*. UEFA *83*. Fairs *67, 71*
Valencia – CC *72*. CWC *68, 80, 81*. UEFA *73, 79, 82, 83*. Fairs *62, 63, 64, 65, 66, 67, 69, 70, 71*
Zaragoza – CWC *65, 67*. UEFA *75, 76*. Fairs *63, 64, 66, 68, 69*

SWEDEN

Aik Solna – CWC *77*. UEFA *74, 76*. Fairs *66, 69*
Atvidaberg – CC *74, 75*. CWC *71, 72*. UEFA *73*
Brage – UEFA *83*
Djurgardens – CC *56, 66, 68*. CWC *76*. UEFA *72, 75, 77*. Fairs *65, 67*
Elfsborg – UEFA *72, 79, 81*
Gais – UEFA *76*
Halmstads – CC *78, 81*
IFK Gothenberg – CC *59, 60, 62, 71*. CWC *80, 83*. UEFA *81, 82*
Kalmar – CWC *79, 82*. UEFA *80*
Landskrona – CWC *73*. UEFA *78*
Malmo FF – CC *65, 67, 69, 72, 73, 76, 77, 79*. CWC *74, 75, 81*. UEFA *78, 80, 82*. Fairs *66, 68, 70, 71*
Malmo IFK – CC *61*
Norrkoping – CC *57, 58, 63, 64*. CWC *69, 70*. UEFA *73, 79, 83*
Orgryte – Fairs *65, 67*
Oesters Vaxjo – CC *70, 80, 82, 83*. CWC *78*. UEFA *74, 75, 76, 77*

SWITZERLAND

Basle – CC *68, 70, 71, 73, 74, 78, 81*. CWC *64, 76*. UEFA *72, 77, 79*. Fairs *65, 66, 67, 69*
Basle (City Select XI) – Fairs *58, 60, 61, 62, 63 (w)*
Chaux de Fonds – CC *65*. CWC *62*
Grasshoppers – CC *57, 72, 79, 83*. UEFA *72, 74, 75, 76, 77, 78, 80, 81, 82*

Lausanne – CC *66*. CWC *63, 65, 68, 82*. UEFA *73, 79*. Fairs *58, 60, 61 (w), 62 (w), 64, 67, 69, 70, 71*
Lugano – CWC *69*. UEFA *72*
Luzern – CWC *61*
Neuchatel Xamax - UEFA *82*
St Gallen – CWC *70*
Servette – CC *56, 62, 63, 80*. CWC *67, 72, 77, 79*. UEFA *75, 78, 81, 83*. Fairs *64, 65, 66, 68*
Sion – CWC *66, 75, 81, 83*. UEFA *74*
Young Boys Berne – CC *58, 59, 60, 61*. CWC *78, 80*. UEFA *76*
FC Zurich – CC *64, 67, 69, 75, 76, 77, 82*. CWC *71, 73, 74*. UEFA *78, 80, 83*. Fairs *68, 70*

TURKEY

Adanaspor – UEFA *77, 79, 82*
Altay Izmir – CWC *68, 69, 81*. UEFA *78*. Fairs *63, 70*
Ankaragucu – CWC *73, 74, 82*
Besiktas – CC *59, 61, 67, 68, 83*. CWC *76, 78*. UEFA *75*
Boluspor – UEFA *75*
Bursapor – CWC *75*
Eskisehirspor – CWC *72*. UEFA *73, 74, 76*. Fairs *71*
Fenerbache – CC *60, 62, 65, 66, 69, 71, 75, 76, 78*. CWC *64, 80*. UEFA *72, 73, 74, 77, 78, 81*
Galatasaray – CC *57, 63, 64, 70, 72, 73, 74*. CWC *65, 66, 67, 77, 83*. UEFA *76, 79, 80*
Goztepe Izmir – CWC *70, 71*. Fairs *65, 66, 67, 68, 69*
Orduspor – UEFA *80*
Trabzonspor – CC *77, 78, 80, 81, 82*. UEFA *83*

USSR

Ararat Erevan – CC *75*. CWC *76*. UEFA *73*
Chernomoretz Odessa – UEFA *76*
Dynamo Kiev – CC *68, 69 (w), 70, 73, 76, 77, 79, 82, 83*. CWC *66, 75*. UEFA *74, 78, 80, 81*
Dynamo Moscow – CWC *69 (w), 72, 78, 80*. UEFA *75, 77, 81, 83*
Dynamo Tbilisi – CC *80*. CWC *77, 81, 82*. UEFA *73, 74, 78, 79, 83*
Karpaty Lwow – CWC *71*
Ska Rostov – CWC *82*
Schakhtyor Donetsk – CWC *79*. UEFA *77, 80, 81*
Spartak Moscow – CC *71, 81*. CWC *67, 73*. UEFA *72, 75, 76, 82, 83*
Torpedo Moscow – CC *67, 78*. CWC *68, 70, 74, 83*. UEFA *76, 79*
Tska Moscow – CC *72*. UEFA *82*
Zarya Voroshilovgrad – CC *74*
Zenit Leningrad – UEFA *82*

WEST GERMANY

Bayern Munich – CC *70, 73, 74, 75, 76, 77, 81, 82*. CWC *67, 68, 72, 73*. UEFA *78, 80*. Fairs *63, 71*
Berlin City (Select XI) – Fairs *62*
Borussia Dortmund – CC *57, 58, 64*. CWC *66, 67*. UEFA *83*. Fairs *65*
Borussia Moenchengladbach – CC *71, 72, 76, 77, 78*. CWC *61, 74*. UEFA *73, 75, 79, 80, 82*
Eintracht Braunschweig – CC *68*. UEFA *72, 77, 78*
Eintracht Frankfurt – CC *60*. CWC *75, 76, 82*. UEFA *73, 78, 80, 81*. Fairs *65, 67, 68, 69*
Frankfurt (City Select XI) – Fairs *58*
Fortuna Dusseldorf – CWC *79, 80, 81*. UEFA *74, 75*
Hamburg – CC *61, 80, 83*. CWC *64, 68, 77, 78*. UEFA *72, 75, 76, 81, 82*. Fairs *69, 71*
Hanover – Fairs *60, 61, 62, 66, 68, 69, 70*
Hertha Berlin – UEFA *72, 76, 79*. Fairs *64, 65, 70, 71*
Kaiserlautern – UEFA *73, 77, 80, 81, 82, 83*
Kickers Offenbach – CWC *71*
Koln (City Select XI) – Fairs *58 (w), 60*
FC Koln – CC *63, 65, 79*. CWC *69, 78*. UEFA *72, 73, 74, 75, 76, 77, 81, 83*. Fairs *61, 62, 64, 66, 68, 71*
MSV Duisburg – UEFA *76, 79*
Munich 1860 – CC *67*. CWC *65*. Fairs *66, 68, 69, 70*
Nurnberg – CC 62, 69. CWC *63*. Fairs *66, 67*
Rot-Weiss Essen – CC *66*
Schalke – CC *59*. CWC *70, 73*. UEFA *77, 78*
Stuttgart – UEFA *74, 79, 80, 81, 82*. Fairs *65, 67, 70*
Tasmania Berlin – Fairs *63*
Viktoria Koln – Fairs *63*
Werder Bremen – CC *66*. CWC *62*. UEFA *83*
Wuppertaler SV – UEFA *74*

YUGOSLAVIA

Belgrade (City Select XI) – Fairs *60, 61*
Bor FK – CWC *63, 67*. UEFA *72, 73, 74*
Borac Banja Luka – CWC *76*
Dynamo Zagreb – CC *59, 83*. CWC *61, 64, 65, 66, 70, 74, 81*. UEFA *72, 77, 78, 80*. Fairs *62, 63, 67, 68, 69, 71*
Hajduk Split – CC *72, 75, 76, 80*. CWC *68, 73, 77, 78*. UEFA *79, 82, 83*. Fairs *71*
Napredak – UEFA *81*
Nogometni Rijeka – CWC *79, 80*
Novisad FK – Fairs *62*
OFK Belgrade – CWC *63, 67*. UEFA *72, 73, 74*. Fairs *64, 65, 69*
Olimpia Ljubljana – CWC *71*. Fairs *67, 69*
Partizan Belgrade – CC *56, 62, 63, 64, 66, 77, 79*. UEFA *75*. Fairs *68, 70, 71*
Radnicki Nis – UEFA *81, 82*
Red Star Belgrade (Crvena Zvezda) – CC *57, 58, 60, 61, 65, 69, 70, 71, 74, 78, 81, 82*. CWC *72, 75, 83*. UEFA *73, 76, 77, 79, 80*. Fairs *62, 63, 66, 67*
Sarajevo – CC *68*. UEFA *81, 83*
Slobodo Tusla – UEFA *78*
Tresnjevka Zagreb – Fairs *64*
Vardar Skopje – CWC *62*
Velez Mostar – CWC *82*. UEFA *74, 75*
Vojvodina Novisad – CC *67*. UEFA *73, 76*. Fairs *63, 65, 68, 69, 70*
Zagreb (City Select XI) – Fairs *58, 60, 61*
Zagreb NK – Fairs *65, 66, 70*
Zeljeznicar Sarajevo – CC *73*. UEFA *72*. Fairs *71*

WORLD CLUB CHAMPIONSHIP

Played annually up to 1974 and intermittently since then between the winners of the European Cup and the winners of the South American Champions Cup – known as the Copa Libertadores. In 1980 the winners were decided by one match arranged on neutral territory in February 1981 and the venue was the same in December 1981.

1960 Real Madrid beat Penarol 0-0, 5-1
1961 Penarol beat Benfica 0-1, 5-0, 2-1
1962 Santos beat Benfica 3-2, 5-2
1963 Santos beat AC Milan 2-4, 4-2, 1-0
1964 Inter-Milan beat Independiente 0-1, 2-0, 1-0
1965 Inter-Milan beat Independiente 3-0, 0-0
1966 Penarol beat Real Madrid 2-0, 2-0
1967 Racing Club beat Celtic 0-1, 2-1, 1-0
1968 Estudiantes beat Manchester United 1-0, 1-1
1969 AC Milan beat Estudiantes 3-0, 1-2
1970 Feyenoord beat Estudiantes 2-2, 1-0
1971 Nacional beat Panathinaikos 1-1, 2-1
1972 Ajax beat Independiente 1-1, 3-0
1973 Independiente beat Juventus 1-0
1974 Atlético Madrid beat Independiente 0-1, 2-0
1975 Independiente and Bayern Munich could not agree dates; no matches.
1976 Bayern Munich beat Cruzeiro 2-0, 0-0
1977 Boca Juniors beat Borussia Moenchengladbach 2-2, 3-0
1978 Not played
1979 Olimpia beat Malmö 1-0, 2-1
1980 Nacional beat Nottingham Forest 1-0
1981 Flamenco beat Liverpool 3-0
1982 Penarol beat Aston Villa 2-0

WORLD CLUB CHAMPIONSHIP – BRITISH FINALISTS

1967

18 October

Celtic (0) 1 *(McNeill)* *Ref:* Gardeazabel

Racing Buenos Aires (0) 0 103,000

Celtic: Simpson; Craig, McNeill, Gemmell, Murdoch, Clark, Johnstone, Lennox, Wallace, Auld, Hughes.
Racing Buenos Aires: Cejas; Martin, Perfumo, Basile, Diaz, Rulli, Mori, Maschio, Cardenas, Raffo, Rodriguez.

1 November

Racing Buenos Aires (1) 2 *(Raffo 2)* *Ref:* Esteban Marino

Celtic (1) 1 *(Gemmell pen)* 80,000

Racing Buenos Aires: Cejas; Martin, Perfumo, Basile, Chabay, Rulli, Maschio, Cardoso, Cardenas, Rodriguez, Raffo.
Celtic: Fallon; Clark, Craig, McNeill, Gemmell, Murdoch, O'Neill, Johnstone, Wallace, Chalmers, Lennox.

4 November
Play-off in Montevideo

Racing Buenos Aires (0) 1 *(Cardenas)* *Ref:* Osorio

Celtic (0) 0 65,172

Racing Buenos Aires: Cejas; Martin, Perfumo, Basile, Chabay, Rulli, Maschio, Cardoso, Cardenas, Rodriguez, Raffo.
Celtic: Fallon; Clark, Craig, McNeill, Gemmell, Murdoch, Auld, Johnstone, Lennox, Wallace, Hughes.

1968

Estudiantes de la Plata (1) 1 *(Conigliaro)* *Ref:* Miranda

Manchester U (0) 0 65,000

Estudiantes: Poletti; Suarez, Medina, Malbernat, Pachame, Madero, Ribaudo, Bilardo, Conigliaro, Togneri, Veron.
Manchester U: Stepney; Dunne, Foulkes, Sadler, Burns, Crerand, Stiles, Charlton, Morgan, Law, Best.

Manchester U (1) 1 *(Morgan)* *Ref:* Machin

Estudiantes de la Plata (1) 1 *(Veron)* 60,000

Manchester U: Stepney; Dunne, Foulkes, Sadler, Brennan, Crerand, Charlton, Morgan, Kidd, Law (Sartori), Best.
Estudiantes: Poletti; Malbernat, Suarez, Medina, Bilardo, Pachame, Madero, Ribaudo (Echecopar), Conigliaro, Togneri, Veron.

1981
11 February at National Stadium, Tokyo

Nacional (Uruguay) (1) 1 *(Victorino)*

Nottingham F (0) 0 62,000

Nacional: Rodriguez; Moreira, Blanco, Enriquez, Gonzalez, Milar, Esparrago, Luzardo, Morales, Bica, Victorino.
Nottingham F: Shilton; Anderson, Lloyd, Burns, Gray F., Ponte (Ward), O'Neill, Gray S., Robertson, Francis, Wallace.

1982
13 December at National Stadium, Tokyo

Flamengo (Brazil) (3) 3 *(Nunez 2, Addilo)*

Liverpool (0) 0 62,000

Flamengo: Raul; Leandro, Junior, Mozer, Marinho, Adilio, Tita, Andrade, Nunes, Zico, Lico.
Liverpool: Grobbelaar; Neal, Lawrenson, Thompson, Kennedy R., Hansen, Dalglish, Lee, Johnston, McDermott (Johnson), Souness.

1983
12 December at National Stadium, Tokyo

Penarol (Uruguay) (1) 2 *(Jair, Silva)* *Ref:* Siles (Costa Rica)

Aston Villa (0) 0 62,000

Penarol: Fernandez; Olivera, Guitierrez, Diogo, Bossio, Morales, Ramos, Saralegui, Morena, Jair, Silva.
Aston Villa: Rimmer; Jones, Williams, Evans, McNaught, Mortimer, Bremner, Cowans, Shaw, Withe, Morley.

SUPER CUP 1982

Jan 19

Barcelona (0) 1 *(Marcos)*

Aston Villa (0) 0

Barcelona: Urruti; Alesanco, Sanchez, Migueli, Julio Alberto, Victor, Schuster, Alonso M. (Urbano), Marcos, Quini (Alonso A.), Carrasco.
Aston Villa: Spink; Jones (Gibson), Evans, McNaught, Williams, Bremner, Mortimer, Cowans, Shaw, Withe, Morley.

Jan 26

Aston Villa (0) 3 *(Shaw, Cowans pen, McNaught)*

Barcelona (0) 0

Aston Villa: Spink; Williams, Gibson, Evans, McNaught, Blair, Bremner, Cowans, Shaw, Withe, Morley (Walters).
Barcelona: Urruti; Alesanco, Sanchez, Migueli, Julio Alberto, Alonso M., Schuster, Victor, Urbano, Carrasco (Quini, Manola), Marcos.

Previous Matches
1972 Ajax beat Rangers 3-1, 3-2
1973 Ajax beat AC Milan 0-1, 6-0
1974 Not contested
1975 Dynamo Kiev beat Bayern Munich 1-0, 2-0
1976 Anderlecht beat Bayern Munich 4-1, 1-2
1977 Liverpool beat Hamburg 1-1, 6-0
1978 Anderlecht beat Liverpool 3-1, 1-2
1979 Nottingham F beat Barcelona 1-0, 1-1
1980 Valencia beat Nottingham F 1-0, 1-2
1981 Not contested

IRISH FOOTBALL 1982–83

After the euphoria of the World Cup in which the Irish FA made a profit of £320,000, the 1982–83 season continued to be a commendable year for Northern Ireland's international squad with home victories over West Germany, Turkey and Albania and a draw in the away game with Albania at the bizarre, hermit-like capital of Tirana. The only game they lost in this series was the 2-0 defeat by Austria in Vienna when the side had not recovered its motivation after Espana, 82.

However, the same could not be said of the domestic season in which the standard of football was generally mediocre, attendances fell in all competitions and the Linfield-Glentoran Irish Cup Final at Windsor Park, Belfast, was marred by violence when rival fans staged a battle on the pitch at the finish.

Glentoran, who won the Irish, Ulster and Gold Cups, started the season in invincible fashion but, on their own admittance, lack of commitment and character midway through the championship lost them the Irish League championship won by Linfield who conceded only 13 goals, a record. Nevertheless, Glentoran got the Team of the Year award and with consistency could have made it a clean sweep.

Irish League officials, concerned at the crowd slump, were convinced of the need for a change and an end to the stereotyped set-up, and decided to increase the number of clubs from 12 to 14. They admitted Newry Town, who withdrew in 1939 at the beginning of the Second World War, and Carrick Rangers, affluent B Division clubs backed by flourishing social centres.

They also increased the clubs competing in the Irish Cup first round to 32, an innovation which proved a winner with Portadown being eliminated by Milford Everton in the first round and Cliftonville beaten by Ballyclare Comrades in the third round. RUC, who got to the third round, retained the British Police championship with a 1-0 extra time triumph over Metropolitan, while Northern Ireland took the British Universities title.

Work is shortly to begin on the new multimillion pound stand at Windsor Park, Northern Ireland's international headquarters, while Distillery have embarked on a fund-raising project to wipe out the £150,000 debt accrued primarily by building the new stadium at Lambeg, County Antrim.

This November Irish FA chief executive Billy Drennan, MBE, retires after almost 40 years in the post. He started as the youngest secretary in the world; now he leaves as the longest-serving, the elder Statesman. His contribution to the game, not only in Ireland, has been immense.

SMIRNOFF IRISH LEAGUE CHAMPIONSHIP

Winners – £5500; *Runners-up* – £2800; *Third* – £1100; *Fourth* – £600. *Irish League* £1000

	P	*W*	*D*	*L*	*F*	*A*	*Pts*
Linfield	22	15	5	2	43	13	35
Glentoran	22	14	2	6	49	21	30
Coleraine	22	11	6	5	44	25	28
Portadown	22	10	6	6	29	17	26
Crusaders	22	11	3	8	35	26	25
Cliftonville	22	10	4	8	30	24	24
Ards	22	9	4	9	40	41	22
Ballymena	22	8	4	10	32	41	20
Distillery	22	7	4	11	23	46	18
Glenavon	22	6	4	12	26	37	16
Larne	22	6	3	13	31	40	15
Bangor	22	1	3	18	17	68	5

GUINNESS PLAYER OF THE MONTH

September	John O'Connor (Ards)
October	Jeff Blair (Ballymena U)
November	Gerry Mullan (Glentoran)
December	Michael Keenan (Portadown)
January	Dermot Keely (Glentoran)
February	Lindsay McKeown (Linfield)
March	George Dunlop (Linfield)
April	Paul Carland (Larne)

SMIRNOFF FAIR PLAY LEAGUE

£200 per month

December	Portadown
January	Coleraine
February	Coleraine
March	Portadown
April	Distillery
Overall Winner (£500)	Distillery

IRISH LEAGUE CHAMPIONSHIP WINNERS

1891	Linfield
1892	Linfield
1893	Linfield
1894	Glentoran
1895	Linfield
1896	Distillery
1897	Glentoran
1898	Linfield
1899	Distillery
1900	Belfast Celtic
1901	Distillery
1902	Linfield
1903	Distillery
1904	Linfield
1905	Glentoran
1906	Cliftonville/Dist
1907	Linfield
1908	Linfield
1909	Linfield
1910	Cliftonville
1911	Linfield
1912	Glentoran
1913	Glentoran
1914	Linfield
1915	Belfast Celtic
1920	Belfast Celtic
1921	Glentoran
1922	Linfield
1923	Linfield
1924	Queen's Island
1925	Glentoran
1926	Belfast Celtic
1927	Belfast Celtic
1928	Belfast Celtic
1929	Belfast Celtic
1930	Linfield

1931 Glentoran
1932 Linfield
1933 Belfast Celtic
1934 Linfield
1935 Linfield
1936 Belfast Celtic
1937 Belfast Celtic
1938 Belfast Celtic
1939 Belfast Celtic
1940 Belfast Celtic
1948 Belfast Celtic
1949 Linfield
1950 Linfield
1951 Glentoran
1952 Glenavon
1953 Glentoran
1954 Linfield
1955 Linfield
1956 Linfield
1957 Glentoran
1958 Ards
1959 Linfield
1960 Glenavon
1961 Linfield
1962 Linfield
1963 Distillery
1964 Glentoran
1965 Derry City
1966 Linfield
1967 Glentoran
1968 Glentoran
1969 Linfield
1970 Glentoran
1971 Linfield
1972 Glentoran
1973 Crusaders
1974 Coleraine
1975 Linfield
1976 Crusaders
1977 Glentoran
1978 Linfield
1979 Linfield
1980 Linfield
1981 Glentoran
1982 Linfield
1983 Linfield

MORANS ULSTER CUP

Winners – £1000; *Runners-up* – £600; *Third* – £400; *Fourth* – £300; *Fifth* – £200.

	P	*W*	*D*	*L*	*F*	*A*	*Pts*
Glentoran	11	9	1	1	31	13	19
Linfield	11	7	2	2	27	10	16
Coleraine	11	7	1	3	24	16	15
Ballymena	11	4	5	2	18	15	13
Ards	11	4	5	2	18	15	13
Crusaders	11	5	3	3	21	21	13
Cliftonville	11	4	3	4	16	17	11
Larne	11	3	4	4	13	17	10
Glenavon	11	2	3	6	10	17	7
Portadown	11	3	1	7	15	25	7
Distillery	11	2	3	6	12	24	7
Bangor	11	0	1	10	10	33	1

Winners

1949 Linfield
1950 Larne
1951 Glentoran
1952
1953 Glentoran
1954 Crusaders
1955 Glenavon
1956 Linfield
1957 Linfield
1958 Distillery
1959 Glenavon
1960 Linfield
1961 Ballymena U
1962 Linfield
1963 Crusaders
1964 Linfield
1965 Coleraine
1966 Glentoran
1967 Linfield
1968 Coleraine
1969 Coleraine
1970 Linfield
1971 Linfield
1972 Coleraine
1973 Ards
1974 Linfield
1975 Coleraine
1976 Glentoran
1977 Linfield
1978 Linfield
1979 Linfield
1980 Ballymena U
1981 Glentoran
1982 Glentoran

HENNESSY GOLD CUP

Winners – £1500; *Runners-up* £1000; *Second placed sectional teams* – £500; *Third placed* – £350.

Section A

	P	*W*	*D*	*L*	*F*	*A*	*Pts*
Linfield	5	3	2	0	9	4	8
Ards	5	3	2	0	8	4	8
Bangor	5	3	1	1	9	8	7
Distillery	5	1	1	3	7	8	3
Portadown	5	1	0	4	4	8	2
Glenavon	5	1	0	4	6	11	2

Section B

	P	*W*	*D*	*L*	*F*	*A*	*Pts*
Glentoran	5	5	0	0	13	2	10
Ballymena	5	3	1	1	10	8	7
Crusaders	5	1	3	1	10	9	5
Cliftonville	5	2	1	2	7	9	5
Coleraine	5	1	1	3	8	10	3
Larne	5	0	0	5	5	15	0

Play-off (*at The Oval, 22 September 1982. Attendance 10,000*)
Glentoran 2 *(Jameson 2)*, **Linfield 0**

Glentoran: Patterson; Neill G., Connell, Keely (capt), Harrison, Cleary, Jameson, Bowers, Manley, McDaid (sub McCreery 43 mins), Morrison.
Linfield: Dunlop; Hayes, McCartney, Walsh (capt), Jeffrey, McKeown, Gibson, Doherty, McGaughey, Murray, Whitten (sub Anderson 45 mins).

Referee: Hugh Wilson (Belfast).
Manager of Tournament: Ronnie McFall (Glentoran)
Player of Final: Jim Cleary (Glentoran)

Winners

1912 Celtic
1914 Distillery
1915 Shelbourne
1920 Distillery
1921 Linfield
1922 Linfield
1923 Cliftonville
1924 Linfield
1925 Distillery
1926 Celtic
1927 Linfield
1928 Linfield
1929 Linfield
1930 Distillery
1931 Linfield
1932 Coleraine
1933 Cliftonville
1934 Portadown
1935 Celtic
1936 Linfield
1937 Linfield
1938 Portadown
1939 Celtic
1940 Celtic
1941 Celtic
1942 Glentoran
1943 Linfield
1944 Celtic
1945 Celtic
1946 Celtic
1947 Celtic
1948 Linfield
1949 Linfield
1950 Linfield
1951 Glentoran
1952 Portadown
1953 Ards
1954 Glenavon
1955 Linfield
1956 Glenavon
1957 Linfield
1958 Coleraine
1959 Linfield
1960 Glentoran
1961 Linfield
1962 Glentoran
1963 Linfield
1964 Derry City
1965 Linfield
1966 Glentoran
1967 Linfield
1968 Linfield
1969 Coleraine
1970 Linfield
1971 Linfield
1972 Portadown
1973 Linfield
1973–74 Ards
1974–75 Ballymena U
1975 Coleraine
1976 Glentoran
1977 Glentoran
1978 Portadown
1979 Linfield
1980 Cliftonville
1981 Linfield
1982 Glentoran

* Switched to league principle.

BASS IRISH CUP 1982–83

Winners – £3000; *Runners-up* – £2000; *Defeated semi-finalists* – £1000 each; *Personality of each round* – £250 each – First Round – Gerry O'Kane (Coleraine); Second Round – Gary McCartney (RUC); Third Round – Andy Dougan (Ballyclare Comrades); Semi-finals – Peter Dornan (Linfield); Final – Johnny Jameson (Glentoran).

First Round (22 January)

Glentoran v Ballymena U			4-0
Portadown v Milford Everton			01
Dundela v Ballyclare Comrades		2-2	2-0
RUC v Tobermore U		1-1	6-2
Newry Town v Cliftonville			0-2
Banbridge Town v Ulster Poly			3-0
Omagh Town v Coleraine		1-1	0-8
Distillery v Linfield			2-3
Limavady v NUU		1-1	3-0
Ballymoney U v Stranmillis College			4-2
Bangor v Ards			0-1
Glenavon v Crusaders			0-2
Brantwood v Larne			1-2
Dunmurry Rec v Carrick Rangers			0-4
Roe Valley v Cookstown U	0-0	1-1	2-0
POSC v Dungannon Swifts			0-4

Note: This was the first season in which 32 teams were included in the opening round draw. There was no seeding.

Second Round (12 February)

Ballyclare Comrades v Milford Everton		3-2
Ballymoney U v Glentoran		0-2
Banbridge Town v Larne	1-1	1-2
Cliftonville v Carrick Rangers		3-1
Crusaders v Coleraine		1-2
Dungannon Swifts v Ards		0-3
Limavady U v RUC	1-1	1-6
RoeValley v Linfield		0-5

Third Round (5 March)

Ards v Larne		2-1
Ballyclare Comrades v Cliftonville	1-1	0-1
Coleraine v Glentoran		2-3
Linfield v RUC		3-1

Semi-finals (25 March, Windsor Park, floodlights)

Glentoran v Ballyclare Comrades 3-0

Saturday 26 March (The Oval)

Ards v Linfield 1-2

FINAL (at Windsor Park, 30 April, attendance 10,000)

Glentoran 1 *(Mullan)*, **Linfield 1** *(McKeown* pen*)*

Glentoran: Patterson; Neill G., Keely (capt), Harrison, Connell, Cleary, Jameson, Bowers (sub Morrison 80 mins), Manley, Mullan, Neill D.

Linfield: Dunlop; Hayes, Crawford, Gibson, McKeown (capt), Walsh (sub Garrett 84 mins), McKee, Dornan, Doherty, McGaughey, Anderson.

Referee: H. Wilson (Belfast)

Replay *(at the Oval, 7 May. Attendance 8000)*

Glentoran 2 *(Jameson 2)*, **Linfield 1** *(McGaughey)*

Glentoran: Patterson; Neill G., Connell, Keely (capt) (sub Morrison 68 min), Harrison, Cleary, Jameson, Strain, Manley, Mullan, Neill D.

Linfield: Dunlop; Hayes, Crawford, Walsh, Gibson, McKeown (capt), McKee, Doherty (sub Anderson 58 mins), McGaughey, Dornan, Murray.

Referee: H. Wilson (Belfast).

Footnote: Jim Cleary (Glentoran) was ordered off 12 minutes before the end for tackle on Dornan.

IRISH CUP FINALS (from 1946–47)

1946–47	Belfast Celtic 1, Glentoran 0
1947–48	Linfield 3, Coleraine 0
1948–49	Derry City 3, Glentoran 1
1949–50	Linfield 2, Distillery 1
1950–51	Glentoran 3, Ballymena U 1
1951–52	Ards 1, Glentoran 0
1952–53	Linfield 5, Coleraine 0
1953–54	Derry City 1, Glentoran 0
1954–55	Dundela 3, Glenavon 0
1955–56	Distillery 1, Glentoran 0
1956–57	Glenavon 2, Derry City 0
1957–58	Ballymena U 2, Linfield 0
1958–59	Glenavon 2, Ballymena U 0
1959–60	Linfield 5, Ards 1
1960–61	Glenavon 5, Linfield 1
1961–62	Linfield 4, Portadown 0
1962–63	Linfield 2, Distillery 1
1963–64	Derry City 2, Glentoran 0
1964–65	Coleraine 2, Glenavon 1
1965–66	Glentoran 2, Linfield 0
1966–67	Crusaders 3, Glentoran 1
1967–68	Crusaders 2, Linfield 0
1968–69	Ards 4, Distillery 2
1969–70	Linfield 2, Ballymena U 1
1970–71	Distillery 3, Derry City 0
1971–72	Coleraine 2, Portadown 1
1972–73	Glentoran 3, Linfield 2
1973–74	Ards 2, Ballymena U 1
1974–75	Coleraine 1:0:1, Linfield 1:0:0
1975–76	Carrick Rangers 2, Linfield 1
1976–77	Coleraine 4, Linfield 1
1977–78	Linfield 3, Ballymena U 1
1978–79	Cliftonville 3, Portadown 2
1979–80	Linfield 2, Crusaders 0
1980–81	Ballymena U 1, Glenavon 0
1981–82	Linfield 2, Coleraine 1
1982–83	Glentoran 2, Linfield (after replay)

OTHER IRISH TROPHIES AND COMPETITIONS

	Winners	*Runners-up*
County Antrim Shield	Linfield	Glentoran
Irish League 'B' Division		
Section I	Carrick Rangers	Dundela
Section II	Linfield Swifts	Ballymena U Res
George Wilson Cup	Ards Seconds	Larne Olympic
Steel Cup	Dundela	RUC
County Antrim Junior Shield	1st Bangor	Ballynafeigh
Smirnoff 'B' Division Knock-out Cup	RUC	Newry Town
Irish FA Junior Cup	Crewe Utd	Newry Shamrocks
Irish FA Youth Cup	Ards Colts	Glenavon III
Irish FA Intermediate Cup	Chimney Corner	Dundela

Ulster Footballer of the Year (Promoted by Castlereagh/Glentoran Supporters Club)	Jim Cleary (Glentoran)
Northern Ireland Footballer of the Year (FWA)	George Dunlop (Linfield)
Young Footballer of the Year	Raymond McCoy (Coleraine)
NIPFA Player of the Year	Jim Campbell (Ards)
Ulster Personality of the Year	Gerry Armstrong (Northern Ireland & Watford)
Most Promising Newcomer	Raymond McCoy (Coleraine)
Mullan-Stewart Award for Meritorious Service	Len Hiller (Linfield Physiotherapist)
Manager of the Year (Coaches Assoc.)	Roy Coyle (Linfield)

WELSH FOOTBALL 1982–83

WELSH FOOTBALL LEAGUE

PREMIER DIVISION

	P	W	D	L	F	A	Pts
Barry Town	34	26	3	5	103	35	81
Blaenrhondda	34	18	12	4	62	35	66
Newport YMCA	34	18	8	8	52	38	62
Maesteg Park	34	18	7	9	52	34	61
Lake United	34	17	8	9	61	43	59
Merthyr Tydfil	34	17	6	11	84	63	57
Sully	34	14	10	10	55	49	52
Caerleon	34	12	10	12	45	46	46
Ton Pentre	34	13	7	14	49	50	46
Pontllanfraith	34	12	9	13	61	49	45
Haverfordwest County	34	12	9	13	40	39	45
Brecon Corinthians	34	11	11	12	37	49	40†
Pontardawe Athletic	34	10	5	19	33	57	35
Pembroke Boro'	34	9	7	18	46	63	34
Milford United	34	9	6	19	41	76	33
Cardiff Corinthians	34	8	7	19	46	72	28*
Llanelli	34	7	6	21	42	77	27
Ammanford Town	34	6	7	21	37	71	25

*Denotes 3 points deducted. †Denotes 4 points deducted.

DIVISION ONE

	P	W	D	L	F	A	Pts
Abercynon Athletic	32	22	7	3	70	33	73
Caerau	32	19	11	2	63	28	68
Taffs Well	32	17	8	7	65	40	59
Morriston Town	32	17	7	8	61	36	58
Spencer Works	32	14	11	7	56	38	53
Treharris Athletic	32	15	8	9	62	45	53
BP (Llandarcy)	32	14	9	9	66	45	51
Cwmbran Town	32	13	8	11	60	48	47
Ferndale Athletic	32	10	10	12	47	48	40
Clydach United	32	10	10	12	50	52	40
Ebbw Vale	32	10	7	15	44	58	37
South Glamorgan Institute	32	16	5	11	71	54	33*
Pontlottyn	32	8	5	19	53	77	29
Bridgend Town	32	7	4	21	40	92	25
Briton Ferry Athletic	32	5	8	19	43	78	23
Trelewis	32	6	5	21	40	82	23
Afan Lido	32	5	5	22	41	78	20

*Denotes 20 points deducted.

DIVISION TWO

	P	W	D	L	F	A	Pts
Tondu Robins	32	23	7	2	76	21	76
Port Talbot Athletic	32	22	7	3	70	23	73
Garw	32	20	7	5	73	29	67
Seven Sisters	32	19	6	7	64	38	63
Carmarthen Town	32	18	7	7	60	35	61
Blaenavon Blues	32	15	12	5	68	39	57
Tynte Rovers	32	14	7	11	73	56	49
Tonyrefail Welfare	32	14	6	12	51	45	48
Abergavenny Thursdays	32	10	11	11	44	50	41
Panteg	32	9	9	14	45	60	36
Swansea University	32	10	6	16	43	58	36
Ynysybwl	32	8	10	14	45	59	34
Pontyclun	32	8	10	14	49	66	34
Blaina West Side	32	7	8	17	41	60	29
Skewen Athletic	32	5	7	20	29	66	22
Lewistown	32	4	6	22	30	92	18
Aberaman	32	2	2	28	38	102	8

S. A. Brain Challenge Cup – *Winners:* Barry Town; *runners-up:* Merthyr Tydfil

THE WELSH FOOTBALL LEAGUE (NORTH)

DIVISION ONE

	P	W	D	L	F	A	Pts
Colwyn Bay	22	16	4	2	66	27	36
UCNW	22	14	3	5	54	30	31
Llandudno	22	14	1	7	67	45	29
Greenfield	22	11	6	5	47	21	28
Rhos United	22	9	4	9	28	30	22
Blaenau Ffestiniog	22	10	2	10	36	45	22
Conwy United	22	7	7	8	33	26	21
Rhyl	22	7	7	8	34	42	21
Flint Town United	22	6	7	9	34	44	19
Bangor City	22	5	5	12	33	44	15
Pwllheli & District	22	2	9	11	30	54	13
Caer T.	22	3	1	18	22	78	7

HONOURS LIST

League Champions: Colwyn Bay
Cookson Cup Winners: Greenfield
Alves Cup Winners: UCNW Bangor
Barritt Cup Winners: Welshpool

OTHER WELSH HONOURS

Welsh National League (Wrexham Area): Brymbo Steel Works *(Champions and League Cup Winners)*
Welsh National League (Central Wales): Caersws *(Champions and League Cup Winners)*
Welsh Youth Cup winners: Newport County
South Wales FA Senior Cup: Ton Pentre
South Wales Intermediate Cup: Sea View *(Barry)*
North Wales Coast Challenge Cup: Colwyn Bay
North East Wales Challenge Cup: Brymbo Steel Works
Gwent County FA Senior Cup: Llanfrechfa Grange
Gwent County FA Amateur Cup: Tredegar Town
Central Wales FA Challenge Cup: Aberystwyth Town
J. Emrys Morgan Cup: Bow Street
West Wales FA Senior Cup: Pontardawe
West Wales FA Intermediate Cup: West End *(Swansea)*
S. B. Williams Inter-League Cup: Carmarthenshire AF League

WELSH CUP 1982–83

First Round

Llandudno Amateurs v Conwy U	0-3
Flint Town U v UCNW Bangor	0-0, 2-1
Porthmadog v Bala T	0-2
Brymbo Steel Works v Lex XI	2-1
Chirk AAA v St Mary's Ruabon	2-1
Gresford Ath v Druids U	3-0
Ruthin T v Buckley	0-3
Brecon Cor v Welshpool	3-0
Kidderminster H v Aberystwyth T	4-0
Stourbridge v Montgomery T	3-0
Caersws v Oswestry T	2-6
Llandrindod Wells v Knighton T	2-1
Blaenrhondda wo Tredomen Works	scr
Clydach U v Milford U	2-3
Ebbw Vale v Cheltenham T	1-3
Cwmbran v South Glamorgan Inst	1-4
Aberaman v Afan Lido	1-5

Second Round

Gresford Ath v Colwyn Bay	0-3
Pwllheli & District v Brymbo Steelworks	2-1
Bala T v Rhyl	1-6
Chirk AAA v Conwy U	1-7
Blaenau Ffestiniog v Flint Town U	2-5
Connah's Quay U v Caernarfon T	1-3
Greenfield v Buckley	3-3
Brecon Cor v Presteigne St Andrews	6-1
Newtown v Oswestry T	2-2, *8-6
Llanidloes T v Stourbridge	3-1
Llandrindod Wells v Towyn	11-0
Kidderminster H v Worcester C	3-1
Milford U v Taffs Well	3-4
Newport YMCA v Pontardawe Ath	2-2
Cheltenham T v Sully	3-1
Bridgend T v Afan Lido	6-0
Ammanford T v South Glamorgan Inst	1-1
Llanelli v Pembroke Borough	4-1
Lake U v Barry T	1-1
Pontllanfraith v Maesteg Park Ath	0-0
Spencer Works v Caerleon	2-1
Haverfordwest Co v Blaenrhondda	2-1
Abercynon v Ton Pentre	2-1
Merthyr Tydfil v BP Llandarcy	5-2
Cardiff Cor v Briton Ferry Ath	2-1

*After penalties

THIRD ROUND

Llandrindod Wells v Bangor C	1-6
Caernarfon T v Greenfield	3-0
Flint Town U v Pwllheli & District	2-5
Rhyl v Shrewsbury T	1-1, 0-3
Colwyn Bay v Conwy U	2-1
Brecon Cor v Kidderminster H	3-4
Wrexham v Oswestry T	4-0
Llanidloes T v Hereford U	1-1, 0-7
Cardiff Cor v Haverfordwest Co	0-2
Newport Co v Cardiff C	1-0
Llanelli v Cheltenham T	0-2
Merthyr Tydfil v Taffs Well	0-1
Bridgend T v Newport YMCA	3-1
Maesteg Park Ath v Barry T	2-3
South Glamorgan Inst v Abercynon Ath	1-2
Spencer Works v Swansea C	0-3

FOURTH ROUND

Bangor C v Colwyn Bay	1-2
Bridgend T v Kidderminster H	1-1, *6-4
Cheltenham T v Pwllheli & District	6-0
Haverfordwest Co v Barry T	2-1
Hereford U v Abercynon Ath	6-0
Swansea C v Shrewsbury T	2-1
Taffs Well v Caernarfon T	2-3
Wrexham v Newport Co	4-1

*After penalties.

FIFTH ROUND

Colwyn Bay v Haverfordwest Co	0-0, 2-1
Swansea C v Hereford U	3-1
Wrexham v Cheltenham T	3-2
Bridgend T v Caernarfon T	1-2

Semi-finals

Colwyn Bay v Swansea C	0-1, 0-3
Caernarvon T v Wrexham	0-2, 0-0

Final, First Leg: Wrexham 1, Swansea C 0

(At Wrexham, 10 May, 1983)

Wrexham: Niedzwiecki; King, Hill, Savage, Dowman, Keay, Cunnington, Buxton, Hunt, Muldoon, (Evans), Gregory.
Swansea C: Sander; Lewis, Richards, Charles, (Pascoe), Stevenson, Rajkovic, Stanley, James, Gale, Kennedy, Latchford.
Scorers: Dowman (Wrexham), Latchford and Gale (Swansea C)

Final, Second Leg: Swansea C 2, Wrexham 0

(At Swansea, 17 May, 1983)

Swansea C: Sander; Marustik, Richards, Charles, Kennedy, Lewis, Pascoe, (Stevenson), James, Gale, Stanley, Latchford.
Wrexham: Niedzwiecki; King, Bater, Savage, Evans, Keay, Hill, Buxton, Hunt, Muldoon, (Savage), Edwards.
Scorers: Latchford 2 (Swansea)

WELSH INTERMEDIATE CUP 1982–3

First Round

Porthmadog v Prestatyn	0-1
Rhos U v Bethesda Ath	4-0
Llanfairpwll v Nantlle Vale	7-0
Bont v Bow Street	6-1
Llanfair Caereinion v Guilsfield	8-4
Abermule Amateurs v Llanwddyn	1-2
Llantwit Fardre v Llanelli Steel	1-1, 1-3
Porthcawl T v Abercwmboi Ath	4-1
Ely Rangers v South Gower	1-1, 1-2

Second Round

UCNW Bangor v Pwllheli & District	2-1
Prestatyn v Llanfairpwll	2-2, 2-3
Holywell T v Rhos United	0-3
Buckley v St Mary's Ruabon	1-3
Chirk AAA v Rhos Aelwyd	1-3
Gresford Ath v Coedpoeth	3-0
Rhostyllen Villa v Llay Welfare	3-1
Llangedwyn v Barmouth & Dyffryn U	3-4
Dolgellau Ath v Llanfyllyn	2-3
Aberaeron v Berriew	0-4
Bont v Llanwddyn	3-3, 3-0
Montgomery T v Harlech T	2-2, 3-0
Llanfair Caereinion v Knighton T	1-1, 1-0
Fields Park v Pontyclun	4-2
Llanelli Steel v Pontardulais T	1-1, 1-2
Ebbw Vale v Tondu Robins	0-2
South Gower v Porthcawl T	2-2, 0-3
Hirwaun Welfare v Cardiff Cosmos	2-1

Third Round

Pilkingtons v Bala T	3-1
Rhos U v Hawarden Rangers	3-2
Abergele U v Llanfairpwll	0-1
Flint Town U v Connahs Quay Nomads	4-3
UCNW Bangor v Conwy U	0-1
Llandudno Amateurs v Llanberis Ath	3-3, 3-4
Blaenau Ffestiniog v Greenfield	1-3
Rhos Aelwyd v Llangollen	0-1
Lex XI v Rhostyllen Villa	0-0, 6-5
Brymbo Steelworks v St Mary's Ruabon	2-0
Mold Alexandra v Gresford Ath	1-2
Denbigh T v Ruthin	2-2, 2-0
Cefn Albion v Druids U	5-2
Bont v Llanfair Caereinion	0-2
Montgomery T v Presteigne St Andrews	4-0
Welshpool v Llandrindod Wells	3-0
UCW Aberystwyth v Barmouth & Dyffryn U	7-0
Berriew v Newtown	2-1
Llanidloes T v Aberystwyth T	0-1
Llanfyllin v Caersws Amateurs	2-3
Towyn v Rhayader T	0-0, 0-6
Taffs Well v Pontardulais T	4-0
Treharris Ath v Tonyrefail Welfare	4-0
South Glamorgan Inst v Cardiff Cor	1-4
Caerau v Afan Lido	3-0
Aberaman v Bryntirion Ath	0-2
Tondu Robins v Newport YMCA	1-1, 0-4
Hirwaun Welfare v Abergavenny Thursdays	4-1
Fields Park v Porthcawl T	2-1
Cwmbran T v BP Llandarcy	0-1
Newport Cor v Clydach U	1-2
Caldicot T v Llantwit Major	2-0

Fourth Round

Greenfield v Denbigh T	1-1, 3-1
Pilkingtons v Montgomery T	2-1
Gresford Ath v Welshpool	1-2
Llangollen v Conwy U	1-1, 1-3
Berriew v Llanfair Caereinion	0-0, 4-2
Lex XI v Cefn Albion	1-1, 3-1
Brymbo Steel Works v Llanfairpwll	1-0
Llandudno Amateurs v Rhos U	1-0
Flint Town U v Rhayader T	5-1
Taffs Well v Caerau	2-1
Treharris Ath v Caersws Amateurs	1-0
Caldicot T v BP Llandarcy	2-0
Newport YMCA v Aberystwyth T	0-1
Fields Park v UCW Aberystwyth	4-3
Bryntirion Ath v Hirwaun Welfare	1-2
Clydach U v Cardiff Cor	3-1

Fifth Round

Aberystwyth T v Llandudno Amateurs	5-2
Brymbo Steel Works v Pilkingtons	7-2
Welshpool v Taffs Well	3-3, 2-0
Greenfield v Clydach U	1-1, 3-2
Treharris Ath v Berriew	5-2
Caldicot T v Hirwaun Welfare	0-2
Flint Town U v Fields Park	2-2, 2-5
Lex XI v Conwy U	0-1

Sixth Round

Brymbo Steel Works v Aberystwyth T	2-1
Conwy U v Fields Park	2-0
Greenfield v Welshpool	2-3
Hirwaun Welfare v Treharris Ath	0-0, 0-3

Semi-finals

Treharris Ath v Welshpool *(at Rhayader)*	*3-5
Brymbo Steel Works v Conwy U *(at Denbigh)*	4-0

Final

Brymbo Steel Works v Welshpool *(at Oswestry)*	*3-4

*after extra time

WELSH INTERMEDIATE CUP 1975–83

(replacing Welsh Amateur Cup)

1975–76	Cardiff Coll of Ed 2, Shifnal T 1
1976–77	Welshpool 4, Whitchurch Alport 1
1977–78	Caernarvon T 1, Llanidloes T 0
1978–79	Flint Town U 0, Pontllanfraith 1
1979–80	Blaenau Ffestiniog 3:1, Brymbo Steel Works 3:0
1980–81	Connah's Quay Nomads 1, Newport YMCA 0
1981–82	Conwy U 1, Blaenau Ffestiniog 0
1982–83	Brymbo Steel Works 3, Welshpool 4

NON-LEAGUE FOOTBALL 1982–83

FA CHALLENGE TROPHY 1982–83

Preliminary Round

Curzon Ashton v Bridlington Trinity	2-1
Emley v Fleetwood Town	5-3
Alfreton Town v Accrington Stanley	1-3
Hednesford Town v Rhyl	2-2
Heanor Town v Bootle	2-3
Darlaston v Boston	1-2
Arnold v Long Eaton United	3-0
Dudley Town v Spalding United	0-0
Lye Town v Redditch United	1-1
Cheshunt v Boreham Wood	1-0
Banbury United v Dunstable	1-4
Tilbury v Cambridge City	6-0
Milton Keynes City v Wembley	0-5
Sudbury Town v Hillingdon Borough	0-2
Hounslow v Hampton	5-2
Sittingbourne v Folkestone	1-4
Metropolitan Police v Ashford Town	4-0
Feltham v Sheppey United	3-1
Canterbury City v Farnborough Town	1-0
Walton & Hersham v Kingstonian	0-5
Melksham Town v Andover	2-1
Maesteg Park v Bromsgrove Rovers	1-1
Welton Rovers v Ton Pentre	0-0
Salisbury v Barnstaple Town	1-1

Replays

Rhyl v Hednesford Town	1-0
Spalding United v Dudley Town	1-2
Redditch United v Lye Town	1-0
Bromsgrove Rovers v Maesteg Park	2-0
Ton Petre v Welton Rovers	1-0
Barnstaple Town v Salisbury	2-0

First Round Qualifying

Durham City v Formby	5-1
West Auckland Town v North Shields	1-3
Workington v Bootle	2-0
Netherfield v Burscough	1-2
South Liverpool v Mexboro' Town Ath	4-0
Consett v Crook Town	4-1
Goole Town v Evenwood Town	9-1
Rossendale United v Tow Law Town	0-0
Southport v Billingham Synthonia	2-1
Penrith v Accrington Stanley	5-0
Horden Colliery Welfare v Willington	4-1
Shildon v Horwich RMI (*at Bishop Auckland*)	2-2
Gateshead v Whitley Bay	3-1
Emley v Hyde United	3-8
Matlock Town v Prescot Cables	3-2
Stourbridge v Rhyl	0-0
Nantwich Town v Brereton Social	3-1
Buxton v Curzon Ashton	0-2
Colwyn Bay v Leek Town	2-1
Oswestry Town v Bilston	0-1
Moor Green v Macclesfield Town	3-0
Highgate United v Bromsgrove Rovers	0-2
Eastwood Town v Grantham	4-1
Ilkeston Town v Gainsborough Trinity	3-1
Boston v AP Leamington	1-1
Tamworth v Belper Town	1-1
Glossop v Arnold	1-1
Ashton United v Droylsden	0-0
Bedworth United v Sutton Coldfield Town	7-3
Sutton Town v Worksop Town	3-2
Redditch United v Dudley Town	1-1
Enderby Town v Hounslow	4-2
Witney Town v Chelmsford City	2-2
Corby Town v Oxford City	1-0
Hayes v Billericay Town	2-1
Wellingborough Town v Dunstable	2-1
Aveley v St Albans City	2-1
Kings Lynn v Lowestoft Town	5-0
Hornchurch v Ware	1-0
Tilbury v Chesham United	1-1
Cheshunt v Hillingdon Borough	1-1
Wembley v Harrow Borough	2-3
Poole Town v Feltham	2-0
Thanet United v Folkestone	2-2
Canterbury City v Crawley Town	2-2
Maidenhead United v Bognor Regis Town	3-2
Basingstoke Town v Lewes	0-2
Fareham Town v Kingstonian	2-3
Worthing v A'stone & Weybridge Town	1-0
Bromley v Welling United	3-2
Dover v Epsom & Ewell	1-1
Metropolitan Police v Staines Town	5-0
Waterlooville v Chatham Town	2-1
Tonbridge AFC v Wokingham Town	1-2
Mangotsfield United v Bridgend Town	0-2
Frome Town v Taunton Town	4-1
Barnstaple Town v Keynsham Town	2-3
Cinderford Town v Weston-super-Mare	1-2
Bideford v Ton Petre	1-1
Bridgwater Town v Dawlish	2-0
Shepton Mallet Town v Melksham Town	1-1
Clandown v Bridport	1-0

Byes

Ferryhill Athletic and Hertford Town

Replays

Tow Law Town v Rossendale United	3-1
Horwich RMI v Shildon	1-3
Rhyl v Stourbridge	2-0
AP Leamington v Boston	6-0
Belper Town v Tamworth	4-1
Arnold v Glossop	2-3
Droylsden v Ashton United	1-1
Dudley Town v Redditch United	2-0
Chelmsford City v Witney Town	1-0
Chesham United v Tilbury	0-1
Hillingdon Borough v Cheshunt	2-0
Folkestone v Thanet United	8-0
Crawley Town v Canterbury City	2-1
Epsom & Ewell v Dover	0-2
Ton Petre v Bideford	0-2
Melksham Town v Shepton Mallet Town	2-1

Second Replay

Droylsden v Ashton United	1-5

Second Round Qualifying

Ferryhill Athletic v Tow Law Town	1-4
Consett v South Liverpool	2-2
Penrith v Shildon	4-1
Horden CW v Durham City	5-0
Goole Town v North Shields	4-2
Southport v Gateshead	2-0
Matlock Town v Hyde United	5-2
Workington v Burscough	0-0
Bilston v AP Leamington	3-0
Rhyl v Glossop	3-1
Sutton Town v Dudley Town	3-0
Eastwood Town v Colwyn Bay	2-2
Enderby Town v Ashton United	2-1
Corby Town v Curzon Ashton	2-0
Bedworth United v Bromsgrove Rovers	1-2
Ilkeston Town v Nantwich Town	2-0
Belper Town v Moor Green	4-1
Hillingdon Borough v Bromley	0-1
Harrow Borough v Wellingborough Town	3-2
Kings Lynn v Dover	2-0

Metropolitan Police v Folkestone	1-0
Chelmsford City v Aveley	2-2
Worthing v Hornchurch	2-1
Crawley Town v Hertford Town	4-2
Maidenhead United v Hayes	0-3
Wokingham Town v Tilbury	2-3
(*1st tie abandoned, 64 mins – fog – 1-0*)	
Kingstonian v Lewes	0-1
Poole Town v Melksham Town	3-0
(*1st tie abandoned, 80 mins – fog – 5-0*)	
Keynsham Town v Bridgwater Town	0-2
Bideford v Frome Town	2-0
Waterlooville v Clandown	4-2
Weston-super-Mare v Bridgend Town	2-0

Replays

South Liverpool v Consett	3-0
Burscough v Workington	2-0
Colwyn Bay v Eastwood Town	3-2
(*at Rhyl FC*)	
Aveley v Chelmsford City	0-1

Third Round Qualifying

Penrith v South Bank	1-0
Spennymoor United v Southport	5-0
Goole Town v Morecambe	1-0
Burscough v Lancaster City	4-1
Tow Law Town v Horden Colliery Welfare	3-1
Whitby Town v South Liverpool	2-1
Sutton Town v Chorley	1-1
Witton Albion v Ilkeston Town	1-1
Alvechurch v Stalybridge Celtic	2-2
Winsford United v Matlock Town	0-2
Frickley Athletic v Colwyn Bay	1-1
Burton Albion v Belper Town	2-0
Rhyl v Enderby Town	2-1
Bilston v Walthamstow Avenue	2-1
Kettering Town v Barking	2-2
Hitchin Town v Corby Town	1-4
Kings Lynn v Bromsgrove Rovers	3-0
Chelmsford City v Harrow Borough	1-1
Barnet v Metropolitan Police	2-1
Hendon v Tilbury	0-3
Hayes v Harlow Town	1-0
Crawley Town v Croydon	1-6
Bromley v Trowbridge Town	4-0
Leatherhead v Waterlooville	2-5
Gravesend & Northfleet v Maidstone United	1-1
Carshalton Athletic v Worthing	1-0
Poole Town v Dulwich Hamlet	0-1
Lewes v Tooting & Mitcham United	1-0
Gloucester City v Minehead	4-1
Bideford v Weston-super-Mare	2-2
Bridgwater Town v Dorchester Town	0-1
Merthyr Tydfil v Cheltenham Town	1-2

Replays

Chorley v Sutton Town	4-0
Ilkeston Town v Witton Albion	3-1
Stalybridge Celtic v Alvechurch	2-0
Colwyn Bay v Frickley Athletic	2-0
(*at Rhyl FC*)	
Barking v Kettering Town	0-0
Harrow Borough v Chelmsford City	2-1
Maidstone United v Gravesend & Northfleet	3-0
Weston-super-Mare v Bideford	3-2

Second Replay

Barking v Kettering Town	0-2

First Round Proper

Ashington v Burscough	1-0
Bishop Auckland v Nuneaton Borough	1-3
Penrith v Stalybridge Celtic	1-2
Colwyn Bay v Chorley	1-5
Bangor City v Kings Lynn	1-1
Barrow v Rhyl	2-1
Matlock Town v Tow Law Town	0-1
Spennymoor United v Bilston	2-1
Corby Town v Altrincham	1-1
Goole Town v Mossley	1-1
Boston United v Marine	3-0
Kidderminster Har v Northwich Victoria	0-3
Whitby Town v Blyth Spartans	2-3
Burton Albion v Telford United	0-1
Runcorn v Scarborough	0-1
Stafford Rangers v Ilkestone Town	2-2
Yeovil Town v Sutton United	2-4
Waterlooville v Carshalton Athletic	1-2
Wycombe Wanderers v Wealdstone	2-1
Hastings United v Croydon	0-2
Maidstone United v Aylesbury United	1-0
Tilbury v Cheltenham Town	2-1
Lewes v Dartford	0-2
Dorchester Town v Gloucester City	3-2
Slough Town v Dagenham	0-1
Harrow Borough v Bromley	2-0
Hayes v Leytonstone/Ilford	0-1
Weston-super-Mare v Weymouth	0-0
Woking v Barnet	0-2
Enfield v Bishop's Stortford	2-1
Bath City v Worcester City	1-2
Dulwich Hamlet v Kettering Town	4-2

Replays

Kings Lynn v Bangor City	0-2
Altrincham v Corby Town	6-0
Mossley v Goole Town	2-0
(*1st replay aband after 45 mins – 1-0*)	
Ilkeston Town v Stafford Rangers	3-2
(*at Eastwood Town FC*)	
Weymouth v Weston-super-Mare	1-0

Second Round Proper

Stalybridge Celtic v Scarborough	1-3
Dorchester Town v Enfield	2-3
Wycombe Wanderers v Boston United	0-0
Tow Law Town v Altrincham	2-2
Carshalton Athletic v Tilbury	2-3
Barnet v Ilkeston Town	1-2
Weymouth v Leytonstone/Ilford	1-0
Worcester City v Dagenham	0-3
Harrow Borough v Sutton United	4-1
Spennymoor United v Telford United	0-0
Maidstone United v Dulwich Hamlet	2-2
Ashington v Barrow	1-1
Blyth Spartans v Nuneaton Borough	3-2
Chorley v Dartford	0-0
Northwich Victoria v Croydon	1-0
Bangor City v Mossley	1-0

Replays

Boston United v Wycombe Wanderers	1-1
Altrincham v Tow Law Town	3-0
Telford United v Spennymoor United	2-1
Dulwich Hamlet v Maidstone United	0-3
Barrow v Ashington	1-0
Dartford v Chorley	aet 3-0

Second Replay

Wycombe Wanderers v Boston United	0-2
(*at Kettering Town FC*)	

Third Round Proper

Barrow v Harrow Borough	1-1
Dagenham v Weymouth	3-0
Northwich Victoria v Bangor City	1-1
Ilkeston Town v Enfield	1-5
(*abandoned 76 mins – match awarded to Enfield FC*)	
Boston United v Maidstone United	2-1
Dartford v Tilbury	2-0
Blyth Spartans v Altrincham	2-0
Telford United v Scarborough	3-0

Replays

Harrow Borough v Barrow	1-1
Bangor City v Northwich Victoria	2-2

Second Replays

Barrow v Harrow Borough	0-2
(*at Stafford Rangers FC*)	
Northwich Victoria v Bangor City	1-0
(*at Wrexham FC*)	

Fourth Round Proper

Telford United v Dartford	4-1
Blyth Spartans v Northwich Victoria	1-1
Dagenham v Boston United	2-1
Harrow Borough v Enfield	5-1

Replay

Northwich Victoria v Blyth Spartans	3-2

Semi-Finals – First Leg

Telford United v Harrow Borough	0-2
Northwich Victoria v Dagenham	3-2

Semi-Finals – Second Leg

Harrow Borough v Telford United	aet 1-5
Dagenham v Northwich Victoria	0-1

(*Telford United won 5-3 on aggregate*)
(*Northwich Victoria won 4-2 on aggregate*)

Final

Northwich Victoria v Telford United	1-2
(*at Wembley Stadium*)	

THE ALLIANCE PREMIER FOOTBALL LEAGUE

BOB LORD CHALLENGE TROPHY 1982–83

First Round

Stafford Rangers v Nuneaton Borough	0-1, 2-0
Bangor City v Kettering Town	6-1, 1-1
Maidstone United v Yeovil Town	4-1, 3-1
Bath City v Wealdstone	0-1, 2-0
Barnet v Trowbridge Town	3-0, 2-0
Altrincham v Frickley Athletic	0-2, 5-0

Second Round

Runcorn v Stafford Rangers	3-0, 1-1
Barrow v Bangor City	2-0, 1-3
(*Bangor win on away goals*)	
Maidstone United v Bath City	2-0, 1-1
Dagenham v Enfield	3-2, 2-4
Worcester City v Telford United	1-0, 2-0
Barnet v Weymouth	2-0, 1-0
Northwich Victoria v Altrincham	3-2, 2-1
Boston United v Scarborough	0-5, 1-3

THIRD ROUND

Runcorn v Barrow	1-2, 2-0
Maidstone United v Enfield	1-3, 1-2
Worcester City v Barnet	0-2, 3-3
Northwich Victoria v Scarborough	1-2, 1-1

SEMI-FINALS

Runcorn v Enfield	2-3, 3-1
Worcester City v Scarborough	0-3, 3-2

Final – First Leg: Runcorn 1, Scarborough 1
Attendance 912

Second Leg: Scarborough 2, Runcorn 2
Attendance 1706

Winners for Season 1982–83: **Runcorn F.C.**
(Score 3-3 on aggregate after extra time, on away goals (5-4)

ALLIANCE PREMIER LEAGUE CHALLENGE SHIELD 1982

Runcorn 4, Weymouth 0
(at Runcorn, August 1982)
Played between 1981–82 champions (Runcorn) and the Bob Lord Trophy winners (Weymouth)

ALLIANCE PREMIER LEAGUE

	P	*W*	*D*	*L*	*F*	*A*	*W*	*D*	*L*	*F*	*A*	*Pts*
Enfield	42	16	3	2	57	21	9	6	6	38	27	84
Maidstone U	42	17	1	3	55	13	8	7	6	28	21	83
Wealdstone	42	13	5	3	45	17	9	8	4	35	24	79
Runcorn	42	15	5	1	50	21	7	3	11	23	32	74
Boston U	42	14	5	2	46	25	6	7	8	31	32	72
Telford U	42	16	3	2	46	17	4	8	9	23	31	71
Weymouth	42	13	6	2	37	14	7	4	10	26	34	70
Northwich Vic	42	15	5	1	48	22	3	5	13	20	41	64
Scarborough	42	10	6	5	39	23	7	6	8	32	35	63
Bath C	42	12	3	6	41	25	5	6	10	17	30	60
Nuneaton Bor	42	11	6	4	36	20	4	7	10	21	40	58
Altrincham	42	13	5	3	40	17	2	5	14	22	39	55
Bangor C	42	8	9	4	33	29	6	4	11	38	48	55
Dagenham	42	5	9	7	30	26	7	6	8	30	39	51
Barnet	42	9	3	9	37	39	7	0	14	18	39	51
Frickley Ath	42	11	6	4	41	25	1	7	13	25	52	49
Worcester C	42	10	7	4	43	33	2	3	16	15	54	46
Trowbridge	42	9	5	7	31	30	3	2	16	25	58	43
Kettering T	42	9	5	7	45	37	2	2	17	24	62	40
Yeovil T	42	10	4	7	37	36	1	3	17	26	63	40
Barrow	42	7	4	10	26	35	1	8	12	20	39	36
Stafford R	42	4	8	9	22	30	1	6	14	18	45	29

ISTHMIAN LEAGUE

PREMIER DIVISION

	P	*W*	*D*	*L*	*F*	*A*	*Pts*
Wycombe W	42	27	7	9	79	47	85
Leytonstone/Ilford	42	24	9	9	71	39	81
Harrow Bor	42	24	7	11	91	58	79
Hayes	42	23	9	10	63	41	78
Sutton U	42	20	8	14	96	71	68
Dulwich Hamlet	42	18	14	10	59	52	68
Slough T	42	18	13	11	73	36	67
Bognor Regis T	42	19	8	15	53	48	65
Tooting & Mitcham U	42	18	9	15	58	56	63
Billericay T	32	17	10	15	54	51	61
Croydon	42	17	9	16	68	58	60
Hendon	42	18	6	18	68	61	60
Bishop's St	42	17	9	16	61	58	60
Barking	42	14	14	14	47	55	46
Bromley	42	14	12	16	51	50	54
Carshalton Ath	42	15	9	18	58	60	54
Wokingham T	42	13	9	20	37	51	48
Walthamstow Ave	42	12	11	19	48	64	47
Staines T	42	12	11	19	62	79	47
Hitchin T	42	11	9	22	49	77	42
Woking	42	6	6	30	30	79	24
Leatherhead	42	4	5	33	36	121	17

SOUTHERN LEAGUE

PREMIER LEAGUE

	P	*W*	*D*	*L*	*F*	*A*	*Pts*
AP Leamington	38	25	4	9	78	50	79
Kidderminster Harr	38	23	7	8	69	40	76
Welling U	38	21	6	11	63	40	69
Chelmsford C	38	16	11	11	57	40	59
Bedworth U	38	16	11	11	47	39	59
Dartford	38	16	8	14	48	38	56
Gosport Bor	38	14	13	11	47	43	55
Fareham T	38	16	7	15	73	82	55
Dorchester T	38	14	12	12	52	50	54
Gravesend & Northfleet	38	14	12	12	49	50	54
Gloucester C	38	13	12	13	61	57	51
Witney T*	38	12	13	13	60	48	47
Alvechurch	38	13	8	17	60	66	47
Stourbridge	38	12	11	15	48	54	47
Corby T	38	12	11	15	58	67	47
Hastings U	38	11	11	16	48	61	44
Enderby T	38	11	9	18	44	62	42
Waterlooville	38	10	9	19	62	83	39
Poole T	38	9	9	20	57	73	36
Addlestone & Weybridge T	38	5	10	23	24	62	25

** Witney T – 2 points deducted for ineligible player.*

NORTHERN PREMIER LEAGUE

	P	*W*	*D*	*L*	*F*	*A*	*Pts*
Gateshead	42	32	4	6	114	43	100
Mossley	42	25	9	8	77	42	84
Burton Albion	42	24	9	9	81	53	81
Chorley	42	23	11	8	77	49	80
Macclesfield Town	42	24	8	10	71	49	80
Marine	42	17	17	8	81	57	68
Workington	42	19	10	13	71	55	67
Hyde United	42	18	12	12	91	63	66
King's Lynn	42	17	13	12	62	44	64
Matlock Town	42	18	10	14	70	65	64
Witton Albion	42	17	12	13	82	52	63
Buxton	42	17	9	16	60	62	60
Morecambe	42	16	11	15	75	66	59
Grantham	42	15	13	14	49	50	58
Southport	42	11	14	17	58	65	47
Goole Town	42	13	7	22	52	66	46
Gainsborough Trinity	42	11	9	22	60	71	42
Oswestry Town	42	10	8	24	56	99	38
South Liverpool	42	7	15	20	57	91	36
Tamworth	42	7	8	27	44	97	29
Worksop Town	42	5	10	27	50	98	25
Netherfield	42	2	9	31	28	129	15

President's Cup – Winners: King's Lynn, Runners-up: Burton Albion.
Challenge Shield – Winners: Gainsborough Trinity, Runners-up: Mossley.

ISTHMIAN LEAGUE

DIVISION ONE

	P	*W*	*D*	*L*	*F*	*A*	*Pts*
Worthing	40	25	6	9	76	39	81
Harlow T	40	21	14	8	84	55	74
Farnborough T	40	20	13	7	69	39	73
Hertford T	40	20	11	9	70	61	71
Oxford C	40	19	13	8	70	49	70
Boreham Wood	40	21	6	13	62	42	69
Metropolitan Police	40	19	9	12	77	57	66
Walton & Hersham	40	17	6	17	65	59	57
Hampton	40	15	10	15	62	60	55
Wembley	40	14	10	16	62	61	52
Aveley	40	15	7	18	52	62	52
Kingstonian	40	13	12	15	53	53	51
Tilbury	40	12	10	18	41	47	46
Feltham	40	11	12	17	45	54	45
Chesham U	40	13	6	21	43	70	45
Epsom & Ewell	40	10	14	16	44	49	44
Lewes	40	12	8	20	47	71	44
Cheshunt	40	10	13	17	41	49	43
Hornchurch	40	11	8	21	45	74	41
Maidenhead U	40	10	10	20	47	87	40
St Albans C*	40	10	9	21	52	79	37

** 2 points deducted.*

DIVISION TWO

	P	*W*	*D*	*L*	*F*	*A*	*Pts*
Clapton	42	30	4	8	96	46	94
Windsor & Eton	42	27	7	8	98	43	88
Barton R	42	26	6	10	86	48	84
Leyton Wingate	42	25	8	9	111	41	83
Basildon U	42	23	13	6	92	42	82
Uxbridge	42	22	12	8	80	42	78
Hungerford T	42	22	10	10	82	39	76
Corinthian Cas	42	23	6	13	95	48	75
Egham T	42	21	8	13	77	67	71
Tring T	42	20	10	12	86	59	70
Letchworth Garden C*	42	18	13	11	68	53	66
Southall	42	18	7	17	81	80	61
Molesey	42	17	9	16	73	56	60
Dorking T	42	16	9	18	56	75	54
Hemel Hempstead	42	12	14	16	53	59	50
Rainham T	42	14	4	24	57	94	46
Eastbourne U	42	10	6	26	54	104	36
Epping T	42	6	8	28	29	89	26
Ware	42	6	6	30	34	97	24
Finchley	42	4	12	26	28	92	24
Horsham	42	5	7	30	32	106	22
Harwich & Parkestone	42	5	7	30	42	130	22

** 1 point deducted.*

SOUTHERN LEAGUE

MIDLAND DIVISION

	P	*W*	*D*	*L*	*F*	*A*	*Pts*
Cheltenham T	32	22	5	5	65	29	71
Sutton Coldfield T	32	21	7	4	62	24	70
Forest Green R	32	21	3	8	68	32	66
Merthyr Tydfil	32	17	7	8	64	45	58
Willenhall T	32	17	6	9	74	49	57
Oldbury U	32	16	6	10	52	49	54
Banbury U	32	15	3	14	59	55	48
Bridgend T	32	12	11	9	46	37	47
Wellingborough T	32	13	7	12	49	37	46
Bromsgrove R	32	13	5	14	47	47	44
Dudley T	32	12	7	13	40	45	43
Bridgwater T	32	12	6	14	42	43	42
Aylesbury U	32	12	5	15	37	51	41
Redditch U	32	8	6	18	51	73	30
Taunton T	32	5	7	20	30	64	22
Minehead	32	5	7	20	24	62	22
Milton Keynes C	32	0	4	28	22	90	4

SOUTHERN DIVISION

	P	*W*	*D*	*L*	*F*	*A*	*Pts*
Fisher Ath	34	23	5	6	79	34	74
Folkestone	34	22	6	6	79	41	72
RS Southampton	34	21	7	6	66	30	70
Dunstable	34	19	5	10	57	39	62
Hillingdon Bor	34	14	11	9	41	30	53
Salisbury	34	14	10	10	58	49	52
Crawley T	23	14	9	11	51	43	51
Ashford T	34	13	10	11	51	41	49
Tonbridge AFC	34	14	5	15	57	57	47
Hounslow	34	11	12	11	46	47	45
Canterbury C	34	12	9	13	52	63	45
Cambridge C	34	12	5	17	56	63	41
Dover	34	11	7	16	35	52	40
Thanet U	34	10	5	19	30	61	35
Basingstoke T	34	8	10	16	37	56	34
Woodford T	34	6	9	19	29	57	27
Andover	34	6	8	20	28	53	26
Erith & Belvedere	34	5	9	20	26	62	24

ALLIANCE PREMIER LEAGUE 1982–83

	Altrincham	Bangor C	Barnet	Barrow	Bath C	Boston U	Dagenham	Enfield	Frickley Ath	Kettering T	Maidstone U	Northwich Vic	Nuneaton Bor	Runcorn	Scarborough	Stafford R	Telford U	Trowbridge T	Wealdstone	Weymouth	Worcester C	Yeovil
Altrincham	—	2-0	3-0	2-2	0-0	2-2	2-0	2–2	2-2	3-1	0-2	3-0	1-2	2-1	2-1	4-0	1-0	2-0	0-1	1-0	2-0	4-1
Bangor C	1-0	—	1-0	2-2	0-0	0-1	1-1	0-0	1-0	4-2	2-2	1-1	5-2	1-2	0-3	1-0	1-1	4-3	2-2	4-3	0-2	2-2
Barnet	2-1	1-3	—	2-1	2-1	1-4	2-2	1-3	4-1	2-3	1-3	4-2	1-0	2-0	2-3	1-0	0-2	1-3	0-0	1-2	3-1	4-4
Barrow	2-2	1-5	0-1	—	0-1	1-1	1-2	0-3	2-0	2-0	0-3	0-0	2-2	1-2	1-2	2-1	0-5	3-2	0-2	3-0	2-0	3-1
Bath C	0-2	1-2	0-2	4-1	—	3-2	3-1	2-2	4-3	2-1	0-1	3-0	3-0	2-1	2-3	5-1	0-0	2-0	3-2	0-1	0-0	2-0
Boston U	3-0	4-3	1-0	2-1	2-2	—	3-3	0-2	2-1	2-1	1-0	1-0	1-1	2-4	1-0	1-1	4-0	3-0	0-0	3-2	4-1	6-3
Dagenham	1-1	1-1	1-2	0-0	0-1	1-1	—	1-0	4-1	2-3	0-1	3-1	0-0	3-1	1-1	3-3	1-1	0-1	1-2	1-2	3-3	3-0
Enfield	2-1	6-2	5-0	2-0	3-0	4-2	2-1	—	2-2	5-2	1-0	2-1	1-1	0-0	5-3	0-1	6-2	2-0	0-1	2-1	4-0	3-1
Frickley Ath	3-0	3-3	0-1	1-1	2-1	2-0	1-2	5-2	—	3-2	2-1	0-0	2-1	0-2	2-1	3-0	2-2	2-2	2-2	1-2	2-0	3-0
Kettering T	3-2	3-4	3-1	3-1	4-2	2-0	1-2	0-2	4-1	—	1-3	1-4	0-0	3-1	2-2	2-2	1-2	1-1	1-3	1-1	4-1	5-2
Maidstone U	3-2	6-1	2-0	2-0	0-1	2-0	1-3	1-1	4-0	5-1	—	1-0	2-0	2-0	6-0	1-0	1-0	6-0	0-3	3-0	5-0	2-1
Northwich Vic	2-1	1-4	1-0	1-0	3-0	1-1	3-0	3-1	2-1	2-1	2-1	—	2-2	2-0	1-1	2-1	2-1	6-3	3-3	1-1	3-0	5-0
Nuneaton Bor	3-1	2-1	1-0	1-1	5-0	1-2	1-1	0-2	5-1	0-0	2-2	2-1	—	0-2	0-2	1-1	2-1	2-0	1-1	2-0	2-0	3-1
Runcorn	1-0	1-2	2-0	2-1	1-0	3-2	5-1	2-2	3-3	6-0	1-1	1-1	3-1	—	2-1	4-1	0-0	3-2	2-1	1-0	3-1	4-1
Scarborough	1-1	2-0	0-2	1-1	0-1	0-0	1-1	0-2	1-2	3-0	2-1	5-1	3-0	3-2	—	2-1	1-1	5-2	1-2	2-0	4-1	2-2
Stafford R	2-3	1-1	1-0	2-0	1-1	0-2	1-2	0-3	1-1	1-1	2-3	1-1	1-2	0-1	0-0	—	1-1	3-2	2-1	1-2	0-0	1-3
Telford U	1-1	2-0	3-0	1-3	2-0	3-2	3-0	4-3	1-1	2-1	3-1	3-0	2-0	4-0	0-2	2-0	—	3-1	0-0	2-0	2-0	3-2
Trowbridge T	3-2	3-2	0-2	2-1	1-1	1-2	2-2	2-1	2-0	2-1	0-2	0-2	0-2	1-2	1-1	5-3	2-0	—	0-0	0-0	2-3	2-1
Wealdstone	1-1	2-0	6-0	4-0	1-1	0-0	3-1	1-3	2-0	4-0	0-0	2-1	1-2	1-0	2-2	3-2	2-0	4-0	—	2-4	2-0	2-0
Weymouth	2-0	2-1	1-3	1-1	1-0	4-2	0-1	1-0	0-0	1-1	0-0	3-0	3-0	1-1	2-0	0-0	0-0	2-1	4-1	—	4-2	2-0
Worcester C	1-0	1-1	4-2	2-1	1-4	1-1	1-4	1-1	4-4	2-0	1-1	3-0	1-1	1-0	1-3	3-0	1-0	4-1	1-3	3-3	—	2-1
Yeovil T	2-1	3-2	4-2	2-2	1-0	0-4	2-0	1-3	2-1	2-1	0-0	2-4	6-2	1-1	2-1	0-0	3-4	0-1	1-5	0-2	3-0	—

SOUTHERN LEAGUE PREMIER DIVISION 1982–83

	Addlestone & Weybridge T	Alvechurch	AP Leamington	Bedworth U	Chelmsford C	Corby T	Dartford	Dorchester T	Enderby T	Fareham T	Gloucester C	Gosport Bor	Gravesend & Northfleet	Hastings U	Kidderminster Harr	Poole T	Stourbridge	Waterlooville	Welling U	Witney T
Addlestone & Weybridge T	—	0-3	0-2	0-0	0-1	1-1	0-2	2-1	1-2	1-2	1-2	0-3	3-0	1-1	0-0	1-2	0-1	2-0	2-0	1-1
Alvechurch	4-0	—	2-3	2-0	1-1	0-2	1-0	2-2	4-2	1-2	1-1	1-0	1-4	4-1	2-1	2-1	0-5	4-2	3-1	3-1
AP Leamington	2-0	3-2	—	2-0	2-4	1-0	2-1	4-2	1-0	3-2	2-2	2-1	2-2	1-0	1-3	4-1	2-1	2-1	3-1	1-0
Bedworth U	0-0	3-1	0-0	—	0-0	3-1	0-1	1-0	2-0	2-1	1-0	2-2	1-1	2-1	0-0	2-0	0-1	2-2	2-0	1-2
Chelmsford C	0-0	4-0	1-2	0-1	—	1-3	0-2	0-0	1-0	3-0	3-1	1-0	2-3	1-2	0-1	2-0	1-1	1-1	2-3	1-1
Corby T	5-1	4-2	3-2	2-0	0-3	—	2-1	1-0	3-3	1-1	1-2	0-0	0-3	0-2	0-1	3-1	3-4	3-3	0-2	3-3
Dartford	3-0	2-0	1-3	2-0	0-2	3-0	—	1-2	1-0	1-1	1-0	4-0	0-2	2-1	1-2	0-1	1-0	1-1	2-0	4-1
Dorchester T	2-0	3-1	2-4	0-1	2-4	2-2	1-1	—	1-1	3-1	1-1	0-0	2-0	0-0	2-0	0-0	0-0	3-2	2-1	2-2
Enderby T	0-0	2-1	2-2	2-2	0-2	0-1	1-2	2-3	—	4-3	0-1	1-1	1-0	1-2	3-1	2-0	1-1	1-1	0-0	0-3
Fareham T	1-0	3-1	2-1	1-4	3-2	2-0	2-2	1-4	3-2	—	0-0	1-5	4-0	2-3	4-0	4-3	1-0	2-1	0-3	2-3
Gloucester C	3-3	2-2	2-1	0-1	2-2	1-1	1-0	3-1	0-2	3-4	—	1-0	3-4	4-0	1-2	3-1	1-0	2-2	0-2	2-2
Gosport Bor	1-1	3-1	0-1	2-0	0-1	1-1	1-0	0-0	4-1	4-2	0-5	—	2-1	0-0	1-0	1-0	2-2	0-2	0-3	2-0
Gravesend & Northfleet	1-0	0-0	1-0	2-0	0-0	1-2	1-1	2-0	0-1	1-0	0-2	1-1	—	1-4	0-0	6-3	3-0	1-3	2-0	0-6
Hastings U	2-1	0-4	0-3	1-1	1-3	3-3	1-1	0-1	3-0	2-2	2-1	3-0	0-0	—	0-3	0-1	5-3	2-4	1-0	1-1
Kidderminster Harr	2-0	3-1	2-1	4-1	3-0	3-2	1-1	3-0	5-1	3-5	3-1	1-2	2-1	2-1	—	2-0	1-0	2-0	0-0	2-2
Poole Town	1-2	1-1	3-0	1-1	2-3	2-2	2-3	0-2	0-2	2-2	3-3	1-1	1-1	3-1	2-4	—	1-2	6-2	1-2	3 1
Stourbridge	1-0	1-1	2-1	2-1	0-4	2-1	0-0	1-3	3-1	1-2	2-2	0-2	1-1	1-1	1-1	1-3	—	2-1	1-2	2-0
Waterlooville	5-0	2-1	2-8	0-4	3-1	2-1	3-0	0-2	0-1	2-2	1-2	1-3	1-2	1-1	2-4	3-2	2-1	—	0-2	1-1
Welling U	3-0	1-0	1-2	2-4	0-0	0-1	2-0	3-1	3-0	4-2	4-1	1-1	1-1	2-0	1-0	1-1	2-1	6-3	—	3-1
Witney T	2-0	0-0	1-2	1-2	0-0	5-0	1-0	3-0	1-2	7-1	1-0	1-1	0-0	1-0	0-2	1-2	1-1	3-0	0-1	—

ISTHMIAN LEAGUE PREMIER DIVISION RESULTS 1982–83

	Barking	Billericay	Bishop Stortford	Bognor Regis	Bromley	Carshalton Athletic	Croydon	Dulwich	Harrow Borough	Hayes	Hendon	Hitchin	Leatherhead	Leytonstone & Ilford	Slough Town	Staines Town	Sutton United	Tooting & Mitchum	Walthamstow	Woking	Wokingham	Wycombe Wanderers
Barking	—	1-0	2-2	0-0	0-4	2-2	2-0	0-1	1-2	1-0	0-0	0-2	4-0	0-3	1-1	1-1	2-1	1-2	3-0	3-0	1-0	3-2
Billericay Town	2-0	—	1-0	1-0	0-2	1-1	1-0	1-0	1-2	1-0	5-0	3-1	0-0	0-1	0-0	3-0	0-2	2-1	1-1	2-2	1-1	1-2
Bishop Stortford	5-0	1-2	—	2-3	0-1	1-2	0-3	1-0	3-2	2-4	2-3	2-1	4-2	0-4	0-0	0-0	2-2	3-1	0-0	2-0	3-1	3-1
Bognor Regis	2-0	4-0	0-0	—	0-0	3-2	1-6	1-0	3-1	1-1	2-0	0-3	1-0	2-1	2-0	2-3	2-1	2-0	2-0	0-0	1-1	0-4
Bromley	0-0	1-1	0-1	2-1	—	4-1	2-1	1-2	0-0	2-4	0-0	0-0	2-0	1-1	0-0	2-1	2-3	0-2	2-2	2-0	0-0	0-3
Carlshalton Athletic	4-1	2-1	5-2	0-1	0-1	—	5-1	1-1	1-1	0-2	1-0	2-2	2-2	3-1	2-2	1-2	1-5	1-0	1-1	3-0	0-1	0-1
Croydon	2-1	0-2	2-1	2-2	2-0	0-1	—	1-4	0-1	0-0	2-1	1-1	3-1	1-0	1-1	2-3	0-0	1-0	1-2	4-1	3-0	2-0
Dulwich Hamlet	2-0	3-3	2-2	2-1	3-2	0-1	1-1	—	3-1	0-0	1-5	2-1	1-0	2-1	1-0	2-1	1-3	2-1	2-0	1-1	1-2	2-1
Harrow Borough	0-0	4-0	4-0	2-1	3-3	2-0	4-3	4-2	—	2-1	3-1	5-1	3-0	1-2	1-0	2-1	5-3	2-2	3-1	2-0	1-0	4-2
Hayes	1-2	1-0	1-1	1-0	0-0	2-0	2-1	1-2	1-0	—	2-0	1-2	3-1	2-2	2-1	2-1	4-3	1-0	2-0	3-1	1-0	4-1
Hendon	2-1	1-0	1-2	1-0	0-1	2-4	2-4	0-0	3-1	2-1	—	0-1	4-0	0-0	3-0	6-2	0-2	0-0	4-1	2-0	2-0	3-4
Hitchin Town	1-1	0-3	0-2	2-0	0-2	1-0	1-1	3-1	1-1	0-2	1-6	—	2-2	0-2	1-3	2-1	1-4	1-1	2-0	1-2	1-2	0-3
Leatherhead	0-1	1-2	1-2	0-2	1-5	1-0	2-5	2-3	1-5	1-1	1-2	1-4	—	1-5	0-1	1-0	1-4	0-8	0-2	2-1	2-1	0-3
Leystone & Ilford	0-0	2-2	1-0	1-0	4-2	2-0	3-2	2-0	3-2	0-0	1-0	4-1	2-0	—	2-1	2-1	0-2	0-1	2-0	2-0	2-0	2-3
Slough Town	1-1	2-1	2-0	2-0	1-2	4-0	0-0	0-0	4-2	0-1	6-0	1-1	5-1	1-0	—	1-1	6-0	5-0	7-2	3-0	0-1	2-3
Staines Town	2-2	4-1	1-0	0-2	1-0	1-3	1-1	1-1	2-2	2-1	2-4	3-1	2-2	1-1	0-2	—	4-5	1-1	0-1	5-1	1-0	1-1
Sutton United	1-1	1-1	1-0	1-1	3-0	1-0	3-4	2-2	2-3	2-0	4-2	4-2	11-1	2-3	0-2	4-0	—	3-1	1-1	1-2	2-4	1-2
Tooting & Mitchum	3-1	2-1	2-5	1-2	2-1	2-0	0-2	1-1	0-4	4-2	0-0	3-2	2-1	1-3	2-1	5-0	2-2	—	2-0	2-1	1-1	1-0
Walthamstow Avenue	1-2	1-2	0-1	4-1	2-1	1-1	2-1	1-1	2-0	2-2	0-1	1-0	3-2	0-1	0-1	3-1	2-3	2-2	—	5-2	0-1	1-1
Woking	0-1	0-2	0-0	0-2	2-1	0-1	1-2	0-2	0-2	1-2	1-4	1-2	2-1	1-1	1-1	2-3	0-1	1-2	0-1	—	1-0	0-2
Wokingham	1-2	0-2	0-1	0-3	2-0	1-4	1-0	0-0	2-1	0-1	2-1	2-0	3-1	2-2	0-2	0-2	2-0	1-2	0-0	0-2	—	1-1
Wycombe Wanderers	2-7	4-1	1-3	1-0	1-0	1-0	2-1	1-1	2-1	0-1	1-0	2-0	5-0	1-0	1-1	4-3	2-0	3-0	2-0	1-0	1-1	—

HITACHI CUP, 1982–83

Preliminary Round

Uxbridge v Leyton W	2-2, 1-0

First Round

Tilbury v Billericay T	1-2
Boreham W v Basildon U	0-1
Lewes v Harlow T	1-4
Farnborough v Uxbridge	3-1
Aveley v Barking	0-3
Bromley v Dorking T	2-1
Dulwich H v Epsom & E	3-0
Tooting & M v Slough T	1-0
Horsham v Chesham U	0-1
Barton R v Wokingham T	1-0
Clapton v Kingstonian	2-2, 1-4
Cheshunt v Eastbourne U	3-1
Rainham T v Carshalton Ath	2-3
Wycombe W v Harrow	2-1
Staines T v Egham T	2-2, 3-0
Met Police v Bishop's Stortford	4-1
Maidenhead U v Windsor & Eton	3-4
Oxford C v Feltham	1-0
Leatherhead v Molesey	0-2
Hampton v Southall	3-0
Worthing v Harwich	8-0
Sutton U v Ware	6-1
Corinthian Cas v Hertford T	0-1
Hitchin T v Tring T	5-1
Leytonstone v Walton & H	0-1
Bognor Regis v Wembley	2-1
Hendon v Hemel Hempstead	3-1
Finchley v Walthamstow	1-2
Letchworth v Hornchurch	1-3
Epping T v Woking	0-3
Hungerford T v Hayes	0-3
St Albans v Croydon	4-2

Second Round

Billericay v Basildon U	3-2
Harlow T v Farnborough	0-2
Barking v Bromley	2-2, 1-0
Dulwich H v Tooting & M	1-1, 0-2
Chesham U v Barton R	1-0
Kingstonian v Cheshunt	1-0
Carshalton Ath v Wycombe W	3–4
Staines T v Met Police	0-4
Windsor & Eton v Oxford C	3-1
Molesey v Hampton	1-2
Worthing v Sutton U	1-2
Hertford T v Hitchin T	1-0
Walton & H v Bognor Regis	2-4
Hendon v Walthamstow	2-0
Hornchurch v Woking	2-1
Hayes v St Albans	3-0

Third Round

Billericay v Farnborough	1-2
Bromley v Dulwich H	4-2
Chesham U v Kingstonian	0-1
Wycombe W v Met Police	3-2
Windsor & Eton v Hampton	4-1
Sutton U v Hertford T	3-0
Bognor Regis v Hendon	3-1
Hornchurch v Hayes	3-0

Fourth Round

Farnborough v Bromley	1-1, 0-1
Kingstonian v Wycombe W	0-1
Windsor & Eton v Sutton U	3-4
Bognor Regis v Hornchurch	2-1

Semi-finals

Bromley v Wycombe W	0-2
Sutton U v Bognor Regis	2-0

Final

Wycombe W v Sutton U	0-1, 1-1

SOUTHERN LEAGUE CHALLENGE CUP 1982–83

First Round (2 legs)

Alvechurch v Willenhall T	4-2, 2-0
Corby T v Banbury U	5-1, 0-1
Bridgend T v Dorchester T	0-1, 0-3
AP Leamington v Sutton Coldfield T	0-1, 2-0
Gloucester C v Forest Green R	1-2, 2-3
Dudley T v Oldbury U	0-1, 1-1
Redditch U v Witney T	0-1, 0-1
Cheltenham T v Bromsgrove R	3-2, 3-1
Merthyr Tydfil v Minehead	4-2, 1-0
Aylesbury U v Milton Keynes C	0-0, 1-1, 3-1
Bridgwater T v Taunton T	2-1, 2-1
Kidderminster Harriers v Stourbridge	2-0, 0-1
Bedworth U v Enderby T	5-2, 2-1
Gosport Bor v Basingstoke T	2-2, 1-0
Folkestone v Erith & Belvedere	1-0, 1-0
RS Southampton v Fareham T	0-2, 1-1
Fisher Ath v Hillingdon Bor	1-0, 1-1
Gravesend & Northfleet v Dartford	1-3, 0-2
Canterbury c v Ashford T	2-0, 2-2
Woodford T v Addlestone & Weybridge T	1-1, 1-1, 0-1
Hastings U v Chelmsford C	1-1, 1-1, 3-2
Crawley T v Thanet U	4-0, 3-1
Dunstable v Cambridge C	4-0, 1-0
Welling U v Hounslow	1-1, 2-3
Dover v Tonbridge AFC	1-1, 0-3
Andover v Salisbury	1-2, 1-2
Poole T v Waterlooville	3-2, 1-4

Bye: Wellingborough T.

Second Round

Alvechurch v Wellingborough T	3-3, 6-1
Corby T v Dorchester T	3-0
AP Leamington v Forest Green R	1-1, 5-3
Witney T v Cheltenham T	1-2
Merthyr Tydfil v Aylesbury U	2-1
Kidderminster Harriers v Bedworth U	2-1
Gosport Bor v Folkestone	0-0, 1-3
Fareham T v Fisher Ath	2-5
Dartford v Canterbury C	1-2
Addlestone & Weybridge T v Hastings U	0-2
Crawley T v Dunstable	0-2
Hounslow v Tonbridge AFC	2-2, 3-2

Byes: Oldbury U, Bridgwater T, Salisbury, Waterlooville.

Third Round

Alvechurch v Corby T	3-0
AP Leamington v Oldbury U	5-1
Cheltenham T v Merthyr Tydfil	2-1
Bridgwater T v Kidderminster Harriers	1-3
Folkestone v Fisher Ath	2-1
Canterbury C v Hastings U	0-2
Dunstable v Hounslow	1-1, 6-5
Salisbury v Waterlooville	2-4

Fourth Round

Alvechurch v AP Leamington	2-0
Cheltenham T v Kidderminster Harriers	0-0, 1-0
Folkestone v Hastings U	3-2
Dunstable v Waterlooville	1-3

Semi-Finals (2 Legs)

Alvechurch v Cheltenham T	1-0, 2-2
Folkestone v Waterlooville	0-3, 3-2

Final (2 Legs)

Alvechurch v Waterlooville	6-1, 1-1

THE FOOTBALL COMBINATION

	P	W	D	L	F	A	Pts
Queens Park R	42	29	8	5	113	47	66
West Ham U	42	26	11	5	102	53	63
Tottenham H	42	25	10	7	92	46	60
Watford	42	22	10	10	78	56	54
Ipswich T	42	20	12	10	74	53	52
Arsenal	42	17	13	12	65	46	47
Chelsea	42	19	7	16	80	61	45
Norwich C	42	14	17	11	59	58	45
Fulham	42	16	10	16	54	52	42
Oxford U	42	18	6	18	72	76	42
Bristol R	42	13	12	17	62	85	38
Swansea C	42	14	8	20	51	60	36
Luton T	42	13	9	20	58	63	35
Brighton & HA	42	10	15	17	53	65	35
Millwall	42	9	17	16	63	77	35
Charlton Ath	42	11	13	18	60	77	35
Birmingham C	42	13	9	20	51	76	35
Leicester C	42	11	12	19	65	84	34
Swindon T	42	12	10	20	52	85	34
Southampton	42	10	13	19	66	77	33
Crystal Palace	42	10	11	21	55	86	31
Reading	42	9	9	24	52	94	27

THE CENTRAL LEAGUE

FIRST DIVISION

	P	W	D	L	F	A	Pts
West Bromwich A	30	19	6	5	53	18	44
Aston Villa	30	20	3	7	71	33	43
Everton	30	17	8	5	47	20	42
Manchester U	30	18	5	7	60	28	41
Sheffield W	30	16	6	8	59	39	38
Liverpool	30	16	5	9	63	37	37
Stoke C	30	14	6	10	54	57	34
Newcastle U	30	12	9	9	41	34	33
Blackburn R	30	12	6	12	49	53	30
Sheffield U	30	11	8	11	42	48	30
Leeds U	30	6	11	13	30	49	23
Bury	30	8	6	16	44	66	22
Coventry C	30	7	5	18	34	63	19
Huddersfield T	30	6	5	19	32	53	17
Blackpool	30	7	1	22	35	74	15
Wolverhampton W	30	3	6	21	19	61	12

SOUTH-EAST COUNTIES LEAGUE

	P	W	D	L	F	A	Pts
Norwich City	28	20	8	0	79	16	48
West Ham United	28	18	4	6	79	33	40
Queens Park Rangers	28	15	6	7	88	36	36
Watford	28	15	4	9	68	56	34
Ipswich Town	28	10	12	6	51	43	32
Chelsea	28	10	9	9	53	53	29
Charlton Athletic	28	12	5	11	52	54	29
Tottenham Hotspur	28	12	5	11	51	53	29
Millwall	28	8	7	13	40	51	25
Gillingham	28	7	10	11	46	57	24
Arsenal	28	8	7	13	40	59	23
Orient	28	6	9	13	49	71	21
Southend United	28	8	5	15	37	68	21
Portsmouth	28	5	8	15	28	64	18
Fulham	28	2	9	17	25	72	13

NORTH WEST COUNTIES LEAGUE

FIRST DIVISION

	P	W	D	L	F	A	Pts
Burscough	38	26	7	5	93	45	59
Rhyl	38	23	11	4	76	30	57
Horwich RMI	38	22	10	6	77	35	54
Stalybridge Celtic	38	17	15	6	60	32	49
Winsford U	38	18	10	10	72	48	46
Darwen	38	17	12	9	68	46	46
Lancaster C	38	17	11	10	69	54	45
Congleton T	38	13	14	11	52	35	40
Penrith	38	17	6	15	68	61	40
Accrington S	38	13	12	13	56	55	38
Leek T	38	14	9	15	42	44	37
Curzon Ashton	38	14	8	16	46	47	36
Ashton U	38	13	10	15	55	69	36
Bootle*	38	14	6	18	55	79	32
Prescot Cables	38	9	13	16	50	60	31
Formby	38	10	8	20	48	68	28
Leyland Motors	38	7	10	21	34	74	24
Glossop	38	6	11	21	29	67	23
St Helens T	38	5	10	23	29	80	20
Nantwich T	38	6	5	27	43	93	17

* *Two points deducted for fielding ineligible player.*

SECOND DIVISION

	P	W	D	L	F	A	Pts
Radcliffe Bor	38	33	4	1	110	25	70
Caernarfon T	38	28	7	3	85	27	63
Wren Rovers	38	23	7	8	84	38	53
Eastwood Hanley	38	23	7	8	81	42	53
Kirkby T	38	22	3	13	80	60	47
Irlam T	38	17	8	13	79	52	42
Chadderton	38	18	6	14	55	51	42
Rossendale U	38	15	10	13	75	68	40
Ford Motors	38	18	4	16	61	59	40
Ellesmere Port & N	38	17	5	16	56	68	39
Skelmersdale U	38	13	11	14	70	63	37
Fleetwood T	38	12	8	18	54	80	32
Atherton LR	38	11	9	18	52	70	31
Lytham	38	11	5	22	54	71	27
Great Harwood T	38	8	10	20	54	76	26
Salford	38	10	6	22	43	86	26
Droylsden	38	11	5	22	49	71	25
Prescot BI	38	10	5	23	46	81	25
Padiham	38	8	6	24	41	74	22
New Mills	38	7	4	27	39	106	18

NORTHERN COUNTIES EAST LEAGUE

PREMIER DIVISION

	P	W	D	L	F	A	Pts
Shepshed Charterhouse	38	24	8	6	109	34	56
Eastwood T	38	21	11	6	71	41	53
Belper T	38	21	10	7	75	32	52
Spalding U	38	19	14	5	69	44	52
Guiseley	38	21	9	8	72	35	51
Winterton R	38	20	9	9	55	32	49
Thackley	38	18	11	9	62	42	47
Arnold	38	17	12	9	77	56	46
Heanor T	38	17	12	9	50	43	46
Emley	38	14	11	13	74	58	39
Appleby-Frodingham Ath	38	15	9	14	59	61	39
Guisborough T	38	16	6	16	59	59	38
Alfreton T	38	16	3	19	47	55	35
Sutton T	38	12	10	16	59	64	34
Ilkeston T	38	10	11	17	50	73	31
Boston	38	10	11	17	53	91	31
Bridlington Tr	38	10	3	25	39	89	23
Skegness T	38	5	8	25	46	82	18
Bentley Vic Wel	38	6	2	30	44	107	14
Wexborough T Ath	38	2	2	34	32	104	6

Resigning: Shepshed Charterhouse, Skegness Town.

DIVISION ONE (NORTH)

	P	W	D	L	F	A	Pts
Scarborough	26	17	6	3	53	20	40
North Ferriby U	26	14	10	2	48	24	38
Farsley Celtic	26	13	8	5	53	30	34
Harrogate T	26	12	10	4	42	23	34
Garforth Miners	26	13	6	7	38	30	32
Ossett T	26	13	5	8	43	30	31
Ossett A	26	8	10	8	41	38	26
Liversedge	26	8	9	9	35	35	25
Bradley R	26	8	7	11	41	51	23
Leeds Ashley Rd	26	7	6	13	30	44	20
Hatfield Main	26	6	5	15	31	50	17
Bridlington T	26	3	10	13	28	49	16
York Railway Inst	26	4	6	16	39	64	14
Hall Road R	26	4	6	16	22	56	14

DIVISION ONE (SOUTH)

	P	W	D	L	F	A	Pts
Lincoln U	26	16	7	3	55	25	39
Staveley Works	26	16	4	6	50	30	36
Sheffield	26	12	8	6	48	34	32
Frecheville Com	26	12	7	7	35	28	31
Denaby U	26	11	8	7	54	41	30
Maltby Miners	26	10	9	7	50	43	29
BSC (Parkgate)	26	9	6	11	37	37	24
Arnold Kingswell	26	8	8	10	43	46	24
Norton Woodseats	26	10	3	13	32	37	23
Hallam	29	9	5	12	31	44	23
Harworth Colliery Inst	26	5	12	9	34	35	22
Long Eaton U	26	8	6	12	33	40	22
Brigg T	26	4	7	15	26	59	15
Kimberley T	26	3	8	15	29	58	14

DIVISION TWO (NORTH)

	P	W	D	L	F	A	Pts
Rowntree Mackintosh	26	18	6	2	73	29	42
Pontefract Coll	26	18	4	4	63	29	40
Tadcaster A	26	15	5	6	48	34	35
Yorkshire Amateur	26	9	9	8	48	38	27
Pilkington Rec	26	10	7	9	44	44	27
Grimethorpe MWES	26	8	10	8	36	32	26
Collingham and Linton	26	10	6	10	40	43	26
Phoenix Pk (Bradford)	26	11	3	12	43	44	25
Fryston Coll Wel	26	9	5	12	45	47	23
Thorne Coll	26	9	5	12	37	57	23
Brook Sports	26	8	6	12	32	47	22
Selby T	26	8	5	13	38	46	21
Pickering T	26	7	6	13	26	40	20
Harrogate Rlwy Ath	26	2	3	21	19	62	7

DIVISION TWO (SOUTH)

	P	W	D	L	F	A	Pts
Woolley Miners Wel	26	19	4	3	61	13	42
Borrowash Vic	26	16	8	2	57	20	40
Worsborough Bdge Miners Wel	26	15	3	8	47	40	33
Oakham U	26	14	4	8	51	44	32
Stocksbridge Works SS	26	12	6	8	41	26	30
Graham Street Prims	26	12	5	9	49	33	29
Kiveton Park	26	11	6	9	52	40	28
Long Eaton Grange	26	9	6	11	40	45	24
Blidworth Wel	26	10	3	13	40	46	23
Rolls-Royce Wel	26	7	9	10	45	59	23
Creswell Coll	26	8	3	15	37	60	19
Retford Rail	26	6	4	16	29	57	16
Wombwell Sporting Ass	26	3	8	15	18	44	14
Sutton Tr	26	3	5	18	19	59	11

Resigning: Cresswell Colliery.

DRYBROUGH'S NORTHERN LEAGUE

FIRST DIVISION

	P	W	D	L	F	A	Pts
Blyth Spartans	36	23	11	2	92	31	80
Whitby T	36	23	9	4	80	34	78
Horden Coll Wel	36	21	5	10	65	35	68
Bishop Auckland	36	17	13	6	69	34	64
Spennymoor U	36	17	10	9	70	53	61
Billingham Synth	36	16	12	8	71	43	60
North Shields	36	17	7	12	73	46	58
Tow Law T	36	16	10	10	71	63	58
Consett	36	15	10	11	53	37	55
Crook T	36	16	7	13	54	47	55
South Bank	36	14	12	10	56	32	54
Ferryhill Ath	36	14	12	10	53	42	54
Whitley Bay	36	13	8	15	56	50	47
Shildon	36	9	11	16	48	71	38
Evenwood T	36	9	8	19	49	67	35
Ashington	36	9	6	21	36	73	33
Durham C	36	4	8	24	32	83	20
West Auckland T	36	5	3	28	37	110	18
Willington	36	2	2	32	26	140	8

FA CHALLENGE VASE 1982–83

Extra Preliminary Round

Maine Road v St Dominics	1-3
Stratford Town v Coleshill Town	2-1
Whitehawk v Hailsham Town	4-1

Preliminary Round

Harrogate Town v Eppleton CW	0-2
Brandon United v Gretna	1-0
High Pit Social v Ryhope CA	2-0
Heaton Stannington v Billingham Town (*wo for Billingham Town FC*)	
Appleby v Dormans Athletic	2-8
Seaham CW Red Star v Wigton	4-1
Roker c Cleator Moor Celtic	3-1
Bedlington Terriers v Nunthorpe Ath	0–0
Ryhope CW v Stockton Town	0-2
Norton & Stockton Anc v Darlington RA	4-2
Chester-le-Street v Haig Colliery	4-0
Percy Main Amateur v Wingate	3-1
Redcar Albion v Peterlee Newtown	3-5
Annfield Plain v Pickering Town	2-1
South Shields v Windscale	3-0
Yorkshire Amateur v York RI	3-1
Easington Colliery v Hebburn Reyrolle	6-1
Atherton LR v Bradley Rangers	1-2
Fryston CW v Stork	3-1
Maghull v Garforth Miners	2-3
Burnley Belvedere v St Dominics	0-6
Padiham v Pilkington Recreation	2-3
Rylands v Grimethorpe MW	1-1
Grasmere Rovers v Ossett Town	2-0
Warrington Town v Wren Rovers	1-2
Milton v Denaby United	1-6
Atherton Collieries v Heswall	3-1
New Mills v Tadcaster Albion	2-3
North Withington v Hoylake Athletic	0-0
Ford Motors (L'pool) v Kiveton Park	5-1
Norton Woodseats v Prescot BI	6-1
Waterloo Dock v Lytham	1-4
Hatfield Main v Linotype	1-2
Salford v BSC (Parkgate) (*wo for BSC (Parkgate) FC*)	
Birkenshawe Rovers v Chadderton	1-5
Woolley MW v Wythenshawe Amateurs	3-1
Skelmersdale United v Sheffield	6-2
Bentley Victoria v Prestwich Heys	4-1
Holbeach United v Clipstone Welfare	2-0
Brigg Town v Hall Road Rangers	3-1
Immingham Town v Newhall United	2-0
North Ferriby Utd v Boots Athletic	2-0
Barton Town v Clay Cross Works	0-1
Stapenhill v Sutton Trinity	3-4
Kimberley Town v Bourne Town	aet 2-3
Appleby Frodingham v Hucknall CW	5-1
Louth United v Melton Town	0-2
Malvern Town v Birstall United	0-3
Atherstone United v Graham St Prims	5-0
Northfield v Oakham United	2-3
Eastwood Hanley v Arnold Kingswell	2-2
Anstey Nomads v Blakenall	2-0
John Player v Mile Oak Rovers & Youth	0-2
Oldbury United v Long Eaton Grange	3-2
Gresley Rovers v Oadby Town	4-0
Racing Club Warwick v Trent Rovers (*wo for Racing Club Warwick FC*)	
Milton Keynes Borough v Coventry Sptg	1-1
Boldmere St Michaels v Lutterworth Tw	1-1
Rothwell Town v Wolverton Town	2-1
Paget Rangers v Bridgnorth Town	1-2
Bicester Town v Ledbury Town	1-3
Quorn v Wolverhampton United	2-3
Stratford Town v Rushall Olympic	1-1
Abingdon Town v Smethwick Highfield	aet 6-2
VS Rugby v Wootton Blue Cross	3-1
Tividale v Solihull Borough	2-0
Ampthill Town v Kidlington	aet 3-0
St Neots Town v Gt Yarmouth Town	0-5
Diss Town v Ransomes	2-3
Wisbech Town v Yaxley	4-4
Hadleigh United v Bungay Town	2-1

Arlesey Town v Ely City	3-1
Histon v Mirrless Blackstone	3-1
Somersham Town v Chatteris Town	2-4
Brantham Athletic v Harwich & Parkstone	5-2
Watton United v Wivenhoe Town	0-3
Sandy Albions v March Town United	aet 1-4
Crane Sports v Ramsey Town	1-0
Stotfold v Witham Town	3-1
Felixstowe Town v Coggeshall Town	2-2
Biggleswade Town v Epping Town	1-1
Hoddesdon Town v Soham Town Rangers	1-0
Heybridge Swifts v Finchley	2-0
Clacton Town v Haverhill Rovers	aet 4-6
Shillington v Stansted	2-2
Stowmarket Town v East Thurrock United (*wo for Stowmarket Town FC*)	
Clapton v Maldon Town	1-2
Tansley v Waterlows	0-1
Letchworth GC v Bowers United	3-1
Barkingside v Brightlingsea United	0-1
Saffron Walden Town v 61 Luton	0-1
Edgware v Braintree	3-1
Beckton United v East Ham United	3-1
Ford United (London) v Vauxhall Motors	2-1
Royston Town v Crown & Manor	2-0
Chalfont St Peter v Old Esthameians	0-0
Winslow United v Woodford Town	1-0
Selby v Highfield	3-5
Canvey Island v Kingsbury Town	aet 3-1
Stevenage Borough v Uxbridge	1-1
Pirton v Crockenhill	0-0
Berkhamsted Town v Midland Bank	2-1
Sawbridgeworth Town v Tring Town	3-3
Hazells (Aylesbury) v Beaconsfield Utd	4-0
Baldock Town v Corinthian-Casuals	0-2
Norsemen v Slade Green	3-2
Horley Town v East Grinstead	0-0
Chessington United v Herne Bay	1-2
Peacehaven & Tels C v West Wickham	3-2
Old Salesians v Cobham	3-0
Chertsey Town v Dorking Town	2-3
Ringmer v Whitstable Town	3-2
Faversham Town v Chobham	1-0
Banstead Athletic v Egham Town	0-0
Greenwich Borough v Hastings Town	2-1
Fisher Athletic v Camberley Town	4-0
Ash United v Eastbourne United	1-0
Hythe Town v Wick	1-1
Swanley Town v Littlehampton Town	2-4
Erith & Belvedere v Redhill	2-1
Tunbridge Wells v Whitehawk	aet 1-2
Frimley Green v Bexhill Town	1-3
Beckenham Town v Darenth Heathside	2-1
Lingfield v Southwick	0-7
Kew Asso v British Aerospace (Weybridge)	1-2
Bracknell Town v Horsham YMCA	aet 3-2
Malden Town v Pagham	1-0
Horsham v Brockenhurst	1-1
AFC Totton v Farnham Town	1-1
Shoreham v Steyning Town	0-4
Horndean v Eastleigh	0-0
Burgess Hill Tw v Guildford & Worplesdon	2-0
Merstham v Portfield	3-1
Maidenhead Town & Youth v Arundel	0-1
Amesbury Town v Chichester City	4-2
Pirelli General v Romsey Town	aet 0-1
Didcot Town v Amersham Town	2-2
Abingdon United v Chipping Norton Town	0-3
Flackwell Heath v Warminster Town	3-1
Portway Bristol v Larkhall Athletic	4-0
Avon Bradford v Lydney Town	1-0
Robinsons DRG v Thame United	1-4
Matson Athletic v Chippenham Town (*wo for Chippenham Town FC*)	
Bristol Manor Farm v Clanfield	2-1
Old Georgians v Portishead	3-1
Sharpness v Glenside St Gabriels	5-0
Evesham United v Odd Down	0-0
Wallingford Town v Wilton Rovers	5-0
Glastonbury v Cirencester Town	2-0
Calne Town v Fairford Town	2-6

Hengrove Ath v Imm Bristol St George	4-1
Paulton Rovers v Lydbrook	1-2
Imperial Bristol v Moreton Town	0-9
Westbury United v Yate Town	5-5
Swanage & Herston v Peasedown Ath	4-0
Exmouth Town v Radstock Town	4-1
Torrington v Wadebridge Town	1-1
Wimborne Town v Ottery St Mary	aet 2-1
Flight Refuelling v Newquay	1-2

Replays

Nunthorpe Athletic v Bedlington Terrs	1-2
Grimethorpe MW v Rylands	3-0
Hoylake Athletic v North Withington	2-1
Arnold Kingswell v Eastwood Hanley	3-1
Coventry Sporting v Milton Keynes Boro	aet 1-2
Lutterworth Tw v Boldmere St Michaels	aet 2-4
Rushall Olympic v Stratford Town	3-1
Yaxley v Wisbech Town	2-2
Coggeshall Town v Felixstowe Town	4-0
Epping Town v Biggleswade Town	2-1
Stansted v Shillington	5-0
Old Eshameians v Chalfont St Peter	1-2
Uxbridge v Stevenage Borough	1-1
Crockenhill v Pirton	3-1
Tring Town v Sawbridgeworth Town	aet 3-1
East Grinstead v Horley Town	5-1
Egham Town v Banstead Athletic	4-1
Wick v Hythe Town	3-0
Brockenhurst v Horsham	1-0
Farnham Town v AFC Totton	1-2
Eastleigh v Horndean	2-0
Amersham Town v Didcot Town	0-2
Odd Down v Evesham United	1-2
Yate Town v Westbury United	1-2
Wadebridge Town v Torrington	2-1

Second Replays

Wisbech Town v Yaxley	3-2
Stevenage Borough v Uxbridge	aet 3-5
(*Bye – Clitheroe*)	

First Round

North Ferriby Utd v Leeds Ashley Rd	1-3
Annfield Plain v Brandon United	0-2
Dormans Athletic v Easington Colliery	aet 2-3
Norton & Stockton Anc v Peterlee N'town	0-1
Stockton Town v High Pit Social	0-3
Percy Main Amateur v Tadcaster Albion	2-1
Chester-le-Street v Billingham Town	1-2
Yorkshire Amateur v Seaham CW Red Star	2-3
Eppleton CW v Roker	7-2
Bedlington Terriers v South Shields	1-2
Grasmere Rovers v Woolley MW	aet 4-3
Norton Woodseats v Denaby United	3-1
Irlam Town v Pilkington Recreation	aet 1-2
Wren Rovers v BSC (Parkgate)	aet 2-1
St Dominics v Bradley Rangers	1-0
Hoylake Athletic v Fryston CW	2-4
Clitheroe v Ford Motors (Liverpool)	aet 2-1
Garforth Miners v Lytham	1-0
Grimethorpe MW v Skelmersdale United	aet 3-2
Chadderton v Thackley	2-2
Congleton Town v Linotype	0-1
Winterton Rangers v Atherton Collieries	2-1
Bentley Victoria v Wednesfield Social	2-4
Arnold Kingswell v Clay Cross Works	5-0
Lincoln United v Melton Town	3-3
Brigg Town v Anstey Nomads	1-1
Gresley Rovers v Immingham Town	1-1
Shepshed Charterhouse v Oakham United	6-1
West Midlands Police v Friar Lane OB	3-5
Birstall United v Walsall Borough	4-1
Wolverhampton United v Sutton Trinity	2-0
Tividale v Oldbury United	0-1
Appleby Frodingham v Holbeach United	2-0
Boldmere St Michaels v Bridgnorth Town	2-2
Rothwell Town v Knowle	aet 4-2
Wigston Fields v Wisbech Town	3-1
Chatteris Town v Bourne Town	2-4
March Town United v Milton Keynes Boro'	4-2
Rushden Town v Desborough Town	1-0
Hinckley Athletic v Atherstone United	1-2
Mile Oak Rovers & Youth v VS Rugby	1-2
Rushall Olympic v Racing Club Warwick	4-3
Haverhill Rovers v Ampthill Town	1-1
Hadleigh United v Rainham Town	2-1
Crane Sports v Tiptree United	2-3
Stowmarket Town v Coggeshall Town	2-0
Wivenhoe Town v Ford United (London)	aet 5-3
Great Yarmouth Town v Stansted	aet 4-2
Ransomes v Brightlingsea United	2-0
Histon v Brantham Athletic	0-3
Uxbridge v Arlesey Town	aet 1-2
Canvey Island v Hazells (Aylesbury)	1-0
Berkhamsted Town v Southall	0-2
Letchworth GC v Winslow United	3-2
Waterlows v Hemel Hempstead	aet 0-2
Highfield v Maldon Town	3-1
Stotfold v Harefield United	0-1
Heybridge Swifts v Chalfont St Peter	5-0
Norsemen v Haringey Borough	0-0
Tring Town v Beckton United	0-1
61 Luton v Royston Town	2-2
Epping Town v Edgware	aet 2-1
Hoddesdon Town v Buckingham Town	0-1
Whitehawk v Corinthian-Casuals	aet 3-4
Wick v Flackwell Heath	1-0
Bexhill Town v Southwick	2-2
Dorking Town v Ash United	0-1
Peacehaven & Tels Cliffs v Old Salesians	3-3
Three Bridges v Herne Bay	1-0
Crockenhill v Erith & Belvedere	0-0
Marlow v Eastbourne United	2-1
Bracknell Town v Greenwich Borough	2-1
Beckenham Town v Burnham	0-2
Ringmer v Fisher Athletic	1-3
East Grinstead v Faversham Town	aet 0-1
Malden Vale v Littlehampton Town	1-2
Amesbury Town v Brockenhurst	1-0
Egham Town v Malden Town	1-2
Eastleigh v British Aerospace (Wey)	3-1
AFC Totton v Newport (IOW)	3-1
Romsey Town v Burgess Hill Town	2-1
Sholing Sports v Steyning Town	aet 2-1
Merstham v Arundel	aet 0-1
Hengrove Athletic v Lydbrook	aet 2-3
Evesham United v Didcot Town	4-1
Avon Bradford v Fairford Town	aet 3-2
Bristol Manor Farm v Ledbury Town	4-0
Chippenham Town v Chipping Norton Town	2-1
Wallingford Town v Westbury United	8-2
Old Georgians v Portway Bristol	4-4
Moreton Town v Thame United	0-3
Abingdon Town v Port of Bristol	3-2
Shortwood United v Sharpness	2-1
Glastonbury v Wadebridge Town	1-2
Newquay v Swanage & Herston	3-2
Wimborne Town v Exmouth Town	1-2

Replays

Thackley v Chadderton	3-0
Melton Town v Lincoln United	0-1
Anstey Nomads v Brigg Town	2-0
Immingham Town v Gresley Rovers	1-3
Bridgnorth Town v Boldmere St Michaels	1-0
Ampthill Town v Haverhill Rovers	aet 2-4
Haringey Borough v Norsemen	0-4
Royston Town v 61 Luton	2-0
Southwick v Bexhill Town	2-2
Old Salesians v Peacehaven & Tels C	2-5
Erith & Belvedere v Crockenhill	2-4
Portway Bristol v Old Georgians	3-1

Second Replay

Bexhill Town v Southwick	0-2

Second Round

Guisborough Town v Fryston CW	aet 4-1
High Pit Social v Easington Colliery	0-2
South Shields v Peterlee Newtown	1-1
(*abandoned after 90 minutes*)	
Norton Woodseats v Ossett Albion	0-3
Brandon United v Guiseley	6-0

Leeds Ashley Road v Blue Star	0-1
Seaham CW Red Star v Percy Main Ama.	aet 1-2
Eppleton CW v Billingham Town	1-1
Clitheroe v Whickham	aet 3-2
Rainworth MW v Thackley	3-0
Gresley Rovers v Grimethorpe MW	0-2
Hallam v Anstey Nomads	2-1
Skegness Town v Shepshed Charterhouse	0-2
Frecheville Community v Lincoln Utd	aet 1-0
Wren Rovers v St Dominics	6-4
Linotype v Pilkington Recreation	2-2
Appleby Frodingham v Arnold Kingswell	aet 2-1
Winterton Rangers v Staveley Works	0-1
Garforth Miners v Grasmere Rovers	4-0
Rushden Town v VS Rugby	aet 2-5
Atherstone Utd v Willenhall Town	1-0
Birstall United v Wigston Fields	2-0
Halesowen Town v Bridgnorth Town	1-0
Rothwell Town v Wolverhampton Utd	1-2
Irthlingboro' Diamonds v Wednesfield Soc	2-1
Oldbury United v Shifnal Town	0-2
Rushall Olympic v Friar Lane OB	0-1
Haverhill Rovers v Gorleston	2-2
March Town Utd v Gt Yarmouth Town	0-4
Hadleigh United v Ransomes	0-2
Stamford v Canvey Island	4-0
Bourne Town v Barton Rovers	0-3
Hemel Hempstead v Wivenhoe Town	3-3
Beckton United v Stowmarket Town	2-3
Kempston Rovers v Norsemen	1-2
Harefield United v Royston Town	aet 2-3
Ruislip Manor v Heybridge Swifts	0-1
Grays Athletic v Leyton-Wingate	3-1
Brantham Athletic v Southall	aet 1-0
Epping Town v Letchworth Garden City	0-4
Arlesey Town v Highfield	3-1
Tiptree United v Basildon United	1-3
Marlow v Southwick	2-1
Littlehampton Town v Wick	3-2
Molesey v Faversham Town	1-0
Burnham v Malden Town	3-1
Windsor & Eton v Fisher Athletic	2-2
Alma Swanley v Cray Wanderers	aet 2-4
Ash United v Three Bridges	2-3
Arundel v Crockenhill	1-2
Peacehaven & Tels C v Bracknell Town	1-1
Corinthian-Casuals v Whyteleafe	2-1
Avon Bradford v Forest Green Rovers	1-2
Thame United v Devizes Town	0-2
Eastleigh v Portway Bristol	3-2
Chippenham Town v Abingdon Town	0-3
AFC Totton v Wallingford Town	1-0
Sholing Sports v Newbury Town	2-3
Almondsbury Greenway v Lydbrook	1-3
Buckingham Town v Evesham United	aet 1-0
Amesbury v Shortwood United	2-2
Hungerford Town v Romsey Town	aet 3-4
Wadebridge Town v Newquay	1-0
Exmouth Town v Bristol Manor Farm	0-2

Replays

Peterlee Newtown v South Shields	3-0
Billingham Town v Eppleton CW	1-2
Pilkington Recreation v Linotype	2-1
Gorleston v Haverhill Rovers	5-1
Wivenhoe Town v Hemel Hempstead	3-0
Fisher Athletic v Windsor & Eton	1-2
Bracknell Town v Peacehaven & Tels Cliffs	1-0
Shortwood United v Amesbury	aet 0-0

Second Round Second Replay

Shortwood United v Amesbury	1-0

Third Round

Clitheroe v Ossett Albion	1-0
Percy Main Amateur v Peterlee Newtown	3-0
Grimethorpe MW v Easington Colliery	1-2
Blue Star v Wren Rovers	1-0
Brandon United v Hallam	3-1
Guisborough Town v Eppleton CW	3-0
Birstall United v Frecheville Community	1-3
Wolverhampton Utd v Pilkington Rec	2-2
Shepshed Charterhouse v Garforth Miners	5-2
Rainworth MW v Shifnal Town	3-3
Staveley Works v Appleby Frodingham	3-2
Barton Rovers v Halesowen Town	aet 1-2
Buckingham Town v Friar Lane OB	3-2
Atherstone United v Arlesey Town	aet 2-1
VS Rugby v Abingdon Town	1-0
Irthlingborough Diamonds v Stamford	1-1
Grays Athletic v Wivenhoe Town	1-2
Royston Town v Ransomes	7-2
Letchworth GC v Gt Yarmouth Town	2-5
Norsemen v Brantham Athletic	0-2
Stowmarket v Basildon United	3-2
Gorleston v Heybridge Swifts	0-3
Crockenhill v Bracknell Town	1-1
Littlehampton Town v AFC Totton	1-5
Molesey v Windsor & Eton	0-3
Marlow v Corinthian-Casuals	0-3
Three Bridges v Romsey Town	3-2
Burnham v Cray Wanderers	aet 3-2
Eastleigh v Newbury Town	aet 4-2
Devizes Town v Bristol Manor Farm	2-0
Shortwood United v Lydbrook	aet 5-3
Wadebridge Town v Forest Green Rovers	2-2

Replays

Pilkington Rec v Wolverhampton Utd	0-1
Shifnal Town v Rainworth MW	4-1
Stamford v Irthlingborough Diamonds	0-1
Bracknell Town v Crockenhill	1-0
Forest Green Rovers v Wadebridge Town	5-1

Fourth Round

Blue Star v Guisborough Town	aet 2-1
Easington Colliery v Percy Main Ama	1-1, 2-0
Frecheville Comm v Brandon United	0-1
Clitheroe v Staveley Works	4-1
Shepshed Charterhouse v Shifnal Town	2-1
Atherstone United v Buckingham Town	4-0
Halesowen Town v Wolverhampton United	4-1
Irthlingborough Diamonds v VS Rugby (*Match ordered to be replayed*)	0-1
Irthlingborough Diamonds v VS Rugby	1-2
Royston Town v Brantham Athletic	0-1
Wivenhoe Town v Stowmarket	4-1
Heybridge Swifts v Great Yarmouth Town	0-1
Bracknell Town v Three Bridges	1-0
Burnham v Eastleigh	aet 2-1
Windsor & Eton v Corinthian-Casuals	1-0
Shortwood United v Forest Green Rovers	0-2
AFC Totton v Devizes Town	1-0

Fifth Round

Percy Main Amateur v Brandon United	0-2
Clitheroe v Atherstone United	0-1
Shepshed Charterhouse v Blue Star	2-1
Forest Green Rovers v AFC Totton	1-0
Gt Yarmouth Town v Bracknell Town	6-0
Brantham Athletic v VS Rugby	1-2
Halesowen Town v Windsor & Eton	2-0
Burnham v Wivenhoe Town	2-1

Sixth Round

VS Rugby v Atherstone United	2-0
Burnham v Forest Green Rovers	4-0
Halesowen Town v Shepshed Charterhouse	3-1
Great Yarmouth Town v Brandon United	2-0

Semi-Finals – First Leg

Halesowen Town v Burnham	2-1
VS Rugby v Great Yarmouth Town	2-1

Semi-Finals – Second Leg

Burnham v Halesowen Town	1-2
Great Yarmouth Town v VS Rugby	1-1

(*Halesowen Town won 4-2 on aggregate*)
(*VS Rugby won 3-2 on aggregate*)

Final

Halesowen Town v VS Rugby (*at Wembley Stadium*)	0-1

David Clarke *Blyth Spartans*

Keith Barrett *Enfield*

STARS OF ENGLAND'S SEMI-PROFESSIONAL SQUAD

Alan Cordice *Wealdstone*

Mickey Joyce *Sutton United*

WEST MIDLANDS (REGIONAL) LEAGUE

PREMIER DIVISION

	P	W	D	L	F	A	Pts
Halesowen T	38	28	6	4	124	37	62
Hinckley Ath	38	24	7	7	59	32	55
Hednesford T	38	22	4	12	64	53	48
Shifnal T	38	19	9	10	78	48	47
Atherstone U	38	21	5	12	73	46	47
Bilston	38	19	7	12	82	50	45
VS Rugby	38	17	10	11	69	36	44
Armitage	38	18	8	12	61	51	44
Gresley R	38	15	11	12	69	52	41
Tividale	38	18	5	15	52	48	41
Wednesfield Soc	38	17	7	14	47	47	41
Wolverhampton U	38	14	12	12	50	47	40
Lye T	38	13	10	15	50	49	36
Rushall Olympic	38	12	8	18	59	66	32
Blakenall	38	8	13	17	45	61	29
Coventry Sporting	38	7	14	17	40	64	28
Oldswinford	38	6	11	21	46	78	23
Brereton Soc	38	8	6	24	43	89	22
Ledbury T	38	6	7	25	45	117	19
Malvern T	38	6	4	28	40	125	16

UNITED COUNTIES LEAGUE

PREMIER DIVISION

	P	W	D	L	F	A	Pts
Irthlingborough	34	19	11	4	61	27	49
Rushden	34	19	9	6	65	38	47
Stamford	34	14	13	7	46	40	41
Bourne	34	14	12	8	55	40	40
Potton	34	13	13	8	48	36	39
Desborough	34	16	6	12	58	46	38
Long Buckby	34	13	12	9	56	44	38
Wootton	34	12	13	9	61	55	37
Arlesey	34	14	9	11	49	48	37
Buckingham	34	13	8	13	42	51	34
Newport Pagnell	34	7	17	10	42	41	31
Stevenage	34	10	10	14	51	56	30
Holbeach	34	9	11	14	60	55	29
S & L Corby	34	9	11	14	44	54	29
Ampthill	34	10	7	17	57	66	27
Rothwell	34	10	9	15	40	55	27
Eynesbury	34	7	8	19	28	60	22
Kempston	34	4	7	23	39	90	15

EASTERN COUNTIES LEAGUE

	P	W	D	L	F	A	Pts
Saffron Walden T	42	31	6	5	107	40	68
Gorleston	42	27	9	6	97	50	63
Yarmouth T	42	26	9	7	101	52	61
Brantham Ath	42	25	8	9	96	46	58
Sudbury T	42	21	15	6	101	57	57
Colchester U Res	42	24	8	10	104	42	56
Lowestoft T	42	22	9	11	85	49	53
Felixstowe T	42	19	15	8	70	50	53
Wisbech T	42	22	7	13	83	67	51
Newmarket T	42	16	14	12	70	60	46
March T U	42	14	16	12	63	53	44
Bury T	42	16	11	15	68	57	43
Tiptree U	42	13	10	19	61	71	36
Stowmarket	42	13	10	19	62	84	36
Haverhill R	42	13	9	20	64	71	35
Chatteris T	42	11	10	21	65	85	32
Soham T Rangers	42	11	9	22	54	75	31
Braintree	42	9	8	25	48	102	26
Histon	42	9	6	27	53	101	24
Clacton T	42	8	8	26	44	100	24
Thetford T	42	7	6	28	36	109	20
Ely C	42	2	3	37	21	129	7

SOUTH-WESTERN LEAGUE

	P	W	D	L	F	A	Pts
St Blazey	38	28	6	4	114	33	62
Torrington	38	24	5	9	105	53	53
Wadebridge	38	21	9	8	85	41	51
Millbrook	38	21	7	10	87	49	49
Bugle	38	22	5	11	77	53	49
Launceston	38	19	8	11	68	36	46
Newton Abbot	38	15	13	10	69	58	43
Plymouth CS	38	17	9	12	65	56	43
Teignmouth	38	18	5	15	93	69	41
St Austell	38	15	11	12	63	55	41
Penzance	38	18	5	15	62	65	41
Torpoint	38	15	8	15	69	72	38
Newquay	38	15	8	15	61	64	38
Appledore	38	14	9	15	68	75	37
Bodmin T	38	8	10	20	56	97	26
Tavistock	38	8	10	20	43	86	26
Holsworthy	38	7	11	20	43	80	25
Plymouth Command	38	6	9	23	53	112	21
Clyst R	38	6	8	24	55	105	20
Truro C	38	3	5	30	36	110	11

MIDLAND COMBINATION

DIVISION ONE

	P	W	D	L	F	A	Pts
Bridgnorth T	38	29	6	3	102	30	64
Moor Green	38	27	6	5	106	44	60
Boldmere St Michaels	38	25	7	6	60	36	57
Highgate U	38	20	12	6	74	38	52
Cinderford T	38	21	7	10	76	51	49
Paget R	38	17	9	12	63	40	43
Stratford T	38	15	11	12	59	62	41
Mile Oak R	38	15	10	13	58	50	40
Hurley Daw Mill	38	13	10	15	60	62	36
Evesham U	38	13	10	15	52	58	36
Cradley T	38	14	7	17	62	74	36
West Midlands Police	38	10	13	15	66	73	33
Racing Club Warwick	38	12	9	17	52	65	33
Coleshill T	38	13	7	18	45	58	33
Walsall Bor	38	10	9	19	34	67	29
Smethwick Highfield	38	8	12	18	38	58	28
Northfield T	38	10	6	22	53	81	26
Chipping Norton T	38	7	11	20	32	59	25
Solihull Bor	38	6	8	24	43	83	20
Knowle	38	6	8	24	43	89	20

GREAT MILLS WESTERN LEAGUE

PREMIER DIVISION

	P	W	D	L	F	A	Pts
Bideford	38	26	9	3	67	32	61
Frome T	38	23	10	5	75	34	56
Dawlish	38	20	8	10	68	47	48
Clandown	38	19	9	10	54	39	47
Saltash U	38	14	18	6	50	39	46
Falmouth T	38	16	13	9	63	57	45
Plymouth Arg	38	15	14	9	67	41	44
Barnstaple T	38	18	6	14	67	57	42
Liskeard Ath	38	16	9	13	69	47	41
Weston-super-Mare	38	15	11	12	57	46	41
Shepton Mallet T	38	15	4	19	50	55	34
Devizes T	38	12	9	17	50	58	33
Chippenham T	38	12	8	18	40	54	32
Clevedon T	38	9	12	17	36	56	30
Bridport	38	8	13	17	49	60	29
Exmouth T	38	10	9	19	40	59	29
Melksham T	38	8	13	17	43	63	29
Wellington	38	8	12	18	46	74	28
Keynsham T	38	7	11	20	32	68	25
Portway-Bristol	38	8	4	26	35	72	20

HELLENIC LEAGUE

PREMIER DIVISION

	P	W	D	L	F	A	Pts
Moreton T	30	20	8	2	78	21	48
Almondsbury Greenway	30	18	4	8	70	37	40
Abingdon T	30	15	9	6	59	33	39
Wallingford T	30	17	4	9	52	42	38
Thame U	30	14	9	7	40	35	37
Didcot T	30	14	7	9	42	33	35
Fairford T	30	12	9	9	44	43	33
Wantage T	30	9	13	8	41	33	31
Northwood	30	11	9	10	34	36	31
Bicester T	30	12	6	12	35	34	30
Clanfield	30	10	6	14	41	44	26
Abingdon U	30	11	3	16	42	49	25
Maidenhead T & Youth	30	10	3	17	36	65	23
Hazells (Aylesbury)	30	8	4	18	36	52	20
Shortwood U	30	6	3	21	30	65	15
Lambourn Sports	30	2	5	23	17	75	9

WELSH LEAGUE

PREMIER DIVISION

	P	W	D	L	F	A	Pts
Barry Town	34	26	3	5	103	35	81
Blaenrhondda	34	18	12	5	62	35	66
Newport YMCA	34	18	8	8	52	38	62
Maesteg Park	34	18	7	9	52	34	61
Lake U	34	17	8	9	61	43	59
Merthyr Tydfil	34	17	6	11	84	63	57
Sully	34	14	10	10	55	49	52
Caerleon	34	12	10	12	45	46	46
Ton Pentre	34	13	7	14	49	50	46
Pontllanfraith	34	12	9	13	61	49	45
Haverfordwest Co	34	12	9	13	40	39	45
Brecon Corinthians*	34	11	11	12	37	49	40
Pontardawe Ath	34	10	5	19	33	57	35
Pembroke Bor	34	9	7	18	46	63	34
Milford U	34	9	6	19	41	76	33
Cardiff Corinthians†	34	8	7	19	46	72	28
Llanelli	34	7	6	21	42	77	27
Ammanford T	34	6	7	21	37	71	25

** 3 points deducted. † 4 points deducted.*

SOUTHERN LEAGUE SOUTHERN DIVISION 1982–83

	Andover	Ashford T	Basingstoke T	Cambridge C	Canterbury C	Crawley T	Dover	Dunstable	Erith & Belvedere	Fisher Ash	Folkestone	Hillingdon Bor	Hounslow	RS Southampton	Salisbury	Thanet U	Tonbridge AFC	Woodford T
Andover	—	1-5	0-1	3-2	1-2	2-1	0-2	1-3	0-0	0-2	2-3	0-2	2-0	0-0	0-0	0-3	1-0	3-0
Ashford T	1-1	—	2-0	1-1	7-0	0-0	0-1	0-1	1-0	2-0	0-3	0-0	1-1	1-1	1-3	1-0	1-1	0-2
Basingstoke T	2-0	1-1	—	0-0	2-2	1-1	1-1	2-3	2-0	1-1	1-2	0-1	1-1	0-2	0-2	1-0	5-5	2-0
Cambridge C	2-1	1-3	2-0	—	3-0	1-1	2-0	0-2	1-0	4-0	2-4	0-2	1-1	1-2	2-3	0-2	4-2	4-1
Canterbury C	2-2	1-3	2-1	1-3	—	0-2	2-0	3-1	1-0	1-1	0-1	1-1	2-3	2-1	4-0	2-1	2-1	3-2
Crawley T	2-0	1-3	4-1	5-0	2-0	—	4-0	2-1	2-1	0-4	1-1	1-1	1-1	0-0	1-2	3-1	3-0	1-1
Dover	0-2	0-2	2-1	1-0	1-1	1-0	—	0-1	1-3	0-3	2-1	0-3	1-0	1-1	2-2	0-1	3-0	2-0
Dunstable	3-1	0-1	3-0	2-1	3-2	1-0	4-1	—	1-1	2-0	1-3	1-0	4-0	0-1	2-2	2-1	2-1	1-1
Erith & Belvedere	1-0	0-0	1-1	1-3	2-2	1-0	0-0	1-3	—	0-4	2-3	0-1	2-5	1-2	0-0	1-0	1-2	3-2
Fisher Ath	1-0	4-3	3-0	3-1	3-0	4-0	3-1	5-2	3-0	—	5-1	1-1	2-3	3-0	3-2	6-1	4-1	1-0
Folkestone	2-0	2-3	4-1	4-1	3-1	3-0	2-3	2-1	1-0	1-1	—	4-2	4-1	3-1	3-1	6-1	3-0	1-0
Hillingdon Bor	2-2	1-0	3-0	0-0	0-0	1-2	2-1	2-1	0-0	0-2	2-1	—	0-0	0-0	1-0	5-0	0-1	1-0
Hounslow	3-3	3-0	1-1	2-3	1-3	3-2	0-0	1-0	2-0	0-2	1-1	1-2	—	1-1	1-1	3-0	3-0	0-1
RS Southampton	2-0	2-0	2-0	6-2	2-1	0-1	1-3	2-1	7-1	4-0	1-0	2-1	3-1	—	3-2	6-0	2-0	2-0
Salisbury	2-0	5-1	1-2	2-0	3-1	2-2	1-1	0-0	2-1	3-1	3-3	3-2	0-1	1-4	—	6-1	3-2	0-2
Thanet U	0-0	0-4	0-1	3-1	2-2	1-3	2-0	0-0	2-1	0-2	1-1	1-0	2-0	2-0	0-1	—	1-2	1-0
Tonbridge AFC	1-0	3-2	2-4	3-1	3-4	4-1	2-1	2-3	7-0	0-0	0-0	3-0	1-2	1-1	2-0	1-0	—	3-0
Woodford T	1-0	1-1	2-1	2-7	2-2	1-2	5-3	0-2	1-1	0-2	0-3	2-2	0-0	0-2	0-0	0-0	0-1	—

SOUTHERN LEAGUE MIDLAND DIVISION 1982–83

	Aylesbury U	Banbury U	Bridgend T	Bridgwater T	Bromsgrove R	Cheltenham T	Dudley T	Forest Green R	Merthyr Tydfil	Milton Keynes C	Minehead	Oldbury U	Redditch U	Sutton Coldfield T	Taunton T	Wellingborough T	Willenhall T
Aylesbury U	—	3-3	1-0	2-1	2-0	0-2	4-1	2-0	0-1	1-1	0-1	3-4	2-1	0-1	3-0	2-2	1-0
Banbury U	3-0	—	2-3	5-1	3-2	2-3	0-2	1-3	3-5	3-0	4-1	1-2	1-1	1-3	1-2	1-0	3-1
Bridgend T	1-1	1-4	—	2-3	1-1	1-1	3-0	1-2	1-1	5-2	0-0	0-2	2-1	0-1	2-0	1-1	2-1
Bridgewater T	1-3	2-1	2-2	—	2-1	0-2	1-0	0-0	0-0	2-0	0-0	2-3	1-0	2-1	0-0	3-1	1-1
Bromsgrove R	2-0	0-3	0-3	2-3	—	1-3	2-1	0-1	0-1	6-2	4-1	1-1	2-2	1-3	1-3	2-0	3-1
Cheltenham T	3-0	4-2	2-0	1-0	1-0	—	3-0	2-0	1-2	2-0	2-0	0-0	3-0	1-0	6-0	0-0	0-0
Dudley T	1-0	2-0	0-0	2-1	0-2	2-2	—	0-1	2-0	4-0	5-0	0-0	1-3	1-1	1-2	1-0	3-3
Forest Green R	2-0	2-0	0-2	2-0	3-0	5-3	3-0	—	5-2	4-0	4-2	5-1	3-0	1-1	4-1	2-0	0-2
Merthyr Tydfil	2-0	0-1	1-1	4-2	2-2	4-0	1-2	1-0	—	3-0	2-0	2-1	6-4	3-3	3-1	1-3	4-0
Milton Keynes C	1-3	0-1	2-3	1-7	0-2	0-2	0-0	0-3	2-4	—	1-1	1-3	0-1	0-1	2-2	1-3	1-3
Minehead	0-1	2-0	0-2	0-3	0-0	1-3	0-2	2-1	0-1	2-0	—	0-1	1-3	2-2	0-0	0-6	1-2
Oldbury U	3-0	2-3	0-3	1-0	1-0	1-2	1-1	0-2	3-1	1-0	2-1	—	3-1	0-2	0-0	5-2	4-4
Redditch U	2-3	1-2	2-3	2-0	1-2	2-7	2-3	1-6	2-2	3-2	2-0	3-1	—	0-1	4-2	1-2	2-2
Sutton Coldfield T	3-0	1-1	0-0	1-0	1-2	4-1	2-1	3-0	4-1	4-0	1-0	4-1	4-0	—	2-0	0-0	3-1
Taunton T	1-0	1-2	0-0	0-1	0-1	1-2	1-2	1-3	0-0	6-3	0-3	1-2	0-0	2-3	—	0-3	0-1
Wellingborough T	0-0	0-1	1-0	1-0	1-3	0-1	3-0	0-0	2-1	2-0	1-1	1-2	4-2	0-2	5-1	—	4-1
Willenhall T	8-0	5-1	3-1	2-1	1-2	1-0	4-0	4-1	0-3	3-0	7-2	3-1	2-2	2-0	4-2	2-1	—

FA SUNDAY CUP 1982–83

First Round

Windscale v Newbiggin Sports Centre	1-2
Hartlepool Lion Hotel v Framwellgate Moor & Pity Me WMC	2-3
Winlaton West End v Cumberland Star	4-3
Ossie's Bar v Murton Victoria	3-2
Newbiggin Dolphin v Sunderland Humbledon Plains Farm WMC	2-0
Deborah United v Byron Athletic	0-5
Fantail v Eden Vale	aet 3-2
Grassendale United v Greyhound Bilston	0-0
Swanfield v East Levenshulme CC	aet 2-4
Aireville v Cobblers	0-1
Shirley Crusaders v Inter-Volante	3-2
Adelaide Park v Northampton Abington Athletic	0-1
Park Rangers (Wednesfield) v Sandwell	3-5
Girton Eagles v Slade Celtic	3-1
Marston Sports v Old Horns	2-1
Brereton Town v Ely Crusaders	5-1
Springfield Social v Hoval Farrar	4-2
Hobbies v Corby Kingfisher	aet 2-1
Wergs Crown United v Sartan United	1-0
Willmotts Sports v Quality Carpets	5-2
Beaufort v Four-In-Hand	3-0
Sandwell Insurance v Halesowen Harriers	3-1
Lodge Cottrell v Hanham Sunday	3-1
Townsend Transport Sunday v Lakeside	2-0
Sunbury Park v Leatherhead (Sunday)	2-0
North Stoneham v Ollis Transport Combined	1-5
Rediffusion Bedminster Down v Hallen Sunday	2-0
Wrythe Athletic v Laverstoke Park Albion	1-4
Artois United v Bowsport	1-0
Breaks v Rainham WMC	2-1
Green-Man-Bracme v Caribb	1-2
Scruttons Social v Odhams OB	2-1
Sun v Lucas Sports	9-3
Clifda v Carlton United	0-1
Woodmans Hall v Leigh Billet	0-1
Forresters United v Continental	0-5
Pools United v Panthers	
w.o. for Panthers – Pools United withdrew	

Replay

Greyhound Bilston v Grassendale United	1-3

Byes to the Second Round

Acorn, AD Bulwell, Boldon Shack SC, Colden Common, Dortmund, Evergreen, Hartlepool Workmen, Highgate, Lion Rangers, Mackadown Counts, Mackintosh, Oxford Road Social, Pelican, Quebec Rovers, St Joseph's (South Oxhey), Sheffield House Rangers, Shildon Elm Road WMC, Sportsco, Undeb United, Wessex

Exemptions to the Second Round

Arras, Dingle Rail, Eagle, Lee Chapel North, Olympic Star, Twin Foxes, Two-Seven-Nine

Second Round

Hartlepool Workmen v Shildon Elm Road WMC	aet 2-1
Winlaton West End v Ossie's Bar	1-1
Newbiggin Sports Centre v East Levenshulme CC	1-3
Highgate v Pelican	2-1
Fantail v Boldon Shack SC	2-1
Dingle Rail v Newbiggin Dolphin	0-4
Framwellgate Moor & Pity Me WMC v Eagle	0-2
Shirley Crusaders v AD Bulwell	1-2
Sandwell v Grassendale United	1-0
Brereton Town v Marston Sports	3-0
Mackadown Counts v Lodge Cottrell	1-4
Byron Athletic v Sandwell Insurance	aet 1-2
Acorn v Twin Foxes	0-2
Scruttons Social v Lee Chapel North	0-1
Springfield Social v Olympic Star	4-3
Quebec Rovers v Breaks	1-2
Mackintosh v Cobblers	aet 2-1
Continental v Girton Eagles	5-2
Carlton United v Hobbies	2-0
Sportsco v Lion Rangers	0-2
St Joseph's (South Oxhey) v Dortmund	3-1
Leigh Billet v Wergs Crown United	2-0
Evergreen v Northampton Abington Athletic	aet 1-0
Willmotts Sports v Sheffield House Rangers	3-1
Beaufort v Laverstoke Park Albion	2-0
Townsend Transport Sunday v Golden Common	6-0
Oxford Road Social v Sun	1-2
Rediffusion Bedminster Down v Artois United	1-2
Two-Seven-Nine v Panthers	6-1
Wessex v Caribb	6-2
Undeb United v Ollis Transport Combined	1-0
Sunbury Park v Arras	6-3

Replay

Ossie's Bar v Winlaton West End	1-2

Third Round

Fantail v Hartlepool Workmen	2-0
Eagle v Winlaton West End	2-1
East Levenshulme CC v AD Bulwell	3-0
Highgate v Newbiggin Dolphin	4-4
Breaks v Twin Foxes	0-1
Sandwell Insurance v Mackintosh	2-1
Lee Chapel North v Brereton Town	aet 3-2
Lion Rangers v Sandwell	2-1
Springfield Social v Continental	3-0
Carlton United v Lodge Cottrell	1-2
Evergreen v Sunbury Park	1-0
Wessex v Willmotts Sports	4-2
Beaufort v Artois United	3-1
Leigh Billet v Sun	3-0
Townsend Transport Sunday v Undeb United	1-3
Two-Seven-Nine v St Joseph's (South Oxhey)	3-1

Replay

Newbiggin Dolphin v Highgate	5-0

Fourth Round

East Levenshulme CC v Newbiggin Dolphin	2-1
Fantail v Eagle	2-3
Beaufort v Two-Seven-Nine	1-3
Springfield Social v Sandwell Insurance	2-1
Lee Chapel North v Evergreen	3-0
Twin Foxes v Wessex	2-0
Lion Rangers v Leigh Billet	0-1
Lodge Cottrell v Undeb United	1-2

Fifth Round

East Levenshulme CC v Eagle	0-4
Undeb United v Springfield Social	1-1
Leigh Billet v Twin Foxes	3-1
Lee Chapel North v Two-Seven-Nine	aet 1-0

Replay

Springfield Social v Undeb United	5-0

Semi-Finals

Springfield Social v Eagle	1-2
(at Willenhall Town FC)	
Leigh Billet v Lee Chapel North	0-2
(at Basildon United FC)	

Final

Eagle v Lee Chapel North	aet 1-1
(at Runcorn FC)	

Replay

Lee Chapel North v Eagle	1-2
(at Walthamstow Avenue FC)	

UNIVERSITY FOOTBALL

ASSOCIATION FOOTBALL CHAMPIONSHIP 1982/83

NORTHEAST GROUP

	P	W	D	L	F	A	Pts
Newcastle	3	3	0	0	6	1	6
Hull	3	1	0	2	7	5	2
Durham	3	1	0	2	3	5	2
York	3	1	0	2	3	8	2

Newcastle and Hull qualify.

EAST MIDLANDS GROUP

	P	W	D	L	F	A	Pts
Nottingham	3	2	0	1	6	4	4
Leeds	3	2	0	1	7	7	4
Bradford	3	1	1	1	6	5	3
Sheffield	3	0	1	2	4	7	1

Nottingham and Leeds qualify.

NORTH WEST GROUP

	P	W	D	L	F	A	Pts
Manchester	5	4	0	1	18	6	8
U.M.I.S.T.	5	3	1	1	4	4	7
Keele	5	3	0	1	11	6	6
Liverpool	5	1	1	3	6	8	3
Salford	5	1	1	3	7	12	3
Lancaster	5	1	1	3	5	15	3

Manchester and U.M.I.S.T. qualify, Keele qualify for Divisional Play-off.

WEST MIDLANDS GROUP

	P	W	D	L	F	A	Pts
Warwick	4	3	0	1	9	2	6
Loughborough	4	2	1	1	10	5	5
Birmingham	4	2	0	2	11	7	4
Leicester	4	2	0	2	5	5	4
Aston	4	0	1	3	3	19	1

Warwick and Loughborough qualify. Birmingham qualify for Divisional Play-off.

Western Division Play-Off:
Keele v Birmingham 2–5 Birmingham qualify.

South West Group

	P	W	D	L	F	A	Pts
Exeter	4	3	0	1	10	3	6
Bristol	4	2	1	1	9	7	5
Southampton	4	2	1	1	5	8	5
Reading	4	2	0	2	5	6	4
Bath	4	0	0	4	1	6	0

Exeter and Bristol qualify.

South East North Sub-Group

	P	W	D	L	F	A	Pts
Brunel	4	2	2	0	10	2	6
East Anglia	4	3	0	1	9	5	6
Essex	4	1	1	2	6	6	4
U.C. London	4	0	2	2	4	10	2
City	4	0	1	3	4	10	1

Brunel and East Anglia qualify for South East Group Play-offs.

South East South Sub-Group

	P	W	D	L	F	A	Pts
Kent	3	3	0	0	14	3	6
Sussex	3	1	0	2	3	5	2
Surrey	3	1	0	2	4	8	2
L.S.E.	3	1	0	2	5	10	2

Kent and Sussex qualify for South East Group Play-offs.

South East Group Play-Offs:
Brunel v Kent 1–3
Brunel and Kent qualify.
East Anglia v Sussex 2–2 U.E.A. won on penalties.
East Anglia qualify for Divisional Play-offs.

Southern Divisional Play-Off:
Southampton v East Anglia 1-4
East Anglia qualify.

Challenge Round

Nottingham v Birmingham	0-1
Aberystwyth v Brunel	2-0
Newcastle v Loughborough	4-1
Manchester v Bristol	0-2
Kent v East Anglia	2-3
Exeter v U.M.I.S.T.	2-1
Warwick v Hull	4-2
Bangor v Leeds	4-2

Quarter-Finals

Birmingham v Aberystwyth	aet 1-0
Newcastle v Bristol	1-3
East Anglia v Exeter	1-0
Warwick v Bangor	2-0

Semi-finals
At Lilleshall National Sports Centre
Birmingham v Bristol 4-0
At Bisham Abbey National Sports Centre
East Anglia v Warwick 0-1

Final
At West Bromwich Albion Football Club Ground
Birmingham v Warwick aet 1-2

Welsh Group

	P	W	D	L	F	A	Pts
Bangor	5	4	1	0	19	4	9
Aberystwyth	5	4	0	1	23	12	8
Swansea	5	2	2	1	7	2	6
Cardiff	5	1	2	2	12	14	4
U.W.I.S.T.	5	0	2	3	5	11	2
Lampeter	5	0	1	4	2	25	1

Bangor and Aberystwyth qualify.

British Universities Sports Federation Tournament held at Surrey Universities

	Pool A
Cambridge v Wales	0-2
U.A.U. I v Scotland	1-0
Wales v Scotland	0-1
Cambridge v U.A.U. I	1-2
Wales v U.A.U. I	0-1
Scotland v Cambridge	5-1

	Pool B
London v N. Ireland	0-1
U.A.U. II v Oxford	1-3
N. Ireland v Oxford	2-0
London v U.A.U. II	0-1
N. Ireland v U.A.U. II	1-1
Oxford v London	0-0

Play-offs

1st and 2nd Place: U.A.U. I v N. Ireland	0-1
3rd and 4th Place: Scotland v Oxford	1-0
5th and 6th Place: Wales v U.A.U. II	3-0
7th and 8th Place: Cambridge v London	aet 2-1

Representative Matches

U.A.U. lost to British Polytechnics	0-1
U.A.U. lost to a Football Association XI	0-4
U.A.U. lost to British Colleges	1-2
U.A.U. lost to Irish Universities	0-1
U.A.U. drew with Athletic Union League (Dublin)	1-1
U.A.U. lost to Stoke City	1-4

YOUTH FOOTBALL 1982–83

FA YOUTH CUP 1982–83

Preliminary Round

Westerhope CA Juniors v Guisborough Town	1-3
Yorkshire Amateur v Bradford City	6-3
Farsley Celtic v Elland Athletic	0-1
Chorley v Barrow	5-3
Wigan Athletic v Preston North End *Wigan Athletic received w.o.*	
Tranmere Rovers v Rhyl	6-1
Crewe Alexandra v Hednesford Town	3-1
Brigg Town v Stamford *Brigg Town received w.o.*	
Oldbury United v Enderby Town	2-2, 2-3
Wigston Fields v Syston Juniors	3-0
Northampton Town v Tamworth	4-1
Northfield Town v Bedworth United	1-0
Coventry Sporting v Nuneaton Borough	1-2
Corby Town v Banbury United	2-0
Amersham Town v Abingdon United	0-2
Witney Town v Milton Keynes City	3-0
Welwyn Garden v Cambridge City	3-1
Stevenage Borough v Colchester United	1-5
Hendon v 61 FC (Luton)	4-0
Ford United v Letchworth Garden City	5-1
Harefield United v Hillingdon Borough	0-4
Hampton v Hounslow	1-2
Addlestone & Weybridge Town v Burnham	5-2
Walton & Hersham v Maidenhead United	2-2, 1-3
Folkestone v Southwick	7-0
Hastings United v Ringmer	3-0
Gravesend & N'fleet v Carshalton Ath	2-1
Epsom & Ewell v Croydon	1-8
Woking v Waterlooville	1-1, 1-2
Newport County v Bournemouth	5-0
Melksham Town v Gloucester City	2-3
Torquay United v AFC Bournemouth	0-1

First Round Qualifying

Guisborough Town v Consett	3-1
Smith's Dock v Darlington	2-3
Yorkshire Amateur v Halifax Town	1-2
Huddersfield Town v Elland Athletic	3-1
Chorley v Chadderton	2-3
Irlam Town v Wigan Athletic	1-8
Tranmere Rovers v South Liverpool	1-0
Marine v Crewe Alexandra	1-0
Brigg Town v Scunthorpe U	3-2
Spalding United v Grimsby Town	1-2
Enderby Town v Paget Rangers	0-0, 3-1
Willenhall Town v Wigston Fields	2-1
Northampton Town v AP Leamington	2-3
Alvechurch v Northfield Town	0-2
Nuneaton Borough v Wellingboro' Town	4-1
Kettering Town v Corby Town	1-0
Abingdon United v Chesham United *(at Chesham United FC)*	3-2
Wokingham Town v Witney Town	2-1
Welwyn Garden v Royston Town	10-1
Stotfold v Colchester United	1-3
Hendon v Harlow Town	2-3
Hertford Town v Ford United	3-1
Hillingdon Borough v Southall	1-2, 2-3
Staines Town v Hounslow	1-1, 2-3
Addlestone & Weybridge Town v Brentford	1-6
Sutton United v Maidenhead United	2-2, 1-2
Folkestone v Faversham Town	1-0
Bromley v Hastings United	0-2
Gravesend & N'fleet v Greenwich Boro'	3-0
Molesey v Croydon	0-1
Waterlooville v Camberley Town	3-2
Worthing v Leatherhead	0-0, 0-4
Newport County v Swindon Town	1-0
Trowbridge Town v Gloucester City	1-1, 2-4
AFC Bournemouth v Taunton Town	3-3, 1-0
Exeter City v Dorchester Town	0-0, 2-1

Second Round Qualifying

Guisborough Town v Darlington	1-3
Halifax Town v Huddersfield Town	2-0
Chadderton v Wigan Athletic	0-3
Tranmere Rovers v Marine	3-0
Brigg Town v Grimsby Town	0-6
Enderby Town v Willenhall Town	0-1
AP Leamington v Northfield Town	2-2, 4-2
Nuneaton Borough v Kettering Town	2-1
Abingdon United v Wokingham Town	2-1
Welwyn Garden v Colchester United	1-5
Harlow Town v Hertford Town	1-0
Southall v Hounslow	2-0
Brentford v Maidenhead United	6-2
Folkestone v Hastings United	3-2
Gravesend & N'fleet v Croydon	2-2, 1-2
Waterlooville v Leatherhead	1-1, 1-4
Newport County v Gloucester City	2-0
AFC Bournemouth v Exeter City	1-2

First Round

Oldham Athletic v Barnsley	0-2
Tranmere Rovers v Doncaster Rovers	6-1
Blackpool v Halifax Town	3-0
Lincoln City v Formby	4-0
York City v Grimsby Town	1-0
Rotherham United v Hull City	3-1
Liverpool v Bury	3-0
Darlington v Blackburn Rovers	1-1, 2-2, 2-1
Hartlepool United v Wigan Athletic	1-1, 3-4
Notts County v Sheffield United	0-1
AP Leamington v Willenhall Town	1-2
Wrexham v Nottingham Forest	2-1
Shrewsbury Town v West Bromwich Albion	2-3
Hereford United v Chesterfield	2-1
Nuneaton Borough v Port Vale	1-2
Sutton Coldfield Town v Mansfield Town	0-1
Cambridge United v Oxford City	19-0
Luton Town v St Albans City	7-2
Ipswich Town v Colchester United	4-2
Norwich City v Southend United	6-0
Southall v Harlow Town	4-1
Orient v Haringey Borough	6-0
Loughton Boys v Abingdon United	1-3
Oxford United v Barking	2-1
Gillingham v Dover	5-2
Windsor & Eton v Wimbledon	1-6
Welling United v Gravesend & N'fleet	0-1
Crystal Palace v Brentford	2-1
Reading v Folkestone	1-3
Leatherhead v Dartford	3-2
Brighton & Hove Albion v Maidstone United	1-2
Bristol Rovers v Swansea City *(at Swansea City FC)*	3-2
Bristol City v Plymouth Argyle	3-3, 2-1
Newport County v Exeter City	2-1

Second Round

Newcastle United v Rotherham United	3-1
Leeds United v Manchester City	3-2
Bolton Wanderers v Liverpool	2-2, 1-0
Burnley v Wigan Athletic	4-0
York City v Sunderland	0-2
Darlington v Blackpool	3-3, 0-0, 1-2
Barnsley v Middlesbrough	2-0
Sheffield Wednesday v Chester	3-0
Everton v Stoke City	3-1
Coventry City v Sheffield United	2-2, 1-0
Willenhall Town v Derby County	1-2
Mansfield Town v Wrexham	0-0, 1-3
Port Vale v Lincoln City	1-1, 4-3
Wolverhampton Wanderers v Leicester City	0-2
Birmingham City v Tranmere Rovers	0-3

West Bromwich Albion v Manchester United	0-1
Hereford United v Aston Villa	1-3
Gravesend & N'fleet v Fulham	1-0
Orient v Wimbledon	3-0
Queen's Park Rangers v Ipswich Town	4-0
Arsenal v Norwich City	2-2, 2-4
Millwall v Watford	1-2
Crystal Palace v Maidstone United	4-2
Leatherhead v Chelsea	0-2
Charlton Athletic v Southall	4-1
Folkestone v West Ham United	0-6
Gillingham v Tottenham Hotspur	1-5
Luton Town v Cambridge United	2-1
Oxford United v Cardiff City	3-0
Bristol City v Bristol Rovers	1-1, 1-2
Portsmouth v Newport County	2-3
Abingdon United v Southampton	0-4

Third Round

Manchester United v Derby County	2-2, 1-0
Bolton Wanderers v Sunderland	0-1
Everton v Port Vale	1-1, 1-0
Barnsley v Burnley	3-0
Blackpool v Sheffield Wednesday	3-4
Tranmere Rovers v Leeds United	0-1
Wrexham v Newcastle United	1-0
Leicester City v Coventry City	1-0
Charlton Athletic v Oxford United	1-1
West Ham United v Crystal Palace	7-1
Bristol Rovers v Tottenham Hotspur	1-4
Chelsea v Southampton	3-0
Norwich City v Aston Villa	5-2
Orient v Queen's Park Rangers	1-1, 1-1, 1-2
Newport County v Luton Town	0-2
Watford v Gravesend & N'fleet	4-2

Fourth Round

Wrexham v Sheffield Wednesday	2-2, 1-3
Sunderland v Chelsea	0-1
Everton v Tottenham Hotspur	5-0
Leeds United v Barnsley	0-2
Queen's Park Rangers v Manchester United	0-0, 0-4
Norwich City v Watford	3-1
West Ham United v Leicester City	2-3
Luton Town v Oxford United	2-2, 3-0

Fifth Round

Everton v Barnsley	2-0
Luton Town v Leicester City	2-0
Sheffield Wednesday v Chelsea	4-2
Manchester United v Norwich City	0-1

Semi-Finals
1st Leg

Sheffield Wednesday v Everton	0-2
Luton Town v Norwich City	1-3

2nd Leg

Everton v Sheffield Wednesday	7-0
Norwich City v Luton Town	0-0

Everton won 9-0 on aggregate
Norwich City won 3-1 on aggregate

Final
1st Leg

Norwich City v Everton	3-2

2nd Leg

Everton v Norwich City	3-2

Aggregate score 5-5

Replay

Everton v Norwich City	0-1

FA COUNTY YOUTH CUP 1982–83

First Round

West Riding v Cumberland	5-0
Westmorland v Durham	0-2
Sheffield & Hallamshire v Lancashire	0-3
Manchester v Cheshire	2-3
Staffordshire v Leicestershire & Rutland	3-1
Shropshire v Birmingham	1-3
Nottinghamshire v Norfolk	3-7
Suffolk v Hertfordshire	0-1
Sussex v London	0-1
RAF v Berks & Bucks	0-9
Royal Navy v Gloucestershire	0-3
Worcestershire v Herefordshire	2-1
Wiltshire v Cornwall	4-1

Second Round

West Riding v Northumberland	2-2, 1-0
Durham v East Riding	3-2
Lancashire v North Riding	4-1
Cheshire v Liverpool	2-2, 0-2
Staffordshire v Lincolnshire	3-1
Birmingham v Derbyshire	1-5
Norfolk v Northamptonshire	2-0
Bedfordshire v Huntingdonshire	0-4
Hertfordshire v Middlesex	4-2
London v Surrey	4-3
Army v Kent	2-4
Berks & Bucks v Cambridgeshire	1-0
Gloucestershire v Hampshire	3-1
Worcestershire v Oxfordshire	2-0
Devon v Dorset	6-0
Wiltshire v Somerset & Avon (South)	5-2

Third Round

Durham v West Riding	2-2, 0-2
Liverpool v Lancashire	1-2
Derbyshire v Staffordshire	1-2
Huntingdonshire v Norfolk	1-5
Hertfordshire v London	1-1, 1-5
Kent v Berks & Bucks	4-1
Devon v Worcestershire	1-0
Wiltshire v Gloucestershire	1-3

Fourth Round

West Riding v Norfolk	2-1
Lancashire v Staffordshire	2-1
London v Devon	1-0
Gloucestershire v Kent	5-0

Semi-Finals

Gloucestershire v West Riding	2-1
at Sharpness FC	
London v Lancashire	4-1
at Barking FC	

Final Tie

Gloucestershire v London	0-3
at Gloucester City FC	

SCHOOLS FOOTBALL 1982–83

FACTS AND FIGURES – SEASON 1982–83

The England Under 18 Squad achieved their best ever result when defeating Wales 5-0 at Shrewsbury in May – but it was not enough! The match was part of the Centenary Shield competition which Scotland won because of their 2-1 win over England at Falkirk. England finished second with two points from two games while Wales were third, their solitary point coming from a 1-1 draw with Scotland at Cwmbran. The match at Shrewsbury was a personal triumph for centre-forward Gary Lund from Humberside who recorded a first-half hat-trick against the Welsh.

The Schoolboys FA Cup, now known as the Gillette Trophy, became the property of the North-East this season when Middlesbrough and Sunderland drew 4-4 in the two-legged final. Middlesbrough led 4-2 at the end of the first leg but a second goal in the dying minutes of the second leg by defender David Wilson put the aggregate scores level. This is only the sixth time since the competition began in 1905 that the two finalists came from the same ESFA Division.

The British Home Stores Inter County Competition has already proved of great benefit to schoolboy representative football in this its first season. As a result of the four area competitions, **Berkshire**, **Essex**, **Merseyside** and the **West Midlands** will go into the draw for the first National Semi-Finals and Final which will be held in the autumn.

In the Associated Biscuits Trophy, a competition for individual school teams at Under 16 level, last year's winners from Wales, Fitzalan School, Cardiff, again qualified for the National section of the competition but were eliminated in Round Two by the Avon representatives, Grange School, Warmley. This season's final was played at Wimbledon in May and resulted in a win for Raynes Park High School, from Surrey, over the Merseyside team, Bishop Challoner School, Birkenhead, by 3-1.

The North-East also came out on top in the Under 19 Individual Schools' Championship when St Mary's Sixth Form College, Middlesbrough, overcame Handsworth Grammar School, Birmingham, 4-2 in an exciting match played at West Bromwich in early May. It is pleasing to note that schools' football will again benefit when the sponsorship of this competition is undertaken by Barclays Bank Ltd next season.

County Football also receives the support of sponsorship from Bukta. This takes the form of an Inter-County competition at Under 19 level. Last year's winners Humberside again reached the final which was played at Hull in April. However, on this occasion they lost 3-2 to Greater Manchester but they fought hard after being 3-0 down at one stage.

THE ESFA GILLETTE TROPHY 1982–83

Fifth Round

East Berkshire v Newham	2-1
South East Sussex v Blackheath	0-1
High Wycombe v South London	1-1, 1-3
Slough v Vale of White Horse	0-3
Newport v Southampton	1-3
Swindon v Poole	3-0
Warrington v Middlesbrough	0-3
Nottingham v Manchester	2-1
Sheffield v Leicester	2-1
Mid Cheshire v Bootle	2-1
Derby v North Sefton	4-2
Sunderland v Solihull	1-0
Liverpool v Bolton	0-0, 3-2
Doncaster v Leeds	0-2
Norwich v Chelmsford	1-3
Dacorum v Ipswich & South Suffolk	0-3

Sixth Round

East Berkshire v Blackheath	0-0, 1-0
South London v Vale of White Horse	2-0
Southampton v Swindon	2-1
Middlesbrough v Nottingham	5-2
Sheffield v Mid Cheshire	1-4
Derby v Sunderland	1-1, 1-2
Liverpool v Leeds	1-1, 1-4
Chelmsford v Ipswich	0-1

Quarter-Finals

East Berkshire v South London	2-3
Southampton v Middlesbrough	1-4
Mid Cheshire v Sunderland	1-5
Leeds v Ipswich	3-3, 2-2, 3-1

Semi-Finals

South London v Middlesbrough	0-1
Sunderland v Leeds	1-1, 1-1, 3-1

Final

Middlesbrough v Sunderland	4-2, 0-2

First Leg of Final played at Ayresome Park, Middlesbrough F.C. Ground on Tuesday, 26 April, 1983.
Second Leg played at Roker Park, Sunderland FC Ground on Tuesday, 10 May, 1983.
Joint Winners: Middlesbrough and Sunderland Schools' FAs. Aggregate Score 4-4.

ENGLISH SCHOOLS' TROPHY FINALISTS 1905–83

	Winners	*Runners up*
1905	London	Sheffield
1906	Sheffield	Manchester
1907	West Ham	Sunderland
1908	Derby	Oxford
1909	Sheffield	Birmingham N
1910	Sunderland	Walsall
1911	Chester-le-Street	Tottenham
1912	West Ham	Birkenhead
1913	Watford	Sunderland
1914	Sheffield	West Ham
1915	Cardiff	Manchester
1916	Bradford	West Ham
1917	West Ham	Grimsby
1918	Liverpool	West Ham
1919	Grimsby	Sunderland
1920	Reading	Grimsby
1921	Liverpool	West Ham
1922	S London	Grimsby
1923	Sheffield	Birmingham
1924	N Staffs	Reading
1925	Sheffield	Brighton
1926	Grimsby	Liverpool
1927	E Northumberland	Rotherham
1928	N Staffordshire	Brighton
1929	S Northumberland	Southampton
1930	Newcastle	Chesterfield
1931	Islington	Wolverhampton
1932	Manchester*	Southampton*
1933	Sunderland	Edmonton
1934	Manchester	Swansea
1935	Manchester	Swansea
1936	Preston*	West Ham*
1937	Liverpool	Blyth (Northumberland)
1938	Manchester	Bootle
1939	Swansea	Chesterfield
1940	Abandoned	
1941–5	No Competition	
1946	Leicester	Stockton-on-Tees
1947	Salford	Leicester

	Winners	*Runners up*
1948	Stockport*	Liverpool*
1949	Barnsley	Derby County
1950	Swansea	Manchester
1951	Liverpool	Brierley Hill & Sedgeley
1952	Ilford	Swansea
1953	Swansea	Chesterfield
1954	Liverpool	Southampton
1955	Swansea	Manchester
1956	Liverpool	Brighton
1957	Southampton*	Barnsley*
1958	Bristol	Swansea
1959	Brierley Hill, Sedgeley & Tipton*	Doncaster*
1960	Manchester	East London
1961	Barnsley	Liverpool
1962	Stoke	Liverpool
1963	Stoke	Bristol
1964	Erdington and Saltley	Chester-le-Street
1965	Swansea*	Leicester*
1966	East London	Oxford
1967	Liverpool	East London
1968	Manchester*	Waltham Forest*
1969	Liverpool	Swindon
1970	Liverpool	East London
1971	Huyton	Stoke
1972	Chelmsford	Oxford
1973	Liverpool	Chelmsford
1974	Manchester	Oxford
1975	Barking	Havering
1976	Liverpool	Slough
1977	South London	Islington
1978	Newham	Ealing
1979	Bristol	Croydon
1980	Middlesbrough	Reading
1981	High Wycombe	Sunderland
1982	Sheffield	Coventry
1983	Middlesbrough*	Sunderland*

*Joint winners

THE ESFA ASSOCIATED BISCUITS TROPHY 1982–83

Second Round

Hampshire A v Middlesex B	3-2
Wiltshire v Hampshire B	4-0
Somerset v Devon B	5-0
Avon v South Glamorgan	1-0
Essex A v Northamptonshire	1-2
Norfolk v Essex B	1-4
Middlesex A v Kent A	0-1
Inner London v Surrey	3-3, 1-2
Northumberland A v South Yorkshire	1-2
Cleveland v West Yorkshire B	2-1
Lincolnshire A v Derbyshire	2-0
Leicestershire v Humberside B	2-1
Cumbria v Merseyside A	0-1
Lancashire B v Greater Manchester B	2-3
West Midlands A v Clwyd	5-1
Staffordshire v Hereford & Worcs	0-2

Third Round

Hampshire A v Wiltshire	1-1, 1-4
Somerset v Avon	1-2
Northants v Essex B	1-7
Kent A v Surrey	0-3
South Yorkshire v Cleveland	1-0
Lincolnshire A v Leicestershire	0-1
Merseyside A v Greater Manchester B	3-1
West Midlands A v Hereford & Worcs	4-0

Fourth Round

Wiltshire v Avon	2-
Essex B v Surrey	0-
South Yorkshire v Leicestershire	0-
Merseyside A v West Midlands	3-

Semi-Finals

Wiltshire (Ridgeway School, Wroughton, Swindon) v Surrey (Raynes Park High School) 0-

Leicestershire (King Edward VII College, Coalville) v Merseyside A (Bishop Challoner Schoo Birkenhead) 1-

Final

Surrey v Merseyside A 3-

Final played at Wimbledon FC Ground on Monday May, 1983.

Winners: Raynes Park High School. (Surrey Coun Schools' FA)

Runners-Up: Bishop Challoner School, Birkenhea (Merseyside County Schools' FA)

THE ESFA UNDER 19 INDIVIDUAL SCHOOLS' CHAMPIONSHIP 1982–83

Second Round

West Glamorgan v Gloucestershire	2-0
West Midlands A v Buckinghamshire	3-1
Dorset v Hampshire	1-0
Devon v Somerset	6-2
Sussex B v Kent B	1-3
Inner London B v Surrey A	5-1
Hertfordshire B v Essex B	1-1, 0-1
Middlesex A v Hertfordshire A	3-1
South Yorkshire B v Humberside B	4-0
Derbyshire v Humberside A	6-0
Durham B v Northumberland B	2-2, 0-0, 2-1
Durham A v Cleveland	1-3
Northamptonshire v Cambridgeshire	3-1
Nottinghamshire v Warwickshire	1-2
Greater Manchester B v Merseyside B	1-1, 0-1
Merseyside A v Greater Manchester A	2-2, 2-4

Third Round

West Glamorgan v West Midlands A	1-6
Dorset v Devon	0-1
Kent B v Inner London B	3-1
Essex B v Middlesex A	2-1
South Yorks B v Derbyshire	1-2
Durham B v Cleveland	2-6
Northamptonshire v Warwickshire	0-3
Merseyside B v Greater Manchester A	1-0

Fourth Round

West Midlands A v Devon	1-0
Kent B v Essex B	3-2
Derbyshire v Cleveland	2-4
Warwickshire v Merseyside B	1-0

West Midlands A (Handsworth Grammar School, Birmingham) v Kent B (Maidstone School)	**2-0**
Cleveland (St Mary's College, Middlesbrough) v Warwickshire (North Warwicks College, Nuneaton)	**2-1**

Final

West Midlands A v Cleveland	2-4

Final played at West Bromwich Albion FC Ground on Monday, 9 May, 1983.
Winners: St Mary's Sixth Form College, Middlesbrough. (Cleveland County Schools' FA)
Runners-Up: Handsworth Grammar School, Birmingham. (West Midlands Metropolitan Schools' FA)

ESFA BUKTA COUNTY CHAMPIONSHIPS 1982–83

Regional Champions

Region I: Durham
Region II: Greater Manchester
Region III: Humberside
Region IV: Inner London
Region V: Dorset

First Round

Durham v Greater Manchester	1-2

Semi-Final

Humberside v Dorset	4-1
Greater Manchester v Inner London	4-1

Final

Humberside v Greater Manchester	2-3

Final played on the Hull City FC Ground on Thursday 28 April, 1983.
Winners: Greater Manchester County Schools' FA
Runners-Up: Humberside County Schools' FA

ENGLISH SCHOOLS INTERNATIONALS

ENGLAND UNDER 15 PLAYING RECORD

(Up to 31 May)

Southampton, 26 February
England 4, N Ireland 0 *(White, Goddard, Rimmer, Scott)*

Wembley, 27 March
England 1, West Germany 0 *(Rimmer)*

Hoogeveen, 16 April
Netherlands 1, England 2 *(Rimmer 2)*

Stoke-on-Trent, 30 April
England 1, Scotland 1 *(Peacock)*

Newport, 7 May
Wales 0, England 5 *(Peacock, White 2, Bogie, Parsons)*

	P	*W*	*D*	*L*	*F*	*A*	*Pts*
England	5	4	1	0	13	2	

Scorers: *Rimmer 4, White 3, Peacock 2, Bogie, Goddard, Parsons, Scott.*

VICTORY SHIELD (Under-15) 1982–83

Southampton, 26 February
England 4, N Ireland 0

Edinburgh, 10 March
Scotland 4, Wales 1

Greenock, 19 March
Scotland 4, N Ireland 0

Flint, 22 April
Wales 3, N Ireland 0

Stoke-on-Trent, 30 April
England 1, Scotland 1

Newport, 7 May
Wales 0, England 5

FINAL TABLE

	P	*W*	*D*	*L*	*F*	*A*	*Pts*
Scotland	3	2	1	0	9	2	5
England	3	2	1	0	10	1	5
Wales	3	1	0	2	4	9	2
N Ireland	3	0	0	3	0	11	0

Trophy to be shared by England and Scotland

UNDER 18 PLAYING RECORD

Doncaster, 23 April
England 0, Scotland 0

Falkirk, 7 May
Scotland 2, England 1 *(Philliskirk)*

Shrewsbury, 14 May
England 5, Wales 0 *(Lund 3, Philliskirk, Gordon)*

	P	*W*	*D*	*L*	*F*	*A*	*Pts*
England	3	1	1	1	6	2	

Scorers: *Lund 3, Philliskirk 2, Gordon.*

CENTENARY SHIELD (Under-18) 1982–83

Cwmbran, 25 March
Wales 1, Scotland 1

Falkirk, 7 May
Scotland 2, England 1

Shrewsbury, 14 May
England 5, Wales 0

FINAL TABLE

	P	*W*	*D*	*L*	*F*	*A*	*Pts*
Scotland	2	1	1	0	3	2	3
England	2	1	0	1	6	2	2
Wales	2	0	1	1	1	6	1

UNDER 18 REPRESENTATIVE MATCH

Burton-on-Trent, 16 March
England XI 6, Combined Services Youth XI 1
(Lund 2, Harvey 2, Gordon, Ashton)

COACHING AND THE COACHES

The coaching structure of English football which is organised by the Football Association through their Coaching Department is going through a brand new phase and within the next twelve months, considerable changes are planned. After the retirement of Allen Wade, the former Director of Coaching, who rendered a sterling service for a number of years, the task of carrying on and holding and developing the Department has been assumed by the very capable and forward looking Assistant Director of Coaching, Charles Hughes. The National Team Manager, Bobby Robson, is involved with the scheme as is his newly appointed assistant, Dave Sexton. All are based at the FA's Headquarters at 16 Lancaster Gate, London W2.

The present Coaching Awards available in descending order are the Full Coaching Award, the Preliminary Coaching Badge, the Youth Team Manager's Certificate and the Teacher's Certificate. In addition the FA have devised an award for school children known as the Super Skills Award.

On the administrative side, there are 43 County Coaching Associations plus the three Armed Services, all with County Secretaries who deal with the day to day running of Coaching at the lower levels and various delegated aspects of the system.

Around the country there are various Regional Coaches supported by Coaching Organisers and each Regional Coach or Organiser has under his control a number of Coaching Associations formed for the purpose of bringing Coaches together to discuss fresh coaching ideas and to take part in practical sessions as well as refresher courses.

The Regional Coaches and Coaching Organisers are:

Regional Coaches

North-East Region: Jack Detchon, Second Floor, 22 High Street, Sheffield S1 2GD.
North-West Region: Richard Bate, 31a Wellington Street (St John's), Blackburn, Lancs BB1 8AU.
Midlands-West Region: Kevin Verity, 25 Gresham Chambers, 14 Lichfield Street, Wolverhampton WV1 1DG, Staffs.
Midlands-East Region: Keith Wright, 29b High Street, Oakham, Rutland.
Mid-West Region: David Burnside, 9 Brunswick Square, Bristol B23 4PE.
London Region (North): Colin Murphy, c/o The FA Regional Offices, 16 Lancaster Gate, London W2 3LW.
London Region (South): Robin Russell, c/o The FA Regional Offices, 16 Lancaster Gate, London W2 3LW.

COACHING ORGANISERS

East Anglia Region: Graham Morgan, Roundwell Cottage, 1 Grove Road, Hethersett, Norwich, Norfolk.
South-West Region: Peter Amos, 20 Tuckers Meadow, Crediton, Devon.

The aforementioned are supplemented by the Staff Coaches who are awarded that status for their efforts and hard work in relation to coaching. The staff coaches are:
Adams J. W.; Adamson J.; Ainsley G.E.; Allen D.; Armfield J.; Bate R.; Beaglehole E. W.; Blunt K. R. W.; Bond C. E.; Bramley J.; Brown A.; Brown A. W.; Burnside D.; Burton K.; Calvert J. S.; Cann S. T.; Cartwright J.; Casey T.; Charlton J. OBE; Churchill T.; Curtis G.; Detchon J.; Dobson C.; Furphy K.; Goodwin J. W.; Gordon J.; Gradi D.; Greaves I. D.; Greenwood R.; Hardisty J. R. E.; Hassall H. W.; Henderson J. R. E.; Hill J. W. T.; Houghton R.; Howe D.; Hughes C. F. C.; Jago G.; Jarman J. E.; Jones C.; Kelly M. J.; Lawrence T. E.; Lee B. R.; Lewis R.; McCluskey E.; MacAnearney J.; Mansell J.; Megson D. H.; Mercer J. OBE; Minshull R.; Nicholson W. E.; Powell E. W.; Robson R. W.; Saunders T. W.; Sayer C.; Sexton D. J.; Shannon L.; Shoulder J.; Sirrel J.; Slater W. J.; Smith G. C.; Smith M. J.; Summers G.; Taylor G.; Tranter T. G.; Truman J. B.; Wade A.; Waiters A. K.; Walker M.; Wardle G.; Watson T.; Welton P.; Wigmore S. T.; Wilkinson H.; Williams B.; Woosnam P.; Worthington E. S.; Wright W. A. CBE.

LAWS OF THE GAME

The Laws of the Game and Decisions of the International Board that follow are reproduced with the special permission of FIFA, and the text is the official text as published by FIFA.

LAW I
THE FIELD OF PLAY

The Field of Play and appurtenances shall be as shown in the following plan:

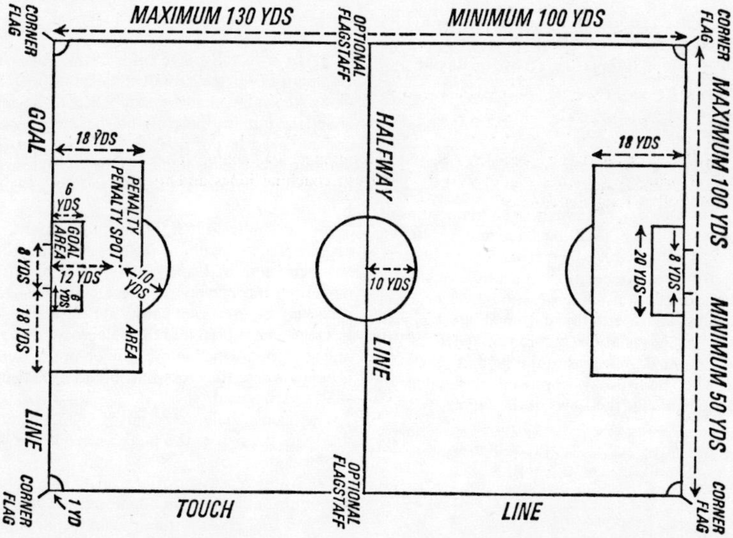

(1) **Dimensions.** The field of play shall be rectangular, its length being not more than 130 yards nor less than 100 yards and its breadth not more than 100 yards nor less than 50 yards. (In International Matches the length shall be not more than 120 yards nor less than 110 yards and the breadth not more than 80 yards nor less than 70 yards.) The length shall in all cases exceed the breadth.

(2) **Marking.** The field of play shall be marked with distinctive lines, not more than 5 inches in width, not by a V-shaped rut, in accordance with the plan, the longer boundary lines being called the touch-lines and the shorter the goal-lines. A flag on a post not less than 5ft high and having a non-pointed top, shall be placed at each corner; a similar flag-post may be placed opposite the halfway line on each side of the field of play, not less than 1 yard outside the touch-line. A halfway-line shall be marked out across the field of play. The centre of the field of play shall be indicated by a suitable mark and a circle with a 10 yards radius shall be marked round it.

(3) **The Goal-Area.** At each end of the field of play two lines shall be drawn at right-angles to the goal-line, 6 yards from each goal-post. These shall extend into the field of play for a distance of 6 yards and shall be joined by a line drawn parallel with the goal-line. Each of the spaces enclosed by these goal lines and the goal-line shall be called a goal-area.

(4) **The Penalty-Area.** At each end of the field of play two lines shall be drawn at right-angles to the goal-line, 18 yards from each goal-post. These shall extend into the field of play for a distance of 18 yards and shall be joined by a line drawn parallel with the goal-line. Each of the spaces enclosed by these lines and the goal-line shall be called a penalty-area. A suitable mark shall be made within each penalty-area, 12 yards from the mid-point of the goal-line, measured along an undrawn line at right-angles thereto. These shall be the penalty-kick marks. From each penalty-kick mark an arc of a circle, having a radius of 10 yards, shall be drawn outside the penalty-area.

(5) **The Corner-Area.** From each corner-flag post a quarter circle, having a radius of 1 yard, shall be drawn inside the field of play.

(6) **The Goals.** The goals shall be placed on the centre of each goal-line and shall consist of two upright posts, equidistant from the corner-flags and 8 yards apart (inside measurement), joined

by a horizontal cross-bar the lower edge of which shall be 8ft from the ground. The width and depth of the goal-posts and the width and depth of the cross-bars shall not exceed 5 inches (12cm). The goal-posts and the cross-bars shall have the same width.

Nets may be attached to the posts, cross-bars and ground behind the goals. They should be appropriately supported and be so placed as to allow the goal-keeper ample room.

Footnote

Goal nets. The use of nets made of hemp, jute or nylon is permitted. The nylon strings may, however, not be thinner than those made of hemp or jute.

Decisions of the International Board

(1) In International matches the dimensions of the field of play shall be: maximum 110×75 metres; minimum 100×64 metres.

(2) National Associations must adhere strictly to these dimensions. Each National Association organising an International Match must advise the visiting Association, before the match, of the place and the dimensions of the field of play.

(3) The Board has approved this table of measurements for the Laws of the Game:

130 yards	... 120 metres
120 yards	... 110
110 yards	... 100
100 yards	... 90
80 yards	... 75
70 yards	... 64
50 yards	... 45
18 yards	... 16.50
12 yards	... 11
10 yards	... 9.15
8 yards	... 7.32
6 yards	... 5.50
1 yard	... 1
8 feet	... 2.44
5 feet	... 1.50
28 inches	... 0.71
27 inches	... 0.68
9 inches	... 0.22
5 inches	... 0.12
¾ inch	... 0.019
½ inch	... 0.0127
⅜ inch	... 0.010
14 ounces	... 396 grams
16 ounces	... 453 grams
15 lb/sq in	... 1 kg/cm^2

(4) The goal-line shall be marked the same width as the depth of the goal-posts and the cross-bar, so that the goal-line and goal-post will conform to the same interior and exterior edges.

(5) The 6 yards (for the outline of the goal-area) and the 18 yards (for the outline of the penalty-area) which have to be measured along the goal-line, must start from the inner sides of the goal-posts.

(6) The space within the inside areas of the field of play includes the width of the lines marking these areas.

(7) All Associations shall provide standard equipment, particularly in International Matches, when the Laws of the Game must be complied with in every respect and especially with regard to the size of the ball and other equipment which must conform to the regulations. All cases of failure to provide standard equipment must be reported to FIFA.

(8) In a match played under the Rules of a Competition, if the cross-bar becomes displaced or broken, play shall be stopped and the match abandoned unless the cross-bar has been repaired and replaced in position or a new one provided without such being a danger to the players. A rope is not considered to be a satisfactory substitute for a cross-bar.

In a Friendly Match, by mutual consent, play may be resumed without the cross-bar provided it has been removed and no longer constitutes a danger to the players. In these circumstances, a rope may be used as a substitute for a cross-bar. If a rope is not used and the ball crosses the goal-line at a point which in the opinion of the Referee is below where the cross-bar should have been he shall award a goal.

The game shall be restarted by the Referee dropping the ball at the place where it was when play was stopped.

(9) National Associations may specify such maximum and minimum dimensions for the cross-bars and goal-posts, within the limits laid down in Law I, as they consider appropriate.

(10) Goal-posts and cross-bars must be made of wood, metal or other approved material as decided from time to time by the International FA Board. They may be square, rectangular, round, half-round or elliptical in shape. Goal-posts and cross-bars made of other materials and in other shapes are not permitted.

(11) 'Curtain-raisers' to International Matches should only be played following agreement on the day of the match, and taking into account the condition of the field of play, between representatives of the two Associations and the Referee (of the International Match).

(12) National Associations, particularly in International Matches, should

— restrict the number of photographers around the field of play,
— have a line ('photographers' line') marked behind the goal-lines at least two metres from the corner flag going through a point situated at least 3.5 metres behind the intersection of the goal-line with the line marking the goal area to a point situated at least six metres behind the goal-posts,
— prohibit photographers from passing over these lines,

— forbid the use of artificial lighting in the form of 'flashlights'.

LAW II – THE BALL

The ball shall be spherical; the outer casing shall be of leather or other approved materials. No material shall be used in its construction which might prove dangerous to the players.

The circumference of the ball shall not be more than 28in and not less than 27in. The weight of the ball at the start of the game shall not be more than 16oz nor less than 14oz. The pressure shall be equal to 0.6–1.1 atmosphere, (=600–1"100gr/cm^2) at sea level. The ball shall not be changed during the game unless authorised by the Referee.

Decisions of the International Board

(1) The ball used in any match shall be considered the property of the Association or Club on whose ground the match is played, and at the close of play it must be returned to the Referee.

(2) The International Board, from time to time, shall decide what constitutes approved materials. Any approved material shall be certified as such by the International Board.

(3) The Board has approved these equivalents of the weights specified in the Law: 14 to 16 ounces = 396 to 453 grammes.

(4) If the ball bursts or becomes deflated during the course of a match, the game shall be stopped and restarted by dropping the new ball at the place where the first ball became defective.

(5) If this happens during a stoppage of the game (place-kick, goal-kick, corner-kick, free-kick, penalty-kick or throw-in) the game shall be restarted accordingly.

LAW III – NUMBER OF PLAYERS

(1) A match shall be played by two teams, each consisting of not more than eleven players, one of whom shall be the goalkeeper.

(2) Substitutes may be used in any match played under the rules of a competition, subject to the following conditions:

(a) that the authority of the international association(s) or national association(s) concerned, has been obtained,

(b) that, subject to the restriction contained in the following paragraph (c), the rules of a competition shall state how many, if any, substitutes may be used, and

(c) that a team shall not be permitted to use more than two substitutes in any match.

(3) Substitutes may be used in any other match, provided that the two teams concerned reach agreement on a maximum number, not exceeding five, and that the terms of such agreement are intimated to the Referee, before the match. If the Referee is not informed, or if the teams fail to reach agreement, no more than two substitutes shall be permitted.

(4) Any of the other players may change places with the goalkeeper, provided that the Referee is informed before the change is made, and provided also, that the change is made during a stoppage in the game.

(5) When a goalkeeper or any other player is to be replaced by a substitute, the following conditions shall be observed:

(a) the Referee shall be informed of the proposed substitution, before it is made,

(b) the substitute shall not enter the field of play until the player he is replacing has left, and then only after having received a signal from the Referee,

(c) he shall enter the field during a stoppage in the game, and at the half-way line.

Punishment:

(a) Play shall not be stopped for an infringement of paragraph 4. The players concerned shall be cautioned immediately the ball goes out of play.

(b) For any other infringement of this law, the player concerned shall be cautioned, and if the game is stopped by the Referee, to administer the caution, it shall be restarted by an indirect free-kick, to be taken by a player of the opposing team, from the place where the ball was, when play was stopped. If the free-kick is awarded to a side within its own goal-area, it may be taken from any point within that half of the goal-area in which the ball was when play was stopped.

Decisions of the International Board

(1) The minimum number of players in a team is left to the discretion of National Associations.

(2) The Board is of the opinion that a match should not be considered valid if there are fewer than seven players in either of the teams.

(3) A competition may require that the referee shall be informed, before the start of the match, of the names of not more than five players, from whom the substitutes (if any) must be chosen.

(4) A player who has been ordered off before play begins may be replaced only by one of the named substitutes. The kick-off must not be delayed to allow the substitute to join his team.

A player who has been ordered off after play has started may not be replaced.

A named substitute who has been ordered off, either before or after play has started, may not be replaced (this decision relates only to players who are ordered off under Law XII. It does not apply to players who have infringed Law IV).

(5) A player who has been replaced shall not take any further part in the game.

(6) A substitute shall be deemed to be a player and shall be subject to the authority and jurisdiction of the Referee whether called upon to play or not. For any offence committed on the field of play a substitute shall be subject to the same pun-

ishment as any other player whether called upon or not.

LAW IV – PLAYERS' EQUIPMENT

(1) A player shall not wear anything which is dangerous to another player.

(2) Footwear (boots or shoes) must conform to the following standard:

(a) Bars shall be made of leather or rubber and shall be transverse and flat, not less than half an inch in width and shall extend the total width of the sole and be rounded at the corners.

(b) Studs which are independently mounted on the sole and are replaceable shall be made of leather, rubber, aluminium, plastic or similar material and shall be solid. With the exception of that part of the stud forming the base, which shall not protrude from the sole more than one quarter of an inch, studs shall be round in plan and not less than half an inch in diameter. Where studs are tapered, the minimum diameter of any section of the stud must not be less than half an inch. Where metal seating for the screw type is used, this seating must be embedded in the sole of the footwear and any attachment screw shall be part of the stud. Other than the metal seating for the screw type of stud, no metal plates even though covered with leather or rubber shall be worn, neither studs which are threaded to allow them to be screwed on to a base screw that is fixed by nails or otherwise to the soles of footwear, nor studs which, apart from the base, have any form of protruding edge rim or relief marking or ornament should be allowed.

(c) Studs which are moulded as an integral part of the sole and are not replaceable shall be made of rubber, plastic, polyurethane or similar soft materials. Provided that there are no fewer than ten studs on the sole, they shall have a minimum diameter of three-eighths of an inch (10mm). Additional supporting material to stabilise studs of soft materials, and ridges which shall not protrude more than 5mm from the sole and moulded to strengthen it, shall be permitted provided that they are in no way dangerous to other players. In all other respects they shall conform to the general requirements of this Law.

(d) Combined bars and studs may be worn, provided the whole conforms to the general requirements of this Law. Neither bars nor studs on the soles shall project more than three-quarters of an inch. If nails are used they shall be driven in flush with the surface.

(3) The goalkeeper shall wear colours which distinguish him from the other players and from the Referee.

Punishment: For any infringement of this Law, the player at fault shall be sent off the field of play to adjust his equipment and he shall not return without first reporting to the Referee, who shall satisfy himself that the player's equipment is in order; the player shall only re-enter the game at a moment when the ball has ceased to be in play.

Decisions of the International Board

---

(1) The usual equipment of a player is a jersey or shirt, shorts, stockings and footwear. In a match played under the rules of a competition, players need not wear boots or shoes, but shall wear jersey or shirt, shorts, or track suit or similar trousers, and stockings.

(2) The Law does not insist that boots or shoes must be worn. However, in competition matches Referees should not allow one or a few players to play without footwear when all the other players are so equipped.

(3) In International Matches, International Competitions, International Club Competitions and friendly matches between clubs of different National Associations, the Referee, prior to the start of the game, shall inspect the players' footwear, and prevent any player whose footwear does not conform to the requirements of this Law from playing until such time as it does comply.

The rules of any competition may include a similar provision.

(4) If the Referee finds that a player is wearing articles not permitted by the Laws and which may constitute a danger to other players, he shall order him to take them off. If he fails to carry out the Referee's instruction, the player shall not take part in the match.

(5) A player who has been prevented from taking part in the game or a player who has been sent off the field for infringing Law IV must report to the Referee during a stoppage of the game and may not enter or re-enter the field of play unless and until the Referee has satisfied himself that the player is no longer infringing Law IV.

(6) A player who has been prevented from taking part in a game or who has been sent off because of an infringement of Law IV, and who enters or re-enters the field of play to join or rejoin his team, in breach of the conditions of Law XII, shall be cautioned. If the Referee stops the game to administer the caution, the game shall be restarted by an indirect free-kick, taken by a player of the opposing side, from the place where the ball was when the Referee stopped the game. If the free-kick is awarded to a side within its own goal-area, it may be taken from any point within that half of the goal-area in which the ball was when play was stopped.

LAW V – REFEREES

A Referee shall be appointed to officiate in each game. His authority and the exercise of the powers granted to him by the Laws of the Game commence as soon as he enters the field of play.

His power of penalising shall extend to offences committed when play has been temporarily suspended, or when the ball is out of play. His decision on points of fact connected with the play shall be final, so far as the result of the game is concerned. He shall:

(a) Enforce the Laws.

(b) Refrain from penalising in cases where he is satisfied that, by doing so, he would be giving an advantage to the offending team.

(c) Keep a record of the game, act as timekeeper and allow the full or agreed time, adding thereto all time lost through accident or other cause.

(d) Have discretionary power to stop the game for any infringement of the Laws and to suspend or terminate the game whenever, by reason of the elements, interference by spectators, or other cause, he deems such stoppage necessary. In such a case he shall submit a detailed report to the competent authority, within the stipulated time, and in accordance with the provisions set up by the National Association under whose jurisdiction the match was played. Reports will be deemed to be made when received in the ordinary course of post.

(e) From the time he enters the field of play, caution any player guilty of misconduct or ungentlemanly behaviour and, if he persists, suspend him from further participation in the game. In such cases the Referee shall send the name of the offender to the competent authority, within the stipulated time, and in accordance with the provisions set up by the National Association under whose jurisdiction the match was played. Reports will be deemed to be made when received in the ordinary course of post.

(f) Allow no person other than the players and linesmen to enter the field of play without his permission.

(g) Stop the game if, in his opinion, a player has been seriously injured; have the player removed as soon as possible from the field of play, and immediately resume the game. If a player is slightly injured, the game shall not be stopped until the ball has ceased to be in play. A player who is able to go to the touch or goal-line for attention of any kind, shall not be treated on the field of play.

(h) Send off the field of play, any player who, in his opinion, is guilty of violent conduct, serious foul play, or the use of foul or abusive language.

(i) Signal for recommencement of the game after all stoppages.

(j) Decide that the ball provided for a match meets with the requirements of Law II.

Decisions of the International Board

(1) Referees in International Matches shall wear a blazer or blouse the colour of which is distinct from the colours worn by the contesting teams.

(2) Referees for International Matches will be selected from a neutral country unless the countries concerned agree to appoint their own officials.

(3) The Referee must be chosen from the official list of International Referees. This need not apply to Amateur and Youth International Matches.

(4) The Referee shall report to the appropriate authority misconduct or any misdemeanour on the part of spectators, officials, players, named substitutes or other persons which take place either on the field of play or in its vicinity at any time prior to, during, or after the match in question so that appropriate action can be taken by the authority concerned.

(5) Linesmen are assistants of the Referee. In no case shall the Referee consider the intervention of a Linesman if he himself has seen the incident and from his position on the field, is better able to judge. With this reserve, and the Linesman neutral, the Referee can consider the intervention and if the information of the Linesman applies to that phase of the game immediately before the scoring of a goal, the Referee may act thereon and cancel the goal.

(6) The Referee, however, can only reverse his first decision so long as the game has not been restarted.

(7) If the Referee has decided to apply the advantage clause and to let the game proceed, he cannot revoke his decision if the presumed advantage has not been realised, even though he has not, by any gesture, indicated his decision. This does not exempt the offending player from being dealt with by the Referee.

(8) The Laws of the Game are intended to provide that games should be played with as little interference as possible, and in this view it is the duty of Referees to penalise only deliberate breaches of the Law. Constant whistling for trifling and doubtful breaches produces bad feeling and loss of temper on the part of the players and spoils the pleasure of spectators.

(9) By para. (d) of Law V the Referee is empowered to terminate a match in the event of grave disorder, but he has no power or right to decide, in such event, that either team is disqualified and thereby the loser of the match. He must send a detailed report to the proper authority who alone has power to deal further with this matter.

(10) If a player commits two infringements of a different nature at the same time, the Referee shall punish the more serious offence.

(11) It is the duty of the Referee to act upon the information of neutral Linesmen with regard to incidents that do not come under the personal notice of the Referee.

(12) The Referee shall not allow any person to enter the field until play has stopped, and only then, if he has given him a signal to do so, nor shall he allow coaching from the boundary lines.

LAW VI – LINESMEN

Two Linesmen shall be appointed, whose duty (subject to the decision of the Referee) shall be to indicate when the ball is out of play and which side is entitled to the corner-kick, goal-kick or throw-in. They shall also assist the Referee to control the game in accordance with the Laws. In the event of undue interference or improper conduct by a Linesman, the Referee shall dispense with his services and arrange for a substitute to be appointed. (The matter shall be reported by the Referee to the competent authority.) The Linesmen should be equipped with flags by the Club on whose ground the match is played.

Decisions of the International Board

(1) Linesmen, where neutral, shall draw the Referee's attention to any breach of the Laws of the Game of which they become aware if they consider that the Referee may not have seen it, but the Referee shall always be the judge of the decision to be taken.

(2) National Associations are advised to appoint official Referees of neutral nationality to act as Linesmen in International Matches.

(3) In International Matches, Linesmen's flags shall be of a vivid colour, bright reds and yellows. Such flags are recommended for use in all other matches.

(4) A Linesman may be subject to disciplinary action only upon a report of the Referee for unjustified interference or insufficient assistance.

LAW VII – DURATION OF THE GAME

The duration of the game shall be two equal periods of 45 minutes, unless otherwise mutually agreed upon, subject to the following: (a) Allowance shall be made in either period for all time lost through accident or other cause, the amount of which shall be a matter for the discretion of the Referee; (b) Time shall be extended to permit a penalty-kick being taken at or after the expiration of the normal period in either half.

At half-time the interval shall not exceed five minutes except by consent of the Referee.

Decisions of the International Board

(1) If a match has been stopped by the Referee, before the completion of the time specified in the rules, for any reason stated in Law V it must be replayed in full unless the rules of the competition concerned provide for the result of the match at the time of such stoppage to stand.

(2) Players have a right to an interval at half-time.

LAW VIII – THE START OF PLAY

(a) **At the beginning of the game,** choice of ends and the kick-off shall be decided by the toss of a coin. The team winning the toss shall have the option of choice of ends or the kick-off. The Referee having given a signal, the game shall be started by a player taking a place-kick (i.e., a kick at the ball while it is stationary on the ground in the centre of the field of play) into his opponents' half of the field of play. Every player shall be in his own half of the field and every player of the team opposing that of the kicker shall remain not less than 10 yards from the ball until it is kicked-off; it shall not be deemed in play until it has travelled the distance of its own circumference. The kicker shall not play the ball a second time until it has been touched or played by another player.

(b) **After a goal is scored,** the game shall be restarted in like manner by a player of the team losing the goal.

(c) **After half-time:** when restarting after half-time, ends shall be changed and the kick-off shall be taken by a player of the opposite team to that of the player who started the game.

Punishment: For any infringement of this Law, the kick-off shall be retaken, except in the case of the kicker playing the ball again before it has been touched or played by another player; for this offence, an indirect free-kick shall be taken by a player of the opposing team from the place where the infringement occurred, unless the offence is committed by a player in his opponent's goal-area, in which case the free-kick shall be taken from a point anywhere within that half of the goal-area in which the offence occurred. A goal shall not be scored direct from a kick-off.

(d) **After any other temporary suspension:** when restarting the game after a temporary suspension of play from any cause not mentioned elsewhere in these Laws, provided that immediately prior to the suspension the ball has not passed over the touch or goal-lines, the Referee shall drop the ball at the place where it was when play was suspended and it shall be deemed in play when it has touched the ground; if, however, it goes over the touch or goal-lines after it has been dropped by the Referee, but before it is touched by a player, the Referee shall again drop it. A player shall not play the ball until it has touched the ground. If this section of the Law is not complied with the Referee shall again drop the ball.

Decisions of the International Board

(1) If, when the Referee drops the ball, a player infringes any of the Laws before the ball has touched the ground, the player concerned shall be cautioned or sent off the field according to the seriousness of the offence, but a free-kick cannot be awarded to the opposing team because the ball was not in play at the time of the offence. The ball shall therefore be again dropped by the Referee.

(2) Kicking-off by persons other than the players competing in a match is prohibited.

LAW IX – BALL IN AND OUT OF PLAY

The ball is out of play:

(a) When it has wholly crossed the goal-line or touch-line, whether on the ground or in the air.

(b) When the game has been stopped by the Referee.

The ball is in play at all other times from the start of the match to the finish including:

(a) If it rebounds from a goal-post, cross-bar or corner-flag post into the field of play.

(b) If it rebounds off either the Referee or Linesmen when they are in the field of play.

(c) In the event of a supposed infringement of the Laws, until a decision is given.

Decisions of the International Board

(1) The lines belong to the areas of which they are the boundaries. In consequence, the touch-lines and the goal-lines belong to the field of play.

LAW X – METHOD OF SCORING

Except as otherwise provided by these Laws, a goal is scored when the whole of the ball has passed over the goal-line, between the goal-posts and under the cross-bar, provided it has not been thrown, carried or intentionally propelled by hand or arm, by a player of the attacking side, except in the case of a goalkeeper, who is within his own penalty-area.

The team scoring the greater number of goals during a game shall be the winner; if no goals, or an equal number of goals are scored, the game shall be termed a 'draw'.

Decisions of the International Board

(1) Law X defines the only method according to which a match is won or drawn; no variation whatsoever can be authorised.

(2) A goal cannot in any case be allowed if the ball has been prevented by some outside agent from passing over the goal-line. If this happens in the normal course of play, other than at the taking of a penalty-kick: the game must be stopped and restarted by the Referee dropping the ball at the place where the ball came into contact with the interference.

(3) If, when the ball is going into goal, a spectator enters the field before it passes wholly over the goal-line, and tries to prevent a score, a goal shall be allowed if the ball goes into goal unless the spectator has made contact with the ball or has interfered with play, in which case the Referee shall stop the game and restart it by dropping the ball at the place where the contact or interference occurred.

LAW XI – OFF-SIDE

(1) A player is in an off-side position if he is nearer to his opponents' goal-line than the ball, **unless:**

(a) He is in his own half of the field of play, or

(b) There are at least two of his opponents nearer their own goal-line than he is.

(2) A player shall only be declared off-side and penalised for being in an off-side position, if, at the moment the ball touches, or is played by, one of his team, he is, in the opinion of the referee

(a) interfering with play or with an opponent, or

(b) seeking to gain an advantage by being in that position.

(3) A player shall not be declared off-side by the referee

(a) merely because of his being in an off-side position, or

(b) if he receives the ball, direct, from a goal-kick, a corner-kick, a throw-in, or when it has been dropped by the referee.

(4) If a player is declared off-side, the referee shall award an indirect free-kick, which shall be taken by a player of the opposing team from the place where the infringement occurred, unless the offence is committed by a player in his opponents' goal-area, in which case, the free-kick shall be taken from a point anywhere within that half of the goal-area in which the offence occurred.

Decisions of the International Board

(1) Off-side shall not be judged at the moment the player in question receives the ball, but at the moment when the ball is passed to him by one of his own side. A player who is not in an off-side position when one of his colleagues passes the ball to him or takes a free-kick, does not therefore become off-side if he goes forward during the flight of the ball.

LAW XII – FOULS AND MISCONDUCT

A player who intentionally commits any of the following nine offences:

(a) Kicks or attempts to kick an opponent;

(b) Trips an opponent, i.e., throwing or attempting to throw him by the use of the legs or by stooping in front of or behind him;

(c) Jumps at an opponent;

(d) Charges an opponent in a violent or dangerous manner;

(e) Charges an opponent from behind unless the latter be obstructing;

(f) Strikes or attempts to strike an opponent;

(g) Holds an opponent;

(h) Pushes an opponent;

(i) Handles the ball, i.e., carries, strikes or propels the ball with his hand or arm. (This does not apply to the goalkeeper within his own penalty-area);

shall be penalised by the award of a direct free-kick to be taken by the opposing side from the place where the offence occurred, unless the offence is committed by a player in his opponents' goal-area in which case, the free-kick shall be taken from a point anywhere within that half of the goal-area in which the offence occurred.

Should a player of the defending side intentionally commit one of the above nine offences within the penalty-area he shall be penalised by a **penalty-kick.**

A penalty-kick can be awarded irrespective of the position of the ball, if in play, at the time an offence within the penalty-area is committed.

A player committing any of the five following offences:

(1) Playing in a manner considered by the Referee to be dangerous, e.g., attempting to kick the ball while held by the goalkeeper;

(2) Charging fairly, i.e., with the shoulder, when the ball is not within playing distance of the players concerned and they are definitely not trying to play it;

(3) When not playing the ball, intentionally obstructing an opponent, i.e. running between the opponent and the ball, or interposing the body so as to form an obstacle to an opponent;

(4) Charging the goalkeeper except when he

(a) is holding the ball;

(b) is obstructing an opponent;

(c) has passed outside his goal-area;

(5) When playing as goalkeeper and within his own penalty area,

(a) from the moment he takes control of the ball with his hands, he takes more than four steps in any direction whilst holding, bouncing or throwing the ball in the air and catching it again, without releasing it into play, or, having released it into play before, during or after the 4 steps, he touches it again with his hands, before it has been touched or played by another player, or

(b) indulges in tactics which, in the opinion of the Referee, are designed merely to hold up the game and thus waste time and so give an unfair advantage to his own team – shall be penalised by the award of an **indirect free-kick** to be taken by the opposing side from the place where the infringement occurred, unless the offence is committed by a player in his opponents' goal-area, in which case the free-kick shall be taken from a point anywhere within that half of the goal-area in which the offence occurred.

A player shall be **cautioned** if:

(j) he enters or re-enters the field of play to join or rejoin his team after the game has commenced, or leaves the field of play during the progress of the game (except through accident) without, in either case, first having received a signal from the Referee showing him that he may do so. If the Referee stops the game to administer the caution the game shall be restarted by an indirect free-kick taken by a player of the opposing team from the place where the ball was when the Referee stopped the game. If the free-kick is awarded to a side within its own goal-area it may be taken from any point within the half of the goal-area in which the ball was when play was stopped. If, however, the offending player has committed a more serious offence he shall be penalised according to that section of the law he infringed;

(k) he persistently infringes the Laws of the Game;

(l) he shows by word or action, dissent from any decision given by the Referee;

(m) he is guilty of ungentlemanly conduct.

For any of these last three offences, in addition to the caution, an **indirect free-kick** shall also be awarded to the opposing side from the place where the offence occurred unless a more serious infringement of the Laws of the Game was committed. If the offence is committed by a player in his opponents' goal-area, a free-kick shall be taken from a point anywhere within that half of the goal-area in which the offence occurred.

A player shall be **sent off** the field of play, if:

(n) in the opinion of the Referee he is guilty of violent conduct or serious foul play;

(o) he uses foul or abusive language;

(p) he persists in misconduct after having received a caution.

If play be stopped by reason of a player being ordered from the field for an offence without a separate breach of the Law having been committed, the game shall be resumed by an **indirect free-kick** awarded to the opposing side from the place where the infringement occurred, unless the offence is committed by a player in his opponents' goal-area, in which case, the free-kick shall be taken from a point anywhere within that half of the goal-area in which the offence occurred.

Decisions of the International Board

---

(1) If the goalkeeper either intentionally strikes an opponent by throwing the ball vigorously at him or pushes him with the ball while holding it, the Referee shall award a penalty-kick, if the offence took place within the penalty-area.

(2) If a player deliberately turns his back to an opponent when he is about to be tackled, he may be charged but not in a dangerous manner.

(3) In case of body-contact in the goal-area between an attacking player and the opposing goalkeeper not in possession of the ball, the Referee, as sole judge of intention, shall stop the game if, in his opinion, the action of the attacking player was intentional, and award an indirect free-kick.

(4) If a player leans on the shoulders of another player of his own team in order to head the ball, the Referee shall stop the game, caution the player for ungentlemanly conduct and award an indirect free-kick to the opposing side.

(5) A player's obligation when joining or rejoining his team after the start of the match to 'report to the Referee' must be interpreted as meaning 'to draw the attention of the Referee from the touch-line'. The signal from the Referee shall be made by a definite gesture which makes the player understand that he may come into the field of play; it is not necessary for the Referee to wait until the game is stopped (this does not apply in respect of an infringement of Law IV), but the Referee is the sole judge of the moment in which he gives his signal of acknowledgement.

(6) The letter and spirit of Law XII do not oblige the Referee to stop a game to administer a caution. He may, if he chooses, apply the advantage. If he does apply the advantage, he shall caution the player when play stops.

(7) If a player covers up the ball without touching it in an endeavour not to have it played by an opponent, he obstructs but does not infringe Law XII para. 3 because he is already in possession of the ball and covers it for tactical reasons whilst the ball remains within playing distance. In fact, he is actually playing the ball and does not commit an infringement; in this case, the player may be charged because he is in fact playing the ball.

(8) If a player intentionally stretches his arms to obstruct an opponent and steps from one side to the other, moving his arms up and down to delay his opponent, forcing him to change course, but does not make 'bodily contact' the Referee shall caution the player for ungentlemanly conduct and award an indirect free-kick.

(9) If a player intentionally obstructs the opposing goalkeeper, in an attempt to prevent him from putting the ball into play in accordance with Law XII, 5(a), the Referee shall award an indirect free-kick.

(10) If after a Referee has awarded a free-kick a player protests violently by using abusive or foul language and is sent off the field, the free-kick should not be taken until the player has left the field.

(11) Any player, whether he is within or outside the field of play, whose conduct is ungentlemanly or violent, whether or not it is directed towards an opponent, a colleague, the Referee, a Linesman or other person, or who uses foul or abusive language, is guilty of an offence, and shall be dealt with according to the nature of the offence committed.

(12) If, in the opinion of the Referee a goalkeeper intentionally lies on the ball longer than is necessary, he shall be penalised for ungentlemanly conduct and

(a) be cautioned and an indirect free-kick awarded to the opposing team;

(b) in case of repetition of the offence, be sent off the field.

(13) The offence of spitting at opponents, officials or other persons, or similar unseemly behaviour shall be considered as violent conduct within the meaning of section (n) of Law XII.

(14) If, when a Referee is about to caution a player, and before he has done so, the player commits another offence which merits a caution, the player shall be sent off the field of play.

LAW XIII – FREE-KICK

Free-kicks shall be classified under two headings: 'Direct' (from which a goal can be scored direct against the offending side), and 'Indirect' (from which a goal cannot be scored unless the ball has been played or touched by a player other than the kicker before passing through the goal).

When a player is taking a direct or an indirect free-kick inside his own penalty-area, all of the opposing players shall remain outside the area, and shall be at least ten yards from the ball whilst the kick is being taken. The ball shall be in play immediately it has travelled the distance of its own circumference and is beyond the penalty-area. The goalkeeper shall not receive the ball into his hands, in order that he may thereafter kick it into play. If the ball is not kicked direct into play, beyond the penalty-area, the kick shall be retaken.

When a player is taking a direct or an indirect free-kick outside his own penalty-area, all of the opposing players shall be at least ten yards from the ball, until it is in play, unless they are standing on their own goal-line, between the goal-posts. The ball shall be in play when it has travelled the distance of its own circumference.

If a player of the opposing side encroaches into the penalty-area, or within ten yards of the ball, as the case may be, before a free-kick is taken, the Referee shall delay the taking of the kick, until the Law is complied with.

The ball must be stationary when a free-kick is taken, and the kicker shall not play the ball a second time, until it has been touched or played by another player.

Notwithstanding any other reference in these Laws to the point from which a free-kick is to be taken, any free-kick awarded to the defending side, within its own goal-area, shall be taken from any point within that half of the goal-area in which the free-kick has been awarded.

Punishment. If the kicker, after taking the free-kick, plays the ball a second time before it has been touched or played by another player an indirect free-kick shall be taken by a player of the opposing team from the spot where the infringement occurred.

Decisions of the International Board

(1) In order to distinguish between a direct and an indirect free-kick, the Referee, when he awards an indirect free-kick, shall indicate accordingly by raising an arm above his head. He shall keep his arm in that position until the kick has been taken and retain the signal until the ball has been played or touched by another player or goes out of play.

(2) Players who do not retire to the proper distance when a free-kick is taken must be cautioned and on any repetition be ordered off. It is particularly requested of Referees that attempts to delay the taking of a free-kick by encroaching should be treated as serious misconduct.

(3) If, when a free-kick is being taken, any of the players dance about or gesticulate in a way calculated to distract their opponents, it shall be deemed ungentlemanly conduct for which the offender(s) shall be cautioned.

LAW XIV – PENALTY-KICK

A penalty-kick shall be taken from the penalty-mark and, when it is being taken, all players with the exception of the player taking the kick, and the opposing goal-keeper, shall be within the field of play but outside the penalty-area, and at least 10 yards from the penalty-mark. The opposing goalkeeper must stand (without moving his feet) on his own goal-line, between the goal-posts, until the ball is kicked. The player taking the kick must kick the ball forward; he shall not play the ball a second time until it has been touched or played by another player. The ball shall be deemed in play directly it is kicked, i.e., when it has travelled the distance of its circumference, and a goal may be scored direct from such a penalty-kick. If the ball touches the goalkeeper before passing between the posts, when a penalty-kick is being taken at or after the expiration of half-time or full-time, it does not nullify a goal. If necessary, time of play shall be extended at half-time or full-time to allow a penalty-kick to be taken.

Punishment

For any infringement of this Law:

(a) by the defending team, the kick shall be retaken if a goal has not resulted.

(b) by the attacking team other than by the player taking the kick, if a goal is scored it shall be disallowed and the kick retaken.

(c) by the player taking the penalty-kick, committed after the ball is in play, a player of the opposing team shall take an indirect free-kick from the spot where the infringement occurred. If, in the case of paragraph (c), the offence is committed by the player in his opponents' goal-area, the free-kick shall be taken from a point anywhere within that half of the goal-area in which the offence occurred.

Decisions of the International Board

---

(1) When the Referee has awarded a penalty-kick, he shall not signal for it to be taken, until the players have taken up position in accordance with the Law.

(2) (a) If, after the kick has been taken, the ball is stopped in its course towards goal, by an outside agent, the kick shall be retaken.

(b) If, after the kick has been taken, the ball rebounds into play, from the goalkeeper, the cross-bar or a goal-post, and is then stopped in its course by an outside agent, the Referee shall stop play and restart it by dropping the ball at the place where it came into contact with the outside agent.

(3) (a) If, after having given the signal for a penalty-kick to be taken, the Referee sees that the goalkeeper is not in his right place on the goal-line, he shall, nevertheless, allow the kick to proceed. It shall be retaken, if a goal is not scored.

(b) If, after the Referee has given the signal for a penalty-kick to be taken, and before the ball has been kicked, the goal-keeper moves his feet, the Referee shall, nevertheless, allow the kick to proceed. It shall be retaken, if a goal is not scored.

(c) If, after the Referee has given the signal for a penalty-kick to be taken, and before the ball is in play, a player of the defending team encroaches into the penalty-area, or within ten yards of the penalty-mark, the Referee shall, nevertheless, allow the kick to proceed. It shall be retaken, if a goal is not scored.

The player concerned shall be cautioned.

(4) (a) If, when a penalty-kick is being taken, the player taking the kick is guilty of ungentlemanly conduct, the kick, if already taken, shall be retaken, if a goal is scored.

The player concerned shall be cautioned.

(b) If, after the Referee has given the signal for a penalty-kick to be taken, and before the ball is in play, a colleague of the player taking the kick encroaches into the penalty-area or within ten yards of the penalty-mark, the Referee shall, nevertheless, allow the kick to proceed. If a goal is scored, it shall be disallowed, and the kick retaken.

The player concerned shall be cautioned.

(c) If, in the circumstances described in the foregoing paragraph, the ball rebounds into play from the goalkeeper, the crossbar or a goal-post, the Referee shall stop the game, caution the player and award an indirect free-kick to the opposing team from the place where the infringement occurred.

(5) (a) If, after the referee has given the signal for a penalty-kick to be taken, and before the ball is in play, the goalkeeper moves from his position on the goal-line, or moves his feet, and a colleague of the kicker encroaches into the penalty-area or within 10 yards of the penalty-mark, the kick, if taken, shall be retaken.

The colleague of the kicker shall be cautioned.

(b) If, after the Referee has given the signal for a penalty-kick to be taken, and before the ball is in play, a player of each team encroaches into the penalty-area, or within 10 yards of the penalty-mark, the kick, if taken, shall be retaken.

The players concerned shall be cautioned.

(6) When a match is extended, at half-time or full-time, to allow a penalty-kick to be taken or retaken, the extension shall last until the moment that the penalty-kick has been completed, i.e. until the Referee has decided whether or not a goal is scored.

A goal is scored when the ball passes wholly over the goal-line.

(a) direct from the penalty-kick,

(b) having rebounded from either goal-post or the cross-bar, or

(c) having touched or been played by the goalkeeper.

The game shall terminate immediately the Referee has made his decision.

(7) When a penalty-kick is being taken in extended time:

(a) the provisions of all of the foregoing paragraphs, except paragraphs (2)(b) and (4)(c) shall apply in the usual way, and

(b) in the circumstances described in paragraphs (2)(b) and (4)(c) the game shall terminate immediately the ball rebounds from the goal-keeper, the cross-bar or the goal-post.

LAW XV – THROW-IN

When the whole of the ball passes over a touch-line, either on the ground or in the air, it shall be thrown in from the point where it crossed the line, in any direction, by a player of the team opposite to that of the player who last touched it. The thrower at the moment of delivering the ball must face the field of play and part of each foot shall be either on the touch-line or on the ground outside the touch-line. The thrower shall use both hands and shall deliver the ball from behind and over his head. The ball shall be in play immediately it enters the field of play, but the thrower shall not again play the ball until it has been touched or played by another player. A goal shall not be scored direct from a throw-in.

Punishment:

(a) If the ball is improperly thrown in the throw-in shall be taken by a player of the opposing team.

(b) If the thrower plays the ball a second time before it has been touched or played by another player, an indirect free-kick shall be taken by a player of the opposing team from the place where the infringement occurred, unless the offence is committed by a player in his opponents' goal-area, in which case, the free-kick shall be taken from a point anywhere within that half of the goal-area in which the offence occurred.

Decisions of the International Board

---

(1) If a player taking a throw-in, plays the ball a second time by handling it within the field of play before it has been touched or played by another player, the Referee shall award a direct free-kick.

(2) A player taking a throw-in must face the field of play with some part of his body.

(3) If, when a throw-in is being taken, any of the opposing players dance about or gesticulate in a way calculated to distract or impede the thrower, it shall be deemed ungentlemanly conduct, for which the offender(s) shall be cautioned.

LAW XVI – GOAL-KICK

When the whole of the ball passes over the goal-line excluding that portion between the goal-posts, either in the air or on the ground, having last been played by one of the attacking team, it shall be kicked direct into play beyond the penalty-area from a point within that half of the goal-area nearest to where it crossed the line, by a player of the defending team. A goalkeeper shall not receive the ball into his hands from a goal-kick in order that he may thereafter kick it into play. If the ball is not kicked beyond the penalty-area, i.e., direct into play, the kick shall be retaken. The kicker shall not play the ball a second time until it has touched – or been played by – another player. A goal shall not be scored direct from such a kick. Players of the team opposing that of the player taking the goal-kick shall remain outside the penalty-area whilst the kick is being taken.

Punishment:

If a player taking a goal-kick plays the ball a second time after it has passed beyond the penalty-area, but before it has touched or been played by another player, an indirect free-kick shall be awarded to the opposing team, to be taken from the place where the infringement occurred, unless the offence is committed by a player in his opponents' goal-area, in which case, the free-kick shall be taken from a point anywhere within that half of the goal-area in which the offence occurred.

Decisions of the International Board

---

(1) When a goal-kick has been taken and the player who has kicked the ball touches it again before it has left the penalty-area, the kick has not been taken in accordance with the Law and must be retaken.

LAW XVII – CORNER-KICK

When the whole of the ball passes over the goal-line, excluding that portion between the goal-posts, either in the air or on the ground, having last been played by one of the defending team, a member of the attacking team shall take a corner-kick, i.e., the whole of the ball shall be placed within the quarter circle at the nearest corner-flag post, which must not be moved, and it shall be kicked from that position. A goal may be scored direct from such a kick. Players of the team opposing that of the player taking the corner-kick shall not approach within 10 yards of the ball until it is in play, i.e., it has travelled the distance of its own circumference, nor shall the kicker play the ball a second time until it has been touched or played by another player.

Punishment:

(a) If the player who takes the kick plays the ball a second time before it has been touched or played by another player, the Referee shall award an indirect free-kick to the opposing team, to be taken from the place where the infringement occurred, unless the offence is committed by a player in his opponents' goal-area, in which case the free-kick shall be taken from a point anywhere within that half of the goal-area in which the offence occurred.

(b) For any other infringement the kick shall be retaken.

ADDRESSES

The Football Association: 16 Lancaster Gate, London W2 3LW

Scotland: Ernie Walker, 6 Park Gardens, Glasgow G3 7YE

Northern Ireland (Irish FA): W. J. Drennan, J.P., M.B.E., 20 Windsor Avenue, Belfast BT9 6EG

Wales: A. Evans, 3 Fairy Road, Wrexham LL13 7PS

Republic of Ireland (FA of Ireland): P. J. O'Driscoll, 80 Merrion Square, Dublin 2

International Federation (FIFA): S. Blatter, FIFA House, Hitzigweg 11, CH-8032 Zurich, Switzerland

Union of European Football Associations: H. Bangerter, PO Box 16, CH-3000 Berne 15, Switzerland

THE LEAGUES

The Football League: R. H. G. Kelly, F.C.I.S., The Football League, Lytham St Annes, Lancs. FY8 1JG. *0253-729421. Telex 67675*

The Scottish League: J. Farry, 188 West Regent Street, Glasgow G2 4RY. *041-248 3844/5*

The Irish League: J. H. Long, 16 Donegall Square South, Belfast

Alliance Premier League: P. D. Hunter, 24 Barnehurst Road, Bexleyheath, Kent DA7 6EZ. *Crayford 22616*

Athenian League: B. W. Hitchings, 18 Tany's Dell, Harlow, Essex. *0279 39757*

Central League: D. J. Grimshaw, 118 St Stephens Road, Deepdale, Preston, Lancs., PR1 6TD. *Preston 55898*

North West Counties League: C. R. Mahood, Burscough Nurseries, Ring O'Bells Lane, Lathom, Ormskirk, Lancs L40 5US. *Rufford 822688*

Eastern Counties League: Dr G. Cubbin, 19 Emmanuel Road, Cambridge. *0223 315099*

Football Combination: T. P. R. Kirkup, 15 Oulton Rise, Spinney Hill, Northampton NN3 1EW. *0604-47831*

Hellenic League: D. A. G. Harrison, 107 Thame Road, Haddenham, Aylesbury, Bucks. *Haddenham 290590*

Kent League: D. Baker, 17 Sterling Road, Sittingbourne, Kent. *Sittingbourne 25105*

Lancashire Amateur League: H. Heap, 'Maraldo', Carlton Road, Hale, Altrincham, Cheshire, WA15 8RH. *061-980 2344*

Lancashire Football League: H. E. Lambert, 3 Cravans Avenue, Ewood, Blackburn BB2 4LB. *Blackburn 58561*

Leicestershire Senior League: P. Henwood, 63 Carisbrooke Rd, Leicester LE2 3PF. *Leicester 705475*

London Spartan: D. Cordell, 44 Greenleas, Waltham Abbey, Essex. *Lea Valley 712428*

Manchester League: F. J. Fitzpatrick, 102 Victoria Road, Stretford, Manchester. *061-865 2726*

Midland Combination: L. W. James, 175 Barnet Lane, Kingswinford, Brierley Hill, West Midlands. *Kingswinford 3459*

Mid-Week Football League: Frank P. White, 11 Tulip Way, Clacton-on-Sea, Essex. *Clacton 32750*

Nemean Amateur League: W. Chivers, 58 Laurel Avenue, Potters Bar, Herts. EN6 2AB. *Potters Bar 54969*

Northern Intermediate League: F. R. Vicary, 12 Holmefield Avenue, Thornes, Wakefield, Yorks WF2 7AF. *Wakefield 75013*

Northern League: G. Nicholson, 99 Watling Road, Bishop Auckland, Co. Durham. *Bishop Auckland 2167*

Northern Premier League: R. D. Bayley, 22 Woburn Drive, Hale, Altrincham, Cheshire WA15. *061-980-7007*

North Midlands League: G. Thompson, 7 Wren Park Close, Ridgway, Sheffield

Old Boys Football League: B. Aldous, Clemitis Cottage, Ongar Road, White Roding, Dunmow, Essex. *White Roding 278*

Peterborough and District League: A. V. Brown, 27 Gloucester Road, Old Fletton, Peterborough

Isthmian League: N. Robinson, 226 Rye Lane, Peckham SE15. *01-653 3903*

Southern Amateur League: F. J. Banner, 10 Oakwood Road, Orpington, Kent. *Farnborough 58720*

South-East Counties League: R. A. Bailey, 10 Highlands Road, New Barnet, Herts. EN5 5AB. *01-449 5131*

Southern League: D. J. Strudwick, 49 Woodlands Way, Southwater, Horsham, West Sussex, RH13 7HT

South Midlands League: C. Moyse, 33 Markham Crescent, Dunstable, Beds. LU5 4SS. *Dunstable 64682*

South Western League: G. Gazzard, 6 Coastguard Crescent, Penzance, Cornwall. *Penzance 61397*

United Counties League: G. Ellitson, 2 St Marks Close, Rushden, Northants. *Rushden 313106*

Wearside: M. G. Gordon, 9 Cliffe Road, Seaburn, Sunderland. *0783 490414*

Western League: J. Veale, 5 Everest Road, Bristol BS16 2BX. *0272-652699*

The Welsh League: Anthony W. Griffiths, 13 Llynfi Road, Maesteg, Bridgend, Mid Glamorgan CF34 9DS. *0656 734096*

West Midlands Regional League: K. H. Goodfellow, 152 Garrison Lane, Small Heath, Birmingham. *021-772-0375*

West Yorkshire League: W. Keyworth, 2 Hill Court Grove, Branley, Yorks. L13 2AP. *Pudsey 74465*

Northern Counties (East): B. Wood, 5 Restmore Avenue, Guiseley, Nr Leeds, LS20 9DG. *Guiseley 4558 (home); Bradford 29595 (9 a.m. to 5 p.m.)*

COUNTY FOOTBALL ASSOCIATIONS

Bedfordshire: P. Burns, 13 Wendover Way, Luton, Beds. LU2 7LS. *Luton 30829*

Berks and Bucks: W. J. Gosling, 15a London Street, Faringdon, Oxon. *0367 22099*

Birmingham County: W. F. Pennick, County F.A. Offices, Rayhall Lane, Great Barr, Birmingham B43 6JE *021-357-4278*

Cambridgeshire: R. E. Rogers, 20 Aingers Road, Histon, Cambridge. *Histon 2803*

Cheshire: F. Foden, 549 Crewe Road, Wistaston, Crewe, CW2 6PU. *Crewe 69429*

Cornwall: W. Parnell, 12 Higher Tremena, St Austell PL25 5QQ. *St Austell 3236*

Cumberland: R. Johnson, 72 Victoria Road, Workington, Cumberland. *Workington 3979*

Derbyshire: H. L. P. Holmes, 82 Friar Gate, Derby. *Derby 25835*

Devon County: C. H. Norsworthy, 8 Belair Road, Peverell, Plymouth PL2 3QH. *Plymouth 73550*

Dorset County: P. Hough, 110 Dorchester Rd, Oakdale, Poole, Dorset BH15 3SD *0202 746244*

Durham: G. L. Pearce, 'Codeslaw', Ferens Park, Durham DH1 1JZ. *Durham 3653*

East Riding County: C. Branton, 83 Belvedere Road, Hessel, Hull HU13 9JH *Hull 649294*

Essex County: M. S. Jeffers, 54A Eastwood Road, Goodmayes, Ilford, Essex. *01-590 7893*

Gloucestershire: E. J. Marsh, 46 Douglas Road, Horfield, Bristol BS7 0JD. *Bristol 46430*

Guernsey: R. Trustum, Carleeta, Marette Du Haut, St Martins, Guernsey C.I. *0481-36529*

Hampshire: R. G. Barnes, 367 Winchester Road, Southampton. *Southampton 766884*

Herefordshire: E. R. Prescott, 7 Kirkland Close, Hampton Park, Hereford. *0432-268904*

Hertfordshire: G. W. Daulby, 158 Hazelwood Drive, St Albans, Herts. AL4 OU2

Hunts County: M. M. Armstrong, 1 Chapel End, Great Giddings, Huntingdon, Cambs. *Winwick 262*

Isle of Man: Mrs R. Raley, 129 Bucks Road, Douglas, I.O.M.

Jersey: Miss S. Mourant, Racqueberg Farm, Samares Lane, St Clement, Jersey, C.I.

Kent County: K. T. Masters, 69 Maidstone Road, Chatham, Kent ME4 6DT. *Medway 43824*

Lancashire: J. Kenyon, 31A, Wellington St, St John's, Blackburn, Lancs. BB1 8AU *Blackburn 64333*

Leicestershire and Rutland: R. E. Barston, 67 Melton Road, Leicester

Lincolnshire: F. S. Richardson, 9 The Avenue, Lincoln. *Lincoln 24917*

Liverpool County: S. A. Rudd, 23 Greenfield Road, Old Swann, Liverpool 13. *051-526-9515*

London: A. F. Monger, 4 Aldworth Grove, London SE13 6HY. *01-690-9626*

Manchester County: S. Holliday, 87 Hart Road, Fallowfield, Manchester 14. *061-224-5185*

Middlesex County: A. L. Smith, 68 Squires Lane, London N3 2AP *01-346 7565*

Norfolk County: R. Kiddell, 39 Beaumont Road, Costessey, Norwich NR5 0HG. *Norwich 742421*

Northamptonshire: B. Walden, 37 Harding Terrace, Northampton. *Northampton 39584*

North Riding County: P. Kirby, 254 Linthorpe Road, Middlesbrough. *0642-818767*

Northumberland: J. A. Forster, 30 St Mary's Place, Newcastle upon Tyne, NE1 7P2. *Newcastle 610779*

Nottinghamshire: W. T. Annable, 7 Clarendon Street, Nottingham. *Nottingham 48954*

Oxfordshire: P. J. Ladbrook, 3 Wilkins Road, Cowley, Oxford

Sheffield and Hallamshire: G. Thompson, Clegg House, 253 Pittsmoor Road, Sheffield 3. *Sheffield 27817*

Shropshire: A. W. Brett, High Street Chambers, 10–11, High Street, Shrewsbury

Somerset & Avon (South): L. G. Webb, 32 North Road, Midsomer Norton, Bath BA3 2QQ. *Midsomer Norton 3176*

Staffordshire: T. Myatt, County Offices, Miller Street, Newcastle-under-Lyme ST5 1HB. *Newcastle-under-Lyme 622585*

Suffolk County: B. A. H. Collings, 15 Taunton Close, Henley Rise, Ipswich IP1 6NL. *Ipswich 714676*

Surrey County: L. F. J. Smith, 2 Fairfield Avenue, Horley, Surrey RH6 7PD *Horley 4945*

Sussex County: R. F. Reeve, County Office, Culver Road, Lancing, Sussex BN15 9AX

Westmorland: J. R. Plumbe, 24 Crescent Green, Kendal LA9 6DR *Kendal 23227*

West Riding County: R. M. Robin, 77 Great George Street, Leeds LS1 3DR

Wiltshire: F. J. Peart, 161 Grange Drive, Stratton St Margaret, Swindon. *Stratton St Margaret 2239*

Worcestershire: P. Rushton, 84 Windermere Drive, Warndon, Worcester WR4 9JB. *Worcester 51166*

OTHER USEFUL ADDRESSES

Amateur Football Alliance: W. P. Goss, Room 33, 3rd Floor, 6 Langley Street, London WC2 *01-240 3837/8*

English Schools FA: A. Rice, 4A Eastgate Street, Stafford ST16 2NN. *0785-51142*

Oxford University: Sir Harold Thompson, C.B.E., F.R.S., St John's College, Oxford

Cambridge University: Dr S. C. Aston, O.B.E., St Catherine's College, Cambridge CB2 1RL

Army: Major A. Dobson, M.B.E., Ministry of Defence (A.S.C.B.), Clayton Barracks, Aldershot, Hants.

Royal Air Force: Sq/Ldr A. V. Heron, 105 Bradenham Beeches, Walters Ash, High Wycombe, Bucks HP14 4XN

Royal Navy: Lt-Cdr H. A. Sheppard, R.N. Sports Office, H.M.S. Nelson, Portsmouth, Hants. PO1 3HH

niversities Athletic Union: Alun Evans, U.A.U., 28 Woburn Square, London WC1 *01-637 4828*

Central Council of Physical Recreation: General Secretary, 70 Brompton Road, London, SW3 1HE. *01-584 6651*

British Olympic Association: 6 John Prince's Street, W1M 0DH *01-408 2029*

National Federation of Football Supporters' Clubs: Lottery Office: 1 Saville Row, Bath, Avon BA1 2QP *0225-312247*. General Secretary: Malcolm Gamlen, 69 Fourth Avenue, Chelmsford, Essex *0245-63305*

National Playing Fields Association: Col R. Satterthwaite, O.B.E., 578b Catherine Place, London, SW1

The Scottish Football Commercial Managers Association: J. E. Hillier (Chairman), c/o Keith FC Promotions Office, 60 Union Street, Keith, Banffshire, Scotland

Professional Footballers' Association: G. Taylor, 124 Corn Exchange Buildings, Hanging Ditch, Manchester M4 3BN. *061-834 7554*

Referees' Association: O. J. Venning, Summerhill, Kingswinford, West Midlands

The Association of Football League Referees and Linesmen: J. B. Goggins, 1 Tewkesbury Drive, Lytham St Annes, Lancs, Lancs FY8 4LN

Women's Football Association: Miss C. Whitehead, 11 Portsea Mews, Portsea Place, London W2. *01-402 9388*

The Association of Provincial Football Supporters' Clubs in London: E. Norfolk, 79 Dellow Close, Ilford, Essex

The Association of Football League Commercial Managers: G. H. Dimbleby, Secretary WBA FC, The Hawthorns, Halfords Lane, West Bromwich B71 4LF

The Association of Football Statisticians: R. J. Spiller, 5 Hempstalls, Basildon, Essex. *0268 282556*

The Football Programme Directory: David Stacey, 'The Beeches', 66 Southend Road, Wickford, Essex SS11 8EN.

England Football Supporters Association: Hon. Publicity Officer, David Stacey, 66 Southend Road, Wickford, Essex SS11 8EN

The Football League Executive Staffs Association: PO Box 52, Leamington Spa, Warwickshire

The Ninety-Two Club: 104 Gilda Crescent, Whitchurch, Bristol BS14 9LD

FOOTBALL LEAGUE FIXTURES 1983–4

Subject to alteration; copyright of the Football League Limited, and may not be reproduced in whole or in part without their consent.

DIVISION ONE

	Arsenal	Aston Villa	Birmingham C	Coventry C	Everton	Ipswich T	Leicester C	Liverpool	Luton T	Manchester U	Norwich C	Nottingham F	Notts Co	QPR	Southampton	Stoke C	Sunderland	Tottenham H	Watford	WBA	West Ham U	Wolverhampton W
Arsenal	—	18.2	27.12	15.10	19.11	10.3	28.4	10.9	27.8	6.9	24.9	22.10	21.1	4.2	31.12	7.4	5.11	21.4	17.12	3.12	7.5	24.3
Aston Villa	29.10	—	15.10	7.4	7.5	17.12	19.11	21.1	4.2	3.3	10.9	17.3	28.4	31.12	24.9	12.11	29.8	27.12	21.4	27.8	3.12	25.2
Birmingham C	23.4	31.3	—	5.11	2.1	17.9	1.10	5.5	10.3	28.1	10.12	26.12	24.3	14.4	12.5	6.9	26.11	22.10	3.9	18.2	14.1	11.2
Coventry C	31.3	28.1	3.3	—	3.9	1.10	17.9	10.12	5.5	26.12	12.5	24.4	6.9	12.11	26.11	18.2	2.1	24.3	14.1	22.10	11.2	14.4
Everton	14.4	10.12	24.9	31.12	—	17.3	18.2	3.3	15.10	5.5	26.11	12.11	4.2	12.5	31.3	27.8	26.12	21.1	22.10	10.9	29.8	23.4
Ipswich T	12.11	12.5	21.1	4.2	6.9	—	22.10	26.11	31.3	10.12	23.4	14.4	31.12	15.10	18.2	10.9	5.5	27.8	24.3	24.9	3.3	26.12
Leicester C	26.11	14.4	4.2	21.1	29.10	25.2	—	24.4	31.8	12.11	31.3	5.5	27.8	26.12	15.10	24.9	12.5	10.9	3.3	31.12	17.3	10.12
Liverpool	11.2	17.9	3.12	7.5	5.11	28.4	27.12	—	29.10	2.1	24.3	3.9	17.12	25.2	6.9	19.11	1.10	10.3	28.1	21.4	7.4	14.1
Luton T	14.1	1.10	12.11	3.12	7.4	28.1	24.3	18.2	—	11.2	6.9	2.1	21.4	3.3	22.10	7.5	3.9	19.11	28.4	18.12	27.12	17.9
Manchester U	17.3	5.11	7.4	21.4	3.12	7.5	10.3	24.9	10.9	—	4.2	29.8	27.12	27.8	21.1	31.12	25.2	17.12	19.11	15.10	28.4	29.10
Norwich C	2.1	11.2	7.5	17.12	28.4	27.12	19.10	31.8	17.3	1.10	—	17.9	10.3	29.10	5.11	21.4	14.1	3.12	7.4	19.11	25.2	3.9
Nottingham F	25.2	7.9	21.4	28.12	10.3	19.11	4.12	31.12	24.9	24.3	21.1	—	16.10	10.9	27.8	28.4	29.10	4.2	7.5	7.4	17.12	5.11
Notts Co	17.9	26.11	30.8	17.3	1.10	3.9	14.1	12.5	26.12	23.4	12.11	31.3	—	5.5	14.4	22.10	10.12	18.2	11.2	3.3	2.1	28.1
QPR	1.10	3.9	19.11	10.3	17.12	7.4	21.4	22.10	5.11	14.1	18.2	11.2	3.12	—	24.3	29.11	17.9	28.4	6.9	7.5	28.1	2.1
Southampton	3.9	2.1	17.12	28.4	28.1	29.10	7.4	17.3	25.2	17.9	3.3	14.1	19.11	29.8	—	3.12	11.2	7.5	27.12	12.11	21.4	1.10
Stoke C	28.1	10.3	17.3	29.10	14.1	11.2	2.1	14.4	10.12	3.9	26.12	26.11	25.2	23.4	5.5	—	31.3	5.11	17.9	29.8	1.10	12.5
Sunderland	3.3	24.3	28.4	24.9	21.4	3.12	18.12	4.2	31.12	22.10	27.8	18.2	7.5	21.1	10.9	15.10	—	7.4	12.11	27.12	19.11	7.9
Tottenham H	26.12	23.4	25.2	29.8	17.9	14.1	11.2	12.11	14.4	12.5	5.5	1.10	29.10	26.11	10.12	3.3	28.1	—	2.1	17.3	3.9	31.3
Watford	12.5	26.12	31.12	27.8	25.2	30.8	5.11	31.3	26.11	14.4	15.10	10.12	10,9	17.3	24.4	21.1	10.3	24.9	—	4.2	29.10	5.5
WBA	5.5	14.1	29.10	25.2	11.2	2.1	3.9	26.12	12.5	31.3	14.4	28.1	5.11	10.12	10.3	24.3	23.4	7.9	1.10	—	17.9	26.11
West Ham U	10.12	5.5	27.8	10.9	24.3	5.11	6.9	15.10	17.4	26.11	22.10	12.5	24.9	31.3	26.12	4.2	14.4	31.12	18.2	21.1	—	10.3
Wolves	29.8	22.10	10.9	19.11	27.12	21.4	7.5	27.8	21.1	18.2	31.12	3.3	7.4	24.9	4.2	17.12	17.3	15.10	3.12	28.4	12.11	—

DIVISION TWO

	Barnsley	Blackburn R	Brighton & HA	Cambridge U	Cardiff C	Carlisle U	Charlton Ath	Chelsea	Crystal Palace	Derby Co	Fulham	Grimsby T	Huddersfield T	Leeds U	Manchester C	Middlesbrough	Newcastle U	Oldham Ath	Portsmouth	Sheffield W	Shrewsbury T	Swansea C
Barnsley	—	23.4	26.11	26.12	4.2	12.5	14.4	10.12	18.2	31.3	27.8	27.9	15.10	22.10	31.12	10.9	24.9	5.5	17.3	3.3	21.1	12.11
Blackburn R	28.12	—	24.9	31.12	7.5	24.3	3.3	7.9	17.10	10.9	29.4	4.12	27.8	12.11	21.1	7.4	20.4	22.10	19.11	4.2	16.10	18.2
Brighton & HA	28.4	2.1	—	18.2	3.12	17.9	1.10	3.9	21.4	6.9	27.12	7.4	5.11	24.3	10.3	7.5	17.12	14.1	8.10	22.10	19.11	11.2
Cambridge U	21.4	3.9	29.10	—	10.3	14.1	17.9	11.2	8.10	5.11	3.12	27.12	18.10	7.4	17.12	19.11	28.4	1.10	25.2	17.3	7.5	2.1
Cardiff C	1.10	10.12	5.5	12.11	—	8.10	14.1	31.3	2.1	23.4	19.2	3.9	26.11	11.2	29.8	3.3	18.10	14.4	17.9	12.5	16.3	26.12
Carlisle U	17.12	29.8	21.1	27.8	7.4	—	17.3	22.10	7.5	4.2	15.10	28.4	24.9	3.12	19.11	21.4	27.12	18.2	12.11	31.12	10.9	3.3
Charlton Ath	19.11	5.11	4.2	21.1	27.8	6.9	—	18.2	27.12	24.9	7.5	10.3	31.12	16.12	15.10	3.12	7.4	24.3	21.4	10.9	28.4	22.10
Chelsea	7.5	16.3	31.12	10.9	15.10	25.2	29.10	—	19.11	27.8	7.4	17.12	4.2	28.4	3.12	24.9	12.11	3.3	27.12	21.1	21.4	6.12
Crystal Palace	29.10	12.5	26.12	1.4	25.9	11.12	23.4	14.4	—	15.10	11.9	25.2	17.3	3.3	27.8	4.2	21.1	12.11	27.9	26.11	31.12	5.5
Derby Co	8.10	11.2	17.3	3.3	27.12	1.10	2.1	14.1	7.4	—	21.4	29.10	25.2	19.11	28.4	12.11	3.12	17.9	9.5	29.8	17.12	3.9
Fulham	14.1	26.11	23.4	5.5	28.10	31.3	10.12	8.10	11.2	26.12	—	2.1	14.4	17.9	17.3	27.9	3.3	12.5	3.9	11.11	25.2	1.10
Grimsby T	24.3	5.5	15.10	23.4	31.12	26.11	12.11	12.5	22.10	18.2	24.9	—	31.3	6.9	4.2	21.1	10.9	10.12	3.3	26.12	27.8	14.4
Huddersfield T	7.4	14.1	3.3	24.3	28.4	2.1	3.9	1.10	6.9	22.10	19.11	8.10	—	21.4	27.12	17.12	7.5	11.2	3.12	18.2	12.11	17.9
Leeds U	25.2	10.3	29.8	14.10	10.9	5.5	12.5	26.11	5.11	14.4	21.1	17.3	26.12	—	24.9	31.12	27.8	24.4	29.10	31.3	4.2	10.12
Manchester C	3.9	17.9	12.11	12.5	24.3	14.4	31.3	5.5	14.1	26.11	7.9	1.10	23.4	2.1	—	22.10	18.2	26.12	11.2	10.12	3.3	8.10
Middlesbrough	11.2	8.10	10,12	14.4	5.11	26.12	5.5	2.1	1.10	10.3	24.3	17.9	12.5	3.9	25.2	—	6.9	31.3	14.1	23.4	29.10	26.11
Newcastle U	2.1	26.12	12.5	26.11	25.2	23.4	8.10	10.3	17.9	5.5	5.11	11.2	10.12	14.1	29.10	17.3	—	3.9	1.10	14.4	29.8	31.3
Oldham Ath	3.12	25.2	27.8	4.2	19.11	29.10	27.9	5.11	10.3	21.1	17.10	7.5	10.9	27.12	20.4	15.10	31.12	—	28.4	24.9	7.4	17.3
Portsmouth	6.9	14.4	31.3	22.10	21.1	10.3	26.12	24.4	24.3	10.12	31.12	5.11	5.5	18.2	10.9	27.8	4.2	26.11	—	15.10	24.9	12.5
Sheffield W	5.11	1.10	25.2	6.9	17.12	3.9	11.2	17.9	28.4	24.3	10.3	21.4	29.10	8.10	7.5	27.12	19.11	2.1	7.4	—	3.12	14.1
Shrewsbury T	17.9	30.3	14.4	10.12	6.9	11.2	26.11	26.12	3.9	12.5	22.10	14.1	10.3	1.10	5.11	18.2	24.3	8.10	2.1	5.5	—	24.4
Swansea C	10.3	29.10	10.9	24.9	21.4	5.11	25.2	24.3	3.12	31.12	5.2	19.11	20.1	7.5	7.4	27.4	15.10	6.9	17.12	27.8	27.12	—

DIVISION THREE

	Bolton W	Bournemouth	Bradford C	Brentford	Bristol R	Burnley	Exeter C	Gillingham	Hull C	Lincoln C	Millwall	Newport Co	Orient	Oxford U	Plymouth Arg	Port Vale	Preston NE	Rotherham U	Scunthorpe U	Sheffield U	Southend U	Walsall	Wigan Ath	Wimbledon
Bolton W	—	28.4	7.1	3.12	4.2	27.9	17.3	7.4	18.10	14.2	2.1	15.10	5.11	27.12	10.3	25.2	17.12	24.9	21.1	7.5	29.10	10.9	21.4	27.8
B'mouth	26.11	—	12.5	18.2	27.9	7.1	31.12	24.9	5.11	4.2	21.1	26.12	23.4	22.10	8.10	5.5	27.8	1.11	14.4	24.3	10.3	3.3	10.9	31.3
Bradf'd C	3.9	17.12	—	28.4	24.3	21.4	1.10	2.11	7.9	7.5	12.11	28.1	14.1	3.3	3.12	11.2	2.1	18.2	8.10	7.4	17.9	22.10	27.12	7.3
Brentford	14.4	29.10	26.11	—	31.3	24.9	20.4	4.2	15.10	10.9	27.8	31.12	10.3	17.3	5.11	18.10	7.1	27.9	5.5	25.2	14.2	12.5	21.1	26.12
Bristol R	1.10	7.4	15.10	6.9	—	12.11	17.9	27.12	17.12	28.4	8.5	14.1	11.2	21.4	3.3	28.1	1.11	6.3	22.10	3.12	3.9	18.2	3.1	17.3
Burnley	31.3	3.9	26.12	11.2	10.3	—	14.2	15.10	14.1	25.2	17.3	6.9	5.5	28.1	1.10	26.11	5.11	14.4	31.12	17.9	18.10	23.4	29.10	12.5
Exeter C	8.10	7.5	3.2	27.12	21.1	2.11	—	3.3	3.12	28.9	17.12	22.10	17.2	2.1	21.4	5.11	28.4	10.9	7.1	10.3	23.3	27.8	7.4	24.9
Gill'ham	6.9	11.2	14.2	1.10	23.4	24.3	18.10	—	3.9	5.11	29.10	5.5	31.3	17.9	28.1	14.4	8.10	26.11	12.5	14.1	26.12	10.3	25.2	31.12
Hull C	3.3	6.3	31.3	24.3	12.5	27.8	14.4	7.1	—	24.9	10.9	12.11	26.11	18.2	22.10	31.12	21.1	23.4	26.12	8.10	5.5	1.11	4.2	27.9
Lincoln C	2.11	1.10	31.12	28.1	26.11	22.10	31.3	7.3	11.2	—	15.10	3.3	7.9	14.1	17.9	12.5	18.2	5.5	12.11	3.9	23.4	26.12	17.3	14.4
Millwall	5.5	17.9	11.3	15.1	30.12	9.10	12.5	19.2	28.1	24.3	—	1.11	26.12	11.2	3.9	6.9	21.10	3.3	26.11	1.10	11.4	14.4	5.11	23.4
Newp't	24.3	21.4	10.9	7.5	27.8	7.4	25.2	2.1	10.3	18.10	14.2	—	8.10	28.4	27.12	29.10	27.9	4.2	24.9	17.12	5.11	22.1	3.12	7.1
Orient	6.3	27.12	27.8	12.11	23.9	2.1	29.10	27.9	28.4	7.4	21.4	17.3	—	7.5	17.12	14.10	3.12	20.1	9.9	18.10	26.2	7.1	14.2	4.2
Oxford U	20.4	25.2	19.10	8.10	26.12	10.9	5.5	21.1	29.10	27.8	24.9	26.11	31.12	—	24.3	10.3	4.2	12.5	31.3	5.11	14.4	28.9	7.1	15.2
Plym'th A	12.11	17.3	14.4	6.3	18.10	4.2	26.12	10.9	25.2	21.1	7.1	20.4	12.5	15.10	—	14.2	24.9	30.3	27.9	29.10	31.12	5.5	27.8	26.11
Port Vale	22.10	2.1	24.9	3.3	10.9	28.4	5.3	3.12	7.5	17.12	7.4	18.2	24.3	12.11	31.10	—	21.4	7.1	27.8	27.12	8.10	4.2	26.9	21.1
Prest NE	12.5	14.1	5.5	3.9	14.2	6.3	26.11	17.3	17.9	29.10	25.2	30.3	14.4	1.10	11.2	26.12	—	12.11	23.4	28.1	6.9	31.12	15.10	18.10
Roth'm U	11.2	14.2	29.10	7.4	5.11	3.12	28.1	28.4	27.12	2.1	18.10	1.10	17.9	17.12	6.9	3.9	10.3	—	24.3	21.4	14.1	8.10	7.5	25.2
S'thorpe	16.9	3.12	17.3	2.1	25.2	7.5	3.9	17.12	21.4	10.3	27.4	10.2	27.1	7.9	7.4	13.1	27.12	15.10	—	14.2	30.9	5.11	18.10	29.10
Sheff U	31.12	15.10	27.9	22.10	14.4	21.1	12.11	27.8	17.3	7.1	4.2	12.5	3.3	6.3	18.2	23.4	10.9	26.12	1.11	—	26.11	31.3	24.9	5.5
S'thend U	17.2	11.11	20.1	31.10	6.1	2.3	15.10	20.4	2.1	27.12	19.9	12.3	21.10	2.12	7.5	16.3	6.4	27.8	3.2	28.4	—	24.9	17.12	10.9
Walsall	28.1	18.10	25.2	17.12	29.10	27.12	14.1	12.11	14.2	21.4	3.12	17.9	3.9	7.4	2.1	1.10	7.5	17.3	6.3	6.9	11.2	—	28.4	15.10
Wigan A	26.12	28.1	23.4	17.9	5.5	18.2	6.9	22.10	1.10	8.10	6.3	14.4	1.11	3.9	14.1	31.3	24.3	31.12	3.3	11.2	12.5	26.11	—	12.11
Wim'don	14.1	6.9	5.11	21.4	8.10	17.12	11.2	7.5	7.4	3.12	27.12	3.9	1.10	1.11	28.4	17.9	3.3	22.10	18.2	2.1	28.1	24.3	10.3	—

DIVISION FOUR

	Aldershot	Blackpool	Bristol C	Bury	Chester C	Chesterfield	Colchester U	Crewe Alex	Darlington	Doncaster R	Halifax T	Hartlepool U	Hereford U	Mansfield T	Northampton T	Peterborough U	Reading	Rochdale	Stockport Co	Swindon T	Torquay U	Tranmere R	Wrexham	York C
Aldershot	—	5.5	22.10	10.9	10.3	31.12	23.4	31.3	12.5	24.3	18.2	7.1	27.8	4.2	1.11	5.11	26.12	26.11	3.3	27.9	21.1	8.10	24.9	14.4
Blackpool	2.1	—	1.11	7.4	24.3	22.10	7.1	24.9	5.11	10.3	7.5	27.12	28.4	27.9	10.9	3.12	27.8	8.10	18.2	21.1	17.12	21.4	3.3	4.2
Bristol C	25.2	14.2	—	7.1	31.12	26.11	31.3	20.4	10.3	5.11	8.10	10.9	4.2	27.8	14.4	29.10	27.9	13.3	26.12	5.5	24.9	24.3	21.1	18.10
Bury	28.1	6.9	3.9	—	14.4	23.4	3.3	13.11	11.4	11.2	18.9	18.2	24.3	8.10	5.5	1.10	26.11	26.12	1.11	12.5	6.3	15.1	22.10	31.12
Chester C	5.11	15.10	7.5	3.12	—	7.3	4.2	10.9	17.3	28.4	2.11	3.3	7.4	27.12	27.8	17.12	24.9	18.2	22.10	7.1	28.9	2.1	21.4	21.1
Ches'field	7.5	25.2	28.4	27.12	5.11	—	24.9	7.1	29.10	18.10	2.1	7.4	27.9	21.4	4.2	10.3	21.1	24.3	8.10	27.8	14.2	3.12	17.12	10.9
C'chester	27.12	3.9	6.9	18.10	1.10	11.2	—	29.10	14.1	14.2	17.12	3.12	7.5	10.3	15.10	21.4	5.11	17.9	28.1	25.2	28.4	7.4	2.1	17.3
Crewe A	6.9	11.2	28.12	10.3	28.1	3.9	18.2	—	17.9	16.12	3.3	1.11	21.4	7.5	22.10	7.4	23.3	14.1	30.9	8.10	2.1	28.4	2.12	5.11
Darl'gton	17.12	6.3	12.11	27.9	8.10	18.2	27.8	21.1	—	27.12	28.4	21.4	3.3	3.12	7.1	2.1	4.2	22.10	24.3	10.9	7.4	1.11	8.5	24.9
D'caster	15.10	12.11	6.3	24.9	26.11	3.3	1.11	12.5	24.4	—	21.10	21.1	11.9	7.1	26.12	17.3	31.3	5.5	31.12	14.4	4.2	18.2	27.8	27.9
Halifax T	29.10	31.12	17.3	21.1	14.2	4.5	11.5	18.10	25.11	25.2	—	23.9	7.1	9.9	27.9	15.10	13.4	23.4	9.3	30.3	27.8	4.11	4.2	26.12
Hart'pl U	3.9	20.4	28.1	29.10	19.10	7.9	14.4	15.2	26.12	17.9	11.2	—	5.11	25.2	31.12	14.1	12.5	31.3	5.5	10.3	17.3	4.11	4.2	26.12
Heref'd U	14.1	26.11	1.10	15.10	7.9	31.3	31.12	26.12	19.10	28.1	3.9	7.3	—	29.10	12.11	17.9	5.5	14.4	23.4	15.2	25.2	11.2	17.3	12.5
M'sf'ld T	1.10	31.3	14.1	17.3	24.4	26.12	12.11	31.12	14.4	3.9	28.1	22.10	18.2	—	12.5	11.2	3.3	1.11	6.9	26.11	15.10	17.9	6.3	5.5
N'th'mp'n	14.2	28.1	3.12	2.1	14.1	1.10	24.3	25.2	3.9	21.4	7.4	10.4	11.3	18.12	—	27.12	9.10	11.2	18.9	6.11	18.10	6.9	28.4	29.10
P'boro' U	7.3	14.4	18.2	4.2	12.5	12.11	26.12	28.9	5.5	8.10	23.3	27.8	21.1	24.9	24.4	—	2.11	3.3	26.11	31.12	10.9	22.10	7.1	31.3
Reading	21.4	14.1	7.4	28.4	11.2	17.9	7.3	14.10	1.10	7.9	2.12	17.12	2.1	19.10	16.3	15.2	—	28.1	3.9	29.10	27.12	7.5	12.11	25.2
Rochdale	28.4	17.3	17.12	21.4	29.10	15.10	21.1	27.8	25.2	2.1	27.12	27.9	3.12	14.2	24.9	18.10	10.9	—	5.11	4.2	7.5	10.3	7.4	7.1
St'ckp't	17.10	29.10	21.4	13.2	24.2	16.3	9.9	3.2	15.10	7.5	11.11	2.1	27.12	6.4	20.1	27.4	6.1	5.3	—	23.9	2.12	16.12	26.9	27.8
Sw'don T	7.4	17.9	2.1	17.12	3.9	14.1	22.10	18.3	28.1	3.12	6.9	12.11	1.11	29.4	6.3	7.5	18.2	1.10	11.2	—	21.4	3.3	27.12	15.10
T'quay U	17.9	12.5	11.2	5.11	31.3	2.11	26.11	5.5	7.9	1.10	14.1	8.10	22.10	24.3	3.3	28.1	23.4	31.12	14.4	26.12	—	3.9	18.2	10.3
Tr'mere R	17.3	26.12	14.10	27.8	5.5	14.4	26.9	26.11	13.2	29.10	5.3	3.2	23.9	20.1	30.3	24.2	30.12	12.11	12.5	17.10	6.1	—	10.9	23.4
W'xham	11.2	18.10	16.9	25.2	26.12	12.5	5.5	14.4	31.12	14.1	1.10	24.3	8.10	5.11	26.11	3.9	10.3	6.9	30.3	20.4	29.10	28.1	—	14.2
York C	3.12	1.10	3.3	7.5	17.9	28.1	8.10	6.3	11.2	8.4	21.4	28.4	17.12	2.1	18.2	6.9	22.10	3.9	14.1	24.3	12.11	27.12	1.11	—

THE FOOTBALL ASSOCIATION 1983–84 FIXTURES

1983

August

13 Opening Day of Season
20 FA Charity Shield
31 FL Milk Cup 1st Round 1st Leg

September

3 FA Challenge Cup Preliminary Round
7 Iceland v England (U16)
10 FA Challenge Trophy Preliminary Round
FA Challenge Vase Extra Preliminary Round
FA Youth Challenge Cup Preliminary Round*
14 European Cups 1st Round 1st Leg
FL Milk Cup 1st Round 2nd Leg
17 FA Challenge Cup 1st Round Qualifying
Scotland v Iceland (U16)
19 England v Iceland (U16)
20 England v Denmark (U21)
21 England v Denmark (EC)
Northern Ireland v Austria (EC)
Norway v Wales (EC)
28 European Cups 1st Round 2nd Leg

October

1 FA Challenge Cup 2nd Round Qualifying
FA Youth Challenge Cup 1st Round Qualifying*
2 FA Sunday Cup 1st Round
5 FL Milk Cup 2nd Round 1st Leg
England v Scotland (U16)
8 FA Challenge Vase Preliminary Round
11 Hungary v England (U21)
12 Hungary v England (EC)
Scotland v Belgium (EC)
Turkey v Northern Ireland (EC)
15 FA Challenge Cup 3rd Round Qualifying
19 European Cups 2nd Round 1st Leg
Scotland v England (U16)
22 FA Challenge Trophy 1st Round Qualifying
FA Youth Challenge Cup 2nd Round Qualifying*
26 FL Milk Cup 2nd Round 2nd Leg
29 FA Challenge Cup 4th Round Qualifying
FA County Youth Cup 1st Round*
30 FA Sunday Cup 2nd Round

November

2 European Cups 2nd Round 2nd Leg
5 FA Challenge Vase 1st Round
9 FL Milk Cup 3rd Round
16 Luxembourg v England (EC)
East Germany v Scotland (EC)
West Germany v Northern Ireland (EC)
Bulgaria v Wales (EC)
19 FA Challenge Cup 1st Round Proper
FA Youth Challenge Cup 1st Round Proper*
23 UEFA Cup 3rd Round 1st Leg
26 FA Challenge Trophy 2nd Round Qualifying
27 FA Sunday Cup 3rd Round
30 FL Milk Cup 4th Round

December

3 FA Challenge Vase 2nd Round
7 UEFA Cup 3rd Round 2nd Leg
10 FA Challenge Cup 2nd Round Proper
FA Youth Challenge Cup 2nd Round Proper*
FA County Youth Cup 2nd Round*
13 Northern Ireland v Scotland (BC)
14 Wales v Yugoslavia (EC)
17 FA Challenge Trophy 3rd Round Qualifying
31 FA Challenge Vase 3rd Round

1984

January

7 FA Challenge Cup 3rd Round Proper
FA Youth Challenge Cup 3rd Round Proper*
8 FA Sunday Cup 4th Round
14 FA Challenge Trophy 1st Round Proper
18 FL Milk Cup 5th Round
21 FA Challenge Vase 4th Round
FA County Youth Cup 3rd Round*
28 FA Challenge Cup 4th Round Proper

February

4 FA Challenge Trophy 2nd Round Proper
FA Youth Challenge Cup 4th Round Proper*
5 FA Sunday Cup 5th Round
8 FL Milk Cup Semi-Final 1st Leg
11 FA Challenge Vase 5th Round
15 FL Milk Cup Semi-Final 2nd Leg
18 FA Challenge Cup 5th Round Proper
25 FA Challenge Trophy 3rd Round Proper
28 Scotland v Wales (BC)
29 France v England (F)

March

3 FA Challenge Vase 6th Round
FA Youth Challenge Cup 5th Round Proper*
FA County Youth Cup 4th Round*
7 European Cups 3rd Round 1st Leg
UEFA Cup 4th Round 1st Leg
10 FA Challenge Cup 6th Round Proper
11 FA Sunday Cup Semi-Final
17 FA Challenge Trophy 4th Round Proper
21 European Cups 3rd Round 2nd Leg
UEFA Cup 4th Round 2nd Leg
24 FL Milk Cup Final
FA Challenge Vase Semi-Final 1st Leg
31 FA Challenge Vase Semi-Final 2nd Leg

April

4 England v Northern Ireland (BC)
7 FA Challenge Trophy Semi-Final 1st Leg
FA Youth Challenge Cup Semi-Final*
FA County Youth Cup Semi-Final*
11 European Cups Semi-Final 1st Leg
14 FA Challenge Cup Semi-Final
FA Challenge Trophy Semi-Final 2nd Leg
25 European Champions' Cup Semi-final 2nd Leg
28 FA Challenge Vase Final
29 FA Sunday Cup Final

MAY

2 Wales v England (BC)
5 FA Youth Challenge Cup Final
FA County Youth Cup Final
9 UEFA Cup Final 1st Leg
12 FA Challenge Trophy Final
16 European Cup-Winners' Cup Final
19 FA Challenge Cup Final
22 Wales v Northern Ireland (BC)
23 UEFA Cup Final 2nd Leg
26 Scotland v England (BC)
30 European Champions' Cup Final

JUNE

12–27 European Football Championship Finals, in France